Dictionary of the Middle Ages

AMERICAN COUNCIL OF LEARNED SOCIETIES

The American Council of Learned Societies, organized in 1919 for the purpose of advancing the study of the humanities and of the humanistic aspects of the social sciences, is a nonprofit federation comprising forty-six national scholarly groups. The Council represents the humanities in the United States in the International Union of Academies, provides fellowships and grants-in-aid, supports research-and-planning conferences and symposia, and sponsors special projects and scholarly publications.

MEMBER ORGANIZATIONS

AMERICAN PHILOSOPHICAL SOCIETY, 1743
AMERICAN ACADEMY OF ARTS AND SCIENCES, 1780
AMERICAN ANTIQUARIAN SOCIETY, 1812
AMERICAN ORIENTAL SOCIETY, 1842
AMERICAN NUMISMATIC SOCIETY, 1858
AMERICAN PHILOLOGICAL ASSOCIATION, 1869
ARCHAEOLOGICAL INSTITUTE OF AMERICA, 1879
SOCIETY OF BIBLICAL LITERATURE, 1880
MODERN LANGUAGE ASSOCIATION OF AMERICA, 1883
AMERICAN HISTORICAL ASSOCIATION, 1884
AMERICAN ECONOMIC ASSOCIATION, 1885
AMERICAN FOLKLORE SOCIETY, 1888
AMERICAN DIALECT SOCIETY, 1889
AMERICAN PSYCHOLOGICAL ASSOCIATION, 1892
ASSOCIATION OF AMERICAN LAW SCHOOLS, 1900
AMERICAN PHILOSOPHICAL ASSOCIATION, 1901
AMERICAN ANTHROPOLOGICAL ASSOCIATION, 1902
AMERICAN POLITICAL SCIENCE ASSOCIATION, 1903
BIBLIOGRAPHICAL SOCIETY OF AMERICA, 1904
ASSOCIATION OF AMERICAN GEOGRAPHERS, 1904
HISPANIC SOCIETY OF AMERICA, 1904
AMERICAN SOCIOLOGICAL ASSOCIATION, 1905
AMERICAN SOCIETY OF INTERNATIONAL LAW, 1906
ORGANIZATION OF AMERICAN HISTORIANS, 1907
AMERICAN ACADEMY OF RELIGION, 1909
COLLEGE ART ASSOCIATION OF AMERICA, 1912
HISTORY OF SCIENCE SOCIETY, 1924
LINGUISTIC SOCIETY OF AMERICA, 1924
MEDIEVAL ACADEMY OF AMERICA, 1925
AMERICAN MUSICOLOGICAL SOCIETY, 1934
SOCIETY OF ARCHITECTURAL HISTORIANS, 1940
ECONOMIC HISTORY ASSOCIATION, 1940
ASSOCIATION FOR ASIAN STUDIES, 1941
AMERICAN SOCIETY FOR AESTHETICS, 1942
AMERICAN ASSOCIATION FOR THE ADVANCEMENT OF SLAVIC STUDIES, 1948
METAPHYSICAL SOCIETY OF AMERICA, 1950
AMERICAN STUDIES ASSOCIATION, 1950
RENAISSANCE SOCIETY OF AMERICA, 1954
SOCIETY FOR ETHNOMUSICOLOGY, 1955
AMERICAN SOCIETY FOR LEGAL HISTORY, 1956
AMERICAN SOCIETY FOR THEATRE RESEARCH, 1956
SOCIETY FOR THE HISTORY OF TECHNOLOGY, 1958
AMERICAN COMPARATIVE LITERATURE ASSOCIATION, 1960
MIDDLE EAST STUDIES ASSOCIATION, 1966
AMERICAN SOCIETY FOR EIGHTEENTH-CENTURY STUDIES, 1969
ASSOCIATION FOR JEWISH STUDIES, 1969

Dictionary of the Middle Ages

JOSEPH R. STRAYER, *EDITOR IN CHIEF*

Volume 13

INDEX

Prepared by Wm. J. Richardson Associates, Inc.

CHARLES SCRIBNER'S SONS
MACMILLAN LIBRARY REFERENCE USA
Simon & Schuster Macmillan
NEW YORK

Simon & Schuster and Prentice Hall International
LONDON • MEXICO CITY • NEW DELHI • SINGAPORE • SYDNEY • TORONTO

Library of Congress Cataloging in Publication Data
Main entry under title:

Dictionary of the Middle Ages.

Includes bibliographies and index.
1. Middle Ages—Dictionaries. I. Strayer, Joseph Reese, 1904–1987

D114.D5 1982 909.07 82-5904

ISBN 0-684-16760-3 (v. 1)	ISBN 0-684-18274-2 (v. 8)
ISBN 0-684-17022-1 (v. 2)	ISBN 0-684-18275-0 (v. 9)
ISBN 0-684-17023-X (v. 3)	ISBN 0-684-18276-9 (v. 10)
ISBN 0-684-17024-8 (v. 4)	ISBN 0-684-18277-7 (v. 11)
ISBN 0-684-18161-4 (v. 5)	ISBN 0-684-18278-5 (v. 12)
ISBN 0-684-18168-1 (v. 6)	ISBN 0-684-18279-3 (v. 13)
ISBN 0-684-18169-X (v. 7)	ISBN 0-684-19073-7 (set)

Charles Scribner's Sons
An imprint of Simon & Schuster Macmillan
1633 Broadway, New York, NY 10019-6785

7 9 11 13 15 17 19 20 18 16 14 12 10 8

PRINTED IN THE UNITED STATES OF AMERICA.

The *Dictionary of the Middle Ages* has been produced with support from the National Endowment for the Humanities.

The paper in this book meets the guidelines for permanence and durability of the Committee on Production Guidelines for Book Longevity of the Council on Library Resources.

In Memory of

Joseph R. Strayer (1904–1987)

and

R.M. Lumiansky (1913–1987)

Editorial Board

Advisory Committee

Editorial Staff

Managing Editors

MARSHALL DE BRUHL *(1977–1984)* JOHN F. FITZPATRICK *(1985–1989)*

Assistant Managing Editor

H. ABIGAIL BOK *(1983–1984)*

Assistants

CAROLYN G. PATTON *(1977–1983)*

PETER C. BENEDICT ELIZABETH ELSTON STEPHEN A. SAYRE

BRIGITTE M. GOLDSTEIN RUSSELL J. HANDELMAN SANDRA D. KELLY MARYLOU H. MANTLO

Copy Editors, Researchers, Bibliographers

JEFFREY L. BENEKE ILENE COHEN ROBERT K. HAYCRAFT
JOEL HONIG *(Chief, 1980–1983)* IRINA RYBACEK ELIZABETH I. WILSON

W. CUNNINGHAM BISSELL GEOFFREY B. GNEUHS MIRIAM ROSEN WILLIAM K. WEST

LESLEY ANN BENEKE WINIFRED M. DAVIS CASEY D. FINCH
ROBERT HALASZ PAMELA NICELY CHARLES PATTERSON
JONATHAN ROSE TERENCE WALZ

Proofreaders

EDWARD FERRARO *(Chief, 1982–1986)*

EMILY GARLIN

W. KIRK REYNOLDS JACK RUMMEL SAM TANENHAUS

Picture Researchers

LUCY BARBER BARBARA SCHULTZ JOHN SCHULTZ
DEBBIE TAYLOR MIMI THOMPSON

DAVID J. BABIN *(Assistant)*

Cartographers

SYLVIA LEHRMAN PATRICIA A. RODRIGUEZ JOSEPH STONEHILL

Indexers

JAN BLAKESLEE
(Editor)

SUSAN D. COERR ALAN GREENBERG BARBARA LONG
TY KOONTZ KATHLEEN McCOOL IRINA RYBACEK

Production Managers

JANET HORNBERGER
(Designer)

MATTHEW M. KARDOVICH ANJU MAKHIJANI

Production Assistants

DANIEL J. CALTO BETH ANN McCABE

FREDERICK A. AIESE NANCY NIEVES

Scribner Reference Staff

G. MICHAEL McGINLEY
(Editorial Director, 1985–1987)

JONATHAN G. ARETAKIS WILLIAM L. C. BROADDUS JOHN CANTRELL
CHRISTIANE L. DESCHAMPS NORMA FRANKEL LAURA D. GROSS
JAMES F. MAURER DAVID WILLIAM VOORHEES JOAN ZSELECZKY

Contents

Accessus: Using the Dictionary—Using the Index xiii

Index 1

List of Contributors 567

Errata 607

Accessus

USING THE DICTIONARY—USING THE INDEX

Our editor, the late Joseph R. Strayer, described the Index as the most important volume of the *Dictionary of the Middle Ages*. Experience had taught him that medieval culture was too broad and diverse to break easily into even as many as 5,000 discrete articles. As the Index demonstrates, there are more than 100,000 persons, places, and concepts that, while not themselves the subject of individual Dictionary articles, are nevertheless legitimate objects of scholarly interest. In the Dictionary this material has been organized into long and short essays according to the paradigms of medieval scholarship in dozens of overlapping disciplines, each with its own customs and nomenclature. Thus persons may be known under more than a single name, and broad cultural movements, such as Islam or the Gothic, may subsume many languages and nationalities. The decade-long publication process of the Dictionary has itself demanded different practical choices in individual volumes. And the Index offers a mode of structuring the material that differs from that of the Dictionary in several respects. The table below is intended to set forth some of the most salient organizing features of the Dictionary and the Index. We hope thereby to offer an equivalent of the medieval *accessus ad auctores*—a delineation and categorization of the writings at hand.

Obviously the difficulties of organizing any large body of material are greatly magnified when dealing with a thousand-year era during which the Latin (and Greek) culture of antiquity gave way (variously over time in different lands) to our modern vernaculars. Even today, the results of this shift are by no means "final," as may be seen in different styles that survive in European and American custom for alphabetizing such particles as "de" and "von."

Dictionaries need to present persons and things by their names. In the Middle Ages names kept changing, and today any well-known medieval person is likely to be known by three of them. There is the common vernacular of everyday life for all; the Latin appellation of record for rulers, churchmen, and scholars; and the modern English form for those figures whose fame endures. Jhenne/Jhannette from Domrémy became Jeanne d'Arc and Joan of Arc. Gualterius Anglicus is Walter the Englishman. Furthermore, identification is not always certain. Roger of Helmarshausen has been found to be the probable author of the mechanical treatise commonly ascribed to (and still informally known as) "Theophilus." For an extreme example of the difficulties, one need only consult the Dictionary article in volume 11 that begins as follows: "**SWINESHEAD** (*Suicet, Suincet, Suisseth, Swyneshed*, and various other forms). There may well have been three men with this name. . . ." (Actually there were more than three, and some of them are more commonly known by first name, as "John of" or "Richardus de" Swineshead.) Rulers pose special problems, for the complex ties of subinfeudation, intermarriage,

and conquest often led to titles of extraordinary complexity. "Charles III of Anjou" signifies a son of a count of Gravina who was actually raised in Hungary and who is also known as Charles of Durazzo after the duchy he inherited in Albania. "King of Naples" is his most important title, but he was also (as Charles II) king of Hungary. It need scarcely be added that the orthography of the Islamic world—expressed in Arabic, Turkish, Persian, and even Mongolian terms—poses special problems of its own.

The 1,300 contributors to the Dictionary, themselves reflecting a variety of languages and disciplines, have inevitably chosen different forms of names for some of the same people. The editors, while enforcing a degree of standardization, have deemed it wise not to insist absolutely on, for example, the vernacular or the English form of a name (though most prominent Western monarchs are given in the familiar English version). Variant forms of names are common throughout the Dictionary. To the difficulties posed by such diversity a thorough system of cross-referencing is the only answer. The Index supplements (but does not entirely replace) the existing systems of parenthetical and blind-entry headings and *see also* references at the end of articles. It also provides a new perspective on some of the topics. Boethius, for example, was a supremely influential figure in music and literature as well as philosophy. The main index entry under his name (with volume, page, and column citations appearing in **boldface**) directs the reader to the principal Dictionary article in volume 2. The scores of Index subentries graphically demonstrate his significance in a way that no single essay could accomplish. The article provides the context; the Index multiplies the examples. Where the Dictionary articles supply knowledge in the expected places, the Index entries offer a continuing fund of surprises: "Muḥammad, accused of being a poet, 8:20b"; "Depression, morbid. *See* "Melancholy"; "Slapping games, 5:347a-b." For the fullest access to the hidden riches of the *Dictionary of the Middle Ages* the reader should consult both sources, as described below.

JOHN F. FITZPATRICK

Alphabetization

DICTIONARY

Articles are arranged according to the word-by-word method. "Hus, John" comes before "Ḥusayn." The chief exception involves prominent persons of the same name. These are arranged in a hierarchical system of (1) saints, (2) popes, (3) patriarchs, (4) emperors, and (5) kings in order to facilitate the comparative study of, say, the popes named John or the French kings called Charles. Thus (St.) John Chrysostom and (St.) John of Ōjun are grouped before the Byzantine emperors. The emperors named John appear in their numerical sequence, with family names or epithets (Tzimiskes, Komnenos, Palaiologos) appearing after the numeral. Following the numbered kings are listed all other figures of the same name in word-by-word order. "Of" is treated as a word. Although many bishops, counts, and princes are also identified by number, these figures are not treated in hierarchical fashion and their numerals do not form part of the article headings.

The Norse and English letters Þ/þ (thorn) and Đ/ð (eth) are treated as if spelled *th*.

Greek χ/ϰ (chi) is alphabetized as *x*.

INDEX

Arrangement is word by word, as in the Dictionary, but the hierarchical system described above is not used. The only exceptions to word-by-word sequence are as follows:

1. Numbered rulers of the same state are grouped together by number.
2. In addition to the usual English words, the following foreign prepositions and particles are ignored in the alphabetical sorting:

al-	del	den	di	l'	les
da	della	der	die	la	von
de	dem	des	du	le	

3. Þ/þ (thorn) and Đ/ð (eth) are alphabetized after *th*.
4. Greek χ/ϰ (chi) is alphabetized as *x*.

Arabic

DICTIONARY/INDEX

Arabic is generally transliterated according to the system of the *Encyclopedia of Islam* except that the dictionary uses *q* instead of *ḳ*, and *j* instead of *dj*. The initial "Al-" (the) and "Ibn" (son of) are inverted to final position for sorting. The reader should search under the next element of the name. It should be noted that the words "Arabic" and (more often) "Islamic" are used in headings as a shorthand for "in the Arabic/Islamic world."

Art and Artists

DICTIONARY

Technical terms (apse, intonacco) and iconographic types (Resurrection, Eleousa) receive brief definitional entries, generally accompanied by a single illustration. The same is true for individual artists. Anonymous masters normally appear under the title of their most famous work (Playing Cards, Master of the).

The major treatment of art history occurs in the survey articles. For the mainstream of Western European art and architecture these are generally studies of periods or movements: Early Christian, Celtic, Migration Period, Pre-Romanesque, Romanesque, Gothic, Trecento. Byzantine and Islamic art receive separate treatment, and the latter is also broken down by dynasties (Abbasid, Mamluk, Umayyad). The arts of other regions are surveyed according to national style (Armenian, Bulgarian, Sasanian) or, as in the case of the Iberian Peninsula, regional variation (Hispano-Mauresque, Mozarabic, Mudejar).

INDEX

The Index essentially reflects the contents of the Dictionary. For the anonymous masters the prime Index entries have been consolidated in a "Master" section, with cross-references at the titles of principal works. Certain national styles that are not the subject of Dictionary articles are indexed separately, allowing a different means of access to the material. There has been no attempt, however, to index the French and Italian national styles, since these are so thoroughly intertwined with the discussions of Gothic and Romanesque. Illustrations are identified in the Index (*illus.*) in order to grant access to numerous pictures (including color frontispieces) not otherwise readily discoverable. Thus while the article on Simone Martini in volume 11 has only a single illustration, the Index identifies other pictures by this artist that accompany the articles on the Annunciation (volume 1) and Petrarch (volume 9).

Cross-References

DICTIONARY

The two principal modes of cross referencing are (1) *blind entries*, which are major headings directing the reader toward an essay under an alternative or variant title ("Martini, Simone. *See* Simone Martini"), and (2) *see also* references, which follow various articles and direct the reader to related topics. As the Dictionary was published serially over the course of a decade and many changes were implemented during those years, *see also* references are generally more copious in the later volumes.

INDEX

See and *see also* are used in the conventional fashion. *See* reflects an indexing decision that the item in question be cited under a name or spelling other than might be expected (sometimes a form different from that used in the Dictionary). The *see also* references are for basic search and are not intended to duplicate the more copious and suggestive cross-references in the Dictionary itself.

Languages

DICTIONARY

The major medieval languages are treated separately. English is divided into Old English Language and *M*iddle English Language. There are separate essays on *L*atin and *V*ulgar Latin. Celtic languages and Slavic languages are grouped together, but French, Picard, and Provençal are treated separately. There is also a general overview of Indo-European languages.

INDEX

Detailed indexing and cross-referencing point to secondary discussions of less familiar languages and dialects.

Law

DICTIONARY

The major treatment of national bodies of law occurs in the twenty-six "Law" essays in volume 7. Cross-references point to definitional entries on numerous subtopics.

INDEX

National bodies of law are indexed not under *L* but by nationality: English Law, French Law, etc.

Literature

DICTIONARY

Discussions are grouped by language, with English literature divided into separate essays on *A*nglo-Saxon and *M*iddle English. Byzantine Greek literature is under *B*. There are separate essays, of various lengths, on all the major authors and many of the minor ones as well.

INDEX

Treatment is generally the same as in the Dictionary, but Anglo-Saxon and Middle English have been indexed together at *E*. See also "Titles" below.

Music

DICTIONARY

Music, musical instruments, and musical notation are treated primarily at *M* in twenty-eight separate essays. Special subjects like Gregorian Chant, Harmony, and Rhythm are treated separately.

INDEX

National schools of music are indexed by name: Armenian Music, Byzantine Music, etc.

Titles

DICTIONARY

Most literary works receive their primary discussion under the heading of their author. The chief exceptions are anonymous works and those which, like the *Roman de la Rose,* have two or more authors. Certain compilations, such as the *Golden Legend,* are also cited by title when the fame of the work is greater than that of the compiler.

INDEX

Anonymous works are cited by title. With the exceptions noted above, all others are indexed primarily under the author, with cross-references under the title. "De" and other introductory prepositions are considered part of the title for purposes of alphabetization, but definite and indefinite articles are generally inverted so as not to affect the sorting. Cross-referencing by title not only guarantees identification for readers uncertain of authorship but also serves to provide a partial catalog of medieval texts on a given subject. Even a brief consultation with the long "De" section of the Index reveals, for example, something of the range of authors who wrote treatises *De musica* or *De natura*. Although such series of listings are limited to those works which receive significant mention in the Dictionary, the sampling is large enough to offer a useful supplement to present-day medieval studies.

Medieval titles are often imprecise, casual, arbitrary, or generic. Inevitably modern scholars have referred to the same text under a variety of names.

ACCESSUS

As the Dictionary has not sought to impose absolute uniformity, the Index user should be aware of some of the most common rubrics by which medieval authors and their modern editors have chosen to designate their texts:

Against	Contra
Art of	Ars
Book of	Liber de, Libellus de, Kitāb, Sefer
Chronicle	Chroniques, Crónica
Deeds	Gesta
Letter	Epistola
Life	Vie, Vita
Mirror	Speculum
On (about)	De
Romance	Roman
Song of	Cantar, Carmen, Chanson
Summa	Summa
Treatise	Tractatus

Dictionary of the Middle Ages

Index

A

A Bella Venus. *See* Via, Francesc de la
A.E.I.O.U. (Emperor Frederick III's motto), 2:9a
"A solis ortus cardine." *See* Sedulius
"A la stagion che 'l mondo foglia e fiora." *See* Compiuta Donzella of Florence
A terzaruolo system. *See A zenzile* system
A zenzile system, 11:235a
Aachen, **1:1a–2b**, 12:313b–314a
  after collapse of Carolingian empire, 1:1b
  art renaissance at (pre-Romanesque), 10:306b
  building projects, 1:2a
  captured by William of Holland, 4:59b
  cathedral of, 10:106a
  center of religious reform, 1:1b
  coronation of Otto I at, 1:1b, 4:426b
  government, citizen role, 1:2a
  imperial protection, 1:1b–2a
  palace chapel, **1:2b–3b**, 5:593b–594b
    building of, 10:91a, 94a
    building plan, 1:2b–3b (*illus.*)
    Byzantine characteristics, 1:3a
    consecration, 1:2b
    coronation site, 1:1a, b
    design of, 1:2b–3a, 4:347a, 10:91a
    foreign artists and, 12:152b
    influence on architecture, 1:3a-b
    services of, 3:676b–677a, 4:274a
  palace school, Alcuin of York and, 1:142b, 143a
  pilgrimages to, 1:1a
  Roman military establishment, 1:1a
  royal residence at, 1:1a-b
  symbolic role in German monarchy, 1:1a
Aachen, Council of (816–817), 2:170b
  abbots' conference, 10:286a
  Divine Office and, 4:230a
  Institutio canonicorum, 4:117b
  reorganization of clergy and, 3:375a
  women's orders and, 12:683b
Aachen, Diet of (818), on blasphemy, 2:272a
Aachen, Synod of (809), 6:306b
Aargau
  Habsburgs and, 11:540a
  Kyburgs and, 11:539b
  vs. Bern, 11:544a-b
Aarhus Cathedral, altarpiece, 9:186b (*illus.*)
Aaron ben Amram, 7:107a
Aaron ben Elijah the Younger, 7:210b
Aaron ben Jeshua, 4:539b, 7:210b
Aaron ben Joseph the Elder, 7:210b
Aaron ben Joseph ha-Levi, 7:81a
Aaron ben Moses ben Asher, 7:104b
Aaron ben Samuel of Baghdad, origins of Ashkenazi Hasidism, 9:578b, 581b
Ab bet din (rabbinic court chairman), 10:243a
"Ab la dolchor del temps novel." *See* William IX of Aquitaine
Aba family, 6:343a
Abacus, 8:206b (*illus.*)
  computation on, 8:206b
  description of, 8:206a-b
  Exchequer and, 4:531b, 533a
  Gerbert of Aurillac, 8:207b, 209a
  Roman numerals and, 10:470a
  Sylvester II and, 11:552b
  texts on, 8:207a-b
  see also Mathematics
Abāḍīya. *See* Ibadites
Abandonment of land. *See* Deserted villages; Plagues; Reclamation of land
Abaqa, Ilkhanid ruler, 1:453a, 6:420a, 603b
  khanate of, 8:474a
Abarshahr. *See* Nishapur
Abas of Armenia, king (928–952/953), 1:482a
Abasgia. *See* Georgia
^{c}Abbādān, Zanj and, 12:739a
^{c}Abbās, al-, 1:401a
^{c}Abbās I, Safawid shah
  Isfahan under, 6:562a
  Mosque of the Ruler and, 4:569b (*illus.*)
^{c}Abbās ibn ^{c}Abd al-Muṭṭalib ibn Hāshim, al-, **1:3b–4b**
  control of *siqāya* and *rifāda,* 1:4a
  relations with Muḥammad, 1:4a-b
^{c}Abbās ibn Aḥmad ibn Ṭūlūn, 3:209a
Abbas Siculus. *See* Nicolaus de Tudeschis
^{c}Abbasāh (sister of Hārūn al-Rashīd), Ja^{c}far ibn Yaḥyā and, 2:110b
Abbasid art and architecture, **1:5a–6b**, 6:596b–601b
  Aghlabid art and, 1:69b
  characteristics of early phase, 1:5a
  glassmaking of, 5:546a–547a
  lusterware, 1:5b
  medallions, 1:6b
  miḥrab, 1:6a (*illus.*)
  monuments
    from early phase, 1:5a
    from late phase, 1:6a-b
  Samarra phase, 1:5a-b
    figure style in painting, 1:5b
  stucco decoration, 1:5a (*illus.*)
  see also Malwiya; *Miḥrāb*
Abbasids, **1:6b–12b**
  ^{c}Abd Allāh (governor of Khorāsān) and, 11:575a
  administration, 3:43b–44a, 44b–45a, 6:589a-b, 590a-b, 591a, 10:608b
    centralization of, 1:8a
    decentralization of, 1:9b
    muḥtasib, 8:527a
    provincial, 3:44b, 45a, 49b
    quasi-feudal state, 1:11b
    removal of tribal sentiments, 1:8a
    Sasanian influences on, 3:42a
  alliance with Abū Muslim, 1:7a-b
  Almoravids and, 11:140a
  ancestors of, 4:596b
  archon ton archonton and, 1:449a
  Arcrunis and, 1:451a
  Armenia and, 1:479a–480a
  Banū ^{c}Abd al-Madān and, 9:55b
  Basra and, 2:127b
  black slaves, 2:268a-b
  Buyids and, 2:435b–436a
  in Cairo, 6:591b
  caliphate of, 3:42a–51b
    legal powers, 3:47b–48a
    Mālik ibn Anas and, 8:58b
    succession, 8:534b–535a
  caliphate of al-Rāḍī, 10:245b–246b
  capital at Samarra, 1:11a, 10:641a–643b
  cavalry, Turkish slave troops, 12:552b
  ceramics, 7:223b
    lusterware, 7:689b, 690a
  civil conflicts, 1:7b, 6:108a
    al-Amīn and al-Ma$^{\supset}$mūn, 1:10a
  coinage of, 8:422a–423a
  commander of the faithful title, 3:488b–489a
  conquests of, 6:570b
  control of Mecca, 8:240a
  court of, 3:45a-b
  cultural ferment in the early period, 10:345a
  in Damascus, 4:81b–82a, 83a
  decline of, 1:11a, 2:46b–47a
    proliferation of centers of learning and, 11:83b
  diplomacy of, 4:200a
  dissolution of caliphate, 10:609b–610a
  dynastic succession, 1:9a-b

Abbasids (*cont.*)
dynastic succession (*cont.*)
9th through 10th centuries, 8:534b–535a
power struggles over, 3:42b–43a
problem of legitimacy, 3:46a-b
economic problems, 1:11a
exilarch and, 4:552a
foundation of Cairo, 3:13b
foundation of dynasty, 11:226b–227a
gastronomy and, 3:584a-b
goals of Islamic reform movement, 3:41b, 42a, 45b–46a
governorships
to family members, 1:9b
to military commanders, 1:10b
Hamdanids and
loss of authority in Mesopotamia, 6:83b
sharing of government, 6:83b–85a
House of Wisdom translation center, 12:128b
hunting and, 6:355a-b
Ibrāhīm ibn al-Aghlab and, 6:391b
in Ifrīqiya, 1:70a, 6:414b
Ikhshidids and, 6:416b
ᶜImād al-Dawla and, 6:424a, b
imperial style, 1:8b
revision of history, 1:9a
imprisonment of Barmakids, 1:10a
in Iran, 6:501b, 502a
in Iraq, 6:512a–513b, 514a
Islamic law and, 7:486b
Ismailism and, 6:615b
Jews under, 7:107a–108a
jund rebellion, 1:70a
Kaysānīya movement and, 11:136a
Kharijite sects and, 11:139a
Khorāsān revolt, 10:608b
al-Kufa under, 7:307b
library development, 7:561a
loss of Egypt, 4:405b
in al-Maghrib, 8:15a
and the Mamikonean family, 8:79a
maritime trade and, 11:246b
mawālī, 1:8a
military forces
amīr al-umarāᵓ, 1:11a
cost of allegiance, 1:11a
intervention in political affairs, 1:9a, 10a, 10b–11a
Khorāsānis, 1:8a
power of, 1:8a, 11a-b
rival factions, 1:10a-b
Turkish slave regiments, 1:10b
veto power of generals, 1:11a
military slaves, 8:69a
military victories
Fatimids, 8:535a
Qarmatians, 8:535a
millennialism and, 8:389a
al-Muᶜizz and, 12:744b
music and, 8:566a–568a
al-Muᶜtaḍid, Egypt's Tulinids and, 12:224b
al-Muᶜtazila and, 6:583a, 583b, 8:655a-b
naval power of, 9:74b–75a
opponents of, al-Baḥrayn used as power base, 2:50b
origin of their name, 1:6b
overthrow of Umayyads, 1:7a, 9:686a
paper varieties named for, 12:698a
polemic with Shiites, 1:4a
political role of early Islamic state, 1:6b–7a
political tutors, role in shadow government, 6:107a, 108a
power
basis of, 3:46a
ideological challenges to, 3:46a-b, 47a
power of military under, 3:49b
Quraysh tribe and, 10:242b
religious policies, 3:47b–48a
revolts against rule, 3:49a
Buyids, 1:11a
Fatimid dynasty, 1:11b
heresy and social conflict, 1:8b
provincial conflicts, 1:9a, 9b
questions of legitimacy, 1:9a
revolutionary groups
governing responsibility, 1:7b
Hāshimiyya, 1:7a
Round City, 1:8b
Sājī guard, 10:246a
Sasanian influence, 1:8b
scholarship under, 3:45a
ṣinf under, 11:308a
sultanate
creation of, 1:11b
seizure of titles and prerogatives, 1:12a
support of Thomas the Slav's rebellion, 12:36b
supported by religious authorities, 1:12a
Syria and, 11:560b
system of clientage, 8:89a-b
Tahirids and, 11:574a-b
Toghrıl-Beg and, 12:66b
trade with Southeast Asia, 9:85a
translations of Greek scientific treatises and, 11:82b
vizierate and, 6:589b
vs. Byzantines, 1:9b–10a
in Anatolia, 6:572a
vs. Fatimids, on Red Sea, 11:247a
vs. Ḥimṣ, 6:230a
vs. Idrīs ibn ᶜAbd Allah, 6:413a
vs. Mongols, 6:504b
Nāṣīr al-Dīn and, 11:228a
Yaᶜqūb ibn Layth and, 12:716a
al-Yaᶜqūbī on, 12:718a
Yemen and, 12:724a
see also Abbasid art and architecture; Baghdad; Barmakids
ᶜAbbāsiyya, al-
fortified wall, 1:70a
transfer of power to, 1:70a
Abbat, Per, *Cantar de mío Cid* and, 3:79b
Abbess
Cistercian, 12:686a
Council of Frankfurt (794) and, 12:683b
Fontevrault, 12:686b
selection of, 12:685a
Abbey, definition, 8:454a
Abbey Pannonhalma/Martisberg, 6:341a
Abbey of Sts. Peter and Paul. *See* St. Augustine (monastery: Canterbury)
Abbeys. *See* Monasticism
Abbo
Carolingian Latin poetry and, 3:103b
see also Adbo of St. Germain-des-Prés
Abbo of Fleury (Floriacensis), **1:12b–13b**
Anglo-Norman *Passiun* and, 1:261a
Apologeticus, 1:13a
Collectio, 7:407a
Commentary on the Calculus of Victorius, 1:12b
cult of, 1:13a
election as abbot, 1:13a
Epitome of Popes' Lives Down to Gregory, I, 1:13a
Excerpts from the Fathers, 1:13a
on Letald of Micy, 7:552b
Passio sancti Eadmundi, 1:13a, 7:363a, 10:16a
as a source for *Passiun Seint Edmund,* 1:261a, 9:448b
as a source for *Vie St. Edmund le rei,* 12:415a
Quaestiones grammaticalae, 1:13a
support for religious reforms, 1:12b–13a, 13b
Syllogismi dialecti, 1:12b
verse life of St. Dunstan, 4:311b
year 1000 and, 12:723a
Abbo of St. Germain-des-Prés. *See* Adbo (Abbo) of St. Germain-des-Prés
Abbot
Benedict of Nursia on, 2:169b
Benedictine
commendatory, 2:175b
episcopal benedictions, 2:178a
Cistercian, 12:686a
election of, 2:173a-b, 4:421b, 424a–425a
in England, 4:424a, 425b
in German principalities, 5:499b
Premonstratensian, 12:685b
Abbreviation marks, in Latin, 7:354b
Abbreviations
as means of identifying MSS, 9:338b
see also Nomen sacrum
Abbreviator, **1:13b–14a**, 3:253a
college of, 1:14a
duties, 1:13b
fees received, 1:13b
history of office, 1:13b
limit on numbers, 1:13b–14a
presidents of the greater enclosure, 1:14a
ABC des simples gens, L'. See Gerson, John
ᶜAbd Allāh (9th century; brother of Ṭalḥa), reign of, 11:575a
ᶜAbd Allāh, Andalusian Umayyad ruler, accession to power, 12:276b–277a
ᶜAbd Allāh, Fatimid caliph. *See* ᶜUbayd Allāh al-Mahdī, Fatimid caliph
ᶜAbd Allāh (Grenada Zirid), 12:745a
ᶜAbd Allāh ibn al-ᶜAbbās, Koranic lexicographies, 4:442a
ᶜAbd Allāh ibn ᶜAlī, 3:46a

  al-Manṣūr and, 8:88b, 89a
ᶜAbd Allāh ibn Ḥamdān
  governorship of Mosul, 6:83b, 84a
  murder of, 6:84b
ᶜAbd Allāh ibn Iskandar, 2:397a
ᶜAbd Allāh ibn Muᶜāwiya, 7:307a
  Iran occupied by, 8:165a-b
ᶜAbd Allāh ibn Muḥammad al-Kātib, 12:744a
ᶜAbd Allāh ibn Qays, Muslim admiral, 9:74a
ᶜAbd Allāh ibn Saᶜd ibn Abī Sarḥ, governor general of Egypt, 1:237a, 9:74a
  vs. Byzantines in Ifrīqiya, 1:15b
ᶜAbd Allāh ibn Ṭāhir, governor of Khorāsān, 11:575b
ᶜAbd Allāh ibn Yāsīn al-Jazūlī, Almoravids and, 1:198a-b
ᶜAbd Allāh ibn al-Zubayr, **1:15a–16b**, 3:39b, 10:242a
  battle with al-Ḥajjāj ibn Yūsuf, 8:166a
  as caliph of Egypt, Iraq, and the Hejaz, 1:16a
  consolidation of power, 1:16a
  control of Mecca, 8:166a
  defense of ᶜUthmān, 1:15b
  efforts to secure political independence of Mecca, 8:240a
  family background, 1:15a-b
  al-Ḥusayn and, 6:370a
  involvement in Meccan party, 1:15b
  military campaigns, 1:15b
  rebellion against Umayyads, 1:15b, 16a
  recognition of Muᶜāwiya ibn Abī Sufyān, 1:15b
  vs. ᶜAbd al-Malik, 1:16a, 12:269b
  vs. ᶜAlī ibn Abī Ṭālib, 1:15b
  vs. Umayyads, 3:38b, 6:511b
  vs. Yazīd, 1:15b–16a, 12:721b–722a
ᶜAbd al-Aziz, 7:111b
ᶜAbd al-Ḥakam, Ibn
  contribution to historiography, 4:407b
  on defeat of Kulthūm ibn ᶜIyāḍ, 12:552a
ᶜAbd al-Ḥaqq, Marinid sultan
  Jews and, 7:99b
  reign of, 8:140b
ᶜAbd al-Jabbār, 7:150b
  summa, 9:568b
ᶜAbd al-Laṭīf al-Baghdādī
  account of Egyptian flora, 6:185a
  on famine in Egypt, 5:2a
ᶜAbd al-Laṭīf (Ulugh Beg's son), 12:57b
ᶜAbd al-Madān (clan)
  conversion to Islam, 9:55b
  in Najrān, 9:55a
ᶜAbd al-Majīd. *See* Ḥāfiẓ, al-
ᶜAbd al-Malik. *See* Marwān, ᶜAbd al-Malik ibn
ᶜAbd al-Malik ibn Nūḥ, Samanid ruler, Alptigin and, 1:220a
ᶜAbd al-Malik al-Muẓaffar, murder of, 12:278a
ᶜAbd al-Muᵓmin, Almohad caliph, 1:194a-b, 200b, 12:745a
ᶜAbd al-Muṭṭalib, **1:14a–15a**
  alliance with tribe of Khuzāᶜa, 1:14b–15a
  control of *siqāya* and *rifāda,* 1:14b
  election as head of Hāshim clan, 1:14b
  Muḥammad and, 1:15a
ᶜAbd al-Qādir, 8:566b, 610a, 611a, 611b, 612a, 612b
  on idiophones, 8:613b
ᶜAbd Rabbih, Ibn, *ᶜIqd al-farid, al-,* 4:445a, 6:233b
ᶜAbd al-Raḥmān I, Andalusian Umayyad ruler, 11:382b
  as founder of Córdoban Umayyad dynasty, 12:275a
  journey to Spain, 12:275a
  reuniting of clan in Spain, 12:275b
  slaves of, 2:268a
  tribal infighting during reign of, 12:275b
ᶜAbd al-Raḥmān II, Andalusian Umayyad ruler, 11:382b, 12:276a-b
  administrative and fiscal reforms of, 12:276b
  crucifixion of Rabīᶜ by, 12:276a
  military campaigns of, 12:276a
  relations with Abbasids, 12:276a-b
  Seville and, 11:213b
ᶜAbd al-Raḥmān III, Andalusian Umayyad caliph, 1:627a, 11:337a, 382b
  coinage of, 8:423a
  concentration of power by, 12:277a-b
  development of Islamic navies, 9:75a
  foreign policy of, 12:277a
  Madīnat al Zahrāᵓ, 6:234b
  reign of, 12:277a-b
  rivalry with Abbasids, 3:488b
  science and, 10:472a
ᶜAbd al-Raḥmān, Abbasid vizier, 10:246a
ᶜAbd al-Raḥmān Ghāfiqī of Spain, emir, 9:715b
ᶜAbd al-Raḥmān ibn Aḥmad Jāmī, *Nafaḥat al-uns,* 9:40a
ᶜAbd al-Raḥmān ibn Muᶜāwiya, established emirate in Córdoba, 3:598a
ᶜAbd al-Raḥmān ibn Rustam, 11:139a
ᶜAbd al-Raḥmān Sanchuelo, named heir to caliphate, 12:278a
ᶜAbd al-Raḥmān al-Ṣūfī, 1:623a
  Ṣuwar al-kawākib al-Thābita, 6:407b
    illumination of, 8:115a-b
ᶜAbd al-Razzāq, 7:111b
ᶜAbd al-Wahhāb, 7:111b
ᶜAbdallāh Anṣārī, 9:40a
  Munājāt, 9:41a
Abdallah el Tarjumí. *See* Turmeda, Anselm
ᶜAbdān, 6:615b, 616a
ᶜAbdarī, al-, 9:651b
Abdinghof Abbey, Paderborn, 10:500a
ᶜAbdishoᶜ bar Berīkha, 11:565b
  Book of the Pearl, 9:107b
Abdišoy (Syriac bishop), 5:540a
Abdlmseh, St., 1:520a
Abdulmesiani. See Ione Šavteli
ᶜAbdūn, Ibn, 11:213b
Abel of Denmark, king, 4:154a,b
Abel, duke of Slesvig. *See* Abel of Denmark, king
Abelard, Peter, **1:16b–20a**, 7:366a-b
  abbacy of St. Gildas, 1:17b
  Anselm of Laon and, 1:315b, 316a
  Anselm of Laon's theology school and, 12:20b–21a
  antifeminism of, 1:323b–324a
  Aristotle and, 1:460b
  attack on William of Champeaux, 12:637b
  Bernard of Clairvaux and, 2:192a
  castration and seclusion, 1:17a
  Cistercian reforms and, 8:643a
  Commentary on the Epistle to the Romans, 9:616b–617a
  condemnations of, 1:17a, 3:322b, 10:531b
    by the pope, 1:18a
    effect on legacy, 1:19b
  criticism of, in *Capitula haeresum Petri Abaelardi,* 12:191a
  derivation of cognomen, 1:16b
  Dialectica, 4:169b
  Dialogue of a Philosopher with a Christian and a Jew, 1:18a, 10:3b
  Ethica, 1:18a, 19a
  as exegete, 2:213b, 4:543b, 9:593a
  Expositio in Hexaemeron, 1:17b, 5:396b
  Gilbert of Poitiers and, 5:528a
  Heloise and, 1:16b–19b
  Historia calamitatum, 1:16b, 17b, 2:237a, 6:263b
    antifeminism in, 1:323b–324a
  Hugh of St. Victor and, 6:322b
  hymns and liturgical poetry, 6:383a, 384a, 9:713a
    Hymnarius Paraclitensis, 6:381b–382b, 9:714b
  Le Paraclet
    convent at, 1:17b
    organization of dependencies, 1:17b–18a
  Logica ingredientibus, 10:271b–272a
  as master at University of Paris, 9:404a
  in "Metamorphosis Goliae," 7:367a
  on Nile, 9:138a
  on Paul's Epistle to the Romans, 1:18a
  philosophy and theology
    adoptionism and, 1:58a
    Christology of, 3:322a
    conceptualism, 3:510a
    on Creation, 1:17b
    definition of sacrament, 9:602b
    dialectic and, 4:169b–170a
    heretical propositions, 6:198a
    interior penance, 9:604a
    knowledge of Greek masters, 9:617a
    on nature of universals, 1:18b
    nominalism of, 1:18b, 9:155a-b, 12:191a, 281b
    original sin, 9:600b
    orthodoxy of views, 1:19a
    personal intention, 9:594a
    on reason and faith, 1:18b
    terminology of, 9:616b–617a
    on the Trinity, 9:598b
    vox significativa, 1:18b

Abelard, Peter (*cont.*)
planctus cycle, 9:693a
preaching of, 10:76a
Problemata, 1:17b
pseudo-Abelardian *De generibus et speciebus,* 10:271a
Robert of Melun and, 10:434b
Rolandus and, 10:448b
Scholastic learning and, 3:357b
Sic et non, 1:17b, 18b, 4:170a, 11:57b
as a model for Peter Lombard, 9:517a
studies, 1:16b
Theologia christiana, 1:17b, 10:272a
on Trinitarian doctrine, 12:192b
Theologia "Scholarium," 1:18a
Theologia "Summi boni," 1:17a
doctrine of Trinity, 10:531b
theology school of, 12:21a-b
Thierry of Chartres and, 12:27a
Thomas Aquinas and, 1:365a
on Trinity, 1:18b–19a
Aberdeen, University of, 11:112a, 12:290b
Aberffraw, as a center of learning under Rhodri Mawr, 10:366a
Aberkios, St., as *isapostolos,* 6:560b
Abgar V (the Black) of Edessa, king, 11:562b
as saint, 1:519b
Abgesang, 5:437a-b, 8:413b
Abgitir Crabhai. See Fenian Poetry
Abi 'l-Jawād, Koran and, 1:71a
^{c}*Abīd*
ethnic makeup, 1:70a
under Ibrāhīm II, 1:71b
see also Slavery, Islamic, military service
Abiell, Guillermo, **1:20a**
cathedral at Gerona, 1:20a
Abingdon, abbey of, 2:174b
Ethelwold and, 4:518a
knights of, 7:278a
Abitur, Ibn, rabbi, on marriage, 4:607a
Abjad (Arabic alphabetic symbols), 1:383b–384a, 386b–387a
Abjuration, asylum and, 1:631b
Abkhazia. *See* Georgia
Ablaing, Willem Matthias d', *Summa Codicis Trecensis,* 6:324a
Ableiges, Jacques, d', 3:279b
Ablutions. *See* Refectory
Abner of Burgos, 3:577b, 7:82a
Teacher of Righteousness, 10:5b
Abo of Tbilisi, 5:413b–414a
Abode of Islam—Abode of War, **1:20–21**, 7:110a-b
Abode of Convenant, 1:21a
Abode of Truce, 1:21a
concept of *jihād* and, 1:20b
diplomacy and, 1:20b, 4:197a–198a
evolution of, 1:20b
Islamic Egypt, protection of Christian and Jewish population, 4:405b
law and, 1:20b–21a, 6:581a
Muslims in *Dār al-Ḥarb,* 4:199a
non-Muslims in *Dār al-Islām,* 4:198a-b
Ottomans and, 9:306a, 306b
political aspects of, 1:21a-b
relations between the two spheres, 4:198a–199a
slavery and, 11:332a, 333a
taxation system and, 1:20b
tribute payment and, 1:21a
Abortion
Christian attitudes to, 3:573a
Islamic attitudes to, 3:575b
Abrabanel, Isaac ben Judah, **1:21b–22a**, 10:6b, 75a
division of Scripture into chapters, 1:22a
exegesis, 1:21b, 4:540a-b
on Pentateuch and Prophets, 1:22a
Isaac ben Moses Arama and, 6:560b
messianic and philosophical works, 1:21b, 22a
salvation theology, defense of rabbinic concept, 1:21b
service to Ferdinand and Isabella, 1:21b
Abraham bar Ḥiyya, **1:22a**, 7:81a, 10:74b
defense of astrology, 11:91b
handbooks on astronomy, 11:91a
Hegyon ha-Nefesh, 1:22a, 4:540a
influence on Ashkenazi Hasidism, 9:579b
Jewish calendar and, 11:90b
Liber embadorum, 8:212b, 9:704b–705a, 10:472a, 11:92a
Megillat ha-Megalleh, on divine spark in man, 1:22a
scientific writings and translations, 12:135a
distribution to Christian world, 1:22a
Tower of Faith, 11:92a
Abraham bar Lipah, 11:568a
Abraham ben David of Posquières, **1:22b–23a**, 3:1b, 7:92a-b, 11:585b
Ba^{c}alei ha-Nefesh, 1:22b
cabala and, 1:23a
characteristics of writing, 1:22b, 23a
contributions to halakhic literature and methodology, 1:22b, 23a
criticism of Maimonides, 7:492a-b
hassagot and, 1:22b–23a
Hebrew translations of philosophic-scientific works, 1:23a
Ibn Gabirol and, 1:460a
law codes, 1:22b
Talmudic commentary, 10:259b
see also Jewish law
Abraham ben Meïr ibn Ezra, **1:23a-b**, 7:92b, 99a, 151b
Arabic numerals and, 10:473a, 473b, 474a
astrological works, 11:91b
challenged by Moses Naḥmanides, 9:53b
commentaries, 2:212a, 4:540a
on Exodus, 9:580a
Old Testament, 1:23b
subjects of, 1:23b
influence on Ashkenazi Hasidism, 9:579b
on Jewish calendar, 11:90b
Kli ha-Niḥoshet, 11:91a
liturgical poetry, 1:23a
mathematical works, 11:92a
piyyutim of, 7:621b
Reshit Hokhmah, 12:135b
scientific treatises, 1:23b
secular poetry, 1:23a-b
Abraham of Bet Rabban, Nestorianism and, 9:106b
Abraham (drama). *See* Hrotswitha von Gandersheim
Abraham ibn Daud, **1:24a**, 7:92b, 11:306b
chain of rabbinic tradition, 6:256b
collaboration with Dominicus Gundissalinus, 12:135a-b, 140b
historical work, 1:24a
Sefer ha-kabbalah, 6:255b, 11:583b
transfer of rabbinic authority to Spain, 6:256b–257a
translation of Ibn Sīnā's *De anima,* 12:135a-b, 140b
works by, 8:23b
Abraham and Isaac (Brome), 4:285b
Abraham of Kashkar, 3:312b, 11:564b
Abraham, *kat^{c}olikos,* vs. Kiwrion of Georgia, 1:499b, 509a
Abraham (Northampton), 4:285b
Abraham (patriarch)
circumcision and, 3:401a
Dome of the Rock and, 6:593b
Muḥammad on, 6:577a, 9:498a
in *Piers Plowman,* 7:336a
Abrégé de la cour des bourgeois, 1:599b
Abrégé des États (representative assemblies of Béarn), 10:327a
Abrogans, 5:426b, 9:233a
Abruzzi, liturgical drama in, 6:636a
Absalon of Lund, archbishop, 4:153b, 154b
in chronicles, 10:678b
commissioning of *Gesta Danorum,* 10:676a
Absidiole, **1:24a**
Absolution
from excommunication, 4:537b, 538a
Wyclif on, 12:708a
see also Confession
Abtar, al-, descendants of, 2:185b
Abū Aaron (character in Aḥima'aẓ's chronicle), 8:24a
Abu 'l-^{c}Abbās ^{c}Abd Allāh ibn Hārūn. *See* Ma$^{\supset}$mūn, al-
Abu 'l-^{c}Abbās Aḥmad ibn Abī Ya^{c}qūb. *See* Ya^{c}qūbī, al-
Abu 'l-^{c}Abbās, Marinid sultan
reign of, 8:140a
reunification of Tunis, 6:54a
Abu 'l-^{c}Abbās al-Saffāḥ, Abbasid caliph, 6:512a, 8:389a
consolidation of family rule, 1:7b
in al-Kufa, 7:307b
succession to, 3:42b
Abū ^{c}Abd Allāh. *See* Mustanṣir bi'llāh, al-
Abū ^{c}Abd Allah (emissary of the Mahdī), preaching against Aghlabids, 1:72a
Abū ^{c}Abd Allāh Muḥammad IX, 5:653b
Abū ^{c}Abd Allāh Muḥammad ibn ^{c}Abd Allāh al-Mahdī. *See* Mahdī, al-

Abū ᶜAbd Allāh al-Shīᶜī, 5:24b–25a, 6:615b
Abū ᶜAbd al-Raḥmān al-Sulamī, 9:141a
Ṭabaqāt al-ṣūfīya, 9:40a
Abū ᶜAbdallāh Musharraf ibn Muslih Saᶜdī of Shīrāz. *See* Saᶜdī of Shīrāz
Abū Aḥmad ᶜAbdallāh. *See* Mustaᶜṣim, al-
Abū ᶜAlī Aḥmad ibn al-Afḍal Kutayfāt, 5:29a
Abū ᶜAlī al-Ḥasan, 6:424b
Abū ᶜAlī al-Ḥasan ibn Alī ibn ᶜUmar al-Marrākushī, 3:457b
Abū ᶜAlī al-Ḥassan ibn ᶜAlī ibn Isḥāq al-Ṭūsī. *See* Niẓam al-Mulk
Abū ᶜAlī al-Ḥusayn ibn ᶜAbdallāh ibn Sīnā. *See* Sīnā, Ibn
Abū ᶜAlī al-Khayyāṭ, 9:704b–705a
Abu 'l-Aswār Shāwur, Shaddadid ruler, 11:217b
Abu 'l-Atāhiya, 1:400b
Abu 'l-Aᶜward, Muslim general, 9:74a
Abu 'l-ᶜAysh Ahmad, 6:413b
Abū Bakr, **1:24a–25b**, 3:488a, 6:576b, 577b
  challenge from tribal groups, 1:25a
  collection of taxes, 1:25a-b
  conversion to Islam, 1:24a
  designation of successor, 1:25b
  emigration to Medina, 1:24b
  government of, *ḥājib,* 6:54a
  Khālid ibn al-Walīd and, 7:235a-b
  Koran recension and, 7:294a
  mathematical theory, 8:212b
  military campaigns
    against Byzantines, 1:25b
    in Arabia, 6:567b–568a
    in Arabian Peninsula, 1:25b
    in Euphrates region, 1:25b
    in Syria, 1:25a, 25b
    for Valencia, 3:384b, 385b, 387b
  pilgrimage to Mecca, leadership of, 1:24b
  Quraysh and, 1:24b, 25a, 25b
  relation to Muḥammad
    election as successor, 1:24b–25a
    role in political career, 1:24b
    through marriage, 1:24a-b
  relations with ᶜAlī, 1:172a
  religious persecution of, 8:523a
  reunion of Hafsid dynasty, 6:53b–54a
  selection as first caliph, 1:373b, 3:32a, 33b
  Shīᶜa and, 11:226b
  Sufism and, 6:585b
  sunna and, 11:510b, 513b
  vs. Tamar, 11:587a
Abū Bakr al-Ḥasan, 9:705a
Abū Bakr ibn Jahān Pahlawān, 6:419b
Abū Bakr ibn Muḥammad ibn al-Ḥusayn. *See* Karajī, al-
Abū Bakr ibn Mujāhid, 7:294b
Abū Bakr ibn ᶜUmar, chief of the Lamtūna, 1:198b–199a
Abū Bakr Muḥammad al-Kalābādhī, *Kitāb al-taᶜarruf,* 9:40a
Abū Bakr al-Muṭahhar Jamālī, *Farahnāma,* 4:445b
Abū Bakr of Ricote, 8:562b
Abu 'l-Baqāᵓ al-Balawī, 9:651b
Abū Dāwūd, collection of *ḥadīth,* 6:47b
Abu 'l-Faḍl ᶜAbd al-Raḥmān ibn Abī Bakr Jalāl al-Dīn. *See* Suyūṭī, al-
Abu 'l-Faḍl Aḥmad ibn Abī Ṭāhir Ṭayfūr, *Kitāb Baghdād,* 8:436a
Abu 'l-Faḍl Bayhaqī, *Taᵓrīkh-i Masᶜūdī,* 6:251a
Abu 'l-Faḍl ibn Mubārak, *ᶜIyār-i Dānish,* 6:508b
Abu 'l-Faraj. *See* Bar Hebraeus
Abu 'l-Faraj al-Iṣfahānī, *Kitāb al-aghānī,* 1:381a, 8:566b
Abu 'l-Fidāᵓ, 5:333a
  governorship of Ḥamā, 6:82b
  on Zakᶜarē, 1:485b
Abū Firās, 1:403a
Abū Firās Tammām ibn Ghālib. *See* Farazdaq, al-
Abū Ḥafṣ ᶜUmar, chief of the Hintāta, 1:194a, 194b, 195a
Abū Ḥalim. *See* Elias III, patriarch
Abū Ḥāmid al-Andalusī, 5:393b
Abū Ḥāmid al-Gharnāṭī, 5:332a
Abū Ḥanīfa al-Nuᶜmān ibn Thābit ibn Zūṭā, **1:26a–27a**, 6:581b
  ancestry, 1:26a
  dietary laws and, 4:179b
  imprisonment, 1:26a
  on interest-bearing loans, 12:340a
  Islamic creeds and, 11:511b
  legal doctrines, 1:26a-b
    comparison with contemporaries, 1:26b
    personal judgment and analogical reasoning, 1:26b
    on precedents of the Prophet, 1:26b
  as proponent of Murjiᵓism, 1:26b
Abu 'l-Ḥasan ᶜAlī ibn Būyeh. *See* ᶜImād al-Dawla
Abu 'l-Ḥasan, Marinid caliph
  expansionism, 8:139b–140a
    occupation of Tunis, 8:139a
Abu 'l-Ḥasan, Marinid sultan, relations with Hafsids, 6:54a
Abu 'l-Hasan Meir ibn Kamniel, 7:98b
Abū Hāshim, Shīᶜa and, 11:226b–227a
Abū Hāshim al-Jubbāᵓī, 8:655b
Abū Ḥātim al-Rāzī, Ḥamīd al-Dīn al-Kirmānī and, 6:616b
Abu 'l-Hayjā, Hamdanid ruler, administration of Mosul, 8:500b
Abū Ḥayyān, 5:653a
Abū Ḥayyān al-Tawḥīdī, *Kitāb al-imtāᶜ wa'l-muᵓānasa (The Book of Enlivenment and Good Company),* 1:381a
Abu 'l-Hudhayl al-ᶜAllāf, 8:655b
Abu 'l-Ḥusayn Aḥmad ibn Abi Shujāᶜ. *See* Muᶜizz al-Dawla
Abū ᶜInān, Marinid sultan, 2:130b
  assumption of *amīr al-muᵓminīn* title, 8:140a
  military conquests, 8:140a
Abū ᶜĪsā of Isfahan, 7:209b
Abū Isḥāq Ibrāhīm ibn Yaḥyā al-Naqqash. *See* Zarqālī, al-
Abū Isḥāq Īnjū, patronage of Ḥāfiẓ, 6:51b
Abū Isḥāq Muḥammad. *See* Muᶜtaṣim, al-
Abū Jaᶜfar. *See* Manṣūr, al-
Abū Jaᶜfar Manṣūr. *See* Mustanṣir, al-
Abū Jahl, chief of Makhzūm clan, Battle of Badr and, 2:42b, 43a
Abū Kālījār, Buyid ruler, Istakhr and, 11:252a
Abū Kāmil, 7:212a
Abu 'l-Kāsim al-Zahrāwī, *Chirurgia,* translated by Gerard of Cremona, 8:249a
Abu 'l-Khayr Ḥammād al-Dabbās, 7:111b
Abū Lahab, 6:576b
Abu 'l-Maᶜālī, loss of Aleppo emirate, 6:86a
Abū Maᶜshar, 1:385b, 386b
  on astronomy, 1:616b, 617b, 618b
  Introductorium maius in astronomiam, 10:473b, 12:139a
  Kitāb al-madkhal ᶜilmᵓaḥkām al-nujūm, 1:618b
Abū Mikhnaf (*d.* 774), 7:307b
Abū Mina, 3:585b–586a
Abu 'l-Misk Kāfūr, governorship of, 4:405b
Abū Muḥammad ᶜAbd al-Wāḥid al-Ḥafṣī, appointment as viceroy of Ifrīqiya, 6:52b
Abū Mūsā al-Ashᶜarī, 6:569a, 11:284b
Abū Muslim
  alliance with Abbasids, 1:7a-b
  assassination of, 1:7b
  al-Manṣūr and, 8:88b
  the reemergence of Mazdakism and, 8:238a
  revolt against Marwān II ibn Muḥammad, 12:274a
Abū Naṣr ᶜAbd Allāh ibn ᶜAlī al-Sarrāj, *Kitāb al-lumaᶜ,* 9:40a
Abū Naṣr Manṣūr ibn ᶜIrāq, teacher of Bīrūnī, 2:248b
Abū Nuᶜaym al-Iṣfahānī, *Ḥilyat al-awliyāᵓ,* 9:40a
Abū Nuwās, **1:27a–28b**, 1:400b, 401a, 403a
  death of, 1:27b
  jail terms, 1:27b–28a
  licentious behavior, 1:27b
  panegyrics, 1:27b
  patronage of work, 1:27b
  poetry
    diction and imagery, 1:28a
    drinking songs, 1:28a
    hunting poems, 1:28a
    love poems, 1:28a-b
  religious beliefs, 1:27b
  stories about in *Thousand and One Nights,* 12:50a
  teachers, 1:27a-b
  zajel and, 8:563b
Abu 'l-Qāsim, 4:582a, 9:705a
  on equatorium, 11:98a
  on lajvard, 7:319b
Abu 'l-Qāsim ᶜAbd al-Karīm al-Qushayrī, *Al-Risālat al-Qushayrīya,* 9:40a
Abu 'l-Qāsim Anūjūr, 6:417a
Abu 'l-Qāsim Bābur (nephew of Ulugh-Beg), 12:57b
Abu 'l-Qāsim ibn ᶜAbbād, ruler of Seville, 11:213b
Abu 'l-Qāsim al-Junayd, 9:40b

Abu 'l-Qāsim al-Qushairī, 9:141a
Abu 'l-Rayḥān, **2:248–251**
Abū Sa^c^d al-^c^Alā^ɔ^ ibn Sahl, optical theory, 9:242a
Abū Sa^c^d ^c^Ali al-Mukharrimī, 7:111b
Abū Sa^c^d Ibrāhīm al-Tustarī, 5:357b
Abū Sa^c^īd ibn Abi'l-Khayr, 7:238b
Abū Sa^c^īd, Ilkhanid ruler, 6:420b
death of, 6:505a, 8:475a
Abū Sa^c^īd al-Jannābī, 6:616a
Abu Sa^c^īd al-Sizjī, astrolabe of, discussed by Bīrūnī, 2:250a
Abū Sa^c^īd, Timurid ruler, 12:57b–58a
honorary title of *küregen* and, 12:58b
Uzun Ḥasan and, 12:342b
Abū Sa^c^īd ^c^Uthmān II, Marinid caliph, cultural advances, 8:139b
Abū Sa^c^īd ^c^Uthmān III, Marinid caliph
Moroccan principalities, 8:140a
murder of, 8:140a
Abū Salama
assassination of, 1:7b
relations with Abbasids, 1:7b
Abu Sarga, church of, 3:588b
Abū Sufyān, **1:28b–29b**
battles
Badr (624), 1:28b–29a, 2:42b
Ḥunayn, 1:29a
al-Khandaq (627), 1:29a
Uḥud (625), 1:29a
Yarmuk, 1:29b
biographical information, 1:28b
conversion to Islam, 1:29a
relations with Muḥammad, 1:29a
boycott of Prophet's clan, 1:28b
"conciliation of hearts," 1:29a
Abu 'l-Su^c^ūd. *See* *Fatwā*
Abū Ṭālib, **1:29b–30a**, 6:576a, 576b
protection of Muḥammad, 1:29b–30a
rule of Hāshim clan, 1:29b
spurious biographical material on, 1:30a
Abū Ṭālib Muḥammad ibn ^c^Alī al-Ḥārithī al-Makkī, *Qūt al-qulūb*, 9:40a
Abū Ṭālib (potter), decorative schemes on bowls, 1:68b
Abū Tammām al-Ḥabīb ibn Aws, 1:400b, 617b
on capture of Amorium, 8:500b
Abu l'-Ṭayyib Aḥmad ibn al-Ḥusayn. *See* Mutanabbī, al-
Abū ^c^Ubayd Allāh Mu^c^āwiya ibn ^c^Ubayd Allāh (al-Mahdī's vizier), new system of taxation, 8:47a
Abū ^c^Ubayd al-Thaqafī, 6:568b
Abū ^c^Ubayda ibn al-Jarrāḥ, 6:568a, 568b
Beirut and, 2:164a
Abū al-Walīd Muḥammad ibn Aḥmad. *See* Rushd, Ibn
Abū Yaḥyā Abū Bakr, occupation of Fēs, 8:138a
Abū Ya^c^qūb Yūsuf, Almohad caliph
expedition to Spain in 1171–1172, 1:194b
philosophical interests, 10:571b
Seville and, 11:213b
Abū Yazīd, 12:744a
Abū Yazīd (Nukkār chief), 11:139b
Abū Yūsuf, Islamic dietary laws and, 4:179b
Abū Yūsuf Ya^c^qūb, Almohad caliph, 10:42b
against the Maliki school, 1:195a
victory over Castile in 1195, 1:195a
Abū Yūsuf Ya^c^qūb ibn Isḥaq. *See* Kindī, al-
Abū Yūsuf Ya^c^qūb al-Manṣūr, construction of Casbah, 8:151a
Abū Yūsuf Ya^c^qūb, Marinid sultan
assumption of *amīr al-Muslimīn* title, 8:138b
military conquests
Marrakech, 8:138b
siege of Tlemcen, 8:139a
Spain, 8:139a
Abū Zakarīya^ɔ^ al-Rāzī, Ḥamīd al-Dīn al-Kirmānī and, 6:616b
Abū Zakariyā^ɔ^ Yaḥyā, governor of Salé
alliance with *shurafā^ɔ^*, 8:140a-b
Portuguese campaign, 8:140a-b
Abū Zakariyā^ɔ^ Yaḥyā, Hafsid ruler
government of, nepotism, 6:53a
military exploits
capture of Tlemcen, 6:53a
losses in Spain, 6:53a
rule of Ifrīqiya, 6:52b–53a
trade treaties, 6:53a-b
Abubacer. *See* Ṭufayl, Ibn
Abulafia, Abraham ben Samuel, **1:27a**, 3:2b
promotion of ecstatic cabala, 1:27a
Abulafia, Meir, 11:585b
Talmudic commentary, 10:259b
Abulafia, Samuel ben Meir ha-Levi, 7:82a
Abulafia, Todros ben Joseph ha-Levi, 7:71a, 81b
love poetry, 6:127a
Abulafia, Todros ben Judah ha-Levi, Hebrew *muwashshaḥs*, 11:447b
Abułamrenc^c^ family, church of S. Grigor in Ani in Širak, 1:292a-b (*illus.*)
Abusahl (*fl.* 972), 1:482b
descendants of, 1:483a
Abydos, battle at (989), 2:118b
Abyssinia, **1:30a–33a**
Aethiopia credet Deo, 1:32a
alliance with anti-Monophysite Christians, 1:32a
ancient history, 1:30a-b
boundaries, 1:30b, 31a (map)
Christianization, 1:30b
Greco-Roman, 1:31b–32a
crusade against Saracens, 1:32b
Greek cultural influence, 1:32a
maritime trade, 1:30b
Muslim ambitions in the Red Sea and, 9:74b
Najrān and, 9:55a
Prester John in, 10:118a–119b
relations with Europe, 1:32a–33a
alliance against Islam, 1:32b
attempt at Christian unity, 1:32b–33a
pilgrimages to Jerusalem, 1:32a
Portugal, 4:562a
rise of Islam, 1:30b
coastal region, 1:31a
through *jihad*, 1:31a-b
Solomonid dynasty, 1:32b
South Arabian expedition, 1:32a
successor to the kingdom of Axum, 2:17a
under Emperor Ezana, 1:30b
Zagwe dynasty and ecclesiastical revival, 1:32a-b
Abyssinia, church of
Alexandrian rite in, 1:155a–156a
litanies of, 7:590b
Abyssinian alphabet. *See* Alphabets, Ethiopic
Acacian Schism. *See* Schisms, East-West church
Acacius of Constantinople. *See* Akakios, patriarch of Constantinople
Acacius of Melitene, bishop, 5:540a-b
Armenian church and, 1:498b, 507b
Academia Isotropolitana, 6:348b
Acallam na Senórach, **1:33a–34b**, 6:528b, 531a-b, 549a
Bóraime Laigen, 1:34a
Cath Finntrága, 1:34a
development of ballad form and, 1:33b
dinnshenchas, 1:33b
frame-tale, 1:34a
plot summary, 1:33b
in-tales, 1:33b–34a
on Finn and Fiana, 1:33b–34a
motivation for, 1:34a
preservation, 1:34a
romantic interludes, 1:34a
Acardus of Arroasia, *Solomon's Temple*, 7:365a
Ačars, 5:403b
Acca of Hexham, bishop, Bede and, 2:154a
Acca Larentia. *See* Jacopo della Quercia
Accademia Pontaniana (Naples), 9:59b
Accent (phonetics). *See* Ictus
Accentus acutus. *See* *Virga*
Accentus gravis. *See* *Punctum*
Acceptatio of Mainz (1439), 3:367a, 526a, 654a
Accessus ad auctores, **1:34b–35a**
applications of, 1:35a
formulations, 1:34b
source of procedure, 1:34b
topics, variation in, 1:34b
verbal vs. speculative and practical disciplines, 1:35a
see also Conrad of Hirsau
Accho. *See* Acre
Acciaiuoli
company in Florence, 2:77a, 78b
vs. Catalans, 7:379b
Acciaiuoli, Antonio, 7:381b
Acciaiuoli, Francesca, 7:381b
Acciaiuoli, Nerio
conquest of Athens and, 3:157a
death of (1394), 7:381b
as lord of Corinth, 7:381a
purchase of Vostitsa, 7:380a
Acciaiuoli, Nerio II (*d.* 1451), 7:381b
Acciaiuoli, Niccolò, grand seneschal at the Naples Angevin court, Boccaccio and, 2:287a, 288b–289a
Accidence, Latin. *See* Latin language

Accident, **1:35a-b**
Accidental (music), 8:598b–599a, 600a
Acclamation. *See Laudes*
Acclamations, **1:35b–36a**
  ceremonial salutes, *Vive le roi,* 1:36a
  chanting of laudatory phrases, 1:35b–36a
  in coronation ceremonies, 1:35b
  derivation
    Franks, Goths, and Anglo-Saxons, 1:35b
    Germanic, 1:35b, 36a
    Roman, 1:36a
    Viking customs, 1:35b
  in electoral process, 1:35b, 36a
Accounting, **1:36a–43a**
  arrangement of entries, 1:40b
  Charlemagne's system of, 8:428a-b
  commercial
    factors, 1:40b
    partnerships, 1:40b
    types of, 1:40a-b
  double-entry method
    account book of *massari* of Genoa, 1:41a
    advantages of, 1:41b–42a
    in Italy, 1:41a, 42a
    origin of, 1:41a
    requirements for, 1:41a-b
    rise of capitalism and, 1:42a-b
  efficiency of, 1:42a
    Avignon papacy, 1:39a
    French exchequer, 1:38b–39a
  English pipe rolls and, 9:662a–663b
  in estate management, 1:39a-b, 4:513b–514a, 601b
    "extents," 1:39b–40a
    household account, 1:40a
    land account, 1:39b
    reeve or bailiff, 1:39b
    standardization of, 1:39b
    stock account, 1:39b, 40a
    works account, 1:39b
  examples
    budget of Roman church from 1480–1481, 1:39a
    commercial account book, 1:40a-b
    French account of 1221, 1:39a
    manorial, 1:39b
    murage and pavage accounts in Shrewsbury (England), 1:39a
  in Exchequer, 1:37b–38a, 4:531b–532a
    Capetian, 1:38a
    English kings, 1:37b–38a
    Flemish, 1:38a
    Norman, 1:38a
    process of, 1:37b
    special commissioners, 1:38a
  extractus memorandorum, 1:38b
  fraud in, 1:37a
  information required for, 1:38b
  manorial, 12:533b
  papal
    cameral council, 1:37a
    cameral treasurer, 1:37b
    camerarius, 1:37a, 38b
    centralization of, 1:39a
    depository, 1:37b
    liber censuum, 1:38b
    use of envoys, 1:37a
    personal responsibility, 1:37a
  profit calculations, 1:40a, 40b
  purpose of, 1:40b
    justification process, 1:36a-b
  stewardship
    audit, 1:36b
    charge and discharge, 1:36b
    prescription for, 1:36b–37a
    purpose of, 1:36b
    to *missi,* 1:37a
  subdivision of accounts, 1:41b
  Teutonic Knights
    account books of factors, 1:40b
    inventories of assets and liabilities, 1:38a
    records kept by *Treszler,* 1:38a
  town and city administrations, 1:38a-b
  see also Exchequer; Pipe rolls
Accroachment treason. *See* Kingship; Treason
Accursius
  Glossa ordinaria, 2:29a, 5:567b–568a, 6:326b
    influence of on Peter Lombard, 9:517a
  glosses on *Corpus iuris civilis,* 11:691b
  Innocent IV and, 6:465b–466a
  legal maxims, 8:232a
  Rogerius and, 10:444a
Accusatio, 6:478b, 479a-b
Acequieros, 6:557b, 558a
Acerba, L'. See Cecco d'Ascoli
Achaea (Latin principality), 7:379a, 381a
  relations with
    Latin Empire of Constantinople, 7:346b, 347a
    Naples, 7:381b
Achaemenid Empire, 6:505b
  conquered by Alexander the Great, 5:18a
  proto-Georgians in, 5:419b
  rule over Caucasia, 3:195b
  seals of, 11:122a
Achaemenids
  divine legitimacy, 10:611b–612a
  Parthians and, 9:443b
  rock carvings at Naqsh-i Rustam, 9:61a
  Sasanians and, 1:451b, 10:666a
Achaia-Morea. *See* Latin states in Greece
Achard, missing works by, 12:22a
Achard (Aichardus), **1:43a-b**
  building of Cistercian church at Himmerod, 1:43a
Achilles Tatius of Alexandria, *Leucippe and Kleitophon,* as a source for Boccaccio, 2:278a, 282b
Ackermann aus Böhmen, Der, **1:43b–45b**, 8:356b
  development of New High German, 1:44b
  humanism and, 1:44b, 45a
  Johannes of Teplá, 1:43b
  Latin influence, 1:44a, 44b
  plowman, prototype for Renaissance characterization, 1:44b
  preservation in manuscripts, 1:44a
  relation to other genres, 1:45a
  relation to *Tkadleček,* 1:44a-b
  sources for, 1:44a
  style and form
    Aristotelian rhetoric, 1:44a
    notarial literary mannerism, 1:44b
  theological influences
    mysticism and medieval sermon, 1:44b
    Peripatetic doctrine of eternity, 1:45a
Acolyte, 3:441a, 442a
  see also Clergy
Acominatus, Niketas. *See* Niketas Choniates
Acoustics
  Gerbert of Aurillac on, 8:640a
  in musical treatises, 8:640a
  Pythagorean, 8:636b, 648b
"Acquisition" (Islamic doctrine), 6:584a
Acre
  as capital of Latin Kingdom, 4:25a–26b
  conquered by
    Mamluks, 2:19a, 4:32b, 54b, 11:562a
    Saladin, 4:31a
    Third Crusade, 2:23b, 4:31b, 409b
  criminal exile to, 9:660a
Acre, Battle of (1191), 10:626a
Acre Bible, 2:219a
Acre (unit of measure), **1:45b**
  English, 12:585a
  regional variation, 1:45b, 12:588b
  Scots, 12:585a
  standardization of, 1:45b
Acrocorinth
  besieged (1397), 7:381b
  seized by Geoffroi de Villehardouin, 7:378a
Acrostics—wordplay, **1:45b–46b**, 1:218a
  diagonals, 1:46a
  Latin hexameters, 1:45b–46a
  in Latin literature, 7:362b
  relation between meaning and being and, 1:46a-b
Acta Archelai, 8:84a
Acta sanctorum, arrangement of, 2:519a
Acta sanctorum Hiberniae. See Colgan, John
Actes des apôtres, performance of at Bourges, 4:284a-b
Acton Burnell, Statute of (1283), 11:468b
Acton (garment), 1:524b
Actors
  costumes for, 4:270b
  names for, 4:278b
  professional
    in England, 4:270b
    in France, 4:266a
  traveling troupes, 4:286a, 287b
Acts of the Apostles (Latin epic). *See* Arator
Acts of the Apostles (tapestry), 11:596b
Acts of the Bishops of Auxerre. See Radulphus Glaber
Acts of Peter, on Simon Magus, 8:33b
Acts of Ravennika (1210), Villehardouin and, 12:448b
Acts of Thomas. See Apocrypha, Irish

Actualism, **1:46b**
  in Christianized Aristotelianism, 1:46b
  Neoplatonized version, 1:46b
Actus beati Francisci et sociorum eius, 6:660a
Acute arch. *See* Arch
Ad abolendam. See Lucius III, pope
Ad adolescentes, quomodo possint ex gentilium libris fructum capere. See Basil the Great of Caesarea, St.
Ad candidam casam, 9:139a
"Ad Eustochium." *See* Jerome, St.
Ad extirpanda. See Innocent IV, pope
Ad extra. See Trinitarian doctrine
Ad intra. See Trinitarian doctrine
Ad nostrum. See Vienne, Council of
Ad pauca respicientes. See Oresme, Nicole
Ada group. *See* Pre-Romanesque art, Carolingian renaissance
Adab, 3:574b, 6:590a, 7:243a
Adab al-kabīr, al-. See Arabic literature, prose
Adab al-kātib. See Qutayba, Ibn
Aḍab al-samāʿ. See Khurdādhbih, Ibn
Adalard of Corbie, abbot, statutes of, 4:512a
Adalbero of Augsburg, bishop, *Chronica* revision by, 10:290a
Adalbero of Laon, **1:46b–47a**, 10:317a
  Carmen ad Robertum regem, 1:46b
Adalbero of Rheims, archbishop, Sylvester II and, 11:552b
Adalbert II of Calw, monastery of Hirsau and, 6:231a-b
Adalbert of Bremen, **1:47a-b**, 7:543a
  acquisition of diocesan territories, 10:684b
  in Adam of Bremen's *Gesta Hammaburgensis ecclesiae pontificum,* 1:50a
  archbishopric of, 1:47a
  Billungs and, 2:235a
  decline of papacy and, 1:47a
  evangelization of Scandinavians and northern Slavs, 1:47a
  exile in Hamburg-Bremen, 1:47a-b
  patronage of Henry IV, 1:47a
Adalbert of Mainz, archbishop, on the study of medicine, 8:256b
Adalbert, St., **1:47b**, 9:719a, 723b
  conversion of Eastern Europe and, 9:302a
  life of, 7:118b
  martyred by Old Prussians in 997, 2:64b
  Stephen I of Hungary and, 11:477b, 478a
Adalbert of Samaria
  ars dictaminis and, 10:358b
  Praecepta dictaminum, 4:174a-b
  school of rhetoric, University of Bologna, 2:312b
Adalbert of Trier, mission to the Kievan Rus, 12:435b
Adalbold of Utrecht, **1:47b–48a**, 9:701b
  on Boethius, 10:270b
  literary works, 1:47b
  Sylvester II and, 11:552b
Adalgar, count (9th century), 9:143a
Adalgisel-Grimo clan, Pepin I (of Landen) and, 9:499a
Adam of Balsham. *See* Adam of the Little Bridge
Adam de la Bassée, **1:48a**
  Ludus super Anticlaudianum, 7:369a
  use of music in, 1:48a
Adam le Bossu. *See* Adam de la Halle
Adam of Bremen, **1:49b–51a**, 5:297a, 397b
  on the Balts, 2:62a, 7:602b–603a
  Gesta Hammaburgensis ecclesiae pontificum, 1:49b–50b, 4:152a, 12:457b
    on Adalbert of Bremen, 1:50a
    derivations of, 10:535a-b
    Descriptio insularum aquilonis, 1:50a-b
    on Nordic history, 1:50a
    on Saxon history and culture, 1:50a
    as source for *Gesta Danorum,* 10:677a
    on Vinland, 12:428a
  historical method, 1:50b
  on missionary activities, 6:151b–152a
  on pagan idols at Uppsala, 12:417b
  sources used, 1:50b
  on Swedish kingship, 11:530a
Adam of Buckfield (*d.* before 1294), Robert Grosseteste and, 1:461b
Adam of Dryburgh, *Fourfold Exercise of the Cell,* 9:19a
Adam of Fulda, 3:658a, 8:648a-b
Adam de la Halle, **1:48a–49b**, 3:536b
  in Bamberg manuscript, 2:68b
  biographical material on, 1:48a-b
  Congé, 1:48b
  courtly song, 5:283a
  Fines amouretes ai, 12:458b
  Jeu de la feuillée, 1:48b, 49a, 4:264a, 577a, **7:62a-b**
    elimination of stage/audience barrier, 5:264b
    setting, 9:636a-b
    taverns in, 6:475a, 476a
    transposition of lyric congé, 5:264a
    use of language in, 5:264b
    use of proverb in, 10:191b
  Jeu du pèlerin, 1:48b
  Jeu de Robin et de Marion, 1:49a, 4:264a, 283b, **7:62b**
    dramatization of *pastourelle,* 5:264a-b, 9:636b
    prologue, 9:636b
  polyphonic works, 1:49a-b
  service to Robert II of Artois, 1:48b
  singing career, 1:48b
  songs, 1:49a
  study in Paris, 1:48b
  "Viderunt omnes" and, 12:411a
  see also Bodel, Jean
Adam of the Little Bridge, **1:51b–52b**
  Anselm of Laon's theology school and, 12:20b
  Ars disserendi, 1:52a, 4:170a
  canon of Notre Dame, 1:52a
  De utensilibus, 1:52a
  use of Aristotle, 4:170a
Adam Lock. *See* Lock, Adam
Adam de Marisco. *See* Marsh, Adam
Adam Marsh. *See* Marsh, Adam
Adam óenathair na ndóene, 6:542a
Adam (OT character), in Manichaeism, 8:85a
Adam of Parma. *See* Salimbene
Adam de Parvo Ponte. *See* Adam of the Little Bridge
Adam of Perseigne, 10:76a
Adam Precentor. *See* Adam of St. Victor
Adam le Roi. *See* Adenet le Roi
Adam of St. Denis, abbot, Suger and, 11:502b, 503a, 503b
Adam of St. Victor, **1:51a-b**, 9:714a
  hymns of, 7:365b
  poetry, 1:1b
  sequences, 1:51a-b, 6:381b, 11:167a, 12:211a
Adam Scotus, 10:87a
Adam Wodeham
  nominalism and, 9:157a
  Ockham and, 9:209b, 212b
Adamitism, 6:375b
Adamnan, St., **1:52b–53a**, 11:113b
  on Columba, 7:362a
  conversion of northern Irish, 1:52b
  De locis sanctis, 1:53a
  hagiographic style of, 6:542b
  Lex innocentium, 1:52b
  role in Easter controversy, 1:52b
  Vita Columbae, 1:52b–53a, 6:258a
  works attributed to, 1:53a
Adamus Parvipontanus. *See* Adam of the Little Bridge
Adana, Council of (1316/1317), 3:394b
Adarga, 1:528a-b
Adarnase I Bagratuni of Ḳʿartʿli-Iberia, king, 5:405b
Adarnase II of Kʿartʿli-Iberia, king
  Ašot II and, 1:482a
  vs. Smbat I, 1:481b
Adarnase IV of Kʿartʿli-Iberia, king, 2:48b, 5:405b
Adarnase of Tao, 4:113b
Adbo (Abbo) of St. Germain-des-Prés, **1:53a-b**
  Bella parisiacae urbis, 1:53a-b, 7:354b, 362b
Adda bar Ahaba, computing *tekufot,* 3:27a
Adelaide (daughter of Rudolf II of Burgundy, wife of Lothar), 5:476a
Adelard of Bath, **1:53b–54a**, 1:611b, 11:273b–274a
  De eodem et diverso, 1:53b–54a, 10:271a
    on philosophical dualism, 4:298a
  on different parts of the brain, 2:244a
  falconry treatise, vernacular translations of, 12:140b
  metaphysical thought, 1:53b–54a
  Quaestiones naturales, 1:53b
    Hebrew adaptation of, 12:134b
  scientific works, 1:53b
  studies in Spain, 7:561b
  translations by, 12:137b, 138a
  travels of, 12:160b
Adelard of Ghent, *Vita Dunstani,* 4:311b
Adelelmus. *See* Aléaume

Adelheid of Poland, marriage to Géza, 8:443a
Adelhelm, count, Robert the Strong and, 3:89b
Adelman of Liège, **1:54b**
Adelperga (daughter of the Lombard king Desiderius), Paul the Deacon and, 9:467a, 467b
Adelwîp. *See* Hadewijch of Antwerp
Adémar of Chabannes, **1:54b**
on the apostolicity of St. Martial, 10:298a
cult of St. Martial, 1:54b
Historiae, 10:247a
Adémar of Le Puy, bishop, 3:449b
Tancred and, 11:589b
Ademar (scribe), *Aesop,* 4:572a
Aden, 12:724a
maritime trade and, 11:247a
Adenet le Roi, **1:54b–55a**
Berte aus grans piés, 3:261b, 9:634a
depiction of women, 1:55a
Buevon de Conmarchis, 1:55a, 3:261b, 9:634a
Cleomadés, 1:55a
sources for, 9:634b
Enfances Ogier, 6:275a-b, 9:634a
source for, 1:55a
roi des ménestrels of Guy of Dampierre, 1:55a
Adgar, **1:55a-b**
Gracial, 1:55b
Adhān, 8:560a, 561b
development of, 8:521b
Jewish and Christian influences, 8:521b
when issued, 8:521a
Adhemar of Monteil, 7:535a
Adīb, writing of encyclopedias and, 4:444b–445a
ᶜĀḍid, al-, Fatimid caliph, 5:29a-b
ᶜĀdil, al-, Ayyubid sultan, in Damascus, 4:83b
ᶜĀdil Ṭūmān Bāy, al-, Mamluk sultan, vs. al-Suyūṭī, 11:520b
ᶜĀdiliyya, al- (Ayyubid mausoleum in Damascus), 2:21b
Adiši Gospels, 5:411 *(illus.)*
ᶜAdīy. *See* Imruᵓ al-Qays
Adjustable sling (armor). *See* Guige
Admetus de Aureliana, Robert de Handlo and, 8:646b
Administration, Islamic. *See* Islamic administration
Administration, royal. *See* Household, royal
Administrative records
as demographic evidence, 4:137a–139b
in royal household, England, 6:300b, 301a
wardrobe and, 6:302a
see also Secretariat
Admiral, **1:55b–56a**
derivation of the term, 1:55b
duties of, 1:56a
in Northern Europe, 9:83a
origins of, 9:80b–81a
Admiralty, court of, **1:56a–57a**
establishment of, 1:56a
"laws of Oléron" and, 1:56a-b
opposition to, 1:57a
settlement of piracy claims, 1:56b
under Edward III, 1:56b–57a
Admonitio generalis, 3:108b, 109b
Ado of Vienne, martyrology, 8:162a
Adolf II of Holstein, count
foundation of Lübeck by, 5:632b–633a
refounding of Lübeck, 7:680a
Adolf of Nassau, king of Germany
deposition by electors, 5:492a
German representative assemblies and, 10:330a
Matteo Visconti and, 12:464b
treaty with Edward I, 4:209b
Waldstätte and, 11:541b
Adolf of Schauenburg, count, dispossession of, 5:460a
Adolph of Liège, bishop, regulation of wine sales, 12:120a
Adonias saga, 10:395a
description of a beautiful woman in, 10:396a
Adonis, cult of, 9:1b
Adopted children. *See* Children
Adoptionism, **1:57b–58a**
against Trinitarian doctrine, 12:190b
Armenian Paulicians and, 9:469b
Christology and, 3:321b
condemnnation of, 1:57b, 143a
Migetius' teachings on Trinity, 1:57b
Nestorianism and, 1:57b
Peter Abelard and, 1:58a
in Spain, 3:677a
suppression of
by Charlemagne, 9:62b
by St. Paulinus of Aquileia, 9:470a
see also Leo III, pope
"Adoro te devote," 6:382a
Adrevald de Fleury, 1:110a
Adrian I, pope
canon law and, 3:349a
Charlemagne and, 8:377a, 9:374a
independence of papacy maintained by, 3:110a
Jews and, 7:95a
martyrs' burials and, 3:154b
Roman aqueducts and, 10:519b
Roman nobility and, 10:521b
Roman Office and, 4:230a
Adrian II, pope, 3:632a
Boris of Bulgaria and, 2:403a
Cyril and Methodios and, 2:299b, 4:73b
Nicholas I and, 9:121b
Adrian IV, pope, **1:58a-b**
abbacy of St. Rufus, 1:58a
Arnold of Brescia and, 1:58b, 540a
coronation of Frederick I Barbarossa, 1:58b, 5:480a
death of, 5:480b
Henry II of England and, 6:517a-b
Laudabiliter, 1:58b
reorganization of Scandinavian church, 1:58a
vs. Frederick I Barbarossa, 1:58b, 2:180a
William I of Sicily and, 1:58b, 5:480a
Adrian V, pope, suspension of *Ubi periculum,* 3:524a
Adrianople, **1:59a**
sacked by Samuil, 2:119a
Adrianople, Battle of (378), 2:90b, 3:201a, 6:352b, 12:469b
in Robert de Clari's *Conquête de Jerusalem,* 10:431b–432a
Adrianople, Battle of (1205), 7:347a, 9:116a
Adriatic Sea, Venice and, 12:386a-b
Adso of Montier-en-Der
on millennialism, 8:385b
treatise on Antichrist, 1:321b
ᶜAḍūd al-Dawla, Buyid emir, 2:436a, 6:424b, 513b, 11:252b
invasion of Mesopotamia, 6:85b
Adufe, 8:563a
Adulis, control of Red Sea trade, 1:30b
Adultery
in courtly love, 3:668a–669b, 672a-b
in Icelandic saga, 4:613a
Islamic law and, 4:598b
shivaree and, 8:28b
Ādur Gušnasp, sacked (622), 12:715a
Ādurbād ī Mahraspandān, religious ordeal, 10:601a
Advaita Vedanta, correspondences with Druzism, 9:3b
Advent, **1:59a-b**
fasting, four-day tradition, 1:59b
Adventus. See Entry into Jerusalem; Translation of saints
Adversus haereses. See Irenaeus
Adversus Jovinianum. See Jerome, St.
Adversus Judaeorum inveteratum duritiem. See Peter the Venerable
Adversus nationes. See Arnobius the Elder
Advocate, **1:59b–60a**
compensation of, 1:59b
in dealings with land grants, 1:59b
Advowson. *See* Presentation
Adz, in shipbuilding, 11:243b
Ælla (Ælle). *See* Ella
Ælnoth, *Vita et passio,* 11:522b
Æsir, **1:62b–63b**, 8:395b
conflict with Vanir, 1:63a
doom of the gods (*Ragnarǫk*), 1:62b
etymology, 1:62b–63a
Freyr, 5:297a
in *Gylfaginning,* 11:354a
Njǫrðr and, 9:146b
Skaði and, 11:325a
see also Scandinavian mythology; Vanir
Ættarfylgja, 5:335b
Ættartölur, in *Sturlunga saga,* 11:497a, 498a
Áed Find, king of Dál Riata, 4:78b
Áed Sláne, **1:60b–61a**
kingship of Tara, 1:60b
rule of his descendants in Brega, 1:60b–61a
successors and, 12:242a
see also Uí Néill
Áedán mac Gabráin, **1:60a-b**, 4:78a-b
alliance with Áed mac Ainmuirech, 1:60a
battle of Degsastán (603), 1:60a
succession to kingship, 1:60a
Aeddi (Eddius Stephanus), **1:61a**
Life of Wilfrid, 1:61a, 6:67b
as source for Frithegod, 5:302a

Aedesius of Cappadocia, 9:97b
Aedicula, **1:61a**
Aegean islands
relations with
Latin Empire of Constantinople, 7:346a, 346b
Venice, 7:376b, 377a
Aegidius Romanus. *See* Egidius Colonna
Aelfled. *See* Ethelfled
Aelfric, **1:61b–62b**, 1:281b
Bible translations, 2:215a, 221a
Catholic Homilies, 1:61b, 4:546a, 549b–550a
account of St. Benedict, 1:62a
dating of, 1:275b
manuscripts of, 1:276b, 281b, 284b, 285a
Colloquy, 5:650a, 7:352a
as exegete, 4:548b, 549a
Latin grammar of, 1:285b
Letter to Sigeweard, 4:549a
letters
of instruction, 1:61b
of pastoral care, 1:285a
liberal arts and, 4:578b
Life of St. Edmund and, 7:363a
on the manufacture of plows, 12:81b
Metrical Paraphrase of the Pentateuch and Joshua, 1:273b, 10:109a
music and, 8:558a
paraphrase of the Hexateuch, depiction of vehicles in, 12:372b–373a
Questions on Genesis, 2:221a
religious life, 1:61b
saints' lives, 1:61b, 285a
Katherine Group and, 7:225b–226a
Oswald, 1:62a
scientific treatises of, 1:285b
sermons of, 1:284b
sex aetates mundi and, 11:215a
studies with Ethelwold, 1:61b
style and diction, 1:62a
translations
Basil's *Admonitio,* 1:62a
biblical, 1:61b–62a
Hexameron, 1:61b, 285b
Treatise on the Old and New Testaments, 2:221a
Aelfric Bata, **1:62b**
Aelfric of Eynsham, abbot, 5:650a
Aelius Gallus, capture of Najrān, 9:55a
Aelius Theon, *Progymnasmata,* 1:505b
Aelred. *See* Ethelred
Aelurus, Timothy. *See* Timothius Aelurus
Aeneas Sylvius Piccolomini. *See* Pius II, pope
Aeneid. See Vergil
Aenigmata. See Tatwine of Canterbury
Aes dána, 6:553a
Aesop, 4:572a
beast epic and, 2:140a
in Byzantine folklore, 8:18b
scenes from fables in Modena Cathedral, 10:501a
Aestii. See Balts
Aetas Ovidiana. See Ovid, literary influence
Aetas Vergiliana, 12:394a
Aeterna et incommutabilis. See Alexander III, pope
Aethelbert. *See* Ethelbert
Aethelflaed. *See* Ethelfled
Aethelwig of Evesham, 2:173b
Aethelwold. *See* Ethelwold
Aethelwulf. *See* Ethelwulf
Aethicus Ister
De cosmographia, 6:237a
fanciful alphabet of, 1:217b
Aethiopes (Greek generic term), 12:739a
Aetios of Amida (Byzantine physician)
influence of in the Palaiologan era, 8:246a
Sixteen Books on Medicine, 8:245a
Aëtius (Roman general), 12:470b
Burgundians and, 11:536b
Hunnish mercenaries and, 2:92b
murder of, 12:355a
Aevia, **1:63b**
Af Upplendinga konungum, 12:7a
Afanasii Nikitin, 11:347b
Afḍal, ibn Badr al-Jamālī al-, Fatimid vizier
al-Mustaᶜlī and, 6:617a
Tancred and, 11:589b
Afḍal, Kutayfāt al-, 6:617a
Afḍal Shāhanshaah, al-, Fatimid vizier, 5:28a-b
Afer. *See* Arnobius the Elder
Afflighem, John of. *See* John of Afflighem
Afghanistan, **1:63b–66a**
artistic renaissance, 1:65a
boundaries, 1:64 (map)
economics, 1:65b
foreign domination, 1:65a
Ghaznavid period, 1:64b–65a
Hindu-Shahi dynasty, 1:64a
intellectual history, 1:65a-b
in Islamic conquests, 6:570b, 572a
local dynasties, 1:64a-b
Muslim conversion, 1:64b
pre-Islamic era, 1:64a
regions of, 1:63b–64a
religious movements
Ismailism, 1:65a
Karramiya, 1:65a-b
rule of Shansabani family, 1:65a
Sebüktigin and, 11:133b
Timurid era, 1:65a, 65b
under Saffarids, 1:64b
Afghans, in Isfahan, 6:562a
Afhending (a *rímur* meter), 10:405b
Afonso I of Portugal, king
aims of, 10:39b, 41a
founder of the Order of Aviz, 2:16b
independence of Portugal and, 10:41a-b
Latin church and, 10:42a-b
Muslims and, 10:41b–42a
parents of, 10:39b
as prisoner of son-in-law, 10:42a
wars waged by, 10:41a
Afonso II of Portugal, king
excommunication of, 10:44a
Muslims and, 10:44a-b
Order of Aviz and, 2:17a
Portuguese law and, 10:43b
royal patrimony and, 10:43b–44a
Afonso III of Portugal, king
accession of, 10:45b–46a
accomplishments of, 10:47a
appointment as keeper of the kingdom, 4:160a
excommunication of, 10:47b
Latin church and, 10:47a-b
marriages of, 10:46b
Muslims and, 10:46a-b
peace with Castile and, 10:46b–47a
prerogative under, 10:47a
Afonso IV of Portugal, king
da Recco and, 4:558b
reign of, 10:50b–51a
Afonso V of Portugal, king
abdication of, 10:55a
Azores and, 4:559b
Guinea and, 4:561b
marriage of, 9:111b
reign of, 10:54b–55a
Afonso VI of Portugal, king, area ruled by, 10:39a
Afonso de Paiva, 4:562b–563a
Afreet, 7:112b–113a
Afri barbari. See Moors
Africa
Belisarios and, 2:165a
circumnavigation of, 4:398a
slave trade, disease and, 9:682b
Africa. See Petrarch
Africa, exarchate of, 4:530a
see also Ifrīqiya
Africa Proconsularis, Vandals and, 12:354b–355a, 355b
African Code, in *Synagoge in Fifty Titles,* 9:158b
Africans
in Europe, 9:682b
see also Blacks; Zanj
Afshīn, al- (9th century), trial of, 8:653b–654a
Afshin ibn Abu 'l-Sāj
rebuilding of Dwin by, 4:324a
vs. Smbat I the Martyr, 11:351a
Aga khan (Nizari title), 6:618a
Against the Emperor Constantius. See Hilary of Poitiers, St.
Against Eunomius. See Gregory of Nyssa, St.
Against the Galilaeans. See Julian the Apostate, Roman emperor
Against Jewish Blindness. See Oliver, Bernard (Bernat)
Against Jewish Disbelief. See Peter of Blois
Against the Paulicians. See John of Ōjun, St.
Against the Phantasiasts. See John of Ōjun, St.
Against the Sects/De Deo. See Eznik of Kołb
Against Those Who Say Two Natures. See Timothius Aelurus
Agape, **1:66a**
in early church, 3:338b
Agatᶜangełos, **1:66a–67b**, 1:510b, 5:371b, 7:299a
on Armenian saints, 1:517b, 518a, 519b
center of Armenian Christianity and, 9:458a
on early Bagratids, 2:48a

Gregory the Illuminator and, 5:668a-b
History of the Armenians, 1:66a–67a, 452a, 508a, 5:668a
literary tradition used, 6:239a
pre-Christian history, 1:66b–67a
on the reign of Trdat, 1:66b
on St. Nino, 9:140a
"Teaching of St. Gregory," 1:66b, 8:202b
on Hṙipᶜsimē, 6:309a
on Mamikonean *sparapets,* 11:460b
on St. Trdat III (IV) the Great, 12:164a-b
see also Łazar Pᶜarpecᶜi; Pᶜawstos Buzand
Agathias, **1:67b–68a**
on Beirut, 2:163b, 164a
Cycle, 1:67b
Daphniaca, 1:67b
historical works, 2:512a
Histories, 1:67b
continuation by Menander Protector, 8:273b
on the Sasanian king Kawād, 8:236b, 237b
Theophylaktos Simokattes' *Histories* and, 12:25a
on Xusrō I, 12:714a
Agaw, Abyssinian capital moved to, 1:30b
Agde, Council of (506), 6:356b, 9:62b
Agen Bridge, 10:420b
construction of, 10:421a
financing of, 10:416b, 418a
Agenda (a designation of ritual in Germany), 10:408a
Aggareia, 11:604a
Aggregati, 11:281b
Aghkand ware, **1:68a-b**
bowl by Abū Ṭālib, 1:68b (*illus.*)
production in southern Caucasus, 1:68b
Aghlab ibn Sālim al-Tamīmī, al-, 6:391b
Aghlabids, **1:70a–72a**
ᶜ*abīd* bodyguard, 1:70a, 71b
administration, Christians in, 1:71a-b
art, **1:69a–70a**, 6:610b
bookbinding technique, 1:69b
minarets, 1:69a
mosques, 1:69 (*illus.*)
Tunisian art and, 6:600a, 600b
coins of, 8:423b
conquest by Abū ᶜAbd Allah, 1:72a
constitutional conflict, 1:71a
founded, 6:391b
in Ifrīqiya, 6:414a, 414b
Islamization under, 1:71b
Jews under, 7:97b–98b
jund rebellion, 1:71b
law under, 1:71a
origin, 1:70a
overthrow of Banū Ḥumayd family, 1:71a
reign of Ibrāhim II, 1:71b
Sicily and, 1:70b, 11:261b, 264b
trade and commerce, 1:70b
transfer of capital to Raḳḳada, 1:71b
vs. Byzantines, in Sicily, 6:572b
vs. Fatimids, in North Africa, 6:608a
Aghri Dagh. *See* Ararat, Mount
Aghts. *See* Ałcᶜ
Agilolfings, in Bavaria, 2:94b, 134a
Agincourt, Battle of (1415), **1:72a-b**, 3:273a, 6:332a
cavalry tactics at, 3:205b
Agiographia. See Huguccio
Agius of Corvey, **1:72b**, 7:362b
biography of Hathumoda, 1:72b
see also Poeta Saxo
Agnarr (saga character), 5:676a-b
Agnellus of Pisa, **1:72b–73a**
Franciscans in England and, 1:73a
Agnellus of Ravenna, St., **1:73a**, 10:263b
De ratione fidei, 1:73a
marble ambo of, 4:361b
Agnes. See Peter Riga
Agnes of Poitou
marriage to Henry III of Germany, 6:162b
regency of Henry IV of Germany, 6:163a
Agnes, St.
martyrium of, 8:161b, 10:297a
in poem by Hrotswitha, 6:315a
Agnesa of Montepulciano, 9:14a
Agnolo di Ventura, **1:73b**
Tarlati tomb at Arezzo, 1:73b
Agnus chant, **1:73b**
Agnus Dei (in art), **1:74a**
banned in Byzantium, 1:74a
Agnus Dei (music), **1:74a–75a**
in Communion rite, 1:74b, 8:194b–195a
earliest reference to, 1:74a
local variations, 1:74b
settings of, 1:75a, 5:662b
in Syrian liturgy, 1:74a-b
tropes, 1:74b, 12:209a
Agobard of Lyons, bishop, **1:75a–76a**, 3:118a, 620b, 8:638b
Contra objectiones Fridugisi, 5:300a, 9:585b
on Jews, 1:75b, 7:75b–76a, 76b, 77a, 86a, 88a, 89b
letters of, 10:2b, 74b
on liturgy, 7:629a
opponent of Amalarius of Metz, 1:228a
religious opinions, 1:75b, 76a
on slavery, 11:200b
Slavic slaves, 11:336b–337a
support for Frankish constitutionalists, 1:75b
writings of, 1:76a
Agone, 10:517b
Agostino, Giovanni d', **1:76b**
Tarlati tomb at Arezzo, 1:73b, 76b
Ağri Daği. *See* Ararat, Mount
Agri (permanent fields). *See* Agriculture; Reclamation of land
Agricola (Georg Bauer), *De re metallica,* 4:329a, 8:401a
Agricola, Rodolphus, *De inventione dialectica,* 4:171a
Agriculture
arable land
Asia Minor and Balkans, 1:76b–77a
increase under Arab domination, 1:81a
island of Patmos, 1:77a
common lands, laws governing, 1:79a-b
crop capacity, 1:83a-b
Byzantine, 1:78a-b
crop rotation, triennial, 1:83b
dry farming, 1:80b, 82a, 85a, 86b
fertilizers and additives, 1:81b
mineral, 1:105a
organic, 1:78b, 98a, 101a, 105a
vegetable matter, 1:105a
grazing, 1:92a
interculture, 1:84a, 86b
irrigated gardens, 1:84a, 85a, 85b
land reclamation
by colonists, 10:278a
labor requirements, 10:277a-b
meat production, 1:91b–92a
mixed farming, 1:92a
Nubia, 9:199a
open fields, 1:80b, 91b
plagues and, 9:673a, 676a-b, 684b, 685b
polyculture, 1:77b, 82b, 86b
dry farming, 1:85a
huerta cultivation, 1:86b–87a, 87b
interculture and, 1:88a
purpose of, 1:87a-b
terraced, 1:85b
protein sources
animal, 1:95b–96a
vegetable, 1:95a
soil, exhaustion of, 1:97b
tillage, 1:77a-b
cooperative, 1:94a
evolution of, 1:97b
hand cultivation, 1:77b
slash and burn, 1:96b, 97a-b, 98b
strip cultivation, 1:91a-b
vitamins and minerals, 1:96a
water mills and, 8:392b–393a
see also Animals, draft; Crop rotation; Dairy products; Famine; Field systems; Grain crops; Irrigation; Peasants; Reclamation of land; Tenure of land; Tools, agricultural; Wine and winemaking
Agriculture, Byzantine, **1:76b–79b**
pronoiai, 2:496a
state control, 2:475b
technology, 11:634b–635a
village communities, 2:476b–477a, 479b–480a
financial inventories, 2:480a-b
see also Farmer's Law
Agriculture, Islamic world, **1:103a–106b**
adaptations to rainfall, 1:103b–104b
agricultural vs. pastoral economies, 1:103a-b
animal husbandry, 1:103b
decline in 11th century, 1:105a-b
Egypt, 10:453a
Egyptian, Nilometer and taxation, 12:223b
farming manuals, 1:105a, 105b–106a
ḥimā, 1:103b
Ifrīqiya, 6:392a
Iraq, 6:509b, 511b–512a, 513a, 514a
land use, 1:104b–105a
large estates, 1:105b
in Ottoman Empire, 9:309b

Agriculture, Islamic world (*cont.*)
principal crops, 1:104b
slavery and, 11:331b
Syria, under Umayyads, 11:560b
taxation of revenues, 11:625a
technology, 11:639b
food preservation, 11:639b
milling and refining, 11:639b
oil presses, 11:639b
Agriculture, Mediterranean region, **1:79b–88b**, 12:445b
Asturias-León, 1:629b
cotton cultivation, 3:626b–627a
French Midi, 1:85a–86a
Italy, 1:86a–87b
Kingdom of Jerusalem, 11:561b
Portugal, 1:84b–85a
Sicily, 11:275b
Sicily and Sardinia, 1:87b–88a
Spain, Christian, 1:83a–84b
use of ard, 12:75a
see also Agriculture, Islamic world; *Mesta;* Tools, agricultural, Islamic world
Agriculture, Northern Europe, **1:89a–96a**
in Baltic lands, 2:63a-b
demesne farms, 11:675b–676a, 677a-b
demographic changes, 1:94a
diet and climate, 1:89a
effect of Norse and Magyar raiders, 1:94a
8th through 10th centuries, 1:92b–93a
enclosure movement, 9:455b–456a
environmental adaptation, 1:89b
history, 1:89a-b
increases in productivity, 1:93a-b
Kievan Rus, 1:99a, 99b
mansus, 11:675a
Norway, 9:179b–180b
partibility, 11:678b
peasant society, 1:94a-b
Poland, 9:716b, 722a, 728a-b
sources of carbohydrates, 1:94b–95a
Agriculture, Slavic world, **1:96b–103a**
animal husbandry, 1:98b, 99b, 100b
apiculture, 1:98b
Balkans, 1:98b–99a
dependent, 11:674a-b, 679b
East Slavs, 1:99a–102b
forest industry, 1:99b
Hungary, 6:341a, 345a
technological advances of German colonists, 1:96b–97a
tillage, 1:97b
use of *sokha,* 12:75a
West Slavs, 1:96b–98b
Agriculture, Western Europe
agricultural investments, 5:117a-b
apiculture, 6:283b
Benedictine monasteries and, 2:174a-b
in Bohemia-Moravia, 2:301b
in Burgundy, 2:427b
in Celtic mythology, 6:546a, 546b
corvée in, 3:613a
crop rotation systems, 5:116a
Denmark, 4:149a
early Germanic, 2:89b
effects of climate on, 3:452a–453a, 454a-b, 456a
environmental effects, 5:133b
expansion of after 12th century, 4:140b
Great Clearances, 4:140b
high farming, 12:532b
Ireland, 6:553b
kitchen garden, 2:347b–348a
Rome, 10:460a
see also Colonate
taxation of, France, 11:619a
technological innovations, 11:651a
units of land, 11:676b
Carolingian dissolution of estates, 11:676b
village organization, 12:442a
Agridi, battle at (1232), 6:389b
Ágrip, 4:617b
Orkneyinga saga and, 9:279b
Ágrip af Nóregs knounga sǫgum, 9:176a
Agron, 7:163b
Ague. *See* Plagues, European, malaria
Aḥa of Shabḥa, *Sheᵓiltot,* 10:74b, 11:584b
Aḥadith. See Ḥadīth
ᶜAhd, 3:39a
under Abbasids, 3:42b
Aḥdāth, 6:591a
"Ahi lasso, or è stagion di doler tanto." *See* Guittone d'Arezzo
Ahimaaz ben Paltiel, 7:91a, 92b
Aḥima'aẓ of Oria, *Megillat Aḥima'aẓ,* 8:23b–24a
Ahl as-sunna. See Sunnites
Ahl al-bidaᶜ, 11:513a
Ahl al-farāᵓiḍ. See Inheritance, Islamic
Ahl al-kitāb. See People of the book
Ahl al-ṣuffa. See Ṣuffa
Ahli Shīrāzī, 11:252b
Ahlspiess, 7:324 (*illus.*), 325a
Aḥmad al-Anṣārī al-Matatabbib, illuminated Koran, 8:114 (*illus.*)
Aḥmad Bāba, 12:55b
Aḥmad Tegüder. *See* Tegüder
Aḥmad ibn Abī Duᵓād, 3:44b
Aḥmad ibn ᶜAlī ibn Thābit. *See* Khaṭīb al-Baghdādī, al-
Aḥmad ibn Ḥanbal. *See* Ḥanbal, Aḥmad ibn Muḥammad ibn
Aḥmad ibn Mājid (Muslim pilot), 4:563a, 5:394a, 9:87a, 11:247b
Ahmad ibn Mūsā. *See* Banū Mūsā
Aḥmad ibn Ṭūlūn
achievements of governorship, 4:405b
administration and economic policies, 12:223b–224a
Egyptian fleet strengthened by, 9:75a
expansion of Cairo, 3:13b, 6:599a-b
military power of, 12:223b
revenues and trade under, 12:223b–224a
Aḥmad ibn Uwais, sultan, 7:181b
Aḥmad, Ikhshidid ruler, 6:417a
Aḥmad Mūsā, **1:106b–107a**
Aḥmad, Samanid emir
assassination of, 10:638a
conquest of Seistan, 10:638a
Aḥmad (son of al-Mustanṣir). *See* Mustaᶜli, al-
Aḥmad (Tegüder). *See* Tegüder
Aḥmadīya confraternity, 4:407a
Aḥnaf ibn Qays, al-, 6:569b
Ahriman (Zoroastrian god). *See* Angra Mainyu
Aḥsan al-Taqāsīm fī Maᶜrifat al-Aqālīm. *See* Muqaddasī, al-
Ahura Mazda (Zoroastrian god), 1:451b, 8:237a-b, 12:746b, 747b, 748b, 749a
in art, 11:597a, 597b
legitimacy of Achaemenids and, 10:611b–612a
temple of in pagan Armenia, 1:290a
in *Vendīdād,* 2:15a
in *Vidēvdād,* 12:411b–412a
Ahuras, 12:746b
Ahvāz, Zanj and, 12:739a
Aianeoeane. See Noeannoe
Aichardus. *See* Achard
Aid (feudal). *See* Feudalism
Áidán. *See* Áedán
Aidan of Lindisfarne, St., **1:107a–108a**
in Bede's *History of the English Church and People,* 1:107a
mission to Lindisfarne, 1:107a
missionary work of, 8:440a
students of, 1:107b
Aided Óenfir Aife, 6:548b
Aides (taxation), 10:319b, 321b, 322b, 11:579a, 624b
Aigion. *See* Vostitsa
Aigues-Mortes, construction of, 5:169a, 7:339b, 675a
Aikilisenē. *See* Anahit
Ailette, 1:525a, 530b
Ailill, Connachta king (saga character), 6:548a, 548b, 550b
Ailly, Pierre d', **1:108a–109a**
on astrology, 1:608b
conciliar theory of, 3:511b–512a, 513a–514b
Concordantia astronomiae cum historica veritate, 1:608b
Concordantia astronomicae veritatis cum theologia, 1:608b
Dit de Franc Gontier and, 12:482b
Gabriel Biel and, 2:234a
Gerson and, 5:512a-b
Hus and, 3:650a, 6:369a
Imago mundi, 1:109a
Nicholas of Clamanges and, 9:122b
nominalism and, 9:157a, 12:44a
Ockham and, 9:214a
philosophical and theological works, 1:109a
predestination and, 3:371a
role in conciliar movement, 3:646a, 647a, 648a
role in Great Schism, 1:108b
Tractatus de ecclesiastica potestate, 3:519b
treatise on calendar reform, 3:23a
via moderna and, 12:407b, 408a
Ailred of Rievaulx. *See* Ethelred of Rievaulx, St.
Aimeric of Angoulême, *Ars lectoria,* on Arator, 1:422b
Aimerus, *De practica artis musicae,* 1:545a
Aimery of Cyprus, king, 4:70b, 71b
Aimoin de Fleury, **1:109b–110a**

Chronographia, 5:653b
Historia Francorum, 1:109b, 5:653b
Liber historiae, 5:653b
Miracula sancti Benedicti, 1:110a
Vita Abbonis, 1:109b–110a
see also André de Fleury
Aiol, 4:318b
Aipgitir Chrábaid, 6:526b, 541b
Airbertach mac Coisse, **1:110a–111a**
poems
on kings of Jerusalem, 1:110b
on Psalms, 1:110b
possible authorship of *Saltair na Rann,* 1:110b
school of Ros Ailithir, 1:110a
work on geography of ancient world, 1:110a-b
Airdena Brátha, **1:111a–112a**
Airdena inna Cóic Lá nDéc ria mBráth, sources for, 1:111b
Apocalypse of Thomas, 1:111a, 112a
Collectanea, 1:111b
"Fifteen Signs" tradition, 1:111b, 112a
Liber Flavus Fergusiorum, 1:111b
Pseudo-Bedan type, 1:111b
Saltair na Rann, 1:111a-b, 112a
Airdrinn, 6:534b
Airec Menman Uraird meic Coisse, similarities to *Aislinge meic Con-Glinne,* 1:114a
Airgialla peoples, burial of St. Patrick, 9:465b
ᶜĀᵓisha, **1:112a–113b**
"affair of the lie," 1:113a
after Muḥammad's death, 1:113a-b
in Arabic literature, 1:113b
Battle of the Camel (656), 1:113b, 172b
conflict with ᶜUthmān, 1:113a-b
financial status, 1:113a
marriage to Muḥammad, 1:112b
opposition to ᶜAlī ibn Abī Ṭālib, 1:113b, 172b
revolt by, 3:35b
Aislinge meic Con-Glinne, **1:113b–114a,** 6:527b
similarities to *Aired Menman Uraird meic Coisse,* 1:114b
two surviving versions, 1:114a
Aistian. *See* Balts
Aistulf, Lombard king, 7:657b, 9:501b, 502a
reign of, 8:377a
vs. Rome, 10:521b
Aitesis. See Litany, in the Greek Byzantine rite
Aithallah of Edessa, bishop, 1:508a
Aix, inns in, 6:469b, 471a, 471b, 472a–473b, 474b, 475a
Aix, University of, 12:285a
Aix-la-Chapelle. *See* Aachen
ᶜAjāride, 11:139a
Ajax saga, 10:395b
Ajímez, **1:114a-b**
surviving Islamic examples, 1:114b
in Visigothic Spain, 1:114b
Ajnādayn, battle at, 6:568a
Ajtony, chief of the "black Magyars," subjugated by St. Stephen I of Hungary, 11:478b
Ajuda, Cancioneiro da, 11:450a
Ajwad ibn Zāmil, ruler of al-Baḥrayn, splendor of the court of, 2:51a
Akakios, *katᶜołikos* of Seleucia-Ctesiphon, 9:106b
Akakios, patriarch of Constantinople
Henotikon and Akakian schism, 6:154b
Peter Mongus and, 1:508b
Akathistos, **1:114b–115a,** 2:511a, 6:378b, 7:292b, 613a, 8:554a
associated with historic occasions, 1:114b
in Lenten services, 1:114b
Marian hymns and, 6:381b
with musical settings, 1:114b
poetic form, 2:524b
Romanos Melodos and, 10:516b
Western liturgical poetry and, 9:714a
'Aḳedat Yiẓḥaḳ. See Isaac ben Moses Arama (ᶜAramah)
Akhīs, 11:308b–309a
Akhlāṭ. *See* Xlatᶜ
Akhlāṭ-shah. *See* Shāh-Arman
Akhṭal, al-, **1:115a-b,** 1:400a
adaptations of Arabic poetic conventions, 1:115b
assertion of Monophysite Christianity, 1:115a
at the Umayyad court, 1:115a
Bedouin virtues praised, 1:115b
dispute with Jarīr, 7:47b
satiric poetry, 1:115a
Akilisene, Peace of, 3:308a
Akiva ben Joseph, 2:210b, 7:159b, 168b
in midrashic legends, 8:22b
Akko. *See* Acre
ᶜAknin, Ibn. *See* Joseph ben Judah ben Jacob ibn ᶜAknin
Akoimetoi, in Studios Monastery, 11:494b
Akolouthia. See Canticle
Akolouthiai. See Koukouzeles, Joannes
Akoluthos (commander of Varangian Guard), 12:359b
Akova, seized (1395), 7:381a
Akritai, **1:115b–116a**
decline of, 1:116a
organizational structure, 1:116a
origin of, 1:116a
relation to Byzantine army, 1:115b–116a
Akropolites, George, 1:614a, 3:642a, 7:127b
history of Nicene Empire, 2:516a-b, 6:247a
continuations of, 2:516b
teacher of Theodore II Laskaris of Nicaea, 12:14a
Aksum. *See* Axum
Aksumite art. *See* Axumite art
Aktuarios, John, medical works by, 8:246a
"Al cor gentil rempaira sempre amore." *See* Guinizzelli, Guido
"Al poco giorno e al gran cerchio d'ombra." *See* Dante Alighieri
Al-. *See* next element of name
Āl-i Afrāsiayāb. *See* Qarakhanids
ᶜAlāᵓ al-Dawla, 11:303a
ᶜAlāᵓ al-Dīn Beg, 7:214a
vs. Bāyazīd I, 2:136b
ᶜAlāᵓ al-Dīn Ḥusayn, 5:526b
ᶜAlāᵓ al-Dīn Kay-Kubād I. *See* Kayqubād I
ᶜAlāᵓ al-Dīn Muḥammad, 5:527a
ᶜAlāᵓ al-Dīn and the Wonderful Lamp, in *Thousand and One Nights,* 12:50a, 50b
Ála flekks saga, **1:116b–117a,** 10:395b
Mírmanns saga and, 8:432b
ᶜAlāᵓ ibn Mugīth, al-, rebellion against ᶜAbd al-Raḥmān I, 12:275b
Ala-ed-Din mosque (Konya), 7:223b
Alaholfingians, 5:506a, 11:525b, 526a
Alain de Lille. *See* Alan of Lille
Alaman family, 2:128b
Alamanni, **1:117a–118a,** 2:94b, 11:525a–526b
assault on Roman imperial territory, 1:117a
Christianization of, 1:117b, 11:526a-b
Clovis and, 2:94b, 3:466b–467a
first cited in literature, 1:117a
Italy plundered by in late 3rd century, 2:89b
laws of, 1:117b
leaders of, 1:117b, 5:508a
Merovingians and, 5:506a, 8:278a
in Noricum, 2:133b
opponents of, 11:525b–526a
Pepin II's campaign against, 5:506a
protection by Ostrogoths, 5:506a
Rhine settlements, 1:117a
territorial expansion of, 11:537a
vs. Franks, 1:117a-b, 118a, 5:506a, 11:537a-b
ᶜAlamayn, 9:651a
Alamūt, **1:118a–119a,** 11:137b
construction of, 1:118b
headquarters of Ismaili Assassins, 1:118a-b
remains of, 1:118b
seized (1090), 6:617a
surrender to Mongols, 1:118b
Ałan Arcruni, Łazar Pᶜarpecᶜi and, 1:508b
Alan Crooked-Beard, Breton ruler, Vikings and, 12:431b
Alan of Lille, **1:119a–120b,** 7:372a
Anticlaudianus, 1:119b, 120a, 182a, 183a-b, 188b, 7:366a, 8:582b, 590b
description of House of Fortune, 5:146b
on perfection of man, 1:119b
source for Heinrich von Neustadt's *Gottes Zukunft,* 2:230b
antiheretical treatises, 1:119a
De planctu Naturae, 1:119a-b, 183a, 188b, 7:366a, 368a, 12:475b
Tesoretto and, 7:383a
De virtutibus et vitiis, 1:120a
theologia moralis, 9:594b
development of "thematic" sermon, 10:362b
Dionysian tradition and, 1:119b
Distinctiones, 1:120a
doctor universalis, 1:119a
"Exceptivam actionem," 6:384a

Alan of Lille, **1:119a–120b** (*cont.*)
Gilbert of Poitiers and, 1:119a, 120a, 12:21b
handbooks and manuals, 1:120a
Ludus super Anticlaudianum and, 7:369a
preaching of, 10:76a, 77a
Prophetia Anglicana Merlini Ambrosii Britanni, 1:567b
"Quoniam homines," 1:119b
Rhythmus de incarnatione, 8:582a
Summa de arte praedicatoria, 1:555b–556a, 557b
Theologicae regulae, 1:119b
theology
Nature and the divine, 1:119a, 119b
negativity of language, 1:119b–120a
Alan de la Roche, founding of Rosary Confraternity, 4:251a
Alan of Tewkesbury, life of St. Thomas Becket, 12:35b
Alan of Walsingham. *See* Walsingham, Alan of
Alani, **1:120b–121b**
alliance with Vandals, 1:121a
armor of, 1:522a, 534b (*illus.*)
assimilation into Western culture, 1:121b
Burgundians and, 2:422b
Christianization, 1:121b
in Constantinople, 1:121a-b
evidence of, 1:121b
in Iberian Peninsula, 10:36a
movement into Western Europe, 1:121a
Roman Empire and, 1:120b–121a, 3:200b, 201a, 10:465a
Sarmatian confederacy, 10:653a
Vandals and, 12:354b
vs. Huns, 1:121a, 6:352b
Alanus Anglicus, 3:516b
canon law compilation by, 7:415b
on the Doctrine of Two Swords, 12:234b
Alanus de Insulis. *See* Alan of Lille
Alarcos, Battle of (1195), 1:195a, 9:70b, 11:383b
Alard de Cambrai, *Moralités des philosophes,* 9:638b
Alardus, Master, missing works by, 12:22a
Alaric I, Visigothic king, **1:122a-b**, 2:90b, 12:470a
agreement with Flavius Stilicho, 1:122a
military campaigns
against Constantinople, 1:122a
against Rome, 1:122a-b
invasion of Thrace, 1:122a, 2:485b
in North Africa, 1:122a-b
multiethnic composition of his army, 1:122a
Alaric II, Visigothic king, 12:470b, 472a
early Germanic law codes and, 7:469b–470a
sapphire seal ring of, 11:125a
Alaude, 8:562b
Alaverdi, **1:122b**
ᶜAlawids. *See* Nuṣayrīs
Alazani, 7:309b
Alb. *See* Vestments
Alba, **1:122b–123a**, 5:441a
in Provençal literature, 10:164b
troubadour, 12:218a
see also Aubade
Alba Bible, 2:215b
Alba Regia. *See* Székesfehérvár
Ałbak, Arcrunis in, 1:451a
Alban, St., lives of, 1:261b
Albania (Balkan), 11:473a, 475a
acquired by Stefan Uroš IV Dušan of Serbia, 11:475b
Skanderbeg in, 11:324a
see also Serbia
Albania (Caucasian), **1:123a–125a**
alphabet, 1:123b, 125a
boundaries, 1:123a-b, 124 (map)
Christianization, 1:123b
church, Ašot I and, 1:480b
conversion to Islam, 1:125a
destruction of, 3:195b
Iranian vassalage, 1:123b
Mihrānid rule, 1:123b–124a, 125a
Kabala, 7:205a
major cities, 1:124b–125a
Mongol and Tartar invasions, 1:125a
origin, 1:123b
pan-Caucasian Georgian empire, 11:631b
plundering by Khazars, 1:124a-b
rebellions against Muslim domination, 1:125a
relations with Armenia and Iberia, 1:123b
religion, ties with Armenian church, 1:123b
see of, 1:482b
Smbat I and, 1:481a
social structure
azat class, 1:123b
dynastic princes, 1:123b
peasants, 1:123b
terms Arrān and Ałwankᶜ replaced by Azerbaijan, 1:125a
trade, 1:124b–125a
under Faḍl II, 11:217a, 217b
see also Azerbaijan; Bardhaᶜa; Derbent
Albanian language, 6:434b, 435a, 437b, 443b
Latin loanwords in, 6:438b
Albanus, Godzin of Mainz on, 5:571a
Albarelli, 1:561b
Albarus of Córdoba, 6:381a
Albategnius. *See* Battānī, al-
Albergati, Nicolas, cardinal, in art, 4:567b
Alberic of Besançon, *Alexandre,* 1:150a, 5:283b–284a, 10:179b
Alberic of London, 7:368b
Alberic of Monte Cassino, **1:125b**
Breviarium de dictamine, 4:174a, 10:358a
Dictaminum radii, 4:174a, 10:358a
Liber dictaminum et salutatione, 1:125b
revival of classical culture, 1:125b
Alberic of Rheims, Anselm of Laon's theology school and, 12:20b–21a
Alberic of Rome, 10:522b, 525a
Alberic of Spoleto, 10:522b
Alberic of Trois Fontaines, 5:398a, 10:118b
Alberich von Bisinzo, Lamprecht and, 7:322b
Alberico da Barbiano, Muzio Attendolo and, 11:216a
Albericus de Porta Ravennate, Hugo and, 6:324a
Albero I of Liège, bishop, 10:253a
Albert, *see also* Albrecht
Albert I of Germany, emperor
assumption of imperial status, 6:42a
death of, 11:542a
expansion of Habsburgs into Austria, 6:42b
fiefs of, 11:540b
reign of, 5:487b
vs. Zurich, 11:541b, 543a
Albert II (Habsburg) of Germany, emperor, 6:347b
reign of, 5:489b
Albert I of Hungary, king. *See* Albert II (Habsburg) of Germany, emperor
Albert of Aix, legend of Peter the Hermit, 9:523a
Albert (German *advocatus* in Poland), 9:722b, 724a
Albert the Great. *See* Albertus Magnus
Albert von Halberstadt, *Metamorphoses,* translation of, 9:314a
Albert of Morra. *See* Gregory VIII, pope
Albert of Pisa, leadership of Franciscans, 5:199b
Albert of Prague, 6:382b
Albert of Riga, bishop, 2:64b
Albert of Saxony, **1:125b–126a**
dialectic and, 4:170b
Jean Buridan and, 1:464b
Liber alchimie Hermes, 1:137a
nominalism and, 12:44a
Perutilis logica, 4:170b
physics and mathematics, 1:125b–126a
Albert von Stade, *Troilus,* 7:369a, 12:733a
Albert of Vercelli, St., Carmelites and, 3:96b
Albertano da Brescia, 3:671a
Alberti family, 7:326b
Alberti, Leon Battista, **1:126a-b**, 1:438a
adviser to Pope Nicholas V, 1:126a-b
architectural projects, 1:126b
on the construction of bridges, 10:419b
De pictura, 1:126b, 580a
De re aedificatoria, 1:126b, 5:365a
Della famiglia, 1:126b
relations with Florentine intellectuals, 1:126a, 126b
Albertus of Brudzewo, on astronomy, 1:614b
Albertus Gandinus, 10:62a
Albertus Magnus, St., **1:126b–130b**
Alkimia minor, 1:137a
as arbitrator in Dominican litigations, 1:127b, 128a
astrology and, 1:607b
at Cologne

establishment of *studium generale,* 1:127b, 3:481b
lector emeritus at, 1:129a
attribution of *Secreta Alberti* (*Liber aggregationis*) to, 8:35a
biographies of, 1:129a
as bishop of Regensburg, 1:128b–129a
Book of Minerals, on brass alloy, 8:286a
canonization, 1:129a
condemnation of William of St. Amour, 1:128a
on contraception, 3:573b
crusade mission, 1:128b
cult of, 1:129a
De animalibus, 1:128b, 2:243b–244a
De mineralibus, 1:137a
De natura boni, 1:127a
De unitate intellectus contra Averroistas, 1:128a
De vegetabilibus et plantis, 2:242a, 5:360b
disciples, 1:129a-b
as doctor of the church, 4:234b
Dominicans and, 4:246b, 7:368b
followers of, *via moderna* and, 12:407a–408a
on heresy of the Free Spirit, 5:217a
In octos libros Topicorum, 4:170a
influence of, 1:129a-b
knowledge of Plato's philosophy, 9:700b–701a, 702b
mastership in theology, 1:127a-b
Meteora, on alchemy, 1:137a
Nicholas of Cusa and, 9:123a
Parva naturalia, 1:128a
patron saint of natural scientists, 1:129a
on *perspectiva,* criticized by Roger Bacon, 2:39a
on Peter Lombard's *Sentences,* 1:127a, 9:517b
on Pharaoh's rods-turned-into-snakes, 8:38a
provincial of Teutonia, 1:127b–128b
on Pseudo-Dionysius, 1:127a
Quaestiones super de animalibus, 2:243b–244a
ratio studiorum of the Dominicans, 1:128a-b
on science and natural history
on the antipodes, 5:398b
celestial bodies and demons, 8:38a
classification of plants, 2:246a
on making a lawn, 5:364a-b
theoretical zoology, 2:244a
theory of vision, 9:248a, 251b–252a
on scriptural interpretation, 4:544a
Semita recta, 1:137a
Siger of Brabant and, 1:463a, 11:286a
Summa Parisiensis, 1:127a-b
Theodoric of Freiberg and, 12:18a
theology of
Aristotelian elements, 9:596a
Christology, 3:323b
nominalism and, 9:155b
original justice, 9:600b
on sacramentality of marriage, 9:604a-b
on Seven Deadly Sins, 11:56b, 211b
Trinitarian doctrine, 12:194b–195a, 196b
on the Trinity, 9:599b
Thomas Aquinas and, 1:127a, 127b, 129a, 12:39a
Thomas of Cantimpré and, 12:34a-b
translations of Aristotle, 1:462a-b
De anima, 1:128a
De plantis, 1:128a
Metaphysics, 1:128b–129a
Physics, 1:127b
universities and, 9:157a
on Virgin Mary, 12:460a, 461a
Western European geography and, 5:397a
Albi
bridge at, 10:418b, 419b
construction of, 10:420a
maintenance of, 10:421b
inquisition in, 6:487b
riot in (1234), 6:487a
Albi Cathedral, rood screen in, 11:118 (*illus.*)
Albigensians, **1:130b**
beguins and, 2:162b
Bogomils and, 2:296b–297a
crusade against, 3:188a–189b, 353a, 6:198a, 7:339b, 10:252a, 12:215a
Children's Crusade and, 4:15a
Eastern crusades and, 4:17b
effect on Provençal literature, 10:173a–178b
Innocent III and, 4:239b, 6:464b–465a
interdict and, 6:496a
poets, 12:215a
Provençal language and, 6:435b, 442a
punishment by, 6:483b
role of papal legates in, 7:535a
Docetism and, 4:233b
Dominic and, 4:239b, 243b
opposition to
Third Lateran Council, 12:509b
Waldensians, 12:509a
Paulician influence on, 9:469a
Simon de Montfort as leader of, 11:296b
Toulouse and, 12:91a, 91b
Trinitarian doctrine and, 12:191a
under Capetians, 7:340b
victory of Roman ecclesiology over, 4:376a
see also Cathars; *Chanson de la croisade contre les Albigeois*
Albinus of Canterbury, archbishop, Bede and, 2:155b
Albion, 1:613a
"Albion" (Richard of Wallingford's astronomical instrument), 10:387b
Albizzi family, conflict with the Medici, 8:242b
Albo, Joseph
on astronomy, 11:91a
as exegete, 2:212b
Sefer ha-Ikkarim, 7:166a, 10:6a
Albogón, 8:563a
Alboin, Lombard king, 2:95b, 7:654b–655a, 11:335b
campaign into Italy, 8:376b
Albon, counts of, 4:107b
Alborada, 11:449b
Albornoz, Gil, cardinal, **1:130b–131b**
administration of papal states by, 9:386a
Angevin-Guelph alliance and, 1:131a
war with Lombard lords, 1:131a
Albrant, 4:579b
Albrecht I of Austria, king (Albert I of Germany, king), 2:7b
Albrecht II of Austria, duke, 2:8a
Albrecht III of Austria, duke, 2:8b
Albrecht V of Austria, duke (Albert II of Germany, Bohemia, and Hungary, king), 2:8b
band of, 8:416a
Albrecht IV (the Wise) of Bavaria, duke, 2:135b
Albrecht I (the Bear) of Brandenburg, margrave, acquisition of Nordmark, 2:360b
Albrecht III of Mecklenburg, king of Sweden, 2:247a, 11:532b
Albrecht of Brandenburg, Grand Master of Teutonic Knights, 3:306a
Albrecht von Eyb
Ehebüchlein, 8:360a
Guiscard und Sigismunda, 8:360b–361a
Marina, 8:361a
translations of Plautus, 8:361a
Albrecht von Halberstadt, **1:131b–132a**
courtly epic tradition, 1:132a
translation of Ovid's *Metamorphoses,* 1:131b–132a
Albrecht von Johansdorf, **1:132a–133a,** 5:441b
crusade songs, 1:132b–133a
Wolfger von Erla and, 12:673a
Albrecht von Kemenaten
Goldemar, 5:572b
Virginal and, 12:462a
Albrecht von Scharfenberg, **1:133a–134a**
fraw Eren hof, 1:133b
hunting and, 6:359a
Jüngerer Titurel, 4:452b, 12:679b
attributed to Wolfram von Eschenbach, 1:133b
dating of, 1:133b
Grail history and Old French tradition, 1:133b–134a
Merlin
dating of, 1:133b
Grail history and Old French tradition, 1:133b–134a
Seifrid de Ardemont, 1:133b
in Ulrich Füetrer's *Buch der Abenteuer,* 1:133a-b
Albret line of Navarre, Bourbon dynasty and, 9:72a
Albucasis. *See* Abu 'l-Qāsim
Albumasar. *See* Abū Ma^{c}shar
Albuquerque, Alfonso de, 11:247b
attack on Malacca, 8:445b
opposition to Pedro I, 3:137a
Alburanus, **1:134a**
Ałc^{c}, **1:134a-b,** 1:493a-b, 495a

Alcáer do Sal, recapture of by Afonso II of Portugal, 10:44b
Alcaicería, 11:213b
Alcalá, University of, 12:287a
Alcántara bridge, 10:410a
rebuildings of, 10:418b
Alcanyís, Lluís, in Valencia, 12:348b
Alcaovas, Treaty of (1479), 3:63a
Alcázar, 11:213b
Alchemy, **1:134b–140b**
allegorical
Christian symbolism, 1:135b–136a, 138b
hermetic-allegorical tradition, 1:141a, 141b
apparatus, 1:135b, 139a-b
Ars alchemie, 1:136a–137a
aurification, 1:135b
Aurora consurgens, 1:138b
biological model, 1:140a, 140b
calcination, 1:139b
ceration, 1:139b
Chaucer and, 4:580a
cited in encyclopedias, 1:137a
classification of elements, 1:134b
coagulation, 1:139a
definition of, 1:134b, 140b, 8:32a
distillation, 1:136a, 139b
of alcohol, 1:135b, 138a, 11:639a
doctrine of universal sympathy, 1:135b
elixir, 1:134b, 141b
etymology, 1:134b, 140b
15th century, 1:138b–139a
in Spain, 11:441b
fixation, 1:139b
four elements of nature, 1:136a, 141a, 141b
gold lettering, 11:635b
gold production, 1:137b, 138a, 141b
hierarchy of metals, 1:139b–140a
Islamic, **1:140b–142a**, 8:21b, 11:83b, 87a
origin, 1:141a
sources of, 1:140b
translations under the Umayyads, 11:82b
treatises, 1:136a-b
literature, 11:635a
materials, 1:139a
of Arabic origin, 1:139b
mathematical descriptions, 1:138a
medical connections, 1:134b, 141a
mercury, 1:136b, 138a
mystical aspects, 1:134b–135a, 135b, 138b
opposition to, 1:137b
origins
Greco-Epyptian, 1:135a–136a
Greco-Roman, 1:140b, 141a
interconvertibility of elements, 9:621b
paint coloring, 11:635b
philosophical tradition, 1:135b, 136a, 138a, 141a
Aristotelian-Galenic influence, 1:136b, 140a
poetry, 1:138b–139a
recipes, Leyden Papyrus X, 11:635b
related disciplines, 1:135a
solution, 1:139b
sublimation, 1:135b, 139b
sulfur, in formation of metal, 1:136a, 136b, 138a, 138b
theoretical problems, 1:139b–140a
theories on structure of matter, 1:134b, 135b–136a
theory and practice, 1:139a
13th and 14th centuries, 1:136b–137a
transmutation
cloth dyeing and, 1:135b
color change in, 1:139b
Greek recipes for, 1:135b
rule of elixir in, 1:134b
spiritual and philosophical aspects, 1:135b, 136a
theory of primal matter, 1:136b, 137a
treatises, 1:135a, 135b, 137b, 140a
use of heat, 1:139a
Alchymey teuczsch, 4:579a
Alcira, 12:346a, 346b
Royal Canal, 6:557b
Alcobaça (church: Portugal), 10:489a
Alcohol
distilled liquors, 4:219a–220a
origins of distillation, 12:649a
in perfumes, 2:147a
Alcuin of York, **1:142a–143b**, 2:173b, 3:438a, 4:542b
adoptionism and iconoclasm, 1:143a
Bede and, 2:154a
Carolingian Renaissance and, 3:433a, 7:362a, 562b
Charlemagne and, 4:458b, 12:151b
on Christian-Jewish polemics, 10:3a
on confirmation, 3:536a
Contra Felicem, 1:57b
coronation of Charlemagne and, 1:143a-b, 3:110a
development of scriptorium at Tours, 1:143a
Dialectica, 4:169a
Disputatio de rhetorica et de virtutibus, 10:355a
Gregorian sacramentary and, 2:168a
Hrabanus Maurus and, 6:306a
hymns of, 6:381b
influenced by Vergil, 12:394a
Interrogationes et responsiones in Genesin, 2:213a, 4:549a
kingship theories of, 7:260a-b
Liber Alcuini contra haeresim Felicis, 12:190b
liber comitus, 1:143a
Life of Willibrord, 3:100b–101a
liturgical reform and, 8:638b
on manuscript book production, 8:102b
mirror of princes and, 8:434a
Paulinus of Aquileia and, 9:470b
poetry of, 3:100b–101b
debates, 7:367a
poem on the church at York, 1:254b
pseudonyms, 3:100a
revision of the Vulgate, 2:211b
role in *translatio studii,* 1:142a, 142b
saints' lives, 1:143b
school of, Aristotelian *Categories,* 9:585b
spread of Hebrew language and, 3:313b
textbooks, 1:142b
theological innovations, 9:585b
on Viking attack on Lindisfarne, 1:254b, 12:424b
on Virgin Mary, 12:461a
Vulgate and, 12:495b
works attributed to, 7:627a-b, 628a, 629a
Alda. See William of Blois
Aldeigjuborg, 4:555a
Aldermen, **1:143b–144a**
duties of, 1:144a
in German town councils, 5:463b
land grants to, 7:659a
London, 1:143b–144a
corruption among, 7:664a
duties of, 7:665b
office for life, 7:664a-b
in provincial towns, 1:144a
see also Ealdorman; Mayor
Alderotti, Taddeo, distilled liquors and, 4:219b
Aldhelm, **1:144a-b**, 3:229a, 7:354b
De virginitate, 1:254b, 7:362a
influenced by Vergil's *Aeneid,* 12:394a
Epistola ad Acircium, collection of riddles in, 10:398a, 398b
on fingernails, 2:149b
in Latin pedagogy, 7:353a
works of, 1:144b, 278a
Aldobrandesca da Siena, 9:14a
Aldobrandino da Siena, 5:306b
Äldre Västgötalagen, 7:524b, 525b–526a
Aldred of Lindisfarne, prior, 7:583a
Ale and beer
amount consumed, 2:374b
brewing of, 2:374b–375a
taxation of, 2:375b
trade in, 5:125b–126a
see also Brewing
Aléaume, **1:144b–145a**
Alegre, Francesc, translations of, 3:169a-b
Alehouses. *See* Taverns
Alemannic language, 6:437a
Alembic (alchemy apparatus), 1:139a-b, 5:556b (*illus.*)
Aleppo, **1:145a–146a**
administration (from 1200), 1:145b
Ayyubids in
fortifications of, 2:21a
mausoleum of, 2:21b
emirate of, Hamdanid control, 6:85b–86a
fall of (1260), 6:329a
Islamic art in, 6:607a, 607b
al-Lāhdiqiya and, 7:316a
Mamluk rule, 1:145b
Mongol conquest, 1:145b, 8:473a
Ottoman Empire and, 1:145b–146a
overwhelmed by Tamerlane (1400), 8:75a
religious freedom under Arab rule, 1:145a
Shī^{c}a and, 11:228b
sūq, 11:514b
Aleppo, Battle of (1516), 11:145b

Aleppo Codex. *See under* Bible, Hebrew
Alesso di Guido Donati, 6:654b–655a
Alethia. See Victor, Claudius Marius
Alevisio Novyi, Arkhangelsky Cathedral and, 8:497a
Alexander. See Lamprecht; Ulrich von Eschenbach
Alexander III, Byzantine emperor, Nikolaos I Mystikos and, 9:135b
Alexander I (the Great) of Georgia, king, 2:49a
Alexander III (the Great) of Macedon, king
  in *Aristoteles und Phyllis,* 1:455a
  in epic poem by Alberic (of Briançon?), 10:179b
  fictitious letters of, 7:365a
  legends of, Waq-waq Islands, 12:545b
  Secretum secretorum and, 11:135a
  Zoroastrianism and, 12:746b
  see also Alexander romances
Alexander II, pope, **1:146a-b**
  Benzo of Alba and, 2:182b
  Camaldolese order and, 3:56a
  Gregory VII and, 1:146a, 146b, 5:669b
  indulgences and, 6:448b
  Jews and, 7:88a, 11:210a
  on the payment of tithes, 12:63a
  reforms of, 1:146a, 147a, 9:377a-b
Alexander III, pope, **1:146b–147a,** 3:637b–638a, 10:250b
  Aeterna et incommutabilis, 6:68b
  Becket and, 2:151b, 152a
  on canonization, 3:68a, 68b
  canonization of Knud Lavard, 7:280b
  on clerical degradation, 4:133b
  decretals of, 1:147a, 4:129b–130a
  Eskil and, 5:480b
  Ethelred of Rievaulx and, 4:517a
  evasions of the ban on interest-taking, 12:338a
  Frederick I Barbarossa and, 5:213a-b, 480b, 7:652b, 11:278b
  in a fresco by Spinello Aretino, 11:464a-b (*illus.*)
  heretics and, 6:198a, 483a
  In apostolicae sedis, 10:86b
  lay taxation and, 11:608b
  legal eminence, 3:352b
  Licet de vitanda, 3:94b
  Notre Dame de Paris and, 9:190b
  right of presentation and, 10:118a
  Rolandus and, 10:448b
  Sententiae, 12:21a
  service to Adrian IV, 1:58b
  subsidy and, 11:606b
  support of Henry II of England for, 4:517a
  treatment of Waldensians, 12:509b
  views on evangelical poverty, 6:197a
  William of Grosseto and, 2:143a
Alexander IV, pope
  Augustinian friars and, 1:659b
  Brancaleone and, 10:523b
  Bulla Cypria, 4:72b
  Dominican women's orders, 12:687b
  Dominicans and, 4:251b
  inquisition and, 6:485a
  Jews and, 7:109b
  Quasi lignum vitae, 9:408b
  on superstitious practices, 8:30b
  witchcraft and, 12:662a
Alexander V, antipope, **1:147a-b,** 3:647a
  adviser to Gian Galeazzo Visconti, 1:147b
  appointment as cardinal of Milan, 1:147b
  commentary on Peter Lombard's *Sentences,* 1:147b
  death of, 3:366a
  liturgical works, 1:147b
  Zybněk and, 6:368a
Alexander VI, pope, 12:348a
  afflicted with syphilis, 9:682b
  on Greenland, 12:427b–428a
Alexander I of Scotland, king, David I and, 4:110b
Alexander II of Scotland, king, 11:106b, 107b, 108a
Alexander III of Scotland, king, 11:106b, 107b, 108a
  aftermath of his death, 11:108a-b
Alexander of Alexandria, bishop, 3:627b
  Arius and, 1:453b
Alexander of Alexandria, St., use of the term *Theotokos,* 12:25b
Alexander of Aphrodisias, 4:170b
  interpretation of Aristotle, 9:95b
  al-Kindī and, 1:458b
Alexander of Ashby
  De modo praedicandi, 1:556a
  development of "thematic" sermon, 10:362b
Alexander, Byzantine emperor
  Epanagoge and, 4:493a
  Symeon of Bulgaria and, 2:404b, 11:555a
  in *Theophanes continuatus,* 12:23a
Alexander and Dindimus, 8:332a
Alexander the Good
  monastery at Baia, 12:505a
  Polish suzerainty, 12:502a
  religious tolerance, 12:502a
Alexander the Great. *See* Alexander III (the Great) of Macedon, king
Alexander of Hales, **1:148a-b**
  Aristotle and, 1:461b
  disputed questions, 1:148a
  as exegete, 4:544a
  on Peter Lombard's *Sentences,* 1:148a
  Summa Fratris Alexandri, 1:148a-b
  Trinitarian teaching of, 12:193b
Alexander of Lincoln, bishop, 10:443a-b
Alexander, Meister (13th century), 8:414a
Alexander of Roes, **1:148b–149b,** 7:148a, 149a
  defense of German Empire, 1:148b–149a
  Memoriale de prerogativa Romani imperii, 1:148b–149a
  Noticia seculi, 1:148b, 149a
  Pavo, 1:148b
Alexander Romance. See Wauquelin, Jean
Alexander romances, **1:149b–152a,** 8:225b–226a
  Alexander as courtly prince, 1:151a-b
  Alexander as pagan, 1:150a
  alliterative poems in Middle English, 8:320b
  Anglo-Norman versions, 1:266a-b
  Armenian and Latin versions, 1:149b
  by Lamprecht of Trier, 5:450a
  Byzantine versions, 2:522b
  constant elements in, 1:151b
  courtly tradition in, 1:151a-b
  French versions, 9:634b
  in German literature, 10:544a-b
  Greek versions, 1:149b
  of Hebrew origin, 1:150a
  Interpolated Quintus Curtius, 1:149b
  Iranian literature and, 6:507a, 507b, 508b
  Islamic, 1:176a
  prose versions, 12:579b
  sources of, 5:445b
  Spanish, 11:453b
    ballads, 11:428a
    lost works, 11:443b
  12th century, 7:365a
  Ulrich von Eschenbach, 12:249b–250a
  Vraie ystoire dou bon Roi Alexandre, depiction of astronomical sighting tube, 11:100b
  in Western European vernacular, 1:150a, 151b
  see also Alexander III (the Great) of Macedon; *Alexanders saga; Alexandre, Roman d';* Hay, Sir Gilbert; Lamprecht, *Alexander; Roman de toute chevalerie*
Alexander of Stavensby, 4:245a
Alexander of Tralles (Byzantine physician), 8:244b
  influence in the Palaiologan era, 8:246a
  Twelve Books on Medicine, 8:245a
Alexander de Villa Dei
  Carmen de algorismo, 8:209a
  Doctrinale puerorum, 3:434b, 5:649b, 7:351b, 365b
    parody of, 9:440a
Alexanderlied
  Kudrun and, 7:304b
  Wolfram von Eschenbach and, 12:674b
Alexanders geesten. See Maerlant, Jacob van
Alexander's Letter to Aristotle, 1:286a, 7:354b
Alexanders saga, **1:152a,** 10:389b
  translated by Brandr Jónsson, 10:391b
Alexandre, Libro de, **1:152b–153a,** 8:281b, 282b, 11:412a-b, 457b
  Berceo and, 2:187a
  cuaderna vía in, 4:63a,b
  manuscripts, 1:152b
  sources for, 1:152b
Alexandre, Roman d', 4:63a, 5:243b, 8:226a
  Alexander de Paris version, 1:151a
  influence on *mester de clerecía* movement, 11:412a
  Roman de toute chevalerie and, 10:453a
  sources for, 1:151a
  use of fantasy, 1:151a
Alexandreis, Czech version of, 11:344a
Alexandreis. See Walter of Châtillon

Alexandria, **1:153a–155a**
administration
under Arab rule, 1:153b
under Mamluks, 1:153b
architecture, 1:153b
attack by Amalric, 1:153b
bishops of, 9:458b
Christian community, 1:154b
conquered
by ᶜAmr ibn al-Aṣ (642), 6:569b
by Arabs, 1:153a
by Peter of Lusignan, 4:55a
destruction of library, 1:153a
harbor, 1:154a
invasion by Peter of Lusignan, 1:153b
Islamic trade and, 12:107b
Jews in, 1:154b
legal system, 1:153b
library of, 7:558b, 559a
mint at, 8:420a
murder of Hypatia by a Christian mob (415), 11:82a
as a naval base under the Umayyads, 9:74a, 74b
Neoplatonic school. *See* Alexandrian school
patriarch of, 2:459b, 9:459a
pentarchy and, 9:495b–496a
presence at the permanent synod, 9:505b
as a pirate base, 1:153b
population, 1:154b
sacked by the Cypriots (1365), 8:74b
scientific tradition of, 11:88a
sculpture workshops, 3:587b
topography, 1:153b–154a
trade, 1:154a-b
with Byzantine Empire, 12:102b, 103a, 103b
with Venice, 12:111b
Alexandria, Synod of (430), condemnation of Nestorius, 9:108b
Alexandria, 10:511b
Alexandrian rite, **1:155a–157b**
anaphora
eucharistic, 1:155b
of Mark, 1:155b, 156b
of St. Basil, 1:155b
structure of, 1:156a-b
baptism, 1:156b–157a
consecrated elements, 1:156b
Dair Balāᵓ izeh, 1:155a
disciplina arcani, 1:155b
Divine Office, 1:157a
Epiclesis, 1:156a-b
in Ethiopia, 1:155a–156a
Eucharist, 1:155b, 156b
euchologion, 1:155a
intercessions, 1:156a
liturgical language, 1:155b–156a
modern use of, 1:155a
monastic elements, 1:155b
ordinary, 1:155b
prayers of the faithful, 1:156a
scriptural reading, 1:156a
Alexandrian Schism. *See* Schism, Alexandrian
Alexandrian school, 9:95a, 98a-b
biblical exegesis, 2:214a
Christianization of, 9:565b
Christology in, 3:320a
influence of, 9:99b–100a
philosophical studies, 9:565a-b
representatives of, 3:336a
theology of, 3:336a
Alexandrine Baths (Rome), 10:517b
Alexandrine verse, 4:653a-b
estrabot and, 4:515a
see also Cuaderna vía
Alexandru, Nicolae, see of Ungro-Walachia and, 12:501a
Alexiad. See Anna Komnena
Alexios I Komnenos, Byzantine emperor, **1:157b–159a**, 7:127a, 131b
Anna Komnena and, 1:303a
Bogomils and, 2:295b, 296a
Bohemond I and, 2:308b, 309a-b
caesar superseded by *sebastokrator,* 3:9a, 11:132a
coins during rule of, 8:420b–421a
family of, 1:158b, 4:595b
financial administration, 1:158b
First Crusade and, 1:158b, 2:494b–495a, 4:30a, 34a-b, 35b
hyperpyron and, 6:386a
John Italos' trial under, 9:698a
Kantakouzenoi family and, 7:208b
Khanate of Tmutarakan and, 12:66a
Kořikos and, 7:298a
military victories, 2:493b
against Turks, 2:495b
capture of Antioch, 1:158a-b
over Pechenegs, 1:158a
Nikephoros Bryennios and, 9:133a
peace with Turkish sultan, 1:157b
problems of succession, 1:158b
reign of, 7:283b–284a
religious beliefs, 1:158b
Seljuks of Rum and, 11:156b
support of Doukas family for, 4:263a
Synopsis of Histories, 11:330a
Tancred and, 11:589a, 589b
Venice and, 4:556a, 12:103a
Vlachs and, 12:483b
vs. Robert Guiscard, 1:157b–158a
Zonaras and, 12:746a
Alexios II Komnenos, Byzantine emperor, 7:284a
strangled by Andronikos I, 1:245a
Alexios III Angelos, Byzantine emperor, 1:251b
Byzantine-Armenian church unity and, 9:104b
deposition of Isaac II Angelos, 6:560a
Fourth Crusade and, 4:45a-b, 46a-b
recognition of first Cilician king, 3:391a
Serbia and, 11:173b
Theodore I Laskaris of Nicaea and, 12:13b
Alexios IV Angelos, Byzantine emperor, 1:251b
Fourth Crusade and, 2:497a, 6:560a, 12:389b
Geoffroi de Villehardouin and, 12:448b
Alexios V Doukas, Byzantine emperor, 1:251b, 6:560a
Niketas Choniates and, 9:134a
Alexios I of Trebizond, emperor, **1:159a**
Black Sea empire, 2:498a
Alexios III of Trebizond
chrysobull of 1364, 8:458b
monasticism and, 8:458b–459a
Alexios III of Trebizond, grand *komnenos,* 12:169b
Alexios Apokavkos, 12:742b
anti-Kantakouzenian rising, 2:501a
Alexios Komnenos Palaiologos, 9:331a
Alexios Komnenos the Protosebastos, 1:245a
Alexios Slav, 2:409a
Alexios Strategopoulos, 7:349b
Alexis of Moscow, **1:159a-b**
reunion of metropolitanate, 10:593b
Alexis Romanov, serfdom and, 11:198a
Alexis, St.
in art, 10:504b
legend of, 11:566b
in *Vie de St. Alexis,* 12:412a–413a
Žale Matki Boskiej, 11:345a
Alexius. *See* Alexios
Alexius. See Konrad von Würzburg
Alf layla wa layla. See Thousand and One Nights
Alfarabius. *See* Fārābī, al-
Alfarrobeira, Battle of (1449), 10:54b
Alfasi, Isaac ben Jacob (RIF), 2:212a, 7:98b, 162b, 11:585b
on law, 7:169b–170a
Sefer ha-Halakhot, 7:169b–170a, 11:586a
Alfonsine Tables, **1:159b–160a**, 1:162a, 614b, 3:23a, 11:415a
Isaac Israeli's work and, 11:90b
Jewish translators and, 12:135b–136a
surviving manuscripts, 1:160a
see also Astronomy, Ptolemaic; Toledan Tables
Alfonso I (the Battler) of Aragon, king, **1:160a–161a**, 9:69b, 70a, 10:255b
Angevins and, 11:273a
claims to Castile, 1:160b
clerical support of "reconquest," 1:407a-b
dispute over will, 1:161a
Ebro campaign, 1:160b–161a
expansion of Aragon under, 1:406a–407b
marriage to Urraca of Castile, 1:160b
Mudejars and, 11:376a, 376b
on Muslim emigration, 11:377b
Naples and, 11:275a
papal support for wars of conquest, 1:406a
Sicily and, 11:273b
siege of Saragossa, 1:160b
victories of, 1:406a-b
Alfonso II of Aragon, king, 10:256a
acquisition of Valencia by, 1:409a-b
consolidation of territories by, 1:409b
in Occitan political conflicts, 3:187a
Spanish alliances of, 1:410a
success in Provence of, 1:409b–410a
successes of supervisory advisers, 1:408b–409a
Alfonso III of Aragon, king, 1:414b, 3:611b
church taxation and, 11:608b
Alfonso IV of Aragon, king, 1:415b
Jews and, 7:81b–82a

Alfonso V (the Magnanimous) of Aragon, king
  Catalonian resistance to, 1:417b, 418a-b
  conquest of Sicily, 1:417b–418a, 9:59b
  courtly lyrics and, 11:451a
  Jordi de S. Jordi in court of, 7:150a
  Mediterranean successes of, 1:417b
  self-exile from Spain, 1:418a
  Spanish poets at Neapolitan court of, 11:424a
  urban improvement of Naples initiated by, 9:59b
  van Eyck and, 9:140b
Alfonso I of Asturias, king, Portugal and, 10:37a
  reign of, 1:626a-b
Alfonso II of Asturias, king
  church built by, 10:113b
  Portugal and, 10:37a
Alfonso II of Asturias, king, reign of, 1:626b
Alfonso III of Asturias, king
  Chronica, 11:406a
  illuminations and, 10:113b–114a
  Portugal and, 10:37b
  reign of, 1:627a
Alfonso V of Asturias-León, king, reign of, 1:628a-b
Alfonso VI of Castile and León, king, 9:69b, 70a
  Almoravids and, 1:199b
  Mudejars and, 11:376a, 376b
  reconquest of Toledo, 12:68a
  relations with Cid, 3:73a, 76a, 383b–387a
  rule of, 3:129a-b
  successors of, 3:129b–130a
Alfonso VII of Castile and León, king, 6:318a
  chronicle of his rule, 11:406b, 435b
  military campaigns of, 3:130a
  reclaiming of imperial title, 1:160b
  successors of, 3:130b
  Treaty of Tudellén and, 3:130a-b
  wars waged by, 10:41a
Alfonso VIII of Castile, king
  betrothal of daughters, 3:76b–77a
  defeat of Muslims, 11:378a
  kingdom of Navarre and, 9:70a, 70b
  Las Huelgas and, 12:686b
  marriage of, 3:130b
  rule of, 3:130b
  successors of, 3:133b
Alfonso IX of Castile and León, king, 3:610b
  Infante Don Juan Manuel and, 3:135a
  intervention in municipal government, 3:139a
  invasion of Portugal by, 10:44a
  marriage of, 3:77a
  rule of, 3:131a, 134b–135a
  tax collection and, 3:132a
Alfonso X (the Learned) of Castile and León, king, **1:161a–162b**, 7:430a
  Abū Bakr and, 8:562b
  on astronomy and astrology, 1:162a
  calendar reform, 3:23a
  Cantigas de Santa María, 1:162a, 3:85a, 85b, 5:341b, 8:563a, 645a, 11:415a, 450b–451a
    author's portrait in, 11:416 (*illus.*)
    musical instruments in, 8:601a, 602 (*illus.*)
  Castilian language and, 3:142a
  codification of secular laws and, 7:430a, 522a–523a
  compared with Peter IV (the Ceremonious), 9:510b
  conflicts with France and Aragon, 1:161b
  court of, 11:379b, 390b
  Crónica general, 1:161b
    biographies in, 11:433a
  cultural achievements of his reign, 11:414a–415a
  election as king of Germany, 1:161b, 4:428a-b
  Estoria de España, 11:415a, 435a, 435b
    15th-century reworkings of, 11:420b–421a, 425b
    reference to lost epic works in, 11:442b
    reworkings of, 11:418b
  Fuero real, 5:310a, 11:414b
  games and, 5:347a
  Grande e general estoria, 1:161b–162a, 11:415a, 415b, 435b
    Biblia Escurialense and, 11:432a
    Troy story in, 11:457b, 458a
  hermandades against, 6:209b
  historical works of, translated into Catalan, 9:511a
  hunting and, 6:358a
  Jewish scientific activity and, 11:161b
  Jews and, 7:81a-b
  Lapidario, 7:342b
  Latini and, 7:382b
  Libro de la ochava esfera, 11:414b
  Libros de acedrex dados e tablas, 5:352a
  Libros del saber de astronomía
    on equatorium, 11:98a
    on globe making, 11:96a
  links to school of Toledo, 1:162a
  lost works of his "school," 11:443a
  on man and universe, 1:161b
  in a miniature in *Cantigas de Santa María,* 11:416 (*illus.*)
  Navarre and, 9:70b
  nobility and, 3:136a-b
  patronage
    Bible translations, 2:215
    of learning, 3:140a
    of troubadours, 1:162a, 7:340b
  patronage of learning, 11:642b
  poetry of, 11:450a, 450b–451a
  protection of *mestas,* 8:280a
  rule of, 3:134a-b
  satirical poems by, 11:454a
  Setenario, 11:414b–415a
  Seville and, 11:214a
  Siete partidas, 1:162a, 11:282a-b, 414b–415a
  Tablas alfonsíes, 9:511a
  tercias and, 11:610a
  Toledan school of translators and, 11:456b, 12:68b
  translation activities at court, 1:161b, 12:135b–136a, 137b
    Arabic works, 11:456b–457a
    Picatrix, 8:37b
Alfonso XI of Castile and León, king
  cortes and, 3:610b, 611b
  Don Juan Manuel and, 8:94a, 94b, 95a, 96a
  Jews and, 7:82a
  Libro de la montería and, 11:415b, 441b
  in literary works, 11:418a
  literature of his reign, 11:415b–418a
  in *Poema de Alfonso XI,* 1:162b–163a
  rise of Spanish ballad and, 11:417b
  Spanish law and, 7:523a-b, 11:282b
  Spanish prose version of *Roman de Troie* commissioned by, 11:415b
  taxation of the *mestas,* 8:280a-b
  translation of Benoît commissioned by, 11:457b
Alfonso III of Catalonia, king, Bible translations for, 3:166b
Alfonso I (the Battler) of Navarre, king. *See* Alfonso I (the Battler) of Aragon, king
Alfonso of Aragon, marquis of Villena, 12:449a
Alfonso de Espina, *Fortress of the Faith,* 10:6b–7a
Alfonso Fadrique (son of Frederick of Sicily), 7:379b
Alfonso de Palencia, *Gesta Hispaniensia,* 11:407a
Alfonso, Peter. *See* Petrus Alfonsi
Alfonso Raimúndez. *See* Alfonso VII of Castile and León, king
Alfonso de Valladolid, 7:82a, 11:416b
  De las batallas del señor, 11:443a
Alfonso XI, Poema de, **1:162b–163a,** 11:438a
  description and metaphor, 1:163a
  form, 1:162b
  influence of oral epic on, 1:162b
  prosody of, 11:459a
  relation to clerical poetry, 1:163a
  sources for, 1:162b–163a
  surviving manuscripts, 1:162b
Alfred the Great, **1:163b–164b**
  Anglo-Saxon law and, 7:473b
  artistic renewal under, 1:272b
  Asser and, 1:593a
  on coins, 7:659a, 659b
  Danelaw treaty and, 4:91a
  on decline of learning, 1:274b, 7:363a
  fairs and, 4:586b
  law code, 1:164a-b
  line of succession, 4:456b
  in literature, 4:456a
  London
    land grants, 7:659a
    reconquest of, 4:456b, 7:659a-b
  Ottar and, 9:179a
  Paris Psalter and, 4:549b
  Peace of Chippenham, 1:164a
  pilgrimage to Rome, 12:151a
  recruitment of foreign scholars, 12:153b

Alfred the Great (*cont.*)
shipbuilding and, 9:79b
shire and, 11:253a, 253b
support of Christianity, 4:458b–459a
taxation, 11:611a-b
translations from Latin, **1:164b–167b,** 284a–285b, 2:221a, 6:439b
Augustine's *Soliloquies,* 2:184a
Pastoral Care of Pope Gregory I, 1:165a, 165b–166a, 274b, 276a, 281a, 284a
purpose of, 1:165a
sequence and dates of, 1:165a-b
treaty with Guthrum, 1:164a
unification of England, 4:456a-b
urbanism under, 12:322b–323b (*illus.*)
victory at Edington (878), 12:431b, 432b, 433a
West Saxon language and, 6:437a, 439b, 440b
Alfred Jewel, 10:108a
Alfred of Sareshel
De mineralibus, 1:136b
De motu cordis, criticism of physicians, 8:257a-b
Algarve, kingdom of the, 10:46b
Algazel. *See* Ghazālī, al-
Algebra, 8:212a-b
alphabetic notation, 8:213b–214a
analytical, 8:218b
geometrical demonstrations, 8:212a
Islamic achievements, 11:86b, 88b
Italian algebraists
arte della cosa, 8:214b
scuole d'abbaco, 8:214b
mensurational techniques, 8:212b, 213a
number-theoretical, 8:213b
rule of three, 8:212a-b
solution paradigms, 8:212a
symbols, 8:213b–214a
in university curricula, 8:212b
see also Karajī, al-
Algeciras, attacked by Vikings, 12:431a
Algemeen Rijksarchief (Holland), 1:448a
Alger of Liège, **1:167b–168a**
on liturgy, 7:631a
On Mercy and Justice, 1:167b
On the Sacrament of the Lord's Body and Blood, 1:167b
Algeria. *See* Maghrib, al-
Algiers, Great Mosque of, 1:196 (*illus.*), 197a
Algirdas of Lithuania, Great Prince, 2:67a, 7:606a-b
rivalry with Muscovy, 7:606a
Algorism, *See* Arabic numerals
Algorismus vulgaris. See John of Holywood
Algorismus vulgaris. See John of Sacrobosco
Alhambra, **1:168a–171b**
Alcazaba, 1:168a, 168b
annex, 1:168b
architecture of, 6:612a
labyrinths, 6:235a-b
construction of, 1:168b
Court of the Lions, 1:168b, 169 (*illus.*), 170a
Court of the Myrtles, 1:168b, 169b
decorative motifs, 1:171a
etymology, 1:168a
gardens, 1:170a
Great Mosque, 1:168b
Hall of the Abencerrajes, 1:168b, 170a
Hall of the Ambassadors, 1:168b, 170a
Hall of the Two Sisters, 1:168b, 170a
Jehoseph bar Najralla's palace, 1:168a
muqarnas, 1:170a, 171a
naqsh ḥadīda decoration in, 9:60a
poetic inscriptions, 1:170a-b
residential complex, 1:168b
royal funerary precinct, 1:168b
stucco and tilework, 1:171a
Tower of Comares, 1:170a
use of contrasts, 1:169a-b, 170b–171a
use of water, 1:170b
wood ceilings, 1:171a
Alhambra vase, 10:65a–66a (*illus.*)
Alhazen. *See* Haytham, Ḥasan ibn al-
Alhóndiga, 6:470b, 11:213b
ʿAlī ibn Yūsuf, Almoravid ruler, 1:200a
ʿAlī Bābā and the Forty Thieves, in *Thousand and One Nights,* 12:50a, 50b
ʿAlī al-Harawī, 9:652a
ʿAli ibn Aḥmad al-ʿImrānī, horoscope, 9:705a
ʿAlī ibn al-ʿAbbās
Kāmil al-malikī, 12:138b
Pantegni, 8:250b
translated by Constantine the African, 8:248a, 248b
ʿAlī ibn Abī Ṭālib, **1:171b–174a,** 6:577b, 10:242a
ʿAbd Allāh ibn al-Zubayr and, 1:15b
accession to caliphate, 1:172b–173a, 3:35a, 35b, 6:108b, 582b, 12:266b
ʿAmr ibn al-ʿĀṣ and, 1:237b
as *asās,* 6:615b
association with Muḥammad, 1:172a
Battle of the Camel (656), 1:172b
Battle of Ṣiffīn, 12:267a
conversion to Islam, 1:171b
death of, 1:173b
descendants of, 1:173b, 174b, 11:226b
great schism of Islam and, 11:135b–138b
Ismaili interpretations of, 6:588a
knowledge of law, 1:173b
al-Kufa and, 6:511b, 7:307a, 307b
Muʿāqiya and, 12:267a
Nuṣayrīs and, 9:3b, 4a, 4b
opponents of, 11:513a
Kharijites, 1:173a, 173b
questions of his legitimacy, 3:35b
relations with caliphs
Abū Bakr, 1:172a
ʿUmar, 1:172a
ʿUthmān, 1:172a-b, 6:108b
role in Medina, 1:171a–171b
Shīʿa and, 6:586b, 11:226b, 227a
speeches and discourses, 1:173b
Sufism and, 6:585b
supporters of, 6:503a
tomb of, 6:513b
vs. Muʿāwiya, 1:172b–173b, 4:188a
at Ṣiffīn, 11:283b–284b
sunna and, 11:510b
wars against, and Muslim doctrine, 6:205a
see also Alids
ʿAlī ibn al-Faḍl, 6:615b
ʿAlī ibn Ḥammūd, 6:413b
ʿAlī ibn Hilal. *See* Bawwab, Ibn al-
ʿAlī ibn al-Ḥusayn. *See* Zayn al-ʿĀbidīn
ʿAlī ibn ʿĪsā, 10:246a
ʿAlī ibn Ismāʿīl al-Ashʿarī, *sunna* and, 11:512a, 512b
ʿAli ibn Khalaf, development of the astrolabe and, 10:387b
ʿAlī ibn Muḥammad al-Ṣulayḥī, 6:617a
ʿAlī ibn Muḥammad, Zanj ruler, 12:739a
ʿAlī ibn ʿUmar, 6:413a
ʿAlī ibn ʿUthmān al-Jullābī al-Hujwīrī, *Kashf al-maḥjūb,* 9:40a
ʿAlī, Idrisid ruler (*fl.* 836–849), 6:413a
ʿAlī Mashhadi, sultan
calligraphy by, in *Language of the Birds,* 9:65b (*illus.*)
on scribes, 3:54a
ʿAlī Qāpū palace, 6:562b
ʿAlī al-Riḍā, heir apparent of al-Maʾmūn, 8:80b
ʿAlī Tegin, ruler of Transoxiana
origins of the Seljuks and, 11:151a
vs. Yūsuf Qadir Khan, 10:230b
ʿAli, Zirid ruler, 12:745a
Alia eorundem. See Second Shepherds' Play
Alia musica, 6:317a, 8:639a-b
modal theory, 8:450b
Aliae regulae. See Guido of Arezzo
Alibech, tale of, in Boccaccio's *Decameron,* 2:284b, 286a
Alice of Schaarbeek, 9:11b, 12a
Alids, **1:174b–175b**
Abbasids and, 1:7a, 9a, 175a, 374b
ancestors of, 4:596b
Barmakids and, 2:110b–111a
Buyids and, 2:435b, 436b
control of Mecca, 8:240a-b
driven out of Iraq, 1:175a
al-Farazdaq's sympathies with, 5:12b
first generations of, 1:174b
Hāshimiyya, 1:7a
al-Maʾmūn and, 8:80a-b
al-Manṣūr and, 8:58b, 89a
massacre of in 786, 1:174b
as object of popular reverence and respect, 1:175a-b
persecuted by Hārūn al-Rashīd, 1:174b
supported by al-Kufa, 2:45a
under the Fatimids, 1:175b
vs. ʿAbd Allāh, 11:575a
in Yemen, 1:374b
Zaydis and, 1:175a, 11:138b, 12:741b, 742a
see also Shīʿa
Alienation of land. *See* Tenure of land
Alimentary rights, 6:460a
Alimpi, **1:175b–176a,** 6:411a
Alisaunder of Macedoine, 8:332a
Aliscans, 3:259a
Alix of Cyprus, queen, 3:249a

Alixandre, Libro de. See Alexandre, Libro de
ᶜĀliya, al-. *See* Fēs
Aljamiado literature, **1:176a-b**
dating of, 11:418a
verse and prose narratives, 1:176a
see also Kharja
Ałjnik, 1:472a-b
Aljustrel tables, 8:403a
Alkimia speculativa, vs. *alkimia practica,* 1:137a-b
All Fools' Day, 5:36a
All Martyrs' Day (Armenian calendar), 1:518a
All Saints (church: Northamptonshire), western tower, 10:681b (*illus.*)
All Saints' Day, **1:176b**
in art, 4:566b
in Celtic church, 7:615b
established by the 8th century, 1:176b
origin of, 1:176b
All Souls' Day, **1:177a**
origins of, 1:177a
Allah, **1:177a–178b**
attributes of, 1:178a-b
creative power of, 1:177b
free will and, 1:177b
in Koran, 1:177b
Last Day and, 1:177b–178a
in pre-Islamic times, 1:177b
prophets of, 1:178a
transcendence of, 1:178b
uniqueness of, 1:178a
see also Islam; Liturgy, Islamic
Allāhu akbar, in Islamic liturgy, 7:617a-b
All'antica, **1:177a**
Allegoresis, 1:180a–182b
Allegoriae. See Isidore of Seville, St.
Allegoriae in universam sacram Scripturam. See Hrabanus Maurus
Allegory, **1:178b–188a**
in Alexander stories, 1:153a
in banquet dishes, 5:35a
Bede, 2:154b
in bestiaries, 2:243b
in biblical exegesis
Christian, 1:180a, 2:213b, 224a-b, 12:708b
Jewish, 2:212b
Boethius' *Consolation of Philosophy* and, 1:182b
in "Canterbury Classbook" glosses, 7:352b
in *Castle of Perseverance,* 1:186a
courtly love as, 3:670b
in *De actibus apostolorum,* 1:422b
definition of, 1:188a
by Dante, 1:178b, 179a–180a
in early Christian authors, 1:188a
in ecclesiastical literature, 9:278a
etymology of, 1:178b
in *Everyman,* 1:186a-b
Four Ages of Man, 5:35a
the four senses of interpretation and, 10:362a
French, **1:188a–189b**, 6:23a
Songe d'enfer, 10:258a
see also Fauvel, Roman de; Ovide moralisé; Roman de la Rose
in Hildegard of Bingen's *Scivias,* 9:10a
Italian. *See* Italian literature
in Johann von Würzburg's works, 7:117b
journeys to otherworldly places and, 1:185b
lawsuit format, 1:43b–44a
in *Libro de Alexandre,* 1:153a
in *Livre de seyntz medicines,* 7:635b
in love poetry, 1:184a
main types of, 1:178b–179b
medieval view of bridges and, 10:410b
metaphor and, 1:179a-b
in Middle English poetry, 8:335b
in *Milagros de nuestra señora,* 2:187b
in *Minnereden,* 8:410b
moral, 1:180b–181a
of Nile, 9:138a
Ovid and, 1:183b–184a, 189a-b, 9:314a-b
in *Pearl,* 1:186a-b
Petrarchan, 9:534a
in *Philomena* (Peckham), 7:369a
philosophical, 1:181a
political
in art, 11:280b
in *Vox Clamantis,* 7:370a
Prudentius' *Psychomachia* and, 1:180a, 181a–182a, 7:361a
as reification, 1:179a-b, 181a, 184a
religious, *De planctu naturae,* 1:119a-b
Roman de la Rose and, 1:184a–185a, 189a-b
sources of, 1:180b
in Spanish sentimental romances, 11:455a
in *Tesoretto,* 7:383a
in *Tristan und Isolt,* 5:636a
in 12th century, 1:183a
as typology, 1:179b
use of pagan material, 1:181a
in vernacular drama, 4:286b–287a
in works by the Rhétoriqueurs, 10:365a
Wyclif on, 12:708b
see also Bestiary; *Everyman;* German literature; Prudentius; specific works, e.g., Langland, William, *Piers Plowman*; Unicorn; Vergil; Visions
Allelengyon, **1:189b–190a**, 11:604b
see also Epibolé
Alleluia of the Mass, sequence and, 11:162b, 164a
Alleluia (music)
example, 8:571
jubilus of, 8:187b
neuma and, 9:109a-b
see also Mass cycles; Plainsong
Alleluia trope. *See* Trope
"Alleluia year" (1233). *See* "Year of the alleluia" (1233)
Allemanno, Johanan, 7:110a
Allerly Matkel, 4:328a
Alliteration
in *areithiau,* 1:452b
in *dróttkvætt,* 11:317b, 320a
in Icelandic *rímur,* 10:404b
in Middle English literature, 8:319b–321a, 326b–333b, 342b–344b
in *Mírmanns saga,* 8:432b
in Old English, 8:327a–328b
decline of after 1000, 8:328b
patterns of, 8:342b
in translated *riddarasögur,* 10:393b
in *Ynglingatal,* 12:726a
Allocutio christiana. See Arnald of Villanova
Allocutio super Tetragrammaton. See Arnald of Villanova
Allod, **1:190a-b**, 11:674b
in Bohemia-Moravia, 2:301a
decline of, 1:190b
etymology of, 1:190a
ministerials and, 8:405a
origins of, 1:190a
peasant, 11:676a
Alma redemptoris mater, 8:571b
Almagest. See Ptolemy, Claudius
Almain, Jacques
conciliar theory of, 3:519b, 520b–521a
Tractatus de auctoritate ecclesiae et conciliorum generalium, 3:521a
Almanach pereptuum. See Zacuto, Abraham
Almanacs, astrology and, 1:609a
Almansa (Spain), arched dam, 12:577a
Almanzor. *See* Manṣūr, Ibn Abī ᶜĀmir al-
Almaric of St. Amand, student riot at Oxford Castle and, 9:424a
Almela, Diego Rodríguez de, *Conpilación de los miraglos de Santiago,* 11:440a
Almemar. See Bimah
Almería, sacking of, by Genoa, 5:384b
Almogávares, **1:190b–191a**
Andronikos II Palaiologos and, 1:246a
described by
Bernat Desclot, 1:190b
Ramón de Muntaner, 1:191a
in the early 14th century, 1:191a
under Berenguer de Entenza, 1:191a
under Roger de Flor, 1:190b–191a, 246a
Almohads, **1:193b–196a**, 10:464b, 11:140b
administration of, 1:194b
art, **1:191a–193b**
decoration in, 1:193a
geometric ornament, 6:235a
in Marrakech, 1:191b–193a (*illus.*)
secular architecture, 1:193a
building and construction
Casbah (Marrakech), 8:151a
Kutubīya Mosque (Marrakech), 8:151a
Caños de Carmona and, 11:214a
coins of, 8:423b
dinar, 8:423b, 424 (*illus.*)
dirham, 4:215b
conquest of Meknes, 8:267b
in Ifrīqiya, 1:194a, 6:415a
Jews and
in Muslim Spain, 7:97a
in North Africa, 7:99a
persecution, 11:161b

Almohads, **1:193b–196a** (*cont.*)
in al-Maghrib, 8:15b
Marinid rebellion, 8:138a
in Marrakech, 8:151b
Maṣmūda and, 2:186a
massacre of the shaykhs, 8:151a
millennialism and, 8:389b
Mudejars and, 11:377a
opposed to Almoravids, 1:193b
origins of, 1:193b
patronage of Fēs, 5:50b–51a
relations with Hafsids, 1:194b–195b
conflicts, 6:53b
loss of importance, 6:55a
origin of dynasty, 6:52b
role in army, 6:53a
role in government, 6:54a
Sancho I of Portugal and, 10:42a-b
science under, 10:472b, 11:84a
in Seville, 11:213b, 214a
social base of the regime, 1:195b
in Spain, 1:194a-b, 6:610b, 611b, 10:42a
capture of Caltrava (1195), 3:16b
defeat at Las Navas de Tolosa, 1:195a
in Granada, 5:652a
Muslim kingdoms and, 11:383b
as rulers of Córdoba, 3:600a-b
subject peoples of, 1:194b
Almoin of Fleury. *See* Aimoin de Fleury
Almond
marzipan, 9:550b
in Mediterranean region, 5:305b, 306b–307a
milk, 9:550b
as mood elevator, 9:550b
Almoravids, **1:198a–201a**, 10:464b, 11:140a-b
Almohads and, 1:193b, 200a
architecture
mosque typology, 1:196b–197b (*illus.*)
secular, 1:197b
army, 12:552b
art, **1:196a–197b**, 6:234b–235a, 610b
decoration, 1:197b
embroidered silks, 11:718a
Banū Ghāniya, rulers of Balearic Islands, 1:194a
in Catalonia, 3:178a-b
coins of, 8:423b
conquest of Fēs, 5:50b
cultural life under, 1:200b–201a
decline of, 1:200a
early campaigns of, 1:198b
etymology of the name, 1:198a
Jews and
in Muslim Spain, 7:96b–97a
in North Africa, 7:98b–99a
in al-Maghrib, 8:15b
end of their rule, 1:200b
Marrakech, Great Mosque, 8:150b
Marrakech founded, 8:150b
in Morocco under Yūsuf ibn Tāshfīn, 1:199a
Mudejars and, 11:377a
in Sahara and sub-Saharan Africa, 1:199a, 200b
Ṣanhāja Berbers and, 2:186a
science, 10:472a
in Spain, 1:199b
in 11th century, 3:384a–385b
Muslim kingdoms and, 11:383b
Seville, 11:213b
Sunni orthodoxy of, 3:488b
vs. Cid, 1:199b, 3:129b
Zanāta confederation and, 1:198a-b
Zirids and, 12:745a
Alms, in common law, 9:546b
Alms tax, Islamic, **1:201b–202b**
beneficiaries of, 1:202a
collection and distribution of, 1:201b–202a
doctrine of, 1:201b
during the lifetime of Muḥammad, 1:201b
exemptions, 1:202a
obligation to pay, 1:201b
replaced by Mongol taxes, 1:202b
Zakāt al-fiṭr, 10:254b–255a
Almsgiving, Islamic, 6:582a
Almshouses
insane and, 6:490b
London, 7:665b
Almush ibn Shilkī, *yıltavar,* 12:488a
Almyros, in the 12th century, 12:102b
Alnage, **1:202b–203a**
Alnwick, William, bishop of Lincoln, 7:582b–583a
Alod. *See* Allod
Alodia, 9:197b
bishoprics of, 9:198b
independence of, 9:198b
Alonso de Covarrubias, 9:694a
Alonso de Espina, *Fortalitium fidei contra Judaeos,* 9:111b
Alonso de Hojeda, 9:112a
Alonso de Monroy, biography of, 11:433b
Alonso de Oropesa, 9:111b
Alovania. *See* Albania
Alp Arslan, **1:203a-b**, 11:155a
conquest of Ani in Širak, 1:290b, 484b
military campaigns of, 11:152b
Niẓām al-Mulk and, 6:606a, 9:144a
plans to conquer Syria, 11:152b
rise to power, 1:203a, 11:152a-b
Romanos IV Diogenes and, 10:516a
Toghrıl-Beg and, 12:67a
Turkomans and, 12:227a
victory at Manazkert (1071), 8:81a
see also Malikshāh
Alpego, Andrea, 11:306b
Alpert of Metz, **1:203b–204a**
Alpetragius. *See* Biṭrūjī, al-
Alpha and omega, **1:204a**, 1:217b
in illustrations of Apocalypse, 1:343b
Alphabet of Ben Sira. See Ben Sira
Alphabet of Piety. See Aipgitir Chrábaid
Alphabetization
in antiquity, 1:204a
classical Rome, 1:204a-b
concordance to the Latin Bible, 1:205b
in exempla and florilegia, 1:204b, 206a
history of, **1:204a–207a**, 7:599a, 601a-b
Slavic, 9:687a
indexes
of patristic works, 1:205b, 206a
Robert Kilwardby's concordance, 1:206a
to Aristotle's works, 1:205b
introduction of printing and, 1:207a
in libraries, 1:206a-b, 7:564a
in Papias' dictionary, 1:204b–205a
principles of
by first letter only, 1:204b–205a
by the first three letters, 1:204b–205a
by initial word, 1:204b
prior to 1050, 1:204b
in scriptural commentary, 1:205a-b
used by Italian banking houses, 1:206b
Alphabets, **1:207b–218b**
ancient views on the origin of, 1:218a
Arabic, 1:209a–210b (*illus.*), 9:332b–334a
adopted for other languages, 1:209b
consonantal alphabet of, 1:376b–377a
development of Arabic script, 2:54a
evolution of script, 1:376b
expansion of, 1:209a-b
for New Persian language, 6:506a
numerology and, 3:55a, 6:588a, 615a-b
suras and, 6:578a
thuluth, 12:53b, 54 (*illus.*)
see also Naskhī; Nastaᶜlīq
Armenian, 1:214 (*illus.*), 477a, **1:491b–498b**, 506b, 507b, 4:114a, 8:202a
creation of, 1:559b
Greek influence on, 1:214a-b
Łazar Pᶜarpecᶜi on, 7:529b
letters as numerals, 1:492b (*illus.*)
propagation of Christianity and, 5:405a
changes during the Middle Ages, 1:207b–208a
Coptic, 1:212a, 213a (*illus.*)
Cyrillic, 1:216a–217a (*illus.*), 4:73b, 11:341b
in Bulgaria, 11:554b
Dado-Romanian texts in, 6:436a
earliest surviving inscriptions in, 1:216a
influenced by the Greek alphabet, 1:216a-b
Romanian language and, 10:510a
as decorative motifs, 1:217b–218a
definition of, 1:207b
demotic, 10:455a
Ethiopic, 1:209b, 211a (*illus.*)
fanciful, 1:217b
Georgian, 5:405a, 414b
χucᶜuri, 5:414b
Glagolitic, 1:216a–217a (*illus.*), 4:6a, 73b, 5:658b, 11:341a-b
in Bulgaria, 11:554b
earliest manuscripts and inscriptions in, 1:216a
Gothic, 1:212a-b, 213a (*illus.*)
Ulfilas and, 12:469a
Greek, 1:209b, 211b–212a (*illus.*)
Armenian alphabet and, 1:492a, 492b

for Bactrian, 6:505b
influence of on other alphabets, 1:209b, 212a-b
Hebrew, 1:208 (*illus.*)
in Judeo-French language, 7:174a
in Judeo-Italian language, 7:175b
in Judeo-Latin language, 7:176a
in Judeo-Spanish language, 7:179a
origins of, 1:218a
used for other languages, 1:208a
for Yiddish, 6:441b, 12:725a
Latin, 1:212b, 213b–214a (*illus.*)
addition of runes to, 1:212b, 214a
literacy in classical Rome and, 7:598a
origin of, 1:212b
spread of, 1:212b
metaphysics of, 1:218b
nonliterary uses of, 1:217b
North Italic, 10:560b
Ogham, 1:216a-b (*illus.*), 9:222b–223a
as organizing principle in dictionaries, 7:351b, 363b, 370a
Pahlavi, 6:505b
Persian, 9:333b–334a
Polish, 9:729b
runic. *See* Runes
Slavic, 9:687a
symbolism of letters, 1:217b
Syriac, 1:208a–209a (*illus.*), 6:506a
of tales, 4:551a,b
see also Paleography; Translation and translators
Alphanus of Salerno, **1:218b–219a**, 7:363b, 8:256a
hymns of, 6:381b
Alpharts Tod, **1:219a-b**
Buch von Bern and, 2:395b
contents of, 1:219a
form of, 1:219b
Alphege, St., murdered, 3:82a
Alphonse, *see also* Afonso; Alfonso
Alphonse Jourdain, count of Toulouse, 7:339a
Montauban and, 2:128a
Alphonse of Pecha, *Epistola solitarii ad reges,* 9:15b
Alphonse of Poitiers, count of Toulouse, 12:91a, 91b
death of, 7:339b
inquisition and, 6:486a
Alphonsus of Liguori, St., as doctor of the church, 4:234b
Alpirsbach abbey church, 10:487b
Alps
mining in, 8:399a
passes, 12:150 (map)
steelmaking in, 11:471b
Álptafjörþr clan, in *Eyrbyggja saga,* 4:568a
Alptigin, **1:219b–220b**
described by Niẓām al-Mulk, 1:220a
early career of, 1:220a
as governor of Khorāsān, 1:220a
origins of Ghaznavids and, 10:638b–639a
Sebüktigin and, 11:133b
ᶜAlqāmī, Ibn al-, 8:651b
Alsace, Swiss Confederation and, 11:544a, 545a
Alta, 8:416b
Altaic language, 6:352b
Ałtᶜamar, **1:220b–221a**, 1:484b, 12:362a
Armenian architectural sculpture at, 1:220b, 495b, 496a (*illus.*)
building program under Gagik II, 12:361b
construction of, 1:221a
frescoes of, 1:220b
see of, 1:501b, 503b–504a
see also Van, Lake
Altar, **1:221a–225b**
apparatus, 1:222b–225a
in Slavic Orthodox churches. *See Pelena*
tabernacle, 10:335b–336a
trulla and ewer, 12:221b–222a
see also Paten; Retable
consecration of, 1:426b
dedication, saints' relics and, 12:145a
furniture, 5:316b–317a
location of in early churches, 4:335b
origin of, 1:221a-b
portable, 1:221b, **1:225a-b**
by Roger of Helmarshausen, 10:442 (*illus.*)
of St. Blaise, 10:442a, 500a
of Stavelot, 10:500 (*illus.*)
of Sts. Kilian and Liborius, 10:500a
reredos, 10:334b–335a
saints' relics and, 10:297b
shapes of, 1:221b–222a
superstructures of, 1:222a
see also Antependium; Pala d'Oro; Paliotto of S. Ambrogio
Altar cross, 4:9a
Altar screens, 11:117a
at Armazi, 5:411a
Georgian, 5:410a-b
Altare, glassmaking in, 5:555b
Altarpieces, **1:225b**
Aarhus Cathedral, 9:186b (*illus.*)
Breslau, 9:710 (*illus.*)
by Bouts, 5:86b, 611a (*illus.*)
by Campin, 3:61 (*illus.*), 5:86a
by Hugo van der Goes, 5:571b (*illus.*)
by Isenmann, 6:55b (*illus.*), 561 (*illus.*)
by Johann Koerbecke, 7:281b–282a (*illus.*)
by Joos van Ghent, 7:148 (*illus.*)
by Juan de Flandes, 7:156a (*illus.*)
by Konrad von Soest, 5:610a-b, 7:286b (*illus.*)
by Lochner, 7:639 (*illus.*)
by Lorenzetti, 5:604b (*illus.*)
by Mariotto di Nardo, 8:141 (*illus.*)
by Martorell, 8:159a (*illus.*)
by Marzal de Sax, 8:168 (*illus.*)
by Master of Moulins, 8:509a (*illus.*)
by Master of St. Bartholomew, 10:614 (*illus.*)
by Master of Wittingau, 12:667b, 668a (*illus.*)
by Nicholas of Verdun, 4:0 (frontispiece)
by Nicolas Froment, 5:304a (*illus.*)
by Nisart, 9:140a (*illus.*)
by Pacher, 5:611a, 9:324 (*illus.*)
by Pleydenwurff, 9:710 (*illus.*)
by Rossello, 10:536 (*illus.*)
by Simone da Bologna, 11:299a (*illus.*)
by Tilman Riemenschneider, 10:399 (*illus.*)
by Witz, 5:609 (*illus.*), 12:668a, 669 (*illus.*)
development, in 14th and 15th centuries, 5:604a
Dijon, Chartreuse de Champmol, 5:628b
Guimera altarpiece, 10:265a–266a (*illus.*)
polyptych in, 10:29a
predella of, 10:83a
relics and, 1:225b
St. Bartholomew in the church of St. Columba (Cologne), 10:614 (*illus.*)
St. Ursula Altarpiece (Rexach), 10:343a (*illus.*)
triptych, 12:198b
see also Baçó, Jaime; Pala d'Oro; Paliotto; Retable
Altdeutsche Exodus, 2:227a
Altdeutsche Genesis, 2:226b–227a
Alten Weibes List. See Schampiflor
Altenberg, Cistercian church at, 5:424a
Altera, 8:628a
"Ältere Not," 9:114a
Þiðreks saga and, 12:31a
Alternation (architecture), **1:225b–226a**
Altfrid of Münster, **1:226a**
Althing, 6:393b–394a, 396a, 12:423b
literature and, 4:618b
Altichiero, **1:226b**
frescoes by, 5:294b, 295b, 607a, 12:175b–176b (*illus.*)
Giusto de Menabuoi and, 5:542a
St. George Saved from the Wheel, 5:293 (*illus.*)
see also Avanzo, Jacopo
Altomanoviç, Nikola, 11:180a, 180b
Altsächsische Genesis, 2:225a
Altswert, Meister (14th century), love discourses of, 8:412a
Altuna (Sweden), carving of Thor and Midgard, 12:45a-b
"Altus prosator," 6:308a, 381a
Aluanki. *See* Albania
Alum
as papal monopoly, 4:327a
sources of, 4:327a
in textile manufacture, 11:276a
use in dyeing, 4:327a
in Western European trade, 12:111b, 115b
Aluredus. *See* Amerus (*fl.* 1271)
Alusianos, 2:407b
Alv Erlingsson, in ballads, 11:7a
Álvarez of Scala Coeli, freestanding Stations of the Cross and, 11:467b
Alvaro de Luna, John II of Castile and, 3:138a
Álvaro, Pablo, of Córdoba, 10:2b
Alvaro Pelayo, kingship theories of, 7:268b
Alvarus. *See* Alvaro Pelayo
Alvarus of Córdoba, bishop, 8:562a

Alvarus of Córdoba, bishop (*cont.*)
Arabization of Christian youths and, 6:233a
Indiculus luminosus, 11:406a
Alvastra (church: Sweden), 10:489a
Alvíssmál, **1:226b–227a**
order in Codex Regius, 4:386b–387a
on Thor, 12:46a
Vǫlundarkviða and, 12:491a
ᶜAlwa. *See* Alodia
Alypius (3rd/4th century), 8:636b
Ama Choluim Cille. See Forgaill, Dallá
Amadas et Ydoine, **1:227a-b,** 1:267a
Amadé family, 6:343a
Amadeo VI of Savoy, count, recapture of Gallipoli, 4:56a
Amadeo VII of Savoy, count, Achaea and, 7:381a
Amadeo VIII of Savoy, duke, 10:675a
artistic patronage, 10:675b
see also Felix V, antipope
Amadís de Gaula, **1:227b–228a,** 1:573a, 576b, 11:416a, 443b, 453b
authorship of, 1:227b
late 15th-century reworking of, 11:423b
popularity of, 1:227b
Amalar, bishop of Trêves, accusations of heresy, 1:75b
Amalaric, Visigothic king, 12:471a
Amalarius of Metz, **1:228a,** 4:542b, 8:638b
antiphonary of, 8:301b
on Divine Office, 4:222b–223a, 230a-b
dramatization of the liturgy and, 4:274a
Gottschalk of Orbais and, 5:638b
on gradual, 5:644a
heretical teachings, 6:194a
influence of, 7:628b, 630a
Liber officialis, 7:628a-b
early sequence and, 11:164a
editions of, 7:628b
liturgical treatises of, 7:628a-b
on liturgical vestments, 12:400a
Amalasuntha, Ostrogothic princess
guardianship of Athalaric, 9:291b
marriage to Theodahad, 9:292a
Theodora I and, 12:12a-b
Amalfi
commerce, 4:556a, 11:275a
consolidation of Norman rule and, 9:58a
lateen sail and, 11:233a
slave trade in, 11:336a-b
trade with Byzantine Empire, 12:101b
vs. Islamic Sicily, 11:263a
Western European trade and, 12:111a
Amalric I of Jerusalem, king
Church of the Nativity and, 4:24b
siege of Alexandria, 1:153b
vs. Muslims, 4:38b–39a
Amalric of Bène, **1:228a-b,** 3:640b
condemnation of dualistic views of, 4:297b
Neoplatonism and, 9:100b
Amalric (Cypriot pretender), 4:71a
Amalricians, 1:228b
influence on heresy of the Free Spirit, 5:216a-b
preaching and practices
human deification, 5:216b
pantheism, 5:216a-b
Amalu/Noravank. *See* Noravankᶜ at Amału
Amān, 4:198a–199a
"Amando con fin core e con speranza." *See* Piero della Vigna
Amarcius, **1:228b–229a**
Amasya, manuscripts of, 6:614a
Amatorium carmen. See Málsháttakvæði
Amatus of Monte Cassino, **1:229a**
on Normans, 7:363b
Amatus of Ostia, 11:266b
Amaury of Toulouse, count, 3:189a
Ambarvalia, as possible precursor of Lesser Rogations, 7:592b
Ambassador
accounts of, 4:212a
Bernard du Rosier on, 4:205a
ceremonies for, 4:212a-b
Comines on, 4:207a
dress of, 4:212a
functions of, 4:206b–208a
gifts to, 4:212b
legatus and, 4:205a
for Louis XI, 4:208a
Machiavelli on, 4:208a
for Martin V, 4:207a-b
nuncius and, 4:205a-b, 206b
resident, 4:206a-b
security of, 4:211a
term of, 4:205a
to vassals and subjects, 4:206a
to Venice, from dependencies, 4:205b–206a
of Treviso, 4:205b
Amber, demand for, 2:61b
Ambervale. See Ambarvalia; Litany, Lesser
Ambo, **1:229a,** 1:442b, 443 (*illus.*), 444a-b
in the Mass, 8:188a
solea and, 11:360b
Ambraser Heldenbuch, **1:229b–230b,** 7:304a
Biterolf, 2:253a
sources of, 1:230a
see also Heinrich von dem Türlin
Ambrogio, Giovanni d'. *See* Giovanni d'Ambrogio
Ambrogio, Maitani. *See* Maitani, Ambrogio
Ambrogio, Traversari. *See* Traversari, Ambrogio
Ambroise d'Évreux, *Estoire de la Guerre Sainte,* 3:331a
Ambrose, St., **1:230b–232a**
against Arianism, 1:231a
in art, 12:682a
Augustine of Hippo and, 1:231a-b, 647a-b
Bede and, 2:154a
biography of, by Emperor Anspert, 8:377b
De mysteriis, 8:381b
depicted in the St. Ambrose Church (Milan), 8:288 (*illus.*), 289a
as doctor of the church, 4:234a
elected bishop of Milan, 1:230b
"Gigas geminae substantiae," 6:383a
Glossed Gospels and, 4:547b–548a
Hexameron, 10:269b
on hymns, 8:572a, 579b
hymns of, 6:381a, 383a, 7:360b, 9:713a-b
Hymn at Cockcrow, 7:374b
on interest charging, 12:336a
Liber notitiae sanctorum Mediolani, 8:381b
on liturgy, 7:626a
Milanese rite and, 1:231a, 231b
octagon as symbol of Resurrection, 4:336a
Physiologus and, 2:204a
as possible author of Athanasian Creed, 1:231b
support of Priscillian, 10:129a, 129b
theology of, 3:336a
see also Ambrosian chant
Ambrosian Bible, 8:111 (*illus.*)
Ambrosian chant, **1:232a–233b,** 3:402a, 402b, 406b, 6:379a-b
analyzed by Bede, 10:379a
borrowed forms in, 1:232b
classification of, 8:448b
early history of, 1:232b
modern editions of, 1:233a
musical style of, 1:233a-b
Tropes to the Proper of the Mass and, 12:211a
see also Ambrose, St.; Gregorian chant; "Veni creator spiritus"
Ambrosian Republic
beginning of, 8:380a
collapse of, 11:216a
Ambrosian rite. *See* Milanese Rite
Ambrosiani (hymns), 1:231a
Ambrosius Aurelianus. *See* Aurelianus, Ambrosius
Ambrosius Autpertus. *See* Autpertus, Ambrosius
Ambulatory, **1:234a**
at St. Denis, 10:616b
part of chevet, 3:300b
radiating chapel church plan. *See* Church architecture
sculpture, French Romanesque, 10:493 (*illus.*)
Ambulatory property. *See* Property
Ambush. *See* Travel and transport, dangers of; Warfare
Amelius Gentilianus, 9:96b, 97a
Amenap'rkičᶜ church, architecture and decoration, 10:648a
Amenapᶜrkičᶜ stele. *See Xačᶜkᶜar*
Amentia, 6:489b
America
Basques and, 2:127a
discovery of, 4:555a
Vinland sagas and, 12:456b
European diseases and, 9:673b, 682a-b
rediscovery of, 4:559b–561a
Amerindians, in Europe, 9:682a-b
Amersfoort, Brethren of the Common Life at, 2:367a
Amerus (*fl.* 1271), *Practica artis musicae,* 8:644b

Amesha Spentas (Zoroastrian gods), 12:747a
Ameto. See Boccaccio, Giovanni
Amhrán, 6:532b–533a
Ami et Amile, **1:234a-b,** 1:267a, 3:259a, 8:316a
  versions of, 1:234a
Amice. *See* Vestments, liturgical
Amicus og Amilíus rímur, skáhenda meter in, 10:406b
Amida. *See* Diyarbakir
Amidah, 7:619b–620b
Amidī, al-, *Kitāb al-muwāzana,* on poetical decorum, 10:346a
Amiens, office of mayor in the 12th century, 8:234b
Amiens Cathedral, **1:234b–235b,** 5:84a (*illus.*), 594a (*illus.*), 599b
  central portal of, 5:618b (*illus.*)
  jamb figures of, 5:622a-b
  nave of designed by Robert de Luzarches, 10:432b (*illus.*)
  photoelastic modeling of, 3:567b–568a (*illus.*)
  style of, 5:623a
  west facade of, 1:235a (*illus.*)
  see also Thomas de Cormont
Amíkus saga ok Amílius, 10:391b
Amīn, Muḥammad al-, Abbasid caliph, 2:46b, 8:79b–80a, 653b
  vs. Ṭāhir ibn al-Ḥusayn, 11:574a, 575a
Amīr, Mamluk dynasty and, 2:272b, 273a
Āmir, al-, Fatimid caliph, 5:28b
  administration of, 6:591a
  murder of, 6:617a, 11:138a
Amīr Khusrau, Niẓāmī and, 6:507b
Amīr al-mu$^{\supset}$minīn. See Commander of the Faithful
Amīr al-umarā'. See Islamic administration, supreme commander
Amiran darejaniani, 5:418a, 11:256b
Amirspasalar, **1:235b,** 5:529b
  etymology of, 1:235b
Amis et Amiloun. See Ami et Amile
Amlóþa saga, Svarfdæla saga and, 11:521b
Ammianus Marcellinus, **1:235b–236a**
  on Arsacids, 1:476a
  on bards, 8:558a
  description of Persians, 10:664b–665a
  on historiography, 10:456a, 463a
  on Iranian king, 10:611b
  on libraries, 7:559a
  reference to Sapaudia, 10:674a
  Res gestae, 1:235b–236a, 7:559a
  on Roman carriages, 12:369a
Ammonius of Alexandria, Cassiodorus and, 8:638a
Ammonius Saccas, 9:95b
  professorate at Alexandria, 9:565a-b
  as teacher of Origen, 9:98b
Ammonius (son of Hermias), 1:457b
  Alexandrian Neoplatonic school and, 9:98a, 98b
  Boethius and, 9:99a
Amoiroutzes, George, at Council of Ferrara-Florence, 12:169b
Amor. *See* Courtly love
"Amor fa una donna amare, L'." *See* Compagnetto da Prato
Amor de lonh. See Jaufré Rudel
"Amor non vole ch'io clami." *See* Iacopo da Lentini
"Amor, tu vedi ben che questa donna." *See* Dante Alighieri
Amoraim, 11:583a, 584a
Amorbach Sermon. See Otloh of St. Emmeram
Amorians, **1:236a**
  see also Michael III, Byzantine emperor
Amorion, **1:236a-b**
  attacked and captured by the Arabs, 1:236b
  as a communication center, 10:424b
  crusaders' route and, 10:423b
  fall of (838), 8:653b
    oral epic tradition and, 8:19a
  as headquarters of Anatolikon theme, 1:242a
  monasteries, 8:457b
Amorós, Carles, printing of *Libro en el qual se contienen cincuenta* romances, 11:429b
Amorosa visione. See Boccaccio, Giovanni
Amoureuse prise, L'. See Jean Acart de Hesdin
Amphissa, Thomas of Autremencourt and, 7:376a-b
Amphitruo. See Plautus
Amphitryo. See Vital of Blois
Amphoras, use of, 2:114a
Ampulla, **1:236b,** 5:320a-b
^{c}Amr ibn ^{c}Adī (*fl.* 3rd century), 7:320b
^{c}Amr ibn al-^{c}Āṣ, **1:236b–238a,** 6:568a, 569b, 11:284b
  administrative and political skills of, 1:237b
  conquests
    Egypt, 1:237a, 4:403b
    Palestine, 1:237a
    Syria, 1:237a
  early career of, 1:236b
  as governor of Egypt, 1:237a-b
  Mu^{c}āwiya and, 1:237a-b, 11:284b
^{c}Amr ibn Layth, 12:716a, 716b
^{c}Amr, Saffarid ruler, 11:252b
  expansion of dynasty, 10:609a-b
  vs. Muḥammad ibn Ṭāhir, 11:575b
Amra Choluim Chille, 6:525b–526a, 541a, 541b
Amram Gaon, prayer book of, 7:620b, 621a
Amṣār, 12:551b–552a
Amsterdam, Sephardic community in, 11:161b
Ämter. See Peasants, German, bailiwicks
Amu Darya
  border between two Timurid states, 12:58a
  see also Transoxiana
Amulets
  use of in Islam, 8:21a
  see also Reliquary
Amulo, 10:2b
Ana 'l-Ḥaqq, 6:585a
Anabasis. See Xenophon
Anabolagium. *See* Vestments, liturgical
Anacletus II, antipope, 1:330b–331a, 3:636b–637a, 7:93b
  Roger II and, 11:267a, 10:440b–441a
Añafil, 8.563a
Anahit, Syrian March and, 1:514b
Anāhitā (Zoroastrian goddess), 1:451b
  in art, 11:597a, 597b
  Erzincan and, 4:508b
Analdi. *See* Arnoldi, Alberto
Analecta Bollandiana. See Bollandists
Analecta hymnica medii aevi, 6:380b
  edition of sequence texts, 11:162b
  medieval rhymed offices published in, 10:366b
Anales toledanos primeros, 1:576a
Analoi, **1:238a**
Analytica posteriora. See Aristotle
Analytica priora. See Aristotle
Anan ben David, 7:162b–163a, 209b–210a
  biblical exegesis, 2:212a
Anania Mokk^{c}ac^{c}i, *kat^{c}ołikos* of Armenia, 1:483b, 510b
Anania Narekac^{c}i, vardapet, 1:510b, 511a
Anania Sanahnec^{c}i (11th century), 1:511a
Anania Širakac^{c}i, **1:238a-b**
  Armenian magical texts, 8:16b
  on Byzantine and Persian weights and measures, 12:97a
  calendar reform and, 3:31a
  genealogical list of human races, 6:239a-b
  Geography of the World, 1:509b
  mathematical texts, 1:238b
Ananites, 7:107b, 209a
Anaphora
  in Armenian rite, 1:516a-b
  Basilian, 2:120b–121a
Anaphora of the Twelve Apostles, 11:567b
Anastas, *kat^{c}ołikos* of Armenia, revision of the Armenian calendar and, 1:238a
Anastasima stichera. *See* Sticheron
Anastasis, **1:239**
  iconology of Macedonian renaissance, 10:307a
  in Jerusalem, 4:336b–337a
  Ravenna cathedral, 10:262a
  representations of, 1:239a
  see also Resurrection cycle
Anastasis Mosaic (S. Marco, Venice), 1:0 (frontispiece)
Anastasius I, Byzantine emperor
  coins during rule of, 8:419a
  currency reforms, 10:461a
  Edict of, translated into Armenian, 1:508b
  Monophysite controversy, 1:499a, 2:486a
  as patron of Priscian, 10:128a
  Sutton Hoo and, 11:519b
Anastasius III, pope, Nikolaos I Mystikos and, 9:135b
Anastasius Bibliothecarius, **1:239a-b,** 7:570a
  Landolfus and, 7:328a
  Nicholas I and, 9:121a

Anastasius Bibliothecarius (*cont.*)
Pseudo-Dionysius the Areopagite's *The Celestial Hierarchy* and, 1:250a
translation of Theophanes Confessor's *Chronographia,* 12:22b
Anastasius of Esztergom, archbishop, 11:479b
Anastasius the Librarian. *See* Anastasius Bibliothecarius
Anastasius, quaestor, 7:133a
Anastasius, St., Bede's lost life of, 2:155a
Anathema, 4:537a
interdict and, 6:494b
Anathomia. See Henry de Mondeville
Anatoli, Jacob ben Abba Mari
Malmad ha-Talmidim, 10:74b
translations by, 12:134a, 135b, 11:91a
Anatolia, **1:239b–242a**, 1:240 (map)
Arab invasions, 1:240b–241a
architecture, *kümbet,* 6:28a-b
art, textiles, 11:718a-b
crusaders' route and, 10:423a
Danishmendids in, 4:91b, 93a
iconoclasm and, 1:241a
Ilkhanids and, 6:420a
in Islamic conquests, 6:572a
madrasas in, 8:12a
Malikshāh and, 8:60a
mints and money in, 8:424a-b
Ottomans and, 1:241b–242a, 8:76a, 536a
Persian invasions, 1:240b
plagues
of 542, 1:240a
of the 740's, 1:241a
Pontus in, 10:31a
restoration to Byzantine rule by First Crusade, 4:344a
roads in, 10:424a-b
Seljuks in, 1:241a-b, 11:152b
art and architecture, 11:148a–149b
private mausolea, 11:147a
ṣinf in, 11:308a, 309a
through the 6th century, 1:239b–240a
Tulinid rule of, 12:224a-b
Turkicization, 10:555a
Turkomans and, 1:242a-b, 9:306b, 12:226b–227a
Umayyad raids, 3:38a
under Selim I, 11:145a-b
urban centers of, 1:239b
see also Karamania; Ottomans; Sebaste; Seljuks; Seljuks of Rum
Anatolian language, 6:433b
Anatolikon, theme of, **1:242a-b**, 12:9b
Anatomia Mundini. See Mondino dei Luzzi
Anatomy, treatises on, 8:462b–463a
Anāzat. See Ramik
Anbār, al-. *See* Ḥadīth
Anchialo, 2:410a, 412b
Anchialo, Battle of (917), 2:405a, 11:555a
Anchiskʾati Icon, 2:164b
Anchorites, **1:242b**
common worship, 8:460b
definition, 8:459b
Egypt, 8:460b
origin of, 8:460a-b
see also Ancrene Riwle
Anchovy (*Engraulis encrasicholis*), fishing of, 5:70b
Anciens usages d'Artois, 4:515b
Ancient of Days, **1:242b–243a**
Ančisxatʿi triptych, 5:410b (*illus.*)
Ancona, attacked by Muslims, 6:572b
"Ancor che l'aigua per lo foco lassi." *See* Guido delle Colonne
Ancrene Riwle, **1:243a-b**, 7:225b, 8:314a-b, 317b, 330a-b, 9:280b
compared with *Brut,* 8:316a
eight parts of, 8:314b
English, French, and Latin versions of, 8:314b
English mysticism and, 9:18b
translations into French and Latin, 1:243a
see also Anchorites
Ancrene Wisse. See Ancrene Riwle
Ancyra. *See* Ankara
Andachtsbild, **1:243b**
imago pietatis and, 6:425b
Andain (land measure), 12:587a
Andalò di Negro (Genoese astronomer), 1:613a, 2:278a
Andalusia, **1:243b–244a**
art in, 11:380a
boundaries of, 11:382a (map)
Christian Spanish states in, 11:375a
conquests of, 11:377a
culture of, 11:384b–385a
effect of Castilian conquest, 3:135b–136a
emirates in, 11:382b–383a
ethnic groups in, 11:384a-b
history of, 11:381b
interpretive problems, 11:385a–387b
Ibrāhīm ibn al-Aghlab and, 6:391b
immigration to Fēs, 5:50b
Jews in, 7:82b, 95b–97a
literary culture of, 6:127a
under the "Party kings," 7:96a-b
Muslim tribal rivalries in, 3:598a
navy of, 9:75a, 11:382b
reconquest of, Order of Caltrava in, 3:17a
trade of, 11:385a
transhumance, 8:280a
under Ibn Abī ʿĀmir al-Manṣūr, 8:89b–90b
Andeli, Henri d'. *See* Henri d'Andeli
Anders Sunesøn, archbishop, 4:153b, 154a
Andra rímur, 6:312a
Andra saga, 6:312a
András I of Hungary, king, 6:340a
András II of Hungary, king, 3:306a
in Fifth Crusade, 4:49b
Golden Bull and, 3:334a, 6:335b
military organization, 12:500a-b
reign of, 6:341a-b
András III ("the Venetian") of Hungary, king
death of, 6:344a
reign of, 6:343a
Andravida, under Latins, 7:378b
André le Chapelain. *See* Capellanus, Andreas
André de Fleury, **1:244a**
Miracula Sancti Benedicti, continuation by Radulphus Tortarius, 10:247a
André (Guigues VI). *See* Guigues VI of Burgundy
André de la Vigne, 10:364b, 365a
Vie de St. Martin, 4:265a
Andrea da Barberino, prose romances of, 6:639a
Andrea Bonaiuti da Firenze. *See* Andrea da Firenze
Andrea di Cione. *See* Orcagna, Andrea
Andrea of Crete, bishop. *See* Andrew of Crete, St.
Andrea da Fiesole. *See* Andrea da Firenze
Andrea da Firenze, **1:244a-b**
frescoes of, 5:294b
Triumph of the Church, 5:607a
Andrea Pisano. *See* Pisano, Andrea
Andrea da Pontedera. *See* Pisano, Andrea
Andreas, 1:279a, 8:327a
Andreas Capellanus. *See* Capellanus, Andreas
Andreas de Isernia, 11:274a
Andreas Lopadiotes, *Lexicon Vindobonense,* 11:53b
Andrés Magnússon, *Mírmants rímur,* 10:403a
Andrés Marzal de Sax. *See* Marzal de Sax, Andrés de
Andrew, *see also* András
Andrew the Chaplain. *See* Capellanus, Andreas
Andrew of Crete, St., 6:379a
Great Kanōn, 2:511b, 7:208b, 613a
on Virgin Mary, 12:460a
Andrew cross, 4:9a, 11a (*illus.*)
Andrew of Prague, bishop, conflict between church and laity, 2:304a
Andrew of St. Victor, **1:244b**, 3:313b
biblical exegesis, 2:213b, 9:593b
Hugh of St. Victor and, 6:322a
Peter Comestor and, 9:514a
theology school of, 12:21b–22a
Andrew of Sens, 8:103b
Andrew of Wyntoun, *Original Chronicle of Scotland,* 10:435b
Andria. See Terence
Andrieu, Michel, on church dedication, 4:130b–131a
Androgynos. See Menander
Andronikos I Komnenos, Byzantine emperor, **1:244b–245b**, 7:284a-b
anti-Latin bias, 2:496a-b
assumption of regency by, 1:245a
coinage of, 8:421a
foreign affairs under, 1:245a
Isaac II Angelos and, 6:559b
Niketas Choniates and, 9:133b
relations with other Komnenoi, 1:245a
conspiracy against Manuel I Komnenos, 2:495b
Isaac Komnenos and, 4:70b
Andronikos II Palaiologos, Byzantine emperor, **1:245b–246a**

Asia Minor policy of, 1:245b–246a
Catalan Company's support of, 3:156a
coinage of, 8:421a
deposition of, 1:246a, 2:500b
domestic policies, 2:499b
inheritance and, 6:452a
John Laskaris and, 7:343a
marriages of, 1:245b
Nikephoros Gregoras and, 9:133b
Nymphaion and, 9:203a
relations with Venice and Genoa, 1:246a
religious policies, 2:499b
Roger de Flor and, 10:441b
Serbia and, 11:176a, 177a
Stefan Uroš II Milutin of Serbia and, 11:186a
Theodore Metochites and, 12:15a
union with Rome and, 1:245b, 246a
Andronikos III Palaiologos, Byzantine emperor, **1:246a-b**, 7:128a
assumption of throne, 2:500b
campaigns in Asia Minor, 1:246b
coinage of, 8:421a
Epiros and, 4:500a
military victories, 2:500b–501a
as president of the permanent synod, 9:505b
Serbia and, 11:177a, 178a
union with Rome and, 1:246b
Andronikos IV Palaiologos, Byzantine emperor
Chioggia War and, 2:502b
plot against father, 2:502a-b
Andronikov monastery (Moscow), cathedral, architectural style, 10:581a-b
Andvaranaut ring, 4:581b
Anecdota/Secret History. See Procopius
Ânée (unit of measure), 12:587a
Anegenge, **1:246b–247a**, 2:228a
Aneirin, **1:247a-b**
Historia Brittonum and, 11:581b
on minstrels, 8:558a
Y Gododdin, 1:247a-b, 564b–565a, 12:602a-b
oral transmission, 12:602b–603a
plot summary, 12:602b
poetic devices, 12:597b
two versions, 12:597b, 602b–603a
Aneirin, Book of, 12:602b
Anejir, 8:562b
Anesthesia, in surgery, 2:99a
Angantýr (mythological character), 6:385b
Angaria (Frankish carting vehicles), 12:370a
Angeł-tun. *See* Ingilenē
Angela of Brescia, St. *See* Angela Merici, St.
Angela of Foligno, **1:251a**
Istruzioni salutifere, 9:14b
Memoriale de fra Arnaldo, 9:14a
Angela Merici, St., 1:250b–251a
Angelenē. *See* Ingilenē
Angelic Doctor. *See* Aquinas, Thomas, St.
Angelic Salutation (Hail Mary). *See* Ave Maria
Angelica de Christi resurrectione, 12:648a
Angelico, Fra. *See* Giovanni da Fiesole
Angelo Clareno
Exposition of the Rule, 5:203a
History of the Seven Tribulations of the Order of the Minors, 5:203a
Angelo da Orvieto, **1:251a-b**
Angeloi
Byzantine expansion, 2:498a-b
Niketas Choniates and, 9:134a
Angelology, **1:249a–250b**
in Duns Scotus, 1:250b
in Peter Lombard, 1:250a
in Pseudo-Dionysius the Areopagite, 1:249b–250a
in Thomas Aquinas, 1:250b
two traditions of, 1:249b
see also Angels; Archangel
Angelomus of Luxeuil, **1:251b**
Angelos, **1:251b**
commerce under, 12:103b
see also Michael I of Epiros
Angelram of St. Riquier, **1:252a**
Angels, **1:247b–248b**
in art, 1:248a, 4:119a (*illus.*), 6:405b, 10:508a (*illus.*)
cherub, 3:297b
in hierarchy of supernatural powers, 8:36a
Islamic, **1:248b–249a**
jinn, 7:112a–113a
in the New Testament, 1:248a, 249a-b
in the Old Testament, 1:247b, 249a
in Pseudo-Dionysius the Areopagite, 1:248a, 249b–250a
see also Angelology; Paradise, Western concept of; Seraph
Angelus, **1:252a–253a**
see also Ave Maria
Angelus bell. *See* Bells
Angelus Clarenus. *See* Angelo Clarenus
Angelus Silesius, influenced by Meister Eckhart, 9:32a
Angelus Urbsveterensis. *See* Angelo da Orvieto
Angerdörfer, 12:446b
Angers Cathedral, 10:481a
Angevins, **1:253a–254a**
duchy of Naxos and, 9:91a
empire of, 9:167a–168a
collapse, 5:483a
in England, 4:461a, 7:675b
family conflicts, 5:161b
in France, 6:157a, 7:675b
control over Normandy, 4:463a
rule over Brittany, 2:379b–380a
support of Charles VII, 5:188
vs. Philip II Augustus, 4:467b, 5:161b
Welf-Angevin alliance, 4:467a
in Hungary, 6:344a–346a
in Italy, 7:8a, 10a-b
Boccaccio at court of Naples, 2:278a-b, 288b–289a
Naples and, 9:59a-b
Rome, 10:524a
Sicily, 11:272a–273a
in Malta, 8:67b
office of seneschal and, 11:160a
Philip of Savoy and, 7:379a
Poland and, 9:724a, 725a
under Henry II, 4:469a-b
vs. Catalans, 7:379b
vs. Michael VIII Palaiologos, 2:499a
Anghiera, Pietro Martire d', 11:425b
"Anghososa partença, L'," 6:657b
Angier, **1:254a**
Angilbert of Milan, **1:254b**
carroccio and, 3:117a-b
Paliotto of S. Ambrogio commissioned by, 8:288 (*illus.*), 289a
peace between Louis I the Pious and Lothair, 8:377b
Wolvinus and, 12:682a
Angilbert, St., **1:254a**, 10:94a
Carolingian Latin poetry and, 3:100b, 101b, 7:362a
on hunting, 6:356a
Nithard and, 9:142b, 143a-b
Ordo for St. Riquier, 4:117a-b, 7:592b
Angiolieri, Cecco, 6:650a
Angł, 1:515a
Angł-tun. *See* Ingilene-Anzitenē
Angles, 1:289a
language of, 6:437a
migration of, 8:363a
to England, 2:96b
surviving runic inscription in alliterative verse, 8:327a
Anglesey, ravaged by the Danes (855, 874), 10:366a
Anglicae historiae. See Polydore Vergil
Anglo-Norman architecture
churches, 1:255b–256a, 257 (*illus.*)
distinctive features of, 1:255b–256a
influences on, 1:255b–256a
Anglo-Norman art, **1:255b–259a**
distinctive features of, 1:255b–256a
illuminated books, 1:257b (*illus.*), 258a
influences on, 1:255b–256b
painting, 1:256b–258b
parallels between England and northeastern France, 1:256b, 258a-b
sculpture, 1:256 (*illus.*)
see also Scroll, inhabited
Anglo-Norman dialect, 1:259a–260a, 271b
characteristics of, 1:259b
Fourth Lateran Council and, 1:263a
grammar of, 1:259b
modern scholarship on, 1:271b–272a
original meaning of the term, 1:255b, 259a
vocabulary of, 1:259b–260a
Anglo-Norman law, 4:464a-b, 7:433a-b
Norman Inquest, 7:435b–436b
see also English common law
Anglo-Norman literature, **1:259a–272b**, 9:558b
antifeminism in, 1:269b
chronicles, 5:340b–341a, 12:628b
courtoisie, 1:268b–269a
definition of, 1:260b
drama, 1:269b–270a
fabliaux, 1:269b
homiletic texts, 1:262b–264a
lais, 1:268a-b

Anglo-Norman literature, **1:259a–272b** (*cont.*)
lyric poetry, 1:269a-b
modern scholarship on, 1:271a–272a
moral and didactic writing, 1:264a-b
Polistorie, 10:9b
Quatre livres des reis, 10:239a
romances, 1:266a–268a, 6:115b
saints' lives, 1:261a-b
source for *Gui de Warewic,* 6:8a
version courtoise of Tristan legend, 12:201a, 202a-b
Anglo-Saxon art, **1:272b–274a**
Celtic art and, 3:218a, 219b
cinerary urn, 3:236b (*illus.*)
cloisonné jewelry, 3:219b
influenced by
Utrecht Psalter, 1:273b, 12:342a
Viking art, 12:418b
Missal of Robert of Jumièges, 10:434a (*illus.*)
monumental sculpture in, 1:256a
under St. Dunstan, 1:273a
see also Hiberno-Saxon art
Anglo-Saxon Chronicle, 3:331a, 6:262b, 439b
accomplishments of William I of England, 4:461b–462a
on Alfred the Great's military campaigns, 1:163b
as a basis of Gaimar's *Estoire des Engleis,* 1:264b
on London Bridge, 10:414b
Parker manuscript, 1:276b, 284a-b
Peterborough Chronicle and, 8:328a, 328b
poems, 1:278b
on the death of King Edward, 8:327a
historical (937 to 1086), 8:327b–328b
reign of Egbert, 4:455b
Roger of Salisbury and, 10:443b
southern copies of, 8:328a
on Vikings, 12:432a, 432b, 433a
first record, 12:424b
Worcester Chronicle and, 8:328a, 328b
Wulfstan of York and, 1:281b, 12:704b
Anglo-Saxon language. *See* English language, Old English
Anglo-Saxon law
church influence on, 7:473b
early codes, 7:473a-b
wergild, 12:617b
Anglo-Saxon literature. *See* Old English literature
Anglo-Saxons
culture, evidence for, 1:274a
described by Bede, 1:189a
in England, 10:465a
hair color of, 2:146b
magical rituals of, 8:34b
military organization
after Alfred the Great, 12:556a-b
fyrd, 12:556a-b
thegns and huscarls, 12:556b
origins and migration, **1:288b–290a,** 2:96a–97a, 10:682a-b
Humber, 4:454a-b
language development, 9:226b
Thames estuary, 4:452b–454a
the Wash, 4:454a
see also Thegn
raids into Cumbria, 11:490b
use of Christian era in reckoning calendar, 3:19b
vs. Charles the Simple, 9:160a
weapons of, 1:522a
"Anglo-Scandinavian" dialect, 12:434a
Ango, 1:522a
Angora. *See* Ankara
Angoulême Cathedral, 10:481b (*illus.*), 481a, 495a, 496a (*illus.*)
Angoumois, battle at (844), 9:143b
Angra Mainyu (Zoroastrian god), 1:451b, 8:237b, 12:746b, 747b, 748b, 749a
in *Vidēvdād,* 12:411b
Ani, Bagratid kingdom of
Aristakēs Lastiverc^{c}i on, 1:511a
imperial annexation, 9:544a-b
Ani, Council of (969), 1:482b, 500b
Ani in Daranalik^{c}, **1:290a-b**
Ani in Širak, **1:290b–291b,** 11:311a-b
annexed by Alp Arslan, 1:203b, 11:152b
as Armenian capital, 1:482b, 483a, 485b, 503b
Armenian trade and, 12:97b–99b
captured by Mongols, 1:291a
churches of, 1:494a
city elders of, 1:490b
establishment of Georgians in, 1:291a
fortifications of, 1:291a, 292 (*illus.*)
monuments of, 1:291a, **1:291b–292b,** 292b (*illus.*)
Trdat's church architecture, 12:164b–165a (*illus.*)
see also Tigran Honenc^{c}
occupied by David the Builder (1123–1126), 1:485a-b
population of, 1:291a
reconquered (1199), 1:485b
Sargis Zak^{c}arean and, 12:736b
Seljuks and, 1:484b, 485a
Shaddadids and, 1:290b–291a, 513b, 514a, 11:217a, 217b, 12:98b
Tamar and, 11:587a
Theme of Iberia and, 1:484a
under the Bagratids, 1:290b, 292a
under Zak^{c}arids, 1:291a-b, 292a
urban growth under Bagratids, 12:98a
Ani in Širak Cathedral, 1:494a, 494b (*illus.*), 12:164b–165a (*illus.*)
Ani-Kamaχ. *See* Ani in Daranalik^{c}
Anian of Bangor, bishop, rite of Bangor and, 2:72a
Anianos, chronography of, 3:18b
Anianus of Orléans, St., Sidonius and, 11:277b
Aniconism, **1:293a**
Animal style, **1:293a**
characteristics of, 8:365a
lacertine ornament and, 6:497b, 7:314a
Lombard art, 7:649b, 650b
Styles I, II, III, 8:365a–367b
Animal substances, in perfumes, 2:147a
Animals
in Alexander Neckham's work, 9:92a
in art, inhabited scrolls, 11:119 (*illus.*)
in bestiaries, 2:204b–206b
breeding, Switzerland, 11:540b
in Celtic mythology, 9:48a-b
cruelty to opposed, 10:268a
in depictions of the Nativity, 9:66a
designs of in Timurid bookbinding, 8:100a
in fables, 4:573b, 6:508b, 7:366b
Herger and, 11:462a
in *Vox Clamantis,* 7:370a
in folklore, 2:204b–205a
in Hebrew manuscript illumination, 8:111 (*illus.*)
human ecology and, 9:673a–674a
in literature
Trecentonovelle, 6:661a
see also Beast epic; Huginn and Muninn
motifs of in Viking art, 12:417b
mythical
in art, 6:408a
see also Unicorn
in *Reginsmál,* 4:581b
study of, 2:240b–241a, 242a–244b
bestiary and, 2:243a-b
classification of, 2:243a
encyclopedic approach, 2:242a-b
hunting manuals, 2:242b, 244b
low status of, 2:242a
symbolism of, 2:206b
see also Hunting; Insects; Rodents; Veterinary science
Animals, draft, **1:293a–299a,** 12:77b
in grain mills, 1:77b
in Islamic regions, 12:83b, 84a, 84b
threshing, 12:85a
land reclamation and, 10:277a-b
origin of the use of, 1:293a
oxen, 12:77b
rights of pasture and, 9:455a-b
species of during the Middle Ages, 1:293a-b
see also Ass; Camel; Cattle; Horse; Mule; Ox; Vehicles, European; Water buffalo
Animals, food, **1:299a–302a**
beef powder as military staple, 1:300a
Bulgaria, 1:78b
butchering, 1:297 (*illus.*), 299b, 9:679b
barrow houses, 5:123b–124a
disposal of waste, 5:123b–124a
health hazards, 5:123b
scalding houses, 5:123b
slaughterhouses, 9:679b
degeneration of domestic breeds, 1:301b–302a
as disease intermediaries, 9:673a–673b, 674a
factors affecting kinds raised, 1:299b
factors affecting quantities raised, 1:299a
foraging, 5:131b
pannage, 5:129b
game animals, 1:300b–301a
as gifts to liege lords and monks, 1:299b–300a
grazing, 1:92a
Byzantium, 1:77b
Christian Spain, 1:83a-b

Islamic world, 1:103b
long-distance migrations, 1:78b–79a
Sicily, 1:87b–88a
transhumance, 1:78a, 83a-b
hunting as source of, 1:299a, 300b–301a
indoor maintenance, 1:78b
investment in, 5:117a
Jewish dietary rules for, 4:181a–183a
mutton, price of, 5:122b–123a
Northern Europe, mixed farming, 1:92a
Norway, 9:180b
price increases, expanded production and, 5:117a
prohibitions and taboos, 1:300a-b
Romans, 1:91b–92a
trade in, 5:122b–124a
sale of unwholesome animals, 5:123a
transportation problems, 5:124a
types eaten, 5:122b
at feasts, 3:581b
Animals, pack, 12:148a, 158a, 159b
in France, 12:375b
see also Vehicles, Islamic
Animals, riding, 1:295a–296b
see also Camel; Horse; Mule
Anime, 1:531b
Animism, Arab, 6:575a
Anjewacᶜikᶜ, separatism of, 1:503b
Anjit. *See* Anzitenē
Anjou
gained by Philip II Augustus, 9:417b
Geoffrey Plantagenet and, 9:166b
relations with Normandy, 9:168a
William I of England and, 9:164b
see also Angevins
Ankara, **1:302a-b**
as a communication center, 10:424b
crusaders' route and, 10:423b
extent of Islamic influence, 1:302b
Seljuks of Rum and, 11:157a
ṣinf in, 11:309a-b
under Byzantine Empire, 1:302a-b
under Ottomans, 1:302b
Ankara, Battle of (1402), 1:242a, 8:92a, 11:472b, 588a
Ankh, 4:9a, 11 (*illus.*)
see also Cross, forms of
Anlautgesetz, 9:189b
Anmchara (Irish "soul-friend"), penance and, 9:488b
Anna, **1:303a**, 2:118b, 12:485b
Anna Komnena, **1:303a–304b**, 5:660b, 7:127a
Alexiad, 1:303b–304a, 2:514b–515a, 6:246a-b, 9:133a, 12:483b
on astrology, 8:18b
on Basil the Bogomil, 2:295b
continuations of, 2:515a, 516a-b
conspiracy to seize imperial throne, 1:303a-b
histories of, 7:596b, 597a
on knights, 7:278a-b
on monks, 8:458b
Niketas Choniates and, 9:134a
Anna von Munzingen, *Vitae sororum,* 9:13b
Anna, ruler of Bulgaria, 11:177a, 177b
Anna (wife of Michael Šišman), 2:411b–412b
Annafir. See Añafil
Annalen der lateinischen Hymnendichtung, 6:380b
Annales. See Einhard
Annales Bertiniani. See Flodoard of Rheims
Annales Cambriae, 5:388b–389a
Arthurian references in, 1:564b–565a, 577a
on Bishop Elfoddw, 2:71a-b
on Maelgwn, 8:13a
Annales Fuldenses, 3:202a
Annales de gestis Carolii Magni. See Poeta Saxo
Annales Poloniae. See Długosz, Jan
Annales de Saint Louis, use of organ, 9:274b
Annales seu cronicae incliti regni Poloniae. See Długosz, Jan
Annales typografici. See Panzer, Georg
Annales typographici. See Maittaire, Michael
Annals of the Four Masters, 6:521a
Annals of Hersfeld. See Lambert of Hersfeld
Annals of Ireland
on the death of St. Patrick, 9:465b
on Muireadhach Albanach, 9:205a
Annals of Loch Cé, on Tadhg, 9:206a
Annals of St. Bertin (839), on "Rhos" (Rus), 12:434b
Annals of Ulster, on the death of St. Patrick, 9:465b
Annate, **1:304b–305b**, 11:606a-b
collection of, 1:305a-b
common services and, 1:305a-b
exemptions from, 1:305a-b
opposition to, 1:305a
papal, 1:304b–305a
Anne. See Noeannoe
Anne de Beaujeu, passion for hunting, 6:357b
Anne of Bohemia, queen of England, 10:384b
introduction of sidesaddle in England, 12:377a
wardrobe of, 12:375b
Anne of Brittany, queen
Jean Lemaire de Belges and, 7:54b, 55a
Rhétoriqueurs and, 10:364b
Anne, St., in Aarhus Cathedral altarpiece, 9:186b (*illus.*)
Anne of Savoy (wife of Emperor Andronikos III Palaiologos), 1:246b, 7:128a-b
Anneau (wood measure), 12:590a
Anno, **1:306a**
Anno II of Cologne, archbishop, 3:481a
glorification in *Annolied,* 1:306a
Anno Shrine (St. Michael's). *See* St. Michael (church: Sieburg)
Annolied, **1:306a**, 8:349a
Wolfram von Eschenbach and, 12:674b
Annuerus. *See* Amerus (*fl.* 1271)
Annular vault. *See* Vaults, types of
Annulment of marriage. *See* Marriage, annulment of
Annulus. See Rupert of Deutz
Annulus (matrix of Roman seal), 11:124a
Annunciation, **1:307b–308a**, 4:24b
in art
by Campin, 3:61a (*illus.*)
by Giovanni da Fiesole, 5:533a (*illus.*)
by Juan de Burgos, 7:155 (*illus.*)
by Koerbecke, 7:282a (*illus.*)
by Simone Martini, 1:307 (*illus.*)
crozier (Limoges), 4:13a (*illus.*)
drawing of in *Bois Protat,* 2:309b–310a
miniature in the *Missal of Robert Jumièges,* 10:434a (*illus.*)
in S. Isidoro church at León, 10:506 (*illus.*)
Tremussen chalice, 9:130 (*illus.*)
Visitation and, 12:478b
conjunction with images of the Fall of Man, 1:308a
in literature. *See* Play of Herod
Protevangelium of James as source for images, 1:307b–308a
unicorn legend and, 6:362b, 12:280b
Annunciation (cathedral: Moscow), iconostasis, 1:444 (*illus.*)
Annunciation (church: Nazareth)
enlarged, 4:24b
St. Thomas Capital (detail), 4:25a (*illus.*)
Annunciation, Order of, 12:688b
Annunziata, Order of the, 3:307a
Annunzione, L'. See Belcari, Feo
Annwfn (Annwn) (the otherworld in Welsh mythology), 9:47b
Anointing, **1:308a–309a**, 7:256b, 258a
of *basileus,* 2:123a
celestial unction of French kings, 1:308b
ceremony of, 10:16b
with chrism, 1:308b–309a
in church dedication, 4:130b, 131a
Gregorian reform of, 1:308b
investiture controversy and, 1:308b
in Middle English prophecies, 10:148b–149a
with olive oil, 1:308a-b
persona mixta of kings and, 1:308b
see also Extreme unction; Holy oil; Kingship, coronation rituals; Ordination, clerical; Unction of the sick
Anomoeanism, 1:453b, 2:121a
Anonimalle Chronicle, 1:265b, **1:309a**
Anonymous I, 7:38a
Anonymous II, alphabetic notation and, 8:614b
Anonymous IV (music theorist), **1:309a–310b**, 3:532a-b
on counterpoint, 1:309b–310a
De mensuris et discantu, 8:563b, 645a
identity of, 1:309a-b
John of Garland's influence on, 1:309b
on Leoninus, 7:548b–549b
on musical notation, 1:309b
Notre Dame school and, 9:191a
on the origin of clausula, 9:507a

Anonymous IV (music theorist), **1:309a–310b** (*cont.*)
on Perotinus, 9:506a-b
on rhythmic modes, 1:309b, 310a
as source of historical information, 1:310a-b
on types of compositions, 1:310a
"Viderunt omnes" and, 12:410b
see also Magnus liber organi
Anonymous of Bologna, *ars dictaminis* and, 10:358b
Anonymous of St. Emmeram, 1:545a
Anonymous of York. *See* York Tractates
Anonymus Mellicensis, *De scriptoribus ecclesiasticis,* 2:239b
Áns rímur bogsveigis, 1:310b
Áns saga bogsveigis, **1:310b–311a**
analogues for narrative, 1:310b–311a
place in the *Hrafnistamannasögur,* 1:311a
supernatural in, 1:311a
Ansāb al-ashrāf. See Balādhurī, Abū Ḥasan Aḥmād ibn Yahya ibn Jābir al-
Ansano, St., Siena and, 11:278a
Ansar
raiding expeditions, 8:524a-b
with Muḥammad, 8:524b
Ansate tablet. *See Tabula ansata*
Ansbach, margraves of, Nuremberg and, 9:202b
Ansegis of Fontenelle, abbot, Benedictus Levita and, 2:178b
Ansegisel (son of Bishop Arnulf of Metz), 9:499a, 499b
Anseïs de Metz. See Lotharingian cycle
Anselm II of Lucca, St., **1:311a**
Collectio canonum, 7:409b–410a
on enemies of church, 4:16b
Anselm of Aosta. *See* Anselm of Canterbury, St.
Anselm of Baggio, Milanese civil war and, 8:378a-b
Anselm of Bec. *See* Anselm of Canterbury, St.
Anselm of Besate, **1:311b**
Anselm of Bovisio, archbishop of Milan
preaching of Crusade (1101), 4:36a
taking up of cross by, 8:378b
Anselm of Canterbury, St., **1:311b–315b,** 2:174a, 3:82b–83a, 10:272a
at Abbey of Bec, 1:311b
biography by Eadmer, 4:330b–331a
canonization initiated by Thomas Becket, 1:311b
contributions to English culture, 4:466b
Cur Deus homo, 1:312b, 314b
De casu diaboli, 1:312a, 314b
De conceptu virginali et de originali peccato, 1:313a, 314b
De concordia praescientiae et praedestinationis et gratiae Dei cum libero arbitrio, used by Thomas Usk in *Testament of Love,* 12:334b
De fide Trinitatis et de incarnatione Verbi, 12:191a
De grammatico, 1:311b, 314a-b, 4:169b
De incarnatione Verbi, 1:312b, 314b, 10:531b
De libertate arbitrii, 1:312a, 314b
De processione Spiritus Sancti contra Graecos, 12:190b–191a, 192a-b
De veritate, 1:312a, 314b
dialogues of, 1:311b–312a, 314a-b
as doctor of the church, 1:311b, 4:234b
English mysticism and, 9:18b
Guibert of Nogent and, 6:9a
idea of personal reform, 10:284b
investiture as archbishop of Canterbury, 1:312a
reception of pallium, 1:312a-b
investiture conflict and, 1:312b–313b
Meditatio redemptionis humanae, 1:313a, 314b
Monologion, 1:311b, 314a, 9:588a, 10:269a
preaching of, 10:76a
Proslogion, 1:311b, 314a, 9:588a
Quintilianus and, 10:356b
realism of, 12:281b
relations with
Henry I, 1:313a-b, 4:466a, 6:155a
relatives, 1:311b
Thomas, archbishop-elect of York, 1:313b
William Rufus, 1:312a-b
Reply to Gaunilo, 1:311b
Rome, journeys to, 1:312b, 313a
on Roscelinus' doctrine of the Trinity, 10:531a-b
sources for writings of, 1:315a
theology of, 9:587b–588a
Christology, 3:322a
dialectic and, 4:169b–170a
existence of God, 9:588a, 598a
original sin, 9:600b
synthesis of faith and reason, 9:587b–588a
theory of redemption, 1:19a
theology school of, 12:20b
treatises of, 1:313b
on Virgin Mary, 12:460a, 460b
Anselm of Havelberg, church's use of force and, 3:356b
Anselm of Laon, **1:315b–316b**
Abelard and, 1:315b, 316a
Anselm of Canterbury's theology school and, 12:20b
as exegete, 4:543b
as fountainhead of *summa* and disputed questions, 1:315b–316a
Peter Lombard and, 9:516b
as pioneer of scientific theology, 1:315b
theology school of, 12:20b–21a
works credited to, 1:315b–316a
writings reattributed to School of Laon, 1:316a
see also Pseudo-Anselm of Laon
Anselm of Liège, **1:316b**
Anselm of Lucca, St., 8:222b, 10:257b
Anselm Marshal, 6:518b
Anselm of Milan, archbishop, exile of, 8:377b
Anselm of St. Rémi, 3:634a
Anselm of Tournai, bishop, 12:733a
Anselm Turmeda. *See* Turmeda, Anselm
Anselmi, Giorgio, *De musica,* 8:648a
Anselmus Peripateticus. *See* Anselm of Besate
Ansgar, St., 8:441b
Denmark and, 4:151a
life by Rimbert, 10:401a
mission to Birka, 2:247b, 248a
Anspert, *missus* (868–881), 8:377b
Answering Angel, The (cabalistic work), 3:3a
Antakya. *See* Antioch
Antalya, liturgical silver hoard from, 4:361b
Antapodosis. See Liutprand of Cremona
Antelami, Benedetto. *See* Benedetto Antelami
Antependium, 1:222a, **1:316b**
Antetheme, 10:80b
Anthemios of Tralles, **1:317a,** 4:339a, 7:202a
Archimedes and, 1:434a
construction of Hagia Sophia (Constantinople), 6:56a
Isidoros of Miletos and, 6:566b
Anthemius, Roman emperor, Sidonius and, 11:277a
Anthimus, *De observatione ciborum,* 12:494b
Anthologia latina, **1:317a,** 1:318b, 7:360b
Anthologia Palatina, 2:507a
Anthologies, **1:317a–320b**
anonymity of verse in, 1:318a-b
Bohemian anthologies (15th century), 1:319b–320a
booksellers' influence on, 1:320a
commonplace books, 1:320a, 3:492b–493a
English satirical anthologies (13th century), 1:319b
etymology of term, 1:317a-b
flowering of Latin anthologies in 13th century, 1:319a
of John Shirley, 1:320a
of John Wilde, 1:319b
of Latin poetry, 7:368b, 370b
methods of compilation of, 1:318b
prose, 1:318a
Bellifortis, 1:318a
reasons for compilation, 1:320a
related terms, 1:317a-b
"Saint Gatien," 1:319a
Vernon Manuscript, 1:319b
verse, 1:318a–320b
see also Anthologia Latina; Cambridge Songs; *Carmina Burana;* Florilegia
Anthology. See Vettius Valens
Anthony of Egypt, St., 3:342b, 595a, 10:455a
asceticism of, 6:213a
foundation of eremitic monasticsm, 6:217a
founding of anchorites, 8:460b
life of, 8:460b
Anthony the Hermit (Armenian saint), 1:518b, 519b
Anthony of Padua, St., **1:320b–321a**
at "Chapter of Mats" in Assisi, 1:320b–321a
biography of, 1:508b

canonization, 1:321a
as doctor of the church, 4:234b
journey to Sicily, 1:320b
sermons by, 1:321a
Anthropomorphism
in Cabala, 3:3a
in Judaism, Karaite opposition to, 7:163a-b
in Koran, 6:583a, 583b
al-Mu^ctazila and, 8:655a
Shī^ca and, 11:228b
Anti-intellectualism. *See* Philosophy and theology, debate between
Anti-Semitism, **1:338b–342a**, 4:564b, 7:88b–89b, 9:652b
Bernard of Clairvaux and, 2:192a
Black Death and, 2:263b
Catholic Church and, 7:75a–79b
in Christian Spain, 7:82a–83a
fundamental Christian stance, 1:339b
genocidal intent of German crusaders, 1:340a
Host desecration libel, 1:341a
inappropriateness of term for Middle Ages, 1:388b
Jew seen as foe of Christendom, 1:339b–341b
Jewish rejection of conversion and, 1:340a
Jews charged with deicide by Christians, 1:339a
medieval Jewish predicament and, 7:93b–94a
in music, 8:565a, 579b
of the Pastoureaux, 9:454a-b
plague blamed on Jews, 1:341b
preached by flagellants, 2:263b
ritual murder allegation and, 1:340a-b
roots in Jewish monotheism, 1:338b–339a
roots of northern European excesses, 1:339b
in Russia, 7:100b
separation of early Christians from other Jewish sects, 1:339a
use of *quaestiones,* 2:213a
in Valencia, 12:349a-b
Vincent Ferrer and, 12:453a
Visigoths and, 12:472b–473a
well-poisoning accusations against Jews, 1:341a-b
see also Blood libel; Flagellants; Polemics; Sephardim
Antichrist, **1:321a–322b**
beguins and, 2:162a
coming of, treated in Roger Bacon's *Opus maius,* 2:40a
death of, 1:322b
development of myth, 1:321b–322a
end of Roman Empire and, 1:322b
expectations of in Byzantium, 8:20a
in the Islamic doctrine of resurrection, 10:341a
Jerome's biblical exegesis and, 7:58b
in the Jewish Book of Zerubbabel, 1:345a
in liturgical drama, 7:678b
meaning of term in medieval times, 1:321a-b
in millennialism, 8:385b, 12:723a
in *Muspilli,* 8:650a
popular tracts on, 1:321b–322a
reign of, 1:321b, 322a-b
Sibylline oracles and, 11:257a
sources of doctrine, 1:321b
witnesses against, 1:322a
Antichrist, Der. See Frau Ava
Antichrist (Tegernsee). *See* Tegernsee *Antichrist*
Anticlaudianus. See Alan of Lille
Anticlericalism
of Peire Cardenal, 9:484a–485a
in *Ysengrimus,* 12:733b
Antidotarium. See Nicolaus Salernitanus
Antifeminism, **1:322b–325b**
in Andreas Capellanus, 3:89a
in Anglo-Norman literature, 1:269b
in *Arcipreste de Talavera,* 11:420a
in *Aristoteles und Phyllis,* 1:455b
Aristotle as antifeminist authority, 1:323a-b
in Boccaccio's *Elegia di Madonna Fiammetta,* 2:282b
Chaucer's treatment of, 1:325a
Christine de Pizan on, 1:324a
of church fathers, 1:322b–323a
of clerics, 1:322b–324a
coquetry and, 1:324b–325a
in courtly society, 1:324a–325a
Eve and, 1:322b–323a
in Holly and Ivy carols, 1:324b
of Jean de Meun, 7:53a
in Juan Rodríguez del Padrón's *Triunfo de las donas,* 11:419b
in Latin literature, 7:367b, 368a, 368b
in Middle English poetry, 8:338b
in *Njáls saga,* 9:145b
in punctuation poems, 1:324b–325a
in *Quinze joies de mariage,* 10:240a
relics veneration and, 10:296b–297a
in *Roman de la Rose,* 10:451b, 452a, 452b
of St. Jerome, 7:58a
in satires, 1:323b–324a
scientific and medical sources of, 1:323a-b
in Spanish satirical literature, 11:454a
as theme of debates in courtly literature, 1:324b
Theophrastus as source of authority for, 1:323a, 324a
Triunfo de las donas and, 10:439a
see also Boccaccio, Giovanni, *Corbaccio* and *Zibaldone laurenziano;* Fabliau
Antiga Casa da Corōa, 1:448b
Antikythera, 11:95a
Antinoë rinceaux silks, 3:590a
Antinomianism, in Nusayrī community, 11:228a
Antioch, **1:325b–326a**
bishops of, 9:458b–459a
designation as patriarch, 9:459a
captured
in 969, 9:132b
in 1268, 2:138b, 7:315b
by Alexios I Komnenos, 1:158a-b
by Heraklios, 1:325b–326a
by Normans, 1:326a
churches in. *See* Golden Octagon
Cilicia and, 3:391b
crusaders' route and, 10:423b
destruction by Mamluks, 1:326a
disasters in 6th century, 1:325b–326a
in First Crusade, 2:495a, 4:30a,b, 35a-b
gilt silver chalice from, 4:361b
John II Komnenos in, 7:127a
al-Lādhiqiya and, 7:316a
mint at, 8:417b
patriarch of
pentarchy and, 9:495b–496a
presence at the permanent synod, 9:505b
regency of, 11:589b
schism of, Basil the Great and, 2:120b
see of, Syrian music and, 8:578a
siege of (1098), Tancred and, 11:589b
Syrian rites and, 11:567b
theological school of. *See* Antiochene school
Thomas the Slav's rebellion and, 12:36b
under Arab rule, 1:326a
vs. Xusrō I, 12:714a
see also Bohemond I of Antioch; Leo I/II of Cilician Armenia, king
Antioch, Battle of (1211), 12:13b
Antioch of Mygdonia. *See* Nisibis
Antioch in Pisidia, early bishops of, 9:459a
Antioch, Song of. See Chanson d'Antioche
Antiochene rite, **1:326b–328b**
in Armenian church, 1:327b
Chaldean rite and, 1:326b
distinctive characteristics, 1:328a-b
division into western and eastern rites, 1:326b
early usages, 1:326b–327a
eucharistic anaphora of, 1:328a
exegesis, historical interpretation, 9:564a
John Chrysostom's homilies and, 1:327a
litany of, 1:328b
liturgical autonomy of, 1:327a
Maronite rite and, 1:326b, 328a
Monophysite schism and, 1:327a-b, 328a
Nestorian movement and, 1:327a
rite of Jerusalem and, 1:326b
in the Roman Empire, 1:327b–328a
Antiochene school
biblical exegesis at, 2:214a
Christology in, 3:320a
Nestorianism and, 9:105a-b
Nestorius and, 3:629a, 9:108a-b
representatives of, 3:336a
Theodoret of Cyr and, 12:17a
theology of, 3:336a
Antiochus of Ascalon, 9:95b
Antipater of Thessaloniki, on water mills, 8:390a
Antiphon, **1:328b–329a**
in choir Psalters, 10:201a-b
classification of melodies by *finalis,* 8:450a
in clerical ordinations, 9:266b
East Syrian, 11:568a
in gloria, 5:564a-b

Antiphon (*cont.*)
in introit, 6:498b
noeannoe and, 9:152b
processional or votive antiphons, 1:329a
responsorial "refrains" and, 1:329a
rhyme scheme of, 10:372b
Sarum chant, 10:654b
tonaries and, 12:70a-b
see also Psalm tones; Rhymed offices; Sticheron; *Variatio*
Antiphonal (antiphoner, antiphonary), **1:329a–330a**, 9:680b, 688a, 689a, 692a-b
Antiphonale missarum sextuplex, 9:689a-b
antiphonaria missarum and, 1:329b
catalog descriptions of, 1:330a
in *Corpus antiphonalium officii,* 5:663a
differentia in, 4:185a
Divine Office and, 4:224b–225a
Dominican, 8:643a
Ethiopian and Coptic, 1:155b
in Irish liturgy, 7:614b
of Metz cathedral, 8:642b
in missal, 8:437b
organization of books, 1:329b
in procession, 8:184b
Roman, Benevantan choral manuscripts and, 2:181a
Solesmes method of plainsong, 11:361b–362a
as a source for rhymed offices, 10:376a
see also Mass cycles; Plainsong
Antiphonale missarum sextuplex. See Hesbert
Antipodes
al-Bīrūnī and, 5:393a
in European geographic thought, 5:398a-b
Antipope, **1:330a–331b**
earlier equivalents of term, 1:331a
Great Schism and, 1:331a
inadequacy of legal definition, 1:331a
line of succession and, 1:331a
Mercati's list of, 1:330a-b
types of, 1:330b
see also Avignon papacy; Pope; Schism, Great
Antiquarianism, **1:331b–338b**
epigraphic studies, 1:336a-b
excavation of King Arthur's burial site, 1:337a-b
Irish literature and, 6:521b, 524b–525a, 531a
manuscript preservation, 1:335b–336a
medieval collectors and collections, 1:335a–336a
as precursor to archaeology, 1:331b–332a
Roman art and, 10:306a
search for Christian relics and, 1:336b–337b
12th-century renaissance and, 10:307b–308a
see also Archaeology; Spolia
Antique art. *See* Art, renaissances and revivals; Spolia
Antiquiores consuetudines monasterii Cluniacensis. See Ulrich of Zell
Antiquities of the Jews. See Josephus
Antirrhetici. See Nikephoros, patriarch
Antoine de la Sale. *See* La Sale, Antoine de
Anton Pilgram. *See* Pilgram, Anton
Antoni Bagrationi, *katᶜolikos, Martirika,* 5:414a
Antoni de Ginebreda, Catalan adaptation of *Speculum historiale* and, 9:511a
Antoni, St. (founder of the Pecherskaya Lavra), 9:481a, 10:595a
Theodosius of the Caves and, 12:19b
Antonine Constitution, 10:461a, 466a
Antonines
erection of hospitals, 6:294a
foundation of, 4:109b
Antoninus, St., **1:342a-b**
as archbishop of Florence, 1:342b
early life and education, 1:342a
Summa moralis, 4:248a, 12:42a
Antonio degli Orso, tomb of in Florence Cathedral, carving by Tino di Camaino, 12:59b–60a (*illus.*)
Antonio da Ferrara. *See* Beccari, Antonio
Antonio di Francesca da Venezia. *See* Antonio Veneziano
Antonio di Francesci di Andrea, Wandering Jew legend, 12:543a
Antonio of Lucca, *Ars cantus figurati,* 8:648a
Antonio de Nebrixa. *See* Nebrija, Antonio de
Antonio da Tempo, *Summa artis rithimici vulgaris dictaminis,* 6:665a
Antonio Veneziano, **1:342b–343a**
influences on the art of, 1:343a
works by, 1:342b–343a
see also Vanni, Andrea
Antonio da Vincenzo, **1:342b**
Antonios of Mount Athos (11th century), 8:443b
Antonius Andreas, John Duns Scotus and, 12:44a
Antonius de Leno, 3:657b
Regulae de contrapuncto, 8:647a
Antonius of Lérins, 4:491b
Antonius de Romagno, 9:702b
Antrustiones, **1:343a-b**
Antsha Gospels, 2:164b
Antwerp
fairs at, 4:586b, 12:108b
in 15th century, 12:112b
Antwerp Songbook, 4:321a
Anulus or Dialogue Between a Christian and a Jew. See Rupert of Deutz
Anwār-i Suhaylī. See Ḥusayn Vāᶜiz ᶜ*Anwatan,* 11:667b
Anzitenē, 1:472b
Anzy-le-Duc (church: Burgundy), 10:475b
Aonghus (Irish god), 6:546a
Aorsi, Alani domination of, 10:653a
Apa Apollo (Bawit), 3:585b
paintings at, 3:592b
Apa Jeremiah (Saqqara), paintings at, 3:592b
Apel, Willi
ars subtilior and, 1:558b–559a
"mannerist" school and, 1:550a
Apgitir Chrábaid, analogies with *De duodecim abusivis,* 4:312b
Aphorismi de gradibus. See Arnald of Villanova
Aphraates, 1:508a
Aphrahat (Syriac writer), 11:565b
Aphrodisias, 12:306a
Aphrodito papyri, 10:466a
Aphthartodocetism, nature of Christ in, 6:191a
Aphthonius
Progymnasmata, 1:505b
in the West and in Byzantium, 10:357b
"Apicius," *De re coquinaria,* 12:494b
Apiculture
Byzantium, 1:79a
charm for, 3:274a
Slavic world, 1:98b
Russia, 1:100a
Apocalypse
in Druzism, 9:3a
French translations of, 2:219a
Apocalypse. See Heinrich von Hesler
Apocalypse, illustration of, **1:343b–344a**
Beatus Manuscripts, 8:513a-b
Byzantine, 1:344a
early examples, 1:343b–344a
Heavenly Jerusalem, 6:125a
miniatures, 1:344a
motifs, 1:344a
post-Byzantine, 1:344a
in Romanesque art, 10:492b
"Second Coming of Christ," 1:343b (*illus.*)
see also Beatus manuscripts
Apocalypse (tapestry), 2:129b, 11:591b, 594b, 596a, 596b
Apocalypse of Thomas, Airdena Brátha and, 1:111a, 112a
"Apocalypsis Goliae," 7:367a
Apocalyptic literature
Byzantine commentaries, 9:564b
visions and, 12:476a
Apocalyptic literature, Jewish, **1:344b–346b**
cabalistic, 1:345b–346b
hatred of Rome expressed in, 1:344b
influence of Pahlavi literature on, 9:326b–327a
in Muslim Spain, 7:96b
myth of ten lost tribes in, 1:346a-b
in North Africa, 7:99a
sex aetates mundi and, 11:215a-b
Story of the Ten Martyrs, 1:344b
"Treatise on the Emanations on the Left," 1:346a
see also Book of Zerubbabel; Magic and folklore, Jewish
Apocalyptic literature, Zoroastrian, 9:326b–327a, 12:746b
Apocalyptic movement, Jewish, **1:344b–346b**
messianic movements, 1:345a–346b
of rationalistic philosophers, 1:345b
Apocrypha
New Testament, translations into Old English, 1:285b

  Virgin Mary and, 12:459b
Apocrypha, Irish, **1:346b–347b**, 6:542a-b
  Acts of Thomas, 1:347a
  after 1100, 1:347b
  categories of, 1:347a
  eschatology in, 1:347b
  as extensive source, 1:346b–347a
  fís genre, 1:347b
  Hiberno-Latin, 1:347a
  immram and, 6:552a
  Middle Irish, 1:347a-b
  sources for, 10:635a
Apocryphal literature, Romanian, 10:511a-b
Apodeipnon, 3:67a
Apographeis, taxation and, 11:604b
Apokatastasis, 5:667a
Apollinarianism, use of *azymes* and, 2:31b
Apollinaris of Clermont, bishop, 11:277b
Apollinaris, St. *See* S. Apollinare Nuovo (church: Ravenna); S. Apollinare in Classe (church: Ravenna)
Apollinaris Sidonius, 4:590b
Apollinarius, **1:348a-b**
  Christology of, 1:348a
  writings of, 1:348a
Apollonios Dyskolos, 5:651a, 11:52a
Apollonius of Perga
  Conics, 1:438b, 439a
    Jewish mathematics and, 11:92a
  works of translated into Arabic, 11:83a
Apollonius of Tyana, **1:348b**
  Book of the Secrets of Creation, 1:136a
    formation of metals, 1:136a
Apollonius of Tyre, in literature, *Gesta Appollonii,* 5:514a
Apollonius of Tyre, Old English translation of, 1:285a
Apollonius von Tyrland. See Heinrich von Neustadt
Apologetic Book against the Pelagians. See Orosius
Apologetics. *See* Polemics
Apologeticum fidei. See Julianus of Toledo
Apologeticus major. See Nikephoros, patriarch
Apologeticus martyrum. See Eulogius of Córdoba
Apologhi verseggiati, 4:572b
Apologia pauperum. See Bonaventure, St.
Apologue
  in bardic poetry, 6:535a
  Gofraidh Fionn and, 9:204b
Apology. See Aristides of Athens; Eunomius
Apolonii Gesta. See Gesta Apollonii
Apolonio, Libro de, **1:348b–349b**, 8:281b, 11:413a, 456b
  Apollonius as intellectual hero, 1:349a-b
  author's identification with Apollonius, 1:349a-b
  Christianization of original story, 1:349a
  Historia Apolonii Regis Tyri as source, 1:349a
  medievalization of original story, 1:349a
  structure and language of, 1:348b
  Tarsiana's prayer, 11:450a
Apophthegmata, 1:204b
Apostasy, **1:349b**
Apostles (church: Cologne), 10:488b
Apostles' Creed, in religious instruction, 10:300a, 300b, 301a
Apostles (Italian sect), 6:488b
Apostolic Brethren, Joachim of Fiore and, 7:114a
Apostolic Constitutions, **1:349b–350a**, 7:625b
  appearance in other collections, 1:350a
  on the feast of the Ascension, 1:582a
  Greek litanies and, 7:589a–590a
  on Kyrie sung by children, 7:593b
  on Simon Magus, 8:33b
  sources of, 1:349b–350a
Apostolic poverty. *See* Poverty, apostolic
Apostolic See. *See* Papacy
Apostolic succession, **1:350a–351a**
  Clement of Rome and, 1:350b
  collegial church organization and, 1:350b
  in early church, 3:338b
  False Decretals and, 4:125a, 126b
  Humbert and, 6:329b
  as means of controlling heresy, 1:350b
  monarchical church organization and, 1:350b
  treasure doctrine and, 6:447a
  see also Papacy
Apostolic Tradition. See Hippolytus of Rome
Apostrophos, 8:617a, 617b
Apothecary pound, 10:67a
Apothegm. *See Sententiae*
Apotheosis. See Prudentius
Appanages, **1:351a-b**, 8:427a
  Artois, 5:170b
  changing conception of monarchy and, 1:351a-b
  county of Poitou, 5:169a, 170b
  defined, 1:351a
  Maine and Anjou, 5:170b
  for women, 1:351b
Apparatus. See Innocent IV, pope
Apparatus (collection of glosses), 4:127b
Appeals of treason. *See* Treason
Appellants. *See* Lords Appellant
Appendix Laterani concilii, 4:123b
Appendix probi, 6:621b, 12:494b
Appendix Vergiliana, 7:360b, 9:440b
Appenzell, Swiss Confederation and, 11:544b
Appetizer. See Hungrvaka
Apple
  growth of, 1:84a
  in Mediterranean region, 5:306a, 307a
Apportionment, estates representation. *See* Representative assemblies
Apprenticeship
  family life and, 4:602b–603a
  see also Guilds and métiers
Aprise/Aprisio, 6:479b, 11:677a
  in Catalonia, 3:174b–175a
Apse, **1:352a**
  Aegean polygonal in Ravenna, 10:263a-b
  early Christian decoration of, 4:354b, 358b
  in Gothic cathedral, 5:590a
  mosaics, Tsromi church, 12:222b
  part of chevet, 3:300b
  see also Ambulatory; Pastophory
Apse echelon, **1:352a**
Apsidal chapel. *See* Chapel
Apuleius Barbarus, *Herbarium,* 2:245a
Apuleius of Madaura
  Aristotle and, 1:460b
  Peri hermeneias, 4:168b
Apulia
  raided (1017), 11:264a
  Robert Guiscard and, 10:433a
  Roger I and, 10:440a
  Roger II and, 11:267a
ApʿχazetʿI. *See* Georgians
Aq Qoyunlu, **1:352a-b**, 6:505a
  capture of Kars, 7:221b
  in Iraq, 6:514b
  Mamluk dynasty and, 8:75b
  in Tabrīz, 11:571a
  Timurid ruler Abū Saʿīd and, 12:57b–58a
  Trebizond rulers and, 12:169a
  Turkoman tribal confederation of, 12:227a
  vs. Qara Qoyunlu, in Armenia, 1:486a, 514a
  see also Azerbaijan; Qara Qoyunlu; Uzun Ḥasan
Aq Sunqur, ruler of Xlatʿ, 11:220a
ʿAqāʾid. See Resurrection, Islamic
Aqedat Yitzḥaq. See Arama, Isaac
ʿAqīl, Ibn, *Wāḍiḥ,* 11:67b
ʿĀqila. See Islamic law
Aqmar, al- (mosque: Cairo), 6:608b, 609 (*illus.*)
Aqqa. *See* Acre
ʿAqrabāʾ, Battle of (633), 6:568a, 7:235a
Aqrābādhīn. See Kindī, al-
Aqṣā, al- (mosque: Jerusalem), 6:594a, 600b
Aqsaq Timür. *See* Tamerlane
Aqua Gregoriana. See Lustration
Aqua Vergine, 10:519b
Aquamanilia, 8:286a
Aqueduct system, Roman, 10:517b, 519b–520a
  see also Caños de Carmona
Aquileia, as ecclesiastical center, 12:385b
Aquileia, rite of, **1:352b–353b**
  abolition of, 1:353a
  early liturgical evidence, 1:352b
  Eastern liturgy and, 1:353a
  Roman-Ravennan rite and, 1:353a
Aquinas, Thomas, St., **1:353b–366b**, 3:573b, 608b, 11:56b
  Abelard's concept of morality and, 1:365a
  Albertus Magnus and, 1:127a, 127b, 129a, 353b
  on analogous names, 1:359b–360b, 361a-b, 362a–363a

Aquinas, Thomas (*cont.*)
antifeminism of, 1:323b
appointed *magister regens,* 1:354a
Aristotle and, 1:356a–357b, 462b–463a, 10:19b–20a
commentaries, 9:607a, 621a
introduction to works of, 1:353b
Posterior Analytics, 1:462b
synthesis of, 6:198b
on astrology, 1:607b
canonization, 1:365a, 463b
Catena aurea, 4:547b
on celestial bodies and demons, 8:38a
commentaries
on Job, 1:364a
on Peter Lombard's *Sentences,* 9:517b
on Plato's *Book of Causes,* 1:357b
on commercial practices, 12:119a
condemnation by Robert Kilwardby, 7:253b
the *correctorium* controversy and, 10:388b
De aeternitate mundi contra murmurantes, 1:356b, 12:40a
De ente et essentia, 1:358a-b
medieval ontology and, 2:36a
De potentia, 9:612a
De regimine principum, 10:19b
De regno, 7:266a, 8:435a
De unitate intellectus, 1:356b–357a, 12:39b
on death, 4:119b
on demons, 8:36a
disciples of, 9:609a, 12:195b
Dominicans and, 4:246a–247a, 7:368b
early life and education, 1:353b
ecclesiology of
on church and state, 1:465a
on indulgences, 6:449b
on interdict, 6:496b
empiricism of, 1:361a
as exegete, 4:544a
on fables, 4:572b
Frederick II and, 11:274a
on Holy Spirit, 2:177b
hylomorphism of, 1:358b–359b, 361b–362a
hymns of, 6:382a, 384b
Verbum supernum prodiens, 8:572a
Isidore of Seville and, 6:566a
on Jews, 7:78b, 88b, 90a
kingship theories of, 7:266a
lectures on Peter Lombard's *Sentences,* 1:353b–354a
Liber de causis and, 9:100a
liturgical poetry of, 9:714b
moderate realism of, 1:358a
on morality, 1:364a–365a
on mysteries, 1:355b
in Paris, 1:354a
philosophy and theology of, 1:361b–362a, 9:601a-b
absolution of sin, 9:604a
on cardinal and intellectual virtues, 1:364b
Christology, 3:323b, 4:375b–376a, 9:602a
conflict between the two, 1:354a–355a
creation, 9:600a
on equity, 4:501a-b
on equivocal terms, 1:360a
esse, 3:323a-b, 9:596a
on essence and existence, 1:361b–362a, 4:510a-b
grace, 9:600a
on immateriality, 1:361b
on knowable and revealed truth, 1:355b–356a
on knowledge and knowing, 1:355b, 360b–361b
on natural law, 1:364b–365a
on necessity, 1:361b
nominalism and, 9:155b
original justice, 9:600b
on Paradise, 9:397a-b
penance, 9:491b
Platonism and, 1:357b–358b, 9:700b–701a, 702b
on primary analogate, 1:360b
on Prime Mover, 1:356b, 362b
principle of individuation, 9:596b–597a
on proofs of God, 1:362b
on the Resurrection, 4:366a
on substances, 1:358b–359b
on substantial change, 1:358b–359b
substantial form, 9:597b
Thomistic synthesis, 1:354b–355a
on the Trinity, 9:599b
on universals, 1:357b–358b
on univocal terms, 1:360a
on unknowability of God's essence, 1:362a–363a
vocabulary, 1:359b–360b, 361a-b
on Plato and Aristotle, 4:298a-b
posthumous influence of, 1:365a-b
preaching and, 6:664a
preambles of faith, 1:355a-b
Quaestiones disputatae, 1:363b
reportationes (*lecturae*) and *ordinationes* (*expositiones*) by, 1:363b
sacraments, theology of, 9:603a
Eucharist, accident of quantity, 9:603b
extreme unction, 4:565a-b
Office of Corpus Christi, 9:603b
on sacramentality of marriage, 9:604a-b
on Sacred Scripture, 1:363b–364a, 2:224a-b
Siger of Brabant and, 1:463a, 11:286a, 286b
Spanish prose life of, 11:439b
Summa contra Gentiles, 1:354b, 363b, 462b, 4:252b, 10:266b
Summa theologiae, 1:354b, 363b, 462b, 9:601b
analysis of heresy, 6:203b–204a
Jews in, 7:78b, 88b, 11:210a
John of Paris and, 7:136b
Morale, addition of, 12:454a
on the nature and powers of angels, 1:250b
political ideas in, 10:19b
Tauler and, 11:602a
William de la Mare's *Correctorium* and, 12:40b
terms for "reform" used by, 10:284b
theological method of
Aristotelian elements, 9:596a
first principles, 9:596a
as a scientific discipline, 9:608b
Thomas of Cantimpré's *De natura rerum* and, 12:34a
translated by Kydones, 4:135b
on Trinitarian doctrine, 12:195a-b
on universality of human nature, 12:281b
views of purgatory, 10:216b–217a
on Virgin Mary, 12:460a, 461a
vs. Latin Averroists, 1:356b–357a
vs. Theodoric of Freiberg, 12:18b
works of at St. Jacques (Paris), 8:103b
see also Thomism; *Via moderna*
Aquisgranum. *See* Aachen
Aquitaine, **1:366b–369b,** 1:367a (map)
acquired by Franks in 507, 2:91a
administration of, 1:368b
bastides in, 2:128b
Bordeaux acquired by, 2:327b–328a
counts of Poitiers and, 2:126b
early tonaries in, 12:69b–70a
Eleanor as duchess of, 1:367b
England and, 6:331b, 332b, 333a
English kings as vassals of France and, 1:368b–369a
French kings and, 1:367b–368a, 369a
genesis of, 1:366b
king-duke's control over, 1:368b
Languedoc and, 7:339a
musical composition, school of, 10:618a-b, 651a
Peace of God movement and, 9:473b
reversion from kingdom to duchy, 1:367a
Richard I (the Lionhearted) and, 10:383a
Viking raids in (799), 12:429b
warfare between Toulouse and Aragon and, 12:91b
wealth of, 1:368a-b
Aquitanica Secunda, Visigoths and, 12:470a
Aqwāl al-dhahabīya, Al-. *See* Ḥamīd al-Dīn al-Kirmānī
Arab-Khazar war (721–737), 7:241a
Araba (Islamic vehicle), 12:380a
Arabesque, **1:369b**
^{c}Arabī, Ibn al-
description of *mi^{c}rāj,* 6:233b–234a
mystical philosophy, 9:572a
pantheistic mysticism of, opposition to, 11:630b
on the unity of being, 6:585b–586a
^{c}Arabī, Muḥyi 'l-Dīn ibn, 9:43a–44a
Arabia
Islamic, 1:372 (map), **1:373a–376b,** 6:571 (map)
Abbasid dynasty, 1:374a-b
contributions to science and philosophy, 1:377b
cosmopolitan influence of non-Arab pilgrims, 1:373b–374a
crusaders and, 1:375b
expansion under Umayyad dynasty, 1:374a
factional strife, 1:374a, 375a
Ghassanids, 5:514b–515b

horse breeding in, 1:295a
Jews and Christians in 12th-century Yemen and Najrān, 1:375b
Portuguese in, 1:376a
Quraysh tribe in, 10:241b–242b
rebellions, 1:374b
Alids vs. Abbasids, 1:374b
religious conflicts between Shiites and Sunnites, 1:374a
trade in, 12:105a-b
ᶜUmar's extension of Islamic empire, 1:373b
under ᶜUthmān, 1:373b
see also Bab al-Mandab
Jews in, 7:101a–103a
pre-Islamic, **1:369b–373a**, 1:372 (map)
central and northern culture, 1:370b–371b
Christianity in, 9:55a
collapse of northern and southern kingdoms, 1:371b–372a
Dedan (Al-ᶜUlā) records, 1:371a
early inscriptions in north and central, 1:370b–371a
geographical conditions of, 1:369b–370a
intertribal feuding, 1:370b, 373b
Jewish-Christian conflict in south, 1:371b
links with Hellenistic-Roman-Byzantine civilization, 1:370b
prehistoric inhabitants, 1:369b–370a
Quraysh tribe in, 10:241a-b
religion in south, 1:370b
social structure in north and central, 1:371a
southern civilization, 1:370a-b
Yūsuf (Himyarite ruler), 1:371b
see also Najd; Najrān
Arabian March (Armenia), 2:140b
Arabian Nights' Entertainment, The. See Thousand and One Nights
Arabic alphabet. *See* Alphabets, Arabic
Arabic language, **1:376b–378b,** 6:574a
absence of vehicular vocabulary, 12:379b, 380b
adequacy of for translations from Greek, 12:129b–130a
Berber language and, 2:186b
Castilian language and, 3:141b
ceramics and, 6:603a
changes due to invasions in 8th century, 1:377a-b
in Coptic church practice, 3:591a
court language of caliphate, 3:42a
development of Islamic science and, 11:81b–82a
Dominican missionary study of, 10:266b
early linguistic analysis of, 1:377b
European difficulties with, 1:376b–377a
formation of neologisms in, 1:377a-b
grammar, 5:650b
-iyyah termination in, 1:377a-b
case system of nouns in, 1:378a
in al-Kufa, 7:307b
in Granada, 5:653a
Hebrew borrowings from, 12:134b–135a
in Iran, 6:501b, 506a
in Islamic administration, 6:589a
Islamic furniture and, 5:313b–314a
Italian and, 6:625b–626a
Karaite literature in, 7:210a-b
in Koran, 1:583a, 7:294b
Latin grammar and, 12:137a
limitations due to bedouin origins, 1:377a
as *lingua franca,* 12:148a
Maltese as dialect of, 1:378b
musical terminology, 8:561b
oral tradition of, 1:377a
pre-Islamic extent of, 1:376b
replacement of Greek by, 4:405a
schism between formal and popular speech, 1:377b–378a
in Spain, 1:378b, 6:434a, 442b
Alvarus of Córdoba on, 8:562a
spread of
in north Africa and Syria, 1:378a
in Persia, Turkey, and the East, 1:378a-b
translations
from ancient sources, 12:128a–133a
of Hellenistic texts, 1:377b
into Greek, 12:126b
into Latin, 12:140a
Western influences on, 1:378b
see also Judeo-Arabic language; Mozarabic language; *Naskhī; Nastaᶜlīq;* Paleography, Arabic and Persian; Translation and translators
Arabic literature
ᶜAbd Allāh of Khorāsān and, 11:575a
book of monasteries, 4:117a
concept of courtly love influenced by, 3:671b–672a
Egyptian contribution, 4:407a-b
floral terminology in, 6:185a
al-Ḥallāj and, 6:80b
in Ibn al-Nadīm's *Al-Fihrist,* 9:51b
influence on Hebrew writers, Muslim Spain, 6:125b–126a, 127a
Platonic thought in, 9:669a–700b, 694b–696a
poetry, **1:398a–403b**
adaptation of contemporary themes, 1:115b
conventions and stock phrases in, 1:402b–403a
dīwān, 7:701a
elegies, 1:401b–402a
form of, 1:398a-b
fortitude (*ṣabr*) as virtue in, 1:399a
fragments (*qiṭᶜa*), 1:398b
ghazal, 7:48a
golden age of, 1:400b–402a
heroic ethos broken by Islam, 1:400a
impiety in, 1:401a-b
individualism in, 1:403a
Iranian poetry and, 6:506b, 507a
Islamic, 1:400a–403a
kharja, 7:239a-b
looseness of composition in, 1:402b
love poems, 1:400a–401a
muwashshaḥ and *zajal,* 6:234a
mystical, 1:402a
odes (*qaṣīda*), 1:398b–400a
oral tradition of, 1:398b
panegyrical, 1:400b, 402a
pious exhortation in, 1:401b
plagiarism in, 1:403a
pre-Islamic, 1:398b–400a
as propaganda, 10:142b
qaṣāᵓid fī-al-gharīb and *nawādir,* 4:442b
qaṣīda, 8:514b
rhetoric in, 1:400b
rhyme in, 1:398a
richness of description in, 1:399b–400a, 401b
Romance lyrics and, 8:563b–564a
satire, 1:402a, 7:47a-b
scenes of pleasure in, 1:399a, 401a
sensibility stressed in love poetry, 1:401a
similes in, 1:399b–400a
Spanish lyric poetry and, 11:446a–447b
stagnation of, 1:402a-b
"ᶜUdhrī love" motif, 1:400a-b
Umayyad period, 1:400a-b
see also Rhetoric, Arabic
prose, **1:379a–382b**
adab, 1:379a–380b
al-Adab al-kabīr, 1:379a
anecdote books, 1:380b
autobiographies, 1:381a-b
belles lettres, 1:380b–382a
development of, 7:43a
fiction, 1:381b
genesis of, 1:379a
al-Hamadhānī's invention of *maqāmāt,* 1:381b
in humanities, 1:380b–381b
on love, 1:381b
maqāma (genre of fiction), 1:381b
popular narrative cycles, 1:382a-b
see also Encyclopedias and dictionaries, Arabic and Persian
Shuᶜūbīya movement, 7:43a
in Sicily, 11:263a
Tāhir ibn al-Ḥusayn and, 11:574b
see also Biography, Islamic; Judeo-Arabic literature; Mozarabic literature; Rhetoric, Arabic; *Thousand and One Nights*
Arabic numerals, **1:382b–398a**
in astronomy, 1:622a-b
derivation of *algorismus* as term, 1:395b
ghubār (Toledan) numerals, 1:387b–395a
absorption into Latin algorisms, 1:388b–389b
comparisons with other forms, 1:388a–389a (*illus.*)
date of development, 1:392b–395a
deformation by rotation, 1:390a
derivation of name, 1:390a-b
development of, 1:391a–392b, 395b
diffusion via Spain, 1:392b
early appearance of in Arabia, 1:387b–388a
evolution of symbols, 1:388b–389a, 393b–394a, 394b

Arabic numerals (*cont.*)
ghubār (Toledan) numerals (*cont.*)
Hindu-Arabic origins of, 1:392b–393a
lack of early diffusion to Byzantine culture, 1:391b–392a
modifications of, 10:471b
uniqueness to western Arabs, 1:388a–390b
Visigothic origins of, 1:393a
Islamic mathematical science and, 11:86a
in medieval Arabic tradition, 1:384a–387b
Ibn Khaldūn's works and, 1:384b–385b, 386b
inconsistent notation by scribes, 1:387b
low esteem of practical mathematics and, 1:384a-b
neglect of mathematical sciences, 1:384b
parallel sequences of *abjad* symbols and *zimām* numerals, 1:386b–387a
persistence of *abjad* (alphabetic symbols) in records, 1:384a–386b
prevalence of "magical" orientation to numbers, 1:384b–385a
use in astrology, 1:385b–387b
origins and early reception of, 1:382b–384a
calculation methods, 1:382b–383a
Indian origins, 1:382b, 383a (*illus.*)
initial lack of zero, 1:383b
persistence of *abjad* (alphabetic symbols) in records, 1:383b–384a
significance of place value in, 1:383a-b
slow reception by astronomers and astrologers, 1:384b
uniqueness of Hindu-Arabic system, 1:383a
Roman numerals and, 1:394a–395a, 10:470a, 472b–474a
spread in medieval Europe, 1:395a–397a
in astronomy, 1:611a–612b
struggle for acceptance, 1:396a-b
use of mathematics in science and, 1:396b–832a
use in divination, 1:385a, 396a-b
ᶜArabiyya, al-, 7:171b
Arabs. *See* Arabia; Islam
ᶜArafat, pilgrimage rites at, 9:651a
Aragon
black slaves in, 2:268b
Catalan language in, 3:157b
Catalonia and, 3:178b
cortes in, 3:610b
hermandades in, 6:210a
history (800–1137), **1:403b–407b**, 1:405 (map)
Christian settlement in the Ebro Valley, 1:407a
decline of Muslim threat, 1:403b–404a
dynastic involvement with Navarre, 1:404a
expansion of, 1:404a, 405a–407b
religious revival in, 1:404b
rise of kingdom, 1:403b–404a
rule of Alfonso I (the Battler), 1:160a-b, 406a-b
inquisition in, 6:488a
Jews in, 7:80b, 81a-b
Languedoc and, 7:339a
Old Spanish dialects in, 11:400a–401a
as papal fief, 6:464b
relations with Muslims
partnership with Tunis, 6:54a
seizure of Jerba and Kerkenna Islands, 6:53b
see also Navarre, kingdom of
Aragon, Crown of (1137–1479), **1:408a–421b**, 1:409 (map)
age of James the Conqueror (1213–1276), 1:411a–413b
chronicle of, 9:511a-b
class struggles, 1:419b–420a
conflict between oligarchic rule and urban society, 1:419a
codification of secular law and, 7:430a
control of Montpellier, 8:482b
culture of, 1:420a, 9:510b–511b
demographics, 1:419a-b
effect of Black Death, 1:419b
early count-kings (1137–1213), 1:408a–411a
Malta and, 8:67b
Mediterranean expansion (1276–1336), 1:413b–415b
annexation of Sicily, 1:413b–414a
conveyance of Sicily to Holy See, 1:414b
Mudejars and, 11:377b
Ordinances of 1344, 9:511a
religious disharmony, 1:419b
Sicily and, 7:7b, 11:273a-b
Simon de Montfort and, 11:296b
social and economic aspects, 1:419a–420a
succession of, Vincent Ferrer and, 12:453a
three official languages of, 9:511b
Toulouse and, 12:91b
trade imbalances, 1:419b
under Pedro IV the Ceremonious and successors (1336–1410), 1:415b–417a
under the Trastámaras (1412–1479), 1:417a–419a
see also Barcelona; Manuel, Don Juan; Valencia
Arakelocᶜ (church: Sewan Island), 11:214b
Araks River, **1:421b**, 1:470b
see also Naχčawan
Araldo, Antonio, 6:636b
Arama, Isaac
Aqedat Yitzḥaq, 10:75a
on lottery system, 11:92a-b
ᶜAramah. *See* Isaac ben Moses Arama (ᶜAramah)
Aramaic language
influences on Arabic script, 9:333a
Middle Iranian languages and, 6:505b
Syriac language and, 11:562a
Zohar written in, 3:2a-b
Arán. *See Egils saga einhenda ok Asmundar Berserkjabana*
Ararat, Mount, **1:421b–422a**, 1:470b
Ararat (Province). *See* Ayrarat
Arator, **1:422a-b**
De actibus apostolorum, 1:422a, 422b, 7:361a
Epistula ad Vigilium, 1:422a-b
in Latin pedagogy, 7:353a
Vergil and, 12:394a
Aratrum (ard), 12:72b, 73a, 75b
Aratus, *Phainomena*, 10:110b
Araxes/Erasx. *See* Araks River
Arbalests, 3:179b (*illus.*)
Arbeo of Freising, **1:422b–423a**
Arbor des batailles. See Bonet, Honoré
Arbor consanguinitatis et affinitatis, glossed by Vincentius Hispanus, 12:456a
Arbor vitae crucufixae Iesu. See Ubertino of Casale
Arbre des batailles. See Bonet, Honoré
Arbroath, Declaration of (1320), 9:439a, 10:427b
Arcade
in Gothic cathedral, 5:591b–592a, 593a–594b
tribelon, 12:187b
Arcade, blind. *See* Arch
Arcadia, Geoffroi de Villehardouin and, 7:378a
Arcadius, Roman emperor, 12:469b
Arcana deorum. See Walsingham, Thomas
Arcaχ, 1:472b, 473b
Arčēš, **1:423a**, 12:362a
Armenian trade and, 12:97b
Catepanate of Basprakania and, 1:484a
silk route to the Far East, 12:99a
Arch, **1:423b–425a**, 1:424a (*illus.*)
centering, 3:234b–235a
diaphragm, 5:592a
in Gothic cathedral, 5:591b–592b
horseshoe, 8:511b
Islamic, 8:512a-b
S. Maria de Melque, 8:512a (*illus.*)
in Visigothic art, 12:465b
ogival, origins, 11:656a
pishtaq, 9:670b–671b (*illus.*)
pointed, 3:563b
in Provençal Romanesque architecture, 10:481b
rounded, as Romanesque feature, 10:475b
spandrel, 11:389b
triumphal, early Christian church, 12:205b–206b (*illus.*)
types of, 1:423b, 424a (*illus.*)
see also Archivolt; Intrados; Rib; Vaults; Voussoir
Archaeology, **1:331b–338b**
artifact collection, 1:333b–336a
antiquities brought to Europe by crusaders, 1:334b–335a
gem and cameo collections, 1:335a-b
legislation against collecting spolia, 1:334a
looting of conquered territories, 1:334b–335a

manuscript preservation, 1:335b–336a
protection and restoration of Roman architecture, 1:334a-b
Roman monuments treated as quarries, 1:333b–334a
statuary collections, 1:335a
vase collections, 1:335b
England. *See* Sutton Hoo
epigraphic studies, 1:336a-b
fortuitous discoveries, 1:336b
grave finds, evidence on metalworking, 8:291b–292a
of medieval monuments, **1:425a–433a**
17th to 18th centuries, 1:427b–428b
19th century, 1:428b–430a
20th century, 1:430a–432a
England, 1:428b, 429a
France, 1:429a-b
Germany, 1:428b–429a, 429b
Italy, 1:429a
technology of, 1:431a–432a
traditional, 1:425b–427a
see also Church architecture
planned excavation, 1:336b–337b
prerequisites for, 1:332a
remnants of agricultural tools, 12:72b–73a
roots in respect for ancient authorities, 1:331b–332a
study of ancient writings, 1:331b–332a
travelers and their accounts, 1:332a–333b
village excavations, 12:444a
see also Antiquarianism
Archangel, **1:433a**
Archangel Michael (church: Kiev), mosaics, 10:583b–584a
Archard, Geoffroi d'Ainai and, 5:391b
Archbishop. *See* Clergy
Archdeacon. *See* Clergy
Archdeacon, Court of the (Canterbury), 1:433b
Archembaud de St. Amand, 3:304a
Archery
games, 5:348b–349a
see also Arrow; Bow
Arches, Court of, **1:433b**
Archiepiscopal cross, 4:9a
see also Cross, forms of
Archil
in Canary Islands, 3:62b
production of as dye, 4:326b
Archil II of Georgia, king, 7:223a
Archimandrite, **1:433b**
Archimedes, **1:433b–440a**
Cattle Problem, 1:434a
Gaurico's edition of *Tetragonismus,* 1:439b
Greek texts, 1:434a-b, 437a
Liber de speculis comburentibus. See Haytham, Ḥasan ibn al-
mathematical theory, interpretation of, 8:210b
On Conoids and Spheroids, 1:437b, 438a
On the Equilibrium of Planes, 1:434a, 434b, 438a, 439b
On Floating Bodies, 1:434a, 437a, 438a, 439a, 439b
Arabic translations, 1:434b
On the Measurement of the Circle, 1:434a, 435b, 439b, 8:210b
Arabic translations, 1:434b
Latin translations, 1:435a, 437b, 438a
On the Method of Mechanical Theorems, 1:434a, 434b, 436b
On the Quadrature of the Parabola, 1:434a, 434b, 439b
On the Sphere and the Cylinder, 1:434a, 435b, 437b, 438a
Liber de curvis superficiebus Archimenidis and, 1:436a-b
On Spirals, 1:434a, 437a-b, 438a
Sandreckoner, 1:437a, 439a
Stomachion, 1:434a, 434b
translations of, 8:210b, 9:705a
Arabic, 1:434b, 11:83a
Latin, 1:435a-b, 436b–438a, 439a
on water clocks, 11:641a-b
Archimenides. *See* Archimedes
Archipelago, duchy of the, 7:380b, 381a
Archirie și Anadan, 10:511b
Architect
design concept, implementation of
on-site changes, 8:177b
plans and elevations, 8:177b
templates, 8:177a-b
tracing house, 8:177b
use of consultants, 8:177b
design programs, literary tradition and, 8:175b
as master masons, 1:440b
professional, in Byzantine Empire, 4:338a
status of, **1:440a–441a**, 9:665b–666b
Geoffoi d'Ainai, 5:391b
Geoffrey of Noyers, 5:390b
personal, 8:174a
political, 8:173b
travels of, 12:152b–153a, 160b
wages, 8:174a-b
see also Parler family
Architecture
collar beam, 3:479b (*illus.*)
column figure, 3:487a, 487b (*illus.*)
decoration in, Cosmati work, 3:614a
liturgical aspects, **1:441b–445a**
solea, 11:360b
Spain, 12:465a-b, 466a
see also Church architecture; Screen; Synagogue, art and architecture in; Synthronon
music of the spheres and, 8:585b–586a
naval, 11:232a
as propaganda, 10:137b
Romanesque, military, 10:489b
theory
geometric experimentation under Justinian, 4:338a-b
geometry of interior spaces, 4:331b, 341b
see also Arch; Construction; Finial; First Romanesque; Fleuron; Flèche; Flushwork; Gallery; Urban architecture
Architecture, early Christian, **4:331a–337a**
annular crypt, 9:237a
apse in, 1:352a
cathedral of S. Marco, 10:484b
construction materials, 4:331b
continuity and change in, 4:331b
definition of, 4:331a
in Ravenna, 10:262b–264b
Romanesque architecture and, 10:478a, 481a
secular survivals, 4:333b
transenna screen, 12:125a
transept, 9:237a
triumphal arch in, 12:205b–206b (*illus.*)
use of spolia, 11:464a-b
see also Parekklesion
Architrenius. See John of Hauville
Archives, **1:445b–449a**
in ancient Rome, 1:445b
Austria, 1:448b
Belgium, 1:447b
Bolognese, popular poetry in, 6:657b
Church of Rome, 1:446a, 448a
compared with libraries, 1:446b–447a
England, 1:448b
France
establishment of permanent, 5:163a
importance in development of, 1:447a-b
Germany, 1:448b
Hungary, 1:448b–449a
Italy, 1:448a
medieval forms, 1:445b, 446a-b
notarial, 1:446a
Portugal, 1:448b
private, 1:446b
Scandinavia, 1:449a
Spain, 1:448b
spread of literacy and, 7:600b–601a
Switzerland, 1:447b
wardrobe and, 6:302a
see also Libraries; Seals and sigillography, Western European
Archivolt, **1:449a**, 5:617a, 618a-b, 622a
see also Vaults; Voussoir
Archon ton archonton (prince of princes), **1:449a-b**, 481a
Gagik II and, 12:361b
Archpoet, **1:449b–450b**
"Confessio Goliae," 1:150a, 449b, 5:575b, 7:367a, 375b
"Imperial Hymn" for Frederick I Barbarossa, 1:449b–450a, 10:252b
language and style of, 1:450a
Latin parody and, 9:441a
"Minor Confession," 1:449b
Arcipreste de Talavera. See Martínez de Toledo, Alfonso
Arcn, **1:450b–451a**
Armenian trade and, 12:97b, 98a
sack of, by Seljuks, 7:215a
Arçonnage. See Bowing
Arcosolium, **1:451a**
Arcrunis, **1:451a-b**, 1:475b, 479b
Ašot I and, 1:480b
capital on Ałtᶜamar, 12:353b
historians of, 1:510b–511a
Mongols and, 12:737a

Arcrunis, **1:451a-b** (*cont.*)
in Vaspurakan, 12:361b–362a
see also T^covma Arcruni
Arculf, bishop
Bede and, 2:154b
on fair in Jerusalem, 4:589a
pilgrimage to Holy Land, 4:553b
Ard, 12:73a-b, 74 (*illus.*), 75a, 445b
in French Midi, 12:82b
in Mediterranean regions, 12:77a
in Scandinavia, 12:77a
see also Agriculture; Reclamation of land; Tools, agricultural, European
Arda (wife of Baldwin of Boulogne), 4:22b
Ardā Wirāz Nāmag, 9:327a
Ardabīl, in Islamic conquests, 6:569a
Ardagh chalice, 3:220b–221a, 222 (*illus.*), 6:516a, 8:373a
Ardashir I. *See* Ardešīr I, Sasanian ruler
Ardawān V of Armenia, king, 1:451b
overthrown by Ardešīr I, 9:443b
Ardebīl, Armenian trade and, 12:97b
Ardengus, Master, William of Auxerre's theology school and, 12:22a
Ardešīr I, Sasanian ruler, **1:451b–452a**
bas relief of at Naqsh-i Rustam, 10:611b–612a
conquests, 10:666b
legend of, 1:451b–452a
in *Kārnāmag-i Ardešīr-i Bābagān,* 7:220b–221a
overthrow of Arsacids and, 9:443b
patronage, 10:666b
political testament of, translated by Balādhurī, 2:54a
praised in *Letter of Tansar,* 7:552b–553a
šāhan-šāh, 10:666b
seizure of power, 1:451b
see also Fīrūzābād
Ardešīr II, Sasanian ruler, bas relief of, 10:658a
Ardešīr-Khurra. *See* Fīrūzābād
Ardre VIII, *Vǫlundarkviða* and, 12:490b
Ardre pictorial stone, 10:695a
Ardvī Sūrā Anāhitā (goddess), 12:720b
Areithian prose (prose rhetorics), **1:452a-b**
Areithiau, 12:608b
Arena (Scrovegni) Chapel (Padua), **1:453a**
Giotto's frescoes in, 1:453a, 9:153b–154 (*illus.*), 447a, 10:340a-b, 12:462b (*illus.*)
Areopagite. *See* Pseudo-Dionysius the Areopagite
Arethas, archbishop of Caesarea, 3:431a
Platonism of, 9:697b
Arethas, St., 9:55a
Aretino, Spinello. *See* Spinello Aretino
Aretinus. *See* Bruni, Leonardo
Arévalo, Rodrigo Sánchez de, political works by, 11:422b
Arezzo
inns in, 6:475a
vs. Siena, Ansano and, 11:278a
Arezzo, University of, 12:285b
Argenteuil Priory, acquired by Suger of St. Denis, 11:503a-b
Arghun. *See* Argun
Argos
capture of
by Theodore Palaiologos, 7:381a
by Villehardouin, 7:378a
sack of (1397), 7:381b
Venice and, 7:380b
Argote de Molina, 11:390b
Arguim, Portuguese trade and, 4:561a-b
Arguments. See Moses of Salerno
Argun, **1:453a**, 11:563b
reign of, 6:420a
Argun, khan
military alliances, 8:474b
religious beliefs, 8:474a
Argutinskiĭ-Dolgorukids, Zak^carids and, 12:737a
Argyll, Gaelic Scottish literature and, 11:113a, 113b, 114a
Argyropoulos, John, Platonistic teachings, 7:1a
Ari the Learned. *See* Ari Þorgilsson
Ari (Norwegian synoptic), 9:177a
Ari Þorgilsson, 4:618a
Eyrbyggja saga and, 4:568a
Íslendingabók, 6:352a, 9:175b, 11:329a, 497a
Kristni saga and, 7:303a
Ynglingatal and, 12:726a
Landnámabók and, 7:327b, 328a
on Vinland, 12:428a
Arianism, **1:453a–454b**, 2:459b, 460a
Agnellus of Ravenna and, 1:73a
Aripert I and, 8:377a
Athanasius of Alexandria and, 1:453b
attitude of Armenian church toward, 6:187b
Augustine of Hippo and, 1:654a
Basil the Great and, 2:121a, 121b–122a
of Burgundians, 2:92a
Byzantine, 4th century, 9:560b
Cappadocian fathers and, 1:454a
Cathars and, 3:183b
as a Christian movement, 6:193b–194a
condemnation of at First Council of Nicaea, 3:628a
Constantine I and, 1:453b, 3:545b
defeated in East, 11:44a
Gothic missionaries and, 10:465b
Goths and, 1:454a-b, 12:469a
Gregory of Nazianzus and, 5:666a
Gregory of Nyssa and, 5:666b
imperial support for, 2:485a
of Lombards, 7:656b
destruction of, 7:657a
Nicene Creed and, 2:453b
opposed by St. Ambrose, 1:231a
opposed by St. Nersēs I the Great, 9:102a
organized resistance to, 6:225a
Ostrogothic, 9:291a-b
Sirmium council and, 11:311b
struggle against, 3:676b
support of Ethiopian Christians, 1:32a
Trinitarian doctrine and, 12:189a–191b
of Vandals, 2:91b, 12:355b
of Visigoths, 2:90b–91b, 12:470b, 471b
architecture and, 12:465b, 466a
see also Anomoeanism; Pneumatomachianism; Theodoric the Ostrogoth
Aribert II of Milan, archbishop, 3:557b–558a
peace with Conrad II, 8:378a
revolt against, 8:378a
Aribo (11th century), *De musica,* 8:642a
^c*Arīd,* 6:590b
Ariminium (Rimini), Council of (359), 3:225b
Arinbjarnarkviða. See Egill Skallagrímsson
Ariosto, Ludovico, *Orlando furioso,* 6:639b, 670a, 8:225b
Aripert I, Lombard king, 7:657a
Arianism and, 8:377a
Aristakēs Lastiverc^ci, **1:454b–455a**, 1:511a
on annexation of Ani in Širak, 1:484a
Aristakes Rhetor (13th century), 1:512a
Aristandros and Kallithea. See Constantine Manasses
Aristas, origins of the kingdom of Navarre and, 9:67b
Aristides of Athens, 9:697a
Apology, 1:508a
in the Greek version of *Balavariani,* 2:54b
De musica, 8:566a
Aristides Quintilianus, 8:636b, 637a, 11:362b
Aristocracy. *See* Class structure; Feudalism; Nobility and nobles
Aristocratic chronicles, 3:327b–328a
Aristote, 7:317a
Aristoteles (Magister Lambertus). *See* Lambertus, Magister
Aristoteles und Phyllis, **1:455a-b**
Aristotelianism
Aristotelian revolution, 9:696a
at University of Paris, 11:285b–286a, 286b
Augustinian, 1:461b, 465b–466a
in philosophy of Duns Scotus, 1:464a
Averroist, 1:463a–464a, 465a, 467b–468a
at University of Paris, 9:408b–409a
Siger of Brabant on, 11:286a
in Western European philosophy, 9:597b–598a
condemnation of forms of (1277), 4:309a
dominance of in 13th-century philosophy, 9:612b
Duns Scotus and, 4:309a, 310a
Islamic philosophy and, 1:458a–459b
Jewish philosophy and, 1:459b–460a, 7:167a-b
Neoplatonism and, 1:457b–458a
Nicholas of Autrecourt and, 9:122a
nominalist. *See* Nominalism
Ockham and, 9:209b, 212a, 214a
orthodox, 1:462a–463a
see also Albertus Magnus; Aquinas, Thomas, St.

Platonic thought and, 9:697a–700a, 701a, 702a-b, 703b
comparatio, 9:701a
George of Trebizond, 9:703b
realism and, 10:271a
scholastic. *See* Scholasticism
Scotistic, 1:463b–464a, 466b–467a
Syrian Christianity and, 11:566b
Theologia Aristotelis, 9:699a, 700a
Thomistic. *See* Thomism
in universities, 1:461a–463a, 465a
varieties of, 1:465b–468a
via antiqua and, 9:157a
see also Classical literary studies; Philosophy and theology; Platonism

Aristotle, **1:456a–469a**
Alexander of Aphrodisias on, 9:95b
alphabetical indexes to the works of, 1:205b–206a
alternative interpretations of, 9:613b
Amalric of Bène and, 1:228b
Analytica posteriora, 1:456a, 460b, 461b, 462b, 4:168b, 12:138b–139a
Grosseteste's commentary on, 6:1b
truths of faith, 9:595b
Analytica priora, 1:456a, 4:168b–169a
as antifeminist authority, 1:323a-b
Arabic commentaries on, 10:572a, 572b
in Arabic Spain, 1:459a
astrology and, 1:604b
on astronomy, 1:614b
Basil the Great and, 2:120a
belief and understanding, formulas for, 9:584a
biological writings of, 8:251b
on the main organs of the body, 8:251b–252a
study of animals, 2:243b–244a
Boethius and, 8:637a
in Byzantine education, 9:565b
Categories, 1:456a, 460b
Armenian translations, 1:505b
Boethius' translation of, 11:688b
Latin versions, 9:585b
Notker Teutonicus and, 9:189a
Porphyry of Tyre's *Isagoge* and, 9:97a
censorship of, 1:461a, 462a
Chapter of the Elements. See Israeli, Isaac
Christian synthesis, 6:198b
commentaries on
by Ibn Rushd, 9:571a-b
by Theodore Metochites, 12:15a
translations of, 11:689a-b
condemnations of 1277 and, 10:388b
Constitution of Athens, 1:456b
critiques of logic, 6:118a
David the Invincible and, 4:114a-b
De anima, 1:128a, 456b, 457a, 458a, 460b
Arabic translations, 8:566a
theory of single intellect, 11:689b
De interpretatione, 1:456a, 460b, 4:168b
Armenian translations, 1:505b
Boethius' translation of, 11:688b
De mundo, 1:460b
De sophisticis elenchis, medieval *disputatio* and, 10:357a
definition of theology, 9:582b
dialectic and, 4:168a-b
early period, 1:460b–461a
Egidius Colonna and, 4:400a-b
on equity, 4:501a
on essence and existence, 4:510a
ethical works, commentaries on, 9:595a
Eudemian Ethics, 1:456b
fictitious letters of, 7:365a
form and matter, 9:575b–576a
four types of changes, 9:621b
nonliving substances, 9:621b
in French literature, 4:575a
in the Greek world, 1:457a–458a
History of Animals, 11:274a
in hymns, 6:383b
Ibn Gabirol's work on, 11:370b
Ibn Sīnā and, 11:304a–305a
influence of
on Christian thought, 9:594b–595a, 610b, 615a
on Italian Renaissance, 7:1b
"invasion of," 9:100b
Islamic syntheses, 1:458a–459b
Jean Buridan and, 2:430a-b
in Jewish philosophy and theology, 1:459b–460a, 9:573a
exegesis and, 4:540a
John of Salisbury and, 7:139b–140a
kingship theories and, 7:266b–267a
late medieval developments, 1:464a–465b
Liber de causis. See Liber de causis
library development and, 7:565b
Livre des secrets. See Secretum secretorum
logical works, commentaries and *quaestiones,* 9:613a-b
Magna Moralia, 1:456b
Marsilius of Padua and, 4:132a, 132b, 10:22b
Matthew of Aquasparta and, 8:227b
Metaphysics, 1:128b–129a, 456b
on music, 8:580a
Meteorology, 1:456b
rainbows, 9:242b
on music, 8:580a, 580b, 581b
Neoplatonism and, 1:457b–458a
Nestorianism and, 9:105b
Nicomachean Ethics, 1:456b, 461a, 461b, 7:267a
Grosseteste on, 1:461b
intellectual virtues, 9:610a
Li livres dou trésor and, 7:383a
translations of, 6:2a, 631b, 7:601b, 11:457a
William of Moerbeke's translation, 12:141a
nominalism and, 1:467a-b
nominalist vs. realist interpretations, 9:613a, 614a–615a
On Generation and Corruption, 1:456b
On the Heavens, 1:456b, 457b, 461a, 461b
Organon, 1:456a, 457b, 458a, 460b, 462b, 464a, 464b
basis for Islamic logic, 7:640a-b
in logic curriculum, 11:688b
Syrian Christianity and, 11:566b
Peri hermeneias, Notker Teutonicus and, 9:189a
Physics, 1:127b, 456b, 457b, 458a, 460b, 464a, 464b
commentaries on, 6:1b, 9:623b–623b
Poetics, 1:456b, 460b, 461a
popularity in 15th century, 10:363b
translations of, 6:208b
Politics, 1:456b, 461a, 7:266b, 267a, 9:699b
in *Defensor pacis,* 8:154b
translations of, 7:601b
principle of causation, 9:575b–576a, 595b
Problemata, Arabic translations, 8:566a
reception at universities, 1:461a–463a
Rhetorica, 1:456b
translations of, 6:208b
virtually unused in the Middle Ages, 10:356b, 357a
Secretum. See Secretum secretorum
on slavery, 11:334a
Sophistical Refutations, 1:456a
subaltern science model, 9:608b
Syrian Christianity and, 1:458a
Ṭawq al-ḥamāma, 6:118b
theological school of Antioch and, 9:105b
theory of creation, 9:607a, 612a
theory of the universe, 9:620b–623a
eternal universe, 9:621a
final cause, 9:622a
First Mover, 9:620b–621a
heavenly spheres, 9:620b
limits of cosmos, 9:621a
sublunar realm, 9:621a-b
vacua, 9:624b
violent motions, 9:622b
Thomas Aquinas and, 1:356a–357b
Topica, 1:456a, 4:168a-b, 169a
medieval *disputatio* and, 10:357a
translations of, 4:298a, 11:274a
Arabic, 11:83a, 12:130b
Armenian, 1:505b
by Albertus Magnus, 1:127b, 128a, 128b–129a
by Boethius, 2:292a
by Leonardo Bruni, 2:391a
Byzantine, 12:126b
from Arabic into Spanish, 11:689a
Latin, 1:127b, 128a, 128b–129a, 460b–461a, 468a, 10:356b, 12:641a
12th and 13th centuries, 9:97a, 11:689a
in Western Europe, 12:138a-b, 140a, 141a
on universals, 1:54a
in university curriculum, 11:688a-b, 689a-b
vision theory, 9:242b, 248a
intromission, 9:242b, 251a
light and color, 9:249a-b
rainbows, 9:252b–253a
Western European political theory after 1100 and, 10:19a–20a

Chapter of the Elements (*cont.*)
  works attributed to
    Book Concerning the Pure Good (Book of Causes), 9:100a
    Theologia Aristotelis, 9:100a
  works of, 1:456b
  Xusrō I and, 12:714a
  see also Bacon, Roger; Fārābī, al-; Levi ben Gershom; Neoplatonism; Philosophy and theology; Plato and Platonism; Thomism; Universals; *Via moderna*
Aristoxenians, 8:636b
Aristoxenus of Tarentum (*fl. ca.* 300 B.C.)
  Harmonica, 8:566a
  Principles and Elements of Harmonics, 8:636b
Arithmetic. *See* Mathematics
Arithmetic curriculum. *See* Seven liberal arts
Arithmetica. See Jordanus de Nemore
Arithmos, 11:573a
Aritmetica. See Diophantus
Arius, 1:453a-b, 3:627b
  Christology of, 3:336a
  condemnation of, 3:336a
  readmittance into church, 3:628a
  Trinity and, 3:339a
Ark of the Covenant, **1:469a-b**
  in Lateran, 7:345a
  see also Torah ark
Arkhangelsky Cathedral. *See* Moscow Kremlin
Arles, inns in, 6:469b, 472b, 473a, 474b
Arles, kingdom of, 4:107b
  first seals of, 11:126a
Arles, Synod of (314), 3:225b
  Donatism and, 4:259b–260a
Arles, Synod of (*ca.* 1041–1043), Truce of God and, 9:474a
Arles and Vienne, kingdom of, 4:108b, 109a
Arlotto of Prato, Peter John Olivi and, 9:515a
Arm reliquary. *See* Reliquary, *brachium*
Arma Christi, **1:469b**
  see also Angel
Armagh, **1:469b–470a**, 12:256a
  monastery of, 6:554a
  Patrick and, 9:463a, 464b, 465b
  see also Malachy, St.
Armagh, Book of. *See* Book of Armagh
Armagnac party in France
  Charles of Orléans and, 3:272b–273a
  Charles VII and, 3:270b, 5:188a
  civil war with Burgundians, 5:187b
Arman-shāh. *See* Shāh-Arman
Armarius. See Librarian
Arme Bäcker, Der. See Folz, Hans
Arme Heinrich, Der. See Hartmann von Aue
Armenia
  administration, 9:288b–289a
  Anatolian principalities, 9:648a-b
  annexation of Ani, 9:544a-b
  Arabs in, 1:473b, 512b–513a
    see also Armenia, Muslim emirates; Islam, conquests of, Armenian campaign
  Basil II and, 2:119a, 119b
  Baybars and, 2:138b
  boundaries, 1:471 (map), 472a-b, 474b–475a
    after Arab conquests, 1:473b
    after the fall of the Bagratids, 1:473b
    partitioning of, 1:483a
    reorganized under Emperor Justinian I, 1:473a
  Byzantine invasion, 8:518b
  Byzantine-Persian partition, 11:629a
  cavalry, 3:198b–199a
  Christianization of, 1:66a, 67b, 517b, 10:660b, 12:1
    Dominican missions, 4:252b
    magic and folklore and, 8:16a
  Cilician, struggle for independence, 2:495a
  Cilician settlement, 10:540a
  crusaders' route and, 10:423b
  cultural identity, 10:660b
  economy
    development of, 1:491a
    under Bagratids, 12:98a-b
    under Mongol domination, 12:99a
  geography, **1:470b–474b**
    Greater Armenia, 1:472a-b, 473a, 475a
    Lake Van, 12:353a-b
    Lesser Armenia, 1:472b, 475a
    Pontus, 10:31b
    topography, 1:470b
    see also Ayrarat; Manazkert; Melitene; Urmia, Lake; Vanand; Vaspurakan
  hazārabad in, 6:116b
  history, **1:474b–488a**
    Arsacids/Aršakuni dynasty in, 1:559a-b
    in Matthew of Edessa's *Chronicle*, 8:228b
    reunion of (in 884), 1:480b
    revolt of 450, 4:433b
    revolt of 451, 1:498b, 518b
    sources, 1:454b–455a, 475a-b
    treatises, 9:256b
    under Arabs, 1:478a–480a
    under Byzantine Empire, 1:477a–478a, 490a
    under Rome, 1:475a, 475b, 476a
    see also Anania Širakacᶜi; Ani in Širak; Avarayr; Bagratids (Bagratuni), Armenian; Bahrām V Gōr; Historiography, Armenian; Łewond; *Patmutᶜiwn Tarōnoy;* Pᶜawstos Buzand; Tᶜovma Arcruni; Tᶜovma Mecopᶜecᶜi; Vanand; Van, Lake; Vaspurakan
  importance in Byzantine Empire, 4:343b
  Inner, 11:598a
  Islamic conquests of, 6:568b, 572a
  Italian migration, 2:492a
  Justinian I and, 1:515b–516a
  marzpanate, 8:169a-b
  Maurice and, 8:230b
  Mongol alliance, invasion of Syria, 8:472b–473a
  Muslim emirates, **1:512b–514b**, 2:20b
    Arab emirates, 1:512b–513b
    attitude to Christians, 1:514a-b
    Iranian emirates, 1:513b
    Tarōn and, 11:599b
    three periods of, 1:512b
    Turkization of the area, 1:513b–514a
    see also Melitene (emirate)
  partitioning of, 3:195b
  population, 1:485a
  relations with
    Azerbaijan, 1:482a-b
    Byzantine Empire, 1:483b
    Georgia, 1:485b
    Rome, 10:463a-b
  satrapies of, 1:472b, 475a, 475b, 476a
  social structure, 1:476b, **1:488a–491b**
    classes, 1:488b
    high nobility, 1:488b–489b
    Iran and, 1:488a-b
    lower classes, 1:488b, 489b–490a
    lowest estate, 10:255a
    office of *tanutēr*, 1:488b–489a
    origins of the *naχarar* system, 1:488a
    šinakan, 11:307b
    under Byzantines, 1:490a-b
    under Zakᶜarids, 1:490b
    see also Nobility and nobles, Armenian; *Sepuh;* Sparapet; Tanutēr
  social structure of. *See Azat*
  trade with Southeast Asia, 9:85a
  Turkish invasions, 2:493a
  under Zakᶜarids, 12:737a
  vs. Mongols, siege of Mayafariqin, 8:472b
  see also Artašat; Berkri; Parthians; Trade, Armenian; Uzun Ḥasan
Armenia, Kingdom of Lesser. *See* Cilicia
Armeniakon, 1:474a
Armeniakon, theme of, **1:491b**, 12:9b
Armenian alphabet. *See* Alphabets, Armenian
Armenian architecture, 1:493a–494a
  in Aštarak, 1:601a-b
  by Trdat, 12:164b–165a (*illus.*)
  cathedral at Ani in Širak, 1:494 (*illus.*)
  central-plan church structures in, 1:493b, 4:343b
  churches
    domed, 11:665a-b
    free-standing cruciform, 8:202a
  construction materials, 4:343b
  domed hall church, 6:286a
  earliest extant Christian structures in Armenia, 1:493a-b
  influence on later Byzantine architecture, 4:343b
  secular, 1:494a
  stylistic affinities, 4:337b
  vaulting, 6:77a-b
Armenian art, **1:493a–498a**
  Armenian seals and, 11:122b
  at Gełard, 5:373a-b
  at Glajor, 5:544a
  at Gošavankᶜ, 5:579b
  Cilician school, 10:652b
  creative periods of, 1:493a
  figural sculpture, 9:224a

*gawit*ᶜ, 5:371a-b
manuscript illumination, 1:496b–497b (*illus.*), 10:652b (*illus.*)
minor arts, 1:497b
painting, 1:496a–497b
monumental, 1:496a
sculpture, 1:494a–496a
early period, 1:494b–495a
on the island of Ałtᶜamar, 1:495b, 496a (*illus.*)
in Skewŕa, 11:326a (*illus.*)
see also Ałtᶜamar; Ani in Širak, monuments of; Betania; Tigran Honencᶜ; Tᶜoros Roslin; Tᶜoros Tarōnecᶜi
Armenian church
after the fall of Bagratids (1045), 1:503b–504a
Albanian church and, 1:123b
Arab conquest and, 1:478b
architecture, by Trdat, 12:164b–165a
Armeno-Georgian schism, 5:540a-b
Ašot I and, 1:480b
Ašot III and, 1:482b
canons, 10:611a
cathedral of Ējmiacin, 4:417a-b
christological disputes, 1:519a
devotion to Virgin Mary, 1:502a
doctrines and councils, **1:498a–502b**, 4:324a
Christology of Theodore of Mopsuestia, 6:187b
council of Šahapivan, 7:388a
Council of the Three Chapters, 6:188a
hellenizing tendencies, 6:189a
influence on culture, 8:169a
Koriwn, 7:299a
schism with Constantinople, 6:188a
see also Dwin, Council of (555); Nersēs II Aštarakacᶜi (Bagrewandacᶜi); Nersēs Lambronacᶜi; Šahapivan, Council of (444)
Gregorid patriarchs of, 5:665a-b
history, 1:475b–476a
sources, 1:455a
in *History of the Armenians,* 1:508a
Hŕomklay and, 6:311b–312a
inauguration of, 1:475b–476a
*Knik*ᶜ *Hawatoy,* 7:279a-b
litanies of, 7:589a, 589b, 590b
Monophysitism and, 1:499a, 6:188a, 8:479a-b, 9:561b, 562b
Monothelitism and, 1:499b–500a, 8:480b
Nersēs I and, 5:665a-b
Nestorianism and, 1:498b–499a
Paulicians and, 9:469a-b
relations with Cilician kingdom, 3:393b
sacraments of, 1:502a
Sahak I and, 5:665a-b
saints, **1:517b–521b**
building of first martyria, 1:518a
commemoration codified in the *Lectionary,* 1:520a-b
movable feast days of, 1:520b–521a
non-Armenians, 1:520a
revolt against the Persians (451), 1:518b
in synaxaria, 1:521a
unauthenticated, 1:519b
veneration of relics, 1:518a
virgin martyrs, 1:517b
see also Armenian literature, hagiography; Łazar Pᶜarpecᶜi; Thaddeus legend; Vardan Mamikonean, St.
schisms
anti-Chalcedonian, 1:123b
Armeno-Georgian, 1:499b
structure, **1:502b–505a**
celibacy and, 1:504a
ecclesiastical hierarchy, 1:504a-b
katᶜołikos, 1:502b–503a, 4:324a, 7:226b–227a
metropolitans, 9:256b
principles of, 1:502b
role of bishops, 1:503a-b, 504a
see also Vardapet
under Byzantine Empire, 1:477b
under *marzpans*, 1:477a
union with Rome, 9:104b
Zenob Glak on, 1:510b
see also Bible, Armenian; Law, canon, Armenian; Schism, Armenian
Armenian Geography/Asχarhacᶜoycᶜ, 1:472a, 478b
on Ayrarat, 2:20a
Armenian Hellenizing School, **1:505a–506a,** 1:509a
beginnings of, 1:505b
dating of texts, 1:505b–506a
Armenian language, **1:506a–507b,** 6:433b
ancient influences, 1:506a
Classical Armenian, 1:506b–507a
consonants, 1:506b
differences between spoken and written language, 1:506b–507a
importance of Armenian Hellenizing School, 1:506b
introduction of the alphabet, 1:506b
loanwords in, 1:491b, 507a
Middle Armenian, 1:507a
translations from Greek, 12:126a–127a
Septuagint, 2:211a
see also Alphabet, Armenian; Bible, Armenian
Armenian law, **7:388a–390a**
civil law, 7:388a-b
council of Šahapivan and, 7:388a
courts, 7:389b
Dawitᶜ of Ganjak's penitential, 7:388b
during Arsacid dynasty, 7:388a
during Sasanian, Byzantine, and Arab domination, 7:388b
Mχitᶜar Goš and, 7:388b–389b, 8:656b
Nersēs Lambronacᶜi and, 7:388b–389b
persons protected by, 7:389b
punishments under, 7:389b
role of churchmen in, 1:504a
Smbat Sparapet and, 7:389a-b, 11:351b
Syro-Roman code and, 7:388a–389a
translations from Syrian and Byzantine texts, 7:389a
see also Law, canon, Armenian
Armenian literature, **1:507b–512b**
Bagratid period, 1:510a–511a
biblical exegesis, 2:214b
chronicles, 1:511b
development of, 10:611a
early period, 1:507b–510a
epistolary, 1:508b, 509a, 510a-b
folk epic, social context of, 4:112b
Girk Tᶜłtᶜocᶜ, 5:540a-b
hagiography, 1:508a, 510a, 511a
importance of Armenian Hellenizing School, 1:506a
later period, 1:511a–512b
magical texts, 8:16a-b
poetry, 1:509b, 511b–512a
translations, 1:507b–508b
see also Armenian church, saints; Łazar Pᶜarpecᶜi; Vardan Arewelcᶜi
Armenian music, **8:551a–553b**
hymns by Nersēs IV Šnorhali (the Graceful), 9:103b
sacred, 8:551a–553a
secular, 8:553a
Armenian numerals, 1:492b (*illus.*)
Armenian Pentarchy, **1:514b–516a**
origins of, 1:514b–515a
under the Romans, 1:515a-b
Armenian rite, **1:516a–517b**
anaphoras in, 1:516a-b
Byzantine rite and, 1:516a-b
Divine Office, 1:516b–517a
latinization of, 1:516b
Syriac and Greek influences, 1:516a
Armenians
in Georgia, 4:112a, 5:405a
in Isfahan, 6:562a
Armes Brydein, 5:388a
Armes et blazons de chevalliers de la Table Ronde, 6:176b
Armes Prydein, 12:515b, 597b
Armet, 1:530a
Armet *à rondelle,* 1:527b (*illus.*), 530a
Armies. *See* Warfare
Armiger. See Squire
Armillary sphere, **1:521b,** 11:95a-b, 102 (*illus.*)
Islamic, 11:86b
Sylvester II and, 11:100a, 100b, 552a
Arming doublet, 1:525b
Armīniya
administration, 9:288b
see also Islam, conquests of, Armenian campaign
Armorial de la Toison d'Or, 6:176b
Armorica
five tribes of, 2:377b
population of, 10:464b–465a
Romanization of, 2:377b
Armorium judicium (trial by arms)
in literature, 7:367b
see also Combat, trial by; Ordeal
Arms and armor, **1:521b–536b**
alla tedescha, 1:530b, 535 (*illus.*)
all'antica, 1:535 (*illus.*)
ambient heat and, 1:524a, 524b–525a
ax, 1:522a, 522b
barbarian, 1:522a
body armor, 1:524a-b

Arms and armor (*cont.*)
breastplates, 1:526b, 528a, 528b, 530a, 530b, 534–535 (*illus.*)
Byzantine
Varangian Guard, 12:359b
see also Stratiotai
crusades and, 1:524a, 524b
Danish axe, 12:564b
decoration, 1:536a-b
design technology, 11:659a-b
development of, 1:522a–532b
etching and, 4:516a,b
for European cavalry, 3:205b–206a
firearms and, 1:531b–532a
fluted, 1:531a
francisca, 12:556b
Frankish, 12:556b–557a
from Sutton Hoo, 11:519a, 519b, (*illus.*)
Gothic, 1:529b–530a, 531a
halberd, 12:565b
helmet, 1:524a, 526a-b, 527 (*illus.*), 531a-b, 534–535 (*illus.*)
horizontal style, 1:530b–531a
for horses, 1:525a, 529a, 529b
importance of Milan, 1:528b–529b
of knights, 7:276a–278b
lamellar, 1:522a-b, 525a
lance, 1:526b
leg armor, 1:524b, 525b
mail shirt, 12:564b
manufacture, 1:529a-b, 533b, 536a
monetary value of, 1:522b, 533a
pavise, 1:528a, 528b (*illus.*)
pike, 12:565b
plate armor, 1:522a, 529a-b, 535b (*illus.*), 3:205b–206a
manufacture of, 1:533b, 536a
pot-helm, 12:564b
progress in metallurgy, 3:561a
repoussé, 10:315b
of the Ripuarian Franks, 8:283a-b
shields, 1:522b–524a (*illus.*), 525b
suit of, 1:528b–529a
three-quarter, 1:531b
for tournaments, 1:525b, 526a, 532b–533a, 5:350a
working of iron and steel, 8:293b–294a
see also Daggers; Guns and gunpowder; specific weapons; Steelmaking; Swords
Árna saga biskups, **1:537a**
author of, 1:537a
see of Skálholt and, 1:537a
Arnald of Villanova, **1:537b–538b,** 8:252b, 11:380a
alchemical treatises, 1:138a
Allocutio christiana, 1:538a
Allocutio super Tetragrammaton, 1:537b
Aphorismi de gradibus, 1:538a
on bad wines, 12:119b
beguins and, 2:162a, 162b, 163a
Catalan writings, 3:157b, 165a
condemnation of, 1:537b
De adventu antichristi, 1:537b
on fruits grown in Mediterranean region, 5:306a-b
imprisonment of, 1:537b–538a
influence of, 1:538a
knowledge of Arabic, 1:538a
life of, 1:537b
medical career, 1:537b
as physician to Pedro III of Aragon, 1:537b
medical theory of, 1:538a
misattribution to, 10:289a
Recetario de diversas enfermedades, 11:441b
Regimen sanitatis, 5:306a-b, 7:366a
support for Franciscan Spirituals, 1:537b, 5:202b
theological views of, 1:538a
in Valencia, 12:348b
Arnaldo da Foligno, 9:14a
Arnalte y Lucenda. See San Pedro, Diego de
Arnamagnaean collection, 7:232a
MS 748 I 4°, collection of Eddic poetry, 4:385b
Arnau de Torrelles, *Chronicle of the Kings of Aragon and Counts of Barcelona* and, 9:511b
Arnaut Daniel, **1:539a,** 10:175a–176b, 179a, 251a, 252a
comparison to Bernart de Ventadorn, 10:175a-b, 176a
Dante and, 6:641a, 648b, 669b
in Dante's *Purgatorio,* 10:175a, 175b
dating of his work, 1:539a
fin'amors in poetry of, 10:176a-b
formalism of, 10:175b–176a
joi in poetry of, 10:176a
Marqués de Santillana on, 11:446a
refinement in verse of, 10:176b
satirized by Peire de Vic, 10:176b
as self-conscious exemplar of troubadour love poetry, 10:176a
sestina of, 10:175b–176a
trobar ric of, 10:179a
troubadour poetry of, 12:215a-b
Arnaut Guilhem de Marsan, *Ensenhamen,* 3:665a-b
Arnaut, Henri, of Zwolle, 8:608a, 608b
Arnaut de Mareuil, *Ensenhamen,* 3:664b–665a
Arnaut of Prat, his rhymed office for St. Louis, 10:374a
Arnegunde, queen, burial of, 4:328a
Arngrím of Thingeyrar, abbot, on Iceland, 6:394b
Arngrímr Brandsson
Guðmundar saga D, 6:34a
Thómas saga erkibyskups and, 12:36a
Arngrímur Jónsson lærði, 11:328a
Arna rímur, 10:403a
Skjǫldunga saga and, 9:176a
Árni Helgason, attribution of *Árna saga biskups,* 1:537a
Árni Jónsson
Guðmundardrápa, influenced by *Líknarbraut,* 7:580b
Hálfdans rímur Eysteinssonar, 10:403a
Árni Laurentiusson
Dunstanus saga, **4:311b–312a,** 7:387a
sources for, 4:311b
Árni Magnússon, 5:673a
collection of Icelandic manuscripts, 6:145b
Árni Þorláksson, bishop of Skálholt, 1:537a, 6:396a
Arnobius the Elder, **1:539a-b**
Adversus nationes, 1:539a
Arnobius the Younger, **1:539b**
Commentarii in Psalmos, 1:539b
Conflictus de Deo trino et uno, 1:539b
Expositiunculae in Evangelium, 1:539b
Arnold Amalric, Cathars and, 3:187b–188a
Arnold of Brescia, **1:539b–540b**
condemnation of, 1:539b–540a
death of, 1:540a
followers of, 1:540a
leadership of Roman commune, 6:196a
return to *vita apostolica,* 6:196a
revolt against church, 1:58b, 540a
Rome and, 10:523a
Arnold of Guînes, siege of Bourbourg castle, 3:145a
Arnold of Liège, *Alphabetum narrationum,* 1:206a
Arnold of St. Emmeram, **1:540b**
De memoria beati Emmerammi, 1:540b
De miraculis beati Emmerammi, 1:540b
see also Manfred of Magdeburg
Arnoldi, Alberto, **1:540b–541a**
Arnoldists, 1:540a
Arnolfo di Cambio, **1:541a-b,** 9:669b
in Florence, 1:541a
influence of, on Giotto di Bondone, 5:531a
sculpture by, 12:170b–171a
style of, 1:541a
Arnulf II of Milan, archbishop, crowning of Henry II, 8:378a
Arnulf of Bavaria, Magyars and, 6:338b
Arnulf of Carinthia, duke
Italian expeditions, 3:114a
opposition to, 5:474a
rule of, 3:114a-b
Arnulf (chaplain of Robert of Normandy), Tancred and, 11:589b
Arnulf, East Frankish king and emperor, **1:541b**
defeat of Vikings, 1:541b
vs. Rudolph of Auxerre, 11:537b
Arnulf of Lisieux, 7:366b
Arnulf of Metz, bishop, 9:498b, 499a
Arnulf of Milan (historian), **1:541b–542a**
Gesta archiepiscoporum Mediolanensium, 1:541b–542a, 8:378b
investiture controversy and, 1:541b
Arnulf of Orléans
Allegories on the Metamorphoses, 1:183b
on classics, 7:366a
Lidia, 4:283a
Arnulf (the Bad) of Bavaria, duke, 5:509a
Conrad I and, 5:507b
defeat of Magyars, 5:507b
Arnulfingians, 9:148a, 499a
of Austrasia, 8:278b
mayors of the palace, 8:236a

Aromanian language, 10:509b
Arons saga, in *Sturlunga saga,* 11:500b
Arostalēs, 5:665a
Árpád, Hungarian ruler, 6:338a, 338b
Arpent (unit of measure), **1:542a,** 12:583b
  journal and, 7:153a
  standards of, 1:542a
Arraby Moor. See Portugal; Rabbinate
Arragel, Moses, of Guadalajara, Alba Bible and, 2:215b
Arrān, Shaddadids in, 7:310b
Arran. *See* Albania
Arras
  development of drama in, 4:264a
  first seals of, 11:126a
  literary circles in, 5:283a
  in literature, 9:633b, 636a-b
  tapestry of, 11:596a-b
Arras, Mathieu d'. *See* Mathieu d'Arras
Arras, Treaty of (1435), 5:188b, 6:332b, 7:699b
  Eugenius IV and, 6:334b
Arrest. *See* Trespass
Arrêt, king's council, role of, 9:262a
Arrêt de Conflans, 2:380a
Arrha (betrothal money), 2:207b
Arrian, on Roman cavalry, 3:200b
Arriccio, **1:542b**
  sinopia over, 11:311a
Arrigo Testa, Iacopo da Lentini and, 6:387b
Arrow
  broad, 2:351 *(illus.)*
  cloth-yard shafts, 2:351b
  fletchings, 2:351a-b
  heads
    Asiatic, 2:351b
    European, 2:351b
  hunting, big game, 2:351 *(illus.)*
  length of
    English longbows, 2:351b
    Mongol bows, 2:351b
  quivers, 2:352a
  range, 2:351b
  see also Bow
Arruda, Diogo, monastery of Christ at Tomar, 5:630a
Arruda, Francisco de, 5:630a
Ars alchemie, alchemical procedures, 1:136b–137a
Ars amatoria. See Ovid
Ars antiqua, **1:542b–547a,** 10:380b–381b
  ars nova and, 1:548b
  composers of, 1:543b
  composition in, 1:545b–546a
  contemporary treatises and, 1:544a
  definition of, 1:542b
  divisions of, 1:543a-b
  forms of
    clausulae, 1:546a-b
    conductus, 1:546b
    discant style, 1:546a-b
    motet, 1:546b–547a
    organa, 1:546a-b
    organal style, 1:546a
  Franco of Cologne and, 1:544b–545a
  French, 12:177b
  from Notre Dame, 1:543a-b
  John of Garland and, 1:544b–545a
  mensural notation, 1:544b–545a
  modal notation and, 1:544b
  musical achievements of, 1:543a-b
  practice of, 1:542b
  Scholastic influences on, 1:543a–544a
  solo sections of, 1:546a-b
  sources transmitting, 1:545a-b
  styles influenced by, 1:547a
  texts associated with, 1:544a
  use of, 1:542b–543a
  "Viderunt omnes" and, 12:411a
  see also Leoninus; Melisma
Ars arengandi (theory of secular speech), 10:363b
Ars cantus figurati. See Antonio of Lucca
Ars cantus mensurabilis. See Franco of Cologne
Ars compendiosa inveniendi veritatem. See Lull, Ramon
Ars dictaminis, 4:173b, 10:357b–359b
  in Boccaccio's *Decameron,* 2:285a
  in law schools, 7:513a
  in monastic schools, 11:76a
  as a new medieval genre of rhetoric, 10:355b
  see also Dictamen
Ars dictandi. See Dictamen
Ars disserendi, See Adam of the Little Bridge
Ars epistolandi, 4:176b
Ars epistolaris ornatus. See Geoffrey of Eversley
Ars grammatica, ars poetriae and, 10:359b
Ars grammatica. See Donatus (Aelius Donatus)
Ars gromatica, 8:207b–208a, 213a
Ars lectoria. See Aimeric of Angoulême
Ars magna. See Lull, Ramon
Ars maior. See Donatus
Ars medicinae. See Articella; Constantine the African
Ars minor. See Donatus (Aelius Donatus)
Ars moriendi, **1:547b–548a**
  description of, 1:547b
  Everyman and, 4:527b
  influence on vernacular plays, 4:286b
  John Gerson's *Opus tripartitum,* 10:302a
  longer version of, 1:547b
  shorter version of, 1:547b–548a
Ars motettorum. See Petrus of Picardy
Ars musica. See Egidius de Zamora
Ars musica. See Johannes de Grocheo, *De musica*
Ars notaria, 4:174b, 176a
  ars dictaminis and, 10:359a
Ars nova, **1:548a–553b,** 10:381b–382a
  ars antiqua and, 1:548b
  ars subtilior and, 1:550b, 558a
  circle and dot system of, 1:549b–550a
  coloration system of, 1:549b
  double leading-tone cadence in, 1:551b–552a
  examples of, 1:548b
  flourishing of, 1:548b
  formes fixes, 10:528b–529a
  forms of
    ballades, 1:552a-b
    ballata, 1:553a
    caccia, 1:553a
    lais, 1:552b
    madrigal, 1:552b–553a
    rondeau, 1:552a-b
    virelai, 1:552a-b
  French
    compared with Italian trecento music, 12:177b–178a
    repertoire of, 1:550–552a
  Italian
    notation of, 1:550a-b
    repertoire of, 1:552b–553a
  Jehan des Murs and, 7:56b–57a
  keyboard performance of, 1:553a
  mensural notation in, 1:549a–550a
  notation of, 1:548a-b, 549 *(illus.)*
  performance practice of, 1:552a-b
  Philippe de Vitry and, 1:548a, 12:482a
  polyphonic repertoire of, 1:551a
  principles of, 1:548b–550a
  rhythmic and notational innovations, in Mass of Tournai, 8:199a
  sources for, 8:126a
  see also Ballata
Ars nova. See Vitry, Philippe de
Ars poetica, **1:553b–555a**
  classic texts as source of, 1:553b–554a
  description of, 1:553b
  in Froissart's *Prison amoureuse,* 5:269a
  of Geoffrey of Vinsauf, 1:554a–555a
  origin of, 5:268b
Ars poetriae, as a new genre of rhetoric, 10:355b
Ars praedicandi, **1:555b–558a,** 10:76a
  as aid to improve quality of pastoral care, 1:556b
  of Alan of Lille, 1:555b–556a, 557b
  development of, 10:79a
  formats of, 1:555b
  as guides for writing thematic sermons, 1:556a
  manuals
    early handbooks, 1:556a-b
    of 13th century, 1:556b
  as a new genre of rhetoric, 10:355b
  preaching in Spain and, 11:456a
  synoptic form of, 1:556b
  textual traditions of, 1:555b
  treatises on, 1:555b
  understanding of, 1:557b–558a
  see also Preaching
Ars de pulsatione lambuti, 8:563b
Ars rethorica. See Grüner, Vincent, of Zwickau
Ars subtilior, **1:558a–559a**
  composers of, 1:558b
  definition of, 1:558a-b
  Franco-Italian, trecento, 12:178b, 180a
  French compositions, 1:558b
  impact of, 1:559a
  Italian, *gallica* notation, 12:178b
  music, 1:558b–559a
  origin of, 1:550b
  style of, 1:558b
  see also Ballade

Ars Tatvini. See Tatwine of Canterbury
Ars versificatoria. See Matthew of Vendôme
Ars veterum/vetus. See Ars antiqua
Arsacids
conversion to Christianity, 10:668a-b
Iranian reunification, 10:666a
lineage, 10:666a
monarchy, titles, 10:611b
Sasanian allegiance, 10:668a
Arsacids/Aršakuni, Armenian, 1:475a, 476a-b, **1:559a-b**
Arcrunis and, 1:451a
Armenian law and, 7:388a
Bagratids and, 2:48a
Basil I and, 1:481a, 2:117a
cavalry of, 3:198b–199a
conversion of by St. Gregory the Illuminator, 9:457b
fall of, 2:49b
in Georgia, 5:405a
Greater Armenia and, 1:472a-b
in *Kārnāmag-i Ardešir-i Bābagān,* 7:221a
in Łazar P⊂arpec⊂i's *History of Armenia,* 7:529b
naχarars and, 9:90b
office of sparapet and, 11:460a-b
Parthian, vs. Sasanians, 1:451b
Parthian language and, 6:506a
P⊂awstos Buzand's *History of Armenia* and, 9:472b
in Širak, 11:311a
Trdat III (IV) the Great, 12:164a
vs. Sasanians, 1:475b
in *Yačaxapatum Čaṙk⊂,* 1:508b–509a
see also Ayrarat; Bahrām VI Čōbēn of Persia, usurper; Kaminakans; Mamikonean; Parthians; Vanand
Aršak II of Armenia, king, 1:476a, **1:559b–560a**
imprisonment of, 1:560a
Nersēs I the Great and, 9:101b
reign of, 1:559b–560a
Sasanians and, 1:560a
Aršak III of Armenia, king, 1:476a
end of Roman branch of Arsacid dynasty, 1:559b
in P⊂awstos Buzand's *History of Armenia,* 9:472b
Aršak, leader of the Parni tribe, 9:443b
Arsam, Orontid king of Sophene, Aršamunik⊂ and, 11:599a
Aršamunik⊂, 11:599a
Aršarunik⊂
Bagratids and, 1:480a
principality of, 2:20a
Vanand and, 12:353b, 354a
Arsen II, *kat⊂ołikos* of Armenia, *Lives of the Thirteen Syrian Fathers,* 5:416b
Arsen Ikalt⊂oeli, 5:417a, 6:416a
Arsenal, origin of the term, 9:74a, 81a
Arsenal Bible, 2:215a
Arsenale (Venetian shipyard), 12:388a
Arsenite schism, 1:245b, 560b
support of Laskarids, 7:343a
Arsenius Autorianus, patriarch of Constantinople, **1:560a-b,** 3:620b
John Laskaris and, 7:343a
Arslan Isrā'īl ibn Seljuq, Seljuk sultan
origins of the Seljuks and, 11:151a
Turkomans and, 12:227a
Arslan Shāh, Eldigüz and, 6:419a, 419b
Arslanshāh, Seljuk ruler of Kirmān, 11:155a
Aṙstakēs, 5:668a
Arsukisdze (Armenian architect), 11:523b
Art
commercial trade of, **1:560b–563a**
commissioned art, 1:561a–562a
domestic painting and statuary, 1:561b
embroidery, 1:561a
high art, 1:562b
majolica, 1:561b
marketing of, 1:562a-b
minor arts, 1:560b
monumental brasses, 1:562a
noncommissioned art, 1:562a
tapestries, 1:561a-b
renaissances and revivals, **10:304b–312a**
see also Drawings; Gothic art; Iconoclasm; Romanesque art
Art. See Lull, Ramon
Art de dictier. See Deschamps, Eustache
Art de vénerie. See Twiti, William
Arta, 4:500a
Artabanus V, Arsacid pretender. *See* Ardawān V of Armenia, king
Artanuč, Armenian trade and, 12:97b
Artašat, **1:563a–564a,** 10:236b
as capital of Armenia, 1:563b
dye industry in, 1:563b–564a
excavations of, 1:563a
founding of, 1:563a-b
importance of, 1:563b
mint at, 8:417b
textile manufacture in, 12:98a-b
trade route from Ectabana to Black Sea, 12:96b–97a
see also Ayrarat
Artašat, Council of (449), 1:498b
Artawazd II of Armenia, king, 3:198b
Artawazd of Erašχawork⊂, prior, *Life* of Vahan of Gołt⊂n, 1:519a, 6:240a
Artaxata. *See* Artašat
Artaxeres. *See* Ardešīr
Artaxiads, coins of, 8:417b
Arte dei Meidici e Speziali, Lorenzetti as member of, 7:668a
Arte dei Popolo Minuto. *See* Ciompi
Arte dei Tintori, 11:714b
Arte del biscanto misurato. See Jacobus of Bologna
Arte della cosa, 8:214b
Arte della Lana
divieto, 11:714a, 714b
regulation of dyeing fees, 11:713a
Artes poeticae, on skaldic poetry, 11:320b
Artevelde, Jacob van
Edward III of England and, 5:82b
power of Ghent under, 3:503a, 5:523a-b
Arthour and Merlin, 1:574a, 8:316a
Arthur, king
excavation of his burial site (1190), 1:337a-b
historical, 1:564a–565b, 8:223b
hunting and, 6:358b
see also Arthurian legend
Arthur (son of Geoffrey of Brittany)
John of England and, 7:129a-b
succession question, 4:468a
Arthur (son of Henry VII of England), marriage festivities of, 4:287b
Arthurian legend, 8:223b–224b
Alani influences, 1:121b
Ambrosius Aurelianus and, 2:3a
in Catalan literature, 1:573a, 3:173a
Celtic tradition and, 1:565b–567b
chastity tests in, 8:507a
Christianization of, 5:285a, 286a-b
in chronicles, 3:327a
in Dutch literature, 4:318b, 319a
earliest accounts of, 1:564a
early allusions to, 1:565b–566a, 572b
in French literature, 1:568a–581b, 5:284a, 285a, 287a-b
Galaad, 5:259a-b, 286a
Gauchier de Dourdan, 5:367b
Gerbert de Montreuil, 5:423b
Guinglain romances, 10:315a-b
Jaufré, 10:179a–181a
lais, 7:316b
Méraugis de Portlesguez, 10:257b–258a
Roman de Brut, 12:496b
romances, 1:568b–571b
Vulgate cycle, 5:259a-b, 285b–286a
see also Chrétien de Troyes
Geoffrey of Monmouth and, 7:365a
in German literature, 1:571b–572b, 5:428b–429a, 447a–449b, 7:642b–643a, 9:708a-b
characters in, 5:448b–449a
Gottfried von Strassburg, 5:634a–637b
Hartmann von Aue, 6:103b–105a
Heinrich von dem Türlin, 6:135a
Konrad von Würzburg, 7:287a-b
Tristan of Ulrich von Türheim, 12:253a-b
Ulrich Füetrer's *Buch der Abenteuer,* 12:248b
Wirnt von Grafenberg's *Wigalois,* 12:657a
in Irish bardic poetry, 6:537a
in Italian literature, 1:572b–575a, 6:637b, 638a, 638b–639a
Karlamagnús saga and, 7: 217b
in literature, **1:564a–575b**
in Middle English literature, 1:573a–575a
ballads, 2:60a
Brut, 2:393a-b
Gawain and the Green Knight, 5:369a–370b
Modena Cathedral and, 10:501b
in *Nine Heroes* tapestry series, 11:596a (*illus.*)
origins and spread of, 8:223b–224a
parodies
by Ulrich von Leichtenstein, 12:251a
Renard the Fox stories, 2:141b, 10:313a
in Picard literature, 9:634a
political uses of, 5:244a

in Portuguese literature, 11:416a
in Provençal literature, 10:179a
in Scandinavian literature
Icelandic *riddarasögur,* 10:395a
Lancelot in, 10:304a
Möttuls saga, 10:391a
translations into Norwegian, 10:390a–391b
in Spanish and Portuguese literature, 1:573a, **1:575b–576b, 11:416a, 453b**
lost works, 11:443b
see also Amadís de Gaula
spread of in Europe, 1:564a, 567b–568b, 571b–573a
Tristan story and, 12:199b–200a, 202a-b, 204b–205a
Vulgate cycle, based on Robert de Boron's work, 10:431a
in Welsh literature, 1:565b–567b, **1:576b–578b,** 6:440b, 12:600a, 602a, 603b–604a, 611a, 611b
Cadoc in, 3:7a-b
Geoffrey of Monmouth and, 5:388b–389a
mabinogi tales, 7:705b
see also Excalibur; Grail, legend of; *Ívens saga;* Malory, Sir Thomas; *Parcevals saga; Perlesvaus;* Prophecy, political, Middle English; Prose Lancelot; Robert de Boron; Tintagel; Ulrich Füetrer; Ulrich von Zazikhoven; Vulgate cycle
Arti Maggiori
control of reorganized government, 11:714b–715a
see also Arte della Lana
Arti di Tintori e Saponai, formation of, 11:714b
Articella, 8:248a-b, 256b
at Montpellier, 8:249b
at the University of Paris, 8:249b
Artichoke, growth of, 1:86a, 87a
Articles of the Barons, 4:469a
see also Magna Carta
Artiller. *See* Trebuchet
Artillery, 3:151b–152a
catapults, 3:150b
categories of, 3:179a
effect on castles and fortifications, 3:151b–152a
field, 3:66a
first use of, 3:151b
Guido da Vigevano on, 11:644b–645a
siege, 3:65a-b
see also Cannon; Trebuchets
Artisans, 3:422b
Irish. *See Aes dána*
Nubian, 9:199a-b
status of, 10:499a, 11:643a
Islamic world, 11:636b
wealth of, 3:419b, 420a
in Ypres, 12:731a, 732a
Artists
artist-engineer, 11:647b
guilds
apprentice system, 6:21b
in Italy, 6:22a
officers, 6:21a-b
regulations, 6:21a, 21b
restricted membership, 6:21a, 22a
stifling of creativity, 6:211b–222a
manuals. *See* Manuals, artistic
status of, **1:578b–580a**
concept of the artist and, 1:578b–579a
Dante Alighieri on, 1:579b
Second Council of Nicaea (787) and, 1:579a
travels of, 12:152b–153a, 160b
Artophorion. *See Darokhranitelnitsa*
Artrí mac Cathail, 4:493a
Arts de seconde rhétorique, Rhétoriqueurs and, 10:365a
Arts, seven liberal. *See* Seven liberal arts
Artugids/Artukids. *See* Ortuqids
Artuq ibn Aksab, Ortuqid descendants of, 9:283b
Artushof, 1:572b
Arukh. See Nathan ben Jehiel
Arundel MSS
hymns and, 6:384b
MS 268, 10:473b
Arundel Psalter, 1:262b, **1:580b**
Arundel, Thomas, archbishop of Canterbury
appointed chancellor, 9:429a
career of, 12:143a
Constitutions, 12:709b
on vernacular Scripture, 7:647a
violation of Oxford's autonomy, 7:646a
Arzachel. *See* Zarqālī, al-
Arzanenē. *See* Ałjnik
Arziz. *See* Arčēš
As a Midsummer Rose. See Lydgate, John
Asaak, ever-burning fire at, 9:443b
Asad clan. *See* Quraysh
Asad ibn al-Furāt, invasion of Sicily, 1:70b
Asadī al-Ṭūsī
Garshāsp-nāma, 6:507a
Lughat-i-Furs, 4:444b
Asaph the Physician, 11:90a
Asās, 6:615b
Asās al-balāgha. See Zamakh-sharī
Ascanians, duchy of Saxony and, 5:511a
Ascension of Christ, **1:580b**
in art, 4:24a
Drogo Sacramentary, 6:463a (*illus.*)
ivory, 4:352b (*illus.*)
Tuotilo's ivory book cover, 12:225b–226a (*illus.*)
feast of the, **1:582a-b**
customs, 1:582b
dramatic interpolations, 1:582a
German plays, 1:582b
processions, 1:582a
in literature. *See* Hrotswitha von Gandersheim, "Ascension of the Lord"
in sculpture, French Romanesque, 10:493b–494a
seraphim in, 11:167b–168a
Ascension (church: Kolomenskoe), architectural elements, 10:581b–582a
Ascension (church: Mileševo), wall paintings, 2:446b
Ascension (church: Žiča), wall paintings, 2:446b
"Ascension of the Lord, The." *See* Hrotswitha von Gandersheim
Ascension of Muḥammad, **1:581a-b**
allegorical interpretations of, 1:581b
Burāq and, 2:419b
Dante Alighieri's *Divine Comedy* and, 1:581b
debate on place of, 1:581a
depiction of, 1:581b (*illus.*)
Koranic commentaries on, 1:581a-b
Ascensius, edition of Vergil's *Aeneid,* 4:262b
Ascetica. See Basil the Great of Caesarea, St.
Asceticism
advocated by Bogomils, 2:294a
among continental women mystics, 9:8b
among pilgrims, 9:654a, 658a, 659b–660a
Basil the Great and, 2:120a, 121b
in dualistic philosophies, 4:297b
Georgian, 5:414a
Irish, 6:515b, 516a
Islamic
Paradise as reward for, 9:394a
see also Fasting, Islamic; Sufism
Jerome as advocate of, 7:57b, 58a
martyrdom for, 8:160a
see also Reform, idea of
Ascetism
aquatici, 10:616a
of Robert d'Arbrissel, 10:429a-b
Ascius (son of Remus), 11:278a
Asclepiad, Lesser, 7:375a
Asen I (John Asen) of Bulgaria, tsar, 2:407b–408a, 9:509b–510a, 12:483b
Asen, John II. *See* John Asen II of Bulgaria, tsar
Asgard, in Scandinavian mythology, 11:29a-b
Ashᶜarī, Abu 'l-Ḥasan ᶜAlī ibn Ismaᶜīl al-, **1:582b–585b**
life of, 1:582b–583a, 6:583b–584a, 8:656a
Muᶜtazilites and, 1:583a-b
theology of, 1:583a–585a
on predestination, 1:584b–585a
theory of justice, 9:569a-b
use of the term "acquisition," 1:584b
Ashᶜarī theology, rise of the Almohads and, 11:140b
Ashᶜarite school, 1:585a-b, 5:515b
al-Ghazālī and, 5:516a, 9:41b
Ashᶜarites, al-Muᶜtazila and, 8:656a
Ashᶜath, Ibn al-
al-Kufa and, 7:307a
revolt of, 6:72b, 511b, 11:513b
Ashburnham Pentateuch, 9:496b, 12:467a
contents page from, 4:356a
narrative miniatures in, 4:356b
Asher ben Jehiel, 5:512a, 7:82a, 11:586a
Asherik/Anastasius, in Hungary, 11:478a, 479b
Ashes, benediction of, 2:177b, 178a
Ashi, Babylonian Talmud and, 11:583a

ᶜÂshıqpasha-zâde, chronicle of Ottoman history, 6:251a
Ashkanians. *See* Parthians
Ashkenaz, **1:585b–586a**, 7:91a
  foundations of, 7:162b
  growth of, 1:585b–586a
  illuminated manuscripts, 7:67a-b
  institutions and mores of, 1:586a
  liturgical rite of, 7:622b
  movement into Spain, 7:82a
  in Poland, 1:586a
  Sephardim and, 11:162a
  use of term, 1:585b
  Yiddish and, 12:725b
Ashkenazi Hasidism, 9:578a–582a
  Kalonymus family and, 7:207a
  origins, 9:578b
  sources of, 9:579b–580a
  theology and ethics, 9:580a–581b
Ashlar, in Visigothic architecture, 12:465a, 468a
Ashmunein, el-, church at, 3:586a
Ashrāf, 1:175b
  role in caliphate, 3:34a
  under Muᶜāwiya, 3:36b–37a
  unreliability in Second Civil War, 3:38b
Ashraf, al-, Mamluk sultan, Acre and, 11:562a
Ashraf Qāᵓitbāy, al-. *See* Qāᵓitbāy, al-Ashraf (the Illustrious), Mamluk sultan
Ashrafti (gold coin), 8:424a
  based on Venetian ducat, 4:301b
Ashtarak. *See* Aštarak
ᶜĀshūrāᵓ, 5:39b
  fasting on, 6:577a
  modeled on the Jewish Day of Atonement, 9:497b
  passion play held on, 6:371a
  see also Fasting, Islamic
Asia
  European explorations, 4:556a–557b
  plagues and, 9:678a, 684b
Asia Minor
  Byzantine rule of, 9:331a-b
  Empire of Trebizond, 12:168a–170a (map)
  Mongol rule of, 9:306a
  roads in, 10:424a-b
Asinarius, 7:369a
Asinius Pollio, library of, 7:558b–559a, 567b
ᶜAskar al-Mahdī. *See* Rušāfah, al-
ᶜAskarī, Abū Hilāl al-, *Two Crafts,* 10:345b
Askeri, in Ottoman social structure, 9:309b
Askia Muḥammad, ruler of Songhai Empire, 12:54b–55a
Askold, attack on Constantinople (860), 7:247a-b
Aṣmaᶜī, al-, *Kitāb al-khalq al-insān,* 4:443a
Asmatikon, **1:586b**, 8:554b
  Psaltikon and, 1:586b
  Slavs and, 8:556b
  surviving manuscript of, 1:586b
  see also Psaltikon
Ásmundar saga kappabana, **1:586b–587b**
  dating of, 1:586b
  death song in, 1:587a-b
  fornyrðislag stanzas in, 1:587b
  Hildebrand's death song, 6:227a-b
  plot of, 1:586b–587a
  surviving manuscript of, 1:587b
Ásmundr the Berserks' Killer. *See Egils saga einhenda ok Asmundar Berserkjab ana*
Ásmundr of Húnaland, king (saga character), 11:290a-b
Asołik. *See* Stepᶜanos Asołik Taronecᶜi
Ašot I Mec (the Great) of Armenia, king, **1:587b–588b**, 2:48a-b, 5:405b
  as *archon ton archonton,* 1:449a, 588b
  foreign policy of, 1:588a-b
  goals of, 1:588a
  Prince Šapuh on, 1:510b
  reign of, 1:480a–481b, 588a-b
  son of, 11:351a
Ašot II Erkatᶜ of Armenia, king, **1:588b–589a**
  as *archon ton archonton,* 1:449a, 588a, 588b
  diplomatic mission of, 1:588b
  reign of, 1:482a, 588a-b
  Yūsuf of Azerbaijan and, 1:588b–589a
Ašot III Ołormac (the Merciful) of Armenia, king, 1:482a, **1:589a-b**
  cession of Vanand, 7:221a
  coronation of, 1:589a-b
  descendants of, 1:483a
  epithet of, 1:589b
  independent kingdom of Kars and, 12:354a
  John I Tzimiskes and, 1:482b
  in Matthew of Edessa's *Chronicle,* 8:228b
Ašot IV Kᶜaĵ (the Brave) of Armenia, king
  death of, 1:484a
  vs. Yovhannēs-Smbat, 1:483a, 484a
Ašot I Bagratuni of Kᶜartᶜli-Iberia, prince (*r.* 813–830), 5:405b
Ašot Bagratuni (*fl.* 685–688), as *išχan,* 1:478b
Ašot Bagratuni (*fl.* mid 9th century), 1:500a, 500b
  Armenian literature and, 1:510a
Ašot Gagik. *See* Ašot III Ołormac (the Merciful)
Ašot Msaker (the Man-eater), 1:479b, 7:208a
Ašot, *sparapet* (cousin of Ašot II Erkatᶜ), 1:482a
Aspacures III (380–394), 3:308a
Aspakunikᶜ, 11:599a
Aspalaton. *See* Split (Dalmatia)
Aspar, Alan ruler, 1:121b
  defeated by Vandals, 12:354b
  vs. Zeno, 12:743b
Asper (silver coin), 8:421a
Aspramonte. See Andrea da Barberino
Aspurakani. *See* Vaspurakan
Ass
  as draft animal, 1:295b
  as pack animal, 1:295b
  as a symbol of the devil, 2:243a
"Ass and the Lion's Skin, The." *See* Avianus
Assanton, Arnaud, 6:472b
Assarting, 12:446a
Assassination, punishment for, 4:133b
Assassins, **1:589b–593a**, 6:617a
  at Alamūt, 1:118a, 118b
  crusades and, 1:590a-b
  Ikhwān al-Ṣafāᵓ and, 9:4b
  information about, 1:591a
  interpretations of term, 1:591b–592b
  as Ismaili sect, 1:589b–590a
  Mongol conquest of, 8:472a, 651b
  Nizārīs and, 11:137b
  in Persia, 1:591b
  references to, 1:590b–591b
  study of, 1:592b–593a
  see also Ḥasan al-Ṣabbāḥ
Assemblées des Commis des États. *See* Dauphiné
"Assembly of Harkᶜ" (974), 1:483b
Asser, **1:593a-b**
  Alfred the Great and, 1:593a
  Annales rerum gestarum Alfredi, 2:239b
  Life of Alfred, 1:593a, 7:261b–262a, 363a
Asser of Lund, bishop, Scandinavian church and, 4:153a
Assise au Comte Geoffroy, L', dismemberment of fiefs forbidden by, 2:382a
Assisi, San Francesco. *See* S. Francesco (church: Assisi)
Assize, **1:594a–596a**
  development of, 1:595a-b
  English, **1:596a–598b**
    creation of, 1:598a
    darrein presentment, 7:439b–440a, 9:546b–547a, 548a
    distress, 4:220b–221a
    grand, 1:597b–598a, 6:481b–482b, 7:440b–441a
    inquest and, 6:481a–482b
    in land disputes, 4:470b
    law and, 1:598a-b
    possessory, 1:596b–597b, 6:481b, 7:438a–440a
    proceedings of, 1:596b–597a
    process of, 1:597a-b
    purpose of, 1:597a
    utrum, 1:596b, 7:439a
    see also Clarendon, Assize of; English common law; Northampton, Assize of; Petty assizes, English; Seisin, disseisin; Woodstock, Assize of
  French, 1:595b–596a
    prévots and, 1:594b–595a
  Grand, 7:184a
  Italian, 5:214b
  see also Statute
Assize of Arms, 7:184a, 11:612a
Assize of Cloth (1196), 12:122a
Assize of the Forest (1184), 5:133a, 7:184a
  renewal of, 5:133b
Assize of Measures (1196), 12:118b
Assize sur la ligece, 1:599a
Assizes of Ariano, Roger II and, 10:441a

Assizes of Jerusalem, **1:598b–600a**
description of, 1:598a
Jean d'Ibelin (of Jaffa) and, 6:390a
Livre de forme de plait, 9:558a-b
works concerned with burgess courts, 1:599b
works concerned with High Court, 1:598b–599a
Assizes of Romania, **1:600a,** 7:378b
Associations, as heirs, 6:451a
Assonance, **1:600a–601a**
in *Cantar de mío Cid,* 3:72a-b
in *chansons de geste,* 3:261a-b
in epics, 1:600b
in French, 1:600b
in Germanic languages, 1:600a-b
in Italian, 1:600b
in Old Portuguese, 1:600b
in Old Provençal, 1:600b
in romances, 1:600b
in *Song of Roland,* 10:446a, 446b
in Spanish, 1:600a-b, 11:458b
ballads, 11:428b
villancico, 12:447b
in Wittenwiler's *Ring,* 12:667a-b
Assumption (church: Most [Brüx]), 5:598b (*illus.*), 601a
Assumption of the Virgin, **1:601a,** 12:460b
in Byzantine art, 1:601a, 7:282b
celebration of, 1:601a
see also Koimesis
Assumptus theory, 3:323a
Assunzione, L'. See Belcari, Feo
Assyro-Chaldean rites. *See* Syrian rites, East
Aštarak, **1:601a–602a**
church of Ciranawor in, 1:601a-b
church of S. Karmrawor in, 1:601 (*illus.*)
church of S. Marinē in, 1:601a-b
Asthianenē, 1:472b, 515a, 515b
Aštišat, Council of (365), 1:498a-b
Astrakhan, fur trade in, 5:333b
Astrarium, 3:461b–462a
see also Dondi, Giovanni de'
Astrolabe, **1:602a–604a,** 8:211a, 9:89b–90a, 11:96b–97b (*illus.*)
Abraham ibn Ezra on, 11:91a, 12:135b
Abu 'l-Qāsim on, 9:705a
in astronomy
Islamic, 1:622b–623a
Western European, 1:611a-b
al-Bīrūnī on, 2:250a
by Radolf of Liège, 10:246b
Hebrew, 1:603b
Islamic, 1:603a-b, 11:86b
Latin, 1:603 (*illus.*)
mariner's, 1:603a
mechanism of, 1:602a-b, 3:28b–29a
oldest known, 1:603a
polar sighting tube and, 11:100a-b
problems solved by, 1:602b
quadrant and, 10:237a
rete of, 1:602a-b
Richard of Wallingford's *Tractatus albionis* and, 10:387b
Sanskrit, 1:603b
surveying and, 11:515b
surviving, 1:603b
three types of, 11:96b
treatises on, 1:603b, 11:634a-b
universal, 1:602b–603a
used on Arabic ships, 9:86a
Western European geography and, 5:397a
Astrolabe-quadrant, 11:98a
Astrology
Sabaeans and, 9:4a-b
see also Astronomy
Astrology, Byzantine, 1:606a, 8:17b–18a
Astrology, Islamic, **1:616b–624b,** 8:21b, 11:83b
Abū Maᶜshar, 1:616b, 617b, 618b
attacks on, 1:617b–618b
al-Bīrūnī on, 1:618a, 619b
classifications of, 1:616b–617a
contrast with astronomy, 1:618b, 619b
definition of, 1:616b
foretelling of the future, 1:618a, 619b
al-Ghazālī on, 1:618a-b
history of, 1:617a
horoscopic, 1:619a-b
katarchai, 1:619a
Nuṣayrīs and, 9:3b–4a
Ptolemy and, 1:619a
religious reaction to, 1:617b, 618b
texts on, 1:617a-b
world and year's cycles in, 1:619a-b
see also Toledan Tables
Astrology, Jewish, 11:91b–92a, 12:135b
Astrology, Western European, **1:604a–610a**
almanacs and, 1:609a
in antiquity, 1:604a-b
at the court of Peter IV (the Ceremonious), 9:510b, 511a
Black Death and, 2:264b, 8:253b
calendars and, 1:609a
Carolingian, 1:606b
definition of, 1:604a
during and after Renaissance, 1:608b–609b
ecclesiastical condemnation of, 1:605b–606a, 607a-b, 608a
forbidden by the church, 8:26a
Greek manuals on, 1:604b–605a
humanism and, 1:609a
Islamic influences on, 1:606b–607a
Judaism and, 1:605a–606b
medicine and, 8:251b
Michael Scot and, 8:305a
opposition to, 1:605a, 605b
powers of the heavenly bodies, 8:36a-b
in Rome, 1:605a
Scholasticism and, 1:607a
theology and, 1:607a–608b
13th-century revival, 1:607b
translations of works of, 1:606b
use of Arabic numerals, 1:385b–387b
Astronomical clock, 3:461a–462a, 462b
by Jean Fusoris, 5:335a
Astronomicon. See Manilius, Marcus
Astronomy, *see also* Astrology; Scientific instruments; Seven liberal arts
Astronomy, Byzantine, 1:613b–614a
Astronomy, Islamic, **1:616b–624b,** 11:83b, 85a-b, 87a-b, 88a
achievements of, 11:86b
astrolabe and, 1:622b–623a
al-Bīrūnī on, 1:620b, 622a
classification of, 1:616b–617a
constellations and, 1:623a
contrast with astrology, 1:618b, 619b
criticisms of, 1:620b–621b
decline of, 11:88b
Hellenistic tradition of, 1:620a
iconology of, 6:407b–408a, 408b
mawaqqits and, 1:623a-b
observational, 1:622a
observatory
at Maragheh, 11:84a
origins of, 11:84b–85a
reform of Ptolemy, 1:621b–622a
religion and, 1:623a-b
texts on, 1:620a-b
tradition of, 1:619b–620a
translations of Sanskrit and Pahlavi works into Arabic, 11:82b
treatises on astrolabe, 1:622b–623a
see also Toledan Tables
Astronomy, Jewish, 11:90a–91b, 93a-b
writings and translations, 12:134a, 135a–136a
Astronomy, Ptolemaic, **10:206a–211b**
conflicts with Aristotle, 10:211a
De spera treatises
epicycle and equant in, 10:207b
John of Holywood's (Sacrobosco's), 10:207a-b
motion of the sun, moon, and planets in, 10:207a-b
precession in, 10:207b
emphasis on coherence, 10:210b–211a
geocentric model of, 10:206b
historical development of, 10:206a–207a
Plato's *Timaeus* as precursor, 10:206b
tables and instruments of, 10:210a-b
Alfonsine tables, 10:210b
Campanus of Novara's equatorium, 10:210b
independent genre of, 10:210a-b
Islamic, 10:210b
Theorica planetarum treatises, 10:207b–210a
Campanus of Novara, 10:210b
eccentric deferent in, 10:209a–210a
ecliptic in, 10:210a
motion of the sun in, 10:208 (*illus.*), 208a–209a
planetary motion, 10:209 (*illus.*), 209b–210a
precession in, 10:210a
Toledan Tables, 12:67b
see also Alfonsine Tables; Ptolemy, Claudius
Astronomy, Western European, **1:610a–616b,** 9:624a
ancient heritage, 1:610a
Arabic impact on, 1:611a–613b
astrolabe and, 1:610a-b
astronomical tables, 1:611b, 612b–613a
at Bologna, 1:613a
at the court of Peter IV (the Ceremonious), 9:511a
calendars and, 1:614a
Copernicus on, 1:615a, 616a

Astronomy, Western European (*cont.*)
  cosmological discussions in, 1:615a–616a
  development of, 1:610a
  equinox, 9:620a
  instruments of, 4:12a-b
    see also Equatorium
  Jean Buridan on, 2:430a-b
  Latin works, 1:610b
  limits of universe, 9:621a
  literature
    Alfonsine Tables, 12:135b
    Libros del saber de astronomia, 12:135b–136a
    Pseudo-Dionysius' *De caelesti hierarchia,* 12:139a
  manuals of, 1:610b–611a, 612a
  moving-earth system, 9:624a
  Muslims on, 1:614a
  new ideas in, 1:614a–615a
  Oresme on terrestrial motions, 9:271b
  physics and, 9:625a
  planetary theory, 1:611b–612a
  planets, rotation of, Aristotelian theory, 9:620b
  Roger Bacon on, 2:38a-b
  scholarship, 1:612b–613b
  in Spain, King Alfonso X's academy, 12:135b–136a
  teaching of, 1:613b
  Vienna school, 1:613b
Astuacacin. See Virgin Mary, in Armenian church
Astuacatur-Maxož (6th-century martyr), 1:518b–519a
Asturian Bible, 12:467a
Asturians, vs. Romans, 2:126a
Asturias
  Reconquest and, 10:280a
  see also Navarre, kingdom of; Spanish law
Asturias-León, **1:625a–631a**
  art, **1:624b–625a**, 1:630b–631a
    monuments of, 1:624b
    S. Miguel de Escalada, 8:511a-b
    Victory Cross of Oviedo, 1:624b–625a (*illus.*)
  Castile and, 3:125b, 127a, 131a
  church in, 1:630b
  civil wars in, 1:627b–628a
  culture of, 1:630b–631a
  economy of, 1:629a-b
  feudalism in, 1:629a
  history of, 1:625b–629a
  institutions of, 1:630a-b
  military organization, 12:562b–563a
  Muslims in, 1:625b–626a
  Navarre and, 1:628b
  Old Spanish dialects in, 11:399a-b
  population growth of, 1:626a-b
  seignorial system in, 1:629a
  social structure of, 1:629b–630a
  Visigoths and, 12:474b
Asṭurlābī, ʿAlī ibn ʿĪsā al-, on astrology, 1:617b–618a
Aswad al-ʿAnsī, al- ("false prophet"), 6:568a
Aswar, al-. *See* Nuʿmān, al-
Ašχarhacʿoycʿ (*World Atlas*), 1:509b, 6:239a
Asylum, right of, **1:631a–632a**
  choices of, 1:631b
  ecclesiastical sanctuary and, 1:631b–632a
  modification of, 1:632a
  rejection of choices, 1:631b–632a
At the Departyng of Thomas Chaucyer on Ambassade into France. See Lydgate, John
At-ṭabl, 8:563a
  see also Ṭabl
Atabeg, **1:632a**
  in Georgia, 1:632a
  Seljuk and Turkoman, 12:227a
  Seljuks and, 1:632a
ʿAṭaʾī, *Burzū-nāma,* 6:507a
Atapuerca, Battle of (1054), 3:128b, 9:69b
Atari, 8:561b
Ataulf, Visigothic king, 2:102a
Atelier, **1:632b**, 10:105a
Atenis Sioni, **1:632b**
Athalaric, Ostrogothic king
  Arator and, 1:422a
  guardianship of, 9:291b–292a
Athanagild, Visigothic king, 11:389b
Athanaric, Visigothic leader, 12:469a
Athanasian Creed
  in *Piers Plowman,* 7:333b
  Trinitarian Doctrine and, 12:190a
Athanasians, **1:632b–633a**
Athanasios (920-1002; founder of Great Lavra), education of, 7:595b
Athanasios (Mt. Athos monk), founding of Great Meteoron, 8:299b
Athanasius I, patriarch of Constantinople, **1:633b**
  canonization of, 1:633b
Athanasius II, Syrian Orthodox patriarch, 11:566b
Athanasius of Alexandria, St., **1:633a-b**, 3:627b, 628a, 10:454b
  anti-Arian struggle, 2:459b
  attribution of Armenian anaphoras to, 1:516b
  Christianization of Abyssinia and, 1:31b–032a
  commentaries on Old Testament, 1:633b
  Council of Serdica and, 3:225b, 11:189b
  Discourses Against the Arians, 1:633b
  as doctor of the church, 4:234a
  exile of, 1:633a
  languages of his works, 10:455a
  Life of St. Anthony, 1:633b, 6:58a, 66a, 213a, 8:460b, 461b
    influence on later works, 2:518a
  Monophysite theology, 8:477a
  on salvation, 1:633a
  supporters of, 1:632b–633a
  Theotokos and, 12:459b
  Trinitarian doctrine, 3:339a, 9:560b
Athanatoi, 11:573b
Athanios, in art, 7:282b–283a
Athankip, battle at (1270), 6:518b
Athanor (in alchemy), 1:139a
Athaulf, Visigothic king, 12:470a
Athelstan, Anglo-Saxon ruler, 12:433b
  bells and, 2:166b
  coinage of, 9:495a
  depicted in Bede's *Life of St Cuthbert,* 11:119b (*illus.*)
  reconquest of Danelaw, 4:456b
Athelstan Psalter, 10:108a
Athenogenes, bishop, relics of, 1:518a
Athens, 12:306a
  archives, 1:445b
  Catalan Company and, 3:156b–157a, 7:379b
  conquest by Ottomans (1456), 6:443b
  disputed ownership of, 7:381b
  duchy of, held by Almogávares, 1:191a
  Guy de la Roche and, 7:378a
  Latin Empire of Constantinople and, 7:346b
  Neoplatonic school of, influence of, 9:99a-b
  Otto de la Roche and, 7:376b
  Platonic Academy, 1:606a, 9:98a
  scientific tradition of, 11:88a
  in 12th century, 12:102b
Athens-Thebes. *See* Latin states in Greece
Atherington (Devon), wooden screen by Roger Down, 4:263b (*illus.*)
Athīr, Ibn al-, **1:634a–635b**, 5:332a
  on art prose, 10:347b
  Ḍiyāʾ al-Dīn Abu 'l-Fatḥ Naṣr Allāh, 1:634b–635a
  family of, 1:634a
  ʿIzz al-Dīn Abu 'l-Ḥasan, 1:634a-b
  Majd al-Dīn Abu 'l-Saʿādāt Mubārak, 1:635a
  references to Scandinavia, 10:707b
  used by Bar Hebraeus, 2:108b
Athis et Prophilias, civilization portrayed, 5:284b
Athis, Peace of (1305). *See* Athis-sur-Orge, Treaty of (1305)
Athis und Prophilias, **1:635b–636a**
  author of, 1:635b
  influence of, 1:630a
  plot of, 1:636a
  source of, 1:635b
Athis-sur-Orge, Treaty of (1305), 5:81b–82a, 522b
  Bruges' penalty, 12:156a
Athlaích, 6:541a
Athos, Mount, **1:636b–637b**
  biblical exegesis and, 2:214b
  Chilandari Monastery, icon of Christ Pantokrator, 2:447b–448a
  Church of the Protaton, fresco by Manuel Panselinos, 8:93 (*illus.*)
  influenced by Studios Monastery, 11:495a
  monasteries at, 1:636b–637a, 4:333b, 8:457a
    architectural design, 4:341b
    founded by St. Athanasius the Athonite, 1:636b
    influences on Serbian architecture, 4:347b, 11:188a
  monastery translation center, 12:127a
  monuments of, **1:637b–638a**, 1:637b–638a
  nomocanon and, 9:158b
  Russian pilgrimage to, 9:653a–654a
  Sava and, 11:173b

Serbian monastery of Hilandar and, 10:672b, 11:186a-b
Stefan Uroš IV Dušan of Serbia and, 11:178a, 475b
Vlachs and, 12:483b
Walachian patronage of Koutloumousiou, 12:504b
see also Meteora; Theodosius of the Caves, St.
Atik Mustafa Pasha Djami (Constantinople), design of, 4:341a
Atlakviða, **1:638a-b**, 9:114a, 11:293a
Atlamál and, 1:638b–639a
characterization of, 1:638b
language of, 1:638b
murder of Atli, precursor in *Guðrúnarkviða II,* 6:37a-b
plot of, 1:638a-b
relation to *Haraldskvæði,* 6:97b
as source for *Guðrúnarhvǫt,* 6:35b
sources of, 1:638a-b
story of Gudrun in, 6:35a
Vǫlsunga saga and, 12:489a
Atlamál, **1:638b–639b**, 9:114a, 11:293a
Atlakviða and, 1:638b–639a
characterization of, 1:639a
language of, 1:639a
plot of, 1:638b–639a
surviving manuscript of, 1:639a
Vǫlsunga saga and, 12:489a
Atlante Farnese, 11:95b
Atlas Mountains, **1:639b–641a**, 1:640 (map)
Almohads and, 1:641a
Almoravids and, 1:641a
extent of, 1:639b–640a
Fatimids and, 1:641a
ranges of, 1:639b
see also Almohads; Almoravids; Maghrib, al-
Atli
in *Atlakviða,* 1:638a
in *Guðrúnarkviða II,* 6:37a-b
Atom (5th-century Armenian general), 1:519b
Atom Anjewacʿi (martyred 853), 1:519b
Atonement, Islamic Day of. *See* ʿAshūrāʾ
Atrium, **1:641a**
in basilica, 2:124b
Atropatene. *See* Azerbaijan
Atsiz (1127–1156), 7:244a
as ruler of independent Khwārizm, 6:504a
Attainder
Henry IV's use of, 6:428a
numbers of, 6:428a-b
origins of, 6:427b–428a
in outlawry proceedings, 6:427b
reversal of, 6:428a-b
see also Impeachment
Attalea, Byzantine sea routes and, 10:423 (map), 424b
Attaleiates, Michael, **1:641b**
Historia, 1:641b
ʿAṭṭār, Farīd al-Dīn, 9:42b, 43a, 141a
Ilāhī-nāma, 6:507b
Mantiq al-ṭayr, 6:507b
nastaʿlīq script in, 9:65b (*illus.*)
Attendolo, Muzio. *See* Sforza, Muzio Attendolo
Atticism, classical literary studies and, 3:430b
Attila (Hunnic leader), 2:92b–93a, 6:354a
Atlakviða and, 1:638a
capture of Aquileia (452), origins of Venice and, 12:383a
death of, 2:93a
Etzel and, 9:114a
invasions of, slavery and, 11:335a
in literature
epic poetry, 12:535a
German heroic tales, 12:29b
Þiðreks saga, 12:30a, 30b
sparing of Paris by, 9:401a
sparing of Rome by, 7:541b, 9:370b
Attire. *See* Costume
Attis, cult of, 9:1a, 1b
Atto, cardinal of S. Marco, *Defloratio canonum,* 7:409b
Atto of Vercelli, **1:641b**
De pressuris ecclesiasticis, 1:641b
Polypticum, 1:641b
on resistance, 10:17a
Atto of Vich, bishop, Sylvester II and, 11:552b
Attone of Milan, archbishop, election of (1072), 8:378b
Attorney, power of. *See* Law; Representative assemblies
Atur Gushnasp, sanctuary of, 11:628a
Aubade, **1:642a**, 5:441a-b
courtly love and, 1:642a
definition of, 1:642a
performance of, 1:642a
Auban, St. *See Vie de St. Auban*
Aube. *See* Aubade
Auberi le Bourguignon, Picard origins, 9:634a
Aubert, David, **1:642b**
Chronique des empereurs, 1:642b
Chroniques et conquêtes de Charlemagne, 1:642b
Perceforest, 1:642b
Aubusson carpets, weaving technique, 10:547a
Aubusson, Pierre d', 3:304a
Aucassin et Nicolette, **1:642b–644a**, 5:264a
chanson de geste and, 1:642b–643a
composition of, 1:642b
literary classification, 9:635b
only known *cantefable,* 1:642a
pastorelle in, 1:643b
plot of, 1:642b–643a
poetic form, 9:635b
repudiation of 12th-century literary genres, 5:256a
romance in, 1:643b
sources for, 9:635b
style of, 1:643b
Tristan legend in, 1:643b
Auchinleck Manuscript, 11:312a
Audacht Morainn, De duodecim abusivis and, 4:312b
Audefroy le Bastard, "Fin amours en esperance," 8:631 (*illus.*)
Audelay, John, carols and, 3:116a
Audenarde, tapestry of, 11:596b
"Audite omnes amantes." *See* Sechnall
Auditing
Exchequer and, 4:531a–532a, 6:302a
royal wardrobe and, 6:305a
see also Accounting
Audivimus. See Gregory IX, pope
Audoin, Lombard king, 7:654b
Audraduz Modicus, **1:644a**
Audrey, St., Bede on, 2:155b
Aufgesang, 5:437a-b
Augen of Clysma, mar. *See* Awgen of Clysma, mar
Auger, breast. *See* Breast auger
Augsburg
diet (1077) not held, 3:69a, 69b
manufacture of scientific instruments in, 11:102b–103a
production of portable sundials, 11:509b–510a
Augsburg Bible, 2:215a-b
Augsburg Cathedral, stained glass in, 5:548b (*illus.*)
Augsburg, Diet of (1209), 12:672b
Augsburg, Diet of (1214), Wolfger von Erla and, 12:673a
Augusta, **1:644a-b**
Augustale, 8:421b, 430a
Augustalis, 11:271b
Augustine of Ancona. *See* Augustinus Triumphus
Augustine of Canterbury, St., **1:644b–645b**, 3:81b
baptism of Ethelbert, 8:440b
concept of paradise of, 9:395b–396a, 397b–398a
Gregory the Great and, 2:172a
life of, 1:644b
missions of, 7:362a, 12:151a-b
to England, 1:288b, 644b–645a, 4:458a
papal library and, 7:559b
Regula sancti Benedicti and, 2:170a
Augustine of Dacia, on the fourfold division of senses, 2:224a, 224b
Augustine of Hippo, St., **1:646a–659a**, 3:540a, 573a
African clergy and, 10:121b
Ambrose and, 1:647a-b
on angels, 1:249b
anti-Manichaean polemics of, 8:84a
on astrology, 1:605b
at Cassiciacum, 1:648a
Augustinism and, 1:660a–661a
on baptism, 1:648a, 3:675b
baptized by St. Ambrose, 1:231a-b
Benedict of Nursia and, 2:170a
as bishop, 1:649a–650a
Boethius and, 2:292a-b
Cassian and, 3:122b
Cassiodorus and, 3:123b, 8:638a
Categoriae decem, 9:585b
City of God, 1:654a–655a, 3:336b, 342b, 4:118b, 8:434a
on demons, 8:36b
on "fall of Rome," 10:467b
on folk healing remedies, 8:26a
influence on later works, 9:303a
Old English translation of, 1:284a
as a polemic against pagans, 2:91a
relation to patristic church, 4:372a-b

Augustine of Hippo, St. (*cont.*)
classical influence, 9:584a
clerical household of, 1:648a, 660b
on concubinage, 3:530a
Confessions, 1:646a, 3:342b
Christian Platonism, 9:616a-b
Neoplatonism and, 9:99a
Contra epistolam Parmeniani, 6:496a
on conversion of Victorinus, 12:409b
dating of Easter, 3:228b
De consensu evangelistarum, Bede and, 2:154a
De cura pro mortuis gerenda, 4:118b–119a
De diversis quaestionibus, realism and, 10:270a
De doctrina christiana, 1:556b, 3:342b, 432a, 7:559b, 10:75b
ars praedicandi and, 1:556b, 10:361b–362a
Bede and, 2:154a
as a major rhetorical work, 10:353a-b
use of parataxis, 6:259a-b
De haeresibus, 6:565a
De musica, 8:637a
Aribo and, 8:642a
on rhythm and meter, 10:378b
De quantitate animae, 1:648b, 10:271b
unity and multiplicity of souls, 9:586a
on death, 4:118b–119a
death of, 12:354b
defense by Prosper of Aquitaine, 10:153b–154a
as doctor of the church, 4:234a
Donatists and, 1:651b–652a, 4:260a
early libraries and, 7:559b
Ennarationes, translated into French, 2:219a
on equality of people, 10:14b
Eugippius and, 4:521a
Free Choice, 1:648b
Glossed Gospels and, 4:548a
on heresy, 6:197b
Arianism, 1:654a
refutations of Manichaeism and Arianism, 6:193b
Hrabanus Maurus and, 10:355b
Immortality of the Soul, 1:648a
Instruction of the Uneducated, 1:655a
on interest charging, 12:336a
Isidore of Seville and, 6:565a, 565b, 566a
on Jews, 7:75b
jubilus and, 8:571a
on just war, 4:15b
kingship theories of, 7:260a
on liberty and liberties, 7:557a
life of, 1:646a-b
light and vision theory, 9:247a
on magic and miracles, 8:33b–34a
Manichaeans and, 1:650b–651b, 8:84a, 85b
Meister Eckhart and, 9:32b
millennialism, 8:385a-b, 12:723a, 723b
monastery at Hippo, 8:461b
monastic directory attributed to, 10:85a-b
Monica, mother of, 1:646a, 647a–648a
moral teaching of, 1:655a-b
Morals of the Catholic Church, 1:648b
Morals of the Manichees, 1:648b
music and, 8:580b, 581b, 587b, 589a
Notker Teutonicus and, 9:189a
Ockham and, 9:212b
on the origin of the Hebrew alphabet, 1:218a
pagans and, 1:650a-b
on Paradise, 9:395b–396a
Pelagians and, 1:652a–654a, 3:336b
Pelagius and, 9:486a, 486b
Peter Lombard and, 9:517a
philosophy and theology, 1:646b–647b, 3:342a-b
acceptance of philosophical dualism, 4:298a
on casuistry, 3:153a
Christology of, 3:321b, 6:258b
definition of terms, 9:616a
eternal happiness, 9:583b–584a
faith and understanding, 9:584a
Filioque doctrine, 5:62b
on God, 1:656b–657b
Heavenly City image, 5:586a, 10:283b–284a, 285a
original sin, 9:600b
predestination doctrine, 9:486b, 600b
on punishment of the innocent, 6:494b, 496a
rejection of theological dualism, 4:297b–298a
on the soul, 1:656a-b
on things, 1:655b–656a
three types of theology, 9:616b
Trinitarian doctrine, 12:189b–190a, 192a–193a, 195a, 195b
Psalm Against the Donatists, 7:360b
on purgatory, 10:215b–216a
realism of, 12:281b
reform ideas of, 10:283b–284a
rhymed offices to, 10:370b
Roman education and, 7:360a
sex aetates mundi and, 11:215b
on singing without words, 8:269a
on slavery, 11:334b
Soliloquies
Alfred the Great and, 2:184a
prose translation of into Old English, 1:167a, 284a
True Religion, 1:655a
on Virgin Mary, 12:460a
Walter Hilton and, 9:23b
on witchcraft, 12:660b
works attributed to
De dialectica, 4:168b
De vera et falsa poenitentia, 9:491b
works of, 1:648b–649a
Wyclif and, 12:708a, 709a, 709b
see also Aristotelianism, Augustinian; Augustinian Rule
Augustinian Aristotelianism. *See* Aristotelianism, Augustinian
Augustinian canons, **1:659a-b**
in Armagh, 1:470a
at Fontevrault, 12:686b
at Prouille, 12:687b
cult center of St. Andrews, 10:612b
founding of, 1:649a-b
Gilbertine rite and, 5:528a
hermits and, 12:686a
monastic churches, London, 7:660b
Premonstratensians and, 12:685b
Ruusbroec and, 9:36b
schools of spirituality arising from, 1:659b
sponsorship of hospitals, 6:294a
traditional ministries of, 1:659b
Augustinian friars, **1:659b–660a,** 5:297b
Alexander IV and, 1:659b
constitution of, 1:660a
founding of, 1:659b
monasteries established by, 1:660a
preaching churches, London, 7:663b
proponents of theology, 14th century, 9:611a
Sapaudian foundations, 10:675b
scholasticism and, 1:465a
in Scotland, 11:105a
theologians of, 1:660a
Augustinian Rule, 1:657b, 658b, 659a, 660b
acceptance of by Friars of the Sack, 10:604a
Devotio Moderna and, 4:166b
Divine Office and, 4:222a
Dominicans and, 4:239a-b, 243b
in the Fontevrault order, 10:430b
Premonstratensians and, 10:85a-b
Robert d'Arbrissel's community and, 10:429a
Augustinianism. *See* Augustinism
Augustinism, **1:660a–661b,** 9:583b–584b, 585b
at University of Paris, 4:309a
description of, 1:660a-b
Gottschalk of Orbais and, 5:638a–639a
method in theology, 9:595b–596a
mysticism in, redefinition by Hadewijch, 6:44a
philosophical, 1:660b
revival of, 9:610b–611a
by Henry of Ghent, 6:166a
unity and multiplicity of souls, 9:586a
in views of Duns Scotus, 4:309a, 309b, 310a
see also Aristotelianism, Augustinian
Augustinus Triumphus, **2:1a-b**
kingship theories of, 7:268b
life of, 2:1a
papal support by, 10:21a–22a
Summa de ecclesiastica potestate, 2:1a-b, 10:21b
Augustus, Roman emperor
Roman civil regions and, 10:517b
vs. Basques, 2:126a
"Auld Alliance," 11:109a, 112b
Auliver, "En rima greuf a far, dir e stravolger," 6:656b
Aulnay, church at, 10:481a
Aulularia. See Plautus; Vital of Blois
Auraicept na nÉces, **2:1b–2a,** 5:650a, 6:440b
influenced by Latin grammar, 2:2a
Aurea Capra. *See* Simon Chèvre d'Or
Aurelian of Arles, women's orders and, 12:682b

Aurelian of Réôme, **2:2b**, 11:362b
  Berno and, 8:641b
  Musica disciplina, 8:639a
    modal theory, 8:449b, 450b
    on *noeannoe,* 9:152a
  Tonary of, 12:69b
  on tremolo, 8:632a
Aurelian, Roman emperor, Dacia and, 10:509b
Aurelianus, Ambrosius, **2:2b–3b**
Aurelianus of Arles, hymns and, 6:379b
Aurelianus Reomensis. *See* Aurelian of Réôme
Aureoli, Peter, theory of declarative theology, 9:609a
Auricept na nÉces. See Auraicept na nÉces
Aurora. See Peter Riga
Aurora consurgens, 1:138b
Ausculta fili, **2:3b–4a**
Ausgesperrte Ehemann, Der. See Folz, Hans
Ausonius, 7:361a
  Cena nuptialis, Latin parody and, 9:440b
  Paulinus of Nola and, 9:471a
  Paulinus of Pella and, 9:471b
Auspicius of Toul, **2:4a**, 7:361b
Aussee saltworks, 10:629b, 633b–634a
  royal control, 10:632a
  technological improvements, 10:632b–633a
Austin friars. *See* Augustinian friars
Austrasia
  establishment of, 8:278a
  Pepin I (of Landen) and, 9:499a
  Pepin II (of Herstal) and, 9:499b–500a
Austria, **2:4b–9a**, 2:5 (map)
  Albert of Habsburg and, 11:540b
  history (5th to 10th centuries), 2:4b
  in Johann von Würzburg's works, 7:117a-b
  land reclamation and German settlement (11th century), 2:6b
  Swiss Confederation and, 11:544a, 544b
  tenurial development, 11:684a
  under the Babenbergs, 2:6a–7b
  under the Carolingians, 2:4b, 6a
  under the Habsburgs, 2:7b–9a
  under the Saxon dynasty, 2:6a
  see also Avars; Babenberg family; Bavaria
Austria, House of. *See* Habsburg dynasty
Austrian literature
  Danubian *minnesang,* 10:293a-b
  influences on, 12:618b
Austro-Hungarian Empire. *See* Habsburg dynasty
Austrogauts. *See* Ostrogoths
Authari, Lombard king, 7:656a
  election of, 8:377a
Authenticum, Hugolinus and, 6:326b
Authority, political. *See* Power, political
Auðunar þáttr vestfirzka, 12:2b, 4b
Autier, Peter, Inquisition and, 3:190b
Auto de la huida a Egipto, 11:425a
Auto de los reyes magos, **2:9a-b**, 4:267a, 282b, 11:410a-b, 437a, 452b
  prosody of, 11:458b
Autobiography
  Book of Margery Kempe, 9:25a
  first German (Heinrich Suso's *Life*), 9:34b–35a
  Oswald von Wolkenstein, 9:295a, 295b
  Otloh of St. Emmeram, 9:299a
  in Thietmar von Merseburg's chronicle, 12:28b
  see also Petrarch
Autocephalos, **2:9b–10b**
  in the early church, 2:10a
  in the Latin West, 2:10a
  in the Orthodox East, 2:10a
  see also Patriarch
Autocrator, **2:10b**, 2:122b–123a
Automata, 11:636b (*illus.*), 649a
  Magnaura Palace, 11:633b, 634a
  textbooks, 11:636b
  treatises, 11:641a
  in water clocks, 3:28a
Automata. See Jazarī, al-; Philo of Byzantium
Autpertus, Ambrosius, **2:11a-b**
  Expositionis in apocalypsin, 2:11a
Autrèche, church at, 10:481a
Autun, city gates, 10:479b
Auvergne
  administration of, office of bailli, 2:53a
  Peace of God and, 9:474b
  provincial estates and assemblies, 10:321a
  Visigoths and, 11:277a
Auvergne, counts of, Toulouse and, 12:91a, 91b
Auxerre Cathedral, stained glass in, 5:552a
Auxilius, **2:11b**
Auðunn rauði, bishop of Hólar, 7:387a
Ava inclusa. See Frau Ava
Avag, 5:544a
Avalon, Emain Ablach and, 6:552a
Avanzo, Jacopo, **2:11b–12a**
  see also Altichiero
Avarayr, **2:12a**
Avarayr, Battle of (451), 1:476b, 12:360a
Avarice, in literature, 7:366b
Avars, **2:12a–13a**
  allied with Lombards, 2:12b
  assimilated by Magyar tribes, 8:46a
  in Austria, 2:4b
  in the Balkans, 2:12b, 4:1a, 6:437b, 443b, 10:459a
  Bulgars and, 2:399a, 401a
  Carolingians and, 2:12b, 12:617a
  ethnic identification of, 2:12a
  Indo-European languages and, 6:434a
  introduction of water buffalo into Western Europe, 1:298a
  invasion of Constantinople, 2:487a
  jewelry of, 5:377a-b
  in Kazakhstan, 6:352b
  in Poland, 9:716b
  Russian invasions, 10:576a
  Serdica and, 11:189a
  settlement in Pannonia, 2:12b
  siege of Thessaloniki, weaponry, 11:660a-b
  Sirmium under, 11:311b
  Slavs and, 2:399a, 11:348b
  territorial expansion, east of Elbe-Salle, 12:616b
  treasures of, carted into Aachen, 12:370a
  use of stirrup, 3:202a
  vs. Krum, 7:303b
  vs. Rome, 10:465a
Ave Maria, **2:13a–14a**, 10:300b
  in Angelus, 1:252a-b
  Angelus bell and, 2:166a
  first printing of the complete text, 2:13b–14a
  origins of, 2:13a
  repeated recitation of, 2:13b
  see also Beaumanoir, Philippe de
Ave Maria en roumans. See Huon le Roi de Cambrai
"Ave maris stella," 6:381b
Ave Virgo gloriosa, parody of, 9:441a
Avempace. See Bājja, Ibn
Avendaño, Martin Ruiz de, 3:61b
Avendauth. *See* Abraham ibn Daud
Avenzoar. *See* Zuhr, Abū Marwān ibn
Averroës. *See* Rushd, Ibn
Averroism, Latin. *See* Aristotelianism, Averroist
Avesta, **2:14a–15b**, 6:505b, 12:747a
  Ardešīr and, 1:452a
  in *Dēnkard,* 2:14b, 4:148b
  etymology of the term, 2:14a
  Gāthās in, 2:14b–15a, 5:366a-b
  Ka^{c}ba of Zoroaster and, 7:204b–205a
  nasks, 8:204b
  redaction of ordered by King Valaχš, 9:443b
  sacred sites in, 10:661b–662a
  Sasanian seals and, 11:122b–123a
  seven climes, 10:661b
  Vendīdād, 2:15a
  Xusrō I and, 12:714a, 714b
  Yasna (sacrifice liturgy), 2:14b
  Yašts (hymns of praise), 2:15a
  see also Letter of Tansar; Vidēvdād
Avestan language, Younger Avestan, in *Yašts,* 12:720b
Avianus, **2:15b**, 4:572a,b, 573a
  "Ass and the Lion's Skin," 9:131a
  Fables, 7:360b
  in Latin pedagogy, 7:352b
Aviaries, in gardens, 5:363b
Avicebrol/Avicebron. *See* Solomon ben Judah ibn Gabirol
Avicenna. *See* Sīnā, Ibn
Avignon, **2:15b–16a**
  Black Death in, 2:260b
  bridge at
    brotherhood initiated by St. Bénézet, 10:413b
    free passage on and under, 10:417a
  corruption in, 2:16a
  during Hundred Years War, 2:16a
  first seals of, 11:126a
  inns in, 6:469b, 473a, 473b
  library of, 7:563b
Avignon 101 (Roman ritual), 10:408a

Avignon Cathedral, 10:481b
Avignon papacy, 3:362a–365a
  abuses by, 3:364b–365a
  Amadeo of Savoy and, 7:381a
  attempts to return to Rome, 9:555a
  Birgitta and, 2:247a
  bureaucratization of, 3:363b–364a
  Catalan Company and, 3:156b, 7:379b
  centralization of Latin church and, 3:377a
  church organization under, 3:377a
  court of, 3:363a
  depiction of, 3:362b
  discontent with, 3:365a
  French monarchy and, 3:362b–363a
  International Style at court of, 5:627b
  John XXII's reforms of, 7:125b
  Languedoc and, 7:341a,b
  Latin church and, 3:362a–365a
  liturgy of, 9:380a-b
  music at court of, 10:382a
  nepotism under, 3:363a
  palace of, 4:377a
    Chambre du Cerf, 6:361b
    decorated by Simone Martini, 2:16a
  papal coronation, 3:604b
  papal provision system of, 3:364a-b
  pontificates in, 3:362a-b
  Roman curia at, 12:160a
  servitia and, 11:606a
  turning point of medieval church, 3:361a-b
Avignon School. *See Ars subtilior*
Avignon, Synod of (1337), condemnation of shivarees, 8:29a
Avignon, University of, 12:285a
Avignonet, inquisitors killed at, 6:487a
Avionnets. See Fables
Avision-Christine. See Christine de Pizan
Avitacum, 11:277b
Aviticitas, 6:345a
Avitus, Eparchius, Roman emperor, Sidonius and, 11:277a
Avitus, St., **2:16b**
Avitus of Vienne, bishop, 7:361a, 592b
  true cross and, 4:553a-b
Aviz dynasty, founding of, 2:17a
Aviz, Order of, **2:16b–17a**
  founding of, 2:16b–17a
  houses of, 2:17a
Avoirdupois pound, 10:67a
Awak (son of Iwanē Mχargrzli), 12:737a
Awāl. *See* Baḥrayn, al-
Awan, 1:477b
Awdl. See Welsh literature, poetic meter
ᶜAwfī, 5:333a
Awgen of Clysma, mar, 11:564b
Awntyrs of Arthure, The, 8:332a
Awrāba Berbers, Idrīs ibn ᶜAbd Allah and, 6:413a
ᶜAwwām, Ibn al-, 6:558a
Awzāᶜī, al- (*d.* 774), Beirut and, 2:164a
Awzalagh. *See* Fārābī, al-
Awzān, 8:611a
Ax, 1:522a
  Danish, 1:522b
  in shipbuilding, 11:243b
  see also Barten
Axiochus, 9:703a
Axum, kingdom of, 1:30a, 31a, 2:17a-b
  conversion to Christianity, 2:17a-b
Axumite art, **2:17a–18a**
  monumental palaces, 2:17b
  stelae, 2:17b
¡Ay, Iherusalem!, **2:18a-b,** 11:413b–414a
  dating of, 2:18a
  form of, 2:18b
Aya Sofya MS, Arabic numerals in, 1:385b–386a
Ayādgār ī Zarērān (Memorial of Zarēr), 9:443b
Ayala, Pedro López de. *See* López de Ayala, Pero
Aᶜyān, 6:591a
Āyās, **2:19a-b,** 7:546b
  Genoese merchants in, 12:111b
  sacked by Mamluks, 2:19a
  trade route to Tabrīz and, 12:99a
Ayasuluk. *See* Ephesus
Āyāt al-kursī, 3:55a
Aybak. *See* ᶜIzz al Dīn Aybak, Mamluk sultan
Aydakīn, blazon of, 2:272b
Aȝenbite of Inwyt, 9:280b, 10:301b
  see also Lorens d'Orléans, *Somme le roi*
Aymard, 3:469a
ᶜAyn Jālūt, Battle of (1260), 2:138a, 6:329a, 591b, 8:73b
ᶜAyn al-Quḍāt al-Hamadānī, 9:42a-b
Aynard of St. Èvre, **2:19b**
Ayr, parliament at (1315), 9:438b
Ayrarat, 1:472b, 473a, 473b, **2:19b–20b**
  district of Vanand and, 12:353b
  origin of the term, 2:19b
  Širak in, 11:311a
Ayrer, Jakob, 4:272a
Ayrivanecᶜi, Mχitᶜar, 5:373b
Aysa, 6:618a
ᶜAyyārūn, 2:437a, 6:591a
Ayyub (11th-century military commander), vs. Roger I, 10:440a
Āyyūb ibn Shadhi (*d.* 1173), 7:310b
Ayyubids, **2:22b–25a,** 3:14a
  administration of, 2:24b
  in Aleppo, 1:145b, 2:23b
  alliance with Badr al-Dīn of Mosul, 2:43b
  in Arčēš, 1:423a
  armed forces of, 2:24b
  in Armenia, 1:513b
  art and architecture, **2:20b–22b,** 4:408a
    brass objects, 2:22 (*illus.*)
    ceramics, 22a-b, 2:21a (*illus.*)
    in Egypt, 2:21b–22a
    fortifications, 2:21a
    influence of on Mamluk art, 8:70b
    manuscript illumination, 2:22b
    mausoleums in Syria, 2:21b
  conquest of Jerusalem, 4:32a
  continuity with Zangids, 2:22a
  control of Ḥimṣ, 6:230a-b
  in Damascus, 4:82b, 83b, 84a, 85a, 10:625b
  decline of, 2:138a
  economic basis of their state, 2:24b–25a
  in Egypt, 2:24a
  Ismailism and, 6:618a
  Jews and, 7:84a
  khānqāh and, 7:238b
  Kurds and, 7:310b
  maritime trade and, 11:247a
  Mongol vassalage, 8:472b
  origins of, 2:23a
  provincial governments, Sanᶜa, 10:647a-b
  rise of dynasty, 10:625b
  rise of the Mamluk dynasty and, 8:73a-b
  Seljuks of Rum and, 11:154a-b
  Shāh-Arman and, 11:220a, 220b
  slave trade under, 11:339a
  taxation policy, military estates, 11:626b
  title of sultan and, 11:505a
  under Saladin, 2:23a-b
  use of *mamlūks,* 4:406a-b
  vs. crusaders, 4:31b
  in Xlatᶜ, 1:485a, 12:713b
  in Yemen, 2:23b, 12:724a
ᶜAyyūqī, *Warqa u Gulshāh,* 6:507a, 8:116b
Azāda, 6:408a
Āzādān, Xusrō I and, 12:714a
Azalais de Porcairagues, trobairitz, 12:207a
Azambuja, Diogo de, 4:562a
Azania, 12:739b
Azarie (Romanian chronicler), 10:510b
Azario, chronicle of Guelph-Ghibelline conflict, 6:7a
Azarquiel. *See* Zarqālī, al-
Azat, 1:488b, 490b, **2:25b**
  judicial role of priests, 1:504a
Azbuka, 8:574b
  see also Diletsky, Nikolai; Mezenets, Aleksandr
Azerbaijan, 1:125a, **2:25b–27b,** 26 (map)
  Alp Arslan and, 11:152b
  Hulagu and, 6:329a
  Ildegizids in, 6:419a, 419b
  Ilkhanids in, 2:27a, 6:420b, 504b
  Malikshāh and, 8:60a, 11:153a
  medieval population of, 2:26a-b
  military conflicts
    Jalāl-al-Dīn, 8:469b
    Mongols, 8:469b
  relations with Armenia, 1:482a-b
  Seljuk art and, 11:147a
  settlement of Turkic tribesmen in, 2:27a
  Smbat I the Martyr's clashes with, 11:351a
  Timurids and, 12:57a
  under the Arabian caliphate, 2:27a
  under Iranian dynasties, 2:27a
  under the Sasanians, 2:26b
  vs. al-Kufa, 7:306b
  Zoroastrian division, 10:662a
  see also Tabrīz; Uzun Ḥasan
Azhar, al- (mosque: Cairo), **2:27b–28a,** 6:608a, 11:514a
  establishment of, 4:407a
  original construction of, 2:27b–28a
  see also Mosques

ᶜAzīz biᵓllāh Nizār Abū Manṣūr, al-, Fatimid caliph, **2:28a-b**, 5:26a-b, 12:744a
  life of, 2:28a
  new style army created by, 2:28a
  as patron of the arts, 2:28b
  political and economic achievements, 2:28a-b
Aznárez, Fortún, 6:557b
Aznauri, **2:28b–29a**
  see also Azat; Nobility and nobles, Georgian
Azo, **2:29a-b**, 2:418a
  Bolognese School and, 5:567b
  disciples of, 2:29a
  Innocent IV and, 6:465b
  Laurentius Hispanus and, 7:385b
  Lectura codicis, on Rogerius, 10:444a
  Summa "Cum multae essent partes iuris" and, 10:444b
Azores, **2:29b–30b**, 2:30 (map)
  discovery of, 2:29b, 9:87b, 89a
  exploration of, 4:559a-b
  Flemish settlers in, 2:29b–30a
ᶜAzrāᵓīl. *See* Angels, Islamic
Azraq, Nāfiᶜ ibn al-, 11:138b
Azraqīs, 11:138b
Azulejo, **2:30b–31b**
  colors in, 2:31a
  tile from Seville (16th century), 2:31a (*illus.*)
Azymes, **2:31b–32a**, 7:610b

B

Baalbek, conquered by Muslims, 6:568a
Baarlam. *See* Barlaam
Bāb, **2:32a**
Bab al-Mandab, **2:32a–33a**, 32b (map)
  derivation of the name, 2:33a
  navigational difficulties in, 2:32b–33a
Bābā Fighānī, 11:252b
Bābā Isḥlāq (Turkoman religious leader), 11:154b, 157b, 12:227a
Baba preachers. *See* Islam, religion
Babai the Great, 11:563a, 565b
  East Syrian rite and, 11:567b
  Persian church and, 3:312b
  synthesis of Nestorian doctrine and, 9:105a
  Tractate on the Divinity and Humanity and on the Person of the Union, 9:107a
Babai of Kashkar. *See* Babai the Great
Babak (*fl.* 809–837)
  vs. Abbasids, 1:479b
  vs. al-Muᶜtaṣim, 8:653b
Babawīya confraternity. *See* Aḥmadīya confraternity
Babees Book, 3:661a
Babenberg family, **2:33a-b**
  Bavaria and, 2:134a, 134b
  inheritance conflict, 2:7b
  in Johann von Würzburg's works, 7:117a-b
  origins of, 2:6a
  power of, 5:508a
  Prêmysl Ottokar II of Bohemia and, 2:300a
  Reinmar der Alte and, 10:293b
  Reinmar von Zweter and, 10:295a
  Wolfger von Erla and, 12:672b
Baberon (castle), Lambron and, 7:322a
Babgēn, *katᶜołikos,* 1:508b, 5:540a
  Henotikon and, 1:499a
Babio, 4:283a, 7:367b
Babrius, 4:572a
Babylon
  image of, 2:34a
  introduction of magic and, 8:20b
  as a symbol
    for Baghdad, 2:34a
    for Cairo, 2:34a
    for pagan Rome, 2:34a
    for papal Avignon, 2:34a
Babylon (Egypt), siege of, 6:569b
Babylonia
  Jewish academies in, 10:337b–338b
  Jews in, 7:104b, 106a–108a
  Talmud and, 10:464a
Babylonian Captivity, **2:33b–34b**, 3:361b, 362b
  Catherine of Siena and, 9:14b
  flowering of mysticism and, 9:18a
  origins of the term, 2:34a-b
  see also Avignon papacy
Babylonian rite, in Spain, 7:621a
Babylonian Talmud. *See* Talmud
Babylonians, dyeing of textiles, 4:325b
Bacaudae
  in Armorica, 10:464b
  Flavius Merobaudes and, 8:276b
Bacchius the Elder, 8:636b
Backgammon, 5:349a (*illus.*), 351b, 353b
Backstaff, 4:12b
Baçó, Jaime, **2:34b–35a**
  compared with Juan Rexach, 10:342b
Bacon, Francis
  Of Gardens, 5:363a
  science and human technology, 11:650b–651a
Bacon, Roger, **2:35a–42a**, 3:314a
  Archimedes and, 1:435a
  on astrology, 1:607b–608a, 2:35b, 38b
  Augustinianism of, 2:36a-b
  biblical exegesis, 2:214a
  on calendar reform, 3:23a
  called "Doctor mirabilis," 2:35b
  Communia naturalium, 2:39a, 40b, 41a
  Compendium studi philosophiae, 2:35a, 37b, 40b
  criticism of magic, 2:38a, 38b
  De multiplicatione specierum, 2:38a, 39a
  De signis, 2:38a
  De speculis comburentis, 2:39a
  early thought of, 2:35b–37a
  Epistola de secretis operibus artis et naturae et de nullitate magiae, against false magic, 8:30b
  explanation of evil eye action, 8:38a
  on foreign language study, 12:137a
  Franciscans and, 7:369a
  on geometry, 2:38a
  Grosseteste and, 1:461b
  influences on, 2:35b
    Ibn al-Haytham, 2:39a, 39b
  later thought of, 2:37a–40b
  life of, 2:35a-b
  Moralis philosophia, 9:596a
  music and, 8:582a
  Opus maius, 2:35a, 36a, 37a–41a
    on the calendar and world geography, 2:38b
    De perspectiva, 2:38b–39b
    on experimental science, 2:39b
    on the four obstacles to wisdom, 2:37b
    on the importance of grammar, 2:37b–38a
    on mathematics and theology, 2:38a, 38b
    on moral philosophy, 2:40a
    on optics, 2:38b–39b
    on philosophy and theology, 2:37b
  Opus minus, 2:35a, 40b
  Opus tertium, 1:137a-b, 2:35a, 39a, 40b
    alkimia speculativa vs. *alkimia practica,* 1:137b
    on translation, 12:139b–140a
  philosophy and theology
    on the composite unity of human soul, 2:36b
    ontology of, 2:36a
    on positive unity of matter, 2:36b
    theology as experimental science, 9:596a
    theory of hylomorphism, 2:35b, 36a, 36b
  rediscovery of by Elizabethans, 2:41a
  reform of education and society, 2:37a
  scientific studies, 2:37a
    alchemical treatises, 1:137b
    on experimental science, 2:244a
    on the magnifying lens, 7:539a-b
    Western European geography and, 5:396b–397a
  Secretum secretorum and, 8:435a, 11:135b
  Speculi almukefi compositio and, 1:438b
  Speculum doctrinale and, 8:645a
  styles of his works, 2:40b–41a
  Summulae dialectices, 4:170b, 9:613b
  on transportation technology, 11:652a
  on the value of magic, 8:37a
  vision theory
    experimental methods, 9:249a
    geometrical modes of propagation, 9:250a-b
    intromission, 9:252a-b
    mathematical tradition, 9:248a
    multiplication of species, 9:249b
    rainbows, 9:253a
  Vulgate and, 12:495b
Bacteria. *See* Plagues
Bactrian language, 6:505b
Badajoz, Treaty of (1267), 10:46b
Badakhshan, founded, 6:616b
Bādgīr, **2:42a-b**

*Badi*ᶜ*, al-*. *See* Karajī, al-
Bādīs, Ibn, *Book of the Staff of the Scribes and Implements of the Discerning,* 12:698a, 698b
Bādīs, Zirid leader, 12:744a, 744b, 745a
Bādiya, **2:42b**
Badoer, Giacomo, 11:339b–340a
Badr, Battle of (624), **2:42b–43b,** 6:577a
  importance of, 2:43a
  referred to in Koran, 2:43a
  religious significance, 8:524b
  role of Abū Sufyān, 1:28b–29a
Badr al-Dīn Hasan, 12:724a
Badr al-Dīn Luᵓluᵓ of Mosul, ruler, **2:43b–44a**
  accession to power, 2:43b
  diplomacy of, 2:43b
  as patron of arts, 2:43b, 6:607a
Badr ibn Ḥasanawaih, as patron of schools, 11:65b–66a
Badr al-Jamālī, Fatimid ruler, **2:44a-b,** 5:27b–28a
  early career of, 2:44a
  rebuilding of Cairo fortifications, 12:553b
  tomb of, 6:608b
Baducing, Biscop. *See* Benedict Biscop, St.
Bær, Battle of (1237), 11:357a
Baebius Italicus. *See* Pindarus, *Ilias latina*
Baeda. *See* Bede
Baena, Juan Alfonso de, *Cancionero,* 11:419a
Baerze, Jacques de, **2:44b**
Báetán mac Cairill, king of the Ulaid, 4:78a-b
Baeza, siege of (1368), referred to in ballads, 11:418a
Bagawan, silk route to the Far East and, 12:99a
Bagh. See Rauḍa
Baghdad, **2:44b–47b**
  Abbasid caliph in, 2:435b
  art and architecture, 1:5a, 6:605b–607a
    palace complex, 2:45b
  Basra and, 2:127b
  besieged (1393, 1401), 6:514b
  Buyids in, 1:11a-b, 2:436b–437a, 6:424b, 513b
  called Babylon in the medieval West, 2:34a
  compared to Constantinople by Benjamin of Tudela, 12:102a-b
  conquered by al-Maᵓmūn, 11:574a
  cultural and scientific development in, 11:95a
  described in *Investigation of Commerce,* 12:105b–106a
  devastation of in the 9th century, 2:46b
  factionalism in, 6:512b
  founding of, 2:44b, 45a-b, 3:42a, 6:512a, 8:89a
  Great Mosque, 1:5a
  as heir to Alexandrian and Athenian scientific traditions, 11:88a
  Hulagu and, 2:47a
  as Islamic business center, 12:107b
  Islamic roads and communications and, 10:426a
  Jalayirids in, 6:514a
  Jews in, 7:107b, 108a
  al-Khaṭīb al-Baghdādī in, 7:239b–240a
  in *Kitāb al-buldān,* 12:718a
  al-Kufa and, 7:307b
  libraries of, 7:561a
  madrasas in, 8:11b
  manuscript copying and selling in, 11:84b
  Mongol conquest, 1:12a, 7:112a, 8:472b, 501a
  al-Mutawakkil in, 8:654b
  Niẓāmiyas, 8:11a-b
  occupied by
    Ottomans (1534), 6:514b
    Seljuks (1055), 6:513b, 12:66b
  plagues in, 9:684b
  population of, 2:47a
  Round City, 2:45a–46a, 6:596b–597b (*illus.*), 8:89a
    Abbasid rule and, 1:8b
    al-Fusṭāṭ and, 6:608a
  sacked (1258), 6:329a, 514a
  Shammasīya observatory, 11:99a
  Shīᶜa and, 11:227b–228a
    Twelver Shiite scholarship in, 11:136b
  size of, 2:47a
  Taq-i Bostan and, 11:597b
  Thirst Market area, 2:46a
  in *Thousand and One Nights,* 12:49b–50a
  Toghrıl-Beg and, 11:152a
  as a translation center, 11:81a, 82b, 12:130a–131b
  Tuesday Market area, 2:45a-b, 46a
  under Hārūn al-Rashīd's successors, 8:79b–80b
  under al-Mahdī, 8:47a
  under al-Mustanṣir, 8:650b–651a
  under al-Muᶜtaṣim, 8:653b
  vs. Alids, 8:80b
  vs. Mongols, 8:651b
  see also Barmakids
Baghdadi tables, 5:314 (*illus.*)
Bagpipe, 8:558b, 602 (*illus.*), 603b, 604a, 605a (*illus.*), 607a (*illus.*)
  Middle Eastern, 8:612b
  performance on, 8:635a
Bagrat II Bagratuni of Taron, prince, as *archon ton archonton,* 1:449a, 480a
Bagrat III of Georgia, king, 2:47b, 49a, 5:406a
  Basil II and, 4:113b
  Dīvān of Kings, 5:417b
Bagrat IV of Georgia, king, Liparit IV Orbēlean and, 7:586b
Bagratids (Bagratuni), Armenian, 1:473b–474a, 475b, 2:20b, **2:47b–48b**
  after the fall of Arsacids, 2:48a
  annexation of Ani, 9:544a-b
  archon ton archonton and, 1:449b
  Arcrunis and, 1:451a, 12:361b
  Armenian trade and, 12:97b–98b
  control of Lōṙi, 7:672a-b
  during *marzpanate,* 1:476b
  Dwin under, 4:324a
  in Georgia, 5:405b–406a
  Grigor Magistros and, 5:675a
  historical works, 1:511a, 6:240a
  John I Tzimiskes and, 7:127a
  junior branches of, 1:480b
  Kamsarakan and, 7:208a
  Kars and, 7:221a-b
  literature and, 1:510a–511a
  Mamikoneans and, 8:79a
  in Matthew of Edessa's *Chronicle,* 8:228b
  Naxčawan and, 9:90b
  origins of, 2:47b–48a
    Davidic descent claimed by, 2:47b, 48b
  Siwnikᶜ under, 11:315a
  Smbat I the Martyr, 11:351a
  *sparapetut*ᶜ*iwn* and, 1:490a
  in Stepᶜanos Asołik Tarōnecᶜi's *History,* 11:477a
  *t*ᶜ*agadir* and, 1:489a
  Tarōn and, 11:599a
  under Arabs, 1:478b, 480a, 513a, 513b
  under Ašot I, 1:480b–481a, 587b–588b
  under Ašot II, 1:482a, 588b–589a
  under Ašot III, 1:589a-b
  in Vanand, 12:354a
  vs. Byzantine Empire, 1:483b
  vs. Faḍl, 11:217a
  vs. Mamikonean dynasty, 1:479a
  vs. Sājids, 1:513b
  see also Ani in Širak; Łewond
Bagratids (Bagratuni), Georgian, **2:48b–49a**
  Dwin under, 4:324b
  geography and ethnology, Tao/Taykᶜ, 11:629a
  history of, 5:417b
  in the late 11th and 12th centuries, 2:49a
  Širak under, 11:311a
  vs. Faḍl, 11:217a
Bagrat's Cathedral, **2:47b**
Bagratuni. *See* Bagratids
Bagrewand, Bagratids and, 1:480a
Bagrewand, Battle of (775), 1:479b
Bahāᶜ-i Walad, 10:556a
Bahāristān, influence of *Gulistān* on, 6:27a
Baḥr al-Muḥīt, **2:49b**
Bahrain. *See* Baḥrayn, al-
Bahrām I, Sasanian ruler
  Kartīr and, 7:221b
  Mani and, 8:84a
Bahrām II, Sasanian ruler
  depicted
    in rock reliefs, 10:658a
    in silverwork, 10:658a
Bahrām V Gōr, Sasanian king, **2:49b–50a**
  in epic literature, 10:669a
  hunting and, 6:354b, 408a
  theory of monarchy, eternal flame, 11:628b
  wuzurg framadār and, 12:705b
Bahrām VI Čōbēn, anti-Sasanian usurper, **2:50a-b**

attempt to usurp throne, 10:670b
Hormizd IV and, 12:715a
vs. Xusrō, in art, 11:598a
Bahrām Shāh, minaret of, 5:519b
Baḥrayn, al-, **2:50b–51a**
as a base for anti-Abbasid activity, 2:50b–51a
Qarmatians in, 6:616a, 617a
set up by Qarmatians, 11:137a
Baḥrī Mamluks. *See* Mamluk dynasty
Baḥrīya regiment (in the Mamluk army), 8:73a
Baybars and, 2:138a
Baḥya ben Asher ben Ḥlava, 5:346b
Kad ha-Kemaḥ, 10:74b–75b
mysticism and, 4:540a
Baḥya ben Joseph ibn Paqūdā, **2:51a-b,** 7:151b
Hidāya ᵓ*ila farā*ᵓ*iḍ al-qulūb, Al-,* 7:96b, 167a
Ḥovot ha-Levavot, 4:540a
Neoplatonism of, 7:166b
personal God of history, 9:577b
Sufi influence, 9:573a
Bail à ferme, 4:513a
Bail à part des fruits, 4:513a
Bailada, 11:452b
Dinis and, 4:190a
Bailan Pass. *See* Cilician Gates
Baile in Scáil, 6:547a, 547b
Bailiff, **2:51b–52a**
English, 2:52a
estate management and, 4:514a,b
France, 7:675a
meaning of the term, 2:51b
in Valencia, 12:348a
see also Bailli
Baille (capacity measure), 12:584a
Baillehaut, Jean, *Sottes chansons,* 9:637a
Bailli, 1:594b, **2:52a–53b**
in county of Savoy, 10:674b–675a
emergence of provost of Paris from office of, 10:197a
in forest administration, 5:133a, 134b
grand, 2:53a-b
holding of assizes, 5:162b
in Normandy, 2:53a, 5:164b
origins of the Parlement of Paris and, 9:417b
petty, 2:52b
recruitment of, 2:53a-b
salary of, 2:53a
in Vermandois, 12:396a
see also Bailiff; Seneschal
Bailliages, 2:53a
in Burgundy, 2:426a, 427a-b
Bailly, Jean-Sylvain, 9:705a
Baird. See Bard
Baiuvarii, 2:133b
Bājja, Ibn, 2:433a
on Aristotle, 1:459a, 464b
Neoplatonic writings, 9:571a
Bākbāk, as Tulinid dynasty forefather, 12:223b
Baker, Gilbert, frescoes of, 5:610a
Bakhtiyār-nāma, 6:508b
Bakócz, Tamás, archbishop, 6:349a
Bakr tribe, Imruᵓ al-Qays and, 6:430a
Bakrī, al-
on Meknes, 8:267b
references to Scandinavia, 10:707b
Bakur of Georgia, king, Nino and, 9:140a
Balaam
early German tale of, 2:227b
star of Jacob and, 4:498b
Balaban of Xlatᶜ, ruler, 11:220a
Balabitenē, 1:472b, 515a, 515b
Balada
in Provençal literature, 10:164b
see also Dance
Balādhurī, Abū Ḥasan Aḥmād ibn Yahya ibn Jābir al-, 1:473b, 478b, **2:54a-b**
Ansāb al-ashrāf, 6:250a
Armenian historians and, 1:478a
Genealogies of the Nobles Among the Arabs, 2:54a-b
on Muslim conquests, 2:54a
on Naxčawan, 9:90b
Balahovit. *See* Balabitenē
Balance of power. *See* Power, political
Balavar and Būdasaf. See Balavariani
Balavariani, **2:54b–55a**
contents of, 2:54b
two recensions of, 2:54b
see also Barlaam and Josaphat; Euthymios
Balbi, Giovanni
Catholicon, 4:248a, 449b–450a, 547a, 7:352a, 368a, 564a
printing of, 6:33a
Balbulus, Notker. *See* Notker Balbulus
Balbus, John. *See* Balbi, Giovanni
Baldachin, **2:55a** (*illus.*)
Balder. *See* Baldr
Balderich of Bourgueil. *See* Baudri of Bourgueil
Baldishol (tapestry), 11:593a
Baldo degli Ubaldi da Perugia. *See* Baldus
Baldr, 1:63a, **2:55a–56a,** 5:301a, 11:25b, 27b, 32b, 33a
according to Snorri, 2:55a-b
in *Baldrs draumar,* 2:55a, 56a-b
interpretation of myth, 2:55b
in *Málsháttakvæði,* 8:66b
Skaði and, 11:325b
see also Scandinavian mythology
Baldrs draumar, **2:56a–57a**
compared with
Helgakviða Hundigsbana, 2:56b
Þrymskviða, 2:56b
Vafþrúðnismál, 2:56b
Vǫluspá, 2:56b
concept of *hel,* 6:147b
Grógaldr and, 11:524b
inclusion in medieval manuscripts, 4:385b
"Odin's question" and, 12:344b
Bald's Leechbook (Old English), 1:286a
Baldus, **2:57a–58a,** 10:61b
commentaries on civil law, 7:423b–424a
consilia of, 2:57b
influenced by Bartolo da Sassoferrato, 2:116a
legal maxims, 8:232a
public offices of, 2:57b
university teaching of, 2:57a
writings of, 2:57a-b
Baldwin (13th-century translator), 2:142a
Baldwin I (Iron-arm) of Flanders, count, **2:58a,** 2:386a, 5:77b–78a
against the Vikings, 2:58a
Baldwin II of Flanders, count, 2:386a, 5:78a-b
Baldwin V of Flanders, count, 5:79a
Baldwin VIII of Flanders, count, 5:80b–81a
Baldwin IX of Flanders, count. *See* Baldwin I, Latin emperor of Constantinople
Baldwin I of Jerusalem, king, **2:58b**
Bohemond I of Antioch and, 2:309a
capture of Edessa by, 4:384a
capture of Hṙomklay, 6:311b
in crusades, 4:30a, 30b, 36b
marriage of, 10:440b
Tancred and, 11:589a, 589b
Baldwin II of Jerusalem, king, 3:304a-b
Baldwin III of Jerusalem, king, diplomacy of, 4:38b
Baldwin I, Latin emperor of Constantinople, **2:58b–59a,** 4:48b, 5:81a, 12:389b
capture of, 7:347a
death of, 9:116a
election of, 7:346a
Geoffroi de Villehardouin and, 12:448b
Kalojan and, 7:206b
Baldwin II, Latin emperor of Constantinople, 7:131a
Asen and, 7:347b
Baldwin of Hainaut and, 4:556a-b
contempt for Greeks, 7:348b–349a
ineptitude as ruler, 7:346b
ousted from power, 7:349b
Baldwin of Bologna, *ars dictaminis* and, 10:358b
Baldwin of Canterbury, archbishop, Nigel of Longchamp and, 9:131a
Baldwin of Edessa, count. *See* Baldwin I of Jerusalem, king
Baldwin of Hainaut, explorations of Asia, 4:556a, 556b
Baldwin (of Viktring), *Liber dictaminum,* 4:175b
Bale, John, 7:371a
King Johan, allegory in, 4:287a
on *Piers Plowman,* 7:330a
Walter Map and, 7:364b
Bale (unit of measure), 12:592a
product variations, 12:584b
Balearic Islands
attacked by Muslims, 6:572b
captured by
Almohads, 1:195a, 200b
Almoravids, 1:200a
irrigation of, 6:558a
liturgical drama in, 11:437a
occupied by Vandals, 12:354b
ruled by Almoravid Banū Ghāniya, 1:194a, 200b
Valencia and, 12:346a
Balīnās. *See* Apollonius of Tyana
Balinger, 11:243a
Balkans
Basil I and, 2:117b–118a

Balkans (*cont.*)
as Byzantine province, 2:485a, 486b, 494a, 498a
Hungarian defense and, 6:346b–347a, 347b
invasions of (6th-7th cent.), 4:1a
languages of, 6:443b, 444b
mining in, 8:399a
Ottoman control of, 2:502b
roads in, 10:422b–424a
Vlach-Bulgarians in, 2:496b
see also Bosnia; Bulgaria; Croatia; Serbia; Walachia
Balkh
Islamic mysticism and, 9:39b
seized, 6:570b
Ball games, 5:348a
Ball, John
liberated by Wat Tyler's rebels, 9:479a
in Peasants' Revolt, 7:645a
Ball-flower, **2:61b**, (*illus.*), 8:454 (*illus.*)
definition, 8:453b
Ballad romances, Faroese. *See* Faroese ballads
Ballade, **2:59a-b**, 4:86b, 492a
in *Ars nova,* 1:552a-b
chant royal, 3:263b
French, Italian ballata and, 12:177b
origins of, 2:59a
standardized by Guillaume de Machaut, 2:59a, 8:6b–7b
without music, 2:59a-b
see also Ballette
Ballade at the Reverence of Our Lady. *See* Lydgate, John
"Ballade des dames du temps jadis." *See* Villon, François
"Ballade des pendus." *See* Villon, François
"Ballade pour Robert d'Estouteville." *See* Villon, François
Ballads
Middle English, **2:59b–60b**, 8:325a-b
canon of, 2:59b
meter of, 8:345a-b
Robin Hood and, 10:436a
see also Middle English literature, lyric
Norwegian *Draumkvæde,* 4:290a-b
origin of Icelandic *rímur* and, 10:403a-b
Romanian, 10:513b
Scottish, 11:113b
Spanish
in *Cancionero general,* 11:424b
from the Trastámaran wars, 11:418a
rise of under Alfonso XI, 11:417b
see also Fenian poetry
Ballata, 1:553a, **2:60b–61a**, 3:116a, 4:86b, 6:640b, 641a, 651a, 668b–669a, 12:177b, 179a
Arabic lyrics and, 8:563b
compared with madrigal, 8:12b
Italian, trecento, 12:177b, 179a
of Landini, 7:326b–327a
of Lapo Gianni, 6:649a
lauda and, 6:662b, 669a
virelai and, 12:458a
Ballette, **2:61a-b**
in Anglo-Norman literature, 1:269a
see also Ballade
Balliol, Edward, 11:110a
Balliol, John, 11:108a, 108b, 109a, 109b
Scottish parliament and, 9:438a-b, 439a, 439b
Ballista, 3:179 (*illus.*), 180a
Ballo, 4:89a-b, 8:595b
Ballock knife. *See* Daggers
Ballon (French unit of measure), 12:592a
product variations, 12:584b
"Balloon guitar." *See Pipa*
Ballot, secret. *See* Representative assemblies, French
Ballymote, Book of, 6:523a, 524b
Balša Balšiç, ruler of Zeta, Stefan Lazareviç of Serbia and, 11:473a
Balšiçi family of Serbia, 11:179a, 180a, 180b
Balsora. *See* Basra
Balthasar (magus), 4:498a
Balthasar of Mecklenburg, *Dresdener Heldenbuch* written for, 4:292b–293a
Balthasar Walter (Romanian chronicler), 10:510b
Baltic countries, **2:61b–68b**, 2:63 (map)
border warfare (10th to 13th centuries), 2:64a
Christianization of, 2:64a–67a
importance of amber, 2:61b
military conflicts, 7:684a-b
Poland and, 9:716b
settlement of German farmers in, 2:66a
trade, 6:91a-b
with Hanseatic League, 2:67a-b
see also Lithuania; Teutonic Knights
Baltic languages, 6:434b, 438a
Baltic Sea
Bornholm, 5:632a
Gotland, 5:631b–633a
Öland, 5:632a
ports, 9:718b
Balts, **2:61b–68b**
earliest records of, 7:602b
pre-Christian religious beliefs of, 7:609a
response to crusaders, 2:65a
Second Golden Age (10th to 12th centuries), 2:62b–64a
Baluchistan, Ghaznavid expansion and, 11:133b
Balxī, al-, on Xusrō I, 12:714a
Bamberg
bishopric of, Nuremberg and, 9:.202b
foundation of, 5:476a
literature in (1050–1170), 8:347b–348a
ministerials, 8:405a, 406b
Bamberg Cathedral
choir of, 5:621a (*illus.*)
Ezzolied and, 4:571b
modern scholarship on, 1:430b
photogrammetry of, 1:432a
Bamberg manuscript, **2:68b–69a**
Bamberg, Staatliche Bibliothek, Lit 115, 2:68b
motet texts, 8:506b
Bamberg Surgery, 8:250b
Bambergensis (decretal collection), 4:123b
Bamyan, Mongol siege, 8:467b
Ban, **2:69a-b**
capitulary and, 3:91a
excommunication and, 4:536a, 538a
exilarch and, 4:552a
husbands and, 4:606b, 607a
tenant labor and, 4:513a
violated pledge and, 4:606a
Bana, **2:70a**
Banalité, **2:69a-b**, 11:619b, 676b
four most common kinds of, 2:69a-b
origin and evolution of, 2:69b
Banana, growth of, 1:81b
Banat, **2:70a-b**
Bancherii, role of in Genoese banking, 2:73a-b
Banco San Giorgio, support of Genoese government, 5:386a
Bandamanna saga, **2:70b–71a**, 4:613b, 614a
comic dialogue in, 2:70b–71a
dating of, 2:71a
flyting in, 9:173b
manuscripts of, 2:71a
þættir related to, 12:2b
Banderesi, 10:524a, 524b
Banderia. *See* Knights and knight service, Hungarian
Bandinelli, Orlando (Roland). *See* Alexander III, pope
Bandini, Domenico, 2:287a
Bandīr, 8:563a, 613a
Bandits
pilgrims and, 9:657a–658a
see also Jacquerie
Bands, town. *See* Town bands
Bangor Antiphonary, 3:230b–231a, 7:361a, 362a, 614b, 8:118b
Bangor, pontifical of, 2:72a
Bangor, rite of, sources on, 2:72a
Bangor (Wales), **2:71a-b**
Banians, 11:250a
Banishment
of Jews. *See* Jews, expulsion of
in Norman administration, 9:161b
Banjska Monastery, church of St. Stephen, 11:186b
Banking, European, **2:72b–79a**
at Bruges, 2:387a
creation of commercial credit, 2:74b
deposits *a discrezione,* 2:73b
in England, 2:74a
exchange banks, 2:73b–74a
exchange contracts (*cambium*), 2:78a
experiments with public banks, 2:75b–76a
foreign exchange dealings, 2:77b
in-bank payments, 2:73b
interest rates, 2:73a-b
international banking, 2:76a–78b
Italian, 2:76a–78b
in Castile, 4:557b
Renaissance houses, 7:8b
in Languedoc, 7:339b
London, merchants' guilds, 7:664b
money markets, 2:78b
in Nuremberg, 9:202b
oral orders of transfer, 2:74a, 75a

origins of, 2:72b–73a
partnership in mercantile banking companies, 2:76b–77a
role of the Medici, 8:242a–243b
Roman, 10:526a
supported by the papacy, 2:77b
trade and, 12:118a
use of written orders (*polizze*), 2:75a
in Valencia, 12:348b
Venetian commerce and, 12:388a-b
see also Trade, Western European; Usury
Banking, Islamic, **2:79a–80b**
credit arrangements in, 2:79b
merchant banking in, 2:80a-b
money changing in, 2:80a
trade and, 12:106a-b
see also Usury, Islamic law
Banking, Jewish
in Europe, **2:80b–82a**, 7:89b–90b
in England, 2:80a-b
interest rates, 2:81a-b
Louis IX of France and, 2:81b
modern scholarship on, 2:81b
in Papal States, 7:109b
scriptural proscriptions of usury, 2:80b
varieties of lending, 2:81a
see also Banking, European; Usury, Jewish law
in Middle East, 7:107a
Banneret, **2:82a-b**
number of men commanded by, 2:82a
royal household and, 6:302b
Banners, in churches, 5:319b
Bannockburn, Battle of (1314), 2:102a, 10:427a, 11:110a
defeat of cavalry at, 3:204b
in literature, 7:370a
Banns, 4:610b
Bannum, in Carolingian Empire, 3:107b
Bannus. See Ban
Banquets, protocol at, 3:581a–582a
Bansenchas, **2:82b**, 6:531a, 542a
Bantu language, Zanj and, 12:739a
Banū Mūsā, 1:620b
on astronomy, 1:620b
Calculation with the Hindu Numerals, 8:208b
Kitāb al-ḥiyal, 11:636b, 641b
automata vessel, 11:636b (*illus.*)
water-lifting device, 11:642a (*illus.*)
tomb of, 11:252b
translations of Greek scientific treatises into Arabic, 11:82b
Verba filiorum, 1:435b–436a, 8:210b
Banū (tribe). *See* next element of name
Banus, **2:82b–83a**
see also Banat
Baphaeon, Battle of (1301), 9:288a
Baptism, **2:83a–86b**
administration of, 2:85a
adult
oil for catechumens, 2:177a, 177b
religious instruction and, 10:300a
among Bogomils, 2:297a
among Cathars, 2:297a
Augustine of Hippo and, 1:648a
baptismal font, St. Barthélemy at Liège, 10:253 (*illus.*)
of bells, 2:166a
by unworthy priests, 6:193b, 194b
Carolingian liturgical treatises on, 7:627a-b
in Celtic church, 2:381b–382a, 3:229a, 7:614a
of Christ, **2:86b–87a**
Byzantine representations of, 2:86b
early representations of, 2:86b
see also Epiphany, feast of
church dedication and, 4:131a
confirmation and, 3:536a
in early church, 3:675a-b
Easter vigil and, 4:367a-b
effects of, 2:85a
Epiphany and, Eastern-Western differences, 4:497a
formula of, 2:84b
heretical ideas on, 6:195b
infant, 2:85a-b, 10:300a-b
Pelagius' doctrine and, 9:486a
institution of, 2:84b
interpretation of, 2:84a
liturgy of, 3:675a–676a
in Byzantine church, 7:610a
for Holy Saturday, 6:279a
Old High German/Old Saxon vows, **2:87a-b**, 9:233b
place of, 2:85b–86a
predestination and, 5:639a
preparation of converts during Lent, 7:541a
records as demographic evidence, 4:138b
resurrection of Christ and, 4:366a
rites of, 2:83a–84a
bells during, 5:321a
candles at, 5:318b
compared with pagan initiation rites, 9:2a
series of four ceremonies, 2:83b
role of sponsorship in, 2:86a
sin and, 6:447a, 449b
Syro-Armenian, 1:516a, 4:497a-b
theology of, 2:85a
time of, 2:85b
water of
benedictions and, 2:177a, 177b
as essential symbol, 2:84b
vessels for, 5:320a
see also Catechism; Liturgy; Liturgy, treatises on
Baptism of blood (martyrdom), 2:84b
Baptism of desire, 2:84b
Baptistery, 2:85b–86a, **2:87b–88a**
at Dura Europos, 4:349 (*illus.*)
development of, 4:336a
octagonal plan, 2:87b–88a, 4:336a
Florence, 10:667b–668a (*illus.*)
S. Maria in Cosmedin, 10:263a
Baptistery of the Arians (Ravenna), 2:86b, 10:263a
cupola decorations of, 4:359a
mosaics, 4:352a
Baptistery of the Orthodox (Ravenna), 1:423b, 5:594a, 10:263a
decorative style, 4:352a
interior decorations of, 4:359a
Baptistery of St. John (Naples), 9:58a
Bāqillānī, al-, 10:345a
defense of Sunnis, 3:50b
Bāqir, Muḥammad al-, 11:136a, 138a
Imāmīs and, 11:227a
Baqṭ, 9:198a, 198b
Bar Hebraeus, **2:108a-b**, 11:565b, 566a
astronomical works of, 12:130a
Chronography, **2:108a-b**
early life of, 2:108a
Kitāb al-aghānī, 2:238b
in Melitene, 8:269b
Bar Ḥiyya. *See* Abraham bar Ḥiyya
Bar Kokhba, 6:575b
rebellion of (132–135), 7:159b
Bar Sauma (13th century), embassy of, 6:420a
Bar Ṣauma, bishop of Nisibis (*ca.* 420–*ca.* 490), 9:106b
Persian church and, 3:312a
Bar tracery (bar branch), **2:116b**
Bar-sur-Aube, fairs, 4:590b
Bar-sur-Seine, count of (13th century), 9:149a
Barada River, irrigation and, 6:556b
Baraita di-Mazalot, 11:90a
Baraita di-Shemuel, 11:90a
Baraka (spiritual power of Sufi saints), 9:44b
Barānis, 2:185b
Baraq, 6:420a
Barbar. *See* Berbers
Barbarians, land ownership, 11:674a
Barbarians, invasions of, **2:88a–97b**
art and, 8:363a-b
in Britain, 2:96a
character of on the Continent, 2:96a
decline of literacy and, 7:599a-b
decline of travel during, 12:153a-b
4th and 5th centuries, 2:90a–94b
Gallic life described by Paulinus of Pella, 9:471b
Italy, 9:220b–221a
kingdom of Lombards, 2:95a–96a
military organization, 12:555a-b
Poland, 9:716b, 721a-b
slavery and, 11:335a-b
3rd century, 2:89b–90a
urbanism and
destruction of churches, 12:314a-b
topographical changes, 12:314b–315a
urban fortification, 12:314b–315a
see also German law, early Germanic codes; Germanic peoples; Vandals
Barbaro, Ermolao, Greek studies of, 7:1b
Barbaro, Josafa, 5:333b
Barbarossa. *See* Frederick I Barbarossa of Germany, emperor
Barbaṭ, 8:565b, 610a-b
Barbato da Sulmona (jurist), 2:278a
Barber-surgeons, **2:97b–101a**
as government employees in Italian city-states, 2:100b
guilds of, 2:99a–100a
religious and social functions of, 2:99b
popular attitudes to, 2:101a
services provided by, 2:99a, 100a-b
social position of, 2:100a
13th-century surgery, 8:250b–251a
see also Beauty aids
Barberini diptych, portrait of emperor, 4:354a

Barbero, Giosophat
as early antiquarian, 1:332b
journey to Persepolis, 1:332b
Barbieri, Giovanni Maria, 11:259a
Barbotine, **2:101a–102a**
jug (1st century), 2:101b (*illus.*)
in Mesopotamia and Syria, 2:101b
three styles of, 2:101b
Barbour, John, **2:102a**
The Bruce, 8:317a, 10:427b–428a, 428b
Barbute, 1:527a (*illus.*), 530a
Barč/Bolč, 7:241a
Barca, Bedouins and, 12:744b
Barcarola, 11:452b
Barcelona, **2:102a–105a**
administration of
in 13th century, 2:103b
in late 14th century, 2:104b
Arab occupation of (717–801), 2:102b
arsenal of, 9:81a
Benjamin of Tudela on, 2:103b
Berenguer Oller's revolt (1285), 2:104a
black slaves in, 2:268b
clash between the Busca and Biga parties, 2:104b
Deeds of the Counts of Barcelona, 10:256a
growth of in the 12th century, 2:103b
irrigation of, 6:558a
Jews in, 7:80a, 81a, 9:705a
Jewish quarter (*Call*), 2:103a, 104b
al-Manṣūr's invasion of, 2:102b, 103a, 3:175b
money changers in, 2:74a
plagues in, 9:681a
population of, 2:103a, 103b, 104a, 105a
prosperity of, 3:178a
religious foundations, 2:104a
social classes (13th century), 2:103b–104a
Taula de Canvi, 2:75b
under the Visigoths, 2:102a-b
administration of, 2:102b
churches, 2:102b
as vassal of Sancho III of Navarre, 9:69a
villanovas of, 2:103a, 104a
Barcelona Cathedral, 2:103a
Pietà by Bartolomé Bermejo, 2:189b
use of iron grilles in, 8:286a
Barcelona disputation (1263), 7:81b, 9:53b, 10:4b–5a
Barcelona, University of, 12:287a
Barclay, Alexander, 10:435a
Wynkyn de Worde and, 12:712a
Bard, **2:105b–106a**
apprenticeship, 12:605a
hereditary associations, 12:599a, 605a
household, 12:598b, 604b–605a
informal poetry, 12:605a-b
instruction of, *gramadegau,* 12:599b
itinerant, 12:607b
music of, 8:558a
musical prowess of, 2:105b
professional organization, 12:608a
social status, 12:605a
training of, 2:105b
Welsh, 12:597b
poetic conventions, 12:604b
see also Mac Lonáin, Flann; Scottish literature, Gaelic
Bardas Caesar, **2:106a-b**, 9:697a
Basil I and, 2:117a
educational reforms, 3:431a
Ignatios and, 6:415b, 11:42b
Michael III and, 8:302a
support of Photios, 11:42b
Theodora II and, 12:12b–13a
see also Leo the Mathematician
Bardas Phokas, **2:106b**
David of Tao and, 1:483b, 5:406a
suppression of the revolt of, 12:359a
vs. Basil II, 2:118b, 4:113b, 8:2b
see also Bardas Skleros
Bardas Skleros, **2:106b–107a**
Basil II and, 2:118b, 4:113b, 8:2b
David of Tao and, 1:483b
see also Bardas Phokas
Bardd. See Bard
Bardd teulu, 12:604b–605a
see also Bard, household
Bardesanes of Edessa, 11:567b
Bardhaᶜa, 1:124b, 125a, **2:107a**
Armenian trade and, 12:97b
Baylakān and, 2:139b
under Arabs, 1:479a, 4:323b
Bardi bank, 2:77a, 77b, 78b
bankruptcy of (1346), 12:118a
collapse of, 2:287a
employer of Boccaccio's father, 2:277b
Hundred Years War and, 6:333b
Languedoc and, 7:341a
Villani and, 6:634a
Bardic grammars, **2:107a-b**
poetic conventions, 12:604b
poetic meter, 12:605b, 607a, 612a
see also Auraicept na nÉces; Bard; Scottish literature, Gaelic
Bardic poetry. *See* Irish literature
Bardic schools, descriptions of, 2:107a-b
Bardic songs
form of, 2:105b
themes of, 2:105b
Bardings of mail. *See* Mail, bardings
Barford, St. Michael's Church, 1:256a, 257b (*illus.*)
Barge, 11:239b, 243a
Bargeboard, **2:107b–108a**, (*illus.*)
Bari, **2:108b**
acquired by Byzantines (875), 2:118a
Carolingian reconquest of, 7:4a-b
commerce, 11:275a
First Crusade and, 2:308b
occupied by Muslims, 6:572b
Robert Guiscard and, 10:433a
Western European trade and, 12:111a
Bari, Battle of (1071), 11:265b
Bari Cathedral, 10:486b
bishop's throne, 10:501b
Bari, Imperial Diet of (1195), Wolfger von Erla and, 12:672b
Barīd, 3:45a, 10:60b–61b
Barinel (Italian ship), 9:89a
Baris. *See* Ararat, Mount
Barisanus of Trani, **2:109a**, 8:284b
Barjawān (military regent for al-Ḥākim), 6:73b
Barjr Haykᶜ, 1:472a
under Byzantines, 1:473a
Barkiyāruq. *See* Berkyaruq
Barlaam of Calabria, **2:109a-b**, 2:278a, 3:632b
condemnation of, 2:109b
Gregory Palamas and, 5:672b
on hesychasm, 6:218a, 9:7b
Barlaam and Josaphat, listed among the Catholic saints, 2:109a
Barlaam and Josaphat, **2:109a**, 6:444b, 12:714b
Byzantine version of, 8:18b–19a
in Don Juan Manuel's *Libro de los estados,* 8:96a, 11:417a
Everyman and, 4:528a
Învăţăturile lui Neagoe Basarab and, 10:510b
Romanian translations, 10:511b
Spanish literature and, 4:551b
Spanish translations of, 11:439b
transmission of, 8:23b
see also Balavariani, vie des anciens pères, La
Barlaam of Seminara, 1:614a
Barlaam und Josaphat. See Rudolf von Ems
Barlas tribe, Timurids and, 12:58a
Barley
as cereal crop, 1:86b, 98b
growth of, in Western Europe, 5:645b
Barmakids, **2:109b–111a**
imprisonment of, 1:10a
influence in Abbasid court, 6:107b, 590a
al-Mahdī and, 8:47a-b
origins of, 2:109b
as typical Abbasid clients, 2:110a
Barna da Siena, **2:111a**
frescoes of, 5:294b, 607a
Giovanni da Milano and, 5:535a
Passion, 5:607a
Spinello Aretino and, 11:463b
see also Vanni, Andrea
Barnaby, John, Hugh of St. Albans and, 6:320b
Barnes, Julyans, Dame. *See* Berners, Juliana, Dame
Barnet, Battle of (1471), 9:450b
Barnet-Tewkesbury campaign. *See* Wars of the Roses
Barnis, descendants of, 2:185b
Barnsdale, Robin Hood and, 10:436a, 436b, 437b
Barolinus de Benincasa de Canulo, commentary on Cicero, 10:356a
Baronius, Caesar, *History of the Church,* year 1000 and, 12:723a
Barons, **2:111a-b**
definitions of, 2:111b
England
disputes with John, 4:469a
Exchequer and, 4:531a, 532b, 533b, 534a
formation of parliament, 4:481a-b
knight-baron distinction, 9:150b
Langton and, 7:338a-b
as sheriffs, 11:225a
support of Matilda, 4:463a

Barons' War, **2:111b–112b**, 4:395b–396a
arbitration of King Louis IX of France, 2:112a
causes of, 2:112a
negotiations with Henry III, 6:159a
peace terms of the Dictum of Kenilworth, 2:112b
Simon de Montfort the Younger in, 11:297b–298a
in *Song of Lewes,* 11:372b
see also Magna Carta
Baronzio, Giovanni, **2:112b–113a**
Barozzi, Francesco, 1:439a
Barqa, Islamic conquest of, 6:572a
Barqūq, al-Sulṭān al-Malik al-Ẓāhir Sayf al-Dīn, **2:113a-b**, 3:398a-b, 399a-b, 8:74b
changes in the Mamluk army under, 2:113b
early career of, 2:113a
rebellion of Syrian emirs, 2:113a-b
threatening letter from Tamerlane, 2:113b
Barr, descendants of, 2:185b
Barra of Cork (literary character). *See* Bran mac Febail (literary character)
Barrel (measure), **2:113b–114a**
Barrel vault. *See* Vault, types of
Barrels, **2:114a-b**
invention of, 2:114a
spread of the use of, 2:114a
Barrientos, Lope de, burning of Enrique de Villena's books and, 11:420b
Barrilli, Giovanni (jurist), 2:278a
Barrio de la Mar (Seville), 11:214a
Barroso, Pedro Gómez, attribution of the lost *Voz del grillo,* 11:443a
Barsaumas (monastery: Melitene), 11:565a
Barsbay al-Ashraf, Mamluk sultan, 8:75a, 75b
Barshchina, 11:191b, 193a
Barten, 1:522a
Bartholomaeus Anglicus
De proprietatibus rerum, 4:448b, 602a, 7:369a, 8:645a, 12:34a
on animals, 2:205a
John Trevisa's translation, 12:187a
medieval study of plants and, 2:245b
Bartholomaeus Brixiensis, 5:657b, 7:122a
Decretum Gratiani and, 4:127b
Bartholomaeus of Salerno, 8:248b, 249a, 256b
Bartholomew, apostle, 1:510a, 519a
Bartholomew of Lucca, as defender of Thomism, 12:42a
Bartholomew of Pisa, *Book of the Conformity of the Life of St. Francis to the Life of the Lord Jesus,* 5:205a
Bartia, 2:63 (map), 67a
Bartoli, Antonio, Ethiopians and, 10:119a
Bartolino da Novara, **2:114b**
Bartolismo, 2:116a
Bartolo di Fredi, **2:116b**
Garden of Eden frescoes, 5:361a-b
Spinello Aretino and, 11:463b
Taddeo di Bartolo and, 11:572b
see also Vanni, Andrea
Bartolo de Michele, 5:524b
Bartolo, Nanni di. *See* Giovanni (Nanni) di Bartolo
Bartolo da Sassoferrato, **2:114b–116a**, 10:19a, 61b
Baldus and, 2:57a, 116a
on citizenship in city-states, 2:116a
commentaries
on civil law, 7:423b–424a
on *Corpus iuris civilis,* 2:115a-b
early life of, 2:114b–115a
jurisprudence of, compared with Cino da Pistoia's, 2:115b
kingship theories of, 7:268b
public offices of, 2:115a
studies of at Bologna, 2:115a
Bartolomaeus Anglicus. *See* Bartholomaeus Anglicus
Bartolomeo di Capua, 11:274a
Bartolomeo, Michelozzo di. *See* Michelozzo di Bartolomeo
Bartolus. *See* Bartolo da Sassoferrato
Barton, John, compiler of *Donait françois,* 1:270b
Baruch ben Isaac, 7:105b
Bas-de-page, **2:117a**
Basarab I, Walachian voivode
Battle of Posada, 12:500b
Charles Robert and, 10:514b
Walachian territories, 12:500b
Basarab dynasty, 12:484b
Dąneşti and Drąculeşti factions, 12:502a
origins, 12:500b–501a
Basean, Vanand and, 12:353b, 354a
Basel, 11:543b
bishopric of, 11:538a
bridge damaged by floods, 10:416b
Henry III of Germany and, 11:538a
persecution of Jews during Black Death, 2:263b
"Rudolphians" in, 11:538a
see of, 11:537a
Swiss Confederation and, 11:542b, 545b
vs. Rudolph of Habsburg, 11:540a
Basel Cathedral, 10:106a
antependium, 10:106 (*illus.*)
nave organ, 9:274a (*illus.*)
Basel, Compacts of, 6:377a
Sigismund and, 11:287b
Basel, Council of (1431–1449), 10:331a
calling of, 10:24a
church taxation and, 11:610a
Communion under both kinds and, 3:505b
conflict with Eugenius IV, 3:652b–653a, 653b–654a
endorsement of *Frequens,* 4:378a
great powers and, 3:654a
Hussites and, 2:305a
manuscript book production and, 8:104b–105a
Metropolitan Isidore of Kiev at, 6:563a
negotiations with Greek church, 3:653a
Nicholas of Cusa and, 9:123a, 123b
Nicolaus de Tudeschis and, 9:129a
opening of, 3:366a
organization of, 3:651b–652a
Pragmatic Sanction of Bourges and, 10:69a
recommendations for calendar reform, 3:23a-b
reforms of, 3:652a-b
Rodríguez del Padrón and, 10:438b
split of, 10:24b
universality of, 9:124b
Basel, Peace of (1499), 11:544b–545b
Basel, University of, 12:288b–289a
via moderna and, 12:408a
Baselard, 11:550 (*illus.*)
Bashkent, Battle of (1473), 12:343a
Bashmouric Rebellion, 3:594b
Bashshār ibn Burd, 1:400b
Basian, Battle of (1203/1204), 11:587a
Basil, *History of Queen Tamar,* 5:417b–418a
Basil I (the Macedonian), Byzantine emperor, **2:118a**, 3:553a
Arsacids and, 1:481a
artistic patronage, 2:453b
Ašot I and, 1:480b
Bardas Caesar and, 2:106a-b
biographies of, 2:453b
Byzantine law and, 7:390b–391a
cultural developments under, 2:489b
destruction of the Paulician state and, 9:468a
Epanagoge and, 4:493a
as founder of the Macedonian dynasty, 8:2a
Ignatios and, 6:415b, 11:43b
in *Imperial Histories,* 5:382a
in legends and prophecies, 8:20a
Methodios and, 4:74a
Michael III and, 8:302a
Photios and, 6:406a
Samosata and, 4:512a
in *Theophanes continuatus,* 12:23a
tribute paid to Slavs, 4:2b
vs. Armenia, 1:483b
Basil II (Killer of Bulgars), Byzantine emperor, **2:118b–119b**, 11:189a
allelengyon, 1:189b, 11:604b
alliance with John Vladimir of Duklja, 11:170b
Armenia and, 1:483b–484a
artistic patronage, 2:442a
attempt to control *dunatoi,* 4:307a
Croatia and, 4:5b
David of Tao and, 4:113b, 5:406b
Gagik I of Armenia and, 5:338b–339a
Karin under, 7:215a
Menologion of, 8:274 (*illus.*)
Nikephoros II Phokas and, 9:132b
Ochrid and, 9:208b
origins of Varangian Guard, 12:359a
pressure on Caucasia, 7:586a-b
Samuil of Bulgaria and, 2:406b–407a, 490a, 10:645a
Senek^cerim-Yovhannēs Arcruni and, 1:484a
Sennacherib of Vaspurakan and, 12:362a
struggle for throne, 2:490b
Theophano and, 12:24a

Basil II (Killer of Bulgars), Byzantine emperor (*cont.*)
  title of girdled patrician and, 5:539b
  Vladimir I of Kievan Rus and, 7:248a
  see also Bardas Skleros; Macedonians
Basil (Bogomil teacher), burned at the stake, 2:295b
Basil (the Great) of Caesarea, St., **2:119b–122b**
  Ad adolescentes, 2:121a, 122a, 9:696b
  anaphora and, 1:516a-b
  Arianism and, 1:454a
  Ascetica, 2:120b, 121b, 122a
  Carmelites and, 3:96b
  commemorated, 2:122a
  confused with St. Nersēs I by P⊂awstos Buzand, 9:473a
  Contra Eunomium, 2:121a
  correspondence, 2:121a
  De baptismo, 2:120b
  De fide, 2:120b
  De judicio Dei, 2:120b
  De Spiritu Sancto, 2:120b, 121a
  Divine Liturgy, 1:507b, 2:121a, 122a
  as doctor of the church, 4:234a
  establishment of *Basileias,* 6:287b, 292b
  Greek eucharistic liturgy and, 7:610b
  Gregory of Nazianzus and, 5:666a
  Hexaemeron, 1:507b, 2:121a, 122a
  homilies, 2:121a, 122a
  influence of, 2:122a
  institutional monasticism, 6:213b
  issues addressed, 2:121b–122a
  liturgy of, Virgin Mary and, 12:460b
  monastic rule of, 8:456b, 461a
  Neoplatonism and, 9:98b
  nomocanon and, 9:158b
  Philokalia, 2:120b, 9:7a
  in poem by Hrotswitha, 6:315a
  preaching of, 10:350b
  on punishment of the innocent, 6:494b
  Regulae morales, 2:120b
  resolution of Nicene controversy and, 3:628b
  rule of in Studios Monastery, 11:495a
  Trinitarian thought and, 12:189b
  writings, 2:120b–121a
Basil of Ialimbana, 5:400a
Basil the Parakoimomenos, 2:118b
Basil (the Pilgrim), bishop, 9:653b
Basil (the Robber). *See* Goł Vasil
Basileia. See Genesios, Joseph
Basileia tōn Romaiōn, 2:484a
Basileus, **2:122b–123b,** 4:154a, 10:11a
  see also Autocrator; Theophano, Byzantine empress
Basiliada, 2:120a
Basilica, **2:123b–125a,** 2:124 (*illus.*)
  adaptation for religious use, 4:335a-b
  architectural revivals of
    Fulda, 10:306 (*illus.*)
    Monte Cassino, 10:309a
  architecture in Ravenna, 10:262b–264b
  Armenian, 1:493b
  at Fulda, 10:92b, 94a
  in Coptic architecture, 3:585b–586b
  disappearance of, 4:343a
  double-ended, 3:378b–379a
  early Christian
    Old St. Paul's, 10:309a
    Old St. Peter's, 10:306b, 309a
  early Christian decoration of, 4:358a-b
  in Georgian architecture, 5:408b
  Isidore of Seville's concept of, 5:586a
  practical design for church, 4:335b
  styles of, in 5th century, 4:337b
  three-nave, 5:408b
  see also Church architecture; Ereroyk⊂; Narthex; Nave
Basilica Constantina. *See* Lateran
Basilica of Constantine (Jerusalem), 9:657 (*illus.*)
Basilica Eufrasiana (Parenzo), apse decorations, 4:354b
Basilica Sancti Salvatoris (Rome)
  ordination ceremonies at, 3:602b–603a
  see also Lateran
Basilics, 2:117b, **2:125a-b**
  Synopsis major, 2:125b
  see also Leo VI (the Wise), Byzantine emperor
Basilika, inheritance in, 6:451b
Basilikon doron. See James I of England, king
Basilius (manuscript illuminator), 4:23a
Basilius (mosaicist), 4:24b
Basinet, 1:526a-b, 527 (*illus.*), 530a
Baṣīr, Joseph ben Abraham ha-Kohen ha-Ro'eh al-, 7:210b
Basīṭ, 8:566b
Basket capital. *See* Capital
Basler Alexander, 7:323a
Basmala, 7:295b
Basmenoye delo, **2:125b**
Basprakania. *See* Vaspurakan
Basprakania (Byzantine theme), 1:474a
Basprakania, katepanate of, 1:484a
  see also Berkri
Basque language, 3:141b, 6:434a, 435a, 442a, 442b
Basque law, 2:126b
Basques, **2:125b–127a,** 12:471a
  geography of Basque region, 2:125b–126a
  history, 2:126a-b
  Latin church among, 2:126a
  see also Navarre, kingdom of
Basra, **2:127a–128a**
  as a center of Kharijite movement, 11:138b–139a
  community of Ikhwān al-Ṣafā⊃ in, 9:4b
  demilitarized, 6:511b, 7:307a
  founded, 6:511a
  as Islamic center, 6:570a
  Ismailism in, 6:616a
  al-Kufa and, 7:306b, 307b
  maritime trade of, 6:512b
  sacked, 6:512b, 513a
  wealth of, 3:42a
  Zanj and, 12:739a
Bassa, Ferrer, **2:128a**
  frescoes of, 5:611b (*illus.*), 612a
  works in International Style, 5:627b
Baṣṣāl, Ibn al-, 6:558a
  on agricultural tools, 12:84b, 85a
  on grafting fruit trees, 12:85b
  on rice husking, 12:85b
Bassām, Ibn, on the Cid, 3:386a-b
Basse lisse. See Looms, low-warp
Basse-Auvergne, provincial estates and assemblies, 10:326a
Basse-Navarre, 2:126b
Bassedanse, 4:87b (*illus.*), 88b–89b
Basset, Thomas, *Defense Against Detractors of Richard Rolle,* 9:20b
Bassora(h). *See* Basra
"Bastard sword grip." *See* Swords, grips
Bastards. *See* Children, illegitimate
Bastide, **2:128a–129b,** 12:324a-b
  growth of Toulouse and, 12:90b
  Provençal, 2:129b
  villages and, 12:444b
Bastille, building of, 9:406a
Bastions, description of, 3:152a
Bastoche, theatrical productions by, 4:266a
Baston, Robert, 7:370a
Baston-course, 5:349b
  armor for, 1:533a
Baszko, Godisław, *Chronica Poloniae Maioris,* 9:723a-b
Bat (animal), in literature, 6:655a
Bata. *See* Aelfric Bata
Baṭā⊃iḥ, 6:509b
Bataille d'Aliscans, La, 12:678b
Bataille (military unit), 3:204a
Bataille, Nicholas, **2:129b–130a**
  Apocalypse and, 11:596a
Bataille des sept arts, La. See Henri d'Andeli
Batalha (monastery), tomb of Philippa of Lancaster, 8:585a (*illus.*)
Batarde (script), 7:601b
Bate, Henry. *See* Henry Bate of Malines
Bath, Order of the, 3:307a
Baths, Umayyad, 6:594b–595b (*illus.*)
Bāṭin, 6:586b, 617b
Battānī, al-, 9:704b
  astronomical tables of, 11:91a
  influence on Maimonides, 11:90b
  Toledan Tables and, 12:67a
Battering ram and cat, 3:146b, 148a, 149 (*illus.*)
Battle Abbey (Senlac), 11:657b
Battle ax. *See* Ax
Battle of the Books, as literary genre, 5:255a
Battle of Brunanburh, The 1:278b
  Tennyson's translation of, 1:287b
Battle, judicial. *See* Judicial combat
Battle of Maldon, The, 8:327a
  compared to *Bjarkamál,* 2:254b
  metrical rules of, 1:277a
  text from, 1:279a
Battle of San Romano, The. See Uccello, Paolo
Battle of the Seven Arts. See Henri d'Andeli, *Bataille des sept arts*
Battre, H., music by in Trent codices, 12:183a
Baṭṭūṭa, Ibn, 1:382a, **2:130a–131a,** 5:653a
  akhīs and, 11:309a
  on al-Baḥrayn, 2:50b, 51a
  on Basra, 2:127b

on the Bulgars, 5:333a
on Caesarea, 3:9b
on Erzincan and Karin, 12:99a
kamkhā production, 7:207b
in Kilwa, 12:740a
on al-Kufa, 7:308a
on Mecca, 8:240b
on the Nile, 9:138a
on Nisibis, 9:142a
Riḥla, 2:130a, 130b–131a
edited by Ibn Juzayy, 9:651b
on Timbuktu, 12:55a
travels of, 5:393b
Batu, **2:131a-b,** 5:572b
alliance against, 8:470b
appanage, 8:469a
conquests of, 2:131b
Golden Horde, 8:471b
territory under control, 8:471b
vs. Hungary, 6:342a
Batuids, vs. Ilkhanids, 6:420a
Batyi. *See* Batu
Baucis et Thraso, 7:367b
Baude Cordier, 8:587a
Baude Fastoul, 3:536b
Baudoin de Condé, court lyrics, 9:637a
Baudouin de Lannoy, in art, 4:567b
Baudri of Bourgueil, **2:132a,** 7:364a, 367b
Historia Hierosolimitana, 2:132a
hymns of, 6:382a
imitation of Ovidian epistles, 9:313a, 440a
Itinerarium, 2:132a
poem for William the Conqueror's daughter Adèle, 8:255b
on Robert d'Arbrissel, 10:429b
Baudri of Dol, 5:514b
Baudricourt, Robert de, 7:114b
Bauernhochzeit, Die, **2:132a-b**
Baugulf of Fulda, abbot, 5:311b
Baumgarten geistlicher Herzen, 8:354b
Bava de-maruta, exilarch and, 4:552b
Bavaria, **2:132b–135b,** 2:133 (map)
duchy of, 5:474b
Eastern March, 2:134b
Latin church in, 2:134a
Otto I the Great in, 5:575a-b
stem duchies in, 5:506b–507b
under Wittelsbachs, 12:665a
see also Austria
Bavaria-Straubing (duchy), founded, 2:135a
Bavarian language, 6:437a
Bavarian law, *Schwabenspiegel* and, 11:80b
Bavarians, 2:94b–95a
first mentioned by Jordanes, 2:94b
settlement of in the Danube valley, 2:4b
vs. Alamanni, 11:526a
Bavo, St., 5:521a
Bawit, sculptures from, 3:587b (*illus.*), 588a
Bawwāb, Ibn al-, **2:135b–136a**
Islamic calligraphy and, 3:54b, 6:606b
reforms of Arabic script, 9:65a
Bay system, 2:125a, **2:139b**
in Gothic architecture, 5:596b
pre-Romanesque, 10:477b
as Romanesque distinction, 10:475b
Speyer Cathedral, 10:487b–488a
see also Alternation; Vault
Bayʿa, 3:33a
under Abbasids, 3:42a
under Umayyads, 3:39a
Bayāḍ wa Riyāḍ, nāʿūra, 9:67b (*illus.*), 67a
Bayān wa 'l-tabyīn, Al-. See Jāḥiẓ, Abū ʿUthmān ʿAmr ibn Baḥr al-
Bāyazīd I Yildirim, Ottoman sultan, **2:136a-b,** 7:214a
Battle on Kosovo Pole and, 11:181a
Byzantine campaigns, 2:502b
siege of Constantinople, 2:503a
conquest of Anatolia, 1:242a
Ikonion and, 6:418b
Manuel II Palaiologos and, 8:92a
military campaigns, Eastern Europe, 9:307a
royal titles, *Sultan al-Rūm,* 9:308b
Stefan Lazareviç of Serbia and, 11:472b
vassalage of Balkan princes, 2:503a
vs. crusaders, 9:129b
vs. Tamerlane, 2:503a, 11:588a
see also Mehmed I, Ottoman sultan; Selim I
Bāyazīd II, Ottoman sultan, **2:137a-b**
capture of Chilia and Cetatea Albà, 12:503b
Baybars I (the Panther), Mamluk sultan, 1:524b
Baybars II, sultan (early 14th cent.), deposed, 3:398b
Baybars al-Bunduqdārī, Mamluk sultan, **2:138a-b,** 3:399b, 8:73b–74a
al-Azhar and, 2:27b
Islamic postal service and, 10:61a
Ismailism and, 6:618a
al-Lādhiqiya and, 7:315b
Mongol conflict
alliance with Hülegü, 8:473b
battle at ʿAyn Jālūt (1260), 8:473b
relationship with al-Manṣūr Qalāʾūn, 10:224b–225a
Seljuks of Rum and, 11:158a
tomb of, 6:607b
Baybarsīya (Sufi convent: Egypt), 11:520b, 521a
Bayḍāwī, al-, *Lights of the Revelation,* 7:297a
Bayerische Chronik. See Ulrich Füetrer
Bayeux Tapestry, 1:273b, **2:139a,** 11:591a
detail, 2:0 (frontispiece)
examples of
armor, 1:523a
chasuble, 12:400a-b
European cavalry, 3:202b, 6:111b (*illus.*)
hair styles, 2:149b
horse harrowing, 1:93b
wheeled plow, 12:77a
whippletree, 12:372a
Romanesque art and, 10:508b
Baylakān, **2:139a-b**
see also Pʿaytakaran
Bayonne, seal of (1298), 11:128a (*illus.*)
Bayrūt. *See* Beirut
Baysān, conquered, 6:568a
Baysunghur (brother of Ulugh-Beg), 12:57b, 59a
Bayt, **2:140a**
in *muwashshaḥ,* 11:446b
see also Riwāq
Bayt al-Ḥikma, 6:512a, 8:566a, 11:84b, 12:128a-b
scholarship under Abbasids, 3:45a
translation of Greek scientific treatises into Arabic, 11:82b
see also Maʾmūn, al-, Abbasid caliph
Bayṭār, Ibn al-, pharmacological writings, 6:179a, 185b
Bazaar
of Isfahan, 6:562a-b
sūq and, 11:514a
Bazzazistan. See Bedestan
Bdešχ, **2:140a-b**
Be kanishta. See Synagogue
Beakers, 5:554a–555a (*illus.*), 557a–558b
Bear, in *Schrätel und der Wasserbär,* 11:79a
Bearbaiting, 5:350b
Beard. *See* Hair
Béarn
Abrégé des États, 10:327a
villages of, 12:443b–444a
"Bear's Son Tale," 2:184b
Beast canon table. *See* Canon table
Beast epic, **2:140b–142b**
Archpoet's "Confession" and, 1:450a
Dutch, 2:141b–142a
German, 2:141b, 142a
Renard the Fox, 10:312a–315a
Van den Vos Reinaerde, 4:319a
wolf-fox antagonism, 4:369a-b
see also Bestiary; *Ecbasis captivi;* Renard the Fox
Beast fables. *See* Animals, in fables
Beatific vision, in Islam, Muʿtazilite beliefs, 6:583a, 583b
Beatification, **2:142b–143a**
see also Canonization
Beatrice of Burgundy, 11:539a
Beatrice of Castile, 10:46b
Beatrice (daughter of Guigues V), Dauphiné and, 4:109a
Beatrice d'Este, Matthias Corvinus and, 6:348b
Beatrice (*Divine Comedy* character), 4:94b, 96a–97a, 101a, 6:647a, 648a
Beatrijs, 4:320a
Beatrijs van Nazareth, 2:161a, 9:11b, 12a
Van zeven manieren van heiliger minnen, 2:160b, 4:319a-b
Beatritz. *See* Comtessa de Dia
Beatrix (daughter of Philip of Swabia), 12:672b, 673a
Beatrix (wife of Frederick I Barbarossa), 5:480a
Beatus commentaries. *See* Emeterius of Tábara
Beatus of Liébana, 10:114a
Commentary on the Apocalypse, 2:143b, 10:115b (*illus.*), 11:406a
decorated letters in, 6:462b
depiction of Heavenly Jerusalem in, 6:125a-b

Beatus of Liébana (*cont.*)
map of, 4:553b
see also Beatus manuscripts
Beatus manuscripts, **2:143b**, 8:54a (*illus.*), 107b, 10:508b
Dominicus (scribe), 4:255b
illustrations, 4:450b (*illus.*), 8:513a-b, 9:44b, 10:115b (*illus.*), 11:657b (*illus.*)
Last Judgment, 8:513b
influence on Iberian world, 8:513a
Obeco and, 9:208a-b
see also Maius
Beaucaire, 7:339a
fairs of, 7:341b
Beaufort, Edmund, duke of Somerset, 12:570a, 570b
conflict with Richard of York, 12:570a
council of Leicester, 12:570a-b
Beaufort, Margaret (mother of Henry VII of England), 9:434b
Wynkyn de Worde and, 12:712a
Beaugency, bridge, 10:416b, 418b
Beaujeu, Anne and Pierre de, regency of, 5:189b
Beaujeu, Guillaume de, 3:304b
Beaujeus, French representative assemblies and the, 10:323a-b
Beaumanoir, Girard de, 2:144a
Beaumanoir, Marguerite, 2:144a
Beaumanoir, Philippe de, **2:143b–145a**, 7:458a–459b
Coutumes de Beauvaisis, 2:144a–145a, **3:674b–675a,** 7:458a
on the classification of roads, 10:412b, 413a
Corpus iuris civilis and, 7:423a
on transport of goods, 12:375a
on inquests, 6:479b
Jehan et Blonde, 2:145a
Manekine, 2:145a
see also French law, in north
Beaumont-en-Argonne, charter of, 3:500b, 12:440a
Beaumont-le-Roger, population, 4:141b
Beaune, wine trade, 12:650a, 650b, 651a, 654a
Beauneveu, André, **2:145a-b**, 5:627b, 7:52b, 8:109b
Beauty aids, **2:145b–150b**
cosmetic preparations, 2:146b–149a
evidence for, 2:146a-b
mechanical devices, 2:149a–150b
Trotula minor treatises on cosmetics, 12:214a-b
Beauvais
church at, Speyer Cathedral and, 10:487b
self-governing commune, 3:496a-b
Beauvais, School of, 9:705b–706a
Beauvaisis, Jacquerie atrocities in, 7:36b
Beaver
described by Albertus Magnus, 2:244a
etymology of name, 2:204b–205a
in medieval bestiaries, 2:243a
Bebo of Bamberg, **2:150b–151a**
Beccari, Antonio, 6:653a-b
Bechin Castle, 5:597 (*illus.*), 601a
Becket prophecy, 8:320a
Becket, Thomas, St., **2:151a–153a**
clerical rights and, 3:409a, 410a
compared with St. Stanislaus of Poland, 10:371a
episcopate of, 2:151a, 3:83a
John of Salisbury and, 7:139b
Latin and French lives of, 1:261a
by Guernes de Pont-Ste.-Maxence, 2:236a
murder of, 2:152b, 9:518a
in literature, 7:364b, 367a
as martyrdom, 8:159b
Nigel of Longchamp and, 9:131a
Office of in Sarum use, 12:70b
oil of the Virgin, 4:475b, 476b
personality, 2:151a-b, 152b–153a
pilgrimage to Canterbury and, 12:156a-b
relations with Henry II, 6:157b
rhymed offices to, 10:367a, 368a-b
distribution of, 10:369b, 370b–371a
in English manuscripts, 10:371a
Robert of Melun and, 10:434b
support of church authority, 4:471a
Thómas saga erkibiskups and, 4:311b
translation date commemoration, 12:145a
see also Thómas saga erkibyskups; Vie de St. Thomas Becket
Beckingham, Elias, 7:188a-b
Bede, **2:153a–156a**, 3:7b–8a
on Aidan of Lindisfarne, 1:107a
on Ambrosius Aurelianus, 2:2b–3a
analysis of Ambrosian hymns, 10:379a
on Anglo-Saxons, 2:96b
as elect of God, 6:262a
political history, 1:289a, 4:454b
their conversion to Christianity, 4:458
on astrology, 1:606a-b
on astronomy, 1:610b
on Augustine of Canterbury, 1:645a-b
as author of alphabetic acrostics, 1:218a
Benedict Biscop and, 2:168a
biblical exegesis, 2:212b
on Cædmon, 1:277b
calendar reckoning, 3:19b
dating of Easter, 3:228b
use of *annus Domini,* 6:259a
on Canterbury, 3:81b
Carmina vulgarium poetarium, 8:572a
classical literary studies and, 3:432b
on Clonard, 3:465b
collection of riddles wrongly attributed to, 10:398a
computation, finger reckoning, 8:206a
on Dál Riata, 4:78a
De arte metrica, 2:154b
De computo vel loquela digitorum, 8:206a
De locis sanctis, 2:154b
De natura rerum, 2:154b, 4:448a
De orthographia, 2:154b
De sex aetatibus mundi, 2:155b, 11:215a
De temporibus, 2:154b
De temporum ratione, 1:606a, 610b, 6:259a
Death Song, 1:276a
as doctor of the church, 4:234b
Ecclesiastical History of the English Church and People, 2:155a-b, 6:259a, 262b, 7:362a
appendix, 2:153a-b
Brut and, 2:393a
dating of, 1:275b
preface, 2:154a
source for Celtic church history, 3:480a, 485a, 485b
translation into Old English, 1:165a, 165b, 166b, 284a
visions and, 12:475b
education of, 2:153b–154a
as exegete, 4:542b, 547b–548a, 548b, 9:585a
first historical martyrology, 6:65b, 8:162a
on French monasteries, 12:683a
on Hiberno-Saxon saints, 6:67a
History of the Abbots of Wearmouth and Jarrow, 2:155a, 6:262b
as hymnodist, 9:713b
Latin hymn on Judgment Day, 1:254a
influence on Christology, 3:321a
influence of, 2:155b–156a
kingship theories of, 7:260a
Latin treatise on tropes and figures, 10:352b
Life of St. Cuthbert, 10:108a
miniature with an inhabited scroll, 11:119 (*illus.*)
on London, 7:658a-b
Manfredi carmina and, 8:83b
on millennialism, 8:386a-b, 12:723a
on Ninian, 9:139a
Ormulum and, 4:546a
as paradigm, 2:174a
Paris Psalter and, 4:549a
Penitential of, 9:489a, 489b
on portable altars, 1:225a
recommendation to study Vergil, 12:394a
relics of, 2:156a
Robert Mannyng and, 8:87a
scientific work of, 1:285b
Vulgate and, 12:495b
writings of, 2:154a–155b
Bede/Egbert, Double Penitential of, 9:490a, 490b, 491a
Bedestan, **2:156a–157a**
see also Hān
Bedford Master, 5:615b
Bedlam, **2:157a-b**, 6:490b
Bedouins
in al-Akhṭal poetry, 1:115b
Arabic language and, 1:377a
in al-Baḥrayn, 2:51a
beverages of, 2:208b
Hafsids and, 6:415a
influence on Islamic furniture, 5:315b
in Iraq, 6:511a, 513a, 514a
Mamluks and, 9:198b
plagues and, 9:686a
vs. Muslims, under Muḥammad, 6:577b
vs. Zirids, in Barca, 12:744b
Yarmuk and, 12:719b
Beds

in Islamic furniture, 5:315a-b
in Western European furniture, 5:323a
Bedthegn. See Chamberlain, England, Anglo-Saxon
Bedüün Noyan, conquest of Kurdistan, 8:470a
Bee
praise of in Easter liturgy, 2:177b–178a
see also Apiculture; Honey
Beer. *See* Brewing
Beg domain. *See* Atabeg
Beggars. *See* Migration; Penance; Pilgrimage
Beghards. *See* Beguines and beghards
Begtimur of Xlat^{c}, ruler, 11:220a
Bégudes. See Provence, inns in
Beguinage, 2:158a
Beguines and beghards, **2:157b–162a**
beghard, etymology, 2:159a
beguine, etymology, 2:158b–159a
erection of hospitals, 6:294a
in France, 5:175b
in Germany, 2:160a, 5:216b–217a, 217b–218a
inquisition and, 6:488a
legislation concerning, 2:159b
living arrangements of, 2:158a
Low Countries, 2:160a
Mary of Oignies, 7:39b
mysticism of, 6:198b–199a
occupations of, 2:160a
prosecution of, 5:218a
in Ruusbroec's work, 9:37a
synodal decree of 1306, 5:217b
Tauler and, 9:34a
tenets of, Council of Vienne, 5:216a
see also Mechthild von Magdeburg; Pikarts
Beguins, **2:162a–163b**
Behaim, Martin, terrestrial globe of, 11:96a
Behistun, relief of Mihrdāt II, 9:443b
Being, theories of. *See* Essence and existence; Realism
Beirdd y tywysogion. See Gogynfeirdd
Beirdd yr uchelwyrf, in Welsh literature, 12:606a
Beirut, **2:163b–164b**
as bastion of Sunnism, 7:532a
Jean d'Ibelin and, 6:389a, 389b
merchant colonies in, 7:533a
siege of (1230), 6:389b
silk cloth and jewelry manufactured in, 12:100b
spice trade and, 7:533a
Bek, Thomas, of Castleford, 5:389b
Bek^{c}a Opizari, **2:164b**
Bekhor Shor, Joseph, as exegete, 2:212b
Bektashīs (dervish order), 11:158b
"Bekynton Anthology," 1:319a-b
Bel inconnu, Le. See Renaut de Beaujeu
Bel, Jean le, *Chronique,* 3:333a
Béla I of Hungary, king, 6:340a
Béla II of Hungary, king, royal household and, 6:340b
Béla III of Hungary, king, 6:341a
crown of St. Stephen and, 11:483a
Béla IV of Hungary, king, 6:342a
Vlachs and, 12:483b
Belbello da Pavia, works in International Style, 5:628a
Belcari, Feo, 6:636b
Belém, church at, 5:630a
Belgrade
crusaders' route and, 10:422b
fall of (1521), 6:349b–350a
Hungary and, 6:346b, 347b
siege of (1456), 6:364a, 7:124a
Belisarios, **2:165a,** 7:201a-b, 10:262a
conflict with Narses, 9:292a
defeat of Vandals, 12:355b
lagoons of Venice and, 12:383b–384a
occupation of Rome, 9:292a
Ostrogoths and, 7:2b, 9:292a-b
portrayal by Procopius, 10:134a, 135a
Theodora I and, 12:12a
in Theophanes Confessor's *Chronographia,* 12:22b
use of bridges, 10:411b
victory over Vandals (530), 2:91b
vs. Mundhir III, 7:320b
Belisarios, style and language, 2:523a
Bell ringers, 2:166b
Bell tower. *See* Campanile; Cupola
Bell Tower of Ivan the Great (Kremlin), 8:497b
Bella parisiacae urbis. See Adbo of St. Germain-des-Prés
Bellarmine, Robert, St., as doctor of the church, 4:234b
Bellator, 7:277a
Belle dame sans merci, La. See Chartier, Alain
Bellême family, 9:164b
Bellerman Anonymous, 11:362b
Belles heures. See Limbourg brothers
Belleville Breviary, 2:371a (*illus.*), 5:614b, 8:109a-b
Bellica tuba, 8:558b
Bellicorum instrumentorum liber. See Giovanni de Fontana
Bellifortis. See Kyeser, Konrad
Bellin, George, author of Chester Plays MS, 3:299a
Bellini, Gentile, 2:165a
Bellini, Giovanni, 2:165a
Bellini, Jacopo, **2:165a-b**
sketchbook of, 4:292a
Bellows, illustrations of in carvings and manuscripts, 8:296b
Bells, **2:165b–167a,** 8:606a
altar, 1:225a
Angelus, 2:166a
bronze and brass, 2:384b
casting of, 2:166a, 8:289a-b, 12:24b
chime, 8:606a
church, 1:225a, 5:320b–321a
consecrated to saints, 2:166a
jingle, 8:562b
Middle Eastern, 8:613b
in reckoning of time, 3:28b
see also Campanulae pro melodia; Steelmaking; Tower
Bellum Avaricum. See George of Pisidia
Bellum civile, Ly hystore de Julius Cesar. See Jean de Thuim of Hainaut
Bellum Iugurthinum. See Sallust
Bellum Troianum. See Joseph Iscanus
Belorussian language, 11:342b
Belos, ban, Bosnia and, 6:340b
Belt (sword). *See* Swords
Belted knights. *See* Knights
Beltram II, magister of Humiliati, 12:687a
Belvoir Castle, 4:24b
Bema, **2:167a**
Ravenna, S. Vitale, 10:264 (*illus.*)
solea and, 11:360b
see also Bimah; Chancel; Naos; Pastophory
Bembo, Bonifacio, International Style of, 5:628a
Ben Sira (Sirach, pseudo-Ecclesiasticus), *Alphabet of Ben Sira,* 8:23a, 9:579a
Benabila, 1:515a
Benaton (unit of measure), 12:587a
Benavente, Alfonso de, *Ars et doctrina studendi et docendi,* 11:441a
Benches, 5:323a
Benci, Tommaso, 6:636b
Bencivene de la Chitarra. *See* Cenne de la Chitarra
Benckels, Willem, "invention" of salted herring, 10:630b
Bene of Florence, 4:174b
Benedetti, Giovanni Battista, 1:438a
Benedetto Antelami, **2:167a,** 10:502a
Benedetto di S. Andrea, *Cronaca,* 6:638a
Benedicamus Domino, **2:167b–168a,** 3:532a-b
assignment to feasts, 10:619a
double-texted, 10:619a
musical notation, 10:619a
polyphonic settings, 10:618b, 619a
tropes, 6:381b
Benedict II, pope, Julianus of Toledo and, 7:181b
Benedict III, pope, Nicholas I and, 9:120b
Benedict VIII, pope, 3:677a
Bebo on, 2:150b
Normans and, 11:264a
Rodolph of Tosny and, 11:263b
Benedict IX, pope
reign of, 11:517b
Synod of Sutri and, 11:517a
Benedict XI, pope, 3:643b
Arnald of Villanova and, 1:537b–538a
Dante and, 4:99a-b
reign of, 3:362a
Benedict XII, pope
church union with Byzantium and, 2:109b
constitutions for Franciscan friars, 5:204a
curial staff of, 3:364a
Dauphiné and, 4:109a, 110a
inquisition and, 6:487b–488a
reorganization of monasteries, 3:377a
simple life of, 3:363a
Benedict XIII, antipope, 3:646a, 649a
election of, 3:365b
Gregory XII and, 5:512b
Jews and, 7:79a
Libro de las consolaciones de la vida humana, 11:418b, 456a
Nicholas of Clamanges and, 9:122b

Benedict XIII, antipope (*cont.*)
refusal to abdicate, 11:40b, 41b
Spanish and Scottish support for, 11:42a
surviving sermon of, 11:420a
Vincent Ferrer and, 12:452a-b, 453a
Benedict XIV, pope, Lateran and, 7:344b
Benedict of Aniane, **2:168a-b**, 2:170b, 8:638b
adviser to Louis, Carolingian emperor, 3:111b
church reform efforts, 3:347b
Gregorian sacramentary, 2:178a-b, 10:605b–606a
idea of monastic reform and, 10:285b–286b
liturgy and, 2:172b
Narbonne rite and, 9:62b
Office of the Dead and, 4:117b
order of Cluny and, 3:468b
women's orders and, 12:683b
Benedict Biscop, St., 2:153b, 155a, **2:168a**, 5:555b, 7:584b
Saxon church construction, 10:679b
Wearmouth and Yarrow, 10:680b
Benedict (canon of St. Peter's), *Mirabilia urbis Romae* and, 10:520b
Benedict the Deacon (Levite). *See* Benedictus Levita
Benedict of Nursia, St., **2:168b–171a**
in art, 2:170b–171a
canticles and, 3:84b
cenobitic monasticism and, 10:285a–286a
Coptic influences on Rule of, 3:595a
cult of, 2:170b
on eremitic life, 6:213b
library development and, 7:560a
monastic houses, 8:462a
monastic Office of, 4:229b–230a
Rule of the Master and, 3:343a
schools and, 2:173b
training of monks, 11:74b
Benedict of Peterborough, abbot
passio of St. Thomas Becket, 12:35b, 36a
rhymed office to St. Thomas Becket, 10:367a, 369b
Benedict the Pole, 7:138a-b
Benedict of St. Peter and St. Paul Monastery, abbot, Bede and, 2:153b
Benedictine church plan. *See* Church architecture, echelon apse
Benedictine Rule, **2:171a-b**, 8:462a, 12:682b
architectural precepts, 8:455a
at Fontevrault, 12:686b
Benedict of Aniane and, 2:168a
Camaldolese order and, 3:56a
canonical hours and, 3:67a
Cistercians and, 3:402a, 403a, 404b, 406a-b
Cluniac order and, 3:468b
compline and, 4:229a
conformity to, 3:347b
Divine Office and, 4:222a
English translations, 4:518a
in the Fontevrault order, 10:430b
in Frankish monasteries, 12:683a
Gregory the Great on, 2:169a
Humiliati and, 12:687a
influence on monastic orders, 8:462a
influence on Western technology, 11:643a, 652b
Institutio sanctimonialium and, 12:683b
interpretation of, 8:481a
on Kyrie eleison, 7:591a
matins and, 4:228b
Office of the Dead in, 4:117b
Order of Aviz and, 2:17a
Regula monachorum and, 6:565a
St. Bernard of Clairvaux and, 2:191a
Smaragdus of St. Mihiel on, 11:351a
sources, 2:170b, 171a-b
translation into Old English, 1:286a-b
attributed to Ethelwold, 1:281b
written in West Saxon dialect, 1:276b
travel discouraged by, 12:152a
Treaty of Verdun and, 12:684a
Wulfstan of York and, 12:704a
see also Fasting, Christian
Benedictines, **2:171b–176b**, 9:663b
Ambrosian hymns of, 9:713a-b
in Bavaria, 2:134a
bells and, 2:165b–166a
birth of sigillography and, 11:130a
Carthusian rule and, 3:118a, 118b
as chapter of cathedral canons, 3:375a
chronicles of, 3:326a
by Jocelin of Brakelond, 7:116a
decline of, 2:174b, 175a-b
in England, 2:175b
preservation of medieval spiritual texts and, 9:27b
foot washing and, 5:41b–42a
glassmaking, 5:556a
in Hungary, under St. Stephen I, 11:479a
idea of monastic reform and, 10:285b–286b
income of, 2:174b
lay brothers, 12:639a
manuscript book production, 8:102b
recruits of, 2:173a, 175b
rhymed offices and, 10:370b
Sapaudian foundations, 10:675a-b
in Scotland, 11:105a
self-sufficiency of, 2:172b–173a
Solesmes method of Gregorian chant, 5:663b–664a
survival of philosophy in monasteries, 9:587a
technological innovations and, 11:651b
under Lombards, 12:682b
Utrecht, 10:245b
vs. Wyclif, 12:706b
Welsh monasticism and, 12:517a
see also Fasting, Christian; Paschasius Radbertus of Corbie, St.
Benedictional, **2:176b–177a**, 2:176b (*illus.*)
see also Pontifical
Benedictions, **2:177a–178b**
episcopal, 2:178a
Jewish, 7:619a-b, 620a
see also Tones, reading and dialogue
Benedictus Levita, **2:178b–179a**
forged capitularies of, 4:125a
kingship theories of, 7:260b–261a
Benediktbeuern (monastery), 3:97b
Benediktbeuern Passion, 4:267a, 281b
Benefice
charistikion, 3:268a
ecclesiastical, **2:179a-b**, 9:715b, 730a, 11:674b
chaplain, 3:264a-b
Innocent IV and, 6:466a, 467a
inquest and, 6:481b
for military service, 12:558a
organization of Latin church and, 3:377a-b
praemunire and, 10:67b–68b
Pragmatic Sanction of Bourges and, 10:69a-b
taxation of, 11:606a-b
travel to obtain, 12:160a, 161b
see also Parish; Provisions, ecclesiastical
lay, **2:179b–180a,** 11:674b
for military service, 12:558a
missi dominici, 8:437b–438b
praemunire and, 10:67b–68b
Pragmatic Sanction of Bourges and, 10:69a-b
see also Fief
military, Frankish, 12:558a
Spain, 12:563a
Beneit of St. Albans, *Vie de Saint Thomas Becket,* 12:35b, 414a
Beneventan minuscule, 9:344a (*illus.*)
Beneventan rite, **2:180a–181a**
sources, 2:180b–181a
Benevento, Troia Cathedral, bronze doors, 8:285b
Benevento, Battle of (1053), 11:265a, 279b
Benevento, Battle of (1266), 4:60b, 95b, 9:59a
Benevento, Council of (1091), 2:178a
Beneventua of Friuli, 9:14a
Beneventum, triens of, 8:428a
Bénézet, St.
bridge at Avignon and, 10:416b, 419b
bridge-building brotherhood at Avignon and, 10:413b
devil as a bridge destroyer and, 10:410b
Benini, Matteo, 6:472b
Benintendi dei Ravignani, chancellor of Doge Andrea Dandolo, 12:392a
Benjamin ben Moses al-Nahāwendī, 4:539a
Benjamin of Tudela, **2:181b**, 7:83b, 105b, 108b, 10:119a
on al-Baḥrayn, 2:51a
on Constantinople and Baghdad, 12:102a-b
description of Barcelona, 2:103b
Ibn Baṭṭūṭa and, 2:130a
on Jewish dyers in Jerusalem, 4:328a
on the Nile, 9:138a
Sefer massao't, 2:181b
Benne (unit of measure), 12:587a
Benno of Osnabrück, **2:182a**
Beno de Rapiza (11th-century Roman butcher), 10:504b

Benoît, life of St. Thomas Becket, 1:261b
Benoît of Marseilles, bishop, on sorcery as heresy, 8:30b
Benoît de Sainte-Maure, **2:182a**
  Chronique des ducs de Normandie, 2:182a, 3:331a
  Roman de Troie, 2:182a, 5:243a, 455b, 7:290a, 8:225b, 11:258b, 12:496b
    recasting in Picard codex, 5:255b
    reinterpretation, 6:182b
    reworkings and translations of, 12:220b–221a
    reworkings and translations of, Byzantine, 12:127a
    as a source for Boccaccio's *Filostrato,* 2:279a
    sources of, 12:219b–220a
    Spanish romances and, 11:416b, 457b
    story of, 12:219–220b (*illus.*)
Bentivenga of Gubbio, "Spirit of Liberty" and, 5:217b
Benvenuto da Imola, 2:289a
Benzo of Alba, **2:182a-b**
Beograd, Stefan Lazareviç of Serbia and, 11:182a
Beowulf, 1:274b, 278a, **2:182b–185b,** 6:445a
  alliteration in, 8:327a, 342b
  dating of, 1:275b, 2:184a-b
  flyting in, 9:173b, 175a
  Grettir and, 4:615b
  modern criticism of, 2:183b–184a
  Nibelungenlied and, 9:112a
  19th-century edition of, 1:287a
  opening lines of, 8:310a-b
  overlord's throne in, 5:321b
  Sinfjǫtli in, 11:310a
  Skjǫldungs and, 6:311a-b
  sources, 2:184a
  textual analysis of, 1:276b, 277a
  West Saxon modifications of, 6:439b
  Ynglingatal and, 12:726a
Bequests
  Islamic, 6:452b–453a
  see also Charitable bequests
Berakhot, 7:619a-b
Berber language, 2:186a, 186b
Berbers, **2:185b–186b**
  attacked by ᶜAmr ibn al-ᶜĀṣ, 1:237b
  cavalry of, 3:208b–209a
  defeat of Kulthūm ibn ᶜIyāḍ, 12:552a
  in Ifrīqiya, 6:414a, 414b
  invasions of
    Mudejars and, 11:377a
    North Africa, 6:232b
  Kharijite sects and, 11:139a-b
  Kutāma, 2:186a
  Meknes and, 8:267b
  Muḥammad ibn Tūmart and, 1:193b
  revolts of, 12:722a
  rule of Fēs, 5:50b–51b
  Ṣanhāja, 2:185b, 186a
  in Sicily, 11:262a
  in Spain, villages, 12:443a
  in Syria, 11:561a
  Timbuktu and, 12:55b
  Twelver Shiism and, 11:137a
  vs. Muslims, 6:572a
  see also Awrāba Berbers; Kutāma Berbers; Maghrib, al-
Berceo, Gonzalo de, **2:186b–188a,** 8:282b, 11:456b
  attribution of *Libro de Alexandre* to, 11:412b
  doctrinal works, 11:412b, 413a
  Duelo de la Virgen, 2:187b
  ¡Eya velar!, 11:458b
  hagiographic works, 11:412b–413a, 433a
  Loores de Nuestra Señora, 2:187a-b
  Marian poems, 11:412b, 413a
  Martirio de San Lorenzo 2:188a, 11:439a
  mester de clerecía and, 8:281b
  Milagros de Nuestra Señora, 2:187b, 11:413a
  religious lyrics, 11:449b
  Sacrificio de la Misa, 2:187a
  Signos del Juicio Final, 2:187a
  Vida de San Millán de la Cogolla, 2:186b–187a, 11:412b, 439a
  Vida de Santa Oria, 2:187b–188a, 11:439a
  Vida de Santo Domingo de Silos, 2:187a, 11:439a
  visions and, 12:477a
Berchán's Prophecy, 7:229b
Berchem, Louis de, 5:381a
Berchorius, Petrus. *See* Bersuire, Pierre
Berchtesgaden, saltworks, struggle for control of, 10:630a
Berdiche, 7:324 (*illus.*), 325a
Bereford, William, 7:190a-b
Berengar I of Friuli, Frankish king of Italy
  seal wax impression of, 11:125a
  vs. Arnulf, 6:338a
Berengar II, Frankish king of Italy, 5:476a
  Genoa charter of (958), 5:383b
Berengar of Tours, **2:188a-b,** 3:634b, 635a
  controversy on the Eucharist, 7:630b
    on transubstantiation, 6:194a, 9:587b
  De sacra coena, 2:188a
  Eusebius Bruno and, 4:523b
  as exegete, 2:213a, 4:543a
  John Wyclif and, 12:710a
  Leo IX and, 7:543b
  vs. Humbert of Silva Candida, 6:330a
  vs. Lanfranc of Bec, 7:328b
Berengaria (wife of Richard I the Lionhearted), 10:383b
Berengarii imperatoris gesta, **2:188b,** 4:496a, 7:363b
Berenguela of León, queen, 2:270b
  marriage to Alfonso IX, 3:77a
  rule of Castile, 3:133b
Berenguer de Entenza, 1:191a
Berenguer Oller, revolt of (1285), 2:104a
Berenguer de Palol, 3:164b
Berenguer Ramon II of Catalonia, count, 3:177b–178a
Berenguer Ramon of Provence, 10:255b
Bergbüchlein, 4:579b
Bergen
  commerce, 9:181a
  Hanseatic merchants and, 9:185a
  population, 9:184b
  runic sticks, 10:567a
Bergen op Zoom, fairs, 4:586b
Berghe, Jan van den, 4:322b
Bergr Gunnrsteinsson, translation of Robert of Cricklade's vita of St. Thomas Becket, 12:35b
Bergr Sokkason, 4:311b
  Thómas saga erkibyskups and, 12:36a
Berke
  conversion to Islam, 8:472a
  Golden Horde under, 5:572b–573a
  succession to khanate, 8:471b
  vs. Ilkhan, 6:329a
Berkeley, William, **2:188b**
Berkri, **2:189a,** 12:362a
  Armenian trade and, 12:97b
  Catepanate of Basprakania and, 1:484a
Berkyaruq, Seljuk ruler, 11:153a-b, 220a
  defeat of Tutush of Syria, 11:155a
  vs. Sökmen I, 11:220a
Berlinghieri, Berlinghiero, panel painting of, 5:605b
Berlinghieri, Bonaventura, **2:189a-b**
  St. Francis retable panel, 5:603b (*illus.*), 606a
Bermejo, Bartolomé, **2:189b**
  Nuño Gonsalves and, 5:577a
  Pedro de Córdoba and, 9:483b
Bermudo III of Asturias-León, king, 1:628b
Bern, 11:543a
  Charles the Bold and, 11:545a
  founded, 11:539a
  Fribourg and, 11:543a, 543b, 544a
  Holy Roman Empire and, 11:528a, 539b
  Peter of Savoy and, 11:539b, 540a
  Rudolph of Habsburg and, 11:540b
  Swiss Confederation and, 11:543b
  vs. Aargau, 11:544a-b
  Waldstätte and, 11:543b
Bernage, 9:162a
Bernard of Angers, *Liber miraculorum sancte fidis,* 10:112a
Bernard of Auvergne, as defender of Thomism, 12:41b
Bernard of Bologna
  ars dictaminis and, 10:358b
  Introductiones prosaici dictaminis, 4:175a
Bernard of Chartres, **2:189b–190b,** 3:434a, 8:255b, 9:702a
  brother of Thierry of Chartres, 2:189b
  lost commentary on Porphyry's *Isagoge,* 2:190a
  philosophical terminology, 9:588b
  Quintilianic education plan and, 10:356b
  theory of participation, 9:588b
  views on classical scholars, 2:189b
Bernard of Clairvaux, St., **2:190b–194b**
  Abelard and, 1:18a, 2:192a, 9:617a
  Arnold of Brescia and, 1:539b–540a
  at Cîteaux, 3:403b
  canonization of, 2:192a, 192b
  on cardinals, 3:94b
  Cloud of Unknowing and, 9:22a-b

Bernard of Clairvaux, St. (*cont.*)
criticism of St. Denis abbey, 11:503b
crusades and
preaching of, 3:356b
Second Crusade, 4:20b, 12:405a
in Dante, 4:94b
De conflictu Vitiorum et Virtutum, 6:632a, 651a
De consideratione, 4:129b, 10:523a
death of, 3:355a
as doctor of the church, 4:234b
on the Doctrine of Two Swords, 12:234a
in *Duelo de la Virgen,* 2:187b
English mysticism and, 9:18a, 18b
Epistola, 11:365b
Ethelred of Rievaulx and, 4:517a
as exegete, 2:213b, 4:543a
foundation of abbey, 10:478b
friendship with St. Malachy, 8:55a
Gilbert of Poitiers and, 5:528a
Hadewijch and, 9:12a
on humility, 2:193a
hymns of, 6:382a, 7:366b, 9:714b
the idea of personal reform and, 10:284b, 287a
Irish monasticism and, 6:554a
on Jews, 2:192a, 7:76b, 78b
kingship theories of, 7:264a
letters of, 2:191a-b
liturgical reform and, 8:642b
on martyrdom, 8:160a
Mechthild von Magdeburg and, 8:241b
opposed by Robert of Melun, 10:434b
papal authority and, 3:352b
Peter Lombard and, 9:516b
preaching against heresy, 3:186a
Prologus in antiphonarium, 8:642b
revision of Cistercian hymnal, 3:402b
on Roger II, 10:440b
Rolandslied and, 10:448a
Savigniac-Cistercian union, 10:673a
sermons of, 2:191a, 10:76a
in *Kaiserchronik,* 7:205b
on the Song of Songs, 2:191a, 193a–194a, 213a
on Song of Songs, 8:241b
on stained glass, 5:549a
Suso and, 9:35a, 11:517a
Templars and, 3:304b
theology of
Christology, 3:322b
on the four stages of love, 2:193b
on God as love, 2:192b–194a
Scholastic thought and, 3:357b–358a
Trinitarian doctrine, 12:191a, 192b–193b, 196a
vernacular language of, 10:77b
on Virgin Mary, 12:460a, 460b
on warfare, 4:17a-b
William of St. Thierry and, 12:642a
works of, 2:191a-b
Bernard of Cluny
De contemptu mundi, 7:366b, 373a
Piers Plowman and, 8:319a
Bernard of Fleury, *De excidio Troiae,* 12:219b
Bernard of Gordon
lecturing at Montpellier, 8:257 (*illus.*)
Lilium medicinae, 8:252b
Gaelic version of, 11:116a
Bernard of Gui. *See* Gui, Bernard
Bernard of Marmoutier, abbot, revision of *Gesta Francorum* and, 5:514b
Bernard of Meun
Flores dictaminum, 4:175a
Summa dictaminis, 4:175a
Bernard of Parma
Glossa ordinaria, 7:416b
Laurentius Hispanus and, 7:385b
Bernard of Pavia
Breviarium extravagantium, 7:415b, 427b
Compilatio prima, 4:123b–124a, 7:415b, 427b, 8:232a
glosses to, 9:519a
Glossa ordinaria, 7:416a-b
legal writings, 7:415a-b
Parisiensis secunda, 4:123b
Summa de electione, 4:123b
Bernard Prim, Innocent III and, 6:465a
Bernard of Santiago, **2:194b**
Bernard of Septimania, 3:174b
Bernard Silvester, **2:194b–195b**, 3:434a
Cosmographia, 1:183a, 2:194b, 195a, 7:366a, 9:702a
De cura et modo rei familiaris, 4:579a
De mundi universitate, 1:607a
Mathematicus, 2:195a, 7:364a, 366a
mistaken identification with Bernard of Chartres, 2:189b, 194b
Tesoretto and, 7:383a
on Vergil, 12:395a
Bernard of Soissons, **2:194b**
west facade of Rheims Cathedral, 10:344 (*illus.*)
Bernard of Tiron, 3:354b
Bernard de Tremelay, 3:304b
Bernard of Trille, as defender of Thomism, 12:41b
Bernard of Verdun, invention of torquetum attributed to, 11:98b
Bernardino da Feltre, 7:88b
on Jews, 7:76b
Bernardino of Siena, St., **2:195b–196b**, 11:281a-b
on contraception, 4:144a
early life of, 2:195b
with his plaque, 2:196a (*illus.*)
Observant Franciscans and, 7:124a
sermons of, 5:205a, 6:664b
for Lent (1424–1425), 2:196a
women's orders and, 12:688b
Bernardo de Brihuega, saints' lives of, 11:415a
Bernardo Ciuffagni. *See* Ciuffagni, Bernardo
Bernardo del Carpio, 11:411b, 438a
Bernardo da Venezia, **2:196b–197a**
Bernardus à Mallinckrodt, 10:127a
Bernart de Ventadorn, **2:197a-b**
"Can vei la lauzeta mover," 10:171b
cansos of, 10:171b, 172a
comparison with Arnaut Daniel, 10:175a-b, 176a
as epitome of *fin'amors* singers, 10:170b
joi as ideal of, 10:172a-b
life of, 10:170a-b
love as basis of poetic composition, 10:171a-b
melodies of, 3:576b
participation in courtly life, 10:172a
on physical and spiritual love, 3:669a, 669b
quest for meaning of, 10:172a-b
tensos of, 10:171b
vida characterization of, 10:170b
Bernat Descoll, *Chronicle of the Kings of Aragon and Counts of Barcelona* and, 9:511b
Bernat de So, *Vesió,* 3:173b
Berne riddles, 10:397b–398a
Bernelinus of Paris, 8:640a
Berners, Juliana, Dame, 6:361a
Berners, Lord, chronicle translations by, 3:325a
Bernerton (stanza), in *Virginal,* 12:462a
Bernhard I of Saxony, duke, 2:235a
recognition of Henry II, 10:684b
Bernhard II of Saxony, duke, 2:235a
Bernhard of Anhalt, count, acquisition of Saxon tribal duchy, 10:685b–686a
Bernicia, kingdom of, 11:489b
Berno of Cluny, abbot, 3:469a
Berno of Reichenau, abbot, 8:641b
Cistercians and, 8:643a
hymns of, 6:381b
on the liturgy of the Mass, 7:629b
rhymed offices of, 10:372a
Bernold of Constance, **2:197b**
dispensation and, 4:217a-b
Micrologus, 7:629b–630a
Bernorinus, **2:197b**
Bernward, St., **2:197b–198a**, 10:101a-b, 107a
beatification of, 2:143a
rhymed office of, 10:370a-b
Bernward, St., monastic goldsmith, 8:289a
Beroldus of Milan, on liturgy, 7:630b
Berolinensis prima, 4:123a
Béroul
Tristan legend and, 12:200a–201a, 202a-b
see also Tristan, Roman de
Berruguete, Pedro, **2:198a**, 5:612a
Berserks, **2:198a-b**
in Icelandic *riddarasögur,* 10:395b
in *Sturlaugs saga Starfsama,* 11:496b
Bersuire, Pierre
Ovidius moralizatus, as exemplum, 4:544b
Philippe de Vitry and, 12:481b
Reductorium morale, 7:369b
Bert῾ai Gospels, 5:411a
Berte aus grans piés. See Adenet le Roi
Bertha of Swabia, queen, 11:538a
Bertharius, **2:199a**
Berthold V of Zähringen, 11:527b, 539a, 539b
Berthold von Henneberg
imperial reform movement and, 5:493a
Maximilian I and, 10:331a
Berthold von Holle, **2:199a-b**
Crane, 2:199a-b
Darifant, 2:199a-b

Demantin, 2:199a-b, 5:454b
Berthold Missal, 8:108b (*illus.*)
Berthold von Regensburg, **2:199b–201a**
on marriage, 3:359b
referred to in *Schwabenspiegel,* 11:80b
sermons of
in German, 2:200b
in Latin, 2:200a-b
problems of authenticity, 2:200a, 200b
travels of, 2:200a
Berthold of Rehinfelden, duke of Swabia, 11:527a-b
Berthold, St. (*fl.* 1155), 3:96b
Berthold of Zähringen (11th century), 11:527b
Berthold of Zähringen (12th century), Frederick I Barbarossa and, 11:538b–539a
Bertin, St., rhymed antiphon to, 10:371b
Bertken Zuster, 4:321a
Bertold. See Giulio Cesare (della) Croce
Bertrada of Montfort, widow of Philip I of France, seal of, 11:126a
Bertrada (wife of Fulk), 3:449a
Bertram, Meister, **2:201a-b**
Grabow Altarpiece, 5:610a
Bertran de Born, **2:201b–202a,** 10:175a
in Dante's *Divine Comedy,* 2:202a
hunting and, 6:358b
as master of *servientes,* 10:175a
polemical poems of, 11:313a
Richard the Lionhearted and, 2:201b, 202a
social origins of, 5:434a
Bertrand de Bar-sur-Aube, **2:201b**
Bertrand de Got. *See* Clement V, pope
Bertrand du Guesclin. *See* Guesclin, Bertrand du
Bertrand of Poggetto, cardinal, vs. Galeazzo Visconti, 12:464b
Bertrandon de la Broquière, praising of Hungarian chariots, 12:378a
Bertuccio, **2:202b**
Berwick, burgh of, Scottish-English relations and, 11:108a
Berwick, Treaty of (1357), **2:202b,** 4:111a
Berytus. *See* Beirut
Berzé-la-Ville, priory at, 10:506b–507a
Besague, 1:530b
Besant, **2:203a**
Bescheidenheit. See Freidank
Bescia (unit of measure), 12:586b
Besestan. See Bedestan
Bessarion, **2:203a-b**
at Council of Ferrara-Florence, 12:169b
George of Trebizond and, 5:400b
In calumniatorem Platonis, 9:699a, 703a-b
promotion of humanistic studies, 7:1a
as Roman cardinal, 11:51a
Bestiaire d'amour. See Richard de Fournival
Bestiaire divin. See Guillaume le Clerc
Bestiary, **2:203b–207a,** 2:204a (*illus.*), 205a (*illus.*), 205b (*illus.*)
in Anglo-Saxon literature, 1:280b
derivation of the term, 2:203b
French, 5:281a
of Philippe de Thaon, 9:558b
German, 5:428a-b
illustrations of, 2:206a-b, 8:108a
Italian, 6:645a
of Gubbio, 6:632a
medieval study of animals and, 2:243a-b
Middle English, 8:316b, 330a
Proverbia quae dicuntur super natura feminarum and, 6:630a
Waldensian, 2:205b–206a
see also Unicorn
Bestiary. See Jāḥiẓ, Abū ᶜUthmān ᶜAmr ibn Baḥr al-
Bet Alfa synagogue, 7:65b
Bēt keneset. See Synagogue
Bet Yosef. See Caro, Joseph
Betania, **2:207a**
Beth ᶜAbe (monastery: Iraq), 11:564b
Beth din, 7:74b
see also Jewish communal self-government
Beth ha-. See Schools, Jewish
Beth Qardū. *See* Corduene
Béthencourt, Jean de, 3:62a–63a, 4:559a
see also Canary Islands
Bethlehem
shrine of the Nativity, 4:336b, 337a
Tancred and, 11:589b
Bethlehem Chapel (Prague), Hus at, 6:364b–365a, 366a
Bethlehem Royal Hospital. *See* Bedlam
Bethu Brigte, 2:376b
see also Brigit (Brigid), St.
"Betrogene Gatte, Der." *See* Herrand von Wildonie
Betrothal, **2:207b–208b**
among Germanic tribes, 2:207b
Byzantine, 4:594b
Christian, 4:610a-b
in classical Rome, 2:207b
Germanic, 4:599b
Islamic, 4:597b
Jewish, 4:606a
mythical, in Irish saga, 6:547a
Beues of Hamtoun, Sir. See Sir Beues of Hamtoun
Beuves de Haumtone. *See* Boeve de Haumtone
Beverages, 12:648b
Islamic, **2:208b–209b**
dietary laws on, 4:178b
nonalcoholic, 2:209a-b
see also Ale and beer; Brewing; Distilled liquors; Wine
Beverley, Corpus Christi plays, 4:285b, 8:658b
Bevers saga, **2:209b–210b,** 10:391b
compared with *Sir Beues of Hamtoun* and *Ystorya Bown de Hamtwn,* 2:209b–210a
dating of, 2:210a
manuscripts of, 2:210a
Bevor, 1:527a (*illus.*), 530a
Beylerbeyi. See Ottomans, armed forces
Beyliks. *See* Turkomans
Beyşehir, carpets of, 6:613a
Beza, Theodore, *Du droit des magistrats* (1574), 3:521b
Bezant. *See* Solidus
Bezborodyi, Markel, 8:573b
Béziers
Albigensians in, 7:340b
bridge construction, 10:419a
massacres at, 3:108a
Bezprym of Poland, king, 9:719b
Bezzeztan. See Bedestan
Bhagavata Purana, Vǫluspá and, 12:492a
Bhariya, 8:561b
Bhāskarā, perpetual-motion machines, 11:652a
Bianca of Savoy, Book of Hours, 5:536b
Bianchi (religious movement), *lauda* and, 6:663a
Biancifiore (character in Boccaccio's *Filocolo*), 2:279b–280a, 6:660a
Bible, **2:210b–217a**
Apocalypse of St. John, 12:475b
Wirnt von Grafenberg's *Wigalois* and, 12:657a
year 1000 and, 12:722a
Arsenal, 2:447a
Asturian. *See* Asturian Bible
chapter/verse divisions, 3:83b
Cistercian, 2:213b, **2:218a-b**
completed in 1109, 2:218a
Stephen Harding and, 2:218a
concordances, 6:321a
crusader, 4:25b, 26a (*illus.*)
Decalogue, *more judaico* oath and, 9:207b
earliest versions, 2:210b–211a
Epistle to the Galatians, Ilarion on, 6:418b, 419a
Exodus, sorcery in, 8:33a, 33b, 38a
glosses and commentaries
alphabetization of, 1:205a-b
Glossa interlinea, 10:239a
Glossa ordinaria, 10:239a
Irish, **2:220a-b**
Gospel of James, on Virgin Mary, 12:459b
Gospel of John, Aelfric on, 4:550a
Hebrew
Aleppo Codex, 8:181a
Christian study of, 3:313b
language study and, 6:128a
Leningrad Codex, 8:181a
philosophical view of, 9:577a
poetic language and, 6:131a
Rabbinic, 8:181b
study of, Masoretic, 8:180a–181b
texts in Cairo genizah, 3:15b
Tiberian, 8:181a
see also Exegesis, Jewish
Hungarian, 6:337a
hunting and, 6:358b
hymns and, 6:384a-b
illustration of, 4:355b, 357a
Acts of the Apostles (5th century), 4:356a
Book of Kings (Berlin MS), 4:351b
catacomb paintings, 4:350a
in early Christian period, 4:350a, 351b
Genesis (Cotton MS), 4:351b, 356b
Genesis (S. Paolo fuori le Mura), 10:99b (*illus.*)

Bible (*cont.*)
illustration of (*cont.*)
Genesis (Vienna MS), 4:356b
Gospel of John (Italian, 5th century), 4:355b–356a
Gothic, 6:434b, 435a, 436b
initials in Richard II's Bible, 6:463a
Karaite MS, 7:66a
Master Hugo, 6:324b (*illus.*)
in migration period art, 8:368b
New Testament cycles, 4:356b–357a
Roman imperial conventions adapted to, 4:354b
Second Bible of Charles the Bald, 6:462b
Sephardi, 8:110b (*illus.*)
Syriac MS (6th century), 4:356b, 357a
Syrian (6th century), 8:105b, 106 (*illus.*)
illustration of, Joshua Roll, 7:152 (*illus.*)
impact on daily life, 2:216a-b
influence of on political thought, 2:216a-b
interpretation of, **2:223b–224b**
by Rashi, 10:259a–260a
centonization, 3:235b
idea of personal reform and, 10:282b–284a
Pentateuch, 10:259b
quaestiones, 10:238a-b
see also Religious instruction
Job
Bonvesin and, 6:631a
German translation of (in the Mergentheim codex), 2:232a
in Latin epic, 7:361a
of León (920), Vimara and, 10:114a, 12:452a, 452b (*illus.*)
Livres dou trésor and, 7:383a
Lollard, 2:222a, 4:548a, 7:648a-b
manuscript production, Rome, 10:508a
as matter of epic, 6:150a-b
medieval scholarship, 2:216b
Muslim exegesis of, 2:214b–215a
mystery plays and, 8:660a
New Testament
canon of established in the 2nd century, 2:211a
casuistry in, 3:153a
Christian-Jewish polemics and, 10:1b–2a
commented on by Muslims, 2:215a
in Coptic manuscripts, 3:590b–591a
English, 4:547b
Georgian translations of, 5:416b
included in the Septuagint, 2:211a
in Ireland (early 9th century), 2:220a
in Middle English, *Glossed Gospels,* 2:222a
synagogue and, 11:556a
tapestry and, 11:591b
translation into Czech, 2:307b
translation into West Saxon (10th century), 2:221a
Virgin Mary in, 12:459b, 460a
of Niketas, model for, 2:454b
of 960, 10:114a
Old Testament
Christian-Jewish polemics and, 10:1b
kingship in, 10:15b, 16b
Masoretic text of, 2:210b
mirrors of princes and, 10:15b
tapestry and, 11:591b
Oriental exegesis, 2:214b
origins of libraries and, 7:559a
Pentateuch
Arabic, 4:539a
Isaac Israeli and, 6:620b
Peshitta translation of, 1:208a
plainsong chants and, 9:688a–693a
"pocket" manuscripts (13th century), 8:103a
poor people's. *See Biblia pauperum*
in popular literature, 2:216b
popularization of, 2:216a
pre-Vulgate, *Versio italica,* 10:239a
production of, 6:32a, 32b, 33a
readings from in lectionaries, 7:534a
readings in liturgy, 2:216a
Septuagint, 2:210b–211a
Armenian translation, 1:507b
final text established in the 9th century, 2:214a
Syro-Hexapla translation, 11:565a
term "patriarch" introduced, 9:458b
translations of, 2:211a, 215b
Song of Solomon (Song of Songs), 5:427b–428a
in Byzantine church, 9:278a
commentaries on, 9:278a-b, 593a
metrical commentary by Brun von Schönebeck, 2:229a-b
in music, 8:546b (*illus.*), 565a
sermons on by St. Bernard of Clairvaux, 2:193a-b
Suso and, 11:517a
as a source of parody, 9:440b
study of, theology curriculum, 11:690b
Tobias, 7:322b
translations, Western European theory and traditions, 12:139a-b
translations in Psalter, 10:200a
verse, 4:546a–547a
see also Aurora; Petrus Riga
versions, 2:211a–212a
Anglo-Norman, 1:262b
Arabic, 4:539a,b
Aramaic, 2:210b
Armenian, 1:507b, **2:217a–218a,** 4:570b, 7:299a, 8:202b
Catalan, 2:215b, 3:166b–167a, 11:432a
Czech, 2:216a
Dutch, 2:215a
English, 2:215a
French, 2:215a, **2:218b–219b,** 2:219a, 4:546b, 10:239a
German, 2:215a-b, 224b–232b
Gothic, 2:211b–212a, 10:465b
Greek, 2:210b, 4:571a, 9:278a
Hungarian, 2:216a
Italian, 2:215b
Judeo-Persian, 7:177b
Judeo-Spanish, 7:179b
Latin, 7:360b, *see also* Theodulf of Orléans; Vulgate
Middle English, **2:221b–222b,** 4:544b, 549a
Near Eastern, 10:463b
Old Church Slavonic, 10:509b–510a
Old English, 1:279b–280a, 285a-b, **2:220b–221b**
Old Latin, 2:211a, 12:494b, 495b
prose, 4:547a-b, 548b
Provençal, 2:215a
Romanian, 10:511a, 512a, 513b
Scandinavian, 11:17b–18a
Slavic, 11:347b
Spanish, 11:161b, 415a, 432a-b
Syrian, 11:565a
Syro-Hexapla, 11:565a
Vulgate, 2:211a, **12:495b–496b**
diffusion of, 2:211a-b
early success of, 12:495b
exegesis of, 4:542a-b, *see also Correctoria*
Gallican, 2:211b
in Ireland, 2:220a
Jerome and, 7:57b, 58a
known to St. Patrick, 9:464a
Latin of, 6:438b
Latin spelling and, 7:358b
Latin syntax and, 7:356a
Middle English literature and, 4:545b
"Paris versions" of, 2:213a
revised by Theodulf of Orléans, 2:211b
revised under the Carolingians, 2:211b
revision of by Alcuin, 2:211b
successive corrections of, 12:495b–496a
version of Isidore of Seville, 2:211b
Western European political theory and, 10:14a-b
Waldensian versions, 12:510b–511a
in Flemish, 2:215a
in Italian, 2:215b
in Provençal, 2:215a
Wyclif on, 12:708a-b, 709a, 709b, 710b
Wycliffite, 2:222a-b, 12:710a
al-Yaᶜqūbī and, 12:718a
see also Canticle; Exegesis; Gospels; Lectionary; Octateuch; Psalm; Psalter
Bible of Alba, 11:432b
Bible of Charles the Bald, 2:211b
Bible historiale, 2:219a-b
Bible moralisée, **2:222b**, 2:223a (*illus.*), 5:614a
illumination of, 8:109a
illustrated by Limbourg brothers, 7:581b–582a
see also Biblia pauperum
Bible of Niketas, model for, 2:454b
Bible of Piscator, 12:720b
Bible of St. Louis, 4:26a (*illus.*)
Bible de sapience. See Herman de Valenciennes
Bible of the Thirteenth Century, 2:219a, 219b
Biblia Escurialense, 11:432a

Biblia parva. See Pasqual of Jaén, bishop
Biblia pauperum, 2:216a, **2:223a** (*illus.*), 10:302a, 12:693a
printed as a block book, 2:275a, 275b
tapestry and, 11:591b
see also Bible moralisée
Biblia sacra (1604), 12:496a
Bibliographies, Islamic, 9:652b–953a
Biblionomia. See Richard de Fournival
Biblioteca. *See* Libraries
Bibliotheca. See Photios, patriarch
Bibliotheca sanctorum, 6:71a
Bibliothèque Nationale, Paris, origin of, 7:567a
Bichetée (unit of measure), 12:587a
Bidāyat al-mujtahid. See Rushd, Ibn
Bideford Bridge, 10:418b
construction of, 10:420a
corporation of, 10:417a
endowed with lands, 10:415a
Bidenhander swords. *See* Swords
Bidpai, *Fables,* 6:607b
Biduino, **2:233b**, 10:503a
Biel, Gabriel, **2:233b–234b**, 3:324a
Brethren of the Common Life and, 2:233b, 234a
establishment of chapter houses, 2:368b–369a
Collectorium, 2:234a
Devotio Moderna and, 4:167a
early life of, 2:233b
Expositio, 2:234a
influence of, 2:233b–234a
on the liturgy of the Mass, 7:633a
nominalism and, 9:157b, 12:44a
predestination and, 3:371a
via moderna and, 12:408a-b
Bien Advisé et Mal Advisé, 4:265a
Bifolia
in book production, 8:101a-b
see also Folio; Manuscript books, binding of
Big Geoffrey. *See* Seifín Mór
Biga party, in Barcelona, 2:104b
Biga (vehicle), 12:367a
Bigorre, hunting in, 6:356b
Bigotian Penitential, 9:489a
Bihzād (Timurid painter), 6:605b, 12:59a
Bijloke, 5:523a
Bijns, Anna, 4:322b–323a
Bijoux indiscrets, Les. See Diderot, Denis
Biket, Robert, *Lai du cor,* 1:568a, 7:317b
Biklarish, Jonah ibn, drug glossary of, 11:92b
Bilāl (first muezzin), 8:560a
Bilbais, conquered, 6:569b
Bilbao, 2:127a
Bilbao region, steelmaking in, 11:471b
Bilingualism
Byzantine, 7:597a
Western European, 7:598b–599a
see also Interpreters; Translation and translators
Bill of exchange, fair letter and, 4:584b
Bill (lance), 7:324 (*illus.*), 325a
Billon trachy, 8:421a
Billungs, **2:235a-b**
division of property, 10:685a
duchy of Saxony and, 5:510b–511a
foundation of duchy, 10:684a-b
Bimah, 10:556a (*illus.*), 557a
Bimaristan. See Hospitals, Islamic
Binchois, Gilles
Philip the Good and, 8:635a
portrait of, 4:567b
Bind (unit of measure), 12:592a
Binham, William, vs. Wyclif, 12:709b
Binne (unit of measure), 12:592a
Biography
dictionaries of, Ibn Khallikān, 7:236a
French, **2:235b–237b**
biographies of Julius Caesar, 2:236b
by Joinville, 7:143b–144a
chivalric biographies, 2:236b–237a
lives of Provençal poets, 2:237a
royal biographies, 2:236a-b, 239b, 240a
secular, 2:236a–237a
12th century, 6:8b, 9b
Icelandic. *See* Bishops' sagas
Islamic, **2:237b–239a**
concept of *ṭabaqāt* and, 2:237b, 238a
historical information in, 2:238b
Ibn Khallikān, 7:236a-b
al-Khaṭīb al-Baghdādī, 7:239b–240a
literary form of, 2:238a
religious. *See* Hagiography
royal, 6:263b
secular, **2:239a–240b**
Jerome's *De viris illustribus* and, 2:239a
in Latin, 2:239a–240a
in the vernacular, 2:240a-b
see also Theganus; Vidas
Biology, **2:240b–246b**
Jewish, 11:93a
origin of the term, 2:240b
as part of physics, 2:241b
Thomas of Cantimpré's encyclopedias and, 12:34a-b
Biondo, Flavio, idea of Middle Ages, 8:308b–309a
Birch bark documents, 9:195b–196a, 12:699a
Birds
classified by Frederick II Hohenstaufen, 2:244b
trapping of, 6:358b, 361a
vs. dogs, in *Jugement de chiens et d'oisiaus,* 6:360a-b
see also Hawking; Sakers
Bird's beak molding, 8:453b
Birger, earl, 11:530b–531a
Birger Gregersson, hymns of, 6:382b
Birger Magnusson of Sweden, king, 4:505b
fall of, 11:532a
Birgham, Treaty of (1290), 9:438a, 439b
Birgitta, St., **2:246b–247b**, 12:689a
Catherine of Siena and, 9:15a
early life of, 2:246b
Margery (Burnham) Kempe and, 7:229a, 9:25b
pilgrimages of, 2:247a
Revelations, 2:247a, 5:604a
Campin and, 3:61a
translated into English, 9:27a
writings of, 9:15b
Birgittines, Order of the, 12:689a
Biringuccio, Vannoccio, *Pirotechnia,* 4:329a
Birka, **2:247b–248a**, 12:423a, 424a
founded, 11:530a
Sigtuna and, 11:530b
see also Swedish law
Birth. *See* Childbirth
Birth control. *See* Contraception
Birth, noble. *See* Nobility and nobles; Prestige
Birth rates. *See* Demography
Bīrūnī, Muḥammad ibn Aḥmad Abu 'l-Rayḥān al-, **2:248a–251b**, 5:393a-b, 9:653a
Astrolabe, 2:250a
on astrology, 1:619b
on astronomy, 1:620b, 622a
at the court of Maḥmūd, 2:248b
Āthār al-Bāqiyah ᶜan al-Qurūn al-Khāliyah, Al-, 2:248b, 249a
computational devices produced by, 11:95a
as court astrologer, 2:248b
early life of, 2:248b
Elements of Astrology, 2:250a-b
Gems, 2:250b
Ghaznavids and, 2:248b
Ibn Sīnā and, 2:251a
India, 2:249a
Kitāb al-jamāhir fī maᶜrifat al-jawāhir, on Turkomans, 12:226b
on the Manichaeans, 8:237b
Mathematical Geography, 2:249a-b
on paper mills and gold-ore crushing, 12:85b
patrons of, 11:83b–84a
Pharmacology, 2:250b–251a
Qānūn al-Masᶜūdī, Al-, 2:248b, 249b
against astrology, 2:250b
references to Scandinavia, 10:707a
Shadows, 2:250a
Warning Against the Craft of Deceit, 2:250b
on waterpower, 11:637a
works of, 2:249a–251a
Bisat. *See* Rugs and carpets, Islamic
Bisclavret, 1:568a
see also Marie de France
Bishapur, **2:251b–252a**
art and architecture, 10:600a-b
Sasanian rock reliefs, 10:658a
statue of Šābuhr, 10:600b
Sasanian residence in, 10:600a
Bishop, 3:441a, 442a
in Armenian church, 1:503a-b, 504a
association with royal chanceries, 3:252b
authority of, False Decretals and, 4:125b–126a
Byzantine, 3:446a-b, 9:265a-b
dress of, 3:616a
chaplain of, 3:264b
consecration of, 3:229a, 4:422b
in early church, 3:340b–341a, 602b
election of, 3:537a, 4:421a–425a

Bishop (*cont.*)
election of (*cont.*)
in Carolingian and Capetian France, 4:421b
in England, 4:424a-b
Henry II and, 4:466a-b
in Italy, 4:424a
papal oversight, 4:424a
reforms in, 4:422b
rights of cathedral chapters, 4:423b
royal influence on, 3:537a, 4:421a-b, 422b–423
in German principalities, 5:499b
German representative assemblies and, 10:332b–333b
Jewish. *See* Rabbinate
ministerials appointed as, 8:406b
miter worn by, 3:624a-b
ordination of, 3:602b–603a, 9:265b
personal seals and, 11:125a-b
as precursor to papacy, 9:365a-b
role in clerical ordination, 9:268a
temporal responsibilities, 3:373a
translation of, 12:142b–143a
see also Clergy; Parish
Bishop of Rome. *See* Papacy
Bishops' sagas, **2:252a–253a**
biographies of Guðmundr Arason, 6:33b, 11:498b
classification of, 10:610b
see also Thómas saga erkibyskups
Bishr ibn al-Ḥārith, on *sunna,* 11:512a
Bishr ibn al-Mu^{c}tamir (*d.* 825), 8:655b
Bīsitūn. *See* Behistun
Bîspel, 5:429b
in Middle High German literature, 8:353a
typology, 8:127b
Bissolo, Bellino, 7:369a
Bisṭāmī, Abū Yazīd al-, Islamic mysticism and, 9:40b
Biterolf und Dietleib, **2:253a-b**
Bithynia
Latin Empire of Constantinople and, 7:346a, 347b
Ottoman conquest of, 1:246a, 246b
rebellion against Andronikos I, 1:245a
Bitlis, Armenian trade and, 12:97b
Bitonto Cathedral, 10:486b
Biṭrīq, Yaḥyā ibn al-, *Secretum secretorum* and, 11:135a
Biṭrūjī, al-, 11:84a
Astronomy, translated into Hebrew, 11:91a
on concentric orbits, 1:614b
Bitshvinta (Pitsunda), **2:253b**
Bjarkamál, **2:254a–255a**, 6:311a
dating of, 2:254b
preservation in *Eddica minora,* 4:388a
sources of, 2:254a-b
Bjarkarímur, 6:311a
Bjarköarätt, 7:525b
Bjarnar saga Hítdœlakappa, **2:255a-b**, 4:612b, 613a
dating of, 2:255b
Bjarni Herjólfsson
discovery of Vinland, 12:428b
Nova Scotia and, 4:555a
in Vinland sagas, 12:457a
Bjarni Kolbeinsson, **2:255b–256b**
attribution of *Málsháttakvæði,* 2:256a, 8:65b
Jómsvíkingadrápa, 2:256a
Björn, *Geðraunir,* 10:402b
Björn Jónsson of Skarðsá, *Skarðsárbók,* 7:327b
Blachernitissa, **2:256b–257a**, 2:257a (*illus.*)
see also Platytera
Bláchoi. See Vlachs
Black, source of black dyes, 4:326a
Black Book of the Admiralty, The
duties of admirals, 1:56a
establishment of court of the admiralty, 1:56a
Black Book of Carmarthen, 1:565b, 577a-b
Gogynfeirdd poems, 12:606a
poetic contents, 12:598a
religious poems, 12:614a
Black Book of Chirk, 12:599b
Black Death, **2:257a–267b**, 3:12b
anti-Semitism and, 1:341b, 2:263b, 7:82a, 89a-b
arrival in Europe, 2:258b
art style, 12:124b, 175a-b
in Boccaccio's *Decameron,* 2:283b
in Bohemia, 2:264a, 303b
in the British Isles, 2:261b–262b
Carthusians and, 3:119a
Cistercians and, 3:405b
Clement VI and, 3:439b
clergy and, 5:181a, 204b
contemporary explanations of, 2:264b–265a
decline of Mamluk dynasty and, 4:406b
demographic effects, 4:142a-b
France, 5:177b–178a, 9:556a
German towns, 5:465a
London, 7:664b
Norway, 9:180a
on urbanism, 12:318b–319a
Dominicans and, 4:245a, 253b
in Eastern Europe, 2:264a
economic effects, 2:265a–266a, 4:484b
France, 5:178a
grain crops, Western European, 5:647b
increase in poverty caused by, 6:297a
on trade, 6:93b, 12:115a
urban guilds, 6:18a
in Egypt
Alexandria, 1:154b
Cairo, 3:14b
in England, 4:398b
London (1348–1350), 2:262a-b
in Europe, 9:677a, 678a, 728a
fatalities from, 2:257a, 3:561a
flagellants and, 2:263a
in Flanders, 2:261a
in France, 2:260b–261a
Champagne, 3:250a
Paris, 9:405b
Paris (1348–1349), 2:261a
Rouen, 10:538b
Toulouse, 12:90b
in Germany, 2:262b–264a
in Greenland (1350), 2:261b
in Iberia, 2:263b–264a
Aragon, 1:419b
Valencia, 12:348b
in Iceland, 2:261b, 6:396b
in Iraq, 6:514a
in Ireland, 6:519b
Irish literature, 6:524a
in Islamic world, 9:684b–685a, 686a
in Italy, 2:259a–260b
art and, 5:606b–607a
Naples, 9:59b
Siena, 2:260a, 11:280a
Venice, 2:100b, 12:392a
lament of Guillaume de Machaut, 8:4a
in Languedoc, 7:341a
lauda and, 7:384a
Mamluk dynasty and, 8:74b, 75b
manorial system and, 3:596b, 4:514b
medical response to, 2:264a–265a, 8:253b
mining and, 8:401b
mysticism and, 9:13b, 18a, 31a
in Netherlands, 2:261a
in Northern Europe, effect on peasant society, 1:94b
in Norway, land rents and, 9:182a
origins of, 2:258a-b
contemporary theories, 2:264b, 265a
peasant rebellions and
Jacquerie, 9:478a
Peasants' Revolt (1381), 9:480a
in Portugal, 10:51a-b
psychological changes caused by, 2:267a
religious and cultural effects of, 2:266a–267a
remedies for, distilled liquors, 4:220a
in Scandinavia, 2:261a-b
in southern Asia, 2:258b
spread of, 2:258b–259a
in Sweden, 11:532b
in Syria, 11:562a
theory of sorcery and, 8:30a
winemaking and, 12:649b, 652a, 653a
see also Flagellants; Plagues
Black Guelphs. *See* Guelphs and Ghibellines
Black land, Russian, 11:191a
Black lead, as writing material, 12:699b
"Black money," 8:428b
Black monks. *See* Benedictines
Black Prince, Order of the, 4:398a
"Black" Russian peasants. *See* Peasants
Black Sea
Byzantine trade and, 12:101a-b, 103a
sea routes, 10:423 (map), 424b
Genoese trade and, 9:503a-b, 12:111b
Ottoman occupation of, 2:137b
Trebizond Empire and, 12:168a–170a (map)
Black Sheep Turkomans. *See* Qara Qoyunlu
"Blackbird by Belfast Loch, The," 6:527b
"Blackbird Calling from the Willow, The," 6:527b
Blackfriars, Council of (1382), 12:706b–707a, 709b

condemnation of Wyclif's teachings, 6:199b
Blacks, **2:268a–270b**
see also Slavery and slave trade; Slavery, Islamic
Blacksmith shop, 11:470 (*illus.*)
Blades, as agricultural tools, 12:80b
Blagoveshchensky Cathedral. *See* Moscow Kremlin
Blaise de Monluc, 11:282a
Blaise, St.
in art, 10:507a
Spanish prose life of, 11:439b
Blanche of Bourbon, mistreatment of by Pedro I of Castile, 3:137a
Blanche of Castile, queen of France, **2:270b–271a**
administrative skills of, 2:270b, 271a
Baldwin II and, 7:349a-b
influence on French government, 5:166b
opposition to crusade of 1248–1254, 2:271a
Pastoureaux and, 9:454a
regency for Louis IX, 2:270b, 7:674b
religious values of, 2:270b
Blanche of Lancaster, 7:135a
Chaucer's *Book of the Duchess* and, 3:281b–282b
Blanche of Navarre, 3:247b, 9:71b–72a
currus (four-wheeled vehicle) of, 12:376a
Blanchefleur (romance character). *See* Floris
Blancheflour et Florence, 1:268b, **2:271a-b**
Boccaccio's *Filocolo* and, 2:279a
see also Floris
Blandin de Cornouailles, 1:569a
Blanks (diplomacy), 4:208b–209a
Blanquerna. See Lull, Ramon
Blasphemy, **2:271b–272b**
compared with heresy, 2:271b, 272a
infrequent prosecution for, 2:272a
medieval definitions of, 2:271b
punishments for, 2:272a
Blast furnace, 8:393b
development of, 8:285b, 292b
Blazon, **2:272b–273b**
compared with coat of arms, 2:273a-b
denoting the status of individuals, 2:273a
origins of the use of, 2:272b
on a Syrian mosque lamp, 2:273a (*illus.*)
Bleda (Hunnic leader), 6:354a
Bleddyn Fardd, praise poem to Llywelyn ap Gruffydd, 12:604b
Blegywryd, Book of, 12:599b
Bleheris, 1:567b–568a
Blekinge runic stones (Sweden), 10:562a
Blemmydes, Nikephoros, 1:614a
Theodore II Laskaris of Nicaea and, 12:14a
Blemmyes (in Egypt), 10:453b
Blessed Virgin Mary, Little Office of, 2:13a, 13b, **2:273b–274a**
in book of hours, 2:326a
development of, 2:325b
Blickling homilies, 1:276b, 281b, 284b
Bliemetzrieder, Franz, conciliar theory of, 3:514b
Bligger von Steinach, **2:274a-b**
lyric poems ascribed to, 2:274b
Blind Harry. *See* Henry the Minstrel
Blind Tigris. *See* Dijla al-ᶜAwrā
Blindman's buff, 5:347a
Block book, **2:275a-b**, 12:693a
appearance of, 2:275a
number of surviving titles, 2:275a
recent research on, 2:275b
see also Bois Protat
Block capital, 3:90b (*illus.*)
Block-book Passion, 12:692b
Bloemardinne of Brussels, wrongly identified with Hadewijch, 9:12a
Blois, Jews murdered in (1171), 7:30b
Blómstrvalla saga, 10:394b, 395b
Blondel, David, False Decretals and, 4:126a
Blondel de Nesle, **2:276a**
melodies of, 3:576a, 576b
Blood group. *See* Extended family
Blood libel, 1:340b–341a, **2:276a-b,** 7:88b
origins of, 2:276a
repudiation of by Frederick II, 1:340b–341a
spread of, 2:276a
Blood money, Islamic law, **2:276b–277b**
scale of payments, 2:276b–277a
Bloodbath of Cannstadt (746), 11:526b
Bloodbath of Stockholm (1520), 11:533b
Bloodletting, in medical practice, 8:252b
Bloody flux. *See* Plagues, enteric, dysentery
Blore Heath, Battle of (1459), 12:570b
Blue, sources of in dyeing, 4:325b
Blue Mosque of Tabriz, kashi in, 7:224a (*illus.*)
Blue Tomb of Marāgha, 6:602a
Blue-threaded glass, 5:558b
Blues (demes). *See* Demes
Bluthirse, 5:647a
Bnabeł. *See* Benabila
Board games, 5:351a
Boat mills, 8:391b
Bobbio
center of Celtic art, 3:219a
monastery of
founding of, 12:682b
library of, 7:652b
Bobbio Missal, 3:230a, 8:118a, 9:491a
liturgy of Pavia texts, 9:62a
Mozarabic litanies in, 7:591b
Bobbio Penitential, 9:489a, 491a
Böblinger, Mathäus (15th-century architect), 1:429a
Bobyli, 11:194a
Bocados de oro, 11:415b
Bocage, 12:445b
Boccaccino di Chellino, 2:277b
bankruptcy of, 2:287a
Boccaccio, Giovanni, **2:277b–290b**
allegory as a source of comedy, 2:285b
Ameto, 2:281a
as a precursor of *Decameron,* 2:281a
Amorosa visione, 2:281a–282a, 6:651b, 670a, 12:477a
Buccolicum carmen, 2:280b–281a, 287b
Caccia di Diana, 2:278a-b
civic offices of, 2:287b–288a
compositions of 1340–1350, 2:280b–283a
Corbaccio, 2:267a, 285b, 6:660a, 12:477a
De casibus virorum illustrium, 2:239b, 286a-b
John Lydgate's *Fall of Princes* and, 8:323b
tragedies of Fortune in, 5:146a, 148a
De genealogia deorum gentilium, 1:180b, 183b, 2:283a-b
De montibus and, 2:286b
on the morality of fiction, 10:345b
De montibus..., 2:286b
De mulieribus claris, 2:239b, 286b–287a
De vita et moribus Domini Francisci Petracchi, 2:288a
Decameron, 2:266b–267a, 283b–285b, 4:551b, 577a, 6:651b, 660a-b, 661a, 7:10b–11a
on Black Death, 2:259a–260a, 267a
compared with *Schüler von Paris,* 11:80a
Disciplina clericalis and, 6:659a
dissemination of, 2:285b
gardens in, 5:362a-b, 363b, 365a
Grettis saga Ásmundarsonar and, 5:673a
inns and, 6:471b, 472a, 475a
Irregang und Girregar and, 6:555b
mention of Michael Scot, 8:305a
revision of, 2:289b
sources of, 2:284b–285a
decision to give up all wordly pursuits, 2:288a
early works of, 2:278a–280b
Elegia di Madonna Fiammetta, 6:660a
considered a precursor of modern psychological novel, 2:282a-b
Juan de Flores' romances and, 11:454b–455a
Epistola consolatoria a messer Pino de' Rossi, 2:287b
Esposizioni sopra la Comedìa di Dante, 2:289b, 6:651b, 660a
Filocolo, 2:279a–280a, 6:660a
sources of, 2:279a
Filostrato, 2:278b–279a, 6:670a, 8:225b
Roman de Troie and, 2:182a
friendship with Petrarch, 2:286b, 288a, 288b, 289a-b
his half brother Jacopo and, 2:283b, 287b, 288b
illegitimacy of, 2:277b
influence of
on Álvaro de Luna, 11:440a
on Chaucer, 3:283a
on Juan de Flores, 5:107b
later life of, 2:287a–289b
later works of, 2:285b–287a
Latin works of, 7:369b

Boccaccio, Giovanni (*cont.*)
lectures on Dante, 2:289b
lyric poetry and, 6:651b–652a
mistreated by Niccolò Acciaiuoli, 2:288b–289a
in Naples, 2:277b–278b, 288b–289a
nascent humanism and, 2:287b
Ninfale fiesolano, 2:282b–283a, 6:670a
Olympia compared with *Pearl,* 8:320a
Specchio di vera penitenza and, 6:664b
Speculum stultorum and, 9:131a
studies of, 2:277b
taking of minor orders by, 2:288b
Teseida della nozze d'Emilia, 6:660a, 670a
tragedies of Fortune, 5:146a
Teseida delle nozze d'Emilia, 2:280a-b
as an answer to Dante's *De vulgari eloquentia,* 2:280a
translation of Livy's *Decades,* 2:287b
translations of
by Chaucer, 3:287b–289a
into Catalan, 3:169a-b
Trattatello in laude di Dante, 2:240a, 288a, 4:102b, 6:651b, 660a
Tuscan dialect and, 6:443b, 624b, 626b, 627a, 629a
Zibaldone laurenziano, 2:278a, 280b, 287a
antifeminism in, 2:286a
Zibaldone magliabechiano, 2:287a
Boccanegra family, 4:558a
Boccanegra, Guglielmo, in Genoa, 5:385a-b
Boccanegra, Simone, 5:385b–386a
Bochka, **2:290b**
Bodel, Jean, **2:290b–291a**, 3:536b
Aucassin et Nicolette, 5:255a
Chanson des Saxons, 2:291a, 5:255a
amorous subplot, 5:241a
poetic form, 9:634a
Congés, 2:290b
"De Gombert et des deus clers," 6:555b
exaltation of Charlemagne, 5:244a
fabliau and, 4:574b
Huon de Bordeaux, 5:258b
Jeu de St. Nicolas, 2:290b–291a, 4:264a, 5:255a, 256b, 264a, 8:431b, 9:633b, 636a
inns in, 6:468b
on romance narrative, 5:445a
Bodin, Constantine, crowned tsar of the Bulgarians, 11:171b–172a
Bodisattva legend, as a basis for *Barlaam and Josaphat,* 8:18b
Bodleian Library Laud Misc. 610 (manuscript). *See* Laud Misc. MS, 610
Bodmer, Johann Jakob, 5:443b
Parzival and, 12:679b–680a
Bodo-Eleazar (Spanish Christian convert to Judaism), 7:95b, 10:2b
Bodonitsa, Pallavicini and, 7:376a
Body corporate. *See* Corporation
Body and the Soul, 8:316a
Boece, Hector, 11:112a
chronicle by, 11:116b
Boecis, 6:442a
dialectical origin of, 10:156b
Boendale, Jan van
Brabantsche yeesten, 4:319b
Leken spieghel, 4:319b
Bœrings saga, 10:394b, 395b
Boerden, 4:320a
Boethius, Anicius Manlius Severinus, **2:291a–293a**
Archimedes and, 1:434b
Aristotle and, 1:460b
Cassiodorus and, 8:638a
Categoriae, 9:189a
Ciconia and, 8:646a
commentaries on, by Gilbert of Poitiers, 5:528a
Consolation of Philosophy, 2:292b, 6:443a, 7:361b, 9:700b, 701a, 10:354b, 11:302a
Anglo-Norman adaptation of, 1:264a
Augustinian philosophy, 9:616b
concept of fortune in, 5:145b–146a, 146b, 12:625a
form of, 1:182b
glosses on, 10:303a
humanistic rationalism, 9:585a
as literary source, 6:169b
meter of, 7:372a
Nicholas Trevet on, 12:186b
Notker Teutonicus and, 9:188b, 189b
precursors of, 1:182b
purpose of, 1:166b
realism and, 10:269b–270a
references to pagan themes in, 1:182b
*Speculum music*e and, 8:582b
Tesoretto and, 7:383a
translations into Old English, 1:165a, 166b–167a, 280b, 284a
Contra Eutychen et Nestorium, 3:321a
realism and, 10:271b
Cosmographia and, 7:366a
De hebdomadibus, influence on ontology, 2:36a
De hypotheticis syllogismis, 2:292a
De institutione arithmetica, 2:291b, 8:206a, 605a (*illus.*), 637a, 10:237a, 12:139b
realism and, 10:270b
De institutione musica, 2:291b, 7:38a, 8:579a, 637a-b
on alphabetic notation, 8:614a
commentaries on, 7:38b
Gerbert of Aurillac on, 8:640a
Giorgio Anselmi and, 8:648a
psychic and cosmic harmony, 6:100a-b
De interpretatione, 9:189a
De plana musica and, 8:643b
De topicis differentiis, 4:169a, 170a, 10:354b–355a
De Trinitate, 4:298a
Notker Teutonicus' lost treatise on Trinity and, 9:189a
realism and, 10:269b, 271b
on dialectic and rhetoric, 10:355a
Dialogus and, 8:640b
education of, 2:291a
Euclid's *Elements,* translations of, 8:208a
execution of ordered by Theodoric the Ostrogoth, 12:19a
Gaffurius and, 8:649a
Glarean and, 8:649a
glossators and, 10:272a
Commentum in Boethii de Trinitate, 10:270b
Guido of Arezzo and, 8:641a
Heinrich of Augsburg and, 8:642a
Hrotswitha and, 6:314a
Hucbald and, 8:626b
imprisonment and execution of, 2:291b, 9:291b
In Isagogen Porphyrii commenta editio secunda, 10:271a-b
In topica Ciceronis, 4:169a, 10:238a
influenced by John the Deacon, 2:292a
Johannes de Grocheo and, 7:118b–119a, 8:644b
Liber quomodo Trinitas unus Deus ac non tres dii, 12:192a
Maximos Planudes' translation of, 12:127a
monochord and, 8:606b, 625–626a (*illus.*)
on music, 5:106b, 6:317a, 317b, 8:581a, 582a-b, 593b
theories of harmony, 6:100a-b
Musica disciplina and, 8:639a
Neoplatonism and, 9:99a
Opuscula sacra, 2:292a
commented on by Gilbert of Poitiers, 12:21b
philosophy of, 2:241a-b, 9:584b–585a
definition of person, 9:599a
effort to reconcile Plato and Aristotle, 4:298a
on essence and existence, 4:510b
quadrivium of disciplines, 9:585a
standardization of vocabulary, 9:584a
Plato and, 9:700b–702a
Porphyry's *Isogoge* and, 9:97a
public career of, 2:291b
Questiones super librum Topicorum, 4:170a
Ramos de Pareja and, 8:648b
Reichenau school and, 8:641b
tonoi, treatment of, 8:450b
translations
of Aristotle, 1:460b, 4:169a–170a, 11:688b, 12:126b
of Greek philosophers, 9:584b
verbum de verbo method and, 12:139a-b
translations of
by Chaucer, 3:283b–284a
into Catalan, 3:168b
Ugolino of Orvieto and, 8:647b
University of Paris and, 1:461b
Usk and, 12:334b
Utrum Pater et Filius et Spiritus Sanctus..., 12:192a
Vincent of Beauvais and, 8:645a
works of, 2:291b–292b
Boethius of Dacia
higher light of faith, 9:598a

On the Eternity of the World, rights of philosphers, 9:607b
speculative grammar and, 10:359b
Boeve de Haumtone, 1:267a-b, **2:293b**
manuscripts of, 2:210a
translated into Norwegian, 10:391b
see also Bevers saga
Bog-iron ore, 8:402a
Bogdan I of Moldavia, voivode, 10:514b
territorial expansion, 12:501b
Bogoliubskii, Andrei, **2:293b**
creation of empire, 8:538b–539a
Mother of God of Vladimir and, 6:411a
Vladimir (city) and, 12:486b
Bogomilism, **2:294a–297b**
Angevins and, 6:345b
biblical tales and, 2:297b
in Bosnia, 2:296b
in Bulgaria, 9:510a
alleged role in political affairs, 2:295a
Catharism and, 3:182a-b, 183b–184b, 6:196b
condemned in 1211, 2:294a
in Constantinople, 2:295b–296a
Docetism and, 4:233a-b
doctrine of, 2:294a, 295a, 296a
dualistic theology, 6:192a
Interrogatio Johannis, 2:294b, 297b
in Macedonia, 2:294b, 296a-b
other heresies and, 2:294b, 296b–297a
Paulicians and, 9:469a
rise of, 2:405b
sectarian elements, 2:467a
in Serbia, 2:296b
sources on, 2:294a, 294b
spread of, 2:295b
Bohemia
administration of, 2:301a
Austria and, 2:7a-b
Black Death in, 2:264a, 303b
celebration of St. Stanislaus' office and, 10:371a
Christianization of, 2:299a, 299b, 303b–304a, 8:443a
Czech literature, 11:343a–344b
Frisian traders and, 9:88b
glassmaking in, 5:558a
Gothic art in, painting, 5:610a
history, Samo's state, 12:617a
internal independence established, 2:300a
jewelry of, 5:377b
mining areas in, 8:398b–399a
origin of the name, 2:297b
Přemyslid dynasty in, 10:87b–89a
raised to the status of kingdom, 2:299b
representative assemblies in, 10:329a
Slavic language in, 11:341a-b
Slavs in, 11:348b
under Charles IV, 2:300b
under George of Podêbrady, 5:489b–490a
under Matthias Corvinus, 5:490a
under Sigismund, 5:489b, 11:287b
Wenceslaus II and, 10:330a-b
see also Great (or Old) Moravia
Bohemia-Moravia, **2:297b–305b**, 2:298 (map)
economy of, 2:301b–303a
Poland and, 9:717a–718b, 720a, 728a
political developments (9th–15th centuries), 2:299b–300b
royal towns in, 2:302b–303a
Silesia and, 9:720a
social patterns of, 2:301b–303b
see also Luxembourg dynasty
Bohemian Brethren, **2:305b–308a**
changes in the second generation, 2:307a-b
division of in the 1490's, 2:307b
Martin Luther and, 2:307b
origin of, 2:306b–307a, 6:377b
persecuted by George of Poděbrady, 2:306b
reinterpretation of sacraments, 2:307a
Bohemian school of painting, 5:610a
Bohemond I of Antioch, prince, **2:308a–309b**
claim to Antioch, 1:158b
crusade against Byzantines, 2:494a
in crusades, 2:308b–309a, 4:20a, 30b, 34a,b, 35a-b
imprisoned, 2:309a, 4:36b, 91b
siege of Antioch, 2:495b
Tancred and, 11:589a, 589b
vs. Alexios I Komnenos, 1:158a, 2:308b, 309a-b
vs. Byzantines, 7:284a
Bohemond III of Antioch, prince, Tarsus and, 11:599b
Bohemond VI of Antioch, prince
vs. Aleppo, 6:329a
al-Lādhiqiya and, 7:315b
Bohemond of Sicily. *See* Bohemond I of Antioch, prince
Bohemond of Tarentum. *See* Bohemond I of Antioch, prince
Bohuslän
Norwegian unification and, 9:182b
Old Norse kingdom and, 9:179b
Boiardo, Matteo, *Orlando innamorato,* 6:639b, 670a, 8:225b
Boileau, Étienne
appointed provost of the guilds, 4:328b
Livre des métiers, 4:328b
on 13th-century chariots, 12:375a
on wheelwrights' guild, 12:374a
Boinebroke of Douai, Jean, wool trading, 11:711b–712a
Bois Protat, **2:309b–310a**, 12:690a
discovery of, 2:309b
Boisseau (unit of measure), **2:310a-b**, 12:587a
Bojador, Cape, 4:561a
Boke of Cupide, The. See Clanvowe, Sir John
Boke of Curtasye, 3:661a
Boke of Kervinge. See Wynkyn de Worde
Boke of Nurture. See Russell, John
Boke of St. Albans, 6:176b, 361a
Bokenham, Osbern, Lives of women saints, 6:63a
Boleslav I of Bohemia, prince, 10:88a
Boleslav II of Bohemia, prince, 8:443a
Bolesław I (the Brave) of Poland, king, 9:719a-b
coronation of, 9:628a-b
Erik the Victorious and, 11:530a
Bolesław II (the Bold) of Poland, king, 9:720a
Bolesław III (the Wry-mouthed) of Poland, king, 9:720a-b, 723b
division of regnum, 9:628b
Boleslaw Chrobry of Poland, Stephen I of Hungary and, 11:480a
Bolg an tsoláthair, 6:525b
Bolgarin, Gregory, metropolitan of Russia, affiliation with Constantinople, 10:594b
Bolingbroke, Henry. *See* Henry IV of England, king
Boll (unit of measure), **2:310b**
of bear's sowing, 12:586b
water of Tay and, 12:589a
see also Peck
Bolla þáttr, 7:528b
Laxdœla saga and, 12:2b, 4a, 4b
Bolland, Jean, *Acta sanctorum,* 6:70b
Bollandists, *Analecta Bollandia,* 6:70b
Bolnisi Seon, **2:311a**
architecture of, 5:408b
cruciform piers, 2:311a
inscription at, 5:416a
transverse section and ground plan, 2:311 (*illus.*)
Bologna
Camera actorum, 6:657b
as a center of dictaminal art, 10:358b–359a
civil war, in popular poetry, 6:658a
inns in, 6:474a, 474b
liturgical drama in, 6:637a
revolt of, 3:439b
sericulture in, 11:295a
Visconti rule of, 8:379b
war with Venice (1273), 5:4b
Bologna, Concordat of (1516), 5:181b
Bologna, University of, **2:311b–313a**, 7:512b–514b
ars notaria in, 12:284a
astronomy at, 1:613a
communal tradition, 2:312b
course of study, 7:515a
daughter universities, 2:312b
decline of, 12:284b
development of *studium,* 12:284a-b
dictamen of, 4:174b
dissections of cadavers at, 8:252a, 259b
division into nations, 7:514a, 12:284b
economic power of students, 12:284a
faculty of art and medicine, 2:312a
famous masters of, 12:283b–284a
influence on other universities, 2:312b
law school, 2:312a, 5:565b, 8:158a-b, 9:671a–672b
Bulgarus at, 2:417b
curriculum, 11:691a
Gratian's method of teaching, 7:513b
histories of, 9:221b
Irnerius' lectures, 7:513b
ius commune and, 7:513b–514a
law codes of, 7:429a
origins of, 5:566b–567a

Bologna, University of (*cont.*)
law school (*cont.*)
as paradigm of European law schools, 7:512b–513a
pragmatic approach to law, 5:567b–568a
quaestiones disputatae, 7:515b
textual emphasis of, 5:567a-b
manuscript book production and, 8:103a, 103b
migrations from, 7:514a
notarial studies, 2:312b
preeminence of, 7:514b
school of rhetoric, 2:312b
secessions from, 12:284a
statutes, 2:311b
student-teacher relations, 7:514a
student-town problems, 7:514a
teaching doctors, hiring of, 2:311b–312a
teaching methods, 7:513b, 515a-b
universitas scholarium, 2:311b–312a
see also Universities; Vacarius
Bolorgir, 1:492a-b
Bolotnikov, Ivan, 11:197b
Bolsena, miracle of, 6:636a
Bolsena Cathedral, frescoes, 6:636a
Bol'shoi znamenny. See Znamenny, large
Bombarde, 8:603b
Bona, Giovanni, 2:171b
Bona of Savoy (widow of Galeazzo Maria Sforza), 11:216b
Bonaccorso of Milan, writings of, 3:182a
Bonadies, Johannes, 4:580a
Bonafed, Solomon ben Ruben, Christian-Jewish polemics and, 10:6a-b
Bonagiunta da Lucca
Dante on, 6:387b, 645b
Guinizzelli and, 6:646a
Bonagiunta Orbicciani, 6:643b–644a
Bonagratia of Bergamo, Ockham and, 9:209b
Bonanno of Pisa, 9:666a
Bonatti, Guido, 1:607b
Bonaventure mizzen, 11:237a
Bonaventure, St., **2:313a–319b**, 3:641b, 642a
Apologia pauperum, 2:318a, 10:122b
Aristotle and, 1:462a
biography of St. Francis, 2:316b–317a, 5:201a
Breviloquium, 2:314b, 9:601a
Christology of, 3:323b
Collationes de decem praeceptis, 2:317b
Collationes in Hexaëmeron, 2:318b
Collationes de septem donis Spiritus Sancti, 2:317b–318a
commentary on Peter Lombard's *Sentences,* 2:313b, 314a-b, 9:517b
concept of paradise of, 9:397a-b
Contemplatio, 3:167a
De mysterio Trinitatis, 2:313b
De perfectione evangelica, 2:315a
De perfectione vitae ad sorores, 2:316a
De reductione artium ad theologiam, 2:314b, 6:321b
De regimine animae, 2:317b
De scientia Christi, 2:313b
defense of Franciscan friars, 5:200b
as doctor of the church, 4:234b
as exegete, 2:313b–314a, 4:544b
as Franciscan minister general, 2:315a-b
general chapter at Narbonne, 5:201a
hymns of, 6:382a
influence of, 12:194a-b
on the N-town plays, 9:50a
"intelligible cross" ecclesiology, 4:375b
mystical works
De triplici via, 2:316a
Itinerarium mentis in Deum, 2:315b–316a
Lignum vitae, 2:316a
Soliloquium, 2:316a
nominalism and, 9:155b
nomination as archbishop of York, 2:317a
nomination as cardinal bishop, 2:318b–319a
opposition to philosophy, 9:607a-b
original justice, 9:600b
on Paradise, 9:397a-b
pilgrimage to La Verna, 2:315b
as poet, 7:369a
posthumous titles, 2:319a
reunion with Greek church and, 2:318b, 319a
sermons, 2:315b
on the Gospel of the day, 2:314b–315a
Siger of Brabant and, 1:463a
Thomas Aquinas and, 12:39b
Trinitarian doctrine and, 12:193b–194a, 195a
University of Paris philosophers and, 11:286a
on unorthodox teaching, 2:317b–318a
Urban IV and, 12:688b
on Virgin Mary, 12:460a, 461a
Boncompagno of Signa, **2:320a-b**
dictamen of, 2:320a, 4:174b, 10:358b
Libellus de malo senectutis et senii, 2:320b
Liber de obsidione Ancone, 2:320a-b
Orléans school and, 2:320a
Rhetorica antiqua sive Boncompagnus, 2:320a
Rhetorica novissima, 2:320b, 10:355b
Tractatus virtutum, 2:320a
Wolfger von Erla and, 12:673a
X tabulae salutationum, 2:320a
Bondie Dietaiuti, 6:643b
Bondol, Jean, **2:320b–321a**, 8:109b
Apocalypse tapestry and, 11:591b–592a
Bataille and, 2:129b
works in International Style, 5:628b
Bondone, Giotto di. *See* Giotto di Bondone
Bone dame, la. See Gute Frau, Die
Boner, *Edelstein,* 4:572b
Bonet, Honoré
Arbre des batailles, 3:205b, 6:334b
chivalry handbooks and, 3:302a
Bonet de Lattes, 7:110a
Bonfils, Immanuel ben Jacob, of Tarascon, 1:613a
mathematical works of, 11:92a
Six Wings, 11:91a
Bonfini, Antonio, 6:348b
Boni homines, in communes, 3:500b, 501b
Boniface VIII, pope, **2:323a–324b**, 3:643b, 9:709a
Angevins and, 10:524a
on Armenian-Roman church union, 3:394b
Arnald of Villanova and, 1:537b
Augustinus Triumphus and, 2:1b
Ausculta fili, 2:3b–4a
canon law code commissioned, 7:416b, 428a
canonization of Louis IX, 5:171b
charges of heresy, 4:483b
clash with Philip IV of France, 3:438b, 515a, 4:218a, 259a, 10:21a–22b, 317b
arrest of, 9:554b–555a
humiliation of, 9:385b
immunity of church, 5:172a
jurisdictional issues, 7:267a-b
taxation of clergy, 2:323b, 324a, 5:171a–172a, 11:609b–610a
Clericis laicos, 2:323b, **3:447b-448a;** 11:609a, 609b
condemnation of dismemberment, 4:120b
Dante and, 4:98b–99a
deposition of, 2:324a
Etsi de statu, 11:609b–610a
Franciscan Second Order and, 12:688b
income of, 10:525b
indulgences and, 6:447a
interdict and, 6:495b, 496a, 496b–497a
Jacopone da Todi and, 6:651a
John of Paris and, 7:136b–137a
kidnapping and death of, 5:172a
Liber sextus, 2:324a, 3:523b, 642a, 4:133b, 7:428a, 8:232a
limitations on mendicant orders and, 8:274a
Matthew of Aquasparta and, 8:227a-b
Nogaret and, 9:153a
opposed by Jacopone da Todi, 7:34a
papal conclave and, 3:523b
power of pope and, 10:32a
Quaestio in utramque partem attack on, 10:238a
reign of, 3:354a
taxation controversy, 11:621a-b
tercias and, 11:610a
theory of papal authority, 4:376a
Unam sanctam, 2:324a, 4:376a, 8:227b
on the Doctrine of Two Swords, 12:234b
vs. Colonna family, 2:323b–324a, 3:95b
Boniface IX, pope
jubilee of 1400 and, 10:526b
refusal to abdicate, 11:40b–41a
Roman commune and, 10:524a-b
Zabarella and, 12:735a
Boniface, Count, defeated by Vandals, 12:354b

Boniface Ferrer, Carthusian master general, 12:453a
Boniface of Montferrat, **2:323a**
  in Byzantine Romania, 7:376a, 376b
  disliked by Robert de Clari, 10:431b
  in Fourth Crusade, 4:42b–43a, 44b–45a, 46b, 47a, 48b
  Greek campaigns, 12:638a
  patron of Raimbaut de Vaqueiras, 10:251a
  Thessaloniki and, 7:347a, 12:26b
Boniface, St., 2:172a, **2:321a–322b,** 7:362a
  anointing of Pepin III, 9:501a
  Bede and, 2:155b
  Christianization of Germans, 4:458b
    Bavaria, 2:134a, 322a
    Frisia, 2:321a-b, 322b
    Hesse, 2:321b
    organization of church, 2:322a, 322b
    Thuringia, 2:321b–322a
  church reform of, 3:347b, 373b, 9:501b
  classical literary studies and, 3:432b–433a
  establishment of Fulda and, 2:322a, 5:311b
  establishment of Salzburg bishopric, 2:4b
  Frankish church and, 12:683a
  Latin riddles by, 1:254b
  martyrdom, 8:159a-b
  missions of, 3:344b–345a, 8:441a-b, 12:151b
  Regula sancti Benedicti and, 2:170a-b
  secular powers, protection of, 2:322a-b
  Tatian manuscripts and, 11:600b
Boniface VIII, pope, *Clericis laicos,* 2:323b, **3:447b–448a**
Bonino da Campione, **2:324b**
  monument of Bernabò Visconti, 2:324b
  tomb of Signorio della Scala, 2:324b
Bonis brothers, 6:469a
Bonizo of Sutri
  on the earliest altars, 1:221b
  Liber de vita christiana, 3:358b, 7:410b
  on the liturgy, 7:629b
  on penance, 9:491b
Bonnano (Bonnanus) da Pisa, **2:324b–325a,** 8:284b
  Pisa Cathedral and, 2:324b, 10:503a
Bonnet (sailmaking), 11:241a-b
Bonoeil (monastery), 12:685b
Bonsenyor, Jaruda, 3:168a
Bonsignori family, 2:76b, 77b
  failure of, 11:280a
  Guelf supporters, 11:279b
  papacy and, 11:279a
Bonus socius. *See* Nicholas, Master
Bonvesin de la Riva, 3:665a
  De magnalibus urbis Mediolani, 6:631a
  De quinquaginta curialitatibus ad mensam, 3:665a, 6:631a
  De vita scholastica, 6:631a
  Disputatio rosae cum viola, 6:631a
  Laudes de Virgine Maria, 6:631a
  Libro delle tre scritture, 6:631a, 651a
Bonvicino da Riva. *See* Bonvesin de la Riva
Book. *See* Manuscript books
Book of the Anchorite. See Llyvyr Agkyr Llandewivrevi
Book of Animals. See Jāḥiẓ, Abū ʿUthmān ʿAmr ibn Bahir al-
Book of Argument and Proof in Defense of the Despised Faith. See Judah Halevi, *Sefer ha-Kuzari*
Book of Armagh, 2:220a, 4:526b (*illus.*)
  appended material in, on two Patricks, 9:465b
  sayings attributed to St. Patrick, 9:463b–464a
  see also Patrick, St.
Book of Ballymote, preservation of, 3:224b
Book of Beliefs and Opinions, The. See Saadiah Gaon, *Kitab al-amānātwa-lʾiʿtiqādāt*
Book of Brome, 3:299b
Book of Calculations. See Swineshead, Richard
Book of Ceremonies, 2:516a, 8:557a
Book of Cerne, liturgical play in, 4:280b
Book of Chastity. See Ishoʿdnaḥ
Book of Clarity. See Sefer Bahir
Book of the Conformity of the Life of St. Francis to the Life of the Lord Jesus. See Bartholomew of Pisa
Book of the Consulate of the Sea. *See* Celelles, Francis, *Llibre del consolat de mar*
Book of Contemplation. See Lull, Ramon
Book of Contention (anonymous), 10:4a
Book of the Courtier, The. See Castiglione, Baldassare
Book of the Covenant. See Kimḥi, Joseph
Book of Creation. See Sefer Yezirah
Book on the Creation of the Angels, 4:525b
Book of Curtesye (*Lytel John*), 3:661a-b
Book of Cyfnerth, 12:599b
Book of the Dean of Lismore, 6:535b, 11:113b, 114a, 115a-b
Book of Deer, 3:407a, 11:113b
Book of Definitions. See Israeli, Isaac
Book of Demonstrations. See Eutychios the Melchite, *Kitab al-burhān*
Book of Doctrines and Beliefs. See Saadiah Gaon, *Kitab al-amānātwa-l-ʾiʿtiqādāt*
Book of the Duchess. See Chaucer, Geoffrey
Book of Durrow
  art in, 3:220a (*illus.*)
  Book of Kells and, 7:228b
  carpet pages of, 8:370b–371a (*illus.*)
  Northumbrian scriptorium as source, 3:219b
Book of Eloquence and Exposition. See Jāḥiẓ, Abū ʿUthmān ʿAmr ibn Baḥr al-
Book of Emperors (*Der keiser und der kunige buoch*), 7:478b–479a
Book of the Eparch. See Eparch, Book of the
Book of Excerpts. See Richard of St. Victor
Book of the Gentile and the Three Wise Men. See Lull, Ramon
Book of Glendalough, 6:540a-b
Book of Government. See Niẓām al-Mulk
Book of Governors. See Thomas of Margā, *Book of Superiors*
Book, guide. *See* Guidebooks
Book of the Holy Hierotheos, The, 11:566a
Book of hours, **2:325a–327b,** 3:67b
  of Catherine of Cleves, 9:707b (*illus.*)
  contemporizing of, 2:327a
  on the Continent, 2:326a
  derivation of name, 2:325a-b
  in England, 2:326a
  format, 2:326a-b
  in France, 2:325b
  Giovanni di Benedetto as artist, 5:536b (*illus.*)
  illustration of, 2:325 (*illus.*), 326b–327a
    engraved, 2:327a
  of Isabella of Portugal, 5:367a
  Jean Pucelle's *Hours of Jeanne d'Évreux,* 10:212a (*illus.*), 212b
  of Mary of Burgundy, 5:615a (*illus.*), 615b
  miniature by Claeys Spierinc, 11:463 (*illus.*)
  Office of the Virgin, 2:274a, 325b
  popularity of, 2:326a
  Psalter-hours, 2:325b
  religious instruction and, 10:301b
  replacement of, by psalters, 5:615b
  rhymed offices and, 10:377a
  secular manuscript book production and, 8:104a
  surviving manuscripts, 2:326b
  see also Limbourg brothers; Master of the Boucicaut Hours; Master of the Rohan Hours; *Très riches heures*
Book of Hours of Isabella of Portugal. See René I of Anjou
Book of Ingenious Devices. See Banū Mūsā, *Kitāb al-ḥiyal*
Book of Joseph the Zealot, 10:4a
Book of Kells. *See* Kells, Book of
Book of Knowledge of Ingenious Mechanical Devices. See Jazārī, al-
Book of Lamentations. See Grigor Narekacʿi, St.
Book of Laws. See Mxitʿar Goš
Book lectern
  Muslim. *See Kursī*
  Turkish. *See* Rahle
Book of Leinster, 6:522a, 522b, 541a
  martyrology of Tallaght, 8:162b
  Táin bó Cúailnge and, 11:580b
Book of Letters. See Girkʿ Tʿltʿocʿ
Book of Lights and Watchtowers. See Kirkisānī, Yūsuf Yaʿūb al-
Book of Llandaf, Privilege of Teilo, 12:609b

Book of Long Narratives. See Dīnawarī, Abū Ḥanīfa Aḥmad ibn Dāwūd al-
Book of the Lover and the Beloved. See Lull, Ramon
Book of Marvels. See Polo, Marco, *The Travels of Marco Polo*
Book of the Marvels of the World, A, 8:38b
Book of Misers. See Jāḥiẓ, Abū ᶜUthmān ᶜAmr ibn Baḥr al-
Book of Musical Modes, The. See Ṣafī al-Dīn
Book of One Thousand Judgments, The. See Mātakdān Ī Hazār Dātastān
Book on Optics. See Haytham, Ḥasan ibn al-, *Kitāb al-Manāẓir*
Book of the Order of Chivalry. See Lull, Ramon
Book of Pericopes, 10:102b–103a (*illus.*), 104a-b
Book of Plants. See Dīnawarī, Abū Ḥanīfa Aḥmad ibn Dāwūd al-
Book of Preaching Against the Jews. See Lull, Ramon
Book of Radiations or the Theory of Magic. See De radiis
Book of Revelation. *See* Bible, *Apocalypse* of St. John
Book of Roots. See Joseph Albo
Book of the Secrets of Creation. See Apollonius of Tyana
Book of Songs. See Abu 'l-Faraj al-Iṣfahānī
Book of Speculation, 3:2a
Book of Splendor. See Zohar
Book of the Staff of the Scribes and Implements of the Discerning. See Bādīs, Ibn
Book of Steps, 11:566a
Book of Superiors. See Thomas of Margā
Book of Taliesin, 1:566a, 577a-b, 11:581b–582a, 12:597a, 602a
  poetry on classical subjects, 12:598b
  religious poems, 12:598a
Book of the Three Virtues. See Christine de Pizan
Book of Truth. See Suso, Heinrich, *Büchlein der Wahrheit*
Book of the Two Principles, 3:182a
Book of Uí Mhaine, 6:523a, 523b, 525b
  Donnchadh Mór and, 9:204a
Book of Vices and Virtues, 10:301b
  see also Lorens d'Orléans, *Somme le roi*
Book of Zerubbabel, 1:344b–345a
  literary influences on, 1:344b
  as prototypical work, 1:345a-b
  see also Apocalyptic literature, Jewish
Booke of Gostlye Grace, The (translation of *Liber specialis gratiae*), 9:11a
Books of secrets, 8:35a
Boon works, 4:512b
Boot, Order of the, 3:307a
Boots, 11:255b
Boquetaux Master, 5:615a
Borbas. *See* Ciwnkert
Bordars. *See* Cottars
Bordeaux, **2:327b–329b**
  ancient civilization, 2:327b
  Aquitaine and, 2:327b–328a
  churches and cathedrals, 2:328a
  French conquest, 2:328b
  Gascon War (1294–1303), 2:328b
  Gascony and, 2:327b
  government, 2:328a-b
    Établissements de Bordeaux, 2:328a
  siege of, by Alfonso VIII of Castile, 2:328a
  trade and commerce
    stagnation (15th century), 2:328b
    wine industry, 2:328b, 12:649b, 650a
Bordeaux, University of, 2:328b, 12:285b
Bordelais, bastides in, 2:128b
Borel of Barcelona, count, Sylvester II and, 11:552b
Borerim (Spanish Jewish electors), 7:70b
Borgia, Cèsar (son of Pope Alexander VI), 12:348a
Borgia, Rodrigo. *See* Alexander VI, pope
Borgo San Donnino Cathedral, Benedetto Antelami and, 2:167a
Boril of Bulgaria, tsar
  condemnation of Bogomilism and, 2:294a, 294b
  reign of, 2:408b–409b
  Serbia and, 11:174a
Boris I of Bulgaria, tsar
  Symeon and, 11:554b
  vs. Serbia, 11:168b
Boris II of Bulgaria, tsar, 9:510a
Boris of Bulgaria, khan, **2:329a-b**
  abdication of, 2:404a
  acceptance of Christianity, 2:329a, 402a-b
  administration of, 2:329b
  Adrian II and, 2:403a
  assimilation of Bulgars, 2:329b
  boyars and, 2:402b–403a
  Byzantine church and, 2:403a-b
  Byzantines and, 2:402a
  conversion to Christianity, 8:302a
  legal concerns of, 2:402b, 403a
  military campaigns, 2:329a
  monasticism under, 2:403b–404a
  Nicholas I and, 2:403a
  overthrow of Vladimir, 2:329b
  return of, as ruler, 2:404a
  Slavic assimilation and, 2:403b
  successors of, 2:404a
Boris Godunov of Russia, tsar, serfdom and, 11:197a
Boris of Kiev, St., 12:720a
  cult of, 8:159b–160a
  feast of, 8:574b
  Khanate of Tmutarakan and, 12:66a
Bořivoj of Bohemia, prince, 10:87b
Borna, Croatian prince (*ca.* 810–821), reign of, 4:2a
Bornholm, 5:632a
  archaeological sites, 10:688b
Bornhöved, Battle of (1227), 4:154a
Borough, Hungary, 6:345b
Borough (England-Wales), **2:329b–332a**
  after Norman Conquest, 2:330a
  Anglo-Saxon, 2:330a, 4:457b–458a
  burgage tenure in, 2:330b, 420b–421a
  burghal courts, 2:331a
  charters, 2:330b, 331b
  councils, 2:331a
  customs of Breteuil, 12:517a
  guild merchants and, 2:330b
  land tenure, 2:331b
  municipal officials, 2:331a
  Norman period
    borough courts, 4:465a
    economic revival, 4:465a
    self-government, 4:465b, 469b–470a
  representation in Parliament, 2:331a
  rights and privileges, 2:330a-b
    incorporation, 2:331b
  royal recognition of, 2:330b–331b
  source of income, 2:330a
  taxation, 2:331a
    for corporate purposes, 11:617a
    seignorial, 11:617a
Borough-English, **2:332a-b**
  etymology, 2:332b
  in Glanville, 2:332a
  in manorial law, 2:332a
  primogeniture and, 2:332a-b
  sheriff and, 11:225b
Borrassá, Luís, **2:332b**
  influence on Jaime Ferrer I (the Elder), 5:49b
  works in International Style, 5:627b
Borre style, **2:332b–333b,** 12:418a-b
  cross-slab with ring-chain motif, 2:333a (*illus.*)
  gripping beast pendant, 2:333a (*illus.*)
Borrell, Raymond, count of Barcelona and Girona, 3:175b
Borromini, Francesco, Lateran and, 7:344b
Bortz, Cuman duke, conversion to Christianity, 4:252b
Bósa saga ok Herrauðs, **2:333b–334a**
  dating of, 2:333b
  sources for, 2:334a
  structure, 2:333b–334a
  themes and motifs, 2:333b–334a
Bosch, Hieronymus, 5:87b, 611b–612a
Böse Frau, authorship, 12:596b
Bosnia, **2:334a–341b**
  administration of. *See* Banus
  art and architecture
    gravestones, 2:341a
    metalwork, 2:341b
    stone fortresses and palaces, 2:341b
  bans
    Dabiša, 2:337b
    rule of, 2:335b
    suzerainty, 2:334a-b
  Bogomilism in, 2:296b
  boundaries, 2:335 (map)
  Catholic diocese, 2:334a
  Croatian invasions, 2:334b
  derivation of name, 2:334a
  Donji Kraji, 2:336b
  economy, 2:336b–337a, 339a, 340a–341a
    peasant, 2:340a
  Franciscan vicariate, 2:334b, 336b
  Hercegovina founded, 2:339a
  history (6th through 15th centuries), 2:334b–339b

Hum, 2:335b–336a
annexation of, 2:336b
invaded by Ottomans in 1461, 11:474a
mines in, 2:336b, 340a, 340b, 4:300a
under Stjepan Kotromaniç, 11:486a
Ninoslav, rule of, 2:336a
nobility
council of, 2:337b
courts of, 2:341a
deposition of Ostoja, 2:337b–338a
knez, 2:340a, 340b
territorial control, 2:340a
Ottoman invasions, 2:339a, 339b
Ottoman mercenaries in, 2:338a, 338b, 339a
principalities, 10:649b
Ragusan role in financial administration, 2:336b–337a, 340a-b
regionalism, 2:335a-b, 337b
relations with
Croatia, 4:5a
Hungary, 4:8a, 6:340b, 348a
Serbian control, 2:334b
Slavic settlement, 2:334b
suburban castles, 2:341a
trade and commerce, 2:340b
commercial routes, 2:341a
customs duties, 2:340b–341a
under Hungarian suzerainty, 2:334b, 335b–336a, 339b
under Kulin, 7:309a
županas, 2:334a, 335a
see also Serbia; Tvrtko I; Tvrtko II
Bosnian church, **2:341b–343b,** 7:309a
assigned to Hungarian archbishopric, 2:336a, 342a
Bogomils and, 2:296b
church-state relations, 2:342b
development, 15th century, 2:338b
djed, 2:342a
forced conversion, 2:339b, 343a
lack of organization in, 2:342b
monastic character, 2:342a-b
need for reform, 2:336a
nobility and, 2:342b
separation from Rome, 2:336a, 342a
Stefan Tomaš of Bosnia and, 11:474a
texts
Gospel manuscripts, 2:342b
Gost Radin, 2:342b
theology, 2:342a
dualism, 2:343a-b
under archbishop of Dubrovnik, 2:341b–342a
Boso of Vienne, count, 2:428b
Boson, Nicholas. *See* Nicole Bozon
Boson of Provence, seal wax impression of, 11:125a
Bosporus, **2:343b–344a**
crusaders' route and, 10:423a
Dardanelles and, boundaries, 2:343 (map)
fortress construction, 2:344a
invasion of Constantinople and, 2:344a
trade and commerce, 2:344a
Boss, **2:344a-b**
ceiling, Château of Blois, 2:344b (*illus.*)
see also Tierceron
Bossuet, Jacques, 3:521b
Bostra. *See* Busra
Bosworth, Battle of (1485), 12:572a
death of Richard III at, 10:385b
Botadeo. *See* Wandering Jew legend
Botany, **2:344b–349a**
academic tradition in, 2:345a-b
agriculture and, 2:347b–348a
alimentary uses of plants, 2:347a-b
botanic gardens, European, 5:360b
data
classes of, 2:346a–348a
organization of, 2:344b–345a
Dīnawarī on, 4:188a
domestic and economic uses of plants, 2:347b
floral iconography, 2:348b
folk, 2:345a, 348a
horticulture, 2:347b–348a
in literature, 2:348a-b
medicinal uses, 2:347a
nomenclature, 2:346b
philosophic, 2:346b–347a
doctrine of four elements, 2:347b
ritual and symbolic uses, 2:348a
sources for
literary, 2:345b–346a
nonliterary, 2:346a
taxonomy, 2:346b
treatises, 9:220a-b
see also Herbs
Bote, Hermann, *Ulenspiegel,* 8:360b
Botta, Leonardo, 4:214a
Bottega, **2:349a**
identification of artistic works by, 2:349a
Bottle (unit of measure), 12:592a
Bottles, glass, 5:561a-b
Botu family, inns and, 6:472b
Bouche, 1:525b
Bouchée (unit of measure), 12:592a
Boucher, Guillaume, **2:349b**
silver tree, 2:349b
Boucicault, Jean. *See* Jean Boucicaut
Boucicaut Master. *See* Master of the Boucicaut Hours
Boudolf, Jan. *See* Bondol, Jean
Boundary of Mecca. *See* ᶜ*Alamayn*
Bourbon dynasty, Albret line of Navarre and, 9:72a
Bourbourg, wooden castle at, 3:145a
Bourdichon, Jean, **2:349b–350a,** 5:615b
Bourgeoisie. *See* Class structure, Western European
Bourges Cathedral, 1:427a, 3:568a
construction of west window, 6:39a
Notre Dame de Paris and, 9:191a
Bourges, Statutes of (1407), use of organ music, 9:274a-b
Bourges, University of, 12:285b
Bourgneuf Bay saltworks, 10:630b
technological improvements, 10:632b
Bourret, Étienne, bishop of Paris, revocation of Étienne Tempier's censures, 12:41a
Boutaric, Julien, 6:475a
Boutillier (Bouteiller), Jean
Somme rurale, 4:515b, 7:460a
on inquests, 6:479b
Bouts, Dirk, **2:350a**
Altarpiece of the Holy Sacrament, 2:350a, 5:611 (*illus.*)
Altarpiece of Mary, 5:86b
Deposition Triptych, 5:86b
Gathering of Manna, 5:86b
influences on, 5:86b
style, Haarlem manner, 2:350a
see also Flemish art, painting; Liédet, Loyset; Master of the Life of Mary
Bouvier, Gilles Le, *Le livre de la description des pays,* 12:162b
Bouvines, Battle of (1214), 5:522a, 9:553b
cavalry tactics at, 3:204a
changes in Capetian royal domain after, 5:164b–165a
impact on literature, 5:165b
Bovattieri, 10:526a
Bovo II of Corvey, **2:350b,** 9:701a-b, 10:270a-b
Bow, **2:350b–354b**
brassards, 2:353a
composite, 2:351 (*illus.*)
in Europe, 2:352b
material and construction, 2:350b
reflex curve, 2:350b
compound, Ottoman use of, 9:307a-b
drawing, method of, 2:352b
English longbow
drawbacks of, 2:352b
in Wars of the Roses, 12:565b
history of, 2:352a-b
Europe, 2:352b
Greeks and Romans, 2:352a
horsemen-archers, 2:352a
in hunting, 2:353a, 6:357a
longbow
for archery games, 5:348b
armor and, 1:532a
cavalry and, 3:205a-b
in Hundred Years War, 6:332b, 333b
pellet, 2:353a
self-, 2:351 (*illus.*)
material and construction, 2:350b
in the *Smithfield Decretals,* 9:83 (*illus.*)
in sport, 2:352b–353a
Flemish archers' guilds, 2:352b–353a
strings, 2:350b
weatherproofing, 2:351a
Bow (musical instrument), origins, 11:660a
Bow and Shield. See Simeon ben Zemah Duran
Bower, Walter, *Scotichronicon* and, 10:435b
Bowing (textile manufacture), cotton bow, 11:696b–697a
Bowling, 5:348a, 351a (*illus.*)
Bowls
glass, Western European, 5:559a
see also Hanging bowl
Boyars, **2:354b–355b,** 2:402b–403a, 406a
administrative and military responsibilities, 2:354b, 4:305b
Bulgaria
revolt against Christianity, 2:329a

Boyars (*cont.*)
Bulgaria (*cont.*)
weakening of, 2:329b
duma and, in Russian principalities, 4:305b
land tenure and, 11:190b
in Muscovy
duties of, 4:306a
14th and 15th centuries, 2:355a
lengthy apprenticeship of, 4:306a
under Donskoi and his successors, 4:306a
Vasilii II and, 4:306a
in Novgorod, 9:194b, 195a, 196b
number of, 2:355a
perquisites of, 2:354b–355a
restrictions on, 2:355a
right of departure, 2:354b, 355a
social composition, 2:355a
Walachian, 12:485a
Boyle, Abbey of, Donnchadh Mór and, 9:204a
Boyle, Robert
foundation of chemistry, 11:651a
thermoluminescence and, 1:431b
Boytac, Diogo, church of Jesus (Setúbal), 5:630 (*illus.*)
Bozen Passion play, 4:270a, 10:245a
staging diagram for, 4:266b (*illus.*)
Božidarević, Nikolas, 4:300b
Bozon (Bozoun), Nicholas. *See* Nicole Bozon
Brabant, fairs, 4:586b
Brabantinus, Thomas. *See* Thomas of Cantimpré
Brabantsche yeesten, Die. See Boendale, Jan van
Brabazon, Roger, 7:193a
Braccio da Montone, Andrea
military tactics, 3:531b
plunder of central Italy, 3:651a
Rome and, 10:524b
Brace (tool), in shipbuilding, 11:243b
Bracelets, 5:378 (*illus.*)
Brachium. See Reliquary
Bracket capital. *See* Capital
Bracteates, **2:355b–356b**
Byzantine, 4th century, 2:355b
categories of, 2:355b
etymology, 2:355b
half-, 2:355b, 356a
migration-period, 2:355b–356a
runic, 10:561b
Denmark, 10:561b (*illus.*)
Scandinavian, 2:356a (*illus.*)
Bracton, Henry de, **2:356b–357b**, 7:443b
Bracton's Note-Book, 2:357a
judicial career, 2:356b, 7:191b
kingship theories of, 7:266a
legal maxims, 8:232a
on markets, 8:145a
maxim *Quod omnes tangit* and, 9:425a
Mirror of Justices and, 8:433b
On the Laws and Customs of England, 2:356b, 4:533b, 5:544a, 7:443b
Coutumes de Beauvaisis and, 2:144b
difficulties in interpretation, 2:357a-b
Roman influence, 2:357a, 7:423a
treatises on, 2:382b
use of cases in, 2:357a
writs, 2:357a, 9:311b
see also English common law
Bradshaw, Henry, 10:127a
Bradwardine, Thomas, 1:464b, **2:357b–359a**
Archimedes and, 1:435a
De causa Dei contra Pelagium et de virtute causarum, 2:358a-b
sources for, 2:358b
De continuo, 2:358a
De insolubilibus, 2:358a
De proportione velocitatum in motibus, 2:358a, 11:534a
Edward III and, 2:358b
election to see of Canterbury, 2:358b
Geometria speculativa, 8:215b
nominalism and, 12:44a
predestination and, 2:358b, 3:371a
scientific theories, 2:358a
effects of motion measured, 9:626a
ratios and proportions, 9:625a-b
Secretum secretorum and, 11:135b
Swineshead and, 11:534b, 535a, 535b
theological works, 2:358a-b
Tractatus de proportionibus, forced motion, Aristotelian theories of, 8:217b–218a
Braga, Councils of
First (561), 1:606a, 10:36b
condemnation of dualism, 4:297b
on liturgical tunicle, 12:398b
Third (675), 10:298a
on the use of stole, 12:402a
Braghenda (a *rímur* meter), 10:405b
Bragi Boddason the Old, **2:359a–360a**, 5:372a-b, 11:23a
drótkvætt stanzas by, 4:295a
Ragnarsdrápa, 7:230b, 11:320a
description of *Hamdismál,* 6:88a
diction and metrical structure, 2:359b
shield motif, 2:359a, 359b
in *Snorra Edda,* 2:359a
on Thor's encounter with Midgard, 12:45b
version of *Hjaðningavíg* in, 6:267b
in *Skáldatal,* 11:316b
in *Skáldskaparmál,* 11:354b
see also Þjóðólfr ór Hvini
Bragi (deity), 11:26b
in *Skáldskaparmál,* 11:323b–324a, 353a
Bragða-Mágus saga. See Mágus saga jarls
Brahe, Tycho, 1:613a-b, 615a
scientific instruments developed by, 11:103a
Brailes, William de, **2:360a**, 8:104a
Bran mac Febail (literary character), 6:530a, 530b, 551b
Brancaleone degli Andalò, 10:523b
Branches (series of stories), 2:141b
Brandenburg, **2:360a–362a**
Altmark, 2:360b
Ascanian colonization, 2:360a
boundaries, 13th century, 2:360b, 361 (map)
division of, 2:360b
dynastic changes in, 5:493b
Frederick VI and, 9:202a
Germanization, 2:360b
in Golden Bull of 1356, 2:361b
history, 10th–15th centuries, 2:360a–362a
Hohenzollern governorship, 2:362a
Nordmark, 2:360b
representative assemblies in, 10:329a
serfdom in, 11:207b
suzerainty over Pomerania, 2:360b
vs. Denmark, Rügen and, 12:668b
Wittelsbach rule of, 2:361a-b
Brandeum, **2:362a–363a**
nonspiritual function, 2:362a, 363a
relic veneration and, 10:296a, 297a
as saintly relic, 2:362a–363b
origin of, 2:362b
see also Relics
Brandkrossa þáttr, Droplaugarsona saga and, 12:4a
Brandr Jónsson
attribution of *Alexanders saga* to, 1:152a
translations
of *Alexanders saga,* 10:391b
of *Gyðinga saga,* 6:41b
Brandr Kolbeinsson, lament for, in *Sturlunga saga,* 11:500a
Brandr Sæmundarson, 11:497b
Brands þáttr ǫrva, 12:2b, 4a
Brandy, 4:220a
Braničevo, 11:176a
Branimir (*fl.* 879–892), reign of, 4:2b
Branković, George, Hunyadi and, 6:363b
Brankoviçi, 11:180a, 180b
in surviving chronicles, 11:182b
Brant, Sebastian, **2:363a–364a**
Narrenschiff, 2:363b–364a, 8:322a, 361b
Robin Hood and, 10:435a
Branwen Daughter of Llȝr, 1:567a
Braquemont, Robert de, admiral, 3:62a
Brass. *See* Bronze and brass
Brattahlíð (Greenland), 12:427a-b
Brattishing, **2:364a**
detail of, Shrine of St. Anno, 2:364a
Braulio of Saragossa, St., **2:364b**, 6:381a, 11:406a
Isidore's *De ecclesiasticis officiis* and, 7:626a
Renotatio, 6:564a, 565a
Vita Beati Aemiliani, 2:364b
Vida de San Millán de la Cogolla and, 2:187a
Braun, Peter, of Kirchheim, *via moderna* and, 12:408a
Braunschweigische Reimchronik, 4:505b
Brautmystik
among women mystics, 9:9a, 11a, 12a
in Thomas of Hales, 9:19a
Brautwerbungsschema, 9:293b
Brawler (unit of measure), 12:592a
Brazilwood, 2:148a
production of as dye, 4:328a
Breacadh, 6:534b

Bread, **2:364b–365a**
  baking of, from consumer's grain or dough, 5:121a
  barley, Byzantium, 1:78a
  controlling bakers' profit, 5:121b
  distribution of in Byzantine Empire, 2:478a
  flour, grinding, 2:364b–365a
  income and type of bread consumed, 5:122a-b
  in Jewish dietary rules, 4:183a
  millet and bran, Serdica, 1:78a
  Northern Europe, effect of mill technology on, 1:94b
  offertory
    leavening, 8:189b–190a
    making of, 8:190a
  percent of monthly income spent on, 5:121a
  quality control
    assizes, 5:121b
    size of loaves, 5:122a
    stamps and seals, 5:121b–122a
  specialty products, 5:122b
  trade in, 5:121a–122b
  types of, 2:364b–365a, 5:122a-b
  water mills used for processing flour, 8:393a
  wheat, 5:646a-b
Breast auger, in shipbuilding, 11:243b
Breastplate, 1:526b, 528b, 530a, 530b, 534a (*illus.*)
  colletin and, 1:530a
  "peascod," 1:531a, 531b
Breath deodorizer, 2:147b
Brehon law. *See* Irish law
Breiðabólstaðr, Battle of (1221), 11:357a
Breitinger, Johann Jakob, 5:443b
Bremen
  archbishopric of, 11:530b
  Billungs and, 2:235a
Bremre, Nicholas, Thomas Usk and, 12:333b–334a
Brendan, St., 6:515b, 552a
  immrama tradition of sea voyages and, 12:428a
  lorica of, 3:231a
Brenhinnedd y Saesson, 3:300a
Brentano, Clemens
  Des Knaben Wunderhorn, 7:300b
  minnesingers and, 5:443b
Bres (mythical Irish king), 6:546b, 547b
Brescia, in early Middle Ages, 12:320b
Brescia reliquary chest (ivory), 4:352a
Breslau, Mongol invasion of, 5:461a
Breslau altarpiece, *Descent from the Cross,* 9:710 (*illus.*)
Bressanone, bishopric of, Nicholas of Cusa and, 9:123b
Breta sǫgur, **2:365b–366a**, 5:389b, 10:389b
  authorship, 2:365b
  epilogue, 2:365b
  Hauksbók redaction, 2:365b
  Merlínusspá and, 2:365b, 8:275b–276a
  Rémundar saga keisarasonar and, 10:304a
  translation, 2:366a
  Trójumanna saga and, 12:207b
Bretèche, 3:146b
Brethren of the Common Life, **2:366a–370a**
  after Reformation, 2:369a-b
    Protestant conversion, 2:369a
  attacks on, 3:649a
  Bible, Low German New Testament, 2:369a-b
  common ownership of property, 2:366a-b, 367b
  daily routine, 2:367a
  Devotio Moderna and, 3:369a, 4:166a–167a
  expansion, 15th century, 2:367a
  formation of, 3:368b
  functions of
    book copying, 2:366b
    preparation of liturgical texts, 2:367b
  Gabriel Biel and, 2:233b, 234a
  Geert Groote and, 2:366b, 5:680b
  Gerson and, 5:512b
  houses of, 2:366b, 367a
    St. Peter at Einsiedel, 2:368b
    under direction of Windesheim, 2:367b
  humanist movement and, 2:368b–369a
  meditation, 2:367b–368a
    chiropsalterium, 2:368a
    on Communion, 2:368a
  monastic influence, 2:366a-b, 367a-b
  Nicholas of Cusa and, 9:123a
  Ruusbroec and, 9:38a
  schools, 2:366b, 367a, 369a
  women mystics in the Low Countries and, 9:11b
  see also Thomas à Kempis
Brethren of the Free Spirit, 12:661a
Brethren of the Sword, 11:549a
Brétigny, Treaty of (1360), 3:269b, 5:185b, 6:331b, 332a, 9:427b
  King John II's ransom, taxation and, 10:319a-b
  in *Piers Plowman,* 7:332b
  travel safe-conduct, 12:161b
Břetislav I of Bohemia, prince
  Conrad II and, 2:299b
  Henry III and, 6:162a
Breton dialect, 3:234a, 6:436b, 442a
Breton lays. *See Lai*
Breton literature, **2:370a-b**
  Arthurian legends, 8:223b–224a
  folktales, Tristan legend and, 12:200b
  influence of, 2:370a
  oral tradition, 2:370a
  poetry
    love, 2:370a
    versification of, 2:370a
  texts, 15th century, 2:370a-b
  see also Lai, lay
Breton (unit of measure), 12:594a
Bretons
  in Armorica, 10:464b–465a
  vs. Charles the Simple, 9:160a
Brevary of Chester History. See Rogers, Robert
Breve, 8:629 (*illus.*)
  in *Ars nova,* 1:548b–549b, 550b
Brevi (Synod of North Britain), penance and, 9:488b
Breviari d'amor. See Ermengaud, Matfre
Breviarium, Berno of Reichenau and, 8:641b
Breviarium. See Wipo of Burgundy
Breviarium ab urbe condita. See Eutropius
Breviarium de dictamine. See Alberic of Monte Cassino
Breviarium extravagantium. See Bernard of Pavia
Breviarium regum Francorum. See Notker Balbulus
Breviarium sive ordo officiorum per totam anni decursionem
  origin of breviary and, 2:371a-b
  saints and seasons, propers of, 2:371b
Breviarum. See Nikephoros I, patriarch
Breviary, **2:370b–373a, 9:688b**
  collectariums, 2:371a
  complexity of, 2:326a
  development of, 3:67b
  Divine Office, 4:225a-b
    reorganization of Papal Chapel, 2:371b–372a
  Franciscan, 2:372a-b
  Monte Cassino MS, 2:371a-b
  ordo, simplification of, 2:370b–371a, 372a
  origin of, 2:370b–371b
  printing of, 2:373a
  Roman, 2:372b
  Romano/Franciscan, 2:372b–373a
  size of, 2:371a
  as a source for rhymed offices, 10:376a
  see also Plainsong
Breviary of Alaric, **2:373a-b,** 7:469b–470a, 520a, 12:471b, 472a, 473a
  Codex Theodosianus and, 3:475b
  Corpus iuris civilis and, 7:418b
  illustrations in, 2:373b (*illus.*), 373a-b
  see also German law, early Germanic codes; Spanish law
Breviary of Queen Isabella of Spain, 8:607a (*illus.*)
Breviary-missals, for Divine Office, 4:225a
Breviatio canonum, 7:400a
Breviloquium. See Bonaventure, St.
Brevis, 8:588b, 628 (*illus.*)
  in *ars nova,* 10:381b
  in Augustine's *De musica,* 10:378b
  in the *perfectio,* 10:380b–381a
  see also Perfectio
Brevis compilatio in arte musica. See Marchettus of Padua
Brevis et vera descriptio rerum..., 10:510b
Brevis historia regum Dacie. See Sven Aggesen
Brevis introductio ad dictamen. See Giovanni di Bonandrea
Breweries
  castle, 2:374b–375a
  England, 2:374b–375a
  France, 2:374b
  Germany, 2:375a
  monastic, 2:374a
  North Central Europe, 2:374b
Brewing, **2:373b–375a,** 4:219a–220a

Brewing, **2:373b–375a** *(cont.)*
ale
ingredients used, 5:125b
spoilage, 5:125b
tasters, 5:125b–126a
women brewers, 5:125b
in ancient Egypt, 2:373b–374a
beer, commercialization of, 5:126a
fermentation
cold or bottom, 2:375a
yeast in, 2:374a
flavorings and additives, 2:374a, 374b
"hopping," 2:374a, 374b
hops, antibiotic effect, 1:94b–95a
Latin *cervesia,* 2:374a
in literature, 2:374a-b
mead, 2:374a, 6:284a
medical purposes, 2:373b
technology, hydraulic trip-hammer, 11:651b
water mills used to produce beer mash, 8:393a
water quality, 2:375a
see also Beverages, Islamic
Breydenbach, Bernhard, *Peregrinationes in terram sanctam,* 6:299a
Brézé, Jacques de, "Chasse," 6:357a
Brian Boru, 6:553a
Battle of Clontarf (1014) and, 6:516b, 8:531b, 12:425b
claims to high kingship of Ireland, 3:397a
in *Cogad Gáidel re Gallaib,* 6:539b
reign of, 4:77b
suzerainty over Uí Néill, 8:531b
Brick, **2:375a-b**
architectural adaptation, 2:375b
climatic factors in production of, 2:375a-b
in early Christian architecture, 4:331b
in Islamic architecture, 6:602a, 606a, 607a
mortaring, 2:375b
patterned brickwork, Bukhara mausoleum, 10:636b
in Polish architecture, 9:723b, 730a
size and thickness, standardization of, 2:375b
"Bricriu's Feast." *See Fled Bricrenn*
Brid, John, fraudulent baker, 5:122a
Bride Mysticism. See Brautmystik
Bridge, Battle of the (7th century), 6:568b–569a
Bridge mills, 8:391b–392a
Bridges
in Ani in Širak, 1:292a-b
Roman
construction of, 10:419a, 419b
length of arches and, 10:420b
Western European, **10:409b–422b**
arches of, 10:420b–421a
asymmetry of, 10:421b
bridge building as a pious activity, 10:413a-b
bridge corporations and, 10:413b–414a
chapels in association with, 10:414a
collapse of a bridge over the Seine (1499), 9:419b
collection of tolls and, 10:415b, 416a
construction of, 10:419a–421b, 12:578a-b
houses on, 10:411a
early medieval, 10:411a-b
11th through 14th centuries, 10:413a–418a
as a focus of town life, 10:409b
funding for, 10:416b–417a
maintenance of, 7:660a, 10:412b
medieval view of, 10:410a–411a
parochialism of bridge building, 10:421a, 421b
role in warfare, 10:411b
Roman heritage, 10:410a
Romantic view of, 10:410b
royal support for, 10:417b–418a
stone, 7:661a, 10:416b
surviving medieval bridges, 10:418a–419a
tolls and maintenance, 10:411a-b, 417a-b
urban and secular support of, 10:416b–417b
Brief Chronicle. See George the Monk
Brief Chronological Expositions, 2:513a
Briefbüchlein. See Suso, Heinrich
Briefmaler, 12:691b
Brieven. See Hadewijch of Antwerp
Brig of Ayr, 10:418b
Brigandage, *taille* and, 11:579a
Brigandine, 1:526b, 528a
Brigands. *See* Bandits; Travel and transport, dangers of
Brigata (company), in Boccaccio's *Decameron,* 2:284a-b, 285b
Brigit (Brigid), St., **2:376a–377a**, 3:227b
claimed as patroness by Fothairt, 7:536a
cult of, 2:377a
hagiographic works on, 2:376b, 6:542b
in Latin poems, 2:376b, 377a
lives of, 2:376b, 377a
monastery at Cell-dara
foundation and administration, 2:376a
in literature, 2:376b
in mythology and folklore, 2:376a-b
in *Triadis thaumaturgae acta,* 6:525a
Brihtheath, bishop of Worcester, Wulfstan of Worcester and, 12:703a
Briones, Treaty of (1379), 9:71b
Bristol
Black Death in, 2:262a
sheriff and, 11:225b
Bristol Cathedral, Harrowing of Hell in, 10:110a
British church
development of, 3:225b–226a, 227a
Easter dating in, 3:228a
see also Celtic church
British Isles
Romans in, 2:96a-b
steelmaking in, 11:471b, 472a
British language. *See* Celtic languages
Brito di Brettagna. See Pucci, Antonio
Brito, William, *Summa Britonis,* 4:450a
Brittanie de Engleter. See Livre de Reis. . .
Brittany, Celtic, **2:381a–382b**
art
christianized menhirs, 2:382a
religious iconography, druidic traditions, 2:382a-b
church of, 3:227a, 232a
Celtic vs. Roman rites, 2:381b–382a
monastic influence, 2:381a
government, 2:382a
law
codification of, 2:382a
inheritance, 2:382a
place-names, prefixes of, 2:378a, 381b
Brittany, duchy of, **2:377b–381a**
administrative and legal system
Assize of Geoffrey, 2:379b, 382a
French influence, 2:379b–380a
reforms under John IV, 2:380a-b
Anglo-Norman suzerainty, 2:379b–380a
art and literature, influences on, 2:379a
assimilation of, by France, 2:380b–381a
boundaries, 2:378 (map)
Briton migrations, 2:377b–378a
Carolingian authority, 2:378b–379a
Celtic vs. Latin traditions, 2:377b
civil war, 2:380a
clerical reform in, 10:429a
expansion, 9th century, 2:379a
factionalism in, 2:379a
feudal institutions, 11th century, 2:379b
Gallo-Roman society, 2:377b
internal colonization, 2:379b
military campaigns, 2:379b
place-names, 2:378a
population, 2:379b
relations with
England, 6:332a
Normandy, 9:164a, 167a
representative assemblies in, 10:327a
royal power in, 2:380a
trade and commerce, 2:379b
urban centers, 2:377b, 379b
Viking raids, 2:379a
Britton, **2:382b**
on Exchequer Court, 4:533b
see also Fleta
Brixworth, abbey church, architectural features, 10:680b–681a
Brjáns þáttr, Njáls saga and, 9:145b
Brno, 2:302b
Broad Manner (engraving style), 4:489a
Brocard, Carmelite prior, 3:96b
Brocarda, 4:127b
Brocardus, 1:591a
Broederlam, Melchior, **2:383a**, 5:85a-b
altarpiece by, 5:608b
at court of Philip the Bold, 2:383a
International Style of, 5:628b
Master of Wittingau and, 12:667b
style of, 2:383a
surviving works of, 2:383a
see also Baerze, Jacques de
Broeter Hanze. *See* Bruder Hans
Brokerage, innkeepers and, 6:474a
Brokers, trade regulations and, 12:121a-b
Bromflet. *See* Carver, William

Brömsebro, Treaty of (1645), 5:633a
Bromyard, John
Summa praedicantium, 4:250b, 7:370a, 10:190a
Bronze and brass, **2:383a–385a**
in Carolingian period, 2:384a
casting of, under the Carolingians, 8:283b
Florence Baptistery doors, 10:667b (*illus.*)
making of, 2:383a-b
metallurgy, 8:286a-b, 297a-b
production of, 8:401b
St. Barthélemy baptismal font, 10:253 (*illus.*)
surviving work of, 2:384b–385a
use of
bells, 2:384b
in church buildings, 2:384b
coins, 2:383a, 384b
memorial brasses, 2:384b
working of, 2:384a-b
8:294b-295a
see also Theophilus; Torel, William
Brooches, 5:380a–381a
Burgundian gold, 5:381a (*illus.*)
migration period, Frankish gold disk brooch, 8:367 (*illus.*)
Brot af Sigurðarkviðu. See Sigurðarkviða in forna
"Brotherhood of the Gonfalone," 6:636b
"Brotherhood of St. Thomas Aquinas," 6:636a
"Brotherhood of Sts. Jerome and Anna," 6:637a
Brothers and Sisters of the Common Life. *See* Brethren of the Common Life
Brothers and Sisters of the Free Spirit, 3:370a
Brothers of the Sword
absorbed by the Teutonic Order, 2:65b
Estonians and, 2:65b
founding of, 2:64b
Broun, Robert, **2:385a**
Brucato, hunting in, 6:357b
Bruce, Edward
attack on Dublin, 4:299b
recognized by parliament, 9:439a
in Ulster, 6:518b
Bruce, Robert. *See* Robert I (the Bruce) of Scotland, king
Brude, Pictish king
conversion to Christianity, 9:642b
military campaigns, 9:642b
Bruder Hans, **2:385a–386a**
Marienlieder, 2:385a-b
Bruges, **2:386a–388a**
as artistic center for Flemish masters, 2:387b–388a
castle at, 2:386a
Christianity in, 2:386a
churches in, 2:386a-b
as commercial center, 2:386b–387a
banking in, 2:74a–75a, 387a
money changers in, 2:74a, 74b
protectionist measures, 6:93b–94a
decline of, 2:387b
development of, 2:386a
échevinage in, 2:386b
fairs at, 12:108b
Guild of St. Luke, 8:104b
Hospital of St. John, painting by Hans Memling, 8:272 (*illus.*)
inns in, 6:469b–470a
manuscript book production in, 8:104b
as a market for Madeira sugar, 8:10b–11a
merchant guild in, 2:386b
patricians in, 2:386b
Philip IV and, 2:387b
pilgrimage penalty and fines, 12:156a
as residence of counts, 2:386a-b
ruling elite in, 9:461a
self-government of, 2:386b
tapestry of, 11:596b
as trading center, 12:112b
under Carolingians, 2:386a
under Merovingians, 2:386a
wine trade, 12:650a
Brugge, Jacob van (Flemish settler in the Azores), 2:29b
Brúilingeacht, 6:535a, 535b
Brun (*d.* 880), 5:507b
Brun von Schönebeck
allegory of, 5:429b–430a
commentary on the Song of Solomon, 2:229a-b
Brunanburh, Battle of (937), poem on in Anglo-Saxon Chronicle, 8:328a
Brunechildis, Merovingian queen, Brünhild and, 9:114a
Brunelleschi, Filippo, **2:388a–390b,** 5:101a-b
architecture of, 2:388b
biography of, 2:390a-b
construction techniques
influence of, 11:648a
S. Maria del Fiore dome, 11:647b–648a
Cosimo de' Medici and, 8:243a
Donatello and, 2:388b
Dufay and, 8:585b
Florence Duomo, 4:236a, 9:56a
capping of, 2:388b–389 (*illus.*)
Ghiberti and, 2:388b
influence of, 2:390b
mathematical system of, 2:390b
Ospedale degli Innocenti, 2:388b, 390a
Pazzi Chapel of Santa Croce, 2:389b (*illus.*), 390a
refusal to join stoneworkers' guild, 6:21b–22a
rise of humanism and, 5:101a-b
Sacrifice of Isaac, 2:388 (*illus.*)
San Lorenzo church, 2:390a
Santa Maria degli Angeli, 2:390a
Santo Spirito interior, 2:389 (*illus.*), 390a
style of, 2:388a-b
surviving work of, 2:390a
Uccello and, 12:237a
Brunetto Latini. *See* Latini, Brunetto
Brünhild (epic character), 7:305a, 9:112b, 113b, 114a
see also Brynhild
Brunhilde (leader of Merovingian reforms), 3:104a, 8:278a-b
"Brünhildenlied," 11:289b
Bruni, Leonardo, **2:390b–391b,** 3:654b, 9:703a
at Pisan curia, 2:391a
Basil the Great and, 2:122a
Cosimo de' Medici and, 8:243a
Historia florentini populi, 2:391a
idea of Middle Ages, 8:308b–309a
Laudatio florentinae urbis, 2:390a
On the Right Way of Translating, 12:141a
propaganda for Florence, 2:390b
translations, 7:369b
of Aristotle, 2:391a, 11:457a
wealth of, 2:391a
Brunia (coats of mail), used by the Franks, 8:283a
Brunkeberg, battle at (late 15th century), 11:533b
Brunner, Heinrich, on European cavalry, 3:201a-b
Bruno I of Cologne, archbishop, 3:481a
Gandersheim and, 6:313b–314a
Bruno the Carthusian, St., **2:392a-b**
Carthusian rite and, 3:118a
foundation of order, 2:392a, 3:118a-b, 354b, 4:109b
Gregorian reform and, 2:392a
influence on future Urban II, 12:302b
Bruno of Cologne. *See* Bruno the Carthusian, St.
Bruno of Egisheim. *See* Leo IX, pope
Bruno of Magdeburg, **2:391b**
at court of Archbishop Werner of Magdeburg, 2:391b
De bello saxonico liber, 2:391b
martyred by Old Prussians in 1009, 2:64b
Bruno of Querfurt, St., **2:391b**
martyrdom of, 2:391b, 7:603b
on the subjugation of Ajtony in Hungary, 11:478b
Bruno of Segni, St., **2:392a**
at Monte Cassino, 2:392a
on Concordat of Sutri, 2:392a
theology of, 2:392a
works of, 2:392a
Bruno of Toul, bishop. *See* Leo IX, pope
Bruno of Würzburg, St., **2:392a**
as exegete, 4:543a
Brunsberg, H(e)inrich von, **2:392b**
Parlers and, 2:392b
Brunswick, duchy of
creation of, 5:499b
princely fiefs and, 5:499b
Brunswick (town: Germany)
governing body in, 5:458b
population of, 5:458a
Brusa, **2:392b–393a**
Byzantium and, 2:392b
Ottoman sultans at, 2:392b
sack of, by Tamerlane, 2:393a
Theodore I Laskaris at, 2:392b
Brussels, tapestry of, 11:596b, 597a
Brut d'Engleterre, Le, 5:389b
Brut, the, 1:264b, 265a, 265b, 565a-b, **2:393a–394b,** 8:316a, 318b, 329a, 330a, 330b, 332b
alliteration in, 8:343a
Arthurian legend in, 2:393a-b

Brut, the (*cont.*)
author of, 2:393a
compared with *Ancrene Riwle,* 8:316a
continued in *Anonimalle Chronicle,* 1:309a
dating of, 2:393b
as epic, 2:393b–394a
popularity of, 3:329b
Robert Mannyng's *Rimed Story of England* and, 8:317a
sources for, 2:393a-b
surviving manuscripts of, 2:393b
use of rhyme in, 8:343b
see also Layamon
Brut y Brenhinedd, 12:600b
Brut y Tywysogion, 5:389b
Gruffydd ap Llywelyn, 12:516b
Welsh rulers, 12:516a
Bryennios, Joseph, on Byzantine medicine, 8:246a
Brykhulle. *See Blancheflour et Florence*
Brynhild, **2:394b–395a**
in Eddic poems, 2:394b–395a
in German literature, 2:395a
in *Grípisspá,* 5:678a
in *Guðrúnarkviða* cycle, lament of, 6:36a-b
in *Oddrúnargrátr,* 9:216b
Sigurd and, 11:289a, 289b
in *Sigurðarkviða in forna,* 11:291b, 292a
in *Sigurðarkviða in meiri,* 11:292a-b
in *Sigurðarkviða in skamma,* 11:293a-b
Svipdagsmál and, 11:524b
see also Laxdœla saga; Lied vom hürnen Seyfrid, Das
Brynhildar, 11:293b
Brynolf Algotsson, hymns of, 6:382b
Brythonic language. *See* British language
Bū ᶜAlī. *See* Sīnā, Ibn
Bubonic plague
population decline and, 10:457a-b
see also Black Death; Plagues
Buccio di Ranallo, *Chronicle of Aquila,* 6:633b
Bucelin, Alemannic duke, 11:526a
Bucentaur, **2:395b**
Buch der Abenteuer. See Ulrich Füetrer
Buch von Bern, Das, **2:395b–396b**
Alpharts Tod and, 2:395b
author of, 2:396a
dating of, 2:396a
Nibelungenlied and, 2:396a
Rabenschlacht and, 2:395b
surviving manuscripts of, 2:395b–396a
theme of, 2:396a
Þiðreks saga and, 12:29b
see also Alpharts Tod
Buch der göttlichen Tröstung. See Eckhart, Meister
Buch der Könige, source for *Lohengrin,* 7:643a
Buch der Natur. See Conrad of Megenberg
Buch von den natürlichen Dingen. See Konrad von Megenberg
Buchanan, George, *De jure regni apud Scotos,* 3:522a
Büchlein, 8:408b–409a
Büchlein. See Klage
Büchlein der Ewigen Weisheit. See Suso, Heinrich
Büchlein von der Fialen Gerechtigkeit. See Roriczer, Mathes
Büchlein der Wahrheit. See Suso, Heinrich
Buckler, 1:528a
Buckles, Visigothic, 12:467b
Bucolicum (Buccolicum) carmen. See Boccaccio, Giovanni; Petrarch
Buda, **2:396b**
Béla IV and, 6:342b
captured (1541), 6:350a
during Turkish War, 2:396b
importance of, 2:396b
New Palace of Sigismund, 6:347a
under Ottomans, 2:396b
Budai-Nagy, Antal, 6:347a
Budakha. *See* Paikuli
Buddha
in *Balavariani,* 2:54b
in *Barlaam and Josaphat,* 2:109a
in Manichaeism, 8:85a
in Rudolf von Ems's *Barlaam und Josaphat,* 10:543a
statue of found in Sweden, 12:110a
Buddhism, Tibetan, correspondences with Druzism, 9:3b
Buerse family, inns and, 6:470a
Buevon de Conmarchis. See Adenet le Roi
Buffe, 1:531b, 534a (*illus.*)
tilting, 1:533a
Buffet, 5:324a
Bughā the Elder, vs. Armenian magnates, 1:479b, 513a
Buhlūl ibn Rāshid, Ibrāhīm ibn al-Aghlab and, 6:391b
Buḥturī, al-, 1:400b, 403a
al-Mutawakkil and, 8:654b
Búi Andríðsson, 7:274a
Buik of King Alexander the Conquerour. See Hay, Sir Gilbert
Builders. *See* Masons and builders
Building. *See* Construction
Building of the Ark, 8:661a
Buildings. See Procopius
Buile Shuibhne, 6:528b–529a, 547b
Buinne, 8:558b
Buisine, 8:602 (*illus.*), 603b, 604a, 605a (*illus.*), 607a
Buke of Bataillis. See Hay, Sir Gilbert, *Buke of the Law of Armys, The*
Buke of the Howlat, The, 8:332a
Buke of the Law of Armys, The. See Hay, Sir Gilbert
Bukhalāᵓ, Al-. See Jāḥiẓ, Abū ᶜUthmān ᶜAmr ibn Baḥr al-
Bukhara, **2:396b–397b**
Arab conquest of, 2:397a
embroidered silks, 11:717b–718a
fairs, 4:589a
growth of, 2:397a-b
importance of, 2:397a
mausoleum
building plan, 10:636b
patterned brickwork, 10:636b
Mongol conquest of, 2:397a
Muslims in, 2:397a
pre-Islamic rulers of, 2:397a
Samanid court
library, 10:638b
model for, 10:638b
palace school, 10:638b
under Qarakhanids, 2:397a
under Samanids, 2:397a
Bukhārī, Muḥammad ibn Ismāᶜīl al-, **2:397b–399a**
biographical dictionary of, 2:398b
ḥadīth study of, 2:397b, 6:580b, 7:616b
Ṣaḥīḥ, 2:398b–399a, 6:47b
Sunnites and, 2:397b–399a
as traditionalist, 2:397b–398a
travels of, 2:398b
Bulbous dome. *See* Dome
Bulgaria, **2:399a–414a,** 2:400 (map)
animal husbandry, 1:78b
Basil II and, 2:118b–119b, 407a
Bogomilism and, 2:294a–297b
boyar aristocracy
revolt against Christianity, 2:329a
weakening of, 2:329b
Bulgars in, 2:329b
Byzantine church in, 2:117b, 403a-b
Byzantine Empire and, 2:401a-b, 402a, 404b–405b, 4:4b, 5b, 8:133b–134a, 9:509b
annexation to, 2:490b
resistance to, 2:406b–407b, 488a-b
Byzantine sea routes and, 10:423 (map), 424b
capital of
at Pliska, 2:399b
at Trnovo, 2:408a
Christianity in, 2:329a, 401b–402b, 464a, 489b
civil wars of, 2:401a
crusaders' route and, 10:423a
culture of, 2:413b–414a
ethnic population of, 2:399a-b
First Bulgarian State (681–1018), 2:402b–403a
hesychasm in, 2:413b
Isaac II Angelos and, 6:559b
John Asen II and, 7:131a
Kalojan and, 7:206a-b
Kometopouloi expansion, 10:645a
land ownership, 11:669b–670a
literature in, 11:345a-b
Magyars and, 2:404b, 6:338a
national consciousness in, 2:407a
Nicaean Empire and, 2:409b–411a
Nikephoros I and, 9:132b
Nikephoros II Phokas and, 9:133a
peasants in, 2:405b–406a
Pecheneg raids on, 2:407b
prominence of, 2:399b, 401a
relations with
Croatia, 4:4b, 5b
Ottomans, 2:136b, 413a-b
papacy, 2:408b
Serbia, 2:409a, 411b–413a, 11:345b–346a
religion, Old Church Slavonic, 12:504a
roads in, 10:424a
Russians in, 2:406a
Second Empire of. *See* Vlach-Bulgarian Empire
Slavic language in, 2:403b

  Slavic mission in, 2:403b
  Slavs in, 2:399a-b, 401a, 403b
  states of, 2:410b
  Stefan Uroš IV Dušan of Serbia and, 11:475a-b
  Theodore II Laskaris and, 7:348a, 12:14a
  Turkish raids on, 2:414a
  under Krum, 7:303b–304a
  vassalage in, 2:413a
  vs. Sübüdey, 2:131b
  see also Avars; Magna Bulgaria; Mesembria
Bulgarian art and architecture, **2:414b–417b**
  Byzantine influence, 2:417a
  ceramics, 2:417a
  churches, 2:417a
  gold vessel, 2:415 (*illus.*)
  Kalojan and wife (portraits), 2:416 (*illus.*)
  painting, 2:417a-b
  palace designs, 2:414b
  patrons of, 2:414b
  reliefs, 2:414b
  Sasanian influence on, 2:414b
  Vlach-Bulgarian Empire, 2:417a
Bulgarian church
  Nicenes and, 9:117b
  title of patriarch and, 9:459b
Bulgarian Empire, Second. *See* Vlach-Bulgarian Empire
Bulgarian language, 6:438a, 443b
  Middle Bulgarian, 6:439a
Bulgarian law, codes, 7:303b
Bulgarian literature, 11:345a-b
  Symeon and, 11:554b
Bulgarophygon, Battle of (897), 11:554b
Bulgars
  attacks by
   on Avars, 2:401a
   on Serbs, 2:409a
  Avars and, 2:401a
  in Balkans, 6:437b, 443b
  Boris and, 2:329b
  Constantine V's campaigns against, 2:401a
  conversion of, Nicholas I and, 9:121b
  Franks and, 2:401b
  Greek liturgy and, 12:484a
  Indo-European languages and, 6:434a
  Justinian II and, 7:202b
  Onogur, 2:399a-b
  Russian fur trade and, 5:332a, 333a
  Serdica and, 11:189a
  Sirmium under, 11:311b
  Slavs and, 2:401a, 403b
  Vlachs and, 12:483b, 484a
  vs. Emperor Henry, 12:448b
  vs. Romanos I Lekapenos, 10:515b
  vs. Rome, 10:465a
  see also Bulgaria
Bulgarus, **2:417b–418a**
  as adviser to Frederick I Barbarossa, 2:418a
  Azo and, 2:29a
  Bolognese School and, 5:567b
  Hugo and, 6:323b
  Johannes Bassianus and, 6:326b
  on law, 2:417b
  legal interpretation, role of equity, 8:158a
  legal maxims, 8:231b–232a
  life of, 2:417b–418a
  Rogerius and, 10:444a
  teaching of summarized in Vacarius' *Apparatus glossarum,* 12:343b
  tract on Roman procedure, 7:503b
  see also Jacobus (de Porta Ravennate)
Bulghar (tribal confederation), 12:487b–488a
Bulghar Turkic language, 12:488b
Bull (animal), in *Táin bó Cúailnge,* 11:580b
Bull, papal, **2:418a-b**
  format of, 2:418a-b
  power of pope and, 10:32a
  rescinding of, 2:324a
  seals for, 2:418b
  surviving MSS of, 2:418b
  Western European seals and, 11:124a
Bull of Union, Armenian-Roman, 3:395b
Bulla Cypria. See Alexander IV, pope
Bullae, 11:127b
  application to document, 11:128b
  Byzantine usage of copied in the West, 11:124b
  seal technique and, 11:127a
Buluggīn ibn Zīrī, 12:744a
Bunch (unit of measure), 12:592a
Bundahishn, **2:419a**
  creation account in, 2:419a
Bundle (unit of measure), 12:592a
Bundos (predecessor of Mazdak), 8:236b, 237b
Bunduqdārī, al-. *See* Baybars al-Bunduqdārī
Bunyan, John, *Pilgrim's Progress,* 10:362b, 12:477a
Buon, Bartolomeo, **2:419a-b**
  Giovanni (Nanni) di Bartolo and, 5:536a
Buon, Giovanni, **2:419a-b**
  Giovanni (Nanni) di Bartolo and, 5:536a
Buonaccorsi, Phillip, *Historia de rege Vladislao,* 9:730a
Buonaccorso da Montemagno, *Controversia de vera nobilitate,* as a source for Henry Medwall's *Fulgens and Lucres,* 8:262b
Buonacorso, Nicolo di. *See* Niccolò di Buonaccorso
Buoncompagno of Signa. *See* Boncompagno of Signa
Buondelmonti, Esau, Epiros and, 4:500a
Buondelmonti-Uberti (Guelph-Ghibelline) rivalry, 5:94b–95a
Buonsignori family. *See* Bonsignori family
Būq, 8:561b, 563a, 612b, 613a (*illus.*)
Burāq, 1:581a, **2:419b–420a**
  depiction of, 2:420a (*illus.*)
  iconology of, 6:407b
Burchard II of Alamannia, 5:508a
Burchard II of Swabia, duke, 5:509a, 11:527a
  Rudolph II and, 11:538a
Burchard III of Swabia, duke, 11:527a
Burchard von Hall, 5:582a-b
  Chronicle, opere Francigeno, 9:254b
Burchard of Mount Sion, 4:246b, 253a
Burchard of Rhaetia, margrave, 5:508a
  execution of, 11:526b–527a
Burchard of Worms, **2:420a-b**
  on canon law, 7:407b–408a
  on confession, 2:420b
  on contraception, 3:572a-b
  Decretum (Burchardus), 2:420b, 3:349a, 4:128b, 7:407b–408a, 9:490b
   on baptismal sponsorship, 2:86a
  on witchcraft, 12:660a
  works of, 2:420a-b
Burchard of Würzburg, bishop, Pepin III and, 9:501a
Burckhardt. *See* Burchard
Burdigala. *See* Bordeaux
Bureaucracy, Islamic. *See* Islamic administration
Burel, Geoffrey, peasants' crusade, 9:523a-b
Burgage tenure, **2:420b–421a**
  dating of, 2:421a
  definition of, 2:330b, 420b
  Ireland, 11:685b
  other free tenures and, 2:420b–421a
  territory using, 2:421a
Bürgermeister, 3:502a
Bürgermeister und Königssohn. See Kaufringer, Heinrich
Burgesses, England, rights and privileges, 4:465a-b
Burggraf, 3:481a-b
Burgh. *See* Borough
Burgh, de (family), **2:421a–422a**
  factional fights among, 2:422a
  in Ireland, 2:421b
  members of, 2:421b–422a
  prominence of, 2:421a-b
Burgh, Hubert de, 2:421b
  as justiciar, 7:200b
  regent for Henry III, 6:158b
  Welsh incursion, 12:519b
Burgh, Richard de, 2:421b–422a
Burgh, Walter de, 2:421b
Burgh, William de, 2:421b–421a
Burghausen, Hanns von, **2:422a**
  works of, 2:422a
Burghers. *See* Citizens; Class structure; Trade; Urbanism
Burgonet, 1:527b (*illus.*), 531b
  light. *See Zischägge*
Burgos Cathedral
  Juan de Burgos at, 7:155a (*illus.*)
  Juan de Colonia at, 7:153b
  Simón de Colonia at, 7:153b, 154 (*illus.*)
Burgundian law, 2:423a
Burgundian party in France
  alliance with England, 5:188a
  Charles VII and, 3:270b–271a
  Charles of Orléans and, 3:272b–273a
Burgundian Penitential, 9:489a
Burgundian school
  Entombment of Christ and, 5:402a
  see also Ballade
Burgundian Wars, Swiss military tactics, 12:565b
Burgundians, 2:92a-b, **2:422b–423b**
  Alani and, 2:422b
  Arianism and, 1:454b

Burgundians, 2:92a-b (*cont.*)
  in Basel, 11:538a
  coins issued by, 8:427b
  defeated by Huns, 2:92a
  fall of in "Niflunga saga," 12:30b–31a
  Frankish history and, 2:423b
  in Gaul, 2:423a
  migration of, 2:422b
  in *Nibelungenlied,* 9:113a, 114a
  origin of, 2:422b
  Roman Empire and, 2:422b–423a
    accepted as federate allies, 2:92a
    emperors established by, 2:422b
  rulers of, 2:423a
  in Sapaudia, 11:536b
  vs. Alamanni, 11:526a
  vs. Roman Empire, 12:470a
Burgundio of Pisa, **2:423b–424a**
  Frederick Barbarossa and, 2:423b
  influences on, 2:423b
  translations
    of *De fide orthodoxa,* 2:423b, 9:517a
    of Galen's works, 8:249a
  on *verbum ex verbo* translation, 12:139b
  works of, 2:423b
Burgundy, county of, **2:424a–426b,** 2:425 (map)
  area of, 2:424a
  baillages in, 2:426a
  churches in, 2:426b
  economy of, 2:426a-b
  enfranchisements of towns in, 2:426a
  establishment of, 8:278a
  Frankish conquests, 10:674a
  Frederick Barbarossa and, 11:539a
  Hohenstaufen dynasty and, 2:424b
  monasticism in, 2:426b
  pagi in, 2:424a
  rulers of, 2:424a-b
  Sapaudian settlements, 10:674a-b
  Treaty of Verdun (843) and, 2:424a
  Valois dukes of, 2:426b
Burgundy, duchy of, **2:427a–428b,** 9:710b
  agriculture in, 2:427b
  area of, 2:427a
  bailliages in, 2:427a-b
  Chambre des Élus, 10:327a
  chivalry in, 2:428a
  culture in, 2:428a-b
  Dauphiné and, 4:108a-b
  enfranchisements of towns in, 2:427b
  gamay grape and, 12:654a
  Latin church in, 2:427b–428a
  pagi in, 2:427a
  the Peace of God movement and, 9:473b
  relations with
    England, 6:332a
    France, 6:332b
  rulers of, 2:427a-b
  tapestry of, 11:596b
  under Conrad II, 5:476b
  under John the Fearless, 10:320b
  Valois dynasty in, 2:427a-b
  vs. Swiss Confederation, 11:544b–545a
  wine trade, 12:649b–650a, 650b
Burgundy, kingdom of, 2:423a, **2:428b–430a**
  annexations of, 2:429b
  Conrad II and, 11:538a
  county of Savoy, 10:674b
  creation of, 2:428b
  division of, 2:428b
  law codes, after conquest by Franks, 7:470b–471a
  Lothair and, 11:538b
  rulers of, 2:428b–429b
Burhān al-Dīn, Bāyazīd I and, 2:136b
Būrī, 8:612b
Burial. *See* Death and burial
Burial grounds. *See* Cemeteries
Buridan, Jean, 1:608a, **2:430a–432a**
  academic career of, 2:430a-b
  Albert of Saxony and, 1:464b
  on Aristotle, 1:464b, 2:430a-b
  on astrology/astronomy, 2:430a-b
  on astronomy, 1:615b
  influence of, 2:431b
  logical treatises of, 2:430a-b
  nominalism and, 12:44a
  philosophy of, 2:430b–431a
  on physics, 2:430a-b
  theory of motion, 1:615b, 2:430b–431a, 9:623b
  via moderna and, 9:157a, 12:406a, 408a, 408b
  William of Ockham and, 2:430a-b
Burin, **2:432a** (*illus.*)
  see also Engraving
Burjī Mamluks. *See* Mamluk dynasty
Bürk Mangolt, 6:325a
Burkhard von Hohenfels, 8:414a
Burleigh, Walter. *See* Burley, Walter
Burley, Walter, **2:432b–433b**
  Averroism and, 2:433a
  in Avignon, 2:432b
  De intensione et remissione formarum, 2:433a
  De potentiis animae, 2:433a
  De suppositionibus, 2:433a
  Expositio super libros de anima, 2:433a
  Ibn Rushd and, 2:433a
  kingship theories of, 7:267a
  lectures on Aristotle, 9:612b–613a
  as logician, 2:432b–433a
  Questiones circa tercium de anima, 2:433a
  Treatise on the Activity of Forms, 9:613b
  William of Ockham and, 2:433a
Burmus. *See* Barnis
Burnellus the Ass, 9:441a
Burning
  ordeal of, 9:259a
  as punishment
    in Albigensian Crusade, 6:483b
    by inquisition, 6:485b–486a, 486b
Burning Bush, in art, 9:130 (*illus.*)
"Burnt Candlemass" (English attack on Scotland in 1356), 11:110a-b
Bursa, art and architecture of, 6:612b, 613b
Bursario. See Rodríguez del Padrón, Juan
Burṭās, Russian fur trade and, 5:331b
Burtʿel, Armenian prince, St. Astuacacin church and, 9:159a
Burthegn. See Chamberlain
Burtius, Nicolaus, 8:646a, 648b
Burton-on-Trent, brewery at, 2:375a
Būrū, 8:561b, 612b
Bury Bible, 6:324b (*illus.*)
Bury St. Edmunds, plagues in, 9:678b, 680a
Bury St. Edmunds, abbey of
  chronicle of, 7:116a
  fire at, 3:458b
  Manière de langage, 8:86b
  manuscript illumination in, 8:108a
Bury St. Edmunds cross, 7:23a (*illus.*), 24a, 10:0 (frontispiece)
Burzōi (physician of Xusrō I), 12:714b
Burzū-nāma. See ʿAṭaʾī
Busant, Der. See Bussard, Der
Busca party, in Barcelona, 2:104b
Buscheto of Pisa, **2:433b,** 9:665b–666b
Būs'hāq, 11:252b
Bushel, **2:433b,** 10:238b
  in Byzantine weight system, 12:581b
  definition of, 2:433b
  monastery, 12:581b
  tax, 12:581b
  trade, 12:581b
  see also Boisseau; Peck
Business correspondence. *See* Letter writing
Buskenblaser, 4:321b
Busnois, Antoine, Adam of Fulda and, 8:648b
Buṣr ibn Abī Arṭah (Muslim naval officer), 9:74a
Busra, conquered, 6:568a
Buss (ship), 11:240b, 241b (*illus.*), 242a
Bussard, Der, **2:433b–434a**
  influences on, 2:434a
  plot of, 2:433b–434a
  theme of, 2:434a
Bussi, Giovanni Andrea, 10:124b
Būstān. See Saʿdī of Shiraz
Bustanai, exilarch, 4:552a, 7:106b
But, John, on *Piers Plowman,* 7:329b
Butāḥ, al-, battle at, 6:568a
Butchers, guilds of, 5:123a
Buðli (saga character), 1:586b–587a
Butkhana. *See* Paikuli
Buṭlān, Ibn, *Tacuini sanitatis. See Tacuinum sanitatis in medicina*
Butler, **2:434a-b**
  in England, 2:434b, 6:301a-b
    Anglo-Saxon, 6:300a
    office of, 6:304a
  in France, 2:434b
  seneschal and, 11:160a
Butler, Edmond, Laud Misc. 610 and, 6:524b
Butler family, 6:518a, 519b
Butr, 2:185b
Buttery, royal. *See* Pantry and buttery, royal
Buttress, 1:424a (*illus.*), **2:434b–435a,** 9:730a
  bay system and, 10:475b
  exterior, 2:435a
  flying, 2:435a (*illus.*)
    in Notre Dame de Paris, 9:190b
  see also Vault

Buwayhids. *See* Buyids
Buxheimer Orgelbuch, notation of, 8:634a
Buyids, **2:435a–437b**
Abbasids and, 2:435b–436a, 6:590a, 10:246a
Alids and, 2:435b
area ruled by, 2:435a-b, 436b–437a
army, Turkish troops, 8:529a
Baghdad under, 3:50a, 6:85b
caliphate and, 6:590b
central government of, 2:437a-b
conquest of, by Maḥmūd the Ghaznavid, 2:436a
culture of, 2:435b, 437a
Daylamīs
Buyids and, 2:435a-b
in Vaspurakan, 1:484a
vs. Kurds, in Armenia, 1:513b
Zaydis and, 12:742a
Daylamīs and, 2:435a-b, 8:528b–529a
deposed by Toghrıl, 11:152a
diplomas of investiture, 8:529a
economic decline of, 2:437a
in Fārs, 2:435b, 5:18a
founding of dynasty, 2:435a, 6:424a
Hasanuyids and, 7:310b
Ibn Sīnā's service to, 11:302b
influence of, 2:436a-b
in Iran, 6:501b
in Iraq, 1:11a-b, 2:435b, 6:513b, 606a
siege of Baghdad, 8:529a
Isfahan under, 6:562a
Islamic postal service and, 10:61a
al-Kufa under, 7:307b–308a
political instability of, 2:437a-b
al-Qāᵓim and, 10:221b
Shiism of, 2:436b, 11:136b, 228a
spread of *nāᶜūras,* 9:67a
Sunnites and, 2:436a-b
Buzākha, al-, battle at, 6:567b
Buzandaran Patmutᶜiwnkᶜ. *See* Pᶜawstos Buzand
Buzkashi, 5:354a
Buzurg ibn Shahriyār, 5:393a
Bycorne and Chychevache. *See* Lydgate, John
Byelorussian language, 6:438a, 444a
Bylina (Old Russian folk epic), 6:444a, 445a
Byrele. *See* Butler, in England, Anglo-Saxon
Byrhtferth of Ramsey, 2:174a
Handboc (*Manual*), 1:284a, 285b
life of St. Dunstan by, 4:311b
Byrhtnoth of Essex, earl, celebrated in *Battle of Maldon,* 1:279a
Byrnie, 1:522a
in Bayeux Tapestry, 1:523a
Byzantine architecture, **4:337a–348a**
in Bulgaria, 2:414b–417b
church as highest expression of, 4:335a
classical traditions in, 2:457b
Constantinople, regulations concerning, 3:554a
definition of, 4:331a
dome in, 4:234b
influence in northern Europe, 4:346b–347a
Mistra, 8:446b
palaces, loss of, 4:334b
Serbian architecture and, 11:186a–187b
see also Architecture, early Christian; Church architecture
Byzantine art
Assumption of the Virgin in, 1:601a
in Balkans, 2:446b–447a, 450b
church control of, 2:438b
after Iconoclasm, 2:439a
church decoration, 8:489b–490a
church of S. Maria de Mur and, 10:505b
church of Sant'Angelo in Formis and, 10:505a
classical traditions in, 4:352b–353a, 353b
crusader style, 2:447a-b
Deesis in, 4:131b
depiction of Pentecost, 9:497a, 497b (*illus.*)
Dionysios of Furna's manual, 4:191b–192a
enamel, 2:453b
cloisonné, 4:437b, 441a
glass bowl with mythological figures, 2:456b (*illus.*)
production methods, 2:455a-b
reliquaries, 4:438a
figure style
background elements, 2:445a-b
draperies, 2:445a-b
facial expression, 2:445a-b
precious artifacts, 2:454a-b
"volume," 2:446a
fish motifs in, 5:66a
foreign influences, 2:443b, 447a, 457a-b
ban on barbarian products, 2:457a
Islamic, 2:440b
Georgian art and, 5:411a
in Great Mosque at Córdoba, 6:601a
in Greece, 2:447b
history (843–1453), **2:437b–452a**
iconoclasm and, 2:439a, 451a, 488a, 6:397b–399b
icons and, 6:399a
imperial patronage of, 2:452b–453b
minor arts, 2:452b–453a
individual artists, identification of, 2:438b
signing of works, 2:443b
influence of
on Bulgarian art and architecture, 2:417a
on French Romanesque fresco, 10:506a, 506b, 507a
on German Romanesque manuscript illumination, 10:508b
on Islamic manuscript illumination, 8:115b
on later art forms, 10:578b–579a, 583a, 586b–587a
on pre-Romanesque art, 10:105a
Italian Romanesque art and, at Palermo, 10:503b
jewelry, 5:375a-b, 377b–378a
in Kariye Djami, 7:215b–216a
Komnenian period, 2:443b–446a
Constantinopolitan, 2:443b–444a
paintings, 2:444a–445a, 445b
Latin occupation of Constantinople and, 2:446a–447b
Macedonian dynasty, 2:439a–443b
imperial patronage, 2:440b
manuscript illumination, 5:612a-b
minor arts, **2:452b–458b**
bronze doors, 2:453a-b, 456a
cameos, 2:457a, 457b (*illus.*)
crown of St. Stephen and, 11:482b
dating of artifacts, 2:454b
destruction of, 2:453a-b
Greek artists, 2:457a
ivory, 2:456a, 12:144 (*illus.*)
manufacture, nonaulic, 2:452b–453a
motifs in, 2:456b
ostentatiousness of, 2:454b–455a
provincial imitations, 2:457a
purpose of, 2:453b, 454b–455a
silver, 12:221b–222a
steatite, 2:456a
stylistic development, 2:453a, 454b–455a
triptychs, 12:198b
monastic influence, 2:439a
Hosios Lukas, 2:442b
painting, in Serbia, 11:184b–186a (*illus.*)
Palaiologan dynasty, 2:447b–451a
imperial patronage, 2:447b
monumental art, 2:448a
panel painting, 5:605a-b
platytera, 9:705a-b
prependulia, 10:89a-b
problems in interpretation, 2:451a-b
fragmentation of material, 2:438a
proskynesis in, 10:153a
Rainer of Huy and, 10:500a
regionalism, 2:451a
renaissances
legitimacy of, 2:451a-b
models for, 2:457b
Romanesque wall decoration and, 10:504b
schools of, 2:442a, 451a
sculpture, Dormition of Mary, 7:282 (*illus.*)
timelessness of forms, 2:438a-b
tomb sculpture, 2:448b–450b
Visigothic architecture and, 12:466b
Visigothic metalwork and, 12:467a
Western manuscript production and, 10:508a
workshops, 2:438b
see also Ivory carving; Macedonia renaissance; *Maniera greca;* Palaiologoi, art under
Byzantine church, **2:458b–471b**
after Arab conquest, 2:462b
Alexandria, archbishop of, control of civil dioceses, 2:459b
Antioch, exegetical tradition, 2:460a
architectural styles. *See* Church architecture, Byzantine
Arian dispute, 2:459b, 460a, 484b
imperial support, 2:485a
in Bulgaria, 2:403a-b
charistikion, 3:268a
Christianization of East, 2:458a
Christmas and, 3:318a

Byzantine church (*cont.*)
church-state relations, 2:458b–459b
theoretical definition, 2:459a
clergy in, 3:446a–447b
confession in, 3:533b, 534a
confirmation in, 3:536a
Constans II and, 3:544b
councils of, 3:631b–632b
Crete and, 3:678a
on Cyprus, 4:72b–73a
Djvari, 4:231b–232a
doctors of the church, 4:234a
Glagolitic rite in, 5:542b–543a
Greek language and, 6:436a
hesychast tradition, 6:217b–218a
revival of, 2:469b
hierarchy, monastic role, 8:458b
hymnography, 2:468a–469a
iconography, Old Testament Trinity, 12:198a-b, 199 (*illus.*)
imperial role, 3:10a–11a
election of patriarch, 2:461b
emperor as viceregent of God, 2:484b–485a
"equal to the apostles," 2:459a, 481b
orthodoxy requirement, 2:459a
powers exercised, 2:459a-b
John of Damascus and, 7:124b
John Skylitzes and, 11:330a
Justinian I and, 7:202a
kanōn in, 7:208b
katholikos, 7:226b–227a
kontakion, 7:292b
Latin occupation of Constantinople and, 2:469a
liturgy of. *See* Liturgy, Byzantine
marriage and, 4:594b
mysticism in, 9:5b–6a
oikonomia, origin of, 2:467b
papacy and, *plenitudo potestatis,* 9:709b
patriarchate, 3:556a, 9:459b
in 14th century, 9:618a-b
plainsong in, 9:686b–688a
plashchanitsa shroud, 9:693b–694b (*illus.*)
poor relief (*ptochika*), 6:288b–289a
priests' clothing, 3:615b–616a
primacy of Constantinople in, 3:555b–556a, 4:630a
in canon 28, 2:460a-b
jurisdiction, 2:460b
Roman interpretation, 2:460b, 464b, 485b–486a
property
expropriation of by crusaders, 7:348a
Nikephoros II Phokas and, 9:133a
Nikolaos Kavasilas on secular abuse of, 9:135a
reunion with Latin church, 2:465b–466a, 470a, 499a, 502a, 503b–504a, 9:331a-b
Council of Ferrara-Florence, 8:143b
opposition to, 8:143b
Third Council of Constantinople, 8:480a
royal confessors in, 3:534b
Russian pilgrimage and, 9:653a–654b
saints, in Canossa missal, 2:181a
schisms, 2:462a-b
anti-Chalcedonian, 2:459b–460a, 8:477a-b
contributing factors, 2:464b–465b
Laurentian, 9:291b
Sergios I and, 11:209a
in Slavic countries, 2:463b–464b
under Ottoman Turks, 2:469b–470a
Trinitarian doctrine and, 12:191b, 198a-b
troparion hymnographic text, 12:208a
under Ottomans, 9:310a
see also Autocephalos; Ferrara-Florence, Council of; Hagia Sophia (church: Constantinople); Iconoclasm, Christian; Law, canon, Byzantine; Literacy, Byzantine; Liturgy, Byzantine church; Patriarch; Pentarchy; Permanent synod; Philosophy and theology, Byzantine; Russian Orthodox church; Schisms, Eastern–Western church; Schism, Photian
Byzantine Empire
Abu 'l-Aswār Shāwur and, 11:217b
agriculture, 1:76b–79b
abstemiousness of diet, 1:78a
apiculture and fishing, 1:79a
with decreasing population, 1:79a
dough machine, 1:77b
effect of Islamic conquest, 1:76b
famines, 1:79b
land use, 1:79a-b
stockbreeding, 1:78b–79a
Arčēš and, 1:423a
archon ton archonton and, 1:449a
Arcrunis and, 1:451a
army
estimated numerical strength, 12:10a
mobile field units, 12:548b
size of, 12:548a
supplies and provisions, 12:548a
Asian provinces, invasion of, 2:487a, 493a-b, 495a-b, 496b, 500a
Ašot II of Armenia and, 1:482a
astrology in, 1:606a
augusta in, 1:644a
bureaucracy, **2:471b–475a**, 4:239a, 7:696a
at Nicaea, 2:474a
centralization of, 2:484b, 487a-b, 492b
characteristics of, 2:471b–472a
chartularioi, 2:473a
comes rei privatae, 2:472a
costs of, 2:475b
count of the sacred largesses, 2:472a
court functionaries, 2:474a
court hierarchy, treatises on, 9:617b–618a
curopalates, 4:66b
decentralization of power under Palaiologoi, 9:331b
despot, 4:165a
dia logou, offices of, 2:472b
domestic, 4:239a
dual civil-military jurisdictions, 2:472b
dux in provinces, 4:323a
educational requirement, 2:471b
eunuchs, positions held by, 2:473a
exploitation of poor, 2:476a
financial officers, 2:473a, 473b–474a
growth of, 11th century, 2:493b
history, 2:472a–475a
honorific offices, 2:474a, 474b
imperial *comitatus,* 2:472a
insignia, offices of, 2:472b
katepano, 7:224b–225a
kuaistor, 2:473b
legal officials, 2:472a, 473a-b
logothete, 2:487a, 7:642a
logothete of the drome, 4:194b–195a
megas logiarist, 2:473b
mesazon, 2:473b
military administration, 2:473b, 4:295b
models for, 2:471b
number of bureaucrats, 2:472b
orphanotrophos, 9:281b–282a
postal and intelligence services, 10:58b–60a
praetorian prefect, 10:68b–69a
prefects, 3:553b–554b
protoasekretis, 2:473a
provincial governors, 2:472b, 484b, 496b
rank consciousness, 2:474a
reforms of Emperor Andronikos III Palaiologos, 1:246b
regional favoritism, 2:474b
rival factions, 2:474b
stratarch class, 2:473b
struggle with landowners, 2:492a-b, 4:306b–307a
thematic administrations, 2:473b, 474b
training, 2:474a
vestiarion, 2:474a
see also Anatolikon, theme of; *Autocrator; Basileus;* Exarchate; Protospatharios; *Magister officiorum; Magistros;* Pseudo-Kodinos; Strategos; Themes
caesar in, 3:9a
Catalan Company and, 3:156a-b
cavalry in, 3:199a, 199b
civil wars
dynastic struggles, 2:481a, 501a
ethnic rebellions, 2:491b–492a
of generals, 2:492a
popular participation in, 2:492b
under Palaiologoi, 9:333b
classical literary studies in, 3:430b–431b
coinage, 8:418a–421b
nomisma, 4:301a (*illus.*)
conquest of, in Catalan literature, 3:166a, 171b
continuity with classical civilization, 2:481b
Coptic church and, 3:594a-b
costume styles in, 3:614a–616a
court of, girdled patrician at, 5:539b
Crete and, 3:678a-b
crusades and

First, 2:494b–495a
Second, 2:495a
Third, 2:496b–497a
Fourth, 2:497a
cultural influence, 4:344b–345a
in Dalmatia, 4:2b
defeat by Syro-Egyptian fleet (655/656), 9:74a
diplomacy in, 4:193b–194a
division of, 4:499 (map)
economic life and social structure, **2:475a–481b**
decline of, 10th–14th centuries, 2:480a-b
financial demands, 2:475b
guild organization, 6:20a-b
hereditary positions, 2:475b–476a, 478a
imperial reforms, 2:475b, 476b, 477b, 481a
munera, 6:20a, 20b
peasants, 2:475b–477b
social immobility, 2:475b, 476a
village communities, 2:476b–477a, 479b–480b
see also Farmers' Law; Paroikoi; Penetes; Pronoia; Tenure of land, Byzantine
emperor
sacred character of, 2:481b, 484b–485a
title of, *see Autocrator; Basileus*
ethnic diversity, 2:481b, 487b
factional struggles (1025–1204), 2:492a-b, 495b–496a
pro- vs. anti-Latin, 2:496a-b
feudalization of nobility in, 3:553a-b
finance, Nikephoros I and, 9:132b
foundation of, 2:484a-b
dating of, 2:475a-b
frontiers
collapse of, after Justinian, 2:486b
contraction of, 4:345b–346a
costs of defense, 2:475b, 486b
invasion of Danube-Sava area, 2:492b
Gagik II of Armenia and, 11:315b
German migrations, 2:485a, 485b
Ghassanid *symmachoi,* 5:515a
Golden Age of, 2:489a–490b
Greek language in, 5:660b, 6:444b
Hārūn al-Rashīd's expeditions (780, 782), 8:47b
Heraklid rulers, 6:171a
higher education in, 12:302a
history (330–1025), **2:481b–491b**
history (1025–1204), **2:491b–498a**
history (1204–1453), **2:498a–505a**
in Iberia, 5:405b
imperial role, meaning of "porphyrogenitos" in, 10:32b–33a
imperial succession
12th century, 2:496a
Angeloi, 2:496a
Macedonian dynasty, 2:481b
Italian territories, 7:2a–5a
Justinian's Plague and, 9:675a-b, 684a
Kantakouzenoi in, 7:208b–209a
Kekaumenos on, 7:227b
Komnenoi in, 7:283b–284a
al-Lādhiqiya and, 7:315a-b
Latin massacre of 1182, 2:496b
Lombard invasions, 9:293a
loss of Italy, 3:546a
Macedonian dynasty, provincial struggles, 2:492b–493b
Mamikonean family and, 8:78b–79a
Mediterranean navigation and, 9:87b–88a
Milan and, 8:376b
military
administration, 2:473b, 474a
mercenaries, 2:476b
Monothelitism and, 3:344a
Muslim attacks on, 3:544b
nadir of, 4:339b–340a
navy
battle depicted, 9:73 (*illus.*)
decline of in 11th century, 9:80a
Nogaj raid against, 2:410b
Palaiologan renaissance, 7:1a
Palestine under, 9:352b–353a
political system, 2:481b
political theory in, 10:9b–12a
Pontus in, 10:31b
in Ravenna, 10:262b–264b
reconquest of Cyprus (874), 2:118a
relations with
Armenia, 1:472b, 473a, 477a, 483b
Bulgaria, 2:118b–119b, 329a, 401a-b, 402a, 404b–405b, 406a–407b, 4:4b, 5b
Croatia, 2:119b, 4:1b, 2b, 4b, 5b, 6a
crusaders, 4:34a–35a, 45a–49a
Dalmatia, 4:79b–80a
Danishmendids, 4:93a
Fatimids, 6:608a, 12:744b
Franks, 2:488b
Georgia, 5:405b, 406a, 416b
Hungary, 6:339a
Kievan Rus, 4:555a, 588a
Latin church, 3:344a, 355b–357a
Magyars, 6:338a
Marwanids, 7:310b
Ottomans, 2:136b, 9:331b
papacy, 4:30a, 6:400b
Seljukids, 4:27b
Serbia, 11:345b–346a
Sicily, 11:261b, 263a, 264b, 265a
Tayk^{c}, 4:113b
Venice, 4:556a, 12:383b–385a
Visigoths, 12:471a
Vlachs, 12:483b
reorganization, in 7th through 9th centuries, 2:487a–489a
Roman aqueducts and, 10:519b
Roman army, 10:521a, 521b
Samuil and, 2:406b–407a
Serdica and, 11:189a
slave trade in, 11:338b
social structure. *See Paroikoi*
soldiers' portions in, 11:359b–360a
superstitious nature of society, 8:18b
Syrian Orthodox Church and, 11:563a
Tarōn and, 11:599a
taxation, *epibolé,* 4:495b
territorial losses of, 6:501b
trade and commerce
Pisan and Genoese domination, 2:496a
Venetian domination, 2:494b
under Palaiologoi, 9:331a-b
urbanism, 10:458b
vs. Abbasids, 10:246a
vs. Arabs, 2:487a, 4:339b
on Mediterranean, 11:230b
vs. Bagratids, 1:483b
vs. Bulgarians, 7:131a
vs. emir of Melitene, 2:117b
vs. Fatimids, near Antioch, 2:119a
vs. Frederick I Barbarossa, 2:496b–497a
vs. Goths, 9:292a–293a
vs. John of Gravina, 7:380a
vs. Kalojan, 7:206b
vs. Krum, 7:303b–304a
vs. Lakhmids, 7:320b
vs. Latins, in Morea, 7:380b
vs. Muslims, 6:573a
in Anatolia, 6:572a
in Egypt, 6:569b
in Mediterranean, 6:572b
in North Africa, 6:572a
in Syria, 6:568a
vs. al-Mu^{c}taṣim, 8:653b
vs. Normans, at Bari, 11:265b
vs. Ostrogoths, 6:443a
vs. Ottomans
Asia and Asia Minor, 2:493a-b
Battle of Myriokephalon/Kırkbaş pass, 10:235b
Bithynia, 2:500a
Brusa, capture of, 2:500a
Gallipoli, 2:501b
Kosovo, 2:502b
Manzikert, Battle of (1071), 2:493a
Nicaea, occupation of, 2:493a
Palestine, 2:495a-b
Pecheneg-Hungarian expedition, 2:492b
pleas for Western aid, 2:501b–502a, 503a-b, 503b–504a
Serbia, 2:502a
vs. Robert Guiscard, 11:266a
vs. Roger I of Sicily, 10:440a, 441a
vs. Sasanians, 10:670b
in Armenia, 1:476b, 478a
over Nisibis, 9:142a
vs. Seljuks
at Myriokephalon (1176), 8:657a
over Ikonion, 6:418a
vs. Seljuks of Rum, 10:235a
vs. Symeon of Bulgaria, 11:554b–555a
vs. Umayyads, 3:38a
vs. William II of Sicily, 11:269a
vs. Xlat^{c}, 12:713b
vs. Yaroslav, 12:720a
see also Anatolia; Constantinople; Trade, Byzantine; Urbanism, Byzantine
Byzantine law, **7:390a–393a**
administrative law, 7:390b, 391a-b, 392b
Assizes of Romania, 1:600a
Basil I (the Macedonian) and, 7:390b–391a
codes of, 4:382b–383a

Byzantine law (*cont.*)
Corpus iurus civilis and, 7:390a
Eclogue and *Ecgloga* handbooks, 7:390b
guilds, 6:20a
handbooks, 7:391b
Hellenization of Byzantine empire and, 7:390a
history (600–800), 7:390a-b
history (800–1100), 7:390b–392b
history (1100–1400), 7:392b
John VIII on, 7:126a-b
Justinian I and, 7:201b–202a
law school, 7:392a
lay legislation, codifications, 6:99b
legal texts, evidence on literacy, 7:596a
Leo VI and, 7:391a-b
protection of peasantry from landholders, 7:391b–392a
Purification of the Old Laws (*Anakatharsis palaion nomon*), 7:391a
soldiers' portions, 11:360a
Tetragamy quarrel, 7:391b
translators of, 12:126b
see also Eclogue; Farmers' Law; Law, canon, Byzantine; *Procheiros nomos; Pronoia;* Theodore Balsamon
Byzantine literature, **2:505a–521a**
"Akritic" ballads, 8:19b
autobiographies, 2:518a
biography, 2:517b–519b
purpose of, 2:518a
secular, 2:518a
see also Hagiography, Byzantine
Bulgarian translations, Symeon and, 11:554b
classical influence, 2:505a
atticist ideology, 2:523b
Homeric language, 2:506a-b, 507b
renaissance, 11th through 12th centuries, 2:507b
revivals, 2:514a, 519a, 523b
romances, 2:508a
Trojan stories, 2:509b
definition, 2:505a
epic poetry, 2:506a, 524a
Digenis Akritas, 4:185a–186a
romances, 2:508b
epistolography, 2:519b–520a
collections, 2:520a
didactic or dogmatic, 2:519b–520a
rhetorical, 2:519b
as status indicator, 2:519b
themes, 2:519b, 520a
genres, 2:505a-b
historical, 2:511b–517b, *see also* Chronicles; Historiography, Byzantine
history, Sozomen, 11:374a
oral epic tradition, 8:19a-b
poetic forms, **2:523b–525b**
poetry, personal, 2:523a
poetry, secular, 2:506a–510a
classicizing, 2:506a-b
demotic, 2:509a
epigrammatic, 2:506b–507a, 524a
historical, 2:509a-b
moralizing and confession, 2:510a
romances, 2:508a-b, 509a
short mythological, 2:506a
short occasional, 2:506a, 506b, 507a
themes, 2:507a, 510a
Western influence, 2:509a
popular, **2:521a–523b**
animal fable, 2:523a
defined, 2:521a
development of, 2:521b–522a
folk elements, 2:508b, 522b
forms, 2:521a-b, 524b
Homeric elements, 2:522b
influences on, 2:524b–525a
lament, 2:523a
oral tradition, 2:521b, 523a
origin, 2:521b
Ptochoprodromos poems, 2:521b
romances, 2:508a, 522a-b
Western patronage, 2:522b–523a
translation and translators, 12:126a–127a
vernacular, origin of, 2:509b
verse forms
classicizing, 2:506a-b, 523b
eight-syllable, 2:524a
fifteen-syllable (political verse), 2:507b, 521a-b, 524b–525a
hexameter, 2:524a
iambic trimeter, 2:505b–506a, 506b, 524a
metrical developments, 2:523b–524a
stress accent, 2:524a
subliterary purposes, 2:508a
twelve-syllable, 2:524a
see also Encyclopedias and dictionaries, Byzantine; Literacy, Byzantine; Liturgical poetry, Byzantine
Byzantine music, **8:553b–558a**
akathistos hymn, 9:714a
chant, 8:556b
classical styles, 8:554a–555b
influence of, 8:556b–557a
notation, 8:556a-b
plainsong, 9:686b–688a
postclassical style, 8:555b–556a
sacred, 8:553b–557a
secular, 8:557a-b
troparion books, 12:208a
see also Sticheron
Byzantius. See Besant
Bznunik^{c}. *See* Van, Lake

C

Cabala, 1:345b–346b, **3:1a–3b**
in Ashkenazi Hasidic theology, 9:581b–582a
biblical exegesis and, 2:212b
contributions of Eleazar ben Judah of Worms, 4:420b
development, influences on, 8:498a-b
ecstatic, 1:27a, 3:2b
Jewish apocalyptic movement and, 1:345b–346b
merkavah mystics, hymns and liturgies, 6:130a
Moses Naḥmanides and, 9:53b
as a mystery religion, 9:5a
Neoplatonism and, 9:100a
Pico della Mirandola and, 9:101a
problem of evil, 3:2a
in Renaissance, 3:3a-b
see also Magic and folklore, Jewish
Cabalga Diego Laínez, 3:389a
Cabalism
effect of Spanish expulsion, 3:3a
religious goals, 7:169a-b
Caballeros villanos, 12:563b
in Castile, 3:131a-b
"Caballus Constantini," 7:345a
Cabannes. See Provence, inns in
Cabarets, wine trade and, 12:651b
Cabasilas, Nikolaos. *See* Nikolaos Kavasilas
Cabasset, 1:531b
Cabbage, growth of, 1:96a
Cabochien riots, 5:187b
Cabot, Sebastian, variation of compass and, 3:507a
Caccia, 1:553a, **3:4a-b**, 6:641a, 653b, 669b–670a, 12:177b, 179a
compared with madrigal, 8:12b
trecento, 12:177b, 179a
virelai and, 12:458b
see also Italian literature; Jacobus of Bologna
Caccia di Diana, La. See Boccaccio, Giovanni
Cachet, Western European seals and, 11:124a
Cadastre, 10:29b
Byzantine taxation and, 11:603a, 603b
Cade, Jack
origins, 3:4b
rebellion of, **3:4b–5b**, 12:570a
Cadeaux (art), 6:463b
Cadell Ddyrnllug dynasty, 10:365b
Cadels. *See Cadeaux*
Cadence (language), 4:67a
Cadence (music), **3:5b–6b,** 8:589b–590a
differentia, 4:185a
EVOVAE and, 4:185a, 529a
14th-century changes, 3:6a-b
illustrated, 3:6a
Landini and, 7:327a
musica ficta and, 8:599a, 599b
in oral tradition, 8:569b
in psalm tones, 10:199a-b
psalmodic, 8:642a, 643a
Cadi. *See* Qadi
Cadira del honor. See Rodríguez del Padrón, Juan
Cadoc, St., **3:6b–7b**
lives of, 3:6b
monastic foundations, 3:7a
origins, 3:6b–7a
travels, 3:7a
Cadwaladr, 6:386b
Cadwallon, Gwynedd king, territorial expansion, 12:514b

Cadzand, Treaty of (1492), 5:523b
Cædmon, 2:221a-b, **3:7b–8a**
Hymn, 8:327a
dating of, 1:275b
Northumbrian version, 1:276a, 277b
quoted, 3:7b–8a
Old English poetry and, 4:550b
paraphrase of Genesis, 10:109a
illustrated at Canterbury, 1:273b
portrayed by Bede, 1:277b
traditional techniques and Christian content, 3:8a
Caecilian of Carthage, bishop, absolved by St. Rheticius of Autun, 10:344b
Caelius Aurelius
De medicina, 8:247a
translation of Soranus, 8:247a
Caemar, 8:563b
Caen, **3:8b**
Black Death in, 2:261a
controlled by dukes of Normandy, 3:8b
loss of prominence, 3:8b
Caen, University of, 3:8b, 12:285b
founded, 9:169b
Caesar, **3:8b–9a**
see also Sebastokrator
Caesar, Gaius Julius
De bello gallico
on the institutions of Germanic peoples, 2:89a
on the religion of Celts, 9:45b–46a
on Veromandui, 12:395b
in French secular biographies, 2:236b
on Gallic vernacular, 6:445a
Germanic peoples and, 2:88b
romances about, 7:53b–54a
see also Fet des Romains, Li
Caesarea, **3:9a-b**
captured by Baybars, 2:138b
as a communication center, 10:424b
crusaders' route and, 10:423b, 424a
early bishops of, 9:459a
ecclesiastical importance, 3:9a
Khwand Khātūn complex, 11:148b
sacking of, 3:9a, 9b
see of, Armenia and, 1:499a
silk route to the Far East and, 12:99a
Talmud and, 10:463b
under Turkish rule, 3:9a
see also Seljuks of Rum
Caesarius of Arles, St., **3:9b**, 3:573a, 12:682b
concept of purgatory, 10:216a
hymns and, 6:379b
sermons on penance, 9:488a
spread of Lesser Litany and, 7:588a
tithe payment and, 12:63b
Visigothic church and, 9:62a-b
women's orders and, 12:682b
Caesarius of Heisterbach, **3:10a**, 3:405a
Dialogus miraculorum, 6:69b, 7:369a
Vie des anciens pères and, 12:415a
exempla and, 4:551a
Libri miraculorum, 6:69b
on theater performance, 4:278a
Caesaropapism, **3:10a–12a**
defined, 3:10a
in Greek church, 3:10a–11a
in Latin church, 3:11a-b
revival during Reformation, 3:11b
Caffa, **3:12a-b**
Armenians in, 1:486a
Black Death and, 2:258b
fur trade in, 5:333a
restoration by Özbeck, 8:475b
as trading center, 3:12b
Caftan, **3:12b–13a**
origins, 3:12b–13a
as woman's robe, 3:13a
Cage (unit of measure), 12:592b
Cahors
origin of pawnbroking and, 2:76a
wines of, 12:649b
Cahorsin, 2:76a, 12:649b
Caílte mac Rónáin (saga character), 6:549a
Patrick and, 6:540b
Cáin Adamnáin. See Lex innocentium
Cairo, **3:13a–15a**, 6:608a
architecture of, 6:599a-b
Abbasid mausoleum in, 2:22a
Ayyubid fortifications, 2:21a
Fatimid walls, 3:14a
palaces and mosques, 5:21b–23a
see also Badr al-Jamālī
called Babylon in the medieval West, 2:34a
ceramic style in, 6:608a
decline of, 3:14b–15a
expansion under Saladin, 3:14a
Fatimids in, 6:608b
fortress of, 2:25a
foundation of, 3:13a-b, 5:21b, 6:608a
House of Science, 11:83b
Ibn Ṭūlūn, 8:68a
al-Ikhshīd in, 6:416b
as Islamic center, 3:14b, 6:570a
Islamic trade and, 12:107b
Ismailism in, 6:616a
libraries in, 7:273b, 561b, 11:84b
madrasas in, 8:11b–12a
Mamluk dynasty and, 3:14b, 8:70b–76b
army in, 8:72b
end of rule (1517), 8:76b
as military center, 3:13b
mixed Arab-Muslim and Coptic society, 3:13b
mosques in, 1:196b–197a
origins of. *See* ᶜAmr ibn al-ᶜĀṣ
sectors of
al-ᶜAskar, 3:13b
al-Fusṭāṭ, 3:13a-b
al-Ḥusaynīya, 3:15a
al-Mansuṣūrīya (al-Qāhira), 3:13b–14a
al-Qaṭāᵓiᶜ, 3:13b
sūq, 11:514b
under al-Naṣīr Muḥammad, 8:74a
Cairo genizah, **3:15a–16b**, 7:562a
administrative documents, 7:72b–73a
horoscopes in, 11:91b
material preserved, 3:15b
origins of, 3:15a
piyyutim in, 7:621a
source documents
for international trade, 9:75b
for Islamic furniture, 5:313a-b
for Islamic trade, 2:80a, 12:106a, 107b
for Jewish culture, 3:15b, 16a, 620a-b
for Jewish history, 5:357a
for Judeo-Arabic language, 7:171b
for Palestinian rite, 7:620b
Cairuan Codex, 8:564b (*illus.*)
Caithréim, 6:537a
Caithréim Chellacháin Chaisil, 6:539b
Cajetan, cardinal (Tommaso de Vio)
De comparatione auctoritatis papae et concilii (1511), 3:520b
as defender of Thomism, 12:39a, 42a, 42b
Cajetan of Thiene (1387–1465), 1:465a
Calabria
as center of Greek culture, 7:4a, 4b
Robert Guiscard and, 10:433a
Roger I and, 10:440a
rule of *strategos,* 7:4b
Calais, siege and capture of (1346–1347), 3:64b, 6:331b, 333a
Calais, Treaty of (1360), 6:334b
Calamarium, 12:699b
Calamus, 12:699b
Calatrava, Order of, **3:16b–17a**
Order of Aviz and, 2:17a
Calaverra, Ferrán Sánchez de, in *Cancionero de Baena,* 11:419a
Calbulus, **3:17a**
Calcario, 10:520b
Calcidius, translation of Plato's *Timaeus,* 1:610b, 9:700b
Calculation with the Hindu Numerals. See Khwārizmshāhs
Çaldiran, Battle of (1514), 7:215b, 11:145a
Cale, Guillaume, leader of the Jacquerie, 9:478a
Calendar of 354, *tabula ansata* and, 11:571b
Calendar, **3:17a–30b**
Armenian, 1:518a, 519b, 520a, 520b–521a, **3:30b–31b**
eras in, 3:30b–31a
reform of, 3:31a
solar calendar, 3:30b
see also Anania Širakacᶜi
bases for, 3:17a-b
Byzantine, Alexandrian era, 3:18b
Christian, 3:18a–24b
days of the week in, 3:23b
division of the day in, 3:23b–24a
division of month in, 3:21a
equal vs. unequal hours, 3:23b–24a
era systems, 3:18a–19a
feast days in, 3:21b–22a
indiction cycle, 3:18a-b
reconciliation of solar and lunar years, 3:20b, 22a
reform of, 3:22b–23b
saltus lunae, 3:22a-b
computus, 3:19a (*illus.*), 509a-b
decorated initials in, 6:462b
Dionysius Exiguus and modern system, 4:192b–193a
Germanic, 3:20b
Icelandic, 3:20b
Islamic, 3:27a-b

Calendar (*cont.*)
Islamic (*cont.*)
based on lunar year, 3:27a
beginning of, 7:203b
divisions of time in, 3:27b
eras in, 3:27a-b
feast days, 3:27b
pilgrimage, 9:650b–651a
prayer hours in, 3:27b
Ramadan, 10:253b–255a
Jewish, 3:24b–27a, 26a (*illus.*), 11:90a, 90b
computations of days of the week, 3:25b
computations for seasons, 3:26b–27a
eras in, 3:24b–25a
feast days, 3:27a
reconciliation of solar and lunar years, 3:25a
Jewish pilgrimage, 9:652a–653a
Jubilee year, 9:660b
Julian, 2:155a
definition of era in, 3:18a-b
division of year, 3:19b
liturgical, 9:688b–690b
Agiographia and, 6:327b
at Synod of Whitby (664), 3:81b–82a
Becket and, 2:152b
Canossa missal and, 2:181a
Celtic vs. Roman practice, 12:626a-b
iconostasis and, 6:409b
Irish, 6:543a
lauda and, 6:635b
Laurea sanctorum and, 6:325b
Nicholas of Cusa and, 9:123a-b
Proper of the Saints, 5:662b
Proper of the Time, 5:662b
sacre rappresentazioni and, 6:636a
saints' days and, 3:68a
separate chapels for saints and, 1:445a
synaxary and, 11:557b
see also Liturgy; Mass cycles
lunar systems, 3:17b
lunar year, 3:17b
reform of, 3:17b
runic, 10:567a
September, 3:22 (*illus.*)
solar systems, 3:17b
Spanish era, 11:389b
West Slavs, agricultural terms in, 1:96b
Zoroastrian, 1:452a
see also Astrology/Astronomy; Indiction; Sundials; Toledan Tables
Calendar of Córdoba, 1:82b
Calendar of Óengus, 6:543a
Calendžiha, church of, Manuel Eugenikos and, 8:93a
Calicut, Portuguese colonization and, 4:563a
Calila e Digna (Dimna), **3:31b–32a,** 11:456b
Spanish version of, 11:414a, 414b
Calimachus. See Hrotswitha von Gandersheim
Calimala, inns in, 6:473b–474a
Caliphate, **3:32a–51b**
administrative centers, Samarra, 10:641a–643b
Arabs in, preeminence under Abbasids, 3:42a
authority of, 8:500b
constitutional basis, 3:33a
decentralization of, 6:107b–108a
delegation of, 3:44a-b
limits to, 3:45b
in religious matters, 3:43a-b
in secular matters, 3:43a
bureaucracy of, 3:37b
capital of, attempt to move to Damascus, 6:85a-b
ceremonial aspects, 3:37a-b, 42b, 45a-b
civil conflicts, 1:7b, 10a
commander of the faithful title, 3:488a–489a
competing caliphs, 3:50a, 488b
decline of, 1:11a, 12a, 3:48b–51a, 6:590b, 10:245a–246b
definition of term, 3:32a
deposition of caliph, 3:39a-b, 43a
Dīnawarī on, 4:188a
diplomatic protocol, 4:200a-b
dynastic principle of succession, 3:38b–40a, 42b
early prestige, 3:33b
economic concerns, 8:35b
economic and political considerations, 1:10a
Egyptian, 1:12a
elevation to, 3:33a-b, 42b
al-Fārābī on reform of, 9:699b
First Civil War (656–661), 3:35b–36a, 6:570a, 12:266b–268b
imamate and, 6:425b, 616a
importance of, 3:48b, 50a
as Islamic institution, 3:39b–40a, 47a-b, 48b
Islamic political theory and, 10:13a
Islamic postal and intelligence services and, 10:60b
Mamluk dynasty and, 8:71a-b, 72a
Muḥammad and, 6:577b
al-Mustanṣir and, 8:650b, 651a
al-Mustaᶜṣim and, 8:651a
non-Arabs under, 3:40b–41a, 42a
non-Muslims under Abbasids, 3:43b
obsolescence of institution, 3:51a
origins of institution, 3:32a
Ottoman state as, 9:309a
palace court, 3:37a-b
political tutors' role in shadow government, 6:107a, 108a
provincial administration, 3:34a
purpose of, 3:33a
Quraysh tribe and the, 10:242a
rāshidūn, 3:33a, 35b
religious role, 3:34a, 46b
residences
Baghdad, 6:597a-b
Samarra, 6:597b, 598a, 605b
Second Civil War (681–692), 3:38b, 8:388a, 12:268b–270a
Shīᶜa and, 11:226b, 227b, 228a
strife between Qays and Kalb factions, 6:230a
sunna and, 11:510b, 513b–514a
Third Civil War, 3:41b
transfer of power in, 3:35a, 42b–43a
transferred from Arabia to Iraq, 3:35b–36a
Tulinid dynasty and, 12:223b–224b
umma and, 3:32b
under Umayyads, 6:589a, 589b
vs. Byzantines, 6:107a
weaknesses under Muᶜāwiya, 3:38a
Yaᶜqūb ibn Layth and, 12:717a
see also Abbasids; Fatimids; Sultan; Umayyads; Umayyads of Córdoba
Calixtine Church (Prague). *See* Prague Utraquist Church
Calixtinus, St., a rhymed office for, 10:368a
Calixtus I, pope, on penitential practice, 9:366a-b
Calixtus II, pope
Concordat of Worms and, 12:697a
First Lateran Council and, 3:352a
Gregory VIII and, 1:296b
Jews and, 7:88a, 109a
Sicut Iudaeis, 7:88a
synods, 3:636a-b
Vital of Savigny and, 12:480a
Calixtus III, pope, 7:115b, 12:126a, 348a
Callan, battle at (1261), 6:518b
Calligraphy
Berber. *See* Tifinagh
cursive, disappearance of in the early Middle Ages, 7:599a-b
Islamic, **3:51b–55b**
in Baghdad, 6:606b
Fatimids' monumental, 5:23a (*illus.*)
in al-Ḥīra, 7:321a
in al-Kufa, 7:307b
styles of, 3:54a-b
thuluth and, 12:53b, 54 (*illus.*)
under Umayyads, 6:596b
see also Khaṭṭ al-mansūb; Kūfī; Naskhī; Nastaᶜlīq
Western European. *See* Caroline minuscule script
see also Initial; Musical notation; Paleography
Callimachus
catalog of Greek writers, 3:430a
as a source for *Suda,* 11:501b
Callimachus. *See* Buonaccorsi, Phillip
Callinicum
battle at (531), 7:320b
Byzantine-Sasanian trade and, 12:97a
Callinicus, 5:659b
Callis, Jaume, 3:611b
Calo, Maestro. *See* Kalonymus family
Calot, Laurence, *Title and Pedigree of Henry VI,* translations of, 7:692a
Calpurnius Siculus Titus, **3:55b**
Caltabellotta, Treaty of (1302), 3:156a, 11:273a, 273b
Calvary cross, 4:9a
Calvin, John
catechism translated into Gaelic, 11:114a
excommunication and, 4:538a
Treatise on Relics, 10:299a
vernacular and, 6:442a
on Virgin Mary, 12:461a

Calvinism. *See* Protestantism
Calvo, Laín, descendants of, 3:383b
Camail, 1:526b, 527a (*illus.*)
Camaldolese, Order of, **3:55b–56b**
foundation, 10:527a
monastic reform and, 12:163b
Camaldoli, Sacro Eremo di, 3:56a
Cambium (exchange contract), description of, 2:78a
Cambrai
first seals of, 11:126a
revolutionary commune, 3:496a
Cambrai Homily, analogies with *De duodecim abusivis,* 4:312b
Cambrai, Peace of (1529), 11:217a
Cambridge Psalter, 1:262b
Cambridge Songs, 1:318b–319a, **3:57a–58b**
"Canterbury Classbook" and, 7:352b
hymns and, 6:384b
love lyrics in, 7:368a
sources, 7:363b
Wipo and, 12:656a
see also Anthologies; "Later Cambridge Songs"
Cambridge, University of, **3:58b–60a,** 12:290a-b
King's College Chapel, stone carvings by Thomas Stockton, 11:486 (*illus.*)
King's Hall, 3:59b
Peterhouse, 3:59b
see also Vertue, Robert
Cambuskenneth indenture (1326), 9:438b
Camel
in Islamic warfare, 12:551b
as object of mockery in Europe, 1:296b
roads in Islamic world and, 10:425a-b
in transport, 1:296a-b, 12:148a, 379b, 380a-b
see also Animals, draft
Camel, Battle of the (656), 1:15b, 113b, 172b, 2:127a-b, 3:35b, 11:513a
Camel of Lombardy. *See* Pietro di Pavia
Cameo glasses, 5:547a
Camera actorum. See Bologna
Camera curie. See Chamber (finance), England, Norman
Camera (papal finance), 3:94a, 4:66a, 66b
archives of, 1:448a
church taxation and, 11:610b
Cameracensis. *See* Ailly, Pierre d'
Camerarius
defined, 3:242a
see also Chamberlain, England, Anglo-Saxon
Camino francés, 11:412a
Camisia. *See* Vestments, liturgical
Campania, controlled by Naples, 9:56b–57a, 58a
Campanian Gospel, 2:180b
Campanile, **3:60a-b**
Florence Duomo, 9:667b–668a
Campanology. *See* Bells
Campanulae pro melodia, 8:606a
Campanus of Novara
De proportione et proportionalitate, 8:215b
Euclid's *Elements,* recension of, 8:209b
Theorica planetarum, 4:500b, 11:103a
on equatorium, 11:98b
Campbell of Glenorchy, Sir Duncan, poems by, 11:115a
Campeador. *See* Cid
Campin, Robert, **3:60b–61b,** 5:86a, 611a
invention of Flemish style by, 5:86a
Mérode Altarpiece, 3:61a (*illus.*), 61b, 5:86a, 12:198b
Campion, Jean, Philippe de Vitry and, 12:482b
Campo, Alonso del, *Auto de la Pasión,* 11:425a
Campsores, 10:526a
Can Grande della Scala, Dante and, 4:103a
Canaanites, descendants of, 2:185b
Cañada (transhumance routes in Spain), 8:280a, 280b
Canals, Antoni, works of, 3:167b
Canals, irrigation. *See* Irrigation
Canary Islands, **3:61b–63a,** 3:62 (map)
discovery of, 9:87b, 89b
exploration of, 4:558b, 5:398a
relations with
Portugal, 4:558b, 559a
Spain, 4:559a
Cancellarius, defined, 3:251b–252a
Cancelli, 5:317a
Cancioneiro da Ajuda, 3:87a, 4:190a, 5:341b
Cancioneiro da Biblioteca Nacional, 5:341b, 11:450a
Cancioneiro geral. See Resende, Garcia de
Cancioneiro da Vaticana, 5:341b, 11:450a
Cancionero, 3:140a, 11:450a-b
Cancionero de Baena, 3:86b, 5:342a, 6:428a, 11:419a, 451a
Cancionero general, **3:63a-b,** 11:424a-b, 425a, 425b, 451a
ballad texts in, 11:429a
Obras de burlas provocantes a risa, 3:63b, 11:424a
Cancionero de Herberay des Essarts, 11:424a, 451a
Cancionero de Marciana, 11:424a
Cancionero musical e poético da Biblioteca Públia Hortênsia, Spanish ballads and, 11:429b–430a
Cancionero musical de palacio, 3:85b, 11:419a, 424b, 451a
ballad texts in, 11:429a
villancico and, 12:447b
Cancionero de Roma, 11:424a
Cancionero de romances, 11:429b
Cancionero de Stúñiga, 11:424a
Cançun d'Antiocha. See Grégoire Béchada
Cancun d'Antioche. See Chanson d'Antioche
Candiani (Venetian noble family), 12:386a, 387a
Candida Casa (monastery: North Britain), 6:515a
Candidus of Fulda (Bruun), **3:63b–64a**
Dicta Candidi, on the Trinity, 9:585b
students of, 9:585b
Vita Eigilis, 3:64a
Candlemas, parallel with pagan Amburbale or Lupercalia, 10:131a-b
Candles
on altars, 1:224b
at baptism, 5:318b
at funerals, 5:319a, 320b
at mass, 5:318b–319a
benediction of, 2:177b, 178a
in chandelier, 5:318b
see also Lighting devices
Candlesticks. *See* Lighting devices
Canines. *See* Dogs
Canisius, Peter, St., 4:234b
Cannabis. *See* Hemp
Canne (unit of measure), 12:584a
Cannibalism
witchcraft and, 12:660b
see also Famine
Cannon, **3:64a–66a** (*illus.*), 11:660b
bellmaking and, 2:166b
breech-loaded, 3:65a
in carrack, 11:237a
cast in iron, 8:285b
effect on castles and fortifications, 3:151b
Islamic, 11:638a (*illus.*), 638b
midfaᶜ, 11:638b
master gunner's handbooks, 11:645b
multiple-barreled, 11:649a
muzzle-loaded, 3:64b–65a
portable, 11:638b
siege, in Hundred Years War, 6:333a
in siege of Metz, 12:566b
stone cannonballs, 12:567a
use of on ships, 9:84a
see also Artillery; Steelmaking
Caño entero, 8:562b
Canon. See Euclid
Canon. See Sīnā, Ibn
Canon (canticle). *See Kanōn*
Canon (clergy), 12:683b–684a
Canon episcopi, witchcraft and, 12:660a
Canon (Mass liturgy)
dominical gestures, 8:192b–193a
emphasis on, 8:191b
epiclesis, 8:192b
intercession, first
communicantes, 8:192a-b
Hanc igitur, 8:192b
memento of the living, 8:192a
length of, 8:191b
memento of the dead, 8:193a
method of recitation, 8:191b
Nobis quoque, 8:193a-b
per quem haec omnia, 8:193b
prayers, 8:193a
Qui pridie, 8:192b
Canon of Medicine. See Sīnā, Ibn
Canon (musical instrument), 8:562b, 607b
Canon (rhythmic instruction), 6:619b
Canon table, **3:66a-b,** 3:66 (*illus.*)
in Lindisfarne Gospels, 7:584a
see also Libraries, information service
Canones Wallici, 3:229b
Canoness, 12:683b, 684a
Canonical hours, **3:66b–67b**

Canonical hours (*cont.*)
Armenian, 1:516b–517a
bells for, 2:165b, 3:28b
Byzantine, music for, 8:554a
reckoning of time and, 3:24a
see also Benedicamus Domino; Lectionary; Liturgy, Byzantine church; Rhymed offices
Canonical inquest. *See* Inquest
Canonization, **3:67b–69a**
Armenian, 1:520a
rhymed offices and, 10:366b
translation of saints and, 12:144a–145b
veneration of relics and, 10:298b–299a
Canons. *See* Law, Canon
Canons of the Apostles, against interest charging, 12:335b
"Canons of Nersēs and Neršapuh," 9:102b
Canons Regular of St. Quentin, Beauvais, 7:21b
Canons regular. *See* Monasticism
Canopies, in churches, 5:319b
Caños de Carmona, 11:214a
Canossa, **3:69a-b**
see also Gregory VII, pope; Henry IV of Germany, emperor; Matilda of Tuscany, countess
Č^cans. *See* Laz
Canso, **3:69b–70b**
canzone and, 6:668a
in Provençal literature, 10:164b, 165b–166a
of *sirventes,* 11:312b
sonnet and, 11:260a-b
trobairitz and, 12:207a-b
see also Provençal literature; *Vers*
Cant espiritual. See March, Ausiàs
Cantabrians
dialect of, 3:141b
vs. Romans, 2:126a
Cantacuzeni. *See* Kantakouzenoi
Cantar de Bernardo de Carpio, 11:442b
Cantar del Sancho II y del cerco de Zamorra, 11:409b, 411b, 437b–438a, 442b
Cantar de mío Cid, 1:600b, **3:70b–80b**, 3:133a, 142a, 386b–388b, 10:280a, 11:410a, 437b, 453a
author of, 11:410b
author's and protagonist's restraint (*mesura*) in, 11:411a
Castilian expansion and, 6:442b
character of hero, 3:387b
compared with European epics, 11:410b–411a
Doña Ximena's prayer, 11:449–450a
double-hemistich line, 10:528b
fact and fiction in, 3:387a–388a
knowledge of geography in, 4:579a
Nibelungenlied and, 9:112a
prosody, 3:72a–73a, 11:428b, 458b, 459a
sources, 3:76b–78b
lost Spanish original postulated, 11:438a
modern interpretations, 3:78b–79b
synopsis, 3:73a–74a
text transmission, 3:70b–72a
themes, 3:74a–75a
"two poets" theory, 11:442b
vocabulary, 3:71b–72a
Cantar de Roncesvalles. See Roncesvalles
Cantares de las caçurias, 11:446a
Cantatorium, **3:80b–81a**
Cantefable. See Aucassin et Nicolette
Canterbury, **3:81a–84a**
archbishops of, 3:82b–83a, 83b
Audience Court, 1:433b
primacy over archbishops of York, 4:466a
Augustine and, 3:81b
ecclesiastical assemblies at, 3:82a
ecclesiastical courts of, 1:433b
ecclesiastical province, inclusion of Wales, 12:517a, 524a
incorporated, 3:83b
Irish church reform and, 6:517a
manuscript book production in, 1:258a, 273b, 8:108a
monastery of St. Augustine, Reginald of Canterbury and, 10:289a-b
as pilgrimage center, 3:83a, 12:627a
Roman settlement, 3:81a
Viking raids, 3:82a
William I and, 3:82b
see also Theodore of Canterbury, St.
Canterbury Cathedral, 1:256a, 3:83a-b, **3:84a-b**, 3:84a (*illus.*)
aisles, 10:680b
Bell Harry tower, 12:575b (*illus.*)
capitals, 3:90b
choir, 1:426a, 426b, 3:539a-b, 4:508a
reconstruction (1179–1184), 12:645a
clerestory (detail), 4:67b (*illus.*)
early clock in, 3:29b
founded, 3:81b
Gervase of Canterbury and, 5:513b
Gothic architecture in, 5:582b, 584a
Henry Yevele and, 12:724b
monastic rite, 10:654a
Old Hall MS and, 9:232a
pilgrimage treasury of, 9:659b
rebuilding (1174), 12:643a
Romanesque paintings, 10:507a
stained glass in, 5:549a, 553a
tomb of Edward the Black Prince, 1:526a
triforium passage, 12:188a
water supply, 11:515b, 12:577b
windows, 11:215a
"Canterbury Classbook," 7:352b, 353a
Canterbury, convocations of
1279, 11:608b, 609a
1283, 11:608b
1377, 11:609a
1383, 11:609a-b
Canterbury Psalter, 3:56b (*illus.*), 57a
levying tolls, 11:611b (*illus.*)
Canterbury Tales. See Chaucer, Geoffrey
Canterbury Troper, Winchester Troper and, 12:648a
Canterini, 6:638a-b
Cantica veteris et novi tentamenti. See Notker Teutonicus
Canticle, **3:84b**, 9:692a
see also Plainsong
Canticle of the Sun (*Cantico delle creature; Cantico di Frate Sole*). *See* Francis of Assisi, St., *Laudes creaturarum*
"Canticum amoris." *See* John of Howden, hymns of
Cantiga, **3:84b–86b**
Alfonso X and, 8:601a
Arabic lyrics and, 8:563b
Razón de Amor, 10:268b–269a
sacred, 3:85a–86a
secular, 3:86b–87a
Cantigas de amigo, 11:450a-b, 452b
compared with *kharjas,* 11:408b
Cantigas d'amigo
of Dinis, 4:190b
in Galican-Portuguese poetry, 5:341b
villancico and, 12:447a, 447b
Cantigas d'amor, 11:412a, 450a-b
of Dinis, 4:190a-b
in Galican-Portuguese poetry, 5:342a
Cantigas d'escarnho e de maldizer, 11:412a, 450a-b, 452b, 454a
of Dinis, 4:190b
Cantigas de meestría, 11:450b
Cantigas de refran, 11:450b
Cantigas de romería, 11:452b
Cantigas de Santa María, 3:85a–86a
see also Alfonso X (the Learned) of Castile and León, king; *Cantiga*
Cantilena
carol and, 3:116a
chansons de geste and, 3:259b–260a
Cantilena. See Wipo of Burgundy
Cantilena of Ezzo. *See Ezzolied*
Cantilène, **3:87b**
Cantillation
Byzantine, 10:516b
Islamic. *See Qirā^ɔa bi'l-alḥān; Tilāwa*
Jewish, 8:564a, 564b
neume and, 8:624a
Cantio, hymns and, 6:380a
Cantle, 1:529a, 532b
Cantor, **3:87b–88a**
contrasted with music theorist, 8:579a
Jewish, 8:564b
see also Paraphonista; Precentor
Cantuagium. See Heinrich Eger von Kalkar
Cantum quem Cisterciensis, 3:402b
Cantus, 1:551a
Cantus firmus motet. *See* Motet
Cantus prius factus, 10:241a
Cantus supra librum, 8:644b
Canute. *See* Cnut
Canvas, **3:88a-b**
Canzicrans, 8:591a
Canzone
Dante on, 6:640b, 665b, 668a-b
envoi of, 6:668b
minnesinger's lyrics and, 8:413b
sonnet and, 6:669a
Canzone a ballo. See Ballata
Canzoniere. See Petrarch
Canzuna, sonnet and, 11:260a
Cão, Diogo, 4:562a
Cape Verde Islands, exploration of, 4:561b
Čapek, John, 6:375a
Capella, Martianus. *See* Martianus Capella

Capella Palatine (Palermo), 10:505a
Capella regia (Sicily), 11:267b, 274b
Capellani, in Carolingian Empire, 3:107b–108a
Capellanus, Andreas, **3:88b–89a**
courtly love treatise of, 1:572b
De amore libri tres, 1:189a, 3:88b–89a, 669b, 7:367b
codification of courtly love, 3:671a-b
Eleanor of Aquitaine and, 4:419b–420a
popularity of, 3:670b–671a
on pure love, 3:669b
relation to contemporary marriage customs, 3:672a-b
Roman de la Rose and, 10:449b
influence of Ovid on, 3:671b–672a
similarities with Meinloh von Sevelingen, 8:265b
Capes, 3:624b
Capetians
accession to throne, 5:154a
acquisition of Toulouse, 12:91b
administration of provinces, 5:168a–170a
communes, 5:169b
great fiefs, 5:170b–171a
Languedoc, 9:475a
in Burgundy, 2:429b
characteristics of government
authoritarianism, 5:174a
feudalism, 5:173a–174a
consecration of heirs, 5:159a
court
composition of, 5:158a-b
itinerant nature of, 5:158a
cultural changes under
economic, 5:174a-b
religious and educational, 5:175a-b
definition of territorial boundaries
Gascony, 5:171a
Lyonnais, 5:171a
development of French language under, 5:234b
alliance with ecclesiastical centers, 5:237b–238a
disintegration of authority, 7:673b
documents and charters
change in character of, 5:158a
charters of privilege, 5:159b–160a
registration of outgoing, 5:163a
as dukes of Burgundy, 5:158a
ecclesiastical support, 5:157a
in annexed provinces, 5:169a
control over ecclesiastical appointments, 5:160b
oaths of fealty, 5:158b
perpetuation of dynasty, 5:159a
regalian sees, 5:158b
renunciation of royal privilege, 5:162a
revenues collected, 5:158b
economic history, 11:619a-b
enquêteurs
fiscal duties, 5:173b, 11:621b
identification of problems, 5:170a
restitution for illegal seizures, 5:170a
family origins, **3:89a–90a**, 5:152b, 9:148b
derivation of name, 5:156a
influence of Champagne family, 5:162a
in Languedoc, 7:340a-b
regnal dates, 5:154b
representative assemblies and, 10:316b
rights of hospitality, 5:170a
rise of Paris and, 10:412a
royal administration
of annexed territories, 5:164b
conseil, 5:162a
entourage, 5:158a, 160a, 162a
governmental tasks of, 5:160a
household officers, 5:160a, 162b–163a, 173b–174a
recordkeeping and archives, 5:163a
reorganization under Philip II, 5:162b
vicomtes, 5:164b
royal domain, 7:673b
addition of Amiénois, Artois, and Vermandois to, 5:164a
division of authority in, 5:157b
fragmented nature of, 5:157b
management of resources, 5:157a
reconstruction of, 5:159a–161a
royal ideology, 5:171b–172a
holy monarchy, 5:172b
royal wardship of Flanders and Troyes, 5:165a
struggle with principalities, 5:158b, 161a–162b
support of papacy, 5:171b
Aragonese Crusade of 1285, 5:171b
vs. Angevins, 2:429b
see also individual rulers; Valois dynasty
Capgrave, John, **3:90a**
saint's Lives, 6:63a
Capilla mayor, **3:90a**
Capistrum Judaeorum. See Martini, Raymond
Capital (architecture), **3:90a–91a**
in Gothic cathedral, 5:598b–599a
Capital punishment
abolished for offenses against forest law, 9:522b
for blasphemy, 2:272a
in *Eclogue*, 4:383a
Forest Charter of 1217, 9:522b
outlawry and, 9:311b
Peter the Chanter on, 9:522a, 522b
reformers, 9:522a
Capital sins. *See* Seven Deadly Sins
Capitals (government), peripatetic medieval government and, 12:159a–160a
Capitanei, 3:557b
Capitol (Rome), 10:519b
stormed (1143), 10:523a
Capitula
in collectarium, 3:480a
of the eyre, 7:185a-b
Capitula Angilramni, 7:405a
Capitula haeresum Petri Abaelardi, 12:191a
Capitula iudiciorum, 9:489b, 490b
Capitula regum Francorum, 10:113b
Capitulare, 7:409b
Capitulare ecclesiasticis ordinis. See Ordines romani
Capitulare missorum, on hunting, 6:356b
Capitulare de villis, 5:358b
prescription for stewardship accounting, 1:36b–37a
Capitularia Benedicti Levitae. See Capitulary, forged
Capitularia missorum, 8:438a
Capitulary, **3:91a–92a**
Carolingian
on the ban, 2:69a
of Charlemagne, 10:76b
for *missi dominici*, 8:438a
forged, Benedictus Levita and, 2:178b–179a, 7:405a
Capitulary aquisgrense, on transport of nobles' equipments, 12:370a
Capitulary of Herstal, 3:91b, 108b, 109a
Capitulary of Quierzy, 3:114b
Capitulary of Thionville, 3:91b, 108b
Capitulatio of 1352, 3:95b
Capitulum, as alternative designation of *þættir*, 12:1b
Capitulum monasticum. See Monasticism, Rule of St. Benedict
Capodistria, homage to Venice (932), 12:386a
Cappadocia, **3:92a–93a**
Cappadocian fathers, 9:6b, 7a, 98b, 696a, 698a-b
Athanasian theology, 9:560b
Platonist philosophy, 9:563a
Cappadocians, Trinitarian doctrine and, 12:189b
Cappella Palatina (Sicily), 6:408b
Capponi family, mass cycles, 8:199a
Capponi, Gino, *Sollevazione de' Ciompi* and, 6:634b
Capreolus, John, *Defensiones theologiae divi Thomae*, 12:42a
Capsa. See Reliquary, chasse
Captain of the people. *See* Commune, Italian; Podesta
Capua
Byzantine rule challenged, 7:4b
triumphal arch, 11:271b
Caput ecclesiae, 10:21b
Čar (son of Master Umek), 12:99a
Carabisiani, theme of, 12:9b
Caracalla. *See* Marcus Aurelius Antoninus (Caracalla)
Caradoc of Llancarfan, life of St. Cadoc, 3:6b–7b
Caradoc Strong-arm (literary character), 7:318b
Carat (unit of measure), 12:594a
Caravans
in art, 6:606b (*illus.*)
routes, fairs and, 4:589a, 589b
see also Han; Trade, Islamic; Travel and transport, Islamic
Caravansary (caravanserai). *See* Han; Khan (building)
Caravel, 9:89a, 11:237a
Carbon-14 dating, in climatology, 3:453b
Carbonell, Miquell, poetry of, 3:171a
Carbury castle, 6:518b
Carcassonne, 7:339a, 12:324b
bridge at, 10:420b

Carcassonne (*cont.*)
bridge at (*cont.*)
cutwaters of, 10:421a
inquisition in, 6:487b
occupied by Muslims, 6:572b
walls of, 2:128b (*illus.*), 12:325 (*illus.*)
Cárcel de amor. See San Pedro, Diego de
Card games, 5:352a-b
see also Games
Cardigan. *See* Ceredigion
Cardinal sins. *See* Seven Deadly Sins
Cardinal virtues. *See* Virtues and Vices
Cardinals, college of, **3:93b–96a**
administration of justice and, 10:522b
administrative reforms, 3:377a
in Augustinus Triumphus' work, 2:1b
authority of, 4:374b
canonization and, 3:68a, 68b
conciliar theory and, 3:511b, 516b, 517a
development of, 4:65b–66b
in Great Schism
anathematization of Urban VI, 11:39b
choice not to convene general council, 11:39b–40a
unification of colleges, 11:41b
Urban VI's attack on, 11:39b
organization of Latin church and, 3:377a
papal administration and, 9:387b
in papal states, 9:387b
papal succession and, 3:604a-b, 634b, 638b, 642a
Peter Damian and, 9:508b–509a
responsibilities of, 3:94b–95a
as successors to the Apostles, 3:517a-b
vs. Innocent VI, 3:95b
Zabarella on, 12:735b
see also Leo IX, pope
Carding, 11:698 (*illus.*)
advantages over combing, 11:695b
banning of, 11:696a
cards, 11:695b
metal, 11:696a-b
in cotton industry, 11:695b
regulation of, 11:696a-b
sliver, 11:695b
teasel, 11:696a
of warps, 11:696a, 696b
Caresini, Raffiano, on Venice, 7:380b, 12:393a
Carew, Sir George, 6:524b
Carillo, Alonso, archbishop of Toledo, 9:111b
Carinthia
duchy of, 5:510a-b
inherited by Přemysl Ottokar II of Bohemia (1269), 2:300a
see also Austria
Caritas (wine measure), 12:589b
Carloman, king of the West Franks (*d.* 884), rule of, 3:114b–115a
Carloman (son of Charles Martel), 9:500b, 501a
territory inherited, 3:106a
vs. Alamanni, 11:526b, 537b
Carlos. *See* Charles
Carmel, Mount, 3:96b
Carmelite rite, **3:96a**
Carmelite Water, 2:147a
Carmelites, **3:96a–97a**
as principal order of friars, 5:297b
rhymed offices and, 10:370b
Carmen ad Lingonensem episcopum. See Godfrey of Rheims
Carmen de algorismo. See Alexander de Villa Dei
Carmen de bello Lewensi. See Song of Lewes
Carmen de bello Saxonico, **3:97a-b**
Carmen campidoctoris, 3:76b
compared with *¡Ay, Iherusalem!,* 2:18b
Carmen Campidoctris, 11:409b, 437b
Carmen de divina providentia. See Prosper of Aquitaine (Prosper Tiro)
Carmen de morte Sanctii regis, 11:409b, 437b
Carmen paschale. See Sedulius
Carmen de ponderibus. See Priscian
Carmina Burana, 1:319a, **3:97b–99a**
authors of, 3:98b
Cambridge songs and, 3:57a
compared with *Carmina Rivipullensia,* 11:406b
hymns and, 6:384b
love lyrics in, 7:368a, 376a
lyrics by Peter of Blois, 9:518a
manuscripts of, 3:97b, 5:436a, 7:368b
Neidhart "von Reuental's" poems and, 9:93a
Ovidian influence, 9:314a
play texts in, 4:277a, 281b
popular music in, 8:570b
prosody, 3:99a
religious drama in, 7:367b
taverns in, 6:475b
see also Anthologies
Carmina Cantabrigiensia. See Cambridge Songs
Carmina figurata
of Eugenius Vulgarius, 4:521a
of Hrabanus Maurus, 6:307b
Carmina Rivipullensia, 11:406b, 410a
Carmina vulgarium poetarium. See Bede
Carniola
inherited by Přemysl Ottokar II of Bohemia (1269), 2:300a
see also Austria
Carnival, **3:99a-b,** 8:29b
municipal co-optation of, 8:29b
origins of, 8:28a
plays
German, 4:271a, 10:245a
political topics, 10:534b
sexual topics, 10:534a
Caro, Joseph
Bet Yosef, 11:586a-b
on law, 7:170a-b, 492b
Shulḥan Arukh, 7:170a-b, 492b, 11:585a, 586b
Carol. *See* Carols
Carol (dance song), 4:86b
Carole, 3:116a
Caroline (Carolingian) minuscule, 7:362a-b, 9:341b (*illus.*), 345a-b, 10:305b
contribution to Western literacy, 11:652b–653a
introduction of, 7:599a
in Lorsch Gospels, 1:213b (*illus.*)
manuscripts written in, 8:102b
neume and, 8:638b
pens and, 12:699b
Carolingian architecture. *See* Pre-Romanesque architecture
Carolingian art. *See* Pre-Romanesque art
Carolingian Empire, **3:104a–115b**
administration of, 3:91a-b, 107a–108b
chancery in, 3:252b
dukes in, 4:303b
office of advocate, 1:59b
power of ban, 2:69a
use of commendation in, 3:491a-b
see also Baldwin I of Flanders
architecture, 10:91b–92b, 94a
arms and armor, 1:522b
Arnulf of Metz and, 3:104a–106b
art
decline of, 10:99b–100a
illuminations, 10:97a–100a
influence on Ottonian art, 10:310a
jewelry, 5:377a
metalwork, 2:384a
mosaics, 10:96b–97a
paintings, 10:97a
sculpture and metalwork, 10:100a–101a
astrology in, 1:606b
Austrasian nobility and, 5:474b
boundaries of, 3:105 (map)
Brittany under, 2:378b–379a
Bruges under, 2:386a
Burgundy and, 2:428b–429b
cavalry in, 3:202b–203a
classical literary studies in, 3:432b–433b
conquest of Saxony, 10:683a-b
eastern, 3:114a-b
emergence of, 8:236a
erosion of authority
growth of principalities, 5:152b–154a, 156b
lack of economic and technical resources, 5:156b
estate management, scarcity of tools, 12:82a
Frankish kingdom and, 5:474a-b
geographic division of (843–870), 3:113 (map)
Jews and, 7:85a, 86a
kingship in, 7:259b–262a
lack of naval forces, 9:79b
languages of, 6:437a, 9:143a
Languedoc and, 7:339a
Latin church in, 3:108b–110a, 373b–374b
Divine Office, 4:230a-b
ecclesiastical support, 5:157a
Jonas of Orléans, 7:146a
tithes, 12:62b
linguistic reforms in, 5:221b, 233a
Magyars and, 6:338a
maintenance of roads and bridges, 10:411a, 411b
mints and money of, 8:428 (*illus.*)
missi dominici in, 8:438a

music in, 11:164a–165a
neume and, 8:624a
Normans and, 9:161b–162a
origins of, 3:104a–106a
parceling-out of, 5:221b
Switzerland and, 11:537b
Pepin the Elder and, 3:104a–106b
political theory of, 10:16a-b, 17b–18a
privileges of international merchants, 12:117b
propaganda for, 10:139b
putative Jewish principality in, 9:64b
relations with
Austria, 2:4b, 6a
Avars, 2:12b
representative assemblies and, 10:316b
restoration of (898), 5:153a–154a
revival of education and culture, 7:688b
rulers of
collapse of regalian power, 5:154a
coronations, 7:256b–257b
early kings, 3:106a–107a
elections, 4:425b–426a
functions of kingship in, 9:473b
last rulers, 5:156b–157a, 474a
successors of Charlemagne, 3:111a–112b, 114a
sanctions against interest taking, 12:336a
seals of, 11:125a, 129a
settlement patterns, 11:675b
slavery in, 11:334b
stem duchies, 5:474a, 506b–507a
Stephen II's alliance with, 8:377a
taxation, 11:619a
tonaries, 12:69b–70a
trade of, 12:109b
travel and transport, 12:151b–153a, 157a-b
urbanism in, 12:313b–314a
church construction and repair, 12:314a
decline of urban palaces, 12:313b
later Carolingian urban repairs, 12:314a
withdrawal of royal authority, 12:314a
vehicles, 12:370a, 371b–373a
Venice and, 12:385a-b
in Vermandois, 12:395b
Viking raids, 5:156b, 12:429b–431a
western, 3:114b–115b
see also Charlemagne; German law, post-Carolingian; Strasbourg oaths
Carolingian Latin poetry, **3:99b–103b**
beginning of, 3:99b–100a
examples of, 3:100a–103b
Germanic legends, 12:535b
Hrabanus Maurus and, 6:308a
liturgical poetry, 9:713b–714a
Carolingian renaissance, 3:100a
Ada group, 10:305b–306a
Court Schools, 10:97a–99b, 100a, 101a, 110b–111a, 306a
drama in, 4:274a
Latin literature and, 7:362a-b
library development and, 7:562a-b
manuscript book production, 8:102a
musical instruments, 8:601a
musical treatises of, 8:638b–640a
punctuation and, 10:213b
Remigius of Auxerre's role, 10:303a
Roman art and, 10:504b
Swabian monasteries and, 11:526b
Carolingians. *See* Carolingian Empire
Carols, 8:572a
in Christmas celebration, 3:319a
Franciscans and, 8:579b
in Judeo-Provençal language, 7:178b
Middle English, **3:116a–117a**, 8:325a, 339a-b, 12:180b
Romanian, 10:513b
villancico and, 12:447a
Carpaccio, depiction of shoes by, 11:255b
Carpatho-Ukraine, Hungary and, 6:337b
Carpenter, Alexander, *Destructorium viciorum,* 3:459b
Carpentras, inns in, 6:474b
Carpet page, **3:117a**, 4:317b (*illus.*)
of Book of Durrow, 8:370b–371a (*illus.*)
in Celtic art, 3:219a
in Gospelbooks, 5:579b–580a
in Hebrew manuscript illumination, 8:110b (*illus.*)
in Lindisfarne Gospels, 3:220b, 7:0 (frontispiece), 8:370b–371b, 372 (*illus.*)
Carpets. *See* Rugs and carpets
Carpini, John of Plano. *See* John of Plano Carpini
Carrack, 9:89a, 11:234 (*illus.*), 237a, 245a
Carrand diptych (ivory), 4:352a
Carrata (unit of measure), 12:592b
Carrión, Antonio de, *Batalla de la riquesa et pobreza,* 11:443a
Carrión family, *Cantar de mío Cid* and, 3:76b–77a
Carroccio, **3:117a-b**
Carrot, growth of, 1:96a
Carruca (four-wheeled vehicle), 12:368b, 369b
Carruca (plow), 12:72b, 73a, 75b
Carta Pisana (portolan chart), 10:33 (*illus.*)
Carta puebla, 5:309a
Cartage. *See* Animals, draft; Travel and transport; Vehicles
Cartagena, captured by Vandals, 12:354b
Cartagena, Alfonso de, 11:420b
Defensorium unitatis christianae, 11:421b
Leonardo Bruni's translation of Aristotle's *Ethics* and, 11:457a
Cartagena, Teresa de, 11:420b
Carthage
African exarchate and, 4:530a
captured (696), 6:414a
mint at, 8:420a
Tunis and, 6:414b, 415a, 8:15b
Vandals and, 8:15a, 12:354b
Carthage, Councils of
(401), *Item placuit,* 3:67b–68a
(411), excommunication of Celestius and, 9:486a
(416), Pelagianism and, 9:486b
(418), condemnation of Pelagius, 9:486b
Carthaginians, Berber language and, 2:186a
Carthusian rite, **3:118a**
Benedictine borrowings, 3:118a
influence of Lyonese rite, 3:118a
sources for, 3:118a
Carthusians, **3:118a–120a**
artistic patronage, 10:613b
Dijon, Chartreuse de Champmol, 4:186a
English translations of continental mystical works and, 9:26b–27a
exemption from tithe payments, 12:65a
founding of, 2:392a, 3:118a-b
library of, 7:562b–563a
monasteries of, 3:118b–119a, 8:456a
isolation of monks, 8:456a
monastic reform unneeded by, 10:287b
reformation and, 3:119a
religious contribution, 3:119a
rigorous practices, 3:118b, 119b
Ruusbroec and, 9:36a–37b
women's orders and, 12:687a
Cartography
Byzantine. *See* Communications, Byzantine; Roads, Byzantine
early, 4:553b
in guidebooks, 1:333a-b
Islamic, 9:77a
al-Balkhī school, 5:392b–393a
travel and transport and, 12:147a–148a
zonal world map, 5:392a (*illus.*)
see also Geography, Islamic
Roman. *See* Tabula Peutingeriana
Western European
Ebstorf map, 5:397a
Hereford map, 5:397a, 8:121a (*illus.*)
Hugh of St. Victor's concepts, 5:397a-b
Italian, 4:559a
O-T maps, 5:397b, 8:121a
Peutinger map, 5:397a
portolan chart and, 5:398b–399a, 10:33a–35a
Psalter map, 5:397a-b
religious elements in mapmaking, 5:397a-b
shape of European coasts, 9:89b
Vinland maps, 12:429b, 430 (*illus.*)
Zeno map, 5:399a
see also Geography, Western European; Mappa mundi; Roads, Western European; Scientific instruments
Cartoixà. See Joan Roís de Corella
Cartulary, **3:120a-b**
in chancery, 3:253a
Irish, 10:620a
Cartulary of Heming, 1:286b
Carucage, 4:90b, 7:200b, 11:612a-b
Carver, William (Bromflet), **3:120b**
Casa dels Folls (psychiatric hospital: Valencia), 6:490b, 12:348b
Casal Imbert, 6:389b
Casbah, **3:120b–121a**
of Marrakech, headquarters for Christian militia, 8:151a

Casbah (*cont.*)
of Tunis, rule of Abū Zakariyāᵓ from, 6:53a
of Udaya (Rabat), 1:192a, 193a (*illus.*)
Casbah Mosque (Marrakech), 1:191b, 193a
minaret, 8:151a
Casbhairdne, 6:534b
Cashel, **3:121a-b**
Éoganachta and, 6:547b
kings of, 3:121a-b
see of, 1:470a
Cashel, Synod of (1172), 6:517b
Divine Office in Ireland and, 7:614a
Casimir I (the Restorer) of Poland, king, 9:719b–720a
Casimir II (the Just) of Poland, grand prince, 9:723a
Casimir III (the Great) of Poland, king, 9:724b–725b
corona regni Poloniae, 9:629a
education and, 9:729a-b
territorial acquisitions, 9:629a
Casimir IV (Jagiellończyk) of Poland, king, 9:727b–728a, 729a
marble tomb of by Veit Stoss, 11:487a
Novgorod and, 9:196b
Časlav of Serbia, 11:170a-b
seizure of part of Bosnia, 4:5a
Casnodyn, **3:121b–122a**
Caspar (magus), 4:498a
Caspe, Compromise of (1412), 12:349a
Caspian Sea
expansion of the Rus and, 12:436a
Western knowledge of, 4:556b
Cassian of Imola, St., 6:317a
Cassian, John, **3:122a–123a,** 7:560a
Augustine's followers and, 3:122b
Benedict of Nursia and, 2:170a
Carmelites and, 3:96b
Collationes (*Conferences*), 1:653b, 3:122b, 343a
De incarnatione, 3:122b
Dominic and, 4:239b
Egyptian travels, 3:122b
Germanus and, 3:122a
Gregory the Great and, 3:122b
Hrabanus Maurus and, 6:307a
Institutiones, 3:122b, 343a
monasticism and, 3:122a-b, 6:213b, 8:462a
ordination of, 3:122a
Pelagianism and, 9:486b
on Seven Deadly Sins, 11:211b
Cassiciacum, Augustine of Hippo at, 1:647a–648a
"Cassino depositions." *See Placiti cassinesi*
Cassiodorus Senator, Flavius Magnus Aurelius, **3:123a–124b,** 10:353b–354a, 354b
Arator and, 1:422a
Archimedes and, 1:434b
Augustine's sermons and, 3:123b
on Boethius, 2:291b
on bookbinders' patternbooks, 4:291b
Chronica, 3:123a
Theodoric the Ostrogoth in, 9:291a
Codex grandior, 4:357a, 7:584a
De anima, 3:123b
dialectic and, 4:169a
early Germanic law and, 7:471a
educational interests, 3:124a
Expositio Psalmorum, 3:123b
Gothic History, 7:149b
Institutiones, 3:124a, 432b, 4:447b–448a, 6:443a, 7:560a, 8:156a, 637b–638a, 9:585a, 10:354a
on medical treatises, 8:247a
Isidore of Seville and, 6:546a
library development and, 7:560a
on medicine, 8:255a
monastery at Vivarium, 3:123b–124a
on music, 8:579a-b, 581b, 586a, 10:378b–379a
Musica disciplina and, 8:639a
Notker Teutonicus and, 9:189a
political troubles, 3:123b
protection of Jews, 5:383b
recommendation to study Vergil, 12:394a
religious studies of, 3:123b
on Roman buildings, 10:517a
School of Nisibis and, 11:564b
Theodoric and, 3:123a-b, 7:471a
translations from Greek at Vivarium, 12:126b
Variae, 3:123b, 10:358a
Vulgate and, 12:495b
Cassone, 5:325b
Castanets, 8:563a
Castel Nuovo (Naples), 9:59b
Castel Sant'Angelo (Rome), 10:525a
Casteleyn, Mathys, *De conste van rhetoriken,* 4:322b
Castelfranco Veneto, founding of, 12:325a
Castellan, **3:124b–125b,** 9:721b
in Catalonia, 3:176b–177a
in Champagne, 3:245b
in county of Savoy, 10:674b
government by, 11:619a
loss of power under Louis VI, 5:159b
recruitment of household officers from ranks of, 5:160a
rise of, 11:577a
under Capetians, public functions, 5:157b
Ypres, 12:731a
Castellani, Castellano, 6:636b
Castellón de la Plana, irrigation of, 6:557a, 558a
Castellón (Valencia), 12:346a
Castelloza (trobairitz), 12:207a, 215a
Castellum Volandum. *See* Oḷakan castle
Castelvecchio, bridge at, 10:421b
Castia-gilos. See Raimon Vidal de Besalú
Castigas y doctrinas que un sabio dava a sus hijas, 3:663b
Castiglione, Baldassare, *Book of the Courtier,* on the status of the artist, 1:580a
Castigos e documentos del rey don Sancho, 11:415b
Castigos y ejemplos de Catón, 8:281b
Castile, **3:125b–141a,** 3:127 (map)
Almoravids and, 1:199b–200a
anti-Castilian alliances, 3:131a
Asturias-León and, 1:627b–628a, 3:125b, 127a, 131a
black slaves in, 2:268b
boundaries of, 3:126 (map), 127 (map)
caballeros villanos in, 3:131a-b
Canary Islands and, 3:61b–62a, 63a
in *Cantar de mío Cid,* 3:75a
church in, 3:133a, 139b–140a
cities of, 3:132a
claim of Alfonso I of Aragon to, 1:160b
conquest of Murcia, 11:378b
conquests, of Seville, 3:135b–136a
converso problem in, 3:137b, 138b, 139b
culture of, 3:133b, 140a
curia regis in, 3:132b
economic crises
inflation in, 3:135a-b
in 13th century, 3:135b–136a
economic structure of, 3:131a-b, 139b
expansion of, 3:128b–129a
to south, 3:131b
feudalism in, 3:132b
geographic influences on, 3:125b, 127a
government of, 3:132b–133a
centralization of, 3:139a
cortes in, 3:138b–139a, 610b, 611b, 612a
financial administration, 3:139a-b
judicial officials, 3:139a
municipal, 3:139a
royal authority in, 3:132a-b
royal bureaucracy in, 3:132b
tax collection, 3:132a-b, 138b
hermandades, 3:134b, 137b, 139a, 6:209b–210a
history (800–1037), 3:125b–128b
history (1037–1212), 3:128b–133b
history (1212–1350), 3:133b–136b
history (1350–1474), 3:136b–140a
political developments, 3:138b–139a
independence of, 3:128a
irrigation of, 6:558a
Jews in
massacres of, 3:137b
rab de la corte office, 10:243b
status of, 7:79b–81a, 82a-b
taxation of, 10:243b
John of Gaunt's claim to, 3:137b, 7:135a
in Juan de Mena's *Laberinto de Fortuna,* 8:273a
legend of origins, 3:128a
merino in, 3:132b–133a
monasteries in, 3:127a
reform of, 3:129a-b
Mudejars in, 11:378a-b
Muslim subjects of, 3:129b
Mudejar revolt, 3:134a, 135a
nobility, 3:136a-b, 139b
counts, 3:127a–128a
Old Spanish dialects in, 11:399b–400a
pilgrimages to, 3:131b–132a
reign of Alfonso X, 1:161a-b
relations with, Portugal, 10:41a-b, 45b, 49a-b, 52a-b
settlement of, 3:125b, 126a–127a

  social structure, 3:131a-b
    ethnic mix of, 3:125b
    free peasants in, 3:127a-b
  Trastámaras in, 3:136b–139a
  unification of, 3:128a
  vs. Muslims, 3:131a
    Almoravid invasion of, 3:129b
    al-Manṣūr's attacks, 3:128b
  see also *Fernán González, Poema de; Mesta;* Navarre, kingdom of; Spanish law; Spanish literature
Castilian language, **3:141a–142b**
  Arabic influences, 3:141b
  evolution of, 3:141b–142a
  French influences, 3:142a
  Greek influences, 3:141a
  influence of Alfonso X, 1:161b, 3:142a
  Latin language and, 3:141a-b
  literature in, 3:142a
  origins of, 3:141a-b, 6:435b, 442b
  Spanish language and, 3:141a
  see also Spanish language
Castilian literature, 3:133a-b, 140a, 142a
  evolution of, 3:133a-b, 142a
  in 14th century, 3:140a
  Galician-Portuguese poetry and, 5:342a
  see also Spanish literature
Castillo, Diego Enríquez del, *Crónica del Enrique IV,* 11:422a
Castillo, Hernando del, *Cancionero general* and, 11:424a
Castillo, Luis de, possible author of *Crónica de don Miguel Lucas de Iranzo,* 11:433a
Castillon, Battle of (1453), 3:65b–66a, 6:332b
Castle of Perseverance, The, 1:186a, **3:142b–143a,** 8:484a, 10:362b
  Everyman and, 4:528b
  performance of, 4:286b
Castles and fortifications, **3:143a–152b**
  Armenian, 1:515a
    see also Lambron
  artillery and, 3:151b–152a
  at Bruges, 2:386a
  at Brusa, 2:392b–393a
  at Prague, 10:70a
  at Salces, 3:152a
  Ayyubid, 2:21a
  in Baltic lands, 2:64a
  battering ram and cat in attacks on, 3:146b, 148a, 149 (*illus.*)
  in Buda, 2:396b
  by Matteo Gattaponi, 5:367a
  Byzantine
    Justinian's building program, 4:334a
    survival of, 4:333b
  Byzantine-Armenian, 1:477a, 482b
    see also Hṙomklay
  cannon and, 3:65b
  Carthusians and, 3:119b
  casbah, 3:120b–121a
  castellan, 3:124b–125a
  construction of, 3:143a
    in England, 3:562a
  crenels in, 3:146a-b, 147 (*illus.*), 149 (*illus.*)
  crusader, 4:22a-b, 24b, 25a-b, 32b
  curtain walls, 3:150b
  Danish. *See* Danevirke
  Derbent, 4:162a-b
  doors to, 3:146b, 148a
  double-enceinte system of walls, 4:333b
  drawbridges in, 3:150b
  dungeons in, 3:148b, 150a, 4:308a-b
  early medieval villages and, 12:443a
  English
    Roger of Salisbury and, 10:443a
    as treasuries, 6:301b
  facade of, 3:149 (*illus.*)
  family life and, 4:601a
  Frederick II and, 11:274b
  in Granada, 5:651b
  Hungarian, 6:342b, 344a, 346b
  Islamic, 12:551b–552a, 553a
  Kořikos, 7:298a-b
  masonry fortifications, 12:564a-b
  merlons, 3:147 (*illus.*), 148a, 149 (*illus.*)
  Mistra, 8:446a-b
  motte-and-bailey type, 3:144a–145a (*illus.*), 6:554a, 12:564a
  noble class and, 3:412b–413a
  Nubian, 9:199b
  obsolescence, 3:151a–152a
  platforms in, 3:146b
  portcullis in, 10:33a
  purpose of, 3:143a
  replacement of, 3:152a
  Richelieu and, 3:152a
  in Roman Empire
    castrum, 3:152b
    types of, 3:143b–144a
  Rome, 10:525a-b
  shell-keep type, 3:144 (*illus.*)
  siege techniques, 3:150a-b, 6:333a, 12:564a-b
    sapping, 3:144 (*illus.*), 146a
  specialization of, 3:150b–151a
  stone, 3:145a–146a, 148b
  surviving walls of, 3:151a-b
  Swedish, 11:531b–532a
  urban, 3:151a
  waterworks, 12:577b
  weapons and, 3:143a-b, 148a-b, 150a-b
  wooden, 3:145a
  Ypres, 12:731a, 731b, 732b
  see also Bastide; Castrum; Châtelet; Jacquerie; Machicolation; Palaces, architecture; Tower
Castorius, Tabula Peutingeriana and, 11:572a
Castra, Florentine poet, 6:656b
Castra Regina, 2:133a
Castracani, Castruccio
  attacks on Florence, 5:97a
  Siena and, 11:280a
Castro, Giovanni di, discovery of alum in Italy, 4:327a
Castro y Bellvis, Guillén de, *Mocedades del Cid,* 3:388b
Castro-Jeriz, Juan García de, Spanish version of Egidius Colonna's *De regimine principium,* 11:441b
Castrum, **3:152b,** 12:446a
  in crusader architecture, 4:22b, 24b
  Polish *gród,* 9:716b–717a, 721b
  see also Castles and fortifications
Castrum doloris, 5:320b
Casuistry, **3:153a–154b**
  definition of, 3:153a
  in Latin church, 3:153a-b
  popularity of, 3:153b
Casus, 4:127b
Casus sancti Galli. See Ekkehard IV of St. Gall
Catacomb of Hermes (Rome), 2:170b
Catacombs, **3:154a–155b**
  art in, 3:155b, 4:350a
    chalice depictions, 3:241b–242a
  Christian cult relics and, 9:658a
  cubiculum in, 4:63b–64a
  definition of, 3:154a
  excavation of, 1:337a
  form of, 3:155a-b
  historical development of, 3:154a-b
  martyrs in, 3:154b
  preserved, 3:155a-b
  Roman, 3:154a–155a (*illus.*)
  tombs in, 3:155a
  see also Commodilla catacomb; S. Callisto (church: Rome) catacomb; Via Latina catacomb
Catalan Company, **3:156a–157a**
  Avignon papacy's opposition to, 3:156b
  destruction of, 3:156b–157a
  formation of, 3:156a
  in Greece, 3:156a-b, 7:379b
    capture of Athens, 2:500a
    rule of Athens, 3:156b–157a
  politics of, 3:157a
  Roger de Flor and, 3:156a, 10:441b
  in Walter de Brienne's service, 3:156a
Catalan drama, extant texts, 11:436a-b
Catalan language, **3:157a–164a,** 6:442b
  Bible translations in, 2:215b
  classification of, 3:157a-b
  documents in, 3:157b
  dominance of, 3:157b
  Jordi de S. Jordi and, 7:150a
  morphosyntax, 3:160a–163a
  origins of, 6:435b
  other Romance affinities, 3:158a
  phonetics of, 3:159a–160a
  Provençal and, 6:442a
  similarities to Occitan, 3:158a-b
  vocabulary in, 3:163a-b
  vocalic mutation in, 3:158b–159b
  writers using, 3:157b–158a
  written, 3:158b–159a
Catalan law, maritime code. *See* Celelles, Francis, *Llibre del consolat del mar*
Catalan literature, **3:164a–173a,** 10:252a-b
  Anselm Turmeda and, 12:227b–228b
  Arthurian legend in, 1:573a
    earliest references, 1:575b–576a
  on contemporary life and customs, 4:416b
  development of, Ramon Lull, 7:686b–687a
  end of, 3:172a
  French influence on, 3:171a-b, 173a
  Italian influence on, 3:171a
  origins of, 3:164a
  poetry, 3:157b

Catalan literature (*cont.*)
poetry (*cont.*)
to 1300, 3:164a-b
after 1300, 3:170a–172a
prose, 3:157b–158a
belles lettres, 3:169a–170a
chronicles, 3:165a–166b
cookbooks, 3:168b
didactic texts, 3:168a–169a
law books, 3:169a
novels, 3:170a
origins of, 3:164b–165a
philosophical texts, 3:168a–169a
practical texts, 3:168a–169a
religious and devotional texts, 3:166b–168a
scientific works, 3:168b
translations, 3:168b–169a
travel texts, 3:169b–170a
saints' lives in, 3:167a-b
theology in, 3:167b–168a
Troy story in, 11:458a
under Peter IV (the Ceremonious), 9:511a
in Valencia, 12:349a
verse narrative, **3:173a–174a**
Arthurian themes in, 3:173a
in *codolades,* 3:173a-b
courtly love in, 3:173a-b
humorous, 3:173b
masterpieces of, 3:173b–179a
in *noves rimades,* 3:173a-b
satiric, 3:173b
subjects of, 3:173a-b
Catalan rite. *See* Narbonne rite
Catalaunian Fields, Battle of (451), 2:92b, 12:470b
Catalogus baronum, 11:268b, 275b
Catalonia, **3:174a–179a**, 3:176 (map), 177 (map)
Almoravids in, 3:178a-b
aprisio in, 3:174b–175a
Aragon and, 3:178b
Berenguer dynasty, 3:178a-b
black slaves in, 2:268b
boundaries of, 3:177 (map)
Castellan aristocracy in, 3:176b–177a
Civil War of 1462–1472, 2:104b
collapse of in 11th century, 3:176a-b
commerce, 4:557b
cortes in, 3:610b, 612a
Corts, based on the Peace and Truce statutes, 9:475a
culture in, 3:175a-b, 11:452a
Frankish protectorate of, 3:174a-b
frescoes in, 10:113b
Guifred the Hairy as founder of, 3:174b–175a
Hispano-Gothic refugees in, 3:174a-b
independence of, 3:177a
inns in, 6:468a, 473b
invasions of
by al-Manṣūr, 3:175b, 8:90a-b
by Moors, 3:175a
irrigation in, 6:558a, 558b
Jews in, 7:80b
Latin church in
Gregorian reform movement, 3:177b
monasticism, 3:175a
Narbonne rite and, 9:63a
Moorish Spain and, 3:175b–176a
national formation of, 3:174b
New and Old, 3:178b
origin of, 3:174a
Peace and Truce of God and, 9:474b, 475a
settlement of Valencia and, 12:346b
in 12th century, 3:178b
vs. Genoa in Sardinia, 5:386b
working of iron, 8:285b–286a
see also Almogávares; Barcelona
Catania, captured by Normans (1072), 11:265b
Catania, University of, 12:286b
Cataphracti, **3:179a-b**, 11:635a
in Armenian cavalry, 3:199a
in European cavalry, 3:200a-b
Catapults, 3:150b, **3:179b–181a**
Cataracts, operations for, 2:99a, 8:249b (*illus.*)
Catchword. *See* Manuscript books, production of
Câteau-Cambrésis, Treaty of (1559), 10:675a, 11:282a
Catechetical Homilies. See Symeon the New Theologian, St.
Catechetical Lectures. See Cyril of Jerusalem
Catechetical School (Alexandria), 3:593b–594a
church fathers and, 3:335b
Catechism and catechetical manuals
for children, 10:302a
early medieval, 10:300a
Lay Folks' Catechism, 10:301b
see also Religious instruction
Catechumens. *See* Baptism, adult; Religious instruction, for baptism
Categoriae. See Boethius
Categoriae decem. See Augustine of Hippo, St.
Categories. See Aristotle
Catena, compilers of, 9:564a
Catena aurea. See Aquinas, Thomas, St.
Catepan. *See Katepano*
Caterinati, 9:14b
Cath Fionntrágha, 11:116a
Cath Maige Tuired, 6:546a-b, 547b, 548b
Cathach initials, 8:370a
Cathach of St. Columba, 2:220a, 3:218b (*illus.*)
decorated initials in, 6:461b
Cathal mac Finguine, 4:493a
war with Uí Néill, 8:531a, 12:242a-b
Cathal Ó Conchobhair, king of Connacht, 6:523a
Cathars, 1:130b, **3:181b–191a**, 6:196a
Arianism and, 3:183b
beliefs of, 3:182a–183b, 6:196a
concept of creation, 6:196b
dualism, 4:297b
goal of the Perfect, 3:185a–186a
rejection of Passion and Resurrection, 6:196b
rejection of worldliness, 5:175b
Trinitarian doctrine, 3:184b
Bogomilism and, 2:296b–297a, 3:182a-b, 183b–184b
Bonaccorso of Milan on, 3:182a
church organization, 3:185b–186a, 6:196a
formation of bishoprics, 6:196b
council at St. Felix-de-Caraman, 3:183b
denunciatio and, 6:478b
destruction of, 3:190a-b
geographical distribution, 3:186a-b
in Germany, 5:484b
history of, 3:182a
inquisition and, 3:189b–190b, 6:483a, 484b, 486a, 487b, 488a, 488b
liturgy of, **3:181a-b**
Lombers debate, 6:196b
in Milan, 8:379a
names for, 3:181b–182a
numbers of, 3:186a
opposition to, 3:640a, 640b
origins of, 4:374b, 6:196b
papacy and, 3:186b
Innocent III, 6:465a
persecution of, 3:186b–188a
Peter of Blois on, 9:518a
politics and, 3:186b–187a
practices of
celibacy, 3:185a
consolamentum, 3:185a-b
fasting, 3:185a, 185b
public confession, 3:185b
refusal to play tithes, 12:64b
rituals of, 3:182a
Satanic myths concerning, 3:184a–185a
status of women, 3:185b
Toulouse and, 12:91a, 91b
witchcraft and, 12:661a, 661b
writings of, 3:182a
see also Albigensians
Cathay. *See* China
Cathedra, **3:191a-b**
Cathedral, **3:191b–192b**
architectural significance, 3:192a-b
bells and, 2:166b
chapel in, 3:192a-b
chapter, 3:191a–192a, 265b–266a, 266b
as representative assembly, 10:328b, 332b–333a
choir in, 3:192a-b
clocks in, 3:29b
construction of, 3:564a–569a
campaigns for, 3:191b–192a
cult served by, 5:589a-b
designers of, 1:440b
double, 3:378b
ecclesiological significance, 3:191a
educational role of, 3:638b
French type, 3:192b
ground plans of
apse, 5:590a
basic, 5:589b–590a
transept, 5:590a–591a
height of, 5:598a
Italian type, 3:192b
Norman designs for, in Italy, 4:346b
organ building and, 8:604b–605a
pointed arches in Gothic style, 1:425a
present state of, 5:589b
schools in, 3:433b–434a
at Rheims, 10:303a
in England, 4:471b–472a
France, 7:363b, 364a, 9:313a
German literature and, 8:347b

in 13th century, 7:368a
use of organs, 9:273a
see also Beauvais, School of; Chartres, School of
sculptural ornamentation in
acanthus leaf, 5:598b
crocket capital, 5:598a–599a
figural sculpture, 5:599a-b
foliage, 5:598a–599a
tracery system, 5:599b, 601a
sexpartite system in, 5:595b
structure of
arcade, 5:591b–592a, 593a–594b
arches, 5:591b–592b
bay system, 5:596b
ceiling, 5:594b–595b
columns, 5:592b–594b
crossing, 5:592a
inner wall system, 5:591a
pier dimensions and slenderness ratios, 3:569a (*table*)
vaulting, 5:595b–596a
wall mass, 5:596a-b
study of, 5:589b
terminology used to describe, 5:598a
see also entries on architectural styles and particular cathedrals; Parekklesion
Cathedral office, 1:516b–517a
Cathemerinon. See Prudentius
Catherine of Alexandria, St.
depicted by Hans Memling, 8:272 (*illus.*)
evidence for existence, 6:68a
rhymed offices to, 10:371a
Spanish prose life of, 11:439b
see also Vie de Ste. Catherine d'Alexandrie
Catherine of Austria, 4:490b
Catherine of Bologna, St., displayed in her glass coffin, 10:299a
Catherine (daughter of St. Birgitta), 2:247a
Catherine of Genoa, St., 9:14b–15a
Catherine of Siena, St., 9:14b, 11:281a
Birgitta of Sweden and, 9:15a
compared with Gertrude the Great, 9:11a
on contraception, 3:572b
Dialogue of Divine Providence, 4:248b
as doctor of the church, 4:234b
as Dominican lay sister, 4:254b
Dominican mysticism and, 4:248b
Letters, 6:660a
monasticism and, 3:368b
William Flete and, 9:26b
writings of, 9:14b
in English, 9:27a
Catherine of Valois, 7:380a
marriage to Henry V of England, 6:332a
Owen Tudor and, 12:222b–223a
Catherning (St. Catherine's Day), 5:37a
Cathmail. *See* Cadoc, St.
Catholic Homilies. See Aelfric
Catholic League, in Hussite wars, 6:372a
Catholicon. See Balbi, Giovanni
Catholicus. *See Katholikos*
Cato's Distichs, 7:352b, 355b, 360a
Anglo-Norman versions of, 1:264a
Bonvesin and, 6:631a
Latin, **3:193a-b**
Notker Teutonicus and, 9:189b
Old French, **3:193b**
Proverbia quae dicuntur super natura feminarum and, 6:630a
Splanamento de li proverbii de Salamone and, 6:630b
Catraeth, Battle of, 12:602b
Cattle
beef powder as military staple, 1:300a
degeneration of domestic breeds, 1:301b
as draft animals, 1:293b–294a
as food animals, 1:299a-b, 300a, 301b
Hungarian gray longhorn breed, 1:301b
milk yield of, 1:301b
selective breeding of, 1:293b, 294a
trade in, Hungarian, 6:345b
see also Animals, draft; Animals, food
Cattle Problem, The. See Archimedes
Cattle Raid of Cooley, The. See Táin bó Cúailnge
Caucasia, **3:193b–195b**
Armenian church and, 1:500b
boundaries of, 3:193b–194 (map), 195a
campaigns of Alp Arslan and, 11:152b
conquered by Arabs, 1:478b
ethnic groups in, 3:195a
Hulagu and, 6:329a
Kipchak alliance, 8:468a
Mongol invasions, 8:468a, 470a
North, 3:195a-b
South, 3:195b
struggles over between Persia and Russia, 3:308a
Sultan Malikshāh I and, 11:153a
see also Liparit IV Orbēlean
Caucasian language group, 5:404a
Caucasus Mountains, **3:195b–196a**
as border of Georgia, 5:402b, 405a
as divider of Caucasia, 3:193a-b
invasions through, 3:195b–196a
in Islamic conquests, 6:572a
Cauda, **3:196a**
Caudati, 7:373b
Caulier, Achille, *Cruelle femme en amours,* 9:637a
Causa reformationis, 5:489a
Causa unionis, 5:489a
Causality, Ockham on, 9:211b–211a
Çavacequia, Peter Raymond, 6:557b
Cavaillon, 12:442b
Cavalca, Domenico, 6:660a, 664b
Cavalcanti, Guido, **3:196a–197b**
ballata by, 6:668b–669a
Cino da Pistoia and, 3:397b
courtly love in, 3:196b–197a
Dante and, 3:196a-b, 4:98b
dolce stil nuovo and, 6:649a, 649b
"Donna me prega," 3:196b, 6:647b, 666b–667a
early life of, 3:196a-b
importance of, 3:196b
politics of, 3:196b
psychology of love in, 6:647a-b
theory of images, 3:197a-b
works of, 3:196b
Cavalier (coin), 5:680a
Cavallero del Cisne, El, 11:453b
Cavallero Zifar, Libro del, **3:197b–198a**, 11:443b, 453b
Cavallini, Pietro, **3:198a-b**
Annunciation, 3:198a
frescoes of, 3:198a, 5:292a, 606a
Giotto and, 3:198b
identity of, 3:198a
Last Judgment, 3:198 (*illus.*)
Life of the Virgin, 3:198a
Madonna and Child, 3:198a
Cavalry, Armenian, **3:198b–199a**
of Arsacids, 3:198b–199a
of Artawazd II, 3:198b
in Byzantine army, 3:199a
nobility and, 3:198b–199a
payment of, 3:199a
in Sasanian army, 3:199a
use of, 3:198a
Cavalry, Byzantine, **3:199b–200a**
besieging a tower, 12:548 (*illus.*)
cataphracti, 3:179a-b
importance of, 3:199b
stirrup and, 3:202a
in thematic armies, 3:199b–200a
units in, 3:199b–200a
see also Magister militum; Themes
Cavalry, European, **3:200a–208b,** 9:715b
at Hastings, 3:203b
in battle on Dyle, 3:202a
in Carolingian Empire, 3:202a–203a
chivalry and, 3:203a–204a
clibanarii in, 3:200b
in crusades, 3:203a
decline of (1300–1500), 3:204a–206b
defeats of, 3:204b–205b
depiction in art, 3:202b
dispute over Dark Ages expansion of, 3:201a–202a
English, 3:205a-b
equine veterinary medicine and, 3:206b
feudalism and, 3:201a-b
Flemish, 3:204b
Frankish, 3:201a–202a, 12:556a, 557a-b, 558a
freemen in, 12:558a
French, 3:205a-b
in Germanic kingdoms, 3:201a
knight in, 3:203a–204a
lance units in, 3:206b
Lombard campaigns, 12:556a
longbow and, 3:205a-b
of Magyars, 3:203a
method of payment, 12:558b
missile weapons and, 3:205a
purpose of, 3:200a
in Reconquest Spain, 3:203a
Roman armored auxiliaries, 1:522a, 531b
in Roman Empire, 3:200a–201a
Saxon tribute and, 3:202a
Scottish, 3:204b–205a
social status, 12:558a
Spanish light, 12:563b
Swiss, 3:204b–205a
tactics, 3:200a–202b, 206b

Cavalry, European (*cont.*)
tactics (*cont.*)
feigned retreat, 3:203b
guerrilla warfare, 3:206a
raiding, 3:202b
reconnaissance role, 3:202b
as shock force, 12:557b
transition period (100–1066), 3:200a–203a
Visigoths, 12:555a-b
weapons and equipment
armor, 3:205b–206a
cost of, 12:557b–558a
high-backed saddle, 3:202b
lance, 3:206a
stirrup, 3:201b–202a, 12:557b (*illus.*)
see also Knights and knight service; Squire
Cavalry, Islamic, **3:208b–210a**
Berber tribesmen, 12:552a
in Egypt, 3:209b
equipment, 3:209a
stirrup, 3:208b
evolution, 12:551a
in Mongol empire, 3:209b
mounted archers, 12:552b, 553a
in North Africa, 3:209b
Persian tradition and, 12:552a
regular and irregular, 12:552b
rise of, 3:208a
in Seljuk armies, 3:209a-b
Spain and Central Asia, 12:552b
Turkish slave troops, 12:552b
Cavalry, Parthian, 9:444a
Cavalry, Persian, Alexander the Great against the Zangids, 12:551b (*illus.*)
Cavendish, John, 7:193b
Caviar, 5:68b
Çavuşin, Great Pigeon House, 3:92b
Caxico, Master, Carmona aqueduct and, 11:214a
Caxton, William, **3:210a–211b**, 3:661a-b, 662b, 8:325b–326a
apprenticeship of, 3:210a
codification of English spelling and, 8:309b–310a
early life of, 3:210a
English translations by, 8:326a
Henry Medwall's *Fulgens and Lucres* and, 8:262b
History of Reynard the Fox, 10:314b
influence of, 3:211a
Malory's *Morte Darthur* and, 3:211a, 8:60a-b, 61b–62b
as manuscript shipper, 3:210b
Merchant Adventurers Company and, 3:210a
move to England, 3:210b
on origins of printing, 10:126a-b
printing operations of, 3:210b
prologues of, 3:211a
published works of, 3:210b–211a
Reinaert II and, 2:142a
on Scandinavian loanwords, 6:440b
translations by, 3:210b
Golden Legend, 5:574a, 6:62b
Vitae patrum, 6:62b
Troy story, 12:221a
Wynkyn de Worde and, 12:712a
Cazola, Treaty of (1179), 3:130b
Cecaumenus. *See* Kekaumenos
Cecco Angiolieri, **3:211b–212a**
Dante Alighieri and, 3:211b
early life of, 3:211b
satire of, 3:212a
Sienese piety and, 11:281a
sonnets of, 3:211b–212a
vulgar language of, 3:211b–212a
Cecco d'Ascoli, 1:613a
Acerba, 6:632b
Čechy. *See* Bohemia
Cedrenus, Georgius. *See* Kedrenos, Georgios
Cefalù Cathedral, 10:486b, 11:274b
mosaics, 10:505a
Céle Dé, 3:228a
Čelebi Ḥusām al-Dīn Ḥasan
leadership of Mawlawīya, 10:556b
relationship with Rūmī, 10:556b
Celelles, Francis, *Llibre del consolat del mar,* 3:570b, 9:511a
Celery, growth of, 1:96a
Celestina, La, **3:212a–213b**, 11:423b–424a
composition of, 3:212a
Fernando de Rojas and, 3:212b–213a
innovations of, 3:213a-b
Juan de Flores as harbinger, 5:107b
literary elements in, 3:213a-b
popular lyrics in, 11:449a-b
popularity of, 3:212b
satire in, 3:212b–213a
second edition of, 3:213a
Celestine I, pope, **3:213b–214a**
consecration of St. Patrick, 9:464b
election of, 3:213b
Irish missions and, 6:514b, 9:463a, 464a
letter to bishops of Gaul, 3:214a
Nestorius and, 3:214a, 9:105b, 106a, 108a-b
Pelagianism and, 3:214a
Celestine III, pope
church of Scotland and, 11:107a
Innocent III and, 6:464a, 464b
Kulin and, 7:309a
opposition to reducing Rome's power, 5:482a-b
Wolfger von Erla and, 12:672b
Celestine V, pope, **3:214a-b**, 3:642a, 9:709a
early life of, 3:214a
election of, 6:214a
monastic life of, 3:214b
Poor Hermits of, 5:202a
resignation of, 2:323a-b, 3:214a-b, 4:160a, 483b
Ubi periculum and, 3:524a
Celestines, **3:214b–215a**
constitutions of, 3:215a
discipline of, 3:215a
foundation of, 3:214a, 214b
in France, 3:214b
prestige of, 3:214b
Celestius (follower of Pelagius), 9:486a-b
Celibacy, **3:215a–218a**
among Cathars, 3:185a
civil war in Milan and, 8:378a
in dualistic philosophies, 4:297b
in early monasticism, 8:460a
Islam and, 4:597a
Judaism and, 4:605b
marriage or, 4:609a
medieval attitudes about, 3:216a-b
Sufism and, 6:585b
see also Leo IX, pope
Celibacy, clerical, 9:522a-b
ambivalence of Anglo-Saxon clergy toward, 4:459a
in Armenian church, 1:504a, 504b
in Byzantine church, 3:215b, 446a
as criterion for ordination, 3:443b
in Danish church, 4:153a
eclipse of in Dark Ages, 3:216b–217a
Gregorian reform and, 3:217a-b
imperial laws reinforcing, 3:215b–216a
in Latin church, 3:215b–216a
laxity of in 14th and 15th centuries, 3:217b
in monasteries, 3:216b
motives for instituting, 3:215b
origins of, 3:215a-b
parish development and, 9:413b, 414b
penalties for not observing, 3:216a, 217a
Peter the Chanter on, 9:522a-b
reform in Brittany and, 10:429a
rulings by Lateran councils, 3:217a-b
see also Nicolaitism
Celje family. *See* Cilli family
Cellachán of Cashel, 4:493a
in *Caithréim Chellacháin Chaisil,* 6:539b
Cellarius, Christoph, *Historia medii aevi,* 8:309a
Cellier, Jacques, Rheims Cathedral, nave-floor labyrinth, 7:50b (*illus.*)
Celsus
Christian movement and, 3:334b–335a
De medicina, 8:247b
Celtes, Conrad. *See* Celtis, Konrad
Celtic art, **3:218a–225a**, 8:369b–371b
Anglo-Saxon influence on, 3:218a, 219b
artistic revolution in, 3:220a
calligraphic decorations, 8:370a
carpet pages, 3:219a, 8:370a–371a (*illus.*), 372 (*illus.*)
ceramics, 6:89b–90a
continuity in, 3:218a-b
definition of, 3:218a
Derrynaflan hoard, 3:220a, 221a
development
in 5th to 8th centuries, 3:218a
in 9th to 10th centuries, 3:221a
hanging bowls, 3:219 (*illus.*), 8:369b–370a
Hiberno-Saxon style of, 3:218a, 219b–220a
La Tene artistic tradition in, 3:219a, 8:369b–370a
Mediterranean influences on, 8:371b
metalwork
Dalriada, 3:224a
ecclesiastical, 3:218b
masterpieces of, 3:223a
secular, 3:218b
silver brooches, 3:221a
Tara brooch, 3:220b, 222 (*illus.*)

Pictish influence on, 3:223a-b
revival of in Ireland, 3:224b
Ringerike style of, 3:223a
Romanesque influence on, 3:218b, 223a
Scottish influence on, 3:223b–224a
Urnes style of, 3:223a
Viking impact on, 3:221a-b, 223a, 12:418b
in Wales, 3:224a-b
see also Lindisfarne Gospels
Celtic church, **3:225a–232b**
baptismal rites, 2:381a–382a
British church as model, 3:227a
British delegations to early councils, 3:225b
Brittany
abbey-bishopric, 2:381b
monastic influence, 2:381b
chant in, 5:661b
clergy in, 3:227b
Clonard, 3:465b–466a
confession in, 3:230b, 533a
decline of, 3:232a
definition of, 3:225a-b
development of, 3:225b–226b
discipline of
baptism, 3:229a
canonical legislation, 3:229a-b
Easter dating, 3:228a-b
penitentials, 3:229b–230a
private penance, 9:488b
tonsure, 3:228b–229a
druids and, 6:544b
education in, 3:231b–232a
end of Northumbrian dominance, 1:107b
geographic boundaries of, 3:225b
influence of Celtic social structure, 3:227a
intellectual life in, 3:231b–232a
liturgy of
calendar, 12:626a-b
consecration, 3:229a
definition of, 3:230a
Divine Office, 3:230a-b
Mass, 3:230a
sacraments, 3:230b–231a
in Stowe Missal, 8:183a
missions of, 3:226a-b, 12:151b–152a
monasticism in, 3:226a-b, 227b
organization of
bishop, 3:227b
Culdee movement, 3:228a
origins of, 3:225b
peculiarities of, 3:226b–227b
Pelagianism in, 3:226b
penitentials and, 9:489a-b
peregrinatio pro Christo and, 12:426a, 426b
reform in, 3:232a
in Roman Empire, 3:227a
royal confessors drawn from, 3:534b
sacramentaries, 10:606a-b
secularization of, 3:601b–602b
spiritual life in, 3:231a-b
structure of, 7:615a
tonsure, 2:381b, 12:626b
women's role in, 2:382a
see also Bangor (Wales); Bible, glosses and commentaries (Irish); Irish church; Liturgy, Celtic; Manuscript books, Celtic liturgical; Nechtan; Patrick, St.; Scotland, history; Welsh church
Celtic cross, 4:9a
Celtic languages, **3:232b–234a**, 6:436a-b, 11:489b
Breton dialect of, 3:234a
Brittonic, 2:381b
Cornish dialect of, 3:234a
Cumbric dialect of, 3:233b–234a
earliest cultures using, 3:232b
earliest evidence of, 3:233b
Gaulish, 2:381a-b
glossary of, *Sanas Cormaic,* 3:602a
grammar, in *Auraicept na nÉces,* 2:2a
inscriptions in, 6:434b
Insular group, 6:436a, 440a
descendants of, 3:232a
Latin loanwords in, 6:438b
Leabhar Breac, 7:614b
litanies in, 7:615a
Pictish associations, 9:641b–642a
Scots Gaelic, 6:436a
as separate dialect, 3:233a
translations, 12:140b–141a
vocabulary, in poetry, 6:534b
Welsh, 3:233b
see also Bard; Breton dialect; Hisperic Latin; Irish language
Celtic literature
Arthurian legend in, 1:565b–567b
see also Irish, Scottish, Welsh literature
Celtic music, **8:558a–559b**
Celtic mythology, **9:45b–49b**
concept of otherworld in, 9:47b
earliest information on, 9:45b–46a
god with boar (Gallo-Roman sculpture), 9:48a (*illus.*)
gods and goddesses in, 9:48b
hagiography and, 6:530b
lay aristocracy and, 8:27b
narrative tradition, motifs, 7:705b
quest for the Holy Grail and, 9:2a
sources on
Celtic writings (in Ireland and Wales), 9:46b–48b
inscriptions, 9:46a
swine god, 7:705b
voyage tales and, 6:550a-b
zoomorphic elements in, 9:48a-b
see also Cycles of the Gods (Irish sagas); Rhiannon
Celtis, Konrad, 6:314a, 9:202b, 729b–730a
Celts
Brython. *See* Aneirin
conversion of, 8:369a
on Danube, 2:133a
in Gaul, 10:465a
Hellenism and, 10:458a
land ownership, 11:674a
tenurial development, 11:685a-b
Rome, 10:464b–465a
settlement of Iceland, 12:426b
use of wheeled vehicles, 12:367b, 368a
see also Anglo-Saxons
Celure, 5:323a
Cely Letters, 8:323a
Cemeteries
consecration of, 3:540b–541b
looting. *See* Relics; Translation of saints
reconsecration of, 3:541a
rites at, 4:120b–121a
see also Catacombs; Death and burial
Cena e Passione. See Castellani, Castellano
Cena Trimalchionis. See Petronius, *Satyricon*
Cenci family, 10:525a
Cencius, cardinal, *Liber censuum romanae ecclesiae,* Peter's Pence listed in, 9:526b
Čeněk of Vartemberk, lord, 6:373b, 375b
Cenél Comgaill, 4:78a
Cenél Gabráin, 4:78a-b
Cenél Loairn, 4:78a, 78b
Cenn Faeladh, 6:526a-b, 540b
Cenne de la Chitarra, 6:649b
Cennétig mac Lorcáin, king of Dál Cais, 4:77a-b
Cenni de Francesco, frescoes of, 5:295b
Cennini, Cennino, **3:234a-b**, 12:692b
Agnolo Gaddi and, 3:234b
early life of, 3:234a
fresco buono and, 5:291b
Giotto di Bondone and, 3:234b
Libro dell' arte, 3:234b, 8:90b–91a
on panel painting, 9:360a-b
works of, 3:234a-b
Cennrigmonaid. *See* St. Andrews
Cenobitic monasticism. *See* Monasticism
Censorinus
Cassiodorus and, 8:638a
De die natali, 1:605a
Censorship, of German religious drama, 4:267b
Censuales, 11:204b
Census (monastic dues), 11:605b
Census sancti Petri. See Peter's Pence
Cent ballades, authorship, 9:637a
Cent nouvelles nouvelles, **3:235a-b**, 9:192b
exemplum and, 4:551b
fabliau and, 4:577a
l'esprit gaulois, 5:275b
Cent (unit of measure), 12:592b
Centering, **3:234b–235a**
"Cento." *See* Proba
Centonization, **3:235b–236a**
of Bible, 3:235b
in Byzantine music, 8:555a, 592b
of chant melodies, 3:235b
definition of, 3:235b
responsory, 10:336b
of Vergil's works, 3:235b
in Western music, 8:592b
Centuriation, villages and, 12:443b
Ceolfrid of Wearmouth, St., 3:229a, 9:91b
Bede and, 2:153b, 154a
Ceolwulf, king, Bede and, 2:155b
Cephalicus, 8:620 (*illus.*)
Cephalonia, Orsini and, 7:376a
Cephissus, Battle of (1311), 1:191a

Ceprano, Treaty of (1230), 5:215a, 11:270b
Ceramics
  Armenian, from Dwin, 12:98a
  in Bulgaria, 2:417a
  Byzantine, 6:608a
  Caucasian, 6:608a
  European, **3:236a–238a**
    archaeological evidence, 7:659a-b
    development of, 3:236a
    glazed bowls, 3:237b
    golosniki, 5:576a
    Islamic influence on, 3:236a
    lead glazing in, 3:236b–237a
    lusterware bowls, 3:238a
    maiolica arcaica, 3:237b
    mezza maiolica, 3:237b
    red-bodied ware, 3:237a-b
    salt-glazed stoneware, 3:238a
    sgraffito, 3:237 (*illus.*)
    in Valencia, 12:348b
    whiteware, 3:237a
    see also Majolica
  Islamic, **3:238a–240a**
    Anatolian, 6:613b
    Chinese models for, 3:238b
    Chinese porcelain in, 3:240a
    in Europe, 3:238b–239a
    frit body, 3:239b
    Gabri ware, 5:337a
    glass, 5:545a–548a
    glazed beaker (Iranian, 13th century), 6:0 (frontispiece)
    Golden Horn ware, 5:574a
    inscriptions, 10:636b
    Iranian, 6:603a
    in Italy, 3:239a
    Kashan as center of, 7:223b
    kashi, 7:223a–224a (*illus.*)
    lajvardina ware, 3:240a
    lusterware, 7:689b–690b
    manufacture of, 11:639a
    Minai ware, 3:240a, 8:396a
    origin of, 3:238a-b
    Persian *chārbāgh* design, 10:261b
    Persian influence on, 3:239b
    Raqqah lusterware, 10:259a
    reaction of ores and, 3:239b–240a
    of Seljuks, 11:147b
    of Seljuks of Rum, 11:149a
    slip-painted earthenware, 10:636a (*illus.*), 636b, 641a
    Spanish, 6:612a
    stylized designs, 10:636b
    Syrian, 6:607b–608a
    underglaze formula in, 3:239a-b
    see also Cuerda seca; Faience; Frit; Lajvard; Laqabi ware; Mamluk art; Pottery; *Minai* ware
Cerbottana. See Guns and gunpowder, blowgun
Cercamon, **3:240a-b**
  identity of, 3:240a-b
  lament for William X of Aquitaine, 3:240b
  preserved works of, 3:240a
Cerchi family of Florence (leader of Whites), 5:96a-b
Cerddorion. See Gogynfeirdd
Ceredigion, 4:329b
  Hywel and, 6:386b
  Rhodri Mwr and, 10:365b
Céret Bridge (over the Tech), 10:420b
Ceretic. *See* Coroticus
Certaldo (Boccaccio's retreat), 2:287b, 288b, 289a-b
Cesarini, Giuliano, 3:652b
  in crusade against Murad, 4:56a
Cesarius of Prüm, abbot, 10:274a
Cétamon. See "May Day"
Ceylon, importance in Indian Ocean navigation, 9:85a
Chace
  music. *See* Caccia; Trecento music
  virelai and, 12:458b
Chace au mesdisans, La. See Vidal, Remon
Chace dou cerf, La, 6:359b
Chacón, Gonzalo, *La Crónica de don Álvaro de Luna,* 11:421b, 433b
Chaghatai, appanage, 8:469a
Chaghatai (Turkic literary language), emergence of, 12:59a
Chaghatayids (Chaghatais)
  Tamerlane and, 11:588a
  Timurids and, 12:58a-b, 59a
Chaghrı, Seljuk leader, 11:156b
  origins of the Seljuks and, 11:151a, 151b
  succeeded by his son Alp Arslan, 11:152a
  Toghrıl-Beg and, 12:66b
Chaillou de Pesstain. *See Fauvel, Roman de*
Chained books, **3:240b**
  binding of books and, 8:97b
Chains, pilgrimage in, 12:156a
Chains (jewelry), 5:381a-b
Chair of the Koran. *See Kursī;* Rahle
Chairete, **3:240b–241a**
  definition of, 3:240b
  depictions of, 3:240 (*illus.*)
  the Resurrection cycle and, 10:340a
Chairs
  in Islamic furniture, 5:315a-b
  in Western European furniture, 5:322a (*illus.*), 323a-b
Chaitivel. See Marie de France
Chalcedon, metropolitan of, presence at the permanent synod, 9:505b
Chalcedon, Council of (451), 1:477b, 3:629a–630a, 7:542a, 8:477a-b, 10:453b, 455a, 11:44b
  Armenian church and, 1:498b–499a, 500a
  condemned by Nersēs II Aštarakacᶜi, 9:102b
  Constantinople's position clarified by, 3:555b
  on the Divine Word, 9:561a
  Eutychianism and, 4:524a
  on heresy, 3:336a, 6:188a
  Melchites and, 4:525a, 8:268a, 11:564a
  Monophysites and, 3:630a, 6:191a
  on the nature of Christ, 2:459b, 3:320a, 629a–630a, 6:190b
  Near Eastern cultures and, 10:463b
  Nestorianism and, 9:106a
  patriarch of Constantinople and, 2:10a
  recognition of Byzantine clergy, 3:446b
  on simony, 11:301a
  Syrian Orthodox Church and, 11:563b
  Theotokos and, 12:26a
  Timothy Aelurus' treatise against, 7:279b
  in *Yačaxapatum Čaṙkᶜ,* 1:509a
  see also Chalcedonianism
Chalcedonianism
  in Armenia, 1:475a, 477a, 477b, 478a, 482b, 483b, 499b
    Council of Širakawan (862) and, 1:500a
    literature of, 1:506a
  Copts' rejection of, 3:594a
  in Syria, 11:568a
Chalcidic Peninsula, acquired by Stefan Uroš IV Dušan, 11:475b
Chalcidius. *See* Calcidius
Chaldean language, translations, 12:138b
Chaldean Oracles
  Iamblichus and, 9:97b
  impact of Christianity on Neoplatonism and, 9:98b
  Porphyry of Tyre and, 9:97a
Chalder, **3:241a-b**, 10:238b
Chaldia, Trebizond Empire and, 12:168b–170a
Chalice, **3:241b–242a**
  depictions of in catacombs, 3:241b–242a
  illustrations of, 1:222b
  shapes of, 1:223a
  silver, with apostles, 3:241b (*illus.*)
  sizes of, 1:222b–223a
  symbol of, for Hussites, 3:505a-b
Chalice capital, 3:90b
Chalk, as cosmetic base, 2:147a
Chalkokondyles, Demetrios, 11:51a
Chalkokondyles, Laonikas, historical works, 2:517b, 6:247a
Challenge poetry. *See* Partimen
Chalon, Councils of
  (647-653), on private penance, 9:489b
  (813), condemnation of penitentials, 9:489b
Châlon-sur-Marne, MS 3.J.250, motet texts, 8:505b
Châlon-sur-Saône
  fairs, 4:585b, 590b
  inns in, 6:471a
    fairs and, 6:475b
Chalon-sur-Saône, Council of (813), women's orders and, 12:683b
Châlons. *See* Catalaunian Fields
Chamber, royal. *See* Camera, papal (finance); Household, royal
Chamber, royal (English financial office)
  Anglo-Saxon, 6:300b
  Edward II and, 6:303b
  Edward III and, 6:304a, 305b
  Exchequer and, 4:530b, 532b
  John and, 6:301b, 302a
  Norman, 6:301a
  Richard II and, 6:305b
Chamber serfdom, 7:87b
Chamberlain, **3:242a–243a**
  administrative duties of, 3:242a-b
  authority of, 3:242a

England, 3:242b
Anglo-Saxon, 6:300a
Exchequer and, 3:242b–243a
financial responsibilities, 3:242b, 4.464a
Norman, 6:301a
French, 3:242a-b
origin of title, 3:242a
seneschal and, 11:160a
Sicilian, 11:268b
Chambre du Cerf. *See* Avignon papacy, palace
Chambre des Comptes, 2:427b, 3:242b
butlers and, 2:434b
origin of, 5:182a
party associated with, 5:184a
Philip IV's reforms of, 9:554b
tax collection, 11:624b
under Philip IV, 5:182b
Chambre des Élus. *See* Burgundy, duchy of
Chambrée (unit of measure), 12:590a
Chamēlē, 8:617b
Chamfrain (chamfron), 1:529a, 534b (*illus.*)
Chamorro (head of Toledo's Jewish community), 9:111b
Champagne, **3:243a–250b**, 4:591 (map)
administrative districts of, 3:245b
Black Death and, 3:250a
boundaries of, 3:243a, 244 (map)
Charles IV of France and, 3:249b–250a
consolidation of by Hugh, 3:244a–245a
count of Bar-sur-Seine and, 9:149a
counts of Meaux-Troyes in, 3:243b–244a
counts of, 3:245a–250a
economic development of, 3:245a-b
English campaigns against, 3:250a
fairs. *See* Fairs, of Champagne
feudal organization of, 3:245b
castellanies in, 3:245b, 248 (map)
fiefs in (late 12th century), 3:246 (map), 249b
serfdom, 11:207a
formation of county, 5:161b
Frankish invasion of, 3:243a-b
history (to 1152), 3:243a–245a
history (1152–1284), 3:245a–250a
history (after 1285), 3:250a
Hundred Years War and, 3:250a
Joinville's administration of, 7:143b
Latin church in, 3:245b–246a
legal system, 7:457b, 458b, 459b
loss of independence, 3:249b
nobles' revolt in, 3:250a
Nogaret and, 9:153a
office of seneschal and, 11:160a-b
political authority in, 3:243b
under duchy of Burgundy, 3:243b
under Roman rule, 3:243a
urban franchises in, 3:248b–249a
see also French law, in north
Champain, Cicely, rape of, 3:286b
Champart, Robert. *See* Robert of Jumièges
Champion des dames. See Martin le Franc
Champion of England, 3:251a
Champion in judicial combat, **3:250b–251b**
civil cases, 3:250b–251a
criminal cases, 3:250b–251a
definition of, 3:250b
examples of, 3:251a
in *Fled Bricrenn,* 6:527a
see also Combat, trial by; Ordeal
"Champion's portion," in Irish saga, 6:549a
Champlevé enamel. *See* Enamel, champlevé
Chancel, **3:251b**
furniture, 5:316b–317a
transept and, 12:125b
see also Bema; Nave
Chancel screen. *See* Screen, chancel; Transenna
Chancellor
cestui que use and, 7:454b
equity of, and common law, 7:455a
petitions of grievance and, 7:454b–455a
see also Chancery
Chancellor of the Exchequer, 4:532b
Chancery, **3:251b–254b**
cancellarius, 3:251b–252a
Carolingian, 3:252b
clerks of, in diplomacy, 4:210a
definition of, 3:251b
development of, 3:252a
documents
division of labor in preparing, 3:253a
language of, 3:253a
script styles in, 3:253b
subdivisions of, 3:253a
England, 6:301a
enrollments under Henry II, 4:469b
equity law and, 4:502a-b
Exchequer and, 4:534a
Provisions of Oxford (1258) and, 10:194b–195a
royal wardrobe and, 6:302b, 303a
expansion of, 3:253a
France, registration of outgoing charters, 5:163a
functions of, royal charters, 5:160a
Hungary, 6:341a, 347a
imperial, Middle High German in, 6:441a-b
inns of. *See* Inns of Court
Islamic, 6:589b, 592a
under Abbasids, 6:590a
languages used by, 6:438b, 440b
officials involved in, 3:253b–254a
papal, 4:66a
cursus and, 4:67a-b
development of, 7:543a-b
indulgences and, 6:450a
Lateran and, 10:522b
under John of Gaeta, 3:253b
see also Datary, apostolic
registers, 3:252b–253a
as archives, 1:448a, 448b
Roman model for, 3:252a-b
seal of, 3:254a
study of, 3:252a, 254a
see also Seals and sigillography, Western European
Chancery Slavic. *See* Slavic, Chancery
Chandelier
candles in, 5:318b
in churches, 5:318b
Chandlery, royal, 6:304b
Chandos, John, "Life of the Black Prince," 6:334b
Chanson, **3:254b**
canzone and, 6:668a
combinative, 10:241a
definition of, 3:254b
Landini's ballate and, 7:326b–327a
polyphonic, Philippe de Vitry and, 12:482a
types of, 3:254b
Chanson d'Antioche, **3:254b–255a,** 3:331a
author of, 3:254b–255a
as example of crusade cycle poem, 5:240b
Picard origins, 9:634a
revision of, 3:255a
Chanson d'Aspremont, 10:391b
Chanson de Basin, 7:216b
Chanson à carole, 3:116a
Chanson de la croisade contre les Albigeois, **3:255a-b,** 10:181a, 182b–183b
cobla capcaudada form in, 10:183a
cobla capfinida form in, 10:183a
content of, 10:182b
precursors of, 10:181a
Chanson de Guillaume
artistic merit of, 3:261b
description of, 3:258b–259a
Chanson de Jérusalem, 3:331a
Chanson d'Otinel, 10:391b
Chanson de Roland. See Roland, Song of
Chanson de sainte Foy d'Agen, 10:161a–162b
compared with *Boecis,* 10:156b–157a
Occitanian sense of time and place in, 10:162a
paganism portrayed in, 10:161b, 162a
reasons for survival of, 10:161b–162a
Chansonnier, **3:255b–257a**
monophonic, 3:255b–256a
motet texts, 8:506a
performance of, 3:255b–256b
polyphonic, 3:256a-b
preserved, 3:256b
troubadour lyric songs in, 12:214b–215a
writing of, 3:256a-b
Chansonnier d'Arras, preservation of, 9:636b
Chansons d'amour, 3:254b
Chansons de femme, 3:254b, **3:257a,** 11:259b
Chansons de geste, 3:254b, **3:257a–262b**
Anglo-Norman literature and, 1:266a–268a
artistic merits of, 3:260b–261b
in *Aucassin et Nicolette,* 1:642b–643a
binary oppositions, 5:242b
cantilène and, 3:87b
categories of, 5:240a–241a
classification by Bertrand de Bar-sur-Aube, 2:201b
crusade cycle, 5:240a

Chansons de geste (*cont.*)
chronicles and, 3:330b
clerkliness, 5:241a
dating of, 6:71b
definition of, 3:257a-b
Elis saga ok Rosamundu and, 4:432a
epics and, 3:257a-b
in 14th century, 5:258b
geste du roi, 5:240a
history and, 3:259b–260a, 5:242b
ideals and values in, 5:241b
gesta Dei per francos, 5:241b
in Italy, 6:637b, 638a, 638b–639a
Karlamagnús saga and, 7:216b
Karlmeinet and, 7:219b
laisse and, 7:319a
manuscripts of, 3:257b–258a
Matter of France and, 8:224b–225b
narrative form
conventions used, 5:242b
cycles in, 3:259a-b
generic dynamism, 5:240a, 241a
mixed tonality, 5:241a-b
monotony in, 3:261b
on Ogier de Danemarche, 6:275a
origins of, 3:259b, 5:236b–237a
Bédierist vs. romantic views, 5:236b–238a
crusader legends, 5:237a-b
performance of, 3:259b–260a, 7:116b–117a
poetic form, 5:242b
laisse in, 3:261a-b
lyric characteristics of, 3:257b
political elements
exaltation of Charlemagne, 5:244a
propaganda purposes, 5:241b–242a
popularity of, 3:258a
rebellious barons, 5:240a
role of women in, 5:242b–243a
Romanesque sculpture and, 10:490b
saint's lives and, 6:59b, 60a
Saracens in, 5:242b
settings, 5:242b
sources for, oral tradition, 5:237a
Spanish ballads and, 11:427b–428a
supernatural and preternatural in, 5:242b
techniques of, assonance in, 3:261a-b
temporal confusion, 5:238a
political uses of, 5:242a
themes of, 3:257b
titles of, 3:257a–259a
translations of into Norwegian, 10:390a–391b
transmission of, 3:259b–260b
variations in
in foreign vernaculars, 5:243a
graftings and spin-offs, 5:240b
in other genres, 5:243a
with performance, 5:240b
stock formulas, 5:240b, 242b
see also Provençal literature
Chansons de malmariée, **3:262b–263a**, 11:259b
troubadours, 12:218a
trouvères, 12:219b
Chansons de Namur. See Jean Lemaire de Belges
Chansons de toile, **3:263a**
Chant
Byzantine, Slavic music and, 8:572b, 574a
classification of. *See* Mode
farcing, 5:13b–14a
Frankish-Roman, 8:557a
Latin
Byzantine music and, 8:553b, 554b, 556a, 557a
during Carolingian Renaissance, 8:638b
music of the spheres and, 8:586a
musical treatises on, in 13th century, 8:644a-b
performance, 8:592a-b
as popular music, 8:571b
as symbol, 8:579b, 581b
melismatic, 5:663b
neumatic, 5:663b
noeannoe in, 9:152b
paraliturgical, 5:663a
rhyme and, 7:372a
in rhymed offices, 10:366b–377a
musical notation for, 10:376 (*illus.*)
rhythmic indications in, 5:663b
Slavic. *See Znamenny*
Solesmes method of performance of, 5:663b–664a
study of, 2:154b
syllabic, 5:663b
see also Ambrosian Chant; Communion chant; Gregorian Chant; Hymns; Music; Plainsong
Chant books, 3:80b–81a
Carmelite, 3:96a
Chant royal, **3:263b**
envoi and, 4:492a
see also Rhétoriqueurs
Chantecler the cock. *See* Renard the Fox
Chanteloup, bishop of Worcester, on maying, 4:183b
Chanterene, Nicholas, 5:630b
Chantry chapel. *See* Chapel
Chapaize, church of, 10:479a
Chapel, **3:263b–264a**
built on or next to bridges, 10:414a
Carolingian, 3:263b–264a
cathedral, 3:192a-b
chantry, 3:264a
chaplain in, 3:264a
chasovnya, 3:277a
chevet, 3:300b
definition of, 3:263b
development of, 1:444b–445a (*illus.*)
royal, 3:264a
specialized types of, 3:264a
see also Screen
Chapel railing. *See* Transenna
Chapel des trois fleurs de lis. See Vitry, Philippe de
Chapel-de-fer, 1:526a, 527b (*illus.*), 530a, 531a, 532a
Chaperon, 3:623b
Chaplain, **3:264a–265a**
capellani in Carolingian Empire, 3:107b–108a
definition of, 3:264a
functions of, 3:264a-b
Chappes, fair at, 4:590b
Chapter, ecclesiastical, **3:265a–266a**
Benedictines, 3:265a
of Brethren of the Common Life, 2:367b
cathedral, 3:191a–192a, 265b–266a
chapter house, 3:266a–267b
as corporation, 3:266a
definition of, 3:265a
organization of Latin church and, 3:375a-b
powers of, 3:265b
purpose of, 3:265a-b
royal authority in France and, 3:537a
Chapter on the Elements by Aristotle. See Israeli, Isaac
Chapter house, **3:266a–267a**
architecture of, 3:266b–267a
uses, 3:266b
Char (wagon), 12:374b, 375a
decoration of, 12:376b
Chārbāgh. See Ceramics, Islamic; Gardens, Islamic
Charcoal, **3:267a-b**
methods of making, 3:267a-b
purposes of, 3:267a-b
wood used for, 3:267b
see also Steelmaking
Charcoal burners, 3:267a-b
Chardri, **3:267b–268a**
Petit Plet, 1:264b
Vie de Seint Josaphaz, 1:260b, 261b
Vie des Set Dormanz, 1:261b, 11:213a
works of, 3:267b
Charge (unit of measure), 12:594a
Charibert, Frankish king, excommunication of, 5:472b
Chariot, 12:367a, 367b–368a
depicted in Aelfric's paraphrase of the Hexateuch, 12:372b–373a
late medieval, 12:373b, 374b–375a
suspended, 12:376b, 377a-b
Chariot branlant. See Chariot, suspended
Charistikion, **3:268a**
Charitable bequests, 6:458a, 458b
under canon law, 3:607a
Charité-sur-Loire, La, church of, 10:479a
Charity. *See* Almsgiving; Charitable bequests
Charity, Islamic. *See* Alms tax, Islamic
Charivari. See Shivaree
Charlemagne, Holy Roman Emperor, **3:268a–269a**, 9:500b
accounting system of, 8:428a-b
administration of empire, 3:107a–108b
ancestry of, 1:149a
at Aachen, 1:1a-b
Byzantines and, 2:488b
calendar of, 3:21b
capitularies of, 3:91b, 10:76b
in Carolingian legends, 8:224b–225a
cavalry of, 3:202a-b
coinage of, 8:428a
coronation as emperor, 3:110a–111a, 268b, 346b, 5:494b–495a, 7:256a, 10:522a
court of, 3:268b
Court School of, 10:97a–99a, 101b
creation of the Spanish March, 9:62b
death of, omens concerning, 10:410b
deathbed fears of Vikings, 12:429b

decline of, 3:268b–269a
Denis and, 9:690b
economic and social policies
  market legislation, 8:144a
  promotion of domestic dyeing industry, 4:328a
educational reforms, 3:268b, 433a, 5:649a
embassy to Constantinople in 813, 1:228a
Epistola generalis, recommendation to use Paul the Deacon's homiliary, 9:467b
foreign talent and
  artists and architects, 12:152b–153a
  scholars, 12:151b–152a
gift from Hārūn al-Rashīd, 12:110a
hearings on adoptionism, 1:57b
hunting and, 6:356a-b
Iconoclastic Controversy, 3:346b
  Libri carolini, 6:399b
on icons, 6:399b
idea of empire, 5:494b–495a
idealization of, 3:269a
ivories commissioned by his court, 7:25 (*illus.*)
joint kingship with Carloman, 3:268a-b
Jordan of Osnabrück and, 7:149a
on king's duties, 10:18a
languages spoken, 6:442a
Lateran and, 7:345a
Latin church and
  advisers, 4:458b
  alliance with papacy, 3:346a-b
  canon law and, 3:348b–349a, 7:403b
  church organization, 4:373a
  church reform, 3:108b–110a, 347b, 676a, 676b–677a, 6:293a
  on convent morality, 5:433a
  Filioque doctrine, 5:62b
  Libri Carolini, 2:465b
  Purification of Mary established, 10:117a
  relations with papacy, 9:374a-b, 383a
  on the rite of baptism, 2:84a
  role in church affairs, 3:11b
Laudes regiae and, 7:385a
legendary fathering of Roland, 12:413b
Leo III of Germany and, 5:494b
life by Einhard, 4:412a, 412b–413a
in literature
  Benedetto di S. Andrea's *Cronaca,* 6:638a
  Dante, 4:102a
  Dutch romances about, 4:318b
  epics about, 3:250a–259b
  German works, 6:439b, 441a
  Gesta Caroli metrica (Poeta Saxo), 9:712a-b
  Gesta Caroli (Notker Balbulus), 9:187a
  Italian works, 6:637b
  Mágus saga jarls, 8:45a
  Pèlerinage de Charlemagne, 4:576b
  Rolandslied, 10:447b, 448a
  Song of Roland, 10:445a, 446a
  Þiðreks saga, 6:311a
  see also Karlamagnus saga; Karlmeinet; Matter of France
literature at court of, 3:100a, 433a, 5:221b, 233a
  Ovidian influence, 9:313a
manuscript illumination and, 8:106a-b
military campaigns, 3:106b–107a, 268b, 4:15b
  Catalonia, 3:174a
  conquest of Saxony, 10:683a
  defeat of the Avars, 4:1b–2a
  expedition to Spain (778), 9:68a
  siege of Pavia, 8:377a
missi dominici of, 3:268b, 8:438a
missions to Hārūn al-Rashīd, 4:200b–201a
monastic schools under, 11:75b–76a
monetary reforms of, 5:679a, 9:494b
moral purpose of government and, 7:260a
MS of *Regula sancti Benedicti,* 2:170b
organization of Saxons by, 5:506b
Paul the Deacon and, 4:543a, 9:467a, 467b, 468a
Paulinus of Aquileia and, 9:470a-b
payment of tithes and, 12:62b
perfume and, 2:147a
planctus lament for, 9:693a
Rhine-Danube canal, 12:576b
Rome and, 10:521b–522a
in St. Angilbert's poems, 1:254a
serfdom and, 11:202b
shoes and, 11:254b
slavery and, 11:200a, 200b–201a
successors of, 3:111a–114a, 268b
in Theganus' life of Louis I the Pious, 12:8a
Theodulf of Orléans and, 12:20a
title of patrician and, 9:460a
towns and, 12:313b
translation of empire and, 12:143a-b
travels of, 12:153b
vs. Lombards, 6:435a, 443a
vs. Tassilo III, 2:4b, 134a
vs. Vascones, 2:126a
Vulgate and, 2:211b
water clock of, 3:28a
see also Aachen, palace chapel; Leo III, pope
Charles II (the Bald), Holy Roman Emperor, 9:500a, 10:245b
  Alamannia and, 11:526b
  Bible of, 2:211b
  Burgundy and, 2:424a, 428b
  capitulary and, 3:91b
  Codex Aureus and, 8:106b
  Court School of, 7:25b, 10:99a-b, 100a, 101a, 110b–111a
  Hucbald's poem on baldness of, 6:317a
  inheritance of Spanish Marches, 3:114a
  irrigation projects authorized, 6:558b
  manuscripts owned by, 6:462b
  Milo of St. Amand and, 8:395b
  music treatises and, 8:639a
  Robert the Strong and, 3:89b
  Strasbourg oaths and, 11:488a
  throne of St. Peter, 7:25b
  Toulouse and, 12:90b
  treatise by Ratramnus of Corbie, 9:446b
  use of bridges against Vikings, 10:411b
  Usuard's martyrology and, 12:335a
  Viking raids and, 12:430a, 431a
Charles III (the Fat), Holy Roman Emperor
  Alamannia and, 11:526b
  Burgundy and, 2:428b
  deposed (887), 3:115a
  Liutward and, 9:187b
  Notker Balbulus and, 9:187a, 188a
  Paris under, 9:401b
  rebellion against, 5:474a
  rule of, 3:114a, 115a
  succeeded by Arnulf, 1:541b
Charles IV of Bohemia, king. *See* Charles IV of Germany, emperor
Charles II (the Bald) of France, king. *See* Charles II (the Bald), Holy Roman Emperor
Charles III (the Simple) of France, king
  Herbert II of Vermandois and, 12:395b–396a
  Normans and, 9:159b–160a, 163b
  political program of, 3:115a
  prerogative and, 10:89b
  Viking settlement of Normandy and, 12:431b
Charles IV of France, king
  Champagne as wife's dower, 3:249b–250a
  conflicts with Edward II of England, 5:182b–183a
  conquest of Guienne, 5:183a
  death of, 6:331b
  financial policies, 5:172b–173a
  Philippe de Vitry and, 12:481a
  taxation, war subsidies, 11:621b
  travels and frequent relocation of, 12:159a
Charles V (the Wise) of France, king, **3:269a–270b**, 12:352b
  Beauneveu and, 2:145a
  biography by Christine de Pizan, 3:317a
  Carmelite Water and, 2:147a
  Dauphiné and, 4:109a
  entertainment of Emperor Charles IV, 5:34b–35a
  Étienne Marcel and, 10:319a
  financial policies, 3:269b–270a, 5:186b
  in *Grandes chroniques de France,* 5:654a
  Great Schism and, 3:269b, 270a
  Guillaume de Machaut and, 8:3a
  in Hundred Years War, 3:270a, 6:332a
  hunting and, 6:358a, 360b
  inherited advantages, 5:186a
  Jacquerie and, 7:35b–36b, 9:478a
  Jean de Liège and, 7:52b
  Languedoc and, 7:341b
  legacy of, 3:270a-b
  library of, 5:629a, 7:567a, 601b
  nobility and, 3:269b–270a
  opposition to, 5:186b
  Paris under, 5:185b, 9:406a

Charles V (the Wise) of France, king (*cont.*)
patronage of learning, translations under, 12:137b
Philippe de Vitry and, 12:481a
portable clock of, 3:462a
portrait of, 5:625b
preparation of *Somnium Viridarii* and, 11:371a
problems facing, 3:269b
relations with Estates, 10:318b–319b, 320b, 324a–325a, 326b–327a
revival of monumental art under, 5:625b
taxation policy, 11:623b
Charles VI of France, king, 12:352b
Cabochien riots and, 3:3b–4a
Enguerrand VII of Coucy and, 4:491a
excommunication of, Nicholas of Clamanges and, 9:122b
in *Grandes chroniques de France,* 5:654a
influence of Marmousets on, 5:187a, 8:148a
insanity of, 5:187a, 6:492a, 9:406a
marriage festivities of, 4:287b
minstrels at court of, 8:416a
Paris under, 9:406a-b
privileges of University of Paris abolished by, 9:409b
relations with Estates, 10:319b–321a, 324a–325a
weakness of rule, 9:406a-b
Charles VII of France, king, **3:270b–272a**
abilities, 3:271a, 271b
Alain Chartier and, 3:275a
Armagnac party and, 3:270b
Burgundian party and, 3:270b–271a
conciliarism of, 3:367a
Council of Ferrara-Florence, 3:653b
coronation of, 7:258b
Estates and, 10:321b–322b, 324a-b, 326b, 327a
fairs and, 4:585b
gilt clock of, 3:462b
in *Grandes chroniques de France,* 5:654a
Hundred Years War, heavy guns, 12:567a
Jacques Coeur and, 7:37a
Joan of Arc and, 3:271a, 7:114b–115a, 12:352b
Languedoc and, 7:341b
legacy of, 3:271b
military expeditions, 5:188–189a
military reforms of, 3:206a-b, 271b
creation of standing army, 12:565a
nobility and, 3:271a-b
Paris under, 9:406b
political struggles of, 3:271a-b
Pragmatic Sanction of Bourges of, 10:69a
relations with
Burgundy, 5:188b
England, 5:188b–189a, 6:332a
tax system of, 3:271b, 11:623b–624a
taille, 11:579a
University of Paris and, 9:409b
Vermandois and, 12:396a
vs. Henry VI, 3:65a
Charles VIII of France, king, 9:682b
complainte by Greban, 3:508a
Gian Galeazzo Sforza and, 11:216b
Italian campaign, 12:566b
Jem Sultan and, 2:137a
Lyons and, 7:700a
military expeditions, against Florence, 5:103a
representative assemblies and, 10:323a-b
Rhétoriqueurs and, 10:364b
University of Paris under, 9:410a
Charles II/III of Germany. *See* Charles II/III, Holy Roman Emperor
Charles IV of Germany, emperor, 2:8a, 10:88b–89a
archbishopric established in Prague, 2:304a
Bavaria and, 2:135b
Bohemian nobility and, 2:301a-b
church reform and, 6:365b–366a
coronation of, 9:530a
elections of kings and, 5:488b–489a
entertainment by Charles V of France, 5:34b–35a
"golden age" of Bohemia and, 11:344a
Golden Bull of, 3:334a-b, 4:428b, 5:499a
Master Theodoric and, 12:17a
Nuremberg and, 9:202a
Prague under, 10:70a-b
Prague University and, 6:365a
rebuilding of Prague bridge, 10:418a
reign of, 5:488b
Siena and, 11:280a
Sigismund and, 11:287a
visit to France in 1378, 12:378b
vs. Zurich, 11:544a
Charles V of Germany, emperor, 5:496a-b, 6:43a
Christian II of Sweden and, 11:533b
Francesco II Sforza and, 11:217a
grant of Malta to the Knights Hospitalers, 8:67b
imperial knights and, 5:498a-b
regulation of trade and, 10:331b
Siena and, 11:282a
Charles I (Charles Robert) of Anjou, king of Hungary (*d.* 1342), 9:724a
Battle of Posada, 12:500b
coronation of, 6:344a, 11:483a
and Stjepan Kotromaniç of Bosnia, 11:485b–486a
Visegrád congress and, 6:345a
Walachia and, 10:514b
Charles II of Anjou, king of Naples (*d.* 1309), 7:379a
Sicily and, 11:273a
Charles III of Anjou-Durazzo, king of Naples and (as Charles II) Hungary (*d.* 1386), 6:346a, 7:381a, 11:273a
Provence and, 10:187b
Charles II (the Bad) of Navarre, king, 9:71a-b
death of, 12:649a
Enguerrand VII and, 4:490b
Jacquerie and, 7:36b, 9:478a-b
John II and, 5:184b
Machaut and, 8:3a
Normandy and, 9:169b
Paris under, 9:406a
Charles III (the Noble) of Navarre, king, 9:71b
courtly lyrics and, 11:451a
Charles I of Savoy, duke, 12:185a
Charles I of Anjou, king of Sicily (*d.* 1285), 1:253b
accession of, 6:335b
alliance against Michael VIII Palaiologos, 2:499b
Arnolfo di Cambio and, 1:541a
at Tagliacozzo, 11:279b
Burgundy and, 2:429b
capture of Dyrrachium, 4:330a
Celestines and, 3:214b
coalition against Byzantium, 11:175b
death of, 11:273a
Epiros and, 4:499b
financed by Italian merchant bankers, 2:77b
invasion of Italy (1265–1266), 9:385b
library of, 1:437a
Louis IX's crusades and, 4:54a
Michael VIII Palaiologos and, 8:302b
papal politics and, 4:60b–61a, 95b–96a
peace with Hafsids, 6:53b
as podesta of Florence, 5:95b
projected restoration of Latin Empire, 3:641b
Provence under, 10:187b–188a
reign of, 11:272a–273a
as Roman senator, 10:524a
salt tax, 10:631a
Sicilian Vespers and, 11:261a
Tuscan merchants and, 11:275b
William II and, 7:379a
Charles VIII of Sweden, king, reign of, 11:533b
Charles of Anjou, Valois, and Maine, count, triumph of Blacks in Florence, 5:96b
Charles (the Bold) of Burgundy, duke
assassination of, 5:490a
Battle of Nancy, 12:566a
Claeys Spierinc and, 11:463a
Comines and, 3:333b, 487a
court of, 7:634a
Lathem and, 7:345b
military campaigns of, 7:676b
representative assemblies and, 10:325b
revolt of Ghent against, 5:523b
Rhétoriqueurs and, 10:364b
Sigismund of Habsburg and, 11:544b–545a
standing army, 12:565b
Vermandois and, 12:396a
War of the Public Weal, 5:189a
see also Baldwin I of Flanders
Charles of Calabria, duke, elected lord of Florence, 5:97a
Charles College (University of Prague). *See* Prague, University of
Charles of Durazzo. *See* Charles III of Anjou, king of Naples and Hungary (*d.* 1386)
Charles (the Good) of Flanders, count, 5:79a-b

assassination of, 3:497a, 12:731a, 731b
Erembalds and, 9:149a
Charles du Fresne, sieur du Cange, *Lexicon,* 8:309a
Charles Martel, **3:272a-b**, 6:572b, 9:500a, 500b, 669b
at Battle of Poitiers (732), 9:715b, 12:557a
at Battle of Tours, 3:345b
Austrasian nobility and, 9:148a
cavalry of, 3:201a-b
church missionaries and, 3:272a-b
church reforms, 3:108b
consolidation of Carolingian Empire, 3:106a
death of, 5:506a
defeat of Muslims, 272a
in *Girart de Rosselhon,* 10:180a
military reorganization, 12:558a
nickname of, 3:272a
office of the mayor of the palace and, 8:236a
patricius and, 10:522a
successors of, 3:106a, 272b
vs. Alamanni, 11:526b, 537b
Charles of Normandy, duke. *See* Charles V of France, king
Charles of Orléans, **3:272b–273b**
early life of, 3:272a
François Villon and, 12:450a
in French civil wars, 3:272b–273a
imprisonment of, 3:273a
Joan of Arc and, 3:273a
literary patronage, 5:265a
poetry of, 3:263b, 273a, 5:265b
Charles the Rash. *See* Charles (the Bold) of Burgundy, duke
Charles Robert of the Sicilian Angevins. *See* Charles I (Charles Robert) of Anjou, king of Hungary
Charles (son of Pepin III), defeat of Lombards, 7:657a
Charles le Téméraire. *See* Charles (the Bold) of Burgundy, duke
Charles of Valois, count, the Ponts-de-Lé and, 10:417a
Charles of Valois (son of Philip III)
Aragon and, 4:61a
Florence and, 4:98b, 99a
Charles of Viana
death of, 3:171b
in Navarrese succession struggle, 9:72a
Charlier, Jean. *See* Gerson, John
Charlieu, church of, 10:479a
Charlotte (wife of Louis of Savoy), 4:71a
Charms
Old English, 1:281a, 286a
"For a Swarm of Bees," 6:284a
Old High German, **3:273b–274b**
characteristics of, 3:273b–274a
examples of, 3:274a
Second Merseburg Charm, 5:301a
Charolais, count of, 4:208a
Charonton, Enguerrand, **3:274b**
Coronation of the Virgin, 5:609a
Pietà, 5:608b
Charrette (vehicle), 12:373b
Charroi de Nîmes, 3:258b–259a
Charroux, Council of (989), Peace of God movement and, 9:473b
Charruée, 11:676b
Charta caritatis, See Harding, Stephen, St.
Charte aux Normands, 9:169a
Charter, **3:274b–275a**
cartulary, 3:120a-b
definition of, 3:274b
ducal, *vicinia* and, 12:438b
parts of, 3:275a
production of, 3:274b–275a
villages and, 12:440a
see also Handfæstning; Seals and sigillography, Western European; Statute
Charter of the Forest, 9:424b
Charter of freedom. *See* Franchises
Chartier, Alain, **3:275a–276a**
audience of, 5:273b
Belle dame sans merci, 5:273a-b
responses to, 9:637a
Charles VII of France and, 3:275a
courtly love and, 3:275b
ecclesiastical benefices of, 3:275a
"Excusacion aux dames," 5:273b
lai and, 7:317a
Latin works of, 3:275b
life of, 3:275a, 5:272b–273a
Livre des quatre dames, 5:273a
poetry of, 3:275b
precursor to Renaissance humanism, 5:273a
prose works of, 3:275b
Quadrilogue invectif, foolishness of war and chivalry, 5:273a
Chartophylax (legal adviser to Byzantine patriarch), 12:14b
Chartoularios, themes and, 12:10a
Chartres Cathedral, 3:192b, **3:276a–277a**
additions to, 5:620b–621a
aerial view of, 3:276b (*illus.*)
ambulatory and choir screen, 3:0 (frontispiece)
building of, 3:276a
capitals, 3:91a
of main nave arcade, 5:590a (*illus.*), 598b
central door of, 5:593a (*illus.*), 599a
clerestory wall, 5:584b (*illus.*), 599b
design of, 5:590b, 7:50b
Gothic architecture of, 3:276a-b
ground plan of, 5:583 (*illus.*)
jubé, 1:442b, 443b (*illus.*), 444a
nave of, 5:583 (*illus.*), 584b (*illus.*), 586b (*illus.*)
quadripartite vaults in, 12:366a
school of, 11:64b
sculptures, 3:276b, 10:498a–499b (*illus.*)
Annunciation image on north portal, 1:308a
column figures, 3:487b (*illus.*)
Elders, 5:618a-b
Last Judgment, 5:620a-b
Nativity of Christ, 5:618b
Presentation in the Temple, 5:618b
Virtues and Vices in, 12:462b
Sébastien Roulliard on, 1:428a
shafts in, 5:596a-b
stained glass in, 5:549a, 551a, 552a–553a
sundial on the south tower, 11:509b (*illus.*)
transepts, 5:260a-b, 623a
western portal of, 5:616b (*illus.*), 617b–618a
windows, 10:504b
Chartres notation. *See* Musical notation, Chartres
Chartres, school of, 9:701b–702a
classical literary studies at, 3:433b–434a
composition of rhymed offices and, 10:372a
music and, 8:581b
Neoplatonism and, 1:183a, 9:200b
study of medicine at, 8:255a-b
influenced by Salerno, 8:256b
see also Ivo of Chartres, St.
Chartreuse de Champmol. *See* Dijon, Chartreuse de Champol
Chartreuse (Grande Chartreuse)
destruction of (1132), 3:119a
prior of, 3:118b
Chartreux, use of. *See* Carthusian rite
Chartularioi (*chartularius*), 11:573b, 603b
Chasovnya, **3:277a**
"Chasse, La." *See* Brézé, Jacques de
Chasteau d'amour. See Grosseteste, Robert
Chastelaine de Vergi, La, **3:277a-b**
plot summary, 5:258b
Chastellain, Georges, 10:364b, 365a
Chronique des ducs de Bourgogne, 3:333a, 9:638a
didactic works, 9:639b
lyric poetry, political purposes, 9:637a
Chastiemusart, Proverbia quae dicuntur super natura feminarum and, 6:630a
Chastity
devices for testing, 6:135b
in literature, 7:317b, 318a-b
tests of, in *Möttuls saga,* 8:507a
vows of, 4:611b
see also Celibacy
Chastoiement des dames. See Robert of Blois
Chasuble
in a fresco in S. Clemente in Rome, 12:400a–401b (*illus.*)
in Landulf Pontifical, 12:402 (*illus.*)
see also Vestments
Château Gailliard, 10:416a
Château de Pierrefonds, 3:148a, 151b (*illus.*)
Château-neuf-le-Rouge, inns in, 6:468b
Châtelain, échevins and, 4:379a
Châtelain de Coucy, **3:277b–278a**
Guy de Thourotte in, 9:635a
Châtelet, **3:278a–279b**
attacked by the Pastoureaux, 9:454a
courts, 3:279a-b
provost of Paris and, 10:197a-b
inquest in, 6:479b, 480a
jurisdiction of the prévots in, 3:278b–279b

Châtillon
fines for using wrong weights, 12:118b
wine trade, 12:650b
Chaucer, Geoffrey, **3:279b–297b**, 3:572b, 8:321a–322a
Alan of Lille and, 7:366a
alchemy and, 4:580a
algorismus, 10:474a
alliterative verse and, 8:331a
Anelida and Arcite, prosody of, 8:346b
antifeminism and, 1:325a
astronomical interests, 3:290b
birthdate of, 3:279b–280a
Boccaccio and, 2:279a, 280b, 286b, 3:283a, 7:369b
translations of, 2:287a, 3:287b–289a
Boethius translations, 3:283b–284a
Book of the Duchess, 3:281b–282b, 8:321a, 321b
compared with *Pearl,* 8:320a-b
use of octosyllabic couplet in, 8:344b
Canterbury Tales, 8:321b–322a
Canon's Yeoman's Tale, 3:294b
Canterbury and, 3:83a
characters in, 3:285 (*illus.*), 290b–291a
Clerk's Tale, 3:294b–295a, 8:346a
Cook's Tale, 3:293a
dramatic aspects of, 3:295b
exempla in, 3:294a–295b, 4:551b
fabliaux in, 3:292b–294a, 4:557a, 572b
framing device of, 3:290b
Franklin's Tale, 3:292a, 8:32b, 35b
genres in, 3:291b
glosses, 5:564b
inns and, 6:469a, 475a
Knight's Tale, 2:280b, 3:292a-b, 302b
lais in, 1:568b
language of, 8:312b
Man of Law's Tale, 3:291b
Manciple's Tale, 3:294a-b
Merchant's Tale, 2:149b, 3:293b–294a
Miller's Tale, 2:147b, 149b, 3:292b–293a
Monk's Tale, 2:286b, 3:294a, 5:146a, 8:346b
Nun's Priest's Tale, 3:295a-b
order of stories in, 3:291a
Pardoner's Tale, 3:295a, 12:543a
parody of Geoffrey of Vinsauf, 10:360a
Parson's Tale, 3:295b–296a, 8:314b, 10:301b–302a
Physician's Tale, 3:294a
Piers Plowman and, 7:333a
pious tales in, 3:291b
Prioress' Tale, 3:291b
Reeve's Tale, 3:293a, 6:555b, 10:281a
Renard and Chantecler in, 10:314a-b
romance tales in, 3:291b–292b
Second Nun's Tale, 3:291b, 6:63a
Shipman's Tale, 3:293b
Squire's Tale, 3:291b, 8:39a
Summoner's Tale, 3:293a-b
Tale of Melibeus, 3:294a
Tale of Sir Thopas, parody of popular romances in, 8:346a
use of iambic pentameter couplet in, 8:344b–345a
vetula in, 7:367b
Wife of Bath's Tale, 3:292a
Charles of Orléans and, 3:273a
chivalry and, 3:302b
Clanvowe and, 3:408a
"Complaint to His Lady," use of terza rima in, 8:345b
"Compleynt unto Pite," 8:338a
as controller of the custom, 3:283a-b
crusades and, 4:57a
Dante's influence on, 3:282b–283a
development of English and, 8:311a-b
Disticha Catonis and, 7:360a
drawing of, 3:280a (*illus.*)
Dunbar and, 4:307b
early life of, 3:280a-b
early poems of, 3:281a-b
equatorium and, 4:500b
Guillaume de Lorris and, 3:281b
Guillaume de Machaut and, 8:3a
House of Fame, 3:284a-b, 8:321a, 321b
use by Gavin Douglas, 4:262b
indulgences and, 6:450a
influence on 15th-century Scottish poets, 8:324a-b
Jean de Meun and, 3:281b
John of Gaunt and, 3:281a, 290a, 7:135b
later life, 3:290a-b
Legend of Good Women, 3:289a-b, 8:321b, 12:476a
Lydgate and, 7:694a-b, 8:323a, 323b
marriage of, 3:280b–281a
meter in works of, 3:286a
minstrels in, 8:415b
miscellaneous writings of, 3:284b, 286a-b
Nicholas Trevet and, 12:186b
Parliament of Fowls, 3:286b–287b, 8:321a, 321b
music and, 8:583a
Peasants' Revolt (1381) and, 3:290a
Petrarch's influence on, 3:282b–283b
rape of Cicely Champain and, 3:286b
on rhyme in English, 8:346a
Richard II of England and, 3:283b, 290a
Roman de la Rose and, 10:452a
Romaunt of the Rose, use of octosyllabic couplet in, 8:344b
royal appointments, 3:290a
in 17th century, 12:477a
Speculum stultorum and, 9:131a
tales in the Ovidian tradition, 9:313b (*illus.*)
travels of, in north and abroad, 3:280b–283a
Treatise on the Astrolabe, 1:603b, 3:29a, 290b, 11:98b
Troilus and Criseyde, 3:287b–289a, 8:225b, 321b
Gower and, 5:639b
inspired by Boccaccio's *Filostrato,* 2:279a
Roman de Troie and, 2:182a
sequels to, 6:169a
as source of Usk's *Testament of Love,* 12:334b
use of "rhyme royal" in, 8:346a
Troy story and, 12:221a
use of proverbs, 10:191b
Chaucer, Philippa, 3:280b–281a
Chauve-souris. See Korseke
Checkers, 5:353b
Cheetah, 6:355b
Chekker. See Eschaquiel
Chelandion, 11:231b
Chelčický, Peter, 6:377b
Net of Faith, 2:306a-b
On Spiritual Warfare, 2:306b
On the Triple Divison of Society, 2:306b
Chelles, Jehan de. *See* Jean de Chelles
Chelles (monastery: France), 12:683a
Chemistry, Islamic, 11:638b–639a
Chêng, 8:612b
Cherasco, founding of, 12:325b
Chernibon. See Trulla
Chernigov
Khanate of Tmutarakan and, 12:66a
ravaged by Mongols, 2:131b
Chërnye Klobuki, formation of, 10:577a
Cherry, in Mediterranean diet, 5:306a
Cherson (Byzantine theme), occupied by Vladimir of Kiev, 2:118b
Cherub, **3:297b**
definition of, 3:297b
in MS of Nicholas of Lyra, 3:298a (*illus.*)
tetramorphic, in silver liturgical fan, 3:298a (*illus.*)
see also Seraph
Cherubim, in *Majestas Domini,* 8:54b
Chess, 5:351b–352a, 353b–354a (*illus.*)
in allegory, 5:430b
discussed by Alexander Neckham, 9:92a
Chester, sheriff of, 11:225b
Chester Plays, **3:298a–299b**, 8:658a, 659a, 660a, 661b
Corpus Christi and, 3:298a-b
cycle of, 3:298b–299b
"Late Banns," 3:298b–299a
performance of, 3:298b, 4:284a-b
staging for, 8:662a
Stanzaic Life of Christ and, 4:547a
suppression of, 8:663a
see also Towneley Plays
Chester, Treaty of (973), **3:299b–300a**
Chestnut, growth of, in Mediterranean region, 5:305b
Chests
in Islamic furniture, 5:316a
in liturgical furniture, 5:319b–320a
in Western European furniture, 5:321b (*illus.*), 322b–323a
Chétifs, 3:331a
Chetmno. *See* Culm
Cheualere Assigne, 8:332a, 332b
Chevage, 11:203b
abolition of, 11:204a
Chevalerie

Chrétien de Troyes' concept of, 5:249b–250a
in French romances, 5:244b
Froissart's concept of, 5:270b–271a
in *Grandes chroniques,* 5:260a
repudiation of, 5:279b
restoration of, 5:265b, 266a
Chevalerie d'Ogier, *Cantar de mío Cid* and, 3:72a
Chevalier. *See* Knights and knight service
Chevalier au cygne et enfances Godefroi, 3:331a
Chevalier au Lion, Le. See Chrétien de Troyes, *Yvain*
Chevalier de la Charrette, Le. See Chrétien de Troyes, *Lancelot*
Chevalier à l'épée, Le, 1:570a
Chevalier du Papagau, similarities with *Eckenlied,* 4:380a-b
Chevalier qui fist parler les cons, Le, 4:575a
Chevauchée, 3:206a
Chevet, **3:300b–301a**
of Canterbury Cathedral, 3:84a
in floor plan, 3:300b (*illus.*)
see also Ambulatory
Chi-Rho monogram. *See* Christogram
Chiaroscuro
engraving and, 4:490a
etching and, 4:516b
Chichele, Henry, archbishop, 3:83b
Chichester-Constable chasuble, opus anglicanum embroidery, 9:255a (*illus.*)
Chichil Dukhtarān (mausoleum at Damghan), 11:147a
Chicken
changes in size, 5:150a-b
as fertility symbol, 5:150a
introduction to Europe, 5:150a
in Northern Europe, 1:95b
religious importance, 5:150a
typical production, 5:150b
Chierheit der gheestelike brulocht, Die. See Ruusbroec, Jan van
Chievrefeuil. See Marie de France
Chifonie, 8:608a
Chilandari monastery. *See* Hilandar Monastery
Childbirth
midwives and, 4:600b
rituals of, 3:382b–383a
interdict and, 6:494a
see also Circumcision; Communion, infant
Childebert I, Frankish king, 9:499b
Germanus of Paris and, 5:472b
Paris under, 9:401b
Childeric I, Merovingian king, 2:94a, 8:277a
golden seal ring of, 11:124b
Childeric II of Austrasia, king, 9:499b
Childeric III, Frankish king, 8:236a
Pepin III (the Short) and, 8:278b, 9:501a
tonsuring of, 4:158b–159a
Children
adoption of, 4:597a, 6:451b
clothing styles, 3:626a
of concubines, 6:451b
disinherited, 6:451b
education of, 4:600b, 603a, 604a, 607b
instruction in courtesy, 3:661b–663b
in Jewish schools, 11:69a
through allegory, 4:287a
in Germanic tribes, 4:599b–600a
guardianship of, 4:601a
illegitimate, 4:597a
inheritance and, 6:457b
intestate, 6:452a, 460a
Islamic, 4:598b
pilgrimage and, 9:650a
Jewish, 4:607a-b
as laborers, 4:602a
in monasteries, as oblates, 10:285b
mortality, 4:595a, 595b
nurses and, 4:602a
plagues and, 9:676b, 678a–679a
infantile diarrhea, 9:681b
measles, 9:674b
smallpox, 9:674a-b
religious instruction
catechism and catechetical manuals, 10:302a
family, 10:300a, 301a
Tractatus de parvulis trahendis ad Christum, 10:302a
of the remarried, 4:594b
role in urban families, 4:144a
in Sacchetti's works, 6:661a
Children's Crusade. *See* Crusades
Chiliasm. *See* Millennialism
Chilidonius of Besançon, bishop, deposition of, 5:471b
Chilperic I, Merovingian king, 6:381a
Christian-Jewish disputation and, 10:3a
Edict of, on inheritance by daughters, 6:457b
Chime bells. *See* Bells, chime
Chimneys
back-to-back hearth, 6:120b
building materials
brick and stone, 6:122a
plaster, 6:122b, 123a
wattle and daub, 6:122b
wooden, 6:122b
caminus, evolution of, 6:120a
changes effected by
in building construction, 6:121a, 123b
class distinctions, 6:124a
in life-style, 6:121b, 123a, 125a
construction of, 6:122b–123a
draft control, 6:120b–121a, 123a
elements of, 6:119a
evidence of
in art, 6:124a
in documents, 6:124b–125a
flue systems
Greek and Roman, 6:119a
metal, 6:122b
multi-flued, 6:120b
shape of, 6:120b–121a
shaft, 6:120b
to enhance environment
guest houses, 6:124a
hospitals and almshouses, 6:124b
in urban projects, 6:123b–124a
see also Fireplace
Chin, **3:301a**
Chin (Chinese dynasty)
Mongol conflicts
alliance with Tatars, 8:465a
Genghis Khan, 5:382b, 8:465b–466a
siege of Ning-hsia (1227), 8:468b
China
Christianity in, 3:642a
Italian trading colony, 7:15a
Kirghiz and, 7:272b
in *Mandeville's Travels,* 8:82a
Manichaeans in, 8:85b
Marco Polo and, 4:557a
paper from, 12:128a
plagues and, 9:678a
silk in, 11:293b–294a
strife with Islam, in Transoxiana, 12:145b
Syriac language and, 11:562b–563a
technological innovations, 11:660a–661b
trade with Europe, 9:85a
Chinchilla, Pedro de, translation of Guido delle Colonne, 11:458a
Chindaswinth, Visigothic king, 12:471b
Eugenius II and, 4:520b
Chinese, vs. Muslims in Iran, 6:570b
Chinese art, at Takht-i Sulaymān, 6:603b
Chinese ceramics
porcelain, 3:240a
stoneware, 3:238b
tomb figure, 3:620a (*illus.*)
Chinggis Khan. *See* Genghis Khan
Chinggisids
Timurids and, 12:58b
see also Mongol Empire
Chioggia (Venice), 12:383b, 385a, 392b
Chioggia War (1378–1381), 5:4b, 7:8a-b
Andronikos IV and, 2:502b
Chios
alum mines at, 12:111b
Byzantine sea routes and, 10:423 (map), 424b
churches on, 4:345a
Chip carving, **3:301a**
in migration period art, 8:365a-b, 366b
Chirino, Alfonso, *Menor daño de medicina,* 11:441b
Chironomic neume. *See* Neume
Chirugia magna. See Guy de Chauliac; Lanfranchi, Guido
Chirurgia. See Henry de Mondeville
Chivalry, **3:301b–303b**
in Burgundy, 2:428a
champion in judicial combat, 3:250b–251a
Christian ideals and, 3:302a-b
in chronicles, 3:301b
coats of arms and, 3:302a
courtesy books and, 3:660b
in epics, 3:302b
etymology of, 7:276b
family life and, 4:601a
handbooks on, 3:302a
in *Klári saga,* 7:274b–275a
legacy of, 3:303a

Chivalry (*cont.*)
literature of, 3:302b
meanings of, 3:301b
in Middle High German literature, 8:350a
models of, 3:303a
nobility and, 3:303a
orders of, crusader states, 12:561b
origin of, 3:301b
religious, 3:302b
in Scandinavian literature, 10:303a–304b
in *Song of Roland,* 3:301a, 302b
in Spervogel's poetry, 11:462b
in *Tristan und Isolt,* 5:636a–637a
warfare and, 3:302a
see also Knights and knight service; Squire; individual orders of chivalry
Chivalry, orders of, **3:303b–307b**
Alfonso the Battler and, 9:70a
swords of, 11:549a
Chlamys, Byzantine, 3:615a-b
Chlodomer, 2:423b
Chlothar II, Frankish king, 8:288a
Choice Stories (ᶜ*Uyūn al-akhbār*). *See* Qutayba, Ibn
Choir, **3:307b**
in cathedral, 3:192a-b
church, triclinium plan, 12:188 (*illus.*)
see also Gregorian chant; Nave; Plainsong; Screen
Chola Empire, Muslim trade and, 11:246b
Cholera. *See* Plagues, enteric
Chorasmia. *See* Transoxiana
Chorasmian language, 6:505b
Chorbishop, *chorepiskopos*
Armenian, 1:504a
see also Clergy, Byzantine
Chordophones
Arabian bowed, 8:561b, 611b–612a
Middle Eastern, 8:610a–612a
Chorea, dementia and, 6:490a
Choriamb, 7:375a
Chormaqan Noyan, conquest of Azerbaijan, 8:469b
Choroi. See Lighting devices, Byzantine
Chorus (musical instrument), 8:558b–559a
Chōsarioi, 10:60a
Chosrau. *See* Xusrō
Chosroids (Mihranids), **3:307b–308b**
Albanian rule, 1:123b–124a, 125a
extinction of, 2:49a, 5:405b
origins of power, 3:307b–308a
rule of, 3:308a
Sasanians and, 3:308a
Chothar II, Merovingian king, 8:236a, 278b
Pepin I (of Landen) and, 9:499a
Choumnos, John, on gout, 8:246a
Chrétien de Troyes, **3:308b–311b,** 8:224a, 224b
Arthurian legend and, 1:568b–569a, 3:309b–310a
depiction of King Arthur, 5:250a
elaborations on, 5:249b–250a
Arthurian romances, sources for, 12:611a
attribution of *Guillaume d'Angleterre,* 1:267b
Chevalier au Lion. See Yvain
chivalric ideals in, 3:309a–311a
on *clergie,* 5:249b
Cligés, 3:308b–309b, 5:246b, 246a, 448a
Engelhard and, 7:289b
Legend of Tristan and, 12:200a, 202a, 203a
sources for, 1:568b–569a
Conte du Graal (*Perceval*), 3:110b–311a, 308b, 5:248b, 249b
Arthurian legend and, 1:570b–571a
continuations of, 5:258b–259a, 367b, 423b, 451a
Grail quest in, 5:645a
Icelandic saga and, 4:613a
mystical aspects, 5:285a
as source of *Parcevals saga,* 9:399a
translated into Norwegian, 10:390a, 390b
Vilmundar saga viþutan and, 12:451b
courtly aspects, 5:249b–250a
courtly love in narratives of, 1:569a
Érec et Énide, 3:308b–309a, 4:574b, 5:248a, 447b
Erex saga and, 4:504b, 505a, 613a
hunting in, 6:358b
prologue, 5:249b
romance in, 1:571b, 643b
translated into Norwegian, 10:390a, 390b
influence of, 3:311a, 5:248b, 448a
Lancelot (*Le chevalier de la charrette*), 5:248b, 448a
Chaucer and, 8:321b
on organs, 9:273a
on riding in a wheeled vehicle, 12:370a
Vulgate cycle reworking of, 5:259a
Wolfram von Eschenbach and, 12:674b
life of, 3:308a, 5:248a-b
myth of poetry, 5:250b–251a
natural behavior and, 5:451a
origination of romances, 5:283b
Ovidian translations by, 3:308b
Provençal lyric and, 5:251a, 282b
recasting of romances, in Picard codex, 5:255b
Roman de Brut and, 12:496b
settings, 5:249b
themes and motifs, 5:250a-b, 251a, 446b, 447b–448a
translation of *Ars amatoria,* 9:314a
Tristan legend in, 5:246a
trouvère poetry, 12:218b
use of proverbs and *sententiae,* 10:191a-b, 192a-b
Wolfram von Eschenbach and, 5:448a, 451b, 12:677b
Yvain (*Le chevalier au lion*), 1:586b, 643b, 3:308b, 309b–310a, 5:248b, 446b, 448a
adaptations of, 7:104a
compared with similar European romances, 1:571b
Eufemiavisor and, 4:520a
Icelandic saga and, 4:613a
translated into Norwegian, 10:390a-b
see also Ívens saga
Chrism, 2:177a-b
Chrismatories, 5:320b
Chrismon, **3:311b**
Christogram, 3:319b
Christ (Exeter Book), sections of, 1:280a
Christ II (Old English poem). *See* Cynewulf, *Christ*
Christ Church Cathedral (Canterbury). *See* Canterbury Cathedral
Christ, Order of, 3:305 (*illus.*), 306b
Christ Pantokrator (monastery: Constantinople)
sarcophagi, 2:444a
south church, decorations, 2:443b–444a
Christ and Satan (Old English poem), 1:280b, 2:221b
Christburg, Treaty of (1249), 2:66b
Christherre-Chronik, 2:229a
Christian I of Denmark, Norway, and Sweden, king, 4:156a
Christian II of Denmark, Norway, and Sweden, king, 4:156a-b
reign of, 11:533b–534a
Christian architecture, early. *See* Architecture, early Christian; Byzantine architecture
Christian art, early. *See* Art, early Christian
Christian Hebraists, **3:313b–314a**
contribution of, 3:313b
decline of, 3:314a
Dominican translations and, 4:246a-b
early, 3:313b
Peter Schwartz and, 4:246a-b
Christian of Lilienfeld, 6:382b
rhymed offices by, 10:373b, 376b
Christian of Oldenburg, vs. Charles VIII, 11:533b
Christian of Prachatice, 6:373b, 376b
Christian of Prussia, bishop, proselytization among Old Prussians, 2:66a-b
Christian of Stablo (Stavelot), **3:311b–312a,** 4:542b
Christian Topography. See Cosmas Indicopleustes
Christian-Jewish relations
in Arabia, 1:371b, 375b
biblical exegesis and, 2:213a, 213b, 214a
collaboration on Bible translations in Spain, 2:215b
moneylending and, 2:81b
responsum literature and, 10:338a, 339a
see also Jews, Catholic church and; Polemics, Christian-Jewish
Christian-Muslim relations
in Arabia, 6:575b–576a
in Armenian Muslim emirates, 1:514a-b
in Egypt
discrimination against, 6:74a
under Ikhshidids, 6:417b
in al-Ḥīra, 7:321a

in Ifrīqiya, 6:414b
in Iran, under Ilkhanids, 6:420a
in Iraq, 6:511a, 513a
in Islamic administration, 6:590b–591a
Islamic sumptuary laws and, 11:508b
Sicily, 11:262a
in Spain, 8:520b
formal cultural borrowing, 11:379b–380a
in late Middle Ages, 11:380a-b
Mudejars, 11:375b–377b
problems of interpretation of, 11:374b–375b
regional evolution, 11:377b–379b
Valencia, 12:346b, 349a-b
see also Toledo
under the Fatimid caliph al-ᶜAzīz, 2:28b
under the Mamluk dynasty, 8:71b, 72a
see also Abode of Islam—Abode of War; Crusades; Crusader states; Islam, conquests of
Christiani, Pablo, debate of, 10:4b–5a
Christianus Druthmarus. *See* Christian of Stablo
Christiern Pedersen, sermons, 11:17b
Christiern Svensen, 11:522a
Christina of St. Trond. *See* Christine of St. Tronde
Christine of Gandersheim, abbess, 6:313b,.316a
Christine de Pizan, 1:324a, **3:315b–317a**, 3:662a, 664b, 665b–666a, 672b
Avision-Christine, 3:315a–316b
biography of Charles V, 3:269a, 317a
Cité des dames, condemnation of misogynist writers, 5:271a
courtesy books by, 3:662a, 664b, 665b–666a
education of, 3:316a
Enseignemens à son filz Jean de Castel, 3:662a
Epistre au Dieu d'Amours, 10:452b
Epître d'Othea à Hector, 3:666a
historical works of, 3:316b–317a
influenced by Guillaume de Machaut, 8:3b
Jean de Meun and, 3:316b
lai and, 7:317a
Livre du duc des vrais amants, 8:415b–416a
Livre des fais et bonnes meurs du sage roy Charles V, 2:240a
Livre de la mutacion de fortune, 6:475b
Livre des trois vertus, 3:664b, 672b
marriage and widowhood of, 3:316a
poetry of, 3:316b
prose works, 3:333a, 5:271a
religious and didactic works of, 3:316b
retirement to convent, 3:317a
Roman de la Rose and, 3:316b
Christine of St. Tronde, 9:11b, 27a
vision of purgatory, 6:69b
Christine of Stommeln, 9:11b, 12a
Christmas, **3:317a–319b**
as beginning of calendar year, 3:19b–20a
celebration of, 3:317a–318a, 319a, 8:339a-b
cycle of feasts for, 5:35a-b, 37a-b
dating of, 3:317a-b, 394b
in Eastern churches, 3:318a
feasting during, 3:319a
Latin hymns, *Puer natus* introit with tropes, 12:211b, 213 (*illus.*)
liturgical plays for, 4:281a
German, 4:268a-b
Play of Daniel, 9:705b–706a
liturgy of, 3:318a–319a
music for, 3:319a
pagan celebrations and, 3:317a–318a
significance of, 3:318a
see also Feasts and festivals, European
Christogram, **3:319b**
chrismon, 3:311b
decorated, 6:462a (*illus.*), 462b
on labarum, 7:313b
silver chalice with, 3:319b (*illus.*)
Christology, **3:319b–324b**
acceptance of doctrine and, 3:324a
adoptionism, 3:321b, 6:194a
in Antiochene church, 6:187b
Arianism and, 3:320b, 336a
Aristotelian concept of unity, 9:595b
Augustine of Hippo and, 3:321b
Byzantine church, Antiochene interpretation, 2:460a
christological nihilism in Peter Lombard's teaching, 9:517b
of church fathers, 3:320b–321b, 336a, 339b
controversy between Eastern and Western churches, 11:44b
Dominicans and, 3:323b
dual nature of Christ, 6:190b
in East, 3:3320a-b
efforts of Heraklios to find compromise, 6:171b
Franciscans and, 3:323b
heresies, Trinitarian Doctrine and, 12:189a–191b
hypostatic union, 8:477a
of iconoclasts, 6:401a-b
later medieval, 3:324a
Leo I and, 3:320b–321a
main concerns of, 3:319b–320a
of Maximus the Confessor, 8:233a-b
merits of Christ and, 3:324a
Monophysitism and, 3:320a–321a
"Phantasiast" of Julian of Halikarnassos, 6:188a
philosophy of being
doctrine of substantial forms, 9:597b
threefold distinction, 9:597a
subsistence theory, 9:598b
theology and, 9:601b
theology of icons and, 6:397b–398a
Theotokos as epithet for Mary, 6:190b
of Thomas Aquinas, 12:40a
in West, 3:320b–324b
see also Nestorianism; *Theotokos*
Christopher I of Denmark, king, 4:154b
Christopher II of Denmark, king, 4:154b, 155a
Christopher of Bavaria, king of Denmark, Norway, and Sweden, 4:156a
Sweden and, 11:533b
Christopher of Mytilene, epigrams, 2:507a
Christopher, St.
in art, woodcut, 12:691b (*illus.*), 691a
in hymns, 6:384a
Christos (church: Veroia), paintings of, 5:399b
Christus, Petrus, **3:324b–325a**
influences on, 3:324b, 5:86b–87a
Madonna with Sts. Francis and Jerome, carpet in, 10:551b
works of, 3:324b
Christus und die Samariterin, 2:226a, **3:325a**, 9:233b
Chrodegang of Metz, bishop, 3:108b, 5:578b, 8:301b, 638b
Rule of, 1:286b
Chromaticism
in Byzantine music, 8:555a, 556a
Marchettus of Padua and, 8:646a
Chronica. *See* Cassiodorus Senator; Hélinand of Froidmont; Regino of Prüm
Chronica Adefonsi imperatoris, 11:406b, 435b
Chronica Boemorum. *See* Cosmas of Prague
Chronica breviter scripta Stephani, 10:510b
Chronica gentis Scotorum. *See* John of Fordun
Chronica Hungarorum. *See* Thuróczi, Johannes
Chronica majora. *See* Matthew Paris
Chronica mundi. *See* Isidore of Seville, St.
Chronica Poloniae Maioris. *See* Baszko, Godisław
Chronica Polonorum. *See* Janko of Czarnków; Kadłubek, Wincentry
Chronica principum Poloniae. *See* Peter of Byczyna
Chronica Slavorum. *See* Helmold of Bosau
Chronicle of Ahimaaz, 10:3a
Chronicle of Alfonso III, 11:435a
Chronicle of Aquila. *See* Buccio di Ranallo
Chronicle of the Days When the Land of Moldavia Was Founded by the Will of God, 12:505a
Chronicle of the Kings of Aragon and Counts of Barcelona, 3:166a, 9:511a-b
Chronicle of Melrose, source of early Scottish history, 6:258a
Chronicle of Morea, 7:378b
Chronicle of Morigny, on Suger of St. Denis, 11:504a
Chronicle of Nájera, 11:435a, 435b
Chronicle of Partenope, 6:633b
Chronicle of the Princes, 12:613a
Chronicle of San Juan de la Peña, 11:435b
Chronicle of Silos, 11:435a
Chronicle to the Year, 1234, 11:566a

Chronicle of Twenty-Four Generals, on Roger Bacon, 2:35b
Chronicles, **3:325a–330b**
accuracy of, 3:326b
Anglo-Norman, Geffrai Gaimar, 5:340b–341a
Anglo-Saxon, 3:299b–300a
aristocratic, 3:327b–328a
Armenian, 6:240b
Arthurian legend in, 3:327a
Benedictines and, 3:326a
biographies in, 3:328a-b
Byzantine
Dark Ages, 2:513a
local, 2:517a
political vs. theological emphasis, 6:244a-b
style and language, 2:522b
world, 2:512a-b, 513a-b, 515b, 517a, 6:246b–247a
Catalan, 3:165a–166b
under Peter IV (the Ceremonious), 9:511a-b
chivalry in, 3:301b
clerical, 3:326a–327a
crusade, 3:328a, 4:20a
English, 3:329b
French, **3:330b–334a**, 5:253a
audience for, 3:330b
chansons de geste and, 3:330a, 5:243a
crusades in, 3:331a–332a
French history and, 3:331b–332a
Grandes chroniques de France, 3:327a-b, 5:653b–654b
Marco Polo's travels, 3:332b
of Philip II Augustus, 6:24a
poetry in, 3:332b
production of, 3:331b
regional, 3:333a-b
subject matter of, 3:331a
translations of Latin histories and, 3:331b
in vernacular prose, 3:333a
see also Historia regum Francorum; Picard literature; Rigord; Robert de Clari
Georgian, 5:404b, 417b–418a
German, 3:329a
interpretation of history and, 3:329b–330a
Islamic
with biography, 6:253b
reproduction of existing, 6:252a
Italian, 10:627a–628a
Moldavian, 10:511b–512a
Romanian, 10:510b
Scandinavian, 10:535a-b
Scottish Gaelic, 11:116b
sources for, personal observations, 10:628a
Spanish, of Pero López de Ayala, 11:418b
translations of, 3:325a-b
types of, 3:325b
universal, 6:263b–264a
urban, 3:328b–329b
vernacular, 3:330b–333b
world, 8:135a, 10:542b, 544b
Sachsenspiegel, 10:602b–603a
see also Anonimalle Chronicle; Scandinavian literature, rhymed chronicles; individual national literatures
Chronicon. See Eusebius of Caesarea; Guillaume de Nangis; Hugh of St. Victor; Otto of Freising; Richard of Devizes; Spechtshart, Hugo
Chronicon comitis Petri. See Historiography, Polish
Chronicon Lethrense. See Lejre Chronicle
Chronicon maius, 6:248
Chronicon maius. See Makarios Melissenos
Chronicon minus. See George Sphrantzes
Chronicon monasterii Casinensis. See Leo of Ostia
Chronicon Paschale, on processions, 7:588b
Chronicon S. Vincentii Vulturnensis. See Johannes of St. Vincent
Chronique annale. See Jean Lemaire de Belges
Chronique de Baudouin d'Avesnes, time period covered, 9:638a
Chronique des ducs de Normandie. See Benoît de Sainte-Maure
Chronique des empereurs. See Aubert, David
Chronique d'Ernoul et de Bernard le Trésorier, 9:638a
Chronique de Flandre. See Froissart, Jehan
Chronique de Reims. See Récits d'un ménestrel de Reims
Chronique rimée. See Philippe Mousket
Chronique rimée des rois de France, La, 3:332b
Chroniques. See Froissart, Jehan
Chroniques abrégées de Baudouin d'Avesnes, derivation of, 9:638a
Chroniques d'Engleterre, 5:389b
Chroniques et conquestes de Charlemagne, 7:55b
Chroniques et conquêtes de Charlemagne. See Aubert, David
Chroniques de Hainaut. See Liédet, Loyset; Wauquelin, Jean
Chroniques de Londres, **3:334a**
Chroniques de Tournai, sources for, 9:637b
Chronographia. See Psellos, Michael
Chronologies
of Bede, 2:154b–155a
of Dionysius of Tel-Mahré, 4:193a
Chrotta, 8:558a
Chrysanthos of Madytos, 8:556a, 616b–617a
Chrysippus, dialectic and, 4:168b
Chrysobullon, **3:334a-b**
in Byzantine Empire, 3:334a
in Western Europe, 3:334a-b
Chrysocheir, vs. Basil I, 2:118a
Chrysoloras, Manuel, 1:580a
Greek studies in Italy and, 7:1a
Chrysostom, John, St. *See* John Chrysostom, St.
Chuds, in Russian *Primary Chronicle,* 12:434b
Chuonradus, 10:103a
Chur, bishopric of, 11:539a
Church
early, **3:337a–343b**
agape and, 3:338b
apostolic succession in, 3:338b
beginning of, 3:337a-b
bishops in, 3:340b–341a
clergy in, 3:340b–341a
concept of primitive church, 10:121a-b
confirmation in, 3:535b
Constantine I and, 3:337a-b
definition of *ekklesia,* 3:338a
domus ecclesiae at Dura Europos, 4:313a
dualism and, 3:340a-b
election of bishops in, 3:602b
evil and, 3:340a
furnishings for churches, 4:361a-b
hierarchy in, 3:338b
medieval Latin church and, 3:343a
monasticism in, 3:342b–343a
Monophysitism in, 3:339b–340a
New Testament and, 3:338a
Old Testament Trinity, 12:198a-b, 199 (*illus.*)
papacy in, 3:341b–342a
Parousia (Second Coming) and, 3:337b
preaching and sermon literature, 10:75b–81b
sacraments in, 3:338a-b
theologians of, 3:342a-b
Trinitarian doctrine in, 3:339a-b, 12:189a-b
see also Nestorianism; Nestorius; Papacy, origins and development of; *Parousia*
as heir, in Byzantine Empire, 6:451a, 452a
nature of
Wyclif on, 6:366b, 12:708a
state and, 10:462a, 462b
Aquinas on, 1:465a
in Armenia, 1:504b, 505a
caesaropapism, 3:10a–11b
in England, 3:409b–410a
Frankish protectorate, 10:522a
Marsilius on, 4:132b–133a
in Siena, 11:278a-b
see also Disputatio inter clericum et militem
types of, pilgrimage, 10:621b
see also Primitive church
Church of the Annunciation. *See* Annunciation (church: Nazareth)
Church architecture, 1:441b–445a, **3:378a–383a**
in Aegean area
basilicas, 4:337b
cross-in-square churches, 4:341a-b
decorative elements, 4:337b
ambulatory/radiating chapel, 10:475b–477a, 476b (*illus.*), 478b
apse in, 1:352a
Armenian, 1:493a–494a, 494b (*illus.*), 6:309b (*illus.*)
atrium, 1:641a

basilica, 3:585b–586b (*illus.*), 12:187b–188a (*illus.*)
Bavarian, 3:379a
bronze and brass in, 2:384b
Bulgarian, Round Church plan, 2:414b, 415a (*illus.*)
Cappadocian, 3:92a–93a (*illus.*)
Carthusian monastery design, 3:119b
chancel, 3:251b
chapel, 3:263b–264a
choir, 3:307b
Cistercian, 3:404b, 5:114b–115a, 10:483a–484a
  monasteries, 8:455b
  spread of, 10:489a
clerestory, 3:440a
conch type, 3:378a, 380 (*illus.*)
Coptic, 3:585b–587a
Croatian, 4:8b
cross-domed type, 3:378b, 380a (*illus.*)
cross-in-square type, 3:378b, 380 (*illus.*), 5:408b, 6:286b, 10:578a (*illus.*), 12:222a-b
  in Italy, 4:346b
  variations of, 4:345a-b
cruciform, 12:125b
  Spain, 12:466a-b
crusader, 4:22b
diaconicon, 4:167b
dome, 4:234b–236a
dome of heaven, 4:236b–237a
domed-hall type, 1:494a
domed-octagon type, 3:378b, 379a, 380b (*illus.*), 381b (*illus.*), 4:341b
double-cathedral type, 3:378b, 381a (*illus.*)
double-ended basilica type, 2:124b, 3:378b–379a, 381a (*illus.*)
early period, 1:442a-b
echelon apse, 1:352a, 10:475b, 476 (*illus.*)
Egyptian, 9:199a
fireproofing, 11:656b
flying buttress construction, 3:565a-b
gallery, 5:343a-b
*gawit*ᶜ, 5:371a-b
Georgian, 5:407b (*illus.*), 407b–409b, 408a (*illus.*), 408a–409a, 409a (*illus.*)
Gothic, 3:379b
Greek-cross type, 3:379a, 381 (*illus.*), 6:286b
hall type, 1:427a, 3:379a-b, 381b (*illus.*)
  in Poitiers, 10:481a
  in southern France, 10:481b
Hrabanus Maurus on, 5:589a
interiors, Eucharist houses, 10:336a
Isidore of Seville on, 5:589a
in Italy, 4:337b
  narrative decorations, 4:337b–338a
later period, 1:442b, 444a–445a
Latin-cross type, 2:124b, 3:379b, 382a (*illus.*)
lighting, 11:655b–656a
liturgical aspects
  Byzantine, 1:442b–445a (*illus.*)
  differences between Eastern and Western church, 1:442a-b, 444b
  early phase, 1:443 (*illus.*)
locus sanctus, 7:640a
monastic, 10:476a-b
  in Georgia, 5:409a-b
nave, 3:564a (*illus.*)
  cross sections, 3:564b (*illus.*)
in Near East
  cut-stone construction, 4:337a-b
  decorative elements, 4:337b
Nubian, 9:199a
ornamentation
  Eastern vs. Western views, 11:664a
  treatises on, 11:643b–643a
pilgrimage type, 2:124b, 3:379b, 382a (*illus.*)
  in France, 10:482b–483a
  in Jerusalem, 4:22b
as propaganda, 10:137b
reredos altar screen, 10:334b–335a
rib vaulting, in Durham Cathedral, 4:315b
Roman, 1:442a, 443a (*illus.*)
Romanesque, 3:379a, 379b, 10:475a–489a
  crossing tower in, 4:347a
Russian
  composite style, 10:579b–580a
  cross-in-square, 10:578a (*illus.*), 579a
  domed square, 10:580b
sacristy, 10:607a-b
Saxon, in Scandinavia, 10:489a
Scandinavian, 3:379b, 382b (*illus.*)
in Serbia, 4:347a-b
structure, pre-Romanesque, 10:91a–92b, 94a–96a
tent, 10:581a (*illus.*)
tithe, 10:578b
triclinium, 12:188 (*illus.*)
triple church, 5:408b
urban religious buildings, 12:329a
vaulting, 3:234b–235a
Villard de Honnecourt and, 8:588b (*illus.*)
Visigothic, 12:465a–466b (*illus.*)
in Walachia, 12:505b
windows, 11:656b
see also Archaeology of medieval monuments; Architecture, liturgical aspects; Baptistery; Basilica; Bema; Crypt; Exonarthex; Narthex; *Papert;* Parekklesion; Prothesis; Synagogue, art and architecture in
Church architecture, Byzantine, 1:442b, 3:378a, 378b, 379a
  Basil I and, 2:117b
  cross-in-square type, 2:442b, 4:341a-b
  decorative elements, 4:339b, 341b, 343a, 345b
  5th-century expansion in, 4:337a
  Greek-cross type, 4:340b–341a
  iconostasis in, 4:344a
  imperial patronage of, 4:343a-b
  innovations in Mistra churches, 4:345a
  interior plan, 1:443 (*illus.*)
  Justinian's innovations, 4:338a-b
  Komnenian period, 4:344a-b
  monasteries
    compared with Western monasteries, 4:333b
    formulas for, 4:333a-b
  monastic influences, 4:343a
  palace architecture and, 4:343a
  Palaiologan period, 4:344b–345b
  regional styles, 4:337a
  separation of lay areas from sanctuary, 4:343b–344a
  three-zone formula, 6:286b–287a
  see also Kastoria
Church architecture, early Christian
  basilica as model for, 4:335a-b
  decorative elements, 4:354b–355b, 357b, 361a
    destruction of, 4:357a-b
  domus ecclesiae, 4:313a
  doors, 4:361a
  floor decorations, 4:359b, 360a
  imperial patronage of, 4:335a
  regional variations in, 4:335b
  shrine in, 4:336a-b
  survival of, 4:335a
  see also Basilica
Church dedication, **4:130a–131b**
  Gallican, 4:131a
  incense and, 6:432a
  mandated by councils, 4:131a
  plainsong and, 9:690b
  precedents for, 130a-b
  Roman, 4:130b–131a
  see also Relics; Shrines, Christian
Church of the East. *See* Nestorianism
Church elections. *See* Bishop, election of; Papacy, election of pope
Church fathers, **3:334b–337a**
  Alexandrian school, 3:336a
  antifeminism of, 1:322b–323a
  Antiochene school, 3:336a
  Armenian, 1:498a
    Chalcedonianism and, 1:499a
  in art, 6:410a
  Beowulf and, 2:183b
  Cappadocian, 3:92a
    Arianism and, 1:454a
  Catechetical School established at Alexandria, 3:335b
  Christology of, 3:320b–321b, 336a, 339b
  Clairvaux edition of the works of, 8:102b
  on contraception, 3:573a
  first, 3:334b–335a
  Gnosticism and, 3:335a
  Greek
    Acta concilii ephesini, 12:190b
    perichoresis teaching of, 12:189b, 194a
    Theophilus of Antioch, 12:198a
  heresy and, 3:335a–336a
  legacy of, 3:336a–337a
  literacy of, 7:598b
  literature, 10:335b
    see also Realism; Reform, idea of
  music and, 8:587b
  recognition of, 3:334b
  their use of the term "pericope," 9:504b
  Theotokos and, 12:25b–26a
  translations
    Armenian, 1:507b
    by Ambrogio Traversari, 12:163a-b

Church fathers (*cont.*)
Trinitarian doctrine and, 12:189a-b, 190b, 191b, 198a
Western, 3:336a-b
Wyclif and, 12:708a, 709b
see also particular Fathers; *Vitae patrum*
Church History. See Evagrius Scholasticus; John of Ephesus; Socrates Scholasticus
Church of the Holy Sepulcher, Jerusalem. *See* Holy Sepulcher (church: Jerusalem)
Church of the Nativity (Bethlehem). *See* Nativity (church: Bethlehem)
Church reform, 3:347a–349a, 367b–371b
Arnold of Brescia, 1:539b–540a
Bohemian, 6:365b–366a
Carolingian, 3:68a, 108b–110a
development of the parish, 9:412b–413a
penitentials, 9:489b–490a
women's orders and, 12:683a–684b
celibacy, 3:217a-b
in Celtic church, 3:232a
conciliar theory and, 3:511a-b
elections of higher clergy and, 4:421b, 422a
England, Wulfstan of York and, 12:704a
as enhancement of papal power in 11th century, 9:375b–376a
excommunication and, 4:536a-b
Humbert of Silva Candida and, 6:330a
Hungarian, 6:341a
Icelandic, 6:394a-b
investiture conflict and, 6:499a
Irish, 6:517a
literature and, 6:541b, 542a
Italy, Normans and, 11:265a
in Latin church
to 1054, 3:347a–349a
1305–1500, 3:367b–371b
lauda and, 6:635a
monastic
Cluniac, 12:154a, 155b
pilgrimage and, 12:155b
Nicholas of Clamanges and, 9:122b
Norman, 9:163a-b
parish and, 9:414a–415b
right of presentation, 10:117a–118a
Synod of Sutri and, 11:517a
under Pepin III, 9:501b
Wyclif on, 6:366b, 367a, 12:708b
see also Councils; Liturgy, reform of; Monasticism, reform of; Papacy, church reform and
Church of the Savior (Rome). *See* Lateran (basilica: Rome)
Church of the Virgin, Studenica. *See* Virgin (church: Studenica)
Churche, Daniel, *Liber urbani,* 3:661a
Churching of women, **3:382b–383a**
Churchscot, 11:616a-b
Chuvash, Volga Bulgars and, 12:487b
Ci nous dit. See Composition de la Saincte Escripture
Ciacco dell'Anguillaia, "O gemma laziosa," 6:656b
Ciampini, Giovanni, *De sacris aedificiis a Constantino Magno constructis,* 1:428a
Ciarán, 6:521a
Ciborium, 1:222a, **3:383b**
Cicero, Marcus Tullius
Aristotle and, 1:460b
Catalan translations of, 3:168b
on Celtic music, 8:558a
compared with Boethius, 10:354b
compilations of excerpts, 6:49a
continuing influence of in the Middle Ages, 10:355b–364a
in Dante's *Divine Comedy,* 10:355b
De divinatione, 1:605a, 4:572a
De inventione, 10:351a–352b, 353a, 353b
on the discovery of the "issue," 10:351b
Latini and, 6:631b
De officiis, 8:434a
De oratore
on decorum and style, 10:346a
in the Renaissance, 10:351b, 356a
unknown in the Middle Ages, 10:355b–356a
on the five parts of rhetoric, 10:351b
Isidore of Seville and, 6:564a
Latini and, 7:383a-b
medieval commentaries on his work, 10:356a
Rhetorica nova. See Rhetorica ad Herennium
Rhetorica secunda. See Rhetorica ad Herennium
Roger Bacon on, 2:40a
on slavery, 11:334a
Somnium Scipionis, 12:475b
influence on Petrarch's *Africa,* 9:534b
Macrobius on, 7:360a-b
Topica, 1:460b
Boethius on, 2:292a
influence of on Boethius, 10:351a
used by St. Augustine, 10:353b
Ciconia, Johannes, 12:180a
ars subtilior and, 1:558b
Cid, the, history and legend of, **3:383b–390b**
in *Mocedades de Rodrigo,* 8:447a–448a
pseudo-translation of an Arabic chronicle by Ibn al-Faraj, 11:457a
in Spanish epic poetry, 11:410b–411a, 437b–438a
Cid, Le. See Corneille, Pierre
Cid, the
achievements of, 3:129b
Alfonso VI and, 3:383b–384a, 384b
ballads about, 3:388b–399a
banishment, 3:384a, 384b
conquest of Sharq al-Andalus (Valencia), 3:385b–386a, 11:376a-b, 12:346a
critics of, 3:386a
cult of, 3:76a
family of, 3:76a
origins, 3:383b
in service of al-Muqtadīr, 3:384a
supporter of Sancho II, 3:383b
victories over the Almoravids, 1:199b, 3:384a-b
see also Cantar de mío Cid
Cidellus (Joseph Ferruziel or Ferrizuel), 7:80b
Cielo d'Alcamo, 6:656a-b, 11:259a-b
"Rosa fresca aulentissima," 6:643a, 11:259b
Cieza de León, Pedro, 8:445b
Cilicia, 3:392 (map)
adoption of Western feudal law, 3:393b
conquered (965), 9:132b
crusades and, 4:55b
kings of, 6:39a-b
languages, 3:393a
Mamluk threat, 6:219a
Mongols and, 3:391b, 6:219a
Muslim attacks on, 3:391b, 393a
see of, 1:504a
strategic location, 3:391a
Tancred and, 11:589b
as trade center, 3:393a
westernization of, 3:393a-b
Cilician Chronicle, Armenian cavalry in, 3:199a
Cilician church
union with Roman church, **3:394a–395b**
see also Leo I/II of Cilician Armenia, king
Cilician Gates, **3:390b,** 3:391a
Byzantine system of beacons and, 10:425a
crusaders' route and, 10:423b
Lambron and, 7:322a
Cilician Kingdom, 1:241b, **3:390b–394a**
absorbed by the Mamluk dynasty, 8:74a
Armenian literature and, 1:511b
Armenian rule of, 8:418b
Kořikos in, 7:298a-b
Lusignan rule, 7:689a-b
Manuel I Komnenos and, 8:91b
manuscript illumination
T^{c}oros Roslin's Crossing of the Red Sea, 12:87 (*illus.*)
see also T^{c}oros Tarōnec^{c}i
Rubenids in, 10:540b, 541a
Seljuks of Rum and, 11:154b, 157a, 157b
Sīs in, 11:313b–314a
Skewřa in, 11:326a
Smbat Sparapet's defense of, 11:351b
trade, 12:98b
Vahka Castle and, 12:344b–345b (*illus.*)
see also Ayās; Leo I/II of Cilician Armenia, king; Leo V/VI of Cilician Armenia, king
Cilician law, 3:393b
Cilli family, 6:346a
Cilli, Ulrich, 6:347b
Cimabue, Cenni di Pepi, **3:395b–396b**
crucifix, 3:396a (*illus.*)
Duccio and, 4:301b, 302a
frescoes by, 3:396a-b
Crucifixion, 5:293a
panel painting of, 5:605b
style, 3:396b
Cimbri, defeated by Marius, 2:88b

Cináed mac Ailpín. *See* Kenneth I Mac Alpin
Cincture. *See* Vestments, liturgical
Cinéal Eóghain, **3:396b–397a**
  see also Uí Néill
Cinnamus. *See* John Kinnamos
Cino da Pistoia, **3:397a–398a**, 10:19a, 61b
  at University of Naples, 2:278a
  dolce stil nuovo and, 6:648b–649a
  education of, 3:397a
  friendship with Dante, 3:397b
  Henry VII and, 3:397b
  influence of on Bartolo da Sassoferrato, 2:115a, 115b
  legal commentaries of, 3:397b, 7:515b
  vernacular love poetry, 3:397b–398a
Cinque Ports, 4:90b, 9:81b
  "compositions," 11:617a
  ship keels supplied to king by, 11:240b–241a
Cinquedea, 11:550b (*illus.*), 551a-b
Ciompi
  abolition of, 11:714b
  Black Death and, 2:266a
  revolt of, 5:99b–100a, 11:714b
  see also Florence; Guilds and métiers
Cipangu. *See* Japan
Ciprianus, St. *See* Cyprian, St.
Ciranawor, 1:601a
Circa instans. See Platearius, Matthaeus
"Circassian regime," 8:71a
Circassians, **3:398a–400b**
  dominance of Mamluk society, 3:399a, 399b–400a
  in Mamluk army, 2:113a-b, 3:398b, 8:68b
  Mamluk dynasty and, 8:71a, 74b–75a
  origins, 3:398a
  Red Sea trade and, 11:247a
  Sultan Barqūq and, 3:398b
Circuli quadratura, 1:437a-b, 8:210b
Circumcision
  female, 3:401a
  Islamic, **3:400b–401a**
    age at, 3:400b–401a
    methods, 3:400b
    rules governing, 3:400b
    see also Feasts and festivals, Islamic
  Jewish, **3:401a–402a**
    ceremony of, 3:401a-b
    derivation of, 3:401a
    in Islamic Jewish communities, 3:401a
    medieval innovations, 3:401b
    naming of child and, 3:401b
    poems for, 3:401b
    ritual impurity of mother, 3:401b
Circus Flaminius, 10:521b
Circus parties. *See* Demes
C^{c}irk^{c}oli, church at, 5:409a
Cirta, Vandals and, 12:354b
Cirugia. See Peter of Ulm
Cisiojanus, 3:21a-b
Cisjurane Burgundy. *See* Burgundy, kingdom of
Cisne, Caballero del, 11:416a
Cistercian chant, **3:402a–403a**
  Milanese influence, 3:402a, 406a-b
  musical treatises and, 8:642b–643a
  principle of authenticity, 3:402a
  revised melodies, 3:402b–403a
  revision of liturgical books, 3:402b
  survival into 17th century, 3:403a
Cistercian order, **3:403a–406a**
  architecture. *See* Church architecture, Cistercian; Romanesque architecture
  Benedictines and, 2:174b
  in Burgundy, 2:428a
  in Byzantine Empire, 7:348a
  calendar and, 3:20a
  Cistercians of the Strict Observance (Trappists), 3:403a
  Cluniac order and, 3:471a
  Conceptualists and, 12:688b
  decline of, 3:405b
  economic activities, 3:404a
  educational reforms, 3:405a
  Ethelred of Rievaulx and, 4:516b–517a
  exemption from tithe payments, 12:65a
  Exordium Cistercii, 10:287a
  Exordium parvum, 10:287a
  expansion of, 3:403b
  foundation of, 3:403a-b
  Gilbertine rite and, 5:528a
  idea of monastic reform and, 10:286b–287a
  in Ireland, 6:517a, 8:55a
  Latin literature and, 7:364a, 366b
  lay brothers in, 3:404a
  library of, 7:562b
  liturgical rite, 3:406a-b
  manuscript book production and, 8:102a, 102b
  monasteries of, 3:403b, 8:455b
  monastic reform and, 3:403a
  pioneers in undeveloped areas, 3:404a
  preaching churches, London, 7:663b
  Premonstratensians and, 10:86a
  Raimon de Cornet and, 10:251a
  reasons for formation, 6:68b
  rhymed offices and, 10:370b
  in royal and ecclesiasatical administrations, 3:405a-b
  Sapaudian foundations, 10:675b
  satirized, 7:366b
  Savigniac union, 10:673a
  scholarship in, 3:404b–405a
    Hebrew language study, 3:313b
  Sergius of Radonezh and, 11:209a
  severity of rule, 3:403a
  supported by Rhys of Deheubarth, 10:378a
  Tintern Abbey and, 12:60b
  tonary of, 12:71a
  Vulgate and, 2:213a-b
  Welsh settlement, 12:517a
  women mystics and, 9:11b
  women's orders and, 12:686a-b
  see also Bernard of Clairvaux, St.; Bible, Cistercian; Birgitta, St.; Harding, Stephen, St.
Cistercian rite, **3:406a-b**
  Premonstratensian rite and, 10:83b–84a
Cita et vera divisio monochordi in diatonico genere, 8:640a
Cîteaux, 3:355a, 403b
  abbey church, 10:483b
  Bernard of Clairvaux and, 2:190b
  founding of, 6:213b
  wine and, 12:650a
Cîteaux Bible, 2:213b, 218a
Cithara, 8:558a, 558b, 559a, 600b, 606a
  Greeks and, 8:601a
Cithara anglica. See Harp
Cithara teutonica. See Lyre
Cities, imperial. *See* Germany, towns; Holy Roman Empire
Citizens
  class differences, 3:417a
  feudal order and, 3:416a–417a
  Islamic. *See A^{c}yān*
  Italian, podesta and, 9:711a–712a
  marriage and, 4:145b–146a
  Roman, 10:461a-b
    client states and, 10:466a
  status of
    in bastides, 2:129b
    in Cyprus, 4:72a-b
  subdivisions among, 3:422a–423b
  see also "Collective seigneurial" status
Citizenship. *See* Political theory; Representative assemblies; Suffrage
Citole, 8:602 (*illus.*), 608a
Citrus, cultivation of, 1:87a
Cittadella, founding of, 12:325b
City. *See* Urbanism
City dwellers. *See* Citizens; Towns; Urbanism
City of God. See Augustine of Hippo, St.
City planning. *See* Urban planning
City-state
  authority of, defined by Bartolo da Sassoferrato, 2:115b
  see also Communes; Towns
Ciuffagni, Bernardo, **3:406b–407a**
Civadier (grain measure), 12:588b
Civadier (land measure), 12:588b
Civic music. *See* Town bands
Cividale, siege of (1331), 3:64a-b
Civil trespass. *See* Trespass
Civitas
  in Carolingian Empire, 3:107b
  in commune, 3:493b
  in Germany, 5:483b
  villages and, 12:442b
Civitavecchia, Rome and, 10:526a
Ciwnkert, 11:599a
Clairmarais, plans for, 5:391b
Clairvaux Abbey, 10:483b
  foundation, 10:478b
  water-operated machines, 11:656b–657a
Clamanges, Nicholas of. *See* Nicholas of Clamanges
Clan. *See* Extended family
Clandestine marriage. *See* Marriage, secret
Clann Sínaigh
  Armagh and, 1:470a
  Ó Brolcháin and, 9:203b
Clanranald, Black and Red Books of, 11:115b, 116a-b
Clans, Scottish, **3:407a-b**
  cattle raiding, 3:407b
  definition of, 3:407a

Clans, Scottish (*cont.*)
feuds, 3:407b
territorial aspects of, 3:407b
Clanvowe, Sir John, **3:408a-b**
at court of Richard II, 3:408a
biography, 3:408a
Boke of Cupide, 3:408a-b
Two Ways, 3:408b
Clanvowe, Sir Thomas, *Cuckoo and the Nightingale,* 8:316a
Clappers, 8:605a (*illus.*)
Clare, Gilbert, Caerphilly castle, 12:521b
Clare, Richard Fitzgilbert de, 6:517b
Clare, St., foundation of Poor Clares, 12:688a
Clarenbaud of Arras, 9:702a
vs. Gilbert of Poitiers's theology school, 12:21b
Clarence. *See* George, duke of Clarence
Clarendon, Assize of, **3:408b–409b,** 7:44a, 442a
accusation procedures, 7:182a-b
administration of criminal justice and, 3:408b–409a
grand jury, 3:409a
inquest and, 6:481a
juries, outlawry cases, 9:311a
novel disseisin, 3:409a
Clarendon, Constitutions of, 1:596a, 2:151b–152a, **3:409b–410b**
circumstances surrounding, 3:409b
compurgation and, 3:508b
definition of church-state relations, 4:471a, 6:157b
development of English common law and, 7:439a
election of bishops, 4:422b–423a
inquest and, 6:481a
praemunire and, 10:67b
purpose of, 3:409b
utrum, 9:546a-b
Clarendon, Council of (1164), 2:151b
Clári saga. See Klári saga
Clarion, 8:603b
Claris (romance character). *See* Floris
Clarisses. *See* Poor Clares
Class structure, Armenian, 1:488a–491a
Class structure, Byzantine
costume and, 3:614b
taxation and, 11:604b
Class structure, Iranian, 10:663b
Armenia and, 1:488a-b, 489a, 489b
social mobility, 10:663b
Class structure, Islamic
costume and, 3:618a
in Ottoman Empire, 9:309a-b
Class structure, Jewish, costumes and, 3:620a-b
Class structure, Russian
in Novgorod, 9:194b–195a
see also Muscovy, rise of
Class structure, Western European
artisans, 8:173a–174b
in Bohemia-Moravia, 2:302a
conflict within, 3:428a–429a
costume and, 3:621b–622a
in Cyprus, 4:72a-b
defined, 3:410b, 421b
development
1000–1300, **3:410b–419a**
1300–1500, **3:419a–429b**
to 1000. *See* Feudalism
distribution of wealth, 7:9a, 666a, 683b
Italy, 11:683b
effects of Black Death and, 2:265b–266a
emergence of lay aristocracy and, 8:27b–28a
in England
London, 7:664b, 666a
Robin Hood and, 10:436b
see also Thegn
in France
bourgeoisie, 10:318b
estates concept and, 10:316a, 317a-b, 318b, 324b, 325b
Jacquerie and, 9:478b
Languedoc, 7:339a-b
Lyons, 7:698b
Germanic, law codes and, 7:475b
in Germany
imperial knights, 5:497a–498b
Lübeck, 7:682b–683a
representative assemblies and, 10:328a–329b, 332a–334a
Saxony, 10:682b–683a
housing, 10:533a
income distribution, 8:174a-b
Irish, 6:553a-b
in Italy, 7:9a-b, 16a-b
podesta and, 9:711a–712a
signori, 9:711b
land reclamation and, 10:276a, 278a–279a
literacy and, 12:140b
merchants and, 12:149b, 162a
middle class and, 12:160a
ministerials, 8:404a–406b
in Norway, 9:181b–182b
parodied in Renard the Fox stories, 10:312b–314b
plagues and, 9:678a–679b, 685b–686a
population and, 4:142b–144a
Praeloquia conduct guide, 10:260b
as reflected in seals, 11:129a–130a
rise of bourgeoisie, 7:668b
Roman, 10:461a-b, 465b
in Scandinavia, as described in *Rígsþula,* 10:400a-b
in Sicily, 11:276a
sumptuary rules reflecting, 3:583a
in Sweden, 11:531b
textile workers, 11:715a
in towns, *see also* Patrician, urban
urbanization and, 3:416a-b
in Walachia/Moldavia, 12:505b–506a
witchcraft and, 12:663b–664a
in Zurich, 11:542b
see also Knights and knight service; Nobility and nobles; Representative assemblies; Serfs and serfdom, Western Europe; Sumptuary laws, European
Classe, port of, mosaic representations of, 10:263b
Classical Armenian language. *See* Armenian language
Classical Latin language. *See* Latin language
Classical literary studies, **3:430a–436b**
advocated by Bernat Metge, 8:300b
Alexander Neckham and, 9:92a
Arab world, 9:699a–700a
at Alexandria, 3:430a-b
at Chartres, 3:433b–434a
at Orléans, 3:434a
atticism and, 3:430b
of Bede, 3:432b
Bernard of Chartres and, 2:190a
Boccaccio's *Genealogy of the Pagan Gods,* 2:283a-b
Byzantine, 3:431a–432a, 9:696a–699a
Suda and, 11:501b–502a
translation and translators, 12:126a–127a
in Carolingian Empire, 3:432b–433b
of Chaucer, 3:280a
Christianity and, 10:462b
Clement of Alexandria and, 3:430b
defense of, 9:696a-b
development in 9th-15th centuries, 3:431a–436a
in early church, 3:430a-b
elementary, 7:352b–353a
England, 12th-century renaissance, 4:471b
of Erasmus, 3:436a
grammar in, 3:432b–433a
Greek learning, in Italian Renaissance, 7:1b–2a
of Hildebert of Lavardin, 6:226b
Homeric, Bardas University, 10:307a
hymns and, 6:383b
influence of
on Chrétien de Troyes, 5:250a-b
decline in, 5:255b–256a
on Marie de France, 5:249a
Italy, Byzantine influence, 7:1a-b
Jewish, 9:700a-b
of John of Salisbury, 3:434a-b
Latin epic poetry, 4:495b–496a
in Latin West, 3:432a-b, 432b–434a
manuscript copies of classical writers, 8:102b
mirror of princes, 8:434a–436a
Neoplatonism and, 9:696a–698a, 699b–700a, 702b, 703a-b
Origen and, 3:430b
of Petrarch, 3:435a-b, 9:534b–535b, 538a
Roman triumphal processions, 9:540b
tradition of, 3:430a
translations in, 3:432a-b, 434a-b, 12:141a
see also Alberic of Monte Cassino; Aristotelianism; Greek literature; Latin drama; Latin literature; Ovid; Plato and Platonism; Translation and translators; Vergil
Classicism in architecture, Coptic, 3:585b, 588a-b
Classicism in art
Coptic sculpture, 3:587a-b
early Christian adaptations, 4:348a, 348b, 349a
influence of, 9:669b–670 (*illus.*)
"pagan revival" of 5th century, 4:350b–351a
persistence of in Byzantine art, 4:353b

survival of, 4:362b, 363b
"Theodosian revival," 4:352a
under Heraklios, 4:353a
under Justinian, 4:353a
see also Antiquarianism; Art, renaissances and revivals
Claude de Beauffremont, on the French monarchy, 10:316b
Claudian (*ca.* 400)
De raptu Proserpinae, 7:360b
In Rufinum, 1:182a, 183a
Phoenix, 7:360b
Claudius Clemens. *See* Clemens Scotus
Claudius of Turin, **3:436b–437a,** 4:542b, 7:146b
Claus de Werve. *See* Werve, Claus de
Clausula, 1:546a-b, **3:437a-b**
in Bamberg MS, 2:68b
definition of, 3:437a-b
in *Magnus liber organi,* 7:549b, 8:44a
modal notation and, 8:621 (*illus.*), 622a
Notre Dame school and, 9:191b
polyphonic, origins of, 9:507a
in "Viderunt omnes," 12:411a
works in MS. Pluteus 29.1, 5:104b–105b
see also Melisma; Perotinus
Clauwaerts, 2:387a-b, 5:522b
revolt of, 11:713b
Clavecin. See Harpsichord
Clavi (strips on liturgical vestments), 12:398a, 399a, 400a
Clavicembalo. See Harpsichord
Clavichord, 8:608b
Clavicytherium, 8:608b
Clavijo. *See* González de Clavijo, Ruy
Claymore swords. *See* Swords
Cleanness, 4:547a, 8:319b, 320a
in Cotton Nero MS, 9:476a
Cleansing, magical, 8:34a
Clef, **3:438a**
Clef d'amour, 1:189a
Clemence of Barking, *Life of St. Catherine,* 1:261b
Clemens Scotus, **3:438a-b**
Clement (9th-century disciple of Cyril and Methodios), 9:208b, 209a
Clement I, pope
depicted in Aarhus Cathedral altarpiece, 9:186b (*illus.*)
initiator of claim for apostolic succession, 1:350b
relics of, 4:73b
Clement II, pope
appointment of, 3:348b
Synod of Rome and, 11:517a
Clement III (Guibert of Ravenna), antipope, 3:635a, 4:165b
coronation of Henry IV of Germany, 6:163b
investiture conflict and, 6:499b
vs. Urban II, 11:606b
Clement III, pope
Innocent III and, 6:464a
Order of Grandmont and, 5:655a
Premonstratensians and, 10:86b
Roman commune and, 9:385a, 10:523b
Clement IV, pope
approval of Dominican rite, 4:242a
Charles of Anjou and, 4:60b
church taxation and, 11:607b
Dominican women's orders and, 4:254b, 12:687b
Roger Bacon and, 2:35a, 37b
William II and, 7:379a
Clement V, pope, **3:438b–439a,** 3:643b–644b
annate and, 11:606b
appointment of cardinals, 3:94b
Arnald of Villanova and, 1:538a
attempt to return to Rome, 9:555a
church finance and, 11:610a
Constitutiones Clementinae, 7:417a, 428a, 11:691b
Council of Vienne and, 3:438b
Dante and, 4:99b
death of, 3:349a
ecclesiastical benefices and, 2:179b
education of, 3:438b
educational interests, 3:439a
Edward I of England and, 9:425b, 11:608a
election of, 3:362a, 438b
Exivi de paradiso, 9:515a
Fidei catholicae fundamento, Peter John Olivi's views and, 9:515b
Franciscans and, 5:202b, 9:515a
Henry VII and, 4:102a
on heresy of the Free Spirit, 5:217b
inquisition and, 6:487b
move to Avignon, 2:15b–16a
Ne Romani, 3:524a
nepotism and, 3:363a
Nogaret and, 9:152a
pro-French policies, 3:362a, 438b
religious life of, 3:438b
Rex gloriae, 2:324a
slave trade and, 11:339a
Templars and, 3:304b, 362a
University of Montpellier and, 11:692a
Clement VI, pope, **3:439a–440a**
Black Death and, 2:265a, 3:439b
number of plague victims calculated, 2:264a
Bologna revolt and, 3:439b
calendar reform and, 3:23a
Cola di Rienzo's removal, 3:478b–479a
crusade preaching of, 4:20b–21a
extravagances of, 3:363a, 439a-b
Hundred Years War and, 3:439b
Jews and, 3:439b
bull protecting, 2:263b
Licet in consuetudine, 3:524a
Nicholas of Autrecourt and, 9:122a
"Petre Clemens/Lugentium" and, 12:482b
Philippe de Vitry and, 12:481a
on *plenitudo potestatis,* 9:709b
successors of, 3:363a
suppression of flagellants, 2:263a, 3:439b, 5:77a
Unigenitus Dei filius, 6:446b–447a
Clement VII, pope
Charles V of France and, 3:270a
election of, 3:95b, 365a, 11:39b
first Avignonese pope, 3:365a-b
in Great Schism, 11:40a
Clement VIII, pope, Jews and, 7:109a
Clement of Alexandria, St.
on appropriate forms of art, 4:349a-b
Cassiodorus and, 8:637b–638a
Christmas celebration and, 3:317b
as church father, 3:335b
classical literary studies and, 3:430b
Docetism and, 4:233a
on liturgy, 7:625b
Paidagogos, 7:315a
on *Physiologus,* 2:203b
Clement of Ireland, St. *See* Clemens Scotus
Clement of Llanthony, *Unum ex quattuor,* 4:547b
Clement of Ochrid, 11:345b
Clement of Rome, St. *See* Clement I, pope
Clement Scottus. *See* Clemens Scotus
Cléomadès. See Adenet le Roi
Cleonides, 8:636b
Introductio harmonico, 8:566a
Cleph, Lombard king, 7:656a
death of, 8:376b
Clepsydra. *See* Clocks, water
Clerecía poets. See *Mester de clerecía* poets
Clerestory, **3:440a,** 3:440b (*illus.*)
in Auvergnat Romanesque architecture, 10:480b
of Canterbury Cathedral (detail), 4:67b (*illus.*)
passage, 10:482b, 484a
in priory church of St. Étienne, 10:480a
triforium and, 12:188b
Clergie
in French literature, 5:243b, 244b, 270a
in *Grandes chroniques,* 5:260a-b
in works of Marie and Chrétien, 5:248b, 249b–250a, 250b
Clergy, **3:440a–446a**
admission to, 3:443a–444b
Albanian (Caucasian), 1:503a
apostolic succession of, 1:350a–351a
archives and, 1:445b
Armenian
hierarchy of, 1:502b–503a
as social element, 1:488b, 489b
beguines and, 2:159a
beguins and, 2:163a
Burgundian, Concordat of Worms and, 12:697a
Byzantine, **3:446a–447b**
celibacy of, 3:446a
development of, 3:446a
inheritance and, 6:451a
lower clergy, 3:447a
marriage of, 3:446a
office of patriarch and, 9:459b
patriarchates, 3:446b–447a
Petrine foundation and, 3:446b
recognition of by Chalcedon Council, 3:445b
regional primacies, 3:446a-b
social obligations of, 3:447a-b
see also Archimandrite; Literacy, Byzantine; Permanent synod; *Synkellos*
in Carolingian Empire, 3:109b
Catalan, Pedro III and, 11:609b

Clergy (*cont.*)
celibacy of. *See* Celibacy, clerical
in Celtic church, 3:227b
chaplain, 3:264a-b
clerk, 3:448b
costume of, sandal, 11:254b
degradation of, **4:133a–134b**
Becket and, 2:151b, 152a
causes for, 4:133b
procedure of, 4:134a
see also Reform, idea of
degrees of, 3:441a-b
development of, 3:440b–441a
Divine Office and, 4:221b–231a
in early church, 3:340b–341a
education of
as children, 10:301a
Fourth Council of Toledo and, 6:563b
Hrabanus Maurus and, 6:306b, 307a
English
at Cambridge University, 3:59b
at Canterbury, 3:82b–83b
Honorius III and, 11:607a
Innocent IV and, 6:467a, 11:606b
Lanfranc's reforms, 4:466a
rights of, 3:409b–410a, 9:547a, 548a
royal duties, 4:464a
satirized, 7:370a
excommunication and, 4:536b
in First Crusade, 4:34a
Frankish
False Decretals and, 4:125b
in Moravia, 4:73b–74a
French
in 13th century, 5:181a-b
Innocent IV and, 6:466b–467a
reform synod (1049), 4:421b
Rouen, 4:519b
social class of, 5:181a
functions of, 3:444b
German
as authors, 8:350b
Concordat of Worms and, 12:697a
hierarchical ranks of, 3:441a-b
historiography, 12:554b
Iberian, 1:503a
indulgences and, 6:449b
interdictions of, 3:444b–445a
interstices, 3:442b–443a
Irish, as parliamentary proctors, 9:435b, 436a
irregularities of, 3:444a-b
Italian, Concordat of Worms and, 12:697a
in judicial proceedings, 6:465a
liturgical seating for, 5:317a-b
major orders of, 3:442a-b
marriage of, 3:215a-b, 216a, 443b, 4:609a,b, 610a, 611b
reform papacy and, 6:499a
Sigebert and, 11:285a
in York tractates, 12:730a
see also Nicolaitism
military service, 12:558a
minor orders of, 3:441a, 442a
mystery plays and, 8:661b
Norwegian, national unification and, 9:183b
Novgorodian, 9:194b
obligations of, 3:444b–445a
ordination of, 3:441b–442b
origin of term, 3:440a-b
papal jurisdiction over, *plenitudo potestatis,* 9:708a–710a
penalties for misbehavior, 4:133b
poetry by, 3:140a
preaching and sermon literature, 10:75b–76a
privileges of, 3:445a-b
protection under feudalism, 5:55a-b
reorganization of in 9th century, 3:374b–375a
representative assemblies of. *See* Representative assemblies
rights of
Benedictus Levita on, 2:178b–179a
in England, 2:151b, 152a
in Hungary, 6:341b–342a
Nigel of Longchamp and, 9:131a
Roman
in development of college of cardinals, 3:93b–94a
lay nobility and, 10:522a, 524b
as royal administrators, 3:251b–254a, 6:300a, 300b
salaries of, corruption and, 10:285b, 288a
satirized
by Protestants, 7:371a
in Renard the Fox stories, 10:312b–314b
serfdom and, 11:201b, 206b
as social class, 3:417a–418a, 421b–422a
sumptuary laws and, 11:507a-b
as syndics, 11:558a
taxation of, 3:447b, 640b, 4:61b
annates, 11:616b
by papal order, 11:614b, 616b
clerical tenth, 11:615a, 621b, 624a
France, 9:554a
Innocent III and, 6:464b
rejection of, 3:640a
unauthorized, 6:495b
valuations, 11:614b
visitation and service taxes, 11:616b
titles of, 3:444b
in villages, 12:442a
women, as Waldensian priests, 12:512b–513a
Wyclif on, 6:366b, 12:708b
see also Papacy, origins and development of; Reform, idea of; Religious instruction; Schools, monastic; Vestments, liturgical
Clerical chronicles, 3:326a–327a
Clericis laicos. See Boniface VIII, pope
Clerics. *See* Clergy
Clerk, **3:448b–449a**
change in role of, 3:448b
definition of, 3:448b
jongleurs and, 12:161a
privileges of, 3:445a-b
tests for, 3:448b
travels of, 12:160b–161b
Clermont, Council of (1095), **3:449a–450a**, 3:635b, 12:303b–304a
appeal to recover Holy Sepulcher, 3:449b
Fulcher of Chartres' report on, 5:311a
indulgences and, 6:448b
Office of the Blessed Virgin Mary and, 2:274a
Peace and Truce of God and, 9:474b
reform legislation issued at, 3:449b
Urban II and, 3:449a-b, 12:303b–304a
Clermont, Council of (1130), on the practice of medicine, 8:256b
Clermont family, in Carolingian legends, 8:225a-b
Clermont poems, 5:234a
Passion of Ruggieri and, 6:657a
Clermont-Ferrand Cathedral, 7:54a
crypt, Aléaume and, 1:144b
Cletorologion. *See* Philotheos (*fl. ca.* 900), *Kleterologion*
Clibanarii, 3:200b
in European cavalry, 3:200b
in Parthian army, 9:444a
Clientage
Roman, 10:466a-b
see also Citizens, Roman
under al-Manṣūr, 8:89a-b
see also Feudalism
Cligés. See Chrétien de Troyes
Climacus, 8:619 (*illus.*), 625 (*illus.*)
Climate, volcanoes and, 10:456b–457a
Climatology, **3:450a–457a**
"big optimum," 3:453a
carbon-14 dating in, 3:453b
chronology of European weather, 3:455b–456a
climate shifts, 3:452b–453a
in 12th century, 3:454b–455a
in 16th century, 3:455b
climatic zones
frigid northern, 3:451b, 452b
Mediterranean, 3:451b–452a
middle temperate, 3:451b–452b
dendrochronology in, 3:450b–451a
European, land reclamation and, 10:272b–273a
grain crops and climate, in Western Europe, 5:647a-b
importance of, 3:450a-b, 456b
"little optimum," 3:454a–455b, 4:140b
medieval theories, 5:396a
phenology in, 3:451a-b
pollen counts, 3:451b, 453b–454a
rural society and, 3:456a-b
see also Famine
Climax of Paradise. See John Klimakos, St.
Clinis. See Clivis
Clipeus (*clipeatus*), **3:457a**
Clito, William, 3:497a
rule of Flanders, 7:673b–674a
Clivis, 8:619 (*illus.*), 624b, 625 (*illus.*), 629a
"Cloak, The," 7:317b
Clock of Wisdom. See Suso, Heinrich, *Horologium sapientiae*
Clocks, **3:457a–464b**, 11:654 (*illus.*)
anaphoric, 3:457b–458a
astronomical, 11:644b
at Lulon and Constantinople, 10:425a

changing conception of magic and, 8:39a
in churches, 5:321a
clockmaking, 3:463a–464a
coiled steel springs, 11:658b
crossbow production and, 11:658a-b
earliest weight-driven, 3:29a-b
fusee, 3:29b
Islamic, 11:87b
manufacture of scientific instruments and, 11:103a-b
mechanical, 3:459a-b, 461 (*illus.*), 463a, 11:664a
at Norwich Cathedral, 3:460b–461a
deterrents to, 3:463a
development of, 3:459a-b
escapements, 11:652b
first, in Europe, 3:460a
illustration of, 3:459b, 461a (*illus.*)
with months and phases of moon, 3:463a (*illus.*)
musical notation and, 8:622b
origin of, 3:460a-b
public, 3:460b
treatises on, 11:644b
metalworking for, 3:463b
planetary machines, 3:461b–462a, 464b–465a
Richard of Wallingford's, 10:388a
portable, 3:462a–464a, 464a
public, 3:29b, 460b
reckoning of time and, 3:24a-b
sandglass, 11:652b
skills required for making, 11:658a
spring-powered chamber clock, 3:462a-b
water, 11:642a, 652b
automata in, 3:28a
construction of, 3:458b
early use of, 3:457a–458a
European, 3:458a-b
fires and, 3:458a
irrigation and, 6:556b
Islamic, 3:28a
of al-Jazarī, 3:458a (*illus.*)
market for, 3:458b–459a
mechanisms of, 3:28a
monastic, 3:458b–459a (*illus.*), 459b–460a
parastatic, 3:28a
prestige of, 3:27b
treatises, 11:641a-b
Vitruvius on, 3:28a
weight-driven, 11:652a-b, 658a-b
see also Sundials; Time glasses
Clockwork, planetary, **3:464b–465a**
Cloisonné enamel. *See* Enamel, cloisonné
Cloister, **3:465a-b**
Clonard, **3:465b–466a**
abbeys at, 3:466a
decline of, 3:466a
fires at, 3:466a
founding of, 3:465b
in Irish church controversy, 3:465b–466a
prominence of, 3:465b
pupils at, 3:465b
Clonmacnoise (monastery), 6:521a, 521b, 554a
Clontarf, Battle of (1014), 4:106a,b, 6:516b, 553a, 12:425b
in *Darraðarljóð*, 9:172a
Valkyries in, 12:351a
Clos de Vougeot, winepresses of, 12:653b
Clotaire, Frankish king. *See* Chlothar II, Frankish king
Cloth. *See* Textiles
Cloth hall, in Ypres, 5:583 (*illus.*), 587a
Cloth of St. Gereon (tapestry), 11:593a
Clothar, Frankish king. *See* Chlothar II, Frankish king
Clothing. *See* Costume
Cloud of Unknowing, 3:368b, 8:317b, 9:18a, 19a, 19b, 22a–23a
criticism of Richard Rolle in, 9:20b
six cognate treatises of, 9:22a, 22b–23a
Walter Hilton and, 9:23a, 23b
Clove (measure), **3:466b**
Clovesho, Council of (747), Divine Office and, 4:230a
Clovis, Frankish king, 2:94a-b, **3:466b–467b**, 8:277b–278a
acceptance of Roman Catholicism, 2:94b
Alamanni and, 1:117a-b, 3:466b–467a, 11:526a
Arianism and, 1:454b
baptism of, 2:147a, 3:243b, 8:277b, 439a
Burgundian unrest and, 2:423a
conversion of the Franks, 3:344a
expansion of kingdom, 3:466b
founding of empire, 3:104a
justifications for legitimacy of, 4:158a
law code of, 3:467a-b, 7:471b–472a
reconciliation of Gallo-Roman and Germanic subjects, 3:467a
role in church affairs, 467a
seal ring of, 11:125a
successors of, 3:467b
title of patrician and, 9:460a
vs. Visigoths, 3:467a, 7:339a
Cloyne (monastery)
founded, 6:526a
literary activity of, 6:540b
Cluain-Iraird. *See* Clonard
Cluniac order, **3:468b–471b**
abbeys of, 3:469b–470a
All Souls' Day and, 1:177a
in Asturias-León, 1:628b
charter for, 3:468b–469a
church reform and, 3:347b–348a, 470b, 4:374a-b
in Burgundy, 2:428a
Cistercians and, 3:471a-b, 9:524a
customs of, 12:639b
decline of, 3:469a-b, 471a-b
domestic architecture, Romanesque, 10:489b
First Crusade and, 3:356b, 470b
founded, 2:170b
Gorze and, 5:578b
Hirsau movement, 6:231a-b
holy abbots of Cluny, 9:524a
Hugh of Semur and, 6:318b
influence of, 3:468b–469a
internal organization of, 3:469b–470a
in the kingdom of Navarre, 9:69a
Lambert and, 7:321a,b
last rites in, 4:120b–121a
library of, 7:562b–563a
manuscript book production and, 8:102a
monastic independence and networking of, 10:286a-b
monastic reform and, 10:286a-b, 12:154a, 155b
Muslims and, abbot kidnapped for ransom, 12:153a
nature of spirituality, 3:470b
origins of, 3:468b
papacy and, 3:470a-b
in art, 10:507a
Peace of God and, 3:470b
pilgrimage and, 9:656a-b, 10:280a
propaganda by, 10:139b
the Reconquest and, 10:280a
reforms
of Odilo, 9:217b
of Odo, 9:220a
Romanesque sculpture and, 10:495a-b
size of, 2:173a
as social movement, 3:470b–471a
Spanish rulers and, 3:470b
success of, 3:469a
wine and, 12:650a
women's orders and, 12:684b–685a
year 1000 and, 12:723b
Cluniac rite, **3:467b–468a**
knowlege of, 3:467b
liturgy of, 3:467b, 468a
masses in, 3:467b
processions in, 3:467b–468a
psalms in, 3:467b
Cluny Abbey
management of, 2:174b
Peter Damian on, 2:172b
Cluny, Abbey Church, **3:468a-b**
building of, 3:468a-b
capitals, 10:490b
Cluny II, 2:175a, 10:479a
German Romanesque architecture, 10:487b
Swiss Romanesque architecture, 10:488b
Cluny III, 10:479 (*illus.*)
dedication of, 1:426b
Monte Cassino and, 10:486a
ogival arches, 11:656a
sculpture, 10:495a-b, 496b (*illus.*)
construction and design, 6:221a
destruction of, 3:468a
Hugh of Semur and, 6:318b
influence of, 10:478b
serfdom and, 11:203a-b
Cnut I (the Great) of Denmark, king, **3:471b–472a**, 4:151b–152a, 153a, 12:434a
consolidation of power of, 3:471b
death of, 3:472a
domination of Baltic by, 5:632b
journey to Rome, 3:472a
Knýtlinga saga and, 7:281a
Latin church and, 3:472a, 8:442a
law and, 3:472a
heriot, 6:207b
Malcolm II of Scotland and, 8:56a
naval empire of, 9:79b
pilgrimage to Rome, 12:151a

Cnut I (the Great) of Denmark, king (*cont.*)
prevented from passing under the London Bridge, 10:411b
rule of England, 4:457a, 457b
Witherlogh and, 11:522a
Wulfstan of York and, 12:704a
Cnut II (the Holy) of Denmark, king, *Knýtlinga saga* and, 9:177b
Cnut IV of Denmark, king, 4:152b, 11:522a
Cnut VI of Denmark, king, 4:153b, 154a
Cnut Lavard. *See* Knud Lavard
Cnut, St. *See* Cnut II (the Holy) of Denmark, king
Coal
mining and use of, **3:472b–473b**
see also Steelmaking
records of, 3:472
sea, 3:473a
sources of, 3:472b–473a
Coats of arms
kingdom of Jerusalem, 6:172b
origin, 6:172b
rules of composition, 6:172b
see also Heraldry
Cobalt oxide, in Lajvard, 7:319b
Coblas capfinidas/doblas/unissonans. See Troubadours
Coblenz Bridge
asymmetry of, 10:421b
indulgences issued for, 10:414b
Cocas, 11:236a
Coccus cacti. See Cochineal
Coccus ilicis. See Grain (dye); Qirmiz
Coche, 11:236a
Cochineal, 11:595b, 12:445b
Cock in the North, The. See Thomas of Erceldoune
"Cocked hat" pommel. *See* Swords, pommels
Cockfights, 5:350b
Cod (*Gadus morhua*), fishing of, 5:71b–72a
Códax, Martín, 5:341b
cantigas of, 3:86a
Coddus (unit of measure), 12:584a
Code of chivalry. *See* Chivalry
Codex, **3:473b–474b**
classical education and, 10:462b
development of, 3:473b–474a
earliest Hebrew (894 or 895), 8:118b
intellectual transformation caused by, 3:474b
introduction of, 4:355b
Islamic bookbinding and, 8:98a
pocketbooks, 9:711a
quire binding of, 10:240a
spread of Christianity and, 3:474b
Western European literacy and, 7:598a
see also Libraries; Manuscript books, binding of (European); Manuscript books, production of; Manuscript illumination; Mχitᑦar Goš; Rabula Gospels
Codex Ambrosianus, carpet page decoration, 3:219a
Codex Amiatinus, 12:700a
Ark of the Covenant in, 1:469a-b
library depiction in, 7:567b
as a model for the Lindisfarne Gospels, 7:584a
Codex Argenteus, 1:212b
Codex Arnamagnaean, 11:326b
Codex Aureus, **3:474b**, 3:474b (*illus.*), 8:106b, 107a (*illus.*), 10:103a-b, 105a-b
decorated initials in, 6:462b
Codex Aureus aus St. Emmeram in Regensburg. See Liuthard
Codex Aureus Epternacensis, 10:102b, 104b
Codex Barberinus, 1:516b
Codex Buranus, 1:319a, 7:368b
see also Carmina Burana
Codex Calixtinus (Liber Sancti Jacobi), 8:558b
hymns in, 6:382a
pilgrim's guide in, 9:661b, 662 (*illus.*)
polyphonic compositions in, 9:506b–507a
school of Santiago de Compostela, 10:650b–651a
Codex Egberti, 8:107a
miniature from, 10:102a (*illus.*), 104b
Codex Florentinus, 3:609a
Codex Grandior. *See* Cassiodorus
Codex Gregorianus, 3:608b
Codex Hermogenianus, 3:608b
Codex of Huesca, 3:611b, 7:430a
Codex iuris canonici, 7:417b
Codex Justinianus. *See Corpus iuris civilis*
Codex legum Langobardorum, 10:113a-b
Codex Neapolitanus, illustrations in, 6:178a
Codex Regius, 2:256a, 8:65b, 11:288b, 291a-b, 292a, 326b
contents and location of, 4:385a-b
lost poems, 4:387a
Norna-Gests Þáttr and, 9:171a
order of poems in
heroic poems, 4:386a-b
mythological poems, 4:386b–387a
Sigurðarkviða in skamma in, 11:293a
version of *Grottasǫngr* in, 6:3a
Codex Salernitanus, *De aegritudinum curatione,* 10:213b–214a
Codex Salmasianus, 7:360b
Codex Sinopensis, 8:105b
Codex Theodosianus, **3:475a-b**, 3:608b
compilation of, 3:474a-b
Corpus iuris civilis and, 7:418b
inheritance in, 6:451a
on librarians, 7:560b, 570a
on mule-drawn vehicles, 12:369a-b
on posthumous veneration of relics, 10:297a
on public maintenance of roads and bridges, 10:411a
reliance of Roman state on guilds, 6:14b
status of Jews under, 7:69a, 75b, 85a
Theodosius II and, 12:19b
use of, 3:475a-b
see also Lydus
Codex Usserianus I, 2:220a, 220b
Codex Vatican latini 3793, 11:259b
Codex Vigilianus, miniature of Visigothic bishops, 12:403b (*illus.*)
Codex Wittekindeus, 10:101b
Codice Atlantico. See Leonardo da Vinci
Codicellus multarum litterarum. See Hugo von Trimberg
Codicology, **3:475b–478a**
definition of, 3:475b
gloss, 5:564b–565a
importance of, 3:477a-b
in paleographic classification, 9:338b–339b
in studying book production, 3:476a–477a
in studying cultural history, 3:475b–476a
terminology of, 3:476a
Trent codices, 12:182b–184b
Western European
quire analysis and, 10:240a
see also Block book; Libraries; Manuscript books, binding of; Manuscript books, production of; Manuscripts, Hebrew; Stichometry
Codolades, in Catalan narrative in verse, 3:173a-b
Coelho, Estevam, "Sedia la fremosa seu singo torcendo," 4:190a
Coemptio, 11:603b–604a
Coenae tuae mirabili, Tou deipnou sou and, 8:557a
Coene, Jaques, **3:478a**, 5:628a
Coffee, introduced in the Yemen (15th century), 2:209b
Cofferdams, in bridge-building, 10:420a-b
Cofferer, royal, England, 6:302b, 305a
Cofferers, Guild of, 5:325a
Cog, 9:81b–82b (*illus.*), 11:234 (*illus.*), 236a-b, 239a, 239b
carrack and, 11:237a
development of, 11:241a–242b (*illus.*)
by the Hanseatic League, 9:88b–89a
in the Mediterranean, 9:83b, 88a
modification of, 11:244a-b
as warship, 11:242a
Cogad Gáidel re Gallaib, 6:539b
Cogitosus, hagiographic works on St. Brigit, 2:376b
Cognition, Ockham and, 9:211b, 212a, 212b
Cóhir Anman, 6:531a
Coif
basinet and, 1:526a-b
in Bayeux Tapestry, 1:523a
Coimbra, University of, 12:287a
Coinage. *See* Mints and money
Coirpre, kingdom of, 12:241a
Coislin notation. *See* Musical notation, Coislin
Coke, Humphrey. *See* Cook, Humphrey
Col, Gontier and Pierre, "querelle de la Rose" and, 10:452b
Cola di Rienzo, **3:478a–479a**
biography of, 6:633a, 660a
coup d'état in Rome, 3:478b
declaration as tribune, 9:529a
early life of, 3:478a-b

as founder of modern archaeology, 1:336b
influence of, 3:479a
murder of, 3:479a
policies of, 3:478b
removal by Clement VI, 3:478b–479a
Roman nobles and, 3:478b
Rome and, 10:524a
visions of a regenerated world, 2:34a
Colas, Antoine, Troyes Cathedral and, 1:426a
Colchester
parliamentary burgesses, 9:432a
in 1485, 9:434a-b
Colchis. *See* Georgians
Colección de poesías castellanas anteriores al siglo XV. See Sánchez, Tomás Antonio
Colet, John, Morton and, 3:83b
Colette Corbie, St., 12:688b
Colgan, John, 6:525a
Colin Muset, **3:479a-b**
débat and, 4:122a
lai and, 7:316b
sirventes of, 11:313a
Colin, Philipp, *Neue Parzival,* 5:452b, 12:679b
Collar beam, **3:479b**
Collaterales, 7:372b
Collatio, 10:79b
Collationes. See Cassian, John
Collationes de decem praeceptis. See Bonaventure, St.
Collationes in Hexaëmeron. See Bonaventure, St.
Collationes de septem donis Spiritus Sancti. See Bonaventure, St.
Colle Val d'Elsa, Battle of (1269), 4:96a
Collect, in the liturgy of the Mass, 8:186b–187a, 196b
Collectae. See Liturgy, stational
Collectanea, "On the Fifteen Signs Preceding Judgment Day," 1:111b
Collectarium, **3:479b–480a**
capitula in, 3:480a
Divine Office and, 4:223b
Dominus vobiscum, 8:186b
early, 3:479b
intentions, 8:186b
later, 3:479b–480a
orationes, 8:186b
post-Communion, 8:196b
Orationes super populum, 8:196b–197a
Collectio Andegavensis II, 7:402a-b
Collectio Angelica, 7:409a
Collectio Anselmo dedicata, 7:406a
Collectio Arelatensis, 7:398b
Collectio Britannica, 7:409a-b
Collectio Caesaraugustana, 7:412a
Collectio canonum. See Deusdedit, cardinal
Collectio canonum hibernensis, 3:229a, 7:403a, 484a
analogies with *De duodecim abusivis,* 4:312b
Collectio canonum regesto Farfensi inserta, 7:409a
Collectio Dacheriana, 7:404a
Collectio Dionysiana, 7:399a-b
additions and abbreviations, 7:400a-b
see also Dionysius Exiguus
Collectio Dionysio-Hadriana, 7:403b–404a
see also Dionysius Exiguus
Collectio duorum librorum, 7:404b
Collectio Gratianopolitana "Ricardus mutuam pecuniam accepit," Hugo and, 6:324a
Collectio Herovalliana, 7:402b
Collectio hispana, 7:398a-b, 401a-b
Collectio hispana gallica Augustodunensis, 7:405a
Collectio hispana gallicana, 7:404a
Collectio hispana systematica, 7:404a
Collectio Lanfranci, 7:412a
Collectio Novariensis, 7:401a
Collectio Parisiensis "Mandaui procuratori ut fundum uenderet," Hugo and, 6:324a
Collectio Quesnelliana, 7:399b
Collectio Sanblasiana, 7:400a
Collectio Sangermanensis, 7:402b
Collectio Vaticana, 7:400a
Collectio vetus gallica, 7:402a-b
Collection des anciens alchimistes grecs, 1:135b
Collection in Five Books, 7:408a-b
depictions of bishops wearing miters, 12:404a
Collection of the Fundamental Doctrines of Religion. See Muᵓtaman Abū Isḥāq Ibrāhīm ibn al-ᶜAssāl, al-
Collection of Laon, 7:404b
Collection in Nine Books, 7:406b
penitentials, 9:490b
Collection of Rheims, 7:410b–411a
Collection of Rome Bibl. Vallicelliana Tom. XVIII, 7:406a-b
Collection of St. Amand. See Ordines romani
Collection in Seventy-four Titles, 7:409b
Collection in Three Books, 7:410a-b
Collection of Vatican S. Pietro H 58, 7:406b
"Collective seigneurial" status, 6:334a
Collector. See Hugo von Trimberg, *Samener*
Colleganza. See Commenda
Colleges
development as autonomous communities, 12:291a
early hospices, 12:291a
English, 12:292a
in Cambridge, 12:292a
in Oxford, 12:292a
French, 12:291a-b
administration of, 12:291b
for foreign students, 12:291b
Navarre, 12:291b
in Paris, 12:291a-b
provincial, 12:291b
for regular clergy, 12:291a-b
Sorbonne, 12:291b
German, 12:292b–294a
in Cologne, 12:293a
in Erfurt, 12:293a-b
in Freiburg im Breisgau, 12:293b–294a
in Greifswald, 12:293b
in Heidelberg, 12:293a
in Ingolstadt, 12:293b
in Leipzig, 12:293a
in Prague, 12:292b
in Rostock, 12:293b
uniqueness of, 12:292b
in Vienna, 12:292b
Hungarian, 12:294a-b
Italian, 12:292b
College of Spain, 12:292b
libraries of, 12:298a-b
in the Low Countries, 12:294a
Polish, 12:294a-b
Scottish, 12:292a
Spanish, 12:292a-b
see also Student; Universities
Collegi de l'Horta, 6:558a
Collegio di Spagna, 5:366a (*illus.*)
Collegium, organization and purpose of, 6:14a-b
Collegium Norbertinum, 10:87a
Colletin, 1:530a, 530b, 532a
Colletine Poor Clares, 12:688b
Colliget. See Rushd, Ibn
Colloquies. See Erasmus
Colloquium. See Kingship, holding court
Colloquy. See Aelfric
Colloquy of the Ancients, The. See Acallam na Senórach
Colman of Lindisfarne, bishop, **3:480a-b**
influence of, 7:362b
Synod of Whitby, 12:626a
Colmán mac Lénéni (Léiníne), 6:526a, 537b, 541a-b
Colmar *Liederhandschrift,* 8:358a
Colmar Song Codex, *Wartburgkrieg,* 12:573b
Colobium, **3:480b**
in Crucifixion scenes, 4:13a
Colocasia, growth of, 1:81b
Cologne, **3:480b–482b**
area of, 3:480b–481a
beguines in, 2:160a
bourgeois control in, 3:497b–498a
as center of religious and cultural development, 3:481b–482a
as commune, 5:459b
economy of, 3:481a, 5:458a
first seals of, 11:126a
Frankish invasions of, 3:481a
Geschlechter conflicts in, 3:481b–482a
guilds in, 5:458b
Jews in, 3:482b
joining with Baltic ports (1369), 12:113a
Kronenbursa, 12:293a
manuscript illumination and, 8:107b
merchants in, 3:481a, 482a
miniature painting in, 10:102b
revolt in, 3:481a, 482a, 497b
seal of, 3:497b
studium generale of Albertus Magnus, 1:127b
trade and commerce, trading privileges, 6:91a
Viking destruction of, 3:481a
Cologne, archbishopric
acquisition of Saxon tribal duchy, 10:685b
representative assemblies and, 10:333a
Cologne Cathedral, 5:424a

Cologne Cathedral (*cont.*)
Apostles and Virgin (statues) at, 5:625a
chevet at, 5:631b
completed, 1:428b–429a
Kuene and, 7:305b
Shrine of the Three Kings, 8:496a, 9:127b
Wooden Gero Cross in, 9:447a
Cologne school, soft style of, 5:610b, 627b–628a
Cologne, University of, 12:288a
nominalism and, 9:157b
via moderna and, 12:407b–408a, 408b
Coloman (the Bookman) of Hungary, king
Croatia and, 4:7a, 8a
reign of, 6:340a, 340b
seal of, 11:129b
Colombe, Jean, **3:482a-b**
Trés riches heures, 5:615a-b
Colombe, Michel, **3:482b**
Colonate, 10:460a
Colonia, crusaders' route and, 10:423b
Colonia, Juan de. *See* Juan de Colonia
Colonia, Simon de. *See* Simon de Colonia
Colonization, internal. *See* Reclamation of land
Colonization of land. *See* Reclamation of land
Colonna family, deposed by Boniface VIII, 3:95b
Colonna, Francis, *Dream of Poliphilus,* 4:248a
Colonna, Odo. *See* Martin V, pope
Colonus, **3:482b–483b**, 11:673b
after 7th century, 3:482b–483a
bound, 11:673b–674a
in Byzantine Empire, living conditions, 2:476b
evolution of, 3:483a
lease contract, 11:673b
serfdom and, 11:202a
tenure of land by, 3:483a-b, 11:673b
see also Paroikoi
Colophon, **3:483b–484a**
in Irish manuscripts, 6:523b–524a
"Color" (music), 6:619a, 619b
Colors
liturgical, **3:484a–485a**
in *Leabhar Breac,* 7:614b
Lotario's catalog of, 3:484b–485a
use of, 3:484a-b
see also Vestments, liturgical
restriction on wearing of, 4:327b
sources of, for dyeing textiles, 4:325a–328a
see also individual colors
Columba, St., **3:485a-b**
Altus prosator, 7:362a
attributions to, 6:381a, 525b
bards and, 6:537b
biography of, 1:52b–53a
Celtic church expansion and, 3:226a
Celtic liturgy and, 7:614b
death of, 8:558b
literary works of, 3:485b
in literature, 6:540b
Amra Choluim Chille, 6:541a, 541b
Triadis thaumaturgae acta, 6:525a
missions of, 3:226a-b, 485a-b, 6:516a, 8:369a, 440a
monks of Iona, Christianization of Northumbria, 1:107a
a poem of praise to, 10:405a
wine and, 12:649b
Columbanus, Rule of, 3:230a-b
Regula sancti Benedicti and, 2:170a
Columbanus, St., **3:485b–487a**
Alamanni and, 11:526a
Celtic church expansion and, 3:226a
De saltu lunae, 3:486b
De sollemnitatibus et sabatis et neomeniis, 3:486b
on Divine Office, 3:230b
Easter dating of, 3:228b
education of, 3:486a
expulsion from Gaul, 3:486a
Gall and, 5:342b
hymns of, 7:362a
letters of, 3:486b–487a
missions of, 8:440a
Irish, 6:516a
Lombard, 7:656b
to Alamanni, 1:117b
to the Continent, 9:489b, 489a
monasteries, 3:486a, 12:682b
Penitential of, 9:489a
Regula sancti Benedicti and, 2:170a
writings of, 3:486b
Columbus, Christopher, 4:559b–561a, 9:682a-b
caravels of, 9:89a
Guinea and, 4:562a
influenced by *Mandeville's Travels,* 8:82a
Marco Polo and, 4:557a
support for voyages of, 12:349b
variation of compass and, 3:507a
Columcille, St. *See* Columba, St.
Column, in Gothic cathedral, 5:592b–594b
Column figure, **3:487a**, 3:487b (*illus.*)
in Gothic sculpture, 5:625b
Rheims Cathedral, Visitation Group, 10:309b–310a (*illus.*)
Colyn, Thomas, Thomas Poppehowe and, 10:32b
Comacchio, sacked by Venice (886), 12:386a
Comb, 2:149a (*illus.*), 149b
Combat, judicial. *See* Champion, in judicial combat; Combat, trial by
Combat, trial by
banned by Parlement of Paris in 1259/1260, 9:418a
in Germanic law, 7:476a
see also Champion, in judicial combat
Combing
advantages over carding, 11:695b–696a
of long-stapled wools, 11:695b–696a
Comedia. See Comoedia
Comedìa delle ninfe fiorentine. See Boccaccio, Giovanni, *Ameto*
Comedies. *See* Drama
Comes Armeniae, 1:476a-b, 477a
Comes orientis, 4:191b
Comet, destruction of Jerusalem and, 1:605a
Comines, Philippe de, **3:487a–488a**
on ambassadors, 4:207a, 210a, 212a
on the Battle of Montlhéry, 5:279a
French chronicles of, 3:333b
hatred of war, 5:279a
interest in human potential, 5:279b
lack of Greek or Latin training, 5:279b–280a
Mémoires, 2:237a, 240a-b, 3:327b, 333b, 487b, 5:272a-b, 279a-b
rejection of chivalric myths, 5:279b
on the role of Providence, 3:488a
in service of Louis XI, 3:487a
Comitatenses, 10:459b
description of, 3:201a
Comitatus, 9:717a
among Germanic peoples, 2:89a
royal household and, 6:300a
witenagemot and, 12:665b
Comites, in Carolingian Empire, 3:107a-b
Comitia. See Representative assemblies
Commagene, coins of, 8:417b
Commander of the faithful, **3:488a–489a**
as caliphal title, 3:488b
later use of, 3:488b–489a
origin of, 3:488a-b
see also Caliphate; ᶜUmar I ibn al-Khaṭṭāb; ᶜUmar II ibn ᶜAbd al-ᶜAzīz
Commandino, Federigo, 1:439a, 439b
Commemoratio brevis, 6:317a, 8:448b
Daseian notation in, 8:618a, 639b
tonaries and, 12:70a
Commenda, **3:489a-b**, 12:106b
colleganza and, 12:388a-b
definition of, 3:489a
Islamic counterpart of, 3:489b
origins of, 12:101a
use of, 3:489a-b
usury injunction in Jewish law and, 12:341a
see also French law, in south
Commendam, **3:489b–490a**
Commendatio animae. See Death and burial, in Europe
Commendation, **3:490a–491b**
Carolingian, 3:491a-b
Germanic, 3:490b
Merovingian, 3:490b–491a
origin of, 3:490a-b
purpose of, 3:490a
result of, 3:490a
in Roman Empire, 3:490a
Commendatory abbot. *See* Abbot, commendatory
Commentaria in quattuor libros Sententiarum. See Durand of St. Pourçain
Commentarii in Psalmos. See Arnobius the Younger
Commentarius, 8:641b
Commentary on 1 Kings. See Gregory I (the Great), pope
Commentary on the Apocalypse. See Beatus of Liébana
Commentary on the Book of Job. See Hesychius
Commentary on the Digest. See Odofredus

Commentary on the Epistle to the Romans. See Abelard, Peter
Commentary on the Hexaemeron. See Grosseteste, Robert
Commentary on the Measurement of the Circle. See Eutocius of Ascalon
Commentary on the Sentences of Peter Lombard. See Fishacre, Richard
Commentary on the Somnium Scipionis. See Macrobius
Commentary on the Sphere and the Cylinder. See Eutocius of Ascalon
Commentators. *See* Postglossators
Commentum in Boethii de Trinitate. See Pseudo-Eriugena; Thierry of Chartres
Commentum in Martianum Capellam. See Remigius of Auxerre
Commerce. *See* Trade
Commercial law
  fairs and, 4:584a-b, 586b, 592a-b
  in France, 7:465a–466a
  Hungary, 6:347a
  market jurisdiction, 8:146a-b
  in southern France, municipal statutes, 7:466a
Commodian, 7:360a
Commodilla Catacomb (Rome), fresco in, 4:261b–262a
Common bench, court of. *See* Common pleas, court of
Common Penny tax. *See* Taxation, Germany
Common pleas, court of, **3:491b–492b,** 4:502a, 502b, 7:186b–190b, 446a–448b
  bench and, 3:492a-b
  early history of, 3:492a
  Exchequer court and, 3:492a
  justices, 7:187b–189b
  in Magna Carta, 3:492a-b
  Magna Carta and, 12:159b
  in Norman-Angevin England, 4:470a
  origin of, 3:491b–492a, 7:443a
  pleas heard by, 7:187b
  term of, 7:187b
  transformation in, 7:185b–186a
  see also English common law; Justices of common pleas
Common services. *See* Annate
Common (Westminster) accounting. *See* Westminster accounting
Commonitorium. See Orientius
Commonplace books, **3:492b–493a**
  examples of, 3:493a
  literary merit of, 3:493a
  pocketbooks, 9:711a
  popularity of, 3:493a
Commons (in villages), rights of pasture and, 9:455a-b
Communal archives. *See* Archives, notarial
Commune civitatis, forming of, 8:378b
Communes, **3:493a–503b**
  in Burgundy, enfranchisements, 2:426a, 427b
  charters for, 3:494b
  of Cologne, 5:459b
  definition of, 3:493a
  England, 3:498a–499a
    London, 7:661b, 662a–663a
  etymology of term, 3:493a-b
  feudal system and, 3:495a-b
  France
    alliance with monarchy, 5:169b
    charters of privileges, 7:674a
    first, 3:495b–497a
    Lyons, 7:699a
    shift to municipal oligarchy, 5:175a
  Germany, 3:497a–498a
    of Goslar, 5:459b
  government in, 3:500b–502b
  Italy, 3:416b, 499a–500a, 7:5b–6a
    administrative and judicial bodies, 7:16a
    appointment of teaching doctors, 2:312a
    capitano del popolo, 9:711b
    chronicles and, 6:632b–633a
    decay of in 13th century, 9:385b–386a
    extension of authority, 7:14b
    in Florence (1138–1250), 5:93a–94a
    of Genoa, 5:384a-b
    Guelphs and Ghibellines in, 6:6a
    lyric poetry and, 6:644a, 649b
    oath, 7:14b
    of Pisa, 9:663b–665b
    podesta and, 9:711a–712a
    Roman, rise of, 9:385a
    Siena, 11:278b–281a
    southern cities, 7:14a
  Jewish. *See* Jewish communal self-government
  local rule in, 3:493b
  Low Countries, 3:497a–498a
  merchant and craft guilds, 6:15b, 18b
  merchants in, 3:500b–512b
  Milanese, 8:378a
  oath and, 9:207b
  political autonomy of, 3:502b–503a
  Rouen, 10:537b–538a
  rural, 3:500a-b
  Slavic, land ownership, 11:670a, 671a
  syndic and, 11:558a
  taxation in, 3:501b–502a
  town councils in, 3:502a-b
  urban privileges, early, 3:493a–495a
  urban revival in, 3:493b–494b
  villages as, 12:440a, 441a
  see also Liberty and liberties; Urbanism, Western European
Communicantes, 8:192a-b
Communications
  Byzantine, **10:422b–425a,** 10:423 (map)
    postal and intelligence services, 10:58a
    sea routes, 10:423 (map), 424b
    system of beacons, 10:425a
    "telegraph system" under Theophilos I, 10:59a
    see also Trade, Byzantine
  disease patterns and, 9:678a
  Islamic world
    coreligionist pilgrimage and, 9:651b
    in Ummayad caliphate, 3:37b
    water routes, 10:425a
  see also Warfare
Communion
  ablutions, 8:196b
  Agnus Dei, 8:194b–195a
  blessing of the people, 8:194a
    of the clergy, 8:195a
  commingling of bread and wine, 8:194a-b, 195a
  consecrated species, disposal of, 8:196a-b
  De corpore et sanguine domini, 10:261a
  fraction, importance of, 8:194b
  frequency of
    annual, 6:465a
    Matthew of Janov and, 6:366a, 372b
  as image of Christ, 6:223b, 398a, 398b, 399a, 401b
  incense and, 6:431b
  infant, Hussites and, 6:374a
  in the Mass of the faithful, 8:193b–196b
  of the people
    communicant's response, 8:196a
    frequency of, 8:195a-b
    placement of host, 8:196a
    position assumed, 8:195b
    receiving the chalice, 8:196a
  Pikart, 6:375b, 376a
  prayers for the celebrant, 8:195a
  preparation, 8:193b
  see also Eucharist
Communion chant, **3:504a-b,** 8:196a
  melodies of, 3:504a
  Tu es Petrus, 9:689a–690b, 690a (*illus.*)
  use of, 3:504a
  see also Liturgical poetry; Mass cycles; Plainsong
Communion under both kinds, **3:504b–505b**
  Bohemian reformers and, 3:504b–505a
  Council of Basel (1433) and, 3:505b
  debates over, 3:505a
  modes of, 3:504b
  origin of, 3:504b
  recognition of, 3:505b
  see also Hussites; Utraquism
Community board (*kahal*), 7:69a
  legal theory of, 7:69b–70a
Commutation of penance. *See* Penance
Commynes, Philippe de. *See* Comines, Philippe de
Comneni. *See* Komnenoi
Comoedia, 7:364a, 367a-b
  definition of, 4:278b
  Ovidian influences on, 9:313a-b
  in 13th century, 7:368b
Compagnetto da Prato, 6:643a, 11:259a-b
  "Amor fa una donna amare," 6:656b
  "Per lo marito c'ho rio," 6:656b
Compagni, Dino, 6:651b
  Cronica delle cose occorenti ne' tempi suoi, 6:633b–634a, 659b
Compagnies d'ordonnance, 3:206b, 271b
  establishment of, 5:189a
  opportunities for employment, 5:189a-b
Companies of Adventure. *See* Great Companies

Comparatio Platonis et Aristotelis. See George of Trebizond
Compass, magnetic, **3:506a–507b**, 11:100b–101b, 102 (*illus.*)
in Arabic ships, 9:86a
azimuth, 3:507b
compass card in, 3:506b–507a
compass needle in, 3:506b
determining polarity, 9:520b
development of, 3:506b
dry, 11:101a, 102 (*illus.*)
improvement of, 3:507a-b
"magnetic variation" of, 3:507a
maritime, 11:638b
in the Mediterranean, 9:89a-b
origins of, 3:506a, 11:101a
portolan chart and, 10:34a
problem of true north, 3:507a
references to, early, 3:506a-b
Western European geography and, 5:396b–397a, 399a
wind rose in, 3:506b–507a
Compendium artis motectorum Marchecti. See Petrus of Amalfia
Compendium grammaticae. See John of Garland (*ca.* 1195–*ca.* 1272)
Compendium of the Logic of al-Ghazālī. See Lull, Ramon
Compendium Salerni, 4:219b
Compert Con Culainn, 6:548b
Compiègne
assembly of the Estates (1358), 7:35a
bridge of the canons of St. Corneille, 10:416a
inns around, 6:470a
Compiègne, Council of (1329–1330), condemnation of shivarees, 8:29a
Compilatio. See Bernard of Pavia
Compilatio antiqua, 7:426b
Compilatio prima. See Bernard of Pavia
Compilatio quarta. See Johannes Teutonicus
Compilatio tertia. See Johannes Teutonicus
Compilationes antiquae, 7:416a-b
Laurentius Hispanus and, 7:385b, 386a
Compiuta Donzella of Florence
"A la stagion che 'l mondo foglia e fiora," 6:643b
"Lascia vorria lo mondo e Dio servire," 6:643b
Complaint of the Black Knight. See Lydgate, John
Complaint (*querela*). *See* Trespass
Complainte, **3:507b–508a**
characteristics of, 3:507b
funèbre, 3:507b–508a
origin of, 3:507b
subject matter of, 3:507b–508a
used by Chaucer, 8:335a
used by Machaut, 8:4a-b
see also Planctus
Complant, 11:677a
Compline, 3:67a, 4:229a
Composers, hymn. *See* Hymns
Composition de la Saincte Escripture, 5:289a
Compositiones ad tinguenda, 4:328a
Compositiones Lucenses, 1:135b
Compositiones variae, 11:643a-b
Compositor. See Translation and translators
Composizione del mondo, La. See Ristoro d'Arezzo
Compostela. *See* Santiago de Compostela
Compromise of Bec, 4:422a
king's presence at church elections, 4:422b
Compurgatio canonica, 9:207a
Compurgation, **3:508a–509a**, 7:476a
canonical purgation and, 7:450b
in early Germanic codes, 7:476a
in English common law, 3:508b–509a
Assize of Clarendon and, 3:409a
erosion of trust in, 3:508b
oaths in, 3:508a-b
in ordeals, 9:259a
in Scandinavia, 10:705b
wergild and, 12:617b
Computus, **3:509a-b**
of Dionysius Exiguus, 4:192b–193a
Computus. See Helperic of Auxerre; Notker Teutonicus
Comtessa de Dia, **3:509b–510a**, 10:168a, 12:207a, 215a
eroticism in love poetry of, 10:168a
love songs of, 3:509b–510a
Comyn family, 11:108b, 109b, 110a
Comyn, John, earl of Buchan, defeated by Robert I of Scotland, 10:427a
Comyn, John, lord of Badenoch, murdered by Robert I of Scotland, 10:426b
Conaire Mór, king of Tara (saga character), 6:546b–547a, 547b
Conall Corc, 4:492b, 6:547b
Cashel and, 3:121a
Conall Gulbann, story of in Gaelic, 11:116a
Conception Nostre Dame, La. See Wace
Conceptualism, **3:510a-b**
Cistercians and, 12:688b
Ockham and, 9:156a
realistic. *See* Nominalism
"Concerning Arłun-Łan and Buła." *See* Frik
Concerning the Education of the Clergy. See Hrabanus Maurus, *De institutione clericorum*
Concerning the Jews and Their Lies. See Luther, Martin
Conch, 3:378a
triconch architectural plan (triclinium), 12:188 (*illus.*)
Conchobor mac Nessa, Ulaid king, 6:547b, 548a
Concilia, in medical studies at Bologna, 8:260a
Conciliabulum of Pisa, 3:367a
affirmation of conciliarism, 3:654a–655b
Conciliar movement
in Germany, *Reichskonzilien* assembly concept, 10:331a
in political theory, 10:23b–24b
Pragmatic Sanction of Bourges and, 10:69a-b
Conciliar theory, 3:366a-b, **3:510b–523b**, 9:729b
career of, 3:518b–521a
church reform and, 3:511a-b
college of cardinals and, 3:511b, 516b
commonality of forms of, 3:512a
Council of Constance and, 3:648b
Decretists and, 3:516a–517a
definition of, 3:510b
differences in forms of, 3:512a-b
Great Schism and, 3:511b, 518a
holiness in, 3:510b–511a
influence on 15th-century church, 4:377b–378a
legacy of, 3:521a–522a
maturity of, 3:510b
nature of, 3:510b–514b
of Nicolaus de Tudeschis, 9:129a
origin of, 3:514b–518b
papal authority and, 3:511b–512a, 516a-b
plenitudo potestatis, 9:708a–710a
papalists' attacks on, 3:512b–513a
reunion with Greek church and, 2:466b
"silver age" apologists in, 3:520b
sources of, 3:365b
strict, 3:516a–517a
unity of the church in, 3:510b–511a
vision of ecclesiastical constitution, 3:517a
Concilium, use of term, 3:633a
Concilium Arelatense II, 7:398b
Concilium in Monte Romarici, Roman de la Rose and, 10:449b
Conclave, papal, **3:523b–525a**
deviation from procedure of, 3:524b
effect of, 3:524b–525a
first, 3:523b
Great Schism and, 3:524b, 649a
origin of, 3:523b
procedure of, 3:523b–524b
Ubi periculum and, 3:94b–95a
Conclusa et preposita, non vota. See Groote, Geert
Concordance of Discordant Canons. See Gratian, *Decretum*
Concordance of Sacred Scripture and the Fathers. See Grosseteste, Robert
Concordances, Bible. *See* Bible
Concordantia astronomiae cum historica veritate. See Ailly, Pierre d'
Concordat, **3:525a–527a**
effects of, 3:526b
etymology of, 3:525a
formal need for, 3:525a-b
Franco-papal (1472), 3:525b
implementation of, 3:526a
legal validity and enforceability of, 3:525b
multipurpose documents, 3:525b
with princes, 3:525b–526a
topics covered in, 3:526b
types of, 3:525a-b
Concorde des deux langages. See Jean Lemaire de Belges
Concorde du genre humain. See Jean Lemaire de Belges
Concordia canonum Cresconii, 7:400a-b
Concordia discordantia canonum. See Gratian, *Decretum*
Concordiae, 7:113b
Concressault, fortification of, 3:151b

Concrete, use in early Christian architecture, 4:331b
Concubinage
  Byzantine, inheritance and, 6:451b
  Islamic, **3:527a–529b**
    children in, 3:528a-b
    definition of, 3:527a-b
    importance of, 3:529a
    Koran and, 3:527a
    marriage and, 3:529a
    mother of children in, 3:528b
    slave women in, 3:527b–528a, 11:333a
    in upper echelons of society, 3:528b–529a
    Western concubinage and, 3:527a, 528a
  monastic, reform of, 10:285b, 287b–288a
  Western, **3:529b–530b**
    Augustine on, 3:530a
    canon law and, 3:530a
    clerical, 3:530b, 6:499a
    Gratian on, 3:530a
    Islamic concubinage and, 3:527a, 528a
    marriage and, 3:530a
    origins of, 3:529b
    see also Prostitution
Conde Arnaldos, El, Rodríguez del Padrón and, 10:439a
Conde Dirlos, El, ballad texts in, 11:429a
Conde Lucanor, El, exempla and, 4:551b
Conde Partinuplés, El, 11:423a
Condesa traidora, La, 11:409a, 442b
Condottieri, **3:531a-b**
  chessboard military tactics, 12:566a-b
  diplomacy and, 4:206a
  effects on Italy, 7:9a
Conduct of the Inquisition. See Gui, Bernard
Conductus, 1:546b, **3:531b–533a,** 8:594a
  in Bamberg manuscript, 2:68b
  by Adam de la Halle, 1:49a
  cum caudis, 1:546b
  in Germany, 3:533a
  in Las Huelgas MS, 6:318a
  in *Magnus liber organi,* 8:43a-b
  modal notation and, 8:622a
  Notre Dame school and, 9:191b, 192a
  political or topical, 3:532b
  religious, 3:532a
  rondellus, 10:529b
  styles of settings, 3:532b
  trecento music, 12:180b
  Winchester polyphony and, 12:696a
  see also Perotinus
Conductus (commerce), 4:584a
Çonesa, Jaume, translation of Guido delle Colonne into Catalan, 11:458a
Conferences. See Cassian, John
Confessio, 1:221b
Confessio Amantis. See Gower, John
"Confessio Goliae." *See* Archpoet
Confession, **3:533a–534b**
  absolution
    deathbed, 4:119b–120a
    indulgences and, 6:447a-b
    unauthorized, 6:449b–450a
  annual, 6:465a
  Burchard of Worms on, 2:420b
  in Celtic church, 3:230b
  deathbed, 4:119b–120a, 565a, 565b
    in *Everyman,* 4:527b
  in early church, 3:533a
  frequency of, 3:533b
  guides to
    John Gerson's *Opus tripartitum,* 10:302a
    Summa de poenitentia (*Raymundina*), 10:266b
    summae confessorum, 10:300b
  indulgences and, 6:447a, 450a
  Peter the Chanter's views, 9:522a
  private penance and, 9:488a-b, 489a
  religious instruction and, 10:301a, 302a
  rites associated with, 3:533b–534a
  Symeon the New Theologian and, 11:553b
  theological justification for, 3:534a
  see also Penance; Religious instruction
Confession et testament de l'amant tréspassé. See Pierre de Hauteville
Confession of Faith. See Ilarion
Confessions. See Augustine of Hippo, St.
Confessor
  royal, **3:534b–535b**
    religious duties, 3:535a
    secular responsibilities, 3:535a
  saint, **3:535b**
Confirmation, **3:535b–536a**
  age at, 3:536a
  in Byzantine liturgy, as a part of baptismal rite, 7:610a, 611a
  in Celtic church, 3:230b
  in Latin West, 43:536a
  origin of, 3:535b–536a
Confiscation of property. *See* Property
Conflictus, see also Débat
Conflictus de Deo trino et uno. See Arnobius the Younger
Confoederatio cum principibus ecclesiasticis (1220), 5:501a
Confraternities, religious, *lauda* and, 6:662a-b, 7:384a, 384b
Confraternity of St. George, Nisart and, 9:140b
Confrérie, **3:536b**
  for fabliaux performance, 5:274b
  of *joglars,* 7:117a
  in Paris, 5:274a
  of trouvères, 12:218b
  see also Puy
Confrérie de la Passion, 4:264a
Congé, **3:536b**
Congé d'élire, **3:536b–537a**
  in Compromise of Bec, 4:422b
Congo, exploration of, 4:562a, 562b
Congregatio generalis. See Representative assemblies
Congregation of Friars Pilgrims for Christ Among the Gentiles, 4:253a
Congregation of the Holy Office, inquisition and, 6:488b
Congregation of Monte Corona. *See* Monte Corona, Congregation of
Congregation of St. Maur. *See* St. Maur, Congregation of
Congregavit chant. *See* Feet, washing of
Conhort, Lo. See Ferrer, Francesc
Conics. See Apollonius
Coniuratores. See Oath helpers
Conn Cétchathach, 6:547a
  descendants of, 6:551a
Conn of the Hundred Battles. *See* Conn Cétchathach
Conn na mBocht, descendants of, 6:521a
Connacht, **3:537a–538a,** 6:518a
  de Burgh in, 2:422a
  control of Munster, 8:532a
  Irish literature and, 6:523a
  ruling dynasties of, 3:537a-b
  see also Mac Lonáin, Flann; Uí Néill
Connachta, 6:548a
Conon de Béthune, **3:538a-b,** 10:294a
  imitations of, 5:441b
  life of, 3:538a
  "Mout me semont Amours que e m'envoise," illustration of lyric triangle, 5:251b–252a
  Picard dialect of, 9:630a
  poetry of, 3:538a-b
Conopaeum, 5:316b
Conquête de Constantinople, La. See Robert de Clari; Villehardouin, Geoffroi de
Conrad I of Germany, emperor, 5:507b
  election of, 4:426a, 5:474b
  Erchanger and, 11:527a
  seal impression in wax, 11:125a
Conrad II of Germany, emperor, 2:424a
  administrative policies, 3:558a
  Bohemia and, 2:299b
  Burgundy under, 2:429a, 5:476b, 11:538a
  Constitutio de feudis, 3:557b–558a
  constitution of 1038, 10:522b
  crowning of, 8:378a
  election of, 4:426b–427a
  invasion of western Hungary, 11:480a
  Leo IX and, 7:543a
  Matilda of Tuscany and, 8:222b
  ministerials and, 8:405a
  in song, 3:57b
  vs. Ernest II, 11:527a
  Wipo and, 12:655b, 656a
Conrad III of Germany, emperor, 2:6b
  election of, 4:427a-b, 5:479a, 6:273a
  Nuremberg and, 9:201a
  reign of, 5:479a-b
  seal of, 11:127b–128a
  in Second Crusade, 4:30b, 37b, 38a
  Swabia and, 11:539a
  vs. Henry X of Saxony, 2:134b
Conrad IV of Germany, emperor
  death of, 4:60a, 5:485b, 6:466b, 11:272a
  election of, 4:428a, 5:485a, 6:273b
  Jean d'Ibelin and, 6:389a, 389b
Conrad of Franconia. *See* Conrad I of Germany, Emperor
Conrad of Gelnhausen, 3:646a
  Epistola concordiae, 3:511a-b, 514b
  on Great Schism, 10:23b

Conrad of Hainburg, 6:382b
Conrad of Hirsau, *Accessus ad auctores,* 7:368a
Conrad of Marburg, as inquisitor, 6:483b–484a
Conrad of Masovia, duke, 2:66b
Conrad of Mazovia, duke, 9:721b
Conrad of Megenberg, **3:539a**
  Buch der Natur, 3:539a
  Deutsche Sphaera, 3:539a
  Oeconomica, 3:539a
Conrad of Montferrat, 1:590b
Conrad of Prague, archbishop, 6:373b
Conrad, prior of Canterbury Cathedral, **3:539a-b**
  reconstruction of cathedral, 3:83b
Conrad the Red, 5:509b
Conrad (son of Rudolf I), 2:429a
Conrad of Wittelsbach, archbishop of Mainz, coronation of King Leo I/II of Cilicia, 3:394a, 7:546a
Conrad of Zabern (*d. ca.* 1480), 8:648a
Conrad of Zähringen, duke
  charters for communes and, 3:494b
  Lothair and, 11:538b
Conradin of Swabia, duke
  claim to Sicilian throne, 6:273b, 466b
  crusade against, 4:60b, 95b–96a
  death of, 11:272a, 279b
    Swabian succession and, 11:528a
Conradins, feud of, 5:508a
Conrois, 3:204a
Consacramentales. See Oath helpers
Consanguinity, **3:539b–540b**
  definition of, 3:539b
  inheritance and, 3:539b–540a, 6:451b, 458a
  marriage and, 3:540a-b
Conscience, The Remorse of. See Aȝenbite of Inwyt
Conscription of armies. *See* Warfare
Consecration
  of bells, 2:166a
  benedictions and, 2:177a
  of cemeteries, **3:540b–541b**
  of church officers. *See* Ordination, clerical
  royal. *See* Kingship
Consecration cross, 4:9a, 131a
Conseil à un ami. See Pierre de Fontaines
Conserva, 11:236a
  see also Convoys
Consilia, 10:63a-b
Consilia. See Nicolaus de Tudeschis
Consilia (medical judgments), 8:252a
Consistoire de Gai Saber, 10:251b
Consistori de la Gaya Ciènca, 3:170b
Consistorium, **3:541b**
  development of, 3:93b, 94b, 95a
Consolat de mar (Valencian maritime law), 12:348a
  see also Consulate of the sea
Consolation of Philosophy. See Boethius
Consolation des trois vertus, La. See Chartier, Alain
Console figures, 5:617b
Consonance/dissonance, **3:541b–542b**
  Boethius on, 8:637b
  counterpoint and, 8:647a
  diaphonia, 4:172a-b
  Isidore of Seville on, 8:638a
  Johannes Gallicus and, 8:643b
  Odington and, 8:645a
  in plainsong, 3:5b
  Prosdocimus and, 8:647a-b
Constable, term used for grand bailli in Auvergne, 2:53a
Constable, local, **3:542b–543b**
  of castles, 3:542b–543a
  of the hundred, 3:543a
  of the township, 3:543a
Constable, master, Sicily, 11:269a
Constable of the realm, **3:543b–544a**
  in England, 3:543b, 6:301b
  in France, 3:543b–544a
  origin of title, 3:543b
  responsibilities of, 3:543b
Constance, 11:543b
  bishopric of, 11:526a-b
  see of, 11:537b
Constance of Aragon, marriage to Henry VI of Germany, 11:269b
Constance Christmas Play, prologue to, 4:269b (*illus.*)
Constance, Council of (1414-1418), 1:147b, 3:647b–651a, 9:726b, 729b, 10:331a, 11:42a, 12:142b
  d'Ailly and, 1:108b–109a
  calling of, 10:24a
  Communion under both kinds and, 3:504b
  conciliar theory and, 3:514b
  concordats of, 3:525a
  condemnation of John XXIII, 3:648a-b
  condemnation of Utraquism, 6:200a
  decrees of, 3:366a, 648b
  ending of Great Schism and, 3:366a
  Frequens, 3:366a, 650b, 651a, 4:377b–378a, 10:24a
  Gerson on, 5:512b–513a
  Haec sancta synodus, 3:366a, 648b, 4:377b–378a, 10:24a, 12:735a
  Henry V of England and, 6:161a
  Hugo von Montfort and, 6:325a
  Hus and, 6:366b, 369a
    condemnation of, 3:649a–650a
    death of, 5:489b
  Hussites and, 6:372a, 372b, 373b
  impact on manuscript book production, 8:104b–105a
  importance of, 3:366a, 647b
  main factions, 4:377b
  papal power limited by, 11:42a
  procedures of, 3:648a
  Sigismund and, 3:647b, 5:489a, 11:287b
  tasks confronting, 3:647b
  Tractatus artis bene moriendi and, 1:547b
  Vincent Ferrer and, 12:453a
  Wyclif and, 6:199b, 12:407a, 707a
  Zabarella and, 12:735a, 735b
Constance (daughter of Manfred of Sicily), 11:261a, 273a
  marriage to Peter III, 4:61a
Constance Gradual, 5:663a
Constance, Peace of (1175), conditions of, 4:203b
Constance, Peace of (1183), 7:15a, 652b–653a, 8:379a
  rights of local government, 7:15a
Constance, Treaty of (1153), 5:479b
Constance (wife of Emperor Henry VI), 11:269a, 269b
  marriage to Henry VI of Germany, 5:481a
  Naples and, 9:58a
Constance (wife of John of Gaunt), 7:135a
Constans I, Roman emperor, Council of Serdica and, 11:189b
Constans II, Byzantine emperor, **3:544a–545a**
  Armenia and, 1:478a-b, 500a
  Italian campaigns, 7:2b
  Maximus the Confessor and, 8:233a-b
  mints established by, 8:420b
  Monothelitism and, 3:630b
  Nersēs III Išχanecʿi (Šinoł) of Armenia and, 9:102b
  Typos, 3:630b, 8:233b
    nature of Christ, 6:191a, 8:480a
Constantia, history of, 4:70b
Constantine I (the Great), Roman emperor, **3:545a-b**
  Arianism and, 1:453b
  building program in Constantinople, 2:484a, 3:549b–551a
    plans for, 4:331b
  Christianity and, 10:462a
  church-building program of, 4:335a
  coinage of, 8:419a-b
  conversion to Christianity, 3:10a-b, 545a
    theological basis for, 2:484a-b
  Dacia and, 10:459a
  Donation of. *See* Donation of Constantine
  Donatist church and, 4:259b–260a
  early church and, 3:337a-b, 545a-b
  economic reforms, 10:460b
  Edict of Toleration, 6:292b
  ex voto churches and, 4:529b
  on interest payments, 12:335b
  as *isapostolos,* 6:560b
  Lateran and, 7:344b
  in *Lectionary of the Church of Jerusalem,* 1:518b
  in legends and prophecies, 8:20a
  limitanei and, 7:582b
  military reforms, 3:545b
  monogram, 3:319b
  Nino legend and, 9:140a
  political reorganization, 2:484b
  praetorian prefect and, 10:68b
  reform of coinage, 12:581a
  revival of the term "patrician," 9:460a
  seizure of power, 3:545a
  Serdica and, 11:189a
  support of imperial library, 7:560b–561a
  tetrarchy, 10:458b
  in Theophanes Confessor's *Chronographia,* 12:22b
Constantine IV, Byzantine emperor, **3:546a**
  condemnation of Monothelitism, 3:630b, 8:480a
Constantine V, Byzantine emperor, **3:546a-b**

convening of council of Hiereia, 6:223a
"Donation of Pepin" and, 9:501b
dual nature of Christ, 6:223
in iconoclastic controversy, 3:11a, 631a, 6:397a, 398a, 400b, 401a, 402a
Karin under, 7:215a
in legends and prophecies, 8:20a
Patriarch Nikephoros and, 9:131b, 132a
Paulicians and, 9:469b
Slavic pirates and, 12:101a
Studios Monastery and, 11:494b
tagmata and, 11:573b
vs. Bulgars, 2:401a, 488a-b
see also Leo III, Byzantine emperor
Constantine VI, Byzantine emperor
claims of Thomas the Slav and, 12:36b
regency, 6:520b
second marriage, 12:15b
Tarasios and, 11:598b
Constantine VII, Byzantine emperor, classical scholarship under, 11:49a
Constantine VII Porphyrogenitos, Byzantine emperor, **3:546b–548a**, 3:614b (*illus.*)
agrarian legislation of, 3:547a
artistic works of, 2:452b
astrology and, 8:18a
boyars and, 2:403a
condition of "porphyrogenitos," 10:33a
on Croatian history, 4:4a, 4b, 5a
De administrando imperio, 1:483a, 4:195a, 196a, 446b, 10:59b, 515b
on Pechenegs and Rus, 12:435b
on Serbs, 11:168a, 168b
De ceremoniis, 4:194b, 446b, 7:593a, 8:557b, 9:617b
depicted on St. Stephen's crown, 11:482 (*illus.*)
encouragement of scholarship, 3:547a-b
evidence on Byzantine themes and, 12:10a
Excerpts, as a source for *Suda,* 11:501b
on Great Moravia, 2:299a
humanism and, 9:697b
Imperial Histories and, 5:382a
influence on Byzantine historiography, 6:244b–245a
ivory representation of, 7:26b
legal works by, 7:391b
life of Basil, 2:453b
in Menologion, 11:554a
on Moravia, 5:658a
Nikephoros II Phokas and, 9:132 b
Novels, 6:452a
parents of, 7:545b
as patron of the arts, 2:440b, 490a
as patron of historical writings, 2:513b–514a, 516a
proaristocratic policy, 3:546b–547a
regency council of, 2:403b
Romanos I Lekapenos and, 10:515a-b
soldiers' portions and, 11:359b–360a
Symeon of Bulgaria and, 11:555a
tetragamy and, 9:135b
Theophanes continuatus and, 12:23a
Theophano and, 12:24a
throne of Solomon, 2:440b
on Tomislav of Croatia, 12:69a-b
works by, 7:391b
see also Macedonians
Constantine VIII, Byzantine emperor, 2:118b
Basil II and, 2:119b
see also Theodora the Macedonian, Byzantine empress
Constantine IX Monomachos, Byzantine emperor, **3:548a**
attempt to seize Ani, 5:339a
creation of law school by, 7:392a
Patriarch Michael Keroularios and, 8:304b
as patron of the arts, 2:443a
Pope Leo IX and, 7:543b
schism of 1054 and, 3:349b
Zoë the Macedonian and, 12:745b
see also Macedonians
Constantine X Doukas, Byzantine emperor, 4:263a
kingdom of Kars and, 12:354a
Naṣr al-Dawla ibn Marwān and, 7:310b
rebuilding of fortifications at Melitene and, 8:269b
Constantine XI Palaiologos, Byzantine emperor, **3:548a**
defense of Constantinople, 2:504a-b
George Scholarios and, 5:401a
Patras and, 7:381b
reunion of Latin and Byzantine churches, 2:504a
Constantine XI Palaiologos,Byzantine emperor, crowning of, 8:446b
Constantine II/IV of Cilicia, king, relation to Guy of Lusignan, 6:39a
Constantine III/V of Cilicia, king
murdered, 3:393a
Tarsus and, 11:600a
Constantine the African, 2:173b, **3:548b–549a**, 11:274b
Ars medicinae, 11:692a
at Salerno, 8:248a–249a
introduction of Greek medicine to the West and, 8:247a
medical practices of, *Trotula* treatises and, 12:214a-b
translations by, 3:548b, 8:256a, 12:138a
Treatises on the Eye, 9:247b
Constantine the Armenian, **3:549a**
Constantine Bodin, 2:407b
Constantine Doukas, betrothal to Anna Komnena, 1:303a
Constantine Doukas Angelos, 6:559b
Constantine of Erznka, 1:511b
Constantine of Fleury, Gerbert of Aurillac and, 11:100b
Constantine Hermoniakos, Homeric poems, Greek paraphrases of, 2:523a
Constantine Manasses
Aristandros and Kallithea, 2:508a
poetry of, 2:508a
World Chronicle, 2:515b
Constantine Payl, 11:351b
Constantine, Peace of (312-323), 8:439a
Constantine the Philosopher. *See* Cyril of Alexandria, St.
Constantine, pope, *camelaucum* (episcopal cap) of, 12:404a
Constantine of Preslav, 11:345b
Constantine of Serbia, king, 11:176b–177a
Constantine (son of Basil I the Macedonian), death of, 2:118a
Constantine Stilbes, epigrams of, 2:507b
Constantine of Thessaloniki, St. *See* Cyril, St.
Constantine Tih of Bulgaria (1257-1277), reign of, 2:410a
Constantine-Silvanos (alleged founder of the Paulician sect), 9:468b, 469a
Constantinian Excerpts, 4:446a
Constantinople, **3:549a–557a,** 3:549a–557a, 550 (map), 12:304b–305b (map), 306a-b
administration of, 3:553b–554b, 4:493b
see also Eparch
archbishop of
assumption of ecumenical patriarchate, 4:383a-b
jurisdiction of, 3:631b
Arianism and, 1:454a
art in, 6:614a
attacks on, 3:38a, 551b–552b, 6:572a, 7:544b, 9:74a-b
by Arabs, 7th century, 2:487a
by Arabs, 8th century, 2:488a
by Prince Igor of Kiev (941), 12:435a-b
by Thomas the Slav, 2:401b, 12:36b–37a
by Vikings (860), 12:435a
see also Ottomans
Benjamin of Tudela on, 12:102a-b
blockaded by Bāyazīd, 2:136b
Bogomils in, 2:295b–296a
Brusa and, 2:392b
Chora monastery. *See* Kariye Djami
churches in
shrines, 4:337a
styles of, 4:337b, 341b
cisterns of Justinian, 4:334a-b
as a communication center, 10:422b–425a
Constantine's plans for, 4:331b
crusader influences, 2:446a–447b
decline of, 12:306a-b
demes, 3:554a-b
during crusades, 3:552a
education and cultural life, 3:556b–557a
schools in, 7:595b
establishment of Pera-Galata and, 9:503a
fairs in, 12:101b
fall of (1453), Vlad Ţepeş and, 12:484b
foreigners in, restrictions on, 3:554b–555a
forum in, 4:332a
foundation of, 2:484a-b, 3:549a–551a
Byzantine political theory and, 10:9b

Constantinople (*cont.*)
Fourth Crusade and
capture and pillage, 1:241b, 334b, 4:31b, 45a–49a, 7:561a, 9:698b
capture and pillage of2.389b
in *Parzival,* 12:676a
Frederick I Barbarossa and, 6:559b
Golden Horn, 5:573b–574a
Great Palace, 3:552b–553a, 4:334b
mosaic pavements, 4:353b, 362b, 363 (*illus.*)
guild structure, 6:15a
hippodrome, 4:331b, 12:304b
as imperial city, 3:552b–553b
imperial palace, 12:304b
Imperial palace, Lateran and, 10:518b
industry and commerce, 3:554b–555b
Justinian I in, 7:201a–202a
Justinian II in, 7:203a
Karaite settlements in, 7:210a
land walls of, 4:333b–334a, 12:304b–305a
Latin occupation of, 2:469a-b, 497a, 498a, 4:344b–345a
recaptured by Byzantines (1261), 7:349b, 378b, 9:117b, 331a
recovery by Michael VIII Palaiologos, 2:499a, 8:302a-b
libraries of, 7:561a
liturgical stations in, 4:333a
liturgy development and, 7:610a
Liutprand of Cremona on, 7:634b
Miklagarðr in Icelandic sagas, 9:442b
mint at, 8:419b–420b
monasteries, 8:457a, 457b
Ottomans and, 2:470a, 4:56a-b
conquest, 2:504a-b, 3:65a-b, 6:247b–248a, 443b, 7:685a, 8:264a
recovery by John V Palaiologos, 2:502b
patriarch of, 2:460a-b, 3:10a-b
early, 9:459a
pentarchy and, 9:495b–496a
pilgrimage and, 9:653a
plagues and, 9:675a–676a, 684b
plan of, 12:304b
Platonic studies in, 9:697a-b
population, 3:551b, 10:457a
position in Byzantine church, 3:555b–556b, 630a, 631b
position in Byzantine Empire, 3:551a–552b
provisioning of, 12:101b, 102a
riot against Western merchants (1182), 12:103a
in Robert de Clari's *Conquête de Jerusalem,* 10:431b
Roman capital moved to, 9:331a-b
size of, 12:304b
social structure of, 12:304b
Symeon of Bulgaria and, 11:555a
Theotokos Church of Constantine Lips, 1:445a (*illus.*)
under Andronikos I Komnenos, 1:245a
under Macedonian dynasty, 3:552a
Venetian trade and, 12:111b, 388b
water supply, 12:576b
see also Trade, Byzantine; Urbanism, Byzantine
Constantinople, Councils of
First (381), 1:454a, 9:459a
archbishop of Constantinople's position, 9:505b
Arianism and, 3:336a
Basil the Great and, 2:120b, 121a
Constantinople's intrachurch position clarified by, 3:555b
heresy and, 3:594a
Nicene Creed, 9:560b
reaffirmation of Nicene faith, 3:628a-b
Second (553)
Armenian church and, 1:499a
Christology and, 3:320a
condemnation of Nestorianism, 9:106b
condemnation of Origen and Evagrius Ponticus, 9:6b
Monophysite problem and, 3:630a-b
Theodoret of Cyr and, 12:17a
Third (680), 3:630b, 8:480a
endorsement of the doctrine of Christ's two wills, 8:233b
Fourth (869-870), 11:43b
acts of, 3:632a, 633a
Basil I and, 2:117b
see also Trullo, Synod in (692)
Constantinople, Histoire de la conquête de. See Villehardouin, Geoffroi de
Constantinople, Latin Empire of. *See* Latin Empire of Constantinople
Constantinople, Synod of (448), 4:524a
Constantinus Cephalas, *Anthology,* as a source for *Suda,* 11:501b
Constantinus of Fleury, Gerbert of Aurillac and, 8:640a
Constantius II, Byzantine emperor
Arianism and, 1:453b, 454a, 2:485a, 11:311b
Aršak II and, 1:559b–560a
building construction, 2:485a
Council of Serdica and, 11:189b
persecution of the Nicenes, 3:628a
Constantius III, Roman emperor, 10:263a
Constantius of Lyons, 5:472a
Constituta usus et legis, 7:428b
Constitutio de feudis (1037), **3:557b–558a**, 8:378a
Constitutio pro Iudaeis. See Innocent III, pope
Constitutio romana (824), 10:522a, 525a
Constitution of Athens. See Aristotle
Constitutiones Aegidianae, 1:131a
Constitutiones apostolicae, 7:397b
Constitutiones Clementinae. See Clement V, pope
Constitutions of Melfi. *See* Melfi, Constitutions of
Constitutum Constantini. See Donation of Constantine
Construction
building materials, **3:558a–564a**, 6:79b
ashlar, 10:253b
brick, 2:375a-b
bridge-building and, 10:419a–421b
chimneys and fireplaces, 6:122a
concrete, 4:331b
stone, 7:660b–661a
stone, in Islamic architecture, 6:607a-b
stonecutting, 8:177a-b
terra cotta, in Islamic architecture, 6:606a
wood in church architecture, 10:578b, 580b, 680a
see also Rib; Spolia; Vault
engineering, **3:564a–569b**, 6:87a-b, 11:645a
bridge building and, 10:419a–421b
building contractors, 8:178b
Byzantine, 6:56a, 56b
centering, 3:234b–235a
design concept, 8:177b
design problems, 3:566b, 8:177a
geometrical elements, 8:179a
geometry of, 3:565b
hollow-tube vaulting, 10:263a–264b
ogival arch, 11:656a
photoelastic modeling, 3:567b
reduction of masonry mass, 11:656b
structural problems of masonry building, 3:567a-b
templates, 8:177a-b
treatises, 10:530b
use of consultants, 8:177b
vaulting, 11:655b–656a
water mills used in, 8:393b
see also Vault
half-timber cottage, 6:80a (*illus.*)
standardization and prefabrication, 3:562a-b
Consubstantiation of Son and Father, 3:627b–628a
Consuetudines. See Customary
Consuetudo Bononiensis, 3:21a
Consulate of the sea, **3:569b–570b**
duties of admirals, 1:56a
maritime law in Valencia and, 12:348a
see also Celelles, Francis, *Llibre del consolat de mar*
Consulates
in France
as municipal government, 7:462b
revival of Roman law and, 7:462b
see also Consuls; French law, in south
Consules ordinarii, 10:521a
Consuls, **3:570b–571b**
Byzantine, Stephanos II of Georgia and, 12:222a
definition of, 3:570b
in Florentine commune (1138-1250), 5:93a
in France, 3:570b–571a, 571b
in Italy, 3:570a, 571a-b
podesta and, 9:711a–712a
loss of authority, 3:571a-b
rise of urban centers and, 3:571a
Contarini, Ambrogio, Russian fur trade and, 5:333b–334a
Contarini, Zaccaria
meeting with king of France, 4:212a
relazione of, 4:209b
Conte d'amours. See Beaumanoir, Philippe de
Conte del Lello Orlandi, **3:572a**

Conte del tumbeor Nostre Dame, derivation of, 9:633b
Conte de fole largece. *See* Beaumanoir, Philippe de
Conte du Graal. *See* Chrétien de Troyes
Contemplació de la Santa Quarentena. *See* Eiximenis, Joan
Contemplatio. *See* Bonaventure, St.
Contemplation of Experience, The (*Kitāb al-i^c tibār*), 1:381a-b
Contemptus mundi, 8:348a
in Jorge Manrique's *Coplas por la muerte de su padre,* 8:88a
Contes de Cupido et Atropos. *See* Jean Lemaire de Belges
Contes moralisés. *See* Nicole Bozon
Conti de antichi cavaliere, 6:659a
Conti morali, 6:659a
Continens. *See* Rāzī, Abū Bakr Muḥammad ibn Zakarīya al-
Contra astrologos conjunctionistas eventibus futurorum. *See* Henry of Langenstein
Contra curiales et officiales clericos. *See* Nigel of Longchamp
Contra epistolam Parmeniani. *See* Augustine of Hippo, St.
Contra Eusebium et Epiphanidem. *See* Nikephoros I, patriarch
Contra Eutychen et Nestorium. *See* Boethius
Contra Graecorum opposita. *See* Ratramnus of Corbie
Contra haereticos. *See* Hugh of Rouen, archbishop
Contra iudices. *See* Theodulf
Contra Nicetam. *See* Humbert of Silva Candida
Contra objectiones Fridugisi. *See* Agobard
Contra Petrobrusianos. *See* Peter the Venerable
Contra quattuor labyrinthos Franciae. *See* Walter of St. Victor
Contra turrim traiectensem. *See* Groote, Geert
Contraception
European, **3:572a–573b**
among Cathars, 3:572b
Bernardino of Siena on, 4:144a
Catherine of Siena on, 4:144a
in Chaucer, 3:572b, 573b
means of, 3:572a
motives for, 3:572b
theological treatment of, 3:573a-b
Islamic, **3:574a–575b**
magical, 3:574b
male, 3:574b
methods of, 3:574a
sanctioned by law and tradition, 3:574a, 575a
Contrafactum, **3:575b–576b**
in *Cantigas de Santa María,* 3:86a
earliest use of term, 3:576a
Contrafacture, 5:438b
Contrapposto, classical. *See* Column figure; Gothic art, sculpture
Contrapunctus. *See* Prosdocimus de Beldemandis
Contrasto del povero e del ricco, Il, 6:636b
Contratenor, 1:551a, **3:576b–577b**
isorhythm and, 6:619a-b
kinds of, 3:577a
Contrediz Franc Gontier, Les. *See* Villon, François
Controller, royal, England, 6:302b, 305a
Controversia de mensibus, 6:631a
Contubernium, 11:335a-b
Contumacy, excommunication and, 4:536a, 536b
Convent. *See* Beguinage; Monastery
Convento do Cristo (Tomar, Portugal), 10:489a
Conventuals, John XXII and, 7:125b
Conventus. *See* Kingship, holding court
Conventus generalis. *See* Representative assemblies
"Conversation between Arthur and Gwenhwyfar," 1:578a
Conversi (Cistercian lay brothers), economic importance of, 3:404a
Conversi (converted Jews), **3:577b–578a,** 7:93b, 100a
in Castile, 3:137b, 138b, 139b
Jewry law and, 7:500a
persecution of, 11:421b
in Spanish literature, 11:420a-b, 454b
Conversion
process of, 8:442b
see also Missions and missionaries
Conversion of Georgia. *See* Grigor the Deacon
Conversion of Iberia, 5:413a
Converts
from Zoroastrianism, 11:563a
to Christianity, in Arabia, 6:575b–576a
to Islam, 11:563b, 564a
in Iran, 6:502a-b
in Iraq, 6:513a
in Islamic conquests, 6:573b
Koran and, 6:579b
in Sicily, 11:262a
see also Conversi (converted Jews)
Conviction by the king's record. *See* Treason
Conviction by notoriety. *See* Treason
Convivio. *See* Dante Alighieri
Convocation of Canterbury, **3:578a–579b**
Convocation of York, **3:578a–579b**
Convoys
Christian pilgrimage, 9:660a, 661a
in Indian Ocean, 11:249b
in Mediterranean, 11:230b
see also Caravans; *Conserva;* Crusades; Pilgrimage, mass; Trade; Travel and transport
Conway, Peace of (1277), **3:579b–580a,** 7:637b
Welsh rights, 12:522a, 526b
Cook (Coke), Humphrey, **3:580b**
Cookery
European, **3:580b–583b**
bread, 2:364b–365a
cooking pots, 1:95a
decorative, 3:582a-b
fruits and vegetables, 2:347a-b
kitchens, 3:583b
pulse, 1:95a
symbolic aspects of foods, 3:582b
Islamic, **3:584a-b**
basic ingredients, 3:584a
beverages, 3:584a
regional traditions, 3:584a
study of, 3:584a
rose petals, 9:551a
Cooke's Ordinary, 6:176b
Cope. *See* Vestments, liturgical
Copenhagen, University of, 12:290a
Copernicus, Nicholas, 11:103a
on astronomy, 1:615a, 616a
theories of, 1:609a
Copho (11th-century anatomist)
Anatomia porci, 8:249a
anatomical studies of, 8:256a
Cop^c k^c Šahuni. *See* Sophenē
Copla, **3:584b–585a**
see also Spanish literature, versification and prosody
Copland, Robert, Wynkyn de Worde and, 12:712a
Coplas de arte mayor, 11:459b
Coplas de arte menor, 11:459a
Coplas de ¡Ay panadera!, 11:421b
Coplas del Provincial, 11:422a
Coplas por la muerte de su padre. *See* Manrique, Jorge
Coplas de Yoçef, 8:281b–282a
Copper
alloys with, 2:383a
importance of, 2:383a
imported from West into Egypt, 12:107b
mining of, 8:397b–398a
production of, 8:402a
source of, 8:401b
see also Mints and money
Copperplate engraving. *See* Engraving
Coppo di Marcovaldo, **3:585a**
influence on Cimabue, 3:396b
Coppo Stefani, Marchionne di, *Chronicle,* 6:634b
Coptic alphabet. *See* Alphabets, Coptic
Coptic architecture, 3:585b–587a
Coptic art, **3:585b–593b**
Egyptian ship (12th century), 9:77 (*illus.*)
illuminated Acts of the Apostles (4th–5th centuries), 8:105b
Islamic bookbinding and, 8:98b–99a
Islamic influences, 3:588b
manuscript illumination, 3:590a–591b
Islamic influences, 8:114a
motifs, 3:590b
painting, 3:591b–593a
early wall painting, 3:591b–592a
sculpture, 3:587a–588b
Ahnās style, 3:588a
classical motifs in, 3:587a
sources of, 4:348b
textiles, 3:588b–590a, 11:716b
decorative motifs, 3:589b–590a
Hellenistic features, 3:589b–590a
preservation of, 3:589a-b
styles of, 3:589b
Coptic church, **3:593b–595b**
Alexandrian rite, 1:155a–157a
Anaphora of St. Basil, 1:155b
biblical exegesis, 2:214b
calendar, 3:18b
Difnar, 1:155b

Coptic church (*cont.*)
Divine Office of, 7:590a
Ethiopia, 8:479a
Fatimids and, 9:52b
taxation of, 11:625b, 626a
theological development, 8:478b–479a
writings, 13th–14th centuries, 8:479a
traditional architectural form, 1:157a
Coptic language, 10:455a
Bohairic dialect in Alexandrian rite, 1:156a
in Nubian liturgy, 9:198b–199a
translation of Septuagint into, 2:211a
translation and translators, 12:126a-b
see also Egypt, late Roman
Copts
etymology of name, 3:593b
in Islamic Alexandria, 1:154b
Islamization of, 3:594b
missionary endeavors, 3:595b
religious freedom under Islam, 3:594b
repression under Mamluks, 3:594b–595a
Copula, **3:595b–596b**
Copyhold, **3:596b–597a**
Cor, 7:317a
Coracle (Irish boat), 9:89a
Coram rege. See King's Bench
Corbaccio. See Boccaccio, Giovanni
Corbacho, El. See Martínez de Toledo, Alfonso, *Arcipreste de Talavera*
Corbechon, Jean
Creation and the Fall, 5:361b
Des proprietez des choses, 5:361b
Corbeil, Treaty of (1258), 5:171a, 7:675b
Corbel, 3:149 (*illus.*), **3:597a**
see also Machicolation
Corbel table, **3:597b**
in Romanesque architecture, 10:487b, 487a
Corbie, abbey of, 2:173a, 174b–175a
False Decretals and, 4:124b, 125b
foundation of, 12:11a
Radbertus of Corbie and, 9:446a
westwork of, 10:92a (*illus.*)
Corbinian, St., bishop of Freising, 1:422b, 2:134a
Corbridge lanx, 7:342a
Corde (unit of measure), 12:583b–584a, 590a
multiple uses for, 12:585b
types of, 12:584a
Córdoba, **3:597b–601a**
caliphate of, 3:50b, 6:414a
capture by Ferdinand III, 3:600b
Castilian settlers in, 3:600b
cordovan leather, 11:255a
decline of, 3:600b
emirate of, 3:598b
Great Mosque of, 1:196b, 6:234a-b, 235 (*illus.*), 600b–601b (*illus.*), 10:234 (*illus.*)
additions to, 6:234b
horseshoe arch, 8:512b
mosaics, 6:234b
orientation of, 10:235a
polychrome glazed tiles in, 2:31a
Roman and Visigothic *spolia,* 6:234a-b
as intellectual center, 3:599a-b, 11:452a
Jews in, 3:600a, 600b
libraries in, 7:273b, 561b
Muslim-Christian relations in, 3:598b
pre-Islamic history, 3:597b
religious censorship in, 3:599b
revolts in, 3:598b, 678a
role of non-Muslims in, 3:599b
slave trade in, 11:337a
strategic location of, 3:598a
under ᶜAbd al-Raḥmān II, 3:598a, 598b–599a
under Almohads, 3:600a-b
under Ibn Abī ᶜĀmir al-Manṣūr, 8:90a-b
see also Umayyads of Córdoba
Córdoba Cathedral, *Annunciation* altarpiece by Pedro de Córdoba, 9:483b, 484 (*illus.*)
Córdoba, Pedro de. *See* Pedro de Córdoba
Cordovan. *See* Leather and leatherworking
Corduene, Kurds and, 7:310a
Coresi (Romanian deacon), 10:511a, 512a
Corfe Castle, William Wynford and, 12:711b
Corfu
captured by Roger II (1147), 10:441a
relations with, Venice, 7:380b
Robert Guiscard and, 10:433a, 11:265b
taken by Venice (1206), 7:376b
Corinth, 12:307a
Byzantine sea routes and, 10:423 (map), 424b
disputed ownership of, 7:381b
glassmaking in, 5:557a–558a, 12:102b
Corippus, Flavius Cresconius, **3:601a**
Johannis, influenced by Vergil's *Aeneid,* 12:394a
Cork, monastery at, literary activity of, 6:540b
Cormac mac Airt, king of Tara, **3:601a-b,** 6:547b
Cormac mac Carthaig, 4:493a
in *Caithréim Chellacháin Chaisil,* 6:539b
Cormac mac Cuillennáin, king of Munster, **3:601b–602b**
death of, 4:493a
influence on Irish literature, 3:602a
Sanas Cormaic (*Glossary*), 3:602a, 8:558a
Cormont, Regnault de. *See* Regnault de Cormont
Cormont, Thomas de. *See* Thomas de Cormont
Corn (musical instrument), 8:558b
Cornaro, Caterina, 4:71a
Corneille, Pierre, *Le Cid,* 3:388b, 11:438a
Corneto, Rome and, 10:526a
Cornett, 8:603b, 604a, 607a (*illus.*)
in civic music, 8:597a
Cornificians, opposed by Thierry of Chartres, 12:27a
Cornish language, 3:234a, 6:4336b
Coron, Venice and, 7:376b, 380b
Corona vault. *See* Vault
Coronant, Armenian, 1:489a
Coronation. *See* Coronation, papal; Kingship, coronation rituals
Coronation charter
of Henry I, 4:462a, 6:155a, 7:338a
baronial support of, 4:469a
of Stephen, count of Boulogne, 4:463a
Coronation Gospels, 4:136a, 8:106b
Coronation, papal, **3:602b–605a**
Byzantine period, 3:603a-b
Carolingian period, 3:603b
German influence in, 3:603b–604a
in later medieval period, 3:604a–605a
Coronation Sacramentary, decorated letters in, 6:462b
Coronel, 1:534a (*illus.*)
Coroner, **3:605a–606a**
Corónicas navarras, 11:410b
Coroticus, British chieftain
Patrick's letter to his soldiers, 9:462b
problems of identification of, 9:465a
reproved by St. Patrick, 11:489b
"Corpi celesti e tutte l'altre stelle." *See* Serdini, Simone
Corporate body, rights of the. *See* Representative assemblies
Corporation, **3:606a–608a**
chapter as, 3:266a
Christianity as stimulus to, 3:607a
common features of, 3:606b
ecclesiasatical, 3:607a
in Roman law, 3:606b
under Code of Justinian, 3:607a
variety of medieval corporate institutions, 3:606a
see also Universitas (collectivity)
Corpse
dismemberment, 4:120a-b
embalming, 4:120a
funeral rites and, 4:120a–121a
Corpus agrimensorum romanorum, 11:515a-b
Corpus antiphonalium officii. See Hesbert
Corpus areopagiticum, 9:563a
Corpus carminum færoensium (CCF). See Faroese ballads
"Corpus Christi carol," 8:339b, 340b
Corpus Christi College Gospels, 5:580a
Corpus Christi, Feast of, **3:608a-b,** 9:714b
Cistercian rhymed office for, 10:370b
establishment of, 3:359a
Hugh of St. Cher and, 6:321a
hymns for, 6:382a
importance of, 3:608b
origin of, 3:608a
plays for, 3:298a-b, 608b, 4:268a, 284b–285b, 8:657b, 658b–659a
rhymed offices and, 10:366b
in Spain, 11:437a-b
York Plays and, 12:727b, 728b
see also Towneley Plays
Corpus Gabirianum, 1:141a
Corpus iuris canonici, 7:417a-b, 428a
Clementines and, 3:645a
decretals of Gregory IX in, 4:124a
Decretum Gratiani and, 4:129a, 130a

papal succession rules in, 3:642a
see also Law, canon
Corpus iuris civilis, 3:474a, 475b, **3:608b–610b**, 10:61b
Bartolo da Sassoferrato on, 2:115a-b
Basil I and, 2:117b
Bologna *studium,* 7:419a–421b
books of, 11:691a-b
Breviary of Alaric and, 7:418b
Cino da Pistoia on, 3:397b
Codex Florentinus MS, 7:418b–419a
Codex Theodosianus and, 7:418b
consilia, 7:423b–424a
corporation under, 3:606a, 607a
Digest, 5:565b, 567a, 7:418a–420a
brought to Bologna, 7:419a-b
difficulties of text, 7:419b
rediscovered, 7:418b–419a
early summae, 7:420a-b
in England, 7:423a
in *Établissements de St. Louis,* 4:515b
evidence on literacy in, 7:596a
format of, 3:609b
"four doctors" (Irnerius' students), 7:419a-b
in France, 7:422b–423a
in Germany and the Low Countries, 7:423a-b
Glossa ordinaria of Accursius, 7:419b
glossators, 5:565b, 567a, 568a, 11:691b
Bolognese, 5:567a-b
interpretations of, 7:419b–421a
Placentinus, 9:671b–672b
Gratian's influence, 7:421b–422a
Hugo and, 6:323b–324a
"humanist jurisprudence," 7:424a
influence on legal procedure, 2:486a, 3:609a, 609b–610a
church courts, 7:422a
inheritance in, 6:451a, 451b, 455a
Institutiones, 7:418a–419a
Irnerius and, 6:554b–555a
in Italy
outside Bologna, 7:422a-b
scholarship after Accursius, 7:423b–424b
ius commune (common law) created, 7:424a-b
on judicial torture, 12:89a-b
in later Middle Ages, 7:424b
in law curriculum, 11:691b
laws for guildsmen, 6:20a
legal maxims and, 8:231b–232b
on liberty and liberties, 7:556b–557a
loss in early Middle Ages, 7:418a-b
notary and, 1:446a
Novels (Novellae), 7:418a-b
Ordo judiciarius and, 7:422a
Pandects, 7:418a–420a
on *paroikoi,* 9:441b
private law and procedures, 7:421b
in Provence, 7:422b
revival and spread, 3:609a, **7:418a–425b**, 7:503b, 513b
Rogerius and, 10:444b, 444a
Siete partidas and, 11:283a
in Spain, 7:422b, 522a
struggle between empire and papacy and, 7:421a
study of, 2:312a
summarized by Vacarius, 12:343b
system building in the 14th century, 7:423b–424a
on trade with Sasanians, 12:97a
translation of, 12:126b
as transmitter of Roman law, 3:609b
see also French law; Law, civil; Law codes; Law, schools of
Corradino da Padova, Bolognese School and, 5:567b
Corral del Carbón, 5:653a
Çorraquin Sancho, 11:442a-b
Corrector sive Medicus, 7:407b
Correctoria, 4:543a, 6:321a
Correctoria corruptorii Thomae, 12:41a
Correctorium controversy, Richardus de Mediavilla and, 10:388b
Correspondence. *See* Letter-writing
Corrogationes Promethei. See Neckham, Alexander
Čorrord Hayk^{C}, 1:472a
Corsi family, 10:519b, 525a
Corsica, Pisa and, 9:664a-b
Corsini family, 7:326b
Cortebarbe, "Les trois aveugles de Compiègne," 4:575b, 577a
Cortes, **3:610b–612b**
in Aragon under Pedro IV the Ceremonious, 1:417a
in Castile, 3:138b–139a
ecclesiastical estate, 3:610b–611a
functions of, 3:611a-b
king and, 3:611a
origin of term, 3:610b
role in taxation, 3:611b–612a
sessions of, 3:611a
in Valencia, 12:348a
Corvée, **3:612b–613b**, 11:619b
bridge maintenance in England and, 10:415a
development of, 11:675b
for maintenance of roads, 10:412b
money payments, 3:612a
tasks of, 3:613a
tenant, 12:152b, 157a-b
see also Taxation, Byzantine, secondary; Travel and transport, Western European
Corvey. *See* Corbie
Corvinian Library, 6:348b
Corvinus. *See* Matthias I Corvinus of Hungary, king
Corycus. *See* Kořikos
Cosmas II, patriarch of Constantinople, accused of Bogomilism and deposed, 2:296a
Cosmas (Bulgarian priest), on Bogomilism, 2:294a, 294b, 295a, 296a
Cosmas Indicopleustes, **3:613b**
on Byzantine trade, 12:100a
Christian Topography, 3:613b
representation of *parousia,* 9:442a
on Nubian Christianity, 3:314b
used by the author of *Paschale chronicon,* 9:446a
Cosmas of Prague, **3:614a**, 11:343b
Chronica Boemorum, 3:614a, 10:87b
Cosmati work, **3:614a**, 10:504b
see also Opus alexandrinum; Vassallettus
Cosmetics. *See* Beauty aids
Cosmetics box, porcelain, 2:146 (*illus.*)
Cosmogony, Ismaili, 6:615a-b, 617b
Cosmographia. See Bernard Silvester
Cosmography
in Alan of Lille's works, 1:183a-b, 184b
in Bernard Silvester's works, 1:183a-b, 184b
Cosmology
Averroist, 1:468a
Greek, Basil the Great and, 2:121a
Ismaili, 6:588a
in Levi ben Gershom, 7:554a
of the Sabaeans of Ḥarrān, 9:4b
School of Chartres and, 1:183a
Ṭayyibī, 6:588a
see also Astrology; Astronomy; Essence and existence; Ontogeny; Philosophy and theology
Costa ben Luca. *See* Qusṭa ibn Lūqā
Costa, Soeiro da, 4:561b
Costin, Miron, 10:512a
Costrel (unit of measure), 12:584a
Costume
in art, 4:13a-b
Byzantine, **3:614a–616a**
belted tunic, 3:614
court garb, 3:615b
hierarchical distribution of, 2:456a
imperial garb, 3:614b–615a
imperial regalia, 2:123a-b
priests' garments, 3:615b–616a
purple in, 4:327b
see also Maphorion; Paludamentum; Stikarion; Tablion
caftans, 3:12b–13a
colobium, 3:480b
Islamic, **3:616a–618b**
Arabic styles, 3:618a
basic attire, 3:616b, 617 (*illus.*)
distinguishing dress for non-Muslims, 3:616b
fabrics used, 8:530a
as gifts, 3:618a
luxury of, 3:616b
Mamluk styles, 3:618a-b
origins, 3:616a
Persian influences, 3:616a
pilgrim, 9:650b
robes, 3:616b–618a
Turkish styles, 3:618a
see also Qalansuwa; Sumptuary laws, Islamic
Jewish, **3:618b–621b**
in Babylonian Talmud, 3:618b–619a
in Christian states, 3:620b–621a (*illus.*)
cloaks, 3:619a
depicted on Chinese ceramics, 3:619b–620a
head covering, 3:619b, 620b
Islamic sumptuary laws and, 11:508b
in Muslim states, 3:619b, 620b
ornamentation of, 3:619a-b
ṣīṣīt, 3:619a
Russian
pilgrim, 9:653b
pokrov veil, 9:716a

Costume (*cont.*)
Western European, **3:621b–626b**
after Black Death, 2:265b–266a
court costume, 3:622 (*illus.*)
differences between men's and women's, 3:624b, 625a
in 14th century, 3:622b–623a
hats, 3:623a (*illus.*)–624b
jewelry, 5:380a–381b
laws governing, 3:622a
leper, 9:677b
for mystery plays, 8:662b
penitential, 12:156a
pilgrim, 9:656b, 12:156b
robes, 3:625a
royal, from 6th-century grave, 4:328a
shoes, 3:625b–626a
status and, 3:621b
see also Paludamentum; Sumptuary laws, European; Vestments, liturgical
Cota, Rodrigo, *Diálogo entre el Amor y un viejo,* 11:424b
Cotehardie, 3:624b
Cotelette, 3:624b
Cottars, 4:512b
Cotton, **3:626b–627a**
bowing, 11:696b–697a
carding, 11:695b
cultivation of, 1:82a, 104b
Islamic world, 11:716a-b
in sailcloth, 11:234b
spinning, India, 11:699a
Cotton Caligula MS A.xiv, Winchester troper and, 12:647b
Cotton, John. *See* John of Afflighem
Cotton Nero MS A.x, 5:369a, 8:319b, 9:476a
Cotton, Sir Robert, 6:524b
Cotton Tiberius Psalter C.vi, 10:110a
Cotton Vespasian MS A.ii, 10:473 (*illus.*)
Cotton Vespasian MS D.viii, N-town plays in, 9:49b
Cotton Vespasian MS S.xiv, 8:310b
Cotton Vitellius MS A.xv, 2:184a
Coucy Castle, 3:146b, 150a (*illus.*)
Guy de Thourotte and, 3:277b–278a
Coucy, Châtelain de. *See* Châtelain de Coucy
Coucy, Enguerrand de. *See* Enguerrand VII of Coucy
Coucy, Robert de. *See* Robert de Coucy
"Council of a Hundred Chapters" (1551), *Stoglavyi sobor,* 8:573b
Council of July 920, 3:632a
Council of lords (Novgorod). *See Soviet gospod*
Council of Remiremont, 7:367a
Council of the Wise (Sapientes), 3:499b
Councils
Armenian. *See* Armenian church, doctrines and councils
Byzantine (859–1368), **3:631b–632b**
ecumenical (325–787), 3:337b, **3:627a–631b**, 10:462a
as center of church authority, 3:341a-b
christological controversies, 3:320a–321b, 9:560a
concept of, 3:633a
influence of Byzantine emperors, 3:10b
theological issues, 3:338b–339a, 9:560a-b
Trinitarian doctrine and, 12:189b
see also individual councils, under name of city
exempla and, 4:551b
Western
crusades and, 4:19b–20a, 36a, 56a, 59a
history (869–1179), **3:632b–639b**
history (1215–1274), **3:639b–642b**
history (1311–1449), **3:642b–656b**
see also individual councils, under name of city
Counterfeiting, German law and, 7:480a
Counterpoint, **3:656b–658a**
classification of consonances and, 8:647a
discant in, 3:657a
innovations in, 3:657b
in *Magnus liber,* 9:191b
structural components, 3:657b
theory of, 3:656b–657a
three-voice works, 3:657b
see also Faux-bourdon; Gymel; Music, polyphonic
Counterpoises
Arab adaptation, 11:633a
bronze, 11:633a
glass, 11:633a
see also Weights and measures, Byzantine
Counts
in Carolingian Empire, 3:107a-b
in England, 3:659a
in France, 3:658b–659a
in Germany, 3:659a
County, **3:658a–659a**
Carolingian, Normans and, 9:162a
England
hide and, 11:253b
sheriff and, 11:225a
origin of term, 3:658a
see also Palatinates
Cour du Petit Scel, 7:464b
Courland. *See* Kurland
Couronne Margaritique. See Jean Lemaire de Belges
Couronnement de Louis, 3:258b–259a
Couronnement de Renart, 10:314a
Course of the Exchequer. See Fitz Nigel, Richard, *Dialogue of the Exchequer*
Courson (Courçon), Robert of, **3:659a-b**, 10:76b
against interest-taking, 12:336a
indulgences and, 6:449a
on Jews, 7:77b, 89b
University of Paris statutes, 11:689b, 690b
Courson, Robert of, Andrew of St. Victor's theology school and, 12:21b–22a
Court of Aids. *See* Taxation, French
Court of the Archdeacon (Canterbury). *See* Archdeacon, Court of the (Canterbury)
Court of Arches. *See* Arches, Court of
Court of Canterbury. *See* Arches, Court of
Court of Chivalry, treason definition and, 12:167b–168a
Court, holding. *See* Kingship
Court, Imperial Cameral. *See* Holy Roman Empire
Court leet, **3:659b–660b**
Court School
of Charlemagne, 10:97a–99a, 110b
see also Pre-Romanesque art
of Charles II (the Bald), 10:99a-b, 100a, 101a, 110b–111a
Court Style. *See* Gothic architecture, Rayonnant Style
Courtenay, William, archbishop of Canterbury
lay taxation and, 11:609b
vs. John Wyclif, 12:706b
Courtesy books, **3:660b–667a**
Anglo-Norman, 3:661a
for children, 3:661b–662a
courtly love and, 3:672b
for daughters, 3:662b–663b
English, 3:661a–662a
for household officials, 3:661b
Latin, 3:661a
for noblemen, 3:665a-b
for sons, 3:662a
Courtly literature
hunting and, 6:358b
Iranian, 6:507a, 508a-b
Irish, 6:536a
in Netherlands, 6:441a
parodied, in *Irregang und Girregar,* 6:556a
Provençal, Iacopo da Lentini and, 6:388a-b
in vernacular, 6:440a, 442a-b, 443a
Courtly love, **3:667a–674b**
Alain Chartier, 3:275b
in allegory, 3:670b
Andreas Capellanus' Latin treatise on, 1:572b
in Anglo-Norman literature, 1:268b–269a
in *Arcipreste de Talavera,* 8:157b
associated conventions, Spain, 8:157b
at court of Eleanor of Aquitaine, 4:419b–420a
aubade and, 1:642a
in *cansos,* 3:70a-b
in Castilian poetry, 11:419a-b
in Catalan poetry, 3:173a-b
in Cavalcanti's work, 3:196b–197a
in *Celestina,* 3:213a
in *chansons de malmariée,* 3:262b–263a, 5:245b
Charles of Orléans and, 3:273a
in *Chastelaine de Vergi,* 3:277a-b
chivalric class and, 3:302b
in Chrétien de Troyes's narratives, 1:59a
Comtessa de Dia, 3:509b–510a
definitions, 3:667a–668a
in Der von Kürenberg, 4:161a-b
in Der Pleier, 9:707a–708b
in Dinis, 4:190a-b
domna viewpoint, trobairitz and, 12:207a-b
farcical treatment of, 8:488a

fin'amor, Raimon de Miraval on, 10:252a
in Francisco Imperial, 6:429a
in French lyrical verse, 5:251b
in French narrative verse
ideal courtly lady, 5:245a
knight's sense of mission, 5:245a
variations on courtly theme, 5:245b
in Friedrich von Hausen, 5:300a
in Gaelic Scottish poetry, 11:115a
Gaston Paris's use of term, 3:668a
in German allegory, 5:431a–432a
in German lyric poetry, cult of *hôhiu minne,* 12:536b–537a
in German romance literature, 5:447a–449b
in Gottfried von Neifen, 5:633b
in Gottfried's *Tristan,* 5:636a–637a
in Guillaume de Lorris, 6:23a-b
Heinrich Suso and, 9:35b
in Iacopo da Lentini, 6:388a
in Italian poetry, 6:641a-b, 656a
in Jorge Manrique's poetry, 8:87b
in *Klári saga,* 7:275a
in *lai,* 7:316b
Latin influences, 3:671b–672a
Latin literature of, 7:367b–368a
in *Minnereden,* 8:410b–411a
minnesingers and, 8:413a
Moorish influences, 3:671b–672a
Ovidian influence, 9:314a
parodied, 6:656a
in *Pearl,* 9:476a
poetry, by Reinmar der Alte, 10:292b–294a
as reflected in Icelandic *mansöngvar,* 10:406a
relation to real life, 3:672a-b
Rodríguez del Padrón and, 10:438b–439a
sexuality in, 4:574b
vs. spirituality, 3:669a-b
in Sicilian poetry, 11:258a
social and literary influence, 3:673a-b
in Spanish literature
Razón de amor, 10:268b–269a
sentimental romances, 11:455a
in Spervogel's poetry, 11:462b
in Thibaut de Champagne's lyric, 12:27a
Tristan legend and, 12:201a, 202a
troubadours
individual poets, 12:215a
subjects, 12:215b–216a, 216b–218a
trouvères
individual poets, 12:218b
subjects, 12:218b–219a
in Welsh poetry, 12:606b
see also Capellanus, Andreas; Partimen; Provençal literature; Spanish literature, courtly lyrics
Courtois d'Arras, **3:674b**, 4:264a
blending of sacred and secular theater, 5:264a
fabliau and, 4:576b–577a
inns in, 6:468b
manner of presentation, 9:636a
Courtrai, Battle of (1302), 5:522b
defeat of cavalry at, 3:204b
Courts, law. *See* Law
Courts of love, 3:672b–673a
Courts, rulers'. *See* Curia, lay
Courtyards. *See* Gardens, Islamic
Couse, 7:324a
Coussemaker, Edmond de, *Speculum musicae,* publishing of, 7:38a
Coustellier, Simon le, 3:3b–4a
Coutumes, 12:439b
Coutumes de Beauvaisis. See Beaumanoir, Philippe de
Coutumier, très ancien. See Custumals of Normandy
Covarrubias, Alonso. *See* Alonso de Covarrubias
Covenant of Omar, 11:563a
exilarch and, 4:552a
Coventry plays, 8:658a
N-town plays and, 9:49b
Covilhão, Pero da, 4:562b–563a
Cowter, 1:525b, 529b–530a, 532b, 534a (*illus.*)
Cowton, Robert, Duns Scotus and, 12:44a
Crabgrass, as grain crop, 5:647a
Craft of Dying, Book of the. See Ars moriendi
Craft of Venery, The. See Twiti, William, *Art de vénerie*
Cramp rings, 7:256a
Cranks. *See* Technology, mechanical
Crann toruidh croch an Choimdhe, 6:538a
Craon, forest of, Robert d'Arbrissel's community and, 10:429a
Crassus, Marcus Licinius, invasion of Parthia (54 B.C.), 9:443b
Crateuas, herbal of, 6:177b
Cravant, church of, 10:481a
Creation
in Ibn ᶜArabī's teaching, 9:43a-b
in Ismaili theology, 6:615a, 618a
in Peter Lombard's *Sententiae,* 9:517a
in Proclus' theology, 9:98a
in *Vǫluspá,* 12:491b
vs. Aristotle's concept of eternity, 12:39b–40a
in Zoroastrianism, 12:747a, 747b
in Zurvanism, 12:748b–749a
Creationism. *See* Trinitarian doctrine
Crèche
Christmas celebration and, 3:319a
as liturgical furniture, 5:319b
Crécy, Battle of (1346), 4:398b–399a, 6:331b, 9:478b, 555b–556a
arms and, 1:532a
artillery used at, 3:151b
cavalry at, 3:205a-b
death of John of Luxemburg, 8:3a
Credence (church furnishing), 5:318a
Credentia. See Credence
Credenza of St. Ambrose, 8:379a
Credo. *See* Creeds, liturgical use of
Credran, battle at (1257), 6:518b
Creed play, 12:727b
Creeds
Apostles', 3:676a, 10:300a
Athanasian, 12:190a
baptismal, in early church, 3:675a-b
in the eucharistic liturgy, 3:676b
Islamic, 3:52b
sunna and, 11:511b–512a
liturgical use of, **3:675a–677b**
Nicene-Constantinopolitan. *See* Nicene Creed
Old Roman, 3:676a
religious instruction in, 10:300a-b
Cremona, vs. Milan, 8:378b
Crenels, in castles and fortifications, 3:146a-b, 147 (*illus.*), 149 (*illus.*)
Crescas du Caylar, 7:178a-b
Crescas, Ḥasdai, **3:677b–678a**, 5:346b
Aristotle and, 1:460a
Or Adonai, 3:677b
Refutation of the Principles of the Christians, 10:5b
Crescentius of Iesi, denunciation of Spirituals, 5:199b–200a
Crescenzi family, 10:522b
vs. Benedict IX, 11:517b
Crescenzi, Pietro de
on fruits grown in Mediterranean region, 5:305b
on making a lawn, 5:364b
on menageries in gardens, 5:363b
Ruralium commodorum liber, 5:362a
Crespine, 2:150a
Cresques, Abraham, 10:34b
Catalan Atlas, 2:29b
Crestià, Lo. See Eiximenis, Francesc
Crete, **3:678a-b**
Byzantine Empire and, 3:678a-b
Byzantine sea routes and, 10:423 (map), 424b
Byzantine trade and, 12:103a
Córdoban refugees in, 3:678a
Greek literature in, 2:523a
monastic population, 8:457b–458a
Muslim conquest of, 3:678a, 6:572b, 9:74b
recaptured by Byzantines (961), 9:75a, 75b, 132b
Romanos II and, 10:515b
Venice and, 7:376b, 380b
Cretin, Guillaume, 7:54b, 10:364b, 365a
Débat de deux dames, 6:360b
Criers, wine sales and, 12:121b–122a
Crimea
Armenians in, 1:486a
Caffa as colony in, 3:12a-b
Jews in, 7:100b
Karaites in, 7:210a
Seljuks of Rum and, 11:157b
Crimea, Khanate of, **3:678b–680b**
foundation of, 3:678b
incorporation into Russia, 3:679b
political structure, 3:679b–680a
relations with Moscow, 3:679a-b
Turkish rule, 3:678b–679a
Crimean Gothic language. *See* Gothic language
Crimean Tatars
in Ottoman army, 3:679a
raids into Russia, 3:679b
Criminal justice
canonical inquest in, 6:478b
ecclesiastical. *See* Clergy, degradation of; English common law; Excommunication; Homicide; Pilgrimage, Western European, as punishment for crime
England, 3:409a–410b
for clergy, 3:410a

Criminal justice (*cont.*)
  France, sentences, 3:279a
  hundred (land division) and, 6:330b
  insanity and, 6:491a
  interdict and, 6:495b–496a, 496b
  Jewish, exilarch and, 4:552a
  Russia, *Sobornoe ulozhenie* and, 11:198b–199a
Criminals, wills of, 6:451a
Crimson. *See* Dyes and dyeing; Qirmiz
Crinet, 1:529a
Criophore. *See* Good Shepherd
Crispi family, 7:381a
Crispin, Gilbert
  Disputation, 10:3a-b
  Joseph Kimḥi and, 10:4a
Crispina, abbess of St. Maria and St. Peter, 12:682b
Crist ist erstanden, 7:593b
Cristallo, 5:560b
Crivelli, Carlo, 5:535a
Croatia, **4:1a–8b**, 4:3 (map)
  administration of. *See* Banus
  art, 4:8b
  Basil II and, 2:119b
  early history, 4:1a–4a
  invasion of, by Symeon of Bulgaria, 2:405a
  Latin church in, 4:4b–5a, 6a
  literature, 11:345b–346b
  power of nobility in, 4:5a, 7b–8a
  relations with
    Bosnia, 4:5a
    Bulgaria, 4:4b, 11:555a
    Byzantine Empire, 4:1b, 2b, 4b, 5b, 6a
    Franks, 4:1b–2a, 2b
    Hungary, 4:5b, 6b–8a, 6:337b, 340a-b, 346a
    Magyars, 4:4a
    Slavonia, 4:6a-b
    Venice, 4:5b
  Slavic church in, 4:6a
  society of, 4:8a-b
  under Tomislav, 4:4a-b
  see also Dalmatia; Pannonia; Serbia; Tomislav
Croatian language. *See* Serbo-Croatian language
Croatians
  assimilation with Slavs, 4:1a-b
  Byzantine influences on, 4:1b, 2a
  Dalmatian, 4:1b, 2a, 79b–80a
  Magyars and, 4:4a
  origins of, 4:1a
  Pannonian, 4:1b, 2a
  rebellions against Frankish rulers, 4:2a, 2b
Crocket, **4:8b**
Crocket capital, 3:90b–91a (*illus.*), 5:598a
Crocus, 9:551a
  medical-cosmetic function, 6:183b
C^{C}romi, church of, 5:407b (*illus.*), 408b
Cronaca. See Benedetto di S. Andrea
Cronaca altinate, on the origins of Venice, 12:383a, 383b
Crône (Krone), Diu. See Heinrich von dem Türlin
Crónica. See Muntaner, Ramón
Crónica Albedense, 8:513a
  Christian Reconquest, Mozarabic commitment to, 8:512a
Crónica de Alfonso XI, 11:418a
Cronica di Anonimo Romano, 6:660a
Cronica delle cose occorenti ne' tempi suoi. See Compagni, Dino
Cronica domestica. See Velluti, Donato
Cronica de gestis principum ac regum Poloniae. See Kadłubek, Wincentry
Crónica de Juan II, 11:421a
Crónica de la población de Ávila, 11:414a
Crónica de San Juan de la Peña. See Chronicle of the Kings of Aragon and Counts of Barcelona
Crónica de Sant Joan de La Penya. See Chronicle of the Kings of Aragon and Counts of Barcelona
Crónica de veinte reyes, 3:71a, 71b
Cronicae et gesta ducum sive principum Polonorum. See Gallus Anonymous
Cronicles. See Trevet, Nicholas
Cronique des ducs de Bourgogne. See Chastellain, Georges
Crop failure. *See* Agriculture; Grain crops
Crop rotation
  biennial
    Christian Spain, 1:83a, 84a
    French Midi, 1:85a
    Islamic Spain, 1:82a
    Mediterranean region, 1:80b
    in open-field villages, 1:91a
    Russia, 1:99b
    Toulouse region, 1:85b–86a
  Sardinia, 1:88a
  summer crops, Islamic world, 1:104b
  triennial
    advantages of, 1:92b–93a
    Christian Spain, 1:83a
    French Midi, 1:85a
    increases in productivity with, 1:97b
    intensification of plowing, 1:92b–93a
    Latium, 1:86b
    Mediterranean region, 1:80b
    Northern Europe, 1:92a–93a
    second and third year, 1:92a-b
    soil and water requirements, 1:92b
    Toulouse region, 1:86a
    West Slavs, 1:97b
  two-field, Byzantium, 1:77a
  wheat-bean, French Midi, 1:85a-b
  wheat-fallow-woad-fallow, 1:86a
  see also Agriculture; Reclamation of land
Crosby, John, house of, 7:665b–666a
Cross
  in church architecture, 3:378a-b, 379a, 379b
  forms of, **4:9a–11b**
    Ankh, 3:591 (*illus.*)
    Tree of Life, 12:182 (*illus.*)
  in Hiberno-Saxon art, 8:371b, 373a-b
  high
    Celtic, 3:221b, 222 (*illus.*), **6:225a**
    of Dalriada, 3:223a
  Holy. *See* Cross, true
  ordeal of, 9:259b
  in painting by Hans Schüchlein, 11:79b (*illus.*)
  Pictish, 9:640b–641a
  in poetry, 6:307b–308a
    see also Holy cross hymns
  processional, 1:224a, **4:12a**, 5:319b
  true
    cult of in Anglo-Saxon England, 1:279a
    discovered by Helena, 8:20a
    legendary discovery of, 7:59a
    pilgrimage and, 4:553a-b
    Reliquary of, 2:455b (*illus.*), 455a, 4:435a (*illus.*)
    restoration of relics to Jerusalem, 6:171b
    in Stavelot Triptych, 10:500 (*illus.*)
    veneration of relics, 10:298b, 302a
    Xusrō II and, 12:715a, 715b
    see also Helena, St.; Relics
  veneration of in Easter rites, 4:366b
  see also Sign of the Cross; Swords, cruciform
Cross, Cape, 4:562a
Cross-domed church, 3:378a-b
Cross-in-square church, 3:378b
Cross-staff, **4:12a-b**, 11:101b
  invention of, 4:12a, 7:553b, 11:91b
  uses of, 4:12b
Cross-stone, Armenian. *See Xač^{C}k^{C}ar*
Crossbow, **2:350b–354b**
  for archery games, 5:348b
  armor and, 1:525a, 532a
  banning of, 2:354b, 11:658a
  bolt, 2:351 (*illus.*), 11:659a-b
    fletching of, 2:353b–354a
    quivers for, 2:354a-b
  clockmaking technology and, 11:658b
  construction of, 2:353a
  cranequin, 2:353b (*illus.*)
  earliest illumination depicting, 11:657b (*illus.*)
  gilded steel, 11:658a
  in hunting, 6:357a
  nut and trigger, 2:353b (*illus.*), 353a
  parangi, 11:657b
  range, 2:354a
  repeating, 2:354b
  on ships, 9:83b
  spanning implements, 2:353a–354a (*illus.*)
    calibration skills, 11:658a
    cranked conical spindle, 11:658b
  technology of and ethics, 11:657a–659b
  trigger, 11:657b
Crossing, **4:12a**
  in Auvergnat Romanesque architecture, 10:480b
Crowd (musical instrument), 8:558a, 606a
Crowley, Robert, *Piers Plowman* and, 7:329b
Crown, mural, **4:12b**
Crown technique, in glassmaking, 5:562a
Crowning, 7:256b–257b
  see also Kingship, coronation rituals
Croxton Play of the Sacrament, performance of, 4:286a, 286b
Crozier, **4:12b**, 4:13a (*illus.*)

Cruachain. *See* Rath Cruachain
Crucible (in alchemy), 1:139a
Cruciferi (rhyme form), 7:372b
Crucifixion, **4:12b–13b**
in art
Andrea Vanni's altarpiece, 12:357 (*illus.*)
at Studenica (Church of the Virgin), 11:185 (*illus.*)
basic images of, 4:12b–13a, 14 (*illus.*)
colobium in, 3:480b (*illus.*)
drawing in *Bois Protat,* 2:309b–310a
earliest representations of, 4:13a
imago pietatis and, 6:425b
Jellinge stone, 12:418b, 419a (*illus.*)
loincloth in, 4:13a-b
of Lorenzo Monaco, 7:671b (*illus.*
of Master I.A.M. of Zwolle, 6:389a (*illus.*)
of Niccolò da Bologna, 9:118b (*illus.*)
panel painting by Cimabue, 3:396a (*illus.*)
of Rodrigo de Osona, 10:437b–438a (*Illus.*)
Siena pulpit of Nicola Pisano, 9:670 (*illus.*)
symbols associated with, 4:13b
Western images of, 4:13b
legends, Wandering Jew, 12:542a–543a
in mystery plays, 8:660b
see also Alpha and omega; Deposition from the Cross; Passion cycle; Seraph
Cruciform architecture. *See* Church architecture
Cruets, 1:223a-b
Cruit (musical instrument), 8:558a, 558b
Crul, Cornelis, 4:322b
Crupper, 1:529a
Crusade and Death of Richard I, 1:265a, **4:18b**
Crusader states, **4:27a–54b**, 4:28–29 (map)
art and architecture of, **4:21b–27a**, 10:489a, 489b, 508a-b
Baybars and, 2:138b
Cairo, 3:14a
Carmelites and, 3:96b
explorations and, 4:556a
Near East, **4:27a–33a**
Battle of Acre, 10:626a
Kingdom of the Crusaders reestablished under Richard I (the Lionhearted), 10:626b
Saladin and, 10:625b–626a
stabilization of after Second Crusade, 4:38b–39a
status after First Crusade, 4:37a-b
see also Antioch; Baldwin I of Jerusalem; Bohemond I of Antioch, prince; Edessa; Jerusalem, Kingdom of; Latin Empire of Constantinople; Latin states in Greece; Lebanon; Leo I/II of Cilician Armenia, king; Syria; Tripoli
Crusades
First, 2:494b–495a, 4:16a, 19a, 30a-b, 33b–33a, 12:155b
Alexios I Komnenos and, 1:158b, 4:34a–35a
in Anatolia, 4:344a
Baldwin I of Jerusalem and, 2:58b
Beirut and, 2:164a
Council of Clermont and, 3:635b
Danishmendids in, 4:91b
Fulcher of Chartres's chronicles of, 5:311a
Genoa in, 5:384a
indulgences and, 6:448b
Karaites and, 7:210a
leadership of, 4:33b–34a
march across Anatolia, 4:35a
origins of, 4:33b
Peace and Truce of God and, 9:474b
peasants' crusade, 4:34a
Pisa and, 9:664a
Raymond IV of Toulouse and, 12:91b
siege of Antioch, 2:495a, 4:35a-b
siege of Jerusalem, 4:35b–36a
southern branch of crusaders' route and, 10:423a-b
success of, 3:356b
Syria and, 11:561a-b
Tancred and, 11:589a
Second, 2:495a, 4:30b–31a
attack on Damascus, 4:38a
Bernard of Clairvaux and, 2:192a
Conrad III of Germany and, 4:37b–38a
launching of, 3:356b
Louis VII of France and, 4:37b–38a
Manuel I Komnenos and, 8:91a-b
origin of, 4:37b
preached at Vézelay (1146), 12:405a
route followed by, 10:423 (map), 424a, 424b
Ysengrimus and, 12:733a
Third, 4:31a-b, 10:626a
Acre and, 4:25a
battle at Ḥiṭṭīn, 6:265b–266b
death of Frederick Barbarossa, 4:40a
English-French rivalry, 4:40a-b
fall of Jerusalem, 4:39b
Paulicians and, 9:468b
Qılıj Arslan II and, 11:154a
Richard I (the Lionhearted) and, 4:40a, 40b, 467b, 10:383b
route followed by, 10:423 (map), 424a, 424b
Saladin, 4:39a–40a
Seljuks of Rum and, 10:236a
Fourth, 4:31b, **4:41b–49a**, 10:251a
Boniface of Montferrat and, 4:42b–43a
Byzantine trade and, 12:103b
conquest of Constantinople, 2:497a, 498a, 4:44a–49a
conquest of Zara, 4:44a-b
Constantinople at time of, 3:550a-b (map)
Crete and, 3:678a-b
duchy of Naxos and, 9:91a
French participation in, 4:55a, 59b
Innocent III and, 6:464b
Isaac II Angelos and, 6:560a
Latin Empire of Constantinople and, 7:346a
Niketas Choniates and, 9:134a
origins of, 4:41b–42a
perversion of, 3:356a-b
in Robert de Clari's *Conquête de Constantinople,* 10:431b
Simon de Montfort in, 11:296b
Thessaloniki and, 12:26b
Venice and, 4:42a-b, 43a–44b, 12:111b, 389a–390a
Villehardouin and, 12:448b
see also Baldwin I, Latin emperor of Jerusalem
Fifth, 4:49a–51a
Innocent III and, 6:465a
papal initiatives, 3:639b, 4:49a-b
peace proclamation, 3:640b
siege of Damietta, 4:50a-b
Eighth, 4:396a
armor, 1:524a, 524b, 526a
art and architecture, **4:21b–27a**
in Jerusalem, 7:60b–61a
jewelry, 5:380a
in Syria, 6:609a
Assassins and, 1:591a-b
in the Baltic lands, 2:64b–67a
Byzantine Empire and, 4:34a–35a, 45a–49a
Cantar de mío Cid and, 3:75a
Catherine of Siena and, 11:281a
Children's, **4:14a–15a**, 9:661a
conventional view of, 4:14a
French popular movement, 4:14b–15a
German popular movement, 4:14b
ideals of, 4:15a
Master of Hungary and, 9:454a
Christian missions and, 8:445a-b
in chronicles, 3:328a
French, 3:331a, 332a, 5:514a-b
church sponsorship, political motives for, 12:567a-b
cog and, 11:242b
concept of, **4:15b–18b**
Crusade of 1101, 4:36a–37a
crusade of Frederick II, 4:51a-b
crusades of Louis IX, 4:52b–54a
capture of Louis, 4:53a-b
Egyptian campaigns, 4:52b–53a
Palestinian campaigns, 4:53b
Tunisian campaigns, 4:53b–54a
decline of crusading movement, 3:643a-b
Ephesus and, 4:495a
European cavalry in, 3:203a
Fachschrifttum and, 4:579a
Fatimid naval power and, 9:75b
financing of
church taxation and, 11:605b, 606b–607a, 608a
France, 11:621a
taxes, 11:614a
French, 4:42a, 55a, 59b
in *Graf Rudolf,* 5:644b–645a
Greek wine and, 12:649a
historiographical treatment of, 6:263a
history

Crusades (*cont.*)
history (*cont.*)
to 1192, **4:33a–41b**, 12:643b
1198–1204, **4:41b–49a**
1212–1272, **4:49a–54b**
to 1464, **4:54b–57b**
Hungarian-Burgundian, 4:56a
Iberian Reconquest and, 10:280a
indulgences for, 6:448b
initiation of, 3:449a
Islamic administration and, 6:591a
Italian ships and, 11:232b
Jerusalem and, 7:60b–61a
al-Lādhiqiya and, 7:315b
in literature, 7:365a
Song of Roland, 8:225a
Lyons as point of departure for, 7:698a-b
Maronites and, 11:564a
martyrdom of crusaders, 8:160a
Mediterranean maritime traffic and, 9:80a
mercenary troops, 12:559a, 561b
as military pilgrimages, 9:396b
military resources, 12:561a-b
military weapons and, 3:145b
Near East, **4:27a–33a**
Assizes of Jerusalem, 1:598a–599b
Trebizond, 12:168b–170a
of Nicopolis (1396), 2:136b
origin of, 4:33a-b
papal bulls concerning, 4:19b–20a
participation of Eleanor of Aquitaine, 4:419a-b
Peasants', 4:34a, 9:523a-b
as penance, 6:485b
pilgrimage and, 9:653b, 658a, 661a
poetry of, 4:20a-b
by Reinmar der Alte, 10:294a
political, **4:57b–62a**, 6:345b
against Frederick II, 4:58b–60a
against Sicily, 4:58a-b, 60a–61a
effect upon papacy, 4:61b–62a
of Innocent IV, 6:466a-b
precedents for, 4:15b
propaganda, **4:18b–21b**, 4:54b–55a, 10:138a-b, 140b
based on the Bible, 2:216a
of Gregory IX, 4:59a
sirventes, 11:313a
see also Berthold von Regensburg
religious orders and, 3:356b
rise of Italian merchants and, 12:111a
Roger II and, 11:268b
Rolandslied and, 10:448a
role of papal legates in, 7:535a
routes, 10:423a-b, 424 (map)
songs of, 3:538b, 4:20a-b, 5:441b, 12:541a
by Albrecht von Johansdorf, 1:132b–133a
see also ¡Ay, Iherusalem!
Syrian Orthodox Church and, 11:563a
13th century, Assizes of Jerusalem, 1:598a–599b
timber use and, 3:145b
see also Albigensians, crusade against; Ayyubids; Palestine; Pilgrimage
Crusado, based on Venetian ducat, 4:301b
Crusies. *See* Lighting devices, Western European
Crutched Friars, 5:297b
preaching churches, London, 7:663b
Crux
ansata. See Ankh
commissa. See Tau cross
fourchette, 4:9a, 11 (*illus.*)
gammata. See Gammadion
gemina. See Double cross (religious symbol)
gemmata, 4:9a, 11 (*illus.*)
hasta, 4:9a
pattée, 4:9a, 11 (*illus.*)
see also Cross, forms of
"Crux de te volo conqueri." *See* Philip the Chancellor, hymns of
Cruz cruzada, panadera, 11:448a-b
Crwth, 8:558a, 558b
Cryfftz, Johan. *See* Krebs, Johan
Crypt, **4:62a-b**
liturgy and, 1:442b
in Ottonian architecture, 10:477b
in pre-Romanesque architecture, 10:92a-b
Crypt of Lucina, depiction of Last Supper in, 7:343b
Crypto Jews. *See* New Christians
Csák family, 6:343a
Ctesibius, inventions by, 11:640b
Ctesiphon, **4:62b–63a**
built by the Parthians, 9:443b
Church of the East and, 11:563a
compared with Baghdad, 2:47a
East Syrian rite and, 11:567b
ethnic makeup, 10:660b–661a
etymology of name, 10:660b
Nestorianism in, 9:106b
pillaged (637), 6:511a
under Sasanians, 6:510b
Ctesiphon, Council of (410), 7:226b
Nisibis and, 9:142a
Ctesiphon school, 3:312b
Ctesiphon, Synod of (410), 11:567b
Cú Chulainn (saga character), 6:537a, 546a, 548a-b, 550b–551a, 11:580b
reincarnation of god Lug, 9:48b
tiompan and, 8:558a
in *Wooing of Emer,* 12:199b
Cuaderna vía, **4:63a-b**, 11:411b–413b
in Juan Ruiz' *Libro de buen amor,* 10:552b–554b, 11:417b
Latin influences on, 4:63a
meter for learned poetry, 4:63a, 63b
in Pero López de Ayala's *Rimado,* 11:418b
in *Poema de Fernán González,* 11:411b
Spanish hagiography and, 11:438b–439a
used by *mester de clerecía,* 8:281a-b
in work of López de Ayala, 7:667b
see also Spanish literature, versification and prosody
Cuaresma, Doña (character in *Libro de buen amor*), 10:553a
Cuba, discovered, 4:561a
Cubānids, vs. Jalāyirids, in Armenia, 1:486a
Cubic capital. *See* Block capital
Cubicularius. See Chamberlain, England, Anglo-Saxon
Cubiculum, **4:63b–64a**
see also Hypogeum
Cubit (unit of measure), 12:588a
Cuchulain. *See* Cú Chulainn (saga character)
Cuckoo and the Nightingale, The. See Clanvowe, Sir Thomas
Cucurbit, 5:556b (*illus.*)
Cuerda seca, 3:237b, **4:64a-b**
Cuirass, 1:529a, 530a, 531b, 532a
tilting, 1:532b
see also Anime
Cuishe. *See* Cuisse
Cuisle, 8:558b
Cuisse, 1:525b, 529b, 534a (*illus.*)
Culdee movement, in Celtic church, 3:228a
Culemann fragment, 2:142a
Culhwch and Olwen, 1:566a-b, 5:389a, 7:705a, 705b, 12:600a, 610a
Culi, Jacob, *Me'am Lo'ez,* 7:179b
Culinary practice. *See* Cookery
Culm, 2:63 (map), 66a
foothold of the Teutonic Order, 2:65b
invaded by Poles and Pomeranians, 2:65a
Cult of relics. *See* Relics
Cult of saints. *See* Saints
Cum de quibusdam mulieribus. See Vienne, Council of (1312–1313)
Cuman language, 4:556a
Cuman-Kipchaks, Möngke and, 2:131b
Cumania, geographic location, 12:500a
Cumans, 7:248b–249a
bishopric, 12:505a
formation of dynasty, 10:577a
in Hungary, 6:342a, 343a, 343b, 344b
invasions of Russia, 10:576b–577a
Kipchak tribal union, 10:577a
Mongol conquest, 10:577a
Volga Bulgars and, 12:488b
see also Russia, nomadic invasions of
Cumbria. *See* Strathclyde, kingdom of
Cumbric dialect, 3:233b–234a, 6:436b
in *Gododdin,* 1:247a
Cumdach, **4:64b**
Cumineus Longus, bishop of Clonfort, 9:489a-b
Easter dating of, 3:228b
Penitential of, 9:489a, 489b
Cummean (Cummian). *See* Cumineus Longus, bishop of Clonfort
Cunedda Wledig, **4:64b–65a**, 8:12b–13a
Cunicpert, Lombard king, 7:657a
schism with church and, 8:377a
Cupboards, 5:323b–324a (*illus.*)
Cupola, **4:65a**
see also Qubba
Cupola church. *See* Church architecture
Cupper, 3:400b
see also Mohel
Cur Deus homo. See Anselm of Canterbury, St.
Cura animarum. See Religious instruction
Cura pastoralis. See Gregory I (the Great), pope, *Pastoral Care*

Curadmír. See "Champion's portion"
Curate, as a clerical leader of a parish, 9:414b–415a
Curfew, **4:65a**
Curia. See Kingship, holding court; Representative assemblies, German
Curia, lay, **4:65a-b**
in Champagne, 3:88b
in Cyprus, 4:71b
in England. *See* Exchequer
hundred (land division) as, 6:330b–331a
Latin literature and, 7:364b
membership of, 4:65a
parallels with papal curia, 4:66a-b
purpose of, 4:65b
in Sicily, 11:268b, 271a, 273b
to 1300, 4:480b–481a
see also Household, royal
Curia, papal, **4:65b–66b**
of Benedict XII, 3:364a
chancery, 4:66a
church architecture and, 1:442a
college of cardinals and, 4:65b–66a
Franciscan modifications, 2:372a–373a
of John XXII, 3:363b
legal offices, 4:66a
liturgy of, **9:379b–380b**
Abelard's view of, 9:379b
addition of martyr-popes to, 9:380a
development of, 9:380a-b
as liturgy of Roman church, 9:380a
vs. the liturgy of the canons of the Lateran, 9:379b
membership of, 4:65a
parallels with lay curia, 4:66a-b
Roger II and, 11:267b
Roman nobility and, 10:522b
see also Datary, apostolic; Legate, papal
Curia regis
as antecedent of the Scottish parliament, 9:438a
in Castile, 3:132b
court of common pleas and, 3:491a
Curial e Guelfa, 3:170a
Curial, Le. See Chartier, Alain
Curopalates, **4:66b**
Nersēs III Išχanecʿi (Šinoł) and, 9:102b–103a
Curragh, 9:89a, 11:238b–239a, 239b
Curriculum. *See* Seven liberal arts; Universities
Currus (luxury vehicle), 12:369b
"Cursed Daunsers," story of, 5:433b
Cursor mundi, 4:546b, 8:316b
on Middle English dialects, 8:312b
sex aetates mundi and, 11:215a
Cursus
cursus velox, 3:253b
use in papal chancery, 4:67a
see also Cuaderna vía
Cursus (grammar), **4:66b–67b**
accentual patterns in, 4:67a
ars dictaminis and, 10:358a, 359a
Cursus publicus. See Postal and intelligence services, Roman imperial
Curtain walls, 3:150b
Curtea de Argeş (monastery: Romania), 10:510b
Curule, 5:323b
Curzoya, Battle of (1298), 12:391a
Cushion capital. *See* Block capital
Cusp, **4:67b–68a**, 4:67b (*illus.*)
quatrefoil, 10:239a
Custom of the Fairs. *See* Fairs
Customary, **4:68a**
of Carthusians, 3:118a, 118b–119b
Customs. *See* Tolls
Customs of Barcelona, in Greece, 7:379b
Custos, **4:68a**
Custumals of Normandy, **4:68b–69b**, 7:458b
Conseil à un ami, 9:644b
Frankish content of, 9:162a
on inquest, 6:479b
Philip Augustus and, 9:168b
provincial status and, 9:169a, 170a
Summa de legibus, 4:68b
Très ancien coutumier and, 4:68b
Cuthbert of Jarrow, on Bede, 2:155b
Cuthbert of Lindisfarne, St.
ascetic life, 6:67a-b
Bede on, 2:155a, 155b
Lindisfarne Gospels and, 7:583a, 584a
Cuthbert reliquary, 7:228b
Cuvier, Le, 4:265b
Cybele, cult of, 9:1a
Cycles of the Gods (Irish sagas), 6:545b–546b
Cycles of history (Ismaili doctrine), 6:587b–588a, 615b
Cycles of the Kings (Irish sagas), 6:546b–547b
Cydnus River, silting of, 11:599b
Cyfarwydd, areithiau and, 1:452b
Cyfarwyddyd, Triads of the Island of Britain and, 12:600b
Cyfranc Lludd a Lleuelys, Celtic mythology and, 9:47a
Cyhydedd hir. See Welsh literature, poetic meter
Cyhydedd naw ban. See Welsh literature, poetic meter
Cymbala. See Bells, chime
Cymbals, 8:606a, 613a (*illus.*)
Cymeriad. See Welsh literature, poetry
Cynan Garwyn, Powys chieftain, poetry written for, 12:597a, 602a
Cynddelw Brydydd Mawr, **4:69b–70a**, 12:606a
bardic career, 4:69b
Gogynfeirdd and, 4:69b
praise poem to Madog ap Maredudd, 12:604b
Cynewulf
Christ, 1:278a, 2:221b, 4:500b
Elene, 8:327a
Exeter Book riddles wrongly attributed to, 10:398b
identification of, 1:278a
Cynfeirdd, 12:598b
legendary poetry, 12:603b–604a
panegyric, 12:604a
political prophecy, 12:604a
religious verse, 12:604a
Cynghanedd, 12:597b, 599a
alliteration and internal rhyme, 12:607a-b
evolution in Welsh verse, 3:121b
Cyprian of Carthage, bishop. *See* Cyprian, St.
Cyprian (Gallic poet, *ca.* 400), *Heptateuchos,* 7:361a
Cyprian of Russia, metropolitan, occupation of see, 10:594a
Cyprian, St., **4:70a-b**
heresy and, 3:335b
on liturgy, 7:625b
Novatian schism and, 9:366b
on portable altars, 1:225a
position on Roman primacy, 9:367a
Cypriot art, 4:73a
early Christian silver plates, 4:350b (*illus.*)
classical motifs, 4:351b, 353a
made for Heraklios, 4:353a, 362a
MS illuminations as model for, 4:357a
Cypriot law, 4:71a–72b
Cyprus
Byzantine sea routes and, 10:423 (map), 424b
Byzantine trade and, 12:101a, 103a
Genoese merchants in, 12:111b
see also Lazarus, raising of
Cyprus, kingdom of, **4:70b–73a**
administration of, 4:71b
Byzantine loss of (1191), 2:497a
Byzantine recapture of
in 874, 2:118a
in 965, 9:75a, 132b
church history, 4:72b
economy of, 4:72a
as feudal monarchy, 4:71a-b
Frederick II of Germany and, 4:70b–71a
Jean d'Ibelin and, 6:389a, 389b, 9:558a
legal system of, 4:71b–72a
Lusignan rule, 7:689a
Muslims and, 4:70b, 6:572b, 9:74a
nobility of, 4:72a
occupied by the Mamluk army (1426), 8:75a
rebellion of Isaac Komnenos, 1:245a, 4:70b
religious communities in, 4:72b
Richard I of England and, 4:70b, 10:383b
sack of Alexandria (1365), 8:74b
social classes in, 4:72a-b
strife over lordship of, 4:71a
Turkish pirates and, 4:71a
Venetian possession, 7:689b
wealth of, 4:72a
Cyriacus, St., 1:520a, 6:317a, 317b
Cyril of Alexandria, St., 3:629a, 629b, **4:74b–75b**, 10:454b
against Nestorius, 4:75a, 9:105b, 106a, 108a-b
anaphora and, 1:516b
Astuacacin and, 1:502a
Christology of, 4:74b–75a
Monophysite theology and, 8:477a
De incarnatione unigeniti dialogus, 1:506a
Divine Word, formula for, 9:561a

Cyril of Alexandria, St. (*cont.*)
  as doctor of the church, 4:234a
  ecclesiastical career, 4:74b
  education of, 7:595b
  Eutyches and, 4:524a
  Five Books Against the Blasphemies of Nestorius, 9:108b
  lexicon attributed to, 11:52b, 53a
  Syrian Orthodox Church and, 11:563b
  Theotokos and, 12:25b–26a
  translations of, into Armenian, 1:507b
  writings of, 4:75a
Cyril of Jerusalem, St., 1:518b
  Alexandrian school and, 3:336a
  Catechetical Lectures, 1:507b
  Christology of, 3:320a
  as doctor of the church, 4:234a
Cyril, St., **4:73a–74b**, 4:73a-b, 9:687a, 12:26b
  Chartres notation and, 8:556b
  Czech literature and, 11:343a-b
  disciples of, 2:464a
  Glagolitic alphabet, 2:463b, 489a
  missionary work of, 8:442b
  Moravian mission, 2:299a, 463b, 489a-b
  Slavic language and, 11:341a-b
  Slavonic language and, 5:658b, 6:436a
  Slavonic liturgical texts, 10:591b
  translations
    of Glagolitic rite, 5:542b
    of Septuagint, 2:215b
Cyril of Turov, 11:347a
Cyrillic alphabet. *See* Alphabets, Cyrillic
Cyropaedeia. See Xenophon
Cyrus II (the Great) of Persia, king
  romantic tradition surrounding, 7:221a
  Zoroastrianism and, 12:746b
Cyrus of Alexandria, governor, 6:569b
Cyrus of Edessa, 11:565b
Cyrus River. *See* Kura River
Cysat, Rennward, 4:267b, 270a-b
Cysegrlan Fuchedd, 12:614b
Cywydd meter, 4:76b, 6:500b, 12:599a, 607a
Cywyddwyr
  foreign influence, 12:599a
  language, 12:599a
  major poets, 12:599a, 599b
Czech Brethren. *See* Bohemian Brethren
Czech drama, 11:344a
Czech language, 6:438a, 444a, 11:341b, 342a
  Bible translation by John Hus, 2:216a
  translation of *Schwabenspiegel* into, 11:80b
Czech literature, 11:343a–344b
Czechs, 2:299a
  in Bohemia, 6:365b, 366b
  Poland and, 9:721a
Czepko, Daniel, influenced by Meister Eckhart, 9:32a

D

Da Costa Hours, 1:297 (*illus.*)
Daʿāʾim al-islām fi'l-ḥalāl wa'l-ḥarām. See Nuʿmān, Abū Ḥanifa
Dabdāb. See Ṭabl al-markab
Dabil. *See* Dwin
Dabo family, 9:149a
Dąbrówka, Jan, 9:729b
Dacheriana, 9:490a
Dach'i (522–534), 3:308a
Dacia
  Constantine I and, 10:459a
  Goths and, 2:89b–90a, 90b, 12:468b
  Vlachs and, 12:484a
  vs. Roman Empire, 10:509b
Daco-Romanian language, 6:435b–436a
Dactylici tripertiti, 7:373a
Daddi, Bernardo, **4:75b–76a**
  Madonna and Child with Eight Angels, 4:75b (*illus.*)
  paintings by, 12:175a
  Virgin and Child, tabernacle for, 9:258a
Dadolychau. See Welsh literature, poetry
Dafni, church of. *See* Daphni, church of
Dafydd ap Edmwnd, codification of canonical meters, 12:599b, 608b
Dafydd ap Gwilym, **4:76a–77a**
  debate with Gruffudd Gryg, 12:608a-b
  innovation in poetry of, 4:76a-b
  Iolo Goch and, 6:500a, 500b
  llatai poems, 12:599b, 606b
  love poetry, 4:76b, 12:606a–607a
  mastery of *cywydd* meter, 4:76b
  poetry, 12:599a-b
Dafydd ap Llywelyn, Welsh prince
  homage to Henry III of England, 12:520b
  rebellion against Edward I of England, 12:522a-b
  rebellion of Welsh and marcher lords, 12:520b
Dagger of Faith. See Martini, Raymond
Daggers
  types of, 11:550 (*illus.*), 551a, 551b
  see also Swords
Dagmar of Denmark, queen, in ballads, 11:7a
Dagobert I, Merovingian king, 8:278b, 9:499a
  creation of Aquitaine by, 1:366b
  Paris under, 9:401b
  seal of, 11:129a
  tomb of, 5:623a-b
Dāʿī. See Daʿwā
Dailamites, 7:310b
Daily Office. *See* Divine Office
Dair Balāʾizeh, 1:155a
Dair Qunni (monastery: Iraq), 11:564b–565a
Dāʾira, 8:561b, 610b (*illus.*), 613a
Daire, 8:561b
Dairy products
  butter cross, 5:126a
  cheese, Northern Europe, 1:95b–96a
  cheesemaking, 5:126a-b
  trade in, 5:126a-b
Dál Cais, **4:77a-b**
  control of Munster, 8:531b
  Irish kingship and, 6:516b
  kings, 8:531b–532a
  origins of, 4:77a
  role in Munster politics, 4:77a-b
  vs. Eóganacht, 4:493a
Dál Riata, **4:77b–78b**, 11:113a, 113b
  colonization of Scotland by, 12:255b–256a
  early history of, 4:77b–78a
  Nechtan and, 9:91b
  ruling dynasties, 4:78a-b
  sources for history of, 4:78a
  Viking attacks on, 7:229b
  see also Strathclyde, kingdom of
Dalalagen, 7:525a
Dalālat al Ḥāʿirīn. See Maimonides, Moses
Dalarna. *See* Dalecarlia
Dalecarlia, rebellions of, 11:533b
Dalimil's Chronicle, 11:344a
Dallán Forgaill
  Amra Choluim Chille, 6:525b–526a, 541a
    on death of St. Columba, 8:558b
Dalle Masegne, Jacobello, **4:78b–79b**
  Tomb of Giovanni da Legnano, 4:79a (*illus.*)
Dalle Masegne, Pierpaolo, **4:78b–79b**
  Tomb of Giovanni da Legnano, 4:79a (*illus.*)
Dalmatia, **4:79b–80a**
  Basil I and, 2:117b
  Basil II and, 4:5b
  as battleground for Hungary and Venice, 4:8a
  as Byzantine province, 4:2b, 4b, 79b
  Croatians in, 4:1b
  Frankish invasions, 4:23
  Hungary and, 4:79b–80a, 6:337b, 341a, 346a
  Norman invasion of (1081–1085), 12:111a-b
  Slavic liturgy in, 4:6a
  Tomislav of Croatia and, 4:4a, 12:68b–69a
  Venice and, 4:5b, 79b, 80a, 12:386a-b
Dalmatian language, 6:435b
Dalmatic, **4:80a-b**, 12:398b, 399a–400a (*illus.*)
Dalmaú, Luis, **4:80b**
  Huguet and, 6:328a
  Juan Rexach and, 10:342b
  Virgin of the Councillors, 5:612 (*illus.*)
Dalmau Ses Planes, 9:511a
Dama y el pastor, La, 11:429a
Damascene, John. *See* John of Damascus, St.
Damascening, 1:536a
Damascus, **4:80b–85b**
  administration of, 4:84a-b

Ayyubids and
fortifications of, 2:21a
mausoleums in, 2:21b
sieges, 10:625b
Beirut and, 2:164a
captured (1260), 7:315b
ceramics of, 6:608a
culture, 4:84b–85a
geography, 4:80b–81b
Great Mosque, 6:403b, 407a, 593a, 593b, 12:263b–264a (*illus.*)
ḥadīth travel and, 12:147b
history, 4:81b–82b
hospital at, 6:607a
Ilkhanid conquest of (1300), 6:420b
Islamic art in, 6:607a, 607b
Islamic conquest of, 6:568a
Islamic mysticism and, 9:39a
libraries of, 7:561a
mint at, 8:417b, 421b
Mongol invasions, 6:329a, 8:473a, 11:630b
al-Mutawakkil in, 8:654b
Qasilynn observatory, 11:99a
Second Crusade and, 4:31a, 38a, 39b
Shīrāz and, 11:252a
sword production in, 11:471a
Tamerlane and, 8:75a, 11:588a
topography, 4:82b–84a
Damasus I, pope
enhancement of papal power by, 9:367b–370a
pretensions of Constantinople and, 9:370a
as founder of papal library, 7:559b
Jerome and, 12:495b
Vulgate, 2:211a
martyrs' burials and, 3:154b
recognition of authority by Optatus of Mileve, 9:367b, 370a
Dame à la licorne (tapestry), 6:362b
Dame loyale en amour, debate on *La belle dame sans merci* and, 9:637a
Dame Siriȝ, 8:316b
Dāmghān, mosque of, 6:599a
Damian of Preslav, patriarch, 2:406b
Damietta, crusades and, 4:31b–32a, 50a-b, 52b–53b, 6:390a
Ḍamīma. See Rushd, Ibn
Dammartin, Drouet de. *See* Drouet of Dammartin
Dammartin, Guy de. *See* Guy of Dammartin
Damnonii, 11:489b
Damoiseau, 11:465b
Dampierre, Guillaume, Pastoureaux uprising and, 9:452b–453a
Dams
arch, 12:577a
Muslim, 12:577a
Siena reservoir, 12:577b–578a
Dámusta saga, 10:395b
Dán díreach, 6:532a, 532b, 534a, 535a, 535b, 537a
Dança general de la Muerte, **4:85b–86a**, 11:420a
reworkings of, 11:422a
Dance, **4:86a–90a**
dancing songs of Neidhart "von Reuental," 9:94a-b
estampida, 10:251a
instrumental dance songs, 4:88a-b
music for, 8:595b–596a, 603a
instruments, 4:68b, 8:635a
as pastime, 5:350b
poetry for, 6:658b
in religious context, 4:86a-b
round, 10:529a
Scandinavian ballad dances, 11:3a-b
trecento music and, ballata, 12:179b
troubadour songs, *balada* and *dansa,* 12:218a
vocal dance songs, 4:87a-b
see also Bassedanse; Ductia; Estampie
Dance of death, 4:93b (*illus.*), 121b
see also Danse macabre; *Dança general de la Muerte*
Dance Statute (1521), 9:202a
Dancus rex, 6:359b
Dandānqān, Battle of (1040), 11:151b
Dandolo, Andrea, doge of Venice, 9:330b, 12:392a-b
on foundation of Venice, 12:382a-b, 385b
Dandolo, Enrico, doge of Venice, 4:204a, 12:387b
Fourth Crusade and, 4:42a-b, 43b–44a, 44b, 45a, 45b, 47a-b, 12:389a-b
vs. Ioannitsa, 7:347a
Dandolo, Giovanni, doge of Venice, 12:391a
Dandolo, Marino, 7:377a
Dandolo (Venetian noble family), 12:390a
Danegeld, **4:90a-b**
amounts of, 4:90a-b
assessment and collection of, 4:90b
Ethelred the Unready and, 4:517b, 12:434a
following Battle of Maldon, 4:457a
survival as tax, 4:90b
Viking raids on Francia and, 12:431a
Danehof, 4:155a
Danelagh. *See* Danelaw
Danelaw, **4:91a-b**, 4:92 (map), 12:432b
distinctive features of, 4:91a-b
Dunstan and, 3:82b
language spoken in, 9:227b
reconquest of, 4:456b
urbanization, 4:458a
Danes
in *Beowulf,* 2:183a
in England, 4:91a-b, 12:432a–434a
Battle of Hastings and, 9:165a
ravaging of Anglesey in 855 and 874, 10:366a
shire and, 11:253b
tribute to, 4:90a-b
Wulfstan of York and, 12:704a, 704b
in Gotland, 11:532b
in Skåne, 11:532b
see also Danegeld; Danelaw
Danevirke, 11:522b, 12:424a
Daniel ben Eleazar ben Hibat Allāh, 7:72b
Daniel ben Moses al-Qūmisī, 4:539a-b, 7:107b, 163a, 210a
Daniel von dem blühenden Tal. See Stricker, Der
Daniel (Israelite prophet)
in art, 1:495a
in literature. *See* Play of Daniel
Daniel of Morley
Arabic numerals and, 10:474a
Arundel 268 and, 10:473b
Daniel (Old English poem), 1:280a, 4:550b
Daniel, Pierre, 3:476b–477a
Daniel da Pisa, 7:109b
Daniel, St. *See* Deiniol, St.
Daniel (Syriac bishop), 1:492a
Daniil Chernyi, collaboration with Andrei Rublev, 10:541b
Danilo, biographer of Milutin, 11:186b
Danish ax. *See* Ax
Danish church, Sweyn Estridsen and, 4:152b, 153a
Danish language, of Copenhagen, 6:437a
Danish law, **7:431a–433a**
abolition of judicial ordeal, 7:431a
absence of church law from, 7:432a
corporation laws, 7:432b
grammatical form of legal statements in, 7:432a
guild laws, 7:432b
influences in early development of, 7:431a
Jutland laws, 7:431b–432a
range of subjects, 7:432a
"Thord's articles," 7:432a
lèse majesté and, 7:431a-b
maritime and commercial regulations, 7:432b
Skåne laws, 7:431b
town regulations, 7:432b
Vederlov corporation laws, 7:432b
Zealand (Sjælland) laws, 7:431b
interrelation of laws and law texts, 7:431b
Danish literature
ballads, influence of, 6:36b, 37b
see also Scandinavian literature
Danishmendids, **4:91b–93a**
in Anatolia, 1:241b
Bohemond I of Antioch and, 2:309a
capital at Sebaste, 11:132a
in First Crusade, 4:91b
Ikonion and, 6:418a
John II Komnenos and, 7:127a
in Melitene, 8:269b
origins of, 4:91b
Qılıj Arslān and, 10:235b
Seljuks of Rum and, 11:154a, 157a
Vahka Castle and, 12:345a
vs. Seljuks, 1:485a, 514a, 4:93a
Dānishnāma (*Dānishnāma-i ᶜAlāʾī*), 4:445b
see also Sīnā, Ibn
Daniști, 10:514b
Dannīya. See Qalansuwa
Dansa, in Provençal literature, 10:164b
Danse macabre, **4:93a**, 4:93b (*illus.*)
by Huss, 9:680a (*illus.*)
by Notke, 9:186b
Danske Rimkrønike, 11:20b–21a
Dante Alighieri, **4:94a–105a**
alleged membership in Fedele d'Amore, 9:2b
in Arezzo, 4:99b

Dante Alighieri (*cont.*)
on artists' status, 1:579a-b
on assassins, 1:590b
Beatrice Portinari and, 4:96b–97a
Boccaccio on, 2:289b
Cavalcanti and, 3:196a-b
Cecco Angiolieri and, 3:211b
Cino da Pistoia and, 3:397b
comic poetry and, 6:649b
Convivio, 4:99b–101a, 6:648b
on Latini, 7:382b
music and, 8:583a
De monarchia, 5:488a, 7:268a
De vulgari eloquentia, 4:99b, 100a, 6:443b, 626a-b, 648a-b
Castra in, 6:656b
Cielo d'Alcamo in, 6:656a
on Guido delle Colonne, 11:258b
on Guittone, 6:644a-b
on Iacopo da Lentini, 6:387b, 11:259b
influence of Guido Guinizzelli on, 6:24b–25a
on Lapo Gianni, 6:649a
on Latini, 7:382b
on lyric poetry, 6:640b–641a
on poetry, 6:665a-b, 666b, 667a
on Sicilian poetry, 11:257a
Divine Comedy, 4:94a–95b (*illus.*)
Arnaut Daniel in, 10:175a
Bertran de Born in, 2:202a
Boccaccio and, 6:651b
in Bologna archives, 6:657b
Bonagiunta in, 6:644a
Cicero's place in, 10:355b
compared with *Pearl,* 8:320a
concept of paradise in, 9:395b, 398a
Convivio and, 4:101a
Dezir a las syete virtudes and, 6:429a
encyclopedic nature of, 4:449a
on the fate of usurers, 12:337b
Fazio and, 6:632b
four senses of allegory in, 1:186a
French literature and, 4:101b
Giacomino da Verona and, 6:651a
Gratian in, 9:517b
Guinizzelli in, 6:25a, 647a
Hugh of St. Victor in, 9:514a
Iacopo da Lentini and, 6:387b
Inferno, 6:658a, 7:382a, 382b, 383b
Istoria fiorentina and, 6:633b
lauda and, 6:663a
lyric poetry and, 6:648b
Mechthild von Magdeburg as Matelda in, 8:241b
metrics of, 6:665b–666a
Michael Scot in, 8:305a
music and, 8:583a
nature of Fortune, 5:146a
Nile and, 9:137b
Paradise in, 9:395b, 398a
parodied by Boccaccio in *Corbaccio,* 2:286a
Peter Comestor in, 9:514a
Peter Lombard in, 9:517b
Piero della Vigna in, 11:258b
popularity of, 4:94b
Purgatory, 6:645b
Siger in, 11:285b
style of, 4:100a-b
terza rima in, 6:670a, 8:345b
theories of harmony, 6:100a
Thomistic theology in, 12:42a
Tuscan dialect and, 6:626a, 626b, 627a, 629a
Urbino Codex, 12:394 (*illus.*)
Vergil and, 12:394a-b
visions and, 12:476b
on dowries, 4:145b–146a
early years, 4:96a-b
education of, 4:97b
eulogy to, 5:97b
exile of, 4:99a, 103b–104a, 5:96b
family, 4:104a
in Florence, 4:95b–98b
in Forlì, 4:99a
Ghibelline ideologies, 6:6b
imperialist views of, 4:101b–103a
influence of
on Boccaccio, 2:285a, 288a
on Chaucer, 3:282b–283a
involvement in Guelph factionalism, 4:98b–99b
Latin works of, 7:369b
Latini and, 6:651b
letter to Can Grande della Scala, 4:103a-b
on allegory, 1:178b, 179b–180a
lyric poetry and, 6:647b–648b, 656b
lyrics and odes, 4:98b–99a, 6:648b
Monarchia, 4:102b–103
on papal power, 10:22a-b
Peire Cardenal and, 9:485a
political career of, 4:97b, 98a–99b
in Ravenna, 4:103b–104a
Roman de la Rose and, 4:101b, 6:631b, 669b
on Sicilian poetry, 11:274b
Te lucis ante terminum, 8:572a
theological and moral concerns of, 4:94a
translations of, into Catalan, 3:169b
in Verona, 4:99a, 103a, 103b, 104a
views of purgatory, 10:217a
visit to France, 4:101a-b
Vita nuova, 4:96b–97a
Breviari d'amor and, 4:506b
Cavalcanti and, 6:647a, 648a
Guinizzelli and, 6:24b, 647a, 648a
on poetry, 6:665a
Dante da Maiano, 6:645a
Danu (Celtic goddess), 9:46a, 47a
Danube River
as boundary between the Roman world and Germanic peoples, 2:88b
crossed by the Goths in the 3rd century, 2:89b
medieval trade and, 12:115a
see also Austria
Danza di Salomè, La, 6:636a
Danzig, population of, 5:458a
Daphni, church of, 4:553a (*illus.*)
Christ Pantokrator, bust of, 2:444a
mosaics
Crucifixion, 2:444b (*illus.*)
figure style, 2:444a
use of line, 2:444a
Daphnusia, Venetians at, 7:349b
Dapifer. See Steward, royal, England
Daqāʾiqī of Marv, *Bakhtiyār-nāma,* 6:508b
Dar al-bazzaziyah. See Bedestan
Dār al-Ḥarb. See Abode of Islam—Abode of War
Dār al-Ḥikma, 6:74a
Dār al-ʿIlm, 11:83b
Dār al-Islām. See Abode of Islam—Abode of War
Dār al-Khilāfah (in Baghdad), 2:46b
Dara, 8:561b
Dārāb-nāma, 6:508b
Darabukka, 8:613a
Darazī, al-, Druze prophet, 4:295b–296a
death of, 4:296a
Ḍarb, 8:561b
Darband. *See* Derbent
Darbazi, in Georgian architecture, 5:408a-b
Dardanelles, **4:105a-b**
Byzantine sea routes and, 10:423 (map), 424b
Dardic languages, 6:505b
Daredevils of Sasun, The. See *Sasna Cṙer*
Dares Phrygius, 4:496a, 5:445b, 7:360b
De excidio Troiae, 12:220a, 221b
Trójumanna saga and, 10:389b
on Trojan War, 2:182a, 8:225b
Daret, Jacques, **4:105b**
Campin and, 3:60b, 61a
Darius I of Persia, king
palace of, 11:252a
tomb of at Naqsh-i Rustam, 9:61a-b
Darokhranitelnitsa, **4:105b**
Darraðarljóð, **4:105b–106b**
Njáls saga and, 4:105b–106a
origin of, 4:106a-b
Valkyries in, 9:172a, 12:351a
Darrein presentment, assize of, 6:481b
Darts. *See* Spears
Darvīsh. See Dervish
Dastin, John, alchemical treatises, 1:138a
Dastūr dastūrān. See Mōbadān mōbad
Datarius, 3:253b–254a
Datary, apostolic, **4:106b–107b**
establishment of, 4:106b
fees and, 4:107a
responsibilities of, 4:107a
Datastanagirkʿ, 11:351b
Dātastānnāmak, 8:204b
Date, 9:199a
in Mediterranean region, 5:306a, 307a-b
in pre-Islamic Arabia, 1:371a
Dating, radiocarbon. *See* Radiocarbon dating
Datini, Francesco (merchant of Prato), 1:446b, 562a-b, 2:77a, 12:112b
Daud, Ibn, *Sefer ha-kabbalah,* order of the rabbis, 6:256a
Dāʾūd ibn Sukmān, capital at Ḥiṣn Kayfā, 9:283b
Daugava (western Dvina) River Valley, Christianization of Balts and, 2:64b
Dauphin, **4:107b–108a**
Paris under, 9:405a–406a, 406b

Dauphiné, **4:108a–110b**, 4:108b (map)
early history, 4:108a-b
economy, 4:110a
French absorption of, 4:107b, 109a
government, 4:109b
Holy Roman Empire and, 10:320a, 321a
provincial estates and assemblies, 10:320a, 321a, 325a-b
relations with
France, 4:109a-b
Holy Roman Empire, 4:108b
Davanzati, Chiaro, 6:632a, 645a
David II (IV) (the Builder) of Georgia, king, 2:49a, **4:111b–112a**
Ani and, 1:291a, 485a-b
campaigns against Seljuks, 4:406a-b, 5:420a
capture of Tbilisi, 11:631b
construction of Gelatᶜi, 5:374a
ecclesiastical reforms of, 5:413b
in *Kᶜartᶜlis Cᶜχovreba,* 7:223a
Zakᶜarids and, 12:736a
David I of Scotland, king, **4:110b–111a**, 11:104b–105a, 107b
Ethelred of Rievaulx and, 4:516b, 517a
family origins, 4:110b
initiation of burgh at Edinburgh, 4:393a-b
invasions of Northumbria, 4:316a-b
land grants of, 4:111a
monastic foundations, 11:105a
parliament and, 9:438a
religious interests, 4:101b
sheriff and, 11:226a
David II of Scotland, king, **4:111a-b**, 10:427b, 11:110a-b, 111a
Edward III and, 2:202b, 4:111a
nobility and, 4:111b
parliament and, 9:438b, 439a, 439b
release from captivity, 11:110b
David Anhołin (the Landless), Loṙi-Tašir and, 1:484b
David ap Gruffudd, treason execution of, 12:165b–166a
David (Armenian Neoplatonist), 1:505b
David of Augsburg, 9:31b
mysticism of, 8:355a
referred to in *Schwabenspiegel,* 11:80b
work in English, 9:27a
David ben Abraham al-Fāsī, 4:539b, 7:210b
Hebrew-Arab biblical lexicon, 6:129a
David ben Daniel, 7:105a
David ben Se'adel ibn al-Hītī. *See* Hītī, David ben Se'adel ibn al-
David (Dawitᶜ) Soslan (consort of Queen Tamar), 5:406b–407a, 11:587a
David of Dinant
condemned in 1210 and 1215, 1:228b
Neoplatonism and, 9:100b
David fitz Gerald, bishop of St. David's, 5:421a
David of Garedja, monasteries and, 4:116a
David of Georgia, king, 1:235b
David, Gerard, **4:114–115**, 5:611b, 7:155b
Baptism Triptych, 5:87b
Virgo Inter Virgines, 4:115 (*illus.*)
see also Flemish art, painting
David of Harkᶜ, 4:114b
David Hypatos, 4:114b
David the Invincible, **4:114a-b**
in Armenian magical texts, 8:16b
commemorated as Armenian saint, 1:520a, 520b
identity of, 4:114b
philosophical works of, 4:114a
David of Israel, king, in art, 1:497a
David Kimḥi, as exegete, 4:541a-b
David Komnenos, ruler of Paphlagonia, vs. Theodore I Laskaris, 9:116a
David, St.
church foundations in Dyfed, 4:329b
putative rivalry with Cadoc, 3:7a
Thomas Becket office and, 10:371a
David of Sasun, **4:112a–113a**
David of Sinope, 10:59b
David of Tao, Georgian Bagratid prince, 2:49a, **4:113b–114a**, 5:406a, 7:215a
alliance of Gagik I with, 5:338b
Basil II and, 1:483b
capture of Manazkert and, 8:81a
rule of Taykᶜ, 11:629a
Xaχuli and, 12:713a
David of Tarōn. *See* David of Harkᶜ
Davidiz, Sisnando, governor of Toledo, 12:68a
Davis, John (*fl.* 1590), inventor of backstaff, 4:12b
Daw, John, **4:115a-b**
Daᶜwā, 6:615a, 615b
Fatimid, 6:616a
of Ḥamīd al-Dīn al-Kirmānī, 6:616b
of Ḥasan-i Ṣabbāḥ, 6:617a
Qāḍī Nuᶜmān and, 6:616b
Dawāt, **4:115b–116a**, 4:116 (*illus.*), 12:698b
Dawāwīn. *See* Fatimids
Dawid-Garedja, **4:116a**
martyrs of, 5:414a
Dawitᶜ Alawkayordi, 1:512a
Dawitᶜ (son of Gurgēn), Armenian campaigns, 7:672b
Dawla, al-, Buyid emir, al-Kufa and, 7:308a
Dawlat al-atrāk. *See* Mamluk dynasty
Dawn song. *See* Alba; Aubade
Dawtᶜak (Armenian poet), 4:114b
on Jewanšēr, 1:509b
Dāwūd ibn Marwān al-Muqammiṣ, **4:116b–117a**, 7:151b
Twenty Treatises, 10:2b
Day
definition of, 3:18a
determination of in Jewish calendar, 3:25b
division of in Christian calendar, 3:23b–24a
in Islamic calendar, 3:27b
names for in Jewish calendar, 3:25b
Day of Atonement, *see also* Fasting, Islamic
Day of Atonement (Jewish ritual), adopted by Muḥammad, 9:497b
"Day of the Ditch" (787), 12:67b–68a
Day Office, 4:229a
Dāy, Idrisids in, 6:413b
Daylamīs. *See* Buyids
Dayr, **4:117a**
Dayyan (Jewish law, rabbinic judge), 7:74b
De, see also Book of; Kitāb; Liber de; On; Sefer; Tractatus de
De actibus apostolorum. *See* Arator
De administrando imperio. *See* Constantine VII Porphyrogenitos
De adventu antichristi. *See* Arnald of Villanova
De amore libri tres. *See* Capellanus, Andreas
De anima. *See* Aristotle; Cassiodorus Senator; Sīnā, Ibn
De anima ad Odonem Bellovacensem. *See* Ratramnus of Corbie
De anulo et baculo. *See* Donizo
De aquis urbis Romae. *See* Frontinus
De arca Noe morali. *See* Hugh of St. Victor
De arca Noe mystica. *See* Hugh of St. Victor
De architectura. *See* Vitruvius
De arithmetica. *See* Boethius
De arte honeste amandi. *See* Capellanus, Andreas, *De amore libri tres*
De arte mensurandi. *See* Jehan des Murs
De arte metrica. *See* Bede
De arte rhetorica. *See* Notker Teutonicus
De arte venandi cum avibus. *See* Frederick II of Germany, emperor
De aspectibus. *See* Kindī, Abū Yūsuf Yaᶜqūb ibn Isḥāq al-
De Babilonia. *See* Giacomino da Verona
De baptismo. *See* Basil the Great of Caesarea, St.
De bello saxonico liber. *See* Bruno of Magdeburg
De bono pacis. *See* Rufinus
De Burgo family, Muireadhach Albanach and, 9:205a
De caelesti hierarchia. *See* Pseudo-Dionysius the Areopagite
De caelo. *See* Oresme, Nicole
De canonio, 1:438a
De cantu et correctione antiphonarii, 8:643a
De cantu et musica sacra. *See* Gerbert, Martin
De cantu figurato. *See* Hothby, John
De cantu organico, 8:646b
De casibus monasterii S. Galli. *See* Ratpert of St. Gall
De casibus virorum illustrium. *See* Boccaccio, Giovanni
De casu diaboli. *See* Anselm of Canterbury, St.
De causa Dei contra Pelagium et de virtute causarum. *See* Bradwardine, Thomas
De ceremoniis. *See* Constantine VII Porphyrogenitos
De civili dominio. *See* Wyclif, John
De civitate Dei. *See* Augustine of Hippo, St., *City of God*
De claris mulieribus. *See* Boccaccio, Giovanni

De clementia. See Seneca
De clerico faciendo. See Tonsure
De clericorum institutione. See Hrabanus Maurus
De cognitione baptismi. See Ildefonsus, St.
De communi mathematica scientia. See Iamblichus
De comparatione auctoritatis papae et concilii. See Cajetan
De compendiosa doctrina. See Nonius Marcellus
De computo vel loquela digitorum. See Bede
De conceptu virginali et de originali peccato. See Anselm of Canterbury, St.
De concordantia catholica. See Nicholas of Cusa
De concordia Ypocratis Galieni et Surani, 8:255b
De conflictu Vitiorum et Virtutum. See Bernard of Clairvaux, St.
De coniuge non ducenda, 7:368b
antifeminism in, 1:323b
De consecratione. See Gratian, *Decretum*
De consensu evangelistarum. See Augustine of Hippo, St.
De conservanda bona valetudine, 4:579b
De consideratione. See Bernard of Clairvaux, St.
De consolatione Philosophiae. See Boethius, *Consolation of Philosophy*
De conspiculis. See Maurolico, Francesco
De contemplando deo. See William of St. Thierry
De contemptu mundi. See Bernard of Cluny; Innocent III, pope, *De miseria humanae conditionis*
De continuo. See Bradwardine, Thomas
De corpore Christi. See Ockham, William of
De corpore et sanguine domini. See Ratramnus of Corbie
De cosmographia. See Aethicus Ister
De cultu imaginum. See Jonas of Orléans
De cura et modo rei familiaris, 4:579a
De cura pro mortuis gerenda. See Augustine of Hippo, St.
De definitione. See Notker Teutonicus
De dialectica. See Augustine of Hippo, St.
De differentia animae et spiritus. See Qusṭa ibn Lūqā
De differentiis. See Serlo de Wilton
De diversis artibus. See Theophilus
De diversis quaestionibus. See Augustine of Hippo, St.
De divinatione. See Cicero
De divisione musicae secundum Alpharabium. See Jerome of Moravia, *Tractatus de musica*
De divisione philosophiae. See Domingo Gundisalvo
De docta ignorantia. See Nicholas of Cusa
De doctrina christiana. See Augustine of Hippo, St.
De doctrina spiritali. See Otloh of St. Emmeram
De dogmate philosophorum. See John of Salisbury
De dominio divino. See Wyclif, John
De dono timoris. See Humbert of Romans
De duabus lineis semper approximantibus sibi invicem et nunquam concurrentibus, 1:438b
De dubiis nominibus, **4:298b**
De duodecim abusivis saeculi, **4:312a-b**
Irish origin of, 4:312a, 312b
on kingship, 4:312b
links with *Collectio canonum hibernensis,* 4:312b
other Old Irish analogies with, 4:312b
popularity of, 4:312a
sources of, 4:312a
style of, 4:312b
De ecclesia. See Hus, John; Wyclif, John
De ecclesiastica potestate. See Egidius Colonna
De ecclesiasticis officiis. See Isidore of Seville, St.
De eerste bliscap van Maria, 4:322a
De electione romani pontificis. See Gozzadini, Giovanni
De eodem et diverso. See Adelard of Bath
De erroribus Guillelmi a Conchis. See William of St. Thierry
De eruditione filiorum nobilium. See Vincent of Beauvais
De eruditione praedicatorum. See Humbert of Romans
De essentiis. See Hermann von Carinthia
De eucharistia. See Wyclif, John
De excidio Britanniae. See Gildas, St.
De excidio et conquestu Brittaniae, 12:597b
De excidio Troiae. See Bernard of Fleury; Dares Phrygius; Josephus Iscanus
De fide. See Basil the Great of Caesarea, St.
De fide catholica contra Judaeos. See Isidore of Seville, St.
De fide orthodoxa. See Burgundio of Pisa
De fide Trinitatis et de incarnatione Verbi. See Anselm of Canterbury, St.
De figuris numerorum. See Priscian
De la Gardie 4-7 (Norwegian codex), version of *Elis saga ok Rosamundu,* 4:432a
De genealogia deorum gentilium. See Boccaccio, Giovanni, *Genealogy of the Pagan Gods*
De generibus et speciebus, falsely attributed to Adelard of Bath, 10:271a
De gloria confessorum. See Gregory of Tours, St.
"De Gombert et des deus clers." *See* Bodel, Jean
De grammatico. See Anselm of Canterbury, St.
De gratia Dei. See Faustus of Riez
De gratia et libero arbitrio contra collatorem. See Prosper of Aquitaine
De gubernatione Dei. See Salvian of Marseilles
De harmonia musicorum instrumentorum. See Gaffurius, Franchinus
De harmonica institutione. See Hucbald of St. Amand, *Musica*
De Heinrico (Henrico), 9:234a
source and provenance, 6:145b
De heretico comburendo, 12:709b
De hierarchia. See Pseudo-Dionysius the Areopagite
De Ierusalem. See Giacomino da Verona
De imagine mundi. See Honorius Augustodunensis
De incarnatione. See Cassian, John
De incarnatione unigeniti dialogus. See Cyril of Alexandria, St.
De incarnatione Verbi. See Anselm of Canterbury, St.
De incendio monasterii sancti Amandi. See Ghislebert of St. Amand
De ingeneis. See Mariano di Jacopo (il Taccola)
De ingratis. See Prosper of Aquitaine
De insolubilibus. See Bradwardine, Thomas; Roger de Swyneshed (14th century)
De institutione arithmetica. See Boethius
De institutione clericorum. See Hrabanus Maurus
De institutione laicali. See Jonas of Orléans
De institutione musica. See Boethius
De institutione regia. See Jonas of Orléans
De intellectu. See Kindī, al-
De intensione et remissione formarum. See Burley, Walter
De interpretatione. See Aristotle; Boethius
De invectionibus. See Gerald of Wales
De inventione. See Cicero
De inventione dialectica. See Agricola, Rodolphus
De inventione et usu musicae. See Johannes Tinctoris
De inventoribus rerum. See Vergil, Polydore
De investigatione Antichristi. See Gerhoh of Reichersberg
De itinere deserti. See Ildefonsus, St.
De iure et statu Menevensis Ecclesiae. See Gerald of Wales
De iure personarum. See Rogerius
De iure Teutonico, 9:722a-b
De iuris et facti ignorantia. See Hugo
De Jona et de Ninive, 4:547a
De judicio Dei. See Basil the Great of Caesarea, St.
De jure regni apud Scotos. See Buchanan, George
De jurisdictione spirituali et temporale. See Gerson, John
De la Mare, Peter, impeachment and, 6:427a
De lapidibus. See Marbod of Rennes

De laude Anastasii imperatoris. See Priscian
De laude Hispaniae. See Isidore of Seville, St.
De laudibus beatae Virginis Mariae. See Richard of Laurent
De laudibus Dei. See Dracontius
De laudibus divinae sapientiae. See Neckham, Alexander
De laudibus sanctae crucis. See Hrabanus Maurus
De legibus et consuetudinibus Angliae. See Bracton, Henry de, *On the Laws and Customs of England*
De libertate arbitrii. See Anselm of Canterbury, St.
De lingua latina. See Varro
De locis sanctis. See Bede
De machinis. See Mariano di Jacopo (il Taccola)
De magistratibus rei publicae romanae. See Lydus
De magnalibus urbis Mediolani. See Bonvesin de la Riva
De magnete. See Nikephoros I, patriarch
De mandatis divinis. See Wyclif, John
De materia medica. See Dioscorides
De maximis pretiis. See Diocletian, Roman emperor
De memoria beati Emmerammi. See Arnold of St. Emmeram
De mensibus. See Lydus
De mensura astrolabii. See Herman von Reichenau
De mensura fistularum. See Eberhard of Freising
De mensurabili musica. See John of Garland (music theorist)
De mensurabili positio, 8:643b
De mensuris et discantu. See Anonymous IV
De metris fabularum Terentii. See Priscian
De mirabilibus mundi, 7:363a
De mirabilis urbis Romae, first mention of carnival in, 8:28a
see also Gregory, Master
De miraculis beati Emmerammi. See Arnold of St. Emmeram
De miraculis sancti Maximini. See Sigehard of St. Maximin
De miseria humanae conditionis. See Innocent III, pope
De missarum mysteriis. See Innocent III, pope
De moderno dictamine. See Merke, Thomas
De monarchia. See Dante Alighieri
De morali principis institutione. See Vincent of Beauvais
De motettis componendis. See Egidius of Murino
De motibus celorum. See Michael Scot
De motibus naturalibus. See Roger de Swyneshed
De motu octauae sphaerae. See Thābit ibn Qurra
De mulieribus claris. See Boccaccio, Giovanni
De mundi universitate. See Bernard Silvester
De mundo, translated, 1:460b
see also Pseudo-Aristotle
De munitionibus castrorum. See Hyginus Gromaticus
De musica, 8:563a
De musica. See Adam of Fulda; Anselmi, Giorgio; Aribo; Aristides; Augustine of Hippo, St.; Engelbert of Admont; Heinrich von Augsburg; Johannes de Grocheo; Nicomachus of Gerasa; Notker Teutonicus
De musica cum tonario. See John of Afflighem
De musica mensurabili, 8:646a
De mysteriis. See Ambrose, St.
De mysteriis ecclesiae. See John of Garland
De mysterio missae. See Hildebert of Lavardin
De mysterio Trinitatis. See Bonaventure, St.
De die natali. See Censorinus
De nativitate Christi. See Ratramnus of Corbie
De natura. See Zeno
De natura et dignitate armoris. See William of St. Thierry
De natura humana. See Nemesius
De natura rerum. See Bede; Isidore of Seville, St.; Thomas of Cantimpré
De naturis rerum. See Neckham, Alexander
De neocosmo. See Honorius Augustodunensis
De nihilo et tenebris. See Fridugisus of Tours
De nugis curialium. See Map, Walter
De numeris datis. See Jordanus de Nemore
De numeris harmonicis. See Levi ben Gershom (Gerson)
De numero indorum, algoristic theory, 8:208b–209a
De nuptiis. See Theophrastus
De nuptiis Philologiae et Mercurii. See Martianus Capella
De obligationibus. See Roger de Swyneshed
De observatione ciborum. See Anthimus
De officiis. See Cicero; Pseudo-Kodinos
De officiis ecclesiasticis. See John of Avranches
De opificio hominis. See Gregory of Nyssa, St.
De ordine creaturarum, borrowings from *De duodecim abusivis,* 4:312b
De origine officiorum. See Isidore of Seville, St., *De ecclesiasticis officiis*
De origine potestatum et jurisdictionum. See Durand of St. Pourçain
De ornamentis verborum. See Marbod of Rennes
De ornatu. See Trota and *Trotula*
De orthographia. See Bede
De ortu et auctoritate imperii Romani. See Pius II, pope
De ortu et obitu patrum. See Isidore of Seville, St.
De ortu scientiarum, al-Fārābi and, 8:563a
De ostentis. See Lydus
De oto religioso (religiosorum). See Petrarch
De pace fidei. See Nicholas of Cusa
De partibus logicae. See Notker Teutonicus
De passionibus mulierum. See Kraut, Georg
De penitentia. See Gratian, *Decretum*
De perceptis artis musicae. See Guillelmus Monachus
De perfectione evangelica. See Bonaventure, St.
De perfectione vitae ad sorores. See Bonaventure, St.
De petitione hereditatis. See Hugo
De pictura. See Alberti, Leon Battista
De plana musica. See John of Garland (music theorist)
De planctu Naturae. See Alan of Lille
De Platonis pluribus libris compendiosa expositio, 9:700b
De potentia. See Aquinas, Thomas, St.
De potentia absoluta, in Gabriel Biel's theology, 2:234a-b
De potentia ordinata, in Gabriel Biel's theology, 2:234b
De potentiis animae. See Burley, Walter
De potestate regia et papali. See John of Paris
De practica artis musicae. See Aimerus
De praedestinatione. See John Scottus Eriugena
De praedestinatione dei. See Ratramnus of Corbie
De predicatione sanctae crucis. See Humbert of Romans
De prerogative romani imperii. See Jordan of Osnabrück
De pressuris ecclesiasticis. See Atto of Vercelli
De primitius ecclesia et synodo Nicena, 4:124b
De principiis. See Origen
De probatione auri et argenti, 1:434b
De processione Spiritus Sancti contra Graecos. See Anselm of Canterbury, St.
De proportione et proportionalitate. See Campanus of Novara
De proportione velocitatum in motibus. See Bradwardine, Thomas
De proportionibus proportionum. See Oresme, Nicole
De proprietatibus rerum. See Bartholomaeus Anglicus
De pugna. See Savigny, Friedrich Karl von
De pugna spirituali. See Bernard of Clairvaux, St.
De quadratura circuli. See Franco of Liège
De quadratura circuli tractatus. See Archimedes, *On the Measurement of the Circle*
De quadripartita specie nuptiarum. See Innocent III, pope
De quantitate. See Ockham, William of

De quantitate animae. See Augustine of Hippo, St.
De quarta vigilia noctis. See Gerhoh of Reichersberg
De quatuor virtutibus vitae honestae. See Hildebert of Lavardin
De querimonia et conflictu carnis et spiritus seu animae. See Hildebert of Lavardin
De quinquaginta curialitatibus ad mensam. See Bonvesin de la Riva
De radiis
influence of, 8:37b, 38a, 39a
on various magical effects, 8:37b
De raptu Proserpinae. See Claudian
De rationali et de ratione uti. See Sylvester II, pope
De re aedificatoria. See Alberti, Leon Battista
De re coquinaria. See "Apicius"
De re diplomatica. See Mabillon, Jean
De re metallica. See Agricola (Georg Bauer)
De re militari. See Valturio, Roberto
De rebus bellicis, military inventions, 11:641a
De rebus a se gestis. See Gerald of Wales
De rectoribus christianis. See Sedulius Scottus
De recuperatione Terre Sancte. See Pierre Dubois
De reditu suo. See Rutilius Claudius Namatianus
De reductione artium ad theologiam. See Bonaventure, St.
De regia potestate et sacerdotali dignitate. See Hugh of Fleury
De regimine animae. See Bonaventure, St.
De regimine christiano. See James of Viterbo
De regimine principum. See Aquinas, Thomas, St.; Egidius Colonna; Ptolemy of Lucca
De regimine vitae et sanitatis. See Bissolo, Bellino
De regno. See Aquinas, Thomas, St.
De remediis utriusque fortune. See Petrarch
De reparatione kalendarii. See Nicholas of Cusa
De reprobatione eccentricorum et epiciclorum. See Henry of Langenstein
De rerum naturis. See Hrabanus Maurus
De ruina ecclesiae. See Nicholas of Clamanges
De sacerdotio. See John Chrysostom, St.
De sacra coena. See Berengar of Tours
De sacramentis. See Hugh of St. Victor
De sacramento altaris. See Ockham, William of
De sacris aedificiis a Constantino Magno constructis. See Ciampini, Giovanni
De saltu lunae. See Columbanus, St.
De sancta Trinitate et operibus eius. See Rupert of Deutz
De scientia Christi. See Bonaventure, St.
De scientia stellarum. See Plato of Tivoli
De scientiis. See Fārābī, al-, *Iḥṣā᾽ al-ʿulūm*
De scriptura aurea/negra/rubra. See Bonvesin de la Riva, *Libro delle tre scritture*
De scripturis et scriptoribus sacris. See Hugh of St. Victor
De secreto conflicto curarum mearum. See Petrarch, *Secretum meum*
De septem diebus. See Thierry of Chartres
De septem ordinibus, clerical orders, 9:265a
De sevenste bliscap, 4:322a
De sex aetatibus mundi. See Bede
De sobrietate. See Milo of St. Amand
De sollemnitatibus et sabatis et neomeniis. See Columbanus, St.
De somno et visione. See Kindī, al-
De speculis comburentibus. See Speculi almukefi compositio
De sphera. See Grosseteste, Robert
De Spiritu Sancto. See Basil the Great of Caesarea, St.; Faustus of Riez
De statu innocenciae. See Wyclif, John
De sui ipsius et multorum ignorantia. See Petrarch
De summa temporum. See Jordanes
De suppositionibus. See Burley, Walter
De syllogismis. See Notker Teutonicus
De temporum ratione. See Bede
De terre en grec Gaulle appellée. See Vitry, Philippe de
De thematibus, 4:446b
De topicis differentiis. See Boethius
De triangulis. See Jordanus de Nemore
De trigono balistario. See Fontana, Giovanni
De trina mersione. See Martin of Braga
De Trinitate. See Boethius; Richard of St. Victor; Walter of Mauretania
De triplici via. See Bonaventure, St.
De triumphis ecclesiae. See John of Garland
De universo. See Hrabanus Maurus, *De rerum naturis*
De universo aut rerum naturis. See Hrabanus Maurus, *De rerum naturis*
De utilitatibus astrolabii. See Herman von Reichenau
De vanitate mundi. See Hugh of St. Victor
De vegetabilibus. See Albertus Magnus
De velitatione bellica. See Nikephoros II Phokas
De vera et falsa poenitentia, attribution of to St. Augustine, 9:491b
De veritate. See Anselm of Canterbury, St.
De veritate sacrae scripturae. See Wyclif, John
De vetula, 7:367b
Ovidian influence, 9:314a
De villis, 4:511b
De virginitate. See Aldhelm
De virginitate S. Mariae. See Ildefonsus, St.
De viribus herbarum. See Odo of Meun
De viris illustribus. See Gennadius of Marseilles; Ildefonsus, St.; Isidore of Seville, St.; Jerome, St.; Petrarch; Sigebert of Gembloux
De viris religiosis. See Mortmain, Statute of
De virtutibus. See Pseudo-Aristotle
De virtutibus et vitiis. See Alan of Lille
De virtutibus herbarum. See Macer Floridus
De visione Dei. See Durand of St. Pourçain; Nicholas of Cusa
De vita curiali. See Chartier, Alain
De vita et obitu eiusdem. See Poeta Saxo
De vita scholastica. See Bonvesin de la Riva
De vita solitaria. See Petrarch
De vulgari eloquentia. See Dante Alighieri
De Wrake van Ragisel, 1:572a
Deacon, 3:441a, 442a
Roman, 10:519a
see also Clergy
Dead, Office of the, **4:117a–118a,** 4:117b (*illus.*), 120a
in art, of Rohan Master, 10:445b (*illus.*)
hours of, 4:118a
introduction of, 4:117a-b
as recited in catacombs, 4:350a
see also All Souls' Day
Dead Sea Scrolls, 3:15b
Deadly sins. *See* Seven Deadly Sins
Death and burial, **4:118a–122a**
Ars moriendi, 1:547b–548a
in art, 4:121a-b, 9:677b–678a, 679b, 680a (*illus.*)
after Black Death, 2:266b
of Rohan Master, 10:445b (*illus.*)
Triumph of Death (Pisa), 9:677b
Augustine on, 4:118b–119a
catacombs, 3:154a–155b
in Celtic church, 3:231a
cemeteries, consecration of, 3:540b–541b
church regulations of, 8:25a
early Christian view of, 4:118b
in *Everyman,* 4:527b
evidence of beauty aids in graves, 2:146a-b
fear of, 4:119b
Greek, translation of saints, 10:297a
iconology, *Triumph of Death* (Pisa), 12:124a–125b (*illus.*)
in Kievan Rus, described by Ibn Fadlan, 12:435b–436a
Latin, Theodosian Code, 10:297a
liturgical formularies and, 4:119a-b
Magyars and, 6:338b
in Middle English lyric, 8:341a-b
plagues and, 9:677b
posthumous veneration of relics, 10:297a
in pre-Christian Baltic regions, 7:609a-b
relics
reliquary chasse, 10:302b (*illus.*)
translation of saints and, 12:144b–145a
rites of, 4:120b

extreme unction, 4:565a-b
graveside, 4:120b–121a
last, 4:119b–121a
postburial, 4:121a
theories of, 4:118b–119b
use of funerary vehicles, 12:367b, 370b–371a
zāwīya and, 12:741a
see also Arcosolium; *Ars moriendi;* Black Death; Crypt; Cubiculum; Danse macabre; Deposition from the Cross; Lamentation; Mausoleum; Mortality under classes of persons, e.g., Children, mortality; Plagues; Purgatory; Tombs; Translation of saints; Unction of the sick
Death and burial, Islamic
inequality of *qubba* mausoleums, 10:239a-b
Rauḍa, 10:261a, 262b
Death Fragment, 8:329b
Death and Life, 8:332a, 333a
Death-song of Hjálmar, The, insertion in *Hervarar saga ok Heiðreka konungs, 6:215a*
"Death's head" helmet. *See* Burgonet
Débat, 4:122a
see also Owl and the Nightingale, The
Débat du cuer et du corps. See Villon, François
Débat de deux dames. See Cretin, Guillaume
Débat du laboureur, du prestre, et du gendarme, Le. See Gaguin, Robert
Debate Between the Vices and Virtues, 8:314b
Debate of the Horse, Goose, and Sheep. See Lydgate, John
Debate poem, *see also* Partimen
Debate poems
in Latin literature, 7:367a
in Middle English literature, 8:315b–316a, 338b
in Spanish literature, 11:413b
Debra Damo, monastic church of, 2:17b (*illus.*)
Debt
in England
compurgation and, 3:508b–509a
Exchequer court and, 4:534b
Exchequer of the Jews and, 4:535a-b
imprisonment for, 7:450b, 455b
king's courts and, 7:447b
legal reforms, 7:450a-b
inheritance and, 6:459a
interdict for, 6:496a
in Russia, 11:192a, 194a
Decameron. See Boccaccio, Giovanni
Décaméron, Le. See Heptaméron, L'
Dečani Monastery, 4:347a
frescoes, 2:450b
in Holy Savior church, 11:187 (*illus.*)
Vita of Kotor and, 11:187a, 12:478b
Decembrio, Pier (Piero) Candido, 9:702b–703a
Latin version of *Iliad,* 11:458a
Decembrio, Uberto, 9:702b–703a
Decima collatio, Hugolinus and, 6:326b
Decir, **4:122b**, 11:451a, 451b
Decius, Roman emperor, persecution of Christians, 11:212b–213a
Declaratio musicae disciplinae. See Ugolino of Orvieto
Decorated Style. *See* Gothic architecture
Decretales. See Gregory IX, pope
Decretals, **4:122b–124a**
after Gratian, 7:414b–417b
of Alexander III, 1:147a
collections of, 4:123a-b
from Bologna, 7:415a–416a
commission of, 5:671a-b
compilation of, by Raymond of Peñafort, 10:266b
concept of primitive church and, 10:121b–122a
courses on decretal law, 7:415a–416a
Gratian's definition of, 4:122b
Lateran III and, 4:123b
legal authority of, 4:122b–123a
property rights and, 10:15a
as supplement to canon law, 4:123a
systematization of, 4:123b
see also Baldus; Bernard of Pavia; Leo IX, pope; Maxims, legal; Raymond of Peñafort; Rescripts
Decretals, False, **4:124a–127a**, 4:124b (*illus.*), 128a, 7:405a-b
Benedictus Levita and, 2:178b–179a
content of, 4:125b–126a
effects on ecclesiastical structure, 4:373a
influence of, 4:126a-b
kingship theories of, 7:260b–261a
manuscripts of, 4:125a-b
Nicholas I and, 9:121a-b
origin of, 4:125b
Decretists, **4:127a–128a**
basic types of glosses, 4:127a-b
conciliar theory and, 3:516a–517a
development of the summa, 4:127b–128a
dispensation and, 4:217a
Italian, 10:545b
on papacy, 10:20a-b, 22a-b
plenitudo potestatis debate and, 9:708b–709b
teaching activities, 4:127b
Decretum. See Burchard of Worms; Gratian; Ivo of Chartres; Johannes Andreae
Decretum Gelasianum (494), 2:204a-b
Decuriones, 10:461a-b
inheritance and, 6:451a
Decussate principle, Roman numerals and, 10:470b
Dedication of churches. *See* Churches, dedication of
Dedication Homily, 11:17a
Deeds of the Bishops. See William of Malmesbury
Deeds of the Counts of Barcelona. See Barcelona
Deeds of the Emperor Conrad. See Wipo of Burgundy
Deeds of the English Kings. See William of Malmesbury
Deeds of the Franks, 6:263a
Deeds of Frederick Barbarossa. See Otto of Freising
Deer, Book of, 11:113b
Deesis, **4:131b**
in the church at Peć, 11:185b
iconostasis and, 6:409b
in Psalter of Queen Melisende, 4:22a (*illus.*), 23a
see also Zvenigorod Deesis
Deesis Master. *See* Master of the Deesis
Defenses, fixed. *See* Castles and fortifications
Defensor (*ca.* 700), 7:560b
Defensor minor. See Marsilius of Padua
Defensor pacis. See Marsilius of Padua
Definitions of Hermes Trismegistos to Asclepius, 1:505b
Deggwa, relation to Coptic *Difnar,* 1:155b
Degik. *See* Digesenē
Degradation of clergy. *See* Clergy
Deguileville, Guillaume de, 1:185b, 186a, 189b, 6:382b
Pèlerinage de l'âme, 12:476b
Pèlerinage de la vie humaine, 4:545b, 5:430b, 12:476b
Roman de la Rose and, 10:452b
translated by Lydgate, 7:692a
Deheubarth, kingdom of (Wales), 10:378a
Dehqān, Firdawsī and, 11:221a
Deibhidhe, 6:534a-b
Deiniol, St., founder of Bangor monastery, 2:71a-b
Deir el-Abiad, church of, 3:588a
wall paintings, 3:593a
Deir es-Suriani, church of, wall paintings, 3:593a
Deirdre (saga character), 6:549a
Déisi, as Irish aristocracy in Dyfed, 4:329a-b
Dekate, 11:604a
Del Buono, Niccolò di Bartolo, 2:281a, 287b
Delaune, Étienne, 1:536b
Delights, Book of. See Henri de Ferrières, *Livre des deduis*
Deljan, 2:407b
Della caducità della vita umana, 6:631a, 651a
Della famiglia. See Alberti, Leon Battista
Della Robbia, Andrea, **4:134b–135a**
Della Robbia, Giovanni, **4:134b–135a**
Della Robbia, Luca, **4:134b–135a**
cooperation with Michelozzo di Bartolomeo, 8:308a
Florence Duomo, *cantoria,* 4:134b (*illus.*)
Della Torre family
support of Guelphs, 8:379a
vs. Visconti, 12:464a, 464b
Delmedigo. *See* Elijah ben Moses Delmedigo
Delphi, oracle of, 12:149b
Delw y Byd, 12:613a
Demanda del Sancto Grial, 11:443b
Demantin. See Berthold von Holle
Demarchs, 4:135a
Dementia. *See* Insanity
Demes, 3:554a-b, **4:135a-b**
fall of Emperor Maurice and, 8:230b

Demesne
management of, 12:533b–534a
peasant tenure
consolidation of holdings, 11:680b
terms, 11:677a-b
Wales, 12:528a
see also Estate management; Tenure of land; Villages
Demestvennoe penie, 8:575b
Demestvennyi chant, 8:575a
Demetre I of Georgia, king, 1:235b
loss of territory, 5:406b
Demetrios Chalkokondyles. *See* Chalkokondyles, Demetrios
Demetrios Kydones, **4:135b**
translations by, 12:127a
Demetrios of Thessaloniki, St.
in art, 4:529b, 11:570b
fairs at Thessaloniki and, 12:102b
miracles of, evidence for Slavic invasion of Greece, 6:57b
patron of Thessaloniki, 12:26a, 26b
Demetrios Triklinios. *See* Triklinios, Demetrios
Demetrius of Phalerum, 4:572a
Demography, **4:136a–148a**
birth rates, 4:143b
factors influencing, 4:144a-b
population and, 4:143b, 144a
Black Death and, 2:257a–264a, 265a–266a
data sources, 4:136b–139b
dependency ratio, 4:145a
England, plagues and, 9:676b, 678a–680b, 681b–682a
equilibrium model of demographic behavior, 4:144b
European population, 3:560b
historical sources
documentary records, 4:137a–139b
field data, 4:136b–137a
serial records, 4:139a
Islamic world
plagues and, 9:685a–686a
population transfers, 12:147b
life tables for medieval society, 4:145a
of Ottoman conquests, 9:306b
polyptych, 10:29a-b
population density
land reclamation and, 10:276b–277b, 278b
plague cycles and, 4:142a-b, 143a-b, 9:672b–674a, 675a, 676a-b, 677b–682a, 683a, 685a–686a, 12:160b
Polish towns, 9:728b
Trebizond's Pontic coastland, 12:169a-b
population explosion in Scandinavia (*ca.* 800), 12:423b–424a
proxy demographic data, 4:136b
of villages, 12:438a, 442b, 446b
of witchcraft, 12:664a
see also Mortality under classes of persons; subheading Population under geographic headings; Refugees; Urbanism, Western European
Demonic possession, 6:490a, 492a
Demons
according to 13th-century philosophers, 8:38a-b
in Armenian magic and folklore, 8:16b–17a
controlled by Simon Magus, 8:33b
in the hierarchy of powers, 8:36a
in Manichaeism, 8:84b–85a
Seven Deadly Sins and, 11:211b, 212a
Demonstratio de minutiis. See Jordanus de Nemore
Denain, Wauchier de. *See* Gauchier de Dourdan
Denarius
silver coinage and, 8:428b
see also Penny
Dendrochronology
in climatology, 3:450b–451a
in dating of monuments, 1:431b
Dengi, 8:426b, 427a
Denier (coin), 8:426b
see also Penny
Denier (unit of measure), 12:594a
Denis, *see also* Dinis
Denis the Carthusian, 3:119a
hymns of, 6:382b
scholastic and mythical theology, synthesis of, 9:611a
Denis, St.
biographies of, 6:67b–68a
Historia regum Francorum, 3:332a
martyrdom of, depicted by Jean Malouel, 8:66 (*illus.*)
Mass and Office for, 5:662b
Dēnkard, **4:148a-b**
on Mazdak, 8:238a
origin of Judaism, 10:662a-b
on Šābuhr I, 10:600b
Sasanian medicine, 10:665a
as source of *Škand-gumānīg Wizār,* 11:324b
summary of Avesta, 2:14b
Tansar in, 1:452a
treatise on horses, 10:665a
on Xusrō I, 12:714b
see also Letter of Tansar (Tōsar)
Denmark, **4:148b–156b**, 4:150 (map)
art, Psalter of Queen Ingeburge, 12:181b–182a (*illus.*)
chronicles, *Gesta Danorum,* 10:676a-b, 678a-b
Cnut the Great and, 3:472a
council of state, 4:155a, 155b
described by St. Rimbert in his *Vita Anskarii,* 10:401a
economy, 4:149a-b
foreign incursions, control of Wendish cities, 6:93a, 96a
foreign policy, 4:154a, 155a
geography, 4:148b–149b
Gotland and, 5:632b–633a
Hanseatic League, Peace of Stralsund (1370) and, 6:94b
history, 4:151b–156b
history, 400–600, 10:688a–691b
archaeological evidence, 10:688b–691a
depopulation theories, 10:688b–689a
golden objects, 10:690a-b
guldgubber, 10:690b, 691a
jewelry, 10:690b
silver hoards, 10:691a
weaponry, 10:689a–690a
history, 600–800, 10:691b–692b
animals in graves, 10:692a
archaeological evidence, 10:691b–692a
theories for absence of findings, 10:692a-b
chronicles, 10:535a-b
sources, 4:152a
monarchy
in chronicles, 10:676b
chronology, 10:678a-b
older and younger dynasties, 10:677b
political and legal organization, 10:698b
population, 4:149b
relations with
Estonia, 4:154a, 155b
Hanseatic League, 4:149b, 155b, 7:682a
Holy Roman Empire, 4:154a
Lübeck, 4:155a
Norway, 9:182b, 185a, 185b
papacy, 4:153b, 154b
Sweden, 4:156a-b, 11:528b–529a, 530a, 530b, 533a
reunification, 4:155b
runic alphabet, 10:558a, 563a, 565a-b
sea empire of, 5:632b
tenurial development, *forlov* and *vornedskab,* 11:685a
under Knud Lavard, 7:280a-b
Viking raids on England and, 12:432a–434a
vs. Brandenburg, Rügen and, 12:668b
vs. Estonia, 11:531a
vs. Germany, in *Brevis historia regum Dacie,* 11:522b
see also Bjarkamál; Lejre Chronicle; Scandinavia; Vikings
Dental care
dentifrice, 2:147b–148a, 150a-b
hygiene, 2:150a-b
surgeries, 2:99a
Denunciatio, 6:478b, 479a
Denys, hierarchies of, 4:375b
Deor, 1:278b, 8:327a
classified as a lyric poem, 8:334b
Kudrun and, 7:304b
Deorham (Dyrham), Battle of (577), 1:290a
Deotisalvi. *See* Diotisalvi
Departing Soul's Address to the Body, The, 8:329a
Depopulation. *See* Demography; Plagues; Refugees
Depositio martyrum, dating of Christmas and, 3:317b
Deposition of clergy. *See* Clergy, deposition of
Deposition from the Cross, **4:157a** (*illus.*)
Breslau altarpiece, 9:710 (*illus.*)
see also Passion cycle
Deposition of rulers
Edward II of England, 9:426a, 426b–427a
Richard II of England, 9:429b, 10:384b

theories of, **4:157b–161a**
church fathers on, 4:158a-b
development, 4:157b–160b
in Germanic tribes, 4:157b–158a
Gregory VII, 4:159a-b
Innocent IV, 4:160a
Isidore of Seville, 4:158a-b
John of Salisbury, 4:159b
national constitutional, 4:160b
papacy, 4:160a
Pepin, 4:158b–159a
tonsuring the king, 4:158b–159a
war leaders as kings, 4:158a
Deprecatio Gelasii. See Gelasius I, pope
Deprecationes. See Litany, in the West
Depressed arch. *See* Arch, segmental
Depression, morbid. *See* Melancholy
Der von Buwenburg, 5:435a
Der von Kürenberg, **4:161a–162a**
love lyrics of, 5:433b–434a
Nibelungenlied and, 9:114b
poetic rivalry, 8:351a
poetry as minnesong, 8:413b
Derashah. See Derush
Derbent, **4:162a-b**
Arabs in, 1:478b, 479a, 4:162a
Armenian trade and, 12:97b
fortifications of, 4:162a-b
in Islamic conquests, 6:569a
Mongols in, 4:162b
Seljuks in, 4:162b
Shirvan and, 4:162b, 11:254a
territory of, 4:162a-b
Derbfine, 11:674a
Derivationes. See Huguccio
Dermot MacMurrough, king of Leinster, 6:517b, 7:536b
Anglo-Norman lords and, 6:554b
Derry. *See* Columba, St.
Derrynaflan chalice, 3:221a
Dertusensis prima, 4:123a
Derush, 10:73b–74a
Dervish, **4:162b–163b**, 6:585b
etymology of, 4:162b–163a
impact on Islamic community, 4:162b–163a
monasticism and, 4:163a
music and, 8:560b
role in Ottoman westward expansion, 9:306b
Sufism and, 4:163a
under the Seljuks of Rum, 11:158b
whirling, 4:163a
Des Champs, Jean. *See* Jean des Champs
Des Champs, Pierre. *See* Pierre des Champs
Des Entkrist vasnacht, 4:268b–269a
Des Knaben Wunderhorn. See Brentano, Clemens
Des Minnesangs Frühling. See Heinrich von Rugge
Des Teufels Netz, 5:432a
Desa, ruler of Serbia, 11:173a
Descant, English style, in Old Hall MS, 9:232a
Descent from the Cross. *See* Deposition from the Cross
Descent into Limbo. *See* Anastasis
Deschamps, Eustache, **4:163b–164a**
Art de dictier, influence on 15th-century writers, 5:268a-b
chant royal and, 3:263b
Christine de Pizan and, 3:317a
lai and, 7:317a
life of, 4:163b
Machaut and, 4:163b
ballade on his death, 5:266a, 8:3b
Miroir de mariage, on suspended chariots, 12:377b
musique artificielle and *musique de bouche,* 5:268a
on poetry and music, 8:583b
poetry of, 4:163b–164a
Roman de la Rose and, 10:452b
satires, 4:164a
theory of poetry, 5:268a
expansion of subject range, 5:268b
Desclot, Bernat, 11:435b, 12:349a
chronicle of, 3:165b
description of Almogávares, 1:190b
Libre de rei En Pere d'Aragó e dels seus antecessors passats, 3:165b
Descort, **4:164a-b**, 10:251a
definition of, 4:164a
lai and, 7:316b
troubadour, 12:218a
see also Discordo
Descriptio Kambriae. See Gerald of Wales
Descriptio orbis romani. See George of Cyprus
Descrissions des relegions, La. See Huon le Roi de Cambrai
Desert markets. *See* Fairs, Turkish
Desert monasticism. *See* Hermits; Monasticism
Deserted villages, 4:136b
in Byzantine Empire, 2:480b
causes of, 5:178a
Desiderius (Desiderio), Lombard (Langobard) king, 7:657a
attack on Rome by, 9:383a, 10:521b
in literature, 6:637b
invasions by, 8:377a
Paul the Deacon and, 9:467b, 467a
Desiderius of Monte Cassino, **4:164b**
basilica of, 11:266b
church decoration and, 10:505a
Dialogue on the Miracles of St. Benedict, 4:164b
Ethelred of Rievaulx and, 4:517a
Gregory VII and, 4:164b
Guiscards and, 11:265b
Henry IV and, 4:164b
Hugh of Cluny and, 2:173b
papacy of, 4:164b
see also Victor III, pope
Desio, Battle of (1277), 8:379a, 12:464a
Desiré, 7:317a
Desmond family, Gofraidh Fionn and, 9:204b
Desmond Geraldines. *See* Fitzgeralds
Despars, Jacques, 8:10b
Despencers, conviction of, 6:427b
Despot, 2:122b, **4:165a-b**
see also Autocrator; Sebastokrator
Desprecio de la fortuna. See San Pedro, Diego de
Dessaisine. See Seisin, disseisin
Destorrents, Ramón, **4:165b**
Consecration of St. Anianus by St. Mark, 4:165a (*illus.*)
Peter IV and, 4:165b
Simone Martini and, 4:165b
Destructio destructionis. See Rushd, Ibn
Destruction of Troy, The, 8:332a, 332b, 333a
Destruction de Troye, La. See Milet, Jacques
Destructorium viciorum. See Carpenter, Alexander
Desvalers, Francesco, 4:559a
Desyatinnaya (church: Kiev), architectural elements, Byzantine influence, 10:578b
Detinue, 3:509a
Detto d'amore, 6:631b
Detto del Gatto lupesco, 6:631b, 651a-b
Deulo de la Virgen. See Berceo, Gonzalo de
Deus amanz. See Marie de France
Deus incrementorum. See Catechumens, oil for
Deus qui humanae substantiae, 8:190b
Deusdedit, cardinal, **4:165b–166a,** 4:177b
Collectio canonum, 4:165b, 7:410a
Libellus contra invasores et symoniacos, 4:165b
on universal synods, 3:633a-b
Deusdedit, doge of Venice, 12:384b–385a
Deusdona (relic-procurer), 1:337a
Deuterius, Arator and, 1:422a
Deutsche Sphaera. See Conrad of Megenberg
Deutschenspiegel, 7:481a
influence of *Sachsenspiegel* on, 10:603b
as a source for *Schwabenspiegel,* 11:80b
Deux amants, Les. See Marie de France
Develtos, taken by Krum (812), 7:303b
Deventer
Brethren of the Common Life at, 2:367a
fairs, 4:586b
Devil
as a bridge destroyer, 10:410b
in Byzantine folklore, 8:20a
Catharism and, 12:661a, 661b
concept of, 8:26b–27a
field of action of, 8:27a
in Manichaeism, 8:84b
personification of. *See* Renard the Fox
symbols of
ass, 2:243a
hedgehog, 2:206b
in the theory of sorcery, 8:30a
in the Towneley Plays, 12:94b–95a
witchcraft and, 12:658b, 661a
see also Angra Mainyu (Zoroastrian god)
Devil (Islam). *See* Iblīs
Devlet Giray, khan of Crimea, burning of Moscow, 3:679b
Devonshire Hunts (tapestries), 6:361b, 11:596b
Devotio Moderna, **4:166a–167b**
adherents of, 4:167a

Devotio Moderna (*cont.*)
Brethren of the Common Life and, 3:369a, 4:166a–167a
Dutch religious literature and, 4:320b
emphasis on private devotion, 5:629b
followers of Ruusbroec and, 9:38a
Geert Groote and, 4:166a–167a
Gerard Zerbolt of Zutphen and, 4:166b
hymns and, 6:382b
influence of, 3:369a-b, 4:167a
monastic influence, 2:366a
origin of, 1:659b, 4:166a
personal piety, 8:160a-b
revival of monastic scriptoria and, 8:105a
Rule of St. Augustine and, 4:166b
Rule of the Third Order of St. Francis and, 4:166b
Thomas à Kempis and, 9:27b
Windesheim Congregation and, 4:166b
women mystics and, 9:11b
see also Bohemian Brethren; Brethren of the Common Life; Thomas à Kempis
Devotional, women's. *See* *Quinze joies de Nostre Dame*
Devshirme, 7:46b, 8:69a
Mehmed I's rule and, 8:263b
Dexippus, Publius Herennius (Athenian), 10:466b
Dextre (unit of measure), 12:588b
Dezir al nacimiento del Rey Don Juan. *See* Imperial, Francisco
Dezir a las syete virtudes. *See* Imperial, Francisco
Dhahabī, al-, *Taʾrīkh al-Islām,* 6:250b
Dhikr, 6:585b, 8:560b, 9:44a-b
Dhimmīs, 9:498b
exilarch and, 4:552a
interest-bearing loans and, 12:340a-b
taxation of, 11:667b–668a
Dhol, 8:561b
Dhow, 9:85b–86a, 11:248a
lateen sail and, 7:344a
Dhu 'l-Nūn al-Miṣrī, Islamic mysticism and, 9:39b
Dhu 'l-Nūnid dynasty (in Toledo), 12:68a
Dhu Nuwās, 7:101b
Dhu 'l-Yamīnain. *See* Ṭāhir ibn al-Ḥusayn
Dhuoda, book of precepts, 2:211b
Diabology. *See* Devil
Diabolus in musica, **4:167b**
Diaconiae. *See* Deacon
Diaconicon, **4:167b–168a**
in St. Savior in Chora (Constantinople), 9:453 (*illus.*)
Diacritical marks
Arabic. *See* Arabic language
German, 9:189b
Diadochus of Photice, 9:7a
Diagonal arch. *See* Arch
Dialect, **4:168a**
dictamen and, 4:176a
politics of, 4:168a
Umberto Cassuto on, 7:175b
see also names of individual languages
Dialectic, **4:168a–171b**
approach to theology, 4:170a
Aristotelian, 14th century, 9:614b
development
in 6th–7th centuries, 4:169a-b
in 10th century, 4:169b
in 13th century, 4:170b
in 14th century, 4:170b–171a
dialecticians vs. antidialecticians, 9:587a-b
disputations, in universities, 4:170a-b
influences of, 4:171a
Jewish, shift from exegesis to, 10:259b
Jewish opposition to, 9:579b
logic manuals, 4:170b
logic in university curriculum, 11:688b–689a
medieval understanding of, 4:168a-b
Plato and, 4:168a
practice of, 4:170a-b
quaestiones, 10:238a-b
quodlibet, 10:238b, 241a
rhetoric and, 10:355a, 357a
Stoic influence on, 4:168b
teaching of, 10:531a-b
terminist, 11:686a-b
textbook commentaries, 11:688a
trivium study of, 12:206b–207a
Dialectica. *See* Abelard, Peter; Alcuin of York; Ramus, Petrus
Dialectica Alexandri. *See* Adam of the Little Bridge
Dialecticae disputationes. *See* Valla, Lorenzo
Dialefe, 6:666a
Diálogo de la lengua. *See* Juan de Valdés
Dialogue. *See* Petrus Alfonsi
Dialogue Between the Rich and the Poor, on *penetes,* 9:493b
Dialogue of Divine Providence. *See* Catherine of Siena, St.
Dialogue of the Exchequer. *See* Fitz Nigel, Richard
Dialogue on Miracles. *See* Caesarius of Heisterbach
Dialogue on the Miracles of St. Benedict. *See* Desiderius of Monte Cassino
Dialogue of a Philosopher with a Christian and a Jew. *See* Abelard, Peter
Dialogue de Saint-Julien et son disciple, 1:264a
Dialogue of Solomon and Saturn, Old English translation of, 2:184a
Dialogue with Trypho. *See* Justin Martyr
Dialogues. *See* Gregory I (the Great), pope
Dialogus (...) in arte musica. *See* Hothby, John (*d.* 1487)
Dialogus. *See* Ockham, William of
Dialogus cum rege Henrico. *See* Peter of Blois
Dialogus familiaris. *See* Chartier, Alain
Dialogus miraculorum. *See* Caesarius of Heisterbach
Dialogus de musica, 8:614b, 640b–641a
Cistercians and, 8:643a
Guido of Arezzo and, 8:641a
Dialogus Salomonis et Marcolfi
description of, 11:366b–367a
vernacular versions from, 11:367a–368b
Dialogus de Scaccario. *See* Fitz Nigel, Richard, *Dialogue of the Exchequer*
Dialogus super auctores. *See* Conrad of Hirsau, *Accessus ad auctores*
Dialogus de tribus quaestionibus. *See* Otloh of St. Emmeram
Diaper pattern, **4:171b–172a**
Diaphonia, **4:172a-b**
Diaphragm arch. *See* Arch
Diarmaid Ó Duibhne (god), 6:546a
Diarmait Mac Murchada. *See* Dermot MacMurrough
Diarrhea. *See* Plagues, enteric
Dias, Bartholomew, 4:560b, 562b
Dias, Dinis, 4:561a
Diastematic neume. *See* Neume
Diastemy, **4:172b–173a**
Diatessaron. *See* Tatian
Diatonicism, in Byzantine music, 8:555a
Díaz, Bernal, 8:445b
Díaz, Fernán, *Instrucción del relator,* 11:421b
Díaz de Montalvo, Alonso, on Spanish law, 7:523b
Díaz, Rodrigo. *See* Cid, the
Dībāj, **4:173a-b,** 4:173 (*illus.*)
Dice, 5:350b–351a
Dicker (unit of measure), product variations, 12:584b
Dicta Candidi. *See* Candidus of Fulda
Dicta Pirminii (Scarapsus). *See* Pirmin, St.
Dictamen, **4:173b–177a,** 10:357b–359b
ars arengandi, 2:320b
ars dictaminis, 2:320a, 320b
Bohemian, 4:176a
Bolognese, 4:174b
as business course, 4:175a-b
decline of use of, 4:176a-b
English, 4:175a-b
epistolary, 4:173b
five parts of the letter, 10:358b, 359a
format of, 4:173b–174a
French, 4:175a
humanists and, 4:176b
Italian, 4:174b–175b
Matthew of Vendôme's *Epistolarium,* 8:229b
origin of, 4:174a
of Peter of Blois, 7:364b, 9:518a
Piero della Vigna and, 11:258a-b
Polish, 4:176a
private letter formulary of Richard de Bury, 10:386a
in 16th century, 4:176b
Spanish, 4:175b
Thomas of Capua on, 7:368a
writers using, 4:174a–175a
see also Seals and sigillography, Western European
Dictamina (formularies), 4:173b
Dictaminis epithalamium. *See* Gil de Zamora, Juan
Dictaminum radii. *See* Alberic of Monte Cassino
"Dictatus of Avranches," 4:177b
Dictatus papae. *See* Gregory VII, pope

Dictio I. See Marsilius of Padua
Dictio II. See Marsilius of Padua
Dictionaries. *See* Encyclopedias and dictionaries
Dictus magister, translators, 12:137b
Dictys Cretensis, 5:445b, 7:360b, 370a
  Ephemeris belli Troiani, 12:220a
  on Trojan War, 2:182a, 8:225b
Dicuil, **4:178a-b**, 4:553b, 7:362a
Didache, 7:397a-b, 559a, 625b
  doctrine of early church fathers and, 3:334b
Didascalia, on Simon Magus, 8:33b
Didascalia apostolorum, 7:397b
Didascalicon. See Hugh of St. Victor
Diderot, Denis, *Bijoux indiscrets,* 4:575a, 577a
Didot Perceval, 1:570b
Didrikskrönikan (translation of *Þiðreks saga*), 12:31a
Diebold of Passau, bishop, 12:672a
Diederic van Assenede, *Floris ende Blanchefloer,* 4:318b
Diederik III of Rijnland, count, Vlaardingen ditches, 12:577b
Diego de Azevedo, bishop of Osma, 4:239b, 254a
  Cathars and, 3:187b
Diego Rodríguez Porcelos, Castile and, 3:128a
Diego de Valencia, in *Cancionero de Baena,* 11:419a-b
Dienstrecht, 8:405a
Dieprecht, 7:117a
Dies irae, 4:120b, 6:382a
  rhythmic stress in, 10:380a
  Thomas of Celano and, 4:121b, 7:369a
Diesbach, 11:545a
Diet (*Dieta*). *See* Representative assemblies
Dietari del capellà d'Alfons el Magnànim. See Miralles, Melcior
Dietary laws
  Islamic, **4:178b–180a**
    food regulations and, 4:178b
    formulation of, 4:178b
    hadīth literature on, 4:179a-b
    Koran prohibitions, 4:178b–179b
    see also Beverages, Islamic
  Jewish, **4:180a–184a**
    agricultural rules, 4:180a–181a
    animal rules, 4:181a–183a
    development of, 4:180a
    foods processed by Gentiles, 4:183a-b
  see also Cookery
Dietlieb, in *Biterolf,* 2:253a
Dietmar von Aist, **4:184a-b**
  poetry as minnesong, 8:413b
  songs attributed to, 4:184a-b
  sources of information about, 4:184a
Dietrich von Bern (epic character), 6:227b, 8:353b, 12:461a, 461b, 705a
  in *Biterolf,* 2:253a
  in *Þiðreks saga,* 10:391b, 12:29a-b
  see also Alpharts Tod; Eckenlied; Ermenrîkes dôt; Theodoric the Ostrogoth
Dietrich von Freiberg. *See* Theodoric of Freiberg
Dietrich of Meissen, duke. *See* Heinrich von Morungen
Dietrich of Meissen, markgraf, bridge construction, 10:416a-b
Dietrich von Moers, archbishop, tomb of, 7:305b (*illus.*), 306a
Dietrich of Niem, 3:515b
Dietrichs Flucht. See Buch von Bern, Das
Dietricus, notation treatise of, 1:545a
Díez de Games, Gutierre, *Victorial,* or *Crónica de don Pero Niño,* 11:421a, 433a, 433b
Diez mandamientos de amor. See Rodríguez del Padrón, Juan
Differentia, **4:185a**
  in tonaries, 12:70a, 70b
  see also Cadence (music); Variatio
Differentiae. See Isidore of Seville, St.
Diffidatio. See Feudalism; Kingship
Difnar (Coptic antiphonary), 1:155b
Digby MS 23, 10:446a
Digenis Akritas, **4:185a–186a**, 7:285b, 8:19a-b
  dating of, 4:185b
  different versions, 2:508b
  division of, 4:185b
  hero of, 4:185a
  sources for, 2:521b
    folk poems, 2:508b
  textual problems of, 4:185b–186a
Digesenē, 1:515a
Digest. *See Corpus iuris civilis*
Digestum novum. See Corpus iuris civilis
Digestum vetus. See Corpus iuris civilis
Digit (unit of measure), 12:587b–588a
Diglossia, in Italy, 6:622a, 624a, 626b, 629b
Dijla al-ᶜAwrā, 6:511a
Dijon
  appointment of brokers, 12:121b
  enfranchisement of, 2:427b
  hostelries, 12:651b
  taverns, 12:651a, 651b
Dijon, Chartreuse de Champmol, **4:186a-b**, 5:623b (*illus.*), 625b–626a, 627b, 628b
  Claus Sluter's work at, 11:349a
  Jean Malouel's painting of St. Denis, 8:66 (*illus.*)
Dikeraton, 11:603b
Dilatatio, 10:18a
Diletsky, Nikolai, *Azbuka,* 8:576a
Dill, pharmaceutical uses, 9:549a, 549b, 550a
Dimashq. *See* Damascus
Dîme de pénitence, La. See Jean de Journi
Dimma, Book of, 7:614a
Dinanderie, 2:384a, **4:186b**, 4:186b (*illus.*), 8:286b
Dinant, metalworking in, 2:384a
Dinar, **4:187a-b**
  Almohad, 8:423b, 424 (*illus.*)
  Fatimid, 8:423b, 424 (*illus.*)
  fractional, 4:187b
  gold, 8:422a-b (*illus.*)
  kinds of, 4:187b
  Mediterranean trade and, 8:430a
  origin of, 4:187a
  standards for, 4:187a-b, 8:425a
  "standing caliph," 8:422a (*illus.*)
  tetartemorion and, 8:419b
  see also Penny
Dinas Powys, metalworkers at, 3:219a
Dīnawarī, Abū Ḥanīfa Aḥmad ibn Dāwūd al-, **4:187b–188b**
  Book of Long Narratives, 4:188a
  Book of Plants, 4:188a
  early life of, 4:187b–188a
  philological writings of, 4:188a
  work on herbs, 6:185a
Dindshenchas, **4:188b–189b**, 6:531a
  sources for, 4:188a-b
  texts of, 4:188b–189a
Dingestow Court Manuscript, 5:389b
Dinghöfe, 11:682a
Dining hall, monastery. *See* Refectory
Dinis I of Portugal, king, **4:189b–191a**
  accession of, 4:189b
  cantigas d'amigo, 4:190b
  cantigas d'amor, 4:190a-b
  cantigas d'escarnho e de maldizer, 4:190b
  Castile and, 10:49a-b
  culmination of courtly style, 4:190a
  death of, and decline of Galician-Portuguese poetry, 4:191b
  economy under, 10:50a
  foreign trade under, 10:50a-b
  growth of Portugal under, 10:48b–49a
  Pessagno and, 4:558b
  poetic activity fostered by, 4:189b–190a
  poetry of, 4:190a-b, 11:450a
  Portuguese language under, 10:50b
  reconciliation with father, 10:47b
  royal authority under, 10:50b
  Templars and, 10:49a–50a
Dinnshenchas. See Dindshenchas
Dínus saga drambláta, 10:395b
Dio Cassius, *Epitome historiarum* and, 12:746a
Diocesan assemblies. *See* Representative assemblies
Diocese
  ecclesiastical, **4:191a-b**
    clergy in, 3:373a
    early, 3:372b
    origins of, 9:411a
    in provinces, 3:372b–373a
    see also Province, ecclesiastical; Vicar
  secular, **4:191b**
Diocletian, Roman emperor
  armies of, 3:201a
  De maximis pretiis, 10:460b
    use of pack camels and, 10:425a-b
  Dominate and, 10:458b
  Edict on Maximum Prices (301), 12:108b
    on camel transport, 12:379b
    price of wagons and, 12:368a
  Egypt and, 10:454a
  Iberian Peninsula under, 10:36a
    vs. Basques, 2:126a
  imperial cabinet of, 3:541b

Diocletian (*cont.*)
Lesser Armenia and, 1:472b
Manichaeans and, 8:85b
office of vicar and, 12:409a
palace of, 5:591b
persecutions under, 4:259b, 10:462a
support of imperial library, 7:560b–561a
Trdat III (IV) the Great and, 12:164a
Diodorus Siculus
on Celtic music, 8:558a
Historical Library, 3:330a
Diodorus of Tarsus
development of Nestorianism and, 9:105a, 564a
translation of works into Syriac, 9:106b
Diogenes Laertius, as a source for *Suda,* 11:501b
Diogo Fernandez, 10:37b
Diogo Pires the Younger, 5:630a-b
Dioikesis, 11:603a
Dionigi da Borgo San Sepolcro (Augustinian theologian), 2:278a
Dionysiana, 3:229b
Dionysio-Hadriana, 3:349a, 4:124b
Dionysios of Fourna, **4:191b–192a**
Hermeneia, 4:191b–192a, 8:91a
Dionysios the Greek, **4:192a-b**
frescoes, Arkhangelsky Cathedral, 8:497a
icons, church of the Nativity of the Mother of God, 10:590a
Last Judgment, 4:192b (*illus.*)
Dionysios the Pseudo-Areopagite. *See* Pseudo-Dionysius the Areopagite
Dionysius bar Ṣalibi (*d.* 1171), 11:565b
West Syrian rite and, 11:568a
Dionysius the Carthusian. *See* Denis the Carthusian
Dionysius Exiguus, **4:192b–193a**
calendar of, 4:193a
invention of *annus Domini,* 6:259a
canon law compilation, 7:399a-b
celibacy and, 3:216a
Collectio Dionysiana, 4:193a
Easter tables of, 3:18b, 22a
importance of, 4:192b
Little Denis, 3:348b
translations of, 4:193a
Dionysius of Tel-Mahré, **4:193a-b,** 7:152a
Annals, 4:193a
Dionysius Thrax, 5:675b
Grammar (*Technē grammatikē*), 1:505b, 4:114a, 11:51b
Dionysus, cult of, 9:1a, 1b
Diophantine analysis, 7:212a-b
Diophantus of Alexandria
Aritmetica, 7:212a-b
mathematical theory, number-theoretical algebra, 8:213b
works of translated into Arabic, 11:83a
Diorthōsis. See Gloss; Translation and translators
Dioscorides
Bīrūnī's *Pharmacology* and, 2:250b
on cosmetics, 2:147a
De materia medica, 2:345a, 6:177b, 7:342b
earliest known donor portrait, 4:262a
influence on Middle Eastern plant studies, 6:185a
Juliana Anicia Codex, 4:326b (*illus.*), 327b (*illus.*), 353a, 353b, 355b, 6:177a, 178a
manuscripts of, 6:178a
popularity of in the Middle Ages, 2:245a, 246a
Spanish study of, 6:185b
translations, Arabic, 6:178b, 185a, 8:115b
translations of, 9:284a
Dioscoros I, patriarch of Alexandria
acceptance of Eutychianism, 6:190b
endorsement of radical Monophysitism, 9:106a
Eutyches and, 4:524a, 9:561a
"Robber Council" and, 3:594a, 629b, 8:477a
Dioscorus of Aphrodito, 10:455a
Diotisalvi, **4:193b**
Diplē, 8:618a
Diploma Adreanum, 6:342a
Diplomacy
Byzantine, 3:252a-b, **4:193b–197a**
agencies of, 4:194b–195a
Byzantine Empire and, 4:193b–194a
Byzantine political theory and, 10:11a-b
defense of frontiers and, 4:194b
emperor and, 4:194b, 195b
envoys in, 4:196a
expense of, 4:196a-b
formalization of, 4:194a-b
ideology of, 4:194a
intelligence services, 4:195a, 10:59b–60a
interpreters and, 12:127a-b
logothete of the drome and, 4:194b–195b
missionaries in, 4:196a
strength of, 4:196b
treaties in, 4:195b–196a
uses of, 4:196b
wartime, 12:550a-b
charter, 3:274b–275a
interpreters and
Byzantine, 12:127a-b
clerical counciliar, 12:138a
see also Translation and translators
Islamic, **4:197a–201b**
in Abbasid period, 4:199b
amān, 4:198a–199a
beginnings of, 4:199a-b
for contacts, commercial and cultural, 4:201a-b
emissaries in, 4:199b–200a
relations between Muslim and non-Muslim rulers, 4:201a
royal marriage and, 12:224b
under caliphate, 4:200a-b
see also Abode of Islam—Abode of War
ransom, King John II of France and, 10:318b–319b
Western European, 3:252b, **4:201b–214b**
ambassador in, 4:205a–208a
ceremonies of, 4:211b–212b
chancery clerks in, 4:210a
clerics in, 4:210a
expenses of, 4:210b–211a
immunities in, 4:211a-b
letters of, 4:208a–209a
in Merovingian period, 4:202a
nuncius, 4:201b–203a
oratory in, 4:212a-b
papal. *See* Legate, papal; Nuncio, papal
personnel in, 4:209b–210b
Peter of Blois's missions, 9:518a
plenipotentiary in, 4:203a–205a
procurator in, 4:203a–205a
ratification of treaties and agreements, 4:213a–214a
reports of, 4:209a-b
royal marriage and, 10:320b
treaties from, 4:212b
Diplomata, 10:16b
Diplomatic pouch, 4:208a-b
Diplomatics, 3:252a
in archaeological studies, 1:427b
Dipsacus fullonum. See Carding
Diptych, **4:214b–215a**
consular, **4:215a-b**
of consul Justinian, 4:215b (*illus.*)
tabula ansata and, 11:571b
definition of, 10:29a
funerals and, 4:120a
of Honorius, 4:215a
of Justin, 4:215a
Justinian as Defender of the Faith, 7:24b (*illus.*)
religious, 4:214a
secular, 4:214a
see also Altarpieces; Ivory carving
Diptychs, altar screens and, 5:410a
Ḍirār ibn ᶜAmr, 1:584a
Direct, the. *See* Custos
Direction of prayer, Islamic. *See* Qibla
Directory of the Inquisition. See Eymeric, Nicholas
Dirham, **4:215b–216a**
alloys in, 8:425a
evolution of, 4:215b
introduction by Almohads, 4:215b
minting of, 4:215b–216a
reintroduction of, 8:424a
in Russia, 4:587b
silver, 8:422a (*illus.*)
Ayyubid, 8:424a (*illus.*)
standard for, 8:425a
in Sweden, 4:555b
varieties in, 4:216a
weight of, 4:215a
see also Penny
Dirk, 11:550b (*illus.*), 551a
see also Daggers
Dirk of Herxen
meditation, methods and material, 2:368a
statutes for Brethren of the Common Life, 2:367a
Dirrīj, 8:612b–613a
Dis dou cerf amoreus, Li, 6:359a
Disabitato, 10:520a-b

Disagreements of Scholars. See *Dissensiones dominorum*
Discant
  Notre Dame school and, 9:191b–192a
  theory of, 3:657a
Discant style, in *ars antiqua,* 1:546a-b
Discantor, **4:216a-b**
  diaphonia and, 4:172a-b
Discantus positio vulgaris, 8:620a, 621a, 643b
Discessa di Gesù all'Inferno, 6:636b
Discharging arch. *See* Arch
Disciplina clericalis. See Petrus Alfonsi
Disciplinants. *See* Flagellants
Disciplinarum libri IX. See Varro
Disciplines. See Varro, *Disciplinarum*
Discordo, 6:640b
Discourse on the Birth of Christ. See Petros of Siwnikʿ, bishop
Discourse on Faith. See Petros of Siwnikʿ, bishop
Discourse on Light. See Haytham, Ḥasan ibn al-
Discourse on the Nativity of Christ. See Gregory Thaumaturgus
Discourse of the Sons of Moses. See Banū Mūsā, *Verba filiorum*
Discourses Against the Arians. See Athanasius of Alexandria, St.
Discourts politique des diverses puissances (1574), 3:522a
Discthegn. See Seneschal, England, Anglo-Saxon
Discussion Concerning the Law Between Simon a Jew and Theophilus a Christian, 10:2a
Disease
  classifications of, 9:673–674a
  as divine judgment, 9:676a, 677a-b
  immunity and epidemic, 9:673b–675a, 683a, 685a-b
  Islamic world, history of, 9:684a–686a
  quarantine and, 9:676b–677b, 679b
  refugee flight from, 9:685a
  trade patterns and, 9:664a-b, 673b–674a, 676b, 678a, 682b, 685b–686a
  see also Black Death; Demography; Leprosy
Disinherited children. *See* Children
Dísir, Norns and, 9:171b
Dismemberment. *See* Corpse
Dispensation, **4:216b–218a**
  Bernold of Constance on, 4:217a-b
  Council of Trent and, 4:218a
  decretists on, 4:217a
  definition of, 4:216b–217a
  granting of, 4:217a-b
  Innocent III on, 4:217a-b
  Ivo of Chartres on, 4:217a-b
  power to dispense, 4:217b
  Reformation and, 4:217b–218a
  sale of pilgrimage vow, 9:660a
  types of, 4:217a
Dispensations, papal. *See* Rescripts
Disputa del alma y el cuerpo, 11:413b, 456b
Disputa del clérigo y el caballero. See Elena y María
Disputa de l'ase, La. See Turmeda, Anselm
Disputació d'En Buc ab son cavall, 3:173b
Disputatio. See Polemics
Disputatio aque et vini, 6:658b
Disputatio de auctoritate concilii supra pontificem maximum. See Major, John
Disputatio inter clericum et militem, **4:218a–219a**, 7:267b, 11:371b
  clergy's duty to king in, 4:218a-b
  language of, 4:218a-b
Disputatio rosae cum viola. See Bonvesin de la Riva
Disputation. See Crispin, Gilbert; Elijah Ḥayyim ben Benjamin
Disputationes adversus astrologos. See Pico della Mirandola
Disputations. *See* Polemics
Dissections, human, reintroduction into medical studies, 8:259b
Disseisin. *See* Seisin, Disseisin
Dissensiones dominorum, 7:420b
  Hugolinus and, 6:326b
Dissimilarianism. *See* Anomoeanism
Dissonance. *See* Consonance/dissonance
Dissuasio Valerii ad Rufinum. See Map, Walter
Disticha Catonis. See Cato's Distichs
Distillation, method of, 4:219b
Distilled liquors, **4:219a–220b**
  Black Death and, 4:220a
  brandy, 4:220a
  methods, 4:219a-b
  Paracelsus' test for, 4:219b–220a
  regulations against, 4:220a
  use of, 4:219b–220a
  whiskey, 4:220a
  wine, 4:219a-b
Distinctiones, 4:127b
  of Hugo, 6:324a
Distinctiones super Psalterium. See Philip the Chancellor
Distraint. *See* Distress
Distress, **4:220b–221a**
  chattels in, 4:220b–221a
  law of, 4:220b–221a
  Magna Carta and, 4:221a
Dit, **4:221a**
  in Guillaume de Machaut's works, 8:3b, 4b, 5a
Dit de l'alerion. See Machaut, Guillaume de
Dit du cerf blanc, Le, 6:359a
Dit dou Lyon. See Machaut, Guillaume de
Dit de Franc Gontier. See Vitry, Philippe de
Dit des trois mors et des trois vifs, Le, 4:121b
Dite de hosbondrie, La. See Walter of Henley
Dites ditatus. See Walsingham, Thomas
Dittamondo. See Fazio degli Uberti
Diu minne lât. See Walther von der Vogelweide
Dīvān of Kings. See Bagrat III of Georgia, king
Dīvān of Shams-i Tabrīzī. *See* Rūmī
Diversarum artium schedula. See Theophilus
Diversorum patrum sententie, 7:409b
Divination
  Byzantine treatises on, 8:18a
  definition of, 8:31b–32a
  in Islam, 8:21a
Divinatory science. *See* Astrology; Geomancy
Divine Book. See ʿAṭṭār, Farīd al-Dīn, *Ilāhī-nāma*
Divine Comedy. See Dante Alighieri
Divine Liturgy. See Basil the Great of Caesarea, St.
Divine Office, **4:221b–231a**
  abbreviated Roman Office of Innocent III, 4:231a
  in Alexandrian rite, 1:157a
  Amalarius of Metz on, 4:222b–223a, 230a-b
  Armenian, 1:516b–517a
  canticles in, 3:84b
  in Carolingian Empire, 4:230a-b
  Carthusian practices, 3:118a
  in Celtic church, 3:230a-b
  choral, dispensations from, 2:372b
  in collectarium, 3:479b
  Council of Aachen on, 4:230a
  Council of Clovesho on, 4:230a
  day Office, 4:229a
  development of, 4:229b–231a
  external sources of
    canon law regulations, 4:222a-b
    liturgical commentaries, 4:222b–223a
    rules pertaining to religious orders and groups, 4:222a
  formulaic sources of
    antiphonaries, 4:224b–225a
    breviaries, 4:225a-b
    breviary-missals, 4:225a
    collectiariums, 4:223b
    homilaries, 4:224b
    hymnaries, 4:224b
    lectionaries, 4:224a-b
    legenda, 4:224b
    libelli with complete offices, 4:225a
    liber ordinarius, 4:225a
    ordines, 4:225a
    passionalia, 4:224b
    Psalters, 4:223b–224a
    responsories, 4:224b–225a
    sacramentaries, 4:223a-b
  Franciscans and, 4:231a
  Gloria in, 5:564a
  Gregorian chant in, 5:662b–663a
  Gregorian reform of, 4:225b
  Hrabanus Maurus on, 4:223a
  Hugh of Fosse and, 10:83b
  hymns, 6:379b, 380a
  incense and, 6:432a
  in Ireland, as prescribed by the Synod of Cashel, 7:614a
  Isidore of Seville on, 4:222b
  Ivo of Chartres on, 4:230b
  liturgical poetry
    Historia, 9:714a
    versifications and, 9:714a-b
  monastic Office, 4:229b–230a
  night Office, 4:228a-b

Divine Office (*cont.*)
in the "Non-Sleepers" monastery in Constantinople, 7:611a
perpetual recitation in Studios Monastery, 11:494b
plainsong, 9:688b
Office for St. Gall, 9:691b–692b (*illus.*)
prayer schedules of, 5:662a-b
Premonstratensian rite and, 10:83b–84a
Pseudo-Germanus on, 4:222b
recitation of, 2:372b, 3:67a-b
reforms of, 2:370b–371a
Roman, 5:662b
reorganization of, 2:371b–372a
Rule of Columbanus, 4:222a
Rule of St. Augustine, 4:222a
Rule of St. Benedict, 4:222a
Sarum use, 10:656a
as a source of parody, 9:440b
structure of, 4:225b–229a
supererogatory Offices, 4:230b
in tonaries, 12:70b
treatises, 10:570a
use of organ in, 9:274b
versified, 6:380b
Walafrid Strabo on, 4:223a
see also Benedicamus Domino; Cathedral Office; Lectionary; Litany; Liturgy, treatises on; Monastic Office; Resurrection office; Rhymed offices; Tones, musical; Tones, reading and dialogue; Vestments, liturgical
Divine providence. *See* Providence, divine
Divisament dou Monde. See Polo, Marco, *Travels of Marco Polo*
Divisio regnorum, 3:111a
Divorce
Byzantine, 4:594a, 594b
Islamic, 4:598a
Jewish, 4:605b, 607a, 607b, 7:495b, 497a
see also Marriage, annulment of
Dīwān, 6:589a
as imperial bureacracy, 3:37b
Roger II and, 11:268b
Samanid, 6:590b
under Abbasids, 3:44a, 6:590a
Dīwān al-jaysh, 6:590a-b
Dīwān al-kharāj, 6:589b
Dīwān al-khātam. See Seal, department of, Islamic
Dīwān al-maẓālim, 6:589a-b
Dīwān al-rasāʾil. See Chancery, Islamic; Egypt, Islamic
Dīwān translations. *See* Translation and translators, Islamic
Dīwān al-wazīr, 6:589b
Diya. See Blood money, Islamic law
Ḍiyāʾ al-Dīn Abu ʾl-Fatḥ Naṣr Allāh, 1:634b–635a
Diyala Plains, 2:45b, 47a
Diyarbakir, **4:231b**
Armenian trade and, 12:97b
Artukids and, 1:485a
Marwanids in, 7:310b
see also Amida
Djazīrat al-Maghrib. See Maghrib, al-
Djenné (Jenné), 8:58a
Timbuktu and, 12:55a-b
Djerids. See Spears
Djime (Thebes), 3:585b
Djruji Gospels, 5:411a-b
Djurdjevi Stupovi (church: Serbia), 11:183b, 184a
Djurhuus, Jens Christian, 4:581a
Djvari, **4:231b–232a,** 5:408b
see also Mcᶜχetᶜa
Długosz, Jan
Annales Poloniae, 9:730a, 11:345a
on the rhymed office of St. Stanislaus, 10:367a
on Vytautas the Great, 7:608a
Dmitar Zvonimir, king of Croatia, Dalmatia and, 4:79b
Dmitrii, False, 11:195b
Dmitrii Ivanovich Donskoi, **4:232a-b**
coinage of, 8:426b
Jagiełło of Lithuania and, 7:606b
minority of, 4:306a
predecessors of, 4:232a
reign of, 4:232a-b
Sergius of Radonezh and, 11:209a
succession plans, 8:543a
suzerainty of recognized, 8:542a
Tatar raids, 8:476a
victory over Tatars, 8:540a-b, 542a-b, 11:347b
Dmitrii, Second False, 11:197b
Dnieper River, Novgorod and, 9:193a
Dobriner Order, founded by Konrad of Masovia, 2:66b
Dobrotica, 2:412b
Docetism, **4:233a-b**
Albigensians and, 4:233b
Bogomil sect and, 4:233a-b
Clement of Alexandria on, 4:233a
doctrine of, 4:233a
Gaianites and, 4:233a
Gnosticism and, 4:233a
Hippolytus on, 4:233a
in Manichaeaism, 4:233a-b
Paulicians and, 4:233a, 9:469b
Doctor, **4:233b–234a**
Doctor solidus, title traditionally accorded to Richardus de Mediavilla, 10:388b
Doctor and Student. See St. German, Christopher
Doctors of the church, **4:234a-b,** 9:715a
St. Jerome, 7:57b–58a
Doctors (of medicine), 9:677a, 679a
leprosy and, 9:677a
see also Disease; Medicine; Plagues; Public health
Doctrina duodecim apostolorum, 7:397a-b
Doctrina patrum de incarnatione Verbi, philosophical terminology, 9:566a
Doctrinale. See Vincent of Beauvais
Doctrinale puerorum. See Alexander de Villa Dei
Doctrine of Addai
Armenian translations, 1:519b
Thaddeus legend and, 12:1a
Documenti d'amore. See Francesco da Barberino
Documents
as archaeological evidence, 1:426a-b, 427b, 428a
as demographic evidence, 4:137a–139b
see also Archives; Birch bark documents
Documentum de modo de arte dictandi et versificandi. See Geoffrey of Vinsauf
Dodecachordon. See Glarean, Heinrich
Dodici avvertimenti che deve dare la madre alla figliuola quando la manda a marito, 3:663a-b
Dodos Rka (monastery: Georgia), 4:116a
Doge
of Genoa, 5:385b–386a
of Venice
authority of, 3:499b, 12:387a-b
origins of the office, 12:384b–385a
Dogmatika stichera. *See* Sticheron
Dogs
charm to protect, 3:274a
diseased, 6:358a, 360a
lawing of, 6:356b
in *Livre de chasse,* 6:361a
vs. birds, in *Jugement de chiens et d'oisiaus,* 6:360a-b
see also Salukis
Dog's tooth molding, 8:454 (*illus.*)
Dohl, 8:561b
Dolce stil nuovo, 3:196a-b, 6:645b–649a
anticipated by Peire Cardenal, 9:485a
in Boccaccio's *Caccia di Diana,* 2:278b
in Cecco Angiolieri's work, 3:211b
imitators of, 6:651b–652a
parodied in Boccaccio's *Decameron,* 2:285a
Dolceaque Bridge (over the Nervia), 10:418b
Dolcino of Novara, 6:488b
Dôle, University of, 12:285a-b
Dolgorukii, Yurii
attacks on Kiev, 8:538b
territorial expansion, 8:538a
Dolopathos, fabliau and, 4:576a
see also John of Alta Silva
Dom zu Köln. *See* Cologne Cathedral
Domagoj, prince (864–876), reign of, 4:2b
Domaine éminent, tenure of land, 11:678b
Dome, **4:234b–236b**
on basilica, 2:124a
Byzantine, 6:56a-b
buttressing, 6:56b
design of, 4:339a
on Hagia Sophia, 4:236a
component parts of, 4:235 (*illus.*)
description of, 4:234b, 236a
double-shell, 4:235 (*illus.*), 236a
in French Romanesque architecture, 10:481a
of Gelatᶜi, 5:374b
Georgian, Tsromi church, 12:222a-b
helmet, 10:579a-b
hollow-tube, Ravenna baptistery, 10:263a

  in mosque architecture, 6:602a, 602b, 604b, 608a
  onion, 4:235 (*illus.*), 236a, 10:579b, 580b
  pendentive, 4:235 (*illus.*), 236a
  pumpkin, 4:236a
  saucer, 4:236a
  semi, 4:236a
  stilted, 4:236a
  Theodoric the Ostrogoth's mausoleum in Ravenna, 10:263b
  as a type of vault, 12:365a
  see also Arch, rounded; Pendentive; Rib; Squinch
Dome of heaven, **4:236b–237a**, 4:236b (*illus.*)
Dome, Islamic. *See Qubba*
Dome of the Rock (Jerusalem), 3:40b, **4:237a-b**, 4:237a (*illus.*), 6:593b–594a (*illus.*), 7:60a, 61a, 103b, 12:263b–264a
  ᶜAbd al-Malik and, 11:560b
  building of, 9:354a
  decoration of, 6:403b, 407a
  dedicated as Templum Domini, 4:24a-b
  ground plan, 6:595a (*illus.*)
  Qalāᵓūn's tomb and, 6:608b
  qubba of, 10:239a
  Templar Romanesque architecture, 10:489a
  use of iron grilles in, 8:286a
  vegetal motifs, 6:186b
Domed octagon church, 3:378b
Domed tomb. *See Turba*
Domenec, Jaume, Catalan adaptation of *Speculum historiale,* 3:166b, 9:511a
Domenichi, Domenico de', 3:519b
Domenico di Cambio, 1:562b
Domenico Fiolario, 5:556a
Domesday Book, **4:237b–239a**, 4:238 (*illus.*)
  on beekeeping, 6:284a
  boroughs and burgesses, 2:330a-b
  breweries, 2:374b
  county descriptions in, 4:238a-b
  as demographic evidence, 4:137b–138a, 139b
  in English law, 7:436a-b
  as evidence of tenure, 4:533a
  forests described, 5:131b
  Great Domesday, 4:238a
  heriot, 6:207b
  inquest and, 6:481a, 7:436a-b
  manor descriptions in, 4:238b
  organizational structure of, 4:238b
  as polyptych, 10:29b
  pound in, 10:67a
  records in, 4:461b
  tax collection and, 4:238b
  tide mills in, 8:392a
  town descriptions in, 4:238b
  use of, 4:238b
  villages and, 12:443a
  water mills in, 8:391a
  William I's Great Survey and, 4:237b–238a
Domestic, **4:239a**
Domestic management. *See* Household management
Domestic production. *See* Economic production, family and
Domhnall Óg O'Donnell, 6:532a
Domical vault. *See* Vault
Domicellus, 11:465b
Dominate, The. *See* Roman Empire
Dominatus, 10:14b
Domingo Gundisalvo, 11:441a
  De divisione philosophiae, 2:241b, 8:563a, 10:357b
  translations by, collaboration with Abraham ibn Daud, 12:135b, 140b
Domini, 7:277a
Dominic of Flanders
  as defender of Thomism, 12:42a
  Summa divinae philosophiae, 12:42b
Dominic Gundissalinus. *See* Domingo Gundisalvo
Dominic, St., **4:239a–240a**
  Albigensians and, 4:239b, 243b
  canonization of, 4:240a
  death of, 4:245a
  in Denmark, 4:239b
  Dominican mysticism and, 4:248a
  early life of, 4:239a-b
  fetters of venerated, 10:298b
  founding of Dominican order, 4:239a-b, 243b
  influence of, 4:240a
  Innocent III and, 6:465a
  introduction of Dominican rite, 4:241b
  invention of rosary, 10:530b
  John Cassian and, 4:239b
  religious life of, 3:355a
  a rhymed office of, 10:369a, 370a
  rule for Dominican nuns, 4:254a
  Spanish prose life of, 11:439b
  travels of in later life, 4:239b–240a
  women's orders and, 12:687b
Dominic of Silos, St., Spanish prose life of, 11:439b
Dominical letter, in Christian calendar, 3:23b
Dominican chant, **4:240a–241b**
  characteristics of, 4:241a
  first use of, 4:240a
  principles used in preparing, 4:240b–241a
  revisions of, 4:240a-b
  version of plainchant in, 4:240a–241a
Dominican rite, **4:241b–242b**
  chapter of 1254 on, 4:242a
  characteristics of, 4:242b
  Clement IV and, 4:242a
  continuity in, 4:242a
  development of, 4:241b–242a
  Humbert of Romans' revision of, 4:241b–242b
  John of Vercelli and, 4:242a
  sources of, 4:242b
  Tridentine rite and, 4:242b
Dominicans, **4:242b–255b**, 9:714b
  apostolic element in order, 4:243a, 248b–252a
  Aquinas and, 4:246a–247a
  in Armagh, 1:470a
  in Barcelona, 2:104a
  beguines and, 2:158b, 159a, 161a, 161b
  biblical exegesis, 4:544a
  Black Death and, 4:245a, 253b
  in Byzantine Empire, 7:348a
  Carmelites absorbed into, 3:96b
  changes in (1054–1305), 3:355b
  chapter of 1221, 4:244a
  chapter of 1228, 4:244a-b
  Christology and, 3:323b
  church approval of, 5:196b
  churches of, 4:250b
  communities of lay sisters, 4:254a–255a
  concept of primitive church, 10:122b
  conflict with secular clergy, 4:251a–252a
  Congregation of Friars Pilgrims for Christ Among the Gentiles, 4:253a
  constitutions of, 4:244b
  contemplative elements in, 4:243a
  correctorium controversy, 10:388b
  crisis of, 4:251a–252a
  decline of, 4:253a-b
  educational system of, 4:245a–248a
  expelled from Sicily, 9:59a
  founding and growth of, 4:240a-b, 243b, 245a, 6:68b, 10:76b
  functions of, 3:355a-b
  general chapter of, 4:244a
  Germany, Ludwig of Bavaria and, 11:516a
  habit of, 4:254a
  Honorius III and, 4:239b, 243b, 245a
  hymns and, 6:382a
  Innocent IV and, 6:467a
  Jews and, 7:77a–78a, 88b
  laity in, 4:243a, 251a
  Latin literature and, 7:368b
  lauda and, 6:635b
  litigation
    against William of St. Amour, 1:128a
    archbishop of Cologne and city burghers, 1:127b
  manuscript book production, 8:103a, 103b
  Martin V and, 4:253b–254a
  master generals of, 4:244b–245a
  membership of, 3:355a
  ministries, 4:248b–252a
    to laity, 3:359a
    to women, 4:251a
  missions of, 4:243b–244a, 252a–253a
    in Armenia, 3:394b, 395a-b
    to Cumans, 12:505a
  motto of, 4:243a
  Muslims and, 4:253a
  mystics, 4:248a-b, 9:31b–35b
    women, 9:11b, 12b–13a, 14a
  Nicene church and, 7:348b
  nuns, 4:221b (*illus.*), 254a–255a
    instructions for, 9:31b
  organization of, 4:244a–245a, 249a-b
  papal support of, 4:251b
  parish system and, 9:416b
  in Pera-Galata, 9:503a
  in *Piers Plowman,* 7:355a
  preacher general in, 4:249b–250a
  preaching churches, Blackfriars, London, 7:663b

Dominicans (*cont.*)
preaching of, 6:663b–664b
books for, 4:250a-b
exempla in, 4:551a-b
penitential preachers, 4:250a
as principal order of friars, 5:297b
Protestantism and, 4:254a
provinces of, 4:244b
Teutonia, 1:127b–128a
Raymond of Peñafort and, 4:247a-b
redaction of constitution by Raymond of Peñafort, 10:266b
reform of, 4:253b–254a
religious instruction and, 10:301a
rhymed offices and, 10:369b, 370a-b
Rule of St. Augustine and, 4:239a-b, 243b
scholarship of
Aristotelianism and, 1:461b–462a
as exegetes, 2:214a, 4:544a
ratio studiorum, 1:128a-b
studium generale at Cologne, 1:127b
translations, 4:246a-b
scholasticism and, 1:465a
Simon de Montfort and, 4:239b
Spirituals, 4:253b
Theodoric Borgognoni and, 4:247b–248a
theology of, 4:246b–248a
Third Order of Penance of St. Dominic, 4:254b
Thomism and, 1:463b
tonary of, 12:71a
Unifiers of St. Gregory the Illuminator, 4:253a
University of Naples and, 9:58b–59a
use of rosary, 10:530b
vow of poverty, 4:253b–254a
vs. heretics, 6:483b, 484a, 487a-b, 488a
William of Moerbeke and, 4:247b
women's orders and, 12:687b–688a
"year of the alleluia" and, 6:662a
see also Fratres Unitores; Preaching; Religious instruction; Theodoric of Freiberg; Thomism
Dominici, Giovanni, cardinal, 3:649a
Regola del governo di cura famigliare, 1:561b
Dominicus, **4:255b–256a**
Dominicus de Clavasio, *Practica geometrie,* 8:211b
Dominus vobiscum, 8:186b, 197a
attributions of, 7:627b
in liturgy, 12:71b
Domitian, Stadium of (Rome), 10:517b
Domitius Domitianus (3rd century), 10:453b
Domna. See Courtly love; Trobairitz
Domnizo. *See* Donizo
Domus cultae, 10:522a
Roman nobles and, 10:525a
Domus ecclesiae, **4:256a**
see also Dura Europos
Don Juan Manuel. *See* Manuel, Don Juan
Don Quixote, Grettir and, 4:615b
Donait français, 1:270b
Donal MacMurrough, king of Leinster, 6:518b
Donald III (Donaldbane) of Scotland, king, **4:256a-b**
David I and, 110b
fall of, 4:256a-b
selection of, 4:256a
Donaldbane. *See* Donald III (Donaldbane) of Scotland, king
Donatello, **4:256b–257b**, 5:101b
as assistant to Ghiberti, 5:524b
Brunelleschi and, 2:388b
Cosimo de' Medici and, 8:243a
Giovanni (Nanni) di Bartolo and, 5:536a
International Style in works of, 5:628a
rise of humanism and, 5:101b
stiacciato relief of St. George and the Dragon, 11:484b, 485 (*illus.*)
work for the Duomo at Florence, 9:56a
Donati, Corso, enemy of Cavalcanti, 3:196b
Donati family of Florence (leader of Blacks), 5:96a-b
Donati, Forese, 6:649b
Donati, Gemma, 4:96a
Donation of Constantine, 3:346a, **4:257b–259b**, 5:136b, 7:263a, 9:373 (*illus.*), 10:18a
authorship of, 4:258a
Doctrine of Two Swords and, 12:234a-b
False Decretals and, 4:124b–125a
grant of *plenitudo potestatis,* 9:708b–710a
Michael Keroularios and, 8:304b
opposition to, 12:539a
papal primacy and, 4:373a, 9:374a
papal states (Republic of St. Peter) granted by, 9:374a, 382b
political uses of, 4:258b–259a
terms of, 4:258a
transmission of, 4:258b
use by Protestants and radical reformers, 4:259a
Waldensian interpretation, 12:511a
Donation of *Dagome iudex,* 9:718b
Donation of Pepin. *See* Pepin III (the Short)
Donatism, **4:259b–260a**
Arab conquest of North Africa and, 4:260a
Augustine of Hippo and, 1:651b–652a
beliefs of, 4:260a
condemned by St. Rheticius of Autun, 10:344b
Constantine I and, 4:259b–260a
origins of, 4:259b
strength in North Africa, 4:260a
validity of sacraments, 6:193b
Waldensian, 12:510a-b
Donatus (Aelius Donatus), 7:352a, 353a, 10:352b
Ars grammatica, 4:504a
in grammar curriculum, 11:688b
Ars minor, 7:351b
in grammar curriculum, 11:688b
as a source of parody, 9:440a
classical literary studies and, 3:432a
on Latin grammar, 5:648b–649b
Smaragdus of St. Mihiel's commentaries on, 11:351a
on Terence, 7:352b, 360a
Donatus of Besançon, St., women's orders and, 12:682b
Donatus of Fiesole, **4:260a-b**, 7:362b
as architect of Lund Cathedral, 10:489a
life of St. Brigit, 2:377a
Donatus (founder of Donatism), 4:259b
Donatus of Melun, count, Robert the Strong and, 3:89b
Donatus, Tiberius Claudius, commentary on Vergil's *Aeneid,* 12:393b, 394a, 395a
Donatz proensal, 10:181b
Dondi, Giovanni de'
academic career of, 4:260b
astrarium of, 3:461a–462a, 4:260b–261a
Gian Galeazzo Visconti and, 4:260b
Tractatus astrarii, 11:644b
Dondi, Jacopo de', astronomical clock by, 3:29b, 464b
Doneldey, Arnold, 4:579b
Döner Kümbet (mausoleum: Kayseri), relation to Iranian tomb tower, 6:28 (*illus.*)
Dongola
as capital of Makuria, 9:198a
population, 9:199b
Donin, Nicholas, 7:77b
Donizo, **4:261a-b**
on Countess Matilda, 7:365b
De anulo et baculo, 10:257b
Vita Mathildis, 4:261a-b, 8:223a
Donkey, as pack animal, 12:148a
Donna angelicata. See Woman, idealized
"Donna me prega." *See* Cavalcanti, Guido
Donna de Paradiso. See Jacopone da Todi
"Donna, di voi mi lamento." *See* Pugliese, Giacomino
Donnchad of Munster, king, 4:77b
"Donne ch'avete intelletto d'amore." *See* Dante Alighieri
Donnei des amants, 1:268b, **4:261b**
Donnino, St., 10:410b–411a
Donor portrait, **4:261b–262a**
Donoratico family, in Pisa, 9:664b
Dönsk tunga, 12:423b
influence of on Old English, 12:434a
Donskoi, Dmitrii Ivanovich. *See* Dmitrii Ivanovich Donskoi
Donzel, 11:465b
Donzella Teodor, La, 11:425b
Doon, 7:317a
Doon de Mayence, 8:225a
Doors
for early Christian churches, 4:361a
Florence baptistery, 9:667a–668a (*illus.*)
Gniezno cathedral, 9:723b
see also Pishtaq; Portal
Dop^{c}ean (*naχarar* family), 1:485b
Doqaq, Seljuk ruler, 11:155a
Doquz Khatun (wife of Hulagu), 6:329a
Vardan Arewelc^{c}i and, 12:360a
Dorestad
in early Middle Ages, 12:321a

trade with Denmark and, 12:424a
Doria, Pietro, Genoese admiral, 12:392b
Döring, Matthias, *Probate spiritus,* against St. Birgitta of Sweden, 9:15b
Dormition Cathedral (Moscow)
iconostasis, 6:409b (*illus.*)
Vladimir Virgin and, 6:411a, 411b (*illus.*), 12:486b
Dormition Cathedral (Vladimir)
architectural elements, 10:580a
frescoes, Last Judgment, 10:588a
Dormition Cathedral (Zvenigorod)
architectural elements, 10:581a
north facade, 10:581b (*illus.*)
Dormition (church: Daphni), mosaics, 8:492b
Dormition (monastery: Nicaea), mosaics, 2:439a
Dormition of the Virgin. *See* Koimesis
Dorothea of Montau, St.
Margery Kempe and, 9:25b
as patroness of Prussia, 9:13b–14a
Dorotheus of Gaza, rule of in Studios Monastery, 11:495a
Dorothy, St., a rhymed office to, 10:373a
Dortmund, origins of, 5:458a
Dorylaeum
as a communication center, 10:424b
crusaders' route and, 10:423b
Dorylaeum, Battle of (1097), 2:309a, 495a
European cavalry charge at, 3:203a
Seljuks defeated at, 4:30a
Dos libros de las armellas, 11:642b
Dotawo
independence of, 9:198b
language of, 9:199a
Double cathedral, 3:378b
Double cross (religious symbol), 4:9a-b, 10 (*illus.*)
"Double truth" doctrine, 11:286b
Double-ended basilica, 3:378b–379a
Double-shell dome, 4:235 (*illus.*), 236a
Doublet, 1:528a
see also Arming doublet
Douglas, Gavin, **4:262a–263a**, 8:324b, 332a, 11:112b, 12:476b
career of, 4:262a-b
Eneados, 4:262b
Palice of Honour, 4:262b, 5:639b, 10:435b
Douglas, Sir James, 10:427b
Doukas, **4:263a**
chronicle of, 2:493a, 495b, 496a, 517b
Doukas, Andronikos, 7:545b
Dove's Necklace, The. See Ḥazm, Abū Muḥammad ᶜAlī ibn Aḥmad ibn Saᶜīd ibn, *Ṭawq al-ḥamāma*
Dovetailed wefts, in tapestry, 11:594b, 595 (*illus.*)
Dower
confiscation of dower rights, 6:486b
English, 6:457b
Islamic, 4:598a
Western, *see also Gerade*
Down, Patrick's mission and, 9:464b
Down, Roger, Hyll and, 6:378a
Dowry
Byzantine, 4:594a, 6:452a
Christian, 4:610a
demography of, 4:145b–146a
feudal, 4:601a
in France, 7:466b–467b
Jewish, 4:606a,b, 607b
as patrimony, 6:455b, 457b–458a
Roman, 6:456a
Slavic, 11:670b–671a
Western, 4:610a
see also Betrothal
Doxology
in hymns, 6:383a
in Sarum use Tonary, 12:70b
Doze sabios, 11:441a
Drachma, Islamic silver, 8:421b
Drachme (unit of measure), 12:594a
Dracontius, 4:520b
De laudibus Dei, 7:361a
Vergil and, 12:394a
Dracula tale. *See* Vlad III Ţepeş
Drăculeşti family, 10:514b, 12:484b
Dracy, hunting in, 6:357b
Drage, 5:646b
Dragma, 8:646a
Dragmaticon. See William of Conches
Dragon, Order of the, 3:305 (*illus.*), 306b, 6:346a
"Dragonskin pattern" swords. *See* Swords, pattern-welded
Dragoş, Vlach voivode, 10:514b
seat of government, 12:501b
Dragutin of Serbia, king, 11:175a–176b, 474b–475a
Drama, liturgical, **4:272b–277b**
Antichrist legend, 7:678b
in *Carmina burana,* 3:98a-b
characteristics of, 4:281a
for Christmas, 4:281a
defined, 4:272b
earliest extant play, 4:280b
Fleury plays, 4:282a
in 14th-century France, 5:273b–274a
Holy Week, 6:277a-b, 278a–279a
importance in history of theater, 4:277a
Italian, 6:635a, 636a–637a, 663a, 7:384b
last emperor, legend of, 7:678b
Latin verse, mystery plays, 7:677b–678b
mystères de la Passion, 5:274a
occasions for, 4:276b–277a
Play of Daniel, 9:705b–706a
Play of Herod, 9:706a-b
prophet plays, 4:281a-b
terms for, 4:278b
Vigil Raber collection, 10:244b–245a
see also Visitatio sepulchri
Drama (Macedonia), acquired by Stefan Uroš IV Dušan, 11:475b
Drama, Western European, **4:277b–289b**
allegorical plays, 4:286b–287a
at court of Charlemagne, 4:274a
audience for, 4:282b, 287b
censorship of, 4:284b–285a
characteristic features, 4:280a-b
as civic ceremonial, 4:284a, 285b
commercialization of, 4:285b
community and, 4:283b
competing critical theories of, 4:280a
detachment from liturgy, 4:277a-b
development of, 4:279b–280a
emphasis on preaching and, 4:286a
farces, 4:279a
folk plays
characteristics, 4:283b
origins, 4:283b
as a game, 4:279a
interludes, 4:279b
Italian. *See* Italian drama
mime in, 4:283a
participatory nature of, 4:280a-b
Paternoster plays, 4:285a-b
patronage of, 4:280a, 284b, 287b–288a
as private entertainment, 4:287a–288a
professional performances of, 4:287b
religious elements, 4:284a
religious instruction and, 4:285b–287a, 10:301b
Roman influence on, 4:277b–278a
separation of text from action in, 4:278a
social functions of, 4:264b, 287a
staging of, 4:280a, 284b
special effects, 4:286b
terms for, 4:278b, 279a
texts of, 4:284b
urbanization and, 4:284a
see also Comoedia; Fleury Playbook; Miracle plays; Morality plays; Mystery plays; N-town plays; Passion plays; Roman architecture, theater; York plays
Drang nach dem Osten
in 12th–13th centuries, 5:460b
to the Baltic lands, 2:66a
Drápa. See Bjarni Kolbeinsson; *Flokkr;* Leiðarvísan; *Líknarbraut; Málsháttakvæði*
Draper
market, 11:706b (*illus.*)
merchant-draper, 11:713a
weaver-draper, 11:712a-b
employees of, 11:714a
income, 11:712b–713a
Drapery (in sculpture)
at Dijon, 12:620a (*illus.*)
at Laon, 5:620a
at Senlis, 5:619a, 620a
Drápur, 11:358b
Drauma-Jóns saga, **4:289b–290a**
origin of, 4:289b
Draumkvæde, **4:290a-b**
characteristics of, 4:290b
composition of, 4:290b
Draw pipe. *See* Sackbut
Drawboys, 11:296a
Drawbridge, 3:148a, 149 (*illus.*)
Drawings, **4:290b–292b**
artists' sketchbooks, 4:292a
English use of, 4:292b
as manuscript illustrations, 4:292a-b
media for, 4:290b–291a
use of, 4:291a, 292b
see also Model books
Drawloom, 11:295b–296a
Drazark, monastery of, 6:312a
Dream of Poliphilus. See Colonna, Francis

Dream of the Rood, text from, 1:280a-b
Dream vision. *See* Visions
Dredge, 5:646b
Dresdener Heldenbuch, **4:292b–293b**
contents of, 4:292b, 293a
verse forms in, 4:292b
version of *Eckenlied* in, 4:380a
Dress. *See* Costume
Dressers, 5:323b–324a, 325a (*illus.*)
Drest/Drust. *See* Tristan, Legend of
Dreux of Haut-Villers, 7:369b
Dreux, Jean. *See* Jean, Dreux
Drîboc, in Wolfram von Eschenbach's *Willehalm,* 12:676a
Drinking horns, in literature, 7:317b–318b
Drinking songs, Middle English, 8:339a-b
Driyosan jadagow (Zoroastrian advocate of the poor), 10:663b–664a
Drogheda, parliaments at (15th century), 9:436b
Drogo of Haut-Villiers. *See* Dreux of Haut-Villers
Drogo of Metz, archbishop, first school of Metz and, 7:25b
Drogo of Ostia, cardinal, on liturgy, 7:631a
Drogo Sacramentary, 8:301b
depiction of subdeacons in albs, 12:398b
historiated initials, 6:463a (*illus.*), 10:607a
Resurrection scene in, 10:340a
Drogo (son of Pepin II of Herstal), 9:500a
Droighneach, 6:534b
Drollery (*drolerie*), 4:293 (*illus.*), **4:294a**, 8:109a
Drome, taxation and, 11:603b
Dromon, 9:76a, 11:230a, 231b
Drone
instrumental, in Celtic music, 8:558b
vocal, in Byzantine music. *See Ison*
Droplaugarsona saga, **4:294a-b**
affinities with *Gísla saga Súrsonar,* 4:294b
Brandkrossa þáttr and, 12:4a
preservation of, 4:294a
see also Fljótsdæla saga; Þorvaldr Ingjaldsson
Dróttkvætt, **4:294b–295a**
flokkr praise poems, 5:91a-b
Geisli, 4:411b
kenning in, 7:230a-b
pagan period, 4:410b
in skaldic poetry, 11:317b–318a, 319b–320a, 321a
see also Egill Skallagrímsson; Eyvindr Finnsson Skáldaspillir; Leiðarvísan; *Líknarbraut*
Drouart La Vache, 1:189a
Drouet of Dammartin, **4:295a-b**
Dijon, Chartreuse de Champmol, 4:186a
Druids
bardic poetry and, 6:536a-b
in Celtic mythology, 9:45b
confrontation with St. Patrick, 9:463a
filid and, 6:544b
Hellenism and, 10:458a
in Irish society, 6:553a
in voyage tales, 6:550a, 551a, 551b
Drum, 8:561b, 563a, 567b
long, 8:605b
Middle Eastern, 8:610b (*illus.*), 613a (*illus.*)
playing of, 8:635a
in processions, 8:595b
see also Kettledrum; Snare drum
Drungarios, **4:295b**, 11:573a
Druzes, **4:295b–297a**
differences from Islamic mainstream, 4:296b
foundation of, 6:587b
al-Ḥākim and, 6:206a-b, 616b
hierarchy of, 4:296a
Ikhwān al-Ṣafāʾ and, 9:4b
Ismailism and, 11:137b, 227b
in Lebanon, 7:532b–533a
marriage practices, 4:296b
as a mystery religion, 9:3a-b
origins of, 4:295b–296a
rituals of, 4:296b
role of *ʿuqqal* in sect, 4:296b
scriptures of, 4:296a
secretiveness of, 4:296a-b
seven commandments of, 4:296b
Drużyna. See Comitatus
Drych yr Ufudd-dawd, 12:614b
Drypoint, 12:699b
of Master of the Housebook, 6:299 (*illus.*)
Držić, Marin, 4:300b
Du droit des magistrats. See Beza, Theodore
Du Guesclin, Bertrand. *See* Guesclin, Bertrand du
Du'a, Chaghatayid prince, Tamerlane and, 11:588a
Dualism, **4:297a–298b**
in Council of Hiereia doctrines, 6:223b
definition of, 4:297a
in early church, 3:340a-b
heresy, Docetism, 4:233a-b
in kingship theories, 7:265b–267a
in Manichaeism, 6:193b, 8:84a-b
in Mazdakism, 8:237a-b
in monastic movements of 12th century, 6:194b–195a
orthodox Christian view, 4:297b
philosophical
definition of, 4:298a
reconciliation of types of, 4:298a
in six Eastern churches, 2:297a
theological
definition of, 4:297b
in human life, 4:297b
see also Bogomilism; Manichaeism; Paulicians
Duan Albanach, 11:113b
source of early Scottish history, 6:258a
Duarte of Portugal, king, 4:559a, 10:53b–54a
Dubbing, 9:150a
oath and, 9:207b
Dublin, **4:298b–300a**
Anglo-Norman invasion of, 4:299a
attack by Scots, 4:299b
Christianization of, 4:299a
citizenship in, 4:299b
English government at, 4:299b, 6:517b, 519a, 519b
as European commercial center, 4:299a
exports of, 4:299b
history, 6:516b–517a, 517b
integration into Gaelic Ireland, 4:299a
origin of, 4:298b–299a
parliaments at (15th century), 9:436b
see of, 1:470a
Viking kingdom of York and, 12:433a-b
as Viking settlement, 4:299a, 12:425a-b
see also Pale, the
Dubois, Pierre. *See* Pierre Dubois
Dubrovnik, **4:300a-b**
Byzantine rule over, 4:300a
city hall clock, 11:658b
culture in, 4:300b
Hungary and, 4:300b, 6:340b
independence of, 4:80a
Kulin and, 7:309a
metal and maritime trade in, 4:300a
Normans and, 4:300a
origin of, 4:300a
Ottoman rule over, 4:300b
as patrician city-republic, 4:300a
public buildings in, 4:300b
public health services in, 4:300b
salt monopoly of, 11:476a
siege of (867), 2:117b
Slavic influences, 4:300b
Stjepan Kotromanić of Bosnia and, 11:485b, 486a
under Uroš of Serbia, 11:175a
Venetian rule over, 4:300a, 300b
Ducat, **4:301a-b**, 8:430b
circulation of, 8:430b
Egyptian dinars and, 8:424a
importance of in international trade, 4:301a-b
inscriptions on, 4:301b
popularity of, 8:430b
standard for reform of coinage, 4:301b
trade and, 8:421b
weight, 4:301a
see also Penny
Ducato, based on Venetian ducat, 4:301b
Duccio di Buoninsegna, **4:301b–303a**, 5:628a, 12:175b
Cimabue and, 4:301b, 302a
Madonna of the Franciscans, 4:302a
Maestà (Palazzo Pubblico, Siena), 4:302a, 11:280b
Maestà (Siena Cathedral), 4:302 (*illus.*), 302b, 303a (*illus.*), 5:606a, 9:447a, 10:29a, 83a
Resurrection scene in, 10:340a
paintings by, 10:83a, 12:172b
panel paintings by, 9:361a
Rucellai madonna, 4:301b
Simone Martini and, 11:299a
Temptation of Christ on the Mountain, 12:0 (frontispiece)
workshop of, 4:302b–303a

see also *Maestà;* Segna di Bonaventura
Duchy, **4:303b–304a**
see also Dukes
Duck, domestication of, 5:150b
Ductia, 4:87a,b, 88b
Ductus, defined, 9:336b
Dudo of St. Quentin, **4:304a**
Duecento art. *See* Dugento art
Duels
in *accusatio,* 6:478b
in canonical inquest, 6:479a
judicial, as ordeal, 9:259a
see also Judicial combat
Duèse, Jacques. *See* John XXII, pope
Dufay, Guillaume
Adam of Fulda and, 8:648b
Florence Duomo and, 8:585b
melody in part music and, 8:271b
motets, 8:504a
synthesis of traditions, 8:504b
music in the Trent codices, 12:183a–184b
Philip the Good and, 8:635a
Duff, 8:561b, 563a, 566a, 567b, 613a
Dugdale, William, 1:428a
Dugento art, **4:304a-b**
Duhamel de Monceau, on charcoal burning, 3:267b
Duhull, 8:561b, 613a
Dukes
in England, 4:304a
ethnic or tribal military leaders, 4:303b
in France, 4:303b–304a
in Merovingian Francia, 4:303b
suppression under Carolingians, 4:303b
as territorial rulers, 4:303b
see also Duchy
Duklja. *See* Serbia
Dukus Horant, **4:304b–305a**
Kudrun and, 7:304b
language of, 4:304b
oral-formulaic style, 4:305a
verse form of, 4:305a
Dulceflorie, compared with *Sperber,* 11:461a
Dulcimer
Arab, 8:611a
Persian, 8:562a
Dulcitius. See Hrotswitha von Gandersheim
Dulmo, Fernão. *See* Olmen, Ferdinand van
Duma, **4:305b–306b**
boyars as permanent members of, 4:305b
conflicting views of, 4:305b
duties of members, 4:305b
in Muscovy
authority in 15th century, 4:306a
evolution of, 4:305b–306a
membership in, 4:306a
prince's authority over, 4:306b
Dumbarton
sheriff and, 11:226a
taken by the Vikings, 11:490a
see also Strathclyde, kingdom of
Dun Cow, Book of the. See Lebor na hUidre
Dunash ben Labrat (Dūnash ibn Labraṭ), 2:212a, 7:96a
criticism of *Maḥberet,* 6:128b
innovations in Hebrew prosody, 7:622a
poetry, adoption of Arabic features, 6:131b
Dūnash ibn Tamīm, 7:98a, 166b
comparative philology, 6:129a
Dunatoi, **4:306b–307a**
acquisition of land by, 4:307a
imperial attempts to control, 4:307a
increase in power of, 4:307a
see also Penetes
Dūnāy, 8:612a
Dunbar, William, **4:307a–308a,** 11:112b, 12:476b
career of, 4:307a-b
Chaucer and, 4:307b
as court poet, 4:307b
"Flyting of Dunbar and Kennedie," 4:307b
"Lament for the Makaris," 4:307b
poetic corpus of, 4:307b
Resurrection of Christ, prosody of, 8:346b
"Tretis of the Tua Mariit Wemen and the Wedo," 4:307b, 8:324b, 332a
Duncan I of Scotland, king, 4:256a, **4:308a**
killed by Macbeth, 8:1a
Duncan of Fife, earl, 11:106b
Dungal (Irish poet), at court of Charlemagne, 7:362a
Dungeon, 3:150a (*illus.*), **4:308a-b**
of Philip Augustus of France, 3:148b
purpose of, 3:148b
Duniry, Great Book of, 6:523a
Dunois, Jean, Bastard of Orléans, 3:273a
Duns Scotus, John, **4:308b–311a,** 9:701a, 702a
academic career of, 4:308b
Aristotelianism of, 4:309a, 310a
Augustinianism of, 4:309a, 309b, 310b
commentaries on Peter Lombard's *Sentences,* 4:308b, 9:517b
differences from Aquinas, 4:310b
education of, 4:308b
followers of, 12:44a
Henry of Ghent and, 6:166a
on Immaculate Conception, 4:311a, 12:43a
on Jews, 7:78b
known as *doctor subtilis,* 4:309a
on the nature of angels, 1:250b
nominalism and, 9:155b
Ockham and, 9:210a, 212b–213b
Ordinatio, 4:308b
Peter Aureoli and, 9:513b
philosophy of
being in, 4:309a-b
on divine will, 4:310b
formal distinction, 4:310a
formalitates, 4:309b
forms of matter, 4:309b–310a
matter and form, 4:309b
passion for unity in, 4:310a
on powers of the human soul, 4:310a
primary object of human intellect, 4:309a
principle of individuation, 4:309b
proof for existence of God, 4:310b
subtlety in solutions of, 4:309a
"thisness" of being, 4:309b
predestination and, 3:371a
Reportata Parisiensa, 4:608b
Reportatio Cantabridgensis, 4:308b
Richardus de Mediavilla and, 10:388b
on Trinitarian doctrine, 12:192a, 194a-b, 196b–197a
on universality of human nature, 12:281b
via moderna and, 12:406b
on Virgin Mary, 12:460b
vs. Thomism, 12:39a
see also Aristotelianism, Scotistic
Dunstable, John
melody in part music and, 8:271b
music of, in Trent codices, 12:183b
Dunstan, Life of, **4:311b**
Dunstan, St., 3:347b
Anglo-Saxon art and, 1:273a
Ethelwold and, 4:517b, 518a
goldsmiths and, 8:289a, 289b
life of
by Byrhtferth, 4:311b
Dunstanus saga, 4:311b–312a
liturgy and, 2:172b
monastic reform and, 7:363a
music and, 8:558a
political importance of, 3:82a-b
popularity in Scandinavia and Iceland, 4:311b
Regularis concordia, 4:274a, 276b, 518b
ashes and, 2:178a
earliest text of *Quem quaeritis* in, 4:280b
election of abbots, 4:421b
Winchester Troper and, 12:648a
Dunstanus saga. See Árni Laurentiusson
Duomo (Florence). *See* Florence, Duomo
Duophysitism, Armenian church and, 1:499a
Duple time. *See* Musical notation
Duplum, 1:546b, **4:312b–313a**
in *Magnus liber organi,* 9:506b, 507a
Dupplin Moor, Battle of (1332), 6:331b
Dūr, Imam, tomb of, 8:534b
Dūr al-ṭirāz, 11:716b
Dura Europos, **4:313a-b,** 11:556b
archaeological importance of, 4:313a
baptistery frescoes, image of Resurrection in, 10:340a
domus ecclesiae, 4:313a, 335a, 349 (*illus.*)
baptistery, 2:87b, 4:349b, 350a, 358a
synagogue, 4:313a
art in, 7:63a–65b, 64 (*illus.*), 8:111b
Duran, Simeon ben Ẓemaḥ
Bow and Shield, 10:5b–6a
Holy War, 10:6b
responsum literature and, 10:339a
Durand, Guillaume, **4:314a–315b**
on bells, 5:321a
on benedictions, 2:178a, 178b
as bishop of Mende, 4:314a, 314b

Durand, Guillaume (*cont.*)
on bishop's miter, 3:624a-b
career as papal judge and administrator, 4:314a
codification of judicial procedures, 7:504b
on consecration of cemeteries, 3:541a
De modo generalis concilii celebrandi, 3:517b–518a, 645b
diocesan instructions and statutes of, 4:314b
education, 4:314a
legal studies, 4:314b
on liturgy, 7:632a–633a
on papal authority, 3:517b–518a
Pontificale Guilelmi Durandi, 10:30b
Rationale divinorum officiorum, 4:315a, 5:586b, 7:593b, 632a–633a
revision of Roman Pontifical, 4:131a, 315a
Speculum iudiciale, 4:314b, 7:118a, 422a, 504b
decretist glossators, 9:519a
Durand of Huesca, Innocent III and, 6:465a
Durand of St. Pourçain, **4:313b–314a**
career of, 4:313b
Commentaria in quattuor libros Sententiarum, 4:313b
condemnation of, 4:313b
De origine potestatum et jurisdictionum, 4:313b
De visione Dei, 4:313b
doctrines of, 4:313b
nominalism and, 9:156a
Durandus, **4:315b**
marble relief of at Moissac cloister, 10:308 (*illus.*)
Durante, *Fiore,* 6:651b, 669a-b
Durayd, Ibn, *Kitāb al-Jamhara,* 4:444a
Durazzo. *See* Dyrrachium
Durendal, 11:546a
Dürer, Albrecht, 9:202ab
armor and, 1:536a
designs for glass, 5:551a
Mair von Landshut and, 4:490a
Master of the Housebook and, 6:299a
Schongauer and, 4:489a
The Syphilitic, 9:683a
Wolgemut and, 12:681b
woodcuts, 12:692a-b
in *Narrenschiff,* 2:363b
Durham
sheriff of, 11:225b
treaties of, **4:316a-b**
Durham Cathedral, **4:315b–316a,** 4:316a (*illus.*), 10:484a, 484b, 485 (*illus.*)
Anglo-Saxon embroideries in, 1:274a
Bede's tomb, 2:156a
groin vaulting, 2:125a
priory, 2:175a
ribbed vaults, 1:429b
Durham Gospels, Book of Kells and, 7:228b–229a
Durham Ritual, written in Northumbrian dialect, 1:276a
Durovernum. *See* Canterbury
Durrow, Book of, 2:220a, 3:219a–220a (*illus.*), **4:316b–318a,** 7:614b
carpet page, 4:317b (*illus.*)
decoration of, 4:316b–317a, 6:461b
German influences, 4:317b
Matthew, 4:317a (*illus.*)
metalwork exemplars for, 4:317b
as a model for the Lindisfarne Gospels, 7:583a-b
origin of, 4:318a
precedents for motifs in, 4:317b
Durum, 5:646a
Dusägge, 11:547 (*illus.*), 551a
Dūst Muḥammad, 7:181b
Dutch art. *See* Flemish art
Dutch drama
rederijkers, 4:322a
religious
morality plays, 4:322a
mystery plays, 4:321b–322a
in vernacular, 4:321b
secular
beginnings of, 4:321a
farces, 4:321b
Hulthem MS, 4:321a
Dutch language
Bible translation, 2:215a
emergence of, 4:318a-b
Frisian and, 6:441b
Middle Netherlandic, 6:441b
origin of, 6:437a
Dutch literature, **4:318a–323a**
allegory in, 4:319a
chambers of rhetoric, 4:322a-b
chronicles, 4:319b
Devotio Moderna and, 4:320b
first vernacular texts, 4:318a-b
Latin devotional writings and, 4:320b
morality play, 8:484a
mysticism in, 4:319a-b, 320b
poetry
classical influences, 4:322b
popular ballads, 4:321a
secular collections, 4:320b
prose, 4:319a
vernacular, 6:44a
Renard the Fox stories, 10:314b–315a
romances
subject matter of, 4:318b
translations from French, 4:318b–319a
saints' lives, 4:320a
verse tales, 4:319b–320a
Dutch way. *See* Travel and transport, Western European
Duties of the Heart. See Baḥya ben Joseph ibn Paqūdā, *Ḥovot*
Dux, 2:89a, **4:323a-b**
among Alamanni, 1:117b
Byzantine, 2:484b, 4:323a
definition of, 5:505a
Polish tribal, 9:716b–717a
in Roman Empire, 4:303b
see also Themes
Dwarfs, in Icelandic *riddarasögur,* 10:395b
Dwin, 2:20a, **4:323b–325a**
administration of, 4:324b
Ani in Širak and, 1:482b
annexed to Georgia, 11:587a
Armenian trade and, 12:97b, 98a
Byzantine attacks on, 1:482a, 483b, 4:323b
capture of
by Arabs, 1:478a, 478b
by Sājids, 1:513b
control disputed between Kurds and Daylamites, 1:513b
decline of, 4:324b, 325a
described by Procopius, 12:97a
during "Iranian Interlude," 4:324a
as early capital of Armenia, 1:563b, 4:323b
earthquake (893/894), 1:481b, 4:324a
economic significance, 4:324b–325a
elders of, 1:490b
finds of Sasanian seals and, 11:122b
foundation of, 4:323b
kat^{c}*ołikoi* in, 1:477a, 477b
mint in, 1:481a, 4:324b
Mongol invasions and, 4:324b
as Muslim emirate, 4:324a
population, 1:485a
Queen T^{c}amar and, 1:485b
reconquered (1203), 1:485b
religious importance, 4:323b–324a
sculpture of, 1:494a
Shaddadids in, 7:310b
Smbat I's martyrdom at, 11:351a
textile industries in, 4:324b
trade and, 1:564a
under Arabs, 1:479a, 513b, 4:323b
under Bagratids, 1:481a, 4:324a
under Kurds, 4:324a-b
under Persians, 1:476a, 4:323b
under Shaddadids, 11:217a, 217b
under Turks, 4:324b
under Zakarids, 4:324b, 325a
Vaspurakan and, 12:361a
see also Naχčawan
Dwin, Councils of
(551/552), 9:102b
(554), 1:499a
(555), 9:102b
condemnation of Nestorianism, 6:187b
condemnation of Paulicians, 6:189a
"Oath of Union," identification of Paulicians with Nestorians, 9:469a
(607), 1:499b
(648/649), 1:500a, 9:103a
(719/720), 1:501b, 7:125a
condemnation of Phantasiast Christology, 6:188a
Dyes and dyeing, **4:325a–329a**
animal sources, 4:326b, 327a
Armenia, *qirmiz,* 10:236a-b
in Artašat, 1:563b–564a
Babylonian, 4:325b
chemistry of, 4:326a-b, 327a
dyers' guilds, 4:328b–329a
eau sure, 11:709a-b
Egyptian, 4:325b
of hair, 2:148b
impact of crusades on, 4:328b
methods, 4:325b (*illus.*)
mineral colors, 4:325a-b
mordant, 11:709b
murex shell imitation, 11:635a
in northern Europe, 4:328a
of paper, 12:698a-b

in the piece, 11:709a
recipes for, 4:328a
regulations governing, 4:328a
revival of under Charlemagne, 4:328a
for tapestry, 11:595a-b
vegetable origins for dyes, 4:325b–326a, 328a
of wool, 11:709a, 12:694b–695a
see also Archil; *particular colors*
Dyfed, **4:329a-b**
annexation by Hywel Dda, 4:329b
extent of, 4:329b
Irish aristocracy of, 4:329a-b
Norman conquest of, 4:329b
origins, 12:514a
as spiritual and cultural center, 4:329b
Dyle, battle on (891), 3:202a
Dynastic archives. *See* Archives, private
Dynna runic stone, 10:565b (*illus.*)
inscription, 10:565a
Dyo kentēmata, 8:617a
Dyrrachium, **4:329b–330a**
attacked by Robert Guiscard, 10:433a, 11:265b
as a communication center, 10:424b, 424a
Norman conquest of, 11:171b
Roman military and administrative center, 4:329b
Samuil and, 2:119a
Serbia and, 11:171a
under Byzantines, 4:329b, 330a, 11:172a
under Ottomans, 4:330a
under Venetians, 4:330a
Dysentery. *See* Plagues, enteric

E

"E·lla Zerbitana retica," 6:657b
Eadfrid (Eadfrith) of Lindisfarne, bishop, Lindisfarne Gospels and, 7:583a, 8:370b, 371b
Eadmer of Canterbury, **4:330b–331a**
Anselm and, 3:82b
Historia novorum, 4:331b
Immaculate Conception and, 12:460b
Life of Anselm, 6:263b
life of Oda "the Good," 9:215b–216a
Vita sancti Oswaldi, 9:216a
Eadred of England, king, Ethelwold and, 4:518a
Eadwine (scribe), Psalter, 2:218b, 3:56b (*illus.*), 57a
Eagle, in heraldry, 6:175a
Ealdorman, 11:225a, 253a
see also Aldermen; Earl
Eanbald of York, archbishop, 1:142b
Eanbald II of York, Alcuin of York and, 1:142b
Eanes, Gonçalves, 4:562a
Earl
sheriff and, 11:225a
see also Aldermen; Ealdorman
Early Christian art, **4:348a–364b**
abandonment of classical naturalism, 4:353b
achievement of, 4:363a-b
aristocratic patronage of, 4:351a, 351b, 362a
Byzantine art and, 10:310b
in catacombs, 4:350a
church furnishings, 4:361a-b
classical traditions and, 4:351a-b, 363b
conventions for depicting sacred hierarchies, 4:355a-b
diversity of, 4:348b
end of classicism in Italy, 4:352a-b
function of, 2:438a-b
Good Shepherd image in, 5:577b
iconoclasm and, 6:191b
Jewish origins of, 7:63b, 65a-b
mosaic of Theodora I, 12:11 (*illus.*), 12b
phases of, 4:348a
portable objects, 4:348b
for private use, 4:362a-b
propriety of images questioned, 4:348a
purposes of, 4:351b–352a
regional traditions in, 4:348b
reliquaries, 10:302b–303a (*illus.*)
Resurrection cycle and, 10:339b–340b
Roman imperial conventions adapted to, 4:353b–355b
Romanesque art and, 10:308b–309a
situla, 11:314b
social and political change and, 4:348b–349a
sources of, 4:363a
symbolism in, 4:349b
Traditio legis, 12:123a–124b (*illus.*)
Transfiguration, 12:125b–126a
Earrings, Byzantine, 5:375b, 376b (*illus.*), 378a-b
Earthenware, in early medieval Western European trade, 12:110a
Earthly paradise. *See* Gardens, Islamic; Paradise
Earthquake Council (1382). *See* Blackfriars Council (1382)
Earthquakes
Beirut (551), 2:163b–164a
Dwin (893/894), 1:481b
Getik (1191), 8:656b
in al-Lādhiqiya, 7:315b
Lombardy (1117), 10:485a, 500b
in Rome (896), 7:344b
Tabrīz, 11:570b
East Africa, Ismailism in, 6:614b
East Angles, kingdom of, 4:454a
East Franconian language, 6:437a, 441b
East Frankish language, Tatian manuscripts and, 11:601a
East Franks, kingdom of, in 843, 5:473a–474a
East Germanic language. *See* Gothic language
East Goths. *See* Ostrogoths
East Middle German language. *See* East Franconian language
East Slavic languages. *See* Slavic languages
East Syrian rites. *See* Syrian rites
Easter, **4:364b–368a**
baptism and, 2:85b, 177b
as beginning of calendar year, 3:20a
benedictions of, 2:178a
blessing of Paschal candle, 2:177b
chants, 9:110 (*illus.*), 713a, 714a
connection with spring renewal, 4:367b
contribution to art and drama, 4:367b–368a
cycle of feasts for, 5:35b–36a
dating of, 3:21b–22a, 4:365a, 8:586a-b
in Armenian church, 3:395a
at Nicaea, 3:628a, 7:611b
in Celtic church, 3:228a-b, 7:614a
introduced into Pictland, 9:91b
Notker's *Computus,* 9:189a
Quartodeciman controversy, 7:396a
Synod of Whitby and, 8:369a
tables by Dionysius Exiguus, 3:18b
derivation of name
English sources, 4:364a
Latin sources, 4:364a–365a
Old High German sources, 4:365a
duration, 4:365a-b
feast of Pentecost and, 4:365b
Eucharist, 4:366a, 366b, 367b
Good Friday services, in Mozarabic rite, 7:591b
incense and, 6:432b
interdict and, 6:494a
liturgy for, 4:274a-b
Byzantine, 2:468b
see also Tones, reading and dialogue
Mass, description in *Ordo romanus,* 6:279b
meaning
forms of Christ, 4:365b–366a
for lay people, 4:365b
pace-egging, 5:36a
Paschal candlesticks, 7:579a
penance, 9:487b
public, 9:491a
plays, German, 10:245a
proclamation, 4:367a
Quem quaeritis in, 4:272b–273a
rites
fasting, 4:366a-b
foot washing, 4:366a-b
in Jerusalem, 4:367a-b
paschal vigil, 4:366b–367b
Scripture reading, 4:367a-b
triduum, 4:366a–368a
significance of in Byzantine liturgy, 7:611b–612a
Tenebrae service, 7:591b–592a
theatrical performances during, 4:267b
"Victimae paschali laudes" sequence, 9:714a
Vigil litany, in *Ordines romani,* 7:592b
see also Holy Week; Lent; Passion cycle; Passion plays
Easter sepulcher, 5:316b
Easterling moneyers, in Norman England, 9:495a

Eastern Orthodox church. *See* Byzantine church
Easton, Adam, 6:382b
  Defensorium, Birgitta of Sweden and, 9:15b
Ebarcius of St. Amand, **4:368a**
  Scripturarum claves iuxta traditionem seniorum, 4:368a
Ebedjesu. *See* ^{c}Abdisho^{c} bar Berīkha
Eberhard of Béthune. *See* Evrard of Béthune
Eberhard of Franconia, 5:508a, 509b
Eberhard of Freising, *De mensura fistularum,* 8:642a
Ebner, Christine, *Von der Gnaden Ueberlast,* 9:13a
Ebner, Margaret
  Diarium, 9:13a
  Johannes Tauler and, 9:33b
  letters from Heinrich von Nördlingen, 8:356a
  Revelations, 8:356a
Ebo of Rheims, **4:368a-b**
  Denmark and, 4:151a
  False Decretals and, 4:125b
  Gospelbook of Épernay made for, 4:368a-b, 10:98a
  manuscript illuminators of, 10:98a
Ebreo, Guglielmo. *See* Guglielmo da Pesaro
Ebro Valley
  Christian immigation into, 11:376b–377a
  kingdom of Navarre and, 9:67b, 68b
  opening of by Aragon, 9:69b
Ebroin, mayor of the palace, 9:499b
Ebstorf map, 5:397a
Eburnant group, 10:101b
Ecbasis captivi, 2:141a, **4:369a–370a,** 4:496a, 7:363b
  monastic connections, 4:369b
  time of composition, 4:369a
  wolf-fox antagonism, 4:369a-b
Ecce homo, **4:370a-b,** 4:370b (*illus.*)
Ecchellensis, Abraham, *Eutychius,* 4:525b
Ecclesia primitiva. *See* Primitive church, concept of
Ecclesia and Synagoga, **4:370b–372a,** 4:371a (*illus.*), 5:620b–621a
  at Chartres, 5:620b–621a
  in *Auto de los reyes magos,* 11:410b
  contrast between old and new covenants, 4:370b–371a
  disappearance after Counter-Reformation, 4:371b
  fixed attributes, 4:371b
  personifications, 4:371a-b
  see also Auto de los reyes magos
Ecclesiastical architecture. *See* Church architecture
Ecclesiastical capitulary. *See* Capitulary
Ecclesiastical Hierarchy. *See* Pseudo-Dionysius
Ecclesiastical Histories, The. *See* Gregory of Tours, St.
Ecclesiastical History. *See* Eusebius of Caesarea; Hugh of Fleury; Ordericus Vitalis; Sozomen
Ecclesiastical penal law. *See* Criminal justice, ecclesiastical
Ecclesiastical reform. *See* Church reform
Ecclesiastical rights. *See* Clergy, rights of
Ecclesiasticus cadence. *See* Cadence (language)
Ecclesiology, **4:372a–378b**
  Ambrosius Autpertus' interpretation of the Apocalypse, 2:11a
  angelic hierarchy, 9:602a
  Avignon papacy, 4:376a–377a
  canons, 9:602a
  Carolingian period, 4:373a–374a
   false decretals, 4:373a-b
  Christ's headship, 9:602a
  communion of saints and of holy gifts, 4:372b, 373a, 375b
  England
   interrelations with parliament, 4:483b
   theories of papal heresy, 4:483b
   under Henry II, 4:471a
   under Richard I and John, 4:471a-b
  Franciscan and Thomist theologies, 4:375b–376a
  patristic period, 4:372a-b
  Roman primacy in church. *See* Papacy
  sacraments, 4:373a, 9:601b–602a
  universalism, 4:372a
   during reign of Charlemagne, 4:373a
  see also Church, early; Conciliar theory; Latin church; Liturgy, treatises on; Papacy; Schism, Great
Ecclesius of Ravenna, bishop, 10:263a
Ecgfrith, accession to Mercian kingship, 4:455a
Echaid Airem, Irish king (mythical), 6:546b
Echelon apse church plan. *See* Church architecture
Echemata, 8:639a
  neuma and, 9:109a
  noeannoe and, 9:152a
Échevin, 3:502a, **4:378b–379b**
  Carolingian period, 4:378b–379a
  function as local government, 4:379a
  in Ghent, 5:521b–522a
  monopoly by the rich, 4:379a-b
  see also Mayor
Échevinage, 3:502a, 12:731b, 732a
  in Bruges, 2:386b
Échiquier. *See* Eschaquiel
Echmiadzin. *See* Ējmiacin
Échoppe, **4:379b**
Echternach, monastery at, 10:104b
Echtrae, 6:550a–551b, 552a
Echtrae Airt maic Cuinn, 6:552a
Echtrae Conli, 6:550b, 551a
Echtrae Cormaic maic Airt i tír tairngiri, 6:550b, 551a-b, 552a
Echtrae Fergusa maic Léti, 6:550b, 551a
Echtrae Laegairi maic Crimthainn, 6:550b, 551a
Echtrae Nerai, 6:550b
Eckbert of Schönau, description of Catharist group, 6:196a
Eckenlied, **4:380a-b**
  borrowing from *Lied,* 8:354b
  construction of, 4:380a
  courtly associations of, 4:380a-b
  origins, 4:380a
  Þiðreks saga and, 12:30a
Eckhart von Hochheim. *See* Eckhart, Meister
Eckhart, Meister, **4:380b–382b**
  beguines and, 2:160b
  career of, 9:31b–32a
  central themes in writings, 4:382a
  doctrines of, 9:32b–33a
  as Dominican, 3:368b
  Free Spirits and, 5:218b
  German mysticism and, 4:248b
  German works, 4:381a, 9:32b, 32a
  on good works and salvation, 4:382a-b
  heresy trials, 4:381a, 9:32a
  importance to mystical thought, 4:380b, 381a, 381b–382a
  influenced by Neoplatonism, 9:100b
  language of, 4:381b, 9:33a-b
  languages used by, 8:356a
  Latin works, 4:381a-b, 9:32a-b
  man's knowledge of God and, 9:32b–33a
  as scriptural commentator, 4:246a
  Suso and, 11:516a, 516b, 517a
  Tauler and, 9:33b, 11:602a, 602b
  in a treatise by Jan van Leeuwen, 9:37b
  on Trinitarian doctrine, 12:195b
Eclectic Aristotelianism. *See* Aristotelianism, Augustinian
Ecloga Theoduli. *See* Gottschalk of Orbais; Theodolus
Eclogue, **4:382b–383a,** 4:594a
  basis for, 4:383a
  denunciation of, 4:383a
  evidence on literacy in, 7:596a
  simplification of laws, 2:488a
  on social structure, 9:493b
  see also Byzantine law; Russian (Muscovite) law
Economic development
  boroughs and, 6:345b
  capital and, 3:419b–420a
  estate management and, 4:512b
  fairs and, 4:582b, 584b–585a
  fostered by Cistercians, 3:404a
  France, in 14th century, 11:680a-b
  growth of towns and, 3:416b
  nobility and, 9:151a-b
  population and, 4:143b
  Russia, 11:192a, 192b
  serfdom and, 11:199b–200a
  speculation and, 3:419b–420a
  villages and, 12:444a
Economic production
  estates and, 4:601b
  family and, 4:595a, 597a, 600b, 604a
  women and, 4:603b
Economy, principle of. *See* Reductionism
Ecstatic experiences. *See* Mysticism
Ectabana, 12:96b, 97a
  Sasanian culture, 10:661a
Ecthesis. *See Ekthesis*
Ectors saga, 10:394b, 395b
Ecumenical patriarch. *See* Patriarch, ecumenical
Edda, meaning and etymology, 4:385b
Eddic meters, **4:384a–385b**

basic unit and alliteration, 4:384a-b, 388a-b
changes in, 4:385a
derivation, 4:388a
dróttkvætt, 6:112b, 10:403b
Eddic vs. skaldic, 4:389a
fornyrðislag, 4:384a-b, 10:403b
in *Grípisspá,* 5:678a
in *Hyndluljóð,* 6:385a
kviðuháttr and, 7:311b
in Old Norse poetry, 4:388b
in *Reginsmál* and *Fáfnismál,* 10:290a-b
in skaldic poetry, 4:389a
in *Vǫlundarkviða,* 12:490a-b
in *Vǫluspá,* 12:491a
see also Grottasǫngr
galdralag, in Old Norse poetry, 4:388b
Grímnismál, 5:676a–677a
in *Grims saga loðinkinna,* 5:677b
in *Ketils saga Hængs,* 7:232a
kviðuháttr, 6:112b
in *Háleygjatal,* 4:570b
ljóðaháttr, 6:112b
development of, 4:390b–391a
in *Grímnismál,* 5:676a
in Old Norse poetry, 4:388b
in *Reginsmál* and *Fáfnismál,* 10:290a-b
málaháttr, 4:384a-b
in Old Norse poetry, 4:388b–389a
in *Merlínússpá,* 8:276a
Old Norse, 4:388b–389a
in *Skírnismál,* 11:327a
strophic characteristics, 4:385a
transitional forms, 4:389a
Eddic poetry, **4:385a–392b**
blame literature, 7:643a-b
Brynhild in, 2:394b–395a
characteristics of, 11:317a
comic dialogue, 6:98a
dating
advent of Christianity, 4:389b
archaeological and historic criteria, 4:389b
linguistic criteria, 4:389a-b
relation to foreign poetry, 4:389b
effect of Christianity on, 4:391a
elegies, theme of love transcending death, 6:35a-b, 36a
fragments of lost poetry, 4:387a-b
Guðrúnarkviða cycle, 6:3a-b, 36a
heroic, 6:149a
fragments in Eddic appendix, 4:387b–388a
German influence, 4:390b
history and genres of, 4:390a-b
organization of, 4:386a-b
praise poems, 4:411a, 414b
provenance, 4:390a
retrospective style, 4:390b
Scandinavian influence, 4:390a-b
Hyndluljóð and, 6:385a
influence on *rímur,* 10:403b
midgard serpent in, 8:362a-b
mythological
fragments in Eddic appendix, 4:387a-b
history and genres of, 4:391a
organization of, 4:386b–387a
provenance, 4:389b–390a
Nibelungenlied and, 9:114a
on Njǫrðr, 9:146a
noncourtly, 4:391b
Norna-Gests þáttr and, 9:171a
oral tradition, 4:391b
praise poems, 6:97b
Ragnarǫk and, 10:248a-b
surviving manuscripts, 4:385a–388a
þættir and, 12:4b
vernacular in, 6:445a
Vǫlsunga saga and, 12:488a, 489a
Vǫlundarkviða and, 12:490a
Vǫluspá and, 12:491a
see also Baldrs draumar; Bjarkamál; Rígsþula; Scandinavian mythology; Snorri Sturluson; Úlfr Uggason; *Vafþrúðnismál*
Eddica minora, preservation of heroic poetry in, 4:388a
Eddius Stephanus. *See* Aeddi
Edelstein. See Boner
Eden, Garden of. *See* Gardens; Paradise
Edessa, **4:384a**
Armenian population, 4:384a
captured by Romanos I Lekapenos, 10:515b
as a center of Nestorianism, 9:106b
First Crusade and, 4:30a, 30b, 37a-b
capture by Baldwin I of Jerusalem, 2:58b
Mandylion, 8:82b–83a
School of the Persians and, 9:142a
schools of, 11:564b
Syriac language and, 11:562a
Syrian rites and, 11:567b
under T^coros, 1:484b
Edgar of England, king (*r.* 959–975)
coinage of, 9:495a
reforms, 4:457a
coronation of, 3:82b
Ethelwold and, 4:518a
monastic reform and, 1:273a, 10:285b
poems on in Anglo-Saxon Chronicle, 8:328a
reforms of, 3:347b, 4:456b–457a, 459a
Treaty of Chester and, 3:299b–300a
Edict of King Rothar. *See Leges Rotharis*
Edict on Maximum Prices. See Diocletian, Roman emperor, *De maximis pretiis*
Edict of Theodoric. *See Edictum Theodorici*
Edict of Union. *See* Zeno the Isaurian, *Henotikon*
Edictum Theodorici, 7:469b, 11:335a, 12:472a
Edigú, Golden Horde under, 5:573a
Edinburgh, **4:392b–394a**
castle of, rebuilt by Robert II of Scotland, 10:428b
dating of remains, 4:392b–393a
English assaults on, 4:393a
etymology of name, 4:392b
evolution as capital, 4:393a-b
growth and population, 4:393b–394a
immigration, 4:393b
royal residence in, 4:393a
stone city wall, 4:393b–394a
town council, 4:393b
trade and commerce, 4:393b
Edinburgh, Treaty of (1328), 9:438b
Edington, Battle of (878), 12:431b, 432b, 433a
Edirne, manuscript illumination style, 6:614a
Edith of Polesworth, St. *See Vie de Ste. Modwenne*
Edmund of Abingdon, St.
Anglo-Norman lives of, 1:261a
Merure de seinte église, 1:261b, 263a, 8:279a
compared with Robert of Greatham's *Corset,* 10:433b
Edmund of East Anglia, king
cult of, 4:456a
rhymed office to, 10:372b
Vikings and, 12:432a
see also Passiun Seint Edmund, La; Vie St. Edmund le rei, La
Edmund Ironside, king of England, sons of in Hungary, 12:373a
Edmund (son of Henry III of England), Sicily and, 11:272a, 607b
Edmund of Wessex, king, Malcolm I of Alba and, 8:55b
Edmyg Dinbych, 12:597b
Édouard le Confesseur, Vie d'. See Vie d'Édouard le Confesseur
Education. *See* names of particular schools; Classical literary studies; Universities
Education of children. *See* Children
Education of clergy. *See* Clergy
Education of women. *See* Women
Edward I of England, king, **4:395b–397a**
accession to throne, 4:475a-b
Adolf of Nassau and, 4:209b
Barons' war and, 2:112a-b
bastides and, 2:128b
bodyguard of, 6:302b
Clericis laicos and, 3:448a
Confirmations of the Charters, 8:42a, 9:424b–425b
as earl of Chester, 12:521a
financing of the Agen bridge, 10:418a
foreign conflicts, 4:396a
with Philip the Fair, 5:171a, 11:609b
furs for, 5:325b
Henry III and, 4:395b–396a
Ireland and, 6:519a
Jews and, 4:564a, 7:77b, 89a, 90a
legal reforms, 7:44b, 9:425b
concerning distress, 4:221a
court of common pleas, 3:492a, 7:188b–189b
Exchequer Court, 4:534a-b
King's Bench court, 7:191a-b
petty jury, 7:183a
Statutes of Westminster, 12:622a-b
military tactics of, 3:205a, 6:332b
parliament and, 4:396b, 481b–483a, 9:423b–425b
in Peter Langtoft's *Chronicle,* 9:516a
prince of Wales and, 4:108a
Rabban Sauma and, 1:453a
regulation of gold and silver manufacture, 8:290a

Edward I of England, king (*cont.*)
rights of London lost under, 7:662b–663a
Robert I of Scotland and, 10:426b–427a
royal wardrobe and, 6:302a, 302b
Scotland and, 4:396a-b, 11:107b, 108a–110a
shipbuilding and, 9:81b
Simon de Montfort the Younger and, 11:298a-b
in *Song of Lewes,* 11:372b
statute and, 11:468b
taxation, 4:484a, 11:615a
on church, 11:608a, 608b–609a, 614b–615a
on movables, 11:614a-b
scutage, 11:120b
touching for king's evil, 7:256a
treason definition and, 12:165b
Welsh conflict, 7:637b
campaign of 1277, 12:522a, 526b
marcher jurisdictions, 12:526b
military strategies, 12:565a
rebellion of Madog ap Llywelyn, 12:523a
reorganization of territory, 12:522b
Welsh overlordship, 12:528b–529a
Wulfstan of Worcester and, 12:703a
Edward II of England, king, **4:397a-b**
accession to throne, 4:475b
competence as a ruler, 4:397a-b
deposition of, 4:160b, 397b, 475b, 476a
effect on kingship, 4:476b
effect on parliament, 4:483a
diplomatic communications, 4:208a
Exchequer and, 4:534b
inauguration as Prince of Wales, 12:523a
Ireland and, 6:519a
legal system under, 7:44b
court of common pleas, 7:188b
in Middle English prophecies, 10:148a
Ordinances of 1311 and, 9:426b, 426a
parliament and, 4:483a, 9:425b–427a
prerogative and, 10:89b–90a
Robert I of Scotland and, 10:427a, 427b
Statute of York (1322) and, 9:426b, 426a
touching for king's evil, 7:256a
treason definition and, 12:165b
Edward III of England, king, **4:398a-b**
accession to throne, 4:475b, 9:426b, 427a
ban on Flanders wool, 5:523a
Bedlam and, 2:157a
claim to French throne, 5:183a-b, 6:160b, 9:555b
default on loans from Italian merchants, 12:118a
Enguerrand VII and, 4:490b
Iolo Goch and, 6:500b
Latin literature and, 7:370a
legal system under, 7:44b
court of common pleas, 7:189b–190a
justices of the peace, 7:196b–197a
King's Bench court, 7:193a-b
on leprosy, 7:550b
marriage of, 6:332a
in Middle English prophecies, 10:148a
military activities, 4:398a
Battle of Crécy, 2:358b, 3:205b
financial needs generated by, 4:484a-b
in Hundred Years War, 6:331b, 334a
siege of Calais, 3:64b
Normandy and, 9:169b
Ordinances of the Staple (1353) and, 9:428a
parliament and, 4:398a-b, 9:427a–428b
Good Parliament, 6:427a
participation of barons in administration, 4:398a
Piers Plowman and, 7:331a, 332b
prerogative and, 10:90a-b
royal wardrobe and, 6:304a
sons of, 7:134b–135a
treason definition and, 6:428a, 12:166a–167a
Treaty of Berwick and, 2:202b
vs. David II, 2:202b, 4:111a-b, 11:110a-b
Edward IV of England, king
accession to throne, 4:478a-b, 6:162a
Barnet-Tewkesbury victories, 12:571b
coronation, 12:571a
on the "French pox," 9:682a
Household Ordinances, 8:416a
Ireland and, 6:520a
marriage to Elizabeth Woodville, 12:571b
in Middle English prophecies, 10:146b
Owen Tudor's execution, 12:223a
parliament and, 9:429b, 430b–431a
infrequency of parliaments under, 9:434a
in Ireland, 9:436b
Paston brothers and, 9:450b
Richard III and, 10:385a-b
siege train, 12:567a
taxation, benevolences, 11:616a
victory at Towton, 12:571a
Edward V of England, king, 9:431a
deposition of, 4:160b
Richard III and, 10:385a-b
Edward VI of England, pretender, Irish parliament and, 9:437a
Edward II of York, duke, translation of *Livre de chasse,* 6:360b
Edward the Atheling, succession to St. Edward the Confessor, 4:395a
Edward the Black Prince, **4:398b–399a,** 7:135a, 9:716a
military career, 4:398b–399a
opposition to John of Gaunt, 4:399a
Richard II and, 10:384a
rule of Aquitaine by, 1:368a
tomb of, 1:526a, 6:334b
victory at Poitiers, 4:398a, 6:332a
consequences, 5:185a
Wyclif and, 12:706b
Edward the Confessor, St., **4:394a–395b**
agreement with Macbeth, 8:1a
biographies of
Anglo-Norman lives, 1:261a-b
anonymous vita, 7:261b–262a
Vie d'Édouard le Confesseur, 12:412a
character, 3:535b
coinage of, 9:495a
establishment of Westminster Abbey and, 1:286b
great seal and, 6:300b
healing miracle by, 7:255a
marriage of, 4:394b–395a
naval defense and, 4:90b
Normans and, 9:165a, 165b
Old English poem on the death of, 1:278b
relics of, 4:517a
restoration of Anglo-Saxon dynasty, 4:457a
Romanesque architecture and, 10:484a
seal of, 11:127b, 128b, 129b
succession controversy, 4:394a-b, 461a
threats to authority, 4:395a
tomb of in Westminster Abbey, 12:621b
unification of England, 4:452b
vs. Stigand, 3:82b
Edward Fitz Odo of Westminster (goldsmith), 8:289b
Edward, king (son of Alfred the Great), reconquest of Danelaw, 4:456b
Edward (the Elder) of Wessex, king, Vikings and, 12:433a
Edward (the Martyr) of England, king (*d.* 978), murder of, 4:457a
Edwin of Northumbria, king, conversion of, 4:458a-b, 12:331b
Een schoon liedekens boeck. See Antwerp Songbook
Effects of Good Government, The. See Lorenzetti, Ambrogio
Effossores, 10:520b
Eftimie (Romanian chronicler), 10:510b
Egbert of Liège, **4:399b**
Fecunda ratis, 4:399b
Egbert of Trier, **4:399b,** 10:101b–102a
Egbert Codex, 4:399b
donor portrait in, 4:262a
Egbert of Wessex, king, reign of, 4:455a-b
Egbert of York, penitential of, 9:489a, 489b
Egen von Bamberg, 8:411b
Eger, carnival plays at, 4:271b
Egeria
Itinerarium Egeriae, **7:19a-b,** 7:350b, 12:494b
authorship, 7:19b
on baptism, 3:675b
on Christmas in Palestine, 3:318a
dating of, 7:19b
on dismissal litanies in Jerusalem, 7:590b
on Kyrie sung by children, 7:590b, 593b
origin of the Stations of the Cross and, 11:467b
on the Palestinian rite, 7:626a
survival in manuscript, 7:19b
Eggja runic stone (Norway), 10:562a
Eggplant, growth of, 1:81b
Eghri Dagh. *See* Ararat, Mount
Egidius Colonna, **4:400a-b,** 9:709a

condemnation by bishop of Paris, 4:400a
Contra gradus et pluralitates formarum, 12:40b
De ecclesiastica potestate, 7:268a, 10:21a
De regimine principum, 6:658b, 7:266b, 601a, 8:435a-b, 10:21a
Spanish version of, 11:441b
ecclesiology, 4:400a-b
influences on work, 4:400a-b
papal support by, 10:21a–22a
theory of kingship, 4:400b, 7:266b–267a
via moderna and, 12:407b
Wyclif and, 12:710a
see also Augustinus Triumphus
Egidius Morini. *See* Egidius of Murino (Morino)
Egidius of Murino (Morino)
De motettis componendis, 8:646a-b
Quatuor principalia musice and, 8:646b
Egidius of Zamora
Ars musica, 8:645a
definition of harmony, 6:100b
Egill One-Hand. *See Egils saga Einhenda ok Asmundar Berserkjabana*
Egill Skallagrímsson, **4:400b–401b,** 11:356a
Arinbjarnarkviða, 4:401a, 403a, 7:312a
description of, 4:401a
dróttkvætt stanzas, 4:401a-b
Hǫfuðlausn, 4:401a, 403a
form and content, 4:401a
lausavísa and, 7:387b
on Norse gods, 9:146a-b
Skarkaðr legend and, 11:467a
Sonatorrek, 4:401a, 403a, 616a, 7:312a
story of in literature, 4:400b–401a
see also Egils saga Skallagrímssonar
Egils saga Einhenda ok Ásmundar Berserkjabana, **4:401b–402a**
resemblance to other stories, 4:401
treatment of gods in, 5:142a
Egils saga Skallagrímssonar, **4:402a–403b,** 4:612b, 614a, 5:677b
authorship of, 4:403a
berserks and, 2:198b
date written, 4:403a-b
goddess Rán in, 10:257a
historical events in, 4:402b
preservation in manuscripts, 4:403b
see also Egil Skallagrímsson
Egino Gospels, 7:651a
Egla. *See Egils Saga Skallagrímssonar*
Egloga de calvis. See Hucbald of St. Amand
Egrisi. *See* Georgians
Egypt
calendar in, 3:18b
Copts in, 3:593b
decline of agriculture, 3:594b
glassmaking in, 5:545a–546a
Hellenism and, 10:457b
in Islamic conquests, 6:569b–570a
Nile and, 9:138a-b
plagues in, 9:675a, 684a–685b, 686a
shipments of grain to Roman Empire, 12:108b
textile manufacture in, 3:588b–589a, 4:325b
Egypt, Islamic, **4:403b–408b,** 4:404 (map)
administration of, 6:590b–591a, 591b
art and architecture, 4:408b
Ayyubid, 2:21b–22a
bowl, 3:239b (*illus.*)
bookbinding in, 8:98b
boundaries, 4:404a
as business center, 12:107b
Cairo as commercial and military center for, 3:13a–14a
conquered and ruled by ᶜAmr ibn al-ᶜĀṣ, 1:236b–237b
conversion of, 4:405a-b
cultural contributions, 4:407a–408a
Dīwān al-rasāᵓil correspondence department, 12:224a
dockyards in, 9:74a
invasions of, 11th through 16th centuries, 4:406b–407a
Ismaili community in, after 1171, 11:138a
Jews in, 7:83a–84b
illuminated manuscripts, 7:66a-b
under the Fatimids, 9:52b–53a
mercenary seizure of control, 9:305b–306a
mints and money in, 8:421b, 423b–424b
navies in, 9:74b–75a
political history, 4:405b–407a
relations with
Nobadia, 9:198a
Nubia, 9:197b
scientific achievements, 4:407b–408b
Sicilian trade and, 11:262b
slave trade in, 11:339a
taxation policy
assessment and collection, 11:626a-b
rates, 11:626b–627a
ushr and *kharāj,* 11:625b–626a
textiles, 11:717a, 11:718b
Tulinid dynasty and, 12:223a–225a
12th-century struggle for control of, 3:14a
under the Ayyubids, 2:24a–25a
under the Fatimids. *See* Badr al-Jamālī
under Ikhshidids, 6:416b, 417b
see also Mamluk dynasty
Egypt, late Roman, **10:453a–456a**
economy, 10:454b
geography, 10:453a-b
government, 10:454a
languages, 10:455a
population, 10:453a-b
relations with
Nubia, 10:453b
Rome, 10:463a-b
revolutions, 10:453b
Egyptian church
Christmas and, 3:318a
Eutychios and, 4:525a
history, 10:454b–455a
see also Coptic church
Egyptian language, Demotic script, 10:455a
Ehebüchlein. See Albrecht von Eyb
Ehrenbote vom Rheim. See Reinmar von Zweter
Ehrenbrief. See Püterich von Reichertshausen, Jacob III
Ehrenreden. See Suchenwirt, Peter
Eideshelfer. See Oath, helpers
Eigel, **4:408b,** 5:311b
Eigen, Habsburgs and, 11:539b
Eight Orations. See John Chrysostom
Eight-mode classification. *See Octoechos*
Eighteen Benedictions, 7:160a
Eighth Age of the World. *See Sex aetates mundi*
Eike von Repgowe, **4:408b–409b,** 10:330a
royal succession, 4:428a
Sachsenspiegel, 2:144b, 5:491b, 499a, 7:426b, 479b–481a, 8:354a, **10:602b–604a**
codes modeled on, 10:603a-b
commissioning of, 10:602b
Dutch version of, 10:603a
historical influence, 4:409a-b
illuminations, 10:603b
importance to German law, 10:602b
papal condemnation of, 10:603b
princes' electoral rights, 4:428a
printing of, 10:603b
punishments in, 7:480
Saxon influence, 10:602b
as a source for *Schwabenspiegel,* 11:80b
sources and achievements, 4:409a
Sachsische Weltchronik, 10:602b
see also German law, post-Carolingian
Eilardus de Oberge. *See* Eilhart von Oberg; *Tristrant*
Eilat, Gulf of, Franks in, 11:247a
Eilhart von Oberg, 6:359a
romance literature of, 5:453a-b
Strassburger Alexander and, 7:323a
Tristrant, 5:450b, 634b–635a, 8:408b, 12:202b, **12:204a–205b**
relation to *Eneide,* 6:144b
version commune of the legend of Tristan, 12:200b–201a
Eilífr Goðrúnarson, **4:409b–410b**
Þórsdrápa
religious aspects, 4:410a
on Thor's encounter with Geirrøðr, 12:45b
uniqueness of kennings, 4:410a
Ein-Sof, 3:1a
Einang rune stone, 10:557b
Einar fóstri, *Skíða ríma,* problems of authorship, 10:402b–403a
Einar Gilsson, *Ólafs ríma Haraldssonar,* 10:402b, 403b
Einar Hafliðason, *Laurentius saga,* 7:386b–387a
Einarm, 3:179 (*illus.*), 180a
Einarr Helgason Skálaglamm, **4:410b–411a**
Vellekla
meaning of name, 4:411a
texts of, 4:410b
Einarr Skúlason, **4:411a–412a**
Geisli, 11:317a, 317b–319b, 321b, 358b

Einarr Skúlason (*cont.*)
Geisli (cont.)
drápa form, 4:411b
mythological kennings, 4:411b–412a
see also Líknarbraut
Einhard, **4:412a–413a**, 7:362a
Annals, 5:654a, 9:712a
Asser and, 7:363a
on the burning of Charlemagne's bridge over the Rhine, 10:410b
Candidus of Fulda and, 3:64a
coronation of Charlemagne, 3:111a
on hunting, 6:356a, 356b
as judge, 2:173b
Latin works, 4:412b
relations with Louis the Pious, 4:412a-b
on riding, 12:370a
service to Charlemagne, 4:412a
Translatio et miracula SS. Marcellini et Petri, 12:145a
translation of relics by, 12:154a
triumphal arch reliquary, 10:306b
Vita Caroli Magni, 2:236a, 239b, 4:412b–413a, 5:654a, 6:262b, 9:712a
on early Balts, 7:602b
Gesta Caroli and, 9:187a
imitation of Suetonius, 5:233a
influence on Theganus, 12:7b
Song of Roland and, 10:445b
Einherjar (dead Scandinavian heroes)
in Valhalla, 12:350b
Valkyries and, 12:351a
Einkorn, 5:645b–647a
Einold of Toul, archdeacon, 5:578b
Einon ap Gwalchmai, **4:413a-b**
elegy on Nest, 4:413a-b
Einschildig, 5:499a
Einsiedeln, abbey of, 11:540b, 542a
Einungen. See Representative assemblies, German, estates unions
Eirene, Byzantine empress, 7:127b
Eirík the Red
Christianity and, 8:442b
discovery of Vinland, 12:428b
Greenland and, 4:554b
settlement of Greenland, 12:427a-b
Eiríkr Bloodaxe of Norway, king
arrival in Valhalla, 12:350b
death of in 954, 12:433b, 434a
defeat by West Saxons, 4:456b
in *Eiríksmál* and *Hákonarmál,* 4:414b
poems dedicated to, 4:401a
Eiríkr Oddsson, **4:413b–414a**
Hryggjarstykki, 4:618a, 9:176a
setting and purpose, 4:413b
sources of, 4:414a
Eiríkr sigrsæli, king, Yngvarr and, 12:726b
Eiríks saga rauða, 4:613b, 12:428a-b, 456b
on Leif Eriksson's discovery of America, 12:422a
Eiríksdrápa, 7:281a
Eiríksmál, **4:414b–415a**, 4:570a
in Eddic-skaldic transitional poetry, 4:389a
importance as historical source, 4:415a
preservation in manuscripts, 4:415a
on Valhalla, 12:350b
Eisagogē arithmetica. See Nicomachus of Gerasa
Eisteddfod, **4:415a-b**, 12:518b
Cardigan Castle, 4:415b, 12:608a
Carmarthen, 12:608a
conferences at Carmarthen and Caerwys, 4:415b
Eiximenis, Francesc, **4:416a–417a**, 12:349a
association with royal family, 4:416a
Catalan writings of, 3:157b
compared with Bernat Metge, 8:301a
Crestià, 4:416a-b
on fruits grown in Mediterranean region, 5:305b
guide to preaching, 11:456a
kingship theories of, 7:269b
Latin works, 4:416b
Libre dels angels, 4:416b
Libre de les dones, 4:416b
Regiment de la cosa pública, 4:416b
supported by Peter IV (the Ceremonious), 9:510b
Vida de Jesucrist, 4:416b
Eiximenis, Joan, *Contemplació de la Santa Quarentena,* 3:167b
Ēǰmiacin, **4:417a-b**
cathedral, 1:493b
founding of, 4:417a
naχekełecʿi and added structures, 4:417a-b
see of, 1:502a
Ekełeacʿ. *See* Anahit
Ekkehard I of St. Gall, **4:418a**
Vita Waltharii manufortis, 4:418a
Ekkehard II of St. Gall, hymns of, 6:381b
Ekkehard IV of St. Gall, **4:418a-b**, 12:225a-b
Cantica veteris et novi testamenti and, 9:189a
Casus sancti Galli, 4:418b, 12:225a-b
on Tuotilo, 12:225a-b
on flute, 8:604a
hymns of, 6:381b
Magyars and, 6:338b
Ekkehard of Aura, **4:417b–418a**
Frutolf of Michelsberg and, 5:307b
Ekphonetic notation. *See under* Musical notation
Ektene. See Litany, in the Greek Byzantine rite
Ekthesis, **4:418b–419a**, 8:233a
Monothelite doctrine, 8:478a-b, 480a
on nature of Christ, 6:191a
Sergios I and, 11:209a
see also Sergios I, patriarch of Constantinople
El-kengüz. *See* Shams al-Dīn Eldigüz
Elaphron, 8:617b
Elatikon, 11:603b
Elazar ben Natan, on women, 4:607b
Elbian Slavs, rebellion of, 5:475a
Elbing Vocabulary of 1300, 6:438a
Elbistan, Battle of (1277), 11:158a
Elbow-cop. *See* Cowter
Elckerlijc, 4:286b, 322a, **4:419a**, 8:484a
Everyman and, 4:527a-b
Eldad ha-Ḍani, legend of Ten Lost Tribes of Israel and, 8:23b
Eldefonsus of Spain, bishop. *See* Ildefonsus, St.
Eldigüzids. *See* Ildegizids
Eleanor of Aquitaine, **4:419a–420b**
besieged by Arthur of Brittany, 7:129b
marriage to Henry II of England, 2:126b, 4:419b, 463a, 5:161b
marriage to Louis VII of France, 5:161a
participation in Second Crusade, 4:419a-b
patronage of literature, 4:419b–420a, 12:215a
Richard I (the Lionhearted) and, 10:383a
seal of Louis VII of France and, 11:128b
wine trade and, 12:649b
see also Aquitaine; Bernart de Ventadorn
Eleanor of Castile, queen of England, tomb effigy of by William Torel, 12:86b (*illus.*)
Eleanor de Montfort, marriage to Llywelyn ap Gruffydd, 12:521b–522a
Eleanor of Provence, queen
marriage to Henry III, 6:158b
prevented from passing under London Bridge, 10:411b
Eleazar ben Judah of Worms, **4:420b–421a**
pietistic writings, 6:109b, 7:157a-b
individual eschatology, 6:110b–111a
prayer commentaries, 9:579a, 581b
Sefer ha-Roqeaḥ, 4:420b, 6:111a, 9:579a
Sode Razayya, 9:579a
Eleazar ben Kallir, "Kallirian" style and, 7:621b, 622a-b
Élection jurisdiction. *See* Taxation
Elections
senatorial, in Rome, 10:523b
see also Representative assemblies; Suffrage
Elections, church, **4:421a–425a**
auctoritas papae-administratio imperatoris, 10:546a
Concordat of Worms and, 12:697a
optimates militiae and, 10:522a
see also Abbot; Bishop, election of; Papacy, election of pope
Elections, Islamic, 6:501b
of imam, 6:425b
Elections, royal, **4:425a–429a**
among Franks, 4:425b–426a
blood right vs. hereditary succession, 4:425b–427b
in Carolingian Empire, 4:425b–426a
in England, by lay assembly, 4:476b
Fourth Council of Toledo and, 6:563b
in Germany
Sachsenspiegel on, 10:603b
1254-1493, 5:488b–490a
in Holy Roman Empire
Bavarian dukes and, 2:134a, 135a-b
Conrad II, 4:426b–427a

double elections, 4:425a, 427b, 428a, 428b
first, 4:425a-b
Frederick Barbarossa and, 4:427b
Golden Bull (1356), 4:428b
Henry of Saxony, 4:426a-b
kur, 4:427a, 428a
princes' electoral rights, 4:427b, 428a-b
Jordan of Osnabrück and, 7:149a
papal rights, 4:427b–428a, 428b
principle of suitability, 4:427a, 427b
Sweden, 11:529b
translation of empire and, 12:143a-b
Electoral College, 5:487a-b, 492a-b
Adolf of Nassau deposed by, 5:492a
conflict between empire and papacy and, 5:491a-b
consequences for German politics, 10:329a–331b
economic collaboration, 5:493a
"electoral union" of, 5:488b
establishment of, 5:492a-b
factional elections of 13th century, 5:492a
function of, 5:492b
Habsburg dynasty and, 5:487b
identity of, 5:491b
imperial reform movement and, 5:493a
members of, 5:487a-b
political power of, 5:492b–493a
rights of Rhenish archbishops, 5:491b–492a
rights to principalities (*Kurland*), 5:492b, 493a, 499a-b
Rudolf of Habsburg's election, 5:492a
Sachsenspiegel on, 5:491b
secular, 5:492b
Electrum trachy, 8:421a
Elegia di Madonna Fiammetta. See Boccaccio, Giovanni; Flores, Juan de
Elegies. See Maximian (6th century)
Elementa super demonstrationem ponderum. See Jordanus de Nemore
Elementarium doctrinae rudimentum. See Papias
Elementorum philosophiae libri IV. See William of Conches
Elements. See Euclid
Elements, Book on the. See Israeli, Isaac
Elements of Theology. See Proclus (410-485)
Elena y María, 11:413b, 454a
Elende Knabe, Der, 8:412a
Elene, 1:279a
name of Cynewulf at the end of, 1:278a
rhyme in, 1:277a
Eleonore of Austria, **4:429a-b**
Pontus und Sidonia, 4:429a-b
Eleousa, **4:429b–430a** (*illus.*), 5:568b
see also Iconography, *umilenie; Vladimir Virgin*
Elephant, in bestiaries, 2:205b (*illus.*), 243a
Elephant, Philip, *Philosophia,* on alchemy, 1:138a
Eleusis, cult of, 9:1a, 1b
Eleutherius, St., martyrdom of, miniature in Basil II's Menologion, 8:274 (*illus.*)
Elevation of the Holy Cross, **4:430a-b,** 4:430b (*illus.*)
Elevations of the saints. *See* Translation of saints
Elfheah, archbishop. *See* Alphege, St.
Elfoddw, bishop of Bangor, 2:71a-b
Elias III, patriarch, 11:567b
Elias bar Shināyā of Nisibis, 11:565b, 566a
Conferences, 9:107b
Elias, Brother
construction of basilica at Assisi, 5:198a
excommunication of, 5:199a-b
lay status, 5:198b
leadership of Franciscans
administration, 5:198b
autocratic tendencies, 5:198b–199a
support of theological studies, 5:198b
Elias of Dereham. *See* Nicholas of Ely
Elias (OT prophet), in *Muspilli,* 8:650a
Elias Salomo, 11:365b
Elidir Sais, **4:430b–431b**
poems for noblemen, 4:431a
Éliduc. See Marie de France
Elie de St. Gille. See Elis saga ok Rosamundu
Eliezer of Beaugency, 4:541a
biblical exegesis, 2:212b
Eliezer ben Yose ha-Gelili, 4:539a
Eligius (goldsmith; *d.* 660), 8:288a, 288b, 292a
Elijah ben Moses Bashyazi, 7:210b
Elijah ben Moses Delmedigo, 9:700a-b
Elijah Ḥayyim ben Benjamin, *Disputation,* 10:6b
Elijah (OT prophet)
in art, 6:411a
Carmelites and, 3:96a, 96b
in circumcision rite, 3:401b
Elijah de Pomis, 7:109a
attacked by Paulinus of Aquileia, 9:470a
theory of Trinity, 1:57b
Elis saga ok Rosamundu, **4:431b–432b,** 10:390a, 392a
Icelandic continuation of, 10:392a-b
Norwegian version, 4:431b–432a, 10:390a
preservation in pre-Reformation manuscripts, 4:432a
Rémundar saga keisarasonar and, 10:304b
stylistic characteristics, 4:432a-b
translations of, 4:431b, 12:203b
Elisabeth of Nassau-Saarbrücken, **4:432b–433a**
Eleonore of Austria and, 4:429a
Huge Scheppel, 4:432b–433a
literary connections, 4:432b
Loher und Maller, 4:432b
Sibille, 4:432b
translation of *Lion de Bourges,* 4:432b
Ełišē, 1:476b, 518b, **4:433a–434a**
commemorated as saint, 1:520a, 520b
history of Hephthalites, 6:170a
History of Vardan and the Armenian War, 1:509a, 4:433a-b, 12:360b
sources for, 6:239a
wuzurg framadār and, 12:705b
use of letters and speeches, 4:433b
see also Łazar Pʿarpecʿi
Elisha (OT prophet), curing by, 11:301a
Elizabeth I of England, queen, standard measurements and, 5:346a
Elizabeth (Eliška) (daughter of Wenceslaus II of Bohemia), 10:88b
Elizabeth of Hungary, St., 6:342a
perfume and, 2:147a
Thuringian history, *Wartburgkrieg,* 12:573b
Elizabeth of Hungary (sister of Casimir III), queen, rule of Poland, 9:725b
Elizabeth of Hungary (widow of Albert of Habsburg), queen, vs. Władisław III of Poland, 6:347b
Elizabeth of Schönau, 9:8a, 10b, 31b
Visiones de resurrectione Beatae Mariae Virginis, 9:10b
works in English, 9:27a
Elizabeth of Spalbeek, 9:11b
vita in English, 9:27a
Elizabeth of Vohburg, margravine of Heitstein, in *Parzival,* 12:676a
Elizabeth of York (wife of King Henry VII of England), tomb of by Pietro Torrigiano, 12:88b
Elizavetpol. *See* Arrān
Ell (unit of measure), 12:585a, 588b
Ella of Northumbria, king, killing of, 12:7a
Ellac (son of Attila), 6:354a
Elmham, Thomas, 7:370a
Elmuahym, 8:563b
Elmuarifa, 8:563b
Elne Cathedral, 10:481b
Eloi d'Amerval, *Livre de la deablerie,* 9:639a
Elucidarium, **4:434a–435b,** 12:614b
attributed to Honorius Augustodunensis, 12:20b
expansion of subject matter, 4:434b
as illustration of period, 4:434b–435a
purpose of, 4:434a
Scandinavian translations of, 11:18a
translations, 4:434b
see also Seifried Helbling
Élus, tax collection, 11:624b
Elvira, under Zirids, 12:745a
Elvira, Synod of (300), 6:400a
images prohibited in churches, 4:349a
on Jewish-Christian relations, 11:161b
Visigothic sculpture and, 12:467a
Ely, abbot's legal dispute, 7:436a
Ely Cathedral
arches of, 1:423b
Lady Chapel, 3:264a
Wysbeck and, 12:712b
Elyot, Sir Thomas, *Boke Named the Governour,* 8:436a
Émail brun, **4:435b** (*illus.*)
Émail-en-ronde-bosse enamel, 5:380b–381a
Emain Ablach, 6:552a

Emain Macha, 6:548a
Patrick and, 9:464b
see also Ulster
Emanation theory
Averroës and, 1:459b
Avicenna and, 1:458b, 459b
al-Fārābī and, 1:458b
Grosseteste and, 1:461b
Ibn Gabirol and, 1:459b–460a
Isaac Israeli and, 1:459b
Levi ben Gershom and, 1:460a
Platonism and, 9:699b–700a
Plotinus and, 1:457b
Proclus and, 1:457b
Emancipation, inheritance and, 6:450a, 458a, 458b
Emanuel I of Portugal, king. *See* Manuel I of Portugal, king
Emaré, 7:317a
Embalming. *See* Corpse
Ember days, **4:435b–436b**
expansion throughout Europe, 4:436a
purpose, 4:436a
source of custom, 4:435b–436a
Embossing, of armor, 1:536a
Embriachi family, 7:24a
Embricho of Mainz, **4:436b**
on Muḥammad, 7:363b
Vita Muhameti, 4:436
Embroidery
commercial trade of, 1:561a
see also Tapestry; Textiles
Embuchi, 8:561b
Emerich of Hungary, king. *See* Imre of Hungary, king
Emesa. *See* Ḥims
Emeterius of Tábara, **4:436b–437a,** 10:114a-b
Beatus commentaries, 4:436b
manuscript illumination, 11:657b (*illus.*), 657a
Emilia in Her Garden, 5:359 (*illus.*), 364b
Emir, **4:437a**
function under Abbasids, 4:437a
Sicilian, 11:268a
Emmanuel, **4:437a-b**
Emmer, 5:645b
Emmeram of Poitiers, Arbeo and, 1:422b
Emmeram, St., life of by Manfred of Magdeburg, 8:83b
Emmeran-Munich Codex, Hrotswitha von Gandersheim and, 6:314a
Empire, Governing Council of the (*Reichsregiment*). *See* Representative assemblies, Holy Roman Empire
Empiricism, Ockham and, 9:212a
En Amanieu de Sescas
Ensenhamen, 3:665b
Ensenhamen de la donzela, 3:663b–664a
En echelon plan. *See* Apse echelon
"En rima greuf a far, dir e stravolger." *See* Auliver
Enactments of Shum. *See* Jewish law
Enamel, **4:437b–439b**
basse-taille, 4:440a (*illus.*), **4:441a,** 5:380a
origin, 4:439a
technique for making, 4:438a
Byzantine, 2:453b
gold ground, 2:455a
production methods, 2:455a-b
Celtic, 8:370a
in Celtic art, 3:218b
champlevé, 4:440a (*illus.*), **4:441a**
opus lemovicense, 4:438b
technique for making, 4:438a
cloisonné, 4:440b (*illus.*), **4:441a-b,** 5:377b
connections between Byzantine and Western, 4:437b
laqabi ware and, 7:342b
reliquaries, 4:438a
on triptych in Xaχuli, 5:410b
development of enameling techniques, 8:295a-b
émail-en-ronde-bosse, 5:380b–381a
encrusted, 4:438a, 439a
in glassmaking
Islamic, 5:547a–548a
stained, 5:550b
Western European, 5:556b
Godefroid of Huy, 5:569b–570a, 10:500b (*illus.*)
gold, 4:439a
Italian, 16th century, 4:439b
Limoges, 4:440b (*illus.*), **4:441b**
15th century renaissance, 4:439a-b
history, 4:438b
millefiori, 3:219b, **4:441b,** 4:441b (*illus.*)
Mosan, 4:438b–439a
Netherlandish, 4:439a
painted, 4:438a
plite, 4:438a-b
relationship between Byzantine and Western work, 4:437b
reliquaries, 4:438a, 10:302b–303a (*illus.*)
repoussé, reliquary, 10:302a (*illus.*)
vermiculé, **4:441b–442a,** 4:442a (*illus.*)
Visigothic tradition in, 1:631a
see also Theophilus
Enamels, of *Codex Aureus,* 10:105a
Enantiophanes, *Nomocanon in Fourteen Titles,* 9:158b
Enarrationes in Evangelium Matthaei. See Pseudo-Anselm of Laon
Encaustic, **4:442a**
Enchiridion. See Nichomachus (Greek music theorist)
Enchiridion sive stella orientalis occidentali splendens. See Milescu, Nicolae
Encina, Juan del, 11:425a
Arte de poesía castellana, 11:424b, 441b, 459b
Enclosure, rights of pasture and, 9:455b–456a
Encolpium (Encolpion), **4:442a-b**
Encyclopedia of the Pure Brethren, 12:228a-b
Encyclopedias and dictionaries, Arabic and Persian, **4:442b–446a**
amthāl (parable) books, 4:442b
dictionaries
arranged by roots, 4:444a
biographical, of Ibn Khallikān, 7:236a
earliest Persian, 4:444b
Koranic commentaries, 4:442b
phonetically arranged, 4:443b–444a
secular, 4:442b
thematic, 4:443a, 443b
dictionaries, biographical
arrangement of, 2:237b
length of biographical notices, 2:238a
origins of, 2:237b
encyclopedias
Aristotelian influence, 4:445a
classification of sciences, 4:445a-b
collective works, 4:445a
of Ikhwān al-Ṣafā'1, 9:4b
influence of Islamic religion on content, 4:445b–446a
Persian language, 4:445b
professional guides, 4:444b–445a
see also Nadīm, Ibn al-
Encyclopedias and dictionaries, Byzantine, **4:446b–447a**
of Constantine VII, 3:547b, 4:446b–447a
lists of offices, 4:447a
military handbooks, 4:447a
Suda, 11:501a–502a
zoological excerpts, 4:447b
see also Pseudo-Kodinos
Encyclopedias and dictionaries, Hebrew, arranged by roots, 6:128a
See also Hebrew language, study of
Encyclopedias and dictionaries, Western European, **4:447b–450b**
alphabetization and, 1:204b–207a
ancient Roman, 4:447b
botanical information, 2:345b
dictionary of the Royal Spanish Academy, 11:391a
early works on rhetoric and, 10:353b–354b
etymology, 4:447b–448a, 449b–450a
glossaries, 4:449b
Hrabanus Maurus and, 6:307a
of Huguccio, 6:327b
Latin, 7:351b–351a, 365b, 368a, 370b
Latin-English, 7:352a
library development and, 7:564a
Libros del saber de astronomía, 12:135b–136a
of music, 8:638a, 645a, 648b
as preachers' aids, 10:363a
in Spain, 11:441b
spread of literacy and, 7:599a, 600b–601a
Stephen Langton's Hebrew-Latin vocabulary of biblical terms, 2:213b
to 1100, 4:447b–448a, 449b
translation aids, 12:136b–137a
translation of Bartholomaeus Anglicus' *De proprietatibus rerum,* 12:187a
vocabularies, 4:450a
see also Thomas of Cantimpré
Ende, **4:450b** (*illus.*)
Endelechius, **4:451a**
Endowments
Byzantine, 6:452a

Islamic. *See* Waqf
Eneados. See Douglas, Gavin
Enéas, Roman, d', **4:451a**, 8:225b
Eneide. See Hartmann von Aue; Heinrich von Veldeke
Enfances Ogier, Les. See Adenet le Roi
Enfant de neige, L', 4:574b–575a
Enfants de Maintenant, Les, 4:265a
Engagement, nuptial, 4:606a
Engelar, Master, 7:24a
Engelberg, abbey of, 11:540b, 542a
Engelbert of Admont, **4:451b–452a**
  De musica, 8:645a, 11:364b
  De ortu . . . et fine romani imperii, 4:451b
  kingship theories of, 7:268a
  political theory, 4:451b–452a
  unity of the Christian people, 4:452a
Engelbert of Cologne, 5:484a, 12:539a
Engelbrekt Engelbrektsson, 7:220a, 11:533a
Engelbrektskrönikan, 11:22a
Engelhard. See Konrad von Würzburg
Engelmodus, **4:452a-b**
Engineering
  Islamic world
    civil, 11:638a
    status of, 11:636a, 638a
  Western European
    artist-engineer, 11:647b
    status of, 11:645a
  see also Construction—engineering
Engineering, Western European, structural, 11:655b–656b
England
  Anglo-Saxon migrations to, 2:96b–97a
  astronomy in, 1:613a-b
  banking in, 2:74a
  Black Death in (1348-1350), 2:261b–262b
  boundaries and territories
    Norman-Angevin, 4:59b, 460 (map)
    1216-1485, 4:474 (map)
  Christianization of, 4:453a–454b, 458a–459a, 8:439b (map), 441a
  communes, 3:498a–499a
  coronations in, 7:257b–258a
  education, ninth century, 1:165a
  financial history, in pipe rolls, 9:662a–663b
  history (Anglo-Saxon), **4:452b–459b**
    Anglo-Saxon heptarchy, 9:227a-b
    economic development, 4:457b–458a
    invading tribes, 9:226b
    political divisions, 4:452b–454b (map)
    West Saxon domination, 4:455a–457a
  history (Norman-Angevin), **4:459b–472b**, 9:165a–168a
    cultural changes, 4:466b, 471b–472a
    internal strife, 12:636a
    mercenary troops, 12:560b–561a
    see also Angevins
  history (1216–1485), **4:472b–486b**
    Barons' war (1263-1266), 2:111b–112b
    kingship and succession rights, 4:472b–479b
  Jews in, 7:71a-b, 86a, 87a
    communal self-government and, 7:90b
  languages of, 6:436a, 437a, 437b, 439b, 440b–441a
  military obligation of freemen, 11:612a
  monarchy, income, 12:569b
  monetary system in, 8:429a, 430b–431a
    beginning of standardized coinages, 9:495a
    groat, 5:680a
    penny, 5:680a
  navy
    in Norman-Angevin period, 9:81b
    office of admiral, 9:81a-b
  nobility. *See* Nobility and nobles, in England
  Norman conquest of
    in literature, 5:244a, 9:260b–261a
    papal attitudes, 9:165b
  as papal fief, 6:464b
  paper introduced into, 9:390a
  plagues in, 9:676b, 678a–680b, 681b–682a
  population, 4:141a-b
  relations with
    Aquitaine, 6:331b, 332b, 333a
    Brittany, 6:332a
    Burgundy, 6:332a
    France, 7:364b, *see also* Hundred Years War
    Hungary, 6:339b
    Ireland, 6:517a–520b, 537b, 554a-b
    Netherlands, 6:332a
    Normandy, 6:331b, 332b, 9:165a–168a, 166a, 166b–168a
    Scotland, 8:56b
  Roman, 1:288a
  royal control of forest, 5:133a
  taxation, 11:612a–613a
    Lancastrian policies, 11:616a
  tenure of land. *See* English common law; Tenure of land, Western European
  town planning, 12:322b–323b (*illus.*), 324b–325a
  trade and commerce, Merchant Adventurers, 6:95a
English architecture
  church, transept, 12:125b
  Early English style, 4:472a
  Gothic
    Decorated Style, 5:626b
    Norwich Cathedral, 10:256b
    Old St. Paul's Cathedral, 10:256b–257b (*illus.*)
    Perpendicular Style, 5:630b–631a, 10:256b–257b (*illus.*)
English art
  glassmaking, 5:555a-b, 558b–559a
  Gothic
    International Style, 5:628a
    painting, 5:609b–610a
    sculpture, 5:625a–626a
  ivory carving, Romanesque cross, 10:0 (frontispiece)
  see also Hiberno-Saxon art
English common law
  ad omnia placita (general eyres for all pleas), 7:442b
  Anglo-Norman, 4:464a-b
  on betrothal, 2:208a
  cestui que use, 7:454a-b
  church property, 8:488b
    inalienability of, 8:489a
  clergy, 7:437a
    benefit of clergy expanded, 7:450b–451a
  compurgation in, 3:508b–509a
  contempt for law and, 7:455a-b
  copyhold, 3:596b–597a
  coram rege pleas, 7:443a
  coroner in, 3:605a–606b
  court leet, 3:659b–660b
  courts, 4:470a-b, 7:445b–448a
    of appeal, 7:446a
    borough, 4:465a, 7:434b
    county (Anglo-Saxon), 7:434a-b
    decline of local courts, 7:447a–448a
    domanial court (Anglo-Saxon), 7:433b–434a
    hundred court, 7:434a
    manorial, 4:138b, 7:433b–434a
    parliamentary, 4:481b–483a
    shire court, 7:434a-b
    system (before 1272), 7:433a
  criminal law, 6:282a, 7:441b–443a
    civil procedure and, 7:44b
  customs and services litigation reform, 7:451a-b
  in Danelaw, 4:91a
  development (to 1272), **7:433a–445b**
    after Henry II, 7:443b–445a
    Anglo-Saxon system, 4:464a, 7:433b–435b
    baronial rebellion and, 7:444b
    before Henry II, 7:436b
    belief in antiquity of, 7:455b–456a
    customary, 4:480a-b
    Ine's laws (*ca.* 694), 11:616a
    introduction of feudalism and, 7:433a-b
    legal texts in Old English, 1:286a-b
    Roman influence, 4:464a
    under Henry II, 3:409a-b, 4:470a-b, 6:157a, 7:436b–443a
    under John, 4:470b
    under Stephen, 7:436b
  development (after 1272), **7:445b–457a**
    adaptability versus continuity, 7:456a-b
    law report collections, 7:450a
    reform and adaptation, 7:450a–455a
    rules of law, 7:448b–450a
    spread of literacy and, 7:450b–451a
    statutes, 4:482b–483a
    weaknesses and strengths, 7:455a–456b
  distress, 4:220b–221a
  due process, 7:455b
    Magna Carta and, 7:444a-b
  equity and, 4:502a, 502a–503a, 503a-b
  eyre system, 7:442a-b

English common law (*cont.*)
eyre system (*cont.*)
decline of, 7:446b
felony penalties reformed, 7:450b–451a
forest law and, overlapping of, 5:127b, 128b
forms of action, 7:451a-b
Glanville's text, 5:544a–545a
growth of professional literature, 7:450a
Henry III's role, 7:443b, 444b–445a
homicide, 12:618a
ideal of government by, 7:456a
influence on Scots law, 7:517a-b
inquest, 6:482b–483a
Anglo-Norman, 7:435b–436b
popular, 7:436a
sworn, origins of, 7:435b–436a
as used by William I, 7:436a-b
jury trial, 4:470b, 6:157a
justice commissions, 7:445b–446a, 446b–447a
justices, under Henry II, 7:443a
king's role in
king's council, 4:502a-b, 503a
kingship theories and, 7:264b–265b
pleas of the crown, 7:441b–442a
royal rights eroded before Henry II, 7:436b–437a
land tenure, 12:622b
law of gage, 2:81a
lawyers, 7:448a-b
London, 7:664b–665a, 665a
regulations, 7:448a
role defined, 7:448a
Magna Carta and, 7:444a-b
nisi prius commission, 7:446b
outlawry in, 9:311a–312b
oyer and terminer, settlement of piracy claims, 1:56b–57a
plaint (querela) or procedure without writ, 7:444a
plea rolls, 2:357a
postmedieval collections of, 1:287a
procedure, 7:449a-b, 505a–506a
reforms in, 7:451a–452a
property, 7:449a
alms, 9:546b
copyholds and villein tenures, 11:682b
land dispute rules elaborated, 7:449a
lay fee, 9:546b
tenement, 9:546b
protection of foreign merchants, 12:120b
public health ordinances, 9:679b
recorder, 7:662b
replevin
expansion of, 7:451b
king's courts and, 7:447a-b
Roman influence, 4:464a, 466b
royal courts, 4:470a, 480b–481a, 7:446a
jurisdiction expanded, 7:447a
under Henry II, 7:441b, 442b–443a
separation of church and lay courts, 4:464b, 7:434a
serjeants, 7:448a-b, 662b
special pleading elaborated, 7:449b
"starr" type of contract, 2:81a, 81b
statute collections, 7:450a
testimony, 7:436a
torture not used, 12:90a
trespass, 7:447b–448a, 452a, 12:185a–186a
trial by combat eliminated, 7:440b
writs
"common form," 7:438a, 439a
during Anglo-Saxon period, 7:434b–435a
during Henry I's reign, 7:435b
during Henry II's reign, 7:434b, 440a–441a
during William I's reign, 7:435a-b
of entry, 7:443b–444a
of gage, 7:443b
in grand assize, 7:441a
of outlawry, 9:311b
praecipe, 7:440a–441a, 444a
returnable writs, 7:438a, 441a, 444a
of right, 7:440a–441b
royal, 7:433a
to reseise, 7:437a-b
see also Assize, English; Attainder; Bailiff; Common pleas, court of; Englishry, presentment of; Exchequer, court of; Felony; *Fleta;* Impeachment; Inns of Court; Inquest, English; Liberty and liberties; Ordinance; Parliament, English; Petty assizes, English; Prerogative; Seisin, disseisin; Statute; Tenure of land
English drama, 4:284b–285b
allegorical plays, 4:287a
Castle of Perseverance, 3:142b–143a
Chester Plays, 3:298a–299b
Corpus Christi plays
content of, 4:284b
form of, 4:285a
performances of, 4:284b–285a
interludes, 4:279b, 287a
masque, origins of, 4:279b
as means of religious instruction, 4:286a–287a
mummings, 7:692a-b
mystery plays, 8:324b–325a
public theaters, 4:288a
see also Actors; Morality plays; Mystery plays
English government
concept of corporation and, 3:606b
constable of the realm, 3:543b
growth of parliament, 4:479b–486a
King in Council, 4:502b
kings' travels and, 12:159a–160a
local constables, 3:542b–543b
local government, Anglo-Saxon, 4:457b–458a
municipal, *burh,* 2:330a
Norman-Angevin period
entourage and council, 4:463b–464a
financial administration, 4:464a
French feudal aristocracy, 4:463b
great and small councils, 4:469b, 470a, 470b
taxation, 4:469b
office of seneschal and, 11:160b
record-keeping, 12:534b
role of bailiffs, 2:52a
see also County; Mayor; Sheriff; Shire
English language
Old English, 1:281a, 284a, **9:226a–231a**
alliterative verse in, 8:327a–328b
Bible translations, 2:221a-b
borrowed words, 9:230a-b
characters, 9:228a
compared with Middle English, 8:310b–311b
definite articles, 9:229a
dialects of, 1:276a-b, 8:312a, 9:227a–228a
dialects of, variation in, 9:226b
differences from modern English, 8:310a
exegesis and, 4:550a-b
French influence, 9:228a
Germanic origins, 9:226a-b
grammar, 5:650a, 9:228b–230a
homily on the phoenix, 8:310b
inflection, 8:310a, 9:228b–230b
influenced by *dönsk tunga,* 12:434a
Kentish dialect, 6:439b
magical recipes and charms in, 8:34b
Mercian dialect, 6:439b
Northumbrian dialect, 6:439b, 8:312a
periods of development, 9:226a-b
phonological characteristics, 9:227a
political influence on, 9:227a-b
postmedieval dictionaries of, 1:287a
pronunciation, 9:228a-b
runes in, 1:275a, 10:562b
Tatian manuscripts and, 11:601a-b
texts, 9:227a
Viking influence, 9:227b
vocabulary, 9:230a-b
West Saxon dialect, 6:437a, 439b, 8:312a, 312b
Winchester and, 4:518a-b
word order in, 8:310a, 9:229a
Middle English, **8:309b–313b**
compared with Old English, 8:310b–311b
dialects of, 8:311b–312a, 312b–313a
diphthongs in, 8:311a
evidence of Paston letters, 9:451a–452a
first stages of, 8:310b
grammar, clausula, 3:437a-b
great vowel shift, 8:309b, 324a
influence of Danish Vikings, 12:433b–434a
John Trevisa's translations into, 12:187a
London English, 8:310a, 313a
merging of declined forms in, 8:311b
Midlands dialect, 8:312b, 313a
Northern dialect, 8:312b
phonetic spelling of in *Ormulum,* 8:315a
Received Standard English and, 9:280b
time boundaries of, 8:309b
Wynkyn de Worde and, 12:712a

loanwords in, 6:445a-b
Old English
Mercian dialect, 8:312a
rhyme in, 1:277a
English language, Old English
Kentish dialect, 8:312a, 312b
in *Azenbite of Inwyt,* 8:317a
English literature. *See* Middle English literature; Old English literature
English music
Caedmonic songs, 3:7b–8a
carols, 3:116a-b
discant, 12:180a-b
liturgical, Trent codices, 12:183a–184a
see also Old Hall MS
English Psalter. See Rolle, Richard
English Tower pennyweight, 9:495b
English wheat, 5:646a
Englishry, presentment of, **4:487a-b**
murder and, 4:487a
rules governing, 4:487a
Englyn unodyl union, 12:605b
Englyn/englynion, 3:121b
in Old Welsh, 12:603a
of Llywarch Hen, 12:598a, 603a-b
style and diction, 12:605b
Englynion y Beddau, 12:598a
Engraving, **4:487b–490b**
burin, 2:432a (*illus.*)
earliest engravers, 4:487a-b
first surviving, 4:488b
goldsmiths and, 4:488a
innovations in technique, 4:488b–489a
origins, 4:487a
other artistic media and, 4:489a–490a
painters and, 4:490a
playing cards, 9:706b–707b (*illus.*)
use as models, 4:489a-b
woodcut and, 12:690a, 692b
see also Block book; *Bois Protat;* Burin; Master E.S.; Metallurgy; Niello
Enguerrand VI of Coucy, 4:490b
Enguerrand VII of Coucy, **4:490b–491a**
Enguerrand of Coucy, *Livre du lignage de Coucy,* 9:638a
Ennaton (monastery: Alexandria), 11:565a
Ennodius, Magnus Felix, **4:491b**, 7:361b
Arator and, 1:422a
hymns of, 6:379b, 381a
Enns River, *see also* Austria
Enoria, 11:603a
Enquête par turbe, 6:479b–480a
Enquêteurs, See Capetians, *enquêteurs*
Enquêteurs-reformateurs, 6:480a-b
Enquiry into Plants. See Theophrastus
Enravota of Bulgaria, 2:402a
Enrique. *See* Henry
Enrique de Aragón. *See* Villena, Enrique de
Ensaladas, ballad texts and, 11:430a
Ensamples. See Filippo degli Agazzari
Enseignemens, Les. See Louis IX of France, king
Enseignemens à son fiz Jean de Castel. See Christine de Pizan
Enseignement des princes. See Robert of Blois
Ensenhamen. See Arnaut Guilhem de Marsan; Arnaut de Mareuil; En Amanieu de Sescas; Garin lo Brun
Ensenhamen de la donzela. See En Amanieu de Sescas
Entail, 6:459b, 460a, 460b, 7:452a–453b
Enteric diseases. *See* Plagues, enteric
Entheticus. See John of Salisbury
Entry into Jerusalem, **4:491b–492a,** 4:492a (*illus.*)
in Passion cycle, 9:447a
Envoi, **4:492a-b**
Envoi, used by Chaucer, 8:335a, 346a
Envoi, *see also* Tornada
ᶜEnyānā, 8:578a
Enzo (son of Emperor Frederick II), *scuola siciliana* and, 11:259a
Eógan Már, 4:492b
Eóganacht, **4:492b–493a**
branches of, 4:492b–493a, 8:531a
in Irish saga, 6:547b
rule over Munster, 4:492b–493a, 8:531a
tribal groupings under, 6:553a
vs. Dál Cais, 4:77b
Epanagoge, 2:117b, **4:493a-b**, 7:391a
description of ecumenical patriarch in, 4:383a-b
Eparch, **4:493b**
of Constantinople, responsibilities, 2:473a-b
of Nobadia, 9:198a
Eparch, Book of the, 3:554b, 7:391a-b, **4:493b–494b**
guild initiation ceremonies, 6:20b
on internal Byzantine trade, 12:101b–102a
structure of Byzantine guilds, 6:15a, 20a
weights and measures, 12:580b
see also Byzantine law; Leo VI (the Wise), Byzantine emperor
Épée. See Sword
Epektasis, 5:667a
Epereiai, 11:604a
Épernay, fairs, 4:591a
Ephemeris belli Troiani. See Dictys Cretensis
Ephesus, **4:494b–495a,** 12:305a-b
as Byzantine trade center, 12:100b, 101a
cathedral of, 1:240a
Christianization of, 12:305b
contested council of (401), 7:122b
continuity and transformation in, 12:305a-b
plan of, 12:305a
see also Urbanism, Byzantine
Ephesus, Councils of
First (431), 3:594a, 628b–629a
Church of the East and, 11:563a
condemnation of Nestorius, 2:459b, 6:190a, 9:105a, 105b, 106a, 108b
Divine Word, Antiochene formula, 9:561a
Eznik and, 4:571a
heresy and, 3:594a
on humanity of Christ, 3:320a
Monophysitism and, 8:477a
Theotokos and, 12:26a, 460a
Second (449), 3:629b, 4:524a, 9:106a
Armenian church and, 1:498b
deposition of Nestorius, 3:594a
Leo I and, 7:542a
reinstatement of Eutyches, 9:561a
"Robber Synod," 3:629b
Ephesus, Seven Sleepers of. *See* Seven Sleepers of Ephesus
Ephraem the Syrian, St., 1:508a, 6:213a, 7:612b–613a, 9:142a, 11:565b, 566a
against Manichaeism, 8:84a
as doctor of the church, 4:234a
East Syrian rite and, 11:567b
madrāshā and, 8:578a
translators of, 12:126b
Ephraim
verse chronicle, 2:517a
see also Ephraem; Ephrem
Ephraim of Bonn, 7:78b
chronicle of Second Crusade, 6:257a
Ephrem (artist), 4:24b, **4:495a-b**
Ephrem of Edessa, St. *See* Ephraem the Syrian, St.
Ephrem the Less. *See* Epᶜtemi Mcᶜire
Ephthalites, Ouar-Khounni and, 6:352b
Epibolé, **4:495b**, 11:603a
Byzantine, village communities, 2:476b–477a, 480a
Epic Histories. See Pᶜawstos Buzand
Epiclesis, in Alexandrian rite, 1:156a-b
Epics
chivalry in, 3:302b
French. *See Chansons de geste*
German
distinguished from romances, 5.444b
Theodoric the Great in, 8:353b
see also Dietrich von Bern
Latin, **4:495b–496b**
characteristics, 12:535b
from Germanic legend, 12:535b
Gesta Caroli metrica, 9:712a-b
Troy stories and, 12:219b–221b (*illus.*)
see also Berengarii imperatoris gesta
Picard, Lotharingian cycle, 9:634a
Russian folk, 9:653b
swords in, 11:546b
vs. chronicles, 3:325b
see also Arthurian legend
Epicurus, 7:164a
Epidemics, infectious. *See* Disease; Plagues
Epigraphy
Islamic, 3:52a, 52b, 53b, 55a
in ᶜAli Qāpū palace, 6:562b
Epilepsy, dementia and, 6:490a, 492a
Epiphanii Premudryi (the Wise), hagiographic works, 11:347b
Epiphanius of Pavia, Ennodius and, 4:491b
Epiphanius of Salamis, 1:507b
Epiphanius the Wise, 9:654a
Epiphany in art, **4:497b–498b**
Epiphany, feast of, **4:496b–497b**
baptism and, 4:497a-b
in Byzantine church, 4:497a, 7:612b
date for, 4:496b
liturgy for, 3:318a

Epiphany, feast of (*cont.*)
  origins, 4:496b
  Play of Herod, 9:706a-b
Epiphonus, 8:620 (*illus.*)
Epiros
  acquired by Stefan Uroš IV Dušan of Serbia, 11:178b, 475b
  Byzantine classical scholarship in, 11:50a
  Visigoths in, 12:469b, 470a
Epiros, despotate of, **4:499a–500a,** 4:499 (map)
  Battle of Pelagonia (1259) and, 9:487a
  origin after Fourth Crusade, 4:499a
  population, 4:595b–596a
  regime of Michael Angelos, 2:498a
  relations with
    Constantinople, 4:499b–500a, 7:347a
    Serbia, 11:174a, 174b, 175a, 473b
    Venice, 7:349a, 12:103b
  Turkish conquest of, 4:500a
Episcopellus, election of in Gerona, 11:437a
Episcopi
  concept of witches' sabbath and, 8:30a-b
  on devil's ways, 8:27a
Epistemology. *See* knowledge, theory of
Epistle Against Jovinian. See Jerome, St.
Epistola ad Berengarium magistrum. See Eusebius Bruno
Epistola ad fratres de Monte Dei. See William of St. Thierry
Epistola ad Hasen regem, 1:136b
Epistola Alexandri Macedonis ad Aristotelem, 1:149b–150a
Epistola de armonica institutione. See Regino of Prüm (Regino Prumiensis)
Epistola concilii pacis. See Henry of Langenstein
Epistola concordiae. See Conrad of Gelnhausen
Epistola consolatoria super morte filii. See Vincent of Beauvais
Epistola de ignotu cantu. See Guido of Arezzo
Epistola de magnete. See Peter Peregrinus of Maricourt
Epistola Michaeli monacho de ignoto cantu. See Guido of Arezzo
Epistola de nihilo et tenebris. See Fridugisus of Tours
Epistola pacis. See Henry of Langenstein
Epistola de permissionis bonorum et malorum causis. See Otloh of St. Emmeram
Epistola Petri Peregrini. . . . See Peter Peregrinus of Maricourt
Epistolae. See Virgil the Grammarian
Epistolarium. See Matthew of Vendôme; Pons of Provence
Epistre au Dieu d'Amours. See Christine de Pizan
Epistre d'Othéa. See Christine de Pizan
Epistula ad Leudefredum, clerical orders, 9:265a
Epistula ad Rufinum de gratia et libero arbitrio. See Prosper of Aquitaine
Epistula ad Vigilium. See Arator
"Epitaph of Seikilos," 8:636b
Epitaphios. *See* Death and burial; *Plashchanitsa*
Epithalamioi, in Byzantine rhetoric, 10:350a
Epithalamium beatae Mariae Virginis. See John of Garland
Epitoma Chronicon. See Prosper of Aquitaine
Epitomae. See Virgil the Grammarian
Epitome Dindimi in philosophiam. See Hugh of St. Victor
Epitome hispanica, 7:401a
Epitome historiarum. See Zonaras, John
Epitome kanonon. See Harmenopoulos, Constantine
Epitrakhil, **4:500a**
Épître d'Othea à Hector. See Christine de Pizan
Épître du roi à Hector de Troie. See Jean Lemaire de Belges
Épîtres de l'amant vert. See Jean Lemaire de Belges
Epona (Celtic goddess), 9:48b, 49a (*illus.*)
Ep^{c}temi Mc^{c}ire, 5:417a
  on Symeon Metaphrastes, 11:554a
Equatorie of the Planetis. See Chaucer, Geoffrey
Equatorium, **4:500b,** 4:500b (*illus.*), 11:98a-b
  of Campus of Novara, 10:210b
  described by Isaac al-Ḥadīb, 11:91a-b
  Islamic, 11:86b
  see also Astronomy, Ptolemaic
Equestrian games, 5:347b–348a
Equilateral arch. *See under* Arch
Équitan. See Marie de France
Equity, **4:501a–504a**
  Aquinas' view, 4:501a-b
  in England
    Chancery and, 4:502a-b
    distinguishing characteristics of, 4:502b
    Exchequer and, 4:534b–535a
    king's particular responsibility for, 4:501b
    remedies in, 4:502b–503a
    subjects of concern, 4:503b
  growth of humanism and, 4:502a
  legal definition of, 4:501a
  Martinus Gosia vs. Bulgarus on, 8:158a-b
  Rogerius and, 10:444a
Era
  in Armenian calendar, 3:30b–31a
  in Christian calendar, 3:18a–19a
  in Islamic calendar, 3:27a-b
  in Jewish calendar, 3:24b–25a
Eracle. See Gautier d'Arras
Eraclius, *De coloribus et artibus Romanorum,* 8:90b
Eraclius. See Ott
Eranspahbad. See Sparapet
Erasistratos of Chios (physician; *b. ca.* 290 B.C.), 8:244a
Erasmus, Desiderius, 9:682b
  on Brethren of the Common Life, 2:369a
  classical literary studies and, 3:436a
  Colloquies, pilgrimage satire, 10:299a
  Devotio Moderna and, 4:167a
  Institutio principis christiani, 8:436a
  Latin language and, 7:357a, 370b
  letter writing and, 10:363b
  Vulgate and, 12:496a
  Wynkyn de Worde and, 12:712a
Erašx. *See* Araks River
Erasxajor (in Ayrarat), 2:20a
Erblandesvereinigung. See Tenure of land, in Germany
Erchambert of Freising, **4:504a**
Erchanger, count palatinate
  defeat of Magyars, 5:508a
  execution of, 11:527a
Erchenbert of Monte Cassino, **4:504a-b**
Erçiş. *See* Arčēš
Érec et Énide. See Chrétien de Troyes
Erek. See Hartmann von Aue
Erembald family, rise of, 9:148b–149a
Eremiticae regulae. See Rudolph, Camaldolese prior (1074–1089)
Eremitism. *See* Hermits
Ereroyk^{c}, **4:504b**
Erex saga, **4:504b–505a,** 10:390a, 390b, 391a, 11:491b
  Chrétien de Troyes' *Érec* and, 4:504b–505a
  derivatives of, 8:507b
  Icelandic adaptations in, 4:505a
  revision of the original translation, 10:392a
  see also Ívens saga
Erfurt
  Maria Gloriosa bell, 2:166b
  siege of (1203), Wolfram von Eschenbach and, 12:676a
Erfurt Cathedral, stucco retable in, 10:342a
Erfurt, University of, 12:288a
  via moderna and, 12:408b
Erfurter Moralität, 4:269a
Erghom, John, 7:370a
Ergotism, 5:5b
  see also Famine, in Western Europe; Plagues, European, ergotism
Eric I of Denmark, king, 4:152b, 153a, 7:280a
  poem about, 7:281a
Eric II of Denmark, king, 4:153a, 7:280b
Eric IV of Denmark, king, 4:154b, 155a
Eric V of Denmark, king, 4:154b
Eric VI of Denmark, king, 4:155a
  occupation of Rostock, 6:93a
Eric VII of Denmark, king. *See* Eric of Pomerania, king of Scandinavia
Eric III of Norway, king. *See* Eric of Pomerania, king of Scandinavia
Eric IX of Sweden, king, Christianity and, 8:442a
Eric XIII of Sweden, king. *See* Eric of Pomerania, king of Scandinavia
Eric of Pomerania, king of Scandinavia, 4:156a, 7:220a
  Sweden and, 11:533a-b
  trade with Norway, 6:95b
Eric the Red. *See* Eiríkr the Red
Eric, Visigothic king, law code of, Recared I's reforms of, 7:520a
Eric's saga. See Eiríks saga rauða

Erigena. *See* John Scottus Eriugena
Erik II of Norway, king, wedding of, 8:559a
Erik, duke (brother of King Birger Magnusson of Sweden), 11:532a
Erik Magnusson, duke, 4:505b, 520a
 in *Erikskrönikan,* 4:505b
Erik, St., dynasty of, 11:530b
Erik (the Victorious) of Sweden, king, vs. Denmark, 11:530a
Erikskrönikan, **4:505b–506a,** 11:19b–20a, 21a-b
 Karlskrönikan and, 7:220a-b
 Scandinavian descendants of, 11:22a
Erinnerung an den Tod. See Heinrich von Melk
Erispoë of Brittany, seal wax impression of, 11:125a
Eristʿaw, **4:506a**
Erla, 5:435a
Erlembald, 3:499b
Erlösung, Die
 contents of, 2:229b–230a
 courtly features of, 2:229b, 230a
 poetical qualities of, 2:232b
 see also Heinrich von Hesler
Erlung von Würzburg, 3:97a
Ermanaric (epic character), 4:507a
 in *Þiðreks saga,* 12:29b
Ermanaric, Ostrogothic king, defeat by Huns, 9:289a
Ermanrich (epic character), in *Alpharts Tod,* 1:219a-b
Ermbert of Freising, bishop, Arbeo and, 1:422b
Ermengarde of Brittany, countess, letter from Robert d'Arbrissel, 10:430a
Ermengaud, Matfre, **4:506b–507a**
 Breviari d'amor, 4:506b, 10:181b
Ermenrich of Ellwangen, **4:507a,** 7:362b
 hymns of, 6:381b
Ermenrîkes Dôt, **4:507a-b**
 relation to *Hamðismál,* 6:88a
Ermentarius of Noirmoutier, on Viking raids, 12:430b
Ermentrude uten Hove, 5:523a
Ermentrude (wife of Charles the Bald), 3:89b
Erminrekr (saga character), 12:29b
Ermoldus Nigellus, **4:507b–508a,** 7:362b
 Carolingian Latin poetry and, 3:103a
 Life of Louis the Pious, 2:236a-b
Ernest of Pardubice, archbishop of Prague, conflict between church and laity and, 2:304a-b
Ernst II of Swabia, duke, vs. Conrad II, 11:527a
Ernst, Herzog. *See* Herzog Ernst
Ernulf, **4:508a**
Eroticism
 in Baudri of Bourgueil, 2:132a
 see also Ribald literature; Sexuality
Erotokritos, 2:523a
Eruditio regum et principum. See Gilbert of Tournai
Erusin. See Betrothal, Jewish
Erwin, Master, **4:508a**
 Strasbourg Cathedral and, 11:488a
Erythraean sibyl, in art, 11:257a
Erzincan (Erzinjan), **4:508b**
 Armenian trade and, 12:97b
 Seljuks and, 1:485a
 silk route to the Far East and, 12:99a
Erzinjan. *See* Erzincan
Erzurum. *See* Theodosiopolis
Es fügt sich. See Oswald von Wolkenstein
Es ist ain altgesprochner rat. See Oswald von Wolkenstein
Esayi Ncʿecʿi, 1:512a, 5:543b (*illus.*), 544a
 Tʿoros Tarōneciʿi and, 12:88a
"Escape of a Captive Treated Allegorically." *See Ecbasis captivi*
Escarbuncle, 1:522b
Escartons. See Representative assemblies, French
Escavias, Pedro de, *Hechos del condestable Miguel Lucas de Iranzo* and, 11:422b, 433a
Eschaquiel, 8:562b, 608b–609a
Eschatology
 Christian, *sex aetates mundi* and, 11:215b
 Islamic
  in art, 6:593a
  in doctrine of resurrection, 10:340b
 in Italian poetry, 6:630b–631a, 651a
 Western European, resurrection theology, 9:604b
 Zoroastrianism and, 12:746b
Escheat, escheator, **4:508b–509b**
 French royal, representative assemblies and, 10:324a
 in Hungary, 6:344a
 origins of office, 4:509a
 procedures, 4:509a-b
 sheriff and, 11:225b, 226a
 treason and, 12:165a-b
Eschequier. See Eschaquiel
Eschwege, land reclamation around, 10:273a
Esclave, etymology of, 11:200b
Escobar, Pero de, 4:561b
Escomb abbey church, architectural features, 10:680a
Escoufle, L'. See Renart, Jean
Escuage. *See* Scutage
Escudier. See Squire
Escuier. See Squire
Eşfahān. *See* Isfahan
Eskil, archbishop, 4:153a, 153b
Eskimos
 Thule culture, 11:329b
 Viking settlement of Greenland and, 12:427b
Eskişehir. *See* Dorylaeum
Esmoreit, 4:321a-b
Eşnaf. See Şinf
Esoteric religions. *See* Mystery religions
Espada. See Sword
Espéculo, 7:522b
Espéculo de las leyes. See Libro del fuero
Espine, 7:317a
Espinette amoureuse. See Froissart, Jehan
Espionage. *See* Postal and intelligence services
Esposizioni sopra la Comedia di Dante. See Boccaccio, Giovanni
Espurgatoire St. Patrice, **4:509b–510a**
 dating of, 8:136a
 plot summary, 8:137a
 sources of, 8:136a, 137a, 10:620a-b
Esquire. *See* Squire
Essence and existence, **4:510a-b**
 in Islamic theology
  Averroës, 1:459b
  Avicenna, 1:458b
  proofs of causality, 9:596b
  al-Rāzī on Plato and, 10:267b–268a
  Sufism, 6:585b–586a
 mathematical *quadrivium* disciplines and, 10:237a-b
 in Western European theology, 9:588a, 597b, 598a
  Duns Scotus, 1:467a, 9:701a, 702a
  Gilbert of Poitiers, 9:588b, 702a
  John Italos, 9:698a
 see also Aristotle; Plato; Realism
Essentia. See Ousia; Trinitarian doctrine
Essex
 Mercian conquest of, 7:658b
 settlement in 6th century, 4:454a
Essex, John, **4:510b–511a**
Esslingen, Frederick II and, 11:528a
Essyllt. *See* Tristan, Legend of
Establishment of the Royal Household, 6:301a
Estampida, 5:434b
Estampie, 4:87a-b, 88a, 88b
 sequence and, 8:571a
 see also Dance
Estat et maintien, L'. See Gilles li Muisis
Estate management, **4:511a–515a**
 Anglo-Saxon, manorial reeve and, 10:281a
 Carolingian, 4:511b–512a
 direct management, 12:533b–534a
 domus cultae as, 10:522a
 English, 4:512a-b, 513a-b, 514a-b
  Paston letters on, 9:450a-b
 land reclamation and, 10:274b, 278a-b
 manorial extent, 12:533a-b
 polyptych, 10:29a-b
 Roman, 4:511a-b
 social status of managers, 12:533a
 surveys in, 4:137b, 512b, 513b
 treatises on, 4:513b, 12:532b–534a
 winemaking and, 12:652a–653a
 women and, 4:601a-b
 see also Household management; Tools, agricultural, European
Estate (status). *See* Status
Estates General of France, 12:162a
 Charles V and, 3:269b
 Charles VII and, 3:271b
 history and development of, 10:316a-b, 317b–324a
 ordinance of March 1357, 5:185b
 relations with aristocracy, 5:185a-b
 taxation policy, 5:187b, 189b, 11:622a, 622b–623a
  reimposition of *aides* and *gabelle,* 11:624a
 see also Representative assemblies, French

Estates, legal and social. *See* Class structure
Estates, political. *See* Representative assemblies
Estates satire. *See* Satire
Estelin (unit of measure), 12:594a
Estêvão Soares da Silva, archbishop of Braga, 10:44a
Estoc, 11:549b
Estoire des Engleis. See Gaimar, Geffrei
Estoire de Griseldis, 4:287b
Estoire de la Guerre Sainte. See Ambroise d'Évreux
Estoire des rois d'Angleterre et de Normandie, 3:332a
origins, 9:638a
Estoire des rois de France, origins, 9:638a
Estoire del Saint Graal, 1:574a
Estonia, 2:63 (map)
Denmark and, 4:154a, 155b
early Christian missions to, 2:64b
sold to the Teutonic Order, 2:65b
vs. Denmark, 11:531a
Estonian language, 6:434a
Estonians, 2:62a, 64a, 64b, 65a-b, 68a
rebellion of 1223, 2:65b
Estoria del Cid, 3:71b, 76a
Estoria de dos amadores. See Rodríguez del Padrón, Juan
Estoria de España, 3:71b
Estoria de los quatro dotores de la santa eglesia, 11:440a
Estorie del euangelie, La, 4:546b
Estorie des Englés. See Gaimar, Geffrei
Estouteville, Guillaume d', cardinal, 7:115b
university reform, 11:690a
Estrabot, **4:515a**
Estrangelo alphabet. *See* Alphabets, Syriac
Estreito (Portuguese settler in Madeira), 4:560a
Estremadura, transhumance and, 8:280a
Estúñiga, Cancionero de, 11:451a
Esus (Celtic divinity), 9:46a
Esztergom, metropolitan see of, 11:478a
Eszterhazy, archbishopric of, 11:479a
Établissement, ordinance and, 9:262a
Établissements de Rouen, form of government, 10:537b–538a
Établissements de St. Louis, **4:515a-b**, 9:262a
Livres de Jostice et de Plet and, 7:635b
Étangs. See Fishponds
Etching, **4:516a-b**
of armor, 1:536a
see also Drypoint
Eternal Gospel. See Gerard of Borgo San Donnino
Etesian wind, 9:137b, 138a
Eth, in Old and Middle English, 8:310b, 311a
Ethelbald of Mercia, king, London trade privileges and, 7:658b
Ethelbert of England, Jutish king, Germanic law codes and, 10:465b
Ethelbert of Kent, king
Augustine of Canterbury and, 1:645a-b
baptism of, 8:440b
Canterbury and, 3:81a-b
contacts with Frankish kingdom, 4:453a-b
Ethelfled of Mercia, queen, Vikings and, 12:433a
Ethelred II (the Unready) of England, king, **4:517b**
danegeld and, 4:90a-b
Danes and, 12:434a
jury and, 7:182a
law code of, 9:436a
marriage of, 9:165a
recalling of, 3:471b
reign of, 4:457a
Winchester Troper and, 12:647b
Wulfstan of York and, 12:704a
Ethelred I of Wessex, king, Vikings and, 12:432b
Ethelred of Rievaulx, St., **4:516b–517b**
as abbot, 4:516b–517a
on Edward the Confessor, 1:261b
Genealogy of the Kings of England, 4:517a
Letter to His Sister, 9:18b
Life of Edward the Confessor, 4:517a, 12:412a
Mirror of Charity, 4:517a
Mirror of Love, 9:18b
On the Soul, 4:517a
On Spiritual Friendship, 4:517a
Rule of Life for a Recluse, 4:517a
translation of works into English, 9:26b
Vita Niniani, 9:139a, 139b
"When Jesus Was Twelve Years Old," 4:517a
works of, 3:405a
Ethelwold, **4:517b–518b**
benedictional of, 1:273a, 2:176b (*illus.*), 8:107b
as bishop of Winchester, 4:518a
liturgy and, 2:172b
monastic foundations, 4:518a
monastic reform and, 7:363a
Regularis concordia, on *visitatio sepulchri,* 12:478a
teacher of Aelfric, 1:281b
translations of, 4:518a-b
Winchester Troper and, 12:647b, 648a
Ethelwulf, *Lives of the Abbots,* 1:254b, 7:363a
Etheria. *See* Egeria
Ethics
Abelard and, 9:155b
casuistry in, 3:153a-b
Catalan-language works on, 3:168b
Ockham and, 9:214a
Ethiopia. *See* Abyssinia
Ethiopian language, translation of Septuagint into, 2:211a
Ethiopian Orthodox church
Alexandrian rite, 1:155a–157a
traditional form, 1:157a
Étienne de Vignolles (La Hire), suit signs in cards, 5:352a
Étienne-Henri of Champagne, count, fairs and, 4:591a
Etiquette
for knights, 3:666b
rules of, *see also* Courtesy books
table manners, 3:665a
Etruria, Rome and, 10:526a
Etsi de statu. See Boniface VIII, pope
Ettichone dynasty, 11:526a
Etymologiae. See Isidore of Seville, St., *Etymologies*
Etymologicum genuinum, 11:53a
Etymologicum gudianum, 11:53a
Etymologicum magnum, 11:53a
Etymologies. See Isidore of Seville, St.
Etzel, king of Hunland (epic character), 9:113a, 113b, 114b
Attila and, 9:114a
Euboea
Latin Empire of Constantinople and, 7:347a
see also Negroponte
Eucharist
accident of quantity, 9:603b
altar apparatus and vessels for, 1:222b–223b
Aquinas on, 4:375b
in Carolingian age, 4:373a
in Celtic church, 3:230b
chalice in, 3:241b–242a
chant, 3:504a
commentaries on, 8:182a
compared with pagan rites, 9:2a
confession and, 3:533b
for Corpus Christi, 3:608a-b, 9:603b
dogmatic controversies, 8:181a
in early church, 3:338a-b, 4:372b, 8:200b
furniture for, 5:316b
in John of Paris' doctrine of impanation, 4:451b
last. *See* Viaticum
in Last Supper iconography, 7:344a
legal status, 8:182a
Lenten, 4:105b
liturgical use of creeds in, 3:676a–677a
liturgical variations (Byzantine-Latin), 7:610b
Office of Corpus Christi, 8:182a
pietistic practice and devotions, 8:182a
predestination and, 5:639a
primacy of, 8:181b–182a
Radbertus of Corbie on, 9:446b
reservation of the Host. *See* Sacrament, reservation of
sign and reality, 9:603b
Symeon on, 9:7b
transubstantiation, 9:603b
Peter Comestor on, 9:514a
use of *azymes* and, 2:31b
veneration of, 6:399a
William of Ockham on, 9:213b
see also Communion; Easter, Mass for; Fasting, Christian; Mass, liturgy of
Eucharisterios, in Byzantine rhetoric, 10:350a
Eucherius of Lyons
Formularium spiritualis, contents page illustrations, 4:356a
letters from St. Paulinus of Nola, 9:471a
Euchologion, 7:595b

Euclid, 1:435a
attribution of *On the Balançe,* 1:434b
Boethius and, 8:637a
Canon, 8:566a
Catoptrics, 9:240b
Elements, 1:433b, 436b
Arabic translations of, 8:209b, 11:82b, 12:128a-b, 129b–130b
Latin translations of, 8:208a, 209b
ratio and proportion, 8:216a, 217b
in Islamic science, 11:86a
mathematical theory, ratio and proportion, 8:215a, 216b
Optics
influence on Islamic optics, 9:241b
translations, 11:274a
theory of perspective, 9:251a
translations into Arabic, 11:83a
Eudemian Ethics. See Aristotle
Eudes III of Champagne, count, fairs and, 4:590b–591a
Eudes of France, seal wax impression of, 11:125a
Eudes of Montreuil, **4:518b–519a**
Eudes Rigaud, **4:519a-b,** 12:376a
as adviser to Louis IX, 4:519a-b
visitations of, 4:519b
Eudes of Sully, statutes of, 10:408b
Eudo of Aquitaine, duke, 9:715b
Eudokia (daughter of Basil II), 2:491b
Eudokia, empress (widow of Constantine X Doukas), 10:516a
Eudokia Ingerina (9th century), 2:117a, 118a
Eudoxia, Byzantine empress, vs. John Chrysostom, 7:122b–123a
Eudoxus of Cnidus, method of exhaustion, 8:215a
Eufemia of Norway, queen, 4:519b, 520a
Eufemiavisor, **4:519b–520b**
Eugenios of Clysma, St. *See* Awgen of Clysma, mar
Eugenius III, pope
Bernard of Clairvaux and, 2:191a, 3:352b
canonization and, 3:68a
Cistercian background of, 3:405b
councils, 3:637b
preaching of Second Crusade, 12:405a
Quantum praedecessores, 4:19b
regularization of sainthood, 6:68b
Second Crusade and, 2:192a, 3:356b, 4:20b, 37b
Eugenius IV, pope
Constantinople and, 4:56a
Council of Basel and, 3:652b–653a, 653b–654a, 6:563a
endorsement of *Haec sancta,* 4:378a
hostility to conciliar reform, 3:651b
Hundred Years War and, 6:334b
Laetentur coeli, 3:519a, 520b
legacy of, 3:367a-b
Nicholas of Cusa and, 9:123b
reign of, 3:366a-b
Rome and, 10:524b
Ut sacra, 5:205b
Eugenius II of Toledo, **4:520b,** 11:406a
Julianus of Toledo and, 7:181a
Eugenius III of Toledo, hymnodist, 6:381a
Eugenius, emir, 11:274a
Eugenius Vulgarius, **4:520b–521a**
Eugippius, **4:521a**
Eulalia, St., 4:521a-b
Eulalie, La Séquence de Ste., **4:521a-b**
chanson de geste form, 6:59b
Picard dialect, 9:629b–630a
use of vernacular, 5:233b–234a, 288a, 9:633a
Eulalios, Church of the Holy Apostles, Constantinople, mosaics in, 2:438b
Eulogius of Córdoba, 3:598b, **4:521b,** 6:381a, 11:406a
Eulogius, patriarch of Alexandria, Christology of, 3:320b
Eulogy on the Holy Theotokos. See Petros of Siwnik^{c}, bishop
Eunapius (Byzantine historian), 6:242b–243a, 10:467b
Zosimus and, 12:748a
Eunomians, 2:121b
Eunomius, *Apology,* 2:121a
Eunuchs, in Byzantine Empire, 2:472b–473a
EUOUAE. *See* EVOVAE
Euphemia, Byzantine empress, 7:201a
opposition to marriage of Justinian and Theodora, 12:12a
Euphemia, St., shrine of, in Chalcedon, 4:337a
Euphemiai, 7:385a
Euphrates River, **4:521b–523b,** 4:522 (map), 6:509b
in Armenia, 1:470b
Islamic communications and, 10:426a
in Islamic conquests, 6:568b
see also Baghdad
Eupolemius, 4:496b, **4:523a**
Euric, Visigothic king, 12:470b
law code of, 7:469b, 520a, 12:471b, 472a
Sidonius and, 11:277a
Euryalus. See Pius II, pope
Euryalus und Lucretia. See Niclas von Wyle
Eusebius Bruno, **4:523b**
Eusebius of Caesarea, **4:523b**
Abgar V and, 11:562b
Aenigmata and, 11:601b
Alexandrian school and, 3:336a
Basil the Great and, 2:120a
canon table of, 3:66a
Chronici canones, commented on by Alfonso Fernández de Madrigal, 11:420b
Chronicle, 1:507b, 6:238b, 259a
history as a linear progression, 6:242b
concept of primitive church and, 10:121b
Ecclesiastical History, 6:238b
on Armenia, 1:475b
Bede and, 2:154b, 155b
continuations of, 9:617b, 11:358a, 374a, 12:17a
derivatives of, 8:510a
life of Origen, 9:277b
precedent for later histories, 6:242b, 261a
icons and, 6:397b
Isidore of Seville and, 6:564b
Life of Constantine, 6:242b
on labarum, 7:313b
Macedonian political theory and, 1:483a
Michael the Syrian and, 8:306a
riddles by, 7:362b
Roman hierarchy, 9:265a
Eusebius of Emessa, 1:507b
Eusebius (identified with Hwaetberht, abbot of Wearmouth), collection of riddles, 10:398a
Eusebius of Nicomedia
Arianism and, 1:453b, 454a
Athanasian Trinitarianism, 9:560b
Constantine I and, 10:462a
Ulfilas and, 12:469a
Eustace, St.
hunting and, 6:358b, 361a
Spanish prose life of, 11:439b
Eustache de Beaumarchais, 11:160b–161a
Eustache Deschamps. *See* Deschamps, Eustache
Eustathios Boilas, 2:455a
Eustathios Kataphloros. *See* Eustathios of Thessaloniki, archbishop
Eustathios of Mc^{c}χet^{c}a, Martyrdoms of, 5:413b
Eustathios Makrembolite, 2:508a
Eustathios of Sebaste, 2:120a, 121a, 121b, 122a
development of Nestorianism and, 9:105a
extremist doctrines of, 6:192a
Eustathios of Thessaloniki, archbishop, 3:431b
as an orator, 10:350b
on the capture of Thessaloniki, 2:516a
commentary on Homer, 11:49a, 54a-b
Eustathius Rhomaios, *Peira,* 7:392a
Eustochius, editions of Plotinus' works, 9:96b
Euthaliana, 1:507b
Euthanasia. *See* Mercy killing
Euthymios of Iviron
biography of, 5:417a
Greek translation of *Balavariani,* 2:54b, 5:417a
literary career of, 5:417a
monastery founded by, 5:414a
Euthymios, patriarch of Constantinople, 7:545b
Nikolaos I Mystikos and, 9:135b
Euthymios of Trnovo, patriarch, 2:413b
Euthymios Zigabenos, *Panoplia dogmatica,* 9:562b
on Bogomilism, 2:295b, 296a
Eutihije. *See* Eutychios
Eutocius of Ascalon
on Archimedes, 1:434a, 434b, 435b
Commentary on the Conics, 1:438b
Commentary on the Measurement of the Circle, 1:437a, 439a
Commentary on the Sphere and the Cylinder, 1:437b, 438a
Eutropius, *Breviarium ab urbe condita,* 7:328a
Eutyches, archimandrite, **4:523b–524b,** 7:541b–542a

Eutyches, archimandrite (*cont.*)
Christology of, 8:477a
on divinity of Jesus, 3:629a-b
"Robber Synod" of Ephesus, 8:477a
Eutyches (grammarian), 7:351b
Eutychianism, 3:594a
nature of Christ in, 6:190b
see also Monophysitism
Eutychides (*fl.* 296 B.C.), 4:12b
Eutychios, 2:448a, **4:524b**
Eutychios the Melchite, **4:525a-b**
Discussion Between the Heretic and the Christian, 4:525b
Kitab al-burhān, 4:525b
Naẓm al-jawhar, 4:525a
Yahya and, 12:716a
Eutychius, patriarch of Constantinople, *On the Distinction of Nature and Person,* 1:505b–506a
Evagrios. *See* Evagrius Scholasticus
Evagrius Ponticus, 1:507b, 9:6a-b, 7a
ascent to perfection, 9:563b
on deadly sins, 11:211b
prayer of the mind, 6:217a
Evagrius Scholasticus, 11:566a
Church History, 7:132b
ecclesiastical histories, 2:513a
Evangeliary, **4:525b–526a**
in Celtic liturgy, 7:614b
of the Sainte Chapelle, historiated initials in, 6:462b
see also Lectionary; Pericope
Evangelienbuch. See Otfrid von Weissenburg, *Christ*
Evangelist symbols, **4:526a-b**, 4:526b (*illus.*)
Christ in Majesty, 10:607a
in Lindisfarne Gospels, 7:584a
Evangelium secundum Marcam argenti, 9:440b
Evangelorum libri IV. See Juvencus
Evangheliar, 10:512a
Eve (OT character)
in art, in St. Lazare church in Autun, 10:498 (*illus.*)
in Manichaeism, 8:85a
Eve of St. Martin, 9:11b
Everaert, Cornelis, 4:322b
Everard the German. *See* Evrard the German
Everhard of Wampen, 4:579b
Evernew Tongue, The
description of Doomsday, 1:111a
influence on Irish literature, 1:111a
Evervinus of Steinfeld, description of Catharist group, 6:196a
Everyman, 1:186a, **4:527b–529a**
doctrinal content, 4:527b–528a
early editions, 4:527b
parallels in other literatures, 4:528a
performance of, 4:286b, 528b
in modern times, 4:526b–527a
relationship to *Elckerlijc,* 4:527a-b
see also Elckerlijc
Evesham, Battle of (1265), 2:112b
in Robert of Gloucester's *Chronicle,* 8:317a
Evfimii of Trnovo, 11:346a
Evfimiya, panegyric to Lazar Hrebeljanovič, 11:346a
Evida (saga character), 4:505a
Evil
Cabalistic studies of realm of, 3:2a
early church and problems of, 3:340a
see also Dualism
Evil eye, in medieval magic, 8:38a
Evora, Pedro da, 4:562a
EVOVAE, 4:185a, **4:529a**
tonaries and, 12:70a, 70b
Évrard of Béthune, *Graecismus,* 3:434b, 7:351b, 365b, 12:137a
Evrard the German, 7:368a
Laborintus, 7:372b, 373a, 373b, 10:359b, 360b
Evrenoz Bey, Bāyazīd I and, 2:136b
Ewer, trulla and, 12:221b–222a
Ewrān, Akhī, *Laṭā'if al hikme,* 11:309a
Ex herbis femininis, 6:181a
Ex secrabilis. See John XXII, pope
Ex te lux oritur, 8:559a
Ex voto, **4:529b**
Exabeba, 8:562b
Exact Exposition of the Orthodox Faith. See John of Damascus, St.
Examination of the Three Faiths. See Kammūna, Ibn
Exaquir. See Eschaquiel
Exarch, title used at Council of Nicaea (325), 9:458b
Exarchate, **4:529b–530a**, 10:459b–460a
of Africa, 4:530a
created by Emperor Maurice, 8:230a
jurisdiction of, 4:529b
of Ravenna, 4:529b
Exarchos, definition of, 4:529a
Excalibur, **4:530a**, 8:291b, 11:546a
Exceptiones legum Romanarum. See Petri Exceptiones
"Exceptivam actionem." *See* Alan of Lille
Excerpts from a Book of David (of Menevia), on penance, 9:488b
Excessus, in St. Bernard of Clairvaux's conception of love, 2:193b–194a
Exchange banks
failures of, 2:74b
spread of, 2:73b–74a
Exchange, bill of. *See* Bill of exchange
Exchequer, **4:530b–533a**
England, 4:502b
accounting methods, 4:531b–532a
in Caen, 3:8b
Chamber of, 4:534b
chamberlain and, 3:242b–243a
efficiency of, 4:532a
escheat and, 4:509a
of the Jews, 4:534a, 535a-b
Lower, 4:530b–531a
made independent by Provisions of Oxford (1258), 10:194b–195a
origin of name, 4:533a
pipe rolls, 9:662a–663b
of Pleas, 4:534a
responsibilities, 4:469b
Roger of Salisbury and, 10:443a
royal chamber and, 6:301a, 305b
royal wardrobe and, 4:532b, 6:302a, 302b, 303b
in England, sheriff and, 11:225b
England
under Henry I, 4:464a
under Henry II, 6:157a
under John, 6:301b, 302a
Upper, 4:531a–532b, 533b
Winchester treasury and, 6:301a
king's evil and, 7:255b–256a
Norman, 4:532a, 5:168a, 9:167b, 168a, 169b
Parlement of Paris and, 9:169a, 420b
Philip Augustus and, 9:168b
Rouen Parlement and, 9:170a
as supreme court, 7:459b
Scotland, under Robert II, 10:428b
see also Accounting; Banking, European
Exchequer, court of, 3:492a, **4:533a–535a**
Britton on, 4:533b
in circuit justice, 7:187a
common pleas and, 4:534b, 7:187a
court of appeal for, 4:534b
as court of equity, 4:534b–535a
emergence as supreme court, 7:446a
established by Henry II, 4:470a
grounds for intervention by, 4:534b
jurisdiction of, 4:533b–534a
officials of, 4:534a
records of, 4:534a
see also English common law
Exchequer of the Jews, 2:80a-b, **4:535a-b**, 7:71a-b
Excitatori de la pensa a Déu. See Oliver, Bernard
Exclusio propter dotem. See Dowry
Excommunicamus et anathematisamus. See Gregory IX, pope
Excommunication, **4:536a–538b**
absolution from, 6:450a
appeal against, 4:537b
at Second Lateran Council, 3:445a
bells and, 2:166a
crimes subject to, 4:537a
definition of, 4:536a
for heresy, 6:484b
interdict and, 6:494b, 495a, 496a, 496b
as penalty for tithe evasion, 12:65a
penance and, 6:447b, 9:487b
phases in development of, 4:536a-b
power to excommunicate, 4:536b–537a
public. *See* Interdict
purpose of, 4:537b
reconciliation of the excommunicate, 4:537b–538a
rites of, 4:537a
secular authorities and, 4:538a
of *universitas,* 6:467b
Wyclif on, 12:708a
Excubitors, 11:573a
"Excusacion aux dames." *See* Chartier, Alain
Execrabilis. See Pius II, pope
Executor, 6:459a
Exedra, **4:538b**
Exegesis, Byzantine, 2:214a-b
Antiochene school, 9:564a
catenae, 9:564a
commentaries, 9:564a-b
eratopokriseis, 9:564a
literal vs. allegorical, 9:563b–564a
Exegesis, Islamic

Ismaili. *See Ta'lwīl*
in al-Kufa, 7:307b
Tafsīr and, 11:570a
Exegesis, Jewish, 2:212a-b, **4:538b–542a**
by Rashi, 10:259a–260a
Franco-German school, 2:212a-b
French, 4:540b–541b
galut, 5:346a–347a
Gaonic, 4:539a
Hugh of St. Victor and, 6:322a
influence of Islamic folklore on, 8:23a
Italian, 4:541b
in Judeo-Arabic literature, 7:172b
Judeo-Spanish school, 2:212a
Kairouan school, 2:212b
Karaite, 4:539a-b
Maimonides, 9:577a
Provençal, 4:541a-b
shift to dialectic, 10:259b
Spanish, 4:539b–540b
universality of biblical teachings, 9:576b
see also Rabbinate; Talmud, exegesis and study of
Exegesis, Latin, 2:212b–214a, **4:542a–545a**
Bede and, 2:154a-b
"fourfold" allegory and, 1:180a
in Irish monasteries, 2:220a
in the Mergentheim codex, 2:232a
monastic, 4:542b–543a, 6:307a-b
Nicholas of Lyra, 10:260a
origins, 9:278a
Ovidian influence, 9:314a
in prose Bible versions, 4:547a-b
scholastic, 4:543a–544b
Smaragdus of St. Mihiel, 11:351a
in the 12th century, 2:213a-b
under the Carolingians, 2:213a
in verse Bible versions, 4:546a–547a
see also Gloss; Glossators
Exegesis, Middle English, **4:545a–548a**
influence of Latin exegesis, 4:545a-b
in prose Bible versions, 4:547a-b
in verse Bible versions, 4:546a–547a
Wycliffite, 4:544b, 547b–548a
Exegesis, Old English, **4:548b–551a**
glosses in Latin bibles, 4:548b
in prose Bible translations, 4:548b
Exegesis, Oriental, 2:214b–215a
Exegesis, Syrian Christian, 11:565b
Exemplum, **4:551a-b**
alphabetical arrangement of, 1:206a
church's disapproval of unseemly exempla, 4:551a-b
in *Disputatio aque et vini,* 6:658b
in Don Juan Manuel's *Conde Lucanor,* 11:417a
Eastern, in Spain, 4:551b
Eyrbyggja saga as, 4:568b
in *Fiore di virtù,* 6:632a
hagiographical, *see also Vitae patrum*
in Jacques de Vitry's *Historia,* 7:369a
in *Novellino,* 6:659b
in *Proverbia quae dicuntur super natura feminarum,* 6:630a
religious instruction and, 10:301a
in Robert Mannyng's *Handlyng Synne,* 8:87a
in sermons, 6:663b, 664b, 664a
as a source for early Icelandic *rímur,* 10:402b
sources for, 4:551a
in Spanish literature, 11:419b–420a
in Spanish preaching, 11:456a
in *Specchio di vera penitenza,* 6:660a, 664b
in Thomas of Cantimpré's *Bonus universale de apibus,* 12:34b
used in preaching, 10:363a-b
see also Apologue
Exercitus Romanus, 10:521b
Exeter Book, 8:327a
metrical fragment of *Physiologus* preserved in, 2:204b
riddles in, 10:398a-b
Riming Poem, use of rhyme in, 8:343a
on the use of plow, 12:75b
Wanderer, 1:282a–283b (*illus.*)
Exeter Cathedral, early clock in, 3:29b
Exiit qui seminat. See Nicholas III, pope
Exilarch, **4:551b–552b**
in Babylonia, 7:107b
dispute with Palestinian yeshiva, 7:105a
family life and, 4:605b
hereditary nature of, 4:552a
income of, 4:552a
office of nagid and, 9:52a, 52b
in Persia, 7:106a-b
responsibilities of, 4:552a-b, 7:73a, 73b, 74a
under Muslim rule, 4:552a
see also Nasi
Exile. *See* Galut
Existence, theories of. *See* Essence and existence; Realism
Exivi de Paradiso. See Vienne, Council of
Exodus (Old English poem), 1:279b, 4:550b
Exonarthex, **4:552b–553a**, 4:553a(*illus.*)
Exorcism, 3:441a, 442a
oil for, 2:177a, 177b
Exordium Cistercii. See Cistercian Order
Exordium parvum. See Cistercian Order
Expeditio Persica. See George of Pisidia
Explanation of the Platonic Chariot-driving of Souls. See Hermeias
Exploration, by Western Europeans, **4:553a–563b**
of Africa, 4:561a–562a
crusades and, 4:556a-b
effect of Turkish conquests, 4:557b
infectious disease and, 9:673b, 674b, 682a–683b
Marco Polo, 10:27a–28a
Norse voyages, 4:553b–555b, 11:329a-b
pilgrimages and, 4:553a-b
portolan chart, 10:33a–35a
Prester John, 10:118a–119b
search for western routes to Asia, 4:558a–563b
see also Azores; Blacks; Cartography; Geography; Vikings
Expositio brevis antiquae liturgiae gallicanae. See Germanus of Paris, St.
Expositio in cantica canticorum. See William of St. Thierry
Expositio in cantica canticorum. See Williram von Ebersberg
Expositio dominicae orationis. See Huguccio
Expositio in Hexaemeron. See Abelard, Peter
Expositio Hymnorum, 10:654b
Expositio in libros physicorum. See Ockham, William of
Expositio officiorum, 11:568a
Expositio Psalmorum. See Cassiodorus Senator
Expositio super libros de anima. See Burley, Walter
Expositio super libros Elenchorum. See Ockham, William of
Expositio symboli apostolorum. See Huguccio
Exposition of the Rule. See Angelo Clareno
Expositiunculae in Evangelium. See Arnobius the Younger
Exposito aurea. See Ockham, William of
Expugnatio Hibernica. See Gerald of Wales
Exsultet. See Exultet
Extended family, 4:604b
Byzantine, 4:595a-b
cycles in, 4:146b
Germanic, 4:599b, 600a
as household, 4:599a-b
Islamic, 4:596b
Extents (manorial surveys). *See* Manorial surveys
Extravagantes communes. See John XXII, pope
Extremadura, established in Aragon by Alfonso I, 1:407a
Extreme unction, **4:565a-b**
Armenian church and, 1:501a
see also Anointing; Unction of the sick
Exultet, 2:177b–178a
incense and, 6:432b
Exultet roll, **4:565b**, 10:113a
illuminations on, 6:279a
Eyck, Hubert van, **4:566a–567b**
Ghent Altarpiece, 5:523b–524b (*illus.*), 10:29a
Madonna with Canon van der Paele, 10:551b
Eyck, Jan van, **4:566a–567b**
Arnolfini Wedding Portrait, 4:567a
Campin and, 3:61b
Ghent Altarpiece, 5:85b–86a, 524a (*illus.*), 10:29a
Adoration of the Lamb, 5:85b–86a
grisaille technique of, 5:678b
influence of
on Hugo van der Goes, 5:571b
on Juan Rexach, 10:342b
on Petrus Christus, 3:324b
Madonna in a Church, 5:85b, 610b (*illus.*), 611b
Nisart and, 9:140b
oil painting, 9:223b
Portrait of a Man in a Red Turban, 4:567b

Eyck, Jan van (*cont.*)
as portrait painter, 4:567a-b
as servant of Philip the Good, 4:566a-b
symbolism of, 5:85b
techniques of, 4:566b, 5:85b
Three Marys at the Tomb, 4:566b, 567 (*illus.*)
Turin-Milan Hours, 5:85b
see also Flemish painting
Eyebrows. *See* Hair
Eyeglasses, **7:538b–541a**
invention of, 7:539b–540a, 11:650a-b
transparent reliquaries and, 11:650b
lenses
concave, 11:650b
convex, 11:650b
Eylhart. *See* Eilhart von Oberg; *Tristrant*
Eymeric, Nicholas, 4:247b
Directory of the Inquisition, 6:487a
Eymundar þáttr Hringssonar, Yngvars saga víþförla and, 12:727a
Eyrbyggja saga, **4:568a-b**, 4:613b, 614a
compared with *Þórðar saga Hreðu,* 12:49a
compared with *Vatnsdœla saga,* 12:363b
goddess Rán in the, 10:256b
Kjalnesinga saga and, 7:274a
Njáls saga and, 9:145b
references to Oddr and Óspakr, 2:71a
sources for, 4:568a
Eyre justices. *See* Justices, itinerant (in eyre)
Eysteinn Ásgrímsson, **4:568b–569a**
identity of, 4:569a
Lilja, 4:568b–569a
influenced by *Líknarbraut,* 7:580b
Eyvān, 2:140a, **4:569b–570a**, 4:569b (*illus.*), 9:671a, 10:219b (*illus.*)
architectural plan, 4:408a
at Taχt-i Suleiman, 11:628b
in Ayyubid mausoleums, 2:21b
barrel-vaulted, 6:607b, 612b
in Cairo madrasas, 2:21b–22a
in Ghaznavid architecture, 4:519a
madrasa and, 8:11b–12a
in mosque architecture, 6:602a, 602b–603a, 604b
in Seljuk architecture, 11:146b
of Taq-i Bostan, 11:597a
see also *Qāᶜa;* Ṣuffa
Eyvindr Finnsson Skáldaspillir, 4:415a, **4:570a-b**
dróttkvætt verse, 4:570b
Hákonarmál, **4:414b–415a**, 4:570a
in Eddic-skaldic transitional poetry, 4:389a
importance as historical source, 4:415a
preservation in manuscripts, 4:415a
Háleygjatal, 4:570a-b, 7:312a
lausavísa and, 7:387b
Ezana of Abyssinia, emperor, 1:30b
Eznak the Priest, list of kings, *marzpans,* and *katᶜołikoi,* 6:239a
Eznik of Kołb, 1:508a, **4:570b–571a**, 7:298b
Against the Sects, 6:187b
Ełcałandocᶜ, 4:571a
letter to Maštocᶜ, 7:279b
Ezr, *katᶜołikos,* Heraklios and, 1:500a
Ezra, Ibn. *See* Abraham ben Meïr ibn Ezra
Ezzolied, 2:226b, **4:571b**, 8:347b, 348b, 349a
cathedral schools and, 8:347b
Ezzos Gesang. See Ezzolied

F

Faba, Guido, *dictamen* of, 4:174b–175a
Fabian, election of, 3:602b
Fabiola, *xenodochium* of, 6:292b–293a
Fables, **4:572a–573a**
Byzantine transmission of, 8:18b–19a
in Der Stricker's work, 11:492b
French, **4:573a-b**
collections of, 4:573a-b
Renard the Fox, 10:312a–314a
themes of, 4:573b
Georgian, 5:418a
Latin, 7:366b–367a, 369a
Romulus, 10:527b
Oriental, Jewish transmission of, 8:23b
sources for, 4:572a
vernacular, 4:572b
see also Avianus; Bidpai
Fabliau, **4:574a–577b**
adultery theme, 9:636a
in Anglo-Norman literature, 1:269b
attitude to women in, 4:575a
Castia-gilos, 10:252b
in Castilian literature, 3:31b
characteristics of, 5:275b, 9:635b–636a
in Chaucer's *Canterbury Tales,* 3:292b–294a
comedy in, 4:574b–575a
connection with bourgeoisie, 4:574a-b
conventions, 5:257b
courtly literature and, 4:574a-b
disappearance as genre, 4:577a
dramatizations of, 5:273b
influence on Welsh poetry, 12:607a
joglars in, 7:116b
in *Kotzenmäre,* 7:300a-b
lais as, 7:317a
Mären and, 8:131b
as model for carnival plays, 4:272a
moral in, 4:575a-b
origins of, 4:576a-b, 9:636a
in *Owl and the Nightingale,* 9:316a
in *Quinze joies de mariage,* 10:240a-b
range of types and experiences, 5:257a-b
"Saint Pierre et le jongleur," 7:116b
sexual explicitness of, 4:574b
social analysis in, 5:257b
translated into Norwegian, 10:391a
verse form, 5:257b
see also Bodel, Jean; Nouvelle; Picard literature, fabliaux
Fabliau du mantel mautaillé, German adaptations of, 6:135b
Fabri, Felix, 4:246b, 6:473b
Fabriano, paper manufacture in, 12:699b
Fabrics. *See* Textiles
Facade construction
Ottonian, 10:477b
Romanesque, 10:481b–482a, 482b
Facade, screen. *See Pishtaq*
Facetus moribus et vita, 8:408b
Fachschrifttum, **4:577b–580a**
chief subjects of, 4:577b
geographic writings, 4:579a
housekeeping manuals, 4:579a
hunting manuals, 4:579a-b
magic and necromancy in, 4:579b
medical treatises, 4:579b
miḷitary writings, 4:579a
seven liberal arts in, 4:577b–578a
seven mechanical arts in, 4:578a, 578b
use of vernacular in, 4:578b
Facundus, 10:114b
Faderfio, 6:457a
Faḍl I, Shaddadid ruler, 11:217a
Faḍl II, Shaddadid ruler, 11:217b
Faḍl III, Shaddadid ruler, 11:217b
Faḍl ibn Sahl, al-, Ṭāhir and, 11:574a
Faḍl ibn Yaḥyā, al-, relationship to the Alids, 2:110b–111a
Faḍlān, Aḥmad ibn
mission to the Volga region, 5:331b, 393a, 12:488a
on a Russian funeral, 12:435b–436a
Færeyinga saga, **4:580b–581a**, 9:176b
Faènza. *See* Faience
Faenza Codex, **4:580a-b**, 8:632b, 633b
musical notation, 12:178a
Faerie Queene. See Spenser, Edmund
Faeroese ballads. *See* Faroese Ballads
Fáfnir, **4:581a–582a**
Fáfnismál, **10:290a–291b**
Fáfnir and, 4:581b
Norns and, 9:171b, 172a
Surtr and, 11:515a
Fagrskinna, 4:617b, 9:176a, 177a-b
Eyvindr Finnsson and, 4:570a, 570b
Hlaðajarla saga and, 9:177a
preservation of *Haraldskvæði* in, 6:97b
Fahd. See Cheetah
Faḥl, conquered, 6:568a
Faidit, Gaucelm, 9:693a
Faience, **4:582a-b** (*illus.*)
in pottery, 10:65a
see also Lajvard
Fair letters, 4:584b
Fairies, in Anglo-Norman literature, 7:317b, 318a
Fairs, **4:582b–590b**, 12:117a-b
administration of, 4:584a-b, 585a
African, 4:589a-b
at Beaucaire, 7:341b
at Ephesus, 12:101a
at Geneva, 2:78b
at Lyons, 2:78b, 7:699b–700a
at St. Gilles, 7:339a-b

at Thessaloniki, 12:101a, 102b
at Trebizond, 12:97b
at Ypres, 12:732a
Byzantine, 4:588a-b, 12:101b
of Champagne, **4:590b–593b**, 7:339b, 341a, 12:108b, 110b, 117b
abandonment of, 10:416a
credit instruments for, 4:592b–593a
Custom of the, 4:592a
cycle of, 4:592a
decline of, 4:593a
development of banking and, 2:74b, 76b, 78a
inns and, 6:468a-b
locations, 4:590b
mercantile policies of counts, 4:590b–591a
Nuremberg and, 9:202b
Siena and, 11:279a
transport of goods and, 12:375a, 375b
travel and, 12:157b–158b
Ypres and, 12:732a
in Cyprus, 12:101a
defined, 4:583a
in early medieval Europe, 12:110b
English, 4:586b–587a
of Flanders, 12:108b, 110b
French, 4:585b–586a
German, 4:586a-b
Italian, 4:587a
of Languedoc, 7:339b
legal privileges, 4:584a
Low Countries, 4:586b
of Lyons, book trade, 7:700a
Scandinavian, 4:587b
seal of, 4:592b
Slavic, 4:587b–588a
Spanish, 4:587b
Turkish, 4:589b
Western European, travel and transport and, 12:157b–158b
Fairy tales. *See* Magic and folklore
Fait, preservation of matter of Rome, 5:256b
Faits des Romains. See Fet des Romains, Li
Faiyūm, occupation by ᶜAmr, 6:569b
Fakhkh, battle at (786), 6:413a
Fakhr al-Dīn II ibn Maᶜn of Beirut, emir, 2:164b
Fakhr al-Dīn Gurgānī, *Wīs u Rāmīn,* 6:507a
Fakhr al-Dīn al-Rāzī, 1:618b, 7:296b–297a
Ḥadaᵓ iqu'l-anvār fī ḥaqāᵓiqi'l-asrār, 4:445b
philosophic commentaries, 9:571b
Fakhrī, al-. See Karajī, al-
Falāsifa. See Philosophy and theology, Islamic
Falchion, **4:593b**, 11:547 (*illus.*), 551a
Falconry
Adelard of Bath on, translations of, 12:140b
Frederick II of Germany on, 2:244b
Henri de Ferrières on, 6:360a
in Islamic world, 6:355b
in *Le jugement de chiens et d'oisiaus,* 6:360a-b
Slavic world, 1:98b
treatises on, 6:359b
women and, 6:357a
Falier, Marin, doge of Venice, 12:392b
Falier, Ordelaffo, doge of Venice, 9:330a
Falier (Venetian noble family), 12:390a
Faliscan language, 6:434b
Falkirk, Battle of (1298), 11:109a
tactics at, 3:205a
Fall of Princes. See Lydgate, John
Fall of Troy, The. See Josephus Iscanus, *De excidio Troiae*
Falsa musica, 8:646a
False Decretals. *See* Decretals, False
Famagusta, history of, 4:71a, 72a
Familia regis. See Household, royal
Familia sancti Petri, 10:525a
Familiares, in Anglo-Saxon royal household, 6:300a
Familiares. See Petrarch, *Rerum familiarium libri*
Familiaritas, 6:345a
Familiars (witchcraft), 12:663a-b
Family
Byzantine, **4:593b–596a**
demography of, 4:595b–596a
schooling of children and, 7:595a–596a
demography of, 4:144a-b, 145a–146b
extended. *See* Extended family
Islamic, **4:596b–599a**
concubinage, 3:527a–529a
Jewish, **4:605b–608a**, 7:92a-b
dowry rules, 7:30a
Gershom ben Judah on, 5:511b–512a
Jutish, 4:599b
nuclear. *See* Nuclear family
serf, 11:201b
status of women. *See* Women, status of
stem. *See* Stem family
village, 12:438a, 438b
Visigothic, 12:473b–474a
Western courtesy books for, 3:661b–663b
Western European, **4:599a–605b**
aristocratic, 4:602a-b
clerical celibacy and, 3:417b
concubinage, 3:529b–530b
consanguinity and, 3:539b–540b
in Florence, 4:144a-b
Germanic, 4:599b–600a
in High Middle Ages, 12:316b
inheritance and, 6:460b–461a
peasant, 4:146a-b, 595a-b, 603b–604a
size of, and land reclamation, 10:278b
urban, 4:602b–603b
vs. class consciousness, 3:411b, 412b–413a
see also Marriage, Western European; Paston family, letters; Patrician, urban
see also Betrothal; Children; Divorce; Genealogy; Household management; Marriage; Men; Women
Family archives. *See* Archives, private
Family law, Jewish, **4:605b–608a**
Family names, inheritance and, 6:459b
Family sagas, Icelandic, **4:612a–619b**
biographic, 4:612b–613b
chronicles of community feuds, 4:613b–614a
classification of, 10:610b
erotic elements in, 4:612b–613b
ethical outlook, 4:614b–615a
form, 4:617b–618a
kings' sagas and, 4:618a
origins, 4:616b–618a
as reflection of Icelandic society, 4:618a-b
relation to oral tradition, 4:616b–617b
revelation of character in, 4:615b–616b
skald sagas, 6:29b
in skaldic poetry, 11:321b
Skjǫldunga saga, 11:328a-b
as sources for early *rímur,* 10:402a-b
use of prose in, 4:617b–618a
violence in, 4:614a-b
Famine
in Byzantium, 1:79b
in Germany, 14th century, 1:94b
in Islamic world, **5:1a–3a**, 9:685b
cannibalism and, 5:2a
causes of, 5:1a-b, 2b
death rates and, 5:1b
economic effects, 5:1b
economic and political causes, 5:2b
effects on children, 5:2b
effects on family and society, 5:1b–2a, 2b
effects on peasants, 5:1a-b
in Fatimid empire, 5:27a-b
plagues and, 5:1a, 2b
prostitution and, 5:2a
religion and, 5:2a-b
role of Nile River, 5:1a, 2a
population decline and, 4:142a
in Western Europe, **5:3a–9b**, 9:676b
cannibalism and, 5:6a, 7b
causes of, 5:3a–4a, 5a–9a
climate and, 5:3a-b, 6b
crime increase and, 5:8a
death rates and, 5:6a-b, 7b–8a
effect on fertility, 5:5a
effect on population levels, 5:3a, 5a-b, 8a–9a
in English microeconomy, 5:8b
famine of 1315-1317, 12:318b
grain monoculture and, 5:3a-b, 6b
history, 5:5a–9a, 174b, 177b, 179b, 647b
Italy, 14th century, 7:8b
livestock depletion and, 5:8a
medieval diet and, 5:4b–5a
in Paris (1314-1317), 9:405b
social problems due to, 5:4a-b
town food supplies, 5:3b–4a
transportation system and, 5:3b, 6a-b
wheat prices and, 5:4a-b, 7a-b
Fan vault. *See* Vault
Fanāᵓ, al- (nothingness), in the Islamic doctrine of resurrection, 10:341a
Fangot (unit of measure), 12:592b
Fann (fairy), 6:550b–551a
Fanon. *See* Vestments, liturgical

Fantasmata, 8:26b, 27a
Faqīr. *See* Dervish
Fārābī, al-, **5:9b–12a**, 6:584a, 7:151b, 10:13b
  Arabic rhetoric and, 10:345b
  on astrology, 1:617b
  Catalog of the Sciences, 11:441a
  commentaries on Aristotle, 5:10a, 10:357b, 11:84b
  commentaries on Plato, 5:10a
  contribution to Islamic logic, 7:640b
  on *dūnāy,* 8:612b
  eschatology of, 5:10b
  al-Ghazālī and, 1:459a
  on harp, 8:611b
  Ibn Sīnā and, 11:304a, 305b
  *Iḥṣā*ᵓ *al-*ᶜ*ulūm,* 4:445a-b, 5:11b, 8:563a
    optical theory, 9:242a
  influence on other scholars of, 5:10b
  Ismailism and, 6:618a
  *Kitāb iḥṣā*ᵓ *al-īqā*ᶜ*āt,* 5:11b, 6:501a
  *Kitāb al-īqā*ᶜ*āt,* 5:11b, 6:501a
  Kitāb al-mūsīqī al-kabīr (*Grand Book of Music*), 5:11b, 6:500b–501a, 8:563a, 610a, 611b
  on knowledge, 1:458b, 459a
  on music, 5:11a–12a, 8:566a, 566b
    *īqa*ᶜ theory, 5:11b
  musical treatises of, 8:640a-b
  Neoplatonic views of, 5:10a-b, 9:100a, 699b
  philosophical writings, 5:9b–10b, 9:569b–570a
  political theories of, 5:10b
  on revelation, 5:10b
  schooling, 5:9b
  tone system, 8:122a
  on virtue, 5:10b
Faraḥnāma. *See* Abū Bakr al-Muṭahhar Jamālī
Faraj ben Solomon. *See* Ferragut
Faraj, Ibn al-, attribution of Arabic chronicle of the Cid, 11:457a
Faraj, al-Nāṣir, Mamluk sultan, 8:74b–75a
  reign of, 3:399b–400a
Faral, Edmond, Latin texts published by, 1:553b–554a
Farāmarz-nāma, 6:507a
Faras, Nubian Christian site, 3:315a
Faras Cathedral, murals, 9:199a
Farazdaq, al-, 1:400a, **5:12a–13b**
  Alid sympathies of, 5:12b
  enemies of, 5:12b
  Jarīr and, 5:12b
  origin of his name, 5:12a
  poetry of, 5:12b–13a
  as recorder of Islamic history, 5:13a
  Umayyad caliphs and, 5:12b–13a
Farces, **5:13b**
  France, 4:265b
Farcing, **5:13b–14a**
  Tropes to the Proper of the Mass and, 12:211b
  troping and, 5:13b
Farḍ, 7:616b
Fardalfus Abbas, **5:14a**
Faremoutiers (monastery: France), 12:683a
Farghānā, **5:14a–15a**
  appanage system in, 5:14b
  cities of, 5:14b
  conquered by al-Mahdī, 8:47b
  Kāsān (major city), 5:14b
  Muslim conquest of, 5:14b
  rule by *dahāqīn,* 5:14b
  socioeconomic attributes, 5:14a-b
  under Karakhanid Turks, 5:14b
  under the Mongol Genghisids, 5:14b–15a
  under the Mongol Qara Khiṭāy, 5:14b
Farghānī, Muḥammad ibn Kathīr al-, 1:620b
  astronomical summary
    translated into Hebrew, 11:90b
    translated into Latin as *Rudimenta astronomica,* 1:612a
Fargot (unit of measure), 12:592b
Farhād (general of Xusrō II Abarwēz), 11:597b–598a
Fāriḍ, Ibn al-, allegorical odes of, 1:402a
Fārisī, Kamāl al-Dīn al-
  astronomical tables of translated into Hebrew, 11:91a
  Kitāb al-manāẓir, commentary on, 9:241b
  on the rainbow, 9:246a, 11:87a
  Tanqīḥ al-manāẓir, 9:245b–246a
    influence of, 9:246a-b
Farlati, on Tomislav, 4:5a
Farmers' Law, **5:15a-b**, 7:390b
  attributed to Justinian II, 5:15a
  Byzantine social structure and, 5:15a-b
  derivation of, 1:99a
  see also Byzantine law
Faroe Islands
  colonized, 4:554b
  in literature, 4:580b–581a
  Viking navigation and, 12:420a, 420b, 426a, 426b
Faroese ballads, **5:15b–17b**, 7:218b
  characters and plots, 5:15b
  compiled by Ulricus Hammershaimb, 5:16a, 17a
  dance and, 11:3b
  Danish influences on, 5:17a-b
  discovered by P. E. Müller, 5:16a
  earliest texts of, 5:16a-b
  Folkesangen paa Færøerne, 5:16b
  Føroya kvæði: Corpus carminum færoensium, 5:16a–17b
  Grundtvig and Bloch's compendium, 5:16a–17b
  Icelandic influences on, 5:17a-b
  kempuvísa (heroic ballad), 5:15b
  Nordic influences on, 5:16b–17a
  origins of, 5:16b–17b
  satirical ballads (*tættir*), 5:17b
  Sigurd and, 11:290a
  "Sjúrðar kvæði," 5:16a–17a
  village social life and, 5:15b–16a
  see also Scandinavian literature, ballads
Farquhar Maccintsacairt, earl of Ross, 11:106b
Farrukhī, 6:507b
Fārs, **5:17b–18a**
  decline of, 5:18a
  during Buyid dynasty, 2:435b, 5:18a
  pre-Islamic rule, 5:17b–18a
  under Iskandar Sulṭān, 12:57a
Fās. *See* Fēs
Fasani, Ranieri, 6:635a-b, 662b
Fascicule (unit of measure), 12:590a
Fascinatio. *See* Evil eye
Fashion. *See* Costume
Faṣl al-maqāl. *See* Rushd, Ibn
Fasti. *See* Ovid
Fasting
  Christian, 3:580b–581a, **5:18a–19b**
    before the Eucharist, 5:18b
    by catechumens, 5:18b
    development of medieval discipline, 5:18a-b
    during Lent, 5:18b
    easing of rules, 5:18b, 19a-b
    exemption from, 5:19a
    monastic, 5:19a-b
    other seasonal and occasional fasts, 5:18b–19a
    as penitential discipline, 5:18b, 19a, 6:448a
    Rule of St. Benedict, 5:19a
    see also Ember days; Fishponds; Lent; *Quattuor temporum*
  Islamic, **5:19b–21a**, 6:582a
    ᶜĀshūrāᵓ, 10:254a
    by pilgrims, 5:19b–20a
    Day of Atonement, 10:254a
    during Ramadan, 5:19b, 20a-b, 7:618a-b, 10:254a–255a
    exemptions from, 5:20a-b
    intention (*nīya*), 10:254a, 255a
    obligatory fasts, 5:19b
    as penance, 5:19b
    recommended fasts, 5:19b–20a
    stipulations and requirements, 5:20a
    taqwā (heedfulness of God) and, 5:20a
  see also Feasts and festivals; Hermits
Fastnachtspiel
  in secular German drama, 4:271a, 11:367b
    content of, 4:272a
  Wunderer as, 12:704b, 705a
Fastolf, Sir John, John Paston I and, 9:450b
Fatāwā. *See* *Fatwā*
Fate. *See* Fortune
Fates of the Apostles, The, Cynewulf and, 1:278a
Fatḥ ibn Khāqān, al-, al-Mutawakkil and, 8:654b
Fath al-Rabbani, al-. *See* Jīlānī, ᶜAbd al-Qādir al-
Fatḥ-nāma. *See* Imrānī
Father, authority of. *See* Power, paternal
Fathers of the church. *See* Church fathers
Fathom (unit of measure), 12:588a
Fatiḥ MSS, Arabic numerals in, 1:386a-b
Fatimid art and architecture, **5:21a–24a**
  in Cairo, 5:21b–23a (*illus.*)
  decorative arts, 6:609b
  influence of, 5:21a
  jewelry, 5:379a
  mashhads (funerary monuments), 5:21b

monumental Arabic writing, 5:23a (*illus.*)
mosque of Ṣāliḥ Ṭalaᵓiᶜ, 5:21b
palace architecture, 6:608a-b
Palatine Chapel paintings, 5:22a (*illus.*), 23b
private arts, 5:22a-b (*illus.*), 23b
religious, 6:608b
style of, 5:23a-b
textile arts, 5:23b–24a
Fatimids, **5:24a–30a**, 11:137a–138a
Abbasids and, 6:590a
administration of, 6:590b–591a
dawāwīn (ministries), 5:25b
reforms, 5:25b
vizier's role, 2:44b, 5:27b–28a
Armenians and, 1:485a
army, 12:552b
Assassins and, 5:28b
Beirut and, 2:164a
Berbers and, 11:561a
in Cairo, 3:13b–14a, 5:21b, 25b
caliphate of, 3:50a-b, 6:73b
cavalry, 3:209a
Christians under, 5:26b–27a
coins of, 8:423b, 424 (*illus.*)
conquest of Egypt, 3:50b, 4:405b–406a
costumes, 3:618a
in Damascus, 4:82a, 83a
defeat by Saladin, 10:625a
derivation of name, 5:24a
Egypt under, 1:11a, 5:24a, 25b, 26a-b
empire of, 5:24a, 29a-b (map)
end of influence in Muslim West, 5:28a
establishment of schools, 4:407a
famines suffered by, 5:27a-b
Idrisids and, 6:413a-b
in Ifrīqiya, 6:414b, 415a
Islamic navies and, 9:75a-b
Ismailism and, 6:587b, 614b, 616a–618a, 11:137a-b, 227b
Jews under, 5:26b–27a, 7:83b–84a, 97b–98a, 104a
communal self-government and, 7:73b–74a
origin of office of nagid, 9:52b
Kharijite insurgence against, 5:25a
Kutāma Berbers and, 2:186a
last caliphs, 5:29a-b
last viziers, 5:29a-b
libraries under, 7:273b, 561b
mamlūks and, 5:26a-b
Mecca and, 8:240b
millennialism and, 8:389a-b
Muḥammad ibn Ismāᶜīl and, 5:24b, 6:615a
Nizār's dispossession, 5:28b
origins of, 1:175a, 375a, 5:24a-b
Palestine and, 5:26b, 28a
as patrons of the arts, 5:21a-b
propaganda mission (*daᶜwa*), 5:25b, 28a
al-Qāᵓim, Abbasid caliph, and, 5:25a
al-Qayrawān under, 10:233a
rejection of Abbasid legitimacy, 1:9a, 11b
relations with
Byzantine Empire, 5:26b, 28a, 12:744b
Yemen, 12:724a
Zirids, 12:744a, 744b
Saladin and, 2:23a, 4:31a, 39a
in Sanᶜa, 10:647a-b
Seljuks of Syria and, 11:155a
Sicily and, 11:262a, 262b
Sunnis under, 5:26b–27a, 28a
Syrian rule of, 5:26a-b, 28a, 6:82b
ṭirāz formulas and, 12:61a-b (*illus.*)
trade route to India and, 2:33a
use of the title sultan, 11:504b–505a
vs. Abbasids, on Red Sea, 11:247a
vs. Basil II, 2:119a
vs. al-Ḥasan al-Aᶜṣam, 5:26a
vs. Ikhshidids, 6:416b, 417a
vs. Qarmatians, 5:26a
vs. Umayyads, in al-Maghrib, 6:413a-b
see also ᶜAzīz biᵓllāh, Nizār Abū Manṣūr, al-; Badr al-Jamālī; Lebanon;
Fatrasies. See Beaumanoir, Philippe de; Trouvères
Fatt (unit of measure), 12:584b
Fatwā, **5:30a–32a,** 6:581b, 8:58b
Abu 'l-Suᶜūd as *shaykh al-islām,* 5:32a
authority of muftis and qadis, 5:30b
decline of importance of, 5:32a
development of new law by means of, 5:30a-b, 31a
divorce, 11:631a
handbooks and manuals created, 5:31a-b
ijtihād as requirement for issuing, 5:31a
in Islamic schools, 11:67b
not used as legal precedents, 5:31b
office of *futyā* instituted, 5:31b
under Ottoman sultans, 5:31b–32a
see also Muftis
Faucard, 7:324 (*illus.*), 325a
Fauchard. *See Faucard*
Fauchée (unit of measure), 12:587a
Faula, La. See Torroella, Guillem de
Faust theme, first appearance of in Byzantine texts, 8:19a
Faustinianus, legend of, in *Kaiserchronik,* 7:205b–206a
Faustus of Byzantium. *See* Pᶜawstos Buzand
Faustus of Riez, **5:32b**
Fauvel, Roman de, 1:189b, 545b, 548b, 553a, **5:32b–33b,** 9:711a
intended audience of, 5:33a
lais in, 7:316b
musical interpolations of, 5:32b–33a
Philippe de Vitry and, 12:482a
as underground document, 5:33a
versions
by Chaillou de Pesstain, 5:33a
by Gervais du Bus, 5:32b–33a
Faux-bourdon, Guillelmus Monachus on, 8:648a
Favolello. See Latini, Brunetto
Fawānīs. See Lighting devices, Islamic
Fayᵓ, 11:667b
Fazārī, al-, Zanj and, 12:739a
Fazienda de Ultra Mar, 11:414a, 432a
Fazio degli Uberti, 6:651b
Dittamondo, 6:632a-b, 670a
Fealty, oaths of, under William I of England, 4:461b
Feast of Asses, 5:36a
Feast days
in Islamic calendar, 3:27a
in Jewish calendar, 3:27a
in reckoning calendar, 3:21b–22a
Feast of Fools, 5:36a
celebration of, 8:28b
Feast of Immolation, 8:560b
Feast of the Nativity. *See* Christmas
Feast of the Sacrifice (Islam), 7:618b
Feasts and festivals
allegorical banquet dishes, 5:35a
Byzantine, iconostasis and, 6:409b–410a
Charles V of France and Emperor Charles IV, 5:34b–35a
courses, 3:581b–582a
Eastern church, Twelve Great Feasts, Transfiguration, 12:125b–126a
ecclesiastical, 3:580b
entertainment during, 4:287a-b
Islamic, **5:38a–41a,** 5:38b (*illus.*)
alms (*zakāt* and *ṣadaqa*) given at, 5:38a–39a
ᶜaqīqah, 5:39a, 40b
associated with Muḥammad, 5:39b–40a
associations with pilgrimage, 5:39a-b
Christian festivals celebrated by Muslims, 5:40a
circumcision (*khitān, ṭahāra*), 5:40b
customs and practices of the *ᶜīd,* 5:38b
in Egypt, 4:589b
fairs and, 4:588b
family celebrations, 5:40b
ᶜīd al-fiṭr after Ramadan, 10:254b
khuṭba at, 5:38a
New Year's days, 5:40a-b
Nile River flooding, 5:40b
prayer during, 5:38a-b, 39b
sacrifices during, 5:39a
Sufi practices at, 5:40a
travel to and from the *muṣallā* during, 5:38b–39a
protocol of, 3:581a-b
service at, 3:583b
songs for, 5:440b
Western European, **5:33b–38a,** 5:34a (*illus.*)
commercial effects of, 5:33b–34a
disruption of work by, 5:33b–34a, 36a
excesses during, 5:34a-b
fairs and, 4:582b, 583b, 584a
fertility rites, 5:35a-b
interdict and, 6:497a
jurisdiction concerning, 5:34a
pagan rites adapted to, 5:34b–36b
playacting at, 5:34b–35a, 36a, 37b
political fetes, 5:34b–35a
wassailing at, 5:35a-b, 37b
widespread persistence and identity of, 5:34b
see also Carnival; Cookery; Fasting

Feate of Gardeninge, The. See Gardener, Jon
Febrer, Andreu, 3:171a
Fecunda ratis. See Egbert of Liège
Fedele d'Amore (Italian secret society), 9:2b
Federates of the Roman Empire. *See* Roman Empire, federate allies
Fee simple, forfeiture of, 6:428a
Feet, washing of, **5:41a–42b**
artistic expression of, 5:42a-b
baptism and, 2:83b, 5:41b
in Celtic church, 3:230b
Christ's *mandatum,* 5:41a-b
cleansing of sins and, 5:42a
clerical spirituality and, 5:42a
condemnation by Council of Elvira, 5:41b
Congregavit or *Ubi caritas* chant and, 5:42a-b
Holy Thursday *mandatum,* 5:42a
incense and, 6:432a
in Last Supper iconography, 7:344a
mandatum fratrum, 5:41b–42a
mandatum pauperum cotidianum, 5:41b
as monastic ritual, 5:41b–42a
in sacramental theology, 5:42a
on Saturday before Palm Sunday, 5:42a
Feidlimid mac Crimthainn, 4:493a
war with Uí Néill, 12:242b
Felim O'Connor of Connacht, king, 6:518b
Félin (unit of measure), 12:594a
Félire Oengusso Céli Dé, 7:615a-b
see also Martyrology, Irish
Felix II, pope
Gelasius I and, 5:374a
imperial power and, 3:11a
Felix V, pope, 3:653b–654a
election of, 3:366b
extension of Savoyard rule by, 7:9b
Felix culpa, Exsultet and, 2:178a
Felix, Minucius, Christian movement and, 3:334b
Felix of Nola
Bede on, 2:155a
homilies on by St. Paulinus of Nola, 9:471b
Felix of Toledo, bishop, biography of Julianus of Toledo, 7:181b
Felix of Urgel, bishop, defense of adoptionism, 1:57b, 6:194a, 12:190b
Felix Vita Guthlaci. See Guthlac, St.
Felony, **5:42b–43b**
emergence of, 5:42b
enlargement of category, 5:43a
Henry II of England and, 5:43a
origin of term, 5:42b–43a
punishment for, 5:42b–43a
treason and, 12:165a-b, 166b–167a
trespass and, 12:185b
trial, 12:168a-b
Felucca, lateen sail, 7:344a
Femegericht, 9:296a
Feminism
Christine de Pizan's espousal of, 3:662a
Hadewijch of Antwerp, 6:44a
Jerome and, 7:57b, 58a
see also Antifeminism; Women, status of
Femme sole, 4:603a
Fen Country. *See* Fenland
Fenari Isa Camii, marquetry work, 2:455a
Fencing, 5:348a-b
swords and, 11:549a, 551b
Fenestellae, in containers of relics, 1:221b
Feng-huang. *See* Phoenix
Fenian poetry, **5:43b–47b**, 6:549a
Battle of Ventry tale, 5:45a
bruidhean (supernatural) tales, 5:44b–45a
Cailte mac Rónáin in, 5:44a
as central concern of Fenian heroes, 5:45a-b
conflictual realities in, 5:44b
early manuscripts containing, 5:43b, 46b–47a
examples of, 5:46a–47a
fían (Finn mac Cumaill's band), 5:44a–45a
fili (poet, seer) in, 5:45a-b
Finn mac Cumaill in, 5:44a, 45b–46a
in Gaelic folklore, 5:43b
laoithe (ballads), 5:43b–44a, 46b–47a
lyrical and nature poetry, 5:46a-b
mantic utterances in, 5:45b–46a
Oisín as author of, 5:44a
oral and literary traditions, 5:43b–44a, 46b–47a
otherworld and, 5:44b–45b
Patrick as recipient of, 5:44a
pre-Christian roots of, 5:43b
rites of passage and, 5:44b–45a
roscada, 5:45b–46a
similarity to *dindshenchas* and "hermit" poetry, 5:46a
similarity to other heroic tales, 5:44a
social values in, 5:45b
Táin bó Cúailnge and, 11:580a
unconventional nature of, 5:45b–46a
way of life presented in, 5:44b–45a
Fenland, drainage of, 6:559a
Fenn, John (editor of Paston letters), 9:448b–449a
Fenollar, Mossèn Bernat, 3:171b
Fenrir. *See* Fenris wolf
Fenris wolf, **5:47b–48a**, 11:26a-b, 28a
confusion about name, 5:47b
in *Ragnarǫk,* 10:248a
Thor and, 12:45a
in *Vafþrúðnismál,* 12:344a
Feoda Campanie, 3:245b
Feodor Krestianin, 8:573b
Feodosiya. *See* Caffa
Feofan Greek. *See* Theophanes the Greek
Ferdinand I of Aragon, king
difficulties in Catalonia, 1:417b
election of, 1:417b
successes of, 1:417b
Vincent Ferrer and, 12:453a
Ferdinand II of Aragon, king. *See* Ferdinand V of Castile, king
Ferdinand I of Castile and León, king, 2:126b, 9:682b
art under, 10:114b–115a
ivory carvings made for, 7:27b
kingdom of Navarre and, 9:69a, 69b
Portugal under, 10:38b
rule of, 3:128b–129a
Ferdinand II of Castile, king, Seville and, 11:213b
Ferdinand III of Castile, king
church taxation and, 11:610a
conquests of, 3:135a
of Mudejars, 11:378a
fuero and, 5:309b–310a
Genoese and, 4:557b
grandfather of Don Juan Manuel, 8:94a
Jews and, 7:81a-b
as a patron of poetry, 11:450a
rule of, 3:133b–134a
Siete partidas and, 11:282b
Spanish law and, 7:521b–522a
sword of, 11:549a
vernacular legal works and, 11:414a
Ferdinand IV of Castile, king
Don Juan Manuel and, 8:94a-b
literary production of his reign, 11:415b, 416a
Moors and, 11:378b
rule of, 3:134b
Ferdinand V of Castile, king
chronicles of reign, 11:436a
in Hernando del Pulgar's chronicle, 11:434a
inquisition and, 6:488b
Jews and, 4:564b, 7:77b, 83a, 9:111b, 112a
kingdom of Navarre and, 9:72a
literary developments and, 11:422a–425a
marriage to Isabella, 3:138b
Castilian Spanish and, 6:435b
Mudejars and, 11:380b
Order of Calatrava and, 3:17a
Spanish law and, 7:523b
Valencia and, 12:347b, 349a-b
Ferdinand I (Habsburg) of Germany, emperor
Hungary and, 6:349a, 350a
rule of Austria, 6:43a
Ferdinand I of Portugal, king
alliance with England, 10:52a-b
war with Castile, 10:52a-b
Ferdinand de Antequera. *See* Ferdinand of Aragon, Valencia, and Catalonia, king
Ferdinand of Aragon, Valencia, and Catalonia, king, victories in Granada, 3:138a
Fergana. *See* Farghānā
Fergus, 1:267b
Fergus of Dál Riata, king, 4:78b
Fergus of Galloway, rebellion of 1160 and, 11:107a
Fergus Mór mac Eirc, 4:78a
Ferguut, 1:572a, 4:318b
"Ferm voler, Lo." *See* Arnaut Daniel
Ferme leases, terms of contract, 11:680b
Fernán González of Castile, count
rule of, 3:128a
unification of Castile by, 3:128a

Fernán González, Poema de, **5:48a-b**, 8:281b, 11:409a, 411a, 411a-b, 412b, 438a, 453a
anomaly of, 5:48a
authorship of, 5:48a
Castilian history and, 5:48a-b
meter of, 5:48a
prayer of the Christians, 11:450a
Fernández de Constantin, Juan, 3:63b
Fernández de Heredia, Juan, 11:418b
historical works of, 9:511a
translations into Aragonese Spanish, 11:457a
of Guido delle Colonne, 11:458a
Fernández de Jerena, Garci, in *Cancionero de Baena,* 11:419a
Fernández, Lucas, 11:425a
Fernández de Minaya, Lope, *Libro de confesión,* 11:443a
Fernando de la Cerda (*d.* 1270), sword of, 11:549b
Fernando of Córdoba, 11:407a
Fernando of Portugal, prince, Hurtere and, 4:559b
Fernando de Rojas. *See Celestina, La*
Ferragut (Faraj ben Solomon), translations by, 12:135b
Ferrand of Portugal, count of Flanders, 5:81a, 522a
Ferrara
Sephardic community in, 11:161b
war with Venice and, 12:391b
Ferrara Cathedral, Nicholaus da Verona and, 10:501b–502a (*illus.*)
Ferrara, University of, 12:286a
Ferrara-Florence, Council of (1438–1447), 1:32b, 2:504a, **5:48b–49b**, 9:709b, 11:47a, 12:163b, 169b
attempts at reuniting church, 10:594a
condemnation of dualism, 4:297b
definiton of papacy at, 10:32a
Ferrara sessions, 5:48b–49a
Florence sessions, 5:49a
Greek church and, 2:465b–466a, 469b–470a, 3:366b, 653b, 9:562b
humanism and, 7:1a
importance of, 5:49b
John VIII Palaiologos at, 7:129a
Laetentur coeli, 9:709b
papal authority and, 3:518b–519a
significance of, 3:653b
Mark Eugenikos and, 8:143b
Maronites at, 7:532b
Metropolitan Isidore of Kiev at, 6:563a
Novgorod and, 9:196b
papalist doctrine of succession, 4:378a
Patriarch Joseph II at, 7:150b
see also Bessarion
Ferrer I (the Elder), Jaime, **5:49b–50a**
Last Supper, 5:50a-b (*illus.*)
Ferrer II (the Younger), Jaime, 5:49b
Ferrer Bassa. *See* Bassa, Ferrer
Ferrer, Boniface, Bible translation, 2:215b, 3:167a
Ferrer, Francesc
Conhort, 3:173b
Romanç del setge de Rodas, 3:171b
Ferrer, Vincent, St. *See* Vincent Ferrer, St.
Ferret, domestication of, Northern Europe, 1:95b
Ferretti, Paolo, centonization by, 3:235b
Ferrús, Pero, in *Cancionero de Baena,* 11:419a
Ferskeyt (a *rímur* meter), 10:404b–405a
compared with Latin and Gaelic meters, 10:405a
Ferteth of Strathearn, rebellion of 1160 and, 11:107a
Fertile Crescent. *See* Mesopotamia
Fertilizer
in winemaking, 12:653a
see also Agriculture
Fēs, **5:50a–51b**, 8:15a, 15b
ʿAbd al-Ḥaqq rules, 5:51b
as Al-ʿĀliya, 5:50a-b
Almoravid rule of, 1:199a, 5:50b
al-ʿAṭṭārīn Madrasa, *naqsh ḥadīda* decoration in, 9:60a-b (*illus.*)
Berber rule of, 5:50b–51b
colleges created by Marinids, 5:51a
conflicts over, 5:50b
conquered by ʿAbd al-Muʾmin, 1:194a
construction of Fās al-Jadīd (New Fēs), 5:51a
founded by Idrīs ibn ʿAbd Allah, 5:50a
Idrisids in, 6:413a, 414a
role of *shurafāʾ* (nobles) in, 5:51a-b
importance of, 5:50b
Jewish community in, 5:51a
madrasas in, 6:611b
Marinid occupation, 8:138a, 139b, 140a-b
as Marinids' capital, 5:51a-b
patronage
by Almohads, 5:50b–51a
by Umayyads of Córdoba, 5:50b
shurafāʾ, 8:139b
sūq, 11:514b
trade routes important to, 5:50a, 51a
Wattasid rule of, 5:51b
see also Meknes
Festival of Weeks. *See* Shavuot
Festivals. *See* Feasts and festivals
Fet des Romains, Li, 2:236b, **5:51b–52a**
Caesar's biography in, 5:51b–52a
didactic intent of, 5:52a
political use of, 5:52a
purpose for translation, 5:290b
Fetch. *See Fylgja*
Fethiye Camii (monastery: Constantinople), parekklesion, mosaics, 2:448b–449a
Feu. *See* Tenure of land
Feudal dominus. See Feudalism; Kingship
Feudal incidents, escheat, 4:509a
Feudalism, **5:52a–57a**
abuse of by lords, 5:53b
aids, 5:53a-b, 55a, 173a
lord's ransom, 10:319a-b
armed retainers and, 5:52b–53b
Armenia, 1:489a
church, 1:503b, 504b
Asturias-León, 1:629a
Bohemia-Moravia, 2:300b–301a, 302a
breakup of Roman Empire and, 5:52b
Byzantine *pronoia* and, 10:136a
Capetian monarchy, 5:173a–174a
concepts of justice, 5:173a
feudal army, 5:173a
regalian rights, 5:173a
Castile, law and, 7:521b
Cilicia, 3:393b
Constitutio de feudis, 3:557b–558a
county and castellany government, 5:53b, 54b–55a
courtly love terminology and, 3:668b
Croatia, 4:8a-b
Cyprus, 4:71a–72a
under Lusignans, 7:689a
decline of
land reclamation and, 10:278a–279a
petty assizes, 9:547b
difficulties proving ownership, 5:55b
end of fragmentation, 5:55b
England, 5:54b–55b
"bastard," 7:664a
brought by William I, 7:433a-b
of church, 2:173b
common law and, 7:433a-b, 437b, 441b
Norman-Angevin, 4:463b, 470a
see also Magna Carta; Mainmort; Thegn
etymology of "feudal," 5:52a-b
family life and, 4:600b–601a, 608b
fief in, 5:52b–53b
fragmentation of political authority and, 5:52b–53b
France, 5:54a
knight-castellan relationship, 11:619a
representative assemblies and, 10:316b, 319a
southern French law and, 7:462a, 467a
frankalmoin, 5:209b–210a
Georgia, 5:407a, 419b, 11:587b
patroni and *qmani* in, 10:236b
see also Aznauri; Patronqmoba
Germany, 5:54a
early law codes and, 7:476b, 10:603a
post-Carolingian law and, 7:480a-b
under Frederick I Barbarossa, 5:213b
Hundred Years War and, 6:333a-b
Hungary, 6:339a, 341a, 349b
see also Familiaritas
influence in later centuries, 5:52b, 56a-b
inheritance and, 6:459a-b
inherited government and, 5:52b–53a
Iran, 6:504a
Italy, 5:54a-b
Jean d'Ibelin on, 6:390a-b
Kievan Rus, 1:100a-b, 7:249b, 251b
king's power, 5:53b–54a
knights' role and obligations, 5:53a, 54a, 7:276a–277b
legal procedures under, 5:55b
local lords and vassals, 5:52b–53b

Feudalism (*cont.*)
military
after Charlemagne, 12:558a-b
crusader states, 12:561a-b
England, 12:560b–561a
France, 12:559b
Germany, 12:561b–562a
Italy, 12:562a-b
Normans, 12:560a–561a
outside France, 12:559b–560a
Spain, 12:562b–563b
mining law and, 8:402a-b
modern state and, 5:56b
Morea, 7:378a-b
Navarre, 9:69a, 69b
Norman, 5:54a-b
French monarchy and, 9:164a, 168a-b
French provinces and, 9:164a-b
under Rollo, 9:161a
William I and, 9:166b
origins of
commendation, 3:490a–491b
role of cavalry, 3:201a-b
outside Europe, 5:56b
papal states, 9:387a
parish churches and, 9:413b–414a
parodied in Renard the Fox stories, 10:312a–314a
pilgrimage and, 9:656a-b
in poetry, 12:217a-b
Poland, 9:728b
prerogatives of lords, 5:53a-b
proof of *seisin* (possession), 5:55b
proprietary churches and, 9:412a
protection of clergy under, 5:55a-b
rear-fief defined, 5:56a
reconsolidation of sovereign states, 5:55b–56a
Scotland, 4:111a, 11:105b–107b
seigneurial taxation, 11:613a-b
serfdom and, 11:202a–203b
Sicily, 11:266a, 267b
slavery and, in Islamic world, 11:332b
Spain, 1:629a, 5:54b
hidalgos and *caballeros,* 12:563a
subinfeudation (rear-fief) problems, 5:55a
Sweden, 11:531b
terminology of, Italo-Romance language, 6:624a
Thessaly, 2:479a
travel and, serf escort duties, 12:152b, 157a-b
treason concept and, 12:165a-b
two levels of, 5:53b–54a
uniformity of, 11:203a
urbanization and, 3:416a-b
vassal rights, *diffidatio,* 12:165a
versus landlordism, 5:56a-b
Wales, marcher lords, 12:526a
wardship of underage and female heirs, 5:53b
Wendish, 12:617a
see also Ban; Fief; Liberty and liberties; Manorial system; Palatinates; Scutage; Vassals
Feuds, Icelandic sagas, 4:613b–614a
Feuerwerksbuch, 4:579a, 11:645b
Feurs, town walls of, 12:326a-b (*illus.*)
Fever. *See* Disease; Malaria; Plagues, European
Fez. *See* Fēs
Fez numerals. *See* Greek numerals
Ffordd y Brawd Odrig, 12:613a
Fiammetta (Boccaccio's literary character)
Amorosa visione, 2:281b
Elegia di Madonna Fiammetta, 2:282a-b
Filocolo, 2:279a–280a
Fian, 6:531a-b
Fibonacci, Leonardo, 1:436a, 9:664b
accounting functions, 1:38b
Flos, 8:213b
Frederick II and, 11:257b, 274a
influence on spread of Arabic numerals, 1:396a
Kuber quadratorum, 8:213b
Liber abaci, 1:38b, 396a, 8:213a, 10:474a
life of, 8:213a
Practica geometriae, 8:213a, 9:705a
Fibula, **5:57a-b**, 5:57b (*illus.*)
Carolingian, 5:377a
Dorestad, 5:377a
Frankish, 5:375b, 376b (*illus.*)
in migration period art, 8:364a-b (*illus.*), 365b (*illus.*)
Merovingian round gold, 8:368a
Ottonian, 5:377a
Roman, 5:375a
Visigothic, 12:467b
Fichet, Mamert, computus-type calendar by, 3:19a (*illus.*)
Ficino, Marsilio, 11:55a
Cosimo de' Medici and, 8:243a
Neoplatonism and, 9:95a, 101a
spiritual magic and, 8:39a-b
translator of Plato, 9:698b, 703a-b
Fiddle, 8:602 (*illus.*), 605a (*illus.*), 606b–607a, 12:180b
Jerome of Moravia on, 8:645a
Fideicommissary, 6:458b, 459b–460a
Fiedler, Veit, possible illustrator of *Ambraser Heldenbuch,* 1:229b
Fief, **5:57b–59b**
alodial property and, 5:59b
Champagne, 3:246 (map), 249a-b
confiscation of by lord, 5:59a
definition of, 5:53a, 57b
duties of fief holder, 5:59a
in England, *see also* Thegn
England as, 5:58b
estate as, 5:58a
etymology of, 5:57b, 7:353b
extent of in Europe, 5:59b
female heirs and, 5:58a-b
inheritance and, 5:53a-b, 58a-b, 6:459b
intangible rights of, 5:58a
Iranian, 6:504a
Irish, 6:518b
kingdom as, 5:58b
knights holding, 7:276a
military, Frankish, 12:558a
ministerials and, 8:405a
money, 5:58b, **5:59b–60b**
defined, 5:59b
demise of, 5:60b
as diplomatic instrument, 5:60a
feudal relations widened by, 5:60b
military service obtained by, 5:60a
payment of, 5:60a-b
persistence of feudalism and, 5:60b
Normandy as, 5:59a
papal, 5:58b
Innocent III and, 6:464b
rear-fief defined, 5:56a
Russia, 5:59b
Scotland as, 5:58b
Sicily as, 5:58b
as social and economic entity, 5:59a
soyurghal in the Timurid state, 12:57b
subinfeudation problems, 5:55a
see also Benefice; Feudalism; Scutage
Fief-rente. See Fief, money
Fiefs de service, 11:205b
see also Sergeant
Field systems, **5:60b–62b**
common-field, 5:61a-b
crop rotation and, 5:61a
defined, 5:60b–61a
documentation of, 5:61b–62a
East Anglian, 5:61a
evolution of rules governing, 5:61b
flexibility of, 5:61a
grazing rights and, 5:61a-b
increasing conformity of, 5:62a
infield-outfield, 5:61a-b, 12:445b
influence of lawyers on, 5:62a
Kent, 5:61a
northern England and Scotland, 5:61a
origins of, 5:61b
polyptycha, 4:511b
rundale, 5:61a
"sun division" and, 5:61b
villages and, 12:439b, 444b–446a
Wales, 5:61a
see also Pasture, rights of
Fierabras, 10:182b
Fieschi, Ottobono, cardinal. *See* Hadrian V, pope
Fieschi, Sinibaldo. *See* Innocent IV, pope
Fiesole, founding of in Boccaccio's *Ninfale fiesolano,* 2:282b
Fiesole, Andrea da. *See* Andrea da Firenze
Fiesole, Giovanni da. *See* Giovanni da Fiesole
Fig, growth of, 1:82b, 5:306a, 307b
Fight at Finnsburh, The, relation to *Beowulf,* 1:278a-b
Figural sculpture
Romanesque, 10:492b
on Chartres Cathedral, 10:499b (*illus.*)
Figure poems. See *Carmina figurata*
Fihrist, Al-. See Nadīm, Ibn al-
Fila, 6:556b
Filanger, Richard, 6:389b
Filelfo, Francesco, 9:703a
Fili (Irish poets), 2:105b
Filid, 6:543a, 544b
Filigree technique, 8:366a
Filioque, 4:74a, **5:62b–63a**
at First Council of Lyons, 3:642a
Byzantine exegesis and, 2:214b
in Byzantine rite, 3:632a
conflict over, 2:464b–465a, 489b

in Eastern-Western schism, 3:349a, 351a, 9:562a, 11:46a-b
evolution of doctrine, 5:62b–63a
Greek opposition to, 5:62b–63a, 9:599b
in Latin rite, 3:346a, 632b, 677a
Photian schism, 9:562a
substantiation of, patristic citations, 12:190a–191a, 195a
see also Leo III, pope; "Veni creator spiritus"
Filippi, Rustico, 6:649b
Filippo degli Agazzari, *Ensamples,* 11:281b
Fillastre, Guillaume, **5:63a-b**
appointed cardinal, 3:647a
at Council of Constance, 3:648a
Fille du conte de Ponthieu, adventure elements, 9:635a
Filocolo. See Boccaccio, Giovanni
Filostrato. See Boccaccio, Giovanni
Filotei (Romanian hymn writer), 10:510b
Fimbul winter, **5:63b–64a**
Gregory the Great on, 5:63b–64a
origin of myth, 5:63b
in *Ragnarǫk,* 10:248a
similarity to Persian mythology, 5:63b
Fimbulvetr. See Fimbul winter
"Fin amours en esperance." *See* Audefroy le Bastard
Fin'amor, 3:668a
in albas, 1:123a
Icelandic *mansöngvar* and, 10:406a
in Provençal language, 10:158b, 166b–167a, 171a, 176a-b
Raimon de Miraval on, 10:252a
in *Razón de amor,* 10:268b–269a
sexuality and, 3:669a-b
see also Courtly love
Finance
fairs and, 4:584a, 585b, 592b–593a
see also Banking
Finance, Islamic, 6:589a
under Abbasids, 6:590a
under Umayyads, 6:589b
Finance, royal
in England, 4:530b–533a
France, 4:532a
see also Taille
Hungary, 6:341a, 348b, 349b
Sicily, 4:532a, 11:268b
see also Financing under names of wars; Taxation
Find (Celtic god). *See* Lug
Fine, Oronce, 1:439a
Fines amouretes ai. See Adam de la Halle
Fingal Rónáin, 6:547b
Finger (unit of measure), 12:588a
Finial, **5:64a,** 5:64b *(illus.)*
Finiguerra, Maso, engraving and, 4:488b
Finland
north European trade and, 9:88b
relations with Sweden, 11:531a
Finn mac Cumhaill. *See* Fionn mac Cumhaill
Finnboga saga, **5:64a–65a**
Ála Flekks saga and, 1:116b
Kjalnesinga saga and, 7:274b
origins of, 5:64b
style of, 5:64b–65a
Þorsteinn goði in, 5:64b
Vatnsdæla saga and, 5:64b
Finnboga saga ramma. See Finnboga saga
Finnian of Clonard, 9:489a
Finnian of Moville
authorship of penitential, 9:489a
in literature, 6:540b
Finnian, Penitential of, 9:489a
Finno-Ugric languages, 6:434a, 444b
Hungarian and, 6:336b, 337a
Fionn mac Cumaill (mythical character), 6:525b, 528b–529a, 537a
in *Acallam na Senórach,* 6:531b, 549a
Fionn mac Cumhaill, 9:47b
Fionnlagh Ruadh, poems to a MacGregor chief, 11:115a
Fioravanti, Aristotele, **5:65a**
rebuilding Kremlin, 5:65a
Uspensky Cathedral, 8:496b
Fiore, paraphrase of *Roman de la Rose,* 6:631b–632a
Fiore, Il. See Durante
Fiore di virtù, 6:632a
Romanian translations, 10:511b
Fiorentino, Giovanni, *Pecorone,* 6:661a
Fioretti di San Francesco. See Actus beati Francisci et sociorum eius
Fiori e vita di filosafi ad altri savi ed imperadori, 6:659a
Fiorino, 8:421b
Fipple flute, 8:558b
Fiqh, 6:581a-b, 10:12b
in Islamic law, 7:485b
Fiqh al-absat, al-, 11:511b
Fiqh al-akbar, al-, 11:511b
Fír catha, 6:548b
Fír flathemon, 4:312b, 6:547b, 548b
Firdause. *See* Firdawsī
Firdaws, mosque at, 6:603a
Firdaws, al- (mausoleum: Aleppo), 2:21b
Firdawsī, Abu 'l-Qāsim al-
Gushtāsp and Katayoun, 7:285b
Shāhnāma and, 11:220b, 221a
see also Shāhnāma
Fire
building construction affected by, 3:560a-b
death by. *See* Burning
Firearms
armor and, 1:531b–532a
Ottomans and, 11:562a
Fireplace, 6:119b *(illus.)*
couvre-feu, 6:121b
danger of fires from, 6:121b
drying shelves, 6:122a
enclosed, 6:121b
hood, 6:121a
angle brackets for, 6:121b
integration with flue and stack, 6:121a
warming cupboards, 6:122a
Firi Aragonum. See Codex of Huesca
Firlot (unit of measure)
Edinburgh, 12:589a
Linlithgow, 12:589a
water of Tay and, 12:589a
Firmicus Maternus, Julius, **5:65b**
Matheseos libri VIII, 1:605a
Firmin de Belleval, treatise on calendar reform, 3:23a
Firmiter credimus. See Lateran Councils, Fourth
First Grammatical Treatise. See Grammatical Treatise, First
First Ottonian Tune. See Walther von der Vogelweide
First Philip's Tune. See Walther von der Vogelweide
First Romanesque, **5:65b**
Firūz Shāhnāma. See Shāhnāma
Fīrūzābād, **5:66a**
architecture of, 5:66a
founded by Ardešīr I, 5:66a
location of, 5:66a
Sasanian palace, 2:140a
Fīrūzābādī, al-, *Al-Qāmūs al-muḥīṭ,* 4:444a
Fís Adamnáin, 1:347b
Fisc, tax collection, 11:625b
Fiscal surveys, 4:137b–138b
Fish
trade in, 5:124a–125a
types and prices, 5:124a–125a
Fishacre, Richard
Aristotelian and Averroist precepts, 9:595a
Commentary on the Sentences of Peter Lombard, 4:246b
Fisheries, marine, **5:66a–73a**
economic role of, 5:66b–67a
fish products, 5:69a
fermented fish, 5:68b–69a
fish oil, 5:69a
fishing gear, 5:67b–68a, 69b–72a
fishing methods, 5:67a–68a, 69b–72a
Icelandic trade, 6:396b, 397a
mass fishes, 5:69a
Mediterranean methods and gear, 5:68a
Norway, 9:180b
preservation, 5:68a-b
salting, 5:68a-b, 124a, 10:630b
smoking, 5:68a
stockfish, 5:124a
terms for preserved fish, 5:68b
wind-drying, 5:68b
regulation of, 5:124a
Scandinavian trade with Baltic Germans, 6:91b
sources of information on, 5:66a-b
archaeological sources, 5:66b, 67b *(illus.)*
artistic and heraldic sources, 5:66a-b
written sources, 5:66a
stockfish trade, Norway, 9:181a, 185a
trade, 5:67a-b (map), 69a-b
before the Middle Ages, 5:69a
by fishmongers, 5:69b
central European, 5:69b
mass fishes and, 5:69a
northern European, 5:69a-b
Fisherman and the Jinnee, The, in *Thousand and One Nights,* 12:50b
Fishing
Byzantium, 1:79a
Fachschrifttum and, 4:579b
Russia, 1:100a

Fishlake, Thomas, translation of Walter Hilton's *Scale of Perfection* into Latin, 9:23b–24a
Fishponds, **5:73a–74b**
before the 12th century, 5:73a-b
carp (*Cyprinus carpio*) in, 5:73b
commercial, 5:73b–74b
design of, 5:73b–74a
distinguished from fisheries, 5:73a
Eastern European, 5:74a
English, 5:74b
fish other than carp in, 5:74a-b
importance during fasting, 5:73a
production methods for, 5:74a
Roman, 5:73a
specialized enterprises using, 5:74a
Western European, 5:73b–74a
Fitniki, 8:574b
Fity, 8:574b
Fitz Mary, Simon, 2:157a
Fitz Neale, Richard. *See* Fitz Nigel, Richard
Fitz Nigel, Richard, 5:544b
Dialogue of the Exchequer, 1:37b, 4:469b, 530b, 7:184a, 10:443b
Fitz Ralph, William, 11:160a
Fitz Waryn. See Foukes le Fitzwarin
Fitzgeralds, **5:74b–76a**, 6:517b, 518a, 519b
Desmond house, 5:75a, 8:532a
1st earl, 5:76a
3rd earl, 5:76a
end of, 5:76a
Lancastrian-Yorkist struggle and, 5:76a
Thomas, 5:75a, 6:524b
Kildare house, 5:75a–76a
conflict with de Burgh family, 5:75a
Garret Oge, 5:75b
Gerald, 5:75a
Great Earl (8th earl Gerald), 5:75b
John Fitzthomas, 5:75a-b
Maurice (grandson of Maurice I), 5:75a
pretenders Lambert Simnel and Perkin Warbeck, 5:75b
rebellion and decline of, 5:75b–76a
Thomas (Silken Thomas), 5:75b–76a
Thomas (son of Fitzthomas), 5:75b
under Henry VII, 5:75
Maurice I, 5:75a
Fitzgilbert, Richard de Clare. *See* Clare, Richard Fitzgilbert de
Fitzneal (Fitzneale), Richard. *See* Fitz Nigel, Richard
Fitzpeter, Geoffrey, as justiciar, 7:200b
Fitzralph, Richard, bishop of Armagh
John Wyclif and, 12:707b, 710a
Summa in quaestionibus armenorum, 4:548a
Fitzwalter, Robert
letter to William d'Albini, 7:662a
opposition to royal tallage, 7:661b
Fixed defenses. *See* Castles and fortifications
Fiziolog. See Physiologus
Fiziologul, 10:511b
Fjǫlsvinnsmál, 11:524a, 524b
Mímir in, 8:395b–396a
Fjósa ríma, illustration of the *ferskeyt* meter, 10:404b
Flabellum, 1:224b–225a, 3:298 (*illus.*), **5:76b**
Flacius Illyricus, Matthias, 7:371a, 12:670b
Flagellants, **5:76b–77a**
anti-Semitism and, 2:263a-b, 5:77a
Black Death and, 2:263a
condemned by Clement VI, 5:77a
Disciplinants of Santa Maria della Scala, 2:195b–196a
heretical, 5:77a
in Italy, 5:76b
of Abruzzi, 6:636a
at Perugia, 5:76b
at Siena, 6:636b–637a, 11:281a
Umbrian, 6:635a-b, 662b
in Jacopone da Todi's poetry, 7:34b
lauda and, 6:662a-b, 7:384a
in northern Europe, 5:76b–77a
in response to plague, 5:76b–77a
ritual performed by, 5:77a
suppression by Clement VI, 3:439b
Flail
as early medieval innovation, 12:80a
Islamic, 12:85a
Flambard, Ranulf, 7:199b
Flamberges, 11:549b
Flamboyant Style. *See* Gothic architecture
Flamenca, Romance of, **5:77b**, 10:183b–184b
anticlerical attitude in, 10:184a
fin'amor in, 10:184a
Flancards, 1:529a
Fland, Robert, on Swineshead, 11:535b
Flanders, county of, **5:77b–83a**, 5:78a-b (map)
alliance with John of England, 5:81a
Black Death in, 2:261a
in Carolingian Empire, 5:77b
cities
political power of, 5:80a
rivalry of, 5:82a
during Hundred Years War, 5:82a-b
expansion in 9th and 10th centuries, 5:78a–79b
fairs, 4:584b, 585a-b, 12:108b, 110b
government structure in 12th century, 5:79b
guilds, 12:119a
history
to 10th century, 5:77b–78b
in 11th and 12th centuries, 5:79a–81a
in 13th century, 5:81a-b
in 14th century, 5:81b–82b
homage to Louis VI, 7:673b–674a
land reclamation, 12:579a
Leliart-Clauwaert struggle, 5:81b–82a
linguistic frontier in, 5:78a-b
local government, 4:379a-b
recovery of jurisdiction, 5:159b
medical literature, 10:289a
neighboring states and, 5:80a-b
office of seneschal and, 11:160a-b
Pastoureaux uprising (1251), 9:452b–453a
peace of 1312, 11:713b
Peace of God and, 9:474b
plagues in, 9:679a, 681b–682b
reclamation of sea land in, 5:80a
relations with
England, 5:78a, 79a, 6:332a
France, 2:387b, 5:80b–82a, 82b, 12:732a
Scotland, 11:112a
royal wardship of, 5:165a
Sluter in, 11:349a
taxation, rebellion against, 5:186b
tenurial development, 11:681a-b
textile industry
export-oriented, 11:707a, 711b
fulling mills, 11:707a
guilds, 11:713a–714a
industrial conflict, 11:713a–714a
textiles trade, 12:153b–154a, 157b–158a
trade and commerce
with Baltic Germans, 6:91b
revival in 10th–11th centuries, 5:79b–80a
wool, 5:80a, 81a, 82a
treaty with Philip IV, 8:137b
under Burgundian dukes, 5:82b–83a
Ypres and, 12:731b
urban rebellions and civil war, 11:714a
village comital revenues, 10:274a
waterworks, 12:577a-b, 578b
weakness of German and French lords, 5:79a
see also Bruges; Flemish art; Vermandois
Flateyjarbók
Eddic poetry preserved in, 4:387b
Færeyinga saga and, 4:581a
Grœnlendinga saga and, 12:456b
Hyndluljóð and, 6:385a
Oláfs saga Tryggvasonar and, 9:177b
Orkneyinga saga, 9:279a
preservation of *Helga Þattr Þórissonar,* 6:148a
text of *Hallfreðar saga* in, 6:81a
þættir in, 12:3b, 4b
Vǫluspá and, 12:492a
Flathemon, 6:548a
Flavian, patriarch
Eutyches and, 3:629a, 4:524a
Pope Leo I (the Great) and, 7:542a
Flavian Tome. See Leo I (the Great), pope
Flavio di Giola of Amalfi, 3:506b
Flavius of Châlon-sur-Sâone, bishop, 6:381a
Flavius Claudius Julianus. *See* Julian the Apostate
Flavius Petrus Sabbatius Justinianus. *See* Justinian I, Byzantine emperor
Flax, **5:83b–84a**
cultivation of, 5:83b
for textiles, 6:154a
exported from Egypt, 12:107b
hemp and, 3:88a-b
linen weaving from, 5:83b–84a
production of, 5:83b
products derived from, 5:83b
see also Linen
Flax breaker, mechanical, invention of, 7:585a

Flea, as host of plague bacillus, 2:257b, 258a
Flèche, **5:84a**, 5:84a (*illus.*)
Fleck, Konrad, **5:84a-b**, 5:454b
Floire und Blanscheflur, 5:84a-b
influences upon, 5:84b
see also Floris
Fled Bricrenn, 6:527a-b, 549a
Flemings, in Azores, 4:559a-b
Flemish art
Haarlem school of painting, 9:312b
painting, **5:85a–87b**
in Bruges, 2:387b–388a
by Pleydenwurff, 9:710a-b (*illus.*)
commissions by Claus Sluter, 5:85a-b
"Flemish" defined, 5:85a
Ghent-Bruges school, 8:167b
Gothic style, 5:603b, 611a–612a
iconic character, 12:623b
influence of on Pedro de Córdoba, 9:483b
manuscript illumination and, 8:109b–110a
oils, 9:223b
under Philip the Bold, 5:85a-b
under Philip the Good, 5:85b–86b
woodcut and, 12:691b
sculpture, Richard de Beauchamp's tomb and, 7:321b
woodcut, 12:692b, 693a
Flemish language, Bible translated into, 2:215a
Fleta, **5:88a**
authorship of, 5:88a
Britton and, 5:88a
on Exchequer Court, 4:533b
origins of English parliament and, 4:483a, 9:422b
Seneschaucy in, 4:513b
sources of, 5:88a
Flete, William, 9:14b
De remediis contra temptaciones, 9:26a-b
English translations of, 9:26b
Fleuron, **5:88a-b**
Fleury, abbey of, 10:247a
Fleury Penitential, 9:489a, 491a
Fleury Playbook, 4:263b, **5:88b–89a,** 9:706b
contents of, 5:88b
dates of composition, 5:88b
liturgical dramas, 5:88b
origin of, 5:88b–89a
Flexa, **5:89a**
see also Clivis
Flexa resupina. See Porrectus
Fliessende Licht der Gottheit, Das. See Mechthild von Magdeburg
Fljótsdæla saga, 4:613b, **5:89a-b**
anachronisms in, 5:89b
Droplaugarsona saga and, 5:89a-b
expansion of older sagas, 5:89a-b
Hrafnkels saga and, 5:89a-b
Flóamanna saga, **5:89b–90b**
Christian sources, 5:90a
date composed, 5:90b
dream episodes in, 5:90a-b
Floarea darurilor (Albinuşa), 10:511b
Flock (unit of measure), 12:592b
Flodden Hill, Battle of (1513), 11:110b, 112b
Flodoard of Rheims, **5:90b–91a**
Theganus' life of Louis I (the Pious) and, 12:8a
Floire et Blancheflor (Blancheflur), 1:643b
translated into Norwegian, 10:391a-b
see also Flores och Blanzeflor; Flores y Blancaflor; Flóres saga ok Blankiflúr; Floris
Floire und Blanscheflur. See Fleck, Konrad
Flóki Vilgerðarson (legendary discoverer of Iceland), 6:392b, 12:426b
Flokkr, **5:91a-b,** 11:319b
history of, 5:91a
versus *drápa,* 5:91a-b
Floors, for early Christian churches, 4:360b
Flor de enamorados, 11:429b
Floreffe Bible
illustrations
figure style, 8:495a-b
Three Theological Virtues and Seven Gifts of the Holy Spirit, 8:495b (*illus.*)
treatment of space, 8:495a-b
Florence, **5:91b–104a**
art
fresco painting, 5:294a-b, 295b
panel painting in, 9:361b–362a
Sienese styles and, 4:301b
of trecento, 12:171b–172b (*illus.*), 175a-b, 176b
bankruptcy of banks in the 1340's, 12:118a
baptistery, 10:502b
Black Death in, 2:259a–260a
catasto, 5:100b–101a
chronicles, 6:633b–634b, 659b–660a
of Filippo Villani, 2:240a
of Giovanni Villani, 5:97a-b
Ciompi regime, 5:99b–100a
civil strife
Blacks vs. Whites, 5:96a-b
Cavalcanti in, 3:196b
conflict between magnates and guilds, 5:96a
factions and internal tensions (1340–1382), 5:98b
cloth workers in, 5:99a-b
coinage of, florin, 4:301a (*illus.*)
communal government of, 5:93a–94a
conflicts with Henry IV, 12:230b–231a
as cultural capital of Italy, 5:103a
description, 4:137a
Duomo, 9:667a–668a
Arnolfo di Cambio's sculpture for, 12:170b–171a
baptistery, 5:524b, 9:667b–668a (*illus.*)
Brunelleschi's cupola for, 2:388b–389 (*illus.*), 12:365a
campanile, 3:60b (*illus.*), 11:581a, 581b (*illus.*)
cantoria (detail), 4:134b (*illus.*)
Ciuffagni and, 3:407a
Dufay motet and, 8:585b
facade, 1:429a
Giotto di Bondone and, 12:172b
Landini and, 7:326a
Luca della Robbia and, 4:134b
Nanni di Banco and, 9:56a
sculptures, 9:643b (*illus.*)
stained glass designs for, 5:525a-b
tomb of Antonio degli Orso by Tino di Camaino, 12:59b–60a (*illus.*)
see also Jacopo di Piero Guidi
dyeing industry in, 4:328a
economy, 12:112a
before 1100, 5:91b, 92a
1100-1250, 5:92b
recessions, 5:97b–98a, 6:18b
education in, 5:97b
classical schooling, 5:101a
electoral system (1340–1382), 5:98b
expansion, 15th century, 5:100a-b, 7:9b
as exporter of alum, 12:115b
financial institutions
Acciaiuoli company, 2:77a, 78b
banchi a minuto, 2:75a-b
Bardi company, 2:77a, 77b, 78b
money changers in, 2:74a
Peruzzi company, 2:77a, 77b, 78b
food supply problems, 5:3b–4a
"freedom of Italy" movement, 7:8b
glassmaking in, 5:555b
government
expansion of bureaucracy (1382–1434), 5:100b
under Medici, 8:242a–243b
Guelph-Ghibelline conflict, 5:94b–97a, 6:6b
decline of Guelph aristocracy, 5:96a
Ghibellines' appeal to Henry VII, 5:96b
Guelph houses gain control, 5:100a
Latini and, 7:382b
guild regimes, 5:98a-b, 98b–99a
first, 5:95b–96a, 97a
second, 5:98a-b
guilds
Arte dei Medici e Speziali, 2:99b
dyers' associations, 4:328b, 329a
power in commune, 5:94b–95a
history (to 1100), 5:91b–92a
rise of the margraves, 5:92a
history (1100–1250), 5:92b–95a
disintegration of traditional structures, 5:92b–93a
growth of urban power, 5:92b–93a
sources, 5:92a
history (1250–1340)
institutional reforms, 5:97a
Ordinances of Justice enacted, 5:96a
papal interference, 5:95b
zenith of golden age (1338), 5:97a-b
history (1340–1382), 5:97b–100a
post-1378 regime, 5:99b–100a
history (1382–1434), 5:100a–101b
history (1434–1537), 5:101b–103b
hospital of S. Maria Nuova, 8:253a-b
humanism in, 5:101a-b, 7:1a
late 15th century, 1:126a-b
imperial power in
conflict with papacy, 5:93a
end of, 5:94b

Florence (*cont.*)
imperial power in (*cont.*)
under Frederick Barbarossa, 5:94a
under Henry VI of Germany, 5:94a
inns in, 6:468a, 469a, 470b, 472b, 474a
lauda in, 7:384b
legation of St. Peter Damian to, 9:509a
liturgical drama in, 6:636b
manuscript book production in, 8:104b
Medicis, 12:231a-b
mint at, 8:430b
Neoplatonism in, 9:101a
Palazzo Medici-Riccardi, 8:307a-b (*illus.*)
plague in, 5:97b–98a
podesta, as chief magistrate, 5:94a
Ponte Vecchio, 10:418b, 420b
population, 4:138a, 141a, 145a
growth (1100–1250), 5:92b
primo popolo
emergence of, 5:94b–95a
entrepreneurial activities of, 5:95a
factors in establishment of, 5:95a
guild regime, 5:95b–96a, 97a
struggle with magnates, 5:96a
relations with
Milan, 5:102a
Naples and Rome, 5:95b
Pisa, 9:664a–665b
rise to dominance, 5:93b
siege of (1312), 4:102a
silk-throwing mills in, 11:295b
Sixtus IV's interference in, 5:102b
slavery in, 11:336a
social structure, 5:92b
textile industry, industrial strife, 11:714a–715a
vs. Siena
after fall of the Nine, 11:281b
at Colle di Val d'Elsa, 11:279b
to Battle of Montaperti, 11:279a-b
wars, 5:99a
with Milan and Naples, 2:390b, 5:100a
with neighboring city-states, 5:94a
with papacy, 5:102b
tax burdens of, 5:99a
see also Boccaccio, Giovanni; Medici family; Tuscany
Florence Antiphonary, 7:368b
Florence, Biblioteca Mediceo-Laurenziana, MS Pluteus 29.1. *See* Notre Dame School, MS Pluteus 29.1
Florence, Council of. *See* Ferrara-Florence, Council of
Florence of Holland, count, 4:209b
Florence de Rome, 3:77a, 259a-b
Florence, University of, 12:286a
Francesco Zabarella and, 12:735a
Florence of Worcester, 12:703b
Florence-Ferrara, Council of. *See* Ferrara-Florence, Council of
Florensian order, founding of, by Joachim of Fiore, 7:113a
Florent of Hainault, Achaea and, 7:379a
Florentine Chronicle. See Naddo da Montecatini
Florentines, in Seville, 11:214a
Florentius, **5:107a**
Florentius, Georgius. *See* Gregory of Tours, St.
Flores Bernardi. See Florilegia
Flores dictaminum. See Bernard of Meun
Flores historiarum. See Roger of Wendover
Flores, Juan de, **5:107a–108a**
Boccaccio's influence, 5:107b
Grimalte y Gradissa, 5:107a-b, 11:423a-b, 454b–455a
Grisel y Mirabella, 5:107a-b, 11:423a-b, 454b–455a
probable author of *Coronación de la señora Gracisla,* 11:423b
Triunfo de Amor, 5:107b, 11:423b
Flores musicae omnis cantus Gregoriani. See Spechtshart, Hugo
Flores och Blanzeflor, 4:519b, 520a
Flóres saga konungs ok sona hans, **5:108a-b**, 10:389b, 394b, 395a, 395b
rímur versions, 5:108a
sources of, 5:108a
Flóres saga ok Blankiflúr, **5:108b–109a**, 10:391a, 395a
corruption of, 5:108b
Floire et Blancheflor as source, 5:108a
patronage for, 5:109a
style of, 5:109a
Swedish version and, 5:108b–109a
see also Floris
Flores sanctorum, 3:167a
Flores y Blancaflor, 11:423a, 425b
Floretum. See Lollards, texts
Floridin. See Fullers' earth
Floridus aspectus. See Peter Riga
Florilegia, 1:317b–318a, **5:109b–110a**, 9:594a
of the Bible, 2:211b
etymology of term, 5:109b
as exegesis, 4:542b
of liturgical explanations, 7:625a
moral doctrine, 9:594a
popularity of, 5:110a
prose, 1:317b
proverb collections, 1:317b
as reference works, 7:564a
of Seneca's works, 1:317b
as sources for historians, 5:109b–110a
sources of, 5:109b
summae as, 1:317b
as teaching tools, 1:317b–318a
types of, 5:109b
verse, 1:317b–318a
see also Anthologies
Florilegium Angelicum, 1:317b
Florin, 4:301a (*illus.*), **5:110b**
circulation of, 5:110b, 8:430b
gold, 8:430b (*illus.*)
prestige of, 5:110b
value of, 5:110b
see also Penny
Florio (character in Boccaccio's *Filocolo*), 2:279b–280a
Floris and Blancheflour, 8:316a
Floris ende Blanchefloer. See Diederic van Assenede
Floris (romance character), **5:110b–111b**
"aristocratic" and "popular" versions, 5:111a
translations of, 5:111a-b
see also Flóres saga ok Blankiflúr
Florus of Lyons, 4:542b, **5:111b–112a**, 5:638b, 7:362b
as debater, 5:111b–112a
epistles, Ovidian influence, 9:313a
hymns of, 6:381b
on liturgy, 7:629a
martyrology, 8:162a
Peter Lombard and, 9:516b
as scholar, 5:111b
Flos. See Fibonacci, Leonardo
Flos medicinae, 7:366a
Flote, Pierre, 7:137a, 340a
death of, 9:152a
Flounder (*Platichthys flesus*), fishing of, 5:70a
Floure and the Leafe, The, 5:364a
Flóvents saga, 10:391b, 395b
Flower of Courtesy. See Lydgate, John
Floyris (Dutch), 4:318b
Floyris et Blanchefleur (French), 4:520a
Flushwork, **5:112a**, 5:112b (*illus.*)
Flute, 8:561b, 562b, 602 (*illus.*), 604a
Arab, 8:610b (*illus.*)
Flûte douce. See Recorder
Flute, fipple. *See* Fipple flute
Fluted armor. *See* Arms and armor
Flying buttress. *See* Buttress
Flyting, 9:173a
"Flyting of Dunbar and Kennedie, The." *See* Dunbar, William
Focagium. See Fouage
Foci. See Hearth lists
Foclut, forest of, 9:462b, 463b
Foederati, tagma of, 11:573a
Foederati. See Roman Empire, federate allies
Fóganacht dynasties, Cashel and, 3:121a
Fogassot, Joan, on imprisonment of Prince Charles of Viana, 3:171b
Foil patterns. *See* Quatrefoil; Tracery; Trefoil
Foils. *See* Swords
Foix, counts of, 7:339a
Foix-Navarre, house of, Pyrenees provinces of, 10:325b
Folcwin of Lobbes, **5:112a-b**
Fólgin nöfn (concealed names), in *rímur,* 10:404a-b
Folgòre da San Gimignano, 6:649b, 669a
Foliage motif, in Western European furniture, 5:324b
Folies Tristan, **5:112b–113a**, 12:201a, 202b
Folio, **5:113a**
quire and, 10:240a
Foliot, Gilbert, bishop of London, 2:151b
Folkeviser, Kudrun and, 7:304b
Folklore
Byzantine, 8:18b–20a
imperial legends and prophecies, 8:20a
oral epic tradition and, 8:19a-b

relic of the True Cross and, 8:20a
ritual lament (*threnos*) and, 8:19b
Theotokos and, 8:19b–20a
transmission of classical and Oriental motifs, 8:18b–19a
Islamic, 8:20b–22a
magical object in, 8:21b–22a
Jewish, talmudic heritage and, 8:22b
plant lore, 2:345a, 348a
Folktales, as sources for early Icelandic *rímur,* 10:402b
Folkung family, in ballads, 11:7a
Folle Bobance, 4:265b
Follis (bronze coin), 10:460b, 461a
Follis (copper coin), 8:419a
Folly. *See* Insanity
Folquet de Marseilles, **5:113a**
Folz, Hans, 4:271b, **5:113b–114b**, 8:359b
Arme Bäcker, 8:129b
Ausgesperrte Ehemann, 8:129b
comic vignettes, 5:114b
couplets, 5:114
Fastnachtspiel, 11:367b
Gebrauchsliteratur, 10:535a-b
historical *Töne,* 5:114a
Köhler als gedungener Liebhaber, 8:129b
literary works
form and content, 5:113b
on religious subjects, 5:113b
Mären, 8:129b, 131b
Meisterlieder, 5:113b, 114a
printing and publishing activity, 5:113b
Salomon und Markolf, 5:114a
Shrovetide plays, 5:114a
"sworn master," 5:113b
Fomoiri (Fomorians), 6:546a-b
in Celtic mythology, 9:47a
Fondaco dei Tedeschi (Venice), 12:113a
Fondicarii (*Fondiguiers*), 6:474a
Fons Evraldi. *See* Fontevrault
Fons vitae. See Solomon ben Judah ibn Gabirol
Font. *See* Baptism
Font de la Vila (Palma), 6:558a
Font of Wisdom. See John of Damascus, St.
Fontaine amoureuse. See Machaut, Guillaume de
Fontana, Giovanni, *De trigono balistario,* 1:437b
Fonte Avellana, 3:56a
Peter Damian and, 9:508a, 508b
Fonte Gaia (Siena), 11:281b
Fontenay Abbey, **5:114b–115a**, 10:483b (*illus.*)
banded barrel vault in, 12:365a
cloister, 5:115a (*illus.*)
Fontenoy, Battle of (841), 3:112b, 9:143a
Fontevrault Abbey
bridge maintenance and, 10:417a
church, 10:481a
education of Suger and, 11:502b
monastic kitchen, 8:0 (frontispiece)
Fontevrault order, 10:429b–430b, 12:686b
see also Robert d'Arbrissel
Food
water mills used for processing, 8:392b–393a
see also Cookery
Food animals. *See* Animals, food
Food for Entertainment (*Nishwār al-muḥāḍara*), 1:380b
Food restrictions. *See* Dietary laws
Food trades, **5:115a–127b**
assizes, 5:119b–120a
for beverages, 5:125a, 125b
of bread, 5:121b
cereal from Egypt, 12:100a, 100b
control of food supply
during famine, 5:119a
grain crops, 5:121a
Italy, 5:118b–119a
regulation of sales, 5:124b
distribution systems, 12:152b, 153b, 157b, 159b
see also Travel and transport
early Middle Ages, 5:115b–116b
effect of new agricultural techniques on, 5:116a
in England, price controls and, 12:118b
export of goods
dried fruits and nuts, 5:126b
from fair of St. Denis, 5:116a
grain exports, 12:108b, 111b, 117b–118a
food rents, 5:115b
forestalling and regrating, 5:121b
fraud, 5:122a, 123b
Hanseatic League and, 12:113a
hoarding, 5:119b, 121a, 9:673a, 685b
import-export regulations, 5:119a
in local markets, 12:117a–118a
long-distance, 5:116a, 124b
cheese and butter, 5:126b
redistribution points, 5:125a
luxury consumption, 5:116a, 116b
market officials, 5:24b, 120a
meat, slaughtering of meat animals, 1:297a-b (*illus.*)
middlemen, 5:126a, 126b
profits of, 5:118b
municipal control, 5:118b–119b, 119b–120a
guild participation in, 5:120a-b
place of sale, 5:120b
price fixing, 5:123a
plagues and, 9:673a, 676a-b, 685b
price control
Carolingian capitularies, 5:116a
ceilings, 5:25a
enforcement of, 5:120a
national legislation, 5:121b
seasonal price and demand fluctuations, 5:123a
tying to raw materials, 5:125b
price fluctuations, 5:123a
effect on demand, 5:116b
primary producers, 5:118a
quality control, 5:123a-b
enforcement of, 5:120a, 123b, 125a-b, 126a
measures, 5:126a
national legislation, 5:121b
stamps and seals, 5:121b–122a
regrators and hucksters, 5:119b, 126a
regulation of, 8:146a
retailers, 5:118b
Rome, 10:526a
rural, 5:116b–118a
exchange for services, 5:118a
monetization of peasant economy, 5:117b–118a
peasant involvement in, 5:117b
response to market conditions, 5:117b
rising population and expansion in, 5:116b–117a
Sicily, 11:275b
standards of measure, 12:586b
storage and transportation, 5:115b–116a
carting services, 5:116a
subsistence needs, 5:115b
taxation and fees, 5:120b
urban, 5:118a–121a
see also Agriculture; Animals, food; Famine; Fisheries, marine; Fish, trade in
Fool's boxes. *See Tollkisten*
Fool's cap, 3:624b
Foot combat, 5:349b
Football, 5:348a
Footbridge, 3:148a
Footwashing. *See* Feet, washing of
Footwear
Western European, 3:625b–626a
see also Shoes and shoemakers
For the Defense of the Holy Hesychasts. See Gregory Palamas
Fora, 10:519a-b
"Forbidden years," 11:196b, 197a
Forcadel, Pierre, 1:439b
Fore-and-aft sail. *See* Sail
Forest Charter of 1217, 5:128a, 134a
abolition of capital punishment, 9:522b
Forest eyre
decline of, 5:130a
origin of, 5:128b
penalties assessed, 5:128b–129a, 130a, 134a
Forest law, **5:127b–131a**
administration of, 5:128a
forest officials, 5:129a-b
attachment court, 5:129b, 133a, 134a
corporal punishment, 5:128b, 133a
determining royal areas, 5:127b–128a
England, 6:356b
common law and, 5:127b, 128b
evidence used, 5:129a-b
fines
pannage, 5:129b
revenue generated by, 5:128b–129a
foresters, 5:129a
general inquisition, 5:130a-b, 136a
Germanic codes, 5:131b
history, 5:128a
justices, function of, 5:129b–130a
local courts, 5:128b, 129a
regard, 5:129b
swanimotes and forest hundreds, 5:129b
Markgenossenschaft, 5:132b
ordeal by cold water, 5:128b
ordinance of 1346, 5:134b, 135a
purpose of, 5:127b, 130b
Robin Hood and, 10:437a

Forest law (*cont.*)
Roman, 5:132a
trailbastons, 5:130a
verderers, 5:130b
see also Forest eyre
Forest-fallow cycle. *See* Agriculture; Forests; Reclamation of land, swidden
Forests, European, **5:131a–136b**, 9:664a
administration of
baillis and *prévôts,* 5:133a, 134b
England, 5:133b–134a, 136a
France, 5:134a-b
gruerie system, 5:134b
magister forestarius, 5:135b
maîtres des forêts, 5:134b, 135a
receveur général des eaux et forêts, 5:135a
regarders, 5:129b, 134a
seigneurial officials, 5:135b
souverain-maître des eaux et forêts, 5:135a
"beasts of the forest," protection of, 5:133a
clearing of, for building materials, 3:560b–561a
decentralization of control
France, 5:132b
Germany, 5:132b
disafforestment, 5:128a, 136a
ducal forests, 5:133a
as economic resource, 5:133b
Germany and France, 5:135b
effect of agricultural expansion on, France and Germany, 5:133b, 136a
etymology of "forest," 5:131b
functions of, 5:132a
in early Middle Ages, 5:131b
garenne, 5:132b
history of, 5:131a-b
hunting in, 6:356b
royal privileges, 5:132a, 133a
king's ban, 5:132a-b
Mediterranean basin, shipbuilding and, 11:230b
monastic use of, 5:132a
parks and chases, 5:128a
political events and (15th century), 5:135b–136a
reforestation, 5:135b
royal control over
Angevin kings, 5:133a
Capetian kings, 5:132b
Carolingian period, 5:132a
Merovingian kings, 5:131b
Norman kings, 5:128a
political opposition, 5:130b, 134a
Saxon and Salian kings, 5:132a
seigneurial rights, 5:132b–133a, 135a-b
taxation of, 5:135a, 168b
town expansion and destruction of, 5:133b
see also Lumber trade; Reclamation of land
Forez, hunting in, 6:357b–358a
Forfeiture of possessions, treason and, 12:166b
Forgaill, Dallá, *Amra Choluim Cille,* 3:233a
Forgery, **5:136b–137a**
by monks, 5:136b
explanations for, 5:137a
canonical inquest for, 6:478b
Donation of Constantine as, 4:257b–259b
extent of, 5:136b–137a
golden age of, 5:136b
methods used, 5:136b
propaganda purposes, 5:136b
see also Decretals, False; *Pseudo-Turpin*
Forgiveness for sins. *See* Penance
Fori Valentiae, 7:430a
Forks, digging, 12:78a–79a, 81b
Forma compoti, 4:513b
Forma dictandi. See Gregory VIII, pope
Formáli, in *Sturlunga saga,* 11:497b, 498b
Formariage, 11:201b, 203b
abolishment of, 11:204a, 206b
Formeret, **5:137a-b**
Formigny, Battle of (1450), 3:66a, 6:332b
Formosus, pope
Arnulf of Carinthia and, 1:541b, 3:114a
election of, 2:11b
Eugenius Vulgarius and, 4:520b
head of papal mission to Bulgaria, 2:403a
Formschneider, 12:690b
Formula vitae honestae. See Martinus Braga
Formulae Marculfi, 10:358a
Formulae Salomonis. See Salomo of Constance
Formulae Sangallenses miscellaneae. See Notker Balbulus
Formularies, in chancery, 3:252b–253a
Formularium spiritualis. See Eucherius of Lyons
Formulary of Marculf, 3:253a
Fornaldarsögur, **5:137b–143b**
absence of historical authenticity, 6:215a
adventure tales
on farming families, 5:138b
listing of, 5:138b
vs. hero legends, 5:138a
ancient custom and rituals in, 5:141b–142a
battle accounts, 5:141a-b
blood brotherhood, 5:139a
classical saga and, 4:618a
common character roles, 5:139a-b
dating of, 5:142b–143a
description of hero, 5:139b
character and country of origin, 5:140b
composite features, 5:140b–141a
transformation of unpromising youth, 5:139b–140a
deviations from conventional pattern, 6:77b–78a
Gull-Þóris saga and, 6:27a
in *Harðar saga Grímkelssonar,* 6:101b
hero legends
common features, 5:138a
listing of, 5:138a-b
historical value, 5:142b
Icelandic *riddarasögur* and, 10:395b, 396a
Íslendingasögur and, time differences, 5:137b
later forms, 5:143a
lygisögur (lying tales) and, 6:267a
common features of, 5:137b
mythical elements, 5:142a
quests
categories, 5:138b–139a
obstacles confronting hero, 5:138b
success of, 5:139a
Rafn's edition of, 5:138b
romantic themes, 5:141b
setting, 5:140a-b
influence of foreign models, 5:141a
Skáldatal and, 11:316a-b
Skjǫldungar saga and, 11:328a-b
as a source for *Víglundar saga,* 12:416b
sources for, 5:137b–138a
use of language in, 6:267a
in verse, 5:142a-b
Fornaldarsögur norðrlanda
as sources for early *rímur,* 10:402a
term for certain *riddarasögur,* 10:389b
Fornaldarsǫgur. See Fornaldarsögur
Fornsögur suðrlanda, term for certain *riddarasögur,* 10:389b
Fornyrðadrápa. See Málsháttakvæði
Fornyrðislag (Eddic meter), in *Merlínússpá,* 8:276a
Føroya kvæði: Corpus carminum færoensium (CCF), 5:16a–17b
Forseti, 11:27a
Fortalitium fidei contra Judaeos. See Alonso de Espina
Fortescue, Sir John, **5:143b–145a**
alliance with Lancastrians, 5:144a
De laudibus legum Angliae, 5:144b
De natura legis naturae, 5:144a, 144b
exile, 5:144a
Governance of England, The, 5:144b–145a
on inns of court, 6:477a-b
on Irish sovereignty, 6:520a
as justice of the King's Bench, 7:194a
kingship theories of, 7:270a
legal commissions, 5:143b
legal works
necessity of fundamental law, 5:144b
proposals for constitutional revision, 5:145a
statute law vs. natural law, 5:144b
negotiations with Louis XI, 5:144a
pardon of, 5:144b
on prerogative, 10:90b
principles of parliamentary privilege, 5:143b–144a
succession arguments, 5:144a-b
Declaracion . . . upon Certayn Wrytinges, 5:144b
Thorpe's Case, 5:143a
on Wars of the Roses, 12:572b
Fortress of the Faith. See Alfonso de Espina
Fortuna. See Nivardus of Ghent
Fortunate Islands
Vinland sagas and, 12:457b
see also Canary Islands

Fortunatianus, Consultus, compendium on rhetoric, 10:353a, 354a
Fortunatus, 8:361b
Fortunatus, Venantius, on *raeda* and *pilentum* (luxury vehicles), 12:369b
Fortunatus (Venetian ecclesiastic), 12:385a
Fortune, **5:145b–147b**
depictions of, 5:147a, 12:751 (*illus.*)
Roman, 5:146b
derivation, 5:145b
in *Dezir al nacimiento del Rey Don Juan,* 6:429a
duality and instability of, 5:147a
Henry of Settimello on, 7:365b
in literature, 5:146a
Italian Renaissance, 5:147a
Latin lyric poetry, 5:146b
Old Spanish concept, **5:147b–148a**
divine providence and, 5:147b–148a
individual's responsibility for fate, 5:148a
in literature, 5:147b
optimistic vs. pessimistic view, 5:147b–148a
other names for, 5:147b
personification of, 5:145b
in proverbs, 5:146b
with rise of Christianity, 5:145b
see also Wheel of Fortune
Fortune-telling, 5:352b
Oracles of the Apostles and, 8:26b
use of Scriptures for, 8:26a
Forty Saints of Sebaste, 1:518b
Forum judicum. See Leges Visigothorum
Foscari, Paolo, archbishop of Patras, Achaea and, 7:381a
Fóstbrœðra saga, 4:612b, 613a, **5:148a–149a**
Bjarkamál and, 2:254a
dating of, 5:148b
plot summary, 5:148a-b
preservation in manuscripts, 5:148b
Saga of Saint Olaf and, 5:148b
style and construction, 5:148b–149a
"Þorgeirsdrápa," 5:148b
Fother (unit of measure), 12:585b
Fouage, 3:269b–270a, 11:578a-b, 579b, 624a
France, 11:621a
Languedoc, 11:622a, 623b
Fougères, lords of, Vital of Savigny and, 12:480a
Foukes le Fitzwarin, 1:267b–268a, **5:149a**
Foulque le Jeune, count of Anjou, Robert d'Arbrissel and, 10:430a
Fountain of life, **5:149a-b**
examples of, 5:149b
four rivers of paradise and, 5:149b
origin of, 5:149a
Fountain of Life. See Solomon ben Judah ibn Gabirol, *Fons vitae*
Fountains, 5:391b
ablutional, 10:281b
Fontana Maggiore (Perugia), 9:669b–670a
in gardens, European, 5:363a-b
see also Baptism; Baptistery; Gardens
Fountains Abbey (Yorkshire)
architectural plan, 8:455a-b (*illus.*), 456a
passageway, 8:585a (*illus.*)
Fouquet, Jean, **5:149b–150a**
panel painting in France and, 5:609a-b
portrait of Charles VI, 5:606a (*illus.*)
portrait of Eugenius IV at Rome, 5:149b
Four Articles of Prague, 3:505a
Four Books of Kings. *See Quatre livres des reis*
"Four Doctors." *See* Bulgarus; Hugo; Jacobus (de Porta Ravennate); Martinus Gosia
Four Gospels of Gelatᶜi, 5:411b
Four Sons of Aymon, The, 8:225a
Fourée (unit of measure), 12:586b
Fournier, Jacques, bishop of Pamiers. *See* Benedict XII, pope
Fowl, domestic, **5:150a–151a**
Byzantium, 1:79a
as food source, 1:301a
Fowling, **5:151b–152a**
list of species, 5:151b
methods of, 5:151b
purposes of
dietary needs, 5:151b
for domestication and taming, 5:152a
for feathers, 5:151b–152a
to protect stock, 5:152a
for sport, royal privilege, 5:152a
see also Hunting and fowling, Western European
Fox stories. *See* Renard the Fox
Fox and the Wolf, 8:316b, 10:314a
Foxtail millet, 5:647a
Fra Angelico. *See* Giovanni da Fiesole
Fractio modi. See Rhythm
Fraga, Battle of (1134), 9:70a
Fragment de Valenciennes. See Jonas fragment
Frame
in manuscript illumination, 10:491b
in Romanesque sculpture, 10:491b
Frame saw, in shipbuilding, 11:243b
Frame stories
Iranian, 6:508b
Irish, 6:549a, 551b
France
administration of, *see also* Mayor
astronomy in, 1:612b–613a
bridge building, 10:413a
brigandage, 11:623b
demographic effects, 5:178a-b
economic consequences, 5:178a-b, 185a
écorcheurs, 5:188b
efforts to combat, 5:185a, 186a
Cabochien riots, 3:3b–4a
Capetian rule, 5:157a–165b
cavalry in, 3:201b
Christian missions to, 8:441b (map), 442a
communes, 3:495b–497a
charters of privileges, 7:674a
conquest of Normandy, 5:164b
coronations in, 7:258a
Dante and, 4:101a-b
demographic trends
in 13th century, 5:174b
in 14th century, 5:176b–178b
dukes in, 4:303b–304a
dyeing industry in, 4:328a, 328b
economic trends
in 13th century, 5:174b
in 14th century, 5:178b–180a, 11:680a-b
glassmaking in, 5:558b–559a
Hebrew manuscripts produced in, 8:119b–120a
history (to 987), **5:152b–154b**
see also Barbarians, invasions of; Carolingian Empire
history (987–1223), **5:154b–166a**
extension of royal control, 5:159a–161a
political disintegration, 5:156b–157a
principalities, 5:152b–154a
sources of, 5:156a
see also Peace of God
history (1223–1328), **5:166a–176b**
control of provinces, 5:168a–170b
emergence of modern nation, 5:166b
history (1314–1494), **5:176b–190b**
see also Hundred Years War; Valois dynasty
Jews in, 7:86b, 87a
languages of, 6:435a-b, 441b–442a
mining areas in, 8:398b
mints and money in, 8:429a, 430b–431a
papermaking in, 9:389b
plagues and famines, 9:675b–676b, 681a-b
Black Death in, 2:260b–261a
economic and social effects of, 5:174b, 177b, 178a, 178b, 179b–180a
population, 4:140a, 141b
pre-Romanesque art in, 10:110a
regional particularism, 5:181b
relations with
Burgundy, 6:332b
Dauphiné, 4:109a-b
England, 5:183b–184a, 185a, 186a-b, 7:364b, *see also* Hundred Years War
Flanders, 12:732a
Gascony, 2:328b
Navarre, 9:71a–72b
Normandy, 9:163b–164a, 166a, 168a
Scotland, 6:331b, 11:111b
roads in, 10:412b–413a
Roman roads, 10:411b–412a
silk industry in, 11:296a
social classes, 5:180a–181b
standing army, 11:623b, 624a
Templars in, 3:644a
tenurial development, 11:680b–681a
métayage, 11:681a
territorial boundaries, 5:171a, 189b–190a
in 987, 5:153a-b (map)
in 1206, 5:155a-b (map)
in 1300, 5:167a-b (map)
in 1491, 5:177a-b (map)

France (*cont.*)
territorial boundaries (*cont.*)
establishment of, 5:171a
town planning, bastides, 12:324a-b
travel and transport in, 12:149a, 151a, 155b, 158a
universities, 12:161b, 285a-b
urban power struggles in High Middle Ages, 12:317a
Valois dynasty, 5:183a–190a
see also Feudalism; Francia; French government; Gaul; Midi; Representative assemblies, French; Taxation
Francés, Nicolás, 5:612a
Franceschino degli Albizzi, in *Trionfo d'Amore,* 6:640b
Francesco I Sforza, ruler of Milan, 8:380a
Francesco II Sforza, duke of Milan, 8:380b–381a
Francesco da Barberino
Documenti d'amore, 3:665b, 6:632b, 665a
Reggimento e costumi di donna, 3:664a-b, 6:632b
preservation of Guido Guinizzelli's work in, 6:24b
Francesco da Colle, influence on Cino da Pistoia, 3:397a
Francesco delgli orghany. *See* Landini, Francesco
Francesco di Giorgio Martini
ball-and-chain governor, 11:662a
Trattati de archittetura, ingegneria e arte militare, 11:648b
Francesco, Maestro, 6:643b
Francesco da Rimini, **5:190b**
fresco cycle, 5:190b
Francesco di Valdambrino, **5:190b–191a**
Francesco di Vannozzo, 6:653b
Franche-Comté
in Burgundian-Swiss war, 11:545a
see also Burgundy, county of
Franchises, serfdom and, 11:204b, 206a, 207b
Franchises, urban, in Champagne, 3:248b–249a
Francia
administration of, 2:52b
divisions of, 8:278a
royal revenues of, collected by *prévôts,* 2:52b
Viking raids and, 12:429b–431a, 431b
Francien dialect. *See* French language
Francis II of Brittany, duke, tomb of, 3:483a (*illus.*)
Francis I of France, king, 9:682b
armor and, 1:529b
vernacular and, 10:178b
representative assemblies and, 10:323b, 324b, 327b
Francis of Assisi, St., **5:191a–192b,** 12:170a, 238a-b (*illus.*)
Anthony of Padua and, 1:321a
in art, 7:349b, 12:173b
asceticism, 8:160a
attempt to convert Muslims, 5:191b–192a, 196b, 197a
biographies of, 6:69a
Acts of St. Francis, 5:204a-b
Bonaventure, 2:316b
Book of the Conformity of the Life of St. Francis to the Life of the Lord Jesus, 5:205a
burning of, 5:201a
by general chapter of Narbonne, 5:201a
commissioned by Crescentius, 5:200a
Little Flowers, 5:204b
Mirror of Perfection, 5:204a-b
canonization of, 5:198a
Canticle of the Sun, 7:384a
conformity to Christ, 5:195b, 204b, 205a
description of ideal friar, 5:204b
Francis as the Second Christ, 5:205a
influence on Italian panel painting, 9:361a
John of Plano Carpini and, 7:137b
lauda and, 6:635a, 7:384a
Laudes creaturarum, 6:635b, 650b, 661b–662a, 667b
military expeditions, 5:191a
missionary work of, 8:444b–445a
mystical experiences, 8:160a
stigmata, 5:192a, 197b–198a
organization of followers, 5:191b
on possession of works of learning, 11:77b
religious conversion, 5:191a-b, 195b
religious life of, 3:355a
remains of, basilica for, 5:198a
a rhymed office to, 10:370a
rights to his body for posthumous veneration, 10:298b
Rule of 1221
composition of, 5:192a
redrafting of, 5:204a-b
Testament, 5:198a
original liturgical practice in, 5:192b
travels to Egypt, 3:357a
veneration of the crèche, 5:197b
women's orders and, 12:687b
Francis von Coudenberg, Ruusbroec and, 9:36a, 36b
Francis de Sales, St., as doctor of the church, 4:234b
Francis of Siena, *Antidotarium,* 9:551b
Francisc, 1:522a
Francisca, 12:556b
Franciscan rite, **5:192b–194b**
Capitularium, 5:194a
clerics and laymen in, 5:193a, 196b
Exposition on the Rule, 5:199b
First Rule (*Regula non bullata,* 1221), 5:193a-b, 197b
legislative elaboration, 5:193a
literacy question, 5:193a
liturgical books, reworking of, 5:193b–194a
Martyrologium, 5:194a
origins, 5:192b–193a
Second Rule (1223), 5:193a-b
glossing of, 5:198a-b
possession of breviaries, 5:193b
Tabula Parisiensis, 5:194a
testament, language in, 5:192b–193a
Tonale tonorum communium, 5:194a
Franciscans, **5:194b–206b,** 5:297b
Aristotelianism and, 1:461b, 465b
in Armagh, 1:470a
in Barcelona, 2:104a
beguines and, 2:158b, 159a, 159b, 161a, 161b
beguins and, 2:162b, 163a
Black Death and, 5:204b
Bosnian vicariate, 2:334b, 336b, 338b
breviarium romanae curiae, 2:372a-b
in Byzantine Empire, 7:348a
carol and, 8:572a
Celestines and, 3:215a
changes in, 3:355b
Christology and, 3:323b
clerics vs. laymen, 5:199a
concept of primitive church and, 10:122a-b
correctorium controversy, 10:388b
development of Middle English lyric and, 8:340a
difference from other orders, 5:194b, 195b–196a
Divine Office recitation, 4:231a
ecclesiology of, 4:375b
in England
intellectual tradition, 1:73a
introduced by Agnellus of Pisa, 1:73a
see also Peckham, John
Eudes Rigaud and, 4:519a
expansion outside Italy, 5:198b
first attempts, 5:196a
North Africa, 5:197a
Spain and Portugal, 5:204b
expelled from Sicily, 9:59a
founding of, 10:76b
Fraticelli, 6:199a, 488b
functions of, 3:355a-b
General Assembly of 1356, 7:683a
general chapter
at Assisi, 2:318a
at Lyons, 2:318b
at Narbonne, 2:316a-b
at Paris, 2:317a-b
Gregory IX and, 5:671a
Holy Circulus in Jerusalem and, 11:467b
housing of, 5:198b
hymns of, 6:382a, 9:714b
Ibn Gabirol and, 1:460a
imitation of the Apostles, 5:195b
imprisonment of leaders, 5:201b, 203b
Innocent III and, 3:353a-b, 6:465a
Innocent IV and, 6:467a
Irish, 6:525a, 536a, 543a
Jews and, 7:76b, 77a, 88b
Joachim of Fiore and, 7:114a
John XXII and, 3:363b, 7:125b, 10:122b
in Latin Empire of Constantinople, 7:349b
literature and, 7:368b–369a
Anglo-Latin poetry, 1:255a
influence on *Owl and the Nightingale,* 9:316b–317a
lauda, 6:635b, 662a, 7:384a, 8:579b
in *Piers Plowman,* 7:334a

liturgy of papal curia adopted by, 9:380a
in London (Newgate), 7:663b
manuscript book production and, 8:103a
membership of, 3:355a
mendicant ideal, 5:298a
ministry to laity and, 3:359a
missionaries
in Armenia, 3:394b
in Tunis, 6:53b
Nicene church and, 7:348b
Observants and Conventuals
division into separate orders, 5:205a–206a
election of vicars, 5:205a-b
"four pillars of the Observance," 5:205a
see also Bernardino of Siena, St.
Ockham and, 9:209a, 209b, 210a, 212b, 213a
opposed by Siger of Brabant, 2:317b
orders of, 2:161a, 161b, 5:195a, 11:663b, 12:688a-b
organization of, 5:191b
in Italy, 5:197a
provincial subdivisions, 5:198b
origin of, 5:195a–198a, 6:68b
papal rulings on, 5:195b
Cum inter nunnullos, 5:203b
Exiit qui seminat, 5:201b, 203a-b
Exivi de paradiso, 5:202b
Ite et vos, 5:206a
Ordinem vestrum, 5:199b–200a
Quo elongati, 5:198a
Quorundam exigit, 5:202b–203a
Sancta romana, 5:203a
Ut sacra, 5:205b
parish system and, 9:416b
in Pera-Galata, 9:503a
poverty vows, 4:375b, 377a
justification for, 5:203a-b
papal attitude toward, 6:199a
Peter John Olivi's views, 9:514b–515a
preaching of, 6:664b
exempla in, 4:551a-b
prestigious members, 5:194b
property issue, 4:377a
construction of convents, 5:198b, 200b
donation of Bologna house, 5:197a-b, 298a
ownership vs. use, 5:198a-b, 200b, 203b, 205a-b
use in right and use in fact, 5:201b
religious instruction and, 10:301a
rhymed offices and, 10:369b, 370a
Ruusbroec and, 9:38a
scholarship of
attitude toward learning, 5:199a
Augustinian philosophy, 9:610b
Averroism and, 1:463a
biblical exegesis, 2:214a, 4:544a-b
scholasticism and, 1:465a
Scotism and, 1:467a
Spirituals, 2:163a, 315a, 3:369b, 6:199a, 488b
attempts to separate, 5:202a
conflict with carnal church, 6:199a
defeat of, 5:201a–203b
emergence of, 5:199b
hermitages, 5:204b
hunted by Inquisition, 5:204a
Joachim of Fiore and, 7:114a
John XXII and, 7:125b
Matthew of Aquasparta and, 8:227a
Peter John Olivi and, 9:515a
Poor Hermits of Pope Celestine, 5:202a
settlement of 1312, 5:202b
see also Jacopone da Todi
split within, 3:644b–645a
Stjepan Kotromanić of Bosnia and, 11:486a
theory of papal authority, 4:376b
Third Order of St. Francis, 2:161b, 162a, 11:663b
Trinitarian doctrine, 12:193b, 196b–197a
in University of Paris dispute, 5:200a-b, 9:408b
vs. heretics, 6:484a, 488a
women mystics in Italy and, 9:14a
"year of the alleluia" and, 6:662a
see also Beguines and beghards; Preaching, Western European; Religious instruction
Francisco de Mello, 1:439b
Francke, Master. *See* Franke, Meister
Franco of Cologne, **5:206b–207b**
Ars cantus mensurabilis, 1:544b, 5:208b, 8:628b, 644a
concern with triple meters, 5:207a
dating of, 5:207a-b
sources for, 5:206b
use of *perfectio,* 9:504b
Compendium discantus, 5:207b
Franconian notation, 5:207a, 208b
Jehan des Murs and, 8:645b
Jerome of Moravia and, 8:645a
Marchettus of Padua and, 8:645b–646a
musical notation, division of breves, 9:545a
musical notation and, 8:622a-b, 628b, 629b
Notre Dame school and, 9:191b
Quatuor principalia musice and, 8:646b
rhythmic notation and, 8:588b, 594a
see also Ligature
Franco of Liège, **5:207b**
De quadratura circuli, 8:208b
Questiones in musica and, 8:642b
Franco of Polonia, invention of torquetum attributed to, 11:98b
Franco Teutonicus. *See* Franco of Cologne
Franco-Provençal. *See* French language; Provençal language
Franco-Saxon school, **5:208a-b**
initial to Book of Genesis, 5:208a (*illus.*)
Franco-veneta language, 6:638b–639a
Franconia, tenurial development, 11:681b–682a
Franconia, duchy of, Otto I (the Great) and, 5:475a-b, 9:300b
Franconian dialects, 6:437a
Franconian motet, **5:208b–209b**
collections of, 5:209a-b
intermingling of modes, 5:209a
longa and *brevis,* 5:208b
parts of, 5:208b
secular texts, 5:208b
Francorum. See Gregory of Tours, St.
Frangipani family, 3:94a, 10:525a
Frankalmoin, **5:209b–210a**
exemption from secular jurisdiction, 5:210a
method of payment
England, 5:210a
Normandy and Scotland, 5:209b–210a
Franke, Meister, **5:210b**
St. Barbara Altarpiece, 5:610a, 629a
St. Thomas Altarpiece, 5:610a, 629a
works in International Style, 5:629a
Frankenspiegel, influenced by *Schwabenspiegel,* 11:81a
Frankenstein Castle (Silesia), Benedict Ried and, 10:399a
Frankenturm (Trier), 10:489b
Frankfurt
bridge of, 10:417b
fairs, 4:586a
generale parlamentum, 10:330a
Frankfurt an der Oder, University of, 12:289a
Frankfurt Capitulary, 3:91b
Frankfurt, Council of (794)
Paulinus of Aquileia and, 9:470a
women's orders and, 12:683b
Frankfurt Passion, 4:270a
performance of, 4:284b
Frankfurter, Philipp, *Pfarrer vom Kahlenberg,* 8:360b
Frankincense, production in southern Arabia, 1:370a
Frankish language, 6:442a
Italo-Romance and, 6:623b–624a
Frankish law, *lex salica,* 8:278a
Frankish penitentials, 9:489a, 490a
Frankish Royal Annals, 6:262a-b
Frankish states
early Germanic law and, 7:471b–473a
government, 1:75b
Italy, 12:556a
military feudalism, 12:557a
military organization in Near East, 12:561a
taxation, 11:618b
Viking raids, 12:558b
Frankish states in Greece. *See* Latin states in Greece
Frankpledge, 4:138b
Franks, 2:89b, 94a-b
anointing ceremony of, 7:256b
attack on Cologne, 3:481a
Bohemia and, 2:299a, 299b
Boniface and, 12:683a
Bulgars and, 2:401b
Clovis and, 3:466b
conquest of Saxony, 10:683a
coronations of, 7:257a
in Croatia, 4:1b–2b, 4a
defeat at Casilinum, 12:556b
expansion of territory, 2:94a-b
as federate allies, 2:94a
francisca, 12:556b

Franks (*cont.*)
in Gaul, 10:465a
German expansion, 12:616b
in Gulf of Eilat, 11:247a
invasion of Champagne, 3:243a-b
in Italy, 8:377a-b
jewelry of, 5:375b, 377a, 8:367b (*illus.*)
Jordan of Osnabrück and, 7:149a
languages of, 6:435a, 436b, 437a
law codes of, 7:471b–473a
Merovingian, 7:472a
Salian, 7:472a–473a
state and, 7:471b
in Lombard army, 12:556a
migration of, 8:363a-b
in Milan, 8:377a-b
military organization, 12:556b–557a
in Noricum, 2:133b
Pepin I (of Landen) and, 9:499a
Pepin III (the Short) and, 9:501a
Rhine River and, 10:459a
Rome and, 10:521b–522b
stem duchies, 4:303b, 5:505b–506b
vs. Alamanni, 11:526a, 526b, 537a-b
vs. Burgundians, 11:536b
vs. Visigoths, 12:471a
Apollinaris and, 11:277b
under Alaric II, 12:470b
weapons of, 1:522a
Wendish overlordship, 12:617a
Franks Casket
depiction of Wayland the Smith, 8:292a (*illus.*)
Vǫlundarkviða and, 12:490b
Frásǫgn, as alternative designation of *þættir,* 12:1b
Frater. *See* Refectory
Fratres militae Christi. *See* Brothers of the Sword
Fratres unitores, 3:395b
Fratrum predicatorum. See Dominicans
Frau Ava, **5:210b–211b**
Antichrist, 5:211a
Ava inclusa, 5:210b
Johannes, 5:210b
Jüngstes Gericht, 5:211a
Leben Jesu, 2:227a, 5:210b–211a
poetry of, 5:211a
Frauen Buch, Der. See Ulrich von Liechtenstein
Frauenbewegung
women mystics and, 9:8a, 12b
see also Feminism
Frauendienst, 9:296a
Frauendienst. See Ulrich von Liechtenstein
Frauenfrage (women's question), women mystics and, 9:8a, 12b
Frauenlied, in German literature, 10:293a-b
Frauenlist, **5:211b–212a**
Frauenlob. See Heinrich von Meissen
Frauentreue, synopsis of, 8:128a
Fraumünster Abbey (Zurich), 11:541a
Fravashis, 12:721a
Fraw Eren hof. See Albrecht von Scharfenberg
Frawenpreiss armor workshop, 1:529b
Frayre de Joy e Sor de Plaser, 3:173a
Frechulf, **5:212a**
Fredebern, Johan, 7:220b
Fredegarius, **5:212b**
Chronicle, sources for, 5:212b
continuations of, 5:212b
Frederick III of Aragon, king of Sicily, 11:273b
Frederick I of Austria, duke, Wolfger von Erla and, 12:672b
Frederick II (the Quarrelsome) of Austria, duke, 2:33b
Neidhart "von Reuental" and, 9:93a
outlawed by Emperor Frederick II, 2:7a
Tannhäuser and, 11:590a, 590b
Frederick II of Brandenburg, 5:468b
Frederick VI of Brandenburg, elector, Nuremberg and, 9:202a
Frederick I of Denmark and Norway, king, 4:156b
Frederick I Barbarossa of Germany, emperor, **5:212b–214a**, 9:672a, 711a
Alexander III and, 3:637b–638a, 5:480b, 481a
appointments to Swabia and Lorraine, 6:273a-b
in Archpoet's "Imperial Hymn," 1:449b–450a, 10:252b
assertion of imperial power, 5:478b, 479b
in Italy, 5:94a
attempt to build territorial kingdom, 5:213a-b
Bohemia and, 2:134b
Bulgarus as adviser to, 2:418a
Burgundio of Pisa and, 2:423b
Burgundy and, 2:429a-b, 11:539a
chandelier of, 5:318b
chronicles of, 9:303b
coronation of, 5:479b, 479b–480a
death of, 4:40a, 58a
Denmark and, 4:153a
election of, 4:427a-b, 5:479b
German domains, 5:478b, 480a
development of German state, 5:481a-b
feudalization of Germany, 5:213b
Gesta Friderici, 7:365b
Continuatio, 10:249b–250a
Henry the Lion and, 4:153b, 5:480a, 481b, 511a, 6:168a, 7:680b
Hildegard of Rupertsberg and, 2:173b
Hohenstaufen-Welf feud and, 5:479b–480a, 485a
Hungary and, 6:340b
idea of empire, 5:495b
Ikonion and, 6:418a
imperial ministerials and, 8:405b
imperial princes and, 5:499a
Isaac II Angelos and, 6:559b
Italian policies, 6:273a
alienation of Lombardy, 5:213a
appointment of podestas, 7:652a
campaign of 1166, 5:480b–481a
claims of *regalia,* 7:652a
Lombard agreement, 5:481a
Matildan lands of, 5:481a
origin of Guelphs and Ghibellines, 6:6a
siege of Alessandria, 7:652b
land-peace ordinance of, 7:479a
limits on knighthood, 3:414a
Manuel I Komnenos and, 7:284a, 8:91b
marriage of, 5:480a
in Milan, 8:378a–379a
military feudalism, 12:561b
mining rights of, 8:402b
Nuremberg and, 9:201a
Otto of Wittelsbach and, 12:665a
as patron of poetry, 5:435a
Peace of Constance (1183), 7:652b
Peace of Venice (1177), 7:652b
planctus for, 9:693a
prestige of, 5:481b–482a
Qılıj Arslan II and, 11:154a
Rainald of Dassel and, 10:252b
Ramon Berenguer IV and, 10:256a, 444a
recognition of King Leo I/II of Cilicia, 7:546a
recognition of Vladislav II of Bohemia, 2:300a
relations with church, 3:353a, 5:480a
Adrian IV and, 1:58b, 2:180a
Alexander III and, 11:278b
alliance with Eugenius III, 5:212b–213a
antipapal policies, 10:252b
confrontations with papacy, 5:480a-b
influence on Roman politics, 10:523b
investiture and, 12:697b
papal legates to, 4:209a
reconciliation of 1177, 5:481a
role in church elections, 4:422a
schism, 5:213b
support of antipope Victor IV, 1:146b–147a, 5:213a
representative assemblies and, 10:329b
seal of Cologne and, 3:497b
Stefan Nemanja of Serbia and, 11:173b
Swabia and, 11:527b, 539a
Tegernsee *Antichrist* and, 4:268b, 282a
Third Crusade and, 5:214a, 441b
William II of Sicily and, 11:269a
Frederick II of Germany, emperor, 3:640b, **5:214a–215b**, 10:295b
addressed in Thomasin von Zerclaere's *Welsche Gast,* 12:38a
agreement for return of Jerusalem, 5:215a
antique art revival of, 10:310b
Assizes of Capua, 5:214b
banning of craft and merchant guilds, 6:17b
Burgundy and, 2:429b
Catalan Company's support of, 3:156a
centralization of kingdom, 5:215a
coinage under, 8:430a
Constitutions of Melfi and, 7:505a, 8:268b
coronation of, 5:214b, 11:270a, 12:61b
court of, 11:257b, 274a
crusade of, 4:32a, 51a-b, 11:270a, 270b
cultural achievements, 5:215b

Cyprus and, 4:70b–71a
Dante and, 4:101b–102a
De arte venandi cum avibus, 2:244b, 5:215b, 6:359b, 360a, 11:257b, 274a
death of, 5:485b, 11:272a
election of, 5:214b, 483a, 6:273b, 12:539a
excommunication of, 11:270b, 272a
fines for using false weights and measures, 12:118b
Golden Bull of Sicily (1212) and, 2:300a
Guelph-Ghibelline rivalry under, 5:94b–95a, 6:6a
Habsburgs under, 6:42a-b
Iacopo da Lentini and, 6:387b
in Italy, 5:214b
Naples and, 9:58b–59a
policies in Lombardy, 5:215a, 7:653a
Jean d'Ibelin and, 6:389a-b
Jews and, 7:87b, 11:210a, 210b
repudiation of blood libel allegations, 1:340b–341a
law and
abolition of ordeals, 7:505a
codification of secular law and, 7:429b
punishment for heresy, 6:483b
Liber Augustalis, 5:215a, 11:257b, 271a, 271b
Louis I and, 2:134b–135a
Malta and, 8:67b
marriage of, 11:269b
Nuremberg and, 9:201b
Otto IV and, 12:676a
patronage of art, 5:435a, 624a
commission of Psalter, 4:25b
patronage of law schools, 7:514b
patronage of Michael Scot, 8:305a
poetry of, 5:435a
principalities and, 5:499b–500a
public health code, 5:215b
recognition of, 12:537b
regency of, 5:214a
reign of, 11:269b–272a
relations with church, 5:495b
conflict with papacy, 3:353a, 5:461b
crusade against, 4:58b–59b, 6:448b
deposition by Council of Lyons, 3:641a-b, 5:215b
excommunication of, 4:32a, 52a, 59a, 537b, 5:214b, 215a, 484b–485a, 671b, 6:466a-b
failure to lead crusade, 5:214b
Innocent III and, 5:484a, 6:464a
Innocent IV and, 5:215b, 6:466a-b
Roffredus and, 10:439b
Roger de Flor and, 10:441b
Rome and, 10:523b
Rudolph of Habsburg and, 11:540a
scuola siciliana and, 6:25a, 624b, 641a, 643a
seizure of diplomatic envoys and, 4:211b
Sicily and, 11:273b
Swabia and, 11:527b–528a
trade agreements with Hafsids, 6:53a
translation patronage by, 12:135b
treaty with sultan of Egypt, 3:357a
troubadours and, 7:340b
Waldemar II and, 4:154a
Waldstätte and, 11:541a
Wolfger von Erla and, 12:673a
Zähringens and, 11:539a-b
Frederick III of Germany, emperor, 10:330a-b
A.E.I.O.U. motto, 2:9a
acquisition of Austrian land, 6:42b–43a
Conrad of Zabern and, 8:648a
crown of St. Stephen I of Hungary and, 11:483b
crowning of, 7:257b
Hungary and, 6:347b, 348a
Nicholas of Cusa and, 9:123b
reign of, 5:489b
retinue of, 6:472a, 473a
ride into Frankfurt, 12:378b
Frederick III (the Wise) of Saxony, duke, Adam of Fulda and, 8:648b
Frederick IV of Wettin, duke of Saxe-Wittenberg, enfeoffment of, 10:686a
Frederick III of Sicily, king, Arnald of Villanova and, 1:538a
Frederick I Hohenstaufen, duke of Swabia, 6:272b
Henry IV and, 11:527a
Frederick VI Hohenstaufen, duke of Swabia, in Third Crusade, 4:40a
Frederick of Antioch, as podesta of Florence, 5:94b
Frederick of Büren, Swabia and, 11:538b
Frederick (the Fair) of Habsburg, 2:7b–8a, 5:488a
Frederick of Habsburg, duke
Waldstätte and, 11:542a
Zurich and, 11:544b
Frederick of Liège (adviser to Pope Leo IX), 7:543a
Frederick of Lorraine, mission to Constantinople, 3:349a
Frederick (the Victorious) of the Rhine, count palatine, armor of, 1:528b
Frederick Roger of Sicily. *See* Frederick II of Germany, emperor
Frederick of Styria, duke. *See* Frederick III of Germany, emperor
Frediano, St., bishop of Lucca, Lucchese reclamation project, 12:576b
Free Choice. See Augustine of Hippo, St.
Free Spirit, heresy of, 2:161a, **5:216a–219b**
belief in human deification, 5:218b–219a
circumvention of sacramental authorities, 5:219b
criticized by Johannes Tauler, 9:34a
description of tenets, 5:216a
determinatio, 5:217a
existence of, 6:198b–199a
in Germany, 5:216b–217a, 217b–218a
influence on Hussites, 5:218b
in Italy, 5:217b
lack of common doctrine, 5:216a
Margaret Porete and, 9:12b
mystical beliefs, 5:217a, 219a
antinomianism, 5:218a
precursors of, 5:216a–217a
Ruusbroec and, 9:36a
social class of members, 5:219b
trials of alleged heretics, 5:218a, 218b
writings of, 5:218b
Free will
in Pelagius' doctrine, 9:486a
vs. predestination. *See* Predestination
Freedom, charter of. *See* Franchises
Freemen, 3:424a
proto-Polish, 9:716b
serfs and
France, 11:202b–203a
as one class, 11:203b, 205a
Freer Gospels, 8:97b
Freiburg im Breisgau, 5:460a
founded, 11:539a
Reichstag of 1498 at, 10:331b
Freiburg im Breisgau, University of, 12:288b
Collegium Sapientae, 12:293b–294a
Freidank, **5:220a-b**
Bescheidenheit
contemporary issues treated, 5:220a
preservation of, 5:220b
sources for, 5:220a
Fremdstofflieder, use in dating Eddic poetry, 4:389b–390a
French architecture. *See* Gothic architecture; Pre-Romanesque architecture; Romanesque architecture
French art. *See* Gothic art; Pre-Romanesque art; Romanesque art
French drama, **4:263b–266b**
actors in, 4:266a
allegory in, 4:286b–287a
by clerks of Parlement of Paris, 9:420a
during Reformation, 4:266a
early beginnings, 5:253a
elaborate staging, 4:264b
fabliau and, 4:576b–577a
farces, 4:265b, 5:13b, 274b
influences on later theater, 4:266a
liturgical origins, 4:263b–264a
major genres, 4:264b
miracle plays, 5:264a, 273b
social types and experiences, 5:257a-b
verse form, purpose of, 5:257b
morality plays, 4:265a-b
mystery plays, 4:279a, 5:273b–274a
ban by government, 5:274b
European adaptations, 5:274b
popularity of, 5:274a-b
nativity plays, 9:636a
Passion plays, 4:264a, 264b–265a
patronage of, 4:266a, 9:636b
religious, 5:273b–274b
secular, 5:273b, 274b–275a
urban origins of, 4:264a
staging of, 4:265b–266a
in 13th century, 5:264a-b
see also Miracle plays; Picard literature, theater

French government (*cont.*)
authoritarian nature of, 7:675a
bailiffs, 7:675a
bourgeoisie as officeholders, 5:180b
Capetian rule, 5:173b–174a, 174a
constable of the realm in, 3:543b–544a
consuls and consulates, 3:570b–571b
decentralization in 14th century, 5:190a
enquêteurs, 7:675a
estates, local, 5:174a
feudal characteristics of, in 13th century, 5:173a–174a
great offices of the crown, 7:674a
kings' travels and, 12:153a, 159a-b
local jurisdiction
division of, 5:157b
recovery by principalities, 5:159b
monarchy
origins, 9:552b
Salic Law, 9:555a, 555b
municipal, 7:675a
office of admiral (1246), 9:81a
Philippe de Rémi's documentation of, 3:674b–675a
reorganization under Philip II, 5:162b–165b
representative assemblies, 5:181b–182a
royal control over great fiefs, 5:170b–171a
royal revenues, 10:319b–320a, 323a
taxation authority, 10:320b, 326b–327b
see also Chambre des Comptes; Estates General of France; Parlement of Paris; Peace of God; Representative assemblies, French
French language, **5:220b–231b**
in Anglo-Norman England, 1:260a-b
consonants, symbols, 5:223a
dialects, 9:629b
in England, 6:441a, 8:313b
influence of, 8:309b
teaching of, 1:270a-b, 271a, *see also Manière de langage*
first documentary evidence for, 5:220b, 233b–234a
Francien dialect, 4:168a, 5:222a, 9:630a
development under Capetians, 5:234b
glosses of Latin texts, 5:221b
Greek influence on, 5:221a, 229b–230a
of Guernes de Pont-Ste.-Maxence, 4:168a
history, 5:220b–222a, 232a–236a
Gallo-Roman period, 5:221a-b, 232a
Merovingian and Carolingian dynasties, 5:221b, 232b
influence of, 5:231b
in Italy, 6:625b, *see also Franco-veneta* language
outside France, 5:222a, 234b, 235b–236a
of Jean de Meun, 4:168a
labialization, 5:224a
langue d'oc, in Tuscany, 6:645a
langue d'oc and *langue d'oïl,* 5:222a, 231a-b, 232a-b, 234a-b, 235a-b
in the late Middle Ages, 7:601a
learning of by foreigners, 7:601a-b
local speech variants
influence of invaders, 5:221b
northern and southern Gaul, 5:221a-b
Maistre Pierre Pathelin and, 8:52a
morphology and syntax, 5:225b–229b
nasalization, 5:224a-b
symbols, 5:222b
Norman dialect, in England, 5:222a
Old French, 5:221b–222b, 231b
borrowing from other languages, 5:235b
comparison to Provençal language, 10:157a
contribution to nationalism, 5:236a
courtly literature in, 6:442a
glosses in Aelfric's linguistic works, 1:285b
in literature, 5:232a
origin of, 5:234b
Rashi and, 10:260a
standard for other literary vernaculars, 5:236a
surviving texts, 5:222b
trouvère songs vocabulary, 12:214b–215a, 218b–219a
written form, evolution of, 5:235b
origin of, 6:435a-b, 442a
orthography, 5:224b–225a
palatization, 5:223b–224a, 232a
Rhétoriqueurs and, 10:365a
Romance vernaculars, 5:232a–236a
sound system, 5:223a–224b
Strasbourg oaths and, 11:488a-b
stress accents, 5:223a-b
teaching and study of, 12:137a
treatises, 12:530b–531a
triumph of Francien dialect, 4:168a, 6:442a
use of vernacular
by clergy, 5:233a-b, 288b
in legal procedures, 5:222a
official recognition of, 5:233a
Viking words and, 12:432a
vocabulary, 5:229b–230b
see also Anglo-Norman dialect; Bible, versions, French; Bodel, Jean, *Jeu de St. Nicolas;* Judeo-French language; Picard language; Provençal language
French law
appeal by combat abolished, 9:418a
appellate system, 5:171a, 173b
customary, treatises on, 9:644b
Établissements de St. Louis and, 4:515b
inquest in, 6:479b
lawyers, 7:457b–458a
in north, **7:457a–460b**
appeal by combat, 7:459a
assize, 1:594a–596a
basic procedure, 7:459a
charters of settlers, 7:458a
courts, appellate, 7:457b
courts, neighborhood, 7:457b
creation of new ordinances, 7:459b–460a
early treatises and collections, 7:458a–459a
general vs. local law, 7:460a
"good men" as deciding voice, 7:457b
inquests and the need for legal codes, 7:458b
multiplicity of codes, 7:457a-b
municipal law, 7:458a
non-self-judgment principle, 7:457b
principles of, 7:457b, 459b
south French law and, 7:461a
success of, 7:460b
summary manuals vs. local differences, 7:460a
taxation, 11:622a
written vs. customary law, 7:460a
see also Coutumes de Beauvaisis; Parlement of Paris
property
church, 8:489a
domaine utile, 11:678b
proprietas, 11:678b
in Renard the Fox stories, 10:313b
Rogerius and, 10:444a
Roman law and
forms adopted by crown, 7:464a-b
influence of, 7:638a
revival and spread, 7:462a–464a
terminology of, 7:463a, 466a
vs. custom, 7:464b–465a, 466b–467b, 9:644b
in south, 7:341b, **7:461a–468b**
accapitum or *accaptum,* 7:466a
ad hoc assemblies versus "feudal" relationships, 7:462a
administrative and judicial offices separated, 7:464a
church and testamentary law, 7:466a-b
commenda, 7:465b
communal family property and, 7:467b–468a
contracts, 7:464b–465b
Corpus iuris civilis and, 7:461a-b
Decretum of Gratian and, 7:461b
early codes, 7:461a
early *coutumiers,* 7:465b
early studia, 7:463a-b
early treatises, 7:462b
emphyteusis, 7:466a
emptio venditio, 7:465b
the family and, 7:466a–468a
feudal law and, 7:467a
fragmentation of political power and, 7:461b–462a
frayresque, 7:468a
Gallo-Roman law, 7:461a-b
glossators and, 7:463b
Goth influence, 7:461a-b
guirpitio as means of arbitration, 7:462a
Italian influence, 7:462a-b
iudex maior, 7:464a
justices, 7:464a
king's courts, 7:464b
laudatio parentum, 7:466b
legal scholarship and, 7:463a-b
lex mercatoria, 7:465a–466a
local governments, 7:464a-b

Montpellier as center of study, 7:463a-b
north French law and, 7:461a
paternal authority and, 7:467b–468a
peace assemblies, 7:462a
property law, 7:465b–466a
public character of, 7:461b–462a
purchase and sale, 7:465b
renunciation formulas, 7:465a-b
retrait lignager, 7:466b
Rhône Valley, 7:462b–463a, 464a
"right of the eldest," 7:467a
right of free disposition, 7:466a-b
Roman and Italian influences, 7:461a
royal influences, 7:464a–465b
societas terrae, 7:465b
summary of, 7:468a
taxation, 11:622a
see also Seneschal
see also Bailli; Ban; Inquest, in French law; Liberty and liberties; Ordinance; Peace of God; Seisin, disseisin
French literature
allegory. *See* Allegory, French
amour naissant theme, 6:170b
at court of Burgundy, 5:278b
autobiography, 2:237a
poetic, 5:267b, 269a
chansons de femme, 3:257a
chansons de geste, 3:257a–261b
chansons de malmariée, 3:262b–263a
chansons de toile, 3:263a
chant royal, 3:263b
chronicles, 5:253a
comoedia, Ovidian influence, 9:313a-b
complainte, 3:507b–508a
congé, 3:536b
courtliness, ideal of, 5:245a-b, 249b–250a
didactic, 5:252b, **5:281a-b**
bestiaries, 5:281a
lapidaries, 5:281a
materia medica, 5:281a
dits, 4:221a, 9:639a
judgment, 5:267a, 273a
love, 5:267b
epic poetry
Cantar de mío Cid versification and, 3:72a, 73a, 77a, 77b, 78a, 78b, 79b
see also Laisse
fables, 4:573a-b
fabliaux, 4:574a–577b
first surviving Old French poem, 5:235a
grands rhétoriqueurs, 5:268b, 278b, 282a, 283a
popularity of, 5:278b
history (to 1200), **5:232a–254a**
history (after 1200), **5:254a–281a**
in 13th century, 5:255a–265a
in 14th century, 5:254b, 265b–272a
in 15th century, 5:254b–255a, 272a–280a
influence of on Catalan literature, 3:171a-b, 173a
Italian influences, 5:278b
Italian prose and, 6:659a
lais, love in, 5:284b–285a
lyric, 5:252b, **5:281b–283b**
abstraction of material, 5:282a
ars nova and, 12:177b–178a
aubade, 1:642a
courtly, 1:123a
divorce of music and text, 5:281b–282a
expansion of subject range, 5:268a
forms, 5:282a, 283b
grand chant courtois, 5:251a, 252a
historicocultural achievement, 5:252a-b
jeu parti, 5:267a
models for, 5:251a, 282a-b
pastourelle, 5:264b
refinement and restructuring by Machaut, 5:266b, 267a
roman expérimental, 5:269a
rondeau, 10:528b–529a
subject matter, 5:282a
in 13th century, 5:282b–283a
verbal and musical levels, 5:251b
see also Ballade; *Débat; Estrabot*
"lyric triangle," 5:251b–252a, 262a-b
in Deschamps's theory of poetry, 5:268a
refinements of, 5:266b–267a
Middle French, 5:272b
narrative, 5:236a–243a
national self-consciousness and, 5:236a, 237b, 260b
"orphan verse," 7:319a
patronage of, 5:265a-b
prizes, Violette d'Or, 10:251b
prose
beginnings of, 5:253a
encyclopedic works, 4:449a
fiction, 5:275a-b, 287b
medical writings, 10:289a
realistic genres, in 13th century, 5:257a-b
religious, 5:233a-b
Renard the Fox stories, 10:312a–314a
Renard poems, 5:257b–258a
romances, 4:419b, 5:243a–253a, **5:283b–288a**
allegory in, 5:287a-b
amalgamations and *incidences,* 5:285a-b
Arthurian legend in, 1:568b–571b
at Norman-Angevin court, 5:244a
audience written for, 5:243b, 284b
believability of myths, 5:244b
courtly, 5:244b, 245a–246a, 258b
criticism of, 5:255b–256a
form, 5:243a-b
Grail legend in, 1:570b–571a
historical reevaluation in, 5:244a-b
Icelandic saga and, 4:617b
influence of hagiography on, 6:60a
influence on other literary genres, 5:260a-b
influence on Spanish literature, 11:423a
Latin sources, 5:284a, 290a
legend of Alexander, 5:284a
major cycles, 5:285b–286b
moral obligation of writer, 5:243b
non-Arthurian, 5:258b, 284a, 287a-b
origin of, 5:283b
portrayal of love, 5:269a, 284b–285a
purpose of, 5:284b
translated into Norwegian, 10:390a–391b
translatio studii, 5:244b, 260a
Tristan story in, 1:569b–570a
Trojan themes, 5:284a
use of lyric imagery, 5:249a, 251a–252b
see also Arthurian legend; Chrétien de Troyes; Floris; Marie de France; Prose Lancelot; *Roman de la Rose; Tristan, Roman de*
romans antiques, 5:243a-b, 256b
saints' lives, 2:235b–236a, 5:239a, 239b–240a, 240a
clerkly witness, 5:239a-b, 240a
combination of lyric and, 5:239b
concept of *imitatio Christi,* 5:238b–239a
dramatic adaptations, 5:256a
epic and, 5:236a-b
goals of, 5:240a
Latin sources, 5:288b
lay vs. clerical audience, 5:236b
Marian cult, 5:239b
mythopoetic concept, 5:242b
St. Mary the Egyptian legend, 5:239b
surviving texts, 5:239b
scientific works, 5:252b
translations, **5:288a–291b**
French to Latin, 5:289a
influence of patrons, 5:289b–291a
Latin to French, 5:288b–289a
legal and scientific texts, 5:289b
philosophic works, 5:289b
prose, 5:290b–291a
religious works, 5:288b–289a
saints' lives, 5:288b–289a
Tristan legend in, 12:200a–201a, 202a-b, 202b–203a
troubadour generation of 1200, 10:251a
12th-century renaissance, influence on Spanish literature, 11:412a
see also Anglo-Norman literature; *Ars poetica;* Bible, versions, French; Biography, French; *Chansons de geste; Chevalerie; Clergie; Ovide moralisé;* Picard literature; Provençal literature; Tristan, legend of; Troubadour; Trouvère
French music
ars antiqua, 12:177b
ars nova, 12:177b–178a
chansons de geste, 3:257a–261b
evolution of contratenor in, 3:577a
Landini and, 7:326b–327a
motet enté, 10:241a
trouvères in, Conon de Béthune, 3:538a-b
women troubadours (*trobairitz*), 12:207a-b, 215a
French pox. *See* Venereal diseases, syphilis
Frequens. See Constance, Council of

Frère Lorens. *See* Lorens d'Orléans
Frere, William (publisher of Paston letters), 9:449a
Fresco buono, **5:291b**
Fresco painting, **5:291b–296b**, 9:355b
Abbasid, at Jawsaq al-Khāqānī, 6:597b
Armenian, 1:496a
arriccio, 1:542b
at Kumurdo, 5:411a
at S. Clemente, 10:112b
at Vincenzo, 10:112b
Byzantine
iconostasis and, 6:409a
portrayal of emotion, 2:445a
in Catalonia, 10:113b
dancing depicted in, 4:86b
of Dawid-Garedja, 4:116a
of Eutychios, 4:524b
in 14th century, 5:292a-b
Francesco Traini and, 12:124a–125b (*illus.*)
French Romanesque, 10:506a–507a
Garel frescoes, 9:708b
Italian
allegorical, 7:668b
at Campo Santo, Pisa, 5:294b
Florentine, 5:294a-b, 295b, 12:171b–172b, 175a-b
of Giotto, 9:153b, 154 (*illus.*)
of Niccolò di Pietro Gerini, 9:119a
Paduan, 12:175b–176a (*illus.*)
in S. Croce in Florence, 5:294a
in S. Francesco of Assisi, 5:293a (*illus.*), 294a
in St. Martin Chapel, 5:294a
Sienese school, 7:668b, 670b, 12:172b–175a (*illus.*), 175b
of Ugolino di Prete Ilario, 6:636a
in Kalenderhane Djami, 7:349b
method of, 5:291b, 292b–293a
Michael Astrapas, 8:303a-b (*illus.*)
panel painting and, 5:296a
picture cycles in, 5:293a-b
preliminary drawings for, 4:291a
of saints' lives, 5:293a–294a, 295b
in 13th century, 5:292a
Umayyad, 6:594b–595b (*illus.*)
see also Mural painting; Sinopia
Fresco secco, 5:291b, **5:296b**
use by Cimabue, 3:396a-b
Frescobaldi banking company, 2:77b
Frescobaldi, Dino, 6:649a
Frescobaldi, Matteo, 6:651b
Frese nouvelles, 8:571b
Fresne, Le. *See* Marie de France
Fressant, Hermann, *Mären,* **5:296b**
Fret (stringed instrument part), 8:563b
Freuchulph. *See* Frechulf
Freyja, 11:27b, 12:356a, 356b
Frigg and, 5:301a
in *Hyndluljóð,* 6:385b
member of the Vanir, 5:296b
Njǫrðr and, 9:146a
Norns and, 9:171b
in *Sturlaugs saga Starfsama,* 11:496b
in *Þrymskviða,* 12:52b
see also Scandinavian mythology
Freyr, **5:296b–297b**, 11:26a, 12:356a, 356b, 423b
characteristics of, 5:297a
fertility statue of, 5:297a
in *Gísla saga Súrssonar,* 5:297a
in *Hrafnkels saga,* 5:297a
meaning of, 5:296b
member of the Vanir, 5:296b–297b
Mímir and, 8:395b
Njǫrðr and, 9:146a, 146b
role in *Lokasenna,* 7:643b
in *Skírnismál,* 5:297b, 11:326b–327a
in *Víga-Glúms saga,* 5:297a, 12:416a
in *Ynglinga saga,* 5:297a
see also Scandinavian mythology
Friar Daw's Reply, 8:332a
Friar Robert. *See* Robert, Brother; *Tristrams saga ok Ísöndar*
Friars, **5:297b–298b**
definition of, 5:298a
Dominican. *See* Dominicans
France, employment as *enquêteurs,* 7:675b
Francis of Assisi and, 5:298a
Franciscan. *See* Franciscans
monks and, 5:298a
preaching churches, London, 7:663b
principal orders of, 5:297a
see also Carmelites; Mendicant orders; Sack, Friars of the
Friars of the Blessed Mary. *See* Pied Friars
Friars Minor. *See* Franciscans
Friars Preachers. *See* Dominicans
Frías, Gonzalo de, lost collection of sermons by, 11:456a
Fribourg
Bern and, 11:543a, 543b, 544a
Holy Roman Empire and, 11:539b
Kyburgs and, 11:539b
Rudolph of Habsburg and, 11:540a
Swiss Confederation and, 11:544b, 545a
Friday, Islamic, compared to Jewish Sabbath and Christian Sunday, 7:617b
Friday prayer (Islamic), **5:298b–299b**
description of, 7:618a
excellence of Friday, 5:299a
historical development of, 5:299a-b
ᶜ*id* prayers and, 5:299b
khuṭba, 5:299b, 10:246a
legal status of, 5:298b–299a
Muḥammad's institution of, 5:299a-b
observance of, 5:298b–299a
Fridegodus. *See* Frithegod
Fridugisus of Tours, **5:299b–300a**
De nihilo et tenebris, 5:300a, 9:585b
Friedberg, fairs, 4:586a
Friedrich der Freidige of Thuringia, count, 4:269a
Friedrich von Hausen, **5:300a-b**, 5:440b–441a
career of, 5:300a
courtly love songs of, 5:300a
crusade poetry of, 10:294a
"Ich muoz von schulden sin unfro," 5:300b
lyrics, 8:413b
"Min herze den gelouben hat," 5:300b
"Min herze und min lip diu wellent scheiden," 5:300b
"Si welnt dem tode entrunnen sin," 5:300b
Friendship of Amlyn and Amig, 12:612a
Frigate mackerel (*Auxis thazard*), 5:69b
Frigg, **5:301a-b**, 11:27a-b
in the Baldr myth, 2:55a-b
characteristics of, 5:301a
divine functions, 1:63a
Freyja and, 5:301a
in *Grímnismál,* 5:301a
in *Lokasenna,* 5:301a
Lombard legends, 5:301a
in Second Merseburg Charm, 5:301a
in *Sturlaugs saga Starfsama,* 11:496b
in *Vafþrúðnismál,* 12:344a
see also Scandinavian mythology
Frigidian. *See* Frediano
Frik, **5:301b–302a**
"Concerning Arłun-Łan and Buła," 5:301b
education of, 5:301b
Mongols and, 5:301b–302a
poetry of, 5:301b–302a
Frisia
coastal trade of, 9:88b
early medieval northern European trade and, 12:110a
Germanic migration into Britain and, 1:289a-b
missionaries in, 9:500a
Viking raids on, 12:429b, 430a
Frisian language, 6:441b
Frisians, vs. Franks, 6:436b
Frisius, (Reiner) Gemma, 3:464a
armillary sphere of, 11:95b
Frit, 4:582a
Frit body, 3:239b
Frithegod (Frithegode, Fridegodus), **5:302a-b**
Aeddi and, 5:302a
Life of Saint Wilfrid, 5:302a, 7:363a
Oswald of Ramsey and, 5:302a
Friðþjófs saga frækna
romantic elements, 5:141b
as a source for *Víglundar saga,* 12:416b
Þorsteins saga Víkingssonar and, 12:47a
Fritigern, Visigothic king, 2:90b, 12:469a, 469b
Friulian spetum, 7:325a
Frobisher, Martin, influenced by *Mandeville's Travels,* 8:82a
Frode the Peaceful. *See* Frotho the Peaceful
Froissart, Jehan, **5:302b–304a**
on Beauneveu, 2:145a
benefactors of, 5:302b
Chronique de Flandre, 5:303b
Chroniques, 3:327b, 5:303a-b, 6:264b, 334b
characteristics of, 3:332b–333a
concept of chivalry in, 5:270b–271a
criticisms of, 5:270a-b
depiction of chariot, 12:377b
on King Leo V/VI of Cilicia, 7:547a
miniature by Loyset Liédet, 9:82a-b (*illus.*)
scope of, 5:270b

sources for, 9:638b
dits of, 5:302b–303a
early life of, 5:302b
Espinette amoureuse, 5:269a-b
on flagellants, 2:263a
on the Jacquerie, 9:478a
on Jean de Vienne's campaign against Scotland (1385), 10:428b
Joli buisson de Jonece, 5:269b–270a
lai and, 7:316b
Lay de Nostre Dame, renunciation of poetry in, 5:270a
lyric poetry, 9:637a
Machaut's influence, 5:303a, 8:3b
Méliador, 5:266a, 303a, 9:635b
number of plague victims estimated by, 2:264a
Orloge amoureus, 5:269a
on the Peasants' Revolt, 9:479a
poetry of, 5:268b–270a, 302b–303a, 8:583b
Prison amoureuse, 5:269a
prose writings, 5:270a–271a
Temple d'Onnour, Le, 5:303a
visions and, 12:475b
Froment, Nicolas, **5:304a-b**
Altarpiece of the Burning Bush, 5:304a-b (*illus.*), 609a
Fromund of Tegernsee, **5:304b**, 7:363a
Frontier land settlement. *See* Reclamation of land
Frontinus, Julius
De aquis urbis Romae, 11:515b
Strategamata
in *Cantar de mío Cid,* 3:77a
translation of, 9:510b
Frontispiece, Islamic arch. *See Pishtaq*
Frotho the Peaceful of Denmark, 10:676b
in legends, 10:677b
in literature, 6:3b
Frotula noiae moralis. See Pateg, Girard, *Noie*
Frowin of Engleberg, missing works by, 12:22a
Fructuosus, **5:304b**
prayer book of Sancha, 5:304b–305a (*illus.*)
Fruits and nuts, **5:305a–307b**
acorns, 1:95a
in Mediterranean region
in cooking, 5:306b–307a
in diet, 5:305a
information about, 5:305b–306b
medical literature on, 5:306a-b
variety of, 5:305a–306a
to prevent drunkenness, 9:550b
trade in, 5:126b–127a, 307a
uses of, 5:126a
see also Grapes
Fruits and vegetables
availability of, 3:581b–582a
Kievan Rus, 1:100b
medicinal aspects, 3:582a
nutritive value, 1:96a
truck gardens, 1:78a
variety of, 1:78a, 81b, 84a, 86a, 87a, 96a, 98b, 104b
see also Grain crops; Legumes
Frumentius, Christianization of Abyssinia and, 1:31b–32a
Frutolf of Michelsberg, **5:307b–308b**
Berno and, 8:641b
chronicles of, 5:307b–308a
influence of, 9:303a
Ekkehard of Aura and, 5:307b
Fuchs. *See* Renard the Fox
Fuel
coal, and air pollution, 6:122a
competition for, 6:122a
increased need for fireplaces, 6:121b–122a
wood, and deforestation, 6:121b–122a
Fuero, **5:308b–310a**
codification by Alfonso X, 5:310a
decline of, 5:310a
Ferdinand III's grants of, 5:309b–310a
function of, 5:308b–309a
Jewish privileges in, 7:80a
long, 5:309b
oldest local, 5:309a
regional, 5:309b
short, 5:309a
statutory compilations of, 5:309a
in Valencia, 5:309b, 12:348a
see also Spanish law
Fuero antiguo, in the kingdom of Navarre, 9:70b
Fuero general, in the kingdom of Navarre, 1:576a, 9:71a, 71b
Fuero juzgo, 5:310a, 7:522a-b, 11:414a
Fuero de las leyes. See Fuero real
Fuero de los fijosdalgo. See Fuero viejo de Castilla
Fuero real, 5:310a, 7:430a, 522a–523b
contents of, 7:522b
extent of acceptance, 7:522b
importance under Alfonso XI, 7:523b
Fuero viejo de Castilla, 7:523a
Fuerteventura, 3:62a-b
Füetrer, Ulrich. *See* Ulrich Füetrer
Fugger family, Hungary and, 6:349a
Fulanis, Timbuktu and, 12:55b
Fulbert of Chartres, **5:310a–311a,** 7:363b, 10:246b
cathedral construction, 10:478b
on church-state relations, 5:310b
correspondents of, 5:310b
education of, 5:310a-b
as exegete, 2:213a
hymns of, 6:381b, 384a
poem attributed to, 3:58a
rhymed offices and, 10:372a
sermons of, 10:3a
Sylvester II and, 11:552b
works of, 5:310b–311a
Fulcher of Chartres, 3:356a, **5:311a-b**
chronicles of, 5:311a-b
on crusaders, 4:20a
description of Constantinople, 1:332b–333a
Gesta Francorum used by Matthew of Edessa, 8:228b
Historia Hierosolymitana, 5:311a
Fulco of Rheims, archbishop
assassination of, 10:303a
Hucbald and, 6:317a
Fulda, **5:311b–312b**
abbots of, 5:311b–312a
basilica at, 10:92b, 94a
church, apse in, 3:378b–379a
decline of, 5:312a
establishment of, 2:322a, 5:311b
Hrabanus Maurus and, 6:306a
illuminations made at, 10:101b
imperial politics and, 5:312a
library of, 7:565a
Michaelskirche at, 5:312a
as missionary training center, 5:311b, 312a
numbers of monks at, 2:173a
royal and papal support of, 5:311b
Salvator basilica at, 5:311b–312a
students at, 5:312a
Tatian manuscripts and, 11:600b
Fulgens and Lucrece. See Medwall, Henry
Fulgentius, Fabius Planciades
Baudri and, 7:364a
De continentia vergiliana, 12:395a
Mythologies, 1:183b
Fulgentius metaphoralis. See Ridevall, John
Fulgentius of Ruspe, St., 3:321a
Liber de Trinitate ad Felicem, 12:189b–190a
Fulk of Jerusalem, king, crowned, 4:22b
Fulk of Neuilly
against interest taking, 12:336a
preaches Fourth Crusade, 4:41b
Full-rigged ship, 11:244b–245a
evolution of, 11:234 (*illus.*)
Fullers' earth, 11:705a
Fulling
foot, 11:705b
of luxury-grade woolens, 11:712b
hand, 11:705b
mill, 11:706a–707a
opposition to, 11:707a
stages of process, 11:705a-b
Fulrad of St. Denis, abbot, 9:690b
Pepin III and, 9:501a, 502a
Funduq, **5:312b–313a**
definition of, 5:312b
design of, 5:313a
khan and, 7:237b
Funeral liturgy. *See* Dead, Office of the
Funerals. *See* Death and burial; Funerary rituals
Funerary rituals
candles, 5:319a, 320a
Coptic funerary paintings, 3:591b–592a
funeral banquets, 4:336a
liturgical furniture, 5:320b
see also Death and burial
Fünfkirchen. *See* Pécs
Fuqahāʾ, 11:85a
see also Fiqh
Fur trade. *See* Furs and fur trade
Furlong management, villages and, 12:439b, 445a
Furlong (unit of measure), 12:585a
Furniture
Islamic, **5:313a–316a**
Bedouin traditions, 5:315b
beds, 5:315b
chests, 5:315b–316a
height of, 5:314b–315a
Koran lectern (*rahle*), 10:250a-b (*illus.*)

Furniture (*cont.*)
Islamic (*cont.*)
social rank and, 5:315a
sources of information about, 5:313a–314a
surviving examples, 5:316a
in Syrian court, 5:315a
tables, 5:314a-b (*illus.*), 315b
thrones, 5:315a-b
see also Kursī
liturgical, **5:316b–321a**
altar enclosures, 5:316b–317a
chests and boxes, 5:319b–320a
credence, 5:318a
for the Eucharist, 5:316b
funeral, 5:320b
lights, 5:318a–319a
liturgical seating, 5:317a-b
misericord, 8:437a
musical devices, 5:320b–321a
oil vessels, 5:320a-b
praesepe, 5:319b
prie-dieu, 5:318a, 10:120a
processional apparatus, 5:319b
for readings, 5:317b–318a
signaling devices, 5:320b–321a
textiles, 5:319a
timing devices, 5:320b–321a
Tuscan Romanesque, 10:502b
wall and columnar furnishings, 5:319a-b
water vessels, 5:320a
see also Sedilia
Western European, **5:321a–325b**
beds, 5:323a
benches, 5:323a
carving design on, 5:324b
chairs, 5:322a (*illus.*), 323a-b
chests, 5:321b (*illus.*), 322b–323a
dressers, 5:323b–324a, 325a (*illus.*)
English, 5:325a
Flemish, 5:325a
foliage motif of, 5:324b
forms and materials of, 5:324a-b
French, 5:325a
information about, 5:321a–322a
Italian, 5:325a-b
joinery, 5:324b
painting of, 5:324b
paneled framing, 5:324b–325a
social rank and, 5:322a-b
tables, 5:324a
see also Inns, structure and furnishings
Furor teutonicus, in Germanic mythology, 2:198b
Furs and fur trade, **5:325b–335a**
in Baghdad and Iraq, 12:105b
Eastern European, 5:326 (map)
with Central and Western Europe, 5:328a–330b
with Far and Middle East, 5:330b–334a
types of furs, 5:327a
Hanseatic League and, 12:113a
Kievan Rus and, 12:435b
Russian merchants in Constantinople, 12:101b
Russian money system in, 8:426b
Siberian, in Transoxiana, 12:146a
taxation of, 5:327b–328a
uses of furs, 5:325b
Vikings and, 12:110a
Western European, 5:325b, 327a
Furs de València, 12:348a
Fursa, missions of, 3:226a-b
Fürstenspiegel, 7:261a, 264b, 267a
see also Mirror of princes
Fusee, invention of, 3:29b
Fusoris, Jean, 3:462b, **5:335a**
achievements of, 5:335a
on astronomy, 1:612b
clocks and scientific instruments made by, 11:103b
Libellus de seccione mukefi, 1:439a
life of, 5:335a
Fust, Johann, 10:124a
Fusṭāṭ, al-, 3:13a-b
mosque of, 4:408a
naval base, 9:74a, 75a
transfer of Egyptian capital to, 4:405b
Tulinid dynasty and, 12:223a-b, 224b
see also Cairo
Fuṣūl wa 'l-Ghāyāt, Al-. See Maᶜarrī, Abu 'l-ᶜAlāᵓ Aḥmad al-
Futhark, 1:215a
see also Runes
Futhark, Older, 10:558b–559b, 561a–562a (*illus.*)
Futūḥ al-Buldān. See Balādhurī, Abū Ḥasan Aḥmād ibn Yahya ibn Jābir al-
Futuh al-Ghayb. See Jīlānī, ᶜAbd al-Qādir al-
Fütüvvetname literature, 11:308b
Futuwwa, 5:518a, 11:308b–309a
Futyā. *See Fatwā*
Fylgja, **5:335a–336a**
categories of, 5:335b
etymology of term, 5:335b
in *Njáls saga,* 5:335b–336a
in *Víga-Glúms saga,* 5:335b–336a
Fylgjukona, 5:335b–336a
Fylke (Scandinavian local unit), 10:699a-b
Fyn (in Denmark), 12:423a
Fyrd, 11:612a
Anglo-Saxon England, 12:556a-b
Norman England, 12:560b
Fyslawe, Thomas. *See* Fishlake, Thomas

G

Gabelle, **5:336a–337a,** 10:319b, 631a-b, 11:624a
Estates-General and, 5:336b
evasion, penalties, 10:631b
exemption from, 10:631b
forms of, 5:336a, 336b
imposed by John II, 10:319b
initiation of, 11:623a
for military purposes, 10:631a-b
models for, 10:631a
opposition to, 11:623b
petit and *grande,* 10:631b
Philip VI of France and, 5:336a-b
Rome, 10:526a
variation between principalities, 10:631b
Gabelliers, 5:336b
Gabirol, Ibn. *See* Solomon ben Judah ibn Gabirol
Gabri ware, **5:337a**
bowl, 5:337a (*illus.*)
description of, 5:337a
Gabriel (archangel), 1:249a-b, 433a
in Islam, 1:248b
equated with Sarōsh, 1:249a
Muḥammad and, 6:576b
Gabriel Biel. *See* Biel, Gabriel
Gabriel de Mussis, on Black Death in south Asia, 2:258b
Gabriel Qatraya bar Lipah, 11:568a
Gabriel, ruler of Melitene, 1:484b
Gace Brulé, **5:337b**
attribution to of an alba, 1:123a
poetry of, 5:337b
Gace de la Buigne
Roman des deduis, 6:360b
on Philippe de Vitry, 12:481b
Gad (British linear measure), 9:504a
Gaddesden, John, *Rosa angelica,* 9:674b
Gaddi, Agnolo, **5:337b**
Cennini and, 3:234b
Coronation of the Virgin, 5:337b
frescoes of, 5:295b–296a, 337b
Giovanni d'Ambrogio da Firenze and, 5:532b
Legend of the True Cross, 5:295b, 337b
Life of the Virgin, 5:295b–296a, 337b
Madonna and Child with Saints, 5:337b
Gaddi, Gaddo, **5:338a**
Gaddi, Taddeo, **5:338a-b,** 12:174b–175a
Entombment, 5:338a-b
frescoes of, 5:294b, 338a-b
Life of the Virgin, 5:338a
Madonna and Child with Four Angels, 5:338b
Meeting of St. Joachim and St. Anne, 5:338a (*illus.*)
Niccolò di Pietro Gerini and, 9:119a
Gaddo di Zanobi. *See* Gaddi, Gaddo
Gadifer de la Salle, 3:62a-b
Gaelic art. *See* Celtic art
Gaelic language
as separate dialect, 3:233a
see also Celtic languages
Gaels, sons of Míl, 9:47a
Gaeta, Western European trade and, 12:111a
Gaetani, Benedict. *See* Boniface VIII, pope
Gaffurius, Franchinus, 8:649a
Giorgio Anselmi and, 8:648a
Gag(a)raljóð (*rímur* meter), 10:405b
Gagik I of Ani, king, 1:482a, 483a, **5:338b–339a**
army of, 5:338b
Basil II and, 1:483b, 5:338b–339a
Church of the Holy Cross and, 1:495b, 496a (*illus.*)

Church of St. Grigor Lusaworič^{c} and, 1:292a, 5:339a, 12:165a
David of Tao and, 4:113b, 5:338b
death of, 1:482b
marriage of, 11:315a-b
statue of, 5:339a
tax policies, 5:338b
Gagik II of Ani, king, 1:290b, **5:339a-b,** 12:361b
Ani in Širak and, 1:484a
Byzantines and, 11:315b
Constantine IX Monomachos and, 5:339a-b
Grigor Magistros and, 5:675a
migration of, 1:485a
murder of, 1:484b
resignation of, 5:339a
Gagik Arcruni of Vaspurakan, king of Armenia
Ałt^{c}amar, 1:220b
as *archon ton archonton,* 1:449b
Smbat I and, 1:481b, 482a
Gagik of Atom in Anjewac^{c}ik^{c}, prior, 1:511a
Gagik of Kars, king, **5:340a-b**
Vanand and, 12:354a
Gagik-Abas II of Kars, king, 7:221a
migration of, 1:485a
Seljuks and, 1:484b
Gagik/Xač^{c}ik-Gagik of Vaspurakan, king, **5:339b–340a**
alliance with Yūsuf of Azerbaijan, 5:339b
building activities of, 5:340a
Gospel of Queen Mlk^{c}ē commissioned by, 5:340a
letters of, 5:339b–340a
see also T^{c}ovma Arcruni
Gaguin, Robert
Le débat du laboureur, du prestre, et du gendarme, 9:638b
translations from Latin, 9:638b
Gahanbar (Sasanian feasts), 10:664a, 664b
Gaianites
Docetism and, 4:233a
see also Aphthartodocetism
Gaillard, Château, 10:384a
Gaimar, Geffrei, **5:340b–341a**
chronicles of, 5:283a, 340b–341a
Estoire des Engleis, 1:261a, 565a, 3:331a, 5:389b
account of St. Edmund's death, 9:448b
contents of, 1:264b–265a
modern edition of, 1:271a
Geoffrey of Monmouth and, 5:389a-b
translations of, 5:340b
Gaiseric. *See* Genseric
Gaius Sollius Apollinaris Sidonius. *See* Sidonius Apollinaris
Galahad, 8:224b
in Thomas Malory's *Morte Darthur,* 8:63b–64a
Galaktotrophousa. See Lactatio
Galata. *See* Pera-Galata
Galata, tower of, 4:45a-b
Galata War, 2:501b
Galatia, origin of name, 6:436a
Galba, Martí Joan de, 12:349a
Galbaio, Giovanni, doge of Venice, 12:385a
Galbert of Bruges, 2:386b, 3:497a, 9:149a
Galen
Ad Glauconem, 8:247a
Aristotle and, 1:457a
Ars medica (*Tegni*), translated by Constantine the African, 8:248a, 248b
Ars parva, 8:256b
Book of Fevers, inadequacy of during Black Death, 2:264a
on cosmetics, 2:147a
criticized by Maimonides, 11:92b
criticized by al-Rāzī, 10:267a
De alimentis, translated by William of Moerbeke, 12:641a
De sectis, 8:247a
Epidemics, Ḥunayn's translations of, 12:132b
influence on Byzantine medicine, 8:244a-b
on the main organs of the body, 8:251b–252a
Metategni, translated by Constantine the African, 8:248a
Natural Faculties, Ḥunayn's Arabic translation of, 12:131b
On Treatment of Diseases, 12:132b
Synopsis of the Platonic Dialogues, 9:699a
Tegni. See Galen, *Ars medica*
Therapeutics, recommended by Cassiodorus, 8:247a
translations of
by Burgundio of Pisa, 8:249a
by Gerard of Cremona, 8:249a
by Ḥunayn ibn Isḥāq, 12:128b, 130a, 131a–132b
by Nicholas of Reggio, 8:251b
into Arabic, 11:83a
into Hebrew, 12:134a
into Syriac, 11:566b
vision theory, 9:251a
Words of Hippocrates, 12:132b
Galeran de Bretagne, **5:341a-b**
author of, 5:341a
inspiration for, 5:341a
Galerius, Roman emperor, 10:462a
Thessaloniki and, 12:26a
Galfredus de Vinosalvo. *See* Geoffrey of Vinsauf
Galfridus Arturus (Monemutensis). *See* Geoffrey of Monmouth
Galib (Galippus), 5:422b
Galicia
relations with Hungary, 6:340b, 341b
Santiago de Compostela, 9:656a, 659a-b, 661b–662a
Galician language, 6:442b
origins of, 6:435b, 442b
Galician literature, poetry, 3:86b, 87a
Galician music, song, 3:84b–87a
Galician-Portuguese literature
Arthurian legend in, 1:576a
poetry, **5:341b–342b**
Alfonso X the Learned and, 11:415a
Castilian literature and, 5:342a, 11:419a
compilations of, 5:341b
musical texts of, 5:341b
Provençal literature and, 5:341b
Razón de amor, 10:268b–269a
rhyme forms, 5:341b–342a
secular texts of, 5:341b
Galilee, Tancred and, 11:589b
Galilei, Alessandro, Lateran and, 7:344b
Galilei, Galileo
Averroism and, 1:468a
Gerald of Brussels' *Liber de motu* and, 1:436b
Galindia, 2:63 (map), 66a
Gall, St. (Gallus), **5:342b–343a,** 11:526a
Columbanus and, 5:342b
influence of, 5:342b–343a
missionary work of, 8:440a
vita by Strabo, 9:691b–692b
Vocabularius Sancti Galli and, 12:487b
Gall-ghàidhil, 11:490b
Galla Placidia, Roman empress, 10:262b–263a, 12:470a
mausoleum at Ravenna, 4:236a, 5:361a, 10:263a
seized as hostage by Visigoths, 2:91a
Gallego, Fernando, **5:343a,** 5:612a
Gallego language. *See* Galician language
Gallery, **5:343a-b**
tribune, 12:187b–188a (*illus.*)
triforium, 12:188a
Galleys
Aragonese, 11:235b
Byzantine, 11:231b–232a
classical, 11:229b
eastern Mediterranean, 11:233a-b
English, 11:243a
Genoese, 9:89a
great, 11:235a-b
in Hundred Years War, 9:81b
Mediterranean, 9:80b, 88a
navies and, 11:237a
Northern European shipbuilding and, 11:242b–243a
oar power and, 11:233b, 235a
see also Dromon
Gallia Narbonensis, 4:108a
Gallica notation. *See Ars subtilior;* Musical notation
Gallican chant, **5:343b–344a**
definition of, 5:343b
diversity of, 5:343b
examples of, surviving, 5:343b–344a
Latin rites and, 5:344b
processionals and, 5:343b–344a
Stephen II and, 5:343b
suppression of, 5:661b
Gallican rite, **5:344a–345b,** 8:301b
clerical orders, 9:265b
Communion, 8:195b
blessing of the people, 8:194a
described, 7:627a
differences from Roman, 8:182b
dismissal, 8:197a
Expositio brevis antiquae liturgiae gallicanae and, 5:344b–345a
incense and, 6:431b
Kyrie in, 7:593b
lectionaries for, 5:344b
libellus for, 10:605a

Gallican rite (*cont.*)
litanies of, 7:591b
Mass, 5:344b–345b
offertory, 8:190a-b
origin of Advent and, 1:59a-b
origin of, 5:181a-b, 345a-b, 8:182b
Quem quaeritis in, 4:273b
sacramentaries for, 5:344b, 10:606a
Solesmes method and, 11:361b
sources of, 5:344b
see also Metz, use of; Narbonne rite
Gallicanism
importance of, 10:69b
Pragmatic Sanction of Bourges and, 10:69b
Gallicanus. See Hrotswitha von Gandersheim
Gallicus, Johannes. *See* John of Garland
Gallienus, cavalry of, 3:201a
Gallinarius. See Wipo of Burgundy
Gallipoli, contested by Ottomans and Europeans, 4:55b–56a
Gallnuts, medicinal and dyeing uses, 4:326a
Gallo-Romance language, 6:437b, 442a
Gallon (unit of measure), **5:345b–346a**, 10:238b
definition of, 5:345b–346a
English, 5:346a, 12:585a
Scottish, 5:346a, 12:585a, 589a
standard for, 5:346a
Gallowglasses. *See* Mercenaries, in Ireland
Gallus. *See* Gall, St.
Gallus Anonymous, 11:345a
Cronicae et gesta ducum sive principum Polonorum, 9:723a
Galut, **5:346a–347a**
God and, 5:346b–347a
as means for spreading of Judaism, 5:346b
as punishment, 5:346a-b
as sacrifice, 5:346b
Gama, Vasco da, 11:247b
Calicut and, 4:563a
navigation techniques, 11:650b
Gamay grape, 12:654a
Gambacorta, Pietro, 9:664b
Gamber, Klaus, 4:224b–225a
Gambling
dice, 5:350a–351a
in inns, 6:474a
in Islam, 5:353b
Latin church's view of, 5:350b–351a
taverns and, 12:651a
Game (hunting). *See* Hunting
Game warrens. *See* Warrens
Games, **5:347a–353a**
Alfonso X (the Learned) on, 5:347a
archery, 5:348b–349a
backgammon, 5:349a (*illus.*), 351b
ball games, 5:348a
bearbaiting, 5:350b
board games, 5:351a-b
bowling, 5:348a, 351a (*illus.*)
card games, 5:352a-b, 9:706b–707b (*illus.*)
chess, 5:351b–352a
equestrian battles, 5:347b–348a
fencing, 5:348a-b
hoodman blind (blind man's buff), 5:347a
Islamic, **5:353a–354b**
backgammon, 5:353b
chess, 5:353b, 354a (*illus.*)
children's games, 3:353a-b
condemnation of, 3:353a
field sports, 5:353b
hawking, 5:354b (*illus.*)
horse racing, 5:354a
military training and, 3:353b–354a
polo, 5:354a
restrictions on, English, 5:348a
sitting games, 5:347a, 350b–351a
slapping games, 5:347a-b
tennis, 5:348a
tournament, 5:347b (*illus.*), 349a–350b
wrestling, 5:348a-b
Gamla burial mounds, 10:693b
Gamla krönikan, 7:220b
Gamla Uppsala Cathedral, 10:489a
Gamli Kanóki, **5:354b–355b**
compositions of, 5:354b–355a
Harmsól, 5:355a, 11:358b
as a model for *Líknarbraut,* 7:580a
kennings of, 5:355a
Gammadion, 4:9b, 11 (*illus.*)
Gamut, 8:640b
musica ficta and, 8:597b
Gandersheim, abbey of, 6:313a-b, 314a, 316a
Ganelon, 8:225a, 225b
"Gangolfus." *See* Hrotswitha von Gandersheim
Gangra, Council of (*ca.* 340), condemnation of dualism, 6:192a
Gangrene. *See* Leprosy; Plagues
Gania Sophia (church: Trebizond), wall paintings, 2:447a
Ganjak, **5:355b–356a**
annexed to Georgia, 11:587b
founding of, 5:355a
Mongols' sacking of, 5:355b
as Muslim stronghold, 5:355b
prosperity of, 5:355b
Shaddadids in, 1:513b, 7:310b, 11:217a, 217b
Ganjak of Atropatene, **5:356a**
identification with Zintha, 5:356a
location of, 5:356a
names of, 5:356a
sack of by Heraklios, 5:356a
Sasanians in, 5:356a
Ganjak of Atropatene, Battle of (591), 2:50a
Gano da Siena, **5:356b**
Virgin and Child Between Saints, 5:356b
Gansfort, Johann Wessel
Devotio Moderna and, 4:167a
nominalist theology, 2:368b
Ganzag-i Shīzīgān. *See* Ganjak of Atropatene
Ganzak. *See* Ganjak of Atropatene
Ganzha. *See* Ganjak
Gao (capital of Songhai Empire), 12:54b–55a, 55b
Gaol delivery. *See* Jail delivery
Gaol fever. *See* Plagues, enteric; Plagues, typhus
Gaon, 11:583b–585a
leadership of Jewish communities by, 5:356b–357a
office of nagid and, 9:52a, 52b
see also Schools, Jewish
Gaonic period, **5:356b–358a**
biblical exegesis during, 2:212a
Epistle of Sherira Gaon as source for, 7:98a
geonim, 5:356b–357a, 7:161a-b
law in, 7:491a-b
messianic movements in, 5:357b–358a
mystic literature in, 7:168b
name of, 5:356b
in Palestine, 7:104b–105a
responsum literature in, 10:337b–338b
talmudic studies, 5:357b–358a
Garai family, 6:346a
Garbage. *See* Public health, sanitation
García III Sánchez of Navarre, king, 2:126b, 9:69a-b
death at Atapuerca, 3:128b
García IV Ramírez (the Restorer) of Navarre, king, 9:70a
García de Salazar, *Bienandanzas,* 11:443b
García of Toledo, canon, *Garsuinis* (*Tractatus de Albino et Rufino*), 11:406a-b, 410a
Garçon et l'aveugle, 4:264a, **5:358a**
bourgeois realism, 9:636a
Gardar, diocese of (Greenland), 12:427a-b
Gardar (legendary discoverer of Iceland), 12:426b
Garden of Chosroes carpet, 10:547b
Garden of Deduit (miniature from *Roman de la Rose*), 10:450 (*illus.*)
Garden of Eden
Paradise and
Islamic, 9:392b
Western, 9:395b
see also Gardens; Paradise
"Garden of Mensural Music, The." *See* Marchettus of Padua, *Pomerium in arte musicae mensuratae*
Garden of Truth, The. See Sanāʾī, *Hadīqat al-ḥaqīqat*
Gardener, Jon, *Feate of Gardeninge, The,* 5:362b–363a
Gardens, European, **5:358a–365b**
church's importance in, 5:361a-b
features of
enclosures, 5:361b–362b
fountains and water jokes, 5:363a-b
lawns, 5:364a–365a
menageries and aviaries, 5:363b
paths, 5:363a
raised beds, 5:362b–363a
statues, 5:363a
topiary, 5:363a
turf seats, 5:363b–364a
"flowery mede," 5:364b–365a
literary references to, 5:358a-b
in monasteries, 5:352b, 358b–359b, 361a
in paintings, 5:361b
religious elements in, 5:361a-b
in religious illustrations, 5:361a-b

in *Roman de la Rose,* 1:184b, 189a
St. Gall plan, 5:358b–360a
sources for knowledge of, 5:358a-b, 360b–361a
university botanic, 5:360a
Gardens, Islamic
in Alhambra, 1:170a
herbal, 6:186a
inspired by concept of Paradise, 9:392b–393a
in the Persian manner, 6:186a
see also Rauḍa
Garel von dem (vom) blüenden Tal. See Pleier, Der
Gargoyle, **5:365b–366a**
on Cathedral of Milan, 5:366a (*illus.*), 10:265b (*illus.*)
definition of, 5:365b
Garigliano, Battle of the (915), 10:522a
Garin lo Brun, *Ensenhamen,* 3:664a
Garin le Loherain, 3:261b
see also Lotharingian cycle
Garinē. *See* Gaurenē
Gariopontus, *Passionarius,* 8:247b–248a, 256a
Garlande family, 11:160a
Garlandian notation, 1:544b–545a
see also John of Garland (music theorist)
Garments. *See* Costume
Garni, temple at, 1:493a
Garniture, 1:533a
Garshāsp-nāma. See Asadī of Ṭūs
Garter, Order of, 3:307a, 6:334b, 7:278b
Garum, production of, 5:68b–69a
Garzo, *Proverbi,* 6:632a, 651a
Gascon Bertrand de Got. *See* Clement V, pope
Gascon War (1294–1303), 2:328b
Gascony, 1:367a (map)
confiscation by Philip VI (1337), 6:331b
English settlers in, 2:129a
French invasion (1294), 4:396a-b
kingdom of Navarre and, 9:67b, 68a
Labourd and, 2:126b
Sancho III of Navarre and, 9:69a
see also Aquitaine
Gaston III of Foix, count
Livre de chasse, 6:360b–361a, 361b
vs. Charles V, 7:341a-b
Gastronomy. *See* Cookery
Gasull, Jaume, 3:171b
Gates of Paradise, 5:524b–525b (*illus.*)
Gāthās, **5:366a–367a**
author of, 5:366a-b
translation of, 5:366b
transmission of, 5:366b
see also Avesta; Zoroaster
"Gathering bag" (Irish manuscripts). *See Bolg an tsoláthair*
Gathic Avestan language, Zarathustra and, 12:720b
Gathic dialect. *See* Avesta
Gato, Juan Álvarez, political satire by, 11:454b
Gattaponi, Matteo, **5:367a-b**
Gattilusio, Francesco, John V Palaiologos and, 7:380a
Gattinara, irrigation of, 6:558b
Gatto lupesco. See Detto del Gatto lupesco
Gaucelm Faidit, importance of troubadour poetry of, 10:175a
Gaucher de Rheims, Rheims Cathedral and, 10:344b
Gauchier de Dourdan, **5:367b**
Second Continuation of *Conte du Graal,* 5:367b
Gaudentius, 8:636b
Cassiodorus and, 8:637b
Gaufrid (Gaudfred) Malaterra, **5:367b**
Historia Sicula, 5:367b
Gaufridi, Raymond
influenced by Roger Bacon, 2:41a
release of imprisoned Spirituals, 5:202a
Gaufridus Anglicus. *See* Geoffrey of Vinsauf
Gaufridus of Jerusalem, prior, 7:365b
Gaul
Burgundians in, 2:423a
Caesar's conquest of, 2:88b
Celts in, 10:465a
Christianity in, 8:439a
pre-Roman roads in, 10:409b, 410a
Roman bridges in, 10:410a
travel in, 12:149a
Visigoths in, 12:470a–471a, 473b
see also France
Gauntlet, 1:530a, 532b, 534a (*illus.*)
Gaurenē, 1:515a
Gauriel von Muntabel. See Konrad von Stoffeln
Gauti of Götaland, 5:368b
Gautier d'Arras, **5:368a**
Eracle, 5:368a
hero's gifts, 9:634b–635a
Ille et Galeron, 5:284b, 285a, 368a, 9:635a
Gautier de Châtillon. *See* Walter of Châtillon
Gautier de Coinci, **5:368a**
beguines and, 2:159b
Miracles de Nostre Dame, 5:368a, 9:633b
fabliau and, 4:574a, 576b
Vie de sainte Léocadie, 9:633b
Gautier le Cordier de Tournai, *Gilles de Chin,* 9:635a
Gautier de Dargies, *lai* and, 7:316b
Gautreks saga konungs, **5:368a–369a**
character of Refr Rennisson, 5:140a
confrontation of Thor and Odin, 5:142a
dating of, 5:368a-b
description of Starkaðr in, 5:139b–140a
episodes of, 5:368b–369a
Hrólfs saga Gautrekssonar and, 6:310b
Skarkaðr legend and, 11:466b–467a
Gauts. *See* Goths
Gauzlin, abbot (11th century), 9:143b
Gauzlin of Jumièges (9th century), 2:173b
Gavelkind, 3:424b
Gaveston, Piers
conviction of, 6:427b
death of, 7:370a
celebrated in a parody, 9:441a
Edward II and, 4:397a, 9:426a
Gavitᶜ, 1:494a
Gawain
in Arthurian legend, 5:448b–449a
Excalibur and, 4:530a
in Thomas Malory's *Morte Darthur,* 8:64b
in Wolfram's *Parzifal,* 12:677a
see also Valven, Sir
Gawain and the Green Knight, Sir, **5:369a–371a,** 8:319b, 320a, 320b, 332a, 332b
alliteration in, 8:343a
antifeminism in, 1:324b
armor in, 1:526a
beheading game, and folk play tradition, 4:283b
on the celebration of Christmas, 8:339a
composition of, 5:369a
in Cotton Nero MS, 9:476a
Fled Bricrenn and, 6:527a
game paradigms in, 4:279a
hunting in, 6:359a
narrative structure of, 5:370a
opening lines of, 8:312b
play in, 4:279b
plot of, 5:369a–370a
rhyme in, 5:370b, 8:343b–344a
symbolism of three in, 5:370a-b
tone of, 5:370a
Gawitᶜ, **5:371a-b**
at Gełard, 5:373b (*illus.*)
at Gošavankᶜ, 5:579b
definition of, 5:371a
interior reliefs, 6:286a
types of, 5:371a-b
vaulting in, 5:371a
Gawrēk. *See* Gaurenē
Gaychatores. See Waits
Gayianē (Armenian virgin martyr), 1:517b, 518a
Gayianē (church: Vałaršapat), 1:493b, **5:371b**
erection of, 5:371b
martyrium at, 5:371b
Gaykhatu, Ilkhanid ruler, 6:420a
Gayrard, Raymond, **5:371b–372a**
St. Sernin church, 10:622a
Gayrard of Toulouse. *See* Gayrard, Raymond
Gaza, synagogue at, 7:65b
Gazza, Yabhalaha II and, 11:567b
Gdańsk, 9:728b
Gear, invention of, 3:458a
Gebehart. *See* Herger
Geber, *De investigatione perfectionis,* 1:138a
see also Jābir ibn Aflaḥ; Jābir ibn Ḥayyān
Geberge la Flamande. *See Pilgrim's Guide*
Gebhard of Constance, bishop, 11:527b
Geblümter Stil, 8:411b
Gecaerde lakenen, 11:696b
Gedicht vom heiligen Kreuz, Das. See Heinrich von Freiberg
Gediminas of Lithuania, ruler, 2:67a, 7:605b–606a
letters to Pope John XXII, 7:605b
successors of, 7:606a

Gedymin. *See* Gediminas
Geert Zerbolt van Zutphen. *See* Gerard Zerbolt of Zutphen
Geertgen tot Sint Jans, 5:87a-b, **5:372a**
Gerard David and, 4:114b
innovations of, 5:87a
Master I.A.M. of Zwolle and, 6:388b
Nativity, 5:372b (*illus.*)
Geese, domestication of, 5:150b
Geffrei Gaimar. *See* Gaimar, Geffrei
Gefjon, **5:371a–373a**
myths about, 5:372b–373a
in *Ragnarsdrápa,* 5:372a-b
role in *Lokasenna,* 7:643a
Zealand and, 5:373a
Gegenbach, Pamphilus, *Die zehn Alter dieser Welt,* 8:484b
Geghard. *See* Gełard
Geheimrat, 5:502b
Geiler, Johannes, *Narrenschiff,* 8:361b
Geirmundar þáttr heljarskinns, in *Sturlunga saga,* 11:498b
Geirrøðr (Scandinavian giant)
Thor and, 12:45b, 48a
in *Þorsteins þáttr bæjarmagns,* 12:48a
Geisli. See Einarr Skúlason
Geisslerlied
carol and, 8:572a
Spechtshart and, 8:647a
Gełam. *See* Sewan, Lake
Gełard, **5:373a–374a**
gawitᶜ at, 5:373b (*illus.*)
main church of, 5:373b (*illus.*)
outside walls of, 5:373b
purchase by Pṙoš, 5:373b
as religious and pilgrimage center, 5:373a
sack of, by Arabs, 5:373a
Gełarkᶜuni. *See* Sewan, Lake
Gelasian Sacramentary, 8:368a, 386b (*illus.*)
on funerals, 4:120b
Gelasius I, pope, **5:374a**
Deprecatio Gelasii, 7:591a, 593b
Felix II and, 5:374a
"Gelasian Renaissance" in canon law, 7:399a
on imperial and papal power, 3:11a
influence of, 5:374a
on papacy's role, 10:17b, 20a–21a
recognition of the Vulgate by, 2:211b
temporal vs. spiritual authority, 4:374a, 9:371a
works of, 5:374a
Gelasius II, pope, 3:636a
cursus and, 4:67a
Gelassenheit (letting-go), in Johannes Tauler's mystical doctrine, 9:34a
Gelatᶜi, 4:112a, **5:374a–375a,** 7:311b
academy of, 5:374b, 417a
bell tower of, 5:374b
builder of, 5:374a
collection of homilies for, 6:61a
dome of, 5:374b
Four Gospels of, 5:411b
scriptorium of, 5:374b
wall decorations, 5:374b
Gelds, collection of, 11:611b
Gellért. *See* Gerard of Csanád
Gellert, Christian, *Renner* and, 6:326a
Gellone Sacramentary, 10:605b
Gelmírez of Santiago, archbishop, 11:435b
Gematria, 10:74a
Gemeine Pfennig. See Taxation, German, common penny
Geminus, Thomas, manufacture of scientific instruments and, 11:103a
Gemistos Plethon, Georgios, **5:375a,** 9:95a, 99b, 11:51a, 55a
Isidore and, 6:563a
Platonic thought and, 9:698b–699a
Platonism of, 7:1a
as teacher of classical literature, 3:432a
Gemma ecclesiastica. See Gerald of Wales
Gems and jewelry, **5:375a–382a**
basse-taille enamel, 5:380a
belt buckle, 5:380a
Bohemian, 5:377b
bracelets, 5:378a
Iranian, 5:378b (*illus.*)
brooches, 5:380a–381a
Burgundian, 5:381a (*illus.*)
Byzantine, 5:375a-b, 377b–378a, 379b–380a
earrings, 5:376b (*illus.*)
cameos, 5:380b (*illus.*), 381a
Carolingian, 5:377a
chains, 5:381a-b
in chivalric age, 5:380a
earrings, 5:378a-b
fibula, 5:375b, 376b (*illus.*)
Frankish, 5:375b, 377a
from crusades, 5:380a
of Germanic tribes, 5:375b, 377a
in hair, 5:381b
Islamic, 5:378b–379b
jasper carving with Christ, 5:376a (*illus.*), 377b–378a
of Justinian, 5:375a
Kievan, 5:378b–379a
kolt, 5:376 (*illus.*), 379a
lapidaries, 5:281a
of Nasrid Spain, 5:379b
necklaces
Byzantine, 5:376a (*illus.*)
Hispano-Mauresque, 5:379b (*illus.*)
Ottonian, 5:377a
pectoral cross, 5:375a-b
pendants, 5:375 (*illus.*), 379a, 381a-b
pomanders, 5:381b
ring brooch, 5:380a-b
rings, 5:380b
Schaffhausen onyx, 5:380 (*illus.*)
as sign of rank, 5:380a-b
silver and gilt coatings, 11:635a
symbolism of the pearl in *Pearl,* 9:477a
Western Europe as center for, 5:379b–381b
see also Metalsmiths, gold and silver
Gems and precious stones, Thomas of Cantimpré's work and, 12:34a-b
Genâde, 8:413b
Genealogie deorum gentilium. See Boccaccio, Giovanni
Genealogy
consanguinity in, 3:539b–540a
Icelandic, in *Landnámabók,* 7:327b
Irish, 6:539a-b
in Old Norse poetry, 7:312a
pipe rolls and, 9:662a–663b
Genealogy of the Kings of England. See Ethelred of Rievaulx, St.
Genealogy of the Pagan Gods, The. See Boccaccio, Giovanni
General Admonition, 3:91b, 108b, 109b
Gènesi de Scriptura, 3:167a
Genesios, Joseph, **5:382a**
Imperial Histories, 2:514a, 5:382a, 6:245a
on the Paulicians, 9:468a
Theophanes continuatus and, 12:23a
Genesis, relief by Lorenzo Maitani, 8:53 (*illus.*)
Genesis. *See* Bible
Genesis and Exodus (Middle English poem), 2:221b, 4:546b
Genesis (Old English paraphrase), 1:279b
alliterative verse, 9:233b
Genesis A, 4:550b
Genesis B, 2:225a, 4:550b
connection with *Heliand,* 6:150a, 151a
Genet, Jean-Philippe, 8:435a
Genetics, Mediterranean, gene pools and disease, 9:673b–674a
Geneva, 11:543b
Berchtold of Zähringen and, 11:539a
fairs, 4:585b
Otto I and, 11:538a
Swiss Confederation and, 11:542b, 545b
Geneva, Lake, in art, 12:668a
Geneviève, Ste., as patron saint of Paris, 9:401a
Genghis Khan, **5:382a–383a**
Chin dynasty and, 5:382b
conquests of, 5:382b–383a
death and burial, 8:468b–469a
descendants of, 6:329a, 420a
in *History of the Nation of the Archers,* 5:674b
Kereyid and, 5:382b
military conquests
Afghanistan, 8:467b
Caucasus, 8:468a-b
Chin, 8:465b–466a, 468b
Hsi-hsia, 8:465b, 468b
Khwārizmshāh, 6:504a-b, 8:466b–468a
Qara Qitai, 8:466a-b
reorganization of army, 8:465b
rise to power, 5:382b
struggle for recognition, 8:465a
title of, 7:237a
vs. Abbasids, 6:514a
vs. Khwārizmshāhs, 6:504b
vs. Nishapur, 9:141a
Genghisids
Tamerlane and, 11:587b, 588a, 588b
see also Farghānā (Fergana); Mongol empire
Genikon, taxation and, 11:603b
Genizah
definition of, 3:15a
see also Cairo genizah
Gennadios II. *See* George Scholarios
Gennadius of Marseilles, 2:239a

De viris illustribus, 2:180a
Statuta ecclesiae antiqua, 3:441a
Gennaro, St.
catacombs of in Naples, 9:57a
cult of in Naples, 9:58a
Genoa, **5:383b–387a**
after Lombard invasion, 5:383b
Andronikos III Palaiologos and, 1:246b
Annals of, 5:384a
beautification of, 5:384a
Boccanegra's rule of, 5:385b–386a
building of, 5:383b
Catalans and, 5:386b
charter of (958), 5:383b
colonies of, 5:386b
Caffa, 2:258b
in Crimea, 3:12a, 7:380a, 12:98b
in Lebanon, 7:533a
as commune, 5:384a-b
conquest by King Rothari, 8:377a
decline of in the 15th century, 12:115b
defense of, 5:384a
diarchy of, 5:385b
dogeship in, 5:385b–386a
economic rise of, 5:384b, 7:14b, 12:111a–112a
financial institutions
Casa di San Giorgio, 2:75b–76a, 7:17b
money changers, 2:73a, 74a
origins and development of, 2:73a–74b, 75b–76b, 78b
First Crusade and, 5:384a
Frederick II and, 11:269b, 270a, 272a
Gelata War, 2:501b
Genoese counts in Malta and, 8:67b
Guelph-Ghibelline rivalry in, 5:385a
isolation of, 5:383b
Jews in, 5:383b
Lombard invasion of, 5:383b
maritime trade routes and, 9:88a-b, 12:114b–115a
merchant ships of, 9:88a (*illus.*)
mint at, 8:430b
Muslim raids on, 5:383b–384a
naval development of, 9:80a
navigators of, in the Atlantic Ocean, 9:87b
Phokaia mines, 5:386b
piracy and, 11:230b
podestà in, 5:385a-b
relations with
Cyprus, 4:71a
Pisa, 9:664b
Rome, 10:523a, 525b
Seville, 11:214a
Venice, 1:246a, 7:8a-b, 9:84a, 12:112a, 390b–391a, 392a, 392b–393a
sack of Almeria, 5:384b
sacked by a Fatimid fleet (934), 9:75b
Sforza rule of, revolt against, 8:380a-b, 11:216b
shipbuilding in, 5:384b
silk industry in, 5:386b
trade in
alum, 11:158b, 12:111b, 115b
food, 11:275b
slaves, 11:338b–339a
trade of, 4:557b–558a, 5:384b–385a
with Alexandria, 1:154a
with Byzantine Empire, 12:103a–104a
with Cilicia, 7:546b
rivals, 5:385a
Sebaste and, 11:132a
Visconti invasion, 7:7b
Visconti rule of, 8:379b
voluntary associations in, 5:386a
see also Pera-Galata
Genovino, 8:430b
Gens nouveaux, Les, 4:265b
Gens du roi, 9:419b
Genseric, Vandal king, 2:91b, 12:354b–355a
Gentile da Fabriano, **5:387a**, 9:666b
Adoration of the Magi, 5:387a
Bellini and, 2:165a
Coronation of the Virgin, 5:387a
inspired by Bartolo di Fredi, 2:116b
Madonna and Child with Two Saints, 5:387a, 387b (*illus.*)
works in International Style, 5:607a-b, 628a
Gentile da Foligno, 8:251b, 260a
Gentile di Niccolò Massio. *See* Gentile da Fabriano
Gentile of Spoleto, 5:204a
Gentiles, Jewish dietary laws and, 4:183a-b
Genuflexorium, 5:318a
Geoffrey V Plantagenet, count of Anjou, 1:253a, 9:693b
Henry II and, 9:167a
itineracy of, 9:167a-b
marriage of, 9:166b
Geoffrey of Auxerre, 2:192a
Geoffrey of Charni, 3:666a
Livre de chevalerie, 3:666a
Geoffrey of Coutances, bishop, writ from William I, 7:435b
Geoffrey of Eversley
Ars epistolaris ornatus, 4:175b
dictamen of, 4:175b
Geoffrey Le Tor, 1:599a
Geoffrey de Lucy, 5:545a
Geoffrey of Monmouth, **5:387b–390b**
Arthurian literature and, 5:388b–389a
on Canterbury, 3:81a
Historia regum Britanniae, 3:327a, 4:471b, 5:340b, 388a-b, 6:264a, 8:224a
accuracy of, 7:365a
Arthurian legend in, 1:565a-b, 572a, 5:447a
Brut and, 2:393a
Excalibur and, 4:530a
influence of, 5:389b
Lludd and Llefelys, 12:610b
as model for Gaimar's *Estoire des Engleis,* 1:264b
Skjǫldungar saga and, 11:328b
translated into Norwegian, 10:389b
translations of, 2:365b, 5:244b, 389a-b
Trójumanna saga and, 12:207b
Welsh versions, 12:600b, 612b–613a
life of, 5:387b
Merlin, sources for character, 12:603b
prophecy of Six Kings, 10:148a-b
Prophetiae Merlini, 1:565a, 2:365b–366a, 5:387b–388a
translated into Old Norse, 8:275b–276a
as a source for Robert Mannyng's *Story of England,* 8:87a
Vita Merlini, 5:389b, 398b
Wace and, 5:389a-b, 12:496b
see also Prophecy, political
Geoffrey of Noyers, **5:390b**
work attributed to, 5:390b
Geoffrey of Sablé, founding of Solesmes by, 11:360b
Geoffrey of Vendôme, 7:364a
criticism of Robert d'Arbrissel, 10:429b
Geoffrey of Vinsauf, **5:390b–391a**
Documentum de modo et arte dictandi et versificandi, 5:391a, 7:366a, 10:359b
influence of, 5:391b
John of Garland's works and, 7:134a
life of, 5:390b
Poetria nova, 1:255a, 452b, 5:390b–391a, 6:659b, 7:365b–366a, 10:359b, 360a, 360b
invention in, 1:554a
opening of, 1:554a
organization in, 1:554a-b
on proverbs, 10:189b
verbal expression in, 1:554b–555a
Summa de coloribus rhetoricis, 5:390a
supplanted by humanist literary theories, 10:363b
Geoffrey of Viterbo, *Pantheon,* derivatives of, 10:544b
Geoffrey of York, archbishop, lay taxation and, 11:608b
Geoffroi II of Achaea, prince, 7:378a
Geoffroi d'Ainai (Aignay), **5:391b**
Archard and, 5:391b
architectural style of, 5:391b
works of, 5:391b
Geoffroi de Fontaines. *See* Godfrey of Fontaines
Geoffroi de Villehardouin. *See* Villehardouin, Geoffroi de
Geoffroy de La Tour-Landry, 2:149b
courtesy book of, 3:662b
Geography
Byzantine, *see also* Communications, Byzantine; Roads, Byzantine
Islamic, **5:391b–395a**
al-Balkhī school, 5:392b–393a
al-Bīrūnī and, 5:393a
cultural information, 8:533a
dictionaries, 5:393b
Ibn Khurdādhbih, 7:242b–243b
Indian influences on, 5:392a
Iranian influences on, 5:392a-b
Iraqi school of, 5:392b
literature of, 5:394a
marine, 5:394a
Ottoman, 5:394a
Persian influences on, 5:393a-b
pre-Islamic roots, 5:391b
travel accounts, 5:393a-b

Geography (*cont.*)
Islamic (*cont.*)
travel and transport and, 12:147a–148a
value of, 5:394a-b
world geography of al-Idrīsī, 5:393b
see also Bab al-Mandab; *Baḥr al-muḥīt;* Maghrib, al-
literature, Bouvier's *Livre de la description des pays,* 12:162b
Roger II of Sicily and, 6:412a-b
Western European, **5:395a–399a**
classical sources for, 5:397b–398a
climate zone problems, 5:399a
expansion of knowledge, 5:398b
geocentric universe, 5:395b–396a
magnetic compass and, 5:396b–397a, 399a
portolan chart and, 10:33a–35a
scientific vs. traditional, 5:396a-b
spherical universe, 5:396a
texts and encyclopedias, 5:396a
treatises, 9:535b
see also Roads, Western European
see also Guidebooks
Geography. See Ptolemy, Claudius
Geography of the World. See Ašxarhacᶜoycᶜ
Geomancy, 9:705a
Geometres, John, poetry of, 2:506b–507a
Geometria Boethii, 8:208a
Geometria culmensis, 8:212b–213a
Geometria deutsch. See Roriczer, Mathes
Geometria speculativa. See Bradwardine, Thomas
Geometry, 9:705b
Archimedean, 8:210b
in building construction, 8:177b–178a
curriculum. *See* Seven Liberal Arts
Euclidean, 8:209b–210a
Islamic achievements, 11:86b
Jewish, 11:90a
methods of approximation, 8:211b
notion of direct measurement, 8:208b
rhetorical presentation, 8:210a-b
Roman tradition, 8:207b–208a
suppositions, 8:211b
theory and practice, 8:208a-b, 210a, 210b–211a, 211b
see also Mathematics
Geonim. *See* Gaonic period
Geoponica, 4:446b, **5:399b**
estate management and, 4:511a
on farming techniques, 11:634b–635a
on horse care, 11:634b–635a
overlapping of theory and lore, 6:178b
Georg of Ehingen, 4:579a
George II Balšić, ruler of Zeta, Lazar Hrebeljanović and, 11:181a
George II, *katᶜołikos,* Ašot I and, 1:480b
George III of England, king, Paston letters and, 9:449a
George of Arbela, *Expositio officiorum* and, 11:568a
George, bishop of Arab tribes (*d.* 724), 11:565b, 566b
George Castriota. *See* Skanderbeg
George of Cyprus, **5:399b–400a**
dating of works of, 5:399b
Descriptio orbis romani, 5:399b–400a
George (Djuradj) Branković of Serbia, despot, 11:182b–183a
Stefan Lazarević of Serbia and, 11:472b, 473a
George, duke of Clarence, 12:571b
George Kalliergis, **5:399b**
frescoes of, 5:399b
style of, 5:399b
George the Monk, **5:401a–402a**
Brief Chronicle, 2:513b, 5:401a–402a
continuations of, 2:513b
purpose of, 6:244b
religious focus of, 5:401b
as source for *Suda,* 11:501b
sources for, 5:401b
on the Paulicians, 9:468a
George Pachymeres, 11:55a
historical works, 2:516b
George of Pisidia, **5:400a-b**
Hexaemeron, 1:506a, 5:400b
historical epic poems of, 2:513a, 5:400a
poetry
influence of, 2:506b
style and meter, 2:506b
George of Poděrady, king of Bohemia, 2:8b, 5:489b–490a, 6:348a, 377a
persecution of Bohemian Brethren and, 2:306b
George, St., 1:520a
in art, 6:411a, 10:265 (*illus.*), 501b–502a (*illus.*)
Bulgarian icon, 2:416 (*illus.*)
of Nisart, 9:140a (*illus.*)
of Notke, 9:186b–187a
in literature, *Georgslied,* 5:420b
in *stiacciato* relief by Donatello, 11:484b, 485 (*illus.*)
George Scholarios, 3:432a, **5:401a,** 11:55a
Constantine XI and, 5:401a
John VIII Palaiologos and, 5:401a
as patriarch of Constantinople, 5:410a
use of the term "transubstantiation," 7:610b
George Sphrantzes, *Chronicon minus,* 2:517a
George Sursuvul, 2:405a
George Synkellos, world chronicle, 2:513a
George Terter of Bulgaria, tsar, 2:411a-b
George of Trebizond, **5:400b–401a,** 9:699a
Bessarion and, 5:400b
Comparatio Platonis et Aristotelis, 9:703b
Nicholas V and, 5:400b
Paul II and, 5:401a
quarrels of, 5:400b–401a
translations of, 5:400b, 7:1b
George Vojteh of Skopje, 2:407b
Georges Chastellain, 10:364b, 365a
Georges de la Sonnette, **5:402a,** 7:56a
Entombment of Christ, 5:402a
Jean Michel and, 5:402a
Sluter and, 5:402a
work of, 5:402a
Georgia
Arabs in, 5:405b–406a
Arcrunis in, 1:451b
Armenians in, 5:405a
Arsacids in, 5:405a
art and architecture. *See* Georgian architecture; Georgian art
atabeg in, 1:632a
Bagratids in, 5:405b–406a
Basil II and, 2:119b
chronicles of, 5:404b
district of Vanand and, 12:354a
division of, by Persia and Byzantium, 5:405b
environs of, 5:403 (map)
ethnology of, 5:403a–404a
feudalism in, 5:407a, 419b
geography and ethnology, **5:402a–404b**
see also Urbnisi
invaded by Alp Arslan, 1:203b, 11:152b
Mongols in, 5:407a
office of *spaspet,* 11:460b
origins of, 5:404b–405a
patroni and *qmani* hierarchy, 10:236b
people of, 5:403a–404a, 419a–420a
Persians in, 5:405a-b
political history, **5:404b–407b,** 12:580b
Chosroids, 3:307b–308a
in *Kᶜartᶜlis Cᶜχovreba,* 7:222b–223a
Mongol invasions, 8:468a, 469b
pan-Caucasian Georgian empire, 11:631b
Queen Rusudan, 8:469b
tavadoba, 9:466b
see also Amirspasalar; Bagratids (Bagratuni), Georgian; Liparit IV Orbēlean; *Patronqmoba;* Sebēos
relations with
Armenia, 1:485b
Byzantine Empire, 5:405b, 406a, 416b
Seljuks of Rum, 11:157b
Sasanians in, 5:405a
Seljuks in, 5:406a-b
separatism of Iberia, 1:483a
Shirvan and, 11:254a
Širak in, 11:311b
Siwnikᶜ in, 11:315b
states of, 5:402b
Sultan Malikshāh I and, 11:153a
Turkomans in, 8:60a
under David II, 4:112a
under Tamar, 11:587a-b
uniting of, 3:195b
vs. Muslims, at Shamkhor, 11:587a
vs. Seljuks, 4:112a
vs. Sökmen II, 11:220a
see also Trade, Armenian; Uzun Ḥasan
Georgian alphabet, 1:214b–215a (*illus.*), 5:405a, 414b
Georgian Annals. *See Kᶜartᶜlis Cᶜχovreba*
Georgian architecture, **5:408a–409b**
Atenis Sioni, 1:632b
church at Mtsxetᶜa, 4:231b–232a
Djvari, 4:231b–232a
domes, central-plan triconch, 9:287a

Gelat^{c}i, 5:374a-b
Išḫani, 6:562b–563a
piers, cruciform, bundle columns and, 2:311a
Tsromi church, 12:222a-b
under Muslims, 5:408b–409a
see also Bagrat's Cathedral; Bana; Bitshvinta; Church architecture, Georgian; Urbnisi
Georgian art, 5:408a, **5:409b–412a**
altar screens, 5:410a-b
architectural sculpture, 5:409b–410a (*illus.*)
Byzantine influence, 5:411a
deesis relief, cathedral of Oški, 9:287 (*illus.*)
frescoes, 5:411a
Byzantine influences, 5:411a
manuscript illumination, 5:411a–412a (*illus.*)
metalwork, 5:410b–411a
icons, 5:410b (*illus.*)
mosaic, 5:411a
painting, 5:411a
sculpture, 5:409b–410a
see also Betania
Georgian chronicle. *See* *K^{c}art^{c}lis C^{c}χovreba*
Georgian church, 1:477b, **5:412b–414b**
Armenian church and, 1:499b
ascetics in, 5:414a
founders of, 5:414a-b
history of, 5:412b
martyrs in, 5:413b–414a
monasticism in, 5:409a, 412b, 414a-b, 417a
origins, 5:407b, 412b
Orthodox faith and, 5:407b
saints in, 5:412b–413b
Georgian language, 5:404a-b, **5:414b–416a**, 5:419a
dialects of, 5:404a
history of, 5:414b–415a
Laz, 5:404b
Mingrelian, 5:404b
origin of, 5:419a
sound system of, 5:415a
subgroups of, 5:404a
Svan, 5:404a-b
verbal system in, 5:415b–416a
written, 5:414b
Georgian literature, **5:416a–419a**
biblical exegesis, 2:214b
chronicles, 5:417b–418a
decline of, 5:418b
epics, 5:418b
romantic, 5:418b
fables, 5:418a
golden age, 11:631b
Gospel translations, 5:416b
Septuagint, 2:211a
historical, 5:417b
inscriptions, 5:416a-b
lyric, 5:418a
prose, 5:418a-b
saints' lives, 5:416b
secular, 5:418a-b
theology in, 5:417b
translations from Greek, 5:416b–417a
see also Balavariani
Georgians, vs. Xlat^{c}, 12:713b
Georgians (Iberians), **5:419a–420b**
Arčēš and, 1:423a
Byzantine influences, 5:419b–420a
ethnic origins of, 5:419a
governing system of, 5:420a
in Kars, 7:221b
in Kura River Valley, 5:419a
Laz, 5:404a
Mingrelians, 5:403b–404a
Mongols and, 5:420a
Persian influence on, 5:419b–420a
religion of, 5:404a
in Rioni River Valley, 5:419b
Seljuks and, 5:420a
social structure, 5:419b
subgroups, 5:403b
Svans, 5:404a
territorial divisions, 5:420a
tribes of, 5:419a
under P^{c}arnavazi, 5:419b
Georgios Monachos. *See* George the Monk
Georgios Trapezuntios. *See* George of Trebizond
Georgius, *Liber formularum,* 4:176a
Georgius Cedrenus. *See* Kedrenos, Georgios
Georgslied, 3:325a, **5:420b**, 9:233b
Gepids, defeated by Avars, 2:12b
Gerade, 4:600a
Geraint and Enid, 12:611a
Gerald of Aurillac, St., 8:640a
Odo of Cluny on, 7:262a
Gerald of St. Gall. *See Waltharius,* authorship
Gerald of Wales, **5:420b–421b**
on alliteration, 8:330b
autobiography of, 5:421b
as church reformer, 5:421a
as commissary of Peter de Leia, 5:421a
as court chaplain of Henry II, 5:421a
De rebus a se gestis, 5:421b
Descriptio Kambriae, 5:421a, 12:554b
on alliterative poetry, 8:318b
on music, 8:559a
rondellus technique, 10:529b
dispute over St. David's, 5:421a-b
education of, 5:421a
Expugnatio Hibernica, 5:421a, 12:554b
on goliards, 5:574a
on Henry II of England, 4:466b
Itinerarium Kambriae, 5:388a, 421a
on Roman theater at Caerleon, 4:277b
Simund de Freine and, 11:302a
Speculum duorum, 1:260a
Speculum ecclesiae, 7:365a, 366b
Symbolum electorum, 5:421b
Topographia Hibernica, 2:240a, 5:396b, 421a
on music, 8:558b–559a
travels of, 5:421a-b
treatises of, 8:435a
on Welsh culture, 12:518b
see also Map, Walter
Geraldines. *See* Fitzgeralds
Geraldo "Sem Pavor" (the Fearless), 10:41b
Gerard I of Cambrai, bishop, 10:317a
peace oaths and, 9:474b
Gerard II of Cambrai, bishop, 3:496a
Gerard of Abbeville
against St. Thomas Aquinas, 12:39b
opposition to mendicants, 2:318a
Gérard of Angoulême, bishop, Fontevrault order and, 10:430b
Gerard of Borgo San Donnino
Eternal Gospel
condemnation as heretical, 5:200b
description of Franciscan order, 6:199a
Joachimite views, 2:315b
prison sentence, 5:201a
Gerard of Brussels
Archimedes and, 1:435a, 435b
Liber de motu (*On Motion*), 1:436b, 9:625b–626a
Gérard of Clairvaux, St., **5:421b–422a**
murder of, 5:421b
Gerard of Cremona, 1:438a, 438b, **5:422a–423a**, 11:379b
Almagest, 5:422b
Archimedes and, 1:435a
Aristotle and, 1:461a
astronomy of, 5:422b–423a
early life, 5:422b
influence of, 5:423a
lectures of, 5:423a
Liber in quo terrarum et corporum continentur mensurationes, 8:212b
Liber de speculis comburentibus and, 1:437a
socii of, 5:423a
studies in Spain, 7:561b
style of, 5:423a
Toledan translations and, 5:422b–423a, 11:410a
translations, 5:422a-b, 12:138a
of Arabic alchemical texts, 1:136b
Euclid's *Elements,* 8:209b
Ibn Sīnā, 11:306b
medical works, 8:249a
Ptolemy's *Almagest,* 12:140b
Gerard of Csanád, St., **5:422a**, 11:479b
at court of Stephen I of Hungary, 5:422a
canonization of, 5:422a
murder of, 5:422a
pilgrimage of, 5:422a
Gerard the Devil, house of, 5:522b–523a
Gerard of Douai, missing works by, 12:22a
Gerard de Frachet, *Vitae fratrum ordinis Praedicatorum,* 6:69a
Gerard of Hérinnes, 9:36a, 37a, 38a
Gerard of Liège, work in English, 9:27a
Gerard Puella, missing works by, 12:22a
Gerard of York, archbishop, York tractates and, 12:730a
Gerard Zerbolt of Zutphen
Reform of the Soul's Power, 2:368a
Spiritual Ascents, 2:368a
Gerardo di Venezia. *See* Gerard of Csanád, St.
Gerardus falconarius, 6:359b
Geraud de Frachet, 5:654a
Gerba, conquered (1135), 10:441a
Gerberga, abbess of Gandersheim, 6:313b

Gerberga II, abbess of Gandersheim, 6:313b, 314a, 314b, 316a
Gerbert of Aurillac. *See* Sylvester II, pope
Gerbert, Martin, *De cantu et musica sacra,* 5:663a
Gerbert de Metz. See Lotharingian cycle
Gerbert de Montreuil, **5:423b**
  Perceval and, 5:423b
  Roman de la violette, 5:423b, 9:635a
  Tristan menestrel, 12:203a
Gerbert of Rheims. *See* Sylvester II, pope
Gerefa, 1:286a
Gereint Son of Erbin, 1:566b–567a
Geremei family, 6:658a
Gerhaert, Nikolaus, **5:423b–424a**
  Erasmus Grasser and, 5:656b
  Isenmann and, 6:561b
  Syfer and, 11:552a
  work of, 5:423b
Gerhaerts, Nicholas. *See* Gerhaert, Nikolaus
Gerhard of Augsburg, **5:424a**
  Vita Udalrici, 5:424a
Gerhard of Cologne, **5:424a**
Gerhard of Elton, as defender of Thomism, 12:42a
Gerhard of Holstein, count, 4:155a
Gerhard of Soissons, **5:424b**
  Life of St. Romanus, 5:424b
Gerhardo di Jacopo Starnina, **5:424b**
Gerhardus. *See* Gerard of Csanád, St.
Gerhoh of Reichersberg, 4:268b, **5:424b–425b**
  biography of, 5:424b, 425b
  De investigatione Antichristi, 4:282a, 5:425a
  De quarta vigilia noctis, 5:425a
  on drama, 4:282a
  influence of, 5:424b–425b
  letters of, 5:425a
  on millennialism, 8:386b
  Opusculum de edificio Dei, 5:424b–425a
  on papal curia, 4:66a
  style of, 5:424a-b
  theological treatises of, 5:425a
  on tithes, 12:63b
Gerini, Niccolò di Pietro, fresco painting of, 5:295b–296a
Germain, Michel, 1:428a
German art
  manuscript illumination, pre-Romanesque, 10:101a–104b
  painting
    Gothic style, 5:610a–611a
    woodcut and, 12:690b
  pre-Romanesque, 10:101a–107b
  sculpture, Gothic style, 5:623b–624a
  sculpture and metalwork, pre-Romanesque, 10:104b–107b
  woodcut, 12:692b, 693a
German drama, **4:266b–272b**
  Ascension plays, 1:582b
  carnival plays, 10:534a-b
  Erlösung and, 2:230a
  numbers of performances, 4:267a
  Priamel, 10:534a
  public theater and, 8:359a-b
  religious
    actors in, 4:270b
    authors of, 4:267b
    censorship of, 4:267b
    Christmas plays, 4:268a-b
    costs of, 4:270b
    Easter plays, 4:267b
    Lübeck morality plays, 4:269a
    origins of, 4:267a
    Passion plays, 4:267a-b
    play director, 4:270a
    play of the ten virgins, 4:269a
    Resurrection plays, 4:267b–268a
    staging of, 4:269b–270a
    types of, 4:267b
  secular
    carnival plays, 4:271a-b, 272a
    Fastnachtspiel, 4:271a
    local character of, 4:271a
    subject matter, 4:271a
  Shrovetide plays, 5:114a
  staging diagram for, 4:266b (*illus.*)
  in Switzerland, 4:269a
  texts preserved, 4:266b–267a
  in vernacular, 4:267a
  Vigil Raber and, 10:245a
German halberd. *See* Halberd
German language, **5:425b–427a**
  in Berthold von Regensburg's sermons, 2:200b–201a
  Bible translation, 2:215a
  consonants, 9:189b
  definition of, 5:425b–426a
  development of, 5:426a-b
  dialects of, 5:425b
  High German
    consonant shifts, 5:426a
    court poets and, 6:441a
    dialects, 6:437a
    Luther and, 6:441b
  Hungarian and, 6:337a
  letters between Henry of Nördlingen and Margaret Ebner, 9:13b
  Meister Eckhart and, 9:33a-b
  Middle High German, 6:437a
    in Berthold von Regensburg's sermons, 2:200b–201a
    definition of, 5:426b
    description of, 5:426b
    dialects of, 5:426b
    didactic poetry in, 5:441b–443b
    epics in, 5:426b
    lyric poetry in, 5:437a–438a, 443a
    surviving texts, 5:426b
  Middle Low German
    Hanseatic League and, 6:440b
    see also Saxon language, Old Saxon
  mixed with Latin in Middle High German literature, 8:356a-b
  New High German
    development of, 1:44b
    dialects of, 5:426b
    literature in, 5:426b–427a
  Notker Teutonicus and, 9:189b
  Old High German, 6:436b
    definition of, 5:426a-b
    description of, 5:426a
    dialects of, 5:426a-b
    literature in, 5:426a
    surviving texts, 5:426b
    translations from Latin, 5:426b
  Old Prussian, 6:438a
  standardization of, 5:427a
  Strasbourg oaths and, 11:488a-b
  works by Mechthild von Magdeburg, 8:241a-b
  Yiddish and, 12:725a
German law
  Burchard of Worms on, 2:420a-b
  compurgation, 3:508a–509a
  early Germanic codes, **7:468b–477a,** 10:465b
    on agricultural tools, 12:75b
    antrustiones privileges, 7:476b
    before Roman conquest, 7:468b–469a
    on betrothal, 2:207b
    blood feuds and, 7:475a-b
    feudalism and, 7:476b
    Forum judicum, 7:470a-b
    fredus (fee) as punishment, 7:476b
    freedman and, 7:475b
    influence outside Germany, 7:470a
    king's authority, 7:476a-b
    kinship and, 7:475a
    monetary compensation for crimes, 7:475a-b
    in North Africa, 7:471b
    oaths and, 7:476a
    procedures, 7:475b–476a
    public peace and king's peace, 7:476b
    Romanism as facade, 7:470a-b
    rule of more culturally advanced peoples and, 7:469b, 470b, 474a
    Salian Frankish codes, 7:472a–473a
    Sententiae of Paul and, 7:469b–470a
    special characteristics, 7:475a–476b
    summary of, 7:474b–475a
    Theodoric II and, 7:469b
    torture, 12:89b
    women's rights, 7:475b
    see also Ban
  influence of *Sachsenspiegel,* 4:409a-b
  ius Novi Fori Stredense, 9:722a-b
  post-Carolingian, **7:477a–483b**
    "assessors," 7:477b
    authority of written law, 7:477b–478a
    canon law and, 7:478b, 481b
    capital punishment, 7:478a, 482a-b
    cities' independence and, 7:482b
    codes (8th century), 7:478a-b
    codification in the 13th century, 7:479a
    compensation, 7:478a-b
    custom vs. written law, 7:477b–478a, 481a
    distrust of lawyers, 7:481b, 482b–483a
    feudal tenure and, 7:480a-b
    history (8th–15th centuries), 7:478a–483b
    imperial law (8th century) and, 7:478b–479a
    influence of Italian and French law schools, 7:479a-b
    justices, 7:477a-b
    Latin as Carolingian standard, 7:478a
    local courts, 7:477a-b

people's court (*Ding* or *Thing*), 7:477a
punishment, 7:480a, 482a
reverence for law, 7:481a-b
rights of free poor and, 7:479b
sources of, 10:602b–603a
tribal identities and, 7:479b
Two Swords doctrine, 7:480b–481a
vs. Roman codes, 7:481b–482a
see also Schwabenspiegel
property, *ius Theutonicum,* 11:684a
Roman influence, 10:603a
Saxony, codes, 10:683b
Schulz, 11:684a, 684b
German literature
allegory, **5:427b–433a**
Ackerman aus Böhmen, 1:43b–45a
allegorical adventures, 5:429a-b
in Arthurian literature, 5:428b–429a
beast, 5:428a-b
biblical, 5:427b
bispel, 5:429b
chase in, 5:431b
chess game in, 5:430b
conventions in, 5:432b
in epics, 5:428b–429a
in 14th century, 6:140a
in larger narratives, 5:428b–430a
love, 5:431a–432a
Minneburg, 8:407a-b
Minnereden, 8:410b
in mystical texts, 5:428b
religious, 5:429b
romance, 5:429a
sin in, 5:430a-b, 432a-b
Song of Solomon, 5:427b–428a, 430a
stag hunt as metaphor, 6:43b
translations of, 5:430b–436a
types of, 5:429b
verse adaptations, 5:430b–431a
Arthurian legend in, 1:571b–573b
beginning of New High German literature, 8:347a
biblical poetry, **2:224b–233a**, 9:298a
9th century, 2:224b–226a
11th century, 2:226a–228b
14th century, 2:230b–232b
classical and postclassical ages (1170–1300), 2:228b–230b
Herger's poetry and, 11:462a-b
influenced by courtly love lyric, 2:228b
metrical form of the late works, 2:232a
pagan conceptions in *Muspilli,* 2:225a
chronicles, 4:578b
court poetry, 5:434b–435a, 443a
Austro-Bavarian, 5:433b–434a
courtly narratives, 6:143b–144a
didactic verse
composers of, 5:442b
decline of, 5:443b
definition of, 5:441b–442a
form of, 5:442b
in Middle High German, 5:441b–443b
minnesong and, 5:442a
strophes in, 5:442b–443a
epics, in Middle High German period, 8:353b, 357a
Fastnachtspiele, 10:534a
Gebrauchsliteratur, 10:535a
genres of, 5:427a
heroic poetry, 6:227a
Brynhild in, 2:394b–395a
influence on Icelandic sagas, 6:36b, 37b, 38b
Italian Renaissance, influence on, 8:347a
lyric, **5:433a–444a**
alba, 9:296a
audience of, 5:435b–436a
in Austria, 1:132b
collections of, 5:436b
contrafacture in, 5:438b
counterforms to the canzone, 5:440b
crusade songs, 1:132b, 133a
cult of *hôhiu minne,* 12:536b–537a
dance songs, 5:436a, 12:537b
Danubian court poetry, 5:433b–434a, 10:293a-b
dawn songs, 12:537b
dialects, 6:142b–143a
dialogue poetry (*wechsel*), 10:293a
didactic, 5:441b–443b
early, 5:433a–434a
feasting songs, 5:440b
forms of, 5:435b, 438b–441b
Frauendienst, 9:296a
"good one" in, 5:439b
harvest songs, 5:440b
Hohenstaufen emperors and, 5:434a, 435a
indigenous, 5:433a–434a
influence on Eddic poetry, 4:390b–391a
love songs, 6:141b
manuscripts of, 5:436a–437b, 6:143a
Meisterlieder, 5:114b
Meistersingers, 6:137a
melodies in, 5:436a-b, 438a-b
metrics in, 5:436b–437b
in Middle High German period, 8:348b, 349b–350b
minne canzone, 5:439a–440a
minnedienst, 10:293a
minnesingers and, 8:413a–414b
minnesong, 8:148b
patrons of, 5:435a-b
performance of, 5:438b
political poetry, 5:442b–443b
rhetoric in, 5:436a
song chants, 5:433b
Spruchdichters, 6:137a
Sprüche, types of, 8:148b
strophes in, 5:433b, 435b, 436b–438a, 6:164a
themes, 12:629a
in 13th century, 6:138b–139a
troubadour poetry, 5:434a
winileot, 5:433a-b
winter songs, 12:537b
woman's song (*Frauenlied*), 10:293a-b
see also Meistersingers
memento mori theme, 6:138a, 142a
narrative, 7:642a
poetry
in *Carmina burana,* 3:97b, 98a
charms, Old High German, 3:273b–274a
Christus und die Samariterin, 3:325a
preservation of early works, 6:439b
prose, crusade sermons, 6:141b
Reimreden, 10:534b
romance, **5:444a–457b**, 6:135a
adventure in, 5:446b–447a
allegory in, 5:429a
Arthurian legend in, 5:447a–449b
comparisons with Chrétien de Troyes, 5:447b–448a
compilations of, 5:455b
criticism of, in 19th century, 5:455b–456a
definitions of, 5:444b
early, 5:449b–450b
height of, 5:455b
historical events used in, 5:445b
höfisches Epos, 5:444b
Jewish interest in, 4:305a
knightly code in, 5:449a
love in, 5:446b
in Middle High German period, 8:349a-b
narrative poetry, 6:30b–31a
outlaw ballad, 6:216a
structure of, 5:449b
themes of, 5:445a–447a
Tristan legend in, 12:201a
Trojan War in, 5:445b, 446b
Volksepos, 5:444b
satire, 2:363b
secular poetry, 2:228b
verse tales, 6:216b, 10:534a
anecdotes, 6:214b
beast fables, 6:214b
chastity-testing devices, 6:135b
father-son fights, 6:227b–228a
novella, 6:214b
religious legends, 6:214b
see also Middle High German literature; *Minnereden; Sangspruch*
German music
minnesong, 12:180b
contrafactum in, 3:576a-b
German towns, **5:457b–471b**
alliances with knights, 5:464a
Black Death and, 5:465a
communal period of, 5:459b
contributions of, 5:471b
craft and merchant guilds, 6:14b
decline in power of, 5:467b–471a
development to 1300, 5:459a–463b
diversity of, 5:457b, 458b
economy of, 5:465a–466a
influence, 5:459a, 460b
foundation dates of eastern cities, 5:484a
governing body in, 5:458b
guilds and métiers in, 5:460a–461a, 464b, 468b–469b
Hanseatic League and, 5:464b–465a
imperial city concept, 5:461b
leagues of, 5:464a-b, 12:317b
legal codes, 5:458a, 7:482b
merchants in, 5:460a–461a, 464b
monarchy and, 5:461a–462a

German towns (*cont.*)
Mongol invasions of, 5:461a
origins of, 5:458a, 459a-b
political influence of, 5:460b, 463b–465a, 467b–468a
population of, 5:457b–458a
princes in, 5:464a
Protestant Reformation and, 5:467b, 468b, 469b
representation and taxation of, 10:330a, 331b–332a
representative assemblies and, 10:330a, 331b–332a
Rhenish League and, 5:461a–462a
Roman law in, 5:458b
ruling elites, 9:461a
settlement of, 11:684a
social stratification in, 5:458a-b
society of, 5:466a–467b
taxation in, 5:463b–464a
Teutonic Knights and, 5:460b–461a
Thirty Years War and, 5:468b
town council in, 5:462a–463b
townsman-noble interactions in, 5:459b
urban power struggles, 12:317a-b
wealth in, 5:466a–467b
Germania. See Tacitus
Germanias (Valencian brotherhoods), war of the, 12:349b
Germanic languages, 6:436b–437b, 441a-b, 442a, 9:226a
Italo-Romance and, 6:623b, 624a
Latin loanwords in, 6:438b
Germanic peoples
attitude to private property, 2:89a-b
Christian missions to, 8:439a-b, 441b (map), 442a
coins issued by, 8:427b
conversion of, 8:367b
deposition of rulers among, 4:157b–158a
early political organization of, 2:88b–89a
early records about, 2:89a
farming techniques of, 2:89b
first contacts with the Roman world, 2:88a-b
invasion of the Roman world
3rd century, 2:89b–90a
4th and 5th centuries, 2:90a–94b
invasions of Iberian Peninsula, 10:36a
jewelry of, 5:375b, 377a
migrations, 8:363a-b, 12:616a-b
original location of, 2:88a
stem duchies in, 5:505b–506b
wheat varieties used by, 5:646a, 646b
Germanos I, patriarch, **5:471b**
Armenian church and, 1:500a
hymns of, 6:379a
iconoclastic controversy and, 5:471b, 6:397b–398a, 400b, 402a
Leo III and, 5:471b
Step^canos of Siwnik^c and, 1:510a, 5:540b
on Virgin Mary, 12:460a
Germans
in Bohemia, 6:365a, 365b, 367a, 367b
as *foederati,* 10:466b
in Hungary, 6:340b, 342a
as innkeepers, 6:473a-b
in Scandinavia, 6:436b
vs. Rome, 10:465a
Germanus of Auxerre, St., **5:471b–472a**
"Alleluia" victory and, 5:471b
Cassian and, 3:122a
Chelidonius of Besançon and, 5:471b
life of by a son of Urien Rheged, 12:331b
mission of to Britain, 3:214a
ordination of St. Patrick and, 9:463a
Pelagians and, 5:471b–472a
Germanus of Paris, St., **5:472a-b**
Childebert I and, 5:472b
deposition of Promotus, 5:472b
excommunication of King Charibert, 5:472b
Expositio brevis antiquae liturgiae gallicanae, 5:344b–345a, 7:627a
influence of, 5:472b
letter to Queen Brunhilde, 5:472b
Germany
Black Death in, 2:262b–264a
boundaries in 1025, 5:473 (map)
boundaries in 1378, 5:486 (map)
boundaries under Henry III, 6:162a
bridge building in 11th century, 10:413a
cavalry in, 3:201a-b
chronicles in, 3:329a
church in (843–1137), 5:477b–478a
communes, 3:497a–498a
coronations in, 7:257b
culture in, 5:483b
East Frankish kingdom, 5:473a–474a
eastern colonization, 6:151a, 167b
south Baltic coast, 6:90b–91a
economic development in, 5:483b
electors, **5:491a–493b**
representative assemblies and, 10:329b–331b
English missionaries in, 12:151b
feudalism, military, 12:561b–562a
government
kings' travels and, 12:159a-b
ministerials, 8:404a–406b
Hebrew manuscripts produced in, 8:119b–120a
heresy in, 5:484b
history (843–1137), **5:473a–478b**
annexation of Wendish territories, 12:617a-b
Christian conversion, 9:302a
collapse of Carolingian Empire, 5:474a-b
nobility in, 5:474a-b, 477b
rise of ducal power, 5:474b–475b
stem duchies, 5:505a–511a
see also Billungs
history (1138–1254), **5:478b–485b**
failure of royal authority, 5:478b–479a, 483a-b
feudalization, 5:213b
Hohenstaufen dynasty, 5:478b, 479b–480a, 481b, 483b
Privilegium minus, 5:213b
territorial expansion, 5:483b–484a
trade, 5:484a
history (1254–1493), **5:485b–491a**
Habsburg dynasty, 5:487b, 489b–490a
interregnum of 1254–1273, 11:80b
local government, 5:490b–491a
nobility in, 5:490a-b
political confusion during, 5:485b, 487a
power vacuum in, 5:490a-b
idea of empire, **5:493b–497a**
authority for the *Reich,* 5:494a-b
Charlemagne's coronation, 5:494b–495a
Charles V and, 5:496a-b
church-empire conflict over, 5:495b–496a
definition of, 5:494a
during religious wars, 5:496b
Frederick I Barbarossa and, 5:495b
imperial coronations by pope, 9:301b
imperial knights and, 5:497b
Maximilian I and, 5:496a
non-Roman, 12:628a
Otto I and, 5:495a
revival in 10th century, 5:495a
roots of, 5:493b–494a
Saxon overlordship, 9:300b–301a
Sigismund and, 5:496a
imperial knights, **5:497a–498b**
ban on private warfare by (1495), 5:498a
Charles V and, 5:498a-b
collapse of Hohenstaufen imperial system and, 5:497a-b
defensive military leagues of, 5:497b–498a
loyalty of to empire, 5:497b
Maximilian I and, 5:498a
rebellions by, 5:497b
representation and taxation of, 10:332a, 333a
Swabian League, 5:498a
imperial succession, Otto of Brunswick and Philip of Swabia, 12:538a–539a
Jews in, 7:86b–87a
art, 7:67a-b
communal self-government, 7:69b, 70a, 70b–71a, 71b
Hochmeister and, 10:243b
taxation of, 10:243b
manorial organization, 11:676a
decline of, 11:681b
military organization
ecclesiastical contingent, 12:561b–562a
ministerials, 12:562a
mints and money in, 8:429a-b
papal politics and, 4:59b
paper introduced into, 9:389b–390a
peasants' living standards, 1:94a-b
plagues in, 9:675b, 681b
population of, 5:487a
principalities, **5:498b–504b**
12th to 13th centuries, 5:501a-b
in 14th century, 5:501b
in 15th century, 5:501b–502a, 503b–504a
basic unit (*Land*) of, 5:502b
clergy as princes, 5:499b
control of, 5:503b
dispute between nobles and towns, 5:501b

dynastic ordinance of succession in, 5:502a-b
electors in, 5:499a-b
features of, 10:332a
feudal hierarchy, 5:499a
Frederick II and, 5:499b–500a
Hohenstaufen dynasty and, 5:500b–501a
Imperial Chamber Court, 5:504a
instability of, 5:503a
origins of territorial lordships, 5:500a-b
political estates, 5:502a
princely fiefs, 5:499b–500a
prince's role, 5:498b, 503b
private war and, 5:504a
representative assemblies (*Landtage*), 10:329a, 332a–333a
shift to, 5:498b
taxation in, 5:503a
printing in, 10:124a-b
property ownership, 11:674a
roads in the early Middle Ages, 10:412a, 413a
royal succession in, 4:426a–427b
stem duchies, **5:505a–511b**
Alemannia, 5:508b
Bavaria, 5:506b–507b
Brunswick, 10:685b
in Carolingian Empire, 5:506b–507a
definition of, 5:507b
formation of, 5:507b–508b
Franconia, 5:508b
in Frankish empire, 5:505b–506b
French duchies and, 5:508b–509a
in Germanic tribes, 5:505b–506b
Lorraine, 5:508a-b
Lüneburg, 10:685b
meanings of "duchy" (*ducatus*), 5:505a-b
older, 5:506b
origins of, 5:505a, 507a
royal control over, 5:509b–510b
Saxe-Lauenburg and Saxe-Wittenberg, 10:686a
Saxony, 507b–508a, 5:510b–511a, 10:682a-b, 684a-b
subordination of, 9:300b–301a
see also Billungs
Swabia and, 11:527b–528a
tenurial development, 11:681b–682a, 683b–684b
Leibrecht, 11:684a
locator, 11:684a
migrant settlements, 11:683b
territorial expansion, 10:684b
towns. *See* German towns
trade and commerce, 6:92a–96b, 10:632a
expansion of, 6:90b–91b
salt trade, 10:629b–630a
universities, 12:161b, 287a–289a (*illus.*)
Great Schism and, 12:287a-b
vs. Denmark, in *Brevis historia regum Dacie,* 11:522b
see also Feudalism; Investiture conflict
Gernardus, *Algorismus de minutiis,* 8:209b
Gero, 10:101b
Gero Codex. *See* Anno
Gerona, Christmas plays at, 11:437a
Gerónimo de Santa Fé (Joshua Lorki), 7:82b–83a
disputations of, at Tortosa, 10:6a
Refutation of Jewish Disbelief, 10:6b
Gershom ben Judah, **5:511b–512a**
divorce and, 4:607a
influence of, 5:511–512a
literary work of, 5:512a
perush and, 11:585a-b
religious poetry of, 7:622b
responsum literature and, 10:339a
Talmud commentaries of, 7:162b
Gershom ben Solomon, *Sha^{c}ar ha-Shamayim,* 11:93a
Gershom, Levi ben. *See* Levi ben Gershom
Gerson, John, **5:512a–513b**, 9:709b
ABC des simples gens, 10:302a
adviser to Pierre d'Ailly, 5:512a-b
at Council of Constance, 3:648a-b, 5:512b–513a
as chancellor of the University of Paris, 5:512a-b, 9:611a
on church reform, 5:512b–513a
college of cardinals and, 3:511b
commentary on Peter Lombard's *Sententiae,* 9:517b
conciliar theory of, 3:513a–514b, 5:512b–513a
on Council of Pisa, 5:512b
criticism of *Roman de la Rose,* 5:271b–272a, 10:452b
De jurisdictione spirituali et temporale, Durand of St. Pourçain and, 4:313b
De probatione spiritum, against St. Birgitta of Sweden, 9:15b
defense of Brethren of the Common Life, 5:512b
education of, 5:512a
as exegete, 4:544b
Great Schism and, 5:512a-b
on hagiotherapy, 6:492b
Hebrew language and, 3:314a
Hus and, 3:650a, 6:369a
hymns of, 6:382b
Nicholas of Clamanges and, 9:122b
nominalism and, 12:44a
Opusculum tripartitum, 1:547b, 10:302a
Prosperum iter, 6:367a
Ruusbroec's *Espousals* and, 9:38a
spirituality of, 5:513a
as teacher, 5:513a
Tractatus de parvulis trahendis ad Christum, 10:302a
Trilogium astrologiae theologizatae, 1:608b
via moderna and, 12:408a
Vincent Ferrer and, 12:453a
writings of, 5:513a
Gersonides. *See* Levi ben Gershom
Gerðr, 11:26a
in *Skírnismál,* 11:326b–327a
Gertrude the Great, 9:11a-b, 31b
Liber specialis gratiae, 9:10b–11a
Gertrude of Hackeborn, abbess of Helfta, 9:10b
Gertrude of Oosten, 9:11b, 12a
Gertrudis of Hungary, queen, death of, 6:341b
Gerusalemme liberata. See Tasso
Gervais du Bus. *See Fauvel, Roman de*
Gervase of Canterbury, 1:126a, **5:513b**
chronicle of, 5:513b
on Gothic architecture, 5:582b, 584a
Tractatus de combustione et reparatione Cantuariensis ecclesiae, 3:84a
Gervase of Melkley, 7:368a
Ars versificaria, 10:359b, 360a
Gervase of Tilbury, *Otia imperialia,* 7:365a
Geschlechter, 3:481b–482a
Gesellen, definition of, 4:271b
Gesith
replaced by the term "thegn," 12:8a-b
see also Nobility and nobles, Anglo-Saxon
Gesso, **5:513b–514a**
definition of, 5:513b–514a
Gest Historiale of the Destruction of Troy, 8:320b
Gest of Robin Hood
characterization of Icelandic *rímur* and, 10:401b
characters of, 10:437a
date of, 10:436a
geographical setting of, 10:436a-b
Palice of Honour and, 10:435b
Gesta. See Simon of Kéza
Gesta abbatum Gemblaciensium. See Sigebert of Gembloux
Gesta abbatum Trudonensium. See Rudolf of St. Trond
Gesta Apollonii, **5:514a**
Gesta Berengarii imperatoris. See Berengarii imperatoris gesta
Gesta Caroli. See Notker Balbulus
Gesta Caroli metrica. See Poeta Saxo
Gesta Chuonradi imperatoris. See Wipo of Burgundy
Gesta Danorum. See Saxo Grammaticus
Gesta Dei per Francos. See Guibert of Nogent
Gesta ecclesiae Hammaburgensis. See Adam of Bremen
Gesta episcoporum Tungrensium, Trajectensium et Leodiensium. See Anselm of Liège
Gesta Francorum ab origine gentis usque ad annum. See Historia regum Francorum
Gesta Francorum et aliorum Hierosolimitanorum, 4:20a, **5:514a-b**
author of, 5:514a-b
rewriting of, 5:514b
Gesta Frederici. See Otto of Freising
Gesta Frederici continuatio. See Rahewin
Gesta Friderici (anonymous), 7:365b
Gesta Guillelmi ducis Normannorum. See William of Poitiers
Gesta Hammaburgensis ecclesiae pontificum. See Adam of Bremen
Gesta Hungarorum, 6:341a
Gesta de las mocedades de Rodrigo, 3:388b, 389a
Cantar de mío Cid and, 3:71b
hero's early life, 8:447b

Gesta Ludovici. *See* Nicolas de Bray
Gesta Normannorum ducum. *See* William of Jumièges
Gesta Ottonis. *See* Hrotswitha von Gandersheim
Gesta Philippi Augusti. *See* Guillaume le Breton; Rigord
Gesta pontificum Anglorum. *See* William of Malmesbury
Gesta regum Anglorum. *See* William of Malmesbury
Gesta regum Britanniae. *See* Guillaume de Rennes
Gesta Roberti Wiscardi. *See* William of Apulia
Gesta Romanorum, 7:370a, 10:511b
  exempla and, 4:544b, 551a
Gesta Stephani, Roger of Salisbury and, 10:443b
Geste de Burch, 1:265b
Geste de Liège. *See* Jean d'Outremeuse
Geste of Robyn Hood, 8:325a
Gestes de saints. *See* Jean de Mailly
Gestes de Sophy. *See* Jean Lemaire de Belges
Gesù tentato dal diavolo, 6:636a
Gesù tradito, 6:636a
Geta. *See* Vital of Blois
Getica. *See* Jordanes
Gévaudan, Peace of God and, 9:474b
Géza I Magnus of Hungary, king, 6:340a
  depicted on St. Stephen's crown, 11:482a (*illus.*), 482b
Géza II of Hungary, king, 6:340b
Géza of Hungary, grand prince
  missionaries and, 6:339a
  Stephen I of Hungary and, 11:477b
Ghāfiqī, al-
  Kitāb al-jāmiᶜ fi'l-adwiya al-mufrada, 6:179a
  textbook on drugs, 6:185b
Ghaidā, 8:612b
Ghālib, Ibn ᶜAbd al Raḥmān, al-Manṣūr and, 8:90a
Ghana, medieval kingdom of, Timbuktu and, 12:55a, 55b
Ghāniya (banū), rulers of Balearic Islands, 1:194a, 194b–195a, 200b
Gharb. *See* Maghrib, al-
Ghassāni, al-, rule as Hafsid chamberlain, 6:54a
Ghassanids, **5:514b–515b**
  against Muslims, 5:515a-b
  clients of Byzantine state, 5:514b–515a
  as *foederati,* 10:466b
  kings of, 5:515b
  Lakhmids and, 5:515a
  Monophysitism and, 5:515a, 6:575b
  religious architecture of, 5:515a-b
  Rome, 10:464a
  use of *barbaṭ* and, 8:610b
  vs. Mundhir III, 7:320b
Ghawrī, Qānṣūh al-, Mamluk sultan, battle at Marj Dābiq and, 11:145b
Ghaybī, Ibn. *See* ᶜAbd al-Qādir
Ghayṭah. *See* *Surnāy*
Ghazā (Islamic holy war), Mongol threat, 9:305b
Ghazal (Persian poetry), 6:51a, 51b, 52a, 508a
Ghazālī, al-, **5:515b–517a**, 9:41a-b, 41b–42a, 141a
  Ashᶜarī and, 6:583b
  on astrology, 1:618a-b
  at Niẓāmiyya, 5:515b–516a
  Averroës and, 1:459b
  on conception and contraception, 3:575a
  conversion to Sufism, 9:570b
  criticisms of philosophy, 5:516b–517a, 9:570b
  early years of, 5:515b
  on government, 3:50b
  Ḥasan-i Ṣabbāḥ and, 6:617a
  Iḥyāᵓ ᶜulūm al-dīn (*Revivification of the Religious Sciences*), 4:445a-b, 597b, 5:516a-b, 9:41b, 570b
  influences on, 9:40a
  Iqtiṣād fi'l-iᶜtiqād, Al-, 5:516a
  on Islam, 5:515b–517a, 7:616b, 617a-b
  Judah Halevi and, 7:158a
  Kitāb naṣīḥat al-Mulūk, 8:436a
  on logic, 7:641b
  Maqāṣid al-falāsifa, 5:516a
  Mishāt al-anwār, 5:516b
  Munqidh min al-ṭalāl, Al- (*Deliverer from Error*), 1:381a, 5:516a, 9:41b
  Mustaṣfā min uṣūl al-fiqh, Al-, 5:516b
  public burning of his books, 11:140b
  spiritual crisis of, 5:516a
  Sufism of, 5:516a-b
  Tahāfut al-falāsifa (*Incoherence of the Philosophers*), 1:459a, 5:516a, 516b, 9:700a
    occasionalist doctrine, 10:573a
    responses to, 10:572b
  on *ᶜulamāᵓ,* 12:244b
Ghāzān (Khan), Maḥmūd, Ilkhanid ruler, **5:517b–518a**, 6:420b, 504b–505a
  cultural renewal, 8:474b
  foreign policy of, 5:517b
  influence of, 5:517b–518a
  succession to power, 5:517b
  Tabrīz and, 11:571a
Ghāzī, 1:203a, **5:518a-b**, 7:110b
  Byzantine raids, 9:288a
  definition of, 5:518a-b
  Seljuks and, 11:151a-b, 156b
  ṣinf and, 11:308a
  support for Mehmed I, 8:263b
  Turkoman, 12:227a
  under Ottomans, 9:305b–306a
Ghazna
  palace of, 6:603a
  Sebüktigin and, 11:133b
Ghaznavids, **5:520a-b**
  in Afghanistan, 1:64b–65a
  art and architecture, 1:64b–65a, **5:518b–520a**
    metalwork, 5:519b
    palaces, 5:518b–519b
    Persian Islamic influences on, 5:520b
    sources of information about, 5:518b
  conquest of Khwarizm, 2:248b
  foundation of dynasty, 5:520a, 10:639a
  Ghurid attacks on, 5:526a
  in India, 6:572a
  military power, 5:520a
  Niẓam al-Mulk and, 9:144a
  occupation of Sīstān, 10:609b
  origins of Seljuks and, 11:151a, 151b
  rulers of, 5:520a-b
  Seljuks and, 2:436a, 5:520b, 11:155a-b
  Sultan Malikshāh I and, 11:153a
  Toghrıl-Beg and, 12:66b
  see also Alptigin; Sebüktigin
Gheel, shrine of, 6:492a
Ghent, **5:520b–523b**
  conflict with Louis de Mâle, 5:523b
  derivation of name, 5:521a
  échevins in, 5:521b–522a
  fair of St. Bavo in, 5:521a
  government of, 5:521b–522a
  growth of, during 12th century, 5:521a, 522a
  guilds in, 5:522a–523a
  manuscript book production in, 8:104b
  in Merovingian period, 5:521a
  political power in Flanders, 3:503a
  revolt of
    against Charles the Bold, 5:523b
    against Philip the Good, 5:523b
  ruling elite in, 5:521b, 522b–523a, 9:461a
  strategic location of, 5:521a
  structure of *échevinage,* 4:379a
  in 13th century, 12:112b
  town houses, 5:522b–523a
  under Habsburgs, 5:523b
  as Viking base, 12:431b
  wool industry in, 5:521a
Ghent Altarpiece, **5:523b–524b**
  Adam and Eve, 5:524b (*illus.*)
  International Style and, 5:611b
  panels of, 5:523b–524b (*illus.*)
  polyptych in, 10:29a
  van Eycks and, 4:566b
  see also Eyck, Jan van
Gherardesca of Pisa, 9:14a
Gherardo di Zanobi. *See* Gaddi, Gaddo
Ghetto. *See* Jewry law
Ghibellines. *See* Guelphs and Ghibellines
Ghiberti, Lorenzo, **5:524b–525b**
  baptismal font (in Siena), 5:525a
  Commentarii, 5:525a-b
  Filippo Brunelleschi and, 2:388b
  Florence Baptistery doors, 5:525 (*illus.*)
  idea of Middle Ages, 8:308b
  training of, 5:524b
  works in International Style, 5:628b
  see also Michelozzo di Bartolomeo
Ghiberti, Vittorio, 5:525a
Ghichak, 8:561b, 612a
Ghillebert de Lannoy
  Instruction d'un jeune prince, 9:639b
  Voyages et ambassades, 9:639b
Ghilmān, 11:560b, 561a
Ghināᵓ al-raqīq, al-, 8:566a

Ghirbāl, 8:613a
Ghisi family, 7:377a, 380b
Ghislarengo, irrigation of, 6:558b
Ghislebert of St. Amand, **5:526a**
De incendio monasterii sancti Amandi, 5:526a
Ghiyār. *See* Sumptuary laws, Islamic, for non-Muslims
Ghiyāth al-Dīn Jamshīd al-Kāshī, 11:84a
Ghiyāth al-Dīn Kaykhosraw. *See* Qaykhosraw I
Ghiyāth al-Dīn Muḥammad of Ghūr, 5:526b
Ghiyāth ibn Ghawth ibn al-Ṣalt. *See* Akhṭal, al-
Ghouls, 7:112b
Ghubār (Toledan) numerals, 1:387b–395a, 10:471b, 473a, 474a
Ghudār, 7:112b
Ghulām, 8:59b, 11:152b, 155b
Ghunya li Tālibī Tarīq al-Haqq, al-. *See* Jīlānī, ᶜAbd al-Qādir al-
Ghurids, 1:65a, **5:526a–527b**
decline of, 5:527a
Ghaznavids and, 5:520b, 526a-b
in India, 5:526b, 527a
in Khorāsān, 5:526b–527a
legacy of, 5:526b
military campaigns of, 5:526b
occupation of Sīstān, 10:609b
power of, 5:526b
Seljuks and, 5:526a-b
Ghūṭa, 4:81a, 83a-b
irrigation of, 6:556b
Ghuzz Turkomans, vs. Seljuks, 6:504a
Giacomino da Verona
De Babilonia, 6:631a, 651a
De Ierusalem, 6:630b–631a, 651a
Giacomo da Campione, **5:527b**
work of, 5:527b
Giacomo da Lentini. *See* Iacopo da Lentini
Giamboni, Bono
De contemptu mundi and, 6:658b
Libro de' vizi e delle virtudi, 6:632a, 659a
Tresor and, 6:631b
Gianni degli Alfani, 6:649a
Gianni, Lapo, 6:649a
Giannotti, Antonia, 6:636b
Giano della Bella, 5:96a
Giantland (*Risaland*)
in *Þorsteins þáttr bæjarmagns,* 12:48a
in *Þrymskviða,* 12:52b
Giants
in Icelandic *riddarasögur,* 10:395b
in Skarkaðr legend, 11:467a
Gibbons saga, 10:395b
Gibert, Guillem, on death of Prince Charles of Viana, 3:171b
Gibraltar, Strait of
navigation through, 9:89a
trade route to England and, 12:115a
Vikings and, 12:431a
Gibuin of Langres, **5:527b**
Gidino da Sommacampagna, *Trattato de li rithimi volgari,* 6:665a
Gielée of Lille, Jacquemart, *Renart le Nouvel,* 10:314a
Giezi (Gehazi), 11:301a
Giezia, 11:301a
Gifford, John, 6:359b
"Gigas geminae substantiae." *See* Ambrose, St.
Gihon River, Nile and, 9:137b
Gikatilla, Joseph, *Shaᶜare Orah* (Gates of light), 3:2b
Gil de Zamora, Juan
Ars musica, 11:441a
Dictaminis epithalamium, 4:175b, 11:441a
Liber illustrium personarum, 11:433a
Gilbert of Clare, count of Pembroke, heraldic seal of, 11:129b
Gilbert of Clare, earl of Gloucester, in the Barons' War, 2:112b
Gilbert Crispin, bishop of London, arrangement of *Glossa ordinaria* attributed to, 2:213a
Gilbert of Limerick, bishop
church reform by, 3:232a
De statu ecclesiae, 7:614a
Gilbert de Middleton, treason execution of, 12:166a
Gilbert of Poitiers, 3:322b, **5:528a,** 9:702a
Anselm of Laon's theology school and, 12:20b, 21a
Apocalypse prologue, 4:547b
on Aristotle's *Categories,* 9:588b
Bernard of Clairvaux and, 2:192a
career of, 5:528a
commentaries on Boethius, 5:528a
as exegete, 4:543b
heresy accusation, 5:528a
nominalism and, 9:155a
Peter Lombard and, 9:516b
reality of essences, 9:588b
Synod of Rheims and, 3:94b
theology school of, 12:21b
theology of the Trinity, 9:598b, 12:193a-b
Thierry of Chartres and, 12:27a-b
trial of, 1:52a
Gilbert de la Porrée. *See* Gilbert of Poitiers
Gilbert of Sempringham, St., 5:528a, 12:685b
canonization of, 3:68b
Gilbert of Tournai
Eruditio regum et principum, 8:435a
on liturgy, 7:632b
Gilbert the Universal, 4:543b
Anselm of Laon's theology school and, 12:21a
Gilbertine order, *see also* Gilbertine rite
Gilbertine rite, **5:528a-b**
Gilbertus Anglicus, 8:250b, 9:677a
canon law collection, 7:415b
Compilatio prima and, 4:124a
on leprosy, 7:550a
on scrofula, 7:255a
Gilda (Germanic guild), social nature of, 6:14b
Gildas, St., **5:528b–529b**
on Ambrosius Aurelianus, 2:2b–3a
biographies of, 5:529a
De excidio et conquestu Britanniae, 1:564a, 5:528b–529a, 7:362a, 8:558a, 12:597b
as historian, 5:528b
on Maelgwn, 8:13a
penance and, 9:488b
Preface of Gildas on Penance, 3:229b
prologue to *Historia Brittonum,* 6:237b
uncertainty regarding, 5:529a
writings of, 5:528b–529a
Gilding, 8:295b
Giles of Lessines
De unitate formae, 12:40b
as defender of Thomism, 12:41b
Giles de Montaigu, curriculum regulation, 11:690a
Giles of Rome. *See* Egidius Colonna
Giles, St. *See* *Vie de St. Gilles*
Giles of Viterbo, 3:655a
Gilim. *See* Kilim
Gilites, Zaydis and, 12:742a
Gilla Modutu Ua Casaide, *Adam óenathair na ndóene* and, 6:542a
Gilles de Chin. *See* Gautier le Cordier de Tournai
Gilles de Corbeil, on the study of medicine at Montpellier, 8:257a
Gilles li Muisis
didactic literature, 9:639b
Estat et maintien, 9:639b
Gilles de Remi, 2:144a
Gilte Legend. *See* Jacobus de Varagine, *Golden Legend*
Giminiano, St., relics of, 10:500b
Giolla Brighde Mac Con Midhe, 6:532a, 533a
Giordano of Pisa
invention of eyeglasses and, 7:540a
sermons on technological expansion, 11:652b
vernacular sermons, 6:664a
Giorgi III of Georgia, king, 5:420a, **5:529b–530a**
daughter Tamar as coruler, 5:529b
depiction of in Betania, 2:207a
foreign campaigns of, 5:529b
revolt against, 5:406b, 529b
Zakᶜarids and, 12:736b
Giorgi IV Lasha of Georgia, king, 5:407a
Giorgi V (the Brilliant) of Georgia, king, 5:407a, 420a
Giorgi Mtᶜacᶜmindeli, 5:414b, 417a
Giorgi Proχore, 5:414b
Giostra delle Virtù e dei Vizi, 6:651a
Giotto di Bondone, 5:97b, **5:530a–532b**
Adoration of the Magi, 5:530b (*illus.*)
Arena chapel, 1:453a
frescoes, 9:447a, 12:462b (*illus.*)
Bardi chapel fresco cycle, 5:531b–532a
Boccaccio and, 2:278a, 281b
Cavallini and, 3:198b
Cennini and, 3:234b
Coronation of the Virgin, 5:530b
followers of, 12:174b–175a
frescoes of, 5:293a–294a, 530b–532a, 11:275a
in Giovanni Villani's chronicle, 5:97b
Giuliano da Rimini and, 5:542a
grisaille technique of, 5:678b
influence of, 5:530a, 532a, 12:171a, 175b, 176b
on Altichiero, 1:226b

Giotto di Bondone (*cont.*)
influence of (*cont.*)
on Daddi, 4:78b
on Giovanni Baronzio, 2:112b–113a
on Nardo di Cione, 9:63a
on Nicoletto Semitecolo, 11:159a
Isaac and Esau frescoes of, 5:606a
Life of Christ (fresco cycle), 5:530b (*illus.*), 531a-b, 7:530a, 9:153b, 154 (*illus.*)
Life of St. Francis, 5:294a, 530b, 531b–532a
Madonna and Child, 5:530b–531a
Madonna (in Uffizi), 5:530b–531a, 12:172a (*illus.*)
Madonna and Saints, 5:530b
paintings by, 12:171b–172b
Peruzzi chapel fresco cycle, 5:532a
Resurrection cycle and, 10:340a-b
St. Francis Receiving the Stigmata, 5:530b
San Francesco d'Assisi frescoes and, 5:532a
style of, 5:530a, 531b–532a
training of, 5:530a
Virtues and Vices, 12:462b (*illus.*)
see also Maniera greca
"Giotto's bell tower." *See* Florence, Duomo, campanile
Giovanetti, Matteo di, 5:627b
garden scenes of, 5:629b
Giovanna of Naples, queen, Boccaccio and, 2:286b, 288b, 289b
Giovanni d'Agostino. *See* Agostino, Giovanni d'
Giovanni d'Ambrogio da Firenze, **5:532b,** 12:176a
works of, 5:532b
Giovanni d'Andrea. *See* Johannes Andreae
Giovanni of Arcoli, on dental hygiene, 2:150a-b
Giovanni di Balduccio, **5:535b–536a**
works of, 5:535b–536a
Giovanni di Benedetto da Como, **5:536b–537a**
Book of Hours, 5:536b (*illus.*)
Giovanni del Biondo, *St. John the Evangelist,* 2:266b
Giovanni di Bonandrea, *Brevis introductio ad dictamen,* 4:174b
Giovanni Buon. *See* Buon, Giovanni
Giovanni da Campione, **5:532b**
works of, 5:532b
Giovanni da Cascia, 8:646a
Giovanni di Cecco, **5:537a**
work of, 5:537a
Giovanni della Colonne, *Mare historiarum,* Spanish adaptation of, 11:434a
Giovanni da Fiesole (Fra Angelico), **5:532b–535a**
Annunciation, 5:533a (*illus.*), 533b–534a
Coronation of the Virgin, 5:534a, 535a
Deposition from the Cross, 5:534a-b
as Dominican, 5:533a-b
frescoes
in chapel of Nicolas V, 5:534b
in S. Marco convent, 5:534a
influence of, 5:532b–533a, 535a
Lamentation over Christ, 5:533b
Madonna of Humility, 5:533b
Masaccio and, 5:533b
Passion paintings of, 5:361b–362a
polyptych in S. Domenico, Perugia, 5:533b–534a
style of, 5:533a, 607b
Giovanni da Fontana, *Bellicorum instrumentorum liber,* 11:647a-b
Giovanni Gherardi da Prato, *Paradiso degli Alberti,* 7:326a
Giovanni (Giovannino) de' Grassi, **5:535b**
manuscript illuminations of, 5:535b
models for drawings of, 5:629a-b
sculptural work of, 5:535b
sketchbook of, 4:292a
works in International Style, 5:628a
Giovanni Gualberto. *See* John Gualberti, St.
Giovanni da Legnano, tomb of, 4:79a (*illus.*)
Giovanni da Milano, **5:535a-b**
frescoes of, 5:535a
influence on Giusto de Menabuoi, 5:542a
origins of, 5:535a
Pietà, 5:535a
Giovanni (Nanni) di Bartolo, 2:419b, **5:536a-b**
Abdias, 5:536a
association with Giovanni and Bartolomeo Buon, 5:536a
Donatello and, 5:536a
Joshua, 5:536a
Giovanni di Paolo, **5:537a-b**
Christ Carrying the Cross, 5:538 (*illus.*)
Giovanni Pisano. *See* Pisano, Giovanni
Giovanni Scriba, reference to a broker by, 12:121a
Giovanni del Virgilio, *Allegories on Ovid,* 1:183b
Giralda (minaret: Seville), 11:213b
Giraldes, Afonso, *Poema del Salado,* 1:163a
Giraldus Cambrensis. *See* Gerald of Wales
Girart de Rosselhon
resemblance to troubadour poetry, 10:180a
use of Old French materials in, 10:180a
Girart de Roussillon, master of, 7:56b
see also Jean, Dreux
Girart de Vienne, 7:216b
Giraut de Bornelh, **5:539b,** 10:175a, 251a
"Reis glorios, verais lums e clartatz," 1:123a, 10:175a
works of, 5:539b
Giray II Semiz, revolt against Ottomans, 3:679a
Giray, Devlet. *See* Devlet Giray
Giray, Haji. *See* Haji Giray
Giray, Krim. *See* Krim Giray
Giray, Mengli. *See* Mengli Giray
Giray, Muḥammad I. *See* Muḥammad I Giray
Girdled patrician, **5:539b–540a**
Girk Pitoyicʿ. See Aphthonius, *Progymnasmata*
Girk Tʿłtʿocʿ, 1:508b, 509a, 518b, **5:540a-b**
description of, 5:540a
earliest manuscripts of, 5:540a
older section of, 5:540a-b
second part of, 5:540b
Girolamo da Cremona, decorated initials of, 6:463a
Gisela, abbess of Chelles, 9:500b
Giselbert, 5:508b, 509a-b
Gísla saga Súrssonar, 4:613a, 616a, **5:540b–541b**
compared with *Sturlunga saga,* 11:500b
dating of, 5:541b
Droplaugarsona saga and, 4:294b
Freyr in, 5:297a
preserved manuscripts of, 5:541a-b
purposes of, 5:541a
similarities to *Harðar saga Grímkelssonar,* 6:101b
skaldic verse in, 5:541a-b
Gislebert. *See* Ghislebert of St. Amand
Gislebertus, **5:541b–542a,** 10:496b–497a
school of, entrance to St. Laze in Autun, 10:498 (*illus.*)
work of, 5:541b (*illus.*)
Gisleham, William, 7:189a-b, 192b
Gísli Súrsson, *lausavísa* and, 7:387b
Gismirante. See Pucci, Antonio
Gittern, 8:608a
Giudicio finale. See Belcari, Feo
Giuliana Falconiere, 9:14a
Giuliano da Rimini, **5:542a**
Giotto di Bondone and, 5:542a
Madonna and Child Enthroned with Standing Saints, 5:542a
work of, 5:542a
Giulio Cesare (della) Croce, *Bertoldo,* 11:367b–368a
Giustina of Arezzo, 9:14a
Giustiniani, Paul, eremitism and, 3:56a-b
Giustiniani, Tommaso, Lateran V and, 3:655a
Giusto de Menabuoi, **5:542a-b**
Altichiero and, 5:542a
Giovanni da Milano and, 5:542a
work of, 5:542a
Giyorgis of Gaseĉ̣ĉ̣a, Abba, horologion of, 1:155b
Gizur Ísleifsson of Skálholt, bishop, 6:352a, 394a
Gizurr Þorvaldsson, 11:357b, 495b, 499b
Glaber, Raoul. *See* Radulphus Glaber
Gladius, 11:546a-b, 547a (*illus.*), 549b
Glælognskviða. See Þórarinn Loftunga
Gläfe, 7:324 (*illus.*), 325a
Glagolitic alphabet. *See* Alphabets
Glagolitic rite, **5:542b–543b**
Byzantine rite and, 5:543a
description of, 5:542b
Kiev leaflets, 5:542b–543b
missals, 5:543a
translation of
by Cyril, 5:542b
by Methodios, 5:542b–543a

Vienna fragment, 5:543a
Glaive, 7:324 (*illus.*), 325a
Glajor, **5:543b–544a**
closing of, 5:544a
as cultural center, 5:543b
manuscript painting at, 5:543b (*illus.*), 544a
students at, 5:543b–544a
see also Tᶜoros Tarōnecᶜi
Glanville, Ranulf de, **5:544a–545a,** 7:442b, 443b
career of, 5:544a-b
on grand assize, 6:482a
Henry II and, 5:544a-b
influence of, 5:544b
as justiciar, 7:200a
Roman models for, 4:471b
Tractatus de legibus et consuetudinibus regni Anglie, 4:533b, 5:544a–545a, 7:442b
practical orientation of, 5:544b
questions of authorship, 5:544b–545a
Glarean, Heinrich, *Dodecachordon,* 8:649a
Glarentsa, under Latins, 7:378b
Glarus, Swiss Confederation and, 11:543b–544a
Glasgow, bishopric of, 4:110b
Glasgow, University of, 11:112a, 12:290b
Glass
Armenian, from Dwin, 12:98a
Byzantine, tinting, 11:635b
Damascene, 6:608a
eyeglass lenses, 11:650b
Islamic, **5:545a–548a**
of Abbasids, 5:546a–547a
beveled style, 5:546b
cameo cutting in, 5:547a
in Egypt, 5:545a–546a
enameled, 5:547a–548a
grooved ornament style, 5:546b
Hedwig glasses, 5:547a
in Iran, 5:545b, 546b–547a
in Iraq, 5:545b, 546b–547a
Lamm's classification of, 5:547a-b
lamps, 5:545b (*illus.*), 546a
luster, 5:546a
lusterware, 7:689b
manufacture of, 11:639a
regions producing, 5:545a–547a
relief cutting style, 5:545b–547a
Riis's classification of, 5:547b
in Syria, 5:545a
techniques of making, 5:546b
Umayyad, 5:545b–546a
varieties of, 5:545a
weights, 5:546a
wheel-cutting technique, 5:546b–547a
see also Mamluk art
reliquary, 11:650b
stained, **5:548a–554a**
in 13th century, 5:551a, 552b–553a
in 14th century, 5:552a
in 15th century, 5:552a
armature, 5:549b–550a
art of, 5:548a
artists in, 5:551a, 552a-b
in Augsburg Cathedral, 5:548b (*illus.*)
in Auxerre Cathedral, 5:552a
Bernard of Clairvaux on, 5:549a
blank glazed windows, 5:553a
in Canterbury Cathedral, 3:83b, 4:67b (*illus.*), 5:549a, 553a
in Chartres Cathedral, 5:549a, 551a, 552a–553a
colors in, 5:550b, 551a-b
definitions of, 5:550b–551a
designs for, 5:549a-b, 550a-b
development of, 5:549a
enameled glass, 5:550b
Flemish panel painters, 5:552a-b
in France, 5:603b
grisaille, 5:552a, 678b–679a
iconography of, 5:552b–553a
images in, 5:549a
influences on, 5:552a-b
lead in, 5:550b
light and, 5:548b–549a
materials used in, 5:550a
paint used in, 5:550a
production methods, 5:551a
in Rheims Cathedral, 5:549b (*illus.*), 552a
rose windows, 10:532a
in Ste. Chapelle, 5:551b (*illus.*), 553a
in St. Denis, 5:548b, 552b
in St. Urbain, 5:552a
in Sens Cathedral, 5:548a
silver oxide in, 5:550b
Theophilus on, 5:549a
in Westminster Abbey, 5:552b
woodcut and, 12:690b
see also Prudde, John; Thornton, John; Tracery
Western European, **5:554a–564a**
in Anglo-Saxon England, 5:555a-b
at La Seube, 5:559a
beakers, 5:554a–555a (*illus.*), 557a–558b
Benedictines as glassmakers, 5:556a
blue-threaded glass, 5:558b
in Bohemia, 5:558a
bottles, 5:561a-b
bowls, 5:559a
colorless, 5:557a–558a, 559b–560a
crown technique, 5:562a
early burial finds, 5:555a-b
in early medieval trade, 12:110a
enameling of, 5:556b
in England, 5:558b–559a
in France, 5:558b–559a
glass materials in, 5:554b
goblets, 5:556a (*illus.*), 558b–559b
green "forest glass," 5:554b, 560a–561b
history of, 5:554a
lamps, 5:557b (*illus.*), 560b–561a
manufacture of in Corinth, 12:102b
mirrors, 5:562a-b
muff technique, 5:556a-b, 561b–562a
opaque glasses, 5:556b
potash glass, 5:554b–555a, 560a
in Rhineland, 5:554a-b
in Roman Empire, 5:554a-b, 555b–556a
Rüsselbecher beaker, 5:554b–555a
in Spain, 5:559a–560a
Syro-Frankish, 5:556b–557a
technology, 11:650b
Theophilus on, **5:556a-b, 12:24b**
urinals, 5:559b (*illus.*), 561a
utilitarian green glass, 5:557a
in Venice, 5:555b–556a
vessel glass, 5:556b–557a, 561b
Waldglas, 5:554b, 560a–561b
window glass, 5:561b–562a
in Yugoslavia, 5:558a-b
see also Lenses; Lighting devices
window, technology and price decline, 11:656b
Glass mosaic. *See* Mosaic
Glastonbury, excavation at, 1:337a-b
Glastonbury Abbey, military service of, 2:173b
Glastonbury Miscellany, 3:493a
Glaðheimr, Valhalla and, 12:350a
Glatz Madonna, 5:610a
Glavendrup runic stone, inscription, 10:564b–565a
Glazier Codex, 3:590b
Glean (unit of measure), 12:592b
Gleb of Kiev, St., 12:720a
cult of, 8:159b–160a
feast of, 8:574b
Gleb of Tmutarakan, prince, 12:66a
Gleemen. *See* Waits
Gliglois, 9:634b
Globe, 11:95b–96b, 102 (*illus.*)
celestial
built by Gerbert of Aurillac, 11:100b
Christian, 11:96a-b
Islamic, 11:96a
terrestrial, 11:96a-b
Globus cruciger, **5:564a**
Gloria, **5:564a-b**
antiphon in, 5:564a-b
in Divine Office, 5:564a
in the liturgy of the Mass, 8:186a-b
in Mass of Tournai, 8:199a
procession of the clergy, 8:185b
Tropes to the Ordinary of the Mass and, 12:209a
where and when sung, 8:186a-b
Gloria in excelsis, incense and, 6:431b, 432b
"Gloria, laus, et honor tibi sit." *See* Theodulf of Orléans
Gloria Patri
EVOVAE and, 4:529a
in introit, 6:498b
Gloria tibi Trinitas equalis una deitas, 10:371b
musical notation for, 10:374 (*illus.*)
Gloriam virginalem. See Gregory IX, pope
Gloriant, 4:321a-b
"Glorious Choir." *See* Canterbury Cathedral, choir
Glosa, 12:447b
Gloss, **5:564b–565b,** 9:671b–672a
Anglo-Saxon, 5:564b–565a (*illus.*)
in "Canterbury Classbook," 7:352b
definition of, 5:564b
development of the "ordinary gloss," 7:515b

Gloss (*cont.*)
in Ellesmere Chaucer, 5:564b–565a
juridical concepts and, 5:566a
in Lindisfarne Gospels, 5:564b
as linguistic source, for Italian, 6:621b
Notker Teutonicus and, 9:188b
recension (*diorthōsis*), 9:697a
translation aids, 12:137a
use of, 5:564b–565a
see also Bible; Exegesis; Glossators; Proverbs; *Solutiones contrariorum*
Glossa in Epistolas beati Pauli. See Peter Lombard, *Magna glosatura*
Glossa interlinea, 10:239a
Glossa ordinaria, 2:312a, 3:516b, 4:543b, 547b, 10:61b, 239a
arrangement attributed to Gilbert Crispin, 2:213a
authorship of, 7:362b
contributions to, 11:691b–692a
French translations of the Bible and, 2:219a
on *Liber Augustalis. See* Marinus da Caramanıca
Ormulum and, 4:546a
see also Law, civil
Glossa ordinaria. See Accursius
Glossa Palatina, Laurentius Hispanus and, 7:385b–386a
Glossa in Psalmos. See Peter Lombard, *Magna glossatura*
Glossae super Platoneum. See William of Conches
Glossary. *See* Encyclopedias and dictionaries; Gloss; Translation and translators, resources and training
Glossators, **5:565b–568a**
on Boethius and Plato, 10:270a-b
of Bolognese School, 5:566b–567b
of *Corpus iuris civilis,* 5:565b–566a
definition of, 5:565b
function of, 5:565b
glossa ordinaria, 2:312a
importance to juridical science, 5:566b
Jewish. *See* Talmud, Jewish exegesis and study of
law before, 5:566a-b
of Plato's *Timaeus,* 9:700b, 701b–702a, 703b
political theory and, 10:19a
Remigius of Auxerre, 10:303a-b
of Roman law, 5:565b–566a
see also Azo; French law; Gloss; Jacobus (de Porta Ravennate); Law, schools of; Translation and translators
Glossed Gospels, 2:222a, 4:547b, 548a
see also Lollards
Glossolalia. *See* Tongues, gift of
Gloucester Cathedral, **5:568a-b**
architecture of, 5:568a
bronze candlestick, 8:284b, 285a (*illus.*)
crypt of, 5:568b (*illus.*)
use of ribs in, 10:383a
Gloucester, Statute of (1278), 4:396b, 7:192a, 447b, 9:424a, 11:468a
Glúmr Eyjólfsson, 10:343a-b, 12:415b–416a
see also Víga-Glúms saga
Gluttony, church condemnation of, 3:580b
Glxawor episkopos. See Katholikos (*katᶜołikos*)
Glykes, Joannes, 8:555b
Glykophilousa, **5:568b**
Gmünd, Frederick I Barbarossa and, 11:527b
Gnadgott. See Daggers
Gniezno Cathedral, 9:723b
bronze doors of, 8:284b
relief on doors of, 11:337 (*illus.*)
Gnome
definition of, 5:568b
Indic, 5:569a
Irish, 5:569a
triadic, 5:569a
Welsh, 5:569a
Gnomic literature, **5:568b–569b**
antiquity of, 5:569a
Old English, 1:281a, 5:569a-b
Old Norse, 5:569a-b
vernacular, 5:569b
Gnomonics, 11:509a, 510a
Gnostic texts, on angels, 1:249b
Gnosticism
angelic music, 6:100a
Cabalistic schools and, 3:1a, 2a
Catharism and, 12:661a
church fathers and, 3:335a
Docetism and, 4:233a
in Ismailism, 6:587b, 588a
Neoplatonism and, in *Sefer Bahir,* 3:1b
Zoroastrianism and, 12:747b
Zurvanism and, 12:749a
Gnuni family
Arčēš and, 1:423a
hazarapet and, 1:489a
Goats, as food animals, 1:299a-b, 302a
Gobelins tapestries, weaving technique, 10:547a
Gobi Desert, rodents and the plague, 9:678a-b
Goblin, in *Schrätel und der Wasserbär,* 11:79a
Godeffroi Bisot, 3:304a
Godeffroi de St. Omer, 3:304a
Godefroid de Claire. *See* Godefroid of Huy
Godefroid of Huy, **5:569b–570b,** 10:500 (*illus.*)
enamel work, 4:438b–439a
identification of, 5:570a
pedestal of cross made by, 5:570a (*illus.*)
work of, 5:570a
Godefroy de Preuilly, 5:349b
Godegisel, 2:423a
Godescalc of Aix, 3:97a
Godescalc Gospels, 8:106a, 10:305b
miniature from, 10:97b (*illus.*)
Godescalc of Le Puy, bishop, 10:480b
Godfred of Denmark, king
construction of Danevirke and, 12:424a
vs. Charlemagne, 12:423a
Godfrey of Bouillon
in First Crusade, 4:30a,b, 33b–34a, 34b–35a
model of chivalry, 3:303a
Tancred and, 11:589b
see also Baldwin I of Jerusalem
Godfrey of Cambrai, Latin epigrams of, 1:254b
Godfrey of Fontaines, **5:570b**
against Thomism, 12:41b
Aristotle and, 1:463b
philosophy of, 5:570b
Quodlibet IV, philosophy as a scientific discipline, 9:608b
Godfrey mac Fergus, 7:229b
Godfrey of Rheims, **5:570b–571a,** 7:363b
Carmen ad Lingonensem episcopum, 5:570b
elegies, 9:313a
Sompnium Godefridi de Odone Aurelianensi, 5:570b
works of, 5:570b–571a
Godfrey of St. Victor
Adam of the Little Bridge and, 12:20b
Microcosmus, 9:593b
"Planctus ante nescia," 6:382a
Godfrey of Upper Lorraine, duke, rebellion against Henry III, 6:162b
Godfrey of Viterbo, 7:365b
treatises of, 8:435a
Godfrey of Winchester, **5:571a**
epigrams of, 7:363b
influences on, 5:571a
Liber proverbiorum, 5:571a
Gododdin, Y. See Aneirin
Godric of Finchal, St., *Crist and sainte Marie,* 7:594a
Godric (hermit of Finchale), verses of, 8:329b
Godwin of Wessex, earl, Edward the Confessor and, 4:394b–395a
Godzin of Mainz, **5:571a-b**
Passio Albani, 5:571a
Goedendag, 7:325a
Goes, Hugo van der, 5:87a, **5:571b–572a**
Adoration of the Shepherds, 5:571b
Dormition of the Virgin, 5:571b
influences on, 5:87a, 571b
life of, 5:571b
Nativity Altarpiece, 5:571b (*illus.*), 12:198b
panels for the Church of Holy Trinity in Edinburgh, 11:112a
Portinari Altarpiece, 5:87a
see also Flemish art, painting
Goethe, Johann von
beast epic and, 2:142b
Von deutscher Baukunst, 1:428b, 4:508a
Goffredo da Castiglione, protests against, 8:378b
Goffredo da Viterbo, **5:572a**
Pantheon, 5:572a
Gofraidh Fionn Ó Dálaigh, 6:538a
Gog and Magog, Islamic doctrine of resurrection and, 10:340b
Gogarenē, 1:472b
Gogynfeirdd, 2:106a, 4:69b, 8:265a, 12:598b–599a

after Llywelyn ap Gruffudd, 12:604a, 606a
late medieval, 12:606a
major poets, 12:598b
minstrels, 12:599a
poets of the princes, 12:604a–606a
praise poems, 12:604b
style and diction, 12:605b
see also Welsh literature, poetry
Goharinos of Sebastia (Armenian martyr), 1:521a
Goidelic language. *See* Irish language
Gojislav of Croatia, ruler, 4:5b
Gökça. *See* Sewan, Lake
Gokstad ship, 12:424b
Goł Vasil, Armenian prince, 1:484b
Hṙomklay and, 6:311b
Golagros and Gawane, 8:332a
Golan Heights, Yarmuk and, 12:719a
Gold
in alchemy, 1:137b, 138a, 141b
assaying of, 8:290a, 290b
casting of, 8:297a
importance of, 8:401a-b
in Islamic bookbinding, 8:99b
in manuscript illumination, 8:101b, 105b
Islamic, 8:113a, 116b
mining of, 8:397b–398a
in Mali, 8:58a
in pre-Romanesque art
Carolingian, 10:110b–111a
English, 10:110a
German, 10:106a–107b
Spanish, 10:114b–115a
trade in, 9:678a
Guinea, 4:562a
Mali, 8:57b
Wangara, 4:561b
see also Metalsmiths, gold and silver; Mints and money
Goldemar. See Albrecht von Kemenaten
Golden Altar. *See* Pala d'Oro; Paliotto of S. Ambrogio
Golden Bull of 1356
codification of electoral process, 5:488b–489a, 492a-b
diet to be held in Nuremberg, 9:202a
on German electors' definition, 10:329b–330a
German princes and, 5:464a
on hereditary lands partition, 10:329a
rules of royal election, 4:425b
Golden Bull of Andrew II (1222), 6:335b, 341b, 345a
Golden Bull of Eger (1213), abrogation of Concordat of Worms, 5:483a
Golden Bull of Sicily (1212), 2:300a
Golden Fleece, Order of the, 3:305 (*illus.*), 307a, 6:334b
Golden Horde, **5:572b–573b**
Batu and, 2:131a, 8:471b
capitals of, 5:572b
coinage, 8:426b, 475b
definition of, 5:572b
destruction of Nogaj Tatars and, 2:411a-b, 11:474b
divisions, 5:573a
emergence of, 5:572b, 8:471a–475b
end of, 5:573a-b
ethnic makeup, 8:471b
"Great Troubles" of, 5:333a
history, 8:475b–476a
in Hungary, 6:342b
Italian trading cities, siege of, 8:476a
Kasranids and, 11:254a
Muscovite independence and, 4:232a
Russian fur trade and, 5:333a-b
Russian principalities, 8:475b–476a, 540a-b
in Saray, 5:573b
suzerainty over Crimea, 3:678b
territorial disputes
Ilkhanids, 8:473b, 476a
Khwarizm, 8:472a
Qubylai and Qaidu, 8:475b
Tatars, 8:476a
Volga Bulgars and, 12:488b
vs. Ilkhanids, 6:420a
vs. Tamerlane, 8:540b, 11:588a
White Horde, 8:472a
see also Mongol Empire
Golden Horn, **5:573b–574a**
Byzantine defenses of, 5:573b
see also Pera-Galata
Golden Horn ware, **5:574a**
Golden Legend. See Jacobus de Varagine
Golden Octagon (church: Antioch), 4:332a
Golden Psalter of St. Gall, 3:202b
Golden Ring (Basel), 9:13a
Golden section, **5:574b**
Golden Spurs, Battle of (1302), 2:387a, 5:81b
Goldene Tempel, Der. See Hermann von Sachsenheim
Goldsmiths. *See* Metalsmiths, gold and silver
Goldsmiths' guild (Paris), miracle plays and, 8:431b
Goldsmiths, Worshipful Company of, 8:287b, 290a, 290b
Golein, Jean
on French coronation anointing, 7:258a
kingship theories of, 7:269b
Goliardic verse, meter of, 7:367a, 375a-b, 8:345a
Goliards, **5:574b–576a**
"Apocalypse of Golias," 5:575b
decline of, 5:575b–576a
fabliaux and, 4:576b
Gerald of Wales on, 5:574b
Italian comic poetry and, 6:649b
members of, 5:575a–576a
"Metamorphosis of Golias," 5:575b
origin of, 5:574b–575a
Ovid's influence on, 9:313b–314a
parodies of religion, 5:575a
poetry, 7:367a
characteristics of, 6:319a–320a
Sedulius Scotus and, 5:575a
sources of information about, 5:575a-b
in Spain, 11:406a-b
travels of, 12:161a
see also Parody, Latin
Goliath, descendants of, 2:185b
Göllheim, Battle of (1308), 5:487b
Golosniki, **5:576a**
Gołtᶜn, Muslim emirate in, 1:513a
Gomes, Fernão, 4:561b
Gómez Barroso, Pedro, *Libro del consejo e de los consejeros,* 11:416b
Gómez de Zamorra, lost translation of Orosius, 11:443b
Gonçalo Mendes, 10:38a
Gonçalo Trastemires, 10:38b
Gonçalves, Antão, 4:561a
Gonçalves, Lopo, 4:561b
Gonfaloniere, 11:558a
Gǫngu-Hrólfs saga, **5:576a–577a**, 6:312a
dating of, 5:576a
Knýtlinga saga and, 5:577a
Konráðs saga Keisarasonar and, 7:292a
plot of, 5:576b–577a
preservation of, 5:576a
purpose of, 5:142b
settings
description of England in, 5:140a
wedding feast, 5:141a
Sturlaugs saga Starfsama and, 11:496a
Yngvars saga víþförla and, 12:272a
Gonsalves, Nuño, **5:577a**
Bartolomé Bermejo as pupil of, 5:577a
Veneration of St. Vincent, 5:577a
Gonzales, Maria, abbess, 6:318a
González de Clavijo, Ruy, **5:577a-b**
ambassadorship of, 5:577a-b
Historia del Gran Tamorlán (Embajada Tamorlán), 5:577b, 11:421a
in Samarkand, 5:333b
González, Fernán, count of Castile, 1:627b
González de Mendoza, Pedro, translation of *Iliad,* 11:458a
Gonzalo de Berceo. *See* Berceo, Gonzalo de
Good Friday
liturgy, 4:366a-b
see also Holy Week
Good Hope, Cape of, 4:560b, 562b
Good Man and the Devil, 8:316a
Good Parliament (1376), 6:426b, 427a-b, 7:664a
on papal Avignon, 2:34a
Peasants' Revolt and, 9:479a
Piers Plowman and, 7:331a
Wyclif and, 12:706b
Good Shepherd, **5:577b–578a**
appearances of, 5:577b
classical origins of image, 5:577b
statues of, 5:577b
Good Wife Taught Her Daughter, The, 3:662b–663a
Good Wyfe Wold a Pylgremage, The, 3:663a
Gordyenē. *See* Korčēkᶜ
Gorget, 1:532a
Gorhoffedd. See Gwalchmai ap Meilyr; Hywel ab Owain Gwynedd
Gorm (the Old) of Denmark, king, 4:151b
killed by Rhodri Mawr, 10:366a
in legends, 10:677b
Gormont et Isembart, 3:258b, 259b
Goro di Gregorio, **5:578a**

Goro di Gregorio (*cont.*)
tomb of Bishop Guidotto, 5:578a (*illus.*)
Gorze, 3:470a, **5:578b–579a**
Cluniac order and, 5:578b
customs of, 5:578b
founding of, 5:578b
Johannes of St. Arnulf at, 7:121a
reform movement, 5:477b
Hungarian church and, 11:479b
Gōsān, **5:579a**, 9:443b
decline of, 5:579a
social origins of, 5:579a
sources of works of, 5:579a
Gošavank^c, **5:579b**, 8:656b
Armenian art at, 5:579b
founding of, 5:579b
gawit^c at, 5:579b
Goscelin of St. Augustine, hagiography, 6:64a
Goscelin of St. Bertin, 7:255a
Gosforth, cross at, depiction of Thor's encounter with Midgard and, 12:45a-b
Goslar
as commune, 5:459b
Frederick I Barbarossa and, 5:481b
Gospel of 1297, The. See Grigor Tat^cewac^ci
Gospel of 966, 1:496b
Gospel According to the Mark of Silver, 3:352b
Gospel of Ējmiacin, 1:496b
Gospel of King Gagik of Kars, 1:496b
Gospel of Mołni, 1:496b
Gospel of Nicodemus. *See* Nicodemus, Apocryphal Gospel of
Gospel of Prince Vasak, 1:497b
Gospel of Queen Keran, 1:497b
Gospel of Queen Mariun. See Sargis Picak
Gospel of Queen Mlk^cē, 1:496b
Gospel of Thomas, Irish literature and, 6:542b
Gospelbook, **5:579b–580b**
carpet pages in, 5:579b–580a
copies of, 5:579b
Corpus Christi College Gospels, 5:580a
decoration, 8:187b
description of, 5:579b
examples of, 5:580a
Godescalc Gospels, 10:305b
in Hiberno-Saxon art, 8:370a–371b
honoring of, 8:187b
illuminated, 10:615a-b
incense and, 6:431b
kissing of, 8:188b
Lorsch Gospels, 10:305b
Macedonian renaissance, Stavronikita Gospels, 10:307 (*illus.*)
Schatzkammer Coronation Gospels, 10:305b–306b (*illus.*)
see also Psalter
Gospels
Codex Aureus, 3:474b
in Communion chant, 3:504a
concordances of, 3:66 (*illus.*)
Coronation. *See* Coronation Gospels
Hiberno-Saxon illuminated MSS, 3:117a
in Ireland, early manuscripts of, 2:220a
in the liturgy of the Mass
ceremony surrounding, 8:187b
reading of, 8:188a-b
manuscript illumination, 3:66 (*illus.*)
see also Evangeliary; specific manuscripts, e.g., Book of Durrow
Gospels of Judith of Flanders, 10:109a-b
Gospels of St. Augustine, Passion cycle illustration in, 9:447a
Gospels of Ste. Chapelle, 10:102a
Gospels for Speyer Cathedral, miniature from, 10:104a (*illus.*), 104b
Götaland (in Sweden), 12:423a
Gothic alphabet. *See* Alphabets
Gothic architecture, **5:580b–603a**
Ani Cathedral, 1:494a
apse in, 1:352a
buttress in, 2:434b–435a
Canterbury Cathedral, 5:582b, 584a
Chartres Cathedral, 5:583 (*illus.*), 584b (*illus.*), 586b (*illus.*), 7:50b
chevet, 1:144b
compared with Byzantine, 5:596b
construction technique, 3:566a (*illus.*)
Court Style, 5:621b, 10:624a
Decorated Style, **5:626b–627a**
Flamboyant Style and, 5:627a
hallmarks of, 5:626b
Perpendicular Style and, 5:626b
subdivisions of, 5:626b
see also Tierceron; Tracery
definition of, 5:580b–582b
design techniques, treatises, 10:530b
developmental factors for, 3:562a-b
documentary sources for, 5:582b, 584a–585a
Early English style, 4:472a
Early Gothic, 5:580b
in England and Italy, 8:455b
first uses of, 5:580b–581b
Flamboyant Style, **5:627a**, 6:39a
Chartres Cathedral, 7:50b
Decorated Style and, 5:627a
in Paris, 9:406b
rose window in St. Étienne of Sens, 12:96 (*illus.*)
soufflet, 11:373b
in Valencia, 12:348b–349a
see also Tracery
forms of, 5:585b–586a
in France
Aisne Valley, 1:427a
Dauphiné, 4:109b–110a
Gervase of Canterbury on, 5:513b, 582b, 584a
"Heavenly City" image, 5:586a–587a
High Gothic, 5:580b, 582b
Laon Cathedral, 5:587b (*illus.*)
Late Gothic, 5:580b
in lay building, 5:587a–588a
Lincoln Cathedral, 5:390b
Lombard Romanesque and, 10:484b
Manueline Style, **5:630a-b**
origin of, 5:630a
sculptors of, 5:630a-b
masons' lodges, 5:588a
Milan Cathedral, 8:381a
monastic influence, 8:455b
negative connotations of, 5:580b–581b
Norman Romanesque and, 10:482b
opus francigenum, 5:582b
organ in transept, 9:275b (*illus.*)
origins of, 5:582a-b
see also Opus Francigenum
Perpendicular Style, **5:630b–631a**
Decorated Style and, 5:631a
fan vault and, 12:365a-b
Gloucester Cathedral, 5:568a-b
Michael of Canterbury and, 8:305a
origin of, 5:630b–631a
Rayonnant features in, 5:630b–631a
see also Tracery
in Poland, 9:723b
portal trumeau, 12:222a
positive connotations of, 5:581b–582a
post-Parler style, 9:525a
Rayonnant Style, **5:631b**
characteristics of, 10:616b
in exteriors, 5:631b
Flamboyant Style and, 5:627a
in interiors, 5:631b
origin of, 5:631b
Perpendicular Style and, 5:630b–631a
soufflet, 11:373b
wheel window, 12:625b
reredos altar screen, 10:334b–335a
reuse of ancient building elements in, 5:584a–585a
revived, 1:428b
Romanesque architecture and, 5:588b–589a
St. Denis, 5:581 (*illus.*), 584a-b
choir, 11:503a–504a (*illus.*)
Sondergotik, 11:372a-b
soufflet, 11:373b
status of the architect, 1:440a–441a
structural elements, 11:656a-b
Suger on, 5:584a–585a, 586a
in 13th century, 5:586b–588b
in town halls, 5:587a
tracery, trefoil, 12:182b
transepts in, 12:125b
triforium passage, 12:188b
use of wood in, 3:563b
vaulting in, 5:580b–581a
Villard de Honnecourt, 5:587a–588a
westwork, 12:622b
Wimpfen-im-Tal, 5:582a-b
Ypres cloth hall, 5:583 (*illus.*), 587a
Gothic art
International Style, **5:627a–630a**
at Avignon papal court, 5:627b
at Bohemian court, 5:627b
at Burgundian court, 5:628b
at Valois courts, 5:628b
characteristics of, 2:332b, 10:622b
contributors to, 2:349b
definition of, 5:627a-b
diverse themes in, 5:629a
emotionalism in, 5:629b
in England, 5:628a
exhibitions of, 5:627a
first use of, 5:627a
French influences on, 5:627b
Ghent Altarpiece, 5:611b

intermingling of styles in, 5:629b
Italian influences on, 5:627b
Italo-Byzantine influences on, 5:627b
Limbourg brothers, **5:628b–629a**
in Lombardy, 5:628a
in manuscript illumination, 5:615b
in Milan, 5:628a
mysticism in, 5:629b
regional styles in, 5:627b
Renaissance, 10:536a
secularization of, 5:629b
in Siena, 5:628a-b, 11:280b
Sienese tradition, 10:671b
Sluter's use of, 11:349a
"soft style," 5:627b–628a
in Spain, 5:612a
trecento art influences on, 5:627b
in Verona, 5:628a
woodcut and, 12:690a, 693b
Manueline Style, **5:630a-b**
origin of, 5:630a
sculptors of, 5:630a-b
Mudejar art and, 11:380a
painting and manuscript illumination, 4:370a, **5:603a–616a**, 8:108b–109a, 167b
altarpieces, 5:604a, 610a–611a
changes affecting, 5:604a–605a
definition of style of, 5:603a-b
in Flanders, 5:611a–612a
forms of, 5:603b–604a
in France, 5:607b–609b
frescoes, 5:603b, 605a (*illus.*), 606a-b
guilds and, 5:605a
icons in, 5:604a
influence of plague on, 5:606b–607a
panel, 5:603b–604a, 605a–612a
secularization of, 5:604b
"soft style" in, 5:610a-b
in Spain, 5:612a
spatial relationships, 8:167b
stained glass, 5:603b
themes of, 5:604a, 606b
transition from Romanesque, 5:603a
see also Nativity; Panel painting
polychrome style of, 8:364a
revival, 10:309a–310a
sculpture, **5:616b–626b**, 9:668b
arma Christi and, 1:469b
birth of, 5:616b
changes in, 5:619a
classical references in, 10:309a–310a (*illus.*)
classical style, 5:623a-b
column figures in, 5:625b
Court Style, 5:621b
in England, 5:625a–626a
in France, 5:616b–623b
French influence on, 5:626a
gargoyle, 5:365b
in Germany, 5:623b–624a
icons in, 5:617a-b
in Italy, 5:624a-b
late forms of, 5:625a
pleurants, 9:709 (*illus.*), 710a-b
polyptych, 12:198b
portal trumeau, 12:222a
reredos altar screen, 10:334b–335a
Romanesque sculpture and, 5:616b–617a
spread of, 5:516b
see also Ivory carving
shoe design and, 11:255a-b
Style 1200, 5:619a-b, 621b
Virtues vs. Vices in, 12:462b
see also Retable
Gothic History. See Cassiodorus Senator, Flavius Magnus Aurelius
Gothic language, 6:434b
in Crimea, 6:437b
Italo-Romance and, 6:623b
translation of Bible, 2:211b–212a
Gothic scripts, 9:345b–349a
role of in the spread of literacy, 7:600a
types of
characteristics of, 9:345a–346a
cursive, 9:348 (*illus.*)
early textual, 9:346 (*illus.*)
formal, 1:213b (*illus.*)
formal cursive, 9:348b, 349a (*illus.*)
formal textual, 9:346b–347a (*illus.*)
hybrid, 9:348b–349a, 349b (*illus.*)
round textual, 9:347b–348a
round textual Bolognese, 9:348a (*illus.*)
textual Parisian, 9:347 (*illus.*)
textual pearl, 9:347a
Gothic wars, 7:2b
beginning of, 8:376b
Benedict of Nursia and, 2:169a
Rome and, 10:517a-b
Goths, 12:468a-b
acquisition of Dacia, 2:90a, 90b
art of, 8:363b–364a
polychrome technique of, 8:364a
invasions of Balkans in the 3rd century, 2:89b
Roman Empire and, 12:468b
in Sweden, 11:528b, 529a, 529b
swords of (spathas), 8:283a
see also Ostrogoths; Visigoths
Goðorð (Icelandic chieftancy), in *Vatnsdœla saga,* 12:363a-b
Gotland, **5:631b–633b**, 12:423a
archaeological record of, 5:632a-b
carved pictorial stones, 5:632b
coin hoards, 5:632a-b
commerce, 11:531a
Denmark and, 5:632b–633a
economic decline of, 5:633a
fines for touching a woman, 12:423b
foundation of Lübeck and, 5:632b–633a
Hanseatic League and, 12:113a
invaded by Danes, 6:94a, 11:532b
in Kalmar Union, 5:633a
Kurish weapons and ornaments found in, 2:62b
in Late Iron Age, 5:632a
Magnus I Ladulås and, 11:531a
in Migration Period, 5:632b
in 9th century, 5:632b
north European trade and, 9:88b
Novgorod and, 9:195a
political history of, 5:632a
Roman Empire and, 5:632a
Sweden and, 5:631b, 633a
trade and commerce, treaties, 6:90b
Viking art and, 12:418b, 419a (*illus.*)
"Gotland Association," 5:461a
Gottes Zukunft. See Heinrich von Neustadt
Gottesfreunde
influenced by Mechthild of Magdeburg, 9:11a
possible influence of on English mysticism, 9:20a
Ruusbroec and, 9:38a
Suso and, 9:34b
women mystics and, 9:11b, 13a
Gottesgeburt in der Seele. See Eckhart, Meister
Gotteshäuser (houses of God), 9:13a
Gottfried, Alamannic duke, vs. Pepin II, 11:526b
Gottfried of Franconia, *Pelzbuch,* 4:579a
Gottfried von Neifen, **5:633b–634a**
courtly love and, 5:633b
influence of, 5:634a
Minnesang tradition and, 5:633b
songs ascribed to, 5:633a
Gottfried von Strassburg, **5:634a–638a**, 8:224b
on Bligger von Steinach, 2:274b
ceremony and, 9:114a
influence of
on *Mai und Beaflor,* 8:48a
on romance literature, 5:454a-b
Johann von Würzburg and, 7:117b
Konrad von Stoffeln and, 7:287b
Konrad von Würzburg and, 7:288a-b
poetic rivalry, 8:351a
on Reinmar von Hagenau, 5:438a-b
technique of, 5:453b–454a, 637b
themes of, 8:350a
Tristan und Isolt, 9:708a
allegory in, 5:636a
cave of the lovers, 5:429a, 431a, 635b–636a
chivalry in, 5:636a–637a
Chrétien de Troyes and, 5:448a
Christianity in, 5:636a
continuation by Heinrich von Freiberg, 5:454a, 6:136a
continuation by Ulrich von Türheim, 5:454a, 12:253a-b
courtly love in, 5:448a-b, 453b–454a, 636a–637a, 637a
derivatives of, 10:543b
eulogy of Reinmar der Alte, 10:292a
hunting in, 6:358b, 359a
love in, 1:455b, 571b–572a
plot of, 5:635a-b
prologue of, 5:635a-b
structure of, 5:634b
style of, 5:634a-b, 637a-b
Thomas of Brittany as source for, 5:453b, 12:200a–201a (*illus.*), 202a
vs. Eilhart von Oberg's treatment, 5:635a, 8:351a, 12:204a, 205a
vs. Thomas de Bretagne's treatment, 5:634b
see also Tristan, legend of
Wolfram von Eschenbach and, 5:634a-b, 12:674b, 679b
Gottschalk of Aachen, Doctrine of Two Swords and, 12:233b–234a

Gottschalk of Limbourg, 6:381b
Gottschalk of Orbais, **5:638a–639a**, 7:362b
condemned for heresy, 5:638a-b
critics of, 5:638b
early life of, 5:638a
grammar treatises of, 5:639a
Hrabanus Maurus and, 5:638a-b, 6:306b
hymns of, 6:380b, 381b
John Scottus Eriugena and, 7:141b–142a
monastic vows of, 5:638a
poetry of, 5:638a
meter, 7:372a
on predestination, 5:638a–639a, 9:587a
teacher of Augustine's writings, 5:638a
theological treatises of, 5:639a
travels of, 5:638a-b
on Trinity, 5:639a
Gottsched, Johann, *Renner* and, 6:326a
Gournay-en-Bray, shrine of, 6:492a
Governour, The. See Elyot, Sir Thomas
Gower, John, **5:639b–643a**
Cinkante balades, 1:269a, 5:642a-b
Confessio Amantis, 4:551b, 5:641a–642a, 8:322b, 435b, 10:452a, 12:476b
courtly love in, 5:641b
exempla in, 7:641a-b
framing story, 5:641a-b
popularity of, 5:642a
sources for, 5:641b
translations into Portuguese and Castilian, 11:457a
verse version of *Secretum secretorum,* 11:135b
effigy of, 5:642b–643a
friendship with Chaucer, 5:639b, 642a
on Great Schism, 5:640a
historical records of, 5:642b
marriage of, 5:642b
Mirour de l'omme, 1:263b, 8:322a, 322b
allegory of, 5:640a
MS of, 5:639b
sources for, 5:639b–640a, 640a
moral views of, 5:642a
reputation of, 5:639b, 642a
satire of, 5:640a-b
shorter poems of, 5:642a-b
Speculum stultorum and, 9:131a
Traitié . . . pour essampler les amantz marietz, 1:263b, 5:642b
Vox clamantis, 5:640a–641a, 7:370a, 8:322a, 435b
Göyük (13th-century Mongol), 2:131b
Gozbertus, **5:643a-b**
identity of, 5:643a
Gozechin. *See* Godzin of Mainz
Gozwin. *See* Godzin of Mainz
Gozzadini, Giovanni, *De electione romani pontificis,* 3:520a
Gozzoli, Benozzo, 5:534b
Grabar (Armenian literary language), 1:507a
Gråborg hill fort, 10:693a
Grabow, Matthew, 3:649a
Gračanica Monastery, 11:186b
Grace, divine
Duns Scotus and, 9:213a-b
Ockham and, 9:213a-b
Pelagius' doctrine and, 9:486a
treasure doctrine and, 6:446b
Graces (musical ornamentation), 8:631a, 633b–634a
Gradenigo, Pietro, doge of Venice, 12:391a, 391b
Gradierwerk. See Salines
Grado (township of Venice), 12:383b, 385a, 386b
Gradual, **5:643b–644a**
Amalarius of Metz on, 5:644a
in Augustine's time, 5:643b
in Bamberg manuscript, 2:68b
Constance Gradual, 5:663a
definition of, 5:643b
designation of, 5:644a
differentia in, 4:185a
Franciscan, Kyriale, 8:200a
Gregorian, 5:644a
music of, 5:644a
oldest sources of, 5:643b–644a
place in Mass, 5:643b, 11:361a-b
plainsong development and, 9:688b–692b (*illus.*)
see also Mass cycles; Plainsong; "Viderunt omnes"
Graduale romanum, Kyries in, 7:312b
Graecismus. See Évrard de Béthune
Graelant, 7:317a
Graf Rudolf, **5:644a–645a**
crusades in, 5:644b–645a
dialect of, 5:644b
influence of, 5:645b
missing parts of, 5:644b–645a
plot of, 5:644b
reconstruction of, 5:644a-b
Graf Urs, 4:516a (*illus.*), 516b
Grágás, 6:396a
on poetry addressed to women, 10:406a
Grail, legend of, **5:645a,** 8:223b
Christianization of, 5:258b–259a, 285a
French Vulgate cycle, 8:224b
in Old French romances, 1:570b–571a
Palamède, 5:286a
in *Perlesvaus,* 9:505a
in Robert de Boron's *Joseph d'Arimathie,* 10:431a
Roman du graal, 5:286a
Roman de Tristan de Léonois and, 12:202b
similarity of to pagan mysteries, 9:2a-b
Svipdagsmál and, 11:524b
in Thomas Malory's *Morte Darthur,* 8:63b–64a
transubstantiation and, 5:645a
Vulgate cycle, origin of, 5:285b–286a
Wolfram von Eschenbach and, 5:451b–452a
see also Arthurian legend; Chrétien de Troyes; Malory, Sir Thomas; *Parcevals saga;* Prose Lancelot; Wolfram von Eschenbach
Grain crops, **5:645b–648a**
barley, 5:645b
Byzantium, 1:77b–78a
Italy, 1:86b
Slavic world, 1:98b
Black Death and, 5:647b
Byzantium, effect of Islamic conquest, 1:76b
cereals and grains, threshing, 1:77b
changes in growing of, 5:647a-b
climate and, 5:647a-b
crop failure, 9:680a
Eastern European
effect on Western grain prices, 5:116b
Poland, 9:728a-b
French Midi, 1:85a
German trade in, 6:91b–92a
hard wheat
Mediterranean region, 1:81a
Roman Baetica, 1:82a
harvesting, Russia, 1:99b
Islamic, transport of, 12:148a
major crops cultivated, 1:78a, 81a, 83a–84a, 86b, 87b–88a, 94b, 99b, 104b
millet, 5:646b–647a
Byzantium, 1:78a
Christian Spain, 1:83b
Slavic world, 1:98b
milling, 11:637a
national and urban policies, 5:121a
Northern Europe, history, 1:89a-b
in Norway, 9:180b
oats, 5:646b
Byzantium, 1:78a
Christian Spain, 1:83b
Italy, 1:86b
Northern Europe, 1:93a
price fluctuation and production of, 5:116b
professional grain sellers, 5:121a-b
rice
Christian Spain, 1:83b
Islamic Spain, 1:82a-b
Roussillon, 1:85b
rye, 5:646b
Byzantium, 1:78a
Christian Spain, 1:83b
Italy, 1:86a
Sardinia, rotations, 1:88a
Sicily, *diminia,* 1:88a
sorghum
Christian Spain, 1:83b
Islamic Spain, 1:82a
Mediterranean region, 1:81a
trade in, 5:121a–122b
Egypt/Mecca, 11:249a
Iceland and, 6:395a
Norway, 9:181a-b
Novgorod, 9:196a
Roman, 10:460b
vetch, Byzantium, 1:78a
water mills used for processing, 8:393a
in Western Europe, 5:645b–648a
see also Food trades; Reclamation of land
wheat, 5:645b–646b
Byzantium, 1:77b–78a
Christian Spain, 1:83b
Islamic Spain, 1:82a
Slavic world, 1:98b

yields, 5:647b–648a
see also Agriculture; Bread; Famine
Grain (dye), 12:694b, 695a
Grain (unit of measure), 12:594a
Graindor de Douai, 3:331a
Chanson d'Antioche, 3:254b–255a
Gram piant' agl'ochi. See Landini, Francesco
Gramadegau'r Penceirddiaid. See Bardic grammars
Gramática de la lengua castellana. See Nebrija, Antonio de
Grammar, **5:648a–651a**
Cassiodorus on, 10:354a
in classical literary studies, 3:432b–433a
clausula, 3:437a-b
dictamen, 4:173b–176b
Ibn Sīnā's treatises on, 11:303b
John of Garland's treatises on, 7:133b
Latin
codifying of, 5:648b–649a
Donatus on, 5:648b–649a
Priscian on, 5:648b–649a
Priscianic tradition of, 5:649a–650a
Scholastic tradition of, 5:649b–650a
seven liberal arts and, 5:648b–649b
teaching of, 5:648a-b
Old Spanish, 11:396a–398b
Quintilian's definition, 10:352b
Razos de trobar, 10:252a-b
Remigius of Auxerre as grammarian, 10:303a
rhetoric and, 10:353a
Roger Bacon on, 2:37b–38a
speculative, 10:359b, 360b
Bernard of Chartres and, 2:190a
study of Vergil and, 12:394a
textbooks, translation and, 12:136b–137a
treatises
Arabic, 5:650b
Byzantine Greek, 5:650b–651a
Icelandic, 5:650a-b
Irish, 5:650a
Latin, 5:649a
Old English, for Latin, 5:650a
Welsh, 5:650a
trivium study of, 12:206a
university curriculum, textbooks, 11:688b
see also De dubiis nominibus; Literacy, Western European; Scandinavian literature, grammatical; Schools
Grammar. See Dionysius Thrax
Grammar school. *See* Schools, grammar; Trivium
Grammatical Treatise, First, 5:650b, 11:10b–12a
Grammatical Treatise, Fourth, 11:12b–13a
Grammatical Treatise, Second, 11:12a
Grammatical Treatise, Third. See Óláfr Þórðarson
Gran conquista de Ultramar, 11:416a
Gran Tavola dei Bonsignori (bank: Siena), 2:76b, 11:279b
Granada, **5:651b–653b**, 5:652 (map)
Albacín area in, 5:651b
Arabic language in, 5:653a
dialect grammar, 12:137a
architecture in, 5:653a-b
castles and fortifications in, 5:651b
Christian Spain and, 5:653a
decline of power of, 11:384a
fall of, 7:112a
irrigation of, 6:558a
Jewish community in, 7:97a
Marinid sultans and, 5:652b–653a
Mudejars in, 11:378a, 380a-b
Muslim conquest of, 5:651b
Nasrid dynasty in, 5:652a–653b
nobility of, 5:653b
population of, 5:653a
prosperity of, 11:384a
under Almohad rule, 5:652a
sections of, 5:651b
siege of, 5:653b
surrender of, 5:653b
Zirid Alcazaba of, 5:651b
Zirids in, 12:745a
Granarium. See Wethamstede, John, abbot of St. Albans
Grand assize. *See* Assize
Grand Book of Music. See Fārābī, al-, *Kitāb al-mūsīqī al-kabīr*
Grand conseil (French royal council), 9:418a
Parlement of Paris and, 9:420a
Grand coutumier de Normandie, 3:279b, 7:426b–427a
Grand coutumier de Normandie, see also Summa de legibus
Grand jury. *See* Jury
Grand Komnenoi, Empire of. *See* Komnenoi
Grand testament. See Villon, François
Grande Chirurgie. See Guy de Chauliac
Grandes chroniques de France, 2:236b, 3:327a-b, **5:653b–654b**
basis for French historiography, 6:264a-b
French monarchy in, 5:654a-b
initiated by Suger of St. Denis, 11:504a
on Manuel II Palaiologos, 8:92b
origins of, 5:243a
principles of
legitimizing Trojan origins, 5:260b
providential view of history, 5:259b
translatio imperii et studii, 5:260a
produced in secular ateliers, 8:104a
romance narrative similarities of, 5:260a-b
sources for, 5:654a
space-time axis in, 5:260b
translations from Latin in, 5:654a
Grandguard, 1:534a (*illus.*)
Grandmont, order of, **5:654b–656a**
apostolic principles and, 5:654b–655a
approval of, 5:655a
Calvinist occupation of, 5:655b
Clement III and, 5:655a
contributions of, 5:655b–656a
destruction of, 5:655b
early history of, 5:654b
enamels from, 4:438b
expansion of, 5:655a
Gregory VII and, 5:655a
ideal of poverty in, 5:655a-b
John XXIII and, 5:655b
reforms in, 5:655b
revival of, 5:655b
Rule of, 5:655a
schisms in, 5:655b
Strict Observance, 5:655b
under Stephen of Liciac, 5:655a
under Stephen of Muret, 5:654b
Grandson, Battle of (1476), 11:545a
defeat of bowmen at, 2:352b
Granovitaya Palace. *See* Moscow Kremlin
Grantham, Angel (inn), 6:468b
Grants geanz, 1:265b
Granum sinapis, 8:357b
Grapes
in diet of Mediterranean people, 5:305a
wine production and, 12:653b–654a
Graphium. See Stylus
Grasburg, Rudolph of Habsburg and, 11:540a
Grasmetze, Die. See Hermann von Sachsenheim
Grasser, Erasmus, **5:656b**
Morris Dancers, 5:656a (*illus.*)
Gratian, **5:656b–658a**
at Second Lateran Council, 5:656b
clergy and, 3:440b
Concordia discordantium canonum, 7:413a-b, 10:19a-b
Paucapalea and, 9:466b–467a
Quadrifidio ciborum and, 10:448b
concubinage and, 3:530a
Corpus iuris civilis and, 7:421b–422a
in Dante's *Divine Comedy,* 9:517b
De penitentia, Laurentius Hispanus on, 7:386a
Decretum, 2:312a, 3:352b, 516a, 517b, 635a, 636b, **4:128a–130a**, 7:413a–414a, 427a-b, 11:58a, 691b
Abelard's method and, 7:413b
additions to, 5:657a-b, 7:414b
against astrology, 1:607a
Augustine in, 6:496a
canon law influenced by, 3:637a-b
on church elections, 4:421b–422a
classification in, 7:565b
commentaries on, 4:127a–128a, 7:414a-b
commented on by Stephen of Tournai, 11:481b
definition of, 4:122b, 123a, 128a
denunciatio and, 6:478b
on dialectic, 4:170a
on dispensation, 4:217a
on Divine Office, 4:222b
Donation of Constantine in, 4:258b
ecclesiastical duality of authority, 4:374a
in *Établissements de St. Louis,* 4:515b
False Decretals in, 4:126b
glosses, 11:691b
glosses of, 9:519a
Huguccio's apparatus, 7:414b
impact of, 5:657b
importance of, 7:413b–414a
Johannes Teutonicus' apparatus, 7:414b

Gratian (*cont.*)
Decretum (cont.)
Laurentius Hispanus on, 7:385b
literary offshoots of, 7:414a
method of treatment, 7:413b
organization and contents, 5:657a, 7:413b
original form (*Concordia discordantium canonum*), 7:413a-b
on papal power, 10:20a-b
purpose of, 5:656b–657a
scholasticism of, 11:58a
summa of, 4:127b–128a
on tithe payment, 12:63b
uniqueness of, 7:413b
use as textbook, 7:413b–414a
usury defined, 12:336b
Vincentius Hispanus and, 12:456a
see also Law codes, canon law
on enemies of church, 4:16b
French law and, 7:461b
influence of canon law on, 7:410a-b, 411b–412a
life of, 5:656b
method of teaching, 7:513b
on penance, 9:490b, 491b
Peter Lombard and, 9:517a
Roman law and, 5:656b
taxation of clergy and, 3:447b
Vacarius' *Summa de matrimonio* and, 12:343b
Grauer Rock. See Orendel
Grave, The, 8:329b
Graverie, 9:162a
Gray, Sir Thomas, of Heton, *Scalacronica,* 1:265b, 10:686a
Gray's Inn, 6:477b
Great Arbitration of 1258, 3:481b
Great Book of Letters. See Suso, Heinrich, *Grosses Briefbuch*
Great Canon. See Andrew of Crete
Great Catechetical Oration. See Gregory of Nyssa, St.
Great Chronicle. See Matthew Paris
Great Companies, 3:206a, 531a-b
Great Council of Union (879-880), 3:632a
Great Hippodrome
demes and, 4:135a
factions in, 3:554a-b
Great Meteoron, 8:300a (*illus.*)
Great Mosque, Isfahan, 11:146 (*illus.*)
Great Mosque, Marrakech
architecture, 8:150b
orientation, 8:150b
Great North Road (England), Robin Hood and, 10:436b
Great Novgorod. *See* Novgorod
Great (or Old) Moravia, 2:299a-b, **5:658a–659a**, 12:617a
Avars in, 5:658a
history of, 5:658b
independence from Frankish rule, 5:658a-b
Magyars and, 2:299b, 6:338a
name of, 5:658a
prominence of, 5:658a
revisionist history of, 2:299b
Slavonic language in, 5:658b
under Sventopolk, 5:658a-b
Great Poland (Polonia maior). *See* Poland
Great Russian language. *See* Russian language
Great St. Martin (church: Cologne), 10:488b
Great Schism of the West. *See* Schism, Great
Great seal
chancellor and, 6:301a, 302b
royal wardrobe and, 6:303a
Great Session. *See* Welsh law
Great Survey, Domesday Book and, 4:237b–238a
"Great Synaxary," 11:557b
"Great Turkish troubles," in Georgia, 5:406a
Great Urswick cross, inscription, 10:562a
Great wardrobe, 6:302b
office of, 6:304a
Greater Armenia. *See* Armenia: Geography
Greater Perfect System, 8:555a, 626a, 647b
Greater Sophenē. *See* Sophenē
Greave, 1:525b, 529b, 531a, 531b, 534a (*illus.*)
Gréban, Arnoul, **5:659a-b**
Mercadé's divison of Passion cycle and, 5:659a
Mystère de la Passion, 4:264b, 5:272a, 274a, 659a, 9:447b–448a
in Paris, 5:659a
Greban, Simon, *complainte* on Charles VIII, 3:508a
Grecismus. See Evrard of Béthune
Greece
astrology in, 1:604b–605a
crusades and, 4:55b
Latin Empire of Constantinople and, 7:346a, 346b
Latin states in. *See* Latin states in Greece
roads in, 10:424a
Stefan Uroš IV Dušan of Serbia and, 11:178a
Greece, ancient
colonies of in Caucasia, 3:195a
Constantinople's importance in, 3:549b
Greek alphabet. *See* Alphabets
Greek architecture, diaconicon, 4:167b
Greek Book of Agriculture, 1:106a
Greek church, monarchical episcopy of, 9:365a-b
Greek cross, 4:9b, 10 (*illus.*)
Greek fire, **5:659b**
captured in Mesembria by Krum, 8:279b
catapults, 3:180a
definition, 11:633b–634a
harrāqa and, 11:247b
in naval battle, 11:634 (*illus.*)
Sasanian "Median oil," 10:665a
Greek language
Armenian and, 1:506b
Atticism in Byzantine Empire, 3:430b
in Balkans, 6:443b
Byzantine, **5:659b–661a**, 6:444b
bilingualism in, 5:660a, 661a
Christianity and, 5:660a
destruction of Byzantine Empire and, 5:660b
ecclesiastical and administrative use, 6:436a, 439a
historiography, 2:513a-b, 515b
learned, 2:506b, 509a, 509b, 510a
literary, 5:660a
meter, 2:505b
phonetics, 2:505b
Ptochoprodromic poems, 2:508b
role of, 5:659b–660a
spoken, 5:660a
technical, 5:660b
translation and translators, 12:126a–127b
vernacular, 5:661a
vernacular, in literature, 2:508b, 509a, 509b–510a, 521a-b, 522a
see also Byzantine literature; Literacy, Byzantine
Castilian language and, 3:141a
Chairete, 3:240b–241a
in Egypt, 6:589a, 10:455a
grammar
by Chrysoloras, 7:1a
by John Basingstoke, 12:137b
classical, 5:650b–651a
in Latin, 12:136b
in Greece, 6:443b
in Hungary, 6:337a
instruction in grammar schools, 11:63b–64a
John Scottus Eriugena and, 7:142a
Koine, 6:439a
in late Roman Empire, 10:467a
Latin loanwords in, 6:438b
Latin translation and translators
Byzantine, 12:126b–127a
Western European, 12:140a
in Morea, 7:378b
neume and, 8:624a-b
in Nubian liturgy, 9:199a
origin of, 6:433b
replacement of by Arabic, 4:405a
teaching of in Italy, *see also* Manuel Chrysoloras
teaching and study of, 12:137a-b
word lists
Alexander Neckham's *Corrogationes Promethei,* 12:137a
Eberhard of Béthune's *Grecismus,* 12:137a
see also Judeo-Greek language; Loanwords, Greek
Greek literature
Armenian translations, 1:507b–508a
fable, 4:572a
medical corpus, translations into Syriac and Arabic, 12:130a, 133a
original texts, evaluation for translation, 12:131b–132a
Platonic thought in, 9:695a, 696a–699a, 702b–703b
poetry, in Sicily, 11:274b
scientific and philosophical texts
translation into Arabic, 12:128b–130a
translation into Latin, 12:140a
translations into Latin, 6:2a

al-Ya^{c}qūbī and, 12:718a
see also Armenian Hellenizing School; Byzantine literature; Translation and translators
Greek numerals, in Spain, 10:472b
Greek Orthodox Church. *See* Byzantine church; Russian Orthodox Church
Greeks
in Africa, Berber language and, 2:186a
early medieval Western European trade and, 12:110b
in Egypt, 10:453a-b, 454a, 454b
Green dyes, production of, 4:326a
Green Mosque of Mehmed I, 6:612b, 613a (*illus.*)
Green revolution, Arab
cereals and grains, 1:82a-b
cotton, 1:82a
fruit and vegetables, bananas, 1:81b
introduction of new species, 1:82b–83a
Islamic Spain, 1:81b–83a
Mediterranean region, 1:81a–83a
irrigated crops, 1:81a
nonirrigated crops, 1:81a
sugar cane, 1:81b
Green Tomb of Mehmed I, 6:612b
Greene, Katharine and Ralph, tomb of, 11:518 (*illus.*)
Greenland
Black Death in, 2:261b
colonized, 4:554b, 568a
settlement of, 10:704a
Skrælings in, 11:329b
Vikings and, 12:426a, 427a–428a
see also Viking navigation
Greens (demes). *See* Demes
Grega saga, 10:394b, 395b
Grégoire Béchada, *Cançun d'Antiocha,* 10:179b
Gregorian of Aniane, compiler of, 10:605b–606a
Gregorian chant, **5:661a–665a**
cadence in, 3:5b–6b
chants in rhymed offices and, 10:374a–376a
Cistercians and, 3:402a
classification of, 8:448b
authentic and plagal forms, 8:449b
contrafactum in, 3:575b–576a
in daily Masses, 5:662b–663a
development of, 5:662a
in Divine Office, 5:662a–663a
Dominican, 4:240b–241a
Eastern Europe, **9:686b–688a**
first treatise on by Aurelian of Réôme, 2:2b
functions of, 5:661b
graduals, 5:643b–644a
Gregory I (the Great) and, 5:661b
jubilus, 7:156b
liturgy of, 5:662a-b
manuals for, 5:663a
manuscripts of, 5:663a
melody, 5:663b–664a
music for, 5:661a
notation systems, 6:12b
of Jacques de Liège, 7:38b
Old Roman chant and, 9:234b–235b
oral tradition, 9:235b
origins of, 5:661b–662a, 9:235a-b
papal vs. urban rites, 9:235a-b
paraliturgical forms of, 5:662b–663a
publication of first history of, 5:663a
restoration of use of, 5:664a-b
in Roman Office, 5:662b
Solesmes method and, 11:361b
sources of, **9:688a–693a**
tonaries and, 12:69b
trope in, 5:663a
Tropes to the Ordinary of the Mass and, 12:208b–210b (*illus.*)
Tropes to the Proper of the Mass and, 12:210b–213b (*illus.*)
Urban VIII and, 5:664a
use of organa in, 8:43a
in Winchester polyphony, 12:696b–697a
see also Ambrosian chant; *Flexa;* Introit; *Intonatio; Liber usualis;* Musical notation; Plainsong; Psalm tones; Sequence (prosa); Tones, reading and dialogue
Gregorian reform
Bruno the Carthusian on, 2:392a
in Catalonia, 3:177b
celibacy and, 3:217a-b
concept of primitive church and, 10:122a
Divine Office and, 4:225b
in Milan, 8:378b
Order of Cluny and, 3:470b
organization of Latin church and, 3:375a–376a
supported by Amatus of Monte Cassino, 1:229a
turning point of medieval church and, 3:361b
see also Gregory VII, pope; Reform, idea of
Gregoriana, see also Law codes, canon law
Gregorids, 1:489a, 503a, **5:665a-b**
Armenian tradition and, 5:665a-b
cemetery of, 1:518a
Mamikoneans and, 8:78b
members of, 5:665a
origin of, 5:665a
as patriarchs of Armenian church, 5:665a-b
West Tarōn and, 11:599a
see also Nersēs I the Great, St.
Gregorius. *See* Bar Hebraeus
Gregorius. See Hartmann von Aue
Gregory I (the Great), pope, **5:668b–669b**
achievements of, 3:343a
administration of Rome, 10:521a-b
against the heretics, 4:15b
Anglo-Saxon conversion to Christianity, 4:458a
Anglo-Saxon slavery and, 11:200b
Augustine of Canterbury and, 1:644b, 2:172a, 12:151a
Bede and, 2:154a-b
Cassian and, 3:122b
Christ II and, 4:550b
Christian missions and, 8:440b
Christmas celebration and, 3:318a-b
on Christology, 3:321a
on church dedication, 4:130b
Commentary on 1 Kings, 2:169a
conflict with patriarch of Constantinople, 9:371b
in Constantinople, 5:669a
control of central Italian church by, 9:371b
on corporeal relics, Roman view, 2:362b
on craftsmens' groups, 6:14b
Cura pastoralis. See Pastoral Care
Dialogues, 3:167a, 4:551a, 5:669a, 6:67a, 10:297a
Alfred the Great's preface, 1:165b
allegorical vision of a bridge, 10:410b
Angier's translation, 1:254a
on Benedict of Nursia, 2:168b, 169a, 170a
translations into Old English, 1:165a
Vie des anciens pères and, 12:415a
Zacharias' translation of, 12:126b
diplomatic and missionary work of, 9:371b–372a
as doctor of the church, 4:234a, 5:668b
education of, 5:668a
election of, 3:603a
English cult of popes and, 9:372a
English mission, 3:81b
on equality of people, 10:14b
excommunication and, 4:536b
as exegete, 2:212b–213a
feast of, 9:688b–689b
plainsongs for, 9:688b–689b
Greater Litany and, 7:587b, 592a
Gregorian chant and, 5:661b
on images, 4:358a
as initiator of fourfold biblical interpretation, 2:224a
Isidore of Seville and, 6:565a, 566b
Jews and, 7:75b, 76b, 85b
John IV the Faster and, 7:126a
kingship theories of, 7:260a
knowledge of Latin, 7:598b
on Kyrie eleison, 7:593b
life of by Paul the Deacon, 9:467b
liturgical tunicle and, 12:398b
liturgies and, 7:624a
monasticism and, 5:669a, 9:371b, 12:682b
Moralia in Job, 2:212b–213a, 3:167a, 4:542b, 5:669a, 6:307a, 8:434a, 10:14b, 114a
Bebo of Bamberg and, 2:150b
decorated initials in, 6:462b
Notker Teutonicus and, 9:189a-b
translations of, metrical, 7:667b
on obedience to kings, 10:17a
papal library and, 7:559b
papal power under, 5:668b–669a
on paradise, 9:396a
Pastoral Care, 1:165b–166a, 274b, 284a, 556b, 5:669a, 6:307a, 439b, 8:434a, 10:75b
ars praedicandi and, 1:556b
mirrors of princes and, 10:15a
Old English translation of, 1:165a, 165b–166a, 274b, 276a, 276b, 281a, 284a
on the priest, 10:361b

Gregory I (the Great), pope (*cont.*)
  on purgatory, 10:216a
  on Roman buildings, 10:517b
  Roman nobility and, 10:521b
  Roman Office and, 4:230a
  secular administration of, 9:371b
  in Segna di Bonaventura's panel, 11:142a (*illus.*)
  Seven Deadly Sins and, 11:211b
  sex aetates mundi and, 11:215a
  on simony, 11:301a
  title of pope and, 10:32a
  works attributed to, Liturgy of the Presanctified, 7:610b
  Wyclif and, 12:709b
Gregory II, pope
  accomplishments of, 3:345b
  conflict with Emperor Leo III, 9:372a
  defiance of imperial power by, 9:382a
  iconoclasm and, 3:345a
  Roman nobility and, 10:521b
  situation inherited by, 3:345a
  vs. Byzantines, 9:382a
Gregory III, pope
  alliances
    against Lombards, 7:657a-b
    with Charles Martel, 9:372b
  reign of, 3:345b
  vs. Emperor Leo III, 9:372b
Gregory IV, pope, pre-Romanesque art under, 10:112b
Gregory V, pope
  Otto III and, 10:522b
  Sylvester II and, 11:553a
Gregory VI, pope
  Gregory VII in service of, 5:669b
  Synod of Sutri and, 11:517a, 517b
Gregory VII, pope, **5:669b–671a**, 9:378a (*illus.*), 720a
  against lay possession of tithes, 12:63a
  Alexander II and, 5:669b
  Alphanus of Salerno and, 1:218b
  Armenian-Roman church union and, 3:394a
  at Canossa, 5:670b
  Benzo of Alba and, 2:182b
  Bernold of Constance and, 2:197b
  Camaldolese order and, 3:56a
  canon law reform of, 3:355a
  celibacy reform and, 3:217a
  Cluniac order and, 3:470a-b, 9:377b
  death in exile, 9:378b
  on deposition of rulers, 4:159a-b
  Desiderius of Monte Cassino and, 4:164b
  Dictatus papae, 3:351b–352a, 633b, **4:177a–178a**, 5:670a-b, 9:377b, 10:32a
    canon law and, 4:177a
    importance of, 5:670a
    on legal procedure, 7:504a
    papal primacy and, 4:177a-b, 374b
  ecclesiastical reforms, 4:374b, 465b, 473b
  formation of a Christian army, 4:16a
  goals of, 5:670a
  Grandmontine order and, 5:655a
  Gregory VI and, 5:669b
  Guiscards and, 11:265b, 266a
  Henry IV of Germany and, 3:69a-b, 5:477b, 670a-b, 6:499b, 9:378a-b
  Hungary and, 6:340a
  imperial-papal conflict under, 5:670a–671a
  indulgences and, 6:448b
  influence of, 5:669b
  in investiture controversy, 5:671b, 7:262a-b, 9:377b–378a
  Lambert and, 7:321b
  legacy of, 5:670b–671a
  Leo IX and, 3:351a, 5:669b, 7:543a
  Matilda of Tuscany and, 8:222b
  Milanese civil war and, 8:378b
  monastic renewal and, 3:403a
  Nicholas II and, 3:351b
  Norman invasion of Balkans and, 3:356a
  as papal adviser, 3:351a, 351b, 5:669b, 7:543a
  papal councils under, 3:634b–635a
  Paschal II and, 9:444b–445a
  Peter Damian's letter, 9:508b
  Platonism and, 9:701b
  on power of pope, 10:18b
  on punishment of the innocent, 6:494b
  reform
    effect on heretical groups, 6:195a
    Henry IV and, 6:163a
    leadership of, 5:160b
    moral, 10:287b
    of papacy, 5:477b–478a
    political, 9:378b–379a, 10:287b–288b
  register of, 4:165b
  reign of, 3:351b–352a
  on resistance, 10:17b
  Robert Guiscard and, 10:433a
  Sigebert and, 11:285a
  Synod of Sutri and, 11:517b
  Urban II and, 12:302b
  vs. Henry IV, in Rome, 10:523a
  see also Gregorian reform; Reform, idea of
Gregory VIII, pope
  Forma dictandi, 4:67a-b
  Innocent III and, 6:464a
Gregory IX, pope, **5:671a-b**, 10:266b
  alliance with Lombard League, 7:653a
  Angelus bell and, 2:166a
  Aristotelianism and, 1:461a
  Audivimus, 3:68b
  on blasphemy, 2:272a
  cardinals and, 3:94a
  De electione et electi potestate, 4:422b
  death of, 3:523b
  Decretals, 3:516b, 638a, 638b, 641a, 4:124a, 11:210b, 691b
    Apparatus on, 6:466a
    commissioning of, 5:671b, 7:77a, 78b, 416a, 428a
    Nicolaus de Tudeschis on, 9:129a
    punishments for usury, 12:337a-b
    Vincentius Hispanus and, 12:456a
  Doctrine of Two Swords and, 12:234b
  Dominican women's orders and, 12:688a
  Francis of Assisi's canonization, 5:198a
  Franciscan Second Order and, 12:688a
  Franciscans and, 5:197a, 671a
  Frederick II and, 4:32a, 58b, 537b, 5:214b–215a, 484b–485a, 671b, 11:270b
  Gloriam virginalem, 2:158b
  Henry III of England and, 11:607a
  on heresy, 5:671a
  heretics and, 4:134a, 6:198a, 483b
  hymns of, 6:382a
  Innocent III and, 5:671a
  Innocent IV and, 6:466a
  Inquisition and, 12:661b
    Excommunicamus et anathematisamus, 5:671a
  interdict and, 6:495b
  Jews and, 6:467a, 7:77a, 77b, 78b, 81b
  mendicant orders and, 5:671a
  Parens scientiarum
    foundation of University of Paris, 9:408b, 556b–557a
    on university privileges, 12:283a
  Quo elongati, 5:198a, 6:199a
    reaffirmed support for, 5:199b
  Raymond of Peñafort's commission and, 4:247b
  reign of, 3:353b
  in Reinmar von Zweter's *Leich,* 10:295b
  Rome and, 10:523b
  S. Francesco Assisi commissioned by, 1:593b
  Thibaut IV's crusade and, 4:51b, 52a
Gregory X, pope
  Charles of Anjou and, 11:272b
  church taxation and, 11:608a
  Dominican preachers and, 4:251a
  election of, 3:523b
  reforms of, 3:641b–642a, 643b
  reign of, 3:354a
  S. Maria of Mount Morrone Church and, 3:214b
  Ubi periculum, 3:94b–95a, 523b–524b, 641b–642a
Gregory XI, pope
  Armenian-Roman church union and, 3:395a, 395b
  campaign against Turks, 9:307a
  disciple of Baldus, 2:57a
  return of papacy to Rome and, 3:365a, 5:186b, 9:386a
  Salvator humani generis,
    condemnation of *Sachsenspiegel,* 10:603b
  vs. Wyclif, 6:367a, 12:706b
Gregory XII, pope
  meeting with Benedict, 5:512b
  oath to support *via cessionis,* 11:41b
  resignation of, 3:648b–649a
  Stanislav of Znojmo and, 6:367a
  summoning of council, 3:646a
  Wenceslas IV and, 6:367b
Gregory XIII, pope
  calendar reform instigated by, 3:23b
  canon law collections printed, 7:417a
Gregory of Akancʿ. *See* Grigor Aknercʿi

Gregory Akindynos, 3:632b, 5:672b
Gregory of Anawarza, *kat^c^ołikos,* 1:521a
Gregory Asbestas, 11:42b
Gregory Chioniades, accusations of heresy, 9:567a
Gregory of Cyprus, patriarch, education of, 7:595b
Gregory the Decapolite, St., biography of, on Byzantine trade routes, 12:101a
Gregory the Illuminator, St., 1:517b–518a, 519a, 519b, **5:668a-b**
anaphora and, 1:516a
ascent from the pit, 1:518b
as bishop, 5:668a
church of in Ani in Širak, 12:54a
Church of St. Hṙip^c^simē and, 6:309a
consecration of, 1:475b
conversions by, 5:412b, 668a
cult of, 5:668b
curing of King Trdat, 5:668a
descendants of, 5:665a-b
Gełard and, 5:373a
in *History of the Armenians,* 1:66a–67a
lost biography of, 1:508a
martyrium at Gayiané and, 5:371b
missions of, 1:66b, 5:668a-b
in *Patmut^c^iwn Tarōnoy,* 9:457a, 457b
persecution by Trdat III (IV) the Great, 12:164a
see of, 1:503a, 503b
works falsely ascribed to, 5:668b
*Yač̣hxapatum girk^c^* and, 1:508b–509a, 7:279b
Zwart^c^noc^c^ and, 12:749a-b
Gregory Mamikonean, 1:478b
Gregory the Martyrophil, *kat^c^ołikos,* 1:520a, 520b
Gregory, Master, 7:27a, 10:102a
De mirabilibus urbis Romae, 10:520b
Gregory of Narek, St. *See* Grigor Narekac^c^i, St.
Gregory of Nazianzus, St., **5:665b–666a**
anaphora and, 1:516b
as archbishop of Constantinople, 5:666a
Arianism and, 1:454a
Basil (the Great) and, 5:666a
as doctor of the church, 4:234a
Homilies
illustrated copies, 11:634b
manuscript illumination, 6:405a–406a (*illus.*)
Visitation and, 12:478b
neo-Nicene doctrine of, 5:666a
Neoplatonism and, 9:98b
Oration, 2:120a
Philokalia. See Basil the Great of Caesarea, St., *Philokalia*
on Platonist philosophy, 9:563a
preaching of, 10:350b
retreat of, 5:666a
Symeon the New Theologian and, 9:7b
Theological Orations, 5:666a
Theotokos and, 12:25b
translations into Armenian, 1:508b
on Trinity, 5:666a
use of the term patriarch, 9:458b
Gregory of Nyssa, St., **5:666b–667a,** 9:6b
Against Eunomius, 5:666b
Arianism and, 1:454a
as church father, 3:335b
commentary on the Song of Songs, 9:278a-b
creation, fall, and ascent of the soul, 9:563a
De opificio hominis, 1:506a
Great Catechetical Oration, 5:666b
Gregory of Nazianzus and, 5:666a-b
In laudem Basilii, 2:120a
Life of Moses, 5:666b
mystical theology of, 5:666b
neo-Nicene doctrine of, 5:666b
Neoplatonism of, 5:666b–667a, 9:98b
On the Creation of Man, 5:666b
rhetorical training of, 5:666b
Theotokos and, 12:25b
To Ablabius, That There Are Not Three Gods, 5:666b
writings of, 5:666b
Gregory Palamas, 3:632b, **5:672a–673a,** 11:559a
Barlaam the Calabrian and, 2:109b, 5:672b
defense of hesychasm, 5:672b, 9:7b
on divine essence and energy, 6:218a
eastern monasticism and, 5:672a
imprisonment of, 5:672b
In Defense of the Holy Hesychasts, 5:672b, 6:218a
Nikolaos Kavasilas and, 9:135a
opposition to, 5:672b
theology of, 5:672b
on transcendence, 5:672b
vs. Kydones, 4:135b
vs. Nikephoros Gregoras, 9:133b
Zealots and, 12:743a
Gregory of Rimini, **5:671b–672a**
Augustinism of, 5:671b–672a
nominalism of, 5:672a, 9:157a, 12:44a
on omnipotence of God, 5:672a
on predestination, 3:371a, 5:672a
theology of, 5:672a, 9:609a, 610a-b
via moderna at University of Wittenberg and, 12:408b
Gregory of San Chrisogono, *Polycarpus,* 7:410a
Gregory of Sinai, 2:413b, 9:7b
Gregory of Tatew. *See* Grigor Tat^c^ewac^c^i
Gregory Thaumaturgus, St.
Basil the Great and, 2:119b–120a
Discourse on the Nativity of Christ, 1:507b
Gregory of Tours, St., 3:453b, **5:667a–668a**
on Christian-Jewish polemics, 10:3a
on church bells, 2:165b, 5:321a
Ecclesiastical Histories. See History of the Franks
flyting and, 9:175a
on Germanus of Paris, 5:472b
History of the Franks (*Historia Francorum*), 2:184a, 239b, 5:667b, 6:66b, 262a, 468a, 494b–495a, 12:494b
influenced by Vergil's *Aeneid,* 12:394a
on Scandinavia, 10:688a
kingship theories of, 7:259b–260a
on Koimesis, 7:282a-b
Liber in gloria confessorum, 3:540b, 6:66b–67a
Life of St. Denis, 6:67b–68a
liturgical colors and, 3:484b
Martin and, 5:667a
on the mayor of the palace, 8:235b
on saintly patronage, 10:297a-b
sanctification of cloth, 2:362b
Seven Sleepers of Ephesus and, 11:213a
slavery and, 11:200b
travel writings of, 12:149a, 151a
Vitae patrum, 6:66a
writings, 5:667b
Gregory of Xlat^c^. *See* Grigor Xlat^c^ec^c^i
Gregory's Rule, 12:700a-b
Gremi, 5:402b
Grenier (unit of measure), 12:592b
Grenoble, University of, 12:285a
Grettir Ásmundarson, Skarkaðr legend and, 11:467a
Grettis saga Ásmundarsonar, 4:612b, 613a, **5:673a-b**
achievement of, 5:673b
attributed to Sturla Þórðarson, 11:496a, 499b–500a
Beowulf and, 2:184b
Boccaccio's *Decameron* and, 5:673a
dating of, 5:673a
plot of, 5:673a-b
references to Oddr and Óspakr, 2:71a
similarities to *Harðar saga Grímkelssonar,* 6:101b
sources of, 5:673a-b
Tristan legend and, 5:673a
Greutungi. *See* Ostrogoths
Grey, John de. *See* John de Grey
Greyfriars. *See* Franciscans
Greyhounds, 6:360b
Grickland (Greece, in Icelandic sagas), 9:442b
Griffins, in *Kudrun,* 7:304a
Grifo (half-brother of Pepin III), 9:500b, 501a, 501b
Grigor II Vkayasēr, *kat^c^ołikos,* **5:675b–676a,** 9:103a, 328a
as *dux* of Mesopotamia, 5:675b
Grigor III Pahlawuni, *kat^c^ołikos,* 9:103a, 103b, 328a-b
Hṙomklay and, 6:311b
Grigor IV Tłay (the Youth), *kat^c^ołikos,* 1:500b, 511b, 9:328b
Grigor Abasean (13th century), 1:512a
Grigor Aknerc^c^i, 1:511b, **5:674a–675a**
as abbot of Akner monastery, 5:674b
History of the Nation of the Archers, 5:674a-b
Grigor of the Arcruni, bishop, 1:508b
Grigor the Deacon, *Conversion of Georgia,* 5:417b

Grigor Derenik of Vaspurakan, prince, T^{C}ovma Arcruni's *History* and, 12:92a
Grigor K^{C}ert^{C}oł, correspondence, 1:509a
Grigor Lusaworič^{C}. *See* Gregory the Illuminator, St
Grigor Lusaworič^{C} (church: Ani in Širak). *See* St. Gregory (church: Ani in Širak)
Grigor Magistros, **5:675a-b**, 9:328a
- church construction of, 5:675a
- condemnation of Zoroastrianism, 6:188b
- correspondence, 1:510b
- cultural works of, 5:675a-b
- as distinguished secular Pahlawuni, 9:328a
- as *dux* of Mesopotamia, 5:675a
- Gagik II and, 5:675a
- letters of, 5:675a-b
- military enterprises of, 5:675a
- Plato and, 1:511a
- as statesman, 5:675a
- translations of, 5:675b

Grigor Manačihr Ražik, 1:518b
Grigor Narekac^{C}i, St., 1:510b, 512a, 520a-b, **5:673b–674a**
- *Book of Lamentations,* 1:511a, 5:674a, 8:16b
- heresy of, 5:673b–674a, 6:189b
- hymns of, 5:674a
- legends about, 5:673b–674a
- on T^{C}ondrakite heresy, 5:674a

Grigor the Priest, 1:511b, 8:228b–229a
Grigor Tat^{C}ewac^{C}i, 1:512a, 520b
- *Gospel of 1297,* 11:600b
- T^{C}ovma Mecop^{C}ec^{C}i and, 12:93a

Grigor the Theologian, works of, 5:411b
Grigor of Xandzt^{C}a, biographies of, 5:414a
Grigor Xlat^{C}ec^{C}i, 1:511b, 521a
Grigorie Ţamblac (Romanian writer of sermons), 10:510b
Grigoris Ałt^{C}amarc^{C}i, 1:511b
Grigoris of Aršarunik^{C}, chorepiskopos, 1:509b–510a
Grigoris, patriarch of Armenia, 5:665a
Grillius, commentary on Cicero, 10:356a
Grimaldus, *Vita Beati Dominici, Vida de Santo Domingo de Silos* and, 2:187a
Grimalte y Gradissa. See Flores, Juan de
Grimani Breviary, 5:361b
- hunting in, 6:361b

Grimestone, John, 3:493a
Grimm, Edward (eyewitness of St. Thomas Becket's murder), 12:413b
Grimma Bridge, 10:416a, 417b
Grímnismál, **5:676a–677a**
- comparisons with *Grottasǫngr,* 6:3b
- controversy about, 5:676b–677a
- Huginn and Muninn in, 6:323a-b
- *Hyndluljóð* and, 6:385b
- importance of, 5:676b
- inclusion in medieval manuscripts, 4:385b
- location of *hel,* 6:147b
- meter of, 5:676a
- narrative frame of, 5:676a-b
- Odin, contest with Geirrøðr, 9:218b
- on Valhalla, 12:350a-b
- Valkyries in, 12:351a
- *Vǫlundarkviða* and, 12:491a
- *Vǫluspá* and, 12:491b

Grimoald of Benevent, seal wax impression of, 11:125a
Grimoald, Lombard king, 7:657a
Grimoald (son of Pepin I), mayor of the palace, 3:104b, 9:499a, 499b
Grimoald (son of Pepin II), mayor of the palace, 9:500a
Gríms saga loðinkinna, **5:677a–678a,** 6:312a
- *Ketils saga Hœngs* and, 7:231b–232a
- preservation of, 5:677b
- *senna* in, 5:677b
- structure of, 5:677b

Gringoire (Gringore), Pierre, 10:364b, 365a
- *Jeu du Prince des Sots,* 4:265b

Gringonneur, Jacquemin, 5:352a
Grípisspá, **5:678a-b**
- compared with *Merlínússpá,* 8:276b
- composition of, 5:678a-b
- dating of, 5:678b
- *Sigurðarkviða in meiri* and, 5:678a
- structure of, 5:678a

Griplur, as alternate title of *Málsháttakvæði,* 8:65b
Griplur (prose cycles), 6:312a–313a
Gripo, 11:232a
"Gripping-beast motif" (in Viking art), 12:418a
Grisaille, **5:678b–679a**
- artists using, 5:678b
- definition of, 5:678b–679a
- in Hours of Jeanne d'Évreaux, 5:614a
- in Narbonne altar frontal, 5:679 (*illus.*)
- in stained glass, 5:549a–552a (*illus.*)

Grisel y Mirabella. See Flores, Juan de
Grisone, Federico, *Ordini del cavalcare,* 3:206b
Grisons, Swiss Confederation and, 11:545b
Groat, **5:679a–680b**
- in Charlemagne's reign, 5:679a
- distribution of, 5:680a
- first, 5:679b–680a
- in Venice, 4:301a

Grocyn, William, 11:51a
Gród. See Castrum
Groenendael monastery, Netherlandish mysticism and, 9:36a–38a
Grœnlendinga saga, 12:428a-b, 456b
- *see also* Vinland Sagas

Grógaldr, 11:524a, 524b
Groined vault. *See* Vault
Groma, 11:515a
Grooming, personal. *See* Beauty aids
Groote, Geert, **5:680b–681b**
- at Carthusian monastery, 5:680b
- Brethren of the Common Life, 5:680b, 9:611b
- on canon law, 5:680b
- *Conclusa et preposita, non vota,* 5:681a
- *Contra turrim traiectensem,* 5:681a
- conversion to ascetic life, 2:366b
- Devotio Moderna and, 4:166a–167a
- disciples of, 2:366b–367a
- formation of monastic orders and, 3:368b
- von Kalkar and, 8:647a
- preaching of, 5:680b
- Ruusbroec and, 4:320b, 5:680b, 9:37a
- Thomas à Kempis and, 12:33a-b
- translations of, 4:320b, 5:680b–681a, 9:37a
- visit to Groenendael, 9:38a

Gros (French unit of measure), 12:594a
Gros tournois (coin), 5:679b (*illus.*), 680a, 8:429b–430a
Groschen, 8:426b, 430a
Gross (British unit of measure), 12:592b
Gross, Konrad, 9:202a
Grosse Heidelberger Liederhandschrift, 12:654b
Grosse Lucidarius, 4:578b
Grosses Briefbuch. See Suso, Heinrich
Grosseteste, Robert, 1:612a, 4:170b, **6:1a–3a**
- Aristotelian science and cosmology, 9:595a
- on Aristotle, 1:461a, 461b
- on beguines, 2:159b
- *Chasteau d'amour,* 1:263b, 6:1a
- *Concordance of Sacred Scripture and the Fathers,* collaboration with Adam Marsh, 8:153a
- *De iride,* 7:538b–539a
- *De sphera,* 6:1b
- on estate management, 4:513b
- excommunicated, 4:537b
- as exegete, 2:214a, 4:544a
- on heresy, 6:203b
- *Hexaëmeron,* 6:1a-b
  - collaboration with Adam Marsh, 8:153a
- influence of on Roger Bacon, 2:39a, 40a, 41a
- Innocent IV and, 6:467a
- *Mariage des neuf filles du diable,* 1:263b
- on papal reform, 6:2a-b
- philosophy of light, 6:2a, 9:247b–248a
  - influences on, 9:247b–248a
- *Rules* for household management, 12:533a
- scriptural commentary, 9:595b
- on Seven Deadly Sins, 11:211b
- students of, 8:152b–153a
- support for Hebrew studies, 3:314a
- Trinitarian doctrine and, 12:196b
- vision theory, rainbows, 9:253a
- writings
  - instructive, 6:1a-b
  - scientific, 6:1b–2a
  - translations from Greek, 6:2a
- Wyclif and, 12:709b
- *see also* Lenses

Grosso (coin), 5:679b–680a, 8:429b
Grotesque, **6:3a,** 6:3a (*illus.*)
Grottasǫngr, **6:3a–4a**
- different traditions exhibited, 6:3b
- etiological tale in, 6:3b
- literary comparisons, 6:3b–4a
- preservation in Codex Regius, 4:387b

Groundolf, Agnes, 5:642b
Grove of Victory, Synod of the, on penance, 9:488b
Gruffudd ab yr Ynad Coch, **6:4a-b**, 12:606a
  elegy to Llywelyn ap Gruffudd, 12:606a
Gruffudd ap Cynan, 2:71b, **6:4b–5a**, 10:378a
  reconquest of Gwynedd, 6:4b, 12:517b
  see also Meilyr Brydydd
Gruffydd ap Gwenwynwyn, prince of Powys, plot against Llywelyn ap Gruffydd, 7:637b
Gruffydd ap Llywelyn, Welsh ruler, 12:516a-b
Grugur of Nin, bishop, at Council of Split, 4:4b–5a
Grüner, Vincent, of Zwickau, *Ars rethorica,* 4:175b–176a
Grünewald, Matthias, Isenheim Altarpiece, 5:604a
Grunwald (Tannenberg), Battle of (1410), 2:67a, 7:607b, 9:726b
Gruuthuse MS, 4:320b
Guadalajara, Treaty of (1207), 9:70b
Guaiferius of Monte Cassino, 7:363b
Guaire, king of Connaught (mythical), 6:547b
Gual, Domingo, 4:559a
Gualberti, Giovanni. *See* John Gualberti, St.
Gualterius Arsenius, manufacture of scientific instruments at Louvain and, 11:103a
Gualterus Anglicus. *See* Walter of England
Gualterus Wiburnus, 6:382b
Guaram of Iberia, king, 4:231b, 5:405b
Guaramids, extinction of, 2:48b, 5:405b
Guardianship, of minors, 6:458b
Guariento di Arpo, **6:5a**
  influence of on Nicoletto Semitecolo, 11:159a
Guarimpotus. *See* Gariopontus
Guarino da Verona, commentary on Cicero, 10:356a
Guarnerius. *See* Irnerius
Guas, Juan, **6:5a-b**
  decorated gallery by, 6:5b (*illus.*)
  Moorish influence, 6:5b
Guas, Pedro, **6:5a-b**
Güdemann, Moritz, 7:176b
Gudrun. *See Guðrúnarkviða*
Guelphs and Ghibellines, **6:6a–7b**
  duration of conflict, 6:6a, 6b
  in Florence, 2:287b, 4:95b, 96a, 97b, 5:94b–97a, 12:231a
    Guelphs vs. guilds, 5:98b–99b
  in Genoa, 5:385a-b
  Ghibellines
    attacks on Papal States, 7:7b–8a
    defeat at Colle Val d'Elsa (1269), 4:96a
    Siena, 11:278b, 279a, 279b
    support of Milanese archbishops for, 8:379a
    theory of papal authority, 4:376b
    victory at Montaperti (1260), 4:95b
    victory at Montecatini (1315), 4:103b–104a
  Guelphs, 11:527b
    Berthold von Holle and, 2:199a, 199b
    Charles of Anjou and, 11:272b
    Henry IV and, 11:527b
    Latini and, 7:382b
    literary influence of, 8:349b
    in Milan, 8:379a
    in Pistoia, 3:397a, 4:97b
    Robert of Anjou's alliance with, 7:8a
    vs. Manfred, 11:272a
  imperial coronation in 1198 and, 12:538a
  influence on communal government, 6:6a-b
  lack of ideology, 6:7b
  Lambertazzi faction, Guinizzelli family, 6:24b
  Parzival and, 12:678a
  in Pera-Galata, 9:503a
  in Pisa, 9:664b
  Roman preference of Guelphism, 6:7a
  serventesi and, 6:658a
  Vincent Ferrer and, 12:453a
Guenevere
  in Chrétien's *Lancelot,* 3:310a-b
  in Thomas Malory's *Morte Darthur,* 8:62b, 63a, 63b, 64a, 64b
Guernes de Pont-Ste.-Maxence, 4:168a, **6:7b**
  hunting and, 6:357a
  Vie de saint Thomas, 1:261b, 2:236a, 6:7b
    form of, 5:239b–240a
  see also Vie de St. Thomas Becket
Guerrin Meschino. *See* Andrea da Barberino
Guesclin, Bertrand du
  campaigns of, 3:151b, 6:332a
    in Spain, 3:270a
  Charles V of France and, 3:269b, 270a
  guerrilla warfare tactics, 3:206a
  model of chivalry, 3:303a
Gugark^{c}, 1:472b, 473b
Guglielmites, Joachim of Fiore and, 7:114a
Guglielmo. *See also* William
Guglielmo Beroardi, Iacopo da Lentini and, 6:387b
Guglielmo, Fra, **6:8a**
Guglielmo da Pesaro, *De pratica seu arte tripudii vulgare opusculum,* 4:87b (*illus.*), 89a
Guglielmo (Tuscan sculptor, *fl. ca.* 1159–1162), 10:502b
Guglielmo da Verona, **6:8a**
  pediments of S. Zeno, Verona, 6:8a
Guglielmus de Francia, Landini and, 7:326b
Guḥadset, 3:25a
Gui, Bernard, 4:247b, 6:487b
  Conduct of the Inquisition, 6:487a
  divination and spell-casting, 8:30b–31a
  on women's orders, 12:688a
Gui de Cambrai, *Barlaam and Josaphat,* adaptation of, 9:633b
Gui de Warewic, 1:267b, **6:8a-b**
  modern edition of, 1:271b
Guiamar, 11:491b
Guiard de Jouy, 2:144a
Guiart des Moulins. *See* Guyart des Moulins
Guibert of Nogent, **6:8b–10a**, 10:76a
  childhood, 6:8b
  Gesta Dei per Francos, 6:9a-b
  influences on writing, 6:9a
  on Jews, 7:76a, 92b
  Liber quo ordine sermo fieri debeat, 2:224a, 6:9a
    four senses of interpretation and, 10:362a
  Memoirs, 6:8b
  minor works, 6:9b–10a
  monastic life, 6:8b–9a
  Moralia, 6:9a
  On the Relics of the Saints, 10:298a
  "On Virginity," 6:9a
  religious works, 6:9a-b
  on touching for king's evil, 7:255b
Guibert of Ravenna. *See* Clement III, antipope
Guibert of Tournai, 10:77b–78a
Guicciardini, Ludovico, on literacy in Netherlands, 7:600b
Guichard de Beaulieu
  Romaunz de temtacioun de secle, 1:262b
  on St. Alban, 1:261b
Guide of the Perplexed. *See* Maimonides, Moses, *Moreh Nevukhim*
Guide to the Duties of the Heart, The. *See* Baḥya ben Joseph ibn Paquda
Guidebooks
  Mirabilia urbis Romae, 9:658b
  pilgrimage, 9:651b–652a, 657b (*illus.*), 660a, 661b–662a (*illus.*), 12:156a-b
  see also Geography; Pocketbooks
Guido I, prior of Chartreuse, 3:118b–119a
Guido II, prior of Chartreuse, 3:119a
Guido of Amiens, **6:12a**
Guido of Arezzo, 2:98b, 3:438a, **6:12a–13a**, 8:641a-b
  Aliae regulae, 6:12b, 8:641a
    lines for alternate pitches, 11:466a
  alphabetic notation and, 8:614b–615a
  Bartolomeo de Pareja and, 8:648b
  Cistercians and, 8:643a
  Epistola Michaeli monacho de ignoto cantu, 8:641a
    discussion of syllables, 6:12b–13a
  Hucbald of St. Amand and, 8:639a
  Liège school and, 8:642a
  Micrologus, 3:542a, 6:12b, 8:586b (*illus.*), 641a, 642a, 642b, 10:379b–380a, 12:648a
    use of organ, 9:274b
  Regulae rhythmicae, 6:12b, 8:579a, 641a
  solmization and, 11:362b–364a
  staff and, 8:593b
  system of notation, 6:12b
  William of Hirsau and, 8:642a
Guido Augensis. *See* Guy d'Eu
Guido de Baysio, *Rosarium,* 7:386a

Guido de Cariloco. *See* Guy de Cherlieu
Guido Cavalcanti. *See* Cavalcanti, Guido
Guido da Como, **6:10a-b**
pulpit of S. Bartolommeo in Pantano, Pistoia, 6:10b (*illus.*)
Guido delle Colonne, 6:641b, 11:258b
"Ancor che l'aigua per lo foco lassi," 11:258b
Historia destructionis Troiae, 3:166b, 8:225b, 12:221a
Boccaccio's *Filostrato* and, 2:279a
derivative Spanish romances and, 11:416b, 457b, 458a
Middle English versification of, 8:320b
Roman de Troie and, 2:182a
translated by Lydgate, 7:691a, 691b, 693a, 694a, 694b
translated into Catalan, 9:510b
history of the Trojan War, 7:369a
Iacopo da Lentini and, 6:387b
translated by Lydgate, 8:323a
Guido Faba, 8:644a-b
ars dictaminis and, 10:358b, 359a
Guido of Monte Roteiro, *Manipulus curatorum,* 11:407a
Guido Novello da Polenta, 6:651b
Dante and, 4:104a
Guido of Orchelles, on sacrament of Order, 9:602a
Guido di Piero. *See* Giovanni da Fiesole
Guido da Siena, **6:10b–11a**
Madonna and Child panel (Siena Pinacoteca), 6:10b–11a (*illus.*)
Virgin and Child and Four Saints, 6:11a
Guido of Velate, archbishop of Milan, tenure of, 8:378a-b
Guido da Vigevano (da Papia), **6:11b–12a**
Liber notabilium a libris Galieni extractis of (1345), 6:11b
Texaurus regis Francie acquisicionis terre sancte de ultra mare, 6:11b
siege engines, 11:644b–645a
on windmill uses, 8:395a
Guidonian hand, 11:364 (*illus.*)
Guidoriccio da Fogliani of Reggio, equestrian portrait of, 11:280b, 299b
Guifred II of Catalonia, count, 3:175a
Guifred the Hairy, count of the Spanish march, 3:174b–175a
Guige, 1:523a
Guigemar. See Marie de France
Guigo II of Grande Chartreuse, work in English, 9:27a
Guigues, *see also* Albon, counts of
Guigues IV of Dauphiné, count, "dauphin" and, 4:109a
Guigues VI of Burgundy, Dauphiné and, 4:109a
Guigues (the Old) of Albon, Brouchard and, 4:109a
Guild of St. Luke, 5:605a
Guild of St. Luke (Bruges), 8:104b
Guilds
Islamic. *See* Şinf
poetic. *See Confrérie; Puy*
Guilds and métiers, **6:13a–20a**
4th to 11th centuries, 6:14a–15a
11th to 14th centuries, 6:15a–17b
14th and 15th centuries, 6:17b–19a
Anglo-Saxon, 6:14b
apprenticeship system, 6:16b
journeyman training, 6:16b–17a
limitations on membership, 6:18a
see also Artists, guilds of
artisans, masons and builders, 8:175b–178b
artists, **6:21a–22a**
Guild of St. Luke, 5:605a
in Barcelona, 2:103b–104a
of book producers, 8:104b
in Bruges, 2:386b
Byzantine, **6:20a-b**
bakers, 2:478a
Book of the Eparch and, 4:494a-b
entry and initiation, 6:20b
hereditary nature of occupations, 2:475b–476a
inheritance and, 6:451a
regulation of, 2:477b–478a
role in government, 6:20a-b
similarities with Roman *collegia,* 6:15a
structure and laws, 6:20a
violence of, 2:478a-b
cofferers, 5:325a
in Cologne, 3:481a, 482a, 5:468b
in communes, 3:500b–501b
conflict between merchant and craft, 6:17b
confréries in, 3:536b
contributions of, 6:19a-b
control of *échevinages,* 4:379b
as corporations, 3:607a-b
cost effectiveness, 11:654a
craft, 6:13a (*illus.*), 15b–16a
enrollment of artists in, 6:21a
organization of, 6:16b
dyers, 4:328b–329a
England
conflicts with the crown, 7:663b
Corpus Christi plays and, 4:284b
journeymen, 7:664b
leadership of boroughs, 4:465a-b
in London neighborhoods, 7:665a
organization by burgesses, 4:465a
role in government, 2:330b
fairs at Constantinople and, 12:101b, 102a
food trade
brewers, 5:126a
butchers, 5:123a
consumer protection, 5:122a
fishmongers, 5:124b
lack of political power, 5:120a-b
regulation of, 5:120a
vintners, 5:125a
in German towns, 6:14b, 16b
in Nuremberg, 5:468b, 9:202a
social conflict, 5:468b–469b
in Ghent, 5:522a–523a
goldsmiths, in the early Middle Ages, 8:287b
growth of, 6:15b
guild masters of the schools, 6:16b
history, problems in reconstructing, 6:13b–14a
innkeepers, 6:470b, 473a, 473b–474b
internal rules and structure, 6:15b–16a, 17a
Italian, 6:14b–15a, 15b–16a
in Florence, 5:94b–96a
Lombard *ministeria,* 6:15a
12th century, 7:16b
law codes of, 7:429a
manufacture of scientific instruments and, 11:102b–103b
of medical practitioners, 8:257b–258a
merchant, 6:13a, 16a, 12:117b
and decline of long-distance trade, 6:18a-b
Northern European, 6:16a-b
painters, 5:605a
parades and processions, 4:284a
perfumers, 2:147a
Poland, ethnic tensions and, 9:728b–729a
production of agricultural tools and, 12:81b–82a
regional variations, 6:19a
regulations
of competition, 6:15b–16a, 19a-b, 21b
job hierarchy in Arras, 5:122a
of prices, 12:119a
quality control, 12:119a-b
of trade, 12:116b
wage control, 6:18a
religious and social activities, 6:17a
restriction of membership, 6:17b–18a
restrictive policies, effect on urban poor, 5:180b
role in government, 6:17a, 18b, 19a
in Rome, 6:14a-b, 10:525b
schola, 6:15a
ship carpenters, 11:244a
shoemakers, 11:255a
şinf and, 11:307b
of Spanish shepherds, cowboys, and livestock owners, 8:279b–281a
tapestry and, 11:595a, 595b–596a, 596b
technological development, 6:19b
textile workers, 11:713a–714a
Cologne, 11:715a
Flanders, 11:713a–714a
Florence, 11:714a–715a
rebellion of, 11:713a–715a
theatrical performances by, 8:657b, 659a-b, 661a-b
in England, 12:727b, 728a
in France, 4:264a-b, 265b–266a
in Germany, 4:271b
Towneley Plays and, 12:94a
in Valencia, 12:348b
in Venice, 12:390a-b
wheelwrights, 12:374a
wool guild in Naples, 9:59a
worker discontent, 6:18b–19a
written records
notarial, 6:15b
statutes, 6:14a, 21a
Guilhem de Peitieus, 3:509b
Guilhem de Tudela, **6:22a-b**
Guillaume d'Angleterre, attributed to Chrétien de Troyes, 1:267b
Guillaume de Berneville, *Vie de St. Giles,* 12:413b

Guillaume (biographer of Suger of St. Denis), 11:502b, 504a
Guillaume of Bourges, archbishop, conductus for, 3:532b
Guillaume le Breton, **6:23b–24b**
Gesta Philippi Augusti, 2:236b, 240a, 6:24a
Karlotide, 6:24a
Philip II Augustus and, 11:211a
Philippide, 6:24a
Guillaume le Clerc de Normandie
Besant de Dieu, 1:264a
Bestiaire divin, 1:188b, 2:205b
Guillaume de Deguileville. *See* Deguileville, Guillaume de
Guillaume de Dôle, **6:22b**
protorondeaux, 10:529a
see also Renart, Jean
Guillaume d'Ostrevant, 6:358a
Guillaume Du Fay. *See* Dufay, Guillaume
Guillaume Fillastre. *See* Fillastre, Guillaume
Guillaume de Jumièges, *Historia Normannorum ducum,* 5:654a
Guillaume de Lorris, 1:184a-b, 189a, **6:23a-b,** 7:53a
Chaucer and, 3:281b
Minnereden and, 8:410a
vocabulary of, 4:574b
see also Roman de la Rose
Guillaume de Machaut. *See* Machaut, Guillaume de
Guillaume le Maréchal. *See* William Marshal
Guillaume de Nangis
Chronicon, 5:654a
translations of Latin lives, 5:654a
Guillaume de Nogaret. *See* Nogaret, Guillaume de
Guillaume d'Orange, *Bataille d'Aliscans* and, 12:678b
Guillaume de Rennes, *Gesta regum Britanniae,* 5:389a
Guillaume Tardif, *Isopet,* 4:572b
Guillebert of Metz, on Paris taverns, 12:651b
Guillelmine Fanjeux, Dominican prioress, 12:687b
Guillelmus Brito, *Expositiones difficiliorum verborum de Biblia,* 7:599a
Guillelmus falconarius, 6:359b
Guillelmus Monachus (15th century), *De perceptis artis musicae,* 8:648a
Guillem de Berguedà, 3:164b
Guillem de Cabestaing (Cabestany), 3:164b, 12:410a
Guillem de Torroella, *Faula,* 1:576a
Guillemain, Bernard, depiction of Avignon papacy, 3:362b
Guillems of Montpellier, 7:339a
Guillem VII, 10:256a
Guillén de Segovia, Pero, *Gaya ciencia,* 11:424b, 441b
Guilloche, 6:497b
Guinea, exploration of, 4:561b
Guinea fowl, domestication of, 5:151a
Guinefort, St., cult of, 3:360a
Guinevere. *See* Guenevere
Guingamor, 7:317a
Guinglain ou le bel inconnu. See Renaut de Beaujeu, *Li Biaus descouneus*
Guinizzelli, Guido, **6:24b–26a,** 6:646a–647a, 649b
"Al cor gentil rempaira sempre amore"
Dante's reference to, 6:24b
theme of love in, 6:25b
uniqueness of, 6:25a-b
evaluated by Marqués de Santillana, 11:446a
literary works, preservation, 6:24b
Guiot de Provins, 3:506a, **6:26a**
Bible, 6:26a
description of a compass, 11:100b–101a
on greedy physicians, 8:257a
Wolfram von Eschenbach and, 12:677b
Guiraut Riquier, **6:26a-b**
song to the Virgin, 10:182a
Guirlanda esmaltada de galanes. See Fernández de Constantin, Juan
Guisarme, 7:324a, 325a
Guiscard. *See* first name
Guiscard und Sigismunda. See Albrecht von Eyb
Guischart de Beaulieu, **6:26b**
Romanz de temtacioun de secle, 6:26b
Guistizieri Vecchi (Venetian guild), 12:390b
Guitar, 8:602a, 607b–608a
"balloon." *See Pipa*
Guitarra latina, 8:607b, 608a
Guitarra morisca, 8:607b
Guitmund of Aversa, Berengar and, 2:188a
Guittone d'Arezzo, 6:644a–645a
"Ahi lasso, or è stagion di doler tanto," 6:644b
Iacopo da Lentini and, 6:387b
influence on Guido Guinizzelli, 6:25a
in *Purgatory,* 6:645b
in *Trionfo d'Amore,* 6:640b
"Tuttor, s'eo veglio o dormo," 6:667b
Gujarat
Ismailism in, 6:617a
maritime trade of, 11:247a
Gül, 10:549b–550a, 551a
Gül Camii (church: Constantinople), cross-domed design of, 4:344b
Guldin spil, Das. See Ingold, Master
Gulistān. See Sa^{c}di of Shiraz
Gull-Ásu-Þórðar þáttr, 12:3b, 4a
Gull-þóris saga, **6:27a–28a**
see also Beowulf
Gumpold, **6:28a**
Gûmûshtegin, Ghāzī, king, vs. crusaders, 4:36b, 91b
Gunabad, mosque, 6:603a
Gunbad-i ^{c}Alī, architectural elements, *muqarnas,* 8:534b, 535a (*illus.*)
Gunbad-i Surkh, 11:147a
Gunbadh (*kümbet*), **6:28a–29a**
association with earlier traditions, 6:28b
forms of, 6:28a-b
Gunbadh-i Qābūs. *See* Qābūs ibn Vashmgīr
Gunbrī, 8:611a
Gundacker von Judenburg, *Christi Hort,* 2:230a
Gundekar II, bishop of Eichstätt, building of the Old Mill Bridge and, 10:413a
Gundēshāpūr, **6:29a**
hospital at, 6:290b–291a
medical education in, 11:564b
Xusrō I and, 12:714a
Gundisalvo, Domingo. *See* Domingo Gundisalvo
Gundisapur. *See* Gundēshāpūr
Gundissalinus, Dominicus. *See* Domingo Gundisalvo
Gundobad, Burgundian king, 2:92b
Gundolfo, heretical following, 6:194b
Gundstapl. *See* Smbat Sparapet
Gundulf of Rochester, bishop, **6:29a-b**
Tower of London construction, 6:29a
Gundulić, Djivo, 4:300b
Gunnarr, 11:293a
Gunnars þáttr Þiðrandabana, 12:2b, 4a
Gunnlaugr Leifsson, 5:388a, 678b
attribution of *þættir* to, 12:4a-b
biography of Óláfr Tryggvason, 9:176b, 225b
Breta sǫgur, 2:365b–366a
Gunnlaugs saga Ormstungu, 4:612b, **6:29b–30a**
compared with *Bjarnar saga Hítdœlakappa,* 2:255b
romantic theme, 6:30a
Gunnlǫð, 11:30a
Guns and gunpowder, 3:151b
antipersonnel weapons, 12:566b
arquebus, 12:566b–567a
Bosnia, 2:341b
bronze, 12:567a
Byzantine army, 12:549b
Eurasia, 11:660b
first picture of, 12:566b
first use of, 3:151b
handguns, 12:566b
introduction of, Lübeck, 7:684b
invention, 12:566b
in Islamic warfare, 12:553a
origins, 11:660a
recipes, 11:638b, 645b–646a
on ships, 9:83b–84a
weapons, 11:638a (*illus.*)
see also Arms and armor
Guntharic, king of Vandals, 12:354b
Gunther of Bamberg, bishop, *Ezzolied* and, 4:571b
Günther, Ursula, *ars subtilior* and, 1:550a, 558a-b
Gunzo de Baume, 3:468a-b
Gunzo of Novara, deacon, **6:30a-b**
Guote Gêrhard, Der. See Rudolf von Ems
Gūr-i Mīr, 6:605 (*illus.*)
Gurganī, *Visramiani,* 5:418a, 11:256b
Gūrgānīya (Islamic designation of Timurids), 12:58b
Gurgānj, 6:504a
Mongol siege of (1221), 8:467a
Gurgēn Anjewac^{c}i, prince, 1:520a
Gurgen, Georgian king, Išḫani and, 6:562b

Gurgēn (Kiwrikē) I of Lōṙi, king, 1:483a
coinage of, 7:672b, 8:418a
Lōṙi-Tašir and, 1:484b
rule of, 7:672b
Gurgeni I of Iberia, king, 4:113b
Gurians, islamized, 5:403b
Gurkhan, 8:466a
Gurun, 11:492a
Gusan, 8:553a
Gushtasp, 6:408a
Gushtásp and Katayoun. See Firdawsī
Gusmin, 5:524b
Gušnap of Ṭabaristān, king. *See Letter of Tansar*
Güssing family. *See* Köszegi family
Gustavus I (Gustav Vasa) of Sweden, king, 4:156b
accession of, 11:533b–534a
Gutalagen, 7:525a-b
Gute Frau, Die, **6:30b–31a**
love romance theme, 6:30b
Gutenberg, Johannes, **6:31a–33b**
Bible, 6:31b (*illus.*)
forty-two line, 6:32a, 32b
thirty-six line, 6:33a
lawsuits involved in, 6:31a–32a, 32b–33a
movable-type printing, 11:661b
partnerships
Berthold Ruppel and Heinrich Kefer, 6:33a
Johann Fust, 6:32a
Peter Schoeffer, 6:33a
Strasbourg, 6:31b–32a
printing press of, 10:124a
production of *Spiegel,* 6:31a-b
small works produced, 6:32a
Guthfrith I, Viking king of York, 12:433a
Guthlac, St., **6:33b**
vita of, 1:279a
Guthred. *See* Guthfrith
Guthrum of East Anglia, king, 12:432b, 433b
Danelaw treaty and, 1:164a, 4:91a
Guðbrandur Þorláksson, bishop of Hólar, *Eín ny Psalma Bók,* criticism of *rímur,* 10:406b
Guðmundar saga biskups, **6:33b–34b**
older versions, 6:34a
see also Bishops' sagas
Guðmundar saga dýra, in *Sturlunga saga,* 11:499a
Guðmundr Arason (*inn góði*), bishop of Hólar, **6:34b–35a**, 6:394a-b, 395b, 7:146b
biographies of, 6:33b–34a, 34b, 11:498b–499a
conflicts with secular chieftains, 6:34b
consecration, 6:34a
feast day, 6:35a
Guðmundur, *Þjófa rímur,* 10:402b
Guðrún, 1:638b
Guðrúnarbrǫgð, Norna-Gests Þáttr and, 9:171a
Guðrúnarhvǫt, **6:35a–36a**
association with other works, 6:35b
murder of Sigurd, 6:35a-b
relation to *Hamðismál,* 6:88a
Guðrúnarkviða I, **6:36a–37a**, 9:114a, 11:293b
basis in oral tradition, 6:36b
dating, 6:36b
Gudrun's lament, 6:36a
order in Codex Regius, 4:386a-b
relation to German heroic poetry, 6:37b
Guðrúnarkviða II, **6:37a–38b**, 9:114a
dating and ethnic origin, 6:37b
order in Codex Regius, 4:386a-b
setting for, 6:37b
themes, persistence of memory, 6:37b
Vǫlsunga saga and, 12:489a
Guðrúnarkviða III, **6:38a-b**, 9:114a
order in Codex Regius, 4:386a-b
other versions, 6:38a-b
plot summary, 6:38a
relation to other poems in cycle, 6:38b
Guðrúnarrœ. See Guðrúnarkviða II
Guy II of Athens, duke, 7:379a-b
Guy de Bazoches, 7:366b
Guy of Brionne (Burgundy), attempt to replace William I, 9:162b, 12:633b
Guy of Châtillon, as benefactor of Froissart, 5:302b
Guy de Chauliac, 9:679a
on Black Death, 2:264a
Chirurgia magna (*Grande Chirurgie*), 8:462b, 11:692a
lecturing at Montpellier, 8:257 (*illus.*)
on leprosy, 7:550a, 551a
Guy de Cherlieu, *Praefatio,* 8:642b–643a
Guy of Dammartin, 4:295a-b, **6:39a**
chimney in palace at Poitiers, 6:38b (*illus.*)
Guy of Dampierre, count of Flanders, 5:81b
abolishment of *Leliaerts,* 11:713b
Adenet le Roi and, 1:55a
restoration of wool trade, 11:713b
support for Ghent craft guilds, 5:522a-b
vs. Philip IV, 2:387a-b
Guy d'Eu, *Regule de arte musica,* 8:643a
Guy of Lusignan, king of Cilicia (*d.* 1344), 3:393a, **6:39a-b**
assassinated, 3:395a
pro-Latin policy, 6:39a
Guy of Lusignan, king of Jerusalem (*d.* 1194)
at Battle of Acre, 10:626a
battle against Saladin at Ḥiṭṭīn, 6:265b–266b, 10:625b–626a
Cyprus and, 4:70b, 71b, 7:689a
Guy d'Orchelles, Gilbert of Poitiers's theology school and, 12:21b
Guy (papal legate), 3:187b
Guy de la Roche
as duke of Athens, 7:378a
regency of, 7:379a
Guy de Thourotte, *Châtelain de Coucy* and, 3:277b–278a
Guy of Vaux-de-Cernay, abbot, in Fourth Crusade, 11:296b
Guy of Vienne, archbishop. *See* Calixtus II, pope
Guy of Warwick. *See Gui de Warewic*
Guy of Warwick (English romance, *ca.* 1300), 8:316a
Guyart des Moulins, 4:547b
Bible historiale, 2:219a-b
Moralized Bible, produced in secular ateliers, 8:104a
Guyenne
English rule of, representative assemblies and, 10:322a-b
provincial estates and assemblies, 10:321a
King Louis XI and, 10:322b
recettes and, 10:325b
Güyük, khan, 7:138b, 8:471a
Guzmán, Leonor de, Alfonso XI and, 11:418a
Gvímars saga, Strengleikar and, 11:491b
Gwalchmai ap Meilyr, **6:39b–40b**, 8:265a
Gorhoffedd, poetic genre, 6:40a
"Gwalchmai's Dream," 6:40a
Hywel and, 6:387a
odes to Owain Gwynedd, 6:39b–40a, 12:604b
relation to Einon ap Gwalchmai, 4:413a
Gwallawg of Elfed, British king, poetry written for, 12:597a, 602a
Gwasanaeth Meir, 12:615b
Gwawdodyn. See Welsh literature, poetic meter
Gwent, origins, 12:514a
Gwyddbwyll, 5:351b
Gwyde (unit of measure), 12:592b
Gwynedd, 6:386b
geographic location, 12:514b
literary revival, 12:518b
origins, 12:514a
Rhodri Mawr and, 10:365b–366a
rule of Owain Fawr, 12:517b–518a
rule of Rhys ap Gruffydd, 12:518a-b
see also Bangor (Wales); Maelgwn
Gylfaginning. See Snorri Sturluson
Gymel, Guillelmus Monachus on, 8:648a
Gypsies, **6:40b–41a**
derivation of English name, 6:40b–41a
language, 6:40b
laws against, 6:41a
life-style, 6:41a
migration, 6:40b–41a
Balkans, 6:41a
Greece, 6:41a
in Walachia/Moldavia, 12:506a
Gyðinga saga, **6:41b**
Gyula of Transylvania, subjugated by St. Stephen I of Hungary, 11:478b

H

H. of Saltrey. *See* Hugh of Saltrey

Ha-rav. See Rabbinate; Scholarship, Jewish
Haakon. *See* Hákon
Ḥabbs. See Barbotine
Habeas corpus, Golden Bull and, 6:341b
Habermehl, Erasmus, manufacture of scientific instruments and, 11:103a
Ḥabīb ibn Maslama, 7:215a
  capture of Dwin, 4:323b
  Transcaucasia and, 1:478b
Habitus theory, 3:323a
Habrecht, Isaac, 3:465a
Habsburg Castle, construction of, 6:42a
Habsburg dynasty, **6:41b–43a**, 6:337b
  Albertine-Leopoldine division, 6:42b
  ancestry, 6:42a
  archives of, 1:448b
  Austria and, 2:7b–9a
  beginning of, 5:487b
  Burgundy and, 10:325b
  Electoral College and, 5:487a-b
  end of male line, 6:42a
  end of, 5:489b
  expansion
    Austria and Germany, 6:42b
    eastern Alps, 6:42b
    France and Spain, 6:43a
    obstacles to, 6:42b
    Swabian, 6:42b, 11:528a
    through marriage, 6:42a, 43b
    under Rudolf, 6:42a-b
  Hungary and, 6:347b, 349a
  Lucerne and, 11:542b
  nobility and, 9:151a
  Rapperswil and, 11:544a
  representative assemblies and, 10:229b–330b
  Siena and, 11:282a
  Swiss Confederation and, 2:8b–9a, 11:543b, 544a
  Switzerland and, 11:539b–540b
  titles assumed
    archduke, 6:42b
    Holy Roman Emperor, 6:42a
    House of Austria, 6:41b
  vs. Sigismund, Bern and, 11:544a
  Waldstätte and, 11:541a–542a
  Zurich and, 11:543a
Habsburg-Laufenburg line, 11:540a
Hachures, in tapestry, 11:595b–596a
Hacivat, Qaragūz figures and, 10:229a
Ḥadaʾ iqu'l-anvār fī ḥaqāʾiqi'l-asrār. See Fakhr al-Dīn al-Rāzī
Hadamar von Laber, **6:43a–44a**
  ancestry, 6:43b
  hunting and, 6:359a
  Jagd, 5:431b, 8:410b–411b
    difficulties in interpreting, 6:43b
  Labers ton, 6:43a
Hadding (mythical Danish king), 10:677b
Haddock (*Melanogrammus aeglefinus*), fishing of, 5:72a
Hadewijch of Antwerp, 2:160b, 161a, **6:44a–45a**, 9:11b, 12a, 31b
  admired by Ruusbroec, 9:37b
  Brieven, 4:319b, 6:44a
    use of imagery, 6:44b
  definition of mysticism, 6:44a
  literary works, 6:44a
  Natureingang, use of imagery, 6:44b
  poetry
    imagery in, 6:44b
    minnesanc, 6:44a-b
  Strofische Gedichte, 4:319b, 6:44a-b
  Visioenen, 4:319b, 6:44a
    use of imagery, 6:44b
Hadhbānī Kurds, 7:310b
Hādī ila 'l-Ḥaqq Yaḥyā, al-, 12:741b
Ḥadīb, Isaac al-, on equatorium, 11:91a-b
Hadīqat al-ḥaqīqat. See Sanāʾī
Ḥadīth, **6:45a–49a**, 10:242a
  in ʿAli Qāpū palace, 6:562b
  authenticity, 6:46a
  biblical exegesis and, 2:214b–215a
  al-Bukhārī's study of, 2:397b
  chronology
    of Muslim scholars, 6:45a-b, 48a-b
    of Western scholars, 6:45b, 48a-b
  collections, 6:580b
    al-kutub al-sitta, 6:47b–48a
    arrangement of material, 6:47b
    canonized, 6:46b, 47b–48a
    8th century, 6:46b–47a
  cosmological view in, 5:391b
  definition of, 6:45a, 580a-b
  dietary laws and, 4:179a-b
  evolution of, 6:45a, 46a
    and Islamic expansion, 6:46a
  excellence of Friday and, 5:299a
  genres
    faḍāʾil/mathālib, 6:46a-b, 47a
    ḥalāl wa-ḥarām, 6:46b
    tarhīb wa-targhīb, 6:46a, 47a
  in Islamic law
    as legal "root," 6:581b
    as precedent, 6:46b
  in al-Kufa, 7:307b
  al-Mahdi and, 8:388b
  Malīk ibn Anas and, 8:58b–59a
  mirror of princes and, 8:435b
  modern, 6:48a
  as motivation for travel, 12:147a-b
  on Muḥammad's prohibition of luxuries, 11:507b–508a
  music and, 8:559b–560a
  offshoot disciplines, 6:48a
  on resurrection, 10:340b
  science of authentication, 6:47b, 89a
  Shiism and, 6:587a
  on slavery, 11:330b–331a
  as a source on Islamic liturgy, 7:616a-b
  Sufism and, 6:584b
  sunna and, 11:511a
  Sunnites and, 11:513b
  al-Tabarī and, 11:569a
  ṭalab al-ʿilm, 6:47b
  transmission of
    oral, 6:45a, 46a
    quṣṣāṣ, 6:46a
    written, 6:46b, 47b
    see also Isnād
  Yazīd and, 12:721a
  see also Biography, Islamic; Sects, Islamic
Hadoardus, **6:49a**
  compilation of Cicero excerpts, 6:49a
Ḥaḍramawt, **6:49a–50a**
  boundaries, 6:49a-b
  caravan route through Najrān and, 9:54b
  government of, 6:49b
  Ibāḍī communities in, 11:139a
  production of frankincense, 6:49b
  seafaring and navigation, 6:49b
  social structure, 6:49b
Hadrian I, pope
  canon law and, 7:403b
  Collectio Dionysiana given to Charlemagne, 4:193a
Hadrian V, pope, Amerus and, 8:644b
Hadrian of Canterbury, St., 2:153b
  Canterbury school and, 3:82a
  sacramentary and, 2:180b
  Saxon church construction, 10:679b
Hadrian, Roman emperor
  Mausoleum of, 10:519a
    see also Castel Sant'Angelo
  in *Sapientia,* 6:316a
Hadrian's Wall
  building of, 3:143b
  three bridges built by Romans and, 10:410a
Haebler, Konrad, 10:127b
Haec sancta synodus. See Constance, Council of (1414–1418)
Haecceitas, 1:467a
Haegen, Willem van der, 2:29b, 4:559b
Ḥāfiẓ, al-, Fatimid caliph, 5:29a
Ḥāfiẓ (Shams al-Dīn Muḥammad), **6:51a–52b**, 11:252b
  court patronage, 6:51b–52a
  Dīwān, 6:52a
    theme of romantic love, 6:52a
  ghazals of, 6:508a
  influence on Persian literature, 6:51a-b
  patrons, 6:51b–52a
  poetry, 6:51b–52b
Haflidi, Icelandic chieftain, in *Sturlunga saga,* 11:498b, 500b
Hafsids, **6:52b–55a**
  alliance with Marinids, 6:54a
  Arab support for, 6:54b
  armed forces
    Arab tribes in, 6:53a
    contingent of Spanish refugees, 6:53a
  art and, 6:611b
  conquest by Spain, 6:55a
  divisions
    between Tunis and Bejaïa, 6:53b
    under Ibn Tafrāgīn, 6:54a
  foreign trade
    with Christian merchants, 6:53a-b
    with Spain and Italy, 6:53a-b
    tribute to Aragon, 6:54a
  government
    ḥājib, 6:54a
    maḥalla, 6:55a
    nepotism, 6:54a
    qadi, 6:54b
    qāʾid, 6:55a
    religious rulers, 6:54b
    sheikhs, 6:53a
    tribal, 6:53a, 54b
  Ibn Khaldūn and, 7:232b
  in Ifrīqiya, 6:415a
  military conflicts
    with France, 6:53b
    with Spain, 6:53a

Hafsids (*cont.*)
problems of succession, 6:53b
raids in Malta, 8:67b
reunification of dynasty under Abū Bakr, 6:53b–54a
see also Abū Zakariyā⊃
Haft paykar. See Niẓāmī
Hagen (epic character)
in *Kudrun,* 7:304a, 305a
in *Nibelungenlied,* 9:112b–113a, 113b, 114b, 115a
in *Waltharius,* 7:363a, 12:535a, 536a
see also Hǫgni
Hagenauer, Nikolaus, 5:604a, **6:55b**
Isenheim Altarpiece, sculpted statues, 6:55b (*illus.*)
Syfer and, 11:552a
Hagia Sofia (church: Bizye), domed-cross design, 3:340a
Hagia Sophia (cathedral: Kiev), **6:57a,** 6:418b
architectural elements, Byzantine influence, 10:579a, 591b
mosaics and frescoes, 10:583b (*illus.*)
Byzantine influence, 10:583a
Greek associations, 10:583a
music of, 8:573a
west corner of south tribune, 6:57a (*illus.*)
Yaroslav and, 12:720a
Hagia Sophia (cathedral: Novgorod), 8:573a
bronze gates, 10:586b
Hagia Sophia (church: Constantinople), 4:340 (*illus.*), **6:55b–56b,** 7:202a
architecture of, 5:596b
Cappadocian architecture and, 3:92a
ceiling mosaics, 4:359a
ceremonies celebrated at, 4:430a-b
construction difficulties, 6:56b
cross-section drawing, 4:338 (*illus.*)
decoration of, 4:339b
design of, 4:339a-b, 6:56a
detail of capital from, 4:344b (*illus.*)
dome reconstruction, by Trdat, 12:164b–165a
domes of, 4:236a
furnishings for, 4:361a
importance of, 3:555b, 6:56a
interior of, 4:342 (illus.)
Isidoros of Miletos and, 6:566b
liturgy development and, 7:610a, 611a
Michael Keroularios and, 8:304b
mosaics, 2:440a, 6:56b, 10:89b
Deesis, 2:447b–448a, 448 (*illus.*)
figure style, 2:440a
figures, layout of, 2:439b
floor, 8:493b
of Leo VI, 10:152 (*illus.*)
narthex panel, 2:440a
panel, south gallery, 2:443a
theme of, 2:440a
Virgin and Child, 2:439b (*illus.*)
mosaics, wall
Christ enthroned, south gallery, 8:493 (*illus.*)
John II Komnenos panel, south gallery, 8:494a (*illus.*)
music in, 8:554b
patriarch of, 2:461a–462a
pendentives in, 9:493b, 494 (*illus.*)
restoration under Basil II, 2:442a
silver chancel barrier in, 11:118b
structure of, 2:461a
Trdat of Ani and, 1:483a, 494a
Typikon of, 7:589a-b
Hagia Sophia (church: Edessa), dome of heaven in, 4:237a
Hagia Sophia (church: Ochrid), 9:209a
Hagia Sophia (church: Thessaloniki)
Cappadocian architecture and, 3:92a
domed-cross design, 4:340a
Hagii Anargyri (church: Kastoria), 7:224b (*illus.*)
Hagiography, Anglo-Norman, 6:63b
Hagiography, Armenian
Grigor II Vkayasēr, 5:676a
see also Armenian church, saints
Hagiography, Byzantine, 2:505b, **6:57b–59a**
aretalogy, 2:518a
collections, 2:518b
commemoration of monastery founders, 6:58b
encomiums, 6:58a-b
hagiographical calendar, 6:58b
hermits and monks, 2:518b
importance of, 2:519a-b
Lausiac History of Palladios, 9:357a
literary purposes, 2:519a
liturgical use, 2:518b
low- vs. high-level, 2:518b
miracles, 6:57b–58a
Christian healing cults, 6:57b
posthumous, 2:518a-b
monastic compilations of ascetic tales, 6:58a
origin of, 2:518a
passions, 6:57b
popular beliefs and, 8:20a
preservation of history and folklore in, 6:57b
saints' lives, 6:58a-b
during iconoclastic period, 6:58b
Palestinian and Syrian monks, 6:58a
posthumous cults, 6:58b
stylites, lives of, 2:518b
Symeon Metaphrastes and, 11:554a
see also Menologion; Synaxary
Hagiography, English. *See* Hagiography, Middle English
Hagiography, French, **6:59a–60b**
definition, 6:59a
encouragement of by church, 6:59a-b
influence on French literature, 6:60a-b
légendiers
organization of, 6:60a
prose, 6:59b–60a
prose, 6:59b–60a
lives of contemporary saints, 6:60a
recasting of, 6:59b–60a
see also Eulalie, La Séquence de Ste.
verse
collections of, 6:59b
common form, 6:59b
see also Picard literature, hagiography
Hagiography, Georgian, 5:412b–413b, 416b, **6:60b–61b**
collections, 6:61a
hymnographical manuscripts, 6:61a-b
metaphrastic lives vs. *kimeni,* 6:61a
monthly codices, 6:61a
sources of, 6:60b
mravalt^c*avi,* 6:61a
Hagiography, Irish, 6:542b–543a
homily and, 6:541b
lives of St. Patrick, 9:462b–463a
mythology and, 6:530b
Hagiography, Islamic, 9:40a
Shiite, 6:371a
Hagiography, Middle English, 3:82b, 4:546a-b, **6:61b–64b**
Barlaam and Josaphat, 6:62b
lives in Middle English, 6:62b–63b
South English Legendary, 6:61b–62a
women saints, 6:63a
see also South English Legendary
Hagiography, Scandinavian, 11:14b–15b, 16a
Hagiography, Western European, **6:64b–71a**
Alcuin of York's lives, 1:143b
Byzantine sources for, 8:19a
canonization procedures, 6:68a–69a
deposition of relics, 6:68b
first formal, 6:68b
Carolingian lives, fiction in writing, 6:67b–68a
collections of saints' lives, 6:69a-b
concept of saint as patron and, 10:297b–298a
cult of the saints, 6:64b–65b, 68a-b
confessores, 6:65b
desert ascetics, 6:66a, 70a
early saints' lives, 6:66a–67a
borrowing from previous authors, 6:66b
passions, 6:66a
English lives in Latin, 6:63b–64b
Gregory of Tours, 5:667b
Hiberno-Saxon lives, 6:67a-b
Hrotswitha von Gandersheim and, 6:314a, 314b
Hucbald and, 6:317a
in Iceland, 11:497b, 498b–499a
Julian calendar and, 2:155a
lauda and, 6:662a, 662b
martyrologies and legendaries, 6:65b–66a
sources, 6:65b–66a
Merovingian period, 6:66b–67a
new orders, 6:69a
in Norman England, 1:261a-b
origin of, 6:65a-b
as propaganda, 10:137a
purpose of, 6:65a
relic authentication and, 10:298a
rhymed offices and, 10:366b–377a
scientific, 6:70b–71a
in Spain, 11:413b, 438b–440a
translation of saints and, 12:144a–145b
12th century, 6:263b
vitae sororum, 9:13b
women saints, 2:376b–377a, 6:69b–70b
Irish, 6:70a
lives of desert mothers, 6:70a
writing of in monastic schools, 11:76b

see also Biography, French; French literature, saints' lives; Saints, cult of; Scandinavian literature, religious; *Vitae patrum*
Hagioi Sergios and Bakchos (church: Constantinople)
design of, 4:338b
dome of, 4:236a
ground plan and isometric drawing, 4:334 (*illus.*)
octagon shape of, 4:337a
Hagios Demetrios (church: Thessaloniki), 11:570b
mosaics, 4:529b
Hagiotherapy. *See* Saints, cult of, in treatment of insanity
Hague fragment, **6:71a-b**
Ḥahuli. *See* Xaχuli
Hai ben Sherira, 7:168a, 10:338b, 11:584b, 585a
Hail Mary. *See* Ave Maria
Haimo of Auxerre, 4:542b, **6:71b–72a**
as historical source, 6:71b–72a
hymns of, 6:381b
on millennialism, 8:386a-b
Hain, Ludwig, *Repertorium bibliographicum,* 10:127a
Hair, grooming of, 2:148b–150a
Haiti, discovered, 4:561a
Ḥajar al-ᶜAsqalānī, centenary dictionary, 6:253a
Haji Giray, 3:678b
Ḥajj. See Pilgrimage, Islamic
Hajjāj ibn Maṭar, al-, translations by, 12:128a-b
Ḥajjāj ibn Yūsuf al-Thaqafī, al-, **6:72a–73b**, 12:530a
administrative innovations
land development, 6:73a
taxation, 6:72b
construction of Wāsiṭ, 6:73b, 12:574a
Euclid's *Elements,* translation of, 8:209b
governorships, 8:166b
of the Hejaz, 6:72a-b
of Iraq, 6:72b
loyalty to Marwanids, 6:73a
military campaigns
central Asia and Indus Valley, 6:73b
conquest of Mecca, 1:16a, 6:72a, 8:166a
defeat of Ibn al-Zubayr, 12:269b
defeat of Iraqi rebellion, 12:269b
defeat of Kharijites, 6:72b
vs. Ibn al-Ashᶜath, 6:72b–73a, 511b, 7:307a
Ḥajjāj ibn Yūsuf, Umayyad governor of Basra, 11:252a
Hājjī Khalīfa, Ibn al-Nadīm's *Al-Fihrist* and, 9:51a
Ḥajjī, Mamluk sultan, 3:398b
Ḥakam I, al-, Umayyad emir, 11:336b, 12:276a
muwalladūn revolts, 12:67b–68a, 276a
Ḥakam II, al-, Umayyad caliph, 11:382b
military campaigns of, 12:277b
patronage of learning, 3:599a
Hake (*Merluccius merluccius*), fishing of, 5:70a-b
Ḥakham (scholar). *See* Rabbinate, in Christian Spain
Ḥākim bi-Amr Allāh, al-, Fatimid caliph, 5:26b–27a, **6:73b–75a**, 11:137b, 12:744b
administration of, 6:73b, 591a
caliphal library and, 7:561a
claim to be Mahdi, 6:74b
construction of Dār al-Ḥikma, 6:74a
development of Islamic science and, 11:83b
disappearance of, 4:296a, 6:74b
Druzes and, 4:295b–296a, 6:74b, 7:532b, 9:3a
economic reforms, 6:73b
foreign policy, 6:74a-b
Ḥamīd al-Dīn al-Kirmānī and, 6:616b
Ismailis and, 6:587b
religious movement
alienation of Sunnis, 6:74a
organization of *daᶜwa,* 6:74a
social reforms, 6:73b–74a
sumptuary laws and, 11:508a
treatment of Jews and Christians, 6:74a
Yahya and, 12:716b
see also ᶜAzīz biᵓllāh Nizār Abū Manṣūr, al-
Ḥākim, al- (Fatimid mosque), 6:608a, 608b
Hakitía, 7:179a
Hakkāri Kurds, vs. Khwarizmshahs, 6:504b
Hakob of Nisibis, bishop. *See* James of Nisibis, St.
Hákon IV Hákonarson (the Old) of Norway, king
expedition to Scotland (1263), 11:108a
Hákonar saga Hákonarsonar and, 9:177b
Iceland and, 6:395a, 395b, 11:495b
Ívens saga and, 7:20b
Norwegian unification and, 9:182b, 183b
translations from Old French, 10:390a, 390b, 391a, 11:491b, 12:31a
Hákon V Magnusson of Norway, king, administration, 9:184b
Hákon VI of Norway, king, 4:155b, 11:532b
Sweden and, 9:185b
Hákon Aþalsteinsfóstri (the Good) of Norway, king
arrival of in Valhalla, 12:350b
Eyvindr Finnson and, 4:570a
Valkyries and, 12:351a
Hákon galinn, jarl, 11:356a-b
Hákon Gamli. *See* Hákon IV Hákonarson
Hákon inn ríki. *See* Hákon Sigurdson of Norway, ruler
Hákon Magnússon of Norway, king
praised in *Viktors saga ok Blávus,* 10:395a
translation of foreign romances and, 10:390a
Hákon (the Great) of Norway, earl
Eyvindr Finnson and, 4:570a
story of in *Vellekla,* 4:410b–411a
vs. Jómsvíkings, 9:177a
vs. Þrándr, 4:580b
Hákon Pálsson, earl, in *Orkneyinga saga,* 9:279b
Hákon Sigurdson of Norway, ruler (*ca.* 970-*ca.* 995), skaldic poetry and, 11:322a
Hákon Ungi (son of Hákon IV Hákonarson), 10:390a
Hákonar saga Hákonarsonar. See Sturla Þórðarson
Hákonar saga Ívarssonar, **6:75b–76b**
differing versions, 6:76a
preservation of, 6:76a
Hákonarkviða. See Sturla Þórðarson
Hákonarmál
on Valhalla, 12:350b
Valkyries in, 12:351a
see also Eyvindr Finnsson Skáldaspillir
Halakhah
responsum literature and, 10:338b–339b
see also Jewish law
Halakhot Gedolot. See Kayyara, Simeon
Halakhot Pesukot. See Yehuday Gaon
Hałarcin, **6:76b**
monastery complex, 6:76b
Hałbakids, Siwnikᶜ under, 11:315b
Hałbat, **6:77a-b**
as Armenian cultural center, 6:77a, 7:672b
church of St. Nšan, 6:77a (*illus.*)
Hałbat Gospel of 1211, 6:77b
Halbe Decke, Die. See Kotzenmäre, Das
Halberd, 7:323b, 324 (*illus.*), 325a
Halberstadt Cathedral, tapestry of, 11:593a
Hales, Robert, Peasants' Revolt and, 9:479a, 479b
Háleygjatal. See Eyvindr Finnsson Skáldaspillir
Half-Gothic architecture. *See* Church architecture, Cistercian; Romanesque architecture, Cistercian
Half-timber, **6:79b–80a**
Halfdan, Viking leader, Vikings in Northumbria and, 12:432b
Hálfdanar saga Brönufóstra, **6:77b–78a**
deviation from conventional pattern, 6:78a
plot summary, 6:77b–78a
Sörla saga sterka and, 11:373a-b
Hálfdanar saga Eysteinssonar, **6:78b–79a**, 6:312a
plot summary, 6:78b
sources for, 6:79a
Vilmundar saga viutan and, 12:451b
Halfeti, 6:311b
Hálfs saga ok Hálfsrekka, **6:79a-b**
origin, 6:79a
plot summary, 6:79a-b
recurring literary patterns, 6:79b
source for, 6:79b
Hali Meidenhad, 8:314b
Halibut (*Hippoglossus hippoglossus*), fishing of, 5:71b
Halicz. *See* Poland, Ruthenia and
Halil Pasha Çandarlı, Mehmed II and, 8:264a, 264b

Halinard of Lyons, adviser to Pope Leo IX, 7:543a
Halitgar of Cambrai, bishop
  penitential of, 9:490a, 491a
    on medicinal herbs, 8:26a
Hall church. *See* Church architecture
Hall, Joseph, bishop, 12:729b, 730a
Ḥallāj, al-, **6:80a–81a**, 9:40b
  ᶜAbdallāh Anṣārī of Herāt and, 9:41a
  Arabic works, misinterpretation of, 6:80b
  compared with ᶜAyn al-Quḍāt al-Hamadānī, 9:42a
  execution of, 6:80b, 206a, 585a, 8:535b
  on Iblīs, 6:391a
  Kitāb al-ṭawāsīn, 6:80b
  religous pilgrimages, 6:80a
  "Uqtulūnī," 6:80b
Halle
  saltworks, 10:629b
    Halloren, 10:632a
    struggle for control of, 10:632a
Hallein, saltworks, dispute over control of, 10:630a
Hallenkirche. See Church architecture, hall-type
Hällestad runic stone, inscription, 10:564b
Hallfreðar saga, 4:612b, 613a, **6:81a–82a**
  compared with *Bjarnar saga Hítdœlakappa,* 2:255b
  Hallfreðr's death scene, 6:81b
  historical authenticity, 6:81a-b
  preservation in manuscripts, 6:81a
Hallfreðr Ottarsson, poems of, as source for *Hallfreðar saga,* 6:81b
Hallinskiði. *See* Heimdallr
Halloween, 5:37a, 12:660a
Hallstatt
  Celtic language of, 3:232b
  saltworks, industrial complex, 10:633a
Hallur Magnússon, *Vilmundar rímur,* 10:403a
Halo. *See* Nimbus
Halogaland saga cycle, 9:284a-b
Halotti beszéd és könyörgés, 6:337a
Ḥalqa (freeborn soldiers in Mamluk army), 8:73a
Hälsingelagen, 7:525a
Haly Abbas. *See* ᶜAli ibn al-ᶜAbbas
Ham, fortification of, 3:152a
Ḥamā, **6:82a–83a**, 7:316a
  conquest by Arabs, 6:82a
  trade and commerce, 6:82a
    agricultural products, 6:82b
  under Mamluks, 6:82b
Hamadan, Mongol siege of (1221), 8:468a
Hamadhānī, al-, *maqāmāt,* 1:381b, 6:233b
Ḥamāᵓil, **6:83a**
Hamam Bagratuni, prince, 1:511a
Hamartolus, George, *Chronicle,* 5:417a
Ḥamāsa, commented on by al-Marzūqī, 10:347a
Hamazasp Arcruni, martyrdom of, 1:479b, 519a
Hamazasp Mamikonean, 1:478b
Hamboys, John. *See* Hanboys, John
Hamburg
  archbishopric of, 4:151a
  population of, 5:458a
  as port city, 5:460b–461a
  relations with Içeland, 6:397a
Ḥamdallāh, al-Qazqīnī, on silk route to the Far East, 12:99a
Ḥamdān ibn Ḥamdūn
  command of militia, 6:83b
  control of Diyār Rabīᶜa, 6:83b
  return to power, 6:84a
  sons of, 6:83b
Ḥamdān Qarmaṭ, 6:615b, 616a
Hamdānī, al-, on Bab al-Mandab, 2:32b
Hamdanids, **6:83a–86b**
  Abbasid strife with, 10:246a
  Arab-Byzantine war, demographic changes caused by, 6:84b
  Armenia and, 1:482a, 513a
  basis of power, 6:83b–84a
  caliphal authority, conflict with central government, 6:84a
  emirates
    of Aleppo, 6:85b–86a
    dual, 6:85a–86a
    of Mosul, 6:83b–84a
    northern Syria, 6:86a
  end of Ḥamdān control, 6:85a
  in Ḥimṣ, 6:230a
  independence from Baghdad, 6:84b–85a, 85b
  in Mesopotamia, 6:83b, 85b
  in northern Syria, 6:85a
  Nuṣayrīs and, 11:137a
  religious views, 6:83a-b
  rule of Sanᶜa, 10:647a
  tribal affiliation, 6:83a
  Twelver Shiism and, 11:137a
  vs. Ikhshidids, 6:416b
  vs. Romanos II, 10:515b
Häme. *See* Tavasts
Ḥamīd al-Dīn al-Kirmānī
  Al-Aqwāl al-dhahabīya, 6:616b
  Rāḥat al-ᶜaql, 6:616b, 618a
Ḥāmidī, al-, *Kanz al-walad,* 6:618a
Hamlet, in legends, 10:677b
Ḥammād, Zirid ruler, 12:744a-b
Hammadids
  founded, 12:744b
  in Ifrīqiya, 6:414b–415a
  in Málaga, 6:414a
  overthrown by ᶜAbd al-Muᵓmin, 1:194a
Hammām, **6:86b–87a**
Hammer beam, **6:87a-b**
Hammerken. *See* Thomas à Kempis
Hammerness, Battle of (1134), 7:280b
Hamðismál, **6:87b–88b**, 11:293a
  association with *Guðrúnarhvọt,* 6:35b
  Ermenrîkes Dôt and, 4:507a
  legend of Ermanaric, 6:88a
  plot summary, 6:87b–88a
  relations with other Norse poems, 6:88a
  Vọlsunga saga and, 12:489a
Ḥamza ibn ᶜAlī
  founder of Druze faith, 4:296a, 9:3a
  teachings of, 4:296a
Hamzić, Mihajlo, 4:300b
Hān, **6:88b–89a**
  alhóndigas and, 6:470b
  architecture of, 6:602a
  with *eyvān,* 6:603a
  see also Bedestan; Khan (building)
Han dynasty, vs. Hsiung-nu, 6:352b
Ḥanafī legal school, 7:487b, 488b, 11:140a
  dietary laws and, 4:179b
Ḥanafīya, Muḥammad ibn al-, 8:389a, 11:136a
Ḥananel ben Ḥushi'el (RaḤ), 7:98a-b, 11:585a, 585b
  exegesis and, 4:539a
Ḥanbal, Aḥmad ibn Muḥammad ibn, **6:89a-b**, 11:513b
  Hanbalism and Hanbalī, 6:89b
  Islamic fundamentalism, 11:630b
  literary works, 6:89b
  Musnad, 6:89b, 580b, 11:511b
  resistance to Muᶜtazilī, 6:583b
  school of, 6:581b, 582a
  al-Tabarī and, 11:569a
  views on theology, 6:89a-b, 9:568b
Hanbalī legal school, 7:111b, 487b, 488b, 9:568b, 12:244a-b
  Islamic preachers in, 10:73a
  al-Jīlānī and, 7:111b
Hanboys, John, 8:644a
Hanc igitur, 8:192b
Hand (unit of measure), 12:588a
Handball, 5:348a
Handfæstning, 4:155a
Handkerchief, 2:146a
Handlyng Synne. See Mannyng, Robert
Handschriftenkunde, 3:476a
Handwriting. *See* Printing
Handy Tables, 1:621b–622a
Hanes Taliesin, 11:582a
Hanging bowl, 3:219 (*illus.*), **6:89b–90a**
  in Hiberno-Saxon art, 8:369b–370a
Ḥanīfa of al-Kufa, Abū, 11:140a
  creeds attributed to, 11:511b
  see also Ḥanafī
Ḥanīfa tribe, vs. Khālid ibn al-Walīd, 6:568a
Hanina, 7:65b
Hanjit. *See* Ingilene-Anzitenē
Hank (unit of measure), 12:592b
Hankey, John, 3:298b–299a
Hannibal, Artašat and, 1:563b
Hannibaldus de Hannibaldis, as defender of Thomism, 12:42a
Ḥanokh ben Moses, 7:96a
Hans, Bruder. *See* Bruder Hans
Hans Schnepper. *See* Rosenplüt, Hans
Hansas. See Merchants, companies of
Hanseatic League, **6:90a–97a,** 9:88b–89a, 12:112b–113b
  Breslau and, 6:95b
  cog and, 11:242b
  Confederation of Cologne, 6:94b
  decline of, 5:465a-b, 468a, 469b–470a, 6:18b
  embargoes
    Bruges, 6:92b, 94a, 96a
    England, 6:95a
    Flanders, 6:94a, 95b
    Scandinavia, 6:96a
  formation of, 5:460b, 464b, 6:16b, 7:681a
  in German towns, 5:464b–465a
  Kontor

Bruges, 6:93b, 94a, 96a
subordination to collective authority, 6:94a
trade protection for, 6:92a-b
language of, 6:440b
leadership, town council, 6:92b
loss of unity, 6:96a
foreign competition, 6:94b–95b
Margaret of Denmark and, 11:533a
membership and initiation, 6:90a-b
naval force of, 9:82b
organizational structure, 6:92a
diet, 6:94a, 94b, 96b
Peace of Utrecht (1474), 7:684b
precursors
Community of German Merchants Frequenting Gotland, 6:90b
Mercatores de hansa Alemanie, 6:91b
relations with
Denmark, 4:149b, 155b, 7:682a
Iceland and Norway, 6:396b, 397a
Norway, 9:185a
Novgorod, 9:195a-b
religious divisions, 16th century, 7:684b
Russian fur trade and, 5:330a-b
ship tolls, conflict over, 7:684a
Swedish-Russian trade and, 11:532a
Thirty Years War and, 7:684b
trade agreements
England, 6:91a-b, 95a
Flanders, 6:95a-b
infractions of, 6:93b
trade with Baltic lands, 2:67a-b, 68a
trade in
grain, 5:116b–117a
herring, 4:587b
iron ore, 11:471b
trade protection
from Danish intrusion, 6:93a, 94a-b
overseas establishments, 6:92a-b
Visby in, 5:633a
vs. Erik of Pomerania, 11:533a
Waldemar IV and, 9:185a
Wendish cities, 12:616a
Ypres and, 12:732a
Hansen's disease. *See* Leprosy
Haoma sacrifice (in Zoroastrianism), 2:14b
Ḥaqāʾiq, 6:617b
Harald II (Bluetooth) of Denmark, king, 4:151a, 151b
Jellinge stone with Crucifixion and, 12:418b, 419a (*illus.*)
Harald I (Fairhair) of Norway, king, 10:249a
Eyvindr Finnsson and, 4:570a
Iceland and, 6:392b
nine sons of, 12:423b–424a
Norwegian unification and, 9:182b
Rǫgnvaldr heiumhárr and, 12:725b
settlement of Iceland, 12:426b
skalds of, 11:322a
in *Svarfdæla saga,* 11:521b
in *Vatnsdæla saga,* 12:363a, 363b
Ynglingatal and, 12:726a
see also Haraldskvæði
Harald III Hardråde of Norway, king
defeat at Stamford Bridge, 12:434a, 560b
invasion of England, 4:395a
Morkinskinna and, 9:177a
skalds and, 11:322a
þættir and, 12:5a
in Varangian Guard, 12:359a, 435b
Harald Gilli of Norway, king, *Hryggjarstykki* and, 9:176a
Harald gráfeldr of Norway, king, Eyvindr Finnson and, 4:570a, 570b
Harald hárfagri. *See* Harald I (Fairhair) of Norway, king
Harald inn harðráði. *See* Harald III Hardråde
Harald Klak, baptism of, 4:151a
Haraldr. *See* Harald
Haralds saga Hringsbana, 10:394b, 395b
Mírmanns saga and, 8:432b
Haraldskvæði, **6:97a–98a**
influence of, 6:97b
preservation in manuscripts, 6:97a-b
relationship with *Atlakviða,* 6:97b
unity and authorship, 6:97a-b
Valkyries in, 12:351a
Ḥaram al-Sharīf, foundation of, 9:354a
Ḥaramain al-Juwainī, al-, 9:141a
Ḥaramayn. *See* Mecca; Medina
Harāt. *See* Herāt
Hárbarðsljóð, **6:98a-b**
elements of social class, 6:98a
image of Thor in, 6:98a
Örvar-Odds saga and, 9:175a
parallels with *Lokasenna,* 6:98a
poetic irregularities, 6:98a-b
on Thor, 12:45a, 46a
Harcanot et Barcanot, 7:178b
Hardel, William, mayor of London, 7:662a
reply to Richard II, 7:666a
Harding, Stephen, St., 3:403b, 404b, **6:98b**
Charta caritatis, 6:98b
Cistercian Bible and, 2:213b, 218a-b
death of, 12:686a
Metz antiphonary and, 8:642b
Hardwick Hunting Tapestry, 6:362 (*illus.*)
Harem, **6:99a**
of Jawsaq al-Khāqānī, 6:597b
see also Selāmlik
Harğa. *See Kharja*
Harīm Tāhir (palace: Baghdad), 11:574a
Hariolf of Langres, 4:507a
Ḥarīrī, al-
character of Abū Zayd, 6:233b
Maqāmāt, 2:22b, 6:606 (*illus.*), 607b, 610a, 8:115b–116a (*illus.*)
illustrations, 11:630a (*illus.*), 12:575a
miniature of a Muslim merchant ship, 9:86 (*illus.*)
Ḥārith al-Aʿraj, al-, Imruʾ al-Qays and, 6:430a
Ḥārith, al-, Ghassanid ruler, 5:515a, 7:320b
Ḥārith ibn Asad al-Muḥāsibī, Islamic mysticism and, 9:39b
Ḥārith ibn-Kaʿb, al-, in Najrān, 9:55a, 55b
Ḥārith ibn Surayj, conflict with Hishām ibn ʿAbd al-Malik, 6:232a
Hariulf, **6:99a**
drawing of St. Riquier by, 10:94a
history of St. Riquier, 6:99a
on Nithard, 9:143a
Harley, Lord, library of, 3:477a
Harley Manuscript, 1:319b, 5:433b, 8:331b, 336b, 337a, 340a
poems on sexual love, 8:337a–338a
Harley Psalters, 10:108b
Harmenopoulos, Constantine, **6:99a-b**
Epitome kanonon, 6:99b
Hexabiblos, 6:99b, 7:392b
economic definition of the poor, 9:493b
Harmonica. *See* Aristoxenus; Ptolemy
Harmonics. *See* Cleonides, *Introductio harmonico*
Harmonie universelle. *See* Mersenne, Marin
Harmony, **6:99b–101a**
cosmological
angelic music, 6:100a
metaphorical music, 6:99b–100a
psychic, 6:100a
musica ficta and, 8:598b, 599b
musica humana, 6:100a
musical definitions, 6:100a
harmonia simplex vs. *harmonia multiplex,* 6:100b
melody, 6:100b
polyphonic, 6:100a
rational ordering of music, 6:100a-b
numerical proportions, 6:100a
philosophy of, 8:589a-b
Pythagorean ideas of, 6:100a
in Worcester polyphony, 12:695b, 696b
Harmony of the spheres, 8:580a–581a
in art, 8:583b–586a (*illus.*), 587a (*illus.*), 587b (*illus.*), 588a (*illus.*)
Pythagorean ideas of, 8:636b
Harmsól. *See* Gamli Kanóki
Harness, medieval improvements of, 12:371 (*illus.*), 378b
see also Tools, Agricultural
Harold III Hardråde. *See* Harald III Hardråde of Norway, king
Harold of England, king. *See* Harold of Wessex, earl
Harold of Wessex, earl, 4:457a-b
Bayeux Tapestry and, 2:139a
claim to English throne, 6:111a
defeat by William I of England, 4:461a, 6:112a, 9:165b, 12:560b
defeat of Vikings at Stamford Bridge, 6:111b–112a, 12:560b
Wulfstan of Worcester and, 12:703a
Harp, 8:606a, 607a (*illus.*), 12:180b
Arab, 8:611a-b
Celtic, 8:558a-b
keyed. *See Clavicytherium*
nobility and, 8:596a
Norsemen and, 8:601a
Harpsichord, 8:608a-b
Harput, Artukids and, 1:485a
Harpy, in art, 6:408a
Ḥarra, al-, Battle of (683), 12:268b, 722a
Umayyads vs. Quraysh, 10:242b

Ḥarrān, Sabaeans and, 9:4a
Harrāqa, 11:247b
Harrowing of Hell, 8:661a
Harrowing of Hell. *See* Anastasis
Harrows, 12:77b–78a
depicted in a 1372 manuscript, 12:78 (*illus.*)
Islamic, 12:84b
Roman antecendents of, 12:77b
see also Agriculture; Reclamation of land; Technology
Harry, Blind. *See* Henry the Minstrel
Harðar saga Grímkelssonar (ok Geirs), **6:101a–102a**
authorship, 6:101a-b
imagery, 6:101b
plot summary, 6:101b
preservation of, 6:101a
Harðr saga ok Hólmverja. See Harðar saga Grímkelssonar (ok Geirs)
Hartker, Office for St. Gall, 9:691b–692b (*illus.*)
Hartlieb, Johannes, 8:360b
Hartmann IV of Kyburg, count, 11:539b
Hartmann V of Kyburg, count, 11:539b
Hartmann von Aue, 3:11a, **6:102a–107a**, 9:708a
allegory of, 5:429a
Arme Heinrich, 6:31a, 9:677b
as example of God's mercy, 6:106a
narrative style, 6:106a
plot summary, 6:105b–106a
Arthurian epic and, 8:414a
Büchlein, 8:409a
ceremony and, 9:114a
Chrétien de Troyes and, 5:451a
crusade poetry of, 10:294a
education of, 6:102a
epic works, sequence of, 6:102a
Erek, 5:429a, 450b
Arthurian legend and, 1:571b
as mirror of princes, 6:104a
plot summary, 6:103b–104a
Wirnt von Grafenberg's *Wigalois* and, 12:657a
Wolfram von Eschenbach and, 12:674b
French lyric technique of, 8:414a
genres
Arthurian romances, 6:103b–105a
legends and miracle stories, 6:105a–106a
songs, 6:102b–103b
Gregorius, 6:105a
Christian view of divine providence, 6:105b
Gute Frau and, 6:30b–31a
influence on epic writers, 6:106b
Îwein, 5:446b–447a, 450b–451a, 6:104a–105a
Bussard and, 2:434a
issue of faithlessness, 6:104b–105a
Kalogrenant's tale, 12:573b
as mirror of princes, 6:105a
as a model for Der Stricker's *Daniel,* 11:493a
Wirnt von Grafenberg's *Wigalois* and, 12:657a
Wolfram von Eschenbach and, 12:674b, 679b
Yvain of Chrétien de Troyes and, 1:571b
Klage, 6:103a, 8:409a
Konrad von Stoffeln and, 7:287b
literary patrons, 6:102b
location of *Ouwe,* 6:102a
lyrics of, 5:434b
Mai und Beaflor and, 8:48a
minnesingers and, 5:440, 8:413a
morality of, 5:451a
natural behavior vs. formal convention, 5:451a
Nibelungenlied and, 9:114b
preservation of works, 6:106a
professional life of, 8:350b
romances, 5:450b–451b
Schüler von Paris and, 11:80a
Seifrid Helbling and, 11:142b
social class, 6:102a
Sperber and, 11:460b
Wolfram von Eschenbach and, 8:351a
Hartmann, John, charges of heresy, 5:218a
Hartmann of St. Gall, *Humili prece et sincera,* 7:592a
Hartmann the Younger, hymns of, 6:381b
Hārūn ibn Muḥammad ibn ᶜAbd Allāh. *See* Hārūn al-Rashīd
Hārūn al-Rashīd, Abbasid caliph, **6:107a–108a**, 9:657a
Baghdad's zenith, 2:46a-b
Barmakids and, 2:110a–111a, 6:107b
building at Samarra, 10:641b
Charlemagne and, 4:200b–201a, 12:110a
in chronicles, 6:108a
death of, 6:512b
decentralization of government, 1:9b
expeditions against the Byzantines (780, 782), 8:47b
governorships, 6:107a
Ibrāhīm ibn al-Aghlab and, 6:391b
Idrīs ibn ᶜAbd Allah and, 6:413a
literary patronage, of Abū Nuwās, 1:27b
Malīk ibn Anas and, 8:58b
military expeditions, 6:107a
al-Muᶜtaṣim and, 8:653b
partitioning of Islamic empire, 6:107b–108a
perfume and, 2:147a
persecution of Alids, 1:174b
qalansuwa (hat) of, 10:224a
succession provisions, 1:9b, 3:43a, 6:107b, 8:79b
succession to caliphate, 6:107b
Ṭāhir and, 11:574a, 575a
Thousand and One Nights and, 12:49b
translation patronage, 12:128b
translations of Greek scientific treatises and, 11:82b
vizier and, 6:590a
Hārūn al-Wāthiq, Abbasid caliph, development of Samarra, 10:643a
Hārūt (Islamic angel)
as teacher of magic, 8:20b
see also Angels, Islamic
Harvest songs, 5:440b
Harvey Nedellec. *See* Hervaeus Natalis
Harz Mountains, mining in, 8:398b, 401b
Ḥasan ᶜAlī Shāh Maḥallātī, aga khan, 6:618a
Ḥasan al-Aᶜṣam, al-, Qarmatian leader, 5:26a
Ḥasan al-ᶜAskari, Shīᶜa imam, death of, 11:227b
Ḥasan al-Baṣrī, 8:655a
Islamic mysticism and, 9:39b
Ḥasan ibn Aḥmad ibn ᶜAlī al-Kātib, al-, 8:566a
Ḥasan ibn ᶜAlī ibn Abī Ṭālib, al-, 1:174b, **6:108a–109a**, 11:136b
abdication of caliphate, 6:108b–109a
conflicts with Muᶜāwiya, 6:108b
descendants of, 1:175a
religious leadership, 6:108b
in the *taᶜziya,* 6:109a
Ḥasan ibn ᶜAlī al-Kalbī, 11:262b
Ḥasan ibn ᶜAlī ibn Khalaf al-Barbahārī, al-, 11:511b, 512a
Ḥasan ibn ᶜAlī, al-, Zirid ruler, 12:745a
Ḥasan ibn ᶜAmmār, al-, military regent for al-Ḥākim, 6:73b
Ḥasan ibn Hāniᵓ, al-. *See* Abū Nuwās
Ḥasan ibn al-Haytham. *See* Haytham, Ḥasan ibn al-
Ḥasan ibn Sahl, al- (al-Maᵓmūn's viceroy), 8:80a, 80b
Ḥasan ibn Zayd, al-, 12:741b
Hasan Jalalean, 1:485b
Ḥasan Jalāyir, 6:514a
Ḥasan, Mamluk sultan, mausoleum of, 6:609a-b, 610 (*illus.*)
Ḥasan, al-Rukn al-Dawla. *See* Rukn al-Dawla
Ḥasan al-Ṣabbāḥ, 6:588a-b
Nizār and, 6:617a
Hasanuyids, 7:310b
Ḥasanwayh, 7:310b
Ḥasdai Crescas. *See* Crescas, Ḥasdai
Ḥasdai ibn Shaprūṭ, 5:357b
Hebrew poems, 6:126a
secular poetry, 6:131b
Hasdings, 12:354a, 354b
Hasenbraten, 8:130b
Hāshim (banū), 1:175b, 6:576a, 576b
Hāshim ibn ᶜAbd Manāf, **6:109a-b**
descendants of, 4:596b
establishment of commercial trade in Mecca, 6:109a
securing of Syrian markets, 6:109a
Hāshimiyya (Alid cadres), overthrow of Umayyads, 1:7a
Hāshimiyyah, al- (Abbasid administrative center), 2:45a, 45b
Hashish, Nizārīs and, 11:137b
Ḥashīshī, term "assassins" and, 1:592a
Ḥashr, al- (gathering), in the Islamic doctrine of resurrection, 10:341a
Ḥashwīya, 11:513b
Ḥasidei Ashkenaz, 1:345b, **6:109b–111a**, 7:93a, 169a
cabala and, 9:581b–582a
circle of Ben Sira, 9:579a
divine immanence, 9:580a, 580b
divine transcendence, 9:580a
Eleazar ben Judah and, 4:421a
foundation of, 7:91a, 92b

kavod, 9:580a-b
martyrdom (*kiddush ha-shem*), 9:581a
on miracles, 9:580b
opposition to philosophy and dialectic, 9:579b
origins, 9:578b
personal vs. societal salvation, 6:110a
pietism
acts of penance, 6:110a
acts of self-denial, 6:110a
fellowship of, 6:110a
German-Jewish, 6:111a
on prayer, 9:581b
repentance literature, 9:581a-b
sin of pride, 9:578b
sources of
German popular culture, 9:579b–580a
Heikhalot and *Merkabah* literature, 9:579b–580a
Jewish philosophers, 9:579b
theology and ethics, 7:169a, 9:580a–581b
zaddikim, 9:580b
see also Magic and folklore, Jewish
Häslein, Das, **6:50a-b**
compared with *Sperber,* 11:461a
love theme, 6:50a-b
Hasmonean revolt
menorah and, 11:557a
synagogue and, 11:556a
Hasp (unit of measure), 12:592b
Ḥassān Mosque (Rabat), 1:193a
Hašteankᶜ. *See* Asthianenē
Hastings, Battle of (1066), **6:111a–112a,** 9:165a-b, 12:560b, 634a
armor in, 1:523a
in art, 6:111b (*illus.*)
Bayeux Tapestry and, 2:139a
cavalry tactics at, 3:203b
described in Gaimar's *Estoire des Engleis,* 1:265a
military tactics, 6:112a
Wulfstan of Worcester and, 12:703a
Hastings, Lord
executed by Richard III, 10:385b
retainers of in the Commons, 9:432b
Hasungen (monastery), 7:321a
Hathumoda (Hathmodo), abbess of Gandersheim, biographies of, 1:72b, 6:313b
Haðarlag, 11:320a
Ḥātimī, on rhetoric, 10:347a
Hats
Western European, 3:623a-b
men's, 3:624a-b
see also Head covering
Háttalykill, **6:112a-b**
models for other works, 6:112b
organization, 6:112b
Orkneyinga saga, 6:112a
preservation of manuscripts, 6:112b
see also Rǫgnvaldr Kali Kolsson
Háttatal, **6:113a**
in *Snorra Edda,* 11:352a-b
variations of *dróttkvætt* in, 11:319b
Ḥaṭṭīn. *See* Ḥiṭṭīn
Hattock (unit of measure), 12:592b
Hatton manuscripts. *See* West Saxon Gospels
Hätzlerin, Klara, **6:50b–51a**
Liederbuch der Clara Hätzlerin, 6:50b–51a
preservation of copied manuscripts, 6:50a
Hauberk, 1:524b
Haukdœla þáttr, in *Sturlunga saga,* 11:498b
Haukr Erlendsson
Hauksbók, 7:327b, 328a, 8:275b, 12:456b
Kristni saga in, 7:303a
Þáttr af Ragnars sonum and, 12:6b, 7a
variation of *Vǫluspá* in, 4:387a
Vǫluspá and, 12:491a
Haukr Valdísarson, **6:113a–114a**
Íslendingadrápa
dating of, 6:113a
death of Helgi Droplaugarson, 4:294b
kennings, 6:113b
preservation of, 6:113a
style, 6:113b
Vápnfirðinga saga and, 12:359a
Hauksbók. *See* Haukr Erlendsson
Haulte Bourgogne, La, 4:87 (*illus.*)
Hauran, Yarmuk and, 12:719a
Haustlǫng. *See* Þjóðólfr ór Hvíni
Haute lisse. *See* Looms, high-warp
Hauteville family, in Sicily, 11:264b–265a, 266a
Hávamál, **6:114a-b**
as gnomic literature, 5:569a-b
gnomic stanzas, *priamel,* 6:114a
Grógaldr and, 11:524b
Loddfáfnismál, 6:114b
meaning of title, 6:114a
Odin in, 9:218a
seduction of Gunnlǫð, 6:114a
Sigrdrífumál and, 11:288b
Sólarljóð and, 11:358b–359a
Hávarðar saga Ísfirðings, 4:612b, **6:114b–115b**
authorship, 6:115a
heroics and exaggeration in, 6:115a
sources for, 6:114b–115a
Haveloc the Dane
in Gaimar's *Estoire des Engleis,* 1:268a
modern edition of *Lai d'Haveloc,* 1:271a
Havelok the Dane, **6:115b,** 7:317a, 8:316a
preservation of, 6:115b
Ḥawāla (Islamic instrument of credit), 2:79b
Hawāra, 2:185b
Hawatarmat. *See* Yovhannēs Mayragomecᶜi
Hawes, Stephen, 12:477a
Passetyme of Pleasure, 5:639b
Wynkyn de Worde and, 12:712a
Ḥāwī, al-. *See* Rāzī, Abū Bakr Muḥammad ibn Zakarīya al-
Hawking, 5:354b (*illus.*)
Fachschrifttum and, 4:579b
Islamic, 6:355b
women and, 6:357a
Hawkins, Thomas, *Everyman* and, 4:527b
Hawkwood, Sir John, military company, 12:566a
Ḥawqal, Ibn, 3:209a, 11:337b
on Armenian economy, 12:97b, 98b
on Armenians, 1:485a
on Baylakān, 2:139b
illustrations in his treatises, 9:77a
on Islamic trade, 12:106a
on al-Maghrib, 8:15a
on Meknes, 8:267b
on Naχčawan, 9:91a
Ḥawshab Manṣūr al-Yaman, Ibn, 6:615b–616a
Kitāb al-rushd wa'l-hidāya, 6:616a
Hawwāra Berbers, irrigation and, 6:557b
Ḥawwās, Ibn al-, vs. Ibn al-Thumna, 10:440a
Haxaëmeron. *See* Grosseteste, Robert
Hay. *See* Hai ben Sherira
Hay, Jean (John). *See* Master of Moulins
Hay, Sir Gilbert, **6:115b–116b**
Buik of King Alexander the Conquerour, 6:115b
inconsistencies in, 6:116a
sources for, 6:116a
Buke of the Governaunce of Princis, 6:116a
Buke of Knychthede, 6:116a
Ḥaydarān, Battle of (1052), 6:415a, 12:744b
Hayden, Gregor, 11:367b
Haymo of Faversham
leadership of Franciscans, 5:199b
opposition to lay brotherhood, 5:199a
reworking of regula-books
Ordo ad benedicendum mensam, 5:194a
Ordo breviarii, 5:193b–194a
Ordo missae, 5:193b
Haytham, Ḥasan ibn al-, 1:621a, 8:566a, 11:83b
commentary on Ptolemy's *Almagest,* 11:84b
daᶜwā and, 6:616a
Discourse on Light, 9:245a
influence of on Roger Bacon, 2:39a
intromission theory, 9:251b
Kitāb al-manāẓir (*Book on Optics*), 1:436a, 9:241a, 11:86b–87a
behavior of light and color, 9:244b
commentaries on, 9:241b, 245a
influence of, 9:245a-b, 246a-b, 247b
vision theory, 9:242a–244a
On the Configuration of the World, translated into Hebrew, 11:90b
On the Form of the Eclipse, 9:245a
On the Light of the Moon, 9:244b
On Parabolic Burning Mirrors, 9:244b–245a
translated into Latin as *Liber de speculis comburentibus,* 1:437a, 438b
On the Rainbow and the Halo, 9:244b
Perspectiva, 1:438b
pin-hole camera, principles of, 9:245a
psychology of perception, 9:243a–244a, 249b

Haytham, Ḥasan ibn al- (*cont.*)
reflection and refraction, 9:243a-b
restoration of book VIII of Apollonius' *Conics,* 11:92a
vision theory, 9:243b (*illus.*), 245b (*illus.*)
Ḥayy. See Extended family, Islamic
Ḥayy ibn Yaqẓān. See Tufayl, Ibn
Hazaj, 8:565b, 566a
Hazār bāf, 11:147a
Hazārabad (Sasanian title), **6:116b–117a**, 12:705b
classical form, 6:116b
Middle Iranian form, 6:116b
Old Persian form, 6:116b
Hazarapet. See Seneschal, Armenian
Hazelnut
in Mediterranean region, 5:305b, 307a
see also Fruits and nuts
Ḥazm, Abū Muḥammad ᶜAlī ibn Aḥmad ibn Saᶜīd ibn, 1:381b, 401a, **6:117a–118b**
on Aristotelian logic, 6:118a
on astrology, 1:618a
Fiṣal fīʾl-milal waʾl-ahwāᵓ waʾl-niḥal, 6:118a
Iḥkām fī uṣūl al-aḥkam, al-, 6:118a
imprisonments, 6:117a
Islamic-Jewish polemics and, 10:8a
Kitāb al-muḥallā, 6:117b
language theory, 6:118a
legal theory, 6:117b–118a
application to theology, 6:118a
literal philosophy, 9:570b
Taqrīb bi-ḥadd al-manṭiq, 6:118a
Ṭawq al-ḥamāma, 3:672a, 6:117a, 117b
Ḥazzan. See Cantor, Jewish
Head covering, 2:145b–146a
Head of the Jews. *See* Nagid
Head ransom. *See* Egill Skallagrímsson, *Hǫfuðlausn*
Head tax. *See* Chevage
Headache
causes of, 9:550b, 551a
positive medical purposes, 9:551a
treatment of, 9:549a, 550a-b
types of, 9:550b
Healfdene. *See* Halfdan
Healing. *See* Doctors; Medicine
Health. *See* Medicine; Public health
Heap (unit of measure), 12:592b
Hearth lists, 4:138a-b
"Hearth tax." *See Fouage; Kapnikon*
Hearthpenny. *See* Peter's Pence
Heating, **6:119a–125a**
changes effected by
privacy and intimacy, 6:124a
technological revolution, 6:122a, 124b
working hours, 6:123b
closed systems
hypocaust, 6:119a
space, 6:119a
epicaustrium, 6:120b
of inns, 6:471b
open systems
braziers, 6:119a
central hearths, 6:119b–120a
dangers of, 6:121b
ventilation, 6:119b
of worker's quarters, 6:123b
see also Chimneys; Fireplace; Fuel
Heaume, 1:526a, 527a (*illus.*), 534b (*illus.*)
tilting, 1:532b
Heavenly Jerusalem, **6:125a-b**, 6:125b (*illus.*)
in Gothic architecture, 5:586a–587a
Heavenly Ladder. See John Klimakos
Hebrew alphabet. *See* Alphabets, Hebrew
Hebrew language
in Byzantium, 4:539b
Christian study of, 3:313b–314a
dictionary of, 7:163b
Dominican missionary study of, 10:266b
enriched by Arabic language, 12:134b–135a
grammar
in Judeo-Arabic literature, 7:172b
treatises, 5:650b
Italian language and, Moses of Salerno's Hebrew-Italian glossary, 12:137a
Jewish study of, **6:128a–129b**
comparative Semitics, 6:128b–129a
dictionaries and grammars, 6:128a, 10:598b
establishment of scientific method, 6:128b
influence of Latin linguistics, 6:129b
popularization, 6:129a
system of graphic signs, 6:128a
translators, 6:129a
see also Masoretes
in liturgical poetry, biblical connotations, 6:131a
in secular poetry, biblical connotations, 6:126a
in Spain, 4:539b, 540a, 6:434a, 442b
spread of, 3:313b
teaching and study of, 12:137a-b
see also Judeo-Arabic language
Hebrew literature
apocalyptic, influence of Pahlavi literature on, 9:326b–327a
belles lettres, **6:125b–128a**
adaptation of Arabic *maqāma,* 6:127a
Arabic influence, 6:125b–126b
epigrams, 6:126b
golden age, 6:126a–127a
lampoons, 6:126a
muwashshaḥ form, 6:126b
panegyrics, 6:126b
poetry of entertainment, 6:126a
silver age, 6:127a
translations of classics, 6:127b
in Cairo genizah, 3:15b
fable, 4:572b
poetry, **6:129b–132b**
biblical quotations, 6:131a
dictionaries for, 6:128b
from book of Lamentations, 6:130b
of German Jewish pietists, 6:132a
golden age poets, 6:131b–132a
influence of *merkavah* mystics, 6:130a
in Italy, 6:132a
litany, 6:31a
liturgical form, 6:129b–130a
"merit of the ancestors" and *ᶜaqedah,* 6:130b
Mishnah and *ᶜavodah* poems, 6:130b–131a
in Muslim Spain, 7:96a, 96b–97a
muwashshaḥs and, 11:447a, 447b
origin of *hoshaᶜnot,* 6:131a
in Palestine, 7:104b
postclassical school, 6:131b
prosody of, 7:622a
qedushah and *qedushatah,* 6:130a
religious, 10:598a
in the Rhineland, 6:132a
rhymed-prose love stories, 6:127a
rhythm of synagogue poetry, 6:131a
secular, 6:126a–127b
seliḥa, 6:132a
selihot, 6:130b
seven benedictions, 6:130a
shemaᶜ, 6:130b
shivᶜatot, 6:130a
sonnets, 6:132a
sources in Cairo genizah, 3:15b
and Torah readings, 6:130b
yotser, 6:130a
qaṣīda-type, meter, 6:126b
rabbinic, 10:598b
see also Magic and folklore, Jewish; Rhetoric, Hebrew
Hebrides, Vikings and, 12:425a, 425b
Hedeby, **6:132b–133a**, 12:110a, 423a
in contemporary literature, 6:132b
physical layout, 6:133a
runic stones, 10:564b
trade and commerce, 6:132b
archaeological evidence, 6:132b–133a
slaves, 6:133a
see also Slesvig
Hedgehog, in medieval folklore, 2:206b
Hednalagen, 7:524b
Hedwig glasses, 5:547a
Heer (unit of measure), 12:592b
Heerschild, 5:499a
Ḥefez ben Yaẓliᵓah, 7:172b
Heggen Church (Norway), weather vane in Ringerike style, 10:408 (*illus.*)
Hegira, 6:577a
Abū Bakr's role, 1:24b
effect on Meccan leadership, 1:28b
factors responsible for, 1:30a
Islamic calendar and, 3:27a
Koranic suras and, 6:578a
movement of followers, 8:523b
Zaydis and, 12:742a
Hegumenos. See Archimandrite
Hegyon ha-Nefesh ha-Azuvah. See Abraham bar Ḥiyya
Heidelberg Codex Palatinus Germanicus 112, 10:447b
Heidelberg Song Manuscript
Larger. *See* Manesse-Codex
Smaller, 5:436b
Heidelberg, University of, 12:287b–288a
via moderna and, 12:408a, 408b
Heikhalot rabbati, 1:344b
Heilgeschichte, 12:541a
Heiligen Leben, Der, 8:356a
Heiligenkreuz, stained glass at, 5:553a

Heimdalargaldr, fragment of in *Prose Edda,* 4:387b
Heimdallr, **6:133a–134a**, 11:27a
Christian and Celtic influences, 6:133b–134a
dual mythological role, 6:133b
etymology, 6:133b
family history, 6:133a
identified with Rígr in *Rígsþula,* 10:400a
list of *heiti,* 6:133b
in *Þrymskviða,* 12:52b
in *Vǫluspá in skamma,* 6:385b
world tree and, 6:134a
see also Scandinavian mythology
Heimericus de Campo, 9:123a
Heimir (epic character), 12:29b, 30b
Heimliche Bote, Der, 8:408b
Heimskringla. See Snorri Sturluson
Hein van Aken
Rose, 4:319a
Van den Coninc Saladijn ende van Hughen van Tabaryen, 4:319a
Heinrich VI. *See* Henry VI of Germany
Heinrich von Augsburg, **6:135a**
De musica, 8:642a
Heinrich von Beringen, *Schachgedicht,* 5:431a
Heinrich von Burgeis, *Der Seele Rat,* 5:430b
Heinrich Eger von Kalkar, *Cantuagium,* 8:647a
Heinrich von Freiberg, 5:634a, **6:136a–137a**
continuation of Gottfried's *Tristan,* 5:454a, 6:136a
variation from author's style, 6:136a
Eilhart von Oberg's *Tristrant* and, 5:445a, 12:201a, 205a
Gedicht vom heiligen Kreuz, 6:136b
Ritterfahrt des Herrn von Michaelsberg, 6:136b
Schrätel und der Wasserbär, 6:136b, **11:79a**
Heinrich der Glîchezaere, 2:141b
Reinhart Fuchs, 10:314a-b
theme of, 8:350a
see also Beast Epic
Heinrich von Hesler
Apocalypse, 8:356b
Erlösung, 2:231a
metrical form of his work, 2:232a
Heinrich Institoris, *Malleus maleficarum,* 12:662b, 663b, 664b
Heinrich, Kaiser. *See* Henry VI of Germany, emperor
Heinrich von Kempten. See Konrad von Würzburg
Heinrich von Kröllwitz, allegory of, 5:429b
Heinrich von Meissen, 5:438a, **6:137a-b**
audience written for, 6:137a
didactic works, 5:443a, 6:137a
fame of, 8:358a
minnesingers and, 8:414a
order in poetry, 6:137b
origin of nickname, 6:137a
Heinrich von Melk, **6:137b–138b**
Erinnerung an den Tod, 6:137b
theme of memento mori, 6:138a
poetic style, 6:138a
Heinrich von Morungen, **6:138b–139b**, 8:414a
ballad on noble Möringer, 6:139a
Dietrich of Meissen and, 6:138b–139a
influence of, 6:139a
Johannes Hadlaub and, 7:120a
literary works
imagery, 6:139a
interpretations, 6:139b
models for, 6:139a
similarity to Latin songs, 6:139a
reputation of, 5:443b
Schüler von Paris and, 11:80a
Suso and, 11:516b
Heinrich von Mügeln, **6:140a-b**
clerical background, 6:140a
didactic poetry of, 5:443a
fame of, 8:358a
influence of on Michel Beheim, 8:306b
languages used by, 8:356a
Latin analogues, 6:140a
literary works, 6:140a
lyrics of, 5:436b
Meide Kranz, 5:432a, 6:140a
alchemy in, 1:138b
Heinrich von München, continuator of *Christherre-Chronik,* 2:229a
Heinrich von Neustadt, **6:140b–141b**
Apollonius von Tyrland, 5:454b
plot summary, 6:140b–141a
Gottes Zukunft, 2:230b, 5:430a, 6:140b
God's appearances to man in, 6:141a
Visio Philiberti, 6:140b, 141a
Heinrich von Nördlingen
letters to Margareta Ebner, 8:356a
Suso and, 9:34b
Tauler and, 9:33b
translation of Mechthild von Magdeburg's *Das fliessende Licht der Gottheit,* 8:241b, 9:11a
women mystics and, 9:13a, 13b
Heinrich von Rugge, **6:141b–142a**
crusade *Leich,* 6:141b
Des Minnesangs Frühling, 6:141b
lyrics for minnesingers, 8:413b
Heinrich Suso. *See* Suso, Heinrich
Heinrich der Teichner, **6:134a–135a**, 8:357b–358a
background, 6:134a
literary works
sources for, 6:134b
subject matter, 6:134b
on love, 8:411b–412a
Mären, 8:131b
style, 6:134b
Heinrich von dem Türlin, **6:135a–136a**
adaptations of French or German sources, 6:135b
Ambraser Heldenbuch, 6:135b
background and ancestry, 6:135a
Diu Crône, 5:455b, 6:135a
chastity tests in, 6:135b
references to other works in, 6:135b
Wolfram von Eschenbach and, 12:679b
Mantel, 6:135a, 135b
Wirnt von Grafenberg and, 12:656a
Heinrich von Veldeke, **6:142a–144b**, 6:441a
dialect of, 4:318b
education and social status, 6:142a
Eneide, 4:318a-b, 5:446a, 450a, 6:142b, 143b, 182b, 8:408b
battle scenes, 6:144a
influence of medieval rhetoric, 6:144a
relation to other works, 6:144b
transition from classical epic to medieval romance, 6:144a
Wolfram von Eschenbach and, 12:674b
language and dialects, 6:142b–143a
Leven van Sint Servaes, 4:318a, 6:142b
influence on other works, 6:143a
oldest vernacular saint's life, 4:320a
preservation, 6:143a
literary works
chronology and sources, 6:143b
themes, 6:143b
lyrics of, 5:434a, 8:413b
modern opinions on, 6:144a
Nibelungenlied and, 9:114b
patrons, 6:142b
preservation of manuscripts, 6:142b
professional life of, 8:350b
"Stauferpartien," 6:144a
Strassburger Alexander and, 7:323a
Heinrich der Vogler, *Dietrichs Flucht* and, 2:396a
Heinrich von Werl, bishop of Paderborn, 10:441b, 442a, 500a
Heinrico (Henrico), De, **6:144b–145a**
Heinzelein von Konstanz, *Von dem Ritter und von dem Pfaffen,* 8:411b
Heirdom. *See* Inheritance
Heiric, 10:303a
Heiric of Auxerre, 3:433a-b, 4:542b, 7:362b
Hucbald and, 6:317a
Heirmologion, 8:554a, 556b
Slavic music and, 8:574a, 574b
Veterem hominem and, 8:557a
Heirmos, **6:145a**, 6:379a, 8:554a, 556b
collections of, 6:145a
in *kanon,* 7:208b
Heiðarvíga saga, 4:613b, 614a, **6:145b–146a**
dating of, 6:145a
Eyrbyggja saga and, 4:568a
narrative devices, 6:146a
Heiti
in *rímur,* 10:404a-b
in skaldic poetry, 11:318a–319b
in *Skáldskaparmál,* 11:324a, 352b
Hejaz, **6:146a–147a**, 6:146b (map)
beginnings of Islam, 6:146a
early Islamic conquests of, 1:236b–237a
Jews in, 7:101a-b, 102b, 103a
loss of political significance, 6:146b
Muslim pilgrimages, 6:146b
Ottoman conquest of, 11:145b
Seljuk penetration into, 11:153a
trade and commerce, 6:146a

Hejaz (*cont.*)
viticulture in, 2:208b
see also Najrān
Hel, **6:147a–148a**
with advent of Christianity, 6:147b
in the Baldr myth, 2:55b
concepts of afterlife, 6:147a
distinction between Hades and Gehenna, 6:148a
gates of hell, 6:147a
midgard serpent and, 8:362a
as place of punishment, 6:147a
separation from concept of *niflhel,* 6:147b
see also Scandinavian mythology
Heldenbuch, 8:360b
Heledd, sister of Cynddylan ap Cyndrwyn, in Welsh poetry, 12:598a, 603b
Helen. *See* Olga of Kiev
Helena, St.
discovery of True Cross, 4:9a, 8:20a
excavation of Jesus' burial site, 1:336b–337a
portrayed in the Old English *Elene,* 1:279a
see also Cross, true
Helfta (convent), women mystics and, 9:8a, 10b–11b
Helga þáttr ok Úlfs, 12:2b, 4b
Helga þáttr Þórissonar, **6:148a-b,** 12:3a
plot summary, 6:148a
preservation in manuscripts, 6:148a
Helgakviða Hundingsbana II
compared with *Baldrs draumar,* 2:56b
Helgi's return from the grave, source for other works, 6:35b
Helgason, Árni, 1:537a
Helgaud, **6:148b–149a**
history of monasteries, 6:148b
on king as healer, 7:255a-b
Life of King Robert the Pious, 2:236b, 6:148b, 7:262a, 10:17a
Helgi Hundingsbani, Norns and, 9:172a
Helgi poems, **6:149a–150a**
common theme, 6:149a
dating of, 6:149a
flyting in, 9:173b, 174a
Kudrun and, 7:304b
order in Codex Regius, 4:386a
skaldic affinities, 6:149b
Valkyries in, 12:351a
Helgö
commerce, 11:529a
statue of Buddha found at, 12:110a
village finds, 10:693a
Heliand, 1:280a, 2:225a, **6:150a–151b**
afterlife in, 6:147b
alliterative verse, 6:441a, 9:233b
dating of, 6:151a
depiction of Christ, 6:150b
English verse and, 6:150a
fate in, 6:150b
Genesis and, 6:150a, 151a
influence on later works, 6:151a
language of, 6:436b, 439b
native adaptations of Bible story, 6:150a
Hélinand of Froidmont, *Chronica,* 1:607b
Heliopolis (Egypt), battle at (*ca.* 640), 6:569b
Heliopolis (Syria). *See* Baalbek
Hell
in art, 10:508a (*illus.*)
Islamic concept of, doctrine of resurrection and, 10:341a
relief by Lorenzo Maitani, 8:52b (*illus.*)
Western concept of, in *Dança general de la Muerte,* 11:420a
see also Hel
Hellenism
Basil the Great and, 2:120a, 120b
Coptic sculpture influenced by, 3:587a-b
Islam and, 6:583a, 584a-b, 587a, 11:88a-b
revival of in the arabized Middle East, 11:82a
in Roman Empire, 10:457b–458a
imperial survival and, 10:466b–467b
Hellenizing School, Armenian. *See* Armenian Hellenizing School
Hellespont. *See* Dardanelles
Hellinus, abbot, 10:253a
Helluland
discovery of, 4:555a
in Vinland sagas, 12:428b, 457a
Helmbrecht. See Wernher der Gartenære
Helmet, 1:526a-b, 527 (*illus.*), 531a-b, 534 (*illus.*)
English, from Sutton Hoo, 11:519b (*illus.*)
lobster-tail. *See Zischägge*
"Norman," 1:523a, 534a (*illus.*)
plate armor and, 1:526a
Scandinavian, 1:522b–523a
tilting, 1:533a
visor, 1:524a, 526b, 534a (*illus.*)
see also Armet; Barbute; Basinet; Chapel-de-fer; Heaume; *Rennhut;* Sallet; Spangenhelm
Helmingr, Gunnarr, 5:297a
Helmold of Bosau, **6:151b–152a**
Chronica Slavorum, 6:151b
meaning of title, 6:151b
source for, 6:151b
as source for later works, 6:152a
on missionary activities, 6:152a
Helmschmied, Lorenz, armor workshop of, 1:529b, 533a
Heloise
Peter Abelard and
birth of Peter Astralabe, 1:16b–17a
convent at Le Paraclet, 1:17b–18a
death and interment, 1:18a-b
letters, 1:19a-b
love affair, 1:16b
priory of Argenteuil and, 11:503a-b
see also Abelard, Peter
Helperic of Auxerre, **6:152a-b**
Computus, 6:152a
Helreið Brynhildar, **6:152b–153a,** 11:293b
dating of, 6:153a
preservation, 6:152b
self-justification of Brynhild, 6:153a
Helvetii, 11:536b
Hemerken, Thomas. *See* Thomas à Kempis
Hemmel, Peter, 5:551a, **6:153a-b**
glass painting, 6:153b (*illus.*)
Hemming, monk, 12:703b
Hemmo of Halberstadt, bishop, Hrabanus Maurus and, 6:307b
Hemp, **6:153b–154a**
bast fibers, 6:154a
cultivation, 6:154a
flax and, 3:88a-b
textiles made from, 6:154a
see also Linen
Henads, doctrine of (Proclus), 9:98a
Ḥenānā (director of the Nestorian school at Nisibis), 9:107a, 107b
Hendregadredd manuscript, 12:605b
Hendrik van Veldeke. *See* Heinrich von Veldeke
Hengham, Ralph
as justice of the King's Bench, 7:191b–192b, 194a
Summa magna, 7:192a-b
Summa parva, 7:192b
Henna, production of, 4:326a, 326b
Hennin, 2:150a, 3:623b–624a
Henotikon, **6:154b**
Akakian schism and, 6:154b, 8:477b
Monophysites and, 6:191a, 8:477b
rejection by Rome, 8:477b
see also Zeno the Isaurian, Byzantine emperor
Henri d'Andeli
Bataille des sept arts (*Battle of the Seven Arts*), 3:434b–435a, 7:368a, 10:359a, 362b
defense of dialectic, 5:255b
study of classical literature affirmed, 5:649b
"Lai d'Aristote," 1:455b, 4:575a
Henri de Courances, 11:160b
Henri de Ferrières
Jugement de chiens et d'oisiaus, 6:360a-b
Livre des deduis, 6:359b, 360b
Livre du roy Modus et de la royne Ratio, 1:189b, 6:359b–360a
Henricho, clockmaker, 3:463b
Henrico, De. See Heinrico, De
Henricus Aristippus, 9:700b, 11:274a
translations by, Plato's *Meno,* 12:139b–140a
Henricus Pomerius, biography of Ruusbroec, 9:36a
Henriquez, Charles, *Menologium Cisterciense,* 6:70b
Henry I, king of the East Franks, recognition of by Charles the Simple, 3:115a
Henry I of Bavaria, duke, 5:475b
Henry II Jasomirgott of Bavaria and Austria, duke, 2:6b, 134b, 5:479b
Rolandslied and, 10:447b
Henry X (the Proud) of Saxony and Bavaria, duke
as candidate for imperial crown, 5:478b
struggle for duchy of Saxony, 6:167b
Henry II of Castile, king, 10:52a-b
literary developments and, 11:418a-b
rule of, 3:137a-b

Henry III of Castile, king
Canary Islands and, 3:61b
rule of, 3:137b–138a
Henry IV of Castile, king
literary developments and, 11:421b–422a
Moors and, 11:378b
relations with sister Isabella, 3:138a-b
rule of, 3:138a-b
Henry I (the Liberal) of Champagne, count
fairs and, 4:591b
Latin church and, 3:245b–246a
Latin literature and, 7:364b
marriage of, 3:246b–247a
patronage of art, 3:246a-b
rule of, 3:245a-b
Henry II of Champagne, count, 3:247a
Henry III of Champagne, count, 3:249b
Henry I of Cyprus, king, 4:71a
Jean d'Ibelin and, 6:389a
Henry I of England, king, 1:253a, **6:154b–156a**
accession to throne, 6:154b
assaulted by villagers, 9:477b
charters for communes and, 3:494b
in chronicles, 12:628a
coronation charter, 4:462, 6:155a
fairs and, 4:586b
hunting park at Woodstock, 5:363b
influx of Normans and, 11:104b
introduction of scutage and, 11:120a
itinerancy of court, 9:165b–166a
kingship theories and, 7:264a
knights of, 7:278a
legal system and
court of common pleas, 3:491a
eyre system founded by, 7:442a
itinerant justices, 7:183b
justiciar, 7:199b
land dispute stipulations of, 7:434a-b
London law, 7:434b
writ to reseise, 7:437a-b
liberty and liberties and, 7:557a
marriages
to Adelaide, 6:155b
to Matilda, 6:155b
pacification of Normandy, establishment of government, 4:462b, 6:156a
reign of, 9:166b
relations with church, 6:155a
investiture conflict and, 1:313a-b
threatened excommunication, 4:466a-b
Roger of Salisbury and, 10:443a
succession problems, 4:462b, 6:155b
tax policies, 11:612a
villes neuves of, 3:498a
Vital of Savigny and, 12:480a
Henry II of England, king, 1:253a, **6:156a–158b**, 10:256a
administration of
establishment of orderly government, 4:466b–467a
financial, 4:469b
use of councils, 4:469b, 470a
Assize of Arms, 11:612a
Assize of Clarendon and, 3:408b–409a
baronial revolts, mercenary troops, 12:559a
Becket and, 2:151a–152b, 3:83a, 409b–410a
Bertran de Born and, 2:201b–202a
Canterbury pilgrimage treasury and, 9:659b
church-state relations, 7:439a–440a
intervention in church elections, 4:424b
relationship with Thomas Becket, 4:471a
restriction of ecclesial court jurisdiction, 4:471a
coins during rule of, 8:429a
conflict with his son Richard, 10:383a
Constitutions of Clarendon and, 3:409b–410b
continental possessions
arrangement for succession, 4:467a
conflict with Philip Augustus, 4:467b
destruction of adulterine castles, 6:156b
expansion of holdings, 5:161b
Labourd and Soule acquired, 2:126b
Welf-Angevin alliance, 4:467a
education, 6:156b
Ethelred of Rievaulx and, 4:517a
family and political problems, 4:420a
discussed in Peter of Blois's letters, 9:518b
Gerald of Wales as court chaplain, 5:421a
Glanville as servant of, 5:544a-b
hereditary claim to throne, 4:462b, 475a
John of Salisbury and, 7:265a
Latin literature and, 7:364b
legal system and, 1:596a-b, 4:470a-b, 6:157a
assize, 1:594b
classification of felonies, 5:43a
court of common pleas, 3:491a, 7:186b–187a
Exchequer court, 3:492a
homicide laws, 12:618a
innovations, 3:659b, 7:436b–443a, 9:260a
inquest and, 6:481a
itinerant justices, 7:183b–184a
jury, 7:182a
justices of the King's Bench, 7:190b–191a
justiciar, 7:200a
petty assizes, 9:546a–548b
royal vs. feudal courts, 7:441b
trespass, 12:185b–186a
London Bridge and, 10:414b
Malcolm IV of Scotland and, 8:57a, 11:106a
marriage of children, 6:157b
marriage to Eleanor of Aquitaine, 4:419b, 463a, 6:156b, 7:467a
military campaigns
against Philip II Augustus, 6:158a
invasion of England, 6:156b
military expenditures, 12:555a
overlordship of Scotland and, 11:107b
Plantagenet family name of, 9:693b
primogeniture and, 6:459b
Rhys of Deheubarth and, 10:378a
Robert of Melun and, 10:434b
Robert de Veneys and, 2:173b
Roman de Rou and, 12:496b
royal rights reestablished by, 7:436b–437a
scutage and, 11:120a, 613a
sheriff and, 11:225a
stabilization of English frontiers
chronicle of, 7:147b
Ireland, 9:167a
in Wales, vs. Owain Gwynedd, 6:386b
wars with Scotland and Ireland, 4:467a, 6:156b–157a, 517a-b
Stephen of Blois and, 9:166b, 167a
suppression of London's liberties and, 3:498b
tallage, 11:613a
Third Crusade and, 4:40a
travels of, 12:159a–160a
Welsh overlordship, 12:517b–518a
wine trade and, 12:649b
Henry III of England, king, **6:158b–159b**
accession to throne, 4:469a
baronial disputes, 2:111b–112b, 4:481a, 481b, 6:159a
bastides and, 2:128b
Canterbury and, 3:83b
church taxation and, 11:607a-b
commercial policies, 6:91a
defeated by Blanche of Castile, 2:270b
Dictum of Kenilworth, 12:529a
diplomatic blanks of, 4:209a
guardianship, 12:636a
Henry of Avranches and, 7:369a
hereditary claim to throne, 4:472b–473a, 475a
Ireland and, 6:517b
Langton and, 7:338b
legal system and
abuses of distress, 4:221a
justices of common pleas, 7:188a
justices of the King's Bench, 7:191a
justiciar, 7:200a-b
marriage to Eleanor of Provence, 6:158b
military capabilities, 6:158b–159a
military draft, 11:612a
parliament and, 4:481a–482b, 9:423b
Provisions of Oxford and, 10:195a-b
Raymond VII and, 6:486b
regency of, 6:158b
relations with church, 6:159a
interference in elections, 4:423b
revolt against, 4:160b
royal wardrobe and, 6:302a, 302b
Sicily and, 4:60a, 11:272a
Siena and, 11:279a
Simon de Montfort the Younger and, 11:297a–298a
in *Song of Lewes,* 11:372b
Statute of Marlborough (1267) and, 7:444a-b
taxation
of movables, 11:614a
scutage, 11:120b, 613a
tallage, 11:613a

Henry III of England, king (*cont.*)
touching for king's evil, 7:256a
vs. Llywelyn ap Gruffydd, 7:637a
Welsh overlordship, 12:520b–521a
Treaty of Montgomery, 12:521a-b, 529a
Westminster Abbey constructed, 12:621b
Henry IV of England, king, **6:159b**
attainder and, 6:428a
Chaucer and, 3:290a, 290b
coronation ceremony, 4:476b
English as mother tongue of, 1:259a
fur robe of, 5:325b
letter to Prester John, 10:119a
in Middle English prophecies, 10:146b, 147b, 148b–149a
Richard II and, 4:476b, 7:135a, 9:430b–431a, 10:384b
succession confirmed by parliament, 9:429b
Taverner and, 2:157b
Henry V of England, king, **6:160a–161b**
chantry chapel of in Westminster Abbey, 12:29 (*illus.*)
in chronicles, 3:328a
claim to throne, 4:477a
Commons' right to petition and, 9:433b
death of, 3:271b
Hoccleve and, 8:323b
in Hundred Years War, 6:332a
invasion of Normandy, 6:160b, 9:169b
Treaty of Troyes and, 10:320a–321a
John Lydgate and, 8:323a
in literature, 7:370a
membership in king's council, 6:160a
military capabilities, 6:160a
music in household chapel of, 9:232a
naval force of, 9:83a
Order of the Most Holy Savior and, 9:15a, 27a
relations with church, 6:161a
religious and political revolts against, 6:160a
shipbuilding and, 11:244b
Signet correspondence of, 8:313b, 323a
taxation, 11:616a
Vincent Ferrer and, 12:453a
Henry VI of England, king, **6:161b–162a**
assumption of throne, 5:144a
battles with Edward IV, 5:144a
Cade's rebellion and, 3:4b–5b
Canterbury and, 3:83b
claim to throne, 4:477a, 6:161b
parliamentary decree, 4:477b–478a
coronation banquet, 4:477a-b
embassy of, 4:209b
factional struggles during reign, 6:161b
ineffectiveness of leadership, 12:569b
insanity of, 6:161b–162a
recovery described in Paston letters, 9:451a
justices of the King's Bench and, 7:194a
marriage to Margaret of Anjou, 6:161b
parliament and, 9:429b, 430a-b
peasant rebellions against, 12:569b–570a
"readeption" of throne, 6:162a
Richard III and, 10:385a
tomb of, 4:510b
visit to Lynn, 3:90a
vs. Charles VII, 3:65a
Wars of the Roses and, 12:569b–571a
Henry VII of England, king
accession to throne, 4:479a
claim to throne, 4:472b–473a
defeat of Richard III, 10:385b, 12:524b
finance and, 4:533a
gardens of, 5:363a
Ireland and, 6:520a
parliament and, 9:431a-b
Poynings' Law and, 9:437a
rebellion of John de la Pole, 12:572a
shilling and, 11:229a
tomb of by Pietro Torrigiano, 12:88b (*illus.*)
Welsh reforms, 12:524b
Welsh Act of Union, 12:527a
Henry VIII of England, king, 9:682
armor of, 1:529b, 531a
caesaropapism and, 3:11b
dissolution of the monasteries, 2:157a, 157b
fur robe of, 5:325b
Ireland and, 6:520b
parliament and, 10:327b
praemunire and, 10:68b
right of asylum and, 1:632a
Succession Acts of, 9:430a
Welsh administration, control of marcher lords, 12:528b
Henry I of France, king
Leo IX and, 3:634a
Paris under, 9:402b
seal of, 11:129b
Henry II of France, king
armor of, 1:529b
representative assemblies and, 10:324b
Siena and, 11:282a
Henry III of France, king, representative assemblies and, 10:316b
Henry I of Germany, emperor
accession to throne, 4:426a
Burchard II and, 11:527a
duchies and, 5:508a–509b
expansion of authority, 10:682a, 683b
fortification of Saxony, 10:684a
Gesta Ottonis and, 6:316a
Magyars and, 5:475a, 10:684a
military games of, 5:349b
problems facing, 5:475a
"Rudolphians" and, 11:538a
seal wax impression of, 11:125a
in Thietmar von Merseburg's chronicle, 12:28a
vs. Magyars, 6:339a
Henry II of Germany, emperor
alliance with Ljutizi, 10:684b
Bebo and, 2:150b
Benno of Osnabrück and, 2:182a
Billungs and, 2:235a
Burgundy and, 2:429a
coronation of, 3:677a, 8:378a
election of, 4:426b
Evangeliary of Henry II, 12:123 (*illus.*)
foundation of Bamberg, 5:476a
in Italy, 6:468a
Poland and, 9:719a-b
Poppo appointed as abbot of Fulda, 5:312a
reign of, 5:476b–477a
in song, 3:57b
succession principle affirmed, 5:477a
in Thietmar von Merseburg's chronicle, 12:27b–28a
Henry III of Germany, emperor, **6:162a–163a**
alliance of noblemen against, 6:162b
Basel and, 11:538a
Billungs and, 2:235a
Burgundy and, 2:429a
church reform and, 6:499a, 11:265a
death of, 3:351a
Goslar residence, 6:162b, 10:684b
Hungary and, 6:340a
Italian policies, 3:558a
marriage to Agnes of Poitou, 6:162b
Nuremberg and, 9:201a
papal reform and, 3:348b
Peter Damian and, 9:508b
reestablishment of Austrian-Hungarian border, 6:162a
relations with church, 6:162b
Leo IX and, 3:351a, 7:543b
papal appointments, 6:162b
reform of papacy, 5:477b
in song, 3:57b
Synod of Sutri and, 11:517a, 517b
Wipo and, 12:655b, 656a
Henry IV of Germany, emperor, **6:163a-b**
abdication, 6:163b
Benno of Osnabrück and, 2:182a
Benzo of Alba and, 2:182b
Billungs and, 2:235a-b
in *Carmen de bello saxonico*, 3:97a
Desiderius of Monte Cassino and, 4:164b
enfeoffment of Hirsau, 6:231b
escape to Eschwege, 10:273a
excommunication, 10:684b–685a
Frederick I and, 11:527a-b
Italian campaign, 6:163b
Lambert and, 7:321b
recuperation of Saxon territories, 10:684b
regency of, 6:163a
relations with church, 6:163a
Gregory VII and, 3:69a-b, 351b, 5:477b, 670a-b, 9:378a-b, 10:288a, 523a
investiture controversy, 6:499a-b, 7:262a-b
papal elections and, 3:634b
Paschal II and, 9:445a-b
revolt against, 3:481a, 5:477b
Robert Guiscard and, 10:433a
Roman Capitol and, 10:519b
Tuscan communes and, 3:500a
Vratislav II of Bohemia and, 2:299b

vs. Gregory VII, Richard Guiscard and, 11:265b
vs. Rudolf of Swabia, 6:448b
Welfs and, 11:527b
Henry V of Germany, emperor
attack on Cologne, 3:481a
Concordat of Worms and, 12:697a
duchy of Saxony and, 5:511a
invasion of Poland, 9:720b
investiture controversy and, 5:478a, 6:499b, 10:685a
Irnerius and, 6:555a
Matilda of Tuscany and, 8:223a
opposition to, 5:478a
Paschal II and, 3:635b–636a, 9:445b
rebellion against father, 6:163b
release of from prison, 3:498a
Henry VI of Germany, emperor, **6:164a-b**
crowning of, 5:482a
Cyprus and, 4:70b
death of, 4:153b
papal states and, 9:385a
hereditary principle of monarchy and, 4:427b, 5:482a, 491b
Italian campaigns, 5:482a-b
conquest of Sicily, 6:273b
limitation on authority of Florence, 5:94a
literary works, 6:164a
lyrics for minnesingers, 8:413b
Markward of Anweiler and, 11:269b
marriage of, 4:58a, 5:481a
ministerials and, 8:405b
as patron of poetry, 5:435a
relations with church, papacy and, 3:353a, 5:482a
Richard I the Lionhearted and, 10:383b
rise of, 5:482a
Sicilian succession and, 9:58a
Sicily and, 11:269a-b
Henry VII of Germany, emperor
authority of, 5:484b
deposition of, 5:485a
heretics and, 5:484b
regents of, 5:484a
Cino da Pistoia and, 3:397b
Dante and, 4:101b–102b, 103b
election to throne, 6:273b
Italian expedition, 5:96b–97a, 6:11b
Matteo Visconti and, 12:464b
as patron of poetry, 5:435a
reign of, 5:488a
Siena and, 11:279b–280a
taxation for public works approved, 10:418a
Unterwalden and, 11:542a
Henry I of Jerusalem, emperor, in Robert de Clari's *La conquête de Jerusalem,* 10:431b
Henry I of Navarre, king, 9:71a
Henry X (the Proud) of Saxony and Bavaria, duke, vs. Conrad III, 2:134b
Henry IV Probus of Wrocław, duke, 9:721a, 723a
Henry of Albano, cardinal, mission against Cathars, 3:187
Henry of Avranches
Archpoet and, 1:450a
vs. Blaunpayn, 7:369a
Henry Bate of Malines (Mecheln), 9:702b
Henry of Blois, bishop of Winchester
legatine powers of, 7:535a
Vacarius and, 12:343b
Henry of Burgundy, count of Portucale, 10:39a-b
Henry of Cremona, **6:165b**
Henry d'Emondeville. *See* Henry de Mondeville
Henry of Flanders, Latin emperor of Constantinople, 7:346a-b, 347a, 348b
Villehardouin and, 7:378a, 12:448b
vs. Theodore I Laskaris, 7:347b, 9:116b–117a
Henry of Ghent, **6:165b–166b**, 9:702b
against Thomism, 12:41b
Aristotle and, 1:463b
condemnation of (1277), 6:166a
revival of Augustinism, 4:309a, 6:166a, 9:611b–612a
theology of, 6:166a
Henry of Gorkum, as defender of Thomism, 12:42a
Henry of Halle, 4:248a-b, 9:11a
Henry of Harclay, 9:156a
Henry of Hesse. *See* Henry of Langenstein
Henry of Huntingdon, 7:367a
Roger of Salisbury and, 10:443b
Henry of Isernia, *dictamen* of, 4:175a, 176a
Henry Kietlicz, archbishop, 9:721a
Henry of Kirkestede, *Catalogus scriptorum ecclesiae,* 1:206b
Henry of Lancaster, duke, *Livre de seyntz medicines,* 1:263b, **7:635a-b**
Henry of Langenstein, **6:166b–167a**
on astronomy, 1:613b, 614b
conciliarist views, 3:646a
Contra astrologos conjunctionistas eventibus futurorum, 6:166b
De reprobatione eccentricorum et epiciclorum, 1:614b
Epistola concilii pacis, 3:511b, 6:166b
Epistola pacis, 6:166b
on Great Schism, 10:23b
influence of on Michel Beheim, 8:306b
Lecturae super Genesium, 6:167a
Quaestio de cometa, 6:166b
Speculum animae, 6:166b
tenure at University of Vienna, 6:166b–167a
Henry of Langton-by-Wragby, lord, 7:337b
Henry of Lausanne, campaign against corrupt clergy, 6:195b
Henry of Lübeck, as defender of Thomism, 12:42a
Henry of Luxembourg. *See* Henry VII of Germany
Henry the Minstrel, **6:169a**
Wallace, The, 6:169a
Henry de Mondeville, **6:164b–165b**
Anathomia, 6:164b–165a
Chirurgia, 6:165a, 8:251a
medicine as main topic, 6:164b
writing style, 6:165a
Henry the Navigator of Portugal, prince
African trade and, 4:561a
Azores and, 2:29b, 4:559b
Canary Islands and, 3:63a
Cape Verde Islands and, 4:561b
exploration of, 8:445b
Madeira Islands and, 4:559a
settlement of Madeira Islands and, 8:10b
Henry of Nördlingen. *See* Heinrich von Nördlingen
Henry the Pious. *See* Henry (the Pious) of Silesia
Henry Raspe of Thuringia, landgrave, 5:485a
Henry of Reynes, **6:167a-b**
Henry, Roy, identity of, 9:231b
Henry of Saltrey. *See* Hugh of Saltrey
Henry of Settimello, 7:365b
Henry (son of David I of Scotland), 4:316a-b
Henry (son of Frederick II of Germany), 11:270a
alienation of German princes, 5:215a
imprisonment by father, 5:215a
Uri and, 11:541a
Henry of Susa. *See* Hostiensis
Henry (the Bearded) of Wrocław, duke, 9:721a
Henry (the Fowler) of Saxony, duke. *See* Henry I of Germany, emperor
Henry (the Lion) of Bavaria and Saxony, duke, **6:167b–168b**
alliance of Saxon princes against, 6:168b
ancestry, 6:167a
Bavaria and, 2:134b, 6:168a
Denmark and, 4:153b
dispossession of Adolf of Schauenburg, 5:460a
Eilhart as vassal of, 12:204a-b
establishment of trade center, 6:90b
foundation of Munich, 6:168a
Frederick I Barbarossa and, 5:213b, 480a, 481b, 6:168a, 10:685b
heraldic seal of, 11:129b
invasion of Nordalbingia, 6:168a
loss of fiefs, 6:168b
marriage to Matilda of England, 6:168a
opposition to, 5:511a
refounding of Lübeck, 7:680a
Reinfrid von Braunschweig as oldest legend of, 10:292a
return from exile, 5:482a
Rolandslied and, 10:447b
Saxony and, 5:479b, 6:168a, 10:685a
Wendish Crusade, 12:617a-b
Henry (the Pious) of Silesia, vs. Mongols, 2:131b
Henry (the Young King) of England, prince
coronation, 2:152a-b
friendship with Bertran de Born, 2:201b–202a
land inheritance, 4:467a
marriage, 2:151a
revolt against brother John, 4:467b
revolt against father, 7:147b

Henry Totting von Oyta, nominalism and, 9:157a
Henry of Trastámara, civil war with Pedro the Cruel, 9:71b
Henry of Virneburg, archbishop of Cologne
  charges of heresy against Meister Eckhart and, 9:32a
  synodal decree of 1306, 5:217b
Henry of Werl, bishop of Paderborn. *See* Heinrich von Werl, bishop of Paderborn
Henry of Winchester, bishop, Roger of Salisbury and, 10:443b
Henry the Wrangler, guardianship of Otto III, 9:302a
Henryson, Robert, **6:169a-b**, 8:324a-b, 332a, 11:112b, 12:476b
  Fables
    narratives and *moralitates,* 6:169a
    sources for, 6:169a
  influence of Chaucer on, 6:169a
  Orpheus and Eurydice, 6:169b
  Testament of Cresseid, 6:169a
    use of "rhyme royal" in, 8:346a
  Walter the Englishman and, 7:366b–367a
Hephaistion, *Encheiridion,* 11:52a
Hephthalites, **6:169b–170a**
  appearance and social customs, 6:170a
  language, 6:170a
  Sasanian king Kawād and, 8:236b
  vs. Armenians, 6:170a
  vs. Sasanians, 1:476b, 10:669b, 670b
  vs. Xusrō I, 12:714a
Heptaméron, L', **6:170b–171a**
  early editions, 6:170b
  identification of narrators, 6:170b
  theme, 6:170b
  unifying structure, 6:170b
Heptateuchon. See Thierry of Chartres
Heptateuchos. See Cyprian (Gallic poet)
Heraclea, metropolitan of, at the permanent synod, 9:505b
Heracles Papyrus, 4:292a
Heraclias. See George of Pisidia
Heraclius. *See* Heraklios, Byzantine emperor
Herakleides of Tarentum, 8:244a
Heraklids, **6:171a**
Heraklios, Byzantine emperor, 3:630b, **6:171a–172a**, 9:697a
  Armenia and, 1:478a
  attempts to reconcile Monophysites, 6:191a
  classicism in art under, 4:353a
  coinage of, 8:419a
  Cyprus silver plates made for, 4:362a
  depicted in Berthold Missal, 8:108b (*illus.*)
  discussed in the *Patmut^{c}iwn Tarōnoy,* 9:457b
  efforts to reform Christology, 6:171b
  Ekthesis, 8:233a, 478a-b, 9:561a
  execution of Phokas, 6:171b
  Ezr and, 1:500a
  free issues of bread and, 12:100b
  George of Pisidia's writings on, 5:400a
  in legends and prophecies, 8:20a
  military defeats, 6:171b
  mint closings during rule of, 8:420a-b
  Pontus under, 10:31b
  reign of
    described by Sebēos, 11:132b
    in *Paschale chronicon,* 9:446a
  reorganization of army, 6:171b
  sack of Ganjak of Atropatene, 5:356a
  Sergios I and, 11:209a
  Syrian Orthodox Church and, 11:563b
  themata and, 10:460a
  Theophylaktos Simokattes and, 12:24b–25a
  vs. Muslims, 6:568a-b
    in Syria, 11:559b
  vs. Persians (628), 2:487a, 4:339b, 6:171b
    in Syria, 11:559b
  vs. Phokas, 10:453b
  vs. Sasanians, 10:670b
  vs. Xusrō II, 12:715a
  Yarmuk and, 12:719a
Herald of Honor from the Rhine. *See* Reinmar von Zweter
Heraldry, **6:172a–177a**
  after 14th century
    as decorative symbol, 6:175b
    legal significance, 6:175b
  animal motifs, 6:175a
  armorial display, 6:174b (*illus.*)
  arms and badges, 6:173a (*illus.*)
  banners and standards, 6:176a
  Burgundian, in tapestry, 11:597b (*illus.*)
  canting arms, 6:175a
  chivalry and, 3:302a
  classification of heralds, 6:172a
  combining of arms in one shield, 6:175a
    courtoisie, 6:175b
  criteria of true, 6:172a
  definition, 6:172a
  differencing, 6:173b (*illus.*)
  iconography on seals and, 11:129a-b
  lines of partition, 6:174a (*illus.*)
  marks of cadency, 6:175b
  national differences, 6:172a
  occasional roles, 6:176a
  ordinaries, 6:174a (*illus.*), 175a
  origin of, 1:524a
  personal badges, 6:175b–176a
  purpose of, identification in battle, 6:172a
  subordinaries and furs, 6:174a (*illus.*)
  symbolic value of colors, 6:172b
  terminology for describing, 6:172b–175a
    furs and precious stones, 6:173a
    influence of French-speaking crusaders, 6:173a
    tincture of field, 6:173b–175a
  see also Blazon; Coats of arms
Heralds. *See* Heraldry
Herat
  battle at (1270), 6:420a
  as capital of Timurid state, 12:56b–57b
  center of Timurid bookbinding, 8:99b–100a
  conquered by Shaybānī Khan in 1507, 12:58a
  cultural flowering under Ḥusayn Bayqarā, 12:59a
  as Iranian cultural capital, 1:65b
Herb gardens, Western European, 5:359b–360b
Herbals, Arabic, **6:177a–180b**
  alphabetical format, 6:179b
  function
    as guidebooks to useful plants, 6:179b
    library showpieces, 6:179b
    therapeutic, 6:179b–180a
  illustrations, 6:178b
  knowledge of herbal medicine, 6:178b–179a
  overlapping of theory and lore, 6:179a
  for pharmacological and toxological purposes, 6:179a
  translations from Greek, 6:178b
Herbals, Byzantine, **6:177a–180b**
  agricultural and veterinary manuals, 6:178a
  alphabetical format, 6:178a, 179b
  function
    as guidebooks to useful plants, 6:179b
    library showpieces, 6:179b
    therapeutic, 6:179b–180a
  illustrations
    problems with, 6:177b–178a
    source for, 6:177a
    three traditions, 6:178a
  pharmacological, 6:177b
  see also Dioscorides, *De materia medica*
Herbals, Western European, **6:180b–182a**, 8:250a
  De viribus herbarum, 9:220a-b
  decline in popularity, 6:181b
  definition of, 2:345b
  format, 6:181a
    indexes, 6:181a
  French, 5:281a
  illustrations, 6:180b
  information contained in, 6:180b
  language, 6:181a
  for medicinal purposes, 6:180b, 181a
  for monastic study, 6:181b
  recipes for hair care, 2:148b–149a
  see also Plants, medieval study of
Herbarius. See Pseudo-Apuleius
Herber, 5:362a
Herberay des Essarts, Cancionero de. See Cancionero de Herberay des Essarts
Herbert I of Vermandois, count, 12:395b
Herbert II of Vermandois, count, 3:243b, 12:395b–396a
Herbert of Auxerre, William of Auxerre's theology school and, 12:22a
Herbert of Bosham, 3:313b
  commentary on the Psalms, 2:213b
  life of St. Thomas Becket, 12:35b
  on Peter Lombard, 9:516b
Herbert (the Younger) of Meaux-Troyes, count, 3:243b

Herbertian family, 9:148b
Herbort von Fritzlar, **6:182a-b**
authorship of Pilate legend, 6:182b
Liet von Troye, 5:450a-b, 6:182a
source for, 6:182b
Herbs, **6:183a–184b**
as contraceptives
Europe, 3:572a
Islam, 3:574b–575a
dermatological uses, 6:184a
in gargles and antiperspirants, 6:184b
herbal cosmetics
for the complexion, 6:183b–184a
in diet or medicinal form, 6:183a
hair coloring, 6:183b
hair growers, 6:183a
sun-screen lotions, 6:183b
Middle Eastern, **6:184b–187a**
in art, 6:186b
cultivation of, 6:186a
economic importance, 6:186a
floral terminology in literature, 6:185a
illustrations, 6:185b
spices, 6:186a
study of, 6:184b–185b
therapeutic value, 6:185a, 186a
uses of, 6:185b–186b
Herceg, 11:476a
Hercegovina, Stefan Vukčić Kosača and, 11:476a
Heredia, Juan Fernández de, *Grant crónica de Espanya,* 11:435b
Hereditary status. *See* Status
Hereford, mystery plays and, 8:658b
Hereford map, 5:397a
see also Mappa mundi
Hereford, Nicholas, 2:222a
Wyclif Bible and, 8:318a
Wycliffite views, 7:645b–646a
Hereford rite, **6:187a**
transfer to Savoy, 6:187a
Heregeld, 4:90b
see also Gelds
Herem ha-ᶜikkul (Jewish ban on confiscation), 7:70b
Herem ha-yishuv (residency limitation in Jewish communities), 7:70a
Heresies, Armenian, **6:187b–190a**
Arewordikᶜ, doctrine and origin, 6:188b
Arianism, 6:187b
Christology, 6:187b, 188a
Iconoclasm, 6:188b
Nestorianism, 6:187b
Paulicians, 6:188b–189a
Tᶜondrakecᶜi, 5:674a
doctrines, 6:189b
origins, 6:189a
sect leaders, 6:189a
survival of, 6:189b
Heresies, Byzantine, **6:190a–193a**
christological, 6:190a–191b
dualistic, 6:191b–192b
Hellenic, 6:192b
iconoclastic, 6:191b
individual heretics, 6:192b
of John Italos, 7:131b–132a
Origenist, 9:278a
Platonism and, 9:697b–698a
sources of information on, 6:190a
see also Bogomilism; Paulicians; Schisms, Eastern-Western church
Heresies, Islamic, **6:204b–207a**
persecution of under the Mamluk dynasty, 8:71b
threat to Abbasid rule, 1:8a
see also Sects, Islamic
Heresies, Western European, **6:193a–202b**
Abelard and, 12:191a
adoptionism (Gallic), 12:190b
Albigensians, 12:191a
antinomianism, 5:216a
Arianism, 12:189a–191b
Arundel's Constitutions, 7:647a
Cathars, 3:181a–191a
De heretico comburendo, 7:646b
Eckhart von Hochheim, 4:381a
English universities and, 3:59a-b
French, 6:466b
in Germany (1138–1254), 5:484b
Gilbert of Poitiers, 5:528a
Gottschalk of Orbais, 5:638a–639a
Gregorian reform movement and, 6:195a
historiographical concerns, 6:200b–201a
idealist vs. materialist interpretations, 6:200a
interrelation with orthodoxy, 6:193a
clarification of doctrine, 6:193b
Joachim of Fiore and, 12:191a-b, 195b, 196a
learned, 6:194a
Lollards, 7:645a–648b
Macedonianism, 12:189a
of Margery (Burnham) Kempe, 7:229a
nominalism, 12:191a
"of the three languages," 2:463b
Orléans, 12:660b, 661a, 661b
popular
church response to, 6:197b–198a
condemnation at Orléans, 6:194b
11th century, 6:194a
Priscillians, 12:190a
Roman commune, 6:196a
Sabellianism, 12:189a–190a
Scholastic, 6:198a
Trinitarian doctrine and, 12:189a–191b
12th century
movement against corrupt clergy, 6:195a
recurring features, 6:194b–195a
unicity of God, 12:191a, 197a-b
Waldensians, 12:191a, 508a–513a
wandering hermits, 6:195a
war against, 4:15b, 17a,b
see also Albigensians, crusade against
Heresy, Christian, **6:202b–204b**
apostolic succession and, 1:350b
beguines and, 2:159a
beguins and, 2:162a, 162b
and church intervention in canonization, 6:68b–69a
comparison with disease, 6:204a
definition, 6:202b, 203b–204a
Aquinas', 6:203b–204a
denial of transubstantiation as, 7:648a
etymology, 6:202b–203a
false gospels, 6:203a-b
Fourth Lateran Council on, 6:465a
Gregory IX on, 5:671a
growth of mendicant orders and, 5:175b, 200b
hairesis in the New Testament
Acts of the Apostles, 6:203a
in the Latin Vulgate, 6:203a
teaching of St. Paul, 6:203a-b
heretics vs. apostates, 6:204a
interdict and, 6:495b, 496a
interrelationship with orthodoxy, 6:203b
Joachim of Fiore and, 7:114a
John of Ōjun on, 7:125a
in Latin church (1305–1500), 3:367b–371b
organizations for combatting, 3:186b
ownership of vernacular scriptures as, 7:648a
punishment for, 6:204a
first instance of, 1:453b
punishment of, *De heretico comburendo* and, 12:709b
schism and, 6:204a
of sectarian behavior, 6:203a
torture in trials of heretics, 12:90a
witchcraft and, 12:658b, 660a-b
see also Blasphemy; Inquisition
Heresy, Islamic, **6:204b–207a**
abrogation of Muḥammad's law, 6:206a
heresiography, 6:206b
heretical terms, 6:206b
pantheism, 6:206a
political basis for, 6:204b–205a
murder of ᶜUthmān, 6:205a
right of judgment, 6:205a
wars against ᶜAlī, 6:205a
Sunna vs. Shīᶜa, 6:205b
Herger, **11:461b–463a**
education and poetry of, 11:462a-b
identity of, 11:461b
see also Spervogel
Heribert of Cologne, archbishop
Lantbert, 7:342a
in song, 3:57b
Heribert of Eichstadt, **6:207a**
Heribert of Rothenburg, song attributed to, 3:58a
Heribrand, 8:255b
Hericus of Friuli, Paulinus of Aquileia and, 9:470b
Heriger of Lobbes, **6:207a-b**
Herimar of St. Rémi at Rheims, abbot, 3:634a
Heriot, **6:207b–208a**
death levy (12th century), 6:207b
Norman relief and, 6:207b
purposes of, 6:207b
Herland, Hugh, **6:208a**, 12:724b
Hermagoras of Temnos, 10:351b
Herman the German, **6:208a–209a**
historic importance, 6:208a
translations
of Aristotle, 6:208b
of al-Fārābī, 10:357b
from Arabic, 6:208b
Herman of Scheda, 10:3b
Herman de Valenciennes, 4:546b
Bible de sapience, 2:215a, 9:638b

Hermandad de la Marina de Castilla, 6:209b
Hermandades, **6:209a–210a**
of Castile, 3:134b, 137b, 139a
of Castile and León, protective measures used, 6:209b–210a
election of officials, 6:209b
in 15th-century Spain, 6:210a
oath of brotherhood, 6:209a
origins of, 6:209a, 358a
protection of crown, 6:210a
types of
bourgeoisie against oppressive lords, 6:209b
for commercial interests, 6:209b
groups of monasteries, 6:209b
trade associations, 6:209a-b
urban leagues, 6:209b–210a
see also Aragon, Crown of
Hermann I of Swabia, duke, 11:527a
Hermann II of Swabia, duke, 11:527a
Hermann I of Thuringia, landgrave
as patron of literature, 5:435a-b, 6:182a
Wolfram von Eschenbach and, 12:674a, 676a
Hermann Billung of Saxony, 2:235a
Hermann von Carinthia, **6:210b–211a**
Arabic numerals and, 10:473a, 474a
De essentiis, 6:210b–211a
Liber trium judicum, 10:473b
translations, 12:138a, 139a-b, 140a
Fatidica, 6:210b
of the Koran, 6:210b
Planisphere, 6:210b, 211a
Hermann of Cologne, archbishop, Lantbert and, 7:342a
Hermann of Dalmatia, 1:611b
Hermann Joseph, 10:87a
Hermann von Reichenau, **6:211a–212a**
alphabetic notation and, 8:615a, 626b, 627a
with an astrolabe in a miniature, 11:100b
Chronicon, 6:211b
De mensura astrolabii, 1:611a
De utilitatibus astrolabii, 1:611a
hymns of, 6:381b
invention of the cylinder sundial, 3:28b
Musica, 8:641b–642a
musical compositions, 6:211b
Musica, 6:211b
systems of notation, 6:211b
poetry, 6:211b
scientific works, 6:211b
teacher of Meinzo of Constance, 8:266a
Hermann von Sachsenheim, **6:212a-b**
genre and style, 6:212a
Goldene Tempel, 8:412a
Grasmetze, 6:212a, 8:412b
Jesus der Artz, 8:412a
Mörin, 6:212a, 8:361a, 412b
postclassical tendencies, 6:212b
religious works, 6:212a-b
Schleiertüchlein, 8:412b
Spiegel, 8:412b
Unminne, 8:412b
Hermann of Saxony, margrave, 10:684a
Hermann of Swabia, duke, 5:509a
Hermannus Contractus. *See* Hermann von Reichenau
Hermeias, *Explanation of the Platonic Chariot-driving of Souls...,* 9:698a
Hermeneia. See Dionysios of Fourna
Hermeneumata, Vocabularius Sancti Galli and, 12:487b
"Hermeneutic" Latin language. *See* Hisperic Latin
Hermeneutics. *See* Bible, interpretation of; Gloss
Hermes Trismegistus, 1:605a
Hermit poetry. *See* Irish literature, religious
Hermitages, Islamic. *See Zāwīya*
Hermits, **6:212b–214a**, 9:658a
in Celtic church, 3:231b
first hermit, 6:213a
France and Italy, common characteristics, 6:213b
and Gregorian reform, 6:214a
heretical teachings, 6:195a
hermits vs. cenobites, 6:213b
Irish, 6:553b
in Iceland, 6:392a-b
Jerome on, 7:57b, 58a
monastic desert, idea of reform and, 10:285a-b
orthodox view of, 6:213b
Peter Damian's teachings and, 9:508a-b
as preachers, 6:214a
precedents for, 6:212b–213a
revival of eremitism by Camaldolese Order, 10:527a
Robert d'Arbrissel and, 10:429a
Syrian, 6:213a
eccentric behavior of, 6:213a-b
women's orders and, 12:686a
see also Anchorites; *Ancrene Riwle*
Hermits of Morrone. *See* Celestines
Hermits of St. Augustine. *See* Augustinian Friars
Hermits of St. Damian. *See* Celestines
Hermits of St. William. *See* Williamites
Hermogenes, school exercises of translated into Latin, 10:357b
Hermoldus, abbot, identified with Ermoldus Nigellus, 4:507b
Hermóðr, in the Baldr myth, 2:55b
Hernac (son of Attila), 6:354a
Hernando de Talavera, archbishop
lost sermons by, 11:456a
Mudejars and, 11:380b
Herneis *le romanceeur,* 8:104a
Hernia repairs, 2:99a
Hero of Alexandria
Archimedes and, 1:434a, 435a
Automata, 11:641a
Catoptrics, 9:240b
Kamarika, 6:566b
Mechanica (*Mechanics*), 1:434b, 11:633a-b
Arabic translation, 11:641a
Qusṭā ibn Lūqā's translation of, 12:132b–133a
Pneumatica, 5:363b, 11:641a
water-driven theatrical machine, 11:633b (*illus.*)
Herod, king. *See* Play of Herod
Herodian of Alexandria, *Universal Prosody,* 11:51b, 52a
Herodotus, 5:419b
on Kurds, 7:310a
Persian Wars, 7:221a
on Sahara, 2:186a
Herod's Temple. *See* Jerusalem, Temple of
Heroides. See Ovid
Herophilos of Chalcedon, 8:244a
Herpin. See Lion de Bourges
Herr Ivan Lejonriddaren, 4:519b, 520a
Herrad of Hohenberg, abbess
Hortus deliciarum, 4:448b
depiction of vehicles in, 12:373a
illumination of, 12:160b
Herrand of Ilsenburg, 5:578b
Herrand von Wildonie, **6:214a–215a**
"Betrogene Gatte," 6:214b
"Katze," 6:214b
"Nackte Kaiser," 6:214b
songs in *Manessische Liederhandschrift,* 6:214b
"Treue Gattin," 6:214b
Herred (Scandinavian local unit), 10:699a-b, 700a
Herrera, Gabriel Alonso de, *Obra de agricultura,* 1:81b
Herring
Atlantic (*Clupea harengus*), 5:70b–71b
Atlanto-scandic stock, 5:71a-b
bank-stock, 5:71a
down-stock, 5:70b–71a
dwarf (*Culpea harengus membras*), 5:71b
fishing of, 5:67 (map), 70b–71b
Herring cran, 12:586a
Herring trade
at fairs, 4:586a, 587b
Denmark, 4:149b
Hersende de Champagne, Fontevrault order and, 10:429b, 430a
Hersir (title of Norwegian leader), 10:701a
Hertford, Synod of (673), reorganization of English church, 12:13b
Hertig Fredrik av Normandie, 4:519b, 520a
Heruli, 11:335a
Hervaeus Natalis
censure of Durand of St. Pourçain, 4:313b
Defensio doctrinae fratris Thomae, 12:41b–42a
Hervagius, Johannes, 8:643b
Hervarar saga ok Heiðreks konungs, 4:387b, 388a, **6:215a–216a**
dating of, 6:215a
Grógaldr and, 11:524b
Hrómundar saga and, 6:312a-b
"Odin's question" and, 12:344b
older poems inserted in, 6:215a
plot summary, significance of Tyrfingr, 6:215b
preservation of *Hlǫðskviða,* 6:268a-b
sources for, 6:215b
two versions of story, 6:215a-b
Hervé of Bangor, bishop, 2:71b, 72a
Hervis de Metz. See Lotharingian cycle
Herz, Das, 8:411b

Herzeloyde (romance character), 12:675a, 676b–677a
Herzmaere, Das. See Konrad von Würzburg
Herzog Ernst, **6:216a–217a**
Latin versions, 6:216b
plot summary, 6:216a-b
Reinfrid von Braunschweig and, 10:292a
sources for story, 6:216a
Ulrich von Eschenbach and, 6:216b, 12:250a
variants of, 6:216b
Wolfram von Eschenbach and, 12:674b
Hesbert
Antiphonale missarum sextuplex, 9:689a-b
Corpus antiphonalium officii, 9:691b
Hesiod, *Works and Days,* illustrated copies, 11:634b
Hesperinos, in *Akolouthiai,* 8:555b
Hesse
landgraves of, 5:499b
tenurial development, 11:681b
Hesso, on Synod of Rheims, 3:636a-b
Hestia Polyolbos, tapestry of, 3:589b
Hesychasm, **6:217a–218a**, 9:7b
at Mount Athos, 1:636b
in Bulgaria, 2:413b
Byzantine oratory and, 10:350b
controversies about, 6:218a
etymology, 6:217a
Gregory Palamas and, 5:672b
integration of secular and monastic liturgies and, 7:611b
John VI Kantakouzenos and, 7:128b
Kievan monasticism, 10:595a
Macarian writings, 6:217a-b
Nikephoros Gregoras and, 9:133b
Nil Sorsky and, 9:137a
opposition to, 2:501b
origins, 9:562b–563a
prayer of Jesus, 6:217b
prayer of the mind, 6:217a
psychosomatic methods of prayer, 6:217b
revival of, 2:469b
Sergius of Radonezh and, 11:209a
Walachia/Moldavia, 12:504b
Zealots and, 12:743a
see also Barlaam of Calabria
Hesychios of Miletos, biographical dictionary (*Onomatologos*), as source for *Suda,* 11:53b, 501b
Hesychius, *Commentary on the Book of Job,* 1:508b
Het spel vanden heilighen sacramente vander Nyeuwervaert, 4:322a
Hetel, king of Denmark (epic character), 7:304a-b, 305a
Heterodox Aristotelianism. *See* Aristotelianism, Averroist
Heteroousians. *See* Anomoeanism
Heterophony, Western, 8:592a, 593a
Hetoimasia, **6:218a-b**, 6:218b (*illus.*), 10:263a
objects accompanying, 6:218a
Roman imperial and funerary motif, 6:218a-b
Het῾um I of Cilician Armenia, king, **6:219a**
cathedral built by, 11:314a
chronology, 6:220a
Kirakos of Ganjak and, 7:272a
pursuit of Cilician-Mongol alliance, 6:219a
Smbat Sparapet and, 11:351b
Vardan Arewelc῾i and, 12:359b
Het῾um II of Cilician Armenia, king, **6:219a-b**
Armenian-Roman church union and, 3:394b
chronicle by, 6:219b
murdered, 3:391b
retreat to monastery, 6:219a-b
instability caused by, 6:220a
Het῾um Koṙikosc῾i, 1:511b
Het῾umids, 3:391a, **6:219b–220b**
chronology of rulers, 6:220a
formation of alliances, 6:220a
through marriage, 6:220a
founding of family line, 6:219b
intermarriage with Rubenids, 10:540b
Lambron and, 7:322a
Rubenid-Hetu῾mid conflict, 6:219b, 10:540a
Skewṙa and, 11:326a
Smbat Sparapet and, 11:351b
see also Leo I/II of Cilician Armenia, king; Nersēs Lambronac῾i
Heunenweise (strophic form). *See* *Hildebrandston* (strophic form)
Ḥevrot, 7:69a
Hexabiblos. See Basilics; Harmenopoulos, Constantine
Hexachord system, 8:597b, 598a
notation and, 8:626a
in solmization, 11:363b–366a
Hexaemeron, **6:220b–221a**
on Gerona tapestry, 6:220b (*illus.*)
as part of larger narrative sequence, 6:221a
variations in images, 6:221a
Hexaemeron. See Basil the Great of Caesarea, St.; George of Pisidia
Hexagram, 8:419a
Hexaphollon, 11:603b
Hexapla. See Origen
Hexekontabiblos. See Basilics
Hey, Jean. *See* Master of Moulins
Heytesbury, William, 1:464b
nominalism and, 12:44a
Regulae solvendi sophismata (*Rules for Solving Sophismata*), 9:626a, 11:535a
Hézelon of Liège, 3:468b, **6:221a**
Hiberno-Latin, **6:221a–222b**
in Celtic liturgy, 7:614a
Old Irish spelling in Latin writing, 6:221b
sense neologisms, 6:221b–222a
stylistics
sobriety of prose, 6:222a
word order, 6:222a
syntactical Hibernisms, 6:222a
"tres linguae sacrae" motif, 6:222a
use of *scotica et alia barbara,* 6:221b
see also Bible, glosses and commentaries (Irish)
Hiberno-Saxon art, 6:516a, **8:363a–376a**
calligraphic decoration in, 8:370a
carpet pages in, 8:370a–371a (*illus.*)
hanging bowls in, 8:369b
human figures in, 8:373a
La Tène style of, 8:369b–370a
Latin church's influence on, 8:371b
manuscript illumination and, 8:105b–106a
Mediterranean influence on, 8:371b
metalworking in, 8:373a-b
period of, 8:369a-b
stone crosses in, 8:371b, 373a-b
Viking influence on, 8:373b
see also Anglo-Saxon art; Animal style
"Hiccuping" effect (in *ars nova*), 1:551b
Hickling, Robert, **6:222b**
Hidalgos. *See* Nobility and nobles, in Spain
Hidāya ʾila farāʾiḍ al-qulūb, Al-. See Baḥya ben Joseph ibn Paqūdā
Ḥiddushim, 11:585b
Hide (land division), **6:222b–223a**
assessment for military service, 12:556b
etymology, 6:223a
shire and, 11:253b
taxation by, 11:611a-b, 612a-b
assessments, 11:613b
in terms of acres, 6:223a
virgate and bovate, 11:676b
in virgates, 6:223a
Hide (skin). *See* Leather and leatherworking
Hiereia, Council of (754), **6:223a-b**, 7:124b
theoretical foundation for iconoclasm, 6:223b, 398a, 399a
enforcement of, 6:223b
Hiero. See Xenophon
Hierocratic theory, growth of in Western Europe, 10:20a–21a
Hierokles, **6:223b–224a**, 9:697a
Synekdemos, 5:400a, 6:223b–224a
dating of, 6:224a
structure of, 6:224a
Hierro, 3:62b
Higden, Ranulf, **6:224a-b**
Chester Plays and, 3:298b
Historia polychronica (*Polychronicon*), 3:326b, 327b, 4:547a, 6:224a
John Trevisa translation, 8:317a, 12:187a
preservation in manuscripts, 6:224b
sex aetates mundi and, 11:215a
translations, 6:224b
theological works, 6:224a
High cross. *See* Cross, high
High treason. *See* Treason
Highwaymen. *See* Travel and transport, dangers of
Hija del rey de Francia, La, Rodríguez del Padrón and, 10:439a
Ḥijāz. *See* Hejaz
Hijra. See Hegira
Hikanati, 11:573a, 573b
Ḥikma, sunna and, 11:511a, 511b
Hilāl (banū)
defeated by ῾Abd al-Muʾmin, 1:194a

Hilāl (banū) (*cont.*)
in Tripolitania, 6:415a
Hilandar monastery, 11:173b, 186a-b, 473b
Hilarion of Iberia, 5:414a
Hilarion of Kiev. *See* Ilarion of Kiev
Hilarion of Moglen, bishop, Bogomils and, 2:294b, 296a
Hilarion, St., *lavra* and, 7:388a
Hilarius
Play of Daniel, 9:705a
plays of, 4:263b, 281b
Hilary of Arles, bishop, 5:471b
Hilary of Poitiers, St., 3:336a, **6:225a-b**, 9:713b
Against the Emperor Constantius, 6:225a
on baptism, 3:675b
as doctor of the church, 4:234a
hymns of, 6:225b, 381a, 7:360b
literary works, 6:225b
Peter Lombard and, 9:517a
resistance to Arianism, 6:225a
Hilda (spirit), 12:660a
Hilda of Whitby, abbess, 3:7b–8a, 227b, 12:683a
Hildebert of Lavardin, **6:225b–227a**, 10:76a
conflict with William Rufus, 6:225b
De mysterio missae, 6:226a, 7:364a
De quatuor virtutibus vitae honestae, 6:226b
De querimonia et conflictu carnis et spiritus seu animae, 6:226a
election as archbishop, 6:226a
Floridus aspectus and, 7:365b
hymns of, 6:382a
In libros regum, 6:226a
literary works
liturgical commentaries, 7:631a
poems on Rome, 6:226b–227a, 10:520b
prose, 6:226
sermons, 6:226a
verse, 6:226a-b
Mathematicus, 6:226b
poetry, Ovidian influence, 9:313a
Tractatus theologicus, 6:226a
Vita beatae Mariae Aegypticae, 6:226b
Vita santae Radegundis, 6:226a
Hildebert of Le Mans. *See* Hildebert of Lavardin
Hildebrand. *See* Gregory VII, pope
Hildebrandslied, **6:227a–228b**
changes in under Lombard rule, 6:227b
derivation, 9:234a
fate and power of God, 6:150b
flyting and, 9:175a
lack of historical prototype, 6:227b
non-Germanic versions, 6:228a
preservation of, 4:387b–388a, 6:440a
Þiðreks saga and, 12:29b
verse technique, 6:228a
Hildebrandston (strophic form), 10:533a
in *Wolfdietrich,* 12:669b
in *Wunderer,* 12:704b
Hildegar, Fulbert of Chartres and, 5:310b
Hildegard of Bingen, St., 1:607a, **6:228b–229b**, 9:8a, 8b, 31b
allegory of, 5:428b
biblical exegesis and, 2:213b
Causae et curae, 2:245a
compared to St. Birgitta of Sweden, 9:15a
hymns of, 6:382a
Liber compositae medicinae, 6:229a
Liber simplicis medicinae, 6:229a
on millennialism, 8:386b
mystical vision, 6:228b
Physica, 2:245a
political importance, 6:229a
religious works, 6:229a
scientific studies, 6:229a
Scivias, 5:428b, 8:584b, 587b (*illus.*), 9:10a-b
image of Living Light, 6:228b
miniature from, 9:9 (*illus.*)
theory of universe, 9:623a
Hildegard of Rupertsberg, 2:173b
Hildegard (wife of Charlemagne), 11:526b
Hilderic, Vandal king, 12:355a, 355b
Hildesheim
casting of Bernward's column at, 8:283b
see also Bernward
Hildesheim Chronicles
Hrotswitha von Gandersheim and, 6:313b
on St. Stephen I of Hungary, 11:478a
Hildgard of Hürnheim, translation of *Secreta secretorum,* 4:578b
Hilduin of St. Denis, **6:229b**, 7:142a, 10:92b
hymns of, 6:381b
Life of St. Denis, 6:68a, 229b
translation of *Celestial Hierarchy,* 1:250a
Hill, Richard, 3:493a
Hilla, al-, as a center of Twelver Shiism, 11:136b
Hillel II, nasi, reform of Jewish calendar, 3:24b
Hilton, Walter, 4:547b, 9:19a, 19b, 20a
authorship of *The Cloud of Unknowing* and, 9:22a
criticism of Richard Rolle, 9:20b
English works of, 9:23a
Latin works of, 9:23a
Scale of Perfection, 3:368b, 8:317b, 9:18b, 23a, 23b–24a, 28a
Himmelgarten, monastery of, Passion play from, 4:267a
Ḥimṣ, **6:229b–230b**
after Abbasid revolution, 6:230a
Church of St. John, 6:229b
conflagration and decline of, 6:230b
during caliphate, 6:230a
al-Lāhdiqiya and, 7:316a
occupation by Arab forces, 6:229b–230a
settlement of, 6:229b
strategic importance
during crusades, 6:230a
under Ayyubids and Mamluks, 6:230a-b
Ḥimṣ, Battle of (1281), 6:420a
Ḥimyar, Jews in, 7:101a-b
Himyarite dynasty, 1:371b
realm of, 6:49b
rise of in southern Arabia, 1:370a-b
Hinckaert, Jan, Ruusbroec and, 9:36a
Hincmar of Laon, 4:126b
interdict and, 6:495a
Hincmar of Rheims, 5:638b, **6:230b–231a**, 7:141b, 362b
crowning ceremony and, 7:256b
on ecclesiastical structure, 4:373a-b
False Decretals and, 4:125b, 126b
interdict and, 6:495a
kingship theories of, 7:260b–261a
mirror of princes and, 8:434b
Nicholas I and, 9:121a
theological writings, 6:230b
Visio Bernoldi, 12:475b
see also Richer of St. Remi
Hinderbach, Johann, music in honor of, 12:183b–184a
Hindu-Arabic numerals. *See* Arabic numerals
Hindu-Shahi dynasty, control of eastern Afghanistan, 1:64a
Hindus, Islam and, 9:498b
Hinrich von Brunsberg. *See* Brunsberg, H[e]inrich von
Hinrik von Alckmer, 2:142a
Hipparchus, 3:457b
invention of astrolabe and, 11:96b
Hippiatrika, 4:446b–447a, 11:635a
Hippo, Vandals and, 12:354b
Hippocrates
Aphorisms, 8:247a, 255b, 256b
translated by Constantine the African, 8:248a
on cosmetics, 2:147a
De regimine acutorum, 8:248b
influence of on Byzantine medicine, 8:244a-b
Prognostics, 8:255b, 256b
translated by Constantine the African, 8:248a
in university curriculum, 11:692a
works of
Galen's commentaries on, 12:132a-b
translated into Arabic, 11:83a
Hippodrome. *See* Great Hippodrome
Hippolytus of Rome, antipope, 1:330b, 507b
Apostolic Tradition, 2:177a, 3:602b, 675b, 7:397b, 625b
Docetism and, 4:233a
Ḥīra, al-, **6:231a**
Lakhmids and, 7:320a-b, 321a
Najrān and, 9:55a
Ḥirāʾ, Mount, Muḥammad and, 6:576a
Hirgorn, 8:558b
Hirmiz. *See* Qirmiz
Hirsau (monastery), **6:231a-b**, 10:487b
custom of, 2:6b
German Romanesque art, 10:508b
reforms of, Hungarian church and, 11:479b
Hirsvogel atelier, 5:551a
Hirð, 9:182b–183a, 184b, 10:702a
Ḥisdai ibn Shaprut, 7:95b–96a
Ḥisba
definition, 8:526a
manuals, 8:527a
personal responsibility for, 8:526b

Hishām I, Umayyad ruler, 12:275b–276a
Hishām II, Umayyad caliph, 12:277b–278a
Ibn Abī ᶜĀmir al-Manṣūr and, 8:90a
Hishām (historian), 7:307b
Hishām ibn ᶜAbd al-Malik, Marwānī caliph, **6:232a-b**
administration
appointments to office, 6:232a
fiscal, 6:232a
Berber invasion, 6:232b
building projects, 6:232a
military campaigns, 6:232a
religious opposition to, 6:232a
Ḥiṣn al-Akrād. *See* Krak des Chevaliers
Hispana, 3:229b, 4:124b, 125a
Isidore of Seville and, 6:564a
Hispaniola. *See* Haiti
Hispano-Arabic language, **6:232b–233a**
Mozarabs, 6:232b–233a
under Muslim conquerors, 6:232b–233a
Hispano-Arabic literature, **6:233a–234a**
adab, 6:233a-b
in al-Andalus, 6:233a–234a
development of literary theory, 6:233b
maqāmā, 6:233b
Mudejar style, 10:554a
poetry, *qaṣīda,* 6:234a
Hispano-Gothic refugees, in Catalonia, 3:174a-b
Hispano-Latin Literature. *See* Spanish Latin literature
Hispano-Mauresque art, **6:234a–235b**
adoption in Christian Spain, 6:235b
geometric ornament, 6:235a
labyrinths, 6:235a-b
Mudejar art, 11:380a
North African, under Almoravids, 6:234b–235a
tile and carved stucco compositions, 6:235a
vegetal designs
at Aljaferí in Saragossa, 6:234b
horror vacui, 6:234b
see also Alhambra; Córdoba, Great Mosque of; Plateresque style
Hisperic Latin, 3:231b, **6:236a–237b,** 7:354b, 361b, 362a, 362b, 363a
characteristics, 6:236a
defined, 6:236a
elements of diction, 6:236a
pre-7th century, 6:236b
rhythmical poems, 6:236b
faminators, 6:236a
Greek and Greco-Latin words, 6:236a
Ireland
development of diction, 6:237b
eastward spread from, 6:236b–237a
source of vocabulary, 6:236a-b
see also Hisperica famina
Hisperica famina, 7:354b, 361b–362a
contents of, 6:236b
imitations of, 6:237a
word order, 6:222a
Histamena, 8:420b
Histoire ancienne, preservation of clerkly wisdom of Rome, 5:256b
Histoire de Charles Martel, illustrated by Loyset Liédet, 7:572 (*illus.*)
Histoire de la conquête de la toison d'or. See Lefèvre, Raoul
Histoire de Guillaume le maréchal, L', 2:236b
Histoire de Jason. See Lefèvre, Raoul
Histoire de saint Louis. See Joinville, Jean de
Histoire de la toison d'or. See Fillastre, Guillaume
Histoire universelle, 4:26a
Histoires des amans fortunez. See Heptaméron, L'
Histoires de Baudouin
associations, 9:637b
modifications, 9:638a
Historia, in rhymed offices, 10:367a
Historia. See Attaleiates, Michael
História. See Tomich, Pere
Historia de antiquitate regum Norwagiensium. See Theodoricus
Historia Apollonii regis Tyri, 5:514a
see also Apolonio, Libro de
Historia Brittonum, **6:237b–238a,** 10:366a
aliqua excerpta, reference to Welsh poetry, 12:597a
chronological gaps, 6:237b
recensions
Harleian version, 6:237b
prologues of later version, 6:237b
survival of manuscripts, 6:237b
on Urien Rheged, 12:331b
Welsh migrations, Cunedda tribe, 12:514a
see also Nennius
Historia calamitatum. See Abelard, Peter
Historia compostelana, 11:435b
Historia del Gran Tamorlán. See González de Clavijo, Ruy
Historia destructionis Troiae. See Guido delle Colonne
Historia (Divine Office). *See* Divine Office, versified
Historia de don Rodrigo Ponce de León, 11:433b
Historia de la donzella Teodor, 11:415b
Historia ecclesiastica. See Bede, *Ecclesiastical History of the English Church and People*
Historia ecclesiastica. See Eusebius
Historia florentini populi. See Bruni, Leonardo
Historia Francorum. See Aimoin de Fleury; Gregory of Tours, St.; Hugh of Fleury
Historia Hierosolimitana. See Baudri of Bourgueil
Historia Hierosolimitana abbreviata. See Jacques de Vitry
Historia Hierosolymitana. See Fulcher of Chartres
Historia Langobardorum. See Paul the Deacon
Historia de la linda Melosina, 11:423a
Historia majoris Britanniae. See Major, John
Historia monachorum, 6:58a
Historia Mongalorum. See John of Plano Carpini
Historia naturalis. See Pliny the Elder
Historia Normannorum ducum. See Guillaume de Jumièges
Historia Norwegiae, 9:175b–176a
Ynglingatal and, 12:726a
Historia novella. See William of Malmesbury
Historia novorum. See Eadmer of Canterbury
Historia plantarum. See Theophrastus
Historia polychronica. See Higden, Ranulf
Historia pontificalis. See John of Salisbury
Historia de preliis, 1:149b
see also Julius Valerius
Historia de rege Vladislao. See Buonaccorsi, Phillip
Historia regum Britanniae. See Geoffrey of Monmouth
Historia regum Francorum, 2:236b, **6:238a-b**
as model for later chronicles, 6:238a
sources for, 6:238a
translations into French, 6:238a
Historia rerum Anglicarum. See William of Newburgh
Historia rerum in partibus tran-marinis gestorum. See William of Tyre
Historia rerum transmarinarum. See William of Tyre
Historia Roderici, 3:76b, 11:406b, 410a, 435b
Historia romana. See Landolfus Sagax; Paul the Deacon
Historia Salonitana mairo, 4:4b–5a
Historia scholastica. See Peter Comestor
Historia septem sapientum. See John of Alta Silva
Historia Sicula. See Gaufrid (Gaudfred) Malaterra
Historia silense, 11:410b
Historia Theophili. See Marbod of Rennes
Historia Troiana. See Guido delle Colonne, *Historia destructionis Troiae*
Historia troyana polimétrica, 11:416b, 453b, 457b
prosody of and, 11:459a
Historiae. See Adémar of Chabannes
Historiae adversum paganos. See Orosius
Historiae Francorum. See Gregory of Tours, St.
Historiae gothorum vandalorum et sueborum. See Isidore of Seville, St.
Historiarum libri quattuor. See Nithard
Historical cycles (Ismaili doctrine). *See* Cycles of history (Ismaili doctrine)
Historical demography. *See* Demography
Historical Library. See Diodorus Siculus
Historie of the Arrivall of Edward IV in England, 12:554b
Historie van den Grale. See Maerlant, Jacob van
Historie van Troyen. See Maerlant, Jacob van
Historien der alden ê, 2:232a

Històries Trojanes. See Guido delle Colonne, *Historia destructionis Troiae*
Historiography, Armenian, 1:511b, **6:238b–242a**
Bagratid period, 1:510b
epitomes, 6:240a
family histories, 6:240a
regional histories, 6:240a-b
semi-legendary historiographical tradition, 6:240b
universal histories, 6:240a
chronicles
colophons and, 6:240b
14th century, 6:241a
collapse of social order and, 6:240b
court histories, 6:240b–241a
effect of nationalism on, 6:238b–239a
emphasis on supernatural, 6:239a
intellectual environment, 6:239a
lists and genealogies, 6:239b
martyrological works, 6:240a
origin of, 6:238b
historical books of the Bible, 6:238b
purpose of, 6:241a
use of eyewitness accounts, 6:239a
see also P^cawstos Buzand; T^covma Arcruni; T^covma Mecop^cec^ci; Vardan Arewelc^ci
Historiography, Byzantine, **6:242a–249a**, 12:23a
4th through 7th centuries, 6:242a–243b
9th through 10th centuries, 6:243b–245a
11th century, 6:245a–246a
14th century, 6:247a-b
15th century, 6:247b–248a
chronicles
distinction between history and, 6:248a
full-length, 6:243b
political vs. theological emphasis, 6:244a-b
12th century, 6:246b
world, 6:246b–247a
classical tradition, 2:511b–512b, 513a, 514a
contemporary
14th century, 2:516b
Greek manner, 2:512a
ecclesiastical, 2:512b–513a, 517a, 6:242a, 242b
apologetic tone, 6:242a, 244b
Komnenoi, 6:246a-b
Latin writers, 6:243b
Nicene period, 6:247a
partisan tendencies in, 6:247a-b, 248a
glorification of Alexios I, 6:246a
rationalization of Macedonian dynasty, 6:244b–245a
reworking of existing works, 6:244a-b
secular, 6:242a-b
classicizing style, 6:245a, 247b
pagan, 6:243a
time span covered, 6:243a
traditions of classical historiography, 6:242b
Thucydidean model, 6:248a
variation in form, 2:516a
view of historical causation, 2:512a, 514a
see also Bar Hebraeus; Literacy, Byzantine; *Paschale chronicon;* Theophanes Confessor; Theophanes continuatus; Theophylaktos Simokattes
Historiography, Iranian, 8:474b–475a
Historiography, Islamic, **6:249b–255b**
Abbasid revisionism, 1:9a
biographical dictionaries, 6:252b–253b
Bīrūnī's *Chronology* and, 2:249a
compilation of works
methods of *ḥadīth* scholarship, 6:252a
reproduction of existing chronicles, 6:252a
courtly milieu
events of the past as political rules, 6:250b
focus on kings, 6:250b–251a
model for, 6:250a
treatises on art of kingship, 6:250b
use of Persian, 6:250b
cultural significance, 6:249b–251b
forms and structures
blended chronicle and biography, 6:253b
dynastic history, 6:252b
local history, 6:252b
madhhab-oriented collections, 6:253a
universal history, 6:252a-b
ḥadīth evolution, 6:45a, 46a, 47a
historical concepts
akhbār, 6:253b–254a
myth of divine promise, 6:254a
science of culture, 6:254a-b
ta^ɔrīkh, 6:253b
verification of sources, 6:254b
isnād, 12:545a
in al-Kufa, 7:307b
in Ottoman Turkish, 6:251a-b
profession of historian, court vs. scholarly-religious traditions, 6:251b–252a
renaissance of Islam, 8:204a
^culamā^ɔ
differences from courtly milieu, 6:250b–251a
doctrinal problems examined, 6:250a
historical approach, 6:250a
Xwadāy nāmag and, 12:716a
Historiography, Jewish, **6:255b–258a**
of ancient Israel, 6:255b
commemorative scrolls
on dramatic events, 6:257b
kiddush ha-shem, 6:257b
on current political institutions, 6:257a
on families and clans, 6:257a-b
legendary materials in, 8:23b–24a
martyrology, 6:256a
political quietism, 6:256a
rabbinic tradition
chain of transmission, 6:256b–257a
doctrinal truth, 6:256b
legal factors, 6:256a-b
restriction to Israelite history, 6:255b
Second Commonwealth, 6:255b–256a
effect of Rabbinic Judaism, 6:256a–257a
Historiography, Roman, 12:143a-b
Historiography, Syriac, 11:566a
Historiography, Western European, **6:258b–265b**, 8:87a-b
accountability of sources
eyewitness testimony, 6:260b–261a
moral character of informant, 6:261a
oral material, 6:261a
annals in Carolingian period, 6:262a-b
annus Domini, 6:259a
annus mundi, 6:258b–259a
authorial bias, 6:261b
biography
ecclesiastical, 6:263b
secular, 6:263b
of Capetians, 6:24a
Carolingian educational reforms, 6:262b–263a
Catalan, 11:435b
chronicles, 3:325a–330a
concept of the Middle Ages and, 8:308b–309b
crusade histories, 6:263a
crusader states, 12:643b
Danish, 10:676b
sources, 10:678a
definition of *historia,* 6:260b
development of forms, 6:261b–264b
doctrine of the six ages, 6:258b, 262a
English, 1:264b–266a, 6:264b, 8:317a-b
Bede and, 2:155a
episcopal biography, 6:262b
exemplarist, 6:261a-b
figural method, 6:259b–260a
foundations
in biblical study, 6:258b–260a
central thread of time, 6:258b
in Roman rhetoric and literature, 6:260a–261a
Frankish states, 9:715b
French, 1:109b, 6:264a
German, 2:229a, 8:348a, 10:289b–290a
Grandes chroniques de France, 5:653b–654b
historia ab origine gentis, 10:676b
historical education, 6:260b
hypotaxis, 6:259a
Icelandic, *see also* Bishops' sagas
invisibilia Dei, 6:260a
Irish, **6:249a-b**
Annals of Ulster and Inisfallen, 6:249a
dates used, 6:249a
problems of orthography and pronunciation, 6:249a
see also Bansenchas; Irish literature, historical compositions
Italian, 6:264b
see also Italian literature, chronicles
military
clerical bias, 12:554b
lay writers, 12:554b
official documentation, 12:567b
sources for, 12:567b
Moldavian, 10:511b–512a

monastic local chronicles, 6:262b
parataxis, 6:259a-b, 263a
Polish, 9:723a-b, 725b, 729b–730a
Radulphus Glaber and, 10:247a-b
rhetorical treatment of, 6:260a-b, 262b, 263a-b
Romanian, 10:510b
Vlachs and, 12:484a
in sagas, 6:75a-b
Scandinavian, *see also* Norse kings' sagas
Scottish, **6:258a-b**
Gaelic, 11:116a-b
incorporated in Irish annals, 6:258a
king lists, 6:258a
sources of early history, 6:258a
sermo humilis, 6:259b
Sicilian, 11:274b
Spanish, 11:410b
in Alfonso X the Learned's reign, 11:415a
chronicles and, 11:435a–436a
Isidore of Seville and, 6:565a, 565b
Pero López de Ayala's chronicles and, 11:418b
13th-century epics and, 11:410b–411b
of supernatural events, 6:259b
synchronization of Judeo-Christian and pagan dates, 6:259b
theology of history, 6:263b
theology of, 10:247a-b
tribal history, 6:262b–263a
connecting to Bible, 6:261b–262a
dignification of Germanic tribes, 6:261b–262a
universal chronicles, 6:261a, 262b
Latin, 6:263b
models for, 6:261a
written on theological level, 6:264a
vernacular, 6:262b, 264a-b
of villages, 12:437b
Welsh, 12:612b–613a
of witchcraft, 12:658b–659b
see also Anglo-Saxon Chronicle; *Sex aetates mundi*
History. See Kirakos of Ganjak
History of the Abbots of Wearmouth and Jarrow. See Bede
History against the Pagans. See Orosius
History of Alexander. See Pseudo-Callisthenes
History of Animals. See Aristotle
History of the Arcruni House. See Thomas Arcruni
History of Armenia. See Łazar Pʿarpecʿi; Pʿawstos Buzand
History of the Armenians. See Agatʿangełos
History of the Bagratids. See Smbat
History of the Berbers. See Khaldūn, Ibn
History of the Bishops of the Church of Hamburg. See Adam of Bremen
History of the British Kings. See Geoffrey of Monmouth, *Historia regum Britanniae*
History of the Caucasian Albanians. See Movsēs Dasχurancʿi
History of the Church. See Baronius, Caesar
History of the English Church and People. See Bede
History of the Family and the Province of Siwnikʿ. See Orbēlean, Stepʿanos
History of the Five Reigns, 5:418a
History of the Franks. See Gregory of Tours, St.
History of the Goths. See Isidore of Seville, St.; Jordanes
History of Greater Britain. See Major, John
History of Gruffudd ap Cynan, Latin original, 12:612b
History of the Indies. See Las Casas, Bartolomeo de
History of the Invasions of Timur, 5:418a
History of the Muslim Conquest, 2:54a
History of the Nation of the Archers. See Grigor Aknercʿi
History of the Patriarchs of Alexandria, translations of, Arabic, 8:479a
History of Queen Tamar. See Basil
History Regarding the Sufferings Occasioned by Foreign Peoples Living Around Us. See Aristakēs Lastivercʿi
History of the Seven Tribulations of the Order of the Minors. See Angelo Clareno
History of the State of Sisakan. See Orbēlean, Stepʿanos
History of Taron. See Patmutʿiwn Tarōnoy
History of the Two Cities. See Otto of Freising
History of Vardan and the Armenian War. See Ełišē
Historye of the Patriarks, 4:547b
Hitda of Meschede, 10:102b
Hītī, David ben Se'adel ibn al-, 7:210b
Ḥiṭṭīn, Battle of (1187), 5:482a, **6:265b–266b**
treatment of captives, 10:625b–626a
Hittite language. *See* Anatolian language
Hjálmþérs saga ok Ölvis, **6:266b–267b**
characterization of Höðr, 6:267a
dating, 6:267a-b
setting, 5:140b
Hjaðningavíg, **6:267b–268a**
development of mythological elements, 6:268a
differing versions, 6:267b–268a
historical background for, 6:268a
meaning of names in, 6:267b–268a
Old Norse sources, 6:267b
Hjǫrungavágr, Battle of (974–985), 9:177a
Hlaðajarla saga, 9:176b, 177a
Hlǫðskviða, **6:268a–269a**
historical background for, 6:268b
insertion in *Hervarar saga ok Heiðreka konungs,* 6:215a
other versions of legend, 6:268b–269a
plot summary, 6:268b
preservation, 4:387b, 6:268a-b
Hlutr (alternative designation of *þættir*), 12:1b
Hobby horse, 8:562b
Hobnails, 11:255a
Hoc est principium destructionis civitatis Bononiae, 6:658a
Hoccleve, Thomas, **6:269a-b**
Complaint, 8:323b
De regimine principium, 8:323b
Dialogue, Synonyma and, 7:361b
literary works, 6:269a
Male regle, 8:323b
Postilla litteralis and, 4:545b
Regement of Princes, use of "rhyme royal" in, 8:346a
verse version of *Secretum secretorum,* 11:135b
Hochmeister (chief rabbi). *See* Germany, Jews in; Rabbinate
Hochzeit, Die, 5:428a
Hocket, **6:269b–270a**
in Bamberg manuscript, 2:68b
definition, 6:269b
in isorhythm, 6:619b
Magister Lambertus and, 8:643b
in measured music, 7:119a-b
as onomatopoeic device, 6:270a
origins, 6:269b–270a
repertory of works, 6:270a
types of, 6:269b
Hodegetria, **6:270a-b**
"Hodie cantandus est." *See* Tuotilo
Hodo, margrave, 9:718b
Hœnir, **6:270b–271a,** 11:296b
member of divine trio, 6:270b, 271a
in *Reginsmál,* 4:581a-b
scholarship on, 6:270b–271a
Vanir and, 12:356b
Hœnsa-Þóris saga, 4:613b, 614a, **6:271a–272a**
dating of, 6:271b
language and characterization, 6:271b
plot summary, 6:271a-b
relationship to legal clause, 6:271b
Hoes
European, 12:78a–79a
Islamic, 12:84b
Hofer Bestiary, 2:206a
Höfisches epos, 5:444b
Hofstaðir (Mývatnssveit), 11:35b–36a
Hoftag. See Kingship, holding court; Representative assemblies, German
Hǫfuðlausn. See Egill Skallagrímsson
Hoger of Laon, count, *Musica enchiriadis* and, 8:639b
Hǫgni, 1:638b
Hogshead (unit of measure), 12:584b
Hoguine, 1:533a
Hohenfurth Master. *See* Master of Hohenfurth
Hohenstaufen dynasty, **6:272b–274a**
Alsace and, 6:272b
assertion of royal authority by, 5:478b
Babenberg family and, 2:6b, 33b, 6:273a
Burgundy and, 2:424b
chronicles of, 9:303b–304a
collapse of, 5:482b, 485a, 501a
coronation of Philip of Swabia, 12:537b–538a
enfeoffment of Frederick I, 6:272b
expansion of, 5:481b
forest administration, 5:132b

Hohenstaufen dynasty (*cont.*)
Franconian claims, 6:273a
imperial ideal under, 5:479b, 494a
Italian policies, 6:273a-b, 7:15a
male line from Frederick II, 6:273b
ministerials and, 5:132b, 8:405b–406a
Nuremberg and, 9:201a
origin of, 6:272b
Otto of Brunswick and, 12:673a
patronage of literature, 5:434a, 435a, 6:102b, 8:349b
in principalities, 5:500b–501a
Rudolf von Ems and, 8:352b
Sicily and, 11:269a
succession rights, 4:427a-b
in Swabia, 5:510a, 6:272b
vs. Innocent IV, 6:466a, 466b
vs. Welfs, 5:212b–213a, 214a-b, 479b–480a, 6:167b, 273a
in Bavaria, 2:134b
vs. Zähringens, in Swabia, 11:527b–528a, 538b, 539a
Waiblingen and, 6:273a
Wolfger von Erla and, 12:672b
Hohenzeuggestech, 1:533a
Hohenzollern dynasty, Nuremberg and, 9:201a, 202a
Hólar, 2:252a, 12:427a
diocese of, 6:352a, 394a
scholarship at, 4:618a
Holbein, Hans, the Younger
armor and, 1:536a
Dance of Death, 4:93b (*illus.*)
Holcot, Robert, **6:274a-b**
biblical commentaries, 6:274b
as defender of Ockhamism, 12:44a
as exegete, 4:544b
Liber de moralizationibus, 6:274a-b
nominalism and, 9:157a
Oxford and Cambridge regencies, 6:274a
Postilla super librum Sapientiae, 6:274a, 8:435b
predestination and, 3:371a
Sex articuli, 6:274a
theology of, 6:274b
Thomism and, 12:41b
Holewell, Thomas, **6:274b–275a**
Thomas Poppehowe and, 10:32b
tomb of John IV, 6:274b–275a
Holger the Dane. *See* Holger Danske
Holger Danske, **6:275a-b**
chansons de geste on, 6:275a
historical prototypes, 6:275a
Scandinavian translations, 6:275b
Holinshed, Raphael, *Chronicles,* 1:565b
Holkham Bible Picture Book, 1:262b, **6:276a**
scenes from life of Christ, 6:276a (*illus.*)
Holland. *See* Low Countries
Holland, John, earl of Huntingdon, court of admiralty under, 1:57a
Holmgard. *See* Novgorod
Hólmverja saga. See Harðar saga Grímkelssonar (ok Geirs)
Holstein, Denmark and, 4:154a
Holstein, counts of
Margaret of Denmark and, 11:533a
vs. Erik of Pomerania, 11:533a
Holt, Jón, *Thómas saga erkibyskups* and, 12:35b, 36a
Holtrop, Jan Willem, 10:127a
Holy Ampulla, 7:258a
Holy Apostles (church: Constantinople), 4:332a, 9:136a
Holy Apostles (church: Peć)
frescoes, 11:184b, 185b
wall paintings, 2:446b
Holy Apostles (church: Thessaloniki), mosaic decoration, 2:450a
Holy Brotherhood, function of, 6:210a
Holy Chrism, 7:258a
Holy Circulus, in Jerusalem, 11:467b
Holy Cross (abbey: County Tipperary), 6:538a
Holy Cross (church: Ałtᶜamar island), 1:495b, 496b (*illus.*), 519a, 520a
Holy Cross (hospital: Toledo), floor plan, 6:395a-b
Holy Cross hymns, 6:381a, 384a
Holy Cross (monastery: Jerusalem), Shostᶜa Rustaᶜveli and, 11:256a
Holy Cross (monastery: Poitiers), 12:682b
Holy Fraternity of the Resurrection, 8:661a
Holy Ghost (hospital: Lübeck), interior hall, 7:682b
Holy Ghost (hospital: Nuremberg), 9:202a
Holy Ghost (hospital: Tallinn), 9:186b
Holy Innocents, plays of the, 9:706b
Holy Lance, discovered by Peter Bartholomew, 4:35b
Holy Monogram, advocated by St. Bernardino of Siena, 2:196a-b
Holy Mountains, 8:457a
Holy Office. *See* Congregation of the Holy Office
Holy oil
benedictions and, 2:177a
see also Anointing
Holy Roman Empire, 2:133 (map), **6:276a-b**
Bohemia, Hussite revolt, 10:330b
boundaries, 5:494a, 10:660a
in 1254, 5:479a (map)
"citizenship" concept, 10:329a-b
commendation in, 3:490b
declaration of Rense, 7:688a
elective vs. hereditary rulership in, 7:149a
emperor-elect, 10:520a
end of, 5:496b
following investiture conflict, 6:500a
Governing Council of the Empire, 10:331a
Habsburg imperial status, 6:42a
Imperial Cameral (Chamber) Court (*Reichskammergericht*), creation of, 5:504a, 8:231a
imperial succession, Philip of Swabia and Otto of Brunswick, 12:537b–539a
inheritance and, 6:454b
Jordan of Osnabrück and, 7:148a–149a
Normans and, 11:265b
Ottoman Empire and Hungary, 10:330b
Poland and, 9:719b–720b
ecclesiastical independence, 9:718b
relations with papacy, *see also* Investiture conflict
relations with Sicily, 11:269b
representative assemblies of, 10:331a
Dauphiné, 10:320a, 321a
Germany, 10:328b–329b, 331a-b
Imperial Cameral (Chamber) Court (*Reichskammergericht*), 10:329a, 331a
Imperial Circles (*Reichskreise*), 10:331a
imperial cities and towns, 10:330a
Imperial Diet (*Reichstag*), 10:329b–332a
imperial knights, 10:332a, 333a
Salian kings, travels of, 12:159a-b
Swabia and, 11:538a
taxation, Common Penny, 10:330b–331a
translation of bishops and, 12:142b–143a
use of term, 6:276b
Wolfram's *Parzival* and, 12:678a
see also Elections, royal; Electoral college
Holy Sepulcher (church: Jerusalem), 7:59a, 60a, 60b, 9:657 (*illus.*)
copies of in northern Europe, 4:347a
holiest pilgrimage goal, 4:336b
rebuilt by crusaders, 4:22b, 23b–24a (*illus.*)
recovered by Bohemond I of Antioch, 2:309a
Holy Shroud. *See* Turin, Shroud of
Holy Spirit, in art, of Pedro Serra, 11:209b, 210a (*illus.*)
Holy Spirit (hospital: Rome), floor plan, 6:295a
Holy Spirit, Order of, erection of hospitals, 6:294a
Holy Thursday. *See* Holy Week
Holy Translators, Feast of the, 1:520a-b
Holy Trinity (church: Edinburgh), 11:112a
Holy Trinity, feast of. *See* Trinity, feast of
Holy Trinity (monastery). *See* Trinity-St. Sergius
Holy War. See Simeon ben Ẓemah Duran
Holy war. *See* Warfare
Holy war, Islamic. *See* Jihad
Holy Week, **6:276b–280a**
French passion plays and, 9:447b–448a
Good Friday
Mass of the presanctified, 6:278b
Orationes sollemnes, 6:278a
rite of the adoration of the cross, 6:278a-b
Holy Saturday
baptism and confirmation, 6:279a-b
blessing of the paschal lambs, 6:278b
Mother of All Vigils, 6:278b–279a
see also Exultet roll
Holy Thursday
incense and, 6:432a
mandatum service, 6:278a

Mass of reconciliation, 6:277b
Missa chrismalis, 6:277b
Missa in coena Domini, 6:277b
reservation of the host, 6:277b–278a
rites of, 4:366a
service of Tenebrae, 6:277b
incense and, 6:432b
Palm Sunday
ascension ceremony, 6:277a
hymn, 9:713b
laudes episcopi, 6:277a
passion aspect, 6:277a
triumphal procession, 6:277a
plashchanitsa shroud, 9:693b–694a (*illus.*)
see also Easter; Passion cycle
Holy Year, **6:280a–281a**
Holyrood, **6:281a**
Homage
commendation, 3:490a–491b
of procurator, 4:204b
Home industry. *See* Economic production, family and
Homelessness. *See* Migration; Reclamation of land; Travel and transport
Homer
Basil the Great and, 2:120a
Iliad
Milan codex, 4:351a, classical models for illustrations, 4:352b–353a
translated into Spanish by Juan de Mena, 8:273a-b
Vǫluspá and, 12:491b
miniature of in Urbino Codex, 12:394 (*illus.*)
Odyssey, 4:401b–402a
visions and, 12:475b
Homicide
in English law, **6:281a–282a**
definition, 6:281b
excusable, 6:281b, 282a
presentment of Englishry and, 4:487a
reforms under Henry II, 6:281b
system of compensation, 6:281b
in Islamic law, **6:282a–283b**
compensation, 6:282b
definition, Mālikī school, 6:282b
determining liability, 6:282b
discretionary punishment, 6:283b
intentional vs. accidental, 6:282b
proof of offense, 6:282b, 283a-b
prosecution by family, 6:282a-b
qasāma, 6:283a-b
right of retaliation, 6:282b–283a
state prosecution, 6:282a-b
see also Blood money, Islamic law
Homilarium, Divine Office and, 4:224b
Homiletical instruction. *See* Religious instruction
Homilia de monachis perfectis, 11:455b
Homiliaries, exegesis and, 4:542b–543a
Homilies
Icelandic book of, 11:17a-b
in the liturgy of the Mass, 8:188b
Norwegian book of, 11:17a-b
Homily
in preaching, 10:76a
see also Preaching
Homme armé, L', 8:571b
Homme de corps, 11:201b, 204b
Homme juste et homme mondaine, L', 4:265a
Homme pécheur, L', 4:265a
Hommée (unit of measure), 12:587a
Homo quadratus
architecture and, 8:585b
harmony of the spheres and, 8:518a (*illus.*), 580b
Homobonus de Cremona, *Tractatus quaestionum,* Hugo and, 6:324a
Homoeans, 1:454a
Homoiōsis theō. *See Imitatio Christi*
Homologetes. *See* Theophanes Confessor
Homoousios, Basil the Great and, 2:120a
Homosexuality
of Ethelred of Rievaulx, 4:517a
Latini and, 7:383b
in Norse flyting, 9:173b–174a
punishment of, 4:133b
Homs. *See* Ḥimṣ
Honestiores, 10:461a
Honey, **6:283b–284a**
earliest recorded production, 6:283b–284a
used in mead, 8:239a
Honeycomb vault. *See* Vault
"Honeysuckle, The," 7:317b
Hœnir, in *Reginsmál* and *Fáfnismál,* 10:289b
Honoratus (founder of Lirius monastery), 8:461b
Honoratus of Milan, archbishop, 5:383b
Honoré, Master, **6:284b–285a**, 8:104a, 109a
Breviary of Philip the Fair, 5:614a
illumination of Gratian's *Decretals,* 6:284b (*illus.*)
Honorius I, pope, 3:630b
Easter dating of, 3:228b
Honorius II, pope, 1:330b
Benzo of Alba and, 2:182b
bull issued by, 10:83b
Knights Templars and, 3:304b
Roger II and, 10:440b, 11:267a
Honorius III, pope
beguines and, 2:158b
Carmelites and, 3:96b
church taxation and, 11:607a
collection of decretals commissioned, 7:427b
Dominicans and, 4:239b, 245a
Fifth Crusade and, 4:49b
Frederick II and, 4:58b, 11:270b
indulgences and, 6:449a
Intellecto, 6:341b
on Judith, 2:231b
Tancred and, 11:589a
on Teutonic Knights, 2:231b
Wolfger von Erla and, 12:673a
Honorius IV, pope
Edward I of England and, 11:608a
Rabban Sauma and, 1:453a
Honorius Augustodunensis, **6:285a–286a**
borrowings from in *Líknarbraut,* 7:580a
Breviari d'amor and, 4:506b
De luminaribus ecclesiae, 2:239b
De neocosmo, 6:285a
Elucidarium
authorship of, 12:20b
as a source for Peter Peckham's *Lumere as lais,* 1:263b
translated into German, 8:349b
free will, 6:285b
Gemma animae, 7:593b, 631a-b
Imago mundi (*De imagine mundi*), 1:610b, 4:448a, 577b
Incarnation and purpose of creation, 6:285a-b
Inevitabile, 6:285b
optimistic humanism, 6:285a
see also Elucidarium
Honorius of Autun
homo quadratus and, 8:580b
Imago mundi, derivatives of, 10:544b
Honorius, Roman emperor, 10:262b–263a, 12:469b
diptych of, 4:215a
Stilicho and, 12:470a
Honrado concejo de la mesta. *See Mesta*
Hood molding. *See* Molding
Hoods, Western European, 3:623b
Hooked cross. *See* Gammadion
Hopfer family, 4:516b
Horaʾah, 11:583a-b
Horace
Ars poetica, 10:353a
influence of on Metellus of Tegernsee, 8:298b, 299a
miniature of in Urbino Codex, 12:394 (*illus.*)
Odes, meter of, 7:371b, 375a
Hörig, 11:204b
Hormizd IV of Persia, king, 8:230a
deposition of, 12:715a
overthrown by Bahrām VI Čōbēn of Persia, 2:50a
Turkish invasions, 10:670b
Hormuz
importance of as a port, 9:74b, 85b
Persian Gulf trade and, 11:247a, 247b
Horn, Andrew, 8:433a-b
Horn, Georg, *Arca Noae,* 8:309a
Horn (musical instrument), 8:561b, 602 (*illus.*)
Celtic. *See Corn* (musical instrument)
Hispano-Moorish, 8:563a
Middle Eastern, 8:612b
Saracen, 8:603b
Horn (romance character). *See Romance of Horn*
Hörnen Seyfrid, Der. *See* Sachs, Hans
Horns, drinking. *See* Drinking horns
Horologion, 3:67a
Horologium, Sylvester II and, 11:553b
Horologium sapientiae. *See* Suso, Heinrich
Horologium viatorium, 11:509b
Hoṙomos, 5:371b, **6:286a**
remaining structures, 6:286a
Horoscopes, 1:619a-b
in Cairo genizah, 11:91b
see also Astrology
Horse
armor for, 1:525a, 529a, 529b
in Baltic lands, 2:63b–64a

Horse (*cont.*)
breeding of, 1:294b–295a, 12:370b, 378b
care and treatment, 11:634b–635a
Celtic, 1:294a
domestication of, 1:294a
two-wheeled chariots and, 12:367b
as draft animal, 12:77b
in early medieval Western European trade, 12:110a
as food source, 1:299a
Northern Europe, 1:95b
prohibition against, 1:300a-b
Germanic, 1:294b
harness, 1:93a, 12:371 (*illus.*), 378b
migration period, 8:366b
horseshoes, 1:93b, 295a
for knights, 5:350b
for plowing, 1:93a-b
post system, 12:148a, 149b
role in transportation, 12:148a, 156b, 158a, 159b
sacrificial, 1:95b
shoe, medieval improvement of, 12:371a, 378b
stabling of at inns, 6:471a
trade in, Indian Ocean, 11:248b
in transport, 1:295a-b
types of in Europe, 1:294b
Horse and Lion, tapestry, 3:589b–590a
Horse racing, 5:354a
Horseshoe arch. *See* Arch
Horsthegn. See Marshal, royal, England
Hortlied (Treasure poem). *See Fáfnismál; Reginsmál*
Hortulus. See Walafrid Strabo
Hortus deliciarum. See Herrad of Hohenburg, abbess
Hosebanderie
geese production, 5:150b
poultry and egg production, 5:150b
Hosios Lukas (church: Phocis)
domed-octagon design of, 4:341b
wall mosaics, 8:492b
Hosios Lukas (monastery: Thessaly), **6:286b–287a**
architecture, 2:442b
Church of the Theotokos-Panaghia, floor plan and exterior design, 6:286b
Katholikon, mosaic program, 6:286b–287a
mosaics
dating of, 2:442a-b
New Testament narrative scenes, 2:442b–443a
use of line, 2:444a
northern part of narthex, 6:286b (*illus.*)
wall paintings, 2:442b
Hosius of Córdoba, 3:628a
at Council of Serdica, 11:189b
Hosn al-Akrad, 7:302a
Hospices, Roman, 10:519b
Hospices, travelers'. *See* Inns; Travel and transport, facilities for travelers
Hospicium. See Household, royal
Hospital d'Ignoscents. *See* Casa dels Folls
Hospital of St. Mary, Fraternity of, Wolfger von Erla and, 12:672b
Hospitalers. *See* Knights of St. John
Hospitalers of the Holy Spirit, Innocent III and, 6:465a
Hospitalers of Rhodes. *See* Knights of St. John
Hospitality system (form of expropriation), 9:147b
Burgundians and, 2:92b
in late Roman Empire, 2:91a
Hospitals, 12:330b
located on bridges, 10:409b
see also Basiliada; Bedlam; Inns
Hospitals, Byzantine, **6:287a–290a**, 8:244b
archiatros, 6:288a
erection of
by churchmen, 6:287b
by imperial decree, 6:287a-b
by laymen, 6:287b
facilities and medical care, 6:287b–288a
hospital built by Emperor John II Komnenos, 8:245b
medical staff, 6:288a
salaries, 6:288a
monastery of the Pantokrator, 6:287b–288a, 293a
monastic hospitals, 8:458b
outpatient service, 6:288a
services to travelers and aged, 6:288a
size of, 6:287b
Hospitals, Islamic, **6:290a–292a**
administration, 6:291a
Jewish and Christian, 6:290b
Jewish physicians and, 11:93a
major, 6:290b–291a
Muslim, 6:290b–291a
outpatient services, 6:291a-b
physical structure, 6:291a
secular, 6:291a
xenodochium, 6:290b
Hospitals, Western European, **6:292a–297b**, 8:253a
administration, 6:294a-b
bishops' responsibility for, 6:294b
decline of in later Middle Ages, 6:296b
in early church, 6:292b–293a
monasteries, 6:293a, 293b–294a
xenodochia, 6:292b
expansion in 12th century
contributing factor, 6:293b
England, 6:293b
France, under Louis IX, 7:675b
Holy Ghost hospital, Lübeck, 7:682b
for the insane, 6:490b
laws affecting, 6:296b
leprosariums, 6:292b, 295a, 296b, 9:677a-b
in London, 7:660b, 665a
in Nuremberg, 9:202a
in Paris, 9:404a
patrons of, 6:293a
physical arrangement
of beds, 6:295a
floor plans, 6:294a-b
for pilgrims, 6:468a
provision of food and clothing, 6:295b
routine
four sets of customs, 6:295b
monastic model, 6:295b
patient's responsibility, 6:296b
rules and regulations, 6:295b–296a
St. Peter's in York, 6:293a
Santa Maria della Scala (Siena), 11:280b
size of, 6:294b
spitals, uses of, 6:294b
sponsorship of
lay associations, 6:294a
motivations for, 6:293b–294a
religous orders, 6:294a
in Tallinn, 9:186b
under Germanic conquerors, 6:293a
in Valencia, 12:348a-b
see also Leprosy; Tithes
Hospites, in Hungary, 6:340b, 342a, 342b, 343b
Hospodine, pomiluj ny!, 11:343b
Host, elevation of, incense and, 6:431b
Host desecration libel, 1:341a, **6:297b**, 7:88b
see also Blood libel
Hostelry. *See* Inns
Hostelry, right of, 6:474a
Hostels, Rome, 10:526a-b
Hostiensis, **6:298a–299a**
clerical appointments, 6:298a
conflict over election rights, 6:298a-b
Ferrariensi episcopo, 6:327a
Hugh of St. Cher and, 6:446b
kingship theories of, 7:268a
Lectura in quinque libros Decretalium, 6:298a
dating of, 6:298b
on *nuncius,* 4:205a
opposition to William Raleigh's election, 6:298a
papal election of June 1270, 6:298b
on papal *plenitudo potestatis,* 10:20b
relations with Innocent IV, 6:298b
on role of cardinals, 3:517a-b
simony charges, 6:298a, 298b
Summa aurea, 6:298a, 298b
Hôtel dui roi (advisers of Philip II Augustus), 9:418a
Hôtel-Dieu, 6:293a
Hothby, John, 8:647a
Hǫðr, 11:27a
in Baldr myth, 2:55b, 56a
Hotman, François, Estates General history, 10:316b
"Hounskull." *See* Helmet, visor
Houpée (unit of measure), 12:588b
Houppelande, 3:625a-b
Hour
division of, 3:24b
equal, 3:29b
vs. unequal, 3:24a-b
measurement by waterclock, 3:28a
Hourglass, 11:102 (*illus.*)
Houris, in Islamic Paradise, 9:393 (*illus.*), 394a
Hours of Anne of Cleves, 2:275a
Hours, Book of. *See* Book of hours
Hours, canonical. *See* Canonical hours
Hours of Jeanne d'Evreux. See Jeanne d'Évreux

Hours of Mary of Burgundy, manuscript illumination, 7:345b (*illus.*), 346a
Hours of Philip the Good, 7:55b
Hours of Sophia von Bylant. See Master of St. Bartholomew
House of Fame. See Chaucer, Geoffrey
House of Science. *See* Dār al-^{c}Ilm
House of Wisdom. *See* Bayt al-Ḥikma
Household. *See* Family
Household management
  aristocratic. *See* Estate management
  early, 4:600a-b
  Fachschrifttum and, 4:579a
  peasant, 4:603b–604a
Household Ordinance of 1279, 6:302a-b
Household Ordinance of York (1318), 6:303a
Household, royal, **6:299b–306a**
  butler in, 2:434a-b
  Byzantine, 2:473a, 474a
    imperial comitatus, 2:472a
  Capetians, 5:160a, 162b–163a, 173b–174a
  chaplain in, 3:264b
  England
    Anglo-Saxon, 6:300a-b
    domestic functions of, 6:304a-b
    Exchequer and, 4:530b
  Hungary, 6:340b, 341a, 344a
  travels of, 12:152b, 159a–160a
  see also Curia, lay
Housemann, Rüdiguer, bishop of Speyer, Jews and, 7:90a
Houses
  building materials for
    stone masonry, 3:561a–564a
    wood, 3:558a–561a
  construction of
    glass in, 3:564a
    half-buried, 3:558b–559a
    rammed-earth, 3:558a, 561a, 561b–562a
    roofing, 3:559b, 563b
    stone, 3:564a
    wood, 559a–560a, 3:558b
  heating of, 3:561a-b
  long house, 3:559b
  see also Urban architecture, Western European
Houwaert, Jan Baptist, 4:322b
Houxds, 3:146b, 147 (*illus.*)
Ḥovot ha-Levavot. See Baḥya ben Joseph ibn Paqūdā
How a Man Should Believe in God. See Py fodd y dyly dyn gredu
How the Plowman Learned His Pater Noster, 10:425a
How the Wise Man Taught His Son, 3:662a
Howard, William, 7:189b
Howling dervish. *See* Dervish
Hrabanus Maurus, 4:542b, **6:306a–308b**
  as abbot of Fulda, 5:311b
  Allegoriae in universam sacram Scripturam, 6:307b
  Carolingian Latin poetry and, 3:103a
  Christian Hebraists and, 3:313b
  as *clavipotens frater,* 7:558a
  on confirmation, 3:536a
  De institutione clericorum, 1:556b, 4:223a, 6:307a, 307b
    ad nostrum dogmatem convertimus (we shall convert them to our doctrine), 10:355a-b
    ars praedicandi and, 1:556b
  De laudibus sanctae crucis, 6:307b–308a, 10:108a
  De rerum naturis (*De universo aut rerum naturis*), 1:606b, 4:448a, 577b, 6:307b, 10:113b
    Etymologiae and, 7:361b, 362b
    list of vehicles in, 12:369b–370a
    on music, 8:638b
  De universo. See De rerum naturis
  development of medicine and, 8:247b
  on Divine Office, 4:223a
  Epistolae, 10:14b–15a
  as exegete, 6:307a-b
  on Gothic architecture, 5:589a
  Gottschalk of Orbais and, 5:638a-b
  on leprosy, 7:550a
  liturgical treatises of, 7:628b
  penitentials of, 9:490a
  "Rhythmus de fide catholica," 6:308a
  study of animals and, 2:242b
  on the symbolic significance of plants, 2:245a
  Tatian manuscripts and, 11:601a
  "Veni creator spiritus," 6:381b, 12:381b
  see also Meginhart of Fulda
Hrabr', 11:554b
Hradec Králové, 6:376a
Hradiště. *See* Tabor
Hrafn Sveinbjarnarson, in *Sturlunga saga,* 11:499a
Hrafnkels saga Freysgoða, 4:613b, 614a, **6:308b–309a**
  Freyr in, 5:297a
  see also Fljótsdæla saga
Hrafns saga Sveinbjarnarsonar, in *Sturlunga saga,* 11:497b, 499a
Hrazdan. *See* Zanga River
Hreiðars þáttr heimska, in *Morkinskinna,* 12:3b, 4a, 4b
Hrings saga ok Tryggva, 10:395b
Hřip^{c}simē, 1:509b, 517b, 518a
  Nino and, 9:140a
Hřip^{c}simē, Church of St., **6:309a–310a**
Hrokkinskinna manuscript, *þættir* in, 12:3b
Hrólf kraki
  in *Bjarkamál,* 2:254a
  in legends, 10:677b
  in Lejre chronicle, 7:538a
Hrólfs saga Gautrekssonar, **6:310a-b**
  description of hero, 5:139a
  purpose of, 5:142b
Hrólfs saga kraka, **6:310b–311b**
  story of King Fróði in, 6:3b
  see also Bjarkamál; Lejre chronicle
Hřomklay, **6:311b–312a**
  katholikos at, 11:313b
  see also T^{c}oros Roslin
Hřomklay, Council of (1179), 1:500b, 9:104b
Hrómundar saga Gripssonar, **6:312a–313a**
  versions of, 5:143a
Hrotswitha von Gandersheim, **6:313a–316b**
  Abraham, 6:315b–316a, 7:363b
  "Ascension of the Lord," 6:314b
  Calimachus, 6:315b
  drama, 6:315a–316b
  Dulcitius, 6:315b, 7:363a-b
  Gallicanus, 6:315b
  "Gangolfus," 6:314b–315a
  Gesta Ottonis, 6:316a
  "Maria," 6:314b
  Paphnutius, 6:315b, 316a
  poetry, 6:314b–315a, 316a
  Primordia coenobii Gandeshemensis, 6:313a, 316a
  Sapientia, 6:315b, 316a
Hrungnir, 11:32a
  encounter with Thor, 12:45b
  in *Haustlǫng,* 12:32a-b
Hruodlandus. *See* Roland
Hrvatinić family, influence on Bosnia, 2:336b, 337a-b
Hrvoje Vukčić
  relations with
    Ostoja, 2:338a
    Sigismund of Hungary, 2:338a
Hry o vzkříšení Páně, 11:344a
Hry Tří Marií, 11:344a
Hryggjarstykki. See Eiríkr Oddsson
Hrynhent, 11:320a
Hsi-hsia, Mongol invasions, 8:465b, 468b
Hsi-ling Shih, empress, silk cultivation of, 11:293b
Hsüan Tsang, 2:397a
Ḥtmh d^{ɔ}yqr^{ɔ}, 11:122a
Hû von Trimberg. *See* Hugo von Trimberg
Huang Ho Valley, silk cultivation in, 11:293b
Huang Ti, emperor, silk cultivation of, 11:293b
Hubert, St., hunting and, 6:358b, 361a
Hucbald of St. Amand, **6:316b–317b,** 7:362b
  Berno and, 8:641b
  De harmonica institutione, 3:542a
  Dialogus and, 8:640b
  Egloga de calvis, 6:317a
  Gerbert of Aurillac and, 8:640a
  hymns of, 6:381b
  Musica, 6:317a, 8:614a-b, 639a
  Musica enchiriadis and, 8:639b
  musical notation and, 8:626b
  on neuma, 9:109b
  Rheims cathedral school and, 10:303a
  rhymed offices written by, 10:371b
Hucbaldus Elnonensis. *See* Hucbald of St. Amand
Ḥud (banū), 5:652a
Ḥudā^{ɔ}, 8:562b, 565b
Hudra, Išʼyahb II and, 11:567b
Ḥudūd, in Druze religion, 4:296a
Ḥudūd al-^{c}ālam, 5:393b
Hue de Rotelande, **6:317b–318a**
  Ipomedon, 1:266b, 8:330a
  Protheselaus, 1:266b, 8:330a
Huelgas, Las (monastery: Burgos), 12:686b
Huelgas MS, Las, **6:318a-b**

Huelgas MS, Las (*cont.*)
Benedicamus Domino versus in, 2:167b
hymns and, 6:380a
Notre Dame materials in, 6:318a
Huerta, irrigation of, 6:556b, 557b, 558a
Huesca, controlled by Banū Qasi, 9:68a
Huesca, University of, 12:287a
Hüffer, Georg, *Korveier Studien,* 9:712a-b
Huge Scheppel. See Elisabeth of Nassau-Saarbrücken
Huges Capet. See Elisabeth of Nassau-Saarbrücken, *Huge Scheppel*
Hugh II of Cyprus, king, 4:71a
Hugh III of Cyprus, king, 4:71a
Hugh IV of Cyprus, king, 4:71a
Hugh the Abbot, Robert the Strong and, 3:89b
Hugh of Arles, 2:429a
Hugh of Baux, count, Rogerius and, 10:444a
Hugh of Bologna, *ars dictaminis* and, 10:358b
Hugh de Brienne, regency of, 7:379a
Hugh le Brun, count of Lusignan, 7:129b
Hugh Capet
ancestry of, 3:89a–90a
elected as Frankish ruler, 3:115b
election to throne, 5:154a-b, 156a
Sylvester II and, 11:553a
Hugh of Cluny, abbot
Desiderius of Monte Cassino and, 2:173b
expansion of Cluniacs under, 3:348a, 469a
Gregory VII and, 3:69b
in Leo IX's procession, 7:543a
support for First Crusade, 3:356b
Hugh of Fleury, **6:318b–319a**
De regia potestate et sacerdotali dignitate, 6:318b
Ecclesiastical History, 6:318b
Historia Francorum, 5:654a
kingship theories of, 7:264a
see also André de Fleury
Hugh of Floreffe, on Yvette of Huy, 9:11b
Hugh of Fosse
Divine Office and, 10:83b
Premonstratensians and, 10:86a
Hugh the Great (*d.* 956), 3:89b
Hugh de Lacy, 6:518b
Hugh of Lucca, 8:251a, 253a
Surgery, 4:248a
Hugh de Lusignan, Philip II of Taranto and, 7:381a
Hugh de Neville, command of foresters, 5:129a
Hugh of Newcastle, as follower of John Duns Scotus, 12:44a
Hugh of Novocastro, on Antichrist, 1:322a
Hugh of Payns, founding of Knights Templar and, 3:244b, 304a
Hugh (Primas) of Orléans, 5:575a-b, **6:319a–320b**, 7:367a
classical knowledge of, 6:319b
epigrams of, 7:367a
life of, 6:319a-b
as reflected in poetry, 6:319b
sequence and, 6:381b
themes in poetry, 6:319b
Hugh of Provence
Magyars and, 6:338b
Rome and, 10:522b
Hugh de Puiset, bishop of Durham, 7:200a, 10:383b
Hugh of Remiremont (adviser to Pope Leo IX), 7:543a
Hugh Ripelin, *Compendium of Theological Truth,* on Antichrist, 1:321b–322a
Hugh of Rouen, archbishop, *Contra haereticos,* 4:375a-b, 12:21a
Hugh, St., Berzé-la-Ville and, 10:506b–507a
Hugh of St. Albans, **6:320b**
Hugh of St. Cher, 4:246a, **6:320b–321a**
Aristotle and, 1:462a
biblical scholarship and, 4:321a
Commentary on the Sentences, 6:321a
Dominican Bible commentary and, 4:544a
on liturgy, 7:632b
Postillae in Bibliam, as a source for *Bible moralisée,* 2:222b
on sacrament of penance, 9:604a
on treasure doctrine, 6:446b
William of Auxerre's theology school and, 12:22a
Hugh of St. Victor, 3:322b, **6:321b–323a**
admired by Robert of Melun, 10:434b
cartography of, 5:397a-b
Chronicle, 6:264a
in Dante's *Divine Comedy,* 9:514a
De sacramentis christianae fidei, 6:322a, 322b, 7:631b, 9:593a, 12:21b
in Rufinus' *Summa decretorum,* 10:545b
sacrament of Order, 9:601b–602a
theology of the Trinity, 9:598b
definition of sacrament, 9:602b
Didascalicon, 1:607b, 4:448b, 543b–544a, 577b, 6:322a, 7:564b, 8:211a
influence of on Peter Comestor, 9:514a
liberal arts, 9:593a
on magic, 8:37a
on physics, 2:241b
on the threefold division of the senses, 2:224a
as exegete, 2:213b
founder of Victorine spiritual traditions, 6:321b
influence of on *Merure de Seinte Église,* 8:279a
on knowledge, 11:643a
late sequences and, 11:167a
library classification and, 7:565b
liturgical treatises of, 7:631b
mathematical theory, 8:211a
mysticism of, 1:51b
Practica geometrie, 8:211a
preaching of, 10:76a
on 'Pseudo-Dionysius' *Celestial Hierarchy,* 9:593a
scriptural interpretation, 9:593a
spirituality, 9:593a
theology of, 6:321b–322a
philosophy and, 6:322a
theology school of, 12:21a-b
on Trinitarian doctrine, 12:192a-b, 194a-b, 196a
see also Andrew of St. Victor; Richard of St. Victor
Hugh of Saltrey, 4:509b
Tractatus de purgatorio sancti Patricii, 10:620a-b
Hugh of Santalla
on Arabic-Latin translation, 12:140a
Liber trium judicum and, 10:473b
Hugh of Semur, St., **6:318b**
Hugh (son of Thibaut I), 3:244a-b
Hugh (the Black) of Burgundy, duke, 2:427a
Hugh von Trimberg. *See* Hugo von Trimberg
Huginn, **6:323a-b**
and Muninn, 6:323a-b
Hugo (glossator), **6:323b–324a**
De iuris et facti ignorantia, 6:324a
De petitione hereditatis, 6:324a
Four Doctors and, 2:417b
legal career, 6:323b–324a
Vacarius' *Apparatus glossarum* and, 12:343b
see also Jacobus (de Porta Ravennate)
Hugo II of Rouen, archbishop, 5:424b
Hugo IV of Lusignan, king of Cyprus and Jerusalem, Boccaccio's *Genealogy of the Pagan Gods* and, 2:283b
Hugo of Bury St. Edmunds, **6:324b–325a**, 6:324b (*illus.*), 7:24a
Hugo von Langenstein, *Martina,* 8:357a
Hugo, Master. *See* Hugo of Bury St. Edmunds
Hugo von Montfort, **6:325a-b**
lyrics of, secular mixed with spiritual, 8:357b
minnesingers and, 8:414a
privatization and, 8:359b
Hugo Pictor, illuminator, 1:258a
Hugo de Porta Ravennate. *See* Hugo (glossator)
Hugo of Reutlingen. *See* Spechtshart, Hugo
Hugo of Santalla. *See* Hugh of Santalla
Hugo von Trimberg, **6:325b–326b**, 10:258a
attitudes toward law and lawyers, 7:481b
Codicellus multarum litterarum, 6:325b–326a
as didactic author, 6:325b
Laurea sanctorum, 6:325b
Registrum multorum auctorum, 6:325b, 326a, 7:368a
Renner, 6:325b, 326a, 8:355a
as reflection of popular attitudes, 7:481b
Samener, 6:326a
Solsequium, 6:325b

sources, 6:325b
Vita beate virginis Maria rythmica, 6:326a
Hugo van der Goes. *See* Goes, Hugo van der
Hugo de Werna. *See* Hugo von Trimberg
Hugolino. *See* Gregory IX, pope
Hugolino's Rule, 12:688a
Hugolinus, **6:326b–327a**
Hugolinus de Presbyteris, 6:323b
Huguccio, 3:516b, **6:327a–328a**
Agiographia, 6:327b
Bolognese School and, 5:567b
Decretum Gratiani and, 4:127b–128a, 7:414b
identity of, 6:327a
importance of, 6:327b–328a
Innocent III and, 6:464a
Laurentius Hispanus and, 7:385b
Magnae derivationes (*Liber derivationum*), 4:449b, 6:327a, 327b, 7:352a, 365b
description of theater in, 4:278a
survival of, 4:450a
Rosarium, 6:327b
on spiritual and temporal hierarchy, 10:20b
Summa artis grammaticae, 6:327b
Summa Decretorum, 5:657b, 6:327a, 327b–328a
Tractatus de dubio accentu, 6:327a-b
Hugues de Berzé, 3:506a
Hugues le Noir. *See* Hugh (the Black) of Burgundy, duke
Hugues de Puiset, Suger of St. Denis and, 11:502b
Huguet, Jaime, **6:328a-b**, 6:328b (*illus.*)
Huguet de Mataplana, 3:164b
Ḥujr ibn ᶜAdī al-Kindī, 7:307a
Shiite rebellion under, 6:370a
Hulagu, 3:313a, 5:573a, **6:329a-b**
alliance with Baybars, 8:473b
burial site of, 12:332a
Christianity and, 11:563b
death of, 8:473b
descendants of, 1:453a
end of Ayyubid rule and, 2:23b
founding of Ilkhanid dynasty, 6:420a
friendship with Vardan Arewelcᶜi, 12:360a
in Iran, 6:504b
in Iraq, 6:504a
Ismailism and, 6:618a
al-Lādhiqiya and, 7:315b
military conquests
Assassins, 8:472a
of Baghdad, 2:47a, 8:472b
Syria and Egypt, 8:472b–473a
Mongol conquests in Middle East and, 6:329a-b
Naṣīr al-Dīn and, 11:228a
observatory at Maraghen and, 11:99a
siege of Mayafariqin, 8:472b
vs. al-Mustaᶜṣim, 8:651a, 651b–652a
Huld (giantess), 11:495b
Hulda manuscript, *þættir* in, 12:3b
Hulde, 8:413b
Hülegü/Hüleʾü. *See* Hulagu
Hulk (ship), 11:239a-b, 241a
modified, 11:244a-b
Hum (Serbia), acquired by Stjepan Kotromanić of Bosnia, 11:486a
Human sacrifice, witchcraft and, 12:660b
Humanism
on astrology, 1:609a
at Naples in 1320's and 1330's, 2:278a
attitudes to Gothic architecture, 5:581b
Byzantine
Platonism and, 9:696b, 697b–699a
see also Bessarion
Chaucer and, 8:321a
condottieri condemned by, 3:531a-b
dictamen and, 4:176b
diplomacy and, 4:212a-b
English universities and, 3:60a
Enrique de Villena and, 12:449a
equity and, 4:502a
German, 8:359a
in Hungary, 6:347a, 348b
Italian, 7:17b–18a
Agryropoulos and, 7:1a
Christian Platonism and, 9:696b, 702b–703a
class element, 7:11b, 17b
education in, 7:11b
in Florence, 2:287b, 5:101a-b, 7:1a
mastery of Greek learning, 7:1b
militant, 7:11b
origins of, 7:11a
Jerome as model of, 7:58a
Landini and, 7:326b
Latin chronicles and, 6:634b
Petrarchist influence, 9:531a, 533b
in Spain, 11:425a-b
Humanistic scripts, 9:349a–350b
antiqua (formal) script, 9:349a-b, 350a (*illus.*)
cursive script, 9:349b–350b (*illus.*)
round or textual (formal) script, 9:349a-b, 350a (*illus.*)
Ḥumaydī, 11:511b
Humber River, as a linguistic dividing line, 8:312b
Humbert I (the Whitehanded) of Savoy, count
Brouchard and, 4:108b
foundation of House of Savoy, 10:674b
Humbert II of Vienne, dauphin
crusade of, 4:55b
sale of patrimony, 4:107b–108a, 109a
Humbert, cardinal. *See* Humbert of Silva Candida
Humbert de La Tour du Pin, Dauphiné and, 4:109a
Humbert of Moyenmoutier. *See* Humbert of Silva Candida
Humbert of Romans, 3:643b, 10:77a
De dono timoris, 4:250b
De eruditione praedicatorum, 4:250a
De predicatione sanctae crucis, 4:20b, 250a
Dominican antiphonary and, 8:643a
Jews and, 7:88b
preaching books of, 4:250a-b
revision of Dominican liturgy, 4:240b, 241b–242b
sisters of Dominican order and, 4:254b
Humbert of Silva Candida, 3:351a, **6:329b–330b**
adviser to Pope Leo IX, 7:543a-b
Berengar of Tours and, 3:634b
church reform and, 10:287b
Contra Nicetam, 9:128b
Donatist views, 6:195a
investiture conflict and, 6:499a
Libri tres adversus simoniacos, 6:330a
mission of to Constantinople (1054), 8:304b
on papal primacy, 6:329b
papal reform by, 5:477b
Peter Damian and, 9:509a
Roman theology and monastic reform, 4:374a-b
sacramental theology of, 6:330a
Schism of 1054 and, 3:349a
on simony, 7:123b, 11:301b
use of Donation of Constantine, 4:258b
Humbert's Codex, St. Dominic Office, 10:376b
Humiliana, St., 9:14a
Humiliati, 12:687a
acceptance into church, 6:197b
evangelical preaching, 6:197a
Innocent III and, 6:464a
lay preaching, papal restriction on, 5:196a
Poor Lombards, 6:197b
Humiliores, 10:461a
Humors (physiology), in insanity, 6:491b
Ḥunayn, Battle of (*ca.* 631), 7:235a
Ḥunayn ibn Isḥāq al-Ibādī, 1:458a, 11:84a, 566b
Isagoge, 8:248a, 249b, 250a, 256a
al-Ṣafadī on, 12:131a
Ten Treatises on the Eye, translations of, 9:247b
Thābit ibn Qurra collaboration, 12:130b–131a
translations, 8:248a, 11:82b, 83a, 12:130a-b, 130b
criteria and methods, 12:131a–133a
of herbals, 6:178b
of Plato, 9:699a
visual ray theory, 9:241a, 247b
Hund and *hundare* (Scandinavian local units), 10:699a-b
Hundingjaland, in *Sturlaugs saga Starfsama,* 11:496b
Hundred (land division), **6:330b–331a,** 9:194b
administration of, 4:464b
murder fine and, 4:487a
Hundred (unit of measure), **6:331a,** 12:593a
Hundred Years War, **6:331a–335a**
armor and weapons, 12:565b
artillery in, 3:151b
heavy guns, 12:567a
auxiliary services, 6:333b
Beauforts vs. Richard, duke of York, 6:161b–162a
Burgundian War (1417–1435), Lyons in, 7:699b
capture of Rouen, 10:537b

Hundred Years War (*cont.*)
Caroline War of 1369–1389, 5:186a–187a
causes, 6:331a-b, 9:555a
dynastic claims, 5:183b, 184a
Edward III and, 4:398a
cavalry in, 3:205a-b, 6:333a-b
Charles V of France and, 3:269a–270a
Charles VII of France and, 3:270b–271b
Charles of Orléans and, 3:272b–273a
chronicles of, 9:638b
Clement VI, pope, and, 3:439b
Edward the Black Prince in, 4:398b–399a
Edwardian War of 1340–1389, 5:184a–185b
effects of
on Caen, 3:8b
on Champagne, 3:250a
on Cistercian Order, 3:405b
on culture of chivalry, 6:334b
on Ghent, 5:523a
on Languedoc, 7:341a
on Normandy, 9:169b
population decline, 4:142a
on royal power, 6:334a
on theory of war, 6:334b
on trade, 6:93b
on University of Paris, 9:409b
on villages, 12:444b
Enguerrand VII and, 4:490b
financial needs generated by, 10:319a-b
financing of, 4:484a-b
English, 6:333b–334a
France, 6:334a, 11:622a-b
salt tax, 10:631a-b
French cities and, 12:318a
French representative assemblies and, 10:317b, 318a, 324a, 325b
indenture system and, 12:565a
Jacquerie and, 9:478a-b
Lancastrian War of 1415–1435, 1:72a-b, 5:187b–188b
manpower, 6:333a-b
mercenary troops, Genoese crossbowmen, 12:559a
military tactics, 12:565a
land battles, 6:322b
naval battles, 6:333a, 9:81b
sieges, 332b–333a
nobility and, 9:151a
phases of, 5:184a, 6:331b–332b
in *Piers Plowman,* 7:332b
royal wardrobe and, 6:303b–304a, 305b
Scottish soldiers in, 11:110b
Sigismund and, 11:287a
support services, 6:333b
Treaty of Arras (1435), 7:699b
Treaty of Troyes, 10:320a–321a
Welsh bowmen, 12:523a
Hundredweight, **6:331a**
Ḥunduj. *See* Imruʾ al-Qays
Huneric, Vandal king, 12:354b, 355a
Hungarian diet, **6:335b–336a**
frequency of meeting, 6:335b, 336a
nobility in, 6:335b–336a
origins of, 6:335b
under Angevin rulers, 6:335b
under Sigismund, 6:335b
Hungarian Illuminated Chronicle, Basarab, 12:500b
Hungarian language, **6:336a–337b**
German and, 6:337a
indefinite conjugation, 6:336b
Latin and, 6:337a
national identity and, 6:434a
in Romania, 6:443b
Slavic loanwords, 6:336b–337a
stages in development, 6:336b
Hungarian law, Stephen I and, 11:479b
Hungarians
in Bulgaria, Symeon and, 11:554b
See also Magyars
Hungary, **6:337b-351b,** 6:338 (map)
administration of. *See* Banat; Banus
administration under St. Stephen I, 11:478b–479a
Angevins and, 11:273a
Bosnian bannate, 2:334b, 335b–336a, 339b
Buda, 2:396b
Byzantine influences in, 11:478a-b
Christianity in, 8:443a
church, Stephen I and, 6:339a-b
diet, horseflesh consumption, 1:300a-b
economy, Sigismund and, 11:287a-b
Edmund Ironside's sons and, 12:373a
foundation of the Christian kingdom, 6:339a–341a
geography, 6:337b
Hungarian chariots, 12:378a-b
invasion by, of Vidin, 2:412b
invasions of Russia, 10:576b
Manuel I Komnenos and, 8:91b
Moldavian invasions, 12:503b
Mongol invasions, 8:470b–471a
nobility in
baronial rule under Sigismund, 6:346a–347a
growth of, 6:341a–342b
origins, 6:338a–339a
Otto III of Germany and, 9:302a-b
Ottoman rule of, German *Reichstage* and, 10:330b
as papal fief, 6:464b
reconstruction after the Mongol invasion, 6:342b–344a
relations with
Bosnia, 4:8a, 6:340b, 348a, 7:309a
Byzantine Empire, 6:339a
Croatia, 4:4a, 5b, 6b–8a, 6:337b, 340a-b, 346a
Dalmatia, 6:337b, 341a, 346a
Galicia, 6:340b, 341b
Kiev, 6:339a
Poland, 9:629a, 727a, 728a
Romanian principalities, 10:514a, 515a
Venice, 12:386b, 389a, 389b
Serdica and, 11:189a
social mobility in, 6:345a
Tomislav of Croatia and, 12:68b–69a
under Sigismund, 11:287a-b
universities, 12:289b–290a
vs. Mongols, at Mohi, 2:131b
vs. Ottomans, 4:56a, 6:349a–350a, 7:124a
at Mohács, 10:514b
final Ottoman advance, 6:349a–350a
under Bāyazīd I, 2:136a
Vlad Ţepeş and, 12:484b
see also Avars; Magyars; Tvrtko I
Hungary Water, 2:147a
Hungrvaka, **6:351b–352b**
author of, 6:352a
as local chronicle of Skálholt, 6:352b
see also Bishops' sagas
Hunnica, 1:522a
Huns, **6:352b–354b**
Altaic nomads, invasions of Russia, 10:576a
in Balkans, 6:437b, 443b
Bulghar and, 12:488a
Byzantine invasion, 2:485a
defeated at Catalaunian Fields (451), 2:92b
empire of, 2:92b–93a
in Europe, 6:353 (map)
in Gaul, 12:470b
Indo-European languages and, 6:434a
in *Nibelungenlied,* 9:113a, 114a
origins of, 6:352b
in Poland, 9:352b
rulers of, 6:354a
Serdica and, 11:189a
as slaves, 11:335a
society of, 6:354a
vs. Alani, 1:121a
vs. Belisarios, 2:165a
vs. Burgundians, 2:92a, 11:536b
vs. Ostrogoths, 6:352b, 12:468b, 469a
vs. Rome, 3:201a, 6:352b–354a, 10:465a
vs. Visigoths, 12:469a
weapons of, 1:522a
westward migration, 2:485b
as cause for invasions of Roman Empire, 2:90a
see also Hephthalites
Hunt of the Unicorn (tapestry), 6:362b–363a, 11:596b
Hunterston brooch, 3:224a
Hunting dogs. *See* Dogs
Hunting and fowling, Iranian, **6:354b–355a**
in art, 11:597b, 598a
as symbol of royal power, 6:354b–355a
Taq-i Bostan and, 12:715a-b
Hunting and fowling, Islamic, **6:355a–356a**
in art
at Khirbat al-Mafjar, 6:595b
at Quṣayr ʿAmra, 6:595a
Koran on, 6:355a
as training for *jihād,* 6:355a
under Abbasids, 6:355a-b
use of cheetahs, 6:355b
see also Falconry
Hunting and fowling, Western European, 2:244b, **6:356a–363b**
in art, 6:361a-b, 362 (*illus.*)
illuminations of, 6:361b
tapestries, 6:361b, 362a (*illus.*)
at French court, 6:358a
by peasants, 6:357b–358a

by women, 6:357a-b
ceremonies, 6:359a
in courtly literature, 6:358b–359a
early history of, 6:356a–357a
Fachschrifttum and, 4:579a-b
falconry, 5:152a
game animals, 1:301a
hunters' organizations, 6:358a
kings' travels and, 12:159b
laws affecting, 6:356a-b
list of species, 5:151b
in literature, 6:358b–359a
manuals for, 6:359b–361a
as musical theme, 3:4a-b
poaching, 6:357b
reserved for nobility, 6:356a
social consequences, 6:357a
restrictions on, 1:300b–301a
rituals of, 6:359a-b
royal privilege, 5:152a, 6:301b
in Russia, 1:100a
social aspects, 6:357a–358b
as source of animal food, 1:299a, 300b–301a
in Spain, 6:358a, 11:441b
of unicorns, 6:361b–363a
warrens, 6:356b–357a
weapons for, 6:357a
see also Forest law; Reclamation of land
Hunting games, 5:351a-b
Hunting swords. *See* Swords
Hunting weapons, 6:357a
Huntingdonshire, fairs at, 12:117a
Huntington, Ellsworth, on climate and history, 3:450a-b, 452b-453b
Hunyadi, János, **6:363b-364a**
Austria and, 2:8b
crusade against Ottomans, 11:182b-183a
defeated at Battle of Varna (1444), 12:361a, 502b
Hungarian defense and, 4:56a
military career of, 6:363b–364a
as regent of Hungary, 6:347b
Vladislav II and, 12:484b
vs. Ottomans, 6:364a
Walachian invasion, 12:502b
Hunyadi, László, 6:348a, 364a
Huon de Bordeaux, 3:259a
Auberon's role, 9:283a
Huon de Méri, *Tournoiement de l'Antéchrist,* 1:188b
Huon le Roi de Cambrai
ABC, 9:639a
Ave Maria en roumans, 9:633b
Descrissions des relegions, 9:639a
Regrés Nostre Dame, 9:633b
Vair Palefroi, 7:317a, 9:636a
Vie de saint Quentin, 9:633b
Huopussu, 8:562a
Hupomnematismoi. See Theodore Metochites
Hurdy-gurdy, 8:608a, 608b
origins, 11:660b
Hurley, William, **6:364b**
Hurling, 5:348a
Hurmann von Thüringen, 5:450a
Hurmuzān, governor of Khuzistān, 6:569a
Ḥurr ibn Yazīd al-Tamīmī, al-, 6:370b
Hurtere, Joost de, 2:29b–30a, 4:559b
Hus, John (Jan), **6:364b–369b**
at Council of Constance, 6:369a
Bible translation into Czech, 2:216a
Christian Bohemian Nation, 6:200a
church reform and, 3:666a
communion under both kinds (utraquism) and, 3:504b, 6:372b
condemnation of, 3:370a, 649b–650b, 6:369a-b
Czech language and, 6:444a
Czech literature and, 11:344b
Czech nationalism and, 6:365a-b
De ecclesia, 6:200, 368b
and church hierarchy, 4:377a-b
death of, 5:489b, 6:200a, 369a-b
doctrines of, 3:370a-b
education of, 6:364b
excommunication of, 6:200a, 368a, 368b
goals of reformist movement, 6:367b
in hymns, 6:384a
links to England, 10:384b
Lollards and, 7:645b
On Simony, 6:368b–369a
opposition to papal authority, 6:368a-b
realism and, 12:407b
Sigismund and, 11:287b
as teacher at University of Prague, 6:364b–365a
Wyclif and, 6:366b–367a, 368a, 12:707a, 710a-b
Zabarella and, 12:735a
Ḥuṣām al-Dīn, 8:651b
Ḥusayn Bayqarā, Timurid sultan, 12:58a
as patron of art and science, 12:59a
Ḥusayn ibn ᶜAlī, al-, **6:369b–371b,** 11:136a, 136b
claim to caliphate, 6:370a
commemoration of, 11:228b
death of, 6:371a, 586b
Iraq and, 6:511b
descendants of, 1:174b–175a
Ithnā ᶜasharī Shiism and, 6:503a
journey to al-Kūfa, 6:370a-b
in al-Kūfa, 7:307a
Shīᶜa and, 6:370a, 11:226b
significance of rebellion, 6:371a
tomb of, 6:513b, 8:654a-b
Umayyads and, 6:370a
vs. Yazīd, 6:370a, 370b
Ḥusayn ibn Ḥamdān, al-
execution of, 6:84a
governorship of Diyār Rabīᶜa, 6:84a
Ḥusayn ibn Manṣūr. *See* Hallaj, al-
Ḥusayn Vāᶜiz Kāshifī, *Anwār-i Suhaylī,* 6:508b
Husband. *See* Men, married
Husbandry (treatise), 4:513b, 12:533a
Huscarl, 12:556b
Húsdrápa. See Úlfr Uggason
Ḥushi'el ben Elhanan, 7:98a
Húska, Martin, 6:375a
Huskarlestefne, 11:522a
Huss, Mathias, *La grande danse macabre,* 9:680a (*illus.*)
"Hussite Engineer," 8:392b
Hussite League, 6:372a
Hussite (Utraquist) church, 2:306a, 306b, 307b
Hussites, 2:300b, 5:489b, **6:371b–378a**
Albrecht V of Austria and, 2:8b
cannon in wars against, 3:65b
chalice symbol of, 3:505a-b
church reform and, 6:377b
communion under both kinds and, 3:504b–505b
defense measures of, 6:375b–376a
effect on church unity, 4:377a-b
military strength of, 2:304b–305a
millennialism of, 8:387b
negotiations with Council of Basel, 3:652b–653a
Nicholas of Cusa and, 9:123a
nominalism and, 9:157b
Nuremberg and, 9:202a
origins of, 2:303a
political consequences of, 6:376b
Prague University and, 6:371b–372a
radical
center of Hussite religious life, 6:372a-b
defeat of, 6:376b
preaching of, 6:372b
religious communities of, 6:372b, 373b, 374b–375a
religious practices, 6:373a
utraquism of, 6:372a-b, 373b
and Waldensian heresies, 6:372b–373a
repression of, 6:373b
resistance to, 6:374a-b, 375b–376a
revolt after Council of Constance, 3:652b–653a
Romanian literature and, 10:511a
Sigismund and, 6:374b, 375b, 376b, 377a
split within movement, 6:374a–375b
Taborites and, 6:374a–377a
two factions, 6:200a
vs. Sigismund, 11:287b
wars of, Wyclif and, 12:707a, 710b
see also Bohemian Brethren
Hwaetberht of Wearmouth, bishop, 10:398a
Hy Many, Book of. *See* Book of Uí Mhaine
Hyde (monastery: England), military contingent from, 2:173b
Hydraulic wheel. *See Nāᶜūra*
Hydraulics. *See* Technology, hydraulic
Hydraulis. See Organ
Hygiene, *see also* Public health, sanitation
Hyginus Gromaticus, *De munitionibus castrorum,* 11:515b
Hyle Historias, continued in Anna Komnena's *Alexiad,* 1:303b
Hylestad (church: Setesdal), door posts, 4:582a
Hyll, John, 4:263a-b, **6:378a**
Hylomorphism, 11:305b
Aquinas on, 12:40a
Aristotle on, 11:370b
Roger Bacon on, 2:35b, 36a, 36b
Hymir, Thor and, 12:45b, 46a
Hymiskviða, Thor in, 12:45b
Hymn at Cockcrow. See Ambrose, St.
Hymn Before Sleep. See Prudentius
Hymnals
Armenian, *heirmoi* and, 8:556b

Hymnals (*cont.*)
Cistercian, 3:402a
Syriac, Byzantine notation in, 8:556b
Hymnarius Moissiacensis, 6:381b
Hymnarius Paraclitensis. See Abelard, Peter
Hymnarius Severinianus, 6:381b
Hymnody, rhythm and, 10:379a-b
Hymns
Ambrosian, Cistercians and, 8:643a
Armenian, 1:509b
dedicated to saints, 1:520a, 520b
Step^canos of Siwnik^c and, 1:510a
see also Šarakan
Byzantine, **6:378a–379a,** 8:554a–555b
akathistos, 9:714a
authors of, 2:469a
John of Damascus and, 7:124b
kanon, 2:469a, 7:208b
kontakion, 2:469a, 7:292b
literary value, 2:468b–469a
musical signs, 2:469a
regulations for, 2:468b
St. Ephraem and, 11:565b
styles of, 8:554a-b
troparion, 12:208a
see also Liturgy, Byzantine; Sticheron
Hebrew, 8:564a, 565a
Latin, **6:379a–385a,** 7:360b–361a
of Aquinas, 9:714b
Bede on, 2:154b
Bohemia, 6:384a
Carolingian Empire, 6:381b
diversification of, 6:379b–380b
Divine Office and, 4:224b
11th and 12th centuries, 7:365b, 9:714a-b
England, 6:382a
farsa, 12:211b
humanist influences, 9:715b
Iberian Peninsula, 6:381a, 384a
influence of, 6:384b
Ireland, 6:381a
Marian, 9:715b
meter of, 6:382b–383a, 7:371b
music of, 6:382b
paraliturgical, 6:380a
of Peter Abelard, 9:713a, 714b
political events and, 9:714b
popularity of, 8:571b–572a
prosula, 12:210a–211b, 212 (*illus.*)
psalmus idioticus, 11:632a
rhyme and, 7:372a
Scandinavia, 6:382b
sequence development and, 9:714a, 12:210a–211b
as a source for parody, 9:441a
sources, 6:380b–382b
themes of, 6:383a–384b
Tropes to the Ordinary of the Mass and, 12:208b–210b
Tropes to the Proper of the Mass and, 12:210b–213b (*illus.*)
tropus or trope, 12:210a, 211b, 213 (*illus.*)
see also "Veni creator spiritus"
melodic style of, 8:270a, 270b–271a
Slavic, 8:574a-b
Syrian, 8:578a
vernacular, in liturgical drama, 4:274b
see also Liturgical poetry; Mass cycles; Plainsong; Rhymed offices
Hyndluljóð, **6:385a–386a,** 12:492a
date of, 6:385b
meter of, 6:385a-b
plot summary, 6:385b
preservation in *Flateyjarbók,* 4:387b
Hypakoai, 8:554b
Hypathius of Ephesus, on Pseudo-Dionysius the Areopagite, 9:99b
Hypatia, murder of in 415, 11:82a
Hypatius, Empress Theodora I and, 12:12a
Hypatos (Byzantine court title), doge of Venice and, 12:384b
see also Consuls
Hyperbola (geometry), 1:438b
Hyperpyron, **6:386a,** 8:420b–421b
Hypogeum, **6:386a-b**
see also Cubiculum
Hypostasis, 12:189a–190a, 192a
Basil the Great on, 2:121b–122a
in Plotinus' philosophy, 9:95b–96b
Hypostatic union
in Cyril of Alexandria's theology, 4:75a
icons and, 6:398b, 401a-b
see also Trinitarian doctrine
Hypsēlē, 8:617b
Hystoire de Julius Cesar. See Jean de Thuim
Hystoria Gruffudd ap Cynan, 12:600b–601a
Hystorie van Reynaert die Vos, Die, 10:314b
Hywel ab Owain Gwynedd, **6:386b–387a**
death in civil war, 6:386b
Gorhoffedd, 6:386b–387a
poetry of, 6:386b–387a
as ruler of Ceredigion, 6:386b
Hywel Dda, Welsh ruler, 10:366a
annexation of Dyfed, 4:329b
inheritance of Dyfed, 12:515b–516a
Law of, 7:527a, 12:516a, 612a
organization of *Gogynfeirdd,* 12:598b
three groups, 12:599b
Hywel y Fwyall, Sir, Iolo Goch and, 6:500b

I

"I sing of a maiden," 8:340b
Iacopo da Lentini, **6:387b–388b,** 11:259b
"Amor non vole ch'io clami," 6:642b, 11:259b
"Io m'aggio posto in core a Dio servire," 11:259b–260a
life of, 6:387b
"Lo viso—mi fa andare alegramente," 6:642b–643a
as master of Sicilian school of poetry, 6:387b
"Meravigliosamente," 6:642a-b, 666b
poetry of
audience for, 6:388a-b
imagery, 6:388a
sonnet, 6:669a
themes, 6:388a
Iacopo Mostacci, 11:259a
vs. Iacopo da Lentini, 6:387b
Iagailo. *See* Jagiełło
Iâl, 6:386b
Iamblichus, 9:97a–98a
on Aristotle, 1:457b, 505b
De communi mathematica scientia, 9:698b
Iasak, 5:327b
Iatrika. See Theophanes Nonnos
Iatviagi. *See* Yotvingians
Iazyges, migrations, 10:653a
^cIbādāt, 6:581a
Ibadites, 11:139a
African Islamization and, 1:71b
Berber language and, 2:186b
legal procedures, 1:71a
Ibāḍīya. *See* Ibadites
Ibas of Edessa, 3:630a
Armenian church and, 1:499a
Nestorianism and, 9:106a, 106b
Ibelin family, 9:150b
Ibelin, Jean d' (of Beirut), **6:388b–389b**
campaigns in Cyprus, 6:389b
Frederick II and, 4:70b–71a, 6:389a-b
imperial wars, 9:558a
as leader of barons in Latin Kingdom, 6:388b–389a
Ibelin, Jean d' (of Jaffa), **6:389b–390b,** 4:71a
Assizes of Jerusalem (*Livre des assises et des bons usages de Iherusalem*), 1:598b–599a, 4:71a
in crusade of Louis IX, 6:390a
legal writings, 6:390a
on limitations of royal power, 6:390a
treaties with Muslims, 6:390a
Iberia. *See* Georgia
Iberia (Byzantine theme), 1:474a
established, 1:483b–484a
Iberian Peninsula
Albans in, 10:36a-b
Black Death in, 2:263b–264a
Castile and, 3:127 (map)
Castilian language in, 3:141a
Christian missions to, 8:439b
Christianity in, 10:37a, 38b
Christians vs. Muslims, Battle of Río Salado (1340), 9:714b
in 11th century, 3:176 (map)
Germanic invasions of, 10:36a
monasticism in, 10:36b–37a
Muslims in, 8:444a-b, 10:37a
paper introduced into, 9:389b
plagues in, 9:675b, 681a
reckoning of era in, 3:18b
relations with, Italy, 4:557b–558a
Suevi in, 10:36a-b
tribes in, 10:35b
under Asturian rule, 10:37a–38a

under Diocletian, 10:36a
under Ferdinand I, 10:38b
under Roman rule, 10:35b–36a
Vikings in, 10:38a-b
see also Aragon; Asturias-León; Castile; Catalonia; Granada: Hispano-Arabic headings; Hispano-Mauresque headings; Navarre; Portugal; Valencia
Iberian/Georgian March (Armenia), 2:140b
Iberians. *See* Georgians
Ibiza, irrigation of, 6:558a
Iblīs, **6:390b–391a**, 6:579b, 9:40b, 41a
in ^{c}Ayn al-Quḍāt's work, 9:42a
Koranic texts regarding, 6:390b
in Sufi tradition, 6:391a
Ibn. *See* next element of name
Ibrāhīm II, Aghlabid emir, 6:391b
siege of Cosenza, 1:71b–72a
tyranny of rule, 1:71b
Ibrahim Beg, 7:214a
Ibrāhīm ibn Adham, 9:39b
Ibrāhīm ibn al-Aghlab, **6:391b–392a**
Abbasids and, 6:391b
^{c}abīds and, 1:70a
appointment as emir of Ifrīqiya, 1:70a
army revolts against, 6:391b
basis for power, 1:70a
construction of al-^{c}Abbāsiyya, 1:70a
raids against Christians, 6:392a
Ibrāhīm ibn Ya^{c}qūb of Tortosa, 5:393a
on Poland, 9:717b
on Prague, 10:70a
on suspended chariot in Hungary, 12:372b–373a
Ibrāhīm Ināl, 7:215a
Ibrāhīm al-Mawṣilī, 8:567a
Ibrāhīm, ruler of Shāh-Arman, 11:220a
Ibrāhīm, Samanid emir, defeat by Ya^{c}qūb ibn Layth, 10:637a
^{c}Ibrī, Ibn al-. *See* Bar Hebraeus
Ibshīhī, al-, *Mustaṭraf fī kull fann mustaẓraf, al-* (*New Book of Polite Accomplishments*), 1:380b
Icart, Lluís, poetry of, 3:171a
Ice, used for cooling drinks in Cairo, 2:209b
Ice ages, "little ice age," 3:455a-b
Içe (^{c}Isā) de Gebir, *Brebario sunnī,* 1:176a
Iceland, **6:392a–397a**, 6:393 (map)
Black Death in, 2:261b
Christian missions to, 8:442a
Christianity in, 12:427a
cultural influence, 6:394b
Guðmundr sagas and, 6:34a, 34b
Valla-Ljóts saga and, 12:352a
Víga-Glúms saga and, 12:416a
see also Vatnsdœla saga
church in, *see also Kristni saga; Laurentius saga*
colonized, 4:554b
geography, 6:394b, 395a
history of
Árna saga biskups, 1:537a
sources, 7:327b–328a
in *Merigarto,* 8:275b
political and legal organization, 10:702b–704a
chieftaincies, 10:703a-b
constitution, 10:702b–703b
hreppar, 10:703b–704a
local assemblies, 10:703a
national assembly (Althing), 10:702b–703a
Norwegian interference, 10:703b–704a
parochial divisions, 10:703b
Quarters, 10:703a
taxation and tithing, 10:703b
under chieftaincy, 6:392b–394a
relations with Norway, 6:395b–396b, 7:386b
settlement of, 12:426b–427a
Sinfjǫtli story in, 11:310a-b
Sturlungs, 6:34a, 34b
Vinland sagas and, 12:458a
see also Scandinavia; Viking navigation
Icelandic Annals (1121), on Vinland, 12:428a
Icelandic language, grammars, 5:640a-b
Icelandic law, 6:396a
adapted from Norwegian Gulathing, 12:32a
courts, 10:705a, 705b–706a
lǫgrétta (law council), 10:703a
penalties and punishments, 10:706a
procedure of, in *Njáls saga,* 9:145b
Icelandic literature
curse of gold theme, 6:27b
historical writing, 4:441a
literary renaissance, 4:391a
Old Icelandic, 6:440a
sagas
earliest period of, 6:145b
13th century, 6:81a-b
see also Bishops' sagas; Family sagas, Icelandic; *Fornaldarsögur;* Norse kings' sagas; *Riddarasögur*
see also Scandinavian literature; Scandinavian mythology
Icelandic parliament. *See* Althing
"Ich muoz von schulden sin unfro." *See* Friedrich von Hausen
Icocedron. See Odington, Walter
Icon Painters' Manual. See Ikonopisnyi podlinnik
Iconium. *See* Ikonion
Iconoclasm, Christian, 2:462b–463a, 3:10b–11a, **6:399b–402b**, 6:405b–406a, 9:561b
in Anatolia, 1:241a
in Armenia, 6:188b
Armenian/Byzantine church union and, 1:500a
biblical arguments for, 6:401a
Byzantine classical scholarship and, 11:48b
Carolingian, 10:305b
Charlemagne and, 3:346b
christological arguments for, 6:401a-b
church design and, 9:452b
collapse of, 2:489a
condemnation of, 3:320b, 631a, 6:191b
consequences of, 2:463a-b
artistic, 2:439a, 451a, 488a
for monasticism, 2:488a
political, 2:462b
Constantine V's support of, 3:546a-b, 6:400b–401a
destruction of early church decorations, 4:357a
Eastern-Western controversy, 11:45b
exceptions to ban on images, 6:401b
Germanos I and, 5:471b
Gregory II and, 3:345a
Hrabanus Maurus and, 6:307b
Ignatios and, 6:415b
imperial support for, 2:488a–489a, 6:191b
Isaurians and, 6:561a
Islam and, 6:403b–404a
John of Damascus on, 7:124b
Justinian II and, 7:203a
Leo III and, 6:400b
Lombards and, 7:657a
Macedonian renaissance, 8:1a-b
Monophysitism and, 6:402a
Octateuch and, 9:214b
opposition to, 2:463a, 487b–488a, 9:619a
Constantine V, 8:457a
zealots vs. politicians, 2:488b
origins of movement, 6:400a, 9:561b
Paulicians and, 9:468b–469b
precursors of, 4:349a
proponents of in Constantinople, 9:561b
Protestant, 10:299a
refugees from in Italy, 7:4a
reorganization of Byzantine government and, 4:340a
restoration of icons by Empress Theodora II, 12:12b
revival of, 7:545a, 9:561b
social and political explanations for, 6:402a
sources for, Neoplatonism, 9:585b
Studios Monastery and, 11:494b, 495a
Synodikon of Orthodoxy and, 9:561b, 11:558b
Tarasios and, 11:598b
Theodora II and, 12:12b
Theodore of Studios and, 12:16a
theology of, 2:462b–463a, 6:191b, 223b
Christology, 2:463a
Theophanes Confessor and, 12:22b
Thomas the Slav's rebellion and, 12:36b
Visigothic sculpture and, 12:467a
see also Amorians; Leo the Mathematician; Leo III, Byzantine emperor
Iconoclasm, Islamic, 6:397b, **6:402b–404b**, 6:407a, 10:306b
ban on representation in religious art, 6:403b
Byzantine iconoclasm and, 6:403b–404a
criticism of relics veneration, 10:296b
destruction of figural artworks, 6:402b–403a
political propaganda, saint's lives as, 6:58b
theological arguments for, 6:403a, 404a
Iconoclasm, Jewish, 7:63a-b

- Iconoclasm, Zoroastrian, 12:747b
- Iconodule, **6:404b**
  - Macedonian revival and, 10:307a-b
- Iconography, **6:404b–406a**
  - analysis of
    - "contextual" theories, 6:405a
    - Panofsky's theories, 6:404b–405a
    - Weitzmann's theories, 6:405a
  - in bestiaries, 2:206a-b
  - on carved stones, 8:367b
  - Christian, art renaissances and, 10:307a-b
  - Christian, in Islamic metalwork, 6:607b
  - Christogram, 3:319b
  - in Ghent Altarpiece, 4:566b
  - *globus cruciger,* 5:564a
  - *Glykophilousa,* 5:568b
  - Good Shepherd, 5:577b
  - Hagia Sophia, Constantinople, mosaics of Photios, 2:439a-b
  - *Hermeneia,* 4:191b–192a
  - Man of Sorrows, evolution of, 2:456b
  - Meuse Valley, 8:496a
  - in migration period art, 8:367b–369b
  - of Mission of the Apostles, 8:438b
  - mystery plays and, 8:662b
  - Old Testament Trinity, 12:198a-b, 199 (*illus.*)
  - Passion of Christ, 4:370a
  - plants, pictorial record of, 2:346a, 348b
  - *plashchanitsa,* 9:693b–694b (*illus.*)
  - Russian, 10:589b–590a
    - Virgin Mary, 9:716a
  - of Sicilian kingship, 11:217b, 267b–268a
  - in stained glass windows, 5:552b–553a
  - *Traditio clavium,* 12:123 (*illus.*)
  - *Traditio legis,* 12:123a–124b (*illus.*)
  - Transfiguration, 12:125b–126a
    - by Theophanes the Greek, 12:23b (*illus.*)
  - Tree of Jesse, 12:181b–182b (*illus.*)
  - Tree of Life, 12:182 (*illus.*)
  - *umilenie, Vladimir Virgin* and, 12:486b
  - *see also* Baptism of Christ; Blachernitissa; Coptic art; Lamentation; Manuals, artistic; Nimbus; *Noli me tangere*
- Iconography, Jewish, 7:63b–65b
- Iconology
  - defined, 6:405a
  - Islamic, **6:406a–409a**
    - definition of, 6:406a-b
    - literary and scientific themes, 6:407b–408b
    - political power and, 6:408b–409a
    - religious imagery in, 6:406b–407b
- Iconophile. *See* Iconodule
- Iconostasis, 1:444 (*illus.*), **6:409a–410a**
  - arrangement of icons on, 6:409a–410a
  - Cathedral of the Dormition, 6:409b (*illus.*)
  - communion and, 6:399a
  - compared with rood screen, 11:118a
  - *kliros,* 7:276a
  - origins of, 6:409a
  - religious symbolism, 10:588a
  - sanctuary-nave division, 10:587b
  - *see also* Screen, chancel
- Icons
  - Armenian, 1:502a
  - artistic conventions, 6:410a-b
  - Bulgarian, 2:415 (*illus.*), 416 (*illus.*), 417a, 417b
  - Byzantine, popularity over relics, 10:299a
  - Byzantine screen, 1:444 (*illus.*)
  - decorative conventions for, 4:355a
  - early church and, 6:399b–400a
  - from Sinai, 4:362b, 363a
  - Georgian metalwork, 5:410b
  - iconoclasts' attacks on, 4:362b
  - ivory, Virgin and Child, 7:26a (*illus.*)
  - kiot, 7:271b
  - magical qualities attributed to, 4:362b
  - manufacture of, **6:410a–411a**
    - Council of 100 Chapters, 10:589a
    - Hellenistic funerary portraits and, 6:410a
    - materials, 6:410b
    - Moscow school, 10:589a (*illus.*)
    - Novgorod, 10:585a, 586a
    - repoussé, 10:315b
    - Russian schools, 10:589a-b
    - *see also Basmenoye delo; Ikonopisnyi podlinnik*
  - miniature mosaic, 2:449a, 457b
  - origin of, 4:354b
  - painting of, 2:417b
  - in panel painting, 5:604a
  - purpose of, 4:362b–363a
  - Russian, **6:411a–412a**
    - Annunciation Icon, Trinity—St. Sergius Monastery, 10:589a (*illus.*)
    - Byzantine origins, 6:411a
    - Four Saint Icon, 10:589b (*illus.*)
    - growth of native tradition, 10:585a
    - icon-painting tradition in folk art, 10:590b
    - *kleimo,* 7:275b (*illus.*)
    - as miracle-workers, 6:412a
    - Moscow school, 10:589a-b
    - Mother of God, 10:584b–585a
    - Novgorod school, 10:586a (*illus.*), 589a-b
    - Old Testament Trinity, 10:588b
    - painters of, 6:411a-b
    - pre-Mongol period, 10:585a-b
    - Pskov school, 10:589b (*illus.*)
    - role in religious ritual, 10:584b
    - Rublev's Old Testament Trinity, 10:541b (*illus.*)
    - secular themes, 10:590a
    - Theophanes' Mother of God, 10:587a-b
    - Ustiug Annunciation, 10:586a (*illus.*)
    - Virgin of the Sign, 10:585a-b
    - Zvenigorod Deesis, 10:588b (*illus.*), 588b
    - *see also* Alimpi
  - St. George, 2:416 (*illus.*), 417b
  - St. Theodore, 2:415 (*illus.*), 417a
  - sources of, 4:362b
  - styles of, 4:362b–363a
  - theology of, **6:397a–399b**, 6:401b
    - early Christian view of images, 6:397b
    - John of Damascus on, 6:398a, 7:124b
    - Nikephoros of Constantinople on, 6:398b–399a, 9:132a
    - Origen's view of, 6:397b
    - response to iconoclasm, 6:397a-b, 398a-b
    - Theodore of Studios on, 6:398b
  - *Transfiguration* icon by Theophanes the Greek, 12:23b (*illus.*)
  - *see also Proskynesis; Proskynetarion*
- Ictus
  - in *Cantar de mío Cid,* 3:72b–73a
- *ʿĪd al-aḍḥā* (*ʿĪd al-aurban*) (festival of sacrificing), 5:38a, 39a
- *ʿĪd al-fiṭr* (festival of the breaking of the fast), 5:38a–39a, *see also* Ramadan
- *ʿĪd al-naḥr. See ʿĪd al-aḍḥā*
- *ʿĪd* prayers, Friday prayer and, 5:299b
- Ida of Leeuw, 9:11b
- Ida of Louvain, 9:11b
- Ida of Nivelles, 9:11b
- Idatius, bishop, 11:389b
- ʿIdhārī al-Marrākushī, *Kitāb al-bayań al-mughrib fī akhbār al-Andalus wa'l-Maghrib,* 8:151a
- Idiocy. *See* Insanity
- Idiophones, 8:563a
  - Middle Eastern, 8:613a-b
- *Idiota de Mente. See* Nicholas of Cusa
- Idley, Peter, *Instructions to His Son,* 662a
- Idrīs I ibn ʿAbd Allah, imam, 6:413a, 414a, 7:97b
- Idrīs II, imam, 6:413a, 413b, 414a
- Idrīs Ḥakīm Bidlīsī, 7:310a
- Idrīsī, al-, **6:412a–413a**
  - cartographic tradition of, 5:393b–394a
  - life of, 6:412a
  - maps of, 5:392a (*illus.*), 9:77a
  - on Meknes, 8:267b
  - *Nuzhat al-mushtāq fī 'khtirāq al-āfāq,* 5:393b, 6:412a, 412b
  - references to Scandinavia, 10:707b
  - Roger II of Sicily and, 6:412a-b, 11:263a, 274a
  - travels of, 6:412b
  - Zanj and, 12:739a
- Idrisids, **6:413a–414a**
  - characteristics of rule, 6:413b
  - conflicts over succession, 6:413a
  - descendants of, 6:413b–414a
  - establishment of power in North Africa, 6:413a, 8:15a
  - founder of, 1:174b
  - southern branch of, 6:413b
- Ieper. *See* Ypres
- Ifrīqiya, **6:414a–415b**
  - Abbasids and, 1:70a
  - Aghlabid rule, 1:70a–72a
  - Almohads and, 1:194a–195a, 6:415a
  - Arab conquest of, 6:414a
  - Christian population of, 6:414b
  - coastal *ribāṭs, 1:71a*
  - decline in prosperity of, 6:415a
  - Ibrāhīm ibn al-Aghlab and, 6:391b, 392a

Islamization, 1:71a-b
Jews in, 7:97b–98b
Marinid invasion, 8:139b–140a
plagues in, 9:684b
Qayrawān as capital, 6:414b
Raḳḳada, 1:71b
relations with, Sicily, 11:261b–262a
revolts against Umayyads, 6:414b
under Aghlabids, 6:414b–415a
9th-century peace, 1:70b
under Buluggīn, 12:744a
under Hafsids, 6:52b–55a, 415a
division between Tunis and Bejaïa, 6:53b
division under Ibn Tafrāgīn, 6:54a
under Ḥammād, 12:744b
under Zirids, 12:744a–745a
see also Africa, exarchate of; Maghrib, al-; Qayrawān, al-
*Iftā*ᵓ. *See Fatwā*
Iggeret Sherira Gaon. See Sherira ben Ḥanina
Īghār, 6:591a
"Iglesia robada, La," *Milagros de Nuestra Señora* and, 2:187b
Ignatios, deacon, *Life of Tarasios,* 11:598b
Ignatios, patriarch, **6:415b**
Basil I and, 2:117b
Council of Constantinople and, 3:631b–632a
Nicholas I and, 9:121a, 121b
see also Schism, Photian
Ignatios Šnorhali, 9:103a, 103b
Ignatius of Antioch, St., 1:508b
on astrology, 1:605a-b
on Virgin Mary, 12:459b
Ignaure, 7:317a
Ignorantia sacerdotum. See Peckham, John
Ignoti Monachi Cisterciensis S. Mariae de Ferraria Chronica et Ryccardi de Sancto Germano Chronica Priora, 12:542b
Igor of Kiev, grand prince, 7:241b–242a
attack on Constantinople (941) and, 12:435a-b
Iḥrām, **6:415b–416a**
see also Costume, Islamic pilgrim
*Iḥṣā*ᵓ *al-*ᶜ*ulūm. See* Fārābī, al-, on music
*Iḥyā*ᵓ ᶜ*ulūm al-dīn. See* Ghazālī, al-
*Ijmā*ᶜ, 6:581b, 587a, 11:219a, 219b
Islamic law and, 7:487a, 488a
Ijtihād, 6:581b, 582a
Ikalto, **6:416a**
Ikhshīd, al- (title), 6:416b–417a, 417b
Ikhshidids, **6:416b–418a**
in Damascus, 4:82a, 6:85a-b
Egyptian rule, 4:405b–406a
government of, 6:417a
military forces of, 6:417a
under Muḥammad ibn Ṭughj, 6:416b–417a
Ikhwān al-Ṣafā, collective encyclopedia, 4:445a
ᶜ*Ikkuv ha-tefillah* (public accusation), 7:70a-b
Ikonion, **6:418a-b**
ᶜAlāᵓ al-Dīn mosque, 11:149a
art and architecture of, 6:612a-b, 613a-b
Byzantine attacks on, 6:418a
crusaders' route and, 10:423b
early bishops of, 9:459a
Ince Minare madrasa, 11:149a
Karatay madrasa, 11:149a, 150 (*illus.*)
"Konya carpets," 11:149b
Manuel I Komnenos and, 8:91b
Mongol attacks on, 6:418a
Mongol conquest of sultanate, 8:470a
sack of during Third Crusade, 6:418a
Seljuks and, 1:241b, 6:418a, 11:154a
see also Seljuks of Rum
Ikonopisnyi podlinnik, **6:418b**
Il milione. See Polo, Marco, *The Travels of Marco Polo*
Il-deniz. *See* Shams al-Dīn Eldigüz
Ilahi-nama. See ᶜAṭṭār, Farīd al-Dīn
ᶜ*Ilal-ḥisāb. See* Karajī, al-
Ilarion of Kiev, metropolitan, **6:418b–419a**
Confession of Faith, 6:418b
election to metropolitanate, 10:592a
Eulogy, 6:418b, 419a
monastic communities, 6:213a
Sermon on Law and Grace, 10:591b
Slovo o zakone i blagodati, 6:418b, 11:346b
on Yaroslav, 12:720a
Ildefonsus, St., **6:419a**
De virginitate sanctae Mariae contra tres infideles, 11:406a
De virorum illustrium scriptis, 2:239a
Isidore of Seville and, 6:564a
liturgical tract of (845), 7:627b (*illus.*), 628a
Spanish prose lives of, 11:439b, 440a
Ildegizids, **6:419a-b**
in Azerbaijan, 1:514a, 2:27a, 11:147a
collapse of, 6:419b
conflicts over succession, 6:419b
consolidation of rule, 6:419b
origin of, 6:419a-b
Île-de-France, 6:442a
government of, 5:159b–160a
Louis VI's campaigns in, 7:673b
return of royal authority, 5:160b
royal domain under Capetians, 5:158a
sculptural traditions in, 5:617b
serfdom and, 11:204b, 205a, 206b
Suger of St. Denis and, 11:502b
Ilek-khanid. *See* Qarakhanids
Īlghāzī I, Ortuqid dynasty, Mardin branch, 9:283b
Ilias latina, 4:496a, *see also* Pindarus
Ilkhan, vs. Berke, 6:329a
Ilkhanids, **6:420a–421a**
administration of, 6:504b–505a, 591a
Armenia and, 1:486a, 514a
Armenian trade and, 12:99a
in Azerbaijan, 2:27a
Christians under, 6:420a
decline of, 8:476a
Ghāzā (Khan), Maḥmūd, 5:517b–518a
Hulagu and, 6:329a
Iran and, 1:514a
in Iraq, 6:514a
Islamicization of, 6:420b
Kasranids and, 11:254a
manuscript illumination and, 8:116b–117b
military conflicts, Golden Horde, 8:473b
Mongol law enforced by, 6:504b
religious dissension, 8:474a
Seljuks of Rum and, 11:158a
ṣinf under, 11:308a–309a
Tabrīz and, 11:571a
vs. Golden Horde, 6:420a
vs. Mamluks, 6:420a, 420b, 8:74a
Xlatᶜ and, 12:713b
see also Uljaytu Khudabānda
Ille Canal, 6:558b
Ille et Galeron. See Gautier d'Arras
Illegitimacy
datary and, 4:107a
see also Children
Illiberal arts. *See* Mechanical arts
Illuga saga Gríðarfóstra, **6:421a-b**
plot summary, 6:421a
sources of, 6:421a-b
Illumination of manuscripts. *See* Manuscript illumination
Illustrations. See Jean Lemaire de Belges
Illyrian language, 6:437b
Illyricum, **6:421b–424a**, 6:422 (map)
Byzantine rule of, 6:422a-b, 423a-b
Diocletian's reorganization of, 6:433a
invasions of, 6:423a
languages of, 10:509b
Latin church in, 6:423a
papacy and, 4:74a, 6:423a, 423b
Roman province of, 6:421b
Slavic conquest of, 6:423a-b
strategic importance, 6:421b–422a
ᶜ*Ilm al-farā*ᵓ*iḍ. See* Inheritance, Islamic
ᶜ*Ilm al-kalām,* 9:567b–568a
Iltutmish, Shams al-Dīn, 5:527a
ᶜĪmād al-Dawla, 2:435b, **6:424a–425a**
as Buyid title, 6:424a-b
ᶜImād, Ibn al-, *Shadharāt al-dhahab,* 2:238b
Image du monde, L', 5:396a
Image of St. Nicholas (Fleury play), 4:278b
Image of the World. See Honorius Augustodunensis
Imagen de la vida, 11:441b
Images d'Épinal, 12:691b
Imago Clipeatus. See Clipeus (Clipeatus)
Imago Dei, in Walter Hilton's *The Scale of Perfection,* 9:23b
Imago mundi. See Ailly, Pierre d'; Honorius Augustodunensis
Imago pietatis, **6:425a-b**, 6:425a (*illus.*)
Imam, **6:425b–426a**, 7:110b–111a
among the Nuṣayrīs, 9:3b
doctrine of, 6:586b–587a, 588b
Fatimid caliph as, 6:616a
functions of, 3:46b
impeccability and infallibility of, 11:136b
in Ismailism, 6:587a, 587b–588a, 614b–615a, 615b
in *Ithnā* ᶜ*asharī* Shiism, 6:503a
of Kharijites, 11:138b
Koran and, 6:586b
power of taxation, 11:669a
Quraysh tribe and, 10:242a

Imam (*cont.*)
role of in the Friday service, 7:616b, 617a
Shiite doctrine of, 6:426a, 11:227a-b
Sunni doctrine of, 6:425b
tombs as Shiite pilgrimage sites, 9:651a-b
Zaydis and, 11:138a, 12:741b
see also Nāṭiq; Sects, Islamic; *Ta^clīm*
Imāmīs, 6:586b, 587a, 11:227a
Baghdad, 11:227b
Imāmīya. *See* Shī^ca, Twelver
Imāmzāda, **6:426a-b**
Imāmzāda Jafar (Isfahan), 6:426b (*illus.*)
Imastasēr. See John of Ōjun, St.
Imerithia. *See* Georgia
Imerius, St., rhymed office to, 10:373b
Imitatio Christi
Byzantine, *Homoiōsis theō,* 9:696b
concept of, in saints' lives, 5:238b
pilgrimage and, 9:654a, 658a, 659b–660a, 12:157a
Thomas à Kempis' *Imitation of Christ,* 12:33a, 157a
Imitatio Jesucristi, 3:168a
Imitation of Christ. See Thomas à Kempis, *Imitatio Christi*
Immaculate Conception, 12:460b
Immaculate Conception, doctrine of
Augustine of Hippo on, 12:460a
defended by Duns Scotus, 9:513b
defended by Peter Aureoli, 9:513b
in Thomism and competing schools, 12:43a
see also Virgin Mary
Immanuel of Rome, 6:650a, 7:92b, 109b–110a
maqāmāt, 6:127b
sonnets, 6:132a
Immigrants, as innkeepers, 6:473a-b
Immortality of the Soul. See Augustine of Hippo, St.
Immram Brain maic Febuil, 6:530a-b, 550b, 551b
as *echtrae,* 6:550b, 551b
Immram Curaig Maíle Dúin, 6:551b–552a
Immram Curaig Úa Corra, 6:551b, 552a
Immram Snédgusa ocus Maic Riagla, 6:551b, 552a
Immram (voyage tale), 1:262a, 6:550a, 551b–552a, 11:440a, 12:428a
Immunity, diplomatic, 4:211
Impartibility. *See* Partibility and impartibility
Impeachment and attainder, **6:426b–428b**
Good Parliament and, 6:427a-b
origin of, 6:426b–427a
Parliament's role in, 6:426b–427a
treason and, 12:168a
Imperfect time. *See* Musical notation
Imperial Cameral (Chamber) Court. *See* Holy Roman Empire
Imperial Circles (*Reichskreise*). *See* Holy Roman Empire, representative assemblies
Imperial decision. See *Decretum*
Imperial, Francisco, **6:428b–429b**
in *Cancionero de Baena,* 11:419a
Dezir al nacimiento de Rey Don Juan, 6:429a
Dezir a las syete virtudes, 6:429a
life of, 6:428b–429a
"Imperial Hymn." *See* Archpoet
Imperial regalia
German, 9:202a
of Latin Empire of Constantinople, 7:346b
see also Labarum; Votive crown
"Imperial Tune." *See* Walther von der Vogelweide
Imperium, 10:11a–12a
Reich and, 5:494a
Imperium transferre. See Translation of empire
Impetus theory, 1:464b, 2:430b–431a
Francis of Marchia and, 12:44a
Imposition foraine, 11:623a, 624a
Imrānī, *Fatḥ-nāma,* 7:177b
Imre of Hungary, king, 5:422a
reign of, 6:341a-b
Imru^ɔ al-Qays, 1:399a-b, **6:429b–431a,** 7:320b
at court of Justinian, 6:430a
character of, 6:429b
contrasted with Islamic poets, 10:346a-b
death of, 6:430a
poetry of
style and imagery, 6:430a-b
themes, 6:429b, 430a
In agro dominico. See John XXII, pope
In apostolicae sedis. See Alexander III, pope
In artem analyticem isagoge. See Viète, François
In bonum patricium. See George of Pisidia
In calumniatorem Platonis. See Bessarion
In domino confido. See Walter of Châtillon
In Heraclium ex Africa redeuntem. See George of Pisidia
In Hexaemeron. See Basil the Great of Caesarea, St.
In Honor of Louis. See Ermoldus Nigellus
In Isagogen Porphyrii commenta editio secunda. See Boethius
In laudem Basilii. See Gregory of Nyssa, St.
In libros regum. See Hildebert of Lavardin
In libros veteris et novi testamenti prooemia. See Isidore of Seville, St.
In octos libros Topicorum. See Albertus Magnus
In restitutionem S. Crucis. See George of Pisidia
"In singulis regnis." *See* Lateran Councils, Fourth (1215)
In spiritu humilitatis, 8:190b–191a
"In a tabernacle of a toure." *See* "Quia amore langueo"
In topica Ciceronis. See Boethius
"In un boschetto." *See* Cavalcanti, Guido
Incarnation
Armenian church and, 1:498a
icons and, 6:397b, 401a, 401b
in *Knik^c Hawatoy,* 7:279b
music and, 8:582a
in Nuṣayrī theology, 9:3b
in Peter Lombard's *Sentences,* 9:517a
in Pseudo-Macarius, 9:7a
in Thomism and competing schools, 12:43a-b
unicorn and, 6:362b
see also Christology; Philosophy and theology, Western European
Ince Minare *madrasa,* 6:612a-b
Incendium amoris. See Rolle, Richard
Incense, 1:224b, **6:431a–433a**
funeral, 4:120b, 121a
in Gospel ceremony, 8:187b, 188a
handling of, 6:432b
liturgical use, 6:431a–432b
censing of the altar, 8:185a
perfume and, 2:147a
symbolism of, 6:432b
Incipit, 9:689a
formulas in hymns, 6:384b
"Incoherence of the Incoherence, The." *See* Rushd, Ibn
"Incoherence of the Philosophers, The." *See* Ghazālī, al-
Income
imperial, Rome, 10:460a
Islamic. *See* Finance, Islamic
papal. *See* Papacy
royal. *See* Finance, royal
Incubus. See Nightmare
Indentured laborers, Russian, 11:190a
India
Ghurids in, 5:527a
in Islamic conquests, 6:570b–572a
Ismailism in, 6:614b, 618a
observatories in, 11:99b
plagues and, 9:681b, 682b
Sebüktigin and, 11:133b
Tamerlane and, 11:588a
trade by Jews with, 3:16b
Indian literature, translation of, into Latin, 12:136a
Indian Ocean
geography, 11:245b, 250a-b
navigation of, 5:394a, 9:85a-b
ports, 11:247b, 248b
Indic languages, 6:505a-b
Indiction cycle, **6:433a-b**
calculation of, 6:433a
in Christian calendar, 3:18a-b
supplanted by *anno domini* dating, 6:433b
Indictment, inquest in, 6:481a
Indigo, 11:595a
preparation of, 4:325b
Indiscreet Jewels, The. See Diderot, Denis, *Bijoux indiscrets, Les*
Indo-European languages, **6:433b–446a**
Avestan, 2:14a
in Balkans, 6:443b
in Baltic, 6:438a
development of, 6:445a-b
ecclesiastical and administrative use, 6:438a–439b
groups of, 6:434b–438a
Latin and Romance, 6:434b–436b, 441b–443b
origin of, 6:433b

spread of vernaculars, 6:439b–444b
see also Celtic languages; Germanic languages; Greek language; Slavic languages
Indo-Iranian languages, 6:433b, 505a-b
Indra, Scandinavian Thor and, 12:46a
Indulgences, **6:446a–451a**
bridge building and maintenance and, 10:414a-b
Christian pilgrimage and, 9:656b, 658b–659a, 660a-b
church taxation and, 11:610b
for crusaders, 4:16a,b, 17a, 55b, 59a, 6:448b
first, 6:448a-b
official doctrine of, 6:447a
penance and, 6:446b, 447b–448a, 9:490b–491a
plenary, 6:448a-b, 450a
purgatory and, 6:446b, 450a-b
treasury of merits and, 6:321a, 446b–447a, 449a-b
Waldensian denial of, 12:510b
Inertia theory, 1:464b
Ine's laws, 11:616a-b
Inevitabile. See Honorius Augustodunensis
Infant mortality. *See* Children, mortality
Infantes de Lara, 11:438a
Infantry, Islamic
battle formations, 12:552a-b
history, 12:551a-b
regulars and irregulars, 12:552a
slaves in, 12:552a
social structure, 12:551a
see also Warfare, Islamic
Infantry, Western European
Anglo-Saxon, 12:556a
Frankish, 12:556b–557a
postfeudal, 12:564b–565a
see also Warfare, Western European
Inflation, Russia, peasant obligations and, 11:192b–193a
Influenza, 10:673a, 676a, 682a
Information for Pilgrims unto the Holy Land, 12:156a-b
Infortiatum
in *Corpus iuris civilis,* 3:609b
Rogerius and, 10:444b
Inge, William, 7:193a
Ingeborg (daughter of Eufemia, queen of Norway), 4:520a
Ingeborg of Denmark, 6:464b
Ingeborg (Ingeburge) of Denmark, queen of France, Psalter of, 5:612b, 614a, 8:109b, 12:181b–182a (*illus.*)
Ingeld-Starkad episode, 10:677b
Inghilfredi, 6:643b
Inghistera, 5:560a
Ingilenē, 1:472b
Ingilene-Anzitenē, 1:515a, 515b
Ingold, Master, *Guldin spil,* 5:352b
Ingólfs þáttr, in *Víga-Glúms saga,* 12:416a
Ingolstadt, University of, 12:289a
Ingvar runic stones, inscriptions, 10:565b–566a
Inheritance, Armenian, 1:488b, 489b, 490a-b, 515b
Inheritance, Byzantine, **6:451a–452b**
by guild members, 6:451a
by women, 6:451a, 452a-b
division of estates under, 6:452a
documentary sources for, 6:452a
family and, 4:594a, 595a, 6:452a
laws governing, 6:451b
legal treatises on, 6:451b–452a
Inheritance, Islamic, **6:452b–454b,** 11:85a
family and, 4:598b–599a
Koranic prescriptions, 6:452b, 453a-b
naskh and, 6:454a
proto-Islamic, 6:453a, 453b, 454a
rules of, 11:85a
Shiite, 11:228b
Sunni rules for, 6:452b–453a
waqf, 12:543b–544a
Inheritance, Jewish, 4:607a, 607b
Inheritance, Roman, 6:455b–457a, 458a
Inheritance, Sasanian, 8:237a
Inheritance, Slavic
daughters, 11:670b
patrilineal bias, 11:670a-b
in Russian (Muscovite) law, 7:511b
Inheritance, Western European, **6:454b–461b**
accensement à toujours, 11:678b
action of right, 9:547a
age at marriage and, 4:609b
appanages, 1:351a-b
Burgundian, 6:456a
in Celtic Brittany, 2:382a
consanguinity in determination of, 3:539b–540a
England, 6:457b
of land, 7:453b
seisin in common law, 7:433b, 451b, 453b
see also Entail; Thegn
evolution of, 6:457–460b
fee tail, 12:622b
France, 6:459b
fragmentation of property, 7:466b–467a
local variations, 7:460a-b
movable capital, 7:466b
tenure problems, 7:458a-b
Frankish, 6:457b
Germanic, 6:455b–457a
honores and, 6:344a
Hungary, 6:345a
in *Hyndluljóð,* 6:385b
insanity and, 6:491a
Irish, 6:518b
Italian, 6:458b, 459b
land, 6:459a, 11:674a, 678a-b
see also Tenure of land
Lombard, 6:456b, 457b
Mâconnais, 6:459b, 460a
mainmort and, 8:51a
mort d'ancestor, assize of, 9:546b
partible, 9:149a-b
repudiation of, 6:458b, 460a
in Scots law, 7:517b
serfdom and, 11:201b–202a
social status and, 6:454b–455b
succession in, 6:456a, 456b
unfree holdings, 2:332a-b
Visigothic kingship and, 12:470b–471a, 472b
wills in Old English, 1:286b
see also Aviticitas; Fee simple; Mainmort; Primogeniture; *Senioratus*
Inherited status. *See* Status, hereditary
Iñigo Arista, 2:126b
Initials
decorated, **6:461b–462b,** 9:662a (*illus.*)
Bible of S. Paolo fuori le Mura, 10:99b (*illus.*)
Book of Kells, 6:462a (*illus.*)
Carolingian styles, 6:462a-b
continental styles, 6:461b
Coptic styles, 6:461b–462a
Hiberno-Saxon scriptoria, 6:461b
in Lindisfarne Gospels, 7:583a-b
monograms, 6:462b
pictorial elements in, 6:462b
historiated, **6:462b–463a**
Gospelbook of Odbert of St. Bertin, 10:111b (*illus.*)
later Italian styles, 6:463a-b
School of Metz, 6:463a (*illus.*)
Initials, decorated, 8:101b
in Hiberno-Saxon art, 8:370a
sacramentaries, 10:607a
Initiation ceremonies, in mystery religions, 9:1a–5a
Injīl (Arabic word for Gospel), used by Muḥammad, 9:497a-b
Ink, **6:463b–464a,** 12:700a
Islamic writing and, 12:698b
see also Manuscript books, production of
Inkwells, 4:115b–116a
Innascibilitas. See Trinitarian Doctrine
Inner Armenia. *See* Armenia: Geography
Inner Temple, 6:477a
Innocent I, pope
assertion of Roman authority by, 9:370a
excommunication of Pelagius and Celestius, 9:486b
Innocent II, pope
Bernard of Clairvaux and, 2:191b
Carthusians and, 3:118b
councils convened by, 3:636b–637a
reign of, 3:352a-b
Roger II and, 10:440b, 441a, 11:267a
Innocent III, pope, **6:464a–465b**
actions against heresy, 3:189b
on altar candles, 1:224b
archives and, 1:446a, 448a
assumption of title vicar of Christ, 4:374b
Bible commentaries of, 3:167a
canonical inquest and, 6:478a-b, 479a
canonization and, 3:68b, 6:68b
Cathars and, 3:187a–188a, 189b, 353a
character of, 6:465b
church taxation and, 11:606a, 606b
condemnation of Raymond of Toulouse, 3:640a
coronation of, 3:353a, 604b
crusades and, 4:16b
against Albigensians, 4:239b, 243b, 376a, 6:465a, 12:538b–539a
Fifth, 4:49a-b, 6:465a
Fourth, 4:41b, 4:42a, 42b, 43a, 44a-b, 45a, 6:464b

Innocent III, pope (*cont.*)
crusades and (*cont.*)
Sicilian regency and, 4:58a, 58b
De miseria humanae conditionis, 6:464a, 464b, 631a, 658b
De missarum mysteriis, 6:464b–465b
De quadripartita specie nuptiarum, 6:464b
decretal collection commissioned by, 7:415b, 427b
Deliberatio, 4:427b
on dispensation, 4:217a-b
Doctrine of Two Swords and, 12:234b
Donation of Constantine and, 12:539a
enforcement of celibacy legislation, 3:216a
English church and, 3:265b
John of England, 6:464b, 7:130a
excommunication, 4:537b
of John of England, 4:468b
of Philip of Swabia, 12:538a
on forgeries of papal documents, 3:253b
Franciscans and, 3:353a-b
Frederick II of Germany and, 5:484a, 11:269b
Gilbert of Poitiers's theology school and, 12:21b
government of Papal States, 6:464b, 9:387a-b
Gregory IX and, 5:671a
as guardian of Constance's son, 5:482b
hierocratic theory of, 10:20b
Hospital of Santo Spirito and, 10:526b
Huguccio and, 4:128a, 6:327a
imperial succession and, 9:58b
importance of, 6:464a
indulgences and, 6:448b–449a
interdict and, 6:495b
for church elections, 4:424b
of Portugal, 10:43b–44a
Jews and, 7:78a-b, 88a, 11:210a
jurisdiction in temporals of France and, 7:264b
Langton and, 7:338a,b
Lateran IV and, 6:465a
Latin Empire of Constantinople and, 7:348a
on liturgical colors, 3:484b–485a
on liturgy, 7:632b, 633a
missions to Eastern Europe, 6:464b
Otto III of Germany and, 5:482b–483a
Otto IV of Germany and, 5:483a
papal primacy and, 3:639b
Philip II Augustus and, 3:187b–188a, 6:464b, 9:553a
pontificals, 10:30b
prohibition of suspect Bible translations, 2:215a
recognition of first Cilician king, 3:391a
reign of, 3:353a-b
repression of heresy, 6:198a, 465a, 483b
Robert of Courson and, 3:659a
Roman Office and, 4:231a, 9:380a
Roman senatorial elections and, 10:523b
royal elections and, 4:425b, 427b
royal intervention in church elections, 4:423a
Sancha García and, 12:686b
Sicut judaeis non (Constitutio pro Iudaeis), 7:78a-b
protection of Jews and, 7:109a
taxation of clergy, 11:614b
Thomasin von Zerclaere's *Welsche Gast* and, 12:38a
on tiara, 12:403b
trial by ordeal forbidden for clerics, 3:610a, 7:503a
Vacarius and, 12:343b
Venerabilem, 4:427b
Vineam domini Sabaoth, 3:639b
vs. John of England, church taxation and, 11:607a
vs. Languedoc, 7:339b
William of Champlitte and, 7:376b
witchcraft and, 12:661b
Wolfger von Erla and, 12:672b, 673a
Wulfstan of Worcester and, 12:703b
Innocent IV, pope, **6:465b–467b,** 9:709b
Ad extirpanda, 6:198a, 485a, 12:661b–662a
Apparatus, 6:466a, 467b
Armenian church and, 1:501a
at Council of Lyons, 3:641a
bankers of, 2:76b
Brancaleone and, 10:523b
cardinals and, 3:94a
church taxation and, 11:606b, 607a
Cistercian women's orders and, 12:686a
Commentarius super libros quinque decretalium, on corporations, 3:606a
Conrad IV of Germany and, 6:466b
Cyprus and, 4:71a, 72b
deposition of rulers theory and, 4:160a
Dominican women's orders and, 12:687b
Donation of Constantine and, 4:259a
Eastern-Western church union and, 7:348b
Franciscan Second Order and, 12:688a-b
Frederick II of Germany and, 4:58a-b, 71a, 5:215b, 6:466a-b, 11:272a
Henry III of England and, 11:607a-b
hierocratic theory of, 10:20b
indulgences and, 6:448b
inquisition and, 6:486a
interdict and, 6:496a
Jews and, 6:467a, 7:77b–78a
John of Plano Carpini and, 4:556b, 7:138a-b
legislation of, 6:467a-b
concept of corporation, 6:467b
Louis IX and, 4:52b
Manfred and, 4:60a-b
Novellae, 6:467b
opposition to, 6:466b–467a
Ordinem vestrum, 5:199b–200a
on punishment of the innocent, 6:496b
reign of, 3:353b
relations with France, 6:466b
revocation of friars' privileges, 4:251b
Romana ecclesia: Ceterum, 6:467a-b
on interdict, 6:496b
tercias and, 11:610a
Innocent VI, pope
Hundred Years War and, 6:334b
vs. cardinals, 3:95b
Zabarella and, 12:735a
Innocent VII, pope, oath to support *via cessionis,* 11:41b
Innocent VIII, pope
Summis desiderantes affectibus, 12:662b
on sorcerers, 8:30b
Inns, **6:468a–477a**
building design for, 6:470a-b
clientele of, 6:474b–475a
commercial vs. noncommercial hospitality, 6:468a
England, 6:469a, 472b
geography of, 6:468a–470a
in literature, 6:468b, 475a-b
ownership and management, 6:472a–474b
Spain, 6:469a
structure and furnishings, 6:470a–472a
wine and, 12:651a-b
see also Taverns
Inns of Court, **6:477a–478a,** 7:665a
antiquity of, 6:477b
apprentices to serjeants-at-law, 7:448b
chancery, 6:477a, 477b, 7:665a
curriculum of, 6:477a-b
internal organization of, 6:477b
monopoly of legal training by, 6:478a
see also English common law
Inquest
canon law, **6:478a–479a**
aprise and, 6:479b
enhanced role of judge, 6:478b
for heresy, 6:479a
interrogation of the accused, 6:479a
introduction of, 6:478a-b
uses of, 6:478b–479a
English law, **6:480b–483a**
in civil cases, 6:481a
in criminal cases, 6:481a
expansion of, 6:482b
Henry II and, 6:481a-b
as instrument of royal power, 6:482b
jurors in, 6:482a
Norman, 4:464a
origins of, 6:480b–481a
property settlements, 4:470b
under Normans, 6:481a
French law, **6:479a–480b**
canon law model for, 6:479b
enquête par turbe, 6:480a
as mode of proof, 6:480a
procedures for, 6:479a-b
use of torture, 6:479b
Norman law, 6:481a, 9:167b
"of the countryside," 6:479b
Inquisitio comitatus Cantabrigiensis, 4:237b
Inquisitio praeparatoria, 6:479a
Inquisitio solemnis, 6:479a

Inquisition, **6:483a–489b**
in Aragon, Raymond of Peñafort and, 10:266b
beguines and, 6:199a
Capetian, 7:340a-b
Cathars and, 3:189b–190b
cooperation with and resistance to, 6:486b–487a
eradication of heretical movements, 6:198a
evasions from, 6:486b
expenses of, 6:486a-b
as form of canonical inquest, 6:478a, 479a
in France, 3:190a-b, 6:487a-b
Gregory IX and, 5:671a, 12:661b
heretics condemned to pilgrimage, 12:156a
Innocent III and, 3:189b
in Italy, 3:190b, 6:488a-b
Jews and, 7:77a-b, 79a
Joan of Arc's trial and, 7:115a
Lateran IV and, 3:640b, 6:464a
Maimonidean controversy and, 8:48b
origins of, 3:189b–190a, 4:376a
penalties of, 6:485b–486a
Peter Autier and, 3:190b
precedents for, 6:483a-b
procedures of, 6:484a–485b
Raymond VII and, 3:190a
records of, 6:487a
sorcery and, 8:28b, 30b
in Spain, 6:484a
as distinct institution, 6:488b
survivals of pagan practices and, 8:25a
tribunals of, 6:483b–484a
use of judicial torture and, 12:89b–90a
in Valencia, 12:349b
Waldensians and, 12:512a-b
witchcraft and, 12:658b, 659a, 661b–662a, 662b
see also Spanish Inquisition
Inquisition, Islamic
Abbasids and, 6:583b
in Iraq, 6:513a
see also Miḥna
Inquisitiones post mortem. See Death and burial; Plagues
Insanity
legal status of the insane, 6:491a
nomenclature of, 6:489b–490a
psychiatric hospital in Valencia and, 12:348b
tolerance of, 6:490a
treatment of, **6:489b–493a**
by physicians, 6:491b–492a
in families, 6:491a
in institutions, 6:490b
see also Bedlam
Inscriptions
Arabic, on ceramics, 6:603a
as archaeological evidence, 1:426b
Armenian, 1:484b
identifying art, 1:493a, 495b
in Tat^cew, 11:600b
χač^ck^car and, 12:713b
Celtic, 6:434b, 436a
Greek, at Quṣayr ^cAmra, 6:595a
Illyrian, 6:437b
Koranic
in Dome of the Rock, 6:593b
in Ince Minare madrasa, 6:612b
in Medinan mosque, 6:593a
Latin, from Pompeii, 6:621b, 12:494b
North African, 10:464a, 464b
Old Church Slavonic, 6:443b
on Pantheon, 1:426a, 426b
Parthian, 6:506a
Roman numerals and, 10:470b–471a
Sasanian, 1:475b
Scandinavian, 6:436b
Zak^carid, 1:485b
see also Tabula ansata
Insects
as disease intermediaries, 9:679a
fleas, 9:675a, 676a
lice, 9:681b
see also Black Death; Disease; Malaria; Plagues
Insegnamenti a Guglielmo, 6:630a
Insignia, imperial. *See* Imperial regalia
Institoris, Henry, *Malleus maleficarum,* 8:30b
Instituta regularia divinae legis. See Junilius Africanus
Institutes. *See Corpus iuris civilis*
Institutes of Polity, Civil and Ecclesiastical. See Wulfstan of York
Institutio canonicorum. See Aachen, Council of
Institutio oratoria. See Quintilian
Institutio principis christiani. See Erasmus, Desiderius
Institutio sanctimonialium, 12:683b
Institutiones. See Cassian
Institutiones divinarum et saecularium litteratum. See Cassiodorus
Institutiones grammaticae. See Priscian
Instruction on the Error of the Priscillianists and Origenists. See Orosius
Instruction d'un jeune prince. See Ghillebert de Lannoy
Instruction of the Uneducated. See Augustine of Hippo, St.
Instructions to His Son. See Idley, Peter
Instrumentation (music), 8:593a
Instruments, musical. *See* Musical instruments
Instruments of the passion. *See* Arma Christi
Instrumentum conchoydeale, 1:437b
Insular Celtic language. *See* Celtic languages, Insular group
Insular Gospels, Book of Kells and, 7:228a-b
Insular scripts
majuscule, 9:342b–343b (*illus.*)
minuscule, 1:275a
pointed or minuscule, 9:343 (*illus.*)
round or half-uncial, 9:342b–343b (*illus.*)
Insurrection. *See* Treason
Intabulation, in Faenza Codex, 4:580a
Intaglio, **6:493a-b**, 6:493a (*illus.*)
used for sealing, 11:124b, 125a
see also Seals and sigillography, Western European, seal technique
Intarsia, **6:493b**
Integumenta Ovidii . See John of Garland (*ca.* 1195-*ca.* 1272)
Intellect, Siger on, 11:286a
Intellect and will, in Thomism and competing schools, 12:43a, 43b
Intellecto. See Honorius III, pope
Intellectual deficiency. *See* Amentia
Intelligence
Averroës on, 1:459b
in Plotinus' philosophy, 9:96a
Intelligence services. *See* Postal and intelligence services
Intelligenza, 6:632a, 651b
Inter sollicitudines. See Vienne, Council of
Inter vivos gifts, 6:459a, 460a
Interdict, **6:493b–497b**
Boniface VIII and, 6:496b–497a
crimes punishable by, 6:495b–496a
effects of, 6:493b–494a
excommunication and, 6:494b, 495a
heresy and, 6:496a
Innocent IV and, 6:496b
legal views of, 6:496a-b
mitigation of, 6:495a-b, 497a
origins of, 6:494a-b
risks for church in, 6:495a-b
Interest group politics. *See* Representative assemblies
Interest rates
in Jewish banking, 2:81a-b
in 12th-century Genoa, 2:73a-b
of pawnbrokers, 2:76a
of Taula de Canvi of Barcelona, 2:75b
see also Usury
Interlace, **6:497b**
Interlacing arch. *See* Arch
Interludum de clerico et puella, 4:279b
Interludum, defined, 4:279b
International relations. *See* Diplomacy
International Style Gothic. *See* Gothic art, International Style
Interpreters
translators and
Arabic-Latin, 12:140a-b
Western European, 12:138a
see also Diplomacy; Translation and translators
Interrogatio Johannis (sacred Bogomil text), 2:294b, 297b
Interrogation, by inquisition, 6:484b–485a
Interrogationes et responsiones in Genesin. See Alcuin
Intestacy. *See* Testacy and intestacy
Intimates. See Household, royal, England, Anglo-Saxon
Intitulationes (superscriptions), 10:16b
Intonaco, **6:498a**
Intonatio, **6:498a**
Intrados, **6:498a**
see also Rib
Introductio harmonico. See Cleonides
Introductio music secundum magistrum Johannem de Garlandia, 8:643b, 11:365a
Introduction to the Eternal Gospel. See Gerard of Borgo San Donnino
Introductiones in Logicam. See William of Sherwood

Introductiones prosaici dictaminis. See Bernard of Bologna
Introductorium Guidonis, 8:641b
Introductorium maius in astronomiam. See Abū Ma^{c}shar
Introductorium musicae. See Keck, Johannes
Introit, **6:498a-b**, 9:688b–690b
Christmas, *Puer natus* with tropes, 12:211b, 213 (*illus.*)
naming of masses for, 8:185b
procession of the clergy, 8:185a-b
see also Mass cycles; Plainsong; Psalm
Învăţăturile lui Neagoe Basarab către fiul său Teodosie, 10:510b
Invectiva contra eum qui maledixit Italie. See Petrarch
Invectiva contra quendam...hominem.... See Petrarch
Invective contra medicum. See Petrarch
Inverness, sheriff of, 11:226a
Investigation of Commerce, The, on markets in Baghdad and Iraq, 12:105b–106a
Investiture
in Rome, travel for, 12:152a, 154b–155b
serfdom and, 11:205a
translation of bishops and, 12:142b–143a
see also Investiture conflict
Investiture conflict, **6:498b–500a**, 9:720a, 12:154b–155b
in *Annals of Hersfeld,* 7:321a-b
Anselm II's collection of canon law, 1:311a
Arnulf of Milan, 1:541b
Babenberg family and, 2:6b
Benzo of Alba and, 2:182b
canon law and, 7:427a
Canossa incident and, 3:69a-b
chronicled by Bernold of Constance, 2:197b
Concordat of Worms and, 12:697a
consequences of, 3:11b, 6:499b–500a
definition of, 6:498b–499a
ecclesiastical benefice and, 2:179a
election of antipope, 6:163b
in England, 10:443a
compromise of 1107, 9:445a
factors perpetuating, 4:22a-b
in France, 3:536b–537a
compromise of 1106, 9:445a
Gerhoh of Reichersberg, 5:424a–425b
in Germany, 7:479b, 480b–481a
legal discussion of, 7:479b, 480b–481a
Henry I and, 6:155a
Henry IV and, 6:163a, 499a-b
Hugh of Fleury on, 6:318b
kingship theories and, 7:262a–264b
Matilda of Tuscany and, 8:222b–223a
ministerials and, 8:405a
origin of, 5:478b, 7:262b, 8:378b
papal reform of church and, 6:499a
Paschal II's role in, 3:635b–636a
political theory and, 10:17a-b, 18a-b
revival of *Corpus iuris civilis* and, 7:427a
Richard Guiscard and, 11:265b
royal unction and, 1:308b
settlement of, 6:499b
Siena and, 11:278b
Sigebert and, 11:285a
simony during, 11:301b
Swabian monasteries and, 11:527a
Synod of Sutri and, 11:517b
translation of bishops and, 12:142b
see also Leo IX, pope; Two Swords, Doctrine of
"Io m'aggio posto in core a Dio servire." *See* Iacopo da Lentini
Ioan Eclesiarh, 10:510b
Ioane Petric^{c}i, 5:417a-b
Ioane Sabanisdze, *Martydom of St. Abo of Tbilisi,* 5:416b
Ioane of Tbet^{c}i, bishop, Bek^{c}a Opizari and, 2:164b
Ioannes Laurentii Lydus. *See* Lydus
Ioannina, history, 4:500a
Ioannitsa. *See* Kalojan
Iolo Goch, **6:500a-b**
cywydd to Owain Glyndwr, 12:608a
Iona (monastery), 3:485a-b
rebuilt by Margaret, 8:56b
see also Columba, St.
Ione Šavteli, *Abdulmesiani,* 5:418a
Iorwerth, Book of, 12:599b
Ipomedon. See Hue de Rotelande
Ipswich, as commune, 3:499a, 501b
Iqa^{c}, **6:500b–501a**
see also Fārābī, al-, on music
^{c}*Iqd. See* ^{c}Abd Rabbih, Ibn
Iqṭā^{c} (feudal grant), 2:25a, 437a, 6:590b, 591a, 591b, 11:561b
see also Tuyul
Iqtiṣād fī'l-i^{c}tiqād, Al-. See Ghazālī, al-
Iran, 6:502 (map)
Arsacids and, 1:559a-b
Assassins in, 1:591b
bookbinding in, 8:99a-b
cavalry, Turkish slave troops, 12:552b
control of Armenia, 10:668a-b
da^{c}wā in, 6:615b
Dīnawarī on, 4:188a-b
glassmaking in, 5:545b, 546b–547a
history, *see also* Ulugh-Beg
history (before 650). *See* Parthians; Sasanians
history (after 650), **6:501a–505a**
Hulagu and, 6:329a
in Islamic conquests, 6:501b–503a, 570b, 590b
Islamic shrines of, 9:671a
Islamic trade and, 12:107b
Ismailism in, 6:618a
Jewish illuminated manuscripts in, 7:67a
Jews in, 7:106a–108a
Kasranids and, 11:254a
Kharijite rebellions, 8:166a
Lakhmids and, 7:320b
local dynasties in, 6:503a-b
manuscript illumination in, 8:116b
mints and money in, 8:421b
monarchy, symbols of kingship, 10:611b
Mongol culture, 8:474b–475a
Mongol invasions, 6:504a-b, 8:469a-b, 12:553a
nomadic tribes, 10:652b–653a
partition of Greater Armenia and, 1:476a
persecution of religious minorities, 10:601a, 662a
Persian church, 3:312a–313b
reunification of, 6:503b
rise of local dynasties, 6:503a-b
Khwarizmshahs, 6:504a
rule over Georgia (Iberia) and, 3:308a
Sasanian culture, 10:662a
Sasanian reunification, 10:666a
Shiism in, 7:307a, 11:137a
social structure, 10:663b
technology, hydraulic, 11:638a
territorial expansion, 10:600a, 601a
under Buyids, 2:435a–437b, 6:424b
under Ilkhanids, 6:420a-b, 504b–505a
under Seljuks, 6:503b–504a
under Timurids, 12:57a–59a
vs. Byzantine Empire
in Armenia, 1:478a
treaty of 561, 12:714a
vs. Rome, Jews and, 10:463b
vs. Turan, in *Shāhnāma,* 11:223a, 223b
Iranian architecture, *gunbadh/kümbet,* 6:28a
Iranian languages, **6:505a–506b**
affinities of, 6:505a-b
Arabic and, 6:506a
Armenian and, 1:506a
branches of, 6:505b–506a
development of, 10:610a
inscriptions, 10:611b
major literary languages, 6:506a
Middle Iranian, 6:505b, 506a
see also Persian language
Iranian literature, **6:506b–509a**
development of, 10:610a
Gāthās, 5:366a-b
poetry, Shīrāz and, 11:252b
see also Persian literature; Rhetoric, Persian
Iranians, al-Mu^{c}taṣim and, 8:653b
Iraq, **6:509a–514b**
Buyid conquests, 8:529a
cavalry, Turkish slave troops, 12:552b
as center of caliphate, 3:35b, 42a
conquests of
by Khālid ibn al-Walīd, 7:235a-b
Islamic, 6:568b–569a
da^{c}wā in, 6:616b
early Islamic period, 6:511a–512a
geography, 6:509b–510a (map)
glassmaking in, 5:545b, 546b–547a
Islamic administration of, 6:590b–591a
Islamic mysticism and, 9:39b
Islamic trade and, 12:107b
Jews in, 7:106a–108a
center of learning for, 3:16a, 7:108a
late medieval period, 6:514a-b
markets in, 12:105b
military conflicts, 6:108b
mints and money in, 8:421b
opposition to Umayyads, 3:39b
plagues in, 9:684a-b, 685b–686a
revolt against Marwanid rule, 6:72b–73a
in Second Civil War, 6:72a-b

Seljuk penetration into, 11:153a
slave rebellion (868–883), 3:49a
Tahirids and, 11:575b
under Abbasids, 6:512a–513b
under Buyids, 2:435b, 6:424b, 513b
under Hamdanids, 6:85a-b
under Ildegizids, 6:419a-b
under Sasanians, 6:510a–511a
under Seljuks, 6:513b–514a
vs. Syria, at Ṣiffīn, 11:284a-b
ᶜIrāqīka. See Surnāy
Ireland
agricultural economy of, 6:553b
Christianization of, 1:288b, 6:514b–516a, 8:439b (map), 440a
diet, horseflesh consumption, 1:300a-b
earldoms
Desmond, 8:532a
Ormond, 8:532a
earliest legends of, in *Leabhar Gabhála Éireann,* 9:46b–47a
early history, *see also* Bard
English in, 6:537b, 554a-b
advance of settlement, 6:517b
assimilation of, 6:519b
de Burghs, 2:421b
Gaelic resistance to rule, 6:518b
Henry II's invasion of, 6:517b
imposition of English administration, 6:517b–518a
military expeditions to, 6:519a-b, 520a
English royal visits to
John, 9:436b
Richard II, 9:436b
feudalism in, 8:532a
history (to 1155), **6:514b–517a**
beginnings of centralized monarchy, 6:517a
political structure, 6:516a-b
history (after 1155), **6:517a–520b**
see also Fitzgeralds
kings of, in "Lament of the Old Woman of Beare," 6:529a
Latin church in, 3:344a-b, 8:440a
missionaries from, 12:151b–152a
Pale, 6:518a (map), 519b
plagues in, 9:675b
Robert I of Scotland and, 10:427a
scholars from at Carolingian court, 7:141a
Scottish invasions, 4:299b, 6:518b–519a
society, **6:552b–554b**
feudalization of, 6:554a-b
king in, 6:553a
monastic organizations, 6:553b–554a
stratification of, 6:553a-b
tribal groups, 6:553a
see also Irish law
tenurial development, 11:685b
territorial divisions
in 1014, 6:515 (map)
in 13th century, 6:518a (map)
Viking raids, 6:516b, 554a, 12:425a–426a
Welsh settlements, 12:514a
see also Dublin; Leinster; Parliament, Irish; Uí Néill; Ulster
Ireland, John, conciliar theory of, 3:520b
Irenaeus, St.
Adversus haereses, 9:128b
on angels, 1:249b
evangelist symbols and, 4:526a
on millennialism, 8:385a
missionary work of, 8:439a
translations into Armenian, 1:505b
on Virgin Mary, 12:460a
Irene, Byzantine empress (12th century)
Nikephoros Bryennios and, 9:133a
Theodore Prodromos and, 12:16a
Irene, St., Byzantine empress (*ca.* 752–803), 2:478b, 488b, **6:520b–521a**
as *basileus,* 2:123a
council at Nicaea called by, 3:631a
iconoclasm condemned by, 3:11a, 6:401a
Nikephoros I and, 9:132b
overthrow of Constantine VI and, 12:15b
rule of, 3:110a
Tarasios and, 11:598b
Irene (virgin martyr), 6:315b
Irind (church: Armenia), 12:750b
Irish art, before 1155. *See* Hiberno-Saxon art
Irish church
asceticism, 6:67a
development of, 3:226a-b, 227a
Easter dating in, 3:228a
missionaries, 6:516a
monastic organization of, 6:515a-b, 553b–554a
monastic scholars, 9:585a
monastic schools, 11:74b
penance in, 9:488b, 489b
preservation of Irish culture, 6:516a
secularization of, 3:601b
Welsh church's influence on, 3:227a
see also Celtic church
Irish language, 3:233a-b, 6:436a, 436b
dialects of, 3:233a
earliest evidence of, 3:233a
Early Modern, 6:531b–532a, 534a
Middle Irish, 6:531a
Old Irish, 6:530b–531a
periods of, 3:233a
Primitive Irish period, 3:233a
verbal system of, 3:233a-b
see also Celtic languages
Irish law, **7:483b–485a**
antiquarianism and, 7:484b
church influence, 7:484a
conservatism of early lawyers, 7:484a
early tracts, 7:484a–485a
on harpers, 8:558b
influence on canon law, 7:484a-b
kingship and justice, 4:312b
law tracts
as sociological documents, 6:553a-b, 7:484b–485a
textual vs. actual social structures in, 7:484a-b
literature and, 6:526a, 527a
merging of secular and canon law practices, 7:484b
Nemed schools, 7:484a
oral tradition, 7:483b
poet-jurists, 7:483b–484a
poetry and, 6:528a
reform of, 7:484b
replacement by English law, 7:483b
separation of church and secular law, 7:484b
unreliability of, 7:484b
see also Parliament, Irish
Irish literature, 6:440a, **6:521a–534a**
Celtic mythology and, 9:46b–48b
Classical Old Irish period, 6:530b–531a
Cormac mac Airt celebrated in, 3:601a-b
Cormac mac Cuilennáin celebrated in, 3:602a
dinnshenchas, 1:33b
Early Modern Irish period, 6:531b–532a, 534a
gnomic literature, 5:568b–569a
historical compositions, **6:539a–540a**
legends, *Dindshenchas,* 4:188b–189b
manuscripts, 6:521a–533a
authorship, 6:525b–526a
commercial value of, 6:524b
Connacht MSS, 6:523a–524b
English and European, 6:524b–525a
linguistic evidence, 6:526a–527b
marginalia, 6:523b, 525b, 527b, 542a
monastic, 6:522a-b
sources, 6:521a–525b
Middle Irish period, 6:531a
narrative cycles, as source for *Mabinogi,* 7:704a-b
poetry, 6:527b–530b, 531b–533a
elegies, 6:538b
inauguration odes, 6:536b
meter, 6:534a-b, 536a
poetry, bardic, **6:534a–539a**
religious, 6:543a
remuneration for, 6:537b–538a
sources, 6:535b–536a
see also Bard; Bardic grammars
prose, 6:526b–527b
religious, 6:538a, **6:540a–544a,** 10:635a
bardic, 6:543a
exemplary personae of, 6:541a-b
form of, 6:541b
hagiographical, 6:542b–543a
hermit poetry, 6:541b–542a
poetry, 6:538a
on St. Brigit, 2:376b–377a
in school and church, 6:542a-b
saga, 6:526b, 527a, **6:544a–550a**
cycles, 6:545b
roscada and, 6:541b
sovereignty myth, 6:547a
satire, *Aislinge meic Con-Glinne,* 1:113b–114a
see also Duodecim abusivis saeculi, De
"Sign of Doomsday" tradition, 1:111a–112a
voyage tales, 6:529b–530b, **6:550a–552b**
sagas and, 6:545b
St. Patrick's purgatory, 10:620a-b
wooing stories, 7:705b

Irish literature (*cont.*)
see also Auraicept na nÉces; Bansenchas; Fenian poetry; Scottish literature, Gaelic
Irish missionaries. *See* Missions and missionaries, Christian
Irminon of St. Germain-des-Prés, abbot, 10:29b
Polyptyque, 11:202b, 203b
survey of, 4:137b, 140a, 511b
Irnerius, **6:554b–555a**
Bologna school and, 5:567b, 7:419a
Bulgarus and, 2:417b, 6:323b
"Four Doctors" and, 11:691b
glosses by, 6:555a
Hugo and, 6:323b
information about, 6:555a
lectures at Bologna, 7:513b
legal teachings, 2:312a, 3:609b, 6:554b, 11:691b
Martinus Gosia and, 8:158a
revival of *Corpus iuris civilis* and, 7:419a-b
Iron
European agricultural tools, 12:81b
grilles
in Barcelona Cathedral, 8:286a
in the Dome of the Rock, 8:286a
in Italy, 8:286a
in Spain, 8:286a
in Winchester Cathedral, 8:286a
hand-digging agricultural tools, 12:78a–79a
importance of, 2:383a
imported from West into Egypt, 12:107b
mining of, 8:397b–398a, 399a-b, 401a
smelting, 8:285b–286a, 401a
with charcoal, 3:267b
in classical times, 11:469b–470a
in sword manufacture, 11:546b
uses of, 8:285b
in Venetian trade, 12:111b
water mills used in producing, 8:393b
working of, 8:285b–286a, 293a-b
see also Metalsmiths, iron and steel
Iron Age, Celtic, 8:369b
Irony, Tannhäuser and, 11:590b
Irregang und Girregar, **6:555b–556a**
Irrigation, **6:556a–559b,** 12:81a
canals
in China, 12:578b
locks, 12:578b
Rhine-Danube link, 12:576b
sluice gates, 12:578b
centralized, 6:557a
cotton cultivation and, 3:626b–627a
Egypt, 10:453a
France, 6:558b
Islamic, 1:103b
active vs. passive, 11:626b–627a
agriculture, 12:84b
dams, 1:104b
nāᶜūra (noria), 1:104a-b
qanāt, 1:104a
rauḍa, 10:261b
taxation of, 11:626b–627a
in Toledo under al-Maᵓmūn, 12:68a
in Valencia, 12:348b
see also Shadirvan
Italy, 6:558b
use of Ticino River, 8:379a
land reclamation and, 10:278b
legal aspects, 6:556b–557a
Mediterranean region, 1:80b
irrigated meadows, 1:87a
Muslim system, 1:84b, 87b
Northern Europe, 6:559a
officials, Muslim. *See Acequieros*
Roman, 6:556a
in Spain, 6:557a-b
Spain, 6:557a–558a
terminology of, 6:558a, 558b
water mills used in, 8:393b–394a
waterwheel, 11:637b–638a, 12:577a
Irués Canal, 6:557b
ᶜĪsā ben Jābir, 11:379b
ᶜĪsā, Ibn, 7:294b
ᶜĪsā ibn Mūsā
al-Manṣūr and, 8:88b, 89a
succession to Abbasid caliphate and, 8:46b–47a
Isaac I Komnenos, Byzantine emperor, revolt against Michael VI Stratiotikos, 7:283b
Isaac II Angelos, Byzantine emperor, 1:245a, 251b, **6:559b–560a**
Grigor Tłay and, 1:500b
military campaigns, 2:496b–497a
restored to throne, 4:46a
Serbia and, 11:173b
Villehardouin and, 12:448b
vs. Bulgarians and Vlachs, 12:483b
Isaac Abu Ibrahim ibn Yashush, on Genesis, 4:539b
Isaac of Antioch, translation of, 12:126b
Isaac ben Jacob ha-Kohen, apocalyptic literature of, 1:346a
Isaac ben Judah, Rashi and, 11:585b
Isaac ben Moses Arama (ᶜAramah), **6:560a-b**
'Aḳedat Yiẓḥaḳ, 6:560a-b
Isaac ben Moses Profiat Duran, *Ma'aseh efod,* 6:129a
Isaac ben Samuel of Dampierre, 7:30a, 11:585b
Isaac ben Sheshet Perfet, 7:99b
responsum literature and, 10:339a
Isaac ben Solomon Israeli. *See* Israeli, Isaac
Isaac (Çag de la Maleha), 7:81b
Isaac Gorni, link to troubadours, 6:127b
Isaac ibn Barūn, grammatical and lexical cognates, 6:129a
Isaac Komnenos, ruler of Cyprus
Patriarch Michael Keroularios and, 8:304b
Richard I and, 4:40b, 70b
Isaac of Nineveh, bishop, 11:566a, 566b
translation of, 12:126b
Isaac Saggi Nehor (Isaac the Blind), 3:1b
Isaac the Sebastokrator, Proclus' treatises rewritten by, 9:567a
Isaac of Stella, on the Mass, 7:632a
Isabel (daughter of William II of Achaea), 7:379a
Isabel (wife of Dinis I of Portugal), 10:50b
Isabella of Castile, queen
Columbus and, 4:560b
conversos and, 9:111b, 112a
crown of Castile and, 3:138a-b
inquisition and, 6:488b
Jews and, 4:564b, 7:77b, 83a
marriage of, Castilian Spanish and, 6:435b
Mudejars and, 11:380b
see also Ferdinand V of Castile, king
Isabella (daughter of Edward III), 4:490b
Isabella, queen (wife of Edward II), 4:398a
coup against Edward II, 4:397b, 483a-b
Isabella, queen (wife of John of England), 7:129b
Isabelle, Blessed, 2:270b
rule for convent at Longchamps, 12:688a
Isabelle of Jerusalem (consort of Frederick II), 6:389a
Isabellian style. *See* Plateresque style
Isagoge. See Porphyry
Isaiah ben Elijah di Trani (the Younger), 4:541b, 7:92b
Isaiah the Greek, influence on Russian art, 10:586b
Isaiah, patriarch (1321–1332), 1:501a
Isaiah (prophet), in art, 6:405 (*illus.*)
Isapostolos, **6:560b**
Isatis tinctoria. See Woad
Isaurians, **6:560b–561a**
Isembert, Master, London Bridge and, 10:414b
Isengrimus. See Ysengrimus
Isengrin the Wolf. *See* Renard the Fox; *Ysengrimus*
Isenheim Altarpiece. *See* Hagenauer (Hagenower), Nikolaus
Isenmann, Caspar, **6:561b,** 9:710b
Passion Altarpiece, 6:561 (*illus.*)
see also Master of the Life of Mary
Iserninus, St. Patrick's associate, 9:465a
Isfahan, **6:561b–562b**
architecture in, 6:562a-b
Buyids in, 6:424b
captured, 7:306b
Great Mosque of, north dome chamber, 11:146 (*illus.*)
Mosque of the Ruler, 4:569b (*illus.*)
mosques, 6:599a
see also Masjid-i Jāmiᶜ
under Malikshāh I, 11:153a
under Safawids, 6:562a
under Seljuks, 6:562a
Išḫani (monastic center: Georgia), **6:562b–563a,** 12:750b
Isḥāq, Ibn
Sīrat rasūl Allāh, 6:250a
on Xusrō I, 12:715a
Isḥāq ibn Ḥunayn, 1:434b
Euclid's *Elements* translated by, 8:209b
Ishbilīya. *See* Seville
Īshōᶜdād of Merv, 11:565b

Nestorian commentaries on the Bible, 9:107b
Ishoʿdnaḥ, *Book of Chastity,* 11:564b
Ishoʿiabh, *katʿolikos,* Nestorianism and, 9:106b–107a
Isidor, 5:426b
Isidore of Charax, *Mansiones Parthicae,* 9:443b
Isidore, metropolitan of Kiev, **6:563a-b**
at Council of Basel, 6:563a
at Council of Ferrara-Florence, 10:594a
contacts with Italian humanists, 6:563a
imperial sympathies, 8:545b
imprisonment of, 8:545b
support for Latin-Byzantine church union, 6:563a-b
Isidore of Seville, St., **6:563b–566b,** 11:409b, 12:473b
on archives, 1:445b
on astronomy, 1:610b
basilica concept of, 5:586a
on the care of books, 7:560b, 570a
Chronica mundi, 6:564b, 565a
doctrine of the six ages, 6:262a
clergy and, 3:440a-b
climatic circles envisioned by, 5:396a
De ecclesiasticis officiis, 4:222b, 5:344b, 6:565b, 7:626b
clerical orders, 9:264b
De fide catholica contra Judaeos, 6:565a, 566a, 9:233a, 10:2a-b
De laude Hispaniae. See Laus Spaniae
De natura rerum, 1:610b, 4:448a, 6:564b
four elements, 9:622a (*illus.*)
order of creation, 9:622b
sources for, 9:622b
De viris illustribus, 2:239a, 6:564b
on deposition of rulers, 4:158a-b
on dialectic, 4:169a
on diaphonia, 4:172a
Differentiae, 6:564b, 565a, 11:406a
on Divine Office, 4:222b
as doctor of the church, 4:234a
Etymologies, 2:242b, 4:169a, 447b, 448a, 449a, 577b, 6:564a-b, 565b, 10:354a-b, 11:406a
astrology and, 1:606a
astronomy and, 1:610b
bestiary and, 2:205b
decline of usefulness, 12:34a
educational program, 9:585a
Hrabanus Maurus and, 6:307a, 307b
importance of, 7:361b
on king's evil, 7:255a
on Latin, 7:351b, 352a, 353b
Latin genre of history, 6:262a
list of vehicles, 12:369b
on the liturgy, 7:626b
on magicians, 8:36b–37a
on music, 8:638a
on Nile, 9:137b
relation between language and nature, 1:46a
source of Hisperic Latin vocabulary, 6:236b
as exegete, 2:212b, 4:542b, 6:565a-b
on Gothic architecture, 5:589a
on harmony, 6:100a
on the heavenly spheres, 9:622b–623a
on heretical works, 7:560b, 564b
Historiae gothorum vandalorum et sueborum (*History of the Goths*), 6:262a, 564b, 565a, 12:472a
historical works, 6:564b
Hrabanus Maurus and, 6:306a, 307a
influence of, 6:564a, 565b–566a, 7:626b–627a
on Christology, 3:321a
on insanity, 6:489b
Laus Spaniae, 6:564b, 565b, 12:466b
Liber numerorum, 6:565a
Liber rotarum, De natura rerum and, 2:154b
on the liberal arts, 8:156a
Livres dou trésor and, 7:383a
on medicine, 8:247b, 255a
mirror of princes and, 8:434a
on music, 8:579a, 581b, 10:378b–379a
Musica disciplina and, 8:639a
On the Catholic Faith ... Against the Jews. See De fide catholica contra Judaeos
On the Natures of Things. See De natura rerum
on plants, 2:245a
recommendation to study Vergil, 12:394a
referred to in *Schwabenspiegel,* 11:80b
Regula monachorum (*Rules for Monks*), 6:565a, 565b
against love songs, 11:445b–446a
on self-castration of beavers, 2:204b–205a
Sentences, 3:336b, 6:565a
sex aetates mundi and, 11:215a
shrine of, 10:115a
Spanish prose lives of, 11:439b, 440a
on stones, 7:342b
Sturlaugs saga Starfsama and, 11:496b
Synonyma, 6:565a-b, 7:361b, 11:406a
use of sources, 6:565b
version of the Vulgate, 2:211b
Versus Isidori, 6:564a
Vincent of Beauvais and, 8:645a
Visigothic rulers and, 6:564a
Sisebut, 11:314a-b
see also Decretals, False
Isidore of Thessaloniki, *Homilies,* on the *penetes,* 9:493b
Isidoros of Miletos, 4:339a, **6:566b,** 7:202a
Archimedes and, 1:434a
construction of Hagia Sophia (Constantinople), 6:56a
Isidorus Mercator. *See* Decretals, False
Isis and Osiris, cult of, 9:1a, 1b
Iskāfī, Muḥammad ibn ʿAbd Allāh al-, *Mabādiʾ al-lugha,* 4:443a
Iskandar-nāma, 6:508b
Iskander Bey. *See* Skanderbeg
Islam
Arabism and, 3:40b–41a
Aristotle and, 1:458a–459b
astrology in, 1:606b–607a
attitude to Greek pagan learning, 9:3a
campaign of permanent conquest, 3:34a, 7:110b
cavalry, 3:208b–209b
Christian subjects of. *See* Christian-Muslim relations
commander of the faithful title, 3:488a–489a
conquests of, **6:566b–574b,** 6:573 (map)
Afghan campaign, 6:570b
Anatolian campaign, 6:572a
Arabian campaign, 6:567b–568a
Armenian campaign, 1:473b, 478a–480a, 500a, 6:568b, 572a
Battle of Ḥunayn, 1:29a
Battle of Poitiers (732) and, 9:715b–716a
Battle of Río Salado (1340), 9:714b
Berbers and, 2:186a
Byzantine thematic armies and, 12:10b
Caucasian campaign, 6:572a
Chinese opposition to, 12:145b
Church of the East and, 11:563a-b
decline of Najd, 9:54a-b
demise of the pentarchy system, 9:496a
disruption of Armenian trade and, 12:97b
disruption of Byzantine trade and, 12:100b–101a
Egyptian campaign, 6:569b–570a, 9:197b
Fārs campaign, 11:252a
Ghaznavid dynasty and, 11:133a-b
Granada, 5:651b
Ḥimṣ, 6:229b–230a
Iberian campaign, 8:444a-b
Indian campaign, 6:570b–572a
invasions of France, 3:272a
Iran, Jews and, 7:106b–107a
Iranian campaign, 6:502a–503a, 570b
Iraqi campaign, 6:568b, 568b–569a
Kabala, 7:205a
Khālid ibn al-Walīd, 7:235a-b
al-Kufa and, 7:306b
Kulthūm ibn ʿIyāḍ, 12:552a
Malta, 8:67a-b
Mecca, 1:29a
Medina, 1:24b–25a, 29a
Mediterranean campaign, 6:572b
Mediterranean trade and, 11:246b
Middle Eastern trade and, 12:105a-b
naval battle with Byzantines, 9:73 (*illus.*)
North African campaign, 6:572a
Nubian campaign, 9:197b–198a
origins and motivations, 6:567a-b
plague and the, 9:684a, 686a
primary, 6:567b–570a, 571 (map)
Reconquest and, 10:279b–280a
recorded by Balādhurī, 2:54a
religious consequences of, 6:579a-b
Roman Empire and, 10:459a, 464a, 464b
Sasanian Empire, 10:671b
secondary, 6:570a–572b, 573 (map)
shipbuilding and, 11:230b
Sicilian campaign, 10:440a, *see also* Sicily, Islamic
significance of, 6:573a–574a

Islam (*cont.*)
conquests of (*cont.*)
Spanish campaign, 6:572a-b, 9:147b
success of explained, 6:569b–570a
Syrian campaign, 1:25b, 6:567b, 568a-b, 11:559b–560a, 12:719a-b
Transoxianan campaign, 6:570b, 12:145b
travel during, 12:153a-b
Tunisian campaign, 6:572a
Visigoths and, 12:471b, 472b, 474b
Coptic art influenced by, 3:588a-b
costume styles of, 3:616a–618b
diet, prohibition against pork consumption, 1:300b
diplomacy in system of, 4:197a–200a
early development of, 8:58b
games in, 5:353a–354a
in Ghūr, 5:526a
Hindus and, 9:498b
ideal of unitary religious system, 3:32b
Islamization of Anatolia under Seljuks, 11:158a
jewelry of, 5:378b–379b
Jews under, 5:357b, 7:99a
jinn in, 7:112a–113a
Kaaba, 7:203a–204b
Karaites in, 7:209a-b
Latin church and, 3:355b–357a
Latin crusade against, 3:643b
Mali empire and, 8:57b
Manichaeans and, 9:498b
Mongols and, 11:563b
non-Muslims under, 7:72a-b
religion, **6:574b–588b**
antecedents of, 6:575b–576a
attitude toward commerce, 12:107a
baba preachers, 12:227a
changing relationship with caliphate, 3:45b–46a
Christianity and, 9:497a–498b
converts to, 2:137b, 7:99a
Damascus as center in, 4:84b–85a
dervish in, 4:162b–163a
dialogue with Nestorians, 9:107b
dogma of God's unity, 6:205b
Druzes as sect of, 4:296a–297a
exegesis, 2:215a
fasting during Ramadan, 10:254a–255a
finality of Muḥammad's apostleship, 6:205b
founded by Muḥammad, 6:576a–577b
Friday ceremony, 8:498b
Friday prayer in, 5:298b–299a
Friday sermon (*khuṭba*), 10:246a
great schism of, 11:135b–136a
house of worship, 8:498b
Ilkhanids and, 6:420b
importance of Mecca, 8:241a
infidel concept (*kāfir*), 10:254a
influence of on the legend of Grail, 9:2a
Islamic law and, 10:573b
Islamic science and, 11:82a
Judaism and, 7:101b–103a, 9:497a–498b
Koran and, 6:577b–579b, 7:293a–297a
law and worship in, 6:580b–582b
mystical aspects, 6:584b–586a
organizational structure, 6:204b
pilgrimage customs, 9:650a–652a
pilgrimage shrines of, 9:650a–652a, 671a, 671b (*illus.*)
"pillars" of, 6:582a-b
political theory and, 10:12a-b
prayer orientation. *See* Qibla
preaching and sermons, 10:70b–73b
pulpit. *See* Minbar
Ramadan (month), 10:253b–255a
rituals and observances, 6:46b
Sabbath. *See* Friday
Shiism in, 6:586a–588b
Sufism in, 9:44b–45a
sumptuary laws and, 11:507b–509a
theology of, 6:582b–584b
tradition in, 2:397b–398b, 6:579b–580b
Turkoman, 12:227a
on usury, 2:79a-b, 12:339a–340b
wine and, 2:208b–209b, 12:649a
see also Allah; *Ḥadīth;* Liturgy, Islamic; Resurrection, Islamic; Sects, Islamic; *Sunna*
rise of, 8:444a
role of civil government under, 3:43a, 47a
Sabians and, 9:498b
sects. *See* Sects, Islamic
slavery in
abuses of, 11:331a-b
agricultural slave, 11:331b
clientage and, 11:332b
in *ḥadīth,* literature, 11:330b–331a
in Koran, 11:330b–331a
legal status of, 11:331b–332a
training of slaves, 11:332b
taxation, of nonadherents, 3:594b
traditions of. *See Ḥadīth*
tribalism in, 3:32a, 33a, 36b
Zanj and, 12:739b–740a
Zoroastrianism and, 9:498b, 12:746b, 747b
see also Polemics, Islamic-Jewish; Propaganda, Islamic
Islam, meaning of, 6:575a
Islamic administration, **6:588b–592a**
ᶜAbd al-Malik's policies, 3:40a
bureaucracy in, 3:43b–44a, 45b
in Cairo, 3:13b–15a
of conquests, 6:570a-b, 588b
development of rhetoric and, 10:345a-b
early period, as recorded by Balādhurī, 2:54a
emirs, 4:437a
engineers, 11:638a
grievances and complaints, 6:589a-b
ḥisba, 11:639b
kātib, 8:138b
al-Kufa and, 7:306b
maqṣūra, 8:519b
in North Africa, 6:592a
preservation of non-Muslim customs, 3:34a-b
provinces, 8:138b–139a
Taᵓrīkh and, 11:570a
Quraysh tribe and, 10:242a-b
regulatory function
marketplace, 8:526b
public conduct, 8:526b
ṣāḥib al-sūq, responsibilities of, 8:526b–527a
shurṭa, 8:519a-b
supreme commander (*amīr al-umarāᵓ*), 10:246a
tax collection, 11:625b–626b
annual survey, 11:626a
assessment and collection procedures, 11:626b
under Abbasids, 3:44b, 6:589a-b, 590a-b, 591a
under Fatimids, 6:590b–591a
under Mamluks, 6:591b–592a
under Mongols, 6:590b, 591a, 591b
under ᶜUmar, 3:34a-b
under Umayyads, 3:37b, 39b, 6:589a, 589b
in Spain, 6:600b–601b
wazīr, 8:138b
see also Caliphate; Sultan; Vizier
Islamic art and architecture, **6:592b–614b**
Anatolian, 6:612b
Auvergnat architecture and, 10:480b
Beatus Manuscripts and, 2:143b
botanical illustrations, 6:186b
ceramics. *See* Ceramics, Islamic
classical period, 1:5a-b
decoration in, 6:609b–610a
dome, *Qubba* dome, 10:239a-b
Egyptian, 6:608a–610a (*illus.*)
al-Qaṭāᵓiᶜ, 12:223b, 224b
facades, 6:608b
figural representation, 3:53a, 6:602a
glassmaking, 5:545a–548a
in Granada, 5:653a-b
iconoclasm and, 6:403b, 404a
iconology of, 6:406b–407a, 408a
imperial style, 6:593a–594a
Iranian, 6:602a–605b
in Ikonion, 6:612b
Iraqi, 6:598a–600a, 605b–607a
in Egypt, 6:599a–600a
in Iran, 6:598b–599a
in North Africa, 6:600a-b
in Syria, 6:607a, 607b
Italian Romanesque art and, 10:503b
Junayd, 7:181b–182a
khan, 7:237b–238a
khānqāh, 7:238a-b
konàk, 7:284b
Koran as frame of reference for, 6:592b–593a
madrasas, 8:11a–12a
metalwork. *See* Metalworking, Islamic
miḥrāb, 8:376a
minaret, 8:396a–397a
Great Mosque, Marrakech, 8:150b
Mosque of the Casbah, 8:151a
minbar, 8:397 (*illus.*)
mosque, 8:499a-b
orientation of, 10:235a
regional variation, 8:500a
muqarnas, 8:534b
North African, 6:600a-b, 610a-b
palace complexes, 6:594a–595b, 596a, 597b
pishtaq, 9:670b–671b (*illus.*)
ribāṭs, 1:69a, 71a

  sahn, 10:612a
  sculpture
    at Khirbat al-Mafjar, 6:596a (*illus.*)
    iconology of, 6:408b
  Sicilian Romanesque architecture and, 10:486b, 503b
  in Sicily, 11:263a
  Spanish, 6:600b–601b, 610a–612a
  Spanish Romanesque architecture and, 10:487a, 487b
  Syrian, 6:607a–608a
    in Egypt, 6:608b
  Turkish, 6:612a–614a
  under Abbasids, 6:596b–601b
  under Aghlabids, 6:610b
  under Almoravids, 6:610b–611a
  under Fatimids, 6:600a, 608a-b, 609b–610a (*illus.*)
  under Mamluks, 6:608b–609b
  under Ortuqids, 9:283b–284a
  under Ottomans, 6:612b
  under Seljuks, 6:612a-b
  under Timurids, 6:605a-b
  under Umayyads, 6:593a–596b
  Western scholarship and, 1:430a
  see also Alhambra; *Azulejo; Bāb; Bādgīr; Bādiya;* Badr al-Dīn Luᵓluᵓ of Mosul, ruler; Barbotine; *Bayt;* Dome of the Rock; Iconology, Islamic; *Imāmzāda; Malwiya;* Mamluk art; Manuscript books, binding of (Islamic); Manuscript illumination, Islamic; Mosque; *Naqsh; Naqsh ḥadīda;* Palmette; *Qāᶜa;* Qaṣr; Seljuks, art and architecture; *Serdāb;* Ṣuffa
Islamic law, **7:485a–489a**
  abuses under Abbasids, 3:47b
  adhān, accepted phrases, 8:521a
  agreement of the faithful and, 7:488a
  ᶜāqila, definition of, 2:277a
  al-Ashᶜarī and, 1:582b–585b
  as aspect of religion, 7:485a-b
  caliph's administrative authority, 3:43a-b, 47a–48a
  classification of offenses, 2:276b
  on commercial practices, 12:106b, 107a
  concept of, and ruler, 3:32b
  contraception and, 3:574a, 575a-b
  development of, 11:218b–219a
  dietary laws, 4:178b–179b
  as divinely ordained, 7:485b–486a
  divorce, 11:631a
  dress codes, 3:616b, 619b
  early specialization, 7:487a
  in Egypt, 4:407a
  establishment of precedent
    fuqahāᵓ, 6:46b
    "raising" of *isnāds,* 6:47a
    ᶜulamāᵓ, 6:46b, 54b
    see also Sunna
  ethical basis of, 7:486a, 9:569a
  evidence
    circumstantial, 6:283a
    witnesses, 6:283a
  fictitious traditions and, 7:487b
  formative tendencies, 7:485b–486a
  foundations of, 11:219a-b
  Friday prayer, 5:298b–299b
  human reasoning and, 7:486a-b, 488a
  Ibadite sheikhs, 1:71a
  ideology of Mamluk dynasty and, 8:71a-b
  imam and, 6:425b
  jurist's authority, 1:71a, 7:486a-b
  khilāf legal literature, 11:67b
  Koran and, 7:293a–297a, 486a–487a, 488a
  in al-Kufa, 7:307b
  kufr, 10:574a
  land tenure, 11:667a
    kharāj, 11:626a, 667b–668a
    mawāt, 11:668b
  legal existence of fetus, 2:277a
  legal studies, 11:67b–68a
  Mālik ibn Anas' contribution, 8:58b–59b
  Malikite school, 6:392a, 7:234b, 487b, 488b
    taqlīd, 6:117b
  on marriage, 4:598a-b
  as most important social institution, 7:488b
  Muḥammad's role in, 1:26b, 7:486b, 487a, 488a
  murābiṭūn, 1:71a
  Nizārīs and, 6:588b
  no distinction between spiritual and temporal, 3:32b–33a
  non-Muslims and, 7:486a
  origins of, 5:30a-b
  personal character of, 7:486a
  private, 8:204b
  qadi
    adjudicators and, 7:487a
    restriction of competence, 1:71a
  Qāḍī Nuᶜmān and, 6:616b
  qāḍi al-quḍāt, 3:44b
  qiṣāṣ, 2:276b
  qiyās, 1:26b, 7:488a
  raᵓy, 1:26b
  religious, on study of philosophy, 10:573b
  religious idealism of, 7:484b–485a
  "roots" of, 6:581b
  sacred character of, 7:486a
  scope of, 7:485b–486a
  Seljuks and, 11:155a-b
  Shāfiᶜī law, 7:487b–488b
    principles of jurisprudence, 6:117b
  sharīᶜa defined, 7:485a, 486a
  on slavery, 8:68b, 11:332a
  sunna (precedent) and development of, 7:487a, 488a
  Sunni schools of, 6:581b–582a
  al-Tabarī and, 11:569a
  taught in madrasas, 8:11a, 11b
  tradition (*ḥadīth*) in, 7:486b–487b
  traditionalists vs. schools, 7:487a-b
  treatment of in encyclopedias, 4:445a
  umma and, 3:41a
  uniformity and, 7:488b
  universality and, 7:485b
  on usury, 12:106b
    Muḥammad and, 12:339b
  waqf, 12:543b–544a
  Ẓāhirite school, 6:117a, 117b–118a, 9:570b
    codifications, 6:118a
  of Zaydis, 12:742b
  see also Abode of Islam—Abode of War; Blood money; *Fatwā; Fiqh;* Homicide; Qadi; Sects, Islamic; *ᶜUlamāᵓ*
Islamic literature, Platonic thought in, 694b–696a, 9:699a–700b
Islamic music, **8:565a–568a**
  Arab musicians, 8:610b (*illus.*)
    in Spain, 8:562b
  development
    early (to 661), 8:565b
    Umayyad period (661–750), 8:565b–566a
    Abbasid period (750–1258) to 1500, 8:566a–568a
  Ibn Ghaybī on, 8:566b
  influence on non-Western, **8:561a–562a**
  mode, 8:122a-b
  oral tradition and, 8:568b
  Western music and, 8:581b
Isle of Man, under Norwegian sovereignty, 11:108a
Ísleifr Gizurarson, bishop, 2:252a, 6:352a
Íslendinga saga. See Sturla Þórðarson
Íslendingabók. See Ari Fróði; Ari Þorgilsson (the Learned)
Íslendingadrápa. See Haukr Valdísarson
Íslendingasögur
  ethos of *Valla-Ljóts saga* and, 12:351b
  fornaldarsögur and, time differences, 5:137b
  Icelandic literature and, 12:1b
  inspired by bishops' sagas, 2:252b
  Landnámabók and, 7:328a
  as source for *Víglundar saga,* 12:416b, 417a
Islip, Simon, archbishop of Canterbury, Wyclif and, 12:706a
Ismaᶜīl. *See* Ashᶜarī, Abu 'l-Ḥasan ᶜAlī ibn Ismaᶜīl al-
Ismāᶜīl I, shah of Iran
  fall of Mamluk dynasty and, 8:76a
  Selim I and, 11:145a
Ismāᶜīl ibn Jaᶜfar, 1:589b
  origins of Ismāᶜīlīya and, 6:614b–615a, 11:137a
Ismaᶜīl, Samanid emir
  conquest of Tabaristan, 10:637b
  defeat of ᶜAmr the Saffarid, 10:637b
  tomb of, 6:602a, 602b (*illus.*)
  veneration of, 10:638a
Ismāᶜīlīya, 6:587a–588a, **6:614b–619a,** 11:137a–138b, 227b
  in Afghanistan, 1:65a
  Baybars and, 2:138b
  caliphate and, 3:50a-b
  cosmology of, 9:570a
  doctrine of resurrection and, 10:341b
  Druzes and, 11:137b, 227b
  esoteric meaning of Holy Writ, 6:206a
  Fatimid, 6:616a–618a
  formative period, 6:614b–616a
  geographical distribution of, 11:514a
  in Iran, 6:503b
  in Iraq, 6:513a
  post-Fatimid, 6:618a-b
  pure, 6:615a

Ismāᶜīlīya (*cont.*)
  Pure Brethren, 6:617b
  recognition of al-Ḥākim as imam, 6:74a
  religious teaching of, 11:138a
  rise of in Arabia, 1:374b–375a
  Samanid persecution, 10:639a
  schismatic movements, 6:616a, 616b–617a
  suppressed by Saladin, 2:23a
  under the Fatimid caliph al-ᶜAzīz, 2:28b
  under Zirids, 12:744b
  vs. Hulagu, 6:329a
  see also Fatimids
Ismantorp hill fort, 10:692b–693a
Isnād, 6:580a, 580b, 8:59a, 11:219a, 219b
  arrangement of collections by, 6:47b–48a
  arrangement of *ḥadīth* collections, 6:46b–47a
  establishment of *ḥadīth* chronology, 6:48a-b
  fabrications of, 6:47a-b
    isnād criticism, 6:47b
  "growing backward," 6:47a
  origin of, 6:45b
  as precedent for Islamic law, 6:46b–47a
  see also Historiography, Islamic; Scholarship, Islamic
Isocrates, 9:696b
  seven liberal arts and, 12:205b
  To Nicocles, 8:434a
Isogloss, in the study of the Middle English language, 8:312b–313a
Isolde/Isolt. *See* Tristan, Legend of
Ison, 8:557a-b, 617a, 617b
Isopet (Chartres), 4:572b, 573b
Isopet (of Lyons), 4:572b, 573a
Isopet (of Paris), 4:572b
Isopets. See Fables
Isorhythm, 1:551a-b, **6:619a–620a,** 8:591a, 594a
  in *ars nova,* 10:382a
  color, 9:232a
  definition of, 6:619a, 8:503a
  mathematical schemes and number symbolism in, 6:619b
  medieval theorists of, 6:619a
  in motet, 8:503a, 503b
  in Old Hall MS, 9:232a
  panisorhythm, 8:503
  talea, 9:232a
  unipartite and bipartite motets using, 6:619b
  in upper voices, 8:503a, 503b
Isperikh Asparukh of Bulgaria, 2:399a-b
Isrāᵓ, 1:581a
Israeli, Isaac, **6:620a-b,** 7:98a, 151b, 166b, 9:700a
  Aristotle and, 1:459b
  on al-Biṭrūjī's *Astronomy,* 11:91a
  Book of Definitions, 6:620a
  Chapter on the Elements by Aristotle, 6:620a
  On Fevers, 11:92b
  philosophy, Eastern influence, 9:574b
  translated by Constantine the African, 8:248a
  universal substances, 9:75b
  Yesod ᶜOlam, 11:90b
Israhel van Meckenem, **6:620b**
  engraving technique of, 4:488b–489a
Isserles, Moses, Jewish law and, 7:492b
Issoire (church: Auvergne), 10:480a
Istakhr, Shīrāz and, 11:252a
Iṣṭakhrī, al-, 5:331b, 393b
  on Armenian economy, 12:97b
Istämi, Turkish khan, Xusrō I and, 12:714a
İstanbul. *See* Constantinople
Istanpitte. See *Estampie*
Istoria (anonymous Italian poem), 6:630b
Istoria fiorentina. See Malispini, Ricordano
Istria
  Venice and, 12:385b, 386a
  Wolfger von Erla and, 12:672b
Istro-Romanian language, 10:509b
Ísucán alar limm im dísieurtán, 6:543a
Iswardus. *See* Usuard
Išxan išxanacᶜ. See Archon ton archonton
Išχani Cathedral, 5:409a (*illus.*)
Iš'yahb II, katholikos, 11:567b
Ita of Killeedy, abbess, 3:227b
Ītākh, 8:654a
Italian art
  Byzantine influences on, 4:353b
  celebration of common man, 7:11a, 17b
  drawing, 15th century, 9:666a (*illus.*)
  frescoes, Brancacci Chapel, S. Maria del Carmine, 8:169b
  influence on crusader art, 4:26a
  manuscript illumination, pre-Romanesque, 10:113a-b
  mosaics, pre-Romanesque, 10:112a–113a
  painting
    Gothic style, 5:603b–604a, 605a–607b
    Hugh of St. Albans and, 6:320b
    Huguet and, 6:328a-b
    pre-Romanesque, 10:112a–113a
    tapestry and, 11:592b
  panel painting, 9:360b–362a
  pottery, 10:65b–66a
  pre-Romanesque, 10:112a–113a
  religious painting, 7:11a
  sculpture
    Arnolfo di Cambio, 1:541a
    chivalric literature and, 6:638a
    Gothic style, 5:624a-b
  woodcut, 12:692b
  see also Dugento art; Romanesque art; Trecento art
Italian cycle (mass), 8:199a-b
Italian drama, **6:635a–637a**
  liturgical aspects, 6:635a
  sacred plays, 6:636b–637a
  staging, 6:635b–636a
  see also Lauda
Italian language, **6:621a–629b**
  affricates, 6:628b
  articles in, 6:628b
    Italo-Romance, 6:623a
  consonants in, 6:628a
  Dante and, 6:440a, 665a-b
  early Italo-Romance, 6:622b–624a
    consonants, 6:623a
  first literary texts, 6:624a–626a
  Genovese dialect, Raimbaut de Vaqueyras and, 6:624a
  later development, 6:626a–629b
  modern, 6:627a, 629b
  morphology, 6:628b
  nouns, 6:628b
  origin of, 6:435a
  orthography, 6:627b
  phonetics, 6:627b–628b
  plural system, 6:628b
  pronoun, 6:628b
    Italo-Romance, 6:623b
  Tuscan dialect, 6:626b, 628a, 629b
    Divine Comedy and, 6:626a, 626b
    scuola siciliana and, 6:624a, 625a
  vowels, 6:627b–628a, 666a
    Sicilian, 6:625a
  Vulgar Latin and, 6:621a–622a
  see also Judeo-Italian language
Italian law
  canonical inquest, 6:478b, 479a
  codes in city-states, 7:428a–429a
Italian League, 7:10a
  Francesco I Sforza and, 11:216b
Italian literature, **6:629b–670b**
  allegorical and didactic, **6:630a–632b**
    central Italian poets, 6:631b–632b
    lyric poems, 6:651a-b
    northern Italian poets, 6:630a–631b
  Arthurian legend in, 1:572b–573a
  chronicles, 3:329a-b, **6:632b–635a**
    Roman, 6:633a-b
    Sicilian, 6:633b
    Tuscan, 6:633b–634b
  comic realists, 7:10b
  disperata (literary genre), 6:653b
  epic and chivalric, **6:637a–640a**
    Arthurian cycle, 6:637b, 638a, 638b–639a
    Carolingian cycle, 6:637b, 638a, 638b–639a
    characteristic themes, 6:639a-b
    French influences, 6:637b
    performance of, 6:638a-b
    prose romances, 6:639a
  fable, 4:572b
  influence of on Catalan literature, 3:171a
  lyric poetry, **6:640a–656a**
    comic, 6:649a–650b
    didactic-allegorical, 6:651a-b
    dolce stil nuovo, 12:177b
    forms of, 6:640b–641a
    humanistic elements, 9:539b
    importance of Cino da Pistoia, 3:397b
    love poets, 7:10b
    music and, 6:653b–655a
    poetic devices, 6:641b
    religious, 6:650b–651a
    Sicilian school, 6:25a, 624b–625a, 641a–644a, 656a, 667a, 11:257a–260b
    Sicilian school imitators, 6:643b–644a
    theme of successional nobility, 6:25b
    transitional, 6:645a-b

trecento music and, 12:177b, 178b–179b
vernacular, 9:538a-b
medical, 10:289a
Platonism and, 9:698b–699a, 702b–703a
popular poetry, **6:656a–658b**
animal epics, 6:657b–658a
collections of, 6:657b
distinguishing criteria, 6:656a
influence of urbanism, 7:17b
political verse, 6:658a
prose, **6:658b–661b**, 7:10b–11a
Boccaccio and, 6:660a-b, 661a
collections of tales, 6:659a-b
expansion of vernacular, 6:658b
facezie, 7:11a
humanist essays, 5:101a
narrative development, 6:659a
see also Boccaccio, Giovanni
religious poetry, **6:661b–663b**
as means of public instruction, 6:662a
see also Lauda
sermons, **6:663b–664b**
Dominican, 6:663b–664b
Franciscan, 6:664b
versification and prosody, **6:665a–670b**
alexandrine verse, 6:667a-b
composite rhyme, 6:667b
consonance in, 6:667b
hendecasyllabic form, 6:665b–666b, 668b
meter, 6:630a
octave in, 6:639a, 669a, 670a
parataxis, 6:630a
quinario, 6:666a-b
rhyme, 6:667b–668a, 668a
sestet, 6:669a
settenario, 6:666a-b, 668b
Sicilian rhyme, 6:668a
synaloepha, 6:666a
syneresis, 6:666a
tenson (tenzone), 6:640b, 669a
terza rima, 6:670a
trisillabo, 6:666b–667a
see also Sestina; Sonnet
see also Dolce stil nuovo; Sicilian poetry;
Italian millet, 5:647a
Italian music
caccia song form, 3:4a-b
lyric poetry and, 6:653b–655a
trecento
composers, 12:179b–180a
forms, 12:177b, 178a–179b, 181b
instruments, 12:180b
notation, 12:177b–178b (*illus.*)
patronage, 12:179b, 181a
Italian Renaissance
art, naturalism and, 9:666b (*illus.*)
Byzantine influence on, **7:1a–2a**, 9:698b–699a
in education, 7:11b
intellectual life at Pera-Galata and, 9:503a
German literature and, 8:347a
see also Humanism
Italian war chariot. *See* Carroccio
Italians, as innkeepers, 6:473b
Italic languages, 6:434b
Italy
agriculture, 1:86a–87b
cotton cultivation in, 3:626b–627a
15th century, 1:87b
flax field, 1:87a
grani grossi and *grani minuti,* 1:86a-b
pasta and *tria,* 1:86b
Angevin kings of, 7:8a, 10a-b
astronomy in, 1:612b–613a
Byzantine areas of, **7:2a–5a**
Arab conquests, 7:4a, 4b
barbarian invasions, 7:2a
boundaries, 7:3 (map)
Byzantine-Gothic wars, 9:292a–293a
Frankish conquest, 7:4a
Frankish-Byzantine alliance, 7:4a-b
government, 7:2b, 4b
Hungarian raids, 7:4b
invasions of, 2:485a, 486b, 490b, 492b, 494a, 496b
Latin vernacular in, 7:4a
Lombard rule, 7:2b, 4a, 654b–656a
rise of Italian merchants and, 12:110b–111a
Robert Guiscard and, 10:433a
Roman church, influence of, 7:4a
under Macedonian emperors, 7:4b
Venice and, 12:383b–385a
see also Bari; Naples
calendar dating methods, 3:21a
city-states
development of, 7:15a, 15b–16a
finance and government, 7:17a-b
public health regulations, 2:100b
suburban expansion, 7:13b
territorial expansion, 7:14a–15b
class structure, in 14th-15th centuries, 7:9a
colonies, in China, 7:15a
commerce
15th century, 7:8b
with East, 7:13a-b
11th century, 4:556a
England and Flanders, 7:15a
Iberian Peninsula, 4:557b–558a
mercantile banking companies of, 2:76a–78b
culture
in 14th-15th centuries, 7:10b–11a
secularization of, 7:11a, 17b
economic growth
in 8th century, 7:13a
in 14th-15th centuries, 7:8b, 9b
French invasion (1494), 7:10a-b
glassmaking in, 5:555b–556a, 557a–558a
Gothic settlement, 9:290a-b
government, 7:7a-b
communal vs. feudal states, 7:5b–6a
consuls and consulates, 3:570b–571a
weakness in 14th-15th centuries, 7:10b
guilds and métiers, 6:15b–16a, 22a
Hebrew manuscripts produced in, 8:119b–120a
history (1300–1500), **7:5a–12a**
role of the Medici family, 8:242a–243b
see also Guelphs and Ghibellines
imperial authority, challenges to, 7:13a, 14b, 15a
Italian Wars, 7:10a-b
Jews in, 7:85b, 86a, 86b, 87a
art, 7:68a
cabalistic schools, 3:2b–3a
translators, 12:135b
Justinian I's expedition to, 7:201a-b
languages of, 6:335a
Lombard invasions, 5:669a, 7:12b–13a, 9:293a
Magyars in, 6:338a
major states, 7:5b
in 14th-15th centuries, 7:6 (map)
military feudalism, 12:562a-b
military organization, condottieri bands, 12:566a-b
mints and money in, 8:429a-b, 430b
groat, 5:680a
Muslims in. *See* Sicily, Islamic
Normans in. *See* Sicily, kingdom of
papermaking in, 9:389a-b
plagues in, 9:674a, 675b–676a, 679b
Antonine Plague, 9:674a
Black Death, 2:259a–260b
population
in 13th century, 7:15a-b
in 14th-15th centuries, 7:8b–9a
printing in, 10:124b–125a
public clocks in, 3:29b
regional wars, 7:14b
relations with Languedoc, 7:339b
rise of towns in, **7:12b–18b**, 12:110b–112a
cultural effects, 7:17b
decline of Fatimid naval power and, 9:75b
emancipation in High Middle Ages, 12:316b–317a
military operations, 12:562b
north-south distinctions, 7:13b–14a, 15b–16a
origins of banking and, 2:73a
podesta and, 9:711a–712a
ruling elites, 9:461a
urban rivalry, 9:663b–665b
see also particular towns; Urbanism, Western European
Roman roads in, 10:411b
silk industry in, 11:295a, 296a
surviving medieval bridges in, 10:418b
tenurial development, 11:683a-b
customary tenancies, 11:683a
towns
housing in, 12:328b–329a
planning in, 12:325a–326a
universities, 12:285b–286b
urban government
despotism and oligarchy, 7:16b–17a
division of towns into quarters, 12:562b
podesta, 7:16b
popolo, 7:16a-b
revenue, sources of, 7:17a
rights of local, 7:15a
urban warfare, 12:317b–318a
Visigoths in, 12:470a
water transport, 12:578b

Italy (*cont.*)
  see also Communes; Condottieri; Feudalism; Papal States; Tuscany
Iʿtazala, 8:655a
Ite chant (*Ite missa est*), **7:18b**
  close of Mass and, 8:197a
  music used, 7:18b
  prosulas, 7:18b
  Tropes to the Ordinary of the Mass and, 12:209a
Item placuit. See Carthage, Councils of (401)
Iter ad Paradisum, 1:150a
  Lamprecht and, 7:323a
Ithael, 3:224a-b
Ithel ap Robert, deacon of St. Asaph's, Iolo Goch and, 6:500b
Ithnā ʿasharī Shiism, 6:503a, 503b, 586b
  in Baghdad, 6:587b
  in Isfahan, 6:562a
  Mūsā al-Kāẓim and, 6:615a
  See also Shīʿa, Twelver Shiites
Iðunn, **7:18b–19a**, 11:27b
  apples, myth of, 7:19a
  in *Haustlǫng,* 12:32a
Itil
  destroyed by Svyatoslav of Kiev, 12:436a
  fur trade in, 5:331a-b
Itineraries. *See* Guidebooks; Travel and transport
Itinerarium. See Baudri of Bourgueil; William of Rubruck
Itinerarium Egeriae. See Egeria
Itinerarium Kambriae. See Gerald of Wales
Itinerarium mentis in Deum. See Bonaventure, St.
Itinerarium syriacum. See Petrarch
Itinerary. See William of Tripoli
Iudicia Dei. See Ordeals
Iura sequimentorum, 10:523b, 526a
Iuramentum. See Oath
Ius commune (common law). *See* Bologna, University of; Law, civil; Law, schools of
Ius Novi Fori Stredense, 9:722a-b
Ius Quiritium, 11:673a
Iusiurandum. See Oath
Ivajlo of Bulgaria, 2:410b–411a
Īvān. See Eyvān
Ivan I Kalita of Muscovy, grand prince, 5:329b
  canonization of Peter, 8:541a
  Gediminas and, 7:605b
  Metropolitan Peter and, 9:512a
  patrimony, 8:543a
  siege of Tver, 8:539b–540a
Ivan III of Muscovy, grand prince, 5:330b, **7:20a-b**
  annexation of Novgorod, 8:546b
  annexation of Tver, 8:546b
  autocratic rule of, 7:20a
  building programs, 8:547a
  conflict with Andrei the Elder, 8:547b
  expulsion of councillors by, 4:306b
  imperial claims of, 7:20a
  law code of, 11:191b
  Lithuanian wars, 8:546b
  territorial sovereignty, 8:542b
  vs. Mongols, 11:192a
  vs. Novgorod, 9:196a–197a
Ivan IV (the Terrible) of Muscovy, tsar, 9:682b
  building programs, Moscow Kremlin, 8:496b–497a
  as composer, 8:573b
  coronation, 8:546a
  icons and, 6:411b
  land tenure and, 11:192a, 192b
  law code of, 11:191b
  Michael Romanov and, 11:197b
  military families, governorships for, 8:548a
  Oprichnina and, 11:194b–195b
  peasant survey and, 11:196b
  pomestie system, 8:549a
  as "Russian Dracula," 11:347b
  servitors and, 11:196a
Ivan Nos, 8:573b
Ivanē Mxargrzeli. *See* Iwanē Mχargrzeli
Ivanko, 2:408a
Ívars þáttr Ingimundarsonar, in *Morkinskinna,* 12:3b, 4a
Ívens saga, **7:20b–21b**, 10:390a-b, 392b, 394b, 11:491b
  alliteration in, 10:393b
  compared to Chrétien's *Yvain,* 7:21a
  Erex saga and, 4:504b, 505a
  Konráðs saga Keisarasonar and, 7:292a
  manuscripts of, 7:20b, 10:392a
  Rémundar saga keisarasonar and, 10:304a
Ivo of Chartres, St., **7:21b–22a**, 8:255b
  correspondence, 7:22a
  Decretum, 4:128b, 7:411a-b
  dispensation and, 4:217a-b
  on Divine Office, 4:230b
  Gregorian reform and, 7:21b
  investiture conflict and, 7:21b
  legal writings, 7:22a
    excerpta from, 7:411b–412a
  missing works by, 12:22a
  Panormia, 1:607a, 7:22a, 411a-b
  penitentials and, 9:490b
  Peter Lombard and, 9:517a
  Robert d'Arbrissel and, 10:429a
  sermons, 7:22a, 630b–631a
  Tripartita, 4:128b, 7:411b
Ivory carving, **7:22a–28b**
  Byzantine, 4:492a(*illus.*), 7:24b, 26 (*illus.*)
    panels in Palazzo Venezia (Rome), 2:454a (*illus.*)
    pyxis (15th century), 2:458a (*illus.*)
  capsa, 7:22b
  Carolingian, 7:25a–26a (*illus.*)
  centers of, 10:105a
  for church doors, 4:361a
  in Cologne, 7:27a-b
  crusader, 4:23a (*illus.*)
  cut *à jour,* 7:22b, 25b
  diptychs, 4:214a, 7:22b, 23b
  in early Rome, 7:24a-b
  English, Romanesque cross, 7:23, 10:0 (frontispiece)
  evangelist symbols in, 4:526a
  Islamic, 7:26b, **7:29a-b**
    casket from Córdoba (1004), 7:29b (*illus.*)
    decorative patterns of, 7:29 (*illus.*)
    decorative writing in, 7:29b
    oliphant, horn of Ulph, 9:239 (*illus.*)
    workshops, 7:29a
  in Liège, 7:27a-b
  manuscript decoration, 7:22b
  material, 7:22a-b
  for mirror, 2:148 (*illus.*)
  oliphants, 7:22b
  Ottonian, 7:26b–27a
  portable religious objects, 7:23b
  in pre-Romanesque art
    Carolingian, 10:100a-b
    German, 10:104b–105b
    Spanish, 10:115a
  "pricked" style, 7:27b
  pyxes, 7:22b
  Roman, from 5th century, 4:351b–352a
  secular objects, 7:23b
  situla, 7:22b, 27a
  in Spain, 7:27b
  tabula ansata and, 11:571b (*illus.*)
  13th and 14th centuries, 7:28 (*illus.*)
  Western European, Tuotilo, 12:225b–226a (*illus.*)
Īwān. See Eyvān
Iwanē Mχargrzeli, 1:485b, 12:736b, 737a
  Mχitʿar Goš and, 8:656b
  see also Zakʿarids
Iwanē Zedazneli, 5:414a
Iwein. See Hartmann von Aue
ʿIyāḍ ibn Ghanm al-Fihrī, 6:568b
ʿIyār-i Dānish. See Abu 'l-Faḍl ibn Mubārak
Izbornik, 11:345b
Iðdunn, role in mythology, 7:19a
Izlā, Mount (monastery: Persia), 3:312b
Iznik, ceramics of, 6:613b
ʿIzz al-Dīn Abu 'l-Ḥasan, 1:634a-b
ʿIzz al-Dīn Aybak, Mamluk sultan, 2:272b, 8:73b
ʿIzz al-Dīn Ḥusayn, 5:526a
ʿIzz al-Dīn ibn al-Athīr
  courtly tradition of history, 6:251b–252a
  Kāmil fī al-taʾrīkh, al-, 6:251b–252a

J

Jabal ʿAmī, Shīʿa and, 11:228a
Jabala, 5:515b
Jabetz, Joseph, 10:75a
Jābir, al-. *See* Balādhurī, Abū Ḥasan Aḥmād ibn Yahya ibn Jābir al-
Jābir ibn Aflaḥ, 1:621a
  invention of torquetum attributed to, 11:98b
  treatises of translated into Hebrew, 11:90b–91a
Jābir ibn Ḥayyān

Book of Balances, 1:136a
Corpus Gabirianum, 1:141a
Five Hundred Books, 1:136a
Liber misericordiae, 1:136a
Liber de septuaginta, 1:136a
One Hundred Twelve, 1:136a
Jabrā⊃īl. *See* Gabriel (archangel)
Jabrids, in al-Baḥrayn, 2:51a
Jaca, growth of, 1:404b
Jaca Cathedral, 10:487a
Jack Upland, 8:332a
Jacob Anatoli. *See* Anatoli, Jacob
Jacob bar Shakkō, 11:565b
Jacob Baradaios, 11:568a
Jacob ben Asher, 7:82a, 92b
on law, 7:170a-b
mysticism and, 4:540a
Sefer ha-Turim, 7:170a, 11:586a
Jacob ben Elie of Venice, 7:93b
Jacob ben Elijah, 10:5a
Jacob ben Ma⊂hir ibn Tibbon of Marseilles, 1:613a, 12:134a
quadrans novus, 10:237a
Jacob ben Meir, **7:29b–30b,** 7:92b
authority over Jewish community, 7:71b, 90b, 91b
on divorce, 4:607b
on interest taking, 12:341a, 341b
ordinance on dowry, 7:30a
personality, 7:30a
Rashi and, 10:259b
responsum literature and, 10:339a
tosafot and, 11:585b
Jacob ben Nissim ibn Shahin
biblical exegesis, 2:212b
school founded by, 7:98a, 162a
Jacob ben Reuben, 7:210b
Wars of the Lord, 10:3b, 5a
Jacob ben Yakar, Rashi and, 11:585b
Jacob of Capua, translations by, 12:136a
Jacob Corsino, 9:511a
Jacob of C⊂urt⊂avi, *Martyrdom of St. Šušanik,* 5:413a, 416b
Jacob of Edessa, 11:565b, 566b
Jacobite church, 8:478a
religious scholasticism, 8:478b
Jacob Erlandsen, 4:154b
Jacob ibn El⊂āzār, *Kitāb al-kāmil,* 6:128b
Jacob and Joseph, 2:221b, 4:546b
Jacob of Nisibis, bishop, 11:567b
Jacob of Serugh, 11:565b
Seven Sleepers of Ephesus and, 11:213a
Jacob van Maerlant. *See* Maerlant, Jacob van
Jacobite alphabet. *See* Alphabets, Syriac
Jacobite church. *See* Monophysitism
Jacobo de las Leyes, *Flores de derecho,* 11:441a
Jacob's staff. *See* Cross-staff
Jacobus of Bologna, **7:31b–32a**
Arte del biscanto misurato, 8:646a
at the Visconti court, 7:31b
madrigals
manuscript sources of, 7:31b
rhyme scheme of, 7:32a
"Non al suo amante," 8:633 (*illus.*)
Vacarius' *Apparatus glossarum* and, 12:343b
in Verona, 7:31b
Jacobus de Bononia. *See* Jacobus of Bologna
Jacobus of Capua, archbishop, Constitutions of Melfi and, 7:429b
Jacobus de Cessolis, *Solatium ludi scaccorum,* 5:430b
Jacobus Cremonensis, 1:439a, 439b
Jacobus (de Porta Ravennate), 2:417b–418a, 5:567b, 6:323b, **7:30b–31a**
Jacobus de Lentino. *See* Iacopo da Lentini
Jacobus of Liège. *See* Jacques de Liège
Jacobus of Navernia, Robert de Handlo and, 8:646b
Jacobus de Varagine, 5:384a
Golden Legend, 3:167a, 4:247b, **5:574a-b,** 5:604a, 6:59b, 69b, 7:369a
author of, 5:574a
Chester plays and, 3:299b
description of, 5:574a
exempla and, 4:551a
manuscript illumination, 12:493b
N-town plays and, 9:50a
Rappresentazione d'Ognissanti and, 6:636a
saints included in, 6:62b
Scaccabarozzi and, 6:382a-b
as a source for French Passion plays, 9:447b
Spanish versions, 11:438b, 439b, 440a
Stanzaic Life of Christ and, 4:547a
tapestry and, 11:591b, 592a
translations of, 5:289a, 574a, 6:62a-b
Vincent of Beauvais's *Life of St. Alexis* and, 12:413a
see also Caxton, William; *Vie de Ste. Marguerite*
Jacomart Master. *See* Baçó, Jaime
Jacopo d'Avanzi. *See* Avanzo, Jacopo
Jacopo de' Benedetti. *See* Jacopone da Todi
Jacopo da Bologna. *See* Jacobus of Bologna
Jacopo del Casentino, 7:325b
Jacopo di Cione, 5:338a, **7:33a**
see also Nardo di Cione
Jacopo della Quercia, **7:32b–33a**
Acca Larentia, 7:32b (*illus.*)
Fonte Gaia, 11:281b
Jacopo da Forli, 8:251b
Jacopo Franchi, Rosello di. *See* Rossello di Jacopo Franchi
Jacopo di Piero Guidi, **7:33a-b**
Jacopo da Voragine. *See* Jacobus de Varagine
Jacopone da Todi, **7:33b–35a**
Donna de Paradiso, 6:635b, 651a
hymns of, 6:382a
imprisonment, 7:34a-b
laude, 6:662b, 669a, 7:34b–35a, 384a
member of the Spiritual party, 7:34a
mysticism of, 7:34b
opposition to Boniface VIII, 7:34a
probable composer of *Stabat mater,* 7:35a
Proverbia and, 6:632a
Jacquemart de Hesdin, 5:615a, 628b, **7:35a-b,** 8:109b
Jacquerie, 5:180a, **7:35b–36b,** 9:477b–478b
Black Death and, 2:266a
causes of, 7:35b, 9:478a-b
Charles V of France and, 3:269b
Charles II of Navarre and, 9:71a-b
compared with Peasants' Revolt of 1381, 9:480a
consequences of, 5:185b
defeat of, 7:36b
Enguerrand VII and, 4:491a
Étienne Marcel and, 9:406a
feud between towns and nobility and, 7:36a-b
in Languedoc, 7:341a
spread of, 9:478a
Jacques d'Ableiges, *Grant coutumier de France,* 7:460a
Jacques d'Amiens, 1:189a
débat and, 4:122a
Jacques de Baerze. *See* Baerze, Jacques de
Jacques Bonhomme, Jacquerie and, 9:477b
Jacques de Bruges, 4:559b
Jacques du Clercq, *Mémoires,* 9:638b
Jacques Coene. *See* Coene, Jaques
Jacques Coeur, **7:37a–38a**
conviction for treason, 7:37b
in King's Council, 7:37a
Languedoc and, 7:341b
mining operations, 7:37a
papal dispensations, 7:37b
textile business, 7:37a
Jacques de Liège, **7:38a–39b**
influence of Boethius on, 7:38a
on music, 8:579b
as musical conservative, 7:39a
Speculum musicae, 7:38a-b, 8:582b, 645a-b
contemporary practice, 7:39a
on Petrus de Cruce, 9:545a
Jacques de Molay, relocated Templars to France, 3:304b
Jacques de Neuilly, Chartreuse de Champmol, 4:186a
Jacques (participants in the Jacquerie), 9:478a
Jacques de Révigny, 10:19a, 62b
Jacques de Vitry, **7:39b–40b,** 10:77a, 78a
beguines and, 2:158b, 7:39b
on church reform, 10:285a
clerical appointments, 7:39b
collection of exempla, 10:363a
on compass, 11:101a
exempla and, 4:551a
Historia Hierosolimitana abbreviata, 7:40a, 369a
laity and, 3:359b
life of Mary of Oignies, 7:40a, 9:11b
"Sermones," 1:455b
sermons
collections of, 7:39b–40a
innovative techniques, 7:40a

Jadwiga of Poland, queen, 9:725b
  marriage to Jagiełło of Lithuania, 7:606b–607a
Jaén, 11:383b–384a
Ja^cfar. *See* Mutawakkil, al-, Abbasid caliph
Ja^cfar ibn ^cAlī ibn Ḥamdūn, governor of Msila, 12:744a
Ja^cfar ibn Yaḥyā, executed by Hārūn al-Rashīd, 2:110b
Ja^cfar al-Ṣādiq
  death of, 6:586b
  influence on Islamic mysticism, 9:39a
  Ismailism and, 6:614b–615a
  Zayd ibn ^cAli and, 12:741b
Ja^cfariyya, founded, 8:654b
Jaffa
  Jean d'Ibelin and, 6:390a
  recaptured (1268), 2:138b
Jagd, Die. *See* Hadamar von Laber
Jaghāna, 8:613a
Jagiełło dynasty, **7:40b–41a**, 9:730a
  Christianity and, 7:41a, 8:444a
  conquest of Teutonic Knights, 7:140a
  derivation of title, 7:40b
  early Jagiellonian state (1386–1492), 9:725b–728a
  founder of, 7:606b–607a
  nobility and, 7:40b–41a
  Phillip Buonaccorsi and, 9:730a
  Polish-Lithuanian union, 7:40b
  polonization of, 7:41a
Jagiełło of Lithuania, grand duke and king of Poland, 2:67a, 7:40b, 606b–607a
  conversion to Roman Catholicism, 10:594a
  Polish crown, 10:594a
  treaty with Petru I Muşat, 12:501b
Jagiełło, Władysław. *See* Władisław I Łokietek of Poland, king
"Jagiełłonczyk." *See* Władisław I Łokietek of Poland, king
Jahābidha (Muslim bankers), 12:340a, 340b
Jahān Pahlawān, Ildegizid atabeg, 6:419b
  Shāh-Arman and, 11:220a
Jahāngīr (son of Tamerlane), 12:56b, 57a
Jaḥḥāfids, in Armenia, 1:513a
Jāḥiẓ, Abū ^cUthmān ^cAmr ibn Baḥr al-, **7:41a–44a**
  Al-Bayān w'al-tabyīn (*Book on Eloquence and Exposition*), 1:379b, 7:42b, 10:72b
  Al-Bukhalā^ɔ (*Book of Misers*), 1:379b, 7:42b–43a
  Al-Tarbī^c wa'l-tadwīr, 7:43a
  Al-^cUthmānīya, 7:42b
  defense of Arab tradition, 7:41b
  Kitāb al-ḥayawān (*Book of Animals,* or *Bestiary*), 1:379b, 7:42b
    on contraception, 3:574b
  literary works, 1:379a-b, 7:42a–43b
  al-Mutawakkil and, 8:654b
  Mu^ctazilite rulers and, 7:42a
  on poetry, 10:346b
  teaching career, 7:41b
  theology of, 1:379b
Jahm ibn Ṣafwān, on predestination, 1:584a
Jail delivery, **7:44a–45a**
  assize adjudication and, 7:44b
  commissioners
    London, 7:45a
    permanent, appointment of, 7:44b
    special, 7:45a
    trailbastons, 7:45a
  general eyre, 7:44a
  justices
    duties of, 7:44a
    knights as, 7:44b
Jail fever. *See* Plagues, enteric
Jaime Baçó. *See* Baçó, Jaime
Jaime Ferrer the Elder. *See* Ferrer I (the Elder), Jaime
Jaime Serra. *See* Serra, Jaime
Jajca, banat of, 2:70a
Jakemes, 3:277b
Jakoubek of Stříbro, 6:367b, 368a, 372a-b, 373a, 374a
Jalājil. *See* Bells, jingle
Jalāl al-Dīn. *See* Rūmī
Jalāl al-Dīn, khwārizmshāh. *See* Jalāluddin
Jalāl al-Dīn Mengübirdi, 5:383a
  Seljuks of Rum and, 11:157b
Jalāluddin (Jalāl-al-Dīn), khwārizmshāh, 7:244a
  Armenia and, 1:485b
  conquest of Azerbaijan, 8:469b
  defeated by Kayqubād I, 11:154b
  Mongol conflicts
    battle at Parwān, 8:467a
    defeat at Ghazna, 8:467b
  sack of Dwin by, 4:324b
  Seljuk-Ayyubid alliance against, 8:469b
Jalayirids
  bookmaking under, 7:274a
  Iranian art and, 6:605a
  Junayd at court of, 7:181b
  rule over Iraq, 6:514a
  vs. Cubānids, in Armenia, 1:486a
  Xlat^c and, 12:713b
Jalūlā^ɔ, battle at (637), 6:511a
Jālūt. *See* Goliath
Jamal, al-, battle at (656), 7:307a
Jamb, **7:45b**
Jamb figures
  of Amiens Cathedral, 5:622a-b
  influences on, 5:619a
  of Rouen Cathedral, 5:624b
  of Strasbourg Cathedral, 5:622a
  tympanum and, 5:617a-b
Jambeg, conquest of Azerbaijan, 8:476a
James I (the Conqueror) of Aragon and Catalonia, king, 1:411a–413b, 11:377a, 379a
  chronicle of, 3:165a-b
  conquest of Valencia, 1:412a, 12:346a
  control of Montpellier, 8:482b
  early factionalism under, 1:411a-b
  establishment of Valencia, 12:346a, 346b
  Jews and, 7:81a-b
  kingdom of Navarre and, 9:70b
  law codes of, 7:429b–430a
    Code of Huesca, 3:611b
    Furs of Valencia, 5:309b
  Libre de la saviesa o de doctrina, 3:168a
  limited knighthood, 3:414a
  marriage to Iolanda of Hungary, 1:412a
  partition of Aragon by, 1:412b–413a
  peacetime difficulties, 1:413a
  Peire Cardenal and, 9:484b
  renewal of Reconquest by, 1:411b–412a
  setbacks in southern France, 1:412b
  Sicily and, 11:273b
  strengths of his reign, 1:413a-b
  treaty of Corbeil (1258), 1:412b
  troubadours and, 7:340b
James II of Aragon and Catalonia, king
  Catalonian difficulties of, 1:415a-b
  conquest of Sardinia, 1:415a
  irrigation and, 6:557b
  wars in Castile and Murcia, 1:414b–415a
  Libre de paraules de savis e de filòsofs, 3:168a
James I of Cyprus, king, 4:71a
James II of Cyprus, king, 4:71a, 72a
James I of England, king
  Basilikon Doron, 8:436a
  Ireland and, 6:537b
James II of Majorca, king, Morea and, 7:380a
James III of Majorca, king, *Leges palatinae,* translated into Catalan, 9:511a
James I of Scotland, king, 11:111b
  Dunbar as court poet of, 4:307b
  Kingis Quair and, 7:254b, 8:324a
    description of Fortune, 5:147a
  parliament and, 9:438b–439a
James II of Scotland, king, 11:111b
James III of Scotland, king, 11:111b
  marriage to Margaret of Denmark, 11:108a
James IV of Scotland, king, 11:111b, 112a-b
  construction of palace near Edinburgh, 4:393a
  suppression of MacDonald lordship, 11:108a
James V of Scotland, king, parliament and, 9:439a
James of Ascoli, as follower of John Duns Scotus, 12:44a
James of Avesnes, Negroponte and, 7:376b
James of Capua, archbishop, Frederick II and, 11:271a
James of Les Baux, 7:381a
James the Monk, **7:46a-b**
  Homilies, Visitation and, 12:478b
  writings, 7:46a
James, Montague Rhodes, pioneer in codicology, 3:475b–476a
James of Nisibis, St., 1:520a, 9:142a
James, St.
  cult of Santiago, pilgrimage and, 10:280a
  eucharistic liturgy in Jerusalem and, 7:610b
James of Venice, Aristotle and, 1:460b
James of Viterbo, **7:45b–46a**, 9:709a

De regimine christiano, 7:45b–46a, 10:21a
Order of Augustinian Hermits, 7:45b
papal support by, 10:21a–22a
political theory, 7:46a
Jāmī, ᶜAbd al-Raḥmān, 12:59a
Jāmiᶜ al-bayān fī tafsīr al-Qurᵓān. See Ṭabarī, al-
Jāmiᶜ (mosque: Isfahan), 6:562a
Jāmiᶜ al-Qāhira. *See* Azhar, al-
Jāmiᶜ al-tawārīkh. See Rashīd al-Dīn
Jamrāt. See Satan, Islamic stone pillars of
Jämtland, Old Norse kingdom and, 9:179b
Jamuqa, 5:382b
Jan Rokycana. *See* Rokycana, Jan
Jan van Boendale. *See* Boendale, Jan van
Jan van Ruusbroec. *See* Ruusbroec, Jan van
Janibeg, 5:573a
Janissary, **7:46b–47a**
ajemi oghlans, 7:46b
development of, 8:536a
isolation of soldiers, 7:47a
Mehmed II and, 8:264a, 264b
in Ottoman army, 12:553a
Ottoman *gazīs,* 7:47a
purpose of, 7:46b–47a
recruitment of, 7:46b
Selim I and, 11:145a
Jank. See Sanj (harp)
Janko of Czarnków, 9:725b
Chronica Polonorum, 9:730a
Janna (Arabic garden). *See Rauḍa*
János Corvinus, 6:349a
János Hunyadi. *See* Hunyadi, János
János (son of Vata), revolt of, 6:340a
János Zápolyai, king of Hungary. *See* Zápolyai, János, king of Hungary
Jans Enikel, world chronicle by, 2:229a
Janus Pannonius, 6:348b
Japan, Columbus and, 4:559b, 560b
Japheth ben Ali, 7:210b
Japheth ben Ali ha-Levi, 4:539b
Jaque de Cysoing, 7:316b
Jār, al-, port, 11:246b
Jaras, 8:613b
Jarawa of the Aurès Mountains, 7:97b
Jarcha. See Kharja
Jargeau Bridge, construction of, 10:420a
Jarīr, 1:400a, **7:47a–48b**
ᶜAbd al-Malik and, 7:47b
dispute with al-Akhṭal, 7:47b
encomiums, 7:47b
al-Farazdaq and, *al-naqāᵓiḍ* between, 7:47b, 48a
love poetry, 7:48a
satire, 7:47a-b, 48a-b
see also Farazdaq, al-
Jarirīyah (*madhhab:* Egypt), 11:569a
Jarla saga (sögur). See Orkneyinga saga
Jarlmanns saga ok Hermanns, **7:48b–49a,** 10:394b, 395a, 395b
analogues to, 7:49a
authorship of, 7:48b–49a
preservation in manuscripts, 7:48b
Járnsíða, 6:396a, 11:495b
Jarrow abbey
architectural features, 10:680b
founded, 2:168a
Jason and the Golden Fleece, in *Roman de Troie,* 2:182a
Játiva (Valencia), 12:346a, 346b, 348a, 348b
Jaufré, 1:569a, 575b–576a, 10:179b–181a
as chivalric romance, 10:180b
comparison to Chrétien de Troyes's writing, 10:180a–181a
date of, 10:179b–180a
form of, 10:179b
lover-knight theme in, 10:180b
plot summary of, 10:180a-b
as poetic experiment, 10:181a
Jaufré Rudel, 5:438a, **7:49a-b,** 10:168b, 170a
amor de lonh, 10:165b
Marcabru and, 10:168b, 170a
surviving poems, 7:49b
Jauharī, al-, *Tāj al-lugha wa ṣiḥāh al-ᶜarabiya,* 4:444a
Jaume. *See* James
Jaume I of Valencia. *See* James I (the Conqueror) of Aragon and Catalonia, king
Javelins. *See* Spears
Jawhar, campaigns of, 5:25a–26a
Jawsaq al-Khāqānī, al- (palace), 6:597b
wall paintings, 1:5b
Jawzī, Ibn al-, 1:380b, 382a, 10:73a-b
Muntaẓam fī taᵓrīkh al-mulūk wa'l-umam, al-, 6:253b
Jawzīyyah, Ibn Qayyim al-, 1:617b, 618b
Jayn, 8:551b
Jaysh, Tulunid emir, Turks and, 11:561a
Jazāla (style), in Arabic rhetoric, 10:356a
Jazarī, Ibn al- Razzāz al-
Kitāb fī maᶜrifat al-ḥiyal al-handasīya (*Treatise on Automata*), 6:607b, 8:610b (*illus.*), 613a (*illus.*), 9:67a, 284a, 11:636b–637a, 662a
bloodletting device, 11:637a (*illus.*)
influence of, 11:642b
piston-driven paddle wheel, 11:636b (*illus.*)
practical applications, 11:641b–642a
Jazīra, al-, 6:509b, 8:500a
Tāhir and, 11:574a
see also Mesopotamia
Jazūlī, ᶜAbd Allāh ibn Yāsīn al-, rise of the Almoravids and, 11:140a
Jazygs, in Hungary, 6:343b, 344b
Jean I de Chalon-Arlay, count, 2:426a
toll rights granted to, 2:424b
Jean Acart de Hesdin, *Amoureuse prise,* 6:359a
Jean d'André. *See* Johannes Andreae
Jean d'Arras, *Livre de Mélusine,* use of fantasy, 9:634b
Jean de Beauce, **7:50b**
choir screen, Chartres Cathedral, 7:51a-b (illus.)
Jean le Bel, *Vraies chroniques,* 5:303b, 9:638b
Jean of Berry, duke, 5:629a-b, **7:49b,** 8:109b
Beauneveu and, 2:145a
chariot branlant and, 12:377a, 378a
Machaut and, 8:3a
patronage of the arts, 7:49b
Limbourg brothers, 7:581b
projects, architectural, 6:39a
Très riches heures, 7:35a, 49b, 12:185a
Jean Boucicaut, **7:49b–50a**
attacks on port cities of Syria, 8:75a
Jean de Brienne, **7:52a,** 7:346b
in Fifth Crusade, 4:31b, 50a,b
vs. Bulgarians, 7:347b
Jean de Bruges. *See* Bondol, Jean
Jean des Champs, **7:54a**
Jean Charlier. *See* Gerson, John
Jean de Condé, court lyrics, 9:637a
Jean de Cresecque, *Cent ballades,* 9:637a
Jean, Dreux, **7:56b**
Jean le Fère, 8:415b
Jean de Flagy, Lotharingian cycle, 9:634a
Jean de la Fontaine, *Fontaine des amoureux de science,* alchemy in, 1:138b
Jean Hay. *See* Master of Moulins
Jean d'Ibelin. *See* Ibelin, Jean d'
Jean de Jandun. *See* John of Jandun
Jean (Jehan) d'Andeli, **7:50a**
Jean (Jehan) de Chelles, **7:52a**
Jean de Journi, *La dîme de pénitence,* 9:639a
Jean de Lastic, 3:304a
Jean Lemaire de Belges, **7:54a–55b,** 10:364b, 365a
Chansons de Namur, 7:55a
Chronique annale, 7:55a
Concorde des deux langages, 7:55a
Concorde du genre humain, 7:55a
Contes de Cupido et Atropos, 7:55a
Couronne Margaritique, 7:54b
Épître du roi à Hector de Troie, 7:55a
Épîtres de l'amant vert, 7:54b
Gestes de Sophy, 7:55a
Illustrations de Gaule et singularités de Troie, 7:54b, 55a
Légende des Vénitiens, 7:55a
Plainte du désiré, 7:54b
precursor to Pléiade, 5:279a
Regrets de la dame infortunée, 7:55a
Temple d'honneur et de vertus, 7:54b
Traité de la différence des schismes et des conciles de l'église, 7:55a
Jean Lemoyne. *See* Johannes Monachus
Jean de Liège, **7:52b**
Jean de la Loupe. *See* Loup, Jean
Jean de Mailly, *Gestes de saints,* 6:69b
Jean le Maitre, 7:115b
Jean de Marville, 5:625b, 11:349b
Chartreuse de Champmol and, 4:186a
Jean de Meun (Meung), 1:184b–185a, 189a, **7:53a-b**
Alan of Lille and, 7:366a
antifeminism of, 1:324a
Art de chevalerie, source for, 5:290b
beguines and, 2:159b
Chaucer and, 3:281b

Jean de Meun (Meung) (*cont.*)
chivalry handbooks and, 3:302a
Christine de Pizan and, 3:316b
dialect of, 4:168a
Philippe de Vitry and, 12:481b
Roman de la Rose. See Roman de la Rose
translations
of Boethius' *Consolation,* 1:188b
of Vegetius' *Epitoma rei militaris,* 12:366b
Jean Michel, **7:56a**
Jean Miélot, 7:55b, **7:56a**, 7:56a
Jean le Moine. *See* Johannes Monachus
Jean Molinet. *See* Molinet, Jean
Jean de Montreuil
defense of Jean de Meun (Meung), 5:271a-b
"querelle de la Rose" and, 10:452b
Jean de la Motte
Parfait du paon, 9:637a
Regret de Guillaume, comte de Haynneau, 9:637a
Voie d'enfer et de paradis, 1:185b, 9:637a
Jean d'Orbais, **7:50a-b**
Rheims Cathedral and, 7:50b (*illus.*), 10:344b
Jean d'Outremeuse
Geste de Liège, 9:634a
Myreur des histors, 9:638a
Ogier le Danois, 9:634a
Trésorier de philosophie naturelle des pierres précieuses, 9:638b
Jean de Paris. *See* John of Paris
Jean Petit
Gerson and, 5:512b–513a
on tyrannicide, 3:649b
Jean Quidort. *See* John of Paris
Jean de Ravi (Ravy), **7:53b**
Jean de Remi, 2:144a
Jean Renart
Escoufle, 5:258b
Galeran de Bretagne and, 5:341a
Lai de l'ombre, 5:258b
realistic romance, development of, 5:287a
Roman de la Rose, ou de Guillaume de Dôle, 5:258b
Jean de la Rochelle, deadly sins and, 11:211b
Jean de St. Pierre, *Cent ballades,* 9:637a
Jean de Savoie, Philippe de Vitry and, 12:482b
Jean le Sourd. *See* John of Paris
Jean de Sy, Bible of
illustration of, 2:321a
translation encouraged by king, 2:219b
Jean le Tavernier, **7:55b–56a**
Jean le Teinturier, *Mariage des sept arts,* 1:188b, 9:638b–639a
Jean de Thuim, **7:53b–54a**
Hystoire de Julius Cesar, 3:331b, 9:638a
Jean de Vienne, campaign against Scotland (1385), 10:428b
Jean de Vignay, *Légende dorée,* 6:62b
Jean de Vitry, 2:426b
Jean de Werchin, *Songe de la barge,* 9:637a
Jeanne d'Évreux, Book of Hours, 5:614b
Jebe Noyan
Bulgar conquests, 8:470a
invasions
of Georgia, 8:468a
of Qara Qitai, 8:466a-b
pursuit of Khwārizmshāh Muḥammad, 8:467a-b
Jedburgh (monastery: Scotland), 11:105a, 105b
Jednota bratrská. See Bohemian Brethren
Jehan. *See also* Jean
Jehan de Chelles, Notre Dame de Paris and, 9:191a
Jehan et Blonde. See Beaumanoir, Philippe de
Jehan des Murs, **7:56b–57a**, 8:607b
Antonio of Lucca and, 8:648a
on astronomy, 1:612b
on calendar reform, 3:23a
Circuli quadratura and, 1:437a-b
on *color,* 6:619a
Compendium musicae practicae, concept of *perfectio* and, 9:504b
De arte mensurandi, 1:437b, 8:211b
Musica mensurabilis
concept of *perfectio* and, 9:504b
Ugolino of Orvieto on, 8:647b
notation and, 8:645b
Notitia artis musicae, 1:548a
Philippe de Vitry and, 12:481b
Quadripartitum numerorum, 8:212b
Jehan de Saintré. See Sale, Antoine de la
Jehannot de l'Escurel, virelai and, 12:458b
Jehoseph ha-Nagid, 7:96b
Jelena (Helena) (mother of Stefan Uroš II Milutin of Serbia), 11:186b–187a
Jelling dynasty, 4:151b
Jellinge style, **7:57a**, 12:418a-b, 419a (*illus.*)
cup, 7:57a (*illus.*)
runic stones, 10:564a, 12:419a (*illus.*)
see also Mammen style
Jem Sultan, 2:137a
Jena Song Codex, 5:437b–438a
Wartburgkrieg, 12:573b
Jens Grand, 4:154b
Jenson, Nicolas, 10:124b, 126b
Jerba, occupied by Roger II, 12:745a
Jeremiah, Maronite patriarch, 11:564a
Jeremiah Monastery (Saqqara). *See* Monastery of Jeremiah
Jerome of Ascoli. *See* Nicholas IV, pope
Jerome of Moravia, 11:364a, 365a
Dominican antiphonary and, 8:643a
on fiddle, 8:606b
on musical ornamentation, 8:632a-b
Tractatus de musica, 1:544b, 4:247b, 8:563a, 620a, 645a
De mensurabili positio and, 8:643b
Jerome of Prague
against modern logicians, 12:407a
death of, 3:649b
on Prague University, 6:365b
Wycliffism of, 6:367b–368a
Jerome, St., **7:57b–58b**
"Ad Eustochium," 6:383b
Adversus Jovinianum (*Epistle Against Jovinian*), 1:323a, 7:368a
against interest charging, 12:336a
antifeminism of, 1:323a
Bede and, 2:154b
Bible translation, 2:211a, 4:223b–224a, 12:495b
Christmas celebration and, 3:318a
classical translation mode of, 12:139a-b
clergy and, 3:440a
Commentary on Daniel, 6:261b
Coptic education of, 3:595a
De viris illustribus, 7:58a
French secular biography and, 2:236a
as doctor of the church, 4:234a
evangelist symbols and, 4:526a
Hebraica, translation of in the Eadwine Psalter, 2:218b
on king's evil, 7:255a
lives of desert ascetics, 6:66a
in Master Theodoric's painting, 12:17 (*illus.*)
on millennialism, 8:386a-b
on monasteries, 12:682b
Notker Teutonicus and, 9:189a
Paulinus of Nola's letters, 9:471a
Pelagians and, 3:336b
Prologus galeatus, 1:507b
Roman education and, 7:360a
teacher Victorinus and, 12:409b
theology of Western church and, 3:336a
use of libraries, 7:559b
Jerusalem, **7:58b–61b**
Anastasis in, 4:336b
in art, in Bible of Richard II, 6:463a
Byzantine building program in, 4:331a
Christian access to, 9:652b, 656a–658a
Christ's entry into. *See* Entry into Jerusalem
conquered by
Ayyubids, 4:32a
First Crusade, 4:30b, 35b–36a, 11:561b
Frederick II, 4:52a
Khorezmians, 4:32a, 52b
Romans (70), 6:575b
Saladin, 2:23a, 4:39b–40a, 10:625a, 626a, 11:561b
Constantine's basilica in, 4:336b
in crusader thought, 4:17a
fairs, 4:589a
fall of in 1244, *see also ¡Ay, Iherusalem!*
Holy Sepulcher, 1:332b
Islamic construction, 7:60a, 60b, 61a-b
Jewish pilgrimage to, 7:104a, 9:652a–653a
Jews in
Karaite, 7:105b
reestablishment of community in, 9:53a-b
under Muslim rule, 7:103a, 103b, 104a
yeshiva of, 7:104b–105a

in *Mandeville's Travels,* 8:82a
Mosque of ᶜUmar, Tafur and, 11:573a
patriarch of, 2:460a–461b, 9:459a
pentarchy and, 9:495b–496a
presence at the permanent synod, 9:505b
Pisa and, 9:664a
in *Solomon's Temple,* 7:365a-b
Stations of the Cross and, 11:467b
Syrian rites and, 11:567b, 568a
Temple of, 6:593b, 7:59a, 59b–60a
under Muslim rule, 9:652b–963a
under Roman rule, 9:652b, 664a
visit of ᶜUmar I Ibn al-Khaṭṭāb, 9:354a
Jerusalem chandeliers, 7:578 (*illus.*)
Jerusalem, Council of (1651), 1:502a
Jerusalem, Kingdom of, 11:561b
founded, 4:30b, 35a, 37a
High Court, 6:389b, 390a
historiography, 12:643b
history, 4:38b–40b
Jean d'Ibelin (of Beirut) and, 6:388b–389b
Jean d'Ibelin (of Jaffa) and, 6:390a
Manuel I Komnenos and, 8:91b
a "new spiritual Israel" and, 2:216a
nobility of, 9:150b
Tancred and, 11:589b
Venetian merchants and, 12:117b
see also Baldwin I of Jerusalem; Crusader states
Jerusalem (religious community: Prague), 6:366a
Jerusalem Talmud. *See* Talmud
"Jerusalemberg," 11:467b
Jeshua ben Judah, 4:539b, 7:210b
"Jesu dulcis memoria," 6:382a
Jesus der Artz. See Hermann von Sachsenheim
Jesus Christ
in art. *See* specific iconographic types, e.g., Baptism of Christ, Man of Sorrows, Pantokrator
in theology. *See* Christology
Jethro. *See* Shuᶜayb
Jeu, **7:62a**
Jeu d'Adam, 1:260b, 261a, 5:361a, **7:62a**
Christian-Jewish polemics and, 10:2a
dating of, 1:269b
first French vernacular play, 4:264a
liturgical elements in, 4:282a-b
rebirth of French theater and, 5:253a
Jeu de la feuillée. See Adam de la Halle
Jeu parti, 5:434b, **7:63a**
trouvères, 12:218b
see also Débat; Thibaut IV of Champagne, count
Jeu du pèlerin. See Adam de la Halle, *Jeu de Robin et de Marion*
Jeu du Prince des Sots. See Gringoire, Pierre
Jeu de Robin et de Marion. See Adam de la Halle
Jeu de St. Nicolas. See Bodel, Jean
Jewanšēr, prince, in literature, 1:509b
Jewelry. *See* Gems and jewelry
Jewish art, **7:63a–68b**
assimilation of Hellenistic culture, 4:313a
Christian art and, 7:63b, 65a
early Christian art and, 4:350a
iconoclasm in, 7:63a-b
illuminated MSS, 7:66a–68b
Islamic East, 7:66a–67a (*illus.*)
Western Europe, 7:67a–68a (*illus.*)
influence of in Ashburnham Pentateuch, 9:496b
surviving synagogues, 7:68a-b
see also Manuscript illumination, Hebrew; Menorah
Jewish communal self-government
in Christian Spain, power of laity, 7:91a
communal ordinances (*takkanot*), 10:243a
in Europe, **7:68b–72a**, 90b–92a
constitutional status of Jews and, 7:87a–88a
Kalonymus family, 7:206a–207b
in Papal States, 7:109b
rabbinate and, 10:243a–244a
in Spain, 7:80a-b
see also Jacob ben Meir
in Islamic world, 5:356b–358a, **7:72a–75a**
in Babylonia, 7:107b–108a
in Egypt, 7:84a-b
in Qayrawān, 7:98b
rabbinate and, 10:244a-b
see also Nagid
pietist communities, 6:110a
see also Exilarch
Jewish courtiers, 7:96a-b
in Merinid period, 7:99b
Jewish Khazars. *See* Khazars
Jewish law, **7:489a–499a**
acquisition, 7:495b–496a
aḥaronim, 7:493a-b
arbitration, 7:494b
Babylonian and Jerusalem Talmuds, 7:490a
classification of legal branches, 7:497b
codes, 7:491b–492b
in talmudic order, 7:492a
in thematic order, 7:492a
coitus interruptus prohibited by, 3:575a
commentaries, 7:491b
communal enactments, 7:493a, 496b–497a
communal self-government and, 7:68b–71b, 496a-b
conflict of laws, 7:496b
contraception permitted by, 3:573a
courts and Jewish autonomy, 7:494a
creativity and change in, 7:490b, 495b–497b
criminal law and Jewish autonomy, 7:494a, 495a
custom and, 7:496a
divine revelation and, 7:490b
"Enactments of Shum," 7:493a
enactments (*takkanot*), 7:493a
enforcement of, 7:494a-b
evidence, kinship and, 4:606a
exegesis and, 4:539a-b
exilarch and, 4:552b
exile of Jews and, 7:493b–494b
extra-halakhic legislation, 7:496a-b
family law and, 7:497a-b
flexibility of, 7:493a
galut, 5:346a–347a
gaonic judgments, 5:357a
German-Jewish customary, 6:111a
as Halakhah versus Haggadah, 7:489a
halakhic codification, 7:490b, 493a
by Sephardic Jews, 9:573b
as "judgment" law, 7:493a
judicial autonomy, 7:495a-b
lay tribunals, 7:494b–495a
legal study, 11:70b
limiting factors in development, 7:496b–497b
in Maimonides' work, 8:50a
minority rights, 7:496a-b
mishpat ivri, 7:489b, 492b–493a
modes of acquisition, 7:495b–496a
money (*mamona*) vs. ritual law (*issura*), 7:489b–490a
morality and legality, 7:489b
national-religious character of, 7:493b–494b
"Noahide Laws" and, 7:498a
non-Jewish law and, 7:498a-b
courts prohibited, 7:494a–495a
reciprocity with, 7:497b–498a
norms and, 7:489a
novellae, 7:491b
obligation, 7:495b–496a
observance of, religious requirements, 9:577b
pluralism of, 7:492a-b
in Poland, 9:729a
post-talmudic period, 7:490b–493b, 493b–495b
practical application of, 7:493b–495b
public administrative law, 7:496a-b
punishment
banning (*ḥerem*), 7:494a-b
capital, 7:494a
collective, 7:498b
rabbinic
court chairman (*ab bet din*), 10:243a
judge (*dayyan*), 10:243a, 244a
rabbinic period
early scholars, 7:491b–493a
later scholars, 7:493a-b
Rashi's commentary on, 10:260a
religion and legality, 7:489a-b
responsa literature (*sheᵓelot u-teshuvot*), 7:492b–493a, 494a
sources, 7:490a-b
literary, 7:490a, 493b
Torah (Pentateuch) as, 7:489a, 490a-b
tradition (cabala) as, 7:489a, 490a
summary, 7:498b
synagogue and, 11:556b
talmudic law vs. post-talmudic law, 7:490b–491a
taxation and, 7:496b
territoriality limitations, 7:496b–497a
"the law of the land is the law," 7:494b, 496b, 498a-b
theological view of, 9:577b
on usury, 12:340b–341b
five major areas of, 12:341a

Jewish law (*cont.*)
see also Responsum literature, Jewish; Torah
Jewish literature
in Yiddish, *see also Dukus Horant*
see also Hebrew literature
Jewish music, **8:564a–565a,** 9:686b–687a
Jewish mysticism. *See* Cabala
Jewish oath. *See* Oath, *more judaico*
Jewish ordination. *See* Rabbinate
Jewish science. *See* Science, Jewish
Jewish-Christian relations. *See* Christian-Jewish relations
Jewish-Muslim relations, responsum literature and, 10:338a, 339a
Jewry law, **7:499a–502b**
canon law and, 7:499a–500a, 501a-b
"chamber serfdom," 7:500a-b
Christian missionary policies and, 7:501b
defined, 7:499a
diversity of, 7:500b
impact on Jewish society, 7:499a
increasing harshness of, 7:501b–502a
municipal, 7:500b–501a
in Papal States, 7:109a-b
in Poland
residence restrictions (ghetto), 9:729a
Statutes of Nieszawa (1454), 9:729a
profitable regulation, 7:501b–502a
proselytism and, 7:501a
protection of Jewry, 7:500a, 501a
religious oaths and, 7:502a
Roman, 7:499a-b, 501a
secular law, 7:499a–502a
segregation and degradation, 7:501a-b
Jewry oath. *See* Oath, *more judaico*
Jews
in Arabia, 6:575b
in Byzantine Empire, inheritance and, 6:451a-b
Catholic church and, **7:75a–79b,** 7:88a-b, 90b
Augustinian-Paulician view of, 7:75a-b
Clement VI, 3:439b
conversion programs, 7:77a-b
Innocent IV, 6:467a
inquisition, 6:488b
medieval Jewish predicament, 7:93b–94a
papal policies, 7:77b–78b
restrictions on, 3:641a
in Spain, 7:77a-b
theological basis for persecution, 7:75b–76b
see also Jews, in the Papal States
Christian convert translators, 12:135b
in Christian Spain, **7:79b–83a**
at the court of Peter IV (the Ceremonious), 9:510b
Barcelona, 2:103a, 104b
in Castile, 7:80b–81a, 82a-b
communal self-government and, 7:69b, 70a, 70b, 71a, 71b, 90b
conversion of, 6:563b, 565a, 7:79a, 93b
as court physicians, 11:92b
cultural creativity of, 7:92b–93a
early settlements, 7:79b–80a
rab de la corte and, 7:71a
rabbinate and, 10:244a
Reconquista and, 7:80b, 81a, 81b
in Seville, 7:82b, 11:214a
in Toledo, 7:81a, 12:68a
translators, 7:81a, 12:134b–135a
in Valencia, 12:349a-b
Vincent Ferrer and, 12:453a
see also New Christians; Sephardim
costumes of, 3:618b–621b
desert sects, 3:15b–16a
dietary laws, 4:180a–183b
prohibition against pork consumption, 1:300b
in dyeing industry, 4:328a
in Egypt, **7:83a–85a**
Cairo genizah, 3:15a–16b
dietary laws for, 4:180a–183b
discrimination against, 6:74a
government protection of, 4:405b
office of nagid and, 9:52b–53a
pre-Islamic community, 7:83a-b
social services, 6:290b
under Ayyubids, 7:84a
under Fatimids, 7:83b
under Mamluks, 7:84a-b
in England, 2:80b–81a
royal administration of, 4:535a-b
in Europe
before 900, **7:85a–86b**
after 900, **7:86b–94b**
Ashkenaz, 1:585b–586a
Benjamin of Tudela on, 2:181b
Cologne, 3:481b
conversion of, 3:577b–578a, 5:170a, 7:93b, 675a-b
dietary laws for, 4:180a–183b
early medieval trade and, 12:110b
immigration to Poland, 9:729a
Kalonymus family, 7:206a–207b
Nogaret and, 9:153a
Pastoureaux and, 9:454a-b
pietists, 6:109b–111a
population statistics, 7:86b, 87a-b
rabbinate and, 10:243a–244b
spread of Spanish-Jewish culture, 6:127b
see also Banking, Jewish; Blood libel; Jacob ben Meir; Schools, Jewish
expulsions of, 2:81b, **4:563b–565a,** 7:77b
decline of Jewish science and, 11:93a-b
Dominicans and, 7:77a
from Castile, 7:82a
from England, 4:564a, 11:608b
from France, 4:563b–564a, 5:172a, 7:86b, 500b, 9:454a
from Gascony, 4:564a
from Île-de-France, 11:211a
from Medina, 6:577b
from Nuremberg, 9:202a
from Portugal, 4:564b
from Russia, 7:100b
from Spain, 4:564b, 7:83a, 87a, 12:349a-b
motives for, 4:564b, 7:75b–76a, 76b
moving to Thessaloniki, 12:26b
see also Sephardim
in France, taxation of, 10:318a
Frederick II and, 11:210a, 210b
in gaonic period, 5:357b–358a
in Germany
defended by Bernard of Clairvaux, 2:192a
during Black Death, 2:263b
taxation of, 10:331a
Hellenism and, 10:457b
in Islamic world
rabbinate and, 10:244a
religious persecution, 10:601a, 662a-b, 668a
takiya, 8:161a
under the Mamluk dynasty, 8:71b, 72a
see also Jews, in Muslim Spain; Jews, in the Middle East
legal status of, 7:87a–88a
see also Servi camerae nostrae
in the Middle East, 3:16a, **7:101a–108b**
Andalusian literary influences, 6:127b
Benjamin of Tudela on, 2:181b
communal self-government of, 7:73a-b, 74b
establishment of hospitals, 6:290b
influences of Islamic culture on, 5:357b
Iraq, 6:511a, 513a
in Islamic administration, 6:590b
as *jahābidha* and money changers, 12:340b
Karaites, 7:209a–211a
Neoplatonism and, 9:700a-b
pilgrimages of, 9:652a–653a
Yemen, 4:552b
see also Baḥrayn, al-; Palestine
Muḥammad and, 6:577a
in Muslim Spain, 7:79b, 86b, 91b, **7:95a–97a**
Arabic literary influences, 6:125b–126a
Biblical study, 6:128b
Christian reconquest, 6:129a
communal self-government and, 7:73b–74a
in Córdoba, 3:600a, b
cultural assimilation, 8:520b
liturgical creativity of, 7:622a
secular poetry, 6:126a–127b
transfer of rabbinic authority to, 6:257a
see also Sephardim
in North Africa, **7:97a–100a**
alliance with Arab clans, 8:523b–524a
communal self-government of, 7:73b–74b
financial responsibilities, 8:139a, 140b
forced conversions to Islam, 7:99a
Marrakech, 8:151b
in Papal States, 7:78a–79a, 86b, 88a-b, **7:108b–110a**
pilgrimages of, 9:652b
population movements, 7:83b–84a, 86b–87a

role in international trade, 4:555b–566a
Rome, 10:461b, 463b–464a
in Russia, **7:100a–101a**
in Kiev, 12:486a
in Sicily, 11:262a, 267a
the 613 commandments, in Maimonides' *Sefer ha-Mitzvot,* 8:50a
slave trade and, 11:200b, 336b–337b
in Spain, under Visigoths, 12:472b–473a
taxation of, England, 11:612b
witchcraft and, 12:661b
see also Anti-Semitism; Maimonidean controversy; Responsum literature, Jewish
Jidda
importance of as a port, 9:85b
Islamic pilgrimage to, 9:650b
Jihad, **7:110a–111a**
crusades, Battle of Ḥiṭṭin, 10:625b–626b
crusades and, 4:16a, 31a
ghāzīs and, 11:156b
hunting and, 6:355a
as Islamic "pillar," 6:582a
Kharijites and, 7:111a
leadership of, 7:110b
origin of, 6:577a
regular army in, 7:110b–111a
rules of conduct of, 7:111a
Shiites and, 7:110b
Sunnites and, 7:110b
theory of, 7:110a
Umayyads and, 3:40a
volunteers in, 7:110b–111a
see also Ayyubids
Jihān-sūz, 5:526b
Jihānshāh, ruler of Qara Qoyunlu, Uzun Ḥasan and, 12:342b
Jihlava laws, 8:403a
Jijim. See Rugs and carpets
Jīlānī, ᶜAbd al-Qādir al-, **7:111b–112a**
Al-Fath al-Rabbani, 7:111b
Al-Ghunya li Tālibī Tarīq al-Haqq, 7:111b
biographies of, 7:112a
Futuh al-Ghayb, 7:111b
Hanbali-Sufi connection of, 7:111b
al-Mukharrimī and, 7:111b
Qadirīya of, 7:111b–112a
reputation of, 7:112a
Jildakī, Aydamir ibn ᶜAlī al-, alchemical works, 1:141b
Jīlī, ᶜAbd al-Karīm al-, 9:43a-b
Jimena family, in the kingdom of Navarre, 9:68b
Jiménez de Cisneros, cardinal
chapel of Corpus Christi, 8:516b
Counter-Reformation spirituality and, 3:368a
Jiménez de Rada. *See* Ximénez de Rada
Jinn, **7:112a–113a**
afreet, 7:112b–113a
ghoul, 7:112b
illustrations of, 7:113a
in Islamic magic, 8:20b
possession and, 7:112b–113a
social organization of, 7:112b
Jiskra z Brandy, Jan, 6:347b, 348a
Jizya. See Poll tax, Islamic
Joachim of Fiore, **7:113a–114a**
accusations of heresy, 5:201b
apocalyptic views of, 7:114a
Apostolic Brethren and, 7:114a
Arnald of Villanova and, 1:537b
compilation of works, 6:199a
concordiae and, 7:113b
Dante and, 7:113b–114a
foundation of Florensian order, 7:113a
Franciscans and, 7:114a
Guglielmites and, 7:114a
Hugh of St. Cher and, 6:321a
influence of, 7:114a
Franciscan Spirituals, 3:369b
Lateran IV and, 3:640b
on millennialism, 8:386b–387a
orthodoxy of, 7:113b–114a
Peter John Olivi's views and, 9:515b
popularity of ecclesiology, 4:375a
prophecies of, 6:662b
Richard I (the Lionhearted) of England and, 7:113a
Savonarola and, 7:114a
on Scripture, 7:113a-b
theology of history, 9:604b
on Trinitarian doctrine, 7:113b–114a, 12:191a-b, 195b, 196a
Joachimites, 3:369b–370a
Joan of Arc, St., **7:114a–116a**, 8:30a
calling of, 7:114b
canonization of, 7:115b
capture of, 7:115a
Charles VII of France and, 12:352b, 3:271a, 7:114b–115a, 258b
Charles of Orléans and, 3:273a
execution of, 7:115b
first theatrical portrayal of, 4:265a
military victories, 7:114b
Orléans and, 3:150b, 6:332a, 333a
orthodoxy of, 7:114b
portrait of, 7:115a (*illus.*)
role in English defeat, 5:188b
trial of, 7:115a-b
as corruption of inquisition, 6:488a
investigations into, 7:115b
Joan (daughter of Louis X), claim to throne, 5:183a
Joan of Flanders, countess, 5:81a
Joan of Navarre, Philip the Fair and, 4:593a
Joan, pope
legend of, 2:239b
in Boccaccio's *De mulieribus claris,* 2:287a
Joan Roís de Corella
Cartoixà, 3:167a
Psalteri, 3:167a
works of, 3:168a, 171b
Joan (widow of the Black Prince), Wyclif and, 12:706b
Joanna I of Anjou, queen of Naples
execution of, 7:8a
rule of Sicily and, 11:273a
Joanna II of Anjou, queen of Naples, 1:253b
rule of Sicily and, 11:273a
Joanna II of Navarre, queen, 9:71a
Joanna of Achaea, princess, 7:381a
Joanna (sister of Edward III), death of, 4:111b
Joanna (the Mad) of Spain, marriage to Philip I (the Handsome), 6:43a, 8:280b
Joannes Barbucallus, on Beirut earthquake, 2:164a
Joannes de Deo, Huguccio and, 6:327a
Joannes Fuldensis, on *De actibus apostolorum,* 1:422b
Joannes Parvus. *See* Jean Petit
João I (the Great) of Portugal, king. *See* John I (the Great) of Portugal, king
João II (the Perfect) of Portugal, king. *See* John II (the Perfect) of Portugal, king
João das Regas, 10:53a
João de Leão, elegy of, 4:190a
Jobbágy. See Peasants, in Hungary
Joc partir. See Partimen
Jocelin of Brakelond, **7:116a**
chronicle of, 7:116a
offices of, 7:116a
see also Vie St. Edmund le rei, La
Joch, 8:563a
Jochi (father of Batu), 2:131a-b
Jofre, Joan Gilabert, in Valencia, 12:348b
Jogaila. *See* Jagiełło
Joglar/jongleur, **7:116b–117a**
Arabic musical instruments and, 8:601b
in *Chanson de sainte Foy d'Agen,* 10:161b
chansonnier and, 3:255b–256a
chansons de geste and, 3:259b–260a, 5:240b
clerks and, 12:161a
decline of, 7:117a
golden age of, 7:117a
Marcabru, 10:168b–169a
minstrels and, 8:415a
origin of, 7:116b
pejorative connotations of, 7:116b
in Provençal troubadour poetry, 10:164a-b
saints' lives, 6:59a-b
travel and, 12:160b–161a
troubadours and, 12:214b
versatility of, 7:116b
Vie de St. Alexis and, 12:412b
William IX of Aquitaine, 10:166b
see also Minstrels; *Mester de juglaría*
Johanan ben Zakkai, rabbi, 7:168b
Johanitius. *See* Ḥunayn ibn Isḥāq
Johanitsa. *See* John Asen II
Johann von Buch, gloss on *Sachsenspiegel,* 10:603a
Johann von Konstanz, *Minnelehre,* 8:410a-b
Johann von Neumarkt
Michel Beheim and, 8:306b
translations of, 8:356a-b
Johann von Würzburg, **7:117a-b**
allegory of, 7:117b
Gottfried von Strassburg and, 7:117b
Wilhelm von Österreich, 5:429a-b, 7:117a-b
Wolfram von Eschenbach and, 7:117b
Johannes. See Frau Ava

Johannes Andreae, **7:118a-b**
additions to *Speculum iudiciale* of Durand, 7:118a
apparatus glossarum of, 7:118a
Glossa ordinaria, 7:417a
legal writings, 7:118a
Novella, 7:118a
theology of, 7:118a
Johannes Anglicus of Montpellier, mathematical theory, quadrant, 8:211a
Johannes Bassianus, 5:567b
Hugolinus and, 6:326b
legal maxims, 8:232a
as teacher of Azo, 2:29a
Johannes Canaparius, **7:118b**
Adalbert of Prague and, 7:118b
Miracula Adalberti, 7:118b
Translatio, 7:118b
Johannes Ciconia, *Nova musica,* 8:646a
Johannes Corvinus. *See* János Corvinus
Johannes Dacus, *Summa gramatica,* on the nature of the alphabet, 1:218b
Johannes Diaconus. *See* John the Deacon
Johannes von Frankenstein, *Kreuziger,* 2:231a
Johannes Gallicus. *See* John of Garland (music theorist)
Johannes de Garlandia. *See* John of Garland (*ca.* 1195–*ca.* 1272)
Johannes de Grocheo (Grocheio), **7:118b–120a**, 8:570b, 571a
Ars musice, 7:118b–119a
on the categories of music, 7:119a
De musica, 1:545a, 4:50a, 50b, 87a, 87b, 8:644b
on fiddle, 8:606b–607a
on measured music, 7:119a-b
motet, description of, 8:502a-b
on music *non praecise mensurata,* 10:380a-b
Johannes Hadlaub (Hadloub, Hadloube), **7:120a-b**
influences on, 7:120a-b
Minnesang in works of, 7:120b
Steinmar and, 11:476b
Johannes Heynlin aus Stein, commentary on Cicero, 10:356a
Johannes Hispalensis, Latin version of *Secretum secretorum,* 11:135a
Johannes of Imola, on purgatory, 6:450b
Johannes Januensis. *See* Balbi, Giovanni
Johannes of Jenstein. *See* John of Jenstein
Johannes von Lichtenberg
as defender of Thomism, 12:42a
succeeded by Theodoric of Freiberg, 12:18a
Johannes of Liège
ars antiqua and, 1:542b
Speculum musicae, 1:542b, 545a
Johannes de Lignano, Zabarella and, 12:735a
Johannes de Mirfeld, *Florarium,* 1:206a
Johannes Monachus, **7:120b–121a**
apparatus glossarum of, 7:120b
on canon law, 7:120b–121a
ecclesiastical career of, 7:120b
on powers of the cardinals, 3:517a
Johannes de Muris. *See* Jehan des Murs
Johannes Primarius. *See* John of Garland (music theorist)
Johannes of St. Arnulf, **7:121a**
Johannes of St. Paul in Rome, **7:121a-b**
Odo of Cluny and, 7:121a-b
prose of, 7:121a
Johannes of St. Vincent, **7:121b**
Chronicon S. Vincentii Vulturnensis, 7:121b
Johannes Scotus Erigena. *See* John Scottus Eriugena
Johannes of Středa, influence on literary works, 1:44b–45a
Johannes Tauler. *See* Tauler, Johannes
Johannes a Temporibus, 9:171a
Johannes of Teplá, *see also Ackermann aus Böhmen, Der*
Johannes Teutonicus, 5:657b, **7:121b–122b**
Bartholomaeus' recension of work of, 7:122a
on canon law, 7:121b–122a
Compilatio quarta, 7:122a, 427b
Compilatio tertia, 7:122a
decretal collection, 7:416a
disciple of Azo, 2:29a
on Fourth Lateran Council, 7:122a
Glossa ordinaria to *Decretum Gratiani,* 4:127b, 7:122a, 414b
Innocent IV and, 6:466a
Laurentius Hispanus and, 7:385b, 386a
Quaestiones disputatae, 7:122a
on spiritual and temporal hierarchy, 10:20b
Vincentius Hispanus and, 12:456a
Johannes Tinctoris, 8:648b
as defender of Thomism, 12:42a
Liber de arte contrapuncti, 3:657b–658a
on lute, 8:607b
Terminorum musicae diffinitorium, definition of harmony, 6:100b
on *trompette sacqueboute,* 8:603b
Johannes de Tinemue, 1:436a
Liber de curvis superficiebus Archimenidis, 8:210b
Johannes Vetulus, 8:646b
Johannitius of Baghdad. *See* Ḥunayn ibn Isḥāq al-ᶜIbādī
John II of Aragon, king, 1:418b–419a
Catalonian resistance to, 1:418b
courtly lyrics and, 11:451a
quarrel with son Charles, 1:418b
succeeded by his son Ferdinand, 1:419a
John I of Aragon and Catalonia, king, Bernat Metge and, 8:300b
John IV of Brittany, duke, 6:332a
administration of, 2:380a-b
Charles V of France and, 3:270a
John I Tzimiskes, Byzantine emperor, 1:636b, **7:126b–127a**
Armenian Bagratids and, 1:482b, 483b, 7:126b–127a
Ašot III and, 1:589b
athanatoi and, 11:573b
Basil II and, 2:118b
Bulgaria under, 2:406a-b
as hero in Joshua Roll, 7:152b
letter to King Ašot of Armenia, in Matthew of Edessa's *Chronicle,* 8:228b
march on Syria and Palestine, 2:490b
Nikephoros II Phokas and, 9:133a
reign of, 7:126b–127a
Theophano and, 12:24a
treaty with Svyatoslav of Kiev, 12:435b
see also Bardas Phokas; Bardas Skleros; Macedonians
John II Komnenos, Byzantine emperor, **7:127a-b**
capture of Vahka Castle in 1138, 12:345a
Cilician campaign of, 11:313b
Danishmendids and, 4:93a, 7:127a
hospital at Pantokrator monastery, 8:245b
military campaigns of, 7:127a
reign of, 7:284a
Theodore Prodromos and, 12:16a
John V Palaiologos, Byzantine emperor, **7:128a**
Alexios Apokavkos and, 12:742a
coinage of, 8:421a
conversion to Roman Catholicism, 2:465b, 502a
Gattilusio and, 7:380a
as joint ruler, 7:128a
Kydones and, 4:135b
recovery of Constantinople, 2:502b
reign of, 7:128a
rescued, 4:56a
Turkish vassalage
Bāyazīd I, 2:502b
Sultan Murad, 2:502a
vs. Ottomans, 2:501b–502a
John VI Kantakouzenos, Byzantine emperor, 5:672b, **7:128a-b**
abdication of, 7:128b, 9:618b
as adviser to Andronikos III Palaiologos, 1:246b
assumption of throne, 2:501a
coronation of, 7:128a-b
family of, 7:128a
hesychasm and, 7:128b
historical works, 2:516b
History, 6:247b
as joint ruler, 7:128a
kommerkion and, 11:605a
Morea and, 7:380a
Nikolaos Kavasilas and, 9:135a
offices of, 7:128a
Pera-Galata and, 2:501b, 9:503a
Serbia and, 11:178a
Stefan Uroš IV Dušan of Serbia and, 11:475a-b
vs. Ottomans, 2:500b
Zealots and, 2:501b, 12:742b, 743a
John VII Palaiologos, Byzantine emperor
government of Thessaloniki, 2:503b
requests for Western aid, 8:545b
John VIII Palaiologos, Byzantine emperor, **7:128b–129a**
at Ferrara-Florence Council, 7:129a
conciliation with Roman church, 8:545b
George Scholarios and, 5:401a
Isidore and, 6:563a

Joseph II and, 7:150b
Ottoman invasions, pleas for Western aid, 2:503b–504a
Pisanello and, 11:255b
recovery of Peloponnesus, 2:503b
reign of, 7:128b–129a
support of Turkish pretender, 2:503b
vs. Zaccarias brothers, 7:381b
see also Ferrara-Florence, Council of
John I of Castile and León, king, 10:52b–53a
rule of, 3:137b
Spanish era and, 11:389b
John II of Castile and León, king
Alvaro de Luna and, 3:138a, 11:421b
burning of Enrique de Villena's books and, 11:420b
courtly poetry and, 11:419a-b, 451a
Enrique de Villena and, 12:449a
in literature, 6:429a
rule of, 3:138a
John II of Cyprus, king, 4:71a
John II of France, king, 12:352b
capture at Poitiers, 3:269a-b, 4:399a, 490b, 9:716a, 11:622b–623a
consequences of, 5:185a
crusades of, 5:186a
financial measures, 5:184b
fur coat of, 5:325b
in *Grandes chroniques de France,* 6:654a
murder of Charles the Bad, 5:184b
opposition of nobility to, 5:184b
Philippe de Vitry and, 12:481a
ransom of, 5:336b, 11:622b–623a
representative assemblies and, 10:318b–319b
Rodríguez del Padrón and, 10:438b
taxation policy, 11:622a
John III Vatatzes (John Doukas Vatatzes), emperor of Nicaea, **7:127b–128a,** 7:343a
character of, 7:127b
Nicaean expansion, 2:498b
Nymphaion and, 9:203a
relations with, papacy, 7:348a,b
Theodore II Laskaris and, 12:13b–14a
vs. Latin Empire of Constantinople, 7:347b, 9:117a
John IV Laskaris, emperor of Nicaea, 12:14a
deposition of, 7:343a-b
John III Scholastikos, patriarch, 7:133a
possible identification with John Malalas, 8:55b
Synagoge in Fifty Titles, 9:158b
John IV (the Faster), patriarch, **7:126a**
Gregory I the Great and, 7:126a
nomocanon and, 9:158b
John VIII Xiphilinos, patriarch, 7:125a-b, **7:126a-b**
on Byzantine law, 7:126a-b
John Mauropos and, 7:126a-b
on marriage, 4:594b
Michael Psellos and, 7:126b
John I Albert of Poland, king, Moldavian invasion, 12:504a
John I, pope, vs. Theodoric, 1:454b
John VIII, pope, 3:632a
appeals for military defense, 4:18b
emphasis on right of coronation by, 9:374b
missions and, 4:73b, 74a
revolt against, by Emperor Anspert, 8:377b
John X, pope
convenes council in Split, 4:4b
Magyars and, 6:338b
Nikolaos I Mystikos and, 9:135b
Tomislav and, 4:5a
John XI, pope, Cluniacs and, 3:470a
John XII, pope, Otto of Germany and, 10:522b
John XIII, pope, Sylvester II and, 11:552b
John XIX, pope
Cluniacs and, 3:470a
as "senator of all Romans," 10:525a
John XXI, pope. *See* Peter of Spain
John XXII, pope, 3:645a, **7:125b–126a,** 9:709a
administration of, 3:363a-b
annate practice established by, 1:304b
Augustinus Triumphus and, 2:1a
on beatific vision, 7:125b–126a
beguins and, 2:163b
on canon law, 7:125b, 417a, 428a
canonization of St. Thomas Aquinas, 12:41a
cardinals and, 3:94a
church taxation and, 11:60a, 606b
condemnation of Peter John Olivi's views and, 9:515b
Cum inter nunnullos, 5:203b
curial staff of, 3:363b–364a
Declaration of Arbroath and, 10:427b
deposition of, 5:203b
Dominican province of Sultanieh and, 4:253a
election of, 7:125b
Ex secrabilis, 11:606b
excommunication of Can Grande, 4:103a
Extravagantes communes, 7:125b
Franciscans and, 2:163a, 3:363b, 369b, 7:125b, 10:122b
persecution of Spirituals, 5:202b–203b
rejection of poverty, 4:376b–377a, 5:203a
help for Āyās, 2:19a
Humiliatae and, 12:687a
imperial election of 1314 and, 4:428b
In agro dominico, condemnation of Meister Eckhart, 4:381a, 9:32a
legitimacy of elections and, 5:492a
Louis IV of Germany and, 3:515a, 5:488a-b
Marsilius and, 4:132a
nepotism and, 3:363a
Ockham and, 9:209b, 210a
opposition to in *Frankenspiegel,* 11:81a
Peter Aureoli and, 9:513a
policies of, 3:363a
Quorundam exigit, 5:202b–203a, 6:199b
Racio recta, 2:161b
reign of, 7:125b–126a
Sancta romana, 5:203a
simple life of, 3:363a
Spondent quas non exhibent divitias pauperes alchymistae, punishments for alchemy, 1:137b
Super illius specula, 12:662a
on sorcerers, 8:31a
Toulouse province created by, 10:193a
vs. Matteo Visconti, 12:464b
John XXIII, antipope
church reform and, 3:647a-b
Council of Constance and, 3:647b–648b
election of, 3:366a
Francesco Zabarella and, 12:735a
order of Grandmont and, 5:655b
unfitness for papacy, 3:647a
Wenceslas IV and, 6:368b
Zybněk and, 6:368a
John I (the Great) of Portugal, king, reign of, 10:52b–53b
John II (the Perfect) of Portugal, king
Cape of Good Hope and, 4:562b
Columbus and, 4:559b, 560a-b, 562a-b
Guinea and, 4:562a
reign of, 10:55a-b
John VIII of Ravenna, archbishop, Nicholas I and, 9:120b–121a
John II of Trebizond, *komnenos,* 12:168b
John of Abbeville, 10:78a
John, abbot (archanter of St. Peter's in Rome), 2:153b
John of Afflighem, **7:132a-b,** 11:365b
Cistercians and, 8:643a
De musica cum tonario, 7:132a-b, 8:642a-b
on organum, 7:132b
John of Albret, ruler of Navarre, 9:72a
John Alexander of Bulgaria, tsar, 2:412b, 11:177b
John the Almsgiver, St., patriarch of Alexandria
influence of in the Palaiologan era, 8:246a
life of, on Byzantine trade, 12:101a
John of Alta Silva
Dolopathos, 5:286b
Historia septem sapientum, 7:365a
John of Antioch, *Paschal Chronicle,* 6:243b–244a
John (the Solitary) of Apamea, 11:566a
John Apokavkos, 12:742b–743a
John Asen I. *See* Asen I of Bulgaria (John Asen), tsar
John Asen II of Bulgaria, tsar, **7:131a**
Bogomils and, 2:295a
military campaigns, 7:131a
reign of, 2:408b, 410b
Serbia and, 11:174b
Theodore II Laskaris of Nicaea and, 12:14a
vs. Theodore of Epiros, 7:131a, 347b
John of Avranches
De officiis ecclesiasticis, 10:538b
on liturgy, 7:630a, 631b
John Balliol of Scotland, king
renunciation of English overlordship, 4:396a
Robert I of Scotland and, 10:426b

John the Baptist, St.
Armenian Christianity and, 9:457b, 458a
in art, 10:496a, 497b (*illus*)
beheading of, 9:667 (*illus.*)
of Notke, 9:186b (*illus.*)
in literature, 6:542b
liturgical cycle of in the Byzantine church, 7:612b
in a panel by Segna di Bonaventura, 11:142a (*illus.*)
relics of, 1:518a
John of Bassolis, as follower of John Duns Scotus, 12:44a
John of Bavaria, count of Holland, Jan van Eyck and, 4:566a
John of Bedford, duke, John Lydgate and, 8:323a
John Beleth, on liturgy, 7:630b
John of Biclaro, 11:406a
John de Blandy, curriculum regulation, 11:690a
"John of Bridlington," *Prophecy,* 7:370a
John of Bridlington, St., a rhymed office to, 10:370b
John of Brienne. *See* Jean de Brienne
John of Bromyard. *See* Bromyard, John
John (the Fearless) of Burgundy, duke
control of Paris, 5:187b, 188a
encouraged French disorders, 3:4a
Louis of Orléans and, 10:320b
murder of, 3:270b, 5:188a
John of Burgundy (physician), on plague treatment, 2:264b
John of Canterbury, *Polistorie,* 1:265b
John of Capestrano (Capistran), St., **7:124a**
as Franciscan, 7:124a
Franciscan reform proposal, 5:205b
Hunyadi and, 6:347b, 364a
siege of Belgrade and, 7:124a
women's orders and, 12:688b
John of Cappadocia, *Corpus iuris civilis* and, 3:608b
John Chrysostom, St., **7:122b–123a**
anaphora and, 1:516b
Antiochene rite and, 1:327a
Cassian and, 3:122a-b
as church reformer, 7:122b–123a
on *coloni,* 4:511a
De sacerdotio, 7:122b
as doctor of the church, 4:234a
Eight Orations, 7:75b
eucharistic liturgy and, 7:610b
exile of, 7:123a
hospitals and, 6:287b
influence of, 7:123a
on Jews, 7:75b, 76a
Nestorianism and, 9:107a
preaching of, 10:350b
scriptural interpretation, 9:564a
translations of
Ambrogio Traversari, 12:163a
Byzantine, 12:126b
into Armenian, 1:507b
Western European, 12:139b
John Cinnamus. *See* John Kinnamos
John Climacus. *See* John Klimakos, St.
John de Cobham, Rochester Bridge and, 10:415b
John of Cornwall, 5:388a, 9:517a, 12:21b
on the liturgy of the Mass, 7:631b–632a
John Cotton. *See* John of Afflighem
John of the Cross, St., as doctor of the church, 4:234b
John Damascene. *See* John of Damascus, St.
John of Damascus, St., **7:124a–125a**, 7:282b
against the Paulicians, 9:469b
Aristotle and, 1:458a
on astrology, 1:606a
as author of *kanōnes,* 7:613a
on Byzantine liturgy, 7:124b
Christology of, 3:320b
Dialectics, 9:566a
as doctor of the church, 4:234a-b
Exact Exposition of the Orthodox Faith, 2:466a
Fountain of Wisdom, 3:320b, 336b, 7:124b
Greek thought and, 7:124a
hymns and, 6:379a
in iconoclastic controversy, 2:463a, 3:631a, 6:398a, 400b, 401a, 404b, 7:124b, 9:561b
lives of Sts. Barlaam and Josaphat, 8:19a
octoechos, 7:124b, 8:554b
hymns in, 7:612b
Peter Lombard and, 9:517a
Sacra parallela, 7:124b
on Trinitarian doctrine, 7:124b
on Virgin Mary, 12:460a
John of Darlington, 11:607b
John the Deacon, **7:142b–143b**
identity of
John I, pope, 7:142b–143a
John the Deacon of Naples, 7:143a
John the Deacon of Rome (*ca.* 824–before 882), 7:143a
John the Deacon of Rome (mid 12th century), 7:143a
John the Deacon of Venice, 7:143a
influence on Boethius, 2:292a
John of Denmark, Norway, and Sweden, king, 4:156a
John Doukas Vatatzes. *See* John III Vatatzes (John Doukas Vatatzes), emperor of Nicaea
John of Dumbleton, 11:535a
John Duns Scotus. *See* Duns Scotus, John
John of England, king, **7:129a–130b**
accession to throne, 4:468, 7:129a
archives and, 1:448b
Arthur of Brittany and, 7:129a-b
barons and, 4:469a
character of, 7:129b
church-state relations under, 4:423a-b, 468b, 471a-b, 7:129b–130a
interdict, 9:518a
papal legates and, 7:535a
controversy with Lusignans, 5:164a
death of, 7:130b
excommunication of, 7:130a
fairs and, 4:587a
fur prices and, 5:325b, 327a
intervention in church affairs, 3:265b
Irish expedition, 5:421a, 9:436b
Jews and, 2:81a
Langton and, 7:130a-b, 338a-b
legal system under
abuses, 4:470b
court of common pleas, 3:492a
itinerant justices, 7:184b
justices of common pleas, 7:187a-b
justices of the King's Bench, 7:191a
London Bridge and, 10:414b, 421a
London self-government and, 3:499a
loss of continental possessions, 5:164a-b, 7:661b
battle of Bouvines, 5:164b
Magna Carta and, 4:160b, 7:130b
marriages
Isabella of Angoulême, 4:468a
Isabella of Gloucester, 7:129b
mercenary troops, 12:559a
military fiascoes of, 7:129b–130a
mining charter granted by, 8:403a
origins of parliament and, 9:422b, 423b
Philip II Augustus of France and, 5:59a, 7:129a-b, 9:168a, 168b
recovery of Norman lands, 4:468b–469a
revolt against, 7:130b
London's role in, 7:661b
Richard I (the Lionhearted) and, 4:467b, 10:383b
royal household and, 6:301b–302a
Scotland and, 11:107b
scutage and, 11:120a, 120b
successors of, 7:130b
taxation, 11:612b
of movables, 11:614a
Treaty of Le Goulet and, 7:129a
vs. Innocent III, 6:464b
church taxation and, 11:607a
Welsh rebellions, 12:519a-b
William Marshal and, 9:150b, 12:635b–636a
see also Magna Carta
John of Ephesus, **7:132b–133a**, 11:566a
Church History, 7:132b–133a
Lives of the Eastern Saints, 7:133a
missions of, 7:132b
monophysitism of, 7:132b–133a
Nubian Christianity and, 3:314b
John of Epiphaneia, Theophylaktos Simokattes' *Histories* and, 12:25a
John the Evangelist, St.
compared to Symeon the New Theologian, 9:7b
ivory plaque, 7:25a (*illus.*)
John the Exarch
Shestodnev, 11:345b
Symeon of Bulgaria and, 11:554b
John of Falkenberg, on tyrannicide, 3:649b
John of Fordun
Chronica gentis Scotorum (*Scotichronicon*), 10:428b, 10:435b, 11:116b
source of early Scottish history, 6:258a
John of Freiburg, *Summa confessorum,* 1:206a
John of Fruttaria, 2:174a

John of Gaddesden, *Rosa medicinae anglicana, Yellow Book of Lecan* translation of, 12:140b–141a
John of Gaèta. *See* Gelasius II, pope
John of Garland (*ca.* 1195–*ca.* 1272), **7:133a–134b**, 7:368a, 8:643b
Compendium grammaticae, 7:368a
De arte prosayca, metrica, et rithmica, 10:359b, 360a-b
De mysteriis ecclesiae, 7:133b
De triumphis ecclesiae, 7:133b
definition of love by, 1:268b–269a
Epithalamium beatae Mariae Virginis, 7:133b
Exempla honestae vitae, 1:255a
Geoffrey of Vinsauf and, 7:134a
grammar treatises of, 7:133b
Integumenta Ovidii, 1:183b, 7:133b, 368a-b
Matthew of Vendôme and, 7:134a
Morale scolarium, 7:133b
Ovid and, 7:133b–134a
Parisiana poetria, 7:134a
rhetorical technique of, 7:134a-b
Stella maris, 7:133b
supplanted by humanist literary theories, 10:363b
on Vergil, 7:134a
John of Garland (music theorist), **7:134b**, 8:583a
Anonymous IV and, 1:309b
on consonance, 3:542a-b, 596a
De mensurabili musica, 7:134b, 8:643b
earliest known use of *perfectio* as ligature, 9:504b
De plana musica, 7:134b, 8:643b
Jerome of Moravia and, 8:645a
mention of Perotinus, 9:506b
on modal notation, 8:620b, 622a
on musical ornamentation, 8:632b
notation treatise of, 1:544b–545a
Notre Dame school and, 9:191b
Robert de Handlo and, 8:646b
John of Gaunt, **7:134b–135b**, 9:428b
Castile and
claim to, 3:137b
expedition against, 7:135a
Chaucer and, 3:281b, 290a, 7:135b
as duke of Lancaster, 7:135a
expedition against France, 7:135a
marriages of, 7:135a-b
opposition by Edward the Black Prince, 4:399a
Peasants' Revolt of 1381 and, 7:135a, 9:479b
as protector of Wyclif, 7:135a, 12:706b
Tudor claim to throne and, 7:135a
John Gerson. *See* Gerson, John
John Glykys, patriarch, 11:52a
Nikephoros Gregoras and, 9:133b
John of Gmunden, 1:613b, 11:103a
John of Gorce, 7:121a, 561b
John the Grammarian, patriarch, accused of sorcery, 8:18b
John of Gravina, Morea and, 7:380a
John de Grey, bishop of Norwich, 7:130a
election of, 7:338a
John Gualberti, St., **7:123a-b**
monastic view of, 3:354b
reform of Florentine church, 5:92a-b
on simony, 7:123b, 9:508b, 509a
Vallombrosan order and, 7:123a-b
John of Haute-Seille. *See* John of Alta Silva
John of Hauville, *Architrenius,* 7:366b
John of Hexham, bishop, Bede and, 2:153b
John the Historian, *kat*ᶜ*ołikos,* 1:482a
John (the Mild) of Holstein, count, 4:155a
John of Holywood. *See* John of Sacrobosco
John of Howden, 1:255a, **7:135b**
hymns of, 6:382a
Philomena, 7:135b, 368b
poetry of, 7:374b
Rossignol, 1:262b, 7:135b
John de Hunyad (Hunyadi). *See* Hunyadi, János
John Italos, 3:632a, **7:131b–132a**
commentary on Aristotle, 11:55a
Feast of Orthodoxy, trial on, 9:698a
heresy of, 7:131b–132a
indictment of, 9:566b–567a
Neoplatonic theories of, 7:131b
Platonism of, 11:49b
Synodikon of Orthodoxy and, 3:631b, 6:190a, 7:131b, **11:558b–559a**, 11:559a
list of heretics, 6:192b
under Psellos, 7:131b
John of Jandun
Averroist writings of, 1:465a
on Ste. Chapelle, 10:624a
Wyclif and, 12:710a
John of Jenstein, archbishop of Prague, collection of rhymed offices supervised by, 10:376b
John of Jenštejn, archbishop of Prague, conflict with Wenceslaus IV, 2:304b
John of Jerusalem, bishop, 1:508b, 518b
John of Jesenic, 6:367b–368a, 368b
John Judeus, 3:185b
John Kameniates, on Arab capture of Thessaloniki, 2:516a, 6:245a
John Kananos, on siege of Constantinople, 2:517a
John the Kat^cołikos. *See* John of Ōjun, St.
John Kinnamos, **7:132a**
Alexiad, continuation of, 2:55a
histories of, 7:132a
Manuel I Komnenos and, 7:132a
Niketas Choniates and, 9:134a
Vlachs and, 12:483b
John Klimakos, St., **7:123b**, 9:7a
as hermit, 7:123b
Ladder of Paradise, 6:217b, 7:123b, 9:563b
illustrations, 2:442b
John Komnenos Asen, 11:178b, 179a
John Koukouzeles (composer), 8:616b
John Kurkuas, Byzantine general, vs. Xlatc, 12:713b
John of La Rochelle, Aristotle and, 1:461b
John of Lancaster, duke of Bedford
conflicts with Charles VII of France, 5:188a-b
death of, 6:332b
John of Legnano, on warfare, 6:334b
John of Lichtenberg. *See* Johannes von Lichtenberg
John of Lignères
Algorismus de minutiis, 8:209b
on astronomy, 1:612b
modification of the equatorium, 11:98b
John of Lodi, biography of St. Peter Damian, 9:508a
John of Lugio, beliefs of, 3:184b
John of Lusignan, relation to Guy of Lusignan, 6:39a
John of Luxembourg, king of Bohemia, 2:300b, 9:724a-b
as patron of Guillaume de Machaut, 8:3a
John Lydus. *See* Lydus
John of Maiuma, bishop, *Plerophoriai, oktoechoi,* 8:449a
John of Marienwerden, 9:14a
John of Monte Corvino
in Armenia, 3:394b
China mission, 5:202a
in Peking, 3:642a
John Moschos
Pratum spirituale, 6:58a
on Alexandrian merchant, 12:100b
John of Murrovalle, persecution of the Spirituals, 9:515a
John of Murs. *See* Jehan des Murs
John of Naples, teaching of Thomism and, 12:41a, 42a
John of Neumarkt, 4:176a, 5:627b
John of Nevers, vs. Bāyazīd I, 9:129b
John of Nikiu, **7:135b–136a**
chronicle of Arab conquest, 2:513a
monophysitism of, 7:136a
works of, 7:135b–136a
John of Ōjun, St., 1:509b, **7:125a-b**
Against the Paulicians, 7:125a, 9:469a
Against the Phantasiasts, 6:188a, 189a, 7:125a
Ašot I and, 1:480b–481a, 481b
on canon law, 7:393a-b
councils called by, 7:125a
heresy and, 7:125a
History of the Arcruni, 1:481b
*Kanonagirk*ᶜ *Hayoc*ᶜ of, 7:393a–394a
Oratio synodalis, 7:125a
Paulicians and, 7:125a
John of Palermo, 1:438b
John of Paris, **7:136a–137b**, 9:709a, 10:238a
on Antichrist, 1:322a
Aquinas' *Summa theologiae* and, 7:136b
Boniface VIII and, 7:136b–137a
chronological difficulties concerning, 7:136a
on church and state, 1:465a
Correctoria corruptorii Thomae and, 7:136b, 12:41a, 41b
De potestate regia et papali, 7:136b–137a, 267b, 10:22a
Dominicans and, 7:136a–137a
impanation theory of, 4:451b, 7:137a

John of Paris (*cont.*)
kingship theories of, 7:267b–268a
on mendicant orders, 7:137a
on papal power, 4:376b, 483b, 7:136b–137a
Philip IV the Fair and, 7:136b–137a
philosophical writings of, 7:136b
on the political role of the church, 7:137a
Tractatus de potestate regia et papali, 3:517a, 4:376a
on transubstantiation, 7:137a
John of Parma
Joachimite views, 2:315a, 316b
leadership of Franciscans
dispute between friars and secular masters, 5:200a
resignation of, 5:200b
theology of, 7:118a
John Philoponos of Alexandria, 1:457b–458a, 464b, 9:698a
Ammonius's lectures, editing of, 9:565a-b
on Aristotle's *Physics,* 1:458a, 11:634a
description of astrolabe, 11:96b
Ibn Sīnā and, 11:305b
Neoplatonism and, 9:98a, 98b
John of Plano Carpini, 4:556b, 5:398a, **7:137b–139a**
as disciple of St. Francis, 7:137b
Historia Mongalorum, 7:137b, 138b–139a
Innocent IV and, 7:138a-b
Mandeville's Travels and, 8:82a
monasteries founded by, 7:138a
Mongol embassy of, 5:200a, 7:137b–139a
on Mongol fur tributes, 5:332b
offices of, 7:137b–138a
travels of, 10:28a
John of Pontoise, bishop of Winchester, 11:608a
John the Precursor, St. *See* John the Baptist, St.
John Quidort. *See* John of Paris
John of Ragusa, at Council of Pavia, 3:651b
John of Regulus, 9:729b
John Ridevall, 7:370a
as exegete, 4:544b
Fulgentius metaphoralis, 1:183b
Ovidian influence, 9:314b
John of Rila, 2:405b
John of Rupescissa
De consideratione quintae essentiae, distillation of alcohol, 1:138a
Liber lucis, derivation of philosophical sulfur, 1:138a
on millennialism, 8:387a
John Saba (the Elder), 11:566a
John of Sacrobosco
Algorismus vulgaris, 1:612a
Peter Philomena's commentary on, 8:209a
on astronomy, 1:612a-b
Tractatus de computo, 1:612a
Tractatus de sphaera, 1:612a, 11:95b
John, St., May Day Festival and, 5:36b
John of St. Albans, Dominicans and, 4:245a-b
John of St. Amand, parliamentary trial of, 9:424a
John of S. Martín de Albares, **7:140b**
illuminations in Bible of León, 7:140b–141a (*illus.*)
John of Salisbury, **7:139b–140b,** 11:56b, 12:21b
Aristotle and, 7:139b–140a
Becket and, 7:139b
Bernard of Chartres and, 2:189b–190a
on Bernard of Clairvaux, 2:191b
as bishop of Chartres, 7:139b
classical literary studies and, 3:434a-b
De dogmate philosophorum, 7:140b
on deposition of rulers, 4:159b
on dialectic, 4:170a
education of, 7:139b
Entheticus, 7:140b
Henry II of England and, 7:265a
Historia pontificalis, 7:140b
kingship theories of, 7:264b–265b
Life of St. Anselm, 7:140b
Life of St. Thomas Becket, 7:140b, 12:35b, 36a
on medicine, 8:256b–257a
Metalogicon, 3:434a-b, 4:471b, 7:139b–140a, 10:352b, 353a
influence of dialectic and philosophy, 11:688b
on philosophical dualism, 4:298a
the Quintilianic education plan and, 10:356b
on papacy, 7:140b
Papal History, 6:263b, 263a
Policraticus, 1:607a, 4:159b, 471b, 7:139b, 140b, 264b–265a, 364b, 8:434b–435a
antifeminism in, 1:324a
Contra curiales et officiales clericos and, 9:131a
political theory of, 10:18b–19a
Robert of Melun and, 10:434b
as Theobald's secretary, 3:83a
theory of morality, 9:594b
Thierry of Chartres and, 12:27a
on universals, 7:139b–140a, 9:588b–589a
John Scottus Eriugena, 4:542b, **7:141a–142b,** 7:362b, 9:100b, 701a-b, 12:152a
Berengar and, 2:188a
Carolingian Latin poetry and, 3:103a
Charles the Bald and, 7:141b–142a
De divisione naturae, Neoplatonism and, 9:99b
De praedestinatione, 7:141b
disciples of, Remigius of Auxerre, 10:303a-b
Disciplinarum libri IX and, 8:637a
as exegete, 2:224a
false attributions to, 7:142b
Gabriel Biel and, 2:234a
Gottschalk of Orbais and, 5:638b, 7:141b–142a
Greek language and, 7:142a
Hucbald and, 6:317a
idea of personal reform and, 10:284b
Irish origins, 7:141a
Martianus Capella glossed by, 9:586b
misinterpreted by Amalric of Bène, 1:228b
on music, 8:579a
Neoplatonism of, 7:142a
Periphyseon, 4:169b, 7:141b–142a, 8:639b, 10:272a
divisio and *reversio,* 9:586a
philosophy and theology of, 7:141b–142a
Christology, 3:322a, 323b
cosmology, 9:586b–587a
on dialectic, 4:169b, 9:586b
doctrine of the syzygies, 9:586a-b
double predestination, 9:587a
dualistic views of, 4:297b
on Pseudo-Dionysius' *Celestial Hierarchy,* 7:142b
teaching career of, 7:141b
on *The Marriage of Philology and Mercury,* 7:141b
translations, 7:142a, 9:586a
of Pseudo-Dionysius' *Celestial Hierarchy,* 1:250a, 12:139a
John the Scribe, on early banking in Genoa, 2:73a
John of Scythopolis, on Pseudo-Dionysius the Areopagite, 9:99b
John of Segovia, conciliar theory of, 3:513a, 516b
John of Seville
on arabic numerals, 1:388b–389a
on astronomy, 1:612a
translations by, Pseudo-Aristotle's *Regimen sanitatis,* 12:140a
John Sigismund, king of eastern Hungary, 6:350a
John Šišman, ascendancy of, 2:136b, 412b
John Skylitzes. *See* Skylitzes, John
John of Spain, Blessed, 12:687a
John of Sterngassen, as defender of Thomism, 12:42a
John Stracimir, 2:412b–413a
John de Swyneshed, 11:534a
see also Swineshead
John of Thessaloniki, St., 7:282b
John Thoresby of York. *See* Thoresby of York, John
John of Tours
Anselm of Laon's theology school and, 12:21a
missing works by, 12:22a
Peter Lombard's theology school and, 12:21b
John of Treviso, William of Auxerre's theology school and, 12:22a
John of Turrecremata. *See* Torquemada, Juan de
John of Tynemouth, 7:370a
Sanctilogium...Angliae, Wallia, Scotiae, et Hiberniae, sources for, 6:64a-b
John Tzetzes. *See* Tzetzes, John
John Tzurillas (Bogomil heresiarch), 2:295b
John Uroš, father of the Great Meteoron, 8:300a
John of Urtubia, conquest of Thebes and, 3:156b–157a
John of Valle, hermitage at Brugliano, 5:204a, 204b

John of Vercelli, Dominican rite and, 4:242a
John Versor, as defender of Thomism, 12:42a
John of Vicenza, 4:250a
John de Vilars, inns and, 6:469a
John Vladimir, ruler of Duklja, 11:170b
John Vladislav, ruler of Bulgaria, 11:170b
John of Wales
canon law collection, 7:415b–416a
Compilatio secunda, 7:427b
John of Worcester, 12:703b
Roger of Salisbury and, 10:443b
John Xiphilinos, patriarch, 9:697b
John Zápolyai, king of Hungary. *See* Zápolyai, János, king of Hungary
John Zosimus, Calendar of, sources for, 6:60b–61a
John of Zurich, bishop of Strasbourg, actions against beghards, 5:217b
John, *see also* Jean, Jehan, Johann, Johannes; João
Joiner, in European furniture making, 5:324b
Joint family, 4:146b
Jointée (unit of measure), variations in, 12:590a
Joinville family, 11:160b
as seneschals of Champagne, 7:143b
Joinville, Jean de, **7:143b–144b**
armor of, 1:526a
on assassins, 1:591a
Histoire de St. Louis (*Life of St. Louis*), 2:236a, 6:264b, 7:144a
autobiographical focus, 5:260b–261a
evocation of finer age, 5:265a
influence on 16th-century *prosateurs,* 5:261a
origin of, 5:243a
on Saracen instruments, 8:605b
Jean d'Ibelin (of Jaffa) and, 6:390a
Louis IX of France and, 3:332b, 7:143b
Louis X of France and, 7:144a
marriages of, 7:143b–144a
in Second Crusade, 7:143b
on ship maneuvering, 11:236b
Joli buisson de Jonece. See Froissart, Jehan
Jomsborg, Cnut IV Valdemarsen and, 11:522a
Jómsvíkinga drápa, 7:145a
Jómsvíkinga saga, **7:144b–145b**, 9:176b
compared with *Málsháttakvæði,* 8:66a
construction of, 7:145a
dating of, 7:144b
Knýtlinga saga and, 7:281a
plot of, 7:144b–145a
redactions of, 7:145a
style of, 7:145a
see also Bjarni Kolbeinsson
Jómsvíkings, 9:176b–177a
Jón Arason, bishop of Hólar, *Hectors rímur* and, 10:403a
Jón Halldórsson, bishop of Skálholt, translation of *Klári saga,* 7:274b–275a, 10:392a
Jón Loftsson, 11:355b–356a
Jón Ögmundarson, St., bishop of Hólar, 2:252b, **7:145b–146a**
canonization of, 7:146a
saga about, 7:145b–146b
Scandinavian language and, 7:146a
travels of, 7:145b
Jón Ólafsson, retelling of *Heiðarvíga saga,* 6:145b
Jonah Abu 'l-Walīd Merwān ibn Janāḥ, 7:172b
Kitāb al-tanqīḥ, 6:128b
philology of, 4:539b
Sefer ha-Dikduk, 7:96b
Jonah of Gerona, 10:74b
Jonas of Bobbio, *Life of Columbanus,* on private penance, 9:489b
Jonas fragment, 5:288a-b, 9:633a
Jonas of Orléans, **7:146a-b**
career of, 7:146b
De cultu imaginum, 7:146b
De institutione laicali, 7:146b
De institutione regia, 7:146a, 260b, 8:434b
ecclesiological theories, 7:146a
on equality of people, 10:14b
kingship theories of, 7:260b–261a
Jonatus, St., abbot of Marchiennes, 6:317a
Jongleur. See Joglar/jongleur
Jóns saga biskups, on Ovid, 10:406a
Jóns saga helga, **7:146b–147a**
author of, 7:146b
as hagiographical literature, 7:147a
Jón Ögmundarson and, 7:145b, 146b
versions of, 7:146b–147a
see also Bishops' sagas
Jóns saga leikara, 10:395b
Jóns saga postula IV, 5:354b
Jónsbók, 6:396a
Joos van Ghent, **7:147b**
Communion of the Apostles, 7:147b, 148 (*illus.*)
triptych by, 7:147b
Joos van Wassenhove. *See* Joos van Ghent
Jordaens, Willem, 9:36b, 37a, 37b–38a
Jordan Fantosme, 1:265a, **7:147b**
chronicle of, 7:147b
Jordan of Osnabrück, **7:147b–149a**
on Charlemagne, 7:149a
De prerogative romani imperii, 7:148a
on the Holy Roman Empire, 7:149a
Jordan of Quedlinburg, **7:149a-b**
Augustinian Hermits and, 7:149a-b
Vitasfratrum, 7:149b
works attributed to, 7:149b
Jordan River, Yarmuk and, 12:719a
Jordan of Saxony
Dominican liturgy and, 4:240a, 241b
Dominican mysticism and, 4:248a
Life of St. Dominic, 6:69a
Jordanes, **7:149b–150a**, 11:528b
on Bavarians, 2:94b
conversion of, 7:149b
De summa temporum, 7:149b, 328a
on early Balts, 7:602b
History of the Goths (*Getica*), 6:261b
on early Scandinavia, 10:687b–688a
on Russian fur trade, 5:330b
Jordanus de Nemore, 1:436a, 438b
alphabetic notation, 8:213b–214a
Arithmetica, 8:214b
De numeris datis, 8:213b
ratios and proportions, 8:216a
De triangulis, 1:436a, 8:214b
Demonstratio de minutiis, 8:209b
Elementa super demonstrationem ponderum, 8:214a
Liber de proportionibus, 8:215b
Tractatus minutiarum, 8:209b
Jordi de S. Jordi, **7:150a**, 12:349a
in Alfonso V of Aragon's court, 7:150a
followers of, 3:171a-b
love poetry of, 7:150a
Presoner, 7:150a
Stramps, 7:150a
Jorge Inglés, **7:150a-b**
Rogier van der Weyden and, 7:150a-b
Jǫrmungandr. See Midgard serpent
Jornandes. *See* Jordanes
Jörundr of Hólar, bishop, 7:387a
Josep Abaramatia, 1:573a
Joseph II, patriarch, **7:150b**
at Ferrara-Florence Council, 7:150b
see also Ferrara-Florence, Council of
Joseph Albo, 7:92b
Joseph of Arimathea
Deposition from the Cross and, 4:157a (*illus.*)
in the legend of the Grail, 8:64a
Joseph of Arimathie, 1:574a
Joseph d'Arimathie. See Robert de Boron
Joseph ben Abba Mari ibn Kaspi. *See* Joseph ibn Caspi
Joseph ben Abraham al-Baṣīr, **7:150b–151a**
ᶜAbd al-Jabbar and, 7:150b
Kalam Muᶜtazilite and, 7:150b
Karaite law and, 7:150b
treatises of, 7:150b–151a
Joseph ben Gurion, recension of *Yosippon,* 6:255b
Joseph ben Isaac Bekhor Shor, exegesis of, 4:541a
Joseph ben Jacob ibn Ẓaddik. *See* Joseph ibn Saddiq
Joseph ben Judah ben Jacob ibn ᶜAknin, **7:151a**
forced conversion to Islam, 7:99a, 151a
on law, 7:151a
writings of, 7:151a
Joseph ben Noah, 7:210b
Joseph ben Phinehas, 7:107a
Joseph della Reina, 3:3a
messianic endeavor of, 1:346b
Joseph of Exeter. *See* Josephus Iscanus
Joseph von Hammer, *Geschichte der Assassinen aus morgenländischen Quellen,* 1:592b
Joseph the Hymnographer, as author of *kanōnes,* 7:613a
Joseph ibn Caspi, **7:151a-b**
Islamic influences on, 7:151b
Joseph ibn Migash, 11:585b
Joseph ibn Saddiq, **7:151b–152a**, 9:700a
Neoplatonism of, 7:166b
parallelism theory of, 7:151b

Joseph ibn Saddiq (*cont.*)
  Sefer ha-Olam ha-Qatan, 4:540a, 7:151b
Joseph ibn Zabara, narrative in rhymed prose, 6:127a
Joseph (Irish Carolingian poet), 3:103a
  Alcuin of York and, 1:142b
Joseph Kimḥi. *See* Kimḥi, Joseph
Joseph (OT character), in art, 8:106 (*illus.*)
Joseph of Pałin, Eznik and, 4:571a
Joseph of Pałnatun, 7:298b
Joseph, St., hymns and, 6:382b
Joseph the Seer, 11:566a
Joseph of Volotsk, St., defense of monastic wealth, 10:595b–596a
Josephus, Flavius
  Antiquities of the Jews
    translation of, 3:166b
    used by Peter Comestor in *Historia scholastica,* 9:514a
  Bede and, 2:154b
  synagogue and, 11:556a
  Yosippon, 6:256a
Josephus Iscanus, 7:365a
  Bellum Troianum, 7:371b
  De excidio Troiae, 4:496a
Josephus Scotus, use of acrostics, 1:46a
Joshua Roll, **7:152b–153a**, 8:1b
  ivories of the "painterly group" and, 7:26a
  model for, 2:454a
  Roman triumph iconology of, 10:307a-b
  Triumph of Joshua in, 7:152 (*illus.*)
Joshua the Stylite, **7:152a-b**
  chronicle of, 7:152a
Josiah of Judah, king, "Deuteronomic reformation" of, 11:555b
Josue Harloqui. *See* Geronimo de Santa Fé
Jouarre-en-Brie, abbey of, shrine of Potentianus, 10:297b
Jour (unit of measure), 12:587a
Journal, **7:153a**
  arpent and, 7:153a
  definition of, 7:153a
  variant spellings, 7:153a
Journey Beyond Three Seas. See Nikitin, Afanasii
Jousting, 3:204a, 5:349b, 350b
  music for, 8:595b
  see also Games; Tournament
Jouvenel des Ursins, Jean, 5:654a
Jovian, Roman emperor
  Aršak II and, 1:476a
  Nisibis and, 9:142a
Joy, William, **7:153a-b**
Joyn, *kat^{c}ołikos,* 5:371b
Jū^{c}. See Famine, in Islamic world
Juan, *see also* John
Juan de Aragon, archbishop of Toledo, sermon outlines by, 11:455b
Juan de Burgos, **7:155a**
  Annunciation, 7:155 (*illus.*)
  works in International Gothic style, 7:155a
Juan Cardinal de Cervantes, Rodríguez del Padrón and, 10:438b
Juan de Colonia, **7:153b**, 10:124b
Juan Espera en Dios. *See* Wandering Jew legend
Juan de Flandes, **7:155b–156a**
  influences on, 7:155b
  Reina católica altarpiece by, 7:155b, 156a (*illus.*)
  works of, 7:155b
Juan de Flores. *See* Flores, Juan de
Juan Gil de Hontañón, New Cathedral of Salamanca, 9:695 (*illus.*)
Juan Hispano, 11:441a
Juan Manuel, Don. *See* Manuel, Don Juan
Juan Rexach. *See* Rexach, Juan
Juan de San Martín, 9:112a
Juan de Segovia, 11:380a
Juan of Trastámara, kingdom of Navarre and, 9:71b–72a
Juan the Twisted (Castilian prince), Don Juan Manuel and, 8:94b
Juan de Valdés. *See* Valdés, Juan de
Juan-juan/Avars, Ouar-Khounni and, 6:352b
Juana la Beltraneja of Castile, marriage of, 9:111b
Juana (daughter of Henry II of Castile), 12:449a
Jubayr, Ibn, 4:588b–589a, 5:393b, 9:651b, 10:73a
  Genoese ships and, 11:232b
  on al-Kufa, 7:308a
  on Mecca, 8:240b
  on Ramadan in Mecca, 10:254a
Jubé. See Screen, rood
Jubilee, **7:156a-b**
  dates of, 7:156b
  etymology of, 7:156b
  first papal, 3:360a
  indulgences for pilgrims, 6:447a, 450a, 9:660b, 12:156b–157a
  in Old Testament, 7:156a-b
  Roman pilgrimage and, 10:526b
Jubilus, **7:156b–157a**, 8:571a
  construction of, 7:156b
  in tonaries, 12:70a
Judah ben Asher, 7:82a
Judah ben David Ḥayyūj, 7:172b
  triconsonantal stem, 6:128b
Judah ben Elijah Hadassi, 7:210b
Judah ben Jehiel, catalog of rhetorical devices of the Prophets, 10:348a
Judah ben Nissim ibn Malkah, philosophic studies, 9:574a
Judah ben Samuel he-Hasid (the Pietist), 7:92b, **7:157a-b**
  Eleazar ben Judah of Worms and, 4:420b, 7:157a-b
  fellowship of pietists
    interaction with nonpietists, 6:110a
    three groups, 6:110a
  pietistic writings, 6:109b
  political strategies, 6:110b
  Regensburg synagogue established by, 7:157a
  Sefer ha-Kavod, 7:157a, 9:578b
  Sefer Ḥasidim, 7:157a, 176b, 8:24b, 9:578b
    social goals for pietist, 6:110a
  Shir ha-Yiḥud, 9:578b
Judah ben Samuel ibn Bal^{c}am, 4:539b, 7:172b
Judah ha-Kohen, 7:70b
Judah ha-Nasi, 7:159a
Judah Halevi, 5:346b, 7:92b, **7:157b–158b**
  documents in Cairo genizah, 3:16a
  al-Ghazālī and, 7:158a
  kharjas by, 7:179b
  literary skills of, 7:158a
  Moses ibn Ezra and, 7:157b
  opposition to philosophy, 9:574a
  poetry of, 6:127a, 7:96b–97a, 157b–158a, 622a
  rejection of philosophic rationalism, 7:168a-b
  Sefer ha-Kuzari, 7:96b–97a, 158a, 165b–166a, 168a-b, 10:3b
  theology
    divine presence, 9:576b
    Eastern influence, 9:574a-b
    messianic views, 7:99a
    personal God of history, 9:577b
  travels of, 7:157b
Judah al-Ḥarizi
  Taḥkemoni, 6:127a
  translation of Maimonides' *Guide of the perplexed,* 12:134b–135b
Judah he-Ḥasid, *Sefer Ḥasidim,* 10:74b
Judah ibn Quraysh
  Risāla, 6:129a
  study of Hebrew philology, 7:98a, 172b
Judah ibn Tibbon
  library of, 7:562a
  translations by, 12:133b–134a
Judah Leon Mosconi, library of, 7:562a
Judah the Prince, rabbi, Mishnah and, 11:583a
Judah Romano, 7:109b, 176a
Judaism, **7:158b–170b**
  antiphilosophical trends, 7:167b–168b
    see also Cabala; Ḥasidei Ashkenaz; Mysticism, Jewish; Pietism
  Ashkenazic, Gershom ben Judah and, 7:162b
  astrology and, 1:605a–606b
  at al-Qayrawān, 7:162a
  Babylonian academies, 7:161a-b, 162b
  central beliefs of, 7:159b
  Christian converts to, 7:95a-b
  on Christianity, considered idolatry, 8:161a
  geonim, 5:356b–357a, 7:161a-b
  influence of on Muḥammad, 9:497a–498b
  interest-bearing loans, 12:340b–341b
  Karaites, 7:162b–163b, 209a–211a
  of Khazars, 7:241b
  legal codification of, 7:169b–170b
  in modern times, 7:170b
  as a mystery religion, 9:5a
  nature of God, 7:159b
  Palestinian academy, 7:161b–162b
  philosophic defense of, Saadiah Gaon, 7:164b–166b
  popular lore, in *Fazienda de Ultra Mar,* 11:432a
  practice of, 7:160a-b
  prayer in, 7:158b–159a, 160a-b
  preaching and sermons in, 10:73b–75a
  prohibition of usury, 12:335b

rationalist challenge to, 7:164a-b
responsum literature and, 10:337a–339b
Scripture in, 7:158b–159a
sectarian challenge to Rabbinic, 7:162b–163b
spread of Rabbinic, 7:160b–161a
new centers of, 7:161b–162b
temple library tradition, 7:562a
tithes and, 12:62a-b
Torah and, 7:158b
tosaphists and, 7:162b
yeshiva in, 7:162a
Zoroastrianism and, 7:160a, 12:746b, 747b
see also Anti-Semitism; Liturgy, Jewish; Philosophy and theology, Jewish; Polemics, Christian-Jewish; Polemics, Islamic-Jewish
Judaizers (Russian sect), Nil Sorsky and, 9:137a
Judenhut, 3:620b, 621b, 624a
Judeo-Arabic language, 7:96b, **7:171a–172a**
Arabic language and, 7:171a-b
documents in Cairo genizah, 3:16a, 7:171b
Judeo-Arabic literature, **7:172a–173b**
exegetical works in, 7:172b
Hebrew grammar in, 7:172b
in Muslim Spain, 7:96a–97a
philosophical works in, 7:173a-b
Rabbinic literature in, 7:172b–173a
see also Magic and folklore, Jewish
Judeo-French language, **7:173b–174a**
contribution of, 7:174a
Hebrew characters in, 7:174a
Rashi's influence on, 10:260a
study of, 7:174a
Judeo-German language. *See* Yiddish
Judeo-Greek language, **7:174b–175b**
glossaries of, 7:174b
Greek language and, 7:174b
poetry in, 7:175a
translations, 7:174b–175a
Judeo-Italian language, **7:175b–176a**
glossaries of, 7:176a
Hebrew characters in, 7:175b
translations, 7:176a
translators, Hebrew-Italian glossary, 12:137a
Judeo-Latin language, **7:176a–177a**
Hebrew characters in, 7:176a
incantations in, 7:176b
in *Niẓẓaḥon vetus,* 7:176a
prayers in, 7:176b
transmission of, 7:176a-b
Judeo-Persian language, **7:177a–178a**
manuscript collections, 7:178a
texts in, 7:177a-b
Judeo-Provençal language, **7:178a–179a**
disappearance of, 7:178b
phonetic traits of, 7:178b
texts in, 7:178a-b
translators, 12:134b
Judeo-Spanish language, 6:435b, 442b, **7:179a-b**
disappearance of, 7:179a-b
Hebrew characters in, 7:179a
influences on, 7:179a
poetry in, 7:179b
rabbinic literature in, 7:179b
translators
into Hebrew, 12:134b
into Latin, 12:135a–136a
see also Sephardim
Judges, Roman, 10:522b, *see also* Justices
Judicial combat, 6:482a, 482b
see also Duels
Judith, in German biblical poetry, 2:227b
Judith (Old English poem), 1:280a, 2:221b, 4:550b
sources, 2:184a
Jugement d'amour, see also Blancheflour et Florence
Jugement de chiens et d'oisiaus, Le. See Henri de Ferrières
Jugement dou roy de Behaigne. See Machaut, Guillaume de
Jugement dou roy de Navarre. See Machaut, Guillaume de
Julian the Apostate, Roman emperor, **7:180b–181a**, 10:296b
Against the Galilaeans, 7:181a
campaigns of, 7:181a
Christianity and, 9:98b
Franks and, 2:94a
Neoplatonism and, 9:97b–98a
paganism of, 2:485a, 7:180b–181a
Rhine River and, 10:459a
rise to throne, 7:180b–181a
Suda and, 11:501b
vs. Alamanni, 11:525b
Julian of Eclanum, bishop, 1:653b
Pelagianism and, 9:486b
Julian, friar, Russian Magyars and, 6:342a
Julian of Halikarnassos, bishop
conversion of the Nobades, 3:314b
on incorruptibility of Christ, 8:478a
Julian the Hospitaler, St.
hunting and, 6:361a
prayer to, 6:468b
Julian of Le Mans, St., a rhymed office to by Letald, 10:372a, 375b
Julian of Norwich, **7:179b–180b**, 9:18b, 19a-b, 20a, 24a–25a
Margery (Burnham) Kempe and, 7:229a, 9:25b
monasticism and, 3:368b
mysticism of, 7:179b–180b
Revelations of Divine Love, 7:179b–180b, 8:317b–318a, 9:24a-b, 28a
themes of shared by Marguerite d'Oingt, 9:12b
theology of, 7:180b
visions of, 7:180a
Julian solar calendar. *See* Calendar
Julian of Speyer
historia and, 6:380b
hymns of, 6:382a
Juliana, 1:279a-b, 280b
name of Cynewulf associated with, 1:278a
Juliana Anicia Codex. *See* Dioscorides, *De materia medica*
Juliana of Liège (Cornillon), St., 4:248a, 9:11b
authentication of relics by, 10:298b
feast of Corpus Christi and, 3:608a
Juliani, Peter
drug testing methods, 9:551b–552a
on Judaeus' drug treatises, 9:551b
Julianists. *See* Monophysitism
Julianus, leadership of Samaritan revolt, 10:639b
Julianus, Flavius Claudius. *See* Julian the Apostate
Julianus Pomerius, confused with Prosper of Aquitaine, 9:490a
Julianus (Ravenna banker), 10:264a-b
Julianus of Toledo, **7:181a-b**, 9:62b
Apologeticum fidei, 7:181b
as archbishop of Toledo, 7:181b
Benedict II and, 7:181b
biography of, by Felix, 7:181b
in conspiracy against Wamba, 7:181a-b
ecumenical councils and, 7:181b
Eugenius II of Toledo and, 7:181a
Peter Lombard and, 9:517a
writings of, 7:181b
Julin. *See* Jomsborg
Julius I, pope, Arianism and, 1:454a
Julius II, pope
conciliar theory and, 3:519a, 520a, 655a
coronation of, 3:605a
Julius Valerius, *Historia de preliis,* 7:322b, 365a
Juljul, 8:613b
Jumièges (monastery), 9:187b
burned by Vikings, 12:430a
see also Anglo-Norman art
Junayd, **7:181b–182a**
at Jalayirid court, 7:181b
at Timurid court, 7:182a
miniature in the *Dīwān* of Khwāju Kirmānī, 8:117a (*illus.*)
signature of, 7:181b
works of, 7:181b–182a
Junayd, al- (Islamic mystic), rise of the Almoravids and, 11:140a
Junayd Naqqāsh al-Sultāni. *See* Junayd
Jund rebellion, 1:71b
Jüngere Judith, 2:227b
Jüngere Titurel, Der, 12:676b, 679b
authorship of, 1:133b–134a
see also Albrecht von Scharfenberg
Junggorze movement, 5:578b–579a
Jüngstes Gericht. See Frau Ava
Junilius Africanus, *Instituta regularia divinae legis,* 11:564b
Junius Bassus
sarcophagus of, 4:350b
artistic style, 4:351b
pagan motifs on, 4:351a
Junius MS, 1:277a
Junius (scribe), Tatian manuscripts and, 11:601a
Junqueres, in Barcelona, 2:104a
Jupiter, temple of (Damascus), remodeling, 12:529b
Jura Mountains, travel in, 12:162b
Jura de Santa Gadea, 11:442b
Juramentum judaeorum. See Oath, *more judaico*
Jürchen dynasty. *See* Chin
Jurés, 3:502a
Jürgen, Johann, Saxony wheel, 11:699b

Juristic person. *See* Person, juristic
Jurjānī, ^{c}Abd al-Qāhir al-
Arabic rhetoric and, 10:345b, 346b, 348a
Asrār al-balāgha, 10:347a, 347b
Dalā$^{\supset}$il al-i^{c}jāz, 10:346b, 347b
Jurjānīya. *See* Gurgānj
Jury, **7:182a–183b**
definition of, 7:182a
England, 7:441a-b
Anglo-Norman, 7:435b–436b
in Anglo-Saxon law, 6:480b–481a, 7:433a
Assize of Clarendon and, 3:409a
equity cases and, 4:502b
Exchequer Court and, 4:534b
grand, 4:470b
in land tenure disputes, 6:481a
ordeal and, 7:182b–183a, 505b
petty, 7:183a-b
of presentment, 3:659b
procedures of, 7:505a–506a
of recognition, 7:435b–436b, 441a-b
replaced compurgation in trials, 3:508b
trial by, 7:182a–183b
verdicts in homicide trials, 6:281b
France, early law and, 7:459a
Germany, 7:477b
history of, 7:182a
petit (trial) jury, 12:168a-b
procedures, treason and, 12:167b–168b
Wulfstan of York and, 12:704a
see also English common law
Just war. *See* Warfare
Justice
administration of
by villages, 12:440b–441a
serfdom and, 11:203a
sheriff and, 11:225b
Sicily, 11:268a
Justice, criminal. *See* Criminal justice
Justices
of assize, 7:446b
regulations, 7:448a-b
in Carolingian Germany, 7:477a-b
of common pleas, Magna Carta and, 12:159b
ecclesiastical, 6:478b
English, 7:443a, 445b–447a, 448a-b
at Westminster, 6:482b–483a
see also Justices of common pleas; Justices, itinerant, Justices of the King's Bench; Justices of the peace
itinerant
nisi prius, 12:622b
Sir Thomas Trevet, 12:186a
trespass and, 12:185b
"learned," 7:504b–505a
professional *scabini,* 12:153a
in southern French law, 7:464a
vs. *doctor legum,* 7:516a-b
see also Oyer and terminer
Justices of common pleas, **7:186b–190b**
backgrounds of, 7:187b–189b
cases of, 7:187a
in circuit justice, 7:186b–187a
definition of, 7:186a
Exchequer court and, 7:187a
importance of, 7:190b
Magna Carta and, 7:187b
political struggles and, 7:189b–190a
professional pleaders and, 7:189a
Justices, itinerant, 4:469b, 470b, 6:157a, **7:183b–186b**
articles of inquiry and, 7:184a
assizes and, 7:184a-b
capitula of, 7:185a-b
in circuit justice, 7:186b
criticism of, 7:184b
difficulties of, 7:185b–186a
duties of, jail delivery, 7:44a
financial benefits of office, 7:184b
inquiries of, 7:185a-b
power of, 7:184b–185a
sheriff and, 11:225b
transformation of office, 7:185b–186a
Justices of the King's Bench, **7:190b–195a**
corruption of, 7:192b–193b
during Wars of the Roses, 7:194a
importance of, 7:194b
jail delivery, 7:45a
justices of the peace and, 7:198a
king's council and, 7:192a
in political crisis of 1386–1388, 7:193b
purge of (1340–1341), 7:193a
recruitment to ranks of, 7:191b–192a
term of, 7:190b–191a
violence against, 7:193b
Justices of the peace, **7:195a–199b,** 7:446b–447a
administrative powers of, 7:198a
changes in, 7:195b–196a
commissions of oyer and terminer, 7:45a
economic power of, 7:197b–198a
impact of, 7:199a
justices of the King's Bench and, 7:198a
military power of, 7:197b
moral supervision of, 7:198a
selection of, 7:199a
trespass and, 7:195b–196a
under Edward III, 7:196b–197a
see also English common law
Justiciar, **7:199b–201a**
compared with seneschal, 11:160a
creation of, 7:199b
during civil war between Stephen and Matilda, 7:200a
lapse of office, 7:200b
resurrection by Provisions of Oxford (1258), 10:195a
Sicilian, 11:268a, 269a
Frederick II and, 11:271a
under Angevins, 9:167b
Justification
Duns Scotus and, 9:213a-b
Ockham and, 9:213a-b
Justin I, Byzantine emperor, 12:12a
Arianism and, 1:454b
Justin II, Byzantine emperor
additions to Sacred Palace, 3:553a
in John of Ephesus' *History,* 7:133a
ordinance on the Creed, 3:676b
Vardan II and, 1:477a
Justin Martyr
Dialogue with Trypho, 10:2a
on Eucharist, 7:625b
theology
definition of terms, 9:616a
philosophical elements of, 9:583a
Justin, St., Gallican Mass and, 5:345a-b
Justina and Cyprian, Sts., Spanish prose lives of, 11:439b
Justina (mother of Emperor Valentinian II), conflict with St. Ambrose, 1:231a
Justinian I, Byzantine emperor, 2:94a, 95a, **7:201a–202b,** 10:262a, 264a-b
administration
autocratic policies, 2:486a
reforms of, 7:202a
architectural projects, 6:56a
additions to Sacred Palace, 3:552b–553a
at Caesarea, 3:9a
Basilica of St. John at Ephesus, 4:494b
Hagia Sophia, 2:486a
public buildings, 4:334a-b
public works, 7:202a
restoration of Sebaste, 11:131b
Arianism and, 1:454b, 9:291b
Armenia and, 1:477a, 515b
in art, 11:570b
attempt to control *dunatoi,* 4:307a, 7:202a
authority of, 3:343b
Belisarios and, 2:165a, 7:201a-b
calendar reform, 3:18a
church and, 3:556a
on the clergy, 3:215b, 447a-b
councils under, 3:630a
policy toward dissidence, 7:202a
civil law, textbooks, 11:691a-b
closing of the Platonic school of Athens, 9:98a–99a
codification of Roman law, 2:486a, 3:608b–609a, 7:201b–202a, 425b
coinage of, 8:419a
death penalty for blasphemers, 2:272a
as Defender of the Faith, ivory diptych, 7:24b (*illus.*)
definition of poverty, 6:288a-b
Digest, De diversis regulis iuris antiqui, 8:231b–232a
during Justin's reign, 7:201a
Greek language and, 6:436a
Imru$^{\supset}$al-Qays and, 6:430a
on interest payments, 12:335b
intervention in Monophysite controversy, 3:10b
Isidore of Seville on, 6:564b–565a
jewelry of, 5:375a
Karin under, 7:215a
Laodicea under, 7:315a
Lesser Armenia and, 1:472b, 473a
military campaigns, 2:486a-b, 3:179b
destruction of the Vandal kingdom, 9:78b
Italian expedition, 7:201a-b, 9:292a
Persian war, 7:201b
Monophysitism and, 7:202a, 8:477b–478a
Mundhir III and, 7:320b

Nestorianism condemned by, 8:478a
Nika Revolt and, 2:486a
Novellae, 6:451b
see also *Authenticum*
Nubian Melchitism and, 9:197b
opposition to, 7:202b
Verecundus of Junca, 12:393b
palace library and, 7:561a
patronage of art, 4:353a
tradition and innovation under, 4:348a-b
pentarchy and, 9:459a-b, 496a
political aims, 4:353a
portrait in S. Vitale, Ravenna, 4:354a
portrayal by Procopius, 10:134a–135a
Sicily and, 11:264a
silk manufacture and, 12:100a
territory of, 10:459a
tetrarchy, 10:458b
Theodora and, 7:201a
in Theophanes Confessor's *Chronographia,* 12:22b
Vandals and, 12:355b
vs. Ostrogoths, 1:422a, 7:201a-b
water projects, 12:576b
see also Corpus iuris civilis; Theodora I, Byzantine empress
Justinian II, Byzantine emperor, **7:202b–203a**
Armenia and, 1:479a, 500a
Bulgars and, 7:202b
church council under, 3:630b
coinage of, 8:419a
execution of, 7:203a
icons and, 6:400a-b
patron of Leo III, 7:544b
recapture of Constantinople, 7:203a
reign of, 7:202b–203a
Synod in Trullo and, 7:203a
Thessaloniki and, 12:26b
Umayyad caliphs and, 7:202b
see also Farmer's Law
Justinianic Code. *See Corpus iuris civilis*
Justinianopolis, 1:473a
Justinian's Plague. *See* Plagues, Islamic world
Justus of Urgel, 9:62b
Jutes, 1:289a, 2:96b
language of, 6:437a
migration of, 8:363a
Jutland, 12:423a, 424a
Juvencus, 7:361a, 11:405b
Evangeliorum libri IV, 4:496a
modeled on Vergil, 12:394a
in Latin pedagogy, 7:353a
Juvencus *englynion,* 12:603a, 614a
Juwāq, 8:562b
Juwaynī, al-, 5:515b
Juzayy, Ibn, 2:130b, 9:651b

K

Kaaba, **7:203a–204a**
Abraham and, 6:577a
covering of, 7:203b (*illus.*), 204a, 273a-b
destruction of, 7:203b
displays of *ṭirāz,* 12:61b
function of, 7:203a-b
Islamic pilgrimage rites at the, 9:650b–651a
miḥrāb niche of, 10:235a
Muḥammad and, 6:576a, 7:203b–204a
pilgrimages to, 8:522a
in pre-Islamic times, 8:239b
qibla and, 7:203b–204a, 10:235a
Quraysh control of, 10:241a-b
rebuilding of, 7:204a
sacked by Qarmatians in 930, 11:137a
Ka^cba of Zoroaster, **7:204a–205a,** 9:61b
Avesta and, 7:204b–205a
dating of, 7:204b
inscriptions on, 7:221b–222a, 11:374b
in Islamic period, 7:205a
purpose of, 7:204b
in Sasanian times, 7:204b
Kaᶜbah-in Zardusht. *See* Kaᶜba of Zoroaster
Kabala, **7:205a-b**
as Albanian bishopric, 7:205a
Arab conquest of, 7:205a
destruction of, by Tamerlane, 7:205a
as residence of *marzpan,* 7:205a
in Shirvan, 7:205a
Kaballarika themata, 3:199b
Kaballarios, 3:199b
Kabars, Magyars and, 6:338b
Kabbalah. *See* Cabala
Kabinettscheiben, 5:552b
Kabīr, al-. *See* Nāṣir li l-Ḥaqq al-Uṭrūsh
Kābul-shāhs, vs. Yaᶜqūb ibn Layth, 12:717a
Kad ha-Kemaḥ. *See* Baḥya ben Asher
Ḳāḍī. *See* Qadi
Kadkhudā, 6:591a
Kadłubek, Wincentry (Vincent), bishop of Kraków
Chronica Polonorum, 5:389b, 9:723a, 11:345a
Kaffa. *See* Caffa
Kāfī, al-. *See* Karajī, al-; Zaylah, Ibn
Kāfir (infidel). *See* Islam, religion
Kaftan. *See* Caftan
Kāfūr, Abu 'l-Misk, Ikhshidid ruler, 6:416b, 417a, 417b
al-Mutanabbī and, 8:652b
Kāghad (Persian word for paper), 12:698a
Kahal
disciplinary powers, 7:69b–70a
foundations of authority, 7:69a-b
limits to local autonomy, 7:70b
membership of, 7:70b, 71a
responsibilities of, 7:69a
taxing authority, 7:70b
Kāhina, al- (the sorceress), 7:97b
Kai-Khusrau I, Ghiyāth al-Dīn. *See* Qaykhosraw I, Seljuk sultan
Kai-Qubadh I. *See* Kayqubād I
Kairouan. *See* Qayrawān, al-
Kaiserchronik, **7:205b–206a,** 7:478b–479a
author of, 7:205b
composition of, 8:349a
legendary matter in, 7:205b–206a
popularity of, 7:206a
prose version of, 7:206a
style of, 7:205b
Wolfram von Eschenbach and, 12:674b
see also German law, post-Carolingian
Kaiserrecht, 5:495b
Kaǰberunids, Arčēš and, 1:423a
Kalām, 10:3a, 12b
biblical exegesis and, 2:212b, 215a
Kalamata, under Latins, 7:378b
Kalāntar, 6:591a
Kalb tribe, Yazīd and, 12:721a
Kalbite dynasty, in Sicily, 11:262a-b
Kalbs, rivalry with Qays, 8:143a
Kalenda Maya. *See* Raimbaut de Vaqueiras
Kalendar, rhymed offices and, 10:366b
Kalenderhane Djami (church: Constantinople), 7:349b
cross-domed design of, 4:344b
St. Francis of Assisi painting, 2:447a-b
Kaleniç (church: Serbia), 11:188a
Kálfur skáld, *Völsungs rímur,* 10:402b
Kalīla wa-Dimna. *See* Muqaffaᶜ, ᶜAbd Allāh ibn al-
Kalinicos, 10:259a
Kaliz tribe, 11:478b–479a
Kalka River, Battle of (1223), 7:249b
Kaller. *See* Cellarius, Christoph
Kalliergis, mosaics, Church of Christ at Veroia, 2:450a
Kallikan, Ibn. *See* Khallikān, Ibn
Kallimachos and Chrysorrhoe
authorship, 2:509b
fantastic elements, 2:509a
Kallot, 7:161a, 11:584a
Kálmán. *See* Koloman
Kalmar Union, Gotland in, 5:633a
Kalmucks, in Caucasia, 3:195a
Kalojan, **7:206a-b,** 9:510a, 12:483b
brothers of, 7:206a
crowning of, 7:206b
crusaders and, 7:206b
as hostage, 7:206a-b
Latin Empire and, 7:206b, 347a
portrait of, 2:416 (*illus.*)
raids on Byzantine Empire, 7:206b
reign of, 2:408a-b
in Thrace, 7:206b, 348b
Kalonymus family, **7:206b–207b**
as authors of religious poetry, 7:622a-b
founding of Mainz Jewry, 6:109a
prominence in European Jewish community, 7:206b–207a
scholarship of, 7:207a-b
translations by, 12:137b
Kalonymus ben Kalonymus, 12:134b, 135b
translations into Hebrew and, 11:91a
transmission of Ashkenazi Hasidism, 9:578b, 581b
Kalonymus, Meshullam ben, 7:207a

Kalophonic melody, 6:379a, 8:555a, 556b
Kamāl al-Dīn al-Fārisī. *See* Fārisī, Kamāl al-Dīn al-
Kamānja, 8:612a
Kamarika. See Hero of Alexandria
Kamariotissa (church: Constantinople), domed-octagon design of, 4:341b
Kamennaya Baba, **7:207b**
  dating of, 7:207b
  interpretation of, 7:207b
Kāmil, al-, Ayyubid sultan
  negotiates with crusaders, 4:31b–32a
  victory in Fifth Crusade, 2:214a
Kaminakans, 1:515a
Kamkhā, **7:207b–208a**
  origin of, 7:207b
  spread of, 7:207b–208a
Kammerknechtschaft. See Servi camerae nostrae
Kammūna, Ibn, *Examination of the Three Faiths,* 10:8b
Kamrǰajor theological seminary, music and, 8:551a
Kamsarakan, **7:208a-b**
  in Ayrarat, 2:20a-b
  Bagratids and, 1:480a, 7:208a
  decline of, 7:208a
  Mamikonean and, 7:208a
  Pahlawuni and, 7:208a
  Sasanians and, 7:208a
  Širak under, 11:311a
  see also Vanand
Kamsarakan Church (Tᶜalin), 1:493b
Kananos, John, on Ottoman siege of 1422, 6:247b
Kániš, Peter, 6:375b
Kankala, 8:610b–611a
Kanōn, 6:378b, **7:208b**, 7:613a
  of Andrew of Crete, 7:208b
  composers of, 2:511b
  heirmos in, 7:208b
  kontakion and, 7:292b
  language and dialogue, 2:511b
  most famous authors of, 7:613a
  music of, 2:511a, 511b, 8:554a
  ninefold form, 2:524b
  troparion, 7:208b, 12:208a
  see also Heirmos
Kanon (psaltery), 8:562b
Kanonagirkᶜ Hayocᶜ, 7:393b–394a
  supplements to, 7:393b
Kantakouzenoi, **7:208b–209a**
  land holdings, 2:479b
  origin of, 7:208b
  Peloponnesus and, 7:208b–209a
Kanz al-Dawla, 3:315b
Kanz al-tuḥaf, 8:566b, 610a, 610b, 611b, 612a, 612b
Kanz al-walad. See Ḥāmidī, al-
Kapikulu. See Ottomans, armed forces
Kapıkulus, Mehmed I's rule and, 8:263b
Kapnikon, 11:603b, 604a
Kaputan Cov. *See* Urmia, Lake
Ḳarā Muḥammad. *See* Qara Muḥammad
Ḳarā Qoyunlu. *See* Qara Qoyunlu
Kára saga Kárasonar, 10:394b, 395b
Kara Su, 4:522a
Ḳarā Yusuf. *See* Qara Yusuf
Ḳaragöz figures. *See* Qaragūz figures
Karaism
  failure of, 7:162b
  founding of, 7:162b, 209b
  Rabbinic Judaism and, 7:162b–163b, 210b–211a
  reaction against, 7:172b
  Sabbath and, 7:163a
  Saddiah Gaon and, 7:163b, 210a
Karaite-Tatar dialect, 7:210b
Karaites, 3:16a, 7:104b, 162a, **7:209a–211b**
  in Babylonia, 7:107b–108a
  Christian-Jewish polemics and, 10:2b
  in Constantinople, 7:210a
  in Crimea, 7:210a
  dogma of, 7:210b–211a
  in Egypt, 7:84a
  exegesis and, 2:212a, 4:539a-b
  First Crusade and, 7:210a
  illuminated Bible MSS of, 7:66a
  in Jerusalem, 7:105b
  Joseph ben Abraham al-Baṣīr and, 7:150b
  law of, 7:210a-b
  literature of, 7:210a-b
  in Lithuania, 7:210a
  liturgy of, 7:210b
  marriage and, 4:606b, 607a
  missionary journeys, 7:209b–210a
  in Muslim empire, 7:209a-b
  in Palestine and Syria, 7:105b
  practice of, 7:210b–211a
  rejection of Talmud, 7:107b–108a, 210b–211a
  in Russia, 7:100a, 100b, 210a
  schism of, 7:209b
  settlements of, 7:210a
  study of biblical text, 6:128a
  title of nasi, 9:64b
Karajī, al-, Abū Bakr ibn Muḥammad ibn al-Ḥusayn (al-Ḥasan), **7:211b–212b**
  algebraic concepts of, 7:211b–212b
  Badīᶜ, Al-, 7:211b–212b
  contribution of, 7:211b, 212b
  Diophantine analysis and, 7:212a-b
  Fakhrī, Al-, 7:211b
  ᶜIlal-ḥisāb al-jabr, 7:211b
  influences on, 7:212b
  Kāfī, Al-, 7:211b–212b
Karak, al-. *See* Kerak
Karakhanids. *See* Qarakhanids
Karaman Beg, 7:214a
Karamania, **7:214a-b**
  empire of, 7:213 (map)
  Ikonion and, 6:418a
  Mehmed I and, 8:263b
  Mehmed II and, 8:264b
  Mongol empire and, 7:214a
  origin of, 7:214a
  rulers of, 7:214a
Karamans, rule over Caesarea, 3:9b
Karamāt (miracles of Sufi saints), 9:44b
Karaminids, Ottoman conflicts, 8:536b
Karāsī. See Kursī
Karatay (madrasa: Ikonion), 6:612a-b, 11:150 (*illus.*)
Karbalāʾ, Battle of (680), 6:370b, 371a, 7:307a, 12:721b
Karbalāʾ, Shīᶜa and, 11:226b
Karbeas, a leader of the Paulicians, 9:469a
Kardez, 8:418b
Karduchoi, 7:310a
  see also Kurds
Karel ende Elegast, 4:318b
Karelia
  fur trade in, 5:329b
  vs. Sweden, 11:531a, 531b, 532a
Kārgah, **7:214b**
  definition of, 7:214b
  in Mongol period, 7:214b
  ṭirāz and, 7:214b
Karim Khan Zand, Shīrāz and, 11:252b
Karimis, 11:249b
Karin, **7:214b–215b**
  Armenian trade and, 12:97b–99a
  in Ottoman empire, 7:215b
  silk route to the Far East and, 12:99a
  strategic importance of, 7:215a
  under Byzantines, 7:215a
  under Muslim rule, 7:215a
  under Seljuks, 7:215a-b
  Vardan Arewelcᶜi's journey, 12:359b
  see also Theodosiopolis/Karin
Karin, Council of (631 or 632), 1:500a
Karin/Erzurum
  Muslim emirate in, 1:513a
  Seljuks and, 1:485a
Kariye Djami (church: Constantinople), **7:215b–216a**
  architecture, classical elements, 2:457b
  depiction of the Last Judgment, 1:344a
  donor portrait at, 4:261b
  enlargement of, 7:215b–216a
  14th-century Nativity mosaic, 9:66 (*illus.*)
  mosaics, 2:449b–450b
    artistic style, 2:450a-b
    Virgin interceding with Christ, 2:449a (*illus.*)
  Palaiologan art in, 7:215b–216a
  parekklesion, mosaics, 2:449b (*illus.*)
  restored by Theodore Metochites, 12:15a
Karkathiokerta. *See* Angł
Karkh (suburb of Baghdad), 2:45b, 46a
Karkhī, al-. *See* Karajī, al-
Karl. See Stricker, Der
Karl Jónsson, Sverrir and, 9:176a-b
Karl Knutsson Bonde. *See* Charles VIII of Sweden, king
Karl Magnus' Krønicke, source for, 6:275b
Karlamagnús saga, 3:258a, **7:216b–219a**, 10:391b
  chansons de geste and, 7:216b
  dating of *Bevers saga* and, 2:210a
  dating of, 7:216b
  narrative style of, 7:216b
  popularity of, 7:218b
  rímur and, 7:218b
  as a source for *Mágus saga jarls,* 8:45b
  stories of Holger Danske in, 6:275b
  theme of, 7:217b–218a
  translations of, 7:217b–218a
Karlmeinet, **7:219a–220a**
  books of, 7:219a-b
  chansons de geste and, 7:219b
  importance of, 7:219b–220a
  Rolandslied and, 10:448a

sources of, 7:219b
Karlotide. See Guillaume le Breton
Karlskrönikan, **7:220a-b**, 11:22a
authors of, 7:220a-b
Erikskrönikan and, 7:220a-b
linguistic importance of, 7:221b
manuscripts of, 7:220b
Karlštein Castle, Master Theodoric's painting, 12:17 (*illus.*)
Karmir Monastery, 9:103a
Karnai, 8:561b
Kārnāmag-i Ardešīr-i Bābagān, 1:451b–452a, **7:220b–221a**, 9:327b
Arsacids depicted in, 7:221a
on foundations of Sasanian dynasty, 7:220b–221a
Karnoy Kᶜałakᶜ. *See* Karin
Karo, Joseph, as exegete, 2:212b
"Karolus Magnus et Papa Leo," 6:356a
Karr wa 'l-farr, al-, 3:209b
Karrāmīya, 7:238b
in Afghanistan, 1:65a-b
Kars, **7:221a-b**
Armenian trade and, 12:97b–99a
in Bagratid period, 7:221a-b
as capital of Armenia, 1:482b
as a center of Vanand, 12:353b–354a
conquerors of, 7:221b
founding of, 7:221a
Mušeł and, 1:483a
Seljuks and, 1:484b, 485a
separatism of, 1:483a
Kart family, rule of Afghanistan, 1:65a
Kartīr, Zoroastrian high priest, 7:204b, **7:221b–222b**
Bahrām I and, 7:221b
honored by King Šabuhr I, 9:61b
identification of, 7:221b
influence of, 7:222b
inscriptions about, 7:221b–222a
persecution of religious minorities, 10:668a
promotion of Zoroastrianism, 10:600b
record of accomplishments, 10:668a
see also Letter of Tansar
Kᶜartᶜli
Chosroids in, 3:307b–308a
see also Georgia
Kᶜartᶜli-Iberia, 5:419b
Kᶜartᶜlis Cᶜχovreba, 5:404b, 417b, **7:222b–223a**
translations of, 7:222b
Karts, 5:419a
Kᶜartᶜvelbi (Kᶜartᶜvelni). See Georgians
Kartvelian languages, 5:404b, 419a
Karv, 11:240a
Kāsān (Kasansay), 5:14b
Kāsāt, 8:613a (*illus.*), 613b
Kāsatān, 8:563a
Kāshān
ceramics of, 6:603 (*illus.*), 7:223b
lusterware workshops of, 11:147b
Kashf al-Ghumūm, 8:566b, 610a, 610b, 611b, 612b, 613a
Kashfᶜan manāhij al-adilla, al-. See Rushd, Ibn
Kashi, **7:223a–224a**
in Blue Mosque of Tabriz, 7:224a (*illus.*)
characteristics of, 7:223a-b
decline of, 7:223b
as generic term, 7:223b–224a
resurgence of, 7:223b–224a
Kashubian language, 6:438a, 444a
Kaškai, 5:419a
Kaspar von Rhön, *Dresdener Heldenbuch* and, 4:292b, 293a
Kaspars von der Roen Heldenbuch. See Dresdener Heldenbuch
Kasranids, Shirvan and, 11:254a
Kastamunitu (monastery), 12:483b
Kastoria, **7:224b**
churches in, 7:224b (*illus.*)
Katarchai, 1:619a
Kataskopoi, 10:59b
Kategoriai. See Aristotle
Katepanate of Italy, 2:108b
Katepanikion, 7:225a
Katepano, **7:224b–225a**
definition of, 7:224b
katepanikion and, 7:225a
see also Strategos
Katherine von Gebweiler, *Vitae sororum,* 9:13b
Katherine Group, **7:225a–226a**
author of, 7:225b
connection with Aelfric's saints' lives, 7:225b–226a
importance of, 7:225a-b
linguistic consistency of, 7:225b
texts referred to as, 7:225a
tradition of, 7:225b–226a
works included in, 6:62b–63a
Katholikon, **7:226a**
Katholikos (*katᶜołikos*), 1:502b–503a, **7:226b–227a**
in Armenian sources, 7:226b
of Baghdad, under Muslim rule, 4:552a
definition of, 7:226b
earliest application of, 7:226b
in Greek sources, 7:226b
in modern times, 7:226b–227a
move to Hṙomklay, 11:313b
primate of Vaspurakan and, 12:362a
see also Patriarch
Kātib, 8:138b
Kātib al-sirr, 6:592a
writing of encyclopedias, 4:445a
Katᶜolikē (church: Gełhard), 5:373b
Katramidē, 5:339a
"Katze, Die." *See* Herrand von Wildonie
Katzheimer, Lorenz, 4:490a
Kaufringer, Heinrich
Bürgermeister und Königssohn, characterization, 8:129a
Mären, 8:130a, 131b
Kauleas (church: Constantinople), Christ Pantokrator figure, 4:343a
Kaunas, 7:608b
Kaupang on the Vik, as trading center, 12:423a
Kavasilas, Nikolaos, importance of sacraments, 9:563b
Kawād I, Sasanian king
assumption of Iranian throne, 6:170a
deposition and reinstatement to throne, 10:669b–670a
Mazdakites and, 8:236b, 237b, 238a
Kawād II, Sasanian king, Xusrō II and, 12:715a
Kāwil al-malikī. See ᶜAlī ibn al-ᶜAbbās
Kaχeti. *See* Georgia
Kay (Arthurian character). *See* Kei
Kay Kā⊃ūs ibn Iskandar, *Qābūsnāma,* 8:436a
Kayanians (legendary dynasty), 2:50a, 11:221b
Kaykā⊃ūs I. *See* Qaykā⊃ūs I
Kaykhosraw I, Ghiyāth al-Dīn. *See* Qaykhosraw I, Seljuk sultan
Kayqāwūs I, Seljuk sultan, 11:154b, 157b
Kayqāwūs II, Seljuk sultan, 11:157b, 158a
Kayqubād I, ᶜAlā⊃ al-Dīn, Seljuk sultan, 1:241b, 11:154b, 157b
Ikonion and, 6:418a
Seljuk art and architecture and, 11:148b, 149 (*illus.*)
Kaysānīya (Kaysanid sect), 1:174b, 11:136a, 226b
in al-Kufa, 7:307a
Kayseri. *See* Caesarea
Kayyara, Simeon (Simon), *Halakhot Gedolot,* 7:169b, 11:584b, 586a
Kazan
fur trade in, 5:333b
Ivan III of Muscovy and, 7:20a
Kazan Tatars, Volga Bulgars and, 12:487b
Kazania świętokrzyskie, 11:345a
Kebar, arched dam, 12:577a
Keck, Johannes, *Introductorium musicae,* 8:648a
Ked Buga, general. *See* Ketbugha, general
Kedrenos, Georgios, **7:227a**
Historical Compendium or *Synopsis historiōn,* 6:245b–246a, 7:227a
Keel, 11:240b–241a, 242a
Keep. *See* Dungeon
Keeper of the royal wardrobe. *See* Wardrobe, royal, England
Keepers of the peace. *See* Justices of the peace
Kefallinia. *See* Cephalonia
Kei (Arthurian character), 5:448b
Kekaumenos, **7:227b**
on his private library, 7:596b
Strategikon, 7:227b, 12:483b
Kelim. *See* Kilim
Kells, Book of, 6:516a, **7:227b–229a**, 7:614b, 8:106a
Book of Durrow and, 7:228b
dating of, 7:227b
decoration of, 3:223b, 224 (*illus.*), 7:228 (*illus.*), 8:373b–374b (*illus.*)
designs, 3:221a
initials, 6:461b, 462a (*illus.*)
lacertine ornament, 7:314a
Durham Gospels and, 7:228b–229a
Lindisfarne Gospels and, 7:228b
origin of, 3:223a, 7:228a
prefatory texts of, 7:228b–229a
Kells, Synod of (1152), 1:470a
Kemal Pasha. *See* Nymphaion
Kemâlpasha-zâde, *Tevarih-i Al-i Osman,* 6:251a

Kempe, Margery (Burnham), 4:603b, **7:229a-b**, 9:18b, 19a, 19b, 20a, 25a–26a
autobiography of, 7:229a
Book of Margery Kempe, 8:314a, 317b–318a
compared with Julian of Norwich, 9:24b
heresy accusations against, 7:229a
possible influence on by Dorothea of Montau, 9:14a
Kempen, Kuene tabernacle at, 7:306a
Kempuvísa (heroic ballad). *See* Faroese ballads
Kend heiti, 7:230a-b
Kenilworth, Dictum of (1266), 2:112b
Kenneth I Mac Alpin, ruler of Scots and Picts, 4:78b, **7:229b–230a**
"Berchán's Prophecy" and, 7:229b
"Laws of Mac Alpin," 7:230a
reign of, 7:229b
in *Scottish Chronicle,* 7:229b–230a
union of Scots and Picts, 9:643a
Viking attacks on Dál Riata and, 7:229b
Kenneth, king of the Scots, in Treaty of Chester, 3:299b–300a
Kenning, **7:230a–231a**
abbreviated, 7:230b
applications of, 7:230b
in Bjarni Kolbeinsson's *drápa,* 2:256a
definition of, 7:230a
elaborate, 7:230b
of Gamli Kanóki, 5:355a
in *Haustlǫng,* 12:32a
kend heiti and, 7:230a-b
kviðuháttr and, 7:312a
in *Málsháttakvædli,* 8:66b
in *Merlínússpá,* 8:276b
proper, 7:230a
in *Ragnarsdrápa,* 7:230b
in *rímur,* 10:404a-b
skaldic, 11:318a–319b, 323a
in *Skáldskaparmál,* 11:324a, 352b
in *Víglundar saga,* 12:416b
Kenningham, John. *See* Kynyngham, John, friar
Kent, settlement in 6th century, 4:452a–453b
Kentēma, 8:617b
Kentigern, St., **7:231a-b**
commemorative writings about, 7:231a
in folkore, 7:231a
Urien Rheged and, 12:331b
Kentish. *See* English language, Old English
Kentish dialect. *See* English language, Old English
Kentish Psalm, 4:549b
Kepler, Johannes, theory of retinal image, 7:540b
Kerak, 4:24b
Kerbogha, atabeg of Mosul
Bohemond I of Antioch and, 2:309a
Tancred and, 11:589b
vs. First Crusade, 4:35b
Kercz (church: Hungary), 10:489a
Kerdīr. *See* Kartīr
Kereyid, 5:382b
Kerlinc. *See* Herger
Kerling, 5:442a
Kermān. *See* Kirmān
Kermes, 4:328a, 11:595b
production of as dye, 4:326b
Keroularios, Michael. *See* Michael Keroularios, patriarch
Kęstutis of Lithuania, 2:67a, 7:606a-b
murder of, 7:606b
Ketav Tammim. See Taku, Moses
Ketbugha (Ket Bugha; Mongol general), 6:329a
capture by Mamluks, 8:473b
occupation of Syria, 8:472b–473a
Keter Malkhut. See Solomon ben Judah ibn Gabirol
Ketill (saga character), 6:310a, 310b
Ketils saga hængs, 5:677a, **7:231b–232a**
dating of, 7:231b–232a
Eddic meter in, 7:232a
folktale motifs in, 7:232a
manuscripts of, 7:232a
Kettle-hat. *See* Chapel-de-fer
Kettledrum, 8:561b, 563b, 605b, 613a (*illus.*)
Kevin, St., music and, 8:558b
Key of Truth, The, questions of authenticity, 9:469b
Keyed harp. *See Clavicytherium*
Keys, delivery of the. *See Traditio clavium*
Kézai, Simon of. *See* Simon of Kéza
Khadīja (wife of Muḥammad), 6:576a, 576b
Khaḍrāᵓ, al-, 4:83a
Khafājī, al-, on poetic euphony, 10:347a-b
Khakhuli. *See* Xaχuli
Khalaf (ivory carver), 7:24a
Khalaf al-Murādī, al-, *Kitāb al-asrar fī nataᵓij al-afkār,* 11:642b
Khalafīya, 6:615b
Khalandrítsa, under Latins, 7:380a
Khalawāt, 4:296b
Khaldūn, Ibn, 1:382a, 618b, 5:653a, **7:232a–234b**
as administrator of Sufi institutions, 7:234b
on the caliph's titles, 3:488b
on cannon, 11:638b
career of, 7:232b
commentary on *Burda,* 7:232b
conflicts of, 7:234b
cyclical theory of civilization, 7:233b–234b
definition of *adab,* 6:233b
education of, 7:232a-b
on the empire of Mali, 8:57b
on Fatimid naval achievements, 9:75b
on Ibn Baṭṭūṭa, 2:131a
as judge at Malikite school of law, 7:234b
Kitāb al-ᶜIbar (*History of the Berbers*), 2:185b, 186a, 7:233a, 234b
on minstrel paraphernalia, 8:562b
Muqaddima, 1:386a-b, 7:233a–234b, 9:571b, 12:127b
discussion of numerals in, 1:384b–385b
on magic, 8:21a-b
on Nile, 9:138a
retreat from politics, 7:232b–233a
science of culture, 6:254a-b, 9:571b
theory of dynasty, 6:54a-b
Khālid ibn Barmak (Barmakid administrator), 2:109b–110a, 6:590a
Khālid ibn al-Walīd, **7:235a–236a**
Abū Bakr and, 7:235a-b
conversion of, 7:235a
military campaigns of, 7:235a-b
Muḥammad and, 7:235a
in *ridda* wars, 6:567b–568a
in Syria, 7:235b
ᶜUmar ibn al-Khaṭṭāb and, 7:235b
Khālid ibn Yazīd, 1:136a
instruction in alchemy, 1:136a, 141a
Khālid al-Qasrī, al-Kufa and, 7:306b
Khalīl ibn Aḥmad, al-, 1:617b
Kitāb al-ᶜain, 4:443b–444a
Khalīl ibn Aybak al-Ṣafadī, 9:651b
Wāfī bi 'l-wafayāt, al-, 6:253a-b
Khalīl Sulṭān, ruler of Samarkand, 12:56b–57a
Khallikān, Ibn, **7:236a-b**, 7:310a
career of, 7:236a
al-Khaṭīb al-Baghdādī on, 7:240a
on al-Mutanabbī, 8:652a-b
Wafayāt al-aᶜyān (*Biographical Dictionary*), 1:634a, 2:238b, 6:253a, 7:236a-b
Khamr. See Beverages, Islamic
Khamsa. See Niẓāmī
Khan (building), **7:237b–238a**
under Seljuks of Rum, 11:148b–149b (*illus.*)
see also Hān
Khan Tervel, 2:401a
Khan (title), **7:236b–237b**
as conceived by Mehmed II, 8:264b
Khānqāh, **7:238a–239a**
conduct code for, 7:238b
definition of, 7:238a
functions of, 7:238b, 8:499a
spread of, 7:238b
Sufis and, 7:238a-b
Khans of Crimea. *See* Crimea, Khanate of
Khāqānīya. *See* Qarakhanids
Khar-banda. *See* Uljaytu Khudabānda
Kharāj. See Land tax, Islamic
Kharijism, 11:138b–139b
Kharijites
ᶜAli and, 11:284b, 513a
in Arabia, domination of Oman, 1:374b
Azraqite, military conquests, 8:166a, 166b
Berbers and, 2:186a, 186b
geographical distribution of, 11:514a
Ibadite, military conquests, 8:165b
Ibrāhīm ibn al-Aghlab and, 6:391b
jihad and, 7:111a
in al-Kufa, 7:307a
al-Muᶜtazila and, 8:655a
in Najd, 9:54b
Najdīya, military conquests, 8:166a
opposition to caliphate, 3:36a-b, 47b
origins of, 1:374a
rebellions of
against ᶜAlī ibn Abī Ṭālib, 12:267a

  against Umayyads, 12:274a, 721b, 722a
  revolts of, 3:39a-b, 46a, 6:511b
  Shaybānī, military conquests, 8:165a
  vs. Yaʿqūb ibn Layth, 12:717a
  Zanj and, 12:739a, 739b
Kharja, **7:239a-b,** 11:408a-b, 409b, 446b–449a, 452b, 458b
  Arabic, 7:239b
  chansons de femme and, 7:239a
  compared with *cantigas de amigo,* 11:450b
  definition of, 7:239a
  dichotomy of moods, 8:515b
  difficulties of deciphering, 11:447a
  discovery of, 7:239a-b, 8:514b
  early Indo-European poetic tradition and, 11:408b
  importance of, 8:514b
  interpretative problems, 8:515a
  Mozarabic songs, 7:239a-b, 8:515a
  origins, popular-traditional, 8:515a-b
  rhythmic pattern, 8:514b
  Romance, 7:239b
    discovered in 1948, 11:447a
  secular *cantiga* and, 3:87a
  villancico and, 12:447a
  see also Aljamiado literature
Kharpūt gate (Diyarbakir), relief carvings, 11:717a
Kharraqān mausoleum, 11:147a
Khāṣṣakiyah, 2:272b, 273a
Khātam. See Seals and sigillography, Islamic
Khatchkʿar. See Xačʿkʿar
Khaṭīb al-Baghdādī, al-, **7:239b–240b**
  reputation of, 7:239b–240a
  Taʾrīkh Baghdād, 2:237b, 238b, 6:253a
  Taʾrīkh Baghdad, 7:240a
  works of, 7:240a
Khaṭīb, Ibn al-, 5:653a
Khaṭṭ al-mansūb, 2:135b–136a
Khawada Nameh. *See* Xwaday Namag
Khawārij, 6:582b
  anti-Abbasid activity of, 2:50b
Khawāṣṣ, 6:617b
Khayyāṭ al-ʿUsfui, Ibn, Al-Ṭabarī and, 11:569b
Khazar Khaghanate, vs. Magna Bulgaria, 12:488a
Khazars, **7:240b–242b**
  Byzantine alliance, 10:576a
  in Caucasia, 3:195a
  conversion to Judaism, 10:576a
  decline of, 7:242a
  defeat of the Rus and, 12:436a
  documents in Cairo genizah, 3:16a
  foreign invasions, 10:576b
  government, 10:576a
  history of empire, 7:240b–241a
  Huns and, 6:354a
  in international trade, 7:241a
  invasion of Syria, 6:232a
  invasions of Russia and, 10:576a
  Judaism and, 7:100a, 241b
  Kabar revolt, 10:576b
  Khwarizmian protectorate, 10:576b
  Magyars and, 6:338b, 8:46a
  missionaries to, 4:73b
  origin of, 7:240b
  origins of the Seljuks and, 11:151a
  Syrian incursions, 8:164b
  in 10th century, 7:241b–242a
  trade with Georgia and Azerbaijan, 12:97b
  in Transcaucasia, 7:241a
  vs. Arabs, 10:576a
    in Armenia, 1:478b, 479a
Khāzim, Bishr ibn Abī, 1:399b
Khilʿa, **7:242b**
  Mahmūd of Ghazna depicted in, 7:242 *(illus.)*
Khilāṭ. *See* Xlatʿ
Khilendar monastery. *See* Hilandar monastery
Khirbat al-Mafjar, 6:408b, 594b, 595a-b, 12:264b
Khizan, manuscript illumination in, 1:497b
Khizānat al-Ḥikma, 11:82b
Khlatʿ. *See* Xlatʿ
Khoja ʿUbayd Allāh Aḥrār, order of Naqshbandiyya in Transoxiana and, 12:59a
Khorāsān
  conquered by Uzbeks, 12:58a
  cultural achievements under Timurids, 12:59a
  daʿwā in, 6:615b
  Ghurids in, 5:526b–527a
  governed by al-Faḍl ibn Yaḥyā, 2:110b–111a
  independence from Abbasid rule, 3:49a
  in Islamic conquests, 6:570b
  local dynasties in, 6:503a, 503b, 504a
  al-Manṣūr and, 8:88b, 89b
  Mazdakism in, 8:238a-b
  origins of madrasa and, 8:11a
  origins of the Seljuks and, 11:151a-b
  as a power base for al-Mahdī, 8:46b
  private Seljuk mausolea in, 11:147a
  rebellion against Umayyads in, 12:272a-b, 273b
  rise of Islamic mysticism and, 9:39b, 40a
  Sanjar ibn Malikshāh and, 11:153b
  Sasanian provincial capital, 10:661a
  Shiism in, 7:307a
  Tamerlane and, 11:588a
  Timurid descendants of ʿUmar Shaykh and, 12:58a
  Toghrıl-Beg and, 12:66a
  Ulugh-Beg and, 12:57b
  under ʿAbd Allāh, 11:575a
  under Ṭāhir, 11:574b, 575a
  under Tahirids, 11:574b
  vs. Basra, 7:306b
  Yaʿqūb and, 11:575b
  see also Abbasids
Khorāsān Highway, 10:426a
Khorzanē (Khordzianenē), 1:515a
Khosrau. *See* Xusrō
Khosrow ud rēdag, 9:327a
Khotanese language, 6:505b
Khozhenie za tri moria. See Nikitin, Afanasii
Khrabr, on Slavic language, 11:345b
Khram. *See* Xrami
Khuda-banda. *See* Uljaytu Khudabānda
Khuld, al- (near Baghdad), 2:45b, 46a
Khumārawayh, administration and economic policies, 12:224a-b
Khurdādhbih, Ibn, 1:473b, 7:107a, **7:242b–243b**
  Adab al-samāʿ, 7:243a
  careers of, 7:243a
  geography and, 7:243a-b
  Kitāb jamharat ansāb al-Furs wa'l-nawāqīl, 7:243a
  Kitāb al-lahw wa'l-malāhī, 7:243a
  Kitāb al-masālik wa'l-mamālik (Book of Roads and Kingdoms), 4:555b–556a, 7:243a, 11:336b
  Kitāb al-nudamaʾ wa'l-julasaʾ, 7:243a
  Kitāb al-sharāb, 7:243a
  Kitāb al-ṭabīkh, 7:243a
  music and, 7:243a
  on qibla, 7:243a
  references to Scandinavia, 10:706b
Khurradādhbih, Ibn. *See* Khurdādhbih, Ibn
Khushqadam, Mamluk sultan, 3:400a
Khusrau. *See* Xusrō
Khusraw u Shīrīn. See Niẓāmī
Khuṭba, 5:299b, 10:71b
Khutsuri script. *See* Georgian alphabet
Khuzāʿa, Ṭāhirids and, 11:574a
Khūzistān, Christian bishoprics, 10:660b
Khvarenah, 12:721a
Khwadāy nāmag. See Xwadāy nāmag
Khwājū Kirmānī, 6:507b, 7:181b
  Dīwān, 8:117a *(illus.)*
Khwand Khātūn complex (Caesarea), 11:148b
Khwāndamīr, 12:59a
Khwārazm. *See* Gurgānj
Khwarizm
  conquered by Shaybānī Khan, 12:58a
  Mongol invasions, 8:472a
  northern part of seized by Uzbeks, 12:57a
  under Seljuk control, 11:151b
  see also Transoxiana
Khwārizmī, Muḥammad ibn Mūsā al-, 1:383a, 385b, 389a, 389b, 391b, 620a
  astronomical writings translated, 12:135b
  on astronomy, 1:620a
  Calculation with the Hindu Numerals, 1:390b–391a, 395b–396a, 10:471b, 473a, 474a
  influenced by Jewish scientific texts, 11:90a
  Kitāb al-mukhtaṣar fī-ḥisāb al-jabr wa'l-muqābala, 8:212a-b
    translations of, 8:212b
  Latin versions of his works, 11:81b
  successors of, 7:212a
  Toledan Tables and, 12:67a
  See also Banū Mūsā
Khwārizmshāhs (Khwārazmshāhs), 7:243b–244b
  area ruled by, 7:243b
  in Azerbaijan, 2:27a
  decline of, 7:244a
  founder of, 7:244a
  Ildegizids and, 6:419b
  invasions of Armenia and, 12:98b
  in Iran, 6:502 (map), 504a-b
  Mongols and, 7:244a

Khwārizmshāhs (Khwārazmshāhs) (*cont.*)
murder of Mongol envoys, 10:640b
Seljuks and, 7:244a, 11:151b, 153b
Toghrıl-Beg and, 12:66b
Turkomans and, 7:244a
vs. Abbasids, 6:514a
Ḳibla. *See* Qibla
Kibyrrhaeot, theme of, 12:9b
Kiddush ha-shem. *See* Martyrdom, Jewish
Kiddushin. *See* Betrothal, Jewish
Kidnappers. *See* Slavery and slave trade; Travel and transport, dangers of
Kiel (Hanseatic ship), 9:88b
Kieran. *See* Ciarán
Kiev
destroyed (1240), 2:131b
jewelry of, 5:378b–379a
monastic movement, 10:595a–596a
Mongol invasion of, 5:461a
origins of, 4:587b
sacked by Andrei Bogoluibskii (1169), 2:293b
Kiev Cathedral, Greek-cross design of, 4:341a
Kiev leaflets, 5:542b–543a
Kievan notes. *See* Musical notation, Kievan
Kievan Rus, **7:244b–252b**, 7:245 (map)
agriculture, 1:99a–102b
monasteries, 1:101a
appanages, 1:101a
art and architecture, 10:583a-b
attacks on Constantinople, 12:435a-b
Chërnye Klobuki, 10:577a
Christianization of, 7:248a, 8:443b, 10:591a
church-state relations, 10:596b
Cuman/Kipchak tribal union, 10:577a
disintegration of, 8:537b–539a
East Slavs in, 7:245b–246b, 250a
economy of, 7:249b–251b
monastic origins, 10:595a
feudalism in, 7:249b, 251b
Jagiełło dynasty in, Western orientation, 10:594a
Jews in, 7:100a-b
land tenure
black lands, 1:101a-b
votchina estates, 1:102a
language of, 7:244b–245a
literary "golden age" in, 11:346b–347a
mints and money in, 8:425a–427a
Mongol conquest of, 7:249b
music of, 8:572b–573a
Novgorod and, 7:249b
origins of, 7:244b, 246b–247a, 10:591a, 12:434b
peasant society
communal, 1:101a-b
decline in living standards, 1:100a, 101a–102b
dues and obligatory services, 1:101a-b, 102b
effect of Mongol conquest on, 1:100b
restriction of movement, 1:101b
seignorial, 1:101b, 102b
on state lands, 1:102b
Pecheneg migrations, 10:576b
Poland and, 9:719b, 720b
political history of, 7:247a–249b
Polovtsy raids on, 7:248b–249a
pomeshchiki, social class of, 1:101b–102a
in *Primary Chronicle,* 10:120a–121a
princes of, 7:246b
principalities of, 7:249a-b
relations with
Constantinople, 2:118b, 4:555a, 588a
Hungary, 6:339a
Novgorod, 9:193a-b
Rurikides, 10:571a
slave trade in, 11:336b
society of, 7:249b–251b
Tatar overlordship, 1:100b–102b
under Mongols, 11:190a-b
under Yaroslav, 12:720a
Vladimir and, 12:485b
vs. Volga Bulgars, 12:488a-b
written sources for history of, 7:246a-b
see also Lithuania; Tmutakaran, Khanate of
Kievo-Pecherskaya (monastery), 8:443b
Kifāyat al-ᶜĀbidin. *See* Maimonides, Abraham
Kildare family, 6:520a, 520b
Kildare Geraldines. *See* Fitzgeralds
Kildare, monastery of, Uí Dúnlainge and, 7:536a-b
Kildare (shire), 6:519b
Kildrummy castle, David II and, 4:111b
Kilian, St., in art, 10:442a, 500a
Ḳīlīj Arslān. *See* Qılıj Arslān
Kilim, **7:252b–253b**
definition of, 7:252b–253a
earliest, 7:253a
technique of, 7:253a (*illus.*)
weaving technique, 10:547a
Kilkenny, Statutes of (1366), 6:519a-b, 9:436b
Killis, Ibn, 2:28a
Kilwa, Ibn Baṭṭūṭa in, 12:740a
Kilwardby, Richard, view on hylomorphism, 2:35b
Kilwardby, Robert, 4:246b, **7:253b**
Aquinas and, 1:463b
concordance to patristic works, 1:206a, 207a
condemnations of Aristotle of 1277 and, 12:40b
conservatism of, 7:253b
De ortu scientiarum, on magic, 8:37a
Grosseteste and, 1:461b
Kimāk, Russian fur trade and, 5:331b–332a
Kimḥi, David, 2:212a
Sefer ha-mikhlol, 6:129a
Kimḥi, Joseph, 4:541a
Book of the Covenant, 10:3b
on Jewish observance of Ten Commandments, 10:4a
work of, 10:3b–4a
Kimḥi, Moses ben Joseph, *Mahalakh Shevilei ha-Daᶜat,* 7:176a
Kīmkhwā. *See* *Kamkhā*
Kinda (a tribe in Najd), 9:54a
Kindheit Jesu. *See* Konrad von Fussesbrunnen
Kindheitslied. *See* Wilde Alexander, Der
Kindī, Abū Yūsuf Yaᶜqūb ibn Isḥāq al-, **7:254a-b**, 11:305b
Aqrābādhīn, 6:179a
Aristotle and, 1:458b
Arnald of Villanova and, 1:538a
attraction to Greek thought, 11:83b
attribution of *De radiis* to, 8:37b
De aspectibus, Greek influences, 9:241b
De intellectu, 7:254a
De somno et visione, 7:254a
fī al-Falsafa al-Ūlā, 7:254a
Isaac Israeli and, 6:620a
Latin versions of his works, 11:81b
Liber de quinque essentiis, 7:254a
music and, 8:563b, 566a, 566b
on musical instruments, 8:610a
musical treatises and, 8:640a
patrons of, 7:254a
philosophical writing, 9:569b
philosophy of, 7:254a-b
vision theory, 9:241b
clarity of center field, 9:242a
extramission hypothesis, 9:242a
law of equal angles, 9:242a
mirror images, 9:242a
Kindī, al-Ashᶜath ibn Qays al-, on battle of Ṣiffīn, 11:284a
Kindite kingdom, 1:371b
Kinematics, *Liber de motu* and, 1:436b
King Horn, 8:316a, 331a
rhyming couplet in, 8:344b
Romance of Horn and, 10:475a
King lists, Irish, 6:539b
King Olger Danskis Krønicke, source for later works, 6:275b
King sagas, Irish. *See* Cycles of the Kings (Irish sagas)
Kingdom of Jerusalem. *See* Jerusalem, Kingdom of
Kingis Quair, The, **7:254b–255a,** 8:324a
use of "rhyme royal" in, 8:346a
Kings, sagas. *See* Norse kings' sagas
King's Bench, court of, 4:502a,b, 7:190b–194b, 446a
Exchequer Court and, 4:533b
jail delivery, 7:45a
Norman-Angevin England, 4:470a
originated by Henry II, 7:443a
parliament and, 9:424a
see also Justices of the King's Bench
Kings, Book of. *See* *Shāhnāma*
King's Chancellor. *See* Chancery, England
King's Chapel at Clarendon, 3:237a
King's Church (Studenica), 11:186b
King's evil, **7:255a–256a**
Latin term for, 7:255a
leprosy and, 7:255a–256a
touching for, 7:255b–256a, 258a
King's Exchequer. *See* Exchequer
King's Hall. *See* Cambridge, University of
King's Mirror, 5:398a, 9:183b
on Greenland, 12:427b
King's peace. *See* Justices of the peace
Kingship
accroachment, as treason, 12:166a–167a

Anglo-Saxon, Dunstan and, 3:82b
Armenian, 1:489a
in art, 6:408b
Byzantine
Frederick II and, 11:271a
Neagoe Basarab on, 10:510b
see also Basileus
challenges to, *diffidatio,* 12:165a
Cilician, Tarsus Cathedral and, 11:600a
consultative tradition, French representative assemblies and, 10:322b–323b
coronation rituals, **7:256a–259a**
anointing, 4:426a, 7:256b
anointing of Pepin III (the Short), 9:501a
at Aachen, 4:426b
in Carolingian empire, 7:256b–257b
of Charlemagne, 7:256a, 542b
closing with Mass, 7:258b
constitutional aspect of, 7:258b
crowning, 7:256b–257a
of English rulers, 7:257b–258a
of Frankish rulers, 7:257a
of French rulers, 7:258a-b, 10:323a, 344b
of German rulers, 7:257b
in Hungary, 11:483a-b
imperial, and papacy, 9:374b
liturgical character of, 7:257a-b, 258b
of Norwegian rulers, 7:258a
oath of Edward II of England, 9:425b
Thomas Becket's oil of the Virgin, 4:475b, 476b
unction, 4:426a
varieties of, 7:258a-b
Wilton Diptych, 4:476a-b, 477a-b
see also Acclamations
English
conviction by king's record, 12:165b–166a, 167a
problems of weak rulership, 12:572b
treason and royal powers, 12:165a–168a
equity and, 4:501b
Fœreyinga saga and, 4:580b
German
Nuremberg's role, 9:202a
Parzival and, 12:678a
in Sicily, 11:268a
weak monarchy of, 10:329a-b
Wipo and, 12:656a
in Germanic tribes, 4:425b
holding court (*conventus, colloquium, curia*)
German *Hoftag,* 10:329a–330b
see also Representative assemblies
Hungarian, 6:339a-b
Iceland and, 6:392b, 397a
inheritance and, 6:459a, 459b
Iran, symbols of, 10:611b
Irish, 6:516a-b, 517a, 520a
bardic poetry and, 6:536b–537b, 538a-b
in historical compositions, 6:539b
in sagas, 6:545b, 546b–547b
sociology of, 6:553a
see also Tara
lèse-majesté, 12:166a
Persian, caliphate and, 6:501b–502a
royal households, travel of, 12:152b–153a, 159a-b
Russian, *Vladimir Virgin* and, 12:486a
Sasanian, eternal flame and, 11:628b
Sicilian
Frederick II and, 11:270b–271b
iconography of, 11:267b–268a, 271b
Swedish
in Viking Age, 11:530a
Ynglingatal and, 12:726a
taxation authority. *See* Representative assemblies; Taxation
Visigothic, 12:468b, 469b–470a, 470b–471a, 472a-b
Isidore of Seville and, 6:564b
Zanj, 12:739b
see also Curia, lay; Elections, royal
Kingship, theories of, **7:259a–271b**
Aristotelian-Thomist, 4:400b
ascetic view, 7:261b–262a, 264a
authority from the people (French), 10:316a-b, 327b
biblical exegesis and, 2:214a
Carolingian, 7:259b–262a
Christian virtues in, 7:261a-b
deposition of kings, 4:157b–160b
Edward II, 4:475b, 476a
Richard II, 4:476b, 477a, 484b–485a
Disputatio inter clericum et militem, 4:218a-b
dualism, 7:265b–267a
election to throne, 5:156b–157a
England
changes under Normans, 4:473b
declaration by parliament, 4:473a-b, 477b, 478a–479b
descent from Arthur, 4:475a
hereditary right, 4:473a-b, 475a-b, 476a-b
Lancastrian hereditary principle, 4:477a-b
sources of authority, 4:473a-b
title by conquest, 4:478a
farr, 10:668a
French king as a source of law, 9:420a
hereditary rights, 12:570b
impeachment and, 6:427a
influenced by the Bible, 2:216a-b
investiture controversy, 7:262a–264b
Jordan of Osnabrück, 7:149a
Kaiserchronik, 7:205b–206a
kings' duties, 10:16a
kingship as divine ministerium, 10:16a–17a
law and, 7:264b–267a
mirror of princes, 8:434a–436a
national, 7:267a–270b
in Old Testament, 10:15b, 16b
papalists on, 7:262a-b, 264a-b
prince, 10:123b–124a
Quaestio in utramque partem tract, 10:238a
Reconquest in Spain and, 7:269b
Roman law and, 7:265b, 269b
royalists, 7:262a–263b, 264b, 267a-b
sacred character, 5:157a, 171b–172a
in *Somnium Viridarii,* 11:371b
succession, 5:159a
arguments about, 5:144a-b
Salic Law, 9:555a, 555b
of women, 5:182a-b, 183a-b
Tractatus, Lupold of Bebenburg, 7:688b
treason and royal powers, 12:165a–168a
see also Prerogative; *Rígsþula*
Kinnamos, John, on Manuel I Komnenos, 6:246b
Kinship. *See* Family; Genealogy; Marriage
Kinship group. *See* Extended family
Kiosk, **7:271b**
Kiot, **7:271b**
Kip (unit of measure), 12:593a
product variations, 12:584b
Kipchak Steppe, slave markets in, 3:398b
Kipchak Turkic language, 8:71a, 12:488b
Kipchaks
in Kars, 7:221b
Mongol invasions
alliance against, 8:468a
Golden Horde, 8:470a
Kirakos Arewelcʿi. *See* Kirakos of Ganjak
Kirakos Banasēr, *Life of Tʿovma Mecopʿecʿi,* 12:92b
Kirakos of Ganjak, 1:511b, 521a, 5:579b, **7:271b–272a**
on Armenian trade, 12:99a
Hetʿum I and, 7:272a
History, 7:272a
Mongol invasion of Armenia and, 7:272a
on *naχarars,* 1:486a
Vardan Arewelcʿi and, 12:359b
Yovhannēs Vanakan and, 7:271b–272a
Kirān. See Mizhar
Kiranides, allegedly translated by Thomas of Cantimpré, 12:34a
Kircher, Athanasius, *Musurgia universalis,* 8:648b
Kirdēr. *See* Kartīr
Kirghiz, **7:272b–273a**
China and, 7:272b
inscriptions concerning, 7:272b–273a
Islamization of, 7:273a
political structure of, 7:272b
sovereign of, 7:272b
Tien Shan, 7:271b–272a
Uighur khanate and, 7:272b
Yenisei, 7:272b–273a
Kirk Smeaton, Robin Hood and, 10:436b
Kirkeby, Margaret, 9:21a
Kirkisānī, Yūsuf Yaʿqūb al-, *Kitāb al-anwār* (*Book of Lights and Watchtowers*), 7:210b, 10:2b
Kirmān
daʿwā in, 6:615b
Seljuk state in, 11:151a, 155a
vs. Yaʿqūb ibn Layth, 12:717a

Kirmānī, Ḥamīd al-Dīn al-
cosmology of, 6:588a
theology of, 6:616b, 618a
Kirmiz. *See* Qirmiz
Kirovabad. *See* Arrān
Kisāᵓī, al-, 7:307b
Kiss of peace, 8:194b
Pax Domini, 8:194b
Kissé. See Kursī
Kiswa, **7:273a-b**, 11:716a
inscriptions on, 7:273b
Kaaba and, 7:203b (*illus.*), 204a
Kitāb, al-. See Sībawayhi
Kitāb al-aghānī, 8:560b, 561a
depictions of *nāᶜūras* in, 9:67a
frontispieces of Badr al-Dīn of Mosul in, 2:44a
see also Abu 'l-Faraj al-Iṣfahānī
Kitāb al-ᶜain. See Khalīl ibn Aḥmad, al-
Kitāb al-alfāẓ. See Sikkit, Ibn al-
Kitāb al-almānāt wa-al-Iᶜtiqādāt. See Saadiah Gaon
Kitāb al-asrar fī nataᵓij al-afkār. See Khalaf al-Murādī, al-
Kitāb Baghdād. See Abu 'l-Faḍl Aḥmad ibn Abī Ṭāhir Ṭayfūr
Kitāb al-bayān al-mughrib fī akhbār al-Andalus wa'l-Maghrib. See ᶜIdhārī al-Marrākushī
Kitāb al-buldān. See Yaᶜqūbī, al-
Kitāb al-burhān. See Eutychios the Melchite
Kitāb al-faraj baᶜd al-shidda, 7:98a
Kitāb fī al-aghānī. See Yūnus al-Kātib
Kitāb fī maᶜrifat al-ḥiyal al-handasīya. See Jazarīᶜ, al-
Kitāb al-ḥayawān. See Jāḥiẓ, Abū ᶜUthmān ᶜAmr ibn Baḥr al-
Kitāb al-ḥiyal. See Banū Mūsā
Kitāb al-ᶜIbar. See Khaldūn, Ibn
Kitāb iḥṣāᵓ al-īqāᶜāt. See Fārābī, al-
Kitāb al-imtāᶜ waᵓl-muᵓānasa (The Book of Enlivenment and Good Company), 1:381a
Kitāb al-jamāhir fī maᶜrifat al-jawāhir. See Bīrūnī, Muḥammad
Kitāb al-Jamhara. See Durayd, Ibn
Kitāb jamharat ansāb al-Furs wa'l-nawāqīl. See Khurdādhbih, Ibn
Kitāb al-jāmiᶜ fi'l-adwiya al-mufrada. See Ghāfiqī, al-
Kitāb al-khalq al-insān. See Aṣmaᶜī, al-
Kitāb al-lahw wa'l-malāhī. See Khurdādhbih, Ibn
Kitāb al-madkhal ᶜilmᵓaḥkām al-nujūm. See Abū Maᶜshar
Kitāb al-maghāzī. See Wāqidī, Abū al-
Kitāb al-manāẓir. See Haytham, Ḥasan ibn al-
Kitāb al-masālik wa'l-mamālik. See Khurdādhbih, Ibn
Kitāb al-mukhtaṣar fī-ḥisāb al-jabr wa 'l-muqābala. See Khwārizmī, al-
Kitāb murūj al-dhahab wa-maᶜādin al-jawhar. See Masᶜūdī, al-
Kitāb al-mūsīqī al-kabīr. See Fārābī, al-
Kitāb naṣīḥat al-Mulūk. See Ghazālī, al-
Kitāb al-nudamaᵓ wa'l julasaᵓ. See Khurdādhbih, Ibn
Kitāb Rujār. See Idrīsī, al-, *Nuzhat al-mushtāq fī 'khtirāk al-āfāq*
Kitāb al-rushd wa'l-hidāya. See Ḥawshab, Manṣūr al-Yaman, Ibn
Kitāb al-sharāb. See Khurdādhbih, Ibn
Kitāb al-shifāᵓ. See Sīnā, Ibn
Kitāb al-sulṭān. See Qutaybah, Ibn
Kitāb al-ṭabaqāt. See Wāqidī, Abū al-
Kitāb al-Ṭabaqāt al-kabīr. See Saᶜd, Ibn
Kitāb al-ṭabīkh. See Khurdādhbih, Ibn
Kitāb al-tāj, 8:435b–436a
Kitāb al-Taᶜlīm, 4:296a
Kitāb al-tanbīh wa 'l-ishrāf. See Masᶜūdī, al-
Kitāb al-umm. See Shāfiᶜī, al-
Kitābkhāna, **7:273b–274a**
collections in, 7:273b
destruction of books in, 7:274a
maintenance of, 7:274a
Kivorii. See Darokhranitelnitsa
Kiwrakos Vardapet, 1:520a
Kiwrikē. *See* Gurgēn (Kiwrikē)
Kiwrion of Georgia, *katᶜołikos*
Abraham of Armenia and, 1:509a
Armenian church and, 1:499b
Kızılbaş, Selim I and, 11:145a
Kjalnesinga saga, 4:613b, **7:274a-b**
Eyrbyggja saga and, 7:274a
Finnboga saga and, 7:274b
Ǫrvar-Odds saga and, 7:274a
plot of, 7:274a-b
sources for, 7:274a
KK. *See Karlskrönikan*
Klada, Joannes, 8:555b
Klængr Björnsson, 11:357b
Klængr Þorsteinsson, bishop of Skálholt, 6:352a
Klage. See Hartmann von Aue
Klage, Die, in *Nibelungenlied,* 9:113a, 114b
Klage der Minne, Die, 8:411b
Klappvisier, 1:526b, 527a (*illus.*)
Klara Hätzlerin. *See* Hätzlerin, Klara
Klári saga, **7:274b–275b**, 10:392a, 395b
chivalry in, 7:274b–275a
composition of, 7:274b
King Thrushbeard motif in, 7:275a
Latin sources for, 7:275a
metrical version of, 7:275a
preservation of, 7:275a
Sigurðar saga þögla and, 11:290b
Klárus, 7:275a
Kleimo, **7:275b**
in hallmark, 7:275b
in icon painting, 7:275b (*illus.*)
Kleine Kaiserrecht, Das. See Frankenspiegel
Kleine Reimpaargedichte, 8:408a
Klet. See Russian architecture
Kliros, **7:276a**
Klokotnica, Battle of (1230), 2:409b, 7:131a, 347b
Kloster der Minne, Das, 5:431b–432a, 8:411a-b
Kloster Sulz, saltworks, royal control, 10:632a
Klosterneuburg Abbey
archives, 1:448b
enameled altarpiece from, 4:0 (frontispiece), 9:127a–128a (*illus.*)
see also Nicholas of Verdun
Knapwell, Richard, *Correctoria corruptorii Thomae* and, 12:41a, 41b
Knarr, 11:240a-b
Knĕdz. See Dux
Kneecop, 1:524b, 534 (*illus.*)
ailettes and, 1:525a
Knez Lazar. *See* Lazar Hrebeljanoviç
"Knight or clerk" debate. *See Blancheflour et Florence*
Knight in the Panther Skin. See Shotᶜa Rustaveli
Knighton, Henry
on the conflict between Richard II and parliament, 9:428b–429a
on the economic effect of Black Death, 2:265a
Knights of Alcántara, 3:305 (*illus.*), 306b
Knights of Avís, 3:305 (*illus.*), 306b
Knights of Calatrava, 3:305 (*illus.*), 306b
Knights of the Holy Grail, 3:307a
Knights of the Holy Sepulcher, 3:305 (*illus.*), 306b
Knights Hospitalers. *See* Knights of St. John
Knights and knight service, **7:276a–279a**
ancient horsemen and, 1:522a
in Aragon, 10:256a
beneficed, 12:559a
chain as emblem of knighthood, 5:381a
chivalric code, 7:276b
courtesy books about, 3:666a-b
derogation of, 9:150a
dubbing ceremony, 7:276b–277a
duties, *Le roman des ailes,* 10:258a
in England
of Henry I, 7:278a
of William I, 7:277b–278a
see also Thegn
Fatimid, 3:209a
fees, 11:613b, 617a
coinage or income measure, 12:586b
scutage, 11:613a
in feudal hierarchy, 7:276a–277b
baron and, 9:150b
fief holder knights, 7:276a
landless household knights, 7:276a
in Germany, 5:501b–502a, 9:150a
imperial, 5:497a–498b, 10:332a, 333a
household, 12:559a
Hungarian, 6:344b
Italy, knight for the commune, 12:562b
as jurors, 6:482a
in literature, 7:277a
Alexander romances, 1:151a-b
code in Arthurian court, 5:449a
military service of, 7:277a–278b
paid professional, 12:559a
in Poland, 9:720b–721a
rise of, 9:149b–150a
in royal administration, 6:302b
France, 7:674a
to castellan, 11:619b

in tournaments, 5:350a-b, 7:278b
travel, 12:162a
Turkish, 3:209a
urban
in Germany, 5:464a
in Italy, 3:416b
in warfare, 4:15b–16a
Anna Komnena on, 7:278a-b
Battle of Hastings, 1:523a
European cavalry, 3:203a–204a
Hundred Years War, 6:333a-b, 334b
Peace of God movement and, 9:474b
weapons, lance, 7:323b, 324 (*illus.*)
see also Baron; Chivalry; Feudalism; Squire; Warfare
Knights of Malta. *See* Knights of St. John
Knights of Rhodes. *See* Knights of St. John
Knights of the Round Table, 3:307a
see also Arthurian legend
Knights of St. John, 8:486a
Achaea and, 7:381a
art and, 4:21b, 24b, 25a-b, 26a
Geertgen tot Sint Jans as employee of, 5:372a
ban of Severin, 12:500b
as bankers for the papacy, 2:77b
classes of members in, 3:304a
Corinth and, 7:381b
cross of, 3:303b–304a, 305 (*illus.*)
in crusader states, 12:561b
dress of, 3:303b
English headquarters, 7:660b–661a
flag of, 3:303b–304a, 305 (*illus.*)
formation of, 3:303b
hospitals of, 6:294a
in Hungary, 2:70a
Krak des Chevaliers and, 7:302a
al-Lādhiqiya and, 7:315b
Malta and, 8:67b–68a
Mistra and, 8:446b
names of, 3:303b
in Rhodes, 10:365b
Tafur and, 11:573a
vs. Templars, 4:52a,b
Knights of Santiago, 3:305 (*illus.*), 306b
Knights of the Sword of Cyprus, 3:305 (*illus.*), 306b–307a
Knights Templars. *See* Templars
Knikᶜ Hawatoy, **7:279a–280a**
compilation of, 7:279a-b
dating of, 7:279b
purpose of, 7:279b
Knitch (unit of measure), 12:593a
Knitting. *See* Textiles; Wool
Knolles, Sir Robert, Rochester Bridge and, 10:415b
Knorr (Knörr). See Knarr
Knot (unit of measure), 12:593a
"Knowledge confrontation," in Icelandic literature, 12:344b
Knowledge, theory of
Adam Wodeham and, 9:157a
in Augustinian Aristotelianism, 1:465b–466a
Averroës on, 1:459b
Nicholas of Autrecourt and, 9:122a
of Ockham, 9:156a, 211a-b, 212a-b
Duns Scotus and, 9:210a
in Thomism, 1:466a-b
Knud. *See* Cnut
Knud Lavard, 4:152b, 153a, 153b, **7:280a-b**
biography of, 7:280b
canonization of, 7:280b
in *Knýtlinga saga,* 7:281a-b
liturgy of, 11:522b
military campaigns of, 7:280a
murder of, 7:280a-b, 10:535b, 11:522a
successors of, 7:280b
Knutsson, Karl, 7:220a
Knýtlinga saga, **7:281a-b**, 9:177b
author of, 7:281b
Gǫngu-Hrólfs saga and, 5:577a
Heimskringla and, 7:281a
Jómsvíkinga saga and, 7:281a
narrative technique of, 7:281a-b
preservation of, 7:280a
Sigurðar saga fóts and, 11:290b
Skjǫldunga saga and, 7:281a
sources of, 7:281a
Koberger, Anton, 12:692a
Kobold und Eisbär. See Heinrich von Freiberg, *Schrätel und der Wasserbär, Das*
Koerbecke, Johann, **7:281b–282a**
altarpieces of, 7:281b–282a (*illus.*)
Kogge. See Cog
Koh-i-nuh. *See* Ararat, Mount
Köhler als gedungener Liebhaber, Der. See Folz, Hans
Koimesis, **7:282a–283a**
depictions of, 7:216a (*illus.*), 282b (*illus.*)
4th-century account of, 7:282b
origin of, 7:282a-b
see also Dormition
Koimesis (church: Nicaea), 3:378a
Koine. *See* Greek language
Kokizniki, 8:574b
Kokkinobaphos. *See* James the Monk
Kokoshnik, **7:283a-b**, 7:283 (*illus.*)
see also Bochka
Koḷ district, 7:309a
Kollema, **7:283b**
Kollesis, **7:283b**
Kollsbók, 6:312a, 8:507b
Kołm, 8:551b
Kolmarer Liederhandschrift, 12:654b
Koḷmn Tarōnocᶜ. *See* Tarōn
Koloman II of Bulgaria, reign of, 2:410a
Kolskeggr Ásbjarnarson, *Landnámabók* and, 7:327b, 328a
Komitas, *katᶜołikos,* 5:540b, 6:309a, 309b
hymn of, 1:509a-b
Knikᶜ Hawatoy and, 7:279a-b
Kommerkion, 11:605a, 12:103a
Komnenoi, 2:493b–496a, **7:283b–284b**
alliance of, with German emperors, 7:284a
Anatolia and, 1:241b
area ruled by, 7:283b
art under, 2:443a–445a
commerce under rule of, 12:102a–103b
in East, 7:284a-b
expansionism in Asia Minor, 2:498a
government of, 7:284a
literature under, 2:507a-b
military campaigns of, 7:283b–284a
reign of, 2:493b–496a
relations with Latin Empire of Constantinople, 7:347a
Tamar and, 11:587b
of Trebizond, 1:159a
in West, 7:284a
see also Alexios I Komnenos, Byzantine emperor; Trebizond, Empire of
Konàk, **7:284b**
see also Khan
"König Drosselbart" motif, in Icelandic *riddarasögur,* 10:395b
König Laurin, **7:284b–285a**
continuation of, 7:285a
dating of, 7:284b
folk motifs in, 7:285a
preservation of, 7:284b
König Rother, **7:285b–286a**
composition of, 7:285b
Dukus Horant and, 4:304b, 305a
political purpose of, 7:285b
popularity of, 7:285b
relationship to other literary works, 7:285b
Þiðreks saga and, 12:30a
Wolfram von Eschenbach and, 12:674b
"König vom Odenwald," 8:356b
Königsberg
named after Přemysl Ottokar II of Bohemia, 2:66b
St. Catherine play, 4:268b
Königsfelden, stained glass at, 5:553a
Koninc Ermenrîkes Dôt. See Ermenrîkes Dôt
Konrad von Ammenhausen, *Schachzabelbuch,* 5:431a, 8:357b
Konrad Fleck. *See* Fleck, Konrad
Konrad von Fussesbrunnen, *Kindheit Jesu,* 2:228b, 8:350a
Konrad von Heimesfurt, *Urstende,* 2:228b
Konrad of Masovia. *See* Conrad of Masovia, duke
Konrad von Megenberg, *Buch von den natürlichen Dingen,* 8:356b
Konrad, Pfaffe. *See* Rolandslied
Konrad von Soest, **7:286b–287a**
altarpieces of, 7:286b (*illus.*)
Niederwildungen Altarpiece, 5:610a-b
Konrad von Stoffeln, **7:287a-b**
Gauriel von Muntabel, 5:455a, 7:287a-b
literary models, 7:287b
works attributed to, 7:287a
Konrad von Würzburg, 5:634a, **7:287b–291b**
Alexius, 7:289a
Arthurian literature in work of, 7:289a
didactic poetry of, 5:443a
Engelhard, 5:454b, 7:289b
Reinfrid von Braunschweig and, 10:292a
Gottfried von Strassburg and, 7:288a-b

Konrad von Würzburg, 5:634a (*cont.*)
Heinrich von Kempten, 7:288a, 8:129a
Herzmaere, 5:454b, 7:288a-b
influence on *Schüler von Paris,* 11:80a
lyric poetry of, 7:290b–291a
Mären, audience for, 8:132a
as minnesinger, 8:414a
narrative verse of, 7:291a-b
Pantaleon, 7:289a-b
Partonopier und Meliur, 5:454b, 7:289b–290a
popularity of, 7:291b
professional life of, 8:352b
on saints' lives, 7:289a-b
Schwanritter, 7:288b–289a
Silvester, 7:289a
Trojanerkrieg, 7:290a-b
Troy verses by, 12:221a
Turnier von Nantes, 7:289a
Welt Lohn, 7:288b, 12:656b
Wirt and, 12:657b
Konráðs saga keisarasonar, **7:291b–292b**, 10:394b, 395b
Oriental motifs in, 7:292a
Konstantine Filozof, biography of Stefan Lazareviç of Serbia, 11:473a
Kontakarion, Slavic music and, 8:574a, 574b
Kontakion, 6:378a, 378b, **7:292b–293a**, 7:612b–613a, 8:554a, 9:687b
Armenian hymns and, 1:509b
Asmatikon and, 1:586b
composers of, 7:292b
dialogue in, 2:510b
form and content, 2:510b
language of, 2:510b
madrāshā and, 8:578a
music for, 2:510b–511a, 7:292b
origin of, 2:510b, 524b
Romanos Melodos and, 10:516a, 516b
structure of, 7:292b
styles of, 2:510b, 7:292b
for Sunday of Orthodoxy, 6:399a
Kontor, 9:185a
Kontós, 7:323b
Kontsovka, **7:293a**, 7:293a (*illus.*)
Kontsy, 9:194b, 195a
Konya. *See* Ikonion
Koppány (Hungarian pagan lord), 11:479a
Stephen I of Hungary and, 11:478a
Koran, **7:293a–298a**
against usury, 12:339b
anthropomorphism in, 6:583a, 583b
Arabic language of, 1:583a, 7:294b
Arabic rhetoric and, 10:345a
art and, 6:403a, 404a, 592b–593a
Ascension of the Prophet, 1:581a-b
attitude toward clothing in, 3:616a
on the Battle of Badr, 2:43a
blood money, 2:276b, 8:525b
calligraphy, 3:52a-b
in *kūfī* script, 7:308b (*illus.*)
naskhī script in, 9:65a (*illus.*)
chronology of, 7:295b–296b
codification of, 6:45b
on commerce, 12:107a
concubinage and, 3:527a
creation controversy, 6:89a-b, 12:244a-b
criticism of merchants, 8:522b
development of, 7:293b–294a
earlier prophets
Abraham, 8:523b, 525b
punishment stories, 8:523a-b
early format of, 8:98a
"Enjoin the good and forbid the evil," 8:526a
eternality of, 6:205b–206a
fasting and, during Ramadan, 10:254a–255a
first written copy of, 7:294a-b
foods prohibited by, 4:177b–179b
on Friday noon service, 7:617b
games and, 5:353a
gharīb al-Qurᵓān, 4:442a
Ḥafṣ, 7:294b
herbs depicted in, 6:184b–185a
in Ibn al-Nadīm's *Al-Fihrist,* 9:51b
illumination of, 8:112b–115a
Egyptian, 3:53 (*illus.*)
finispiece (copied by Aḥmad al-Anṣārī al-Matatabbib), 8:114 (*illus.*)
suras 38-39 (8th to 9th century), 8:113 (*illus.*)
under the Mamluk dynasty, 8:70a
on inheritance, 6:452b–454a, 8:525b
interpretation of, 7:296b–297a, 9:568b–569a
Islamic law and, 11:218a, 219a, 219b
Islamic mysticism and, 9:38b–39a
jinn in, 7:112b
Kufan, 7:294b
lecterns, *See Kursī; Rahle*
as legal "root," 6:581b
lex talionis, 8:525b
on magic, 8:20b–21a
on marriage, 4:597a, 597b, 8:525b
Medinan passages in, 7:295a-b
on metamorphosis of humans into animals, 8:22a
mirror of princes and, 8:435b
monotheism in, 8:523a
Muḥammad and, 7:293b–294a
music and, 8:559b
Muᶜtazilī doctrine and, 1:583b–584a, 6:583a-b, 8:655b–656a
oldest parts of, 7:295a
origins of, 7:293b
on Paradise, 9:392b
people of the book and, 9:497a
perfume and, 2:147a
prohibition of luxuries and, 11:507b–508a
prohibition of wine and, 2:208b–209a
as propaganda, 10:142b
Quraysh scholarship and the, 10:242a
recensions of, 7:294a
recitation from, 7:617b, 618a-b
on resurrection, 10:340b–341a
revelation of, 10:253a
Night of Power, 10:254b
revelations of Muḥammad, 8:522b
against Jews and Christians, 8:525a-b
rewriting by al-Ḥajjāj, 6:72b
ṣadaqa, 6:290a
on slavery, 11:330b–331a
structure of, 6:577b–578a
Sufism and, 6:584b
suras of, 7:294b–295b
text of, 6:578a-b
theology of, 6:578b–579b
translations of, 6:210b, 7:297a, 9:510b
by Hermann von Carinthia and Robert of Ketton, 12:138a
by Robert of Ketton, 11:379b
into Latin, 3:356b
ᶜUmar II ibn ᶜAbd al-ᶜAzīz's defense of divine preordination, 12:261b
on the unity of God, 9:568a, 569a
uses of, 6:578b
versions of, 7:294b
on worship (*ṣalāt*), 7:616a
zarābiyya, 10:547b
see also Allah; *Āyāt al-kursī;* Islamic law
Koranda, Wenceslas, 6:375a
Korčekᶜ, 1:472b
Korčula Codex, 11:670b
Kořikos, **7:298a-b**, 7:546b
Armenian inscriptions, 7:298b
Koriwn, **7:298b–299a**
on the Armenian Bible, 2:217a
birthplace of, 7:298b
David the Invincible and, 4:114a
Life of Maštocᶜ, 1:492a, 508a, 518b, 7:226b, 298b–299a
historical facts, 6:238b
style, 6:238b
on Mamikonean *sparapets,* 11:460b
on St. Sahak, 1:498b, 518b
Kormákr Ǫgmundarson, 7:299a
lausavísa and, 7:387b
Kormáks saga, 4:612b, **7:299a–300a**
dating of, 7:299a
poetry in, 7:299a-b
preservation of, 7:299a-b
Skáldatal and, 11:316a
Tristan story and, 7:299b
Kormchaya kniga (Pilot's book), 7:506b, 507b
Korone. *See* Coron
Korova, Loggin, 8:573b
Korseke, 7:324 (*illus.*), 325a
Korykos. *See* Kořikos
Köse Dağ (Kösedagh), Battle of (1243), 1:241b, 11:154b, 157b
Kosmas of Maïuma, as author of *kanōnes,* 7:613a
Kosovo, 11:473a
Kosovo, Battle of (1389), 7:529a, 10:514b, 11:180a, 181a-b, 346a
Kostandin the Armenian. *See* Constantine the Armenian
Köszegi family, 6:343a
Koszyce, Charter of (1374), 9:727a
Kota. *See* Kutᶜaisi
Kotatission. *See* Kutᶜaisi
Kotor
possible Romanesque workshop at, 11:184a
see also Serbia
Kotzenmäre, Das, **7:300a-b**
influences on, 7:300b
Koukoulion, 6:378b, 7:292b

Koukouzeles, Joannes, *Akolouthiai,* 8:555b, 556a
Koumbarion, 11:232a
Koumiss, 2:209b
Kouphisma, 8:617a, 617b
Kovrat, Bulgar leader, 2:399a-b
Kozan. *See* Sīs
Kozma the Presbyter, 11:345b
Krafft, Adam, **7:300b**
  Entombment, 7:300b
  self-portrait from Nuremberg, 7:301 (*illus.*)
  "Seven Falls of Christ" in Nuremberg, 11:467b
  Stations of the Cross, 7:300b
Kragehul bog deposit, 10:689b
Krak des Chevaliers, **7:302a-b**, 7:302 (*illus.*), 10:489b
  Baybars and, 2:138b
Krak de Montreal, 4:22b
Kraków (Cracow), 9:720a, 722b, 728b, 729b
  colleges, 12:294a-b
  Jagiellonian University, 12:289b
  smelting in, 9:728b
  works by Veit Stoss, 11:487a
Kranc, Klaus, 8:357a
Kraut, Georg
  De passionibus mulierum, 12:214a-b
  see also Trota and *Trotula*
Krebs, Johan, 9:123a
Krebs, Niclas. *See* Nicholas of Cusa
Kremlin. *See* Moscow Kremlin
Kresimir II of Croatia, king, recapture of western Bosnia, 4:5a
Kresimir III of Croatia, king, 4:5b
Kresimir IV of Croatia, king, 4:6a, 6b
  Dalmatia and, 4:79b
Kress, Hans Wilhelm, Wolfram von Eschenbach and, 12:673b
Kreuziger, Der. See Johannes von Frankenstein
Kreuzlied. See Walther von der Vogelweide
Krewo, Treaty of (1385), 7:606b–607a, 9:725b
Kriemhild (epic character), 9:112b, 113a, 113b, 114b, 115a
Krim Giray, khan of Crimea, 3:679a
  Ukrainian expedition, 3:679b
Kringla, 11:316a
Kristni saga, **7:302b–303b**
  attributed to Sturla Þórðarson, 11:496a
Kristni þáttr, Njáls saga and, 9:145b
Kritovoulos, Michael, **7:303a-b**
  Histories, 6:248a
Krivichians, in Russian *Primary Chronicle,* 12:434b
Króksfjarðarbók, 11:498a
Kronidēs (hermit), 1:519b
Kruismes, 11:550a (*illus.*)
Krum of Bulgaria, khan, **7:303b–304a**
  conquest of Mesembria, 8:279b
  reign of, 2:401a-b
  Serdica and, 11:189a
  vs. Nikephoros I, 9:132b
  see also Leo V (the Armenian), Byzantine emperor
Kruševac, 11:188a
Kuabtaqev, martyrs of, 5:414a
Kūba, 8:610b (*illus.*), 613a
Kuber quadratorum. See Fibonacci, Leonardo
Kublai Khan
  Marco Polo's service to, 10:27b
  Möngke Temür and, 5:573a
Küchlüg, 5:382b
  attack on Buzar of Almaliq, 8:466a
  rule of Qara Qitai, 8:466a-b
Kudanbes of Nubia, king, 3:315a
Kudrun, **7:304a–305b**
  compared with *Biterolf und Dietlieb,* 2:253a
  Dukus Horant and, 4:304b, 305a
  Nibelungenlied and, 7:305a
  plot of, 7:304a-b
  provenance of, 7:304a
  sources for, 7:304b–305a
  version of *Hjaðningavíg* in, 6:267b–268a
Kuene, Konrad, **7:305b–306a**
Kufa, al-, **7:306a–308b**
  Abbasid rule, 8:165b
  administrative center of al-Manṣūr, 2:45a
  Alids established in (815), 8:80a
  architecture of, 6:595a-b
  decline of, 6:512b
  demilitarized, 7:307a
  factionalism in, 6:511b
  founded, 6:511a, 7:306a
  Ḥusayn in, 6:370a-b
  as Islamic center, 6:570a
  Qarmatians in, 6:615b
  rulers of, 7:307b–308a
  Shī^{c}a and, 11:136a, 137b, 226b
  as supporter of the Alids, 2:45a
Kūfī (Arabic script), 1:209b–210b (*illus.*), **7:308b** (*illus.*)
  in Auvergnat architecture, 10:480b
  development of, 9:333b
  in Fatimid *ṭirāz,* 12:61 (*illus.*)
  inscriptions at Karatay madrasa at Ikonion, 11:149a
  see also Naskhī
Kufic script. *See Kūfī* (Arabic script)
Kuhn, Hugo, 8:414a
Kulaynī, 6:587a
Kulikovo Pole, Battle of (1380), 4:232b, 7:606b
Kulin, **7:309a**
Kulliyyāt, al-. See Rushd, Ibn
Kulthūm ibn ^{c}Iyāḍ, defeat by Muslim Berbers, 12:552a
Kūm Ashqūh. *See* Aphrodito
Kümbet. See Gunbadh
Kunegund of Germany, empress, seal of, 11:126a
Künhilt, 7:285a
Kunhutina modlitba, 11:343b
Kūnī, 6:615a
Kunigunde, St., canonization of, 3:68b
Kunstbüchlein, 11:649a-b
Kur
  Hohenstaufen period, 4:427a-b
  princes' rights, 4:428a-b
  Salian period, 4:27a
Kura (Kur) River, 1:470b, **7:309a-b**
  as border of Georgia, 5:402b
  Georgian tribes near, 5:419a
  Vanand and, 12:353b
Ḳuraysh. *See* Quraysh
Kurdābih, Ibn. *See* Khurdādhbih, Ibn
Kurdish language, 6:309b–310a
Kurdistan
  founded, 7:310a
  see also Uzun Ḥasan
Kurds, **7:309b–311a**
  vs. Daylamites, in Armenia, 1:513b
  Xlat^{c} and, 12:713b
  see also Ayyubids; Hakkāri Kurds
Küregen (title of Timurid rulers), 12:58b
Kūrgā, 8:613a
Kurish pirates, 2:62b
Kurland, 2:63 (map)
  descriptions of
    by Adam of Bremen, 2:62a
    by St. Rimbert, 2:62b
    by *Vita sancti Anscharii,* 2:62b
  Viking settlements in, 2:62b
Kurland (electoral principality), 5:492b
Kürnberger, Der. *See* Der von Kürenberg
Kurraj. See Hobby horse
Kurs, 2:62b, 65a, 67b
Kursan, "king" of the Magyars, 6:338b
Kurseyā$^{\supset}$*. See Kursī*
Kursī, **7:311a**
  Koran lectern *kursī miṣḥaf,* 10:250 (*illus.*)
Kūs, 8:613a
Kush, Nubia and, 9:197b
Kushan Empire, Parthians and, 9:443b
Kūshyār ibn Labbān, 1:383a, 384b, 385b, 386a
Kusti (in Zoroastrianism), 10:663a, 664a
Kut^{c}aisi (Kutaisi), **7:311a-b**
Kutāma Berbers
  Ismailism and, 6:615b
  see also Berbers
Kut^{c}at^{c}isi, 5:402b
Kutná Hora
  Benedict Ried and, 10:399a
  Church of St. Barbara, Johannes II Parler and, 9:421b
  silver mines of, 2:300a, 8:400 (*illus.*)
Kutná Hora Decree (1409), 6:367b
Kutná Hora Gradual, 8:400 (*illus.*), 403b
Kutubīya Mosque (Marrakech)
  first, 1:191b, 197b
  minaret, 8:151a
  orientation, 8:11b, 151a
  second, 1:191b–192b (*illus.*)
Kuvrat, khan. *See* Qubrat, khan
Kuwītra, 8:611a
Kuzari. See Judah Halevi
Kvasir, 11:29b
  mead of poetry made from blood of, 11:29b–30a, 30b–31a
  Mímir and, 8:395b
Kvirike Baneli, bishop of Bana, 2:70a
Kviða, origin of, 4:389a-b
Kviðuháttr (meter), 11:320a
  in *Merlínússpá,* 8:276a
  in *Ynglingatal,* 12:726a
Kvæðium Hrómund Gripsson, 6:312a
Kyburg dynasty, 11:539b, 540a
  Rudolph of Habsburg and, 11:541b
Kydones, 4:135b

Kyeser, Konrad, 3:65b (*illus.*)
Bellifortis, 1:318a, 11:645b–646a (*illus.*)
illustrations of crossbow spanner, 11:658b
magical themes, 11:646a
Kyllēnē. *See* Glarentsa
Kyng Alisaunder, Roman de toute chevalerie and, 10:453a
Kyng Orfew. See Sir Orfeo
Kynyngham, John, friar, vs. John Wyclif, 12:709b
Kyot the Provençal, Wolfram von Eschenbach and, 12:677b, 679b
Kyriale, **7:312a-b**, 9:688b
Franciscan Gradual, 8:200a
see also Mass cycles; Plainsong
Kyrie, **7:312b–313b**
in *aitesis,* 7:589b
at the Exaltation of the Cross, 7:590a-b
in Gallican rite, 7:593b
in Greater Litany, 7:588b
in hymns and secular songs, 7:593b
in the liturgy of the Mass, 8:185b–186a
melodies for, 7:312b–313a
in Milanese rite, 7:593b
in *Ordines romani,* 7:593b
in Roman Mass, 8:185b–186a
Sarum chant, 10:654b
in *synapte,* 7:589a
Tropes to the Ordinary of the Mass and, 12:209a, 210a
in the West, first evidence of, 7:590b–591a
see also Litany, in the West
Kyrie prosulae, 7:313a
Kyros. *See* Kura River
Kyssegyrlan Uuched, 12:601a
Kytaia. *See* Kut^{c}aisi
Kyteler, Alice, dame, 12:663a

L

La. See next element in title
La Cava (monastery: Italy), Normans and, 11:266a
La Fontaine, Jean de, fabliau and, 4:577a
Lā ilāha ill' allāh, in ^{c}Ayn al-Quḍāt's interpretation, 9:42a
La Mancha, transhumance and, 8:280a
La Rochelle, Battle of (1372), 6:333a
La Roë, Robert d'Arbrissel's community at, 10:429a, 429b
La Sale, Antoine de
Cent nouvelles nouvelles, 3:235a
false attribution to, 10:240a
Petit Jehan de Saintré, 4:577a, 5:272a, 12:162b
plot summary, 5:275b–276a
role of author/narrator, 5:276a
use of irony, 5:276a
Réconfort de Madame de Fresne, 5:275b
La Tène culture, 10:458a, 467a
artistic tradition of, 3:219a
Celtic language in, 3:232b
Táin bó Cúailnge and, 11:580a
Labarum, **7:313b–314a**
Labers ton. See Hadamar von Laber
Labor, corvées, 3:612b–613b
Labor, child. *See* Children, as laborers
Labor, tenant. *See* Tenant labor
Laborers, Ordinance of (1349), 9:480a
Laborers, Second Statute of (1388), 7:331a
Laborers, Statute of (1351), 7:455b, 9:480a, 11:468b
increased urban immigration following, 6:18a
Laborintus. See Evrard the German
Labourd, history of, 2:126b
Labrador, discovery of, 4:555a
Laccadive Islands, shipbuilding and, 11:246a
Lacertine, **7:314a**
Lacnunga, 1:286a
Laconia, Villehardouin and, 7:378a
Lactantius
De ave phoenice, 7:360b
metrical adaptation in Old English, 1:280b
on millennialism, 8:385a
Lactatio, 3:587a, 590b, **7:314b–315a**
Lacy, Hugh de, monastic foundation at Clonard, 3:466a
Ladder of Paradise. See John Klimakos, St.
Lade, earls of, 4:570a-b
Lādhiqī, al-, 8:566b
Lādhiqiya, al-, **7:315a–316a**
in crusades, 7:315b
earthquakes, 7:315b
origins of, 7:315a
significance for Mediterranean trade, 7:315b–316a
Tancred and, 11:589b
under Muslim rule, 7:315a-b
Ladin (Ladino) language. *See* Judeo-Spanish language
Ladislas I of Hungary, king
defeated by Ottomans at Varna, 12:361a
reign of, 6:340a
see also Władysław III of Poland, king
Ladislas II of Hungary, king, 6:340b
reign of, 6:349a
Ladislas IV ("the Cuman") of Hungary, king, reign of, 6:342b–343a
Ladislas V of Hungary, king, 2:8b, 9a, 5:489b, 6:347b, 348a
coronation of, 11:483b
gift to the French queen, 12:378a
Hunyadi and, 6:364a
Ladislas of Durazzo, Rome and, 10:524b
Ladislas of Naples, king, 11:273a
conquest of Rome and Umbria, 7:9b–10a
Dalmatia and, 4:80a, 6:346a
threat to Rome, 3:647b
vs. Wenceslas IV, 6:368b
Ladle, Eucharistic rite. *See* Trulla
Lady Chapel, 3:264a
Lady of the Fountain, The, 1:566b, 12:611a
Lady Mass, in Wolfenbüttel MS, 12:670b, 671b
Lady with the Unicorn (tapestry), 5:365a, 11:596b
Laetentur coeli. See Ferrara-Florence, Council of
Laethem, Livinus van. *See* Lathem, Liévin van
Lagny, fairs, 4:590b
Lagos, Gil Eanes de, 4:561a
Lagoudera Master, wall paintings of, 2:445b
Lagsaga (Scandinavian administrative unit), 10:699b
Lai d'amours. See Beaumanoir, Philippe de
"Lai d'Aristote." *See* Henri d'Andeli
Lai du chievrefeuil. See Marie de France
Lai du cor, Le, 1:268a, **7:317b–319a**
Lai del Desiré, Le, 1:268a-b, **7:317b**
Lai, Breton, 1:567b–568b
Lai de Lanval, 1:568a
Lai, lay, **7:316a–317b**
in Anglo-Norman literature, 1:268a-b
in *Ars nova,* 1:552b
Arthurian, 1:568a
Breton, 1:567b–568b, 7:317a
"courtly" style, 7:317a
English, 1:568b
French, 1:568a-b
of Guillaume de Machaut, 8:6a
Lai du chievrefeuil, 12:201a, 202b
lyrical, 7:316a–317a
of Marie de France, 1:568a-b
narrative, 7:317a
origin of, 8:136b
planctus and, 9:693a-b
sequence and, 8:571a
see also Nouvelle; *Strengleikar;* Thibaut IV of Champagne, count
Lai de l'ombre. See Renart, Jean
Lai lyrique, 4:164a
Laíd (*laoidh*), 6:549a
Laidh, lai and, 7:316a
Laigin, vs. Eóganacht, 4:493a
Lailat-al-qadr, See Ramadan
Lais. See Marie de France
Lais, Le. See Villon, François
Laisse, **7:319a-b**
in *chansons de geste,* 3:261a-b
variation of, 5:240b
Laity
in cloister, 3:465a
in Latin church, 3:358a–360a
Lajvard, **7:319b–320a** (*illus.*)
Lajvardina ware, 3:240a, 7:319b–320a
Lakhmids, **7:320a–321a**
decline of power, 10:667a
Ghassanids and, 5:515a
Nestorian, 6:575b
Persia, 10:464a
Xusrō II and, 12:715b
Lamb of God. *See* Agnus Dei
Lambert of Auxerre, *Summa,* 4:170b
Lambert de Guines, bishop of Arras, travels of, 12:155a-b

Lambert of Hersfeld, **7:321a-b**
Annals of Hersfeld, 7:321a-b
Carmen de bello saxonico attributed to, 3:97a
Lambert (Laurent) of St. Omer, 1:317b
Liber floridus, 4:448a-b
Lambert "le Bègue," 2:158b
Lambertazzi family, 6:658a
Lambertus, Magister, 11:363a, 365a, 365b
notation treatise of, 1:545a
Quatuor principalia musice and, 8:646b
Tractatus de musica, 8:643b
on organs, 9:275a
use of *perfectio,* 9:504b
Lambesc, inns in, 6:468b
Lambespringe, Bartholomew, **7:321b–322a**
Lambeth Bible, 1:258a, 8:108a
Lambeth, Council of (1222), 3:578b
Lambeth, Council of (1281), 10:300b
Lambeth Psalter, 4:548b
Lambkárr Þorgilsson
Prestssaga Guðmundar góða, 6:33b, 34b
in *Sturlunga saga,* 11:497b, 498b–499a
Lambron, **7:322a**
Lambuleti, Johannes, Sorbonne Mass, 8:198b
Lamellar armor. *See* Arms and armor
Lament, in troubadour poetry. *See* Sirventes, *planh*
"Lament for the Makaris." *See* Dunbar, William
"Lament of the Old Woman of Beare," 6:529a-b, 530b
Lamentation, **7:322a-b**
in Byzantine folklore, 8:19b
in *Carmina burana,* 3:98a
Lamentation on the Holy Cathedral of Vałaršapat. See Orbēlean, Step^c^anos
Lamentations of Matheolus, The, antifeminism in, 1:323b
Laments, public, in Carolingian Latin poetry, 3:100b
Lammas Day, 5:36b
Lamp of the Darkness and Explanation of the Services. See Šams ar-Ri^ɔ^āsa Abu 'l-Barakāt ibn Kibr
Lamprecht, 5:450a, **7:322b–323a**
Alexander, 1:150a, 7:323a
relation to *Eneide,* 6:144b
Tobias, 2:228a, 7:322b
Lamprecht von Regensburg, adaptation of Thomas of Celano's *Life of St. Francis,* 8:354b
Lamps
glass, 5:545b (*illus.*), 546a
Western European, 5:557b (*illus.*), 560b–561a
see also Lighting devices
Lamtūna, 1:198b
Lancastrian party, formation of, 12:570b
Lance, **7:323b–325b**, 7:324 (*illus.*)
infantry, 7:323b
knightly, 7:323b
shock tactics, 12:557b, 564b
Lance, Holy. *See* Holy Lance
Lance rest, 1:528b, 534a (*illus.*), 3:206a
Lance (unit of measure), 3:206b, 12:588b
Lancelot
in Vulgate cycle, 1:571a
see also Arthurian legend; Chrétien de Troyes, *Conte du Graal; Prose Lancelot*
Lancelot (Arthurian character), 8:224b
in Thomas Malory's *Morte Darthur,* 8:63a, 63b, 64a, 64b, 65a
Lancet arch. *See* Arch
Lancet window, **7:325b**
see also Tracery
Lancia, Constance, 7:127b
Land
clearing of, 4:140b
serfdom and, 11:206a
conveyances, as demographic evidence, 4:138b
division of, 3:414b–415a, 424a-b
see also Gavelkind
grant of, Islamic. *See Iqṭā^c^*
inheritance of, 6:459a
see also Entail
lease of, 4:512a–513a, 514b
as means of production, 3:420b
regulation of, 11:679a
revenues
Byzantine Empire, 11:603b
epibolé and, 4:495b
escheat and, 4:509a-b
Land charters, Russia, 11:190b–191a
Land of Cockaygne, 8:316b
Land reclamation and uses. *See* Reclamation of land
Land registers, Russia, 11:196b–197a, 198a, 198b
Land (Scandinavian administrative unit), 10:699b
Land tax, Islamic, 6:589b, 11:625b, 626a, 667b
Copts affected by, 3:594b
see also Tenure of land, Islamic
Land tenure. *See* Tenure of land
Land use
Byzantium, dispersal of houses, 1:79a
Islamic world, overcultivation, 1:105a
Land of Women. *See* Tír na mBan
Landes- und Hochschulbibliothek Darmstadt, 7:219b
Landesherrschaft, 5:490a-b
Landesordnung, 5:490b
Landfreide, 5:500b
Landini cadence. *See* Cadence (music), Landini
Landini, Francesco, **7:325b–327a**, 8:646a
development of ballata and, 2:61a
in Faenza Codex, 4:580a
as Francisco delgli orghany, 7:326a
Gram piant' agl'ochi, 7:327a
Italian trecento music and, 12:180a
madrigal and, 6:654b
Musica son, 7:326b
Landino, Christopher, on Vergil, 12:395a
Landnámabók, 4:554b, **7:327b–328a**, 9:175b, 11:497a
on discovery of Iceland, 12:426b
Eyrbyggja saga and, 4:568a
Grímr loðinkinni in, 5:677b
historical importance, 7:327b
Icelandic saga and, 4:618a
Laxdœla saga and, 7:528a
Njáls saga and, 9:146a
on oaths, 9:146a
as source for *Víglundar saga,* 12:416b
Starkaðr in, 5:368b
Svarfdæla saga and, 11:521a
Vatnsdœla saga and, 12:363b
versions of, 7:327b–328a
on Viking navigation, 12:420a, 420b
see also Haukr Erlendsson; Sturla Þórðarson
Landolfus Sagax, **7:328a**
Historia romana, 7:328a
Landrecht, 10:603a
Landriani of Lodi, bishop, discovery of Cicero's *De oratore* and, 10:363b
Landscape design. *See* Gardens; Irrigation; Reclamation of land
Landscape painting, disappearance in early Christian era, 4:348b
Landshut, founded, 2:135a
Landslag. See Swedish law
Landtage. See Representative assemblies, German principality
Landulf II of Milan, archbishop, 12:464a
uprising against, 8:378a
Landulf of Benevento, in a miniature from Landulf Pontifical, 12:402 (*illus.*)
Lanfranc of Bec, archbishop of Canterbury, 2:173b, 3:82b, 7:199b, **7:328b**, 7:328b (*illus.*)
Berengar and, 2:188a
contributions to English culture, 4:466b
dialectic and, 4:169b
as exegete, 2:213a, 4:543a
Liber de corpore et sanguine Domini, 4:169b
on liturgical vestments, 12:401a
reform of archbishopric, 4:466a
on transubstantiation, 9:587b
Vulgate and, 12:495b–496a
writ from William I, 7:435b
Wulfstan of Worcester and, 12:703b
Lanfranc of Milan, *Cirugía menor,* 11:441b
Lanfranc of Modena, **7:329a**
Lanfranchi, Guido, *Chirugia magna,* 11:692a
"Langarian" language. *See* Latin language, in Hungary
Langland, William, 1:186a, **7:329a–337b**
Disticha Catonis and, 7:360a
Piers Plowman, 8:318b–319b, 332a, 332b, 9:679a, 12:477a
alliteration in, 8:343a
authorship, 7:329a, 330a–331a
on the Black Death, 2:265b
characterization of Icelandic *rímur* and, 10:401b
contents of, 8:319a
date, 7:331a
exegesis and, 4:545b
indulgences and, 6:450b

Langland, William (*cont.*)
Piers Plowman (cont.)
Meed, Lady (allegorical character), 7:330b, 331a, 332a–333a
prophecies in, 10:149a
Robin Hood and, 10:425a, 436a, 437a
synopsis, 7:331a–337a
use of "Lollard" in, 7:645a
versions, 7:329b
Langlois, Jean, **7:337b**
Langmann, Adelheid, *Offenbarungen,* 9:13a
Langobard language, Italo-Romance and, 6:623b
Langobards. *See* Lombards
Langton, Stephen, archbishop of Canterbury, **7:337b–338b**
Andrew of St. Victor's theology school and, 12:21b–22a
election as archbishop of Canterbury, 3:83b, 94b, 265b, 4:423a, 468b
as exegete, 4:544a
Hebrew language study, 3:313b
Hebrew-Latin vocabulary, 2:213b
Innocent III and, 6:464b
John of England and, 4:469a, 7:130a-b, 338a
Magna Carta and, 7:338a-b
on penance, 6:449a
Questiones, 7:337b–338a
summoned Council of Lambeth (1222), 3:578b
suspension of, 3:640a
training of, 10:76b
"Veni sancte spiritus," 6:382a
Language of the Birds, The. See ᶜAṭṭār, Farīd
Language training. *See* Grammar; Translation and translators
Langue d'oc. See Provençal language
Langue d'oïl. See French language
Langue-de-boeuf. See Ox-tongue partisan (pole arm)
Languedoc, **7:338b–342a**, 7:340 (map)
administration of
office of bailli, 2:53a-b
Peace of God and, 9:475a
annexation by France, opposition to, 5:168b–169a
assassination of Peter of Castelnau, 10:174a
Cathars in
crusade against, 10:174a
emergence of, 10:173b
decline of troubadour poetry in, 10:173a–178b
derivation of name, 10:159b
Dominican and Franciscan Inquisitions in, 10:174a-b
economic development, 7:339b
Estates-General, 7:341a, 341b
fairs, 4:586a, 7:339b
incorporation into French kingdom, 10:174b
inquest in, 6:479b
inquisition in, 6:485a
interference by northerners, 10:174a
Languedoil and, separated estates of, 10:318b, 323b–324a
legal system, 7:464a-b
Montpellier, 7:463a-b, 464b–465b, 467a-b
papal "imperialism" in, 10:173b–174a
Parlement of Paris and, 9:419a
provincial estates and assemblies, 10:319b–320a, 322a, 324a-b
deputies apportionment, 10:324b
Raymond VII and anti-French alliance, 10:174b
taxation policy, 11:622a, 622b, 623a, 623b
équivalent, 11:624a
villages of, 12:443b
wars of princes in, 10:174a
see also French law, in south; Midi; Provence; Provençal language; Provençal literature; Toulouse
Languedocian rite. *See* Narbonne rite
Languedoil
Languedoc and, separated estates of, 10:318b, 323b–324a
provincial estates and assemblies, 10:316a, 318b–319a, 320a, 321b, 322b
taxation policy, 11:622a, 623b
L'Anse aux Meadows (Newfoundland), Viking settlement at, 12:429a
Lanseloet van Denemarken, 4:321a-b
Lantbert of Deutz, **7:342a**
Vita Heriberti, 7:342a
Lantern tower, 10:487b
Lantern transept. *See* Transept
Lantfird, Alamannic duke, vs. Charles Martel, 11:526b
Lantfred, *Life of St. Swithin,* Wulfstan of Winchester and, 7:363a
Lanval. See Marie de France
Lanx, **7:342a**
Lanzarote, 3:61b, 62a-b
Lanzelet. See Ulrich von Zazikhoven
Lanzone de Corte, 8:378a
Laodicea. *See* Lādhiqiya, al-
Laodicea, Council of (*ca.* 360), cantor and, 3:87b
Laoidh. See Laíd
Laoithe (ballads). *See* Fenian poetry
Laon Cathedral, 2:125a, 3:565a
drapery at, 5:620a
facade, 11:257a
Gothic architecture in, 5:587b (*illus.*)
sexpartite vaults in, 12:366a
Laon gradual. *See* Gradual; Plainsong
Laonikas Chalkokondyles. *See* Chalkokondyles, Laonikas
Lapapu, 8:562a
Lapidaire chrétien, 5:281a
Lapidario. See Alfonso X (the Learned) of Castile and León, king
Lapidarium, **7:342b**
Anglo-Norman, 5:281a
origin of, 5:281a
Lapis lazuli, *see also* Lajvard
Lappish language, 6:440b
Lapsit exillis, 12:678a
Laqabi ware, **7:342b–343a**, 7:343a (*illus.*)
L'Aquila, founding of, 12:325b–326a
Lärbro tower in Gotland (Sweden), 3:235a
Large, Robert, Caxton and, 3:210a
Largess. *See* Virtues and vices
Larissa, Battle of (1083), 10:433a
Las Casas, Bartolomeo de, *History of the Indies,* 4:560a
Las Huelgas MS. *See* Huelgas MS, Las
Las Navas de Tolosa, Battle of (1212), 1:195a, 3:75a, 76b, 133b, 9:70b, 10:44a, 11:377a, 378a, 383b
Order of Calatrava and, 3:16b–17a
"Lascia vorria lo mondo e Dio servire." *See* Compiuta Donzella of Florence
Lashkari Bāzār, Ghaznavid palace at, 4:569b, 5:519a-b, 6:603a
Laskarids, **7:343a-b**
continuity of Byzantine culture and, 4:345a
expansionism of, 2:498a-b
Laskaris, Constantine, 4:48a, 7:343b, 11:52a
Laskaris, John. *See* John IV Laskaris, emperor of Nicaea
Laskaris, Theodore, 4:48a
Lassus, Jean-Bapiste, Notre Dame de Paris and, 9:191b
Last Judgment
altarpiece by Tilman Riemenschneider, 10:399 (*illus.*)
depicted in German plays, 4:268b–269a
fresco by Cavallini, 3:198b (*illus.*)
in mystery plays, 8:657a, 660a, 662a
Sibylline oracles and, 11:257a
Last rites. *See* Death and burial; Extreme unction
Last Supper (play), 8:661a
Last Supper, The, **7:343b–344a**
in art, Tremussen chalice, 9:130 (*illus.*)
Last (unit of measure), **7:343b**
English, standards for, 12:586a
French, 12:586a
László I of Hungary, king. *See* Ladislas I of Hungary, king
László V Posthumus. *See* Ladislas V of Hungary, king
Latāᵓif al hikme. See Ewrān, Akhī
Latakia. *See* Lādhiqiya, al-
Lateen sail, **7:344a-b**, 9:85b, 11:230a
Amalfi and, 11:233a
in caravel, 11:237a
in carrack, 11:237a
in dhow, 11:248a
in full-rigged ships, 11:244b
in galley, 11:233b
in Muslim ships, 9:77a
used on cogs, 9:83b
"Later Cambridge Songs," 7:368b
Lateran (basilica: Rome), 4:332b–333a, **7:344b–345a**, 10:112b, 517a, 518a-b, 523a
Constantine's design for, 4:335a
Donation of Constantine and, 4:258a, 258b
furnishings for, 4:361a
importance in papal elections, 3:603b
Leonine City and, 10:520a
monasteries and, 10:519b
Monte Cassino and, 10:505a
papal chancellor and, 10:522b

see also Vassallettus
Lateran Councils
First (1123)
calling of, 3:352a
church reform and, 3:636b
married clergy and, 3:217a-b
Second (1139)
banning of crossbow, 11:658a
condemnation of dualism, 4:297b
excommunication, 3:445a
Gratian at, 5:656b
marked end of Schism of 1130, 3:637a-b
married clergy and, 3:217b
on usurers, 12:336a
Third (1179), 3:94b, 12:509b
Alexander III and, 3:638b
Basques and Navarrese and, 2:126b
canon law and, 7:415a-b
Cathars condemned at, 3:187a
church taxation and, 11:608b
decrees of, 3:638a-b
ecclesiastical election, 4:422a
heretics as violators of the Peace of God, 9:475a
importance of, 3:638a
indulgences and, 6:448b
interdictions of clergy at, 3:444b
on lepers, 7:550b
right of presentation and, 6:481b
on stipends for teaching masters, 10:79b
on tithes, 12:63b
on usurers, 12:337a
Fourth (1215), 1:223b, 263a, 12:145a
Berceo and, 2:187b
on canon law, 7:416a
canonization and, 3:68b
church taxation and, 11:607a
condemnation of dualism, 4:297b
confession required by, 3:533b, 6:449b
consanguinity rules changed by, 3:540a
Der Stricker and, 11:493b
Dominican ministry and, 4:248b
on Easter rites, 4:367b
extension of tithe obligation to Jews, 12:64b
Firmiter credimus, 3:640b
grammar schools mandatory for cathedrals, 11:64a
importance of, 3:641a
"In singulis regnis," 2:175b
indulgences and, 6:448b, 449a
Innocent III and, 6:465a, 465b
interdict and, 3:444b, 6:495b
Jeremiah the Maronite and, 11:564a
Joachim of Fiore and, condemnation of, 7:113b–114a
Johannes Teutonicus' commentary on, 7:122a
on the keeping of hosts, 1:223b
laity and, 3:359a
Langton at, 7:338b
lay taxation and, 11:608b
legal decisions of, 3:640a-b
Maronites at, 7:532b
marriage and, 3:217b, 4:610a, 610b
on non-Christian costume, 3:620b
occasion for, 3:639b
Omnis utriusque sexus fidelis, 1:263a
on ordeals and duels, 6:479a, 7:182b–183a, 503a, 9:207a
on penance, 9:491b
penitential manuals, 8:87a, 8:316b
on Peter Lombard's teaching, 9:517b
on preaching, 6:663b, 10:76b
reform constitutions and decrees, 3:640b–641a
religious poetry and, 6:661b
requirements for new religious orders, 5:196b
on reservation of the sacrament, 10:335b
sessions of, 3:640a
on stipends for teaching masters, 10:79b
supreme reality, acceptance of, 9:598b–599a
on surgery, 8:253a
taverns and, 12:651a
Thomasin von Zerclaere and, 12:37a
on tithe revenues, 12:63a
Toulouse and, 12:91b
on transubstantiation, 9:603b
victory over Albigensians, 4:376a
Vincentius Hispanus and, 12:456a
Wolfger von Erla at, 12:673a
Fifth (1512–1517)
conciliarism and, 3:654a–655b
epilogue to general councils, 3:643a
Pastor aeternus, 3:518b–519a
Lateran, Roman Council of (649), Maximus the Confessor's doctrine of two wills of Christ and, 8:233b
Laterani family, 7:344b
Laterculus. See Polemius Silvius
Latgalians. *See* Lettgallians
Lathe (land division). *See* Hundred (land division)
Lathem, Liévin van, **7:345b–346a**
Madonna and Child, 7:345b (*illus.*)
Latifondi, 11:683a
Latimer, William, impeachment of, 6:427a-b
Latin alphabet. *See* Alphabets, Latin
Latin Alphonsine Tables, 1:612b
Latin Averroism. *See* Aristotelianism, Averroist
Latin chant
development of polyphony and, 8:271b
melodic style of, 8:270a-b, 271a
Solesmes method of, 11:361b–362a
sources of, mass cycles, 8:199b
Latin church
administration, customary, 4:68a
architectural styles. *See* Church architecture
in Burgundy, 2:427b–428a
Byzantine Empire and, 3:334a, 355b–357a
canon law and, 3:348b–349a
in Castile, 3:133a, 139b–140a
celibacy in, 3:215b–217a
in Champagne, 3:245b–246a
church-state relations
Bohemia, 6:366b
Hungary, 6:341b–342a
Ireland, 6:516a
Wyclif on, 6:366b–367a, 368a, 372b
Cilician-Roman union, **3:394a–395b**
commemorations, 8:134a
conciliar movement and, 3:366a-b
concubinage and, 3:529b–530a, 530a-b
confession in, 3:533a–534b, 535b
confirmation in, 3:535b–536a, 536a
contraception condemned by, 3:573a-b
creeds in, 3:676a, 676b
in Croatia, 4:6a, 44b–45a
on Cyprus, 4:72b–73a
doctors of the church, 4:234a-b
Easter dating in, 3:228a-b
ecclesiastical structures of, 3:362a–367b
in England
feudalism of, 2:173b
Henry II and, 2:151b, 152b–153a
independence of ecclesiastical courts, 4:470b–471b
organization, 3:375a-b
reforms under William I, 4:465b–466a
under Richard I and John, 4:471a-b
finance
indulgences and, 6:448b
see also Papacy, income of
in France
preservation of public order by, 5:154a
under Capetians, 158b–159a
on gambling, 5:350b–351a
in Germany (843–1137), 5:477b–478a
in Greece, 7:378a, 378b
heresy and, 3:367b–371b
history, reflected in hymns, 6:383b–384a
history (to 1054), **3:343b–350b**
history (1054 to 1305), **3:350b–361a**
history (1305 to 1500), **3:361a–372a**
see also Schism, Great
in Iceland, 6:394a
ideals of chivalry and, 3:302a-b
institutional unity of Christianity and, 3:336a-b
intellectual life in, 3:357a–358a
in Ireland, 3:344a-b, 8:440a
Islam and, 3:355b–357a
Jews and, 4:564a,b
laity in, 3:358a–360a
control of property (Iceland), 6:396a, 7:386b
patronage (in Bohemia), 2:304b
proprietary churches, 2:304a, 9:412b–413a
marriage and, 3:640b, 4:608b–610b
military-religious organizations. *See* Orders of chivalry
musical instruments and, 8:600b–601a
national churches and, 3:366b–367b
in Normandy
ducal power and, 9:163a
organization of, 9:163b

Latin church (*cont.*)
organization, 3:350b–354a, 362a–367b, **3:372b–378a**
centralization of, 3:376a-b
changes in, 3:377b
chapter in, 3:265a–266a
clergy, 3:441a-b
diocese, 4:191a-b
episcopal structure of, 3:372b
feudalization of, 3:347a
geographical differences in, 3:372a
Gregorian reform and, 3:375a–376a
metropolitan clusters, 3:374a-b, 375b
monasticism and, 3:373b
parliamentary institutions in, 3:610b–611a
proprietary churches, 3:373a-b, 374b
provincial synods of, 3:578a–579b
secular, 3:372a
translation of bishops policies, 12:142b–143a
under Carolingian kings, 3:345a-b, 373b–374a
under Merovingian kings, 3:373b
see also Parish; Province, ecclesiastical
pilgrimages and, 3:360a
politics of, 3:362a–367b
in Portugal, 10:42a-b, 44b–45b, 47a-b
primacy of Petrine foundations, 3:446b
property
inheritance and, 6:454a
Italy, 10:521b
Rome, 10:525b
secularization of (in Greece), 7:378a
see also Benefice, ecclesiastical
religious orders in, 3:354a–355b
right of presentation, 10:117a–118a
Roman Empire and, 3:343b–344a
later Roman Empire, 10:461b–462b
transmission of Roman law by, 5:566a
taxation by, 11:616a-b
taxation of, 3:447b–448a
theological flowering in 5th century, 3:336a-b
union with Byzantine church
Isidore and, 6:563a-b
under Latin Empire, 7:348a-b, 349b
see also Andronikos II Palaiologos, Byzantine emperor; Andronikos III Palaiologos, Byzantine emperor
urbanism and, 5:195b–196a
in Venice, 7:380b
vs. Russian Orthodox Church, in Novgorod, 9:196b
see also Avignon papacy; Canonical hours; Cardinals, college of; Church, early; Church reform; Investiture conflict; Papacy; Papal states; Schism, Great; Schisms; Schisms, Eastern-Western church; Schools, monastic
Latin cross, 4:9b, 10 (*illus.*)
see also Cross, forms of
Latin drama
classical models for, 4:282b–283a
influences of, 4:263b–264a, 267b, 283a
Passion plays, 4:281b–282a
purpose of, 4:283a
see also Drama, liturgical
Latin Empire of Constantinople, 7:52a, **7:346a–350a**, 12:389b
Charles I of Anjou and, 11:272b
cultural life of, 7:349b
duchy of Naxos and, 9:91a-b
feudal nature of, 7:346b–347a
founded, 4:31b
John Asen II in, 7:131a
lack of native support for, 7:348b–349a
poverty of, 7:349a-b
relations with
Byzantine successor states, 7:347a–348a
Mongols, 4:556b
papacy, 7:348a
religious issues, 7:348a-b
rulers of, 7:346a-b
vs. Nicaean Empire, 9:115b
Western merchants and, 12:103b–104a
see also Baldwin I, Latin emperor of Constantinople
Latin Kingdom of Jerusalem. *See* Jerusalem, Kingdom of
Latin language, **7:350a–359a**
Armenian and, 1:507b
in Balkans, 6:443b
Carolingian effort to revive, 5:221b, 233a
in Carolingian German law, 7:478a
Castilian language and, 3:141a-b
cathedral school instruction in, 11:61a-b
Classical, 7:353a–358b, 12:494a
conservatism of, 7:351a-b
dialects of, 3:164a, 6:434b
dictamen, 4:173b–176b
direct discourse, 7:356a
early translations of the Bible, 2:211a
Eastern Orthodox Church and, 6:436a
ecclesiastical and administrative use, 6:438a-b, 440a
in Egypt, 10:455a
in England, 8:313b
grammar, 5:648b–650a, 7:355a–357a
accidence, 7:354b–355a
Alexander Neckham on, 9:92a
articles, 7:356a
conjugations, 6:622a
declensions, 6:622a, 623a
influence on *Auraicept na nÉces*, 2:2a
instrumental case, 7:356a
prepositions, 7:356a-b
Priscian on, 10:128a-b
grammar school instruction in, 11:64a-b
grammar textbooks for translators, 12:136b–137a
Hibernisms in, 6:221b, 222a
Hisperic, 3:231b
Huguccio on, 6:327b
in Hungary, 6:337b, 434a
indirect discourse, 7:355b–356a
Italian and, 6:625b, 626b–627a, 627b, 629a
in Italy, 6:443a
jubilee and, 7:156b
Late Vulgar Latin and, 12:494a
in law, Justinian's use of, 3:609a
learning of, 7:599a
liberal arts and, 4:578a-b
literacy and, 7:369b, 598a
medieval changes in, their impact on music, 10:379a
metaphor in word formation, 7:354a
Middle High German literature and, 8:348a-b
neume and, 8:624a-b
in Norman England, 1:260a
phonology
consonants, 6:622a, 7:357b
fricatives, 7:357b
vowels, 6:621b–622b, 7:357a
Portuguese language and, 10:58a
pronunciation, 7:357a-b
rhyme and, 7:372a
prose style, *see also* Cursus
purification of, 6:439a
church and, 6:440a
in Roman Empire, 6:434b–435a
Romanian and, 10:509b, 510a, 512b, 513a, 513b
Salian Frankish law and decline of, 7:472b
sermon texts in, 10:77b
in Spain, Alvarus of Córdoba on, 8:562a
spelling, 7:357b–358b
study of, 7:351b–353a, 360a
translation from Greek, 12:140a
vocabulary, 7:353a–354b
Vulgar Latin, 5:221a, 233a
word formation, 7:353b–354a
local influences, 7:354a-b
see also Hisperic Latin language; Judeo-Latin language; Neo-Latin language; Translation and translators; Vulgar Latin
Latin literature, **7:359a–371b**
allegory, 1:181a–183b
Cato's Distichs, 3:193a-b
Dares, *De excidio Troiae,* 12:220a, 221b
debate genre, 1:44a
Dictys, *Ephemeris belli Troiani,* 12:220a
early medieval, 7:360a–361b
eclogues, 9:534a
elegiac comedies, 9:314a
England, 7:363a, 364b–365a, 369b–370b
epic, 4:495b–496b, 7:361a
modern interpretation of, 7:359b
see also Eupolemius
fable, 4:572a
folk motifs, 10:569a
France, 7:363b–364a, 364b, 369b
Germany, 7:363a-b
influence on *Cantar de mío Cid,* 3:78a-b
Ireland, 7:361b
Italy, 7:363b, 369b
Latinorum penuria translation stimulus, 12:138a

letters, metrical, 9:534a
liberal arts curriculum, realism and, 10:270a
narrative poetry, 10:568b–569a
poetry, 7:361a-b
caesura, 7:372a–373a
collections, *see also Carmina burana*
elision, 7:371b, 374a
in England, 1:254b–255a
hiatus in, 7:317b, 374a
"praise of ladies" genre, 8:124a
postmedieval, 7:370b–371a
Querolus, 10:239b–240a
Rapularius, 10:258a-b
religious poetry, 7:370a
Franciscans and, 7:368b–369a
lai and, 7:316b
rhetoric, influence on German writers, 1:44b
sequence
"regular Victorine," 7:364a, 365b, 368a, 374a, 376a
rhythmical, 7:363a
Spain, 7:361b
translations of into Old English, 1:164b–167a
see also Biography, secular; Classical literary studies; Epic, Latin; Parody, Latin; Translation and translators
Latin meter, 2:4a, **7:371b–376a**
alexandrine verse and, 4:63a
cursus and, 4:66b–67b
dactylic, 7:371a, 372a–373a
elegiac couplets, 7:371b, 373b
iambic dimeter, 7:371b, 374b
Leonine rhyme, 7:372b, 373a
liturgical poetry and, 9:713a-b
nonrhyming verse and, 7:371b–372a
paroxytonic stress, 7:373b
proparoxytonic stress, 7:373b
rhyme and, 7:363a, 372a–373b
in rhymed offices, 10:372b–373a
rhythm and, 7:363a, 364a, 373b, 10:380a
sequence and, 7:375b–376a
spondee, 7:371b, 373b
trochaic septenarius, 7:371b, 374a
see also Auspicius of Toul; Goliardic verse; Sequence; Sequence, late; Tropes
Latin states in Greece, **7:376a–382a,** 7:377 (map), 10:514a
Achaea, 12:638a
Battle of Pelagonia (1259), 9:487a
Catalan Company and, 3:156a-b
Mistra, 8:446a-b
nobility of, 9:150b–151a
Villehardouin and, 12:448b
Latini, Brunetto, **7:382a–383b**
commentary on Cicero, 10:356a
on the compass, 5:396b
in Dante's *Divine Comedy,* 2:285a
Favolello, 6:631b, 651b, 7:383a
Livres dou trésor, 4:449a, 6:631b, 651b, 658b, 7:382b, 383a, 383b, 601a
Cicero's rhetoric and, 10:355b
language used, 5:231b, 235b–236a
Rettorica, 7:382b, 383a
Tesoretto, 6:631b, 651b, 7:382b–383a
Latinisms. *See* Loanwords, Latin
Latinitas, 7:598a
Latinorum penuria. See Translation and translators, Western European, motivations
Latreia, 3:320b
Latrocinium. See Ephesus, Councils of, Second (449)
Latus rectum, 1:438b, 439a
Latvian language, 6:438a, 444b
Latvians, 2:67b, 7:604a
origins of, 2:67b
Laúd, 8:562b
Laud MS Misc. 610, 6:524a-b, 541a
Laud MS Misc. 615, 6:541a
Lauda, 6:650b–651a, **7:384a-b**
carol and, 8:572a
confraternities for religious renewal and, 6:662a-b
Franciscans and, 8:579b
Italian drama and, 6:635a–636a, 663a
lai and, 7:316a
metrical form, 6:669a
see also Jacopone da Todi
"Lauda Sion Salvatorem." *See* Aquinas, Thomas, St., hymns of
Laudario Cortonese (manuscript), 6:650b
Laudatio, 4:137a
Laudatio florentinae urbis. See Bruni, Leonardo
Laudation to a City. See Rosenplüt, Hans
Laudes (acclamations), **7:384b–385b**
see also Tropes to the Ordinary of the Mass
Laudes creaturarum. See Francis of Assisi, St.
"Laudes crucis attolamus," 11:166a-b
Laudes regiae, 7:385a, 385b, 10:16a-b
Laudes de Virgine Maria. See Bonvesin de la Riva
Lauds, 3:67a, 4:229a
time of, 5:662b
Laufáss Edda, 2:254a
Laufen, Rudolph of Habsburg and, 11:540a
Launcelot. *See* Lancelot
Laupen, Battle of (1339), 11:543a
Laura. *See Lavra*
Laura (poetic character), 6:652b
Laure-crans voor Laurens Coster van Haerlem. See Scriverius, Petrus
Laurea sanctorum. See Hugo von Trimberg
Laurentian Library, Cosimo de' Medici and, 8:243a
Laurentius Hispanus, **7:385b–386a**
Laurentius Kálfsson, bishop of Hólar, in literature, 7:386b–387a
Laurentius of Monte Cassino, bishop, **7:386b**
Passio sancti Venceslai, 7:386b
Laurentius saga, **7:386b–387a**
Laurentius Surius, 9:38a
Laus Spaniae. See Isidore of Seville, St.
Lausanne, 11:543b
Berchtold of Zähringen and, 11:539a
Swiss Confederation and, 11:545b
Lausavísa, **7:387a-b**
Lausiac History. See Palladios
Lausor de la Divinitat, 3:167a
Laüstic. See Marie de France
Laute, 8:562b
Lauzengier. See Troubadours
Lavabo. *See* Fountain, ablutional
Lavra, **7:387b–388a**
Palestinian, and beginnings of eremitic monasticism, 6:213a
Law
as autonomous field of studies, 5:567a
of irrigation, 6:556b–557a
lepers and the, 9:677b
maritime, 9:664b
martial, marshal's court, 8:153b
in medieval scheme of knowledge, 5:566a-b
national, class development and, 3:413a–414b
procedure of, 1000–1500, **7:502b–506a**
centralization of governmental authority and, 7:503b–504b
cognitio extraordinaria, 7:503a-b
creation of as a branch of jurisprudence, 7:503b
early tracts, 7:503b
evolution from irrational to rational systems, 7:502b–503a
God's will and, 7:502b–503a
"learned" judges required, 7:504b–505a
papal decretals and, 7:504a
royal authority and, 7:504b
in secular courts, 7:504b–506a
use of torture and, 12:89b–90a
writs and, 7:505b
schools of, **7:512b–517a**
after Bologna, 7:514a–515a
at Bologna, 2:311b–312b
before 12th century, 7:513a
commentators and, 7:515b–516a
curricula, 7:516a
development of European universities and, 7:512b
doctor legum vs. judge, 7:516a-b
effects on legal procedure, 7:504b–505a
in Germany, 7:515a
Islamic, 7:487b
ius commune, 7:513b–514a
ius commune and *ius proprium,* 7:516b
in northern Europe, 7:515a
patronage of, 7:514b
Poland, 9:729a-b
quaestiones disputatae in, 7:515b
rise of *consilia,* 7:516b
Sicily, 11:274a-b
significance of, 7:516a-b
in southern France, 7:514b–515a
teaching methods, 7:513a, 515a–516a
textbooks, 11:691a–692a
trivium rhetoric studies and, 12:206a–207a
see also Bologna, University of, law school; Inns of Court; Islamic law; Montpellier; Universities

Law (*cont.*)
treatises, 4:578a
see also Glossators
Law, canon
to Gratian, 3:348b–349a, **7:395b–413a**
decisions of councils, 7:396b
decrees of bishops or pontiffs, 7:396b
fontes formales (formal sources), 7:396b–412a
fontes materiales (material sources), 7:395b–396a
influence of papacy, 7:409a-b
Libri duo de synodalibus causis et disciplinis ecclesiasticis, 10:289b
material sources vs. formal sources, 7:395b
papal decrees, 7:399a
penitential books, 7:403b
reform and unification (Carolingian period), 7:403a-b, 404b
sources, 7:395b–396b
after Gratian, **7:413a–418a**
auctoritas and *administratio,* 10:546a
glosses, 7:416b
growth of legal business, 7:414a
Innocent III and, 7:415b
Lateran Councils and, 7:415a-b, 416a
Raymond of Peñafort and, 10:266b
Roman-law procedure, 9:519b
study of, University of Bologna, 2:312a
see also Azo; Baldus; Decretals; Gratian
Armenian, **7:393a–394a**
derivation of ecclesiastical rules, 7:393a
Bolognese school on, 5:567a
Byzantine, **7:394a–395b**
apostolic canons, 7:394a-b
canons and civil law, 7:394a
canons of the Fathers, 7:394b
codifications, 2:467b, 6:99b
commentaries, 7:394b–395a
development of, 2:466b
ecumenical council decrees, 7:394a
imperial legislation on ecclesiastical affairs, 7:394b
local council canons, 7:394b
oikonomia, 2:467b, 7:395a
patriarchal decrees, 7:395a
sources, 2:467b–468a, 7:394a–395a
synodal decrees, 7:395a
see also Leo VI (the Wise), Byzantine emperor; *Nomocanon;* Permanent synod
canons of Sardica, 4:373b
casuistry in, 3:153a-b
in Celtic church, 3:229a-b
Charlemagne's use of, 3:348b–349a, 4:373a
church as corporation, 3:606a–607a
church structure and, 3:638b
collections
100–870, 7:396b–397a, 403a–405b
870–1000, 7:405b–407a
1000–1050, 7:407a–408b
of Anselm II of Lucca, 1:311a
decretals, 7:414b–416a
forgeries and spurious collections (Carolingian period), 7:404b–405b
Gallican, 7:398b, 401b–402b, 407a
"Gelasian Renaissance," 7:399a–400a
German (870–1000), 7:406b–407a
Insular, 7:402b–403a
Italian, 7:398b–399a, 400b, 405b–406b, 408b–410b
North African, 7:398a, 400a-b
official vs. private, 7:396b
organizing principles, 7:397a
primitive Western, 7:397b–400a
pseudoapostolic, 7:397a-b
regional and national, 7:400a–403a, 410b–412a
sources of, 7:397a
Spanish, 7:398a-b, 400b–401b
concubinage and, 3:530a
contraception and, 3:573a-b
Coutumes de Beauvaisis and, 2:144b–145a
definition of, 7:395b
Deusdedit and, 4:165b
development of, 5:566b
Summa decretorum, 10:545b
Dictatus papae and, 4:177a
dispensation, 4:216b–218a
Divine Office and, 4:222a-b
dress code for Jews, 3:620b
ecclesiastical travel and, 12:154b–155a
England
contributions of Lanfranc and Anselm, 4:466b
ecclesiastical courts, 4:464b, 471a
equity and, 4:503a
papal heresy, 4:483b
12th century renaissance, 4:471b
see also Arches, Court of; Vacarius
on excommunication, 4:536b
False Decretals, 3:349a
feudalism in papal states and, 9:387a
first compilation of, 3:348b
Gamli Kanóki on, 5:354b–355a
Geert Groote on, 5:680b
governing discipline and administration, 3:628a
Gratian and, 3:637a-b, 5:656a–657b
inheritance and, 6:457b, 458a, 458b
Innocent IV on, 6:467a-b
in Ireland, secular influence on, 7:484a-b
Jewish expertise in, 7:78b–79a, 93a
Jewish status in, 7:75b, 78a–79a, 88a-b, 93b–94a
Papal States, 7:109a-b
John XXII on, 7:125b
Justinian II's contribution to, 3:630b
Leo IX on, 7:549a-b
on liturgical vestments, 12:401a
papal reform and, 3:349a
papal rescripts, 10:335a
parish and, 9:414b
penance and, 9:491b
Piacenzan canons, 3:635a-b
plenitudo potestatis, 9:708b–710a
power of attorney, representative assemblies and, 10:317a
prohibition of *turpe lucrum* (dishonest gain) and, 12:337b–338a
as propaganda, 10:138b
property ownership under, 3:607a
provincial synods and, 3:578b
Quaestio in utramque partem tract, 10:238a
reform of, 3:355a
right of presentation, 10:117a–118a
Roman legal influence, 3:609b–610a, 7:503b–504b
scholasticism in, 11:57b–58a
Siete partidas and, 11:283a
on simony, 11:301b–302a
Spanish compilation of, 3:348b
Sweden, 11:531a-b, 533a
textbooks, 11:691b
on tithes, 12:64a
Traditio legis, 12:123a–124b (*illus.*)
on usury, 12:335a-b, 336b
Wyclif and, 12:710a
see also Decretals; Durand, Guillaume; Equity; Ivo of Chartres; Johannes Andreae; Johannes Monachus; Johannes Teutonicus; Law, procedure of, 1000–1500; Liturgy, treatises on; Ordeals
Law, civil
Burchard of Worms on, 2:420a-b
champion in judicial combat, 3:250b–251a
classical Roman, treason concept and, 12:165b
Codex Theodosianus, 3:475a-b
contraception and, 3:572b
on corporations, 3:606a
court travels and, 12:153a, 159a–160a
dissensiones, 8:158b
dress codes, 3:622a
English, links with criminal procedure, 7:44b
food quality and prices governed by, 3:580b
forfeiture of possessions, 12:166b
glossators' view of, 5:567a
inheritance and, 6:460b
offenses
misprision, 12:167a
treason definition and trial, 12:165a–168b
penalties, expiatory pilgrimage, 12:155b–156a
principle of *Q.o.t.* and, 8:232a-b
regionalization of, 12:162a
trespass, 12:185a–186a
see also Bartolo da Sassoferrato; *Corpus iuris civilis;* Equity; Jewry law; Johannes Andreae; Law codes; Law, procedure of, 1000–1500
Law codes, **7:425b–431a**
before 1000, 7:425b
in Bologna, 7:429a
Byzantine, 2:125a-b
Basil I and, 2:117b
see also Nomocanon
canon law, 7:427a–428a

consent of subjects to, 7:426a
Corpus iuris civilis as model, 7:425b
defined, 7:425b
early codifications, 7:426a
18th century theory, 7:425b–426a
Germanic
on slavery, 11:336a
vicinia and, 12:438b
see also German law, early Germanic codes
importance of law schools to, 7:430a-b
Jewish, *see also* Talmud, law codes of
monarchical activity and, 7:430a-b
in northern Europe, 7:430a
registration of statutes, 7:430a
principles of kingship and, 7:426a-b
private collections, 7:426b–427a
rationales for, 7:426a
of religious corporations, 7:429a
Russian
of Ivan III, 11:191b, 192a
of Ivan IV, 11:192a
Yaroslav and, 12:720a
Swedish, 11:532a
of universities, 7:429a
Visigothic, 9:147b, 12:471b, 472a
of Wulfstan of York, 12:704a
see also Schwabenspiegel
Law, maritime
conservators of truce, 1:57a
consulate of the sea, 3:569b–570b
guardianship of the seas, English claims to, 1:56b
laws of Oléron, 1:56a-b
settlement of piracy claims, 1:56b
see also Admiralty, court of
Law, martial, treason and, 12:166a-b
Law of the Twelve Tables, 12:335b
Law-things, Norwegian, 9:184a
Lawāta, 2:185b
Lawing of dogs. *See* Dogs
Lawns, in gardens, 5:364a-b
Lawrence of Aquileia
dictamen of, 4:176b
Practica sive usus dictaminis, 10:358b
Lawrence of Brindisi, St., as doctor of the church, 4:234b
Lawrence of Durham, 7:363a
Lawrence of Milan, bishop, Arator and, 1:422a
Lawrence, St.
in art, 10:507a
in literature, 7:364a
see also Vie de St. Laurent
Laws. See Plato
Laws, food. *See* Dietary laws
Laws of Henry I, 7:441b, 442b
Laws of Hywel Dda, 8:558b
Lawyers
Islamic, 11:218b
noble class and, 3:413a, 413b
status of, 3:426b
Laxdœla saga, 4:613b, 614a, **7:528a-b**
attributed to Sturla Þórðarson, 11:496a
compared with *Vatnsdœla saga,* 12:363b
continued in *Njáls saga,* 7:528a-b
Landnámabók and, 7:528a
Njáls saga and, 9:145b
possible authors of, 7:528b
related *Bola þáttr* and, 12:4a
Sigurðarkviða in meiri and, 11:292b
as a woman's biography, 7:528a
Lay. *See Lai/lay*
Lay of Bjarki. *See Bjarkamál*
Lay capitulary. *See* Capitulary
Lay curia. *See* Curia, lay
Lay Folks' Catechism. See Thoresby of York, John, bishop
Lay le Freine, 7:317a
Lay of Grímnir. *See Grímnismál*
Lay of Helgi Hjǫrvarðsson. See Helgi poems
Lay of the Host of Igor, The, struggle against Lithuania and, 7:604a
Lay de Nostre Dame. See Froissart, Jehan
Lay of Rígur. *See Rígsþula*
"Lay of the Smithy," 5:46b–47a
Lay of Vafþrúðnir. *See Vafþrúðnismál*
Lay of Vǫlundr. *See Vǫlundarkviða*
Layamon, 2:393a–394a
Roman de Brut and, 12:496b
see also Brut, The
Layas, Layazzo. *See* Āyās
Laylā and Majnūn. See Nizāmī
Layla (vocal genre), 8:562b
Laylat al-barāᵓa (night of quittance), 5:39b
Laylat al-miᶜrāj (night of the ascension), 5:39b
Laylat al-qadr (night of the divine decree), 5:39b–40a
Laylī u Majnūn. See Niẓāmī
Lays de Bretagne, Les, 10:390b–391a
Laysa, 6:618a
Laz language, 5:404a-b
Lazar Brankoviç of Serbia, despot, Stefan Tomaš of Bosnia and, 11:474a
Lazar Hrebeljanović, **7:528b–529a,** 11:180b–181a
canonization of by the Serbian church, 11:181b
panegyric to by Evfimiya, 11:346a
Stefan Lazareviç of Serbia and, 11:472b
Łazar Pᶜarpecᶜi, 1:476b, 508b, 5:668b, **7:529a–530a**
on Armenian saints, 1:518b
David the Invincible and, 4:114a
Ełišē and, 1:509a
History of Armenia
contents of, 7:529b
manuscript sources of, 7:529b–530a
narrow scope of, 6:239a
use of eyewitness accounts, 6:239a
Letter to Lord Vahan Mamikonean, heretics mentioned in, 9:469a
on the Mamikonean family, 8:78b
on Mamikonean *sparapets,* 11:460b
on native heresy, 6:187b
Pᶜawstos Buzand's *History of Armenia* and, 9:472b
Lazarica (church: Kruševac), 11:188a
Lazarus, Feast of (in Byzantium), panegyric on the patriarch, 10:349b
Lazarus, raising of
in art, **7:530a-b**
of Panteón de los Reyes, 10:492a (*illus.*)
Lazika. *See* Georgia: Geography
Lazio, villages of, 12:443b
Le. *See* next element in title
Le Goulet, Treaty of (1200), 7:129a
Le Loup, Jean. *See* Loup, Jean
Le Mans, Synod of (1247), on Ave Maria, 2:13b
Le Paraclet
Hebrew language study, 12:137a
see also Abelard, Peter; Heloise
Le Puy Cathedral, 10:480b
Le Puy, Councils of, Peace of God movement and, 9:473b
Leabhar Branach, 6:535b
Leabhar Breac, 7:614b
Leabhar Gabhála Éireann, 6:542a, 546a, 9:46b–47a
Lead
imported from the West into Egypt, 12:107b
mining of, 8:397b–398a
working of, 8:286b
Lead glazing, 3:236b–237a
League of Lesh, 11:324a
League (measure), **7:530b**
Leander, St., bishop of Seville, 12:473b
Isidore of Seville and, 6:563b
Leaning Tower of Pisa. *See* Pisa Cathedral
Leap (unit of measure), 12:588b
Leasing of land. *See* Land
Leather and leatherworking, **7:530b–532a**
in bookbinding, 8:97b
Timurid, 8:100a
chamois, 7:531a
cordovan, 11:639b
in shoe manufacture, 11:255a
cordwainers, 7:531a
in England, 7:531b
manufacture of, 11:639a
methods of production, 7:530b–531a
in shoe manufacture, 11:255a
supply of raw materials, 7:531a-b
in Valencia, 12:348b
whittawyers, 7:531a
Lebadea. *See* Levádhia
Lebanon, **7:532a–533b** (map)
Arabization of, 7:532a
divisions of, 7:532a
Druzes of, 7:532b–533a
economy of, 7:532b–533a
Maronite church of, 7:532b–533a
Melchites and, 7:532b
Monothelitism and, 7:532b
spread of Islam in, 7:532a
Twelver Shiism in, 11:137a
Leben Jesu. See Frau Ava
Lebey de Batilly, Denis, *Tratié de l'origine des anciens assassins porte-courteaux,* 1:592b
Lebor na hUidre
manuscripts of, 6:521a, 521b, 522b
as ransom, 6:524a
works in, 6:526a, 527b, 540b, 545b
Lebuinus, St., 6:317a
Lecan, Great Book of, 6:523a
Lecan, Yellow Book of, 6:523a
Lecheor, 7:317a

Lechfeld, Battle of (955), 2:6a, 11:477b
in Widukind of Corvey's description, 12:628a
Lectionary, **7:534a**, 9:690a
of the Church of Jerusalem, Armenian translations, 1:508b, 518b, 520a, 520b
Divine Office and, 4:224a-b
evangeliary and, 4:526a
Gallican rite and, 5:344b
missal, 8:437a-b
see also Bible; Pericope
Lectionary notation. *See* Musical notation, ekphonetic
Lector, 3:442a
instruments in ordination of, 9:267a
Lectura in codicem. See Cino da Pistoia
Lectura codicis. See Azo
Lectura in quinque libros Decretalium. See Hostiensis
Lectura super Genesium. See Henry of Langenstein
Ledrede, Richard, 7:370a
Red Book of Ossory and, 7:375b
Ledung (militia system in Scandinavia), 9:79a-b
Leechbook
as botanical source, 2:345b
see also Medicine
Leeuwen, Jan van, 9:37b
Lefèvre, Raoul, **7:534a-b**
Histoire de la conquête de la toison d'or, 7:346a
Histoire de Jason, 7:534b
Recueil des histoires de Troie, 7:534b
Legal personality. *See* Person, juristic
Legate, papal, **7:534b–535b**
compared with papal nuncio, 7:534b, 535b
in England, 7:535a
in Germany, 7:535b
involvement in secular politics, 7:535a
in Italy, 7:535b
powers of, 7:535a
role in crusades, 7:535a
Sicily, 11:266a-b
in Spain, 7:535b
types of, 7:534b–535a, 535b
Legatus, 4:202a
ambassador and, 4:205a
Legend of Good Women. See Chaucer, Geoffrey
Legend of St. George. See Lydgate, John
Legend of St. Thomas, 6:636a
Legenda, in Divine Office, 4:224b
Legenda aurea. See Jacobus de Varagine, *Golden Legend*
Legenda o svaté Kateřině, 11:344a
Legendary Saga of St. Olaf, 9:176b
Legendary sagas. *See Fornaldarsögur*
Légende dorée. See Jean de Vignay
Légende des Vénitiens, La. See Jean Lemaire de Belges
Leges Henrici
presentment of Englishry and, 4:487a
sac and soc, 10:601b
Leges Rotharis, 7:474a-b, 8:377a, 11:335a
Leges Visigothorum, 7:470a-b, 12:471b, 472a
Leges Wallicae, 7:526b
Leggings, Western European, 3:625a
Legislator humanus, 10:22b–23a
Legitim, rights of, 6:458b, 460a
Legname. *See* Madeira Islands
Legnano, Battle of (1176), 3:117b
Legnica. *See* Liegnitz
Legrense, Johannes, *Libelli musicalis de ritu canendi,* 8:646a
Legumes
benefits to soil from, 1:92b
broad bean, 1:86b
growth of, 1:78a
as source of protein, 1:95a
Lebor na hUidre, Táin bó Cúailnge and, 11:580a
Lehre von den Zeichen des Hirsches. See Wittenwiller, Hugo
Leibeigen, 11:204b
Leibeigenschaft, 11:681b
Leibniz, Gottfried Wilhelm
Liber calculationum and, 11:535b
Nicholas of Cusa and, 9:125a
Leich, 5:440b–441a, 7:290b–291a
lai and, 7:316a
in Middle High German literature, 8:354b
in minnesingers' lyrics, 8:413b–414a
See also Reinmar von Zweter; Ulrich von Liechtenstein
Leiden Papyrus, recipes for transmutation, 1:135b
Leiden Riddle, 1:276a
Leif Eriksson (Ericson)
Christianity and, 8:442b
discovery of America and, 12:422a
Vinland and, 4:555a, 12:428b
in Vinland sagas, 12:457a
Leifr Ǫssurarson, 4:580b
Leifsson, Gunnlaugr
Jóns saga helga, 7:146b–147a
Oláfs saga Tryggvasonar, 7:145a
Leile, 8:562b
Leimonarion. See Moschos, John
Leinster, 6:518a, 519a, **7:536a–537a**
contact with Roman world, 7:536a
kingship of, 6:517b, 7:536a-b
in Irish saga, 6:547b
Leinster, Book of. *See* Book of Leinster
Leipsana. See Relics
Leipzig
College of the Blessed Virgin, 12:293a
fairs, 4:586b
Leipzig, University of, 12:287b, 288a
Leire monarchy, 4:151b
Leisure. *See* Games
Leiðangr, 9:184a
Leiðarvísan, **7:537a-b**
contents of, 7:537a-b
form of, 7:537a
as a model for *Líknarbraut,* 7:580a
structure of, 7:537b
Lejre Chronicle, **7:538a-b**
hatred of Germany in, 7:538a
manuscript sources of, 7:538a-b
probable date of origin, 7:538a
Lekaḥ Tov. See Tovia ben Eliezer
Leken spieghel, Der. See Boendale, Jan van
Lekno church, 10:489a
Leliaerts, 5:522b
role in government, 11:713b
Lemaire, William, on church reform, 3:517b, 645b
Lemmata, 1:434b
Lemosi (Limousin), 10:156a
Lendir menn (Norwegian magnates), 10:701a-b
Lendit, fairs, 4:583a (*illus.*), 585a
Leningrad Codex. *See* Bible, Hebrew
Lennox, earl of, addressed by Muireadhach, 11:114a, 114b
Lenses, **7:538b–541a**
lack of theory of, 7:540b
magnifying, 7:539a-b
negative (convex), 7:540a-b
Lent, **7:541a-b**
in Byzantine church, 7:541a, 612a
carnival and, 3:99b
duration, 4:365a-b
hymns for, collected in triodion, 7:612a
public penance and, 9:487b, 491a
in Roman tradition, 7:541a
suppression of, 4:587b
see also Communion; Fasting, Christian; Liturgy, stational
Lenta, irrigation of, 6:558b
Lenzburg, count of, 11:527b
Lenzburg dynasty, 11:538a, 538b
extinction of, 11:539a
Habsburgs and, 11:539b
Kyburgs and, 11:539b
Schwyz and, 11:541a
Unterwalden and, 11:541a
Leo I, Byzantine emperor, **7:544a**
Isaurians and, 6:560b
Theodoric the Ostrogoth and, 12:19a
Zeno and, 12:743b
Leo II, Byzantine coemperor, 12:743b
Leo III, Byzantine emperor, 2:402a, **7:544a–545a**
accession to power, 7:544a, 544b
administrative reforms, 2:488a
breaking of Muslim siege of Constantinople (717), 7:544b
coinage of, 8:419a
defense of Constantinople, 2:488a
Ekloga, 2:117b
as founder of imperial dynasty, 7:544b
Gallican chant and, 5:343b
hexaphollon and, 11:603b
iconoclasm and, 2:462b–463a, 488a, 3:10b, 631a, 6:397a, 397b, 400b, 402a, 7:544a-b, 9:561b
Isaurians and, 6:560b, 561a
legal innovations, 2:488a
in legends and prophecies, 8:20a
in Łewond, 7:554b
palace library and, 7:561a
Paulicians and, 9:469b
power base of in Amorion, 1:236a-b
reform of imperial administration, 3:345a
military and naval reforms, 7:544b
victory over Arabs at Akroinon, 7:544b
Leo IV, Byzantine emperor, death of, 6:520b
Leo V (the Armenian), Byzantine emperor, **7:545a**

icons and, 6:401a, 402a
Theodore of Studios and, 12:16a
in *Theophanes continuatus,* 12:23a
Thomas the Slav and, 12:36b
vs. patriarch Nikephoros, 9:131b
Leo VI (the Wise), Byzantine emperor, **7:545b–546a**
Arab challenge and, 7:545b
astrology and, 8:18a
Basil I and, 2:118a
Basilics. See Basilics
Book of the Eparch, 4:494a
trade regulation, 2:478b
Book of the Prefect and, 12:102a
Bulgarian conflicts, 2:404b, 489b, 7:545b
crown of, 5:377b–378a
deposition of Photios, 11:43b
Epanagoge and, 4:493a
Eugenius Vulgarius and, 4:521a
Italy, reorganization of government, 7:4b
lack of heir, 2:489b–490a
law and, 7:391a-b
on marriage, 4:594b
marriage of, 3:632a, 7:545b
Nikolaos I Mystikos and, 9:135b
Novels, 6:451b–452a
oratorical skills, 10:350b
prostration before Christ, 10:152 (*illus.*)
royal confessor to, 3:534b
Smbat I the Martyr and, 11:351a
Taktika, 10:59b
"tetragamy" of, 7:545b
in *Theophanes continuatus,* 12:23a
Leo I of Cilicia, baron, death of (1140), 3:394a
Leo I/II of Cilician Armenia, king, **7:546a-b**, 11:313b
Āyās and, 2:19a
Cilician-Roman church union and, 1:501a
coronation of, 7:546a, 10:540b
court of, 7:546b
head of Rubenid line, 7:546a
Lambron and, 7:322a
reign of, 3:391a-b, 394a
Leo II/III of Cilician Armenia, king
Āyās and, 2:19a
sought Cilician-Mongol alliance, 3:391b
Yovhannēs VI and, 6:312a
Leo IV of Cilician Armenia, king, murdered, 3:393a
Leo V/VI of Cilician Armenia, king, **7:547a**
imprisonment by Mamluks, 7:689b
reign of, 3:393a, 395a
Leo I (the Great), pope, **7:541b–542a**
assumption of title *pontifex maximus* by, 9:370b
Attila and, 6:354a, 7:541b, 9:370b
authority of, Valentinian III and, 9:370a-b
ban on interest taking, 12:336a
changes brought about by, 3:341b–342a
Christmas celebration and, 3:318a
Council of Chalcedon and, 3:629b, 7:542a, 9:370b, 561a
cursus and, 7:372b
dictums on fasting, 4:436a
as doctor of the church, 4:234a
Eastern churches and, 7:541b–542a
Eutyches and, 4:524a
extant writings of, 7:542a
Huns and, 2:93a
papal definitions during reign of, 10:31b–32a
Priscillians and, 1:605b–606a
as promoter of Roman primacy, 7:541b
on the Roman rite, 7:626a
Tome of Leo (*Flavian Tome*), 3:320b–321a, 7:542a, 8:477a
condemned by Nersēs II Aštarakacᶜi, 9:102b
tracts by Prosper of Aquitaine, 10:154a
unity of Western church and, 3:336b
Vandals and, 7:541b, 12:355a
Leo III, pope, **7:542b–543a**
Apostles' Creed and, 3:677a
Charlemagne and, 3:110a, 346a-b, 5:494b, 7:542b, 9:374a-b
on Frankish rite, 3:677a
Gallican chant and, 5:343b
Germanos I and, 5:471b
introduction of Lesser Litany and, 7:558a
Lateran and, 7:344b, 10:518b
martyrs' burials and, 3:154b
mosaics commissioned by, 10:112a-b
opposed to adoptionism, 7:542b
Leo IV, pope, appeals for Frankish assistance, 4:18b
Leo VII, pope, on Jews, 7:76a
Leo IX, pope, **7:543a–544a**
against lay possession of tithes, 12:63a
against simony and nicolaitism, 7:543a-b
on clerical celibacy, 7:543a
convened Synod of Rheims, 3:634a
defeated by Normans, 7:543b
dubbed "the Apostolic Pilgrim," 7:543a
ecclesiasical appointments and, 3:93b
elevation to papacy, 7:543a
on general councils, 3:633b
Gregory VII and, 5:669b
Humbert and, 6:329a
moral reform by, 9:376b
Patriarch Michael Keroularios and, 8:304b
Peter Damian and, 9:508b
refinement of canon law under, 9:376b–377a
reforming synod, 4:421b
reign of, 3:350b–351a, 354a
a rhymed office to Gorgonius and, 10:372a
Schism of 1054 and, 3:349a-b
vs. Normans, 11:265a
Leo X, pope
Acts of the Apostles and, 11:596b
on clerical celibacy, 3:217a
Innocent VIII and, 8:243b
Ite et vos, primacy of Observants, 5:206a
reign of, 3:367b
Leo Africanus, legends about Timbuktu and, 12:54b–55a
Leo, archpresbyter
Historia de preliis, adaptations of, 6:116a
translations of Alexander romances, 5:445b
Leo Choirosphaktes (Choerosphactes), 4:196a
satire on, 9:566b
Leo the Deacon
History, 2:514b, 6:245a
revival of classicizing style, 6:245a
Leo Marsicanus. *See* Leo of Ostia
Leo the Mathematician, **7:547b**, 9:697a
astrology and, 8:18a
Epitome of Medicine, 8:245b
al-Maᵓmūn and, 1:391b–392a
On the Characteristics of Human Beings, 8:245b
opposition to, 9:566b
Leo of Ostia, **7:547a-b**, 11:266b
Leo, patriarch of Constantinople, lead seal of, 11:121b (*illus.*)
Leo Sgouros, lord of Nauplia, vs. Boniface of Montferrat, 7:376a, 376b
León
attacked by Ibn Abī ᶜĀmir al-Manṣūr, 8:90a-b
irrigation projects, 6:558a
origin of name, 6:436a
see also Castile; Navarre, kingdom of
Leon of Perego, archbishop, Ghibellines and, 8:379a
Leon of Thessalonica, Archimedes and, 1:434a
Leonard of Maurperg, notebook of alchemical formulas, 1:138b
Leonardo Fibonacci. *See* Fibonacci, Leonardo
Leonardo di Ser Giovanni, **7:547b–548a**
St. John the Baptist in prison, altar relief, 7:548a (*illus.*)
Leonardo da Vinci
Archimedes and, 1:439b
armor and, 1:536a
Codice Atlantico, Saxony wheel, 11:699b
homo quadratus and, 8:580b
inventions, rotating spit, 11:662a-b
Last Supper, 8:583b–584a (*illus.*)
letter to Lucovico Sforza, 11:645a-b
Madrid Codex I, 11:649a
mechanical treatises, 11:648b–649a
automation, 11:649a
friction, 11:649a
Naviglio Interno, swinging miter gates, 12:578b
water mills and, 8:390b
Leonine City, 10:517b, 519a
Lateran complex and, 10:520a
walls, 10:520a
Leonine Sacramentary. *See Sacramentarium Veronense*
Leoninus (Leonius, Léonin), **7:548a–549b**, 8:594a
Anonymous IV and, 7:548b–549b, 9:191a, 506a, 506b
ars antiqua and, 1:546a
identification of, 7:548a-b, 8:43a

Leoninus (Leonius, Léonin) (*cont.*)
Magnus liber organi, 9:191b, 192a, 12:671a
influence on motet development, 8:501a
see also Perotinus
revised by Perotinus, 7:549a
works in MS Pluteus, 29.1, 5:105a-b
see also Magnus liber organi
Leonor de Albuquerque, property of, 3:139b
Leonor López de Córdoba
autobiography of, 11:433b
Memorias, 11:421a-b
Leontios Mechanikos, treatise on globe making, 11:96a
Leontius, Byzantine emperor, icons and, 6:400b
Leontius of Byzantium, Christology of, 3:320b
Leonzio Pilato
Boccaccio's *De mulieribus claris* and, 2:28a
commissioned by Petrarch to translate *Iliad,* 2:287b
as informant of Boccaccio, 2:283a
Leopard, in heraldry, 6:175a
Leopold III of Austria, duke, 2:6b, 8b
Leopold V of Austria, archduke, 2:6b–7a, 33b
Leopold VI (the Magnificent) of Austria, duke, 2:7a, 33b
as patron of poetry, 5:435a
Leopold III of Bavaria, margrave. *See* Leopold III of Austria, duke
Leopold of Habsburg, duke
acquisitions of, 11:544a
Waldstätte and, 11:542a
Zurich and, 11:543a
Leovigild, Visigothic king, 10:36b, 12:471a-b
vs. Basques, 2:126a
Lepers, exempt from tithes, 12:65a
Lepperwerk. *See* Salines
Lepra Giezi, 11:301a
Leprosariums, 7:551a–552a, 12:330b
Leprosy, **7:549b–552b**
among upper classes, 7:550a-b
attitudes to, 6:296a, 7:550a, 551a
causes of, 7:549b–550a
cultural importance of, 9:677b
diagnosis of, 7:550b–551a
in Europe, 9:676b–677b
incidence of, 7:550b, 551b
in Islamic world, 9:684a
king's evil and, 7:255a–256a
Lateran III and, 7:550b
leper colonies, in Bodel's *Congés,* 2:290b
manifestations of, 7:550a
Robert I of Scotland and, 10:427b
seclusion of lepers, 7:551a–552a
treatment of, 6:292b, 293b, 295a, 296b
see also Plagues
Lérida, irrigation of, 6:557b
Lérida Ferrer the Elder. *See* Ferrer I (the Elder), Jaime
Lérida, University of, 12:286b
Lérins, Ennodius and, 4:491b
Les Andelys
bridge at, 10:416a
Château Gaillard and, 10:384a
Lesbos. *See* Mytilene
Lèse-majesté. *See* Kingship
Leselieder. *See Pia dictamina*
Lesene. *See* Pilaster strip
Lesser Armenia. *See* Armenia: Geography; Cilician Kingdom
Lesser Asclepiad. *See* Asclepiad
Lesser Sophenē. *See* Sophenē
Lessing, Gotthold, *Renner* and, 6:326a
Lest (unit of measure), 12:593a
Letald of Micy, **7:552b**
rhymed office to St. Julian, 10:372a, 375b
Leth Cam, Battle of (827), 3:397a
Letter from Valerius to Rufinus Against Taking a Wife, antifeminism of, 1:323b
"Letter of Maestro Andreas," 7:93b
Letter of Tansar, 1:452a, **7:552b–553a**, 10:668a
seizure of sacred fire, 10:663a
Letter to the Brethren at Mont Dieu, A. *See* William of St. Thierry
Letter to Gloucester. *See* Lydgate, John
Letter to Posterity. *See* Petrarch
Letter to Sigeweard. *See* Aelfric
Letter writing
business correspondence, 12:158b
crusader, 4:20a
diplomacy, 4:208a–209a
Egypt, Tulinid *Dīwān al-rasāʾil,* 12:224a
papal. *See* Decretals
quattrocento humanist, by Ambrogio Traversari, 12:163b
Roman imperial post system and, 12:148b–149b
see also Dictamen; Postal and intelligence services
Letters
metaphysics of, 1:218b
symbolism of, 1:217b
Letters of Abu 'l-ʿAlāʾ. *See* Maʿarrī, Abū 'l-ʿAlāʾ Aḥmad al-
Letters, Book of. *See Girk Tʿłtʿocʿ*
Letters of Helen and Paris. *See* Baudri of Bourgueil
Lettgallians, 2:65a, 65b, 67b
Lettish language. *See* Latvian language
Lettre de jussion, legislative power of the French king and, 9:420a
Lettres de foire, 12:732a
Lettuce, romaine, 1:86a, 96a
Leudefredus, bishop of Córdoba, 7:626b
Leudus, lai and, 7:316a
Leutharis, Alamannic duke, 11:526a
Levádhia, Acciaiuoli and, 7:381b
Levant. *See* Near East
Levée en masse. *See* Warfare, conscription of nobility
Leven van Sint Servaes. *See* Heinrich von Veldeke
Leven van Sinte Lutgart, 4:320a
Lever, 1:438a-b
Levi ben Gershom (Gerson), 1:460a, **7:553b–554b**
astronomical contributions of, 7:553b, 11:91b
astronomical tables of, 11:91a
commentaries of, 4:541b
De numeris harmonicis, Philippe de Vitry and, 12:481b
as exegete, 2:212b, 7:55b
influenced by
Ibn Rushd, 7:553b–554a
Maimonides, 7:554a
invention of cross-staff, 4:12a, 7:553b, 11:101b
mathematical works, 7:553b, 11:92a
philosophy, 7:553b–554a
Sefer tekunah, 1:613a
Wars of the Lord, as defense of Platonic cosmology, 7:554a
Levirate marriage. *See* Marriage, Jewish
Levita, Elijah, 7:110a
Levon I. *See* Leo I/II of Cilician Armenia, king
Levon II. *See* Leo II/III of Cilician Armenia, king
Lewes. *See Song of Lewes*
Lewes, Battle of (1264), 2:112a
Łewond (historian), 7:298b, **7:554b–555a**
on Arabs in Armenia, 1:478a, 6:240a
on Armenian saints, 1:519a
identification of, 7:554b
Paulicians and, 9:469a-b
Łewond (presbyter), 1:518b
Lex Alamannorum, 11:526b
Lex Baiuvariorum, 5:506b, 7:477b–478a
Schwabenspiegel and, 11:80b
Lex barbara visigothorum, 7:520b–522a
Lex Burgundionum, 2:92b
Lex castrensis. *See* Sven Aggesen
Lex Falcidia, inheritance in, 6:456a
Lex Gundobada, 7:470b
inheritance in, 6:456a
see also German law, early Germanic codes
Lex innocentium, 1:52b
Lex ripuaria, on armor, 1:522b
Lex Romana Burgundionum, 2:92b, 7:470b–471a
Lex Romana Visigothorum. *See* Breviary of Alaric
Lex salica, 8:278a
German translation of, 9:233b
Lex salica emendata, 7:472b
Lex salica karolina (*Lex Saxonum*), 7:472b–473a, 10:683b
pays du droit coutumier and, 7:473a
Lexicons. *See* Encyclopedias and dictionaries; Gloss; Translation and translators, resources and training
Leyden Papyrus X, alchemic recipes, 11:635a, 635b
Leyenda de Cardeña. *See Estoria del Cid*
Leys d'amors, **7:555a**, 11:312b
See also Molinier, Guilhem; Provençal literature
Li biaus descouneus. *See* Renaut de Beaujeu
Liability
collective, 4:584a
inheritance and, 6:456b, 457a
Liakitʿ (church: Caucasia), 12:750b

Libaerts, Elisaeus, 1:536b
Libanius, Basil the Great and, 2:120a
Libelli with complete offices, 4:225a
Libelli (in land tenure), 11:679a-b
Libelli missarum
  arrangement of prayers, 10:605a
  with canon, 10:605a
  for Gallican rite, 10:605a
  for Old Spanish rite, 10:605a
Libelli musicalis de ritu canendi. See Legrense, Johannes
Libellus alter de consecratione ecclesiae Dionysii. See Suger of St. Denis
Libellus de arte dictandi rethorice. See Peter of Blois
Libellus contra invasores et symoniacos. See Deusdedit, cardinal
Libellus de ecclesiastica et politica potestate. See Richer, Edmond
Libellus de institutione morum, 11:480a
Libellus iuris canonici. See Roffredus de Epiphaniis of Benevento
Libellus de malo senectutis et senii. See Boncompagno of Signa
Libellus de modo vivendi hominum simul commorantium. See Zerbolt of Zutphen, Gerard
Libellus de praescriptionibus. See Rogerius
Libellus responsionum, 1:645a-b
Libellus de seccione mukefi. See Fusoris, Jean
Libellus de suis temptationibus. See Otloh of St. Emmeram
Liber abaci. See Fibonacci, Leonardo
Liber de admonitione clericorum et laicorum. See Otloh of St. Emmeram
Liber aggregationis, attributed to Albertus Magnus, 8:35a
Liber Alcuini contra haeresim Felicis. See Alcuin of York
Liber algebra. See Khwārizmī, al-, *Kitāb al-mukhtaṣar fī-ḥisāb al-jabr wa 'l-muqābala*
Liber de anima ad Odonem. See Ratramnus
Liber argumentorum, 8:641b
Liber Arsamithis de mensura circuli. See Archimedes, *On the Measurement of the Circle*
Liber de arte contrapuncti. See Johannes Tinctoris
Liber assumptorum. See Lemmata
Liber Augustalis. See Melfi, Constitutions of
Liber benedictionalis. See Benedictional
Liber benedictionum. See Ekkehard IV of St. Gall
Liber calculationum. See Richard de Swyneshed
Liber de causis, 1:458a, 461a, 4:510b
  influence on Roger Bacon, 2:35b, 40b
Liber chronicarum. See Schedel, Hartmann
Liber de civitatis Florentiae famosis civibus. See Villani, Filippo
Liber compositae medicinae. See Hildegard of Bingen, St.
Liber constitutionum, 7:470b
Liber continens. See Rāzī, Abū Bakr Muḥammad ibn Zakarīya al-
Liber contra sectam sive haeresim Saracenorum. See Peter the Venerable, abbot of Cluny
Liber de corpore et sanguine Domini. See Lanfranc of Bec
Liber de cultura hortorum. See Walafrid Strabo
Liber de cursu spiritali. See Otloh of St. Emmeram
Liber de curvis superficiebus Archimenidis, 1:436a-b, *see also* Johannes de Tinemue
Liber decem capitulorum. See Marbod of Rennes
Liber derivationum. See Huguccio; Osbern of Gloucester
Liber dictaminum. See Baldwin (of Viktring)
Liber de divinis officiis
  incorrectly attributed to Alcuin, 7:629a
  see also Pseudo-Alcuin
Liber embadorum. See Abraham bar Ḥiyya; Plato of Tivoli
Liber Ersemidis in quadratum circuli. See Archimedes, *On the Measurement of the Circle*
Liber evangeliorum. See Otfrid von Weissenburg
Liber ex lege Moysi, 7:403a
Liber Faceti, 3:661a
Liber facetiarum. See Poggio Bracciolini, Gian Francesco
Liber de fine. See Lull, Ramon
Liber Flavus Fergusiorum, prose text on "Fifteen Signs" in, 1:111b
Liber floridus. See Florilegia; Lambert (Laurent) of St. Omer
Liber formularum. See Georgius
Liber gestarum. See Marsilius, Petrus
Liber in gloria confessorum. See Gregory of Tours, St.
Liber glossarum, 4:449b
Liber historiae, Chronographia. See Aimoin de Fleury
Liber hymnorum. See Notker Balbulus
Liber hymnorum (Irish, 11th century), 6:381a, 7:362a
Liber ignium. See Marcus Graecus
Liber iudiciorum, 7:520b–522a
  becomes *Fuero juzgo,* 7:522a
Liber karastonis. See Thābit ibn Qurra
Liber lapidum seu de gemmis. See Marbod of Rennes
Liber legum moralium. See Bissolo, Bellino
Liber mensurationum. See Gerard of Cremona, *Liber in quo terrarum et corporum continentur mensurationes*
Liber miraculorum sancte fidis. See Bernard of Angers
Liber missarum de toto circulo anni, 10:606a
Liber misticus, 10:606a
Liber de moralizationibus. See Holcot, Robert
Liber de motu. See Gerard of Brussels
Liber de natura rerum. See Thomas of Cantimpré
Liber niger, on the history of Lincoln, 7:582b
Liber notabilium a libris Galieni extractis. See Guido da Vigevano (da Papia)
Liber notitiae sanctorum Mediolani. See Ambrose, St.
Liber numerorum. See Isidore of Seville, St.
Liber de obsidione Ancone. See Boncompagno of Signa
Liber ordinarius, Divine Office and, 4:225a
Liber Papiensis, 7:426b
Liber de passione Christi et doloribus et planctibus matris eius, Duelo de la Virgen and, 2:187b
Liber de ponderibus (Archimenidis), 1:437a
Liber de ponderoso et levi, 1:438a
Liber pontificalis
  antipopes and, 1:331a
  on pallium, 12:402b
  paten mentioned (2nd century), 9:456a
  on Pope Leo III, 7:542b
  reference to Agnus Dei, 1:74a
Liber de proportionibus. See Jordanus de Nemore
Liber proverbiorum. See Godfrey of Winchester; Otloh of St. Emmeram
Liber quare, 7:630a
Liber de quinque essentiis. See Kindī, al-
Liber quo ordine sermo fieri debeat. See Guibert of Nogent
Liber in quo terrarum et corporum continentur mensurationes. See Gerard of Cremona
Liber de rebus in administratione. See Suger of St. Denis
Liber de rectoribus christianis. See Sedulius
Liber regum, 11:410b
  Castilian version of, 11:414a
Liber rotarum. See Isidore of Seville, St.
Liber sancti Jacobi. See Codex Calixtinus
Liber scintillarum. See Florilegia
Liber secretorum. See Rāzī, Abū Bakr Muḥammad ibn Zakarīya al-
Liber sextus, 7:416b–417a
  decretals of Innocent IV in, 6:467b
  on dowry, 6:458a
  see also Boniface VIII, pope; Boniface X, pope
Liber simplicis medicinae. See Hildegard of Bingen, St.
Liber specierum, 8:641b
Liber de speculis comburentibus. See Haytham, Ḥasan ibn al-
Liber taediorum. See Salimbene
Liber de Trinitate ad Felicem. See Fulgentius of Ruspe
Liber trium judicum. See Hermann von Carinthia
Liber Urbani. See Churche, Daniel
Liber usualis, 7:555b

Liber usualis (*cont.*)
chant settings of *Agnus Dei,* 1:75a
Kyries in, 7:312a
Liber visionum. See Otloh of St. Emmeram
Liber de vita christiana. See Bonizo of Sutri
Libera me, 4:121b
Liberal arts
Fachschrifttum and, 4:577b–578a,b
in *Tesoretto,* 6:631b
see also Seven liberal arts
Libergier, Hugues, **7:555b–556a**
portrayal of, 7:556a (*illus.*)
Liberius, pope, Christianization of Robigalia and, 7:587b
Liberty and liberties, **7:556b–557b**
biblical exegesis and, 2:213b–214a
the church and, 7:557a
in England, *see also* Magna Carta
as exemptions, 7:557a-b
as franchises, 7:557b
membership in social groups and, 7:556b–557a
Liborius, St., in art, 10:442a, 500a
Libra, 8:428b
Librarian, station of, 7:569a–570a
Libraries, **7:557b–570b**
access to, 7:564b
ancient, 7:558b
architecture of, 7:563b
archives and, 1:445b, 446b–447a
at Alexandria, 1:153a
at Córdoba, 3:599a
at St. Gall, 3:599a
bibliographic control, 7:565a-b
binding of books and, 8:97b
book acquisitions, 7:566b–567a
book circulation, 7:564b
Byzantine, 7:560b–561a
in Cairo, 7:561b
Carolingian revival and, 7:652a-b
catalogs, 7:565a–566a
alphabetization of, 1:206b
Henry of Kirkestede's *Catalogus scriptorum ecclesiae,* 1:206b
cathedral, 7:562b–563a
chained books, 3:240b, 7:564b, 600b
collection categories of, 7:566a-b
in Constantinople, 7:561a
desk arrangements in, 7:568 (*illus.*), 569a
early Christian, 7:559a–560a
sites of, 7:559a-b, 560a-b
early development of, 7:558a, 560a-b
estimates of sizes of, 7:566b
expansion in 12th century, 7:563a-b
funding, 7:567a-b
furnishings of, 7:567b, 569b (*illus.*)
historiography of, 7:557b–558b
impact of printing on, 7:563b
inventory control, 7:565a
Islamic, 7:561a-b, 11:84b
the crusades and, 7:561b
kitābkhāna, 7:273b–274a
in Spain, 7:561b
Judaic
in Italy, 7:562a
in Spain, 7:561b–562a
late medieval, 7:563b–564a
Lateran IV and, 7:565a
medical, 8:259a
monastic, 4:117a, 7:559b–560a
catalogs of, 7:368a
manuscript book production and, 8:102a, 105a
in Ostrogothic Italy, 7:560b
papal, 1:448a, 7:559b, 567a-b
Archimedes in, 1:437a
of Peter IV (the Ceremonious), 9:510b
physical layout of, 7:568 (*illus.*), 569a
public, 7:565a
reference service in, 7:564a
representative authors, 7:566a-b
Roman
imperial, 7:559a
private, 7:558b–559a
terminology, 7:558a
typology of, 7:558b
of universities, 12:298a-b
Venice, Biblioteca Marciana, 9:703b
in Visigothic Spain, 7:560b
see also Literacy, Western European; Richard de Bury
Library of Philosophical Sciences. *See* Khizānat al-Ḥikma
Librate (coinage or income measure), 12:586b
Libre de consells. See Roig, Jaume
Libre del Consolat del mar, 9:511a
Libre del orde de cavalleria. See Lull, Ramon
Libre dels angels. See Eiximenis, Francesc
Libre dels feyts del rey En Jacme, 3:166b
Libre dels tres reys d'Orient, 11:413b
Libre de les dones. See Eiximenis, Francesc
Libre de les dones. See Roig, Jaume, *Spill*
Libre de Fra Bernat. See Via, Francesc de la
Libre de paraules de savis e de filòsofs. See James II of Aragon and Catalonia
Libre de rei En Pere d'Aragó e dels seus antecessors passats. See Desclot, Bernat
Libre de la saviesa o de doctrina. See James I of Aragon and Catalonia
Libre de tres. See Turmeda, Anselm
Libri Carolini, rejection of pagan philosophies, 9:585b
"Libri Catoniani." *See* Cato
Libri duo de synodalibus causis et disciplinis ecclesiasticis. See Regino of Prüm
Libri feudorum, Hugolinus and, 6:326b
Libri memorialium, 6:657b
Libri tres adversus simoniacos. See Humbert of Silva Candida
Libro de Alexandre. See Alexandre, Libro de
Libro de Apolonio. See Apolonio, Libro de
Libro de buen amor. See Ruiz, Juan
Libro de la consolación de España, 11:421b
Libro de' vizi e delle virtudi, Il. See Giamboni, Bono
Libro dei sette savi, 6:659a
Libro del cavallero Zifar, 11:415b–416a
Libro del fuero, 7:522b, 11:282b
Libro del infante don Pedro de Portugal, 11:422b
Libro dell' arte, Il. See Cennini, Cennino
Libro delle tre scritture. See Bonvesin de la Riva
Libro, Il. See Uguccione da Lodi
Libro de la infancia y muerte de Jesús, 11:413b, 438b–439a
Libro de las leyes. See Siete partidas
Libro de las leyes u ordenanzas reales de Castilla, 7:523b
Libro de laude, 6:635b
Libro de los assayamientos de las mujeres, 11:456b
Libro de los buenos proverbios, 11:441a
Libro de los caballos, 11:441b
Libro de los cien capítulos, 11:415b
Libro de los doce sabios, 11:414a
Libro de los engaños, 11:414a, 414b
Libro de los exenplos por a.b.c. See Sánchez de Vercial, Clemente
Libro de los fueros de Castilla, 7:523a
Libro de miseria de omne, 8:281b
hagiographic theme in, 11:439a
Libro siciliano, 11:259a
Libro de la vida de Barlaam e del rey Josapha de India, 11:415b
Libros de acedrex dados e tablas. See Alfonso X (the Learned) of Castile and León, king
Libros del saber de astronomía, 1:613a, 11:642b
translations, Arabic, 11:644b
Libyans, *see also* Berbers
Lice. *See* Insects
Licet in consuetudine. See Clement VI, pope
Licet juris, 5:488b
Licet de vitanda. See Alexander III, pope
Lichfield Chronicle, on the deposition of Edward II, 4:483b, 9:427a
Lichfield Gospels. *See* St. Chad, Book of
Licinianus of Cartagena, bishop, disapproval of popular songs, 11:445b
Lied, in Middle High German literature, 8:354b, 357b, 359b–360a
Lied vom hürnen Seyfrid, Das, **7:571a-b**, 9:114a, 11:289b
compared with *Nibelungenlied,* 7:571a
compared with *Þiðreks saga,* 7:571a-b
Rosengarten and, 7:571a
Liederbuch der Clara Hätzlerin. See Hätzlerin, Klara
Liédet, Loyset, **7:571b–572a**
Chroniques de Jean Froissart, miniature depicting the Battle of Sluis, 9:82 (*illus.*)
collaboration with Lefèvre, 7:534a-b
miniature in *Histoire de Charles Martel,* 7:572 (*illus.*)
Liedform hymns, 6:380a
Liedstrophe, 5:442b
Liège
iron produced in, 8:393b
statutes of 1317, punishments for wine adulteration, 12:120a

statutes of 1332, on remuneration for wine broker, 12:121a-b
Liegnitz, battle at (1241), 2:131b
Lierne, **7:572a**, 7:573 (*illus.*)
as type of vault, 12:365b
Liet von Troye, Das. See Herbort von Fritzlar
Lieue (unit of measure), land and sea measures, 12:585a
Liévin van Lathem. *See* Lathem, Liévin van
Life of Alfred. See Asser
Life of Augustine. See Possidius
Life of the Black Prince. See Chandos, John
Life of Cola di Rienzo, 6:633a-b
Life of Edward the Confessor. See Ethelred of Rievaulx, St.
Life of Euthymios. See Mtᶜacᶜmindeli, Georgi
Life expectancy, 4:145a
Life of Georgia. *See Kᶜartᶜlis Cᶜχovreba*
Life of Grigor of Xandztᶜa. See Merčuli, Giorgi
Life of Henry IV, 6:263b
Life of Heribert, Archbishop of Cologne. See Rupert of Deutz
Life of Ipomydon, The, 8:415b
Life of King Robert the Pious. See Helgaud
"Life of Lucullus." *See* Plutarch
Life of Maštocᶜ. See Koriwn
Life of Methodius, 9:717a
Life of Moses. See Gregory of Nyssa, St.
Life of Our Lady. See Lydgate, John
Life of St. Abdlmseh, 1:520a
Life of St. Alban. See Lydgate, John
Life of St. Alexis. See Vie de St. Alexis
Life of St. Anselm. See John of Salisbury
Life of St. Ansgar, 11:530a
Life of St. Anthony. See Athanasius of Alexandria, St.
Life of St. Edmund. See Lydgate, John
Life of St. Edmund, English King and Martyr. See Abbo of Fleury
Life of St. Eigil. See Candidus of Fulda (Bruun), *Vita Eigilis*
Life of St. Louis. See Joinville, Jean de
Life of St. Oswald, use of organ, 9:274b
Life of St. Pancratius of Taormina, 4:292a
Life of St. Thomas Becket. See John of Salisbury
Life of St. Wilfrid. See Frithegod
Life of Tarasios. See Ignatios, deacon
Life of Willibrord. See Alcuin of York
Lifris, 3:6b–7b
Ligature, **7:573a–574a**
neumatic, 8:627b, 629a, 630b, 9:110a
in Notre Dame discant, 9:192a
numerical, 10:471a, 473a
see also Perfectio; Prolatio; Proprietas; Rhythm
Light
metaphysics of
Franciscans and, 1:461b
see also Neoplatonism; Plato and Platonism
Lighting devices, **7:574a–579b**
Byzantine, 574b–576b (*illus.*)
candlesticks, 7:575 (*illus.*)
choroi, 7:575b–576b (*illus.*)
lampstands, 7:575a
polycandela, 7:575b–576a (*illus.*)
candlesticks, English bronze, Gloucester Cathedral, 8:284b, 285a (*illus.*)
church, 11:655b–656a
Islamic
candlesticks, 7:576b–577a
chandeliers, 7:577 (*illus.*)
Damascene, 6:608a
fawānīs (ceremonial lanterns), 10:255a
lamps, 7:576b–577b (*illus.*)
lampstands, 7:576b
mosque lamp, 5:545b (*illus.*)
polycandela, 7:577a
polycandelon, 10:28b (*illus.*)
Western European, 7:577b–579a
candlesticks, 7:578a–579a
crusies, 7:579a
Jerusalem chandeliers, 7:579 (*illus.*)
see also Chandlery, royal
Lights of the Revelation. See Bayḍāwī, al-
Lignages d'outremer, 1:599b
Lignum vitae. See Bonaventure, St.
Lihyanite kingdom, 1:371a
Líknarbraut, **7:580a-b**
connection to Easter liturgy, 7:580a-b
dating of, 7:580b
influence of, 7:580b
models for, 7:580a
Lilja. See Eysteinn Ásgrímsson
Lilla rimkrönikan, 11:22a
Lille, **7:580b–581b**
as administrative center, 7:581a-b
money changers in, 2:74b
origins of, 7:581a
privileges of, 7:581a
wool industry of, 7:581a
Lily, symbolism of, 2:245a
Lily, The. See Eysteinn Ásgrímsson, *Lilja*
Limbourg brothers, **7:581b–582b,** 8:109b–110a,
illuminated manuscripts by, 5:629b
International Style of, 5:628b–629a
Jean, duke of Berry, and, 7:581b
ransomed by Philip the Bold, duke of Burgundy, 7:581b
Très riches heures, 5:628b, 12:185a
Limbourg, Jean, 6:361b
Limbourg, Pol, 6:361b
Limburgse leven van Jezus, 4:320a
Limes, 2:88b, 89b
of Friuli, broken by Lombards, 2:95b
in North Africa, 8:15a
Vandals and, 2:91b
Limitanei, **7:582b,** 10:459b
see also Magister militum
Limoges, Councils of
(994), Peace of God movement and, 9:473b
(1031), interdict of, 6:495a
Limpieza de sangre, statutes concerning, 3:139b
Linacrẻ, Thomas, 11:51a
Linaje, 3:76b
Lincoln, Corpus Christi plays, 4:285b, 8:658a
Lincoln Cathedral
construction of, 4:472a
Geoffrey of Noyers' work on, 5:390b
use of ribs in, 10:383a
Lincoln, rite of, **7:583b–584b**
Lincoln's Inn, 6:477a-b
Lindau Gospels, 10:100a
Lindholm Høje, grave site, 10:691b–692a
Lindisfarne Gospels, 2:221a, 3:220a-b, 4:458b, **7:583a–584b,** 7:583b (*illus.*)
Book of Durrow and, 7:583b–584a
Book of Kells and, 7:228b
Campanian Gospel list and, 2:180b
carpet pages, 3:220b, 7:0 (frontispiece), 8:370b–371b, 372 (*illus.*)
colophon of, 7:583a
dating of, 7:583a
decorated initials in, 6:461b, 7:583b
glosses in, 4:548b, 5:564b (*illus.*)
Mediterranean influences on, 4:318a, 7:584a-b
modeled on the Codex Amiatinus, 7:584a
quality of, 3:220a-b
St. Matthew portrait, 7:583b (*illus.*), 584a
scribe of, 7:583a
use of colors in, 7:583a-b
written in Northumbrian dialect, 1:276a
Lindisfarne monastery
Viking attack on, 12:424b, 432a
Viking destruction of, 1:254b
Linen, **7:584b–586a**
in ancient Egypt, 7:584b
chief producers of, 7:586a
cost of, 7:586a
early history of, 7:584b
exported from Egypt, 12:107b
Islamic world, 11:16a
manufacture of, 7:584b–585b
bleaching, 7:585b
flax breaking, 7:585a
hackling, 7:585a-b
harvesting of flax plant, 7:585a
retting, 7:585a
spinning, 7:758b
weaving, 7:585b
reasons for popularity of, 7:585b–586a
in sailcloth, 11:234b
in Venetian trade, 12:111b
weaving, 11:701b–702a
wool trade and, 12:115b
see also Flax; Vestments, liturgical
Ling (*Molva molva*), fishing of, 5:72a
Lingua franca. See Arabic language; French language; Translation and translators
Linys, 11:232a
Linzer Antichrist, Der, 2:228a

Lion
in animal tales, 2:205a
in art, 6:408b
as beast epic character, 2:140b
in bestiaries, 2:243a
in folklore, 2:206b
in heraldry, 6:175a
in Icelandic *riddarasögur,* 10:394b
Lion de Bourges
romance themes, 9:634a
see also Elisabeth of Nassau-Saarbrücken
Lion, the Lily, and the Son of Man, The, 10:148a
Lionel of Clarence, in Ireland, 6:519a
Lionello d'Este, Bellini and, 2:165a
Lios Monocus, *Libellulus sacerdotalis,* Hisperic words in, 6:237a
Lipany, battle at (1434), 6:376b
Lipari Islands, 12:162b
Liparit IV Orbēlean of Georgia, ruler, **7:586a-b**
betrayed by Georgian nobles, 7:586b
capture of, 7:586b
Naṣr al-Dawla ibn Marwān and, 7:310b
victory in Arrān (1034), 7:586b
Liparit, prince (*fl. ca.* 1225), S. Karapet church and, 9:159a
Lipmann, Yom Tov, *Book of Contention,* 10:6b
Lippo Memmi, **7:587a-b**, 11:299b
Madonna del Popolo, 7:587a (*illus.*)
see also Maestà; Vanni, Lippo
Lipsanotheca, **7:587b**
Liquescent neume. *See* Neume
Liquors, distilled, 4:219a–220a
Lirius (Lérins), monastery, 8:461b
Lisān al-ᶜArab. See Manẓūr, Ibn
Lisbjerg Retable, 10:342a
Lisbon
Casa de los Escravos, 2:269a
diocese of, Vincentius Hispanus and, 12:456a
Lisbon, University of, 12:287a
Lismore, Book of the Dean of. *See* Book of the Dean of Lismore
Lit de justice, at Parlement of Paris, 9:420a
Litaniae Lauretanae, 7:593a
Litany, **7:587b–588a, 7:588b–594b**
dismissal, in the *Apostolic Constitutions,* 7:589b–590a
etymology of, 7:588b
Greater
course of, 7:587b–588a
origin of, 7:587b, 592a
in the Greek Byzantine rite
aitesis, 7:589b
dismissal litanies, 7:589b–590a
ektene, 7:589b
litē, 7:590a
synapte, 7:589a-b
types of, 7:589a–590b
laudes regiae, 7:593a
Lesser
introduced in Rome, 7:558a
origin of, 7:588a, 592b
spread of, 7:588a
Major. *See* Litany, Greater
origins of, 7:589a
in other Eastern rites, 7:590b
parallel with pagan Robigalia, 10:131a
to the Virgin Mary, 7:593a
in the West, 7:590b–594a
litany of saints, 7:592a–593a
preces, 7:590b–592a
Litany of saints. *See* Litany, in the West
Litē. See Litany, in the Greek Byzantine rite
Litera Florentina. See Corpus iuris civilis, Codex Florentinus MS
Litera hybrida, 8:103b
Literacy
in classical Rome, 7:597b–598a
oral character of, 7:598a
Germanic, 10:465b
Roman, 10:462a
Western European
technological innovation and, 11:645a
translation and the spread of, 12:140b–141a
Literacy, Byzantine, **7:594b–597b**
acquisition of, 7:595a-b
compared with Western European literacy, 7:594b–595a, 597a
evidence on, 7:596a
in foreign languages, 7:597a
ownership of books and, 7:596b
spread of, 7:595a, 595b–597a
Literacy, Western European, **7:597b–602a**
adoption of codex and, 7:598a
church fathers and, 7:598b
compared with Byzantine literacy, 7:594b–595a, 597a
in the early Middle Ages, 7:599a-b
in England
evidence of Paston letters, 9:451a-b
under Alfred, 6:439b
expansion of, 7:600a–602a
Gothic scripts and, 7:600a
Latin language and, 7:598a–599a
pecia system and, 7:600b, 601b
punctuation and, 7:598a
Roman antecedents of, 7:597b
silent reading and, 7:599b–600a
universities and, 7:600b
vernacular languages and, 7:369b, 601a-b
word separation and, 7:599a, 599b–600a
see also Alphabets; Encyclopedias and dictionaries, Western European
Literae florissae, 6:462b
Literature. *See* national literatures and individual authors and works
Lithuania, **7:602a–609b**, 7:603 (map)
administration of, in 14th century, 7:608b
Christianization of, 7:607a, 609a, 9:725a-b
cities of, 7:608b
early political organization of, 7:603a-b
expansion
in the 12th century, 7:604a
into East Slavic lands, 7:605a
first mention of, 7:603b
history, 14th to 16th centuries, 7:40b–41a
Jewish commmunal self-government in, 7:71b
Karaites in, 7:210a
languages of, 6:438a-b
military conversion of, Baltic trade and, 12:113a
military service families, Muscovite suzerainty, 8:548a-b
mints and money in, 8:426b
Muscovite expansion, 8:546b
relations with
Moldavia, 10:515a
Novgorod, 9:196a-b
Poland, 9:721b, 725a, 726a–727b
ruler of, nature of his power, 7:608b–609a
structure of society in, 7:608a–609a
Teutonic Knights in, 8:444a
13th through 14th centuries, 2:67a
tribal confederation of (13th century), 7:604b
vs. Kiev, 7:604a
Lithuanian language, 6:444b
"Lithuanian" targe. *See* Targe
Lithuanians, 2:64a, 64b, 67a, 67b
Litlyngton Missal, Rolf and, 10:449a
Litomyšl, Bohemian Brethren in, 2:307a
Litsy, 8:574b
Litter, Islamic pilgrimage, 9:650b, 12:148a
Littera bastarda, 8:103b
Littera hybrida, 8:103b
Littera mercantesca, 8:103b
Littera vs. sensus. See Translation and translators
Little Book of Eternal Wisdom. See Suso, Heinrich, *Büchlein der Ewigen Weisheit*
Little Book of Letters. See Suso, Heinrich, *Briefbüchlein*
Little Book of Truth. See Suso, Heinrich, *Büchlein der Wahrheit*
Little Denis. See Dionysius Exiguus
Little hours, 3:67a
Little Poland (Polonia minor). *See* Poland
"Little Synaxary," 11:557b
Liturgical calendars. *See* Calendar
Liturgical drama. *See* Drama, liturgical
Liturgical furnishings. *See* Furniture, liturgical
Liturgical poetry, **9:712b–715a**
Byzantine, 2:505b
in classical meter, 2:510a-b
poetic form, 2:524b
troparia, 2:510b
see also Kanōn; Kontakion
Carolingian innovations, 9:713b–714a
early development, 9:713a-b
Hebrew. *See* Hebrew literature, poetry
Historia, 9:714a
later developments, 9:714b–715a
local traditions and, 9:713b
Marian typology, 1:51b
versus, 9:713b–714a
see also Hymns; Mass cycles; Sequence; Tropes
Liturgical prosa. *See* Drama, liturgical
Liturgical year. *See* Liturgy; Mass cycles

Liturgy
architecture and. *See* Architecture, liturgical aspects
Armenian, saints in, 1:519b, 520b
baptismal, Syro-Armenian, 1:516a, 4:497b
bells and, 2:166a
Benedictines and, 2:172a-b
Beneventan. *See* Beneventan rite
for blessing of knight's sword, 3:302b
Campanian, 2:180a-b
cantor and, 3:87b–88a
for Christmas, 3:318a-b
Cistercian, 3:406a-b
of Cluniac rite, 3:468a
collectarium, 3:479b–480a
colors, 3:484a–485a
Communion chant, 3:504a
in coronation, 7:257a-b, 258b
Divine Office and, 4:222b–223a
drama and, 4:263b–264a, 267a, 272b–277b
Durand's commentaries on, 4:315a
early church furnishings for, 4:361a-b
Eastern Orthodox
Old Church Slavonic translations, 8:572b
in Romania, 10:510a
Eastern-Western church union and, 7:348b
for Epiphany, Feast of, 3:318a
EVOVAE in, 4:529a
Gallican, 8:592b
Gloria, 5:564a-b
Greek, Bulgarians and, 12:484a
with Gregorian chant, 5:662a-b
Hrabanus Maurus on, 6:307a
Hussite, 6:373a-b, 374a
incense and, 6:432a–432b
influence on church architecture, 4:335
Isidore of Seville on, 6:565b
John of Damascus on, 7:124b
"marginal." *See* Misic, polyphonic, in *lauda*
Milanese. *See* Milanese rite
monastic
Benedictine, 10:286a
Cluniac vs. Cistercian, 10:287a
Mozarabic, Isidore of Seville on, 8:638a-b
music for, 8:596a
Nubian, 9:198b–199a
Old Church Slavonic, 12:504a
Walachians and, 12:484a
pontificals for, 10:30a
reform of
Cistercians and, 8:642b–643a
under Charlemagne, 8:638b
ring and staff, 10:257b
Roman, 5:661a
Beneventan rite and, 2:180a, 180b
hymns and, 8:572a
Romanian, Coresi and, 10:511a
Romano-Frankish, benedictions and, 2:177b, 178a
Russian, Slavonic translations, 10:591b
seating for, 5:317a-b
sermon and preaching literature and, 10:78b–79a
sign of the cross and, 11:288a
Slavic, 5:658b
in Croatia, 4:6a
in Moravia, 4:73b–74b
Spanish, 6:563b, 564a
Visigothic architecture and, 12:465b, 466a
stational, **7:623b–624b**
cycle of, 7:624a
definition of, 7:623b
in Metz, 8:301b
origins of, 7:623b–624a
processions, 4:333a, 10:132a-b
simplification of, 5:193a
spread of, 7:624a-b
see also Litany
Syrian, 4:343b, 8:578a
see also Syrian rites
treatises on, **7:624b–633b**
allegorical and spiritual commentaries, 7:630b–631a
Amalarius of Metz, 7:628a-b
Carolingian, 7:627a–629a
Irish, 7:627a
Isidore of Seville's works, 7:626a-b
layers of commentaries in, 7:625a
Norman school, 7:630a, 631b, 10:539a
patristic period, 7:625b–626a
pre-Carolingian, 7:626a–627a
usual contexts of, 7:625a
see also Lincoln, rite of; Ritual; Tonary
use of creeds in, 3:675a–677b
uses of organ in, 9:273a–274b
Western European, music in, 11:664a
see also Anaphora; Communion
Liturgy, Byzantine, **7:610a–613b**
Antiochan influence, 2:468a
baptism, 2:468b, 7:610a
Basil (the Great), 2:468a
character of, 7:611b
in city churches, 7:610a–611a
cycles of, 7:611b–612b
daily, 2:468b
Easter, 2:468b
ekphonetic notation and, 8:618b–619a
emphasis on hymnography, 7:611a-b, 612a
Eucharist and, 7:610a-b
Glagolitic rite, 5:542b–543a
Greek rite, 2:465a
hagiographical texts, use of, 2:518b
hesychasm and, 7:611b
Horologion, 2:468b
hymnography, 2:468b, 7:612b–613b
imago pietatis and, 6:425a
integration of secular and monastic liturgies, 7:611a-b
James, St., 2:468a
John Chrysostom, 2:468a
kanōn, 7:208b
kontakion, 7:292b
language, 2:463b–464a, 489a
monastic tradition, 2:468a, 7:611a-b
Neoplatonic elements, 2:468b
orientalizing of, 4:343b–344a
Patriarch Philotheos Kokkinos and, 7:611b
plainsong, 9:687a–688a
role of Hagia Sophia in development of, 7:610a
symbolic interpretation, 2:468b
translations of liturgical books, 7:613b
troparion hymnographic text, 12:208a
vernacular, 74a-b
see also Litany; Synaxary
Liturgy, Celtic, 3:230a–231a, **7:613b–616a**
absence of sanctorale in, 7:615b–616a
antiphonaries and, 7:614b
evangeliaries and, 7:614b
martyrology and, 7:615a
paraliturgical texts, 7:616a
Psalters and, 7:614b
sacramentary texts, 7:614a
terminology of, 7:614b
see also Litany
Liturgy, Islamic, **7:616a–619a**
annual and occasional services, 7:618a-b
daily salats in, 7:616b–617a
Friday service, 7:617b–618a
primary sources on, 7:616a-b
recitation from Koran and, 7:617b, 618a-b
role of mosque in, 7:616b
Liturgy, Jewish, **7:619a–623b**
Amidah and, 7:619b–620b
Ashkenazic rite, 7:622b
Berakhot, 7:619a-b
differences between the Palestinian and Babylonian rites, 7:620b, 621a
efforts to standardize, 7:620b
Kalonymus family, 7:207a
Karaite, 7:210b
in Muslim Spain, 7:622a
responsum literature and, 10:338a
Roman (Italian) rite, 7:622b
Romanian (Byzantine, Greek, Balkan) rite, 7:622b
Sephardic (Spanish) rites, 7:623a
Shema and, 7:620a-b
standard daily services, 7:619b–620b
Liturgy of the Presanctified. *See* Gregory I (the Great), pope
Liturgy of St. Basil. See Basil the Great of Caesarea, St., *Divine Liturgy*
Liturgy, Western European. *See* Liturgy, individual topics
Liudolf of Saxony, duke
abbey of Gandersheim and, 6:313a-b
defense of eastern Saxony, 10:682a, 683b
Gesta Ottonis and, 6:316a
Liudolf of Swabia, duke, revolt of, 5:475b–476a
Liudolfingians
as dukes of Saxony, 5:474b
see also Saxon dynasty
Liutberga of Wendhausen, 9:12a
Liuthard, bishop, at Canterbury, 3:81b
"Liuthard group," ivory carvers, 7:25b, 10:100a-b, 102b
Liuthard (scribe), **7:634a**
Liuto, 8:562b
Liutolf of Swabia, duke, 11:527a
Liutpold. *See* Luitpold

Liutprand of Cremona, 7:363b, **7:634a-b**
Antapodosis, 11:337b
capitula of, 11:335b
embassies to Constantinople, 7:634a-b
inheritance and, 6:457b
on people called "Rhos" (Rus), 12:434b
Relatio de legatione Constantinopolitana, 7:634b
on Viking attack on Constantinople (941), 12:435a-b
on wine, 12:649a
Liutprand, Lombard king, 2:96a, 7:657a-b
capitula, on slaves, 11:335b
in Italy, 10:521b
Pepin III (the Short) and, 9:500b
reign of, 8:377a
Livere de reis de Britannie et Le livere des reis de Engleterre, 1:265a, **7:634b–635a**
Lives of the Abbots. See Ethelwulf
Lives of the Abbots of Wearmouth and Jarrow. See Bede
Lives of the British Saints, The, 6:70b–71a
Lives of the Eastern Saints. See John of Ephesus
Lives of the Egyptian Fathers, Armenian translations, 1:508a, 518a
Lives of the Persian Martyrs, Armenian translations, 1:508a
Lives of the Thirteen Syrian Fathers. See Arsen II, *kat*^{c}*olikos*
Lives of the Two Offas, Beowulf and, 2:184b
Living cross, 4:9b, 11 (*illus.*)
see also Tree of Life
Livingstone, Thomas, conciliar theory of, 3:520b
Livinus van Laethem. *See* Lathem, Liévin van
Livio, Tito, 3:328b
Livländische Reimchronik, 4:505b
Livonia, 2:63 (map), 64b, 65b
military conversion of, Baltic trade and, 12:113a
Livonian Knights. *See* Swordbearers, Order of
Livonian War, 2:68a
Oprichnina and, 11:195a
Livre
esterlin, 12:585b
poids de marc, 12:585b
Livre des assises de la cour des bourgeois, 1:599b
Livre au roi, 1:598b
Livre de chasse. See Gaston III of Foix, count
Livre de chevalerie. See Geoffrey of Charni
Livre du chevalier de La Tour-Landry. See Geoffroy de La Tour-Landry
Livre du ciel et du monde. See Oresme, Nicole
Livre du corps de policie. See Christine de Pizan
Livre du cuer d'amours espris. See René I of Anjou, king of Naples
Livre de la deablerie. See Eloi d'Amerval
Livre des deduis. See Henri de Ferrières
Livre de la description des pays, Le. See Bouvier, Gilles Le
Livre de divinacions. See Oresme, Nicole
Livre des droiz, 4:515b
Livre du duc des vrais. See Christine de Pizan
Livre des estoires, 3:331b
Livre de forme de plait. See Philippe de Novare
Livre de Lancelot del lac, Le, 10:150b–151a
see also Prose Lancelot
Livre de l'espérance. See Chartier, Alain
Livre du lignage de Coucy. See Enguerrand of Coucy
Livre de l'ordre de chevalerie, Le, translations of, 6:116a
Livre de Marco Polo. See Polo, Marco
Livre de Mélusine. See Jean d'Arras
Livre des métiers. See Boileau, Etienne
Livre de la mutacion de fortune. See Christine de Pizan
Livre de la prod'hommie de l'homme. See Christine de Pizan
Livre de prudence. See Christine de Pizan
Livre des quatre dames. See Chartier, Alain
Livre du roy Modus et de la royne Ratio. See Henri de Ferrières
Livre des secrets, 7:346a
Livre de seyntz medicines, Le, **7:635a-b**
use of allegory, 7:635b
Livre de Sibile. See Philippe de Thaon
Livre des trois vertus. See Christine de Pizan
Livre à un sien ami. See Philippe de Novare, *Livre de forme de plait*
Livre (unit of measure), **7:635a,** 12:594a–595a
esterlin, 7:635a
local usage, 7:635a
marchande, 7:635a
medical, 7:635a
poids de marc, 7:635a
Livres dou trésor, Li. See Latini, Brunetto
Livres de jostice et de plet, Li, **7:635b–636a**
adaptations of Roman and canon law, 7:635b–636a
Corpus iuris civilis and, 7:423a, 635b
Établissements de Saint Louis and, 7:635b
Louis IX's reform ordinance, 7:635b
Orléans region, customary law, sources for, 7:363a
provost of Paris, regulation of court procedure, 7:635b
surviving manuscript, 7:635b
Livs, 2:64b, 65b, 67b
allied with crusaders, 2:65a
Livy (Titus Livius)
French translations, 7:369b
Roman History, 3:166b
Līwān. *See Eyvān*
Ljetopis popa Dukljanina, 11:345b
Ljósvetninga saga, 4:613b, 614a, **7:636a–637a**
dating, 7:636b
family feud
debt repayment, 7:636a
slandering of Guðmundr, 7:636a-b
Njáls saga and, 9:145a
preservation, two redactions, 7:636b
standard of conduct in, 7:636b
technical artistry, 7:636b
Ljóðabók. See Marie de France; *Strengleikar*
Ljóðaháttr (meter), 11:327a, 524a, 524b
in *Hákonarmál,* 4:570a
in *Sigrdrífumál,* 11:288b
in *Vafþrúðnismál,* 12:344a
Ljudevit of Pannonia, prince (*ca.* 810–823), reign of, 4:2a
Llandaf, Book of. *See* Book of Llandaf
Lleu of the Skilled Hand. *See* Lug (Lugus)
Llibre del consolat de mar, 3:569b
Llibre vermell, hymns and, 6:380a
Lludd and Llefelys, 12:600a, 610b
see also Mabinogi
Lluís de Fenollet, translations of, 3:166b
Lluís de Santàngel, Columbus' voyages and, 12:349b
Llull, Ramon. *See* Lull, Ramon
Llyvyr Agkyr Llandewivrevi, 12:601a
Llywarch Hen, *englynion,* 12:598a, 603a-b
Llywarch, king of Dyfed, 4:329b
Llywelyn ap Gruffydd, prince of Wales, **7:637a–638a**
death of, 7:637b
Edward I, conflict with, 7:637a-b
elegies to, 7:638a
see also Gruffudd ab yr Ynad Coch
Henry III, opposition to, 7:637a
lordship of Gwynedd, 7:637a
marriage to Eleanor de Montfort, 7:637b, 12:521b–522a
Peace of Conway and, 3:579b–580a
Treaty of Montgomery and, 12:521a–522b
vassalage of Welsh lords, 12:521a-b
Llywelyn (the Great) ap Iowerth, prince of Wales
arranged marriages, 12:520a-b
expansion of overlordship, 12:519a–521a
homage to King John, 12:519a
legal codifications, 12:520a
truce with Henry II of England, 12:519b
Lo Codi, **7:638a-b**
Rogerius and, 10:444a
"Lo viso—mi fa andare alegramente." *See* Iacopo da Lentini
Load (unit of measure), 12:593a
Loanwords
Arabic, in *Shahnāma,* 11:223b
in English, 6:445a-b
Greek, in Latin, 7:353a, 354b, 355a
in Italian language, 6:625b–626a
in Italo-Romance language, 6:623b–624a
Latin, 7:352a
in *Amra Choluim Chille,* 6:541a
in Italian language, 6:629a

in Romanian, 10:513b
vernacular, in Latin, 7:353b
Lob Salomonis, Das, 2:227b
Lobster-tail helmet. *See Zischägge*
Locator, 11:681a-b
Loch Febuil, in *Immram Brain maic Febuil,* 6:551b
Loch Rudraige, in *Echtrae Fergusa maic Léti,* 6:551a
Lochaber axe, 7:324 (*illus.*), 325a
Lochamer Liederbuch, 8:360a
Locher, Jakob, translations by, 8:361b
Lochner, Stephan, 5:610b, **7:638b**
Adoration of the Magi Altarpiece, 7:638b, 639 (*illus.*)
devotional panels, 7:638b
Last Judgment center panel, 7:638b
Presentation in the Temple, 7:638b
Lock, Adam, **7:639a-b**
Loculus, **7:639b**
Locus amoenus, in *Roman de la Rose,* 1:184b
Locus sanctus, **7:640a**
architectural innovations, 7:640a
connection with biblical events, 7:640a
Lodestone, 11:102 (*illus.*)
magnetic compass and, 11:101a
Lodi (Christmas metrical compositions), 3:319a
Lodi, Peace of (1454), 3:367b, 7:10a, 8:243a, 11:216b
Lodi, war with Milan, 8:378b
Lödöse, founded, 11:530b
Lóegaire, kingdom of, 12:241a
Lóegaire m Néill, king of Tara, Patrick and, 9:463a
Lof vanden Heilighen Sacramente. See Roovere, Anthonis de
Lofty Gate palace. *See* ᶜAlī Qāpū palace
Lǫg (Scandinavian administrative unit), 10:699b
Logarike litra, 12:581b
Loggin (unit of measure), 12:593a
Logic, Islamic, **7:640a–641b**
after 13th century, 7:641b
canon of
Isagoge of Porphyry, 7:640b
nine branches, 7:640b
al-Fārābī, 7:640b
Greek origins, 7:640a-b
medical, 7:640b
opuscules of Galen, 7:640a-b
Ibn Rushd, Aristotelian commentaries, 7:641a
Ibn Sīnā, 7:640b–641a, 11:304a
indigenous Arabic treatises, 7:641a
place in Islamic thought, 7:641b
theory of temporal modalities, 7:641a
three phases, 7:640b
Logic, Western European. *See* Dialectic; Trivium
Logica contra Ockham, Aristotelian interpretation, 9:613b–614a
Logica ingredientibus. See Abelard, Peter
Lögmannsannáll, Einar Hafliðason and, 7:387a
Lögmaðr, 11:495b
Logos, **7:641b–642a**
definition, 7:641b
evangelical view of, 7:641b
in Gospel of John, 7:641b
references to in art, 7:642a
Logothesion tou stratiotikou, 11:360a
Logothete, **7:642a-b**
of the agelai, 7:642a
of the drome, 2:473a, 487b, 4:194b–195a
Byzantine postal and intelligence services and, 10:59a-b
of the flocks and herds, 2:473b
of the genikon, 7:642a
grand, 2:473b
influence of, 2:487b
of the oxys, 7:642a
of the *sekreta,* 7:642a
of the stratiotikon, 7:642a
taxation and, 11:603b
see also Strategos
Lögrétta, 6:393a-b, 394a, 396a
Lohengrin, 5:453a, **7:642b–643a**
authorship, 7:642b
French and German versions, 7:643a
influence on later works, 7:643a
Parzival and, 12:679b
polemic dialogue, 12:573b
political purposes of, 7:643a
sources for, 7:643a
variety of genres used in, 7:642b–643a
Loher und Maller, Konráðs saga Keisarasonar and, 7:292a
Loîd, lai and, 7:316a
Loincloth. *See Perizoma*
Loire River, Viking raids and, 12:430a-b, 431b
Loire Valley, tapestry of, 11:597a
Lok, Adam. *See* Lock, Adam
Lokasenna, **7:643a–644a**
flyting in, 7:643b–644a, 9:173b
Frigg in, 5:301a
Hyndluljóð and, 6:385b
parallels with *Hárbarðsljoð,* 6:98a
plot summary and format, 7:643a-b
preservation and dating, 7:644b
Loki, **7:644a–645a,** 11:27a, 27b, 28a, 31a, 32b
in the Baldr myth, 2:55b
in *Fáfnismál,* 10:289b
in *Haustlǫng,* 12:32a
in *Lokasenna,* 7:643a
midgard serpent and, 8:362a
mythological role, 7:644a-b
in *Reginsmál,* 4:581a-b, 10:289b
Skaði and, 11:325b
Thor and, 12:45a, 45b–46a
in *Þrymskviða,* 12:52b
in *Vǫluspá in skamma,* 6:385b
see also Scandinavian mythology
Lollard Bible. *See* Bible
Lollards, **7:645a–649a,** 8:318a-b
Arundel's Constitutions, 7:647a
basis of teachings, 6:199b–200a
beliefs of, 7:645b
"priesthood of all believers," 7:648a
private religion, 7:648a
sacraments, 7:648a
transubstantiation in the Eucharist, 7:648a
vernacular scriptures, 7:648a
worship of images, 7:648a
biblical exegesis and, 4:547a,b, 548a
Clanvowe and, 3:408b
in Coventry and Tenterden area, 7:647b
De heretico comburendo, 7:646b
derivation of, 7:465a
documentation for
bishops' registers, 7:647b
chroniclers, 7:646b
episcopal registers, 7:646b, 647a
secular records, 7:646b
English archbishops and, 3:83b
English universities and, 3:59a-b
Oxford, 7:645b–646a
first use of term, 7:645a
Hussites and, 10:384b
knights supporting cause, 7:646b–647a
in Latin writings, 7:645b
Lollard Disendowment Bill, 7:648b
major trials, 7:647a
merger with Lutheranism, 7:647b
in Norfolk and Suffolk, 7:647b
Oldcastle rebellion, 7:647a-b
in *Piers Plowman,* 7:645a
"poor preachers," 7:647a
"poor priests," 7:645b
Reginald Pecock and, 9:483a
Richard Rolle's English Psalter and, 9:21a
rising of 1431, 7:647b
social class, 7:647a
stages of movement
Wyclif's lifetime to 1401, 7:646a
1401 to Oldcastle revolt, 7:647a
after 1415, 7:647b–648a
texts
in English and Latin, 7:648b
Floretum, 7:646a, 646b
Glossed Gospels, 7:646a-b
Opus arduum, 7:646a
sources for, academic, 7:646a
Twelve Conclusions, 6:200a, 7:648b
Wyclif and, 12:710b
see also Bohemian Brethren; Wyclif, John
Lombard arch. *See* Arch
Lombard art, **7:649a–651b**
animal styles, 7:649b, 650b
Campionesi group, 2:324b
decorative sculpture, 7:650a-b
baptismal ciborium of Calixtus, 7:650b
Ratchis altar, 7:650b, 651 (*illus.*)
influences on
Byzantine Empire, 7:649b
Italian painting and sculpture, 7:649b, 650a
interlace, 7:650a-b
jewelry, 5:375b
manuscript illumination, 7:651a
Mediterranean styles, transmission to other Germanic tribes, 7:649b–650a
metalwork, 7:649b–650a
helmet plaque from Val di Nievole, 7:650 (*illus.*)
objects of personal adornment, lack of human forms, 7:649a-b
painting, 7:650b–651a
dating of, 7:650b

"Lombard art," as a denotation of *ars dictaminis,* 10:359a
Lombard bands, **7:651b–652a**
Lombard League
alliances of, 6:6a
with Gregory IX, 7:653a
battle of Legnano, 12:562b
carroccio and, 3:117b
common army, 7:652b
consulates and, 3:571a
end of, 7:653a
First, 7:652b
formation of, 7:652a-b
fortress of Alessandria, 7:652b
Frederick II and, 11:271b–272a
internal administration, 7:652b
member cities, 7:652a
military organization, payment of troops, 12:562b
Peace of Constance, 5:213b
recognition of imperial sovereignty, 7:652b
rights of renewal, 7:652b–653a
Peace of Venice, 7:652b
precursors to
League of Pontida, 7:652b
Veronese League, 7:652b
Second, 7:653a, 8:379a
vs. Frederick I Barbarossa, 5:213b, 481a, 7:652b
vs. Frederick II, 7:653a
Lombard, Peter. *See* Peter Lombard
Lombard script. *See Scripta Beneventana Lombarda,* 7:426b
Lombards
allied with Avars, 2:12b
Arianism and, 1:454b
attacks on Roman territory, 3:345b–346a, 9:381b–382b, 383a
coins issued by, 8:427b
craft and merchant guilds, 6:15a
defeated by Franks (774), 2:96a
in the 5th and early 6th centuries, 2:95a-b
Frigg and, 5:301a
invasion of Ostrogothic kingdom, 7:471a-b
in Italy, 10:459a, 465a, 12:555a
arrival (568), 2:95b
invasion of Genoa, 5:383b
Italy nobility and, 9:147
linguistic influences, 6:443a
Maurice and, 10:459b
Milan, 8:376b–377b
Normans and, 11:264a
origins of Venice and, 12:383a, 383b
Rome, 10:521a, 521b
Tuscany, 12:229b
vs. Frederick II, 11:271b
laws, 7:473b–474b
under Frankish conquest, 7:474b
as mercenaries in Byzantine armies, 2:95b
original location of, 2:95a
in Sicily, 11:264b
under Roger I, 11:267a, 267b
under Roger II, 11:267a, 267b
slavery and, 11:335a-b
vs. Charlemagne, 6:435a
weapons of, 1:522a
Lombards, kingdom of, 2:95a–96a, **7:654b–658a**
assimilation of Germans and Romans, 2:95b
boundaries, 7:655 (map)
Christianization of, 7:656b, 8:377a
duchies
Archis, assumption of princely title, 7:4a
assumption of monarchy, 7:656a
finance, 7:12b
Friuli and Istria, 7:657a
royal supervision of, 7:657a
Spoleto and Benevento, 7:2b, 4a, 4b, 657a
ethnic background, 7:654b
expansion in 6th century, 7:654b
financial resources, 7:656b–757a
Frankish-Byzantine alliance, 7:4a-b, 656a
gastaldi, authority of, 7:657a
incorporation into Carolingian empire, 7:657b
invasion of Exarchate and Pentapolis, 7:657a
Italian campaign, 7:2b, 12b, 654b–656a, 657a-b
settlements, 7:656b
laws, 8:377a
Edict of 643, 7:656b
wergild, 12:617b
military organization, 7:656b, 12:555b–556a
monarchy
restoration of, 7:656a
royal court at Pavia, 7:657b
sources of revenue, 7:656b–757a
Paul the Deacon on, 9:467a–468a
Pepin's invasion, 7:657b
political and military organization, 2:95b
relations with
Avars, 7:654b–655a, 656a
Byzantine Empire, 7:654b
rulers of, 8:376b–377b
social classes, 7:656b
Lombards (moneylenders), 2:76a, **7:653b–654b**
accumulation of capital, 7:654a
activities of, 7:653b
customers of, 7:654a
first, 7:653b
granting of licenses, 7:654a
interest charges, 7:654a
partnerships, 7:654a
pawns, 7:654a
profit and loss, 7:654a
Lombardy
demesne farms, 11:676a
Gothic art in, International Style, 5:628a
"liturgical strikes" in, 9:508b
papal politics and, 4:58b–59b, 60a
slavery in, 11:336a
towns, architecture in, 12:320a
London, **7:658a–667a**
administration
aldermen, 7:664a-b, 665b
civil service, 7:662b
common clerk, 7:662b
Common Council, election to, 7:663b–664a
commune, 7:661b, 662a–663a
guild control, 7:663b–664a
mayor, 7:661b, 665b
sheriff, 7:665b, 11:225a
wards, 7:662b, 663b
administration, royal, 7:661a-b, 666b
charter of William I, 7:661a
Black Death in, 2:262a-b
bridges
Bridge House Estates, 7:661a
maintenance of, 7:660a
Peter of Colechurch's, 7:661a
see also London Bridge
building construction, 7:659b, 665b
company halls, 7:666a
stone, 7:660b–661a
town houses and inns, 7:663a-b
Cade's rebellion, 3:5a
charitable organizations
almshouses, 7:665b
hospitals, 7:665a
religious, 7:665a-b
charter for, 3:498b
Christian missionaries, 7:658a
chronicles of, 1:265b–266a, 3:334a
churches
monastic, 7:660b
parish, 7:659b, 660b
preaching, 7:663b
citizen status, 7:666a
privileges of, 7:663b–664a
in civil war between Matilda and Stephen, 3:498b
class structure, 7:664b
distribution of wealth, 7:666a
livery, 7:666a
merchants and craftsmen, 7:666a-b
communal activity, 7:659b–660a
corporation of, sergeant and, 11:208b
Cripplegate, 7:659a
English language development and, 6:437a, 441b
fairs of St. Bartholomew and, 4:587a
fires in, 3:560a
guilds
barbers and barber-surgeons, 2:99b
benefits, 7:665a
journeymen, 7:664b
Masons' Company, 8:175a
merchant, 7:663b, 664b–665b
parish, 7:665a
Scriveners' Guild, 8:104b
Stationers' Company, 8:104b
Worshipful Company of Goldsmiths, 8:287b
land grants, King Alfred's, 7:659a
land market, 7:665a
legal system
Anglo-Saxon, 7:658b
common serjeant and recorder, 7:662b
courts, 7:661b
inns of law. *See* Inns of Court
lawyers, 7:665a
Letter Books, 7:662a
manuscript book production in, 8:104b
mayor, 8:235a

merchants, election to Common Council and, 7:663b–664a
Mercian control, 7:658b
Newgate prison, 9:681b–682a
Norman-Angevin period, 7:660a–662a
Norse influence, 7:659b–660a
Peasants' Revolt and, 9:479a-b
plagues in, 9:680a-b, 681b–682a
play performances in, 4:285b
population
after Black Death, 7:664b
expansion in 11th century, 7:660b
in 15th century, 7:666b
port of
archaeological evidence, 7:659b, 660b
continental trade, 7:658b
pre-Christian, 7:658a
public health ordinances, 9:679b
riots against Nicholas Brembre (1384), 12:333b
Roman, 7:658a
Saxon, 7:658a–659a
location of, 7:658b–659a
suburbs, 7:663b, 666b
taxes and tolls, 11:617a
exemption from, 7:661a
John's tallage, 7:661b
national parliamentary, 7:663b
poll, 7:664a
port, 7:659b
trade and commerce, 7:663a, 665b–666a
international, 7:660b
with royal household, 7:663a
under Henry II, 3:498b
under John, 3:499a
under Richard I, 3:499a
Viking conquest, 7:659a
vs. Henry III, 7:662b
vs. Richard II, 7:666a
London Bridge, 10:411b, 416b, 417a, 418b, 419a
in 1630, 10:415 (*illus.*)
construction of, 10:420a, 421a
heavy taxation for, 10:414b
maintenance of, 10:421b
London, Council of (1102), Vital of Savigny and, 12:479b
London English dialect, 8:310a, 312a-b, 313a
London, Tower of, Hurley and, 6:364b
Londres, Chroniques de. *See* Chroniques de Londres
Long (musical notation), 8:629 (*illus.*)
Longa, 8:588b, 628 (*illus.*), 643b
in *ars nova,* 10:381b
in Augustine's *De musica,* 10:378b
in the *perfectio,* 10:380b–381a
see also Perfectio
Longbow. *See* Bow
Longchamp, William, 7:200a, 10:383b
Longchamps (convent: Paris), 12:688a
Longes Mac n-Uislenn, 6:549a
Longinus, Byzantine envoy to Venice, 12:384a
Longinus, missionary to Nubia, 3:314b
Longo Campo, N. de. *See* Nigel of Canterbury
Longobards. *See* Lombards
Longship, 11:242a
Lonja (commercial exchange in Barcelona), 2:74a, 104b
Lonja de Genova (Seville), 11:214b
Lonja de los Paños (Seville), 11:214b
Loom
broadloom, 11:704b–705a
gender of weaver, 11:712b
high-warp, for tapestries, 11:593b (*illus.*), 594a
horizontal treadle, 11:702b–704b, 703 (*illus.*), 705a
advantages of, 11:704a
European version, 11:703a
gender of weaver, 11:712b
heddle harness, 11:703a
limitations, 11:704b
origins, 11:702b–703a
slcy and reed, 11:703b
weaving process, 11:703b–704a
low-warp, for tapestries, 11:593b, 594 (*illus.*)
pedal, 6:395a
two-beam vertical, 11:702b
warp-weighted, 11:701a–702b (*illus.*)
heddle rod, 11:701b
natural and counter shed, 11:701b
shed rod, 11:701a
weft yarn, 11:701b–702a
Loores de Nuestra Señora. See Berceo, Gonzalo de
Lope Diaz de Haro, Sancho IV of Castile and, 3:134b
Lopes, Fernão, **7:667a**
account of Portuguese history, 7:667a
López de Ayala, Pero, **7:667a–668a,** 11:418b
attribution of *Crónica troyana* to, 11:458a
chronicles of, 11:436a
Libro de la caça de las aves, 11:418b, 441b
lost translations by, 11:443b
mester de clerecía and, 8:281b
political importance, 7:667a-b
Rimado de palacio, 11:418b
legend of St. Nicholas in, 11:439a
preservation of, 7:667b
prosody of, 11:459b
satire in, 11:454a
twelve religious songs in, 11:450a
translations, 7:667b, 668a
López de Baeza, Pedro
Dichos de los santos padres, 11:416b
Qué sinifica el hábito de los frailes de Santiago, 11:456a
surviving sermon of, 11:420a
López de Haro, Mécia, 10:45b
López de Salamanca, Juan, *Libro de los evangelios,* 11:456a
López de Villalobos, Francisco, *Sumario de medicina,* 11:441b
Lords, *see also* Class structure; Kingship; Nobility and nobles
Lords Appellant, 6:428a, 9:429a
Thomas Usk and, 12:334a
Lord's Prayer II, The, 4:550b
Lore of places. *See Dindshenchas*
Lorens d'Orléans (Gallus), *Somme le roi (roy),* 1:263a, 547b, 5:290a, 639b, 8:317a, 10:301b
Chaucer's *Canterbury Tales* and, 8:322a
Lorenzetti, Ambrogio, **7:668a–670a**
altarpieces, of S. Procolo, 7:668a
Florentine painters' guild, membership in, 7:668a
frescoes, 5:293b–294a, 606b
Annunciation to the Virgin, 7:668b, 669a
Effects of Good Government, 5:292b (*illus.*), 606b, 7:668b, 668b–669a, 669 (*illus.*), 11:280b, 12:328b (*illus.*)
Marriage of the Virgin, 7:668b
influence of, 12:124b, 171a, 175a
on Francesco Traini, 12:124a–125b (*illus.*)
Madonna and Child, 7:668b
Madonna del Latte, 7:668b, 12:174 (*illus.*)
Maestà, 5:294a, 7:669b
object of art, 7:669b–670a
panels, 10:117b (*illus.*)
life of St. Nicholas, 7:668b
Presentation of the Virgin, 7:668b
Rapolano Madonna, 7:668b
Presentation of Christ at the Temple, 5:606b
pupil of Duccio, 4:302b
see also Nardo di Cione; Vanni, Andrea; Vanni, Lippo
Lorenzetti, Pietro, **7:670a–671a**
Birth of the Virgin, 5:604b (*illus.*)
frescoes, 5:293b, 606b, 7:670b–671a
at S. Francesco (Assisi), 1:593b–594a
Virgin and Child, 7:670b (*illus.*)
influence on Francesco Traini, 12:124a–125b (*illus.*)
Life of Christ cycle, 9:447a
Madonna and Child with Angels, 7:670a
paintings by, 12:173a–174b (*illus.*)
panels
Birth of the Virgin, 7:670a-b, 12:174a (*illus.*)
Carmelite altarpiece, 7:670a
Madonna and Child, 7:670a
Virgin and Saints, 7:670a
pupil of Duccio, 4:302b
see also Nardo di Cione; Vanni, Andrea; Vanni, Lippo
Lorenzo della Volpaia of Florence, clocks and mathematical instruments made by, 11:103b
Lorenzo Monaco, **7:671a–672a**
Agony in the Garden, 7:671b
Annunciation altarpiece, 7:671b
"cutout" crucifix, 7:671b (*illus.*), 9:362a
frescoes of, 5:296a
influence of, 10:536a
Life of the Virgin, fresco cycle, 7:671b
Man of Sorrows, 7:671b
works in International Style, 5:607a-b, 628a
Lorenzo di Niccolò di Martino, **7:671a**
Coronation of the Virgin, 7:671a
S. Bartholomew, 7:671a
Spinello Aretino and, 11:464a

Lorenzo of Orvieto, 8:648a
Lorenzo Veneziano, **7:672a**
Lorenzstadt, founded, 9:201a-b
Loṙi, **7:672a–673a**
Bagratid rule, 7:672a
cultural centers, 7:672b
emergence as independent kingdom, 7:672a
Loṙē, fortified city of, 7:672b
natural resources, 7:672b
Seljuk conquest, 7:672b
trade and commerce, 7:672b
Zakᶜarids and, 12:736b
Loṙi-Tašir
Gurgēn and, 1:483a
under David Anhołin, 1:484b
Lorica, 3:231a
Lorki, Joshua. *See* Gerónimo de Santa Fé
Loros, 3:615a
Lorraine
Otto I (the Great) and, 9:301a
resistance to Conrad of Franconia's election, 5:474b
rule of, 5:508a-b
serfdom and, 11:205a
stem duchies in, 5:508a-b
Lorris, charter of liberty, 11:677b
Lorsch, abbey of, 3:89b
Lorsch, gatehouse at, 10:92b
Lorsch Gospels, 10:100a, 305b
Caroline minuscule in, 1:213b (*illus.*)
uncial letters from, 1:213b (*illus.*)
Los Toros de Guisando, Treaty of (1468), 3:138b
Losengier. See Trouvères
Lotario di Segni. *See* Innocent III, pope
Lote, Stephen, **7:673a**
Lothair. *See* Lothar
Lothair Cross, 10:105b–106a
Lothar I, Holy Roman Emperor
Burgundy under, 2:428b
civil war over Carolingian succession, 3:112b, 114a
Hrabanus Maurus and, 6:306a
Nithard on, 9:143a
patronage of Sedulius Scottus, 11:141a
peace with Louis I the Pious, 8:377b
Lothar II, Holy Roman Emperor
acquisition of Billung duchy, 10:685a
Burgundy under, 2:428b
defeat of imperial forces, 10:685a
election of, 4:427a, 5:478a
Magnus of Denmark and, 4:152b–153a
reign of, 3:114a, 5:478a-b
seal of, 10:100b
selection of margrave, 10:685a
Zähringens and, 11:527b, 538b
Lothar II of Lorraine, king, Nicholas I and, 9:121a, 121b
Lothar of Supplinburg, duke of Saxony. *See* Lothar II, Holy Roman Emperor
Lotharingia, Rudolph of Auxerre and, 11:537b
Lotharingian cycle, 9:634a
Lotharingian reform, Hungarian church and, 11:479b
Lothario dei Segni. *See* Innocent III, pope
Lothian, 8:56a, 57a
Lots (in astrology), 1:619b
"Louage à Marie d'Orléans." *See* Villon, François
Lough Foyle. *See* Loch Febuil
Louis I (the Pious), Holy Roman Emperor, 3:620b, 7:86a
area ruled by, 5:473a
Benedict of Aniane and, 2:168a, 170b
capitularies, 3:91b
on public works, 10:411a
Carolingian Latin poetry and, 3:100b
church reform of, 3:347b
consecrated as king of Aquitaine, 1:366b
coronation of, 7:256b, 9:374b
death of, 5:474a, 6:437a
deposition of, 4:159a
Heliand and, 6:151a
Jews and, 7:76a, 11:210b
life of
by Ermoldus Nigellus, 2:236a, 4:507b
by Theganus, 12:7b–8a
Lothar and
civil war, 3:112b, 114a
conclusion of peace, 8:377b
missi dominici under, 8:438b
monastic reform and, 10:286a
monastic schools under, 11:76b–77a
Nithard on, 9:143a
palace of, 10:97a
relic authentication and, 10:298a-b
Robert the Strong and, 3:89b
rule over Carolingian Empire, 3:111a–112b
Saxon bishoprics, 10:683a
Smaragdus of St. Mihiel's advice to, 11:351a
Theodulf of Orléans and, 12:20a
vernacular and, 6:440a
Viking raids and, 12:429b
Walafrid Strabo and, 6:306a
Louis II, Holy Roman Emperor, Nicholas I and, 9:121a
Louis I of Anjou, duke, 3:270a
Louis I of Bavaria, duke, 2:134b–135a
Neidhart "von Reuental" and, 9:93a
plots against Frederick II, 5:484a
Louis IV of Bavaria, king. *See* Louis IV of Germany, emperor
Louis II of Bourbon, duke, Tunisian crusade of, 4:491a
Louis I de Nevers, count of Flanders
Edward III of England and, 5:82a, 523a
rule of, 3:503a
Louis II de Mâle, count of Flanders
Beauneveu and, 2:145a
Charles V of France and, 3:270a
conflict with Ghent, 5:82b, 523b
Louis V of France, king, last Carolingian ruler, 3:115b
Louis VI (the Fat) of France, king, **7:673a–674b**
charters of privilege, 3:494b, 5:159b–160a, 7:674a
church and, 5:160b, 7:674a
reform of, 3:347b
councils, 7:674a
Garlande family and, 11:160a
government, great offices of the crown, 7:674a
intervention in Flanders, 5:161a
king's evil and, 7:255b
marriage to Bertrada, 7:673a
military campaigns
against Henry I, 7:673b
feudal lords, 7:673b
Odo of Deuil's chronicle of, 7:264a
Paris under, 9:402b–403a
reinforcement of Île-de-France, 5:159b
seal of, 11:127b
siege of Le Puiset, 3:145a
Suger and, 11:502b–503a, 504a
life of, 2:236b, 7:264a
see also Flanders
Louis VII of France, king
alliance with Champagne, 5:161b
changes after crusades, 5:161a, 161b–162a
church reform of, 3:347b
coronation of, 7:258a
imposition of Peace of God on France, 9:475a
marriages
need for male heir, 5:161a
to Adèle, 5:161b
to Eleanor of Aquitaine, 5:161a
office of bailli and, 2:52b
pilgrimage to Canterbury, 3:83a
Renard the Fox stories and, 10:313b
seal of, 11:127b, 128b
in Second Crusade, 4:30b, 37b, 38a
Suger of St. Denis and, 11:504a
taxation, 11:620a
Louis VIII of France, king
conflict with Albigensian heretics, 5:165a
coronation, 9:553b
heretics and, 6:483b
invasion of England, 5:165a
vs. Languedoc, 7:339b
Louis IX of France, king, **7:674b–676a**
abolition of appeal by combat, 9:418a
arbitration activities, 7:675b
armor of, 1:526a
Baldwin II and, 7:349b
Barons' War and, 11:297b–298a
Baybars and, 2:138a
building program of, 9:405a
canonization of, 5:171b, 7:676a
charitable acts, 7:675b
Charles I of Anjou and, 11:272b
church taxation and, 11:609b
construction program, Ste. Chapelle, 10:624a
crusades, 4:25b, 52b–54a, 59b, 7:675a, 676a
financing of, 11:620a
crusades of
demands needed to support, 5:169b–170a
Edward I of England and, 4:396a
financed by Italian merchant bankers, 2:77b
first uprising of the Pastoureaux and, 9:452b–454a
Jean d'Ibelin (of Jaffa) and, 6:390a

presence of opposition leaders on, 5:169a
ships for, 9:80b
William II and, 7:378a
effectiveness of rule, 5:166b
encouragement of dyeing industry, 4:328b
Établissements. See Établissements de St. Louis
Eudes of Montreuil and, 4:519a
Eudes Rigaud and, 4:519a-b
Genoese shipbuilders and, 11:232b
governmental reforms, 7:675a
Parlement of Paris, 7:676a
Innocent III and, 6:466b
instructions to his children, 3:661b
Jews and, 7:77b, 78a, 89a, 675a-b, 11:211a
money lenders, 2:81b
Joinville and, 2:236b, 3:332b, 7:143b, 144a
king's evil and, 7:255b–256a
Les enseignemens, 8:435a
military campaigns, 7:674b–675a
monetary reforms of, 5:680a
origins of the Parlement of Paris and, 9:418a
Paris under, 9:405a
University, 9:405a, 409a
as patron of the arts, 9:405a
Raymond VII of Toulouse and, 6:486b
regency of mother, 7:674b
regulation of mayors' activities and expenditures, 8:235a
reign of, 5:172b
relations with church, 7:675a, 675b–676a
friars and, 7:675b
relationship with mother, 7:675a
religious pieties, 7:675a, 675b
rhymed office for, 10:374a
royal courts and, 6:479b, 480a
serfdom and, 11:206b
veneration of relics of, 10:298b
Vincent of Beauvais and, 12:454a, 454b–455a
William of Rubruck and, 4:556b
see also Blanche of Castile
Louis X of France, king
Charte aux Normands, 9:420b
charters of reform, 5:181b
Jean de Remi and, 2:144a
Jews and, 4:564a
Joinville and, 7:144a
Normandy and, 9:169a
taxation policy, 11:621b
Louis XI of France, king, **7:676a–677a,** 12:352b
ambassadors for, 4:208a
Angelus bell and, 2:166a
arbitration of the Barons' War, 2:112a
Arras and, 11:596b
biography by Philippe de Comines, 2:237a
Botu and, 6:472b
character of, 5:279a
Comines in service of, 3:487a-b
conflicts with Burgundy, 5:189b, 7:676b
Diesbach and, 11:545a
economic policy, 7:676b–677a
fairs and, 4:585b
"gathering in" of territories, 5:189a, 189b
Languedoc and, 7:341b
in literature, 7:676a
Lyons and, 7:699b–700a
princes and
appanages, liquidation of, 7:676b
coalition, concessions to, 7:676b
purchase of Hungarian-style chariot and, 12:378a
reactions to death of, 5:189b
rebellion against father, 7:676b
representative assemblies and, 10:322b–323a, 327b
reversal of father's policies, 5:189a
taille and, 11:579b
University of Paris under, 9:410a
Vermandois and, 12:396a
Louis XII of France, king
as duke of Milan, 8:380b, 12:464b
in Italy, 11:216b
representative assemblies and, 10:323b
Rhétoriqueurs and, 10:364b
tomb of, 4:120a
University of Paris under, 9:410b
Louis XIV of France, king, representative assemblies and, 10:316b
Louis XVI of France, king, serfdom and, 11:207a
Louis I (the German), East Frankish king, Strasbourg oaths and, 11:488a
Louis II (the German), East Frankish king, Nithard on, 9:143a
Louis II (the Stammerer), West Frankish king
Burgundy under, 2:428b
Gauzlin and, 2:173b
rule over Carolingian Empire, 3:114b–115a
seizure of Bari, 2:108b
Louis III (the Younger), West Frankish king, 3:114a, 7:679a
Louis III (the Blind) of Germany, emperor, 2:428b–429a
Louis IV of Germany, emperor
court of, 2:135a
Dominicans and, 11:516a
election of, 4:428b
excommunication of, 7:125b
feud with John XXII, 3:515a, 4:259a, 5:203b, 488a-b, 7:687b–688a
German representative assemblies and, 10:330a
grant of Lithuania to Teutonic Knights, 7:606a
Italian campaign of, 5:488b
laws of influenced by the *Schwabenspiegel,* 11:81a
legitimacy of elections and, 5:492a
Licet iuris, 4:428b
Marsilius and, 4:132a
Nicholas of Autrecourt and, 9:122a
Nuremberg and, 9:202a
Ockham and, 9:209b–210a
reign of, 5:488a-b
removal of, 5:488b
in Rome, 10:524a
Waldstätte and, 11:542a
Louis I (the Great) of Hungary, king, 6:344a, 9:727a
Dalmatia and, 4:80a
Dragoş and, 10:514b
Golden Bull and, 6:335b
Ottomans and, 6:345b
Ruthenian conquest, 12:501b
treaty with Vladislav I of Walachia, 12:501a
Louis II of Hungary, king
diet and, 6:336a
reign of, 6:349a
Louis I of Orléans, duke, 3:272b, 12:353a
assassination of, 5:187b
conflict with Philip of Burgundy, 5:187a-b
Enguerrand VII and, 4:490b, 491a
marriage of, 12:464b
Louis the Bavarian. *See* Louis IV of Germany, emperor
Louis de Berchem. *See* Berchem, Louis de
Louis of Blois, count, killed, 7:347a
Louis of Burgundy, 7:379b
Louis of France, dauphin (son of Louis XI), 12:454b–455a
Louis, St. *See* Louis IX of France
Louis le Sancerre, tomb of, 6:334b
Louis (the Child), East Frankish king
last Carolingian ruler, 5:474a
rule over Carolingian Empire, 3:114b
vs. Magyars, 6:338a
Louis of Toulouse, St., 12:238 (*illus.*)
Richardus de Mediavilla and, 10:388b
Louis van Valbecke, pedal board, invention of, 9:275a
Loup, Jean, **7:677a-b**
Rheims Cathedral and, 7:677a, 10:344b
Louth (shire), 6:519b
Louvain, manufacture of scientific instruments in, 11:103a
Louvain treatises, 11:364a, 365a
Louvain, University of, 12:289a-b
Nicholas of Cusa and, 9:123a
nominalism and, 9:157b
via moderna and, 12:408a
Louvet, Jean, miracle plays of, 8:432b
Louvre
library of, 7:567a
renovation of, 4:295a
"Louvre School" (armor workshop), 1:529b, 536b
Love
in *Breviari d'amor,* 4:506b
three arts of, 8:410b–411a
Love, courtly. *See* Courtly love
Love songs. *See* Troubadours; *Trouvères*
Love-Council of Remiremont, Ovidian influence, 9:313b
Lovell, Thomas, speaker of the 1485 parliament, 9:434a
Low Countries, 5:78 (map)
Black Death in, 2:261a
center of manuscript production, 3:210a-b
commercial development of, 12:112b
land reclamation, 12:579a
local government, 4:379a-b

Low Countries (*cont.*)
paper introduced into, 9:390a
peat bog reclamation, 12:577b
settlement of, 11:681b
trade and commerce
Flanders, 6:96a
in the late Middle Ages, 12:115b
Scandinavia, 6:95b–96a
universities in, 12:289a-b
waterworks, 12:577a-b, 578b
see also Flanders, county of
Low Franconian language. *See* Dutch language
Low German dialects
Frisian and, 6:441b
Protestantism and, 6:44b
Lower Exchequer. *See* Exchequer
Loyalty oaths. *See* Oaths
Lübeck, **7:679b–684b,** 12:112b–113a
bishops, relations with Holstein, 7:681b
building construction, 7:681b
carnival plays, 4:271b
charters granted, 7:680b
churches
St. Catherine's, 7:683a
St. Marys, 7:682b
civic center, 7:682b
class structure, 7:682b–683a
distribution of wealth, 7:683b
patricians, 7:682b, 683a
demographics, 7:682b–683a
after plague, 7:683a
economy of, 5:458a
decline in 16th century, 7:684b
expansion, 14th century, 7:682a
Henry the Lion and, 7:680a
fishing industry, 7:680a
founding of, 5:632b–633a, 7:679b–680a, 9:88b
government, 5:458b, 7:683a, 683b–684a
Holstein, counts of
annexation by, 7:680a
protection agreements with, 7:681a, 681b
Holstentor gate, 7:684b
hospitals, schools, cloisters, 7:682b
imperial rule, 7:680b
"Jerusalemberg," 11:467b
Kalmar Union, 7:684a
laws, 7:680b
legal code, 7:683b
making of, 7:683a
merchants association, control of Lüberg saltworks, 10:630b
merchants in, 5:460a
morality plays, 4:271a, 271b
Old Lübeck, 7:679b–680a
population of, 5:458a
as port city, 5:460b–461a
relations with
Denmark, 4:155a, 6:93a, 7:680b, 681b, 684a
Norway, 6:396b, 397a
relocation by Henry the Lion, 10:685b
renderers, political demands of, 7:683b
rights over its bridge, 10:416b
robber barons, protection from, 7:681a
ship tolls, conflict over, 7:684a
Stecknitz Canal, 7:684a
town plan, 7:681b
trade and commerce, 6:92b, 7:680a-b
with England, 6:91a
hansa membership, 6:90a-b
international, 7:683a
loss of strategic position, 6:95a
routes, protection of, 7:680b–681a
uprisings in, 5:470a
Vitalienbrüder, conflicts with, 7:684a
see also Hanseatic League
Lublin, Union of (1569), 7:40b
Luca di Tommè, **7:677b**
Assumption of the Virgin, 7:677b, 678a (*illus.*)
Crucifixion, 7:677b
Madonna and Child with Saints, 7:677b
Lucan
Arnulf of Orléans on, 7:366a
in Christian hymns, 6:383b
De bello civili
on Celtic divinities, 9:46a
translated by Jean de Thuim, 9:638a
Nile and, 9:137b
Pharsalia, source for *Rómverja saga,* 10:528a
Lucanor. *See* Manuel, Don Juan
Lucas de Iranzo, Miguel, biography of, 11:433a, 433b
Lucas de Penna, 10:62a, 11:274a-b
on equity, 4:502a
Lucas of Túy, bishop, 11:414a
Chronicon mundi, 11:406b
on Laurentius Hispanus, 7:385b
Lucca
bridge over the Sergio, 10:418b, 420b
commune of, 3:500a
money changers in, 2:74a, 74b
Ricciardi company of, 2:76b, 77b
sericulture in, 11:295a
Lucca Cathedral, *Volto Santo* and, 12:489b, 490a (*illus.*)
Lucena, Juan de
Epístola exhortatoria a las letras, 11:425a
Libro de vita beata, 11:422b
Lucena, Luis de, *Repetición de amores,* 11:423b
Lucena, Martín de, gospel translation of, 11:443a
Lucernarium
paschal vigil and, 4:367a
see also Vespers
Lucerne, 11:542b
Last Judgment play, 4:285a
Pfahlburger and, 11:544a
Waldstätte and, 11:543b
Lucerne hammer, 7:324 (*illus.*), 324a, 325a
Lucerne Passion
censorship of, 4:267b
staging of, 4:270a-b
Lucian of Antioch, subordinationism, 9:560b
Lucian of Samosata, on early Christians, 3:334b–335a
Lucić, Hanibal, 4:80a
Lucidario, **4:434a–435b,** 11:415b
see also Elucidarium
Lucidarium in arte musicae planae. See Marchettus of Padua
Lucidarius, Seifrid Helbling's work and, 11:142b
Lucina, crypt of. *See* Crypt of Lucina
Lucius III, pope
Joachim of Fiore and, 7:113a
Ad abolendam, 3:186b
Anno and, 9:127b
grants indulgences to Armenians, 3:394a
heretics and, 6:483b
Humiliati and, 6:464a
subsidy and, 11:606b
Lucretius, Isidore of Seville and, 6:564a
Lucy, St., Spanish prose life of, 11:439b
Lud-Hudibras, 3:81a
Luder von Braunschweig, German version of Books of the Maccabees, 2:231b–232a
Ludford Bridge, Battle of (1459), 12:570b
Ludger, St., biography of by Altfrid of Münster, 1:226a
Ludolf of Sudheim, 4:579a
Ludolph of Saxony, *Vita Christi,* translated into Spanish, 11:422b
Ludus, defined, 4:278b–279a
Ludus de Antichristo, 3:98b, **7:677b–679a**
characterization of Antichrist, 7:678b
dating of, 7:678a
religious drama in, 7:367b
sources for, 7:678b
Ludus Conventriae, 8:325a
Ludus Danielis. See Play of Daniel
Ludus super Anticlaudianum. See Adam de la Bassée
Ludwig. *See* Louis
Ludwigslied, **7:679a-b**
depiction of Louis III, 7:679a-b
genre, 9:234a
language in, 7:679a
theodicean view of history, 7:679a
Lug (British linear measure), 9:504a
Lug (Find), in place names, 6:436a
Lug (Lugus) (Celtic god), 6:436a, 546a, 546b, 547a, 547b, 548b, 9:46a, 48b
Lugdunensis secunda, Normandy and, 9:159b
Lugdunum. *See* Lyons
Luis Dalmaú. *See* Dalmaú, Luis
Luis of Valladolid, on Vincent of Beauvais, 12:453b
Luit, 8:562b
Luitger the Frisian, Alcuin of York and, 1:142b
Luitpold of Bavaria and Austria, margrave, 5:507b
Luitpoldingians
Babenberg family and, 2:6a, 33b
as dukes of Bavaria, 2:134a, 5:474b
Luitprand of Cremona. *See* Liutprand of Cremona
Lukas of Esztergom, archbishop, 6:341a
Lukas Notaras, **7:685a**
defense of Constantinople, 7:685a

Luke of the Convent of the Holy Cross, 5:414a
Luke of Prague, bishop of the Bohemian Brethren, 2:307a-b
Lull, Ramon, **7:685a–687b, 10:181b–182a, 11:407a**
academic chairs, creation of, 7:686a
Arabic sources of, 11:379b
Arnald of Villanova and, 1:538a
Ars magna, 8:445a
Art (Ars compendiosa inveniendi veritatem), versions of, 7:686a
beatification of, 7:686b
Blanquerna, 7:686b, 10:5a
Book of Contemplation, 7:685b
Book of the Gentile and the Three Wise Men, 7:685b, 10:5a
Book of the Lover and the Beloved, 7:686b
Book of Preaching Against the Jews, 10:5a
Catalan literary language and, 7:686b
Catalan writings, 3:157b–158a, 163a-b, 165a
on the circumnavigation of Africa, 5:398a
Compendium of the Logic of al-Ghazālī, 7:685b
crusade literature, 7:686a
Dominican persecution of, 10:181b
exempla and, 4:551b
Félix, 7:686b
Franciscanism of, 10:182a
Franciscans and, 7:685b, 686a-b
guide to preaching, 11:456a
Hebrew language and, 3:314a
Inter sollicitudines and, 3:644b
Islamic influence on, 7:685a-b, 686b
Liber de fine, 7:686a
Libre del orde de cavalleria, 3:666a-b, 7:685b
translations of, 6:116a
martyrdom legend, 7:686a
on missionary activity, 8:445a
missionary work in Tunis, 6:53b
mystical works, 7:686b
Nicholas of Cusa and, 9:123a
philosophical-social novels, 7:686b
philosophy, Neoplatonic realism, 7:687a
poetry of, 3:170b
religious conversion, 7:685a, 685b
Scourge of the Jews, 10:5a
theology
Dignities, 7:686b–687a
reunification of mankind in Christ, 7:686b
theory of correlative principles, 7:687a-b
Tree of Science, 7:687b
Vida coatanea, 7:685b
Lully, Raymond. *See* Lull, Ramon
Lulon, clock at, 10:425a
Lumber supply, shipbuilding and, 11:231b, 246a
Lumber trade, Norway, 9:181a
Lumiere as Lais. See Peter Peckham
Luna, Álvaro de
biography of, 11:433a-b, 436a
execution of, 11:433b
fall of, 11:421b
Libro de las virtuosas e claras mujeres, 11:419b, 440a
Lunacy. *See* Insanity
Lunar year. *See* Calendar
Lund, archbishopric of, 4:153a
Lund Cathedral, 4:153a, 10:189a
astronomical clock at, 3:465a
Lüneburg, salt mines of, 10:629b–630a, 12:113a
transportation network, 10:632b
Lunel, Armand, 7:178b
Lunel de Monteg, 3:665b
Lupold of Bebenburg (Bamberg), **7:687b–688a**
kingship theories of, 7:268b, 688a
papal dispute, involvement in, 7:687b–688a
Tractatus de iuribus regni et imperii romani, 7:687b
Lupus. *See* Wulfstan of York
Lupus of Ferrières, 4:590b, **7:688b–689a**
in Carolingian revival, 7:688b
correspondence of, 7:688b
interest in Latin, 7:688b
Maximinus and, 11:285b
revision of Donatus' commentary on Vergil's *Aeneid,* 12:394a
Lupus Servatus. *See* Lupus of Ferrières
Lupus of Troyes, bishop, 5:471b
Lusatian language, 6:438a, 444a
Lusignan, Guy de. *See* Guy of Lusignan
Lusignans, **7:689a-b**, 9:150b
beginning of rule, 6:220a
of Cilicia, 7:689a-b
complaint against John of England, 5:164a
French branch, 7:689a
as kings of Cyprus, 7:689a-b
as kings of Jerusalem, 7:689a
Levantine branch, 7:689a
of Poitou, legend of Mélusine and, 8:27b
see also Guy of Lusignan; Leo I/II of Cilician Armenia, king; Leo V/VI of Cilician Armenia, king
Luster, in glassmaking, 5:546a
Lusterware, 3:238a, **7:689b–690b**
archaeological evidence
al-Fusṭāṭ, 7:689b
Samarra, 7:689b
Egyptian, 7:690a
Fatimid style, 7:690 (*illus.*)
glass, 7:689b
Iranian, 11:147b, 148 (*illus.*)
miniature style, 7:690b
monochrome, 7:690a
Moorish, 10:65b
origins of, 7:689b
Persian, 7:690b
polychrome, 7:690a
Raqqah, 10:259a
Saᶜd, 10:607b (*illus.*), 608a
Seljuk, 5:379a
Spanish, 7:690b
see also Majolica
Lustration, in church dedication, 4:130b, 131a
Lut, 8:562b
Lute, 8:561b, 562b, 602 (*illus.*), 605a (*illus.*), 607a (*illus.*), 607b, 12:180b
nobility and, 8:596a
Persian, 8:565b, 610b
Turkistani, 8:562a
Lutetia Parisiorum. *See* Paris
Lutgard of Aywières, 9:11b, 12a
devotion to Sacred Heart, 6:69a
Luth, 8:562b
Luther, Martin
admiration for Johannes Tauler, 9:33b, 34a, 11:602b
appeal to general council, 3:655a-b
the art of preaching and, 10:363b
Bohemian Brethren and, 2:307b
commentary on Peter Lombard's *Sententiae,* 9:517b
Concerning the Jews and Their Lies, 7:76b
East Franconian language and, 6:437a, 441b
on excommunication, 4:538a
indulgences and, 6:449b
influenced by Gabriel Biel, 2:234a, 234b
on medieval Roman Christianity, 2:34b
Nuremberg and, 9:202b
on Virgin Mary, 12:461a
Wyclif and, 12:710b
Lutheranism, Romanian literature and, 10:511a
see also Protestantism
Luttrell Psalter
depiction of a carriage, 12:373b, 374 (*illus.*), 376a
depiction of a plow, 12:76 (*illus.*)
Luxembourg dynasty, 2:300b
Nuremberg and, 9:202a
Poland and, 9:724a–725a
Luxeuil minuscule, 9:344b, 345 (*illus.*)
Luxeuil (monastery: Burgundy), 8:440a
manuscript book production and, 8:102a
Luxorius, in *Anthologia Latina,* 1:317a
Luzarches, Robert of. *See* Robert of Luzarches
Lužiči, 12:616a
Luzūmiyyāt, Al-. See Maᶜarrī, Abu'l-ᶜAlāᵓ Aḥmad al-
Luzzi, Mondino dei. *See* Mondino dei Luzzi
Lvov
fur trade in, 5:333b–334a
mint at, 8:426b
Lybeaus Desconus, 10:315b
Lyceum of Aristotle, 1:456a
Lychnidos. *See* Ochrid
Lychnitis. *See* Sewan, Lake
Lydgate, John, **7:690b–696b**, 8:323a-b
As a Midsummer Rose, 7:695a
At the Departyng of Thomas Chaucyer on Ambassade into France, 7:691a
Ballade at the Reverence of Our Lady, 7:695b
Boccaccio and, 7:369b
translation of, 2:286b, 7:692b–693a
Bycorne and Chychevache, 7:692b

Lydgate, John (*cont.*)
Complaint of the Black Knight, 7:694b
Danse Macabre, version of, 7:692a
Debate of the Horse, Goose, and Sheep, 7:693a
Fall of Princes, 7:694a, 8:323b
Flower of Courtesy, 7:694b
French years, 7:692a
Gloucester College, studies at, 7:691a
Henry V, patronage of, 7:691a
Henry VI, patronage of, 7:692a
importance of, 7:695b–696a
as Lancastrian poet laureate, 7:692a-b
Legend of St. George, 7:692b
Letter to Gloucester, 7:693a
Life of Our Lady, 7:695b
Life of St. Alban, 7:693a
Life of St. Edmund, 7:693a
Mumming at Hertford, 7:692b, 694b
mummings, 7:692a-b
Now Is Hay Sometime Was Grass, 7:691b
On the Sudden Fall of Princes in Our Days, 7:692b
Payne and Sorow of Evyll Maryage, 1:323b
Pilgrimage of the Life of Man, 7:692a
poetic style
aureation, 7:695a-b
conception of, 7:693a
influence of Chaucer on, 7:694a-b
language and sentence structure, 7:694a
prolixity, 7:693b–694a
rhetorical amplification, 7:693b
use of humor, 7:694a-b
poetry
civic pieces, 7:692b
commissioned for noblewomen, 7:691b
courtly, 7:694b–695a
instructional and informational, 7:695a
moralizing, 7:693a, 695a
occasional, 7:693a-b
political, 7:691b, 693a
religious, 7:695a-b
Queen Margaret's Entry into London, 7:693a
Reason and Sensuality, 7:694b, 8:603a
Roundell, 7:692a
royal favors granted, 7:691b–692a
saints' lives, 6:63a
Secreta secretorum, 7:693a
Serpent of Division, 7:693a
Siege of Thebes, 7:691b
"Canterbury Prologue," 7:694a
Temple of Glass, 7:694b
Thomas Chaucer and, 7:691a
Title and Pedigree of Henry VI, translation of, 7:692a
Triumphal Entry, 7:692a
Troy Book, 8:323a-b
antifeminist comments of Guido, 7:694b
Chaucerian influence, 7:694a
commissioning of, 7:691a
epilogue, 7:691b
theatrical performance in, 4:278a
use of amplification, 7:693a
Valentine to Her That Excelleth All, 7:691b
verse version of *Secretum secretorum,* 11:135b
Walter the Englishman and, 7:366b–367a
Lydus (Ioannes Laurentii Lydus), **7:696b–697a**
administrative posts, 7:696b
Codex Theodosianus, 10:58b
De magistratibus rei publicae romanae, 7:697a
De mensibus, 7:696b
De ostentis, 7:696b
Peri Diosemeion, 8:17b–18a
on the Persian War, 7:696b
Lygisaga. See Flóres saga konungs ok sona hans
Lygisögur, 10:610b
as pejorative designation of *riddarasögur,* 10:389b, 396a
Lyndsay, Sir David, *Satyre of the Thrie Estaitis,* 4:287a
Lyonese rite, 3:118a, **7:697a-b**
fête des merveilles, 7:697b
primat des Gaules, 7:697a
Lyonnais, seneschalsy of, *plat pays* assembly and suffrage, 10:326a
Lyons, **7:697a–700b**
art and architecture, Romanesque, 7:698a
barbarian invasions, 7:698a
bridge-building brotherhood, 10:413b–414a
in Burgundian War, 7:699b
capital of Gaul, 7:698a
as the crossroads of Gaul, 10:412a
crusades, point of departure for, 7:698a-b
fairs, 4:585b–586a, 7:699b
book trade, 7:700a
French domination in 13th century, 5:171a
government
commune, 7:698b, 699a, 700a
ecclesiastical, 7:698a, 698b–699a
royal control of, 7:699b–700a
Holy Roman Empire, incorporation into, 7:698a
inns in, 6:472b
origin of name, 6:436a
papal councils, 7:698b–699a
Pont-de-la-Guillotière
construction of, 10:420a
rebuilding of, 10:421a
Roman colony, 7:697b–698a
serfdom and, 11:207a
silk-weaving crafts in, 11:296a
social structure, 7:698b
taxes, 7:699a
gabelle, 7:699b
Waldensian heresy, 7:698b
Lyons, Councils of
First (1245), 7:698b
deposition of rulers theory and, 4:160a
Frederick II of Germany and, 5:215b, 6:466b
papal centralization and, 3:361b
on Portugal, 10:45b
taxation of clergy and, 11:606b
Vincentius Hispanus and, 12:456a
Second (1274), 2:161a, 3:94b, 11:272b
church taxation and, 11:607b–608a
failure to end schism, 7:698b–699a
interdict of, 6:495b
mendicant orders and, 5:297b–298a, 7:369a, 10:604b
papal centralization and, 3:361b
use of *plenitudo potestas,* 9:709b
promotion of antifeminism, 1:323b
union between the Greek and Latin churches and, 8:302b
Lyre, 8:558a, 606a
Romans and, 8:601a
Lyric, meaning of the term, 8:334a
Lyric poetry, definition and classification, 11:445a-b
Lyskander, Klaus Kristoffersen, 11:522b
Lytell Gest, 10:436a
Lyubech congress of princes (1097), Vladimir Monomakh and, 12:486a

M

M.N., translator of Margaret Porete's *Miroir des simples ames,* 9:12a, 27b
Ma fin est mon commencement, **7:702b–703a**, 8:7b, 591a
cancrizans composition, 7:702b
rondeau, 10:529a
see also Machaut, Guillaume de
Mā warāʾ al-Nahr. See Transoxiana
Maʿarrī, Abu 'l-ʿAlāʾ Aḥmad al-, 1:381b, 401b, **7:700b–702b**
Al-Fuṣūl wa 'l-Ghāyāt, parody of the Koran, 7:702a
Al-Luzūmiyyāt
personal philosophy in, 7:701b
structural and thematic singularity, 7:701b
death of mother, 7:701a
epitaph, 7:702a
Letters of Abu 'l-ʿAlāʾ, 7:702a
Risālat al-Ghufrān, 7:702a
Saqt al-Zand
commentaries, 7:701a
poetic style, 7:701a
seclusion, 7:701a-b
Maʿarufya (trade monopoly of Jewish merchants), 7:70a
Mabādiʾ al-lugha. See Iskāfī, Muḥammad ibn ʿAbd Allāh al-
Mabillon, Jean
De re diplomatica, 1:427b, 447a, 3:252a
paleographic work, 9:335a-b
study of diplomatics, 6:70b

Mabinogi, 1:566a–567a, **7:703a–706b,** 12:610a–611a
Arthurian tales, 7:705b–706a
Celtic mythological sources for, 7:704b–705a
"Dream of Maxen Wledig," 7:705b–706a, 12:600a, 610a
"Dream of Rhonabwy," 1:566a, 566b, 578a, 12:600a, 611a
four branches, 12:600a, 610a-b, 611b
authorship, 7:703b
characters, interrelationship of, 7:705a
commentaries on, 7:704a-b
Dôn, family of, 7:704a
Irish influences upon, 4:329b
literary style, 12:611a
Mabinogi Jesu, 7:703b
meaning of word, 7:703b
narrative technique, 12:610b–611a
native tales, 7:705a–706a
ordering of episodes, 12:610b
settings, 7:704a
Svipdagsmál and, 11:524b
in Welsh manuscripts, 7:703a
Mabinogion. See Mabinogi
Mac Carthy family, 6:519b
Gofraidh Fionn and, 9:204b
Mac Craith family, Gofraidh Fionn and, 9:204b
Mac Dermot, O'Duignan family and, 6:523a
Mac Donagh, Book of Ballymote and, 6:523a, 524b
Mac Egan family, 6:523a
Mac Firbis, Dubhaltach, 6:524b
Mac Firbis family, 6:523a
Lecan books and, 6:523a
Mac Lonáin, Flann, **8:8b–9a**
legendary persona of, 8:9a
Mac Regol of Birr, Gospelbook painted by, 3:221b
Mac Vuirrich family, Muireadhach Albanach and, 9:205a
Macaire (*chanson de geste*), hunting in, 6:360a-b
Macarie (Romanian chronicler), 10:510b
Macarius, *see also* Pseudo-Macarius
Macarius the Egyptian (the Elder), Spanish prose life of, 11:439b
Macarius (Irish theologian, 9th century), 9:586a
Macarius of Jerusalem, bishop, 1:508b, 5:540b
Macarius, St., biography of, 1:508b
Macaronics, 1:269b, 269a
in the Old English *Phoenix,* 1:280b
Macbeth of Scotland, king, **8:1a**
defeated by Malcolm III of Scotland, 8:56b
Mcᶜbin. *See* Nisibis
MacCarthy. *See* Mac Carthy
MacCraith. *See* Mac Craith
Maccus (or Magnus), king (son of Harold Bluetooth), 3:299b–300a
MacDonald clan, 3:407a, 407b
MacDougall clan, 3:407a, 11:114a
defeated by Robert Bruce, 11:110a
MacDougall of Dunollie, lament for, 11:114a
Macedo-Romanian language. *See* Aromanian language
Macedonia
aristocracy, land holdings, 2:479b
Basil II and, 2:119a
Bogomilism in, 2:294a, 296a-b
Boris of Bulgaria and, 2:329a
division of, after Tzimiskes' death, 2:406b
occupied by Stefan Dušan, 11:178a, 475b
population, 4:595b
ravaged by Catalans, 7:379b
relations with Nicenes, 7:347b
Symeon of Bulgaria and, 11:555a
Theodore of Epiros in, 7:347b, 378a
see also Serbia
Macedonian language, 6:438a, 443b
Macedonian renaissance, 2:117b, **8:1a–2a**
art, 10:306b–307b
Palaiologan revival and the, 10:310b
Cappadocia, 2:441b–442a
classical style
Paris Psalter, 2:441a-b
wall paintings, church at Castelseprio, 2:441b
figure style, 2:454a-b
legitimacy of, 2:440b–442b, 453b–454b
models for, Byzantine vs. classical, 2:441a-b, 454b, 457b
Macedonianism. *See* Heresies, Western European
Macedonians, **8:2a-b**
Anatolia and, 1:241a
Armenia and, 1:481a, 483a-b
in Michael Attaleiates' *History,* 8:304a
return to classical literary studies and, 11:501b
Macer Floridus, *De virtutibus herbarum,* 6:181b
MacEwen poets, 11:114a, 115a
MacGregor chief, 11:115a-b
MacGregor clan, Scottish Gaelic folk song and, 11:116b
MacGurcaigh, Norse influences in poetry, 11:114b
Macha, myth of Epona and, 9:48b
Machaut, Guillaume de, **8:2b–8a,** 8:583b
allegorical characters, 5:267a
ars subtilior and, 1:558b
art and life, inseparability of, 5:267a-b
chansonniers of, 3:256a
codices of work, organization of, 5:266b
collected works of, 8:358a
Confort d'ami, 8:3a, 4b, 7b
consolation poems, 5:267b
Deschamps and, 4:163b
Dit de l'alerion, 5:267b, 8:4b, 5a
Dit dou lyon, 5:267b, 8:4b
dits, 8:5a
judgment, 5:267a
love, 5:267b
structure of, 5:267a
in Faenza Codex, 4:580a
Fontaine amoureuse, 5:267b, 8:3a, 4b
Froissart and, 5:303a
on harp, 8:606b
hocket *David,* 8:6b
influence of, 8:2b–3a
influence on other writers, 5:268a
Jugement dou roy de Behaingne (Behaigne), 5:267a, 8:4a
Jugement dou roy de Navarre, 5:267a, 8:4a
lais, 7:316b
structure of, 8:6a
life of, 8:3a-b
Livre dou voir dit, 8:4b–5a (*illus.*), 7a
lyric poetry, refinement of
introduction of new modes, 5:266a
jeu parti, 5:267a
lyric triangle, 5:266b
use of courtly song, 5:267a
manuscripts of his works, 8:3b
Messe de Nostre Dame, 8:6b, 198a
motets of, 8:6a-b
music of, 8:5b–7b
innovations in, 8:6b–7a
notation and, 8:645b
patrons of, 8:3a-b
Philippe de Vitry and, 12:481b
polyphonic Mass and, 8:594a
Prise d'Alexandrie, 5:267b, 8:5a, 7b, 601b, 608b
Prologue, artistic aims articulated in, 8:3b, 5b
Remède de fortune, 5:267b, 8:4a-b, 5a-b, 6a, 7a, 7b
concept of fortune in, 5:146a
rondeaux of, 8:7a-b
Scholastic-type argumentation, 5:267a
standardization of the ballade, 2:59a, 8:6b–7a
Ugolino of Orvieto and, 8:647b
virelais, 8:7a-b, 12:458b
visions and, 12:475b
Voir dit, poet's love and craft, themes of, 5:267b–268a
see also Ma fin est mon commencement
Machiavelli, Niccolò
on ambassadors, 4:208a
on condottieri, 3:531b
History of Florence, on Cosimo de' Medici, 8:242b
mirror of princes literature and, 10:13a
Prince, 8:436a
concept of fortune, 5:147a
Machicolation, **8:8a-b** (*illus.*)
in Ayyubid art and architecture, 2:21a
Machir, Jacob ben. *See* Tibbon, Jacob ben Machir ibn
Macías
in *Cancionero de Baena,* 11:419a
Rodríguez del Padrón and, 10:438b, 439a
Maciot, 3:62b, 63a
Mackerel (*Scomber scombrus*), 5:70a
Macleans of Mull, 11:114a
Maclodio, Battle of (1427), 8:380a
MacMhuirich family, historical prose written by, 11:116a-b

MacMhuirich poets, 11:114a, 114b–115a, 116a
MacMuireadhaigh, Eóin, *Námha dhomh an dán,* 11:115a
MacNamee family. *See* MicConMidhe
Mâcon, serfdom in, 11:205a, 207a
Macrobius, **8:9a–10a,** 9:701b
on Cicero's work, 1:610b
Commentary on the Dream of Scipio, 4:572a, 7:360a-b, 8:10a, 10:270a, 12:475b
tradition of moral allegory and, 1:181a
education of, 8:9b
grammar textbook by, 8:9b
Hymnarius Paraclitensis and, 6:382a
influence of, 8:9b
Guillaume de Lorris, 6:23a
nightmare and, 12:476b
political career of, 8:10a
Saturnalia, 8:9b, 12:395a
Macrocosmos, 1:694b
Macsó, banat of, 2:70a
MacWilliam of Moray, Donald, defeated by Lachlan, 11:107a
MacWilliams of Moray, defeated by Farquhas Maccintsacairt, 11:106b
Mc$^{c}\chi$et^{c}a, 5:409b, 413a, 419a, **8:238b–239a**
compared with Meteḫi, 8:298b
as a seat of *kat^{c}ołikos,* 8:239a
"Mad Parliament," 11:297b
Provisions of Oxford (1258) and, 10:194b
Madaba map of Palestine and Jerusalem, 7:59b
Mada^{c}in, al-. *See* Ctesiphon
Madara relief, 2:414b
Madayan i Hazar Dadistan, ownership of water resources, 10:661b
Mädchenlieder. See Reinmar der Alte
Madder plant, 4:326b (*illus.*), 11:595b, 12:694b–695a
production of, 4:326b–327a
Madeira Islands, **8:10a–11a**
beginnings of sugar production, 8:10b
discovery of, 8:10a-b, 9:87b, 89b
exploration of, 4:559a
foreign settlers in, 8:10b
settlement of by the Portuguese, 8:10a-b
Madeleine (church: Troyes), tapestry of, 11:592a
Madeleine, La (church: Vézelay), 2:175a, 8:438b, 10:475b, 476a (*illus.*), 479b, **12:404b–405b**
banded barrel vault in, 12:365a
Cistercian architecture, 10:483b
narthex of, 12:405 (*illus.*)
sculpture, 10:496a-b, 497b (*illus.*)
Speyer Cathedral and, 10:488a
Madhhab, 6:581b–582a, 11:569a
Ma^{c}dīkarib, ^{c}Amr ibn, 1:399a
Madīnat al-Salām. *See* Baghdad, Round City
Madīnat al-Ẓāhira, al-, 3:600a, 8:90a
Madīnat al-Zahrā$^{\supset}$, 3:600a, 6:600b, 601b
Mādiyān ī hazār, description of official Sasanian seals in, 11:122b
Madkhal al-Kabīs, al-. See Abū Ma^{c}shar
Madness. *See* Insanity; Mania
Madness of Sweeney, The. See Buile Shuibhne
Madog ap Llywelyn, rebellion against Edward I of England, 12:523a
Madog ap Maredudd
Cynddelw and, 4:69b
praise poetry to, 12:604b
relation to Gwalchmai ap Meilyr, 6:40a
vs. Owain Gwynedd, 6:386b
Madonna. *See* Virgin Mary
"Madonna, dir vi voglio." *See* Iacopo da Lentini
Madonna Lionessa. See Pucci, Antonio
Madrasa, **8:11a–12a**
in Anatolia, 8:12a
architecture of, 6:602a, 608b, 611b, 612a-b, 8:11b
in Ayyubid mausoleums, 2:21b
of Baghdad, 6:606a
in Cairo, 8:11b–12a
in Damascus, 4:83b, 84b–85a, 6:607b
eyvān and, 4:570a
functions of, 8:499a
in Iran, 6:503b, 504a, 8:11a-b
in Iraq, 6:514a
Islamic science and, 11:85a-b
Karatay madrasa at Ikonion, 11:150 (*illus.*)
in al-Maghrib, 8:12a
Nishapur and, 9:141a
origins of, 8:11a
promoted by Niẓām al-Mulk, 11:146b–147a
in Seljuk Anatolia, 11:148b, 149a
in Syria, 8:11b
^{c}ulamā$^{\supset}$ and, 12:245a
see also Niẓāmīya; Schools, Islamic
Madrāshā, kontakion and, 6:378b, 8:578a
Madrid
academy of, 11:392b–393a
Dominican women's religious house, 12:687b
relations with, Milan, 11:217b
Madrid Codex I. *See* Leonardo da Vinci
Madrigal, 1:552b–553a, **8:12a-b,** 12:177b, 178b–179a
distinguished from caccia, 3:4a-b
in Italian literature, 6:640b, 641a, 653b
forms and themes, 6:654b–655a, 669b
terzetto/terzetti pattern of, 12:178b–179a
trecento, 12:177b, 178b–179a
Landini and, 7:327a
structure of, 8:12b
see also Jacobus of Bologna
Madrigal, Alfonso Fernández de (El Tostado), 11:407a
De cómo al ome es necesario amar, 11:420b
Mægth. See Extended family, Germanic
Máel Dúin (literary character), 6:551b–552a
Mael Máedoc Ua Morgair. *See* Malachy, St.
Máel Muire, 6:521a
Máel Sechnaill, king of Uí Néill, 12:242b
Máel-Muire hua Gormáin
martyrology
addition of saints, 8:163a-b
rinnard mor form, 8:163a
Maelgwn, **8:12b–13a**
in *Hanes Taliesin,* 11:582a
Maelwael, Jan. *See* Malouel, Jean
Maerlant, Jacob van, 5:390a
Alexanders geesten, 4:318b
didactic works of, 4:319b
Historie van den Grale, 1:572a
Historie van Troyen, 4:318b
Merlijns Boeck, 1:572a, 4:318b
poetry of, 4:319b
Spieghel historiael, 7:219b
Maestà, **8:13a-b**
by Simone Martini, 12:172b–173b (*illus.*)
in panel painting, 9:361a
Maestro Calo. *See* Kalonymus family
Maeve. *See* Epona
Maforet. See Maphorion
Mag Mell, 6:550b, 551a, 9:47b
Mag Rath, Battle of (637), 6:526a, 540b
Magauran, Book of, 6:535b
Magdalen Altarpiece. *See* Moser, Lucas
Magdalene hymns, 6:384a
of Neckham, 6:382a
of Philip the Chancellor, 6:382a
Magdeburg
governing body in, 5:458b
law code of, 7:482b
Magdeburg Cathedral, 10:94b
Maghīla, 2:185b
Maghrib, al-, 1:622a, **8:13b–15b,** 8:14 (map)
Berbers and, 2:186b
bookbinding in, 8:99b
Byzantine conquest of, 8:15a
conquered by ^{c}Abd al-Mu$^{\supset}$min, 1:194a
economy of, 8:15b
Ibāḍīya in, 11:139a-b
Ibrāhīm ibn al-Aghlab and, 6:391b, 392a
Idrisids and, 6:413a-b
in Islamic conquests, 6:572a
Ismaili community in, 11:138a
Jews in, 7:97b–99b
in legend, 8:13b, 15a
madrasas in, 8:12a
parts of, 8:13b
Rome and, 10:464b, 467a
Ṣufrīya in, 11:139a
see also Meknes
Maghribī, al-, on astronomy, 1:622a
Maghribī, Samau'al al- (physician-mathematician)
Islamic-Jewish polemics and, 10:8a-b
Silencing the Jews, 10:8a
Maghribī, Samuel ben Moses al- (Karaite scholar), 7:210b
Magi
in art, 4:497b–498b (*illus.*)
Epiphany and, 4:496b, 497a

names of, 4:498a
see also Play of Herod
Magi, Shrine of (Cologne Cathedral). See Cologne Cathedral
Magic
definition of, 8:32a
in *Picatrix,* 8:37b
Fachschrifttum and, 4:578a, 579b
forms of, 8:32b
formulas of, 8:35a
later views on, 8:38b–39b
miracles and, 8:33b
pagan elements in, 8:32b
range of magical activities, 8:33a
rituals of, sources on, 8:34a-b
science and, 8:32a
as viewed by medieval thinkers, 8:36b–38b
Magic, black, accusations of Enrique de Villena and, 11:420b
Magic, bookish, Western European, **8:31b–40b**, 12:658a
books of secrets, 8:35a
delineation of, 8:31b
history of, 8:32b
in Icelandic *riddarasögur,* 10:395a-b
influenced by Arabic works, 8:37b
magical texts, 8:32a
natural philosophy in the 13th and 14th centuries and, 8:38a
structure of Christian cosmos and, 8:35b–36b
Magic and folklore
Armenian, **8:15b–17a**
arrival of Christianity and, 8:16a
magical texts, 8:16a-b
methods of, 8:16b
Byzantine, **8:17a–20a**
popular beliefs, 8:18a
sources for the study of, 8:17a-b
gypsies and, 6:41a
instructions for magical cleansing, 8:34a
Irish, 6:67b
Islamic, **8:20b–22b**
concept of authorized and unauthorized magic, 8:21a
Jewish, **8:22b–25a**
cabalism and, 3:3a
transmission of Oriental tales and, 8:23b
pre-Islamic, 8:20b
Western European, **8:25a–31b**
carnivals in, 8:29b
changes in, 8:25b
charms, Old High German, 3:273b–274a
dances in rural cemeteries and, 8:27b
devil and, 8:26b–27a
emergence of lay aristocracy and, 8:27b–28a
fortune-telling and, 8:26a-b
later witchcraft and, 8:30a–31a
medicine and, 8:26a
motifs in, 6:3b, 7:705a-b
music and, 8:586b
natural vs. black magic, 8:30b
practices considered dangerous by the church, 8:25b–26a
in *Ragnars saga loðbrókar,* 10:248b–249b
Rapularius, 10:258a
recipes and charms in Old English, 8:34b
in Romanian literature, 10:511b
runic number magic, 10:559a
Scholasticism and, 8:28a-b
shivarees, 8:28b–29b
swords and, 11:546b
in technological treatises, 11:646a
testimony of inquisition on, 8:25a
transformation of rural space and, 8:27b
urbanism and, 8:7.28a
witchcraft and, 12:658b
see also Prophecy, political, Middle English
Magicians, 8:33a-b
Magister (head of monastery), 12:685b
Magister (title for translators), 12:137b
Magister militum, **8:40b**, 10:459b
origin of themes and, 12:9b
Magister officiorum, **8:40b–41a**
Magistra, 12:685b
Magistretti, Marco, 8:383a
Magistros, **8:41a**
Magius. *See* Maius
Maglocunus. *See* Maelgwn
Magna Bulgaria, founded, 12:488a
Magna Carta, **8:41a–42b**
on bridge building, 10:414b
church's opposition to, 3:640a-b
confirmation of by Edward I, 9:424b
conflict leading to, 12:636a
court of common pleas and, 3:492a-b, 7:187b, 12:159b
distress and, 4:221a
forest law clauses, 5:134a
inheritance and, 9:150b
Jean d'Ibelin's *Assizes of Jerusalem* and, 6:390b
Langton and, 3:83b, 7:338a-b
London, right to government, 7:661b–662a
models for, 4:462a
Articles of the Barons, 4:469a
origins of parliament and, 9:423b
postmedieval attitudes to, 8:42a-b
protection to foreign merchants and, 12:120b
Provisions of Oxford (1258) and, 10:195a
scutage and, 11:120b, 613b
signing by John, 7:130b
to curb royal abuse, 4:470b
translation of, 1:260a
1215 version of, 8:41b
Welsh independence and, 12:519b
see also English common law; Statute
Magna glosatura. See Peter Lombard
Magna Moralia. See Aristotle
Magnae derivationes. See Huguccio
Magnates
Alamannic, vs. Franks, 11:526b
Armenian, 1:475a, 476b, 488a-b
Aršak II and, 1:476a
Ašot I and, 1:481a
migration of, 1:485a, 513a
status of, 1:515a
under Abbasids, 1:479b–480a
under Arabs, 1:479a, 500a, 513b
under Umayyads, 1:478b
vs. John I Tzimiskes, 1:482b
Xusrō II and, 1:477a
see also Bdešχ; individual families, e.g., Mamikonean
bastide and, 2:128b
in Castile, 3:139b
English
as sheriff, 11:226a
treason definition and, 12:166b, 167b
Hungarian, 11:287a
vs. Andrew III, 6:343a
vs. Sigismund, 6:346a
Islamic, 6:591b
knights and, 3:414b
Norman, 9:163a
Battle of Hastings and, 9:165a, 165b
Norwegian, 9:182b–183a
Polish, 9:727a-b
Russian
Oprichnina and, 11:194b–195a
peasants and, 11:196a
under Romanovs, 11:197b–198a, 198b
Sienese, 11:280a, 281a
in Thessaloniki, vs. Zealots, 12:742a
see also Nobility and nobles
Magnaura palace, 9:697a
automata, 11:633b, 634a
Magnaura, School of the, 3:556b
Magnentius Maurus. *See* Hrabanus Maurus
Magnet, in magnetic compass, 11:100b–101a
Magnetism
attraction and repulsion, 9:520b
determining polarity, experiments in, 9:520b
Magnificat, use of organ in, 9:274b
Magnus (priest), Chronicle of Reichersberg, 5:424b–425a
Magnus I Ólafsson (the Good) of Norway, king
invasion of England, 4:395a
Morkinskinna and, 9:177a
þættir and, 12:5a
Magnus VI Håkonsson (the Law Mender) of Norway, king
national unification and, 9:183b, 184a
Sturla Þórðarson and, 11:495b
Magnus VII of Norway, king. *See* Magnus II Eriksson of Sweden, king
Magnus I Ladulås of Sweden, king, 4:505b
Gotland and, 11:531a
Magnus II Eriksson of Sweden, king
German nobility and, 4:155a
Norway and, 9:185a
reign of, 11:532a-b
Swedish law and, 7:525b
Magnus (son of Niels of Denmark), murder of Knud Lavard, 7:280a-b
Magnús Einarsson, bishop, 6:352a
Magnús Hákonarson of Norway, king, translation of *Alexanders saga* and, 10:391b–392a

Magnús Jónsson prúði, *rímur* attributed to, 10:403a
Magnus liber organi, **8:42b–45a**
circulation of, 8:44
manuscripts of, 8:43a, 43b, 44a
three-voice conductus, 10:635b
see also Leoninus; "Viderunt omnes"
Magnús Þorhallson, a *Flateyjarbók* scribe, 12:4b
Magnússona saga, flyting in, 9:173a
Mágus saga jarls, **8:45a–46a,** 10:389b, 391b, 394b, 395a, 395b, 12:542a
manuscripts of, 8:45b
Rémundar saga keisarasonar and, 10:304a
sources of, 8:45a, 45b
two redactions of, 8:45a-b
Magyar language. *See* Hungarian language
Magyars, **8:46a-b**
attack of, on Bulgaria, 2:404b
cavalry of, 3:203a
conversion of to Christianity, 3:355b
defeat of
by Arnulf the Bad, 5:507b
by Erchanger, 5:508a
derivation of the name, 8:46a
destruction of Great Moravia and, 2:299b
Henry I of Germany and, 5:475a
invasions by, 6:338a
travel during, 12:153a-b
Otto I of Germany and, 5:475a
raids in Croatia, 4:4a
in Russia, 6:342a
use of camels and, 1:296b
use of water buffalo and, 1:298a-b
vs. Pechenegs, 6:338a
vs. Swabia, 11:526b, 527a
see also Hungary
Mahalakh Shevilei ha-Daᶜat. See Kimḥi, Moses ben Joseph
Mahasiddhanta (Sindhind), Arabic translation of, 12:128a
Mahaut, (daughter of Florent of Hainault), 7:379a, 379b, 380a
Mahaut of Artois, countess
bequests for repair of roads and bridges, 10:412b
Philippe de Remin and, 2:144a
Mahdī, al-, Abbasid caliph, **8:46b–47b**
accession to power, 8:46b–47a
Barmakids and, 8:47a-b
changes in order of succession, 6:107b
conflict with the Byzantines and, 8:47b
expeditions against Byzantines, 6:107a
fiscal policies of, 8:47a
heretics and, 8:47b
in Khorāsān, 8:46b
second palace complex in Baghdad completed by, 2:46a
sunna and, 11:511a
Mahdi, the, 5:24b–25a, 6:587a-b, 588a, 11:226b, 227b
belief in, 8:388a
Islamic doctrine of resurrection and, 10:340a, 340b
in Ismāᶜīlīya, 6:614b–615a, 615b
Muḥammad's prophecy of, 8:388b
in Sufism, 8:388b
Sunnites on, 8:388a-b
see also Millennialism, Islamic; Tūmart, Muḥammad ibn
Mahdīya, Great Mosque, battlements, 12:553a-b
Mahdīya, al- (Mahdia), 5:384a
conquered by ᶜAbd al-Muᵓmin, 1:194a
decline of, 12:745a
as a Fatimid naval base, 9:75a
fortifications, 12:553a-b
Ismailism in, 6:616a
sacked (1087), 12:745a
siege of, 5:25a
taken by Italians, 4:556a
vs. Roger II, 11:268b
Mahkanaberd, Arcrunis in, 1:451b
Maḥmal. See Litter, Islamic pilgrimage
Maḥmūd II, Seljuk ruler, 11:153b
Maḥmūd al-Āmulī, Muḥammad ibn, *Nafāᵓis al-funūn fī ᶜarāᵓis al-ᶜuyūn,* 4:445b
Maḥmūd ibn Sebüktigin, Ghaznavid ruler, 5:520a, 6:507b, 11:133a, 133b, 302b
Bīrūnī and, 2:248b
expansion of Ghaznavid dynasty, 1:65a
his use of the title sultan and, 11:504b–505a
vs. Buyids, 2:436a
Maḥmūd ibn Zangī. *See* Nūr al-Dīn Maḥmūd
Maḥmūd Shāh of Malacca, maritime laws of, 9:86b–87a
Mahzor, 7:67a-b
Mai und Beaflor, **8:47b–48b**
sources of, 8:47b–48a
"Maiden in the mor lay"(Middle English lyric), 8:339a
Maigelein, 5:560a
Mail
bardings, 1:525a
chausse, 1:524b
manufacture of, 1:533a
mittens, 1:524b
shirt, 1:522a-b, 524a, 524b
see also Byrnie; Hauberk
Maille (unit of measure), 12:595a
Maimon ben Joseph, 7:99a
Maimonidean controversy, 7:81a, 170a, **8:48b–49a**
Maimonides, Abraham ben Moses, 7:84a, **8:49a**
Kifāyat al-ᶜĀbidīn, 7:169a
movement of, 7:169a
Maimonides, Moses, 3:600b, 7:84a, 99a, 108a, **8:49b–50b,** 9:700a
on Apollonius' *Conics,* 11:92a
Aristotle and, 1:460a
on astrology, 11:91b
Commentary on the Mishnah, 7:173b, 8:49b–50a
death of, 10:472b
documents in Cairo genizah, 3:16a
early life of, 8:49b
early works of, 8:49b
Epistle on Resurrection, 8:48b
Epistle to Yemen, 10:9a
as exegete, 2:212a
on Galen, 11:92b
house physician of Saladin's vizier, 8:49b
influence of, 8:49b
Jewish philosophy and, 7:167b
Jewish translators of, 12:134a, 136b
Joseph ben Judah ben Jacob ibn ᶜAknin and, 7:151a
Joseph ibn Caspi and, 7:151b
on *kharjas* in Egypt, 11:447b
on law, 7:170a-b, 492a-b
letters and occasional pieces, 8:50a
Levi ben Gershom and, 7:554a
Maimonidean controversy and, 8:48b–49a
Meister Eckhart and, 9:32b
Mishneh Torah, 7:167b, 170a, 492a-b, 8:50a, 11:586a
first book of banned in northern France, 8:48b
Jewish law, 9:573b
Jewish translations of, 12:134a
order of the rabbis, 6:256a
schools of rabbinic authority, 6:256b
Moreh Nevukhim (*Guide of the Perplexed*), 1:460a, 4:540a, 7:167b, 8:50a-b, 9:577a-b, 10:74b, 11:90b, 12:134a, 135a
on astronomy, 11:91a
banned in northern France, 8:48b
doctrine of personal attributes, 9:577b
knowledge of God, 9:577a-b
nature of immortality, 9:577a
translations of, 11:441a
Moses Naḥmanides and, 9:53b
opposition to Aristotelian views of, 3:677b
philosophy of, 7:173b
rabbinic transmission of authority, Babylonian role, 6:257a
rationalism of, 7:167b
responsum literature and, 10:339a
Sefer ha-Mitzvot, 8:50a
talmudic commentary, 10:259b
in Toledo, 11:410a
on the transcendental character of "pi," 11:92b
translation of his works, 9:510b
Treatise on the Sanctification of the New Moon, 11:90b
Yad ha-Ḥazakah, 7:170a
Maina (fortress), 7:378a, 378b
Maine, county of, William I of England and, 9:164a-b
Mainmort, **8:50b–51b,** 11:201b, 203b
abolition of, 11:204a, 206b
Mainz
as commune, 3:498a
in early Middle Ages, 12:320b
first seals of, 11:126a
Jewish community of, 4:420b
printing in, 10:124a-b
Roman bridge at, 10:410a
synods of (847–852), 6:306a
Mainz Cathedral, 10:488b
Mainz, Diet of (1184), 5:481b–482a
Mainz, University of, 12:289a
Maio of Bari, 11:268b, 269a
Maiolica arcaica, 3:237b

Mair von Landshut, engraving technique of, 4:490a
Mairano, Romano (Venetian shipowner), 12:388a-b
Maire, 3:502a
Maistre Pierre Pathelin, 4:265b, 5:272a, **8:51b–52b**
 authorship of, 8:51b
 characterizations, 5:275a
 dating of, 8:51b
 expressions derived from, 5:275a
 fabliau and, 4:577a
 plot summary, 5:274b–275a
Maitani, Ambrogio, **8:52b–53a**
 Church of S. Ercolano in Perugia, 8:52a (*illus.*), 52b–53a
Maitani, Lorenzo, **8:53a-b**
 Orvieto Cathedral sculpture, 12:171b
 reliefs at Orvieto Cathedral, 8:52b (*illus.*), 53 (*illus.*)
Maître des requêtes de l'Hôtel, 12:481a-b
Maittaire, Michael, *Annales typographici,* 10:127a
Maius (illuminator), **8:54a,** 10:114a
 Commentary on the Apocalypse, 8:54a (*illus.*)
Majd al-Dīn Abu 'l-Sa^{c}ādāt Mubārak, 1:635a
Majestas Domini, **8:54a-b**
 church of St. Pierre, Moissac, 8:453 (*illus.*)
 see also Seraph
Mājid, Ibn, on navigation, 11:638b
Majlis, 8:567b–568a
Majolica, **8:54b–55a,** 8:54b (*illus.*)
 commercial trade of, 1:561b
 origin of, lusterware, 7:690b
Majolus of Cluny, abbot, 3:469a
Major. See Mayor
Major domus. *See* Mayor of the palace
Major, John, 11:112a
 conciliar theory of, 3:519b, 520b–521a
 Disputatio de auctoritate concilii supra pontificem maximum, 3:521a
 Historia majoris Britanniae (*History of Greater Britain*), 1:565b, 10:435b
Majoria. See Mayor
Majorian, Roman emperor, Sidonius and, 11:277a, 277b
Majorissa. See Mayor
Majrīṭī, Maslama al-, 1:385b, 391a
Mākān ibn Kākī, ^{c}Imād al-Dawla and, 6:424b
Makarim, Druzes and, 9:3a, 3b
Makarios Melissenos, *Chronicon maius,* 2:517a-b
Makka. *See* Mecca
Makrān, vs. Ya^{c}qūb ibn Layth, 12:717a
Makuria, 9:197b
 administration, 9:198a
 bishoprics of, 9:198b
 Mamluks and, 9:198b
Malachy, St., 6:517a, **8:55a**
 Armagh and, 1:470a
 Bernard of Clairvaux and, 6:382a
 church reform by, 3:232a
 Irish monasticism and, 6:554a
Malaga, ceramics of, 6:612a
Málaháttr (meter), in *Hákonarmál,* 4:570a
Malalas, John, **8:55b**
 on Beirut earthquake, 2:164a
 chronicles of, 2:512a-b, 6:243b
  compared with *Paschale chronicon,* 9:446a
Malamocco (Venice township), 12:383b, 385a
Malaria, 9:672b–674a, 681b
 see also Disease; Insects; Plagues
Malatesta, Sigismondo, of Rimini, 8:446b
Malatya. *See* Melitene
Malazgirt. *See* Manazkert
Malchus, 11:547b (*illus.*), 551a
Malchus, St., Reginald of Canterbury's epic on, 10:289b
Malcolm I of Alba, king of Scots, **8:55b–56a**
Malcolm II of Scotland, king, **8:56a-b**
 Strathclyde and, 11:490b
 succession of Duncan I and, 4:308a
Malcolm III of Scotland, king, 4:110b, 256a, **8:56b–57a**
 installation by MacBeth, 8:1a
 invasions of England, 8:56b
Malcolm IV of Scotland, king, 4:111a, **8:57a,** 11:104b, 106a-b, 107b
Malcolm Canmore, 11:105a, 106a
Malcolm, Cumbrian king, 3:299b–300a
Maldive Islands, shipbuilding and, 11:246a
Maldon, flyting and, 9:175a
Maldonado, Alonso de, *Hechos de don Alonso de Monroy,* 11:433b
Maleficus (witch), 12:660b
Malevich, Kazimir, icon painting, 10:590b
Mali, **8:57b–58a**
 decline of, 8:57b–58a
 importance of in the 14th century, 8:57b
 rise of, 8:57b
 Timbuktu and, 12:55a-b
Maliasenoi family, land holdings, 2:479a
Mālik ibn Anas, **8:58a–59b**
 arrangement of *ḥadīths,* 6:47b–48a
 on heresy, 8:21a
 Islamic dietary laws and, 4:179b
 law school founded by, 6:581b
 on magic, 8:21a
 Muwaṭṭa$^{\supset}$, 6:580b, 8:59a-b
 revolt against al-Manṣūr, 8:58b
 al-Shāfi^{c}ī and, 11:218b, 219a
 see also Islamic law; Mālikī school of law
Malik al-Mu'ayyad, al-, Mamluk sultan, sumptuary laws and, 11:508b–509a
Malik al-Nāṣir, al-, Mamluk sultan, 3:398b
Malik al-Ṣāliḥ, al-, Mamluk sultan, sumptuary laws and, 11:508b
Mālikī school of law, 7:234b, 8:59b
 Aghlabids and, 6:392a
 Almohads and, 11:140b
 Almoravids and, 11:140a
 favored by the Jabrids of al-Baḥrayn, 2:51a
 opposed by Abū Yūsuf Ya^{c}qūb, 1:195a
 spread of in Africa, 4:407a
Malikshāh I, Seljuk sultan (Great Seljuks), **8:59b–60a,** 11:152b–153a
 Armenia and, 1:485a, 514a
 captivity of Qılıj Arslan I and, 11:154a, 156b–157a
 conquest of Qarakhanids, 10:231a
 death of, 6:504a
 flowering of religious architecture and, 11:146a–148b (*illus.*)
 Isfahan and, 6:562a
 al-Lādhiqiya and, 7:315b
 Niẓam al-Mulk and, 9:144a
Malikshāh, Jalāl al-Dīn, algebraist Omar Khayyām and, 11:84a
Malikshāh, Seljuk sultan (of Rum), 11:154a
Malimir of Bulgaria, 2:402a
Malipiero (Venetian noble family), 12:390a
Malispini, Giacotto, chronicle of Florence, 6:633b
Malispini, Ricordano, *Istoria fiorentina,* 6:633b
Malla, Felip de, *Lo pecador remut,* 3:168a
Malleus maleficarum. See Institoris, Henry
Mallorca (Majorca)
 black slaves in, 2:268b, 270a
 irrigation of, 6:558a
 liturgical drama in, 11:437a
 Miramar college at, 8:445a
 slaves in, 11:339b
Malmad ha-Talmidim. See Anatoli, Jacob ben Abba Mari
Malocello, Lanzarotto, 4:558b, 559a, 5:398a
Malory, Sir Thomas, **8:60a–65b,** 8:323a, 325b
 chivalry and, 3:302b
 historical identity of, 8:60b–61b
 influences on, 8:320b
 Morte Darthur, 12:201b, 203a
  Arthurian legend and, 1:574b–575a
  basis for, 3:327a
  Caxton's modernization of, 3:211a
  Caxton's printing of (1485), 8:60a-b, 61b
  chivalry in, 3:302b
  completion of, 1:564a
  contradictions in, 7:217b
  cornett in, 8:604a
  dialect written in, 8:61a
  influence of, 8:64b–65a
  sources of, 8:61b, 62b, 63a, 63b, 64a, 224b
  structure of, 8:61b, 62a-b
  title of, 8:62a-b
  visions and, 12:475a
  Winchester manuscript of, 8:60a-b, 61b–62a, 63a, 64b
Malory, Sir Thomas, of Newbold Revell, Warwickshire
 imprisonment of, 8:60b–61a
 as possible author of *Morte Darthur,* 8:60b–61a

Malouel, Jean, 8:65b
  Martyrdom of St. Denis, 5:608b, 8:66 (*illus.*)
  Pietà, 5:606b (*illus.*), 608b, 628b
  works in International Style, 5:628b
  see also Limbourg brothers
Malqaf. See Bādgīr
Málsháttakvæði, **8:65b–67a**
  compared with *Jómsvíkinga saga,* 8:66a
  possible attribution to Bjarni Kolbeinsson, 2:256a
  variant titles of, 8:65b
Malta, **8:67a–68a**
  conquered by Muslims, 8:67a-b
  as part of the Crown of Aragon, 8:67b
  under Sicilian control, 8:67b
Maltese cross, 4:9b, 11 (*illus.*)
Maltolte (*maltôte*), **8:68a-b,** 11:612b
  England, 11:615a
Malwiya, **8:68a-b**
Mamai, emir, 4:232b, 5:573a
Mamas, St., shrine of, 6:358a
Mamasaχlisi, tanutēr and, 11:591a
Mambrē Vercanoł, 1:509b
Mamertus of Vienne, bishop, origin of Lesser Litany and, 7:588a, 592b
Mamikonean, 1:475b, **8:78b–79a**
  Bagratids and, 1:479a, 480a, 2:48a
  during *marzpanate,* 1:476b
  Heraklios and, 1:478a
  Łazar Pᶜarpecᶜi and, 1:508b
  Pᶜawstos Buzand and, 9:473a
  portrayed in the *Patmutᶜiwn Tarōnoy,* 9:457b
  sparapet and, 1:489a
  Tarōn and, 11:599a
  Taykᶜ rule, 11:629a
  under Arabs, 1:478b
  Yovhannēs Mamikonean on, 1:510b
  see also Sparapet; Vardan Mamikonean, St.
Mamikonean, Hamazasp, Nersēs III Išχanecᶜi (Šinoł) and, 9:102b–103a
Mamikonean, John (Yovhannēs), *Patmutᶜiwn Tarōnoy* and, 9:457a
Mamlūk, **8:68b–69b**
  definition of, 3:209b
  in the Mamluk army, 8:72b
  Mamluk dynasty and, 8:71a
  origins of the institution of, 8:69a
  under Ayyubids, 4:406a-b
  under Fatimids, 5:26a-b
  usage of the term, 8:68b
  see also Blazon
Mamluk art, 6:608b–609b, **8:69b–70b**
  architecture, 4:408a
  characteristics of, 8:69b–70a
  glassmaking, 5:545a–548a
  manuscript illumination and, 8:114b–115a
  metalwork, 8:70a (*illus.*)
  textiles, 11:718b
Mamluk dynasty, **8:70b–78b**
  administration of, 6:591b–592a, 8:71b, 72a
    Ḥamā, 6:82b
  in Aleppo, 1:145b
  in Alexandria, 1:153b
  army of, 8:72a–73a
    Baḥrīya regiment, 8:73a
    organization of, 8:72b–73a
  astronomy and, 11:87a-b
  Beirut and, 2:164a
  Berke's treaty with, 5:573a
  Black Death and, 8:74b, 75b
  in Cairo, 3:14a-b
  Circassian sultanate after 1382, 8:71a
  coinage of, 8:424a
  conquest of Egypt, 3:14a-b
  contribution to historiography, 4:407b
  Copts under, 3:594b–595a
  costume of, 3:618a-b
  in Damascus, 4:82b, 83b, 84a-b
  decline of, 3:399a-b, 400a, 4:406b–407a
  economic decline under, 8:71b–72a
  establishment of Sufi convents, 4:407a
  ethnic friction under, 3:399b
  fall of Ayyubids and, 2:24a, 25a
  formation of, 10:577a, 11:339a
  history (1260–1517), 8:73b–76b
  Hṙomklay and, 6:312a
  ideology of, 8:71a-b
  influence on Mecca, 8:240b
  intolerance toward Jews and Christians, 8:71b, 72a
  Islamic postal service and, 10:61a
  Jem Sultan and, 2:137a
  Jews and, 7:84a-b
  Karamania and, 7:214a
  Kipchak-Turkish sultanate until 1382, 8:71a
  leadership, 4:406a-b
  in Lebanon, 7:533a
  manuscript illumination under, 8:116b
  military campaigns, vs. Ottomans, 8:142a
  military organization, 12:552b–553a
    firearms, 12:553a
  military strength of, 8:71b
  military technology, use of cannon, 11:638b
  navy of, 9:76a
  office of nagid and, 9:53a
  patronage of arts, 8:71b
  persecution of heresy, 8:71b
  relations with
    Cilicia, 3:391b, 393a
    Circassians, 3:398a–400b
    Mongols, 8:474b
    Nubia, 9:198b
    Seljuks of Rum, 11:158a
  rise of, 2:138a, 3:209b, 4:32a
  ruling coalitions of emirs, 8:72a
  sack of Āyās, 2:19a
  sack of Sīs, 11:314a
  Selim I and, 11:145a-b
  slaves in, 11:339a
  Smbat Sparapet and, 11:351b
  succession to the throne, 8:70b–71a
  sultanate and, 11:631a
  in Syria, 6:507a, 11:562a
  Tamerlane and, 8:75a
  Tarsus and, 11:600a
  title of sultan and, 11:505a
  vs. Argun, 1:453a
  vs. Hulagu, 6:329a
  vs. Ilkhanids, 6:420a, 420b, 504b
  vs. Mongols, 5:517b
    battle at ᶜAyn Jālūt, 8:473a-b
    defeat of 1260, 8:73b
  vs. Ottomans, 3:400a, 9:309a
    under Bāyazīd II, 2:137b
  Yemen and, 12:724b
"Mamma, lo temp'è venuto," 6:657b
Mammen axe, 8:79b (*illus.*)
Mammen style, **8:79a-b,** 12:418a, 418b, 419a (*illus.*)
  see also Ringerike style
Mamoris, Pierre, *Flagellum malificarum,* on the witches' sabbath, 8:30a
Maᵓmūn, al-, Abbasid caliph, **8:79b–81a**
  Alids and, 8:80a-b
  astronomical observations under, 11:99a
  in Baghdad, 2:46b
  Bayt al-Ḥikmah and, 8:566a
  conflict during rule, 1:10a-b
  conflict over caliphate, 1:10a
  encouragement of learning, 4:201a-b
  exilarch and, 4:552a
  Hellenism and, 6:583a
  imprisonment by al-Āmir, 5:28b
  inquisition on creation of Koran, 6:89a-b
  Leo the Mathematician and, 1:391b–392a, 7:547b
  Library of Philosophical Sciences and, 7:273b, 561a, 11:82b
  map of the world, 5:392b
  Mecca and, 8:240a
  miḥna and, 8:655b–656a
  al-Muᶜtaṣim and, 8:653b
  al-Mutawakkil and, 8:654a
  Muᶜtazilite inquisition and, 11:513b
  named governor of Khorāsān, 8:79b
  parentage of, 4:597b
  as patron of arts and sciences, 8:80b, 12:68a-b
    translation, 12:128a-b
  rule in Toledo and, 12:68a
  Sabaeans and, 9:4a
  Ṭāhir and, 6:503a, 11:574a, 574b, 575a
Man in the Panther's Skin. See Shotᶜa Rustaᶜveli
Man of Sorrows. *See Imago pietatis*
Manannán mac Lir, 6:530a, 530b
Manār(a), 8:396b
Manarah. *See* Minaret
Manāret al-Malwiya. *See* Malwiya
Manasija (monastery: Serbia), 11:182a, 188a
  built by Stefan Lazareviç of Serbia, 11:473a
Manasse ibn Ibrahim al-Qazzāz, 7:104a
Manasses, Constantine, *Historical Synopsis,* 6:246b–247a
Manazkert, **8:81a-b,** 12:362a
  Armenian trade and, 12:97b
  Catepanate of Basprakania and, 1:484a
  retaken (990), 1:483b
  silk route to the Far East and, 12:99a
Manazkert, Battle of (1071), 1:203b, 241a, 455a, 484b, 2:493a, 10:516a, 539b, 11:152b, 156b
  factors precipitating, 10:576b
  Sebaste and, 11:131b–132a

Manazkert, Council of (725/726), 1:501b, 7:125a, 8:81b
communion between Armenian and Syrian/Jacobite churches, 9:458a
Mancian tenure, 10:460a
Mancipia, 11:204b
Mancorn, 5:646b
Mandaeans. *See* Sabaeans
Mandakuni family, Aršamunik^{c} and, 11:599a
Mandakuni, John, *kat^{c}ołikos, Call to Repentance,* condemnations of the Paulicians, 9:469a
Mandatum. See Feet, washing of
Mande, Hendrik, 4:166b
Mandeville, Geoffrey de, as sheriff of London, 3:498b
Mandeville, Sir John, of St. Albans
Travels, 1:332b, **8:81b–82b**, 8:322b, 356b
Cleanness and, 4:547a
influence of, 8:82a
manuscripts of, 8:81b
referred to in *Purity,* 8:319b
translations of, 8:322b, 11:422b
Mandora, 8:602 (*illus.*), 608a
Mandorla, **8:82b**
in Islamic bookbinding, 8:99b
in *Majestas Domini,* 8:54b
probable derivation of, 8:82b
Mandrake, 6:184a
illustrations of, 2:245b
pharmaceutical uses, 9:50b
Mandylion, **8:82b–83a**
of Edessa, 4:362b, 384a
Romanos I Lekapenos, 10:515b
Manē (Armenian saint), 1:519b
Manegold of Lautenbach, **8:83a-b**, 9:701b
antidialecticism, 9:587b
on Cicero, 10:356a
dialectic and, 4:169b
on resistance, 10:17b
Manekine. See Philippe de Rémi
Manekine, La. See Beaumanoir, Philippe de
Manes. *See* Mani
Manesse family (of Zurich), 5:436b
Manesse-Codex, 5:436b, 443b
miniature depicting Hêr Nîthart, 9:93b (*illus.*)
Steinmar's songs and, 11:476b
Manfred of Magdeburg, **8:83b**
Manfred of Sicily, king, 6:273b
death of, 11:279b
defeated at the Battle of Pelagonia (1259), 9:487a
defeated by Charles of Anjou, 1:253b
Epiros and, 4:499b
reign of, 4:60a-b, 95b, 11:272a
troubadours and, 7:340b
Manfred of Vercelli, 4:250a
Mangonel, 3:180 (*illus.*)
Mangujaqids, in Armenia, 1:514a
Manhal, al-. See Taghrībirdī, Ibn
Mani
at the Sasanian court, 8:84a
books written by, 8:84a
church of, 8:85a
early life of, 8:83b
on Jesus Christ, 4:233a
Parthian origin of, 9:444a
Šābuhrāgān, presentation to Šābuhr I, 10:600b
three ages of the world, 8:84a-b
Tradition, 8:84a
Mania, treatment of, 6:491b, 492a
Manichaeans, **8:83b–86a**
^{c}Amr ibn ^{c}Adi and, 7:320
Augustine of Hippo and, 1:650b–651b
al-Bīrūnī on, 8:237b
book bindings of, 8:99a-b
in China, 8:85b
George the Monk and, 5:401b
in Ibn al-Nadīm's *Al-Fihrist,* 9:51b
icons and, 6:401b
in Iraq, 6:513a
Islam and, 9:498b
khānqāhs and, 7:238b
in Mesopotamia, 8:85b–86a
origins of, 8:83b–85a
Paulicians and, 9:468b–469a
proscribed by Emperor Diocletian (297), 8:85b
religious persecution, Sasanian culture, 10:662b
rise of Christianity and, 8:85b
script of, 6:506a
in *Škand-gumānīg Wizār,* 11:325a
in the Turkish Uighur kingdom, 8:85b
use of Parthian language, 9:444a
Zoroastrian dualist doctrine, 10:663a
Zurvanism and, 12:749a
Manichaeism
acceptance of opposing elements, 6:191b–192a
disappearance of in the West, 8:85b
Docetism and, 4:233a-b
doctrine of, 8:84a–85a
dualism, 4:297b, 6:193b
early sources on, 8:84a
origins of Mazdakism and, 8:236b
spread of, 8:85a-b
Manichaeus. *See* Mani
Maniera greca, **8:86a-b**
Manière de langage, 1:270b–271a, **8:86b**
Manilius, Marcus, *Astronomicon,* 1:605a
Maniple. *See* Vestments, liturgical, insignia
Manipule (unit of measure), 12:590a
Manipulus florum. See Florilegia
Manises
ceramics of, 6:612a
majolica production and, 8:55a
Manjacoria, Nicholas, text of the Psalms and, 2:213b
Mankala games, 5:353a-b
Mankind, performance of, 4:287b
Mannerist (manneristic) school, 1:550a
see also Ars subtilior
Manners. *See* Etiquette
Mannyng, Robert, of Brunne, **8:86b–87b**
Handlyng Synne, 1:263a, 8:316b, 317a, 317b, 10:301b
compared with John Gower's work, 8:322b
on interludes, 4:279b
Rimed Story of England, 8:87a-b, 317a
sources for, 5:389b
translation of *Manuel des péchés,* 8:96b
translation of Peter Langtoft's *Chronicle* into English, 9:516a
Manorial surveys, 4:137b
see also Domesday Book
Manorial system
England
copyhold affecting, 3:596b–597a
court leet, 3:659b–660b
decline with urbanization, 4:470a
Manosque, poaching in, 6:357b
Manoualia. See Lighting devices, Byzantine, candlesticks
Manrique, Gómez
Coplas para el señor Diego Arias de Ávila, 11:424b
political satire by, 11:454b
Representacion del Naciemiento de Nuestro Señor, 11:425a
Manrique, Jorge, 3:140a, **8:87b–88b**
Coplas por la muerte de su padre, 8:88a-b, 11:424b
Manrique, Rodrigo, 8:88a
Manrusum, 8:551b
Mansā Maḥmūd of Mali, king, 8:58a
Mansā Mūsā of Mali, king, 8:57b
Mansā Sulaymān of Mali, king, 8:57b
Mansā Ulī of Mali, king, 8:57b
Mansǫngskvæði. See Málsháttakvæði
Mansöngur (maid song), as an introduction to *rímur,* 10:405b–406a
Manṣūr, al-, *Judicia,* 1:606b
Manṣūr, Abū Ja^{c}far ^{c}Abd Allāh ibn Muḥammad al-, Abbasid caliph, 5:25a, **8:88b–89b**, 10:259a
army of, 8:89b
Baghdad and, 3:42a, 6:597a
Baghdad as capital, 5:546a-b
execution of Ibn al-Muqaffa^{c}, 8:534a
founding of Baghdad, 2:44b, 45a, 45b
games and, 5:353a
al-Kufa and, 7:307b
legacy of, 11:383a
millennialism and, 8:389a
official hagiography of, 8:89a
residence at al-Khuld, 2:45b–46a
restructuring of government, 1:7b–8a
rise of Abbasids and, 8:88b
rise of, 11:383a
scientific geography under, 5:392a
Manṣūr bi-Allāh, al-. *See* Manṣūr, Ibn Abī ^{c}Āmir al-
Manṣūr, Ibn Abī ^{c}Āmir al-, Andalusian ruler, **8:89b–90b**, 10:38a
Asturias-León and, 1:628a
attack on Castile, 3:128b, 175b
attack on Catalonia, 3:175b
military campaigns against Christians, 8:90a-b, 12:277b–278a
rise to power, 8:90a, 12:277b
Manṣūr Qala$^{\supset}$ūn, al-. *See* Qala$^{\supset}$ūn, al-Manṣūr
Manṣūr al-Yaman. *See* Ḥawshab Manṣūr al-Yaman, ibn
Manṣūr, al-, Zirid ruler, 12:744a
Mansūra, al-
in Fifth Crusade, 4:50b
in Louis IX's crusade, 4:32a, 53a-b

Mansūra, al-, Battle of (1250)
armor in, 1:526a
Baybars and, 2:138a
Mansus
division of, 11:675a-b, 676b
economic and juridical hierarchy, 11:675a
origin and development, 11:675a-b
peasants' legal claim to, 11:675b
Mantegna, Andrea
armor and, 1:536a
Bellini and, 2:165a
engravings of, 4:489a, 490a
Squarcione and, 11:464b
Mantel (a courtly *lai*), 7:317a
Mantel, Der. See Heinrich von dem Türlin
Mantel mautaillié, Le
derivatives of
Icelandic, 8:507a-b
Norwegian, 8:507b
translated into Norwegian, 10:391a
Manthen, Johannes, 10:124b
Mantino, Jacob, 7:110a
translations by, 12:136b
Manṭiq al-mashriqiyyīn. See Sīnā, Ibn
Mantiq al-ṭayr. See ^{C}Aṭṭār, Farīd al-Dīn
Mantling, 1:524a
on heaume, 1:526a
Manuale ad usum percelebris ecclesis Sarisburiensis, 10:408b
Manuale curatorum. See Surgant, Johann Ulrich
Manuale (French designation of ritual), 10:408a
Manuals, artistic, **8:90b–91a**
Manūchihr, Shaddadid ruler, 11:217b
Manūchūhrī, 6:507b
Manuel I Komnenos, Byzantine emperor, 4:165a, 7:127a, 132a, **8:91a–92a**
Armenian-Byzantine church union and, 1:500b
coinage of, 8:421a
conflicts with Western Europeans, 8:91a-b
correspondence with Nersēs IV Šnorhali, 9:103b
dealings with Michael the Syrian, 8:305b
defense of astrology, 8:18a
embellishment of Church of the Nativity, 4:24b
expulsion of Venetians, 12:103b, 388b–389a
Hungary and, 6:340b
Louis VII and, 4:38a-b
military conflicts, 2:493b
defeated at Myriokephalon, 1:241b, 8:657a
Seljuks, 2:495b
as president of the permanent synod, 9:505b
Qılıj Arslān II and, 8:657a, 10:235b–236a, 11:154a
reign of, 7:284a-b
relations with Venice, 2:494b
Seljuks of Rum and, 11:157a
Serbia and, 11:172b–173b
Theodore Prodromos and, 12:16b
Turks and, 8:91b
Manuel II Palaiologos, Byzantine emperor, **8:92a-b**
as an orator, 10:350b
defense of Constantinople, pleas for Western aid, 2:503a-b
in *Grandes chroniques de France,* 8:92b
in Morea, 8:486a-b
Morea and, 7:381b
Ottoman succession struggles and, 2:503b
rule of Thessaloniki, 2:502b
treatises of, 8:92b
in *Très riches heures* of Jean, duke of Berry, 8:92b
vassalage to Bayazid I, 2:502b–503a
Manuel I of Portugal, king, 4:563a
Jews and, 4:564b
Manueline Style and, 5:630a
Manuel I (the Fortunate) of Trebizond, *komnenos,* 12:169b
Manuel Bryennius, 11:363b
Manuel Chrysaphes, 8:556a
Manuel Chrysoloras, **8:92b–93a,** 11:51a, 51b
Erotemata, 8:92b
translator of Plato's *Republic,* 9:698b, 702b
Manuel, Don Juan, **8:94a–96b,** 11:417a
Alfonso IX of Castile and, 3:135a
Crónica abreviada, 11:417a
early life of, 8:94a
Libro de la caza, 8:95a, 96a, 11:417a, 441b
Libro del cavallero et del escudero, 11:417a, 441b
Libro del conde Lucanor et de Patronio, 8:95a, 95b–96a, 11:417a
Libro infinido, 8:95a, 95b, 11:417a, 442b
Libro de las armas (*Libro de las tres cazones*), 11:417a
Libro de los estados, 8:95a, 96a, 11:417a, 441b
lost works of, 11:443a, 443b
political involvements of, 8:94b–95a
Tratado de la Asunción, 11:417a
Manuel Eugenikos, **8:93a**
mural at church of Calendžiha, 8:93 (*illus.*)
Manuel Kalekas, 11:51b
Manuel Kantakouzenos, despot of Morea, 7:209a
Manuel de Lando, Ferrán, in *Cancionero de Baena,* 11:419a
Manuel Moschopulos, 11:54b
Collection of Attic Words, 11:53b
Erōtēmata, 11:51b
Manuel Panselinos, **8:93a–94a**
fresco in Church of the Protaton, 8:93 (*illus.*)
Manuel des péchés, 1:263a, 5:289b, **8:96b,** 8:316b, 317a
religious instruction and, 10:301b
as a source for Robert Mannyng's *Handlyng Synne,* 8:87a
Manueline Style. *See* Gothic architecture
Manumission
conversion to Christianity and, 11:338a-b
in Islamic world, 11:332b–333b
Lombard law on, 11:335b
of serfs, 11:201b, 203b, 206b
Manuscript books
binding of (European), **8:96b–98a,** 8:101b
a quaternio, 10:240a
Byzantine technique, 8:97a
ivory book covers, 12:225b–226a (*illus.*)
the quire, 10:240a
Trent codices, 12:182b–184b
Western technique, 8:97a
binding of (Islamic), **8:98a–100b,** 11:639b
books found in Qayrawān Jāmi^{C}, 8:99a
comparison of Egyptian and Iranian bindings, 8:99b
dating of, 8:98b, 99a
Egyptian and Tunisian bindings, 8:98b–99a
in Harāt, 8:99b–100a
Iranian bindings, 8:99a–100a
Shīrāz bindings, 8:99b
binding of, *see also* Signatures
book fairs, 7:567a
Breton, 3:234a
cartulary, 3:120a-b
Caxton a dealer in, 3:210a–211a
Celtic, 3:233a–234a
liturgical, **8:118a-b,** 8:370a–371b
pontificals, 10:30a-b
chained books, 3:240b
codex, 3:473b–474a
colophon, 3:483b
conservation of, 7:566a
Córdoba as copying center, 3:599a-b
Cornish, 3:234a
determining provenance, 3:477a
diaper pattern, 4:171b–172a
effect of printing press on, 9:350b
geographical attribution of, 9:690b
Georgian, 5:411a–412a
girdle book, 3:19a (*illus.*)
gloss in, 5:564b–565a
Hebrew, **8:118b–120a**
in Byzantine territories, 8:120a
in Islamic territories, 8:119a-b
production of, 8:118b–119a
in Western Europe, 8:119b–120a
Irish, 3:233a-b, 6:554a
as ransoms, 6:524a-b
see also Irish literature
Islamic
kitābkhāna, 7:273b–274a
in Samarkand, 6:605b
in Syria, 6:607b
leechbooks, 9:677a
lending of
in the Byzantine world, 7:596b
see also Libraries
manufacture of, in monastic schools, 11:74a
paper for, 3:599a
kollema, 7:283b
private Mass, 9:690a-b
production of, **8:100b–105a,** 10:554b, 12:700a–702b
at the universities, 8:103a-b
by Benedictines, 2:174a, 175a

in Canterbury, 1:258a
cost of labor, 7:601b
in ecclesiastical settings, 8:102a
introduction of paper and, 11:84b
Jean Miélot and, 7:56a
kollesis, 7:283b
late 7th to mid-13th century, 8:102a-b
Michelsberg, 12:701 (*illus.*)
in monastic communities, 8:102a-b
origin of printing and, 10:124a–127b
ornamentation, 11:693a
owner-produced manuscripts, 8:100b, 101b–102a
pecia system, 8:103a-b, 9:481a-b
pocketbooks, 9:711a
prickings, 10:119b–120a
Romanesque period, 10:507a–508b
in secular shops, 8:102a, 103b
stages in, 8:101a-b
13th century, 8:103a-b
see also Alphabetization, history of; Libraries; Scriptorium; Stichometry; *Volumen*
Romanian, 10:510a-b
scribe at work (15th-century woodcut), 7:569b (*illus.*)
study of (codicology), 3:475b–477b
theft of, 7:566a
value of, 7:562b
Welsh, 3:233b
see also Cumdach; Music manuscripts
Manuscript of the Hussite Wars' Engineer, machine design illustrated, 11:646a-b
Manuscript illumination, 8:101b
ancient, 8:105b
Manuscript illumination, Armenian, 1:496b–497b
in Cilicia, 1:497a, 497b
T^{C}oros Roslin's miniature of the Crossing of Red Sea, 12:87 (*illus.*)
in Tat^{C}ew, 11:600b
T^{C}oros Tarōnec^{C}i's miniature of St. Matthew, 12:88a (*illus.*)
Manuscript illumination, Byzantine, 2:440a-b
decorated initials in, 6:462a
gold ground, 2:455b–456a
influence of, 5:612a-b
Joshua Roll, 7:152b
Macedonian renaissance, 10:307 (*illus.*)
palmette decorations, 9:358 (*illus.*)
see also Octateuch
Manuscript illumination, Coptic, 3:590a–591b
decorated initials in, 6:461b–462a
Nubian pottery and, 9:199b
Manuscript illumination, European, **8:105b–110a**, 12:37b
as artists' examples, 4:292a
Ashburnham Pentateuch, 9:496b
in Asturias-León, 1:631a
in Bohemian court, 5:627b
Book of St. Chad, 10:615b (*illus.*)
in Bulgaria, 2:417b
Carolingian, 8:106a–107a (*illus.*), 10:97a–99a
decorated initials in, 6:462a-b
classicizing influences on, 5:612a-b
decoration of book covers, 8:97b
drolleries, 4:293b (*illus.*), 294a
earliest fragments, 8:105b, 106 (*illus.*)
École Savoyarde, 10:675b
English, 8:107b–108a
Anglo-Saxon, 1:275a, 4:458b
French Romanesque sculpture and, 10:491b
pre-Romanesque, 10:108a–109b
Winchester, 4:518b
Franco-Saxon school, 5:208a
French
in 13th century, 5:614a
Italian influences, 5:614b
pre-Romanesque, 10:110b–111b
Fructuosus, 5:304b
German
pre-Romanesque, 10:101a–104b
Roger of Helmarshausen and, 10:442a
Goffredo da Viterbo, 5:572a
in Gospelbooks, 5:579b–580a
Gothic, 5:612a–615a, 8:108b–109a
decorated letters in, 6:462b
Hiberno-Saxon, 8:105b–106a, 370b–371b
decorated initials in, 6:461b, 462a
lacertine ornament in, 7:314 (*illus.*)
Pictish associations, 9:640b
hunting in, 6:361b
influences on, 5:612a-b
inns in, 6:470a
International Style in, 5:615b
Irish, 3:219a
decline in, 3:221a-b
Italian
decorated letters in, 6:463a
pre-Romanesque, 10:113a-b
Jean Pucelle, 5:614a-b
Jean le Tavernier, 7:55b–56a
John of S. Martín de Albares, 7:140b–141a (*illus.*)
landscapes in, 5:614b–615a
Latin bestiaries, 2:206a-b
Limbourg brothers, 5:629b
Lombard tradition, 7:651a
Machaut's works and, 8:3b
as major art form, 4:348b, 355b
Master Honoré, 614a
Matthew Paris, 5:609b
metalwork exemplars in Book of Durrow, 4:317b
Missal of Robert of Jumièges, 10:434a (*illus.*)
as models for other media, 4:357a
Mosan, 8:495a, 495b (*illus.*)
Mozarabic, 8:513a
in MS Pluteus 29.1, 5:106b
in northern Europe, 5:603b–604a, 612a
opposition to in early church, 4:355b
in Ottonian Germany, 8:107a-b
in pontificals, 10:30b
Rabula Gospel, 9:497b (*illus.*)
realism in, 5:266b
rise in, under St. Louis, 5:614a
Romanesque, 8:108 (*illus.*), 10:507a–508b
decorated letters in, 6:462b
sacramentaries, 10:607a
secular and scientific topics, 4:355b
in Spain, 8:107b, 112a
Spanish, pre-Romanesque, 10:113b–114a
spread of styles, 12:160b
"Style 1200," 8:109a
tables of contents, 4:356a
techniques, 4:356b
uncolored drawings, 4:292a-b
see also Apocalypse, illustration of; *Bas-de-page;* Beatus manuscripts; Bible; *Bible moralisée; Biblia pauperum;* Carpet page; Gothic art, painting and manuscript illumination; Initials, decorated; Initials, historiated; Psalter, illumination of
Manuscript illumination, in Georgia, 5:411a–412a
Manuscript illumination, Hebrew, 8:105b, **8:110a–112b**
Ashkenazi school, 8:111 (*illus.*), 112a
Eastern school, 8:111b–112a
Italian school, 8:110a, 112a
Jewish art and, 7:65b–68a
of Pentateuchs, 9:496b
Sephardi school, 8:110a, 110b (*illus.*), 112a
special characteristics of, 8:110b–111b
Manuscript illumination, Islamic, **8:112b–118a**
in Anatolia, 6:614a
Ayyubid, 2:22b
in Cairo, 6:610a
frontispieces, 8:113b
iconology of, 6:408a-b
influence of
Byzantine art, 8:115b
Sasanian art, 8:114a, 115b
in Iran, 6:604b–605a
in Iraq, 6:606 (*illus.*)
in late 12th and early 13th centuries, 8:115b–116b
Mamluk, 8:70a
Maqāmāt, 8:115b–116b (*illus.*)
in Mozarabic art, 10:114a-b
in Mughal India, 8:117b–118a
in Ottoman Turkey, 8:117b
in the post-Mongol era, 8:117b
secular texts, 8:115a–118a
three main types of, 8:112b–113b
transcriptions of Koran and, 8:112b
under the Ilkhanids, 8:116b–117b
see also Manuscript books, binding of (Islamic)
Manutius, Aldus, Greek translations, 7:1b
Manutius, Paulus, printer of *De passionibus mulierum,* 12:214a
Manwood, John, treatise on royal forest, 5:128a
Manx language, 6:436a
as separate dialect, 3:233a
Manzikert. *See* Manazkert
Manẓūr, Ibn, *Lisān al-^{C}Arab,* 4:444a, 11:330b
Maoileachlainn (son of Seifín Mór), 6:535b
Maona, in Greece, 7:380a

Map, Walter, **8:120a-b**
antifeminism in, 1:323b
De nugis curialium, 7:364b, 366b, 368a
Dissuasio Valerii ad Rufinum (*Letter from Valerius to Rufinus Against Taking a Wife*), 1:323b, 7:368a
on early French translations of the Bible, 2:218b
Mapes. *See* Map, Walter
Maphorion, **8:120b**
Mapmaking. *See* Cartography
Maponos (Celtic name for Apollo), 9:46a
Mappa mundi, **8:120b–122a**, 10:34b
Hereford Cathedral, 8:121b (*illus.*)
material included, 8:121b
O-T schema, 8:121a
origins, 8:121b–121a
Mappae clavicula, 1:135b, 435a, 8:90b, 11:643b
on assaying gold, 8:296b
Maps. *See* Cartography
Maqām, **8:122a-b**, 8:561b
modal system of al-Munajjim, 8:122a
Ṣfiyy al-Dīn al-Urmawī, 8:122b
tone system, al-Fārābī, 8:122a
Maqāmāt, 1:381b, 8:578a
Maqāṣid al-falāsifa. See Ghazālī, al-
Maqdisī, al-. *See* Muqaddasī, al-
Maqrizi, 3:315a
Maqṣūra, 6:407a, 8:519b
Mar Aba, katholikos at Seleucia, 3:312b, 9:106b
Mar Mattai (monastery: Mosul), 11:565a
Mar Zakkai (monastery: Kallinikos), 11:565a
Mar Zutra, exilarch, 7:106a
Marabotto, Cattaneo, 9:15a
Marāgha. *See* Maragheh
Maragheh
Armenian trade and, 12:97b
observatory at, 11:84a, 85a, 99a
work of Ibn al-Shāṭir and, 11:87b
see also Urmia, Lake
Marand, silk route to the Far East and, 12:99a
Marash, under T^c^at^c^ul, 1:484b
Marble
in Byzantine church ornament, 4:337b
in early Christian architecture, 4:331b
Marbod of Rennes, 7:373a, 374b, **8:122b–124a**
criticism of Robert d'Arbrissel, 10:429b
De ornamentis verborum, 8:123b
Floridus aspectus and, 7:365b
Historia Theophili, 8:124a
hymns of, 6:382a
Liber decem capitulorum, 7:364a
chapter summaries, 8:123b–124a
Liber lapidum seu de gemmis (*De lapidibus*), 5:289a-b, 7:342b, 364a
continental versions of, 5:281a
sources for, 5:281a, 8:123a-b
life of, 8:122b–123a
poetry
epistles, 8:124a
religious, 8:123a-b
on sufferings of saints, 8.123a
Marbodus Andecavensis (Redonensis). *See* Marbod of Rennes
Marby rug. *See* Rugs and carpets
Marc (unit of measure), 12:595a
Marc (weight), **8:124b**
Marcabru, 5:441b, **8:124b–125a,** 10:167a, 168a–170a, 294a
admiration for Jaufré Rudel, 10:168b
courtly ideals of, 10:168b–169a
crude vocabulary of, 10:167a
derivative rhymes in poetry of, 10:170a
education in *trobar,* 10:168a
fin joi in poetry of, 10:168b, 169a
fin'amor vs. *fals'amor,* 3:669a
fin'amors in poetry of, 10:169a
form and subject matter, 8:125b
genres of compositions by, 10:168b
life of, in songs, 8:124b
misogyny of, 10:168b
Pax in nomine Domini, 8:124b
"Per savil tenc ses doptanssa," 10:169a
poverty of, 10:168a-b
sirventes of, 11:313a
vida of, 10:168a
Marcadé, Eustache. *See* Mercadé, Eustache
Marcel, Étienne, 7:35b–36a
alliance with Charles (the Bad) of Navarre, 5:185b
Charles V of France and, 10:319a
Jacquerie and, 9:478a
revolt of, 9:406a
Marcellinus, St., Einhard's removal of relics, 12:145a, 154a
Marcellus of Ancyra, Council of Serdica and, 11:189b
Marcellus, Theater of, 10:519a
Pierleoni and, 10:525a
March, Ausiàs, **8:125a-b**, 12:349a
Cant espiritual, 8:125a
followers of, 3:171a-b
poetry, sensuality vs. idealism in, 8:125a
March of Spain. *See* Catalonia
Marche, Arnau, 3:171a
Marche, Jaume, 3:170b–171a
Marche, Olivier de la, memoirs of, 3:333a-b
Marche, Pere, 3:171a
Märchen, 11:328b
Marchettus of Padua, **8:125b–126b**
biographical information, 8:125b
Brevis compilacio (compilatio), 8:125b, 126b, 646a
Lucidarium in arte musicae planae, 8:125b, 646a
musica plana and *musica mensurabilis,* 8:125b–126a
musical intervals, theory of, 8:126a
modal definition and, 10:374b
Pomerium in arte musicae mensuratae, 1:550b, 8:125b, 126a, 645b–646a
Johannes Vetulus and, 8:646b
tempus, concept of, 8:126a-b
Marchfeld, Battle of (1278). *See* Moravské Pole, Battle of (1278)
Marchionni, Bartolomeo, slave trader, 2:269b, 270a
Marcian, Byzantine emperor, 7:542a
Council of Chalcedon (451) and, 3:629b
Marciana, Cancionero de. See Cancionero de Marciana
Marcigny (monastery: France), 12:685a
Marcion, New Testament and, 3:338a
Marco Polo. *See* Polo, Marco
Marcus Aurelius Antoninus (Caracalla), Roman emperor, citizenship, 10:461a
Marcus Aurelius, Roman emperor, in art, 7:345a
Marcus Graecus, *Liber ignium,* gunpowder recipes, 11:645b–646a
Mardānfarrox ī Ohrmazddādān (fictional character), 11:324b
Mardanīsh, Ibn, 1:194a
defeated by the Almohads, 1:194b
Mardānšāh (son of Xusrō II), 12:715a
Mardāwīj, ^c^Imād al-Dawla and, 6:424b
Mardi Gras, 3:99b
Maremma, 9:664a
Mären, **8:126b–133a**
Bussard, 2:433b–434a
characterization and role, 8:129a–131a
bourgeoisie, 8:129b
ecclesiastical hierarchy, 8:129a
monks and nuns, 8:130b
nobility, 8:129a
peasantry, 8:130a
ritter, 8:129a-b
social class distinctions, 8:129a
students and *schrîbaere,* 8:130b–131a
urban life, 8:129b–130a
village priests, 8:130a-b
in Der Stricker's work, 11:492b, 493a-b
distinguishing criteria, 8:126b–127a
literary history, 8:131a–132a, 353a, 357a, 359b
15th century, 8:132a
French fabliau, 8:131b
love theme, exchanging love for animal, 6:50a-b
related terms, 8:127a
settings, 8:127b–128a
subjects written on, 5:114b
synopses of, 8:128a-b
types of, 8:127b–128b
comic stories, 8:127b
see also Fressant, Hermann
Margaret of Anjou, queen of England
alliance with Warwick, 12:571b
battle of St. Albans, 12:571a
council of Coventry, 12:570b
defeat at Tewkesbury, 12:571b
support for Beauforts, 6:161b
Margaret of Antioch, St. *See Vie de Ste. Marguerite*
Margaret of Austria, Jean Lemaire de Belges and, 7:54b–55a
Margaret of Constantinople, 5:680a
Margaret of Cortona, 9:14a
Margaret (daughter of Waldemar IV), 9:185a
Margaret of Denmark, queen regent

marriage to James III of Scotland, 11:108a
Sweden and, 11:532b–533a
Margaret of Faenza, 9:14a
Margaret of Flanders, countess, 4:209a, 5:81a-b
Margaret of France (daughter of Louis VII), 2:151a
Margaret of Hungary, St., 6:342a
recitation of Ave Maria, 2:13b
Margaret of Luxembourg, tomb of, 9:668b, 669a, 12:170b–171b (*illus.*)
Margaret Maultasch of Tyrol, 2:8a
Margaret of Scotland, St., 4:110b
born in Hungary, 11:479b
church reform by, 3:232a
Queen's Ferry for pilgrims at St. Andrews, 10:612b
residence at Edinburgh, 4:392b–393a
Margaret Tudor (daughter of Henry VII of England), journey to Scotland, 12:377a
Margaret, wife of Malcolm Canmore, criticism of Scottish religious customs, 11:105a
Margaret of Ypres, 9:11b
religious order, 6:69a
Margarit i Pau, Joan, *Paralipomenon Hispaniae,* 11:407a
Margaritus of Brindisi, Sicilian admiral, 9:81a
Margherita of Città di Castello, 9:14a
"Marginal" liturgy. *See* Music, polyphonic, in *lauda*
Marginalia
grammatical notes in, 7:351b
of Regiomontanus, 1:439b
of William of Moerbeke, 1:437a
Margrave, marquis, **8:133a-b**
Ancona, 8:133b
Bavarian Ostmark, 8:133b
counts of La Marche, 8:133b
emergence of principalities, 8:133b
etymology, 8:133a
march, types of, 8:133a
prestige and privileges, 8:133a-b
Scotland-England and Wales-England boundaries, 8:133b
Slavic Eastern Europe, 8:133b
Spanish March, 8:133b
Margriet van Meerbeke, 9:36a, 37a, 37b
Marguerite de Angoulème. *See Heptaméron, L'*
Marguerite de Foix, tomb of, 3:483a (*illus.*)
Marguerite d'Oingt, 9:12a-b
Marguerite de Provence, queen of France, Vincent of Beauvais and, 12:455a
Mārī Jāṭa II of Mali, king, 8:57b
Mārī Jāṭa/Sunjata of Mali, king, origins of the Mali Empire and, 8:57b
"Maria." *See* Hrotswitha von Gandersheim
Maria. See Wernher, Priester
Maria (daughter of Constantine IX Monomachos), 12:486a
Maria (daughter of Emperor Maurice), 12:715a
Maria Laach, abbey church at, 10:487b
Maria Lekapena, **8:133b–134a**
marriage to Peter of Bulgaria, 9:510a
María de Molina, 8:94a, 94b
marriage of, 3:134b
opposed by Don Juan Manuel, 8:96a
Mariage des sept arts. See Jean le Teinturier
Marian feasts, **8:134a-b**
Compassion, 8:134b
Conception, 8:134a-b
of expectation, in Mozarabic rite, 8:517a-b
Koimesis, 7:282a–283a
origin of, 8:134b
Presentation of the Virgin, 8:134b
Roman commemorations, 8:134a
Visitation, 8:134b
Western expansion, 8:134a
see also Annunciation; Assumption of the Virgin; Virgin Mary
Marian hymns, 6:382b, 383a-b
akathistos hymn and, 6:381b
of Neckham, 6:382a
Marian *planctus. See Planctus*
Marian poetry
by Gonzalo de Berceo, 11:413a
in Winchester polyphony, 12:696b
see also Middle English literature, lyric
Mariano di Jacopo (il Taccola)
De ingeneis, 8:392a, 394a, 11:648a
De machinis, 11:648a-b
battleships, 11:648a (*illus.*)
sketchbook, "Tartar" pump, 12:579a
Marianos, 7:65b
Greek poems, rewriting of, 2:506b
Marianus Gormanus, abbot. *See* Máel-Muire hua Gormáin
Marianus Scotus, **8:134b–135a**
universal chronicle, 8:135a
Marica, Battle of (1371), 2:413a, 11:180a-b
Marica River, **8:135a-b**
Battle at Černomen (1371), 8:135a
defeat of Theodore of Epiros (1230), 8:135a
see also Lazar Hrebeljanović
Māridāniyya, al- (Ayyubid mausoleum in Damascus), 2:21b
Marie de Bar, 4:491a
Marie carmina. See Walter of Wimborne
Marie de Champagne, **8:135b**
Chrétien de Troyes and, 12:200a
courts of love and, 3:673a
cultural patronage, 8:135b
in *De amore libri tres,* 3:89a
in literature, 8:135b
as regent for son, 3:247a
Marie of Enghien, Argos and, 7:381a
Marie de France, **8:135b–137b**
Aesop's fables, translation of, 5:289b
biographical information, 5:248a
Bisclavret, 8:136b
Chaitivel, 8:136b
Chastelaine de Vergi and, 3:277b
Chievrefeuil, 1:568a, 569a, 8:136b, 12:201a, 202b
Deus amanz, 5:248b, 8:136b
Éliduc, 5:249a, 8:136b
Équitan, 5:248b–249a, 8:136b
Espurgatoire St. Patrice and, 4:509b
Fables, 4:572b, 573a, 574a, 574b, 576a
dating of, 8:136a
sources for, 8:136b–137a, 10:527b
Fresne, 8:136b
Guigemar, 5:249a, 8:136b
variation on courtly theme, 5:245a
hunting and, 6:358b
Icelandic saga and, 4:613a
influence on later writers, 5:248b
Lais, 1:568a-b, 5:248a, 7:317a
Breton oral tradition in, 2:370a
Celtic concepts of supernatural in, 5:249a
dating of, 8:136a
dedications, 8:136a
evoking of ancients, 5:249a
modern editions of, 1:271b
predominant themes, 5:248b–249a
sources for, 8:136a-b
supernatural and folkloric elements, 8:136b
translated into Norwegian, 10:390b
Lanval, 5:341a, 8:136b
Latin sources, 5:288b
Laüstic, 1:568a, 5:249a, 8:136b
on literary process, 5:249a-b
Milun, 8:136b
"modern" aspects of work, 5:249b
signing of works, 8:135b–136a
translated into Old Norse, 11:491b–492a, 12:203b
use of lyric imagery, 5:249a, 251a
see also Espurgatoire St. Patrice
Marie de France, princess, 7:52b (*illus.*)
Marie d'Oignies. *See* Mary of Oignies
Marie de Ponthieu, countess, 5:423b
Marie of Savoy, wedding gown of, 5:325b
Marienkirche (Lübeck), 9:186b
Marienlieder. See Bruder, Hans
Ma^crifat al-madhāhib, 11:511b
Marigny, Enguerran de, **8:137b–138a**
castellan and, 3:124b
conflict with Charles of Valois, 8:138a
counselor to Philip IV, 8:137b
as patron of sculptors, 5:625b
service to Queen Jeanne, 8:137b
Mariken van Nieumeghen, 4:322a
Marina. See Albrecht von Eyb
Marine chronometer, 11:235a
Marine trumpet. *See under* Trumpet
Mariners. *See* Seamen
Marinids, **8:138a–140b**, 11:383b–384a
administration
financial, 8:139a
palace, 8:138b
provincial, 8:138b–139a
Almohads and, 1:195b
art and, 6:611b
culture and education, madrasas, 8:139b, 151b
dynastic expansion, 8:138a-b, 139b
Granada and, 5:652b–653a
Hafsids and
marriage alliance with, 6:54a
seizure of Hafsid territory, 6:53b
in al-Maghrib, 8:15b

Marinids (*cont.*)
military conquests
Fēs, 8:138a
Marrakech, 8:151a
Meknes, 8:267b
Spain, 8:138b, 139a
Tafilelt, 8:138b
Tlemcen, 8:139a
Tunis, 8:139b–140a
Muḥammad al-Jūtī and, 6:414a
New Fēs, construction of, 8:138b
royal titles
*amīr al-mu*ᵓ*minīn,* 8:140a
amīr al-Muslimīn, 8:138b
ancestral claims, 8:138b
tribal origins, 8:138a
see also Fēs
Marinus da Caramanica (de Carmanico), 11:274a
Glossa ordinaria, 7:429b
Mariotto di Nardo, **8:140b–141a**
altarpieces, 8:140b–141a
Coronation of the Virgin, 8:141 (*illus.*)
Marisco, Adam de. *See* Marsh, Adam
Māristān, eyvān, 4:570a
Maritime law. *See* Law, maritime
Maritime trade. *See* Trade, maritime; Trade routes, maritime
Maritime transportation. *See* Ships and shipbuilding
Maríulykill, models, 6:112b
Marius of Avenches, 5:667b
Marius, Roman general, 2:88b
Marius Victorinus. *See* Victorinus
Marj Dābiq, **8:141b–142a**
defeat of the Mamluk army (1516), 8:76b
as military staging area, 8:141b–142a
Marj Rāhiṭ, Battle of, **8:142b–143a,** 12:269a, 269b
Marj al-Suffār, battle at (1304), 6:591b
Marjoram, pharmacological uses, 9:550b
Mark associations, 12:441a
Mark of Ephesus, church union and, 6:563b
Mark Eugenikos, **8:143b**
Byzantine-Latin church reunion opposed by, 8:143b
Mark the Gravedigger, Cathar deacon, 3:183b, 185a
Mark, king. *See* Tristan legend
Mark of Montefeltro, Bonaventure and, 2:315b
Mark, St., foundation of Venice and, 12:382a-b, 385b
Markab (Islamic warship), 9:76a, 76b
Markets, European, **8:143b–147b,** 12:117a–118a
charters, 8:144a
churches and monasteries, 8:144a
feudal lords, 8:144a
responsibilities of holder, 8:144b
commodities sold, 8:143b, 144a (*illus.*)
demographic changes and, 8:144b
fairs and, 4:583a-b, 584a
food supply and, 8:146a
frequency, 8:144b
location, 8:145b
factors determining, 8:145a
London, Cheapside, 7:663a
market rights, 8:143b
owner profits, 8:144a-b, 146b
physical structure, 8:145b, 147a
post-Roman era, 8:144a
proliferation
9th through 11th centuries, 8:144b
12th through 13th centuries, 8:144b–145a
regulation of
distance between, 8:145a
enforcement, 8:146a-b
fines, 8:145b–146a
price, 8:145b, 146a
quality control, 8:145b, 146a
social function, 8:147a
Sunday, 8:144b
taxation and tolls, 8:144a-b
collection of, 8:146b
customs, 8:146b
exemption from, 8:146b
under Charlemagne, 8:144a
villages and, 12:442a
see also Trade, Western European
Markets, Islamic, regulation of, 8:526b, 527b
Markland
discovery of, 4:555a
in Vinland sagas, 12:428b, 457a
Marko, **8:147b**
coronation of, 11:179b, 180a
killed at the Battle of Rovine, 11:181b
succession to throne, 8:147b
in surviving chronicles, 11:181b, 182a
Turkish vassalage, 8:147b
Marks, quire. *See* Signatures
Markward of Anweiler, 5:482b, 8:405b
crusade against, 4:58a-b
Henry VI and, 11:269b
Marlborough, Statute of (1267), 7:444a-b
peace terms of the Barons' War, 2:112b
Marmaras, land expansion, 2:479a-b
Marmion, Simon, **8:147b–148a**
Marmorata, 10:519a
Marmousets, **8:148a-b**
governmental reforms, 8:148a
influence on Charles VI, 5:186b–187a
loss of power, 8:148a-b
members, 8:148a
Marmoutier, Abbey of, tenant labor and, 4:513a
Marner, Der, 5:442a, **8:148b–149a**
Latin songs, 8:149a
minnesongs, characteristics of, 8:148b
Sprüche, religious songs, 8:148b–149a
style and composition, 8:149a
Maron, St.
monastery of, 8:149a
under Muslim rule, 8:149b
see also Maronite church
Maronite church, **8:149a–150a,** 11:564a
acceptance of Monophysitism, 6:191b
Antiochene rite and, 1:326b, 328a
Catholic church and, 8:149b–150a
liturgical differences, 8:150a
foundation of, 8:149a-b
in Lebanon, 7:532b–533a
litanies of, 7:590b
liturgy, 8:149b
Monothelitism and Monophysitism opposed by, 8:149b
Syria, 11:561b
two wills of Christ, 8:149b
West Syrian rite and, 11:568a
Marot, Clément, chant royal and, 3:263b
Marot, Jean, 10:364b, 365a
Marquard vom Stein, *Ritter vom Turn,* 3:662b
Marque (unit of measure), 12:593a
Marquess. *See* Margrave, marquis
Marquetry, **8:150a**
Marrakech, 8:15b, **8:150b–151b**
Almohad art in, 1:191b–193a (*illus.*)
Almohad rule, 8:150b–151a
Berber control, 8:151b
building and construction
Tensift bridge, 8:150b
walls, 8:151b
conquered by ᶜAbd al-Muᵓmin, 1:194a
Dār al-Umma, 8:150b
decline, 8:151b
founding of, 8:150b, 11:383b
Great Mosque, 8:150b
Jews in, in Almoravid period, 7:98b
Kutubīya Mosque, 8:151a
Marinid occupation, 8:138b
religious groups
Christians, 8:151a
Jews, 8:151b
Sufis, 8:151b
strategic importance, 8:150b
under Saᶜdian dynasty, 8:151b
water supply, 8:151a
see also Meknes
Marranos. See New Christians
Marriage. *See* Betrothal; Courtly love; Divorce; Family; Genealogy; Men; Polygamy; Polygyny; Women
Marriage, Byzantine
age at, 4:594a
of clergy, 3:446a
multiple, 4:594b
prohibited, 4:594a, 594b
Marriage, Islamic
among Druzes, 4:296b
concubinage and, 3:529a
contraception, 3:574a–575b
rituals, 4:597b–598a
Shiite, 11:228b
Turkish militia, Abbasid restrictions on, 10:642b
Marriage, Jewish, 7:92a-b
age at, 4:606b
annulment of, 4:607b
laws governing, 7:495b, 497a
levirate, 4:607a, 607b
rituals, 4:606a
Marriage, Sasanian, next-of-kin, 10:664a
Marriage, Western European, **4:608a–612a**
age at, 4:145b, 609b
annulment of, **1:306a–307a,** 4:611a
datary and, 4:107a
divorce and, 1:306b
frequency of, 1:307a
grounds for, 1:306b

jurisdiction for granting,. 1:306b–307a
repudiation of spouse and, 1:306b
antifeminist literature on, 7:368b
of clergy, 3:215a-b, 443b, 9:522a-b
in Celtic church, 3:231a
in early church, 3:215a-b
reform papacy and, 6:499a
concubinage and, 3:530a
consanguinity, 3:539b–540b, 9:522a, 522b
Peter the Chanter on, 9:522a, 522b
contraception, 3:572a–573b
contracts of, in French law, 7:467a-b
De anulo et baculo, 10:257b
financial aspects, 4:145b
inheritance and, 6:457a, 459b
incest taboos, 4:473b–475a
indissolubility of, 1:306b
interdict and, 6:495a, 497a
lepers and, 9:677b
medieval attitudes to, 3:216a-b
minority age and, 1:306b
mixed, 4:597b
multiple, 4:601a, 611b
church and, 4:609a
Norman, 9:162a
in peasant communities, 4:145b
Polish royal, as diplomatic instrument, 9:717b, 719a, 721a, 724a
prohibited, 4:597b, 609b–610a
Quinze joies de mariage, 10:240a-b
ring symbolism and, 10:257b
rituals
Christian, 4:610a
York, 12:729b
as sacrament, 4:611a, 9:604a-b
questioned by Peter John Olivi, 9:514b
Saxony, 10:682b
secret, 4:606b, 610b
of serfs, 11:201b
sexual continence and, in early church, 3:216a
shivaree and, 8:28b–29a
social mobility and. *See* Social mobility
temporary, 6:587a
theatrical depictions of, 4:265b
as virtue, 4:597a
Visigothic, 12:471b
wife purchase, 2:207b
see also French law, in south
Marschhufendörfer, 12:446b
Marseilles, **8:152a-b**
Black Death in (1348), 2:260b
Islamic conquest of, 12:153a
travel and transport to, 12:149a-b
Marsh, Adam, **8:152b–153b**
church reform, 8:153a
correspondence, 8:153a
Quaestio de fluxu et refluxu maris, 8:153a
Robert Grosseteste and, 1:461b, 8:152b–153a
literary collaborations, 8:153a
royal and ecclesiastical commissions, 8:153a
Marshal, **8:153b–154a**
court of, 8:153b, 154a
duties, 8:153a, 154a
England, 8:153b–154a
royal, England, 6:300a, 301b
Marshal, William. *See* William Marshal
Marshalsea Court, procedures, 8:154a
Marshes, uses of. *See* Reclamation of land
Marsili, Luigi, 7:326b
Marsilio Ficino. *See* Ficino, Marsilio
Marsilius von Inghen, 1:464b
influence on Gabriel Biel, 2:234a
nominalism and, 9:157a, 12:44a
via moderna and, 9:157a-b, 12:406a, 407b, 408a, 408b
Marsilius of Padua, **8:154b–155a,** 9:709a
Aristotle's works and, 10:22b
Averroism and, 1:465a
on community's right to enact laws, 3:606a
conciliar theory of, 3:515a-b
Defensor minor, 8:154b
Defensor pacis, 1:465a, **4:132a–133a,** 6:7a, 198b, 10:22b–23a, 11:371b
Aristotelian theory in, 8:154b
emperor as defender of peace and justice, 5:488b
papal condemnation of, 8:154b
plenitude of power, refutation of, 8:154b
political theory underlying, 4:132a
primary purpose of, 4:132a
relation between religious and secular powers, 4:132b
three discourses, synopses of, 8:154b–155a
Dictio I, 10:22b
Dictio II, 10:22b–23a
Ghibelline ideologies, 6:6b
kingship theories of, 7:269b
Louis the Bavarian and, 2:135a, 8:154b
political theory of, 10:22b–23a
republicanism of, 4:132b–133a
theory of papal authority, 4:376b
Wyclif and, 12:707b, 710a
Marsilius, Petrus, *Liber gestarum,* 3:165b
Marston, Roger, Grosseteste and, 1:461b
Martaba, 5:315a-b
Martel, Gonzalo Perez de. *See* Perez de Martel, Gonzalo
Martène, Edmond, publication of *Expositio* by, 5:344b
Martha, St.
Spanish prose life of, 11:439b
taming of an aquatic monster, 8:28a
Martí, Ramón. *See* Martini, Raymond
Martial law. *See* Law, martial
Martial (Marcus Aurelius)
imitated, 7:366b
Isidore of Seville and, 6:564a
Martial, St., cult of, 1:54b, 10:618a
Martianus Capella, **8:155a–157a,** 9:702a, 10:272a
Aristotle and, 1:460b
translations, 1:460b
commentary on, 7:366a
Cosmographia and, 7:366a
De nuptiis Philologiae et Mercurii (*Marriage of Philosophy and Mercury*), 1:182a, 188a-b, 610b, 642b, 3:432a, 4:168b, 7:141b, 360a, 361b, 372a, 8:206a, 637a, 639b, 10:270a, 353b–354a, 12:205b–206a
astronomical value, 8:156a-b
Carolingian period, 8:156a
commentaries on, 8:156a
editions printed, 8:156b
glosses on, 10:303a
influence on Saxo Grammaticus, 10:677a
Notker Teutonicus and, 9:188b–189a
seven liberal arts in, 8:155b–156a, 156b
synopses of, 8:155a-b
value to later authors, 8:156a
Hrabanus Maurus and, 6:307a
Isidore of Seville and, 6:546a
John Scottus Eriugena on, 8:579a
music and, 6:317a
Remigius of Auxerre's *Commentum in Martianum Capellam,* 10:270a–271a
Martígnes, Gerard de, 3:303b
Martin I of Catalonia, king, poetic jousts of, 3:170b
Martin I, pope
Constans II and, 3:10b, 630b, 8:233b
death of, 3:344a
Martin IV, pope
apostolic syndics, 5:202a
Charles I of Anjou and, 11:272b
Dominicans and, 4:251b
Edward I of England and, 11:608a
vs. Peter III, 4:61a
Martin V, pope
ambassadors representing, 4:207a-b
concordats of, 3:526a
Council of Constance and, 3:650b–651a
datary and, 4:106b
death of, 3:366a
on Dominican ownership of property, 4:253b–254a
election of, 3:649a
endorsement of *Haec sancta,* 4:378a
Franciscan reforms, 5:205a
hostility to conciliar reform, 3:651b
Hussites and, 6:375b
pacification of Papal States, 9:386b
Pavia meeting and, 3:366a
reorganization of curia, 4:66b
Rome and, 10:524b
Vincent Ferrer and, 12:453a
Martín of Aragon, king of Sicily, 11:273b
Martin of Braga, St., **8:157a**
De correctione rusticorum, on rural superstition, 8:26b
De trina mersione, 12:190a
denounced contraception, 3:573a
Formula vitae honestae, 11:405b
Martín de Córdoba
didactic works by, 11:422b
guide to preaching, 11:456a
Martin of Dume, St., 10:36a-b

Martin le Franc, *Champion des dames,* 10:675b
Martin, Jean, chancellor to René of Provence, 6:472b
Martin of Laon, *Disciplinarum libri IX* and, 8:637a
Martín of León, St., sermons of, 11:455b
Martin, Master, Gilbert of Poitiers' theology school and, 12:21b
Martín, Pedro, collection of sermons, 11:456a
Martin of Tours, St.
  Benedictines and, 2:172a
  biography of, 5:472a
  cloak of, in court of Carolingian Empire, 3:107b
  Gregory of Tours and, 5:667a-b
  life of by Venantius Fortunatus, 12:381a
  missionary work of, 8:439a
  monastery of, 10:98b
    pilgrimage to, 10:412a
  religious life, 6:67a
  remains of, 5:667a
    Viking raids and, 12:431a
Martina. See Hugo von Langenstein
Martines, Fra Pero
  poetry of, 3:168a
  Spill de la vida religiosa, 3:168a
Martínez de Cala y Jarava, Antonio. *See* Nebrija, Antonio de
Martínez, Ferrán, *Libro del Cavallero Zifar,* 3:197a, 11:415b–416a
Martinez, Ferrante, on Jews, 7:76b, 77b, 82b
Martínez de Toledo, Alfonso, **8:157a–158a**
  Arcipreste de Talavera, 8:157a, 11:420a
    language and rhetoric, 8:157b
    sources for, 8:157b–158a
    treatment of courtly love, 8:157b
  Atalaya de las corónicas, 8:157a, 157b
  ecclesiastical benefices, 8:157b
  hagiographies, 8:157b, 11:440a
  lost works of, 11:443a
  Vida de San Ildefonso, 8:157b, 281b, 11:433a
    versions of, 11:433a
  Vida de San Isidoro, 11:433a
Martínez de Toledo, Alfonso, *Arcipreste de Talavera,* exempla and, 4:551b
Martini, Raymond
  Capistrum Judaeorum, 4:252b
  Dagger of Faith, 10:5a
  Pugio fidei (*Dagger of Faith*), 4:252b, 7:77a, 81b, 10:5a
Martini, Simone. *See* Simone Martini
Martinus Braga, *Formula vitae honestae,* 8:434a
Martinus of Fano (disciple of Azo), 2:29a
Martinus Gosia, 6:323b, **8:158a-b**
  Bolognese School and, 5:567b
  Four Doctors and, 2:417b
  glosses, 8:158b
  legal interpretation
    resolution of antinomies, 8:158a-b
    role of equity, 8:158b
  Rogerius and, 10:444a
  see also Jacobus (de Porta Ravennate)
Martinuzzi, George, 6:350a
Martirio de San Lorenzo. See Berceo, Gonzalo de
Martorana (church: Palermo), 10:505a, 11:267b–268a, 274b
Martorell, Bernardo, **8:158b**
  Huguet and, 6:328a
  Jaime Ferrer II (the Younger) and, 5:49b
  St. George and the Dragon altarpiece, 8:159a (*illus.*)
Martorell, Joanot, 12:349a
  Tirant lo Blanch, 3:170a
  writings in Catalan, 3:157b
Martorelli Bridge, 10:418b, 420b
Martyrdom
  Christian, **8:159a–160b**
    in Armenia, 1:518b
    ascetic, 8:160a
    of assassination victims, in Balkans and Russia, 8:159b–160a
    canonization and. *See* Canonization
    in catacombs, 3:154b
    characteristics of, 8:159b
    church-state conflicts and, 8:159b
    crusaders, 8:160a
    cult of the martyrs, 8:159a
    Georgian, 5:413a–414a
    "green" and "white," 8:160a
    in Najrān, 9:55a
    relics veneration and, 10:296b–297a
    variation in application, 8:159b
    victims of heretics, 8:159b
    of women, 10:296b–297a
  Islamic, Shiite, 6:503a, 11:228b
  Jewish, 7:82b, **8:160b–161a**
    for acceptance of Islam, 8:161a
    commandment of, 8:160b
    ideology of, 7:93a
    public action, 8:160a
    in theology, 9:581a
    "three inviolables," 8:160b–161a
    under persecution, 8:160b
    voluntary, 8:161a
Martyrdom of Polycarp, 10:296b
Martyrdom of St. Abo of Tbilisi. See Ioane Sabanisdze
Martyrdom of St. Šušanik, 5:413a
Martyrium, **8:161a-b**
  Armenian, 1:518a, 518b–519a
  basilica and, 2:124a
  definition of, 4:336b
  earliest preserved, 8:161a-b
  structural form, 8:161b
  tomb of St. Agnes, 8:161b (*illus.*)
Martyrius, 11:566a
Martyrologium Hieronymianum, 7:615a
  historical elements, 8:162a
Martyrology, **8:161b–162b**
  Acts of the Martyrs, 10:669a
  Bede and, 2:155a
  Byzantine, 2:518a
  East Frankish, 8:162a
  Germanic, 8:162a
  historical, 8:162a
  Insular, 8:162a
  liturgical calendar and, 8:161b–162a
  post-Carolingian, 8:162b
  translations of saints and, 12:144a–145b
  vernacular, 8:162a-b
  see also Usuard
Martyrology, Irish, 6:543a, 7:615a, **8:162b–163b**
  development of, 8:162b
  of Donegal, 8:163b
    Ó Brolcháin and, 9:203b
  of Gorman, 6:543a
  Máel-Muire hua Gormáin, "rinnard mor" form, 8:163a
  of Oengus, Ó Brolcháin and, 9:203b
  of Óengus, rinnard form, 8:163a
  Roman dating system, 8:163a
  of Tallaght, 6:543a, 7:615a-b, 8:162b–163a
  Tallaght format, 8:163a
Martyropolis, 1:473a
Marulić, Marko, 4:80a
Mārūt, as a teacher of magic, 8:20b
  see also Angels, Islamic
Marutha of Martyropolis, 11:567b
Marwān I ibn al-Ḥakam, Umayyad caliph, 1:16a, 3:39a, **8:163b–164b**
  advisory role, 8:164a
  alliances against, 8:142b
  ascension to throne, 8:164a
  battle of Marj Rāhiṭ, 8:142b–143a, 12:269a, 269b
  succession arrangements, 8:164a
  tribal conflicts, 8:164a
Marwān II ibn Muḥammad, Umayyad caliph, 3:41b, 7:241a, **8:164b–165b**
  Abbasid invasions, 8:165b
  assumption of caliphate, 8:165a
  defeat of, 12:274a-b
  Kharijite rebellions, 12:274a
    Iraq and Mesopotamia, 8:165a
  military conquests
    Iraq, 8:165a
    Syria, 8:165a
  military reorganization, 8:164b–165a
  Shīᶜa rebellion, 8:165a
  tribal conflicts
    Egypt, 8:165b
    Kalb, 8:165a
    Khazars, 8:164b
  Yemenite revolt against, 12:274a
Marwān, ᶜAbd al-Malik ibn, Umayyad caliph, **8:166a–167b**, 12:269a–270b
  administration of, 11:560b
    centralization of, 8:166b
    Islamizing reforms, 8:167a
  Arab factions under, 12:269a-b, 269b
  Arabic language and, 3:52a, 6:589a
  Arabization policies, 3:40a, 12:270b
  coinage of, 6:403b, 8:167a
  consolidation of power by, 12:270a
  Dome of the Rock and, 4:237a, 6:593b
  Iraq and, 6:511b
  Kharijite rebellions
    Arabia, 8:166a
    Iran, 8:166b
  military conquests
    Iraq, 8:166a
    Mesopotamia, 8:166a

military organization, reliance on Syrian troops, 8:166b–167a
postal service during reign of, 10:60b
promotion of al-Ḥajjāj, 6:72a, 72b
promotion of Islam, 12:270b
reign of, 1:628a
succession arrangements, 3:39a, 8:167a
vs. ᶜAbd Allāh, 1:16a
vs. Byzantines, 8:166a
vs. Zubayrids, 8:166a
Marwānids, 7:310b
in Armenia, 1:513b
Arčēš and, 1:423a
crushed by Malikshāh, 8:60a
in Iraq, 6:85b
rule of al-Ḥajjāj, 6:72a, 72b, 73a
in Shāh-Arman, 11:220a
vs. Byzantine Empire, 1:483b
Xlatᶜ and, 12:713b
Marwazī, 5:331b
Marwysgafn (Welsh deathbed song), by Meilyr Brydydd, 8:265a
Mary. *See* Virgin Mary
Mary of Austria, Louis II and, 6:349a
Mary of Burgundy
Lathem and, 7:345b
marriage to Maximilian I, 6:43a
seal of, 11:128b (*illus.*)
Mary (city). *See* Merv
Mary of Egypt, St., Spanish prose life of, 11:439b
Mary of Hungary, queen, 6:346a
coronation of, 6:335b
Mary legends. *See* Picard literature
Mary Magdalene
in art, *see also* Lamentation
as *isapostolos,* 6:560b
pilgrimage and, 10:496a
Spanish prose life of, 11:439b
Mary Magdalene (play), 4:287a
Mary of Oignies, 2:158b, 9:11b, 12a
followers of, 7:39b
lives of, 6:69b, 9:27a
Margery Kempe and, 9:25b
Marzal de Sax, Andrés, 5:612a, **8:169a**
St. George Altarpiece, 8:168 (*illus.*)
Marzbān-nāma. *See* Varāvīnī
Marzpan, residence of, in Kabala, 7:205a
Marzpanate, 1:476b, **8:169a-b**
after the fall of Arsacid monarchy, 2:20a
in Armenia, 2:48a
cultural evolution, 8:169a-b
Kamsarakan and, 7:208a
marzpan, jurisdiction of, 8:169a
naχarar rebellions, 8:169a
origins of, 2:49b
in Persarmenia, 1:559b
see also Bahrām VI Čōbēn of Persia, usurper; Mamikonean
Marzpetakan gund, 5:338b
Marzūqī, al-, commentary on the *Ḥamāsa,* 10:347a
Masaccio, Tommaso Cassai, **8:169b–170b**
Expulsion from Eden, 5:295a (*illus.*)
figural conception, 8:170a
frescoes, 5:296a, 8:170b
Brancacci Chapel, S. Maria del Carmine, 5:101b, 8:169a
Giovanni da Fiesole and, 5:534b
influence of style, 8:170b
International Style of, 5:628a
Pisa altar, 8:169b
Madonna, dimensional form, 8:170a
rise of humanism and, 5:101b
San Giovenale triptych, 8:169b, 170a
Sant' Ambrogio altarpiece, 8:169b, 170a
spatial perspective, 8:170a
style of, 5:607b
Tribute Money, 8:170 (*illus.*)
Trinity, 5:296a
Maṣāla ibn Ḥabūs, 6:413b
Masālik wa 'l-mamālik, al-, 5:392b
see also Khurdādhbih, Ibn
Māsarjuwayh, referred to by al-Razi, 11:92b
Māsawayh, Ibn, medical aphorisms, translations of, 12:140b
Masdovelles, Guillem de, *Prohemio,* 3:171a
Masegne. *See* Dalle Masegne, Pierpaolo and Jacobello
Masetto, in Boccaccio's *Decameron,* 2:284b
Māshāᵓallāh, *Tractatus astrolabii,* 1:611a-b
Mashhad (city), **8:171a**
Mashhad al-Juyūshī, 6:608b
Mashhad (place of martyrdom), of Fatimids, 5:21b
Mashrabīya, **8:171b**
Masis. *See* Ararat, Mount
Masjid. *See* Mosque
Masjid al-Aqṣā, 1:581a
Masjid al-Ḥarām, 1:581a
Masjid-i-Jāmiᶜ, 6:602b
eyvān and, 4:569b
pishtaq at, 9:671b (*illus.*)
Maslama, 3:33b
Maslin, 5:646b
Maṣmūda, Almohads and, 2:186a
Maso di Banco, **8:171b**
fresco of St. Sylvester, 8:172 (*illus.*)
frescoes of, 5:294b
paintings by, 12:175a
principal works, 8:171b
see also Nardo di Cione
Masolino, **8:171b–172a**
fresco cycles
Brancacci Chapel, 8:171b–172a, 173a (*illus.*)
Man of Sorrows, 8:171b
St. Peter Raising Tabitha, 8:173a (*illus.*)
True Cross, 8:171b
Madonna of Humility, 8:171b
works in International Style, 5:628a
Masons and builders, 5:588a, **8:172a–180a**
Articles and Points of Masonry, 8:175b, 176a, 178b
bridge construction and, 10:419a–421b
building contractors, 8:178b
construction crews, 3:566b
depicted in Bourges Cathedral, 8:178a (*illus.*)
design booklets, 8:179a
education, 8:174b–175b
apprenticeship stages, 8:175a
literacy, 8:174b–175a
oral transmission, 8:175a, 175b
practical training, 8:175a-b
English, 8:305a
Ramsey family, 10:256b–257b (*illus.*)
geometrical skills, 8:178b–179a
itinerancy of profession, 8:173b
master mason
patron-craftsmen connection, 8:177a
pay scale, 8:174b
role of, architectural, 8:177a-b
role of, construction, 8:177b–178a
role of, political, 8:173b
organizations, 8:175b–178b
German, 8:176a
regional assemblies, 8:176a
prefabrication of stone, 3:562a-b
"secret of the masons," 8:179a
social-economic status, 8:173a–174b
personal prestige, 8:174a
political role, 8:173b
wages, 8:174a-b
sources of information on, 8:172a–173a
supervision of, 8:178a-b
technical expertise of, 8:175a-b, 176b–177a
see also Construction, building materials; Thirsk, John; Thomas de Cormont
Masons' lodge
at York Minster, ordinances of, 8:175b
German *Bauhütten*
jurisdictional authority, 8:176b
oath of obedience, 8:176b
Regensburg ordinance, 8:176a-b
rules and customs, 8:176a-b
physical structure, 8:176a
professional functions
continuity of work, 8:176b
transfer of technique, 8:176b–177a
regulations
behavioral, 8:176a
enforcement of, 8:176a
Masorah, 8:564a
Masoretes, 7:104b, **8:180a–181b**
anonymity, 8:181a
Ben-Asher family, 8:181a
function of, 8:180a, 181a
grapheme systems, 8:180b
Masorah tradition, 8:181a
notations
classification of, 8:181a
counting and summing of, 8:180b
instructional, 8:180b
of peculiarities, 8:180b
origins, 8:180a
Mass
Armenian rite, 3:394b
candles at, 5:318b–319a
canticles in, 3:84b
in Celtic church, 3:230a
Christmas, 3:318a–319a
Cistercian rite, 3:406b
feast of Corpus Christi, 3:608a-b
Gallican, 5:344b–345b

Mass (*cont.*)
gradual in, 5:643b
incense and, 6:431a–432a
for lepers, 9:676b
in literature, 7:364a, 365b
liturgy of the, **8:181b–197b**
absolutions, 8:185a
Agnus chant and, 1:73b
announcements and excommunications, 8:188b
Berengar on, 2:188a
Byzantine, 1:516a, 7:610a–613b, 8:553b–554a, 554b, 555b
calendar for Rouen, 10:538b–539a
censing of the altar, 8:185a
De corpore et sanguine domini, 10:261a
discussed in Berno, abbot of Reichenau, 7:629b
dismissal formulas, 7:18b, 8:197a
Dominus vobiscum, 8:186b, 191b
Eucharist veneration, 10:298a-b, 12:221b–222a
general prayer, 8:189a-b, 193a
kissing of the Gospels, 8:185a, 188a, 188b
lections and instruction, 8:187a–189b
low Mass, 8:184a
major Western rites, 8:182a–183b
Mass of the catechumens, 8:184b–189a
Mass of the faithful, 8:189b–197b
Ockham and, 9:213b
prayers of the people, 8:189a
recession, 8:197a-b
responsory, 10:336a-b
sacrament reservation, 10:335a–336a
thanksgiving and post-Mass ritual, 8:196b–197a
in tonaries, 12:70b
trecento music, 12:178a-b, 179b
tropes to the Ordinary of the Mass and, 12:208b–210b (*illus.*)
tropes to the Proper of the Mass and, 12:210b–213b (examples)
types of celebration, 8:183b–184a
"Veni creator spiritus" and, 12:381b
Virgin Mary and, 12:460b
Virtues and, 12:462a
Wyclif and, 12:708b–709a, 710a
York, 12:729a-b
see also Lectionary; *Liber usualis;* Litany; Liturgical poetry; Liturgy, treatises on; Sacraments; Sequence (prosa); Sequence, late; Tones, musical; Tones, reading and dialogue; Vestments, liturgical
Milanese, 8:383b
music, 1:550b–551b, 9:272b–273b, 275a-b
Gregorian chant, 5:662b–663a
Premonstratensian rite in, 10:84a
requiem, 4:120b
chapels and, 1:445a
Roman, 5:662b
votive, **8:200b–201b**
Carolingian era, 8:201a-b
for certain persons, 8:201a
common of saints, 8:200b
for the dead, 8:201a
old Gelasian, 8:200b–201a
origins, 8:200b
for private circumstances, 8:201a
sanctorale, 8:200b
temporale, 8:200b
to the Blessed Virgin Mary, *see also* Blessed Virgin Mary, Little Office of
see also Eucharist
Mass of Barcelona, 8:198b
Mass of Bolsena. See Raphael
Mass cycles
early polyphonic, **8:198a–199b,** 8:596a
compilations, 8:198b–199a
for the Ordinary, 8:198a
origins, 8:198a
parody, 8:198b
for the Proper, 8:198a
solo voice, 8:198a
isorhythmic, 6:619a, 619b–620a
late polyphonic, Trent codices, 12:182b–184b
liturgical calendar, 9:688b–690b
plainsong, **8:199b–200b**
assignment to feasts, 8:200a
Eastern Europe, 9:686b–688a
melodies, 8:199b
musical disunity, 8:200a
Ordinary, 9:688a-b
origin and development, 8:199b–200a
Proper, 9:680b, 688a–689b
troped Ordinary chants, 8:200a
Western Europe, 9:688a–693a
polyphonic, 6:619b–620a, 8:594a
private pocketbooks of, 9:690a-b, 692a (*illus.*)
see also Kyriale
Mass of Toulouse, 8:199a
Mass of Tournai, 8:198b–199a
note-against-note style, 8:199a
Massae. See Tenure of land
Masses of Mone, 10:605a
Massingham, John, **8:201b**
All Souls, Oxford, chapel reredos, 8:201b
Massinissa, 10:457b–458a, 467a
Mastara, **8:202a**
architectural features, 8:202a
dating of, 8:202a
"Master A," *ars dictaminis* and, 10:358b
Master of the Amsterdam Cabinet
Mittelalterliches Hausbuch, 11:647a
Saxony wheel, 11:699b
Master of the Amsterdam Print Room. *See* Master of the Housebook
Master of Ávila, 5:612a
Master of the Avila Bible, **2:16b**
Master of the Bañolas Altar, 5:627b
Master of the Berlin Passion, 4:489a
Master of the Boucicaut Hours, **2:349b**
book of hours, 2:349b
Coronation of the Virgin, 5:614b (*illus.*), 615a
identity of, 3:478a, 5:628b
landscapes, 5:615a
style, 2:349b
Master of the Brussels Initials, 5:629a
Master of Catherine of Cleves, **3:192b–193a**
book of hours, 4:117b (*illus.*), 119a (*illus.*)
Master of the Codex of St. George, swords and, 11:549a
Master of the Death of the Virgin, 4:488a-b
Master of the Deesis
mosaic, Hagia Sophia
dating of, 2:447b
style, influence of, 2:447b–448a
Master E.S., **4:330a-b,** 4:488b–489a, 489b, 9:706b
engraving by, 4:330b (*illus.*)
Master Eckhart. *See* Eckhart, Meister
Master Erwin, Goethe on, 1:428b
Master of Flémalle. *See* Campin, Robert
Master of the Floral Borders, 4:489a
Master of the Frankfurt *Paradise Garden,* 4:489b
Master of Game, The. See Gaston III of Foix, count, *Livre de chasse*
Master of the Girart de Roussillon. *See* Jean, Dreux
Master of Heiligenkreuz, 5:629a
"Master of the *Histories.*" *See* Peter Comestor
Master of Hohenfurth, 5:610a, 627b, **6:272a-b**
panels in cloister of Vyšší Brod, 6:272a (*illus.*)
Resurrection cycle and, 10:340a
Master of the Holy Kinship, 5:552a-b
Master of the Housebook, **6:299a-b,** 6:299 (*illus.*)
engraving technique of, 4:490a
Master of Hungary, leader of the Pastoureaux, 9:453b–454a
Master I.A.M. of Zwolle, **6:388b,** 6:389a (*illus.*)
Mount of the Calvary, 6:389a (*illus.*)
Master LCz. *See* Katzheimer, Lorenz
Master of the Life of Mary, **7:572b**
Annunciation, 7:574 (*illus.*)
Master of Mary of Burgundy, **8:167b**
style, 8:167b
Master of Moulins, **8:508a-b,** 8:509a (*illus.*)
Coronation of the Virgin altarpiece, 8:509a (*illus.*)
Master of Nerezi
influence of, 2:445a
wall paintings, Church of St. Panteleimon, 2:444b–445a
Master of the Nuremburg Passion, 4:489b
Master of the Playing Cards, 4:488b, 489b (*illus.*), **9:706b–707a,** 9:706b–707b (*illus.*)
Master of the Power of Women, 4:488a
Master of the *Registrum Gregorii,* 8:107a-b
Master of the Rohan Hours, 5:629a, **10:445a**
Grandes heures, 10:445a, 445b (*illus.*)
Master of St. Bartholomew, **10:613b**
St. Bartholomew altarpiece, 10:614 (*illus.*)
Master of St. Cecilia, **10:613b–615a**

St. Cecilia Enthroned with Scenes from Her Life, 10:614 (*illus.*)
Master of St. Erasmus, 4:489a
Master of St. George. *See* Martorell, Bernardo
Master of St. Mark. *See* Destorrents, Ramón
Master of St. Severin, 5:552a-b
Master of St. Veronica, **10:622a–623a**
Veronica panel in the church of St. Severin, 10:623a (*illus.*)
"Master of the *Sentences.*" *See* Peter Lombard
Master of Třeboň. *See* Master of Wittingau
Master of Vyšší Brod. *See* Master of Hohenfurth
Master of Wittingau, 5:610a, 629b, **12:667b–668a**
Mästermyr chest, 8:296a
Masties, Numidian ruler, 10:464b, 467a
Maštocᶜ, *katᶜołikos* (*d.* 898), 1:510b
Maštocᶜ, St., 1:508a, 518b, 7:298b, **8:202a–203a**
Ałan Arcruni and, 1:508b
Armenian alphabet and, 1:123b, 214a, 491b, 507b, 559b, 8:202a
Armenian Bible and, 2:217a
canonization, 8:202b–203a
commemorated, 1:520a
Eznik and, 4:570b
Georgian alphabet and, 1:214a-b
missionary work, 8:202b
on St. Nersēs, 1:510b
social status, 8:202a-b
"Teaching of St. Gregory," 8:202b
on Theodore of Mopsuestia, 1:498b
Yačaxapatum cařkᶜ, 1:508b–509a, 8:202b
Masts, Battle of the (655), 8:519a, 9:74a
Masᶜūd I, Ghaznavid ruler, 5:520a-b, 6:507b
Bīrūnī and, 2:248b
ghāzī organization of, 5:518a
origins of the Seljuks and, 11:151b
Masᶜūd I, Seljuk sultan (of Rum), 10:235a, 11:154a
Masᶜūd III, Ghaznavid ruler
minaret of, 5:519 (*illus.*)
palace of, 5:519b
Masᶜūd, Iraqi Seljuk sultan, 11:153b
Eldigüz and, 6:419b
Masᶜud Saᶜd Salmān, 6:507b
Masᶜūd Yūsuf, al-, Ayyubid sultan, Sanᶜa and, 12:724a
Masᶜūdī, al-, **8:203a–204a**
on fur trade, 5:331b
geography as part of history, 5:394b
historical writings, 8:203a
Kitāb murūj al-dhahab wa-maᶜādin al-jawhar, 1:381a
contents, 8:203b
on *Thousand and One Nights,* 12:49b, 50b
Kitāb al-tanbīh wa 'l-ishrāf, topics covered, 8:203b–204a
references to Scandinavia, 10:707a
travels of, 8:203a
on Xusrō I, 12:714b
Zanj and, 12:739a, 739b
Maᶜṣūm imam. *See* Imam
Mātakdān Ī Hazār Dātastān, **8:204a–205b**
authorities cited, 8:204b
compilation of, 8:204a
dating of, 8:204a
organization, 8:204b
survival in manuscripts, 8:204a-b
Matara, palace of, 2:17b
Matazone da Caligano, 6:658a
Mateo da Perugia, 12:180a
Mater patris, 6:318a
Materge, 8:410b
Material for History. See Nikephoros Bryennios
Matfrid of Orléans, count, 7:146b
Math (unit of measure), 12:586b
Mathematical Collection. See Pappus of Alexandria
Mathematics, **8:205a–222a**
agrimensor, development of, 8:210b
algorism, 8:208b–209a
computation of fractions, 8:209b
altimetry, 8:211a, 211b
among Germanic tribes, 8:205a
Arabic tradition, 8:209b, 213b
ᶜilm al-misāḥa, 8:212b, 213a
Ars gromatica, 8:207b–208a, 213a
binomial surds, 8:213a
character of "pi," according to Maimonides, 11:92b
computation
abacus, 8:206a-b
decimal placement-value, 8:213a
written, 8:209a
division, 8:209a
abacus, 8:206b
golden vs. iron, 8:206b
duodecimal system, 8:206b–207a
European achievements, 8:205b, 213a–219a
15th-century madrasa at Samarkand and, 11:84a
Filippo Brunelleschi and, 2:390b
finger reckoning, 8:206a
fractions, abacus, 8:206b–207a
Greek masters, 8:205b, 208a–209a, 210b
Iamblichus' *De communi mathematica scientia,* 9:698b
instruction
oral tradition, 8:207a, 212b
university, 8:212b, 218b
instruments, 8:211a
Islamic, 11:83b
arithmetizing tendency of, 11:88a
order of study of, 11:86a
techniques of computations, 11:86a-b
Jewish, 11:92a-b
al-Karajī on, 7:211b–212b
metaphysics of light and, 6:2a
multiplication
abacus, 8:206b, 207 (*illus.*)
of binomials, 8:212a
doubling, 8:209a
music and, 8:580b–581a, 637b
in nature, theories of, 2:358a
physics and, 9:627a
planimetry, 8:211a, 211b
practical value, 8:214b–215a
Pythagorean number theory, 8:206a
quadrivium curriculum and, 10:237a-b
ratio and proportion
addition and subtraction, 8:217a
commensurability, 8:216a–217b
of continuous quantities, 8:217a-b
denomination, 8:215b–216a
Euclidean, 8:214b–218b
method of exhaustion, 8:215a
parts and units, 8:217b
rational and irrational, 8:217b
ratios of ratios, 8:205b, 216b, 9:271b
rhythm and, 8:588b–589a
Roger Bacon and, 2:38a-b
Roman heritage, 8:205a-b, 206a–208b
stereometry, 8:211a, 211b
subtraction, abacus, 8:206b
Sylvester II and, 11:552a
symbols, 8:208b, 213b–214a
theories of God and, 10:270b
treatises, Boethius' *De arithmetica,* 12:139b
trigonometry
Abraham bar Ḥiyya and, 11:92a
Islamic achievements, 11:86a
unit, definition of, 8:215a
see also Algebra; Anania Širakacᶜi; Geometry; Trigonometry
Mathematicus. See Bernard Silvester; Hildebert of Lavardin
Matheseos. See Firmicus Maternus, Julius
Mathgamain of Munster, king, 4:77b
Mathieu d'Arras, **8:222a-b**
bust of, 8:222a (*illus.*)
in Prague, 10:70b
Prague Cathedral and, 9:421a
Mathnawī-i Maᶜnawī. See Rūmī
Matija Vlačic. *See* Flacius Illyricus
Matilda of Canossa, countess. *See* Matilda of Tuscany, countess
Matilda (daughter of Earl Waltheof), David I and, 4:110b
Matilda (daughter of Henry II of England), marriage to Henry the Lion, 6:157b, 168a
Matilda, dowager empress of Germany
Roger of Salisbury and, 10:443b
Rolandslied and, 10:447b
Matilda (mother of Guigues IV), "dauphin" and, 4:109a
Matilda (mother of Henry II of England), 1:252a
civil war with Stephen (1135–1154), 3:498b, 4:463a, 7:535a
support of David I for, 4:316a-b
as heir of Henry I, 9:166b
marriage of, 6:155a, 156b
seal of, 11:126a
Matilda of Tuscany, countess, 5:481a, **8:222b–223a,** 10:257b
allodial lands of, 8:222b, 223a
dispute over Matildine lands after her death, 9:384b
Gregory VII and, 3:69b
Irnerius and, 6:555a
Lanfranc of Modena and, 7:329a
life by Donizo, 4:261a-b, 7:365b
marriages of, 8:222b

Matilda of Tuscany, countess (*cont.*)
Modena Cathedral and, 10:492a
reconciliation with Emperor Henry V, 8:223a
Matilda (wife of Alfonso III of Portugal), 10:46b
Matins, 3:67a
at Monte Cassino, 4:228a-b
Benedictines and, 4:228b
of Bruges, 2:387b
changes in time of, 4:274a
Eastern, synaxary and, 11:557b
in Milanese rite, 8:383b–384a
Sunday, 1:517a
time of, 5:662a-b
Matmonoc of Landévannec, abbot, 3:229a
Matn, 6:580a
Matres, Norns and, 9:172b
Matrikel taxation. *See* Taxation, German
Matrimony. *See* Family; Marriage
Matteo del Nassaro, stone-polishing mill, 11:654b
Matteo di Giovanelli Gattaponi da Gubbio. *See* Gattaponi, Matteo
Matteo di Giovanetti da Viterbo, 5:608a
Matteo di Giovanni, 5:535a
Matteo of Perugia, *ars subtilior* and, 1:558b
Matteo Raverti. *See* Raverti, Matteo
Matteo da Siena, 5:535a
Matt^cēos Uřhayec^ci. *See* Matthew of Edessa
Matter of Britain, 5:284a
adaptation to French verse, 5:287a
Christianization of, 5:259b
craze for, 1:572b
in France, perceived superficiality of, 5:256a
in German literature, 8:349b
in Italy, 1:572b
Karlamagnús saga and, 7:217b–218b
Karlmeinet and, 7:219a–220a
Middle High German literature and, 8:349b
troubadours and, 1:569a
see also Arthurian legend
Matter of France, 8:224b–225b
Karlamagnús saga and, 7:217b–218b
Karlmeinet and, 7:219a–220a
Matter of Rome
in French literature, 5:256b
Karlmeinet and, 7:219a–220a
preservation of clerkly wisdom, 5:256b
see also Alexander romances
Matthaeus of Grabow, 5:512b
attacks on, 4:166b
Matthaeus Platearius. *See* Platearius, Matthaeus
Matthaeus Silvaticus, 5:360a
Mattheus Hostus, Roman numerals and, 10:470b
Matthew of Aquasparta, **8:227a–228a,** 9:709a
career of, 8:227a-b
epistemology of, 8:227b–228a
works of, 8:227b
Matthew of Boulogne, *Lamentationes Matheoluli,* 7:368b
Matthew of Edessa, 1:482b, 511b, **8:228a–229a**
on Ani in Širak, 1:291a
Matthew of Janov
communion under both kinds and, 3:505a
Jakoubek and, 6:372a, 372b
Rules of the Old and New Testament, 6:366a
Wyclif and, 6:366b, 372b
Matthew Kantakouzenos, Byzantine coemperor, 2:501b
Matthew of Knín, 6:367a
Matthew Paris, 7:369b, **8:229b–230a**
on assassins, 1:591a
beguines and, 2:158b, 159b
Chronica majora, 2:174a, 3:326b
Wandering Jew legend, 12:542b
Estoire de seint Aedward le rei, 12:412a
Latin of, 7:356b–357a
manuscript illuminations, 5:609b
occasional roll by, 6:176b
on St. Alban, 1:261b
on St. Edward the Confessor, 1:261b
on St. Thomas Becket, 1:261b
saints' lives, 6:63b
Vie de St. Auban, 12:413a
Matthew, St.
in art
Lindisfarne Gospels, 7:583b (*illus.*), 584a
miniature by T^coros Tarōnec^ci, 12:88a (*illus.*)
feast of, plainsong manuscript, 9:690a, 691 (*illus.*)
Matthew of Vendôme, **8:229a-b**
Ars versificatoria, 7:365b, 8:229a, 10:359b, 360a
Epistolarium, 4:175a
Grandes chroniques de France and, 2:236b
John of Garland's works and, 7:134a
Milo, 4:283a
Tobias, 7:365b, 8:229a
Vital of Blois and, 12:479b
Matthias I Corvinus of Hungary, king, 5:490a, 6:348a–349a, 364a
Austria and, 2:8b, 9a
Bohemian barons and, 6:377a
crown of St. Stephen and, 11:483b
Maximilian I of Germany and, 8:231a
Moldavian invasion, 12:503b
vs. Vlad Ţepeş, 12:484b
Matthias Flacius Illyricus, on composition of *Heliand,* 6:151a
Matthias the Just. *See* Matthias I Corvinus of Hungary, king
Matthias, Master (spiritual adviser of St. Birgitta of Sweden), 9:15a
Mattocks, 12:78a–79a
Islamic, 12:84a
Māturīdī, al-, 6:583b
theory of justice, 9:569b
Mat^cusała of Siwnik^c, bishop, 1:509a
Matutinales. See Lectionary
Maucraux brothers, 4:515b
Maudith, John, tables of, Richard of Wallingford and, 10:387b
Maund (unit of measure), 12:593a
Maundy Thursday. *See* Holy Week, Holy Thursday
Mauretania, as granary of Rome, 8:267a
Maurice, Byzantine emperor, 7:126a, **8:230a-b,** 10:459b
Armenia and, 1:477b, 499a, 499b
execution of, 1:478a, 8:230b
influence of on Menander Protector, 8:273b
Koimesis and, 7:282b
origins of Serbia and, 11:168a
in the *Patmut^ciwn Tarōnoy,* 9:457b
recapture of Iberia, 5:405b
Strategikon, 10:59b
in Theophylaktos Simokattes' *Histories,* 12:24b–25a
Xusrō II Abarwēz and, 2:50a, 12:715a
Maurice de Craon, 5:455a
Maurice of Sully, 10:77b–78a
missing works of, 12:22a
Notre Dame de Paris and, 9:190b
Peter Lombard's theology school and, 12:21b
Maurists, *Acta Sanctorum ordinis sancti Benedicti,* 6:70b
Maurolico, Francesco, 1:439a, 439b
De conspiculis, 11:650b
On the Sphere and the Cylinder, 1:436b
Mauropus, John, epigrams, 2:507a
Maurus of Salerno, 8:256b
influenced by Aristotle, 8:248b, 249a, 250b
Mausoleum
private, in northern Iran, 11:147a
in Seljuk Anatolia, 11:148b
see also Serbia, art and architecture; Tombs
"Mausoleum of the Exodus" (painting), 3:592a
Mausoleum, Islamic. *See Qubba*
Mautby, Margaret (wife of John Paston I), 9:449b–450a, 450b
Mawālī, 2:110a, 6:502b, 8:89a-b
Mawaṣilī, Isḥaq al-, 7:243a
Mawāt, 11:668b
Mawlawīya, leadership of, 10:556b
Mawlawīya convent (Konya), 12:740 (*illus.*)
Mawlawīya order (*mevlevī*), 4:163a, 9:44b, 11:158b
music and, 8:560b
see also Dervish
Mawlid al-nabī, 5:40a
Mawrids, 8:425a
Mawṣūl, 8:612b
Maxentius, vs. Constantine the Great, Lateran and, 7:344b
Maxima, 8:629 (*illus.*)
Maximian (6th century), *Elegies,* 7:361b
Maximian, West Roman emperor, 4:521b
cathedra of, 4:361b, 7:23a, 24b, 25b
Maximilian I of Germany, emperor, **8:230b–231b**
academy founded by, 8:347a
administrative reforms of, 8:231a
Ambraser Heldenbuch and, 1:229b, 2:253a, 7:304a, 8:347a

armor and, 1:529a-b, 531a, 533a
claims of ancestry, 6:42a
imperial ideal, 5:496a
imperial knights and, 5:498a
Lathem and, 7:345b
losses of, 5:490a
marriage of, 5:490a, 6:43a
military involvements of, 8:231a
as patron of learning and arts, 8:231a-b
representative assemblies and, 10:331a-b
subduing of Ghent by, 5:523b
vs. Swiss Confederation, 11:545a-b
Maximinus of Trier, St., 11:285a-b
Maximos Planudes, 11:52a, 52b
translations from Latin, 3:431b
Maxims. *See Sententiae*
Maxims, legal, **8:231b–233a**
in Justinian's *Digest,* 8:231b–232a
principle of *Q.o.t* and, 8:232a-b
Maximus the Confessor, St., **8:233a–234b**, 9:696a, 698a
Christology of, 3:320b
condemnation and punishment of, 8:233b
as defender of orthodoxy, 8:233a-b
doctrine of deification, 2:467a
exile of, 3:630b
mystical theology, 9:563b
opposition to Monothelitism, 3:630b, 9:561a
Pseudo-Dionysius the Areopagite and, 9:99b
translation of, by John Scottus Eriugena, 7:142a
writings of, 8:233b–234a
Maximus of Ephesus, Julian the Apostate and, 9:97b–98a, 98b
Maximus, Gallic usurper, 1:231a, 231b
May Day, 5:34b, 36a-b
Kalenda Maya, 10:251a
"May Day" (Old Irish song), 6:528b
Maydānī, Aḥmad al-, *Al-Sāmī fī-al-asāmī,* 4:444b
Mayence family, 8:225a-b
Maying, as ancient fertility rite, 4:283b
Mayor, **8:234b–235b**
Bordeaux, election of, 2:328a
in England, 8:235a
in France, 8:234b–235a
London, 9:682b
election of, 7:661b, 665b
see also Provost
Mayor of the palace, **8:235b–236b**
duties of, 8:235b
Merovingian kings and, 3:272a
selection of, 8:235b
see also Pepin I (of Landen); Pepin II (of Herstal); Pepin III (the Short); Seneschal
Mayyāfāriqīn. *See* Martyropolis
Maẓalim, 3:43b
Mazarine gradual. *See* Gradual; Plainsong
Mazdaism. *See* Zoroastrianism
Mazdak (Zoroastrian heresiarch), 7:106a, 106b
ascetic practices of, 8:237a
life of, 8:236b
proposal that women should be held in common, 8:237a
social reforms of, 8:237a, 238a
teachings of, 8:236b–237a
Mazdakism
as an early form of communism, 8:238b
compared with Zurvanism, 8:237b–238a
materialism of, 8:237b
origins of, 8:236b
Mazdakites, **8:236b–238b**
festivals and entertainment, 10:664b
massacred by Xusrō I, 8:238a, 12:714a
in *Škand-gumānīg Wizār,* 11:324b
social theory, 10:670a
status of women, 10:664b
Zoroastrian dualist doctrine, 10:663a
Mâze, 8:350a
Mazhar, 8:613a
Mazyadids
vs. Buyids, 6:513b
vs. Seljuks, 6:514a
Mazzeo di Ricco, 11:259a
Mᶜbin. *See* Nisibis
Mead, **8:239a-b**
making of, 6:284a
in Yemen, 2:208b
Meal (unit of measure), 12:587a
Me'am Lo'ez. See Culi, Jacob
Mease (unit of measure), 12:593a
Measles, 9:673a, 673b, 674b, 676b, 678a
Measured music. *See* Music, measured
Measurement of the Circle. See Archimedes
Meat. *See* Animals, food
Meath, 6:518a, 519a, 519b
Meaux, Jacquerie and, 9:478a
Mec Copᶜk. *See* Sophanenē
Mec Darpas, Smbat Sparapet's membership in, 11:351b
Mec Haykᶜ, 1:473a
Mecatun, 1:485b, 491a
Mecca, **8:239b–241a**
Abbasids and, 8:240a
acceptance of Islam, 8:525a
Alid sharifate and, 8:240a-b
art in, 6:592b
attacks on Medina, 8:524b
Black Stone stolen and returned, 1:375a, 2:51a
commercial importance of, 12:105b
cults at in pre-Islamic Arabia, 1:372a-b
economic resources of, 8:240b–241a
Fatimid caliphs and, 8:240b
Fatimid propaganda in, 5:25b–26a
ḥadīth travel and, 12:147b
Hasanid sharifate established, 1:375a
hunting and, 6:355a
Islamic pilgrimage to, 10:241b
Mamluk dynasty and, 8:240b
Muḥammad in, 6:576b
Muslim occupation of, 1:373a-b
pilgrimage to, 6:146b, 7:203b–204a, 9:650a–652a
plagues in, 9:684b
pre-Islamic importance of, 8:239b
in qibla, 7:616a, 617a
Quraysh tribe and, 6:146b, 10:241a–242a
rebellion against ᶜAlī ibn Abī Ṭālib, 12:267a
rulers of, 1:175a
sacked by Qarmatians, 8:240a, 11:137a
ṣalāt and, 6:582a
sieges of, 12:722a
by al-Ḥjjāj, 8:166a
taken over by the Ottomans, 11:145b
trade and commerce, 6:109a, 8:522a
caravans, 6:109a
fairs, 4:588b–589a
investments, 6:109a
in 12th- and 13th-century accounts, 8:240b
under Abbasids, 8:240a
under Umayyads, 8:240a
urbanization in the 8th century, 8:239b
see also Kaaba; Zamzam
Mechanica. See Hero of Alexandria
Mechanical arts, *Fachschrifttum* and, 4:578a–579b
Mechanical clocks. *See* Clocks
Mechanics. See Hero of Alexandria
Mechthild of Hackeborn, 9:10b–11a, 31b
works in English, 9:27a
Mechthild von Magdeburg, 2:161a, **8:241a–242a**, 9:11a, 31b
allegory of, 5:428b
in Dante's *Purgatorio,* 8:241b
Fliessende Licht der Gottheit, 2:160b, 5:428b, 8:241a-b, 354a, 9:11a
translations of, 9:11a
new spirituality of laity and, 8:354a
work of compared with *Vitae sororum,* 9:13b
Mechthild von der Pfalz, countess, literary circle, 6:212a
Mecklenburg
Margaret of Denmark and, 11:533a
vs. Sweden, 11:532b
Mecopᶜ monastery, Tᶜovma Mecopᶜecᶜi and, 12:92b, 93a
Medalists, Italy, 9:666b
Medardus monastery, 5:424b
Medb. *See* Epona
Medb (wife of King Ailill), 6:548a, 548b, 550b
Medersa. See Madrasa
Media glosatura, 4:543b
Media vita, 8:571b
Median cadence. *See* Cadence (music)
Mediatio, **8:242a**
Medici, Cosimo de', 8:242a, 242b–243b
Ambrogio Traversari and, 12:163a
establishment of Medici regime, 5:101b–102a
as patron of the arts, 8:243a
Siena and, 11:282a
Medici family, **8:242a–244a**
bank of, 2:77a, 8:242a-b
bankruptcy of, 2:78b, 8:243b
staff and branches, 2:78b
conflicts
with the Albizzi family, 8:242b
with the Pazzi family, 8:243a-b, 11:281b

Medici family (*cont.*)
decline of in early 16th century, 8:243b
early resistance to rule of, 5:102a
investments of in manufacturing and trade, 8:242b
origins of, 8:242a
as papal bankers, 8:242b
as patrons of the arts, 5:102b–103a
patrons of Michelozzo di Bartolomeo, 8:308a
Petrucci and, 11:282a
Platonic Academy of Florence, 9:99b, 698b, 703b
principate established, 5:103a-b
rise to power in Florence, 5:101b–102a
in Tuscany, 12:231a-b
see also Florence
Medici, Giovanni di Bicci de', 8:242a-b
Medici, Lorenzo de', 8:242a, 243a-b
as peacemaker in Italy, 5:102b
poetry of, 8:243b
Rappresentazione dei Santi Giovanni e Paulo, 6:636b
rule over Florence, 5:102a–103a
Medici, Piero de', 5:102a, 8:243a
Medici, Piero di Lorenzo, exile of, 8:243b
Medicine, *see also* Anatomy; Insanity, treatment of
Medicine, Byzantine, **8:244a–247a**
attitude toward disease, 8:244b
branches of, 8:244b
history (330–1453), 8:244b–246a
influences on, 8:244a-b
medical education, 8:246a-b
periods of, 8:244b
treatises, translations from Arabic into Greek, 12:126b–127a
Medicine, Greek, physicians, 6:292a
Medicine, Islamic
classical Greek sources of, 12:130a, 133a
contraception, 3:574a–575b
history of, Ibn Sīnā, 11:306a
plagues and, 9:684a-b
al-Rāzī and, 10:267a–268a
Medicine, Jewish, 11:92b–93a
self-teaching from translations, 12:134b
treatises, translations from Arabic into Hebrew, 12:134a-b
Medicine, Roman
nursing facilities, slaveowners', 6:292b
valetudinaria, 6:292a
Medicine, schools of, **8:254b–261b**
at Chartres, 8:255a-b
curricula, 8:258a-b
two phases of, 8:258b–259a
degree requirements, 11:692a
early, 8:254b–255a
founding of the medical faculty at Montpellier, 8:258a
in the 14th century, 8:251a–252b
influence of Alexander of Tralles and, 8:245a
influence of Paul of Aegina and, 8:245a
required clinical work, 8:259b
Sicily, 11:274b
textbooks, 11:692a-b
traditions and trends, 8:260a-b
University of Bologna, 2:312a
use of surgical illustrations preserved by Niketas, 8:245b
see also Universities
Medicine, Western European, **8:247a–254b**
Alexander Neckham on, 9:92a
anatomy at Salerno, 8:248b–249a
Arabic influences, 3:548b
translations of Arabic authors, 8:248a-b, 249a
Arnald of Villanova, 1:537b–538b
astrology and, 11:644b
at Salerno, 4:579b
availability of medical care, 8:254a
Byzantine influences, 8:247a
in the Carolingian period, 8:247a-b
classical influences, 8:247a
differences between Aristotle and Galen, 8:251b–252a
8th- and 9th-century manuscripts, 8:255a
translations, 8:249a–250b
transmission of the Hippocratic-Galenic tradition, 8:255a
contraception, 3:572a–573b
diagnosis, 9:677a
diet and, 3:581a, 582a, 582b
dissection, 6:11b, 8:463a
elements of, 6:295a
fees for medical treatment, 2:99b–100a
folk remedies, 8:26a, 34b
gynecology and obstetrics, *Trotula* treatises on, 12:213b–214b
headache treatment, 9:550a
history of
Regimen sanitatis Salernitanum, 10:289a
translations and translators, 12:138a-b, 140b–141a
women's, 12:213b–214a
importance of Salerno and Monte Cassino, 8:247b–248a
leechbooks, 2:345b, 9:677a
leprosy and, 9:676b–677a
medical practice, 8:252b–254a
medieval distrust of, 2:100b–101a
monasteries and, 2:157b
music and, 8:586b
physics and, 9:624a
plagues and, 9:674b
Black Death, 2:264a–265a
plants, use of, 2:347a
Platonism and, 9:699a-b
practice of, 8:26a
discussed in *Isagoge,* 8:250a
practitioners, guilds of, 8:257b–258a
practitioners of, 8:253b–254a
public health services in Dubrovnik, 4:300b
recipe collections, 2:345b
religious orders and treatment of the sick, 2:157a
surgery, 6:165a, 8:250b–251a
separation of, 2:98a
surgeon as medical innovator, 4:578a
treatises, 4:578a, 579b
Greek, 11:83a
in Old English, 1:286a
school of Salerno, 7:363b, 366a
Scottish Gaelic, 11:116a
in Spain, 11:441b
universities and, 2:98a-b, 8:254b
see also Barber-surgeons; King's evil; Leprosy; Plagues; Technology, medical
Medina, **8:262a-b**
allegiance to Yazīd, 1:15b–16a
Ansar raiding expeditions, 8:524a
besieged (627), 6:577a-b
"Constitution" of, Muḥammad's authority, 8:524a
Fatimid propaganda in, 5:25b–26a
importance of in Islamic law, 8:58b–59b
Jews in, 7:101b, 102a–103a, 8:523b–524a, 9:497b–498a
dispute over *qibla,* 8:525a
expulsion of, 8:525a
see also Yathrib
Meccan sieges against, 8:524b
as model Islamic community, 6:580a
mosque, 6:593a, 593b
Great Mosque of Qayrawān and, 6:600a
Muḥammad in, 6:567a, 576b–577b
Muḥammad's house, poor people encamped in, 11:502a
Quraysh tribe in, 10:241b–242a
revolt in (683), 12:721b
taken over by the Ottomans, 11:145b
tribal conflicts, 8:524a
under Abbasids, 8:240a
see also Hegira; Hejaz
Medio cano, 8:562b
Medio-Bulgarian language, in Romania, 10:510a
Meditatio redemptionis humanae. See Anselm of Canterbury, St.
Meditation of the Sad Soul. See Abraham bar Ḥiyya, *Hegyon ha-Nefesh ha-Aẓuvah*
Meditations on the Life of Christ. See Pseudo-Bonaventura
Mediterranean region
agriculture
Arab contributions, 1:80a-b, 84b, 87b
climate and vegetation, 1:79b–80a
green revolution, 1:81a–83a
labor-intensive technologies, 1:80b
under Romans, 1:80a
variegated planting regimes, 1:80b–81a
climate, 3:451b–452a
diseases. *See* Plagues
gene pools, 9:673b–674a
irrigation of, 6:556a-b
slave trade in, 11:338b–340a
Mediterranean Sea
Byzantine navies in, 9:74a–75a, 78b–79a, 80a-b
Byzantine sea routes and, 10:423–424 (map)
cog in, 9:83b
geography, 10:456a-b

in Islamic conquests, 6:572b, 12:107a-b
Islamic navies in, 9:73b–77b
maritime laws and customs in, 3:569b–570b
rise of Italian merchants and, 12:110b–112a
sea routes in, 9:87b–88b
Western navies in, 9:78b–79a, 80a–81a, 84a-b
see also Trade, Western European
Medium plantum, 11:677a
Medius canon, 8:562b
Medrese. See Madrasa
Medwall, Henry, **8:262b–263a**
Fulgens and Lucrece, 4:287b, 8:262b–263a
Nature, 8:262b, 263a
Megas protosynkellos, 11:558b
Megillat Aḥimaᶜaṣ, as source of community information, 6:257a-b
Megillat Evyatar, purpose of, 6:257a
Megillat Zuta, purpose of, 6:257a
Meginhart of Fulda, **8:263a**
Megrelo-Čans. *See* Zvans
Mehmed I, Ottoman sultan, **8:263b–264a**
architecture and, 6:612b, 613a (*illus.*)
Manuel II Palaiologos and, 8:92a
Stefan Lazarević of Serbia and, 11:182a, 473a
Mehmed II, Ottoman sultan, 7:214a, **8:264a–265a**
administration, 9:309a
Anatolia and, 1:242a
art and architecture and, 6:613a, 614a
Bāyazīd II and, 2:137a
ecclesiastical appointments, 9:310a
ideological claims of, 8:264a-b
Kritovoulos and, 7:303a
legal system, 9:309a
military campaigns, 8:264b, 9:308b
capture of Caffa, 3:12b
Constantinople, 2:504a, 3:65a-b, 4:546a, 5:573b
fall of Pera-Galata, 9:503b
invasion of Morea, 8:486b
Otranto, 9:308b–309a
Stephen the Great, 12:503b
royal titles
Fatih, 9:308b
kayser, 9:308b
Rümeli Ḥiṣār, 2:504a
vs. Hunyadi, 6:364a
vs. Vlad Ţepeş, 12:485b
Mehmed Beg, 7:214a
Ikonion and, 6:418a
Mehmed the Conqueror. *See* Mehmed II, Ottoman sultan
Meide Kranz, Der. See Heinrich von Mügeln
Meier Betz, 2:132a
Meilorius, Thomas, efforts to identify him with Sir Thomas Malory, 8:60b
Meilyr Brydydd, **8:265a-b**
Meinhard II of Tyrol, 5:680a
Meinhard of Bamberg, *Carmen de Bello Saxonico* attributed to, 3:97a
Meinhard of Uxküll (Ikskile), bishop, 2:64b, 65a
Meinloh von Sevelingen, **8:265b–266a**
manuscripts preserved, 8:265b–266a
poetry for minnesingers, 8:413b
Meinzo of Constance, **8:266a**
Meir ben Baruch of Rothenburg, 7:71a
on marriage, 4:606b
responsum literature and, 10:339a
Meir ben Simeon of Narbonne, 7:78b, 93a
Milhemet Mitzvah, 11:211a
Meir Gaon, 7:104b
Meir ha-Levi Abulafia. *See* Abulafia, Meir
Meiri, Menahem ben Solomon, of Perpignan, 4:541b, 7:93b
Meirionnydd
in *Gorhoffedd,* 6:387a
Hywel and, 6:386b
Meissner, Der, 5:442a
Meister Alexander. See Wilde Alexander, Der
Meister Bertram. *See* Bertram, Meister
Meister Eckhart. *See* Eckhart, Meister
Meistergesang. See Meistersingers
Meistersinger von Nürnberg, Die. See Wagner, Richard
Meistersingers, 5:437a, 443a, 443b, 8:359b, 414a
see also Sachs, Hans
Meit, Conrad, **8:266b–267a**
Judith, 8:266b–267a (*illus.*)
Meknes, **8:267a–268a**
agricultural wealth of, 8:267a, 267b
conquered by Marinids, 8:267b
in medieval accounts, 8:267b
sacked by the Almohads, 8:267b
Mekor Ḥayyim. See Solomon ben Judah ibn Gabirol
Melabók, 7:327b
Melancholy, treatment of, 6:491b, 492a
Melanchthon, Phillip, on astrology, 1:609a
Melania the Younger, St., 9:471a
Melchior (magus), 4:498a
Melchites, 2:462b, **8:268a-b**, 11:564a
after the Great Schism of 1054, 8:268a
Islam and, 4:525a
in Lebanon, 7:532b
Nubian Christianity and, 3:314b, 9:197b, 198b
origin of the term, 8:268a
present use of the term, 8:268b
see also Eutychios the Melchite
Melchitism, vs. Monophysitism, in Egypt, 10:455a
Melech Artus, 1:572b
Meleranz. See Pleier, Der
Meles of Bari, 11:264a
Melfi, Constitutions of, 7:429b, **8:268b**, 11:257b, 270b–271a, 271b, 274a
Naples and, 9:58b
public health and, 11:274b
Méliador. See Froissart, Jehan
Melibea (character in *La Celestina*), 11:423b
Melion, 1:568a, 7:317a
Melior et Ydoine, 1:268b, **8:269a**
see also Blancheflour et Florence
Melioratio, 6:457a
Melisende of Jerusalem, queen (*d.* 1161)
arts and, 4:23a-b
crowned, 4:22b
Melisma, 5:663b, **8:269a-b**, 9:689b, 692a-b
in *Magnus liber organi,* 7:549a
musica mensurabilis and, 10:380b, 381b
noeannoe and, 9:152b
in Notre Dame discant, 9:192a
responsory, 10:336b
tonaries and, 12:70a
used by Machaut, 8:7a
in "Viderunt omnes," 12:411a
see also Fity; Litsy; Musical notation; Neuma; Perotinus; Plainsong; Tropes to the Ordinary/Proper of the Mass
Melitene, **8:269b–270a**
contested by Danishmendids and Seljuks, 4:91b, 93a
crusaders' route and, 10:423b
early bishops of, 9:459a
emirate of
Paulicians and, 9:468a
vs. Basil I, 2:117b, 118a
under Abbasids, 1:479b
under Diocletian, 1:472b
under Gabriel, 1:484b
under Justinian, 1:473a
Melkites. *See* Melchites
Mellah, 7:99b
Mellitus, bishop, Christianization of Essex, 7:658a
Melody, **8:270a–271b**
in Armenian chant, 8:551b
in Byzantine chant, composition of, 8:555a
in *Carmina burana,* 3:99a
German, Meistersingers', 10:295a-b
John of Afflighem and, 8:642b
of kontakion, 10:516b
of Kyries, 7:313a
laisse and, 7:319a-b
neume notation and, 9:691a–692b
in oral tradition, 8:569a
plainsong, 9:688a
formulas, 9:689b
plica notation and, 9:710b–711a
in popular music, 8:570b
responsory, 10:336b
"tones" and, 12:71b
in troubadours' songs, 12:216a-b, 217b–218a
in *trouvères*' songs, 12:218b
see also Musical notation; Neume
Melon dome. *See* Pumpkin dome
Meloria, Battle of (1284), 5:386b
Melton, William, on York Plays, 4:286a
Melχisedek, *katᶜolikos,* Sveti Cχoveli and, 11:523b
Memalik-i mahruse, in Ottoman state, 9:308a
Membranophone, Middle Eastern, 8:612b–613a
Memling, Hans, 5:87b, 7:155b, **8:271b–272b**
contempory evaluations of, 8:271b
Mystical Marriage of St. Catherine, 8:272 (*illus.*)

Memling, Hans (*cont.*)
portraits by, 8:272a
Willem Vrelant and, 12:493b
Memmo, Giambattista, 1:439a
Mémoires. *See* Comines, Philippe de
Memoirs of the ... Marquis of Clanricarde, 6:532b
Memoirs. *See* Guibert of Nogent
Memoranda rolls, 4:534a
Memorare, 12:460a
Memoriale sanctorum. *See* Eulogius of Córdoba
Memorialia communis. *See Libri memorialium*
Memory, disorders of, 6:492a
Men
flyting and, 9:173a, 173b–174a
married
ban and, 4:606b, 607a
status of, 4:595b, 598a, 611a
unmarried, 4:600a
Mena, Juan de, **8:272b–273b**, 11:419b
Calamicleos, 8:273a
Coplas contra los pecados del mundo, 11:419b
Laberinto de Fortuna, 8:273a, 11:419b, 421b
prosody of, 11:459b
lost works of, 11:443a, 443b
translation of *Ilias latina,* 11:458a
visions and, 12:477a
Menageries, in European gardens, 5:363b
Ménagier de Paris, 3:663b, 5:362b
Menahem ben Benjamin Recanati, 4:541b
Menahem ben Ḥelbo, as exegete, 4:540b
Menahem ben Saruq, 2:212a, 7:95b–96a
Menahem ben Solomon, *Midrash Sekhel Tov,* 7:176a
Menahem ben Solomon Meiri of Perpignan. *See* Meiri, Menahem ben Solomon, of Perpignan
Menaḥem ibn Sārū, *Maḥberet,* influence in non-Arabic-speaking countries, 6:128b
Menaion, synaxary and, 11:557b
Menander (Athenian dramatist)
Androgynos, medieval version of, 4:283a
in Middle Ages, 4:277b
Menander Protector, **8:273b**
historical works, 2:512a
Theophylaktos Simokattes' *Histories* and, 12:25a
two treatises on epideictic oratory, 10:349b
Mendenitsa. *See* Bodonitsa
Mendicant orders, **8:273b–274a**
absolution and, 6:449b
at Oxford University, 9:321a
at University of Paris, 9:408b
Augustinian friars, 1:659b–660a
Béla III and, 6:342a
Benedictines and, 2:175b
concept of primitive church and, 10:122b
Gregory IX and, 5:671a
Italian chronicles and, 6:633a
John of Paris on, 7:137a
Latin literature and, 7:368b–369a
mirrors of princes and, 8:435a
monastic schools and, 11:77b
opposition to, at Second Council of Lyons, 5:201b, 297b–298a
parish system and, 9:416b
preaching, 6:663b–664b
churches in London, 7:663b
of crusades, 4:20b
principal orders, 5:297b
religious instruction by, 10:301a
religious poetry and, 6:661b
restricted by Council of Lyons, 10:604b
rise of, 8:444b
role in education, 11:77b
in *Roman de la Rose,* 10:451b
sermon handbooks, 4:448b–449a
urban preaching, 10:604b
vs. heretics, 6:484a, 488a
women's orders and, 12:687b–688b
see also Augustinian friars; Carmelites; Dominicans; Franciscans; Friars; Monasticism
Mendoza, Íñigo López de, 3:140a
Coplas de Mingo Revulgo, 11:422a
Coplas de vita Christi, 11:422b
Menelaus, *Sphaerica,* translated into Hebrew, 11:90b
Menginhardus Fuldensis. *See* Meginhart of Fulda
Mengkorn, 5:646b
Mengli Giray, 3:678b, 5:573b
alliance with Muscovy, 3:678b
Mennas, St., 1:520a
Meno. *See* Plato
Menologion, **8:274b**, 8:274 (*illus.*)
of Basil II, 11:557b
illustrations for, 2:438b
imperial sponsorship, 2:442a
Menologion. *See* Symeon Metaphrastes
Menologium Cisterciense. *See* Henriquez, Charles
Menologium (Old English mnemonic poem), 1:281a
Menorah, **8:275a**, 11:557a
Mensa. *See* Altar
Mensura fistularum et monochordi. *See* Sylvester II, pope
Mensuration. *See* Musical notation
Mensuration (music), *lai* and, 7:316b
Mensuration sign (music), isorhythm and, 6:619b
Mental deficiency. *See* Amentia
Mentelin, Johann, *Speculum maius* and, 12:454b
Meo Abbracciavacca da Pistoia, 6:644b
Meo dei Tolomei, 6:650a
Me'or ha-Gola. *See* Gershom ben Judah
Méquinez. *See* Meknes
Méraugis de Portlesguez. *See* Raoul de Houdenc
"Meravigliosamente." *See* Iacopo da Lentini
Mercadé, Eustache, **8:275a**
Passion d'Arras, 5:274a, 8:275a, 9:447b, 636b
Vengeance de Jésus-Christ, 4:265a, 8:275a, 9:636b
Mercantile pound, 10:67a
Mercedarians
in Barcelona, 2:104a
Raymond of Peñafort and, 10:266b
Mercenaries
armor of, 1:536a
Byzantine army, 12:549b
Catalan, *see also* Catalan Company
Christian, used by the Almoravids, 1:200a
crusades, 12:559a, 561b
Frankish, 12:559a-b
French, in Switzerland, 11:544b
Germanic, vs. Isaurians, 6:560b
Gothic, vs. Isaurians, 6:560b
in Hundred Years War, 12:559a
Hunnish, 2:92b
Iranian, in Armenia, 1:513b
in Ireland, 6:517b, 518b
Italy, condottieri, 12:566a
in Languedoc, 7:341a, 341b
in Latin Empire of Constantinople, 7:349a
Lombard, 2:96b
Navarrese, in Achaea, 7:381a
Norman
English conquest, 12:559a
in foreign army, 12:560a
Norman-Angevin England, 12:560b–561a
scutage and, 11:120a
Sicilian army, 12:560a-b
Swiss, 11:545a
see also Almogávares
Mercers' Guild (York), 12:728a
Merchant Adventurers Company, 7:665b
Caxton's membership in, 3:210a
Merchants
Byzantine, *kommerkion* and, 11:605a
Catalan, in Sicily, 11:275b
companies of, 4:584b, 592b
difficulty in defining as class, 3:422b
English, in Exchequer Court, 4:534b
fairs and, 4:583a
family life, 4:602b
Frisian
cog and, 11:239a
wine and, 12:649b
Genoese, Frederick II and, 11:270b
Indian Ocean, 11:249a-b
Italian, 4:593a
chronicles and, 6:633a
in England, 6:427a
lyric poetry and, 6:644a
in Sicily, 11:262b, 270a
Jewish. *See* Trade, Jewish
of Languedoc, 7:339b
Lombard, in Ypres, 12:731b
of London, 7:663b–664b, 665b
Muslim, 11:246b
in East Africa, 11:247a
Stockholm, 11:533b
trade with crusaders and Muslims, 4:32b–33a
Transylvanian Saxon, Vlad Ţepeş and, 12:484b–485a
Tuscan, Charles I of Anjou and, 11:275b
wealth of, 3:419b, 420a
Western European, Byzantine tax exemption of, 11:605a
Ypres, 12:731a, 732a

see also Fairs
Mercia, kingdom of
control of London, 7:658b–659a
formation of, 11:253b
history, 4:454b
8th century, 4:455a
pagans in, 11:338a
Vikings and, 12:432b, 433a
Mercian dialect. *See* English language, Old English
Merciless Parliament, 6:428a
Thomas Usk and, 12:334a
Merčuli, Giorgi, *Life of Grigor of Xandztʿa,* 5:416b
Mercury
in alchemy, 1:136a, 136b, 138a
in cosmetics, 2:149a
imported from the West into Egypt, 12:107b
Mercury (god), Moccus (Celtic name for Mercury), 9:46a, 47a
Mercy killing, of the insane, 6:491a-b
Meregarto. See Merigarto
Meretrix, vs. *publica meretrix,* 10:154b
Merfyn Frych (Vrych)
dynasty of, 4:64b
father of Rhodri Mawr, 10:365b, 366a
Mergentheim, as headquarters of the Teutonic order, 2:231a
Mergentheim Codex, 2:231a–232a
Meriasek, St., Cornish miracle play about, 4:284b
Merigarto, **8:275b**
Merilo pravednoe, 7:507b
Merino (public official), in Castile, 3:132b–133a
Merino sheep, introduced into Spain, 8:280b
Merits, treasury of. *See* Treasury of merits
Merke, Thomas, *De moderno dictamine,* 4:175b
Merlijns Boeck. See Maerlant, Jacob van
Merlin, 1:565a, 566a
Ambrosius Aurelianus and, 2:3a
magical feats of, 8:35b
in *Merlínússpá,* 8:276a-b
in Thomas Malory's *Morte Darthur,* 8:62b–63a
in *Vita Merlini,* 5:389b–390a
see also Arthurian legend
Merlin. See Robert de Boron
Merlin (French prose version), 1:573a, 574a
Merlino. See Paolino Piero
Merlínússpá, 5:678b, **8:275b–276b**
preservation of, 8:275b–276a
translator of, 8:276a
Merlons, 3:147 (*illus.*), 148a, 149 (*illus.*)
Merobaudes, Flavius, **8:276b–277a**
De Christo, 8:276b
Mérode Altarpiece. See Campin, Robert
Merovich, Merovingian ruler, 8:277a
Merovingian cursive script, 9:344b (*illus.*)
Merovingians, **8:277a–279a**
administration of, *see also* Mayor of the palace
after Clovis' death, 8:278a
Alaholfingians and, 11:526a
Alamanni and, 5:506a, 11:526b, 537a
art of
fibula, 8:368a
monastic scriptoria of, 8:368a-b
Bavaria and, 2:134a
Bruges under, 2:386a
Burgundy and, 11:536b
chancery of, 3:252b
Clovis, 3:466b–467b
coinage of, 8:427b–428a
commendation under, 3:490b–491a
construction and maintenance of bridges and, 10:411a, 411b
decline of, 3:345b
defeated by the Arnulfings, 8:278b
deposition of rulers under, 4:158a
diplomacy of, 4:202a
duchies of, 5:505b–506a
dukes under, 4:303b
empire of, 3:104a-b
parceling-out of, 5:221b
expansion of, 8:277 (map), 278a
Ghent under, 5:521a
Jews and, 7:86a
nobility and, 9:148a
organization of church under, 3:373b
seals and, 11:124a, 125a, 129a
status of goldsmiths under, 8:288a-b
trade in quernstone and, 12:109b
travel and transport, 12:149a-b
under Dagobert I, 8:278b
urban forms under, 12:312b
working of iron and steel, 8:294a
see also Franks; German law, early Germanic codes; Hiberno-Saxon Art; Migration period, art; Pepin I (of Landen); Pepin II (of Herstal); Pepin III (the Short)
Merseberg *a* Penitential, 9:489a, 489b, 491a
Merseburg, bishopric of, Thietmar von Merseburg and, 12:28a
Merseburg charms, 2:87a
Second, Frigg in, 5:301a
Merseburger Zaubersprüche. *See* Merseberg charms
Mersenne, Marin, *Harmonie universelle,* 8:648b
Merswin, Rulman, of Strassburg, 8:356a
Merton College, spread of Arabic numerals and, 1:396b
Merton, Council of (1236), 11:468a
Merton mean speed theorem. *See* Physics
Merton, Statute of, 7:444b
Mertonians, 1:464a-b
Cajetan of Thiene and, 1:465a-b
Merure de Seinte Église, **8:279a-b**
Merużan Arcruni, Aršak II and, 1:476a
Merv
in Islamic conquests, 6:569b, 570b
al-Maʾmūn and, 8:80a
Ṭāhir and, 11:574a
Merveilles de Rigomer, 9:634b
Meschinot, Jean, 10:364b, 365a
Mesembria, 2:410a, 411b, 412b, **8:279b**
taken by Krum (812), 7:303b
Mesopotamia, 6:571 (map)
art and culture, textiles, 11:717a-b
Black Death in, 2:259a
Hamdanid rule, 6:83a–86a
Arab-Byzantine war, 6:84b
increasing influence under al-Muqtadir, 6:84a
invasion by Muʿizz and ʿAdūd al-Dawla, 6:85b
in Islamic conquests, 6:568b
Kurds in, 7:310a
Manichaeans and, 8:85b–86a
Tamerlane's invasion of, 3:313a
see also Iraq
Mesopotamia (Byzantine theme), 1:474a
Mesrob, St. *See* Maštocʿ, St.
Mesrop Erēc, biography of Nersēs the Great, 6:240a
Messalianism
dualistic theology, 6:192a
Pseudo-Macarius and, 9:7a, 7b
Symeon the New Theologian and, 11:553b
Messe de Nostre Dame. See Machaut, Guillaume de
Messiad. See Eupolemius
Messiads, 4:495b
Messianism, Islamic. *See* Imam; Mahdi, the
Messianism, Jewish. *See* Apocalyptic literature and movement, Jewish
Messina
autonomy of, 11:276a
Black Death in, 2:259a
commerce, 11:275a
Sicilian vespers and, 11:261a
vs. Byzantines, 11:263a
vs. Roger I, 11:263a, 265b
Mesta, 6:209b, **8:279b–281a**
great assemblies of, 8:280b
judicial and financial organization of, 8:280b–281a
role of in the finances of Castile, 8:280a
Mester de clerecía, 3:140a, 4:63a-b, **8:281a–282a,** 11:411b–413b
compared with *mester de juglaría,* 8:281b, 282a-b
decir and, 4:122b
Spanish hagiography and, 11:438b–439a
surviving poems of, 8:281b
University of Palencia and, 2:187a
Mester de juglaría, **8:282a–283a**
coexistence with *mester de clerecía,* 8:281b
Mocedades de Rodrigo and, 11:438a
schools of, 8:282a
Meta, 6:457a
Metallurgy, **8:283a–287b**
technology innovations, armor design, 11:659a
see also Bronze and brass; Iron; Metalsmiths; Metalworking; Pewter; Steelmaking; Tin
Metalogicon. See John of Salisbury
Metals
in alchemy, 1:139b–140a
mining of, *see also* Silver
Metalsmiths, **8:291a–297b**
agricultural tools and, 12:81b–82a
in ancient folklore and mythology, 8:291a

Metalsmiths (*cont.*)
blacksmiths, wheelwrights and, 12:374a-b, 377b
Celtic, spathas of the Goths and, 8:283a
gold and silver, **8:287b–291a**, 8:295a-b
Bosnia, 2:340b, 341b
clock making and, 8:290a
in England, 8:289b–290a
Georgian, 5:410b–411a
Godefroid of Huy, 5:569b–570a
invention of wiredrawing, 8:295b
Meuse region, 8:496a
in monasteries, 8:288b, 289a
purity standards, 8:290a-b
purity testing, 11:635b
repoussé, 10:315b
secular objects produced by, 8:289b
status of, 8:288a
Theophilus on, 12:24b
tools of, 8:296a–297a
transmutation of base metals, 11:635a-b
under the Merovingians, 8:288a-b
see also Leonardo di Ser Giovanni; Niello; Retable
importance of, 8:291a–292a
instruction manuals, 11:644a
iron and steel, 8:293a–294b
specialization of, 8:294b
Italy, 9:666b–668a (*illus.*)
later medieval, 8:293a
metalworking tools, 8:296a–297a
sources on, 8:296a
mystique of, 11:469b
in nonferrous metals, 8:294b–297b
Nuremberg, 9:202b
specialization of in the early Middle Ages, 8:292b
see also Lighting devices; Visigothic art, metalwork
Metalworking
in Carolingian period, 2:384a, 8:283a-b
in Celtic art
Dalriada, 3:224a
ecclesiastical, 3:218b, 221a
masterpieces, 3:223a
secular, 3:218b
silver, 3:221a
chip carving, 3:301a
for clocks, 3:463b
dinanderie, 4:186b (*illus.*)
in Dinant, 2:384a
engraving and, 4:487b, 488a, 490a
evidence of in grave finds, 8:291b–292a
Ghaznavid, 5:519b
in Hiberno-Saxon art, 8:373a
Islamic
Iranian, 6:603a
Syrian, 6:607b
mining and, 8:400a
in Mosan art, 2:384a
Mosan craftsmen and, 8:284b
in pre-Romanesque art
Carolingian, 10:100b–101a
English, 10:109b–110a
French, 10:111b–112a
German, 10:104b–107b
Spanish, 10:114b–115a
in Roman Empire, 2:384a
water mills used in processes of, 8:393b
see also Émail brun
Metamorphoses. *See* Ovid
Métamorphoses d'Ovide allégorisées, Les, depiction of a vehicle, 12:373a-b
Metamorphosis of humans into animals
in Arab folklore, 8:22a
in Sufism, 8:22a
"Metamorphosis Goliae," 7:367a
Metaphrastes, Symeon. *See* Symeon Metaphrastes
Metaphysics. *See* Aristotle
Metaphysics. *See* Essence and existence; Philosophy and theology
Métayage, 11:681a, 12:651b–652a
Meteḥi, **8:298a-b**
compared with Mc^{c}χet^{c}a, 8:298b
Méteil, 5:646b
Metellus of Tegernsee, **8:298b–299b**
problems of identification, 8:298b–299a
Quirinalia, 8:299a-b
Metempsychosis, 11:228a
Druze belief in, 4:296b
Meteora, **8:299b–300a**, 11:179a
Meteorology. *See* Aristotle
Meter (music)
īqā^{c} as, 6:501a
in Philippe de Vitry's treatise, 1:548b
Meter (poetry). *See* Eddic meters; Latin meter; national literatures
Metge, Bernat, **8:300b–301a**
compared with Francesc Eiximenis, 8:301a
Lo somni, 8:300b–301a, 12:227a
official positions of, 8:300b
Sermó, 3:173b
writings of in Catalan language, 3:157b
Methley, Richard, 9:26a, 26b
Methodios, patriarch, clash with iconoclasts, 11:42b
Methodios, St., **4:73a–74b**, 9:687a
as archbishop of Sirmium, 5:658b
Bible translation and, 2:215b
Chartres notation and, 8:556b
Czech literature and, 11:343a-b
mission to Great Moravia and, 2:299a-b
missionary work of, 8:442b
Slavic language spoken by, 11:341a-b
Slavonic liturgy of, 5:542b–543a, 658b, 10:591b
Slavs and, 6:436a
Thessaloniki and, 12:26b
Métiers. *See* Guilds and métiers
Metrica opuscula. *See* Fardalfus Abbas
Metrics
in German lyric literature, 5:436b–437b
in *leich,* 5:440b–441a
see also entries on versification and prosody in individual languages
Metrologus, 8:641b
Metron, 12:581b
Metropolitan, 3:374a-b, 375b, **8:301a**
compared with the title of exarch, 9:458b
election of patriarch and, 9:459b
emergence of office, 10:193a
in Lithuania, 10:593b
in Russia
Byzantine appointment of, 10:592a, 593a-b
list of (1237–1441), 10:593b
patriarchal control, 2:469b
residence, 10:593b, 594a
Russian appointments, 10:592b, 594a-b
of Siwnik^{c}, 1:503b
see also Synkellos
Mettingham, John, 7:188b
Metz
bridge at, 10:417a
Carolingian art in, 10:99a
first seals of, 11:126a
ivory carvings at, 10:100a-b
siege of (1324), 3:64a
Metz Psalter, 2:218b
Metz, Synod of (863), Nicholas I and, 9:121a
Metz, Tonary of, 12:69b
Metz, use of, **8:301b–302a**
chant tradition, 3:402a, 402b
Metzen hochzit, 2:132a
Wittenwiler's *Ring* and, 12:666a
Metzkanon, 8:562b
Meulan, first seals of, 11:126a
"Meunier et les deus clers, Le," 6:555b
Meuthi (Tatheus), 3:7a
Mevlevi. *See* Mawlawīya order (*mevlevī*)
Mexía, Gonzalo, possible author of *Crónica de don Miguel Lucas de Iranzo,* 11:433a
Mezenets, Aleksandr, *Azbuka,* 8:575b
Mezuzah, discussed in responsum literature, 10:338a
Mezza maiolica, 3:237b
Mezzadria, 11:683a-b
Miasto (miejsce), 9:721b
Mic an Bhaird, 6:535a
Micanon, 8:562b
MicConMidhe, 6:535a
Michael I Doukas. *See* Michael I of Epiros
Michael II, Byzantine emperor, 1:236a, 2:401b
attempt to reconquer Crete, 3:678a
Theodore of Studios and, 12:16a
in *Theophanes continuatus,* 12:23a
Thomas the Slav and, 12:36b
Michael III, Byzantine emperor, 1:236a, **8:302a-b**
advisers of, 2:489a-b
artistic patronage, 2:453b
Basil I and, 2:117a, 117b, 118a
Christian missions to Eastern Europe and, 8:442b
Cyril and Methodios and, 4:73b, 5:658b
in *Imperial Histories,* 5:382a
in legends and prophecies, 8:20a
Nicholas I and, 9:121a
Theodora II and, 12:12b, 13a
in *Theophanes continuatus,* 12:23a
victory over Arabs (859), 4:523a
see also Bardas Caesar

Michael IV (the Paphlagonian), Byzantine emperor
 Ani and, 1:484a
 coinage of, 8:420b
 successor of, 2:407a
 Zoë and, 12:745b
Michael V Kalaphates, Byzantine emperor, Zoë and, 12:745b
Michael VI Stratiotikos, Byzantine emperor
 overthrow of, 8:304b
 revolt against, by Isaac I Komnenos, 7:283b
Michael VII Doukas, Byzantine emperor, 4:263a, 7:131b
 coinage of, 8:420b
 depicted on St. Stephen's crown, 11:482 (*illus.*)
 Robert Guiscard and, 10:433a, 11:265b
Michael VIII Palaiologos, Byzantine emperor, **8:302a–303a**, 9:331a-b
 alliance with Genoa, 5:385a-b
 Angevin alliance against, 2:499a, 499b
 Arsenius Autorianus and, 1:560b
 Battle of Pelagonia and, 9:487a
 Charles I of Anjou and, 8:302b
 coinage of, 8:421a
 Constantinople libraries and, 7:561a
 founding of Pera-Galata and, 9:503a
 John Laskaris and, 7:343a
 Latin Empire of Constantinople and, 7:349b, 11:272b
 reconquest of Constantinople, 2:498b–499a, 3:552a-b
 reestablishment of the empire, 12:390b
 religious policies, 2:499a-b
 reunion with Latin church, 2:465b, 3:641b, 642a
 Sicilian Vespers and, 2:499b, 11:261a, 273a
 slave trade and, 11:339a
 Trebizond and, 12:168b–169a
 vs. William, II, 7:378b
Michael IX Palaiologos, Byzantine coemperor
 Almogávares and, 1:191a
 Catalan Company and, 2:500a
Michael I of Epiros, 4:499a, 7:347a, 347b, **8:303a**
 Arta regime, 2:498a
 Serbia and, 11:174a
 Stefan Prvovenčani and, 11:473b
 vs. crusaders, 7:376b
Michael II of Epiros, despot, **8:303b**
 defeat at Pelagonia, 2:498b, 9:487a
 vs. Nicaea, 4:499a
 vs. Theodore II, 7:348a
 William II and, 7:378b
Michael Aneotes, 8:555b
Michael of Antwerp, St., 10:85b
Michael (archangel), 1:249a-b, 433a
 in bardic poetry, 6:538a
 in Islam, 1:248b
Michael Asen of Bulgaria, reign of, 2:409b–410a
Michael Astrapas, 4:524b, **8:303b–304a**
 Meeting of Joachim and Anne and Birth of the Virgin, 8:303 (*illus.*)
Michael Attaleiates, **8:304a**
 historical works, 2:514b
 histories, 6:245b
 Ponema nomikon, 7:392a
 ring of, 2:455a (*illus.*)
Michael Blaunpayn (the Potter), vs. Henry of Avranches, 7:369a
Michael of Canterbury, **8:305a**
Michael of Cesena
 effort to suppress the Spirituals, 9:515b
 excommunication of, 5:203b
 leadership of Franciscans, 5:202b, 203b
 Ockham and, 9:209b
 as opponent of Peter Aureoli, 9:513a
Michael Choniates, 9:133b
Michael, Dan, of Northgate, *Aȝenbite of Inwyt,* 8:317a
Michael of Ephesus, 4:170b
Michael Glykas
 poetry of, 2:509a
 world chronicle, 2:515b
Michael Keroularios, patriarch, **8:304a–305a**
 early career of, 8:304a-b
 Leo IX and, 6:329b, 7:543b
 role of in Byzantine politics, 8:304b
 Schism of 1054 and, 2:465a-b, 3:349a-b
Michael Kritobulos of Imbros, historical works, 2:517b
Michael de Leone, *Renner* and, 6:326a
Michael (Macedonian artist), 2:448a
Michael of Marbais, speculative grammar and, 10:359b
Michael Panaretos, history of Trebizond, 2:517a
Michael de la Pole, earl of Suffolk, impeached by parliament, 10:384a-b
Michael (the Brave), Romanian ruler, 10:510b, 511b
Michael Romanov, tsar of Russia, 11:195b, 197b
Michael, ruler of Duklja, 11:171a-b
Michael, St.
 in art, 12:701 (*illus.*)
  of Rohan Master, 10:445b (*illus.*)
 see also Michaelmas
Michael Scot, **8:305a-b**
 Aristotle and, 1:461a
 De motibus celorum, 1:614b
 Frederick II and, 11:257b, 274a
Michael Šišman of Bulgaria, tsar, 2:411b–412b
 Serbia and, 11:177a
Michael Synkellos of Jerusalem, 11:52a
Michael the Syrian, patriarch of Antioch, 5:674b, **8:305b–306a**, 11:566a
 Chronicle, 8:306a
 involvement of in church matters, 8:305b
 in Melitene, 8:269b
 Nersēs IV Šnorhali and, 9:103b
 used by Bar Hebraeus, 2:108b
 West Syrian rite and, 11:568a
 works of, 8:306a
Michael of Tarrazona, Aristotelian translations and, 11:689a
Michael of Tver, prince, 4:232b
Michael of Zahumlje, 11:169b, 170b
Michaelmas (St. Michael's feast), 5:36b–37a
Michaelskirche (church: Fulda), 5:312a
Michel Beheim, 5:443a, **8:306a–307b**
 influences on, 8:306b
 lyric poetry of, 5:436b
 patrons of, 8:306a-b
 range of his musical and poetical work, 8:306b
Michel Colombe. *See* Colombe, Michel
Michel, Jean
 Georges de la Sonnette and, 5:402a
 Mystère de la Passion, 9:448a
 Passion play by, 4:264b
Michel de la Tour of Nîmes, biography of Peire Cardenal, 9:484a-b
Michele di Lando, leadership of Ciompi, 11:714b
Michelino da Besozzo, works in International Style, 5:628a
Michelozzo di Bartolomeo, **8:307b–308a**
 Palazzo Medici-Riccardi in Florence, 8:307 (*illus.*)
Michelsberg (abbey: Bamberg), 12:701 (*illus.*)
Michiel (Venetian noble family), 12:388b, 390a
Micmacs, 11:329b
Micon of St. Riquier, 7:362b, **8:308a-b**
 epitaph for Nithard, 9:143b
Microcosm, Book of the. See Joseph ibn Saddiq, *Sefer ha-Olam ha-Qatan*
Microcosmos, 1:604b
Microcosmus. See Godfrey of St. Victor
Micrologus. See Bernold of Constance; Guido of Arezzo
Microtonality, in Byzantine music, 8:555a, 556a
Micy, Abbey of, 2:16b
Middle Ages, concept of, **8:308b–309b**
 in the 15th century, 8:308b–309a
 in Petrarch's view, 8:308b
 in the 16th and 17th centuries, 8:309a
Middle Armenian. *See* Armenian Language
Middle Bulgarian. *See* Bulgarian language
Middle East, plagues in. *See* Plagues, Islamic world
Middle East. *See* Near East
Middle English language. *See* English language, Middle English
Middle English literature, **8:313b–326b**
 alliterative Alexander poems, 8:320b
 alliterative revival, 8:318b–321a
  compared to emergence of Icelandic *rímur,* 10:403a-b
 alliterative verse, 8:318b–321a, **8:326b–333b**, 8:342b–344b
 Arthurian legend in, 1:567b–568b, 573a–575a
 ballads, 2:59b–60b, 8:325a-b
 boundaries of defined, 8:314a
 carols, 8:325a
 development
  Chaucer, Gower, Mandeville, 8:321a–322b
  15th century, 8:323a–326a

Middle English literature (*cont.*)
development (*cont.*)
from *Ancrene Riwle* to John Wyclif, 8:314a–318b
devotional manuals, 8:314b–315a
English mysticism and, 9:20a
exegesis and, 4:545b
historiography, 8:317a-b
influence of Vulgate on, 4:545b
lyric, **8:333b–342a**
ballad, 8:336a
Brut, 2:393a–394a
carol, 8:336a, 337a-b, 338b
classification, 8:336a–337a
drinking songs, 8:339a
imitations of French genres, 8:336a
Marian poems, 8:340a–341a
meaning and usage of the term "lyric," 8:334a-b
native poems, 8:336a–337a
poems on sexual love, 8:337a–339a
religious themes, 8:315a-b, 339b–341a
role of Franciscans and, 8:340a
subject of mortality, 8:341a-b
moralistic poems, 8:315b
poetry, distinction between secular and religious, 8:335b
prosody and versification, **8:342a–347a**
alliteration, 8:318b–321a, 342b–344b
ballad meter, 8:345a
French octosyllabic couplets, 8:315b, 321b
rhyme with optional alliteration, 8:344a-b
rhyming couplet, 8:344b–345b
rhyming stanzaic verse, 8:345b–346b
religious prose, 3:408b
rise of vernacular literature, 4:419b
romance, 8:316a-b
standard created by Wyclif and his followers, 8:318a
time boundaries of, 8:313b
trilinguality of England and, 8:313b
see also Anglo-Norman literature; Bible, versions, Middle English; Prophecy, political, Middle English
Middle French. *See* French language
Middle High German. *See* German language
Middle High German literature, **8:347a–362a**
early (1050–1170)
beginning of, 8:347b
histories in, 8:348a
oral poetry in, 8:348b
prose in, 8:348b–349a
shift away from Latin, 8:348a-b
verse pattern in, 8:348b
classical (1170–1220/1230)
audience of, 8:350b–351a
cleric's works in, 8:350b
hagiography in, 8:350a
ministeriales and, 8:349b, 352a-b
movement toward national literature, 8:351b
rivalry between writers of, 8:351a
textual coherency in, 8:351b–352a
topics of, 8:349b–350a
in vernacular, 8:349b
warning against idealizing and, 8:351b–352a
women's literature in, 8:350b
writers of, 8:350b
late I (1220/1230–1300)
courtliness in, 8:352a
experimentation during, 8:352a
laity's writing in, 8:352a
oral-traditional narrative poetry in, 8:353b
prose in, 8:354a-b
Rede in, 8:353a-b, 355a
regional variety in, 8:352a
religious writings in, 8:354a-b
rhymed couplets in, 8:354b–355a
sermon collections in, 8:354b
strophic composition in, 8:354b
late II (1300–1430), 8:347b
city chronicles in, 8:358b
diversity in, 8:355a
homily in, 8:355a-b
interaction between clergy and laity and, 8:355a-b
Latin-German bilingualism in, 8:356a-b
letters in, 8:358a-b
Lied in, 8:357b
literary public during, 8:358b
lyrical poetry in, 8:358a-b
nonlyrical poetry in, 8:357b
patronage during, 8:358b
Rede in, 8:357a-b
scholastic prose in, 8:356a
secular narratives in, 8:356b–357a
sermon in, 8:355a-b
Sprecher in, 8:357b
translations in, 8:356b
verse-making in, 8:356b
women's literature in, 8:355b–356a
late III (1430–1500)
drama in, 8:359a-b
Latin-Italian novella and, 8:360a
Lied in, 8:359b–360a
Meistergesang in, 8:359b
narrative prose in, 8:360b, 361b
popular culture in, 8:360a-b
printing and, 8:361b
publishers of, 8:361b
Rede in, 8:359b, 361b
social and artistic milieu, 8:361a-b
Athis und Prophilias, 1:635b–636a
Biterolf, 2:253a
end of, 8:347a
epic, 4:380a-b, 5:426b, 9:269b–270a
Spielmannsepik, 9:283a, 293b
Gebrauchsliteratur, 12:619b
Hildebrandston strophe, 9:282b
historiography of, 8:348a
Italian Renaissance influence on, 8:437a
lyric
Buch von Bern, 2:395b–396a
Bussard, 2:433b–434a
Minnereden, 8:408a–412b
minnesingers and, 8:413a–414b
narrative poetry, strophic form, 10:532b
narrative tradition, 9:282b
poetry, Danubian school, 8:265b
saints' legends, characteristics, 9:293b–294a
see also German literature
Middle Hungarian language. *See* Hungarian language
Middle Irish. *See* Irish language
Middle Low German. *See* German language
Middle Persian. *See* Persian language
Middle Platonism
Scholasticism and, 9:100b
see also Classical literary studies; Plato and Platonism
Middle Temple, 6:477a-b
Middlesex, sheriff, 11:225a
Middleton, Richard. *See* Richardus de Mediavilla
Midgard serpent, **8:362a-b**, 11:29a, 32a
in *Ragnarǫk,* 10:248a
Thor and, 8:362a-b, 12:45a-b, 46a
see also Scandinavian mythology
Miʾdhana, 8:396b
Midi, French
agriculture
oulières, 1:85b
Roussillon, 1:85b
Toulouse region, 1:85b–86a
idealized society, 10:159a–160a
legal system, 7:461b–462a, 463a, 464a–465a, 466a, 467a–468a
Midrash. *See* Exegesis, Jewish
Midrash Sekhel Tov. See Menahem ben Solomon
Midsummer Eve, 5:34b
Midsummer Night's Dream, A. See Shakespeare, William
Midwives, 4:600b
Mielno, Treaty of (1422), 9:726b–727a
Miélot, Jean. *See* Jean Miélot
Mieszko I of Poland, king, 8:443a
reign of, 9:717b–719a
territorial acquisitions, 9:628a
Mieszko II Lambert of Poland, king, 9:719a-b
Miftāḥ Maghāliq al-Talmudh. See Nissim ben Jacob
Migetius, teachings on Trinity, 1:57b
Migliaio (unit of measure), 12:593a
Mignano, Treaty of (1139), 10:441a, 11:267a
Migration
in Russia, 11:195a
of serfs, 11:201b, 206a-b
see also Peasants
Migration, internal. *See* Demography; Reclamation of land
Migration period
art, **8:363a–376a**
animal style, 8:365a–367b
carved stones in, 8:367a-b
chip carving and, 8:365a-b, 366b
Christian art and, 8:367b–369b
cloisonné style and, 8:364b–365a
fibulae in, 8:364 (*illus.*), 365b (*illus.*)
filigree technique and, 8:366a
gold collars in, 8:366a-b
jewelry in, 8:364a–365b
liturgical objects in, 8:368a

migrations of Germanic tribes and, 8:363a-b
monumental buildings in, 8:368a–369a
overview of, 8:363b
polychrome style, 8:363b–365a
time frame of, 8:363a
tombs in, 8:363b
see also Animal style; Hiberno-Saxon art
Gotland in, 5:633b
late medieval, villages and, 12:444b
proto-Polish *völkerwanderungen,* 9:716b
travel and, 12:160b
villages and, 12:443a
see also Barbarians, invasions of
Miguel de Morillo, 9:112a
Miḥna, 3:48a
see also Mu^{c}tazilite inquisition
Miḥrāb, 1:193a, 6:603b (*illus.*), **8:376a,** 10:235a
in Ayyubid mausoleums, 2:21b
definition of, 8:376a
in Great Mosque of Algiers, 1:196b (*illus.*)
in Great Mosque of Qayrawān, 1:69b
iconology of, 6:406a
location of, 8:376a
in Medinan mosque, 6:593a
in Seljuk art and architecture, 11:146a, 147b
see also Kaaba
Mihrān ibn Manṣur, translation of Dioscorides, 6:178b
Mihranids. *See* Chosroids
Mihrdāt I, Parthian ruler, 9:443b
Mihrdāt II, Parthian ruler, 9:443b
Mihrnerseh, *wuzurg framadār,* 12:705b
Mijares River, 6:558a
Mīkā$^{\supset}$il. *See* Angels, Islamic
Mikel Mirianisdze, *katholikos,* Tamar and, 11:587a
Miklagarðr (Viking name for Constantinople), 12:435a
Miknās. *See* Meknes
Milagros de Nuestra Señora. See Berceo, Gonzalo de
Milan, **8:376b–381a**
anarchy in, 8:377b
archbishopric, in investiture conflict, 6:499a, 499b
archbishops in, 8:377b–379a
armor manufacture in, 1:528b, 529b
barbarian invasions of, 8:376b
Black Death in, 2:260b
Byzantine Empire and, 8:376b
castles and fortifications in, 8:377b
civil war, 15th century, 7:9b
economic growth in, 8:377b–378a, 378b, 380a
emperors in, 8:377b–379a
expansion of, 7:7a-b, 14b
French domination of, 8:380b–381a
Gradicio River irrigation canals, 6:558b
Grand Canal (1179), 8:379a
hostelries and inns, 6:472b, 12:651b
as intellectual center, 8:376b
Italian League, *entente cordiale,* 7:10a
legation of St. Peter Damian to, 9:509a
as manufacturing center, 12:112a
political power in, 3:499b–500a
political preeminence of, 8:377b
population increase in, 8:377b
rebellion of lay vassals, 3:557b
relations with Venice, 12:393a
revolts against, by Genoa, 8:380a-b
revolts in, by nobility, 8:378a–379a
Sforza rule of, 7:10a, 8:380a–381a
sieges of, 8:378b
social stratification in, 8:378b
Spanish domination of, 8:381a
under France, 11:217b
under Madrid, 11:217a
under Sforzas, 11:216a–217a
Venetian expansion into, 7:9b
Visconti rule of, 7:7a-b, 8:379a–380a, 12:463b–464b
end of, 7:9b
wars, against Lodi, Cremona, and Pavia, 8:378b
written record of, 8:377a
see also Ambrose, St.; Ambrosian Republic
Milan Cathedral, 1:233a, **8:381a-b**
apse of, 8:382 (*illus.*)
construction of, 8:381a
design problems, 8:177b
facade, 1:429a
Francesco I Sforza and, 11:216b
planning and construction of, 5:628a
sculptures, 9:644a, 10:265 (*illus.*)
see also Bernardo da Venezia
Milan, Edict of, 4:351a, 358a
Milanese chant. *See* Ambrosian chant
Milanese rite, 5:661a, **8:381b–384a**
Ambrosian melodies, 8:183a
books of the Office of, 8:381b, 383a
Charlemagne and, 8:377b
described by Beroldus of Milan, 7:630b
description of, 8:381b
Gallican rite and, 5:344a–345b
Kyrie repetitions in, 7:593b
litanies of, 7:591a-b
liturgical year of, 8:383a
liturgy of, 8:381b
Mass in, 8:383b
matins in, 8:383b–384a
Paulinus of Nola and, 2:180b
prayers of the people, 8:189a
preservation of, 8:381b
sacramentaries of, 8:381b, 10:606a
similarities with Roman, 8:183a
spissim, 8:183a
see also Ambrose, St.; Ambrosian chant; Baptism
Milčani, 12:616a
Mile de Noyers, association with Chamber of Accounts, 5:184b
Mile (unit of measure), **8:384a,** 12:585a
definition of, 8:384a
English, 12:588a-b
etymology of, 8:384a
standardization of, 8:384a
Milemete MS, 3:64a, 64b (*illus.*)
Miles-clericus controversy, 8:411b
Milescu, Nicolae, *Enchiridion sive stella orientalis occidentali splendens,* 10:512a
Mileševo, 11:180b
Church of the Ascension
fresco by Theodore, 12:14b, 15 (*illus.*)
fresco with a Resurrection scene, 10:340a
frescoes, 11:184b, 185b, 186a
Milet, Jacques, *La Destruction de Troye,* 4:265a
Miletus, as a communication center, 10:424a
Milevis, Council of (416), Pelagianism and, 9:486b
Milhemet Mitzvah. See Meir ben Simeon of Narbonne
Miliarensis, 8:419a
Milič, John, 6:365b–366a, 366b, 372b
Military. *See* Warfare
Military orders, in Byzantine Empire, 7:348a
Military orders. *See* Chivalry, orders of
Military representative assemblies. *See* Representative assemblies
Military service
Russian land tenure and, 11:192a, 195a
serfdom and, 11:202b, 203a
see also Knights and knight service; Warfare
Milites, 7:276b–277b
emergence of, 7:277a-b
see also Knights
Milites maiores. See Capitanei
Milites minores. See Valvassores
Milites secundi. See Valvassores
Mill Song. *See Grottasǫngr*
Millas, irrigation of, 6:558b
Millau Bridge, 10:417a
shape of cutwaters of, 10:421a
Millefiori. *See* Enamel, Millefiori
Millefleurs. *See* Tapestry, Millefleurs
Millennialism
Christian, **8:384b–388a**
Antichrist and, 8:385b
beguins and, 2:162a
beliefs about, 8:384b
Book of Revelation and, 8:384b–385a
in Byzantium, 8:20a
discrediting of, 8:385a
Hussites and, 8:387b
idea of reform and, 10:282b
inspiration of, 8:387b–388a
late, 8:387a
Lord of the Second Coming, 12:123a–124b (*illus.*)
meaning of, 8:384b
political, 8:385b–386a
Radulphus Glaber on, 10:247b
revolutionary, 8:387a-b
theological, 8:385b–386b
Islamic, **8:388a–389b**
Abbasids and, 8:389a
Almohads and, 8:389b
doctrine of resurrection and, 10:341a-b
eschatology and, 8:388b
Fatimids and, 8:389a-b

Millennialism (*cont.*)
  Islamic (*cont.*)
    Muḥammad's prophecy of, 8:388b
    origin of, 8:388a
    political history of Islaṁ and, 8:389a
    Shīʿa and, 8:388a–389a
    Sunnites and, 8:388a-b
  Sasanian, 12:715a
  see also Year 1000
Millet
  as cereal crop, 1:83b, 98b
  common, 5:647a
  growth of, in Western Europe, 5:646b–647a
Millier (unit of measure), 12:595a
Mills, **8:389b–395a**
  adjustment of, 2:36a
  animal-operated
    Byzantium, 1:77b
    use of asses, 1:295b
  built on bridges, 10:409b
  built under bridges, 10:411a
  French, 12:579a
  fulling, 11:706a-b
  gig, for wool raising, 11:708a
  grain, 1:77b, 11:647b (*illus.*)
  hand, 2:365a
  irrigation and, 6:557a, 558a, 558b
  for papermaking, 9:389b
  principles of, 8:389b
  rotation, ball-and-chain governor, 11:662a
  trade in quernstones and, 12:109b
  vertical mill wheel (*nāʿūra*), 9:67 (*illus.*)
  water-driven hammer, 11:639b, 651b
  water-powered, 11:637a
    boat, 8:391b
    bridge, 8:391b–392a
    building and construction, 8:393b
    Byzantium, 1:77b
    in Domesday Book, 8:391a
    early, 8:389b–390a
    food, 8:391a (*illus.*), 392b–393a
    grain crops and, 5:647a
    horizontal, 8:390a-b
    industrial adaptations of, 8:392b–394a
    irrigation and drainage, 8:393b–394a
    metallurgy, 8:393b
    Northern Europe, 1:94b
    paper, 8:393a-b
    Slavic world, 1:98a, 99b
    technology and, 8:392b
    textiles, 8:393a
    tide, 8:392a
    types of, 8:389b–392a
    vertical, 8:390b–391b
    woodworking, 8:393b
  waterwheels, 12:579a
  windmills
    Byzantium, 1:77b
    early, 8:394a
    employment of, 8:394b–395a
    Eurasia, 11:661b
    in food production, 8:394b
    grain crops and, 5:647a
    history of, 8:394a
    horizontal axle, 11:637b, 652a, 653b (*illus.*), 661a, 661b
    importance of, 8:395a
    in industries, 8:394b–395a
    post mill, 8:394a-b
    Slavic world, 1:98a
    technical imagination and, 8:395a
    tower mill, 8:394b
    types of, 8:394a-b
    vertical axle, 11:661a, 662a
    water drainage, 8:394b
  see also Banalité
Millstätter Exodus. See Altdeutsche Exodus
Milo of St. Amand, **8:395b**
  on Amandus, 8:395b
  Charles the Bald and, 8:395b
  De sobrietate, 6:317a
  Hucbald and, 6:317a
Milun. See Marie de France
Milutin of Serbia, king, 4:524b
  churches built by, 4:347a-b
  marriage to Simonida, 11:186a
  Michael Astrapas and, 8:303b
Mimbar. *See* Minbar
Mime, in medieval theater, 4:278b
Mímir (Mímr, Mími), **8:395b–396a,** 11:29b
  in *Fjǫlsvinnsmál,* 8:395b–396a
  Snorri Sturluson and, 8:395b
  Vanir and, 12:356b
  in *Vǫluspá,* 8:395b–396a
  in *Ynglinga saga,* 8:396a
Mimus, 7:116b
"Min herze den gelouben hat." *See* Friedrich von Hausen
"Min herze und min lip diu wellent scheiden." *See* Friedrich von Hausen
Minā, fairs, 4:588b
Minai ware, 3:240a, 6:603b, **8:396a,** 11:147b
  description of, 8:396a
Minaret, **8:396a–397a**
  Arabic words for, 8:396b
  of Bahrām Shāh, 5:519b
  conventional meaning of, 8:396a-b
  decorations of, 8:397a
    Mosque of the Casbah, 8:151a
  earliest monumental, 8:396b–397a
  from pre-Abbasid times, 8:396b
  Kutubīya Mosque, 8:151a
  in later architecture, 8:397a
  of Masʿūd III, 5:519 (*illus.*)
  in mosques, 8:499b
  paired, 6:604b
    in al-Ḥākim, 6:608b
  practice of calling prayer and, 8:396b
  regional variations of, 8:396b
  spiral, 6:598a, 599b
  square, 6:601a
  surviving, 8:396b
  tall cylindrical, 8:396b
  see also Malwiya; Şerefe
Minbar, 6:593a, **8:397a-b,** 8:397b (*illus.*), 10:235a
  in Ayyubid mausoleums, 2:21b
  function of, 8:498b, 499b
  introduction of, 8:397a
  in Seljuk architecture, 11:146a-b, 149a
  see also Mosques
Minbāriyya, 6:453a
Mind of God, the. *See* Essence and existence; Realism
Mindaugas (Mindovg) of Lithuania, prince, 2:67a
  conversion to Christianity, 7:604b
  murder of, 7:605a
  rise to power of, 7:604b
Ming porcelain, 3:240a
Mingrelian language, 5:404b
Mingrelians, 5:403b, 404b
Miniatures. *See* Gospelbook; Manuscript illumination; Pocketbooks
Minim, 8:629 (*illus.*)
  Johannes Vetulus and, 8:646b
  Philippe de Vitry and, 8:645b
Minima, 8:588b
Mining, **8:397b–404a**
  in Alps, 8:399a
  in Balkans, 8:399a
  Black Death and, 8:401b
  in Bohemia, 8:398b–399a
  in Bosnia, under Stjepan Kotromaniç, 11:486a
  in Britain, 8:398a
  coal, 3:473a-b
  conditions of, 8:399b–401a
  of copper, in Sweden, 6:91b
  distribution of ores mined, 8:398a–399b
  early metals mined, 8:397b–398a
  expansion of, 8:401b
  in Harz Mountains, 8:398b, 401b
  history of, 8:401a–402a
  increase in, 8:401b
  law governing, 8:402a–404a
  lead, Bosnia, 2:336b
  metalworking and, 8:400a
  numbers employed in, 8:403b–404a
  operations, growth of, 8:403b
  origin of, 8:397b–398a
  in Poland, 9:725a, 728b
  of precious metals, in Hungary, 6:344a-b
  regalian rights of, 8:402b–403a
  salt, 9:725a, 728b, 729b
  in Saxony, 8:398b
  in Scandinavia, 8:399a
  in Serbia, 11:175a, 176b
  silver
    Anatolia, 10:236a
    Bosnia, 2:336b, 340a, 340b
  in Slovakia, 8:399a
  smelting and, 8:400a
  social history of, 8:403b–404a
  in Spain, 8:398a-b
  status of miners, 8:403b
  technology, 11:639b
    diving and dredging equipment, 11:639b
    underground and open-cut techniques, 11:639b
  water and, 8:400a–401a
  wheel in, 11:639b
  see also Gold; Iron; Silver; Tin
Ministerials (*ministeriales*), 5:454b, **8:404a–407a,** 9:150a-b, 12:562a
  acceptance of, 8:406a-b
  allods and, 8:405a
  Bamberg, 8:405a, 406b

as bishops, 8:406b
code of, 8:405a
criticized by Seifrid Helbling, 11:142b
decline of, 8:406b
definition of, 7:277b, 8:404a-b
fiefs and, 8:405a
Hohenstaufen dynasty and, 8:405b–406a
imperial, 8:405b
importance of, 8:404b, 405a-b
investiture controversy and, 8:405a
in Middle High German literature, 8:349b, 352a-b
ministeriales regni, 8:405b
monasticism and, 8:406b
nobility and, 8:406a-b
princely, 8:405b–406a
problem of, 8:406a
source of, 8:404b–405a
Styrian, 8:406a
support of Henry IV and Henry V and, 8:405a
in Westphalia, 8:406b
Ministerium, 10:16a–17a
Minne canzones, 5:439a–440a
Minne und Gesellschaft, 8:410a
Minneburg, 5:431a-b, **8:407a–408a,** 8:410b
complexity of, 8:407a
forms of, 8:407a-b
poet of, 8:407a
Minnehof. See Pseudo-Zilies von Sayn
Minnekanzone. See Minne canzones
Minnekind, 8:410b
Minnen loep, Der. See Potter, Dirc
Minnereden, 8:357b, **8:408a–413a**
collections of, 8:412b
debates in, 8:411b
early, 8:409b–410b
genre of, 8:408a
in Germany, 8:408a
minnesong and, 8:408b
other works and, 8:411b–412b
popularity of, 8:408b
precursors of, 8:408b–409b
three arts of love and, 8:410b–411a
Titurelstrophe in, 8:408b
Minnesang. See Minnesingers
Minnesingers, **8:413a–415a,** 8:583a
courtly love and, 8:413a
courtly tradition of, 8:413b–414a
cult of *hôhiu minne,* 12:536b–537a
dawn song, 9:304b
decline of, 8:414a-b
definition of, 5:434b
dependence on troubadours and trouvères, 5:434a-b, 8:413a
employment of, 8:350b
first, 5:434a
frauendienst, 12:537a
Frauenlied and, 8:413b
functions of, 8:413b
ideology of, 8:413b
influence on later writers, 6:139a
language of, 8:413b
lyrics of, 8:413b–414a
Minnesang manuscripts, 6:142b
oral tradition and, 8:568b
realism of, 8:414a
Reinmar von Zweter's melodies and, 10:295a-b
Sicilian school and, 6:641a, 11:258a
styles of, 6:164a
surviving melodies of, 8:414b
trecento, 12:180b
Wechsel, 8:413b, 9:304b
woman's song, 9:304b
Minnesong
audience of, 5:435b–436a
canzone and, 6:668a
as court poetry, 5:35a-b
critics of, 5:440a
dances with, 5:436a
decline of, 5:443b
didactic poetry and, 5:442a
earliest, 8:413b
forms of, 5:435b
aubade, 5:441a-b
counterform, 5:440b
crusade song, 5:441b
exchange, 5:439a
"feasting songs," 5:440b
landscape description, 5:438b–439a
minne canzones, 5:439a–440a
singer as vassal of the lady, 5:439b
Gottfried von Neifen and, 5:633b
influence of on Mechthild von Magdeburg, 8:241b
interest in, 5:443b
Konrad von Würzburg and, 7:290b–291a
leich, 5:440b–441a
in Middle High German literature
late (1220/1230–1300), 8:352b–353a
late (1300–1430), 8:357b–358a
Minnereden and, 8:408b
nobility and, 5:434b–435a
performers of, 5:434a
rhetoric in, 5:436a
romance in, 5:434a–436a
themes of, 5:434a
topoi of, 8:414a
Walther von der Vogelweide's criticism of, 5:440a
Minor excommunication. *See* Excommunication
Minorite order, Berthold von Regensburg and, 2:200a
Minority
in Byzantine law, 6:452a
in Roman law, 6:458b
see also Emancipation
Minstrels, **8:415a–417a,** 8:634b
divisions of, 8:416a
employment of, 8:415b
in feudal court, 8:415b
gōsās, 5:579a
Italian. *See Canterini*
jongleur and, 8:415a
Mynnyddog Mwynfawr and, 8:558a
popularity of, 8:416a-b
references to, in literary works, 8:415b–416a
Reinmar von Zweter's melodies and, 10:295a-b
schools of, 8:603a, 634b
Spanish, 8:562b
travels of, 12:160b–161a
see also Chansons de geste; Joglar/Jongleur; Troubadour
Mint (herb), 6:184a
Minṭāsh, governor of Melitene, rebellion against Sultan Barqūq, 2:113a
Mints and money
coins as evidence of trade routes, 4:553b, 555b, 587b
counterfeit, treason and, 12:167a
currency
manipulation, 11:620a, 623a, 624a
stabilization, 11:619b–620a
Golden Horde, 8:475b
Hungarian, 6:344b
under St. Stephen I, 11:480a
metals used for, 2:383a, 384b
power machines, restrictions on, 11:654b
problems of exchange, 4:592b
Roman
Dominate and, 10:460b–461a
papacy and, 10:523b
solidus of Constantine the Great, 3:545b
Sasanian, astral symbolism, 10:663b
Seljuk, 10:235b–236a
Serbian, 11:176b
under Stefan Uroš II Milutin, 11:475a
Mints and money, Armenian, **8:417a–418b**
Artaxiad coins, 8:417b
at Antioch, 8:417b
at Artašat, 8:417b
at Damascus, 8:417b
Cilician, 8:418 (*illus.*)
earliest coins, 8:417b
geographical position of Armenia and, 8:417a-b
lifestyle of Armenians and, 8:417b
of Tigran II, 1:493a, 494a
under Ašot, 1:481a
under foreign rule, 8:418a
Mints and money, Byzantine, **8:418b–421b**
after Fourth Crusade, 8:421a
bracteates, 2:355b
coin weights, 12:581a-b
of early period, 8:419b–420b
gold coinage in, 8:421a
devaluation of, 2:443a
histories of, 8:419a
icons and, 6:400b
of late Roman period, 8:419b–420b
mint marks on coins, 8:420a
nomisma, devaluation of, 2:493b
officinae on, 8:420a–421a
in 6th century, 8:418b–419a
solidus of Justinian II, 7:203a
in 10th century, 8:420b–421a
trade and, 8:421a-b
see also Besant; *Nomisma; Tetarteron*
Mints and money, Islamic, **8:421b–425b,** 12:574b
Abbasid coins, 3:44b
in Anatolia, 8:424a-b
Arabic inscriptions, 8:167a
at Damascus, 8:421b
coinage reforms, 4:301b
conquered territories and, 8:421b
copper coins, 8:421b–422b
dinar, 4:187a-b
dirham, 4:215b–216a
in Egypt, 8:421b, 423b–424a

Mints and money, Islamic (*cont.*)
Egyptian Tulinid, 12:224a
gold coins, 8:421b–423b, 425a
iconoclasm and, 6:403b
inscriptions on coins, 8:422a-b
in Iraq, silver coins, 6:72b
in Mediterranean area, 8:423b
minting procedures, 8:425a
in North Africa, 8:423a-b
Ortuqid coinage, 9:283b
silver coins, 8:421b, 423a, 425a
in Spain, 8:423a
standards of, 8:424b–425a
standing caliph, 8:422a (*illus.*)
in Syria, 8:421a, 424a
trade and, 8:424b–425a
Umayyad coinage, 3:40a-b
see also Rubāᶜīya; particular dynasties
Mints and money, Russian, **8:425b–427a**
coinless era in, 8:426a-b
earliest coins, 8:425b
end of Rus coinage, 8:427a
foreign influences on, 8:426a
of Golden Horde, 8:426b
identifying and cataloging, 8:427a
in Lithuania, 8:426b
trade and, 8:426a-b
Tverian coins, 8:427a
types, 8:425b–426a
Mints and money, Western European, **8:427b–431b**
alloys of coins, 8:428b
augustal, 8:430a
black money, 8:428b
changes affecting, 8:431a
characteristics of, 8:427b
currency fluctuations, 5:179a–180a
debasing of coinage, 5:174b
development (5th–11th centuries), 8:427b–428b
England, 8:289b–290a, 429a, 430b–431a
Canterbury as coinage center, 3:82a
coinage reforms under Edgar, 4:457a
Exchequer and, 4:531a
King Alfred coins, 7:659a, 659b
London, 7:659b, 660b
pound, 10:66b–67a
silver coinage, 7:659b
France, 8:429a, 430b–431a
écus, 10:319a
fixed *taille* and, 11:577b
fluctuations in, 5:179a–180a
"good money of St. Louis," 5:179a
groat, 5:680a
pied de monnaie formula, 5:179a
reform of 1343, 5:179b
Tournois, 5:179a-b
Germany, 8:429a-b
groat, 5:680a
gold coins, 8:428b, 430a–431a
in Gotland, 5:632a-b
Italy, 8:429a-b, 430b
libra, 8:428b
Merovingian, 8:288a-b
"money of Melgueil," 8:482b
production of coinage, 8:295b
in Scandinavia, bracteates, 2:356a
Sicilian. *See Augustalis*
silver coins, 8:428b, 429b–431a
solidus, 8:428b, 430a
stabilization of coinage, 5:181a
standards for, 8:427b, 431a
trade and, 8:430a, 431a
Trebizond, silver asper, 12:169b
varieties of, 8:427b
Venice, ducat, 4:301a-b
weights of coins, 8:428b
see also Banking, European; Florin; Groat; Penny
Minučihr. *See* Manūchihr, Shaddadid ruler
Minucius Felix, theology, philosophical elements of, 9:583a
Miquel de la Tor. *See* Michel de la Tour of Nîmes
Mīr ᶜAlī Shīr Nawāᵓi, 12:59a
Mīr ᶜAlī al-Tabrīzī, script *nastaᶜlīq* and, 9:65b
Mir Geribert, revolt of, 3:176a-b
Mirabilia, 1:564b–565a
Miracle de Nostre Dame de Saint Alexis, 12:413a
Miracle plays, **8:431b–432a**
decline of, 8:432a
earliest, 8:431b
in England, 8:431b
in France, 4:264a-b, 268b, 8:431b–432a
in Germany, 4:268b
origins, 10:597b
see also Drama; Mystery plays
Miracle de Théophile. See Rutebeuf
Miracles
at Becket's tomb, 3:83a
canonization and, 3:68b
in *Cantar de mío Cid,* 3:77b
magic and, 8:33b
relics and pilgrimage, 9:654b–655a
Russian pilgrimage and, 9:654a
of Virgin Mary, 3:85a
Miracles de Nostre Dame, 4:264a-b, 8:431b
performance of, 4:284b
place in French hagiography, 6:60a
see also Gautier de Coinci
Miracles de Notre Dame. See Jean le Tavernier
Miracles of St. Artemius, on Byzantine merchants, 12:101a
Miracles of St. Edmund, on Viking attack on Thetford, 12:559b (*illus.*)
Miracolo del Corporale, 6:636a
Miracula Adalberti. See Johannes Canaparius
Miracula S. Dionysii, on portable altars, 1:225a
Miracula sancti Benedicti. See Radulfus Tortarius
Miracula sancti Heriberti. See Lantbert of Deutz
Miraculi Nynie episcopi, 9:139a
Miraculum, defined, 4:278b
Miraflores Altarpiece. *See* Weyden, Rogier van der
Miragros de Santiago, 11:439b
Miᶜrāj, 1:581a
Miᶜraj-nāmeh, 9:393 (*illus.*)
Miralles, Melcior, *Dietari del capellà d'Alfons el Magnànim,* 3:166b
Miramar (college: Majorca), 8:445a
Mīrānshāh (son of Tamerlane), 12:56b
honorary title of *küregen* and, 12:58b
Mircea (the Old) of Walachia, prince
anti-Ottoman resistance, 12:501a
territorial expansion, 12:501a
vs. Ottomans, 10:514b
Mirdasids, control of Ḥimṣ, 6:230a
Mireoirs as princes, Le. See Watriquet de Couvin
Mīrī, 11:669a
Mirian III (Meribanes), St., king of East Georgia, 5:405a, 413a
conversion of Chosroids and, 3:308a
Djvari at Mtsxetᶜa and, 4:231b–232a
Mirk, John, *Festial,* 8:315a
Mīrkhwānd (Timurid historian), 12:59a
Mírmanns saga, **8:432a–433a,** 10:394b, 395b
alliteration in, 8:432b
names and motifs in, 8:432b
surviving manuscripts of, 8:432b
Mírmanskvæði, 8:433a
Mírmantsrímur, 8:432b–433a
Miro II of Urgel, count, rule in Catalonia, 3:175a
Miroslav of Croatia, ruler, overthrown, 4:5a
Miroslav (son of Tihomir of Serbia), 11:473a
Mirouer des simples ames. See Porete, Marguerite
Mirozshki monastery, design of, 4:341a
Mirror of Charity, The. See Ethelred of Rievaulx
Mirror of Justices, 7:456a, **8:433a-b**
author of, 8:433a-b
on Exchequer Court, 4:533b
writing of, 8:433a
Mirror of princes, **8:434a–436b**
Alcuin of York and, 8:434a
Arabic, 8:435b–436a
counterparts to, 8:434a
first English, 8:435b
first formal, 8:434a-b
first identifiable, 10:15b
Gower's *Confessio Amantis* as, 8:435b
ḥadīth and, 8:435b
Hartmann's *Erek* as, 6:104a
Hartmann's *Îwein* as, 6:105a
Hincmar of Rheims and, 8:434b
influence on, 8:435b
Isidore of Seville and, 8:434a
Islamic tradition and, 8:435b–436a
Koran and, 8:435b
of mendicant orders, 8:435a
moral exhortation and, 8:435a
in *Moralium dogma philosophorum,* 12:619b
Old Testament and, 10:15b
Persian, 8:436a
political theory and
Islamic, 10:13a-b
Western European, 10:15a–16a
prince in, 10:123b–124a
proliferation of, 8:435a
Renaissance examples of, 8:436a
in Spain, 11:441a-b
Stephen I of Hungary and, 11:480a

under Valois kings, 8:435b
see also Secretum secretorum
Mirror of the Simple Souls. See Porete, Marguerite
Mirrors, 2:148 (*illus.*), 149a, 5:562a-b
Mīrzā Jahān-Shāh, Tabrīz and, 11:571a
Misa de Amor, La, **8:436b–437a**
Misaca, king. *See* Mieszko I of Poland, king
Miscellaneous Agama, The, Everyman and, 4:528a
Misdemeanor, in English common law, 7:197a
Mise of Amiens (1264), 6:159a, 7:675b, 11:297b–298a
Mise of Lewes (1264), 6:159a, 11:298a
Mise roll, 6:302a
Miserere. See Reclus de Mollien
Miserere mei Deus. See Psalm 50
Misericord, **8:437a**, 9:689a
Misericordia. See Daggers, types of
Misha (mattock), in Visigothic illuminations, 12:78b
Mishkāt al-anwār. See Ghazālī, al-
Mishnah
dietary laws and, 4:181a–183a
Maimonides' commentary on, 7:173a
oral tradition and, 7:159a
on public commenting on Scriptures, 10:361a
Talmud and, 11:583a
Mishnah ha-Middot, 11:90a
Mishneh Torah. See Maimonides, Moses
Mishpat ivri. See Jewish law
Mishqar. See Shaqira
Misis, basilica at, 4:357a
Misithra. *See* Mistra
Misjaḥ, Ibn, 8:565b
Miskawayh
on ᶜImād al-Dawla, 6:424b
Tajārib al-uman, 6:251a
Misogyny. *See* Antifeminism
Misprision (official misconduct). *See* Law, civil
Miṣrī, Dhy 'l-Nūn, Sufi teaching, 4:407a
Missaglia, 1:528b
armor workshop, 1:529b
Missaḥarātī, 10:254b
Missal, **8:437a-b**
decoration of, 8:437a
earliest examples of, 8:437a-b, 10:606b
models for, 10:606a
texts of, 8:437b
variations in, 8:437a
see also Mass cycles; Pericope; Plainsong; Ritual
Missal VI 33, 2:181a
Missale Francorum, 10:606a
Missale Gallicanum vetus, 10:606a
Missale Gothicum, 10:606a
Missi dominici, **8:437b–438b**
capitulary and, 3:91b
in Carolingian Empire, 3:108a-b, 114b, 8:438a-b
of Charlemagne, 3:268b
corruption of, 8:438b
instructions to, 8:438a
responsibilities of, 8:438a
Mission of the Apostles, **8:438b**
description of, 8:438b
iconography depicting, 8:438b
in New Testament, 8:438b
Missions and missionaries, Christian, **8:439a–446a**
Anglo-Saxon
reforms of, 12:683a
Regula sancti Benedicti and, 2:170a
Augustine of Canterbury, 1:644b–645a
Bogomil, Catharism and, 12:661a
Byzantine, 9:687a
language used by, 6:436a
to Bulgaria, 4:74a
to Khazars, 4:73b
to Moravia, 4:73b–74b
to Nubia, 9:197b
to Russia, 2:464a-b, 489a
to Serbs, 2:117b
to Slavs, 2:463b–464b, 489a-b, 4:73a–74b
Celtic, 9:663b
Church of the East, 11:563a
conquests of new territories and, 8:445b
Copts, 3:595b
crusades and, 8:445a-b
Dominican, 4:252a–253a
in Cumania, 6:342a
language training, 10:266b
in Eastern Europe (to 1400), 8:442b–444a
English, to Sweden, 11:530b
Frankish, to Croatia, 4:2a, 4b
Genoese, headquartered in Pera-Galata, 9:503a
German, to Slavs, 6:151b–152a
Gothic, 10:465b
Gregory the Illuminator, St., 5:668a
Irish, 6:516a
to Europe, 6:516a
language training (*studia linguarum*), 12:137a
in late Roman Empire, 8:439a–440a
liturgical poetry and, 9:714b
Muslim challenge to (700–1350), 8:444a–445b
of Pope Gregory I, 9:371b–372a
Ramon Lull on, 8:445a
Roman, 10:462b
language used by, 6:438b
to England, 3:81b, 7:362a
to Hungary, 6:339a
teaching with saintly relics, 10:297b
to Anglo-Saxons, 4:458a
to Armenia, 1:507a
to Baltic lands, 2:64a–67a
to China, 5:202a
to Cilicia, 3:394b
to England, 8:439b (map)
to Ethiopia, 2:459b
to the Finnish Zyrians, 10:595a-b
to France, 8:441b (map), 442a
to Germany, 4:458b, 8:441b (map), 442a
Boniface, 2:321a–322b
to Ireland, 8:439b (map), 440a
to Poland, 9:718a
to southern Arabia, 9:55a
Vita Anskarii by St. Rimbert and, 10:401a
in Western Europe (600–1200), 8:440b–442b
see also Augustine of Canterbury, St.; Boniface, St.; Columba, St.; Columbanus, St.; Cyril, St.; Dominicans; Franciscans; John of Monte Corvino; Methodios, St.; Patrick, St.
Missions and missionaries, Islamic
Ismailism and, 6:587b
Sufism and, 6:586a
to Bulgars, 12:488a
see also Daᶜwā
Missorium, **8:446a**
Mistere, defined, 4:279a
Misteri d'Elx, 12:349a
Mistilteinn sword, 6:312b
Mistra, 7:378a, 378b, 379a, 380a, **8:446a-b**
artistic and scholastic achievements, 8:486b–487a
building of, 8:446a-b
as center of late Byzantine religious art, 8:446b
church architecture in later Empire, 4:345a
town planning of, 4:333a
under Ottomans, 8:446b
Misyn, Richard, translations of Richard Rolle's works, 9:20b–21a, 26b
Miter. *See* Vestments, liturgical
Mithra (Mithras), 12:721a, 746b
in mystery religions, 9:1a, 1b
Miðfjarðar-Skeggi (saga character), 12:48b–49a
Mittelalterliches Hausbuch. See Master of the Amsterdam Cabinet
Mittelfränkische Reimbibel (Legendar), 2:228a
Mittelland (Switzerland), 11:536b, 542b
Mitylene, Byzantine sea routes and, 10:423 (map), 424b
Miyyafarqin, Armenian trade and, 12:97b
Miᶜzafa, 8:567b, 611a
Mizhar, 8:610b
Mizmār, 8:612a-b
Mizmār al-jirāb, 8:612b
Mizmār al-muthannā, al-. See Dūnāy
Mizmār al-muzāwaj, al-. See Dūnāy
Mizr (beer), 2:209a
Mizzen, 11:237a, 244b, 248a
Mjǫllnir (Thor's hammer), 11:25b, 26 (*illus.*), 12:45b, 46a
in *Þrymskviða,* 12:52b
Mkhedruli script. *See* Georgian alphabet
Mladá Boleslav, Bohemian Brethren in, 2:307a
Mleh, Rubenid ruler of Armenia
invasion of Cilicia, 10:540b
Lambron and, 7:322a
Moats, **8:447a**
around castles and fortifications, 3:150a
Mōbadān mōbad, **8:447a-b**, 11:597b
duties of, 10:668b
establishment of seminary, 8:447b
functioning of office, 8:447a
Mazdakism and, 8:238a
precursors of, 10:668a
promotion of Zoroastrianism, 10:601a

Mōbadān mōbad (*cont.*)
in Zoroastrian hierarchy, 10:612a
Mobility, social. *See* Social mobility
Moccasin. *See* Shoes and shoemakers
Mocedades del Cid. See Castro y Bellvis, Guillén de
Mocedades de Rodrigo, **8:447b–448b,** 11:409a, 411b, 418a, 438a
descendants of, 8:448a
diffusion by minstrels, 8:448a
diocese of Palencia in, 8:447b–448a
lost predecessor of, 11:443a
meter of, 11:428b
origin of, 8:448a
Mocedades de Rodrigo, Gesta de las. See Gesta de las mocedades de Rodrigo
Modal notation. *See* Musical notation, modal
Modalism, condemnation of, 3:628b
Mode, **8:448b–451a,** 8:561b
in *Alia musica,* 8:639b
Aribo and, 8:642a
Armenian, 8:551b
Byzantine, 8:551b
in the chants of rhymed offices, 10:374a-b
Cistercians and, 8:643a
in *Dialogus,* 8:640b
ecclesiastical
as abstractions, 8:450b
authentic and plagal forms, 8:449b
by *finalis,* 8:450a
by melody types, 8:449a–450a
calendaric assignments, 8:449a
cosmological basis for, 8:449a
eight-mode system, 8:448b
limitations of, 8:450a
origin of, 8:449a
twelve-mode system, 8:449b
eight-mode system, 9:215a
Hermann von Reichenau on, 8:641b–642a
intonatio and, 6:498a
Johannes Gallicus and, 8:643b
John of Afflighem and, 8:642b
noeannoe and, 9:152a
oral tradition and, 8:569a
psalm tones, 8:448a
rhythmic, 8:588a-b, 593b, 594a
Syrian, 8:565b, 578a
Turkestani, 8:561b
white-note octave scales, 8:450b
William of Hirsau and, 8:642a
see also Mediatio; Melody; Rhythm; Tonary; Tones, musical
Model books, for workshop use, 4:291b
Modena, inns in, 6:471a, 471b–472a, 472b, 474a-b
Modena Cathedral, 6:638a
facade, 10:492a, 500b–501a
Lanfranc of Modena and, 7:329a
Wiligelmo's Genesis scenes, 12:630 (*illus.*)
Moderni. See Via moderna
Modestus of Jerusalem, St., 7:282b
Modified nominalism. *See* Nominalism
Modillion, **8:451a**
Modios, 12:581b
Modistae (medieval linguists), 10:359b, 360b
Modoald of Trier, bishop, 9:499a
Modoin, 7:362a, **8:451a-b**
Carolingian Latin poetry and, 3:102b–103a
"Eclogue," 8:451b
Louis the Pious and, 8:451a
Ovidian influence on, 9:313a
poem to Theodulf of Orléans, 8:451b
Modon, Venice and, 7:376b, 380b
Moduin. *See* Modoin
Modus tenendi parliamentum, **8:451b–453b**
dating of, 8:451b–452a
Irish version of, 8:452a, 9:435a
uses for, 8:452a
Modwenna, St. *See Vie de Ste. Modwenne*
Moesia
languages of, 10:509b
Visigoths in, 12:469b
Moghāns and *hērbadān* (in Zoroastrianism), 10:668b
Moghuls, Great, origins, 12:58a
Moguer, Rafael, 9:140b
Mohács, Battle of (1526), 6:350a, 10:514b
Mohammed. *See* Muḥammad
Mohel, 3:401a
see also Cupper; *Sandek*
Moissac Abbey
reliefs in cloister, 4:315b
St. Pierre Church, **8:452b**
Mojmír (Mojmar), 5:658a
founder of Great Moravia, 2:299a
Mokkᶜ, 1:472b, 473a, 473b
Vaspurakan and, 12:361a, 361b
Molad, computation of, 3:25b
Moldavia
administration
foreign influence, 12:505b
logofat and *vistier,* 12:505b–506a
soltuzi and *vornici,* 12:506b
anti-Ottoman resistance, 12:503a-b
Bohemian Brethren in, 2:305b
boundaries, 12:499 (map)
church architecture, exterior painting, 12:505b
class structure, 12:503a, 506a
culture, Byzantine influence, 12:505a-b
Cumans, 12:500a
ethnic make-up, 12:506b–507a
factional strife, 12:503a
geographic location, 12:498a
history, 10:514b–515a
to 1432, 12:501b–502a
after 1432, 12:503a–504a
origins
chronology, 12:501b
Daco-Roman continuity theory, 12:498b–500a
migration theory, 12:499a–500a
Ottoman protectorate, 12:504a
Ottoman tribute, 12:503b
Pocutia conflict, 12:501b–502a, 504a
Polish suzerainty, 12:501b, 502a, 503b–504a
relations with Lithuania, 10:515a
religion, 12:504a–505a
Catholic bishoprics and monasteries, 12:502a
hesychast movement, 12:504b
Latin Christianity, 12:504b–505a
Orthodox Christianity, 12:504a-b
see of Moldo-Vlachia, 12:502a, 504b
representative assemblies, 12:506a
Tatar campaigns, 12:501b
taxation, 12:506a
trade and commerce, 12:502a, 506a–507a
voivode, 12:501b, 503b
functions and privileges, 12:505b
Moldavian language, 10:513b
Molding, **8:452b–454a**
practical applications, 8:453a
ribbing, 8:453a
types of, 8:454a (*illus.*)
see also Stringcourse
Moldo-Vlachia, metropolitan see of, 12:502a, 504b
Molesme (monastery), 12:685a
liturgical reform and, 3:406a-b
Molinet, Jean, 7:54b, 55a, 10:364b, 365a
Art de rhétorique, 5:278b
Chroniques, 9:638a
Moling, in literature, 6:540b
Molinier, Guilhem, *Las leys d'amors,* tenso and partimen, 11:666b
Molla Sadra, tomb of, 11:252b
Mombaer, Jan
hymns and, 6:382b
meditation techniques, 2:368a
Rose Garden of Spiritual Exercises, 2:368a, 4:167a
Mommerie, defined, 4:279b
Mommynge, defined, 4:279b
Monarchia. See Dante Alighieri
Monarchia sicula, 7:535a
Monarchy. *See* Kingship
Monasteries, **8:454a–456b**
Armenia, 1:482b, 512a
Benedictine
France, 12:684b–685a
Germany, 12:685a
Puglia, 12:684b
Byzantine
artistic patronage, 2:439a
on Cyprus, 4:72b–73a
defense needs, 4:333b
as "ideal city" of town planners, 4:333a
secluded location of, 4:333b
taxation and, 11:605a
see also Studios Monastery
Cappadocia, 3:92a
Carolingian, villages and, 12:443b
Celtic
Benedictines and, 2:172a
Regula sancti Benedicti and, 2:170a
cenobitic, 8:454b
census and, 11:605b
cloister, 3:465a-b
composition of rhymed offices and, 10:369b
Coptic, 3:585b
cenobitic communities, 3:595a
paintings in, 3:592b
design of, 8:455a-b
Benedictine Rule and, 8:455a
Carthusians and, 3:119b
refectory, 10:281a-b

double
  Astorga, 12:686b
  England, 12:683a
  France, 12:682b, 683a
  Italy, 12:682b, 687a-b
  Premonstratensians and, 12:685b
England, 4:518a
  Henry VIII and, 2:157a
  hospitality of, 6:468b
  Roger of Salisbury and, 10:443a
as forerunners of guilds and fraternities, 8:288b
founded 601–790, 2:172a
France, 12:684b
  as centers of drama, 4:263b
  Dauphiné, 4:109b
Frankish, 12:683a
  Regula sancti Benedicti and, 2:170b
garden plans, 5:358b–359b, 361a, 362b
Gaul, 7:560b
Georgia, 4:116a
Germany, 12:685a
Hungary, 6:341a
Iceland, 4:618a
Ireland, 6:515a-b, 553b–554a
  Armagh and, 1:470a
  literature and, 6:521b, 522b, 535a, 541b–542a, 545a
Italy, 12:682b
Kievan Rus, as landholders, 1:101a
Latin, in Byzantine Empire, 7:348a
as learning centers, 8:456a
libraries of. *See* Libraries, monastic
literature and, 7:362b
Lombardy, 12:684b
medical functions, 8:458b
medicine and, 2:157a
Melchite, 11:565a
mendicant influence, 8:456a
Morea, 7:378b
Mozarabic, 8:511a
Near East, 4:117a
  see also Lavra
Norman, 9:162b, 163a-b
organ, use of, 9:22b
public services offered by, 4:332b–333a
Romanian, 10:510a-b
Rome, 10:519b
Russian
  land tenure and, 11:190b, 196a
  peasants and, 11:196a
  as pilgrimage shrine, 9:654a
  slaves and, 11:191b–192a
Siwnik^{c}, 11:315a
social status of monks, 8:458b
Spain, irrigation and, 6:558a
Sufi, 6:585b
  architecture of, 6:602a
Swabian, 11:527a
Swiss, 11:537b, 540b
Syrian Christian, 11:564b–565a
tithes and, 12:62b–63a
transport corvées, 12:152b, 157a-b
urban, 8:456a, 457b
Viking damages to, 12:153b
water clocks in, 3:458b–459a (*illus.*), 459b–460a
see also Dayr; Scriptorium

"Monastero Maggiore" (Milan). *See* S. Maurizio (monastery: Milan)
Monastery of the caves. *See* Pecherskaya Lavra
Monastery of Goš. *See Gošavank^{c}*
Monastery of Jeremiah (Saqqara), 7:315a
Monastic chant. See individual entries
Monastic office, 1:516b–517a
Monasticism
  abuses of, 10:285b
  Anglo-Saxon, educational work, 4:459a
  Arianism and, 1:454a
  Armenian, 1:504b, 589b
    Skewṙa, 11:326a
  ascetic practices, 8:460a
  Asia Minor, 8:457a, 461a
  Augustinian friars and, 1:660a
  Augustinism and, 1:660a–661a
  Balkan Peninsula, 8:457a-b
  Brethren of the Common Life and, 2:366a-b, 367a-b
  in Britain, 3:227b
  in Bulgaria
    under Boris, 2:403b–404a
    under Peter, 2:405b
    under Symeon, 2:404a-b
  in Burgundy, 2:426b, 428a
  Byzantine, **8:456b–459a**
    after Persian and Arab invasions, 8:457a
    ascetic practices, 8:456b–457a
    church architecture and, 4:343a
    cultural and social functions, 8:458b–459a
    development of, 2:478b
    education of monks, 7:595b–596a
    golden age, 8:457a-b
    iconoclasm and, 2:488a
    land holdings, 2:477b, 478b, 481a
    liturgies in, 7:611a-b
    monastic centers, 8:457a-b, 461b–462a
    monastic population, 8:457a, 457b–458a
    monks' garb, 3:616a
    on Mount Athos, 1:636b–637b, 637b–638a
    mystical spirituality in, 9:563a
    opposition of Constantine V to, 8:457a
    scholastic pursuits, 2:214a-b, 8:456b
    social and political power, 2:478b–479a
    see also Basil (the Great) of Caesarea, St., monastic rule of; Meteora; *Paterikon;* Patmut^{c}iwn Tarōnoy; Pecherskaya Lavra
  Caesarius of Arles and, 3:9b
  canons regular, 4:230b, 10:287b
  capitulum monasticum, 10:286a
  Cassian and, 3:122a-b
  in Castile, 3:129a-b
  in Catalonia, 3:175a
  celibacy in, 3:216b
  Celtic, 3:226a-b, 227b, 8:462a
    Clonard, 3:465b–466a
    in Ireland, 3:227b
    missionary travels and, 12:151b–152a
    see also Celtic church
  cenobitic, 6:213b, 8:454b, 459b, 460b–461a
  chapter in, 3:265a–266a
  charistikion, 3:268a
  children and, 4:594b, 599b
  children as oblates, 10:285b
  Cistercian general chapter as model for, 3:640b
  common characteristics, 8:459b
  consuetudine texts on monastic rule, 10:285a
  Coptic influence on, 3:595a
  desert or cenobitic, idea of reform and, 10:285a-b
  in early church, 3:342b–343a
  Egyptian, 10:455a, 11:564b
    Benedict of Nursia and, 2:170a
  eremitic
    origins, 6:213a
    Palestinian, 6:213a
  expansion, eastern, 8:461a
  expansion, western, 8:461b
  female, decline of, 10:297b
  in Georgia, 5:409a, 412b, 414a-b, 417a
  glorification of labor, 11:663b
  Gregory I and, 5:669a
  Gregory IX and, 5:671b
  Hrabanus Maurus and, 6:306b
  in Iberian Peninsula, 10:36b–37a
  intellectual life and, 3:357b–358a, 4:543a
  in Ireland
    Céli Dé, 8:162b
    origins, 2:376a
  Islamic, dervish, 4:163a
  in Latin church (1054–1305), 3:354a–355b
  manuscript book production and, 8:102a-b
  medical functions, 8:458b
  migration period art and, 8:368a
  ministerials and, 8:406b
  motivation for, 8:459b–460a
  Nubian, 9:199a
  observant, 3:368a
  oriental provinces, 8:457a
  origins, 8:454b, 456b, **8:459a–462a**
    in the East, 8:460a–461b
    Egyptian, 8:456a-b
    Pepin I and, 9:499a
    Pepin II and, 9:500a
    in the West, 8:461b–462a
    see also Vitae patrum
  Orthodox, Walachia/Moldavia, 12:504b
  peregrinatio pro Christo of Irish monks, 12:426a, 426b
  power and influence
    abuses of, 8:458a-b
    attempts to reduce, 8:458a
    landholdings, 8:458a
    patronage, 8:458a
  recurring characteristics, 6:194b–195a
  reform of, 10:281b–282a, 285b
    at Gorze, 5:578b–579a
    Benedict of Aniane's influence on, 10:285b–286b
    Carmelites and, 3:96b–97a
    Carthusians and, 10:287b

Monasticism (*cont.*)
reform of (*cont.*)
Celestine movement, 3:214b–215a
Cistercians and, 3:403a-b, 10:286b–287a
Cluniac order and, 3:468b–469a, 10:286a-b
Dunstan and, 3:82b
in 8th century, 9:375b
England, 7:363a
Ethelwold and, 4:518a
Grandmont, order of, 5:654b–656a
in Italy, 3:55b–56b
Rule of St. Benedict, 10:285a–287a
simony and, 10:285b, 287b–288a
to 1054, 3:347b–348a
regulation of, 8:457b, 461a-b, 462a
revival of, pilgrimage and, 9:656a-b
Romanesque architecture and, 10:478b
Russia, 8:443b
economic prosperity, 10:595b–596a
origins, 10:595a
religious pilgrimage and, 9:653a, 654a
Sergius of Radonezh and, 11:209a
Sicily, under Roger I, 11:266a
Sinai and Palestine, 8:461a
solitude, forms of, 8:459a-b
Syria, 8:461a
literature and, 11:565b
virtues, *stabilitas,* 12:148a, 151b–152a
Welsh, 12:514b–515a
Benedictine, 12:517a
women's orders, 8:461b
see also Abbot; Anchorites; individual monastic orders
Monasticon Anglicanum, 1:428a
Monasticon Gallicanum, 1:428a
Moncada Canal, 6:557b
Mönch von Salzburg, 8:357b
Mondino dei Luzzi, **8:462a–463a**
Anatomia Mundini, 8:252a, 462b
anatomical vocabulary, 8:462b
importance of, 8:462b–463a
sources for, 8:462b
medical lectures, 8:462b
Monemvasia, **8:463a-b**
foundation of, 8:463a-b
trade and commerce, 8:463b
William II and, 7:378a, 378b
Monenergism. *See* Monoenergism
Moneta of Cremona, 4:247b
Money. *See* Mints and money
Money changers, 2:73a–74b
at fairs, 4:584b, 592b
Moneyer's pound, 10:67a
Moneylending. *See* Banking
Mongán, 6:540b
Monge blanch. See Cistercian order
Möngke, great khan, 2:131b, 6:329a
Hulagu and, 8:651b
Möngke Temür
Golden Horde under, 5:573a
Kublai Khan and, 5:573a
Mongol empire, **8:463b–476b**
administration, 6:590b, 591a, 591b, 8:471b, 474a
financial, 8:474b
Afghanistan, 8:467b
Arčēš and, 1:423a
Armenia and, 1:485b–486a, 514a, 12:98b–99b
negotiations with Smbat Sparapet, 11:351b
army
military tactics, 8:467a
organization and training, 8:465b, 467a
raiding parties, 8:471a
Asia Minor, Turkomans and, 12:227a
Basra and, 2:127b
Baylakān and, 2:139b
boundaries, 8:464 (map)
in Caffa, 3:12a-b
Caucasian campaigns, 8:468a-b
battle at the Kalka (1223), 8:468a-b
Georgia, 8:468a
Kipchaks, 8:470a
Russia, 8:468a-b, 470a-b, 539b
unity of Caucasia and, 3:195a-b
cavalry of, 3:209b
Church of the East and, 11:563b
conquest of Samarkand, 10:640b
Crimea in, 3:678b–680b
in Damascus, 4:82b, 83b–84a
in Derbent, 4:162b
division of, 8:469a
in Eastern Europe, raid on Lithuania, 7:605a
Erzincan and, 4:508b
foundations
Khwārizmshāhs, 7:243b–244a
Kirghiz, 7:272b–273a
Frik and, 5:301b–302a
genealogy of, 5:674b
Genghis Khan and, 5:382a–383a
in Georgia, 5:407a, 420a
Golden Horde as branch of, 5:572b–573b
history of, 5:517b, 7:137b, 138b–139a
Grigor Aknerc^c^i, 5:674a-b
icons and, 6:409a, 411a
Ikonion and, 6:418a
Ilkhan realm, 8:469b, 472a, 473b
Innocent IV and, 6:467a
invasions
of Anatolia, 9:288a
of Armenia, 7:272a
of Bukhara, 2:397a
of Damascus, 5:517b
of East Central Europe, 9:721a-b, 725a, 726a
of Germany, 5:461a
of Kievan Rus, 7:249b
Transoxiana route, 12:145b–146a
in Iran, 6:504b, 507b
architecture and, 6:603b–604b
in Isfahan, 6:562a
Islam and, 11:563b
Ismailism, 6:618a
Sufism, 6:586a
John of Plano Carpini and, 7:138b–139a
Karamanids and, 7:214a
kārgah in, 7:214b
in Kars, 7:221b
Kasranids and, 11:254a
khanate
beginnings of, 8:463b–464a
disintegration of, 8:475a-b
election of Ögödai, 8:469a
succession conflicts, 8:471a-b, 473a, 474b, 540a
Mamluk alliance, 8:474b
Marco Polo's service in, 10:27b
military conquests
Azerbaijan, 8:469b, 476a
Baghdad, 1:12a, 3:50b–51a, 7:112a, 8:472b, 501b, 651b
Bulgars, 8:470a
Chin, 8:465b–466a, 468b
Cumans, 10:577a
Georgia, 8:469b
Greater Armenia, 8:469b–470a
Hsi-hsia, 8:465b, 468b
Hungary, 6:342a-b, 8:470b–471a
Khwārizmshāh, 8:466b–468a, 10:640b
Kurdistan, 8:470a
Sung empire, 8:470a
Syria and Egypt, 8:472b–473a
al-Mustanṣir and, 8:651a
Mu^c^tazila and, 6:583b
origins, 8:463b–465b
confederacy of warrior tribes, 8:465a-b
plagues and, 9:678a
Qara Qitai and, 8:466a-b
Qaraqorum, 8:469a
relations with
Cilicia, 3:391b
Genoa, 5:385b
Latin Empire of Constantinople, 4:556b
papacy, 4:31b, 556b
religion and culture
Islamization, 8:473a, 474a, 474b
religious tolerance, 8:474a, 474b, 10:592b–593a
under Ghazan, 8:474b
in Russia
Nevsky and, 9:111a
Novgorod and, 8:573a
Sweden and, 11:531a
Vladimir-Suzdal, 12:486b, 487a
Russian fur trade and, 5:332b–333a
Russian serfdom and, 11:190a–191a
Sebaste and, 11:132a
Seljuks of Rum and, 11:154b, 157b–158b
Shīrāz and, 11:252b
Širak in, 11:311b
Siwnik^c^ in, 11:315b
struggle for supremacy in, 4:232a
Tabrīz and, 11:571a
trade and, 3:12a, 4:558b, 588a
Uljaytu Khudabānda's movement toward unity, 12:246b
vs. Abbasids, 6:514a
Naṣīr al-Dīn and, 11:228a
vs. Baybars, 2:138a, 138b
vs. Ilkhanids, 9:306a
vs. Ivan III, 11:192a
vs. Kurds, 7:310b
vs. Mamluks, 5:517b
at Elbistan (1277), 11:158a
battle at ^c^Ayn Jālūt (1260), 8:73b, 473a-b
in Egypt, 6:591b
in Syria, 6:591b

vs. Volga Bulgars, 12:488b
vs. Xlat^{c}, 12:713b
vs. Yaroslavl, 12:720b
Zak^{c}arids and, 12:737a
see also Barbarians, invasions of; Genghis Khan; Golden Horde
Monica, St.
an unrhymed office to, 10:368b
a rhymed office to, 10:370b
Moninne, St. *See Vie de Ste. Modwenne*
Monism, Iblīs and, 6:391a
Monk of Salzburg, minnesingers and, 8:414a
Monk-Solitary of Farne. *See* Whiterig, John
Mönke
administrative reforms, 8:471b
death of, 8:473a
election as Great Khan, 8:471b
military conquests, Asia and Iran, 8:472a
Mönke-timur, Qaidu-Qubylai conflict, 8:475b
Monks. *See* Clergy; Monasteries; Monasticism
Monks, white. *See* Cistercian order
Monmouth, abbey of, Geoffrey of Monmouth as prior of, 5:387b
Monochord, 8:606b, 608b, 626a
alphabetic notation and, 8:614a, 614b
Boethius and, 8:637a
in *Dialogus,* 8:640b
marine trumpet and, 8:607a
Notker Teutonicus and, 8:640a
Prosdocimus and, 8:647b
Pythagoreans and, 8:636b
Ugolino of Orvieto and, 8:647b
Monody, in Byzantine rhetoric, 10:350a
Monoenergism, 11:45a
acceptance of, 6:191a
opposed by St. Maximus the Confessor, 8:233a
Monograms, decorated, 6:462b
Monologion. See Anselm of Canterbury, St.
"Monomakh, cap of," 12:486a
Monophonic singing. *See* Plainsong
Monophony, **8:476b**
in Armenian chant, 8:551b
Byzantine, 8:553b, 554b
Slavic music and, 8:572b
Galician, *see also Cantiga*
Italian trecento, 12:179b
lai and, 7:317a
secular music by Machaut, 8:6a
in Western song, 8:594a
see also Melody
Monophysitism, 2:460a, 462a-b, 464b, 486a, **8:476b–479b,** 11:563b–564a
adoption by non-Greek-speaking Christians, 6:191a
after Arab conquest, 9:561b
al-Akhṭal and, 1:115a
Anania Sanahnec^{c}i on, 1:511a
Antiochene rite and, 1:327a-b, 328a
in Arabia, 6:575b
Armenian church and, 1:499a, 500a
in Axum, 2:17b
Christology and, 3:320a–321a
condemnation of, 2:485b, 3:629a-b
by Council of Chalcedon, 6:190b–191a, 8:477a-b, 9:561a, 10:463b
Coptic church condemned for, 3:594a
development after 8th century, 8:478b
Dioscoros of Alexandria and, 9:106a
doctrinal assumptions, 8:477a
Dominican missions and, 4:252b
early church and, 3:339b–340a
Egyptian, 8:477b, 10:453b
schismatic splinter groups, 8:478a
Theodosians, 8:478a
see also Coptic church; Copts
Eutychianism and, 4:524b, 8:477a, 478a
Ghassanids' influence on, 5:515a-b
Girk T^{c}łt^{c}oc^{c}, 5:540a
hypostatic union, doctrine of, 8:477a
icons and, 6:398a, 401b
Jacobite church and, 8:478a, 478b, 11:568a
of John of Ephesus, 7:132b–133a
of John of Nikiu, 7:135b–136a
Justinian I and, 3:10b, 7:202a
Leo I (the Great) and, 7:541b–542a
Maronite position on, 8:149b
Maximus the Confessor and, 8:233a, 233b, 234a
Melchites and, 8:268a
in Melitene, 8:269b
missionary work, 8:479a
Ethiopia, 8:479a
in Najrān, 9:55a
Nestorianism and, 9:105a, 105b
Nicene-Constantinopolitan Creed and, 3:676b
in Nubia, 3:314b, 9:197b, 198b
patriarchal succession, 8:477b
Henotikon viewpoint, 8:477b
pentarchy system and, 9:496a
promotion by imperial initiative, 6:191a
role in East-West schisms, 11:44b–45a
Rome, 10:463b, 464a
in Sasanian Empire, 1:503a
Second Council of Constantinople and, 3:630a-b
sects of
Akephaloi, 6:191a
by leader, 6:190b–191a
Julianists, 6:191a, 8:478a
tritheists, 6:191a
see also Aphthartodocetism
in Syria, 8:477b, 11:559b
after Arab conquest, 8:478b
persecution of, 8:478a
West Syrian rite and, 11:568a
Taghlib tribe, support of Umayyads, 1:115a
Theodora I and, 12:12a, 12b
theological basis for, 8:477a
Cyril's doctrine, 8:477a
vs. Melchitism, in Egypt, 10:455a
Waχtang I Gurgaslani and, 5:413a
Yaḥyā ibn ^{c}Adī, 9:699a
see also Copts; Michael the Syrian; Schisms, Eastern-Western church; Vigilius, pope
Monothelitism, **8:479b–480b**
acceptance of, 6:191a
in Armenia, 1:499b–500a
Byzantine Empire and, 3:344a
condemnation of, 11:45a
Constans II and, 3:544b, 630b
Constantine IV and, 3:546a, 630b
defeat of, 9:561a
divine will, 8:149b
doctrinal assumptions, 8:479b–480a
in the *Ekthesis,* 8:478a-b, 480a
in Lebanon, 7:532b
Maronite position on, 8:149b
Maximus the Confessor and, 8:233a, 233b, 234a
opposition to, 8:480a
revival in 8th century, 8:480b
Sergios I and, 11:209a
supported by Nersēs III Išχanec^{c}i, 9:102b
in Syria, 11:564a
Monreale Cathedral, 10:486b–487a, 503b–504a
donor portrait at, 4:261b
mosaics, 2:445b, 10:505a
Monreale (monastery: Sicily), 11:274b
Monselice (castle), Wolfger von Erla and, 12:672b, 673a
Monsoon, navigation and, 11:245b
Monstrance, 1:223b–224a
Monstrelet, Enguerrand de, 3:328a, 333b
Mont-Saint-Michel
abbey church, 10:111a, 482a, 482b
walls of, 10:489b
pilgrimage to, 10:412a
Montagnac, fairs, 4:586a
Montague. *See* Neville, John, earl of Montague
Montaillou, religious life of, 3:360a
Montalvo, Garci Rodríguez de, reworking of *Amadís de Gaula,* 11:416a-b, 423b
Montaperti, Battle of (1260), 3:117b, 4:95a, 5:95a, 11:279b
Guittone on, 6:644b
Montauban
bastide of, 2:128a-b
bridge, 10:418a
construction of, 10:419a, 419b
founding of, 12:324a
Monte Andrea, 6:644b–645a
Monte Cassino, **8:480b–481b**
abbacy, succession to, 8:481a
abbey church, 10:486a
decorations, 10:505a
plan of, 10:309a
"Ambrosian" choral song and, 2:181a
Bruno of Segni at, 2:392a
destruction of
by Arabs, 8:481a
by Lombards, 8:480b
development of medicine and, 8:247b–248a
first known treatises on letter writing and, 10:358a
founded, 2:169a
incense and, 6:432a
intellectual activities, 8:481a-b
Latin literature and, 7:363b
lauds at, 4:229a
manuscript production, 10:508a
matins at, 4:228a-b

Monte Cassino (*cont.*)
monumental painting at, 10:112b–113a
Naples and, 9:58b
Normans and, 11:266a, 266b
notable occupants, 8:481a
oratories of St. Benedict, 8:480b
Paul the Deacon and, 9:467a, 467b
restoration and construction, 8:480b–481a
Abbot Gisulf, 8:481a
sacked (577), 2:172a
shrine of St. Benedict, pointed arches and vaults, 11:656a
slaves at, 11:336a
see also Bertharius; Leo of Ostia
Monte Cassino Passion, 4:281b
Monte Cassino Penitential, 9:490a
Monte Corona, Congregation of, 3:56a
Montebourg Psalter, 2:218b
Montefeltro, Federigo da, 7:147b
Monteleone, Roger I and, 10:440a
Montepulciano
Duomo, polyptych, 11:572b
Florence and, 11:281b
Montereau, Pierre of. *See* Pierre de Montreuil
Montesino, Ambrosio, religious works by, 11:422b
Montfaucon, Bernard de, *Monuments de la monarchie française,* 1:427b
Montfort (castle), excavated, 1:524b
Montgomery, Treaty of (1267), 7:637a-b
Welsh recognition, 12:521a
Month
definition of, 3:18a
division of, Roman, 3:20b–21a
Germanic names for, 3:20b
Islamic names for, 3:27a
lunar, 3:22a
numbering of days, 3:21a
Monti, 10:517b
see also Disabitato
Montiérender (basilica: Champagne), 10:478a
Montjuic, Jaume de, Bible translation of, 3:166b
Montmajour, church at, 10:481b
Montpellier, **8:481b–483a**
Aragonese-Catalonian domination of, 10:256a
Black Death in, 2:261a
consuls of the sea, 8:482b
Coutûme of Montpellier, 8:482a
decline of, 7:341a, 8:482b–483a
development, 14th century, 8:482b
feudatories, 8:482a
foreign population, 8:482b
government
consular, 8:482a
Guillem family, 8:482a
growth of, 7:339b, 341a, 341b
inns in, 6:469b, 470a, 471a, 471b, 472a, 472b, 473a, 473b
money of Melgueil, 8:482b
origins, 8:481b–482a
schools and universities, 8:482b
trade and commerce, 8:482a, 482a-b
see also French law, in south
Montpellier MS H.159, 8:614b, 615b–616a
Montpellier MS H.196, **8:483a-b**
experimental idioms, 8:483b
motet compositions represented, 8:483a-b
motet texts, 8:506b
Montpellier, University of, 7:340b–341a, 341b, 12:285a
medical school, 8:249b–250a, 252a-b
criticism of, 8:257a-b
dissection sanctioned in 1340, 8:259b
influenced by Salerno, 8:256b–257a
origins of, 8:258a
relation between surgery and medicine, 8:251a
textbook regulations, 11:692a
Placentinus at, 9:671a–672b
Montréal, castellan of, 3:124b
Montségur, Cathars at, 6:486a, 487a
Monumental tombs. *See* Tombs
Monumental wall painting. *See* Panel painting
Monuments de la monarchie française. *See* Montfaucon, Bernard de
Monza, "iron crown" of, 12:492b
Monza, Gradual of, 3:80b
Moor, Arraby. *See* Portugal; Rabbinate
Moors
Ferdinand IV and, 11:378b
as *foederati,* 10:466b
Henry IV and, 11:378b
lusterware of, 10:65b
Rome, 10:464a-b
as slaves, 11:337b–338a
taxes paid by, 11:377b
Moosburg Ordinarium, 1:582b
Mora, Marcos García de, *Memorial contra los conversos,* 11:421b
Moral conduct. *See* Ethics
Morale, Speculum maius and, 12:454a
Morale scolarium. *See* John of Garland (*ca.* 1195–*ca.* 1272)
Moralia. *See* Guibert of Nogent
Moralia in Job. *See* Gregory I (the Great), pope
Moralis philosophia. *See* Bacon, Roger
Moralité, defined, 4:279a
Moralités des philosophes. *See* Alard de Cambrai
Morality plays, 4:279a-b, **8:484a-b**
antecedents, 8:484a
English, *Castle of Perseverance,* 3:142b–143a
French, 8:484a
characteristics of, 4:265a-b
German, 8:484a-b
instructional purposes, 8:484a
in Lübeck, 4:269a
regional variations, 8:484a-b
see also Elckerlijc; Everyman
typical plot, 8:484a
see also Drama; Medwall, Henry, *Nature*
Moralium dogma. *See* William of Conches
Moralium dogma philosophorum, translations, German, 12:619a-b
Morall Fabillis of Esope the Phrygian, The. *See* Henryson, Robert, *Fables*
Morals of the Catholic Church. *See* Augustine of Hippo, St.
Morals on Job. *See* Gregory I the Great, pope, *Moralia in Job*
Morals of the Manichees. *See* Augustine of Hippo, St.
Morant und Galie. *See* Karlmeinet
Morat, Battle of (1476), 11:545a
Peter of Savoy and, 11:540a
Morava school, 11:187b–188b
Moravia, **8:484b–485a**, 9:687a
Bohemian Brethren in, 2:305b
changes in rulership, 8:485a
Christianization of, 2:299a, 463b–464a, 489a-b
ethnic background, 8:484b–485a
government, 8:485a
jewelry of, 5:377b
margravate of, 2:300b
origin of the name, 2:297b
Poland and, 9:717a–718b, 728a
Slavic language in, 11:341a-b
Slavs in, 11:348b
under Sigismund, 11:287b
under Sventopolk, 8:484b
see also Great (or Old) Moravia
Moravian Brethren. *See* Bohemian Brethren
Moravian church, history, 4:73b–74a
Moravian language, 11:341a-b
Moravské Pole, Battle of (1278), 2:7b, 300a, 6:343a, 10:88b
Moray, David I and, 4:110b
Morčaisdze, Ioane, 6:562b
Mordant, in dyeing, 4:327a
Mordaxt, 7:324 (*illus.*), 325a
Mordent, 8:631a
Mordred, 8:62b, 63a, 64a, 64b, 224a
More, Sir Thomas
on Bedlam, 2:157b
on literacy in England, 7:600b
Morton and, 3:83b
portrayal of Richard III, 10:385a
Utopia, 5:364a
Morea, **8:485b**
crusaders in, 7:376b
disputed ownership of, 7:381b
Kantakouzenoi and, 7:208b
Nikephoros I and, 9:132b
nobility of, 9:151a
survival of Byzantine arts in, 2:458a
see also Mistra
Morea, Chronicle of, **8:485b–486a**
French and Greek versions, priority of, 8:485b
lost prototype, 8:485b
Old French version, 2:509a-b
point of view, 2:509a
purpose of, 8:486a
style and language, 2:522b
Morea, despotate of, **8:486a–487a**
conquest of Achaea, 8:486b
development, 15th century, 8:486b
Hexamilion, 8:486a-b
Ottoman invasion, 8:486b
Palaiologan despots, 8:486a
Moreh Nevukhim. *See* Maimonides, Moses

Morel, Eustache. *See* Deschamps, Eustache
Morel, Pierre, **8:487a-b**
choir vault, Celestine church at Avignon, 8:487 (*illus.*)
Morenu ha-rav. See Rabbinate; Scholarship, Jewish
Moresca, 8:595b
Moretum, 7:360b, 9:440b
Morgante. See Pulci, Luigi
Morgengabe, 6:457a
Morgenstern, 7:325a
Morholt. *See* Tristan, Legend of
Moriaen, 4:318b–319a
Moriale, Fra, Siena and, 11:280a
Morienval, 1:429b
Morimond, abbot of, Order of Calatrava and, 3:16b
Mörin, Die. See Hermann von Sachsenheim
Morion, 1:527b (*illus.*), 531a-b, 532a
Moriscos, 11:380b
Moriz von Craûn, 5:455a, **8:487b–488b**
dating of, 8:131a
German influences, 8:488a
hero's identity, 8:488a
place and date of composition, 8:487b–488a
sources for, 8:488a
Morkinskinna, 4:618a, 9:176a, 177a-b
þættir in, 12:3b, 4a
version of *Hákonar saga* in, 6:76a-b
Morley, Thomas, *Plaine and Easie Introduction to Practicall Musicke,* 8:646b
Morocco
conquest of Songhai empire, 12:55b
Idrisids in, 6:413a, 414a
see also Maghrib, al-; Meknes
Moros, Lope de, *Razón de amor,* 11:413b
Morosini, Thomas, elected patriarch of Constantinople, 7:348a
Morosini (Venetian noble family), 12:390a
Morozov, B. I., 11:198a-b
Mórrígan, 9:48b
Morris dancing, 5:36a
Morris game, 5:351a
Mors, 12:671a
Mort d'ancestor, assize of, 3:414a, 6:481b, 482b
Mort Artu, 1:571a, 10:151b
as a source for Thomas Malory's *Morte Darthur,* 8:64a
see also Prose Lancelot
Mort de Garin le Loherenc, 9:634a
Mortality. *See* Death and burial; Demography; Plagues
Morte Arthure (Middle English alliterative poem), 1:573b, 574a, 8:320b, 332a
as a source for Malory's *Morte Darthur,* 8:61b, 63a, 64a
Morte Darthur, Le. See Malory, Sir Thomas
"Morte, perchè m'ài fatta sì gran guerra." *See* Pugliese, Giacomino
Morte di Tristano, 6:670a
Mortifications, in Celtic church, 3:231a-b
Mortimer, John. *See* Cade, Jack
Mortimer, Roger, earl of March
coup against Edward II, 4:483a-b
execution by Edward III, 4:398a
Mortimers, condemned, 6:427a
Mortmain, **8:488b–489b**
England, 8:489a
France, 8:489a
inalienability of, 8:489a
interpretation of, 8:488b
noble derogation and, 9:149b
redistribution of land, 8:489b
restrictions on, 8:489a
seizures and taxation, 8:489a-b
Mortmain, Statute of (1279), 8:489a, 11:468a-b
Morton, John, archbishop of Canterbury, 3:83b
patronage of Henry Medwall, 8:262b
Mosaics
adaptation of manuscript illuminations to, 4:357a
in Ala-ed-Din mosque, 7:223b
apse mosaic, S. Apollinare in Classe, 8:491 (*illus.*)
Ark of the Covenant depicted in, 1:469a
at Khirbat al-Mafjar, 6:595b
at Ravenna, 10:113b, 263a–264b (*illus.*)
church processions, 6:431b
at Thessaloniki, 10:113b
Byzantine
in Hagios Demetrios, 4:529b
Italy, 10:505a
miniature icons, 2:449a, 457b
in Sicily, 2:445b
use of line, 2:444a
see also Daphni, church of; Hagia Sophia (church: Constantinople); Hosios Lukas (monastery: Thessaly)
Byzantine Jewish, 7:65b
in church decorations, 8:489b–490a
crusader, 4:24a (*illus.*)
in Dome of the Rock, 4:237a
earliest known complete, 7:223b
early Christian
examples of, 4:358a
purpose of, 4:359a-b
secular, 4:362a-b
evangelist symbols in, 4:526a
floor, 8:492b–494a
Church of the Pantokrator, 8:492b (*illus.*)
Georgian, 5:411a
in Great Mosque at Córdoba, 6:601b
Hagia Sophia (Kiev), 10:583 (*illus*)
in Kariye Djami (Constantinople), 7:216a (*illus.*), 9:66 (*illus.*)
influence of, 2:450a-b
making of, **8:489b–494b**
differences between workshops, 8:492b
group efforts, 8:492a
heads, 8:492a
main repositories, 8:490a
procedure for, 8:491a–492b
setting bed, 8:489b, 491b
technical vocabulary, 8:492b
underpainting, 8:491b
use of space, 8:490a
see also Tessera
in mausoleum of Uljaytu, 7:223b
mosaicists
division of work, 8:492a
salaries, 8:492a
training of, 8:492b
in mosque of al-Walid, 5:545b–546a
Nea Moni, use of color, 2:443a-b
in Old St. Peter's, Rome, 9:237a
opus sectile, 8:492b
revival of, 11th century, 8:493a
revival of, Carolingian, 8:493b–494a
opus tesselatum, 8:492b–493a
painting and, conventions shared, 8:490a-b
in pre-Romanesque art
Carolingian, 10:96b–97a
Italian, 10:112a–113a
preliminary drawings for, 4:291a
prependulia and, 10:89a-b
Renaissance, 8:490a
S. Marco, Venice, 10:646 (*illus.*)
S. Maria Maggiore (Rome), 12:89 (*illus.*), 199 (*illus.*)
subject matter, patron's role in, 8:490a
tile, in Islamic architecture, 6:602b
of Torriti, 5:606a
Western patrons, 8:494a
in Zāhiriyya madrasa, 6:607b
Mosan art, 8:108b, 284b, **8:494b–496b**
baptismal font, Notre-Dame-aux-Fonts, 8:495a (*illus.*)
boundaries of, 8:494b
classicizing style, 8:495a
cross-media development, 8:495b–496a
goldsmithery, 8:496a
iconography, 8:496a
manuscript illumination, 8:495b (*illus.*)
metalworking in, 2:384a
small-figured ivories, 8:495a
stylistic source, 8:495a
treatment of space, 8:495a-b
see also Retable
Mosburg Gradual, hymns and, 6:380a
Moschi, Lorenzo, 6:653b
Moschos, John
Leimonarion (*Spiritual Meadow*), 12:542b
as a model for *paterika,* 9:457a
Moscow
fur trade in, 5:329b, 330b, 333b
Jews in, 7:100b
mint at, 8:426b
music of, 8:573a-b
relations with Khanate of Crimea, 3:679a-b
Vladimir (city) and, 12:487a
see also Muscovy, Rise of
Moscow, Council of (1503), Nil Sorsky and, 9:137a
Moscow Kremlin
Annunciation (Blagoveshchensky) Cathedral, 8:496b–497a, 10:541a
Ivan III frescoes, 10:590a
Mother of God icon, 10:587a-b
Arkhangelsky Cathedral, 8:497a

Moscow Kremlin (*cont.*)
  art and architecture, **8:496b–498a**, 8:497 (*illus.*)
    style, 8:496b
    towers, 8:496b
    see also Fioravanti, Aristotele
  Bell Tower, 8:497b
  frescoes, 10:583b
  Granovitaya Palace, 8:497a-b
  Mother of God of Vladimir in, 6:411a
  neo-Vladimirian style, 10:582a
  Rizpolozhenie Church, 8:496b
  Uspensky (Dormition) Cathedral, 8:496b
    original church, 9:512a
Mose Xoneli, author of *Amiran darejaniani,* 5:418a-b
Moselle River, in literature, 7:361a
Moselle Valley, population, 4:141a
Moser, Lucas, **8:498a**
  Magdalen Altarpiece, 5:610b, 8:498a
Moses Arragel of Guadalajara, Bible of Alba and, 11:432b
Moses ben Abraham Darʿi, 7:210b
Moses ben Ḥanokh, 7:96a, 162a
Moses ben Jacob of Coucy, 7:92b
Moses ben Maimon. *See* Maimonides, Moses
Moses ben Nahman. *See* Naḥmanides, Moses
Moses ben Samuel of Damascus, 7:210b
Moses ben Samuel ha-Kohen Gikatilla, as exegete, 4:539b
Moses ben Shem Tov de León, 1:346a, 3:2a-b, 7:92b, **8:498a-b**
  apocalyptic symbolism of, 1:346a
  Book of Zohar, 8:498a
Moses of Bergamo (12th century), 7:365b
Moses and the Brazen Serpent, ivory cross, 7:23a (*illus.*), 10:0 (frontispiece)
Moses of Coucy, *Sefer Mitzvot ha-Gadol,* 10:75a
Moses al-Da'ri, 7:99a
Moses ha-Cohen of Tordesillas, *Support of the Faith,* 10:5b
Moses ha-Darshan, 4:541a
Moses ha-Sefaradi of Huesca. *See* Petrus Alfonsi
Moses ibn Ezra, 7:96b
  Book of Discussion and Conversation, 10:348a
  Judah Halevi and, 7:157b
  panegyrics, 6:127a
Moses ibn Tibbon, 4:541a
  translations by, 12:134a
Moses Isserles of Poland
  on law, 7:492b
  Shulḥan Arukh and, 11:585a
Moses of Kiev, 7:100b
Moses of Nisibis, 11:565a
Moses (OT prophet), in Bury Bible, 6:324b (*illus.*)
Moses da Rieti, 7:110a
Moses of Salerno
  Arguments, 10:4a
  Hebrew-Italian glossary, 12:137a
Moshe bar Kēphā, 11:565b
Moshe ben Asher codex, 7:66a
Mosques, **8:498b–500a**
  Almoravid, 1:196a–197b (*illus.*)
  architectural features, 8:499a–500a
    minaret, 8:396a–397a
    minbar, 8:397 (*illus.*)
    organization of space, 8:499b
    variation in style, 8:499b–500a
  architectural features of, 7:616b
  barrel-vaulted, 6:599a
  in Cairo, 3:14a
  columnar, 6:599a
  early, 6:593a–594a
  eyvān and, 4:569b
  functions of, 8:498b–499a
  furniture, ivory decorations of, 7:29a
  al-Hākim, 5:21b. 5.22a (*illus.*)
  iconology of, 6:407a
  Iranian, 6:602b–603a
  in Islamic liturgy, 7:616b–618b
  masjid al-jāmiʿ, 8:498b, 499a
  miḥrāb, 8:499b
  orientation of, 8:499b
  Ottoman, 6:612b–613a
  Prophet's in Medina, 8:262a, 498b, 499 (*illus.*), 524a
    miḥrāb at, 8:376a
  in Qayrawān, 1:69 (*illus.*)
  qibla orientation of, 10:235a
  Ṣāliḥ Ṭalaʾiʿ, 5:21b
  in Seljuk Anatolia, 11:148b
  Umayyad, Zāhiriyya madrasa and, 6:607b
  see also Almohads, art; Madrasa; Urbanism, Islamic
Mosquitos. *See* Insects
Mosul, 1:634a–635a, **8:500a–501a**
  Arab rule, 8:500b
  architecture of, 6:607a
  artists from, 6:607b
  Ayyubid art and, 2:22a
  Kurds in, 7:310a
  Mongol control, 8:501a
  origins, 8:500a-b
  seized by Qılıj Arslan I, 11:154a
  see also Badr al-Dīn Luʾluʾ of Mosul, ruler
Motaqāreb, in *Shāhnāma,* 11:221a
Motet, **8:501a–505a**, 8:590b, 594a
  in *ars antiqua,* 1:546b, 10:381b
  calculation of phrase lengths, 8:502a
  cantus firmus, 8:502a, 503b
    relation of poetry to, 8:502b
    in Winchester polyphony, 12:697a
  conductus, 8:505a-b
  decline in importance, 8:504a-b
  double, 8:501b–502a, 506a
  English, 8:504b
  essential characteristics, 8:502b–503a
  French, 8:502b
    collections of, 8:505b, 506a
  history, 8:501a-b, 505b
  hymns and, 6:380a
  influenced by chants from rhymed offices, 10:375b
  isorhythmic, 6:619a, 619b, 8:503a, 503b
    Egidius of Murino and, 8:646b
  Italian influence, 8:504b
  Latin, 8:502b, 506a
    collections of, 8:506b
  lower voices, 8:504a
  in Machaut's production, 8:6a-b
  Magister Lambertus and, 8:643b–644a
  major composers, 8:502b
  manuscripts, **8:505a–507a**
    appended to other works, 8:506b
    lost volumes, 8:505a
    Montpellier Codex, 5:209a
    ordering of, 8:505a-b, 506b
    self-contained, 8:506a-b
    Trent codices, 12:182b–184b
    in trouvère *chansonniers,* 8:506a
    variation in form, 8:505a
    see also Bamberg manuscript; Notre Dame school (music), MS Pluteus 29.1
  in measured music, 7:119a-b
  melodic imitation, 8:504a-b
  mensuration, 8:504a, 506a
  modal notation and, 8:621 (*illus.*), 622a
  monotextual, 8:504b
  motet enté, 10:241a
  motetus, 8:502b
  Notre Dame school and, 9:191b, 192a
  organ accompaniment, 9:273b–274a
  panisorhythmic, 6:619b, 8:503b
  Perotinus and, 9:507a-b
  pes, in Worcester polyphony, 12:696a, 696b, 697a
  Philippe de Vitry and, 12:482a-b
  pièces d'occasion, 8:504b
  poetic text, role of, 8:501a-b, 502a
  popularity of, 1:550b–551a
  precursors of, 10:619a
  purpose of, 8:503b
  reverse troping, 8:503a
  sectional diminution, 8:504a
  secular, 8:502b, 506a
  short value, 8:502b
  tenor part, 8:501b, 502a, 503a, 503b
  trecento music, 12:179b, 180b
  triplum, Petronian innovation, 9:545b
  upper voices, 8:503b
  verse structure, irregularity of, 8:501b
  "Viderunt omnes" and, 12:411a
  voice
    notation of, 8:502b
    rhythmic differentiation, 8:501b–502a
    two-voice clausulae, 8:501b, 505a, 506a
  see also Melisma
"Mother of the Book," 6:577b
Mother of God. *See* *Theotokos*; Virgin Mary
Mother of God of Vladimir. See Eleousa; *Vladimir Virgin*
Mothers. *See* Women
Mǫðruvallabók
  preservation of *Droplaugarsona saga* in, 4:294a
  text of *Hallfreðar saga* in, 6:81a
  Víga-Glúms saga and, 12:415b
Motion, Ockham on, 9:211b
Motte St. Didier. *See* St. Antoine (monastery: Dauphiné)
Motte-and-bailey castles. *See* Castles and fortifications

Möttuls saga, **8:507a–508a**, 10:391a, 393a, 394b
King Arthur in, 8:507b
magic mantle motif, 8:507a
preservation, 8:507b
rimur version, 8:507b
source for, 8:507a
two redactions, 8:507b
Mouchette, **8:508a**
Vendôme, La Trinité church, 8:508b (*illus.*)
Moulay Idris, 6:414a
Moulins Cathedral, Coronation of the Virgin altarpiece, 8:509a (*illus.*)
Mount Izla (monastery: Syria), 11:564b
Mount of Olives, Jewish pilgrimage and, 9:652b–653a
Mounted combat. *See* Cavalry; Warfare
Mourning. *See* Death and burial
Mourning figures. *See* Pleurant
Mourtzouphlos, 4:47a–48a
"Mout me semont Amours que m'envoise." *See* Conon de Béthune
Mouth organ, 8:612b
Mouvance, in chansons de geste, 3:260b
Movsēs of Cʿurtaw, bishop
Vrtʿanēs Kʿertʿoł and, 1:509a
vs. Kiwrion of Georgia, 1:499b
Movsēs Dasχurancʿi, 1:511a, **8:508b–509b**
on Bahrām VI Čōbēn, 2:50b
History of the Caucasian Albanians, 6:240a-b
compilation of, 8:509b
synopsis of, 8:509a-b
Zwartʿnocʿ and, 12:749a
Movsēs the Grammarian, 1:520a, 520b
Movsēs Kałankatuacʿi. *See* Movsēs Dasχurancʿi
Movsēs, *katʿołikos,* vs. Yovhannēs of Bagaran, 1:499a
Movsēs of Siwnikʿ, bishop, 1:510a
Movsēs Xorenacʿi, 1:510b, 5:540a, **8:509b–511a**
Armenian saints and, 1:519b
Ašχarhacʿoycʿ (*Armenian Geography*), 1:472a, 8:510b
on the Mamikonean family, 8:78b
Patmutʿiwn Hayocʿ (*History of the Armenians*), 1:451a, 510a, 5:579a, 665a, 8:509b–510b
on Armenian magic, 8:15b–16a, 17a
dating of, 6:239b
distortions in, 8:510b
fiction of archives, 8:510a
organization, 6:239b
as a source for Tʿovma Arcruni's *History,* 12:92a-b
sources for, 8:510a
sources and methodology, 6:239b
Moxenē. *See* Mokkʿ
Moyenmoutier, monastery of, 6:329b
Moytura, battles of, 9:47a
Mozarabic art, **8:511a–514a**
architecture, 8:511a–513a
horseshoe arch, 8:511b, 512a-b
Islamic influence, 8:512a
ribbed vaults, 8:512a
roll-corbels, 8:512b
Visigothic influence, 8:511b
manuscript illumination, 8:513a-b, 10:114a-b
political aspects, 8:513b
portrait of St. Luke, 8:513a
schematized style, 8:513a
spatial relationships, 8:513b
use of color, 8:513a, 513b
origins, 8:511a
painting, effect of Roman reform on, 8:513b–514a
prayer book of Ferdinand I and wife Sancha, 10:114b
traditional elements, 10th century, 8:512b–513a
Mozarabic chant, 8:623b
end of use of, 5:661b
Mozarabic Hymnary, 7:361a
Mozarabic language, 6:442b, 7:239a-b
Mozarabic literature, **8:514a–516a**
concept of courtly love influenced by, 3:672a
individualists vs. traditionalists, 8:514a
kharja, 7:239a-b
origins, 8:514a
poetry, 3:672a
romance, 6:233a
differences from Castilian, 6:233a
jarchas, 6:233a
songs
characteristics of, 8:515a
popular tradition, 8:515a-b
speaker, 8:515a
Spanish literature and, 11:408a-b
see also Kharja; Muwashshaḥ; Zajal
Mozarabic rite, **8:516a–517b**
Advent cycle, 8:517a
Byzantine influence, 8:183a
in Castile, 3:129a, 133a
cathedral office, vespers and matins, 8:517a
changes in 6th century, 8:516b
description, 8:516b–517b
development of, 1:630b, 8:516a
dramatization of Sibyl's monologue, 11:437b
Gallican rite and, 5:344a-b
history, 8:516a-b
after Arab invasion, 8:516b
Ildefonsus and, 6:419a
influence of on Narbonne rite, 9:62b
litanies of, 7:591b
Mass, 8:517a
missals and breviaries, 8:516b
monastic office, 8:517a
reflected in Isidore of Seville's *De ecclesiasticis officiis,* 7:626a-b
revival in 16th century, 8:516b
Roman rite and, 8:183a, 516b
sacraments, 8:517a
Spain and France, 8:182b
suppression of, 8:182b–183a, 11:406a
in Toledo, 8:516b
Tropes to the Proper of the Mass and, 12:211a
two traditions, origin of, 8:516b–517a
Visigothic lands, 8:182b
see also Baptism
Mozarabs
Christian Reconquest
attitude toward, 8:511b–512a
influence on architecture, 8:511a
of Córdoba, 3:599b–600a
in Toledo, 12:68a
Mren, summer palace of Čar, son of Umek, 12:99a
Mren (church: Armenia), **8:517b–518a**
figural sculpture, 8:517b, 518a (*illus.*)
Mroveli, Leontius, 5:417b
Mshattā, 12:264b
Msr, vs. Sasun, 4:113a
Msra Melikʿ, 4:112b, 113a
Mstislav of Kiev, grand prince, 7:248b–249a, 604a
as prince of Chernigov, Khanate of Tmutarakan and, 12:66a, 720a
Mtʿacʿmindeli, Georgi, *Life of Euthymios,* 5:417a
Mtkvari. *See* Kura River
Mtsχetʿa, church of Djvari at, 4:231b–232a
Muadwin. *See* Modoin
Muʿallaqa. See Imruʾ al-Qays
Muʿāmalāt, 6:581a
Muʿāwiya II ibn Yāzid, 3:38b–39a
Muʿāwiya, Umayyad caliph, **8:518a–519b**
administration of, 3:37a, 37b, 8:519a-b, 11:560a
Iraq, 6:511b
ʿAmr ibn al-ʿĀṣ and, 1:237a-b
Byzantine conflicts, 8:518b–519a
as caliph, 3:36b
centralizing policies of, 12:267b
consolidation of power, 12:265b–266a
consultative policies, 3:36b–37a
conversion to Islam, 8:518a
designation of successor, 12:267b–268a
diplomatic skills, 8:519b, 12:267a
domain land, 8:519b
establishment of dynastic succession, 3:37a
governorship of Syria, 4:77b, 81b, 8:518b
great schism of Islam and, 11:135b–136a
Mecca and, 8:240a
military organization, 8:518b
parchment and, 12:697b
promotion of naval activity, 9:74a
reestablishment of caliphate in Syria, 3:36b
rise to power, 12:265b–266a, 267b–268a
Shīʿa and, 11:226b
Syrian conquest, 8:518a-b
territorial conquest, 8:519b
Theodore Řštuni and, 1:478a
tribal politics of, 12:267a-b
vs. ʿAlī, 1:172b–173b, 3:36a, 4:188a, 8:519a
arbitration, 1:172b–173a
at Ṣiffīn, 1:172b–173a, 11:283b–284b
sunna and, 11:510b
vs. Ḥasan, 6:108b
vs. al-Ḥusayn, 6:370a
Yazīd and, 12:721a, 722a

Mu⊃ayyad al-Dīn al-ᶜUrḍī, on astronomy, 1:621a-b
Mu⊃ayyad Shaykh, al-, Mamluk sultan, 3:400a, 8:75b
Muayyid al-Dīn Muḥammad ibn al-ᶜAlqāmī, 8:650b
Mubārak, ᶜAbd Allāh ibn al-, 11:511b, 513b
Muḍāraba, 3:489b
Mudejars
  after Reconquest, 11:377a
  Alfonso I (the Battler) of Aragon and, 11:376a
  Alfonso VI of Castile and, 11:376a
  in Aragon, 11:377b
  art, **8:520a–521a**, 11:380a
    after Reconquest, 8:520b–521a
    brick and tile work, 8:520a
    carved stucco reliefs, 8:520b
    exteriors, 8:520a
    figurative painting, Christian and secular themes, 8:520a
    geometric and architectonic motifs, 8:520a
    influence on Jewish synagogue architecture, 7:68b
    origins, 8:520a
    Romanesque architecture, 10:487a
    Toledo, 8:520a
  Berber invasions and, 11:377a
  Castilian, 11:378a-b
  Christian-Muslim relations in Spain and, 11:375b–377b
  disappearance of, 11:380b
  etymology of, 11:376a-b
  Ferdinand of Spain and, 11:380b
  in Granada, 11:378a, 380a-b
  Hernando de Talavera and, 11:380b
  history of, 11:379a-b
  Isabel of Spain and, 11:380b
  liberties of, 11:377b–378b, 380b
  manuscript materials for, 11:377b–379b
  pacts with Christians, 11:376b–377a
  in Portugal, 11:376b, 380b
  revolt of, 3:134a, 135a
  in Valencia, 11:379a-b
Muerte del príncipe don Juan, La, modern discovery of, 11:430b
Muezzin, **8:521a–522a**
  in the Koran, 8:521b
  origins, 8:521a-b
  responsibilities, 7:616b, 8:521b
    call to prayer, 8:521a
  see also Adhān; Şerefe
Muff technique, 5:556a-b, 561b–562a
Muftis, 6:581b, 8:58b
  decline of scholarship, 5:31a
  in modern times, 5:32a
  mujtahids as, 5:31a
  muqallids as, 5:31a
  official appointments of, 5:31b
  origins of, 5:30a-b
  Ottoman, 5:31b
  qualifications for, 5:30b–31a
  shaykh al-islām as chief mufti, 5:31b–32a
  see also Fatwā
Mugaddam ibn Muᶜāfā of Cabra, 8:563b
Mughals
  manuscript illumination under, 8:117b–118a
  pipa and, 8:610b
Mughīth al-Rūmī, capture of Córdoba by, 3:598a
Mughnī, 8:611b
Mughtasilas, 8:83b
Muḥammad, **8:522a–526a**, 9:393 (*illus.*)
  accused of being a poet, 8:20b
  acknowledgment of allegiance, 1:4b
  ᶜAmr ibn al-ᶜĀṣ and, 1:236b–237a
  ascension of, 1:581a-b, 4:237a
    iconology and, 6:407a-b
  in Balādhurī's works, 2:54a-b
  boycott of Hāshim clan, 1:28b, 29b–30a
  Christianity, influenced by, 9:497a–498b
  claim to prophethood, 1:29b
  clan protection, 8:523a
    withdrawal of, 8:523b
  conflict with ᶜAlī, 1:171b–172a
  conquest of Mecca, 1:29a
  Constitution of Medina, 8:524a
  descendants of, 6:369b
  dress code devised by, 3:616b
  early life, 8:522a
  Embricho of Mainz on, 7:363b
  emigration
    to Ethiopia, 8:523a
    to Medina, 1:24b, 28b, 30a, 372b–373b, 8:523b
  family of, 1:174b
  Farewell Pilgrimage, 8:525b
  followers, 8:522b
    Meccan, economic pressure on, 8:523a
  Ḥadīth travel ideal, 12:147a
  imam and, 6:426a
  importance of achievements, 8:525b–526a
  Islamic law and, 11:218a
    property laws, 11:667a
  Islamic-Jewish polemics and, 10:7a-b
  Ismaili interpretations of, 6:588a
  Jews and Judaism
    break with over *qibla,* 8:525a
    influenced by, 7:101b–103a, 9:497a–498b
  Kaaba and, 7:203b–204a
  Khālid ibn al-Walīd and, 7:235a
  Koran and, 7:293b–294a
  life of, 6:576a–577b
    origins, 1:15a
  on magic, 8:20b, 21a
  Master of Hungary and, 9:454a
  in Medina, 8:262a
  military expeditions
    battle of Badr, 8:524b
    Gulf of ᶜAqaba, 8:525a
    hill of Uḥud, 8:524b
  as *nāṭiq,* 6:615b
  nomadic tribes, alliance with, 8:525a
  opposition to
    merchants, 8:522b
    Quraysh boycott, 8:523a
  Pledge of War, 8:523b
  political activity of, 6:567a, 567b
  prayer rituals and, 7:203b
    Friday prayer, 5:299a-b
  prohibition of luxuries, 11:508a
  prophecies of, on al-Mahdi, 8:388b
  Quraysh tribe of, 10:241a–242b
  Ramadan fasting and, 10:253b–254a
  revelations, 8:522b
  succession to, 3:32a-b
  tomb of, *Rauḍa* at Medina, 10:262b
  on trade, 12:107a
  trading journeys, 8:522a
  transmission of teaching, 6:45a
    Companions and Successors, 6:47a
    see also Isnād
  treaties
    with Christians, prohibition of usury in, 12:339b
    with Mecca, 8:524b–525a
    with Najrānites, 9:55b
  unification of Arabia and, 1:373a
  on wine, 2:208b
  see also Allah; Badr, Battle of (624); Liturgy, Islamic; Medina
Muḥammad (13th-century Khwārizmshāh)
  battle at Parwān, 8:467b
  battle at Syr Darya, 8:467a
  defeat and death, 8:467a-b
  great caravan, 8:466b
  siege of Gurganj, 8:467a
Muḥammad I Giray, khan of Crimea, expansionist policies, 3:679b
Muḥammad I, Ottoman sultan. *See* Mehmed I, Ottoman sultan
Muḥammad I, Umayyad ruler, 12:276b
Muḥammad II, Ottoman sultan. *See* Mehmed II, Ottoman sultan
Muḥammad V of Granada, Nasrid sultan, 5:653a, 11:384a
  Alhambra and, 6:612a
Muḥammad of Cabra. *See* Muqaddam ibn Muᶜāfā al-Qabri (of Cabra)
Muḥammad ibn ᶜAbd Allāh, 8:389a
  reign of, 11:575b
Muḥammad ibn ᶜAbdullāh al-Nafs al-Zakiyya, 1:174b
Muḥammad ibn al-Aḥmar, prince of Jaén, 5:652a-b
  founding of Nasrid dynasty, 11:383b–384a
Muḥammad ibn ᶜAlī. *See* Mahdī, al-
Muḥammad ibn ᶜAlī (Abbasid ancestor), marriage of, 9:55b
Muḥammad ibn al-Ḥanafīya, Shīᶜa and, 11:226b
Muḥammad ibn Hūd, Andalusian ruler, 1:195b, 11:383b
Mūhammad ibn Idrīs, Idrisid ruler of Fēs, 6:413a
Muḥammad ibn Idrīs al-Shāfiᶜī. *See* Shāfiᶜī, al-
Muḥammad ibn Ishaq al-Nadīm, 7:308b
Muḥammad ibn Ismāᶜīl, 11:137a, 137b
  disappearance of, 6:587a-b
  as 7th imam, 6:615a, 615b
  as symbol of active intellect, 6:588a
Muḥammad ibn Marwān, Armenia and, 1:479a
Muḥammad ibn Mūsā ibn Shākir. *See* Banū Mūsā
Muḥammad ibn Naṣr. *See* Muḥammad ibn al-Aḥmar, prince of Jaén
Muḥammad ibn Qarā Arslān, Artuqid governor of Āmid, 9:283b

Muḥammad ibn al-Qāsim al-Thaqatī, in India, 6:570b
Muḥammad ibn al-Sā⊃ib al-Kalbī, 7:307b
Muḥammad ibn Shaddād, 7:310b, 11:217a
Muḥammad ibn Sīrīn, 11:513a
Muḥammad ibn Sulayman, Idrisid ruler of Tlemcen, 6:413a
Muḥammad ibn Tāshfīn, campaign for Valencia, 3:384b, 385a-b, 387b
Muḥammad ibn Tekish, Khwārizmshāh, 6:504a-b, 7:244a
Muḥammad ibn Ṭughj
as governor of Egypt, 4:405b
honorary title of *al-Ikhshid,* 6:416b
Muḥammad ibn Tūmart. *See* Tūmart, Muḥammad
Muḥammad ibn ᶜUkāsha, 11:511b
Muḥammad ibn Umail al-Tamimī, *Epistola solis ad lunam crescentem,* 1:136b
Muḥammad al-Jūtī, Idrisid ruler of Fēs, 6:414a
Muḥammad, Khwārizmshāh, 5:382b–383a
Muḥammad al-Nāṣir, Almohad ruler, 1:195a
Muḥammad of Shāh-Arman, ruler, 11:220a
Muḥammad Tapar, Sökmen I and, 11:220a
Muḥammad Taraghay. *See* Ulugh-Beg
Muhi, Battle of (1241), 6:342a
Mühldorf, Battle of (1322), 5:488a
Muḥtasib, **8:526a–528b,** 12:310b
appointment of, 3:44b
assistants, 8:527b
basis of authority of, 3:46b
development of
after Abbasid revolution, 8:527a
ṣāḥib al-sūq, 8:526b
enforcement of sumptuary laws and, 11:509a
municipal functions, 8:528a
municipal functions of
financial, 8:527a
public conduct, 8:526a, 527b
quality control of manufactures, 12:86a
regulatory, 8:527b
spiritual sanctions, 8:527a
power of office, 8:527b–528a
social status and, 8:528b
purchasing of office, 8:527b
qualifications for, 8:527a-b
regional variation, 8:528a
theoretical foundation, 8:526b
see also *Ḥisha*
Muḥyī al-Dīn ibn ᶜArabī, Iblīs and, 6:391a
Muid, **8:528b**
Muᶜīn al-Dīn Sulaymān, 11:154b, 157b–158a
Muirchertach Mac Lochlainn, 6:539b
Muirchertach Ua Briain, king of Munster, 4:77b
in Irish historical compositions, 6:539b
Muirchú, life of St. Patrick, 9:463b, 463a
Muiredach cross, 3:222 (*illus.*)
Muisc, Syrian. *See* Syrian music
Muᶜizz al-Dawla, Buyid ruler of Baghdad, 3:50a, 6:424b, **8:528b–529b**
Baṣra, occupation of, 8:529b
Buyid rule over Iraq established by, 2:435b–436a
Hamdanids and Qarmatians, conflict with, 8:529a-b
invasion of Mesopotamia, 6:85b
Iraqi expeditions, 8:529a
siege of Baghdad, 8:529a
military reorganization, 8:529a
power over caliphate, 8:529a
Shiite festivals, 8:529a
Muᶜizz al-Dīn Muḥammad of Ghazna, 5:526b
Muᶜizz, al-, Fatimid caliph, 12:744a
Ismaili unity and, 6:617a
Qāḍī Nuᶜmān and, 6:616b
Muᶜizz li-Dīn Allāh, al-, 5:25a–26a
see also Fatimids
Muᶜizz, al- (son of Ḥammād), 12:744b
Mujaddid, al-Suyūṭī as, 11:520b
Mujāhid, al-, 5:384a
Mujāhid ibn Jabr, *ḥikma* and, 11:511a
Mujāwir, Ibn al-, 5:393b
Zanj and, 12:739b
Mujtahids, 6:587a
Muḳammis, al-. *See* Dāwūd ibn Marwān al-Muqammis
Mukhaṣṣaṣ. See Sīda, Ibn
Mukhtār, al-, revolt of, 6:511b, 7:307a
Mukhtāra, siege (882), 12:739a
Mukkarnas. See Muqarnas
Mukūs (noncanonical taxes), 2:25a
Mulayka. *See* Imru⊃ al-Qays
Muldenfaltenstil (*Muldenstil*), 5:612b, **8:529b**
Mule, 1:295b–296a
as pack animal, 1:296a
riding animal for women and church dignitaries, 1:296a
role in transportation, 12:148a
see also Animals, draft
Mule sans frein, Le, 1:570a
Mulḥam, **8:530a**
embroidered, 11:716b, 717a
Mulieres sanctae
in Italy, 9:14a
see also Mysticism, Christian, women mystics
Müller, Christoph Heinrich, Wolfram's *Parzival* and, 12:680a
Müller, Johann. *See* Regiomontanus
Mullets (Mugilidae), fishing of, 5:70b
Mulling, Book of, 7:614a-b
Mullion, **8:530a** (*illus.*)
see also Tracery; Trumeau
Mulomedicinae Chironis, 12:494b
Multiloquiorum in Seven Books, 7:409a
Multscher, Hans, **8:530a-b**
Man of Sorrows, Ulm Minster, 8:531a (*illus.*)
Wurzach Altar, 5:610b
Mum and the Sothsegger, 8:319b, 332a
Mumadona Dias, 10:37b–38a
Mumming at Hertford. See Lydgate, John
Munajjim, Ibn al-, 8:565b
Risāla fī al-mūsīqī, 8:122a
Muncaci, bishopric of, 10:511a
München Gladbach, cathedral of, 5:4224a
Münchner Oswald, Der. See Oswald, St., German epics about
Mundhir, al-, Ghassanid ruler, 5:515a-b
Mundhir, Lakhmid ruler (*ca.* 418–452), 7:320b
Mundhir III, Lakhmid ruler (*fl.* 503–554), 7:320b
Mundhir, al-, Umayyad ruler, 12:276b
Mundiucus (Hunnic leader), 6:354a
Mungo. *See* Kentigern, St.
Munich, founded, 2:134b
Munich *Ascension* (ivory), 4:352a, 352b (*illus.*)
Munich, Bayerische Staatsbibliothek Mus. 4775, motet texts, 8:505b
Municipalities, as heirs, 6:451a
Muninn, **6:323a-b**
Munio of Zamora, rule for Dominican laity, 4:254b
Munkar, 11:512a
doctrine of resurrection and, 10:341b
see also Angels, Islamic
Muño, *Vida de Santa Oria* and, 2:187b
Munqidh min al-ṭalāl, Al-. See Ghazālī, al-
Münster (Germany), Brethren of the Common Life at, 2:367a
Münster (Germany), bishopric of, representative assemblies and, 10:332b
Munster (Ireland), **8:530b–532b**
Anglo-Norman settlements, 8:532a
Cashel and, 3:121a
control of
Connacht dynasty, 8:532a
Dál Cais, 8:531b
Eógan Már, 8:530b–531a
earldoms of Desmond and Ormond, 8:532a
rulers of, 4:77a-b, 492b–493a
Viking settlements, 8:531b
Muntaner, Ramón, 11:435b, 12:349a
Crónica, 3:165b–166a
Roger de Flor and, 10:441b
Muntaṣir, al-, assassination of al-Mutawakkil, 8:654b
Muqaddam ibn Muᶜāfā al-Qabri (of Cabra), 11:408a
origins of *muwashshaḥ,* 8:514b, 11:447b
Muqaddam (Jewish local community head under Islam), 7:74b
Muqaddasī, al-, **8:532b–533b**
Aḥsan al-Taqāsīm fī Maᶜrifat al-Aqālīm, 8:532b–533a
cultural information, 8:533a
pattern of description, 8:532b–533a
rhymed prose, 8:532b
on Armenian economy, 12:97b
on Armenians, 1:485a, 513b
on Bab al-Mandab, 2:33a
biographical information, 8:532b
on Bukhara, 2:397b
founder of systematic Arabic geography, 5:392b
on the fur trade, 5:331b
hydraulic project described, 11:638a

Muqaddasī, al- (*cont.*)
information, sources of, 8:533a
Muslim lands, division into regions, 8:532b
on *naʿūras, 9:67a*
religious loyalties, 8:533a-b
Muqaddima. *See* Khaldūn, Ibn
Muqaddimat al-adab. *See* Zamakh-sharī, al-
Muqaffaʿ, ʿAbd Allāh ibn al-, 1:379a, **8:533b–534a**
alienation of caliphate, 8:534a
execution of, 8:534a
imitation of Koran, 8:534a
Kalīla wa-Dimna, 5:418a, 6:508b, 8:23b, 533b, 10:670b, 11:566b, 12:714b
manuscript of, 6:610a
Spanish literature and, 4:551b
Spanish translations, 3:31b
translation of, by Symeon Seth, 12:126b
political advice, 8:534a
prose works of, 1:379a
religious loyalties, 8:533b–534a
Risāla fi 'l-Ṣaḥāba, 8:534a
translation of *Letter of Tansar,* 7:553a
translations from Persian, 8:533b
Sasanid history, 8:533b
Muqalqalāt (Islamic plows), 12:83b
Muqammis, al-. *See* Dāwūd ibn Marwān al-Muqammis
Muqannaʿ, al- (leader in Khorāsān), crushed by al-Mahdī, 8:47b
Muqarnas, 1:191b, 197b, 6:607a, **8:534b**
in Alhambra, 1:170a, 171a
in Ayyubid mausoleums, 2:21b
Gunbad-i ʿAlī at Abarqūh, 8:534b, 535a (*illus.*)
masking of underlying structure, 8:534b
tomb of Imām Dūr at Samarra, 8:534b
Muqātil ibn Sulaymān
ḥikma and, 11:511a
interpretation of Koran, 9:39a
Muqla, Ibn
Ibn al-Bawwāb and, 2:135b
Islamic calligraphy and, 3:54b, 6:606b
Koran and, 7:294b
reforms of Arabic script, 9:65a
Muqla, Ibn, Abbasid vizier, 10:246a
Muqtadīr, al-, Abbasid caliph, **8:534b–536a**
Christian and Jewish *jahābidha* and, 12:340b
execution of al-Ḥallāj, 8:535b
factional conficts, Furāṭids and Jarrāḥids, 8:535b
financial concerns, 8:535b
Hamdanids and, attempted overthrow of, 6:84a, 84b–85a
Volga Bulgars and, 12:488a
war with Muʾnis, 8:535b
Muqtadīr, al-, of Saragossa, emir
Cid and, 3:384a
Sancho IV Garcés of Navarre and, 9:69b
Muqtafī, al-, Abbasid caliph, 6:514a
Muqtanā, ʿAlī Bahāʾ al-Dīn al-, Druze leader, 4:296a
Muqurra. *See* Makuria
Mur, Raymond de. *See* Raymond de Mur
Murad I, Ottoman sultan, 2:413a, **8:536a-b**
ʿAlāʾ al-Dīn Beg and, 7:214a
death of, 2:136b, 11:181a
imperial recognition, 9:307a
Janissary corps, 8:536a
military conquests
Adrianople and Thrace, 8:536a
Anatolia, 8:536a
Balkan states, 8:536a
Balkans and Asia Minor, 9:307a
battle at Kosovo Pole, 8:536a, 11:181a
royal titles
hüdavendigar, 9:308b
padishah, 9:308b
vs. Lazar Hrebejlanović, 7:529a
Murad II, Ottoman sultan, **8:536b–537a**
accession to sultanate, 8:536b
Balkan campaigns, 8:537a
Serbian annexation, 8:536b
Bāyazīd II and, 2:137a
conflict over Salonika, 8:536b
defeat of crusaders at Varna, 8:537a
Karamanid conflicts, 8:536b
Serbia and, 11:182b
Skanderbeg in court of, 11:324a
Stefan Lazareviç of Serbia and, 11:473a
Thessaloniki and, 12:26b
truce at Adrianople, 8:536b–537a
victory at Varna, 12:361a
vs. Hunyadi, 4:56a, 6:363b
vs. John VIII Palaiologos, 7:129a
Murad III, Ottoman sultan
observatory at Damascus and, 11:85a
succession struggles, 9:308a
Murād Su, 4:522a
Mural painting
early Christian, 4:348b
Nubian, 9:199a
see also Fresco painting; Mosaics
Murcia
Castile's conquest of, 11:378b
Don Juan Manuel and, 8:94a
hunting in, 6:358a
plan of Almoravid rural palace preserved in, 1:197b
revolts at, 11:377a
Murder. *See* Homicide
Muret, Battle of (1213), 6:442a, 465a, 7:339b, 12:91b
Provençal literature and, 10:177a-b
Muri (abbey: Eigen), 11:527a, 539b
early Resurrection play from, 4:267b
Murjiʾa, 6:582b, 11:139b–140a
Murjiʾism
Abū Ḥanīfa and, 1:26b
tenets of, 1:26b
Murjiʾites, al-Muʿtazila and, 8:655a
Murūj al-dhahab (*Book on the Meadows of Gold*). *See* Masʿūdī, al-
Mūsā al-Hādī, accession to caliphate, 6:107b
Musa, Ḥayyim ibn, *Shield and Spear,* 10:5b
Mūsā ibn Nuṣayr, 11:382a
consolidation of Muslim conquest in North Africa, 6:572a
in Spain, 6:572b
Mūsā al-Kāẓim, 6:615a
Twelver Shīʿa and, 11:227b
Musa (son of Bāyazīd I), Stefan Lazareviç of Serbia and, 11:473a
Mūsā (son of Seljuk ibn Doqaq), origins of the Seljuks and, 11:151a, 151b
Muṣʿab ibn al-Zubayr, defeat by al-Ḥajjāj, 6:72a
Muṣādara, under Umayyads, 3:39b
Muṣaffaḥāt, 8:613b
Musāfirids
in Dwin, 1:482b
Muḥammad ibn Shaddād and, 11:217a
Musailima, 7:235a
Muṣalla, **8:537a**
Muṣallayāt (Islamic prayer rug), 10:550a
Musaylima, vs. Khālid ibn al-Walīd, 6:568a, 568b
Muscovy
administration of, 4:305b
okol'nichie in, 4:306a-b
advantages of location, 8:541b–542a
duma, 8:549a–550a
duties of, 8:549b
patronage, 8:549b
power of members, 8:549b
struggle for positions, 8:549b–550a
dynastic wars, 7:20a, 8:542b–545a
allegiance of populace, 8:543b
effects of, 8:547a-b
Galich challenge, 8:543a–544a
financial administration, 8:547a
Golden Horde, defeat of, 8:540a-b
government
annexed territories, 8:548a-b
centralization of, 8:547b
crown lieutenants, 8:547b
grand prince
court of, 8:547a–548a
marital rights of brothers, 8:547b
sovereignty of, 8:544a–545a, 547a
succession conflicts, 8:539a-b, 542b–545a, 546a
growth of autocracy in, 4:306b
imperial aspirations, 8:546a
military serving families
annexation of property, 8:548b
court positions, 8:547a-b
grand prince and, 8:547a–548a, 550a
income, 8:547a
Lithuanians and, 8:548a-b
marital alliances, 8:549b
Novgorod and, 8:548b
transfer of allegiance, 8:541b
mints and money in, 8:426b–427a
Novgorod and, 9:196a–197a
peasantry, enserfment of, 8:550a
pomestie system, 8:548b–549a
religious property, 8:549a
princes
court positions, 8:547b–548a
expansion of northern territories, 8:537b–539a

Serpukhov branch, 8:543a
rise of, **8:537b–550b**, 11:347a–348a
to 13th century, 8:537b–539a
13th and 14th centuries, 8:539a–540a
Battle of Kulikovo, 10:594a
boundaries, 8:538 (map)
contributing factors, 8:540b–542b, 545a–546a
Dmitrii Ivanovich Donskoi, 4:232a-b
Metropolitan Peter and, 9:512a
metropolitanate, 10:594a, 594b
Yaroslavl and, 12:720b
see also Lithuania
royal control of Russian church, 3:11b
royal succession, absence of claimants, 8:542a
Tatar overlordship, defeat of, 8:540a-b, 542a-b, 546a
Tatar tribute, 8:542a
territorial expansion
Lithuania, 8:546b
military and administrative requirements, 8:546b–547a
Novgorod, 8:540b, 545a, 546b
Tver, 8:546b, 548a
Viatka, 8:545a
see also Boyars; Russian (Muscovite) law
Mušeļ of Kars, king, 1:483a, 7:221a
Mušeļ Mamikonean, 1:479b
Musha^csha^c revolt, 6:514b
Music
accompaniments, Middle Eastern, 8:567a-b
Armenian. *See* Armenian music
in art, 10:495b, 496b (*illus.*)
Byzantine. *See* Byzantine music
cadence in, 3:5b–6b
Cantus prius factus, 10:241a
cauda, 3:196a
Celtic. *See* Celtic music
centonization, 3:235b–236a
chanson, 3:254b
chants in rhymed offices, 10:374a–376a
chapel and college choirs, 10:655a
Christmas, 3:319a
chronology, 8:593b–594b
civic. *See* Town bands
clausula, 3:437a-b
clef, 3:438a
combinative chanson, 10:241a
conductus, 3:531b–533a
consonance and dissonance in, 3:542b
copula in, 3:595b–596b
counterpoint in, 3:656b–658a
diabolus in musica, 4:167b
discant, 3:657a
discantor, 4:216a-b
15th century, Trent codices and, 12:184a
harmony of the spheres and, 8:580a–581a
importance of *Magnus liber organi,* 8:43b
importance of melody, 12:540b
improvisation, 8:636a
Middle Eastern, 8:567a
ornamentation as, 8:631b
see also Cantus supra librum
influenced by medieval changes in the Latin language, 10:379a
instrumental
church fathers on, 8:587b
Middle Eastern, 8:567b
Western European, 8:594a, 603a
Isidore of Seville on, 8:638a
Islamic. *See* Islamic music
Islamic attitudes toward, **8:559b–561a**
see also Fārābī, al-
for *laudes,* 7:385a-b
as liberal art, 8:581b–582a
liturgical
ars subtilior, 1:558b
at Solesmes, 11:360b–362a
differentia, 4:185a
see also Aurelian of Réôme; Tones, reading and dialogue
manuscript materials of, 8:630a-b
measured
Amerus and, 8:644b
Italian notation of, 8:630a
modal notation and, 8:620b
Parisian theorists and, 8:643a-b
in medieval society, **8:595a–597b**
see also Ligature
melodic styles of, 8:270a
Middle Eastern. *See* Islamic music
monophonic, Eastern European plainsong, 9:686b–688a
motet enté, 10:241a
for mystery plays, 8:662b
non-Western, Islamic influence on, **8:565a–568a**
oral tradition in, **8:568b–570b**
"memorization" model, 8:568b, 569a
"oral composition" model, 8:568b
plays, 9:705b–706b
performance, 8:592a–593a, **8:634a–636a**
caccia, 12:177b, 179a-b
chansonnier, 3:255b–256b
freedom of, 8:635b–636a
of instrumental music, 8:635a-b
Middle Eastern, 8:567a–568a
of minstrels, 8:634b
plainsong notation and, 9:690b–692b
of sacred compositions, 8:634a-b
of secular compositions, 8:634b–635a
troubadours, 12:216a-b
see also Gregorian chant; *Musica instrumentalis;* Plainsong
polyphonic, 9:687b
in *Benedicamus Domino* settings, 2:167b
Byzantine music and, 8:556a
in Celtic music, 8:559a
duplum, 4:312b–313a
earliest monument of, 12:648a
English, 12:695a-b, 12:696a
French, 7:326b, 12:696b
Italian poetry and, 6:640b
for Kyrie eleison, 7:313b
lai and, 7:316b
in *lauda,* 7:384b
in *Magnus liber organi,* 7:549a
measured notation and, 8:627b
melodic styles of, 8:271b
in *Musica enchiriadis,* 8:626b, 639b
musica ficta and, 8:598a
Notre Dame school and, 9:192a
paraphonista in, 9:398b
Parisian theorists and, 8:643b
performance of, 8:635b
popular music and, 8:571a-b
portative organ and, 8:605b
in Renaissance masses, popular tunes and, 8:571b
responsory, 10:336a-b
in Russia, 8:573b
in *sacre rappresentazioni,* 6:636a
sacred, 8:605a, 634a-b
in Slavic music, 8:575b, 576a
Spanish, collections, *see also* Huelgas MS, Las
in *Sumer Is Icumen In,* 11:505a–506a
in treatises, 8:618a
see also Counterpoint; Old Hall MS; Part-music; Trecento music; Worcester polyphony
popular, **8:570b–572b**
Antwerp Songbook, 4:321a
chansonnier, 3:255b–256b
chansons de geste, 3:257a–261b
in England., *See* Middle English literature, lyric
Icelandic *rímur* and, 10:406b
melodic style of secular songs, 8:270a, 270b
minstrels performing, 8:416a-b
Neidhart "von Reuental's" songs, 9:94b
see also Ballade; Ballads, Middle English; Ballata
as practical art, 8:587a–591a
precentor, 10:82b–83a
quodlibet, 10:241a
in rhymed offices, 10:366b–377a
round singing, 10:536b
sacred, 8:591b–592a
German theorists and, 8:648a
oral tradition and, 8:569a
performance of, 8:634a-b
secular, 8:591b, 593a, 594a, 601b, 603a
Johannes de Grocheo and, 8:644b
performance of, 8:634b–635a
Slavic. *See* Slavic music
sociology of, 8:595a–597b
speculative vs. practical, 8:579a–580a
texts, contrafactum, 3:575b–576b
theology of, 8:581a–582b
treatises, 8:586 (*illus.*), **8:636b–649b**
Arabic, 8:566a-b
ars antiqua, 1:542b, 544a, 544b–545a
by Hucbald, 6:317a
Jewish, 8:564b–565a
Russian, 8:574b
on solmization, 11:362b–366a
see also Anonymous IV; Aurelian of Réôme; *Prolatio;* Tonary
underlying other disciplines, 8:582b–587a

Music (*cont.*)
vocal
contratenor, 3:576b–577b
counterpoint, 3:657a-b–658a
dance songs, 4:86b
duplum, 4:312b–313a
in Easter liturgy, 4:275a-b, 276a-b
isorhythmic, 6:619a
paraliturgical, 6:382b
waits, 12:497a-b
Western European, **8:578b–595a**
historiography, 12:225b–226b
Islamic influence on, **8:562a–564a**
see also Dance; Hymns; Troubadours; Trouvères; particular countries
Music manuscripts, 3:80b–81a
German, 3:97b
Italian, *see also* Faenza Codex
Spanish, 3:85a
see also Huelgas MS, Las
see also Kyriale
Music, measured
in *De mensurabili musica,* 7:134b
hocket in, 7:119a-b
Johannes de Grocheo and, 7:119a-b
motet in, 7:119a-b
organum in, 7:119a-b
tempus in, 7:119a-b
Musica. See Hermann von Reichenau; Hucbald of St. Amand; John of Afflighem
Musica disciplina. See Aurelian of Réôme
Musica divina. See Musica mundana
Musica enchiriadis, 3:438a, 6:317a, 8:639b, 10:379b, 11:632b
alphabetic notation and, 8:614b
Daseian notation in, 8:618a, 626b
Dialogus and, 8:640b
Guido of Arezzo and, 8:641a
John of Afflighem and, 8:642b
Winchester Troper and, 12:648a
Musica falsa, 11:365b
Musica ficta, 1:552a, **8:597b–600b,** 11:365b
in performance, 8:635b, 636a
solmization and, 8:626a
Ugolino of Orvieto and, 8:648a
Musica humana, 8:582b, 587b, 589a, 637b
Musica instrumentalis, 8:587a–591a, 637b
Musica mensurabilis. See Jehan des Murs
Musica mensurata (*mensurabilis*), as distinct from *musica plana,* 10:378b
Musica mundana, 8:582a-b, 587b, 589a, 637b
architecture and, 8:585b–586a
Easter and, 8:586b
Musica plana, as distinct from *musica mensurata,* 10:378b
Musica practica. See Ramos de Pareja, Bartolomeo
Musica son. See Landini, Francesco
Musica vera. See Musica ficta
Musical instruments
Celtic, 8:558a-b
for dances, 4:86b, 89b
in illuminated manuscripts, Spanish, 3:85a, 85b
Islamic, **8:610a–613b**
Middle Eastern, 8:610b (*illus.*), 613a (*illus.*)
aerophone, 8:612a-b
attitudes toward, 8:560a
bowed string, 8:611b–612a
chordophone, 8:610a–612a
in Europe, 8:562b–563a, 593b, 600b, 601a-b
idiophone, 8:613a-b
literary sources for, 8:610a
lute family, 8:610a–611a
membranophone, 8:612b–613a
open string, 8:611a-b
terminology for, 8:561b
treatises on, 8:566b
Western European, **8:600b–610a,** 12:180a-b
Celtic, 2:105b
Italian trecento, 12:180b
keyboard, 8:608a–609a
loud, 8:635a
minstrels using, 8:416a-b
percussion, 8:605b–606a
performance of, 8:635a-b
soft, 8:635a-b
stringed, 8:606a–609a
wind, 8:603a–605b
see also Bells; Instrumentation (music); *Serena serenarum*
Musical meter. *See* Meter (music)
Musical notation
mensural
ambivalence of note forms, 5:207a
ars antiqua and, 1:544b–545a
in *ars nova,* 1:549a–550a
rules of, 5:207b
modal, *ars antiqua,* 1:542b–547a
Musical notation, Byzantine, 8:556a-b, **8:616a–618a,** 9:687a–688a
early, 8:616b
ekphonetic, 8:616a
neume and, 8:624a
kondakarian, 9:687b
Koukouzelian, 8:616b
late, 8:616b–617a
middle, 8:616b
origins of, 8:616a
principles of, 8:617a–618a
Musical notation, Greek, 8:613b
Musical notation, Islamic, terminology for, 8:563b
Musical notation, Jewish, 8:564a
Musical notation, Slavic, 8:574a (*illus.*), 575a (*illus.*), 575b
Kievan, 8:575b, 576a, 577a (*illus.*)
plainsong, 9:686b–688a
Musical notation, Syrian, 8:578a
Musical notation, Western European, **8:623a–631a**
alphabetic, 6:317a, **8:613b–615b**
of Boethius, 8:614a
in *Dialogus de musica,* 8:614b, 640b
Guido of Arezzo and, 8:614b–615a, 641a
Hermann von Reichenau and, 8:615a
neumes and, 8:625b–626a, 639a
Scolica enchiriadis and, 8:614a
Aquitanian, 8:627a, 10:618b
ars antiqua, 1:543a, 543b, 544a–545b
ars nova, 1:548a–553a, 5:209a
ars subtilior, 12:178a
bilingual, **8:615b–616a**
in Montpellier H.159 MS, 8:614b, 615b–616a
breve (*brevis*), 12:177b
division of, 8:126a-b
in *cantigas de Santa María,* 3:85b
in *Carmina burana,* 3:99a
Chartres, 8:556a-b, 616b
clef, 3:438a
Coislin, 8:556b, 616b, 9:687b
color in, 8:630a, 645b
custos, 4:68a
Daseian, **8:618a-b,** 8:626a-b, 639b
structure of, 8:618b
in treatises, 8:618a
De musica mensurabili and, 8:646a
diaphonia, 4:172a-b
diastemy, 4:172b
dot (*punctus divisionis*), 12:177b
ekphonetic, 8:551b–553a (*illus.*), 556a, 556b, **8:618a–619a**
first development of, 8:593b
of Franco of Cologne, 5:207a, 208b, 8:628b, 629b, 644a
French, 1:550b–552a
14th century, 8:126b
gallica rules, 12:178b
Greek, 8:636b
of Guido of Arezzo, 6:12b
Hermann von Reichenau and, 8:626b, 627a
Hucbald and, 6:317a, 8:626b
Hufnagel, **8:619a–620a**
Italian, 1:550a-b
Italian and French compared, 8:126a-b
Italian trecento, 12:177b–178b (*illus.*)
of Johannes Gallicus, 8:643b
in Las Huelgas MS, 6:318a
of Latin chant, 8:592b
in *Magnus liber organi,* 8:43b
Marchettus of Padua and, 8:645b–646a
mensural, 9:219b
modal, 8:588a-b, 593b, 594a, **8:620a–623a**
Anonymous IV's treatment, 1:309b
Franco of Cologne and, 8:644a
interpretation of, 8:627b–628a
measured music and, 8:620b, 643b
Notre Dame school and, 8:628a-b, 9:191b, 192a
Perotinus, 9:507b
syllabic music and, 8:622a
see also Mediatio; Rhythm
modal rhythms, 8:199a
motets, 8:502b
in MS. Pluteus 29.1, 5:104a
musica instrumentalis and, 8:587b
musical intervals development, 9:690b–691a
neumes and, 8:623b–625b, 9:691a–692b
Notre Dame, 9:710b–711a
Old Hall Manuscript, 9:231b

oral tradition and, 8:568b, 569b, 570a
of ornamentation, 8:631b–634a
perfect and imperfect time, 12:177b–178a
Petronian, 9:545a-b
Philippe de Vitry and, 12:481b, 482a
of pitch, 8:593a, 623b–627a
plainsong, 9:688a–693a
planctus, 9:693a-b
plica, 9:710b–711a
polyphonic, 8:198a-b
quatre prolacions and, 8:629b–630a
of rhythm, 8:587b–589a, 594a, 627b–630a
see also Musical notation, modal
St. Gall and, 8:624a, 625a
semitone, 8:126a
solmization, 11:362b–366a
staff and, 8:627a
successive, 10:619a
theory and, 8:623a
time signatures, 12:177b–178b (*illus.*)
in treatises, 8:566b, 568b
uses of, 8:623a
of Winchester Troper, 12:647b
see also Flexa; Hocket; Intabulation; Ligature; Neume; *Perfectio; Prolatio; Proprietas;* Staff
Musical ornamentation, **8:631a–634a**
of chant, 8:592b
in Faenza Codex, 4:580a
improvised, 8:631b
Middle Eastern, 8:567b
notated, 8:631b–634a
in oral tradition, 8:569b
in performance, 8:636a
in treatises, 8:632a-b
varieties of, 8:631a
Musical treatises
ancient, 8:636b–637a
Boethius and, 8:637b, 640b
Arabic translations from Greek, 8:566a
of *ars nova* period, 8:645b–647a
of Carolingian renaissance, 8:638b–640a
on chant, 8:644a-b
Cistercians and, 8:642b–643a
Daseian notation in, 8:618a
15th century, 8:647a–648b
of Germans, 8:648a-b
Islamic, 8:640a-b
Italian, 8:640b–641b, 647b–648a
Latin translations from Arabic, 8:563a-b
of Liège school, 8:642a-b
on ornamentation, 8:632a-b
of Reichenau school, 8:641b–642a
13th century, 8:643a–645b
Musices opusculum. See Burtius, Nicolaus
Musicus (theoretical musician), 8:579a
Mūsīqār, 8:612b
Muskatblüt, influence of on Michel Beheim, 8:306b
Muški, 5:419a
Muslim ibn ^{c}Aqīl, al-Ḥusayn and, 6:370a, 370b
Muslim ibn al-Ḥajjāj, *ḥadīth* and, 6:47b, 580b
Muslim-Christian relations. *See* Christian-Muslim relations
Muslim-Jewish relations, responsum literature and, 10:338a, 339a
Muslims. *See* Islam
Musnad. See Ḥanbal, Aḥmad ibn Muḥammad ibn
Múspell, 11:28b
Muspilli, 2:225a, **8:650a-b**
alliterative verse, 9:233b
Otfrid von Weissenburg and, 8:650a
"Mustafa, Pretender," bid for power, 8:263b
Musta^{c}īn, al-, relations with the Cid, 3:384a–385a
Musta^{c}lī, al-, Fatimid caliph, 5:28b, 6:617a, 11:137b, 138a
Musta^{c}līs. *See* Ṭayyibīs
Mustanṣir, al-, Abbasid caliph, **8:650b–651a**
Baghdad under, 8:650b–651a
caliphate and, 8:650b, 651a
al-Mustanṣirīya and, 6:606a, 8:650b
al-Musta^{c}ṣim and, 8:651a
Mustanṣir, al-, Almohad ruler, 1:195b
Mustanṣir bi'llāh, al-, accession to Hafsid throne, 6:53a
Mustanṣir, al-, Fatimid caliph, 1:590a
Ismailism and, 6:617a
Nizārīs and, 11:137b
viziers of, 5:27b–28a
Mustanšir, al-, Fatimid caliph, *see also* Badr al-Jamālī
Mustanṣirīya, al-, 6:606a, 8:650b
Mustaq, 8:612b
Mustaṣfā min uṣūl al-fiqh. See Ghazālī, al-
Musta^{c}ṣim, al-, Abbasid caliph, **8:651a–652a**
caliphate and, 8:651a
executed, 3:51a, 6:329a, 504b, 514a
vs. Hulagu, 8:651a, 651b–652a
Musurgia universalis. See Kircher, Athanasius
Mu^{c}taḍid, al-, Abbasid caliph
Egypt's Tulinids and, 12:224b
return to Baghdad, 2:46b
al-Ya^{c}qūbī on, 12:717b
Mu^{c}taḍid, al-, of Seville, ruler, 11:213b
Mutakallimūn (theologians), on resurrection, 10:341b
Mu$^{\supset}$taman Abū Isḥāq Ibrāhīm ibn al-^{c}Assāl, al-, *Collection of the Fundamental Doctrines of Religion,* 8:479a
Mu^{c}tamid, al-, caliph
Ašot I and, 1:480b
Samanids and, 6:503b
Mu^{c}tamid, al-, king of Seville, love poems, 6:234a
Mutanabbī, al-, 1:401b, 403a, **8:652a–653a**
Kāfūr and, 8:652b
poetry of, 8:652b–653a
Sayf al-Dawla and, 8:652a, 652b
Mutaqārib. See Motaqāreb
Mu^{c}taṣim, al-, Abbasid caliph, **8:653b–654a**
Baghdad under, 8:653b
capital at Samarra
palaces, 10:642a
selection of site, 10:641b
West Bank development, 10:643a
cavalry of, 3:209a
foreign troops and, 8:653b–654a
mamlūk institution and, 8:69a
miḥna and, 8:655b–656a
al-Mutawakkil and, 8:654a
reign of, 6:513a
Samarra and, 2:46b, 6:597b
Turkish guard, 3:49b
Turks and, 11:560b–561a
Mutation, **8:654a**
Mutawakkil, al-, Abbasid caliph, **8:654a-b**
Armenian magnates and, 1:479b–480a
development of Samarra, 10:643a-b
edict on non-Muslim clothing, 3:619b
al-Fatḥ ibn Khāqān and, 8:654b
friendship with Balādhurī, 2:54a
headquarters of, 8:654b
Islamic sumptuary laws and, 11:508b
miḥna and, 8:656a, 11:513b
murder of, 3:49b, 8:654b
Nestorians under, 3:312b
orthodox view of Koran creation, 6:89b
Turks and, 8:654a, 654b
Mutawakkiliyya. *See* Ja^{c}fariyya
Mu^{c}tazila, al-, 6:583a-b, **8:655a–656a,** 11:139b
anthropomorphisms and, 7:163a-b, 164b
Baḥya ben Joseph ibn Paqūdā and, 2:51b
creation of Koran, 6:89a
decline of, 8:656a
doctrines of, 6:513a, 8:655b
ethical theology, 9:568a, 569a
Imāmamīs and, 6:587a
influence of on Muḥammad ibn Tūmart, 11:140b
intellectual achievements of, 8:656a
Joseph ben Abraham al-Baṣir and, 7:150b
Koran and, 1:583b–584a
al- Ma$^{\supset}$mūn and, 8:80b
opposition to, 9:568b
origins, 9:568a
on power, 1:584a
rationalist method, 9:568b
Shī^{c}a and, 11:228b
in *Škand-gumānīg Wizār,* 11:324b–325a
under Abbasids, 8:655a-b
under Umayyads, 8:655a
al-Ya^{c}qūbī on, 12:718a
Zaydis and, 12:742b
Mu^{c}tazili Abu 'l-Wafā$^{\supset}$ ibn ^{c}Aqīl, 7:111b
Mu^{c}tazilite inquisition, 11:65a-b, 511b, 512a, 512b, 513b
al- Mu^{c}tazila and, 8:655b–656a
Mu^{c}tazilite school, Islamic preachers in, 10:72b
Mu^{c}tazilites. *See* Mu^{c}tazila, al-
Mu^{c}tazz, Ibn al-, 1:401b, 402b
Book of Decorative Devices, 10:345a
praised by Ibn Rashīq, 10:346b–347a
Ṭabaqāt al-shu^{c}arā$^{\supset}$, 2:237b
Mutetus. See Motet

Muthannā ibn Ḥāritha, al-, 6:568b–569a
Mutimir of Croatia, prince, 12:68b
  reign of, 4:2b
Muttaqī, al-, Abbasid caliph, relations with Ikhshidids, 6:85a-b, 416b
Muwaffaq, al-, Abbasid regent, vs. Zanj, 12:739a
Muwallad, revolt of, 11:382b, 384b, 386b
Muwalladūn
  rebellions against ᶜAbd Allāh, 12:277a
  in Toledo, 12:67b
Muwaqqit, 11:87b
  astronomical texts written by, 1:623a-b
Muwashshaḥ, 7:239a-b, 8:563b, 11:408a, 446a–449a, 452b
  composition scheme, 8:514b
  organization, 8:514b
  origins, 8:514b
  rhythmic pattern, 8:514b
  Romance poetic tradition and, 11:442a
  speaker, 8:515a
  spread of, role of Jewish poets, 11:447b
  structure of, 11:446b
  see also Aljamiado literature
Muwaṭṭaʾ. See Mālik ibn Anas
Muwattar. See Mizhar
Muzaffar al-Din, atabeg of Tabrīz, 11:571a
Muẓaffar Yūsuf, al-, Rasulid sultan, 12:724a
Muzaffarids, Iranian art and, 6:605a
Muzalon family, as regents for John IV Laskaris, 9:331a
Muzeirib, El, fairs, 4:589a
Muzza (canal), 6:558b
Mχargrdzeli family, Tamar and, 11:587a
Mχitᶜar of Ani, 1:511b
  historiographical handbook, 6:240b
  lost history of, 12:360a
Mχitᶜar Ayrivanecᶜi (13th century), 1:511b
Mχitᶜar Goš, 1:511b, 512a, **8:656a–657b**
  Codex, 5:579b, 7:388b–389b
    editions of, 7:388b
    importance of, 7:389a
    sources for, 7:388b
    translations of, 7:389a
  Smbat Sparapet's work and, 11:351b
  works of, 8:656b
  Yovhannēs Vardapet of Tawuš and, 8:656b
  see also Armenian law
Mχitᶜar Heracᶜi (12th century), 1:512a
Myeur des histors. See Jean d'Outremeuse
Mynyddog Mwynfawr
  at battle of Catraeth, 12:602b
  minstrels and, 8:558a
Mynyw
  mother church of St. David, 4:329b
  scholarship at, 4:329b
Myrddin, 5:388a, 12:603b–604a
  see also Merlin
Myrelaion (church: Constantinople), cross-in-square design of, 4:341a
Myrepsos, Nicholaos, *Pharmacopoieia,* 8:246a
Myriokephalon, Battle of (1176), 1:241b, 6:418a, 7:284a, 8:91b, **8:657a,** 10:235b, 11:154a, 157a
Myrobiblion. See Photios, patriarch of Constantinople
Myrrh, production in southern Arabia, 1:370a
Mystère d'Adam, Le. See Jeu d'Adam
Mystère de la Passion. See Gréban, Arnoul
Mystère du siège d'Orléans, 4:265a
Mystère du Vieil Testament, performance of, 4:284b
Mystères et moralités du manuscrit 617 de Chantilly, dating of, 9:636a
Mystery plays, 4:279a, **8:657a–663b**
  biblical characters in, 8:660a
  Corpus Christi and, 8:657b, 658b–659a
  costuming for, 8:662b
  demise of, 8:662b–663a
  emotionalism of, 8:660b–661a
  guilds and, 8:657b, 659a-b, 661a-b
  in Latin verse, 7:677b–678b
  music for, 8:596b, 662b
  organization of, 8:659a–661a
  origins of, 8:657b–658b
  performance of, 8:661a–662b
  sources for, 8:658a
  staging of, 4:266a, 8:661b–662a
  typology of, 8:660a-b
  in Valencia, 12:349a
  see also Chester Plays; Drama; N-town plays; Towneley plays; York Plays
Mystery religions, **9:1a–5b**
  characteristic features of, 9:1a
  Roman Empire travel and, 12:149b
  within Christianity, 9:1b–2b
  within Islam, 9:2b–5a
  within Judaism, 9:5a
Mystical poetry. *See* Poetry
Mystical Theology. See Pseudo-Dionysius the Areopagite
Mysticism, Christian
  antinomianism, 5:218a
  beguines and beghards, 2:160b, 161a, 6:198b–199a
  Byzantine, **9:5b–8a,** 9:563b
    charismatic, 2:467a
    definition, 2:467a
    doctrine of deification, 2:467a
    hesychasm, 9:7b
    on Mount Athos, 1:636b–637b, 2:490a
  Carthusians and, 3:118a
  Dominican, 4:248a-b
  in Dutch literature, 4:319a-b, 320b
  Eastern tradition of, 9:5b
  English, 8:317b–318a, **9:18a–31a**
    background and precursors, 9:18a–19a
    compilations, 9:27b
    main characteristics of, 9:19a–20a
    orthodoxy of, 9:19b
    Passio Domini concentration, 9:19b
    in the postmedieval period, 9:27b–28a
    secondary figures and works, 9:26a-b
    translations, 9:26b–27b
    writings in vernacular, 9:20a
  Franciscan tradition, 7:686b
  German, **9:31a–36a**
    heretical sects practicing, 5:216a
    Suso and, 11:516b–517a
  in Hugh of St. Victor, 6:322b
  in hymns, 6:382a, 382b
  Low Countries, **9:36a–38b**
    followers of Ruusbroec, 9:37b–38a
    Ruusbroec, 9:36a–37b
  in Middle High German literature, 8:355a-b, 356a-b
  proponents of, 9:611a
  women mystics, continental, 6:44a-b, 69b–70a, 228b, **9:8a–18a**
    campaign against social evils, 9:9b, 11b
    centers of, 9:13a
    characteristics of, 9:8b–10a
    in France, 9:12a-b
    heresy of the Free Spirit, 5:217a-b
    in Italy, 9:14a–15b
    in the Low Countries, 9:11b–12a
    in southern Germany and Switzerland, 9:12b–14a
    in western and central Germany, 9:10a–11b
    see also Birgitta, St.
  see also Richard of St. Victor
Mysticism, Islamic, **9:38b–45b**
  Ascension of the Prophet, 1:581a-b
  ecstatic experiences, 9:40b–41a, 44b
    in Aḥmad al-Ghazālī's work, 9:42a
  hagiographic works, 9:40a
  influences on, Rūmī, 10:556a-b
  khānqāh, 7:238a-b
  in Khorāsān, 9:39b, 40a
  Koran and, 9:38b–39a
  mathnawī in, 9:42b–43a
  role of Iblīs in, 9:40b, 41a
  "sober school" and the "drunken" mystics, 9:41a-b
  Sufi fraternities, 4:407a, 9:44a-b
  al-Suyūṭī and, 11:520a
  see also Sects, Islamic; Sufism; *Ṭarīqa*
Mysticism, Jewish, 7:168b–169a
  in gaonic period, 7:168b
  in Spain, 4:540a
  see also Cabala
Mysticorum expositiones sacramentorum. See Isidore of Seville, St.
Mystras. *See* Mistra
"Mythographus tertius." *See* Alberic of London
Mythography, 7:368a-b, 369b, 370a
  Christian, 1:180b
  in classical times, 1:180b
Mythologia Aesopica. See Nèvelet, Isaac
Mythology, Celtic. *See* Celtic mythology
Mythology, classical, hymns and, 6:383b
Mythology, Scandinavian. *See* Scandinavian mythology
Mytilene, Gattilusio and, 7:380a-b
Mžež Gnuni, marzpan, 1:477a

N

N-town plays, 8:658a, 661b, **9:49b–51a**
  allegory in, 4:287a
  dialect of the scribe of, 9:50b
  listing of, 9:49b–50a
  origin of the manuscript of, 9:49b
  performance of, 4:284b, 286a
  see also Towneley plays
Na-si-pi-na. *See* Nisibis
Nabataean Book of Agriculture, 1:106a
Nabataeans, in pre-Islamic Arabia, 1:371a
Nabīdh. See Beverages, Islamic
Nabuchodonosor, 2:227b
Nacaires, 8:563a
Nachbarschaft, 12:439a
"Nackte Kaiser, Der." *See* Herrand von Wildonie
Naddo da Montecatini, *Florentine Chronicle,* 6:634b
Naddod (legendary discoverer of Iceland), 12:426b
Nadīm, court musician as, 8:567a, 568a
Nadīm, Ibn al-, 1:389b, 390a, 616b, **9:51a–52a**
  Fihrist, 9:51a–52a
    on Arabic numerals, 1:384a
    on magic, 8:21a
    on Manichaeism, 8:84a
  Islamic translation and, 12:127b–128a
  Kitāb al-Fihrist
    on Arabic translators, 12:127b–128a
    on *Thousand and One Nights,* 12:50b
Nafāʾis al-funūn fī ʿarāʾis al-ʿuyūn. See Maḥmūd al-A6mūlī, Muḥammad ibn
Nafīr, 8:561b, 563a, 612b
Naghara, 8:561b
Nagid, 7:73b–74a, **9:52a–53a**
  in Egypt, 7:84a, 84b
  exilarch and, 4:552b
  in Qayrawān, 7:98b
Nagy, Antal Budai-. *See* Budai-Nagy, Antal
Nahapet, tanutēr and, 11:591a
Nahapet Kʿučʿak, 1:512a
Nahʾāwendī, Benjamin ben Moses al-, 7:209b–210a
  as exegete, 2:212a
  on God, 7:164b
  as Karaite leader, 7:107b, 163a
Naḥmanides, Moses, 2:212a, 7:81a, 92b, **9:53a-b,** 11:586a
  Barcelona disputation and, 7:81b
  cabalistic teachings, 3:1b–2a
  debate of, 10:4b–5a
  mysticism and, 4:540a
  ornithological investigations, 11:93a
  preaching of, 10:74b
Naḥmias, Joseph, on astronomy, 11:91a
Nahrawān canal, 6:514a
Nahraý ben Nissim, 3:16a
Nāʾib. See Viceroy, Islamic
Naifty, writ of, 3:415b
Nāʾiḥāt, 8:565b
Nail (unit of measure), 12:588a
Nailhead molding, 8:454a
Naisābūr. *See* Nishapur
Naissance du chevalier au cygne, 3:331a
Naissus, crusaders' route and, 10:422b
Najadāt, 11:138b
Najaf, shrine at, 7:308a
Najāt, al-. See Sīnā, Ibn
Najd, **9:54a-b**
  decline of with the rise of Islam, 9:54a-b
  in pre-Islamic times, 9:54a
Najda ibn ʿAmir, 11:138b
Nájera, Esteban G. de, *Silva de romances,* 11:429b
Najrān, 6:575b, **9:54b–56a**
  as an Arabian martyropolis, 9:55a
  Islam and, 9:55b
  in pre-Islamic time, 9:54b–55a
Nakers, 8:563a, 605a (*illus.*)
Nakīr (Islamic angel), 11:512a
  doctrine of resurrection and, 10:340b
  see also Angels, Islamic
Naloi. See Analoi
Namatianus, Rutilius Claudius. *See* Rutilius Claudius Namatianus
Namrun. *See* Lambron
Namur, counts of, 5:499b
Nancy, Battle of (1477), 5:490a
  Swiss military strategy, 12:566b
Nanni di Banco, **9:56a-b**
  Assumption of the Virgin, 9:57 (*illus.*)
Nanni di Bartolo. *See* Giovanni (Nanni) di Bartolo
Nantes
  Viking raid on, 12:430a
  Viking settlement at, 12:431b
Nantes, University of, 12:285b
Naos, **9:56b**
  see also Nave; Pastophory
Naples, **9:56b–60a**
  Accademia Pontaniana, 9:59b
  Achaea and, 7:381b
  Alfonso I of Aragon and, 11:273b
  Angevins and, 11:273a
  attacked by Muslims, 6:572b
  Baptistery of St. John, 9:58a
  black slaves in, 2:269b
  in Boccaccio's time, 2:277b–280a, 288b–289a
  as capital of kingdom of Sicily, 11:275a, 276a
  cultural life, 9:58b–59a
  dogana (customs), 9:59a
  early history of, 9:56b–58a
  Florentine merchants and, 12:117b–118a
  law school of, 7:514b
  legal education in, 11:274a-b
  library of, 7:567a
  medical education in, 11:274b
  population of, in the 14th century, 9:59b
  seized by the counts of Forlì and Capua, 9:58b
  Siena and, 11:281b
  under Alfonso of Aragon, 9:59b
  under Angevins, 1:253b
Naples Cathedral, Sta. Restituta chapel, 10:504a
Naples, University of, 9:58b–59a, 12:286a
  Frederick II and, 11:257b, 274a
Naqīb, 1:175b
Naqqāra, 8:561b, 563a, 613a (*illus.*)
  see also Ṭabl al-markab
Naqš-i Rustam (Persepolis). *See* Naqsh-i Rustam
Naqsh, **9:60a-b**
Naqsh ḥadīda, **9:60b–61a**
Naqsh-i Rajab, 7:222a
Naqsh-i Rustam, **9:61a–62a**
  bas-reliefs, 1:451b
  Kaʿba of Zoroaster at, 7:204a-b
Naqshbandiyya (Sufi order), 6:585b
  during Timurid period, 12:59a
Nar, 8:563b
Narbonne
  arsenal of, 9:81a
  civil war (1234-1237), 6:487a
  conquered by Pepin III the Short (759), 9:62b
  growth and decline of, 7:339b, 341a
  Jewish traditions concerning, 9:64b
  occupied by Muslims, 6:572b
  Peace of God and, 9:475a
Narbonne, Constitutions of, Franciscan reforms, 5:199b
Narbonne, Council of (990), Peace of God movement, 9:473b
Narbonne, Council of (1054)
  indulgences and, 6:448b
  prohibition of killing, 9:474a
Narbonne rite, **9:62a–63a**
  influenced by Mozarabic rite, 9:62b
  modifications of under the Carolingians, 9:62b
  romanization of, 9:63a
Narbonne, Synod of (1035), 6:448b
Narcissus, in *Roman de la Rose,* 10:450a (*illus.*)
Narcisus, 5:243a
Nardo di Cione, **9:63a–64a,** 12:176b
  frescoes of, 5:295b
  Last Judgment, 5:295b, 9:63 (*illus.*), 12:175a
  panels ascribed to, 9:63a-b
  Paradise and Hell, 5:607a
  see also Jacopo di Cione
Narjot de Toucy, 7:349a
Narni, Ponte d'Augusto, 10:410a, 420b
Narratio de rebus Armeniae, 6:239b
Narrenschiff. See Brant, Sebastian; Geiler, Johannes
Narsai (Nestorian scholar), 9:106b, 11:565b, 567b
  Persian church and, 3:312a
Narses, Byzantine general
  campaign against Ostrogoths, 7:201b
  Italian command, 9:292b
Narses (Narseh), Sasanian king, 1:475b
  Treaty of Nisibis, 10:668a
Narthex, **9:64a-b**
  nave and, tribelon arcade separation, 9:64 (*illus.*), 12:187b
Nasáībīn. *See* Nisibis

Naṣb, 8:565b, 566a
Nāṣer-i Khusraw. *See* Nāṣir-i Khusraw
Nashid, al-, 8:562b
Nashīd al-^{c}ajam, 8:566b
Nashīd al-^{c}arab, 8:566b
Nashki. See Naskhī
Nasi, **9:64b**
  Jewish dynasty of in the duchy of Naxos, 9:91a
Nāṣir, al-, Abbasid caliph, 6:514a, 11:308a
  attempt to restore caliphate, 1:12a, 8:650b
  Persian Gulf trade and, 11:247a
  vs. Seljuks, 7:244a
  vs. Tekish, 6:504a
  wealth acquired by, 8:651a
Nāṣir al-Dawla
  appointment to *amīr al-umarā$^{\supset}$,* 6:85a
  conflicts with Mu^{c}izz al-Dawla, 6:85b
Naṣīr al-Dīn al-Ṭūsī, 1:434b, 6:587a, 11:84a
  Hulagu and, 8:651b
  invention of torquetum attributed to, 11:98b
  Mongols and, 11:228a
  Nasirean Ethics, 9:571b–572a
  observatory at Maraghen and, 11:99a
Nāṣir Faraj, al-. *See* Faraj, Nāṣir al-
Nāṣir li l-Ḥaqq al-Uṭrūsh, 12:742a, 742b
Nāṣir Muḥammad, al-, Mamluk sultan, 3:399b, 8:73a, 73b–74a, 74b
Nāṣir Yūsuf II, al-, Ayyubid sultan, 2:23b, 8:73b
Nāṣir-i Khusraw, 5:393b, 6:507b, 616b
  on Beirut, 2:164a
  establishment of Ismā^{c}īli community, 1:65a
Naskh
  ^{c}ilm al-farā$^{\supset}$iḍ and, 6:454a
  theory of, 9:498a
Naskhī, 1:209b–210a (*illus.*), **9:65a**
  development of, 9:334a
  use in Koran (14th century), 9:65a (*illus.*)
Naṣr Allāh, 6:508b
Naṣr al-Dawla ibn Marwān (*d.* 1061), 7:310b
Naṣr ibn Muzāḥim, 7:307b
Naṣr, Samanid emir
  conquest of Isḥāq ibn Aḥmad, 10:638a
  cultural achievements, 10:638b
  treatment of Ismailis, 10:638a
Nasrids
  art and, 6:611b–612a
  in Granada, 5:652a–653b
Nasta^{c}līq, **9:65b**
  development of, 9:334a
  use in *Language of the Birds,* 9:65b (*illus.*)
Nasturtium, pharmacological uses, 9:551a
Natalis, abbot of St. Maria and St. Peter, 12:682b
Natalis solis invicti, 3:317b
Natanz, mosque, 6:604b
Nathan the Babylonian, report on Babylonian exilarchate, 6:257a
Nathan ben Abraham, 7:105a
Nathan ben Isaac ha-Bavli, 4:552a
Nathan ben Jehiel, 7:109b
  Arukh, 7:176a
Nations, student. *See* Universities
Nāṭiq, 6:615b
Nativita del Signore, La, 6:636a
Nativity, **9:66a–67a**
  in art
    in Benedictional of St. Aethelwold, 2:176b (*illus.*)
    by Schongauer, 4:488a (*illus.*)
  in the Second Shepherds' Play, 11:134b
  see also Epiphany, feast of
Nativity (church: Bethlehem), 4:22b, 24b
  mosaics, 4:495a
Nativity, Feast of the. *See* Christmas
Nativity plays. *See* Drama, liturgical, for Christmas
Natronai bar Hilai (Hilar), gaon of Sura, 10:338a
  list of benedictions, 7:619a, 621a
Natronai ben Ḥavivai, 7:95b
Nattangia, 2:63 (map), 67a
Natura. See Physis; Trinitarian doctrine
Natural Faculties. See Galen
Natural History. See Pliny
Naturalis historia. See Pliny the Elder, *Natural History*
Naturalism in art. *See* Trecento art
Nature poetry
  in Cambridge Songs, 3:58a
  in Middle English literature, 8:335a–337a
Natureingang. See Hadewijch of Antwerp
Nauclerus, 11:233a
Nauheim, saltworks, 10:633b
Naum (9th-century disciple of Cyril and Methodios), 9:208b
Naumburg Cathedral, choir screen at, 5:621b (*illus.*), 624a, 9:447a
Nauplia
  besieged by Boniface of Montferrat, 7:376b
  seized (1210–1211), 7:378a
  Venice and, 7:380b
Nā^{c}ūra, 6:556b, **9:67a-b,** 12:81a
  in Toledo, 12:68a
Nauruz, governor of Khorāsān, 6:420a
Navan Fort. *See* Emain Macha
Navarre, kingdom of, **9:67b–73a,** 9:68 (map)
  Asturias-León and, 1:628b
  as a dominant state in Christian Spain, 9:69a-b
  episcopal sees in 1000, 9:68b
  formation of, 2:126b, 9:67b–68a
  French settlers in, 9:71a
  in the late 15th century, 9:72a
  loss of independence, 9:69b
    annexed to Castile (1512), 9:72a
    as possession of France, 9:71a
  Old Spanish dialects in, 11:400a–401a
  population of in later Middle Ages, 9:71b
Nave, **9:73a**
  decoration of, 4:337b–338a
  narthex and tribelon arcade separation, 9:64 (*illus.*), 12:187b
  Speyer Cathedral, 10:487b–488a (*illus.*)
  transepts and, 12:125b
Navgyvárad, Peace of (1538), 6:350a
Navicularii (Byzantine shipowners), 12:100a
Navidad, 4:561a
Navies, *see also* Ships and shipbuilding; Trade, maritime
Navies, Byzantine, 11:231b
  see also Navies, Islamic; Warfare, Byzantine
Navies, Islamic, 6:572b, **9:73b–78a**
  attack on Constantinople, 2:487a
  decline of, 9:75b–76a
  development, 12:553b
  Egyptian ship, 9:77 (*illus.*)
  land campaigns, 12:553b
  merchant fleets, 9:76b–77b
    in the Persian Gulf, 9:86 (*illus.*)
  piracy, 12:553b
  Tulinid at Acre, 12:224a
  types of ships, 9:76a
  Umayyad, 11:246b
  under Abbasids, 9:74b–75a
  under Fatimids, 9:75a-b
  under Umayyads, 9:73b–74b
  warships, 9:76a-b
  see also Navigation
Navies, Western, **9:78b–85a**
  appearance of cog, 9:81b–82b
  arsenals, 9:81a
  Cypriot, 4:71b
  English, cog and, 11:242a
  galley ship and, 11:237a
  guns on ships, 9:83b–84a
  in Hundred Years War, 6:333a
  leagues of, 4:55b
  in the Mediterranean Sea, 9:80a–81a
  office of admiral, 9:80b–81a
  organization of in Northern Europe, 9:81a-b
  of Pisa, 9:664a-b
  raising of, 9:82b–83a
  Venetian, 4:30b, 31b, 32b, 45a-b, 127b
  Venice and, 12:388a-b
  Viking, 12:558b
  warships, cargo ships contrasted, 9:84a-b
Navigatio sancti Brendani, 6:552a
  Voyage de Saint Brendan and, 12:493a
Navigation
  Byzantine, Mediterranean sea routes, 10:423a-b (map)
  compass, magnetic, 3:506a–507b
  devices for, 11:638b, 650b
    extension of sailing season, 11:655b
  Fachschrifttum and, 4:579a
  Indian Ocean, 5:394a, **9:85a–87a**
    Islamic trade and, 12:107b
  instruments of, 4:12a-b
  laws and customs regulating. *See* Law, maritime
  Mediterranean, 11:234b–235a
    see also Trade, Byzantine
  Persian Gulf, 11:247b
  portolan chart and, 10:34b

Red Sea, 5:394a, **9:85a–87a**, 11:247b
maps and navigational aids, 9:87a
see also Trade, Islamic
solar declination tables, 11:650b
Western European, **9:87a–90a**
maritime codes, *see also Libre del Consolat del mar*
origins of, 9:87a-b
trade and, 12:113b–115a
see also Scientific instruments; Venice; Viking navigation
see also Compass, magnetic; Lateen sail
Naviglio Grande, locks, 12:578b
Nawba, 8:566b
Nawbakhtī, al-, 6:615a
Nawḥ, 8:565b
Naχarar. See Nobility and nobles, Armenian
Naχčawan, **9:90b–91a**, 12:362a
Arab invasions, 12:97b
Muslim emirate in, 1:513a
population, 1:485a
Naxos, duchy of, **9:91a-b**, 12:389b
Sanudo and, 7:377a
Nāy, 8:561b, 567b
Nāy abyaḍ, 8:612b
Nāy mashk, 8:612b
Nāy ṭunbūr, 8:611a
Nāy zunāmī, 8:563a, 612a
Nāy-i narm, 8:612b
Nāy-i safīd, 8:612a, 612b
Nāy-i siyāh, 8:612a
Nāyīn, mosques, 6:599a
Nazarius, Cathar bishop, baptism of in Bulgaria, 2:294b, 297a, 297b
Naẓm al-jawhar. See Eutychios the Melchite
Ne Romani. See Clement V, pope
Nea of Basil I (church: Constantinople), 2:117b, 3:378b
Nea Moni (church: Chios)
domed-octagon design of, 4:341b
mosaics in, 2:443a-b
Neacşu, Walachian boyar, 10:511a
Neagoe Basarab, Walachian ruler, 10:510b
Near East, 4:28–29 (map), 6:502 (map)
under Dominate, 10:463a-b, 464a
Nebridius, bishop of Narbonne, 9:62b
Nebrija, Antonio de
Gramática de la lengua castellana, 11:390b, 425a, 441b
Introducciones Latinae, 11:407a-b
Prosodia i silaba, 11:459b
Vocabularium, 11:441b
Nechtan, Pictish king, **9:91b**
Neckam, Alexander. *See* Neckham, Alexander
Neckham, Alexander, **9:92a**
on castle building, 3:145b–146a, 150b
Corrogationes Promethei, 12:137a
De laudibus divinae sapientiae, 1:255a
De naturis rerum, 1:607a, 4:448b, 5:396b, 9:92a
description of a compass, 11:100b–101a
on lions, 2:205a
on weasels, 2:205a
De nominibus utensilium, 9:92a
goldsmith's preliminary designs, 4:291b
hymns of, 6:382a
in Latin pedagogy, 7:352b
magnetic compass and, 3:506a
Novus Aesopus, 4:573b, 7:365a, 366b, 10:527b
on Roman theater in Paris, 4:277b–278a
Romulus and, 4:572b
on the teaching of medicine at Salerno and Montpellier, 8:257b
works of, 7:364b–365a, 366b
Necklaces, 5:379b (*illus.*)
Neculce, Ion, 10:512a
Nedae, Battle of (454), 6:354a
Nedellec, Harvey, 7:137a
Needlefish (*Belone belone*), fishing of, 5:70a
Negroli armor workshop, 1:529b
Negroponte
crusaders in, 7:376b
relations with Venice, 7:380b
see also Euboea
Nehunyah ben Ha-Kanah, 3:1b
Neidhart the Fox, 9:92b
Neidhart Fuchs, 8:360a
Neidhart "von Reuental," **9:92b–94b**
Bauernhochzeit and, 2:132b
in *Carmina burana,* 3:97b
crusading songs of, 9:92b–93a
dances, 12:537b
Gottfried von Neifen and, 5:633b–634a
identity of, 9:92b
Johannes Hadlaub and, 7:120a
as a legendary peasant foe, 9:92b, 93b (*illus.*)
lyric poetry of, 5:433a-b, 437a, 438a, 440a-b, 443b, 8:358a
manuscript sources of his poems, 9:93a-b
minnesinger style and, 8:414a
patrons of, 9:93a
poetic rivalry of, 8:351a
poetry of, 9:93a–94b
compared with Steinmar's, 11:476b
satirical frolickings of, 8:352a
Summer Songs, 9:94a-b
Tannhäuser and, 11:590b
Winter Songs, 9:92b, 94a-b
Wolfram von Eschenbach and, 12:674b
Neidharte (imitations of Neidhart "von Reuental"), 9:93b, 94b
Neilos, metropolitan (14th century), 9:135a
Neithart Fuchs, 9:93a
Neiton. *See* Nechtan
Nekresi, 5:408b
Nemain (a Celtic goddess), 9:48b
Nemanjiç dynasty, 11:173a–180a
Nemesianus, Calpurnius Siculus and, 3:55b
Nemesius of Emesa, 9:701a
on Aristotle's *On the Soul,* 1:458a
De natura humana, 1:506a
Neoplatonism and, 9:98b–99a
Vepᶜkhistoqaosani and, 11:256a
Nennius, 5:388b, **9:94b–95a**
Arthur references in, 1:564b–565a
on Canterbury, 3:81a
disciple of Elfoddw, 2:71b
Historia Brittonum, 1:564b–565a
on Ambrosius Aurelianus, 2:2b–3a
on Taliesin, 11:581b, 582a
on Urien Rheged, 12:331b
Neo-Latin language, 7:370b
Neon of Ravenna, bishop, 10:263a
Neopatras, captured (1318), 7:379b
Neoplatonic Aristotelianism. *See* Aristotelianism, Augustinian
Neoplatonism, **9:95a–101a**
Aristotle and, 1:457b–458a, 11:370b
Chaldean Oracles, 9:566b
in Christian philosophy and theology, 9:98b–99a, 99a–100a
Aquinas and, 1:357b–358b
at Chartres, 7:366a
Augustinian tradition, 7:687a
Byzantine exegesis and, 2:214a
Byzantine political theory and, 9:585b–586a
cult of icons, 9:585b
division and *reversio,* 9:586a
doctrine of procession, 9:596a
Eckhart von Hochheim and, 4:381b–382a
in Georgia, 5:417b, 11:256b
Greek codex of Pseudo-Dionysius, 9:586a
of Gregory of Nyssa, 5:666b–667a
Jerome and, 7:58b
John Italos, 7:131b
John Scottus Eriugena, 7:142a
Maximus the Confessor, 8:233b–234a
Meister Eckhart, 9:32b
Nicolas of Cusa, 9:703a-b
opponents of, 9:586a
Origen and, 3:335b, 9:6a-b
Pseudo-Dionysius the Areopagite, 1:249b–250a
punishment for the soul, 9:586b
revival, 11th century, 9:566b
in the Scholastic period, 9:100b–101a, 700a
Tauler, 11:602a
Theodoric of Freiberg, 12:18b
development of, 12:641a
Iamblichus, 9:97a–98a
in Islamic philosophy, 9:100a, 699b–700a
among Pure Brethren, 6:617b
Avicenna and, 1:458b
Ismailism, 6:587b, 588a, 615b, 618a, 11:138a
in Jewish philosophy, 7:166b–167a, 9:100a-b, 573a
Baḥya ben Joseph ibn Paqūdā, 2:51b, 7:166b
exegesis, 4:540a
Ibn Gabirol and, 1:459b
Isaac Israeli and, 1:459b, 6:620a
Joseph ben Jacob ibn Ẓaddik, 7:166b
Sefer Bahir influenced by, 3:1b
in Judeo-Arabic literature, 7:173b
in Latini's *Tesoretto,* 7:383a
meaning of the term, 9:95a
music and, 8:581a-b

Neoplatonism (*cont.*)
Platonic schools of Athens and Alexandria, 9:98a-b
Plotinus, 9:95a–96b
Porphyry of Tyre, 9:96b–97a
spread of, 9:563b
study of animals and, 2:242b
survival of, 9:566b
in *Vep^{c}khistqaosani,* 11:256a
visions and, 12:476a
see also Classical literary studies; Plato and Platonism; Pseudo-Dionysius the Areopagite
Neretljani, Venice and, 4:2a-b, 5b
Neri di Fioravanti, **9:101b**
Nero, Roman emperor, Trdat I and, 1:475a
Neroniana, 1:563b
Nerra, Fulk, count of Anjou, 9:656a
Neršapuh, Armenian bishop, 9:102b
Nersēh Kamsarakan, 7:208a
Nersēs I (the Great), St., 5:665a-b, **9:101b–102a**
Aršak II and, 1:560a
assassination of, 1:476a
Council of 365 (at Aštišat) and, 1:498a
exile of, 9:102a
Mesrop on, 1:510b
Nersēs II Aštarakac^{c}i (Bagrewandac^{c}i), **9:102a-b**
Bishop Abdišoy and, 1:508b, 5:540a
Nersēs III Išχanec^{c}i (Šinoł), **9:102b–103a**
Arab conquest and, 1:478b
Patmut^{c}iwn Tarōnoy and, 9:457a
Zwart^{c}noc^{c} and, 12:749a
Nersēs IV Šnorhali, 1:511b, 512a, **9:103a–104a**, 9:328b
commemorated, 1:520b
Confession of Faith, 6:188b
education of, 9:103a-b
as *kat^{c}ołikos,* 9:328b
Michael the Syrian and, 8:305b
negotiations with the Byzantine church, 9:103b
Nersēs Lambronac^{c}i and, 9:104a
poetry of, 9:103b
šarakans and, 8:551b
theological and pastoral writings of, 9:103b
Nersēs (architect), Church at Išḫani, 6:562b
Nersēs of Cilicia, *kat^{c}ołikos,* 1:502a
Nerses Kamsarakan
St. Astuacacin church and, 11:582b
T^{c}alin and, 11:582b
Nerses of Lambron. *See* Nersēs Lambronac^{c}i
Nersēs Lambronac^{c}i, 1:512a, **9:104a-b**
as abbot of Skewṙa, 11:326a
Armenian Bible and, 2:217b
in Constantinople, 1:500b–501a
embassy to Constantinople, 9:104b
Greek-Armenian church union and, 3:394b
Latin Mass and, 1:516b
translations of Syrian legal work, 7:388b–389b
works of, 9:104b
Nersēs Mšec^{c}i, abbot of Glajor, 5:543b
Nerthus, 9:146b
Nesebūr. *See* Mesembria
Nest (unit of measure), 12:593a
Nestor, *Povest vremennykh let* and, 11:346b–347a
Nestorian alphabet. *See* Alphabets, Syriac
Nestorianism, **9:104b–108a**, 11:563a-b
Adoptionism and, 1:57b
after the Council of Chalcedon, 9:106a-b
among Sasanian Christians, 10:669a
Antiochene rite and, 1:327a
Antiochene theological school and, 9:105a-b
in Arabia, 6:575b
Arabic translators of Plato, 9:699a-b
in Armenia
attitude of church toward, 6:187b
opposition to, 9:102b
Babai the Great and, 9:107a
biblical exegesis of, 2:214b
center in Edessa, 4:384a
in China, 3:312b
Council of Ephesus (431) and, 9:105a, 105b, 106a
decline of in the 14th century, 9:107b
derivation of the name, 9:105a
dialogue with Islam, 9:107b
in early church councils, 3:594a
Egypt, 10:454b
Eutyches and, 4:524a
icons and, 6:401a-b
Iranian Christians, 10:669a
medical school and hospital at Gundešāpūr, 6:290b–291a
in Nisibis, 9:106b
in Persia, 3:312a–313a, 6:190a
Monophysites and, 1:499a
reaction of Monophysites to, 8:477a
School of the Persians and, 11:564b
Sogdian language and, 6:506a
Syrian Christianity and, 9:106b–107b
Theotokos and, 9:105b, 106a, 12:25b–26a
unction of the sick, 12:279a
see also Persian church
Nestorians
at Lake Urmia, 12:332a
Dominican missions to, 4:252b
identified with Paulicians, 9:469a, 469b
trade with Southeast Asia, 9:85a
translations from Greek, 8:566a, 11:82b–83a
Nestorius, patriarch of Constantinople, 9:105a, **9:108a–109a**
against the use of *Theotokos,* 9:108a, 561a, 12:25b
Bazaar of Heraclides, 9:106a, 108b
Celestine I and, 3:214a, 9:106a
condemnation of, 2:459b, 485b, 3:312a
at Council of Ephesus (431), 9:108b
Cyril of Alexandria and, 4:74b–75a
East Syrian rite and, 11:567b
exile of, 9:108b
on the humanity of Christ, 3:628b
Tragedy, 9:108b
translation of his works into Syriac, 9:106b
Net vault. *See* Vault
Netherlandic language. *See* Dutch language
Netherlands. *See* Low Countries
Netter, Thomas, *Doctrinale,* 12:709b
Neue Parzival. See Colin, Philipp; Wisse, Claus
Neuma, **9:109a-b**
classes of, 9:109a
sequence and, 9:109b
tonaries and, 12:70a
Neumatic chants, 5:663b
Neume, **9:109b–111a**
Byzantine, 8:616a, 617a-b
Carolingian minuscule and, 8:638b
chironomic, 9:109b
diaphonia and, 4:172a-b
diastemy and, 4:172b, 9:109b–110a
Greek, 8:572b
liquescent, 9:109b
in MS Egerton 857, 9:110 (*illus.*)
ornamenting, 9:109b
in Slavic music, 8:576a, 576b (*illus.*)
sources of, 8:623b–624b, 9:109b
in West Frankish sequence repertories, 11:163b
see also Melody; Plica; Staff
Neustria
establishment of, 8:278a
Pepin I and, 9:499a
Pepin II and, 9:500a
Neustrians, in Carolingian Empire, 3:104b
Nev Šāburh. *See* Nishapur
Nèvelet, Isaac, *Mythologia Aesopica,* 4:573a
Neville, John, earl of Montague, 12:571b
Neville, Richard, earl of Warwick, alliance with Margaret, 12:571b
Neville's Cross, Battle of (1346), 6:332a
Nevsky, Alexander, prince of Novgorod, **9:111a**, 11:347a-b, 12:486b
appeasement of Mongols, 10:593a
vs. Sweden, 11:531a
Nevu'at ha-yeled, 1:346b
New Academy, Neoplatonism and, 9:95a
New Book of Polite Accomplishments (al-Mustaṭraf fī kull fann mustaẓraf), 1:380b
New Christians, 7:82a, 82b, 93b, **9:111a–112a**
Catholic monarchs and, 9:111b–112a
inquisition and, 4:564b, 9:111b–112a
Sephardim and, 11:161b
Spanish literature and, 9:111b
New Church (Tokalı Kilise), 3:92b (*illus.*)
nave, 3:93a (*illus.*)
New Fēs, construction of, 8:138b
New Forest, 5:133a
New Getik (monastery: Armenia). *See* Nor Getik (monastery: Armenia)
New Hungarian language. *See* Hungarian language
New March province. *See* Poland
New Rome. *See* Constantinople
New Testament. *See* Bible; Gospels

New World. *See* America
New Year, Jewish, computation of, 3:25b–26a
Newcastle, mystery play cycle of, 8:658a
Newfoundland, discovery of, 4:555a
Neyshābūr. *See* Nishapur
Neẓāmī. *See* Niẓāmī
Nezikin, 11:583a
Niall of the Nine Hostages (Noígiallach), descendants of, 3:396b, 407b, 6:547a, 547b
Niani (capital of Mali), 8:57b
Nibelungenlied, 5:426b, **9:112a–115b**
action of, 9:112b–113a
author of, at the court of Duke Leopold VI of Austria, 2:7a
betrothal in, 11:292b
Biterolf und Dietlieb and, 2:253a
Brynhild in, 2:394b–395a
Buch von Bern and, 2:396a
compared with *Siete infantes de Lara,* 11:408b
court festivities in, 9:114a
courtly values of, 8:350a
flyting and, 9:173a, 175a
geographic knowledge in, 4:579a
Guðrúarkviða cycle and, 6:36b, 37b, 38b
hunting in, 6:359a
Kudrun and, 7:304a, 305a
motivation in, 9:113a-b
Norna-Gests Þáttr and, 9:171a
prosody of, 9:114b
relation to *Rosengarten,* 10:532b–533a
Sigurd and, 11:289a, 289b
sources for, 9:114a
transmission of, 9:114b–115a
Walter legend in, 12:535b
Wolfger von Erla and, 12:673a
Wolfram von Eschenbach and, 12:674b
Wunderer and, 12:705a
see also Lied vom hürnen Seyfrid, Das; Þiðreks saga
Nicaea
Byzantine classical scholarship in, 11:50a
Byzantine roads and, 10:424a
crusaders' route and, 10:423a
First Crusade and, 4:30a, 35a
as a Seljuk capital, 11:154a
see also İznik
Nicaea, Councils of
First (325), 1:453b, 3:10b
against interest charging, 12:335b
on Arianism, 3:336a, 627b–628a
Athanasian formula, 9:560b
Basil the Great and, 2:121b
date of Easter, 4:365a, 7:611b
episcopal sees recognized, 2:459b
importance of, 9:367a-b
James of Nisibis and, 9:142a
office of metropolitan and, 8:301a
organization of Latin church and, 3:372b
on preaching, 10:361b
role of Constantine at, 3:545b
teachings of Peter and Paul and, 10:2b
Theodosius I and, 10:462a
on the Trinity, 5:666a, 9:105a
Second (787), 7:124b
Armenian church and, 1:502a
on artists' status, 1:579a
Christology and, 3:320b
church control over art imposed, 2:438b
Hincmar's repudiation of, 4:373b
iconoclasm condemned, 3:631a, 6:191b, 397a, 398b, 399a, 399b, 401a
Irene and, 6:520b
patriarch Nikephoros and, 9:131b
restoration of image worship, 9:561b, 585b
Tarasios at, 11:598b
Theotokos and, 12:460b
Nicaea, Empire of, 1:241b, **9:115b–118b**, 9:116 (map)
Battle of Pelagonia (1259), 9:487a
Bulgaria and, 2:409b–410a
intellectual activity of, 9:117b, 11:50a
John Asen II and, 7:131a
Niketas Choniates and, 9:134a
prosperity in, 9:117b–118a
relations with
Latin Empire of Constantinople, 7:347a–348a
Macedonia, 7:347b
Thessalonica, 7:347b, 12:26b
Thrace, 7:347b
Venice, 7:349a
trade relations with Seljuks, 12:103b
under John III Vatatzes, 7:127b, 9:117a-b
under Theodore I Laskaris, 9:115b–117a
vs. Epiros, 4:499a
see also Anatolia; Laskarids; Rhodes
Niccolò d'Angelo. *See* Nicolaus Angeli
Niccolò da Bologna, **9:118b–119a**
Niccolò di Buonaccorso, **9:119a**
Niccolò dalle Carceri, 7:380b
Niccolò di Giacomo. *See* Niccolò da Bologna
Niccolò, Lorenzo di. *See* Lorenzo di Niccolò di Martino
Niccolò de' Niccoli, Ambrogio Traversari and, 12:163a
Niccolò di Pietro Gerini, **9:119a-b**
Entombment, 9:119a
Life of St. Matthew, 9:119a
Resurrection, 9:119a
Spinello Aretino and, 11:464a
Niccolò de' Rossi, 6:651b
Niccolò da Verona. *See* Nicholaus da Verona
Nicene Creed, 2:464b–465a, 5:62b
Arianism and, 1:453b, 454a
Armenian version, 1:498a
"consubstantiation" in, 3:628a
Filioque clause, 4:74a, 7:348b, 9:562a
Armenian church and, 1:501a
Hrabanus Maurus and, 6:306b
formulation of, 9:560b–561a
issuance of, 3:346a
in the liturgy of the Mass, 8:189a
use in Byzantine church, 3:675b–677a
Nicene-Constantinopolitan Creed. *See* Nicene Creed
Nicetas of Remesiana, 9:713a
Niche, **9:119b–120a**
Nicholas I, pope, **9:120a–122b**
Boris of Bulgaria and, 2:403a
canonized, 9:121b
on dress, 3:620b
establishment of papal prerogatives by, 9:120b, 121a-b, 374b–375a
Filioque conflict and, 2:465a
missions and, 4:73b, 74a
in Photian schism, 11:42b
on predestination, 5:638b
restoration of Ignatios, 11:43a
Trajan's aqueduct and, 10:519b
see also Anastasius Bibliothecarius
Nicholas II, pope
Guiscards and, 11:265a, 265b
Humbert and, 6:330a
Lateran synod of, 3:634b
on Nicolaitism, 9:128b–129a
papal elections and, 3:93b, 523b, 9:377a
Peter Damian and, 9:509a
reform canons of, 9:377a
reign of, 3:351a-b
Nicholas III, pope
in Dante, 4:98b
decree on poverty, 4:377a
Edward I of England and, 11:608a
Exiit qui seminat, 5:201b, 10:122b
assistance of Peter John Olivi, 9:514b
justification of poverty, 5:203a-b
papal infallibility, 5:203a-b
Roman senate and, 10:524a
Nicholas IV, pope
Archimedes and, 1:439a
cardinals and, 3:94a
church taxation and, 11:609b
condemnation of Roger Bacon, 2:35a-b
crusades and, 4:54b–55a
Edward I of England and, 11:608a
Lateran and, 7:345a
Matthew of Aquasparta and, 8:227a
Pastoralis officii, 10:49b
Richard Knapwell and, 12:41b
Nicholas V, pope
on Christianization of blacks, 2:268b
Concordat of Vienna and, 3:526a
Council of Basel and, 3:366b, 654a
disabitato and, 10:520b
George of Trebizond and, 5:400b
Giovanni da Fiesole and, 5:534b
Nicholas of Cusa and, 9:123b
translations from Greek and, 2:203a
Nicholas of Autrecourt, **9:122a-b**
Buridan and, 1:464b
opposition to Aristotelianism, 9:122a
Nicholas Boson. *See* Nicole Bozon
Nicholas of Caen, 7:366b
Nicholas of Clairvaux, 9:714b
book lending and, 7:565a
rhymed offices of, 10:372b
Nicholas of Clamanges, **9:122b**
on church reform, 9:122b
De ruina ecclesiae, 9:122b
"querelle de la Rose" and, 10:452b
Nicholas of Cologne, Children's Crusade and, 4:14b

Nicholas of Cusa, 9:703a-b, **9:122b–125b**
on astronomy, 1:615b
Bussi and, 10:124b
calendar reform and, 3:23b
as cardinal, 9:123b
on church unity, 4:378a
conciliar theory of, 3:511b–512a, 515b, 9:124a-b, 10:24a-b
De concordantia catholica, 9:124a-b, 10:24a
De docta ignorantia, 9:124b
De pace fidei, 9:125a
De reparatione kalendarii, 9:123b
De visione Dei, 9:125a
Devotio Moderna and, 4:167a
Donation of Constantine a forgery, 4:257b
hospice of, 9:124a
Idiota de Mente, science and technology, 11:650b
influenced by Neoplatonism, 9:100b
as legate, papal, 7:535b
Meister Eckhart and, 9:32a
On the Peace of the Faith, 10:7a
on the origin of writing, 1:218a
piety and, 3:371a
Quadratura circuli, 1:437b
support for Council of Basel, 3:652b
theology of, 9:124b–125a, 611a
on Trinitarian doctrine, 12:195b
works of, 9:124a
Nicholas of Dresden, 6:372a, 373a
Nicholas Dvali, 5:414a
Nicholas Dybinus of Dresden, 4:176a
Nicholas of Ely, **9:126a**
Nicholas of Guildford, possible author of *Owl and the Nightingale,* 8:315b, 330a
Nicholas Hermansson, hymns of, 6:382b
Nicholas of Hus, 6:375a
Nicholas von Leiden. *See* Gerhaert, Nikolaus
Nicholas of Lisieux, vs. Aquinas, 12:39b
Nicholas of Lyra, **9:126a-b**
anti-Jewish treatises of, 10:5a
Bible commentaries of, 3:167a
Hebrew language study by, 3:313a
Postilla litteralis, 4:544a-b, 545b, 548a
literal sense of Scripture and, 2:224b
Rashi and, 4:540b, 10:260a
Nicholas, Master, *Bonus socius,* 5:352a
Nicholas of Methone, 11:55a
Nicholas of Pelhřimov, 6:376a, 376b
Nicholas Poillevillain. *See* Nicholas of Clamanges
Nicholas of Reggio, translations of Galen, 8:251b
Nicholas, St.
in art, 6:411a
medieval bridges and, 10:414a
Nicholas Segrave, tried before parliament, 9:424a
Nicholas of Strassburg, as defender of Thomism, 12:42a
Nicholas Trevet. *See* Trevet, Nicholas
Nicholas of Verdun, **9:127a–128b**
Klosterneuburg altar, 4:439a, 5:612a-b
Shrine of the Three Kings, 8:496a
shrines of, 5:619b
Nicholaus da Verona, **9:128b**
tympanum relief at Ferrara Cathedral, 10:501b–502a (*illus.*)
see also Guglielmo da Verona
Nichomachus (Greek music theorist), *Enchiridion,* 8:566a
Niclas von Cusse. *See* Nicholas of Cusa
Niclas Krebs. *See* Nicholas of Cusa
Niclas von Wyle
Euryalus und Lucretia, 8:361a
Translatzen, 8:361a
Nicodemus, *Volto Santo* and, 12:489b
Nicodemus, Apocryphal Gospel of, 9:447b
on the Anastasis, 1:239a
the Lamentation and, 7:322a
Old English translation of, 1:285b
Wirnt von Grafenberg's *Wigalois* and, 12:657a
Nicola de Martoni, on Venetian eastern empire, 7:377b–378a
Nicola Pisano. *See* Pisano, Nicola
Nicolaitism, **9:128b–129a**
see also Leo IX, pope
Nicolas de Bray, *Gesta Ludovici,* 2:236b
Nicolás Francés of León, Juan de Burgos and, 7:155a
Nicolaus Angeli, Lateran and, 7:344b
Nicolaus Cancer (Cusanus). *See* Nicholas of Cusa
Nicolaus Hermanni, bishop of Linköping, 2:247a
Nicolaus Rhetor, 1:505b
Nicolaus Salernitatus, *Antidotarium,* 5:306b, 8:250a, 256a
Nicolaus de Tudeschis, **9:129a**
conciliar theory of, 3:512b, 9:129a
Consilia, 9:129a
Francesco Zabarella and, 12:735a-b
Nicole Bozon, **9:129a-b**
Char d'Orgueil, 1:263b–264a
Contes moralisés, 1:264a, 9:129b
De la femme et de la pye, 1:269b
metrical sermons of, 1:262b
saints' lives, 6:63b
see also Vie de Ste. Marguerite
Nicolo da Martoni, 1:333a
Nicoloso da Recco, 3:61b, 5:398a
Nicomachean Ethics. See Aristotle
Nicomachus of Gerasa, 8:636b
De arithmetica, translated by Boethius, 2:291b
De musica, 8:637b
De musica, translated by Boethius, 2:291b
Eisagogē arithmetica, 10:237a
Pythagorean number theory, 8:206a
Nicomedia
crusaders' route and, 10:423a
relations with Latin Empire of Constantinople, 7:347b
Nicopolis, **9:129–130**
retaken by Ottomans, 2:136b
Nicopolis, Battle of (1396), 6:346b, 11:472b
Nicostratus, 4:572a
Nidaros
population, 9:184b
see of, 9:183a
Niederdeutsch, 10:602b
Niello, **9:130a-b**
preparation of described by Theophilus, 8:284a
Niels Ebbesen, 4:155a
Niels Estridsen of Denmark, king, 4:152b, 153a, 7:280a
Nieszawa, Charter of (1454), 9:727b
Nifhel. See Hel
"Niflunga saga," in *Nibelungenlied* and *Þiðreks saga,* 12:30b–31a
Nigel of Canterbury
on medicine, 7:366a
Speculum stultorum, 7:366b, 371b
Tractatus contra curiales, 7:366b
Nigel of Ely, bishop, 10:443b
Nigel of Longchamp, **9:130b–131b**
Contra curiales et officiales clericos, 9:131a
monastic rights, 9:131a
poetry of, 9:131b
Speculum stultorum, 1:255a, 9:130b, 131a, 440b
Middle English literature and, 8:319a, 319b
Nigel Wireker. *See* Nigel of Longchamp
Nigellum, 9:130a
Niger, Peter, 10:6b
Niger River, 8:57b, 58a
Nigg stone, 3:222 (*illus.*)
Night of Destiny. *See* Ramadan
Night Office, 4:228a-b
Night of Power. *See* Koran, revelation of; Ramadan
Nightingale of Hagenau. *See* Reinmar der Alte
Nightingale, Peter, *Tractatus de semissis,* on the equatorium, 11:98b
"Nightingale, The," 7:317b
Nightingales, in literature, 7:369a
Nightmare, 6:492a
Nigri, Petrus. *See* Peter Schwartz
Nihāvand, battle at (642), 6:501b
Nika Revolt (532), 2:486a, 4:135a, 7:202b
Empress Theodora I and, 12:12a
Nikephoros I, patriarch of Constantinople, **9:131b–132b**
"adultery" controversy and, 12:15b–16a
Antirrhetici, 9:132a
Apologeticus major, 9:132a
Breviarium, 6:244a-b, 9:131b–132a
theological perspective, 2:513b
Chronicle, 6:244a-b
chronographic list of, 9:132a
Contra Eusebium et Epiphanidem, 9:132a
De magnete, 9:132a
George the Monk and, 5:401b
on icons, 2:463a, 3:631a, 6:398b–399a
on Leo III, 6:402a
Refutatio et eversio, 9:132a
regulation of monastic establishments, 8:457b
theology of, 9:132a
in Theophanes Confessor's *Chronographia,* 12:22b
works of, 9:131b–132a

Nikephoros I, Byzantine emperor, **9:132b**
allelengyon and, 1:189b
Bulgarian conflicts, 2:401a, 488b
hikanati and, 11:573b
Irene and, 6:520b
patriarch Nikephoros and, 9:131b
Venice and, 12:385a-b
vs. Krum, 7:303b, 304a
Nikephoros II Phokas, Byzantine emperor, **9:132b–133a**
Basil II and, 2:118a
coinage of, 8:419b
De velitatione bellica, 10:59b
described by Liutprand of Cremona, 7:634b
Empress Theophano and, 12:24a
as hero in Joshua Roll, 7:152b
al-Lādhiqiya and, 7:315a-b
reconquest of Crete, 3:678b, 9:75b
reign of, 9:132b–133a
reliquary of the True Cross made for, 7:26b
social and economic policies, 2:490a-b
soldiers' portions and, 11:360a
Tarsus and, 11:599b
tetarteron and, 4:494a
see also Macedonians
Nikephoros III Botaneiates, Byzantine emperor
coinage of, 8:420b
panegyric on by Michael Attaleiates, 8:304a
revolt against, 7:283b–284a
Nikephoros Basilakios, edition of panegyrics, 10:349b
Nikephoros Blemmydes
Byzantine culture and, 9:117b
Filioque controversy, 9:562a
Nikephoros Bryennios, **9:133a**
Alexios I Kommenos and, 9:133a
glorification of Alexios, 6:246a
marriage to Anna Komnena, 1:303a-b
Material for History, 2:514b
Nikephoros Choumnos, 1:246a, 9:698b
Nikephoros Chrysoberges, poetry, 2:507b
Nikephoros Ethikos, 8:555b
Nikephoros Gregoras, 1:246a, 614a, 5:672b, **9:133b**, 9:698b
as an orator, 10:350b
astrolabe treatises, 11:634a-b
Roman History, 2:516b, 9:133b
theological controversy, 6:247a-b
Nikephoros the Hesychast, 9:7b
Nikephoros Kallistos Xanthopoulos, church history, 2:517a
Nikephoros Ouranos, vs. Samuil, 2:119a
Nikephoros Phokas (grandfather of Nikephoros II), 2:118a
Niketas Acominatus. *See* Niketas Choniates
Niketas (Bogomil priest), 3:183b, 185a
Niketas (Byzantine physician), collection of surgical illustrations of, 8:245b
Niketas Choniates, 5:660b, **9:133b–134b**
Alexiad
continuation of, 2:515a
language and style, 2:515b
sources for, 2:515a
view of historical causation, 2:515a-b
collection of panegyrics, 10:349b
histories of, 6:246b, 7:597a, 9:134a
Thesaurus of Orthodoxy, 9:134a
Vlachs and, 12:483b
Niketas of Constantinople
Bogomilism and, 2:296a
organization of Western Cartharism, 6:196b
Niketas of Herakleia, 11:52a
Niketas Stethatos, on the use of azymes in the Eucharist, 2:31b
Nikitin, Afanasii, **9:134b–135b**
Journey Beyond Three Seas, 11:347b
Nikiu, battle at, 6:569b
Niklot of Mecklenburg, conquest of Lübeck, 7:680a
Nikolaos I Mystikos, patriarch of Constantinople, 1:500b, 510b, 2:404b–405a, 5:339b, **9:135a–136a**
first patriarchate of, 9:135b
second patriarchate of, 9:135b
Symeon of Bulgaria and, 11:555a
Tome of Union, 9:135b
see also Macedonians
Nikolaos Kavasilas (Cabasilas), **9:135a**
Life in Christ, 9:7b
Zealots and, 12:743a
Nikolaos Mesarites, **9:136a-b**
on Church of the Holy Apostles (Constantinople), 9:136a
Nikolaus von Bueren, tomb of, 7:306a
Nikolaus von Dinkelsbühl, influence of on Michel Beheim, 8:306b
Nikorcᶜminda, 5:410a (*illus.*), **9:136b**
east facade, 9:136a (*illus.*)
Nikulás saga leikara, 10:395b
Nil Sorsky, St., **9:136b–137a**
defense of monastic poverty, 10:595b–596a
Predanie, 9:137a
Ustav, 9:137a
Nilant, Frédéric, *Romuli fabulae Aesopiae,* 4:573a
Nile River, **9:137a–138b**
in allegory, 9:138a
in *Divine Comedy,* 9:137b
Egyptian character and, 9:138b
flooding measurements, 12:223b
geographical speculations about, 9:137b–138a
al-Ḥākim's project of regulation, 11:83b
information about restricted by al-Muᶜizz, 5:25b
Islamic communications and, 10:426a
Nubia and, 9:197b
observed by travelers, 9:138a-b
see also Famine; Feasts and festivals, Islamic
Nilometer, 9:138a-b
Nilus of Ancyra, St., *Sententiae,* 1:508b
Nilus of Rossano, St., eremitical tradition, 7:4b–5a
Nilus of Sinai, St., writings of Evagrius Ponticus and, 9:6b
Nimbus, **9:138b–139a**
cruciform, 9:138b
in *Majestas Domini,* 8:54b
origin of in art, 4:354b
square, 9:138b
triangular, 9:138b
see also Mandorla
Nine Books on the Romans' Famous Deeds and Sayings. See Valerius Maximus
Nine Heroes (tapestry), 11:596a (*illus.*), 596b
Nine Heroes (woodcut), 12:692b
Nineveh, in Islamic conquests, 6:569a
Ninfale fiesolano. See Boccaccio, Giovanni
Ninian, St., **9:139a-b**
in Bede's *Ecclesiastical History,* 9:139a
cult of, 9:139b
in *Miraculi Ninie episcopi,* 9:139a
missionary work of, 8:439b
Niño, Don Pero
biography by Gutierre Díez de Games, 11:433a
raid on the English coast, 11:421a
Nino, St., 1:519b, **9:140a-b**
Conversion of Iberia, 5:413a
legend of, 5:412b, 413a, 417b
Niphon (Cappadocian monk), imprisoned for preaching Bogomilism, 2:296a
Niš, taken by the Ottomans, 11:181a
Nisart, Pedro, **9:140b**
van Eyck and, 9:140b
Nish. *See* Naissus
Nishapur, **9:140b–141b**, 11:228a
ceramics of, 6:603a
founded, 9:140a
ḥadīth travel and, 12:147b
refounded, 9:141a
taken by Toghrıl, 11:151b
under Arabs, 9:140b–141a
under Sasanians, 9:140b
vs. Yaᶜqūb ibn Layth, 12:717a
Yaᶜqūb and, 11:575b
Nisi prius, **9:141b**
in Statutes of Westminster, 12:622b
see also English common law, development (after 1272)
Nisibis, **9:141b–142b**
besieged by Persians, 9:142a
burned (972), 9:142a
as a center of Nestorianism, 9:106b
commerce of, 9:142a
as transit point in Byzantine-Sasanian trade, 12:97a
Nisibis, Peace of (298), 1:475b, 515a, 5:405a, 10:668a
Nisibis, School of, 11:564b
Nissim ben Jacob ben Nissim ibn Shahin, 7:98a, 172b–173a
Elegant Composition Concerning Relief After Distress, 8:23a
Miftāḥ Maghāliq al-Talmūdh, 7:162a
Nithard, **9:142b–143b**
De dissensionibus filiorum Ludovici Pii, evidence of French language, 5:220b
Historiarum libri IV, 9:142b–143a, 143b
Strasbourg oaths in, 11:488a
on military tactics, 3:202b
Nið, 11:321a

Nítida saga, 10:394b, 395b
Nivardus of Fleury, **9:143b–144a**
Nivardus of Ghent
Fortuna, 12:734b
Ysengrimus, 2:141a-b, 4:496a, 7:366b, **12:732b–735a**
Niwalden, geography, 11:540b
Nīya. *See* Fasting, Islamic
Niẓām al-Mulk, 1:203a, 6:503b–504a, **9:144a-b**
achievements of, 9:144a
Alp Arslan and, 11:152a
Book of Government, 10:13b
al-Ghazālī and, 9:41b
Isfahan and, 6:562a
madrasas and, 6:606a, 8:11a, 11:85a
murder of, 6:617a, 9:144a
as patron of schools, 11:66a
religious architecture and, 11:146a–148b (*illus.*)
Siyāsat-nāma, 6:250b, 8:436a, 9:144a
on Alptigin, 1:220a
under Malikshāh I, 11:153a
see also Malikshāh
Niẓāmī, 6:507a-b, 11:598a
Alexander epic, 11:628b
Haft paykar, 6:507a
Khamsa, 6:408a, 8:117a
cavalry charge of Alexander the Great, 12:551b (*illus.*)
Khusraw u Shīrīn, 6:507a
Laylā and Majnūn (*Laylī u Majnūn*), 5:418a, 6:507a, 11:256b
Sharaf-nāma/Iqbāl-nāma, 6:507a-b
Niẓāmīya, 9:144a
al-Ghazālī in, 5:515b–516a
Nizamiyas. *See* Madrasa
Nizār (son of al-Mustanṣir), 6:617a
followers of, 1:590a-b
Nizārīs, 6:587b, 588a-b, 617a, 618a, 11:137b–138a
Ismailism and, 11:227b
see also Assassins
Nizhni Novgorod-Suzdal grand princes, coinage of, 8:426b
Njáls saga, 4:612b, 613b, 614a,b, **9:144b–146a**
compared with *Sturlunga saga,* 11:500b
dialogue in, 4:617a
flyting in, 9:173a, 173b
fylgja in, 5:335b–336a
historicity of, 9:145b–146a
Kristni saga in, 7:303a
plots of, 9:144b–145a
popularity of, 9:146a
as a sequel to *Laxdœla saga,* 7:528a-b
structure of, 9:145a
Þórðar saga Hreðu and, 12:48b
Njǫrðr, 5:296b, **9:146a–147a,** 11:25b–26a, 12:356a, 356b
Mímir and, 8:395b
Skaði and, 11:325a-b
see also Scandinavian mythology
Noah, Barbar and, 2:185b
Noah's Ark, 1:422a
Hugh of St. Victor and, 6:322b
Nobadia, 9:197b
administration, 9:198a
relations with Egypt, 9:198a
under Ottomans, 9:198b
Nobiles, 7:276a–277b
emergence of, 7:276a-b
see also Knights
Nobility and nobles, **9:147a–152a**
aggrandizement of, 9:149b
Anglo-Saxon, 9:148a
Armenian, 1:488a-b, 489a-b, 490a, 490b, 4:506a, **9:90a-b,** 9:91a
cavalry and, 3:198b–199a
Mongols and, 1:486a
naχarar system, 3:199a, 393b
Nersēs I the Great and, 9:101b
P^{c}awstos Buzand's *History of Armenia* on, 9:473a
rebellion against *marzpans,* 8:169a
under Zak^{c}arids, 1:485b
see also Azat; Tanutēr
Austrasian, 9:148a
in Bavaria, 2:134a-b, 135a, 135b, 9:148a
Nuremberg and, 9:201b
in Bohemia, 2:301a-b
barons, 6:377a
Hussite, 6:372a, 373b–374a, 377a
vs. Wenceslas IV, 6:365a-b
Burgundian, Flanders and, 12:731b
Byzantine
economic expansion, 2:477a-b
family life, 4:595b
Great Palace of Constantinople and, 3:552b–553a
in Macedonia, 2:479b
power of, 2:499b–500a
pro- and anti-Latin factions, 2:496a-b
reforms affecting, 2:487b, 490a
in Thessaly, 2:479a-b
in Thrace, 2:479b
vs. Isaac II Angelos, 6:560a
see also Dunatoi
Cadira del honor and, 10:439a
in Canary Islands, Spanish nobility, 3:63a
Carolingian, 9:148a-b
in Castile, 3:136a-b, 139b, 9:151a
chivalry and, 3:303a
class structure (1000–1300), 3:412a–414b
class structure (1300–1500), 3:419b, 420b–421b, 427b–428a
confessors for, 3:534b–535b
congé d'élire and, 3:536b–537a
constable of the realm and, 3:543b–544a
costume, colors in, 4:328a-b
courtesy books for, 3:660b–667a
in crusades
First Crusade, 4:33b–34a, 36a-b
Fourth Crusade, 4:42a
in Denmark, 4:154a–155a, 155b, 156a
derogation of, 9:149a-b
economic development and, 9:151a-b
in Egypt, 10:453b, 454a
in England
baronial control over wardrobe, 6:303a-b
court leet and justice system, 3:659b–660b
dukes, 4:304a
earls, 3:659a
kings and, 12:569a-b
local constabularies, 3:542b–543b
Magna Carta and excommunication of, 3:640a-b
Wessex, 9:148a
see also Baron
expansion of landholdings, 11:674b
familial longevity of, 9:149b
family life, 4:602a-b
folklore and, 8:27b–28a
in France
baronial rivalry in 12th century, 5:161b–162a
bastide and, 2:128b
Charles V and, 3:269b–270a
Charles VII and, 3:271a-b
factional conflict in 14th century, 5:180b–181a
government policies benefitting, 5:181a
Hundred Years War, 9:151a
opposition to John II, 5:184b
Provençal, 6:475a
revolt of in Champagne, 3:250a
Song of Roland and, 10:445b, 447b
taxation of, 11:622b–623a
troubadours and, 7:340b
Frankish-Roman, 9:147b
in Georgia
erist^{c}aw and, 4:506a
vs. Tamar, 11:587a
in Germany
Denmark and, 4:154b, 155a
growth in power (9th century), 5:474a-b
ministerials and, 8:406a-b
opposition to monarchy, 5:477b
role in government, 5:490a-b
in Granada, 5:653b
in Hundred Years War, 6:333a-b, 334b, 9:151a
in Hungary
Andrew II and, 6:341b
Andrew III and, 6:342b–343b
Angevins and, 6:344a, 344b–345a
barons in, 6:342b–343a, 344a
diet and, 6:335b–336a
hunting as privilege of, 1:300b–301a, 6:356a
in Iberian Peninsula, parliamentary institutions for, 3:611a–612b
ideal of courtly love, 3:668b–669a
Idrisid, 6:414a
ill defined, 9:147a, 150a
interdict and, 6:496a
in Iran, importance of hunting, 6:354b
in Ireland
Anglo-Irish, and bardic poetry, 6:536b–537a
Anglo-Irish, and Gaelic families, 6:519b–520a
Anglo-Norman families, 6:518b, 554a-b
in Italy
condottieri, 3:531a-b
Guelph-Ghibelline conflict, 6:6b
Milan, 8:378a-b
relationship to communes, 3:571a-b
Sienese, 11:278b

Sienese and Guelphism, 11:279b
Jewish, 3:578a
in Kingdom of Jerusalem, 9:150b
knights. *See* Knights and knight service
law codes and, 9:147b
marriage and, 4:145b–146a
Merovingian, 3:658b
minor, 9:148b
music and, 8:595a–596a, 634b–635a
in *Nativitas rusticorum et qualiter debent tractari,* 6:658a
new, 9:150b–151a
Norman, 9:162b–163a
dispersion of, 9:164b
in Norway, 9:181b–182a
Ostrogothic, 9:147b
pages, training of, 3:661a-b
pilgrimage by the feudal, 9:656a-b
private armies, 12:556a
representative assemblies of. *See* Representative assemblies
Roman, 9:147b–148a
Angevins and, 10:524a
domus cultae and, 10:525a
in ecclesiastical hierarchy, 10:522a, 524b
German emperors and, 10:522b
papacy and, 10:521b, 522a–523a
prior to papal state, 10:525a
revolutions of, 10:524b
in Romania, 10:511a
royal representatives, counts, 3:658a–659a
in Russia
Argutinskiĭ-Dolgorukids and, 12:737a
see also Boyars
Saxon, 8:405a
serfs as, 11:205b
in Sicily, 11:261a, 269a, 275b
Charles of Anjou and, 11:272b
Frederick II of Aragon and, 11:273b
Frederick II of Sicily and, 11:270a, 270b, 271a
social mobility and. *See* Social mobility
in Spain, hunting and, 6:358a
Swabian, 11:526b, 527a
in Sweden
Albrecht of Mecklenburg and, 11:532b
church and, 11:531b
Earl Birger and, 11:530b–531a
Erik of Pomerania and, 11:533a
Magnus Eriksson and, 11:532b
royalty and, 11:530b
vs. Birger Magnusson, 11:532a
in Switzerland, 11:538a-b
taille and, 11:579a
Visigothic, 9:147b, 12:472b, 473a
women, courtesy books for, 3:663b–664a, 664a
see also Baron; Dukes; Earl; Knights; Magnates; Parlement of Paris; Parliament, English; Squire; Women, noble
Nobis quoque, 8:193a-b
"Noble sultanate," term used for Mamluk dynasty, 8:71a
Nocturales. See Lectionary
Nocturn. *See* Mass cycles; Monastery; Vigils
Noeane, 8:639a
Noeannoe, **9:152a-b**, 11:363a
antiphons and, 9:152b
creation of, 8:449b
echemata and, 9:152a
melismas and, 9:152b
tonaries and, 12:70a
Noël, 3:116a
Nofri de Giunta, 6:475a
Nogaj Tatars, 2:410b–411b, 11:474b
destroyed by the Mongols, 11:176a
Nogaret, Guillaume de, 7:137a, **9:152b–153b**
arrest of Boniface VIII, 2:324a, 9:554b–555a
Boniface VIII's bull *Ausculta fili* and, 2:4a
Clement V and, 3:644a
kingship theories of, 7:267b
property of, 9:153b
rise of, 9:153a
Nogent-sous-Coucy, abbots, 6:9a
Noghay (Noghai), 5:573a
foreign policy, 8:475b
Golden Horde under, 5:573a
Noie. See Pateg, Girard
Noirmoutier, as Viking base, 12:430a
Nola, mosaics in the churches of, 8:91a
Noli, Antonio da, 4:561b
Noli me tangere, **9:153b–154a**
Resurrection cycle and, 10:340a-b
Nomads
Eastern European, Rome and, 10:465a
Islamic, rugs and carpets of, 10:550b
Near Eastern, Rome and, 10:464a
North African, Rome and, 10:464a
plagues and, 9:685b–686a
Syrian, 4:81a-b
textiles, 11:716a
Nome, Egyptian, 10:454a, 454b
Nomen mentale, 3:510a
Nomen sacrum, **9:154a-b**
Nomenoë, rule of Brittany, 2:378b–379a
Nominalism, 1:464a, 467a-b, **9:155a–158a**
of Abelard, 9:155a-b
at Cologne, 9:157b
at Louvain, 9:157b
at Merton College, 12:44a
at Oxford, 9:157a
at Paris, 1:464b, 9:157a, 157b
of Cajetan of Thiene, 1:465a
compared with Thomism, 12:42b, 43b
of Gregory of Rimini, 5:672a
impact on physics, 9:626b–627a
of Ockham, 9:156a, 210b–211b, 614a–615a
real vs. inhering qualities, 9:614a-b
revived, 9:155b–156a
Roscelinus' theory of universals, 10:531b–532a
terminism and, 11:686b–687a
theology and, 9:155b, 156b
theory of universals and, 12:637b
Thomism in England and, 12:41b
of Walter Burley, 2:432b–433a
see also Biel, Gabriel; Universals; *Via moderna*
Nomisma, 4:301a (*illus.*), 8:418b–419b (*illus.*), 420b, **9:158a**
coin weights and, 12:581a
Constantine I and, 10:460b
see also Solidus
Nomisma hyperpyron. See Hyperpyron
Nomocanon, 7:394b, **9:158a–159a**
codes of, 9:158b
commentary on by Theodore Balsamon, 12:14b
as penitential, 9:158b
translated into Serbian, 11:174b, 473b
Nomocanon in Fifty Titles, 9:158b
Nomocanon in XIV Titles. See Enantiophanes; Photios
see also Law, canon, Byzantine
Nomophylax (head of Byzantine imperial law school), 12:14b
Nomos Rodion nautikos. See Rhodian Sea Law
"Non al suo amante." *See* Jacobus of Bologna
"Non-Sleepers" monastery, Divine Office in, 7:611a
Nonannoeane. See Noeannoe
Nonantola (monastery: Lombardy), 11:336a
Huguccio and, 6:327b
Noncontradiction, principle of, Ockham and, 9:210b, 213a
None (canonical hours), 3:67a, 4:229a
Nonius Marcellus, *De compendiosa doctrina,* 3:432a
Nonnberg (church: Strassburg), 10:507a
"Nonpossessors," Nil Sorsky and, 9:136b
Nor Getik (monastery: Armenia), founded, 8:656b
Noravank^{c} at Amału, **9:159a**
Norbert of Iburg, *Vita Bennonis II episcopi Osnabrugensis,* **9:159a**
Norbert of Xanten, St., 3:354b
canonization of, 10:87a
on the idea of reform, 10:285a
life of, 10:84b–85a
Premonstratensian rite and, 10:83b–84a
Premonstratensians and, 10:84b–87a, 12:685a-b
Norbertine translator of Ruusbroec, 9:36b–37a
Nordic Union, Norway and, 9:185a-b
Nördlingen, Frederick II and, 11:528a
Nóregs konungatal, 7:312a
Norfolk, duke of, John Paston II and, 9:450b
Noria. *See Nā^{c}ūra*
Noricum, 2:4b, 133a-b
Celts in, 10:465a
Norman Anonymous, 7:263b
on married clergy, 3:217a
see also York tractates
"Norman" helmet. *See* Helmet
Norman inquest, 7:435b–436b
Norman law
administration of, 9:166a, 167b, 169a
codes, 4:68b–69b
serfdom and, 11:205a
see also French law, in North

"Norman" shield. *See* Shield
Normandy, duchy of, 9:150b, **9:159a–170b**, 9:160 (map)
administration, 9:161a–162a
office of bailli, 2:53a-b
office of seneschal and, 11:160a
under Carolingians, 9:161b–162a
chronicles, 12:639b
conquest of (1415–1420), 6:332a, 333b
establishment under Carolingians, 5:156b
Exchequer of, 9:420b
pipe rolls, 9:663a-b
financial administration, 10:537b
rights of lordship, 5:168b
under French rule, 5:168a
French monarchy and, 9:163b–164a, 166a, 169a
annexation to Capetian royal domain, 5:164b
conflict with Louis VI, 7:673b
integration into French kingdom, 5:168a-b
Philip II Augustus, 9:168a-b, 417b
geography of, 9:159b
Hundred Years War and, 9:169b
lack of naval forces, 9:79b
Louis XI and, 10:322b–323a
Peace of God and, 9:474b
Philippe de Vitry and, 12:481a
plagues in, 9:678b–679a, 680b–681a
power of, 9:162a–163b
provincial estates and assemblies, 10:324b–325a, 327a
recovery of local jurisdiction, 5:159b
relations with
Anjou, 9:168a
Brittany, 9:164a
England, 6:331b, 332b, 9:165a–168a, 166a, 166b–168a
Poitou, 9:168a
representative assemblies under English rule, 10:320a–321a, 322a-b
Richard I's campaign against Philip II Augustus, 10:384a
settlement of, 12:431b–432a
succession of, 9:162a, 166b–167a
territorial expansion, 9:161a, 164b
in England, 9:165a, 165b
under Angevins, 9:167a–168a
under William I, 9:165a–166b
wealth of, 9:162b
see also Feudalism; French law, in north
Normannensequenz, 6:384a
Normans, **9:159a–170b**
in Byzantine Empire, 6:559b
cavalry tactics at Hastings, 3:203b, 6:111b (*illus.*)
conquest of Dyrrachium, 11:171b
conquest of England, 4:459b–461b, 9:165a-b
Anglo-Norman institutions, 4:461b, 463b–465a
Battle of Hastings, 6:111a–112b, 12:560b
Latin literature and, 7:364b
legitimacy of rule asserted, 5:244a-b
London, building construction in, 7:660b
mercenary troops, 12:559a
proposed again in 1339, 9:169b
questions of dynastic succession, 4:394a-b
unification of, 6:156a
conquest of Sicily, 9:75b, 12:560a
conquest of southern Italy, 4:345b–346a
development of medicine in Salerno and, 8:256a
conquest of Thessaloniki, 12:26b
conquest of Wales, 12:516b–517b, 525b–526b
emigration to England and Scotland, 11:104b
in Italy, 1:229a
Leo IX and, 7:543b
Lombards and, 11:264a
Naples and, 9:58a-b
Romanesque architecture and, 10:486b
Rome, 10:523a
Sicily, 10:440a–441a
vs. Leo IX, 11:265b
language of, 6:437b
mercenary troops, in foreign armies, 12:560a
military campaigns, 6:111a–112a
Byzantium, 2:494b
Thessaloniki, 2:496b
military organization
feudalism, 12:560a–561a
fyrd, 12:560b
size of armies, 12:560a
Ordericus Vitalis on, 9:261a
papacy and, 11:265b
pilgrimages of, 9:656a
Seville and, 11:213b
in Sicily, *see also* Sicily, Kingdom of
taxation, 11:612a–613a
textile industry, fulling mills, 11:707a
Venice and, 12:386b, 389a
vs. Byzantines, at Bari, 11:265b
see also Robert Guiscard
Norna-Gests þáttr, 5:368b, **9:170b–171b**, 12:2b, 4b
Norns, **9:171b–172b**, 11:27b
in *Njáls saga,* 4:106b
Norse flyting, **9:172b–175b**
content of, 9:173b–174a
sexuality in, 9:173b–174a
works containing, 9:172b–173a
Norse kings' sagas, 4:612b, **9:175b–178b**
after *Heimskringla,* 9:177b
by monks of Þingeyrar, 9:176a-b
classification of, 10:610b
early Icelandic, 9:175b
early Norwegian, 9:175b–176a
family saga and, 4:617b, 618a
lost Icelandic texts, 9:176a
modern historiography and, 9:177b
Snorri Sturluson and, 9:177a
as sources for early *rímur,* 10:402a
þættir and, 12:2a
Norse language. *See* Old Norse language
Norse literature
Eufemiavisor and, 4:520a
folktales, Icelandic saga and, 4:617a, 617b
kings' sagas, Sturla Þórðarson and, 11:495b
poetry
divisions of, 11:317a-b
dróttkvætt as chief skaldic meter, 4:294b–295a
meter, 4:388b
see also Scandinavian literature
Norse sagas. *See* Bishops' sagas; Family sagas, Icelandic; *Fornaldarsögur;* Norse kings' sagas; *Riddarasögur*
Norsemen. *See* Vikings
North Africa
cavalry in, 3:209b
da^cwā in, 6:615b–616a
Hellenism and, 10:457b
Ibn Khaldūn on, 7:234a-b
Islamic administration of, 6:592a
in Islamic conquests, 6:572a
mints and money in, 8:423a-b
plagues in, 9:684b
Roger II and, 10:440b, 441a
under Roman Empire, 10:459a, 464a-b
Vandals and, 12:354b–356a
see also Maghrib, al-
North Britain (Brevi), Synod of, 3:229b
North Italian Services of the Eleventh Century, 10:408b
Northampton, charter for, 3:499a
Northampton, Assize of, 7:44a, 182b, 184a
established by Henry II, 7:439a-b, 442a-b
inquest and, 6:481a
Northampton, Battle of (1460), 12:570b
Northampton, John, Thomas Usk and, 12:333b–334a
Northern Homily Cycle, 4:546a, 8:315a
Northumbria
Christian missions to, 1:107a
as cultural center, 4:454b–455a
division of, 11:253b
history and migration, 4:454a-b
invaded by Malcolm III of Scotland, 8:56b
Scottish invasions under David I, 4:110b–111a, 316a-b
Vikings and, 12:432b, 433a
see also Strathclyde, kingdom of
Northumbrian language. *See* English language, Old English
Norton, Thomas, *Ordinal of Alchemy,* 1:139a
Norway, **9:179a–186a**
administration, 9:184b
civil wars, 9:182b
coronations in, 7:258a
economy, 9:180a–182a
finance, royal, 9:184a, 184b
geography, 9:179a-b
history (400–800), 10:695b–697a
archaeological evidence, 10:696a–697a
8th-century expansion, 10:697a
similarities to Denmark and Sweden, 10:697a
kingship, 9:183b
succession, 9:182b, 185a
Magnus Eriksson and, 11:532a

navigation in the North Atlantic and, 9:87b
plagues in, 9:677b
political and legal organization, 10:699a
population, 9:179b–180b, 184a
in towns, 9:184b
relations with
Denmark, 9:182b, 185a, 185b
Iceland, 7:386b
Sweden, 9:185a
royal educational policies, *Trójumanna saga* and, 12:207b
runic alphabet, 10:558a, 565a, 567a
Snorri Sturluson's trip to, 11:356b
social structure, 9:181b–182b, 183b
territorial expansion, 9:179b
trade and commerce, with Germany, 6:91b
unification, 9:182b–185a
hirð and, 9:183a
under Harald Fairhair, 6:97a
union with Iceland, 6:395b–396b
see also Scandinavia; Scandinavian literature; Viking navigation; Vikings
Norwegian church
church-state relations, 9:181b–182a, 182a-b
history, 9:183a-b
national unification and, 9:183a-b
Norwegian language, of Oslo, 6:437a
Norwegian law
codes, 9:183b, 184a
Gulathing, 12:32a
in Iceland, 6:396a
Norwegian literature
poetry, influence on *Guðrúnarkviða* cycle, 6:37b–38a, 38b
see also Sagas; Scandinavian literature
Norwegian synoptics, 9:175b–176a, 177a
Norwegians
in Ireland, 4:554b
in Italy, 4:554b
in Mediterranean, 4:554a-b
in Spain, 4:554b
see also Vikings
Norwich, mystery play cycle of, 8:658a
Norwich Cathedral, 10:484a, 484b
master mason John Ramsey, 10:256b
mechanical clock at, 3:460b–461a
Nosce vias Domini. *See* Hildegard of Bingen, St., *Scivias*
Nostre Dame, Quinze joies de. *See* *Quinze joies de Nostre Dame*
Nota Emilianense, 11:438a
Notabilia, 4:127b
Notabilia ad Compilationem quartam. *See* Peter of Spain
Notarial archives. *See* Archives, notarial
Notaries
at the Châtelet, 3:279a
in Cyprus, 4:71b
papal, 10:526a
Rome, 10:526a
in southern France, 7:462b–463a
validation of documents and, 11:126b–127a
Nöteburg, Peace of (1323), 11:532a
Notger of Liège, **9:186a,** 10:95a
Notitia artis musicae. See Jehan des Murs
Notitia dignitatum, **9:186a-b,** 10:459a, 459b
on Roman cavalry, 3:201b
Notitia ecclesiarum urbis Romae, 10:520b
Notke, Bernt, **9:186b–187a**
Notker Balbulus, 8:640a, **9:187a–188a**
Breviarium regum Francorum, 9:187b
Formulae Sangallenses miscellaneae, 9:187b
Gesta Caroli, 9:187a
on hunting, 6:356a-b
hymns of, 6:381b
Liber hymnorum, 9:187b, 12:211a
dating of, 11:163b
reconstruction of, 11:164a
literary texts of, 9:187a-b
musical texts of, 9:187b–188a
Psallat ecclesia, 9:187b
rhythmical sequence and, 7:363a
"Romanus letters" and, 8:625a
Sancti spiritus assist nobis gratia, 9:187b
sequence and, 7:375b–376a
"Sermo S. Galli," 9:187b
Tuotilo of St. Gall and, 12:225a-b
Vita S. Galli, 9:187b
see also Sequence (prosa)
Notker Labeo. *See* Notker Teutonicus
Notker of St. Gall. *See* Notker Teutonicus
Notker Teutonicus, 2:174a, 5:426b, **9:188a–190b**
Cantica veteris et novi testamenti, 9:189a
Computus, 9:189a
De arte rhetorica, 9:189a
De definitione, 9:189a
De musica, 9:.189a
De partibus logicae, 9:189a
De syllogismis, 9:189a
liberal arts and, 4:578b
patients treated by, 8:247b
Principia arithmeticae, 9:189a
style of, 9:189b
translations, prose style, 9:233a
Noto, fall of (1091), 10:440a
Notoriety, conviction by, 6:427b–428a
Notre Dame (abbey church: Bernay), 10:482a
Notre Dame de la Basse Oeuvre (church: Beauvais), 10:92b
Notre Dame (cathedral: Amiens). *See* Amiens Cathedral
Notre Dame (cathedral: Chartres). *See* Chartres Cathedral
Notre Dame (cathedral: Noyon), 10:488b
Notre Dame (cathedral: Paris), **9:190b–191a**
architects of, 7:52a
late sequence production in, 11:167a
organist, 9:274a
restoration of, 9:191a
rose windows, 8:584 (*illus.*), 12:625 (*illus.*), 626a
sculptors of, 7:53b
sculptures, 1:431a, 9:190b–191a
transept facades, 3:91a
see also Notre Dame School (music)
Notre Dame (cathedral: Rheims). *See* Rheims Cathedral
Notre Dame (cathedral: Senlis), 5:593b, 617 (*illus.*), 619a–620a
exemplar of "Style 1200," 5:619a-b
portal celebrating the Virgin, 5:619a
sculpture
drapery, 5:619a, 620a
naturalistic style in, 5:619a, 621b
Notre Dame (cathedral: Sens), 5:586b, 592b, 593b, 10:475b
stained glass in, 5:549a
Notre Dame (cathedral: Soissons), 10:488b
Notre Dame (cathedral: Tournai), 10:488b
Notre Dame (church: Beaune), 10:479a
Notre Dame (church: Jumièges), 10:482a, 482b
Notre Dame (church: Tartūs), 4:25b
Notre Dame la Grande (church: Poitiers), 10:481a, 495a
Notre Dame notation (musical). *See* Musical notation
Notre Dame (parish church: Paris), 9:190b
Notre Dame du Port (church: Clermont-Ferrand), 10:480a (*illus.*)
Notre Dame School, MS Pluteus 29.1, motet collections, 8:505a
Notre Dame School (music), 2:167b, 8:570a, 594a, **9:191a–192b**
ars antiqua, 1:543a-b
chancellorship, 9:556b
copula in repertory of, 3:596a
De mensuris et discantu and, 8:645a
genres of, 9:191b
manuscript sources of, 9:191b
manuscripts of, discant polyphonic snippets in, 9:507a
measured music and, 8:643a-b
modal notation and, 8:628a-b
motet, development of, 8:501b
MS Pluteus 29.1, **5:104a–107a**
Boethius' division of music illustrated, 5:106b
clausulae in, 5:104b–105b
conductus in, 5:104b, 106a
contents of, 5:104a-b
Léonin's works in, 5:105a-b
modal notation in, 5:104a
motets in, 5:106a-b
organa in, 5:105a-b
ownership of, 5:106b
Pérotin's works in, 5:104a–105a, 106a
Philip the Chancellor's texts in, 5:106a
recomposition examples in, 5:105b
rondeaux (rondelli) in, 5:106b
organum purum, 10:651a
polyphonic genera, *organum,* 9:276b
polyphonic repertory at, 3:532a-b
see also Leoninus; *Magnus liber organi; "Viderunt omnes"*
Notre-Dame-aux-Fonts (church: Liège), baptismal font of, 8:284b, 495a (*illus.*)

Notrgir (Armenian cursive script), 1:492b
Nottingham
granted the right to elect a mayor (1284), 8:235a
Robin Hood and, 10:436a, 436b
Nouvelle, **9:192b**
development of, 5:287b
Nova musica. *See* Ciconia, Johannes
Nova vulgata, 12:496a
Novae machinae. *See* Verantius, Faustus
Novales. *See* Reclamation of land
Novarank^{c} at Amatu, **9:159a**
Novel, first European, 11:423b–424a
Novel disseisin. *See* Seisin, Disseisin
Novella
Boccaccio and, 6:660b–661a
see also Nouvelle
Novellae. *See Corpus iuris civilis*
Novellino, 6:658b, 659a-b
Novellus musicae artis tractatus. *See* Conrad of Zabern
Noves rimades, in Catalan narrative in verse, 3:173a-b
Noves rimades comediades, 3:174a
Novgorod, **9:192b–197a**
administration, 9:194b–195a
Andrei Bogoliubskii and, 2:293b
annexation by Muscovy, 4:306a, 8:540b, 545a, 546b, 9:197a
archaeology of, 9:195b
art and architecture, 10:584a
ecclesiastical, 10:579a-b
icons, 10:589a-b
political disruption, 10:585b
churches
Church of the Savior, 4:341a
St. George monastery church, 9:512b (*illus.*)
Transfiguration Church frescoes, 12:23b
decline of Kievan Rus and, 7:249b
defeated, 9:196a, 196b
founded, 4:555a
geography, 9:193a
industries, 9:195b
Jews in, 7:100b
military aristocracy, Muscovite suzerainty, 8:548b
mint at, 8:427a
music of, 8:573a
pilgrimage and, 9:653b
politics, 9:193b–195a
population, 9:193a
relations with
Karelia, 11:531a
neighboring states, 9:193a-b, 195a-b, 196a–197a
Sweden, 11:531a, 531b, 532a
Vladimir-Suzdal, 12:487a
Rurik's rule of, 7:246b, 10:571a
social structure, 9:194b–195a
Tatar raids, 8:541b
trade and commerce, 4:587b, 9:195a-b
with Baltic, 7:249b, 250b
fur trade, 5:329a–330a, 460b
treaty of 1189, 6:90b
Vikings and, 12:434a–435a
see also Lithuania
Novgorod Cathedral
architectural elements, 10:579a
bronze relief on door of, 12:372a (*illus.*)
Greek-cross design of, 4:341a
south facade, 10:579b (*illus.*)
Novgorod Judicial Charter, 7:507a
civil law in, 7:511b–512a
criminal law in, 7:511a
documentary evidence preferred under, 7:508b
ordeal under, 7:509a
procedure, 7:508b–509b
witnesses, 7:508b–509a
Novo Brdo, 11:180b, 182b
silver mine at, 11:175a, 176b
Novo ordem. *See* Aviz, Order of
Novodevichy Monastery, cathedral, architectural style, 10:582a
Novoprikhodtsy, 11:191a, 191b
Novus Aesopus. *See* Neckham, Alexander
Novus Avianus. *See* Neckham, Alexander
Now Is Hay Sometime Was Grass. *See* Lydgate, John
Nowell Codex, 1:277a
Noyon Cathedral (France), 12:187b–188a (*illus.*)
Nozeroy, Chateau of Chalon-Arlay, 2:426b
Np^{c}kert. *See* Martyropolis
Nuachrotha (*Nuachrutha:* new meters), 6:531b
in religious literature, 6:541b
Nubia, **9:197a–200a**
administration, 9:198a-b
architecture, 9:199b
area of, 3:314a
Christianity in, **3:314a–315b**
Arabic sources for, 3:314b–315a
Coptic missionaries, 3:595b
evidence of, 3:314b–315a
Melkites, 3:314b
Monophysitism, 3:314b
commerce, 9:198a
conquered by Baybars, 2:138b
geography, 9:197a-b
kingdom of, 3:314a-b
kingship, succession, 9:198a
Mamluks and, 9:198b
Monophysite missions, 8:479a
relations with Egypt, 9:197b, 10:453b
Nubian church, 9:198b–199a
Nubian language, 9:199a
Christian church and, 3:315b
Nucio, Martin, printing of *Cancionero de romances,* 11:429b
Nuclear family
Byzantine, 4:593b, 594a
Islamic, 4:596b
Nūḥ ibn Manṣūr, Samanid emir, 11:302b
military threats, 10:638a–639a
Nukkār, 11:139b
Nu^{c}mān II, Lakhmid ruler, vs. Byzantium, 7:320b
Nu^{c}mān III, Lakhmid ruler, 7:320b, 321a
Nu^{c}mān, Abū Ḥanifa (qadi, *d.* 974), *Da^{c}ā$^{\supset}$im al-islām fi'l-ḥalāl wa'l-ḥarām,* 6:616b
Number symbolism
in isorhythm, 6:619b
in *Pearl,* 9:477a
runes, 10:559a
Numbers
in God's mind. *See* Boethius, *De institutione arithmetica*
realism theories and, 10:270b
see also Arabic numerals; Roman numerals
Numenius of Apamea, 9:95b
Numera, 11:573a
Numerology
Arabic alphabet and, 3:55a
in *De actibus apostolorum,* 1:422b
of deadly sins, 11:211b
Ismaili, 6:588a, 615a-b
Numismatics. *See* Mints and money
Nummia, 8:419a
Nuncio, papal, **9:200a-b**
compared with papal legate, 7:534b, 535b
see also Legate, papal
Nuncius
ambassador and, 4:204a-b, 206b
functions of, 4:201b–203a
Hostiensis on, 4:205a
procurator and, 4:205a
to Venice, 4:203a
Nunē, St. *See* Nino, St.
Núñez, Nicolás, sequence to Diego de San Pedro's *Cárcel de Amor,* 11:423a
Núñez, Nuño, Castile and, 3:127b
Nuns. *See* Women's religious orders
"Nun's fiddle." *See* Trumpet, marine
Nuova cronica. *See* Villani, Giovanni
Nuqaira, 8:613a
Nūr al-Dīn Maḥmud, Zangid ruler, 10:259a
Nūr al-Dīn, Zangid atabeg of Aleppo
capture of Edessa, 4:384a
in Damascus, 4:82a-b, 83b, 84a–85a
hospital built by, 6:607a
Hṙomklay and, 6:312a
initiator of mausoleum complexes in Syria, 2:21b
al-Lādhiqiya and, 7:315b
Qılıj Arslān and, 10:235b
renovation of Aleppo, 1:145b
Saladin and, 2:23a
vs. Second Crusade, 4:30b–31a, 38a,b, 39a
Nūr ḥadaqat al-abṣār. *See* Taqī al-Dīn ibn Ma^{c}rūf
Nuremberg, **9:201a–203a**
Adam Krafft's "Seven Falls of Christ" and, 11:467b
artisan poets, 10:533b, 534b–535a
carnival plays from, 4:271a-b
citizenship, 10:533b
city hall, 9:202a
culture in 15th century, 5:113b
economy, 9:202b
guilds in, 5:458b
revolution of, 9:202a
Hauptmarkt, 9:202a
as literary center, 8:359a, 360a
manufacture of scientific instruments at, 11:102b–103a
population of, 5:458a, 9:202b

production of portable sundials, 11:509b–510a
ruling elite in, 9:461a
Sigismund and, 11:287b
trade and commerce, 6:95b
water supply, 12:577b
works by Veit Stoss, 11:487 (*illus.*)
Nuremberg Chronicle (1493), 10:125b
see also Schedel, Hartmann
Nuremberg School, Middle High German literature in, 8:359b
Nurses, 4:602a
Nusaybin. *See* Nisibis
Nuṣayrīs, 9:3b–4a, 11:137a
foundation of, 11:228a
Nut gall, ink from, 6:463b
Nutrition
Byzantine. *See* Agriculture, Byzantine
effects of climate on, 3:452a–453a, 454a
food preservation, 11:639b
Islamic world
dietary laws, 4:178b–179b
see also Agriculture, Islamic world
Jewish, dietary laws, 4:180a–181a
medicinal foods, 3:582a, 582b
Mediterranean region
fruits and nuts, 5:305a–307b
maintaining food supply, 5:119b–119a
see also Agriculture, Mediterranean region
Northern Europe. *See* Agriculture, Northern Europe
Slavic world. *See* Agriculture, Slavic world
Western European
food costs as percent of annual income, 5:115a
maintaining food supply, 5:118b–119a, 121a
town residents, 5:120b–121a
see also Agriculture, Western Europe
see also Famine
Nuts. *See* Fruits and nuts
Nuwayrī, al-, on rhetoric, 10:347b
Nuzha, 8:611b
Nuzhat al-mushtāq fī 'khtirāq al-āfāq. *See* Idrīsī, al-
Nya krönikan, 7:220b
Nymphaeum, **9:203a**
Nymphaion, **9:203a-b**
fall of, 9:203a
Nymphaion, treaties of (1212, 1261), 5:385a-b, 7:347b, 9:203a
Nynias. *See* Ninian, St.
Nyons Bridge, 10:421a
Nyssa, early bishops of, 9:459a

O

O quando in cruce, 8:557a
O Roma nobilis, 7:363b, **9:206b,** 10:520b
O-T maps, 5:397b
Oar power
in galleys, 11:233b, 235a, 243a
in Northern European shipbuilding, 11:242b
in Roman ships, 11:229b
in sailing ships, 11:232a
in Viking ships, 11:240b
Oases, irrigation in, 6:556b, 558a
Oath, 3:388b–389a, **9:207a-b**
of allegiance
in Sufism, 6:585b
Sweden, 11:531a, 531b
in Armenia, 1:489a
bells and, 2:166a
breaking of, 4:573b
in canon law, 9:207a
commune and, 9:207b
in compurgation, 3:508a-b
in *enquête par turbe,* 6:480a
equity law and, 4:502b
of fealty, under William I of England, 4:461b
feudalism and, 9:207b
in German law, 7:480a
in grand assize, 6:482a
helpers, 9:207a
accusatio and, 6:478b
Ismaili, 6:587b
Landnámabók and, 9:146a
mode of proof and, 6:480a
more judaico, **9:207b–208a**
of obedience, excommunication and, 4:537b
peace, 9:473b, 474b
of purgation, 6:478b, 479b
of renunciation, 6:458a
in Roman law, 9:207a
of Romans, 10:523a
serfdom and, 11:201b
in *Sigurðarkviða in forna,* 11:291b
value of, Anglo-Saxon law, 12:617b
see also Compurgatio canonica; Compurgation; German law, early Germanic codes; Vows
Oats
as cereal crop, 1:83b, 86b
growth of, in Western Europe, 5:646b
see also Agriculture; Grain crops
Obadiah. *See* Abū ʿĪsā of Isfahan
Obadiah of Bertinoro, 7:84b
Obadiah the Proselyte, 8:565a
Obazine (Cistercian community), 12:686a
Obeco, **9:208a-b**
Obedience, *see also* Monasticism
Ober-Eschenbach, Wolfram von Eschenbach and, 12:673b
Oberland (Switzerland), 11:543a
Obikhod, 8:574b
Oblates. *See* Children, in monasteries
Obligation (logic), Swineshead and, 11:535a-b
Oboe, 8:561b, 562a
Obole (unit of measure), 12:595a
O'Brien family, 6:517a, 519b
Muireadhach Albanach and, 9:.205a
Obrok, 11:191b
Ó Brolcháin, Maol Íosa, **9:203b–204a**
Ó Bruaḍair, Dáibhidh, 6:533a
Observatory, 11:99a-b
Islamic
creation of, 11:84b–85a
decline of, 11:88b
Óbuda, University of, 6:347a, 12:289b–290a
Obwalden (Switzerland), 11:540b
Ocampo, Florián de, adaptation of *Estoria de España,* 11:425b
Occitan language. *See* Provençal language
Occitan law. *See* French law, in south
Occitania. *See* Languedoc
Occleve, Thomas. *See* Hoccleve, Thomas
Occultation (Shīʿa)
greater, 11:227b
lesser, 11:227b
Ó Ceallaigh of Uí Mhaine, Gofraidh Fionn and, 9:204b
Ochrid, 2:406b, **9:208b–209a,** 11:474b
acquired by Stefan Uroš IV Dušan of Serbia, 11:475a
as autocephalous archbishopric, 9:208b
as Bulgarian patriarchate, 10:645a
churches of, 9:209a
conquered, 9:208b
Peć and, 9:209a
Serbia and, 11:174b
see also Virgin Peribleptos (church: Ochrid)
Ockham, William of, **9:209a–214b**
against Thomism, 12:39a
Aristotelianism of, 1:464a-b, 9:209b, 212a, 214a
Biel and, 9:157b
commentary on Lombard's *Sententiae,* 9:517b
conceptualism, 3:510a
on dialectic, 4:170b
Dialogus, 3:515a
principle *Q.o.t.* and, 8:232b
education of, 9:209a-b
empiricism of, 9:212a-b
epistemology of, 9:212a-b
on ethics, 9:214a
Gabriel Biel and, 2:234a
guiding principles of, 9:210a-b
Hus and, 6:366b
interpretation of reality, 9:614b
Jean Buridan and, 2:430a-b
Landini and, 7:326b
Louis IV and, 2:135a
natural philosophy of, 9:211b–212a
nominalism of, 9:156a–157a, 210b–211b, 12:281b
Aristotelian interpretation, 9:613a, 614a, 614b–615a
impact on physics, 9:626b–627a
opposition to, 9:613b
Ordinatio, 9:209b
Peter Aureoli and, 9:513a
political philosophy of
conciliar theory, 3:515a, 10:23b
kingship theories, 7:268b–269b
on liberty and liberties, 7:556b
theory of papal authority, 4:376b, 10:23b
Reportatio, 9:209b

Ockham, William of (*cont.*)
Summa logicae, 4:170b, 9:157a, 209b, 210a, 613b
theology of, 9:156b, 210a-b, 212b–214a
Christology, 3:324a
on divine power, 9:210b, 213a
predestination, 3:371a
on transubstantiation, 9:209b, 213b–214a
use of philosophy in, 4:311a
theory of the Universal Church, 10:23a-b
Walter Burley and, 2:433a
Wyclif and, 12:710a
see also Via moderna
Ockhamism, 12:39a
compared with Thomism, 12:43b
see also Via moderna
Ockham's razor, 1:464a, 9:156b, 210b, 614b
via moderna and, 12:406a
O'Clery, Michael, 6:525a
martyrology, medieval sources used, 8:163b
O'Connor, Rory, Cinéal Eóghain and, 3:397a
O'Connors, Peter Bermingham and, 6:518b
Octar (Hunnic leader), 6:354a
Octateuch, **9:214b–215a**
iconoclasm controversy and, 9:214b
Octave (music), in art, 10:495b
Octavian (of Rome). *See* John XII, pope
Octavien de Saint-Gelais, 10:364b, 365a
Octoconch church plan. *See* Church architecture, conch type
Octoechos, 8:554b–555a, **9:215a-b**
alteration of music, 8:450a-b
Armenian modes and, 8:551b
calendaric assignments, 8:449a
cosmological basis for, 8:449a
Eastern European, 9:215a-b
eight-mode system, origins, 9:215a
Frankish-Roman chant and, 8:557a
liturgical cycles, 9:215a
melodic formulas, 9:215a
origin of, 8:449a
Slavic music and, 8:572b
traditionally attributed to St. John of Damascus, 7:612b
see also Oktoikh
Oda. See Otaq
Oda of Canterbury, **9:215b–216a**
biographies of, 9:215b–216a
education of Oswald, 9:215b
reforms of, 9:215b
Odal, 11:679b, 685b
Ó Dálaigh, Donnchadh Mór, **9:204a**
poem on Doomsday, 1:111b
Ó Dálaigh, Gofraidh Fionn, **9:204b**
Ó Dálaigh, Muireadhach Albanach, 9:204a, **9:204b–205a**, 11:114a, 114b
O'Daly family. *See* Uí Dhálaigh
Odbert of St. Bertin, abbot, 10:110b
Gospelbook illuminated by, 10:111b (*illus.*)
Oddaverja þáttr, in *Þorláks saga,* 2:252b
Oddr Snorrason, **9:216a-b**
biography of Olaf Tryggvason, 9:176b, 9:216a, 225b
Yngvars saga víðförla and, 9:216b, 12:727a
Oddrúnargrátr, **9:216b–217b**
sources for, 6:35b
Ode (Byzantine hymnody), 6:378b–379a
Odericus. *See* Oderisi, Pietro
Oderisi, Pietro, **9:217b**
tomb of Clement IV, 9:217b
Odilo of Bavaria, duke
resistance to Carolingian rule, 5:506a
submission to Pepin III, 9:501b
Odilo of Cluny, St., 3:469a, **9:217b**, 10:247a
Cluniac reforms, 9:217b
correspondence with St. Stephen I of Hungary, 11:479b
organizational reforms, 3:348a
Otto I and, 7:262a
Truce of God and, 9:474a
Odin, **9:218a–219a**, 11:25a, 29b–31b, 12:423b
in the Baldr myth, 2:55a-b, 56a
cognates of, 9:219a
divine functions, 1:63a
einherjar, 9:218b
in *fornaldarsögur,* 5:142a
Frigg as wife of, 5:301a
in *Grímnismál,* 5:676a-b, 676b–677a, 6:323a
in *Gylfaginning,* 11:354a
in *Hávamál,* 11:359a
in *Lokasenna,* 7:643b
magic powers, 9:218b
mentioned in Old Saxon baptismal vows, 2:87a
midgard serpent and, 8:362a-b
Njǫrðr and, 9:146a, 146b
Norna-Gests Þáttr and, 9:171b
in poetry, 6:113b, 114a
acquisition of power, 6:114b
in *Ragnarǫk,* 10:248a
in *Reginsmál* and *Fáfnismál,* 4:581a-b, 10:289b
relation to Hœnir, 6:270b
seiðr, 9:219a
shamanism, connection with, 9:218b–219a
in *Skáldskaparmál,* 11:353a
in the Skarkaðr legend, 11:466b–467a
Skaði and, 11:325b
in *Sturlaugs saga Starfsama,* 11:496b
Thor and, 12:45a, 46a
in *Urgeschichte,* 11:328b
in *Vafþrúðnismál,* 12:344a-b
Valhalla and, 12:350a-b
Valkyries and, 12:351a
Vanir and, 12:356b
in *Víga-Glúms saga,* 12:416a
warriors, 9:218b
wisdom of, 9:218a-b, 11:31a-b
worship of in Anglo-Saxon England, 1:289a
see also Scandinavian mythology
Odington, Walter, **9:219a-b**
Icocedron, 9:219b
mathematical descriptions of alchemical changes, 1:138a
rondellus technique, 10:529b
Summa de speculatione musicae, 8:645a, 9:219b
theories of harmony, 6:100a
Odo (888–898) of France, king, election of, 5:152b
Odo II of Blois-Chartres-Tours, count, 3:244a
Odo of Arezzo, abbot, 8:640b
Odo of Bayeux, bishop, 2:139a
Vital of Savigny and, 12:479b
Odo of Blois, count, 2:429a
Odo of Cambrai, on liturgy, 7:630b
Odo of Ceriton, prose fables and, 7:365a
Odo of Châteaudun, Angers, and Troyes, count, Robert the Strong and, 3:89b
Odo of Châteauroux, on Jews, 7:77b
Odo of Cheriton, *Fabulae,* Spanish version of, 11:420a
Odo of Cluny, abbot, 7:363b, **9:219b–220a**
biography of, 7:121a-b
Dialogus and, 8:640b
hagiography and, 6:314b
Life of Gerald of Aurillac, 7:262a, 9:220a
monastic reform and, 10:286a-b
music and, 8:563b
office of St. Martin and, 10:372a
as pupil of Remigius of Auxerre, 10:303a
reforms of, 3:469a
Vita Geraldi, 3:469a
Odo of Corbie, as military leader, 2:173b
Odo delle Colonne, 11:259a
Odo of Deuil
chronicle of Louis VI of France, 7:264a
on Frankish atrocities in Greece, 3:356b
Odo the Good Marquis, 11:589a
Odo of Metz, **9:220a**
Charlemagne's chapel, Aachen, 9:220a
Odo of Meun, **9:220a-b**
De viribus herbarum, 9:220a-b
Odo of Ourscamp, theology school of, 12:21b
Odo Rigaldus. *See* Eudes Rigaud
Odo de St. Amand, grand master of the Templars, 3:304b
Odo, West Frankish king, 3:89b, 115a
Odoacer, 2:93a-b, **9:220b–221a**, 11:335a
assassination of, 9:221a
defeat by Ostrogoths, 2:93b, 9:290a, 12:19a
election to kingship, 9:220b
last Western emperor and, 12:355a
military conflicts, 9:220b–221a
title of patrician and, 9:460a
in works of literature, 6:227b
Zeno the Isaurian and, 12:743b
Odofredus, **9:221a-b**
Commentary on the Code, 9:221b
Commentary on the Digest, 9:221b
on Irnerius, 6:554b
political theory, 9:221b
Odomantis, organized as Syrian March, 1:514b

Odoric of Pordenone, *Mandeville's Travels* and, 8:82a
O'Duignan family, 6:523a
Odyssey. See Homer
Œgishjálmr, 4:581b
Oebarsius (Hunnic leader), 6:354a
Oeconomica. See Conrad of Megenberg
Oecumenical councils. *See* Councils, ecumenical
Oecumenical patriarch. *See* Patriarch
Oengobann the Culdee, authorship of *Saltair na Rann,* 10:634b
Óengus (8th-century monk), martyrology, rinnard form, 8:163a
Óengus. *See* Aonghus (Irish god)
Óengus mac Fergus, Pictish king, 4:78b
  victory over King Nechtan, 9:91b
Óengus mac Nad Froích, 4:492b
Offa of Mercia, king
  Beowulf and, 2:184b
  coins bearing his name, 9:495a, 495b
  Peter's Pence and, 11:606a
  summons to witenagemot, 3:82a
  unification of England, 4:455a
Offal. *See* Public health, sanitation
Offa's Dyke, cultural divisions of, 12:514b
Offerimus tibi, Domine, calicem, 8:190b
Offertory, **9:221b–222b**, 9:689a-b, 690b
  conclusion of, 8:191a
  congregational participation, 8:190b
  distribution to the poor, 8:190b
  Gallican rite, 8:190a-b
  incense and, 6:431b
  items offered, 8:189b
  lavabo, 8:191a
  loaves
    leavening of, Eastern and Western church, 8:189b–190a
    making of, 8:190a
  in Milanese Mass, 8:383b
  music, 9:222a
  occasions for, 9:222a
  offerings in kind, 8:189b
  offertorium chant, 8:190b
  Orate fratres, 8:191a
  placement on altar, 8:190b
  prayers
    Deus qui humanae substantiae, 8:190b
    In spiritu humilitatis, 8:190b–191a
    Offerimus tibi, Domine, calicem, 8:190b
    Suscipe sancta Trinitas, 8:191a
    Veni Sanctificator, 8:191a
  presentation of, 8:190a
  reading of diptychs, 8:191a
  reading of names, 8:191a
  regional variations in, 4:335b
  secret, 8:191a-b
  source for, 9:222a
  wine
    adding water to, 8:190a
    regulation of, 8:190a
  see also Mass cycles; Plainsong
Office. *See* Divine Office; Rhymed Offices
Office of the Dead. *See* Dead, Office of the
Office tropes. *See Verbetae*
Officia (several rhymed offices bound together), 10:376a
Officina, on Byzantine coins, 8:420a, 421a
Officium capitula, 4:230b
Officium parvum B.M.V. *See* Blessed Virgin Mary, Little Office of the
Officium regum trium. See Play of Herod
Officium stellae. See Play of Herod
Ofljóst, 11:353a
Ögadai (Ögdai, Ogedei, Ögedei, Ögedey). *See* Ögödai, Great Khan
Ogee arch. *See* Arch
Ogham, 1:216 (*illus.*), 6:439a, **9:222b–223b**
  additions to, historic period, 9:223a
  after introduction of Latin alphabet, 9:223a
  alphabet, 9:222b–223a
  etymology, 9:222b
  inscriptions in, 1:215a
  origins, 9:223a
  surviving examples, 9:222b
  treated in *Auraicept na nÉces,* 2:2a
Oghul Qaimish, role in Mongol succession, 8:471a, 471b
Oghurs, Volga Bulgars and, 12:487b, 488a
Oghuz, 5:518b
  Chërnye Klobuki, 10:577a
  early Seljuks and, 11:151a, 151b, 152a
  Russian migrations, 10:576b–577a
  Seljuks of Kirmān and, 11:155a
  see also Seljuks of Rum
Oghuz Turks. *See* Turkomans
Ogier the Dane, 8:225a
Ogier le Danois. See Jean d'Outremeuse
Ogier Ghislain de Busbecq, 6:437b
Ogier of Laon, count. *See* Hoger of Laon, count
Ogive arch. *See* Arch
Ógláchas, 6:535b
Ǫgmundar þáttr dytts, 12:4a, 4b, 5a
Ognibene. *See* Salimbene
Ögödai, Great Khan
  appanage, 8:469a
  death of, 2:131b, 6:342b, 8:471a
  election to khanate, 8:469a
O'Hara family, Tadhg Dall and, 9:205b
O'Higgins family. *See* Uí Uiginn
Ohrid. *See* Ochrid
Ōhrmazd (Zoroastrian god). *See* Ahura Mazda
Ohrmizd IV (479–490), abolished Chosroid dynasty, 3:308a
Ohthere (traveler to Scandinavia), 1:284a
Ó hUiginn, Philip Bocht, poem on the Judgment, 1:111b
Ó hUiginn, Tadhg Dall, **9:205a-b**
  murder of, 9:205b
Ó hUiginn, Tadhg Óg, **9:205b–206b**
  "Anocht sgaoilid na sgola," 9:206a
  court poetry of, 9:206a
  religious poetry of, 9:206a
  Tadhg Dall and, 9:205b
Oikoi, 6:378b
Oikos ekklesias, 4:256a
Oil, holy. *See* Holy oil
Oil painting, 5:85b, 566b, **9:223b**, 9:360a
Oil trade, Marseilles, 12:149a-b
Oisín (saga character), 6:525b, 531a-b, 549a
Ojun, **9:224a-b**
  figural sculpture, 1:495a-b, 9:224a
  stelae, 6:309b, 9:224a (*illus.*)
O'Kelly, Muircheartach, archbishop of Tuam, 6:523b
O'Kelly, William, 6:523b
Okol'nichie
  in Muscovy, duties of, 4:306a-b
  see also Duma
Oksbøl, houses at, 10:688b
Oktoechos. See Octoechos
Oktoikh, 8:574b
Olaf, *see also* Óláfr
Olaf IV of Denmark and Norway, king, 4:155b–156a
  Danish-Norwegian Union and, 9:185a
Olaf Engelbrektsson, archbishop, revolt of, 9:185b
Olaf, St. *See* Óláfr II Haraldsson of Norway, king
Óláfr I Tryggvason of Norway, king
  biographies of, 9:176b
  Christianization of Iceland and, 12:427a
  Christianization of Norway, 9:225b
  English invasions, 9:227b
  Greenland and, 4:554b–555a
  Grœnlendinga saga and, 12:456b
  in Icelandic saga, 4:618a
    vs. Þrándr, 4:580b
  Leif Ericson and, 12:457a
  in sagas, 9:225a–226a
  ship *Long Serpent* and, 12:424b
  þættir and, 12:5a
  in *Þorsteins þáttr bæjarmagns,* 12:48a
Óláfr II Haraldsson of Norway, king, 2:254a-b, 7:281a, 11:15a, 16a
  in *Bjarnar saga Hítdœlakappa,* 2:255a
  encomium on, 11:316b–317a
  in Icelandic saga, 4:618a, 9:176b, 225b, 11:365a
    vs. Þrándr, 4:580b
  Norwegian unification and, 9:182b, 183a, 183b
  sailing to Greenland and, 12:422a, 422b
  in Snorri Sturluson's *Heimskringla,* 2:254a, 4:581a, 7:281a, 9:176b–177a, 225b
  þættir and, 12:5a
  see also Bjarkamál; Olafs saga helga
Óláfr Þórðarson, 11:354b
  as possible author of *Knýtlinga saga,* 7:281b
  as possible author of *Laxdœla saga,* 7:528b
  Third Grammatical Treatise, 11:10b, 12a-b, 320b
Óláfs saga helga, 2:255b, 4:581a, 9:176b, **9:224b–225a**
  basis for, 9:224b
  Norse redactions, 9:225a
  Olaf, characterization of, 9:225a
  on sailing to Greenland, 12:422a
  versions of, 9:224b–225a
  see also Bjarkamál; Snorri Sturluson

Óláfs saga Tryggvasonar, 9:176b, 177b, **9:225a–226a**
Battle of Svǫldr, 9:226a
conversion of subjects, 9:225b
Færeyinga saga and, 4:581b
influence on later sagas, 9:226a
Jómsvíkinga saga and, 7:145a
Kristni saga in, 7:303a
versions of, 9:170b, 225a
later, 9:216a-b
structural similarities, 9:225b
Yngvars saga víþförla and, 12:727a
Óláfsdrápa. See Einarr Skúlason
Oláh. See Vlachs
Oḷakan castle, 11:599a
Øland, 5:632a
Olanē castle. *See* Oḷakan castle
Old Academy, Neoplatonism and, 9:95a
Old age, in literature, 7:361b
Old Believers, music and, 8:576a
Old Church Slavonic language, 6:434b, 438a, 439a, 11:341b
in Balkans, 6:443b–444a
Byzantine chant and, 8:574b
Old Church (Tokalı Kilise), 3:92 (*illus.*)
Old English (Anglo-Saxon) literature, **1:274a–288b**
beginnings of, 1:274b
Bible translations, 1:285a-b
dating of, 1:275a-b
extant texts in, 1:275a-b
German poetry and, 2:225a-b
gnomic literature, 1:281a, 5:568b–569a
hagiography, 1:285a
identification of scriptoria, 1:275b–276a
interlinear glosses in, 1:275a
legal texts, 1:286a-b
liturgical poetry, Winchester troper and, 12:647b
manuscripts, 1:274b
modern editions of texts in, 1:287a
poetry, 1:276b–281a
adaptations of classical texts, 1:280b
alliterative patterns of, 1:276b–277a
Caedmonic songs, 3:7b–8a
heroic poems, 1:278a-b
influence of exegesis on, 4:550a-b
manuscript sources of, 1:277a
metrical system of, 1:276b–277a
mnemonic, 1:281a
occasional, 1:281a
Old Testament paraphrases, 1:279b–280a
poems on contemporary themes, 1:278b–279a
saints' lives, 1:279a-b
use of rhyme in, 8:343a
wisdom poems, 1:280b–281a
post-Reformation scholarship on, 1:286b
prose, 1:281b–286b
homilies, 1:284b
riddles, 1:281a
scientific works, 1:285b–286a
sources of, 1:275a
see also Beowulf; Bible, versions, Old English; English language
Old English *Martyrology,* 1:276b, 284a
Old French. *See* French language; . French literature
Old Hall MS, **9:231a–232b**
arrangement of music, 9:231b
composers, 9:231b–232a
continental sources, 9:232a
liturgical ordering, 9:232b
notation, 9:231b
social and political influences, 9:231b
styles, 9:232a
Old High German literature, **9:233a–234b**
alliterative verse, 9:233b
in biblical epics, 9:233b
continuity with later periods, 9:234a
derivation of Eddic meter, 4:388a-b
heroic lays, 9:234a
interlinear glosses, 9:233a
Latin influence, 9:233a
Latin-German glossaries, 9:233a
prose style, Latin constructions in, 9:233a
religious works, 9:233b
rhyming verse, 9:233b
secular texts, 9:233b–234a
utilitarian purpose, 9:233a
vernacular oral poetry, 9:233a
see also German literature
Old Hungarian Lament of the Virgin. See *Ómagyar Mária-siralom*
Old Hungarian language. *See* Hungarian language
Old Irish language. *See* Irish language
Old Moravia. *See* Great (or Old) Moravia
Old Norse language, 6:436b, 9:179a
see also Scandinavian languages
Old Occitan. *See* Provençal language
Old Persian language. *See* Persian language
Old Provençal language. *See* Provençal language
Old Prussian language. *See* German language
Old Prussians. *See* Prussians, Old
Old Roman chant, **9:234b–236b**
graduals, 9:234b
Gregorian chant and, 9:234b–235b
office antiphoners, 9:234b
oral tradition, 9:235b
Old Roman Creed, 3:676a
Old Russian language. *See* Russian language
Old Russian literature, 11:346b–348a
Old St. Paul's (cathedral: London)
Chapter House for, 5:631a
master mason William Ramsey, 10:256b–257b (*illus.*)
Old St. Peter's (church: Rome), 2:124 (*illus.*), 124a, **9:236b–237b,** 10:517a, 518a
crypt, 1:442b, 9:236 (*illus.*), 237a
decoration of, 9:237a
exterior, 4:361a
drama in, 6:636b
ground plan of, 5:589b
imperial coronations, 9:237b
ivories of, 10:100b
monasteries and, 10:519b
Monte Cassino and, 10:486a, 505a
mosaics in, 4:338a
pallia, 9:237b
papal coronation at, 3:603a–604b
pilgrimages to, 9:237a
remodeling, 6th century, 9:237a
throne of St. Peter, 12:342a
tombs and relics, 9:237b, 658a-b
transept, 9:237a
water supply, 10:520a
see also Leonine City
Old Sarum, **9:237b**
Roger of Salisbury and, 10:443a
Old Saxon language. *See* Saxon language
Old Spanish rite
libellus for, 10:605a
sacramentaries, 10:606a
Old Testament plays. *See* Drama, liturgical
Old Testament Trinity. *See* Trinity, Old Testament
Old Yiddish. *See* Yiddish
Old-Irish Penitential, 9:489a
Oldcastle, Sir John
charges of heresy, 7:647a
conspiracy of, 6:160a, 200a, 7:647a
trial and execution, 7:647b
Wyclif and, 12:709b
Oldenburg, bishop of, transfer to Lübeck, 7:680a
Oldermanni, 5:463b
Oldest Saga. See Óláfs saga helga
Oldrado da Trezzeno, 8:379a
Oldřich of Bohemia, duke, 10:88a
Oleg of Kiev, grand prince, 8:443b, **9:238a**
Derevlianian tribute to, 5:332a
expansionism, 9:238a
Kievan Rus under, 7:247b
in Tmutarakan, 12:66a
Oleg-Michael of Tmutarakan, prince, coins during rule of, 8:426a
"Oléron, Laws of," 1:56a-b
Oleśnicki, Zbigniew, bishop of Kraków, 9:727a, 730a
Olga of Kiev, 7:248a, **9:238a**
conversion to Christianity, 10:591a, 12:435b
Olgerd. *See* Algirdas
Oliba, **9:238b–239a**
episcopacy of, 9:238b
foundation of Montserrat, 9:238b
initiation of Truce of God, 9:238b
Olif ok Landres, Bevers saga and, 2:210a
Oligon, 8:617a, 617b
Olim (official records of the Parlement of Paris), 9:418b
Oliphant, 7:29a, 8:603b, **9:239a-b**
horn of Ulph, 9:239 (*illus.*)
uses of, 9:239b
see also Ivory carving
Oliva. *See* Oliba
Oliva (ship), 11:234a
Olive, growth of, 1:78a, 82b, 84a
Oliver, in *Pèlerinage de Charlemagne,* 4:576b
Oliver, Bernard (Bernat)
Against Jewish Blindness, 10:5a
Excitatori de la pensa a Déu, 3:168a

Oliver Sutton, bishop of Lincoln, 11:608a
Olivi, Peter John. *See* Peter John Olivi
Olivier de Clippson, leadership of Marmousets, 5:187a
Olivier d'Iscam. *See Pilgrim's Guide*
Öljaitü. *See* Uljaytu Khudabānda
Öljeitü. *See* Uljaytu Khudabānda
Ollamh, 6:534b, 535a, 537b–538a
Ollave. *See Ollamh*
Olmedo, Battle of (1445), 11:421b
Olmen, Ferdinand van, 2:30a
  voyage of, 4:559b–560a, 562b
Olof Eriksson of Sweden, king
  conversion of, 11:530b
  Denmark and, 11:530b
O'Loughlin, Murtagh, 3:466a
Oltenia. *See* Walachia
Oltremare (lands of crusading states), 12:111a-b
Olympia. See Boccaccio, Giovanni
Olympiodorus, 9:699a
  Alexandrian school of Neoplatonism and, 9:98a
  Zosimus and, 12:748a
Om konung Albrekt, 11:22a
Ómagyar Mária-siralom, 6:337a
Oman, Ibāḍī imamate in, 11:139a
Omar I. *See* ᶜUmar I ibn al-Khaṭṭāb
Omar II. *See* ᶜUmar II ibn ᶜAbd al-Azīz
Omar, Covenant of. *See* Covenant of Omar
Omar Khayyam. *See* ᶜUmar Khayyām
Ombre, 7:317a
Omega, in Armenian alphabet, 1:491b
Ommegang, 8:416b
"Omnigenas ergo vocemus Musas," 6:383b
Omnipotence. *See* Power, divine
Omophorion, **9:240a**, 12:401b, 402b
  see also Stikarion
Omurtag of Bulgaria, 7:303b
  reign of, 2:401b–402a
  Thomas the Slav's rebellion and, 12:37a
On . . . , see also De for works cited under their Latin titles
On the Administration of the Empire. See Constantine VII Porphyrogenitos, Byzantine emperor
On Being and Essence. See Aquinas, Thomas, St.
On the Care of the Dead. See Augustine of Hippo, St., *De cura pro mortuis gerenda*
On Christian Doctrine. See Augustine of Hippo, St.
On the Church. See Hus, John, *De ecclesia*
On Conoids and Spheroids. See Archimedes
On the Creation of Man. See Gregory of Nyssa, St.
On the Deaths of Oxen. See Endelechius
On the Distinction of Nature and Person. See Eutychius, patriarch of Constantinople
On the Divine Names. See Pseudo-Dionysius the Areopagite
On the Divine Offices. See Rupert of Deutz
On the Division of the Circle into Seven Equal Parts, 1:434b
On the Equilibrium of Planes. See Archimedes
On the Erection of the Walls of New Ross, 1:265b
On the Error of the Profane Religions. See Firmicus Maternus, Julius
On the Eternity of the World. See Aquinas, Thomas, St.; Boethius of Dacia
On Floating Bodies. See Archimedes
On the Form of the Eclipse. See Haytham, Ḥasan ibn al-
On Generation and Corruption. See Aristotle
On the Government of the Empire, subjects in, 2:516a
On the Heavens. See Aristotle
On Holy Living. See Kyssegyrlan Uuched
On the Intellective Soul. See Siger of Brabant
On Interpretation. See Aristotle
On the Laws and Customs of England. See Bracton, Henry de
On the Laws and Customs of the Kingdom of England. See Glanville, Ranulf de
On the Light of the Moon. See Haytham, Ḥasan ibn al-
On the Measurement of the Circle. See Archimedes
On the Method of Mechanical Theorems. See Archimedes
On Motion. See Gerard of Brussels
On the Nature of Things. See Isidore of Seville
On the Origin and History of the Goths. See Jordanes, *History*
On the Origin and History of the Roman Race. See Jordanes, *De summa temporum*
On Parabolic Burning Mirrors. See Haytham, Ḥasan ibn al-
On the Peace of the Faith. See Nicholas of Cusa
On the Properties of Things. See Bartholomaeus Anglicus
On the Quadrature of the Parabola. See Archimedes
On the Rainbow and the Halo. See Haytham, Ḥasan ibn al-
On Reckoning Times. See Bede, *De temporibus*
On the Relics of the Saints. See Guibert of Nogent
On the Right Way of Translating. See Bruni, Leonardo
On Simony. See Hus, John
On the Soul. See Aristotle; Ethelred of Rievaulx
On the Sphere and the Cylinder. See Archimedes
On Spirals. See Archimedes
On Spiritual Friendship. See Ethelred of Rievaulx
On the State of the Saracens. See William of Tripoli
On the Sudden Fall of Princes in Our Days. See Lydgate, John
On Temperance. See Theodore Meliteniotes
On Themes, 2:516a
On Treatment of Diseases. See Galen
On the Unicity of Intellect. See Aquinas, Thomas, St.
On Vardan and the Armenian War. See Ełišē
On the Victory of the Word of God. See Rupert of Deutz
Onager, 3:180 (*illus.*)
  see also Ass
Once (unit of measure), 12:595b
One Hundred Chapters, Council of, production of icons, 10:589a
O'Neill family, 6:519b
O'Neill kings. *See* Uí Néill
Öngüt confederacy, alliance with Mongols, 8:465b
Onion dome. *See* Dome
Onogur Bulgars, in Bulgaria, 2:399a-b
Ontogeny, of Isaac Israeli, 6:620a-b
Ontology
  Aristotle's ten modes of being, 1:457b, 9:614a
  God as Being, 1:657a, 2:36a, 9:598a
  Ibn Sīnā and, 11:304a-b
  Ockham and "logical being," 9:211a-b
  ontological hierarchy, 9:698a
  unity and being, 9:95b–96a
  see also Philosophy and theology, Islamic; Philosophy and theology, Jewish; Philosophy and theology, Western European
Onulf of Speyer, **9:240a**
  Rethorici colores, 9:240a
Opaque glass, 5:556b
Opere Francigeno. See Opus Francigenum
Opizari, 5:410b
Oppian, *Cynegetica,* miniature of a naval battle from, 9:73 (*illus.*)
Oprichnina, 11:194b–195b
Opsikion, theme of, **9:240a-b**, 12:9b
  Bogomils in, 2:295b
  Nikephoros I and, 11:573b
  territorial jurisdiction, 9:240b
Optics, *see also* Eyeglasses
Optics, see also Haytham, Ḥasan ibn al-
Optics, Islamic, **9:240b–247a**, 11:86b–87a, 88b
  burning mirrors and spheres, 9:242a, 244b–245a
  crystalline humor, 9:243a
  geometrical approach, 9:240b, 244b
  Greek influence, 9:240b–241a, 241b, 242b
  influence of, 9:246a-b
  lack of unified discipline, 9:241a
  light and color, 9:243a, 243b, 244a-b
    lux and *lumen,* 9:249b
    motion of, two components, 9:244b
  mathematical aspects, 9:241a
  perception, 9:243a–244a, 249b
    modes of inference, 9:244a

Optics, Islamic (*cont.*)
  perception (*cont.*)
    sensation and, 9:244a
    three-dimensional space, 9:243b–244a
  philosophical aspects, 9:241a
  pin-hole camera, principles of, 9:245a
  rainbows, 9:244b
    color theories, 9:242b, 246a
    secondary bows, 9:246a
  rectilinear radiation, 9:241b, 244a
  reflection, 9:244a-b
    Alhazen's problem, 9:244a
  refraction, 9:244a-b
  vision theory, 9:241a-b, 243b (*illus.*), 245b (*illus.*)
    clarity of center field, 9:242a
    extramission hypothesis, 9:242a
    Galenic, 9:241a
    mirror images, 9:242a
    straight-line, 9:243a–244a
Optics, Western European, **9:247a–253b**
  animated medium, 9:250b
  burning spheres, 9:251a
  crystalline humor, 9:252a-b
  Franciscans and, 1:461b
  geometry of propagation, 9:249b–251a
    Bacon's modes, 9:250a-b
    sources of, 9:250a
  glass, 5:554a–562b
  image formation, 9:250a (*illus.*)
  John Peckham's treatise on perspective and, 9:482a
  light and color, 9:249a-b
    Aristotelian philosophy, 9:249a-b
    multiplication of species, 9:249b
    Platonic tradition, 9:249a
  methods
    research, 9:248b–249a
    of study, 9:248b
  multiplication of species, 9:625b
  perception, 9:249b
  physics and, 9:625a
  practical applications, 11:650b
  primary and secondary light, 9:250a-b
  rainbows, 9:252b–253b (*illus.*)
  rectilinear radiation, 9:250a
  reflection, 9:250b
    in rainbows, 9:253a
  refraction, 9:250a, 250b–251a, 251b (*illus.*), 252b
    in rainbows, 9:253a
  Roger Bacon and, 2:38b–39b
  as a scientific discipline, 9:608b
  sources
    Greek, 9:247a-b
    Islamic, 9:247b
    Roman, 9:247a–248a
  stained glass in, 5:548a–553a
  thin lenses, theory of, 9:251a
  traditions
    Aristotelian, 9:248a
    medical, 9:248b
    perspectiva, 9:248a-b
    theological, 9:248b
  vision theories, 9:251a–252b
    extramission, 9:251a, 252b
    Galen's visual spirit, 9:251a
    intromission, Aristotle's, 9:251a–252a
    intromission, Bacon's, 9:252a (*illus.*)
    intromission, Ibn al-Haytham's, 9:22a, 251b
  visual cone, 9:252b
  see also Lenses
Optimates militiae, 10:522a
Opus alexandrinum, **9:253b–254a**
  Cosmati work, 9:254 (*illus.*)
Opus anglicanum, 1:561a, **9:254a,** 12:400b
  Chichester-Constable chasuble, 9:255a (*illus.*)
  methods, 9:254a
  pattern books, 9:254a
Opus arduum. See Lollards
Opus Dei, writings of women mystics and, 9:9a
Opus evangelicum. See Wyclif, John
Opus expositionum. See Eckhart, Meister (Eckhart von Hochheim)
Opus Francigenum, **9:254b**
  in Gothic architecture, 5:582b
Opus mixtum, **9:254b**
Opus nonaginta dierum. See Ockham, William of
Opus pontis (a bridge corporation), 10:413b–414a
Opus reticulatum, **9:255a**
  in Western and Byzantine architecture, 9:255a
Opus sancti Eligii. See Enamel, cloisonné
Opus sectile, **9:255a-b**
Opus tertium. See Bacon, Roger
Opus tripartitum. See Eckhart, Meister; Gerson, John
Opus universale. See Vincent of Beauvais
Opusculum de edificio Dei. See Gerhoh of Reichersberg
Opusculum de monochordo. See Conrad of Zabern
Opusculum tripartitum. See Gerson, John
Or Adonai. See Crescas, Ḥasdai
Or San Michele (church: Florence), 5:525a
  painting in, 4:75b (*illus.*)
Oracles, Byzantine, 8:18a
Oracles of the Apostles, used for fortune-telling, 8:26b
Órækja (son of Snorri Sturluson), 11:357a
Orange Cathedral (France), 10:481b
Orange, University of, 12:285a
Orant, **9:255b–256a**
  Christian adaptation, 9:256a
  origins, 9:255b–256a
  Virgin, Monastery of the Savior, Yaroslavl, 9:255b (*illus.*)
  see also Platytera
Orarion, **9:256a**
Orarium. *See* Vestments, liturgical, insignia
Oratio synodalis. See John of Ōjun, St.
Orationes, 8:186b, 196b–197a
Oratorio, *lauda* and, 8:572a
Oratory (chapel), **9:256a**
  chasovnya, 3:277a
Oratory of Divine Love, founded by Catherine of Genoa's followers, 9:15a
Oratory (rhetoric)
  deliberative, 10:349a, 351b
  epideictic, 10:349a, 351b
  forensic, 10:349a, 351b, 352a
  six parts of, according to Cicero, 10:351b–352a
  three types of, according to Aristotle, 10:351b
  see also Rhetoric, Byzantine
Orbais, Jean d'. *See* Jean d'Orbais
Orbēlean family
  Mongols and, 12:737a
  Zak^{c}arids and, 12:736b
Orbēlean, Step^{c}anos, 1:511b, **9:256a–257a**
  ecclesiastical positions, 9:256b
  History of the State of Sisakan, 9:256b
  Lamentation on the Holy Cathedral of Vałaršapat, 4:417b
  on *naχarars,* 1:486a
  Tat^{c}ew and, 11:600a, 600b
Orbeli family, 1:235b, 5:529b
Orbelids, Siwnik^{c} under, 11:315b
Orbelišvili, Bessarion, 5:414a
Orbini, *History of the Slavs,* on Vuk Brakoviç, 11:181b
Orcagna, Andrea, 5:338a, **9:257a–258b**
  Christ in Majesty with Saints altarpiece, 12:175a, 176a
  elements of style, 9:257b, 258a-b
  Niccolò di Pietro Gerini and, 9:119a
  Strozzi altarpiece, 5:607a, 8:438b, 9:257 (*illus.*), 257b–258a
  see also Jacopo di Cione; Leonardo di Ser Giovanni; Nardo di Cione
Orchard, William, **9:258b**
  Magdalen College, construction of, 9:258a
  pendant vaults, Oxford Divinity School, 9:258a (*illus.*), 258b
Orcival (church: Auvergne), 10:480a
Orda (brother of Batu), 2:131b
Ordainers, Lords, Ordinances of 1311 and, 9:426a
Ordeals, 7:503b–504a, 9:207a, **9:259a–260b**
  acceptance by courts, 9:259b
  in *accusatio* and *denunciatio,* 6:478b
  by fire, authentication of relics and, 10:298a-b
  in canon law, 7:502b–503a
  in canonical inquest, 6:479a
  Carolingian, 9:259b
  in civil law, 7:505a
  of cold water, 9:259 (*illus.*)
  duels, 9:260a
  in English law, 7:182b–183a
    Assize of Clarendon, 3:409a
    presentment of Englishry and, 4:487a
  in German law, 7:477a, 480a
  judgments of God, 9:259a
  jury system and, 7:505b
  Lateran IV and, 7:182b
  origins
    in Christian theology, 9:259b
    Germanic, 9:259a

papal opposition to, 7:503a–504a
participation by priests, 9:259b, 260a
Peter the Chanter on, 9:522a, 522b
renunciation of, 9:260a
in Russian law, 7:509a
in Scandinavian legal procedure, 10:705b
townsmen and, 7:505a
types of, 7:182b
see also Compurgation; German law, early Germanic codes; Russian (Muscovite) law
Ordelaffi, Francesco, Boccaccio and, 2:287b
Ordenamiento de Alcalá, 3:135a, 611b, 7:523a-b
Ordenamiento de Montalvo, 7:523b
Ordene de chevalerie, 1:189a, 3:666a
Ordenung. See Seldeneck, Philipp von
Order of Friar Servants of St. Mary. *See* Servites
Order of Friars Minor. *See* Franciscans
Order of the Holy Cross. *See* Crutched Friars
Order of the Most Holy Savior (founded by St. Birgitta of Sweden), 9:15a
Order of Our Lady of Mount Carmel. *See* Carmelites
Order of Penance of Jesus Christ. *See* Friars of the Sack
Order of Penitence, relation to Franciscans, 5:195a
Order of Preachers. *See* Dominicans
Order, sacrament of
angelic hierarchy and, 9:602a
Hugh of St. Cher's doctrine, 9:601b–602a
Order of St. Clare. *See* Franciscans
Order of S. Damiano. *See* Franciscans
Order of the Salamander. *See* Teutonic Knights
Ordericus Vitalis, 1:260a, **9:260b–261a**
Ecclesiastical History, 2:174a, 6:263a, 9:260b–261a
Roger of Salisbury and, 10:443b
Orders of chivalry, 4:17a-b
in Baltic lands, 2:64b–67b
minor, 3:306b–307a
national military, 3:306a-b
origin of, 3:302b
see also Aviz, Order of; Knights of St. John; Lithuania; Templars; Teutonic Knights
Ordinale, **9:261a-b**
of Christ, 9:261a-b
contents, 9:261a
Ordinals. *See Ordines romani*
Ordinance, **9:261b–262b**
arrêt and, 9:262a
for the common good, 9:262a
English usage, 9:261b–262a
king's personal seal, 9:262a
établissement and, 9:262a
French usage, 9:262a-b
king's council and, 9:262a
issues addressed, 9:261b
passage of, 9:261b
provision and, 9:261b–262a
statute and, 9:261b–262a
see also Statute
Ordinances of 1311, 4:397b, 9:261b, 426a, 426b
on royal wardrobe, 6:303a
Ordinarius, liber, **9:262b–263a**
Ordinary chants. *See* Mass; Plainsong
Ordinary (diocesan), canonization and, 3:68a, 68b
Ordinary of the Mass. *See* Mass; Tropes
Ordinatio. See Duns Scotus, John; Ockham, William of; Suger of St. Denis
Ordination, clerical, **9:263a–269a**
actions and gestures, 9:268a-b
allocutions and admonitions, 9:266b–267a
in Celtic church, 3:230b–231a
clerical orders, systems of
Gallican, 9:265a
Roman, 9:265a
Spanish, 9:264b–265a
description in *Ordines romani,* 9:263b
final credo, 9:268b
general instructions, 9:265b
importance of, 9:263a
instruments, 9:267 (*illus.*), 267a–268a
porrection, 9:267a
lectionaries and antiphonalia, 9:264a
libelli
allocution, 9:264a
with ordination directions, 9:263b
prayer, 9:263b
liturgical commentaries, 9:264b
musical portion, 9:266b
ordinands
examination of, 9:266a-b
oath of, 9:266b
place of, 9:265b–266a
pontificals, 9:264a-b
prayers and benedictions, 9:266b
presentation of offerings, 9:268b
as rank, 3:441a-b
rites of, 3:441b–442b
sacramentaries, 9:263b–264a
textual sources, 9:263b–264b
time of, 9:265b
title of, 3:443b–444a
Wyclif and, 12:708a
Ordination, Jewish. *See* Rabbinate
Ordines, 8:383a
in Divine Office, 4:225a
Ordines romani, **9:269a-b**
cantatorium mentioned in, 3:80b
Capitulare ecclesiasticis ordinis, 9:269b
collections, 9:269a-b
copies and modifications, 9:269a
didactic additions, 9:269b
direction for private mass, 8:183b
on Easter Vigil litany, 7:592b
Gallican influence, 9:265a
on Kyrie eleison, 7:593b
on liturgical vestments, 12:397b, 398a, 399a, 400a
missal and, 8:437b
ordo, development of, 9:269a
in pontifical, 10:30b
protopontificals and protorituals, 9:269b
use of Metz and, 8:301b
in Western European preaching literature, 10:79a
see also Baptism
Ordini del cavalcare. See Grisone, Federico
Ordnance
Fachschrifttum and, 4:579a
see also Cannon
Ordo. See Ordines romani
Ordo ad repraesentandum Herodem, 4:282a
Ordo iudiciarius. See Tancred (canonist)
Ordo Predicatorum. See Dominicans
Ordo quod sacerdos debet sacrificare, 7:629b
Ordo Rachelis, 9:706b
Ordo representacionis Adae. See Jeu d'Adam
Ordo Romanus I
Communion
of the clergy, 8:195a
noncommunicants' exit, 8:194a
fraction, importance of, 8:194b
Gospel, ceremonies preceding, 8:187b
lections and instruction, 8:187a
offertory, 8:190b
Ordo romanus XXXIV, clerical orders, 9:265a
Ordo of St. Amand, 7:312b
Ordo virtutum, dramatic use of allegory, 4:286b
Ordonnance cabochienne, 5:187b
Ordonnance de Montil-les-Tours, 7:427a
Ordoño I of Asturias, king
Portugal under, 10:37a-b
reign of, 1:626b–627a
Ordoño II of Asturias, king, reign of, 1:627a-b
Ordulf of Saxony, duke, 2:235a
Oreibasios of Pergamum
Euporista, 8:244b–245a
influence of
in the Palaiologan era, 8:246a
on Theophilos Protospatharios, 8:245b
Oren-Kala, 2:139a
Orendel, **9:269b–270b**
Oresme, Nicole, **9:270b–272a**
Ad pauca respicientes, 1:608a-b
aesthetics and, 8:583b
on astrology and magic, 8:38b
attitude to magic, 8:37b, 38a
De caelo, 1:615b
De proportionibus proportionum, 8:217a, 9:271b
ecclesiastical career, 9:270b
glossed French versions of Aristotle, 7:601b
Livre du ciel et du monde, 9:271a
Livre de divinacions, 1:608b
mathematical theory, theory of commensurability, 8:217a-b, 218a-b
music and, 8:583b
nominalism and, 12:44a
Questiones super de caelo, 1:438a
scientific treatises, 9:270b
on astronomy, 1:615b
distribution of qualities, 9:271b
earth's rotation, 9:271a-b
effects of motion measured, 9:626a

Oresme, Nicole (*cont.*)
scientific treatises (*cont.*)
intensities of qualities, 9:627a-b
on physics, 1:464b–465a
quantity of quality, 9:626b
ratios of ratios, 9:271b
theology, relation of faith and reason, 9:271a
Tractatus de configurationibus qualitatum et motuum, 9:271b
translations, 5:291a
of Aristotle, 9:270b
via moderna and, 12:408b
Orfeo, Sir. See Sir Orfeo
Orff, Carl, *Carmina burana,* 3:99a
Organ, 5:320b, 8:604b–605a, **9:272a–276a**, 11:663b–664a, 12:180a-b
accidentals, 9:275a
bellows, 9:272a-b
conflatorium, 9:275a
in Byzantine court music, 8:557a
in Carolingian renaissance, 9:272b
in the cathedral of Basel, 9:274a (*illus.*)
in the cathedral of Vienna, 9:650a (*illus.*)
Gothic period, 9:275a
keyboard, 9:275a
Landini and, 7:326a
literary references, 9:273a-b
in monasteries, 9:272b
motet, 9:273b–274a
mouth. *See* Mouth organ
pedal board, 9:275a
pipes, 8:640a, 642a
placement of in church, 9:274a
polyphonic settings, 9:274a, 275a
portative, 8:605 (*illus.*)
nobility and, 8:596a
registration, 9:275a
in sacred music, 8:596a, 634b
technological innovations, 9:275a
in transept, 9:275b (*illus.*)
tribune platform, 12:187b
voice accompaniment, 9:273a, 274b
Organal style, 1:546a-b
Organistrum, 8:608a
Organon. See Aristotle
Organum, **9:276a-b**
in *ars antiqua,* 1:546a-b
in Bible and patristic literature, 9:276b
clausula, 3:437a-b
consonance and dissonance in, 3:542a
in contemporary musicography, 9:276b
Daseian notation and, 8:618b
diaphonia and, 4:172b, 9:276b
florid and tenor voices, 9:276b
Guido of Arezzo and, 8:641a
John of Afflighem on, 7:132b, 8:642b
of John of Garland, 7:134b
in Las Huelgas MS, 6:318a
Magister Lambertus and, 8:643b
in *Magnus liber organi,* 8:43a
in measured music, 7:119a-b
modal notation and, 8:622a
Notre Dame school, 9:191b
polyphonic genera, 9:276b
oral tradition and, 8:569b–570a
organicum melos, 9:276b
polyphonic association, 9:276b
in St. Magnus hymn, 8:559a
in Winchester Troper, 12:647b–648a
works in MS Pluteus 29.1, 5:105a-b
see also Leoninus; Perotinus
Orgies, witchcraft and, 12:660b
Orgon, inns in, 6:469b, 472b
Oria, St., Berceo and, 2:187b
Oribasius, *Synopsis,* translations of in the West, 8:247a
Oriel window, **9:277a**
Orientation of Islamic prayer. *See* Qibla
Orientius, **9:277a-b**
Commonitorium, 9:277a
mediation between Theodoric I and Litorius, 9:277a
poems attributed to, 9:277a
Oriflama. See Rodríguez del Padrón, Juan
Origen, 2:223b–224a, 9:5b, 6a-b, **9:277b–279a**
on angels, 1:249b
Basil the Great and, 2:119b, 120b
castration of, 9:277b
as church father, 3:335b
classical literary studies and, 3:430b
condemnation of, 3:630b, 9:278a
De principiis, 9:278a
emendations of New Testament, 2:211a
on great chain of being, 9:278a
Hexapla, 2:211a, 9:278a
Vulgate and, 12:495b
influence on exegesis, 9:278a
Jerome and, 7:57b, 58a
on liturgy, 7:625b
Maximus the Confessor and, 8:233b
on millennialism, 8:385a
Neoplatonists' influence and, 3:335b
Nestorianism and, 9:107a
ordination in Caesarea, 9:277b
Philokalia. See Basil the Great of Caesarea, St., *Philokalia*
on *Physiologus,* 2:203b, 204a
Platonism of, 9:98b, 278a, 278b
prayer of the mind, 6:217a
rabbinical tradition and, 9:278a
on the rule of faith, 9:278a
Septuagint and, 11:565a
subordinationism, 9:560b
use of allegory, 9:278a
on Virgin Mary, 12:459b
Origenism, Seven Sleepers of Ephesus and, 11:213b
Original Chronicle of Scotland. See Andrew of Wyntoun
Origo gentis Langobardum, as a basis for Paul the Deacon's *History of the Lombards,* 9:468a
Origo mundi, 4:546a
Orion of Thebes, 11:53a
Orkhon Turks, 7:236b–237a
Orkney Islands
acquired by Scotland, 11:108a
expedition of Áedán mac Gabráin, 1:60a
Viking attacks on Scotland and, 12:425a
Orkneyinga jarla saga. See Orkneyinga saga
Orkneyinga saga, 9:176b, **9:279a–280a**, 11:328b
additions and revisions, 9:279a
dating and preservation, 9:279a, 279b
in *Flateyjarbók,* 9:279a
Icelandic traditions in, 9:279b
miracles in, 9:279b
relation to *Ágrip,* 9:279b
Snorri Sturluson and, 9:279a-b
Orlandi, Deodato, *Crucifix,* 5:531a
Orlando furioso. See Ariosto, Ludovico
Orlando (in Italian Carolingian legends), 8:225b
Orlando innamorato. See Boiardo, Matteo
Orléans
bridge of, 10:416b
construction of, 10:420a, 420b
free passage on and under, 10:417a, 417b
maintenance of, 10:421b
classical literary studies at, 3:434a
heresy trials of, 12:660b, 661a, 661b
Joan of Arc at, 6:332a, 7:114b
serfdom and, 11:204b
Orléans Cathedral, 10:478a
Orléans, Charles of. *See* Charles of Orléans
Orléans, University of, Parlement of Paris and, 9:419b–420a
Orloge amoureus. See Froissart, Jehan
*Ørlygsstaðir, Battle of (1238), 6:395b, 11:357b
in Sturla Þórðarson's *Íslendinga saga,* 11:499b
Ormazd (Zoroastrian god). *See* Ahura Mazda
Ormr Jónsson, in *Sturlunga saga,* 11:500a
Ormsby, William, 7:192b
Ormulum, 4:546a, 8:315a, 330a, **9:280a-b**
ballad meter used in, 8:345a
composer of, 9:280a
corrections and revisions in manuscript, 9:280a-b
dating and preservation, 9:280a
lexicographic value, 9:280b
scribal features, 9:280b
Ormur
Vilmundar rímur, 10:402b
concealed name in, 10:404a-b
Ormur Jónsson í Gufudal, *Gögu-Hrólfs rímur,* 10:403a
Ormur Loftsson, wrong attribution of a *ríma* to, 10:402b
Ornamentation. *See* Manuscript illumination; Musical ornamentation
Ornamenting neume. *See* Neume
Ornatus difficilis, Wolfram von Eschenbach and, 12:675a
Ornatus mulierum. See Ornement des dames
Orne fragment, 1:262b
Ornement des dames, 2:148a, **9:281a**
Oromantis. *See* Odomantis
Orontid dynasty, 1:514b–515a
Arcrunis and, 12:361b
links to the Bagratids, 2:48a, 48b
Orosius (Paulus Orosius), **9:281a-b**

Apologetic Book Against the Pelagians, 9:281a
Bobbio MS, 3:117a
Historiae adversum paganos, 1:653a, 6:261b, 9:137b, 281a-b, 11:405b
English translation by Alfred the Great, 1:165a, 166a-b, 276b, 284a, 285b, 9:179a
Hymnarius Paraclitensis and, 6:382a
Instruction on the Error of the Priscillianists and Origenists, 9:281a
Livres dou trésor and, 7:383a
sex aetates mundi and, 11:215a
Orphanages, contributions for, 9:281b
Orphanotrophos, **9:281b–282a**
appointment of, 9:281b, 282a
in Constantinople, 9:282a
influence of, 9:281b–282a
Orphans, treatment of, 9:281b
Orphanus, the, 12:678a
Orpheus, cult of, 9:1a, 1b
Orpheus and Eurydice. *See* Henryson, Robert
Orphrey, **9:282a**
Orseille. *See* Archil
Orseoli (Venetian noble family), 12:386a, 387a
Orseolo, Pietro I, doge of Venice, 9:330a
Orsini family, vs. John of Gravina, 7:380a
Orsini, Matteo
Ionian islands and, 7:376a
papal elections and, 3:523b
Orsini, Napoleone, cardinal, Ubertino of Casale and, 12:236a
Orsini, Nicholas, murder of Thomas of Epiros, 4:499b
Orthez, bridge at, 10:421a
Orthodox Aristotelianism. *See* Aristotelianism
Orthodox Eastern church. *See* Byzantine church; Russian Orthodox church
Orthodoxy, Feast of, 9:698a
Orthographia Gallica, 1:270b, **9:282a-b**
Orthography
Italian. *See* Italian language, orthography
Latin. *See* Latin language, spelling
see also Alphabets
Orthros, 2:468b, 3:67a
in *Akolouthiai,* 8:555b
see also Matins, Eastern
Ortliebians
influence on later sects, 5:216b–217a
preaching and practices, human deification, 5:216b
Ortnit, **9:282b–283b**
characterization, 9:283a
popular literary elements, 9:283a
preservation of, 9:282b
style, 9:282b
variants of, 9:283a
Wolfdietrich and, 9:283a, 12:670a
Ortolf of Bayerland, 4:579b
Ortuqids (Artuqids), **9:283b–284a**
architectural monuments, 9:283b–284a
inscriptions, 9:284a
relief sculptures, 9:284a
in Armenia, 1:485a, 514a
coinage, 9:283b
cultural patronage, 9:283b–284a
classical revival, 9:283b
literature, 9:284a
Islamic manuscripts and, 6:607b
Mardin branch, 9:283b
military politics, 9:283b
origins, 9:283b
Seljuks of Syria and, 11:155a
succession struggle after Malikshāh I's death and, 11:153b
Örvar-Odds saga, **9:284a–285a**
compared with two *þættir,* 12:3a
flyting in, 9:173a, 174a-b
Ketils saga Hængs and, 7:232a
Kjalnesinga saga and, 7:274a
plot summary, 9:284b–285a
reference to old Viking laws, 5:141b–142a
Svarfdæla saga and, 11:521b
tragedy of Hjálmarr and Ingibjörg, 5:141b
Orvieto
Black Death in, 2:260a-b, 264a-b
laude of, 6:636a
Orvieto Cathedral, 12:239 (*illus.*)
reliefs by Lorenzo Maitani, 8:52b (*illus.*), 53 (*illus.*)
Osbern of Gloucester
Liber derivationum, 4:449b
Panormia, 7:352a, 365b
Oscan language, 6:434b
O'Scanlain, Patrick, archbishop of Armagh, 1:470a
Osculatorium, 1:224b
Oseberg find, **9:285a–287a**
Buddha bucket, 9:286a-b
burial chamber, 9:285b–286a
funerary vehicle, 12:370b–371a, 374b
identity of the deceased, 9:285a
ship's dimensions and construction, 9:285a
tapestry reconstruction, 12:417 (*illus.*)
textiles in, 4:328a, 9:286b
use of wheeled vehicles and, 12:367b
wood carvings, 9:286a
animal-head post, 9:285b (*illus.*)
wagon panel, 9:286 (*illus.*)
see also Viking art
Ošin of Cilicia, king
foundation of Het῾umid line, 6:219b
Tarsus and, 11:600a
O'Sinaich, Cellach, **9:206b–207a**
Armagh and, 1:470a
Oški, **9:287a-b**
Oški Cathedral, 5:408a (*illus.*), 409a-b
architectural elements, 9:287a
deesis relief, south pastophory, 9:287 (*illus.*)
historical inscriptions, 9:287a-b
Oski (Roman envoy), 1:519a-b
Oslo, population, 9:148b
Osman I, **9:287b–288b**
battle of Baphaeon, 9:288a
beylik, 9:288a
Byzantine raids, 9:287a
creation of dynasty, 9:288a-b
ghāzīs, 9:288a, 305b, 306a
territorial conquests, Bithynia, 9:288a
Osmanlılık (Ottomanism), 9:308a-b
Osmanlis. *See* Ottomans
Osmoglasnik. See Oktoikh
Osmund, St., *Institucio,* 10:655b
Osnabrück, bishopric of, representative assemblies and, 10:332b–333a
Osona, Rodrigo de. *See* Rodrigo de Osona
Ossian (saga character). *See* Oisín (saga character)
Ossianic poetry. *See* Fenian poetry
Ostan-i-Marzpan, 7:205a
Ostasio da Polenta, Boccaccio and, 2:287b
Östgötalagen, 7:525a
Ostikan, **9:288b–289a**
appointment to office, 9:288b
in Naxčawan, 9:90b–91a
residence of, 9:288b–289a
Shaybānī succession, 9:288b
usages, 9:288b
Ostoja of Bosnia, king, 11:474a
overthrow of, 2:337b–338a
relations with Sigismund of Luxembourg, 2:338a
vs. Sandalj, 2:338b
Ostracism. *See* Leprosy
Ostrogoths, 2:92b–94a, **9:289a–293b**
Alamanni and, 5:506a
Arianism of, 9:291a-b
Byzantine wars, 9:292b–293a
battle at Taginae (532), 9:292b
coins issued by, 8:427b
Dacia and, 10:459a
destruction of their kingdom, 2:95a
Fritigern and, 12:469b
Huns and, 6:352b
defeated (375), 2:90a
rule by, 9:289a-b
Illyrian migration, 9:289b
internal dissension among nobility, 9:291b
Italian campaigns, 5:383b, 9:221a, 290a, 292a-b
invasion of Po Valley, 8:376b
Italian kingdom, 6:443a, 7:2b
Jews and, 7:85b
Justinian I and, 7:201a-b
kings, recognition by Rome, 9:289a
language of, 6:435a, 437b
legal system
courts, 9:291a
land distribution, 9:290b
law codes, 7:471a-b
personality of law, 9:291a
migration of, 8:363a
Odoacer and, 2:93b, 9:290a
origin of confederacy, 9:289a
polychrome jewelry of, 8:364a
Ravenna as capital, 7:201b, 9:920b–921a, 10:262b, 263a, 264a
Roman Empire and, 10:466b
assimilation, 9:291a, 293a
recognized as federate allies, 2:93a
settlement of Pannonia, 9:289b
in Sicily, 11:264a
as slaves, 11:335a
in Sweden, 11:528b, 529a
Visigoths and, 12:471a
vs. Belisarios, 2:165a
vs. Huns, 12:468b, 469a

Ostrogoths, 2:92b–94a (*cont.*)
vs. Zeno the Isaurian, 12:743b
see also German law, early Germanic codes; Theodoric the Ostrogoth
Ostromir, *Evangelium,* 6:438a
Ostrovská píseň, 11:343b
Oswald of Northumbria, king. *See* Oswald, St.
Oswald of Ramsey, **9:294b–295a**
Frithegod and, 5:302a
Oswald, St.
Christianization of Northumbria, 1:107a
death at Maserfelth, 1:107b
German epics about, **9:293b–294b**
dating of, 9:294a
Münchner Oswald, 9:293b–294a
Sant Oswald von Norwegen, 9:294a-b
Wiener Oswald, 9:293b–294a
Oswald von Wolkenstein, 8:357b, **9:295a–297a**
at Council of Constance, 9:295a
conflict with Frederick IV, 9:295b–296a
crusade against Hussites, 9:296a
desire for posthumous fame, 9:296b
Es fügt sich, 9:295a
Es ist ain altgesprochner rat, 9:295b
in *Femegericht,* 9:296a
inheritance of, 9:295a
lyric poetry of, 5:436b
minnesingers and, 8:414a
Pisanello portrait, 9:295b (*illus.*)
polyphonic repertoire collection, 12:180b
privatization and, 8:359b
service to Sigismund, 9:295a-b
songs
autobiographical, 9:295a, 295b
popularity of, 9:296b
themes of, 9:296a-b
Oswald of Worcester, bishop, 4:518a
Oswald of York, St., biography of, 12:433b
Oswiu of Northumbria. *See* Oswy of Northumbria, king
Oswy of Northumbria, king
Benedict Biscop and, 2:168a
rule of, 4:454b
Otacher. *See* Odoacer
Otaq, **9:297a-b**
otaq-i humayun, 9:297a
in Ottoman miniatures, 9:297a, 297b (*illus.*)
protective wall, 9:297a
Turkish usage, 9:297b
Ótarr Innsteinsson. *See Hyndluljóð*
Ote tō staurō, 8:557a
Otenē. *See* Utik^{C}
Otfrid von Weissenburg, **9:297b–298b**
allegorical poetry, 5:427b
Evangelienbuch, 5:420b, 426b, 6:439b, 9:233b, 297b–298b
influence of *Heliand* on, 6:151a
Muspilli and, 8:650a
Hrabanus Maurus and, 6:308a
introduction of rhyming verse into German poetry, 2:225b–226a
Liber evangeliorum, 2:225b–226a
on musical instruments, 8:601a
rhyming verse and, 6:441a
Otherworld
in Celtic mythology, 9:47b
in Fenian poetry, 5:44b–45b
see also Paradise
Othman. *See* Osman I
Otho, cardinal, Henry III of England and, 11:607a
Otho de la Roche, in Byzantine Romania, 7:376b, 378a
Otia imperialia. See Gervase of Tilbury
Otloh of St. Emmeram, **9:298b–300a**
Amorbach Sermon, 9:299a
antidialecticism, 9:587b
autobiographical works, 9:299a
De doctrina spiritali, 9:299a
Dialogus de tribus quaestionibus, 9:299a
didactic-pastoral messages, 9:299a
Epistola de permissionis bonorum et malorum causis, 9:299a
hymns and tropes, 6:381b, 9:299a-b
Libellus de suis temptationibus, 9:299a
Liber de admonitione clericorum et laicorum, 9:299a
Liber de cursu spiritali, 9:299a
Liber proverbiorum, 9:299a
Liber visionum, 9:299a
saints' lives, 9:299a
theological messages, 9:299a
Translatio I, 9:299b
years at St. Emmeram's, 9:298b, 299b
Otokar. *See* Přemysl Otokar
Otr, in *Reginsmál,* 4:581a-b
Otranto Cathedral, floor mosaic, 10:501b
Ott, *Eraclius,* 5:450b
Ottar (9th century), northern voyage of, 4:555a
visit to King Alfred's court, 9:179a
Óttarr Innsteinsson (mythological character), in *Hyndluljóð,* 6:385b
Ottava rima. See Italian literature, poetry, octave
Otterburn, Battle of (1388), 10:428b
Otto II of Burgundy, count, 2:424b
Otto IV of Burgundy, count, 2:429b
Otto I (the Great) of Germany, emperor, **9:300a–301b,** 10:260b
alliance with German bishops, 9:300b–301a
annexation of Elbian Slav territory, 10:684a
archbishopric of Magdeburg, 10:684a
Billungs and, 2:235a
Christianity and, 8:442b–443a
in chronicles, 12:628a
church reforms of, 3:347b
compurgation and, 3:508b
coronation of, 1:35b, 5:476a, 8:377b, 9:301b, 10:18a-b, 682a
defense of Saxon duchy, 10:682a
duchies and, 5:508a–509b
election of, 4:426b
enfeoffment of bishops, 5:475b–476a
expansion of authority, 10:683b
Geneva and, 11:538a
Gesta Ottonis and, 6:316a
Hungarian campaigns, battle of the Lechfeld (955), 2:6a, 6:339a, 9:301a, 11:477b
imperial ideal under, 5:476a-b, 495a
intervention in Italy, 5:476a, 9:301b
ivory carvings commissioned by, 7:26b–27a
John XII and, 10:522b
land donations by, 8:378a
Magyars and, 5:475a
marriage of, 5:476a
Nikephoros II Phokas and, 9:133a
Notger of Liège and, 9:186a
problems facing, 5:475a
relations with, Byzantines, 7:634a-b
Rome and, 10:522b
seal of, 11:129a
selection of pope by, 3:604a
subordination of dukes, 9:300a
Sylvester II and, 11:552b
in Thietmar von Merseburg's chronicle, 12:28a
Otto II of Germany, emperor, 9:718b
in Alpert of Metz's history, 1:203b
defeat of, 5:475a
ducal selections of, 5:475b
duchy of Carinthia created by, 5:510a-b
Géza and, 6:339a
Rome and, 10:522b
rule of, 5:476b
in Thietmar von Merseburg's chronicle, 12:28a
Otto III of Germany, emperor, **9:301b–302b**
archbishopric of Gniezno, 10:684b
coronation, 9:302a
Gerbert of Aurillac and, 8:640a
Gospels of, 7:26b, 530a
Poland and, 9:302a-b, 719a-b
regency for, 9:302a
Reichenau Gospels of, 8:107b
relations with papacy, 5:495a, 9:302a-b
Sylvester II and, 3:347b, 11:553a
"Renovatio imperii Romanorum" and, 9:302a
Rome and, 10:522b
rule of, 5:476b
Stephen I of Hungary and, 11:478a
succession to, 4:426b
in Thietmar von Merseburg's chronicle, 12:27b–28a
tutored by Bernward, 2:197b
year 1000 and, 6:339a-b, 12:723b
Otto IV of Germany, emperor
coronation of, in *Willehalm,* 12:676a
election of, 4:25a, 5:214a-b
excommunication of, 5:214b
Gervase of Tilbury and, 7:365a
Innocent III and, 5:483a
Lateran IV and, 3:640b
rule of, 5:483a
vs. Innocent III, 11:269b–270a
Otto I of Wittelsbach, duke, 12:665a
acquisition of Bavaria (1180), 2:134b
Otto III of Bavaria, duke of Wittelsbach (*d.* 1312), 6:344a
Otto of Bamberg, St., **9:300a**
role in Concordat of Worms, 9:300a
Otto von Botenlauben, **9:304a–305a**

Otto of Brunswick
coronation of, 12:538a, 538b
excommunication, 12:538b
imperial claims of, 9:58b
Innocent III and, 6:464b
in song, 12:538b
Wolfger von Erla and, 12:672b–673a
Otto of Freising, 2:6a, 3:405a, **9:302b–304a**
aristocratic background, 9:302b
Arnold of Brescia and, 1:539b
Chronicon, 9:378a (*illus.*)
ecclesiastical career, 9:302b
Gesta Friderici, 2:239b–240a, 9:302b, 303b
Rahewin's continuation of, 10:249b–250a
History of the Two Cities, 6:264a, 9:302b–303a
historical theories, 9:303b
sources for, 9:303a
on Hungary, 6:340b
Metellus of Tegernsee and, 8:299a
on millennialism, 8:386b
origins of Babenberg family and, 2:33a-b
on Roger II, 11:268a
on St. Bernard of Clairvaux, 2:192a
Spanish Alfonsine chronicles and, 11:435b
spread of learning and, 9:303b
on Zurich, 11:538b
Otto of Northeim, revolt against Henry IV, 10:684b
Otto of Saxony. *See* Otto I (the Great) of Germany, emperor
Otto of Zeigenhain, archbishop of Trier, 9:123a
Otto-Guillaume (*d.* 1027), vs. Capetians, 2:424b
Ottokar II of Bohemia, king
in Ulrich von Eschenbach's *Alexander,* 12:249b–250a
vs. Rudolph of Habsburg, 11:540b
Ottoman law
codification of under Mehmed II, 8:264a
Islamic law, 9:309a
secular laws, 9:309a
Ottomans, **9:305a–310b**
Aleppo and, 1:145b–146a
Anatolian principalities, 1:241b–242a, 2:136a, 136b, 8:536a, 9:306b
annexation of, 9:307a, 308b
in Arčēš, 1:423a
armed forces, 12:553a
archers, 9:307a-b
firearms, 12:553a
mamluk institution and, 8:69a
salaries, 9:307b
standing army, 9:307b
see also Janissary
in Armenia, 1:474a, 486a, 514a
patriarch and, 1:504a
art and architecture under, 6:612b
Balkan campaigns, 2:136a, 8:537a, 9:306a–307a
battle at Černomen (1371), 2:502a, 4:56a, 8:135a, 11:180a
battle at Kosovo Polje (1389), 2:502a, 4:56a, 8:536a, 11:180a
Bosnia, 2:338a-b, 339a-b, 11:474a, 476a
Bulgaria, 8:536a
conquest of the Balkan states, 6:347b
Serbia, 8:536a
Walachia and Moldavia, 12:503b
Basra and, 2:127b
Beirut and, 2:164a
bookbinding and, 8:99b
Byzantine Empire as vassal state, 9:331b
capture of Ikonion, 6:418b
capture of Rhodes (1522), 10:365b
civil wars, 9:308a
as classic Islamic caliphate, 9:309a
concept of state, 9:308b
in Crimea, 3:678b–680b
defeated by Mamluk sultan Qāᵓitbāy, 10:222b, 223a
Devlet-i Osmaniyye, 9:308a
devshirme, 8:69a
duchy of Naxos and, 9:91a
dynasty
consolidation of, 9:307b–308a
origins, 9:305a–306b
empire of
boundaries, 9:305 (map)
centralization, 9:308b
historical accounts, 2:517b
Enguerrand VII and, 4:491a
Ephesus and, 4:495a
fiefs, 9:306b, 307b
of Orthodox metropolitans, 9:310a
financial administration
military, 9:309a-b
waqfs, 9:309b
frontier tradition, 9:309a
gazīs, 7:47a
geographic studies in, 5:394a
German representative assemblies and, 10:330b, 331b
ghāzī period, 9:305b–306a
Greek language and, 6:443b
Hungary, 4:55b–56a, 9:306b–307a, 307a
battle at Varna (1444), 6:347b, 363b
Buda under, 2:396b
conquest of, 6:337b, 349a–350a, 10:514b
Hungarian-Burgundian crusade against, 4:56a
vs. Hunyadi, 6:363b, 364a
invasion of Morea, 8:486b
jewelry of, 5:377a
in Karin, 7:215b
in Kars, 7:221b
kul, 9:38b, 306a
Kutᶜaisi and, 7:311b
in Lebanon, 7:533a
Louis I and, 6:345b–346a
Mamluk dynasty and, 2:137b, 3:400a, 8:75b–76b, 142a, 9:309a, 11:145a-b
Manuel II Palaiologos and, 8:92a, 92b
Mistra under, 8:446b
navy, 9:309a
expansion of, 9:307a
Nobadia and, 9:198b
non-Muslims under, 9:309b–310a
dhimmi status, 9:309b
segregation, 9:310a
Ochrid and, 9:208b–209a
origin of, 5:518b, 9:287b
origins of, 11:158a
Qadirīya order and, 7:112a
relations with Romanian principalities, 10:514a-b, 515a
revolt against, by Anatolian begs, 7:214a
rule of Ankara, 1:302b
in Sebaste, 11:132a
Sigismund and, 6:346b
social structure, 9:309a-b
succession arrangements, 9:307b–308b
sultans of, at Brusa, 2:392b
supreme titles, 9:308b
Syria and, 11:562a
Tabrīz and, 11:571a
Thessaloniki and, 12:26b
Uzun Ḥasan and, 12:342b–343a
vs. Byzantines
Bithynia, 2:500a, 500b
capture of Brusa, 2:500b
Gallipoli, 2:501b
siege of Constantinople, 2:504a-b
Western alliance against, 2:501b–502a
vs. Epiros, 4:500a
vs. Kydones, 4:135b
vs. Sigismund, 11:287a
vs. Venetians, 2:137b
vs. Vlad Ţepeş, 12:485a, 485b
William II and, 7:381a
Xlatᶜ and, 12:713b
see also Andronikos III Palaiologos, Byzantine emperor; *Fatwā*
Ottonian architecture. *See* Pre-Romanesque architecture
Ottonian art. *See* Pre-Romanesque art
Ottonian sequence. *See* Sequence
Ottonians. *See* Saxon dynasty
Otᶜχtᶜ eklesia, 5:409b
Ouar-Khounni, Huns and, 6:352b
Oudenaarde. *See* Audenarde
Oukhimerion. *See* Kutᶜaisi
Ounce, **9:310b–311a**
Oungia, 12:581b
Our Lady (church: Nuremberg), 9:202a
Ourma. *See* Vrma giganti
Ousia, Basil the Great on, 2:121b–122a
Ousia (*essentia*). *See* Trinitarian doctrine
Ousiakos, 11:231b
Outlawry, **9:311a–312b**
actions of account, 9:312a
in Anglo-Saxon law, 9:311a
attainder and, 6:427b
excommunication and, 4:536a
inlawing outlaws, 9:311b
in nonfelonious litigation, 9:312a
process of, 9:311a
punishments for, 9:311b
Robin Hood and, 10:436a, 436b–437a
royal writs, 9:311b
in trespass cases, 9:312a
in Viking law, 12:423b
Ouvrée (unit of measure), 12:587a
Ouwater, Albert van, 5:86b, **9:312b**
Raising of Lazarus, 9:312b

Ovid (Publius Ovidius Naso), **9:312b–314b**
Arnulf of Orléans on, 7:366a
Ars amatoria, 7:367b, 368a
influence on Guillaume de Lorris, 6:23a
play based on, 4:283a
translations of, French, 9:313a
Carolingian Latin poetry and, 3:101b
Catalan translations of, 3:169a
on colored hair, 2:147a
Fasti, 9:313a
Heroides, 9:313a
Baudri and, 7:364a
translations of, 9:314a
hunting and, 6:358b
Icelandic *mansöngvar* and, 10:406a
John of Garland and, 7:133b–134a
literary influence
in 12th-13th centuries, 7:367b
on allegory, 1:180b, 183b–184a, 189a-b, 9:314a-b
on comedies, 9:313a-b, 314a
on courtly love, 3:671a–672a
elegaic poetry, 9:313a
English MS illustrations, 9:313b (*illus.*)
on love poetry, 1:184a
on vernacular poetry, 9:314a, 314b
Metamorphoses, 7:367b
Albrecht von Halberstadt's translation, 1:131b–132a, 9:314a
Arcana deorum on, 7:370a
Hrotswitha von Gandersheim and, 6:314a
Integumenta Ovidii and, 7:368a
Reductorium morale and, 7:369b
surviving text, 9:313a
translations of, 9:314a
preservation by monastic copyists, 9:313a
Proverbia quae dicuntur super natura feminarum and, 6:630a
Remedia amoris, 3:671b, 7:368a
translations of, 9:314a
Rodríguez del Padrón's *Bursario* and, 10:439a
Roman d'Enéas and, 8:225b
Roman de la Rose and, 10:449b
Tristia, 9:313a
in Urbino Codex of *Divine Comedy,* 12:394 (*illus.*)
Ysengrimus and, 12:733b
see also Bligger von Steinach
Ovide moralisé, 1:183b, 189b, 9:314a, **9:315a**
Pierre Bersuire's Latin version, 4:544b, 9:315a
Tesoretto and, 7:383a
Ovidian (pseudonymous) works, *De mirabilibus mundi. See De mirabilibus mundi*
Owain Fawr. *See* Owain Gwynedd
Owain Glyn D^{W}1r, Welsh ruler
anti-Lancastrian alliance, 12:523b–524a
Iolo Goch and, 6:500b
religious and educational reforms, 12:524a
revolt of, 12:528a, 528b
Owain Gwynedd (Owain Fawr), **9:315a-b**
Bangor (Wales) and, 2:71b
conflict with Henry II of England, 9:315b, 12:517b
excommunication of, 9:315b, 12:518a
exploits before accession, 9:315a
praise in poetry, 12:604b
sons of, 6:386a
title of prince, 12:518b
Owain of Rheged, king, Taliesin and, 11:582a
Owain (son of Urien Rheged), Arthurian literature and, 12:331b
Owen ap Meredith ap Tider. *See* Tudor, Owen
Owen the Bald of Strathclyde, king, 11:490b
Owl and the Nightingale, The, 8:315b, 330a, **9:315b–319b**
antifeminism, 1:324b
art of song as subject of, 9:316a-b
authorship of, 9:317a-b
debate form and, 8:315b
dialect of, 9:317b
Dunbar's *Flyting of Dunbar and Kennedy* and, 8:324b
Franciscan influence in, 9:316b–317a
manuscripts of, 1:264b
Nightingale's character in, 9:316b, 318b–319a
Owl's character in, 9:316b, 318b–319a
rhyming couplets in, 8:315b, 321b, 344b
sources of, 9:319a
stylistic aspects, 9:317b, 318a
Ox, 1:293b–294a
plow teams, 1:90a, 90b–91a
use in threshing, 1:77b
Ox-tongue partisan (pole arm), 7:324 (*illus.*), 325a
Oxeia, 8:617a, 617b
Oxford
Black Death in, 2:262a
town-gown riot in (1263), 8:317a
Oxford Calculators, 11:534b–535a
effects of motion, alternative measures, 9:626a-b
Oxford Psalter, 1:262a-b, **9:319b–320a**
Oxford University, **9:320a–322a,** 9:320b (*illus.*), 12:284b–285a
administrative organization of, 9:320b–321a
Aristotelianism at, 1:461b, 464a-b
Cambridge University and, 3:59a–60a
chancellorship of, 9:320b–321a
Chichele and, 3:83b
clergy at, 7:369a, 370a
college system, 9:321a-b
curriculum of, 9:321a, 321b
adaptation for changing needs, 9:321b
textbooks, 11:690a-b
difficulties in late Middle Ages, 9:321b
dispersals of, 9:320a-b
faculty of arts, ethical studies, 9:595a
faculty, in 13th century, 6:1a
Hebrew studies and, 3:314a
legal recognition of, 9:320a
library of, 7:563a
Lollard movement, 7:645b–646a
Magdalen College, Sir John Fastolf's estate and, 9:450b
masters of, 9:320a, 321a
Merton College
Aristotle's *Physics* and, 1:464b
spread of Arabic numerals, 1:396b
New College, 12:645a
William Wynford and, 12:711b
Nicholas Trevet and, 12:186a
Ockham and, 9:157a, 209b
origins of, 9:320a
physics research, 9:626a-b
Queens College, brewery at, 2:375a
Richard de Bury's plan to establish a lending library, 10:386b
Roger Bacon and, 2:35a, 41a
statute on the teaching of grammar (*ca.* 1344), 10:352b
Trinitarian doctrine and, 12:194a-b, 196b–197a
Vacarius' *Liber pauperum* and, 12:343b
Wyclif and, 12:706a, 709a, 709b
see also Mertonians
Oxus River. *See* Amu Darya
Oxyrhynchos, 3:588a
Oyer and terminer, **9:322a–323b**
ad hoc commissions, 9:322a–323a
decline of, 9:323a
regulation of, 9:322b–323a
defined, 9:322a
general commissions (trailbastons), 9:323a-b
changing nature of, 9:323a-b
jail delivery, 7:45a
justices, trespass and, 12:185b–186a
treason and, 12:167a, 168a-b
Özbek, restoration of Kaffa, 8:475b
Özbeg, 6:419b
Golden Horde under, 5:573a

P

Pablo Christiani, 7:81b
polemics with Moses Naḥmanides, 9:53b
Pablo de Santa María. *See* Paul of Burgos
Pacem reformare. See Reform, idea of
Pacher, Michael, **9:323b–325a,** 9:324 (*illus.*)
influences on, 9:323b–325a
St. Wolfgang Altarpiece, 5:611a, 9:323b–325a (*illus.*), 10:83a
Pachomius, St., 10:455a
early libraries and, 7:559b
foundation of monasteries, 8:454b
monastic community
at Pebou, 8:461a
at Tabennisi, 8:460b

monastic rule of, 3:595a, 8:460b–461a, 12:152a
in Studios Monastery, 11:495a
Pachymeres, George, histories, 6:247a
Pacino di Bonaguida, **9:325a**
Tree of Life, 9:325b (*illus.*)
Pacio da Firenze, sculptures in the charterhouse of St. Martin at Naples, 9:59b
Pacioli, Luca, *Summa de arithmetica,* double-entry method of accounting, 1:41a, 41b
Pack (unit of measure), product variations, 12:584b
Pact of ᶜUmar, 7:72a-b, 84b
people of the book and, 9:498b
Pactis legis Alamannorum, 11:526b
Pactum dotale. See Dowry
Pactum Lotharii, 11:336b
Pactus legis Salicae, 7:472a
Paderborn, bishopric of, representative assemblies and, 10:332b–333a
Paderborn Cathedral, Roger of Helmarshausen and, 10:442a
Padilla, Juan de, religious poetry of, 11:422b–423a
Padua
Arena (Scrovegni) Chapel. *See* Arena (Scrovegni) Chapel (Padua)
inns in, 6:471a, 471b
relations with, Venice, 12:393a, 673a
trecento painters, 12:175b–176a (*illus.*)
Padua Cathedral, Francesco Zabarella and, 12:735a
Padua, University of, 12:285b–286a
exemplar, 11:692b
Francesco Zabarella and, 12:735a
law school, 7:514a-b
statutes introduced at, 10:80a
Páez de Ribera, Ruy, in *Cancionero de Baena,* 11:419b
Pagan literature. *See* Classical literary studies
Paganism
allegorization of pagan stories, 4:544b
Augustine of Hippo and, 1:650a-b
in Baltic lands, 2:61a–68a
Basque, 2:126a
charms, in Old High German, 3:273b–274a
Christian adaptations of pagan symbols, 4:3349b
Christmas and, 3:317b–318a
fertility-rite survivals, 4:283b
in 4th- and 5th-century Rome, 2:91a
in iconography, Coptic, 3:587a, 589b
Iranian, 12:720b–721a
of Julian the Apostate, emperor, 7:180b–181a
in medieval magic, 8:32b
in Mercia, 11:338a
in Poland, 9:717a-b, 720a
in Scandinavia, 12:2b, 5a
slavery and, 11:338a-b
survival in early Christian art, 4:350b–351a
survival of rituals in Europe, 8:25a-b
Zanj, 12:739b
Pagano della Torre, 8:379a
Paganus, Peter Lombard's theology school and, 12:21b
Paganus Bolotinus, 7:367a
Page, courtesy books for, 3:660b–661b
Pageant money, 8:661b
Pageant wagon, 4:284b, 285a, 8:661b, 662a
for York Plays, 12:728a
Pagi
in Carolingian Empire, 3:107b
see also County, Carolingian
Pagina pastorum. See Second Shepherds' Play
Pagus, **9:325b–326a**
casual meaning of, 9:326a
derivation of "pagan" from, 9:326a
ecclesiastical usage of, 9:326a
political or jurisdictional meaning of, 9:325b–326a
in Vermandois, 12:395b
Pahlavi language. *See* Persian language, Middle Persian
Pahlavi literature, **9:326a–327b**
Arabic translators of, 12:128a, 129a
čāštak, 8:204b
evolution of, 9:326a-b
geographical listings, 10:661a
Kārnāmag-i Ardešir-i Bābagān, 7:220b–221a
oral tradition of, 9:326a
Parthians and, 9:444a
scholarship in, 9:326b
translations in, 9:326b
from Greek and Sanskrit, 10:670b
under Islamic rule, 9:326b, 327a-b
wisdom literature, 9:327a
Xusrō I and, 12:714b
see also Dēnkard; Iranian literature; *Mātakdān Ī Hazār Dātastān;* Sasanian culture
Pahlavi script, 6:505b, 9:326b
Pahlavis, Tabrīz and, 11:571a
Pahlawuni, **9:327b–329a**
churches in Ani in Širak, 1:292a
domains and titles of, 9:327b–328a
Kamsarakan and, 7:208a
katᶜołikoi, 9:328a-b
decline of, 9:328b
Paidagogos. See Clement of Alexandria
Paien de Montdidier, 3:304a
Paigi, in Burgundy, 2:424a, 427a
Paikuli, **9:329a-b**, 9:329b (*illus.*)
inscriptions on, 9:329a
reconstruction of, 9:329 (*illus.*)
Painter's Handbook, paint coloring, 11:635b
Painting, techniques. *See* Fresco painting; Manuscript illumination; Oil painting; Panel painting; Tempera painting
Pairlement Chloinne Tomáis, 6:533a
Paisy Yaroslavov (15th century), 9:137a
Paix (township). *See* "Peace" (township)
Pakuda, Ibn. *See* Bahya ben Joseph ibn Paqūdā
Pala d'Oro, **9:330a–331a**, 9:330 (*illus.*)
as example of cloisonné enamels, 4:438a
see also Paliotto of S. Ambrogio
Palace of the Despots (Mistra), 8:446b
Palaces
Abbasid, in Iraq, 6:606a
architecture
influence on Byzantine church design, 4:343a
triclinium plan, 12:188a-b
churches in, 4:337a
with *eyvān*s, 6:603a
in Samarra, 6:595b, 597b
Umayyad, 6:594a–595b
in Spain, 6:601b
see also Caliphate, residences
Palaiologan art, in Serbia, 2:450b, 11:188a
Palaiologoi, **9:331a–332a**
art under, 2:447b–451a, 9:331b, 10:310b
Byzantine dynastic rule, 2:498b–504b
classical scholarship under, 11:50a
commerce under, 12:104a-b
decentralization of authority under, 9:331b
defeated by Turks, 9:331b
development of medicine under, 8:245b–246a
early family members, 9:331a
rise to power, 9:331a
Trebizond and, 12:168b–169a
Palamas, Gregory, essence of God, 9:563a
Palamism, 5:672b
Palas, khan at, 11:149 (*illus.*)
Palatinates, **9:332a-b**
in England, 4:464b–465a, 9:332a-b
royal authority in, 9:332a-b
in Germany, 9:332a
Louis the Bavarian and, 2:135b
representative assemblies and, 10:329a, 333a
Rhenish, under Wittelsbachs, 12:665a
Palatine Chapel (Palermo), woodwork, 8:562b
Palatine court. *See* Charlemagne
Palazzo del Capitano (Padua), public clock in, 3:29b
Palazzo Venezia, Rome, ivory triptych, 2:454a
Pale, the, 4:299b, 6:519b, 520a
Paleae. See Gratian
Palearium poetarum. See Wethamstede, John, abbot of St. Albans
Palencia, *mester de clerecía* and, 11:412a
Palencia, Alfonso de, 11:436a
Batalla campal de los perros contra los lobos, 11:422a
chronicle of the campaign against Granada, 11:422a
Décadas, 11:422a
translations of his own works, 11:457a
Universal vocabulario en latín y en romance, 11:425a, 441b
Palencia, University of, 12:286b
mester de clerecía and, 2:187a
Paleo-Serbian language, in Romania, 10:510a
Paleodemography. *See* Demography
Paleography
Arabic and Persian, **9:332b–334a**
additional consonants in Persian script, 9:333b

Paleography (*cont.*)
  Arabic and Persian (*cont.*)
    Arabic script, 9:333a
    development of measured writing, 9:333b–334a
    kūfī script, 9:333b
    naskhī and *thuluth* scripts, 9:334a
    nastaᶜlīq script, 9:334a
    thuluth, 12:53b, 54 (*illus.*)
  in archaeological studies, 1:427b
  definition of, 9:334a
  Western European, **9:334a–351b**
    applied, 9:337b–339b
    calligraphic concerns in, 9:336b–337a
    decline of Roman Empire and, 9:342b
    decline of scribes, 9:350b–351a
    development of, 9:335a-b
    early medieval scripts, 9:342b–345a
    elements of individual letters, 9:336b
    influence of printing press on, 9:350b
    library history and, 7:558b
    modern history of, 9:334b–336a
    nomenclature, 9:336a–337b
    as practical necessity for medieval scribes, 9:334b
    predominance of book scripts in, 9:334a-b
    provenance as evidence for place and date of origin, 9:339b, 340b–341a
    purposes of, 9:335a-b
    script classifications, 9:337a-b
    shading defined, 9:336b–337a
    styles defined, 9:337a
    technological aids for, 9:335b–336a
    theoretical paleography, 9:339b–341a
    variations in Latin scripts, 9:334b–335a
    see also Alphabets; Gothic scripts; Humanistic scripts; Insular scripts; Literacy, Western European; Manuscript books; Roman scripts
Palermo, **9:351b–352b**
  art of, 10:503b
  as capital of Norman Sicily, 9:352a
  captured (1072), 11:265b
  commerce, 11:275a
  conquered by
    Arabs (831), 7:4a, 9:352a
    Byzantines, (535), 9:352a
    Normans (1072), 9:352a, 10:440a, 11:265b
    Vandals (440), 9:352a
  economic life of, 9:352a-b
  important Norman monuments of, 9:352a
  Islamic culture of, 11:266b
  Palatine Chapel, 5:22a (*illus.*), 23b
  Roger I and, 10:440a
  slaves in, 11:338b
  under Muslims, 9:352a
  vs. Roger I, 11:263a
Palermo Cathedral, 11:274b
Palestine, **9:352b–355b**
  ban on Jewish settlement in, 9:354a
  Black Death in, 2:259a
  Cabalistic schools in, 3:3a
  conquered by
    ᶜAmr ibn al-ᶜĀṣ, 1:237a
    crusaders (1099), 9:354b
    Muslims, 9:353b, 353b–354a
    Turks (878), 9:354b
  economy of, 9:355a
  evolution of religious importance to Muslims, 9:354a
  Islamic administration of, 6:591b
  Jews in, 3:16a
    illuminated manuscripts, 7:66a–67a
    synagogue art of, 65a-b
    under Muslim rule, 7:103a–105b
  pilgrimage to
    Jewish, 7:104a, 9:652a–653a
    Russian Orthodox, 9:653a-b
    Western European Christian, 4:27b, 7:59a-b, 9:657a-b
  provinces of, 9:352b
  religious persecution in, 7:103a-b, 9:352b–353a, 353a, 10:670b
  Samaritan revolts, 10:639b
  Sasanid invasion (614), 7:103b, 9:353a
  Seljuk penetration into, 11:153a
  Turk, Arab, and Qarmatian warfare over, 9:354b
  under Byzantines, 9:353a
  under crusaders, 9:354b–355a
  under Egyptian Mamluks, 9:355a
  under Imruʾ al-Qays, 6:430a
  under Muslim rule, 9:354a-b
Palestinian notation. *See* Musical notation, Coislin
Palestinian rite, as recorded in Cairo genizah, 7:620b
Palestinian Song. See Walther von der Vogelweide
Palestinian Talmud. *See* Talmud
Palia, 10:511a
Palice of Honour. See Douglas, Gavin
Palimpsest, **9:355b**
  in painting, 9:355b
  in texts, 9:355b
  wall at S. Maria Antiqua in Rome, 9:346 (*illus.*), 355b
Paliotto of S. Ambrogio, 8:288 (*illus.*), 289a, **9:355b–357a**
  commission and design of, 1:254b, 9:355b–356a
  derivation of name, 9:356a-b
  Wolvinus and, 8:289a, 377b, 9:355b, 12:682a
  see also Pala d'Oro
Palisenē, 1:515a
Páll Jónsson, bishop, 11:328b, 12:359a
Palladios, **9:357a**
  Lausiac History, 6:58a, 9:357a
    as a model for *paterika,* 9:457a
Palladius of Auxerre
  mission to Ireland, 3:214a, 6:514b, 9:463a, 464a-b
  Patrick and, 9:463a, 464a, 465b
Palladius of Helenopolis, Nitrian monastic communities, 6:213a
Palladius, Rutilius Taurus Aemilianus (*ca.* 350), 4:511a
  De re rustica
    translated by Ferrer Sayol, 8:300b
    translated into Catalan, 9:510b
    on garden drainage, 5:360b
Pallavicini, Guido, Bodonitsa and, 7:376a
Pallium, **9:357a–358a**, 9:357b (*illus.*), 12:402a–403a
  derivation of, 9:357a
  used at investiture in Rome, 12:152a
Palls, 5:320b
Palm Sunday. *See* Holy Week
Palm (unit of measure), 12:588a
Palma, irrigation of, 6:558a
Palma, *bachiller, Divina retribución sobre la caída de España,* 11:422a
Palma Cathedral (Majorca), 3:568b (*illus.*), 568b–569a
Palmesel, 4:492a
Palmette, **9:358a-b**
Palms, benediction of, 2:177b, 178a
Palmyra, ancient paganism in, influence on the Nuṣayrīs, 9:4a
Pałnatun. See Palisenē
Páls saga biskups, 6:352a, **9:358b–359b**, 11:328b
  authorship of, 9:358b
Pałtasar, 4:112b, 113a
Paltiel, Rabbi, in Jewish legends, 8:24a
Paludamentum, **9:359b–360a**, 9:359 (*illus.*)
  as robe of Jesus before Crucifixion, 9:359b
Palunikᶜ, 11:599a
Pamiers, Statutes of, 7:467a–468a
Pammakaristos (church: Constantinople)
  parekklesion of, 4:345b, 346 (*illus.*)
  sculptural elements, 4:345b
  south facade, 4:345b
Pamphilus de amore, 7:367b, 368b
  Ovidian influence, 9:313b
Pamphilus, Gliscerium et Birria, 7:367b
Pamphlet on the Case of Formosus. See Eugenius Vulgarius
Pamphylos, 9:76a, 11:231b
Pamphylus, 6:630a
Pamplona
  French settlers in, 9:71a
  origins of the kingdom of Navarre and, 9:67b
  taken by Charlemagne (778), 2:126a, 9:68a
Panagia (church: Chios), 4:345a
Panagia tou Arakou (church: Lagoudera), wall paintings, 2:445b
Pañchatantra, 6:508b, 8:23b, 10:670b
  Aristoteles und Phyllis and, 1:455b
  basis of the story of Stephanites and Ichnelates, 8:19a
  Burzōi and, 12:714b
  Spanish version of, 11:414a
  transmission to European literature, 3:31b
Pandects, 5:565b, 567a
Pandemic cycles. *See* Plagues
Pandero, 8:563a
Pandora (musical instrument). *See Ṭunbūr*
Pandulf of Capua, Lombard prince, 11:264b
  Sergius of Naples and, 11:264b

Pandulf, papal legate, Langton and, 7:338b
Panegyric
in Byzantine rhetoric, 10:349b, 350a, 350b
in Gaelic Scottish literature, 11:113b, 114a
Panegyricon Berengarii. See Berengarii imperatoris gesta
Panel painting, **9:360a–362b**
in Bohemia, 5:610a
Byzantine, 5:605a-b
Cennino Cennini on, 9:360a
construction of panel, 9:360a-b
continental influences on, 5:610a
destruction of, 5:604a
early panels, 9:360a
in England, 5:609b–610a
in Flanders, 5:611a–612a
Florentine, 12:171b–172b (*illus.*), 175a-b
in France, 5:607b–609a
fresco painting and, 5:296a
in Germany, 5:610a–611a
half-length Madonna style, 9:362a
innovations in, 5:606a-b
in Italy, 5:603b–604a, 605a–607b
during dugento period, 9:361a
during trecento period, 9:361a-b
Pisan School, 5:605b
polyptychs in, 9:361b, 362a, 10:29a
revival of (12th century), 9:360a
Russian, 6:411a–412a, 10:588b–589b
secular art and, 9:362a
segmented quality of Florentine panels, 9:361b
Sienese, 12:172b–175a (*illus.*)
of Simone Martini, 11:299b–300a
single wingless panels, 9:361b–362a
size of, 9:361a
in Spain, 5:612a, 10:505b
stained glass windows and, 5:552a-b
subject matter, 9:361b
techniques, 9:360a-b
gesso, 5:513b–514a
tempera, 9:360b, 11:666a
undercoating of panel, 9:360b
Pangat simul eia, 6:317b
"Pange, lingua." *See* Venantius Fortunatus
"Pange, lingua gloriosi." *See* Aquinas, Thomas, St., hymns of
Panisorhythmic motet. *See* Motet
Pannage in woods, rights of, 9:455a
Pannartz, Arnold, 10:124b
Pannonhalma/Martisberg Abbey. *See* Abbey Pannonhalma/Martisberg
Pannonia, 2:4b
Croatians in, 4:1b, 2a
Tomislav of Croatia and, 12:69a
Pannonian March, Magyars and, 6:338a
Panodoros, chronography of, 3:18b
Panormia. See Ivo of Chartres, St.; Osbern of Gloucester
Panormitanus. *See* Nicolaus de Tudeschis
Panphilus, 4:283a
Panpipes, 8:604a
Pantaleon. See Konrad von Würzburg
Pantaléon, Jacques. *See* Urban IV, pope
Pantegni. See Constantine the African
Panteón de los Reyes. *See* S. Isidoro (church: León)
Pantheon. See Geoffrey of Viterbo
Pantheon (Rome), 10:519a
archaeology of, 1:426a
conversion to Christian use, 9:690b
Pantokrator (epithet for Christ), **9:362b**
Pantokrator (monastery: Constantinople)
decorative elements in design, 4:344b
design of, 4:344a
floor mosaics, 8:492b (*illus.*), 493a-b
hospital, 8:245b, 246b
Pantoleon
influence of style, 2:438b
Menologion of Basil II, illustrations for, 2:438b
Pantry and buttery, royal, 6:304b
Panuccio del Bagno, 6:644b
Panzer, Georg, *Annales typografici,* 10:127a
Panziera, Ugo, 6:663a
Paolino Piero, *Merlino,* 1:572b–573a
Paolo di Dono. *See* Uccello, Paolo
Paolo di Giovanni Fei, 5:537a, **9:363a**
Presentation of the Virgin, 9:364 (*illus.*)
Paolo Lafranchi da Pistoia, 6:645a
Paolo da Perugia (director of Naples library), 2:278a
Paolo Veneziano, **9:363a**
Death of the Virgin, 9:364 (*illus.*)
Nicoletto Semitecolo and, 11:159a
Pap of Armenia, king, 1:559b, 560a
murder of, 1:476a
murder of St. Nersēs (the Great) and, 9:102a
Papacy
absence from Rome, 10:524a
according to Aquinas, 12:41a
administration
bureaucratization of, 3:637b
datary and, 4:107a
financial office, 1:206b
Angevins and, 11:272a
in ante-Nicene era, 9:365a–367a
archives, 1:446a, 446b
authority over secular rulers, 9:374a
Ausculta fili and, 2:3b–4a
Avignon. *See* Avignon papacy
banking and, 2:77b
beatification and, 2:143a
Benedictines and, 2:175b
Bonsignori bank and, 11:279a
bulls of, 2:418a-b
calendar used in official documents, 3:19b–20a
caliphate and, 8:651a
canonization procedures, 3:67b, 68a-b, 6:68b
Carolingian and Ottonian periods, 9:365a, 372b–375b
centralization of, 12:160a
church reform and, 11:517b
in 11th century, 9:365a, 375b–379a
to 1054, 3:348a–349a
Cluniac order and, 3:470a-b
in art, 10:507a
conciliar theory and, 3:511b–512a, 516a-b
Marsilius of Padua, 4:132b–133a
Nicholas of Cusa, 9:124b
consecration of pope, 3:603a
under Byzantines, 3:603a-b
consistorium of, 3:541b
consultation with cardinals, 3:95a
crisis of monarchy in, Council of Vienne and, 3:643a–645b
crusades
Holy Land, 4:16b–17b, 18a
political, 4:57b–62a
decline of imperial authority in West and, 9:370a-b
decline of papal power, 9:375a
degradation of a pope, 4:134a
deposition of a pope, 4:160a-b
causes for, 3:647a
ecclesiastical benefice and, 2:179b
election of a pope, 3:523b, 603a, 604a-b
cardinals and, 3:94b, 6:499a
Marsilius on, 4:133a
Nicholas II and, 3:93b
English church and, 3:578b
Ennodius and, 4:491b
episcopal benedictions and, 2:178a
False Decretals and, 4:126a, 126b
first papal Jubilee, 3:360a
following investiture conflict, 6:500a
Frederick II and, 11:270a, 272a
German princes and, 5:461a
Germanic invasions and, 9:371a
Gregorian reforms and, 10:287b–288b
Gregory I's Italian policies and, 5:669a
Gregory VII's activist conception of, 5:670a–671a
Guiscards and, 11:265a
Hohenstaufen dynasty and, 5:461a-b
Hundred Years War and, 6:334b
Hungary and, 6:339a-b, 340a, 341b
support for Charles I, 6:344a
income of, 3:94a, 11:605b
Rome and, 10:525b
infallibility of, 5:203a-b
controversy over John XXII, 4:377a
Thomist principles of hierarchy and, 4:375b–376a
interdict and, 6:495b, 497a
Jewish money lenders and, 2:81a
John of Salisbury on, 7:140b
Jubilee indulgences and, 9:660b
lawyer-popes, 1:58b
Maronites and, 11:561b, 564a
marriage and, 4:610a
mendicant orders and, 4:251b
Normans and, 11:265b
origins and development of, 3:523b–525a, **9:363a–379b**
appearance of "chair of Peter" (*cathedra Petri*) concept, 9:367b
early church and patristic period, 3:341b–342a, 9:365b
ecclesiastical travel and, 12:152a, 158b, 160a, 161b–162a
hierocratic theory in, 10:20a–21a
papal vs. secular jurisdiction, 8:155a
in political theory, 10:17b–18b, 20a–21a
pope's title, 9:367b, 10:31b–32a

Papacy (*cont.*)
origins and development of (*cont.*)
rescripts, 10:335a
role of the Medici bankers, 8:242b
Roman terminology borrowed for church, 9:365b–366a
translation of empire and, 12:143a-b
see also Two Swords, Doctrine of
papal supremacy, 3:352a-b, 4:372b, 373a–374a, 373b–374a, 374b, 375b, 376a, 8:154b
advocated by Augustinus Triumphus, 2:1a
Aristotelianism and, 1:465a
debate over, 4:373a–374a, 374b
Donation of Constantine and, 4:257b–259a
Eastern-Western church union and, 7:348b
first defined, 3:653b
Gregory VII's *Dictatus papae* and, 4:177a-b
Irenaeus on, 9:365b
mandate of Peter, 2:460b, 9:363b, 365a
policy toward Jews, 7:75b, 76a-b, 78a–79a, 88a-b, 109a–110a
pope as the vicar of Christ, 4:374b, 375b, 375b–374a
in writings of Egidius Colonna, 4:400a
popes from St. Peter to Pius III (listing), 9:368a–369b
post-Nicene era, 9:365a, 367a–372b
powers of, 3:343b, 377a-b, 10:21a–22b
Boniface VIII on, 3:354a
differences from Byzantine patriarchy, 9:459a-b
False Decretals in, 4:126a
Henry of Cremona on, 6:165b
John of Paris on, 7:136b–137a
royal attacks on, 3:643b–644a
see also plenitudo potestatis
reform of
by Henry III of Germany, 5:477b
by Hildebrand, 5:477b–478a
by Humbert of Silva Candida, 5:477b
in 11th century, 9:375b–379a, 379a
moral emphasis of early reform popes, 9:376b
relations with
Bosnia, 7:309a
Byzantine church, 9:370b
Byzantine Empire, 3:10a-b, 4:30a, 6:400b, 9:331a-b
Denmark, 4:153b, 154b
France, 9:385b
Holy Roman Empire, 3:11b, 353a, 603b–604a, 4:58a, 102b, 103a, 9:370b–371a, 372a-b, *see also* Investiture conflict
Ilkhanids, 6:420a, 420b
John III Vatatzes, 7:348a
Latin Empire of Constantinople, 7:348a
Mongols, 4:31b, 556b
Ravenna, 10:521b
return of to Rome, 3:365a
rights of, conveyance to temporal rulers, 12:161b–162a
rival claimants of 1040's, 9:376a-b
Roger II and, 11:267a, 267b, 268b
Roman communal government and, 10:523a-b
Roman nobility and, 10:522a–523a
succession, 3:634b, 638b, 642a, 4:377b
synods, 3:634a-b
Tancred of Lecce and, 11:269a
taxation by, 12:158b
temporal vs. spiritual authority, 4:373a–374a, 376a–376a, 9:375b–376a
monastic reforms, 4:374a
in writings of Egidius Colonna, 4:400a-b
as touchstone of ecumenicity, 3:633b
Tuscolani family and, 11:517b
via cessionis plan, 3:646a
vs. kingship powers, *Quaestio in utramque partem* tract, 10:238a
women's orders and, 12:686a, 687b
Wyclif on, 6:366b, 367a
Zabarella on, 12:735b
see also Apostolic succession; Coronation, papal; Crusades, political; *Plenitudo potestatis;* Pope; Schism, Great; Taxation, church
Papafava fragment. *See* "Responder voi' a dona Frixa"
Papagomenos, Demetrios, treatise on gout, 8:246a
Pāpakān. *See Kārnāmag-i Ardešīr-i Bābagān*
Papal Book, as source for later histories, 6:261b
Papal conclave. *See* Conclave, papal
Papal cross, 4:9b, 10 (*illus.*)
Papal curia. *See* Curia, papal
Papal elections. *See* Papacy, election of pope
Papal fief. *See* Fief
Papal grant. *See* Indulgences, plenary
Papal History. See John of Salisbury
Papal letters. *See* Decretals; particular bulls and encyclicals, by author
Papal nuncio. *See* Nuncio, papal
Papal *possessio. See Possessio,* papal
Papal States, **9:380b–388b**, 9:381 (map)
administration of, Cardinal Gil Albornoz, 1:130b–131a
Donation of Pepin and, 11:481a
during Avignon papacy, 7:5b, 7a, 7b
effect of papal nepotism on, 7:7a
feudalism in, 9:387a
Norman feudal investitures, 9:384a
founded by Innocent III, 6:464b
in 14th century, 7:5b
Ghibelline allies, 7:7b–8a
governmental institutions in, 9:386b–388a
apostolic chamberlain, 9:387a, 387b
apostolic vicariates, 9:387b
Byzantine and early Roman officials, 9:386b
imperial jurisdiction after 962, 9:386b–387a
regionalism of central Italy in late Middle Ages, 9:388a
history (to 756), 9:381a–382b
Lombard attacks, 9:381b–382b
see also Donation of Constantine
history (756–1046), 9:382b–384a
early power struggles, 9:383b–383a
Frankish and German treaties, 9:383a-b
granting away of church lands and possessions, 9:383b
Lombard attacks, 9:383a
history (1046–1198), 9:384a–385a
imperial administration in papal lands, 9:384b–385a
Matildine lands, 9:384b
opposition to reform papacy, 9:384a
history (1198–1307), 9:385a–386a
decline of imperial authority in, 9:385a-b
expansion of papal territorial administration, 9:385b
history (1307–1447), 9:386a-b
decline of papal power, 9:386a-b
imperial vicars, appointment of, 7:8a
Italian language development and, 6:443a
laws, *Constitutiones Aegidianae,* 1:131a
origins of, 9:501b–502a
political crusades in, 4:57b–62a, 6:466a-b
rulers of, legatine powers of, 7:535b
uncertainty under Roman Empire, 9:380b–381a
under Avignonese popes, 9:386a, 387b
Visconti, conflict with, 7:7b–8a
see also Jews in Papal States
Papal treasury. *See* Camera (papal finance)
Paper
in Baghdad and Iraq, 12:105b
Chinese, 12:697b–698a
colored, 12:698a-b
Genoese, 12:698b
introduction of, 3:54a, 6:32b, **9:388b–390b**, 9:390a (*illus.*)
Muslim empire, 11:661a, 12:128a
Muslim occupation and, 9:389a
replacement of parchment by, 9:400b
watermarks, 12:576a
Islamic science and, 11:84a-b
Islamic writing and, 12:697b–698b
manufacture of
Europe, 12:698a
Fabriano, 12:699b
Islamic world, 11:639a-b, 12:698a, 698b
in Játiva, 12:348b
method of determining origins, 9:388b–389a
nomenclature in Middle Ages, 9:390a-b
production methods, in Italy, 9:389a-b
Samarkand, 12:698a
spread of literacy and, 7:601b
Syrian, 12:698a
use of seals and, 11:126b

water mills used in making, 8:393a-b
Western writing and, 12:699b
woodcut and, 12:690a
see also Manuscript books, production of; Papyrus; Parchment
Papert, **9:390b–391a**
Paphlagonia, Theodore I Laskaris and, 9:117a
Paphnutius. See Hrotswitha von Gandersheim
Papias, 1:204b–205a, **9:391a-b**
definition of *fumarium,* 6:120a
Elementarium doctrinae rudimentum, 4:449b, 7:352a, 363b, 599a, 9:391a-b
date of, 9:391a
sources of, 9:391b
nationality of, 9:391a
Pappus of Alexandria
Archimedes and, 1:434a
Mathematical Collection, 11:633b
Papyrus, **9:392a-b,** 9:392 (*illus.*)
Byzantine trade and, 12:100b
in Islamic trade, 12:105b
Islamic writing and, 12:697b
kollema, 7:283b
kollesis, 7:283b
preservation of, 9:392a
production and grading of, 9:392a
replacement by parchment, 9:392a
Western writing and, 12:699a
Paqūdā, Ibn. *See* Baḥya ben Joseph ibn Paqūdā
Parabiago, Battle of (1339), 8:379b, 12:464b
Parabola (geometry), 1:438b, 439a
Paracelsus, distilled liquors and, 4:219b–220a
Paraclitus. See Warnerius of Basel
Paradise
Islamic concept of, **9:392b–395b,** 9:393 (*illus.*)
in art at Medina, 6:593a
combination of fabulous and familiar in, 9:394a-b
creation of, 9:395a
divine approval as reward in, 9:394b
doctrine of resurrection and, 10:341a
in Druzism, 9:3a
fabulous accounts of, 9:394b–395a
as a garden, 10:261a–262b (*illus.*)
iconology and, 6:407a, 407b
as literary inspiration, 9:395a
sensual pleasures of, 9:394a
springs and rivers in, 9:393b–394a
theological questions, 9:395a
versus hell, 9:393a-b
vision of God (*ruᶜyat Allāh*) as highest bliss of, 9:394b
in Manichaeism, 8:84b–85a
Western concept of, **9:395b–398a**
attainment of heaven on earth, 9:396b
beatific vision in, 9:395b–396a, 397a-b
church construction and, 9:396b
corporeality of, 9:397a
derivation of term, 9:395b
in *Erlösung,* 2:229b–230a
extension to include heaven, 9:395b
iconography, 12:182 (*illus.*)
in Irish voyage tales, 6:550a
liturgy and, 9:396a-b
location of heaven, 9:396a, 397a
official doctrine, 9:398a
otherworldliness and, 9:396b
pilgrimages and, 9:396b
proportion of humanity in, 9:397b–398a
resurrection of the body in, 9:397b
scholastic speculations, 9:396b–398a
see also Purgatory
Paradiso. See Dante Alighieri
Paradiso degli Alberti, Il. See Giovanni Gherardi da Prato
Paradisus Magnus (ship), 11:234a-b
Parakletike, definition, 9:215a
Parallelism (music), 8:592a, 593b
Paraphonista, **9:398a–399a**
as leader of group, 9:398b
as one of Roman schola cantorum, 9:398a-b
Parasites. *See* Animals, as disease intermediaries; Plagues
Parata, 5:319a
Paray-le-Monial, church at, 10:479a
Parcevals saga, **9:399a–400a,** 10:390a, 390b, 391a, 394b, 11:491b
Chrétien de Troyes' *Perceval* as source, 9:399a
compared to other *riddarasögur,* 9:399a
description of *graal* in, 9:399a-b
incompleteness of, 9:399b
redactions of, 9:399b–400a
style of, 9:399b
Valvens þáttr and, 9:399a
Parchment, **9:400a-b**
derivation of term, 9:400a
Muᶜawiya and, 12:697b
palimpsests on, 9:355b
preparation of, 9:400a-b
regulation of, 11:693a
replacement by paper, 9:400b
use of hanging seals and, 11:126b
Western writing and, 12:699a-b, 701 (*illus.*)
see also Manuscript books, binding of (European); Manuscript books, production of; Vellum
Pardon, royal, for the insane, 6:491a
Pardon screen. *See* Screen
Pardoners. *See* Quaestors
Pardulus of Laon, bishop, 7:141b
Parekklesion, **9:400b**
Parement de Narbonne, 2:310a
Pares, John, 4:115a, **9:401a**
Hyll and, 6:378a
Parfait du paon. See Jean de la Motte
Parias, 3:128b
Parigoritissa (church: Arta), domed-octagon design of, 4:345a
Paris, **9:401a–407b**
abbeys of, 9:401b–402a
administrative reforms in 13th century, 5:170a-b, 175a
Black Death in, 2:261a
bridges in, 10:418b, 419a
houses built on (6th century), 10:411a
mills built under (9th century), 10:411a
pre-Roman, 10:409b
washed out in floods, 10:416b
churches of, 9:403a
dyers in, 4328b
economic crises, 9:405b
French language development and, 6:435a, 442a
Geneviève as patron saint, 9:401a
history (to 1180), 9:401a–403a
chosen as capital of Gaul, 9:401b
under Merovingian and Carolingian dynasties, 9:401b–402a
history (1180–1223), 9:403a–404a
history (1223–1314), 9:404b–405a
as cultural center of Europe, 1:548a-b, 5:582a, 9:405a, 408a
history (1314–1470), 9:405a–406b
Hôpital St. Jacques-aux-Pélerins, 8:104b
inns in, 6:469b, 474a, 476a
Left Bank, 9:403b
legend of St. Marcel subduing the dragon, 8:28a
merchants in, 9:402b
Normans and, 9:159b, 402a
office of provost, 10:197a-b
Parlement of Paris and, 9:420a
Pastoureaux uprisings and, 9:454a
plagues in, 9:681a
Black Death epidemic, 9:405b
population, 4:141a, 5:174a, 9:403b–404a, 405a-b
prêvot of, 3:278a–279b
revolt in (1356-1358), 6:332a
serfdom and, 11:204b, 206b
tapestry of, 11:596a
taverns, 12:651b
under Capetians, 5:152b, 157b, 9:402a-b, 10:412a
Viking raids, 3:115a, 12:431b, 431a
walls of, 9:403b, 406a
water supply, 12:577b
Paris, Bibliothèque Nationale, motet texts, 8:506a-b
Paris, Council of (1210), condemnation of dualism, 4:297b
Paris, Council of (829)
condemnation of penitentials, 9:489b
decrees of, and Jonas' treatise, 8:434b
Paris *Isopet,* 4:572b
Paris, Matthew. *See* Matthew Paris
Paris Organum Treatise, 8:626b
Paris Penitential, 9:489a, 491a
Paris Psalter, 2:221a, 4:549a-b, 8:1b, **9:407b**
illumination of, 9:407b, 10:307a
miniature of David, 2:441b (*illus.*), 9:0 (frontispiece)
models for, 2:441a
metrical psalms in, 1:280a
metrical rules of, 1:277a
Paris, Synod of (1074), celibacy rulings at, 3:217a
Paris, Treaty of (1229), 3:189a-b
basis for royal policy, southern provinces, 5:168b–169a

Paris, Treaty of (1229) (*cont.*)
transfer of Toulouse to Capetians, 12:91b
Paris, Treaty of (1259), 7:675b
English control of Gascony, 5:171a
Eudes Rigaud and, 4:519a
Paris, University of, 9:404a-b, **9:409a–410b**, 12:161a-b, 283a-b
Aristotelianism at, 1:127a, 461a-b, 463a
bachelor of arts, requirements for, 11:690a
colleges of, 9:404b, 409a
curricular model of 1215, 10:357a
curriculum, arts
Aristotelian studies, 9:607a
dialectic and disputation (*disputatio*), 10:357a, 12:207a
dominance of, 12:283b
natural philosophy, 9:606b, 11:689b–690a
requirements for master of arts, 11:690a
rhetoric, 10:357a
statutes of 1255, 9:612b
textbooks, 11:689b–690a
treatises on logic, 9:613a
departure of German masters, 9:409b
dispute between friars and secular masters, 5:200a-b, 9:408b
division into nations and provinces, 12:283b
explanation of the Black Death and, 8:253b
faculties of, 9:404b
founding of, 7:563a, 9:404b, 12:283a-b
Great Schism and, 1:108a
guild of masters and students, 12:283b
influence on Paris, 9:404b
Innocent IV and, 6:467a
intellectual preeminence, 5:254a-b
intellectual preminence, 5:255a-b
manuscript book production and, 8:103a-b
measured music and, 8:643a-b
medical faculty at, 8:245a, 249b
as national institution, 9:410b
Parlement of Paris and, 9:419b–420a
political factionalism in, 9:409b
Roger Bacon and, 2:35a, 41a
scholars' societies formed, 9:404a-b
secular party, 5:175b
sermons of members of, 10:78a
Siger and, 11:285b
society of masters at, 9:408a
strike of 1229–1231, 9:556b
student nations
English, 12:161b
English-German, 11:690a
Picard, 12:161b
suspension of classes as political tool, 9:408a-b
theological studies at, 4:245b, 5:175a, 9:557a, 10:80a
in 13th century, 9:606b–607a
requirements for degree, 11:690b
textbooks, 11:690b–691a
Thomas Aquinas and, 12:39a-b
travel to, 12:161a-b
Trinitarian Doctrine and, 12:193b, 194b–195b
unorthodox masters, 2:318b
verdict on the causes of Black Death and, 2:264b
vernacular and, 6:442a
via moderna and, 12:407b, 408a
views on papal succession, 4:377b
witchcraft and, 12:662a
Parish, 3:376a, **9:411a–417b**
in the Carolingian period, 9:412b–413a
characteristics of (*ca.* 1300), 9:414b–415a, 415b–416a
in the early rural church, 9:411a-b
fixing of the boundaries of, 9:414b
late medieval developments, 9:415b–417a
leadership of, 9:414b, 416a
membership of, 9:415b
organization of, 3:376a, 4:191a-b
patrimony of, 9:415a-b
payment of tithes and, 12:62b–63a
population growth after 1000 and, 9:414a
private churches and, 9:411b–412b
reform of after 1000, 9:414a–415a
secularization and feudalization of, 9:413b–414a
see also Province, ecclesiastical
Parisian Articles of 1277, Ockham and, 9:210b
Parisian Gothic. *See* Printing
Parisiana poetria. See John of Garland
Parisiensis secunda (Second Paris Collection), 4:123b–124a, 7:415a
see also Bernard of Pavia
Parker Chronicle. *See* Anglo-Saxon Chronicle
Parker, Matthew, archbishop of Canterbury, 12:729b
Parkoszowić (Parkosz), Jakub, 9:729b, 11:345a
Parlement
early use of the term, 9:418a
in England, 9:422a
Parlement of Paris, 5:173b, **9:417b–421a**
bridge maintenance and, 10:417a
Chambre des Enquêtes, 9:419a
Chambre des Requêtes, 9:419a
characteristics of in the late 13th century, 9:418b
creation of, 7:676a
criminal cases and, 9:419a
French king and, 9:420a
Grand'Chambre, 9:418b–419a, 419b
growth of under Philip IV the Fair, 9:419a-b
influenced by Roman law, 9:419a
jurisdiction of, 9:418a-b, 554b
legislative powers of, 9:420a
nobility and, 9:150a
Norman exchequer and, 9:169a
office of seneschal and, 11:160b
organization of, 5:170a, 9:418b–419a
Philip IV and, 9:554b
police powers of, 9:419b
precedents of under Philip II Augustus, 9:417b–418a
provincial parlements and, 9:420a-b
support by nobles, 5:182a
as supreme court, 7:459a-b
Tournelle, 9:419a
under Louis IX, 9:418a
Parlement of the Thre Ages, 8:319a, 332a
Parler family, 5:588a, **9:421a–422a**
soft style of, 5:627b
Parler, Heinrich (the Elder), 9:421a
Parler, Johannes, 9:421b
Heinrich von Brunsberg and, 2:392b
Parler, Michael, 9:421b
drawing for Strasbourg Cathedral, 11:488b (*illus.*)
Parler, Peter
children of, 9:421b–422a
Heinrich von Brunsberg and, 2:392b
in Prague, 10:70b
vaulting in the St. Vitus Cathedral in Prague, 9:421b (*illus.*)
Parliament
English, **9:422a–434b**
authority to elect kings, 4:484b–485b
baronial support, 4:481a-b
bestowal of the right to rule and, 9:429b–431b
burgesses in, 2:331a
committees and commissions, 9:427a-b
Commons, 9:431b–434b
community of the realm, 4:482b, 485a-b
compared with French Estates General, 10:323b, 327b
deposition of kings and, 4:483b–484a, 9:426b–427a
development (1205–1307), 9:422b–425b
development (1308–1398), under Edward II, 9:425b–427a
development (1308–1398), under Edward III, 9:427a–428b
development (1399–1485), 9:429b–434b
development (1399–1485), under Richard III, 9:422b, 431a
divine rights of, 4:483b–484a
division of into two houses, 9:432b
early use of term, 9:422a
economic expansion and growth of, 4:482a
Edwardian statutes, 12:622a-b
elections to in the 15th century, 9:432a-b
Exchequer and, 4:532b–533a
first recorded dissent in, 9:428b
Henry VIII and, 10:327b
impeachment and, 6:426b–427b, 9:428b–429a
initiation of money bills, 9:433a-b
judicial functions of, 4:481b–482a, 482a–483a, 483b–484a, 7:446a, 9:425a, 429b
knights in, 7:666a
legislative function of, 9:424a
Lords Spiritual, 9:429b, 431b
Lords Temporal, 9:431b, 439b–430a
meetings of, 9:430 (*illus.*), 434a-b

military requirements of Edward I and, 9:424a, 424b, 425a, 425b
number of members (1305), 9:423a
of October 1480, 4:485b
Ordinances of 1311, 4:483a
origins of, 4:479b–480a, 9:422a-b
plague cancellations of, 9:679b, 680b
pleas and appeals of individuals, 9:424a
popular representation in, 9:423b
power of, 12:572b–573a
principles governing, 4:481a-b
procedure in (15th century), 9:433b
as promoter of merchants' and craftsmen's interests, 9:432b
relationship between Commons and Lords, 11:469a
Richard II and, 9:429a-b, 10:384a-b
rights to investigate public accounts, 9:428b
Rolls of, 9:424a-b, 428a
royal intervention, 4:483a
on scutage, 11:120b
speaker's office, 9:432b–433a
statutes and reform, 7:450a-b
structure of, 9:429b–430a
taxation and, 4:484a-b, 6:334a
taxation and, assessment of parishes, 11:615b–616a
treason definitions and, 12:166b–168b
tricameral structure of, 10:328a
under Edward I, 4:396b
under Edward III, 4:398a
under Henry III, 4:481a–482b
witenagemot and, 12:665b
see also Good Parliament; Merciless Parliament; Representative assemblies; Statute
Iberian Peninsula, development of cortes, 3:610b–612b
Icelandic. *See* Althing
Irish, **9:435a–437b**
administrative and quasi-judicial functions of, 9:436b
clerical proctors in, 9:435b, 436a
continuing controversy over the role of, 9:435a
first reference to, 9:435a
as the highest court of the land, 9:436b–437a
importance of for Irish-English relations, 9:437b
jurisdiction of, 9:435a
legislation of, 9:436a-b
number of members in, 9:435b–436a
Poynings' Law and, 9:437a
structure of, 9:435a-b
taxation and, 9:436a
Scottish, **9:437b–440a**
basis of representation, 9:438a-b
commissions of, 9:438b–439a
origins of, 9:438a
ransom money for David II, 11:110b
records of, 9:439b
Robert I of Scotland and, 10:427b
Robert II of Scotland and, 10:428a-b
three estates in, 9:438b
see also Scotland, history
treatises on, 8:451b–452a
in Valencia, 12:348a
see also Representative assemblies
Parliament of Fowls. See Chaucer, Geoffrey
Parliament, Irish, 6:520a, 520b
Parma Baptistery, Benedetto Antelami and, 2:167a, 10:502a
Parma Cathedral, 10:485a-b, 486b
pulpit, 2:167a
Parnas (supervisor of social services), 7:74b
P^carnavazi, primacy within Iberia, 5:404b, 419b
Parochia. See Parish
Parody
fabliaux and, 4:576b
in goliardic poetry, 5:575a
in Neidhart "von Reuental"'s poetry, 9:93b–94b
Parody, Latin, **9:440a–441a**
of the Bible and liturgy, 9:440b–441a
of Vergil, 9:440b
Parody songs. *See Trouvères*
Paroemia. *See* Proverb
Paroikia. See Parish
Paroikoi, **9:441b–442a**, 11:604a
categories of, 9:441b
Paroisien romain. See Liber usualis
Paros, Sanudo and, 7:377a
Parousia, **9:442a**
in early church, 3:337b
Parri Spinelli. *See* Spinelli, Parri
Parrys, John. *See* Pares, John
Pārs. *See* Fārs
Parsis, 12:746b, 747b
Parskahayk^c, 1:472b, 473b–474a
Part-music
Western European, 8:593a, 594a
theory of, 8:593b
see also Music, polyphonic
Partalopa saga, **9:442a–443a**, 10:391b
content of, 9:442b
language of, 9:442b–443a
manuscripts of, 9:443a
Partaw. *See* Bardha^ca
Parténopeus de Blois, 10:391b
Partalopa saga and, 9:442a
Partesnoe penie, 8:575b
Part^cew, Armenian tradition of, 5:665a
Parthénie. See Roulliard, Sébastien
Parthenon, *see also* St. Mary (church: Athens)
Parthian language, 6:505b, 506a, 9:444a
Parthians, **9:443a–444a**
cavalry of, 9:444a
seals of, 11:122a
in *Shāhnāma,* 11:221b
vs. Rome, 9:443b
Zoroastrianism of, 9:443b
Partibility and impartibility, 6:459a-b, 460b
in Byzantine law, 6:452a
in English law, 6:458b
in Islamic law, 6:452b–453a
Partimen, 7:63a, **9:444a-b**
in Provençal literature, 10:164b
tenso and, 11:666b
troubadour, 12:218a
see also Tornada
Partiones duodecim versuum Aeneidos principalium. See Priscian
Partipazi (Venetian noble family), 12:387a
Partisan (pole arm), 7:324 (*illus.*), 325a
Partitiones. See Priscian
Partonopeu de Blois, dreamlike aspects of, 5:284a
Partonopier und Meliur. See Konrad von Würzburg
Parvum sigillum. See Seals and sigillography
Parvus contemptus mundi, 7:366b
Parvus, Joannes. *See* Jean Petit
Parvus tractatulus de modo monocordum dividendi. See Prosdocimus de Beldemandis
Parwa, John. *See* Pares, John
Parwāna, 11:154b, 157b
Parχali, church of, 5:409a-b
Parzival. See Wolfram von Eschenbach
Pascal, Blaise, on casuistry, 3:153b
Paschal I, pope
martyrs' burials and, 3:154b
pre-Romanesque art under, 10:112b
vs. Roman nobles, 10:525a
Paschal II, pope, 3:303b, **9:444b–446a**
Camaldolese order and, 3:56a
councils under, 3:635b–636a
early career of, 9:444b
Emperor Henry V and, 9:445b
First Crusade and, 4:36a
Fontevrault order and, 10:430a, 430b
on lay investiture of clerics, 9:445a
Sigebert and, 11:285a
Paschal III, antipope, selection by Rainald of Dassel, 10:252b
Paschal tables, 2:155a
Paschale chronicon, **9:446a**
arrangement of, 2:512b
audience, 2:512b
motive in writing, 2:512b
Paschasius Radbertus of Corbie, St., 4:542b, 5:639a, **9:446a-b**
De corpore et sanguine Domini, 9:446b
as exegete, 2:224a
Pashan, Battle of (mythical), in art, 11:222 (*illus.*)
Pasión trovada, La. See San Pedro, Diego de
Pasqual of Jaén, bishop
Biblia parva, 3:167b
popularity of, 3:167b
Pasquin (literary character), 7:367a
Passaggerii, Rolandino
dictamen of, 4:174b
Summa artis notariae, 4:174b
Passaggi, 8:631a, 633b, 634a
Passau on the Danube, sword manufacture in, 11:548a
Passavanti, Jacopo, *Specchio di vera penitenza,* 6:660a, 664b
Passeggieri, Rolandino
Bolognese School and, 5:567b
Summa artis notariae, 2:312b
Passetyme of Pleasure. See Hawes, Stephen
Passio Albani. See Godzin of Mainz

Passio sanctae Thaisidis. See Marbod of Rennes
Passio sancti Mauritii et sociorum eius. See Marbod of Rennes
Passio sancti Venceslai. See Laurentius of Monte Cassino
Passio sanctorum martyrum. See Marbod of Rennes
Passion. See Mercadé, Eustache
Passion du Christ, La, chanson de geste form, 6:59b
Passion du Christ (Provençal), 10:160b–161a
Passion de Clermont, La. See Passion du Christ, La
Passion cycle, **9:446b–447b**
in art
arma Christi and, 1:469b
by Isenmann, 6:561 (*illus.*)
Crucifixion, 4:12b–13b, 5:531a, 9:447a
Ecce homo, 4:370b (*illus.*)
Last Supper, 7:344a
in drama. *See* Passion plays
see also Resurrection cycle; Stations of the Cross
Passion des jongleurs, 9:447b
Passion du Palatinus, 4:264a, 9:447b
Passion plays, 4:281b
of Arnoul Gréban, 5:659a
in France, 4:264a, 264b–265a, **9:447b–448a**
appearance of in early 14th century, 9:447b
banned by Parlement of Paris in 1548, 9:448a
staging of, 9:448a
in Germany, 4:267a-b
special effects, 4:270a-b
staging of, 4:270a
subject matter, 4:268a
Vigil Raber and, 10:245a
inns and, 6:475a
mystery plays and, 8:660b
planctus and, 9:693a-b
see also N-town plays; Passion cycle
Passion of Ruggieri. *See* Ruggieri Apugliese
Passion of Saint Genesius of Arles, possible attribution of to Paulinus of Béziers, 9:471a
Passion Ste. Genevieve, 9:447a
Passion de Semur, 9:447b
Passional, 8:357a
Passionalia, Divine Office and, 4:224b
Passiun Seint Edmund, La, 1:261a, **9:448a-b**
see also Vie St. Edmund le rei, La
Passover, date of Resurrection cycle and, 4:365a
Passover Haggadah, 7:67b, 68a
Pastel (dye). *See* Woad
Pastimes. *See* Games
Paston family
letters, 8:323a, **9:448b–452b**
concerned with property, 9:450a-b
on domestic family matters, 9:451a
linguistic value, 9:451b–452a
printing history, 9:448b–449b
on various public events, 9:451a
Paston, John I, 9:449b–450a, 450b
letters by his siblings, 9:450a
Paston, John II, 9:450a
dispute about Sir John Fastolf's will and, 9:450b
in parliament, 9:432a
on the plague, 9:680b
Robin Hood and, 10:435b, 437a
Paston, John III, 9:450a
dispute with William Paston II, 9:451a
spelling changes in his letters, 9:451b
Paston, Margaret, 9:451b
Paston, William I, Paston letters and, 9:449b
Paston, William II, 9:450a, 451a
Paston, William IV, 9:450a, 451a
Pastophory, **9:452b**
in the plan of Myrelaion church, 9:453 (*illus.*) later printings
in the plan of St. Savior in Chora, 9:453 (*illus.*) 1st printing
Pastor aeternus. See Lateran Councils, Fifth
Pastoral Care. See Gregory I (the Great), pope
Pastoralis officii. See Nicholas IV, pope
Pastorela, 11:452b
in Provençal literature, 10:164b, 165a
Pastores, 4:281a
Pastoureaux, 5:169b, 7:81b, **9:452b–454b**
1251 uprising, 9:452b–454a
1320 uprising, 9:454a-b
Blanche of Castile and, 2:271a
social composition of, 9:453a-b
Pastourelle, **9:454b**
in Anglo-Norman literature, 1:269a
in *Aucassin et Nicolette,* 1:643b
influence of on Neidhart "von Reuental," 9:94b
in Italy, 6:643a
Jeu de Robin et Marion as, 7:62b
Maid Marion and, 10:435b
in Marqués de Santillana's poetry, 11:451b
troubadour, 12:218a
Pasture, rights of, **9:455a–456a**
land reclamation and, 10:278a
population pressure and, 9:455b
restrictions on, 9:455a
Pataria, 3:499b
Patarine question
Benzo of Alba and, 2:182b
in Milan, 8:378b
Patarini. *See* Bosnian church
Patecchio, Girardo. *See* Pateg, Girard
Pateg, Girard
Noie, 6:630b, 651a
Splanamento de li proverbii de Salamone, 6:630b, 651a, 667b
Paten, 1:223a, **9:456a-b**
alabaster, from Constantinople (11th century), 9:456b (*illus.*)
relief depicting trulla and ewer, 12:221b–222a
Paterikon, **9:456b–457a**, 11:347a
Theodosius of the Caves and, 12:19b
Paterna, majolica production and, 8:55a
Paternalia, Resurrection cycle and, 10:340a
Paternoster, 8:193b–194a
in Angelus, 1:252a-b
definition, 10:530b–531a
play, 12:727b
Pathelin (drama character), 8:51b–52a
Patience, 4:547a, 8:319b, 320a, 332a
in Cotton Nero MS, 9:476a
Patmutᶜiwn Hayocᶜ. See Movsēs Xorenacᶜi
Patmutᶜiwn Tarōnoy, **9:457a–458b**
contents of, 9:457b
dating of, 9:458a
history of the work, 9:457a
"iconoclastic" interpretation of, 9:457b–458a
"orthodox" interpretation of, 9:457b
Patras
captured (1430), 7:381b
under Latins, 7:380a
Patria Constantinopoleos, 2:512b
Patria potestas. See Power, paternal
Patriarch, **9:458b–460a**
of Antioch, Latin, 8:149b–150a
of Antioch, Maronite
civil role, 8:149b
transfer of, 8:149b
Armenian, 1:489a, 491a, 504a
in Byzantine church, 9:496a
Chalcedonian succession, 8:477b
creation of pentarchy and, 2:461a, 9:459a-b
deposition of, permanent synod and, 9:505b
development of papacy and, 9:459b
early synonymy with the term "exarch," 9:458b
Eastern patriarchates, 2:459b–460a
ecumenical, **4:383a–384a**
after Latin occupation, 2:469a-b
christological controversies, 2:462a
clothing of, 3:615b–616a
Constantinople, archbishop of, 4:383a
dependence on imperial power, 4:383b
election of, 2:461b, 9:505b
functions of, 2:461a-b
imperial dependence, 2:459b
jurisdiction, 4:383b
list of, 2:461b–462a
responsibilities, 2:461a-b
Roman recognition of, 2:462a
under Ottoman rule, 2:470a
Monophysite succession, 8:477b
of Serbia, 11:178a, 475b
title of claimed by Slavic churches, 9:459b
see also Autocephalos; Pentarchy; *Synkellos*
Patriarchal School (Constantinople), 12:301b
Patriarches. See Patriarch
Patrician
girdled, 5:539b–540a
Roman, **9:460a-b**
urban, 3:422a-b, **9:460b–461b**
as an ideal type for historians, 9:461a-b
inadequacy of the term, 9:461b
modernity of the term, 9:460b, 461a
Patricius, 10:522a

Patricius romanorum, title bestowed by Pope Stephen II on Pepin III, 9:502a
in *Acallam na Senórach,* 6:549a
Armagh and, 1:469b
Book of Armagh, 7:614a, 615b, 9:465b
burial of, 9:465b–466a
charges against, 9:462b, 462a
chronology of mission, 9:463a
Confession, 9:462a–463a, 463b, 464a, 464b, 466a
Coroticus and, 11:489b
in *Echtrae Conli,* 6:551a
education of, 9:463b–464a
Espurgatoire St. Patrice and, 4:509b
in Irish literature, 5:44a, 6:540b, 542b
Letter to Coroticus, 9:462b, 465a, 466a
lorica of, 3:231a
northern focus of his mission to Ireland, 9:464b
Picts and, 9:139b
Spanish prose life of, 11:439b
theory of two historical Patricks, 9:463a, 464a-b, 465b
in *Triadis thaumaturgae acta,* 6:525a
voices and visions of, 9:462a-b
Patrick, St., First Synod of (457), 9:488b
Patrikeev family, marital alliances, 8:549b
Patrikios, 10:59b
Patrimony. *See* Inheritance
Patrington, Stephen, 3:535a
Patristic literature. *See* Church fathers
Patronage, Islamic, translation of Greek scientific treatises into Arabic and, 11:82b, 83b
Patroni lord. *See* Georgia; *Qma*
Patronqmoba, 5:420a, **9:466a-b**
Patronus (the term), 11:233a
Pattishall, Martin, 7:188a, 191b
Pattishall, Simon, 7:188a
Paucapalea (jurist), **9:466b–467a**
Decretum Gratiani and, 4:127b
Paul I, pope
martyrs' burials and, 3:154b
vs. Roman nobles, 10:525a
Paul II, pope
carnival and, 3:99b
George of Trebizond and, 5:401a
Paul III, pope, inquisition and, 6:488b
Paul of Aegina, 8:244b, 245a
influence of in the Palaiologan era, 8:246a
Paul of Burgos, *Scrutiny of the Scriptures,* 10:6a
Paul of Burgos, bishop
conversion of, 7:82b, 10:6a, 12:453a
Hebrew studies and, 3:314a
Vincent Ferrer and, 12:453a
Paul the Deacon, 7:362a, **9:467a–468a**
Carolingian Latin poetry and, 3:101b–102a
Deeds of the Bishops of Metz, 6:262b, 9:467b–468a
education of, 9:467a
flyting and, 9:175a
Historia romana, 7:328a
History of the Lombards, 4:504a, 6:261b, 7:654b, 9:467b–468a
homiliary of, 4:543a, 550a
hymns of, 6:381b, 11:363a
jubilus and, 8:571a
King Lion story and, 2:141a
on Monte Cassino, 4:504a, 567a, 10:505a
poetry of, 9:467b
visit to Aachen, 9:467b
see also Alpert of Metz
Paul of Nisibis
Instituta regularia divinae legis and, 11:564b
Nestorianism and, 9:106b
Paul, ruler of Serbia, 11:170a
Paul, St.
art of preaching and, 10:361a
on Jews, 7:75a-b, 88a
missionary work of, 8:439b
in Rome, 9:365b
Tarsus and, 11:599b
in Thessaloniki, 12:26a
Paul of Samosata
Paulician sect and, 9:468b
in Armenia, 9:469b
Paul of Tella, Septuagint and, 11:565a
Paul of Trinci, 5:204b
Paul of Venice
on Aristotle, 1:465a
Logica, popularity of, 9:613a
Paula, Jerome and, 7:57b
Pauldron, 1:525b, 530a-b, 534a (*illus.*)
Paulicians, **9:468a–470a**
accused of Docetism, 9:469b
in Anatolia, 1:241a
in Armenia, 9:102b
church and, 1:501b
origin, 6:188b–189a
condemnation of, 6:187b
dispersion of after 872, 9:468a-b
Docetism of, 4:233a
dualistic theology, 6:192a
early leaders of, 9:469a
iconoclastic tendencies, 6:188b
John of Ōjun and, 7:125a
Key of Truth, 9:469b
military organization, 6:192a
origin of, 6:192a, 9:468a
Armenian theory, 9:469a-b
Greek theory, 9:468b–469a
settlement in Balkans, 6:192a
Sons of Sinfulness, 6:189a
in southern Italy, 9:469b
vs. Basil I, 2:118a
vs. Byzantine Empire, 1:483b, 4:523a
see also Amorians; Bogomilism
Paulinus of Aquileia, St., 7:362a, **9:470a-b**, 12:385b
Carolingian Latin poetry and, 3:101b
Holy Syllabus Against Elipandus, 9:470a
hymns of, 6:380b, 381b
Nicene-Constantinopolitan Creed and, 3:677a
On the Divinity of the Son Against Felix of Urgel, 9:470b
Rule of Faith, 9:470b
Paulinus of Béziers, **9:470b–471a**
Paulinus, Meropius Pontius. *See* Paulinus of Nola, St.
Paulinus of Nola, St., 5:320b, **9:471a-b**, 10:297a
bells and, 2:165b
De arte metrica and, 2:154b
on decoration of basilica at Nola, 4:358a-b
on mosaics in the churches of Nola, 8:91a
poetry of, 7:361a-b
sacramentary of, 2:180a-b
Paulinus of Pella, 7:361b, **9:471b–472a**
Thanksgiving to God in an Account of My Life, 9:471b
Paulinus of Périgueux, 7:361b, **9:472a**
life of St. Martin, 7:361b
Paulinus of York, archbishop, Urien Rheged and, 12:331b
Paulus Alvaro, 7:95b
Paulus Diaconus. *See* Paul the Deacon
Paulus of Heredia, 3:3a
Paulus Orosius. *See* Orosius
Paulus Paulirinus (*ca.* 1460), 8:608b
Pauperistae (canon-law students), 12:343b
Pausikakos of Apameia, ordained by Kyriakos of Constantinople, 8:246b
Pavao Šubić, ban of Bosnia, 2:336a-b
Pavely, John, commander of king's fleets, 1:57a
Pavia
bridge over the Ticino, 10:418b
as capital of Italy, 8:377b
fairs, 4:587a
siege of, by Charlemagne, 8:377a-b
war against, by Milan, 8:378b
Pavia, Battle of (1524), 11:217a
Pavia, Battle of (1525), 8:380b
Pavia, Certosa of
Francesco I Sforza and, 11:216b
see also Bernardo da Venezia
Pavia, First Peace of (755), 9:502a
Pavia, Second Peace of (756), 9:502a
Pavia, Treaty of (1329), 2:135a-b
Pavia, University of, 12:286a
Pavia-Siena, Council of (1423-1424), 3:651a–654a
Martin V and, 3:651b
Pavise, 1:528a, 582b (*illus.*)
Pavle Radenović, murder of, 10:650a
Pawnbrokers, punishments of, 12:337b, 338b
Pawnbroking
development of banking and, 2:74b, 75a-b, 76a
in Italy, 2:76a
in Prague (between 1388 and 1416), 2:303b
Pʿawstos Buzand, 7:299a, **9:472b–473a**
on Armenian church, 1:519a
on Armenian saints, 1:517b, 518a
on Aštišat synods, 1:498a
authorship of *Buzandaran Patmutʿiwnkʿ,* 6:239a
on the Bagratids, 2:48a
Buzandaran Patmutʿiwnkʿ, 1:508a
emphasis on supernatural events, 6:239a
on deportation of Armenians, 12:97a
History of Armenia, 5:579a, 9:472b–473a

P^{c}awstos Buzand, 7:299a (*cont.*)
  History of Armenia (cont.)
    dating of St. Nersēs' pontificate, 9:101b
  on the Mamikonean family, 8:78b
  on the Mamikonean *sparapets,* 11:460b
  Patmut^{c}iwn Tarōnoy and, 9:458a
  Thaddeus legend and, 12:1a
  see also Łazar P^{c}arpec^{c}i
Pax Brede, 1:224b
Pax mongolica, northern trade routes and, 12:103b
Pax in nomine Domini. See Marcabru
Payerne (abbey: Switzerland), 2:175a, 10:488b
  Bertha and, 11:538a
  Frederick I Barbarossa and, 11:539a
  vs. Rudolph of Habsburg, 11:540b
Pays du droit coutumier. See French law, in north; German law, early Germanic codes
P^{c}aytakaran, 1:472b, 473b
  Baylakān and, 2:139a
Pazyryk rug, 10:547b
Pazzi family, assassination plot against Medici, 5:102b, 8:243a-b, 11:281b
"Peace of beasts," as part of Peace of God, 9:475a
Peace of Budziszyn (Bautzen), 9:719a
Peace of God, 3:177a, 4:16a, 5:405b, **9:473a–475b**
  after 1030, 9:474b–475a
  in Aquitaine, 5:154a
  bishops' role in forming, 5:154a
  breach of, interdict and, 6:495a
  bridge-building and, 10:413b
  compared with Truce of God, 9:474a
  development of communes and, 3:495a-b
  influence of, 9:475b
  millennial expectations and, 12:723a
  nonroyal French rulers and, 11:125b
  Order of Cluny and, 3:356a-b, 470b
  origins of, 9:473a-b
  as propaganda, 10:140a
  revival of in the 12th century, 9:475a
  Synod of Tuluges, 9:238b
  trade and, 12:117b
  year 1000 and, 12:723a
  see also French law, in south
"Peace Hymn." *See* Fulbert of Chartres, hymns of
Peace of Kalisz (1343), 9:724b–725a
Peace of Toruň
  first, 9:726b
  second, 9:727b–728a
"Peace" (township), 12:439b–440a
Peace-Fróði, 11:328b
Peacock, uses of, 5:151a
Pear, in cooking, 5:307a
Pearl, 1:186a-b, 8:319b, 320a-b, 332a, **9:476a–477b**
  compared with Boccaccio's *Olympia,* 8:320a
  compared with Dante's *Divine Comedy,* 8:320a
  number symbolism of, 9:477a
  Olympia and, 7:369b
  prosody of, 8:344a
  structure of, 9:476b–477a
  visions and, 12:476a
Pearl fisheries, in al-Baḥrayn, 2:51a
Peasants
  1000–1300, 3:414b–415b
  1300–1500, 3:423b–424b
  in Armenia, 1:489b
    see also Ramik; Šinakan
  in Bohemia, 6:377a
  duke's (*rustici ducis*), 9:722a
  in England, rebellions of, 10:437a
  family life, 4:603b–604a
  "full," 12:440b
  in Germany
    bailiwicks (*ämter*), 10:333b
    representative estates of, 10:333a
  in Hungary, 6:343b
    taxation of, 6:344b
  inheritance and, 6:459a
  in Islamic world, plagues and, 9:685b
  land ownership and, 11:205b
  in Macedonia, family life, 4:595a-b
  marriage and, 4:146a-b
  migration of, *taille* and, 11:576b–577a
  in *Nativitas rusticorum et qualiter debent tractari,* 6:658a
  in Norway, national unification and, 9:183b, 184a
  in Poland, 9:720a, 722a-b, 725b
  Roman, 10:461b
    modern historiography and, 10:468a
  in Russia
    "black," 11:191a, 191b, 199a
    categories of, 11:191a
    as debtors, 11:192a, 194a
    economic condition of, 11:193b–194b
    exportation of, 11:194b, 196a
    as free renters, 11:190b, 191a
    obligations of, 11:191b, 192b–193b
    rights of, 11:191b, 194a-b, 198b–199a
    see also Serfs and serfdom, Russia
  serfdom and, 11:207a
  in Sweden, 3:424b, 11:531b
  in Syria, 10:460a
  see also Agriculture; Class structure; Conversi; Serfs and serfdom
Peasants' Crusade. *See* Crusades
Peasants' rebellions, **9:477b–480b**
  against Gottschalk, 12:617a
  effect on guilds, 6:18b–19a
  England, 11:207b
  France
    Ordonnance cabochienne, 5:187b
    Pastoureaux uprising of 1320, 5:180a
  in Hungary, 6:347a, 349a-b
  in Iraq, 6:513a
  Poland, 9:720a
  Russia, 11:197a-b
  Sweden, 11:533a
  three major causes of, 9:477b
  Wendish, 12:617a
  see also Jacquerie; Pastoureaux
Peasants' Revolt (1381), 3:83b, 424b, 428b, 596b, 7:664a, 9:478b–480b
  causes of, 4:484b
  Chaucer and, 3:290a
  compared with the Jacquerie, 9:480a
  effect on guilds, 6:19b
  English poll tax and, 10:26b, 11:617b
  Gower on, 5:642b
  John of Gaunt during, 7:135a
  lawyers, treatment of, 7:665a
  Lollards in, 7:645a
  low level of violence in, 9:480a
  Piers Plowman and, 7:329a
  Richard II and, 10:384a
Peasants' Wedding. See Bauernhochzeit, Die
"Peascod" breastplate. *See* Breastplate
Peć, patriarchate, 9:209a
Pecador remut, Lo. See Malla, Felip de
Pecha, Pedro Fernández, *Soliloquios,* 11:418b
Pecham, John. *See* Peckham, John
Pechenegs, 11:478b–479a
  Chërnye Klobuki, 10:577a
  Constantine VII's *De administrando imperio* and, 12:435b
  defeated by Alexios I Komnenos, 1:158a
  invasions of Russia, 10:576b
  migration into Pontic steppes, 10:576b
  Serdica and, 11:189a
  Sirmium under, 11:311b
  in Transylvania, 11:480a
  Turkish conflicts, 10:576b
  vs. Hungarians, Symeon and, 11:554b
  vs. Magyars, 6:338a
  vs. Romanos IV Diogenes, 10:516a
  vs. Yaroslav the Wise, 7:248b, 10:583a
  see also Magyars; Russia, Nomadic Invasions of
Pecherskaya Lavra (Monastery of the Caves), 8:573a, **9:481a**, 10:591b
  inventory from, 4:291b
  as a pilgrimage shrine, 9:654a
  see also Theodosius of the Caves, St.
Pecia, 7:563a, 8:103a-b, **9:481a-b**
  spread of literacy and, 7:600b, 601b
Peck, **9:482a**
Peckham, John, 1:461b, **9:482a-b,** 9:714b
  Constitutions of 1281, 12:615a
  on convergence of solar rays, 7:539b
  on creation vs. eternity of the world, 12:39b–40a
  excommunication of Richard Knapwell and, 12:41b
  hymns of, 6:382a
  Ignorantia sacerdotum, 10:300b
  influenced by Roger Bacon, 2:39b, 41a
  Jerarchie, 1:264a
  office of the Trinity, 10:370a
  Perspectiva communis, 7:540b
  Philomena, 1:255a, 7:369a
  Robert Kilwardby and, 12:40b
  Super magistrum sententiarum, 12:196b–197a
Pecock, Reginald, **9:482b–483b**
  career of, 9:482b–483a
  trial for heresy, 9:483a
Pecorone, Il. See Fiorentino, Giovanni
Pécs, 6:345b
Pécs, University of, 12:289b
Pedes, in Worcester polyphony, 12:696a

Pedilavium. See Feet, washing of
Pedralbes (convent: Barcelona), mural, 2:128a
Pedro, *see also* Peter
Pedro I of Aragon and Navarre, king, 1:405a–406b, 9:69b
Pedro II of Aragon, king, 10:252a
administration of, 1:411a
Albigensian crusade and, 3:187b, 188b
Aragonese-papal entente and, 1:410a-b
disaster in Occitania, 1:410b
expansion of Aragon and, 12:344a
killed, 7:339b
opposed by military elites, 1:410b–411a
Simon III de Montfort and, 11:296b
Pedro III of Aragon, king, 1:413b–414b
annexation of Sicily, 1:413b–414a
Aragonese "Union" originated under, 1:414a
Arnald of Villanova and, 1:537b
church taxation and, 11:609b
conquest of Sicily and, 8:67b
consolidation of realm by, 1:413b
crown of Sicily offered to, 4:61a
functions of cortes and, 3:611b
Jews and, 7:81b
quelling of French uprising, 1:414a
seizure of Infantes de la Cerda, 1:413b
Sicilian vespers and, 8:302b, 11:261a, 273a
vs. Martin IV and Philip III, 4:61a-b
Pedro IV (the Ceremonious) of Aragon, king, 1:415b–417a, **9:510b–512a**
astronomy and, 9:511a
Black Death and, 1:416a
Castilian rebellion, 1:416b
Chronicle, 9:511a-b
compared with Alfonso X of Castile, 9:510b
cultural and administrative successes of, 1:417a
destruction of Unions in Aragon and Valencia, 1:416a
interest in history, 9:511a-b
Jews and, 7:81b–82a
literary court of, 3:170b
as patron of arts and learning, 4:165b, 9:510b
Peter de Luna and, 12:452b
poems of, 9:511a
reconquest of Majorca, 1:415b–416a
reliance on *cortes* and *corts,* 1:417a
reunion with Sicily, 1:416b
support for Valencia, 12:348b
uprising in Sardinia quelled, 1:416a-b
Pedro I (the Cruel) of Castile, king
civil war with Henry of Trastámara, 9:71b
historical ballads about, 11:428a, 429a
Jews and, 7:82a
literary developments and, 11:418a
in López de Ayala's chronicle, 11:436a
Pedro IV of Aragon and, 12:348b
revolt against, 3:137a
rule of, 3:136b–137a
Pedro I of Navarre, king. *See* Pedro I of Aragon and Navarre, king
Pedro I of Portugal, king, reign of, 10:51b–52a
Pedro de Alcalá
Arabic grammar in Latin, 12:137a
Arte para ligeramente saber la lengua aráuiga, 11:441b
Vocabulista aráuiga en letra castellana, 11:441b
Pedro de Córdoba, **9:483a**
Annunciation altarpiece in the Cathedral of Córdoba, 9:483b, 484 (*illus.*)
Pedro del Corral, *Crónica sarracina,* 11:419b
Pedro Juliano Rebolo. *See* Peter of Spain
Pedro de Luna. *See* Benedict XIII, antipope
Pedro de Portugal, Dom
Sátira de la infelice e felice vida, 11:423a, 457a
Siervo libre de amor, 11:423a
Pedro Ramírez (son of Sancho), conquests of, 1:405b–406a
Pedro Serra. *See* Serra, Pedro
Pedro (son of João I of Avis), reign of, 10:53b–54b
Pegolotti, Francesco
fruits grown in Mediterranean region, 5:307a
Pratica della mercatura, 4:557a-b
on silk route to the Far East, 12:99a
Peira. *See* Eustathius Rhomaios
Peire d'Alvernha, **9:485b**
Peire Cardenal, **9:483b–485b**
devotional poetry of, 10:182a
sirventes of, 11:313a
Peire de Vic, 10:176b
comic *razos* by, 10:176b
Pos Peire d'Alvernhe a Chantat, 10:176b
satire of formalism in troubadour poetry by, 10:176b
Peire Vidal, **9:485b–486a,** 10:175a
travels of, 12:161a
Peisage (market tax), 8:146b
Peitrel, 1:529a
Pelagianism
Augustine of Hippo and, 1:652a–654a, 3:336b, 9:486b
in British church, 3:225b
Celestine I and, 3:214a
in Celtic church, 3:226b
Germanus of Auxerre and, 5:471b–472a
Jerome and, 3:336b
need for personal salvation, 6:193b
Orosius on, 9:281a
Thomas Bradwardine and, 1:464b
Pelagius, 3:225b, **9:486a–487a**
doctrine of, 9:486a
Pelagiani moderni, treatises against, 2:358a-b
Prosper of Aquitaine's opposition to, 10:153b–154a
used in Irish biblical commentaries, 2:220a
see also Pelagianism
Pelagius II, pope, exarchate and, 4:529b
Pelagius, cardinal
in Fifth Crusade, 4:50a, 50b
Latin Empire of Constantinople and, 7:348b
Pelagonia, **9:487a-b**
Pelagonia, Battle of (1259), 8:303b, 9:117b, 487a
Pelaston, 8:617a
Pelayo, king, 1:625b–626a, 11:435a
Pelayo of Oviedo, *Chronicle,* 11:435a
Pelena, **9:487a-b**
Pèlerinage de Charlemagne, 3:258b, 4:576b, 7:216b, 10:391b
humor in, 5:241b
Pèlerinage de l'âme. See Deguileville, Guillaume de
Pèlerinage de la vie humaine. See Deguileville, Guillaume de
Pelican, in medieval animal tales, 2:205a
Pella. *See* Faḥl
Pellet (unit of measure), 12:595b
Peloponnesus
Byzantine sea routes and, 10:423 (map), 424b
see also Morea
Pelusium, conquered, 6:569b
Pelzbuch. See Gottfried of Franconia
Pemba, al-Mas^{c}ūdī on, 12:739b
Penal law. *See* Criminal justice
Penance, **9:487b–493a**
absolution, 9:604a
barefoot travel, 12:156a-b
casuistry in, 3:153b
in Celtic church, 3:229b–230b
Christian pilgrimage and, 9:655a–657a
commutations of, 6:448a, 9:490b–491a
confession in, 3:533a-b
in Der Stricker's poems, 11:493b
doctrinal development of, 9:491b
Duns Scotus and, 9:213b
excommunication and, 4:537b
fasting and, 5:18b
forms of, 9:487b–489a
granted by inquisition, 6:485a, 485b
indulgences and, 6:446a, 447b–448a
in interdict, 6:494b, 495a, 497a
Lateran IV on, 6:449b
Ockham and, 9:213b
penitentials and, 9:489a–491b
private, 9:481a-b, 488a–489a, 604a
Council of Chalon (647–653) and, 9:489b
public, 9:481a-b, 487b–489a
in Robert Mannyng's *Handlyng Synne,* 8:87a
as sacrament, 9:604a
self-flagellation and, 5:76b
solemn, 9:488b
in *Specchio di vera penitenza,* 6:660a, 664b
tract on by Peter Comestor, 9:514a
see also Advent; Fasting, Christian; Lent; Pilgrimage; Purgatory
Pence. *See* Penny
Pencerdd (chief poet at a Welsh court), 8:265a
see also Gogynfeirdd
Pendant vault. *See* Vault
Pendants, 5:376 (*illus.*), 379a, 381a-b

Pendentive, 4:235 (*illus.*), 236a, **9:493a-b**
in Hagia Sophia in Constantinople, 9:493b, 494 (*illus.*)
see also Vault
Penetes, **9:493b–494a**
legal disability of, 9:493b
Penitence of Jesus Christ, Friars of the. *See* Sack, Friars of the
Penitentiale. See Theodore of Canterbury, St.
Penitentials, **9:487b–493a**
after Gratian, 9:490b
condemnation of in the early 9th century, 9:489b–490a
Continental vs. Insular, 9:491a
description of, 8:442b
harsh and lengthy penances in, 9:490b–491a
incorporation into church-law collections, 9:490a-b
indulgences and, 6:447b–448a
Irish, spread of, 9:488b–489b
Jewish repentance literature, 9:581a-b
magic and, 12:659b
relic veneration and, 10:298b
spread of in the 6th and 7th centuries, 9:489a-b
Summa de poenitentia (*Raymundina*), 10:266b
see also Lent; *Nomócanon;* Penance
Penitents of al-Kufa. *See Tawwābūn*
Penityas, 12:614b
Peniworþ of Witte, 8:316b
Penna, 12:699b, 701 (*illus.*)
Penny, 5:680a, **9:494b–495b**
as basic unit of coinage in Latin Europe, 8:428b
Carolingian silver, 8:428a (*illus.*), 429b
derivation of the term, 9:495b
in England, 9:495a-b
era of, 10:66b
long cross, 8:429a
shilling and, 11:229a
short cross, 8:429a
variations of, 8:428b
Penrose, John, adulterated wine and, 12:120a
Pens
Islamic writing and, 12:698b
Western writing and, 12:699b
Pensionaris, 11:558a
Pentarchy, 9:459a-b, **9:495b–496a**
Pentateuch, **9:496a-b**
carpet page, 7:66b (*illus.*)
importance of in Judaism, 7:158b
more judaico and, 9:207b
see also Jewish law
Pentēchostos. See Pentecost
Pentecost, **9:496b–497a**
in art, 10:496a, 497b (*illus.*)
of Pedro Serra, 11:210a (*illus.*)
conclusion of Easter season and, 4:365b
iconography of, 9:497 (*illus.*)
incense and, 6:432b
ordination of clergy during, 9:265b
see also "Veni creator spiritus"
Pentekostarion, 7:612a
Penula. *See* Vestments, liturgical
People of the book, 7:103a, **9:497a–498b**
Pepin I of Aquitaine, king (son of Louis the Pious), 9:499a
Pepin I (of Landen), **9:498b–499b**
conquest of Ravenna, 7:4a
rule of, 3:104a–106b
Pepin II of Aquitaine (grandson of Louis the Pious), 9:500a
Pepin II (of Herstal), mayor of the palace, 3:272a, **9:499b–500b**
aggressive foreign policy of, 9:500a
campaign against Alamanni, 5:506a
as the greatest landowner in Austrasia, 9:499a
as leader of Austrasians against Neustrians, 9:500a
vs. Alamannic dukes, 11:526b
Willibrord's missionary work and, 8:441a
Pepin III (the Short), mayor of the palace, 8:236a, **9:500b–503a**
accession of, 3:272b
Austrasian nobility and, 9:148a
buried at St. Denis, 3:378b
consecration of, 10:16b
consolidation of kingdom, 9:501b
on deposition of rulers, 4:158b–159a
Donation of Pepin, 3:346a, 9:373b, 501b–502a
Ermoldus Nigellus and, 4:507b
Italian expedition of, 3:201b–202a, 7:657b
leprosy and, 7:550b
love of St. Peter, 9:373a-b
Odilo of Bavaria and, 9:501b
patricius and, 10:522a
payment of tithes and, 12:62b
reform of the Frankish church and, 9:501b
reliquary of, 10:302a (*illus.*)
rise of, 3:345b
Robertinians and, 3:89b
rule of, 3:106a
Salian Frankish law and, 7:472b
Saxon tribute and, 3:202a
Stephen II and, 3:106b, 346a, 9:372b–373b, 460a, 11:481a
strengthening of papal power by, 9:382a-b
vs. Alamannic dukes, 11:526b
Zacharias and, 3:106b, 9:372b
Pepin I of Italy, king (son of Charlemagne), 9:499a
attack on Venice, 12:385a
Pepin the Elder. *See* Pepin I (of Landen)
Pepin the Hunchback (*fl. ca.* 794), revolt of, 3:91b
Pepo, 6:554b
Corpus iuris civilis and, 7:419a
legal teachings of, 3:609b
Pepysian Gospel Harmony, 4:547b
Per quem haec omnia, 8:193b
Pera-Galata, **9:503a-b,** 12:111b
location of, 5:573b–574a
Peraḥya of Regensburg, 7:108a
Peraldus, William
on Seven Deadly Sins, 11:211b
Summa de casibus poenitentiae, 4:247b
Summa de vitiis et virtutibus, 8:316b
Perceforest. See Aubert, David
Perceval. See Chrétien de Troyes
Perceval (Percival). *See* Arthurian legend; French literature; Grail, legend of; Malory, Sir Thomas; Matter of Britain; Matter of France; Matter of Rome
Percevals saga. See Parcevals Saga
Perch (unit of measure), **9:504a,** 12:584a
in measuring acreage, 12:588b–589a
variations in, 12:588a
Perchevael, 1:572a
Percy, Henry, earl of Northumberland, 12:570a, 570b
Pere Gilbert (astronomer at the court of Peter IV the Ceremonious), 9:511a
Pere III of Catalonia. *See* Pedro IV (the Ceremonious) of Aragon, king
Peredur Son of Efrawg, 1:567a, 12:611a
Perego, Camillo, *La regola del canto fermo ambrosiano,* Ambrosian chant and, 1:233a
Peregrín de Atrosillo, 6:557b
Peregrinatio Aetheriae. See Egeria, *Itinerarium Egeriae*
Peregrinatio pro Christo, 3:231b, 7:616a
Peregrinationes in terram sanctam. See Breydenbach
Peregrinus. See Pilgrims
Pereiaslavl'. *See* Pereyaslav
Pereslavl Cathedral, Theophanes the Greek's icon of the *Transfiguration,* 12:23b (*illus.*)
Perestrello, Bartolomeo, 8:10b
Pereyaslav, ravaged by Mongols, 2:131b
Pérez de Guzmán, Fernán
in *Cancionero de Baena,* 11:419a
Generaciones y semblanzas, 11:421a, 433b–434a
hagiographic poems by, 11:439a
poetry of, 11:434a
translations from Latin and, 11:434a
see also Spanish literature, biography
Pérez de Martel, Gonzalo, 3:61b
Pérez, Miquel, writings of, 3:168a
Perfect time. *See* Musical notation
Perfecti
among the Bohemian Brethren, 2:307a
in Bogomilism, 2:295a
in six Eastern dualist churches, 2:297a
in Western dualist heresies, 2:297a
Perfectio, 8:629a, 630 (*illus.*), **9:504a-b,** 10:380b–381a
Perfume, 2:146b–147a
Pergama flere volo, 7:365a
Pergenstörffer monument, 7:300b
Peri Chreias. See Aphthonius, *Progymnasmata*
Peri hermeneias. See Apuleius of Madaura; Aristotle
Perichoresis. See Trinitarian doctrine
Pericope, **9:504b–505a**
see also Lectionary
Pericopes of Henry II. See Henry II of Germany, emperor
Periegesis. See Priscian
Perigord, bastides in, 2:128b

Périgueux, shrines of, 6:492a
Peripatetic philosophy, 11:303a–304a
Peripatetic philosophy, Islamic. *See* Philosophy and theology, Islamic
Periphyseon. See John Scottus Eriugena
Periplus maris Erythraei, on Ethiopian relations with Greco-Roman world, 1:32a
Perisa, Christianity in, **3:312a–313b**
Peristephanon. See Prudentius
Perizoma, 4:13a-b
Perjury, bells and, 2:166a
Perkunas (Baltic god), relation to Thor, 12:46a
Perlesvaus, 1:567a, **9:505a**
Permanent synod, **9:505a–506a**
  membership of, 9:505b
Pero de Tafur. *See* Tafur, Pero de
Perotinus (Pérotin), 8:594a, **9:506a–508a**
  Anonymous IV and, 9:191a
  ars antiqua and, 1:546a
  clausula of, 3:437b
  influence of, 9:507b
  innovations of, 9:507b
  Magnus liber and, 9:192a, 919b
  musical theory, motets, 8:502a
  optimus discantor, 4:216b
  quadrupla of, 9:506a, 506b, 507a
  Sederunt, 12:671a
  tripla of, 9:506a, 506b
  two views of the chronology of his work, 9:506b
  Viderunt omnes, 8:571 (*illus.*), 590 (*illus.*), 12:410b, 671a
  works in MS Pluteus, 29.1, 5:104a–105a, 106a
  see also Leoninus; *Magnus liber organi; Salvatoris hodie*
Pērōz, Sasanian king
  assumption of Iranian throne, 6:170a
  defeat and death, 8:236b, 10:669b
Perpendicular Style. *See* Gothic architecture, English
Perperum. See Hyperpyron
Perpetua servitudo, 11:210a, 210b
Perpetual pilgrimage. *See* Pilgrimage, as punishment
Perpetuus of Tours, bishop, 9:472a
Perpignan, irrigation of, 6:558b
Perpignan, University of, 12:286b–287a
Perrée (unit of measure), 12:595b
Perrers, Alice, 7:331a
Perronet, Jean-Rodolphe, reconstruction of Ponte Vecchio, 12:578a-b
Persarmenia. *See* Mec Hayk^{C}; Parskahayk^{C}
Persefores, Castilian version of, 11:443b
Persepolis, Shīrāz and, 11:252a
Persia
  Nizārīs in, 11:137b
  see also Iran; Sasanians
Persian art
  in Anatolia, 6:614a
  bowls, 3:238b–239a (*illus.*)
  in Damascus, 6:608a
  influence of on Islamic ceramics, 3:239b
Persian church
  decline of, 3:313a
  golden age of, 3:312b–313a
  Nestorianism in, 3:312a-b, 10:669a
  organization of, 3:312a
  persecution of, 10:601a
    Sasanian culture and, 10:662b
  under Babai the Great, 3:312b
  under Mar Aba, 3:312b
Persian Empire
  Byzantine authority in Iberia and, 5:405b
  Georgian kingdom compared with, 5:419b–420a
Persian gardens. *See* Gardens, Islamic
Persian language, 6:505b
  bilingual encyclopedias, 4:448b, 449b
  dictionaries, 4:444a-b
  grammars, 5:650b
  Iranian nationalism and, 6:501b, 503b
  Middle Persian, 6:505b, 506a
  New Persian, 6:506a, 7:309b
  Old Persian, 6:505b
  scientific treatises written in, 11:82a
  see also Iranian languages; Judeo-Persian language
Persian literature
  consequences of Shiite dominance, 6:509a
  epic tradition, 10:669a
  ghazal, 6:51a–52b
  Indian style. *See Sabki-Hindī*
  love poetry, Sufism and, 6:586a
  maqāma genre, 6:26b
  parallel with Norse *Ragnars saga,* 10:249a
  poetry, 6:506b–508a
    lyric forms, 6:507b–508a
    mystical, 6:507b
    narrative forms, 6:507a-b
  prose, 6:508a–509a
    courtly, 6:508a-b
    popular, 6:508b
  romance, 6:507a, 508b–509a
Persian Wars. See Herodotus
Persians
  in Egypt, 10:453b
  Nisibis and, 9:142a
  physical description, 10:664b–665a
  in Syria, 11:559b
Person, Gobelinus, *Tractatus musicae scientiae,* 8:648a
Person, juristic
  inheritance and, 6:456b, 458b
  universitas as, 6:467b
Persona. See Hypostasis; Trinitarian doctrine
Personal grooming. *See* Beauty aids
Perspectiva. See Haytham, Ḥasan ibn al-; Witelo
Perspectiva communis. See Peckham, John
Perspective
  Brunelleschi's system of, 2:390b
  in Hugh of St. Albans, 6:320b
  Masaccio's use of, 8:170a
  Uccello's use of, 12:237a
Perspice christicola, Sumer Is Icumen In and, 11:505b
Perth, Treaty of (1266), western seaboard of Scotland and, 11:108a
Pertussa, Francesc de, 3:168a
Perugia
  architecture, 9:668b
  church of San Ercolano, 8:52a (*illus.*)
  disciplinants of, 6:635a-b
  Fontana Maggiore, 9:669b–670a
Perugia, University of, 12:286a
Perun (Varangian god), 6:411a
  relation to Thor, 12:46a
Perushim, 11:585a
Perutilis logica. See Albert of Saxony
Peruzzi, 2:77a, 77b, 78a
  bankruptcy of (1343), 2:287a, 12:118a
  Hundred Years War and, 6:333b
  Languedoc and, 7:341a
  Villani and, 6:634a
Pervleptos (church: Ochrid), 9:209a
Peryf ap Cedifor, 6:386b
Pes, 8:619 (*illus.*), 624b, 625 (*illus.*), 629a, 11:505a-b
Pes flexus. See Torculus
Pes motet. *See* Motet
Pesaḥ-Peter, 10:6b
Pesaro, Guglielmo da. *See* Guglielmo da Pesaro
Peshitta, 2:211a
  influence of on the Armenian Bible, 2:217b
Pessagno, Bartolomeo, discovery of Madeira Islands and, 8:10a
Pessagno, Carlo, discovery of Madeira Islands and, 8:10a
Pessagno, Lanzarote, 4:559a
Pessagno, Manuel, 4:558b
Pestilence. *See* Disease; Plagues
Pestis puerorum. See Children, plagues and; Plagues
Petaḥia of Regensburg, Benjamin of Tudela and, 2:181b
Petastē, 8:617a, 617b
Peter II of Ravenna, archbishop, palace of, 10:263a
Peter I of Bulgaria, **9:510a**
  Bogomil heresy and, 2:294a, 405b
  Byzantine titles during reign of, 2:403a
  Byzantium and, 2:405a-b
  monasticism under, 2:405b
  rise of, 2:405a
  as ruler, 2:405b
Peter II of Bulgaria, 9:509b–510a
  reign of, 2:407b–408a
Peter I of Cyprus, king
  Landini and, 7:326a
  reign of, 4:71a
Peter II of Cyprus, king, 4:71a
Peter of Abernon. *See* Peter Peckham
Peter of Alexandria, bishop, 1:518b
  Arius and, 1:453b
  correspondence with Acacius of Constantinople, 5:540b
Peter of Alexandria (*fl.* 1342), translation of *Sefer tekunah,* 4:12a
Peter of Amiens, Robert de Clari and, 10:431b
Peter and Asen, Isaac II Angelos and, 6:559b
Peter (Asenović), **9:509b–510a**
Peter Aureoli, **9:513a-b**
  nominalism and, 9:156a

Peter Aureoli (*cont.*)
Scriptum super primum Sententiarum, 9:513a
Peter of Auvergne, as defender of Thomism, 12:41b
Peter Bartholomew, Holy Lance and, 4:35b
Peter of Benevento, *Compilatio tertia,* 7:427b
Peter of Bergamo, *Tabula aurea,* 12:42a
Peter, bishop of Poitiers, excommunication of William of Aquitaine, 12:631a
Peter of Blois, **9:517b–518b**
Against Jewish Disbelief, 10:3b
ars dictaminis and, 10:359a
career of, 9:518a
De fide, 9:518b
Dialogus cum rege Henrico, 8:435a
dictamen of, 4:175a
king's evil and, 7:255b
letters of, 7:364b, 9:518a-b
Libellus de arte dictandi rhetorice, 4:175a, 9:518a
preaching of, 10:76a
work in English, 9:27a
Peter Bordo de St. Superan, 7:381a-b
Peter, bridge master, reconstruction of London Bridge, 10:414b
Peter of Bruis, rejection of infant baptism, 6:195b
Peter of Byczyna, *Chronica principum Poloniae,* 9:729b
Peter of Candia. *See* Alexander V, pope
Peter of Castelnau
in Albigensian crusade, 3:187b–188a
murder of, 3:353a, 6:465a
Raymond VI of Toulouse and, 12:91b
Peter of Celle, 10:76a
Peter the Chanter, **9:521a–522b**, 10:76b
Andrew of St. Victor's theology school and, 12:21b–22a
denunciation of ordeals, 9:260a
as exegete, 4:544a
Innocent III and, 6:464a
as judge legate, 9:521b
on medieval medicine, 2:100b–101a
notable students of, 9:521b
practical moral reforms of, 9:522a-b
promotion to high office, 9:521b
Summa de sacramentis, 9:521b
theology of, 9:521b
Verbum abbreviatum, 9:522a
Peter Chrysologus, St.
as doctor of the church, 4:234a
unity of Western church and, 3:336b
Peter of Colechurch, stone bridge, 7:661a
Peter Comestor, **9:513b–514b**
career of, 9:513b
in Dante's *Divine Comedy,* 9:514a
Historia scholastica, 2:213b, 3:299b, 4:543b, 545a-b, 546b, 547a-b, 5:604a, 9:513b–514a
derivatives of, 10:544b
Nigel of Longchamp on, 9:131a
representation of Ptolemy or Pythagoras, 11:100b
as a source for *Historien der alden ê,* 2:232a
used by Rudolf von Ems, 2:229a
Peter Lombard and, 9:517a
Peter Lombard's theology school and, 12:21b
preaching of, 10:76a
Sententiae de sacramentis, 9:514a
sermons of, 9:514a
Peter de Coninck, 2:387a-b
Peter of Corbeil
Innocent III and, 6:464a
missing works by, 12:22a
Peter of Cornflans, archbishop of Corinth, as defender of Thomism, 12:40b
Peter of Cornwall, 1:205b
Peter of Courtenay, 7:346b, 349a
Peter cross, 4:9b, 10 (*illus.*)
Peter Damian, St., 3:467b, 7:363b, **9:508a–509b**
as advocate of the Office of the Blessed Virgin Mary, 2:274a
antidialecticism, 4:169b, 9:587b
biography of St. Romuald of Ravenna, 9:508a-b
Book of Gomorrah, attack on penitentials, 9:490b
on book handling, 7:566a
Camaldolese order and, 3:56a
canon law reform and, 3:355a
church reform and, 10:287b
church's use of force, 3:356b
on Cluny Abbey, 2:172b
De divina omnipotentia, 9:509a
Dictatus papae and, 4:177b
as doctor of the church, 4:234b
on excommunication, 4:536b
hymns of, 6:381b
kingship theories of, 7:263b–264a
Liber gratissimus, 9:508b
monastic views of, 3:354b
Nicholas II and, 3:351a
on Nicolaitism, 9:129a
papacy and, 3:348a, 9:508b–509a
polemic treatise of, 10:2b
popularity of, 9:508a
priesthood of the laity, 4:375a
reputation as an anti-intellectual, 9:509a
on resistance, 10:17b
on simony, 7:123b, 543b, 9:508b–509a
Peter the Deacon of Monte Cassino, **9:522b–523a**
Registrum Petri Diaconi, 9:522b–523a
Peter della Vigna, 4:204b
Peter of Dusburg, on the Baltic peoples, 2:64a
Peter of Eboli (*d.* 1219/1220), 7:365b
Peter Fetcham. *See* Peter Peckham
Peter the Fuller. *See* Peter Mongus
Peter Getadarz. *See* Petros Getadarj
Peter Helias, commentary on Cicero, 10:356a
Peter the Hermit, **9:523a–524a**
First Crusade, 1:158a
influence on Urban II, 9:523a
preaching of, 4:30a, 33b, 34a, 6:214a
siege of Antioch, 9:523b
siege of Jerusalem, 9:523b
peasants' crusade, 9:523a-b
Peter of Hungary, king, 6:339b
Peter the Iberian, St.
historical narrative of, 5:413b
life of, 5:413a-b
monastery established by, 5:411a
Syriac Life, 5:413b
Peter of Isernia. *See* Celestine V, pope
Peter Ismael, abbot, Innocent III and, 6:464a
Peter John Olivi, **9:514b–516a**, 10:251a
accusations of heresy, 5:201b, 202b
burning of books, 5:202a
Apocalypse commentary, 9:515b
Aristotelianism and, 9:156a, 613b
beguins and, 2:162a, 163a
Bernardino of Siena and, 2:196b
censured by Parisian scholars, 9:514b–515b
doctrine of *usus pauper,* 6:199a
infallibility of Christ, 4:377a
Joachim of Fiore and, 7:114a
professorships, 5:201b
reinterpretation of Franciscan Rule, 5:201b
Richardus de Mediavilla and, 10:388a-b
Ubertino of Casale and, 12:235b
unofficial cult of, 9:515a
Peter, "king" of Croatia (1093–1097), 4:7a
Peter Kresimir. *See* Kresimir IV of Croatia, king
Peter of La Palu. *See* Petrus Paludanus
Peter Langtoft, **9:516a**
Chronicle, 1:265b, 9:516a
Peter de Leia, 5:421a
Peter of Lérida, 9:62b
Peter Lombard, **9:516a–517b**
Burgundio of Pisa and, 2:423b
career of, 9:516b
Collectanea, glosses from in *Biblia Escurialense,* 11:432a
in Dante's *Divine Comedy,* 9:517b
interior penance, 9:604a
Joachim of Fiore's criticism of, 7:113b–114a
Magna glosatura, 4:543b, 547a,b, 9:516b–517a, 593b
translated into French, 2:218b–219a
on the nature of angels, 1:250a-b
Peter Comestor and, 9:513b, 514a
preaching of, 10:76a
on the sacraments, 9:602b
Sentences, 3:322b–323a, 4:170a, 543b, 7:565b, 9:516b, 517a-b, 11:57b, 12:192b–193a
Aquinas and, 1:353a–354a, 11:691a
biblical quotations in, 2:213b
commentaries on, 9:517b, 594a, 612a-b
cost of, 7:567b
dating of, 9:517a
Eudes Rigaud and, 4:519a
Gabriel Biel's lectures on, 2:233b
Ockham on, 9:209b
on penance, 9:491b
Rufinus' use of, 10:545b
scholasticism of, 11:57b
sources for, 9:593b

study of, 11:690b–691a
summary of contents, 9:593b–594a
Tauler and, 11:602a
as theological textbook, 1:148a
Trinitarian doctrine in, 9:598b
sermons of, 9:516b
theology school of, 12:21b
Trinitarian doctrine and, 12:191a-b, 192b–193b
Peter de Luna, cardinal. *See* Benedict XIII, antipope
Peter of Lusignan, king of Cyprus
crusade of, 4:55a-b
invasion of Alexandria, 1:153b
Peter Manducator. *See* Peter Comestor
Peter of Maricourt. *See* Peter Peregrinus of Maricourt
Peter Martyr, St., 6:487a, 8:379a
Catholic confraternities in Italy and, 3:190b
martyrdom, 8:159b
murder of, 3:190b
Peter, Master, **9:513b–514a**
Peter, metropolitan of Kiev, **9:512a-b**
Muscovite conflict, 8:541a
Peter Mongus, Acacius of Constantinople and, 1:508b
Peter of Morrone. *See* Celestine V, pope
Peter Odeljan, 2:407b
Peter Olivi. *See* Peter John Olivi
Peter Orseolo, king of Hungary, 11:480a, 482a
Peter the Patrician (*d.* 565), Roman history, 6:243b
Peter Peckham, **9:520a**
life of Richard of Chichester, 6:63b
life of Richard Wyche, 1:261b
Lumere as lais, 1:263a-b
compared with Robert of Greatham's *Corset,* 10:433b
Lumiere as Lais, 9:520a
Secret des secrets, 1:264b, 9:520a
Vie de saint Richard, 9:520a
Peter Peregrinus of Maricourt, **9:520a–521a**
Epistola de magnete, 3:506a-b, 9:520a-b
on compass, 11:101a
on experimentation, 9:520b
perpetuum mobilium, 11:644a, 652a
Peter Philomena of Dacia, 1:612a
commentary on *Algorismus vulgaris,* 8:209a
Peter of Pisa, 7:362a, **9:519a**
at court of Charlemagne, 9:519a
Carolingian Latin poetry and, 3:101b
friend of Paul the Deacon, 9:467b
Peter of Poitiers, 7:366b
Peter Lombard's theology school and, 12:21b
Peter von Prachtatitz, **9:525a–526a**
atelier at St. Stephen's, 9:525b (*illus.*), 525a
Peter of Prussia, biography of Albertus Magnus, 1:129a
Peter Riga, **9:521a**
Agnes, Hildebert of Lavardin and, 7:364a
Aurora, 7:365b, 9:521a
Floridus aspectus, 1:319a, 7:365b, 9:521a
Susanna, 7:365b, 9:521a
Hildebert of Lavardin and, 7:364a
Peter de Rivaux, royal wardrobe and, 6:302a, 302b
Peter des Roches
as justiciar, 7:200b
regency for Henry III, 6:158b
royal wardrobe and, 6:302a
Peter, St.
in art, 6:405a, 7:153b (*illus.*)
Einhard's translation of, 12:145a, 154a
feast of St. Peter's Chair, 9:689a–690b
as intercessor, 9:658b
liturgy of, 9:691b–692b
Tu es Petrus, 9:689a–690b, 690a (*illus.*)
office of, 6:317b
origins of papacy and, 4:373b–374a, 374b, 9:363b–365a
primacy of
Traditio clavium, 12:123 (*illus.*), 175a
Traditio legis, 12:123a–124b (*illus.*)
Vatican shrine of, 4:337a
Peter of Savoy
Bern and, 11:539b, 543a
Simon de Montfort the Younger and, 11:297b
vs. Rudolph of Habsburg, 11:540a
Peter Schwartz (Niger), 4:246a
Peter of Serbia, ruler, 11:169a-b, 170a
Peter of Sicily, *History of the Manichaeans Called Paulicians,* 9:468b
Peter of Spain (Pedro Juliano Rebolo), election as John XXI, 9:519b
Peter of Spain (the Elder), **9:519a–520a**
Averroism and, 1:463b
Bernard's *Compilatio,* glosses to, 9:519a
early career of, 8:250b
legal treatises, Roman-law procedure, 9:519b
Siger and, 11:286b
Summulae logicales, 4:170b, 8:250b, 9:519b, 11:407a
Thesaurus pauperum, 3:168b, 8:250b, 9:519b
Tractatus, 4:170b
via moderna and, 12:408a
Peter of Spain (the Younger), *Notabilia ad Compilationem quartam,* 9:519b
Peter of Tarentaise, church reform proposals, 3:641b
Peter of Ulm, 4:579b
Peter Urseolus, St., **9:525a**
restoration of S. Marco, 9:525a
Peter the Venerable, abbot of Cluny, 7:366b, **9:524a–525a**
Adversus Judaeorum inveteratum duritiem, 9:524b, 10:3b
Benedictine observance, 9:524a
on Cluniac liturgy, 3:467b
Cluniac order under, 3:469a-b, 9:524a
collection of letters, 9:524b
Contra Petrobrusianos, 9:524b
cult at Clermont, 9:524b
Liber contra sectam sive haeresim Saracenorum, 8:444b
on Muslims, 11:375b
on Peter Abelard, 1:18a
preaching of, 10:76a
translation of Koran, 3:356b, 7:297a
translations of Koran, 8:444b
travels, 9:524a-b
works of, 9:524b
writings against Islam, 9:524b
Peter of Verona. *See* Peter Martyr, St.
Peter of Vinea, 4:174b–175a
ars dictaminis and, 10:359a
dictamen of, 4:174b–175a
Peter (Vlach leader), 12:483b
Peter Waldo. *See* Waldes
Peter Włostowicz of Silesia, 9:723a
Peterborough Cathedral, 10:484a
Peterborough Chronicle, 8:311a, 313b, 328a, 328b
Peterborough (monastery), military service of, 2:173b
Peterhof, Russian fur trade and, 5:330a-b
Peterhouse. *See* Cambridge, University of
Peters, Gerlach, 4:166b
Peter's Pence, **9:526a–527a**, 11:606a
after Roman reform movement, 9:526a-b
alternative names, 9:526a
amount of, 9:526b, 11:616b
origin, 9:526a
papal rights to, 9:526b
payment by Scandinavian church, 1:58a
political conditions affecting, 9:526b
Petit, Jean. *See* Jean Petit
Petit Jehan de Saintré. See La Sale, Antoine de
Petit jury. *See* Jury
Petit Plet, Le. See Chardri
Petite philosophie, La, 1:263b, **9:527a**
modern edition of, 1:272a
sources for, 9:527a
Petitions, papal. *See* Rescripts
Petrajolo dei Negroni da Ello. *See* Missaglia
Petrarch (Francesco Petrarca), **9:527a–543b**, 9:679b
Africa, 9:528b
classical influences, 9:534b
historical importance, 9:535a
humanist elements, 9:533a
integration of Livy's history, 9:535a
Apollo-Daphne myth, 9:542b
in *Canzoniere,* 9:538b
in *Trionfi,* 9:540a, 541a
Arquà residence, 9:530b
artistic patronage, *Ambrosian Vergil,* 9:531b (*illus.*)
ascent of Mt. Ventoux, 12:162a
on the astrarium, 3:461b–462a
authentication of Caesar-Nero documents, 9:530a
Avignon papacy, opposition to, 9:530b, 532a
letters to Benedict XII, 9:528b
petitioning of Clement VI, 9:529a
Barlaam of Calabria and, 2:109b
on Black Death, 2:257b

Petrarch (Francesco Petrarca), **9:527a–543b** (*cont.*)
Boccaccio and, 2:285b, 286b, 288a, 288b, 289a-b
Bucolicum carmen, 9:534a
Canzoniere, 6:652a, 653a, 653b, 9:538a–539b
Christian elements, 9:539a-b
metrical forms, 9:538b
ordering of poems, 9:538a
poem 263 to Laura, 9:538b
sources for, 9:539a
themes and structure, 9:539a
Catalan translations of, 3:169b
Celestine piety of, 3:215a
character of, 9:527b
Chaucer and, 3:282b–283a
Christian ethics, 9:536b–537a
caritas vs. *cupiditas,* 9:539b, 540b
classical studies and, 9:543a
personal glory and, 9:535a, 537b–538a, 538b, 542a
Cicero's letters, 9:529a, 532a
Cino da Pistoia and, 6:649a
classical literary studies and, 3:435a-b
coronation of as poet laureate, 2:288a
De oto religioso, 9:536a-b
De remediis utriusque fortune, 9:536b
De sui ipsius et multorum ignorantia, 9:530b, 533b
De viris illustribus, 2:239b, 9:528b, 535a
intentions in writing, 9:535a-b
sources for, 9:535a
De vita solitaria, 9:536a
ecclesiastical career, 9:528b, 529b
Epistolae sine nomine, 2:34b
Epistole metrice, 9:534a-b
Florentine dialect and, 6:443b
historical importance, 9:531a
historical works, 9:534b–535b
as bridge to antiquity, 9:535b
humanism, 9:531a
Christian dimension, 9:536b–537a, 539b–540a
treatises on, 9:533a
idea of Middle Ages and, 8:308b
illegitimate children, 9:29a
introspective and lyrical works, 9:537a–543a
Invectiva contra eum qui maledixit Italie, 9:533b–534a
Invectiva contra quendam . . . hominem . . . , 9:533b
Invective contra medicum, 9:533a
Itinerarium syriacum, sources for, 9:535b
Landini and, 7:326a
Latin works of, 7:369b
eclogues, 9:534a
first poem, 9:528a
list of, 9:531a
metrical letters, 9:534a-b
Laura
in *Canzoniere,* 9:538b–539a
first encounter with, 9:528a-b
in *Secretum Meum,* 9:537b–538a
in *Trionfi,* 9:541a, 541b–542b
laurel crown, 9:528b
reservations on receiving, 9:537a, 538a
legal studies, 9:528a
Letter to Posterity, biographical elements, 9:527b
letter-writing, 9:529b, 531b–533a, 12:149a
addressees, 9:531b
self-analysis in, 9:532b
lyric poetry and, 6:652a–653b
Marsili and, 7:326b
Non al suo amante, 7:31b
number six, significance of, 9:534b
in *Canzoniere,* 9:539a-b
in *Trionfi,* 9:540b
opposition to
Aristotelians, 9:530b, 533b
clerics, 9:529b
on papal Avignon as Babylon, 2:34a
personal treatises, 9:535b–537a
on isolation, 9:535a
on religious themes, 9:536a
Philippe de Vitry and, 8:645b, 12:481a-b
Platonism and, 9:702b–703a
poetry of, in trecento music, 12:177b, 178b
polemical works, 9:530b, 533a–534b
Psalmi poenitentiales, 9:529b
Rerum familiarium libri, 9:529b
classical influence, 9:532a-b
content, 9:532a
Rerum memorandarum libri, 9:529a
attitude towards antiquity, 9:535b
opening book, 9:535b
Rerum senilium libri, 9:533a
on Richard de Bury, 10:386a
scholarly works, 9:531a–537a
Secretum meum, 9:529a, 537a–538a
Augustine's remonstrations, 9:537b–538a, 538b
self-analysis in, 9:537b–538a
theme of eternal life, 9:537b
as transitional figure, 7:10b
translated by Bernat Metge, 8:300b
Trionfi, 6:640a-b, 670a, 9:528b, 539b–543a, 12:477a
Christian superstructure, 9:540a
concept of love, 9:541a
Dante's influence on, 9:540b
sonnet development, 9:540a
structure and themes, 9:540b–542a
triumphal figures, 9:540b
Trionfo d'amore, on Sicilian poets, 11:257b
Tuscan dialect and, 6:624b, 626b, 627a, 629a
Variae, 9:532a
Venetian residence, 9:530b
Venetian-Genoese war and, 9:529b
vision genre, use of, 9:537b
on wine, 12:650a
Petri exceptiones, **9:544a**
Petrine supremacy. *See* Apostolic succession
Pétronille de Chemillé, Fontevrault order and, 10:429b–430a, 430b, 12:686b
Petronius
Satyricon, 12:494b
wine and, 12:650a
Petros Getadarj, **9:544a-b**
annexation of Ani, 1:290b, 484a, 9:544a-b
hymns, 9:544b
incarceration and exile, 9:544b
Petros, *katᶜołikos,* 5:675a
Petros Philargos. *See* Alexander V, antipope
Petros of Siwnikᶜ, bishop, 1:509a
Petru I Muşat of Moldavia, voivode, submission to Polish suzerainty, 12:501b
Petrucci, Fabio, 11:282a
Petrucci, Federico, mentor of Baldus, 2:57a
Petrucci, Pandolfo, 11:281b–282a
Petrus
Beatus *Commentary,* illustration of, 9:544b
see also Peire; Peter; Piero; Pierre; Pietro
Petrus. *See Petri Exceptiones*
Petrus Alfonsi
Adelard of Bath and, 12:135b
Dialogus contra Judaeos, 3:167b, 10:3a
Disciplina clericalis, 3:167b, **4:216b,** 4:551b, 6:630a, 658b, 659a, 7:365a, 8:23b, 11:406b, 410a, 441a
Anglo-Norman translation of, 1:264a
fabliaux and, 4:576a
preaching in Spain and, 11:456a
Víga-Glúms saga and, 12:416a
Petrus de Alliaco. *See* Ailly, Pierre d'
Petrus of Amalfia, *Compendium artis motectorum Marchecti,* 8:646a
Petrus Apianus, heavenly spheres, 9:620a (*illus.*)
Petrus Bonus, *Pretiosa margarita novella,* 1:138a
Petrus Capuanus. *See* Petrus of Amalfia
Petrus Christus. *See* Christus, Petrus
Petrus de Cruce, 8:644a, **9:545a-b**
Jerome of Moravia and, 8:645a
motets, style, 9:545a-b
musical notation, 5:209a
division of breves, 9:545a
puncti, 9:545a
notation of, 1:550a-b
Philippe de Vitry and, 12:482a
rhythmic notation and, 8:588b, 594a
Robert de Handlo and, 8:646b
in *Speculum musicae,* 9:545a
Petrus Damiani. *See* Peter Damian, St.
Petrus de Ebulo, 9:58b
Petrus frater dictus Palma ociosa, 11:366a
musical theory of, 3:657b
Petrus Helie, 3:434b
Petrus Hispanus. *See* Peter of Spain
Petrus Le Viser, Robert de Handlo and, 8:646b
Petrus Nigri, *Clypeus Thomistarum,* 12:42a
Petrus Olavi, hymns of, 6:382b
Petrus Paludanus, as defender of Thomism, 12:42a
Petrus Peregrinus de Maricourt. *See* Peter Peregrinus of Maricourt
Petrus Phiolarius, 5:556a

Petrus of Picardy, *Ars motettorum,* 8:644a
Petrus Pictor (*fl. ca.* 1100), 7:365b, 372b
  Hildebert of Lavardin and, 7:364a
Petrus Ramus, views on rhetoric, 10:354b
Petrus Riga
  Aurora, 1:319a
  Floridus aspectus, 1:319a
Petrus of Silos, **9:544b**
Petruslied, 9:233b, **9:546a**
  Kyrie in, 7:593b
Petty assizes, English, **9:546a–549a**
  advowsons, 9:547a
  assize of nuisance, 9:546b, 547b
  effect on feudal system, 9:547b
  lay vs. church courts, 9:546b
  mort d'ancestor, 9:546b, 548b
    protective function, 9:547a-b
  quare impedit, 9:548a
  utrum, 9:546a-b
    king's court, 9:547b
    parson's writ of right, 9:548a
    uses of, 9:547a
  see also Assize, possessory; Seisin, Disseisin
Petty jury
  creation of, 7:183a
  member selection for, 7:183a
  problems of, 7:183a-b
  statute on, 7:183a
Petty treason. *See* Treason
Peuerbach, Georg, *Theôricae novae planetarum,* 1:613b, 11:103a
Peutinger, Konrad, 11:572a
Peutinger Table (map), 1:563b, 5:397a
Pewter, working of, 8:286b–287a
Pewterers Company of London, parliament and, 9:432b
Peyrolles, inns in, 6:468b
Pézenas, fairs, 4:586a
Pfaffe Amis. *See* Stricker, Der
Pfaffe im Käskorb, Der, peasantry, characterization of, 8:130a
Pfaffe Konrad. *See* Rolandslied
Pfaffe Lamprecht. *See* Lamprecht
Pfaffenbrief (1370), 11:543b
Pfahlburger, 11:544a
Pfännerschaft. *See* Salt trade
Pfarrer vom Kahlenberg. *See* Frankfurter, Philipp
Pfullendorf, population of, 5:458a
Pfullendorf, count of, 11:527b
Phaedrus (*d. ca.* 50), 4:572a, 572b
Phaletolum. *See* Adam of the Little Bridge, *De Utensilibus*
Phantasiasts. *See* Aphthartodocetism
Phantom's Frenzy, The, 1:567a-b
Pharisees, synagogue and, 11:556a-b
Pharmacognosy. *See* Pharmacopeia
Pharmacopeia, **9:549a–552a**
  action of a compound drug, 9:625b
  balancing agents, 9:551a
  Byzantine, 8:246a
  drug testing, protoscientific method, 9:551b–552a
  galenicals, 9:550a
  medicinal properties of ancient dyestuffs, 4:326a
  medieval study of plants and, 2:244b–246a
  method of preparation, 9:550a
  multilingual drug glossaries, 11:92b
  in Old English, 1:286a
  pharmacodynamic effects, 9:549b–550a
  physician's prescription, 9:550a
  simples, 9:549b
  theriac, 9:549b (*illus.*)
    ingredients, 9:549a
  treatment of Plague and, 2:264b
  see also Almond; Dill; Headache; Mandrake; Medicine; Rose; Toxicology
Pharos lighthouse, 1:154a
Pharsalia, adaptations of, 10:528a
Phelonion, 3:615b
Phenology, in climatology, 3:451a-b
Philanthropia, 8:244a-b
Philaretos Vakhramios. *See* P^cilartos Varažnuni
Philaretus (physician), *De pulsibus,* 8:248b, 256b
Philes, Manuel
  poetry, 2:507b
    use of meter, 2:524a
Philip II (the Bold) of Burgundy, duke
  administration of, 2:427b
  Claus Sluter's work for, 11:349a-b
  commissioning of Chartreuse de Champmol, 4:186a
  as Guillaume de Machaut's patron, 8:3a
  influence in court of Charles VI, 5:186b–187a
  inheritance of Flanders, 5:523b
  marriage of, 2:426a
  Melchior Broederlam at court of, 2:383a
  tomb of, 9:709 (*illus.*), 710b
  Ypres and, 12:732a
Philip III (the Good) of Burgundy, duke, 10:320b
  alliance with Henry V, 6:160b
  authors at court of, 3:235a
  clock built for, 3:29b
  Jan van Eyck and, 4:566a-b
  Lathem and, 7:345b
  music and, 8:635a
  power of, 5:490a
  revolt of Ghent against, 5:523b
  Rhétoriqueurs and, 10:364b
  Vermandois and, 12:396a
Philip I of France, king
  acquisition of territories, 5:159b
  excommunication of, 3:449a
  opposed by Ivo of Chartres, 7:21b
  seal usage by nonroyal rulers and, 11:125b
  touching of, for king's evil, 7:255b
Philip II Augustus of France, king, **9:552b–554a**
  accession to throne, 5:161a
  administration of, 5:162b, 9:403b
    office of bailli, 2:53a
    reforms, 9:553a
    in territories outside royal domain, 5:164b
  assessment of levies, 5:163a
  assize and, 1:594b
  biography of
    by Guillaume le Breton, 2:236b
    by Rigord, 2:236b
  calendar used in chancery of, 3:20a
  Children's Crusade and, 4:15a
  chronicles of, 6:23b–24a
  confiscation of fief of Normandy, 5:59a
  coronation, 9:552b
    evidence of baronial rivalry at, 5:162a
  court rivalries, 9:52b
  divorce of, 6:493b
  dungeons of, 3:148b
  election of Frederick II, 5:483a
  extension of royal domain, 9:403a-b, 417b–418a, 553b
    feudal overlordship, 5:165a-b
  Frederick II and, 11:270a
  history of his reign by Rigord, 10:399a-b
  Innocent III and, 3:187b–188a, 6:464b, 9:553a
  Jews and, 4:563b–564a, 11:211a
  Langland and, 7:338a
  legitimization of heirs, 9:553a
  marriages
    to Agnes of Meran, 9:553a
    to Ingeborg of Denmark, 9:553a
    to Isabella of Hainaut, 9:552b
  mercenary troops, 12:559a
  military acquisitions
    Artois, Vermandois, and Valois, 5:163a-b
    battle of Bouvines, 5:164b
    Brittany and Anjou, 5:164a
    royal wardship of Flanders and Troyes, 5:165a
  military campaigns
    against Henry II of England, 4:467b
    against John, 4:468a-b, 7:129a-b, 581a, 9:168a, 168b
    against Richard I, 4:467b–468a
    conquest of Normandy, 3:8b
  Norman finance and, 4:532a
  Norman law and, 4:69a
  ordinance of 1346, 5:134b, 135a
  Paris under, 9:403a–404a
  Parisian water supply, 12:577b
  perfumers' guilds and, 2:147a
  Richard I (the Lionhearted) and, 10:383a–384a
  Simon III de Montfort and, 11:296b–297a
  in Third Crusade, 4:40a-b, 9:552b–553a
  Thomas of Savoy and, 11:539b
  Vermandois and, 12:396a
  vs. Angevins, 1:253a, 5:161b
    alliance with Arthur against John, 5:164a
    alliance with John against Richard I, 5:163b
    Henry II of England, 6:158a
  vs. Ferrand of Flanders, 5:522a
  wax seal impressions of, 11:127b
  William (the Lion) of Scotland and, 11:107b
Philip III of France, king
  Aragonese crusade of, 7:144a

Philip III of France (*cont.*)
church taxation and, 11:609b
crusade against Peter III, 4:61a-b
effectiveness of rule, 5:166b–168a
Eudes of Montreuil and, 4:518b
Joinville and, 7:144a
Parlement of Paris and, 9:419a
prohibition of wool and grain exports, 12:118a
Somme le roi for, 10:301b
Philip IV (the Fair) of France, king, 2:1b, **9:554a–555b**
administrative reforms
king's council, 9:554b
local government, 9:554b
Beaumanoir and, 2:144a
Bonsignori bank and, 11:280a
breviary of, 5:614a
bridge at Montauban and, 10:418b
domination of German politics, 5:488a
in *Grandes chroniques de France,* 5:654a
growth of the Parlement of Paris and, 9:419a-b, 10:317b
inquisition and, 6:487b
Jews and, 4:564a
expulsion of, 5:172a
John of Paris and, 7:136b–137a
Lull's dedication of works to, 7:686a
Lyons and, 7:699a
marriage of, 3:249b, 4:593a
Nogaret and, 9:153a
Normandy and, 9:169a
overlordship of Flanders, 11:713b
ownership of vehicles and, 12:375b, 376a
Rabban Sauma and, 1:453a
relations with church, 9:646b–647a
Celestines and, 3:214b
Clericis laicos and, 3:447b–448a
conflict with Boniface VIII, 2:324a, 3:438b, 515a, 643b, 4:218a, 259a, 5:171a–172a, 7:699a, 9:554b–555a, 10:21a–22b, 11:609b–610a
conflict with Boniface VIII, *Ausculta fili,* 2:3b–4a
Council of Vienne and, 3:644a
forged papal documents, 5:136b
jurisdiction of French church, 7:267a-b
theory of papal authority, 4:376b
revolutionary policies, 5:168b
spring-powered chamber clock of, 3:462a-b
succession problems, 5:172a-b, 9:555a
taxation
of clergy, 2:324a, 9:554a, 554b
general taxes, 9:554a
taxation policy, 11:621a-b
Templars and, 3:304b, 5:172a, 9:405a, 647a
touching for king's evil, 7:255b
tract in defense of, 10:238a
vs. Edward I of England, 5:171a
vs. Guy of Dampierre, 2:387a-b
Philip V of France, king
accession of, 5:182a-b
administrative reforms, 5:182b
Pastoureaux uprising (1320) and, 9:454a
problems of leadership, 5:172b
representative assemblies and, 10:318a
salt tax, 10:631a
travels of court, 12:159a
wine brokers and, 12:121a
Philip VI of France, king, **9:555b–556a**, 12:352b
claim to throne, 5:183a
conquest of Flemish rebels, 5:183b
court rivalries, 9:555b
English campaigns, 6:331b, 9:555b–556a, 556a
explanation of the Black Death and, 8:253b
in *Grandes chroniques de France,* 5:654a
Philippe de Vitry and, 12:481a, 482b
purchase of Dauphiné, 4:108a, 109a
representative assemblies and, 10:318a-b, 324a
salt tax (gabelle) of, 5:336a-b
succession to throne, 9:555b
taxation policy, 8:68a, 11:621b
travels of court, 12:159a
Philip I (the Handsome) of Spain, king, marriage to Joanna the Mad, 6:43a, 8:280b
Philip I of Taranto, prince of Achaea, 7:379a
Morea and, 7:379b
Philip II of Taranto, 7:381a
Philip VI of Valois. *See* Philip VI of France, king
Philip of Alsace, count of Vermandois, 12:396a
Philip of Antioch, king of Armenia, 3:395a
Philip of Aquila, freestanding Stations of the Cross, 11:467b
Philip the Chancellor, **9:556b–557b**
conflict with University of Paris, 9:556b
Distinctiones super Psalterium, 9:557a
French and Latin poetry, 9:557a-b
hymns of, 6:382a
poetry of, 7:374a
polyphony and, 9:192a
Quaestiones, 9:557a
Summa de bono, 9:601a
Summa duacensis, 9:557a
Summa quaestionum theologicarum, 9:557a
sources for, 9:557a
tenure at Notre Dame, 9:556a
texts in MS Pluteus 29.1, 5:106a
theology, classical influence, 9:557a
Walter of Châtillon and, 7:368b
Philip of Évreux, marriage to Queen Joanna II of Navarre, 9:71a
Philip of Flanders, count, 3:308b, 5:80b
Philip of Germany, emperor
conflict over German throne, 5:214a, 482b, 483a
election of, 4:425a
excommunication, 12:538a
imperial claims of, 9:58b
Innocent III and, 6:464b, 11:269b
as patron of poetry, 5:435a
recognition of first Cilician king, 3:391a
succession to throne, 12:537b–538a
Swabia and, 11:527b, 12:676a
in Walther von der Vogelweide's songs, 12:538a-b
Wolfger von Erla and, 12:672b
Philip of Harvengt, **9:556a-b**, 10:87a
literary works, 9:556a-b
Philip of Heinsberg, archbishop, 3:481a
Philip of Leyden, 10:274a
Philip of Swabia. *See* Philip of Germany, emperor
Philippa of Hainault (Lancaster)
Edward III and, 6:332a
tomb of, 8:585a (*illus.*)
Philippe d'Artois, *Cent ballades,* 9:637a
Philippe de Beaumanoir. *See* Beaumanoir, Philippe de
Philippe de Grève, **9:557b**
Philippe de Mazerolles, Lathem and, 7:346a
Philippe de Mézières, 1:608b, 6:382b
Philippe Mousket (Mouskès), **9:559a-b**
Chronique rimée, 3:258a, 9:559a, 638a
sources for, 9:559a
Wandering Jew legend, 12:542b
Philippe de Novare (Navarre), **9:558a-b**
Assizes of Jerusalem and, 1:599a
French chronicles of, 3:332b
imperial-Ibelin wars, 9:558a
prose history, 9:558a
reconquest of Cyprus, 9:558a
Jean d'Ibelin and, 6:390a
Livre de forme de plait, 6:390a, 9:558a-b
Quatre âges de l'homme, 9:558b
Philippe de Rémi
Coutumes de Beauvaisis, 3:674b–675a, 9:639b
Jehan et Blonde, 5:287a
Manekine, 5:287a
folktale elements, 9:635a
Philippe de Thaon, **9:558b–559a**
Bestiaire, 1:188b, 262a, 9:558b
Latin sources, 5:289a
modern edition of, 1:271a
Compoz, 1:262a, 9:558b
modern edition of, 1:271b, 271a
lapidaries, 5:281a, 9:559a
Livre de Sibile, 5:289a, 9:558b–559a
Philippe de Toucy, 7:349a
Philippe de Vitry. *See* Vitry, Philippe de
Philippicus Bardanes, Byzantine emperor, icons and, 6:400b
Philippide. See Guillaume le Breton
Philippopolis, **9:559b**
Basil II in, 2:119a
Paulicians in, 9:468b
seized by crusaders, 6:559b
Philippus of Caserta, *Tractatus de diversis figuris,* 8:646b
Philippus Tripolitanus, translation of *Secretum secretorum,* 11:135a
Phillippe de Courguilleroy, on hunting, 6:358a
Philo, translations into Armenian, 1:505b
Philo of Byzantium
mechanics manual, 11:633a, 640b

pneumatic inventions, 11:640b–641a
Pneumatica, Arabic translation, 11:641a
Philobiblon. See Richard de Bury
Philodemus of Gadara (*ca.* 110-*ca.* 40/35 B.C.), 8:636b
Philokalia. See Basil (the Great) of Caesarea, St.
Philolaus (Pythagorean), 8:636b
Philology
Byzantine, 9:696b–697a
reason identified with, 8:156a
Philomena. See John of Howden; Peckham, John
Philoponos, John. *See* John Philoponos of Alexandria
Philosophia mundi. See William of Conches
Philosophy, in Georgia, 5:417b
Philosophy and theology
debate between, 9:696a-b, 697b–698a, 700a, 702b
Incoherence of the Philosophers, 9:700a
subordination of philosophy, 9:696a-b
Greek, Zoroastrianism and, 12:746b
see also Cosmology; Ontology
Philosophy and theology, Armenian, *Knik*ᶜ *Hawatoy,* 7:279a-b
Philosophy and theology, Byzantine, **9:560a–567b**
Alexandrian Neoplatonists, 11:54b–55a
Aristotelianism, 9:565b
Athanasian, 9:560b
Christology, 3:320a-b
classical authors studied, 11:49b
classical revival, 13th–14th centuries, 9:567a
dogmatic literature
against Armenian Monophysites, 9:562b
against Islam, 9:562b
against Latins, 9:562b
11th-century renewal, 11:55a
hesychast controversy, 9:562b–563a
hiatus during invasions and internal disputes, 11:55a
iconoclasm, 9:561b–562a
late works on Plato and Aristotle, 11:55a
literal vs. allegorical, 9:564b
literary studies and, 3:431a
Neoplatonism, 9:563a-b
attitudes toward, 9:566a-b
Nestorianism, 9:564a
orthodoxy, 9:560a–563a
basis for, 9:560a
defining the trinity, 9:560b–561a
Divine Word, 9:561a-b
Filioque controversy, 9:562a
origins, 9:560a
Palamas' doctrine, 9:563a
Pauline and Johannine, 9:560a
philosophical terminology, 9:565b–566a
in christological debates, 9:566a
consubstantial, 9:566a
tritheism, 9:566a
philosophy
definition of, 9:564b
education in, 9:565a–566a
opposition to, 9:566a–567a
societal functions, 9:565a
philosophy, schools of, 9:564b
Alexandria, 9:565a-b
Athens, 9:565a
Gaza, 9:565a
Photian schism, 9:561b–562a
Platonism, 9:563a-b, 567a, 695a, 696a–699a
education in, 9:565a
sacraments and sacramentals in, 7:611a
speculative and mystical, 9:563a–563b
Stoicism, 9:563a
theology
framework for, 2:467a
Greek philosophical elements, 2:467a-b
lack of systematization, 2:466a-b
mystical, 2:467a, 490b
perception of God, 2:466a-b
threat of heresy, 11:55a
translation and translators, 12:126a–127b
Trinitarianism vs. subordinationism, 9:560b
see also Councils, ecumenical; Exegesis, Byzantine; Monophysitism
Philosophy and theology, Greek
Islamic transmission of, 6:584b
music and, 8:580a
Philosophy and theology, Islamic, **9:567b–572b**
Andalusian, 9:570b–571b
Aristotle and, 1:458b–459b
al-Ashᶜarī, 9:569a-b, 10:573a
atomism, 9:575a
classical tradition
Aristotelian-Rushdian tradition, 9:571a-b
Latin and Hebrew translations, 9:571b
development, 12th and 13th centuries, 9:571b–572a
ethical voluntarism, 9:569a
Hanbalite, 9:568b
Ibn Sīnā, 10:572b, 574b, 11:302a–307a
Imamite theologians, 9:568b
interaction of, 9:570a-b, 10:573b–574a
Islamic science and, 11:88a-b
Islamic-Jewish polemics, 10:7a–9a
justice of God, 9:568a
theories of, 9:569a-b
language used, 9:568a
al-Māturīdī, 9:569b
Muᶜtazilites, 9:568a-b, 569a
occasionalism, 9:575a
Peripatetic, 11:303a–304a
philosophy, schools of, 6:582b–584b, 9:570b–571a
place of logic in, 7:641b
Plato and, 9:669a–700b, 694b–696a
political, 10:13b–14a
prophets, 9:570a
al-Rāzī and, 10:267a–268a
Sufi, 6:585a
taught in madrasas, 8:11a, 11b
theology, schools of. *See* Muᶜtazila, al-
theory of acquisition, 9:569a-b
theosophy, 9:572a
translations from Greek, 9:569b
see also Creeds, Islamic; Madrasa; Sufism; Sunnites, theology of
Philosophy and theology, Jewish
Aristotelianism in, 7:167a-b
Aristotle and, 1:459b–460a
classical tradition, 9:576b
concept of potentiality, 9:576a
creation, 9:576a-b
creatio ex nihilo, 9:576b
critiques by Ḥasdai Crescas, 3:677b678a
despiritualization of nature, 11:663a
development of, 7:163b, 163b–166b
eternal universe, 9:576a
ethics, 9:582a
freethinkers, 7:164a-b
God
attributes of, 9:577b
attributes of, in miracles, 9:580b
divine will, 9:576b
knowledge of, for common man, 9:577a-b
personal, 9:577b
presence in history, 9:576b
Greek philosophy and, 7:163b–164a
in Islam, in Judeo-Arabic literature, 7:173a-b
in Islamic world, **9:572b–578a**
classical tradition, 9:572b–573a
creation theories, 10:599a
decline of, 9:574a
faith and reason, 9:573a
Latin translations, 9:574a
major philosophers, 9:574a–577a
Platonic thought and, 9:694b–696a, 700a-b
religious texts, philosophical interpretation, 9:573a
Sufi influence, 9:573a
translation and translators, 12:133a–135a
in Judeo-Arabic literature, 7:173a-b, 9:571b
mysticism in, 7:168b–169b
nature of substances
Aristotle's four causes, 9:575b–576a
final cause, 9:575b–576a
Neoplatonism, 7:160b–167a
in Northern Europe, **9:578a–582a**
esoteric writers, 9:579a-b
translations from Hebrew and Arabic, 9:574a
philosophy, opposition to, 7:167b–169b, 9:573b–574a
physical arguments, 9:576b
pietism in, 7:168b–169b
Plato and, 9:694b–696a, 700a-b
prayer commentaries, 9:579a, 581b
numerical structures, 9:581b
preaching and sermons in, 10:73b–75a
prophet-philosopher, 9:577a-b
reality
attempts to explain, 9:574b–576a

Philosophy and theology (*cont.*)
reality (*cont.*)
form and matter, 9:575b
nonsensible objects, 9:575a
singularity of, 9:575b
translunar vs. sublunar world, 9:575b
rejection of, 7:167b–169b
repentance literature, 9:581a-b
scope of, 9:573b, 574b
trends in, 7:166b–167b
see also Ashkenazi Hasidism; Cabala; Maimonides, Moses; Ontogeny
Philosophy and theology, Western European
Anselm of Laon as pioneer of scientific theology, 1:315b
astrology and, 1:607a–608b
attitude toward time, 11:663a
Augustinian, 9:616b
Christian work ethic, 11:663b
Christology, 3:320b–324b
classical tradition
availability of material, 9:606b–607a
see also Aristotelianism; Aristotle; Neoplatonism; Plato and Platonism
classification of disciplines, 2:241a–242a
concepts and terms of, *potentia Dei,* 12:194b
conceptualism, 3:510a
creation and, 9:596b, 624a-b, 12:191b–192a, 197a-b
Aristotelian, 9:607a, 612a
creation of matter, 9:600a
declarative theology, 9:610a
deductive theology, 9:609a, 610a-b
despiritualization of nature, 11:663a
development (to mid 12th century), **9:582b–590b**
after Boethius, 9:585a–586a
dialecticians vs. antidialecticians, 9:587a-b
double predestination, 9:587a
human and divine dialectics, 9:586b
logical doctrine, sources for, 9:584b, 585b
moral doctrine, 9:601a-b
world soul, 9:586a
see also Bernard of Chartres; Bernard of Clairvaux, St.; Bernard Silvester; Pseudo-Dionysius the Areopagite
development (12th century)
ecclesiology, 9:601b–602a
German spirituality, 9:598a
Lombard's *Sentences,* 9:593b–594a
new philosophies, 9:596b–597b
scriptural commentaries, 9:594b
theological summae, 9:594b
Victorine school, 9:592b–593a
development (late 12th century), **9:590b–606b**
development (13th century), **9:606b–608a**
see also Bacon, Roger; Ontology
development (late medieval), **9:608a–615b**
academic excellence vs. spirituality, 9:611a-b
anti-Aristotelianism, 9:613b
anti-Thomist writers, 9:609a
literary works, 6:166b–167a
philosophical-theological division, 9:606b–607b
role of theologian, 9:609b–610a
scriptural studies, 9:608a
theology as a scientific discipline, 9:608a–614a
see also Biel, Gabriel
divine exemplarism, 9:598a
Divine Providence, 9:607a
double truth, 9:607b
eschatology, 9:604b
ethics
disputed and quodlibetal questions, 9:594b
natural vs. supernatural, 9:595a-b
philosophical commentaries, 9:594b
Stoic influence, 9:594a
studies in, 9:595a
transmission of, 9:594a–595b
faith and reason
Anselm's synthesis of, 9:587b–588a
conflict of, 9:597b–598a
in theological debate, 9:609a-b
Filioque theology, 12:190a–191a, 195a
Florentine humanism, 12:163a
God
absolute power of, 9:624b
existence of, 9:596b, 597b
knowledge of, 9:598b
great chain of being, 9:278a
historical orientation, 9:584a
human destiny, 9:600a
Aquinas' doctrine of grace, 9:600a-b
theory of limbo, 9:600b
hymns and, 6:383a
Islamic influences, 9:596b
availability of material, 9:606b–607a
Italian humanists, Plato and, 9:702b–703b
logical doctrine, treatises on, 9:613a
metaphysics and theology, 9:609a-b
music and, 8:581a–582b
original justice and original sin, 9:600b
personal immortality, 9:607a
realism
universalia ante res, 10:269a–270b, 272a
universalia in rebus, 10:269a, 270a–272a
revealed sources, 9:608b
rule of faith, 9:278a
sacred teaching, 9:617a
schools of, Victorine, 9:596b–593a
Siete partidas and, 11:282b–283a
terminology, **9:616a–617b**
Augustinian definitions, 9:616a
de proprietatibus terminorum, 11:686b
disputationes, 10:238b, 241a
quaestiones, 10:238a-b
quodlibet, 10:238b, 241a
writings on, 9:617a
theory of universals, 10:531b–532a
13th century, *esse essentiae,* 6:166a
Trinitarian doctrine, 10:531b
Trinitarian theory, 12:642b
trivium and quadrivium, 9:584b–585a, 588b, 12:205a–207a
University of Paris and, 2:318b
see also Aristotelianism; Augustinism; Dualism; Humanism; Neoplatonism; Nominalism; Ockham, William of; Ontology; Theology, schools of; Trinitarian doctrine; Universals
Philostorgios, **9:617b**
Eusebius' *Ecclesiastical History* continued by, 9:617b
Philotheos (*fl. ca.* 900), **9:617b–618a**
Kletorologion, hierarchy of titles and offices, 9:617b–618a
Philotheos, patriarch, 3:632b, **9:618a-b**
appointment of Cyprian, 10:594a
enthronement, 9:618a-b
liturgy development and, 7:611b
patriarchate, 9:618b
Philoxenus of Mabbug, Syrian Orthodox Church and, 11:563b, 565b, 566a
Phipoctus (14th century), 8:646b
Phlebotomy, 2:99a
Phocaea, alum mines at, 12:111b, 115b
Phoebus (Gaston III). *See* Gaston III of Foix, count
Phoenix
in art, 6:603b
in medieval folklore, 2:206b
Phoenix. See Claudian (*ca.* 400); Lactantius
Phoenix, Battle of (*ca.* 655), 6:572b
Phoenix, The, 4:550b
Old English adaptation of Lactantius' *De ave phoenice,* 1:280b
rhyme in, 1:277a
Phokas, Byzantine emperor, **9:618b–619a**
column of, 10:517b
exarchate and, 4:529b
fall of Emperor Maurice and, 8:230b
vs. Heraklios, 10:453b
Phokas family, 7:126a
Phonology, Latin, 12:495a
Phōs hilaron, 6:378a
Photios, patriarch, 3:631b–632b, 5:540b, **9:619a–620a**
Amphilochia, 9:564b, 619b
Armenian/Byzantine church union and, 1:500a
Basil I and, 2:117b, 6:406a
Bibliotheca, 4:446b, 6:245a, 9:619a, 697a
chapters on medicine, 8:245b
Christianization of Slavs, 2:464a, 489a-b, 4:73b, 74a
on church mosaics, 8:490a
condemnation of, 3:633a, 11:43b
contribution to Byzantine renaissance, 9:619b
design of mosaics, Hagia Sophia, 2:439b–440a
election of, 11:42b–43a
Epanagoge and, 4:493b
as exegete, 2:214b

Filioque controversy and, 2:465a, 9:562a
Homilies, 9:619b
iconoclasm, 6:561a, 9:619a
Ignatios and, 6:415b
lexicon of, 11:52b–53a
Myrobiblion, 7:561a, 564a
Mystagogia, 9:562a, 619b
Nicholas I and, 9:121a, 11:43a-b
Nikolaos I Mystikos and, 9:135a
nomocanon and, 9:158b
Nomocanon in XIV Titles, 2:468a
papal recognition, conditions for, 2:402a
patriarchate, 9:619a-b
succession after Ignatios' death, 11:43b
teacher of Emperor Leo VI (the Wise), 7:545b
on Theophylaktos Simokattes, 12:25a
on Viking raid, 12:435a
see also Schism, Photian
Photogrammetry, in monumental archaeology, 1:432a
Phrase exchange (polyphony). *See* Voice exchange (polyphony)
Phundagiagitae (heretics in the Opsikion), 2:295b
Phylarchate, Justinian I and, 7:320b
Phyllis and Flora, 7:367a
Physicians
licensing of, 2:98b
numbers of in the 15th century, 2:98b
scientific treatises, 11:644b
university training of, 2:100a
see also Barber-surgeons; Medicine
Physics, **9:620a–628a**
Aristotelian theory of universe, in university curriculum, 9:620a–623a
Aristotelianism and, 1:464b–465a
continuity and infinity, 9:627a-b
density, 9:624a-b
distribution of qualities, 9:271b
earth's rotation, 9:271a
ether, 9:620b, 622b
form and matter
movement of, 9:622a-b
properties of matter, 9:621b
four elements, 9:622a
interconvertibility, 9:621b
Isidore of Seville's, 9:622a (*illus.*)
qualities of, 9:621b
Galileo's mean-speed theorem, 9:271b–272a
heavenly spheres
Apian's, 9:620a (*illus.*)
Aristotelian, 9:620b
impetus, 9:623b
interrelation of disciplines
achievements resulting from, 9:627a-b
impact of logic on, 9:626b–627a
Islamic, 11:87a
Jean Buridan on, 2:431a
macrocosm and microcosm, 9:623a
motion
causes of, 9:623b
effects of, 9:625b–626a
force and resistance, 9:625a-b
measurement of, 9:626a-b, 627a
perpetual, 11:652a
relativity of, 9:271a-b
studies of, 12:44a
in a vacuum, 9:624b–625a, 625b
violent, 9:622b
Newtonian, precursors of, 9:625a
Oxford Calculators, 9:626a-b
planets, 9:620b
Platonism and, 9:622b, 701b–702a
rotation of earth, 9:623b–624a
moving-earth system, 9:624a
study of animals and plants and, 2:241b
of Swineshead, 11:535b
theology and
absolute power of God, 9:624b
theory of creation, 9:624a-b
in university curriculum, 9:625a
disputations, 9:627a
Physics. See Aristotle
Physika kai mystika, doctrine of universal sympathy, 1:135b
Physiologus, 2:243a-b
Bern MS of, 4:368b
dating of, 2:204a
deluxe editions of, 2:205a
development of into a bestiary, 2:204b
early Byzantine manuscripts of, 8:18b
first Latin translations of, 2:204b
German versions of, 5:428a–429a
hymns and, 6:384b
Învăţăturile lui Neagoe Basarab and, 10:510b
questions of authorship, 2:204a
Richard de Fournival's *Bestiaire d'amour* and, 2:203b
Romanian translations, 10:511b
Schüler von Paris and, 11:80a
Slavic version (*Fiziolog*), 11:345b
Theobald of Monte Cassino and, 7:363b
on unicorn, 6:362a
see also Bestiary
Physis (*natura*). *See* Trinitarian doctrine
Pia dictamina, 6:380a-b, 382b
Piacenza, Diet of (1236), 11:271b
Piast dynasty, **9:628a–629b**
early Polish state (1025-1138), 9:719b–720b
end of, 9:629a, 723b–725b
internal affairs, 9:629a
Poland, naming of, 9:717a
restoration of monarchy, 9:628b
territorial acquisitions, 9:629a
Poland, 9:628a-b
Piazza Navona. *See* Agone
Pibau, 8:558b
Pibgorn, 8:558b
Picard drama, 9:636a-b
comic, 9:636a-b
patrons and *puys,* 9:636b
religious, 9:636b
Picard language, 4:168a, **9:629b–632b**
church promotion of, 9:630a, 633a
consonant system, 9:631b
development, 9:630a-b
dialects, 9:629b–630a, 632b–633a
foreign influences, 9:629b
metathesis, 9:631b
morphological system, 9:631b
nasalization, 9:630a-b
palatalization, 9:630b
Picardisms, in literature, 9:630a
tonic stress, on vowel system, 9:630b–631a
velarization, 9:631b
verb system, 9:632a
Picard literature, **9:632b–640a**
area of origin, 9:632b
cantefable, 9:635b
chronicles, 9:637b–638a
courtly lyric, 5:251b–252a
didactic, 9:638b–639a
dit, 9:639a
political, 9:639a
translations from Latin, 9:638b
in verse form, 9:639a
epics, 9:633b–634b
fabliaux, 9:635b–636a
courtly elements, 9:636a
hagiography, 9:633a-b, 633b
history, 9:637b–638a
lyric poetry, 9:636b–637a
Belle dame sans merci, 9:637a
Chapel vert association, 9:637a
for political purposes, 9:637a-b
romance, 5:255a-b, 9:634b–635b
adventure elements, 9:635a
Arthurian, 9:634a
folk themes, 9:635a
historico-biographical, 9:635a-b
parodies of, 9:635b
use of fantasy and magic, 9:634b
see also Amadas et Ydoine; Bodel, Jean
Picard nation, student. *See* Universities
Picardy
boundaries, 9:632b
political history, 15th century, 9:630a
Picardy Sweat. *See* Respiratory diseases, influenza
Picatrix
definition of magic in, 8:37b
Ikhwān al-Ṣafāᵓ and, 9:4b
influence of, 8:38a, 39a
Picaud, Aymeri. *See Pilgrim's Guide*
Piccinino armor workshop, 1:529b
Piccolomini, Aeneas Silvius. *See* Pius II, pope
Piccolomini family, 11:279b
Pickage (market tax), 8:146b
Pico della Mirandola, Giovanni, 9:700a-b, 703a
Disputationes adversus astrologos, 1:609a
Hebrew language study by, 3:313a
Neoplatonism and, 9:95a, 101a
Pictish art
animal figures, 9:640a-b
Ardross wolf, 9:640b (*illus.*), 640b
Hiberno-Saxon associations, 9:640a-b, 641a
influence of on Celtic art, 3:223a
silverwork, St. Ninian's Isle treasure, 9:641b (*illus.*), 641a
symbol stones
Class I, II, 9:640a–641a
distribution of Pictish place-names and, 9:642b
relief carving, 9:640b

Pictish art (*cont.*)
symbol stones (*cont.*)
symbols employed, 9:640a
Pictish language, 6:434a
Celtic and non-Celtic Pictish, 9:641b
personal names, 9:642a
Pictish-Gaelic hybrids, 9:641b–642a
in place names, 9:641b–642a
Picts, **9:641a–643a**, 11:113a
acceptance of Christianity, 9:642b
archaeological evidence, 9:642a-b
art, **9:640a–641a**
Christianization of, 1:288b
Dál Riata and, 4:78a-b
defeat of Northumbria, 4:454b
Dicalydones and Verturiones, 9:642a
etymology of "Pict," 9:642a
historical, 9:642b
military campaigns, Scots and Northumbrians, 9:642b–643a
Ninian and, 9:139a, 139b
union with Scots, 9:643a
see also Nechtan; Strathclyde, kingdom of
"Picture poems." *See* Acrostics—wordplay
Pie Powder (Piedpoudre) courts (English merchant courts), 4:586b, 12:120b.
Pie quebrado, 11:459a
Pied Friars, 5:297b–298a
Piedi. *See* Ballata
Piedmont, Savoyan assemblies, 10:675a
Piedpoudre court. *See* Pie Powder (Piedpoudre) courts
Pieds-droits, 7:45b
Piemonte, irrigation of, 6:558b
Piepus, Lake, battle on (1242), 9:111a
Pier. *See* Trumeau
Pier Innocenzo da Faerno, 1:529b
Pierce the Ploughman's Crede, 8:319a, 332a
Pierleone, Peter. *See* Anacletus II, antipope
Pierleoni family, 10:525a
Piero della Vigna, 6:643a, **9:643a-b**, 11:258a-b
"Amando con fin core e con speranza," 11:258b
Constitutions of Melfi and, 8:268b
Frederick II and, 11:271a, 272a, 274a
vs. Iacopo da Lentini, 6:387b
Piero di Giovanni Tedesco, **9:643b–644a**
Florence cathedral sculptures, 9:643b (*illus.*)
Milan cathedral sculptures, 9:644b
Piero Igneo, 9:260a
Piero, Maestro, "Quando l'aria comenza," 8:632 (*illus.*)
Pierre. *See also* Peter; Petrus
Pierre II Legros, sculpture of Ecclesia and Synagoga, 4:371b
Pierre II of Poitiers, bishop
Fontevrault and, 12:686b
Robert d'Arbrissel and, 10:429b, 430a
Pierre d'Abernun. *See* Peter Peckham
Pierre d'Ailly. *See* Ailly, Pierre d'
Pierre de Beauvais
didactic works, 9:639a
Translation et les miracles de saint Jacques, 9:633b
Pierre de Belleperche, 10:62b
Pierre Bersuire, *Ovidius moralizatus,* 1:183b
Pierre de Bourbon, Rhétoriqueurs and, 10:364b
Pierre de la Broce, 3:242b
Pierre Cardinal. *See* Peire Cardenal
Pierre de Chalon, 2:179b
Pierre des Champs (Pierre Deschamps), **9:645a-b**
Pierre de Corbiac, *Tesaur,* 3:657a
Pierre de la Croix. *See* Petrus de Cruce
Pierre Dubois, **9:645b–647a**
De recuperatione Terre Sancte, 9:646a-b
influence on Philip IV, 9:647a
kingship theories of, 7:268a
legal services, 9:645b
political problems dealt with, 9:646b
primacy of French monarchy, 9:646b
rediscovery of works, 19th century, 9:646a
Summaria brevis, 9:645b, 646a-b
Pierre de Fenin, *Mémoires,* 9:638b
Pierre de Fontaines, **9:644a–645a**
Conseil à un ami, 9:644a-b
royal service, 9:644b
Pierre de Hauteville, *Confession et testament de l'amant tréspassé,* 9:637a
Pierre de Lusignan of Cyprus, king, Machaut and, 8:3a-b, 5a
Pierre de Montreuil, 7:52a, **9:645a**
Notre Dame de Paris and, 9:191a
Pierre Olivi. *See* Peter John Olivi
Pierre d'Orgement, 5:654a
Pierre Pelerin. *See* Peter Peregrinus of Maricourt
Pierre le Picard. *See* Pierre de Beauvais
Pierre de Remin, 2:144a
Pierre de St. Cloud
Renard story and, 2:141b
Roman de Renart, 10:312a–313b, 12:200a
see also Renard the Fox
Pierre de Saintes, *Viribus arte minis,* 7:365a
Pierre de Savoy, castle of St. Just, capture of, 7:699a
Piers Plowman. *See* Langland, William
Piers Venables of Derbyshire, Robin Hood and, 10:435a-b
Pieśń o zabiciu Andrzeja Tęczyńskiego, 11:345a
Pietà, **9:647a-b**
by Malouel, 5:606b (*illus.*)
extracted from the Passion cycle, 9:447a
Lamentation and, 9:647a
wood, 14th century, 5:0 (frontispiece)
Pieter van Aelst, *Acts of the Apostles* and, 11:596b
Pietism, Jewish, 7:168b–169b
see also Judah ben Samuel he-Hasid (the Pietist)
Pietro II Orseolo of Venice, doge, campaign against pirates, 12:386a-b
Pietro III Candiano of Venice, doge, campaign against pirates, 12:386a
Pietro d'Abano, 1:613a
on circumnavigation of Africa, 5:398a
Pietro da Barsegapè. *See* Pietro da Bescapè
Pietro da Bescapè, *Sermone,* 6:631a
Pietro dei Cerroni. *See* Cavallini, Pietro
Pietro dei Faitinelli, 6:650a
Pietro Oderisi. *See* Oderisi, Pietro
Pietro di Pavia, cardinal, Renard the Fox allusions to, 10:313b
Pietro Piccolo de Monteforte (jurist), 2:278a
Pietro da Rimini, **9:647b**
statue of St. Francis, 9:648a (*illus.*)
Pietro Spagnuolo. *See* Berruguete, Pedro
Pig, importance of in Celtic mythology, 9:47a
"Pig-faced visor." *See* Helmet visor
Pigeon, 5:150b
Pigs
as food animal, 1:95a-b, 299a-b, 302a
prohibition against, 1:300b
Pikarts, 6:375a-b
Pike. *See* Arms and armor; Lance
Pᶜilartos Varažnuni, duke of Antioch, **9:647b–649a**
Anatolian principality, 9:648a-b
imperial negotiations, 9:648b
military campaigns, 9:648b
principality in Taurus region, 11:156b
Seljuks and, 1:484b
Pilaster, **9:649a**
bay division and, 10:475b
Troia Cathedral, 9:649b (*illus.*)
Pilaster strip, **9:649a**
Pilchard (*Sardinia pilchardus*), fishing of, 5:70b
Pilēnai castle, mass suicide of Lithuanians at, 7:609a-b
Pilentum (luxury vehicle), 12:369b
Pilgerfahrt des träumenden Mönchs, Die, 5:430b
Pilgram, Anton, **9:649b**, 9:650a (*illus.*)
Pilgrimage
1054-1305, 3:60a, 356a
criticism of
Russian clerical, 9:653a–654a
Western European, 9:659b–660b
guidebooks for, 9:652a, 657b (*illus.*), **9:661b–662a**, 9:661b–662a (*illus.*)
Islamic, 6:582a-b, **9:650a–652a**
art and, 6:592b
economic effects of, 9:651a
founded by Muḥammad, 6:577a
imāmzāda and, 6:426a
Indian Ocean travel, 11:249a
navigation in the Red Sea and, 9:85b
to Shīrāz, 11:252b
see also Fasting, Islamic; *Iḥrām*
Jewish, **9:652a–653a**
to Jerusalem, 7:104a
see also Palestine
Russian, **9:653a–654b**
Western European, **9:654b–661b**, 9:676a
barefoot, 12:156a-b

biblical associations and, 2:216a
by the insane, 6:490b, 492a
in Celtic church, 3:231b, 6:515b–516a
Chaucer on, 3:290b–296a
church architecture and, 9:422b, 10:482b–483a
class structure and, 12:155b, 156b
criticism of, 12:152a, 157a
crusades and, 4:16a
development of new routes, 10:412a
economic effects of, 9:659a-b
Fachschrifttum and, 4:579a
fairs and, 4:588b, 589a-b
great galleys and, 11:235b
Imitatio Christi and, 9:654b, 658a, 659b–660a
indulgences and, 6:447a
knights as pilgrims, 9:656a-b
in literature, 7:19a-b
Lollard attitude to, 7:648
Muireadhach Albanach and, 9:205a
origins and appeal of, 9:654b–655b
proxy, 12:155b
as punishment, 6:485b, 9:655a-b, 658b, 660a-b, 12:155b–156a, 155a–156b, 157a
in "Responder voi' a dona Frixa," 6:657a
satire of, in Erasmus' *Colloquies,* 10:299a
as symbolic journey to heaven, 9:396b
to Canterbury, 3:83a, 84a, 4:538a
to Holy Land, 4:27b, 336b, 553a-b, 576b, 7:59b, 61a, 9:656a–658a, 11:479b
to Marian shrines, 12:461a
to Najrān, 9:55a
to Near East, 1:332a-b
Romanesque art and architecture and, 10:482b–483a, 492b–495a
to Rome, 1:333a, 9:237a, 658a–659a, 12:151a, 154b–155a, 156a
to Rome, economic aspects, 10:526b
to Rome, St. Peter's and, 10:519a
to Santiago de Compostela, 1:629b, 3:131b–132a, 9:69a, 659a-b, 10:280a, 480b, 650b, 12:155b
to Vézelay, 10:496a
tourism and, 9:660b–661a
traditional development of, 9:655b–656b
Treaty of Athis stipulation, 12:156a
voluntary, 9:659b–660a
see also Ampulla; Crusades; Taverns; Travel and transport; Vernicle
Pilgrimage church. *See* Church architecture
Pilgrimage, Islamic
Muḥammad's Farewell Pilgrimage, 8:525b
music and, 8:560a, 560b
to Mecca, 8:240a, 240b–241a, 522a
to Medina, 8:262a
see also Hegira
Pilgrimage of the Life of Man. See Deguileville, Guillaume de; Lydgate, John
Pilgrimage songs, German, 12:541a
Pilgrims, guidebooks for, 12:151a, 156a-b
Pilgrim's Castle, 4:24b
Pilgrim's Guide, 9:661b–662a (*illus.*), 10:494a
Pilgrim's Progress. See Bunyan, John
Piling (unit of measure), 12:593a
P^c^ilippos, *kat^c^ołikos* of All Armenians, 1:502a
Pillius de Medicina, 5:567b
Pilltown, Battle of (1462), 6:524b
P^c^ilon Tirakac^c^i, 1:506a
Piloti, Emmanuel, 11:339a-b
Pinar, Florencia, poetry of, 11:424b
Pincée (unit of measure), variations in, 12:590a
Pindarus, *Ilias latina,* 7:360b
Pinot noir, 12:654a
Pint (unit of measure)
English, 12:585a
Scots, 12:585a, 589a
Pintoin, Michel, 5:654a
Pinzón, Martin Alonso, 4:560b
Piotrków, Diet of (1496), 9:728b
Pipa, 8:610b
Pipe (musical instrument), 8:602 (*illus.*), 604b, 607a (*illus.*)
in dance music, 8:595b
Middle Eastern, 8:612a, 612b
Pipe organ. *See* Organ
Pipe rolls, 1:37b–38a, 446a, **9:662a–663b**
English Exchequer and, 4:530b, 531b, 532a, 533a, 534a, 9:662a–663b
French, 1:38b–39a
manorial, 1:39b
military expenditures, 12:555a
see also Accounting
Pipino, on Hugh of Orléans, 6:319b
Pippin. *See* Pepin
"Pir meu cori allegrari." *See* Stefano Protonotaro da Messina
Pīr Muḥammad (grandson of Tamerlane), 12:56b
Piracy
in the 12th and 13th centuries, 9:80b
in Adriatic, Venice and, 12:386a-b
in the Baltic, 9:82b–83a
from Crete, 3:678b
from Malta, 8:67b
Indian Ocean, 11:247b, 249b
Mediterranean, 9:80a, 11:230b
settlement of claims, 1:56b
tithes from the spoils, 12:64b
Viking, 9:79a-b
Piramus, Denis. *See Vie St. Edmund le rei, La*
Pirckheimer, Johann, 9:202b
Pirckheimer, Willibald, 9:202b
Pirenean rite. *See* Narbonne rite
Pirindj būrū, 8:612b
Pirmin, St., **9:663b**
Dicta Pirminii (Scarapsus), 9:663b
Pirotechnia. See Biringuccio, Vannoccio
Pisa, **9:663b–665b**
Campo Santo, frescoes, 5:294b
commune of, 3:500a
defeated by Florence (1406), 12:112a
economic rise of, 12:111a–112a
expansion, 11th through 13th centuries, 7:14b
factional violence in, 9:664a-b
first seals of, 11:126a
food trade, 11:275b
Frederick II and, 11:269b, 270a
Genoa and, 5:385a
law codes of, 7:428b
Mediterranean dominance, 9:664a-b
merchant colonies in Lebanon, 7:533a
navy of, 9:80a
prohibition of imports of woolens, 12:118a
rival cities and, 9:664b–665a
Rome and, 10:523a, 525b
trade with Byzantine Empire, 12:103a-b
trade and commerce of, 4:557b, 9:663b–664b
trecento sculptors, 12:170b–171b (*illus.*)
vs. Islamic Sicily, 11:263a
wool industry, 9:664a
see also Tuscany
Pisa Cathedral, **9:665b–666b**, 9:665 (*illus.*), 10:485b–486a, 486b, 502b
baptistery, 2:87b (*illus.*)
Campanile, 3:60b (*illus.*)
Porta de S. Ranieri, 10:503a
pulpit sculpture, 4:498 (*illus.*), 9:668a–669a (*illus.*)
Rainaldus and, 10:252b–253a
sculpture for, 12:170b–171a
see also Tino di Camaino
Pisa, Council of (1135), 3:637a
Pisa, Council of (1409), 3:645b–647a, 11:41b–42a
calling of, 10:23b
conciliar theory and, 3:514b
deposition of rival popes, 1:108b, 147b, 3:647a
election of Alexander V and, 1:147b, 10:23b
Gerson on, 5:512b
Great Schism and, 11:41b–42a
procedures of, 3:646b
wide support for, 3:646b
Pisa, University of, 12:286a
Pisan School, panel painting in, 5:605b
Pisançon. *See* Alberich von Bisinzo
Pisanello, Antonio, **9:666b**
portrait of Oswald von Wolkenstein, 9:295b (*illus.*)
study of a horse, 9:666a (*illus.*)
Vision of St. Eustace, 11:255b
works in International Style, 5:628a
Pisani, Vettore, war of Venice with Genoa and, 12:392b–393a
Pisano, Andrea, 5:524b, **9:666b–668b**
door panel, 9:667 (*illus.*)
sculpture by, on Florence Baptistery doors, 12:171b
Pisano, Antonio. *See* Pisanello, Antonio
Pisano, Giovanni, **9:668b–669a**, 9:669b
on artists' status, 1:579b
figures of, 5:624b
French influences on, 9:668b
ivories by, 7:24a
Virgin and Child, 7:24a
marble pulpits of, 5:624b

Pisano, Giovanni (*cont.*)
Pisa Cathedral, 4:498 (*illus.*)
pulpit sculptures, 9:668a (*illus.*)
sculpture by
Margaret of Luxembourg tomb, 12:170b–171b (*illus.*)
Pisa pulpit, 12:170a
see also Tino di Camaino
Pisano, Nicola, **9:669a–670b**
Arnolfo di Cambio and, 1:541a
Benedetto Antelami and, 2:167a
figures of, 5:624b
Hercules, 5:624a
Perugia, Fontana Maggiore, 9:669b–670a
Pisa Baptistery pulpit, 5:624a
classical inspiration of, 10:310b
Siena pulpit, 5:624a, 9:670 (*illus.*)
Pisano, Nino, 9:666b, 668a, 12:176a
Piscatura. See Fisheries, marine
Pisciculture. *See* Fishponds
Piscinae. See Fishponds
Písek, Taborites and, 6:373a
Pīsha, 8:612b
Pishdadians (mythical dynasty), 11:221b
Pishtaq, **9:670b–671a,** 9:671b (*illus.*)
Pistill of Susan, The, 8:332a
Pistoia
inns in, 6:474b
waterways, 12:577a
Pistoia, Cino da. *See* Cino da Pistoia
Pit saws, 3:145b
Pitch
notation of, 8:593a, 623b–627a
solmization and, 11:362b–366a
Pitchforks, as agricultural tools, 12:80b
Pithou, Pierre, 3:476b–477a
Pîtres, construction of a bridge at, 12:431a
Pîtres, Edict of (864), 4:512a
Pitsunda. *See* Bitshvinta
Pius I, pope, in the *Annunciation* panel by Pedro de Córdoba, 9:484 (*illus.*)
Pius II, pope
Commentaries, 11:280b
communion under both kinds and, 3:505b
crusade preaching of, 4:21a, 56b
De ortu et auctoritate imperii Romani, 10:24b
Euryalus, 8:361a
Execrabilis, 3:366b–367a, 518b–519a, 654b
on inns, 6:473a
Latin works of, 7:369b
Matthias and, 6:348a
reign of, 3:367b
Pius V, pope
breviary of, 2:373a
Gregorian chant and, 5:664a
Quo primum tempore, 10:79a
reforms of, 3:67b
Jews and, 7:109a
Piyyutim, 7:160a
in Jewish literature, 7:621a–623a
major schools of, 7:621a
origins of, 7:621a
spread of, 7:622a-b
structure of, 7:621a-b
see also Hebrew literature, poetry; Hymns, Hebrew
Place-names, land reclamation and, 10:273b
Placentinus, **9:671a–672b**
Bolognese School and, 5:567b
completion of *Summa codicis* of Rogerius, 9:671b
Cum multae essent partes iuris and, 10:444b
legal maxims and, 8:232a
Questiones de iuris subtilitatibus, 9:672a
Rogerius and, 10:444a
Sermo de legibus, 9:672a
Summa cum essem Mantuae, 9:671b
Summa trium librorum, 9:671b
Placiti cassinesi, 6:621a, 622b, 623b
Placitum, in Venice, 3:499b
Plagiarism, in Arabic poetry, 1:403a
Plagues
in Anatolia, 1:240a, 241a
in art, 2:266b
bubonic, 2:257b, 258a, 9:728a
enteric, 2:257b, 258a, 9:673a, 681b
European, **9:672b–683b**
of 1361, 1374, 5:178a
Antonine Plague, 9:674a
in art, 9:677b, 679b
bubonic, 9:664b, 674b–676b, 678a, 680a-b, 684b–685a
cycles of, 9:676a
ergotism, 9:676b
Justinian's Plague, 9:675a-b, 684a
late medieval, 9:681a–683b
in literature, 9:677b, 679b
malaria, 9:672b–674a, 681b
measles, 9:673a, 674b, 676b, 678a
pneumonic, 9:672a, 673a, 674b–675a, 680a
psychological effects of, 9:679b
St. Anthony's disease, 9:676b
smallpox, 9:674a–675b, 676a-b, 678a, 681a-b
tuberculosis and, 9:677b
typhus, 9:673a, 681b
see also Flagellants
famine in Western Europe and, 5:7a, 9a
Iraq, 6:511b
Islamic world, **9:684a–686b**
cycles of, 9:684a–685a
historical impact of, 9:686a
Justinian's Plague, 9:684a
leprosy, 9:684a
measles, 9:684a
pneumonic, 9:685a-b
smallpox, 9:684a, 686a
in literature, 2:266b–267a
pandemic
first, 9:675a–677b, 684a, 685a-b
second, 9:677b–681a, 684b–685a
pneumonic, 2:257b, 258a
septicemic, 2:257b, 258a
treatment of, 2:264b
venereal diseases, 9:673a, 682a–683b
see also Black Death; Demography; Famine; Leprosy
Plaice (*Pleuronectes platessa*), fishing of, 5:70a
Plainchant. *See* Gregorian Chant; Plainsong
Plaine and Easie Introduction to Practicall Musicke. See Morley, Thomas
Plainsong
in *De plana musica,* 7:134b
Johannes de Grocheo on, 7:119b
melisma, 9:689b, 692a-b
as *musica plana,* 10:378b–380b
notation, plica, 9:710b–711a
sources for, 10:651a
versus ad repetendum, 9:689a, 690a-b
see also Gregorian Chant; Mass cycles; Psalm
Plainte du désiré. See Jean Lemaire de Belges
Planctu Naturae, De. See Alan of Lille
Planctus, **9:693a-b**
by Bertran de Born, 2:201b–202a
in Carolingian Latin poetry, 3:100b
Marian, 6:382a, 9:639a
"Planctus ante nescia," 6:382a
Planctus cygni, 12:211a
Plantus de obitu Karoli, compared with *¡Ay, Iherusalem!,* 2:18b
Planys del cavaller Mataró, 3:173b
see also Abelard, Peter; Complainte; Jean Lemaire de Belges; Lai, Lay; Passion Plays; Sequence; *¡Ay, Iherusalem!*
Planetary clocks, 3:464b–465a
Planetary machines, 3:461a–462a
see also Dondi, Giovanni de'
Planh. See Sirventes
Plank roads, in Germany, 10:413a
Plano Carpini, John of. *See* John of Plano Carpini
Plantagenet, Geoffrey. *See* Geoffrey V Plantagenet, count of Anjou
Plantagenets, **9:693b**
Aquitaine and, 1:368a, 5:185b
claim to French throne, 5:184a
origins of, 1:253a
Planto, in Galician-Portuguese lyrics, 11:450b
Plants
classified by Albertus Magnus, 2:246a
illustrations of in herbals, 2:245b
medieval study of, 2:240b–241a, 244b–246a
low status of, 2:242a
Planudes, Maximos, translations by, 12:127a
Planudes, Maximos. *See* Maximos Planudes
Planus cadence. *See* Cadence (language)
Plashchanitsa, **9:693b–694a,** 9:693b–694b (*illus.*)
see also Blachernitissa
Plat pays assemblies. *See* Lyonnais, seneschalsy of
Plate armor. *See* Arms and armor
Platearius, Johannes(?), *Circa instans,* 8:250a
Platearius, Matthaeus, *Circa instans,* 6:181b
Plateresque style, **9:694a-b,** 11:380a
see also Guas, Juan and Pedro; Hispano-Mauresque art

Plato
  Laws 9:699a-b, 703a
  Meno, translations of, 11:274a, 12:139b–140a
  on music, 8:580a, 580b
  Republic, 9:699b–700b, 702b
    Virtues and, 12:462a
  Timaeus, 9:698a-b, 699a, 700b, 10:462b
    cosmogony, 6:99b–100a
    glosses and glossators, 9:700b, 701b–702a, 10:270a-b
    importance of, 9:701a–702b
    influence on physics, 9:622b
    light and vision theory, 9:247a
    Marsilio Ficino's *Compendium in Timaeum,* 9:703b
    al-Rāzī's cosmogony and, 10:267b–268a
    studies of, 9:698a-b, 699a, 700b–702b, 703b
    Thierry of Chartres's *Tractatus de sex dierum operibus* and, 12:27b
    translators of, 12:139b
  translations of
    Arabic, 11:83a
    Armenian, 1:505b
    Latin, 1:460b
    Spanish, 11:457a
Plato and Platonism, **9:694b–704b**
  Abelard and, 9:155b
  Albertus Magnus and, 1:462b
  apologetical polemics and, 9:701b–702a
  in the Arab world, 9:696a–699a, 699a–700b
  Aristotle and, 1:456a, 457a, 9:697a–700a, 701a, 702a-b, 703b
    comparatio, 9:701a
  at the school of Chartres, 9:588a-b
  Basil the Great and, 2:120a
  Boethius and, 8:637a
  in the Byzantine world, 9:694b–699a
  commentaries by Proclus, 9:98a
  creation theory, 9:701b–702a
  definition of theology, 9:582b
  on dialectic, 4:168a
  dualism and, 4:298a
  of Gemisthos Plethon, 5:375a
  Glossae super Platoneum, 10:270b
  great chain of being, 9:278a
  Grigor Magistros and, 1:511a
  in hymns, 6:383b
  Iamblichus' curriculum of his works, 9:97b
  influence on Aquinas, 1:357b–358b
  Italian study of, 7:1a
  in the Jewish world under Islam, 9:700a-b
  John Italos and, 7:131b
  in the Latin West, 9:694a–696a, 700b–703b, 702a
  Myth of Er, development of allegory and, 1:180b–181a, 185b
  Neoplatonism and, 10:270b
  nominalism and, 9:155a
  Patriarch Cyril of Alexandria and, 9:105b
  universals, 1:54a, 10:269a-b
  Xusrō I and, 12:714a
  see also Bernard of Chartres; Bernard Silvester; Fārābī, al-; Glossator; Levi ben Gershom; Neoplatonism; Translation and translators; Universals
Plato of Tivoli, **9:704b–705a**
  De scientia stellarum, 1:611b
  Liber embadorum, 12:135a
  Liber embadorum and, 10:472a
  Liber Ersemidis in quadratum circuli and, 1:435a
  translations by, 12:135a
Platonic Academy (Florence), 5:375a
  influence of Argyropoulos on, 7:1a-b
Platytera, 2:257a (*illus.*), **9:705a-b**
Plautus, 4:277b
  Amphitruo, 4:283a
    Geta and, 7:367a
  Aulularia, 4:283a, 10:239b–240a
  Nicholas of Cusa and, 9:123a
  Vital of Blois and, 12:479a, 479b
Play of Daniel, **9:705b–706a**
  polyphonic conductus in, 3:532a
  vernacular refrains in Latin text, 4:263b–264a
Play of Herod, **9:706a-b**
Plays. *See* Drama, liturgical; Morality plays; Mystery plays; Passion plays
Pleas of the crown (England), sheriff and, 11:225b, 226a
Plectrude (wife of Pepin II of Herstal), 9:500a
Pleier, Der, **9:707a–708b**
  Garel von dem blühenden Tal, 5:455a, 9:707a-b, 708b
  Meleranz, 9:707a, 708a
  Tandareis und Flordibel, 9:707a–708a
Plena potestas
  in diplomacy, 4:203b–205a
  Irish parliament and, 9:435b
Plenary indulgence. *See* Indulgence
Plenipotentiaries, ratification of treaties and, 4:213b–214a
Plenitudo potestatis, **9:708b–710a**
  arguments against, *Defensor pacis,* 8:154b, 155a
  Innocent III and, 6:464a, 464b
  Matthew of Aquasparta's support of Boniface VIII and, 8:227b
  in political theory, 10:20a-b, 21b–23b
  power of pope and, 10:32a
Plerophoriai. See John of Maiuma, bishop
Plethon. *See* Gemistos Plethon, Georgios
Pleurant, 9:709 (*illus.*), **9:710a-b**
  on tomb of Philip the Bold, 9:710b, 11:349b, 12:620 (*illus.*)
Pleydenwurff, Hans, **9:710b**
  Descent from the Cross, 9:710 (*illus.*)
  Wolgemut and, 12:681b
  see also Master of the Life of Mary
Plica, **9:710b–711a**
Plictho. See Rosetti, Gioanventura
Pliegos sueltos, Spanish ballads and, 11:429a-b
Pliny the Elder
  on cosmetics, 2:147a
  Natural History, 1:610b, 2:345a, 4:447b
  on early Scandinavia, 10:686b–687a
  on the Sahara, 2:186a
  Sidonius and, 11:277a
Pliska
  as capital of Bulgaria, 2:399b
  Great Basilica of, 2:329a
  palace at, 2:414b
  rebuilding of, 2:401b–402a
  sacked (811), 2:401a, 7:303b
Plotinus, 1:457b, 458a, 462a
  attack against the Gnostics, 9:98b
  Basil the Great and, 2:120a
  disciples of, 9:96b–97a
  Enneads, 9:95b–96b, 97a
    edition by Porphyry of Tyre, 9:96b
    Theologia Aristotelis and, 9:100a
  Neoplatonism of, 9:95a–96b, 703b
  translation by Ficino, 9:703b
  Vita Plotini by Porphyry of Tyre, 9:96b
Plow
  in 11th and 12th centuries, 12:76a-b
  ard, 1:77a
    crook, 1:80a
    deep-share, 1:80a
  asymmetrical design of, 12:73b, 74 (*illus.*)
  forked, Slavic world, 1:97b
  from 13th century on, 12:76b
  heavy
    advantages of, 1:90b–91a, 98a
    carruca, 1:90b
    in England, 1:90b
    in Germany, 1:90b
    human labor required, 1:91a-b
    increases in food production with, 1:97b, 5:116a
    Slavic world, 1:90a-b, 97b, 100b
    terminology for, 1:90a-b
  hook, Slavic world, 1:96b
  Islamic, 12:83b–84a
    contruction of, 12:83b–84a
    in late medieval miniature, 12:84a (*illus.*)
  light
    Balkans, 1:98b–99a
    Slavic world, 1:97b–98a, 99b, 100b
  manufacture of, 12:81b
  medieval types of, 12:74 (*illus.*)
  modifications of in late Middle Ages, 12:77b–77a
  moldboard, depicted in Luttrell Psalter, 12:76 (*illus.*)
  origins of, 12:73a-b, 75a-b
  ristle, 12:74b–75a
  scratch
    Northern Europe, 1:89b–90a
    Slavic world, 1:97b
  spread of
    in early medieval period, 12:75b
    scarcity of iron and, 12:81b
  wheeled
    depicted in a 1372 manuscript, 12:78 (*illus.*)
    in literature, 1:90a
    Northern Europe, 1:90a-b
Plow tax. *See* Carucage
Plowing, 12:445a, 445b
  see also Agriculture; Reclamation of land; Technology

Plowman from Bohemia. See Ackermann aus Böhmen, Der
Plowmen. *See* Peasants
Plucked zither. *See* Psaltery
Plum, growth of, 5:306a
Plumpton Correspondence, 8:323a
Plundered art. *See* Spolia
Pluralism, 2:179b
  Gregory X's curtailment of, 3:641b
Plutarch, 9:98a, 699a
  Crassus' invasion of Parthia, 9:443b
  "Institutio Trajani" and, 8:434b
  "Life of Lucullus," 2:140a
  Placita philosophorum, in Byzantine education, 9:565b
Plzeň, Taborites and, 6:375a
Pneumatica. See Hero of Alexandria; Philo of Byzantium
Pneumatomachianism, 2:121a, 121b
Pneumonic plague. *See* Plagues
Po, Fernão do, 4:561b
Po Valley
  canal network in, 12:114a-b, 115a
  Lombards' invasion of, 8:376b–377a
  Ostrogoths' invasion of, 8:376b
Poaching, in Manosque, 6:357b
Poblet (Cistercian monastery), Peter IV (the Ceremonious) and, 9:510b
Pochen, 5:352b
Pocketbooks, **9:711a**
  troper, 12:208a-b
Pocquet, Antoine, writings of, 3:215a
Pocutia, Polish-Moldavian contention, 12:501b–502a, 504a
Podatus. See Pes
Podesta, 3:502b, **9:711a–712a**
  election of, 7:349a
  in Genoa, 5:385b
  in Pera-Galata, 9:503a-b
  see also Jacobus (de Porta Ravennate)
Poel, William, modern performance of *Everyman,* 4:526b–527a
Poem of Joseph. See Poema de Yúçuf
Poema de Almería, 11:409b, 437b
Poema coniugis ad uxorem. See Prosper of Aquitaine
Poema de Fernán González. See Fernán González, Poema de
Poema de mío Cid. See Cantar de mío Cid
Poema morale, 8:315b
  ballad meter used in, 8:345a-b
Poema de Yúçuf, 1:176a, 8:281b–282a
Poet-seer, in Celtic mythology, 9:47a-b
Poeta Saxo, **9:712a-b**
  Annales de gestis Caroli Magni, 4:496a, 9:712a-b
  De vita et obitu eiusdem, 9:712a-b
  see also Agius of Corvey
Poetic Edda
  derivation of name, 4:385a-b
  organization of, 4:385a–387a
  Sigurd and, 11:289a
  see also Eddic poetry
Poetic guild. *See Confrérie; Puy*
Poetics. See Aristotle
Poetria nova. See Geoffrey of Vinsauf
Poetry
  Islamic attitudes toward, 8:559b
  music and, 8:583a-b
Poetry, liturgical. *See* Liturgical poetry
Poets
  social status
    fealty to patrons, 12:539b
    Ireland, 6:531b–532b
    noble attributions, 12:539b–540a
    Norway and Iceland, 11:316a-b, 320a–321a
    Wales, 12:605a
Poets of Princes. *See Gogynfeirdd*
Pogesania, 2:63 (map), 66a, 66b
Poggio Bracciolini, Gian Francesco, 3:654b
  discovery of MS of Vitruvius, 5:588b
  discovery of Quintilian's *Institutio oratoria* (1416), 10:356b, 363b
  influence of on *Cent nouvelles nouvelles,* 3:235a
  Liber facetiarum, 3:235a
  Zabarella and, 12:735a
Pogh, 8:418b
Pogost, **9:715a-b**
Pöhlder Annals, *Rhitmus ad Henricum* and, 12:656a
Poignée (unit of measure), 12:590a
Poillevillain, Nicholas. *See* Nicholas of Clamanges
Poimanenon, Battle of (1224), 9:117a
Point (armor), 1:525b
Pointed arch. *See* Arch
"Poitevin Collections," 7:411a
Poitevin expedition (1242), 11:297a
Poitiers, counts of, 2:126b
Poitiers, Battle of (732), 3:345b, **9:715b–716a,** 12:557a
  Frankish *vs.* Spanish Muslims, 9:715b
Poitiers, Battle of (1356), 3:205b, 6:331b, 9:715b–716a
  Jacquerie and, 9:478a, 478b
  victory of Edward the Black Prince, 4:399a
Poitiers, Council of (*ca.* 1011-1014), Peace of God movement and, 9:473b
Poitiers, University of, 12:285b
Poitou, relations with Normandy, 9:168a
Poker, 5:352b
Pʿokʿr Copʿkʿ. *See* Sophenē
Pʿokʿr Mher, 4:112b, 113a
Pokrov, **9:716a**
Pola casket, 12:492b
Poland, **9:716a–731b**
  Armenians in, 1:486a
  art and architecture, 9:723b, 725a, 730a-b
  Bohemia-Moravia and, 9:717a–718b, 720a, 728a
  Bohemian Brethren in, 2:305b
  celebration of St. Stanislaus' office, 10:371a
  Christian church of
    influence on monarchy, 9:727a
    papacy and, 9:718a-b, 720a
    power of, 9:722a, 727b
    reorganizations and reforms, 9:719a, 721a
    resurrection of, 9:720a
  Christianization and pagan reversions, 9:717b–718a, 720a
  culture
    early medieval, 9:722b–723b
    late medieval, 9:729a–730b
    proto-Polish tribes, 9:716b–717b
  duchies, factional strife, 9:720b–721a
  education in, 9:729a-b
  historiography of, 9:723a-b, 729b–730a
  history
    formation of the state (to 1025), 9:717b–719b
    14th to 16th centuries, 7:40b–41a
    territorial disintegration (1138-*ca.* 1300), 9:720b–721b
    see also Jagiełło dynasty; Piast dynasty
  Hungarian alliance, 9:629a
  immigration in, 9:722a-b
    German, 9:721a-b
    Jewish, 9:729a
  Jewish self-government in, 7:71b
  Lithuania and, 9:721b, 725a, 726a–727b
  Louis I of Hungary and, 6:356a
  Luxembourg family and, 9:724a–725a
  Moldavian alliance, 12:501b, 502a
  Moldavian invasions, 12:504a
  monarchy
    papal authorization, 9:720a
    vs. nobility, 9:719b–720b, 722a, 725b–726a, 727a–728, 729a
  monarchy. *See* Jagiełło dynasty; Piast dynasty
  naming of, 9:717a
  New March, 9:721a-b
  nobles of Little Poland, 7:40a
  Otto III of Germany and, 9:302a-b
  partition of, 9:720a–721b
  peasantry of, 9:720a, 722a-b, 725b
  plagues in, 9:677b, 728a
  regnum Poloniae, 9:628b
  relations with, Romanian principalities, 10:514a, 514b, 515a
  Ruthenia and, 9:725a, 727a, 728a
  Silesia and, 9:717a, 718b, 720a–721a, 722b–723a, 725a
  society and economy
    early medieval, 9:721b–722b
    late Middle Ages, 9:728a–729a
  towns in
    development of, 9:721b, 725a
    ethnic tensions in, 9:728b–729a
    town hall architecture, 9:730a-b
  universities, 12:289b
  see also Lithuania
Polanie tribe, 9:717a
  see also Poland
Polar sighting tube, 11:99b–100b
Pole arms, 7:323b
Pole (British linear measure), 9:504a
Pole, John de la, earl of Lincoln, Battle of Stoke, 12:572a
Pole, Michael de la, earl of Suffolk
  impeachment of, 9:428b–429a
  rise of, 3:426b
Poleax, 7:324 (*illus.*), 325a
Polemics
  Christian-Jewish, 7:93a-b, **10:1a–7a**
    arguments of, 10:1a-b
    Bible and, 10:1b–2a
    characterization of, 10:1a

disputations at Paris and Barcelona, 10:4b–5a
early medieval, 10:2a–3a
effects of, 10:7a
11th to 13th centuries, 10:3a–4b
14th to 15th centuries, 10:5a–7a
Franco-German treatises on, 10:4a-b
literary and artistic genres of, 10:2a
Moses Naḥmanides and, 9:53b
in Muslim Spain, 7:95b
in Russia, 7:100a-b
Trinitarianism in, 10:3b
disputationes, 10:238b, 241a
Islamic-Jewish, 7:101b–102a, **10:7a–9a**
against Jews, 10:7b
Islamic empire and, 10:7b
Karaites and, 7:108a
Muḥammad and, 10:7a-b
see also People of the book
Platonism and apologetical, 9:701b–702a
rhetoric and, 10:357a-b
see also Philosophy and theology; Rhetoric
Polemius Silvius, **10:9a-b**
Laterculus, 10:9a
Polestar, polar sighting tube and, 11:99b–100b
Poleyn. *See* Kneecop
Policraticus. See John of Salisbury
Polish church. *See* Poland
Polish language, 6:438a
Czech and, 6:444a
Polish law, 9:725b
Polish literature, 11:344b–345a
Sodalitas Litteraria Vistulana, 9:730a
see also Historiography, Polish
Polistorie, **10:9b**
Politianos, patriarch of Alexandria, 8:246b
Political authority. *See* Power, political
Political crusades. *See* Crusades
Political theory, citizenship, in Bartolo da Sassoferrato's doctrine, 2:116a
Political theory, Byzantine, 1:483a-b, **10:9b–12a**
ancestral traditions and, 10:10a-b
basis of, 10:12a
Christianity and, 10:9b–10a, 12a
emperor's role in, 10:10a-b
foreign policy and, 10:11a-b
founding of Constantinople and, 10:9b
Hellenistic political thought and, 10:11a
imperial imagery, 10:11a
relations between emperor and patriarch, 10:11b–12a
Roman empire and, 10:9b–10a
Political theory, Islamic, **10:12a–14a**
mirrors of princes and, 10:13a-b
philosophy and, 10:13b–14a
Quraysh tribe and, 10:242a
al-Rāzī and, 10:267b
relation between religion and politics, 10:12a-b
on succession controversy, 10:13a
traditional, 10:12b–13a
Political theory, Western European
development (to 1100), treason and, 12:165a-b
development (after 1100), treason and, 12:165b–168b
Aristotle's works and, 10:19a–20a
assemblies and citizen representation, 10:328b, 329b
Bible and, 2:216a-b, 10:14a-b
citizen suffrage and, 10:328b
custom and law, 9:221b
development (to 1100), **10:14a–18b**
development (after 1100), **10:18b–26a**
papal vs. secular jurisdiction, 8:155a
Disputatio inter clericum et militem, 4:218a-b
dispute of Boniface VIII and Philip IV (the Fair), 10:21a–22b
divide and rule, 10:334a
dominatus in, 10:14b
empire in, 10:17b
equality in, 10:14b
estatist principle of organization, 10:317a–320a, 332a–334a
hierocratic theory in, 10:20a–21a
imperial authority, 9:221b
mirrors of princes and, 8:434a–436a, 10:15a–16a
Norwegian, 9:183b
papacy in, 7:688b, 10:17b–18b
Plato's *Republic* and, 9:699b–700b, 702b
prince's role, 10:123b–124a
private property in, 10:14b–15a
resistance to royal authority, 10:17a-b
Roman law and, 10:19a-b
in *Somnium Viridarii,* 11:371b
taxation without representation, 10:318a
temporal jurisdiction, 7:46a
translatio imperii (translation of empire), 7:688a, 12:143a-b
12th-century discoveries in, 10:19a–20a
tyranny in, 10:15a-b
see also Conciliar movement; Investiture conflict; Kingship, theories of; Ptolemy of Lucca; Suffrage; Taxation
Politics. See Aristotle
Polity. *See* Class structure; Representative assemblies
Poljica Statute
land ownership, 11:670b
patrilineal households, 11:670b
Poll tax
English, **10:26a–27b,** 11:616a
Peasants' Revolt (1381) and, 10:26b
population counts and, 10:26b
French, 11:619b
graduated rates, 11:617b
Islamic, 6:589b, **10:27a**
imposition on Copts of, 3:594b
jizya, 11:667b, 668a, 669a
in al-Lādhiqiya, 7:315b
see also Suffrage
Poll tax, Islamic, 10:27a, 11:667b, 668a, 669a
Pollaiuolo, Antonio, 4:489a
Pollen count, in climatology, 3:451b, 453b–454a
Polo, Maffeo, 4:557a
Polo, Marco, **10:27a–28a**
assassin references by, 1:591b
Columbus and, 4:557a, 559b
Ibn Baṭṭūṭa and, 2:130a
journey to China, 1:332b
in Kublai Khan's service, 10:27b
magnetic compass and, 11:101a
Mandeville's Travels and, 8:82a
Russian fur trade and, 5:332b–333a
silk route to the Far East and, 12:99a
Travels of Marco Polo, 3:332b, 10:27b–28a
William of Rubruck and, 4:556b–557a
Polo, Niccolo, 4:557a
Polo (sport), 5:354a
Połos Tarawnecʿi (12th century), 1:512a
Polovniki, 11:191a-b
Polovtsians. *See* Cumans; Russia, nomadic invasions of
Polycandelon, **10:28b–29a**
bronze, from Constantinople, 10:28b (*illus.*)
definition of, 10:28b
use of, 10:28b
see also Lighting devices
Polycarpus. See Law, canon, to Gratian
Polychrome style, 8:363b–365a
Polychronia, 7:385a
Polychronicon. See Higden, Ranulf
Polycraticus. See John of Salisbury
Polydore Vergil, *Anglicae historiae,* 1:565b
Polygamy
among Vikings, 12:423b–424a
Islamic, 4:598b
Polyglot Bible, 2:215b
Polygyny, Jewish, 4:606b, 607b
Polyphemus, *Hrólfs saga Gautrekssonar* and, 6:310b
Polyphony. *See* Music, polyphonic
Polypticum. See Atto of Vercelli
Polyptych, **10:29a**
diptych, 4:214b
panel paintings, 9:361b, 362a
of Taddeo di Bartolo, 11:572b
triptych, 12:198b
see also Altarpiece
Polyptych of Irminon. *See* Irminon of St. Germain-des-Prés, abbot, survey of
Polyptych (land book), 4:511b, **10:29a–30a**
Polytheism, Arab, 6:575a
Pomanders, 5:381b
Pomegranate, growth of, in Mediterranean region, 5:306a
Pomerania, 2:63 (map), 66a, 66b
see also Poland
Pomerium. See Marchettus of Padua
Pomerium in arte musicae mensuratae. See Marchettus of Padua
Pomeshchiki, 11:190b, 192a-b, 193a, 196a
see also Kievan Rus
Pomestie system, 8:548b–549a
Pomety, 8:575b, 576a
Pommel (sword). *See* Swords
Pompey, Theater of, 10:517b

Pomponazzi, Pietro, *On the Natural Causes of Effects; or, On Enchantments,* influenced by Siger of Brabant, 8:38b
Pomposa (abbey church), 12:480b
Ponce de León, Rodrigo, biography of, 11:433b
Ponema nomikon. See Michael Attaleiates
Ponet, John, *Shorte Treatise of Politicke Power* (1556), 3:521b
Poniard, 11:550b (*illus.*)
Pons of Cluny, abbot, 3:469a
Pons of Provence
  Epistolarium, 4:175a
  Summa dictaminis, 4:175a
    on proverbs, 10:189b
Pont Flavien (St. Chamas), 10:410b
Pont du Gard aqueduct (Provence), 10:410a, 477a
Pont-de-Cahors, 10:418b
Pont-de-la-Guillotière (Lyons), 10:413b–414a
  indulgences issued for, 10:414a
  taken over by the town of Lyons, 10:417b
Pont-Saint-Bénézet (Avignon), 10:420b
  construction of, 10:419a-b, 420a
Pont-Saint-Esprit (St. Saturnin), 10:418b, 420b
  bridge-building brotherhood, 10:414a
  construction of, 10:419a, 419b
  maintenance of, 10:417b
Ponte Vecchio, segmental arches, 12:578a-b
Pontedera, Andrea de. *See* Pisano, Andrea
Ponthieu, count of, William I of England and, 9:164b
Pontic coastland, 12:168b–170a
Pontic Mountains, 1:472a
Pontida, League of, 7:652b
Pontifical, **10:30a–31a**
  at Mainz, 4:131a, 10:30a-b
  definition of, 10:30a
  during Innocent III's reign, 10:30b
  illuminations in, 10:30b
  Insular, 9:264a
  modifications to, 10:30b
  Old Spanish, 9:264a
  Pontificale Guilelmi Durandi
    ordinands, 9:266b, 266a
    ordination rites, 9:264b, 265b
    see also Durand, Guillaume
  Pontificale romano-germanicum
    benedictions and, 2:178a
    ordinands, 9:266a
    ordination rites, 9:264b
  Roman, 9:264a-b
  see also Ritual
Pontigny, abbey church at, 10:483b
Pontoise, first seals of, 11:126a
Ponts-de-Cé
  construction of, 10:420a
  maintenance of, 10:421b
Pontus, **10:31a-b**
  annexed by Rome, 10:31b
  in Byzantine Empire, 10:31b
  patriarchate of, 9:459a
  in Trebizond, 10:31b
Pontus und Sidonia. See Eleonore of Austria
"Poor Catholics." *See* Waldensians
Poor Clares
  church of San Damiano, 5:201a
  forced convent life, 5:201a-b
  legislation for, 2:317a
  massacre by Muslims, 5:202a
  in Naples, 9:59b
  organization of, 5:191b
  relation to Franciscans, 5:195a
  revival of, 5:205b
  see also Franciscans
Poor Hermits of Pope Celestine. *See* Franciscans, Spirituals
Poor Knights of Christ. *See* Templars
Poor of Lyons. *See* Waldensians
Poor Men of Lyons
  branches of, 5:196a-b
  return to Catholicism, 5:196a
Poor Recluses (religious order). *See* Franciscans
Poor relief. *See* Hospitals
Poor relief, Byzantine
  informal dispensations, 6:288b
  monastic communities, 6:289a
  philanthropic institutions, 6:289a-b
  poor
    definition of, 6:288a-b
    percent of population, 6:288b
    social classification, 6:288b
  ptocheia, 6:289a-b
  ptochika, 6:289a
  public works, 6:289b
  through church
    bequests and endowments for, 6:288b–289a
    lists of poor, 6:289a
  see also Penetes
Poor relief, Islamic
  effect of political climate on, 6:290a-b
  family responsibility for, 6:290b
  personal philanthropy
    religious basis for, 6:290a
    waqf, 6:290a
  ṣadaqa and *zakāt,* 6:290a
Poor relief, Western European
  bishops' reponsibility for, 6:292b
  charitable obligations and, 6:292b
  effect of urbanism on, 6:297a
  laws affecting, 6:296b–297a
  response to Black Death, 6:297a
  xenodochia, 6:292b
Poorters (*poorterie*), 5:521b
  role in government, 11:713b–714a
Pope, **10:31b–32b**
  definitions of, 10:31b–32b
  see also Antipope; Papacy; Patriarch
Poperinghe, 12:732b
Popevki, 8:574b
Popolo
  decline of, 7:16b–17a
  definition and purpose, 7:16b
  development of, 7:16a
  in Pisa, 9:664b
  social makeup, 7:16b
  in Venice, 12:390a-b
  see also Florence
Poppehowe, Thomas, **10:32b**
Poppo, archbishop, in song, 3:57b
Poppo of Fulda, abbot, 5:312a
Population
  fertility rates, after Black Death, 2:267a
  Western Europe
    aggregate trends, 4:139b
    causes of catastrophic decline in, 4:142a–144a
    distribution of in Carolingian times, 4:140a
    epidemics and, 4:143b
    in 14th century, 4:141a-b
    increase in 12th century, 4:140b–141a
  see also Demography
Porbeagle (*Lamna nasus*), fishing of, 5:70a
Porcelain, Chinese, 2:146 (*illus.*), 3:240a
Porcupine, Order of the, 3:307a
Porete, Marguerite
  Mirouer des simples ames, 2:160b, 161a, 9:12b
    heresy of the Free Spirit and, 5:218b
    heretical views in, 5:217a-b, 6:198b
    path to mystic union, 5:218b
    translated into English, 5:217a, 9:12b, 27a
Poridat de las poridades, 11:415b, 441a
Porpēs. *See* Ciwnkert
Porphyrius, Publilius Optatianus
  acrostics of, 1:45b–46a
  carmina figurata, 1:218a
Porphyrogenitos, **10:32b–33a**
  rights of, 10:33a
Porphyry of Tyre, 9:96b–97a
  Against Christians, 9:97a, 98b
  Chaldean Oracles and, 9:97a
  introduction to Aristotle's *Categories,* 12:281a
  Isagoge, 1:457b, 505b, 9:97a, 700b–701a
    Aristotle's *Organon* and, 1:457b
    Boethius and, 1:460b
    Boethius' translation theory and, 12:139b
    University of Paris and, 1:461a-b
    Victorinus and, 1:460b
Porrectus, 8:619 (*illus.*), 625 (*illus.*)
Porrée, Gilbert de la. *See* Gilbert of Poitiers
Porta San Lorenzo, battle at (1347), 3:479a
Portable clocks, 3:462a, 464a
Portal
  Islamic *pishtaq,* 9:670b–671b (*illus.*)
  see also Doors
Portal of the Counts. *See* St. Sernin (church: Toulouse)
Portal pier. *See* Trumeau
Portal sculpture
  French, 1:428a, 469b
  French Gothic, 5:617a–628b (*illus.*)
  French Romanesque, 10:492a, 493b–494a, 496a–499a (*illus.*)
  Italian Ronanesque, 10:500b–502a
  Nicholaus da Verona and, 9:128b
Portative organ. *See* Organ, portative
Portcullis, 3:148a, 149 (*illus.*), **10:33a**
Porte-Dieu. See Monstrance
Porter, 3:441a, 442a

Porter and the Three Ladies of Baghdad, The, in *Thousand and One Nights,* 12:50b, 50a
Portiuncula (chapel: Assisi), indulgences and, 6:449a
Porto Pisano, 9:664a-b
Portolan chart, 5:398b–399a, 9:89a, 89b, **10:33a–35b**, 11:234a
  in atlases, 10:35a
  Carta Pisana, 10:33 (*illus.*)
  cartography and, 10:34b–35a
  magnetic compass and, 10:34a
  makers of, 10:34b
  navigation and, 10:34b
  origin of, 10:34b
Portraits
  clipeus, 3:457a
  in early Christian manuscripts, 4:356a-b
  of Roman and Christian emperors, 4:353b–354a
  see also Donor portrait
Portugal, 10:40 (map)
  African slave trade and, 2:268b–270a
  agriculture
    Algarve region, 1:85a
    coltura promiscua, 1:85a
    dual agricultural terminology, 1:84b–85a
    French *bocage* system, 1:84b–85a
  Alans in, 10:36a-b
  Black Death in, 10:51a-b
  Christians in, 10:38b
  cortes in, 3:611b
  discoveries in the Atlantic Ocean, 9:87b
  Germanic invasions of, 10:36a
  history (to 1279), **10:35b–48b**
  history (1279-1481), **10:48b–56b**
    see also Azores
  Iberian tribes in, 10:35b
  Indian trade and, 11:247b
  invaded by Ibn Abī ᶜĀmir al-Manṣūr, 8:90a-b
  Jews in
    Arraby Moor office and, 10:243b
    taxation of, 10:243b
  languages of, 6:435b
  Madeira Islands and, 8:10a–11a
  al-Manṣūr in, 10:38a
  Marinid occupation, 8:140a-b
  monasticism in, 10:36b–37a
  Mudejars in, 11:376b, 380b
  Muslims in, 10:37a
  as papal fief, 6:464b
  penetration of the Indian Ocean, decline of the Mamluk state and, 8:76a
  provinces of, 10:36a
  relations with
    Abyssinia, 4:562a
    Canary Islands, 4:558b, 559a
    Castile, 10:41a-b, 42a-b, 45b, 49a-b
    Italy, 4:557b
  revolution in 1383-1385, 10:53b
  slaves in, 11:338a
  Suevi in, 10:36a-b
  tenurial development, 11:682b–683a
  terra portucalense, 10:38b–39b
  under Asturian rule, 10:37a–38a
  under Ferdinand I of León and Castile, 10:38b
  under Roman rule, 10:35b–36a
  universities, 12:287a
  Vikings in, 10:38a-b
  see also Aviz, Order of
Portuguese art, Manueline Style, 5:630a-b
Portuguese language, 6:442b–443a, **10:56b–58b**
  Latin and, 6:435b, 10:58a
  linguistic unity of, 10:56b
  origins of, 6:435b, 442b, 10:56b–57a
  orthography, 10:56b–57a
  pronunciation in, 10:57a-b
  sound changes from Galician, 10:56b
  syntax in, 10:58a
  texts in, 10:56b
  under Dinis I, 10:50b
Portuguese literature
  fable, 4:572b
  lyric, Galician-Portuguese, 5:341b–342a
  poetry, decline of, 4:190b–191a
  see also Galician-Portuguese literature
Portus, 3:481a
Pos Peire d'Alvernhe a Chantat. See Peire de Vic
Posada, Battle of, Walachian independence and, 12:500b
Posadas. *See* Inns, Spain
Posadniki, 9:194a, 194b, 195a
Posidonios of Apamea
  on Celtic mythology, 9:45b
  as early Platonist, 9:95b
Posidonius of Apamea
  on Celtic bards, 2:105b
  on Celtic poets, 6:526a, 527a
  on Celts and Hellenism, 10:458a
  on Celts and music, 8:558a
Pospolite ruszenie. See Warfare, conscription of nobility
Possessio, papal, Lateran and, 10:520a
Possessory assizes. *See* Assizes
Possidius of Calama, bishop, *Life of Augustine,* 1:648b, 660b
Post mills, 8:394a-b
Post mortem, Inquisitiones. See Death and burial
Postal and intelligence services
  Byzantine, **10:58b–60b**
    counterintelligence, 10:60a
    documentation of, 10:58b
    logothete of the drome and, 10:59a-b
    maintenance of, 10:58b–59a
  Islamic, 6:589b, 591b, **10:60b–61b**
    of Baybars, 2:138b
    Baybars al-Bunduqdārī and, 10:61a
    Buyids and, 10:61a
    caliphate and, 10:60b
    disorganization of, 10:61a
    influence of, 10:61b
    Mamluks and, 10:61a
    post relay system, 12:148a
    resurgence in, 10:61a
    termination of, 10:61b
    under Mongols, 6:591b
    see also Communications
  Roman imperial (*cursus publicus*), 12:148b–149b
  Western European
    postal relay systems, 12:149b
    University of Paris and, 12:161b
  see also Letter-writing
Posterior Analytics. See Aristotle, *Analytica posteriora*
Postglossators, **10:61b–63b**
  consilia of, 10:63a-b
  Corpus iuris civilis and, 10:61b
  definition of, 10:61b
  function of, 10:61b–62a
  humanists' view of, 10:62b–63a
  on Roman law, 10:61b–62b
  Western European political theory and, 10:19a
Postilla litteralis. See Nicholas of Lyra
Postilla super librum Sapientiae. See Holcot, Robert
Postilla super totam bibliam. See Wyclif, John
Pot, Philippe, on the French monarchy, 10:316b, 323a
Pot, wide-brimmed. *See* Chapel-de-fer
Potash glass, 5:554b–555a, 560a
Potestas iurisdictionis, 10:21b
Potestas ordinis, 10:21b
Potter, Dirc
  Minnen loep, 4:320a
  tales of, 4:320a
Pottery, **10:64a–66b**
  centers for making, 10:65b
  European
    ceramics, 3:236a–238a
    in Italy, 10:65b–66a
    lead-glazed, 10:64b–65a
    red-gloss, 10:64a
    Surrey jug, 10:64a (*illus.*)
    unglazed earthenware, 10:64a-b
  faience, 10:65a
  Islamic
    Alhambra vase, 10:65b–66a (*illus.*)
    ceramics, 3:238a–240a
    Moorish lusterware, 10:65b
    in Spain, 10:65a-b
  Nubian, 9:199b
Pou, Pere, 3:171a
Poulain, Jean, commentary on Cicero, 10:356a
Poulaine, 1:530b, 3:625b (*illus.*)
Poulterer, royal, 6:304b
Pound (money), 8:428b, **10:66b–67a**
  in Domesday Book, 10:67a
  etymology of, 10:67a
  history of, 10:66b
  see also Penny
Pound (weight), **10:67a-b**, 10:238b
Poundage. *See* Tolls
Pourpoint. *See* Arming doublet
Pouthieu, battle at (845), 9:143b
Poverty
  apostolic
    beguins and, 2:162a, 162b
    in crusader thought, 4:15a
    in early church thought, 7:360a
    Franciscan Second Order and, 12:688a
    John XXII and, 2:163a
    Ockham and, 9:209b
    Peter Damian and, 9:509a
    in *Piers Plowman,* 7:335b

Poverty (*cont.*)
apostolic (*cont.*)
see also Franciscans; "Nonpossessors"
demography of, 4:143b, 144b
in villages, 12:441a
Povest vremennykh let, 11:346b–347a
Power, divine
absolute/ordained, 9:213a
Ockham and, 9:210b, 212b–213a
in Peter Damian's teachings, 9:509a
Power, Leonel, Old Hall Manuscript, contributions to, 9:232a
Power, paternal
in Byzantine family, 4:593b, 594b, 595a
entail and, 6:460a
in Germanic family, 4:600a, 6:455b, 456a, 456b, 457a
in Jewish family, 4:607a
in Roman family, 6:455b–456a, 456b
in southern French law, 7:467b–468a
Power, political
in art, 6:408b–409a
balance of
in Italy, 4:58a–61b, 10:504b
Mediterranean, 10:441a, 467a, 11:268b, 272b
Norway, 9:185a
in Rome, 10:521a-b
fairs and, 4:582b–583a,b
Francesco Zabarella on, 12:735b
Marsilius on, 4:132b–133a
of nobility, 9:147a
relation to wealth and prestige, 3:411a-b
Wyclif on, 12:707b, 710a
Powers (mathematics), rhythm and, 8:588b
Powys
acquired by Rhodri Mawr, 10:365b
origins, 12:514a
Pox. *See* Disease; Plagues
Poynings' Law (1494), 6:520b, 9:436b, 437a
Poynings, Sir Edward, 6:520a
Pozsony, 6:348b
Pozsony, University of, 12:290a
Pozza Toscannelli, Paolo del. *See* Toscannelli, Paolo del Pozzo
Prachatitz, Peter von. *See* Peter von Prachtatitz
Practica. See Trota
Practica artis musicae. See Amerus (*fl.* 1271)
Practica geometrie. See Dominicus de Clavasio; Hugh of St. Victor
Practica musicae. See Gaffurius, Franchinus
Praecepta dictaminum. See Adalbert of Samaria
Praeceptor Germaniae. See Hrabanus Maurus
Praeexercitamina. See Priscian
Praefatio. See Guy de Cherlieu
Praeloquia. See Rather of Verona
Praemunire, **10:67b–68b**
definition of, 10:67b
first formal pronouncement on, 9:262a
Henry VIII and, 10:68b
Statute of 1353, 9:312a, 10:68a
Praeposita, 12:685b
Praepositus, 12:687a
Praesepe, 5:319b
Praetorian prefect, **10:68b–69a**
Byzantine, responsibilities of, 2:472a-b, 484b
creation of, 10:68b
functions of, 10:68b
rights of, 10:68b–69a
see also Vicar
Praevalitana, 4:79b
Pragmatic Sanction of 554, 10:521a
Pragmatic Sanction of Bourges (1438), 4:378a, **10:69a–70a**
Basel reforms and, 3:654a
conciliar movement and, 10:69a-b
content of, 10:69a-b
definition of, 10:69a
Gallicanism and, 10:69b
papal authority in, 3:526a
reaction to, 5:181b
significance of, 3:367a
Prague, 2:302b, 303a-b, **10:70a-b**
bishopric of
founding of (973), 2:304a
raised to archbishopric (1344), 2:304a
Collegium Caroli, 12:292b
first written records, 10:70a
Hradčany Castle, Vladislav Hall, 10:398a (*illus.*), 399a
Hussites in, 10:70b
"Kulturkreis," Michel Beheim and, 8:306b
manufacture of scientific instruments in, 11:103a
origins of, 10:70a
population of (14th century), 2:303a
prostitutes of, 2:303b
as religious center, 10:70a
social classes of, 2:303a-b
sources of livelihood in, 2:303a
stone bridge in, 10:70a, 418a
under Charles IV, 2:300b, 10:70a-b, 418a
under interdict (1415), 6:373a
see also Ried, Benedikt
Prague Calixtine Church. *See* Prague Utraquist Church
Prague Cathedral, vaulting of completed by Peter Parler, 9:421 (*illus.*)
Prague, Four Articles of, 6:375b, 376b
Prague, University of, 2:303a, 10:70a-b, 12:287b
Charles IV and, 6:365a, 365b
Hus at, 6:364b–365a, 366a, 367b, 368a
Hussites and, 6:371b–372a
utraquism and, 6:373b
Prague Utraquist Church, 6:377a-b
Praguerie, 5:188b
Praise of the Bald. See Hucbald of St. Amand, *Egloga de calvis*
Praise of the Holy Cross, The. See Hrabanus Maurus,
Praises of the Lord. See Dracontius
Pram (ship), 11:239a, 239b
Prata. See Suetonius
Pratica della mercatura. See Pegolotti, Francesco
Prato, canals, 12:577a-b
Pratum spirituale. See John Moschos
Pravosudie mitropoliche (Metropolitan's justice), 7:507b–508a
see also Russian (Muscovite) law
Prayer
concept of formulated by Evagrius Ponticus, 9:6b
creeds in liturgical use, 3:675a–677b
Islamic, 6:582a, 7:617a
secret, 9:690b
see also Angelus; Ave Maria; Mass
Prayer books, *see also* Book of hours
Prayer cylinder, technical innovations, 11:662a
Prayer hymns. *See Pia dictamina*
Prayer rugs, Turkish, 6:613b (*illus.*)
Prazdniki, 8:574b
Pre-Romanesque architecture, **10:91a–96b,** 10:94a–96a
Carolingian, 10:91a–94a (*illus.*), 477b
church plans, 10:91a–92a (*illus.*), 306 (*illus.*)
emphasis on crypts, 10:92a-b
see also Aachen, palace chapel; St. Gall
French, 10:478a, 480b–481a
Germany, 10:487b
Norman, 10:478a-b
relationship between mass and space, 10:94b–95a
as Romanesque source, 10:477b–478b
Southern tier, 10:477a-b, 487a
westwork, 12:622b
Pre-Romanesque art, **10:96b–116b**
attitude to classical art, 10:310a-b
bronze doors at Hildesheim, 8:283b, 284a (*illus.*)
Carolingian
decline of, 10:99b–100a
illuminations, 10:97a–100a
mosaics, 10:96a–97a
paintings, 10:97a
sculpture and metalwork, 10:100a–101a
Egbert of Trier as patron, 4:399b
English, 10:107b–110a
French Romanesque sculpture and, 10:491b
in France, 10:111b–112a
French, 10:110b–112a
German, 10:101a–107b, 491b
stimulus to, 10:101a
Italian, 10:112a–113a
manuscript illumination and, 8:107a-b
Resurrection cycle and, 10:340a
Spanish, 10:113b–115a
term of, 10:96b
see also Carolingian renaissance; Ivory carving, Carolingian; Lombard art; *Parousia;* Utrecht Psalter
Preachers, Order of. *See* Dominicans
Preaching
Byzantine, 10:350a-b
Carolingian vernacular, 8:188b
Dominicans and, 10:301a
English, 10:301b–302a
Azenbite of Inwyt, 10:301b
Book of Vices and Virtues, 10:301b
as a form of entertainment, 8:315a

four senses of interpretation and, 10:362a-b
Franciscans and, 10:301a
French, *Manuel des péchés,* 10:301b
Irish, 6:541b
Islamic, 8:498b, **10:70b–73b**
decline in, 10:73b
during the Friday service, 7:618a
lay preachers, 10:71b
narrative tendency of, 10:71b–72a
special class of preachers, 10:71a-b
Jewish, **10:73b–75b**, 10:360b–361a
anthologies of, 10:74a-b
focus of, 10:74a-b
growth of, 10:75a
Jewish name for, 10:73b–74a
literary form of, 10:74a
in the liturgy, 8:188b
Western European, **10:75b–82b**, 10:360b–363b
in 10th and 11th centuries, 10:75b–76a
ars praedicandi and, 1:555b–558a, 10:76a
audiences of, 10:76b–77b
Bernardino of Siena and, 2:196a
crusade, 4:20b–21a, 6:141b–142a
development, 10:80b–81a
exempla in, 4:551a-b
Gallo-Italian, 6:663b
instructional, 10:79a–80a
Italian. *See* Italian literature, sermons
lay, papal restrictions on, 5:196a-b
liturgy and, 10:78b–79a
orders of friars and, 4:286a
pastoral instruction guides, 10:300b–301a
patterned on Jesus' use of parables, 10:361a-b
poetic penitential sermon, 6:138a
popular, 10:76a-b
preachers' aids, 10:300b–301a, 10:363a-b
as propaganda, 10:138a-b
in Spain, 11:420a, 422b, 455b–456a
study of, 10:81a-b
texts of sermons, 10:77b–78b
to clerics, 10:75b–76a
treatises on (1200-1500), 10:362b
Tuscan, 6:664a
vernacular, 4:286a, 5:233b
see also Guischart de Beaulieu; Religious instruction; Robert of Greatham; Robert d'Arbrissel; Scandinavian literature, religious
Prébayon (monastery: Provence), 12:687a
Precarium, 11:674b
Precentor, **10:82b–83a**
responsibilities of, 10:83a
see also Cantor
Preces
sequence and, 6:379b
see also Tropes to the Ordinary of the Mass
Precession of the equinoxes, 3:17b–18a, 22b–23a
Predanie. See Nil Sorsky, St.
Predella, 1:222b, 4:302a, **10:83a-b**
Predestination
in Augustinus Triumphus' work, 2:1a
baptism and, 5:639a
debates about, 3:321b, 5:638b
double, 5:638b–639a
Duns Scotus and, 9:213a-b
in early Islam, 11:139b
Eucharist and, 5:639a
Gottschalk of Orbais on, 5:638a–639a
Gregory of Rimini on, 5:672a
in Islam, al-Mu^{c}tazila and, 8:655a, 8:655b
John Cassian on, 9:486b
Nicholas I on, 5:638b
Ockham and, 9:212a-b
in *Piers Plowman,* 7:334b
theologians and, 3:371a
Wyclif on, 3:371a, 12:708a
Predestination, in Islam, 6:582b, 583a, 583b–584a
Abu 'l-Ḥasan ^{c}Alī ibn Isma^{c}il al-Ash^{c}ari on, 1:584b–585a
Jahm ibn Ṣafwān on, 1:584a
see also "Acquisition" (Islamic doctrine)
Preemption rights
Byzantine, 4:595a
Romanos I Lekapenos and, 10:515b
Preface of Gildas on Penance. See Gildas, St.
Prefect, Roman, 10:519b, 521a
Preislied, 7:679b
Preller, Der, synopsis of, 8:128b
Premonstratensian rite, **10:83b–84b**
calendar of, 10:84a
chant melodies in, 10:84a
Cistercian rite on, 10:83b–84a
Divine Office and, 10:83b–84a
features of, 10:83b
in Mass order, 10:84a
original form of, 10:83b
Premonstratensian Rule, Dominicans and, 12:687b
Premonstratensians, **10:84b–87b**
Cistercians and, 10:86a
criticism of, 10:86a
decline of, 10:87a
expansion of, 10:85a-b
founding of, 10:84b
intellectual life of, 10:87a
rule of Augustine and, 10:85a-b
women's orders and, 10:85b, 87a, 12:685a-b
Přemysl Otokar I of Bohemia, king, 2:300a, 10:88a
a charter on the rights of the church (1222) and, 2:304a
Přemysl Otokar II of Bohemia, king, defeat by Habsburgs (1278), 5:487b
Přemysl Otokar II of Bohemia, king, 2:300a, 10:88b
Babenberg inheritance and, 2:7b
defeat by Habsburgs (1278), 6:42b, 343a
expedition against Prussians, 2:66b
imperial aspirations of, 2:300a
legal code of, 10:70a
Přemysl the Plowman, 10:87b
Přemyslid dynasty, **10:87b–89a**
Babenbergs and, 2:7a
disputes within, 10:88a-b
dominance of, 10:87b
first recorded residence of, 10:87b
German colonization by, 10:88b
Moravian rule, 8:485a
in Prague, 10:70a
royal towns established by, 10:88b
Rudolf of Habsburg and, 10:88b
see also Bohemia-Moravia
Preneurs, 5:350a
Prentys, Thomas, **10:89a**
Robert Sutton and, 11:518b
Preparatory inquest. *See Inquisitio praeparatoria*
Prependulia, **10:89a-b**
Prerogative, **10:89b–90b**
change in, 10:89b
definition of, 10:89b–90b
expansion of in England, 10:89b
Richard II vs. Parliament, 10:90b
Sir John Fortescue on, 10:90b
Presbeutikos, in Byzantine rhetoric, 10:350a
Presbyter Iudaeorum, 4:535b, 7:71a-b, 90b
Presbyterium, **10:116b**
Presentation, right of, **10:117a–118a**
abuses of, 10:117b
conciliar legislation on, 10:117b
inquest and, 6:481b
reform of, 10:117b–118a
Presentation in the Temple, **10:116b–117a**, 10:116b–117b (*illus.*)
Presentment (law). *See* Jury, grand
Preslav
held by Peter, ruler of Bulgaria, 9:510a
Round Church
ground plan of, 2:415 (*illus.*)
preservation of works of, 2:414b
Symeon of Bulgaria and, 11:554b
Preslav, Council of, 2:404a
Presoner. See Jordi de S. Jordi
Pressura, 1:629b
Pressus, 8:620 (*illus.*)
Prest roll, 6:302a
Prester John, 1:32b, 5:398a, 413b, **10:118a–119b**
communication between Ethiopia and Europe and, 10:119a
disappearance of, 10:119b
Henry IV's letter to, 10:119a
letter attributed to, 10:118b
in *Mandeville's Travels,* 8:82a
in *Parzival,* 12:677a
power and prestige of, 10:118b
Western trade and, 4:558b, 562a,b
Prestige
citizenship and, 3:423a
noble lineage and, 3:420b–421a
Prestssaga Guðmundar góða. See Lambkárr Þorgilsson
Prévôt
assize and, 1:594b–595a
castellan as, 3:124b–125a
in Châtelet, 278a–279b
emergence of office, 5:159b
see also Provost
Priamel. See German drama

Pribina, ban of Lika, Krbava, and Gacka, 4:5a
Příbram, John, 6:376a, 376b
Prices
  Black Death and, 2:265a–266a
  in Bohemia, 2:302b
Pricke of Conscience, 8:317a
Prickings, **10:119b–120a,** 12:700a, 700b
  scribe pricking his manuscript, 7:569b (*illus.*)
Prickle (unit of measure), 12:584a
Pride of Life, 4:287a
Prie-dieu, 5:318a, **10:120a**
Priest
  in church hierarchy, 3:441a
  see also Clergy; Ordination
Priesterleben
  authorship of, 6:137b
  model of good priest in, 6:138b
  style, 6:138b
  theme, 6:138a
  see also Heinrich von Melk
Priesthood
  advancement in, 3:442b–443a
  entrance into, 3:441b, 443a–444b
  order of, 3:441a
  ordination rites of, 3:441a–442b
Priesthood of all believers, Wyclif on, 12:708a
Prilep, 11:474b
Prima pastorum. See Second Shepherds' Play
Primary Chronicle, Russian, **10:120a–121a**
  author of, 10:120b
  on Bulgaria, 2:405b
  contribution of, 10:120b–121a
  Ilarion and, 6:418b
  on Khanate of Tmutarakan, 12:66a
  on Novgorod, 9:192b
  redactions of, 10:120b
  Rurik's Novgorodian expedition, 10:571a
  Slavic living arrangements, 11:669b
  on Varangians, 12:434b
Primary History of Armenia
  also known as "pseudo-Sebēos," 11:133a
  on the origins of Bagratuni, 2:47b
Primas. *See* Hugh (Primas) of Orléans
Primate, metropolitan and, 4:126a,b
Prime (canonical hours), 3:67a, 4:229a
Prime (unit of measure), 12:595b
Primer seisin, 10:90a
Primera crónica general, 3:71b, 11:453a
Primicerius notariorum, notitia dignitatum and, 9:186a
Primitive Christianity, of Bohemian Brethren, 2:306b
Primitive church
  concept of, **10:121a–123b**
    decretals and, 10:121b–122a
    deviant movements in, 10:122a-b
    Dominicans and, 10:122b
    early church and, 10:121a-b
    Franciscans and, 10:122a-b
    Gregorian reform and, 10:122a
    mendicant orders and, 10:122b
  in Rome, 10:461b
Primogeniture
  Basque, 2:126b
  Bavarian, 2:135b
  senioratus and, in Hungary, 6:340a
  vs. partibility, 6:451a, 452a, 459a-b
  see also Ultimogeniture
Primordia coenobii Gandeshemensis. See Hrotswitha von Gandersheim
Prince, **10:123b–124a**
  German, representative assemblies and, 10:329a, 332a–333a
  governance. *See* Representative assemblies
  in political theory, 10:123b–124a
Prince. See Machiavelli, Niccolò
Prince of princes. *See* Archon ton archonton
Princeps, Alberic of Rome as, 10:525a
Princeps Wallie. *See* Llywelyn ap Gruffydd
Principate, in Roman Empire, 10:458b, 10:461a
Principe, discovered, 4:561b
Principia arithmeticae. See Notker Teutonicus
Principles and Elements of Harmonics. See Aristoxenus of Tarentum (*fl. ca.* 300 B.C.)
Prinsault, Clément, *Treatise,* 6:176b
Printing, 9:680a (*illus.*)
  of Archimedes, 1:439b
  archives and, 1:446b
  Armenian literature and, 1:512a
  of Averroës, 1:467b
  Benedictines and, 2:175b
  in Buda, 6:348b
  Caroline minuscule and, 7:362b, 11:652b–653a
  Carthusian presses, 3:119a-b
  of *Catholicon,* 7:352a, 368a
  codification of English spelling and, 8:309b–310a
  decorated letters and, 6:463b
  essential features of, 10:126a-b
  first press, 10:124a
  in France, 5:272b
    first printshop established, 9:409b–410a
  impact on library development, 7:563b
  introduced into Valencia, 12:348b
  Irish literature and, 6:525b
  Italian romance literature and, 6:639a
  Jewish exegesis and, 4:541b
  Latin and, 6:439a
  literacy and, 7:601b
  manuscript book production and, 8:104b–105a, 9:350b
  Marian devotion and, 12:461a
  movable type, 11:693a
  musical notation and, 8:627a
  Nuremberg, 9:.202b
  origins of, **10:124a–128a**
    adjustable mold, 6:32a, 32b
    annotated copies of books, 10:127a
    effects of, 10:125b–126a
    in Germany, 10:124a-b
    in Italy, 10:124b–125a
    Latin texts in, 10:125b
    metal type, 6:32b
    Middle East, 11:661b
    movable type, 6:31a, 32a, 7:700a
    printer's ink, 6:32b
    study of, 10:127a-b
    see also Block book; *Bois Protat;* Caxton, William;
  of *Regimen sanitatis Salerni,* 7:366a
  of Romanian religious texts, 10:511a
  of *Speculum maius,* 12:454b
  of *Vulgate,* 12:496a
  witchcraft and, 12:662b
  woodcut and, 12:692a, 693a
  of Wyclif's works, 12:710b
  of York missal, 12:729a
Prints and printmaking
  burin, 2:432a (*illus.*)
  see also Engraving; Woodcut
Prior Analytics. See Aristotle, *Analytica priora*
Prior de San Juan, El, 11:429a
Priscian, 7:352a, 353a, **10:128a–129a**
  Carmen de ponderibus, 1:434b
  commentaries on, 10:128b
  De figuris numerorum, 10:128b
  De laude Anastasii imperatoris, 10:128b
  De metris fabularum Terentii, 10:128b
  grammatical works of, 10:128a-b
  Institutiones grammaticae, 5:648b–649b, 7:351b, 10:128a-b, 352b
    in grammar curriculum, 11:688b
  life of, 10:128a
  Partitiones duodecim versuum Aeneidos principalium, 5:649a, 10:128b
  Periegesis, 10:128b
  poetry of, 10:128b
  Praeexercitamina, 10:128b
  Roman numerals and, 10:470b
Priscillian of Ávila, bishop, **10:129a-b**
  accusations against, 10:129a
  ascetic doctrine of, 10:129a-b
  dualism of, 4:297b
  execution of, 10:129a
Priscillianism
  Leo I and, 1:605b–606a
  Origen's treatises on, 9:281a
Prise d'Alexandrie. See Machaut, Guillaume de
Prise d'Orange, 3:258b–259a
Prisons, **10:129b–130b**
  alms for prisoners, 12:130a
  for debtors, 12:130a
  ecclesiastical, 12:130a-b
  English, 9:681b–682a
  of inquisition, 6:486a, 486b
  murus largus versus *murus strictus,* 12:130a
  provisions in medieval folklaws, 12:130a
Private archives. *See* Archives
Private excommunication. *See* Excommunication
Privatum sigillum. See Seals and sigillography
Privilege of Teilo. *See* Book of Llandaf
Privilegio de los Votos, Vida de San Millán de la Cogolla and, 2:187a
Privilegium maius (document forged by Rudolf IV of Austria), 2:8a, 5:503a-b

Privilegium minus, conferred by Frederick I Barbarossa on Henry II Jasomirgott, 2:6b
Privy seal, 6:301b
office of, 6:303a
royal wardrobe and, 6:302b, 303a
Priznaki, 8:576a
Proba, *Cento Virgilianus,* 7:361a, 9:440b
Proba centum scripturarum. See Wagner, Leonhard
Probate records, as demographic evidence, 4:139a
Probi. See Boni homines
Problemata. See Aristotle
Probst. See Provost
Probus (1st century), 12:494b
Probus of Antioch, 11:566b
Probus diptych, 4:215a
Proceres exercitus, 10:521b
Procés de la Senyora de Valor contra En Bertran Tudela. See Via, Francesc de la
Processional hymn. *See* Liturgical poetry, *versus*
Processions, liturgical, **10:130b–133b**
accoutrements for, 10:133a
calamities and, 10:131b
chants and psalms for, 10:133a-b
crosses for, 5:319b
of the donkeys, 10:539a
Gallican chant, 5:343b–344a
incense and, 6:432a
indoor, 10:132b–133a
in Jerusalem, 10:131b–132a
Mass, 10:131b–132b
music for, 6:380a, 383a, 8:596a-b, 9:688b
occasions of, 7:592b
pagan practices parallel with, 10:131a-b
on Palm Sunday, 10:131a
participants at, 10:133a
for reception of eminent visitors, 10:133a
Rogation, 10:131a, 131b
roots of, 10:131a
Sarum use, 10:654b–655a, 10:656a
scriptural justification for, 10:131a
to burial or martyrdom sites of saints, 10:131b
to stations in Rome, 10:132a
to ward off Black Death, 2:265a
see also Litany; Liturgy, stational; Mass cycles; Plainsong; Stations of the Cross; *Versus;* Vestments, liturgical
Processions, secular, 8:595b
Processus prophetarum. See Drama, liturgical
Procheiros nomos, 2:117b, 125b, 7:391a, **10:133b–134a**
Epanagoge and, 4:493a-b
Prochoros Kydones, 3:632b, 4:135b
Prochorus (Georgian monk), Holy Cross monastery and, 11:256a
Proclus (410-485), 1:462a, 9:699a, 700b–701a
against Christianity, 9:98a, 98b
attempt to make an equatorium, 11:98b
Elementatio theologica, translations of, 12:641a
Elements of Theology, 1:457b
Liber de causis and, 9:100a
On Plato's Psychogony, 9:697b
Pseudo-Dionysius the Areopagite and, 9:99b
Siger and, 11:286b
Vep^{c}khistqaosani and, 11:256b
vs. John Philoponus, 1:458a
Proclus, patriarch, 5:540a
Armenian church and, 1:498b, 507b
Proconessus, marble quarries, 4:331b
Procop the Shaven, 6:376b
Procopius, **10:134a–135b**, 10:464a-b, 11:528b
Buildings, 10:134b, 135a
incompleteness of, 10:135a
Byzantine intelligence services and, 10:59b
Christianity and, 10:134b
disillusionment with Belisarios and Justinian, 10:135a
on Dwin, 12:97a
on *foederati,* 10:466b
on Justinian's Plague, 9:675a-b
on military techniques, 12:549a
Secret History, 10:58b, 134b–135a
on shipbuilding, 11:230a
Theophylaktos Simokattes' *Histories* and, 12:25a
on Vandals, 12:355b, 356a
Wars, 10:134a-b
continuations of, 6:243a
contradictions in, 6:243a
Proctor, Robert, 10:127b
Procurator
functions of, 4:203b–205a
nuncius and, 4:205a
royal, in France (*procureur général*), 6:479b, 9:419b
Producta. See Punctum
Production, economic. *See* Economic production
Profiat Duran of Perpignan
anti-Christian writings of, 10:5b
Reproach of the Gentiles, 10:5b–6a
Programmatic Capitulary, 3:91b, 108b
Progymnasmata. See Aelius Theon; Aphthonius
Prohemia poetarum. See Walsingham, Thomas
Prohemio. See Masdovelles, Guillem de
Prohemio e carta. See Santillana, Marqués de
Prokhor of Gorodets, **10:135b**
see also Theophanes the Greek
Proklos, patriarch of Constantinople. *See* Proclus, patriarch
Prolatio, 1:549a-b, **10:135b–136a**
see also Quatre prolacions
Prolegomena. *See* Gloss
Prologus in antiphonarium. See Bernard of Clairvaux, St.
Prologus galeatus. See Jerome, St.
Promissione ducale (coronation oath of Venetian doge), 12:387b
Promotio per saltum, 3:442b–443a
Promotus of Chateaudun, bishop, deposition of, 5:472b
Promptorium parvulorum, 7:352a
Pronoia, **10:136a-b**, 11:604b
feudalism and, 10:136a
in Greece, 11:178a
imperial decline and, 10:136b
inheritance of, 10:136b
military use of, 10:136a-b
for monasteries, 10:136b
in Serbia, 11:176b
under Stefan Uroš II Milutin, 11:475a
under Stefan Uroš IV Dušan, 11:475b
versus fief, 10:136a
see also Stratiotai
Pronoia system, 7:284a
Pronunciation, Latin. *See* Latin language
Prooimion, 6:378b, 7:292b
Propaganda, **10:137a–145b**
anticrusade, 10:140b
antipapal and anticlerical, 10:141a
Byzantine, 10:141b–142b
anti-Carolingian, 10:141b
anti-Islamic, 10:141b
anti-Western, 10:142a
iconoclastic, 10:141b–142a
imperial, 10:142a
justification of violent coups d'état, 10:142a
promotion of militant imperial image, 10:142a
role of rhetoric and, 10:350a
Carolingian, 10:139b
Cluniac, 10:139b
during the Trastámaran wars, 11:418a
early Christian, 10:139a
Hundred Years War, 10:141a
Islamic, 10:142b–143a
campaigns of "Pure Brethren," 10:143a
Koran as propaganda, 10:142b
Shiite and Sunnite propaganda, 10:143a
Sufi propaganda, 10:143a
Thousand and One Nights as propaganda, 10:142b–143a
Umayyads vs. Abbasids, 10:142b
Libelli de lite as, 10:138a
medieval vs. modern, 10:137a, 143b–144b
"big lie" technique, 10:143b–144a
effectiveness on elite, 10:144b
nationalism in the 15th century, 10:141a-b
negative and antagonistic, 10:137a
crusade propaganda, 10:138a-b, 140b
speeches and sermons, 10:138a-b
papal
anti-imperial, 10:140b
centralization of authority and, 10:139b–140a
pilgrimage shrines, 9:659a-b
positive and integrative, 10:137a
ceremonies, 10:138b
church councils and canon law, 10:138b
coins, 10:137b
hagiography, 10:137a
iconographic and architectural forms, 10:137b
legends and myths, 10:138a

Propaganda (*cont.*)
positive and integrative (*cont.*)
miracles and exempla, .10:137b
relics, 10:137b
speeches and sermons, 10:138a
visions and prophecies, 10:137a-b
written, 10:137b–138a
secular workers' strikes, 10:141a
12th century, 10:140a-b
Wars of the Roses, 10:141a
see also Bertran de Born
Propaganda, crusade. *See* Crusades
Proper chants. *See* Mass; Plainsong
Proper of the Mass. *See* Mass; Tropes
Property
administration of, counts and, 3:658b
ambulatory, 6:458b
confiscation of, under inquisition, 6:486b
inheritance of. *See* Inheritance
of inns, 6:472a
marital, in Visigothic family, 12:474a
ownership of, under canon law, 3:607a
see also Tenure of land
Prophatius Judaeus. *See* Jacob ben Maᶜhir ibn Tibbon of Marseilles
Prophecy
in Isaac Israeli, 6:620b
in Ismailism, *see also Nāṭiq*
in Koran, 6:579a
in *Merlínússpá,* 8:276a
Prophecy. See "John of Bridlington"
Prophecy, political, Middle English, **10:145b–150a**
authority given to, 10:145b
bans upon, 10:145b
Galfridian symbolism in, 10:146a
Last King of Rome, 10:148a
Merlin and related prophecies, 5:387b–388a, 10:146a-b
in *Piers Plowman,* 10:149a
Sibylline symbolism in, 10:146a
Six Kings, 10:148a-b
Prophetia Anglicana Merlini Ambrosii Britanni. See Alan of Lille
Prophetiae Merlini. See Geoffrey of Monmouth, *Prophecies of Merlin*
Prophets, in art, 6:410a
Proprietary churches, 3:373a-b, 374b
Proprietas, **10:150a,** 11:678b
Propriety (musical notation), 8:629a
Přoš, prince, purchase of Gełard, 5:373b
Prosa. See Sequence (*prosa*); Tropes to the Ordinary of the Mass
Prosa-Lanzelot. See Prose Lancelot
Prosaiska Krönikan, see also Lejre chronicle
Prosdocimus de Beldemandis, 8:598b
Contrapunctus, 8:647a-b
musical theory of, 3:657b
Parvus tractatulus de modo monocordum dividendi, 8:647b
Tractatus musicae speculativae, 8:646a
Prose Edda. See Snorri Sturluson
Prose Lancelot, 8:354a, **10:150b–152b**
adaptations of Chrétien romances, 5:248b
compilation of, 10:150b
popularity of, 10:151b–152a
sources of, 10:150b
translations and spread of, 10:151b–152a
see also Arthurian legend
Proseuchai, 11:556a
Proskynesis, 3:320b, **10:152b–153a,** 10:152 (*illus.*)
iconoclasm and, 10:153a
Proskynetarion, **10:153a-b**
Proslogion. See Anselm of Canterbury, St.
Proso millet, 5:647a
Prosōpon, Theotokos and, 12:25b
Prosper of Aquitaine (Prosper Tiro), 7:361b, **10:153b–154a**
anti-Pelagianism of, 10:153b–154a
Carmen de divina providentia, 10:153b
confused with Julianus Pomerius, 9:490a
De gratia et libero arbitrio contra collatorem, 10:153b
De ingratis, 10:153b
as defender of Augustine of Hippo, 10:153b–154a
Epistula ad Flavianum, 10:154a
Epistula ad Rufinum de gratia et libero arbitrio, 10:153b
Epitoma Chronicon, 10:154a
Isidore of Seville and, 6:565a
on the mission of Palladius of Auxerre to Ireland, 9:464a
Poema coniugis ad uxorem, 10:153b
Tome, 10:154a
Prosperum iter. See Gerson, John
Prosphonetikos, in Byzantine rhetoric, 10:350a
Prostitution, **10:154a–155a**
cosmetics and, 2:147b
early church attitudes toward, 10:154b
England, dress code for prostitutes, 3:623b
Germanic imprecision concerning, 10:154b
in inns, 6:474a-b
in Islamic world, 5:2a
legal status of prostitutes, 10:154b–155a
in Prague, 2:303b
town regulations for, 10:154b
Prosula/prosulae. See Tropes to the Proper of the Mass
Protestantism
Dominicans and, 4:254a
vernacular and, 6:440b, 441a, 441b, 442a, 444b
see also Reformation
Protevangelium. *See* Annunciation
Protheme, 10:76a, 80b
Protheselaus. See Hue de Rotelande
Prothesis, **10:155a-b**
in the plan of St. Savior in Chora in Constantinople, 9:453 (*illus.*)
Protimesis. See Preemption rights
Proto-Romance language, Vulgar Latin and, 12:494a
Proto-Romanian language. *See* Romance languages
Proto-Slavic language, 11:341a-b
Protocuropalates. *See* Curopalates
Protonotario
strategos and, 11:489a
taxation and, 11:603b
Protonotarios, themes and, 12:10a
Protospatharios, **10:155b**
Protosynagogue. *See* Synagogue, origins of
Protosynkelloi, 11:558b
Prouille (monastery), founded, 12:687b
Provençal language, 4:168a, **10:155b–159a**
absence of nasalization of, 10:157b
albas and, 1:123a
Bible in, 2:215a
case system of, 10:157b–158a
Catalan language and, 3:157a–163b
consonantal modifications of, 10:157b
decline of, 10:158b
derivation of "Languedoc," 10:159b
divergence from *langue d'oïl,* 10:156a
Frankish invasion and, 10:156a-b
grammar in Latin, 12:136b
Italian and, 6:625b, 626a
Jordi de S. Jordi and, 7:150a
as *lenga (langue) d'oc,* 10:155b–156a
literary borders of the Midi, 10:160a
medieval terms for, 10:155b–156a
Old Occitan, troubadour songs, vocabulary, 12:214b, 215b–216a
Old Provençal, 6:442a, 10:157a
as a language of poetry, 10:159b–160a
as misnomer, 10:159a
origin of, 6:435a-b
orthographical renderings of, 10:157b
parts of speech, 10:158a
Raimon Vidal on, 10:156a
similarities of, to Catalan language, 3:158a-b
stability of southern Gaul and, 10:156b
substantives, 10:157b
syntax of, 10:158b
of troubadours
artificial standardization of, 10:157a
influence on vocabulary, 10:158b
verb system of, 10:158a-b
Visigothic impact on development of, 10:156a
vowels, 10:157a-b
diphthongs and triphthongs, 10:157a
palatalization of, 10:157b
William IX of Aquitaine on, 10:159b
see also Judeo-Provençal language
Provençal literature
history (to 1200), **10:159a–173a**
history (after 1200), **10:173a–185b**
absence of songs before 1000, 10:160a-b
Albigensian Crusade and, 10:173a–174b
Albigensian heresy and, 10:164a
Arthurian materials in, 10:179a
assimilation into French literature, 10:178a-b
Battle of Muret and, 10:177a-b
beginnings, 10:160a–162b
influences on, 10:163b–164a
Breviari d'amor and, 4:506b
by Catalans, 3:157a–163b, 164a–172a, 173a–174a

canso versus narrative verse, 10:180b–181a
chansons de femme, 3:257a
chansons de geste, 3:257a–261b, 10:179a–181a
tradition of after Albigensian Crusade, 10:182b
chansons de malmariée, 3:262b–263a
chansons de toile, 3:263a
complexity of poetical content, 10:164a
courtly character, 10:172a
esteem for verbal virtuosity, 10:175b
patronage, 10:172a
cultural, not political, coherence, 10:159a-b
demise of, 10:178b
devotional poetry, 10:178b
after Albigensian Crusade, 10:182a-b
early bilingual manuscripts, 10:160b–161a
epic, 10:179a–181a
on Alexander the Great, 10:179b
Roland legend in, 10:179a
fin'amors poetic mode, 10:166b–167b, 168b
codes of love in, 10:170b
jealous husband prototype in, 10:170b–171a
later styles, 10:176a-b
noble protector prototype in, 10:171a
Galician-Portuguese poetry and, 5:341b
genres
cobla (stanza), formal variety, 10:165b
razo, 10:164a–165a, 10:176b–178a
vida, 10:164a–165a, 10:176b–178a
incorporation into French kingdom and, 10:174b
increasing provincialism of, 10:178a-b
influence of French trouvères on, 10:179a
Inquisition and, 10:174a-b
Italian lyric poetry and, 6:640b, 6:645a
Italian popular poetry and, 6:656a, 6:657a
joglars, 10:164a-b
joi
as theme, 10:167a-b, 169a, 172a
in William IX's poetry, 10:166b, 167a-b
language of, 10:159a–160a
Leys d'amors, 10:181b
literary borders of the Midi, 10:160a
as literary heritage, 10:184b–185a
loss of universality, 10:178b
lyric
courtly love in, 3:670a-b
early secular tradition, 10:163a
genres, 10:164b–166b
importance of, 5:252a-b
to 12th century, 5:113a
nonlyric genres, 10:178b–184b
Occitania as a nation, 10:159b–160a
Ordinance of Villers-Cotterets and, 10:178b
poetry as metaphor for civilization, 10:174b–175a, 176a-b
pre-Albigensian Crusade period, 10:175a–176b
protests in poetry against sack of Occitania, 10:174b
rabbinic works, 1:23a
rhyme patterns, 10:165b
scuola siciliana and, 6:625a, 641a, 641b, 11:258a, 260b
sirventes, 11:312b–313a
subjugation of Occitania and, 10:173b–174a
territorial extent of, 10:159a–160a
themes of, 10:167a
troubadour poetry, 10:162b–172b
vernacular prose, 10:181a-b
see also Alba; French literature; Partimen; Provençal language; Tornada; Troubadour; *Vers; Vidas*
Provence, **10:185b–189a**, 10:186 (map)
annexation to France, 10:187b
architecture, 10:188a-b
Avignon school of painting in, 10:188b
birthplace of modern poetry, 3:667b
Cabalistic schools in, 3:1b
courtly love and, 3:668b
cultural boundaries of, 10:185b
early Christian presence in, 10:188a
economy of, 10:186a
imperial sovereignty in, 10:187a
inns in, 6:468b, 473a
legal system, 7:462b–463a, 465b, 468a
legend of Mary Magdalen in, 10:188a
monasticism in, 10:188a
Muslim threat to, 6:572b, 10:186b–187a
political boundaries of, 10:185b–186a
rivalry with Catalonia, 10:187b
rulers of, 2:428b–429a
under the house of Barcelona, 10:187a-b
villages of, 12:442b, 446b
see also Angevins; French law, in south; Midi; Provençal literature
Proverbes en rimes, 10:192a
Proverbi. See Garzo
Proverbia centum. See Wipo of Burgundy
Proverbia (pseudo-Jacoponic), 6:632a
Proverbia quae dicuntur super natura feminarum, 6:630a, 630b
Proverbios morales. See Shem Tov
Proverbios de Salamón, 8:281b
Proverbs, **10:189a–192b**
anthologies of classical proverbs, 10:190a-b
appeal to preachers, 10:190b
Arabic, 9:699a
Aristotle on, 10:189b
biblical anthologies, 10:190a
difference from *sententiae,* 10:189a-b
in drama, 10:191b
English, use of alliteration in, 8:330b–331a
formal properties of, 10:189a
French compendia of, 10:189b–190a
Italian, 6:630a-b, 632a
Latin compendia of, 10:189b
as legal authority, 10:190b
literary variants, 10:191a
in lyric poetry, 10:191b–192a
Scandinavian, in *Málsháttakvæði,* 8:66a–67b
in vernacular literature, 10:190b–191b
vernacular proverbs, 10:190a
see also Sententiae
Proverbs of Alfred, The, 8:315b, 329a, 329b
Proverbs of Hendyng, The, 8:315b, 331a
Proverbs of Solomon. See Sanson de Nanteuil
Providence, divine, icons and, 6:402a
Province, ecclesiastical, 3:373a, **10:193a-b**
in the Americas, 10:193a
ecclesiastical diocese contrasted with Roman diocese, 10:193a
emergence of archbishop or metropolitan, 10:193a
in England and northern Europe, 10:193a
Roman province as model for, 10:193a
spread of Christianity and, 10:193a
Provins, fairs, 4:590b, 593a
Provisions, ecclesiastical, **10:193b–194b**
benefices, 10:194a
by pope's initiative, 10:194a
expectancies, 10:194a
for supplicants, 10:193b–194a
see also Babylonian captivity
Provisions of Oxford (1258), **10:194b–195b**
acceptance by Henry III, 6:159a
baronial control of parliament, 4:481a
committees and councils established by, 10:194b, 195a
Edward I's support for, 4:395b
English parliament and, 9:422b
Exchequer made independent of royal household by, 10:194b–195a
expulsion of Poitevin favorites, 10:194b
implemented in Ireland, 9:435a
independence of chancery and, 10:194b–195a
legal force of, 4:481b
local government changes, 10:195a
resurrection of office of justiciar, 10:195a
Simon de Montfort the Younger and, 11:297b
translation of, 1:260a
see also Barons' War
Provisors, Statute of (1351), 10:68a
Provost, **10:195b–197b**
accounting of, 10:196b
Bordeaux, hereditary element, 2:328a
Carolingian usage, 10:196b
ecclesiastical usage, 10:195b
in educational administration, 10:195b
of estates, 10:196a-b
in forest administration, 5:133a, 5:134b
French and German forms of term, 10:195b

Provost (*cont.*)
functions of, 5:159b
in financial bureau, 5:162b
guild usage, 10:196a
inheritance of office, 10:196b
of merchants of Paris, 10:196a
military usage, 10:195b–196a
municipal usage, 10:196a
of Paris, 10:197a-b
farmer of royal income, 10:197a
office of bailli and, 10:197a
remuneration of, 10:196b
in Roman administration, 10:196a
royal and central governmental usage, 10:196b
see also Bailli; *Prévôt*
Próxita, Gilabert de, 3:171a
Proxy pilgrims. *See* Pilgrimage
Prudde, John, **10:197b–198b**
Beauchamp Chapel glass painting by, 10:197b–198a, 198a (*illus.*)
"Prudent dissimulation" (Ismailism). *See* *Taqīya*
Prudentius (Aurelius Prudentius Clemens), **10:198b–199a,** 11:405b
on church decoration, 4:358b
De arte metrica and, 2:154b
Eulalia and, 4:521a-b
Hrotswitha von Gandersheim and, 6:314a
Hymn Before Sleep, 7:374b
hymns of, 6:379b, 7:360b–361a
in Latin pedagogy, 7:353a
Psychomachia, 1:180a, 181a-b, 4:495b, 496a,b, 6:632a, 651a, 659a, 7:361a, 10:198b (*illus.*)
allegory in, 4:286b
biblical typology in, 1:181b–182a
as a "christianized" *Aeneid,* 1:181b
deadly sins and, 11:212a
depiction of vehicles, 12:372a, 372b
illustrated at Canterbury, 1:273b
source of *Waltharius,* 12:536a
Virtues vs. Vices, 12:462a
on value of art, 4:351a
Vergil and, 12:394a
Prüfening abbey church, 10:507a
Prüm, monastery of
founding of, 9:500b
Regino of Prüm and, 10:289b
Prussia, Bohemian Brethren in, 2:305b
Prussian Union, 9:727b
Prussians, Teutonic Knights and, 8:444a
Prussians, Old, 2:66a
in Adam of Bremen's description, 2:62a
disappearance of, 2:67b
Przemysł II of Great Poland, 9:721a, 9:723b
Psallat eccelesia. *See* Notker Balbulus
Psalle modulamina, 12:211a-b, 212 (*illus.*)
Psalm Against the Donatists. *See* Augustine of Hippo, St.
Psalm tones, **10:199a–200a**
antiphon, 10:199b
Byzantine, 8:555a
canticle, 10:199b
differentia in, 4:185a
inflections in, 10:199a-b
in oral tradition, 8:569b
parts of, 10:199a-b
solo, 10:199b
in tonaries, 12:70a-b
see also Mediatio; Rhythm; Tones
Psalmi poenitentiales. *See* Petrarch
Psalmist (clerical rank), 3:441a
Psalmody, rhythm and, 10:379a-b
Psalms
in communion chant, 3:504
Psalm 22, glossed, 4:549a-b
Psalm 50, glossed, 4:545b–546a, 549b
Psalmus idioticus, 11:632a
Psalter, **10:200a–202a**
of Basil II, 2:442a
Choir, 10:200b–201b
antiphons in, 10:201a-b
doxologies in, 10:201a
commentaries, 4:546a
Divine Office and, 4:223b–224a
division of, 10:200a, 200b, 201 (*illus.*)
English, Richard Rolle and, 9:21a
exegesis of, 4:539b, 547a-b
Ferial, 10:200b–201b
French translations of, 2:218b
from Corbie (Amiens B.M. MS 18), decorated initials in, 6:462a, 462b
Gallican, 10:200a
glossed, 4:548b
illumination of, **10:202a**
Chludov, 2:440b
crusader, 4:22a (*illus.*), 23a (*illus.*), 23b, 25b
English, 3:56b (*illus.*)
importance of in Celtic liturgy, 7:614b
in Ireland (7th century), 2:220a
Itala, 10:200a
in liturgy, 4:529a, 10:200b–201b
lauda and, 6:662a
Laudes creaturarum and, 6:661b
localization of, 10:201b
in music
singing of, 8:634a
see also Introit
numbering of psalms in, 10:200a (*illus.*)
paraphrases of in Old English, 1:280a
pocketbooks, 9:711a
replacement by Book of Hours, 5:615b
Roman, 10:200a
translations
English, 4:547a
German, 9:189a
Latin, 4:223b–224a
see also Gospelbook; Hymns; specific manuscripts, e.g., Lambeth Psalter; Troparion
Psalter of Blanche, 5:614a
"Psalter of Cashel," 3:602a
Psalter of Charlemagne, *octoechos* in, 8:554b
Psalter of Charles the Bald, 10:100a
Psalter of Colum Cille. *See* Laud MS Misc. 615
Psalter of Henry of Blois, 10:508a (*illus.*)
Psalter map, 5:397a-b
Psalter of Queen Ingeburge of Denmark, 12:181b–182a (*illus.*)
Psalter of Queen Melisende, 2:447a, 10:508b
Psalteri. *See* Joan Roís de Corella
Psalterium Aureum, campaign of Joab, 12:557b (*illus.*)
Psaltery, 8:562b, 567b, 605a (*illus.*), 607a (*illus.*), 607b, 12:180b
Arab, 8:611a, 611b
harpsichord and, 8:608b
Psaltikon, 8:554b, **10:202b**
Asmatikon and, 1:586b
Psellos, Michael, 4:170b, 5:660b, **10:202b–203b,** 11:49b, 55a
Aristotelian commentaries, 9:565b
Chronographia, 1:641b, 2:240a, 514b, 9:697a, 10:202b, 203a
arrangement of, 6:245a-b
classical literary studies, 3:431a
Didaskalia pantothape, 8:245b
doubts about astrology, 8:18b
funeral orations of, 10:202b–203a
John VIII and, 7:126b
John Italos and, 7:131b
letter to John Xiphilinos, 9:697b
on monks, 8:458a-b
Neoplatonism of, 9:99b, 566b
political career of, 10:202b
Synopsis ton nomon, 7:392a
Pseudepigrapha, Armenian translations, 1:508a
Pseudo-Albertus, *Book of the Marvels of the World,* 8:38b
Pseudo-Alcuin, *Liber de divinis officiis,* 4:223a
Pseudo-Anselm of Laon, *Enarrationes in Evangelium Matthaei,* 4:546a
Pseudo-Apuleius
Herbarius, 6:181a
Old English translation of, 1:286a
Pseudo-Apuleius. *See* Apuleius Barbarus
Pseudo-Aristotle
De mundo, 1:460b, 505b, 11:566b
De plantis, 1:128a
De virtutibus, 1:505b
Regimen sanitatis, John of Seville's translation, 12:140a
Pseudo-Augustine
Contra Judaeos paganos et Arianos, 1:270a
De spiritu et animae, influence of on Roger Bacon, 2:36b
Pseudo-Bede. *See* Lambertus, Magister
Pseudo-Bonaventura
ars praedicandi of, 1:557a
Meditations on the Life of Christ, 5:604a, 8:660b
Pseudo-Callisthenes
on Alexander the Great, 8:226a
History of Alexander, 1:508b, 511b
as a source for *Thousand and One Nights,* 8:22a
Syriac translations of, 11:566b
Pseudo-Chrysostom, Wyclif and, 12:709a
Pseudo-Clementines, 4:125a
Pseudo-Codinus. *See* Pseudo-Kodinos
Pseudo-Dionysius the Areopagite, 9:99b, 100b, 701a, **10:203b–204b**
Anglo-Saxon literature and, 9:18b

Aristotle's *Organon* and, 1:458a, 459a
on Beirut earthquake, 2:164a
Celestial Hierarchy, 10:204a
on angels, 1:248a, 249b–250a
commentaries on, 9:593a
influence of in Byzantine world, 1:250a
influence of in Latin West, 1:250a-b
on music, 8:584b, 588a (*illus.*)
translations of, 1:250a, 506a, 12:139a
Christology of, 3:321b–322a
Corpus areopagiticum, 9:563a
De hierarchia, 8:584b, 8:588a (*illus.*)
Ecclesiastical Hierarchy, 2:468b, 10:204a
on angelic orders, 1:250a
influence on Byzantine liturgy, 7:611a
Hugh of St. Victor and, 6:322a, 322b
identified with the patron of St. Denis abbey, 11:504a
identity of, 10:203b
influence of, 10:204a
knowledge of God, 9:598a
on liturgy, 7:626a
Meister Eckhart and, 9:32b
Mystical Theology, 9:5b–6a, 6b, 10:204a
influence of on *The Cloud of Unknowing*, 9:22a, 22b
Nicholas of Cusa and, 9:123a
On the Divine Names, 10:203b–204a
sacrament of Order, 9:602a
Sergius of Reshaina and, 11:566b
Suger of St. Denis and, 11:504a
Syriac literature and, 11:566a
translation into Latin, 6:2a
on the two natures of Christ, 8:223a
Vepᶜkhistqaosani and, 11:256b
Pseudo-Dionysius of Tel-Mahré, 11:566a
Pseudo-Egbert
Confessional, 1:286a
Penitential, 1:286a
Pseudo-Eriugena, *Commentum in Boethii De Trinitate*, 4:298a
Pseudo-Geber, *Summa perfectionibus magisterii*, 1:137b–138a
Pseudo-Germanus, on Divine Office, 4:222b
Pseudo-Gregory Penitential, 9:490a, 9:490b
Pseudo-Hugh of St. Victor, 7:631b, 632a
"Pseudo-Isidore." *See* Decretals, False
Pseudo-Kodinos, **10:204b–205a**
authorship of, 10:204b
content of, 10:204b
De officiis, 8:557a
importance of, 10:204b–205a
Pseudo-Macarius, 9:6b–7a
conditions of Christian experience, 6:217a-b
prayer of the heart, 6:217b
homilies, 11:566a
Symeon the New Theologian and, 11:553b
Pseudo-Melito, 7:282b
Pseudo-Methodios, 8:386a
Apocalypse of, 8:19a, 11:566b
Pseudo-Niccolò, **10:205a**
Pseudo-Nonnus, *Scholia*, 1:505b
Pseudo-Odo. *See Dialogus*
Pseudo-Remedius of Chur, 4:125b
Pseudo-Roman Penitential. *See* Roman Penitential
Pseudo-Simon Tunstede, Philippe de Vitry and, 12:481b
"Pseudo-Symeon," 11:555b
Pseudo-Theodore Penitential, 9:490a
Pseudo-Turpin, 3:331b, 5:259b, 654a, 7:217a, **10:205a-b**
Anglo-Norman versions, 12:637a
authorship of, 10:205a
Rolandslied and, 10:448a
Song of Roland and, 10:446b
translations of, 5:290a, 10:391b
Pseudo-Zacharias Rhetor of Mytilene, 11:566a
Pseudo-Zenob Glak, on the conversion of Armenia, 6:240b
Pseudo-Zilies von Sayn
Minnehof, 8:409b
Ritterfahrt, 8:409b
Pseudo-Zonaras, 11:53b
Pskov
annexation by Muscovy, 9:197a
Ivan III of Muscovy and, 7:20a
Pskov Judicial Charter, 7:507a
civil law in, 7:511b–512a
criminal law in, 7:511a
documentary evidence preferred under, 7:509a
ordeal under, 7:509a-b
witnesses, 7:509a-b
Psychomachia. *See* Prudentius
Psychopomp, **10:205b**
Psychotherapy, 6:492a
Ptłni, **10:206a**
Ptochoprodromos, identification of with Theodore Prodromos, 12:16b
Ptochos (indigent), compared with *penetes*, 9:493b
Ptolemaic astronomy. *See* Astronomy, Ptolemaic
Ptolemaïs. *See* Acre
Ptolemy, Claudius
Almagest, 1:604b, 610a, 620a, 8:115a, 10:236b, 11:95a
Arabic translators of, 11:83a, 12:128b, 129b–130b
astronomical observations under al-Maᵓmūn and, 11:99a
description of celestial globe, 11:95b
Jewish translators of, 12:134a-b
price of the manuscript, 11:84b
translation of, 11:82b, 90b, 274a
translations of, 5:422b, 12:137b, 138a, 140b
Analemma, theory of sundial, 11:509a
Aristotle and, 1:457a
on astrology, 1:619b
on astronomy, 1:610a
atlas of printed in 1482, 9:89b
Averroism and, 1:468a
Boethius and, 8:614a
Centiloquium, 1:606b–607a
Geography, 5:392a
on Naχčawan, 9:90b
on the Nile, 9:138a
Handy Tables of, 1:621b–622a
Toledan Tables and, 12:67b
Harmonics, 8:566a, 637b, 640a
psychic and cosmic harmony, 6:100a
translated by Boethius, 2:291b
in *Introductorium maius in astronomiam*, 10:473b
in Islamic science, 11:86a, 88a, 99a-b
Latin versions of works, 11:81b
law of refraction, 9:251a
map of, 5:395 (*illus.*), 397a
Mathematical Compilation, as synthesis, 10:206a
Optics, 9:240b
Quadripartitum, 9:704b
Tetrabiblos, 1:604b, 617a, 619a
Western European astronomy and, 1:614b
Ptolemy of Lucca, **10:211b–212b**
anti-imperialism of, 10:212a
De regimine principum, 8:435a
Italian patriotism of, 10:212a
Public excommunication. *See* Interdict
Public health
in Dubrovnik, 4:300b
laws, 9:677b, 679b
regulations for in Italian city-states, 2:100b
sanitation, plagues and, 9:677a-b, 679b, 681b, 686a
see also Medicine
Public Weal, War of (1464-1465), 5:189a, 7:676b
Public works
Islamic
financing of, 6:589b, 591b
see also Islamic art and architecture
Pucci, Antonio, 6:639a, 650a-b
Carduino, 10:315b
Madonna Lionessa, 6:670a
Pucelle, Jean, 8:109a, **10:212b–213a**
grisaille technique of, 5:678b
Hours of Jeanne d'Évreaux, 3:22 (*illus.*)
Hours of Jeanne d'Évreux, 10:212a (*illus.*), 212b
illuminated manuscripts by, 5:614a-b
Puente Mayor (Orense), 10:418b, 420b
Puente de San Martin (near Toledo), 10:418a-b, 420b
"Puer natus," 6:498b
Pugille (unit of measure), 12:590a
Pugio, 11:550a (*illus.*)
Pugio fidei. *See* Martini, Raymond
Pugliese, Giacomino, 6:643a
"Donna, di voi mi lamento," 6:667a, 11:259a
"Morte, perchè m'ài fatta sì gran guerra," 11:259a
Puig, Guillem de, 12:349a
Pulcheria Augusta (sister of Emperor Theodosius II the Calligrapher), 12:19b
Pulci, Bernardo, 6:636b
Pulci, Luigi, *Morgante*, 6:639b
Pulgar, Hernando del, 11:436a
Claros varones de Castilla, 11:422a-b, 433b, 434a
commentary on *Coplas de Mingo Revulgo*, 11:422a

Pulgar, Hernando del (*cont.*)
Crónica de los reyes católicos, 11:434a
see also Spanish literature
Pullan, Robert, communion under both kinds and, 3:504b
Pullen, Robert, 12:21b
Pullies. *See* Technology, mechanical
Pulpit, sculpture, 9:668a–669a (*illus.*), 669b–670b (*illus.*)
Pulpit, Islamic. *See Minbar*
Pulpit, Islamic. *See* Minbar
Pulpit, synagogue. *See Bimah*
Pulpitum, 5:317a, 318a
Pulse, as protein source, 1:95a
Puly, 8:426b
Pumbedita, Jewish academics in, 11:583b
Pumpkin dome, 4:236a
Punctuation, **10:213a–214a**
appearance of space for pause, 10:213b
in early Scriptures, 7:598a
German, 9:189b
Hebrew, 8:564a
lack of in classical Rome, 7:598a
as means of classifying MSS, 9:338b
regional differences, 10:213b
threefold system of points, 10:213b
Punctum, 8:619 (*illus.*), 625 (*illus.*)
in Franconian notation, 8:628b
Punctus divisionis. See Musical notation, Western European
Punic apple. *See* Pomegranate
Puns and wordplay, in rhymed offices, 10:373a
Punt (ship). *See* Pram (ship)
Pupillary substitution. *See* Substitution (law)
"Pure Ismāʿīlīya." *See* Ismāʿīlīya
Purgation (law), 6:478b
Purgatorio de San Patricio, 11:439b
Purgatory
Islamic concept of, **10:214a–215a**
affinity with concept of underworld, 10:214a
barzakh, 10:214a–215a
believers vs. unbelievers, 10:214b
doctrine of resurrection and, 10:341a
as one of three realms, 10:214a
"torment of the tomb" and, 10:214b
see also Paradise, Islamic concept of
Western concept of, **10:215a–217b**
Black Death and, 10:217b
debt for sins and, 10:215b
degree of suffering in, 10:216b
development from prayers for dead, 10:215a-b
fires of, 10:216a
Greek objections to Latin doctrine, 10:217a-b
Gregorian Masses, 10:216a
guilt and, 10:216b
heretical views, 10:217a
Hussites and, 6:373a
indulgences as suffrages, 10:217a
intercession by suffrages of living, 10:215b, 216a-b, 217a
penance and, 6:446b, 450b, 10:215b
scriptural evidence for, 10:216b
see also Paradise, Western concept of
Purity. See Cleanness (Middle English poem)
Purple dye, 4:327a
Purslane, 6:184a
Pursuit After Diarmaid and Grainne, The, 1:569b
Purvey, John, 4:547b
Wyclif Bible and, 8:318a
Pustules. *See* Plagues
Püterich von Reichertshausen, Jakob III, **10:217b–218b**
antiquarian and literary interests of, 10:218a
Wolfram von Eschenbach and, 12:673b
Ehrenbrief, 10:218a
political career of, 10:218a
Putevoi chant, 8:575a
Puy, 7:117a, **10:218b**
trouvères' confréries, 12:218b
see also Confrérie
Puy d'Arras, poet members of the, 12:218b
Puy, Raymond du, Master of the Knights of St. John, 3:303b
Pwn (unit of measure), 12:593a
Py fodd y dyly dyn gredu, 12:614b, 615a
Pyatiny, 9:194b
Pynson, Richard, **10:218b–219a**
Everyman and, 4:527b
innovations in printing by, 10:218b
as king's printer, 10:218b
notable illustrated books produced by, 10:219a
Wynkyn de Worde and, 12:712a
Pyramus et Tisbé, 5:243a
Pyrenees
provincial estates and assemblies, 10:316a, 325b
see also Navarre, kingdom of
Pythagoras, 8:638a
Guido of Arezzo and, 8:641a
influence of on the Sabaeans of Ḥarrān, 9:4b
Pythagoreans, 8:636b
Boethius and, 8:637b
Marchettus of Padua and, 8:646a
on music, 8:580a
Prosdocimus and, 8:647b
Pytheas of Massilia, on early Scandinavia, 10:686b
Pyx, 1:223b
Pyxis, **10:219a-b**
ivory, from Córdoba (*ca.* 970), 7:27a (*illus.*)
see also Ivory carving

Q

Q.o.t. See Quod omnes tangit debet ab omnibus approbari
Qāʿa, **10:219b–220a,** 10:219b (*illus.*)
eyvāns flanking, 10:219b–220a
Qaʿba. See Kaaba
Qabala. *See* Cabala
Qabīṣī, al-, *Treatise on the Distances and Sizes of the Planets,* 11:90b
Qabul, khan, union of Mongol tribes, 8:463b
Qābūs ibn Vashmgīr, Gunbadh-i Qābūs built by, 6:28a
Qabusnama, 11:308a, 309a
Qadar, 6:615a
Qadarī, political theory, 6:232a
Qadarīya, 3:41a, 11:139b
al-Muʿtazila and, 8:655a
Qadi, **10:220a-b**
appointment of, 3:44b
independence of, 10:220a-b
interest-taking and, 12:340a-b
under Umayyads, 3:39b, 6:589a
see also Islamic law; *Fatwā*
Qaḍīb, 8:567b, 613b
Qadir Khan, Yūsuf, vs. ʿAlī Tegin, 10:230b
Qādir, al-, of Valencia, king, the Cid and, 3:385a, 385b, 386a
Qadirīya, 7:111b–112a
Qādisīya, Battle of (636/637), 6:501b, 511a, 569a, 11:315a
Qādisīya, Battle of (637), Al-Kufa and, 6:596a
Qāhir bi'llāh, al-, Abbasid caliph, **10:220b–221a,** 10:246a
conflict with Muʾnis, 10:220b–221a
imprisonment of, 10:221a
Qāhira, al-. *See* Cairo
Qāʾid Abū Manṣūr Bikhatakīn, al-, elephant silk of, 11:717a-b
Qāʾim, al- (the Resurrector), title of the Mahdi, 10:341b
Qāʾim, al-, Abbasid caliph, 5:25a, **10:221a–222a**
difficulties of last years, 10:221b–222a
exile from Baghdad, 10:221b
marriage to Tughril's daughter, 10:221b
Seljuks and, 11:152a
Qaʾim (riser imam), 11:136b, 227b
Qairawān, al-. *See* Qayrawān, al-
Qais, importance of as a port, 9:74b
Qāʾitbāy, al-Ashraf (the Illustrious), Mamluk sultan, 8:75b–76a, **10:222a–223b**
charities and good works of, 10:223a
domestic policies, 10:222b–223a
early life and training, 10:222a
exile of Timurbughā, 10:222b

historical recognition of, 10:223a
military campaigns, 10:222b–223a
monuments built by, 10:223a
Qajars, Tabrīz and, 11:571a
Qālā, 8:578a
Qalʿa of the Banū Ḥammād, 6:415a, 12:744b
Qalaʿat Rōmaitā. *See* Hṙomklay
Qalāmdan. See Dawāt
Qalansuwa, **10:223b–224b**, 10:224a (*illus.*)
ban against, 10:224a
qalansuwa ṭawīla, 10:224a
Qalaṣādī, al-, 9:652a
Qalʿat al-Muslimīn, Hṙomklay and, 6:312a
Qalʿat Samʿan, church and monastery, 8:454b
Qalʿat Simʿan
church and monastery at, 4:333a-b
pilgrimages to, 4:333b
Qalāʾūn al-Manṣūr, Mamluk sultan, 3:399b, 8:73b–74a, **10:224b–226a**
achievements of, 10:225a-b
al-Lādhiqiya and, 7:315b
as architect of Mamluk state, 10:225b
campaigns of, 10:225a
monuments built by, 10:225a
regiments of, 3:398b
tomb of, 6:608b
Qalonomide family. *See* Kalonymus family
Qalqashandī, al-
encyclopedic manual for clerks, 10:347b
paper and, 12:698b
Ṣubḥ al-aʿshāʾ, 3:54a, 4:445b
Qāʾm. See Mahdi
Qamar, 8:563b
Qāmūs al-muḥīṭ, al-. See Fīrūzābādī, al-
Qannūbīn (monastery: Lebanon), 11:565a
Qānṣūh al-Ghawrī, Mamluk sultan, 8:76a, 76b, **10:226a–227b**
domestic policies, 10:227a
early life and training, 10:226a
failure to win loyalty of troops, 10:226a
military policies, 10:226a–227a
monuments and public works of, 10:227a
Qānūn, 8:562b, 611b
Qanūne yawnāye, 8:578a
Qara Khitāy
conquest of Qarakhanids, 10:231a
defeat of Sanjar ibn Malikshāh and, 11:153b
expansion, Turkoman discontent and, 12:227a
Mongol invasions, 8:466a-b
vs. Sanjar, 6:504a
see also Farghānā
Qara Muḥammad (Mehmed), **10:227b–228a**
alliance with Jalayirids, 10:227b
assassination of, 10:227b–228a
politics of legitimacy and, 10:227b
structure of state led by, 10:228a
see also Qara Qoyunlu
Qara Qoyunlu, 6:505a, **10:228a-b**, 12:227a
Aq Qoyunlu and, 1:352a
in Armenia, 1:486a, 514a
Arčēš and, 1:423a
in Iraq, 6:514b
Tabrīz and, 11:571a
Timurids and, 12:57a
Tʿovma Mecopʿecʿi and, 12:93a
Xlatʿ and, 12:713b
see also Aq Qoyunlu; Azerbaijan; Qara Muḥammad (Mehmed); Qara Yusuf; Uzun Ḥasan
Qara Yusuf, **10:228b–229a**
campaigns of, 10:228b–229a
as exegete, 4:540b
exile, 10:228b
freebooting period, 10:228b
structure of state led by, 10:229a
see also Qara Qoyunlu
Qaragūz figures, **10:229a–230a**
Qaragūz plays and, 10:229b
Qarakhanids, **10:230a–231b**
Alp Arslan and, 11:152b
in Bukhara, 2:397a
conflict with Ghaznavids, 10:230b
conflict with Samanids, 10:230b, 639a
conversion to Islam, 10:230b
division of khanate, 10:230a
in Farghānā, 5:14b–15a
internal strife, 10:230b–231a
Malikshāh I and, 11:153a
origins of the Seljuks and, 11:151a
Toghrıl-Beg and, 12:66b
Qarāmiṭa. *See* Qarmatians
Qarāqūsh, Almohads and, 1:194b
Qaratay (tutor of Kaygāwūs II), 11:157b
Qarawī, Ibrahim al-, 11:337b
Qarawīyīn Mosque (Fēs), 1:197 (*illus.*)
Qardū. *See* Corduene
Qarluqs. *See* Turkomans
Qarmatians, 1:375a, 6:512b–513a, 11:137a
anti-Abbasid activity of, 2:50b–51a
in Bahrain, 6:616a, 617a
Basra and, 2:127b
control of Ḥimṣ, 6:230a
founded, 6:615b
as Islamic sect, 11:137a
in Najd, 9:54b
plunder of Mecca, 8:240a
separation of, 6:587b
Qarna, 8:612b
Qaṣʿa, 8:563a, 613a
Qaṣaba, 8:561b, 612b
Qaṣaba. See Casbah
Qasi, Banu, control of Saragossa, Huesca, and Tudela, 9:68a
Qasī (banū), rebellion of, 11:382b
Qaṣīda, 6:507b–508a, 509a
Qasilynn (observatory: Damascus), 11:99a
Qāsim Gannūn, al-, 6:413b
Qāsim ibn Ḥammūd, al-, 6:413b
Qāsim ibn Ibrāhīm Tabāṭabā al-Rassī, al-, 12:741b
Qāsim ibn Idrīs II, al-, 6:413a
Qāsim ibn Yūsf al-Tujībī, al-, 9:651b
Qaṣr, **10:321b**
Qaṣr al-Ḥayr West, 6:408b
Qaṣr al-Qadīm, al-, 6:391b
Qastamonu, annexed by Ottomans (1392), 2:136b
Qatāda ibn Diʿāma, *ḥikma* and, 11:511a-b
Qaṭāʾiʿ, 11:669a
Qaṭāʾiʿ, al-. *See* Egypt, art and architecture, Islamic
Qaṭr al-Nadā, marriage to Abbasid caliph al-Muʿtaḍid, 12:224b
Qavurd (brother of Alp Arslan), 11:152b, 155a
last bid for power, 11:152b–153a
Qavurd Qara Arslan, Seljuk dynasty of Kirmān and, 11:152a
Qaydu (grandson of Ögödai), 6:420a
Qaykāʾūs I, 10:232a
Qaykhosraw I, Seljuk sultan, **10:231b–232b**, 11:154a-b, 157a-b
death of, 10:232a
first reign and exile, 10:231b–232a
Qılıj Arslān and, 10:236a
Qaykhosraw II, Seljuk sultan, 11:154b, 157b
Qayna, 8:565b
Qayrawān
Great Mosque, battlements, 12:553a
al-Muʿizz and, 12:744b
Qayrawān, al-, 6:414a, 414b, 415a, 7:162a, **10:232a–233b**
Aghlabids and, 6:391b
establishment as capital of Arab West, 10:232b
founding of, 6:572a, 8:15a, 15b
Great Mosque, 1:69 (*illus.*), 70b, 191b, 196b, 6:600a, 600b, 601a, 601b, 610b, 8:395b, 10:232b
bookbindings found in, 8:99a
as a holy city, 10:233b
Iggeret Sherira Gaon and, 11:584b
immigration to Fēs, 5:50b
Jews in, 7:97b, 98a-b
location of original camp, 10:232a-b
reduction to capital of Ifrīqiya, 10:232b
separation of government from mosque in, 10:232b
trade routes through, 10:233a
water sources for, 10:232b–233a
Qays
Battle of Marj Rāhiṭ, 8:142b–143a, 164a
Kalb rivalry, 8:143a
Qays ibn Nushbah, 1:617a
Qayṣarīya, **10:233b–235a**
Qaysite emirs
in Berkri, 2:189a
Mamikonean family and, 8:79a
Qaysites
Arčēš and, 1:423a
in Armenia, 1:481a, 482a, 513a
Xlatʿ and, 12:713b
Qazwīn, mosque of, 6:407a
Qazwīnī, al-, 5:393b
books on rhetoric, 10:347b
Qenneshre (monastery: Iraq), 11:565a
Qibla, 6:577a, 7:616b, 617a, 9:497b, 10:234 (*illus.*), **10:235a**
Bīrūnī's work on mathematical geography and, 2:249b

Qibla, 6:577a (*cont.*)
Ibn Khurdādhbih on, 7:243a
Islamic-Jewish dispute, 8:525a
Kaaba and, 7:203b–204a
in mathematical geography, 11:87a
miḥrāb, 8:376a
transept
in Almohad mosques, 1:191b–192b (*illus.*)
in the Great Mosque of Córdoba, 1:197a
wall, in Medinan mosque, 6:593a
Qılıj Arslān I, Seljuk sultan, 11:154a, 156b–157a
vs. First Crusade, 2:308b–309a, 4:30a, 34a, 35a
Qılıj Arslān II, Seljuk sultan, **10:235a–236a**, 11:154a, 157a
coinage under, 10:235b–236a
Danishmendids and, 4:93a, 10:235b
expansion in Asia Minor, 2:495b
Ikonion and, 6:418a
sons of, 10:236a
vs. Byzantines, 6:418a
vs. Manuel I, at Myriokephalon, 8:657a
Qılıj Arslān IV, Seljuk sultan, 11:158a
Qipčaq. *See* Kipchak
Qirāᵓa-bi'l-alḥān, 8:560a
Qirāḍ, 3:489b
Qirghiz. *See* Kirghiz
Qirmiz, **10:236a-b**, 12:98a-b
Qirqisānī, Jacob al-, 4:539b
Qiṣāṣ. *See* Islamic law
Qiṣṣa-yi Hamza, 6:508b
Qiyāma, al-. *See* Resurrection, Islamic
Qiyās, 6:581b, 11:219a-b
Qızıl Arslan, 6:419b
Qma, **10:236b**
Qmani. *See* Qma
Qom
Shīᶜa and, 11:228a
Shiism in, 7:307a
Quackery, in treatment of insanity, 6:492a
Quaderna via. See *Cuaderna vía*
Quadrant, 8:211a, **10:236b–237a**, 11:97a–98a (*illus.*)
by Jacob ben Machir, 11:91b
Islamic, 11:86b
sundial and, 11:509a-b
Western European geography and, 5:397a
Quadrant arch. *See* Arch
Quadratura circuli. *See* Nicholas of Cusa
Quadrifidio ciborum. *See* Rolandus
Quadriga, meanings of the term, 12:367a
Quadrilogue invectif, Le. *See* Chartier, Alain
Quadrilogus
Old Norse translation of, 12:35b, 36a
Vie de St. Thomas Becket and, 12:414a
Quadripartite vault. *See* Vault
Quadripartitum. *See* Ptolemy
Quadripartitum numerorum. *See* Jehan des Murs
Quadrivium, **10:237a–238a**
Alcuin of York and, 1:143a
Boethius and, 2:291b
classical literature translations and, 12:141a
Fachschriftum and, 4:577b, 578a
in Martianus Capella's work, 10:353b–354a
Pythagorean concept of quantity and, 10:237b
Quadruplum
in Perotinus' work, 9:506a, 506b, 507a
see also "Viderunt omnes"
Quadruvium. *See* Quadrivium
Quaestio, Hugh of St. Victor and, 6:322b
Quaestio de cometa. *See* Henry of Langenstein
Quaestio de fluxu et refluxu maris. *See* Marsh, Adam
Quaestio in utramque partem, **10:238a**
Quaestiones, **10:238a-b**
biblical exegesis and, 2:213a
of Hugo, 6:324a
literature, Nicholas Trevet's *Quaestiones disputatae*, 12:186b
in Peter Comestor's work, 9:514a
in Roger Bacon's work, 2:40b
in the teaching of medicine, 8:252b, 256b, 258b–259a
Quaestiones disputatae
Hugolinus and, 6:326b
see also Aquinas, Thomas, St.; Johannes Teutonicus
Quaestiones de iuris subtilitatibus, 10:444a
Quaestiones legitimae, 7:420b
Rogerius and, 10:444b
Quaestiones mechanicae, theoretical nature, 11:641b
Quaestiones Nicolai Peripatetici, 1:137a
Quaestiones sabbatinae. *See* Roffredus de Epiphaniis of Benevento
Quaestors, 6:449a, 450a, 450b
"Quando l'aria comenza." *See* Piero, Maestro
Quantity of the Soul, The. *See* Augustine of Hippo, St.
Quantum praedecessores. *See* Eugenius III, pope
Quarantine, of penance, 6:448a
Quarantine, disease. *See* Disease, quarantine; Medicine
Quarter, **10:238b**
Quarter Courts, 6:394a
Quarteron (unit of measure), 12:595b
Quarton, Enguerrand. *See* Charonton, Enguerrand
Quaternio, a. *See* Manuscript books, binding of
Quatre âges de l'homme, Les. *See* Philippe de Novare
Quatre fils d'Aimon, Les. *See Renaud de Montauban*
Quatre livres des reis, Li, **10:239a**
Anglo-Norman translation of, 1:262b
Quatre prolacions, 8:629b–630a
Quatrefoil, **10:239a**
see also Tracery; Trefoil
Quatrefoil cusp. *See* Cusp
Quatrefoil of Love, The, 8:332a
Quattuor doctores, 7:30b–31a
Quattuor principalia musicae, 8:563a, 646b
Quattuor temporum, etymology, 4:436a
Qubasar, 5:529b, 11:587a
Qubba, **10:239a-b**
cupola, 10:232a
see also Gunbadh
Qubbat al-Sakhra. *See* Dome of the Rock
Qubilay (son of Toluy), 6:420a
Qubrat, khan, 12:488a
Qubuz, 8:562a
Quḍāᶜa, relations with, Umayyads, 12:721b
Qudāma, *Critique of Poetry*, 10:345b, 346a
Qudayd, Battle of, Karijites vs. Quraysh, 10:242b
Quedlinburg
Annals of, on Lithuania, 7:603b
Thietmar von Merseburg and, 12:28a
Quedlingburg Itala, 8:105b
Queen Margaret's Entry into London. *See* Lydgate, John
Queen Mary's Psalter, 6:357a
Quem quaeritis, 6:498b, 7:363b, 11:436b
acting in, 4:276b
attributed to Tuotilo, 12:225b–226a
in Gallican liturgy, 4:273b
in Germany, 4:274b
importance of, 4:280b–281a
music for, 4:275a-b, 276a-b
origins of liturgical drama in, 4:272b, 280b
origins of, 4:273a–274a
Paris, BN MS 1119, 4:276 (*illus.*)
Paris, BN MS 12044 notation for, 4:273 (*illus.*)
performance of, 4:276a
12th-century expansion of, 4:274b
type II text of, 4:275b–276a
Utrecht MS 406, 4:275 (*illus.*)
visitatio sepulchri and, 12:478a
Quem vere pia laus, 6:317b
Quentovic
trade route center, 12:152b, 157b
Vikings' ruin of, 12:153b
Quercy, estates of, educational support by, 10:326b
Querela. *See* Trespass
Querini family, 7:377a, 381a, 12:391b
Querini-Tiepolo conspiracy, 12:391b, 392a
Quernstone, early medieval Western European trade and, 12:109b
Querolus, **10:239b–240a**
Querolus sive Aulularia, Vital of Blois and, 12:479b
Questals, 11:207a
Queste del saint Graal, La, 1:571a, 10:151a-b
as a source for Malory's *Morte Darthur*, 8:63b
see also Prose Lancelot
Question mark, introduction of, 10:213b
Questione della lingua, 6:626a
Questiones. *See* Langton, Stephen
Questiones circa tercium de anima. *See* Burley, Walter

Questiones de iuris subtilitatibus. See Placentinus
Questiones in musica, 8:642b
Questiones super de caelo. See Oresme, Nicole
Questiones super librum Topicorum. See Boethius
Questions of John, 3:182a
Questions on the "Liber de Causis." See Siger of Brabant
Questions on the "Metaphysics." See Siger of Brabant
Questions to Amphilochios. See Photios
Questions to the pope. *See* Rescripts
Queue (armor), 1:532b
Quevedo, Francisco de, 12:477a
Qui pridie, 8:192b
"Quia amore langueo," 8:340b
in Richard Rolle's mystical lyrics, 9:21a
Quia emptores statute, 7:449a
Quicumque. See Athanasian Creed
Quiercy, Council of (853), Christology and, 3:321b
Quijote. See Cuisse
Quilichinus of Spoleto, 7:365a
Quilisma, 8:620 (*illus.*)
Quillon dagger. *See* Poniard
Quillons. *See* Swords
Quinary meter, in Italian poetry. *See* Italian literature
Quince
in cooking, Mediterranean, 5:307a
preservation of, 5:306a
Quincunx, 3:378b
see also Church architecture, cross-in-square type
Quinisext Synod. *See* Synod in Trullo
Quinque compilationes antiquae, 3:638a
Quinque ecclesiae. *See* Pécs
Quintain, 5:347b–348a
Quintal, regional variations, 12:584a
Quintilian (Marcus Fabius Quintilianus)
on improvised discourse, 10:357b
influence of in the Middle Ages, 10:356b
Institutio oratoria, 5:649a, 10:352b, 356b
on reification allegory, 1:179a-b
Isidore of Seville and, 6:564a
Quintus Curtius Rufus, *Historiae Alexandri,* 1:149b
Quinze joies de mariage, Les, 5:275a-b, **10:240a-b**
exempla and, 4:551b
fabliaux and, 4:577a
Roman de la Rose and, 10:452b
Quinze joies de Nostre Dame, 10:240a
Quire, **10:240b**
see also Manuscript books, binding of; Manuscript books, production of; Manuscripts, Hebrew; *Pecia*
Quire marks. *See* Signatures
Quire (unit of measure), 12:593a
Quiricus of Barcelona, 6:381a
Quirini, Giovanni, 6:651b
Quirini, Vincenzo
support of Lateran V, 3:655a
Tractatus super concilium generale, 3:520b
Quirinus, St., in Metellus of Tegernsee's *Quirinalia,* 8:299a-b
Qulf, in *muwashshaḥ,* 11:446b
Qulzum, al-, as a naval base, 9:74a, 74b
Quo primum tempore. See Pius V, pope
Quo Warranto, Statute of, 7:448b
Quod omnes tangit debet ab omnibus approbari (What touches all ought to be approved by all), 8:232a-b
English parliament and, 9:425a
Quodlibet, **10:241a**
disputationes quodlibetales, 10:241a
literature, Nicholas Trevet's *Quodlibeta,* 12:186b
quaestiones quodlibetales, 10:238b
see also Dialectic; Polemics; Scholasticism
Quodlibeta septem. See Ockham, William of
Quominus, writ of, 4:534b
Qurʾān. See Koran
Quraysh, Imruʾ al-Qays and, 6:429b
Quraysh (Kuraysh), 6:567a, 567b, **10:241a–242b**
ʿAbd al-Muṭṭalib and, 1:14b
ʿAbd Shams tribe, boycott of Hāshim clan, 1:28b
Abū Bakr and, 1:24b, 25a, 25b
ʿAmr ibn al-ʿĀṣ member of, 1:236b
in Balādhurī's work, 2:54a
Battle of Badr and, 2:42b–43a
creation of Islamic empire and, 10:242a
dispersal of the tribe, 10:242a-b
Hāshim clan
control over, 1:14b
rule of Abū Ṭālib, 1:29b
al-Ḥusayn and, 6:370a
imamate and, 6:425b
initial resistance to Muḥammad's mission, 10:241b
Koran and, 10:242a
pre-Islamic, 6:575b
prestige of, 10:241b
rise of, 1:372a-b, 10:241a-b
trading stations of, 10:241b
treaty with Muḥammad, 1:24b, 29a
Qurrāʾ, 11:513b
Qurra (banū), Barca and, 12:744b
Qurṭubī, al-
on contraception, 3:575a
iconoclasm and, 6:404a
Quṣar, al-Ṭūr and, 11:247a
Quṣayr ʿAmra, 6:594b–595a
Quṣayr ʿAmra (Umayyad palace), frescoes, 8:611a, 612b
Quṣayr al-Ḥayr West, 12:264a (*illus.*)
Quṣayy, Quraysh tribal leader, 10:241a-b
Quṣṣāba, 8:610b (*illus.*), 612b
Quṣṣāṣ, 10:71b–72b
Qusṭa ibn Lūqā, 1:458a, 461a-b
Qusṭā ibn Lūqā, Hero's *Mechanica* translated by, 11:641a
Qusṭā ibn Lūqā al-Baʿalbakkī, Greek translations into Arabic by, 12:130b–131a, 132b–133a
Qutayba, Ibn
Adab al-kātib, 4:444b
ʿUyūn al-akhbār (*Choice stories*), 1:379b–380a
Quṭayba ibn Muslim
conquest of Bukhara, 2:397a
in Transoxiana, 6:570b
Qutaybah, Ibn, *Kitāb al-sulṭān,* 8:436a
Quṭb al-Dīn Aybak, 5:527a
Quṭb al-Dīn Hasan, 5:526a
Quṭb al-Dīn al-Shīrāzī, 1:621b
Quṭlugh İnanč ibn Jahān Pahlawān, 6:419b, 11:220a
Qutlumush ibn Isrāʾīl/Arslan
defeated by Alp Arslan, 11:152a-b
four sons of, 11:156b
Seljuks of Rum and, 11:153a
Qutula, khan, attacks on Chin, 8:465a
Quṭuz, Sayf al-Dīn. *See* Sayf al-Dīn Quṭuz, Mamluk sultan
Quzman, Ibn (1086-1160), 1:401a, 8:563b

R

Raabs, counts of, Nuremberg and, 9:201a
Rab de la corte, 7:71a, 80b–81a, 90b, 10:243b
Rabāb, 8:561b, 562a, 606b, 611b–612a
in art, 8:562b
mughnī and, 8:611b
Rabad. See Abraham ben David of Posquières
Raban of Helmstadt, 9:123a
Rabanus Maurus. *See* Hrabanus Maurus
Rabat, Almohad art in, 1:192b–193a (*illus.*)
Rabban Ṣāwmā (Nestorian Mongol monk), 1:453a, 3:313a, 11:563b
Rabbanites, biblical exegesis and, 2:212a
Rabbenu Tam. *See* Jacob ben Meir
Rabbi. *See* Rabbinate
Rabbih, Ibn ʿAbd, 1:380b
Rabbinate, **10:242b–244b**
bestowal of rabbinical title, 10:243b–244a
in Christian Europe, 10:243a–244a
election of rabbis, 10:244a
in Islamic Spain, *ḥakham* and *dayyan,* 10:244a
in Islamic world, 10:244a
Jewish communal self-government and, 7:70b–71b, 91a-b
shift of power to laity from, 7:91a-b
in Slavic countries, 10:244a
talmudic, 10:242b–243a
see also Responsum literature, Jewish
Rabbit, in Northern Europe, 1:95b
Rabbit-hunting with Ferrets (tapestry), 11:592a
Rabelais, François
fabliaux and, 4:577a
"Gothic" as term of abuse, 5:581b
Rabenschlacht. See Buch von Bern, Das

Raber, Vigil, 4:271b, **10:244b–245b**
collection of playbooks, 10:245a
staging diagram by, 4:266b (*illus.*)
as theatrical entrepreneur in Sterzing, 10:245a
Rabī^{c}, count in Córdoba, rebellion against Umayyads, 12:276a
Rābi^{c}a al-^{c}Adawīya, Islamic mysticism and, 9:39b
Rabies, mercy killing and, 6:491b
Rabula of Edessa, bishop, Armenian church and, 1:498b
Rabula Gospels, 5:580a
canon table in, 4:356a
miniature depicting Pentecost, 9:497b (*illus.*)
narrative miniatures in, 4:357a
Resurrection cycle in, 10:340a
Racio recta. *See* John XXII, pope
Rackett, 8:563a
Radbod of Utrecht, 7:362b, **10:245b**
hymns of, 6:384a
Radegunda of Poitiers, 12:682b
True Cross and, 4:553b
Radewijns, Florens, 5:680b, 9:38a
Brethren of the Common Life, leadership of, 2:367a
Deventer community of, 4:166a
formation of monastic orders, 3:368b
Thomas à Kempis and, 12:33a-b
Radhanites, 7:107a
Rāḍī, al-, Abbasid caliph, **10:245b–246b**
decline of caliphate and, 10:245b–246a
al-Ikhshīd and, 6:416b
Rāḍī bi'llāh Abu 'l-^{c}Abbās Aḥmad ibn al-Muqtadir, al-. *See* Rāḍī, al-
Radical Aristotelianism. *See* Aristotelianism, Averroist
Radiocarbon dating, of monuments, 1:431a-b
Radleucher. *See* Jerusalem chandeliers
Radolf of Liège, **10:246b**
correspondence on mathematics, 10:246b, 247b
Radoslav of Duklja, ruler, 11:172b, 173a
Radoslav Pavlović, vs. Sandalj, 2:338b
Radoslav of Serbia, ruler, 11:174a, 174b, 175a, 473b
Radulfus Tortarius, **10:246b–247a**
Miracula sancti Benedicti, 10:247a
Translatio sancti Mauri, 10:247a
see also Ami et Amile
Radulphus, life of Peter the Venerable, 9:524b
Radulphus Ardens, Gilbert of Poitiers's theology school and, 12:21b
Radulphus Glaber, **10:247a-b**
Acts of the Bishops of Auxerre, 10:247a
on Benedictines, 2:175a
on church buildings, 10:476a
criticism of fake relics by, 10:298a
Five Books of Histories, 10:247a
year 1000 and, 12:722b–723a
on Jews, 7:76a
Peace of God movement and, 9:473b
Radulphus of Laon, 4:543b, 12:20b
Rādūyānī, *Tarjumān al-balāgha,* 10:348b
Raeda (luxury vehicle), 12:368b, 369a-b
Raedwald, East Anglian king
grave of, 8:287b, 291a-b
Sutton Hoo and, 11:520a
Raetia, 2:133a
Rafiqah, al-, 2:46b
Raganaldus Sacramentary, liturgical tunic depicted in, 12:399a
Ragimbold of Cologne, **10:247b–248a**
correspondence on mathematics, 10:246b, 247b–248a
Raginfred of Rouen, archbishop, 9:500b
Ragnald, Viking king of York, 12:433b
Ragnarǫk, **10:248a-b**, 11:25b, 27a, 28a, 32b–33b
Æsir and, 1:62b
in *Lokasenna,* 7:643b
parallels to other traditions, 11:33a-b
role of Heimdallr in, 6:133b
Thor's encounter with Midgard, 12:45b
Valhalla and, 12:350a-b
see also Scandinavian mythology
Ragnarr, legendary king of Danes, 10:248b–249b
Ragnars saga loðbrókar, **10:248b–249b**
different versions of, 5:138a
Norna-Gests Þáttr and, 9:170b
parallel with Persian *Shāhnāma,* 10:249a
Vǫlsunga saga and, 10:249b
see also Þáttr af Ragnars sonum
Ragnarsdrápa. *See* Bragi Boddason the Old
Ragusa (Ragusium). *See* Dubrovnik
Ragvaldus, hymns of, 6:382b
Rāḥat al-^{c}aql. *See* Ḥamīd al-Dīn al-Kirmānī
Rahere (jester of Henry I), 4:586b
Rahewin, **10:249b–250b**
Gesta Frederici, Continuatio, 10:249b–250a
history of Frederick Barbarossa, 9:303b
Rahle, **10:250b**, 10:250a (*illus.*)
Raimbaut d'Aurenga, 3:509b, **10:250b–251a**, 10:252a
Raimbaut d'Orange. *See* Raimbaut d'Aurenga
Raimbaut de Vaqueiras, 4:87b, 10:168a, **10:251a**
Contrasto, 6:624a-b
Kalenda Maya, 10:251a
patronage by Boniface of Montferrat, 10:168a
"Savis e fols, humils et orgoillos," 6:657a
Raimbert de Paris, *Chevalerie Ogier de Danemarche,* 6:275a
Raimon de Cornet, **10:251a-b**
versa, 10:182a
Raimon de Miraval, 10:177a–178a, **10:251b–252a**
Battle of Muret and, 10:177a-b
joi as emblem of Occitanian civilization, 10:178a
loss of castle by, 10:177a-b
travels of, 12:161a
Raimon Vidal, 3:164b
Raimon Vidal de Besalú, **10:252a-b**
Castia-gilos, 10:252b
characterization of Provençal language by, 10:156a
linguistic definition of Lemosi, 10:160a
Razos de trobar, 10:252a-b
Raimond Martini. *See* Martini, Raymond
Raimondo de' Liuzzi. *See* Mondino dei Luzzi
Raimundo da Perugia, Bolognese School and, 5:567b
Raimundo of Toledo, archbishop, 11:379b
Rainald of Dassel, 5:480b, **10:252b**
adviser to Frederick I Barbarossa, 5:213a
Archpoet and, 1:449b, 450a
Two Swords doctrine and, 7:481a
Rainaldo e Lesengrino, 6:657b
Rainaldus, 9:665a–666a (*illus.*), **10:252b–253a**
Rainardo e Lesengrino, 10:314a
Rainbow
in Byzantine *Majestas Domini,* 8:54b
theory of, 7:539b
by Kamāl al-Dīn al-Fārisī, 11:87a
see also Optics, Islamic; Optics, Western European
Rainer, cardinal. *See* Paschal II, pope
Rainer of Huy, **10:253a-b**, 10:253b (*illus.*)
baptismal font, 8:495a (*illus.*)
church of St. Barthélemy and, 10:499b–500a
Rainerio Capoccio, hymns of, 6:382a
Rainier of Ponza, 3:187b
Rainier Sacconi
conversion of, 3:182a
Summa on the Cathars and the Poor of Lyons, 3:182a
Rainulf, duke of Gaeta, Sergius of Naples and, 11:264b
Rā$^{\supset}$iq, Ibn, supreme commander of Baghdad, 6:416b, 10:246a
Ra$^{\supset}$īs, 6:591a
Ra$^{\supset}$īs al-ru$^{\supset}$asā, 6:590b
Raising of Lazarus. *See* Lazarus, raising of
Raising (textile technology), 11:707b–708a (*illus.*)
gig mill, 11:708a
handle, 11:708a
Raisins, production in Mediterranean region, 5:306b, 307b
Rakes
as agricultural tools, 12:80b, 81b
Islamic, 12:84b
Rakka. *See* Raqqah
Raḳḳada, Aghlabids and, 1:71b
Raleigh, Sir Walter, influenced by *Mandeville's Travels,* 8:82a
Raleigh, William, bishop of Winchester, 7:188a, 191b
patron of Bracton, 2:356b
Ralph, abbot of Royaumont, Vincent of Beauvais and, 12:454a
Ralph of Fontfroide, 3:187b
Ram (weapon), in galley ships, 11:233b
Ramadan, 6:577a, 582a, 7:618a-b, **10:253b–255a**

  fasting regulations, 5:19b, 20a-b, 10:254a–255a
  the four sacred months and, 5:20b
  ^{c}*id al-fiṭr* festival following, 10:254b
  music for, 8:560b
  Night of Destiny (*lailat-al-qadr*), 5:20b–21a
  pre-Islamic, sacred month of, 10:253b–254a
  Salat of the Pauses, 7:618a-b
  services and prayers, 10:254b
  worship during, 5:20b
Ramādī, Yusuf al-, panegyric to Samuel ibn Nagrella, *kharja* in, 11:447a
Ramazanids, takeover of Cilician Kingdom, 1:241b
Rambam. *See* Maimonides, Moses
Rambert of Bologna, *Correctoria corruptorii Thomae* and, 12:41a, 42a
Rameau, Jean Philippe, *Traité de l'harmonie,* as end of "medieval" music theory, 8:648b
Ṙamik, **10:255a-b,** 11:307b
Ramírez, Sancho, of Aragon and Navarre. *See* Sancho I Ramírez of Aragon and Navarre
Ramiro I of Aragon, king, 2:126b
Ramiro I of Asturias-León, king, reign of, 1:626b
Ramiro of Navarre, prince, marriage to the Cid's daughter, 3:76a
Ramitha, 7:315a
Ramle, Jews in, 7:103b–104a
Rammāḥ, Ḥasan al-, on saltpeter, 11:638b
Rammelsberg mine, 8:401a
Ramon Berenguer I of Barcelona, count, reign of, 3:176a–177a
Ramon Berenguer II of Barcelona, count, reign of, 3:177a–178a
Ramon Berenguer III of Barcelona, count
  marriage to the Cid's daughter, 3:76a
  reign of, 3:178a-b
Ramon Berenguer IV of Barcelona, count, **10:255b–256a**
  administrative strengths of, 1:408b
  eastern Hispanic reconquests of, 10:255b
  founder of Catalonia, 10:255b–256a
  New Catalonian victories of, 1:408a-b
  reign of, 3:178b
  Rogerius and, 10:444a
  role in Aragon, 10:256a
Ramón Destorrents. *See* Destorrents, Ramón
Ramón Llull. *See* Lull, Ramon
Ramón de Muntaner, description of Almogávares, 1:191a
Ramon Vidal. *See* Raimon Vidal
Ramos de Pareja, Bartolomeo, *Musica practica,* 8:648b
Ramsey, John, **10:256b**
Ramsey, William, **10:256b**
  Chapter House of, 5:631a
Råmund unge, 6:312a
Ramus, Petrus, *Dialectica,* 4:171a
Rán, **10:256b–257b**
Randolph, Thomas, earl of Moray, 10:427b
Rangerius of Lucca, **10:257b**
Ranieri Fasani. *See* Fasani, Ranieri
Ranieri da Perugia, school of rhetoric, University of Bologna, 2:312b
Rank. *See* Status
Rannaigheacht, 6:534b
Ransom. *See* Diplomacy; Feudalism, feudal aids; Travel and transport, dangers of; Warfare
Ranulf Higden. *See* Higden, Ranulf
Raoul de Cambrai, 3:258b, 259b
  pipes in, 8:604a
  place of origin, 9:633b
Raoul Glaber. *See* Radulphus Glaber
Raoul de Houdenc, **10:257b–258a**
  Méraugis de Portlesguez, 1:570a, 5:284b, 10:257b–258a
  Roman des ailes, 1:188b–189a, 10:258a
  Songe d'enfer, 1:185b, 10:258a
  Vengeance Raguidel, 1:570a
Raoul de Presles, French translation of the Psalter, 2:218b
Raoul de Remi, 2:144a
Raoul of St. Trond, 8:642b
Raoul le Tourtier. *See* Radulfus Tortarius
Raoul le Tourtier/Tortaire. *See* Radulfus Tortarius
Raoul of Vermandois, count, heraldic seal of, 11:129b
Rape (land division). *See* Hundred (land division)
Raphael, *Mass of Bolsena,* 6:636a
Raphael (archangel), 1:433a
Raphael Sanzio
  Acts of the Apostles tapestry design, 11:596b
  tapestry cartoons by, 8:438b
Rapiers, 11:547b (*illus.*), 551b
Rapperswils, 11:543a
  Habsburgs and, 11:544a
Rappresentazione de Abramo e Isacco. *See* Belcari, Feo
Rappresentazione dei Santi Giovanni e Paulo. *See* Medici, Lorenzo de'
Rappresentazione del figliuol prodigo, La. *See* Castellani, Castellano
Rappresentazione sacra. *See* Italian drama, liturgical
Raptus. *See* Trance
Rapularius, 7:369a, **10:258a-b**
Raqqāda, 6:391b
Raqqah, **10:259a**
  Ayyubid ceramics at, 2:21a (*illus.*), 22a-b
  glassmaking style, 5:547a-b
  Tāhir and, 11:574a
Raqs, 8:561b
Rasā⊃il al-ḥikma, 4:296a
Rashbam, 7:30b
  as exegete, 2:212b, 4:540b–541a
  Rashi and, 10:259b–260a
Rashi, 5:511b, 7:30b, **10:259a–260a**
  on *Bava Mezia* 86a, 11:583a
  challenged by Moses Naḥmanides, 9:53b
  commentaries on the Talmud, 7:162b, 10:259a-b
  as exegete, 2:212a-b, 4:540b
  followers of, 10:259b, 260a
  glosses of, 7:174a
  Hugh of St. Victor and, 6:322a
  impact of on Jewish mentality, 10:260a
  influence of on Christian biblical exegesis, 10:260a
  on interest taking, 12:341a-b
  on marriage, 4:606b
  perush and, 11:585b
  responsum literature and, 10:339a
Rashīd, al-, Andalusian ruler, 1:195b
Rashīd al-Dīn
  Jāmi^{c} al-tawārīkh, 5:517b, 6:252b, 8:474b–475a
  on lajvard, 7:320a
  Uljaytu Khudabānda and, 12:247a
Rāshid al-Dīn Sinān, 11:137b
Rashīd al-Dīn Vatvāt, *Ḥadā'iq al-siḥr fī daqā'iq al-shi^{c}r,* 10:348b
Rāshidūn period, Islamic preaching and sermons in, 10:71a
Rashīq, Ibn, ^{c}*Umda, Al-,* on poetry, 10:346a, 346b, 347a
Raška, 11:473a
  see also Serbia
Rastislav of Great Moravia, ruler, 2:299a, 5:658a-b
  request for missionaries, 4:73b
Rastislav of Moravia, duke, Christianity and, 8:442b
Rasul, anti-Semitic incitations of, 2:192a
Rasulids, 12:724a-b
  as rulers of Yemen, 1:375b–376a
  in San^{c}a, 10:647b
Rat (council), 3:502a
Ratgar of Fulda, abbot, 5:311b
Rath Cruachain, in *Echtrae Nerai,* 6:550b
Rathbreasail, Synod of (1111), 1:470a
Rathcroghan. *See* Rath Cruachain
Rather of Liège. *See* Rather of Verona
Rather of Verona, **10:260a-b**
  hagiography and, 6:314b
  Praeloquia, 10:16a, 260b
Ratification
  of diplomatic documents, 4:213a–214a
  Ratihabitio clause, 4:213b
Rationale. *See* Vestments, liturgical, insignia
Rationale divinorum officiorum. *See* Durand, Guillaume
Ratpert of St. Gall, 7:363a, **10:260b–261a**
  De casibus monasterii S. Galli, 10:260b
  hymns of, 6:381b
  Notker Balbulus and, 9:187b
  Tuotilo and, 12:225a-b
Ratramnus of Corbie, 5:638b–639a, **10:261a**
  Berengar and, 2:188a
  compared with St. Radbertus of Corbie, 9:446b
  Contra Graecorum opposita, 10:261a, 12:190b
  De anima ad Odonem Bellovacensem, 9:586a, 10:271b
  De corpore et sanguine domini, 10:261a
  De nativitate Christi, 10:261a

Ratramnus of Corbie (*cont.*)
De praedestinatione dei, 10:261a
nature of the soul, 9:586a
Rats. *See* Rodents
Ratsherrn, 3:502a
Rauḍa, **10:261a–262b**
carpet design of, 10:261b–262b (*illus.*)
fourfold *chārbāgh* design, 10:261b
Rauf Coilȝear, 8:332a
Rav. See Rabbinate; Scholarship, Jewish
Rav Ashi. *See* Ashi
Ravanica Monastery, 11:181a, 188a (*illus.*)
Ravano dalle Carceri, Negroponte and, 7:376b
Ravenna, **10:262b–265a**
architecture of, 10:263a–264b
captured (540), 2:165a
churches
dome decorations of, 4:359a
early Christian furnishings for, 4:361b
decline of, 12:110b
development of Venice and, 12:383a
early Christian art, examples of, 4:352a
exarchate of, 4:529b–530a
conquered by the Lombard king Aistulf, 9:501b
fall of (751), 12:383b
Gothic building program, 9:290b
mausoleums of, 12:466b
mosaics at, 10:113b
Pepin I's conquest of, 7:4a
relations with
papacy, 10:521b
Rome, 10:521b
under the Ostrogoths, 10:263a-b
see also S. Vitale (church: Ravenna)
Ravenna Cathedral, 10:262b
marble ambo of Agnellus, 4:361b
Ravenna map (7th cent.), 4:553b
Raverti, Matteo, **10:265a**
St. George sculpture, 10:265b (*illus.*)
Ravina I (*d.* 422), Babylonian Talmud and, 11:583a, 583b
Ravina II (*d.* 499 or 501), Babylonian Talmud and, 11:583a, 583b
Rawād, Ibn al-, Tabrīz and, 11:570b
Rawk, 6:592a
Rawlinson MS B 502, 6:522b, 545b
Rawlinson MS G 109, 6:320a
Rawwadids
in Dwin, 1:482b
Kurds and, 7:310b
vs. Shaddadids, 11:217a
Raᵓy, 11:218b, 219b
Ray, etymology, 10:661a
Raymond IV of Toulouse, count, 12:91b
in crusades, 4:34b, 35b, 36b
Languedoc and, 7:339a
Lateran IV and, 3:640a-b
Urban II and, 3:449b–450a
Raymond V of Toulouse, count, 7:339a, 12:90b–91a
writings on Catharism, 6:196b
Raymond VI of Toulouse, count, 7:339a
alliances of, 3:187a-b
excommunication of, 3:188a, 188b
fall of, 3:188a–189a
Peter of Castelnau and, 12:91b
as troubadour patron, 10:251b–252a
vs. Albigensians, 7:339b
Raymond VII of Toulouse, count, 7:339b
inquisition and, 6:486a, 486b–487a
joining of anti-French alliance by, 10:174b
peace with papal forces, 3:189a-b
persecutions of Cathars, 3:199a
Treaty of Paris and, 12:91b–92a
war with Louis IX, 3:190a
Raymond de Béziers, translation of *Calila e Digna,* 3:31b
Raymond of Burgundy, 10:39a-b
Raymond of Capua, 4:253b, 9:14b
Raymond of Fitero, 3:16b
Raymond Gayrard of Toulouse. *See* Gayrard, Raymond
Raymond Lully. *See* Lull, Ramon
Raymond de Mur, **10:265a-b**
Guimera altarpiece, 10:265a–266a (*illus.*)
Raymond de Nogaret, 11:607b
Raymond of Peñafort, St., **10:266a–267a,** 11:407a
as canonist and moralist, 4:247a-b
on casuistry, 3:153b
Decretals, 4:247b, 5:671a-b
Decretals of Gregory IX and, 12:456a
Gregoriana, 7:428a
on Jews, 7:77a
legal maxims and, 8:232a
Liber extra, 7:416a-b
novellae additions to, 7:416b
on penance, 6:449a
revision of Dominican constitutions, 4:244b
on sexuality, 7:92b
Summa de poenitentia, 3:153b, 8:316b, 10:266b
theological dialogue of, 11:380a
Raymond of St. Gilles, Tancred and, 11:589b
Raymond of Toledo, archbishop, 5:422b
literary patronage, Aristotelian translations, 11:689a
Raymond de Vineis, 6:382b
Raymondins (counts of Toulouse), 12:90b, 91a–92a
Raymundina. See Raymond of Peñafort, St., *Summa de poenitentia*
Rayna potentissima, 6:662a
Rayonnant Style. *See* Gothic architecture
Rays (*Raja* sp.), fishing of, 5:70a
Rayy
captured, 7:306b
daᶜwā in, 6:615b
Shīᶜa and, 11:228a
Razdan. *See* Zanga River
Raźden, St., 5:414a
Rāzī, Abū Bakr Muḥammad ibn Zakarīya al-, **10:267a–268b**
al-Ḥāwī (*Liber continens*), 3:574a
cosmogony, 10:267b–268a
Ḥāwī, al-, 10:267a
Liber Almansoris, 8:258b
Liber continens, Ferragut's translation of, 12:135b
Liber secretorum, 1:136a-b
classification of mineral substances, 1:136a-b
medical writings, 10:267a
philosophical writings, 10:267b
references to Māsarjuwayh, 11:92b
transmigration and prophetic revelations, 10:268a
Turba philosophorum, 1:136b, 141a
works of translated by Gerard of Cremona, 8:249a
Razón de amor, **10:268a–269b**
secular song embedded in, 11:448a
Razors, 2:149a, 149b
for parchment preparation, 12:700a
Razos, compared with *vidas,* 12:410a
Razos de trobar. See Raimon Vidal de Besalú
Razzāz al-Jazarīᶜ, Ibn al-, water clock designs, 11:642a
Re Enzo, *scuola siciliana* and, 6:624b–625a, 643a
Reading
in classical Rome, 7:598a, 599b
patterns of among monks, 7:599b
Reading Abbey, *Sumer Is Icumen In* and, 11:505a
Reading Rota. See Sumer Is Icumen In
Realgestech, 1:533a
Reali di Francia, I. See Andrea da Barberino
Realism, **10:269a–272b**
conceptualism and, 3:510a
universalia ante res, 10:269a–270b, 272a
universalia in rebus, 10:269a, 270a–272a
via moderna and, 12:407a
Walter Burley on, 2:432b–433a
Wyclif and, 12:707a-b, 709a
see also Universals
Ream (unit of measure), 12:593b
Reason and Sensuality. See Lydgate, John
Reaya
in Ottoman social structure, 9:309b
military service, 9:307a, 307b
Rebab, 8:602 (*illus.*)
Rebais, fairs, 4:591a
Rebec, 8:561b, 562b, 602 (*illus.*), 606b
Jerome of Moravia and, 8:645a
Rebellions
urban, 12:317b
see also Jacquerie; Peasants' rebellions; Peasants' Revolt (1381); Zanj
Recanati, Menahem, 3:3a
Recared, Visigothic king, 12:471b
conversion of, 9:147b
renunciation of Arianism, 3:344a, 676b
Recceswinth, Visigothic king
crown of, 12:467a, 492b (*illus.*)
law code of, 7:470a-b, 12:472a
S. Juan de Baños and, 12:465b
Recco, Nicoloso da, 4:558b
Recension. *See* Gloss; Translation and translators
Recettes. See Guyenne (France); Taxation, French
Rechiarius, 10:36a

Rechtfertigungsschrift. See Eckhart, Meister
Reciting tone. *See* Psalm tones
Récits d'un ménestrel de Reims, 3:332b, 6:658a
Reclamation of land, **10:272b–279b**
central and eastern Europe, 10:273b
folk culture and, 8:27a-b
High Middle Ages, scale of change, 10:273a
Italy, 12:576b
Mediterranean world and Asia, 10:273a
Netherlands, 12:577b, 579a
novales land, 10:273b
patterns of land use
abandonment, 10:274b–275a, 277b
early period, 10:274a–276b
the great expansion, 10:276b–279a
permanent fields (*agri*), 10:274a–276a, 277a-b
saltus or *wastina* (wasteland), 10:275a–276a, 277a
silva or *nemus* (wilderness), 10:275a, 276a
swidden, 10:274b–275a, 278a-b
socioeconomic effects of, 10:273a–274a, 278a–279a
villages and, 12:444b
see also Tools, agricultural
Reclus de Mollien
Miserere, 9:639a
Roman de carité, 9:639a
Réconfort de Madame de Fresne. See La Sale, Antoine de
Reconquest, 6:572b, 8:444b, **10:279b–280b**
Basques and, 2:126b
Catholic Monarchs and, 11:422a
cavalry in, 3:203a
Cluniac reform and, 3:356b
ideological foundations for, 10:280a
Islamic administration and, 6:591a
kingship theories and, 7:269b
Mozarabic commitment to, 8:511b
Mudejars after, 11:377a
in *Siete infantes de Lara,* 11:409a
villages and, 12:443a, 444a
Recorder, 8:604b
Records, administrative. *See* Administrative records
Recort. See Turell, Gabriel
Recreation for the Person Who Longs to Traverse the Horizons, A. See Idrīsī, al-, *Nuzhat al-mushtāq fī 'kht irāk al-āfāqi*
Recta, 8:628a
Rectangulus, 1:613a-b
Rector, as a clerical leader of a parish, 9:414b–415a
Recueil des histoires de Troie. See Lefèvre, Raoul
Red. *See* Archil; Henna; Kermes; Madder; Scarlet
Red Book of Hergest, 1:566a, 577a, 12:606a
audience compiled for, 12:613a
Mabinogi, 7:703a, 12:610a
Red Book of Ossory, 7:375b
hymns and, 6:380a
Red plague. *See* Plagues, European, smallpox
Red Sea
geography, 11:245b–246a
navigation of, 5:394a, 9:85b–87a
Nile and, 9:138b
Red Tomb of Marāgha, 6:602a
Reddition, in baptismal rite, 3:675b
Rede
in Middle High German literature
1220/1230–1300, 8:353a-b, 355a
1300–1430, 8:357a-b
1430–1500, 8:359b, 361b
Redemptus, on Isidore of Seville, 6:563b
Rederijkers, 4:322a-b
Redolfo (son of Engelar), 7:24a
Reductionism, Ockham and, 9:156b, 210b
Reductorium morale. See Bersuire, Pierre
Reed pipe, 8:563a
Rees (unit of measure), 12:593b
Reeve, **10:280b–281a**, 12:440b
estate management and, 4:514a
justice administration and, 10:280b
manorial, 10:281a
see also Bailiff; Sheriff
Refectory, **10:281a-b**
Reform
idea of, **10:281b–288b**
Augustine's *City of God,* 10:283b–284a, 285a
the "golden age" ideal and, 10:281b
Gregorian church, 10:287b–288b
John Chrysostom on, 7:122b–123a
pre-Gregorian, 10:260b
propaganda for, 10:139b
in reform papacy, 9:375b–379a
relic authentication and, 10:298b
theology and, 10:284a-b
imperial
German, 5:493a
Reichskonzilien, 10:331a
individual
Augustine on, 10:283b–284a, 285a
baptismal regeneration and, 10:282b–283a
Greek concepts of, 10:283a
patristic era, 10:282a–284a, 288b
renewal concepts of, 10:282a-b
Western concepts of, 10:283a–284a
institutional, 10:284b–285b
church, 10:287b–288b
monastic, 10:285a–287b
900-1054, 3:347b–348a
1054-1305, 3:354a–355b
architectural revival and, 10:309a
Benedictine, 10:285b–286b
Carthusian exemption from, 3:119b
Cistercian, 10:286b–287a
Cluniac, 10:286a-b
papal
900–1054, 3:348a-b
1054–1305, 3:351a–354a
royal
900–1054, 3:347a–349a
1054–1305, 3:355b–357a
secular, *pacem reformare,* 10:281b
see also Lutheranism; Protestantism
Reform, church. *See* Church reform
Reform of the Soul's Power, The. See Gerard Zerbolt of Zutphen
Reformatio in melius, 3:347a
Reformatio Sigismundi. See Sigismund of Germany, emperor
Reformation
impact on drama
in France, 4:266a
in Germany, 4:270b–271a, 272a
see also Protestantism
Refraction of light, discussed by Robert Grosseteste, 7:538b–539a
Refrain, villancico and, 12:447a
Refugees, Islamic world, plague, 9:685b
Refundición de las mocedades de Rodrigo. See Mocedades de Rodrigo
Refutatio et eversio. See Nikephoros I, patriarch
Refutation of Jewish Disbelief. See Gerónimo de Santa Fé
Refutation of the Koran. See William of Tripoli
Refutation of the Principles of the Christians. See Crescas, Ḥasdai
Refutation of Sects. See Eznik of Kołb, *Ełc ałandoc*
Regalia. *See* Costume
Regalia, imperial. *See* Imperial regalia
Regalia, right of, *congé d'élire* affecting, 3:537a
Regalia of St. Peter, 9:384a-b
Regenbogen, 8:358a
Regensburg
bridge at, 10:413b, 416a, 416b, 417b
origins of, 5:458a
taxes for improvement of roads and bridges, 10:418a
see also Castra Regina; St. Emmeram (monastery: Regensburg)
Regensburg, Burggraf von. *See* Meinloh von Sevelingen
Regensburg Cathedral, west facade of entrance porch, 10:530a (*illus.*)
Reggimento e costumi de donna. See Francesco da Barberino
Reggio di Calabria, Roger I and, 10:440a
Regimen of Health, 2:149a
Regimen sanitatis Salernitanum, 2:245b, 7:366a, **10:289a**
in medical practice, 8:252b
see also Arnald of Villanova; Pseudo-Aristotle
Regiment de la cosa pública, El. See Eiximenis, Francesc
Reginald of Abingdon, abbot, 1:258a
Reginald of Canterbury, **10:289a-b**
election of, 7:338a
Latin epic on St. Malchus, 1:254b
Vita sancti Malchi, 7:363a, 373b
Reginald of Châtillon, vs. Saladin, 4:39b
Reginald, earl of Cornwall, castle at Tintagel and, 12:60b
Reginar of Lorraine, count, 5:508a-b
Reginn (saga character), in *Reginsmál,* 4:581a, 581b
Regino of Prüm (Regino Prumiensis), 7:406b–407a, **10:289b–290a**, 11:363a
Chronica, 10:289b–290a

Regino of Prüm (Regino Prumiensis) (*cont.*)
Cistercians and, 8:643a
Dialogus and, 8:640b
Epistola de armonica institutione, 8:639b–640a
Incipiunt octo toni, 12:69b
Libri duo de synodalibus causis et disciplinis ecclesiasticis, 9:490a-b, 10:289b–290a
on music, 8:581b
Tonarius, 10:289b
Reginsmál, 5:678a, **10:290a–291b**
Fáfnir and, 4:581a-b
Sigurd and, 11:289b
Vǫlsunga saga and, 12:489a
Regiomontanus (Johann Müller), 1:613b, 11:103a
Archimedes and, 1:436a, 439a, 439b
interest in torquetum, 11:98b
on sundials, 3:28b
Register. See Polemius Silvius, *Laterculus*
Registers, 3:120a
in chancery, 3:252b–253a
Registrum multorum auctorum. See Hugo von Trimberg
Registrum Petri Diaconi. See Peter the Deacon of Monte Cassino
Regnault de Cormont, 1:234b–235a, **10:291b**
Regnum transferre. See Translation of empire
Regola del governo di cura famigliare. See Dominici, Giovanni
Régres Nostre Dame. See Huon le Roi de Cambrai
Regret de Guillaume, comte de Haynneau, Le. See Jean de la Motte
Regrets de la dame infortunée. See Jean Lemaire de Belges
Regula magistri, 4:222a
Regula sancti Benedicti and, 2:169a-b
Regula mixta, 2:170a
Regula monachorum. See Isidore of Seville, St.
Regula pastoralis. See Gregory I (the Great), pope, *Pastoral Care*
Regula Sancti Benedicti. See Benedictine Rule
Regulae de contrapuncto. See Antonius de Leno
Regulae iuris. See Maxims, legal
Regulae morales. See Basil the Great of Caesarea, St.
Regulae de numerorum abaci rationibus. See Sylvester II, pope
Regulae pastoralis. See Gregory I (the Great), pope
Regulae rhythmicae. See Guido of Arezzo
Regulae solvendi sophismata. See Heytesbury, William
Regulae supra contrapunctum. See Hothby, John
Regular sequence. *See* Sequence
Regularis concordia. See Dunstan, St.
Regularis concordia. See Ethelwold
Regule de arte musica. See Guy d'Eu
Rehinlik, 3:679a
Reich
definition of, 5:494a
imperial ideal in Germany, 5:494a-b
Reichenau, 10:101b, 102b
manuscript illumination and, 8:107b
Reichenau Glossary, explanation of biblical terms, 5:221b
Reichenau Gospels of Otto III, 8:107b
Reichenau (monastery)
Carolingian renaissance and, 11:526b
Swiss Confederation and, 11:544b
Reichenhall
saltworks, 10:629b
control by Salzburg bishops, 10:630a
Reichersberg, Chronicle of, 5:424b–425a
Reichsfürstinnen, 12:685a
Reichskammergericht. See Holy Roman Empire, Imperial Cameral Court
Reichskirche, 12:683a
Reichskonzilien, concept of, 10:331a
Reichskreise. See Holy Roman Empire, representative assemblies
Reichsregiment. See Holy Roman Empire, representative assemblies
Reichsritterschaft, 11:528a
Reichstag. *See* Representative Assemblies, German
Reigenlied, 3:116a
Reiher, Der, synopsis of, 8:128b
Reimgebete. See Pia dictamina
Reimreden. See German literature
Reinaert I, 2:141b
Reinaert II, 2:142a
Reinaerts Histoire, 10:314b
Reinalds rímur, internal rhymes in, 10:404b–405a
Reincarnation
in Druzism, 9:3a-b
in Nuṣayrī theology, 9:4a-b
Reine Sebile, see also Sibille
Reinfrid von Braunschweig, **10:291b–292b**
Reinhart Fuchs. See Heinrich der Glîchezaere
Reinke de Vos, 2:142a, 8:360b, 10:314b
Reinmar der Alte, 8:414a, **10:292b–294b**
compared with Meinloh von Sevelingen, 8:265b
crusade poetry of, 10:294a
feud of, 8:351a
Gottfried von Strassburg's eulogy of, 10:292a
hôhiu minne in songs, 12:536b, 537a
lyric poetry of, 5:439a–440a
Mädchenlieder, 5:440a
origin and possible occupations of, 10:293a–294a
praises of, 5:438a-b
school of, 6:141b
secular love poetry (*Töne*), 10:292b–294a
Wechsel, 5:440a
Reinmar von Hagenau. *See* Reinmar der Alte
Reinmar von Zweter, 8:414a, **10:294b–296b**
Frederick II of Austria and, 9:93a
gnomic verse, 10:295a-b
Leich, 10:295a-b
"Reis glorios." *See* Giraut de Bornelh
Reis, Quatre livre des. See Quatre livres des reis, Li
Reis van Sinte Brendaen, 4:318b
Relics, **10:296a–299b**
ambulatories and, 1:234a
arma Christi and, 1:469b
of Armenian saints, 1:518a, 518b
authentication, 10:298a-b, 12:154a
in Celtic church, 7:615a
ceremonial discoveries of, inventions of saints, 12:144a
in church dedication, 4:130b–131a
commerce in
local communities and, 10:297b–298a
saints' bodies and penitential instruments, 10:298b–299a
translation of saints and, 12:144b–145a
corporeal vs. contact, 2:362b
Deusdona's, relic-procurer, 1:337a
enshrinement in churches, 4:130b
Holy Lance, 5:373a
in hymns, 6:384a
incense and, 6:432a
of Magi, 4:498b
of Rome, 9:658a-b
Russian pilgrimage and, 9:653b–654a
tours of, 12:154a-b
in treatment of insanity, 6:492a
veneration, 6:10a
criticism of, 10:296b, 298a–299a
spiritual and historical roots, 10:296a
Western European pilgrimage and, 9:654b–655a, 656a-b, 658a, 661a
zandanījī and, 12:738b
see also Altarpieces; Ampulla; Crypt; Mandylion; names of specific relics, *e.g., Brandeum;* Holy Lance; Maphorion; Vernicle
Relieving arch. *See* Arch
Religious instruction, **10:300a–302**
of adult laity
catechumens, 10:300a
required topics of, 10:300b, 301b–302b
for baptism, 10:300a
by Dominicans and Franciscans, 10:301a
by parish priests
cura animarum and, 10:300a, 301b
guides for, 10:300b–301a
literature, 10:301a–302a
Ignorantia sacerdotum, 10:300b
summae confessorum, 10:300b
oral sermons and, 10:300b–301a
in the parish, 9:414b, 416b
vernacular, *ABC des simples gens. See* Gerson, John
visual arts and, 10:301a-b
Biblia pauperum, 10:302a
see also Children; Confession; Preaching
Religious orders. *See* Mendicant orders; particular orders; Women, religious orders of

Reliquary, **10:302b–303a**, 10:302b (*illus.*)
brachium, 10:302a
early Christian, decoration of, 4:361b
Einhard's triumphal arch, 10:306b
invention of eyeglasses and, 11:650b
silk wrapping, 11:717b (*illus.*)
Stavelot Abbey Triptych, 10:500 (*illus.*), 12:198b
of the True Cross, 4:435a (*illus.*), 438a
see also Lipsanotheca
Reliquary, chasse, 5:316b
Reliquiae. See Relics
Rellach, John, 4:246a
Remanence, Wyclif's doctrine of, 6:367a
Remaniement, 3:260b
Remarriage. *See* Marriage, multiple
Rembert, St. *See* Rimbert, St.
Remède de fortune. See Machaut, Guillaume de
Remedia. See Ovid
Remedium amoris. See Ovid
Remedius of Chur, *Collectio canonum,* 7:406a
Remigio de' Girolami, as defender of Thomism, 12:42a
Remigius of Auxerre (Remigius Autissiodorensis), 3:433a-b, 4:542b, **10:303a-b**
commentaries, *De nuptiis,* 8:156a
Commentum in Martianum Capellam, 10:270a–271a
Disciplinarum libri IX and, 8:637a
Epistola de armonica institutione and, 8:639b
Gerbert of Aurillac and, 8:640a
Hucbald and, 6:317a
John Scottus Eriugena and, 10:303a
on liturgy, 7:629a
Remigius de Fécamp, bishop of Lincoln, 7:583a
Remontrance, legislative power of the French king and, 9:420a
Remorse of Judas, 8:661a
Rémundar saga keisarasonar, **10:303b–304b**, 10:394b, 395b
analogues to *Tristrams saga,* 10:304a
Mírmanns saga and, 8:432b
plagiarisms in, 10:304a
Renaissance
astrology during and after, 1:608b–609b
precursors of, Cavallini, 3:198b
revival of classical languages, 12:141a
see also Italian Renaissance
Renaissance architecture, triumphal arch wall tombs, 12:205b
Renaissance Latin. *See* Neo-Latin language
Renaissances, in art. *See* Art, renaissances and revivals; Carolingian renaissance; Palaiologoi
Renard le contrefait, 2:141b, 6:657b
Renard de Cormont. *See* Regnault de Cormont
Renard the Fox, 2:140a, 141b–142a, **10:312a–315a**
branching of tales, 5:258a
characterization, 5:257b–258a
fables of
Alsatian, 10:314a
Dutch, 10:314b–315a
English, 10:314a-b
Flemish, 10:314b
French, 10:312a–314a
in Italian popular poetry, 6:657b
as literary parody, 5:258a
Marie de France and, 4:572b
Modena Cathedral and, 10:501a
Roman de Renart
Picard origins, 9:635b
sources for, 9:635a
trompeur trompé theme, 9:635b
sources for, 5:257b
see also Ysengrimus
Renard le nouvel, 2:141b
Renardie. See Renard the Fox
Renart le Bestourné. See Rutebeuf
Renart le Contrefait, 10:314b
Renart, Jean
Escoufle, 9:635a
Guillaume de Dôle, folk themes, 9:635a
Lai de l'ombre, 9:635a
Renart le Nouvel. See Gielée of Lille
Renaud II of Burgundy, count, 2:424b
Renaud III of Burgundy, count, 2:424b
Renaud de Montauban, 2:128a, 10:391b
in Carolingian legends, 8:225b
as a source for *Mágus saga jarls,* 8:45a
Renaut, *Galeran de Bretagne* and, 5:341a-b
Renaut de Beaujeu, **10:315a-b**
Li biaus descouneus, 1:570a, 10:315a-b, 12:657a
René I of Anjou, king of Naples, 1:253b
Book of Hours of Isabella of Portugal, 5:363a
Livre du cueur d'amours espris, 5:359 (*illus.*), 364b, 10:551b–552a (*illus.*)
troubadours and, 7:341b
René of Sicily, king, chariots and, 12:376b, 378a
Renier van Thienen, brass paschal candelabrum by, 8:286b
Renner, Der. See Hugo von Trimberg
Rennewart. See Ulrich von Türheim
Rennhut, 1:533a
Renntartsche, 1:533a
Renout van Montalbaen, 4:318b
Renovare. See Reform, idea of
Répartition. See Taxation
Repentance. *See* Penance
Repertorium bibliographicum. See Hain, Ludwig
Repingdon, Philip, Wyclif and, 12:709b
Replacement ratios (population), 4:139a
Reply of Friar Daw Topias to Jack Upland, 10:435a, 437a
Reportata Parisiensa. See Duns Scotus, John
Reportatio, 10:78a
Reportatio. See Ockham, William of
Reportatio Cantabridgensis. See Duns Scotus, John
Repoussé, 5:410b–411a, **10:315b**
Pepin reliquary, 10:302b (*illus.*)
see also Enamel
Representative assemblies
Danish. *See* Danehof
English. *See* Parliament, English
French, 9:554b, **10:316a–328a**
Abrégé des États, 10:327a
archives establishment, 10:326b–327a
Assemblées des Commis des États, 10:327a
bailiwick, 10:323a, 325a, 327a
central, 10:317b–324a
Dauphiné, 4:109b
escarton, 10:325a
in Languedoc, 7:341a,b
monarchy and, 10:326b–327b
origins of, 10:316a–317b
Protestant, 10:316a
secret ballot adoption, 10:324b
seneschal, 10:323a
taille and, 11:578b, 579a
taxation powers, 11:621a, 621b
viguerie, 10:325a
see also Estates General
French officials of the
clerks, 10:326b–327a
deputies, 10:323b, 324b–325a, 327a
élus, 10:318a-b, 319b, 322a-b, 327a
proctors, 10:317a
syndics, 10:326b–327a
treasurers, 10:326b–327a
French regional, 10:316a, 321a, 324a–327b
duties of, 10:326b
growth patterns of, 10:326b–327b
Holy Roman Empire provinces, 10:320a, 321a
German, **10:328a–334b**
bishoprics and, 10:332a–333b
cathedral chapters, 10:328b, 332b–333a
development factors, 10:328b–329b
Electoral Palatinate and, 10:329a, 333a
estates unions (*Einungen*), 10:332a
generale parlamentum, 10:330a
Golden Bull and, 10:329b–330a
Imperial Peace and, 10:329a
political world and, 10:333b–334a
principalities (*Landtage*), 10:332a–334a
tricameral colleges (*curiae*), 10:329b, 331b
government centralization and, 12:160a
Hungarian, 6:335b–336a
Andrew III and, 6:343a
Angevins and, 6:344a
Hunyadi and, 6:347b
Icelandic. *See* Althing
Irish. *See* Parliament, Irish
Norwegian, 9:183b–184a
Novgorodian, 9:194a–195a, 197a
Polish diet, 9:727b, 728b
Roman, 10:523b
Scandinavian, 9:185b
Althing, 12:423b
Scottish. *See* Parliament, Scottish
Spanish. *See* Cortes
Swedish, 11:533b

Representative assemblies (*cont.*)
Western European, development of, 10:328a-b, 333b–334b
see also Parliament
Reproach of the Gentiles. See Profiat Duran of Perpignan
Republic, The. See Plato
Republicanism
Marsilius on, 4:132b–133a
Novgorod, 9:193a–195a
Requests, Court of, 4:503a
Requiem aeternam, 4:120a
Requiem mass. *See* Mass
Rerebrace, 1:525b, 530b, 534a (*illus.*)
Reredos, 1:222a, **10:334b–335a,** 11:117a, 487b–488a (*illus.*)
Rerum familiarium libri. See Petrarch
Rerum memorandarum libri. See Petrarch
Rerum senilium libri. See Petrarch
Rerum vulgarium fragmenta. See Petrarch
Res contra naturam, in Galenic medical theory, 8:250a
Res naturales, in Galenic medical theory, 8:250a
Res non naturales, in Galenic medical theory, 8:250a, 252b
Rescripts, **10:335a**
see also Decretals
Reseda luteola. See Weld (dye)
Reseisin. *See* Seisin, Disseisin
Resende, Garcia de, 3:63b
Reservation of the sacrament, 1:223b, **10:335a–336a**
Reshit Ḥokhmah. See Abraham ben Meïr ibn Ezra
Resistance theories, in Western European political theory, 10:17a-b
Reson and Sensuallyte. See Lydgate, John
Respiratory diseases. *See* Plagues
"Responder voi' a dona Frixa," 6:657a, 658a
Responsa. See Samuel ben ha-Yatom
Responsory, 9:692a-b, **10:336a–337a**
Divine Office and, 4:224b–225a
neuma and, 9:109a
performance of, 10:336a-b
rhyme scheme of, 10:372b
texts and music of, 10:336b
in tonaries, 12:70b
see also Hypakoai; Plainsong; Rhymed offices; Tones, reading and dialogue
Responsum literature
Islamic. *See* Fatwā
Jewish, **10:337a–339b,** 11:584b–586b
after the decline of Babylonian academies, 10:338b–339b
by Rashi, 10:260a
description of, 10:337b
during the Gaonic period, 10:337b–338b
rabbinate and, 10:243b
sheᵓelot u-teshuvot, 10:243b
see also Rabbinate
Respublica Christiana, 10:20a
"Ressurrexi," 6:498b
Restaurare. See Reform, idea of
Resting-Places of the Saints, 6:62a
Restituta, St., translation of remains of from Ischia to Naples, 9:57b
Resurrection
centrality of in the Byzantine church, 7:611b
conception of affected by Black Death, 2:266b
meaning of, 4:365b–366a
Pharisees and, 11:556b
see also Anastasis; Easter
Resurrection cycle, **10:339b–340b**
in art, of Master of Wittingau, 12:668a (*illus.*)
in Byzantine iconography, 10:340a
in Early Christian mosaic, 12:222b
early images of, 10:339b–340a
see also Noli me tangere
Resurrection, Islamic, **10:340b–342a**
centrality of in Koran, 10:341a
different interpretations of, 10:341a-b
doctrine of, 10:340b–341a
Seven Sleepers of Ephesus and, 11:213a
see also Paradise, Islamic concept of
Resurrection Office, 1:517a
Retable, **10:342a**
of Huguet, 6:328b (*illus.*)
in Museo de Arte de Cataluña, 10:505b
Rethorici colores. See Onulf of Speyer
Retrait lignager, 6:457a, 11:678b
Retsina, in wine, 12:649a
Rettorica. See Latini, Brunetto
Reuchlin, Johann, 11:51a
Hebrew language study by, 3:13a
Reuwich, Erhard, Master of the Housebook and, 6:299a
Reveal (in door jamb), 7:45b
Revelación de San Pablo, 11:439b
Revelation, Book of. *See* Bible, *Apocalypse* of St. John
Revelation to Eldefonsus, 7:627b (*illus.*)
Revelationes. See Brigit (Brigid), St.
Revelations. See Ebner, Margaret
Revenue, royal. *See* Finance, royal
Reverdie, **10:342b**
Reverter, general, 1:200a
"Reviho-te Nanan," 7:178b
Revival of the Religious Sciences. See Ghazālī, al-
Revocatio technique, 5:436a
Revolts. *See* Peasants' rebellions
Revolving Mausoleum. *See* Döner Kümbet
Rex caeli Domine, 11:165b
Rex gloriae. See Clement V, pope
Rex Iudaeorum, 7:90b, 91a
Rex pacificus, 7:267b
Rexach, Juan, **10:342a**
compared with Jaime Baçó, 10:342b
St. Ursula altarpiece, 10:342b, 343a (*illus.*)
Reyes Católicos. *See* Ferdinand V of Castile, king; Isabella of Castile, queen
Reykdœla saga, 4:613b, 618a, **10:342b–344a**
Reykjarfjarðarbók, 11:498a
Reyna Pastor de Togneri, 11:376a
Reynaert de Vos, 10:314b
Reynard the Fox
Caxton's translation of, 8:415b
see also Renard the Fox
Reynes, Henry of. *See* Henry of Reynes
Reynolds, Walter, *Vox populi, vox Dei,* 4:483b
Rhadanites, 11:249b
Rhaeto-Romanic dialects, 6:435b
Rhain ap Cadwgan, king of Dyfed, 4:329b
Rhandeia, Treaty of (63), 5:405a
Rhazes. *See* Rāzī, Abū Bakr Muḥammad ibn Zakarīya al-
Rheged, kingdom of. *See* Urien Rheged
Rheims
False Decretals and, 4:125b
inns in, 6:469b, 472a-b
Rheims Cathedral, 1:430b, 3:565a, **10:344a-b**
Annunciation at, 5:622b
arcade of, 5:592a (*illus.*), 599a
choir, design of, 7:50a-b
column figures, Visitation Group, 10:309b–310a (*illus.*)
construction of, 7:677a
coronation of French kings in, 10:344b
impact of, 5:623b–624a
mullions, 8:530b (*illus.*)
Presentation Portal at, 5:617b, 619b (*illus.*), 622b
reconstruction of, 1:431a
stained glass in, 5:549b (*illus.*), 552a
style of, 5:623a
Virgin of the Visitation at, 5:623b–624a
west facade by Bernard of Soissons, 10:344a (*illus.*)
west portal, 12:478b
see also Bernard of Soissons; Libergier, Hugues; Robert de Coucy
Rheims, Council of (1119), 3:636a-b
Irnerius and, 6:555a
Vital of Savigny and, 12:479b
Rheims Penitential, 9:489b
on public and private penance, 9:488b
Rheims, Synod of (1148), 3:94b
Rheinfelden family, 11:527a-b, 538a
Rhenish League
founding of, 5:461b
in German towns, 5:461b–462a
Rhens, Declaration of (1338), 4:428b
Rheticius of Autun, St., **10:344b**
Rheticus (astronomer, 16th century), 1:609a
Rhetoric
ancient Roman, 10:351a–353a
Byzantine, in Theophylaktos Simokattes' *Histories,* 12:24b–25a
definition of the term, 10:351a
Western European
trivium study of, 12:206a-b
see also Victorinus, Gaius Marius
Rhetoric. See Aristotle
Rhetoric, Arabic, **10:345a–347b**
in the 10th and 11th centuries, 10:345b–347b
art prose and, 10:347b
euphony, 10:347a-b
as a formal discipline, 10:347b

influence of
on Hebrew rhetoric, 10:348a
on Western rhetoric, 10:357b
Islamic preaching and sermons, 10:70b–73b
literary, 10:346a–347a
needs of Islamic bureaucracy and, 10:345a-b
rhetorical devices, 10:347a
Rhetoric, Byzantine, 9:697a, **10:349a–351a**
epithalamioi, 10:350a
eucharisterios, 10:350a
influence on other genres, 2:505a-b
monody and, 10:350a
panegyric and, 10:349b
preaching and, 10:350a-b
presbeutikos, 10:350a
prosphonetikos, 10:350a
traditional Greek oratory and, 10:349a-b
see also Literacy, Byzantine
Rhetoric, Hebrew, **10:348a–349a**
Rhetoric, Persian, **10:348a–349a**
Rhetoric, Western European, **10:351a–364b**
Arabic influences on, 10:357b
ars arengandi, 2:320b
ars dictaminis, 2:320a, 320b
ars poetriae, 10:359b–360b
ars praedicandi, 10:360b–363b, 363b–364a
Augustine and, 10:353a-b, 361b–362a
chambers of rhetoric, 4:322a-b
development
5th to 11th centuries, 10:353a–355b
15th century, 10:363b–364a
dialectic and, 10:355a, 357a
dictamen, 4:174a
in early Christian era, 1:181a
"encyclopedists" and, 10:353b–354b
figures of speech and figures of thought, 10:352a
grammar and, 10:353a
Greek influences, 10:357b
historical, 6:260a-b
instruction in, 6:260b, 262b, 263a-b
in *Livres dou trésor,* 7:383a
parts of
according to Cicero, 10:351b
according to Quintilianus, 10:352b
preaching and sermon literature, 10:75b–81b
razos de trobar, 10:252a-b
rhyme and, 7:372a
study of Latin literature and, 7:359b
survival of ancient traditions, 10:355b–357b
three medieval genres of, 10:355b, 357b–363b
use of allegory and, 1:179a
Welsh. *See* Areithian prose, prose rhetorics
see also Ars dictaminis
Rhetorica ad Herennium
ars poetriae and, 10:359b, 360a
influence of, 10:353b, 355b–356a
on Isidore of Seville, 10:354b
wrongly attributed to Cicero, 10:352a
Rhetorica antiqua sive Boncompagnus. See Boncompagno of Signa
Rhetorica novissima. See Boncompagno of Signa
Rhetorica vetus. See Cicero, Marcus Tullius, *De inventione*
Rhetoricale wercken. See Roovere, Anthonis de
Rhetorimachia. See Anselm of Besate
Rhétoriqueurs, 4:322a-b, **10:364a–365b**
Jean Lemaire de Belges as, 7:54a–55b
Rhiannon
marriage to Pwyll, 7:704b–705a
myth of Epona and, 9:48b
Rhieingerddi, 3:121b
see also Welsh literature, poetry
Rhine River
as boundary between the Roman world and Germanic peoples, 2:88b
crossed by Franks in the 3rd century, 2:89b
crossed by Vandals in 406, 2:91b
Julian the Apostate and, 10:459a
medieval trade and, 12:115a
Rhineland
flagellants in, 2:263a
glassmaking in, 5:554a-b
mysticism in, 9:31b
plagues in, 9:675b, 681b
steelmaking in, 11:471b, 472a
Rhineland of Holland. *See* Rijnland
Rhinoceros, confusion with unicorn, 12:280a
Rhinotmetus. *See* Justinian II, Byzantine emperor
Rhipidion. *See* Flabellum
Rhitmus ad Henricum. See Wipo of Burgundy
Rhodanthe and Dosikles. See Theodore Prodromos
Rhodes, **10:365b**
attacked by Muslims (654), 9:74a
Byzantine sea routes and, 10:423 (map), 424b
Rhodian Sea Law, 3:569a, 7:390b, 9:87b
origins of, 12:101a
Rhodri Mawr, Welsh ruler, **10:365b–366a**
overlordship, 12:515b
wars with Vikings and Danes, 10:366a
Rhône Valley
occupied by Muslims, 6:572b
Viking raids and, 12:431a-b
Rhos. *See* Rus
Rhotacism, Romanian, 10:513a
Rhyme. *See* Latin meter, rhyme and
Rhyme royal, in English poetry, 8:346a
Rhymed offices, **10:366a–377b**
arrangements of, 10:369a-b
chants of, 10:374a–376a
compilation of a new office, 10:370a
differences between north and south Europe, 10:372a
known authors of, 10:369b
monastic and secular, 10:369b
monastic subgroups of, 10:370a-b
movement from prose to poetry and, 10:371a-b
poetic texts in, 10:367b–368a
problems of identification of, 10:366b–367a
repertory of, 10:366a-b
sectional nature of, 10:368b–369a
sources for, 10:376a–377a
textual and musical borrowings, 10:369b–370a, 375a
unexplored hagiographical information in, 10:373b
Rhys ap Gruffydd, prince of Deheubarth, 12:518a-b
Rhys ap Maredudd, treason trial of, 12:165b
Rhys of Deheubarth, **10:378a**
vs. Hywel, 6:386b
Rhythm, 8:594a, **10:378a–382b**
in Armenian chant, 8:551b
in Byzantine chant, 8:554b
classical attitude to, 10:378b
in Latin verse. *See* Latin meter, rhythm and
mathematics and, 8:588b–589a
musica mensurabilis, 10:380b–382a
musica plana, 10:378b–380b
neume and, 8:624b–625a
notation of, 8:587b–588b
Perotinus' innovations and, 9:507b
plainsong, 9:690b–691a, 692b
syllabic, 9:690a
plica and *fractio modi,* 9:710b–711a
rhythmic density and, 10:381a-b
variation of accentual meter and, 10:380a
variation of line length and, 10:380a
see also Isorhythm; Mode, rhythmic; *Prolatio; Proprietas*
"Rhythmic offices" (rhymed offices), 10:371b
Rhythmus ad Deum, skáhenda meter of Icelandic *rímur* and, 10:405b
Rhythmus de fide catholica. See Hrabanus Maurus
Rhythmus (hymnody), 6:379b
Rhythmus de incarnatione. See Alan of Lille
Rialto. *See* Venice
Rib, 5:594b, 596a, **10:382b–383a**
diaphragm arch and, 1:423b
in Romanesque architecture, 10:476a–488a (*illus.*)
in St. Philibert at Tournus, 10:621b (*illus.*)
spandrel, 11:389b
see also Tierceron
Rib vault. *See* Vault
Ribā. See Usury, Islamic law
Ribald literature
French, 4:574b–575b
Norse flyting, 9:173b–174a
Ribāṭ, 1:71a, 198a, 198b, 7:110b, 111b, 238b
in Aghlabid art, 1:69a-b
eyvān, 4:570a
of Sousse, Tunisia, battlements, 12:553a
see also Monasteries, Sufi
Ribe, trade in, 4:149a
Ricar hinn gamli, 11:492a
Ricciardi company of Lucca, 2:76b, 77b
Ricciardo da Battifolle, 6:653b

Riccobaldus of Ferrara, on Huguccio, 6:327b
Rice
as cereal crop, 1:83b, 87b
husking of in Islamic world, 12:85b
Ricemarch Psalter, origin of, 3:224a-b
Rich, Edmund
Mirror of Holy Church
English mysticism and, 9:18b
William of Nasington and, 9:26a
translation of *Speculum ecclesiae* into English, 9:26b
Rich, Edmund, archbishop of Canterbury, a rhymed office for, 10:370b
Richard I (the Lionhearted) of England, king, **10:383a–384a**
armistice with Saladin, 2:23b, 10:383b
Bertran de Born and, 2:201b, 202a
Blondel de Nesle and, 2:276a
bridge at Les Andelys and, 10:416a
captivity of, 10:383b
capture of, 2:7a, 5:482a
church-state relations, 4:471a-b
conflict with his father, 10:383a
Eleanor of Aquitaine and, 4:420a
fur prices and, 5:325b
Genoese ships and, 11:232b
Joachim of Fiore and, 7:113a
laments for
by Gaucelm Faidit, 9:693a
by Giraut de Bornelh, 5:539b
legal system and
court of common pleas, 3:491b–492a
itinerant justices, 7:184b
justiciar, 7:200a
literary patronage, 6:26a
military campaigns
against Philip Augustus and John, 4:467b–468a
Third Crusade, 4:40a-b, 70b, 467b, 9:552b–553a, 10:626b
Peire Vidal on, 9:485b
Peter of Blois on, 9:518a
ransom, 11:613b–614a
Sancho VII of Navarre and, 9:70b
scutage and, 11:120a-b
seal of, 11:128 (*illus.*)
self-government of London and, 3:499a
Tancred of Lecce and, 11:269a
Richard II of England, king, **10:384a–385a**
accession to throne, 4:476a
Chaucer and, 3:283b, 290a
criticized by Gower, 8:322b
deposition of, 4:160b, 476b, 10:384b
effect on kingship, 4:477a
Ireland and, 6:519a, 8:532a
justices of the King's Bench and, 7:193b
kingship theory of, 7:270a
manuscripts owned by, 6:463a
parliament and, 6:428a, 9:428b–429b, 433a
as patron of poets, 10:384b
Peasants' Revolt and, 9:479a, 479b
Piers Plowman and, 7:331a, 331b
prerogative and, 10:90a-b
in prophecies, 10:148b–149a
royal chamber and, 6:305b
scutage and, 11:120b
serfdom and, 11:207b
struggle with Lords Appellant, 7:666a
Thomas Usk and, 12:333b
treason definition and, 12:166a, 167b–168a
Richard III of England, king, **10:385a–386a**
act of succession, 4:479a-b, 485b–486a
claim to throne, 4:478b
coronation of, 10:385b
Ireland and, 6:520a
as lieutenant general for northern England, 10:385a
opposition to rule, 4:478b–479a
parliament and, 4:479a, 9:431a
Plantagenet family name, 9:693b
Richard the Redeless and, 8:319b
in Wars of the Roses, 12:571b–572a
Richard I of Normandy, duke, 9:162a, 12:432a
commissioned history of Normans, 4:304a
Ethelred II and, 9:165a
Richard II of Normandy, duke, 6:357a, 9:162a
Rodolph of Tosny and, 11:263b–264a
Richard III of Normandy, duke, 9:162b
Richard de Beauchamp, monument of, 4:510b, 7:321b
Richard de Burgh, 6:518b
Richard de Bury, **10:386a-b**
Philobiblon, 7:370a, 563a, 10:386a, 386b
antifeminism in, 1:324a
Richard of Canterbury, archbishop, 5:421a
Richard of Capua, prince, 11:264b, 265a
Gregory VII and, 11:265b
Robert Guiscard and, 10:433a
Richard of Coggeshall, *Visio Thurkilli,* 7:367b, 370a
Richard of Cornwall, earl
crusade of, 4:32a, 51b, 52a-b
election as king of Germany, 4:428a-b
Richard of Devizes, *Chronicon,* on London pleasures, 4:278a
Richard de Fishacre, Robert Grosseteste and, 1:461b
Richard Fitz Nigel. *See* Fitz Nigel, Richard
Richard Fitzgilbert de Clare. *See* Clare, Richard Fitzgilbert de
Richard Fitzneal. *See* Fitz Nigel, Richard
Richard de Fournival
Bestiaire d'amour, 1:188b, **2:203b,** 2:205b, 9:639a
see also Unicorn
Biblionomia, 7:368a
love treatises, 9:639a
lyric poetry, courtly elements, 9:637a
unicorn and, 6:362a
Richard of Fulda, abbot, 5:312a
Richard of Gloucester. *See* Richard III of England
Richard le Justicier, 2:427a
Richard of Laurent, *De laudibus beatae Virginis Mariae,* 7:368b
Richard Ledrede, 6:382b
Richard de Lucy, 7:200a
Richard of Middleton. *See* Richardus de Mediavilla
Richard the Pilgrim, *Chanson d'antioche,* 3:254b–255a
Richard the Redeless, 8:319b, 332a
Richard of St. Victor, **10:387a,** 12:192a-b, 193b–194a
Book of Excerpts, 4:448b
Cloud of Unknowing and, 9:22a, 22b
De Trinitate, 9:599a, 10:387a
as exegete, 2:213b
Hadewijch and, 9:12a
Hugh of St. Victor and, 6:322b
mystical theology, 9:593a
preaching of, 10:76a
Vincent of Beauvais and, 8:645a
Richard de Swyneshed. *See* Swineshead, Richard
Richard of Thetford
Ars dilatandi sermones, 10:363a
ars praedicandi of, 1:556a
"thematic" sermon and, 10:362b, 363a
Richard de Verdun, 8:104a
Richard of Wallingford, **10:387a–388a**
astronomical clock by, 3:29b, 461a-b, 464b
on astronomy, 1:613a
instrument called Albion, 11:98b
Quadripartitum, 10:387b
Rectangulus, 10:388a
St. Albans grain mill, 11:653b–654a
Tractatus albionis, 10:387b–388a
Tractatus horologii astronomici, 11:644b
weight-driven clock, 11:658a-b
Richard Wyche, bishop of Chichester, 1:261b
Richard of York, duke
claim to crown, 12:570a-b
claim to throne, 4:477b, 6:161b
conflict with Henry VI, 12:570a-b
death at Wakefield, 12:571a
in Ireland, 6:520a
Irish parliament and, 9:437b
parliament and, 9:429b, 430a-b
Richardus de Mediavilla, **10:388a–389a**
on intercourse, 3:573b
on Trinitarian doctrine, 12:196b–197a
Richart le Pélerin, 3:331a
Richbod, abbot (9th century), 9:143a
Richelieu, cardinal, destruction of French castles, 3:152a
Richemont, Arthur de, 3:271a
appointment as constable, 5:188a-b
Richer, Edmond, *Libellus de ecclesiastica et politica potestate,* 3:521a-b
Richer of St. Remi, 8:247b, 255b, **10:389a**
Sylvester II and, 11:552b
Richerzeche, 3:481b, 5:462a
Richeut, 9:636a
Richmond Castle, Scolland's Hall, wall fireplace, 6:121a
Ricos hombres, 12:563a
Rictrude, St., 6:317a

Ricvère de Clastres, 10:85b
Ridda (apostasy), after death of Muḥammad, 3:32a
Ridda wars. *See* Islam, Conquests of
Riddarasögur, **10:389a–397b**
  Icelandic compositions, 10:389b
    borrowings from the Norwegian translations, 10:394a-b
    dismissed as *lygisögur,* 10:396a
    number of extant works, 10:396a-b
    typical motifs and forms, 10:395a–396b
  Icelandic editions of original Norwegian translations, 10:392a–393a
  influence on *Gull-Þóris saga,* 6:27a
  Klári saga, 7:275b–275a
  Mírmanns saga, 8:432a–433a
  prose translations from originals in verse, 10:393a–394a
  as source for *Víglundar saga,* 12:416b
  as sources for early *rímur,* 10:401b–402a
  translations
    as adaptations, 10:392b–393a
    from French, 10:390a–391b
    from Latin sources, 10:391b–392a
    into Norwegian, 10:389b, 390a–394a
    style of, 10:393a–394a
  Tristrams saga ok Ísöndar influence on, 12:203b
  usage of the term, 10:389a
  see also Bevers saga; Mágus saga jarls
Ridder, 5:680a
Riddles, **10:397b–398b**
  in Anglo-Saxon literature, 1:281a
  in Latin literature, 7:362b
  in Scandinavian literature, in *Baldrs draumar,* 2:55a, 56b
Riddles of Gestumblindi, The, insertion in *Hervarar saga ok Heiðreka konungs,* 6:215a
Riderch of Strathclyde, ruler, 11:489b
Ridevall, John. *See* John Ridevall
Riḍwān ibn Muḥammad al-Saᶜtī, repair of Jayrūn Gate water clock, 11:641b
Riḍwān (son of Tutush), 11:155a
Ried, Benedikt, **10:398b–399a**
  Vladislav Hall in Hradčany Castle in Prague, 10:398a (*illus.*), 399a
Ried, Hans, scribe of *Ambraser Heldenbuch,* 1:229b, 2:253a, 7:304a
Riedegg manuscript, Neidhart "von Reuental's" songs and, 9:93a-b
Riemenschneider, Tilman, **10:399a**
  altarpiece from St. Jacob's church in Rothenburg, 10:399 (*illus.*)
RIF. *See* Alfasi, Isaac ben Jacob
Rīfāᶜdīs. See Dervish
Rig-Veda
  Vǫluspá and, 12:492a
  Yašts and, 12:720b
Riga
  allied with Gediminas, 7:605b
  besieged by Kęstutis of Lithuania, 7:606b
  founding of (1201), 2:64b, 7:604a
  Semgallians subjected to, 2:65b
Right of hostelry. *See* Hostelry
Right, writ of, 3:414a
Rights
  alimentary. *See* Alimentary rights
  of clergy. *See* Clergy
  of legitim. *See* Legitim, rights of
  of preemption. *See* Preemption rights
Rigord, **10:399a–400a**
  Gesta Philippi Augusti, 2:236b, 240a
Rígr (Germanic god), 10:400a-b
Rígsþula, **10:400a–401a,** 11:354b
  Hyndluljóð and, 6:385b
  preservation in Snorri's *Edda,* 4:387a
  role of Heimdallr in, 6:133b
Riḥla. See Baṭṭūṭa, Ibn
Rijkel, Denys, conciliar theory of, 3:511b–512a
Rijmkroniek van Holland, 4:319b
Rijnland
  drainage of, 6:559a
  reclamation of land, 12:577b
Rijssele, Colijn van, 4:322b
Rima cara. See Italian literature, poetry, rhyme
Rima ricca. See Italian literature, poetry, rhyme
Rima siciliana. See Sicilian poetry
Rimado de Palacio. See López de Ayala, Pero
Rimbert, St., **10:401a**
  on Kurland, 2:62b
  Life of St. Ansgar, 10:401a
    on the town of Birka, 2:247b
Riming Poem, The (Exeter Book), 8:327a
  rhyme in, 1:277a
Rimmonim, 7:68a
Rímur, **10:401a–407b**
  before 1500, 10:402b–403a
  after 1500, 10:403a
  collections of, 10:401b
  definition of, 10:401a-b
  influenced by Eddic poetry, 10:403b
  introductory *mansöngur* in, 10:405b–406a
  Karlamagnús saga and, 7:218b
  meter of, 10:403b, 404b–405b
  music to, 10:406b
  origin of the term, 10:401b
  origins of, 10:403a-b
  pious objections to, 10:406b
  poetic devices in, 10:404a-b
  presentation of, 10:406a-b
  saga sources of, 10:401b–402b
  subject matter of, 10:401b–402b
  Þrymskviða and, 12:52b
  versions of *Flóres saga konungs ok Sona Hans,* 5:108a
  see also Víglundar saga
Rímur of Clares of Serena, 7:275a
Rinaldo d'Aquino, 6:641a-b
  "Già mai non mi conforto," 6:657b, 11:258b–259a
  Iacopo da Lentini and, 6:387b
Rinaldo degli Albizzi, conflict with Medici, 5:101b–102a
Rinaldo (in Italian Carolingian legends), 8:225b
Ring, Der. See Wittenwiler, Heinrich
Ring, marriage. *See* Donizo, *De anulo et baculo*
Ringerike style, **10:407b,** 12:418a, 418b
  11th-century bronze gilt weather vane, 10:408 (*illus.*)
  in Celtic art, 3:223a
  see also Urnes style
Rings, 5:380b
Rinn, 6:534b
Rinuccini, Cino, 6:653b
  on Landini, 7:326a-b
Rio do Padrã, 4:562a
Río Salado, Battle of (1340), 9:714b
  Don Juan Manuel and, 8:95a
Rioni River Valley, Georgians in, 5:419b
Rionnaird, 6:534b
Riote du monde, purpose of, 9:639a-b
Ripa (medieval port of Rome), 10:519a
Ripley, George, *Componde of Alchemy,* 1:139a
Ripoll (monastery)
  translations of Arabic works and, 11:456b
  Visitatio sepulchri manuscript and, 11:437a
Ripresa. See Ballata
Ripuarians, 2:94a
Riqq, 8:613a
Risāᵓil Ikhwān al-Ṣafā, 12:228a-b
Risāla fi 'l-Ṣaḥāba. See Muqaffaᶜ, ᶜAbd Allāh Ibn al-
Risālat al-Ghufrān. See Maᶜarrī, Abu 'l-ᶜAlāᵓ Aḥmad al-
Risbyle runic stone, inscription, 10:566a
Rishonim, 11:585a–586b
Ristoro d'Arezzo, *Composizione del mondo,* 6:659a
"Rithmus domini Gibuini Lingonensis episcopi de paradiso." *See* Gibuin of Langres
Ritmo giullaresco toscano, 6:624a
Ritmo Laurenziano. See Ritmo giullaresco toscano
Ritornello. *See* Trecento music
Ritter mit den Nüssen, synopsis of, 8:128b
Ritter vom Turn, Der. See Marquard vom Stein
Ritterfahrt. See Pseudo-Zilies von Sayn
Ritterfahrt des Herrn von Michaelsberg, Die. See Heinrich von Freiberg
Ritterschaft, 8:350a
Ritual (book), **10:407b–409a**
  see also Pilgrimage
Ritual elevation of saints. *See* Canonization
Ritual, Islamic. *See* Liturgy, Islamic
Ritual, Jewish. *See* Liturgy, Jewish
Rituale romanorum, 10:408a
Riurik. *See* Rurik
Rivesaltes, water rights, 6:558b
Rivet wheat, 5:646a
Riwāq, **10:409a**
Riyād. See Rauḍa
Rizpolozhenie Church. *See* Moscow Kremlin
Roads
  Byzantine, **10:422b–425a,** 10:423 (map)
    military highway from the Balkans to Syria, 10:422b–424a (map)

Roads (*cont.*)
Byzantine (*cont.*)
postal and intelligence services, 10:58a
telegraph system under Theophilos I, 10:59a
see also Trade, Byzantine
Islamic world, **10:425a–426b**
absence of vehicles, 12:380a-b
of Damascus, 4:81a
improvement of, 10:425b–426a
Khorāsān highway, 10:426a
travel and, 12:147b
see also Trade, Islamic
Roman
in Islamic world, 10:425b
Lateran complex and, 10:518b, 519a
Leonine City, 10:519a
in Tabula Peutingeriana, 11:572a
travel and, 12:148b–149a
Via Aemilia, 9:663b
villages and, 12:443b
Western European, **10:409b–422b**
Camino de Santiago, 9:656a, 659a-b, 661b–662a
in early Middle Ages, 10:411b–412a
medieval trade and, 12:113b–115a (map), 117b
Paris-centered, 12:158a
pilgrimage, 9:656a, 659a-b, 660a, 661b–662a
as pious works, 10:412b
as property of individuals, 10:412b
Roman heritage, 10:409b–410a
in 13th century, 10:412b
tolls and maintenance, 10:412b–413a
trade routes, 12:114 (map)
Viking raids on England and, 12:433a
see also Vehicles, European
Roads and Kingdoms, The Book of. See Khurdadbi, Ibn
Robber barons, in Rhineland, 12:117b
Robber synod. *See* Ephesus, Councils of, Second
Robbia. *See* Della Robbia: Luca, Andrea, Giovanni
Robert II of Burgundy, duke, Dauphiné and, 4:109a
Robert IV (the Strong), West Frankish count, 3:89b
Robert I (the Frisian) of Flanders, count, 5:79a
Robert II of Flanders, count, 5:79a
Robert I of Neustria, king of France, 3:115a
Robert II (the Pious) of France, king, 2:427a
biography of, 6:148b
Helgaud's life of, 2:236b, 7:262a
Jews and, 7:78b–79a
principle of primogeniture, 5:159a
relations with church, 5:157b
Sylvester II and, 11:552b
witchcraft and, 12:660b
Robert I of Normandy, duke, 9:162b
Robert I (the Bruce) of Scotland, king, 4:111a, **10:426b–428a**, 11:107b, 108b, 109b–110a
attack on Dublin, 4:299b
domestic policy of, 10:427b
heirs of, 10:427b
in Ireland, 6:519b
in John Barbour's *Bruce,* 2:102a, 10:427b–428a
letter to Pope John XXII, 10:427b
parliament and, 9:438b, 439a
peace with England and, 10:427a
Robert II of Scotland, king, 10:427b, **10:428a-b**, 11:111a
as lieutenant of Scotland, 10:428a
offspring of, 10:428a
parliament and, 9:439b
renewal of war with England, 10:428b
Robert III of Scotland, king, 11:111a
Robert, abbot, translation of *Elis saga ok Rosamundu,* 4:431b–432a, 10:304a-b, 390a
Robert of Anjou, king of Sicily
Dauphiné and, 4:109a
feudalization of baronage, 7:8a
Guelph alliances, 7:8a
invasion of Sicily, 7:8a
as leader of Florence, 5:97a
Naples and, 9:59a, 11:273a
in Philippe de Vitry's "O canenda," 12:482a-b
Simone Martini's *St. Louis of Toulouse Crowning Robert of Anjou,* 12:173a
Tuscan art and, 11:275a
Robert ap Huw, on Welsh harp technique, 8:558b
Robert d'Arbrissel, **10:429a–431a**
Fontevrault and, 4:374b, 10:429b–430b, 12:686b
letter to Ermengarde, 10:430a
preaching in northwest France, 10:429b
stay in Rennes, 10:429a
women followers of, 10:429b
Robert of Artois, count
Philippe de Remin and, 2:144a
pursuit of Artois, 5:183b
Robert of Basevorn
ars praedicandi of, 1:556a, 557a-b
on preaching, 10:363a
Robert de Beaumont, 7:200a
Robert of Béthune, count of Flanders, 5:81b–82a
Robert of Blois
Chastoiement des dames, 3:664a
Enseignment des princes, 3:665b
Robert de Boron, **10:431a-b**
Joseph d'Arimathie, 1:570b, 8:318b, 332a, 332b
reworking of, Vulgate cycle, 5:259a
Merlin, 1:570b–571a, 5:390a
reworking of, Vulgate cycle, 5:259a
Suite du Merlin, 1:571a
as a source for Malory's *Morte Darthur,* 8:62b
Robert of Bosco, Anselm of Laon's theology school and, 12:21a
Robert le Bougre, as inquisitor, 6:483b–484a
Robert, Brother (Old Norse poet), 5:634b
Elis saga ok Rosamundu translation, 12:203b
translations of
as adaptations, 10:392b
popularity of in Iceland, 10:394b
Tristrams saga ok Ísöndar, 1:572a, 10:304a-b, 390a, 392a, 12:201a, 203a-b
Robert (brother of William Rufus), recovery of duchy, 4:462a
Robert Bruce VIII of Scotland. *See* Robert I (the Bruce) of Scotland
Robert of Bury, St., martyrdom of, 7:116a
Robert of Capua, 11:267a
Robert, Cistercian abbot (*fl.* 1098), establishment of Cîteaux, 3:403b
Robert de Clari, **10:431b–432a**
Conquête de Constantinople, 3:332a, 5:256b–257a, 9:638a-b, 12:448b
French chronicles of, 3:332a-b
Robert le Clerc d'Arras, *Vers de la mort,* 9:639a
Robert of Clermont, count, Beaumanoir and, 2:144a
Robert de Coucy, **10:432a**
Rheims Cathedral and, 10:344b
Robert of Courson. *See* Courson (Courçon), Robert of
Robert of Courtenay, 7:346b, 349a
Robert of Cricklade
vita of St. Thomas Becket, 12:414a
translated into Old Norse, 12:35b, 36a
Robert Curthose of Normandy
conflicts with Henry I, 6:155a
reign of, 9:166b
Robert le Diable, 8:431b–432a, **10:433b**
Robert of Dreux, revolt against Louis VII of France, 11:504a
Robert of Ely, 7:280b
Robert the Englishman. *See* Robertus Anglicus
Robert of Flamborough, on the three types of penance, 9:488b
Robert of Gloucester, 5:389b
Chronicle, 8:317a
Robert of Greatham, **10:433b**
Corset, 1:263b
Evangiles des domnees, 1:262b
Robert Grosseteste. *See* Grosseteste, Robert
Robert Guiscard, 7:284a, **10:433a**
as duke of Apulia and Calabria, 11:265a
father of Bohemond I, 2:308a, 308b
Gregory VII and, 11:265b, 266a
Naples and, 9:58a
Roger I and, 10:440a, 440b
in Sicily, 11:264b–265a, 265a–266a
vs. Byzantines, 1:157b–158a, 2:494a, 11:266a
capture of Bari, 2:492b
Robert de Handlo, 8:644a
Regule, 8:646b
Robert de Ho, *Enseignements Trebor,* 1:264a
Robert of Jumièges, 1:256b, **10:434a-b**

Robert of Ketton, 11:379b, 12:138a
Koran interpretations of, 7:297a
translations by, 12:139a-b
Robert Kilwardby. *See* Kilwardby, Robert
Robert de Luzarches, 1:234b, **10:432a-b**
nave of Amiens Cathedral, 10:432b (*illus.*)
Robert of Melun, 3:322b, **10:434b–435a**
Abelard and, 12:21a-b
Robert of Molesme, St., Cistercian Order and, 3:355a, 10:286b–287a
Robert the Monk (of Rheims), rewriting of *Gesta Francorum* by, 5:514b
Robert of Mortain, count, Vital of Savigny and, 12:479b
Robert of Naples, king. *See* Robert of Anjou, king of Sicily
Robert of Orford
Correctoria corruptorii Thomae and, 12:41a
as defender of Thomism, 12:41b
Robert Paululus of Amiens, on liturgy, 7:632a
Robert Reynes of Acle, 3:493a
Robert of Ruddlan, alliance with Gruffudd ap Cynan, 6:4b
Robert of St. Rémy, *Expeditio Ierosolimitana,* 8:299b
Robert of Sicily, king. *See* Robert of Anjou, king of Sicily
Robert (son of Charles of Anjou), Catalan Company's opposition to, 3:156a
Robert (son of Herbert II, count of Vermandois), 3:243b
Robert de Sorbon. *See* Sorbon (Sorbonne), Robert de
Robert the Strong, count of Neustria, Robertinian-Capetian descendants of, 3:89b
Robert (the Wise) of Sicily, king. *See* Robert of Anjou, king of Sicily
Robert de Veneys, 2:173b
Robertet, Jean, 10:364b, 365a
Robertinians, 9:148b
see also Capetians, family origins; Robert the Strong
Robertsbridge Codex, 8:632b, 633b
Robertus Anglicus, 3:459a, 10:237a
mechanical clocks, 11:644b, 652a-b
quadrans vetus and, 11:97b
Robertus de Sabilone, according to Anonymous IV, 8:42b, 43a
Robes. *See* Costume
Robigalia, Major Litany and, 10:131a
Robin Hood, **10:435a–437b**
audience of, 10:437a-b
ballads on, 2:60a
historicity of, 10:436a
Piers Plowman and, 10:435a
plays of, and fertility rites, 4:283b
Scottish chroniclers and, 10:435b
social status of, 10:436b
Robin Hood and the Monk, 10:436a
Robin Hood and the Potter, 10:436a
Robinson, Robert, on Latin pronunciation, 7:357a
Roccafortis (ship), 11:234a
Roch, St., plague and, 2:265a
Rochester Bridge, 10:415a–416a
construction of, 10:420a
corporation of, 10:417a
maintenance of, 10:421b
Rochester Cathedral, west portal, 8:585b (*illus.*)
Rochet. *See* Vestments, liturgical
Rod (British linear measure), 9:504a
Rodents
plague and, 2:257b
rats, as disease intermediaries, 9:673b–674a, 676a, 678a–679a, 686a
see also Plagues
Roderick, Visigothic king, 11:382a
vs. Ṭāriq ibn Ziyād, 6:572a
Ródhos. *See* Rhodes
Rodighieri, Andrea, 6:658a
Rodolph of Tosny, 11:263b
Rodrigo of Castile, count, rule of, 3:128a
Rodrigo Díaz. *See* Cid, History and Legend of
Rodrigo el último godo, 11:438a
Rodrigo, Mocedades de. See Mocedades de Rodrigo
Rodrigo de Osona, **10:437b–438a**
Rodríguez del Padrón, Juan, **10:438b–439b**, 11:423a
antifeminism, 10:439a
ballad texts, 11:429a
Bursario, 10:439a
Cadira del honor, 10:439a
courtly love and, 10:438b–439a
Diez mandamientos de amor, 10:438b
Estoria de dos amadores, 10:438b
lost works of, 11:443a
Oriflama, 10:439a, 11:443b
Siervo libre de amor, 10:438b, 11:454b
Siete gozos de amor, 10:438b–439a
Triunfo de las donas, 10:439a, 11:419b
troubadours and, 10:438b
Rodríguez de Lena, Pero, *Libro del Passo Honroso,* 11:421a
Rodríguez de Montalvo, Garcí, 11:453b
reworking of *Amadís de Gaula,* 1:227b
Roffredus de Epiphaniis of Benevento, 2:29a, **10:439b–440a**
on canonical inquest, 6:478b, 479a
Frederick II and, 11:271a, 274a
Libellus iuris canonici, 10:439b
Quaestiones sabbatinae, 10:439b
Roffud of Benevento. *See* Roffredus de Epiphaniis of Benevento
Rogaland, grain crops of, 9:180b
Rogation days, parallel with pagan Ambarvalia, 10:131a
Roger I of Sicily, king, **10:440a-b**
conquest of Malta, 8:67b
reign of, 11:266a–267a
Robert Guiscard and, 10:433a
Roger II and, 10:440b
in Sicily, 11:265a–267a
vs. Messina, 11:263a
Roger II of Sicily, king, **10:440b–441b**, 11:263b
al-Idrīsī and, 6:412a-b, 11:263a, 274a
John of Salisbury and, 7:265a
Kerkyra seized by, 2:494a
Manuel I Komnenos and, 8:91a-b
medicine and, 11:275b
Norman attacks and, 7:284a
papacy and, 10:440b
personal qualities, 11:268a
reconquest of Malta, 8:67b
reign of, 11:267a–268b
vs. Muslims of Mahdia, 11:268b
Zirids and, 12:745a
Roger, Book of. See Idrīsī, al-, *Nuzhat al-mushtāq fī 'khtirāk al-āfāq*
Roger Borsa, 11:266a, 267a
Roger of Caen, 7:366b
Roger de Flor, 1:190b–191a, 246a, 7:379b, **10:441b**
assassination of, 1:191a, 2:500a
Catalan Company's formation and, 3:156a
Roger Guiscard. *See* Roger I of Sicily, king
Roger of Helmarshausen, **10:441b–442b**, 10:499b, 500a
attribution to of *De diversis artibus,* 8:90b, 283b, 289a, 10:442a-b, 12:24a
portable altar of Sts. Kilian and Liborius, 10:442a (*illus.*)
see also Theophilus
Roger of Laon, count. *See* Hoger of Laon, count
Roger of Salerno, 2:98b
Roger of Salisbury, 7:199b–200a, **10:442b–443b**
administration, 10:443a
fall of, 10:443b
Roger of Stoke, 3:464b
Roger de Swyneshed
De insolubilibus, 11:534b, 535a
De motibus naturalibus, 11:534b, 535a, 535b
De obligationibus, 11:534a, 535a
see also Swineshead
Roger of Wendover, *Flores historiarum,* Wandering Jew legend, 12:542b
Roger of York, archbishop, 2:152a
Vacarius and, 12:343b
Rogerius, 9:671a–672b, **10:444a–445a**
Bolognese School and, 5:567b
De iure personarum, 10:444a
Enodationes quaestionum, 10:444b
equity and, 10:444a
serfs and, 10:444a
Summa codicis, gloss by Placentinus, 9:671b–672a
Summa 'Cum multae essent partes iuris', 10:444b
works of, 7:420b, 10:444b
Rogers, Robert, archdeacon, *Brevary of Chester History,* on Chester Plays, 3:298b–299a, 4:285a
Roggia di Buronzo, 6:558b
Roggia del Comune di Gattinara, 6:558b
Roggia Marchionale, 6:558b
Rogkerus, Frater. *See* Roger of Helmarshausen
Rognac, inn in, 6:468b
Rögnvaldr, earl, crusade of, in *Orkneyinga saga,* 9:279b

Rǫgnvaldr heiðumhárr, *Ynglingatal* and, 12:725b, 726a
Rǫgnvaldr Kali Kolsson, *Háttalykill,* 11:320b
Rǫgnvalds Þáttr ok Rauðs, 12:2b, 5a
Rögnvaldur blindi, *rímur* attributed to, 10:403a
Rohan Master. *See* Master of the Rohan Hours
Roi de Navarre. See Thibaut IV of Champagne, count
Roig, Jaume, 12:349a
Libre de consells, 3:173b
noves rimades comediades, 3:174a
poetry of, 3:171b–172a
Spill, 3:173b–174a
Roís de Corella, Joan, 12:349a
Rojas, Fernando de
early life of, 3:213b
see also Celestina, La
Rök stone (Östergötland), 7:311b
Rokycana, Jan, archbishop of Prague, Bohemian Brethren and, 2:306b
Rokycana, John, 6:376a, 377b
communion under both kinds and, 3:505b
Roland at Saragossa, 10:182b
Roland of Cremona, 4:246a
Aristotle and, 1:462a
William of Auxerre's theology school and, 12:22a
Roland (epic character), 6:638a
in Italian literature, 6:637b
in *Roncesvalles,* 10:528a
Roland, St., statue at Chartres, 5:620b
Roland, Song of, 7:217a, 8:225a, 10:391b, **10:445a–447b**
acquisition of Durendal, 10:674a
artistic merit of, 3:260b–261b
chivalry in, 3:301a, 302b
compared with Spanish epics, 11:409a
cor sarrazinois in, 8:603b
dating of, 5:236b–237a
description of Charlemagne, 5:238a
description of, 3:258a-b
dulce France, rise of French nationalism and, 5:238a
historical basis for, 9:68a
in Italy, 6:638a
laisse similaire in, 7:319b
manuscript of, 3:257b
motivation in, 10:446b
Nibelungenlied and, 9:112a
Oxford version of, 1:260b, 271a
plot summary, 10:446a-b
redactions, 10:446a
religious and ethical aspects, 10:446b–447a
Rolandslied and, 10:448a
Roncevaux section, 12:611b
in Spanish epic legends, 11:438a
style, 10:446b
vehicles in, 12:375a
see also Turoldus; *Roncesvalles*
Rolando, cardinal. *See* Alexander III, pope
Rolandslied, 5:429a, **10:447b–448b**
Der Stricker's *Karl der Grosse* and, 11:493a
Karlmeinet and, 7:219b
Kudrun and, 7:304b
style of, 10:448a
Rolandus, **10:448b–449a**
Paucapalea and, 9:466b
Quadrifidio ciborum, 10:448b
Sententiae, 10:448b
Rolf, Thomas, **10:449a**
Rolin, Nicolas, 2:427b
Roll. *See Volumen*
Roll (unit of measure), 12:593b
Rollant, 3:304a, 7:217a–218a
Rolle, Richard, 4:547a, 8:317b, 9:19a, 19b, 20a–21b
detractions of, 9:21a-b
Ego dormio, 9:20b
English Psalter, 4:547a
English writings of, 9:21a
Form of Living, 9:18b, 21b, 23b
English translation of, 9:26b
Incendium amoris, 7:370a
English translation of, 9:20b, 21a, 21b, 26b
Judica me Deus, 9:19b, 20b
Latin works of, 9:20b–21a
Melos amoris, 9:19b, 20b
Melos Amoris, alliteration in, 8:331a
monasticism and, 3:368b
personality of, 9:21b
Pricke of Conscience attributed to, 8:317a
Psalter of, 2:221b
rhymed office for, 10:366b
three degrees of love, 9:21a
writings attributed to, 9:21a, 27b
see also Mysticism, Christian, English
Rollo, Viking leader
administration of, 9:161a-b, 162a
Charles the Simple and, 3:115a, 9:160a–161a
settlement of Normandy and, 12:431b
Rom. *See* Gypsies
Roma, Cancionero de. See Cancionero de Roma
Romainmôtier, church of, 10:488b
Romainmôtiers (abbey: Switzerland), Frederick Barbarossa and, 11:539a
Romaioi, 2:484a
Rōmaion koula. *See* Hṙomklay
Roman I, Moldavian voivode, territorial expansion, 12:502a
Roman d'Abladane, Le, authorship, 9:634b
Roman des ailes, Le. See Raoul de Houdenc
Roman d'Alexandre. See Alexandre, Roman d'
Roman architecture
Cluniac sculpture and, 10:495b
dome, 4:234b–236a
Provençal sculpture and, 10:497a
as Romanesque source, 10:477a, 481b–482a
theaters, *scenae frons,* 10:308b–309a
triumphal columns, 10:307b
Roman art
collection of. *See* Antiquarianism
plundered. *See* Spolia
revivals. *See* Art, renaissances and revivals; Classicism in art; Romanesque art
Roman d'Auberon, 3:259a
Roman de Brut. See Wace
Roman de carité. See Reclus de Mollien
Román, *comendador,* religious poetry of, 11:422b
Roman Curia, University of, 12:286a
Roman des deduis. See Gace de la Buigne
Roman Empire, **10:456a–470a**
administration of, 2:91a
in Africa, Berber language and, 2:186a
architecture, triumphal arch, 12:205b
armies and disease, 9:674a
army, 10:459a–460a, 461b
see also Exarchate
Burgundians and, 2:422b–423a
Byzantine political theory and, 10:9b–10a
Byzantine postal and intelligence services and, 10:58a
Byzantine trade and, 12:100a-b
catacombs in, 3:154a–155a
cavalry in, 3:200a–201a
Celtic church in, 3:227a
Champagne in, 3:243a
church and state during, 3:10a
civil wars in, 2:97a
commendation in, 3:490a
communication systems, travel and, 12:148b–149a
corporate legal entities during, 3:606a–607a
culture, 10:462b
decline of, 10:467b
barbarian invasions and, 2:97a-b
plagues and the, 9:674b
trade and, 12:108b–109a
definition of, 5:476b
depopulation of, 4:139b
diocese in, 4:191b
division of, in 5th century, 2:485b
economy, 10:460a–461a
fairs and, 4:583b
federate allies, 10:466b
Burgundians, 2:92a
Franks, 2:94a
Ostrogoths, 2:93a
Vandals, 2:91b
Vandals and, 12:354b, 355b
Visigoths, 2:91a
foreign relations, 10:466a-b
geography, 10:456a-b
Hellenism and, 10:457b–458a
Jerusalem pilgrimage and the, 9:652b
languages of, 6:435a
late
Christian missions of, 8:439a–440a
simony in, 11:300b–301a
slavery in, 11:334a–335a
Latin church and, 3:343b–344a
Mediterranean trade and, 12:107a
metalwork in, 2:384a
naval forces, 9:78b
navigation in the Mediterranean and, 9:87b
Orestes' rebellion against, 9:220b
origins of Venice and, 12:383a-b
Pontus in, 10:31b
population, 10:457a-b
provinces, 10:459a
European, 10:464b–465b

Near Eastern, 10:463a-b, 464a
North African, 10:459a, 464a-b
relations with
Armenia, 1:475a, 475b, 476a
Basques, 2:126a
Dacia, 10:509b
Goths, 12:468b
Gotland, 5:632a
Huns, 6:352b, 354a
Islam, 10:459a, 464a, 464b
Persia, 10:463b
Vandals, 12:354b–355b
Visigoths, 12:469a, 469b
religion, 10:461b–462b
sea-based trade routes, 9:673b–674a
survival of, 10:465b–467b
in Tabula Peutingeriana, 11:572a
territorial expansion, 10:458a-b
Theodoric the Ostrogoth and, 12:19a
title of patrician and, 9:460a
transition to Byzantine, 2:481b–484a
under Dominate, 10:458a–462b
church, 10:462a, 462b
citizenship, 10:461a-b
under Principate, 10:458b
citizenship, 10:461a
see also Armenian Pentarchy; Barbarians, invasions of; Roman law; Themes; Vicar
Roman Empire, German. *See* Germany, idea of empire; Holy Roman Empire
Roman d'Enéas, 5:243a, 245a, 6:358b
adaptations, 6:143b
Roman d'Enéas. See Enéas, Roman d'
Roman de Fauvel. See Fauvel, Roman de
Roman de Filomena, 10:181a-b, 182b
Roman du graal, 5:286a
Hispanic version of, 11:416a
Roman History. See Livy; Nikephoros Gregoras
Roman law
absence of under Anglo-Saxons, 7:473a-b
in Armenia, 1:490a
barbarian customs and, 7:469a-b
codification of, under Justinian I, 7:201b–202a
continuance of late Empire traditions, 5:566a
German towns and, 5:458b
Germanic codes and, 7:469a–475a, 481a-b, 482b–483a
glossators of, 5:565b–566a
Gratian and, 5:656b
influence on European law, 3:609b
influence on Western European political theory, 10:19a-b
kingship theories and, 7:265b, 269b
on mining, 8:402a, 402b
personality of law, 9:291a
postglossators and, 10:61b–62b
reintroduction of procedures, 7:503a-b
under Franks, 7:472a–473a
under Lombards, 7:474a
on usury, 12:335b
Roman numerals, **10:470a–474b**
Arabic numerals and, 10:472b–474a
evolution, 10:470b–471b
Exchequer and, 4:531b
origin of, 10:470b
in Spain, 10:471a, 472a-b
subtractive device of, 10:470b, 471a
Roman Office, 4:230a
abbreviation of, 4:231a
see also Divine Office
Roman Penitential, 9:490a
Roman de Philosophie. See Simund de Freine
Roman, prince of Tmutarakan, 12:66a
Roman de Renard, 2:141b
see also Renard the Fox
Roman de Renart. See Pierre de St. Cloud; Renard the Fox
Roman rite
acceptance of
Italy, 8:182a-b
Spain, 8:182a
canon, fixed formulas of, 8:182b
Communion, 8:195b
dismissal, 8:197a
prayers of the people, 8:189a
style of prayers, 8:182b
unction of the sick, 12:279a
Roman de la Rose, 3:670b, 5:287a-b, 6:23a-b, **10:449a–452b**
alchemy in, 1:138b
antifeminism in, 1:324a, 8:338b, 10:451b, 452a, 452b
autobiographical strain in, 2:237a
beguines in, 2:159b
Chaucer and, 8:321a, 321b
Chrétien de Troyes' influence on, 3:311a
Cleanness and, 4:547a
concept of Fortune in, 5:146a
contents of, 1:184a-b, 185a, 189a, 5:262b–263a
criticism of moral opinions, 5:271
Dante and, 4:101b
encyclopedic nature of, 4:449a
fabliaux and, 4:575a-b
Fiore and, 6:632a
gardens in, 5:360b, 363a, 364b–365a
Guillaume de Lorris as author of, 6:23a–23b
ideological interpretation, 5:263a-b, 271a
influence of, 1:183b, 185a, 10:452a-b
Italian literature and, 6:630a, 631b–632a, 651b, 669b
Jean de Meun as author of, 7:53a
literary importance, 5:263a
literary precedents for, 6:23a
love theme, 5:262a-b
Machaut and, 8:4a
manuscripts of, 1:185a, 189b
mendicant orders in, 10:451b
minnereden and, 8:410a
narrative structure, 6:23b
parts of, 10:449b–452a
personification allegory, 5:263a
protagonist and narrator-poet, relation between, 5:262a
Quarrel of, 5:263a-b, 271a–272a
Reason, representation of, 5:263b
sexuality in, 10:451a, 452a
structure of, 5:262a–263a
lyric-romance, 5:262b
translations
by Chaucer, 1:185b
Dutch, 4:319a
troubadour poetry antecedent, 12:218a
use of language, 5:263b–264a
vetula in, 7:367b
visions and, 12:475b
see also Guillaume de Lorris; Jean de Meun
Roman de Rou. See Wace
Roman scripts, 9:341a–342b (*illus.*)
half-uncial, 9:341b (*illus.*), 342a
later cursive, 9:342 (*illus.*)
rustic capital, 9:341b (*illus.*), 345 (*illus.*)
square capital, 9:341 (*illus.*)
uncial, 9:341b (*illus.*), 342a, 345 (*illus.*)
Roman des septs sages, fabliau and, 4:576a
Roman de Thèbes, 5:243a, 8:225b
audience written for, 5:243b
comments on civil war, 5:244b
Roman de toute chevalerie, 1:266a-b, **10:453a**
Roman de Troie, Spanish version of, 11:415b
Roman de Troie. See Benoît de Ste.-Maure
Roman de la violette. See Gerbert de Montreuil
Romana. See Jordanes, *De summa temporum*
"Romana ecclesia: Ceterum." *See* Innocent IV, pope
Romanç. See Ferrer, Francesc
Romance. *See* French literature; German literature
Romance. See Spanish literature, ballad
Romance genre, *echtrae* and, 6:552a
Romance of Girart de Roussillon, prose versions, 12:579b
Romance of Horn, 1:266b, **10:474b–475a**
König Rother and, 7:285b
a Middle English ballad derived from, 2:60b
modern edition of, 1:272a
Romance, ideal of. *See* Courtly love
Romance languages
origin of, 6:434b, 438b–439a
Vulgar Latin and, 7:350b, 12:494a
see also particular languages
Romance literature, poetry, Arabic lyrics and, 8:563b–564a
Romance and Prophecies of Thomas of Erceldoune, The. See Thomas of Erceldoune
Romance of the Rose. See Roman de la Rose
Romancero, 3:140a, 8:564b
Romanesque architecture, **10:475a–490a**
apse in, 1:352a
banded walls, 7:651b–652a
Benedictines and, 2:175a
Burgundy, 10:478b–480a (*illus.*), 488b
Byzantine influences, 4:346a-b, 347a
centering, 3:234b–235a
Cistercian, 10:483a–484a
spread of, 10:489a
clerestory, 3:440a
Cluny, abbey church, 3:468a-b

Romanesque architecture (*cont.*)
defined, 10:475a-b
England, 10:484a-b, 485 (*illus.*)
French, 10:478b–484a, 488b
antique revivalism and, 10:308b–309b (*illus.*)
influence in Spain, 10:487a, 487b
La Madeleine at Vézelay, 12:404b–405b (*illus.*)
Lyons, 7:698a
Normandy, 10:482a-b, 484a, 486b
Palestine, 10:489a, 489b
Périgord region, 10:481a
Poitiers region, 10:481a
southern, 10:481a–482a
German, 10:487b–488b
Gothic architecture and, 5:588b–589a
harmony of the spheres and, 8:584a, 584b
Italian, 10:484b–487a
Apulia, 10:486b
Lombardy, 10:486b
Sicily, 10:486b–487a
monastic influence, 8:455b
Norman-Angevin England, 4:472a
Palestinian, 10:489a, 489b
pilgrimage churches, 10:482b–483a, 650b
in Poland, 9:723b
portal trumeau, 12:222a
Scandinavian, 10:489a
secular, 10:489a-b
in Serbia, 11:183b–184a
sources, 10:477a–478b
Spanish, 10:487a-b
spread of, 10:488b–489a
Swiss, 10:488b
Tuscan, 10:502a-b
vaulting, 10:621a-b
westwork, 12:622b
see also Anglo-Norman art; Narthex; Pre-Romanesque architecture; St. Gall; Tympanum; Vault
Romanesque art, **10:490a–509a**
Benedictines and, 2:175a
Gothic art and, 5:603a
influence of on Celtic art, 3:218b, 223a
Italian, 10:308b, 503a–504a
La Madeleine at Vézelay, 12:404b–405b
Lyons, 7:698a
manuscript illumination, 8:108 (*illus.*), 10:507a–508b
Anglo-Saxon, 10:508b
Cluniac, 10:508b
German, 10:508b
Italian, 10:508a
Jerusalem, 10:508a-b
Spanish, 10:508b
minor, 10:491a
Meuse Valley, 10:499a–500b (*illus.*)
revival, 10:308b–309a
sculpture
at Moissac, Church of St. Pierre, 5:618a
Auvergnat, 10:497a
Burgundian, 10:495a–497a (*illus.*)
chronology, 10:490b
commissions for, 10:492a
decorative/didactic purpose of, 10:492b
French, 10:308a (*illus.*), 490a, 490b, 491a–499a (*illus.*)
Gothic sculpture and, 5:616b–617a, 620b
Île-de-France, 10:490b, 498a–499a
and inlay, 6:10a
Italian, 10:500b–504a (*illus.*)
Languedoc, 10:492b–495a (*illus.*)
Lombard, 10:500b–502a (*illus.*)
ornamentation, 10:491b
Provençal, 10:497a–498a, 501a
relief, 10:491a-b
S. Zeno, Verona, 6:8a
Spanish, 10:490b, 494a
Tuscan, 10:502a–503a
in Serbia, 11:183b–184a
sources of, 8:108a
wall decoration, 10:504a–507a (*illus.*)
Austrian, 10:507a
English, 10:507a
French, 10:505b–507a
German, 10:507a
Italian, 10:504a–505a
Spanish, 10:505b
see also Anglo-Norman art; Gothic art; Pre-Romanesque art
Romania, languages of, 6:443b, 444a
Romania. *See* Romanian principalities; Walachia/Moldavia
Romania, Byzantine. *See* Latin states in Greece
Romania (Roman way of life), 10:465b–466a
Romanian art, Byzantine influences on, 10:510a
Romanian church
history, 10:514a
Muncaci bishopric and, 10:511a
Romanian language, 6:443b, **10:509a–514a**
grammar, 10:512b–513a
Old Church Slavonic and, 6:439a
oldest text, 10:510b–511a
origin of, 10:509a-b
parts of speech, 10:513a
pronunciation, 10:512b
survival of, 10:509b
vocabulary, 10:510a, 513b
see also Daco-Romanian language
Romanian literature, **10:509a–514a**
didactic, 10:511b
folk, 10:513b
historiography, 10:510b, 511b–512a
romance, 10:511b
translations, 10:511a-b
Romanian principalities, **10:514a–515a**
relations with
Hungary, 10:514a, 515a
Ottomans, 10:514a-b, 515a
Poland, 10:514a, 514b, 515a
Tatars, 10:514a, 514b
Vlachs and, 12:483a
see also Moldavia; Walachia
Romanians
relations with, Bulgars, 7:303b
in Transylvania, 6:343b
Romano-German Pontifical, on private penance, 9:491a
Romanos I Lekapenos, Byzantine emperor, **10:515a-b**
administrative reforms, 2:490a
Arab conquest, 2:490a
attempt to control *dunatoi,* 4:306b–307a
as coemperor, 10:515a
descendants of, 10:515b
Nikolaos I Mystikos and, 9:135b
peace with Rus, 12:435b
on *protimesis,* 4:595a
Romanos II, Byzantine emperor, **10:515b**, 11:360a
Empress Theophano and, 12:24a
in *Theophanes continuatus,* 12:23a
Romanos III Argyros, Byzantine emperor
allelengyon and, 11:604b
Zoë and, 12:745b
Romanos IV Diogenes, Byzantine emperor, 4:263a, **10:516a**
Alp Arslan and, 11:152b
defeat at Manazkert (1071), 8:81a
representation of his coronation, 7:26b
Sebaste and, 11:131b
vs. Ottomans, 2:493a
Romanos Melodos, St., 1:520a, 7:292b, 8:554a, **10:516a–517a**
canonized, 10:516b
kontakion, 2:469a, 6:378b, 7:612b–613a, 10:516a
language and dialogue, 2:510b
music, 2:510b–511a
poetic form, 2:524b
style and imagery, 2:510b
Romans Bridge, construction of, 10:421a
Romans à tiroir, fabliau and, 4:576a
Romansch language, 6:435b
Romanus (6th-century monk), Benedict of Nursia and, 2:168b
"Romanus letters," 8:625a
Romanus of the Tusculans. *See* John XIX, pope
Romanz del infant García, 11:409a, 442b
Romanz de temtacioun de secle. See Guischart de Beaulieu
Rome, **10:517a–527a**
archives, 1:445b, 446a
army, 10:521b
art of, 10:504a–505a
revivals, 10:520b–521a
astrology in, 1:605a
basilicas in, 4:332b
Belisarios and, 2:165a
bishopric, lay nobility and, 10:522a
boundaries, 10:518 (map)
camera urbis, 10:524b
capture by Frederick I Barbarossa, 5:480b
Christian pilgrimage and, 9:656a-b, 658a–659a, 660b, 12:151a, 154b–155a, 156a
Christian replanning of, 4:332a-b
churches, 10:517a, 517b–519a
communal government and, 10:523b
rebuilt, 10:504b
civic maintenance, 10:520b, 521a
civil war, under Innocent III, 10:523b
commerce, 10:525b–526a

communal government
Boniface IX and, 10:524a-b
Capitol and, 10:519b
papacy and, 10:523a-b
compared with Venice, 12:382b
Constans II in, 3:544b
Constantine's building program in, 4:332b, 335a
Dante and, 4:89a,b
early bishops of, 9:458b
early Christian art, examples of, 4:352a-b
in early Middle Ages, 12:320b
economy, 10:525b–526b
fall of (1084), 10:523a
foundation of, Siena and, 11:278a
Germanic threats in the 3rd century, 2:89b
house for Ethiopian pilgrims, 1:32b
inns in, 6:470a, 471b, 473a
Jerome's views of, 7:57a, 58a
Jews in, 7:108b–110a
literacy in, 7:597b
literary guides, 10:520b
liturgical drama in, 6:636b
Lombards' invasion of, 3:345b–346a
monuments
ancient, 10:517a-b, 520b
Christian, 10:517a, 517b–519b
Muslim attacks on, 6:572b
occupied by Louis of Bavaria, 10:524a
papal absence from, 10:524a
Papal Jubilee years and, 9:660b
patriarch of, 9:459a
pentarchy and, 9:495b–496a
Ponte Sant'Angelo, 10:410a
popular government of, during Great Schism, 10:524a
population, 10:517a, 517b, 521a
foreign, 10:526a
primacy of bishopric, *Traditio clavium,* 12:123 (*illus.*)
regions
civil, 10:517b
ecclesiastical, 10:517a, 517b
Greek, 10:521a
see also Disabitato; Lateran; Leonine City
relations with
Genoa, 10:523a, 525b
Pisa, 10:523a, 525b
Ravenna, 10:521b
revolt against church (1148–1155), 1:58b, 540a
revolution (1294), 10:523b
roads, 10:518b, 519a
sack of
in 846, 6:392a, 10:522a
by Vandals (455), 2:91b, 9:78b
by Visigoths (410), 2:90b, 10:467b, 12:470a
see of, Council of Serdica and, 11:189b
Senate, 10:519b, 521a, 523a
Nicholas III and, 10:524a
under Theodoric, 9:290b
see also Senatus
under Angevin protectorate, 10:524a, 525b
under Byzantine protectorate, 10:521b
under Dominate, 10:458b
under Frankish protectorate, 10:522a-b, 525a
under local nobility, 10:522a-b
vs. Tusculum, 10:523a, 523b, 525b–526a
vs. Viterbo, 10:526a
walls, 10:520a
water supply, 10:517b, 519b–520a
Rome, Synod of (313), 10:344b
Rome, Synod of (1046), 11:517a
Rome, Synod of (1059), 3:93b
Rome, University of, 12:286a
Romefeoh. *See* Peter's Pence
Romescot. *See* Peter's Pence
Romuald of Ravenna, St., **10:527a-b**
biography by St. Peter Damian, 9:508a-b
founder of Camaldolese order, 3:55b–56a
monastic views of, 3:354b
on simony, 7:123b, 9:508b
Romuli fabulae Aesopiae. See Nilant, Frédéric
Romulus Augustulus, West Roman emperor
deposed by Odoacer, 2:93a
deposition of, 12:471a
Romulus (fable collection), 2:141a, 4:572a-b, 573a, **10:527b**
Romulus Niveleti. See Walter of England
Romulus and Remus, myth of, depicted on Sasanian seals, 11:123a
Rómverja saga, **10:528a**
two redactions, 10:528a
Rónán, king of Leinster, 6:547b
Roncaglia, Diet of (1158), 2:418a, 5:480b, 7:31a, 10:329b
Hugo and, 6:323b
Roncesvalles, 3:72b, **10:528a-b**, 11:411b, 438a
Roncesvalles Pass, 9:70b
kingdom of Navarre and, 9:67b, 68a, 69a
Roncevaux, Battle of (778), 8:225a
Roncone, 7:324 (*illus.*), 325a
Rondache, 1:528a
Rondeau, **10:528b–529b**
13th-century prototype, 10:528b
in Anglo-Norman literature, 1:269a
in *ars nova,* 1:552a-b
dissociation from music, 10:529a
earliest appearance in literature, 10:529a
in Guillaume de Machaut's work, 8:7a-b
tricks of composition, 10:529a
trouvères, 12:218b
see also Ma fin est mon commencement
Rondeau (dance song), 4:86b
Rondeau (hymnody). *See Rondellus*
Rondellus, 1:547a, 6:380a, **10:529b**
in *Sumer Is Icumen In,* 11:505a–506a
in Worcester polyphony, 12:696a, 696b
Rood screen. *See* Screen
Roof construction, Romanesque, 10:477a
Roofs
lead, 3:563b
slate, 3:563b
thatch, 3:559b, 563b
tile, 3:563b
Rook (unit of measure), 12:593b
Roovere, Anthonis de
Lof vanden Heilighen Sacramente, 4:322b
Rhetoricale wercken, 4:322b
Vander Mollenfeeste, 4:322b
Rope (unit of measure), 12:593b
Roriczer, Conrad, **10:530a**
entrance porch of Regensburg Cathedral, 10:530a (*illus.*)
Roriczer, Mathes, **10:530b**
Gothic design booklets, 10:530b
Rory O'Connor of Connacht, Irish high king, 6:517b
Henry II of England and, 6:517b
"Rosa fresca aulentissima." *See* Cielo d'Alcamo
Rosa medicinae anglicana. See John of Gaddesden
Rosaflorida, Rodríguez del Padrón and, 10:439a
Rosarium. See Guido de Baysio; Huguccio
Rosary, **10:530b–531a**, 12:461a
see also Ave Maria
Rosary Confraternity, founding of, 4:251a
Rosc catha, 6:537a
Roscada, saga and, 6:541b
Roscelinus, **10:531a–532a**
Abelard and, 1:16b, 10:531b
concept of *flatus vocis,* 1:18b
heresy trial, 10:531b
influence on William of Champeaux, 12:637b
nominalism and, 9:155a, 155b, 10:531b
Trinitarian doctrine, 10:531a, 12:191a, 192a
on universals, 12:281a
Rose
in art and literature, 9:550b–551a
in cookery, 9:551a
pharmacological uses, 9:550b–551a
Rose Garden of Spiritual Exercises, The. See Mombaer, Jan
Rose of Lima, St., as Dominican lay sister, 4:254b
Rose (liturgical book). *See Warda*
Rose window, **10:532a**
"Rose of the Winds," 12:467a
Rosemary, as perfume base, 2:147a
Rosengarten, 2:253a, **10:532a–533a**
association with *Nibelungenlied,* 10:532b–533a
see also Lied vom hürnen Seyfrid, Das
Rosengarten zu Worms, Der. See Rosengarten
Rosenplüt, Hans, 4:271b, 8:359b, **10:533a–535a**
carnival plays, 10:534a-b
Des Türken Vasnachtspil, 10:534b
gun-keeping business, 10:533b
instructional verse tracts, 10:534b
"Laudation to a City," 10:534b

Rosenplüt, Hans (*cont.*)
Mären, 8:131b
nom de plume, 10:533b
poetry, 10:533b–534a
political tracts, 10:534b
Priamel, 10:534a
Türkenlied, 10:534b
verse tales, novelistic, 10:534a
Wettstreit der drei Liebhaber, 12:658a
Rosetti, Gioanventura, *Plictho,* 4:329a
Rosetum exercitiorum spiritualim et sacrarum meditationum. See Mombaer, Jan
Rosewater, 2:147a
Rosh ha-golah. See Exilarch
Rosicrucians, 9:2b
Rosier, Bernard du
on ambassador versus *legatus,* 4:205a
personnel for diplomacy, 4:209b
security of ambassadors, 4:211a
Roskilde Cathedral, 10:489a
Roskilde Chronicle, **10:535a–536a**
authorship, 10:535a
Brevis historia regum Dacie and, 11:522b
Knud Lavard in, 7:280b
later additions to, 10:535b
Rossano Gospels, 5:580a (*illus.*), 7:344a
narrative miniatures in, 4:357a
Passion cycle illustrations in, 9:447a
portraits of the evangelists, 4:356b
Rosselli, Francesco, engraving technique of, 4:489a
Rossello di Jacopo Franchi, **10:536a-b**
Coronation of the Virgin altarpiece, 10:536 (*illus.*)
Rossi Codex, trecento composers in, 12:179b
Rossignol. See John of Howden
Rosso. *See* Giovanni (Nanni) di Bartolo
Rostand (papal nuncio), 11:607b
Rostislav of Kiev, khanate of Tmutarakan and, 12:66a
Rostock, University of, 12:288a-b
Rostov, population, 8:537b–538a
Rostov land. *See* Vladimir-Suzdal
Rostov-on-the-Klyazma, Kremlin churches, architectural style, 10:582a
Rosweyde, Heribert, collection of saints' Lives, 6:70b
Roswitha. *See* Hrotswitha von Gandersheim
Rota, **10:536b–537a**
Rothad of Soissons (9th century), 9:121a, 121b
Rothari, Lombard king, 7:656b, 11:335b
conquests of, 8:377a
Genoa, 5:383b
edict of, 7:474a-b
supplements to, 7:474a-b
Rothe, Johannes, chronicles of, 8:358b
Rothenburg
St. Jacob's church, altarpiece by Tilman Riemenschneider, 10:399 (*illus.*)
seized (1385), 11:544a
Rother. *See König Rother*
Rother, Martin, German translation of the Old Testament, 2:215b
Rothesay Castle, rebuilt by Robert II of Scotland, 10:428b
Rotrouenge, **10:537a**
Röttgen Pietà, 5:0 (frontispiece)
Rottweil, Frederick II and, 11:528a
Rotuli, 2:181a, 12:490a
"Rotuli paschales," 2:181a
Rotulus, Joshua Roll, 7:152b (*illus.*)
Rotunda, in building of shrines, 4:337a
Rotundellus. See Round (Music)
Rouen, **10:537a–538b,** 12:328a (*illus.*)
Black Death in, 2:261a
burned by Vikings, 12:430a, 431a
communal government, 10:537b–538a
conversion to Christianity, 10:537b
establishment of arsenal in (1294), 9:81b
fires in, 3:560a
Harelle of 1382, 10:538a
interdict against (586), 6:494b
Norman Exchequer, 10:537b
Normans and, 9:159b
office of mayor in, 8:234b
origins, 10:537a-b
Palais de Justice, 1:431a
Parlement of, 9:420b
Exchequer and, 9:170a
population, 10:538b
prophet plays at, 4:281b
shipyard, 11:243a
supplanting of Caen as government center, 3:8b
synagogue, 1:431a
trade and commerce, 10:538a-b
as Viking capital, 12:431b, 432a
Rouen Cathedral
design of, 7:50a
Flamboyant Style of, 5:627a
jamb figures of, 5:624b
reconstruction of, 1:431a
transepts at, 5:624b
tympanum of, 5:624b
Rouen, use of, **10:538b–539a**
in Hereford liturgical celebrations, 6:187a
introduced in Lincoln, 7:583a
in liturgical books, 10:538b–539a
in liturgical dramas, 10:539a
procession of the donkeys, 10:539a
Sarum chant, 10:654b
York rite and, 12:729a
Rouergue family, Toulouse and, 12:91a-b
Rouge, 2:147b, 148a
Rougiers, hunting in, 6:357b
Roul (unit of measure), 12:593b
Roulliard, Sébastien, *Parthénie,* 1:428a
Roumanz de Julius Cesar. See Jean de Thuim
Round arch. *See* Arch
Round City (Baghdad). *See* Baghdad
Round (music), 4:87a
see also Rondeau (dance song)
Round notation. *See* Musical notation, Byzantine
Round Table, Knights of. *See* Arthurian legend
Roundel, in Islamic manuscript illumination, 8:112b
Roundell. See Lydgate, John
Rouphaiou chala. *See* Hṙomklay
Roussel de Bailleul, **10:539a-b**
Roussillon, irrigation of, 6:558b
Routiers, 3:206a
Rovine, Battle of (1395), 11:181b, 472b
Rowing. *See* Oar power
Roxburgh, taking of in 1460, 11:110b
Roxolani, Sarmatian confederacy, 10:653a
Royal Cilician Chronicle, 1:511b
Royal courts. *See* Kingship
Royal Frankish Annals, Song of Roland and, 10:445a-b
Royal Psalter, 4:548b
Royaumont (Cistercian abbey), Vincent of Beauvais and, 12:454a, 454b
Rozmowa mistrza ze śmiercią, 11:345a
Rozmyšlanie o zywocie Pana Jezusa, 11:345a
Rozzarzneibuch. See Albrant
Rrekontamiento del Rrey Ališandere, 1:176a
Ruan-Ruan, 7:236b–237a
Rubāb, 8:561b, 562a, 611a
Rubāᶜīya, 11:262b
Rubāᶜīyāt. See ᶜUmar Khayyām
Ruben I of Armenia, king, **10:539a–540a**
ancestry, 10:539b
migration, 10:540a
Vahka Castle and, 12:345a
Ruben III of Armenia, king
Lambron and, 7:322a
Tarsus and, 11:599b
vs. Bohemond of Antioch, 10:540b
Rubenids, 3:391a, 7:127a, **10:540a–541a**
anti-imperial faction, 10:539b
in Cilicia, 1:484b, 10:540b
Hetᶜumids and, 7:322a, 10:540b
origins and migration, 10:539b, 540a
rulers of Cilicia (chronography), 10:541a
Sīs under, 11:313b
territorial expansion, 10:540a
Vahka Castle and, 12:344b–345b (*illus.*)
Rubia tinctorum. See Madder
Rublev, Andrei, 6:411b, **10:541a–542a**
collaboration with Daniil Chernyi, 10:588a-b
frescoes
in Annunciation Cathedral, 10:541a
Last Judgment in Dormition Cathedral, 10:588a
icons
Christ in Zvenigorod Deesis, 10:541b, 588a (*illus.*), 588b
Old Testament Trinity, 10:541b (*illus.*), 588b, 595b
influence of, 10:586b, 589a
life of, 10:588b–589a
in literature, 10:541a
use of color, 10:588b
see also Theophanes the Greek
Rubric, in book production, 8:101b
Rubrice breves, 8:126b
Rubruck, William, 2:38b
Ruck (unit of measure), 12:593b
Rudakī (*d.* 940), *qaṣīda* and, 6:507b
Rudder
side, 11:241b

stern-post, 11:236b, 241b–242a, 248a
Rudel, Jaufré. *See* Jaufré Rudel
Rüdiger von Munre, 6:555b
Rudnik, 11:474b
Rudnitz Bridge, construction of, 10:421a
Rudolf IV (the Founder) of Austria, duke, 2:8a
Privilegium maius and, 5:503a-b
Rudolf II of Auxerre, count, Burckhardt of Swabia and, 11:538a
Rudolf I of Burgundy, king, 2:429a
Rudolf II of Burgundy, king, 2:424a, 429a
rule of France, 3:115a
Rudolf III of Burgundy, king, 2:429a
ecclesiastical land grants, 10:674b
Rudolf I of Germany, emperor, 2:7b, 10:88b, 11:540a-b
assumption of imperial status, 6:42a
Bern and, 11:543a
death of, 11:541b
election of, 4:60a, 428b, 5:487b, 492a
expansion of Habsburg dynasty under, 6:42a-b
German representative assemblies and, 10:329b–330a
Ladislas IV and, 6:343a
pacem reformare, 10:281b
Swabia and, 11:528a
Rudolf II of Germany, emperor, manufacture of scientific instruments and, 11:103a
Rudolf IV of Habsburg, assumption of archduke title, 6:42b
Rudolf von Ems, **10:542b–545a**
Alexander, 1:151b, 5:454b
instructional purpose, 10:544a-b
sources for, 10:544a
Barlaam und Josaphat, 10:543a-b
on Bligger von Steinach, 2:274b
classical influence, 10:544b–545a
on Der Stricker, 11:493a
Guote Gêrhart, 10:542b–543a
Hohenstaufen dynasty and, 8:352b
literary innovations, 10:545a
surviving works, 10:542b
Weltchronik, 2:229a
dating of, 10:544b
depiction of chariot in, 12:377a, 378a
sources for, 10:544b
Willehalm von Orlens, 5:454b, 7:289b, 10:545a
in art, 10:544a
Bussard and, 2:434a
dating of, 10:543b–544a
source for, 10:543b
Rudolf von Fenis, lyrics for minnesingers, 8:413b
Rudolf of Fulda, **10:542a**
Translatio S. Alexandri, completed by Meginhart of Fulda, 8:263a
Rudolf of Habsburg, elected king of Bohemia, 2:300a
Rudolf of Rheinfelden, duke of Swabia, 11:538a-b
elected king of Germany, 3:69b, 6:163b, 11:527a
succession to, 4:427a
vs. Henry IV, 6:448b
Rudolf of St. Trond (Sint-Truiden), **10:542a-b**
Gesta abbatum Trudonensium, 10:542a
Rudolph I (Wittelsbach; 1274-1319), 12:665a
Rudolph of Auxerre, count, Lotharingia and, 11:537b
Rudolph of Bruges, Arabic numerals and, 10:473a, 473b, 474a
Rudolph Brun, 11:542b–543a
Rudolph, Camaldolese prior (1074–1089), *Eremiticae regulae,* 3:56a
Rudolph the Elder of Habsburg, count, Waldstätte and, 11:541a
Rudolph (monk), rabble-rousing against Jews by, 7:76b, 77a-b
Ruffo, Marco, Granovitaya Palace, 8:497a-b
Ruffus, Jordanus, on equine veterinary medicine, 3:206b
Rufinus (12th-century canonist), 3:638a, 5:656b, **10:545b–546b**
auctoritas papae-administratio imperatoris, 10:546a
De bono pacis, 10:545b–546a
development of canon law, 10:545b
ecclesiastical offices, 10:545b
glosses, 10:545b
sermons, 10:546a
Summa decretorum, 10:545b
election of bishops, 4:422a-b
theological sources, 10:545b
Rufinus (early Christian scholar), 3:336a
Basil the Great translated by, 2:122a
on Nino, 9:140a
Rufinus (Greek calligrapher), 1:492a
Rugas (Hunnic leader), 6:354a
Rügen
Denmark and, 4:154a
under Wizlaw III, 12:668b
Ruggerone da Palermo, 11:259a
Ruggieri Apugliese, 11:259a
poems, 6:657a-b
Rugieri d'Amici, Iacopo da Lentini and, 6:387b
Rugs and carpets, **10:546b–552a**
almirante carpets, 10:551a
Anatolian pile, 10:549a (*illus.*)
brocaded, 10:547a
Chinese influence, 10:548b, 551a
cut-loop pile, 10:547b
definitions, 10:546b
embroidered, 10:547a
Europe, 10:548a, 550a, 551a–552b
felt rugs, mosaic and appliqué, 10:546b
flat-woven rugs, 10:546b–547a
Flemish, 10:551b
as floor coverings, 10:547b–548a
functions of, 10:550a-b, 551b
Holbein carpets, 10:549b–550a (*illus.*), 551a
Islamic
of Anatolia, 11:718b
iconology of, 6:406b, 407b
in mosques, 10:550a-b
of Seljuks of Rum, 11:149b, 158b
kilim, 7:252b–253a
knotted-pile carpets, animal, 10:548b, 549b
knotted-pile rugs, 10:547a-b
Konya and Beyshehir, 10:548b
in literary sources, 10:547b
Marby rug, 10:549b (*illus.*)
Mediterranean basin, 10:547b
Middle East, 10:548a
origins, 10:546b
pattern designs, 10:547b
Persian garden design, *Rauḍa* and, 10:261a–262b (*illus.*)
Spain, 10:551a
Spanish-knot technique, 10:547b
as status symbols, 10:547b, 548a, 550a, 550b
trade in, 10:550b
Turkish, 6:613 (*illus.*), 10:549b, 551a
see also Tapestry, art of
Rūḥ afzā, 8:611a
Ruiz, Juan, 3:140a, **10:552b–554b**
on guitar, 8:607b
Libro de buen amor, 4:572b, 11:417a-b, 456a
Arabic vocabulary, 10:554a
Archpriest of Hita's prayer, 11:450a
baker-woman's song, 11:448a-b
clerics of Talavera, 10:553b–554a
Cruz segment, 10:553a
didactic purpose of, 10:554a
exempla and, 4:551b
form and unity, 10:553a, 554a
inserted songs in, 11:448a–449a
loco amor vs. *buen amor,* 10:552b
manuscripts of, 10:552b
models for, 10:554a
musical instruments in, 8:601b
organization of, 10:552b–554a
prosody of, 11:458b, 459a
Romulus and, 4:572b
satire in, 11:454a, 454b
secular songs inserted in, 11:448b–449a
use of *cuaderna vía,* 10:552b
mester de clerecía and, 8:281b
mester de juglaría and, 8:282b–283a
on music, 8:604b
religious songs of, 11:449b
textual ambiguity, 10:552b
Ruiz, Martin (of Avendaño), 4:559a
Ruiz de Ulibarri, Juan, copies *Cantar de mío Cid* MS, 3:70b
Rukn al-Dawla, 2:435b–436a, 6:424b
Rukn al-Dīn, sultan of Rum, vs. Tamar, 11:587a
Rule of Columbanus. *See* Columbanus, Rule of
Rule of Life for a Recluse, A. See Ethelred of Rievaulx, St.
Rule of the Master, 3:343a
Rule of the Observants, Conceptualists and, 12:688b
Rule of St. Augustine. *See* Augustinian Rule
Rule of St. Benedict. *See* Benedictine Rule
Rule of St. Sisto, 12:687b
Rule of the Third Order of St. Francis, Devotio Moderna and, 4:166b
Rülein, Ulrich (von Calw), prints *Bergbüchlein,* 4:579a

Rules. *See* Monasticism
Rules of the Old and New Testament. See Matthew of Janov
Rules for Solving Sophismata. See Heytesbury, William
Ruling, **10:554b–555a**, 12:700b, 702a (*illus.*)
ink for, 12:700a
staff notation and, 8:627a
see also Stylus
Rulman Merswin, Johannes Tauler and, 9:33b
Rum, **10:555a-b**
Seljuk government, 10:555a
town and provinces, 10:555b
see also Seljuks of Rum
Ruma state (former Songhai empire), 12:55b
Rumelant, 5:442a
Rümeli Ḥiṣār, construction of, 2:504a
Rūmī, 9:42b–43a, **10:555b–557b,** 11:158b
Arabic titles, 10:555b–556a
Dīvān of Shams-i Tabrīzī, 10:556b, 557a
education, 10:556a
influences on, 9:40a
Kutᶜaisi and, 7:311b
Mathnawī-i Maᶜnawī, 6:507b, 9:43a, 10:556b, 557a
allegory of the travelers and the elephant, 9:43b (*illus.*)
Mawlawīya and, 10:556b
music and, 8:560b
mystical lyrics, 9:572a, 10:556b, 557a
narrative-didactic poems, 10:557a
spiritual unions
Čelebi Ḥusām al-Dīn Ḥasan, 10:556b
Ṣalāh al-Dīn Zarkūb, 10:556b
Shams-i Tabrīzī, 10:556a-b
Sufism and, 6:586a, 9:44b
tomb of, 12:740 (*illus.*)
vs. Xlatᶜ, 12:713b
Rūmī, Ibn al-, 1:402a
Rūmī, Yāqūt al-, description of Baghdad, 2:47a
Rumkale. *See Hṙomklay*
Rundlingen, 12:446a
Runes, 1:215 (*illus.*), 6:439a, **10:557b–568b**
added to Latin alphabet, 1:212b, 214a
Anglo-Saxon
Germanic influence, 10:562a
objects inscribed, 10:562b
stones and crosses, 10:562b
artistic decoration, 10:566a
at Ramsundsberg, 4:582a
bind-rune, 10:559b
bracteates, 10:561b (*illus.*)
Sjælland, 10:561b
Christian influence, 10:566a
chronology, 10:567a
"Danish" Futhark, 10:563a (*illus.*)
development
linguistic changes in the 7th century, 10:561b–562a
simplification and reduction, 10:563b–564a
direction of reading, 10:559b
dotted, 10:566b
earliest surviving example of, 8:327a
English, 10:558b
Frisian, 10:562b–563a
"Helnaes-Gørlev" group, 10:563a
Ingvar stones, 10:565b–566a
inscriptions, 1:215a, 274a
chronology, 10:558b, 564a-b
commemorative, 10:561a, 565b
first use of "rune" in, 10:557b
formulas for, 10:564a
memorial, 10:561b
on movable objects, 10:561a, 561b, 562b
number and distribution, 10:558b
religious, 10:566a, 566b
in younger runes, 10:564a–566a
Jellinge stone inscription, 12:418b, 419a (*illus.*)
late Middle Ages, 10:566a–567a
Latin influence, 10:566a-b
memorial stones, 10:558a, 563a
inscriptions on, 10:561a-b
proliferation in the 9th century, 10:564a
Viking Age, 10:564a–566a
modern usage, 10:557b
mysterious associations, 10:557b
naming of, 10:559a
number magic, 10:559a
Old English Futhorc, 10:562b (*illus.*)
Older Futhark, 10:559b (*illus.*)
development of, 10:558b
inscriptions in, 10:561b–562a (*illus.*)
models for, 10:560a-b
phoneme-grapheme associations, 10:559a
sound value of **E**, 10:559a-b
order of, 10:559b, 566b
place of origin, 10:561a
postmedieval, 10:567a
probable origins of, 1:215a
Rök, 10:563a
runic calendars, 10:567a
runic sticks from Bergen, 10:567a
runology, 10:557b–558a
Scandinavia
Denmark, 10:558a, 563a, 565a-b
11th through 15th centuries, 10:566a–567a
9th century, 10:563a–564a
North Atlantic islands, 10:558b
Norway, 10:558a, 565a, 567a
Sweden, 10:558a, 565b–566a
spacing and punctuation, 10:559b
"Swedish-Norwegian" Futhark, 10:563b (*illus.*), 563a
theories of origin, 10:559b–561a
Greek, 10:560a-b
Latin, 10:560a, 560b–561a
North Italic, 10:560b
Younger Futhark, 10:564a–566a
Runhent
in *Málsháttakvæði,* 8:65b
in *Merlínússpá,* 8:276a
Runka, 7:325a
Runkelstein Castle, 12:205a
Ruodlieb, 4:496a, 7:363b, **10:568b–570a**
depiction of peasant society, 1:94a-b
folk motifs, 10:569a
Greater King, 10:568b, 569b
plot summary, 10:568b–569a
realistic elements, 10:569a-b
surviving manuscripts, 10:568b
Ruodpreht, 10:101b
Rupert of Deutz, 8:642b, **10:570a-b**
Anulus or Dialogue Between a Christian and a Jew, 10:3b, 570a
classical influence, 10:570a-b
hymns and, 6:383b
influence of, 12:196a
Life of Heribert, Archbishop of Cologne, 10:570a
On the Divine Offices, 7:631a, 10:570a
On the Trinity and Its Works, 10:570a, 12:195b–196a
On the Victory of the Word of God, 10:570a
theological treatises, 10:570a
works of, 2:174a
Rupert von Durne, Wolfram von Eschenbach and, 12:674a
Rupert, St.
patron saint of Vienna, 2:6a
in Salzburg, 2:4b, 134a
Ruprecht von Freising, influenced by the *Schwabenspiegel,* 11:80b
Ruralium commodorum liber. See Crescenzi, Pietro de
Rurik, **10:570b–571b,** 12:434b
descendants of, 7:246b, 10:571a
Holmgard and, 4:555a
Novgorodian expedition, 10:571a
rule over Kievan Rus, 7:246b–247a
Rurikid dynasty, 7:241b
Rus
expansion into Caspian Sea regions, 12:436b
in 9th-century sources, 12:434b–435a
slavicization of, 12:436a
Rus kaganate, 7:241b
Ruṣāfah, al-, as center of Abbasid caliphate, 8:47a
Rušāfah, al- (in Baghdad), 2:46a
Rushayd, Ibn, 9:651b
Rushd, Ibn, 7:151b, 9:700a, **10:571b–575b,** 11:84a
Abū Yūsuf Yaᶜqūb and, 1:195a
on afterlife, 10:574a–575a
Agent Intellect and Possible Intellect, 9:597b, 10:574a-b
al-Kashfᶜan manāhij al-adilla, 10:572a-b
al-Kulliyyāt, 10:572a
Albertus Magnus and, 1:462b
Aquinas' rejection of his interpretation of Aristotle, 1:356b–357a
Aristotle and, 1:459a-b, 462a, 467b, 7:641a
commentaries, 10:572b
translation-adaptation of *Poetics,* 6:233b
Arnald of Villanova and, 1:538a
on Ashᶜarite causal theory, 10:573a
on astrology, 1:618b
on astronomy
Islamic, 1:621a
Western European, 1:614b
Bidāyat al-mujtahid, 10:572a

Colliget, 1:459a, 8:251b
commentaries of, 4:170b, 7:641a, 9:571a
condemnation of Averroism by Albertus Magnus, 1:128a
condemnation and exile, 9:571a-b
Ḍamīma, 10:572b
Destructio destructionis, Kalonymus' translation of, 12:135b
on essence, 10:573a-b
eternal universe, 9:621a
Faṣl al-maqāl, 10:572a, 573b
Final Cause, 9:597b
Ibn Sīnā and, 10:574b, 11:303b
"Incoherence of the Incoherence," 1:459b
on individual immortality, 10:574a-b
influence of, 11:379b
on Christian doctrine, 9:597b, 10:575a
on Islamic East, 10:575a
on Jewish thought, 10:575a
Paris faculty of arts, 9:597b–598a
Jewish translators of, 12:134a-b, 136b
Levi ben Gershom and, 7:553b–554a
life of, 10:571b–572a
medical treatises, in university curriculum, 11:692b
Mertonians and, 1:464b
Neoplatonism and, 9:100a
objectivity of value, 9:571a
opposition of European theologians to, 9:597b
philosophical treatises, 9:571a, 10:572a
religion and philosophy, 10:573b–574a
response to al-Ghazālī, 10:572a
on resurrection of the dead, 10:574a, 574b
scriptural interpretation, 10:573b–574a
Siger of Brabant and, 11:286b, 12:39b
Tahāfut al-Tahāfut, 5:517a, 10:572b, 573a
in Toledo, 11:410a
translated by Michael Scot, 8:305a
as transmitter of Platonic thought, 9:701a
via antiqua and, 9:157a
Walter Burley and, 2:433a
see also Aristotelianism, Averroist
Rushworth Gospels, 2:221a
dialects in, 1:276a
Russell, bishop, on the speaker of parliament, 9:433a
Russell, John, *Boke of Nurture,* 3:661b
Russia
calendar in, 3:19b
Christianity in, 2:464a-b, 489a, 8:443b, 9:687b
Crimean relations with, 3:679a-b
economy, in Time of Troubles, 11:195b–197b
furs and fur trade in
with Central and Western Europe, 5:328a–330b
with Near East, Central Asia, and Byzantium, 5:330b–334a
types of, 5:327a–328a
Karaites in, 7:210a
military serving families
allegiance to Moscow, 8:541b
income, 8:547a
origin of, 8:541b
monasticism in, 8:443b
Mongol invasions, 8:470b
alliance of princes, 8:468a-b, 475b–476a
National Assembly, 11:198b
nomadic invasions of, **10:576a–578a**
Altaic nomads, 10:576a
Arabo-Khazar warfare, 10:576a
Cuman/Kipchak tribal union, 10:577a
Cumans, 10:576b–577a, 12:500a
Hungarian tribal union, 10:576b
into Caucasia, 3:195a-b
Khazar Kaganate, 10:576a-b
Oghuz Turks, 10:576b
Pechenegs, 2:493b, 494a, 10:576b
Tatar, 9:687b
through Caucasus Mountains, 3:195b–196a
see also Magyars
paper introduced into, 9:390a
princes
genealogy, 1125–1505, 8:544a-b
grand principalities, 8:540a
succession conflicts, 8:539a-b, 542b–545a, 546a
Tatar approval, 8:539b
principalities
dynastic conflicts, 8:541b–542a
ranking servitors (boyars), 4:305b
role of duma, 4:305b
Yuri of Vladimir, 8:468b
Tatar yoke, 8:476a, 539b
end of, 8:540a-b, 542a-b, 546a
Varangians in, 4:555a
vs. Bulgaria, 2:406a
see also Kievan Rus; Muscovy; Novgorod
Russian architecture, **10:578b–582b**
bas-relief figures, 10:580a
bell cotes, 10:580b
brick structures, 10:578b
Byzantine influence, 10:578b–579a, 583a
churches, 10:578b, 579a–580a
tent, 10:580b, 581a (*illus.*)
votive, 10:581b–582a
dome, 4:236a
drum windows, 10:579b–580a
engaged colonettes, 10:579b–580a
14th century, 10:580b–581a
Greek-cross church type in, 4:341a
helmet domes, 10:579a-b
klet, 10:578b, 580b
kokoshniki, 7:283 (*illus.*), 10:581a, 581b
native Baroque style, 10:582a
neo-Vladimirian style, 8:496b, 10:582a
Novgorodian style, 10:579a–580b, 584a
onion dome, 10:579b, 580b, 582a
pagan influence, 10:583a
stone structures, 10:578b, 580a-b, 584b
imitation of wooden church style, 10:580b–582a
town walls, 10:578b
12th century, 10:579b–580a
two-story buildings, 10:578b
vertical line, 10:579a, 580b
wood structures, 10:578b, 580b
see also Bogoliubskii, Andrei; *Bochka;* Fioravanti, Aristotele; Hagia Sophia (cathedral: Kiev); *Papert;* Pecherskaya Lavra; Peter, Master; Venets
Russian art, **10:582b–591a**
Byzantine influence, 10:583a
conception of, 10:590b
Dionysios the Greek, 4:192a
15th century, 10:590a
Greek influence, 10:586b
Palaiologan style, 10:586b, 587a, 589a-b
icon painting in, *kleimo,* 7:275b (*illus.*)
iconography, 10:589b–590a
influence on later periods, 10:590b
interrelation of disciplines, 10:590b
kontsovka, 7:293a (*illus.*)
mosaics and frescoes, 10:583b–584a (*illus.*), 585 (*illus.*), 590a
pre-Mongol, 10:584b
Muscovite, 10:586b, 589b–590a
Novgorodian style, 10:584a-b, 586a-b
origins, 10:582b
pagan, 10:582b–583a
periods of development, 10:583a
realism, 10:590b
relief sculpture, 10:584b
secular themes, 10:590a
Suzdal, 10:584b
symbolism, 10:590b
13th through 14th centuries, 10:585b–586a
Western influences, 10:585b–586a, 590a-b
see also Icons; *Pelena;* Venets
Russian language, 6:438a, 439a
Christianization of Kievan Rus and, 12:436a
in Crimea, 6:437b
Old Russian language, 6:444a
see also Byelorussian language; Slavic languages and literatures
Russian (Muscovite) law, **7:506a–512b**
bloodwite (fine) payment, 7:510b
church guarantees, 7:508a
civil law, 7:511b–512a
criminal law, 7:510a–511b
Eclogue revised, 7:507b
false accusation and, 7:511a-b
homicide, 7:510a-b
local codifications, 7:507a
Muscovite princes (Ivan III and Ivan IV) and, 7:507a
"On Witnesses," 7:510a
ordeals under, 7:510a
private prosecution, 7:508a-b
procedure, 7:508a–510a
punishment, 7:507b–508a, 510b
revenge and homicide, 7:510a-b
in Smolensk, 7:507a
sources, 7:506b–508a
summary, 7:512a-b

Russian (Muscovite) law (*cont.*)
testimony, 7:509b–510a
theft, 7:508b
wergild (compensation) payment, 7:510b
witnesses, 7:509b–510a
see also Novgorod Judicial Charter; Pskov Judicial Charter; *Russkaya pravda* (Russian truth)
Russian music, 9:687a-b
see also Slavic music
Russian nomads, invasions of
into Hungary, 6:340a
Khazars, 7:240b–242a
see also Russia, nomadic invasions of
Russian Orthodox Church, 2:118b, **10:591a–597b**
anti-Latin sentiments, 10:593a
canonical structure, 10:592a
cathedrals, 10:592a-b
church and state, 10:596a-b
Novgorod, 9:194b
Council of One Hundred Chapters, 10:596a
dioceses
establishment of, 10:592a
Great Russia and Little Russia, 10:592b
during Mongol occupation, 10:592b–594b
economic prosperity, 10:593a
Nil Sorsky-Joseph debate, 10:595b–596a
feasts, Pokrov, 9:716a
Holy Synod of, *znamenny* chant and, 8:576a
Isidore and, 6:563a
land holding, *pomestie* system, 8:549a
liturgical texts
local writers, 10:591b–592a
Slavonic translations, 10:591b, 594a–595a
martyrdom, 8:159b–160a
metropolitanate, 2:469b
of all Russia, 10:594a, 594b, 596b
approval of by Constantinople, 8:541a, 545a-b
approval of by grand prince, 8:545b–546a
division of, 10:593b–594b
Moscow, 8:541a
monastic movement, 10:595a–596b
origins, 10:591a–592b
pilgrimage and the, 9:653a–654b
plainsong, 9:687a-b
property, Nil Sorsky on secularization of, 9:137a
rise of Muscovy and, 2:470a, 8:540b–541a, 545a–546a
spiritual and cultural trends, 10:594b–596a
tax-exempt status, 10:593a, 595b
Third Rome, 10:596b
title of patriarch and, 9:459b
unifying force, 10:593a
views on slavery, 1:100a
vs. Latin church, in Novgorod, 9:196b
see also Metropolitan, Russian
Russian *Primary Chronicle. See Primary Chronicle,* Russian
Russkaya pravda (Russian truth), 7:506b–509a, 510a–512b
abbreviated version, 7:507a
civil law in, 7:511b
expanded version, 7:506b
homicide and, 7:510a-b
inheritance law, 7:511b, 11:670a
Kormchaya kniga and, 7:506b
liability limits in, 7:511b
Novgorod's Judicial Charter and, 7:507a
origin of, 7:506b
patrilineal kinship, 11:670a
procedure, 7:508a–509b
punishment in, 7:510a–511a
revisions and changes in, 7:506b–507a
short version, 7:506b
slavery law, 7:511b
Slavic land boundaries, 11:669b
Sudebnik and, 7:507a
see also Russian (Muscovite) law
Rüssulbecher beaker, 5:554b–555a
Rustam (epic character), 11:221b, 223b
Rustamid dynasty, 11:139a-b
Rusta^{c}veli, Shot^{c}a. *See* Shot^{c}a Rusta^{c}veli
Rustic knights. *See* Knights
Rustici ducis. See Peasants, duke's
Rusticiano, *Tristano Riccardiano,* 1:572b, 6:638b, 659a
Rusticus, Elphidius, on church decoration, 4:358b
Rustum, 6:548b
Rusudan of Georgia, queen (1223–1245), 5:407a
Rūṭah, 8:611a
Rutebeuf, **10:597b**
attention to detail, 5:261b
autobiographical indications in his work, 2:237a
beguines and, 2:159b
complainte on Thibaut V de Navarre, 3:507b
consistency of principles, 5:261b
etymology of, 5:261b
fabliaux and, 4:574a, 576b
lyric mode, transformation of, 5:261–262a
Miracle de Théophile, 4:264a, 5:264a, 8:431b, 10:597b
poetic works
five topical areas, 5:261a-b
variety of genre, 5:261b
Renart le Bestourné, 10:313b
sirventes of, 11:313a
technical excellence, 5:261b
use of vernacular, 5:262a, 264a
Voie de paradis, 1:185b
Ruthenia, Poland and, 9:725a, 727a, 728a
Ruthwell cross, 10:562b
Rutilius Claudius Namatianus, **10:597b–598a**
De reditu suo, 10:598a
Etrurian estates and, 4:511a
Rutland, sheriff of, returns of examined by parliament, 9:432a
Ruusbroec, Jan van, **10:598a**
as Augustinian canon, 3:368b
beguines and, 2:160b
Chierheit der gheestelike brulocht, 4:320b, 10:598a
doctrine of, 9:37b
followers of, 9:37b–38a
Geert Groote and, 5:680b
influenced by Hadewijch, 9:12a
life of, 9:36a-b
on mystical union, 5:513a
relation to Free Spirits, 5:219a
Spiritual Espousals, 9:36b
Vanden blinckenden steen, 4:320b
works in English, 9:27a
writings of, 9:36b–37b
Ruvo Cathedral, 10:486b
Ruwad, al-Ashraf and, 11:562a
Ryazan
Ivan III of Muscovy and, 7:20a
taken (1237), 2:131b
Rye, as cereal crop, 1:83b, 86a
Ryman, James, carols and, 3:116a
Rymington, William, vs. Wyclif, 12:709b

S

Saadiah Gaon (Sa^{c}adya ibn Yūsuf al Fayyūmī), 5:356b, 7:83b, 104b, **10:598b–599a**, 11:584b
Book of Doctrines and Beliefs, 7:108a, 165a–166b, 10:3a, 598b–599a
commentary on *Sefer yezirah,* 10:598b
defense of Orthodoxy, 10:599a
divine unity and, 7:151b
as exegete, 2:212a, 4:539a, 7:172b
impact on Spanish Jews, 6:128b
influence on Ashkenazi Hasidism, 9:579b
on Judaism, 7:165a–166b
on the Karaites, 7:163b, 210a
kavod, 9:580a
Mu^{c}tazilite influence, 9:573a
piyyutim of, 7:622a
prayer book of, 7:620b
Sefer ha-agron, 6:128a, 10:598b
synagogue poetry, 6:131b
theology
created glory, 9:576b
kalam, rejection of, 9:575a
Saarbrücken, Roman bridge at, 10:410a
Sabaeans
of Ḥarrān, 9:4a-b
in Ibn al-Nadīm's *Al-Fihrist,* 9:51b
Islam and, 9:498b
navigation in the Indian Ocean and, 9:85a
translations of Greek scientific treatises into Arabic, 11:83a
Sabaton, 1:525b, 529b, 530b, 534a (*illus.*)
Sabellianism
definition, 9:560b
see also Heresies, Western European

Sabers. *See* Swords
Sabīl, **10:599b**
Sabin, Ibn, Frederick II and, 11:274a
Sabinianus, pope, bells and, 2:165b, 5:321a
Sābiqā, 3:34b
Sabki-Hindī, 6:509a
Sabruguera, Romeu, Bible translation of, 3:167a
Ṣabtī, al-, treatise on divination, 8:21b
Šābuhr I, Sasanian king, 1:452a, **10:599b–600b**
capture of Valerian, 10:666b
cities and palaces named after, 10:600a
founding of Bishapur and, 2:251b–252a
inscription of, on Ka^{c}abapyi Zardušt, 7:221b
Ka^{c}ba of Zoroaster and, 7:204b–205a
Mani and, 8:84a
mentioned on Ka^{c}ba of Zoroaster, 11:374b
promotion of Zoroastrianism, 10:600b
record of conquests, 10:600a
in a relief carving at Naqsh-i Rustam, 9:61 (*illus.*)
Roman wars, 10:599b–600a
Šābuhr II, Sasanian king, **10:600b–601b**
bas relief of, 10:601a, 657b, 658a
Church of the East and, 11:563a
government, centralization of, 10:668a
Gundēshāpūr and, 12:714a
Nishapur and, 9:140b
partitioning of Armenia, 10:668b
persecution of Christians, 10:601a, 662b
Roman wars, 10:601a
vs. Aršak, II, 1:476a
Šābuhr III, Sasanian king, in art, 11:597a
Šābuhrāgān. *See* Mani
Sabunde of Barcelona, Raymond, *Theologia naturalis,* 11:407a
Sabur. *See* Bishapur
Sabutai. *See* Sübüdey
Sac and soc, **10:601b–602b**
cases pertaining to, 10:601b
earliest grant of, 10:602a
lords' right to, 10:601b–602a
royal grants of, 10:601b–602a
Sacchetti, Franco, 1:562a, 6:653b–654b, 669b–670a
inns and, 6:475a
Trecentonovelle, 6:660b–661a
Sacchetti, Giannotto, 6:663a
Sacellarius, 10:522b
Sacerdos, St., bishop of Limoges, 6:318b
Sachs, Hans, 1:455b, 4:272a, 8:412b, 9:202b
Der hörnen Seyfrid, 11:289b–290a
Gebrauchsliteratur, 10:535a-b
Mären, 8:132a
Spruchgedichte, 7:300b
Sachsenspiegel. *See* Eike von Repgowe
Sächsische Weltchronik, 8:354a
authorship of, 10:602b
source for *Lohengrin,* 7:643a
see also Eike von Repgowe
Sack, **10:604a,** 12:593b
Sack, Friars of the, 5:297b, 298a, **10:604a–605a**
abolition of at Council of Lyons, 10:604b
constitutions, 10:604b
establishment of houses, 10:604a-b
origins, 10:604a
Rule of St. Augustine, 10:604a
Sackbut, 8:603b, 12:180b
in civic music, 8:597a
Sacra corona regni Hungariae, 11:483b
Sacra parallela. *See* John of Damascus, St.
Sacralias. *See* Sagrajas
Sacrament, benedictions of, 2:177a
Sacrament, reservation of, **10:335a–336a**
in churches, 10:335b–336a
in homes, 10:335a-b
see also Eucharist
Sacramentaire grégorien, Benedict of Aniane and, 2:178a-b
Sacramentals, in the Byzantine church, 7:611a
Sacramentarium Hadrianum. *See* Sacramentary, Lateran type
Sacramentarium Veronense, 10:605a
ordination prayers, 9:263b
Sacramentary, **10:605a–606b**
of Angoulême, 4:131a
Campanian, 2:180b
Celtic rite, 10:606a-b
in collectarium, 3:479b
Divine Office and, 4:223a-b
Gallican rite and, 5:344b, 10:606a
of Gellone, decorated initials in, 6:461b
Gregorian, 2:168a, 180b–181a
illumination of, **10:607a**
Christ in Majesty, 10:607a
painted initials, 10:607a
incorporation of *libelli* elements, 10:606b
Irish, 7:614a-b, 615b
Lateran type, 10:605b
Milanese rite, 8:381b, 10:606a
in missal, 8:437b
Missal of Robert of Jumièges and, 10:434a (*illus.*)
Old Spanish rite, 10:606a
Paduensis, 10:605b
Reginensis, 10:605b
Roman rite, 10:605b
for St. Gereon, 10:102b
see also Coronation Sacramentary; *Libelli missarum;* Ritual
Sacramentary of Bergamo, 8:381b
Sacramentary of Biasca, 8:381b
Sacraments
in Armenian church, 1:502a
in Byzantine church, 7:611b, 611a
in Celtic church, 3:230b–231a
in *Decretum Gratiani,* 4:129b
Donatist view of, 4:260a
in early church, 3:338a-b
Hugh of St. Victor and, 6:322a, 322b
Hussites and, 6:373a
for the insane, 6:491a
interdict and, 6:493b, 495a, 496b
marriage, rules of consanguinity, 3:540a-b
Ockham and, 9:213b
primacy of, 8:181b
Razón de Amor allusions to, 10:268b–269a
simoniac, 9:508b, 509a
theology of, in 12th century, 9:602b–603a
see also Baptism; Confirmation; Eucharist; Extreme Unction; Marriage; Ordination, Clerical; Penance
Sacramentum. See Oath
Sacre rappresentazioni. *See* Italian drama, liturgical
Sacred Heart, cult of, promoted at Helfta, 9:11a, 11b
Sacrificio de la Misa. *See* Berceo, Gonzalo de
Sacrilegis monachis, 7:366b
Sacristan, instruments in ordination, 9:267a
Sacristy, **10:607a-b**
Sacro Eremo di Camaldoli. *See* Camaldoli, Sacro Eremo di
Sacrosancta, on authority of church councils, 4:483b
Sa^{c}d, **10:607b–608a**
lusterware bowl, 10:607b (*illus.*)
Sa^{c}d al-Dawla, 7:108a
Sa^{c}d ibn Abī Waqqāš, 6:569a, 7:306a
Sa^{c}d, Ibn (*d.* 845), *Kitāb al-Ṭabaqāt al-kabīr,* 6:253a
Sa^{c}da, Zaydis and, 12:742a
Saddle
armored, 1:529a, 532b–533a
highbacked, European cavalry and, 3:202b
Saddlers, Worshipful Company of, 7:531b
Sa^{c}dī of Shiraz
Būstān, 6:508a
Gulistān, **6:26b–27a,** 508a, 11:252b
influence on Persian proverbs and literature, 6:27a
moral point, 6:26b, 27a
Ṣādiq, Ja^{c}far al-, 11:136a-b
Imāmīs and, 11:227a, 227b
Sælden Hort, Der, 2:230b
Sæmundr Sigfússon (the Learned), 9:175b, 177a, 11:328a
Safad, recaptured (1266), 2:138b
Ṣafadī, al-
Al-Wāfī bi'l-wafayāt, 2:237b
biography of Hunayn ibn Isḥāq, 12:131a
Safar-nāma. *See* Nāṣir-i Khusraw
Safawids (Safavids)
in Azerbaijan, 2:27a
Bāyazīd II and, 2:137b
fall of the Mamluk state and, 8:76a-b
in Iran, 6:505a, 509a
in Iraq, 6:514b
Isfahan under, 6:562a
manuscript illumination and, 8:117b
Selim I and, 11:145a
Shī^{c}a and, 11:228a
Tabrīz and, 11:571a
vs. Ottomans, over control of Anatolia, 8:76a

Saffāḥ, Abu ’l-ᶜAbbās al-, Abbasid caliph, **10:608a–609a**
  ancestry, 10:608a
  al-Manṣūr and, 8:88b
  Najrānite clan of Banū ᶜAbd al-Madān and, 9:55b
  problems with succession, 10:608a-b
Ṣaffāra, 8:612b
Saffarids, **10:609a–610a**
  Abbasids and, 6:590a, 10:609b–610a
  control of western Afghanistan, revival of Iranian imperial tradition, 1:64b
  defeat by Samanids, 10:609b
  Ghaznavid control, 10:609b
  language and literature, 10:610a
  military expansion, 10:609a-b
  military organization, 10:610a
  origins, 12:717a
  plebeian origins, 10:609a
  Seljuk suzerainty, 10:609b
  tenure of power, 6:503b
  vs. Muḥammad ibn Ṭāhir, 11:575b
Safflower, 4:327b (*illus.*)
  production of as dye, 4:326a
Saffron, 6:183b
  production of, 4:326a
Ṣafī al-Dīn, 8:611b
  Book of Musical Modes, 8:566a-b
  musical notation and, 8:566b
  Sharafīya, 8:566a
Safīna (Muslim warship), 9:76a, 76b
Saga
  as designation of *þættir,* 12:1b
  Saga af Hálfu ok Hálfsrekkum, as a source for *Mágus saga jarls,* 8:45b
  Saga af Tristram ok Ísodd, 10:391a, 394a-b, 395b
  Saga of Ragnarr Shaggy-Breeches, 10:248a–249b
  Saga of Sigurd Fáfnisbani, 9:171a
  Saga Þorbjarnar ok Hávarðar ins halta, retelling of, 6:114b–115a
Sagas, 4:612a-b
  armor in, 1:523a, 524a
  biblical
    Gyðinga saga, 6:41b
  main categories of, 4:612b, **10:610a-b**
  non-royal subjects, 6:75b–76a
  see also Bishops’ sagas; Family sagas, Icelandic; Fornaldarsögur; Norse kings’ sagas; *Riddarasögur;* Scandinavian literature
Sage, uses of, 6:183b
Sagena, 11:232a
Sagitta, 11:232a
Sagrajas, battle at, 1:199b, 3:129b, 384a-b
Sagristà i la burgesa, El, 3:173b
Šah Ismāᶜil, 2:137b
Šah-i Armen, in Xlatᶜ, 1:485a
Sahak III of Jorapᶜor, *katᶜołikos,* 1:509b
  Byzantine church and, 1:500a
Sahak Arcruni, martyrdom of, 1:479b, 519a
Sahak Bagratuni of Armenia, 2:48a
Sahak (Qaysite martyr; *d.* 808), 1:519b
Sahak, St., 1:518a, 5:540a, 665a-b, **10:610b–611b**
  anaphora and, 1:516b
  Armenian alphabet and, 1:559b
  commemorated, 1:520b
  correspondence with Akakios of Melitene, 10:611a
  dates of pontificate, 10:611a
  ecclesiastical endeavors, 10:611a
  Eznik and, 4:571a
  in Łazar Pᶜarpecᶜi’s *History of Armenia,* 7:529b
  Mamikonean link, 10:611a
  Maštocᶜ and, 1:507b, 518b, 10:611a
  modal classification of, 8:551b
  Proclus and, 1:508a
  rebuilding of cathedral of Ējmiacin, 4:417a-b
  revision of the Bible, 2:217a
  role in Armenian affairs, 10:611a
  on Theodore of Mopsuestia, 1:498b
Sahakanuyš, 5:665b
Sahakduxt (sister of Stepᶜanos of Siwnikᶜ), 1:510a
Šāhan-šāh, **10:611b–612a,** 12:737a
  Arsacid use, 10:666a
  in inscriptions, 10:611b
  kayan χwarrah, 10:611b, 663b
  in non-Iranian cultures, 10:612a
  in Sasanian culture, 10:611b, 660a
  symbols of, 10:611b
  in Zoroastrianism, 10:663b
Šahanšah (son of Zakᶜarē), 1:485b
Šahapivan, Council of (444), 1:498b, 502b, 508a, 518a, 520a
  condemnation of *mcłneutᶜiwn,* 6:187b
  condemnation of heretics, 9:469a
Sahara
  Berbers and, 2:186a
  Mali Empire and, 8:57b, 58a
  tribes, Islamization of, 1:199a, 200b
Ṣāhdōna. *See* Martyrius
Šahē. *See* Sophenē
Ṣāḥib al-sūq, 8:526b–527a
Ṣaḥīḥ. See Bukhārī, al-
Sahl al-Tustarī, disciples of, 6:80a-b
Sahn, 6:592a, **10:612a-b**
Saḥnūn, *Mudawwana,* 1:71a
Šāhpurh. *See* Šābuhr
Šahristānī, on the teachings of Mazdak, 8:236b
Šahristaniha i Eran, major Sasanian towns, 10:661a
Šahuni, Lesser Sophenē and, 1:515a
Saḥūr meal, 10:254b
Sahyun. *See* Saone
Saibante Codex, 6:630b
Saᶜīd, Ibn, 5:393b–394a
Saᶜid ibn Birṭrīq al-Fusṭāṭ. *See* Eutychios the Melchite
Saif al-Dīn Ghāzī I, vs. Second Crusade, 4:38a
Sāᵓiḥ, al-. *See* Nuᶜmān
Sail
  fore-and-aft
    classical, 11:230a
    Northern European, 11:244b
  lateen. *See* Lateen sail
  square, 11:229b–230a
    in carrack, 11:237a
    in cog, 11:236b, 241a
    in full-rigged ship, 11:244b
  see also Bonaventure mizzen; Lateen sail; Mizzen; Spritsail; Staysail
Sailing ship, 11:233b–234b (*illus.*)
  evolution of, 11:234 (*illus.*)
  oar power and, 11:232a
  see also Carrack; Cog; Full-rigged ship; *Knarr*
Sailors. *See* Seamen
S. Abbondio (church: Como), 10:485b
St. Agnes (basilica: Rome), monasticism and, 8:461b
St. Agnes (monastery: Bologna), 12:687b
St. Albans, battles in Wars of the Roses, 12:570b, 571a
St. Albans (abbey: England), 2:173a
  church taxation and, 11:608a
  Richard of Wallingford and, 10:387b
  Walsingham on, 7:370a
St. Albans Cathedral, Crucifixion painting, 12:532a (*illus.*)
St. Albans (Hertfordshire), no citizenship in, 3:423a
St. Albans Psalter, Bury Bible and, 6:324b
St. Amand (abbey: near Valenciennes), 6:317a
S. Ambrogio (church: Milan), 10:484b–485a, 486b
  founding of, 8:377b
  narthex of, 9:64a (*illus.*)
  Paliotto of, 8:288 (*illus.*), 289a, 10:100b–101a
St. Ambrose, Peace of (1258), 8:379a
St. Ambrose, sarcophagus of, 4:354b
S. Ana (church: Granada), 5:653b
St. André-de-Sorède (church: Pyrenees), 10:112a, 493a
S. Andrea (church: Perugia), 9:668b
S. Andreo (monastery: Celio), Innocent III and, 6:464a
St. Andrew cross. *See* Andrew cross
St. Andrew’s (church: Greensted, England), 3:559a (*illus.*)
St. Andrews MS. *See* Wolfenbüttel, Helmstedt MS 628
St. Andrews (Scotland), **10:612b–613b**
  Augustinians, 10:612b
  bishopric, 10:612b
  church of St. Mary of the Rock, 10:612b
  cum universi status, 10:613
  naming of church, 10:612b
  Queen’s Ferry for pilgrims, 10:612b
  revenues, 10:612b
  St. Rule’s Church, 10:612b
  town, economic development, 10:613a
St. Andrews, University of, 10:613a, 11:112a, 12:290b
S. Angelo (church: Formis), 10:113a, 505a
St. Anne (church: Jerusalem), constructed, 4:22b, 23b
St. Anthony, Order of, 3:305 (*illus.*), 307a
St. Anthony’s Disease. *See* Plagues, European
St. Antoine (monastery: Dauphiné), founded, 4:109b
St. Antony’s College (Louvain), 6:525a

S. Apollinare in Classe (church: Ravenna), 10:264b
  apse mosaic, 8:491 (*illus.*)
S. Apollinare Nuovo (church: Ravenna), 7:344a, 9:153b, 10:263b
  interior decoration of, 4:358b
  nave mosaic, 4:358a (*illus.*), 9:447a, 10:340a, 12:493a
St. Astuacacin (cathedral: Ani), 5:339a
  architectural features, 10:647b–648a
St. Astuacacin (church: Siwnik^{c}), 9:159a
St. Astuacacin (church: T^{c}alin), 11:582b
St. Astuacacin (church: Tat^{c}ew), 11:600b
St. Augustine (church: Canterbury), customary, use of organ, 9:273b
  see also Canterbury Cathedral
St. Augustine (monastery: Canterbury)
  architectural features, 10:681a
  founded, 3:81b
  Reginald of Canterbury, 10:289a-b
St. Aurelius (church: Hirsau), 10:487b
St. Barbara (church: Kutná Hora), Johannes II Parler at, 9:421b
St. Barthélemy (church: Liège), 10:499b–500a
  baptismal font, 10:253 (*illus.*)
St. Bartholomew. *See* Master of St. Bartholomew
St. Bartholomew at Smithfield, fairs, 4:586b–587a
St. Bartholomew's (almshouse: London), 6:490b
S. Bartolomeo in all'Isola (church: Rome), 10:504a
St. Basil (church: Moscow), architectural elements, 10:582a
  see also Moscow Kremlin
S. Baudillo de Berlanga (church: Spain), architectural elements, choir, 8:512b (*illus.*)
St. Bavo (cathedral: Ghent), 4:566b
St. Bénigne (church: Dijon), 10:112a, 479a
  William of Volpiano and, 10:247a
St. Benoît-sur-Loire (church: central France), 10:112a
St. Bernard, College of (Paris), founded, 3:405a
St. Bricín (church: Tuam Drecain), 6:540b
S. Callisto (church: Rome), catacombs, 4:350a, 7:343b
S. Cassiano a Settimo (church: Tuscany), 10:503a
St. Castor (church: Coblenz), copper gilt retable in, 10:342a
S. Caterina (church: Pisa), 11:299b
St. Catherine (church: Lübeck), Franciscan order, General Assembly of, 7:683a
St. Catherine (monastery: Sinai), 8:454b
  apse mosaics, 4:354b–355a, 356 (*illus.*)
  doors of, 4:361a
  encaustic panel, 4:355a
  icon of the Annunciation, 2:445b–446a, 446a (*illus.*)
  icon of Christ, 4:35(*illus.*)
  panel painting, 10:505b
"St. Catherine of the Night Brotherhood," 6:637a
St. Catherine's Day. *See* Catherning
S. Cecilia (church: Montserrat), 10:477b
St. Cecilia Master. *See* Master of St. Cecilia
St. Chad, Book of (Lichfield Gospels), **10:615a–616a**
  date and place of origin, 10:615b
  illuminations, St. Luke miniature, 10:615b (*illus.*)
  lacertine ornament in, 7:314b (*illus.*)
  liturgical usage, 10:615a
  scope of original manuscript, 10:615a
  Surexit memorandum, 12:599b
Ste. Chapelle (church: Paris), 3:264a, **10:623b–624b**
  architect, 10:624a
  Beauneveu and, 2:145b
  construction of, 7:675a
  cost of building, 10:624a
  date of construction, 10:624a
  decorative style, 10:624a
  figural sculpture in, 5:599b
  imitations of, 10:624a-b
  interior of, 5:631b
  origins, 10:623b
  relics housed in, 10:624a
  stained glass in, 5:551b (*illus.*), 553a
  statues of Apostles at, 5:623a
  style of, 5:623a
Ste. Chapelle (church: Riom)
  tracery forms, 6:39a
  vaulting in, 10:383a
S. Chiara (church: Naples), 9:59b, 11:275b
St. Chrysogonus (church: Trastevere), 2:170b
St. Clair-sur-Epte, Treaty of (911), 3:115a, 9:160a–161a
St. Clement (church: Ohrid), 7:282b
S. Clemente (church: Rome), 10:485b, 486a, 518b
  decorations, 10:504b–505a
  fresco with chasuble, 12:400a-b, 401 (*illus.*)
  frescoes at, 10:112b
S. Clemente de Tahull (church: Spain), 10:505b
Sts. Cosmas and Damian (church: Rome), donor portrait at, 4:262a
S. Costanza (mausoleum: Rome), 4:336b, 350b
  apse mosaic *Traditio legis,* 12:123a–124b (*illus.*)
  dome mosaics, 4:358a
S. Croce (church: Florence), frescoes in, 5:294a
S. Croce (church: Ravenna), 10:263a
S. Croce in Gerusalemme (church: Rome), 10:517a
St. Cuthbert (church: Edinburgh), history, 4:392b
St. Cyriakus (church: Gernrode), 10:95a-b (*illus.*), 96a
S. Damiano (convent), 5:191b, 12:688a
  founded, 12:687b
St. David's, **10:616a-b**, 12:515a, 516a
  aquatici, 10:616a
  bid for archiepiscopal status, 10:616a
  bishops of Mynyw, 10:616a
  cult of, 10:616b
  Gerald of Wales, dispute over bishopric, 5:421a-b
  independence from Canterbury, 12:524a
St. Denis
  fair of, export of goods from, 5:116a-b
  fairs, 4:585a
St. Denis (abbey church: Paris), 3:237a, **10:616b–617a**
  ambulatory of, quadripartite vaults in, 12:366a
  apse in, 3:378b
  architectural elements, 10:92b, 616b
  Beauneveu and, 2:145a
  construction of, 9:403a
  dedication of, 9:690b
  Gothic architecture, 5:581 (*illus.*), 584a-b, 11:656a-b
  gradual manuscripts, 9:688b–692a (*illus.*)
  Grandes chroniques de France and, 5:654a-b
  ground plan of, 10:93 (*illus.*)
  interior of, 5:631b
  management of lands, 2:174b
  Pepin III and, 9:500b
  Pope Stephen II and, 9:502a
  reconstruction of under Suger, 11:503b–504a (*illus.*)
  sculpture, 10:490b, 498a
  stained glass in, 5:548b, 552b
  tombs
    of Capetian kings, 5:620a (*illus.*)
    of Dagobert at, 5:623a-b
    of Frankish queen, 8:363b
  transept of, 5:623a-b
  Viking raids and, 12:430b
  see also Suger of St. Denis
St. Dimitri (cathedral: Vladimir)
  architectural elements, 10:580a
  frescoes
    Last Judgment, 10:585 (*illus.*)
    political elements, 10:584b
  ground plan, 10:578a (*illus.*)
  south facade, 10:580a (*illus.*)
S. Domingo de Silos (monastery: Burgos), 10:494 (*illus.*)
  Berceo and, 2:187a
St. Donatian (church: Bruges), 2:386a-b
St. Dymphna (shrine: Gheel), 6:492a
St. Elias (church: Gelat^{c}i), 5:374b
St. Elizabeth (church: Marburg), retable in, 10:342a
St. Emmeram (monastery: Regensburg), 2:134a, 174b, 225a
  baptism of 14 Czech nobles and, 2:299a, 299b, 303b–304a
  Codex Aureus, 10:99b
  production of Codex Aureus, 8:106b, 107a (*illus.*)
S. Ercolano (church: Perugia), 8:52a (*illus.*)
St. Erkenwald, 8:320a, 332a
  source and author, 6:63a
St. Étienne (chapter: Troyes), founded by Henry I of Champagne, 3:246a

St. Étienne (church: Caen), 2:125a, 175a, 10:482a (*illus.*), 482b, 483a (*illus.*)
English Romanesque architecture, 10:484a, 484b
quadrant vaults in, 12:365b
St. Étienne (church: Nevers), 10:475b, 479b–480a
Gothic architecture in, 5:585b (*illus.*), 591a
St. Étienne (church: Paris), 9:190b
St. Étienne-de-la-Cité (church: Périgueux), 10:481a
Ste. Eutrope (church: Saintes), 10:495a
Ste. Foy (cathedral: Conques), 3:564b–565a, 10:483a, 495a, 497a
S. Francesco (church: Assisi), **1:593b–594a**
Cimabue's frescoes for, 3:396a-b
commissioning of, 1:593b
decoration of, 1:593b–594a
frescoes, 5:292a (*illus.*), 293a
Coronation of the Virgin, 12:175a
Life of Christ, 12:173b
Giotto di Bondone's involvement in, 5:532a
Pietro Lorenzetti's work in, 1:593b–594a, 9:447a
S. Martin Chapel, frescoes, 5:294a, 11:300a (*illus.*)
Simone Martini's work in, 1:594a
stained glass in, 5:553a
see also Torriti, Jacopo
S. Francesco (church: Pescia), retable by Bonaventura Berlinghieri, 2:189a
"St. Francis Brotherhood," 6:636a
St. Front (church: Périgueux), 10:481a
S. Fructuoso de Montelius (church: Portugal), 12:465b, 466a, 466b
St. Gabriel (church: Provence), 10:481b
St. Gall (city), 11:543a-b
Rudolph of Habsburg and, 11:540a
St. Gall, Feast of, 9:691b–692b(*illus.*)
St. Gall Gospels, 7:228b
St. Gall (monastery: Switzerland), 5:342b–343a, 10:617a–618a
abbot as librarian, 7:570a
apse of church in, 3:378b
architectural plan of, 8:455a
beer mill in, 8:392b
Carolingian renaissance and, 11:526b
discovery of Quintilian's *Institutio oratoria* and, 10:356b, 363b
distinguished abbots, 10:617a
Gallus and, 11:526a
history of, 10:260b
hymnody of, 6:381b, 9:187b
imperial protection, 10:617a
Latin literature of, 7:363a
library of, 7:562b, 10:617a
Magyars and, 6:338b
musical notation of, 8:624b, 625a
Office antiphonal manuscript for, 9:691b–692b (*illus.*)
plan of, 10:306b, **10:617a–618a,** 10:617b (*illus.*), 11:515b
basis for, 10:94a
location of fireplaces, 6:121a
sequence tradition and, 11:163a
Swiss Confederation and, 11:544b
technological innovations
flues and chimneys, 11:651b
heating, 6:120a
hydraulic trip-hammers, 11:651b
Tuotilo and, 12:225a-b
versus processional origination, 9:713b–714a
St. Gall MS. 359, 3:80b
St. Gall Penitential (Tripartite of St. Gall), 9:489a, 489b, 491a
St. Gayianē. *See* Gayianē (church: Vałaršapat)
St. Généroux (church: Loire Valley), 10:481a
Ste. Geneviève (monastery: Paris), 11:481b
St. Génis-des-Fontaines (church: Pyrenees), 10:112a, 493a
St. George (church: Gelat῾i), 5:374b
St. George (church: Kurbinovo), wall paintings, 2:445b
St. George (church: Staraya Ladoga), frescoes, 10:584a (*illus.*)
St. George (church: Staro Nagoričino), 11:186b
St. George (church: Suceava), exterior wall paintings, 12:505b
St. George (church: Thessaloniki), interior decorations of, 4:359a
St. George and the Dragon plays, 5:34b–35a
St. George icon, 2:416 *illus.*, 417b
St. George (monastery church: Novgorod), 9:512b (*illus.*)
St. Georgener Prediger, 8:354b
St. Gereon (church: Cologne), 10:102b, 488b
St. Germain-des-Prés (church: Paris), 10:112a
archaeology of, 1:427b
produce transport corvées, 12:152b, 157a-b
St. Germain-des-Prés (monastery: Paris), serfdom and, 11:202b, 203b
St. German, Christopher, *Doctor and Student,* 4:503a
Ste. Gertrude (church: Nivelles), 10:93b (*illus.*), 94b, 487b
S. Gião (church: Nazaré), 12:465b
St. Gilles, fairs of, 7:339a-b
St. Gilles-du-Gard (church: Provence), 10:481b, 497a, 497b, 499a (*illus.*)
domestic architecture of, 10:489b
Roman *scenae frons* facade of, 10:308b–309b (*illus.*)
S. Giovanni Evangelista (church: Ravenna), 10:263a
S. Giovanni in Monte (church: Bologna). *See* S. Victor (church: Bologna)
S. Giulia (monastery: Brescia), 11:336a
St. Godehard (church: Hildesheim), 10:487b
St. Gotthard Pass, 11:540b–541a, 541b
construction of Pont Ecumant and, 10:416a
St. Gregory (church: Ani in Širak), 5:339a, 12:165a
Zwart῾noc῾ and, 12:749b, 750a, 750b
St. Gregory (church: T῾anahat), 1:495b
frescoes, 1:496a
S. Grigor Lusaworič (church: Tat῾ew), 11:600b
St. Gudule, Jan van Ruusbroec and, 9:36a
St. Guilhem-le-Desert (church: Languedoc), 10:475b
St. Hildevert (shrine: Gournay-en-Bray), 6:492a
St. Hṙip῾simē (church: Vałaršapat), 1:493b, **6:309a–310a,** 6:309b (*illus.*)
St. Hubert Penitential, 9:490a
St. Hubert (shrine: Ardennes), 6:491a
St. Hubrecht (asylum: Bruges), 6:490b
S. Isidoro (church: León), 10:487a
Panteón de los Reyes, 10:492a (*illus.*), 505b, 506 (*illus.*)
portals, 10:494a
St. Ives
fairs of, 12:121a
opposition to royal control, 12:122b
St. Jacques (convent: Paris), Hugh of St. Cher and, 6:320b, 321a
St. Jacques (Dominican house: Paris), Vincent of Beauvais and, 12:453b–454a
St. Jacques-aux-Pélerins (hospital: Paris), 8:104b
St. Jakob an der Birs, Battle of (*ca.* 1444), 11:544b
St. James (church: Sandomierz), 9:723b
St. Jan ten Dullen (asylum: Ghent), 6:490b
St. Jean-d'Acre. *See* Acre
St. Jean-le-Rond (baptistery: Paris), 9:190b
St. John (abbey: Clonard), 3:466a
St. John the Baptist (monastery: Georgia), 4:116a
St. John (basilica: Ephesus), 4:494b, 7:202a
St. John (church: Escomb), architectural elements, 10:680 (*illus.*)
St. John (church: Hoṙomos), 5:371b
St. John (church: Pürgg), 10:507a
St. John (church: Ramla), construction of, 4:24b
St. John (church: Rome), drama in, 6:636b
St. John Lateran. *See* Lateran (basilica: Rome)
St. John (monastery: Arles), 12:682b
St. John the Precursor (monastery: Taron), 1:510b, 9:457a, 457b, 458a
St. John's disease, 6:490a
S. José (church: Granada), 5:653b
St. Jouin de Marnes (church: Poitiers region), 10:481a
S. Juan de Baños (basilica: Palencia), 12:465b, 466a (*illus.*)
S. Juan de los Reyes (church: Granada), 5:653b
S. Julián de los Prados (Santullano) (church: Oviedo), 1:624b, 10:113b
St. Julien (church: Brioude), 10:480a

St. Julien (church: Tours), frescoes in, 4:292a
St. Karapet (church: Sewan Island), 11:214b
S. Karapet (church: Siwnik^{C}), 1:496a, 9:159a
S. Karmrawor (church: Aštarak), 1:601 (*illus.*)
St. Kilian (church: Heilbronn), high altar, 11:552a (*illus.*)
St. Lambert (church: Liège), 10:95a
St. Lawrence (church: Lorenzstadt), 9:201b
St. Lazare (church: Autun), 10:475b, 479a, 496a, 496b, 498 (*illus.*)
St. Leu d'Esserent, beginning of the *Jacquerie* and, 9:478a
St. Lorenz (church: Nuremberg), sculpture by Adam Krafft, 7:300b, 301 (*illus.*)
S. Lorenzo (church: Florence), Landini and, 7:325b, 326a
S. Lorenzo (church: Milan), 4:236a, 10:488b
  octagon shape of, 4:337a
S. Lorenzo (church: Rome), 10:517a
St. Luke's Fair, Beaune, 12:650b
S. Lusaworič^{C} (church: Siwnik^{C}), 9:159a
St. Madeleine (church: Vézelay). *See* Madeleine, La (church: Vézelay)
St. Mamas (monastery: Constantinople), Symeon the New Theologian and, 11:553b
S. Marco (cathedral: Venice), 10:265a, **10:645a-b**, 12:385b
  Byzantine design and decoration, 4:346a, 10:645a
  mosaics in, 4:292a
    Anastasis mosaic, 1:0 (frontispiece)
    Porta S. Alippio, 10:646 (*illus.*)
  Pala d'Oro in, 9:330 (*illus.*)
  plunder from sack of Constantinople, 12:389b
  restoration of, 9:525a
  Romanesque architecture, 10:481a, 484b
  see also Bertuccio
St. Maria ad Martyres (church: Rome), 9:690b
S. Maria Antiqua (church: Rome), 10:519b
  interior decoration of, 4:358b
  palimpsest wall at, 9:355b, 356 (*illus.*)
S. Maria in Capitolio (church: Rome), 10:519b
St. Maria (cathedral: Augsburg), 5:424a
S. Maria (church: Granada), 6:653b
S. Maria (church: Insula), 10:112b
S. María (church: Manresa), 11:209b, 210a (*illus.*)
S. Maria (church: Mount Morrone), 3:214b
S. Maria (church: Quintanilla de las Viñas), 12:465b, 467b, 468a
S. Maria (church: Tarrasa), retable, 6:328b
S. Maria in Cosmedin (baptistery: Ravenna). *See* Baptistery of the Arians (Ravenna)
S. Maria in Cosmedin (church: Rome), 10:519a
  decorations, 10:504b
S. Maria del Fiore (church: Florence), 9:667b–668a (*illus.*)
  marble relief by Nanni di Banco, 9:57 (*illus.*)
S. Maria delle Grazie (church: Milan), refectory, 8:583b (*illus.*)
St. Maria im Kapitol (church: Cologne)
  Pestkreuz (Plague crucifix), 9:447a
  plan, 12:188 (*illus.*)
S. Maria Maggiore (church: Rome), 10:517a
  decorative sculpture, 4:337b–338a
  interior decoration of, 4:358b–359a
  Jacopo Torriti's mosaic, 12:89 (*illus.*)
  monasteries and, 10:519b
  mosaics in, 1:469a, 4:357a, 358b
    Abraham mosaic, 12:199 (*illus.*)
  triumphal arch in, 12:205b, 206a–206b (*illus.*)
S. María de Melque (church: Toledo)
  architectural elements
    nave and choir, 8:512a (*illus.*)
    Visigothic influence, 8:511b
S. María de Mur (church: Spain), 10:505b
S. Maria de Naranco, 1:624b
S. Maria Novella (church: Florence)
  Andrea da Firenze's frescoes in, 1:244a
  in *Decameron,* 6:660a
  Nardo di Cione's *Last Judgment* fresco cycle, 9:63 (*illus.*)
  Rucellai Madonna in, 4:301b
  tomb of Patriarch Joseph II, 7:150b
S. María de Ripoll (monastery: Catalonia), 11:406b
St. Maria and St. Peter (monastery: Alife), 12:682b
S. Maria in Trastevere (church: Rome), icon in, 4:355a
S. Maria in Valle (church: Cividale), panels and stucco figures, 7:650b
S. Marinē (church: Aštarak), 1:601a-b
St. Mark's, Venice. *See* S. Marco (cathedral: Venice)
St. Martial (abbey: Limoges), 10:111a, 482b–483a
  affiliation with Cluny, 10:618a
  foundation of, 10:618a
  sequence tradition and, 11:163a
  as source of earliest *Quem quaeritis,* 4:273b
  Sponsus from, 4:263b
  see also St. Martial school
St. Martial school, **10:618a–619b**
  Aquitanian notation and, 8:627b
  Aquitanian repertories, 10:618b
  cadential melismata, 10:619a
  division of *libelli,* 10:618b
  melodic style, 10:619a
  preserved manuscripts, 10:618b
  tropes and, 6:381b
  Tropes to the Ordinary of the Mass, 12:209a
  see also Benedicamus Domino
St. Martin (abbey: Tours), 10:480b–481a, 482b, 483a
  manuscript book production and, 8:102b
St. Martin (abbey: Trier), rebuilding of, Regino of Prüm and, 10:289b
St. Martin du Canigou (church: Pyrenees), 10:477b
St. Martin, charterhouse of (in Naples), 9:59b
St. Martin (church: Canterbury), 4:453b
  Liuthard at, 3:81b
St. Martin (church: Colmar)
  altarpiece at, 6:561 (*illus.*)
  Madonna in a Rose Arbor, 11:59a (*illus.*)
S. Martín (church: Fromista), 10:487a
St. Martin (church: Landshut), 5:595a (*illus.*), 601a
St. Martin (church: Laon), 10:85b
St. Mary (abbey: Clonard), 3:466a
St. Mary (abbey: Dublin), **10:619b–620a**
  association with Buildwas abbey, 10:619b
  English connections, 10:620a
  land holdings, 10:620a
St. Mary of Bethlehem (asylum: London). *See* Bedlam
St. Mary of Bethlehem (priory: London), 2:157a
St. Mary (cathedral: Valencia), converted from Grand Mosque, 3:386a
St. Mary (church: Athens), 7:381b
St. Mary (church: Kotor), 11:184a
St. Mary (church: Kraków), 9:730a-b
St. Mary (church: Lübeck), construction of, 7:682b
St. Mary (church: Warwick), 7:321b
  Beauchamp Chapel stained glass, 10:197b–198a (*illus.*)
"St. Mary of the Flagellants Brotherhood," 6:637a
St. Mary the Great (cathedral: Dubrovnik), 4:300a-b
St. Mary Magdalene (convents), Dominicans and, 12:688a
St. Mary of the Rock (church: Scotland). *See* St. Andrews
St. Mary-le-Bow (church: London), 1:433b
  Court of Arches and, 1:433b
St. Maur, Congregation of, history of French ecclesiastical foundations and, 1:427b
St. Maurice (abbey: Augaune), 11:536b
St. Mauritius (cathedral: Magdeburg), in an ivory carving (*ca.* 962-973), 7:27 (*illus.*)
S. Maurizio (monastery: Milan), 12:684a
St. Menas (church: Abu Mina), 3:586 (*illus.*)
St. Michael (church: Hildesheim), 2:124b, 10:94b–95a
  bronze doors of, 8:283b, 284a (*illus.*), 10:107 (*illus.*)
St. Michael (church: Sieburg), Anno Shrine, 9:127b
St. Michael (church: Steinbach), ground plan for, 10:91b (*illus.*)
St. Michael (church: Ston), 11:183b, 184a

St. Michael of the Skovorodsky (monastery: Novgorod), architectural style, 10:586b
St. Michael's feast (Michaelmas). *See* Feasts and festivals, European
St. Michel de l'Aiguilhe (chapel: Le Puy), 10:480b
S. Michele Arcangelo (monastery: Florence), 11:336a
S. Miguel de la Escalada (church: Spain), 10:487a
architectural elements, 8:511a-b
S. Millán de la Cogolla (monastery: La Rioja), Berceo and, 2:186b, 187a
S. Miniato al Monte (church: Florence), 10:486a, 502b
foundation of, 5:92a
St. Nectaire (church: Auvergne), 10:480a-b
St. Nicholas (church: Gelat^ci), 5:374b
St. Nicholas (church: Tallinn), 9:186b
St. Nicholas Orphanos (church: Macedonia), 5:399b
S. Nicola (church: Bari), 10:486b
St. Nicolas (church: Angers), 10:481a
St. Nicolas (church: Caen), 10:486b
St. Nicolas (church: Kuršumlija), 11:183b
S. Nicolás (church: Valencia), 10:438a
St. Ninian, Isle of, archaeological find, Pictish silverwork, 9:641a, 641b (*illus.*), 642b
St. Nizier (church: Lyons), 7:698b
St. Omer (town)
charter of, 3:497b, 12:731a-b
first seals of, 11:126a
guild ordinances of, 3:501a
St. Ouen (monastery: Rouen), 9:161b
S. Pablo (church: Vallodolid), 7:153b
St. Pantaleon (church: Cologne), 10:95a
St. Panteleimon (church: Boiana), wall paintings, 2:447a
St. Panteleimon (church: Nerezi), wall paintings, 2:444b–445a
St. Panteleimon (church: Ochrid), 9:209a
S. Paolo (church: Collegarli), 11:572b
S. Paolo fuori le Mura (church: Rome), 10:517a
bronze doors, 2:456a
narrative mosaics in, 4:338a
St. Patrick's Purgatory, **10:620a-b**
legend of, 10:620a-b
versions of, 1:261b
S. Pedro de Arlanza (monastery: Spain), *Poema de Fernán González* and, 11:411a-b
S. Pedro de Cardeña (monastery: Burgos), 3:71b, 76a, 79b
Cantar de mío Cid and, 11:411a
S. Pedro de la Mata (church: Toledo), 12:466a
S. Pedro de la Nave (church: Zamora), 12:465b, 466a, 466b–467a, 467b (*illus.*)
structure of, 8:368b–369a
S. Pedro de Portella (abbey: Urgel), indulgences and, 6:448a-b
S. Pere (church: Casserres), 10:475b
S. Pere de Roda (church: Catalonia), 10:487a
St. Peter (abbey: Clonard), 3:466a
St. Peter in Chains (church: Rome), Nicholas of Cusa and, 9:123b
St. Peter (church: Barton-on-Humber), 5:112b (*illus.*)
St. Peter (church: Saintes), 6:450b
St. Peter (church: Salzburg), 10:104a
St. Peter (church: Utrecht), 10:95a
St. Peter cross. *See* Peter cross
St. Peter, Liturgy of, **10:620b–621a**
adaptation to Eastern liturgy, 10:621a
Greek translation, 10:620b, 621b
Latin text for, 10:620b
original and Gregorian versions, 10:620b–621a
time and place of composition, 10:620b
Sts. Peter and Paul (abbey: Armagh), 1:470a
Sts. Peter and Paul (church: Hirsau), 10:487b
Sts. Peter and Paul (Cluniac abbey). *See* Cluny, Abbey Church (III)
St. Peter, Rome. *See* Old St. Peter's (church: Rome)
St. Peter and St. Paul (monastery: Wearmouth and Jarrow), Bede and, 2:153a-b
St. Peter's Chair, Feast of, 9:689a–690b
St. Philibert (church: Tournus), 10:478b–479a, **10:621a-b**
stone vaulting, 10:621 (*illus.*)
St. Philibert de Grandlieu (church: Loire Valley), 10:481a
St. Pierre (abbey church: Jumièges), 10:478a
St. Pierre (church: Aulnay), 10:495a
St. Pierre (church: Moissac), 5:618a, **8:452a**, 10:494b–495a, 495b (*illus.*)
Majestas Domini, 8:453 (*illus.*)
marble relief figures, 10:308 (*illus.*)
sculptural programs, 8:452b
"Saint Pierre et le jongleur" (fabliau), 7:116b
St. Pierre (monastery: Ghent), 5:521a
St. Pierre sur Dives (church), ceramic tiles at, 3:237a
S. Pons de Corbera (church: Llobregat), 10:487a
St. Pourçain-sur-Sioule, wine trade, 12:158b, 650b–651a
S. Pudenziana (church: Rome)
mosaics of, 4:351b
depiction of Heavenly Jerusalem, 6:125a
SS. Quattro Incoronati (church: Rome), 10:518b, 523a
St. Quentin, wool trade, 12:395b, 396a
St. Quiriace (church: Provins)
founded by Henry I of Champagne, 3:246a
inventory of castellanies, 3:249a
S. Radegonda (monastery: Milan), 12:684a
St. Remi (abbey church: Rheims), 10:478a
S. Reparata (church: Florence), 1:431a
St. Restitut (church: Provence), 10:481b
St. Riquier (monastery)
engraving in, 10:93 (*illus.*), 94a
numbers of monks at, 2:173a
Radbertus of Corbie and, 9:446a
St. Rule's Church. *See* St. Andrews
St. Sabas (church: Gelat^ci), 5:374b
St. Sabas (monastery: Jerusalem), typicon of, 7:611b
S. Sabina (church: Rome), doors in west portal, 4:360 (*illus.*), 361a
S. Salvador (church: Seyre), 10:487a
S. Salvador (church: Toledo), 12:466b
S. Salvatore (church: Bologna), polyptych, 12:480b
St. Sargis. *See* Tekor
St. Saturnin. *See* Pont-Saint-Esprit
St. Saturnin (church: Auvergne), 10:480a
St. Savin-sur-Gartempe (church: Poitiers), 10:505b–506b
St. Savior in Chora (church: Constantinople), plan of, 9:453 (*illus.*)
St. Sebald (church: Nuremberg), 7:300b, 9:201a
S. Sepolcro (church: Pisa), 4:193b (*illus.*)
St. Sergios (martyrium: Dwin), 9:103a
St. Sergius (church: Gaza), 3:378a
St. Sernin (church: Toulouse), 2:125a, 7:341a, 10:483a, 490b, **10:621b–622a, 12:90b**
ambulatory relief, 10:493a–494a (*illus.*)
Gayrard's work at, 5:371b–372a
monastery of St. Pierre and, 10:495a
Portal of the Counts, 10:492a
Porte de Miègeville, 10:493b–494a
Ascension relief, 10:622 (*illus.*)
St. Servatius (church: Maastricht), 10:95a
St. Sever (church: Gascogne), 10:111a
St. Severin (church: Cologne), *Veronica* panel, 10:623a (*illus.*)
St. Severin (church: Speyer), sacristy book, use of organ, 9:273b
St. Severin, Master of. *See* Master of St. Severin
S. Sigismondo (church: Rivolta d'Adda), 10:485a
S. Silvestro in Capite (monastery: Rome), 10:519b
St. Sisto (monastery: Rome), 12:687b
S. Sofia (church: Bonavento), 10:112b
St. Sophia (cathedral: Kiev). *See* Hagia Sophia (cathedral: Kiev)
St. Sophia, Council of (815), *Definition, Refutatio et eversio* and, 9:132a
S. Spirito in Sassia (hospital), 6:465a
St. Stephen (cathedral: Vienna), 2:8a, 9:650a (*illus.*)
south tower, 9:525b (*illus.*), 525a
St. Stephen's Chapel. *See* Westminster Abbey; Westminster Palace
St. Swithin's Day, 5:36b
St. T^cadei Vank^cin (monastery: Armenia), founding of, 12:1a
St. Théodard (abbey: Montauban), lands of, 2:128a
St. Theodore icon, 2:415 (*illus.*), 417a
St. Therapont (monastery: Russia), church of the Nativity of the Mother of God, frescoes, 10:590a
S. Tiurso (church: Sahagún), 10:487a

S. Trinità (monastery: Florence), 7:326a
Ste. Trinitê (abbey church: Caen), 5:588b (*illus.*), 595b
St. Trophîme (church: Arles), 10:481b, 497a, 497b
St. Trudperter Hohelied, 8:349a
St. Tugean (shrine: Brittany), 6:491b
St. Urbain (church: Troyes)
  Langlois and, 7:337b
  stained glass in, 5:552a
St. Vaast (abbey), 10:110b
St. Valentine's Day, 3:408a, 5:35b
St. Veronica, Master of. *See* Master of St. Veronica
St. Victor (abbey: Paris), 6:321b
  Groenendael priory and, 9:36b
  late-sequence production at, 10:623b, 11:166b, 167a
  school of, 11:77a-b
    biblical exegesis and, 2:213b
S. Victor (church: Bologna), 6:323b
St. Victor (church: Xanten), *tref,* 8:286b
St. Victor Manuscript, **10:623b**
  see also Sequence, late
St. Victor (monastery: Marseilles), 12:443b
  survey of, 4:137b, 145b
S. Vincenao a Galliano (church: Galliano), 10:112b
S. Vincente de Castillo (church: Cardona), 10:487a
S. Vincenzo al Volturno (monastery: Farfa), 10:112b, 113a
S. Vincenzo (monastery: near Benevento), Ambrosius Autpertus at, 2:11a
S. Vitale (church: Ravenna), 4:336 (*illus.*), 7:202a, 10:263b–264b (*illus.*)
  apse of, 4:354b, 359b (*illus.*)
  cathedra in, 4:353a
  design of, 4:339a
  dome of, 4:236a
  donor portrait at, 4:261b
  interior decoration of, 4:359a
  mosaic of Empress Theodora I, 12:11 (*illus.*), 12b
  mosaics, 6:431b, 10:89a, 11:570b
    bema vault, 10:264 (*illus.*)
  portrait of Justinian, 4:354a
  sacrifice of Isaac (mosaic), 10:263b–264b (*illus.*)
St. Vitus (cathedral: Prague)
  Benedikt Ried and, 10:399a
  vaulting of by Peter Parler, 9:421b (*illus.*)
St. Vitus' dance, 6:490a
St. Wandrille (monastery), 2:173a
S. Zeno (church: Verona)
  bronze doors of, 8:284b
  Nicholaus da Verona and, 10:501b
Saint-Gatien anthology, 1:319a
Saintonge
  saltworks, 10:630b
    technological improvements, 10:632b
Saints
  canonization of. *See* Canonization
  cult of
    as a replacement for pagan practices, 8:25b
    rise of private churches and, 9:412a
    in treatment of insanity, 6:492a-b
    see also Hagiography; Shrines
  multiplication of pilgrimage, 9:660a
  as protectors of bridges, 10:410b–411a
  Sufi, 6:586a
  veneration of
    composition of rhymed offices and, 10:366b
    hagiographical information in rhymed offices, 10:373b
    visionary appearances, 10:298a, 299b
  see also Relics
Saints' bells. *See* Bells
Saints' lives
  in fresco painting, 5:293a–294a, 295b
  oldest vernacular, 4:320a
  see also Hagiography
Saisine. See Seisin, disseisin
Saisset, Bernard, arrest by Philip IV of France, 9:554b
Saithe (*Pollachius virens*), fishing of, 5:72a
Saiz de Carillo, Don Sancho, tomb painting for, 5:612a
Sajāḥ ("false prophet"), vs. Khālid ibn al-Walīd, 6:567b
Sājī guard. *See* Abbasids
Sājids
  in Armenia, 1:513b
  in Dwin, 1:481b, 4:324a
Sajjāda (Islamic prostration rug), 10:550a
  see also Rugs and carpets
Sakarya River. *See* Sangarius River
Sakas, migration into Drangiana, 10:660b
Sakers, 6:355b
Sakhra, Qubbat al-. *See* Dome of the Rock
Säkingen Abbey, 11:539b
Ṣakk (Islamic promisory notes), 12:106a-b
Sakkākī, al-, books on rhetoric, 10:347b
Sakr ibn Ḥarb. *See* Abū Sufāyn
Sākūra, ruler of Mali, 8:57b
Saladin, 1:634a, 634b, **10:624b–627a**
  administrative reforms, 10:625b
  army, cavalrymen, 12:552b
  capture of Āmid, 9:283b
  capture of Mosul and Aleppo, 10:625b
  in Damascus, 4:82b, 10:625b
  Egyptian expeditions, 3:14a, 10:625a
  founding of Ayyubid dynasty, 4:406a
  glorification of, 10:626b
  house of, 2:23b
  inherited power, 10:624b–625a
  Isaac II Angelos and, 6:559b
  jihad, 10:625b–626b
  Kurds and, 7:310b
  al-Lādhiqiya and, 7:315b
  Nūr al-Dīn and, 2:23a
  occupation of Ḥama, 6:82b
  restoration of naval power under, 9:75b
  service to Nūr al-Dīn, 10:625a
  significance of achievements, 10:626b
  vs. crusaders, 4:31a, 38b, 39a–40b, 10:625b–626b, 11:561b–562a
    Battle of Acre, 10:626a
    Battle of Ḥiṭṭīn, 6:265b–266b, 10:625b–626a
    conquest of Jerusalem, 10:626a, 626b
    rescue of Cairo, 10:625a
    truce with Richard I (the Lionhearted), 2:23b, 10:383b, 626b
  see also Ayyubids
Saladin Tithe, 11:612b
  on clergy, 11:614a, 614b
Ṣalāḥ al-Dīn Yūsuf ibn Ayyūb. *See* Saladin
Ṣalāḥ al-Dīn Zarkūb, relationship with Rūmī, 10:556b
Salamanca, new cathedral, 9:694a, 695 (*illus.*)
Salamanca Cathedral, 10:487b
Salamanca, University of, 12:286b
Salamanes Hermeios Sozomenos. *See* Sozomen
Salamis. *See* Constantia
Salamīya, Ismailism in, 6:616a
Salārids, in Dwin, 1:482b
Salat
  daily performance of, 7:616b–617a
  for the Dead, 7:618b
  of the Eclipse, 7:618b
  of the Feasts, 5:38a-b, 7:618b
  in the Friday service, 7:618a
  of the Pauses, during Ramadan, 7:618a-b
  for Rain, 7:618b
  thirteen "essentials" of, 617a-b
Salatièle, Bolognese School and, 5:567b
Ṣalbāq. See Sanj (harp)
Salces, fortress of, 3:152a
Salerno
  medical school of, 4:579b, 8:247b–249a, 255b–257a, 11:266b, 274b
    anatomical studies at, 8:256a
    criticism of, 8:257a-b
    surgery at, 8:249b (*illus.*)
  medicine at. *See* Alphanus of Salerno
Salerno Cathedral, 10:504a
  mosaics, 11:266b
Salerno medical regimen. *See Regimen sanitatis Salernitanum*
Sales taxes. *See* Taxation
Salghurids of Fārs, 11:147a
Salian dynasty, 2:424b, 8:277a
  Babenberg family and, 2:6b, 33b
  Bavaria and, 2:134a
  in Germany (843-1137), 5:477a-b
  kings' travels, 12:159a
  Nuremberg and, 9:201a
  territorial acquisitions, 10:684b
Salian Franks, 2:94a
Salian (Salic) Law
  Clovis and, 3:467a
  see also Kingship, theories of
Ṣāliḥ ibn Ayyūb, al-, Mamluk sultan
  Baybars and, 2:138a
  beginning of Mamluk dynasty and, 2:272b
  crusaders and, 4:32a, 53a

Ṣāliḥ ibn Ayyūb, al- (*cont.*)
establishment of the Baḥrīya regiment and, 8:73a
introduction of madrasa to Cairo, 2:21b–22a
tomb of, 6:608b
Ṣāliḥ Ṭalaʾiʿ. *See* Mosques
Salimbene, **10:627a–628b**, 12:649b
Chronicle
on Hugh of Orléans, 6:319a
importance of, 10:627a
sources for, 10:628a
entry in Franciscan order, 10:627a, 627b
on Huguccio, 6:327a
Liber taediorum, 6:630b
writings, 10:627b
Salimbeni family, 11:279b
Salines
in antiquity, 10:629a, 633b
briquetage, 10:629b
coastal, 10:629a, 630b–631a
distribution of product, 10:629b–630a
England, 10:630b
fuel used in, 10:632a-b
Holland, 10:630b
inland, 10:629b, 632b, 633a-b
Mediterranean, 10:628a, 631a
monastic, 10:625b–630a
Normandy, 10:633a
solar evaporation, 10:629a, 630b
technological improvements, 10:632a–634a
endless chain pump, 10:633b–634a
Lepperwerk and *Gradierwerk,* 10:633b
preconcentration of brine, 10:633a-b
Schöpfwerk, 10:632b
Sinkwerk, 10:633a
Salins, saltworks, technological improvements, 10:633b–634a
Salisbury, charges against heard at parliament, 9:424a
Salisbury Cathedral, **10:628a-b**, 10:628a (*illus.*)
Salisbury, earl of, 12:570a, 570b
Salisbury, use of. *See* Sarum use
Saljuqids. *See* Seljuks
Sallet, 1:527a (*illus.*), 530a, 531a, 533a
Sallust (Gaius Sallustius Crispus)
Bellum Iugurthinum, adaptations of, 10:528a
in *Cantar de mío Cid,* 3:77a
Catilinae coniuratio, adaptations of, 10:528a
as inspiration for Peter IV (the Ceremonious), 9:510b
Isidore of Seville and, 6:564a
philosophical allegory and, 1:181a
translations of into Spanish, 11:434a
Salman und Morolf. See Solomon and Marcolf
Salmon ben Jeroḥam, 4:539b, 7:210b
Salomo of Constance, **10:629a**
Formulae Salomonis, 10:629a
Salomo, Elias (13th century), *Scientia artis musicae,* 8:644b
Salomon of Hungary, king, 6:340a
Salon, inns in, 6:469b
Salona (castle: Amphissa), 7:376b
Ṣalṣal, 8:613a
Salt trade, **10:629a–634b**
in antiquity, 10:634a
bay salt, 10:630b
Bosnia, 2:339a
duties, 10:631a, 631b
early medieval, 12:109b
Eastern Europe, 10:633a
economic aspects, 10:631a–632a
Germany, 10:629b–630a, 632a
growth of industry, 10:629b–631a
Halloren, 10:632a
Hanseatic League and, 12:113a
medieval need for salt, 10:629a
monastic control, 10:629b–630a
North Sea, 10:630b
Pfännerschaft, 10:632a
Polish mining, 9:725a, 728b, 729b
regalian rights, 10:631b–632a
rock salt, 10:632b, 634a
salted herring, 10:630b
taxation, 10:631a–632a, 12:586b
transportation networks, 10:629a-b, 632b, 634a
Venice, 10:630a, 12:111a
see also Gabelle; Salines
Salt-glazed stoneware, 3:238a
Saltair na Rann, 1:347b, 6:542b, 8:559a, **10:634b–635b**
additional cantos, development of *Airdena Brátha* and, 1:111a-b
authorship, 1:110b, 10:634b–635a
form, 10:634a
God's plan for salvation, 10:635a
sources for, 1:347b, 10:635a
Saltarello, 4:88a
Saltuqids, in Erzurum, 1:514a
Saltworks. *See* Salines
Salu d'amours. See Beaumanoir, Philippe de
Ṣalūbā, Ibn, 7:106b
Salukis, 6:355a, 355b
Salūqī. See Salukis
Sálus saga ok Nikanors, 10:395b
Salut d'amor, 3:173a
Salut a refrains. See Beaumanoir, Philippe de
Salutati, Coluccio, 2:287b, 289a, 390b
as chancellor of Florence, 5:101a
classical literary studies, 3:435b
Šalva Mandaturuxucʿessi of Axalcʿixe, 5:414a
Salvador, El (church: Teruel), belfry tower, 8:520b (*illus.*)
Salvani, Provenzan, 6:657a
Salvator basilica (Fulda), 5:311b–312a
Salvatoris hodie, **10:635b**
three-voice conductus, 10:635b
"Salve, festa dies." *See* Venantius Fortunatus
Salve regina, 12:461a
Salvian of Marseilles, **10:635b–636a**
De gubernatione Dei, 10:636a
see also Paulinus of Béziers
Salvo (Anglo-Saxon monk), 4:507a
Salzburg
bishopric of
elevated to archbishopric (798), 2:4b
established by St. Boniface (739), 2:4b
trade and commerce, saltworks, 10:630a
Salzkammergut, saltworks, technological improvements, 10:632b
Samāʿ (musical recital of Sufi poetry), 9:44a, 44b
Samak-i ʿAyyār, 6:508b
Samanid Tomb (Bukhara), 6:602a-b (*illus.*)
Samanids, 6:503b, **10:637a–639b**
acceptance of Islam, 10:637a
administration of, 6:590b
art and architecture, **10:636a–637a**
Bukhara mausoleum, 10:636b
excavations at Nishapur and Samarkand, 10:636b
Kufic Arabic inscriptions, 10:636b
slip-painted earthenware, 10:636 (*illus.*)
in Bukhara, 2:397a
bureaucracy, 10:638b
Buyid threat, 10:638b
conquest of Seistan, 10:609b, 638a
cultural achievements, Bukhara court, 10:638b
dispute between Naṣr and Ismaʿīl, 10:637b
emir title, 10:638a
family origins, 10:637a
governorship of Khwarizm, 10:637b
internal revolts, 10:638a, 638b
in Iran, 6:424a
origins of the Seljuks and, 11:151a
persecution of Ismailis, 10:639a
Qarakhanid invasions, 10:639a
rule of Khorāsān, 10:637b
Sebüktigin and, 11:133a-b
Shāsh and Samarkand, 10:637a
territorial expansion under Ismaʿīl, 10:637b–638a
Turkish revolt, 10:638b
ʿAbd Allāh of Khorāsān and, 11:575a
vs. Yaʿqūb ibn Layth, 12:717a
see also Alptigin
Samaritans, **10:639b–640a**
church on Mount Gerizim, 10:639b
communities outside Samaria, 10:640a
control of Samaria, 10:639b
Dustāniyya and Kūshāniyya sects, 10:640a
early Muslim rule, 10:639b–640a
revolts against Byzantine rulers, 10:639b
taxation of, 10:639b–640a
Samarkand, 2:397a, **10:640a–641a**
Arab conquest, 10:640b
ceramics of, 6:603a
commercial importance, 10:640b
Great Mosque, 6:605a
introduction of paper manufacture and, 11:84b
Iranian architecture in, 6:605a
mathematics at, 11:84a
observatory at, 11:85b (*illus.*)
Samanid administration, 10:637a-b, 640b
Timurids and, 12:56b, 58a
Turko-Muslim dynasties, 10:640b
under Tamerlane, 10:640b–641a
Samarkand ware, **10:641a**

slip-painted earthenware, 10:636b
Samarra, **10:641a–644a**
as Abbasid capital, 1:11a, 3:49b
architecture of, 1:5a, 6:596b, 597b–598a
in Egypt, 6:599b
in Iran, 6:598b, 599a
city planning, 10:642a-b
decline of, 10:643b
development under Hārūn al-Wāthiq, 10:643a
early settlements, 10:641b
foundation of, 2:46b, 6:513a, 8:653b
Friday mosque, 10:642a, 642b, 643a, 643b
Great Mosque, 1:5b
in *Kitāb al-buldān,* 12:718a
market districts, 10:642a, 643b
mosques of, 8:68a
al-Mutawakkil in, 8:654b
palaces, 10:642a, 643a
separation of ethnic groups, 10:642b
serdaab in, 11:189a
settlement pattern, 10:642a
thoroughfares, 10:642b–643a
around Friday mosque, 10:643a-b
Great Road, 10:642b, 643b
Turkish militia, 10:642a-b
water supply, 10:643b
West Bank development, 10:643a
Samawʾal, al-, Imruʾ al-Qays and, 6:430a
Sambia, 2:63 (map), 66a, 66b
Samener. See Hugo von Trimberg
Samḥ, Ibn al-, equatorium and, 4:500b
Samhenda (a *rímur* meter), 10:405b
Sāmī, fī-al-asāmī, Al-. See Abu 'l-Faẓl Maydānī Nīshāpūrī, Aḥmad ibn Muḥammad
Samʿiyāt, al-. See Resurrection, Islamic
Samo (Frankish merchant), empire of, 2:12b, 299a
Samogitia, 2:63 (map), 65b, 66b
see also Lithuania
Samos, Byzantine sea routes and, 10:423 (map), 424b
Samosata, seized by Byzantines, 2:118a, 4:523a
Sampirus of Astorga, **10:644a**
Sampson, William, excommunicated, 4:537b–538a
Šams ar-Riʾāsa Abu 'l-Barakāt ibn Kibr, *Lamp of the Darkness and Explanation of the Services,* 8:479a
Samson of Bury St. Edmund's, 2:173b, 175b
Samson Killing the Philistines, fresco, 3:155 (*illus.*)
Samsonar saga fagra. See Samsons saga fagra
Samsons saga fagra, 10:394b, **10:644a-b**
magic mantle motif, 8:507b–508a
preservation, 10:644a
rímur versions, 10:644b
Samšvilde, church in, 5:409a
Samuel Aba, count palatine, as king of Hungary, 6:339b
Samuēl of Ani, 1:511b
scientific basis for chronology, 6:240b
Samuel ben ʿĀdiyā, 7:171a
Samuel ben Eli ibn al-Dastūr, 7:72b, 108a
Samuel ben ha-Yatom, *Responsa,* 7:176a
Samuel ben Hophni, 5:356b, 7:168a, 172b, 11:584b
exegesis and, 4:539a
Samuel ben Judah ben Meshullam, translations by, 12:134b
Samuel ben Judah ha-Marsili, Plato translation and, 9:700a-b
Samuel ben Judah ibn Tibbon, 4:541a
Samuel ben Kalonymus, Ashkenazi Hasidic writing, 9:578a
Samuel ben Kalonymus (the Elder) of Speyer
pietist writings, 6:109b
Sefer ha-yir'ah, emphasis on personal salvation, 6:110a
Samuel ben Meir (grandson of Rashi). *See* Rashbam
Samuel ha-Nagid (Ismail ibn Nagrela), 7:91a, 96a-b, 10:8a
panegyric poems, 6:126b
poems on military expeditions, 6:126b–127a
as vizier of Granada, 9:52b
Samuel ibn Nagrela. *See* Samuel ha-Nagid
Samuel ibn Tibbon, translations by, 12:134a, 137b
Samuēl Kamrǰajorecʿi, 1:510b, 511a
Samuel the Moroccan, rabbi, *Epistle,* 10:5a
Samuel (rabbi), computing *tekufot,* 3:26b–27a
Samuil of Bulgaria, 2:406b–407a, **10:644b–645a**
expansion of state, 10:645a
his attack on Duklja, 11:170b
Ochrid and, 9:208b
Vlachs and, 12:483b
vs. Basil II, 2:118b–119a, 10:645a
vs. Byzantines, 4:5b
San Donato, inns around, 6:470a
San Germano, Treaty of (1230), 4:58b
San Juan de la Peña, as religious center, 1:404a
San Pedro, Diego de, **10:645b–646b**
Arnalte y Lucenda, 10:645b, 11:423a
Cárcel de amor, 10:645b, 11:423a, 454b–455a
Crónica incompleta de los Reyes Católicos, 11:423a
Desprecio de la fortuna, 10:646a
lost works of, 11:443b
Pasión trobada, 10:645b, 11:422b, 425a
poetry of, 11:424b
rhetorical style, 10:645b–646a
Sermón, 10:646a
San Salvador, discovered, 4:560b
Sanāʾ al-Mulk, Ibn, 7:239a
on *kharjas,* 11:446b, 447a
on *muwashshaḥs,* 11:447b
Sanʿa (Ṣanʿāʾ), **10:646b–647b,** 12:724a
changing dynastic control, 10:647a-b
provincial governors, 10:646b–647a
Zaydis and, 12:742a
Sanahin, **10:647b–648b**
as Armenian cultural center, 7:672b
chapel of St. Grigor, 10:648a-b
church of Amenap'rkičʿ, 10:648a
church of St. Astuacacin, 10:647b–648a
gawitʿ, 10:648a
library, 10:648a
monastic academy, 1:482b
Sanāʾī, Abu 'l-Majd Majdūd, 9:42b, 43a
Hadīqat al-ḥaqīqat, 6:507b
Sanas Cormaic. See Cormac mac Cuillennáin
Sanasar, 4:112b, 113a
Sancha García, Doña (Cistercian abbess), 12:686b
Sancha (wife of Ferdinand I of Castile and León), prayer book written for, 5:304b
Sánchez de Arévalo, Ruy, *Speculum vitae humanae,* 11:441a
Sánchez, Tomás Antonio, 3:70b
Sánchez de Valladolid, Fernán, chronicles by, 11:418b
Sánchez de Vercial, Clemente
Libro de los exenplos por a.b.c., 4:551b, 11:419b–420a
preaching in Spain and, 11:456a
Sancho I Ramírez of Aragon, king, 9:69b
political success of, 1:404a-b
relations with the Cid, 3:384a, 385a-b
Sancho I of Castile, king, 2:126b, 9:69a
Jews and, 7:79b–80a
reign of, 1:628b
rule of, 3:128b
Sancho II of Castile, king
assassination of, in literature, 11:409b
rule of, 3:129a
Sancho IV of Castile, king, 8:94a
church taxation and, 11:609b
in Don Juan Manuel's *Libro de las armas,* 8:95a, 96a
literary production in his reign, 11:415b
Lope Díaz de Haro and, 3:134b
marriage of, 3:134b
on Moorish musicians, 8:562b
rule of, 3:134b
sword of, 11:549b
Sancho I Garcés of Navarre, king, 9:68b
Sancho III Garcés (the Great) of Navarre, king. *See* Sancho I of Castile
Sancho IV Garcés of Navarre, king, 9:69b
Sancho V Ramírez of Navarre. *See* Sancho I Ramírez of Aragon
Sancho VI (the Learned) of Navarre, king, 9:70a-b
seizure of Castilian territory, 3:130b
Sancho VII (the Strong) of Navarre, king, 9:70b, 70a
Sancho I of Portugal, king
Almohads and, 10:42a-b
area ruled by, 10:38b–39a
development of towns by, 10:42b–43a
excommunication of, 10:43a
wars waged by, 10:43a

Sancho II of Portugal
accession of, 10:44b
decline of Portugal during reign of, 10:45b–46a
Latin church and, 10:44b–45b
Muslims and, 10:44b–45a
suspension of, 4:160a
Vincentius Hispanus and, 12:456a
Sancho of Mallorca, king, irrigation and, 6:558b
Sancho Ramírez of Aragon and Navarre. *See* Sancho I Ramírez of Aragon, king
Sancho de Zamora, 5:612a
Sancti Spiritus assit nobis gratia. See Notker Balbulus
Sancti Thorlaci episcopi officia rhythmica et proprium missæ, alliteration in, 10:405a
"Sancti venite," 6:381a
Sanctilogium . . . . Angliae, Wallia, Scotiae, et Hiberniae. See John of Tynemouth
Sanctius, **10:648b**
in miniature, Bible of Valeránica, 10:648a (*illus.*)
Sanctuary. *See* Asylum, right of
Sanctuary screen, 11:118a
"Sanctum simpliciter patrem cole." *See* Fulbert of Chartres, hymns of
Sanctus, **10:648b–649b**
addition of Benedictus to, 8:192a
development of, 8:192a
melodic style, 10:649a
monophonic, 10:649a
polyphonic, 10:649a-b
tropes and prosulas, 10:649a
Tropes to the Ordinary of the Mass and, 12:209 (*illus.*)
in Western liturgy, 10:648b–649a
Sandal, 11:254b
Sandalj Hranić Kosača, **10:649b–650a**
murder of Pavle Radenović, 10:650a
recognition of Sigismund, 10:650a
Stefan Vukčiç Kosača and, 11:476a
vs. Radoslav, 2:338b
Sandek, 3:401b
see also Mohel
Sandrart, Joachim von, stages of the Italian Renaissance, 5:581a-b
Sandreckoner, The. See Archimedes
Sanduxt, St. (*ca.* 75–110), 1:519a
Sangarius River, Justinian's bridge, 4:334a
Sangspruch, in Middle High German literature, 8:351b, 352b–353a, 354b, 358a, 359b
Sangspruchdichtung, 10:295a
Ṣanhāja
origin of the Almoravids and, 1:198a-b
Timbuktu and, 12:55b
see also Berbers
Sanhedrin, in Palestine, 7:104a-b
Sanitation. *See* Public health
Sanitatis Salernitanum, Regimen. See Regimen Sanitatis Salernitanum
Ṣanj (harp), 8:611a, 611b
Ṣanj (idiophone), 8:613a-b
Ṣanj ṣīnī, 8:611b
see also Ṣanṭūr
Ṣanjāha confederation, rise of the Almoravids and, 11:140a
Sanjar, Seljuk sultan, 5:526a-b
imprisoned, 9:141a
Kurdistan and, 7:310a
rule of Khorāsān and Transoxiana, 11:153b–154a
seized by Turkomans, 12:227a
tomb of (Merv), 6:602a
vs. Ghuzz Turkomans, 6:504a
Sankt Bendt (church: Ringsted), 7:280a
Sankt Trudperter Hohes Lied, 5:428a
Sannazzaro Sesia (church: Lombardy), 10:484b
Sannto, Marino, on violence to ambassadors in Florence, 4:211b
Sano di Pietro, 11:281b
Sanskrit, Arabic translations of, 12:128a, 129a
Sanskrit literature, Western European literature and, 3:31b
Sanson de Nanteuil, **10:650a**
Proverbs of Solomon and, 1:262b, 10:650a
Sant Oswald von Norwegen. See Oswald, St., German epics about
Santa Fé. *See* Gerónimo de Santa Fé
Santa María, Pablo de, 11:420a-b
Edades del mundo, 11:421a
Santarem, Joā de, 4:561b
Santiago, exploration of, 4:561b
Santiago de Compostela, **10:650a-b**
confraternities of, 12:156b–157a
as a cultural center, 11:452a
facade of cathedral, 8:607b
French Romanesque architecture and, 10:482b–483a
Godescalc and, 10:480b
invaded by Ibn Abī ᶜĀmir al-Manṣūr, 8:90b
kingdom of Navarre and, 9:69a
musical repertory of, 2:167b
pilgrimage church at, 2:194b
pilgrimage to, 9:656a, 659a-b, 661b–662a, 10:280a, 412a, 12:156a
manuscripts of *Quem quaeritis* and, 11:436b
promotion of, 12:156b–157a
Provençal love poetry and, 11:412a
Puerta de las Platerías, 10:494a
routes to, 3:379b
tomb of St. James, 10:650a-b
Santiago de Compostela, school of, 8:558b, **10:650b–651b**
monophonic pieces in plainsong, 10:651a
polyphonic pieces, 10:651a
Santiago de Peñalba (church: Spain), 10:487a
architectural elements, 8:512a-b
Santillana, Marqués de, **10:651b,** 11:419b, 451a-b
Bías contra Fortuna, 11:421b
Doctrinal de privados, 11:421b
Favor de Hércules contra Fortuna, 11:421b
Garcilaso de la Vega and, 11:451b
literary criticism by, 11:419b, 446a, 451b
Moçá tan fermosa, 11:459b
as patron of translators, 11:457a
political satire of, 11:454b
Prohemio e carta, 10:651b
religious poetry of, 11:439a, 450a
visions and, 12:477a
Santissima Annunziata (church: Florence), Landini and, 7:326a
Santo. *See* Shem Tov
Santo Spirito (hospital: Rome), 10:526b
Santob de Carrión. *See* Shem Tov
Santorro, Cardinal Giulio Antonio, *Rituale sacramentorum romanorum,* 10:407b–408a
Santuccia of Gubbio, 9:14a
Ṣanṭūr, 8:562a, 611a
see also Ṣanj ṣīnī
Sanudo family, 7:380b
Sanudo, Fiorenza, 7:380b
Sanudo, Marco
Aegean islands and, 7:377b
death of, 7:378a
duchy of Naxos and, 9:91a, 12:389b
Sanudo, Niccolò ("Spezzabanda"), 7:380b
São Jorge da Mina, 4:562a
São Mamede, Battle of (1128), 10:39b
São Thome, discovered, 4:561b
Saone (castle: Syria), 4:24b
Saoshyant, 12:747a, 747b
Sap technique, 3:144 (*illus.*), 146a
Sapaudia. *See* Savoy, county of
Saphea Azarchelis (astrolabe), 10:387b
Sapientia. See Hrotswitha von Gandersheim
Sapor I. *See* Šābuhr I, Sasanian king
"Sappho of the Rhône." *See* Comtessa de Dia
Šapuh Bagratuni, 1:510b
Ṣaqāliba. See Mamlūk
Sāqiyat al-Hawwāra. See Hawwāra Berbers
Sąqt al-Zand. See Maᶜarrī, Abu 'l-ᶜAlāᵓ Aḥmad al-
Sar Mašhad, 7:222a
Saracen horn. *See* Horn (musical instrument)
Saracens, in Italian literature, 6:637b, 639b
Saragossa
bridge at, 10:418b
captured from the Muslims (1118), 1:406a-b, 9:69b
defended by the Cid, 3:384a
emerging kingdom of Navarre and, 9:68a
rebellion against Umayyads, in *Song of Roland,* 12:275b
Saragossa, University of, 12:287a
Sarai. *See* Saray
Šarakan, 8:551a
Sarakhsi, on credit, 2:79b
Šaraknots, 8:551a
Šarāt Canal. *See* Baghdad
Sarāy, **10:651b–652a**
destruction of, 5:573b
fur trade in, 5:333a
Golden Horde in, 5:573b
Sarcinée (unit of measure), 12:595b
Sarcophagus
classical
Biduino and, 10:503a

Rome and, 10:504a
labarum on, 7:313b, 314 (*illus.*)
Sardica (Sardika). *See* Serdica
Sardinia
fall of (827), 6:443a
Pisa and, 9:664a-b
Sardinian language, 6:435a, 443b
Sardis, 12:305b–306a
Church *E,* 4:345a
decline of, 12:306b
Sargis Picak, **10:652b**
Christ's Entry into Jerusalem, 10:652a
Gospel of Queen Mariun, 10:652b
Sargis (Sergius) the General, St., 1:519a, 520a
Sargis Šnorhali, 9:103a, 103b
Sargis (the Great) Zak^c^arean, 12:736b
Sargis T^c^mogveli, 5:418a
Sargis (*vestes*), 1:484a
Sarigüzel sarcophagus, 4:351b
Sarīr, 5:315a
Sarmatians, **10:652b–653b**
armor of, 1:522a, 534b (*illus.*)
art of, 8:364a
association with Goths, 10:653a
in Caucasus and trans-Volga steppes, 3:195a, 10:653a
confederacy, 10:653a
Hunnic conquest, 10:653a
migrations, 10:653a
original habitat, 10:653a
social structure, 10:653a-b
vs. Rome, 10:465a
Sarmiento, Pedro, 9:111b
Sarolt (wife of Géza of Hungary), 11:477b, 478a
Sarracinus, **10:653b**
Sarrāj (banū), 5:653b
Sarrià (church: Barcelona), retable, 6:328b (*illus.*)
Sarum chant, **10:653b–655b**
antiphonal, 10:654b
development of English liturgy and, 10:654a
kyriale, 10:654b
New Ordinal, 10:654b
Norman French influence, 10:654b
oldest manuscripts, 10:654a-b
order of chants, 10:654a
popularity of, 10:654a
preservation of, 10:654a
processional, 10:654b–655a
Sarum use, **10:655b–656b**
Divine Office, 10:656a
extreme unction in, 4:565b
feast of the Transfiguration, 10:656a
liturgical instructions, 10:656a
non-Roman practices, 10:656a
Osmund's *Institucio,* 10:655b–656a
processions, 10:656a
rhymed office to St. Thomas Becket, 10:369b
tonary and, 12:70b
York rite and, 12:729a, 729b
see also Bangor, rite of; Lincoln, rite of
Sarvandik^c^ar, Battle of (1276), 11:351b
Sarzosius of Aragon, Franciscus, treatise on the equatorium, 11:98b
Sasanian art, **10:656b–660a**
3rd and 4th centuries, 10:657a–658b
5th to 7th centuries, 10:658b–659b
architectural remains, 10:658b–659a, 659b
bas reliefs, 10:600a-b
of Ardešīr I, 10:611b–612a
coins, 10:663b
importance for dating, 10:656b–657a
decoration, 10:658b
eyvān and, 4:569b
geographical parameters, 10:656b
Greco-Roman influence, 10:658a-b
influence of, 10:659b
on Bulgarian art, 2:414b
on Islamic manuscript illumination, 8:114a, 115b
molded stucco, 10:659a, 659b
Paikuli monument, 9:329 (*illus.*)
rock reliefs, 10:657b–658a, 659a
royal busts, 10:659a
seals, 10:658b, 659b
silk weaving, 10:665a-b
"Spring of Xusrō," 10:665b
Tepe Hissar villa, 10:659b
Umayyad sculpture and, 6:595b
vessels and plates, 10:659a-b
silver-gilt, 10:657 (*illus.*), 658a-b, 659a, 659b, 664b
Western influence, 10:659b
zandanījī and, 12:738a-b
see also Bishapur; Naqsh-i Rustam; Palmette; Seals and sigillography, Sasanian
Sasanian culture, **10:660a–666a**
astrology, 10:665a
cleanliness, 10:664a
daily life, 10:664a–665a
death rituals, 10:664b
ecological practices, 10:665a
education, 10:664a, 664b
epic tradition, 10:669a
Eran and Aneran, 10:662a
feasts and entertainment, 10:664b–665a
fire temples, 10:663b
gahanbar foods, 10:664b
magic bowls, 10:664a-b
next-of-kin marriage, 10:664a
royal horoscope, 10:665b
science and technology, 10:665a
see also Zoroastrianism
Sasanian Law-Book. *See Mātakdān Ī Hazār Dātastān*
Sasanians
Abbasid caliphate and, 3:42a
administration of, 11:122a-b
resh-galuta, 10:662b
agriculture and food supply, 10:661b
Armenian saints and, 1:518b
army of, office of sparapet and, 11:460a
Aršak II and, 1:560a
artisans, 10:663b
Byzantine trade with, three transit points, 12:97a
cavalry of, 3:199a
Chosroids and, 3:308a
Christians in government service, 10:663b
Church of the East and, 11:563a
division of Iran into quadrants, 10:662a
ethnic groups, 10:660b–661a
in Ganjak of Atropatene, 5:356a
geography, 10:660a-b, 666b–667b (map)
in Georgia, 5:405a
government
clergy in, 10:663b, 669a
service in, 10:663b, 664a
vuzurg-framadār, 10:669a, 670a
history, **10:666a–671b**
Achaemenid associations, 10:666a
Arab conquest, 10:671a
Armenia and, 10:668a-b, 12:360a
Byzantine truce, 10:670a
church and state, 10:668a
5th to 6th centuries, 10:658a
founding of dynasty, 1:451b–452a
Iranian reunification, 10:666a
Siwnik^c^ under, 11:315a
Vaspurakan and, 12:361a, 362a
see also Avarayr; Bahrām V Gōr of Armenia, Sasanian king; Bahrām VI Čōbēn of Persia, usurper; *Letter of Tansar*
horsemanship, 10:665a
influence on Islamic culture, 10:665b
influence of Pahlavi literature on Muslim scholars, 9:327a-b
inheritance laws, 8:237a, 10:664a, 668b
invasion of Afghanistan, 6:72a
in Iraq, 6:510a–511a
Ka^c^ba of Zoroaster and, 7:204b
Kamsarakan and, 7:208a
in *Kārnāmag-i Ardešīr-i Bābagān,* 7:220b–221a
Lakhmids and, 7:320b
language, 6:506a, 10:660b, 665b
literature and philosophy, 10:670b
major cities, 10:660b–661a
Manichaeans and, 8:85b
medicine, 10:664a, 665a
military campaigns, 10:666b, 669b, 670a, 670b
military organization, 10:670a
military titles, 6:116b
monarchy, 10:611b–612a, 660b
Christian favoritism, 10:669a
divine legitimacy, 10:667a-b
proof of capabilities, 10:667b–668a
succession conflicts, 10:669b
traveling encampments, 10:661a
Niẓam al-Mulk and, 9:144a
origins, 10:666b
Parthians and, 9:444a
persecution of Christians, 10:601a
religious policies, 10:662a–663a, 668a
persecution of religious minorities, 10:662a-b, 668b
proselytizing, 10:662b, 663a
toward Christianity, 10:669a
rules described by Sebēos, 11:132b
Sahak I's opposition to, 5:665b
in *Shāhnāma,* 11:221b
Shirvan and, 11:254a
slavery, 10:664a
social structure, 10:663a–664a, 668a, 668b, 670a
class mobility, 10:669b

Sasanians (*cont.*)
  spāhbad in, 11:374a-b
  taxation, 10:670a
    of religious minorities, 10:668b
  territorial expansion, 10:600a, 601a, 666b–667a
  trade and commerce, 10:661a
  transportation, 10:665a
  urban development, 10:661b
  vs. Arabs, 6:501b
  vs. Arsacids, 1:475b, 559a-b
  vs. Byzantines
    in Armenia, 1:476b, 478a
    over Nisibis, 9:142a
  vs. Hephthalite Huns, 1:476b
  vs. Muslims, 6:568b–569b, 573a
  vs. Romans, 10:599b–600a, 601a
  vs. Yemen, 12:714a
  writing of Avesta and, 2:14b
  see also Mamikonean; Seals and sigillography, Sasanian
Sasanids. *See* Sasanians
Sasine, in Scots law, 11:143b, 144a
Sasna Cṙer, 4:112b–113a
Sassetta, 5:537a, **10:671b–672a,** 11:281b
  altar of S. Francesco at Borgo San Sepolcro, 10:671b
  Madonna of the Snows, 10:671b
  St. Francis in Ecstasy, 10:672a (*illus.*)
  works in International Style, 5:628a
Sasun
  rebellion of 849, 4:112b
  under T^{c}ornik, 1:484b
Sasunc^{c}i Dawit^{c}. *See* David of Sasun
Satala, crusaders' route and, 10:423b
Satan
  in Armenian magic and folklore, 8:16b
  Islamic stone pillars of, 9:651a
  in mystery plays, 8:660a, 660b
  sorcery and, 8:30a
  see also Witchcraft, European
Satan (Islam). *See* Iblīs
Sat^{c}enik (legendary Armenian queen), 1:519b
Satire
  Bohemian, 7:370b
  of Cecco Angiolieri, 3:212a
  in *Celestina,* 3:212b–213a
  in early Icelandic *rímur,* 10:402b
  of Franciscans, 7:369a
  in Latin literature, 7:366b–367a, 368b, 370a, 371b
  in Peire Cardenal's work, 9:484a–485a
  in *Piers Plowman,* 7:331b, 332a
  political, in *Garsuinis* (*Tractatus de Albino et Rufino*), 11:406a-b
  rhythmical stanzas for, 7:364a
  in *Roman de Renard,* 2:141b
  "Satire on the estates," 8:322a
  in Spanish literature, 11:454a-b
  in *Ysengrimus,* 2:141a
  see also Parody, Latin
Satisfaction. See Dracontius
Satrapies, Armenian, 1:475a, 476a
  under Byzantium, 1:477a, 477b
  under Rome, 1:475b
  see also Armenian Pentarchy
Saturnalia, Mardi Gras and, 3:99b
Satyricon. See Petronius
Saucer dome, 4:236a
Saucery, royal, 6:304b
Saul, as an alleged burial site of St. Patrick, 9:463a, 465b
Saule, Battle of (1236), 2:65b
Saumur bridge, 10:416b
Sauna, in *Eyrbyggja saga,* 4:568a
Sava, St., **10:672a-b,** 11:174b
  against the Roman church, 11:174a-b
  church at Peç and, 11:185b
  cult of, 10:672b, 11:180b
  father of, 11:173b, 174a
  renovation of Hilandar, 10:672b
  Serbian bishoprics, 10:672b
  see also Stefan Nemanja
Savage, Sir John, 3:298b–299a
Savalo, 7:24a
Savasorda. *See* Abraham bar Ḥiyya
Savigny, **10:672b–673b**
  agricultural development, 10:673a
  Cistercian union, 10:673a
  endowments and foundations, 10:673a
  foundation of, 10:672b, 12:479b, 480a
  notable monasteries, 10:673a
  political influence, 10:673a
  renowned scholars and writers, 10:673a-b
  Savigniac practices, 10:673a
  second abbey church, 10:673a
Savigny, Friedrich Karl von, *Summula De pugna,* 6:324a
"Savis e fols, humils et orgoillos." *See* Raimbaut de Vaqueiras
Savonarola, Girolamo, 4:246a-b, 250a, 6:664b
  as defender of Thomism, 12:42a-b
  influenced by Joachim of Fiore, 7:114a
  on papal infallibility, 4:378a
  S. Bernardino and, 11:281b
  sermon on the plague, 9:679b
  Triumphus crucis, 12:42b
Savoraim, 11:583b
Savoy, county of, **10:674a–675b**
  agricultural resources, 10:675a
  Allobroges settlements, 10:674a
  art and culture, 10:675b
  Burgundian occupation, 10:674a-b
  Burgundians in, 11:536b
  Christianization, 10:674a
  counts of Maurienne, 10:674b
  extension of domain, 7:9b
  Frankish occupation, 10:674a
  geography, 10:675a
  government, 10:674b–675a
  kingdom of Arles and Vienne, 10:674b
  monasticism, 10:675a-b
  Roman conquest of, 10:674a
  Saracen and Magyar invasions, 10:674b
  Switzerland and, 11:545b
Savoy, House of
  Berchtold of Zähringen and, 11:539a
  chronicles, 10:675b
  foundation of, 10:674b
  vs. Rudolph of Habsburg, 11:540a
Saw, frame. *See* Frame saw
Sawād
  irrigation of, 6:556b
  kharāj, 11:668a
Sawīrus ibn al-Muqaffa^{c}
  History of the Patriarchs, 4:525a
    translation of, 8:479a
Sawles Warde, 8:314b
Ṣawm. See Fasting, Islamic
Ṣawma^{c}a, 8:396b
Sawtegin, 11:217b
Sawyer, shipbuilding, 11:243b
Sax (weapon), 1:522a, 522b
Saxnot (tribal god of Saxons), 2:87a
Saxo Grammaticus, **10:675b–679a**
  Ásmundar saga Kappabana and, 1:586b–587a
  contribution to medieval Latin poetry, 10:677a
  Gesta Danorum, 2:184b, 3:327a, 5:368b, 7:281a, 369a, 10:249a, 675b–679a
    Absalon's personal testimony, 10:676b, 678b
    Angers fragment, 10:676a
    on Baldr, 2:55a, 55b
    Brevis historia regum Dacie and, 11:522b
    chronological distortions, 10:676b–677a, 678b
    compendia and quotations from, 10:676a
    dating of, 10:676b
    flyting in, 9:172b
    fornaldarsögur in, 5:143a
    on giant Geirrödr, 12:48a
    historical books, 10:676b–677a, 678a-b
    on Hrólf Kraki, 2:254a-b
    Hrómundar saga and, 6:312b
    Illuga saga Gríðarfóstra and, 6:421a
    Kudrun and, 7:304b
    legendary books, 10:677b–678a
    manuscript fragments and first edition, 10:676a
    meter of, 7:372a
    mythology in, 11:23a, 24a
    secular viewpoint, 10:678a
    Skarkaðr legend and, 11:466b, 467a
    Skjǫldung legends and, 6:311a
    as source for Scandinavian mythology, 11:23a, 24a
    sources, 4:414a, 10:676b
    verses from *Hlǫðskviða,* 6:269a
    on *Witherlogh,* 11:522a
  prose style, 10:677a
  role in 12th-century renaissance, 10:667a
  Skjǫldungar saga and, 11:328b
  Svipdagr and, 11:524b
Saxo, Poeta. *See* Poeta Saxo
Saxon architecture, **10:679a–681b**
  aisles, 10:680b
  building materials, 10:680a
  churches
    chronology, 10:679b
    constructional features, 10:679b
    Kentish type, 10:680a-b
    Northumbrian type, 10:680b
    two-celled, 10:679b–680a
  Greater Saxon and Later Saxon, 10:681a

monastic revival, 10:681a
porticuses, 10:680a, 680b
pre-Conquest, 10:680b
Saxon dynasty, **10:682a**
accession and election of, 4:426a
in Austria, 2:6a
Bavaria and, 2:134a
in chronicles, 12:628a
dukes of Saxony and, 9:148b
end of, 10:684b
influence on papacy, 9:375a-b
invasion of Italy, 7:4b
seals of, 11:129a
territorial expansion, 10:683b
in Thietmar von Merseburg's chronicle, 12:27b–28a
Saxon language, Old Saxon, 6:436b
Saxon law, codification of, 8:354a
Saxon Poet, The. *See* Poeta Saxo
Saxon pound, 10:67a
Saxons, 1:289a, 2:96b
in Canterbury, 3:81a
conquest of Britain, 10:682a
in England, language of, 6:437a
Frankish conquest, 10:683a-b
history, sources, 6:317a
migration of, 8:363a
mythology of, in Old Saxon baptismal vows, 2:87a
nobility of, 8:405a
organization by Charlemagne, 5:506b
tribal assembly, 10:682b
tribal authority under Merovingians, 5:505b
tribal laws, 10:683b
tribal origins, 10:682b
vs. Franks, 6:436b
Saxony, **10:682a–686a**
Christianization, 8:441b, 10:683a
dioceses, 10:683a
internal revolts, 10:683a, 683b, 684b–685a
provincial divisions, 10:682b
representative assembly in, 10:329a
revolt against Salian rulers (1073-1075), 8:405a
social structure, 10:682b–683b
Saxony, duchy of
assembly
non-noble participation, 10:675a
tribal, 10:682b
clergy, 10:684a
division of, 5:510b–511a, 10:685b
foundation of, 5:507a, 508b
German representative assemblies and, 10:329a
Henry I's election as emperor and, 5:475a
imperial recognition, 10:683b–684a
independence from Carolingian control, 5:474b
investiture conflict, 10:685a
later territories, 10:686b
Liudolfingian leadership, 10:683b
Lotharian expansion, 10:685a
monarchy, Salian kings, 10:684b
Otto I's rule of, 9:300b
rejection of antipope, 10:685a
revolt in (1075), 5:477b
road construction, 10:683a-b
selection of margrave, 10:685a
tribal duchy, grant of to archbishop of Cologne, 10:685a
under Henry the Lion, 5:479b
vs. Henry IV, 3:69a, 97a
see also Billungs
Saxony wheel
invention of, 11:699b–700b
labor productivity, 11:700b
Šaχruχadze, *T^{c}amariani,* 5:418a
Say, Lord, 3:5a
Sayf al-Dawla
in Aleppo, 1:145a
immortalization in poetry, 6:83b
al-Mutanabbī and, 8:652a, 652b
professional army of, 6:85b–86a
vs. Byzantines, 4:523a
vs. Ikhshidids, 6:416b, 417a
Sayf al-Dawla Abu 'l-Futūḥ Yūsuf. *See* Buluggīn ibn Zīrī
Sayf al-Dīn Quṭuz, Mamluk sultan, 8:73b
battle at ^{c}Ayn Jālūt, 8:473a-b
Baybars and, 2:138a
death of, 8:473b
Sayf ibn ^{c}Umar (*d.* 796), 7:307b
Sayyid. *See* Cid, the
Sayyida, Arwā al-, Sulayhid queen, 6:617a
Sāz-i alwāḥ-i fūlād, 8:613b
Sāz-i kasāt, 8:613b
Scabbard. *See* Swords
Scabini. See Justices
Scabinus. See Échevin
Scaccabarozzi, Origo
Liber officiorum, 10:376b
liturgical poetry, 6:382a-b, 9:714b
Scala Coeli (monastery), freestanding Stations of the Cross and, 11:467b
Scalacronica, **10:686a-b**
English-Scottish border events, 10:686a
Scale
balance, 12:580b–581a
counterpoise, 12:581a
steelyard, 12:581a
Scale of Perfection, The. See Hilton, Walter
Scaligieri (family), trecento music patronage, 12:179b
Scalloped capital, 3:90b (*illus.*)
Scandicus, 8:619 (*illus.*), 624b, 625 (*illus.*)
Scandinavia
in Arabic sources, **10:706b–708b**
Arabic designations of Scandinavians, 10:706b
example of runic writing, 10:707a
Scandinavias as subgroup of Slavs, 10:706b–707a
Black Death in, 2:261a-b
Christianity in, 8:442a
close connections with England, 4:311b
history (before 800), 4:553b–554a, **10:686b–698b,** 10:687 (map)
archaeological evidence, 10:688b–689b, 691b–694b, 695a-b, 696b
decline of Roman empire and, 10:697a-b
early written records, 10:686b–688a
economic isolation, 10:697b
Heruli, 10:687b–688a
Hunnic expansion and, 10:697b
legendary Amazon state, 10:687a
paganism vs. Christianity, 10:697b–698a
Ptolemaic maps, 10:687b
Sithones, 10:687a
Viking Age, 10:698a
see also Vikings
history (after 800). *See individual countries*
kingship, 10:701b–702b
authority and limitations, 10:700b–701a, 704a-b
dynastic descent, 10:700b
magnetic compass and, 11:101a
mining areas in, 8:399a
political and legal organization, **10:698b–706b**
assemblies, 10:699b–700a, 700b, 701a, 702b, 704b–706a
blood vengeance and feuds, 10:704b
centralization, 10:701b–703b
court life, 10:702a-b
crown lands and plantations, 10:701b
district divisions, 10:699a-b
local leaders, 10:701a-b
military cooperation, 10:701b–702b
organizational units, 10:699a–700a
royal military forces, 10:702a-b
taxation, 10:702a
yeomen, 10:700a-b, 704b
property ownership, *bóndi* and *odal* land, 11:679b
social structure, 10:700a–701b
tenurial development
payment to crown, 11:685a
peasant freeholds, 11:684b–685a
trade and commerce
with Baltic Germans, 6:91b
Norway, 6:95b
universities, 12:290a
see also Denmark; Iceland; Norway; Sweden
Scandinavian languages, **11:1a–3a**
derivation, 11:1a
early inscriptions, 11:1a-b
futhark alphabets, 11:1a
Jón Ögmundarson and, 7:146a
peculiarity of, 7:146a
phonological innovation, 11:2a-b
phonological restructuring, 11:1b–2a
runes
development of, 10:563a–564a
number and distribution, 10:558a-b
origin of, 10:560a-b
separation of dialects, 11:2b
Scandinavian law
codes in vernacular, 6:440b
lack of torture, 12:90a
law codes, 10:704a–706a
lawmen and law-speakers, 10:701a
procedures, 10:705a–706a
see also Compurgation
Scandinavian literature
ballads, **11:3a–10a**
accuracy of history in, 11:7b

Scandinavian literature (*cont.*)
ballads (*cont.*)
of chivalry, 11:7b–8a
Christian themes in, 11:6a-b
collections of, 11:8b–9b
death and escape from death in, 11:7b–8a
development of scholarship, 11:9a
"Dream Ballad," 11:6b
early fragments, 11:4a
early metrical forms, 11:4a-b
erotic themes in, 11:7b
heroic, 11:8a
historical, 11:6b–7b
introductory strophes, 11:5b
jocular, 11:8b
legendary, 11:6a-b, 6b
"Little Karin" stanza forms, 11:4b
melodies, 11:3b–4a
novelistic, 11:8a
"Proud Ellen" stanza forms, 11:4b–5a
quatrains, 11:4b
refrains, 11:5a
similarities to British tradition, 11:3a
sources, 11:3a-b
of the supernatural, 11:5b–6a
theme groupings, 11:5b
see also Faroese ballads
fragments of a bestiary, 2:206a
grammatical, **11:10a–13b**
Christianity and, 11:10a
consonant treatment, 11:11b
"Danish" grammarians in Paris, 11:10a-b
development in Iceland, 11:10b
diphthong treatment, 11:11b
errors in Third Grammatical Treatise, 11:12b
Latin grammar, 11:10a-b
minimal pairs, 11:11a, 11b
nasal vowel treatment, 11:11a-b
phonotactics, 11:12a
vowel system treatment, 11:11a-b
see also Grammatical Treatise
heroic lay, origin of, 4:390a-b
homilies and sermons, 11:16b–17a
patronage of, 4:618b
poetry
heroic, 6:88a
relation to *Guðrúnarkviða* cycle, 6:36b
Preislied genre, 7:679b
religious, **11:13b–19a**
apocrypha, 11:15a, 15b
categories, 11:14a
English influence on, 11:14a, 17a
epic literature, 11:14b–16b
handbooks, 11:18a-b
homilies and sermons, 11:16b–17a, 18a
Icelandic *rímur,* 11:16a
Latin influence on, 11:14a-b
liturgical poetry, 9:714b
Marian literature, 11:15b–16a
otherworldly journeys, 11:16a-b
prayerbooks, 11:18b
revelations, 11:16b
university influences, 11:14b
vernacular in preaching and teaching, 11:14b
visions, 11:16a-b
see also Hagiography, Scandinavian
rhymed chronicles, **11:19a–22b**
in Denmark, 11:20b–21a
"Europeanization" of Scandinavia and, 11:20a
14th-century revival, 11:19b
medieval rhetoric and, 11:21a
politics and the diffusion of, 11:19a-b
propagandistic intent of, 11:19a
sources, 11:20a
sphere of influence of, 11:20a-b
in Sweden, 11:20a-b
see also Eddic poetry; Norse flyting; *Rímur;* Sagas; *Þættir*
Scandinavian mythology, **11:22b–34b,** 12:423b
borrowing from other mythologies, 11:29b
Christian parallels, 11:31b
cosmology, 11:29a-b
creation, 11:28b–29a
dead (*einherhjar*), 11:31b
in Denmark, 4:149b, 151a
diachronic and synchronic aspects, 11:22b–23a
dísir, 11:28a
euhemerism of Snorri, 11:24b–25a
in *Eyrbyggja saga,* 4:568a
forces of evil, 11:28a
Gefjon, 5:372a–373a
giants and giantesses, 11:25b, 27b, 28a
conflicts with Thor, 11:32a
creation of, 11:28b
frost giants, 11:28b
gods and goddesses, 11:24b–28a
creation of, 11:28b
days of week named after, 11:25a, 25b, 26b, 27b
war with Vanir, 11:29b–31a
good vs. evil in, 11:28a
in *Haustlǫng,* 12:32a-b
Indo-European parallels, 11:30a-b
magic in, 11:30b, 31a
mead of poetry, 9:218a, 11:31a
midgard serpent, 8:362a-b
other worlds, 11:29a
pagan, 6:40b
parallel with Persian, 10:249a
in *Reginsmál* and *Fáfnismál,* 10:290a–291a
in *Saga of Ragnarr Shaggy-Breeches,* 10:248a–249b
in Saxo's *Gesta Danorum,* 10:678a
shield poems, 2:359b
"Sigurdliederheft" and "Sigurðar saga" theories, 10:291a
Sinfjǫtli story, 11:310a-b
Skaði, 11:325a-b
in *Skírnismál,* 11:326b–327b
sources
artistic representations, 11:24a
Eddic poetry, 11:23a-b
from other Germanic areas, 11:24a-b
Latin histories and chronicles, 11:24b
pagan religious practice, 11:24a-b
Skáldskaparmál, 11:23b
Yggdrasill (world tree), 10:248a
see also Alvíssmál; Baldr; *Baldrs draumar;* Berserks; Fenris wolf; Fimbul winter; Freyr; Frigg; Njǫrðr; Odin; *Rígsþula;* Surtr; Thor
Scandinavian temples, **11:34b–36b**
Christian persecution of pagans and, 11:35a
hof, 11:34b, 35a–36a
farms as, 11:35b
in Iceland, 11:35b
hǫrgr, 11:36a
lack of vocational priesthood, 11:34a–35b
open-air sites, 11:35a
sacrifice (*blót*), 11:35a
source materials, 11:34a
under Christian churches, 11:36a-b
see also Scandinavian mythology
Scandinavian Union. *See* Nordic Union
Scandinavians
in England, 4:455b–456a, 457a, 6:437b, 440b–441a
Beowulf and, 2:184b
in France, 9:159a-b, 164a
in Ireland, 6:515 (map), 516b
linguistic impact of, 6:531a
Scaramangion, 3:615a
Scarlet, 10:236a-b, **11:36b–37b,** 11:296a
dyestuffs for, 11:37a
dying methods for, 11:37a
as fine woolen broadcloth, 11:36b–37a
variations in color, 11:37a
see also Kermes
Scáthach (Celtic goddess), 9:48b
Sceat, 8:428a
shilling and, 11:228b–229a
Scéla Mucce Meic Da Thó, 6:549a
Sceld (shield), 11:229a
Scena, defined, 4:278a
Scenae frons. See St. Gilles-du-Gard
Schachgedicht. See Heinrich von Beringen
Schachtbrett. See Eschaquiel
Schachzabelbuch. See Konrad von Ammenhausen
Schaffhausen, 11:543a-b
Germany and, 11:528a
Swiss Confederation and, 11:544b
Schaffhausen beakers, 5:558a
Schaffhausen onyx, 5:380 (*illus.*)
Schampiflor, **11:37b–38a**
confusion with *Frau Metze die Käuflerin,* 11:38a
sources and parallels, 11:38a
Schatzkammer Coronation Gospels, 10:306b
St. John, 10:305b (*illus.*)
Schedel, Hartmann, 9:202b
Weltkronik (*Liber chronicarum; Nuremberg Chronicle*), 4:578b, 6:264b, 9:201 (*illus.*)
Michael Wolgemut and, 12:681b–682a
Schedula diversarum artium. See Theophilus

Schefer Ḥarīrī, 12:575a
Scheffler, Johannes. *See* Angelus Silesius
Schembs, 8:563b
Schenk Ulrich von Winterstetten und Schmalenegg. *See* Ulrich von Winterstetten
Scheves, William, archbishop of St. Andrews, 11:112a
Scheyern dynasty, Wittelsbachs and, 2:134b
Schiacciato. See Stiacciato
Schism of 1054. *See* Schisms, Eastern-Western church
Schism of 1130, 3:636b–637a
Schism of 1378. *See* Schism, Great
Schism
  Acacian. *See* Schisms, Eastern-Western church
  Alexandrian, 10:252b
  Armenian-Byzantine, 1:499a-b
  Armenian-Georgian, 1:477b, 499b, 5:540a-b
    epistolary literature and, 1:509a
    Uxtanēs on, 1:510b
Schism, Byzantine
  Nikolaos I Mystikos and, 9:135b
  see also Iconoclasm, Christian; Iconoclastic controversy
Schism, early church
  Laurentian, 9:291b
  pentarchy system and, 9:496a
Schism, Great, **11:38a–42b**
  Ailly and, 1:108b
  Anselm Turmeda's prophecies and, 12:228a
  antipopes during, 1:331a
  attempts at arbitration, 3:646a
  background
    1378 election, 11:39a
    arrangements with secular rulers, 11:38b
    cardinals' privileges under Avignon popes, 11:38b
    conflicts in Papal States, 11:38b–39a
    election of Urban VI, 11:39a-b
    Gregory XI in Rome, 11:39a
  beginnings of, 2:1a
  Bohemia and, 6:367b
  Carthusians and, 3:119a
  Charles V of France and, 3:270a
  church taxation and, 11:610a
  college of cardinals and, 3:95b
  conciliarism and, 3:511b, 518a, 646a
  Council of Constance and, 3:647b–649b
  Council of Pisa and, 1:147b, 3:646a–647a
  crusades and, 4:56a
  deposition of pope and, 4:160a
  deposition of rulers and, 1:147b
  Disputatio inter clericum et militem and, 4:218a
  duration, 4:377a
  effects of, 3:365a–366b, 645b–646a
    on policymaking, 5:181a-b
    on University of Paris, 9:409a-b
  efforts to resolve, 3:646a
  flowering of mysticism and, 9:14b, 18a
  Gerson and, 5:512a-b
  growth of parliament and, 4:484b
  Henry V's role in ending, 6:161a
  history (1378–1395), 11:39b–41a
    division of European princes, 11:40a
    France and, 11:40a-b
    Urbanist consolidation of power, 11:41a
  history (1395–1417), 11:41a–42a
    election of Martin V, 11:42a
    France and, 11:41a-b
  indulgences and, 6:450b
  Italian political instability and, 7:8a-b, 10a
  Nogaret and, 9:153a
  papal conclave and, 3:524b
  papal power and, 9:709b, 11:40a
  Papal States and, 7:8a-b, 9:386a-b
  political factors favoring schism, 11:40a
  Russia and, 8:443b
  Sigismund and, 6:346a
  via cessionis, 1:108b
  via concilii, 1:108b
  Vincent Ferrer and, 12:453a
  see also Avignon papacy
Schism, Photian, **11:42b–44a**
  condemnation of Ignatios and dissidents, 11:43a
  Council of Reconciliation, 9:562a
  dogmatic conflict, 9:561b–562a
  factors precipitating, 9:619a
  long-term effects, 11:43b
  Nicholas I and, 11:43a
  origins of controversy, 11:42b
  see also Amorians
Schisms, Eastern-Western church, **11:44a–47a**
  Akakian schism, 4:491b, 6:154b, 8:477b, 11:44b–45a
  alliance against Turks, 11:47a
  Arab conquests and, 11:45a-b
  Basil the Great and, 2:120b
  Basil I and, 2:117b
  Chalcedonian, 8:477a-b
    attempts at reconciliation, 9:561a-b
  condemnation of "Three Chapters," 11:45a
  crusades and, 11:47a
  differences in ranking, 11:44b
  doctrinal differences, 2:465a–466a
  efforts to reunite, 2:465b–466a, 486a
  election of antipope Victor IV, 1:146b–147a
  Henotikon and, 12:743b
  iconoclastic controversy and, 2:463a-b, 488a–489a
  imprecision surrounding, 11:44a
  John V Palaiologos and, 7:128a
  John VIII Palaiologos and, 7:129a
  Norman and Turkish invasions and, 11:46b, 47a
  Patriarch Michael Keroularios and, 8:304b
  primacy issue, 2:464b–465b, 485b–486a, 489b
  Schism of 1054
    beginnings of, 9:459a-b
    effects of, 3:349b
    events leading to, 3:349a-b
    excommunications of, 11:46b–47a
    Guiscards and, 11:265a
    intellectual causes, 9:562a
  translation and, 12:138a
  Western reform movement and, 11:46b
  see also Azymes; *Filioque;* Schism, Photian
Schisms, Islamic. *See* Sects, Islamic
Schleiertüchlein, Das. See Hermann von Sachsenheim
Schleswig. *See* Slesvig
Schmieher, Peter, *Mären,* characterization, 8:130a
Schnabelflöte. See Recorder
Schneider, Hans, *Mären,* characterization, 8:130a
Schola. See Guilds and métiers
Schola. *See* Solea
Scholae, 11:573a
  Byzantine, **11:47b**
    division into East and West, 11:47b
  Latin. *See* Schools, palace
"Scholar and His Cat, The," 6:527b, 528a
Scholars' Primer, The. See Auraicept na nÉces
Scholarship
  clerical, 4:577b–578a
  Irish, 6:516a
  Islamic
    in Damascus, 4:84b–85a
    in Iraq, 6:512a
    oral transmission *isnād* tradition, 12:147a-b
    pilgrimage and, 9:651b–652a
    Quraysh tribe and, 10:242a
  Italian, Christian humanists and Plato, 9:702b–703b
  Jewish
    ha-Rav (rabbi) title, 10:243a
    Morenu ha-rav (teacher the rabbi) title, 10:243a
    pilgrimage and, 9:652b–653a
    rav (master) title, 10:242b
  monastic
    Bruno of Cologne and, 6:313b–314a
    Near East, 4:117a
  secular, Platonism and, 9:701a
  see also Classical literary studies; Glossators; Translation and translators
Scholarship, Byzantine classical, **11:48a–55b**
  Atticism, 11:48a, 49a-b
  commentaries on ancient authors, 11:53b–54b
  decline of, 11:48b, 50b
  East-West cultural exchange, 11:50b–51a
  effect of Christianization on, 11:48a-b
  grammar, 11:51a–52a
  Greek heritage, 11:48a
  Greek refugees in the West, 11:51a
  history, 11:48a–51a
    Arab conquests and, 11:48b
    breakup of Byzantine Empire after 1204, 11:49b–50a
    challenges to ancient authority, 11:49b
    13th-century polymaths, 11:50a

Scholarship, Byzantine classical (*cont.*)
lexica, 11:52b–53b
meter, 11:52a-b, 52a
philosophy, 11:54b–55a
Scholarship, legal. *See* Glossators; Law, schools of
Scholastica, St., 2:169a
rhymed office to, 10:370b
Scholasticism, **11:55b–58b**
Aristotelian framework, 11:688a
on *ars antiqua,* 1:543a–544a
astrology and, 1:607b
authority of Scriptures in, 11:56b
ban on interest taking and, 12:337a
biblical exegesis and, 2:213a-b
on blasphemy, 2:271b
in canon law, 11:57b–58a
church criticism of magic practices and, 8:28a-b
commentary format, 11:57a
concordia discordantium as goal, 11:56a
departures from Aristotelian authority, 11:56b
derivation of term, 11:55b–56a
disputation, 10:241a
ecclesiastical authorities, 4:375b
effect on 13th-century literature, 4:448b
first Scholastic treatises, 12:21a
French prose and, 5:255b–256a
on God's omnipotence, 8:36a
Ibn Sīnā's influence on, 11:306b
impact of university on, 11:57a-b
innovation and, 1:468a
intellectual life in Latin church and, 3:357b–358a
Jewish translators and, 12:134b
Meister Eckhart and, 4:381b, 9:32b
musical theory, 7:39a
Neoplatonism and, 9:100b–101a, 700a
origins, 9:557a
Anselm of Canterbury, 9:588a
quaestiones, 10:238a-b
question format, 11:57a
quodlibet, 10:238b, 241a
religious orders and, 1:465a
scholastic method, 11:56a-b
basic characteristics, 11:56b
development of, 11:56a-b
importance of Aristotelian logic in, 11:56b
standardization of, 11:57b
as servant of theology, 11:56b–57a
in Spain, 11:407a
Isidore of Seville and, 6:566a
summa format, 11:57a-b
in theology curriculum, 11:691a
theories of government, 4:451b–452a
witchcraft and, 12:658b, 661b
Scholasticus, translators, 12:137b
Scholia. See Pseudo-Nonnus
Scholica enchiriadis, 8:639b
alphabetic notation and, 8:614a, 614b
Daseian notation in, 8:618a
Schöner, Johannes, 1:613b
Schongauer, Martin, **11:58b–59a**
engraving technique of, 4:488b, 490a
Madonna in a Rose Arbor, 11:58b, 59a (*illus.*)
School of Chartres. *See* Chartres, School of
School of the Persians, 9:142a, 11:564b
Schools, 11:63b (*illus.*)
academy, Consistoire de Gai Saber, 10:251b
Byzantine, 7:595a-b
in Constantinople, 3:556b
see also Universities, Byzantine
cathedral, **11:59a–63a**
careers as specialists prepared at, 11:61b
Carolingian reform movement and, 11:60a
as centers of 12th-century intellectual life, 11:60b
Chartres, 12:638b
curriculum of, 11:59b, 61a–62a
early bishops' schools, 11:59b–60a
literature and the arts in, 11:59b
masters of, 11:60b
monastic reform movement and, 11:60a-b
prestige of, 11:62a-b
subservience to scriptures, 11:62a
universities and, 11:62b
see also Theology, schools of
elementary, goals of religious instruction, 10:301a
grammar, **11:63a–64b**
Byzantine, 11:63b
Carolingian reform and, 11:64a-b
fostered by alphabetic script, 11:63a-b
in late Middle Ages, 7:600a-b
religions of the book and, 11:63a
Roman, 11:63b–64a
teacher qualifications, 11:63b
textbooks, 11:64b
trivium studies and, 12:206b
Irish, 6:516a, 544a
manuscript transmission and, 6:545b
for poets, 6:532b, 534b–535a
religious literature in, 6:542a
Islamic, **11:64b–69a**
Arabic or literary sciences or arts, 11:65a
colleges, 11:65a–66b
divisions of knowledge in, 11:65a
exclusion of "ancient (Greek) sciences," 11:65a
fatwā in, 11:67b
home and library studies, 11:66b–67a
Islamic sciences, 11:65a
law, 4:407a
learning methodologies, 11:67a-b
license to teach, 11:67b–68a
madrasa and, 11:66a-b
masjid-khan complexes, 11:65b–66a
memorization in, 11:67a
scholastic method in, 11:67a-b
students, 11:68a-b
for *ᶜulamāᵓ*, 12:245a
university and, 11:64b–65a
see also Azhar, al-; Madrasa
in Italy, closing of in the 6th century, 7:598b
Jewish, **11:69a–72b**
adult study, 11:72b
Ashkenazic educational patterns, 11:69b, 71b
in Babylonia, 7:107b
beginning study of Leviticus in, 11:70a
Bible study and, 11:70b
communal self-government under Islam and, 7:73a-b
curriculum, 11:70a-b
etymology of *ḥeder,* 11:72a
foundings of, 7:162a
gaon (Jewish academy head), 7:73a-b, 74a
in gaonic period, 5:357a–358a
logical prowess and, 11:71a
as mediators of culture, 11:69a-b
in Palestine, 7:104a–105b
prestige of rabbinic masters, 11:71a
"Prince of Torah" ceremony and, 11:69b–70a
in Qayrawān, 7:98a-b
regulation of, 11:69a, 72a
rite of passage into, 11:69b–70a
role in Judaism, 7:162a
Sephardic, 11:69b, 71b
southern vs. northern approaches, 11:71a-b
talmudic (yeshiva), rabbi training and, 10:243b
transmission of rabbinic authority, 6:256b
see also Exegesis, Jewish
minstrels'. *See* Minstrels, schools of
monastic, **11:72b–78a**
antiphilosophical stance of, 11:73b
Benedictines and, 2:173b–174a
in Byzantium, 11:75a
cantus (chant), 11:76a
Carolingian reforms and, 11:60a, 75b–76a
of cenobites, 11:73a-b
computus (counting), 11:76a
contriban model, 11:74b–75a
Latin as language of, 11:75b
literacy tests in monasteries, 11:73b
missionary, 12:137a
monastic histories, 11:76b
notae, 11:76a
post-Nicene monasticism and, 11:73a
pre-Reformation neglect, 11:77a
preservation of scriptures in, 11:76b
psalmi, 11:76a
as repositories of writings, 11:75b
responsibility for Western education, 11:74a-b, 75a-b
rhetoric, 11:76b
silent reading in, 11:73b–74a
studia linguarum, 12:137a
under Saxon emperors, 11:77a
writing and bookmaking in, 11:74a
music and, 8:581b–582a
for nobles, courtesy books in, 3:660b
palace, **11:78a-b**
definition of *schola,* 11:78a
Emperor Heraklios, 9:697a
flowering under Carolingians, 11:78b
Medici Platonic Academy, 9:698b, 703b
replacement of, 11:78b

vocational training at, 11:78a
Roman
Christianity and, 10:462b
Latin literature and, 7:360a
survival of their teaching methods, 10:352b–353a
Syrian Christian, 11:564b
see also Law, schools of; Medicine, schools of; Religious instruction
Schoonhoven, Jan van, defense of Ruusbroec, 9:38a
Schöpfwerk. See Salines
Schrätel und der Wasserbär, Das. See Heinrich von Freiberg
Schreyer-Landauer monument, 7:300b
Schüchlein, Hans, 9:710b, **11:79b**
high altar at Tiefenbronn, 11:79b (*illus.*)
Schule der Ehre, Die, 8:410a
Schüler von Paris, Der, **11:79b–80b**
contents of, 11:80a
three versions of, 11:80a
Schulze, 12:440b
Schützenfeste, 5:348b
Schwabenspiegel, 7:426b, 481a, **11:80b–81a**
influence of *Sachsenspiegel* on, 10:603b
source for *Lohengrin,* 7:643a
sources of, 11:80b
Schwäbisch Gmünd, Parler family and, 9:421a
Schwäbisch-Hall, prehistoric saltworks, 10:633b
Schwanritter, Der. See Konrad von Würzburg
Schwarz (Niger), Petrus. *See* Peter Schwartz (Niger)
Schweinschwert. See Swords
Schweizerdegen, 11:551b
Schweizerdolch. See Daggers
Schwester Katrei, 5:218b
Schwyz
Habsburgs and, 11:540a, 541a, 541b
Lenzburgs and, 11:541a
vs. Zurich, count of Tottenburg and, 11:544b
Sciant artifices alkimie, 1:136b
Science
experimental approach
advocated by Roger Bacon, 2:39b–40a
lack of in the Middle Ages, 2:242a, 244a
Hellenistic, 11:95a
magic and, 8:32a, 12:658a
spread of, translations and, 12:140b–141a
see also Astronomy; Mathematics; Optics; Physics
Science, Islamic, **11:81a–89b**
achievements, 11:86a–87b
ancient heritage, 11:82a–84b
character of, 11:87b–88b
decline of, 11:88b, 93b
Dīnawarī on, 4:187b–188b
flowering of under the Almohads, 11:84a
geography, 5:391b
Greek sources of, 12:128b–130a, 133a
institutions of, 11:84b–86a
Jewish translators and, 12:134a–136a
al-Rāzī and, 10:267a–268a
in Spain, 10:472a-b
system of study, 11:86a
Western science and, 11:95a
see also Bīrūnī, Muḥammad ibn Aḥmad Abu 'l-Rayḥān al-; Translation and translators
Science, Jewish, **11:89b–94b**
astrology, 11:91b–92a
astronomy, 11:90a–91b, 93a-b, 12:134a
biology, 11:93a
delimitation of the term, 11:89b
early works, 11:89b–90a
late medieval decline of, 11:93a-b
mathematics, 11:92a-b
medicine, 11:92b–93a, 12:134a–135a
Scientia artis musicae. See Elias Salomo
Scientific instruments, **11:95a–104a**
of European origin or development, 11:99b–102a
of Greco-Roman origins, 11:95a–97b (*illus.*)
of Indian and Islamic origins, 11:97a–99b (*illus.*)
quadrant, 10:236b–237a
rise of instrument making, 11:102a–103b
Scientific literature. *See Fachschrifttum*
Scissors, 2:149b
Scivias. See Hildegard of Bingen, St.
Sclavus, 11:338b
Scoithín (literary character). *See* Manannán mac Lir (god)
Scolari, Filippo, 6:346b
Sconfitta di Monte Aperto, La, 6:633b
Score (musical notation), 8:627b, 630b
Score (unit of measure), 12:593b
Scorpion. *See* Mangonel
Scotichronicon. See John Fordun
Scotism, 12:39a
compared with Thomism, 12:43a-b, 44a
see also Duns Scotus, John
Scotistic Aristotelianism. *See* Aristotelianism
Scotland, 11:104a (map)
administration under Malcolm IV, 8:57a
Anglo-Norman settlers in, 11:104b, 105b, 106b
Battle of Hastings and, 9:165a, 165b
Black Death in, 2:262b
Flemish settlers in, 11:105a, 106b
geography, 11:104a-b, 109b–110a
Henry II and, 9:167a
history, **11:104a–113a**
contacts with Europe (after 1371), 11:110b–112b
later stability, 11:110b–111b
rebellion of six earls in 1160, 11:107a
social reorganization in the 12th and 13th centuries, 11:106a–108a
wars of independence (1296-1350's), 11:108a–110b
wars of independence, "middling folk" and, 11:109a, 109b, 110b
see also Berwick, Treaty of; Strathclyde, kingdom of
independence of recognized by England (1328), 10:427a
Normans in, 11:104b–105a
Picts and, 9:643a
relations with
England (to 1290), 11:104b–106a
France, 6:331b, 11:109a
Ireland, 6:518b–519a
religion and culture, Scottish sees, 10:613b
"Renaissance" of, 11:112a-b
tenurial development
feu, 11:685b
tack and at will, 11:685b
Treaty of Chester and, 3:299b–300a
universities, 12:290b
Viking attack on, 12:425a
war with England
invasion by Edward I, 4:396a-b
under Edward III, 4:111a-b
see also Nechtan; Parliament, Scottish
Scots
Christianization of, 1:288b
in Ireland, 6:518b–519a
invasion under Robert Bruce, 4:299b
Scots law, **7:517a–518b**
Celtic base of, 7:517a
courts, 7:518b
emergence of central civil, 7:518b
divergence from European norm, 7:517a
English common law and, 7:517a-b
ideal of one law under one monarch, 7:517b–518a
incorporation of Anglo-Saxon inheritance, 7:517b
incorporation of older customary law, 7:517b
under MacDonald lords, 7:518b
see also Parliament, Scottish; Seisin, disseisin
Scott, John, early editions of *Everyman,* 4:527b
Scott, Sir Walter, *Eyrbyggja saga* and, 4:568a
Scottish art, influence of on Celtic art, 3:223b
Scottish Chronicle, 7:229b
Scottish church, history, David I and, 4:110b
Scottish Field, 8:332a, 333a
Scottish language. *See* Celtic languages
Scottish Legendary, sources for, 6:62a
Scottish literature
in the 15th century, 8:324a-b
chronicles, Robin Hood and, 10:435b, 437a
Scottish literature, Gaelic, **11:113a–117b**
dynasties of poets, 11:114a
folk song, 11:116b–117a
hereditary bardic poets, 11:113b–115b
Muireadhach Albanach and, 9:205a
poetry
bardic style and, 6:535b, 537b
manuscript sources, 11:113b, 115b
in postmedieval period, 11:115a-b
praise poetry, 11:115a

Scottish literature, Gaelic (*cont.*)
  prose, 11:115b–116b
    manuscript sources, 11:116a
  records from before 1200, 11:113a-b
  see also Bard; Bardic grammars
Scottish Prophecies, 8:332a
Scotus. *See* Duns Scotus, John
Scourge of the Jews. See Lull, Ramón
Scramasax, 8:283b, 11:550b (*illus.*)
  see also Sax (weapon)
Scratch dial, 3:457b
Screen, **11:117b–118a**
  altar, reredos, 10:334b–335a
  in Chartres Cathedral, 1:442b, 443b (*illus.*), 444a
  transenna, 12:125a
  see also Iconostasis
Screen, altar. *See* Reredos
Screen, chancel, **11:118a-b**
Screen, rood, in Albi Cathedral, 11:118b (*illus.*)
Screens passage, 11:118a
"Scribe in the Woods, The," 6:527b, 528a-b
Scribes
  instruments in ordination, 9:267a
  Islamic, 3:53a–54a
Scrinium, **11:119a**
Script. *See* Calligraphy
Scripta Beneventana, 11:266b
Scriptores post Theophanem
  authorship, 2:514a
  historical conception, 2:514a
Scriptorium, 3:109b–110a, **11:119a**
  of Alfonso X (the Learned), 11:414b
  in Anglo-Saxon England, 1:275b–276a
  at Aachen, 7:25b
  at Tours, 1:143a
  in Book of Durrow, 3:219b
  Carolingian, decorated initials from, 6:462b
  of Gelatʿi, 5:374b
  in Herāt, 8:100a
  Hiberno-Saxon, decorated initials from, 6:461b
  Irish sagas and, 6:544b
  of Mar Mattai, 11:565a
  Merovingian, 8:368a
  monastic, revival of in the 15th century, 8:104b–105a
  regulations on silence in, 7:599b
  Romanesque, 10:507b
  in Studios Monastery, 11:495a
  Timurid, 6:605b
  see also Libraries; Manuscript books, production of; Manuscript illumination, European; Stichometry
Scriptuaries. *See* People of the Book
Scripturarum claves iuxta traditionem seniorum. See Ebarcius of St. Amand
Scripture cross, 3:221b
Scriveners' Guild (London), 8:104b
Scriverius, Petrus, *Laure-crans voor Laurens Coster van Haerlem,* 10:127a
Scrofula. *See* King's evil
Scroll, inhabited, **11:119a-b**
  in Bede's *Life of St Cuthbert,* 11:119 (*illus.*)
Scrope, Geoffrey, 7:194a
Scrope, Stephen, translation of Christine de Pizan, 3:666a
Scrovegni Chapel. *See* Arena (Scrovegni) Chapel (Padua)
Scrovegni, Enrico, 1:453a
Scrupule (unit of measure), 12:595b
Scrutiny of the Scriptures. See Paul of Burgos
Sculpture
  early Christian avoidance of, 4:348b
  see also nationalities and individual artists
Sculpture, classical style. *See* Classicism in art
Scuola siciliana. See Italian literature, lyric poetry, Sicilian school
Scutage, 7:278a, **11:120a–121a**
  crown and, 3:414a
  in France, 11:120b
  origins, 11:613a
  seignorial, 11:613a-b
  sergeant and, 11:208b
Scutifer. See Squire
Scylding dynasty, *Skjǫldunga saga* and, 9:176a
Scythe, 12:79b–80b
Scythians, in Caucasia, 3:195a
Scythopolis. *See* Baysān
Sea, secret, 6:303b
Sea charts, 11:235a
Sea coal, 3:473a
Sea law. *See* Law, maritime
Sea Laws of Visby, 5:633a
Sea trade. *See* Trade, maritime
Sea warfare. *See* Navies
Séadna, 6:534b
Seafarer, The, 1:281a
  classified as a lyric poem, 8:334b
Seafaring. *See* Ships and Shipbuilding
Seal, department of, Islamic, 6:589b
Seal of the fairs. *See* Fairs
Seal of Faith. *See Knikʿ Hawatoy*
Seals, royal, English. *See* Great seal; Privy seal
Seals and sigillography
  Byzantine, **11:121a**
    seal of Patriarch Leo of Constantinople, 11:121b (*illus.*)
  chancery, 3:254a
  Islamic, **11:121a–122b**
    a hematite seal, 11:121b (*illus.*)
  Sasanian, **11:122a–123b**
    a 6th-century jadeite seal, 11:123b (*illus.*)
    Christian iconography on, 11:122b
    religious formulas on, 11:122b
    titles on, 11:122a-b
    uses of, 11:122a
    Zoroastrian motifs on, 11:122b–123a
  Western European, **11:123b–131b**
    application to the document, 11:127b–129a
    heraldic, 11:129b
    history of usage, 11:124a–127a
    iconography, 11:129a–130a
    medieval matrices, 11:127a
    national collections of seals, 11:130a
    of nobility, 11:129b
    as a portrayal of medieval life, 11:129b–130a
    preserved matrices and seal impressions, 11:130a
    replaced by signatures, 11:126b–127a
    seal technique, 11:127a–129a
    terminology, 11:123b–124a
    wax impressions, 11:125a-b, 127b
Seam measure. *See* Quarter
Seamen
  Indian Ocean, 11:249b
  Mediterranean, 11:236b
  Northern European, 11:241a
Seanchaidhean, 11:113b
Seasons of Fasting, 8:327a
Seasons, myths of, in Irish saga, 6:548b
Seax, 11:547b (*illus.*), 551a
  see also Sax (weapon)
Sebaldus, St., tomb of, Vischer and, 12:463b, 464a (*illus.*)
Sebaste, 1:473a, **11:131b–132a**
  Armenian trade and, 12:97b
  crusaders' route and, 10:423b, 424a
  Seljuks and, 1:484b
  silk route to the Far East and, 12:99a
Sebastian, St., martyrdom of, 11:159 (*illus.*)
Sebastokrator, **11:132a-b**
Sebenico, Hungary and, 6:340b
Sebēos, **11:132b–133a**
  on Arabs in Armenia, 1:478a
  Armenian cavalry and, 3:199a
  on Armenian-Byzantine church relations, 1:500a
  on Church of St. Hṙipʿsimē, 6:309b
  History, 1:511a
    unique elements in, 6:239b
  history of Heraklios, 2:513a
  Łazar Pʿarpecʿi and, 1:509b
Sebüktigin, 5:520a, **11:133a–134b**
  early life of, 11:133a-b
  founder of the Ghaznavids, 1:220a, 220b
Sechnall, 9:465a
  "Audite omnes amantes," 6:381a
  hymns of, 7:362a
"Second Battle of Mag Tuired," in *Mabinogi,* 7:705b
Second Bible of Charles the Bald. *See* Bible
Second Bulgarian Empire. *See* Vlach-Bulgarian Empire
Second Coming. *See* Millennialism; Parousia
Second Constantine Gospel, 1:497a (*illus.*)
Second inquest. *See Inquisitio solemnis*
Second Lay of Helgi Hunding's-slayer. See Helgi poems
Second Scottish Prophecy. See Thomas of Erceldoune
Second Shepherds' Play, **11:134a–135a**
  see also Towneley Plays
Secret History. See Procopius
Secret History of the Mongols
  on Genghis Khan's early life, 8:465a
  origin of the empire, 8:463b

Secret marriage. *See* Marriage
Secret des secrets. See Peter Peckham
Secret Supper, 3:182a
Secreta Alberti
attributed to Albertus Magnus, 8:35a
magical formulas of, 8:35a-b
Secretariat, royal
England
Anglo-Saxon, 6:300b
chamber as, 6:301b
Norman, 6:301a
see also Administrative records
Secretum. See Aristotle
Secretum of the eparch, 4:493b
Secretum meum. See Petrarch
Secretum secretorum, 8:37b–38a, 435a-b, **11:135a-b**, 12:138b
Anglo-Norman adaptation of, 1:264b
commentary by Roger Bacon, 2:38a, 39b, 40b
Hoccleve and, 8:323b
manuscripts of, 8:38a
translations of, 4:578b, 6:116a, 7:693a
Sectator Platonis. See Plato and Platonism; Wolfhelm of Cologne
Sects, Christian. *See* Heresies
Sects, Islamic, **11:135b–140b**
Kharijite faction, 6:205a
istiʿrāḍ, 6:205a
on millennialism, 8:389a
Muʿtazilites, creation of Koran, 6:205b–206a
prediction of divisions, 6:206b
see also Alids; Assassins; Ismāʿīlīya; *Ithnāʿasharī,* Lebanon; Shīʿa; Shiism; Sunna
Sects, Jewish. *See* Karaites
Secunda pastorum. See Second Shepherds' Play
Secundinus. *See* Sechnall
Seder Olam Rabbah, 6:255b
Seder Olam Zuta, 7:106a-b
Seder Tanna'im ve-Amora'im, 11:584a
order of the rabbis, 6:256a
Sederunt. See Perotinus (Pérotin)
"Sedia la fremosa seu singo torcendo." *See* Coelho, Estevam
Sedilia, **11:140b–141a**
Sedition. *See* Treason
Sedulius Scottus, 4:542b, 7:362b, **11:141a-b**
"A solis ortus cardine," 6:381a, 384b
Carmen paschale, 4:496a, 7:361a
De actibus apostolorum and, 1:422a
modeled on Vergil, 12:394a
Carolingian Latin poetry and, 3:100b, 103a
De rectoribus christianis, 7:261b, 8:434b, 10:15b
goliards and, 5:575a
Hrotswitha von Gandersheim and, 6:314a
hymns of, 6:384a
kingship theories of, 7:261b
life of written by Meginhart of Fulda, 8:263a
ode on Rhodri Mawr, 10:366a
Seele Rat, Der. See Heinrich von Burgeis
Seelenfünklein. See Eckhart, Meister
Sefer Bahir (Book of Clarity), 3:1b
Sefer ha-agron. See Saadiah Gaon
Sefer ha-Dikduk. See Jonah Abu 'l-Walīd Merwān ibn Janāḥ
Sefer ha-Emunot. See Shem Tov ibn Shem Tov
Sefer ha-Halakhot. See Alfasi, Isaac ben Jacob
Sefer ha-Ḥayyim, 9:579a
Sefer ha-Ikkarim. See Albo, Joseph
Sefer ha-Kabbalah. See Abraham ibn Daud
Sefer ha-Kavod. See Judah ben Samuel he-Hasid (the Pietist)
Sefer ha-Kuzari. See Judah Halevi
Sefer ha-Navon, 9:579a
Sefer ha-Olam ha-Katan. See Joseph ibn Saddiq
Sefer ha-Roqeaḥ. See Eleazar ben Judah of Worms
Sefer ha-Turim. See Jacob ben Asher
Sefer ha-Yashar, 6:255b
Sefer ha-Zohar. See Zohar
Sefer halakhot, 11:586a
Sefer Ḥasidim. See Judah ben Samuel he-Hasid (the Pietist)
Sefer massao't. See Benjamin of Tudela
Sefer Milḥamot Adonai. See Levi ben Gershom
Sefer Mitzvot ha-Gadol. See Moses of Coucy
Sefer pesakim, 11:586a
Sefer tekunah. See Levi ben Gershom
Sefer Yezirah (Book of Creation), 3:1a
astrological references in, 11:91b
commentaries on, 10:598b
Sefirot, 3:1a
Segarelli, Gerard, 6:488b
Segmental arch. *See* Arch
Segna di Bonaventura, **11:141b**
Madonna Enthroned with Saints, 11:141b, 142a (*illus.*)
pupil of Duccio, 4:302b
Segovia, Roman bridge at, 10:410a
Segriá Canal, 6:557b
Seguidilla, 11:459b
Segura, Juan de, *Proceso de cartas de amores,* 11:454b
Seifín Mór, 6:535b
Seifín Óg (son of Seifín Mór), 6:535b
Seifried Helbling, **11:141b–143a**
identification of, 11:141b
Seignorial immunity
France, 11:203a
Russia, 11:191a
Seikilos. *See* "Epitaph of Seikilos"
Seine River
Normans and, 9:159b
Viking raids and, 12:430a–431a, 431b
Seinte Resureccion, La, 1:270a, 4:282b, **11:143a-b**
Seisin, disseisin, **11:143b–144b**
assize of novel disseisin, 1:596b–598a, 6:481a, 481b, 9:546b, 548a-b
expanded, 7:451b–452a
protective function, 9:547a-b
customary law and, 3:413b, 414a
escheat and, 4:509a
etymology and meaning of, 11:143b
heirs and, 7:443b, 451b, 453b
Henry II of England and, 3:409a, 6:481a-b, 7:437a–441b, 438a–439b
Pseudo-Isidorian decretals and, 7:438a
reseisin, 7:437a-b, 438a
versus proprietary right, 7:437b, 440a-b
see also English common law
Sekretikon, on Cyprus, 4:71b
Sekte der Minner, Die, 8:411a
Šełagir, 1:492a
Selāmlik, **11:144b**
Selden, John, *Eutychii Aegyptii,* 4:525a-b
Seldeneck, Philipp von, 4:579a
Seleucia. *See* Ctesiphon
Seleucids, displaced by Arsacids, 9:443b
Seleukis I Nikator, founder of Laodicea, 7:315a
Self-government. *See* Representative assemblies
Self-government, Jewish. *See* Jewish communal self-government
Selīm I, Ottoman sultan, **11:145a-b**
Bāyazīd II and, 2:137a
Crimean khanate and, 3:679a
military campaigns
battle of Marj Dābiq, 8:142a
defeat of ʿAlāʾ al-Dawla, 8:142a
Tarōn and, 11:599b
vs. Mamluks, 2:137b, 4:407a, 8:76a-b, 9:309a, 10:226b–227a, 11:145b
Selion (unit of measure), 12:588b
Seljuk ibn Doqaq, 11:151a
Seljuks, **11:150b–156a**
Arčēš and, 1:423a
in Armenia, 1:484a-b, 485a, 514a, 7:221b, 12:98b
Aristakēs on, 1:455a
army of, 3:209a-b, 11:152b
Arslān Isrāʾīl ibn Seljuq, 12:227a
art and architecture, 6:612a-b, **11:146a–150b**, 11:146a–148b (*illus.*)
domes, 6:28a-b
khan, 7:237b–238a
role of Niẓām al-Mulk, 11:146a–147a
Badr al-Dīn of Mosul and, 2:43b
branches of, 11:150b–151a
būq and, 8:612b
caliphate and, 6:590b
conversion of to Islam, 3:355b–356a
in Derbent, 4:162b
development of madrasas and, 8:11a-b, 11:85a
early history of, in Vardan Arewelcʿi's *Universal History,* 12:360a
Erzincan and, 4:508b
expansion, Asia Minor, 2:495b
First Crusade and, 4:30a
in Georgia, 4:112a, 5:406a-b, 420a
Ghaznavids and, 2:436a, 5:520b
Ghurids and, 5:526a-b
Great Seljuks, 11:151b–154a
Ikonion and, 6:418a
Ildegizids and, 6:419a-b

Seljuks (*cont.*)
in Iran, 6:503b–504a, 12:552b
in Iraq, 1:11b, 6:513b–514a, 606a
Isfahan under, 6:562a
Islamic administration and, 6:591a
Islamic mysticism and, 9:44a
Karamanids and, 7:214a
in Karin, 7:215a
khānqāh and, 7:238b
Khwārizmshāhs and, 7:244a
of Kirmān, 11:151a, 152a, 155a
Kutᶜaisi and, 7:311b
lusterware of, 5:379a
military campaigns
Armenia, 2:493b
Constantinople, 2:493b
Nicaea, 2:493b
al-Naṣir and, 11:247a
Nizārīs and, 11:137b
office of atabeg, 1:632a
office of sultan, 1:11b
origins of, 11:151a-b, 12:145b
patronage of arts, 11:147b–148a
raids by, Arcn, 7:215a-b
relations with
Byzantine Empire, 2:494b, 4:27b
Danishmendids, 4:91b, 93a
Kurds, 7:310b
of Rum, 11:154a-b, **11:156a–159a**
administrative capitals, 10:555a
in Anatolia, 1:241b, 10:555a
arrival in Azerbaijan, 2:27a
art and architecture, 11:148a–149b, 158b
Caesarea as capital for, 3:9a-b
capture of Sebaste, 11:132a
centralized state, 9:287b–288a
decline of, 11:154b, 158a
economy under, 11:158a-b
in Melitene, 8:269b
origins of, 11:156a-b
Qılıj Arslān's sultanship, 10:235a–236a
vs. Mongols, 1:241b
see also Qaykhosraw I, Seljuk sultan
Shaddadids and, 11:217b
in Shāh-Arman, 11:220a
Širak under, 11:311b
sultanate of Konya, Mongol conquest of, 8:470a
sultanate of, 11:151b–154a, 156b, 505a
decline of, 11:153a–154a
in Syria, 4:82a, 83b, 11:151a, 155a
Tabrīz and, 11:571a
Tarsus and, 11:599b
Turkomans and, 12:226b–227a
Turks and, 11:561a
vs. Byzantine Empire, at Myriokephalon, 8:657a
vs. Ḥasan-i Ṣabbāḥ, 6:617a
vs. Romanos IV Diogenes, 10:516a
vs. Theodore I Laskaris, 9:116b
vs. Xlatᶜ, 12:713b
vs. Zakᶜarids, 12:736b
see also Alp Arslan; Malikshāh; Qarakhanids; Toghrıl-Beg
Selmi, resident ambassadors and, 4:206a-b
Šem Ṭob. *See* Shem Tov
Sembi. *See* Prussians, Old
Semblanzas. *See* Spanish literature, biography
Semeca. *See* Johannes Teutonicus
Semejança del mundo, 11:414a, 441a
Semen Gordyi of Muscovy, grand prince, succession plans, 8:543a
Semgallia, 2:63 (map), 65b
Semgallians, 2:65b, 7:604a
Semi-Arians. *See* Homoeans
Semi-Pelagianism, 3:122b
Semibreve, 8:588b, 629 (*illus.*), 643b
in *ars nova,* 10:381b
see also Dragma
Semibrevis minima, 8:628b
Semidome, 4:236a
Semigallians. *See* Semgallians
Semikhah ordination. *See* Rabbinate
Semis, 8:419b
Semitecolo, Nicoletto, **11:159a-b**
St. Sebastian altarpiece, 11:159 (*illus.*)
Semitic languages, Yiddish and, 12:725a
Semivocales. *See* Neume, liquescent
Sempach, Lucerne and, 11:544a
Sempach, Battle of (1386), 11:544a
Sénas, inns in, 6:468b
Senate, Roman. *See* Rome, Senate
Senatus, 10:524b
Senchas Fer nAlban, 11:113b
source of early Scottish history, 6:258a
Senchas Már, 6:526a, 7:484a-b
on abuses of royal power, 4:312b
Seneca
Aristotle and, 1:460b
Catalan translations of, 3:168b, 169b
De clementia, 8:434a
De ira, discussed in Roger Bacon's *Opus maius,* 2:40a
Martin of Braga and, 11:405b
Moral Epistles, translation of into Spanish, 11:434a
on slavery, 11:334a
Senegal, slave trade in, 2:269a
Senekᶜerim-Yovhannēs Arcruni of Armenia, king, 1:451a, 483a, 484a
in Cappadocia, 1:484b–485a
Seneor, Abraham, 7:80b–81a
Seneschal, **11:159b–161a**
Angevins and, 9:167b
Armenian, 1:489a
compared with butler and chamberlain, 11:160a
England, Anglo-Saxon, 6:300a
France, 2:53a, 7:675a, 9:417b, 11:160b
Philip Augustus and, 9:168b
functions of, 5:160a
Henry V and, 9:169b
Norman, 6:301a
two meanings of the term, 11:159b–160a
see also Steward, royal
Seneschaucy, 4:513b, 514a, 12:533a
Senhal (pseudonym), in troubadours' songs, 12:216b
Seniles. *See* Petrarch, *Rerum senilium libri*
Senioratus, primogeniture and, in Hungary, 6:340a
Senius (son of Remus), 11:278a
Senlis Cathedral. *See* Notre Dame (cathedral: Senlis)
Senna, 9:173a
in *Grims saga Lodinkinna,* 5:677b
Sennacherib, king of Vaspurakan, cession of Vaspurakan to Basil II and, 12:362a
Sennar, Nubia and, 9:198b
Sennuccio del Bene, 6:651b
in *Trionfo d'Amore,* 6:640b
Sens Cathedral. *See* Notre Dame (cathedral: Sens)
Sens, Council of (1141), condemnation of Peter Abelard, 3:322b, 6:198a
Sens, Council of (1252), Thibaut IV of Champagne and, 3:249a-b
Sensa. *See* Venice, fairs
Sensus vs. littera. *See* Translation and translators
Sente Servas. *See* Heinrich von Veldeke
Sentences. *See* Proverbs; *Sententiae*
Sententiae, **10:189a–192b**
anthologies of classical *sententiae,* 10:190b
in Chrétien de Troyes, 10:191a-b
Yvain, 10:192a-b
comic value of, 10:192b
difference from proverbs, 10:189a-b
etymology of, 10:189a
in lyric literature, 10:192a
see also Isidore of Seville, St.; Nilus of Ancyra, St.; Proverbs
Sententiae of Paul. *See* German law, early Germanic codes
Sententiae philosophorum. *See* Hadoardus
Sententiarum libri quattuor. *See* Peter Lombard, *Sentences*
Seo de Urgel Cathedral, 10:487a
Separate Saga of St. Olaf. *See* Snorri Sturluson
Sephardic language. *See* Judeo-Spanish language
Sephardim, **11:161a–162a**
Ashkenazim and, 11:162a
biblical exegesis and, 2:212a
hymns of, Spanish ballads and, 11:430a, 430b
liturgical rite of, 7:632a
Sept psaumes allégorisés. *See* Christine de Pizan, religious and didactic works of
Septimania
Languedoc and, 7:339a
Peace of God movement and, 9:473b
Visigoths and, 12:471a, 473b
Septimius Severus, Roman emperor, 3:549b
Egypt and, 10:454a, 454b
Septuagint. *See* Bible, Septuagint
Sepuh, 1:489a, 490a, **11:162a,** 11:591a
see also Azat
Sequeira, Ruy de, 4:561b
Sequence
rhyme scheme of, 10:372b
see also Rhymed offices
Sequence, late, **11:166a–167b**
melodies of, 11:166b–167a
meter in, 11:166a-b

Sequence (plainsong), 6:379b–380a, 381b, 8:571a, 579b, 593b
Cistercians and, 8:643a
development of and liturgical poetry, 9:713b–714a
of Hucbald, 6:317b
lai and, 7:316b
Latin hymns and, 7:365b
Latin meter and, 7:375b–376a
melodic style of, 8:270b–271b (*illus.*), 270a
neuma and, 9:109b
Notker Balbulus and, 9:187a, 187b, 188a
planctus and, 9:693a-b
Sequence (*prosa*), **11:162b–166a**
Alleluia and, 11:162b, 164a
in Cambridge songs, 3:57b, 58b
characteristics of, 11:162b
earliest texts, 11:162b–164a
manuscript sources of, 11:162b–163a
origins of, 11:164a-b
performance of, 11:165a-b
repertory of, 11:162b
in sequence repertories, 11:163b
structure of, 11:164b–165a
three styles of, 1:51a
tropes to the Proper of the Mass and, 12:210a–211b (*illus.*)
two traditions of, 11:163a–164a
see also Adam of St. Victor; Rhythm
Séquence de Ste. Eulalie, La. See Eulalie, La Séquence de Ste.
Sequentia, in sequence repertories, 11:163b
Sequential. *See* Mass cycles; Plainsong
Sequin. *See* Ducat
Seraph, **11:167b–168a**
images of, 11:167b
Serapion, *Breviarium,* translated by Gerard of Cremona, 8:249a
Serapion of Thmuis, St., *Euchologion,* 1:155a
Serapis, cult of, 9:1a
Şerban (son of deacon Coresi), 10:511a
Serbia, **11:168a–183a**, 11:169 (map)
administration of, *župas* and *župans,* 11:168b, 170a, 171b, 172a-b, 173a
Adriatic states and, 4:347a
annexation by Symeon of Bulgaria, 2:405a
annexed by the Ottomans (1441), 11:182b
archbishopric of raised to patriarchate, 11:178a, 475b
art and architecture, **11:183a–188b**
beginnings, 11:183a-b
13th century, 11:184b–186a
14th century, 11:186a–187b
last phase (1371–1459), 11:187b–188b (*illus.*)
fusion of Western and Byzantine styles, 4:347a
Italian Romanesque and, 4:347a
monastic, by Byzantine artists, 2:446b–447a
Morava phase, 4:347b
see also Theodore
Battle on Kosovo Pole, 11:181a-b
Battle of Marica, 11:180a-b
Bogomilism in, 2:296b
Bosnian associations, 10:649b–650a
Bulgaria and, 2:411b–413a, 11:345b–346a
Byzantine influences, 4:347a-b, 11:186a–187b, 345b–346a
church
autocephalous status, 9:208b, 209b, 10:672b
bishoprics, 10:672b
established, 11:184b
Nicenes and, 9:117b
title of patriarch and, 9:459b
crushed by Manuel I Komnenos, 8:91b
disintegration after Stefan Uroš IV Dušan's death, 11:178b–179b
first archbishoprics of, 11:174b
Hungarian suzerainty, 2:334b
invasions of
by Boril, 2:409a
by Bosnians, 2:337a
by Ottomans, 2:502a, 502b, 4:56b, 11:183a
mines in, 4:300a
Ottoman suzerainty over, 11:181b
patriarch of
excommunicated, 11:178b, 180a
recognized by the Byzantines in 1375, 11:181a
patrilineal kinship, 11:670b
Stjepan Kotromanić of Bosnia and, 11:486a
vs. Symeon of Bulgaria, 11:555a
vs. Theodore II, 7:348a
Zealots and, 12:743a
see also Lazar Hrebejlanović
Serbian language, 6:443b
Serbian law, *Zakonik* (1349), 11:178a
Serbian literature, 11:345b–346b
Lazar Hrebeljanović and, 7:529a
Serbo-Croatian language, 6:438a, 439a, 443b
Serbo-Croatian literature, 11:345a–346b
Serbs
conversion of, 2:117b
ethnic origin of, 11:168a-b
Ottomans and, 2:136b
Serdica and, 11:189a
under Byzantine Empire, 2:119b
in Yugoslavia, 6:435b
Sercambi, Giovanni, 6:661a
inns and, 6:475a
Serçe Liman ship, 11:231a, 232a-b
Serdāb, **11:189a**
Serdica, **11:189a**
attacked by Basil II, 2:118b
crusaders' route and, 10:423a
taken by Krum (809), 7:303b
Serdica, Council of (342/343), 3:225b, 442b, **11:189b**, 11:189a
Serdini, Simone, 6:653b
Şerefe, **11:189b**
Serena serenarum, 7:326a
Serena virginum, 12:671a
Sererus, patriarch of Antioch, Monophysite theology, 8:477b–478a
Serfs and serfdom, Baltic lands, 2:67b–68a
Lithuania, 7:608a-b
Serfs and serfdom, Eastern Europe, 11:207b
Poland, 9:722a, 728b
Russia, **11:189b–199b**
consummation of, 11:198b–199a
"forbidden years" and, 11:196b, 197a
Georgian *qmani,* 10:236b
Kievan Rus, 1:101b, 102a
Oprichnina and, 11:194b–195b
peasant obligations and, 11:192b–193b
seignorial immunity and, 11:191a
taxation and, 11:193b
in Time of Troubles, 11:195b–197b
under Boris Godunov, 11:197a
under Mongols, 11:190a–191a
under Romanovs, 11:197b–199a
under *Sobornoe ulozhenie,* 11:198b–199a
under Vasilii Shuiskii, 11:197a
Walachia/Moldavia, 12:506a
Serfs and serfdom, Western Europe, **11:199b–208a**
1000–1300, 3:415b–416a
1300–1500, 3:424a
Brandenburg, 11:207b
civil rights and, 11:201b–202a, 203a-b, 206a
colonus, 3:482b–483b
corvées, 3:612b–613b, 12:152b, 157a-b
degrees of, 11:203b–204a
development, 11:684b
development of, 3:490b
economic development and, 11:199b–200a
England, 11:205a, 207a-b
feudalism and, 11:202a–203b
France, 11:204b, 205a, 206b, 207a
Champagne, 11:207a
emancipation of peasantry, 5:174a
Île-de-France, 11:204b, 205a, 206b
Paris, 11:204b, 206b
Gaul, 11:202a-b
German law, 7:478b, 480b
Germany, 11:204b, 207b
growth of, 11:202a–203b
hunting and, 6:357a
Italy, 11:204b–205a
Lorraine, 11:205a
new settlements and, 11:206a
Norway, 9:182a
Peasants' Revolt of 1381 and, 9:478b–480b
prohibition of travel, 12:148b
Rogerius and, 10:444a
second, 11:206a–207b
slavery and, 11:200a–201a, 205b, 335b, 337b
Spain, 11:204b
suffrage denial to, 10:328b
urbanism and, 11:206a
see also Liberty and liberties; Manorial system; Peasants
Sergas de Esplandián. See Amadís de Gaula
Sergeant, **11:208a-b**
English, royal household and, 6:302b, 304a
grand, 11:208b

Sergeant (*cont.*)
petty, 11:208b
see also Fiefs de service
Sergeant (bailiff). *See* Bailiff
Sergios I, patriarch of Constantinople, 8:233a, **11:209a**
Ekthesis, 3:630b
Theophylaktos Simokattes and, 12:24b–25a
Sergios-Tychikos, 9:469b
as leader of Paulician sect, 9:469a
Sergius III, pope, 1:330b
"cadaveric synod" and, 2:11b
Eugenius Vulgarius and, 4:520b
Lateran and, 7:344b
Sergius (Armenian martyr). *See* Sargis (Sergius) the General, St.
Sergius of Naples, duke, Rainulf and, 11:264b
Sergius of Radonezh, St., 8:443b, 9:654a, **11:209a-b**
hesychast movement, 10:595a
icons of, 10:588b
monastic community, 10:595a
relics of, 11:209a
Sergius of Reshaina, 11:566b
Serglige Con Culainn, 6:548b, 550b, 551a
Sericulture, 11:293b, 294b–295a
Serjeant at law, 11:208b
Serlo de Bayeux, 7:366b
Serlo de Wilton, 7:366b
De differentiis, 7:357a, 357b, 365b, 371b
Serments de Strasbourg. *See* Strasbourg Oaths
Sermini, Gentile, *Novelle,* 11:281b
Sermó. See Metge, Bernat
Sermo de legibus. See Placentinus
"Sermo S. Galli." *See* Notker Balbulus
Sermón. See San Pedro, Diego de
Sermón de amor, 11:456a
Sermon on Law and Grace. See Ilarion of Kiev, metropolitan, *Slovo o zakone i blagodati*
Sermon literature
in Middle English, 8:314b
in Middle High German, 8:354b–355b, 355a-b
Sermon of the Wolf to the English. See Wulfstan of York
Sermone. See Pietro da Bescapè
"Sermones." *See* Jacques de Vitry
Sermones quadraginta. See Wyclif, John
Sermoneta, Giuseppe, 7:175b
Sermons, Byzantine
effect on liturgy, 2:511a
rhetorical influence, 2:505b
Sermons, Western European
ars praedicandi, 1:555b–558a
collections of, Jacques de Vitry, 7:39b–40a
in the liturgy of the Mass, 8:188b
sermo ad status, 7:40a
six essential parts of, 10:362b
use of exempla, 7:40a
see also Preaching
Seron (unit of measure), product variations, 12:584b
Šērōy. *See* Kawād II
Serpent of Division. See Lydgate, John
Serpent, Scandinavian mythological. *See* Fáfnir; Midgard serpent
Serpentini. See Cruciferi
Serpukhov family, 8:543a
Serra, Jaime, **11:209b**
Serra, Pedro, **11:209b**
Serracum (heavy-duty wagon), 12:369b
Serranilla
Galician-Portuguese lyrics and, 11:450b
in Santillana's work, 11:419b, 451b
Serres, Olivier de, 12:653b–654a
Serres (Serrai), 11:178a, 179b, 180b
acquired by Stefan Uroš IV Dušan of Serbia, 11:475b
Servants, family and, 4:601a-b, 604a-b, 606b
Servants, royal. *See* Household, royal; specific offices, *e.g.,* Seneschal, royal
Servatus. *See* Lupus of Ferrières
Serventese. See Italian literature, poetry
Serventois. See Trouvères
Servi camerae nostrae, 7:87a, **11:209b–211a**
perpetua servitudo and, 11:210a-b
tanquam proprii servi and, 11:210b, 211a
tuitio and, 11:210b
Servi casati, 11:204b
see also Slavery and slave trade
Service, chivalrous. *See* Chivalry; Feudalism; Knights and knight service
Servientes regis, Hungarian, 6:341b, 343a
Servites, 5:297b, 6:662a
Servitia, 11:606a, 606b
Servitors, tsarist
Boris Godunov and, 11:197a
land tenure and, 11:192a
peasants and, 11:196a, 198b
under Romanovs, 11:197b, 198a, 198b
Servius, on Vergil, 7:352b, 360a, 12:395a
Sestina, 6:640b
Dante and, 6:641a, 648a, 648b, 669b
double, 6:648a, 648b
invention of, 1:539a
Setam, 11:583a
Setamaim, 11:583a, 583b
Setenario, 7:522a
Setier, **11:211a-b**
wine, 11:211a
Settenario. See Italian literature, poetry
Setúbal, Church of Jesus at, 5:630 (*illus.*)
Seusenhofer armor workshop, 1:529b, 536b
Sevan, Lake. *See* Sewan, Lake
Seven Books of History Against the Pagans. See Orosius
Seven Cities, island of the
Telles and, 4:559b
van Olmen and, 4:559b–560a
Seven cycles of history. *See* Cycles of history (Ismaili doctrine)
Seven Deadly Sins, **11:211b–212b**
in *Ancrene Riwle,* 1:243b
in art, 11:212a
in German allegory, 5:430a-b, 432a-b
in Gower's works, 5:639b–640a, 641a-b, 8:322a-b
in Henry Medwalls' *Nature,* 8:263a
in literature, 11:212a
numerology of, 11:211b
Ó Brolcháin and, 9:203b
penance and, 9:487b–488a
personification of, 11:212a
in *Piers Plowman,* 8:319a
in Prudentius' *Psychomachia,* 1:188a
religious instruction on, 10:300b, 301b–302a
Renner and, 6:326a
in Robert Mannyng's *Handlyng Synne,* 8:87a
in *Songe du castel,* 1:189a
theology of, 11:211b
in Turmeda's *Disputa de l'ase,* 12:228a
Seven liberal arts, **1:580a-b**
in Cassiodorus, 10:354a
convent curriculum and, 2:154b
establishment of, 1:580a
grammar, 5:648b–649b
introduced by Martianus Capella, 9:188b, 10:353b–354a
literary treatment of, 8:155b–156a
Notker Teutonicus and, 9:188b
origin of, 8:155b
personifications of, 1:580a-b
pictorial representations, 8:156b
quadrivium, 10:237a–238a
subjects in, 1:580a
in Thierry of Chartres's *Heptateuchon,* 12:27b
in Thomasin von Zerclaere's *Welsche Gast,* 12:38a
trivium, 12:205b–207a
see also Quadrivium; Trivium
Seven manieren van Minne. See Beatrijs van Nazareth
Seven Portraits. See Niẓāmī, *Haft paykar*
Seven Sages cycle, transmission of, 8:23b
Seven Sages of Rome, The, 5:286b
in Iranian literature, 6:508b
Seven Sleepers of Ephesus, **11:212b–213a**
Chardri's story of, 3:267b
"Sevener" Shī^{c}a. *See* Ismā^{c}īlīya
Seventeen Towns (league), fairs and, 4:592a
Severian of Gabala, bishop, 1:507b
Severin, banat of. *See* Walachia
Severinus of Noricum, St., 2:134a, 4:521a
Severus Alexander, Roman emperor, reliance on guilds, 6:14a
Severus of Antioch, 4:524b
Syrian Orthodox Church and, 11:563b
translations of, 11:566a
Zacharias of Mytilene on, 12:736a
Severus of Ashmunein (*fl.* 10th century). *See* Sawīrus ibn al-Muqaffa^{c}
Severus Sebokht, 11:565b
astronomical works of, 12:130a
Seville, **11:213b–214b**
Alcázar, 11:380a

  black slaves in, 2:268b
  captured by Vandals, 12:354b
  Castilian conquest of, 3:135b–136a
  commerce, 11:213b, 214a-b
  Great Mosque, 1:191b
  irrigation of, 6:558a
  mosques, 11:213b, 214a
  population, 11:213b, 214a
  as seat of the caliph, 1:194b
  sewer system, 11:214a
  under Almohads, 11:213b
  under Almoravids, 11:213b
  walls of, 11:213b
  water supply, 11:214a
Seville Cathedral, Simón de Colonia at, 7:153b
Seville, Councils of, Second (619), Isidore at, 6:563b
Sew Learn, Council of (1113), 1:501b
Sewan Island, 11:214b
Sewan, Lake, 1:470b, **11:214b–215a**
Sex aetates mundi, **11:215a–216a**
  Augustine and, 11:215b
  Christian eschatology and, 11:215b
  chronology, in literature, 10:635a
  eighth age and, 11:215b
  influence of, 11:215a
  Jewish apocalyptic literature and, 11:215a-b
  see also Theodofrid of Corbie
Sex articuli. See Holcot,
Sexpartite vault. *See* Vault
Sext (canonical hours), 3:67a, 4:229a
Sextant, 11:235a
Sextus Amarcius, 7:363b
Sexual abstinence. *See* Celibacy
Sexuality
  abstinence as aid to piety, 3:215b, 216b
  Arabic erotica, 3:574b
  in courtly love, 3:669a-b
  in *De planctu Naturae,* 7:366a, 368a
  for the generation of children, 3:216a
  in Icelandic sagas, 4:612b–613a
  in Irish law, 6:527a
  Islamic, contraception and, 3:574b
  Jewish views of, 7:92a-b
  Latin church's attitude to, 3:572b, 573b
  in marriage, 4:606a, 609a
  in *Roman de la Rose,* 10:451a, 452a
  see also Celibacy; Contraception; Eroticism; Ribald literature
Sézanne, fairs, 4:591a
Sfax
  Great Mosque, 1:70b
  Tamīm and, 12:745a
Ṣfiyy al-Dīn al-Urmawī, tone and modal system, 8:122b
Sforza, **11:216a–217a**
  rule of Milan, 8:380a–381a
Sforza, Francesco I, 11:216a-b
  Filippo Maria Visconti and, 12:464b
  Hunyadi and, 6:363b
Sforza, Francesco II, 11:217a
Sforza, Galeazzo Maria, 11:216b
Sforza, Gian Galeazzo II Maria, 11:216b
  rise of, 8:380a
Sforza, Ludovico (il Moro)
  assault of on Milan, 8:380a-b
  marriage of, 8:380b
  Milan and, 11:216b
  reign of, 8:380b
Sforza, Muzio Attendolo, 3:531b, 11:216a
Sforza, Tristano, 4:204b, 206a
Sgraffito, 3:237 (*illus.*)
Shāanshāh (son of Qılıj Arslan I). *See* Malikshāh, Seljuk sultan (of Rum)
Sha^{c}are Orah. See Gikatilla, Joseph
Shabbāba, 8:562b, 612b
Shaddadids, 7:310a, **11:217a–218a**
  in Albania, 11:217a
  in Dwin, 1:482b, 483a, 484a, 484b, 513b
  in Ganjak, 1:483a, 513b
  in Naxčawan, 9:91a
  Širak under, 1:290b–291a, 485a, 485b, 513b, 514a, 11:311b, 12:98b
  vs. Bagratids, 11:217a
  vs. Sargis Zak^{c}arean, in Ani, 12:736b
Shādhilī, Abu 'l-Ḥasan al- (founder of a Sufi fraternity), 9:44a
Shādhilīyha (Sufi fraternity), 9:44a
Shadirvan, **11:218a**
Shāfi^{c}ī, al-, **11:218a–219b**
  denial of local consensus (*ijmā^{c}*) by, 7:488a
  elevation of Muḥammad and traditions in Islamic law, 7:488a
  Islamic dietary laws, 4:179b
  Islamic law and, 6:580b–582a
  juridical autonomy of non-Muslims, 7:72b
  kitāb al-umm, 11:219b
  on land tenure, 11:668b
  law school, 4:407a
  on *quiyās* (analogical reasoning), 7:488a
  school of
    in Nizamīya madrasas, 11:66a-b
    on traditions in legal theory, 11:219a
  studies of, 11:218b
  sunna and, 6:580a, 11:511a, 511b
  on systematic legal reasoning, 7:488a
Shafiites, Zanj, 12:739b
Shafrā, Muḥammad al-, in Valencia, 12:348b
Shaftment, 12:588a
Shāh-Arman, **11:220a-b**
  in Xlat^{c}, 1:514a
Shāh-nāma, 6:508b
Shāh-Suwār, defeated by Mamluk sultan Qā$^{\supset}$itbāy, 10:222b
Shahāda, 6:582a
  see also Creeds, Islamic
Shahanshah. *See* Šāhan-šāh
Shāhānshāh (Qılıj Arslān's brother), 10:235b
Shahin of Shiraz, 7:177b
Shāhmalik, Oghuz leader, early Seljuks and, 11:151b
Shāhnāma, 6:507a, 7:221a, 10:249a, **11:220b–223b**
  Arabic loanwords in, 11:223b
  on Bahrām VI Čōben, 2:50b
  didacticism in, 11:221b
  fatalism in, 11:223a
  hunting and, 6:354b
  Iranian nationalism and, 6:501b
  manuscript illumination, 6:408a, 8:116b–117a, 11:222 (*illus.*)
  Parthian legends in, 9:443b–444a
  prose, 11:221a
  scenes from on minai vessels, 11:147b
  setting of, 11:223a
  style of, 11:223b
  use of *mathnawī* in, 9:42b
  Xwadāy nāmag and, 12:716a
  Yašts and, 12:721a
  see also Firdawsī
Shahrastānī, al-, on the Sabaeans of Ḥarrān, 9:4b
Shāhrūd, 8:611a, 611b
Shāhrukh, Timurid ruler, 12:56b–57b
  adoption of title of sultan, 12:58b
Shaidurov, Ivan, 8:575b
Shaikh Majd al-Dīn Isma^{c}īl, Ibn Baṭṭūta and, 11:252b
Shajar al-Durr, Ayyubid ruler, 8:73a, 73b
Shakespeare, William
  As You Like It, 6:536b
  Geoffrey of Monmouth and, 5:389b
  Midsummer Night's Dream, 5:364a
  portrayal of Richard III, 10:385a
  sources of *Macbeth,* 8:1a
  Troilus and Cressida
    inspired by Boccaccio's *Filostrato,* 2:279a
    Troy story and, 12:221a
  Wars of the Roses and, 12:572b
Shalāḥī, al- (early 14th century), on *būq,* 8:563a
Shalandī (Muslim ship), 9:76b
Shamkhor, Battle of (1195), 11:587a
Shammasīya (observatory: Baghdad), 11:99a
Shampoo. *See* Soap, in hair care
Shams al-Dawla, Buyid prince, 11:302b
Shams al-Dīn (court painter), 7:181b
Shams al-Dīn Eldigüz, 6:419a-b
Shams al-Dīn Muḥammad. *See* Ḥāfiẓ
Shams al-Dīn Muḥammad Tabrīzī. *See* Shams-i Tabrīzī
Shams al-Dīn Tabrīzī. *See* Shams-i Tabrīzī
Shams-i Qays, *Al-mu^{c}jam,* 10:348b
Shams-i Tabrīzī, 11:158b
  Rūmī and, 9:42b–43a, 10:556a-b
Shanfarā, 1:400a
Shansabanids of Ghur (dynasty in Afghanistan). *See* Ghurids
Shapur. *See* Šābuhr
Shaqira, 8:562b
Sharaf-nāma/Iqbāl-nāma. See Niẓāmī
Sharafīya. See Ṣafī al-Dīn
Sharecropping. *See Metayage;* Tenure of land
Sharī^{c}a. See Islamic law
Sharīf al-Idrīsī, al-. *See* Idrīsī, al-
Shark, fishing of, Greenland, 5:69a, 70b
Sharq al-Andalus, 12:346a
Sharvanshah, 11:254a
Sharwān. *See* Shirvan
Shāsh, conquered, 6:570b
Shashtār, 8:611a
Shāṭir, Ibn al-
  on astronomy, 1:621b, 622b

Shāṭir (*cont.*)
  planetary theory of, 11:87b
Shatt al-Arab. *See* Dijla al-ᶜAwrā
Shavuot, Pentecost and, 9:497a
Shawakānī, al-, Arabic names of days of week and, 5:299b
Shāwar, Fatimid vizier, 5:29b
Shawm, 8:602 (*illus.*), 603b, 604a, 605a (*illus.*), 607a (*illus.*), 12:180b
  bagged. *See* Bagpipe
  in civic music, 8:597a, 604a
  in dance music, 8:595b
  performance of, 8:635a
  in processions, 8:595b
Shaybānī, Abū ᶜAmr al-, *Kitāb al-jīm,* 4:442b
Shaybānī Khan, Uzbek ruler, conquest of Timurid states, 12:58a
Shaybānids, in Armenia, 1:513a
Shaykh (Sufi master), 9:44a-b
Shearing, 11:708a–709a (*illus.*)
  shears, 11:694b, 708b
    as agricultural tools, 12:81a
  wet, 11:707b
Sheᵓelot u-teshuvot, 11:584b
Sheep
  as food animal, 1:299a-b, 301b–302a
  in Slavic world, 1:98b
Sheep raising
  in England, 4:470a, 12:694a-b
  pasture rights and, 9:455b
Sheet, winding. *See Plashchanitsa*
Sheets (book). *See* Folio; Manuscript books, binding of
Sheftiah, Rabbi, in Jewish legends, 8:24a
Shehitah, Jewish dietary laws and, 4:181b–182a
Sheikh Luṭfallāh mosque, 6:562b
She'iltot. See Aḥa of Shabḥa
Shell keep. *See* Castles and fortifications
Shem Tov, 7:82a, **11:224a–225a**
  Proverbios morales, 11:224a-b, 418a
    anonymous commentary on, 11:443a
    prosody of, 11:459a
Shem Tov ben Isaac Shaprut, *Touchstone,* 10:5b
Shem Tov ibn Shem Tov, *Sefer ha-Emunot,* 3:3a
Shema, 7:620a-b
Shemariah ben Elijah ben Jacob, 4:541b
Shemiaka, Dmitrii, anti-Muscovite actions, 8:545a
Shepherd's Chapel (church: Ani in Širak), 1:494a
Shepherds' Plays. *See* Second Shepherds' Play; Towneley Plays
Sheriff, **11:225a–226a**
  court leet and, 3:659b–660a
  Exchequer and, 4:531b–532a
  hundred (land division) and, 6:330b–331a
  local constables and, 3:542b–543b
  London, election of, 7:661a-b, 665b
  loss of powers, 11:225b
  origin as shire-reeve, 10:280b
  pipe rolls of, 9:662a–663b
  responsibilities of, 4:464b
Sherira ben Ḥanina Gaon, 7:98a, 10:338b, 11:585a
  Iggeret, 11:583b, 584a, 584b
    chain of rabbinic tradition, 6:256b
's Hertogenbosch, brass baptismal font at, 8:286b
Sherwood Forest, Robin Hood and, 10:436a
Shestodnev. See John the Exarch
Shetland Islands
  acquired by Scotland, 11:108a
  Vikings and, 12:420a, 425a, 426a
Shīᶜa, 11:136a–138b, **11:226a–228b**
  Abbasids and, 3:50a, 11:227a
  accusations of heresy, 6:205b
    esoteric meaning of Holy Writ, 6:206a
  Aleppo, 11:228a
  among Buyids, 2:436b
  among Safawids in Azerbaijan, 2:27a
  caliphate and, 11:226b, 227b, 228a
  civil service and, 11:228a
  in Daylam, 6:424a
  doctrine of resurrection and, 10:340b
  geographical distribution of, 11:514a
  al-Ḥusayn and, 6:370a, 371a
  Ibrāhīm ibn al-Aghlab and, 6:391b
  Idrisids and, 6:413b
  Iranian literature and, 6:509a
  in Iraq, 6:511b, 512b, 513b
  Islamic pilgrimage and, 9:651a-b, 671a
  Islamic political theory and, 10:12b–13a
  Ismailism and, 11:227b
  Jabal ᶜAmīl, 11:228a
  jihad and, 7:110b
  in al-Kufa, 7:307a, 307b–308a
  millennialism and, 8:388a–389a
  Muᶜtazila and, 6:583b, 11:228b
  Nuṣayrīs and, 9:3b
  opponents of, 11:513a
  origins of, 6:205a-b, 586b, 11:226b
  in Persia, 7:307a, 11:228a
  Qarmatian, Zanj and, 12:739a
  qubba mausoleums of, 10:239b
  religious festivals, 8:529a
  revolts of, 3:46a
  Rightly Guided, 6:205b
  role of the imams, 6:586b–587a
  sects, 11:227b
    derivation of names, 1:173b
    Druzes, 4:295b
    Imamites, 11:227a
    Inamites, opposition to Muᶜtazilites, 9:568b
    Kaysanids, 1:174b, 11:226b
    Zaydi, 1:174b–175a
    Zaydis, 11:227a
    see also Ismāᶜīlīya; *Ithnā ᶜasharī* Shiism
  spread of, 11:227b–228a
  taᵓwīl and, 9:39a
  Twelver Shiites, 1:175a, 6:587a, 11:136b–137a, 227b
    Baghdad, 11:228a
    resurrection and, 10:340b
    al-Yaᶜqūbī on, 12:718a
    Zaydis and, 12:741b
  under Umayyads, 3:39b
  vs. Sunnites, in Iraq, 6:514a
Shield, 1:522b, 523b (*illus.*), 525b, 528a-b, 11:229a
  Byzantine, 1:523b (*illus.*)
  knightly, 1:523b (*illus.*), 524a
  limb armor and, 1:526a
  "Norman," 1:523b (*illus.*), 523a, 524b, 534a (*illus.*)
  Viking, 1:523b (*illus.*)
  see also Renntartsche
Shield boss, 1:522b, 524a
Shield money. *See* Scutage
Shield and Spear. See Banū Mūsā
Shifāᵓ, al-. See Sīnā, Ibn
Shihāb al-Dīn ᶜUmar Suhrawardī, 11:308a
Shiite law, 11:228b
Shiites, al-Muᶜtazila and, 8:655a
Shilling, 8:428b, **11:228b–229a**
  Kentish, 11:228b
  penny and, 11:229a
  sceat and, 11:228b–229a
  see also Penny
Shinbawde. *See* Greave
Shīnī (Muslim ship), 9:76b
Ship carpenter, Northern European, 11:243b, 244a
Ships and shipbuilding
  Arab, 11:230a-b, 232a, 232b
  in Barcelona, 2:104b
  battleships, 11:648a (*illus.*)
  Byzantine, 11:231b–232a
    regulation of *navicularii,* 2:475b, 477b–478a
  Celtic, 11:238b–239a
  crews. *See* Seamen
  financing of, 11:233a, 235b
  Genoa, 11:232b, 233a, 235b, 243a
  Indian Ocean, 11:248a
    tonnage, 11:248a-b
  Islamic, 9:76a-b
    captain and crew of, 9:86a–87a
    description of, 9:85b–86a
  Italian
    in crusades, 11:232b
    great galleys and, 11:235a-b
  Laccadive Islands, 11:246a
  lateen sail, origins, 11:654b–655a
  Maldive Islands, 11:246a
  Mediterranean, 9:87b–88b, 89a-b, **11:229a–238a**
    classical era, 11:229b–230a
    in Genoa, 5:384b
    government intervention in, 11:235b–236a
    Islamic navies and, 9:73b–77b
    in Northern Europe, 11:243a
    northern influences on, 11:236a
    Pisa and, 9:664a-b
    tonnage, 11:233b–234a
    Venetian *Arsenale* and, 12:388a
    see also Navies, Western; Trade, Byzantine
  as metaphor of death, 4:118b
  Northern European, 9:88b–89a, **11:238b–245b**
    cogs, 7:682a
    government intervention in, 11:243b–244a
    Roman influence on, 11:238b
    social status of, 11:245a
    tools for, 11:243a-b
    types, 11:238b–241a
    Vikings, 9:79a-b, 285b

see also Viking navigation
Red Sea and Persian Gulf, **11:245b–251b**
Islamic navies and, 9:74b
see also Navigation, Red Sea
safety measures, 11:235b–236a
"shell-first," 11:230b–231a, 248a
"skeleton-first," 11:230b–231a, 244b–245a, 655a-b
sternpost rudder, 11:655a
Swedish, 11:530a
technology of, 11:638b, 648a (*illus.*), 654b–655a
in Valencia, 12:348b
Venice, 11:233b, 235b
Viking, 12:424a-b
Western European, trade routes and, 12:158a
wood scarcity and, 11:231b
see also Lateen sail; Navies; Travel and transport
Shipwrecks, Indian Ocean, 11:249b
Shiᶜr, 8:561b
Shir ha-Yiḥud. See Judah ben Samuel he-Hasid
Shir (the term), 11:253a
Shira-its-tsi-ish, 11:252a
Shirak. *See* Širak
Shīrāz, **11:252a–253a**
art of, 6:408b–409a
Buyids in, 6:424b
decline of, 5:18a
geography, 11:252a
history, 6:51b, 11:252a-b
Ibn Baṭṭūṭa and, 11:252a, 252b
mosque of ᶜAmr, 11:252b
rulers of, 11:252a-b
see also Fārs
Shīrāz bindings, 8:99b
Shīrāzī, al- (*d.* 1311), 8:566b
Shire, **11:253a–254a**
Anglo-Saxon England, 4:457b
formation from
early settlements, 11:253b
independent states, 11:253b
Norman-Angevin England, administration of, 4:464b
subdivision of, 11:253b
Shīrīn (wife of Xusrō II Abarwēz), 11:597b, 598a
Shirk, 6:585a
Shīrkūh (Kurdish commander), 2:23a
Egyptian military campaign, 10:625a
as Fatimid vizier, 5:29b
Shirley, John
anthology of, 1:320a
rubrics to Lydgate's work, 7:691a
Shirvan, **11:254a-b**
Derbent and, 4:162b
Kabala in, 7:205a
see also Azerbaijan
Shīrwan-Shāhs, vs. Shaddadids, 11:217b
Shivaree, 8:25b, 28b
condemned by the church, 8:29a
fee on, 8:29b
judicial function of, 8:29a
politicization of, 8:29b
Shock (unit of measure), 12:593b
Shoes and shoemakers, **11:254b–256a**
Byzantine, 11:254b
Coptic, 11:254b, 255a
Gothic, 11:255a-b
heel design, 11:255b
Hittite, 11:254b
Irish, 11:254b
moccasin construction, 11:255a
Roman, 11:254b, 255a
Seljuk, 11:255b
toe design, 11:255a-b
turnshoe construction, 11:255a
Western European, 3:625b–626a
Shofar, 8:564a, 564b
Short Treatise of Politicke Power. See Ponet, John
Shotᶜa Rustaᶜveli, 5:418a, **11:256a-b**
Vepᶜkhistqaosani, 5:418a-b, 11:256a-b
Shovels, as agricultural tools, 12:80b
Shrines, Christian, 4:336a-b
competition among, 9:659a–660b
in Constantinople, 4:337a
convent locations of, 10:297b
economics of, 10:299a
forms of, 4:337a
for the insane, 6:491a-b, 492a-b
Jerusalem, 9:656a–658a
late medieval, 9:659a-b
Marian relics venerated at, 10:298b–299a
pilgrimage, 12:151a
competition among, 12:154b, 156b–157a
Inquisition-approved, 12:156a
Rome, 12:151a, 154b–155a, 156a
Santiago de Compostela, 12:154b, 155b
Rome, 9:656a-b, 658a–659a, 660b
Russian pilgrimage, 9:653a–654b
saints' relics venerated at, 10:296b–297a
tourism and, 9:660b–661a
see also Pilgrimage; Saints, cult of
Shrines, Islamic, 9:650a–652a, 671 (*illus.*)
pilgrimage, 12:147a-b
see also Kaaba
Shrines, Jewish, 9:652a–653a
Shrivijaya, Muslim trade and, 11:246b
Shroud of Christ. *See Plashchanitsa*
Shroud, Holy, rhymed office for, 10:370b
Shroud of Turin. *See* Turin, Shroud of
Shrove Tuesday. *See* Mardi Gras
Shrovetide, theatrical performances for, 4:271a
Shuadit, 7:178b
Shuᶜayb, 4:296b
Shuᶜaybīya, 8:612b
Shuᶜba, science of *ḥadīth* authentication, 6:47b
Shujāᶜ, Abū Kāmil ibn, *Algebra,* translated into Hebrew, 11:92a
Shujāᶜ, shah, patronage of Ḥāfiẓ, 6:51b, 52a
Shul. See Synagogue
Shulḥan Arukh. See Caro, Joseph
Shurafāᵓ, power in Fēs, 8:139b, 140b
Shuraḥbīl ibn Ḥasana, 6:568a
Shurfa. *See* Serefe
Shurṭa, 6:590a, 8:519a-b
Shūsh. *See* Sūsa
Shūshtar, in Islamic conquests, 6:569a
Shushtarī, al-, 1:402a
Shūᶜūbīya, 6:503a, 513a
"Si welnt dem tode entrunnen sin." *See* Friedrich von Hausen
Sībawayhi, *Al-kitāb,* 5:650b
Šibenik. *See* Sebenico
Siberia, fur trade, through Transoxiana, 12:146a
Sibert of Beka, 3:96a
Sibille. See Elisabeth of Nassau-Saarbrücken
Sibille la Pourcelette, 6:473a
Sibylline Oracles, **11:257a**
in art, 11:257a
Sibyl's monologue, dramatization of in Spanish literature, 11:437b
Sibyl's Prophecy. *See Vǫluspá*
Sic et non. See Abelard, Peter
Sicard of Cremona, on liturgy, 7:632a-b
Sich hûb vor gotes trône, 2:230a
Sicilian architecture, 11:274b–275a
Sicilian language, 6:624b–625b
Sicilian law, Constitutions of Melfi and, 8:268b
Sicilian poetry, **11:257a–261a**
Dante on, 11:257a, 274b
foreign influences on, 11:258a
Frederick II and, 11:257b, 259a
Petrarch on, 11:257b
Tuscan versions, 11:259a
see also Italian literature, lyric poetry, Sicilian school
Sicilian Vespers, 1:253b, 2:499b, 4:60b–61a, 95b, 7:5b, 7b, **11:261a**, 11:272b–273a
applauded in Malta, 8:67b
Byzantine Empire and, 1:245b
in chronicles, 6:633b
Naples and, 9:59a
role of Michael VIII Palaiologos, 8:302b
Sicily
agriculture
diminia, 1:88a
wheat and grazing pattern, 1:87b–88a
Aragon and, 1:413b–414b
conquered by
Aghlabids, 6:572b
Muslims (902), 9:74b
Islamic, **11:261b–263b**
economy, 11:262b
factionalism in, 11:262a, 265b
al-Muᶜizz and, 12:744b
Norman conquest of, 11:262b–263a, 263b–267a
population, 11:262a
Tamīm and, 12:745a
under Aghlabids, 11:261b, 264b
under Fatimids, 11:262a
under Kalbites, 11:262a-b
under Zirids, 11:262a
Ziyādat Allāh I and, 11:261b
see also Palermo
Lombards and, 11:264b
Muslim raids
in 652, 9:74a
in 9th century, 7:4a
Otto of Brunswick and, 12:673a
relations with

Sicily (*cont.*)
relations with (*cont.*)
Byzantine Empire, 11:261b, 263a, 264b
Ifrīqiya, 11:261b–262a
sericulture in, 11:295a
strategic importance of, 11:261b
see also Malta
Sicily, Kingdom of, **11:263b–277a,** 11:264a (map)
administration, 11:268a-b
appearance of the office of admiral, 9:80b–81a
Arab conquest of, 4:345b
Black Death in, 2:259a
black slaves in, 2:269a, 269b
Catalan Company in, 3:156b
centralization under Frederick II, 5:215a
Charles of Anjou installed as king, 4:60b
commerce, 11:275a
conflict between Philip IV and Peter of Aragon over, 4:61a-b
cultural life, 11:266b–267a, 273b–275a
economy, 11:275b–276a
financial system of, 4:532a
fiscal administration, 11:268b
foreign policy, 11:268b
Innocent III and, 6:464b
law codes, 7:429a-b
Louis I and, 6:345b
military organization, mercenary troops, 12:560a-b
Naples and, 9:58a-b
Norman conquest, 6:443a, 11:263a–267a, 12:560a
population, 11:275a-b
relations with
France, 4:60b–61b
Holy Roman Empire, 4:58a, 11:269b
papacy, 4:58a-b, 60a–61b, 6:466b
Spain, 11:273b
religious life, 11:266a-b, 267a
Robert Guiscard and, 10:433a
royal privileges of, 11:270b
social structure, 11:275a-b, 276a
under Roger I, 10:440b
under Roger II, 10:441a
war between Manfred and Innocent IV, 4:60a
see also Angevins; Palermo
Sickle, 12:79a-b, 80b
Islamic, 12:84b–85a
Siculo, Lucio Marineo, *De laude Hispaniae,* 11:425a
Siculo-Toscani. See Italian literature, lyric poetry, Sicilian school imitators
Sicut iudaeis non (*Constitutio pro iudaeis*). *See* Innocent III, pope
Sicut pia mater, 6:563a
Sicut uetus testamentum, Paucapalea and, 9:466b–467a
Sīd. *See* Cid, the
Sīda, Ibn
on construction of plows, 12:83b–84a
on harrows, 12:84b
Mukhaṣṣaṣ, 4:43a-b
on threshing wheel, 12:85a-b
Sídh (the otherworld in Irish mythology), 9:47b
Sidi ᶜAli C4elebi (Turkish admiral), 9:87a
Sidon
glassmaking in, 5:545a
merchant colonies in, 7:533a
Sidonius Apollinaris, 7:361b, **11:277a-b**
correspondence of, 11:277a
descendants of, 11:277b
lost works of, 11:277b
on Nile, 9:137b
on Paulinus of Périgueux, 9:472a
on travel, 12:148b–149b, 151a
Siege. *See* Castles and fortifications; Warfare
Siege artillery. *See* Artillery; Cannon
Siege of Jerusalem, The, 8:332a
Siege of Thebes. See Lydgate, John
Siege tower, 3:149 (*illus.*)
Siege weapons, 3:143a-b, 148a-b, 150a–152a
battering ram and cat, 3:146b, 148a, 149 (*illus.*)
see also Trebuchet
Siege of Zamora, 11:453a
Siegfried (epic character)
in *Biterolf,* 2:253a
in *Niebelungenlied,* 9:112b, 113a, 113b, 114a, 114b
see also Sigurd
Sien-Pi, 7:237a
Siena, **11:277b–282a**
art in, 9:361a-b, 11:281b
International Style, 5:628a-b
schools of, 4:301b, 302b–303a
in 13th century, 6:10b
trecento painters, 12:172b–175a (*illus.*), 175b (*illus.*)
trecento sculptors, 12:171a-b
bishopric of, 11:278a-b
Black Death in, 2:260a
Bonsignori company of, 2:76b, 77b
Campo, 11:280b, 281b
civic improvements, 11:280a-b
Communal Palace, 11:280b, 281b
commune, 11:278b–281a
economy, 11:279a
urban nobles and, 11:278b
geography, 11:277b–278a
Giovanni di Cecco in, 5:537a
Giovanni di Paolo in, 5:537a-b
government
of the Nine, 11:279b–281a
podestarile, 11:278b
of Twelve Governors, 11:281a
of Twenty-four Priors, 11:278b
Guelphs and Ghibellines, 11:279a-b
painters' guild, 6:21a-b
Palazzo della Signoria, depiction of St. Bernardino of Siena, 2:196a (*illus.*)
Palazzo Pubblico, 11:280b, 299b
Chapel of the Virgin, 11:572 (*illus.*)
Lippo Vanni's fresco, 12:357 (*illus.*)
Simone Martini's *Maestà* fresco, 12:172b–173b (*illus.*)
religious life, 11:280b–281a
territorial expansion, 11:279a
Terzo, 11:278a
under Habsburgs, 11:282a
vs. Arezzo, 11:278a
vs. Florence
after fall of the Nine, 11:281b
at Colle di Val d'Elsa, 11:279b
to Battle of Montaperti, 11:279a-b
vs. Spain, 11:282a
water supply, 11:277b, 279a, 12:577b
reservoir dam, 12:577b–578a
Siena Cathedral, 9:668b, 669b–670b (*illus.*), 11:299b
facade of, 5:622a (*illus.*)
Giovanni Pisano sculpture on, 12:170b
Maestà by Duccio, 4:302 (*illus.*), 302b, 303a (*illus.*)
mosaics, 11:281b
Nine and, 11:280b
style of, 5:624b
Siervo libre de amor. See Rodríguez del Padrón, Juan
Siete gozos de amor. See Rodríguez del Padrón, Juan
Siete infantes de Lara, 11:408b–409a, 410b, 411a, 412b, 442b, 453a
Siete partidas, 1:162a, 5:310a, 7:269b, 430a, 522b–523a, **11:282a–283b, 11:414b–415a**
on the Almogávares, 1:190b
importance under Alfonso XI, 7:523b
influence of, 11:283b
on *juegos de escarnio,* 11:437a
sources of, 11:283a
sumptuary laws and, 11:507b
translated into Catalan, 9:511a
translations of, 11:282b
on water rights, 6:557a
Ṣiffin, Battle of (657), 7:307a, **11:283b–284b,** 11:513a, 12:267a
inconclusive outcome, 3:36a
Sifrei halakhot, 11:584a
Sifrei mevoᵓot, 11:584a
Sigebert of Gembloux, 7:372a, **11:284b–285a,** 11:364a
Chronica, 11:285a
De viris illustribus, 2:239a-b, 11:285a
Gesta abbatum Gemblaciensium, 11:285a
on liturgy, 7:630b
Vita Sigiberti III, 5:653b–654a
Sigehard of St. Maximin, **11:285a-b**
De miraculis sancti Maximini, 11:285a-b
Siger of Brabant, **11:285b–287a**
Aristotelianism, 6:198b
Averroism and, 1:463a, 465a
condemnations of 1270 and, 12:39b
human free will, 9:598a
inquisition and, 11:286b
on magical effects, 8:38a-b
On the Intellective Soul, 11:286a
Questions on the "Liber de Causis," 11:286a
Questions on the "Metaphysics," 11:286a
views on philosophy, 9:607b
Siger of Courtrai, speculative grammar and, 10:359b
Sigeric of Canterbury, archbishop, danegeld and, 4:90a
Sighvatr Sturluson, 11:499a, 499b

Sighvatr Þórðarson, *Knútsdrápa, Þáttr af Ragnars sonum* and, 12:7a
Sigibert III, Merovingian king, 9:499b
Sigillography. *See* Seals and sigillography
Sigillum, Western European seals and, 11:124a
Sigisbert of Gaul, king, Venantius Fortunatus and, 12:381a
Sigismund of Austria, duke, vs. Nicholas of Cusa, 9:123b
Sigismund of Germany, emperor, **11:287a-b**
  at Council of Constance, 5:489a, 11:287b
  in Bohemia, 2:300b, 5:489b, 11:287b
  Central European trade and, 11:287b
  church reform and, 3:650b, 5:489a
    Great Schism, 3:647a
    role in Council of Constance, 648a, 3:647b
  communion under both kinds and, 3:505b
  crusade of, 2:503a
  diet and, 6:335b
  foreign policy, 11:287a
  Hungary and
    pursuit of Hungarian throne, 2:337a-b
    rule of, 6:346a–347a
  Hunyadi and, 6:363b
  Hus and, 3:650a, 6:369a
  Hussites and, 6:372a, 375b–376a, 376b
  imperial ideal of, 5:496a
  Mircea the Old and, 10:514b
  Nuremberg and, 9:202a
  privileges for imperial knights, 5:498a
  Reformatio Sigismundi, 5:489b, 496a
  reign of, 5:489a-b
  representative assemblies and, 10:330a-b
  Stefan Lazareviç and, 11:182a
  Treaty of Narbonne and, 3:649a
  vs. Bāyazīd I, 9:129b
  vs. Habsburgs, Bern and, 11:544a
  vs. Hussites, 11:287b
  vs. Ostoja of Bosnia, 2:338a
  vs. Ottomans, 11:287a
  Vytautas of Lithuania and, 7:608a
  Zabarella and, 12:735a
Sigismund of Habsburg, duke
  Alsace and, 11:544b
  Swiss Confederation and, 11:545a
Sigismund of Hungary, king. *See* Sigismund of Germany, emperor
Sigismund, St., Burgundian king
  abbey of St. Maurice and, 11:536b
  conversion from Arianism, 2:423a
Sigiward of Fulda, abbot, 5:312a
Sigmund Korybut, prince, 6:376b
"Sigmundar kvæþi," *Færeyinga saga* and, 4:581a
"Sigmundar kvæþi nýggja." *See* Djurhuus, Jens Christian
Sigmundr Brestisson, 4:580b
Sign of the Cross, **11:288a**
  religious instruction in, 10:300b
Signa. See Bells
Signatures, **11:288a**
Signboards, of inns, 6:470b–471a
Signet rings
  sealing and, 11:124b–125a
  Western European seals and, 11:124a
Signori. See Class structure, Italian
Signos del Juicio Final. See Berceo, Gonzalo de
Signum, Western European seals and, 11:124a, 124b
Signý, princess (saga character), 11:290a, 290b
Sigrdrífa, 5:678b
Sigrdrífumál, 5:678a, **11:288b–289a**
  as gnomic literature, 5:569a-b
  Norns and, 9:171b
  Sigurd and, 11:289a
  Vǫlsunga saga and, 12:489a
Sigrgarðs saga frækna, 10:395b, 396a
Sigtuna, founded, 11:530b
Sigüenza, University of, 12:287a
Sigurd, 2:394b–395a, **11:289a–290a,** 11:293a-b
  in *Grípisspá,* 5:678a
  in *Guðrúnarkviða* cycle, 6:36, 37a-b
  invasion of Brynhild's fortress, 9:216b, 217a
  in *Reginsmál* and *Fáfnismál,* 10:290a–291a
  Svipdagsmál and, 11:524b
  see also Biterolf und Dietleib; Lied vom hürnen Seyfrid, Das Siegfried
Sigurd poems, order in Codex Regius, 4:386a
Sigurdliederheft, 5:678b
Sigurðar saga, existence of, 4:385b
"Sigurðar saga." *See Reginsmál*
Sigurðar saga Fóts, **11:290a-b**
  Knýtlinga saga and, 11:290b
Sigurðar saga ok Valbrands, 10:395b, 396a
Sigurðar saga þögla, 10:394b, 395a, 395b, 396a, **11:290b–291a**
Sigurðar saga turnara, 10:391a, 396a
Sigurðarkviða, 5:678a
Sigurðarkviða in forna, 9:114a, **11:291a–292a**
  Brynhild in, 2:394b
  rendition in Codex Regius, 4:386a
  Sigurd and, 11:289b
  Vǫlsunga saga and, 12:489a
Sigurðarkviða in meiri, 9:114a, **11:292a–293a**
  Brynhild in, 2:394b–395a
  Sigurd and, 11:289b
  Vǫlsunga saga and, 12:489a
Sigurðarkviða in skamma, 9:114a, **11:293a-b**
  Brynhild in, 2:394b
  dating of, 9:217a
  monologues of, 11:293b
  relation to *Guðrúarkviða I,* 6:36b
  Sigurd and, 11:289b
  sources for, 6:35b
  structure of, 11:293a-b
Sigurðr (epic character), 4:581a, 581b, 9:174b, 12:30b, 30a, 31a
Sigurðr Slembidjákn (saga character), 4:414a
  Hryggjarstykki and, 9:176a
Sigurður blindi, *rímur* attributed to, 10:403a
Sihtric, king of Dublin. *See* Sitric of Dublin, king
Sijilmāsa
  founding of, 8:15b
  Islamic trade and, 12:106a
  occupied by Ṣufrīs in 757, 11:139a
Sijistān, *da^{c}wā* in, 6:615b
Sikkit, Ibn al-, *Kitāb al alfāẓ,* 4:443a
Síl Muiredaig, rule of Connacht, 3:537b
Silencing the Jews. See Maghribī, Samau'al al-
Silesia. *See* Bohemia-Moravia; Poland
Silings (Vandal group), 12:354b, 354a
Silk, **11:293b–296b**
  aristocratic, 11:296b
  Armenian trade and, 12:97a-b
  in Baghdad and Iraq, 12:105b
  Bukhara, 11:717b
  of Bursa, 6:613b
  China, 11:293b–294b
  decoration of book covers and, 8:97b
  diaper-weave, 11:718a
  dībāj, 4:173 (*illus.*)
  drawloom, 11:295b–296a
  dyeing of, 4:328b
  European, *zandanījī* and, 12:738b
  France, 11:296a
  from Beirut and Tyre, 12:100b
  in Genoa, 5:386b
  Huang Ho Valley, 11:293b
  Islamic, 11:716b, 717a–718a
  Italy, 11:295a, 296a
  kamkhā, 7:207b–208a
  lion strangler, 11:718a
  manufacture of
    in Beirut, 2:164a
    Corinth and Thebes, 2:452b–453a
  Mesopotamian, 11:717a-b
  origins of, 11:293b
  process of making, 11:294a-b
  reliquary wraps, 11:717b (*illus.*)
  rugs and carpets, 10:548a
  Spanish, 6:612a
  spinning, 11:700b
  spread of, 11:294b–295a
  textile production of, 11:293b, 294b–295a
    in Byzantine Empire, 12:101a
    in Constantinople, 12:101b
    Italy, Azzo Visconti and, 12:464b
    Sicily, 11:262b
    in Thebes, 12:102b
  throwing for, 11:294b
    by machine, 11:295a-b
  in Timurid bookbinding, 8:100a
  trade in
    Byzantine, 12:714a
    Constantinople, 3:554b
    early medieval, 12:109b, 110a
    imports into Egypt, 12:107b
    route to the Far East, 12:99a
    "silk road," 10:661a
    state monopoly imposed by Justinian I, 12:100a
    Venice and, 12:386a, 387a
    wool trade and, 12:115b
  weaving, 11:703a
  worn in Islam, 3:616b
  yarns, 11:295b
  Zandanī-jī group, 11:718a
  see also Vestments, liturgical
Silkworms, 11:294a

Silos (monastery: Spain), oldest Spanish text of *Quem quaeritis* and, 11:436b
Silveira family, 4:559b
Silver
assaying of, 8:290a, 290b
casting of, 8:297a
deposits of, 8:398a
importance of, 8:401a-b
mining of, 8:397b–398a, 400b (*illus.*), 401a
in Bosnia, 4:300a
in Kutná Hora, 2:300a
in Serbia, 4:300a, 11:175a, 176b
in pre-Romanesque art
Carolingian, 10:110b–111a
English, 10:110a
German, 10:106a–107b
Spanish, 10:114b–115a
production of, 8:402a
smelting, 8:401b–402a
see also Mints and money
Silversmiths. *See* Metalsmiths, gold and silver
Silvester. See Konrad von Würzburg
Silvester. *See* Sylvester
Silvestre de Sacy, Antoine-Isaac, 1:592a
Simeon ben Yoḥai, 3:2a
Simeon ben Zemah Duran, 7:99b
Simēon of Erevan, *katᶜołikos,* 1:520b
Simeon, katholikos of Seleucia-Ctesiphon, 11:567b
Simeon Kayyara. *See* Kayyara, Simeon
Simeon, St. (*fl.* early 5th cent.)
al-Nuᶜmān and, 7:320b
relics kept in Antioch, 10:297a
Simeon, St. *See* Stefan Nemanja
Simeon the Young. *See* Symeon the New Theologian
Simnel, Lambert, 6:520a, 9:437a
crowned king in Dublin, 4:299b
Simon of Bisignano, *Decretum Gratiani* and, 4:127b
Simon of Brion (13th-century papal legate), Siger and, 11:285b
Simon Chèvre d'Or, *Ylias,* 7:365a, 12:219b
Simón de Colonia, 7:153b
Arms of Doña Mencia de Mendoza, 7:154 (*illus.*)
works of, 7:153b
Simon de Covino, on the plague, 2:264b
Simon de Cramaud
agitation for *via cessionis,* 11:41a-b
at Council of Pisa, 3:646b
Simon of Frankfurt, *Yalkut Shimoni,* 10:74b
Simon Kayyara. *See* Kayyara, Simon
Simon of Kéza, *Gesta,* 6:343a
Simon Magus, 8:33a-b, 11:300b–301a
Simon de Montfort (the Elder, *ca.* 1165–1218), 10:252a, **11:296b–297a**
Aragon crown and, 11:296b
on distress, 4:221a
family of, 11:296b
in Fourth Crusade, 11:296b
in Languedoc, 7:339b
Pedro II of Aragon and, 11:296b
Philip II Augustus and, 11:296b–297a
as ruler of Carcassonne, 3:188b
Simon de Montfort the Younger and, 11:297a
support for Dominicans, 4:239b
Toulouse and, 11:296b–297a, 12:91b
two parliaments, 4:481a
Simon de Montfort (the Younger, *ca.* 1200–1265), **11:297a–298b**
Barons' war and, 2:112a-b, 6:159a, 11:297b–298a
charges against, 11:297b
Edward I of England and, 11:298a-b
fame of, 11:298b
Henry III of England and, 11:297a–298a
Llywelyn ap Gruffydd and, 7:637a, 12:521a-b
marriage of, 11:297a
Provisions of Oxford and, 11:297b
reforms of, 11:298a-b
regarded as usurper by the pope, 2:112b
rhymed office for, 10:366b
Robin Hood and, 10:436a
in *Song of Lewes,* 11:372b
Simon of Reading (13th century), 2:173b
Simon Stock, St., 3:96b
Simon of Sudbury, beheaded, 3:83b
Simon Tailler, 8:559a
Simon of Tournai, Gilbert of Poitiers's theology school and, 12:21b
Simon Tunstede. *See* Tunstede, Simon
Simon Ushakov. *See* Ushakov, Simon
Simon du Val, Siger and, 11:286b
Simone da Bologna, **11:299a**
altarpieces of, 11:299a (*illus.*)
Coronation of the Virgin by, 11:299a
Crucifix by, 11:299a
fresco painting of, 11:299a
Simone da Cascia, 6:663a
Simone dei Crocefissi. *See* Simone da Bologna
Simone Martini, **11:299a–300b**
altarpiece of, 5:608a
Annunciation, 1:307 (*illus.*), 11:299b–300a
elements of style, 9:258b
at Avignon, 2:16a, 5:627b, 11:300a-b
at S. Francesco Assisi, 1:594a
Blessing Christ Surrounded by Angels by, 11:300b
Destorrents and, 4:165b
Duccio di Buoninsegna and, 11:299a
Francesco Traini and, 12:124a–125b
frescoes of, 5:293b–294a, 11:299b–300b (*illus.*)
frontispiece for *Ambrosian Vergil,* 9:531b (*illus.*)
influence of, 12:175a, 176b
influence of, on Barna da Siena, 2:111a
Life of St. Martin, 5:606a
Madonna of Humility, 11:300b
Maestà, 5:293b, 606a, 11:280b, 299b, 12:172b–173b (*illus.*)
as a model for Lippo Memmi, 7:587a
miniatures of, 11:300b
panel of St. Louis of Toulouse, 11:300a
pupil of Duccio, 4:302b
school started under, 5:608a
Siena Palazzo Pubblico and, 11:280b
works in International Style, 5:628a
see also Nardo di Cione
Simonetta, Cicco, 11:216b
Simonida (daughter of Andronikos II), marriage to Stefan Uroš II Milutin, 11:176a, 177a, 186a, 474b
Simony, **11:300b–302a**
canon law on, 11:301b–302a
civil war in Milan and, 8:378a
concept of, 11:301a-b
Council of Chalcedon on, 11:301a
crime of, 11:301b
during investiture controversy, 11:301b
France, Capetian kings, 5:158b, 160b
Gregory I on, 11:301a
Gregory VI and, 11:517a, 517b
Gregory VII and, 5:160b
Humbert of Silva Candida on, 6:330a, 11:301b
Hus on, 6:368b–369a
idea of monastic reform and, 10:285b, 287b–288a
Leo IX's condemnation of, 3:634a
"liturgical strikes" against in Italy, 9:508b
Peter Damian and, 9:508b–509a
proof of innocence, 9:259b
reform papacy and, 6:499a
in Roman Empire, 11:300b–301a
theologians' views of, 7:123b
Tractatus de Albino et Rufino, on, 11:406a-b
Simphronius, prefect, 6:315a
"Simple benedictional." *See* Benedictional
Simplicius, 9:701a
Alexandrian school of Neoplatonism and, 9:98b
on Aristotle, 1:457b, 458a, 461b, 9:101a
Simund de Freine, **11:302a**
adaptation of Boethius' *Consolation,* 1:264a
Gerald of Wales and, 11:302a
Roman de Philosophie, 11:302a
Vie de saint Georges, 1:261a, 11:302a
Sin
confession and absolution of. *See* Confession
theology of, 6:446a-b
Sīnā, Ibn, 1:462a, 6:584a, 7:151b, 158a, **11:302a–307b**
al-Najāt, 8:566a
Al-Shifāᵓ, 1:458b, 8:566a
formation of metals, 1:136b
translations of, 1:136b
alchemy and, 11:306a
Aristotle and, 11:304a–305a
Arnald of Villanova and, 1:538a
on astrology, 1:618a
Bīrūnī and, 2:251a
botany of, 11:306a
in Buyid service, 11:302b
Canon, in university curriculum, 11:692b

Canon of Medicine, 1:458b, 8:249a, 249b, 258b
  on contraception, 3:572a
  Jewish translators of, 11:93a, 12:134a–135a
commentaries on, 9:571a
contribution to Islamic logic, 7:640b–641a
cosmology of, 11:304a–305a
Dānishnāma, 11:304a
De anima, 1:136b
  Jewish translators of, 12:135a-b
on dentifrice, 2:147b–148a
Duns Scotus and, 1:464a
early life of, 11:302b
on essence and existence, 4:510b
existence of God, proofs of causality, 9:596b
al-Fārābī and, 11:84b, 304a, 305b
on the first cause, 9:570a
geology of, 11:305b–306a
al-Ghazālī and, 1:459a
in Hamadān, 11:302b–303a
Henry of Ghent and, 1:463b
Ibn Rushd and, 1:459b, 11:303b
influence of, 11:306a–307a, 379b
John Philoponos and, 11:305b
Kitāb al-shifā$^{\supset}$, 11:303a
  Aristotelian doctrine of light, 9:242b
  on rainbows, 9:242b
  translations, Latin, 9:571b
Liber suficientiae, influence on Roger Bacon, 2:35b
logic of, 4:170b, 11:304a
Manṭiq al-mashriqiyyīn, 11:304a
material philosophy of, 11:305b–306a
mausoleum of, 11:303a
medical works of, 11:303a-b, 306a
metaphysics of, 11:304a–395a
musical treatises and, 8:640a
Neoplatonism of, 9:100a, 100b, 699b–700a, 701a
opposition to theory of immortality, 10:574b
pharmacology of, 11:306a
philosophical perspective of, 11:303b–304a
philosophical works, in Persian, 9:570a
psychology of, 11:305a-b
rejection of transmutation, 1:136b
on rosewater, 2:147a
on Scholasticism, 11:306b
scientific works of, 11:303a-b
Siger and, 11:286b
theory of vision, 9:241a
  lux and *lumen,* 9:249b
translations of, 11:306b
  by Bar Hebraeus, 2:108a
  by Gerard of Cremona, 8:249a
Sinād, 8:565b, 566a
Šinakan, **11:307b**
  as *ramik,* 10:255a
Sinān ibn Thābit, history of Abbasids, 6:251a
Sinbad the Sailor, in *Thousand and One Nights,* 12:50b, 51a
Sinbād-nāma, 6:508b
Sind, *da*^{c}*wā* in, 6:616a
Sindbād legend, 8:19a, 11:249a
Sindhind, 1:620a
Sindibad, Book of
  Spanish literature and, 4:551b
  translated into Spanish, 11:414a
Ṣinf, **11:307b–310a**
  in Anatolia, 11:308a, 309a
  in Ankara, 11:309a-b
  of bookbinders, 8:100a
  futuwwa traditions and, 11:308b–309a
  ghāzīs and, 11:308a
  guilds and, 11:307b
  origins of, 11:308a
  Sufi movement and, 11:309a
  under Abbasids, 11:308a
  under Ilkhanids, 11:308a–309a
  under Ottomans, 11:309a-b
Sinfjǫtli, **11:310a-b**
  in *Beowulf,* 11:310a
  etymology of, 11:310b
  in *Vǫlsunga saga,* 11:310a-b
Singers. *See* Minstrels; Troubadours
Singiad. See Cywyddwyr
Singidunum. *See* Belgrade
Singing
  Middle Eastern, 8:567a-b
  Welsh, 8:559a
  see also Song
Sinibuldi, Guittoncino. *See* Cino da Pistoia
Sinie Vody, Battle of (1363), 7:606a
Sinjibū, Turkish khan. *See* Istämi, Turkish khan
Sinkwerk. See Salines
Sinopia, 4:291a, **11:311a**
  with arriccio, 11:311a
  by Francesco Traini, 12:124b
  in fresco painting, 5:292b
  in mosaic making, 8:491a
  uncovering, 5:292b
Sion, Berchtold of Zähringen and, 11:539a
Siôn Cent, jeremiads, 12:608b
Sion Printed Textile, 12:690a
Sipahīs. See Ottomans, armed forces
Sippe. See Extended family, Germanic
Sir ben Abu Béker. *See* Sīr ibn Abī Bakr
Sir Beues of Hamtoun, 8:316a
  see also Bevers saga
Sir Gawain and the Green Knight. See Gawain and the Green Knight, Sir
Sir Gowther, 7:317a
Sīr ibn Abī Bakr, Spanish conquests of, 3:385a
Sir Landevale. See Sir Launfal
Sir Launfal, 7:317a
Sir Orfeo, 7:317a, **11:312a-b**
  love in, 11:312b
Sīrāf
  importance of as a port, 9:74b, 85a-b
  Persian Gulf trade and, 11:247a
Sīrāfī, Abū Zayd al-, 5:393a
Širak, 1:473b, **11:311a-b**
  Bagratids and, 1:480a
  rulers of, 11:311a
Širakawan, Council of (862), 1:500a-b
Sīrat Baybars, 2:138b
Siren (British Library MS Add. 24686), 2:205a (*illus.*)
Siricius, pope
  length of time in orders and, 3:442b–443a
  rescript, 10:335a
Sirmium, **11:311b**
  Rastislav's control of, 5:658a-b
Síros. *See* Syros
Sirr al-asrār. See Secretum secretorum
Sirventes, **11:312b–313b**
  canso of, 11:312b
  on crusade propaganda, 11:313a
  planh lament type, 12:217b
  in Provençal literature, 10:164b
  religious, 11:313a
  subjects of, 11:313a
  of troubadours, 11:313a, 12:217b
  of trouvères, 11:313a
  vers of, 11:312b
  see also Bertran de Born
Sīs, **11:313b–314a**
  church seat transferred to, 3:393b, 394a-b
  churches in, 11:314a
  description by Willebrand, 11:314a
  fortress of, 11:313b
  as religious center, 11:313b–314a
  remains of, 11:314a
  rulers of, 11:313b
  sacked by Mamluks, 3:391b, 393a, 11:314a
  trade at, 11:314a
Sīs Cathedral, 11:314a
Sīs, councils of (1204–1361), 1:501a-b, 521a, 3:394b
Sisakan. *See* Siwnik^{c}
Sisebut, Visigothic king, **11:314a-b**
  Isidore of Seville and, 6:564a, 564b, 11:314a-b
  reign of, 11:314a-b
  writings of, 11:314b
Sisenand, Fourth Council of Toledo and, 6:563b
Sisinnios II, patriarch, *Tomos,* 4:594b
Šišman of Vidin, Serbia and, 11:176a
Sisnando Davidiz, 11:376a
Sīstān
  administrative center, 10:661a
  agriculture in, windmills, 11:637b
  Ghaznavid control, 10:609b
  local dynasties in, 6:503a, 503b
  Mongol invasions, 10:609b
  Saffarids and, 11:575b
  Saminid occupation, 10:609b
  Tahirids and, 11:574b
  Ya^{c}qūb ibn Layth and, 12:716b
Sisters of the Common Life
  common ownership of property, 2:366a
  Devotio Moderna and, 4:166a-b
  Geer Groote and, 5:680b
Site of Durham, The, 8:329a-b
Sitric of Dublin, king, 6:517a
Sitt al-Mulk, regent of al-Ẓāhir, 5:27a
Situla, **11:314b**
  ivory, from the Ottonian period, 7:22b
Sivas. *See* Sebaste
Siward of Northumbria, earl, invasion of Scotland (1054), 8:1a
Siwnik^{c}, 1:472b, 473a, 473b, 484b, **11:315a–316a**

Siwnikʿ (*cont.*)
churches of, 1:495b–496a
devastated by Tatars in 1386, 12:93a
during *marzpanate,* 1:476b
economy of, 11:315a
manuscript illumination in, 1:497b
metropolitans, 9:256b
monasteries in, 11:315a
princes of, Ašot I and, 1:480b
rulers of, 11:315a-b
as Sasanian Persian province, 11:315a
see of, 1:482b, 503b
separatism of, 1:475a, 503b
Tatʿew and, 11:600b
Vaspurakan and, 12:361a
vs. Abbasids, 1:479b
see also Naχčawan
Six Ages of the World. *See* Sex aetates mundi
Six Days of Creation. See Dracontius
"Six Wings," 1:613a
Sixtus III, pope
Lateran and, 7:344b
Roman basilicas of, 4:332b
Sixtus IV, pope
Divina aeterni, rules for abbreviators, 1:13b
Dominicans and, 4:254a
funeral candles for, 5:320b
indulgences and, 6:450b
inquisition and, 6:488b, 9:112a
nuncio and, 9:200b
reign of, 3:367b
Siena and, 11:281b
Vatican Library and, 7:563b
Sixtus V, pope
carnival and, 3:99b
Gregorian chant and, 5:664a
Lateran and, 7:344b
Ṣiyām. See Fasting, Islamic
Siyāsatnāma. See Niẓām al-Mulk
Sizain (unit of measure), 12:595b
Skáhenda (a *rímur* meter), 10:405a-b
Skáld (the word), 9:173b
Skáldasǫgur
Kormáks saga and, 7:299b
þættir and, 12:2a
Skáldatal, 7:299a-b, **11:316a-b**
fornaldarsögur and, 11:316a-b
Kormáks saga and, 11:316a
preservation of, 11:316a
skalds in, 11:316a-b, 321a
transmission of, 11:316a
Skaldic verse, **11:316b–323b**
after *Snorra Edda,* 11:354b
artes poeticae on, 11:320b
in *Bjarnar saga Hítdœlakappa,* 2:255b
on blame and derision, 11:321a
on communication and celebration, 11:320b–321a
dróttkvætt and, 2:359b, 11:317b–318a, 319b–320a, 321a
Eyrbyggja saga and, 4:568a
Gamli Kanóki, 5:354b–355a
Gísla saga Súrssonar, 5:541a-b
heiti, in, 11:318a-b
Icelandic, 4:613b, 618a
influence on Eddic meter, 4:385a, 389a
its influence on *rímur,* 10:403b–404a
kennings in, 7:230a-b, 11:318a–319b, 323a
kings and legendary heroes, 6:113a
meter, *see Kviðuháttr*
metric variation, 6:113a
origin of, 11:316b–317a
preservation of, 11:321a–323a
renaissance of native tradition, 6:112b
sagas in, 11:321b
Skáldatal, 11:316a-b
Skáldskaparmál, in, 11:323b–324a
Sólarljóð, 11:358b–359a
þættir and, 12:4b
Þulur, in, 11:318b
treatises on, 11:320b
varieties of, 11:319b–320a
see also Bjarni Kolbeinsson; *Leiðarvísan; Líknarbraut; Málsháttakvæði*
Skalds, 11:320a–321a
for Hákon inn ríki, 11:322a
for Haraldr inn harðráði, 11:322a
for King Sverrir of Norway, 11:316b
in *Skáldatal,* 11:316a-b
Skáldskaparmál, **11:323b–324a,** 11:352a–353b
heiti in, 11:324a, 352b
Iðunn's apples, myth of, 7:19a
kennings in, 11:324a, 352b
Kudrun and, 7:304b
Skaði in, 11:325a
in *Snorra Edda,* 11:352a–353b
story of, 11:323b–324a
on Thor's encounter with Geirröðr, 12:48a
on Thor's encounter with Hrungnir, 12:45b
on the Vanir, 12:356b
Skálholt, diocese of, 2:252a, 6:351b–352a, 394a, 12:427a
in *Árna saga biskups,* 1:537a
scholarship in, 4:618a
Skálholtsbók, 12:456b–457a
Škand-gumānīg Wizār, **11:324a–325a**
author of, 11:324b
description of, 11:324a-b
sources of, 11:324b
Skanderbeg, **11:324a**
Skåne, invaded by Danes, 11:532b
Skanöor, fairs, 4:587b
Skara, founded, 11:530b
Skarðsárbók. See Björn Jónsson of Skarðsá
Skaði, **11:325a–326a**
Skelton, John, 8:324a, 12:477a
Magnificence, 4:287a
translation of Diodorus Siculus, 3:325a
"Skeltonic" verse, 8:324a
Skepticism, in *Proverbios morales,* 11:224a
Skewŕa, **11:326a-b**
Nersēs Lambronacʿi and, 9:104a, 104b
Reliquary, 11:326a (*illus.*)
Skikkju rímur, sources for, 8:507b
Skin disease. *See* Disease; Leprosy; Plagues
Skírnir, 11:326b–327a
Skírnismál, **11:326b–328a**
Freyr in, 5:297b
poet of, 11:327a-b
preservation of, 11:326b
Svipdagsmál and, 11:327a, 524b
Skive (unit of measure), 12:593b
Skjǫldunga saga, 9:176a, **11:328a–329a**
author of, 11:328a-b
Hrólfs saga Gautrekssonar and, 6:310b–311a
Knýtlinga saga and, 7:281a
oral tradition of, 11:328b
Þáttr af Ragnars sonum and, 12:7a
Skjǫldungs
in *Bjarkamál,* 2:254a
Óttarr and, 6:385b
Sklabos, 11:339a
Skopje
captured (1004), 2:119a
great council at (1346), 11:475b
Stefan Uroš II Milutin and, 11:474b
taken by the Turks, 11:181b
Skrælings, **11:329a-b,** 12:428b, 457a
definition of, 11:329a
in Greenland, 11:329b
references to, 11:329a-b
in Vinland, 11:329a-b
Skuld (Norn), 9:171b, 172a
Skúli, Jarl, 11:356b–357b
Skullcap. *See* Vestments, liturgical
Skylitzes, John, **11:330a,** 12:483b
Alexios I Komnenos and, 11:330a
historical works, 2:514b
on Theophanes Confessor's *Chronographia,* 12:22b
Theophanes continuatus and, 6:245b, 11:330a
Slapping games, 5:347a-b
Slash-and-burn agriculture. *See* Reclamation of land, swidden
Slate, as writing material, 12:699a
Slaughter of the Innocents. *See* Holy Innocents
"Slaughter of the Innocents" (play), 9:706b
Slaughterhouses. *See* Animals, food; Food trades
Slave revolts, Iraq, Zanj and, 12:738b–739a
Slavery, Islamic, **11:330a–333b**
abuses of, 11:331a-b
agricultural, 11:331b
clientage and, 11:332b
in *ḥadith* literature, 11:330b–331a
ideology of, 11:332a-b
in Iraq, 6:513a
in Koran, 6:579a, 11:331a
legal status of, 11:331b–332a
Mamluks and, 2:138a
manumission and, 11:332b–333b
military, 2:268a, 12:552a
Egyptian Tulinids and, 12:223b
al-Maʾmūn and, 8:80b
Ottoman soldiers, 9:307a-b
Ottoman, Bāyazīd I and, 2:136a
pilgrimage and, 9:650a
training of slaves, 11:332b
under Mamluk dynasty, 3:398b, 399a
see also Blacks; Janissary; Zanj
Slavery and slave trade, **11:334a–340b**
Anglo-Saxon, 11:200b
Arab and Jewish merchants, 6:133b
at Hedeby, 6:133a

in Baghdad and Iraq, 12:105b
barbarians and, 11:335a-b
blacks
in Majorca, 2:270a
in Naples, 2:269b
in Portugal, 2:268b
in Sicily, 2:269a-b
in Spain, 2:268a-b, 270a
in Bohemia-Moravia, 2:301b–302a
Byzantine, 11:338b
Canary Islands, 3:62b–63a, 4:561a
Carolingian Empire, 11:334b
Christianity and, 11:200a, 200b, 334b–335a
civil rights and, 11:200a, 201a
Council of Vienna on, 11:339a
depiction of, 11:337 (*illus.*)
disappearance of, 11:340a
dispersion of, 11:201a
early medieval trade and, 12:109b, 110a
in Egypt, 11:338b
Gaul, 11:200b
farm labor, 11:676a
in Genoa, 11:338b–339a
German law and, 7:475b
in German-speaking countries, 10:328b
on Indian Ocean, 11:249a
inheritance and, 6:451a-b, 452a
Jews in, 7:85b, 86a
in Kievan Rus, 1:100a, 11:336b, 12:435b
legal positions of, 11:334a
in Mali, 8:58a
Mamluk dynasty and, 11:339a-b, 12:107b
military service, 12:555b
in 9th through 12th centuries, 11:335b–338a
Norway, 9:182a
pagans and, 11:338a-b
persistence of, 11:338a–340a
plagues and, 9:682b
Portuguese, 4:561a, 562a, 11:338a
Roman, 11:200a, 334a
Russian, 11:190a, 191b–192a, 195b, 12:101b
serfdom and, 11:200a–201a, 205b
servi casati, 11:673b–674a
Slavic, 11:200b
Tartar slaves, 11:662a
traveler kidnapping and, 12:149a, 152b
Turkic, through Transoxiana, 12:146a
in Valencia, 12:348b
Venice and, 11:338b–339a, 12:111a, 386b, 387a
in Verdun, 11:200b, 12:152b
Vikings and, 12:110a
Visigothic, 12:473a-b
Walachia/Moldavia, 12:506a
Wulfstan of Worcester and, 12:703b
see also Blacks; Concubinage; Emancipation; Manumission; Serfs and serfdom
Slavic agriculture. *See* Agriculture, Slavic world
Slavic languages, 6:437b–438a, **11:340b–348a**
alphabets for, 11:341a-b
beginnings of, 11:340a–342a
Bulgaria, 2:329a-b, 403b
Chancery, as administrative language of Lithuania, 7:605a
in Croatia, 4:6a
development of written languages, 11:341a–342a
East Slavic, 11:346b–348a
East vs. West Slavic, 11:342a–343a
foreign influences on, 11:342a-b
Hungarian and, 6:336b–337a
Latin loanwords in, 6:438b
linguistic differentiation in, 11:341a
liturgical literature, 2:463b
missionaries and, 6:436a
Old Church Slavonic, Cyril and Methodios and, 2:299a
Old Slavic, 11:342a-b
proto-Slavic, 11:341a-b
Romanian and, 10:509b–510b, 512b, 513b
South Slavic, 11:345a–346a
syntax differences in, 11:342b–343a
West Slavic, 6:438a, 11:343a–345a
Yiddish and, 12:725a
see also Alphabets, Cyrillic; Alphabets, Glagolitic
Slavic literatures
East Slavic, 11:346b–348a
religious, Romanian translations, 10:511a
South Slavic, 11:345a–346b
West Slavic, 11:343a–345a
Slavic music, **8:572b–577b**
musicians, in art, 8:573a
notation of
Muscovite period, 8:574b–575a (*illus.*)
to 15th century, 8:573b–574b (*illus.*)
plainsong, 9:686b–688a
sources, 17th century, 8:575a–576a
Slavniks, relations with Přemyslids, 8:485a
Slavonia
relations with, Hungary, 4:5b, 6:340a
under
Tomislav, 4:4a
Zvonimir, 4:6a-b
Slavonic language
in Bulgaria, 11:554b
in Great Moravia, 5:658b
in liturgy, 5:658b
Slavs
Avars and, 2:399a, 11:348b
in Balkans, 4:1a, 6:443b, 11:168a
in Bulgaria, 2:399a-b, 401a, 403b, 6:435b
Bulgars and, 2:403b, 7:303b
Christianization of, 2:463b, 489a-b, 4:73a–74b, 6:436a
culture, after German expansion, 12:616b–617a
Elbian, Saxon overlordship, 10:684a
first Slavic state, 12:617a
German invasions, 12:616b
homeland of, 11:348b
land ownership, 11:669b–670a
music of, 8:577a
Old Slavonic, translation and translators, 12:127a
origins of, **11:348a–349a**, 12:616a-b
see also Wends
patrilineal kinship, 11:669b, 670a-b
Polish unification of, 9:717b–719b
revolt against Germans (983), 12:617a
in Russian *Primary Chronicle,* 12:434b
Serdica and, 11:189a
"Seven Tribes," 2:399b
as slaves, 11:200b, 336b–337a
in Thietmar von Merseburg's chronicle, 12:28a
tribal states of, 9:717a-b, 719a
in Ukraine, 11:348b
vs. Rome, 10:465a
Slavs, East, in Kievan Rus, 7:245b–246b, 250a
Šlemon, George Warda and, 11:568a
Slesvig, 4:155b
Ansgar and, 4:151a
trade in, 4:149a
Slesvig, duchy of
Erik of Pomerania and, 11:533a
Margaret of Denmark and, 11:533a
Sligo castle, 6:524a
Sling, adjustable (armor). *See* Guige
Slitki, 8:426a
Sḷkuni family, East Tarōn and, 11:599a
Slovakia
Hungary and, 6:337b
mining areas in, 8:399a
Slovakian language, 6:438a
Slovenian language, 6:438a, 443b
Slovo o ljubve. See Stefan Lazarević
Slovo o pogibeli Russkyia zemli, 11:347b
Slovo o polku Igoreve, 11:347a
Slovo o zakone i blagodati. See Ilarion
Sluis, Battle of (1340), 6:331b, 333a
miniature by Loyset Liédet, 9:82 (*illus.*)
Sluter, Claus, **11:349a-b**
artistic heirs of, 11:349b
Chartreuse de Champmol, 4:186a
Georges de la Sonnette and, 5:402a
Mérode Altarpiece, 5:611a
Philip the Bold and, 11:349a-b
Tomb of Philip the Bold, 9:709 (*illus.*), 710b, 12:620a
Virgin and Child, 5:623b (*illus.*)
Well of Moses, 11:349b, 350 (*illus.*)
work of, 11:349a-b
Smallpox, 9:673b, 674a–676b, 678a, 681a-b, 684a, 686a
see also Plagues
Smallpox and measles, book of. *See* Rāzī, Abū Bakr Muḥammad ibn Zakarīya al-
Smaragdus of St. Mihiel, 4:542b, **11:349b–351a**
on equality of people, 10:14b
kingship theories of, 7:261a-b
life of, 11:349b, 351a
on spiritual and temporal government, 10:15a
Via regia, 7:261a, 8:434a-b
writings of, 11:351a
Smbat, *History of the Bagratids,* 5:417b
Smbat I (the Martyr), Bagratid king of Armenia, 1:481b, 519b, 5:339b, **11:351a**

Smbat I (the Martyr), Bagratid king of Armenia (*cont.*)
as *archon ton archonton,* 1:449a
Ašot III Ołormac (the Merciful) and, 1:589a
martyrdom of, 4:324a, 11:351a
Naχčawan and, 9:90b
Smbat II Tiezerakal (Master of the Universe) of Armenia, king, 1:482a, 482b
Cathedral of Ani and, 1:291b
fortification of Ani in Širak and, 1:292b, 482b
Smbat II of Siwnik^{c}, prince, 1:483a, 11:315a
Smbat Bagratuni (*d.* 775), Mušeł Mamikonean and, 1:479b
Smbat Bagratuni (*fl.* 693), as *išχan,* 1:478b
Smbat Bagratuni (*fl.* late 6th and early 7th centuries)
Armenian church and, 1:499b
correspondence, 1:509a
Xusrō II and, 1:477a
Smbat Bagratuni, viceroy of Hyrcania, 2:48a
Smbat the Confessor, 1:480a
Ašot I Mec (the Great) and, 1:587b
Smbat Sparapet, 1:511b, 512a, **11:351b–352a**
Armenian law and, 7:389a-b
chronicle of, 11:351b
as jurist, 11:351b
law translation of, 11:351b
military career of, 11:351b
S. Karapet and, 9:159a
Smbat Zarehawanc^{c}i, establishment of T^{c}ondrakec^{c}i, 6:189a
Smelting
iron, 8:401a
mining and, 8:400a
silver, 8:401b–402a
Smeredevo, 11:188a
acquired by Bosnia, 11:474a
last capital of Serbia, 11:182b
Smith, Thomas, on bardic poetry, 6:536a
Smithfield Decretals, depiction of a battle between two cogs, 9:83 (*illus.*)
Smiths. *See* Metalsmiths, gold and silver
Snæfellsnes, in *Eyrbyggja saga,* 4:568a
Snare drum, 8:563a
Sneglu-Halla þáttr, 12:2b, 4b
Snjólvskvæði, death of Hildebrand, 6:227b
Snodland Manor, 7:435a
Snorra Edda. See Snorri Sturluson, *Prose Edda*
Snorri goði, 4:568a
Snorri Markusson of Melar, *Melabók* and, 7:327b, 328a
Snorri (son of Þorfinn and Guðríð), 12:457b
Snorri Sturluson, 7:281a, **11:355a–358a**
account of Swedish law, 7:524b
ambition of, 11:355b–356a
at Oddi, 11:355b–356a
attribution of *Þrymskviða* to, 12:53a
Auðunar þáttr vestfirzka, attributed to, 12:4b
characteristics of, 11:355b
children of, 11:357a
connection with *Poetic Edda,* 4:385a-b
Egils saga and, 4:403a, 612b
euhemerism of, 11:24b–25a
Eyrbyggja saga and, 4:568a
family of, 11:355b
feud between Norwegian crown and Oddaverjar and, 11:356b
Gylfaginning, **6:40b**, 11:23b, 325a, 352a, 353b–354a, 515a
argument between Njǫrðr and Skaði, 10:677a
Christian influences, 6:148a
midgard serpent in, 8:362b
Norns and, 9:171b, 172a
personification of Hel, 6:147b
Skaði in, 11:325a
sources for, 11:353b
Surtr and, 11:515a
on Thor, 12:45a, 45b–46a
on *Vafþrúðnismál,* 12:344a, 344b
on Valhalla, 12:350b
Valkyries in, 12:351a
Háttatal, 6:113a, 11:319b
models for, 6:112b
Heimskringla, 5:398a, 9:177a, 177b, 11:322a, 497b
author of, 11:355a
Battle of Svǫldr, 9:226a
Eyrbyggja saga and, 4:568a
Eyvindr Finnsson and, 4:570a,b
Færeyinga saga and, 4:581a
geographic knowledge, 5:398a
Hálfdanar saga svarta, see also Þáttr af Ragnars sonum
Hlaðajarla saga and, 9:177a
Knýtlinga saga and, 7:281a
on Njǫrðr, 9:146a
on Norwegian discoveries, 4:554b–555a
Olaf Haraldsson in, 9:225a
Olaf Tryggvason in, 9:225b
Orkneyinga saga and, 9:279b
St. Olaf and, 2:254a, 9:176b
in *Skáldatal,* 11:316a
Skjǫldungar saga and, 11:328a
sources for, 9:216a
version of *Hákonar saga,* in, 6:76b
see also Eyrbyggja saga; Ynglinga saga
marriage of, 11:356a, 357a
Mímir and, 8:395b
murder of, 11:500b
Norway trip of, 11:356b
Odin theology, 9:218a
Óláfs saga helga, 9:225a, 279a
on sailing to Greenland, 12:422a
Orkneyinga saga, revisions of, 9:279a
as possible author of *Laxdœla saga,* 7:528b
saga about, 11:355b
Separate Saga of St. Olaf, 9:176b
skaldic poetry of, 11:355a-b
Skírnir story and, 11:327a
Snorra Edda, **11:352a–355a**, 11:355a-b
on Baldr, 2:55a-b
Bjarni Kolbeinsson and, 2:256a
composition of, 11:352b
conflict between Æsir and Vanir, 1:63a
Eiríksm2l and *Hákonarmál,* 4:415a
Eyvindr Finnsson and, 4:570a
flyting and, 9:173a
fragments of lost poems in, 4:387a-b
Gefjon story in, 5:372a–373b
Gylfaginning of, 10:248a
Háttatal, 11:352a-b
Haustlǫng and, 12:32a
on Hrólf Kraki, 2:254a
Hrólfr and, 6:311a
Hrómundar saga and, 6:312b
Huginn and Muninn and, 6:323a
Hyndluljóð and, 6:385a
Iceland and, 4:554b
influence of, 11:354b
Kormáks saga, in, 7:299b
midgard serpent in, 8:362a-b
mythology in, 11:23b–24a
on Njǫrðr, 9:146a, 146b
Norna-Gests Þáttr and, 9:171a
Odin, role of, 9:218a
preservation of, 11:352a-b
prologue of, 11:354a
Ragnarsdrápa, 2:359a-b
Rán in the, 10:256b
settlement of Scandinavia and, 11:496b–497a
as skaldic treatise, 11:320b
Skírnir in, 11:327a
Skjǫldungar saga and, 11:328a
as a source of poetic devices for *rímur,* 10:404a
Svipdagr and, 11:524b
on Thor, 12:45b, 45a
version of *Grottasǫngr,* in, 6:3a
version of *Hjaðningavíg,* in, 6:267b
Vǫluspá and, 12:491a
see also Alvíssmál; Baldrs draumar; Háttatal
as source for Scandinavian mythology, 11:23b–24a
Sturla Þórðarson and, 11:495a-b, 499a-b
Swedish trip of, 11:356b
in *Þorsteins þáttr standarhǫggs,* 12:4a
training of, 11:355b–356a
Vǫluspá hin skamma and, 12:492a
Ynglinga saga, 6:311a, 9:177a
Ála Flekks saga and, 1:116b
conflict between Æsir and Vanir, 1:63a
description of Hœnir, 6:270b
etymology of Æsir and, 11:354a
Freyr in, 5:297a
Gefjon story in, 5:372a-b
Huginn and Muninn and, 6:323a
Mímir in, 8:396a
on Njǫrðr, 9:146b
Odin's role, 9:218a-b
Starkaðr in, 5:368b
on the Vanir, 12:356b
Ynglingatal and, 12:726a
see also Scandinavian mythology
Soap
in hair care, 2:149a
manufacture of, 11:639a
Islamic, 11:639a
Sobornoe ulozhenie, 11:198b

Soc. *See* Sac and soc
Social mobility
  church and, 3:417b–418a, 425a-b
  demography of, 4:144b
  marriage and, 3:425b–426a
  noble class and, 3:427a-b
  warfare and, 3:425b
  wealth and, 3:426b
  see also Wheel of fortune
Social structure. *See* Class structure
Societas Ricciardorum. *See* Ricciardi company of Lucca
Socrates Scholasticus, **11:358a-b**
  Constantinople as "Second Rome," 3:551a
  Ecclesiastical History, 1:506a, 11:358a-b
    on Patriarch Nestorius, 9:108b, 108a
  on the First Council of Constantinople, 9:459a
  Sozomen and, 11:374a
Sode Razayya. See Eleazar ben Judah of Worms
Södermannalag, 7:525a
Sodomy. *See* Homosexuality
Soest, Konrad von. *See* Konrad von Soest
Sofia. *See* Serdica
Sogdian language, 6:505b, 506a
Sogdiana. *See* Samarkand
Sǫgn, as alternative designation of *þættir,* 12:1b
Sogur Danakonunga. See Knýtlinga saga
Sohar, importance of as a port, 9:74b, 85b
Sohn des Bürgers, Der, synopsis of, 8:128a-b
Sohrab, 6:548b
Soils, Western European. *See* Reclamation of land
Soiscél Molaise, 3:221b, 223a
Soissons, acclamation of Pepin II as king, 9:501a
Soissons, Battle of (486), 8:277b
Soiture (unit of measure), 12:587a
Soke, 10:602a
Sokemen. *See* Sac and soc
Sokha (type of plow), 12:74b (*illus.*)
  use of draft horse and, 12:77b
Sokhasterion, 5:374b
Sökmen II, Seljuk ruler of Shāh-arman, 11:220a
Sökmen al-Quṭbī, Seljuk ruler of Shāh-arman, 11:220a
Sökmenids, successions struggle after Malikshāh I's death, 11:153b
Solar cycle, 3:17b
  in Christian calendar, 3:23b
Solario, Pietro, Granovitaya Palace, 8:497a-b
Sólarljóð, 6:147a, **11:358b–359b**
  in Eddic-skaldic transitional poetry, 4:389a
  meter of, 11:358b
  Norns and, 9:172a
  preservation of, 11:359a
  sources of, 11:358b
Solatium ludi scaccorum. See Jacobus de Cessolis
Soldanieri, Niccolò, 6:655b, 669b
Soldiers. *See* Warfare
Soldiers' Portions, **11:359b–360b,** 12:10a
  holders of, 11:359b–360a
  law on, 11:360a
  origin of, 11:359b
  statistics on, 11:360a
  see also Stratiotai
Solea, **11:360b**
  description of, 11:360b
Solesmes, **11:360b–362a**
  founding of, 11:360b
  history of, 11:360b–361b
  method of, 5:663b–664a, 11:361b–362a
Soleure
  Bern and, 11:543b
  Swiss Confederation and, 11:545a
Solfège, Guido of Arezzo and, 8:641a-b
Solidus, 8:428b, 430a
Solidus aureus. See Nomisma
Solidus (Byzantine gold coin), 9:495a
Soliloquium. See Bonaventure, St.
Solingen, sword manufacture in, 11:548a
Solís, Jaeme de, *Tratado del juego de Axedrez,* 11:443a
Sollevazione de' Ciompi, 6:634b
Solmization, **11:362b–366b**
  Chrysanthos and, 8:617a
  definition of, 11:362b
  examples of, 11:363–364 (*illus.*)
  Guidonian hand in teaching, 11:364 (*illus.*)
  hexachords in, 11:363b–364a
  monochord and, 8:606b
  musica ficta and, 8:597b, 626a
  origin of, 11:362b
  pitch and, 11:362b–366a
  tetrachords in, 11:362b
  theory of, 11:363b–365b
  see also Solfège
Soloist book. *See* Troper
Solomon ben Abraham Adret, 7:81a, 168b, 11:71b, 586a
  ban on the study of Greek and Arabic works, 8:48b–49a
  responsum literature and, 10:339a
Solomon ben Isaac of Troyes. *See* Rashi
Solomon ben Judah, 7:105a
Solomon ben Judah ibn Gabirol, 1:459b–460a, 7:92b, 151b, 166b, 173b, **11:370a–371a**
  on Aristotle's work, 11:370b
  early life of, 11:370a
  exegesis and, 4:540a
  Fons vitae, 1:459b, 11:370b
    influence on Roger Bacon, 2:35b
    Neoplatonism and, 9:100a-b, 700a
  Keter Malkhut, 7:96b, 11:370a
  meditations on religious themes, 6:127a
  Mekor Ḥayyim, Latin translation of, 7:96b
  philosophical prose writing of, 11:370b
  poetry of, 7:622a, 11:370a
  Source of Life, 6:127a
  will of God, 9:576b
Solomon ben Moses Melgueuil of Provence, translations by, 12:134b
Solomon ben Moses de Rossi, *Testimony of the Lord Is Faithful,* 10:4a
Solomon ben Reuben Bonafed, 10:6a-b
Solomon ben Sampson, 7:78b
Solomon of Constance, bishop, Notker Balbulus and, 9:187b
Solomon ha-Levi (Pablo de Santa María). *See* Paul of Burgos
Solomon ibn al-Mu⊂allim, 7:98b
Solomon ibn Zadok, 7:81b
Solomon and Marcolf, **11:366b–370a**
  Dialogus Salomonis et Marcolfi, 11:366b–368a
  other dialogues in, 11:368a
  tradition of, 11:366b
Solomon (OT king of Israel)
  in art, 6:408b–409a
    in Windmill Psalter, 6:463a
Solomon and Saturn (Old English poem), 1:280b, 11:368a
Solomon's Temple. See Acardus of Arroasia
Solomon's Temple. *See* Jerusalem, Temple of
Solothurn
  Basel and, 11:543a
  Germany and, 11:528a
Solsequium. See Hugo von Trimberg
Solutiones contrariorum, 6:555a
"Solvitur acris hiems." *See* Horace
Somateia. See Guilds and métiers, Byzantine
Somerled, descendants of, 3:407a
Somerset. *See* Beaufort, Edmund
Sommaire philosophique, alchemy in, 1:138b
Sommaripa family, 7:381a
Somme le roy (roi). See Lorens d'Orléans
Somme rurale. See Boutillier
Sommi, Lo. See Metge, Bernat
Somnium Scipionis. See Cicero
Somnium Viridarii, 7:270a, **11:371a–372a**
  dream vision in, 11:371a-b
  sources of, 11:371b
Sompnium Godefridi de Odone Aurelianensi. See Godfrey of Rheims
Somχet⊂i. *See* Gugark⊂
Sona, 8:562a
Sonajas de azofar, 8:563a
Sonatori di varii strumenti, 8:416b
Sondergotik, **11:372a-b**
Sondergotik, example of, 11:372a (*illus.*)
Sonetto. See Italian literature, sonnet
Song
  Armenian. *See Tal*
  Islamic, 8:565b, 566a
    Kitāb al-aghānī on, 8:567a
  see also Singing
Song Against the Blacksmiths, 8:331a
Song of Dermot and the Earl, 1:265b
Song of Hyndla. *See Hyndluljóð*
Song of Lewes, **11:372b**
Song, monophonic. *See* Plainsong
Song of Roland. See Roland, Song of
Song of St. Faith, 2:126b
  copies of, 5:235a-b
Song of the Sun. *See Sólarljóð*

Songe de la barge, Le. See Jean de Werchin
Songe du castel, 1:189a
Songe d'enfer, Le. See Raoul de Houdenc
Songe de pestilence, 6:359b
Songe du vergier, 7:270a, 11:371b
Songhai Empire, 12:54b–55b
Sonnet
first Spanish, by Santillana, 11:451b
Italian, 6:640b, 641a, 643a
double, 6:643b
Iacopo da Lentini and, 6:388b, 642b, 669a, 11:259b–260a
modified sixteen-line, 6:644b
Petrarch and, 6:653a
sources of, 11:260a-b
Sophanenē, 1:472b
Sophenē, 1:472b
Armenian Pentarchy and, 1:514b, 515a, 515b
coinage of, 8:417b
commercial importance of, 12:96b, 97a
Sophistical Refutations. See Aristotle
Sophronius of Jerusalem, patriarch, 3:630b
Monoenergism and, 8:233a
opposition to Monothelitism, 8:480a
Sopoćani Monastery, 11:175b, 184b, 185a (*illus.*), 186a
Soranus (physician), 8:255b
attribution to of *Isagoge,* 8:256a
method of bandaging, 8:245b
translated by Caelius Aurelianus, 8:247a
Sorbian language. *See* Lusatian language
Sorbon (Sorbonne), Robert de, 7:143b, 563a, 567a
Sorbonne
library of
catalog of, 1:206a-b, 7:565b
desk arrangement in, 7:569a
number of volumes, 7:563a, 567a
rules on lending, 7:565a
Sorbonne Mass. *See* Lambuleti, Johannes
Sorbs, 12:616a, 616b
Sorcery
Inquisition and, 12:662a
Malleus malificarum and, 8:30b
witchcraft and, 12:658b, 659b
see also Magic; Witchcraft
Sordello, 10:168a
patronage by Ramon Berenguer IV, 10:168a
Sorghum, 5:647a
as cereal crop, 1:82a, 83b
Sörla saga Sterka, **11:373a-b**
preservation of, 11:373a
story of, 11:373a-b
style of, 11:373b
Sörla þáttr, 7:304b, 11:373a-b
everlasting battle, 5:141b
mythical elements in, 5:142a
Sormen Stratelates, 5:540a
correspondence, 1:509a
Soterichos Panteugenos, 3:632a
Sottes chansons. See Baillehaut, Jean; Trouvères
Sottie des copieurs et lardeurs, 4:265b
Sottie, defined, 4:279a
Sottoposti
in Florentine guilds, 6:18b
in guilds of artists, 6:21a
Sou (unit of measure), 12:596a
Soualia litra (unit of measure), 12:582a
Soudée (coinage or income measure), 12:586a-b
Soufflet, **11:373b–374a**
Souillac, abbey church of, 10:481a, 495a
Soul
Augustine of Hippo on, 1:656a-b
in Iamblichus' philosophy, 9:97a-b
Peter John Olivi's views on, 9:514b
in Plotinus' philosophy, 9:96a
Soul scot, 11:616a
Soule, history, 2:126b
Soulis, 11:250a
Sous, Idrisids in, 6:413b
Sousse
Great Mosque, 1:70b
Tamīm and, 12:745a
South English Legendary, 4:546a-b, 8:315a
saints represented in, 6:6b–7a
British, 6:62a
Old English, 6:62a
sources for, 6:61b–62a
Southampton
in early Middle Ages, 12:320b–321a
raid on (1338), 3:64b
Southampton Castle, William Wynford and, 12:711b
Southampton Plot of 1415, 6:160a
Soviet gospod, 9:195a
Soyurghal. See Tuyul
Sozomen, **11:374a**
Ecclesiastical History, 11:374a
see also Theodoret of Cyr
Sozopetra, captured by Byzantines, 2:118a
Sozzini, Bartolomeo, on inheritance, 6:460a
Spada. See Sword
Spades, 12:78a–79b, 81b
Islamic, 12:84a-b
Spāhbad, **11:374a-b**, 12:705b
sparapet and, 11:374a
see also Sparapet
Spain
agriculture
Andalusia, 1:84a-b
Galicia, 1:83b
Old Castile, 1:83a-b
shift to Mediterranean style, 1:83a–84b
Valencia, 1:83b, 84b
astronomy in, 1:613a
Belisarios in, 2:165a
black slaves in, 2:268a-b
cabalistic schools in, 3:1b–2b
Christian-Muslim relations, **11:374b–381b**
Anselm Turmeda's philosophy and, 12:227a–228b
formal cultural borrowing, 11:379b–380a
Mozarabs, 8:514a
Mudejars, 11:375b–377b
Reconquest and, 10:279b–280a
regional evolution, 11:377b–379b
summary of, 11:380a-b
in Valencia, 12:346b, 349a-b
see also Toledo
Christianity in, 8:444a–445b
"Gothic personality" of, 11:435a-b
city-principalities in, 11:383a–384a
colonization of frontier, 12:563a
feudalism in, 1:629a
glassmaking in, 5:559a–560a
Gothic art in, painting, 5:612a
Jews in
art, 7:66a, 68a, 68b
expulsion of, 3:3a
rabbinate, 10:244a
schools of, 11:70a, 71a-b
languages of, 6:435b, 442a-b
military aristocracy, 12:563a
military orders, 12:563a
military organization, 12:562b–563b
mining areas in, 8:398a-b
mints and money in, 8:423a
Muslim kingdoms of, **11:381b–389b**
Almohads and, 6:132a, 11:383b
Almoravids and, 11:383b
area covering, 11:382a (map)
battles of the Reconquest, 10:255b–256a
Christian-Muslim relations, 6:232b–233a
history of, 11:381b
interpretations of, 11:385a–387b
in Islamic conquests, 6:572a-b
jewelry, 5:379b
Marinid conquests, 8:138b, 139a
narratives of, 11:381b–385a
overthrow of Umayyad caliph, 6:117a
paper exports, 9:389a
refugees from, in France, 6:558b
see also Almoravids; Andalusia; Aviz, Order of; Umayyads of Córdoba
Muslim raids in, transhumance and, 8:280a
Norwegian raids on, 4:554b
pilgrimage in, 9:656a, 659a-b, 661b–662a
plagues in, 9:676a, 681a–682a
relations with
Canary Islands, 4:559a
Italy, 4:557b
sculpture and metalwork, pre-Romanesque, 10:114b–115a
social structure, under Visigoths, 12:473a-b
surviving medieval bridges in, 10:418a-b
tenurial development, 11:679b, 682b–683a
payeses de remensa, 11:682b
right of *aprisio,* 11:677a
universities, 12:286b–287a
urbanism in, under Visigoths, 12:473b
Vincentius Hispanus and, 12:456a
Visigoths in, 12:471a–472a
see also Andalusia; Aragon; Asturias-León; Castile; Catalonia; Feudalism; Hispano-Arabic headings; Hispano-Mauresque headings; Navarre; Reconquest; Valencia

Span (unit of measure), 12:588a
Spandrel, **11:389b**
Ravenna mosaic, 10:263a, 264a-b
Spaneas, use of language, 2:509a
Spangenhelm, 1:522a, 523a, 527a (*illus.*), 534b (*illus.*)
Spangröl, 1:530b
Spanish architecture, Plateresque style, 9:694a-b, 695 (*illus.*)
Spanish art
manuscript illumination, pre-Romanesque, 10:113b–114a
painting
Hispano-Flemish style, 5:612a
pre-Romanesque, 10:113b
pottery, 10:65a-b
textiles, 11:718b
diasper-weave silks, 11:718a
veil of Hishām, 11:718a
Spanish drama, **11:436b–437b**
interludes, 4:279b
La Celestina, 3:212a–213b
lost, 11:443b–444a
secondary evidence about secular plays, 11:437a
under the Catholic Monarchs, 11:424b–425a
see also Auto de los reyes magos
Spanish era, **11:389b**
Spanish Inquisition
in Barcelona, 2:105a
distinguished from papal Inquisition, 6:488b
Jewish conversion to Christianity during, 3:577b–578a
New Christians and, 9:111b
Spanish language, 6:442b–443a, **11:390a–405b**
Alfonso X (the Learned) and, 11:414b
delimitations of, 11:390a-b
dialects of, 3:141b
Asturo-Leonese territory, 11:399a-b
bilingualism and bidialectalism, 11:401a–402a
Navarro-Aragonese territory, 11:400a–401a
Old Castilian territory, 11:399b–400a
zones of, 11:398b–399a
from Romance stock, 11:390a
glossaries, 11:390b–391a
Italian language and, 6:626a
linguistic works, 11:441b
lyrics in Juan Ruiz' *Libro de buen amor* and, 11:417b
Old Spanish
early, 11:396a
grammar forms of, 11:396a–398b
late, 11:396a
standardized or classical, 11:396a
vocabulary forms of, 11:396a–398b
periodization pattern of, 11:395b–398b
in Old Spanish, 11:396a
pronunciation in, 11:402a-b
research on, 11:390b–392a, 392b–395b
spelling in, 11:402a-b
style of Juan de Mena and, 8:273a
Visigoths and, 6:435a
Vulgar Latin and, 11:391a
see also Castilian language; Catalan language; Judeo-Spanish language
Spanish Latin literature, **11:405b–407b,** 11:409b
after the Muslim invasion, 11:406a-b
Julianus of Toledo, 7:181b
12th century, 11:406b
under the Visigoths, 11:405b–406a
Spanish law, **7:518b–524a**
acceptance of *Corpus iuris civilis,* 7:522a
after Ferdinand and Isabella, 7:523b
in Asturias-León, 7:521a-b
acceptance of *Liber iudiciorum,* 7:521a
in Castile, 7:521a–522a
impact of Frankish law and feudal practices, 7:521b
judgment by *albedrío,* 7:521b
rejection of *Liber iudiciorum,* 7:521b
codes, 7:429b–430a,
see also Siete partidas
conflicting ideologies in, 7:518b
development of localized customs, 7:521a-b
dual legal system under Germanic conquerors, 7:519b–520a
early indigenous customs and, 7:519a
fueros, 5:308b–310a, 7:521b–523b
in Galicia, 7:521a-b
Leovigild's reforms of Euric's code, 7:520a
movement toward legal unification, 7:519b–520a
Muslim influence, 7:520b–521a
Roman influence on, 7:519a-b
romanizing influence of legal study, 7:522a
Spain as a legal entity and, 7:518b–519a
under Alaric II. *See* Breviary of Alaric
under Alfonso X, 11:414b–415a
under Visigoths, 7:519b–520b
see also Siete partidas
Spanish literature
Arthurian legend in, 1:575b–576b
ballads, 11:417b, **11:427b–431b,** 11:443a
definition of, 11:427b
first printed collections of, 11:429b
inspired by the Cid, 3:388b–389a
manuscript sources, 11:429a
origins of, 11:428b–429a
in *pliegos sueltos,* 11:429a-b
romances épicos, 11:427b–428a, 428b
romances fronterizos, 11:428a
style of, 11:428a-b
themes of, 11:427b–428a
Bible translations, **11:432a-b**
biography, **11:432b–435a**
15th century, 11:421a-b
semblanzas, 11:433b–434b
works on idealized nobles, 11:433a-b
cancioneros, 11:424a-b, 450a–451a
lost, 11:443b
characteristics of, apparent vs. real, 10:552b
chronicles, **11:435a–436b**
under the Catholic Monarchs, 11:422a-b
clerecía poets, 11:411b–413b
conversos and, 9:111b
conversos and, 11:420a-b
courtly poetry and fiction under Juan II, 11:419a-b
dawn and spring songs, **11:436b,** 11:449b
see also Villancicos
development of, **11:408a–427b**
didactic literature, 11:419b–420a, 422b
Don Juan Manuel and, 8:95a-b
during Trastámaran wars, 11:418a-b
ensaladas, 11:430a
epic poetry, **11:437b–438b**
ballads and, 11:428b, 437b
cantos noticieros, 11:437b
early, 11:408b–409b, 411b, 428b
peninsular tradition, 10:528b
see also Alfonso XI, Poema de; Cantar de mío Cid; Cid, the, legend of
exempla, 4:551b
hagiography, **11:438b–440b**
poems, 11:438b–439a
prose, 11:439b–440a
humanism and postmedieval developments, 11:425a-b
instructional, **11:440b–442a**
Islamic influences, 3:31b
kharja, 7:239a-b
lost works, **11:442a–445a**
counts cycle of early epics, 11:442b
early secular lyrics, 11:442a-b
epic narratives, 11:442b–443a
lyric poetry, **11:445a–452a**
courtly, 11:450a–451a
ecclesiastical, 11:449b–450a
evidence for lost early songs, 11:445b–446a
individualists vs. traditionalists, 8:514a
muwashshaḥs and *kharjas,* 11:446a–449b
origins, 8:514a
secular songs, 11:448a–449b
suppression of secular poetry, 11:445b–446a
traditional, 11:408a-b
see also Villancicos
maiden songs, 8:515
poetry
cancioneros, 3:140a
copla in, 3:584b–585a
Rimado de Palacio, 7:667b
romancero, 3:140a
see also Castillo, Hernando del, *Cancionero general*
popular poetry, **11:452a–453a**
prose
Golden Age, 8:157b
precursors of Renaissance, 10:646a
techniques, 3:31b
religious, 10:645b
rise of vernacular prose in the 13th century, 11:414a–415b
romancero viejo, 11:427b–428b, 429b–430a
modern scholarship, 11:430a–431a

Spanish literature (*cont.*)
romances, 10:645b, **11:4533a-b**
Arthurian legend in, 1:575b–576b
Libro de Apolonio, 1:348b–349b
under the Catholic Monarchs, 11:423a–424a
see also Amadís de Gaula
satire, **11:454a-b**
themes of, 11:454a
scientific, 9:704b–705a
sentimental romances, **11:454b–455b**
sermons, **11:455b–456b**
serranillas, 10:651b
translations, **11:456b–457b**
Trinitarian doctrine in, 12:190a
Troy story, **11:457b–458b**
versification and prosody, 10:552b–554a, **11:458b–460a,** 11:458b, 459a, 459b
see also *Cuaderna vía*
visionary legends, 11:439b–440a
see also Castilian literature; *Mester de clerecía; Mester de juglaría*
Spanish music, trecento style, 12:180a
Spanyol, 7:179a
Sparapet, 1:489a, 490a, **11:460a-b**
spāhbad and, 11:374a
see also Vardan Mamikonean, St.
Sparta
in the 12th century, 12:102b
Villehardouin and, 7:378a
Spaspet. See Sparapet
Spatha, 8:283a, 11:546a, 546b
see also Sword
Spear. *See* Lance
Specchio di vera penitenza. See Passavanti, Jacopo
Spechtshart, Hugo
Chronicon, 8:647a
Flores musicae omnis cantus Gregoriani, 8:646b
Speckled Book. *See* Duniry, Great Book of
Specula principum, 10:15b
Speculator, 7:407b
Speculi almukefi compositio, 1:438b
Speculum animae. See Henry of Langenstein
Speculum artis bene moriendi. See Ars moriendi, longer version
Speculum astronomiae, 1:607b–608a
Speculum doctrinale. See Vincent of Beauvais
Speculum duorum. See Gerald of Wales
Speculum ecclesiae. See Gerald of Wales
Speculum historiale. See Vincent of Beauvais
Speculum Hominis. See Gower, John, *Mirour de l'omme*
Speculum humanae salvationis
Heilspiegel Altarpiece and, 12:668a
Tree of Jesse and Tree of the Cross, 12:182 (*illus.*)
Speculum iudiciale. See Durand, Guillaume
Speculum maius. See Vincent of Beauvais
Speculum meditantis. See Gower, John, *Mirour de l'omme*
Speculum morale. See Vincent of Beauvais
Speculum musicae. See Jacques de Liège
Speculum naturale. See Vincent of Beauvais
Speculum principis, 7:261a-b, 264b, 270b
Speculum regum. See Godfrey of Viterbo
Speculum stultorum. See Nigel of Longchamp
Speculum vitae. See Bissolo, Bellino
Speier, commune of, 3:498a
Spell of Heimdall. *See Heimdalargaldr*
Spells, condemned by the church, 8:26a
Spelt, 5:646a
Spenser, Edmund
Faerie Queene, 7:329a, 10:362b
Geoffrey of Monmouth as source for, 5:390a
Spenta Mainyu (Zoroastrian god), 12:747a, 749a
Sper, Bagratids in, 1:480a
Sperber, Der, **11:460b–461a**
Sperling, 5:442a
Spervogel, **11:461b–463a**
courtly poetry of, 11:462b
identity of, 11:461b
Spesar þáttr, 5:673a
Speyer Cathedral, 5:595a, 10:95a-b, 487b–488a (*illus.*)
Gospels for, 10:104a (*illus.*), 104b
Lund Cathedral and, 10:489a
Speyer, prince-bishopric of, representative institutions and, 10:333b
Sphere and Cylinder. See Archimedes
Sphinx, in art, 6:408a
Sphrantzes, George, histories, 6:248a
Spices
trade in, 12:386a, 387a
by Beirut, 7:533a
early medieval, 12:109b, 110b, 110a
by Egypt, 12:107b, 108a
Hansa, 12:113a
Indian Ocean, 11:248b, 249a
by Venice, 12:111a
Spider, in *Theobaldus-Physiologus,* 2:205b
Spiegel, production of by Johannes Gutenberg, 6:31a-b
Spiegel, Der. See Hermann von Sachsenheim
Spieghel historiael. See Maerlant, Jacob van
Spiel von Frau Jutten, 4:268b
Spielmannsepik, 11:368a-b
Spierinc, Claeys, **11:463a-b**
miniature in the 1486 book of hours, 11:463 (*illus.*)
Spierinc, Nicolas, Lathem and, 7:345b–346a
Spill. See Roig, Jaume
Spill de la vida religiosa. See Martines, Fra Pero
Spinach, growth of, 1:81b, 96a
Spinelli, Parri, 11:463b, 464a
Spinello Aretino, **11:463b–464a**
fresco in the Palazzo Pubblico at Siena, 11:464 (*illus.*)
frescoes of, 5:294b, 295b
Spinning
cross-reel, 11:700b
drop spindle, 11:697a-b
fineness and uniformity, 11:698a
hand, 11:697b–697a, 697a–698a
reeling and winding, 11:700b–701a
spindle, 11:697 (*illus.*)
rock, 11:697a-b
of warp wool, 11:699a-b
wheel, 6:395a, 11:698 (*illus.*), 698a–700b
bans on, 11:699a
productivity, 11:698b
Small and Great, 11:698a-b
in woolen industry, 11:699a-b
Z- and S-twists, 11:697b, 698a
Spinoza, Baruch, on Levi ben Gershom, 7:554a
Spinsters. *See* Women, unmarried
Spira, Johannes de, 10:124b
Spira, Vindelinus, 10:124b
Spiral, 1:437a-b
Spirants, Latin, 12:495a
Spiration. *See* Trinitarian doctrine
Spirinc. *See* Spierinc, Claeys
Spirits, magic and, 8:34a
Spiritual Ascents. See Gerard Zerbolt of Zutphen
Spiritual Ladder. See John Klimakos
Spiritualia (spiritual offices of clerics), investiture conflict and, 9:445a
Spirituals, Franciscan. *See* Franciscans, Spirituals
Splanamento de li proverbii de Salamone. See Pateg, Girard
"Splendida flammifero iam nubit," 6:383b
Split, Kulin and, 7:309a
Split, Councils of (925, 928), 4:4b–5a, 12:69a
Spoils of Annwfn, 5:389a
Spolia, **11:464a-b**
art renaissances and, 10:305a, 307b
Roman, 10:517a
source identification, 10:305a
see also Antiquarianism; Art, renaissances and revivals
Spontoon, 7:325a
Sporran, 11:551a
Sporting games, 5:353b–354a
Sprat (*Sprattus sprattus*), fishing of, 5:71b
Sprecher, Middle High German literature and, 8:357b
Sprenger, James, 8:30b
Spring-powered chamber clock, 3:462a-b
Springolf, 3:179 (*illus.*), 180a
Spritsail, 11:244b
Sproken, 4:319b–320a
Spruch, 7:290b–291a
Spruchdichtung, 2:228b, 5:441b–443b
Sprüche
by Walther von der Vogelweide, 12:540b
mode of performance, 12:540b
Spruchgedicht, in *Dialogus Salomonis et Marcolfi,* 11:367b
Spruchgedichte. See Sachs, Hans
Spruchstrophe, 5:442b
Spur castles. *See* Castles
Spurdog (*Squalus acanthias*), fishing of, 5:69b–70a

Spuria. *See* Forgery; Translation and translators
Spytihněv of Bohemia, duke, 10:88a
  founder of the Přemyslid dynasty, 2:299b
Ṣqāliba, 11:336b–337b, 338b
Squarcialupi Codex, Landini in, 7:326a
Squarcione, Francesco, **11:464b–465a**
Square notes. *See* Musical notation, Kievan
Square sail. *See* Sail
Squinch, 4:235 *illus.*, 9:666a, **11:465a**
  see also Dome
Squire, **11:465a–466a**
Squyr of Lowe Degre, 8:601b
Srebreniki, 8:426a
Srebrnica
  awarded to Stefan Lazareviç of Serbia, 11:182a, 473a
  conflict between Serbia and Bosnia (1448-1450) and, 11:474a
Šruan. *See* Shirvan
Stabat mater, 6:382a
  probable author of, 7:35a
  reinstated by Pope Benedict XIII (in 1727), 11:162b
  see also Sequence, "regular Victorine"
Stabili, Francesco. *See* Cecco d'Ascoli
Stabilitas. See Monasticism
Stacco, sinopias and, 5:292b
Stacy de Rokayle, 7:330a
Städtetage. See Representative assemblies, German, urban
Stadtschreiber, 11:558a
Stadtvogt, 3:481a-b
Stæte, 8:413b
Staff (music), **11:466a**
  diatonicism and, 8:623a
  Guido of Arezzo on, 8:593b, 641a
  neumatic notation and, 8:627a
Staff (unit of measure), 12:593b
Stafford, Humphrey, 3:5a
Stafhenda (*rímur* meter), 10:405b
Stagecraft. *See* Drama
Stagel, Elsbeth, 9:13a, 13b
  Heinrich Suso and, 9:34b, 35a
  Suso and, 11:516b
  Vitae sororum, 9:13b
Stags, 6:358b, 360a
Stained glass. *See* Glass
Stalactite vault. *See* Vault
Stallage (market tax), 8:146b
Stamena, 8:420b
Stammesherzogtum. See Franks, stem duchies
Standard, Battle of the (1138), 4:110b
Stanislav of Znojmo, 6:367a, 368a, 368b
Stanislaw of Kraków, St.
  compared with St. Thomas Becket, 10:371a
  patron of Poland, 9:720a, 722b
  rhymed office to, 10:367a, 371a
Stans, Compromise of (1481), 11:545a
Stantipes. *See* Dance; *Estampie*
Stanza. *See* Liturgical poetry; Musical notation
Stanzaic Life of Christ, 2:222a, 3:299a-b, 4:547a
Staple, Ordinances of the (1353), 9:428a
Star vault. *See* Vault
Starkaðr, **11:466b–467a**
"Starlings," in bridge construction, 10:419b–420a
Starozhiltsy, 11:191a, 191b
State archives. *See* Archives
Statenbijbel, 2:215a
Statics, of Jordanus de Nemore, 1:438b
Stationer
  functions, 11:692b
  oath, 11:693a
  pecia system and, 9:481b
Stationers' Guild (London), 8:104b
Stations of the Cross, **11:467b–468a**
  freestanding, 11:467b
  pictorial representations of, 11:467b
  see also Passion cycle
Statistics, population. *See* Demography; Plagues
Statius
  on the construction of Roman roads, 10:410a
  Vergil and, 12:394b, 394a
Statua ecclesiae antiqua. See Gennadius of Marseilles
Status
  "collective seigneurial." *See* "Collective seigneurial" status
  hereditary, 6:454b, 460b
  see also names of social groups or professions, *e.g.,* Citizens; Prestige; Social mobility; Women
Status, marital. *See* Marriage
Statūs theory, 7:113a–114a
Statuta ecclesiae antiqua, 7:398b
  clerical orders, 9:265a
  on ordinands, 9:266a
  ordination directions, 9:263b
Statuta et consuetudines See *Très ancien coutumier*
Statute, **11:468a–469a**
  De donis conditionalibus, 7:452b
  in English common law, 7:444a-b, 447b, 448b, 452b, 455b
    collections of, 7:450a
    parliamentary, 7:450a-b
  French municipal statutes and commercial law, 7:466a
  issues addressed, 9:261b–262a
  king's personal seal, 9:262a
  ordinance compared, 9:261b–262a
  origin of the term, 11:468a
  passage of, 9:261b
  registration of in northern Europe, 7:430a
  in Russian (Muscovite) law, 7:508a
  in southern French law, 7:466a, 467a–468a
Statute of Gruffudd ap Cynan, as basis for eisteddfod, 4:415b
Statute of treasons of 1352. *See* Treason
Statutes of Nieszawa. *See* Jewry law
Statutes of the Realm, The, 11:468a
Statutum in favorem principum, 5:501a
Staufische Klassik, 8:349b
Stave. *See* Staff
Stave church. *See* Church architecture
Stavelot Triptych, 10:500 (*illus.*), 12:198b
Stavronikita Gospels, 10:307 (*illus.*)
Staysail, 11:244b
Stecknitz Canal, locks, 12:578b
Steel
  forms of transportation of, 11:471b–472a
  Spanish, 11:471a
  in sword manufacture, 11:546b, 548a
    Damascus, 11:471a
Steelmaking, **11:469b–472b**, 11:639b
  amount of production, 11:471b
  annealing, 11:471a, 471b
  "cementation," 11:470b–471a
  described in Theophilus' *De diversis artibus,* 12:24b
  main regions of, 11:471b
  methods of, 11:470a-b
  "natural" process, 11:470b
  postmedieval methods of, 11:471a
  quality of ore and, 11:470a
  tempering and annealing, 11:469b, 471a, 471b
  as a trial-and-error process, 11:469b, 471b
  "wrought" and "cast" iron, 11:469b
  see also Tools, agricultural, European
Stefan Dečanski of Serbia, ruler, 2:412a, 11:176a–177b
  blindness of, 11:176b
  canonization of, 11:177b
  coronation of, 11:176b–177a
  mausoleum church at Dečani Monastery, 11:187a
  mausoleum church of, 12:478b
  murder of, 11:475a
  quarrel with son Stefan Dušan, 11:177b
  Stefan Uroš II Milutin of Serbia and, 11:474b–475a
Stefan Dušan's Code. *See* Stefan Uroš IV Dušan
Stefan Lazarević of Serbia, ruler, 11:181b, 182a-b, **11:472b–473a**
  as patron of arts and literature, 11:182a-b
  Slovo o ljubve, 11:346a
Stefan Nemanja of Serbia, ruler, 11:173a-b, **11:473a-b**
  abdication, 10:672b
  abdication of, 11:173b
  Frederick I Barbarossa and, 11:173b
  monumental church architecture and, 11:183b–184a
  Serbian independence from Byantines, 4:347a
  vs. Isaac II Angelos, 6:559b
Stefan Prvovenčani of Serbia, ruler, 11:173b–174b, **11:473b**
  Roman associations, 10:672b
Ştefan (the Great), Moldavian voivoide. *See* Stephen III (the Great) of Moldavia, voivode
Stefan Tomaš of Bosnia, king, **11:474a**
  Stefan Vukčiç Kosača and, 11:476a
Stefan Tomašević of Bosnia, king, 11:183a, **11:474a-b**
Stefan Uroš II Milutin of Serbia, ruler, 11:175b–177a, **11:474b–475a**
  development of Serbian mines and, 11:176b
  as a patron of art, 11:186a-b
Stefan Uroš IV Dušan of Serbia, ruler, 11:346a, **11:475a-b**

Stefan Uroš IV Dušan of Serbia, ruler (*cont.*)
Bogomils and, 2:296b
coronation, 11:177a, 177b, 178a, 475a
Emperor John VI Kantakouzenos and, 11:178a, 178b
evaluation of his reign, 11:178b
excommunicated by the patriarch of Constantinople, 11:475b
his mausoleum church near Prizren and, 11:187a-b
imperial ambitions of, 11:178b
Ochrid and, 9:208b
public law code, 11:475b, 670a, 670b
quarrel with Stefan Dečanski, 11:177b
title of *sebastokrator* and, 11:132a
Stefan Uroš V of Serbia, ruler, 11:177488b–177179b
disintegration of the Serbian empire and, 11:475b
Vukašin Mrnjavčeviç and, 11:179a-b
Stefan Vojislav of Duklja, ruler, 11:170b–171a
Stefan Vukčić Kosača, **11:476a**
conflict over succession, 2:339a
economic development, 2:339a-b
herceg title, 2:339a
invasion of Hum and Dubrovnik, 2:339b
Stefan Tomaš of Bosnia and, 11:474a
Turkish conflicts, 2:339b
Stefano di Giovanni. *See* Sassetta
Stefano Porcari, Rome and, 10:524b
Stefano Protonotaro da Messina, 6:624b–625a
Iacopo da Lentini and, 6:387b
"Pir meu cori allegrari," 11:259a
Stefano da Zevio, 5:628a
Steinbach church, 10:91b
Steinbach, Wendelin, *via moderna* and, 12:408a
Steingrímr Ǫrnólfsson (saga character), 10:343a
Steinhöwel, Heinrich
adaptation of Boccaccio story, 8:361a
fables and, 4:572b
Steinmar, **11:476b–477a**
Johannes Hadlaub and, 7:120b
Stelae
Armenian
T^calin, 11:582b
see also Xač^ck^car
in the Axum kingdom, 2:17b
of Ōjun, 9:224a (*illus.*)
Steli, 8:551b
Stella, 4:281a
Stella maris. See John of Garland
Stem family, 6:452a
Sten Sture, regent of Sweden, 11:533b
Step (unit of measure), 12:588a
Step^canos Asołik Tarōnec^ci, **11:477a-b**
on Gagik, I, 1:482a
Universal History, 1:510b, 6:240a
see also Łewond
Step^canos Orbēlean. *See* Orbēlean, Step^canos
Step^canos of Siwnik^c, bishop, 1:506a, 510a, 5:540b
Stepennaia kniga, 8:573a
Stephanius, Stephan Hansen, 11:522b
Stephanos II of Georgia, hypatos (consul), 12:222a
Stephanos of Baghdad, translation of Dioscorides herbals, 6:178b
Stephanos of Byzantium, *Ethnica,* 11:52b
Stephanos of Georgia, curopalate, 4:231b
Stephen IV, kat^cołikos, captured, 6:312a
Stephen I of Hungary, king, 5:422a, **11:477b–481a**
administrative reforms and, 11:478b–479a
canonization of, 11:480a-b
Christianity and, 8:443a-b
crowned king, 11:478a, 482a
family of, 11:477b
"mirror of princes" for his son, 11:480a
reign of, 6:339a
"royal" sword of, 11:484a
struggle with Koppány, 11:478a
subjugation of rivals, 11:478a-b
support for the church, 11:479a-b
Sylvester II and, 11:553a
Székesfehérvár and, 11:568b
two books of laws, 11:479b
see also Stephen, Crown of St.
Stephen II of Hungary, king, reign of, 6:340b
Stephen III of Hungary, king, reign of, 6:340b
Stephen IV of Hungary, pretender, 6:340b
Stephen V of Hungary, *junior rex,* 6:342b
Stephen III (the Great) of Moldavia, 10:510b, 515a
anti-Ottoman resistance, 12:503a-b
invasion of Ruthenia, 12:504a
Polish alliance, 12:503b–504a
vs. Bāyazīd II and, 2:137b
Walachian invasions, 12:503b
Stephen I, pope
assertion of Roman authority, 9:366b–367a
Cyprian and, 4:70a, 9:366b–367a
Novatian schism and, 9:366b
Stephen II, pope, **11:481a-b**
alliance of, with Carolingians, 8:377a
Gallican chant and, 5:343b
Pepin III and, 3:106b, 346a, 9:372b–373b, 460a, 501b–502a
travel by, 12:152a
visit to Francia (754), 9:501a
Stephen III, pope, vs. Roman nobles, 10:525a
Stephen IV, pope
coronation of Louis the Pious by, 9:374b
on Jews, 7:76a
Stephen IX, pope
"Ambrosian" choral song and, 2:181a
Humbert and, 6:329b–330a
Peter Damian and, 9:508b
Stephen of Alexandria, 1:614a, 9:99b, 697a, 11:54b–55a
Stephen of Antioch, translations by, 12:138b
Stephen of Autun, attribution of *Tractatus de sacramentis altaris,* 7:632a
Stephen bar Ṣūdhaili, 11:566a
Stephen of Blois, 1:253a
Stephen of Bourbon, 4:250a
Stephen of Cloyes, Children's Crusade and, 4:14b
Stephen, Crown of St., 4:437b, **11:482a–484a,** 11:568b
association with St. Stephen, 11:483a
dating of, 11:482b, 483a
description of, 11:482a–483a (*illus.*)
veneration of, 11:483a-b
see also Stephen I of Hungary, king
Stephen of England, king
anarchy under, 7:436b
civil war with Matilda (1135-1154), 3:498b, 4:463a, 7:535a, 9:166b
English church and, 2:151b
Henry II and, 9:167a
itinerant justices and, 7:183b
Roger of Salisbury and, 10:443b
Vacarius and, 12:343b
Stephen of Garlande
chancellorship and seneschalsy, 7:674a
royal appointments, 5:160a
Stephen Harding. *See* Harding, Stephen
Stephen of Kolín, Hus and, 6:364b–365a
Stephen of Lexington
abbacy of Clairvaux, founder of College of St. Bernard, 3:405a
abbacy of Savigny, 10:673a-b
Stephen of Liciac, 5:655a
Stephen of Liège, 6:381b
historia and, 6:380b
office of the Trinity and, 10:371b
Stephen of Muret, St., 3:354b
Order of Grandmont and, 5:654b
Stephen of Orléans. *See* Stephen of Tournai
Stephen of Páleč, 6:368a, 368b
Stanislav of Znojmo and, 6:367a
Stephen of Patras, archbishop, 7:381b
Stephen, patriarch, 7:545b
Stephen of Perm, St.
refutation of Strigolniki, 10:595b
Zyrian mission, 10:595a-b
Stephen, St. (first martyr), 12:238 (*illus.*)
translation of relics to Constantinople, 12:144 (*illus.*)
Stephen of Sawley
Threefold Exercise, 9:19a
translation of *Speculum novitii* into English, 9:26b
Stephen de Segrave, 7:200b
Stephen of Taron. *See* Step^canos Asołik Tarōnec^ci
Stephen of Tournai, **11:481b**
Decretum Gratiani and, 4:127b
on interdict, 6:495a-b
Stephen of Ulnia (Armenian martyr), 1:519b
Stepped cross, 4:9b, 10 (*illus.*)
Sterling. *See* Penny
Stern-post rudder. *See* Rudder
Sterzing (South Tirol), Vigil Raber's theatrical activities in, 10:244b–245a

Stethaimer, Hanns. *See* Burghausen, Hanns von
Steward
  estate, 4:514a, 4.514b
  royal, England, 6:301a, 304b
  see also Seneschal; *Wuzurg framadār*
Stews. *See* Fishponds
Stiacciato, **11:484a-b**
  Donatello's relief of St. George, 11:484b, 485 (*illus.*)
Sticharion. *See* Stikarion
Sticherarion, 8:554a, 11:484b
  Slavic music and, 8:556b, 574a, 574b
Sticheron, 6:378a-b, 379a, 7:613a, 8:554a, **11:484b**
Stichometry, **11:484b–485a**
Stick (unit of measure), 12:593b
Stickball, 5:348a
Stigand of Canterbury, archbishop
  deposed, 3:82b
  religious pluralism and, 4:459a
Stikarion, 3:615b, **11:485a-b**
Stiklestad, Battle of (1030), 2:254a-b, 9:224b, 11:317a
Stikluvik (a *rímur* meter), 10:405b
Stilicho, Flavius, vs. Visigoths, 1:122a, 12:470a
Stillinga Revolt, Saxon sympathies, 10:683b
Stilnovismo. See Dolce stil nuovo
Stilted arch. *See* Arch
Stilted dome, 4:236a
Štip, 11:474a
Stipes. See Altar
Stirling
  castle of, regained by Robert Bruce at the Battle of Bannockburn, 11:110a
  siege of (1339), 3:64b
Stirling Bridge, Battle of (1297), 11:109a
Stirrup
  effects
    on European cavalry, 3:201b–202a
    on Islamic cavalry, 3:208b–209a
Stjepan, (son of Svetoslav), 4:5b
Stjepan I of Croatia, king, 4:6a
Stjepan Držislav of Croatia, king, reign of, 4:5a
Stjepan Kotroman, 2:336a-b
Stjepan Kotromanić of Bosnia, ruler, 2:336b, **11:485b–486a,** 11:485b
  annexation of Hum, 11:177a
Stoclsturgan, 8:558b
Stock. *See* Animals, draft; Animals, food
Stockholm, vs. Christian II, 11:533b
Stockholm Bloodbath, 4:156a-b
Stockholm Papyrus, recipes for transmutation, 1:135b
Stockings, Western European, 3:625a
Stockton, Thomas, **11:486a-b**
  stone carvings in King's College Chapel, 11:486 (*illus.*)
Stoeffler, John, 3:465a
Stoglavyi sobor. See "Council of a Hundred Chapters" (1551)
Stoicism
  Christianity and, 7:360a
  ethical doctrine, 9:594a
  moral doctrine, 9:601a, 601b
  slavery and, 11:334a
Stojkovic, John, cardinal, 4:248a
Stoke, Battle of (1487), 12:572a
Stoke (unit of measure), 12:593b
Stokton, Dame Elizabeth, 4:603b
Stole, depicted in Landulf Pontifical, 12:402 (*illus.*)
Stollen, 8:413b
Stomachion. See Archimedes
Stone, **11:486b–487a**
  in building construction, 3:562a-b
  limestone as building material, 3:566b
Stone masonry. *See* Masons and builders
Stone-tossing games, 5:348a
Stoner, John, 7:189b–190b
Stonor Letters and Papers, 8:323a
Stora rimkrönikan, 7:220a-b, 11:22b
Storia de l'amat Frondino e de Brisona, 3:173a
Storia di Liombruno, 6:670a
Storia de Merlino, 6:638
Storta, 11:547b (*illus.*), 551a
Story of Bakhtiyār. See Bakhtiyār-nāma
Stoss, Veit, 9:730b, **11:487a-b**
  Rosary Annunciation, 11:487 (*illus.*)
Stourbridge, fairs, 4:587a
Stowe Missal, 7:614a–615b, 627a, 8:118a
  baptism in, 3:230b
  creed in, 3:676b
  litanies in, 7:591b, 592b
  mass in, 3:230a
  metalwork in, 3:221b–223a
Stowell, John, **11:487b–488a**
  remains of a reredos to the Virgin, 11:487b–488a (*illus.*)
Strabo
  Geographica, on the origin of the globe, 11:95b
  on water mills, 8:390a
Strabo (Greek geographer), on Armenian language, 1:506b
Stracimir (son of Tihomir of Serbia), 11:473a
Strambotto, 6:640b
  sonnet and, 6:669a, 11:260a
Stramps. See Jordi de S. Jordi
Strandar strengleikr, 11:492a
Strasbourg (Strassburg)
  burning of Jews of (1349), 2:263b
  commune of, 3:498a
Strasbourg Cathedral, **11:488a**
  astronomical clock at, 3:465a
  Benno of Osnabrück and, 2:182a
  Coronation Portal tympanum, 5:621b–622a
  Ecclesia and Synagoga at, 5:620b–621a
  jamb figures of, 5:622a
  Last Judgment at, 5:618a (*illus.*), 621a
  style of, 5:620b
  west facade of, 5:622b (*illus.*), 625a, 11:488b (*illus.*)
  see also Ulrich von Ensingen
Strasbourg Oaths, 5:221b, 6:434b, 436b, 621a, 622b, 9:233b, **11:488a–489a**
  in *Historiarum libri quattuor,* 9:143a
  use of French vernacular in, 5:220b–221a, 233b, 288a
  Vulgar Latin and, 7:350b
Strassburg, Battle of (357), 11:525b, 526a
Strassburg Bridge (1388), 10:416a
Strassburg Oaths. *See* Strasbourg Oaths
Strassburger Alexander, 7:323a
Strategemata. See Frontinus
Strategikon. See Kekaumenos
Strategos, **11:489a-b**
  Byzantine theme, authority of, 2:487b
  taxation and, 11:603a-b
  themes and, 12:9b, 10a
Strateia, 11:604a
Stratford, John, archbishop, 3:578b
  Edward III and, 6:334a
  quarrel with Edward III, 9:428a
Stratford-on-Avon, medieval streets in, 12:327b
Strathclyde, kingdom of, **11:489b–491b**
  conversion to Christianity, 11:490a
  first mention of, 11:489b
  kings of, 11:490a
  Malcolm II of Scotland and, 8:56a
  relations to the Romans, 11:489b
  under Kentigern, 7:231a
  Viking raids, 11:490a-b
Stratiotai, **11:491a-b**
  see also Limitanei
Stratiotika Ktemata. *See* Soldiers' Portions
Stratiotikon, taxation and, 11:603b
Stratophilos, bishop, 2:253b
Straubing, founded, 2:135a
Straubing family, 2:135a
Streit der vier Töchter Gottes, Der, 5:430a
Strengleikar, 10:390b, 391a, 392a, 394a, **11:491b–492b,** 12:203b
  Icelandic redaction of, 10:392b–393a
  three groups of lays, 11:491b–492a
  see also Marie de France
Stress (phonetics). *See* Ictus
Strez, 2:409a
Stříbro, Jakoubek, communion under both kinds and, 3:504b–505a
Stricker, Der, 8:353a, 355a, **11:492b–494a**
  assumptions about his life, 11:492b
  Daniel von dem blühenden Tal, 5:454b–455a, 9:707a–708a, 11:493a
  didactic and religious poems, 8:131a-b, 11:493b
  Frauenehr, 8:409a
  influence of on Seifrid Helbling, 11:142a
  Karl, Rolandslied and, 10:448a
  Karl der Grosse, 11:493a
  Mären, 8:131a, 11:493a-b
Stringcourse, **11:494a-b**
  on the Château de Vincennes, 11:494b (*illus.*)
Strochnoe penie, 8:575b
Strode, Ralph, vs. Wyclif, 12:709b
Strofische Gedichte. See Hadewijch of Antwerp
Stroma magistri Rolandi, 4:127b
Strongbow (Richard Fitzgilbert de Clare). *See* Clare, Richard Fitzgilbert de
Strophes
  in didactic poetry, 5:442b–443a

Strophes (*cont.*)
in German lyric literature, 5:433b, 435b, 436b–438a
in *kanon,* 7:208b
Strophicus, 8:620 (*illus.*)
Strophische gedichten. See Hadewijch of Antwerp
Strumica, 11:474b
Strzelno, architecture, 9:723b
Strzempiński, Thomas, 9:729b
Stucco, in Islamic architecture, 6:598b, 599a, 599b, 602a, 606a, 607a
Studenica, church at, 4:347a
Studenica Monastery, 11:173b, 174a, 183b–184a
Stefan Nemanja and, 11:473b
Students
distribution of, 3:59b–60a
taverns and, 6:476a
Studia humanitatis. See Humanism; Philosophy and theology
Studia linguarum. See Schools, monastic, missionary
Studios (monastery: Constantinople), 3:556b, **11:494b–495a**
biblical exegesis at, 2:214b
compilation of triodion at, 7:612a
destruction of during the Latin occupation (1204-1261), 11:495a
liturgy in, 7:611a
rule adopted by Pěcherskaya Lavra, 12:19b
see also Theodore of Studios
Studium Generale. *See* Universities
Stuhlweissenburg. *See* Székesfehérvár
Stúñiga, Cancionero de. See Cancionero de Stúñiga
Sture chronicles, 7:220a-b
Sturla of Hvammr, in *Sturlunga saga,* 11:498b, 499a
Sturla Sighvatsson, 11:499a-b
Sturla Þórðarson, 5:673a, 11:354b, 355b, **11:495a–496a**
assumption of the office of *lögmaðr,* 11:495b–496a
friendship with Magnús of Norway, 11:495b, 500b
Hákonar saga Hákonarsonar, **6:75a-b,** 9:177b, 11:495b, 500a
attitude toward writing, 6:75a-b
historical sources, 6:75
kings' saga composition, 6:75b
preservation in manuscripts, 6:75a
Hákonarkviða, 7:312a
Íslendinga saga, 11:497a, 497b–498a, 499a–500a
biography of Guðmundr Arason in, 6:33b
Kristni saga and, 7:303a
Landnámabók, 11:496a
anecdote from *Hálfs saga ok Hálfsrekka,* 6:79a
reference to *Harðar saga Grímkelssonar,* 6:101a
revision of older work, 6:27a
later life, 11:500b
Magnúss saga lagabœtis, 11:495b
opposition to King Hákon of Norway, 11:495b
as possible author of *Laxdœla saga,* 7:528b
Sturlubók, 7:327b, 328a, 11:496a
Svafdœla saga and, 11:521a
Vatnsdœla saga and, 12:363b
Sturlaugs saga Starfsama, **11:496a–497a**
Sturlu saga, in *Sturlunga saga,* 11:498b
Sturlu þáttr, in *Sturlunga saga,* 11:500b
Sturlubók. See Sturla Þórðarson
Sturlunga saga, **11:497a–501a**
ballads in, 11:4a
biographies of Guðmundr Arason, 6:33b
contents of, 11:498b–500b
editions of, 11:498a, 498b
Icelandic history and, 4:614b
manuscript sources, 11:498a
reference to *Hákonar saga* in, 6:75a
Snorri Sturluson in, 11:355b
Sturlungs, 11:497a
in Sturla Þórðarson's *Sturlunga saga,* 11:495b
Sturmi of Fulda, abbot, 5:311b
life of written by Eigel, 4:408b
Sturmsense, 7:324 (*illus.*)
Stuðlafall (a *rímur* meter), 10:405b
"Style 1200," in manuscript illumination, 8:109a
Stylianos Zaützes, 7:545b
Stylites, 8:461a
ascetic practices, 8:456b
Stylus, **11:501a,** 12:699b, 701 (*illus.*)
Styria
Albert of Habsburg and, 11:540b
Hugo von Montfort and, 6:325a
steelmaking in, 11:471b
taken by Přemysl Otokar II of Bohemia (1260), 2:300a
see also Austria; Babenberg family
Styrmir Kárason, 9:176b, 224b
authorship of *Harðar saga Grímkelssonar,* 6:101b
Styrmisbok, Landnámabók and, 7:328a
Styrmisbók. See Styrmir Kárason
Suan pan. *See* Abacus
Suárez, Francisco, 10:7a, 11:56b
Subdeacon, 3:441a, 442a
Ṣubḥ al-aᶜshāᵓ. See Qalqashandī, al-
Šubiçi of Bribir, Stjepan Kotromanić and, 11:485b
Subiecti, 10:461a
Sublime Porte, 9:307b
Sübödai
Bulgar conquests, 8:470a
invasion of Georgia, 8:468a
pursuit of Khwārizmshāh Muḥammad, 8:467b
Subordinationism, proponents of, 9:560a
Subotai. *See* Sübüdey
Subsistence theory, 3:323a-b
Substances, Book of. See Israeli, Isaac
Substantia. See Trinitarian doctrine
Substitution (law), 6:459b–460a
Subtile (ship), 11:235b
Sübüdey, Mongolian general, 2:131b
Succession, political. *See* Kingship; Warfare
Successive counterpoint, 1:551b
Suceava, sacked by Turks, 10:515a
Suchenwirt, Peter
collected works of, 8:358a
Ehrenreden, 8:357b
heraldic poetry of, 8:412a
Suckenies, 3:624b
Suda, 4:447a, 11:53b, **11:501a–502a**
errors and distortions in, 11:501b–502a
sources of, 11:501b
Sudak, fur trade in, 5:332a
Sudan. *See* Nubia
Sudavians. *See* Sudovians
Sudbury, Simon, archbishop of Canterbury, Peasants' Revolt of 1381 and, 9:479b
Sudebnik, 7:507a-b, 11:191b
civil law in, 7:512a
criminal law in, 7:511a-b
Südeli ballads, *Kudrun* and, 7:305a
Süder-Brarup ferrule, runic inscription on, 8:327a
Sudovians, 2:63 (map), 67a
subjugated by Yaroslav the Wise, 2:64b
Suebi. *See* Sueves
Suetonius
influence on French biography, 2:236a
Prata, 6:564a
as probable author of *Life of Vergil,* 12:393b
Sueves, 2:91b, 11:525b
Arianism and, 1:454b
in Iberian Peninsula, 10:36a-b, 12:471a
independent state of, 2:92a
Vandals and, 12:354b
vs. Roman Empire, 12:470a
in Spain, 12:470b
Suevi. *See* Sueves
Ṣuffa, **11:502a**
"Sufficient reason," principle of. *See* Reductionism
Suffield, Walter, bishop of Norwich, 11:607b
Suffolk, duke of
Cade's rebellion and, 3:5a-b
murder of (1450), 9:451a
Suffrage
citizenship and limited, 10:328b
French
bailiwick assemblies and, 10:327b
monarchy and, 10:316b, 327b
representative assemblies and, 10:317b
indirect, by head vs. by order, 10:325a
property qualifications, 10:328b
universal, 10:328b
see also Poll tax; Representative assemblies
Suffrage (congregational), 6:447b
"Suffrages," in the books of hours, 10:377a
Sufism, 6:584b–586a, 9:572a
ascetic nature, 6:80a-b
in Bursa mosque, 6:612b
derivation of name, 6:584b, 9:38b
doctrine of resurrection and, 10:340b
fraternities, 9:44a-b
ghazal and, 6:508a
of al-Ghazālī, 5:515b–517a
ghāzī and, 5:518a-b
on Iblīs, 6:390b–391a
influence of

on cabala, 3:2b
on Druzism, 9:3b
on Islamic society, 4:163a
in Islamic theology, 9:572a
khānqāh and, 7:238a-b
on al-Mahdi, 8:388b
metaphysics of, 6:585a
motif of metamorphosis in, 8:22a
music and, 8:560b
mysticism, ^{c}*ulamā*$^{\supset}$ and, 12:244b
Nizārīs and, 6:588b
origins of, 6:584b
popularity of "letter magic" in, 8:21b
relations with ^{c}*ulamā*$^{\supset}$, 6:54b
spread of, 9:44b–45a
under the late Timurids, 12:59a
zāwiya, 6:54b–55a
Zaydis and, 12:742a
see also Jīlānī, ^{c}Abd al-Qādir al-; Mysticism, Islamic
Ṣufrīya, 11:139a
Suftaja (Islamic letter of credit), 2:79b, 12:106a
Sufyān ibn ^{c}Uyayna, 11:511b, 513b
Sufyān al-Thawrī, *ḥikma* and, 11:511a
Sugar, 1:87b
sugarcane, 1:81b
Sugar industry
crushing mills, 11:637b
on Cyprus, 4:72a
on Madeira, 4:559a, 8:10b
refining, 11:639b
Suger of St. Denis, 1:426a, 427b, 2:173b, 175a, 4:346a, **11:502b–504b**
abbey church of St. Denis, 10:616b
as art collector and patron, 1:335b
assumption of regency, 5:160a-b
biography of, 11:502b, 504a
career of, 9:402b–403a
elected abbot of St. Denis, 11:503a
on Gothic architecture, 5:584a–585a, 586a
Historia gloriosi regis Ludovici septimi, 11:504a
kingship theories of, 7:264a
Libellus alter de consecratione ecclesiae Sancti Dionysii, 10:490b, 11:503b
Liber de rebus in administratione sua gestis, 10:490b, 11:503a
Life of Louis VI, 2:236b
Louis VI and, 11:502b–503a, 504a
missions to the papal court, 11:502b–503a
named regent of France, 11:504a
Ordinatio, 10:490b
on stained glass, 5:548b–549a, 551a, 552b
theory of feudal hierarchy, 5:160b–161a
Vita Ludovici Grossi, 2:239b, 11:504a
Suhrawardī al-Maḳtūl, al-
on angels, 1:249a
illuminationism, Sufi influence, 9:572a
Suibhne Geilt, 6:528b–529a, 540b
Suicide
by Lithuanians at Pilėnai (1336), 7:609a-b
of the insane, 6:491a
Suidas, *Lexikon,* 7:564a
Suit of armor. *See* Arms and armor
Suite du Merlin. See Robert de Boron
Suk^{c}ias (Armenian saint), 1:519b
Sulayhids
control of Ṣan^{c}a, 10:647a
founded, 6:617a
under as-Sayyida Arwā, 1:375a-b
Sulaym al-Aswānī, Ibn, Nubia and, 9:198a, 199b
Sulaymān. *See* Imru$^{\supset}$ al-Qays
Sulaymān II, Seljuk sultan, 11:157a
Sulaymān ibn ^{c}Abd al-Malik, Umayyad caliph
dress of, 3:616b
successors of, 3:39a
Sulaymān ibn Qutlumush, 11:153a, 154a, 156b
defeated by Tutush, 11:155a
Sulaymān al-Mahrī (Muslim captain), 5:394a, 9:87a
Sulaymanids, in Algeria, 6:413a
Suleiman. *See* Süleyman
Suleiman (Indian ocean merchant), 11:249a
Süleyman I (the Magnificent), Ottoman sultan, 11:145b
as caliph of all Muslims, 9:309a
construction program in Jerusalem, 7:61a
Hungary and, 6:349b, 350a
Knights of St. John and, 3:304a
Moldavian protectorate, 12:504a
occupation of Baghdad, 6:514b
tomb of, 7:112a
Xlat^{c} and, 12:713b
Süleyman, ruler of Rumelia (son of Bāyazīd I), Stefan Lazareviç of Serbia and, 11:472b, 473a
Süleyman, Seljuk ruler, Ikonion and, 6:418a
Süleymanname, 8:117b
Sulien, Welsh scribe, 3:224a-b
Sulpicius Severus
letters from St. Paulinus of Nola, 9:471a
Life of St. Martin, 2:236a, 6:261b
Paulinus of Périgueux and, 7:361b, 9:472a
Sultan, **11:504b–505a**
later Timurids and, 12:58b
Mamluk, 8:71a-b
Marinid, administration, 8:139a
Sultan, Ottoman
divine will, 9:307b
kapikulu, 9:307b
military command, 9:307b
religious appointments, 9:310a
succession plan, 9:307b–308a
Sultan al-Rūm, 9:308b
Sulṭāniyya
architecture of, 6:604a
established as Ilkhanid capital, 12:247a
Sulṭānshāh, Seljuk ruler of Syria, 11:155a
Sumak. See Rugs and carpets
Sumer Is Icumen In, 8:336a-b, 340a, 589 (*illus.*), 590a, **11:505a–506b**
harmonic substructure of, 11:505 (*illus.*)
musical genre, 10:536b
Summa. See Lambert of Auxerre
Summa. See Odington, Walter
Summa de arte praedicatoria. See Alan of Lille
Summa artis grammaticae. See Huguccio
Summa artis notariae. See Passaggerii, Rolandino
Summa artis rithimici vulgaris dictaminis. See Antonio da Tempo
Summa aurea. See Hostiensis; William of Auxerre
Summa de bono. See Philip the Chancellor
Summa Britonis. See Brito, William
Summa de casibus. See Raymond of Peñafort, St.
Summa de casibus poenitentiae. See Peraldus, William
Summa on the Cathars and the Poor of Lyons. See Rainier Sacconi
Summa codicis. See Placentinus; Rogerius
Summa Codicis Trecensis. See Ablaing, Willem Matthias d'
Summa de coloribus rhetoricis. See Geoffrey of Vinsauf
Summa contra gentiles. See Aquinas, Thomas, St.
Summa cum essem Mantuae. See Placentinus
Summa "Cum multae essent partes iuris." See Rogerius
Summa decretorum. See Huguccio; Rufinus
Summa dictaminis. See Bernard of Meun; Pons of Provence
Summa duacensis. See Philip the Chancellor
Summa de ecclesia. See Torquemada, Juan de
Summa de ecclesiastica potestate. See Augustinus Triumphus
Summa de electione. See Bernard of Pavia
Summa Fratris Alexandri
character of sacraments, 9:603a
existence of God, 9:598a
moral doctrine, 9:601a
Summa de legibus, 4:68b–69a
see also Custumals of Normandy
Summa logicae. See Ockham, William of
Summa magna. See Hengham, Ralph
Summa moralis. See Antoninus of Florence
Summa parva. See Hengham, Ralph
Summa de poenitentia. See Raymond of Peñafort, St.
Summa praedicantium. See Bromyard, John
Summa in quaestionibus armenorum. See Fitzralph, Richard
Summa quaestionum theologicarum. See Philip the Chancellor
Summa recreatorum, 1:320a, 7:370b
Summa de sacramentis. See Peter the Chanter
Summa sententiarum
influence of on Peter Lombard, 9:517a

Summa sententiarum (*cont.*)
- major and minor sacraments, 9:602b

Summa de speculatione musicae. See Odington, Walter
Summa de sponsalibus et matrimonio. See Tancred (canonist)
Summa theologiae. See Aquinas, Thomas, St.
Summa trium librorum. See Placentinus
Summae confessorum. See Confession; Penance; Religious instruction
Summaria brevis et compendiosa doctrina.... See Pierre Dubois
Summarium libroum Platonis. See De Platonis pluribus libris compendiosa expositio
Summerhart, Conrad, *via moderna* and, 12:408b
Summulae logicales. See Peter of Spain
Summule dialectices. See Bacon, Roger
Sumptuary laws
- European, **11:506b–507b**
  - in the aftermath of Black Death, 2:266a
  - for clothing, 3:622a
  - in Florence, 2:285b
  - foods and, 3:583a
  - late medieval dislocations and, 11:507a
  - three major explanations for, 11:506b
- Islamic, **11:507b–509a**
  - for Muslims, 11:507b–508a
  - for non-Muslims, 11:508a–509a
- ownership of vehicles and, 12:376a

Sumula sumulorum magistri Johannis Wiclif. See Wyclif, John
Sunday of Orthodoxy, 12:12b
Sünden Widerstreit, Der, 5:430a
Sundgau. *See* Alsace
Sundials, 3:28a-b, **11:509a–510a**
- Anglo-Saxon, 3:28b
- on church walls, 3:28b
- Islamic, 3:457a-b, 11:86b
- portable, 3:28b
- quadrant, 10:236b–237a
- Western, 3:457b

Sung Empire, Mongol invasions, 8:470a
Sunifred II of Catalonia, 3:175a
Sunifred of Carcassonne, 3:174b
Sunitai. *See* Siwnikʿ
Sunjata, king. *See* Mārī Jāṭa
Sunna, **11:510a–513a**
- Almoravids and, 11:140a-b
- *as-sunna* and, 11:510b–511a, 511b
- Bishr ibn al-Ḥārith on, 11:512a
- Druzes and, 9:3a
- during *Jāhilīya,* 11:510a
- during "rightly guided" caliphate, 11:510b
- *ḥadīth* and, 11:511a
- *ḥikma* and, 11:511a, 511b
- Islamic creeds and, 11:511b–512a
- Islamic law and, 6:46b, 11:219a
- Mālik ibn Anas and, 8:58a–59b
- Muʿtazilite inquisition and, 11:511b, 512a
- origin of, 6:579b, 580a
- of the Prophet
  - and arrangement of *ḥadīth* collections, 6:48a
  - 9th century, 6:47a
- *see also* Sects, Islamic

Sunni law. *See* Islamic law
Sunnites, **11:513a–514a**
- alienation by al-Ḥākim, 6:74a
- appellatives for, 11:513a-b
- Arabian dynasties
  - Ayyubids, 1:375b
  - Mamluks, 1:376a
  - Rasulids, 1:375b–376a
- in Bukhara, 2:397a
- al-Bukhārī and, 2:397b–399a
- Buyids and, 2:436a-b
- in Cairo, 3:14b
- in Damascus, 4:82a, 84b, 85a
- geographical distribution of, 11:514a
- in Iran, 6:503a, 503b
- in Isfahan, 6:562a
- jihad and, 7:110b
- on millennialism, 8:388a-b
- origins of, 6:583b
- as political partisans, 11:513a
- political theory, 10:12b, 242a
- Shīʿa and, 6:205b
- theology of, 9:568b–569a
- traditionalist interpretation of Koran, 9:568b
- vs. Shiites, in Iraq, 6:514a
- *see also* Fatimids

Ṣunūj al-ṣufr, 8:563a
Sunyer of Catalonia (911–947), 3:175a
Supʿan. *See* Sophanenē
Super illius specula. See John XXII, pope
Super magistrum sententiarum. See Peckham, John
Supererogation. *See* Treasury of merits
Supererogatory Offices, 4:230b
Superstition, 8:25b
- in the Byzantine Empire, 8:18b
- in the countryside, 8:26b
- *see also* Witchcraft

Suppedaneum cross, 4:9b, 10 (*illus.*)
Supplemented Gregorian Sacramentary, Gallican orders, 9:265a
Supplication (or Lament) of Daniel the Exile, 11:347a
Supplices, 8:193a
Support of the Faith. See Moses ha-Cohen of Tordesillas
Supra quae, 8:193a
Suq, **11:514a-b**
Sura, Jewish academies in, 11:583b
Suras, of Koran, 7:294b–295b
Surcoat, 1:524a, 525a
Sūrēn house, 5:665a
Surexit memorandum, 12:599b
Surgant, Johann Ulrich, *Manuale curatorum,* 1:556b
Surgery
- at the Italian universities, 8:251a
- at the School of Salerno, 8:249b (*illus.*)
- chair of, at the University of Pisa, 2:100b
- as a lower-class profession, 2:98b
- textbooks on, 8:260a
- in treatment of insanity, 6:491b
- *see also* Barber-surgeons

Surgery. See Hugh of Lucca
Surhan-David (*d.* 701), 1:519a
Sūrī, Ibn al-, illustrations of plant growth in work, 6:185b
Surnāy, 8:563a, 612a
Surplice. *See* Vestments, liturgical
Surtees Psalter, 4:547a
Surtr, 11:32b, 33a, **11:514b–515a**
- *see also* Scandinavian mythology

Survey of the Times. See Jordanes, *De summa temporum*
Surveying, **11:515a-b**
- irrigation and, 6:558a

Surveyor's transit, 11:515b
Surveys
- as demographic evidence, 4:137a–139b
- in estate management, 4:137b, 512a, 513b
- fiscal, 4:137b–138b
- manorial, 4:137b
- of Russian peasants, 11:196b

Sūrya Siddhānta, on the construction of a celestial globe, 11:95b
Sūsa, in Islamic conquests, 6:569a
Šušanik, St., 1:518b, 5:413a
- Christianity vs. Zoroastrianism in Georgia and, 8:298b

Susanna. See Peter Riga
Susannah (*The Pistel of Swete Susan*), 2:221b
Suscipe sancta Trinitas, 8:191a
Suso, Heinrich, **11:516a–517a**
- *Briefbüchlein,* 11:516b
- *Büchlein der Ewigen Weisheit,* 11:516b
- *Büchlein der Wahrheit,* 11:516b
- conversion of, 11:516a
- as Dominican, 3:368b
- *Grosses Briefbuch,* 11:516b
- *Horologium sapientiae* (*Clock of Wisdom*), 3:462b, 11:516b
- influence of on Michel Beheim, 8:306b
- influenced by Neoplatonism, 9:100b
- language of, 9:35b
- *Life,* 8:356a, 9:34b–35a, 11:516b
- *Little Book of Eternal Wisdom,* 4:248b, 9:35a
- Meister Eckhart and, 9:32a
- mysticism of, 4:248b, 11:516b–517a
- Tauler and, 11:602a
- women mystics and, 9:12b, 13a, 13b
- works of, 9:34b–35b, 11:516a-b
  - in English, 9:27a

"Suspended odes." *See* Imruʾ al-Qays
Sussex, settlement of in 6th century, 4:454a
Susteren (church: Limburg), 10:95a
Sutri, Concordat of (1111), Bruno of Segni's criticism of, 2:392a
"Sutri song." *See* Wipo of Burgundy, *Rhitmus ad Henricum*
Sutri, Synod of (1046), **11:517a–518b**
Sutton Hoo, 1:274a, 8:292a, **11:519a–520a**
- Anglo-Saxon gold belt buckle, 8:366b–367a
- *Beowulf* and, 2:184b
- body of, 11:519a, 520a
- Byzantine silver plate in, 12:101a
- coins of, 11:520a

decorative chainwork (7th century), 8:294b
Germanic jewelry, 8:366b
hanging bowls, 3:219b, 6:90a, 8:369b
lacertine ornament and, 7:314a
purselid, 8:366 (*illus.*), 367a
ship of, 11:519a
see also Lindisfarne Gospels
Sutton, Robert, **11:518b**
Thomas Prentys and, 10:89a
Sutton, Thomas, 12:39a
Correctoria corruptorii Thomae and, 12:41a, 41b
Ṣuwar al-kawākib. See ᶜAbd al-Raḥmān al-Ṣūfī
Suyūṭī, al-, **11:520a–521a**
controversiality of, 11:520b
on *taylasān,* 11:630a
works of, 11:520b, 521a
Suzdal
mint at, 8:426b
political growth of, 7:249a-b
population, 11:190b
Yuri Dolgorukii and, 12:486b
Suzdalia. *See* Vladimir-Suzdal
Suzerain, 9:726a, 728a
see also Kingship
Svan language, 5:404a-b
Svans, 5:404a-b, 419a
Svarfdœla saga, 4:613b, **11:521a-b**
Amlóða saga and, 11:521b
Landnámabók and, 11:521a
Svatopluk of Great Moravia, prince, 2:299b
arrest of Methodios, 4:73b
death of, 6:338a
reign of, 5:658a-b
Svatý Václave, 11:343b
Svear, 12:247b
Sven Aggesen, 11:328b, **11:522a–523a**
Brevis historia regum Dacie, 11:522b
as source for *Gesta Decorum,* 10:677a
on Sven Estridsen's sons, 10:676a, 678b
Lex castrensis, 11:522a
Svend. *See* Sweyn
Sventopolk of Moravia, prince. *See* Svatopluk of Great Moravia, prince
Sverre Sigurdsson of Norway, king
Karl Jónsson and, 9:176a, 176b
Norwegian unification and, 9:182b, 183b
skalds for, 11:316b
Sverrir of Norway, king. *See* Sverre Sigurdsson of Norway, king
Sverris saga, 9:177b, **11:523a-b**
Sveti Cχoveli, 8:239a, **11:523b–524a**
Sveti Ivan Aliturgitos (church: Nesebūr), 2:416 (*illus.*), 417a
Svetoslav of Croatia, king, reign of, 4:5a-b
Sviatoslav. *See* Svyatoslav
Svínfellinga saga, in *Sturlunga saga,* 11:500a
Svipdagsmál, **11:524a–525a**
in "Eddic appendix," 4:387b
Skírnismál and, 11:327a
sources, 11:524b–525a
Svjatoslav. *See* Svyatoslav
Svyatapolk II of Kiev, grand prince, Novgorod and, 9:193b
Svyatopolk I of Kiev, grand prince, vs. Yaroslav, 12:720a
Svyatopolk II of Kiev, grand prince, 12:486a
Svyatoslav I of Kiev, grand prince, 12:485b
in Bulgaria, 2:406a
destruction of Khazar capital, Itil, 12:436a
peace treaty with John I Tzimiskes, 12:435b
reign of, 7:247b–248a
vs. Khazaria, 7:241b–242a
Swabia, **11:525a–528b**, 11:525 (map)
Alamanni and, 11:525a–526b
church in, Henry I and, 11:527a
duchies of, 5:510a
fragmentation of, 11:528a
geography, 11:525a-b
as German dependency, 11:527b–528a
Habsburgs and, 6:42b, 11:528a
Hohenstaufen dynasty and, 5:510a, 11:527b–528a, 538b
in Holy Roman Empire, 11:538a
investiture controversy, 6:272b
poets from, and Henry VII, 5:435a
under Carolingians, 11:526b
under Frederick of Büren, 11:538b
under Rheinfeldens, 11:527a-b, 538a-b
under Saxons, 11:527a
under Zähringens, 11:527b, 538b
vs. Magyars, 11:526b, 527a
Welfs and, 5:510a
Swabian League, 5:464a, 490b
defeat of, 5:501b
formation of, 5:498a
princes in, 5:503b
"Swabian School," Middle High German literature and, 8:352a-b
Swabian Society of the Shield of St. George, 5:498a
Swabian-Rhenish League, 5:464a-b
collapse of, 5:467b
Swamps, uses of. *See* Reclamation of land
Swan, in medieval folklore, 2:206b
Swarog (Swarożyc) cult, 9:717b
Swastika. *See* Gammadion
Sweating sickness. *See* Disease; Malaria; Plagues
Sweden, **11:528b–534b**
administration of, 12th century, 11:530b
Christianity in, 8:442a
civil wars
12th century, 11:530b–531a
14th century, 11:532a
15th century, 11:533b
early historians on, 11:528b
economy, 11:532b, 533a
gold collars from, 10:694b
Gotland, 5:631b–633a
history (400–800), 10:692b–695b
archaeological evidence, 10:692b–694b, 695a-b
similarities to Denmark, 10:695b
language, runic alphabet, 10:558b, 563a, 565b–566a
north European trade and, 9:88b
political and legal organization, 10:698b–699a
relations with
Denmark, 4:156a-b
Finland, 11:531a
Norway, 9:185a
Novgorod, 11:531a, 531b, 532a
Snorri Sturluson's trip to, 11:356b
steelmaking in, 11:471b
tenurial development, 11:685a
transportation, 11:530a, 531b
under Mecklenburg, 11:532b
in Viking Age, 11:529b–530b
vs. Denmark
Erik the Victorious and, 11:530a
Olof and, 11:530b
vs. Karelia, 11:531a, 531b, 532a
see also Birgitta, St; Birka; Scandinavia; Scandinavian literature; Vikings
Swedes
in Russia, 12:434a–436a
see also Varangians
Swedish church
Birger Magnusson and, 11:532a
nobility and, 11:531b
Swedish language, of Uppsala and Stockholm, 6:437a
Swedish law, **7:524b–526b**
in Birka Island, 7:525b
in central and northern provinces, 7:525a
Eskil Magnusson, 7:524b
epsørisbrot and, 7:525b
in Götaland, 7:524b–525a
in Gotland Island, 7:525a-b
lawman's role and qualifications, 7:524b
literary style of, 7:526a
Snorri Sturluson's account of, 7:524b
in Uppland, 7:524b
see also Scandinavia, political and legal organization
Sweyn I Forkbeard of Denmark, king
conquests of, 11:530a-b
English campaigns, 3:82a, 4:151b
seizure of English crown, 12:434a
Sweyn II Estridsen of Denmark, king, 4:152b, 153a
on discovery of Vinland, 12:428a
Sweyn III of Denmark, king, 4:153a
Sweynheym, Conrad, 10:124b
Swidden agriculture. *See* Reclamation of land
Swineshead, **11:534b–536a**
identity of, 11:534b, 535a
as logician, 11:535a-b
as physicist, 11:535b
see also John de Swyneshed; Roger de Swyneshed
Swineshead, Richard, 1:464b
Book of Calculations, 9:626a-b, 11:534a, 535a, 535b
intensities of qualities, 9:627a-b
nominalism and, 12:44a
Świnka, Jakub, archbishop, 9:721a
Swiss, as innkeepers, 6:473b
Swiss Confederation, 11:536a
Basel and, 11:542b, 545b
common domain territories, 11:544b

Swiss Confederation (*cont.*)
development of, 11:543b–544b
Geneva and, 11:542b
Habsburgs and, 11:528a, 544a
internal conflicts of, 11:544b, 545a
territorial expansion of, 11:545b
vs. Burgundy, 11:544b–545a
vs. Maximilian I, 11:545a-b
Waldstätte and, 11:540b, 541b
see also Switzerland
Swiss halberd. *See* Halberd
Swithin, St., in literature, 7:363a
Switzerland, **11:536a–546a**, 11:537 (map)
Alamanni and, 1:117b
Burgundian Wars, 12:565b–566a
cities of, 11:542b–543b
Charles the Bold and, 11:545a
drama in, 4:269a
French-speaking
Berchtold of Zähringen and, 11:539a
Charles the Bold and, 11:545a
Peter of Savoy and, 11:539b
Rudolph of Auxerre and, 11:537b
Savoy and, 11:545b
gaus organization of, 11:537b
geography, 11:536a-b
glassmaking in, 5:557a–558a
lay seignories of, 11:538a-b
military organization, 12:565b–566a
Mitteland, 11:536b
Oberland, 11:543b
population, 11:542b
surviving medieval bridges in, 10:418b
territorial expansion of, 11:545b
unification of Schwyz, Uri, Unterwalden (1291), 2:7b–8a
Waldstätte, 11:540b–542a
administration, 11:540b
Bern and, 11:543a, 543b
cities of, 11:544a
geography, 11:540b
Habsburgs and, 11:541a–542a
Lucerne and, 11:542b, 543b
Swiss Confederation and, 11:540b, 541b
Zurich and, 11:543a, 543b
Zähringen dynasty, 11:538b–539b
see also Swabia; Swiss Confederation
Sword, 1:522b
Sword belt, 1:528a
dupsing, 11:549b
Swordbearers, Order of
defeated at Šiauliai (1236), 6:604b
founding of, 7:604a
subordination to Teutonic Knights, 7:604b
vs. Nevsky, 9:111a
Swords, 8:293b–294a, **11:546a–552a**, 11:547 (*illus.*)
belts, 11:549b
Bidenhander, 11:547 (*illus.*), 549b
blades, 11:548b
Byzantine, 11:548b
Celtic, 11:546b
claymore, 11:547 (*illus.*), 549b, 551a
cruciform, 11:549a
in early medieval trade, 12:110a
executioners', 11:551a
for fencing, 5:348b
grips, 11:549a-b
"half-and-a-half," 11:547 (*illus.*), 549b
hilts, 11:548b
hunting, 11:547 (*illus.*), 551a
long cutting sword, 12:564b
magical, 8:291b
manufacture of, 11:546b, 548a
pattern-welded, 11:546b
pommels, 11:548a-b
"Brazil nut," 11:547 (*illus.*), 548a, 548b
quillons, 11:549a
Roman, 11:546a-b
Sasanian, 11:547 (*illus.*), 548b
scabbards, 11:549b
Schweinschwert, 11:547 (*illus.*), 551a
steelmaking and, 11:471a
tuck, 11:549b
Turkish, 3:54 (*illus.*)
types of, 11:547 (*illus.*)
Viking, 11:547 (*illus.*), 548a, 548b
see also Daggers; Excalibur; Rapiers
Swyneshed. *See* Swineshead
Swynford, Katherine, 3:281b, 7:135a-b
Syagrius (Roman governor), 2:94a
defeated by Clovis (486), 8:277b, 278a
"Sybil of the Rhine." *See* Hildegard of Bingen
Syfer, Hans, **11:552a-b**
Sykai. *See* Pera-Galata
Syllimanus, Martinus, 7:118a
Sylvester I, pope
in Donation of Constantine, 4:258a, 258b
legend of, in *Kaiserchronik,* 7:205b
Sylvester II, pope, 1:611a, **11:552b–553a**
abacus, 8:209a
apices, 8:207a
Arabic numerals and, 1:388b, 390a, 390b, 395b, 10:472b
Berno and, 8:641b
Christianization of Poland and Hungary, 9:302a-b
church reform of, 3:347b, 9:376a
De rationali et de ratione uti, on philosophical dualism, 4:298a
development of medicine and, 8:255a
dialectic and, 4:169b
humble origins of, 3:417b
influence on Otto III, 9:302a
legends about magical performances of, 8:35b
music theory and, 8:640a
Otto III and, 10:522b
policies of, 11:553a
pupils of, 11:552b
Regulae de numerorum abaci rationibus, 8:207b
as scholar, 7:363b
scientific instruments and, 11:552b, 553a
Sententiae astrolabi de Gerbert, drawing of a polar sighting tube, 11:99b–100b
Stephen I of Hungary and, 11:478a, 482a
studies in Spain, 7:561b
on trade in silk and spices, 12:109b
year 1000 and, 6:339a-b
Sylvester III, antipope
Crescenzi family and, 11:517b
Synod of Sutri and, 11:517a
Sylvester de la Guerche, bishop of Rennes, Robert d'Arbrissel and, 10:429a
Sylvester, St. *See* Sylvester I, pope
Symbatios, *protospatharios,* 2:125a
Symbolism
cabalistic, literature of, 3:2b
numerical. *See* Number symbolism
Symbolum electorum. See Gerald of Wales
Symeon of Bulgaria, tsar, **11:554b–555a**
Alexander and, 2:404b
cultural activities of, 11:554b
military campaigns of, 2:405a, 11:554b–555a
monasticism under, 2:404a-b
Nikolaos I Mystikos and, 9:135b
raids on Thessaloniki and, 12:26b
rise of, 2:404a
Serbia and, 11:169a-b, 170a
Serbia's annexation and, 2:405a
Slavic language and, 2:404a
successors of, 2:405a
Tomislav of Croatia and, 12:69a
vs. Byzantines, 2:404b–405a, 489b, 4:4b, 7:545b, 11:554b–555a
Symeon (half-brother of Stefan Uroš IV Dušan of Serbia), Meteora monasteries and, 11:179a
Symeon Hieromonachos, Symeon Metaphrastes and, 11:554b
Symeon the Logothete, **11:555a-b**
chronicle, 2:514b
poetry, political verse, 2:507b
Symeon Metaphrastes and, 11:554a, 554b, 555a
Theophanes continuatus and, 12:23a
Symeon Magister. *See* Symeon the Logothete
Symeon of Mesopotamia
extremist doctrines of, 6:192a
identified with Pseudo-Macarius, 9:7a
Symeon Metaphrastes, **11:554a-b**, 11:557b
chronicle of, 6:244b
hagiographic works, 6:61a
Menologion, 6:58b, 61a, 8:274b, 11:554a
Metaphrastic Lives, 2:519b
Symeon the Logothete and, 11:554a, 554b, 555a
Symeon the New Theologian, St., 2:214b, 9:7a-b, **11:553b–554a**
Catechetical Homilies, 11:553b
Hymns, 6:217b, 11:553b
mystical theology, 9:563b
mystical thought, 2:467a
Sermons, 6:217b
Symeon the Pious, 9:7b
Symeon the New Theologian and, 11:553b
Symeon Seth, 8:18b
Lexicon on the Properties of Foods, 8:245b
story of Stephanites and Ichnelates and, 8:19a

Symeon Stylites the Younger, St., Zenon and, 6:416a
Symeon of Thessaloniki, archbishop, against the Bogomils, 2:296b
Symeon Uroš of Bulgaria, despot of Epiros, 4:500a
Symmachi-Nicomachi diptych, 11:571b
Symmachus, Quintus Aurelius Memmius, 7:149b
  execution of, 12:19a
  Sidonius and, 11:277a
  as tutor of Boethius, 2:291a, 291b
  on Vergil, 12:395a
Symmachus, St., use of the pallium and, 12:402b
Sympatheia, 11:603a
Symphonia (musical instrument). *See Chifonie*
Symphosius, 7:362b
  Aenigmata, 10:397b–398a, 398b
Synadenoi family, land holdings, 2:479b
Synagoge in Fifty Titles. See John III Scholastikos
Synagogue, **11:555b–557a**
  art and architecture in, 7:63a–65b
    medieval Christian architecture and, 1:442a, 7:68a-b
  Ashkenazi, 11:557a
  at Dura Europos, 4:313a
  Byzantine mosaics, 7:65b
  etymology of, 7:353a
  importance of in liturgy, 7:619b
  interiors, 3:619a (*illus.*)
  Italian, 11:557a
  Jewish communal self-government under Islam and, 7:74a-b
  origins of, 11:555b–556a
  Pharisees and, 11:556a-b
  Spain, 11:556a (*illus.*)
  Torah in, 11:556b–557a
  women in, 11:557a
  see also Rabbinate
Synapte. See Litany, in the Greek Byzantine rite
Synaxary, **11:557b**
  Armenian saints and, 1:519b, 520a, 521a
  illustrated, 11:557b
  Yovsēpʿ of Constantinople and, 1:511a, 520a
Syncopation
  in *ars nova,* 10:382a
  see also Hocket
Syndic, **11:558a**
Syndics, French, representative assemblies' growth and, 10:326b–327a
Syneisaktism, 10:429b
Synekdemos. See Hierokles
Synetheia, 11:603b
Synkellos, **11:558a-b**
Synkellos, George
  chronicles, 6:244a
  continuation of Theophanes Confessor's chronicle and, 12:22b
Synod. *See* individual synods under name of city
Synod, provincial
  in England, 3:578b–579b
    membership of, 3:579a
    procedures of, 3:579b
Synod in Trullo. *See* Trullo, Synod in
Synodicus. See Warnerius of Basel
Synodikon of Orthodoxy. See John Italos
Synodos endēmousa. See Permanent synod
Synodus, use of term, 3:633a
Synone, 11:603b
Synonyma. See Isidore of Seville, St.
Synonymorum de lamentatione animae peccatricis libri ii. See Isidore of Seville, St.
Synopsis of Histories. See Alexios I Komnenos, Byzantine emperor
Synopsis historiōn. See Kedrenos, Georgios
Synopsis of the Platonic Dialogues. See Galen
Synopsis ton nomon. See Psellos, Michael
Syntagma in Fourteen Titles, 9:158b
Synthronon, **11:559a**
Syntipas, as the basis of Sindbād legend, 8:19a
Syon Abbey, 9:27a
  women mystics and, 9:14b, 15a
Syphans of Ferrara (late 13th or early 14th century), 8:646a
Syphilis. *See* Plagues; Venereal diseases
Syracuse
  captured (875), 2:118a
  commerce, 11:275a
  under Genoa, 11:275b
Syrgiannes, Serbian invasion of Macedonia and, 11:177b
Syria, **11:559a–562b,** 11:560a (map)
  Arab migration, 6:230a
  Arab-Byzantine war, 6:86a
  Armenian-Mongol invasion, 8:472b–473a
  Ayyubid mausoleums in, 2:21b
  Byzantine sea routes and, 10:423 (map), 424b
  caliphate in, 3:36b
  Druzes in, 4:296a
  early medieval Western European trade and, 12:110b
  economy, 11:559b
  establishment of Arab rule, 6:82a
  First Crusade and, 11:561a-b
  glassmaking in, 5:545a, 547b, 11:639a
  Hamdanid dynasty, 6:84a
  infected by Black Death, 2:259a
  Islamic administration of, 6:590b–591a, 591b
  Islamic conquests of, 6:567b, 568a-b
    ʿAmr ibn al-ʿĀṣ and, 1:237a
    Khālid ibn al-Walīd and, 7:235b
    plagues and the, 9:684a–686a
  Jewish-Christian relations in, 1:231b
  Jews in, 7:105b–106a
  Latin, Pisa and, 9:664b
  madrasas in, 8:11b
  in Michael the Syrian's *Chronicle,* 8:306a
  military campaigns
    Asia Minor, 8:141a
    Egypt, 10:625a
  mints and money in, 8:421a, 424a
  Nizārīs in, 11:137b
  political conditions, 11th century, 4:27b
  population, 11:559b, 562a
  relations with Rome, 10:463a-b
  religion, 11:559b, 561b
  Seljuk penetration into, 11:153a
  social instability, 6:82b
  Syriac religious literature, translations of, 12:126a-b
  taxation policy, "on the threshing floor," 11:627b
  trade and commerce, 6:109a
  Tulunid dynasty and, 12:224b
  Twelver Shiism in, 11:137a
  under Abbasids, 11:560b
  under Mamluks, 11:562a
  under Ottomans, 8:142a, 11:562a
  under Umayyads, 8:143a, 164a, 518a-b, 11:560b
    Ḥarrān as capital, 8:165a
  vs. Iraq, at Ṣiffīn, 11:284a-b
  Yarmuk battle and, 12:719b
  see also Barqūq, al-Sulṭān al-Malik al-Ẓāhir Sayf al-Dīn; Lebanon; Mamluk dynasty
Syriac alphabet. *See* Alphabets
Syriac communities, literacy of, 7:597a
Syriac language, 11:562b–563a
  Bible translations
    Peshitta, 2:211a, 217b
    pre-Peshitta, 2:217b
  biblical exegesis, 2:214b
  Maronites and, 11:564a
  Melchites and, 11:564a
  Nestorianism and, 9:106b–107b
  revival efforts by Bar Hebraeus, 2:108a
  translations of Greek scientific treatises and, 11:83a
  translators into Arabic, 12:127b, 129b–130a
Syriac literature, 11:565a–566b
  Armenian translations, 1:507b–508a
  historiography, 11:566a
  monastic, 11:566a
  12th and 13th centuries, 8:478b
  see also Armenian Hellenizing School
Syrian Christianity, **11:562b–567a**
  after 7th century, 8:478b
  Armenian Paulicians and, 9:469b
  center of in Melitene, 8:269b
  churches of, 11:563a–564a
  Council of Manazkert (726) and, 8:81b
  influence of on Armenia, 9:458a
  Jacobites, 8:478a
  literature of, 11:565a–566b
  monasteries of, 11:564b–565a
  monastic orders
    browsers and stylites, 8:461a
    tree-monks, 8:461a
  Monophysitism, 8:477b, 478a
  Nestorianism and, 9:106b–107b
  Nisibis, School of, 3:312b
  schools, 11:564a
  Theodoret of Cyr and, 12:17a
  see also Maronite church; Melchites
Syrian Gates. *See* Cilician Gates
Syrian March (Armenia), 1:514b–515a, 2:140b
Syrian music, **8:578a-b**

Syrian Orthodox Church. *See* Monophysitism
Syrian rites, **11:567b–568b**
Armenian rite and, 1:516a
Eastern, 11:567b–568a
Maronites and, 11:568a
Western, 11:568a
Syrians
barbaṭ and, 8:610b
in Iraq, 7:307a
Syro-Antiochene rites. *See* Syrian rites, Western
Syros, Sanudo and, 7:377a
Sýslumenn, 9:184b
Syssel (administrative division in Jutland), 10:699a-b
Systemata. See Guilds and métiers, Byzantine
Székely, 11:478b–479a
in Transylvania, 6:343b, 344b, 347a
Székely-Dózsa, György, 6:349b
Székesfehérvár, **11:568b–569a**
annual courts in, 6:335b
crown of St. Stephen I of Hungary and, 11:483b
as seat of St. Stephen I of Hungary, 11:479b, 480b
Szilágyi, Mihály, 6:348a
Szörény. *See* Walachia

T

Tabala, 8:561b
Ṭabaqāt (Islamic concept of classes), 2:237b
Tabard Inn, Southwark, 6:469a
Ṭabarī, al-, 1:634b, **11:569a–570a**
Armenian historians and, 1:478a
on Bahrām VI Čōbēn of Persia, 2:50a
as exegete, 2:215a
ḥikma and, 11:511a, 511b
Jāmiʿ al-bayān fī tafsīr al-Qurʾān, 11:568a, 569b
Koran commentaries, 7:296b
law and, 11:569a
Taʾrīkh al-rusul wa 'l-mulūk, 6:250a, 11:569b
Tabaristān
dew worship, 10:663a
Samanid occupation, 10:637b–638a
Zaydis and, 12:741b
Ṭabāṭabā, Ibn, on poetry, 10:347a
Tabelliones, 10:526a
Tabernacle, Christian, reservation of the sacrament and, 10:335b–336a
Tabernaculum. *See* Monstrance
Ṭabīb, ʿAbda ibn al-, 1:399b
Ṭabl, 8:567b, 612a, 613a (*illus.*)
kāsāt and, 8:613b
see also At-ṭabl
Ṭabl al-markab, 8:613a
Ṭabl al-shāmī, 8:613a
Ṭabla, 8:613b
Tablature, 8:630b
Tables
in Islamic furniture, 5:314 (*illus.*), 315b
in liturgical furniture, 5:318a
in Western European furniture, 5:324a
Tablettes Albertini, 12:355a
Tablion, **11:570b**
Tabor (musical instrument), 8:563a, 602 (*illus.*), 604b, 607a (*illus.*)
in dance music, 8:595b
Taborites, 6:200a, 374a–377a
Tabrīz, **11:570b–571a**
as Armenian capital, 11:570b
Armenian trade and, 12:99a, 99b
Demotte *Shāhnāma* and, 8:116b
geography, 11:570b
as Iranian capital, 11:571a
occupied by Selim I, 11:145a
Rawwadids in, 7:310b
sciences in, 5:517b
silk route to the Far East and, 12:99a
Uzun Ḥasan and, 12:342b
see also Azerbaijan; Urmia, Lake
Tabrīz style, miniature from Rūmī's *Mathnawī,* 9:43b (*illus.*)
Tabula ansata, **11:571b**
of Orestes, 11:571b (*illus.*)
Tabula exemplorum secundum ordinem alphabeti, 10:190a
Tabula Peutingeriana, **11:572a-b,** 12:97a, 99a
Tabula smaragdina, 1:141b
Tabulae Ceratae. *See* Wax Tablets
Tabulae salutationum. See Boncampagno of Signa
Tabularium, 10:519b
Taccola, il. *See* Mariano di Jacopo (il Taccola)
Tacitus, Cornelius
on the Balts, 2:61b–62a, 7:602b
on cavalry, 3:200b
Christian movement and, 3:334b
on *comitatus,* 6:300a
on early Scandinavia, 10:687a
on fertility goddess Nerthus, 12:356b
on Germanic betrothal practices, 2:207b
on Germanic idolatry, 4:151a
on Germanic institutions, 2:89a
on Germanic tribes, 4:157b–158a
on hospitality, 6:468a
on Nerthus, 9:146b
on ships of Northern Europe, 12:424a
on the use of alliteration among Germanic tribes, 6:445a, 8:326b, 330b
Tacuinum of Liège (handbook), 1:297a (*illus.*)
Tacuinum sanitatis in medicina, Lombard miniature, 9:88a (*illus.*), 549b (*illus.*)
Taddeo Alderotti, 8:251b, 252a, 260a
Taddeo di Bartolo, **11:572b–573a**
Farewell of the Apostles, 11:572 (*illus.*)
Tados (monastery), music and, 8:551a
Tafrāgīn, Ibn, domination of Hafsid politics, 6:54a
Tafsīr, 9:39a
Tafsīr bi-l-ma'thūr, 7:296b
Taftazānī, al-, books on rhetoric, 10:347b
Tafur, Pero de, **11:573a**
Andanças e viajes, 11:421a
Tʿagadir. See Coronant, Armenian
Tagelied. See Walther von der Vogelweide
Tageliet, 11:476b
Taghlib tribe
Imruʾ al-Qays and, 6:430a
refusal to pay *jizya,* 11:668a
Taghrībirdī, Ibn, 3:529a
on Circassians, 3:400a
Manhal, 3:399a
Nujūm al-zāhira, 2:238b, 6:25a
Tagilde, Treaty of (1372), 10:52a
Tagliacozzo, Battle of (1268), 11:279b
Tagmata, 4:239a, **11:573a-b**
thematic armies and, 12:9b
Tagrit, Syrian Orthodox Church and, 11:563b
Tahāfut al-falāsifa. See Ghazālī, al-
Tahāfut al-Tahāfut. See Rushd, Ibn
Tāhart, as a center of Ibāḍī activity, 11:139a
Ṭāhir II, reign of, 11:575a-b
Ṭāhir ibn al-Ḥusayn, 6:503a, 8:80b, **11:574a-b,** 11:575a
administrative career, 11:574a
Arabic literature and, 11:574b
military career, 11:574a
Tahirids, 6:503b, **11:574b–576a**
Abbasids and, 6:590a
Islamic historiography and, 11:575b
rise of under al-Maʾmūn, 8:80b
vs. Zaydis, Sanʿa and, 12:724b
al-Yaʿqūbī and, 12:717b
Tahmasp, shah, Xlatʿ and, 12:713b
Taḥrīf ("falsification" of Abrahamic monotheism), in Islam, 9:498a
Taḥrīr al-Majisṭī. See Ṭūsī, Naṣīr al-Dīn al-
Taif, 6:567a
Muḥammad in, 6:576b
Taifa states, 1:198a, 199b–200a
kingdom of Navarre and, 9:69b, 69a
see also Spain, Muslim kingdoms of
Tailed lines. *See Caudati*
Taille, 11:204a, 206b, **11:576a–580a,** 11:624a, 676b
of 1439, 11:579a-b
Charles VII and, 3:271b, 10:321b–322b
Charles VIII and, 10:323a-b
classification of, 11:576b
fixed, 11:577a-b
fouage and, 11:578b, 579b
France, 11:619b
Louis XI and, 10:322b–323a
municipal, 11:577b–578a
regional assemblies and, 11:578b
nobility and, 11:579a
origins, 11:623b
personal, in jurisdictional disputes, 11:576b–577a
royal, 11:578a–579b
seigneurial, 11:576b–577b
territorial, in jurisdictional disputes, 11:577a
see also Representative assemblies, French; *Questals;* Taxation

Taillement, Michault, on Jura Mountains, 12:162b
Táin bó Cúailnge, 6:521b, 522a, 531b, 539a, 546a, 548a, 548b, 554a, 11:116a, **11:580a–581a**
  Echtrae Nerai and, 6:550b
  Recension I, 11:580a, 580b
  on Ulster, 12:255b
Tairdelbach O'Connor, military successes, 3:538a
Tairdelbach Ua Briain, king of Munster, 4:77b
Taisabun. *See* Ctesiphon
Tāj al-lugha wa ṣiḥāh al-ʿarabiya. See Jauharī, al-
Tāj al-Mulk, 6:562a
Takhi-i Sulaiman. *See* Ādur Gušnasp
Takht, 5:315a
Takht-i Sulaymān, 6:603b
  excavations at, 7:320a
Takkanot. See Jewish communal self-government
Takrīt, 6:509b
Takrit. *See* Tagrit
Taktika. See Leo VI, Byzantine emperor
Taku, Moses, *Ketav Tammim,* 9:579a
Tal, 8:553a
Ṭalāʾi ibn Ruzzīk, Fatimid vizier, 5:29a-b
Talbot, Robert, 3:477a
Tale of Bygone Years, The. See Primary Chronicle, Russian
"Tale of Lludd and Lleuelys," in *Mabinogi,* 7:705b
Talea, 6:619a, 619b
Talenti, Francesco, **11:581a-b**
Ṭalḥa ibn ʿUbayd Allāh, revolt of, 10:242a
Ṭalḥa (son of Ṭāhir ibn al-Ḥusayn), 11:575a
Talhaearn, 11:581b
Taliesin, 1:247b, 9:47b, **11:581a–582a**
  legend of, 12:603b
  patrons, 12:597a
  poems addressed to Urien Rheged, 12:331b, 602a
  praise poems, 12:602a
Taliesin, Book of. See Book of Taliesin
Taʿlīm, 6:617a
Tʿalin, **11:582b–583a**
Tʿalin Cathedral, 1:493b, 11:582b
Taʿlīq (Arabic script), 9:65b
Tallage
  assessment of, 11:613a
  England, 11:612b–613a
  seigneurial, 11:616b–617a, 620a
Tallage. *See* Taille
Tallies. *See* Taille
Tallóci brothers of Ragusa, 6:346b
Talmud
  amoraim and, 11:583a, 584a
  Babylonian, 10:337b–338a, 11:583a
    primacy of, 11:584a
  Christian anti-Semitism and, 7:77b–78a
  on clothing
    essential garments, 3:618b
    head covering, 3:619b
  dietary laws and, 4:181a–183a
  dispute over, 10:4b
  exegesis and study of, 2:212a-b, 7:173a, **11:583a–587a**
    Ashkenazic, 11:585a, 585b
    by Rashi, 10:259a–260a
    Gaonic, 5:357a, 11:584a
    ḥiddushim genre, 11:585b
    in *kallot,* 11:584a
    perushim genre, 11:585a
    preaching and sermons, 10:74a
    rabbinate and, 10:243a–244a
    Sephardic, 11:585a, 585b–586a
    tosafistic, 11:585b–586a
    see also Maimonides, Moses; Responsum literature, Jewish; Schools, Jewish
  family and marriage in, 7:92a-b
  as framework for normative Judaism, 7:160b–161a
  geonim and, 11:583b–585a
  Jerusalem, 11:583a
    modern interest in, 11:584a
    Nezikin, 11:583a
  in Jewish schools, 11:70b–71a
  Karaites and, 7:107b–108a, 209a, 210b–211a
  law and, 7:169b, 490a
  law codes of
    Gaonic, 11:584a-b, 586b
    rishonim, 11:586a-b
  Palestinian, 10:463b
  responsa literature of
    Gaonic, 11:584b–585a
    rishonim, 11:586b
  rishonim and, 11:585a–586b
  savoraim and, 11:583b
  two main disciplines of, 8:22b
  see also Jacob ben Meïr; Jewish law
Talmud affair, 7:77b
Talmud Katan. See Alfasi, Isaac ben Jacob, *Sefer ha-Halakhot*
Talmudic schools. *See* Schools, Jewish
Talorc/Talorcan. *See* Tristan, legend of
Tamar of Georgia, queen, 2:49a, 4:112a, **11:587a-b**
  Ani in Širak and, 1:291a, 485b
  coruler with father, 5:529b
  depiction of in Betania, 2:207a
  Dwin and, 1:485b
  historical narrative of, 5:413b, 417b–418a
  Komnenoi and, 11:587b
  military campaigns of, 11:587a
  office of atabeg and, 1:632a
  poetry in honor of, 5:418a
  problems facing, 5:529b
  reign of, 5:406b–407a, 420a
  Shotʿa Rustaʿveli and, 11:256a
  Siwnikʿ and, 11:315b
  Zakʿarids and, 12:736b
Tʿamariani. See Šaχruχadze
Tambourine, 8:561b, 563a, 567b, 605a (*illus.*), 605b–606a, 610b (*illus.*), 613a
  Muḥammad and, 8:560a
Tambura, 8:561b
Tāmdult, Idrisids in, 6:413b
Tamerlane, **11:587b–588b**
  ʿAlāʾ al-Dīn Beg and, 7:214a
  Armenia and, 1:486a, 514a, 12:99b
  Brusa sacked by, 2:393a
  capture of Sebaste, 11:132a
  Chinggisid house and, 12:58b
  in Damascus, 4:82b, 83b–84a
  defeat of Tokhtamysh, 8:540b
  empire of, 11:588a-b
  Erzincan and, 4:508b
  in González de Clavijo's account, 11:421a
  in Iran, 6:505a
  in Iraq, 6:514b
  in Isfahan, 6:562a
  Islamic art and, 6:605a
  Kabala destroyed by, 7:205a
  Kars destroyed by, 7:221b
  Kasranids and, 11:254a
  Mesopotamia invaded by, 3:313a
  Nestorianism and, 9:107b
  occupation of Samarkand, 10:640b–641a
  Shīrāz and, 11:252b
  Siwnikʿ and, 11:315b
  succession dispute after death of, 12:56b–57a
  in Syria, 8:75a
  threatening letter to Sultan Barqūq, 2:113b
  Timurids and, 12:56b
  tomb of, 6:605b (*illus.*), 605a
  in Tʿovma Mecopʿecʿi's *History,* 12:93a
  victory at Ancyra (1402), 1:242a
  vs. Bāyazīd I, 2:136b, 11:588a
  vs. Golden Horde, 11:588a
Tametsi. See Trent, Council of
Tamīm, Zirid ruler, 12:745a
Tʿamtʿa (daughter of Iwanē Mχargrzeli), 1:486a, 12:737a
Ṭanbūr, 8:561b, 562a
Tancred of Bologna. *See* Tancred (canonist)
Tancred (canonist), **11:589a**
  Compilationes and, 11:589a
  on inquest, 6:479a
  Laurentius Hispanus and, 7:385b
  legal codifications, 7:504a-b
  Ordo iudiciarius, 7:504a-b, 11:589a
  Summa de sponsalibus et matrimonio, 11:589a
  Vincentius Hispanus and, 12:456a
Tancred (crusader), **11:589a–590a**
  Bohemond I of Antioch and, 2:309a
  al-Lādhiqiya and, 7:315b
  supported by Naples, 9:58a
Tancred of Hauteville, 11:264b
Tancred of Lecce, Sicilian succession and, 11:269a
Tancred of Sicily, king, 5:482a
Tandareis und Flordibel. See Pleier, Der
Tang dynasty, Muslim merchants and, 11:246b
Tangier, conquered by the Almoravids, 1:199a
Tanḥum of Jerusalem, 7:172b
Tank (coin), 8:418b
Tannenberg. *See* Grunwald
Tanner Collection, 4:123b
Tanners' Guild, triptych of, 5:611a
Tannhäuser, 5:633b, **11:590a-b**
  Frederick II of Austria and, 9:93a
  Leiche of, 11:590a
  minnesinger style and, 8:414a, 11:590a-b

Tannhäuser, 5:633b (*cont.*)
reputation of, 5:443b
satirical frolickings of, 8:352a
Sprüche of, 11:590b
Steinmar and, 11:476b
Tannin, in leather preparation, 4:326a
Tanpula, 8:562a
Tanqīḥ al-manāẓir. See Fārisī, Kamāl al-Dīn al-
Tanquam proprii servi, 11:210b, 211a
Tansar, Letter of. *See* Letter of Tansar
Tansar, Zoroastrian high priest, 1:452a
Tanūkhī, al-, *Food for Entertainment (Nishwār al-muḥāḍara),* 1:380b, 382a
Tanutēr, 1:488b–489a, 490b, **11:591a**
see also Sepuh; Vardan Mamikonean, St.
Tao. *See* Tayk^c
Taormina, recaptured (880), 2:118a
Tapar, Muḥammad
Qılıj Arslan I and, 11:154a
recognized as a sultan, 11:153b
Tapestry
architectural uses of, 11:591b
art of, **11:591a–597a**
commercial trade of, 1:561a-b
design of, 11:592a-b
dyes for, 11:595a-b
Egypt, 11:592b–593a
hunting and, 6:361b, 362b–363a
kilim, 7:252b–253a
materials for, 11:594b–595a
millefleurs, **11:597a**
social uses of, 11:591b
subjects of, 11:591b
Syria, 11:593a
transportability of, 11:591b
weaving centers, 11:596a-b
weaving techniques, 11:593a–594b (*illus.*)
see also Bayeux Tapestry
Tapestry with Arms of Burgundy, 11:595a, 597b (*illus.*)
Taq-i Bostan, **11:597a–598a**
Baghdad and, 11:597b
Xusrō II and, 12:715a-b
zandanījī designs and, 12:738a
Taqī al-Dīn ibn Ma^{c}rūf, 11:85a
Nūr ḥadaqat al-abṣār, 9:246b
Taqīya, 6:615a
Taqlīd, 6:582a
Tar, 8:561b
Ṭār (chordophone), 8:611a
Ṭār (tambourine), 8:561b, 613a
Tara, **11:598a-b**
Áed Sláne and, 1:60b
kingship of, 12:241a-b
in Irish saga, 6:547a-b
Patrick and, 9:464b
see also Uí Néill
Tara brooch, 3:220b, 222 (*illus.*), 8:373a
Tara River, Battle of (1150), 8:91b
Ţara Românească, 12:498a
Ṭarab al-futuḥ, 8:611a
Taranis (Celtic divinity), 9:46a
Tarasicodissa. *See* Zeno the Isaurian
Tarasios, **11:598b**
Tarawn. *See* Tarōn
Tarbī^c wa 'l-tadwīr, Al-. See Jāḥiẓ, Abū ^{c}Uthmān ^{c}Amr ibn Baḥr al-
Tarbīya, 11:332b
Tardus cadence. *See* Cadence (language)
Tarette, 11:232a
Targe, 1:523b (*illus.*), 525b
"Lithuanian," 1:523b (*illus.*)
tilting, 1:532b
in tournaments, 1:526a
Ṭarḥa, legal usage, 11:630a
Tarida, 11:232a
Ta$^\supset$rīkh. See Ya^{c}qūbī, al-
Ta$^\supset$rīkh Baghdad. See Khaṭīb al-Baghdādī, al-
Ta$^\supset$rīkh al-kabīr, Al-. See Wāqidī, Abū al-
Ta$^\supset$rīkh al-rusul wa 'l-mulūk. See Tabarī, al-
Ta$^\supset$rīkh-i Mas^{c}ūdī. See Abu 'l-Faḍl Bayhaqī
Tāriq ibn Ziyād, 7:95a
in Spain, 6:572a-b, 11:381b–382a
Ṭarīqa, 6:585a, 585b
see also Sufism, fraternities
Tarocchi, 5:352b
Tarōn, **11:598b–599b**
Byzantines and, 1:474a, 483b, 484a
Mamikonean family and, 8:78b, 79a
see of, 11:599a
separatism of, 1:475a
see also Patmut^{c}iwn Tarōnoy
Tarot, 5:352b
Tarraconensis, liturgical practices in, 9:62a, 62b
Tarragona
metropolitan see of, 12:348a
restoration of, 3:178a
Tarsaitch, Armenian prince, S. Lusaworič^c and, 9:159a
Tarsus, **11:599b–600a**
Tancred and, 11:589a
see also Nersēs Lambronac^{c}i
Tarsus Cathedral, 11:600a
Tarsus, Council of (1198), 1:501a
Tart (Cistercian community), 12:686a
Tartaglia, Niccolò, 1:439b
La travagliata inventione, 1:438a
Tartars, defeat of, by Dmitrii Donskoi, 11:347b
Tartushi, al- (Arab merchant), on Hedeby, 6:133a, 12:423a-b
Ṭarūn. *See* Tarōn
Tashahāda, in Islamic liturgy, 7:617b
Tāshfīn ibn ^{c}Alī ibn Yūsuf, Almoravid ruler, 1:200a-b
Tāshfīn, Yūsuf ibn. *See* Yūsuf ibn Tāshfīn
Tashkent. *See* Shāsh
Tašir
Georgia and, 1:485b
separatism of, 1:483a
Tasset, 1:531b, 532a, 534a (*illus.*)
tilting, 1:533a
Tassilo III of Bavaria, duke, 2:4b, 94b–95a, 134a, 5:506a-b
Pepin III and, 9:501b
Tasso, *Gerusalemme liberata,* 6:670a
Tasyīr, 1:619b
Tatars
Bāyazīd II and, 2:137a-b
in Caffa, 3:12a-b
in Crimea, 3:679a-b
factional disputes, 8:476a
invasion of Russia, 9:687b
Mongol conflicts, alliance with Chin, 8:465a
Romanian principalities and, 10:514a, 514b
Russian overlordship, 8:539b
approval of princes, 8:539b
end of, 8:546a, 573a
grand principalities, 8:542a
social status, Walachia/Moldavia, 12:506a
Tat^{c}ew, 1:504b, **11:600a-b**
academic hierarchy at, 1:482b
facilities of, 11:600a
T^{c}ovma Mecop^{c}ec^{c}i and, 12:92b
Tatheus. *See* Meuthi
Tatian manuscripts, **11:600b–601b**
Diatessaron, 9:233a
East Frankish language and, 11:601a
German translation, 11:600b–601a
Gospel Harmony, as source for *Heliand,* 6:150b
Old English language and, 11:601a-b
Tats, in Caucasia, 3:195a
T^{c}at^{c}ul (Armenian anchorite), 1:519b
T^{c}at^{c}ul of Marash, ruler, 1:484b
Tatwine of Canterbury, 7:362b, **11:600b**
collection of riddles, 10:398a, 398b
Tau cross, 4:9b, 10 (*illus.*)
Taula de Canvi of Barcelona, 2:75b
Tauler, Johannes, **11:600b–602b**
as Dominican, 3:368b
influenced by Neoplatonism, 9:100b
life of, 9:33b
Meister Eckhart and, 9:32a
mysticism of, 4:248b, 9:33b–34b
spurious works of, 11:602a, 602b
style of, 11:602b
Suso and, 9:34b, 11:516a, 517a
visit to Groenendael, 9:38a
Tauris. *See* Tabrīz
Taurus Mountains, passage through, 3:390b
T^{c}avadoba, 5:420a
Tavadoba (rule of the princes in Georgia), 9:466b
Tavasts, 11:531a
Taverner, Peter, 2:157b
Tavernier, Jean le. *See* Jean le Tavernier
Taverns, **6:468a–477a**
see also Inns
Tavola ritonda, 1:572b, 6:638b
Tawḥīd, 6:586a
Tawḥīdī, Abū Ḥayyān al-, 1:618a
Ta$^\supset$wīl, 6:617b, 9:39a
influence on Jewish biblical exegesis, 2:212b
Tawnapatčar̄, 1:511a
Tawq al-Ḥamāma. See Ḥazm, Abū Muḥammad ^{c}Alī ibn Aḥmad ibn Sa^{c}īd ibn
Tawrāt (Arabic word for Torah), mentioned by Muḥammad, 9:497a
Tawruberan. *See* Turuberan
Tāwūs, Ibn, 1:618b
Tawwābūn march (684), 6:511b, 7:307a
Tax collectors. *See* Taxation, collection of

Taxation
administrative records and, 4:137b–138a
agricultural revenues, 11:625a
Egypt, 11:626a-b
payments in kind, 11:619a, 627a-b
aids
feudal, 11:619b, 621b
seignorial, 11:617a
alnagers and, 1:202b–203a
apportionment, 11:576a
Armenia, Gagik I and, 5:338b
assessment, 11:613b
Egypt, 11:626a-b
England, 11:607b, 608a
municipal, 11:577b, 578a
Austria, salt tax, 10:631b–632a
in Baltic lands, as a complement to Christianization, 2:65b–66b, 67b
Byzantine, **11:603a–605b**
chrysargyron, 6:20a
collective responsibility, 2:476b–477a, 480a
direct, 11:603a–604b
exemptions from, 11:604a-b, 605a
farming out of, 11:604b
geographical units of, 11:603a
jugatio-capitatio, 2:475b
opposition to, 2:496b
oppression of poor, 2:496a, 496b
secondary, 11:604a, 604b, 605a
soldiers' portions, 11:359b–360a
see also Allelengyon; Paroikoi; Pronoia
carucage, 7:200b
Castile, 3:132a-b, 138b
church, **11:605b–611a**
annate, 1:304b–305b
ecclesiastical benefice and, 11:606a
England, 11:607a–609b, 616a-b
lay taxation and, 11:608b, 610b
in Poland, 9:727b
Pragmatic Sanction of Bourges and, 10:69a-b
Western Europe, 11:609b–610a
Wyclif and, 12:706b
see also Annate; Peter's Pence; Tithes
of clergy, 3:447b–448a, 11:614a, 614b–615a
by Philip IV, 11:621a-b
clerical tenth, 11:615a, 624a
papal order, 11:614b, 616b
valuations, 11:614b
collection
Egypt, 11:626a-b
élus and *élections,* 11:624b
enquêteurs, 11:621b
fisc, 11:625b
institutions, 11:624a-b
papal, 11:607a, 607b, 608a, 610b
in communes, 3:501b–502a
for crusades, 11:614a, 614b
currency manipulation, 11:620a, 623a
England, **11:611a–618a**
aids, feudal, 11:613a, 613b, 615a
benevolences, 11:616a
borough taxes, 11:617a
construction and maintenance of bridges, 10:414b–416a
Domesday Book and, 4:238b
Exchequer and, 4:532a
hidage and carucage, 11:612a-b
in Hundred Years War, 6:334a
import and export, 11:615a
issues of representation, 4:484a
Jews and, 4:535b, 11:612b
late, 11:615b–616a
measures of, 6:223a
for military needs, 4:484a-b
on movables, 11:613b–614b
nonroyal, 11:616a–617a
Norman-Angevin period, 11:612a–613b
old custom of 1275, 11:615a
opposition to, 11:617b
parliament and, 7:664b, 9:424a-b, 428a, 11:615a, 615b–616a
Peasants' Revolt and, 9:480a-b
pipe rolls, 9:662a–663b
poll tax, 7:664a, 10:26a-b
poundage, 11:615a, 615b
of property, 2:331b
for ransoms, 11:613b–614a
royal, 11:617a
seizure of wool, 11:615a
sheriff and, 11:225b, 226a
subsidy, 11:615b
tolls, 11:612b
under Henry II, 4:469b
yield, 11:614a, 614b
see also Carucage; Danegeld; Heregeld; Scutage; Tallage
evasion
Egypt, 11:626b
penalties, 10:631b
exemptions, 11:611b–612a, 617b
drafting of, 11:624b
nobility, 11:623b
fees, 11:619b
see also Banalité
feorms, 11:611a
France, **11:618b–625a**
aides, 5:186b, 188b, 10:319b, 321b, 322b, 11:623a, 623b, 624a
aides de l'ost, 11:621a, 621b
attitudes toward, 11:618b, 621a
by representative assemblies, 11:621a, 621b
Chambre des Élus, 10:327a
of clergy, 2:323b, 5:171b, 9:554a, 554b
of consumer goods, 11:578b
Court of Aids, 10:322b
currency manipulation, 11:624a
development of permanent bureaucracies, 10:326b–327b
direct, 10:325b, 11:623b
droit de rève, 11:621b
élection jurisdictions, 10:319b
élu tax collectors, 10:318a-b, 319b, 322a-b, 327a
exemption practices, 5:181a, 10:320a-b
extraordinary, 11:621b, 623a-b
fouage, 3:269b–270a, 5:168a, 186b
gabelle, 5:336b, 336a-b, 7:699b
general taxes, 9:554a
haute passage, 11:621b
indirect, 5:184b, 186b, 187a, 10:325b, 11:622a, 623a
of Jews, 10:318a
maintenance of roads and bridges, 10:412b, 417b
for military purposes, 5:163a, 171a-b, 184a, 185a, 9:554a-b, 556a
national animosity toward, 5:184a
nobility, 11:622b–623a
Normandy and, 9:169a
north-south variations, 11:622a
opposition to, 11:622b, 623b
public vs. private, 11:619a
for ransom of John II, 5:185–186a
for ransoms, 11:622b–623a
recette jurisdictions of Guyenne, 10:325b
reduction, 10:322a
reform, 14th century, 11:623a
regular, 11:622b–624a
revocation, 10:319b
royal authority, 10:319b–320b, 321b–322b, 323b, 11:620a
sales taxes, 10:319b–320a
sergeant and, 11:208b
taille, 3:271b, 5:188b, 10:321b–323b
to control brigandage, 11:623a-b
to stabilize currency, 5:179b
types of, 11:618b
under Charles V, 3:269b, 270a
under Charles VII, 3:271a-b
war subsidy, 11:620b–622b, 624a
of wine, 2:328b
see also Gabelle; *Maltolte*
of furs and fur trade, 5:327b–328a
Germany
Common Penny (*der Gemeine Pfennig*), 10:330b–331a
of imperial knights, 10:332a
of Jews, 10:331a
Matrikel money and troop quotas, 10:330b–331a
in principalities, 5:503a
representative assemblies and, 10:330b–331a
in towns, 5:463b–464a
gifts, 11:618b
government centralization and, 12:160a
Hungary
under Angevins, 6:344b
under Matthias, 6:348a-b, 348b–349a
Iberian Peninsula, as cortes' function, 3:611b–612a
indirect, 11:611b–612a
inflation and, 11:613b
of inns, 6:474b
Ireland, discussed by parliament, 9:435a, 435b, 436a
Islamic, **11:625a–628a**
Abode of Islam and, 1:20b
Abū Bakr and, 6:567b
alms tax, festivals and, 5:38a-b
alms tax (*zakāt al-fiṭr*), 10:254b–255a
assessment of, 1:202a
iqṭa, 11:627b
in Iraq, 6:72b, 512a, 512b
irrigation, 11:626b, 667a
kharāj, 11:667b–668b

Taxation (*cont.*)
Islamic (*cont.*)
in al-Maghrib under the Almohads, 1:194b
maks, 11:627b
military estates, 11:626b
of non-Muslims under Ottomans, 9:309b–310a
Ottoman tax registers, 9:306b
poll tax, 10:27a
rates of, 11:627a
tanzīmāt decrees, 11:669a
tax farms, 11:627b
to encourage agriculture, 1:103a-b
tribute payment, 1:21a
under the Ayyubids, 2:25a
under al-Mahdī, 8:47a
under the Mamluk dynasty, 8:71b
under Mongols, 6:591b
under Umayyads, 6:589b
^{c}*ushr* on *mawa*^{c}*t* land, 11:668b
see also Alms tax, Islamic; *Iqṭā*^{c}*;* ^{c}Umar II ibn ^{c}Abd al-^{c}Azīz
Italy, *gabelle,* 7:17a
in Jewish communities, 7:70b
of Jews, by so-called chief rabbis, 10:243b
justification
coronation expense levy, 10:323a
evident necessity, 10:319b
feudal aid, 10:319a-b
war subsidy, 10:318a
land, 10:273b–274a, 11:625b–626a, 667a–668b
annona, 11:673a
laws, evident necessity, 11:620b, 621a
market, 8:144a-b, 146b
for military purposes, 11:619b, 620a-b
defense of Aquitaine, 11:614a
municipal, as taille, 11:578a
Normandy, 9:162a
Norway, 9:184a
papal, 11:606b, 607a, 12:158b
plagues and, 9:674b, 685b, 10:318b, 324a
Poland, royal, 9:725a
practices
exemption, 10:320a-b
withholding from royal, 10:320a-b
progressive principle, 11:617b
Roman Britain, 11:611a
Romano-canonical
evident necessity, 10:319b
war subsidy, 10:318a
Rome, *see also* Indiction
royal, 11:611a
land use, Scandinavia, 11:685a
Russia
peasants and, 11:193b
pogost centralization of, 9:715a-b
Saladin Tithe, 11:612b, 614a
Scotland, under James I, 9:439b
seignorial, 11:613a-b, 616b–617a, 618b–619a, 620a, 676b
counts, 11:619a
types of, 11:619b
service, 11:611a
Sicily, 9:59a
Charles of Anjou and, 11:272b
Frederick II and, 11:271b
Spain
cortes and, 3:611b–612a
mestas and, 8:280a-b
urban, 12:318a
Visigothic, 12:473a
war, English treason definition and, 12:166b–167a
yields
geld, 11:611b
tolls, 11:612a
see also Chevage; Clergy; Gelds; Maltolte; Political theory; Poll tax; Taille; Tithes; Tolls
Taχt-i Suleiman, **11:628a-b**
in literature, 11:628b
Sasanian monarchy and, 11:628b
Tay River, water of as measurement standard, 12:589a
Tayk^{c}, 1:472b, 473a, 473b, **11:628b–629b**
Aristakēs Lastiverc^{c}i on, 1:455a
Armenian-Georgian rule, 11:629a
Bagratids in, 1:480a, 11:629a
Byzantine-Persian partition, 11:629a
ethnology, 11:629a
Mamikoneans and, 8:78b, 79a
residence of princes, 11:629a
separatism of, 1:475a
trade and commerce, 11:629b
under David, 4:113b
Ṭaylasān, **11:629b–630b**, 11:630a (*illus.*)
Arab adaptation, 11:629b
legal significance, 11:630a
Persian use, 11:629b
treatises on, 11:629b–630a
Taym clan. *See* Quraysh
Taymīya, Ibn, 7:111b, **11:630b–631b**
imprisonment, 11:630b–631a
Islamic fundamentalism, 11:630b
legal works, 11:631a
opposition to Islamic logic, 7:641b
popularity, 11:631b
refutation of Aristotelian logic, 9:568b
vs. Sufism, 6:586a
Ṭayyib, al-, 5:28b–29a, 6:617a-b
Ṭayyib, Ibn al-, 11:565b
Ṭayyibīs, 6:587b, 588a, 617a-b, 618a
Tbilisi, **11:631b–632a**
Armenian trade and, 12:97b
capital of western Iberia, 5:402b
Church of Meteḫi, 8:289 (*illus.*)
cultural center, 11:631b
Liparit IV Orbēlean and, 7:586b
martyrs of, 5:414a
monuments, 11:631b–632a
trade and commerce, 11:631b
under Arabs, 1:478b, 479a
Te Deum, **11:632a-b**
melody, 11:632a-b
in mystery plays, 8:596b
in tonaries, 12:70b
use of organ in, 9:274b
Te lucis ante terminum, 8:572a
Teacher of Righteousness. See Abner of Burgos
Teaching centers. *See* Schools; Universities
Te'amim, 8:564a, 565a
Teasel. *See* Carding
Technical literature. *See Fachschrifttum;* Technology, treatises on
Technology
agricultural, 11:634b–635a, 639b, 651a
food preservation, 11:639b
plowing changes and land reclamation, 10:277a-b
texts, 11:634b
alchemy, 11:635a-b, 638b–639a
attitude of church toward, Eastern vs. Western views, 11:664a
counterpoises, 11:633b
elimination of friction, 11:649a
Hellenistic, 11:95a
hydraulic, 11:656b–657a
hammer, 11:639b, 651b
"Tartar" pump, 12:579a
theatrical machine, 11:633b (*illus.*)
water-lifting device, 11:642a (*illus.*)
waterwheels, 11:637a, 637b–638a, 12:577a, 579a
see also Irrigation
mechanical, 11:633a–634a, 636b–638a
bearings, 11:649a
cam and crank system, 11:651b–652a
crank, 11:660b
cranks and pullies, 11:646b, 651b, 660b, 661b (*illus.*)
double-acting crane, 11:647a (*illus.*)
machine design, 11:642a-b, 645a, 645b
manual, 11:640b
perpetual motion machines, 11:644a, 652a
spring, 11:658b–659a
treatises on, 11:636b–637a, 648a-b
medical
bloodletting device, 11:637a (*illus.*)
surgical techniques, 11:652a
treatises on, 11:644b–645a
military. *See* Warfare, technology of
of monumental archaeology, 1:431a–432a
pneumatic
blowgun, 11:660a
loading devices, 11:660a
post-Roman, 11:659b
religious
mechanical clock, 11:664a
pipe organ, 11:663b–664a
prayer cylinders, 11:662a
spread of. *See* Translation and translators
status of, 11:643a
theaters of machines, 11:649b
transportation, suspension systems, 11:659a
treatises on, 4:329a, **11:640a–650a**
ancient, 11:640b–641a
artistic influence, 11:647a
book of secrets, 11:649b
engineering, 11:645b–649b
European, 8:296b–297a, 11:642a–649b
Gothic design, 11:649a
instrument making, 11:644b
Islamic, 11:641a–642b
Italian school, 11:647a–649a

Latin, 11:643a–645b
magical themes, 11:646a
monastic, 11:643a
recipe books, 11:643b
theoretical subjects, 11:641a, 641b
see also Theophilus
wind power, 11:637b–638a, 652a, 653b (*illus.*), 661a, 661b
Eurasia, 11:661b
pumps, 11:637b–638a
see also Automata; Clocks; Engineering
Technology, Byzantine, **11:632b–636a**
attitude toward, 11:661a
farm tools, 11:634b–635a
Greek fire, 5:659b
mechanics, 11:633a–634a
scientific instruments, 11:634a-b
Technology, Islamic, 11:87a, **11:636a–640a**
ancient influence, 11:641a
attitude toward, 11:661a
civil engineering, 11:638a
economic and cultural factors, 11:636a
Nilometer flood measurement, 12:223b
philosophic discipline, 11:636a
piston-driven paddle wheel, 11:636b–637a, 637b (*illus.*)
reaction to Western innovations, 11:661b–662a
shipbuilding and, 9:76b–77b
wheel, in mining, 11:639b
see also Nāᶜūr
Technology, Western, **11:650a–664b**
ancient influence, 11:640b
attitude toward invention, 11:651a–652b
ball-and-chain governor, 11:662a
charcoal in, 3:267a-b
Christian ethics and, 11:656b–657a, 662b–663a
effects of Black Death and, 2:266a
Eurasian interchange of ideas, 11:659b–662b
glassmaking, 5:554a–562b
interrelationship of inventions, 11:657a–659b
invention of wiredrawing, 8:295b
Islamic influence, 11:644b
mechanical marvels, 8:39b
metalworking and, 6:32b, 8:293a
iron and steel, 8:293a–294b
metalworking tools, 8:296a–297a
mills, 8:389b–395a
mining, 8:401a-b, 403b
origins of printing, 10:124a–127b
science and, 11:650a–651a
social aspects, 11:656b
Theophilus' *De diversis artibus* and, 12:24a-b
time-, labor-, and material-saving, 11:652b–657a
turbi, 11:662a
xylography, 6:32b
see also Bridges, Western European; Richard of Wallingford; Roads, Western European; Steelmaking; Vehicles, European
Tegernsee *Antichrist,* 4:268b
allegory in, 4:286b
political motives for, 4:281b–282a
Tegghia, Angelino del, 4:558b
Tegliacci, Niccolò di Ser Sozzo, **11:664b–665a**
Assumption of the Virgin, 11:665 (*illus.*)
Tegüder, Ilkhanid ruler
murder of, 6:420a
overthrow of, 6:504b
vs. Argun, 1:453a
Teichen. See Fishponds
Tᶜeimuraz I of Georgia, king, 5:418a
Teixeira, Tristão Vaz, 4:559a
Tekfur Saray, Nymphaion and, 9:203a
Tekish, khwārizmshāh, 5:526b, 6:504a, 7:244a
Ildegizids and, 6:419b
Tekor, **11:665a–666a**
Teküder, conversion to Islam, 8:474a
Tekufot, 3:26b–27a
Telemark homesite, 10:696a
Telescope. *See* Polar sighting tube
Telesphorus, pope, Christmas celebration and, 3:317a-b
Telestichs, in Latin literature, 7:362b
Telles, Fernão, 4:559b
Telyn, 8:558b
Temair Breg. *See* Tara
Temesvár diet, 6:335b, 346b
Tempera painting, **11:666a**
in icons, 6:410a, 410b, 411b
see also Panel painting
Tempests, Cape of. *See* Good Hope, Cape of
Tempier, Étienne, bishop of Paris, 1:608a
censure of University of Paris (1270), 6:198b, 9:409a, 607b, 624b, 12:39b
censures revoked in 1325, 12:41a
condemnations of 1277 and, 12:40b
criticism of astrology, 1:608a
opposition to Averroism, 1:463a-b, 9:597b
Siger and, 11:286a, 286b
Templars, 4:17a-b
acknowledgment of, 3:304b
architecture of, 10:489a
art and, 4:21b, 25b
as bankers for the papacy, 2:77b
Bernard of Clairvaux on, 2:191a
church in Laon, 10:489a
Clement V and, 3:362a
cross of, 3:305 (*illus.*)
in crusader states, 12:561b
Cyprus and, 4:70b
Denis I of Portugal and, 10:49a–50a
English headquarters, 7:660b–661a
flag of, 3:304b, 305 (*illus.*)
formation of, 3:244b, 304a-b
fortress of Baghrās, 7:546a
grand masters of, 3:304b
inquisition and, 6:488a
Jem Sultan and, 2:137a
Nogaret and, 9:153a
papal condemnation of, 8:137b
Philip IV of France and, 5:172a, 10:317b
Pierre Dubois on, 9:646a
as a secret society, 9:2b
suppression of, 3:304b, 306a, 643b, 644a-b, 9:405a
vs. Hospitalers, 4:52a, 52b
Temple. *See* Synagogue
Temple of Glass. See Lydgate, John
Temple d'honneur et de vertus. See Jean Lemaire de Belges
Temple d'Onnour, Le. See Froissart, Jehan
Temple of Solomon (religious order), 10:489a
Temple-breed (Armagh), 1:470a
Temple-na-Ferta (Armagh), 1:470a
Templon screen. *See* Screen, chancel
Templum Domini (Jerusalem). *See* Dome of the Rock
Temporale, in Stowe Missal, 7:615b
Temporalia (tangible properties and governmental rights of clerics), investiture conflict and, 9:445a
Tempus, in measured music, 7:119a-b
Tempus, see also Perfectio
Temüjin. *See* Genghis Khan
Ten Commandments. *See* Bible, Decalogue
Ten Lost Tribes of Israel, according to Eldad ha-Dani, 8:23b
Tenant labor
Carolingian, 4:511b–512a
decline of, 4:513a
Roman, 4:511a
see also Corvée; Tenure of land
Tendürük, Mount, 1:470b
Tenement, in common law, 9:546b
Tennis, 5:348a
Tenor, 1:551a, **11:666a-b**
isorhythm and, 6:619a-b
see also Contratenor
Tenorio, Peter, 3:645b–646a
Tenso (*tenson*), **11:666b**
by Cercamon, 3:240b
in Galician-Portuguese lyrics, 11:450b
partimen and, 11:666b
in Provençal literature, 10:164b
trobairitz and, 12:207a-b
in troubadours' songs, 12:217b–218a
in trouvères's songs, 12:218b
see also Débat
Tensone, 5:434b
Tent, portable. *See Qubba*
Tentering. *See* Wool, preparation
Tenths. *See* Tithes
Tenure à champart, 11:679a
Tenure of land, Armenia, 1:489b
Tenure of land, Byzantine
in Asia Minor, under Basil II, 2:119a
charistikion, 3:268a
imperial chrysobull, 2:479b
paroikoi, 2:479b, 496a
patrocinium, 2:476a-b
peasants, attachment of, 2:475b
pronoiai, 2:496a
reforms under Constantine VII, 3:547a
"soldiers' lands," 2:487b, 490a, 492a-b
village communities, 2:476b–477a, 479b–480a
see also Paroikoi
Tenure of land, Islamic, 11:561b, **11:667a–669b**

Tenure of land, Islamic (*cont.*)
Egypt, 10:454b
God's ownership of property, 11:667a, 668b, 669a
non-Muslims, 11:667b
Ottoman rule, 11:669a
under the Ayyubids, 2:25a
Tenure of land, Slavic, **11:669b–671a**, 11:679b
communal ownership, 11:670a
Kievan Rus, 1:101a-b
black lands, 1:101a-b
pomestie estates, 1:101b–102a
princely rights, 1:100a, 102a
votchina estates, 1:102a
Russia, 11:190b, 192a
under Ivan IV, 11:192a
under Mongols, 11:190b–191a
Tenure of land, Western European, 1:596a–598b, **11:671a–686a**
absentee ownership, 11:673a
allod, 11:674b
benefice, 11:674b
in Bohemia-Moravia, 2:300b–301a, 302a-b
burgage tenure, 2:420b–421a
by serfs, 11:205b
cash payments, 11:672a, 677b, 678b–679a
fixed, 11:678a, 682a
in Castile, 3:136a
Celtic, 10:465a
charters of liberty, 11:677b–678a
class formation and, 3:413b
colonus, 3:482b–483b, 11:673b
Conrad II's ordinance, 3:557b–558a
consolidation of holdings, 11:680b, 683a
copyhold tenure, 11:682b
demesne farms, 11:675b–676a, 677a-b
development
6th–9th centuries, 11:673a–676a
9th–12th centuries, 11:676a–680a
distress, 4:220b–221a
domaine éminent, 11:678b
East-Central Europe, 11:684a-b
economic leases, 11:679b
England, 11:682a-b
common law procedures, 7:452b–454b
copyhold, 3:596b–597a
disputes, 6:481a, 7:434a-b, 9:546b
entail, 9:149b
escheat, 4:508b–509b
feudal system and, 7:437b
franchises, 7:448b–449a
high farming, 11:682a-b
primogeniture, 12:622b
right of "incidents," 7:453b–454a
use of land, 7:453b–455a
warranty of land grants, 7:440b
see also Sergeant; Thegn
feu, 11:685b
5th century, 12:148b
France, 11:680a–681a
appanage system, 5:169a, 170b
customary tenure, 5:174a
frankalmoin, 5:209b–210a
Germany, 11:681b–682a, 683b–684a
archiepiscopal *Erblandesvereinigung,* 10:333a
Golden Bull of 1356 and, 10:329a-b
"high farming," 11:682a, 12:532b–533a
Hungary, reforms of St. Stephen I and, 11:478b–479a
inherited, partition custom, 10:329a
Ireland, Scotland, and Wales, 11:685a-b
Italy, 11:683a-b
joint ownership, 11:671a, 680b–681a
kindly tenants, 11:685b
knighthood and, 3:414a-b
labor services, 11:675b, 682a, 683b
Germany, 11:681b
leasehold farms, 11:677b
land use regulation, 11:679a
landlord control, 11:674b, 678a
lessening of, 11:679b
latifondi, 11:683a
leasehold farms, 11:673b, 680a, 681b, 684b–685a
commercial, 11:683a
terms of lease, 11:681a
Low Countries, 11:681a-b
mainmort and, 8:51a
manorial organization, 11:674b–676a
decline of, 11:676b, 680a-b, 681b
market and, 11:679a
military service and, 3:414a-b
ministerials and, 8:404a–406b
Norway, 9:181b, 182a
owner-operators, 11:673a, 676a
partibility, 11:678b, 682a
peasants and, 11:675b–676a
precarium, 11:674b
proof of ownership, 5:55b
regional development, variations in, 11:680a–685b
rental tenure, 11:677a, 677b–679a, 680a
hereditary transfer, 11:678a-b, 681b–682a, 684a
restriction of movement, 11:673b, 684b
right to disposal of wilderness, 10:278a
rights of alienation, 11:678b
Rome, 10:460a
of nobles, 10:525a
see also Mancian tenure
rural depopulation and, 11:683b, 684b, 685a
Scandinavia, 11:684b–685a
free farmers, 11:679b
in Scottish clans, 3:407b
seignorial authority, 11:676b
sergeanty and, 3:414b, 425b
sharecropping, 11:681a, 683a
size of holdings, 11:671a, 673a-b
slaves, 11:673b–674a
Spain and Portugal, 11:682b–683a
squatters, 11:676b–677a
squires in Italy and, 11:465b
tenurial variables, 11:671b–672a (*illus.*)
terms of contract, 11:673b
unit of ownership
fundus, 11:673b
massae, 11:673b
in Valencia, 12:346b
in Vandal state, 12:355b
villae, 11:674b–676a
decline of, 11:682a, 683b
in villages, 12:438a, 438b
villein tenure, 3:415b, 11:678a, 681a
commutation, 11:682b
wage labor, 11:683b, 684b
see also Allod; Colonus; Commendation; Corvée; Demesne; English common law; Fee simple; "Hospitality"; *Manus;* Pasture, rights of; Reclamation of land; Seisin, disseisin; Serfs and serfdom; Status
T^cēodoros K^crt^cenawor, 1:509b
Tephrikē, 9:469a
as capital of a Paulician state, 9:468a
taken (872), 2:118a
Tēr Israyēl, 1:521a
Terce (canonical hours), 3:67a, 4:229a
time of, 5:662b
Tercias, 11:610a
Terem, **11:686a**
Terence, 4:277b, 278a, 282b
Andria, Notker Teutonicus and, 9:189b
Donatus on, 7:352b, 360a
Hrotswitha and, 6:314a, 315a-b, 316a-b
Teresa of Ávila, St., compared to Gertrude the Great, 9:11a
Teresa (wife of Henry of Burgundy), 10:39a, 39b
Terminism, **11:686a–687a**
Aristotelian logic and, 11:686b–687a
nominalism and, 11:686b–687a
origins, 11:686a-b
treatises, 11:686b
university studies in, 11:686b
via moderna and, 12:406a
see also Nominalism
Terminorum musicae diffinitorium. See Johannes Tinctoris
Terra Sigillata, **11:687a**
dish, 11:687b (*illus.*)
Terra-cotta. *See* Construction, building materials
Terrage (market tax), 8:146b
Terres de Beauvais, 3:238a
Territorio portucalense
description of, 10:38b–39b
references to, 10:37b
Terryglass (monastery), 6:521b
Terter, 7:309b
Tertry, Battle of (687), 8:236a, 9:500a
Tertullian
antifeminism of, 1:322b–323a
Christian moralism, 9:583a
Christian movement and, 3:334b
heresy and, 3:335b
hostility to art, 4:349a
on liturgy, 7:625b
philosophy and
elements of in writing, 9:583b
opposition to, 9:583a
on reservation of the sacrament, 10:335b
Roman education and, 7:360a
sign of the cross and, 11:288a

Tervel, Bulgar khan, 7:203a
Tervingi. *See* Visigoths
Terzetto/terzetti. See Madrigal
Terzo. See Siena
Tesaur. See Pierre de Corbiac
Teseida delle nozze d'Emilia. See Boccaccio, Giovanni
Tesoretto. See Latini, Brunetto
Tessera, **11:687a-b**
glass, 11:687a-b
gold, 8:490b
production of, 8:490b
insertion of
interstices, 8:491b–492a
rules for, 8:492a
wall mosaics, 8:491b–492a
materials used, 8:489b
availability of, 8:490b
mother-of-pearl, 8:490b
recycling, 8:490b–491a, 11:687b
stone, 8:490b
terracotta, 8:490b
Testacy and intestacy
in Byzantine law, 6:451a, 452a
Germanic, 6:455b
Roman, 6:456a
see also Will (testament)
Testament. See Vic, Bernat Serradell de
Testament of Cresseid. See Henryson, Robert
Testament of Love. See Usk, Thomas
Testament (will). *See* Will (testament)
Tester, 5:323a
Testimonia, 10:2a
Testimonium septimae, 9:207a
Testimony of the Lord Is Faithful. See Solomon ben Moses de Rossi
Tet River, 6:558b
Tetartemorion, 8:419b, 421a
Tetarteron, 4:494a
Tetartion, 12:582a
Tetrabiblos. See Ptolemy
Tetrachords, in solmization, 11:362b
Tetraconch, **11:687b**
see also Church architecture, conch type
Tetragamy, Nikolaos I Mystikos and, 9:135b
Tetralogus. See Wipo of Burgundy
Tetramorph, **11:688a**
Tetrarchy, imperial, 10:458b
Tetry, Battle of (687), 8:278b
Teufelsnetz, 8:357b
Teutates (Celtic divinity), 9:46a
Teutones, defeated by Marius, 2:88b
Teutonic Knights
accounting system, 1:38a, 40b
Andrew II of Hungary and, 3:306a
in the Baltic lands, 2:65b, 66b–67b
called "new Maccabees" by Pope Honorius III, 2:231b
control of trade, 6:91a, 92a, 94a, 96a
conversions to Christianity, 3:306a
cooperation with Lübeck, 7:681a
cross of, 3:305 (*illus.*)
defeated at Grunwald (Tannenberg), 2:67a, 7:607b
dress of, 3:306a
in East Prussia, 7:604a
English trade boycott, 6:95a
in Estonia, 2:65b
first and second Peace of Toruň, 9:726b, 727b–728a
flag of, 3:305 (*illus.*)
formation of, 3:306a
German biblical poetry and, 2:231a
in German towns, 5:460b–461a
"granted" Lithuania by Emperor Louis IV, 7:606a
in Hungary, 2:70a
Lithuanians and, 8:444a
Margaret of Denmark and, 11:533a
Middle High German literature and, 8:357a
Order of the Salamander dissidents, 9:727b
Peace of Kalisz, 9:724b–725a
in Poland, 9:721b, 723b–725a, 726a–728b, 730a
Prussians and, 6:438a, 8:444a
territory of, 3:306b
in Transylvania, 6:341b
Wolfger von Erla and, 12:672b
see also Baltic countries
Tevah. See Bimah
Texaurus regis Franciae acquisitionis terre sancte de ultra mare. See Guido da Vigevano (da Papia)
Texier, Bartholomew, 4:253b–254a
Texier, Jean, Chartres Cathedral and, 3:276a
Textbooks, **11:688a–693a**
arts curriculum, 11:689b–690a
law, 11:691a–692a
medical, 11:692a-b
pastoral guidance, religious instruction and, 10:300a–302a
quadrivium, 11:688b–689a
regulation and production of, 11:692b–693a
required reading lists, 11:688a
theology, 11:688b, 690b–691a
trivium, 11:688b
Textile technology, 11:639a, **11:693a–711a**
gender issues, 11:712b
loom, 11:639a
productivity gains
with broadloom, 11:704b–705a
with fulling mill, 11:706b
with horizontal treadle loom, 11:704b
with spinning wheel, 11:698b, 700b
qirmiz dye and, 10:236a-b
silk, 11:295a–296a
spindle machine, 11:639a
spinning wheel, 11:639a
quality of thread, 11:654a-b
weaving, technological innovations, 6:395
see also Dyes and dying; Linen; Spinning; Tapestry, art of; Weaving
Textile workers, **11:711a–715b**
dyers and shearers
commercial function, 11:713a
income, 11:713a
family-based, 11:711a-b
fullers, income, 11:714a
gender, 11:711b, 712b, 715a
guilds, 11:713a–715a
in Italy, 14th century, 7:8b
specialization of labor, 11:711b
status of, 11:715a
urban, 11:711b
wages, 11:712b, 714a
piecework, 11:712a
warpers and winders, 11:712a
weaver-draper, 11:712a-b
dyeing industry and, 4:328b
employees of, 11:714a
income, 11:712b–713a
Textiles
Armenian, 12:98a-b
Bosnia, 2:341b
Byzantine, 2:452b–453a
cope (silk, 10th–11th century), 11:0 (frontispiece)
decorative motifs, 2:456a-b
Visigothic sculpture and, 12:466b, 468a
see also Trade, Byzantine
Chinese. *See Kamkhā*
cloth trade, Poland, 9:728b
Coptic, 3:588b–590a
decoration of, 4:362b
cotton cultivation, 3:626b–627a
embroidery, rugs and carpets, 10:547a
Icelandic, market for, 6:395a
importation of, mercantile edicts governing, 3:622a
Islamic, 3:616b–617a, **11:715b–719b**
assignment of, 11:716b
Chinese motifs in, 11:718b
Coptic and Byzantine Egypt, 11:717a
design, 11:717a, 718a, 718b
dībāj, 4:173 (*illus.*)
of Fatimids, 5:23b–24a
felt, 10:546b
human figures in, 11:718a
kamkhā, 7:207b–208a
kārgah, 7:214b
kiswa, 7:273a-b
Mongol Iran, 11:718b
mulḥam, 8:530a
robes of honor, 11:716a
of Seljuks of Rum, 11:149a-b
Spanish peninsula, 11:718a
sumptuary laws and, 11:507b–508b
ṭirāz bands, 11:716 (*illus.*), 716b–717a
uses, domestic, 11:715b–716a
uses, political, 11:716a
woven, 10:546b–547a, 548b–550a
Zandanī-jī group, 11:718a
see also Mamluk art; Rugs and carpets; *Ṭirāz;* Trade, Islamic; Zandanījī
for liturgical furniture, 5:319a
Nubian, 9:199b
printing of, woodcut and, 12:689b–690a, 692b
shroud, *plashchanitsa,* 9:694a–694b (*illus.*)
Sicily, 11:275b–276a
silk, 4:362b
European import of, 10:548a
testing of (alnage), 1:202b–203a
trade in, 12:152b
at fairs, 4:585b, 586a,b, 587a, 592a, 593a
bedestan and, 2:156b

Textiles (*cont.*)
trade in (*cont.*)
early medieval, 12:110a
exchanges in Seville, 11:214b
Flemish, 12:153b–154a, 157b–158a
Frisian, 12:152b
international, 4:327b, 328a
London, 7:665b
Tuscany woolens, 7:8b
in Valencia, 12:348b
water mills used for producing, 8:393a-b
Western European, Islamic trade and, 12:107b
see also Dyes and dyeing; Flax; Hemp; Scarlet
Textualis. See Caroline minuscule
Textus Roffensis, 1:286a, 286b
Tha^{c}ālibī, al-, *Yatīmat al-dahr,* 2:238b
Thābit ibn Qurra, 9:4b, 11:84a
on astronomy, 1:614b–615a, 622a
De motu octauae sphaerae, 1:612b
designer of sundials, 3:28b
Euclid's *Elements,* translation of, 8:209b
Isḥāq ibn Ḥunayn and, 12:130b–131a
Liber karastonis, 1:434b, 438a
scientific works by, 12:131a
translations of Greek scientific treatises into Arabic and, 11:82b, 83a
trepidation theory of, 12:67b
Thaddeus Legend, 1:510a, 519a, 519b, **12:1a**
Thaddeus of Parma, 1:613a
Thaddeus of Suëssa, 3:641a
Thaïs (converted harlot), 6:316a
Thalassion metron (unit of measure), 12:581b
Thalassios modios (unit of measure), 12:581b
Thaleia. See Arius
Thames River, as a linguistic dividing line, 8:312b
Thane. *See* Thegn
Thanksgiving, oil for, 2:177a
Theater. *See* Drama
Theatrum, defined, 4:278a
Thebes (Greece)
Catalans and, 7:379b
disputed ownership of, 7:381b
Guy de la Roche and, 7:378a
Otto de la Roche and, 7:376b
plundered by Michael Palaiologos, 7:378b
as silk manufacturing center, 12:102b
Thèbes, Roman de, 8:225b
Thecla, St., as *isapostolos,* 6:560b
Theganus, **12:7b–8a**
influences on, 12:7b
Thegn, **12:8a–9a**, 12:556b
bells and, 2:166b
during West Saxon hegemony, 12:8b
term *gesith* and, 12:8a-b
witenagemot and, 12:665b
Theinred of Dover, 8:598a
Themes, **12:9a–11a**
administration of, 2:487b
fiscal, 2:474b
katepanikion, 2:474b
protonotarios, 2:473b
in Anatolia, 1:241a
armies of, 3:199b–200a
military efficiency and, 12:10b
numerical strength, 12:10a
decline of, 12:10a-b
dioikesis and, 11:603a
ducal authority, 2:474b
exarchate and, 10:460a
formation of, 12:9a-b
judges, 2:473b
see also Strategos
Themistius, 1:457b, 9:701a
Victorinus and, 1:460b
Theobald, bishop of Arezzo (*d.* 1036), 8:641a
Theobald of Canterbury, archbishop, 2:151a, 3:83a
John of Salisbury and, 7:139b
Vacarius and, 12:343a-b
Theobald of Monte Cassino, *Physiologus* and, 7:363b
Theobaldus-Physiologus, 2:205b
Theodebert II, Frankish king, Sutton Hoo and, 11:520a
Theoderic. *See* Theodoric the Ostrogoth
Theodofrid of Corbie, **12:11a-b**
Theodolus, *Eclogue,* 7:352b–353a, 362b, 367a
Theodonus di Caprio, *De musica mensurabili* and, 8:646a
Theodora I, Byzantine empress, 7:201a, **12:11b–12b**
Antonina and, 2:165a
cosmetics of, 2:147b
marriage to Justinian I, 12:12a
mosaic of in S. Vitale at Ravenna, 10:264b, 12:11 (*illus.*), 12b
Nubian Monophysitism and, 9:197b
Theodora II, Byzantine empress, **12:12b–13a**
Michael III and, 8:302a
owner of trading ships, 12:102a
persecution of Paulicians and, 9:468a
see also Bardas Caesar
Theodora Komnena, *Rolandslied* and, 10:447b
Theodora the Macedonian, Byzantine empress, **12:13a**
Theodore, **12:14b**
Theodore (Greek artist), fresco at Mileševo, 12:14b, 15 (*illus.*)
Theodore I Laskaris, Nicaean emperor, 7:127b, 343a, 347a, **12:13b**
at Brusa, 2:392b
expansion, Asia Minor, 2:498a-b
reign of, 9:115b–117a
vs. Latin Empire of Constantinople, 7:347b
Theodore II Laskaris, Nicaean emperor, 7:127b, 343a, **12:13b–14a**
treatises of, 12:14a
wars of, 7:348a
Theodore II Palaiologos, despot of the Morea, 7:381b
Argos and, 7:381a
Corinth and, 7:381b
Theodore Abū Qurra, iconoclasm and, 6:403a
Theodore Anagnostes, on the capture of Thessaloniki (1430), 2:517a
Theodore Angelos Komnenos Doukas, ruler of Epiros, 2:409a-b, 4:499a
capture of Thessaloniki, 2:498b, 9:117a, 12:26b
defeat at Klokotnica, 2:498a-b, 8:135a
expansion of Epiros by, 7:347b
Serbia and, 11:174b
vs. Latins, 7:378a
Theodore of Antioch, Frederick II and, 11:257b
Theodore Balsamon, **12:14b**
nomocanon and, 9:158b
poetry of, 2:507a
Theodore bar Konai, on Manichaeism, 8:84a, 9:107b
Theodore bar Wahbōn, Michael the Syrian and, 8:305b–306a
Theodore Bestes, *nomocanon* and, 9:158b
Theodore Branas, 7:348b
Theodore of Canterbury, St., 2:153b, 180b, **12:13a-b**
consolidation of Anglo-Saxon church, 4:458b
episcopate of, 3:82a
missions of, 7:362a
on penance, 9:488b, 489b, 490a
Penitentiale, 4:599b, 600b
reorganization of church by, 8:371b
Saxon church construction, 10:679b
Theodore Laskaris. *See* Laskaris, Theodore
Theodore Lector, on the Creed, 3:675b
Theodore Meliteniotes, *On Temperance,* 2:510a
Theodore Metochites, 1:246a, 7:215b–216a, **12:15a**
artistic patronage, 2:449a–450a
Hupomnematismoi commentaries, 9:698b
Kariye Djami mosaic cycle and, 2:450a
Nikephoros Gregoras and, 9:133b
poetry, Homeric, 2:507b
Theodore of Mopsuestia, 3:630a, 4:549a
Armenian church and, 1:498b, 499a
Christology of, 12:25b
Church of the East and, 11:563a
East Syrian rite and, 11:567b
known as "the Commentator," 9:106b
Nestorianism and, 9:105a, 107a, 564a
School of Nisibis and, 11:564b
translations of, 11:566a
used in Irish biblical commentaries, 2:220a
Theodore Prodromos, **12:16a-b**
epigrams, 2:507a-b
poetry, use of meter, 2:508a
Rodanthe and Dosikles, 2:508a, 12:16b
Theodore Psalter, unicorn in, 6:362b
Theodore Řštuni
Arabs and, 1:478a, 478b
Nersēs III Išχanec^{c}i (Šinoł) and, 9:103a
Theodore, St., in art, Bulgarian icon, 2:415 (*illus.*)
Theodore Skutariotes, historical works, 2:517a

Theodore of Smyrna, 11:55a
Theodore the Stratelates, 1:518b
Theodore of Studios, 3:631a, 11:494b, **12:15b–16a**
against charms, 8:18a
against iconoclasm, 12:16a
as author of *kanōnes,* 7:613a
on icons, 2:463a, 6:398b, 404b
kontakion, 2:511a
patriarch Nikephoros and, 9:131b
poetry, 2:506b
on sacraments, 7:611a
Theodore Svetoslav of Bulgaria, 2:411a-b
Theodore of Tarsus. *See* Theodore of Canterbury, St.
Theodoret of Cyr, 3:630a, **12:17a**
Armenian church and, 1:499a
condemnation of, 9:564a
eratopokriseis, 9:564a
Historia religiosa, 6:58a
Nestorianism and, 9:106a, 106b
Theodoric I, Visigothic king, 2:92a-b, 12:470a-b
court in Toulouse, 12:90b
Theodoric II, Visigothic king, 12:470b, 472a
Sidonius and, 11:277b
see also German law, early Germanic codes
Theodoric Borgognoni of Lucca, Dominican scholarship and, 4:247b–248a
Theodoric of Cervia, bishop (medieval surgeon), 2:98a
on leprosy, 7:550a
Theodoric of Freiberg, **12:17b–18b**
conflict with Aquinas, 12:18b
reform of metaphysics, 12:18b
studies of, 12:17b–18a
vision theory
experimental methods, 9:249a
rainbows, 7:539b, 9:253a
works of, 12:18a
Theodoric the Great. *See* Theodoric the Ostrogoth
Theodoric of Lucca (surgeon), 8:251a
medical treatises of, 11:692a
Theodoric, Master, **12:17a-b**
frescoes of, 5:610a
painting in Karlstein Castle, 12:17 (*illus.*)
Theodoric the Ostrogoth, **12:19a**
administrative system, 9:290a, 290b
Alamanni and, 11:526a
amethyst seal ring of, 11:125a
Arator and, 1:422a
Arianism and, 1:454b
assassination of Odoacer, 9:221a, 290a
Boethius and, 2:291b
building program, 9:290b
Byzantines and, 9:289b, 290a
Cassiodorus Senator and, 3:123a-b
Catholic church and, 9:291a-b
chancery of, 3:252a-b
in chronicles, 9:291a
death of, 5:506a
dynastic marriages, 9:290a
dynastic problems, 9:291b
Ennodius and, 4:491b
as hostage in Constantinople, 2:93a
legal system, 7:471a, 9:290b, 291a
early Germanic law and, 7:471a
monastic schools fostered by, 11:74a
in Ravenna, 10:263a-b
Roman education, 9:289b
Roman repairs and, 10:517a
rule of Italy, 9:290a-b
on slavery, 11:335a
Þiðreks saga and, 12:29a-b
title of patrician and, 9:460a
Visigoths and, 12:471a
see also Dietrich von Bern
Theodoric of Rheims, St., 6:317b
Theodoric (son of Triarius), Ostrogothic ruler, 2:93a
Theodoric (Theuderich) III, Frankish king, 9:500a
Theodoric (Theuderich) IV, Frankish king, 3:272b, 8:236a
Theodoricus, *Historia Norwegiae,* 4:618a, 9:175b, 176a
Theodoricus de Campo. *See* Theodonus di Caprio
Theodoricus Teutonicus de Vriberg. *See* Theodoric of Freiberg
Theodoros Meliteniotes, against astrology, 8:18a
Theodorus of Asine, 9:97b
Theodosian Code. *See* Codex Theodosianus
Theodosians. *See* Monophysitism, Egyptian
Theodosiopolis/Karin, 1:473a, 474a
captured by Arabs, 1:478b
partition of Greater Armenia and, 1:476a
refortified by Basil II, 1:483b
retaken (949), 1:483b
under Arabs, 1:479a, 479b
under Justinian I, 1:477a
see also Karin
Theodosios
epitome of Herodian's *Universal Prosody,* 11:51b
Introductory Rules on Inflection of Nouns and Verbs, 11:51b
Theodosios of Trnovo, 2:413b
Theodosius I (the Great), western Roman emperor
Ambrose and, 1:231b
Arianism and, 1:454a, 2:485a
Christianity declared official religion, 3:337b, 10:462a-b
First Council of Constantinople and, 2:485a-b, 3:628b
in *Lectionary of the Church of Jerusalem,* 1:518b
Lesser Armenia and, 1:472b, 476a
missorium of, 8:446a
hieratic style of, 4:353b
patronage of art, 4:352a
Paulinus of Nola on, 9:471b
restoration of Nicene Orthodoxy, 5:666a-b
Thessaloniki and, 12:26a
Vegetius' *Epitoma rei militaris* and, 12:366b
Visigoths and, 12:469b
Theodosius II (the Calligrapher), eastern Roman emperor, 7:542a, **12:19b**
Codex Theodosianus and, 3:475a
convened Council of Ephesus (431), 3:629a
death of, 3:629b
Eutyches and, 4:524a
founder of university at Constantinople, 3:556b
Nestorius and, 9:106a, 108b
palace library and, 7:561a
Seven Sleepers of Ephesus and, 11:212b
Sozomen and, 11:374a
Theodosius III, Byzantine emperor, displaced by Emperor Leo III, 7:544b
Theodosius of the Caves, St., **12:19b**
foundation of Kievan monasticism, 10:595a
Theodosius the Deacon, poem on the recapture of Crete, 2:506b
Theodotus (*primicerius notariorum*), 10:522a
Theodricus, 11:322a
Theodulf of Orléans, 3:573a, 7:362a, 9:713b, **12:20a**
apse built by, 10:97a
Carolingian court and, 3:109b
Contra iudices, 3:102b
"Gloria, laus, et honor tibi sit," 6:381b
imprisonment, correspondence during, 8:451b
Jonas of Orléans and, 7:146a-b
Latin poetry of, 3:102a–103a
revision of the Vulgate and, 2:211b
Theogerus, bishop of Metz (*ca.* 1050-1121), 8:642a
Theognostos, on orthography and grammar, 11:51b
Theognostus of Sarai, bishop, 9:653b
Theoktistos, logothete of the drome
recapture of Crete by, 3:678a-b
Theodora II and, 12:12b–13a
Theologia Christiana. See Abelard, Peter
Theologia Summi boni. See Abelard, Peter
Theological Orations. See Gregory of Nazianzus, St.
Theologos. *See* Ephesus
Theology. *See* Philosophy and theology
Theology of Aristotle, 1:458a, 606a
Theology, schools of, **12:20a–22a**
Theon of Alexandria, 1:613b–614a
Archimedes and, 1:434a
Theon of Smyrna, 9:699a
Theophanes Confessor, **12:22b–23a**
on Battle of Yarmuk, 12:719a
Chronographia, 2:513a-b, 12:22b
continuations of, 2:513b, 514a, 514b
on Nikephoros I, 9:132b
patriarch Nikephoros and, 9:131b
source for later works, 6:244a, 245b
George the Monk and, 5:401b
on icons, 6:402a
inspired by John Malalas, 8:55b
see also Theophanes continuatus
Theophanes continuatus, 3:547b, 5:382a, 6:244a, 244b, **12:23a**
John Skylitzes and, 11:330a

Theophanes continuatus, 3:547b (*cont.*)
on the Paulicians, 9:468a
see also Scriptores post Theophanem; Theophanes Confessor
Theophanes the Greek, **12:23b–24a**
Christ Pantokrator in church of the Transfiguration, 10:587 (*illus.*)
frescoes, 10:595b
style and influence, 10:587a
hesychast influence, 10:587a
influence on Russian art, 10:586b
Mother of God icon, 10:587a-b
Transfiguration icon, 12:23b (*illus.*)
works of, 2:450b–451a
Theophanes Nonnos, *Iatrika,* 4:446b
Theophano, Byzantine empress, 10:515b, **12:24a**
Theophano, Byzantine princess, encouragement of education, 11:77a
Theophano (wife of Nikephoros II Phokas), 9:132b, 133a
Theophano (wife of Otto II), regency for Otto III, 9:302a
Theophany, in art, 6:405b
Théophile. See Rutebeuf
Theophilos, Byzantine emperor, 1:236a, 12:12b
building at Constantinople, 3:553a
coinage of, 8:419a
higher education and, 12:301a
icons and, 2:488b–489a, 6:401a
Leo the Mathematician and, 7:547b
telegraph system of, 10:59a
in *Theophanes continuatus,* 12:23a
title of girdled patrician and, 5:539b
Theophilos Protospatharios (compiler of a medical encyclopedia), 8:245b
Theophilus, 10:505b, **12:24a-b**
De diversis artibus, 2:166a, 5:556a-b, 7:369a-b, 8:90b, 9:273a, 10:442a-b, 12:24a-b
church ornamentation, instructions for, 11:643b–644a
on enamel making, 4:435b, 438b
on glassmaking, 5:556a-b, 561b, 11:656b
influence of, 11:644a
on metalworking, 8:283b–284b, 289a, 296b, 297a
on organs, 8:604b
religious motivation, 11:643b
identity of, 12:24a
on stained glass, 5:549a
on steelmaking, 11:470b–471a
see also Roger of Helmarshausen
Theophilus of Alexandria, 7:122b
Theophilus of Antioch, 12:198a
Theophilus (medical author), *De urinis,* 8:248a, 256b
Theophilus Miracle, 4:268b, 271a, 320b
Theophrastus
as authority for antifeminism, 1:323a, 324a
on charcoal burning, 3:267a
De nuptiis, 7:368a
Historia plantarum, 2:345a, 6:177b
ignored in the Middle Ages, 2:244b–245a
influence of on Byzantine medicine, 8:244a
Theophylact, 10:522a, 525a
Theophylact family, control of papacy in 10th century, 9:383b–384a
Theophylact of Ochrid, archbishop, 2:407a
Theophylact, patriarch, letter on the Bogomils, 2:294a, 294b
Theophylaktos Simokattes, **12:24b–25b**
on Bahrām VI Čōbēn of Persia, 2:50a
on the European Avars, 2:12a
historical works, 2:512a, 6:243a-b
Quaestiones physicae, 12:25a
see also Paschale Chronicon
Theorica planetarum. See Campanus of Novara
Theorica planetarum (anonymous), 1:612a-b
Theoricae novae planetarum. See Peuerbach, Georg
Theoricum opus. See Gaffurius, Franchinus
Theosophy, Islamic, 6:587a
Theotikon, 6:379a
Theotokos, 7:612b, **12:25b–26a**
Athanasius and, 12:459b
Byzantine folklore and, 8:19b–20a
Council of Chalcedon (451) and, 9:106a
Council of Ephesus and, 12:460a
in hymns, 6:383a-b
Nestorius and, 9:105b, 108a-b
see also Virgin Mary
Theotokos Church of Constantine Lips (Constantinople), 1:445a (*illus.*)
Thermoluminescence testing, 1:431b
Thesaurus of Orthodoxy, The. See Niketas Choniates
Thesaurus pauperum. See Peter of Spain
Thessaloniki, **12:26a–27a**, 12:306a
Bulgarian market at, 2:404b
Byzantine classical scholarship in, 11:50a-b
as Byzantine trade center, 12:100b, 101a
conquered, 9:117a, 117b
fairs, 4:588b
in 15th century, 2:503b
historical accounts, 2:516a
influx of Jews into, 12:26b
massacre in 390, 1:231b, 12:26a
mint at, 8:420a
monasteries, 8:457b
mosaics at, 10:113b
Norman invasion, 2:496b
origins of, 12:26a
Ottoman conquest (1430), 6:443b
raids by foreign powers, 12:26b
relations with
Bulgarian empire, 7:347b
Latin Empire of Constantinople, 7:346a,b, 347b
Nicenes, 7:347b
sacked by
Arabs (904), 7:545b, 9:75a
Normans (1185), 1:245a, 6:559b
strategic location of, 10:424a
Symeon of Bulgaria and, 11:555a
Theodore of Epiros and, 7:378a
Turkish invasions, 14th century, 2:502b
under the Palaiologoi, 8:92a, 12:26b
Zealots and, 12:742b–743a
Thessaly
acquired by Stefan Uroš IV Dušan of Serbia, 11:178b, 475b
aristocracy, land holdings of, 2:479a
attacked by Samuil (985-986), 2:118b
reconquered by Basil II, 2:119a
Theodore of Epiros and, 7:347b, 378a
see also Meteora
Theudebald, Alemanni leader, 11:526b
Theudis, Visigothic king, 12:471a
Theudoald, named successor of Pepin II, 9:500a
Thewis of Gud Women, The, 3:663a
Thibaut I of Blois-Chartres-Tours, count, territorial losses of, 3:244a-b
Thibaut II of Blois-Chartres-Meaux, count, 3:244b–245a
appointment as seneschal, 5:162a
Thibaut III of Champagne, count
reign of, 3:247a
succession to, 3:247a-b
Thibaut IV of Champagne, count (Thibaut I of Navarre), 7:63a, 9:70b, **12:27a**
administrative reforms of, 3:249a
in Fourth Crusade, 4:32a, 42a, 42b, 51b–52a
lai and, 7:316b
lyric poetry, 5:282b
reign of, 3:247b–248a
trouvère poetry, 12:218b
wooing of Blanche of Castile, 2:270b
Thibaut V of Champagne, count (Thibaut II of Navarre), 9:70b
complainte on, 3:507b
reign of, 3:249b
Thibaut d'Aussigny, bishop of Orléans, 12:450b
Thibaut of Blois, count. *See* Thibaut II of Blois-Chartres-Meaux, count
Thibaut de Champagne. *See* Thibaut IV of Champagne, count (Thibaut I of Navarre)
Thielt, Battle of (1128), cavalry tactics at, 3:203b
Thierry III, Frankish king, seal impression in wax, 11:125a
Thierry of Alsace, count of Flanders, 5:80b
claim to Flanders, 3:497a
homage to Louis VI, 7:674a
Thierry of Chartres, 9:702a, **12:27a-b**
brother of Bernard of Chartres, 2:189b
commentary on Cicero, 10:356a
Commentum in Boethii de Trinitate, 10:270b
De septem diebus, 9:588b
four elements, 9:588b
Heptateuchon, 9:588b, 10:356a, 12:27b
Tractatus de sex dierum operibus, 12:27b
Thietmar I, abbot of Helmarshausen, 10:441a
Thietmar, Billung count, 2:235a
Thietmar von Merseburg, 9:717b, **12:27b–28b**

Gerbert of Aurillac's astronomical observations and, 11:100a-b
on hospitality, 6:468a
on St. Stephen I of Hungary, 11:478a
on St. Vladimir of Kiev, 12:435b
on Saxon dynasty, 12:27b–28a
on Slavic tribes, 12:28a
Thing (local Scandinavian assembly), 10:700a, 12:423b
"Things," Norwegian. *See* Law-things, Norwegian
Thingvellir (place of Icelandic assembly), 12:426b
Thiódólf of Hvín. *See* Þjóðólfr ór Hvíni
Thiofrid von Echternach, **12:28b–29a**
Third estate. *See* Political theory, Western European, estatist principle of organization; Representative assemblies
Third Order of Penance of St. Dominic. *See* Dominicans
Third Order of St. Francis. *See* Franciscans
Thirning, William, 7:190b
Thirsk, John, **12:29a**
"Thirteen Questions of Love," in Boccaccio, 2:279b, 284a
Thirteen-Year War (1454-1466), 2:67b
"Thirty Dayes Has November" (Middle English lyric), 8:339a
Thirty Years War
effects of
on German towns, 5:468b
on trade, 6:96b
"Thisness." *See Haecceitas*
Thjohild, 8:442b
Thomas the Apostle, St.
in art, 4:25a (*illus.*)
relief panels in St. Domingo de Silos, 10:494 (*illus.*)
Thomas Aquinas. *See* Aquinas, Thomas, St.
Thomas Arcruni, *History of the Arcruni House,* 1:481b
Thomas (Armenian anchorite), 1:519b
Thomas of Autremencourt, Amphissa and, 7:376b
Thomas à Becket. *See* Becket, Thomas, St.
Thomas à Becket's Prophecies, 10:149a
Thomas de Bretagne, 5:453b, 12:200a
hunting in, 6:359a-b
Tristan, 5:634b, 12:200b–201a
Norwegian translation of, 12:203a-b
see also Tristan, legend of
Thomas of Britain (Brittany). *See* Thomas de Bretagne
Thomas of Cantimpré, **12:34a–35a**
Bonum universale de apibus, 6:69b, 12:34a, 34b
De natura rerum, 4:448b–449a, 577b, 12:34a-b
medieval study of plants and, 2:245b
hagiographic works, 9:11b, 12:34a
Thomas of Capua
ars dictaminis and, 10:358b
hymns of, 6:382a
on letter writing, 7:368a
Thomas of Celano
Dies irae and, 7:369a
hymns of, 6:382a
Tractatus de miraculis sancti Francisci, 6:69a
Vita Prima, 6:69a
Thomas de Charlton, bishop of Hereford and chancellor of Ireland, Harley Manuscript and, 8:337a
Thomas of Claudiopolis, bishop, icons and, 6:400b
Thomas de Cormont, **12:33b**
as architect of Amiens Cathedral, 1:234b
Thomas, duke of Gloucester, Richard II and, 10:384a-b
Thomas of Epiros, murdered, 4:499b
Thomas of Erceldoune
mentioned in *The Cock in the North,* 10:147b
prophecies of, 10:146b–148a
Romance and Prophecies of Thomas of Erceldoune, 10:147a-b
four-line stanzas in, 8:345b
Second Scottish Prophecy and, 10:147b–148a
in Waldegrave's *Whole Prophesie of Scottlande,* 10:147b
Thomas of Erfurt, speculative grammar and, 10:359b
Thomas Gallus, *Commentary, The Cloud of Unknowing* and, 9:22b
Thomas of Hales, **12:35a-b**
"A Luve Ron," 9:19a, 12:35a
prose sermon in Anglo-Norman, 1:262b
Thomas of Harkel, 11:565a
Thomas of Ireland, *Manipulus florum,* 1:206a
Thomas à Kempis, 9:38a, **12:33a-b**
Devotio Moderna and, 4:166b
hymns and, 6:382b
Imitation of Christ, 2:368a-b, 4:166b–167a, 8:160b, 9:27b, 611b, 12:157b
attributed to, 12:33a
writings of, 12:33a-b
Thomas of Kent
Roman de toute chevalerie and, 1:266a, 10:453a
on St. Alban, 1:261b
Thomas of Lancaster
condemned, 6:427a
royal chamber and, 6:303b
Thomas Magister, *Selection of Attic Words and Expressions,* 11:53b
Thomas of Margā, *Book of Superiors,* 11:564b
Thomas, Master. *See Romance of Horn*
Thomas of Medzoph. *See* Tʿovma Mecopʿecʿi
Thomas Palaiologos, 7:381b
Thomas de Pisan, 1:608a
Thomas Preljubovič, Epiros and, 4:500a
Thómas saga, Thómas saga erkibyskups and, 12:35b, 36a
Thómas saga erkibyskups, 4:311b, **12:35b–36a**
Thomas of Salisbury, development of "thematic" sermon, 10:362b
Thomas of Savoy, 4:209a
Philip II Augustus and, 11:539b
Thomas of Sens, 8:103b
Thomas the Slav, 2:401b, **12:36b–37a**
claims of, 12:36b
siege of Constantinople, 12:36b–37a
see also Amorians
Thomas of Spalato, archdeacon, on Imre and Andrew, 6:341b
Thomas de Stromoncourt. *See* Thomas of Autremencourt
Thomas van Bellinghen. *See* Thomas of Cantimpré
Thomas of York (13th century)
Grosseteste and, 1:461b
on music, 8:579b
Thomasin von Zerclaere, 5:442b–443a, **12:37a–38b**
Welsche Gast, 3:665a, 12:37a–38a
Thomism, 1:463b, 466a-b, **12:38b–45a**
Aristotelian-Thomist theory of kingship, 4:400b
compared with Ockhamism, 12:43b
compared with Scotism, 12:43a-b, 44a
competing schools and, 12:42b–44b
confidence in reason and, 12:43a
differences with Franciscan theology, 4:375b–376a
Dominicans and, 1:463b, 466a
on Immaculate Conception, 12:43a
on Incarnation, 12:43a-b
on intellect and will, 12:42a
opponents of, 12:39a–40a
condemnations and *correctoria,* 12:40b–41a
Correctoria corruptorii Thomae, 12:41a
medieval Thomists, 12:41a–42b
Richardus de Mediavilla, 10:388b
Robert Kilwardby, 7:253b
see also Via moderna
postmedieval developments of, 12:44a-b
revival in 19th century, 12:44b
in 16th-century Spain, 12:42b
Summa de ecclesia, 4:378a
theology as a scientific discipline, 9:609a
theory of papal authority, 4:376b
in universities, 9:157a
Thor, 11:23a, 25b, 30b, 31b–32a, **12:45a–46b**, 12:423b
in *Alvíssmál,* 1:226b–227a
in the Baldr myth, 2:55b
cult of, 12:46a
as culture hero, 12:45b
divine functions, 1:63a
in *Flóamanna saga,* 5:90a
in *fornaldarsögur,* 5:142a
giant Geirröðr and, 12:48a
giant Hrungnir and, 12:45b
in *Haustlǫng,* 12:32a-b
in *Lokasenna,* 7:643b
midgard serpent and, 8:362a-b, 12:45a-b
mythological function of, 12:45a
in *Ragnarǫk,* 10:248a
in the Skarkaðr legend, 11:466b–467a
in *Sturlaugs saga Starfsama,* 11:496b
in *Þrymskviða,* 12:52b
worship of in Anglo-Saxon England, 1:289a

Thor, 11:23a (*cont.*)
see also Scandinavian mythology
Thoresby of York, John, bishop, *Lay Folks' Catechism,* 10:301b
Thorfinn Karlsefni, 4:555a
Thorismud, Visigothic king, 12:470b
Thorkelin, Grímur Jónsson, *Beowulf* and, 2:184a
Thorkillus, *Illuga saga Gríðarfóstra* and, 6:421a
Thorlák Thorhallson, bishop, 6:394a
Thorn (letter), in Old and Middle English, 8:310a, 310b, 311b
Thornton, Gilbert, 7:192b
Thornton, John, **12:46b**
Great East Window of York Minster, 12:46b–47a (*illus.*)
Thorp, William, chief justice, 7:193a-b
on statute law, 4:482b–483a
Thorpe, William. *See* Thorp, William
Thorvald Ericson, 4:555a
Thousand and One Nights, 1:382a, 8:21b–22a, **12:49a–52a**
afreets in, 7:113a
chronicles of Hārūn al-Rashīd in, 6:108a
Egyptian influences, 4:407b
genesis of, 1:382a
Historia de la donzella Teodor and, 11:415b
Islamic geography and, 5:393a
19th-century editions of, 12:50b
origin of, 12:49a–50a
poems in, 12:50a
as propaganda, 10:142b–143a
six narrative categories of, 12:50a
sources of, 12:50a-b
translation of into European languages, 12:51a-b
Thousand (unit of measure), 12:593b
Thrace
aristocracy, land holdings of, 2:479b
crusaders' route and, 10:423a
devastated (1205-1206), 7:347a
Ioannitsa and, 7:348b
Kalojan in, 7:206b
Krum in, 7:303b
ravaged by Catalans, 7:379b
relations with
Latin Empire of Constantinople, 7:346a, 347a
Nicenes, 7:347b
Symeon of Bulgaria and, 11:555a
Theodore Angelos and, 9:117a
Thraco-Illyrian language, Romanian and, 10:512b
Thrave (unit of measure), 12:593b
Three Chapters, condemnation of, 7:202a
Three Chapters, Council of (553), 1:477b, 499a
Three Children in the Furnace, The, music for, 8:557b
Three curtains. *See* Tribelon
Three Marys, in the Resurrection cycle, 10:340a
"Three Powerful Swineherds of the Island of Britain," 1:577b
Threnos. *See* Lamentation
Threshing, 12:80a
Throne of Christ. *See Hetoimasia*
Throne of the Koran. *See Kursī;* Rahle
Thrones
in *Beowulf,* 5:321b
in Islamic furniture, 5:315a-b
Thrush and the Nightingale, The, 8:315b–316a
Thuir, Royal Canal, 6:558b
Thuluth (Arabic script), **12:53b**, 12:54 (*illus.*)
development of, 9:334a
Thumna, Ibn al-, Roger I and, 10:440a
Thun
founded, 11:539a
Kyburgs and, 11:539b
Thurgau
Hugo von Montfort and, 6:325a
Kyburgs and, 11:539b
occupied by Swiss Confederation (1460), 11:544b
Thurible, 1:224b, 6:432a, 432b
Thurifer, 6:431b
Thurkelby, Roger, 7:188a
Thuróczi, Johannes, *Chronica Hungarorum,* 6:348b
Þættir, **12:1a–6b**
authorship of, 12:4a-b
classification of, 12:2a
dating of, 12:4a
family sagas and, 12:2a
historicity of, 12:5a-b
origins of, 12:3b–4a
short biographies, 12:3a
skaldic verses and, 12:3a
sources of, 12:4b–5a
stories about
Christianization, 12:2b
dreams, 12:3a
family feuds, 12:2b–3a
Norwegian king, 12:2a-b
otherworld journeys, 12:3a
transmission of, 12:3a-b
in the younger redaction of *Mágus saga jarls,* 8:45a-b
see also Sturlunga saga
Þáttr. See Þættir
Þáttr af Ragnars sonum, **12:6b–7b**
Ragnars saga loðbrókar and, 12:6b–7a
Þingeyrar, scholarship at, 4:618a
Þiðrekr. See Þiðreks saga
Þiðreks saga, 9:114a, 10:389b, 391b, 392a, 394b, 395a, 11:292b, **12:29a–31b**
Brynhild in, 2:395a
characters in, 12:29b–30a
compared with *Biterold und Dietlieb,* 2:253a
dating of, 12:31a
flyting and, 9:173a
German heroic epics and, 12:29a-b
Hrólfs saga kraka and, 6:311a
manuscript sources of, 12:31a
Ragnars saga loðbrókar and, 10:249b
Sigurd and, 9:217a, 11:289a, 289b
as a source for *Mágus saga jarls,* 8:45b
structure of, 12:30b
Vǫlsunga saga and, 12:488b
Vǫlundarkviða and, 12:490b, 491a
see also Dietrich von Bern; *Lied vom hürnen Seyfrid, Das*
Þjalar-Jóns rímur, author of, 10:402b
Þjálfi (mythological character), Thor and, 12:45b, 46a
Þjazi (mythological character), in *Haustlǫng,* 12:32a
Þjóðólfr ór Hvini, **12:32a-b**
Haustlǫng, 11:320a, 12:32a-b
Iðunn's apples, myth of, 7:19a
on Thor's encounter with Hrungnir, 12:45b
Ynglingatal, 7:312a, 11:320a, 12:32a, **12:725b–726b**
Hákonarmál and, 4:570a
structure of, 12:726a
Þóra (Sigmundr's daughter), 4:580b
Þórarinn Loftunga, *Glælognskviða,* 7:312a
Þorbjǫn hornklofi. *See Haraldskvæði*
Þorbjǫrn dísarskáld, on Thor, 12:46a
Þorfinn Karlsefni, in Vinland sagas, 12:457a, 458a
Þorgils, (saga character), 5:90a
Þorgils the Harelip, in *Sturlunga saga,* 11:500a-b
Þorgils saga ok Hafliða, 6:312b–313a
reference to *fornaldarsögur* in, 5:142b–143a
in *Sturlunga saga,* 11:498b
Þorgils saga skarða, in *Sturlunga saga,* 11:497b, 500a-b
Þórir of Trondheim, archbishop, 11:356b
Þorlákr the Holy, bishop, 12:359a
Þorlákr Rúnólfsson, bishop, 6:352a
Þorlákr of Skalholt, St., 2:252b, 6:352a
canonization of, 7:146a
Þorlákr Þórhallsson, St. *See* Þorlákr of Skalholt, St.
Þorláks saga, 6:352a
see also Bishops' sagas
Þorlákstíðir. See Sancti Thorlaci episcopi officia rhythmica et proprium missae
Þorleifr Þórðarson, 11:357a
Þorleifr the Wise, Þjóðólfr ór Hvini's *Haustlǫng* and, 12:32a
Þórmóðr Trefilsson, 11:319b–320a
Þórsdrápa. See Eilífr Goðrúnarson
Þórsnes clan, in *Eyrbyggja saga,* 4:568a
Þorstein (brother of Leif Ericson), in Vinland sagas, 12:457a
Þorsteinn, *Hjálmþérs rímur,* 10:402b
Þorsteinn Gyðuson, in *Auðunar þáttr vestfirzka,* 12:4b
Þorsteins saga Víkingssonar, **12:47a-b**
Þorsteins þáttr Austfirðings, 12:3a, 4b, 5a
Þorsteins þáttr Bæjarmagns, 12:3a, **12:47b–48b**
Þorsteins þáttr stangarhǫggs, 4:615a-b, 12:2b, 4a
Þórðar saga Hreðu, **4:48b–49a**
Eyrbyggja saga and, 4:568b
Þórðar saga Kakala, 11:500a
Þórðarbók. See Þórður Jónsson of Hítardalur
Þórðr Narfason, 11:497b–498a, 500b
Þórðr Sturluson (*d.* 1267), 4:568a
Þórðr Þórðarson, *Þórðar saga Hreðu* and, 12:48b

Þórður Jónsson of Hítardalur,
Þórðarbók, 7:327b, 328a
Þórður Magnússon á Strjúgi, *rímur* by,
10:403a
Þorvald (brother of Leif Ericson), in
Vinland sagas, 12:457a
Þorvaldr Ingjaldsson, *Droplaugarsona saga,* 4:612b, 613b
Þorvalds þáttr tasalda, 12:4a, 4b
Þorvaldsson, Björn, 11:357a
Thyra, in *Brevis historia regum Dacie,*
11:522b
Þrændlur, Færeyinga saga and, 4:581a
"Þráinn í haugi," 6:312a
Þrándr í Gǫtu, 4:580b, 9:176b
Þrymr, encounter with Thor, 12:45b
Þrymskviða, **12:52b–53b**
compared with *Baldrs draumar,* 2:56b
dating of, 12:52b
on Thor, 12:45b–46a
Þulur, in skaldic poetry, 11:318b
Tiara. *See* Vestments, liturgical
Tibalians, 5:419a
Tibbon, Jacob ben Machir ibn, quadrant of, 11:91b, 98a
Tibbonid family, 12:137b
translations into Hebrew and, 11:91a
Tiber River, flooding of, 10:521a, 521b
Tiberian Bible. *See under* Bible, Hebrew
Tiberias
Jews in, 7:104a, 104b
Talmud and, 10:463b
Tiberio Galliziani da Pisa, Iacopo da Lentini and, 6:387b
Tibet, technological innovations, prayer cylinders, 11:662a
Tibia, 8:558a, 559a
Tibia utricularis. See Bagpipe
Tiburtine sibyl, 8:386a
Ticino, Swiss Confederation and,
11:545b
Tide mills, 8:392a
Tides
action of, Establishment of Port,
2:155a
theories on, 5:396b
Tie-beam roof, 3:479b (*illus.*)
Tieck, Ludwig, interest in minnesingers,
5:443b
Tiefenbronn, high altar by Hans Schüchlein, 11:79b (*illus.*)
Tien Shan Kirghiz, 7:272b–273a
Tiepolo, Giacomo, doge of Venice,
12:390a-b
Tiepolo (Venetian noble family),
12:390a, 391a, 391b
Tierceron, **12:54a**
in a net vault, 12:365b
in a rib vault, 12:366a
Tifinagh, 2:186b
Tiflis. *See* Tbilisi
Tights, Western European, 3:625a
Tigran II (the Great) of Armenia, king
bdešχ and, 2:140a
coins of, 1:493a, 494a, 8:417b
Syrian March and, 1:514b
Tigran Honencᶜ, **12:54a-b**, 12:98b
church of S. Grigor Lusaworičᶜ and,
1:292a, 495b
dedicatory inscription of, 1:291a
will of, 1:485b
Tigrini, Francesco, mentor of Baldus,
2:57a
Tigris River, 4:522a,b
in Armenia, 1:470b
canal systems, 6:509b
see also Baghdad
Tihomir (Bulgarian rebel), 2:407b
Tihomir of Serbia, ruler, 11:173a, 473a
Tikrit. *See* Tagrit
Tilāwa, 8:560a
Tile
in Islamic architecture, 6:602a-b, 603b (*illus.*), 604a
lead-glazed, 3:236b (*illus.*), 237a
Tillage. *See* Agriculture; Reclamation of land
Tilo von Kulm, *Von siben Ingesigeln,*
2:230b–231a
Timaeus. See Plato
Timber (unit of measure), 12:593b
Timboholm gold hoard, 10:694b–695a
Timbrel. *See* Tambourine
Timbuktu, **12:54b–56b**
as capital of Moroccan Ruma state,
12:55b
origins of, 12:55a
postmedieval development of,
12:55b–56a
textile industry in, 8:58a
Time glasses, 11:101b–102a
Time, reckoning of, **3:17a–31b, 3:457a–464b**
aids to, 3:27b
astrolabe in, 3:28b–29a
astrology and, 1:609a
religion in, 3:18a
Western European astronomy and,
1:614a
see also Calendars; Clocks; Sundials
Time signatures
in *ars nova,* 1:549b
see also Musical notation
Timişoara diet. *See* Temesvár diet
Timoneda, Juan, *Rosas de romances,*
11:429b
Timothius Aelurus, 7:279b
Against Those Who Say Two Natures,
1:505b
Timothy I, Nestorian katholikos,
9:107a-b
Timothy I, patriarch of Antioch,
11:563b
Timothy, patriarch of Constantinople,
3:676b
Tīmūr. *See* Tamerlane
Timur Leng. *See* Tamerlane
Timurbughā, Mamluk sultan, 3:400a,
10:222a
Timurids, **12:56b–59b**
administration, 12:58b–59a
art and architecture, 6:605a-b
renaissance in, 1:65a
book production of, 7:274a
bookbinding and, 8:99b–100a
decline and fall of, 12:58a
descendants of Mīrānshāh in Transoxiana, 12:58a
descendants of ᶜUmar Shaykh, 12:58a
division of dynasty after 1469, 12:58a
four Turkic tribes (Chaghatais) and,
12:58a
Junayd at court of, 7:182a
Mehmed I and, 8:263b
Mehmed II and, 8:264a
Qara Yusuf's campaigns against,
10:228b
title of sultan and, 12:58b
Timurtāsh ibn Īlghāzī, copper coinage,
9:283b
Tin
as alloy, 2:383b
in Bronze Age, 2:383a
imported from the West into Egypt,
12:107b
mining, 8:397b–398a, 401a
working of, 8:287a
Tinibeg, Golden Horde under, 5:573a
Tinmal, Great Mosque, 6:611a-b
Tinne/pipai, 8:558b
Tino di Camaino, 5:535b, **12:59b–60b**
marble carving in Florence Cathedral,
12:59b–60a (*illus.*)
sculpture by, 12:171a-b
Tintagel, **12:60b**
Tristan legend and, 12:199b
Tintern, **12:60b–61a**
Tintinnabula. See Bells
Tiompan, 8:558a
Tióðels saga, 10:394a
Tipografskii Ustav, 8:573b
Tipoukeitos, 2:125b
Tír na mBan, 6:551b
Tír na n'Óg (the otherworld in Irish mythology), 9:47b
Tír Tairngiri (the otherworld in Irish mythology), 9:47b
Tirade. See Laisse
Tirant lo Blanch. See Martorell, Joanot
Ṭirāz, 3:618a, **12:61a–62a**, 12:224a
after the fall of Fatimids, 12:62a
with Kufic inscriptions, 12:61 (*illus.*)
Ṭirāz stuffs
band, 11:716 (*illus.*)
earliest example, 11:717a
material, 11:716b
Tīrdat I, Parthian ruler. *See* Trdat I, Arsacid king
Tiréchán, life of St. Patrick, 9:463a,
463b, 465a, 465b
Tirel, Walter, murder of William Rufus,
6:154b–155a
Tîrgovişte, Vlad Ţepeş and, 12:484b
Tiridates I, Arsacid king. *See* Trdat I, Arsacid king
Tiridates III of Armenia, king. *See* Trdat III (IV) (the Great) of Armenia, St.
Tirmidhī, al-, collection of *ḥadīths,*
6:47b
Tiro, Prosper. *See* Prosper of Aquitaine
Tirol, carnival plays from, 4:271b
Tišemir, ruler of Bosnia, defeated by Peter of Serbia, 11:169b
Tishtrya (Zoroastrian god), 12:721a
Tisserand, Jean, 6:382b
Tithes, **12:62a–65b**
after the Fourth Lateran Council
(1215), 12:63a
Byzantine, 11:604a
clerical, 11:616b
clerical tenth, 11:615a, 621b, 624a
collection of, 12:64b

Tithes (*cont.*)
Denmark, 4:153a
determination of tax base and, 12:64b
disbursement, 11:616b
doctrine of, 12:63a–64a
England, 11:616b
see also Frankpledge
evasions of payments, 12:65a
exemptions from payments of, 12:65a
historical development, 12:62a–63a
Islamic, 6:589b
land reclamation and, 10:273b–274a
in Latin Empire of Constantinople, 7:348b
penalties for nonpayment, 11:616b
types of, 12:64a-b
under the Carolingians, 9:412b–413a, 12:62b
used as gifts, 12:63b–64a
see also Taxation; *Tercias*; *ᶜUshr*
Tithes. *See* Peter's Pence
Titianus, 4:572a
Titles. *See* Nobility and nobles
Tituli, 3:93b
see also Liturgy, stational; Rome, churches
Titurel fragment. *See* Wolfram von Eschenbach
Titurelstrophe, 8:411b, 412b
Minnereden in, 8:408b
popularity of in Middle High German literature, 8:354b–355a
Tjängvide pictorial stone, 10:695a-b
Tkadleček, Ackermann aus Böhmen and, 1:44a-b
Tła Vasil, Hṙomklay and, 6:311b
Tlemcen
conquest of (709), 6:413a
Grand Mosque, 1:197a, 6:407a, 611a (*illus.*)
Tmutarakan, Khanate of, **12:66a-b**
To Ablabius, That There Are Not Three Gods. *See* Gregory of Nyssa, St.
To Nicocles. *See* Isocrates
To the Young. *See* Basil the Great of Caesarea, St., *Ad adolescentes*
Tobias. *See* Lamprecht; Matthew of Vendôme
Tobias ben Moses, 7:150b
Tocco, Carlo, 7:381b
Epiros and, 4:500a
Tochmarc Emire, 6:548b
Tochmarc Étaíne, 6:546b
Togail Bruidne Da Derga, 6:546b–547a, 547b
Togha Temür (*d.* 1353), 6:420b
Toghrıl-Beg, Seljuk sultan, 11:156b, **12:66b–67a**
Abu 'l-Aswār Shāwur and, 11:217b
creation of sultanate, 1:11b
deposition of the Buyids, 11:152a
given the title of sultan, 11:505a
marriage of daughter to al-Qāᵓim, 10:221b
occupation of Baghdad (1155), 6:513b
origins of the Seljuks and, 151b, 11:151a
titles granted by al-Qāᵓim, 10:221b
titles of, 12:66b
Toghrıl II, Seljuk sultan, Eldigüz and, 6:419a
Toghrıl III ibn Arslan Shāh, Seljuk sultan, 6:419b, 11:153b
Toghrıl-Shāh, vs. Balaban, 11:220b
Toghtu, succession to khanate, 8:475b
Toilet water, 2:147a
Toiseach, 3:407a, 407b
Tóka þáttr, 12:2b, 4b
Tokalı Kilise. *See* New Church (Tokalı Kilise); Old Church (Tokalı Kilise)
Tokhtamysh, defeat by Tamerlane, 8:540b
Tolbiac. *See* Zülpich
Toledan Tables, 1:611b, **12:67a-b**
see also Astronomy, Ptolemaic
Toledo, **12:67b–68b**
Gerard of Cremona in, 5:422b–423a
hunting in, 6:358a
irrigation of, 6:558a
in Islamic conquests, 6:572a
Jews in, 7:80b, 81a
Mozarabic community, 8:516b
reconquered by Christians (1085), 11:376b, 12:68a
as a seat of learning, 12:68a-b
seized by Alfonso VI, 1:199b
Spanish language development and, 6:442b
sword manufacture in, 11:548a
synagogues in, 12:68a
translation in, 3:313b, 11:161b, 406b, 410a, 414a, 456b
as Visigothic capital, 12:471a
Toledo Cathedral, Portal of the Lions
Toledo, Councils of
First (400)
concubinage and, 3:530a
condemnation of dualism, 4:297b
Second (527), school system established by, 11:59b–60a
Third (589), 12:471b, 472a
against "lewd songs and dances," 11:445b
Nicene Creed and, 3:676b
private penance and, 9:488a-b
Fourth (633)
Isidore at, 6:563b
on Jews, 9:111b
Fifth (636), deposition of rulers theory and, 4:158b
Twelfth (681), prince's free choice of bishops, 4:421a-b
Seventeenth (694), 12:472a
Toledo, councils of, Julianus of Toledo and, 7:181b
Tolfa, alum mines at, 12:115b
Tollkisten, 6:490b
Tolls
customs, 11:615a
England, 11:612a
England, 11:611b (*illus.*), 611b–612a, 612b
seizure of wool, 11:615a
exemptions from, 11:611b–612a
Islamic, 11:627b
lastage, 11:612b
poundage, 11:615a, 615b
right of prisage, 11:612b
right of purveyance, 11:612b
scavage, 11:612b
tunnage, 11:615b
see also Maltolte
Tolls. *See* Trade, regulation of; Travel and transport
Tolomei family, 11:279b
Tolta (the term), 11:576a
Toltrey (unit of measure), 12:586b
Tolui
appanage, 8:469a
military conquests, Khorāsān and Afghanistan, 8:467b
Tomás de Cuenca, 9:111b
Tomáš ze Štítného, 11:344b
Tómasskinna, Thómas saga erkibyskups and, 12:35b–36a
Tomb of Ismail the Samanid (Bukhara). *See* Samanid Tomb (Bukhara)
Tomb looting. *See* Relics; Translation of saints
Tombs
in catacombs, 3:155a
Iranian, 6:426a
Islamic, 6:602a-b, 608b
see also Crypt; Death and burial; Sarcophagus; Shrines
Tome. *See* Prosper of Aquitaine (Prosper Tiro)
Tome of Leo, 4:524a
Armenian church and, 1:499a, 499b, 500a
see also Leo I (the Great), pope
Tome of Union. *See* Nikolaos I Mystikos, patriarch
Tomich, Pere, *História,* 3:166b
Tomislav of Croatia, king, **12:68b–69b**
coronation of, 12:69a
as patron of literature, 11:345b
reign of, 4:2b, 4a–5a
Tommaso da Missaglia, 1:528b
Tommaso da Modena, Nicoletto Semitecolo and, 11:159a-b
Tonale Sancti Bernardi, 8:643a
Tonarius. *See* Regino of Prüm
Tonary, **12:69b–71a**
of *Alia musica,* 8:639a
of Amerus, 8:644b
Carolingian, 8:638b–639a, 12:69b–70a
differentia in, 4:185a
for ecclesiastical orders, 12:71a
of Frutolf of Michelsberg, 8:641b
Musica disciplina and, 8:639a
of Odo of Arezzo, 8:640b
Regino of Prüm and, 8:639b, 10:289b
of St. Bénique of Dijon. *See* Montpellier MS H.159
of St. Bernard, 8:643a
of Sarum use, 12:70b
see also Variatio
Tᶜondrakecᶜi, 1:482b, 5:674a
Paulicians and, 9:469b
Tone, reciting. *See* Communion chant
Tone, reciting. *See* Psalm tones
Tones, musical, **12:71a-b**
psalm tones, 8:448b
Regino of Prüm's tonary of, 10:289b
tonoi, eight-note modal system and, 8:450b
see also Melody; Plainsong
Tones, reading and dialogue, **12:71b–72a**

Tongues, gift of, Vincent Ferrer and, 12:453a
Tonlet, 1:531a
Tonneau (unit of measure), 12:596a-b
Tønsberg, population, 9:148b
Tonsure
  Celtic, 2:381b–382a, 3:228b–229a, 7:614a
  Celtic vs. Roman custom, 12:626b
  ceremony of, 3:442a
  for clerk, 3:448b
  degredation of clergy and, 4:134a
  deposition of rulers and, 4:158b–159a
  in priestly ordination, 9:268a
  Roman church, 2:381b–382a
Tools
  for building construction, 3:560a
  in grave finds, 8:291b–292a
  metal, 3:561a
  metalworking, 8:296a–297b
  saws, 3:561a
  shipbuilding, 11:243a-b
  writing materials and, 12:700a, 700b
Tools, agricultural, 8:294a-b
  European, **12:72a–83b**
    as capital, 12:82a-b
    hand digging tools, 12:78a–79a
    harrows, 1:98a, 12:77b–78a
    harvest tools, 12:79a–80b
    materials, 12:81a-b
    miscellaneous tools, 12:80b–81a
    plows, 12:72b–77b
    pointed sticks, 1:97b
    production of, 12:81b–82a
    scythes, 1:92a, 98a
    sickles, 1:77b, 98a
    sources of knowledge, 12:72b–73a
    use of ard, 12:77a
    see also Plow
  Islamic, **12:83b–86a**
  Islamic world
    for grafting fruit trees, 12:85b–86a
    harrows and digging tools, 12:84a-b
    harvesting tools, 12:84b–85a
    plows, 12:83b–84a
    rice husking and, 12:85b
    threshing and, 12:85a-b
    winnowing and, 12:85b
  see also Agriculture; Steelmaking
To'oril, 5:382b
Toothpaste. *See* Dental care, dentifrice
Topia, Karl, capture of Dyrrachium, 4:330a
Topiary, 5:363a
Topica. See Aristotle
Topica Ciceronis. See Boethius
Topics. See Aristotle, *Topica;* Cicero
Topkapi *sarāy,* 10:652a
Topographia Hibernica. See Gerald of Wales
Topographical guidebook. *See* Guidebooks; Pilgrims, guidebooks for
Topoteretes, 11:573b
Toqtamish, 5:573a
  vs. Tamerlane, 11:588a
Tor de' Conti (Rome), 10:525b
Torah, 7:69a
  as blueprint for divine plan, 9:576b–577a
  dietary laws and, 4:181a–183a
  Judaism and, 7:158b
  knowable vs. unknowable, 9:577b
  Maimonides' *Mishneh Torah,* 12:134a
  "Mother of the Book" and, 6:578a
  readings of, 7:160b
    and Hebrew literature, 6:130b
    in liturgy, 7:620a
  study of, 7:160b
  synagogue and, 11:556b–557a
  testing devotion to God, 9:581a
Torah ark, 11:557a
Tóraigheacht Dhiarmada agus Ghráinne, 6:546a, 549a
Törbel, irrigation of, 6:559a
Torcello, glassmaking in, 5:555b
Torches. *See* Lighting Devices
Torculus, 8:619 (*illus.*), 624b, 625 (*illus.*)
Torel, William, **12:86b–87a**
  tomb effigy of Eleanor of Castile, 12:86b (*illus.*)
Torgils Knutsson, regent of Sweden, Karelia and, 11:531a
Torna-fuye tactic, 3:203a
Tornada, **12:87a**
  in *Noie,* 6:630b
Tornada, troubadour, 12:215b, 216b
Tornada, *see also* Partimen
Tornada, see also Vers
Tornada (envoy), in Provençal literature, 10:165b
Tornik Mamikonean, Tarōn and, 11:599a
T^{C}ornik, ruler of Sasun, 1:484b
Tornikids, Greater Tarōn and, 11:599b
Toro, church at, 10:487b
T^{C}oros I of Cilician Armenia, king, 11:313b
  vengeance of Gagik II, 10:540a
T^{C}oros II of Cilician Armenia, king, 1:313b, 7:298b
  Byzantine campaigns, 10:540b
  capture of Vahka Castle (1145), 12:345a
T^{C}oros of Edessa, ruler, 1:484b
T^{C}oros Roslin, 1:497 (*illus.*), 3:393b, **12:87a-b**
  Crossing of the Red Sea miniature, 12:87 (*illus.*)
T^{C}oros of Tarōn. *See* T^{C}oros Tarōnec^{C}i
T^{C}oros Tarōnec^{C}i, 5:544a, **12:87b–88b**
Torote, Robert de, bishop of Liège, 3:608a
Torquemada, Juan de, cardinal, 3:515a
  as defender of Thomism, 12:42b
  Defensione, Birgitta of Sweden and, 9:15b
  Dominican theology and, 4:246a, 248a
  Summa de ecclesia, Thomist view of church in, 4:378a
Torquemada, Juan de, *Summa de ecclesia,* 3:519b, 520b, 10:24b
Torquemada, Tomás de, 6:488b, 9:112a
Torquetum, 11:98b–99a
Torre, Alfonso de la, *Visión delectable de la filosofía y artes liberales,* 11:420b, 425b, 441b
Torre del Mangia (Siena), 11:280b
Torre delle Milizie (Rome), 10:525b
Torriano, Gianello, clockmaker, 3:463b
Torrigiano, Pietro, **12:88b–89a**
  tomb of Henry VII of England, 12:88b (*illus.*)
Torriti, Jacopo, **12:89a**
  Lateran and, 7:345a
  mosaic in S. Maria Maggiore, 5:606a, 12:89 (*illus.*)
Torroella, Guillem de, *La faula,* 3:173a
Torroella, Pere, on Prince Charles of Viana, 3:171b
Torsion engines, in Greek and Roman empires, 3:180a-b
Tortelli, Giovanni, list of inventions, 11:659b
Tortosa disputation, 7:82b–83a
Torts origin. *See* Law, civil; Trespass
Torture, **12:89a–90a**
  by inquisition, 6:485a
  in canonical inquest, 6:479a
  Clement V's extension of, 3:644a
  forms of, 12:90a
  in French inquests, 6:479b
  judicial, in Roman law, 12:89a-b
  vs. jury trial, in England, 7:183a
  see also Ordeal
Tosafists, 7:162b
  as exegetes, 4:540b
Tosafot, 7:30a, 11:585b–586a
  see also Talmud, exegesis and study of
Tōsar. *See Letter of Tansar*
Toscannelli, Paolo del Pozzo, 4:559b, 560a
Tostado, El. *See* Madrigal, Alfonso Fernández de
Totila, Ostrogothic king, 7:201b
  Benedict of Nursia and, 2:168a
  siege of Rome, 9:292b
Tottenburg, count of, 11:544b
Tou deipnou sou, 8:557a
Touchstone
  for assaying gold, 8:290b, 296b
  used for testing silver, 8:290b
Touchstone. See Shem Tov ben Isaac Shaprut
Toucy, Council of (860), 5:638b
Toulouges, Council of (1027), Truce of God and, 9:474a
Toulouse, **12:90a–92a**
  acquired by Capetians, 12:91b
  Albigensian Crusade and, 12:91b, 91a
  Albigensians in, 7:340b
  bastides in, 2:128b
  celebrated by Peire Cardenal, 9:485a
  cloisters of, 10:494b–495a
  counts of, 12:91a–92a
    church of St. Sernin and, 10:492a
  decline of, 7:341a
  ecclesiastical province of, created by pope, 10:193a
  growth of, 7:339b, 341a, 341b
  inns in, 6:469a-b, 471a, 472b, 474b
    regulated, 6:468b, 470a-b
  inquisition in, 6:487a, 487b
  made into Visigothic capital, 9:62a-b
  origins of, 12:90a-b
  Parlement of, 9:420b
  Pont-de-la-Daurade, 10:413b
  population of, 12:90b

Toulouse (*cont.*)
  seneschal Eustache de Beaumarchais and, 11:160b–161a
  Simon de Montfort (the Elder) in, 11:296b–297a
  surviving monuments in, 12:90b
  as Visigothic capital, 12:471a
Toulouse Bridge, construction of, 10:419b
Toulouse, Council of (1229), heretics and, 6:483b
Toulouse, counts of, origins, 10:187a
Toulouse, Synod of (1119), condemnation of dualism, 4:297b
Toulouse, University of, 7:341a, 12:91a, 285a
Toulouse-Rouergue, count of, 7:339a
Tour Landry, Knight de la. *See* Geoffroy de la Tour-Landry
Tourette's syndrome, 6:490a
Tourism. *See* Pilgrimage, as tourism; Shrines
Tourmai, in Byzantine thematic armies, 12:10a
Tourmarchs, in Byzantine thematic armies, 12:10a
Tournai
  Chapel vert association, 9:637a
  interdict against, 6:495a-b
  tapestry of, 11:596b
Tournament
  armor for, 1:525b, 526a, 532b–533a, 5:350a
  changes in, 3:204a
  depiction of, 5:347b (*illus.*)
  description of, 3:204a, 5:349a-b
  Hundred Years War and, 6:334b
  knights in, 5:350a-b
  music for, 8:595b
  see also Games
Tournament of Antichrist, The, 1:185b
Touronian Bibles, 10:98b
Tours, Battle of (732). *See* Poitiers, Battle of (732)
Tours Bridge, 10:413b
Tours, Council of (813), on vernacular, 5:233b, 6:439b, 9:630a, 633a
Tours, Council of (1163), on the practice of medicine, 8:256b
Toutiorix (Celtic name for Apollo), 9:46a
Tovia ben Eliezer, *Lekaḥ Tov,* 10:74b
T^{c}ovma Arcruni, **12:92a-b**
  History, completion by others, 12:92b
T^{c}ovma Mecop^{c}ec^{c}i, 1:511b, **12:92b–93b**
  History of Tamerlane and Successors, 12:92b, 93a
Tower, **12:93b**
Tower, bell. *See* Campanile; Cupola
Tower, Leaning (Pisa). *See* Pisa Cathedral
Tower of London
  castellan and, 3:125a
  White Tower, 7:660b
Tower mills, 8:394b
Tower musicians. *See* Town bands
Tower pound, 10:67a
Town bands, 8:596b–597a, 601b, 604a, 635a
Town council, 3:502a-b
  German
    aldermen in, 5:463b
    citizens and, 5:462b–463a
    concept of, 5:462b
    expansion of, 5:463b
    limits of power of, 5:468b
    origin of, 5:462a
    power struggles, 5:463a-b
    uprisings against, 5:468b–469b
    urban patriciate, 5:462b–463a
Town dwellers. *See* Citizens
Town planning. *See* Urban planning
Towneley Plays, 8:658a, 660a, 662b, **12:93b–95a**, 12:93b–94b
  manuscript of, 12:93b
  staging of, 12:94a
  see also Second Shepherds' Play
Towns
  Byzantine
    defense needs, 4:333a
    loss of clearly defined center, 4:333a
    multiplication of ecclesiastical foundations in, 4:333a
  chronicles of, demographic uses, 4:137a
  Coptic architecture, 3:585b
  on Cyprus, charters of, 4:72a-b
  diversity of social classes in, 3:422b
  fires, building construction affected by, 3:560a-b
  French
    local jurisdiction and, 12:162a
    provincial estates and assemblies, 10:325b–326a
    royal taxation shared by, 10:320a-b
  government of. *See* Representative assemblies
  imperial. *See* German towns
  Islamic world
    Cairo, 3:13a–15a
    plagues and, 9:685b–686a
  Jews in, residence restrictions, 9:729a
  motives for founding, 3:416a
  Northern European, fairs and, 12:157b–158a
  particularism of, 3:417a
  political and legal separation of, 3:416b–417a
  public services, in early Christian era, 4:332b
  rise of
    Black Death and, 12:160b
    commercial travel and, 12:154b
    French estates concept and, 10:317a
    municipal promotion through travel, 12:160a
  Russia, pogost settlement, 9:715a-b
  Western European, plagues and, 12:160b
  see also Burgesses; Urbanism
Township, villages and, 12:440a, 442b, 443b
Towton, Battle of (1461), 12:571a
  described in Paston letters, 9:451a
Toxicology
  Antidotarium, 9:551b
  credence testers, 9:551a, 551b
  prevention as antidote, 9:551a-b
Traceried window, 7:325b
Tracery, **12:95a–96a**
  geometrical, 12:95b–96b (*illus.*)
  in ivory carving, 12:226a (*illus.*)
  plate, 12:95b
  quatrefoil, 10:239a
  soufflet, 11:373b
  trefoil, 12:182b
  see also Quatrefoil
Tracery system, 5:599b, 601a
Trachy, 8:421a
Tract, 9:689a-b
  see also Mass cycles; Plainsong
Tractatum criminus. See Jacobus (de Porta Ravennate)
Tractatus astrarii. See Dondi, Giovanni de'
Tractatus astrolabii. See Māshā^{c}allāh
Tractatus de auctoritate ecclesiae et conciliorum generalium. See Almain, Jacques
Tractatus de combustione et reparatione Cantuariensis ecclesiae. See Gervase of Canterbury
Tractatus de computo. See John of Sacrobosco
Tractatus de configurationibus qualitatum et motuum. See Oresme, Nicole
Tractatus contra curiales. See Nigel of Canterbury
Tractatus contra Judaeos. See Walter of Châtillon
Tractatus de diversis figuris. See Philippus of Caserta
Tractatus de dubio accentu. See Huguccio
Tractatus de ecclesiastica potestate. See Ailly, Pierre d'
Tractatus Garsiae Toletani Canonici de Albino et Rufino. See García of Toledo, canon
Tractatus horologii astronomici. See Richard of Wallingford
Tractatus de iuribus regni et imperii romani. See Lupold of Bebenburg
Tractatus minutiarum. See Jordanus de Nemore
Tractatus de modo concilio celebrandi. See Durand, Guillaume
Tractatus de musica. See Jerome of Moravia; Lambertus, Magister
Tractatus musicae scientiae. See Person, Gobelinus
Tractatus musicae speculativae. See Prosdocimus de Beldemandis
Tractatus orthographiae, 1:270b, 9:282a-b
Tractatus de parvulis trahendis ad Christum. See Gerson, John
Tractatus de potestate regia et papali. See John of Paris
Tractatus de purgatorio sancti Patricii. See Hugh of Saltrey
Tractatus quaestionum. See Homobonus de Cremona
Tractatus de schismate. See Zabarella, Francesco
Tractatus de sphaera. See John of Sacrobosco
Tractatus super concilium generale. See Quirini, Vincenzo

Tractatus theologicus. *See* Hildebert of Lavardin
Tractatus virtutum. *See* Boncompagno of Signa
Tractus artis bene moriendi. *See* *Ars moriendi,* longer version
Trade
  archaeological evidence for, 4:553b
  Caffa's role in, 3:12a-b
  "commercial revolution" of 11th century, 5:116a
  East-West, 9:678a
  in Georgia, *see also* Urbnisi
  Indian, Mamluk dynasty and, 8:75b, 76a
  in Mediterranean, 12:107a–108a
    after Arab invasions, 4:555b
    Umayyads and, 11:246b
  plagues and, 9:676a-b, 678a, 685b
  regulation of
    Assizes of Jerusalem, 1:598a–599b
    enforcement in market courts, 8:146a-b
    fines, 8:145b–146a
    Madeira sugar and, 8:10b–11a
    markets, 8:145b–146a
    markets, *ad quod damnum,* 8:145a
    markets, proximity of, 8:145a
    monopolistic practices, 8:145b
    price controls in salt trade, 10:630a
    see also Trade, Byzantine; Trade, Western European
  silk, 11:293b–296a
  slave. *See* Slavery and slave trade
  see also Fairs; Pilgrimage; Slavery and slave trade
Trade, Armenian, **12:96b–99b**
  Artašat, 1:563b
  at Sīs, 11:314a
  decline of, 12:99a-b
  Dwin, 1:564a, 4:324b–325a
  importance of Manazkert, 8:81a
  route through Vanand and, 12:353b
  trade routes, 11:629b
  under Bagratids, 12:97b–98b
  under Zakᶜarids, 12:98b
  see also Āyās
Trade, Byzantine, **12:100a–105a**
  early period, 12:100a-b
  7th century, 12:100b–101a
  8th through 10th centuries, 12:101a–102a
  11th and 12th centuries, 12:102a–103b
  1204 to 1453, 12:103b–104b
  in Constantinople, 3:554b–555b
  importance of Pera-Galata, 9:503a-b
  money system for, 8:421a-b
  regulation of, 102a, 2:475b–476a, 478a, 12:101b
    see also *Eparch, Book of the*
  rise of guilds and, 6:14a-b
  with Russia, 9:238a
  with Sasanians, 12:97a
  standards of measure, 12:580b
  Venice and, 12:385b–386a, 386b–387a
  Western merchants and, 12:103a-b
Trade, Eastern European
  agricultural products, 12:506b
  Bosnia, 2:341a
  Khazars and, 7:241a
  Kievan Rus
    domestic, 1:101a
    foreign, 1:101a
    Novgorod and, 9:193b
  Polish, tribal, 9:716b–717a
  Russia, 1:99a
  Sigismund and, 11:287b
  trade routes, 12:506a-b
Trade, Islamic, **12:105a–108a**
  Abbasids and, 11:246b
  absence of vehicles and, 12:379b–380b
  agricultural, 11:625a-b
  Alexandria, 1:154a
  antecedents of, 12:105a
  caravan routes
    Yemen to Gaza and Damascus, 8:522a
    see also Najrān
  caravan routes, 12:147b–148a
  commercial arrangements, 12:106a–107a
  Egypt to Spain, 1:70b
  fairs and, 4:588b
  funduq, 5:312b–313a
  Hafsid, 6:415a
  in herbs, 6:185b–186a
  importance of al-Maghrib, 8:15b
  Indian Ocean, 11:248b–249a
    organization of, 11:249b–250a
  Isfahan and, 6:562a
  Jewish responsum literature and, 10:337a
  joint ventures, 12:106b
  khan, 7:237b–238a
  Mali and, 8:57b
  with Mecca, 6:109a
  Mediterranean-Chinese-Indian economic sphere, 1:65b
  money system for, 8:424b–425a
  Ottoman Empire, 1:145b
  Persian Gulf, 11:247a
  Quraysh tribe and, 10:241b–242a
  Red Sea
    Ayyubids and, 11:247a
    Circassians and, 11:247a
    Fatimids and, 11:247a
  role of Alexandria, 1:154a-b
  "silk road," 10:661a
  ṣinf in, 11:307b–309b
  with Spain and Italy, 6:53a-b, 55a
  in spices, under the Mamluk sultan al-Ashraf Barsbay, 8:75b
  through Transoxiana, 12:146a-b
  trans-Saharan, Timbuktu and, 12:54b, 55a-b
  Tulinid Egypt and Byzantium, 12:224a
  Venice and, 12:387a
  see also Berkri; Navies, Islamic; Navigation, Indian Ocean; Navigation, Red Sea; Roads, Islamic world; Timbuktu
Trade, Jewish
  Indian Ocean, 11:249b
  in Middle East, 7:107a
  9th–11th centuries, 4:555b–556a
Trade, maritime
  disease patterns and, 9:673b–674a, 682b
  Icelandic, 6:394b–395a, 396b–397a
  Iraqi, 6:512b
  Italian, 4:557b–558a
  Portuguese, 4:558a, 561a–563a
  Spanish, 4:558a
Trade, Roman, Dominate and, 10:460b
Trade routes
  African, 4:561a–563a, 6:413b
  Aren and, 1:450b
  Armenian, 1:423a
    Baylakān and, 2:139a
    Xlatᶜ and, 12:713b
    Zakᶜarids and, 12:737a
  Asiatic, 11:246a-b
  Baltic countries, 7:680b–681a
  Bardhaᶜa-Derbent, Shirvan and, 11:254a
  Bavarian, 2:132b
  commercial trade in art and, 1:560b–561a
  Danish, 4:554a
  early, 4:553b
  east-west axis, 6:95a
  Flemish, Ypres and, 12:731a
  food supply and proximity to, 5:118b
  Frankish-Frisian trade routes, 6:132b
  Hejaz corridor, 6:146a
  Hungary and, 6:337b
  Indian Ocean, 4:562b–563a
  inns on, 6:468b–469b
  Iranian, Shīrāz and, 11:252a
  Iranian-Byzantine treaty and, 12:714a
  Iraqi, 6:512b
  Italian, 4:556a, 557a-b
  maritime, 4:558a-b
    cog and, 11:242b
    Columbus and, 4:559b–561a
    Indian Ocean, 12:724a
    Rome and, 10:525b
    Venice and, 7:380b
  Mediterranean, 4:556a
  north-south, 4:590b
  Norwegian, 4:554a
  overland
    disruption of, 11:247b
    port development and, 11:246a-b
  in Poland, 9:721b
  in pre-Islamic Arabia, 1:370a-b
  Scandinavian, 4:554a-b
    knarr and, 11:240b
  Sicilian, 11:262b
  Slavic, 4:587b
  to Flanders, 4:593a
  to Trebizond, 4:588a
  trans-Saharan, 4:561b
    Berbers and, 2:186a
  Varangian, 4:554a
  west-east axis, 6:95b
  see also Caravans, routes
Trade, Western European, **12:108a–116b**
  Baltic countries, 7:679a, 683a
  Basque, 2:127a
  Birka and, 2:247b–248a
  in Bruges, 2:386b–387a
  Burgundy, 2:426a
  with Central Asia, 12:169b
  in Champagne, 4:590b–591b
  chronological division, 12:108b
  commercial agents and devices, 12:162a

Trade, Western European (*cont.*)
commercial techniques, 12:112a-b
consulates and, 3:571a
"container revolution" and, 2:114a
convent tenants' corvées, 12:152b, 157a-b
Cypriot role in, 4:72a
Danish, 4:149a-b
decline in long-distance (14th century), 6:18b
demographic changes, effect of, 8:144b, 147a
development of markets, 12:117a–118a
early Middle Ages, 12:109a–110b
effects of Black Death, 2:266a
England
charter of liberties, 11:615a
Iceland and, 6:396b–397a
Ephesus and, 4:494b–495a
Eurasian, 11:659b–660a
fairs and, 12:157b–158a
forestalling, 8:145a
from late 10th century, 12:109b
Genoese and, 4:557b, 558a
German
1138-1254, 5:484a
in Baltic, 5:486 (map)
customs fees, 10:331b
east-west alliance, 6:91a-b
with England, 6:91a
with Flanders, 6:91b
Iceland and, 6:396b, 397a
with Scandinavia, 6:91b
in towns, 5:465a–466a
Gotland, 5:632b–633a
Hanseatic League, 12:112b–113b
importance of Malta and, 8:67a
influence of technology on, 11:662b–663a
Irish, 6:553b
Italian domination of, 12:158a-b
Jewish responsum literature and, 10:337a
Kievan Rus, 7:249b, 250b
late medieval, 12:115a-b
localization of, 12:148b
London, 7:658b
Low Countries, 12:112b
Lyons fair, 7:699b–700a
Madeira sugar and, 8:10b–11a
maritime
Mediterranean, 11:232b
Seville and, 11:214a
Mediterranean, Pisa and, 9:664a-b
merchant and carrier travel, 12:152b–153a
millennial revival of, 12:153b–154a
money system for, 8:430a, 431a
Norman, 9:162b, 164a
Northern Europe, 12:108a
Norway, 9:181a-b
Hanseatic League and, 9:185a
Iceland and, 6:396b
Pera-Galata and, 9:503a-b
pilgrimage routes and, 12:156b–157a
"Pirenne thesis" of, 12:109a
regrating, 8:145b
regulation of, **12:116b–123a**
implementation, 12:120b–122b
merchant and craft guilds, 6:15b–16a
packaging, 12:122a-b
prices, 12:118b–119a
quality control, 12:119a–120b
role of church, 12:116b
weights and measures, 12:118a-b
see also Alnage
revivals of, 12:152b–153a
rise of Italian merchants, 12:110b–112a
rise of urban guilds and, 6:15b
role of Alexandria, 1:154a-b
Rouen, 10:538a-b
Russian money system for, 8:426a-b
southern European trade, 12:108b
spread of Islam and, 12:108a
surplus of marketable goods, 6:91a
Swedish/Eastern, 11:529b–530a
Swedish/Russian, 11:531a
Hanseatic League and, 11:532a
taxes and tolls, 11:611b–612a, 615a
textile
drapers' market, 11:706b (*illus.*)
merchant capitalists, 11:711b–712a
time-, labor-, and material-saving, 11:663a
tolls and duties, 10:538a
trade routes, 12:149b
transportation, 12:113b–115a
travel and transport and, 12:157a–159a
Viking, in the kingdom of York, 12:433b
see also Banking, European; Fisheries, marine; Hanseatic League; Markets, European; Navigation, Western European; Travel and transport; Usury; Vehicles, European; Venice
Traders. *See* Merchants
Traditio clavium, **12:123a**
in art, 12:123 (*illus.*), 175a
Traditio legis, **12:123b–124a,** 12:124 (*illus.*)
Traductio. See Italian literature, poetry
Traelborg, slave's fort at, 10:688b
Trahearn ap Caradog, battles against Gruffudd ap Cynan, 6:4b
Trailbaston, **9:322a–323b**
changing nature of, 9:323a-b
derivation of name, 9:323a
disappearance of nickname, 9:323b
initial commissions, 9:323a-b
jail delivery, 7:45a
see also Oyer and Terminer
Traini, Francesco, **12:124a–125a**
frescoes of, 5:294b, 12:124a–125b (*illus.*), 175b
Last Judgment, 5:294b
Triumph of Death, 5:294b
Traité de l'harmonie réduite à ses principes naturels. See Rameau, Jean Philippe
Traitié . . . pour essampler les amantz marietz. See Gower, John
Traitor. *See* Treason
Trajan aqueduct, 10:519b
Trajan, Roman emperor, Dacia and, 10:509b, 12:484a
Trajan's Column, 3:200a, 10:520b
Trakai, 7:608b
seat of Kestutis, 7:606a
Tram (coin), 8:418b
Tramezzo. See Screen, rood
Tramo di Lonardo, 6:636a
Trance, 6:491b, 492a
Trancoso, Battle of (1385), 10:53b
Trani Cathedral, 10:486b
Transcaucasia
art and architecture, 10:656b
silver vessels, 10:658a
Ilkhanids and, 6:420a
Khazars in, 7:241a
see also Caucasia
Transenna, **12:125a**
Transept, **12:125b**
of Chartres Cathedral, 5:620a-b, 623a
in Gothic cathedral, high, 5:590a–591a
lantern, 10:480b
of Rouen Cathedral, 5:624b
of St. Denis, 5:623a-b
of Westminster Abbey, 5:625b
Transfiguration, **12:125b–126a**
Christian iconography and, 12:126a
Eastern church feast of the, 12:126a
Transfiguration (cathedral: Chernigov), architectural elements, 10:578b
Transfiguration (church: Kizhi Island), 7:283a (*illus.*)
Transfiguration (church: Novgorod)
frescoes
Christ Pantokrator, 10:587 (*illus.*)
of Theophanes the Greek, 10:587a-b
wall paintings, 2:450b–451a
Transfiguration (mystery play), 8:659b
Transhumance
Castilian nobility and, 9:151a
North African, 10:464b
in Spain. *See Mesta*
Transit (surveying tool). *See* Surveyor's transit
Transjurane Burgundy. *See* Burgundy, kingdom of
Translatio. See Johannes Canaparius
Translatio et miracula SS. Marcellini et Petri. See Einhard
Translatio imperii. See Translation of empire
Translatio sancti Mauri. See Radulfus Tortarius
Translation of bishops, **12:142b–143**
Translation of empire, 5:495b, **12:143a–144b**
Translation et les miracles de saint Jacques, La. See Pierre de Beauvais
Translation, musical. *See* Musical notation
Translation of saints, **12:144a–145b**
in catacombs, 3:154b
Einhard's *Translatio et miracula SS. Marcellini et Petri,* 12:145a
relics of St. Stephen moved to Constantinople, 12:144 (*illus.*)
Translatio sancti Mauri, 10:247a
see also Death and burial; Relics; Shrines

Translation and translators
Armenian Hellenizing School, 1:505a–506a
Bulgarian, Symeon and, 11:554b
Georgian, from Arabic, 2:54b
into Pahlavi, Xusrō I and, 12:714b
into Russian, Yaroslav and, 12:720a
Melchite, 11:565a
Syriac, 11:565a, 566a, 566b
Translation and translators, Byzantine, **12:126a–127b**
early period (330–641), 12:126a-b
middle period (641–1204), 12:126b–127a
late period (1204–1453), 12:127a-b
centers of, 12:126b, 127a
Greek into Latin, Italian Renaissanace, 7:1a-b
of Plato, 9:694b–696a
translations of liturgical books, 7:613b
Translation and translators, Georgian, 5:416b–417b
Translation and translators, Islamic, 11:81a-b, 82a-b, 83a-b, **12:127b–133a**
adaptations of Ascension of the Prophet, 1:581b
Bayt al-Ḥikmah and, 8:566a
centers of, 12:128b, 131a
Dīwān translations, 12:128a
in Ḥarrān, 9:4b
historical background, 12:127b–129a, 141a
languages and circumstances, 12:129a–130a
patronage
Abbasid, 12:128a-b
Banū Mūsā, 12:128b, 131a
effect on quality and style, 12:131b, 132b
Maᶜmūnī translations, 12:128b
philosophers, classical, 9:571b
philosophers, Jewish, 9:571b
into Latin, 9:574a
of Plato, 9:669a–700b, 694b–696a
role of Syriac, 12:127b, 129b–130a
theories and methods
collaboration, 12:130b–131a, 135a-b, 140b
lacunae policies, 12:132b–133a
evaluation of sources, 12:131b–132b
transliteration, 12:130b
whole sentence, 12:131b
word for word, 12:131a, 139a–140b
translation movement in 9th century, 11:87b
Translation and translators, Jewish, 11:89b, 90b–91a, **12:133a–136a**
centers of, 12:135b–136a
into Arabic, 4:539a
into Hebrew, 12:133a–135a
from Arabic, 12:134b–135a
from Latin, 12:134b
of Karaite Arabic writings, 7:210b
into Latin and vernacular, 12:135a–136b
Peshitta translation of the Bible, 1:208a
of Plato, 9:694b–696a, 700a-b
in Toledo, 7:81a
translation of Ibn Sīnā's *Canon* into Hebrew, 11:93a
Translation and translators, Western European, **12:136a–142a**
in 12th-century Toledo, 11:406b, 441a
adaptations in *riddarasögur* translations, 10:392a–394a
of Arabic astrological works, 1:606b
Arabic into Latin, 12:140a-b
of Aristotle, 9:701a
of *Confessio Amantis,* 5:642a
at the court of Peter IV (the Ceremonious), 9:510b–511a
audience, 12:140b–141b
centers of, 12:136a-b, 137b, 140b–141b
Dominican, 4:246a-b
during the reign of Alfred the Great, 1:164b–167a
England, 4:518a
in English mysticism, 9:26b–27b
of German allegory, 5:430b–431a
gloss, 5:564b–565a
of *Golden Legend,* 5:574a
Greek into Latin, 12:140a
Iberian, 1:573a
influence of Arabic works on Western approach to magic and, 8:37b–38a
of Koran, 7:297a
into Norwegian, 12:203b
Latinorum penuria attitude, 12:138a-b
motivations, 12:138a-b
other professions and, 12:137b–138a
patristic, 12:163a-b
of *Physiologus,* 2:204b
of Plato, Italian humanist, 9:702b–703b
of religious instruction books, 10:301b–302a
resources and training, 12:136b–137b
role of Jews in, 8:23b
Secretum secretorum and, 11:135a-b
Sicilian, from Arabic, 11:263a
Spain, 11:443a-b, 456b–457b, 689a
theories and methods, 12:138b–140b
ad verbum, 9:700b
bowdlerization, 9:696a, 702b
Christianization, 9:696a-b, 702b
recension (*diorthōsis*), 9:697
three kinds of translation, 12:139a–140a
Toledan school, 12:68b
traditions of, 12:139a–140b
training, 12:137a-b
translated *riddarasögur,* 10:390a–394a
translations of *Amadís de Gaula,* 1:227b
writings of women mystics and, 9:8b–9a
into vernacular, 12:135a–136a, 138a, 140b
see also Spanish literature, Bible translations; *Strengleikar*
Translatzen. See Niclas von Wyle
Transliteration. *See* Alphabetization, history of; Translation and translators
Transoxiana, 10:640b, **12:145b–146b**
after death of Ulugh-Beg, 12:57b
Arab control of, 12:145b
as capital of Uzbek khanate, 2:397a
conquered by Uzbeks in 1500, 12:58a
descendants of Mīrānshāh and, 12:58a
in Islamic conquests, 6:570b
Islamic trade through, 12:146 (map)
Mongol invasions through, 12:145b–146a
origins of the Seljuks and, 11:151a
private Seljuk mausolea in, 11:147a
Samanids in, 6:503b
Sanjar ibn Malikshāh and, 11:153b
taken over by the Qara Khitai, 11:153b
Tamerlane and, 11:588a
Timurids and, 12:56b
see also Ulugh-Beg
Transportation. *See* Travel and transport
Transubstantiation
at Lateran IV, 3:640b
in Byzantine eucharistic liturgy, 7:610b
first use of the term, 9:514a
Grail legend and, 5:645a
Humbert and, 6:330a
Innocent III and, 6:464b
John of Paris on, 7:137a
Lanfranc of Bec on, 7:328b
Ockham on, 9:209b, 213b–214a
in 12th-century theology, 9:587b
Wyclif on, 12:708b–709a
see also Eucharist; Remanence
Transverse arch. *See* Arch
Transylvania
Hungary and, 6:337b, 350a
see also "Union of three nations of Transylvania"
Trapezitai, 10:60a
Trapezuntius, Georgius. *See* George of Trebizond
Trapping
Gaston III of Foix on, 6:361a
Henri de Ferrières on, 6:360a, 361a
in literature, 6:358b
see also Hunting
Trastámara, Enrique, 7:82a-b
Trastámaran wars
in Leonor López de Córdoba's *Memorias,* 11:421a
literary developments and, 11:418a-b
Trastámaras
in Aragon, 1:417a–419a
breach of direct succession at Martín's death, 1:417a-b
in Castile, 3:136b–139a
in Navarre, 9:71b
Trastevere, 10:517b
Pierleoni and, 10:525a
Tratado de astrología, 12:449b
Tratado de San Francisco, 11:439b
Trattatello in laude di Dante. See Boccaccio, Giovanni
Trattati de archittetura, ingegneria e arte militare. See Francesco di Giorgio Martini
Trattato de li rithimi volgari. See Gidino da Sommacampagna
Traù, Hungary and, 6:340b

Travagliata inventione, La. See Tartaglia, Niccolò
Travel and transport
caravans, 9:650b
convoys, 9:657a-b, 660a, 661a
pilgrimage, 9:654b–661b
guidebooks for, 9:652a, 657b (*illus.*), 660a, 661b–662b (*illus.*)
Islamic, 9:650a–652a
Jewish, 9:652a–653a
Russian, 9:653a–654b
pocketbooks for, 9:711a
see also Animals; Crusades; Inns; Navies; Pilgrimage; Trade routes; Vehicles
Travel and transport, Byzantine, *see also* Communications, Byzantine; Roads, Byzantine; Trade, Byzantine
Travel and transport, Islamic, **12:147a–148a**
absence of vehicles and, 12:379b–380b
by land, 12:147b–148a
by water, 12:147b
economic characteristics, 12:148a
freedom of, 12:147a–148a
funduq, 5:312b–313a
military, 12:147b
objectives, 12:147a-b
postal and intelligence services, 10:60b–61b
see also Roads, Islamic world; Trade, Armenian; Trade, Islamic
Travel and transport, Western European, **12:148b–163a**, 12:150 (map)
building materials, 3:562a
canals, 12:578b
Carolingian period, 12:151b–153b, 157a-b
class structure and, 12:149b, 160a
convent tenants' corvées, 12:152b, 157a-b
costs of, 12:158b
dangers of, 12:149a, 153a-b
highwaymen and brigands, 12:152b
invasions of Europe, 12:153a-b
kidnappings, 12:149a, 152b
safe conducts, 12:157b–158a, 161b–162a
"Dutch way," 12:158b–159a
Fachschrifttum and, 4:579a
facilities for travelers, 12:147b–148a, 157a
freedom of, 12:148b–149a, 152b, 153a-b, 157a-b
journey timing and duration, 12:148a, 155a-b, 159a
land routes, 12:158a
in late antiquity, 12:149b–150a
literature, 12:148b–149b, 151a, 155a-b
tourist, 12:162a-b
Marco Polo's travel, 10:27a–28a
market development and, 8:145a
Merovingian period, 12:149a-b, 153a
motivations
fairs, 12:157b–158b
missionary work, 12:151a–152a
papal diplomacy, 12:152a, 154a–155b, 160a, 161b–162a
pilgrimage, 12:151a, 155b–157a, 162a
touring of relics, 12:154a-b
trade, 12:153b–154a
patterns and changes in, 12:148b, 159a-b, 162a
religious, 12:149b–152b, 154a–157a
Sweden, 11:530a, 531b
travelers
artists and architects, 12:152b–153a, 160b
church administrators, 12:152a, 154a–155b, 160a, 161b–162a
clerks, 12:160b–161b
feudal serfs, 12:152b, 157a-b
goliards, 12:161a
homeless folk, 12:162a
justices of common pleas, 12:159b
knights, 12:162a
merchants and carriers, 12:149b, 152b, 154a, 157a–159a, 162a
minstrels and jongleurs, 12:152b, 160b–161a
rulers and lay administrators, 12:148b–149a, 153a-b, 159b–160a
students and scholars, 12:161a–162b
tourists, 12:162a-b
town representatives, 12:160a, 162a
troubadours, 12:160b–161b
vagabonds and vagrants, 12:152a, 161a, 162a
water routes, 12:149b, 151a-b, 158b
see also Bridges, Western European; Roads, Western European; Vehicles, European
Travels of Sir John Mandeville. See Mandeville, Sir John
Traversari, Ambrogio, **12:163a–164a**
Camaldolese reform and, 3:56a
church fathers and, 12:163a-b
Council of Basel and, 3:653a
patristic scholarship of, 12:163a
public roles of, 12:163b
Ṭrāz, kārgah and, 7:214b
Trdat I, Arsacid king, 9:443b
in Agatᶜangełos', *History of the Armenians,* 1:66b
coronation by Nero (66), 1:475a, 559a
Trdat III (IV) (the Great) of Armenia, king, 1:475b, 518a, **12:164a-b**
Agatᶜangełos cycle on, 12:164a
Armenian historiography and, 12:164a
in art, 11:582b
conversion to Christianity, 5:668a
Hřipᶜsimē and, 1:517b, 6:309a
in *Patmutᶜiwn Tarōnoy,* 9:457b
Tauris and, 11:570b
Zwartᶜnocᶜ and, 12:749a
Trdat (architect), 1:292a, 483a, 494a, **12:164b–165a**
Armenian church architecture of, 12:164b–165a (*illus.*)
Treason, **12:165a–168b**
attainder and, 6:428a
English
conviction, 12:165b–166a, 167a-b
statute of treasons of 1352, 12:166b–167a, 168a
trial and punishment, 12:165b–166a, 168a-b
Tudor period, 12:168a
Visigothic kingship and, 12:472b
Treasons, Statute of (1352), 6:428a
Treasurer of the royal wardrobe. *See* Wardrobe, royal, England, keeper of
Treasury, France, tax collection, 11:624a-b
Treasury of merits, 6:321a
commutation and, 6:448a
indulgences and, 6:446b–447a, 449a-b
see also Suffrage (congregational)
Treasury, papal. *See* Camera (papal finance)
Treasury, royal
England. *See* Chamber, royal (English financial office); Exchequer
see also Finance, royal
Treaties
Byzantine observance of, 4:195b–196a
ceremonial surrounding, 4:212b
Islamic geography and cartography and, 5:392b
negotiation of, 4:195b
ratification of, 4:213a–214a
Treatise on the Activity of Forms. See Burley, Walter
Treatise Against the Chronic Obstinacy of the Jews. See Peter the Venerable
Treatise on the Astrolabe. See Chaucer, Geoffrey
Treatise on Automata. See Jazarī, al-
Treatise on Calculation with Hindu Numerals. See Banū Mūsā
Treatise on the Laws and Customs of England. See Glanville, Ranulf de
Treatise on the Old and New Testaments. See Aelfric, *Letter to Sigeweard*
Treatise on Spirit and Soul. See Israeli, Isaac
Treatises on the Eye. See Ḥunayn ibn Isḥāq
Trebinje. *See* Serbia
Trebizond
as a communication center, 10:424b
fair at, 4:588a-b, 12:97b
Pontus in, 10:31b
Trebizond, empire of, 1:241b, **12:168b–170a**
Aq Qoyunlu in, 1:352a
Armenian trade and, 12:98b, 99a
extent of, 12:169 (map)
foundation of, 1:159a, 12:169a-b
monasteries, 8:457b
Seljuks of Rum and, 11:154b
Tamar and, 11:587b
Uzun Ḥasan and, 12:342b
Třeboň Master. *See* Master of Wittingau
Trebuchet, 11:646 (*illus.*)
in China, 11:660a
counterweight, 11:660b
description of, 3:180b (*illus.*)
earliest, 3:181a
in Europe, 11:660b
in Hundred Years War, 6:333a
inside castle, 3:150b

- in Islamic warfare, 11:660a-b
- throws of, 3:148a-b, 180b–181a
- traction, 11:660a-b

Trecento art, 9:363a, 667 (*illus.*), 668a–669a (*illus.*), **12:170a–177a**
- Black Death style, 12:124b
- characterization of, 12:170a, 176a-b
- landscapes in, 5:615a
- manuscript illumination, 5:614b
- Northern Italy, Paduan painters, 12:175b–176a (*illus.*)
- painting, Sienese school, 7:668a–670a, 670a–671a, 677b
- panel painting, 9:361a–362a
- Resurrection cycle and, 10:340a
- Tuscan art (to 1348)
  - Florence, 12:171b–172b (*illus.*)
  - Pisan sculpture, 12:170b–171b (*illus.*)
  - Sienese painters, 12:172b–175a (*illus.*)
- Tuscan art (after 1348)
  - Florence, 12:175a-b, 176a, 176b
  - Sienese painters, 12:125 (*illus.*), 175b
- *see also* Lippo Memmi; Paolo Veneziano; Tino di Camaino; Vanni, Andrea

Trecento music, **12:177a–181b**
- composers, 12:179b–180a
- forms, 12:178a–179b
- instruments, 12:180b
- notation, 12:177b–178a

Trecentonovelle. See Sacchetti, Franco

Tree of Jesse, **12:181b–182a,** 12:181b (*illus.*), 182b (*illus.*)
- *see also* Stowell, John

Tree of Life, **12:182a-b,** 12:182 (*illus.*)
- *see also* Pacino di Bonaguida

Tref, 8:286b

Trefoil, **12:182b**
- in German Romanesque architecture, 10:488b
- *see also* Quatrefoil; Tracery

Trefoil cusp. *See* Cusp

Trefologion. *See* Paterikon

Trelleborgs. *See* Castles and fortifications, Danish

Tremissis, 8:419b, 427b

Trémoille, Georges de La, 3:271a

Tremolo, 8:631a, 632a

Tremussen chalice, 9:130 (*illus.*)

Trencavel, Raymond-Roger, viscount of Béziers, opposition to French rule, 5:168b–169a

Trencavels of Béziers-Carcassonne, 7:339a

Trendle (unit of measure), 12:584a

Trent Codices, **12:182b–184b**
- codicology of, 12:182b–184b
- scribes, Puntschucherh, 12:183a

Trent, Council of (1545-1563), 12:194b
- on church dedication, 4:131a
- dispensation and, 4:218a
- Dominican convents and, 12:688a
- on excommunication, 4:538a
- Marian worship and, 12:461a
- on occult practices, 1:609a
- parish system and, 9:414a-b
- removal of sequences from liturgy, 11:162b
- restoration of Gregorian chant, 5:664a
- *Tametsi,* 4:611b
- Vulgate and, 12:495b, 496a
- *see also* Tridentine rite

Trentham manuscript, 5:642a

Treponema diseases. *See* Venereal diseases

Très ancien coutumier de Normandie, 4:68b, 7:426b–427a

Très ancienne coutume de Bretagne, 2:382a, 4:515b

Très belles heures de Notre Dame. See Limbourg brothers

Tres libri codicis. See Corpus iuris civilis

Très riches heures, 8:109b–110a, **12:185a,** 12:185a
- depiction of chariots in, 12:376b
- enclosed gardens illustrated in, 5:362a
- hunting in, 6:361b
- January, 5:34a (*illus.*)
- Jean Colombe's illuminations for, 5:615b
- Limbourg brothers' illuminations for, 5:615a, 628b, 7:582a (*illus.*)
- miniatures of Manuel II Palaiologos in, 8:92a

Treseau (unit of measure), 12:596b

Tresilian, Robert, 7:193b

Trésor. See Latini, Brunetto

Trésor de la cité des dames. See Christine de Pizan

Trésorier de philosophie naturelle des pierres précieuses. See Jean d'Outremeuse

Trespass, **12:185a–186a**
- emergence of, 12:185a-b
- justices of the peace and, 7:195b–196a
- punishment for, outlawry, 9:312a
- role of, 12:168a-b, 185b–186a
- suits in property claims, 9:548b
- *see also* Seisin, disseisin

"Tretis of the Tua Mariit Wemen and the Wedo." *See* Dunbar, William

Tretise of Miraclis Pleyinge, A, 8:660b–661a

"Treue Gattin, Die." *See* Herrand von Wildonie

Trevelyan Papers, 8:323a

Trevet, Nicholas, 4:246a, **12:186a–187a**
- biblical and patristic commentaries, 12:186b
- chronicles of, 1:265b
- *Cronicles,* 12:186a-b
- as defender of Thomism, 12:41b
- historiography by, 12:186b–187a

Trevi Fountain, 10:519b

Trevisa, John, 4:218a, **12:187a-b**
- translations by, 8:317a, 12:187a
- Wyclif Bible and, 2:222a, 8:318a

Treviso, ambassador from, 4:205b

Treytz armor workshop, 1:529b

Trezzo Bridge, 10:420b

Triadis thaumaturgae acta. See Colgan, John

Triads of Ireland, 6:540b

Triads of the Island of Britain, 12:600b

Trial by combat. *See* Combat, trial by; Ordeal

Trial by jury. *See* Jury

Trialogus. See Wyclif, John

Trials, criminal. *See* Criminal justice

Triangle (musical instrument), 8:606a, 607a (*illus.*)

Trias. See Trinity, Old Testament

Tribe, Irish. *See Túatha*

Tribe. *See* Extended family

Tribelon, **12:187b**

Tribonian, 3:608b, 7:201b

Tribunal of Waters, 6:557b

Tribune, **12:187b–188a**
- basilica aisle gallery, 12:187b–188a (*illus.*)
- organ platform, 12:187b
- in Ottonian architecture, 10:478a
- triforium and, 12:187–188a, 188b

Tribute
- *pogost* centralization of, 9:715a-b
- *see also* Taxation

Triclinium, **12:188a-b,** 12:188b (*illus.*)

Triconch. *See* Triclinium

Triconch church plan. *See* Church architecture, conch type

Trictrac, 5:535b

Triens, 8:427b–428a

Trier
- archbishopric of, Nicholas of Cusa and, 9:123a
- first seals of, 11:126a
- Roman bridge at, 10:410a

Trier Cathedral, 5:643a

Trier, University of, 12:288b

Triforium, **12:188b**
- in basilica, 2:125a
- tribune and, 12:187b–188a, 188b

Trigonometry, 8:211b–212a, 213a, 218b
- Richard of Wallingford's *Quadripartitum* and, 10:387b

Triklinios, Demetrios, 3:431b, 11:50a-b, 52b

Trill, 8:631a, 632a-b

Trilogium astrologiae theologizatae. See Gerson, John

Trinitarian doctrine, 7:62b–63a, **12:189a–198a**
- Abelard on, 9:155b
- anti-Trinitarian theology, 12:197a
- antiheretical writings and, 12:189b–191b
- apostolic foundations of, 12:189a-b
- Arius on, 3:339a
- Armenian, 1:498a
  - in *Knik^{C} Hawatoy,* 7:279b
  - in *Yačaxapatum Čaṙk^{C},* 1:508b–509a
- in art. *See* Nimbus, cruciform; Nimbus, triangular
- Athanasius on, 3:339a, 9:560b
- Augustine's *De quantitate animae,* 10:271b
- Basil the Great and, 2:120b, 121b
- breadth and emphases of, 12:189b, 197b–198a
- in Christian-Jewish polemics, 10:3b
- church fathers and, 12:189a-b, 190b, 191b, 194a, 198a
- concepts and terms of, 12:189a-b, 195a
  - *ad extra,* 12:189b, 193a, 194a, 195b–196b, 197a

Trinitarian doctrine, 7:62b–63a (*cont.*)
concepts and terms of (*cont.*)
ad intra, 12:189b, 191b–195b
begotten, 12:192a-b
bonum est sui diffusivum, 12:193b
Filioque, 12:190a–191a, 195a
hypokeimenon (*substantia*), 12:189a
hypostasis (*persona*), 12:189a–190a, 192a
innascibilitas, 12:194a
natural reason, 12:189b, 196b–197b
ousia (*essentia*), 12:189a, 192b
perichoresis, 12:189b, 194a
person, 12:192a-b
physis (*natura*), 12:189a, 194a
properties of divine relations, 12:192b, 195a
spiration, 12:191b, 195a
in Docetism, 4:233a-b
in early church, 3:339a-b, 11:44a
ecumenical councils and, 12:189a, 190a–191b
English mysticism and, 9:18b
foundations of, 12:189a–191b
Gottschalk of Orbais on, 5:639a
Gregory of Nazianzus on, 5:666a
hymns and, 6:383a
indwelling, 9:599b
interpersonal love, 9:599a
John of Damascus on, 7:124b
in Meister Eckhart's works, 9:33a
metaphysical approach, 9:598b
natural reason and, 12:189b, 196b–197b
nature-will and intellect-will, 9:599a-b
Nestorianism and, 9:105a
non est aliquid, 9:598b
Old Testament iconology and, 12:198a-b, 199 (*illus.*)
in *Ordo quod sacerdos debet sacrificare,* 7:629b
Peter Lombard on, 9:517a, 599a
in *Piers Plowman,* 7:336a
Richard of St. Victor's *De Trinitate,* 10:387a
of Roscelinus, 10:531a
see also Filioque; Philosophy and theology, Western European
Trinité, La (church: Caen), 2:175a, 10:482b
Trinité, La (church: Vendôme), west facade, 8:508b (*illus.*)
Trinity (church: Ikalto), 6:416a
Trinity (church: Sopačani), wall paintings, 2:446b, 447a, 447b
Trinity, feast of, 9:714b
rhymed offices and, 10:366b
Trinity, office of, 10:371b
Trinity, Old Testament, **12:198a-b**
Trinity-St. Sergius (monastery: Zagorsk), 9:654a, 10:595a
Annunciation icon, 10:589a (*illus.*)
foundation of, 11:209a
Trinity church
architectural style, 10:581a
Old Testament Trinity, 10:588b
Triodion. *See* Lent, hymns for
Trioedd Ynys Prydein, 1:577b
Trionfi. See Petrarch (Francesco Petrarca)
Trionfo d'amore. See Petrarch (Francesco Petrarca)
Tripartita, 9:158b
Tripartita. See Ivo of Chartres, St.
Tripartite Life, on the Palladian mission in Ireland, 9:464a
Triple church basilica. *See* Church architecture
Triple time. *See* Musical notation, Western
Triplum, 1:546b–547a, 551a
isorhythm and, 6:619a-b
in Perotinus' work, 9:506b, 507a
Tripoli
Buluggīn and, 12:744a
controlled by Qarāqūsh, 1:195a
county of, 4:30b
Zanāta Berbers and, 12:744b
Triptych, **12:198b–199a**
definition of, 10:29a
panel paintings, 9:361b, 362a
trecento, Italian, 12:174a (*illus.*), 176b
see also Altarpiece; Polyptych
Trisagion, 1:501a
Tristan, hunting in, 6:359a
Tristan. See Eilhart von Oberg; Gottfried von Strassburg; Ulrich von Türheim
Tristan, legend of, 8:224a-b, **12:199a–201b**
Estoire as basis of, 12:200a–201b (*illus.*)
French versions, 1:569b–570a, 5:246a–248a
Aucassin et Nicolette, 1:643b
by Thomas de Bretagne, 1:266a, 5:246b, 247b–248a, 634b
characterization of heroes, 5:247a
Donnei des amantz, 1:268b, 4:261b
Iseut in, 5:246a–248a
lost common version, 5:246b
origins of, 5:246a
permutations and innovations, 5:248a
prose *Tristan,* 5:286a
reconstructed plot summary, 5:246b–247a
tragic interpretation, 5:247b–248a
German versions
by Eilhart von Oberg, 5:634b–635a, 12:204a–205b
by Gottfried von Strassburg, 5:634a–637b
in *Grettis saga Ásmundarsonar,* 5:673a
Icelandic saga and, 4:613a
in *Kormáks saga,* 7:299b
later medieval treatments of, 12:201a-b, 203a-b, 204a–205b
origins of
Celtic, 12:199a-b
French, 12:200a-b
Welsh, 12:199b–200a
postmedieval treatments of, 12:201b
Roman de Tristan de Léonois, 12:202b
Thomas branch of, 10:390a
version commune, 12:200b–201a
in Welsh poetry, 12:598a
see also Arthurian legend; Chrétien de Troyes; *Folies Tristan;* Malory, Sir Thomas; Ulrich von Türheim
Tristan love, in Gottfried von Strassburg's *Tristan,* 5:453b–454a
Tristan menestrel. See Gerbert de Montreuil
Tristan, Roman de, **12:202a–203a**
compared with *Vie de Ste. Catherine d'Alexandrie,* 12:414a
modern edition of, 1:271b
as a source for Thomas Malory's *Morte Darthur,* 8:63b
Thomas' version of, 1:266a
Vīs u Rāmīn and, 12:463a
Tristan rossignol. See Donnei des amants
Tristan und Isolt. See Gottfried von Strassburg
Tristano riccardiano. See Rusticiano
Tristano veneto, 6:638b
Triste deleytaçión, 11:423a
Tristia. See Ovid
Tristram. *See* Tristan
Tristrams saga ok Ísöndar, 10:390a, 391a, 392b, 11:491b, 12:201a, **12:203a–204a**
compared with *Víglundar saga,* 12:416b
hunting in, 6:359a
Mírmanns saga and, 8:432b
participial clusters in, 10:394a
Rémundar saga keisarasonar and, 10:303b–304b
semantic variation and antithesis in, 10:393b–394a
Tristrant, 8:408b, **12:204a–205b**
Eilhart von Oberg and, 12:202b, 204a-b
influence of, 12:205a
plot and style of, 12:204b–205a
Wolfram von Eschenbach and, 12:674b
see also Eilhart von Oberg
Tristrem, Sir, hunting in, 6:359a
Tritheism. *See* Trinitarian doctrine
Tritone, 8:599a
Triumphal arch, **12:205b**, 12:206 (*illus.*)
Triumphal columns, Roman. *See* Antiquarianism; Art, renaissances and revivals
Triumphal Entry. See Lydgate, John
Triune God. *See* Trinitarian doctrine
Triunfo de Amor. See Flores, Juan de
Triunfo de las donas. See Rodríguez del Padrón, Juan
Triuwe, 8:350a, 409a, 413b
Trivet, Richard, 7:370a
Trivium, **12:205b–207a**
according to Isidore of Seville, 10:354a-b
at Aachen, 1:142b
dialectic studies, 12:206b–207a
Fachschrifttum and, 4:577b–578a
grammar studies, 12:206a–207a
in Martianus Capella's work, 10:353b–354a
origins of, 12:205b–206a
rhetoric studies, 12:206a-b
Trnovo, 11:177a, 178a
archbishopric of, 9:208b

made Bulgarian capital by Asen, 9:510a
school of, 11:346a
taken by Ottomans (1393), 2:136b
Troas, Latin Empire of Constantinople and, 7:346a, 347b
Trobairitz, **12:207a-b**
Trobar clus, 6:644a, 656b, 8:125a, 10:250b–251a, 252a
Wolfram von Eschenbach and, 12:675a
Trobar leu, 6:645a, 10:252a
Trobar poetry styles. *See* Trouvères, poetry
Trobar ric, 1:539a, 6:644a, 10:175a-b
Trogir. *See* Traù
Troia Cathedral, pilasters, 9:649b
Troianus, Curtius, 1:439b
Troilus. See Albert of Stade
Troilus and Cressida. See Shakespeare, William
Troilus and Criseyde. See Chaucer, Geoffrey
"Trois aveugles de Compiègne, Les." *See* Cortebarbe
Trojan War. *See* Troy story
Trojanerkrieg. See Konrad von Würzburg
Trojanerkrieg, Der. See Ulrich Füetrer
Trójumanna saga, 10:389b, **12:207b**
see also Troy story
Trolls, in Icelandic *riddarasögur,* 10:395b
Trompe, 8:603b
Trompette sacqueboute. See Sackbut
Trøndelag
agriculture of, 9:180b
Norwegian unification and, 9:182b
Trondheim. *See* Nidaros
Troparion, 6:378a, 379a, 7:613a, 8:554a, **12:208á**
in *kanon,* 7:208b
Trope, 8:579b, 592a, 592b
assignment to feasts, 8:200a
Cistercians and, 8:643a
part-music and, 8:593b
Troper, 9:688b, **12:208a-b**
Notre Dame *Magnus liber organi,* 10:336b
Winchester Troper, 10:336b
Tropes, 6:379b, 9:713b
in Agnus Dei, 1:73b, 74b
in Gregorian chant, 5:663a
in introit, 6:498b
for the Kyrie eleison, 7:313a, 313b
of Montauriol, 6:381b
in *Rhetorica ad Herennium,* 10:352a
St. Gall monastery and, 9:187b
to *Benedicamus Domino,* 2:167b
see also Benedicamus Domino; Liturgical poetry; Sequence (prosa)
Tropes to the Ordinary of the Mass, **12:208b–210b**
compared with chants of the Proper, 12:209b–210b
performance of, 12:209b
procedures of, 12:209a-b
terminology and examples of, 12:208b–209 (*illus.*)
Tropes to the Proper of the Mass, 9:688a-b, **12:210b–213b**
compared with chants of the Ordinary, 12:209b–210b
genres of, 12:210b
sequentia, 12:210b–211a
Troping. *See* Farcing
Tropology, in Hugh of St. Victor, 6:322b
Trot, 7:317a
Trota, 8:247b, 256a, **12:213b–214b**
Trota and *Trotula, Trotula* treatises, 12:213b–214b
Trotula. See Trota
Troubadours, 10:173a–178b, **12:214b–218a,** 12:214b–218a
alba, 1:123a
amor de lonh, 7:49b
Breviari d'amor and, 4:506b
canso subjects and expression, 12:216b–217a
of Catalan origin, 3:164b
chanson, 3:254b
chansonnier and, 3:255b–256a
chansons de malmariée, 3:262b–263a
coblas capfinidas/doblas/unissonans, 12:215b
comparison with trouvères, 12:218a–219a
as court entertainers, 8:124b
courtly love, 3:668b–669a, 12:536b–537a, 632a
Dauphiné, 4:110a
descort and, 4:164a
emergence of in Provençal literature, 10:162b–163b
etymology of, 10:164a
expansion of troubadour mode, 10:167b–168a, 170a
fabliaux and, 4:576a
first, 5:434a
French, trecento music and, 12:177b
genres, 10:168a, 12:217b–218a
German lyric literature and, 5:434a
as guardian of worthiness, 10:162b
Guittone d'Arezzo and, 6:644a
Iacopo da Lentini and, 6:642b, 11:259b
influence of
on other literary genres, 5:284b
on Provençal language, 10:157a–158b
on secular *cantiga,* 3:87a
jeu parti poetic form, 63a
joglar/jongleur and, 7:116b–117a
lai and, 7:316a
in Languedoc, 7:340b, 341b
late 13th century, 6:26b
lauda and, 7:384a
literary context, 10:178b–184b
"Matter of Britain" and, 1:569a
minnesingers and, 5:434a-b, 8:413b
oral tradition and, 8:568b
origins and foreign imitations of, 12:218a
patronage of, 10:168a
centers, 12:161a, 215a
Raymond VI of Toulouse, 10:251b–252a
poetic form, 11:666b
poetic persona of, 10:166b–167a
poetic variety, 10:164b–165a
poets, 12:215a
senhal (pseudonym), 12:216b
travels of, 12:160b–161b
trobairitz and, 12:207a-b, 215a
Pugliese and, 11:259a
rise of formalism in, 10:175a–176b
scholarly study of, 10:181b–182a
Sicilian school and, 6:641a, 11:258a
sirventes of, 11:313a
sociocultural climate for, 10:173b
songs, 10:164a
melody and performance, 12:216a-b
structure, 12:215a-b
travels of, 12:160b–161b
virtuosity of, 10:165a
vocabulary, 12:215b–216a
vocabulary of, Sicilian school and, 11:258a
women, 12:207a-b, 215a, 219a
see also Alba; Minstrels; Partimen; *Canso; Reverdie; Vidas*
Trouvères, 12:214b–215a, **12:218a–219b,** 12:218b–219a
comparison with troubadours, 12:218a–219a
courtly love, 12:536b–537a
first, 5:434a
French courtly lyric, models for, 5:251a
genres, 12:218a–219a
minnesingers and, 5:434a-b, 8:413b
Notre Dame school and, 9:192a
patronage centers, 12:161a
poetic form, 11:666b
poets, 12:218b
portrayal of love, 12:632a
Sicilian school and, 11:258a
sirventes of, 11:313a
travels of, 12:160b–161b
trobar clus style, 12:218b
troubadours and, 5:282b
see also Troubadours
Troy Book. See Lydgate, John
Troy pound, 10:67b
Troy story, 7:360b, 365a, 369a, 370a, 8:225b, **12:219b–221b**
in Byzantine literature, 2:509b
Chaucer's telling of, 3:287b–289a
death of Hector, in *Roman de Troie,* 12:219b (*illus.*)
French versions, 2:182a, 12:219b–221a
Grandes chroniques de France, 3:327b
German versions, 12:221a
romance literature, 5:445b, 446b
13th century, 6:182a
other medieval versions, 12:221a-b
Spanish versions, 11:416b, 453b, 457b–458a
ballads, 11:428a
lost works, 11:443b
Trójumanna saga, 12:207b
continuations of, 2:365a
see also Lydgate, John
Troyes, fairs, 4:590b, 591a
Troyes Cathedral, nave, 1:426a
Troyes, Council of (1128), Templars established by, 2:191b

Troyes, Treaty of (1420), 3:271a, 5:188a
French representative assemblies and, 10:320a–321a
see also Hundred Years War
Trpimir I, prince (845–864), 4:2b
Truce of God, 3:176a, 4:16a, **9:473a–475b**
compared with Peace of God, 9:474a
in hymns, 6:384a
indulgences and, 6:448b
influence of, 9:475b
revival of in the 12th century, 9:475a
see also Peace of God
True Cross. *See* Cross, true
True Religion. *See* Augustine of Hippo, St.
Trulla, **12:221b–222a**
Trullan Synod. *See* Trullo, Synod in
Trullo, Synod in (692), 3:630b, 7:610b, 11:45b
on celibacy, 3:215b
icons and, 6:397b, 400a
patriarchate and, 9:459a
pentarchy system and, 9:496a
on preaching, 10:78b
Trumeau, **12:222a**
Trumpet, 8:561b
Celtic, 8:558b
in civic music, 8:597b
in dance music, 8:595b
marine, 8:607a
Middle Eastern, 8:612b
performance on, 8:635a
in processions, 8:595b
Trumscheit. *See* Trumpet, marine
Trunnion, 3:65a
Truss (unit of measure), 12:593b
Tryphonius, on slavery, 11:334a
Tsamblak, Cyprian, 2:414a
Tsamblak, Gregory, 2:414a
Tsḥāq, Awrāba chief, 6:413a
Tsignanes. *See* Gypsies
Tskarostᶜavi Gospels, 2:164b
Tsromi (Cᶜromi), **12:222a-b**
Tu es Petrus. *See* Communion chant; Peter, St., liturgy of
Tu patris sempiternus es filius, 11:632b
Tuaim Drecain (monastery: County Cavan), 6:540b
Tuam, see of, 1:470a
Tuan mac Cairill, 6:540b
Tuaregs, in Timbuktu, 12:55a, 55b
Tuath. *See* Ireland, society
Túatha Dé Danann, 6:546a-b, 9:48b
in Celtic mythology, 9:47a
Tuba, 8:600b
Ṭubaila. See Nuqaira
Tuberculosis. *See* Plagues
Tübingen, Treaty of (1514), 10:332b
Tübingen, University of, 12:289a
Gabriel Biel and, 2:233b–234a
via moderna and, 12:408a-b
Tuchins, 7:341a
Tuck (sword). *See* Swords
Tudela
charter of, 11:376b
controlled by Banu Qasi, 9:68a
Tudellén, Treaty of (1151), 3:130a-b
Tudeschis, Nicholaus de. *See* Nicolaus de Tudeschis
Tudor arch. *See* Arch
Tudor dynasty, first king of, 9:431b
Tudor, Edmund, earl of Richmond, 12:222b–223a
Tudor, Jasper, earl of Pembroke, 12:222b–223a
Henry VI and, 12:524a-b
Tudor, Owen, **12:222b–223a**
execution of, 12:223a
Tudors
parliament and, treason legislation, 12:168a
Welsh, capture of Conway castle, 12:523b
Tuduael, king, vs. Ninian, 9:139a
Tudwal (5th century), 9:139b
Ṭufayl, Ibn
Aristotle and, 1:459a
Ḥayy ibn Yaqẓān, 6:233b, 9:571a
Tughluq Timür, Tamerlane and, 11:588a
Ṭughrïl Bak. *See* Toghrıl-Beg
Tughril Beg. *See* Toghrıl-Beg
Tuḥfa, La. *See* Turmeda, Anselm
Tuḥfat al-arib fi-l-radd ala ahl al-Salib. *See* Turmeda, Anselm
Tuḥfat al-ᶜūd, 8:611a
Ṭulaiṭula. *See* Toledo
Ṭulayḥa ibn Khuwaylid, vs. Khālid ibn al-Walīd, 6:567b
Ṭūlūn, Ibn (mosque: Cairo), 6:599b (*illus.*)
architectural style of, 4:408a
Tulunids, **12:223a–225a**
Abbasids and, 6:590a
control of Ḥimṣ, 6:230a
in Egypt, 4:405b–406a, 12:223a–224b
waning rule and civil strife, 12:224b
Tūmart, Muḥammad ibn, 11:140b, 383b
assumption of the role of Mahdi, 1:193b
claim of descent from Muḥammad, 1:193b
founder of Almohads, 1:193b
Great Mosque of Tinmal and, 6:611a
opposed to Maliki school, 1:193b, 195a
recognized as Mahdi by the Maṣmūda, 1:193b
sumptuary laws and, 11:508a
Tun (unit of measure), 12:649b
English, 12:585b
Scots, 12:585b
Tuna, bluefin (*Thunnus thynnus*), 5:70b
Tuna, skipjack (*Katsuwonus pelamis*), 5:69b
Tuna-Badelunda graves, 10:694a-b
Ṭunbūr, 8:561b, 567b, 611a
Ṭunbūr-i a-yi Turkī, 8:611a
Ṭunbūr-i shirwīnān, 8:611a
Tunicle. *See* Vestments, liturgical
Tunics
Byzantine, 3:614a-b
Western European, 3:624b
Tunis, 8:15a, 15b
Carthage and, 6:414a, 415a
Great Mosque, 1:70b
writers, Anselm Turmeda, 12:227b–228a
Tunisia
in Islamic conquests, 6:572a
loss by Abbasids, 3:49a
in Louis IX's crusades, 4:53b–54a
under Zirids, 12:744b, 745a
Tunisia. *See* Maghrib, al-
Tunnage. *See* Tolls
Tunstede, Simon, 8:646b
Quattuor principalia musicae and, 8:563a
Tuotilo, 7:24a, 10:100b, **12:225a–226b**
artistic work by, 12:225b–226a (*illus.*)
fact and legend concerning, 12:225a-b
"Hodie cantandus est," 6:498b
hymns of, 6:381b
Notker Balbulus and, 9:187b
tropes and music by, 12:225b–226b
Tūr, al-, Quṣar and, 11:247a
Ṭūr ᶜAbdīn, monasteries of, 11:565a
Turan, vs. Iran, in *Shāhnāma,* 11:223a, 223b
Tūrān-Shāh, Ayyubid sultan, death of, 2:138a
Turanshah (brother of Saladin), Yemen and, 12:724a
Turba, in Mamluk architecture, 4:408a
Turba philosophorum, 1:141a
Turba philosophorum. *See* Rāzī, Abū Bakr Muḥammad ibn Zakarīya al-
Turbans
Islamic, 3:616b
non-Arabs forbidden to wear, 3:619b
Turbot (*Scophthalmus maximus*), 5:70a
Turcopoles, in crusade armies, 12:561b
Tureholm gold hoard, 10:694b
Turell, Gabriel, *Recort,* 3:166b
Turf seats, 5:363b–364a
Turgau, Rudolph of Habsburg and, 11:540a
Turgeis, Norse leader, captured by Uí Néill, 12:425b
Türgesh
invasion of Syria, 6:232a
vs. Muslims, in Transoxiana, 6:570b
Turin, Biblioteca Reale, Vari 42, motet texts, 8:506a
Turin, Diet of (1162), 10:444a
Turin, Shroud of, 8:83a
imago pietatis and, 6:425b
Volto Santo and, 12:489b
Turin, University of, 12:286a-b
Turin-Milan Hours, Jan van Eyck and, 4:566a
Türken Vashnachtspil, Des. *See* Rosenplüt, Hans
Türkenlied. *See* Rosenplüt, Hans
Turkey, domestication of, 5:151a
Turkey. *See* Anatolia
Turkish language
Hungarian and, 6:336b
scientific treatises written in, 11:82a
"Turkish regime," term used for Mamluk dynasty, 8:71a
Turkomans, **12:226b–227b**
Abbasid militia, marriage restrictions, 10:642b
Abu 'l-Aswār Shāwur and, 11:217b
Alp Arslan and, 11:152b
Anatolia and, 1:241a-b, 9:287a, 288a, 306b

Armenia and, 1:485a, 512a, 514a, 2:493a, 12:92b, 93a
book production of, 7:274a
carpets, *gül,* 10:549b
cavalry, 12:552b
Jem Sultan and, 2:137a
in Karamania, 7:214a
Malikshāh and, 8:59b–60a
Malikshāh I and, 11:153a
Mongol conquests, 9:306a
rebellion against Qaykhosraw II, 11:154b
relations with
Khwārizmshāhs, 6:504b, 7:244a
Kurds, 7:310b
Mamluks, 9:306a
Safawids, 2:137b
Seljuks and, 11:155a-b, 12:226b–227a
Širak under, 11:311b
Siwnikᶜ under, 11:315b
Timurids and, 12:58a–59a
in Transoxiana, 12:145b–146b
Trebizond rulers and, 12:169a-b
see also Alp Arslan; Cumans; Ghuzz Turkomans; Oghuz; Qara Qoyunlu; Seljuks, origins of; Uzun Ḥasan
Turks
in Anatolia, 6:572a
in Azerbaijan, 6:420b
Caffa seized by, 3:12b
Ikonion and, 6:418a-b
Mamluk dynasty and, 3:398b–399a
Manuel I and, 7:284a
in Morea, 7:381b
al-Muᶜtaṣim and, 8:653b, 654a
al-Mutawakkil and, 8:654a, 654b
in Nishapur, 9:141a
Serdica and, 11:189a
in Shirvan, 11:254a
in Sirmium, 11:311b
as slaves, in Iraq, 6:513a
suzerainty over Crimea, 3:678b–679a
in Syria, 11:560b–561a, 562a
in Tarōn, 11:599a
in Vaspurakan, 1:484a
vs. Catalans, 7:379b
vs. Samanids, ᶜAbd Allāh and, 11:575a
Western trade and, 4:557b, 558a
see also Kabars
Turks, Ottoman. *See* Ottomans
Turks, Seljuk. *See* Seljuks
Turmarch, 11:573a
Turmeda, Anselm, 11:380a, **12:227b–229a**
conversion to Islam, 12:227b–228a
Disputa de l'ase, 12:227b–228a
Libre de tres, 3:168a-b
Tuhfat al-arib fi-l-radd ala ahl al-Salib, 12:228b
Turmeric, production of as dye, 4:326a
Turn (musical ornamentation), 8:631a
Turnier von Nantes, Das. See Konrad von Würzburg
Turnip, the giant. *See Rapularius*
Turnips, growth of, 1:83b, 99b
Turnshoe construction. *See* Shoes and shoemakers
Turnu-Severin. *See* Walachia
Turoldus, **12:229a**
Song of Roland and, 10:446a
Turpin. *See* Pseudo-Turpin
Turres, 5:316b
Turuberan, 1:472b, 473a, 473b, 11:599a
Tuscan art, in Naples, 11:275a
Tuscan Bestiary, 6:632a
Tuscan dialect. *See* Italian language
Tuscany, **12:229a–231b,** 12:230 (map)
Black Death in, 2:259a–260a
Byzantine invasion, 12:229a-b
Charlemagne's invasion, 12:229b
communes, 3:500a
division under Henry II, 12:229b–230a
during Ottonian restoration, 12:229b
emergence of independent communities, 12:231a
Guelphs vs. Ghibellines, 12:231a
imprisonment of Beatrice and Matilda, 12:230b
inns in, 6:468a, 468b
lauda in, 7:384a
"liturgical strikes" in, 9:508b
Lombard period, 12:229b
panel painting in, 9:361b, 362a
politics of (1260-1270), 4:95b–96a
population, 4:141b
trecento sculptors, 12:170b–171b (*illus.*)
under Boniface family, 12:229b, 230a–231a
under Ostrogoths, 12:229a-b
see also Florence; Pisa; Siena
Tuscolo. *See* Tusculum
Tusculan family, papacy and, 9:384a, 11:517b
Tusculum, vs. Rome, 10:523a, 523b, 525b–526a
Tusculum, family of, 10:522b
Tusfun. *See* Ctesiphon
Ṭūsī, Naṣīr al-Dīn al-, *Taḥrīr al-Majisṭī,* 1:620b
Tustari brothers, 7:104a
Ṭusūt, 8:613b
Tutilo. *See* Tuotilo
"Tuttor, s'eo veglio o dormo." *See* Guittone d'Arezzo
Tutush ibn Alp Arslan, Seljuk ruler, 11:155a
in Damascus, 4:82a, 83b
Malikshāh I and, 11:153a
Sulaymān ibn Qutlumush and, 11:154a
Túy, Lucas of, *Chronicon mundi,* 11:435a
Tuyul (*soyurghal*), 6:591a, 12:59a
Tveggia elskanda strengleikr, 11:492a
Tver
annexation by Muscovy, 8:546b
grand princely sovereignty, 8:548a
coinage of, 8:427a
Muscovite-Tatar siege, 8:539b–540a
selection as capital, 8:539b
uprising against Tatars, 8:539b
Tvrtko I of Bosnia, ban, 11:180a, 180b, 486a, **12:231b–232b**
alliances and territorial expansion, 12:232a
annexation of Upper Drina and Lim, 2:337a
exile of, 12:232a
as king of Serbia, 2:337a, 12:232a
rule over
Bosnia and Usora, 2:337b
Croatia and Dalmatia, 2:337a-b
as vassal of Louis I of Hungary, 12:231b
Tvrtko II of Bosnia, ban, 11:474a, **12:232b**
on Bosnian throne, 2:338a, 338b
Hungarians and, 2:338b
Tweede rose, 4:319a
Tweezers, 2:149b, 150 (*illus.*)
Twelfth Night, 5:35a-b, 37a
Twelve Great Feasts, **12:232b–233a**
Koimesis, 7:282a–283a
Transfiguration, 12:125b–126a
see also Pentecost
Twelver Shiism. *See Ithnā ᶜasharī* Shiism; Shīᶜa
Twenty-four Priors, 11:278b
Twilight of the Gods. *See Ragnarǫk*
Twin (spirit of Mani), 8:83b
Twisted-rope pattern. *See* Guilloche
Twiti, William, *Art de vénerie,* 6:359b, 361a
Two Sicilies, kingdom of the, formation of, 11:267b, 273b
Two Swords, doctrine of, **12:233a–235a**
as allegory, 12:233b
attitudes toward in civil law, 12:234b
biblical sources of, 12:233a
evolution of, 12:233b
incorporation into papal hierocratic theory, 12:234a
papalist interpretations of, 12:234b–235a
Rainald of Dassel's version, 7:481a
in *Sachsenspiegel,* 7:480b
in *Schwabenspiegel,* 7:481a
summary, 12:233a
Two Ways, The. See Clanvowe, Sir John
Tyana, crusaders' route and, 10:423b
Tydorel, 7:317a
Tyler, Wat, Peasants' Revolt and, 9:478b–479b
Tympanon, 8:607b
Tympanum, 8:558a, 558b, **12:235a-b**
of Chartres Cathedral, 5:618a-b
definition of, 5:617a
jamb figures and, 5:617a-b
of La Madeleine at Vézelay, 12:405 (*illus.*)
Romanesque, 5:618a
of Rouen Cathedral, 5:624b
sculpture and, 4:121b
of Strasbourg Cathedral, 5:621b–622a
trumeau support column, 12:222a
Tyolet, 1:568a-b, 7:317a
Typhoid. *See* Plagues, enteric
Typhus. *See* Plagues
Typikon, 1:637a-b
Typos. See Constans II, Byzantine emperor
Týr (Scandinavian god), 1:63a, 11:26a-b, 30b
Tyrannicide, debate at Council of Constance over, 3:649b

Tyrant, in Western European political theory, 10:15a-b
Tyre
Ibelins and, 6:389b
Jews in, 7:105b–106a
manufacture of silk cloth and jewelry, 12:100b
merchant colonies in, 7:533a
Palestine yeshiva in, 7:105a
Saladin and, 11:561b–562a
Venice and, 12:389a
Tyrian purple. *See* Purple
Tyrol. *See* Austria
Tysyatskii, 9:194a, 194b, 195a
Tzakisma, 8:618a
Tzamblakoi family, imperial service, 2:479b
Tzetzes, Isaac, 11:52b, 54a
Tzetzes, John, 11:49b, 52b, 54a
poetry of, 2:508a

U

ʿUbāda ibn al-Ṣāmit al-Ansārī, Laodicea and, 7:315a
Ubaldo of Florence, clockmaker, 3:463a
ʿUbayd Allāh ibn Ziyād, governor of Basra, 6:370b, 371a
invasion of Transoxiana, 12:145b
ʿUbayd Allāh al-Mahdī, Fatimid caliph, 5:24b–25a, 6:616a, 8:389b
claim to imamate, 6:587b, 616a
Qāḍī Nuʿmān and, 6:616b
ʿUbayd Allāh (son of ʿAbd Allāh), 11:575a
"Úbeda, Beneficiado de," *Vida de San Ildefonso,* 11:433a, 439a
Ubertino of Casale, **12:235b–236b**
abuses within Franciscan order, 6:199b
accusations of heresy, 5:203a
adherence to *usus pauper* doctrine, 12:235b–236b
Arbor vitae crucifixae Jesu, 5:202a-b, 12:235b–236a
on Angela of Foligno, 9:14b
Bernardino of Siena and, 2:196b
conflicts with popes and Conventuals, 12:235b, 236a
disappearance of, 12:236a
influence of, 12:236a-b
as leader of Franciscan Spirituals, 12:235b
Ubi caritas chant. *See* Feet, washing of
Ubi periculum. See Gregory X, pope
Uc de St. Circ, travels of, 12:161a
Üç Şerefili Mosque, 6:612b–613a
Uccello, Paolo, 5:524b, **12:236b–237a**
Battle of San Romano, 12:236b–237b (*illus.*)
Flood and the Recession of the Flood, The, 12:236b
Uchau (unit of measure), 12:596b
ʿŪd, 8:562b, 566a, 610 (*illus.*)
as accompaniment, 8:567a-b
al-Kindī and, 8:566b
ʿŪd al-shabbuṭ, 8:610b
Udalric, biography of. *See* Gerhard of Augsburg
Udalschalc, rhymed offices of, 10:372a
Udel, 8:427a
Udine Cathedral, St. Nicolas Chapel, 12:480a
Udo of Toul, adviser to Pope Leo IX, 7:543a
Uffo, in *Brevis historia regum Dacie,* 11:522b
Ugedei. *See* Ögödai, Great Khan
Ugieri Apugliese. *See* Ruggieri Apugliese
Uglješa, John, ruler of Serres, 11:179b, 180a
Ugo de Alberico. *See* Hugo
Ugo di Perso, 6:630b
Ugolino dei Conti de Segni, cardinal. *See* Gregory IX, pope
Ugolino di Nerio. *See* Ugolino da Siena
Ugolino of Orvieto, 8:598b
Declaratio musicae disciplinae, 8:598a, 647b
musical treatise of, 11:364b, 366a
Ugolino di Prete Ilario, 6:636a
Ugolino da Siena, **12:237b**
pupil of Duccio, 4:302b–303a
Virgin and Child, 12:238 (*illus.*)
Ugolino di Vieri, **12:238a**
reliquary at Orvieto Cathedral, 12:239 (*illus.*)
Uguccione della Faggiuola
attacks on Florence, 5:97a
Dante and, 4:103b–104a
Uguccione da Lodi, *Il libro,* 6:630b, 651a
Uhlans, 7:325a
Uí Briain. *See* Dál Cais
Uí Briúin, Connacht dynasty, 3:537a-b
Uí Chennselaig, defeated by Uí Dúnlainge, 7:536b
Uí Dhálaigh, 6:535a
Uí Dúnlainge
associated with the monastery of Kildare, 7:536a-b
defeat of, 7:536b
principal rivals of, 7:536a-b
Uí Fiachrach, Connacht dynasty, 3:537a-b
Uí Mhaine, Book of. *See* Book of Uí Mhaine
Uí Néill, 3:396b, 407a-b, 6:547a, 547b, 553a, **12:238a–243b**
achievement of primacy by, 12:242b
capture of Norse leader Turgeis and, 12:425b
conquest of Ulster, 12:256a
decline of, 12:243a
division into Cinéal Conaill and Cinéal Eóghain, 12:241b–242a
dynastic strife of, 12:243a
expansion from Connacht, 12:241a
genealogy of, 12:240 (*illus.*)
kingdoms of, 12:241a
midlands branch, 1:60b–61a
opposition to, 8:531a-b
Patrick and, 9:464b
provenance of, 12:238b–240a
suzerainty, 8:531b
Tara and, 11:598a
vs. Eóganacht, 4:493a
see also Leinster
Uí Uiginn, 6:535a
Uighur kingdom, Turkish
destruction of Kirghiz, 7:272b
Manichaeans and, 8:85b
Ukhuwwa, Ibn al-, *Maʿālim al-qurba,* on Islamic metal tools, 12:86a
Ukraine
Armenians in, 1:486a
Slavs in, 11:348b
Ukrainian language, 6:438a, 444a, 11:342a-b, 346b
Ulagh. See Postal and intelligence services, Islamic, under Mongols
Ulaid, 6:547b–548a
ʿUlamāʾ, 6:591a, 11:227b, 228b, 332b, **12:243b–245b**
alliance with ruling institution, 12:245a
defined, 12:243b–244a
doctrine of uncreatedness of Koran and, 12:244a-b
education of, 12:244a-b, 245a
First Civil War and, 12:244a
influence of
on economy, 12:244b–245a
on Islamic society, 3:41a, 47b, 48a-b, 12:244a-b
Zaydi, 12:742a
see also Sects, Islamic, Twelver Shiism
Ulema. *See ʿUlamāʾ*
Ulenspiegel. See Bote, Hermann
Úlfeðinn. See Berserks
Ulfilas, Arian bishop, 1:454a, 2:90b, 211b–212a, 10:465b, 12:469a
Bible translation, 1:212a
Bible translation of, 6:436b
Visigoths and, 6:436a
Úlfljótr, 9:146a
Icelandic law and, 12:32a
Úlfr Uggason, **12:245b–246a**
Húsdrápa, 11:320a, 12:245b–246a
kennings in, 12:245b–246a
refrain of, 12:245b
on Thor's encounter with Midgard, 12:45b
as wedding poem, 12:245b
Uljaytu Khudabānda, Ilkhanid sultan, 6:420b, **12:246a–247b**
alliance with Christian West, 8:475a
coins of reign, 12:246b
conversion to Shiism, 12:246b
death of, 12:247a
etymology of name, 12:246a-b
mausoleum of, 6:602a, 603b–604b (*illus.*), 7:223b, 12:247a
relations with
Byzantines, 12:247a
European leaders, 12:246b–247a
Mongol leaders, 12:246b
Ullinn. *See* Ullr
Ullr (Germanic god), 11:27a, 325b, **12:247b–248a**
cult of, 12:248a
as hunter and skier, 12:247b–248a
places named after, 12:247b
replaced by Odin, 12:248a

Ulm, Frederick I Barbarossa and, 11:527b
Ulm Minster, Man of Sorrows sculpture, 8:531a (*illus.*)
Ulmannus, *Dreyfaltigkeit,* allegorical alchemy, 1:138b
Ulpian
  definition of prostitution, 10:154a-b
  on slavery, 11:334a
Ulric of Imola, bishop, attitudes on celibacy and, 3:217a
Ulric of Kyburg, 11:539b
Ulrich of Augsburg, canonization, 6:68b
Ulrich von Ensingen, **12:249a-b**
  Strasbourg Cathedral and, 11:488a
Ulrich von Eschenbach, **12:249b–250b**
  Alexander, 12:249b–250a
  early life and education of, 12:249b
  Herzog Ernst D, 6:216a, 12:250a
  praise of Bohemian royal house by, 12:249b–250a
  Wilhelm von Wenden, 12:250a
  Wolfram von Eschenbach and, 12:249b
Ulrich Füetrer, **12:248a–249a**
  Bayerische Chronik, 12:248b
  Buch der Abenteuer, 5:455b, 8:360b, 12:248b, 679b
    Albrecht von Scharfenberg and, 1:133a-b
  renaissance of chivalry and, 12:248b
  surviving frescoes of, 12:248a
  Trojanerkrieg, 12:248b
Ulrich Funk the Elder, possible illustrator of *Ambraser Heldenbuch,* 1:229b
Ulrich von Hutton, 9:682b–683a
Ulrich von Liechtenstein, 5:633b, 634b, **12:250b–252a**
  Frauen Buch, 8:409a-b, 12:251b
  Frauendienst, 5:436b, 438b, 8:409a
    contemporary references in, 12:251a-b
    literary value of, 12:251b
    parallels with Wolfram's *Parzival,* 12:251b–252a
    parody in, 12:251a
    songs and love letters in, 12:251a, 251b
    sources for, 12:251b
  Liech, 12:251a
  love letters (*büechlîn*), 12:251a
  minnesongs, 8:414a, 12:250b–251a
  Steinmar and, 11:476b
Ulrich von Manderscheid, 9:123a
Ulrich von Richenthal, *Konzilschronik,* 6:176b
Ulrich von Singenberg, **12:252a–253a**
  innovations of, 12:252b
  traditionalism of, 12:252b
Ulrich von Strassburg, 1:128b, 129a
Ulrich von Türheim, 5:634a, **12:253a-b**
  Eilhart's *Tristrant* and, 12:201a, 205a
  Rennewart, 12:679b
  sources, 12:253a
  Tristan, 12:253a-b
  Willehalm, 12:253b
Ulrich von dem Türlin, 5:453a, 454a
Ulrich von Winterstetten, 5:634a, **12:253b–254b**
  identification of, 12:253b–254a
  Leiche, 12:254a
  Tagelieder, 12:254a
Ulrich von Zazikhoven, 5:455a, **12:254b–255b**
  Lanzelet, 12:254b–255a
    Hartmann von Aue's *Erek* and, 12:254b
    Wirt von Grafenberg's *Wigalois* and, 12:657a
    Wolfram von Eschenbach and, 12:674b
Ulrich von Zell, *Antiquiores consuetudines monasterii Cluniacensis,* 6:65b
Ulster, 6:518a, **12:255b–256b**
  collapse of earldom of, 12:256a
  Dál Riata colonization of Scotland, 12:255b–256a
  dominated by Cinéal Eóghain, 3:397a
  early Roman records of, 12:255b
  growth of church of Armagh and, 12:256a
  invasion of
    in 1315, 6:518b
    in *Táin bó Cúailnge,* 6:548a
  Norman conquest of, 12:256a
  pre-Celtic population of, 12:255b
  Ulaid kingships, 12:255b, 256a
Ulster, Annals of
  King Nechtan's expulsion of monks, 9:91b
  on Rhodri Mawr, 10:366a
  on Viking raids, 12:425a
Ulster Cycle, 6:547b–549a
  Bible and, 6:542a
  echtrae and, 6:550b
  gods in, 6:546a
Ultimogeniture, 6:459a
Ulugh-Beg, **12:256b–257b**
  accession to power, 12:57b
  adherence to Turko-Mongol traditions, 12:257a
  astronomical tables of, 12:257a-b
  defeated by son, 12:257a
  honorary title of *küregen* and, 12:58b
  installation as ruler of Transoxiana, 12:256b
  as patron of culture, 12:59a, 257b
    madrasa at Samarkand and, 11:84a
    observatory at Samarkand and, 11:85b (*illus.*)
  relations with
    Moghuls, 12:256b
    Shāhrukh, 12:256b
    Uzbeks, 12:256b–257a
  respect for Islam, 12:257a
  as scholar, 12:257a-b
  struggle for throne, 12:257a
ᶜUlūm al-ᶜarabīya, 11:82a
ᶜUlūm al-awāʾil, 11:82a
ᶜUmar I ibn al-Khaṭṭāb, Umayyad caliph, 6:568b–569a, 569b, 577b, 7:106b, 235b, 11:563a, **12:257b–260b**
  achievements of, 3:34a
  administration, 12:259b
    control of governors by, 12:259b
    elective council appointed by, 12:260a
    fiscal structure developed by, 12:259b–260a
  ᶜAmr ibn al-ᶜĀṣ and, 1:237a-b
  assassination of, 10:242a
  cities established
    Basra, 12:259a
    al-Fusṭāṭ, 12:259a-b
    al-Kufa, 12:259a, 259b
  commander of the faithful title, 3:488a
  conversion to Islam, 6:576b, 12:257b
  Dīwān and, 6:589a
  expansion during reign of, 12:258a–259a
  Jerusalem and, 9:354a, 11:560a
  Jews under, 7:103a, 103b
    self-government by, 7:72a-b
  Koran and, 6:578b
  land grants by, 12:260a
  legislation, 12:258a
  military registry system, 12:259b
  Muḥammad and, 12:257b, 258a
  Najrān and, 9:55b
  opposition to seafaring, 12:308b
  Pact of, sumptuary laws for non-Muslims and, 11:508b
  property taxes, 11:667b
  Shīᶜa and, 11:226b
  source of power, 3:33b
  succeeds Abū Bakr, 3:33b–34a
  sunna and, 11:510b, 514a
  Syrian visits of, 12:258b
  weaknesses of caliphate, 3:34b
  Yarmuk and, 12:719b
ᶜUmar II ibn ᶜAbd al-ᶜAzīz, Umayyad caliph, 3:312b, **12:260b–262a**
  administrative innovations, 12:261a-b
  administrative reforms of, 3:41b
  on alms tax, 1:201b
  appointment as governor of Hejaz, 12:261a
  defense of divine preordination by, 12:261b
  in Łewond's *History,* 7:554b
  promotion of Islam, 12:261b–262a
  rebuilding of *masjid* at Medina by, 12:261a
  reputation for piety, 12:261a
  siege of Constantinople and, 12:261a
  sunna and, 11:510a
  taxation policy, 11:668a, 12:261b–262a
  treatment of non-Muslims, 12:262a
ᶜUmar ibn Abī Rabīᶜa, 1:400a
ᶜUmar ibn Ḥafṣūn, revolt against Umayyads, 12:276b
ᶜUmar ibn Saᶜd ibn Abī Waqqāṣ, 6:370b–371a
ᶜUmar Khayyām, 9:141a, **12:262a–263a**
  contemporary neglect of poetry of, 12:262b
  contributions to astronomy and mathematics, 12:262a-b
  patrons of, 11:84a
  Rubāᶜiyāt, 12:262b–263a
    FitzGerald's translation of, 12:262b, 263a
    growth of, 12:263a
ᶜUmar al-Murtaḍā, cultural school of, 8:151a
ᶜUmar (son of Idrīs II), 6:413a

ᶜUmar Shaykh (son of Tamerlane), 12:56b, 57a, 58a
ᶜUmarī, al-, 5:333a
Umayyad art, 6:593a–596b, **12:263a–265a**
combination of influences in, 12:264b
innovations in, 12:264b
Islamic furniture and, 5:315a
as propaganda and proselytism, 12:264a, 264b
sacred architecture, 12:263b–264a (*illus.*)
secular architecture, 12:264 (*illus.*)
in Spain, 6:600b–601b
see also Bādiya
Umayyad Mosque (Damascus), 3:40b
Umayyads, **12:265a–275a**
administration of, 6:501b–502a, 589a, 589b
ṣāḥib al-sūq, 8:526b–527a
apogee of Umayyad era
army factionalism, 12:271b–272b
assertion of caliphal authority, 3:36b
building projects of al-Walīd and Hishām, 12:271a-b
development of market economy, 12:271a
disintegration of tribalism, 12:272a
emergence of Islamic political culture, 12:271b
ideals of Islamic identity and Muslim equality, 12:273a
internal development, 12:271a-b
Islamization and Arabization, 12:272b–273a
literary culture and scholarship, 12:271b
military expansion, 12:270b–271a
urban growth, 12:271a
Arab orientation, 8:166b
Armenian magnates and, 1:478b
Basra and, 2:127b
Beirut and, 2:164a
claim to caliphate, 8:166b
coinage of, 8:422a–423a
collapse of, 1:7a, 198a, 3:40b–41b, 8:15a, 10:608b, 12:273a–274b
final surrender, 12:274b
Hāshimīyad missionaries, 12:273b
rebellions against, 12:273b–274a
rise of internal opposition, 12:273a-b
conquests of, 6:570a
costumes of, 3:616b
in Damascus, 4:81b, 83a
dress restrictions and, 11:508a
First Civil War, 8:519a, 12:266b–268b
foreign policy, 3:40a
glassmaking of, 5:545b–546a
Greek numerals and, 10:472b
Ḥarrān as capital, 8:165a
historiography
contradictory accounts, 12:265a
Dīnawarī's history, 4:188a
non-Islamic sources, 12:265a-b
hunting and, 6:355a, 355b
iconoclasm and, 6:403b
Idrisids and, 6:413b
Ifrīqiya and, 6:414b
in Iraq, 6:511b–512a
Islamic preaching and sermons under, 10:71a
Justinian II and, 7:202b
Kharijites and, 11:138b, 139a
in Arabia, 8:165b, 166a
in Iran, 8:166b
al-Kufa under, 7:307a
last dynasty of, 11:382b
libraries under, 7:273b
Marwanid period, 3:38b–41b
Mecca and, 8:240a
military campaigns, 3:37b–38a, 12:529b
military conquests
Egypt, 8:164a
Iraq, 8:165a
Syria, 8:164a, 165a
military rule of provinces, 3:39b
Murjiᵓa, 11:140a
music and, 8:565b–566a
al-Muᶜtazila and, 8:655a
Najd and, 9:54a-b
navy of, 9:73b–74b
opposition to, 3:39b–40a, 12:721b, 722a
origins of, 1:374a
palace weavers and, 11:716b
palaces of, *see also Bāb*
plagues and, 9:684a-b, 686a
public works of, 3:40b
Qadarīya and, 11:139b
Quḍāᶜa and, 12:721b
Quraysh tribe and, 10:242a-b
rise of Islamic mysticism and, 9:39a
rise to power, 3:36b, 5:545b
early economic power, 12:265b
opposition to Muḥammad and, 12:265b
Second Civil War, 8:163b–164a, 166a, 10:242a-b
Arab factionalism, 12:269a-b
consequences of, 12:269b–270a
effects of, 12:574a
Kharijite and Shīᶜa propaganda, 12:270a
opposition to Umayyad-Quḍāᶜa hegemony, 12:269a
rise of Marwanids, 12:269a
Shīᶜa and, 11:226b
slave trade and, 2:268a
slaves of, 11:337a-b
Sufyanid branch, 12:267a–268a
consolidation of power, 12:268a
shift of caliphate to Damascus, 12:268a
Syria and, 11:560b
taxation policy
provincial governors, 11:627b
redefinition of *ushr,* 11:625b
theology of, 6:582a
ṭirāz formulas and, 12:61a
tribal conflicts, 8:143a
Battle of Marj Rāhiṭ, 8:142b–143a, 164a
Kalb, 8:165a
Khazars, 8:164a
Qays, 8:164a
under ᶜUthmān's caliphate, 3:35a
vs. Abbasids and Tahirids, 11:574a-b
vs. Berbers, 2:186a
vs. Byzantines, 8:166a
in Anatolia, 6:572a
vs. Fatimids, in al-Maghrib, 6:413a-b
vs. al-Ḥusayn, 6:370a, 370b, 371a
vs. Kaysānīya, 11:226b–227a
al-Yaᶜqūbī on, 12:718a
see also Farazdaq, al-; Umayyad art; Umayyads of Córdoba
Umayyads of Córdoba, 3:49a, 50b, 598a, **12:275a–278b**
in Asturias-León, 1:627b–628a
decline and fall, 12:278a
emergence of party kingdoms, 12:278a-b
end of caliphate, 3:600a
internal strife and power struggles, 12:278a
patronage of Fēs, 5:50b
rebellions of Toledan *muwalladūn,* 12:67b–68a
in Seville, 11:213b
vs. Buluggīn, 12:744a
Zāwī ibn Zīrī and, 12:745a
see also Spain, Muslim kingdoms of; Umayyads
Umbo. See Shield boss
Umbraculum. See Ciborium
Umbrella dome. *See* Pumpkin dome
Umbrellas, in churches, 5:319b
Umbrian language, 6:434b
"Umìle sono ed orgoglioso." *See* Ruggieri Apugliese
Umilenie iconography. *See* Iconography
Umiltà of Florence, St., 9:14a
Umma, 8:262a
family and, 4:596b
importance to Islamic concepts of rule, 3:32b
Islamic law and, 3:41a
Kharijite view of, 3:36a
ᶜUmra. See Pilgrimage, Islamic
Umruᵓ al-Qays, kingdom of, 1:371b
Umur of Aydin, 7:128b
Umur Bey (mosque: Brusa), 12:741a
Unam sanctam. See Boniface VIII, pope
Uncial letters, in Lorsch Gospels, 1:213b (*illus.*)
Unconsciousness, treatment of, 6:491b
Unction
in Celtic church, 3:230b
in clerical ordination, 9:268a
effect of, 7:262a
Unction, royal. *See* Anointing
Unction of the sick, **12:278b–279a**
Armenian church and, 1:502a
Byzantine rite, 12:279a
development as Extreme Unction, 12:279a
in extremis, 4:120a
liturgical rites for, 12:278b–279a
see also Anointing; Extreme unction
Under der linden. See Walther von der Vogelweide
"Under-third cadence." *See* Cadence (music), Landini
Underbint, 8:407b, 410b
Ungro-Walachia, metropolitan see of, 12:501a, 504b
Unibos, **12:279b–280a**
date of composition, 12:279b
etymology of name, 12:279b

moral of, 12:279b–280a
Unicorn, 2:243a, 6:361b–363a, **12:280a–281a**
in art, 6:408a, 12:280b
in Islamic writings, 12:280a
Unifiers of St. Gregory the Illuminator, 4:253a
Unigenitus Dei filius. See Clement VI, pope
Unio mystica
in Hildegard of Bingen, 9:10b
in Mechthild von Magdeburg's work, 8:241b
"Union of three nations of Transylvania," 6:336a, 347a
Unions of poets. *See Confrérie; Puy*
Unison chant. *See* Plainsong
Unisoni couplets, 7:372b
Unitas fratrum (Unity of the Brethren). *See* Bohemian Brethren
Universal councils. *See* Councils, ecumenical
Universal History. See Orosius; Step^c^anos Asołik Taronec^c^i
Universals, **12:281a–282a**
Aristotelian tradition of, 12:281a, 281b
in conceptualism, 12:281b
human nature and, 12:281b
Islamic, Umayyads and, 11:560b
in nominalism, 12:281b
Ockham and, 9:211a
Platonic tradition of, 12:281a, 281b
in realism, 12:281b
universalia ante res, realism and, 10:269a–270b, 272a
universalia in rebus, realism and, 10:269a, 270a–272a
Universitas, village as, 12:440a
Universitas Anglorum (Rome), 10:526b
Universitas (collectivity)
excommunication and, 6:467b
see also Corporation; Interdict
Universities, Byzantine, **12:300b–302a**
Bardas University in the Magnaura, 10:307a
classical literary studies in, 3:431a-b
in Constantinople, 3:556b, 12:300b–301b
early higher education, 12:300b
private teachers, 12:301b
see also Literacy, Byzantine
Universities, Islamic. *See* Schools, Islamic
Universities, Western European, **12:282a–300b**
academic dress, 12:298a
academic year, 12:298a
as *alma mater,* 12:299a
Aristotelian studies in, 1:461a–463a, 465a, 9:702a-b
at Naples, 9:58b–59a
Black Death and, 2:266a
botanical gardens in, 5:360a
classical literary studies in, 3:432b–434a
classical translations for, 12:141a
curriculum
arts, 11:688a-b, 689b–690b
building trades, 8:175a
mathematics, 8:212b
optics, 9:248b
physics, 9:623a, 625a
textbooks, 11:688a
doctors of, 4:233b, 376a
England, 12:290a-b
church and, 3:59b
faculty of arts
bachelor of arts, 12:294b
curriculum, 12:294b
license to teach, 12:295a
regent masters vs. nonregents, 12:295a
faculty of canon law, 12:295b
faculty of civil law, 12:295b
faculty of medicine
bachelor and licentiate, 12:295b–296a
curriculum, 12:296a
master, 12:296a
teaching of anatomy, 12:296a
faculty of theology, 12:295a-b
foreign language teaching in, 12:137a-b
formal debate in, 10:238a-b, 241a
foundation of, Gothic art and, 5:604b–605a
foundation types, 12:284b
France, Parlement of Paris and, 9:419b–420a
grammar studies in, 5:648a–641a
Holy Roman Empire, 12:161b
legal status of, 3:606a
manuscript book production and, 8:103a-b
meeting places for, 12:298a
officers
chancellor, 12:297a
conservators, 12:297b
consiliarii, 12:297a
dean, 12:297b
fiscal officers, 12:297b
inrotulator, 12:297b
key holders (*clavigerii*), 12:297a-b
legal officers, 12:297b
librarius or *stationarius,* 12:297b
peciarius and *correctores peciarum,* 12:297b
proctors, 12:297a
rector, 12:297a
reformatores, 12:297b–298a
origins of, 12:282b
"paper," 12:290b–291a
pecia system and, 9:481b
Platonic studies in, 9:702a–703a
Poland, Collegium Maius, 9:729b, 730b
privileges of
exemption from secular jurisdiction, 12:282b–283a
protection of traveling students, 12:283a
universities as third power, 12:282b
salaries of masters, 12:298b–299a
Scotland, 10:613a, 11:112a
Spain, Peter IV (the Ceremonious) and, 9:510b
spread of literacy and, 7:600b
spread of, 12:161b
students
financial obligations of, 12:299a
power of, 2:311b–312a
teaching methods
disputationes, 12:296b
lectiones, 12:296a-b
quolibet, 12:296b
repetitio, 12:296b–297a
travel of teachers and students to, 12:161a–162a, 283a
via antiqua/via moderna controversy in, 9:157a-b
via moderna and, 12:407b–408b
see also Colleges; Law, schools of; Medicine, schools of; Scholasticism; Textbooks
University students. *See* Students
Unminne, Die. See Hermann von Sachsenheim
^c^Unṣurī, 6:507b
Unterwalden
geography, 11:540b
Habsburgs and, 11:540a, 541a
Henry VII of Luxembourg and, 11:542a
Lenzburgs and, 11:541a
Unum ex quattuor. See Clement of Llanthony
Unur, Mu^c^īn, vizier of Damascus, vs. Second Crusade, 4:38a
^c^*Unwān* (chapter heading in Koran), illumination of, 8:113a, 114a
Uplands Rejoinder, 8:332a
Upper Armenia. *See* Barjr Hayk^c^
Upper Exchequer. *See* Exchequer
Upper Monastery of Mar Gabriel (Mosul), 11:564b
Upplandslagen, 7:524b–526a
Uppsala
archaeology of, 11:519b
cult of, 11:530a, 530b
temple at, 11:36a, 12:417b
Uppsala Edda, 11:316a
Uppsala, University of, 12:290a
Uqaylids, al-Kufa and, 7:308a
^c^Uqba ibn Nāfi^c^, in Tunisia, 6:572a
^c^*Uqqal,* 4:296b
Urach dynasty, 11:539b
Uralic languages, 6:434a
Uranius, *On the Death of St. Paulinus,* 9:471a
Urbain le Courtois, 1:264a-b, 3:661a, **12:302b**
Urban II, pope, **12:302b–304a**
Angelus bell and, 2:166a
Byzantine court and, 3:356a
church of St. Sernin and, 10:493a
Cluniac order and, 3:470b
consecration of Cluny III, 1:426b
Cluniac sculpture and, 10:495b
early offices held by, 12:302b
First Crusade and, 4:15b, 16a, 19a, 30a, 33b, 5:670b–671a, 12:303a, 303b
general councils under, 3:635a-b
Council of Clermont, 3:449a-b
Hugh of Cluny and, 3:356b
indulgences and, 6:448b, 9:656b
investiture conflict and, 1:312b–313a, 6:499b
Ivo of Chartres on, 4:128b
Paschal II and, 9:444b–445a
Raymond IV of Toulouse and, 3:449b–450a
reform programs of, 12:303a-b

Urban II, pope (*cont.*)
reign of, 3:352a
Robert d'Arbrissel and, 10:429b
Roger I and, 10:440b, 11:266a
subsidy and, 11:606b
succession as Roman pontiff, 12:303a
vs. Henry IV of Germany, 6:163b
Urban IV, pope
Ave Maria and, 2:13b
Charles of Anjou and, 4:60b
crusade propaganda and, 2:200a
feast of Corpus Christi and, 3:608a
Franciscans and, 12:688b
Isabella of France and, 12:688a
Ottone Visconti and, 12:464a
St. Maria of Mount Morrone Church and, 3:214b
on torture, 6:479a
Urban V, pope
Hundred Years War and, 6:334b
return to Avignon, 9:530b
in Rome, 10:524a
Urban VI, pope
Achaea and, 7:381a
attack on cardinals, 11:39b
attempts to depose, 5:186b
election of, 3:95b, 11:40a
reign of, 3:365a
successors of, 3:365b
Urban VIII, pope
beatification and, 2:143a
Gregorian chant and, 5:664a
Urban architecture, Western European, **12:220a–231a**
commercial buildings, 12:329b
early Middle Ages, 12:320a–322b
collapse of towns, 12:320a-b
housing, 12:328b–329a
market buildings, 12:329b
North Sea trading centers, 12:320b–321a
open spaces, 12:327a-b
palaces, 12:329b
planned towns, 12:322b–326a
grid plans, 12:324a, 324b
hill plans, 12:324b
satellite towns, 12:323b–324a
public buildings, 12:329a-b
streets, 12:327b–328b
alterations in, 12:328a-b
in circular towns, 12:322b
covered walkways or porticos, 12:328b (*illus.*), 328a
in crossroad towns, 12:325a-b
encroachment on, 12:327b
names, 12:322b–323a
paving of, 12:327b–328a
town walls and gates, 12:326a–327a
towns of Roman origin, 12:321b–322a
modification of ancient buildings, 12:321b–322a
refugee settlements, 12:322a
Roman walls as limits, 12:321b
survival of episcopal sees, 12:321b
types of towns, 12:321a-b
Urban chronicles, 3:328b–329b
Urban citizens. *See* Citizens
Urban government, 3:658a–659a
consuls and consulates, 3:570b–571b
see also Communes
Urban planning
in Baghdad, 6:596b–597a (*illus.*)
in Damascus, 4:82b–83b
in early Christian era, 4:331b–333a
changing nature of urban center, 4:332b
cultural changes and, 4:332a, 332b
Roman castrum design, 3:332b
Rome, 10:520b
in Samarra, 6:597b–598a
Siena, 11:280a
see also Bastide
Urbanism
Nubia, 9:199b
Roman Empire, 10:456b, 458a, 458b
imperial survival and, 10:465b–466a
Urbanism, Armenian, 1:490b–491a, 12:98a
Muslim emirates and, 1:513b
Urbanism, Byzantine, **12:304a–307a**
decline of, 12:306a-b
11th and 12th centuries, 12:102a–103a
fortification of cities, 12:306b
late antiquity, 12:304a–306a
regularity of ancient cities, 12:305a
revival of, 12:306b–307a
7th-century invasions and, 12:306a
Urbanism, Eastern European
Bosnia, 2:341a
Hungary, 6:345a
Poland, 9:721b, 725a, 728b–729a, 730a-b
Urbanism, Islamic, 6:591a, 12:106a, **12:307a–311b**
absence of urban institutions, 12:310b–311a
absence of vehicular transport, 10:426a
absence of vehicular transport and, 12:380a-b
architecture and, 6:595b–596a
coastal cities, 12:308b–309a
cohesive forces in, 12:311a
concentration of power and wealth, 12:307b–308b
concerns for privacy, 12:310b
Egyptian, 10:454b
flourishing of, 12:307a-b
food supply, 10:661b
Idrisids and, 6:413b
Iraq, 6:512b
limitations on growth, 10:661b
manuscript illumination and, 8:115b
mosque and marketplace, 12:308a (*illus.*), 309a–311a
central market as Islamic invention, 12:310a
hierarchical order of markets, 12:310a
marketplace structure, 12:310a
other city centers and, 12:309b–310a
North Africa, demand for goods, 1:71b
plagues and, 9:685b–686a
residential and commercial areas, 12:310b
spread of, 12:307a-b
in Syria, 6:82b
Timbuktu and, 12:56a
under late Timurids, 12:59a
Zanj, 12:739b
see also Baghdad; Cairo; *Sūq*
Urbanism, Western European, **12:311b–320a**
architectural aspects, **12:320a–331a**
Bavarian, 2:135a
beguins and, 2:162a
bells and, 2:166b
Bohemia-Moravia, 2:302b–303b
in Carolingian Empire, 12:313b–314a
Celtic, resistance to Hellenism, 10:458a
church and, 5:195b–196a
class struggle, 6:19a
Denmark, 4:149b
drama and, 4:284a
early church and, 9:411a
effect on poor relief, 6:297a
England
Anglo-Saxon period, 4:457b–458a
commercialization of boroughs, 4:465a
effect on countryside, 4:465b
fairs and, 4:584b–585a
food supply, 5:118a, 8:146a
self-production, 5:121a
France
in 15th century, 5:180b
cultural changes, 5:175a
evolution of communes, 5:175a
growth of new towns, 5:174b
migration to towns, 5:178a
urban poor, 5:180b
guilds and, 6:15b
heritage of Roman towns, 12:311b
history, early Middle Ages, 12:311b–313b
castrum, 12:312b
Christian influences, 12:312a-b
civitas, 12:312b
decline of urban education, 12:313a-b
declining role of towns, 12:313a
demographics, 12:313a
Roman vs. barbarian values, 12:311b–312a
urban conditions, 12:312b–313a
urban destruction, 12:312a
vicus, 12:312b
history, 9th and 10th centuries, 12:314a–315a
attacks on fortified towns, 12:314b
history, High Middle Ages, 12:315a–317b
conditions favoring urban growth, 12:315a
crusades and urban expansion, 12:315a-b
demographics, 12:315b–316b
European commercial centers, 12:315b
industrialization, 12:315b
Italo-Byzantine commercial centers, 12:315a
population composition, 12:316a-b
professional organizations, 12:316b
secular authority vs. urban independence, 12:317a
town origins, 12:316a

urban administration and government, 12:316b–317a
history, late Middle Ages, 12:317b–319a
decline of urban expansion, 12:317b
demographic decline, 12:319a
diseases and epidemics, 12:318b–319a
subsistence problems and natural disasters, 12:318a-b
urban military struggles, 12:317b–318a
impact on trade, expansion of cultivated areas, 5:116b
industries, 12:330b
inns and hostels, 6:469b–470a, 12:330a
insane and, 6:490a-b
Ireland, 6:516a, 553b
Italy, serfdom and, 11:204b–205a
law codes and, 3:609a
legal procedure and, 7:505a
manuscript production and, 8:103b–104a
market development and, 8:145a-b
merchant communities, 12:330a
music and, 8:596b–597a, 601b
natural towns, 12:322a-b
at crossroads, 12:322a-b
circular, 12:322a
strip or ribbon towns, 12:322a
neighborhoods, 12:329b–330a
class mix in, 12:330a
ethnic divisions in, 12:330a
ghettos, 12:330a
Norway, 9:184b
parish and, 9:414a
population growth and, 4:141a
rise of urban patricians and, 9:460b–461a
sanctuaries and monasteries, 12:330b
Scotland, 11:105a-b
serfdom and, 11:206a
Sicily, 11:276a
social classes and, 3:416a-b
social system and, 3:416a-b
specialization of metalsmiths and, 8:292b–293a
Switzerland, 11:538a, 542b–543b
Zähringens and, 11:539a
town and countryside, 12:330a-b
villages and, 12:442a-b
see also Bastide; "Collective seigneurial" status; Commune; Communes; Constantinople; Florence; German towns; Italy, rise of towns in; London; Paris; Rome; Venice
Urbanitatis, 3:661a
Urbar of Einsiedeln, 11:540b
Urbino Codex, miniature from *Divine Comedy,* 12:394 (*illus.*)
Urbnisi, **12:331a**
Ureche, Grigore, 10:510b, 511b–512a
Urfa. *See* Edessa
ᶜUrfī Shīrāzī, 11:252b
Urgeschichte, 11:328b
Uri Valley, 11:541a
geography, 11:540b
Habsburgs and, 11:541a, 541b
Urien Rheged, **12:331b–332a**
poetry written for, 12:597a, 602a
Taliesin and, 11:582a
Urinals, glass, 5:559b (*illus.*), 561a
Urinary-tract stones, surgeries for, 2:99a
Úrkast (a *rímur* meter), 10:405b
Urmia, Lake, 1:470b, **12:332a-b**
Urnes style, **12:332b,** 12:418a, 418b
in Celtic art, 3:223a
woodcarving, 12:332b, 333 (*illus.*)
Uroš I of Serbia, grand župan, 11:172b, 473b
Stefan Uroš II Milutin of Serbia and, 11:174b
Uroš II of Serbia, grand župan, 11:172b–173a
Uroš (son of Stefan Nemanja) of Serbia, king, 11:174b, 175a-b
Urraca of Castile, queen
death of, 10:41a
on *juglares,* 8:282a
marriage to Alfonso I (the Battler) of Aragon, 1:160b, 3:129b–130a, 9:70a
Ursicinus of Ravenna, bishop, 10:263b–264b
Urso of Calabria, 8:256a-b
works of, 8:248b, 249a, 250b
Urstende, Diu. See Konrad von Heimesfurt
Ursula von Hohenberg, 6:325a
Ursula, St.
in Elizabeth of Schönau's *Visiones de resurrectione Beatae Mariae Virginis,* 9:10b
in Juan Rexach's altarpiece, 10:342b, 343a (*illus.*)
Ursulines, founded by Angela Merici, 1:250b–251a
Ursus, doge of Venice, 12:384b
Urðr (Norn), 9:171b, 172a
"Usages of the Orléanais," 4:515b
Uşak, carpets of, 6:613b
Usāma ibn Munqidh, *The Contemplation of Experience* (*Kitāb al-iᶜtibār*), 1:381a-b
Usatges of Barcelona, 10:256a
Ushakov, Simon, **12:332b**
Old Testament Trinity icon, 12:333a (*illus.*)
Usher of the royal wardrobe. *See* Wardrobe, royal, England
ᶜUshr, 11:625b, 667b, 667a
on *mawaᶜt* land, 11:668b
see also Tithes, Islamic
Usk, Thomas, **12:333b–335a**
execution of, 12:334a
Testament of Love, 7:331a
attribution of to Chaucer, 12:334b
contents of, 12:334a-b
Uspensky Cathedral. *See* Moscow Kremlin
ʾUsra. See Extended family, Islamic
Ussher, James, archbishop, 6:524b
Ustav. See Nil Sorsky, St.
Usuard, **12:335a**
Uṣūl al-fiqh, 11:219a
Usurpation of royal power (accroachment). *See* Kingship
Usury, 7:89a, 89b, 109b, **12:335a–339a**
enforcement of punishments for, 12:337b, 338b
in patristic writings, 12:335b–336a
permission of interest-bearing loans to enemies, 12:338a
Scholastic writers on, 12:337a
see also Banking, European; Law, canon; Roman law
Usury, Islamic law, 2:79a-b, **12:339a–340b**
Usury, Jewish law, 12:335b, **12:340b–341b**
Uswārī, Mūsā ibn Sayyār al-, 10:72b
Ut de curis. See Trota and *Trotula*
Ut queant laxis, solfège and, 8:641a
"Ut queant laxis resonare fibris," 6:381b
Uta Gospels, miniature from, 10:103b (*illus.*)
Uta of Niedermünster, abbess, 10:103b
ᶜUtba ibn Ghazwān, 6:569a
Utensilibus, De. See Adam of the Little Bridge
Utgard, 11:29a
Útgarða-Loki (giant in Scandinavian mythology), 12:45b–46a
ᶜUthmān ibn ᶜAffān, caliph, 6:572b, 577b, 7:294a
ᶜAmr ibn al-ᶜĀṣ and, 1:237a-b
apparent nepotism of, 12:266a
caliphate of, repudiated by the Kharijites, 11:138b
as candidate for caliphate, 3:35a
centralization of caliph's power under, 3:35a-b
codification of Koran, 6:45b
as founder of Umayyad dynasty, 12:266a
murder of, 3:35b, 6:108b, 511b, 582b, 7:306b, 10:242a, 11:283b, 284a, 284b, 12:266b
effect on Muslim doctrine, 6:205a
opposition to, 8:519a, 12:266b
Shīᶜa and, 11:226b
strife with Egypt and Iraq, 12:266b
sunna and, 11:510b, 514a
"ᶜUthmānic text," 7:294a
ᶜUthmānids
in Armenia, 1:513a
seat of at Berkri, 2:189a
ᶜUthmānīya, Al-. See Jāḥiẓ, Abū ᶜUthmān ᶜAmr ibn Baḥr al-
Utiesenić, George. *See* Martinuzzi, George
Utikᶜ, 1:472b, 473b
Utopia. See More, Sir Thomas
Utraquism, 6:372a-b, 373b, 374a
in Bohemia, 2:306a, 306b, 307b
Wyclif and, 12:710b
Utraquist Church (Prague). *See* Prague Utraquist Church
Utraquists, compromise with papacy, 6:200a
Utrecht Psalter, 1:273b, 4:368b, 7:25b, **12:342a**
copying of, 10:108b
illustrations, 4:292b
Psalm 102, 10:98 (*illus.*)
technological innovations, 11:651a-b
ivories of, 10:100a
musical instruments in, 8:601a

Utrum, 6:481a
Utterström, Gustav, effect of climate on history, 3:450a-b, 455b
Uwāl. *See* Baḥrayn, al-
Uχt. *See* Oaths, in Armenia
Uχtanēs, bishop, 1:510b
on the Armeno-Georgian schism, 6:240a
first mention of Zenob Glak, 9:458a
ʿUyūnids, on al-Baḥrayn, 2:51a
Uzbek. *See* Özbeg
Uzbeks
invasion of Khorāsān, 12:58a
seizure of northern Khwarizm, 12:57a
Uzun Ḥasan, **12:342a–343a**
Aq Qoyunlu and, 1:352a
defeated by Mamluk sultan Qāʾitbāy, 10:222b
Tabrīz and, 11:571a

V

Vacarius, **12:343a–344a**
Apparatus glossarum, 12:343b
Bolognese School and, 5:567b
on equity, 4:501b
Liber pauperum, 12:343b
Vačʿē II of Albania, king, founding of Bardhaʿa and, 2:107a
Václav. *See* Wenceslaus
Václav IV of Bohemia. *See* Wenceslaus IV of Germany, emperor
Vačʿutean, 1:485b
Vadstena (monastery: Sweden), 2:247a
Birgitta of Sweden and, 9:15a, 15b
founded, 12:689a
Vafþrúðnismál, 11:31a, **12:344a-b**
battle of dead warriors and, 12:350b
compared with *Baldrs draumar,* 2:56b
concept of *hel,* 6:147b
Odin's contest of wisdom, 9:218a-b
Surtr and, 11:515a
texts of, 4:385b
Vagrants. *See* Travel and transport, Western European, travelers
Vahagn, shrine of, 11:599a
Vahan of Gołtʿn, prince, 1:519a
Vahan Mamikonean, 1:476b, 477a
construction of cathedral of Ējmiacin, 4:417b
Łazar Pʿarpecʿi and, 1:508b, 7:527b
Vahan of Siwnikʿ, *katʿołikos,* 1:500b
Vahevuni family, West Tarōn and, 11:599a
Vahka Castle, **12:344b–345b**, 12:345 (*illus.*)
Vahnuni family. *See* Vahevuni family
Vahrām Čōbēn, 1:477a
Vahram Pahlawuni, 9:328a
Ani in Širak and, 1:484a
Vahram Rabun, 1:511b, 512a
history of Rubenids, 6:241a
Vainglory, 8:327a
Vair Palefroi. *See* Huon le Roi de Cambrai
Vaison, Council of (529), 7:590b–591a
Vajk of Hungary, king. *See* Stephen I of Hungary, king
Vakhtang Gurgasali. *See* Waχtang I Gurgaslani
Val de Travers (abbey: Switzerland), Frederick I Barbarossa and, 11:539a
Valais, Swiss Confederation and, 11:545b
Valamir, Ostrogothic king, settlement of Pannonia, 9:289b
Vałaršapat
see of, 1:503a, 504a
see also Ējmiacin
Vałaršapat, Council of (1441), 1:502a
Valaxš V, Arsacid pretender, 1:451b
Valdambrino, Francesco di. *See* Francesco di Valdambrino
Valdemar (son of Magnus Ladulås), 4:505b
Valdemar of Sweden, king, coronation of, 11:530b
Valdés, Juan de, *Diálogo de la lengua,* 11:390b
Valdevez, Battle of (1212), 10:44a
Valdimars saga, 10:391a, 395b
Valencia, **12:346a–350a**, 12:347 (map)
administration of, 12:346b–348a
after Reconquest, 11:377a
black slaves in, 2:270a
Cid and, 3:75a, 384b, 385a–386a, 11:376a-b
established as separate kingdom, 12:346a
fruits grown in, 5:305b
irrigation of, 6:557a, 557b–558a
literary golden age, 12:349a
Mudejars in, 11:379a-b
revolts in, 11:377a
Valencia (city)
literary festivals in, 3:171b
metropolitan see of, 12:348a
population of, 12:348b
as printing center, 12:348b
religious orders in, 12:348a-b
Valencia, University of, 12:287a
Valencian law, 12:348a
Valenciennes, first seals of, 11:126a
Valens, Roman emperor, 12:469b
Arianism and, 1:454a
death of, 6:352b
defeated by the Visigoths, 2:90b
Valent. *See* Wayland the Smith
Valentine, first known record of the custom in Paston letters, 9:451a
Valentine to Her That Excelleth All. *See* Lydgate, John
Valentine's Day. *See* St. Valentine's Day
Valentinian I, Roman emperor, Arianism of, 2:485a
Valentinian II, Roman emperor, Ambrose and, 1:231a
Valentinian III, Roman emperor, 10:262a
assassination of, 12:355a
Codex Theodosianus and, 3:475a
Valentinios, 4:196a
Valera, Diego de, 11:436a
didactic works by, 11:422b
Valeránica, Bible of, Florentius and Sanctius, 10:648a (*illus.*)
Valerian, Roman emperor, defeated by King Šābuhr of Iran, 9:61 (*illus.*)
Valerius Maximus, 10:247a
Nine Books on the Romans' Famous Deeds and Sayings, 3:166b
Valery of Bierzo, St., against secular songs, 11:446a
Valhalla, 11:31b, **12:350a-b**, 12:423b
depicted on a picture stone, 12:419a (*illus.*)
etymology of, 12:350b
images of in *Eiríksmál* and *Hákonarmál,* 4:415a
see also Scandinavian mythology; Valkyrie
Valhǫll. *See* Valhalla
Váli, 11:27a
Valkjósandi (name of Odin), 12:351a
Valkyrie, 11:27b–28a, **12:350b–351a,** 12:423b
in *Njáls saga,* 4:106a-b
Norns and, 9:171b, 172a
Valla, Lorenzo, 4:572b, 5:400b
Alfonso of Aragon and, 9:59b
Dialecticae disputationes, 4:171a
Donation of Constantine a forgery, 4:257b
idea of Middle Ages and, 8:308b
Valla-Ljóts saga, 4:612b, **12:351b–352b**
contents of, 12:351b–352a
dating of, 12:352a
"Valladolid laws," Vincent Ferrer and, 12:453a
Valladolid, University of, 12:286b
Vallani, Filippo, biography of Boccaccio, 2:277b
Valle, Laurent. *See* Valla, Lorenzo
Valle Leventina, Uri and, 11:544a
Vallicellian Penitential, 9:489b, 491a
Valois dynasty, **12:352b–353a**
in Burgundy, 2:426a, 427a–428a
factional strife, representative assemblies and, 10:320b–321a, 322b–323a
"gathering in" of territories, 5:189a
International Style at courts of, 5:628b
Joan of Arc and, 7:114b–116a
mirror of princes under, 8:435b
opposition to
Burgundian influence, 5:183b
Évreux family, 5:183a, 184b
noble and bourgeois, 5:183b
origin of, 5:183a, 9:555b
Siena and, 11:282a
threat of alternative dynasties, 5:183b
Valsgärde
archaeology of, 11:519a, 519b
graves, 10:694a
Valturio, Roberto, *De re militari,* 11:649a
Valvassores, 3:557b–558a
Valven, Sir (Gawain), 7:21a
in *Ívens saga,* 7:21a
Valvens þáttr, 10:390a, 390b
see also Parcevals saga
Vambrace, 1:525b, 534a
Vamplate, 1:532b

- *Van den Coninc Saladijn ende van Hughen van Tabaryen. See* Hein van Aken
- *Van Heer Halewijn,* 4:321a
- Van, Lake, 1:470b, **12:353a-b**
  - Ałtᶜamar bishops and, 1:503b–504a
  - Arab occupation of, 1:479a, 481a, 513a
  - Arčēš and, 1:423a
  - Armenian economy and, 12:97b, 98a
  - David of Tao and, 1:483b
  - under Prince Gagik II, 12:361b
- Van Maerlant, Jacob. *See* Maerlant, Jacob van
- *Van 't kind van twalef jaren,* 4:321a
- *Van den Vos Reinaerde. See* Willem
- *Van zeven manieren van heiliger minnen. See* Beatrijs van Nazareth
- Vanakan Vardapet, 5:579b, 674b
- Vanand, **12:353b–354a**
  - *see also* Kars
- Vandals, **12:354a–356a**
  - administration, 12:355a-b
  - in Africa, 10:466b
  - Arianism and, 1:454a, 454b
  - early Germanic law and, 7:471b
  - language of, 6:437b
  - laws of, 7:471b
  - in al-Maghrib, 8:15a
  - Mediterranean conquests of, 12:355a
  - movements of, 12:354a-b
  - in North Africa, 2:91b–92a, 12:354b–356a
  - numbers of, 12:354b
  - origins of, 2:91b, 12:354a
  - piratical fleets of, 9:78b
  - Pope Leo I (the Great) and, 7:541b
  - recognized as federate allies, 2:91b
  - as slaves, 11:335a
  - in Spain, 2:91b
  - vs. Belisarios, 2:91b, 165a
  - vs. Roman Empire, 12:470a
    - sack of Rome (455), 2:91b
    - in Spain, 12:470b
    - treaty with Rome (435), 12:354b
  - *see also* Leo I, Byzantine emperor
- *Vanden blinckenden steen. See* Ruusbroec, Jan van
- *Vanden levene ons Heren,* 4:320a
- *Vanden winter en vanden somer,* 4:321a-b
- *Vander Mollenfeeste. See* Roovere, Anthonis de
- Vanir, 9:146a, 146b, 146b–147a, 11:29b, **12:356a-b**
  - as fertility deities, 5:296b–297b
  - Hœnir and Mímir, 11:29b
  - Mímir and, 8:395b
  - war with Æsir, 11:29b–31a
  - *see also* Æsir; Scandinavian mythology
- Vanni, Andrea, **12:356b–358a**
  - altarpiece with Crucifixion, 12:356b–358a (*illus.*)
  - *see also* Bartolo di Fredi
- Vanni, Lippo, **12:358a**
  - fresco in Palazzo Pubblico, Siena, 12:357a–358a (*illus.*)
- *Vápnfirðinga saga,* 4:613b, 614a, **12:358a–359a**
- Varallo, Calvary of, 11:467b
- Varamin, mosque at, 6:604b
- Varangian Guard, 4:555b, **12:359a-b**
  - Basil II and, 2:118b
  - origins of, 12:435b
- Varangians
  - in Hungary, 11:479a
  - in Near East, 4:555b
  - in Russia, 4:554a, 555a-b
  - in *Russian Primary Chronicle,* 12:434b
- Varāvīnī, *Marzbān-nāma,* 6:508b
- Varaz-Bakur II (380-394), 3:308a
- Varaztirocᶜ, Xusrō II and, 1:477a
- Varazvałan Siwni, 1:476b
- Vard Patrik, 1:477a
- Vardan II Mamikonean, 1:477a, 8:78b
- Vardan Arewelcᶜi, 1:511b, 512a, **12:359b–360a**
  - *Universal History,* 12:359b, 360a
- Vardan Aygekcᶜi, 1:512a
- Vardan Mamikonean, St., 1:476b, 480a, 518b, **12:360a-b**
  - battle of Avarayr and, 2:12a
  - in Łazar Pᶜarpecᶜi's *History of Armenia,* 7:529b
  - martyrdom of, 8:78b
- Vardan Vardapet, *Geography,* on Ayrarat, 2:20b
- Vardapet, 1:504b, 5:544a, **12:360a-b**
- Vardzia. *See* Wardzia
- *Variae. See* Cassiodorus Senator; Petrarch
- *Variatio,* **12:361a**
  - in tonaries, 12:70a-b
- Varna, **12:361a**
- Varna, Battle of (1444), 6:347b, 363b, 8:264a, 11:182b
- Varos (Armenian anchorite), 1:519b
- *Varqeh va Gulshāh,* 11:147a-b
- Varro
  - Aristotle and, 1:460b
  - Cassiodorus and, 8:638a, 10:354a
  - *De lingua latina,* 6:351b
  - *Disciplinarum libri IX,* 4:447b, 8:637a
  - three types of theology, 9:616b
- Varuna (Zoroastrian god), 12:746b
- Vasak Pahlawuni, lord of Bjni, 5:675a
- Vasak of Siwnikᶜ, prince, 1:476b, 11:315a
- Vasallectus. *See* Vassallettus
- Vasari, Giorgio, on Gothic architecture, 5:581a
- Vasconia, 2:127a
- Vasilii I of Muscovy, grand prince
  - annexation of Nizhnii Novgorod, 8:540b
  - succession plans, 8:543b
- Vasilii II of Muscovy, grand prince
  - appointment of metropolitan, 8:545b
  - aristocracy and, 4:306a
  - economic recovery and, 11:192a
  - imperial aspirations, 8:546a
  - imprisonment of Isadore, 8:545b
  - Muscovite sovereignty, 8:544a–545a
  - Novgorod and, 8:545a, 9:196a
- Vasilii III of Muscovy, grand prince, 5:330b
  - Pskov and, 9:197a
- Vasilii Rogov, 8:573b
- Vasilii Shuiskii of Russia, tsar, serfdom and, 11:197a, 197b
- "Vaso Vescovali," 6:408b
- Vaspurakan, 1:472b, 473a, 473b, **12:361a–362b**
  - Arcrunis in, 1:451a, 451b, 12:361b
  - capital on Ałtᶜamar, 12:353b
  - as Catepanate of Basprakania, 1:484a
  - ceded to Byzantine Empire, 12:362a
  - divided, 1:482b, 483a
  - overrun by Turks (1071), 12:362a
  - separatism of, 1:475a, 481b
  - towns and fortresses of, 12:362a
  - vs. Yūsuf, 1:482a
  - *see also* Berkri; Naχčawan
- Vaspurakan (family), Zakᶜarids and, 12:736b
- Vassallettus, **12:362b–363a**
  - Lateran and, 7:344b
- Vassals
  - in Bulgaria, 2:413a
  - Carolingian, 3:491a
  - Conrad II's ordinance concerning, 3:557b–558a
  - definition of, 5:53a
  - feudal, 3:491a-b
  - great lords as royal vassals, 5:54a
  - Merovingian, 3:490b–491a
  - obligations of, 5:53a-b
  - rise of, 8:404b
  - *see also* Feudalism; Serfs and serfdom
- Västmanland, rebellion in, 11:533a
- *Västmannalag,* 7:525a
- Vasxyen, 5:413a
- Vata (*fl.* 1046), revolt of, 6:340a
- *Vaterbuch,* 8:357a
- *Vaterrachelied* (Vengeance poem). *See Reginsmál*
- Vatican, mosaics in (3rd century), 4:349b
- Vatican Library, 7:563b
- Vatican mythographers, 1:183b
- *Vatnsdœla saga,* 4:613b, 614a, **12:363a-b**
  - *Finnboga saga* and, 5:64b
- *Vatnyshyrna, Eyrbyggja saga* and, 4:568a
- *Vaðmál,* 6:394b
- Vaud, in Burgundian-Swiss war, 11:545a
- Vault of St. Georg (Nordlingen), 11:372a (*illus.*)
- Vaults, **12:363b–366b**
  - barrel, 3:562b–563a, 12:364a–365a (*illus.*)
    - origins, 11:656a
  - brick, 4:331b
  - in Byzantine churches, 4:339a
  - centering of, 3:234b–235a
  - construction of, 3:562b–563b
  - dome of heaven, 4:236b
  - early Gothic, sexpartite system, 5:595b
  - fan, 12:365a-b
    - origin of, 1:427a
  - in *gawitᶜ,* 5:371a
  - in Gothic architecture, 5:580b–581a
  - in Gothic cathedral, 5:595b–596a
  - in Greek-cross church type, 4:340b–341a
  - groin, 3:563a, 10:621a, 12:364 (*illus.*), 365b
    - in abbey church of La Madeleine, 10:479b

Vaults (*cont.*)
in Hagia Sophia in Constantinople, 9:494 (*illus.*)
lierne, 12:365b
Monte Cassino, 10:486a
Mozarabic, 8:512a
rib or ribbed, 1:427a, 12:364 (*illus.*), 366a
in Cistercian architecture, 10:483b
in Durham Cathedral, 4:315b
in English Romanesque architecture, 10:484b
Lombardy, 10:484b
modern controversy about, 1:429b
in St. Étienne (Caen), 10:482b
as Romanesque distinction, 10:477a, 479a
in St. Philibert (Tournus), 10:479a
in St. Vitus Cathedral in Prague, 9:421b (*illus.*)
spandrel, 11:389b
in Speyer Cathedral, 10:487b–488a
tierceron, 12:366a
transverse barrel, 10:621 (*illus.*)
types of, 12:364a–366a (*illus.*)
see also Alternation; Arch; Lierne; Pendentive; Rib; Squinch; Tierceron; Voussoir
Vavasor knights. *See* Knights; *Valvassores*
Vecchietta, 11:281b
Veche, 7:249b
Vega, Garcilaso de la, 11:425a
grand-nephew of Santillana, 11:451b
Vegetables
trade in, 5:126b–127a
see also Fruits
Vegetarianism, 3:580b–581a
among Cathars, 3:185a
in Latin church, 3:580b
Vegetius (Flavius Vegetius Renatus), **12:366b**
cavalry tactics of, 3:200b
Epitoma rei militaris, 12:366b
influence on chivalry handbooks, 3:302a
Vegtamskviða. See *Baldrs draumar*
Vehicles
in ancient Middle East, 12:379b
European, **12:367a–379b**
chariot branlant, 12:377a-b
classification of, 12:367a
construction and maintenance of, 12:377b–378a
decline of passenger vehicles, 12:369a–373a
early whippletree, 12:371b–372a (*illus.*)
in England, 12:375a
four-wheeled wagons, 12:81a
in France, 12:374a–375a
history (5th to 12th centuries), 12:369a–373a
history (13th to 15th centuries), 12:373a–378b
legacy from antiquity, 12:367a–369a
litter, 12:377a
ox carts, 12:81a
prejudice against riding in, 12:370a, 372a, 376a
raeda, 12:368b, 369a, 369b
Roman vehicles, 12:368b–369a
as status symbols, 12:376a–377a
see also Roads, Western European
Islamic, **12:379b–380b**
in Indus Valley, 12:380a
in Spain, 12:380a
in Turko-Mongolian steppe, 12:380a
see also Roads, Islamic world
wheeled
cartage, 12:158a
disappearance of, 12:147b–148a
see also Animals, draft; Litter
Veil. *See* Pokrov
Veil, taking the. *See* Cloister
Velbužd, Battle of (1330), 11:475a
Veldener, John, Caxton and, 3:210b
Veleti tribe (Slavs), 9:717b, 719a
Vellekla. See Einarr Helgason Skálaglamm
Vellum, **12:380b**
popularization of by monastic schools, 11:74a
Velluti, Donato, *Cronica domestica,* 6:660a
Velox cadence. *See* Cadence (language)
Velte. See Setier, wine
Velum ianuarium, 5:319a
Venantius Fortunatus, 5:472b, **12:380b–381a**
acrostics, 1:46a
borrowings from in *Líknarbraut,* 7:580a
Hrotswitha von Gandersheim and, 6:314a
hymns of, 6:379b
on music, 8:558a
on musical instruments, 8:601a, 606a
Pange lingua gloriosi, 6:381a, 7:361a, 374a, 12:381a
parody of, 9:441a
Salve, festa dies, 6:383a
travels of, 12:148b–149a, 151a
Vexilla regis prodeunt, 6:381a, 384b, 7:361a, 12:381a
parody of, 9:441a
Vencimiento del mundo, 11:456a
Vendel, archeology of, 11:519a, 519b
Vendel cemetery, 10:693b–694a
Vendīdād. See Avesta; *Vidēvdād*
Veneration of relics. *See* Pilgrimage; Relics; Shrines
Venereal diseases
syphilis, 9:673a
in art, 9:683a
famous people with, 9:682b–683a
theories of origin, 9:682a-b
Venery. *See* Hunting
"Venetian sallet." *See* Barbute
Venetic language, 6:434b
Venets, **12:381a-b**
Veneziano, Antonio, 12:175b, 176b
frescoes of, 5:294b
Life of St. Ranieri, 5:294b
Vengeance de Jésus-Christ, La. See Mercadé, Eustache
Vengeance de Notre Seigneur. See Mercadé, Eustache
Vengeance poem, Scandinavian mythological. *See Reginsmál*
Vengeance Raguidel, La. See Raoul de Houdenc
Veni creator Spiritus, **12:381b–382a**
Hrabanus Maurus and, 6:306b
incense and, 6:432b
translations of, 12:382a
in York rite, 12:729a
Veni, Sancte Spiritus. See Langton, Stephen
Veni Sanctificator, 8:191a
Venice, **12:382a–393b**
ambassadors of, 4:210a, 212b
relazioni, 4:209b
ambassadors to, 4:205b–206a
nuncius, 4:203a
Argos and, 7:381a
arsenal of, 9:81a
Avogadori di Comun (state attorneys), 12:391b
Biblioteca Marciana, Bessarion collection, 2:203a, 9:703b
Black Death in, 2:260b
Black Sea trading posts of, 12:98b
Bolla d'Oro from Byzantine emperor, 12:386b
bucentaur in, 2:395b
Carolingian period, 12:385a-b
Catalans and, 7:379b
coinage of
ducat, 4:301 (*illus.*)
grosso, 4:301a, 5:679b–680a
compared with Rome, 12:382b
Council of Ten, 12:391b, 392b
crusades and, 12:389a-b
currency problems, 4:301a
Dalmatian possessions, 2:338a
destruction of Pera-Galata in 1296 and, 9:503a
during Roman times, 12:383a
economic rise of, 12:111a
early trade and commercial growth, 12:386b–387a
expansion, "lordship of the Adriatic," 7:14b
on mainland, 7:9b, 10a
fairs, 4:587a
financial institutions
development of banking and, 2:73a, 73b–74a, 75b, 76a, 77a, 78b
money changers in, 2:74a
food supply
problems, 5:4a-b
trade agreements, 5:119a
foundation of, 12:382a-b
Fourth Crusade and, 4:43a–44a, 48b, 12:111b
Frederick II and, 11:269b, 272a
German warehouse at, 12:113a
government of
as commune, 3:499b
independence of, 12:385b–386b
Great Council, 12:391a–392a
expense of diplomacy and, 4:210b–211a
Venice ambassadors and, 4:209b
gulf and lagoons, 12:384 (map)
as heir to Roman civilization, 12:383a-b
imports of cloth from Low Countries, 12:112b
industry in

dyeing, 4:328a
glassmaking, 5:555b–556a
silk-throwing mills, 11:295b
inns in, 6:472b, 473b
invasions of, 12:383a–385a
in Lebanon, 7:533a
Major Council. *See* Great Council
medicine in (late 13th century), 2:99b
merchants of expelled from Byzantine Empire, 12:103b, 388b–389a
naval development of, 9:80a
political developments, 12th-14th centuries, 12:387a-b, 390a–391a, 391b–392b
political power in, 3:499b
population of, 12:387b
printing in, 10:124b–125a
Quarantia (Council of Forty), 12:391b
relations with
Byzantine Empire, 1:245b, 4:556a, 12:383b–384a
Byzantine Romania, 7:376a, 376b–378a, 380b
Croatia, 4:5b, 6:337b
Dalmatia, 4:80a, 6:337b
Genoa, 12:122a, 390b–391a, 392a, 392b
Latin Empire of Constantinople, 7:346b, 347a, 349a
Neretljani, 4:2a-b, 5b
Renaissance in, Byzantine influence, 7:1b
ruling elite in, 9:461a
sea trade routes, 12:114b–115a
Byzantine routes and, 10:423 (map), 424b
sea trade routes and, 9:88a-b
Sephardic community in, 11:161b
Signoria (executive committee), 12:391b
slave trade in, 11:338b–339a
Stefan Uroš IV Dušan of Serbia and, 11:178b
Stefan Vukčiç Kosača of Bosnia and, 11:476a
Thessaloniki ceded to, 12:26b
trade, 12:388a
with Alexandria, 1:154a
with Byzantine Empire, 12:101b, 103a–104a
Byzantine privileges, 2:494b, 12:103a, 111a-b, 388b
with Cilicia, 7:546b
in food, 11:275b
with Kingdom of Jerusalem, 12:117b
as leading center, 12:111b–112a, 385b–386b
salt, 10:630b
Uzun Ḥasan and, 12:342b–343a
Villehardouin and, 7:378a
vs. Genoa, 5:385a, 9:84a, 12:392b–393a
war of 1296-1302, 1:246a
vs. Ottomans
alliance with Hungary and the Karamanids, 8:536b
under Bāyazīd I, 2:136a
under Bāyazīd II, 2:137b
war with Mehmed II, 8:264b
vs. Padua and Treviso, Wolfger von Erla as negotiator, 12:673a
vs. William II, 7:378b
see also Chioggia War; Doge of Venice
Venice, Peace of (1177), 5:481a
recognition of Alexander III, 7:652b
Venice, Treaty of (1201), 4:42a-b, 43b
"Venite, polcel' amorosi," 6:658b
Vento, Ugo, 4:557b, 558a
Ventoux, Mount, Petrarch's ascent of, 12:162a
Ventrini. See Collaterales
Ventura. *See* Fortune, Old Spanish
Venturino of Bergamo, 4:250a, 250b
Vepᶜkhistqaosani. See Shotᶜa Rustaᶜveli
Verantius, Faustus
invention of wagon spring, 11:659a
Novae machinae, 8:392a
Verba filiorum. See Banū Musa
Verbae. *See* Tropes to the Ordinary of the Mass
Verbetae, 6:380b
Verbum abbreviatum. See Peter the Chanter
Verbum supernum prodiens. See Aquinas, Thomas, St.
Verbundbrief, 3:482a
Vercelli, irrigation of, 6:558b
Vercelli Book, 1:277a
Vercelli rotulus, 4:291 (*illus.*), 292a
Vercelli, University of, 12:286a
Vercellina (canal), 6:558b
Verdiana, St., 9:14a
Verdun, slave trade and, 11:200b, 337a
Verdun, Treaty of (843), 3:112b, 7:698a, 12:684a
Burgundy and, 2:424a
Verecundus of Junca, **12:393b**
Verethraghna (Zoroastrian god), 12:721a
Verge, Court of the. *See* Marshalsea Court
Vergerio, Pier Paolo
at Council of Constance, 3:654b
Sigismund and, 6:347a
Vergil, Polydore, *De inventoribus rerum,* 11:659b
Vergil (Publius Vergilius Maro), **12:393b–395b**
Aeneid, 12:393b, 394a, 395a
adaptations of, 4:451a, 6:143b
Bernard Silvester on, 7:366a
in German romance literature, 5:445b–446a
influence on Petrarch's *Africa,* 9:534a
translation by Gavin Douglas, 4:262a
visions and, 12:475b
Alexander Neckham on, 9:92a
allegory and, 1:180b
antique manuscripts of works by, 8:102b
Bucolics, Notker Teutonicus and, 9:189b
Calpurnius Siculus and, 3:55b
centonization of lines of, 3:235b
Dante and, 4:94b, 100b, 101a, 12:394b
Eclogues, 7:367a, 10:462b
epic and, 4:495b, 496a, 7:361a
Ermoldus Nigellus and, 4:507b
Hrotswitha and, 6:314a
hunting and, 6:358b
in hymns, 6:383b
Isidore of Seville and, 6:564a
John of Garland and, 7:134a
known as Vergil the Necromancer, 8:35b, 39a
Latin parody and, 9:440b
Metellus of Tegernsee and, 8:298b, 299a-b
as model for early Christian poets, 12:394a
as prophet of Christ, 12:394b
Servius on, 7:352b, 360a
in Urbino Codex of *Divine Comedy,* 12:394 (*illus.*)
Vergilius Augusteus, decorated letters in, 6:461b
Vergilius Maro Grammaticus. *See* Virgil the Grammarian
Verin, Smbat Sparapet's membership in, 11:351b
Vermandois, **12:395b–396b**
Vermicle enamel. *See* Enamel, Vermiculé
Vermudo III of Asturias, León, and Castile, king, 3:128b
Vernacular
literacy and, 7:369b
spread of, 6:439b–444b
as type of musical oral tradition, 8:570a
Vulgar Latin and, 7:350b, 353b, 355a
see also Questione della lingua and individual languages
Vernacular. *See* languages under country names
Vernazza, Ettore, 9:15a
Verneuil, Council of (755), women's orders and, 12:683a-b
Vernicle, **12:396b**
Vernon Golden Legend, 6:62a
sources for, 6:62b
Vernon Manuscript, 1:319b
Verona
in early Middle Ages, 12:320b
Gothic art in, International Style, 5:628a
slavery in, 11:336a
Venice and, 12:393a
Verona Cathedral, 6:638a
Nicholaus da Verona and, 10:501b
west portal, 9:128a (*illus.*)
Verona, Council of (1184)
condemnation of Arnoldists and, 1:540a
interdict of, 6:496a
ruling on mendicant orders, 5:196a
Veronese, Guarino, Isidore and, 6:563a
Veronese League, opposition to Frederick I, 7:652b
Veronica, Veil of, 8:83a
Verrius Flaccus, *De verborum significatu,* 4:449b, 8:571a
Vers, **12:396b**
in Provençal literature, 10:164b, 165b
of *sirventes,* 11:312b
see also Provençal literature
Vers de la mort. See Robert le Clerc d'Arras

Versiculi Familiae Benchuir, meter in, 10:405a
Versio Isidoriana, 7:398b–399a
see also Law, canon, to Gratian
Versio Itala, 7:398b–399a
Versio Italica. See Bible
Versio Prisca. See Versio Itala
Verso de arte mayor, 11:459b
Verso de arte menor, 11:458b
Versum de Mediolano ciuitate, 8:377a
Versus. See Tropes to the Ordinary of the Mass
Versus ad mensam regis. See Wipo of Burgundy
Versus ad repetendum. See Plainsong
Versus Isidori. See Isidore of Seville, St.
Versus (processional hymn), 6:379b, 9:713b–714a
St. Gall monastery and, 9:187b
Versus, Benedicamus Domino, 2:167b
Vertue, Robert and William, **12:396b–397a**
chapel of Henry VII in Westminster Abbey, 12:621b (*illus.*), 622a
lierne vaulting from St. George's Chapel, 7:573 (*illus.*)
Vesió. See Bernat de So
Vespasian Psalter, 2:221a, 4:548b
Vespasiano da Bisticci, 8:104b
Vespers, 3:67a, 4:229a
cathedral, 1:517a
time of, 5:662b
Vespignani, Virginio, Lateran and, 7:344b
Vessel glass, 5:556b–557a, 561b
Vestfold dynasty, *Ynglingatal,* 12:726a
Vestiarius, 10:522b
Vestibule, *see also Pishtaq*
Vestments, liturgical, **12:397a–404b**
alb, 12:397b–398a
amice, 12:397b
anabolagium, 12:397b
anagolaium, 12:397b
biretta, 12:404b
camisia, 12:397b, 398a
chasuble, 12:398b, 399b (*illus.*), 400a-b
cincture, 12:398a-b
cope, 12:400b
early medieval, 12:397a
fanon, 12:397b, 400b, 401a
humerale, 12:397b
insignia, 12:400b–403a
manipie, 12:400b–401b
orarium, 12:401b–402a
pallium, 12:402a–403a
rationale, 12:403a
stole, 12:401b–402b (*illus.*)
miter-tiara, 12:403b–404a (*illus.*)
outer garments, 12:398b–400b
penula, 12:400a, 400b
pontifical gloves, 12:403a
rochet, 12:398a
shoes and stockings, 12:403a-b
skullcap, 12:404a-b
surplice, 12:398b
tunicle, 12:398b–399a, 399b (*illus.*)
undergarments, 12:397b–398b
white, 3:484b
see also Dalmatic; *Epitrakhil;* Pallium; Stikarion;
Veterem hominem, Heirmologion and, 8:557a
Veterinary science, *Fachschrifttum* and, 4:579b
Vetrliði Sumarliðason, on Thor, 12:46a
Vettius Valens, 1:619b
Anthology, 1:605a
Vetula. See Women, aged
Vetus latina, 7:360b, 12:494b
Vetusissimum registrum, on the rite of Lincoln, 7:582b–583a
"Vexilla regis prodeunt." *See* Venantius Fortunatus
Vézelay
revolt of (1152), 12:652a
walls of, 10:489b
Vézelay, Church of La Madeleine. *See* Madeleine, La (church: Vézelay)
Vi et armis. See Trespass
Via Domitia, bridges on, 10:410a
Via Egnatia, 10:424a
Thessaloniki and, 12:26a
Via Flaminia, 10:521a, 521b
Via, Francesc de la
A Bella Venus, 3:173b
Libre de Fra Bernat, 3:173b
Procés de la Senyora de Valor contra En Bertran Tudela, 3:173b
Via Francigena, Siena and, 11:279a
Via Latina catacomb, 4:350b
importance of, 4:363a
pagan motifs in decoration of, 4:351a
Via moderna, 12:44a, **12:406a–409a**
approach to logic, 12:406a-b
at German universities, 12:408a-b
at University of Paris, 12:407b, 408a
Durand of St. Pourçain and, 4:313b
God and humanity and, 12:406b–407a
nominalism and, 9:757b, 12:406a
Ockham's razor and, 12:406b
via antiqua and, 9:157a-b, 12:406a–408b
Via mystica
English mysticism and, 9:19a
in Richard Rolle, 9:21a
treatises on, 9:8b
Via Papalis, 10:519a
Via di Parione. *See* Via Papalis
Via Recta, 10:519a
Via regia. See Smaragdus of St. Mihiel
Via Romea. *See* Via Francigena
Via Triumphalis, 10:520a
Via Valeria, 10:526a
Vialis, Jean, 6:472b
Viaticum, 4:119b, 120a
in *Everyman,* 4:527b
extreme unction and, 4:565a,b
Vic
bishopric of, 3:175a
culture in, 3:175b
settling of, 3:175b
Vic, Bernat Serradell de, *Testament,* 3:173b
Vicar, **12:409a-b**
role of in the parish in late Middle Ages, 9:416a
Vicarius, 4:191b, 10:16a, 17a
Viceroy, Islamic, 6:592a
Vicinia (neighborhood), 12:438b
Victimae paschali laudes. See Wipo of Burgundy
Victime paschali, 8:579b
Victor I, pope
assertion of Roman power, 9:366a
dating of Easter and, 9:366a
Victor II, pope, Humbert and, 6:329b
Victor III, pope
early career of (at Monte Cassino), 8:256a
Latin literature and, 7:363b
Pisan-Genoese expedition against Mahdia and, 3:355b
see also Desiderius of Monte Cassino
Victor IV, antipope, 3:637b, 10:250b
Victor of Capua, bishop, Tatian manuscripts and, 11:600b
Victor, Claudius Marius, *Alethia,* 7:361a
Victorines
founded, 6:321b
Rashi and, 4:540b
Victorinus, Gaius Marius, 4:169a, **12:409b–410a**
Aristotelianism and, 1:460b
commentary on Cicero, 10:353a, 356a
Miserere Domine, miserere Christe, 7:590b
Neoplatonism and, 9:99a
translations of Aristotle, 1:460b
Victory Cross of Oviedo, 1:624b–625a (*illus.*), 10:114b–115a
Vicus (seat of a parish), 9:411a, 411b, 412a
Vida coatanea. See Lull, Ramon
Vida de Jesucrist. See Eiximenis, Francesc
Vida de San Amaro, 11:440a
Vida de San Ginés de la Xara, 11:439b
Vida de San Ildefonso. See Martínez de Toledo, Alfonso
Vida de San Millán de la Cogolla. See Berceo, Gonzalo de
Vida de Santa María Egipciaca, La, 11:413b, 433a, 438b, 456b
Vida de Santa Oria. See Berceo, Gonzalo de
Vida de Santo Domingo de Guzmán, 11:439a
Vida de Santo Domingo de Silos. See Berceo, Gonzalo de
Vidal de Besalú, Raimon. *See* Raimon Vidal de Besalú
Vidal, Peire. *See* Peire Vidal
Vidal, Remon, *La chace au mesdisans,* 6:359a
Vidas, **12:410a-b**
of Bernart de Ventadorn, 10:170b
as historical investigations, 10:178a
identification of poetry and civilization in, 10:176b–178a
importance for development of prose, 10:177a
of Marcabru, 10:168a
of Provençal poets, 2:237a, 240a
in Provençal troubadour poetry, 10:164a–165a
survival of poetry through, 10:178a
of troubadour poets, 12:216b
see also Biography
Viderunt omnes, **12:410b–411a**

see also Perotinus (Pérotin)
Vidēvdād, **12:411b–412a**
religious significance of farming, 10:665a
Zoroastrian Ragha, 10:661a
see also Avesta
Vidimus, 5:549a-b
Vidin
besieged (1002), 2:119a
Hungarian invasion of (1365), 2:412b
Louis I and, 6:345b
Serbia and, 11:176a
Stefan Uroš II Milutin of Serbia and, 11:474b
Vie des anciens pères, La, **12:415a**
translation from Latin, 6:60a
Vie d'Édouard le Confesseur, **12:412a**
Vie de Guillaume le Mareschal, 3:332b
see also William Marshal
Vie de St. Alexis, **12:412a–413a**
authorship of, 5:239a
date and provenance of, 5:238a
Greco-Latin version, 5:238a
monastic elements of, 5:235a
Old French text, 5:238b–239a
plot summary, 5:238a-b
poetic and religious devotion in, 5:239a
recasting of, 6:59b
Vie de St. Auban, **12:413a-b**
Vie de Ste. Catherine d'Alexandrie, **12:414a**
Vie St. Edmund le rei, La, 1:261a, 9:448b, **12:415a-b**, 12:415b
Vie de St. Eustache. See Pierre de Beauvais
Vie de St. Gilles, **12:413b**
Vie de St. Josaphaz, La. See Chardri
Vie de St. Laurent, **12:413b**
Vie di St. Léger, composition of, 6:59b
Vie de St. Legier, 10:160b–161a
Vie de Ste. Léocadie, La. See Gautier de Coinci
Vie de Ste. Marguerite, **12:414b**
see also Wace
Vie de St. Martin. See André de la Vigne
Vie de Ste. Modwenne, **12:414b**
Vie de St. Nicolas. See Wace
Vie de St. Nicolas, La. See Wace
Vie de St. Quentin, La. See Huon le Roi de Cambrai
Vie de St. Richard. See Peter Peckham
Vie de St. Thomas Becket, **12:413b–414a**
Vie de St. Thomas le Martyr. See Guernes de Pont-Ste.-Maxence
Vie des set dormanz, La. See Chardri
Vieille-Brioude Bridge, 10:420b
Vielle. See Fiddle
Vienna
Academy in, 8:347a
bishopric of (1469), 2:9a
Collegium Ducale, 12:292b
granted trading privileges and municipal charter, 2:7a
origin of name, 6:436a
residence of Austrian duke, 2:6b
Vienna, Concordat of (1448), 5:489b, 9:123b
agreement with secular authorities and, 3:526a
as unilateral papal grant, 3:525b
Vienna Penitential, 9:489a
Vienna, University of, 12:287b
astronomy in, 1:613b
foundation of, 2:8a-b
Vienne, Council of (1311–1312), 3:643a–645b, 12:137a-b
Ad nostrum, 2:161a, 161b, 5:216a, 217b
church reform and, 3:364b, 645a-b
circumstances surrounding, 3:643a
Clement V at, 3:438b
conciliar theory and, 3:517b–518a
Cum de quibusdam mulieribus, 2:161a-b
Exivi de paradiso, 3:645a
Franciscan disputes and, 3:644b–645a, 9:515a
Free Spirit heresy and, 6:198b–199a
Hebraic studies and, 3:314a
Inter sollicitudines, 3:644b
Quia contingit, 6:296b
on slave trade, 11:339a
study of Middle Eastern languages and, 8:445a
suppression of Templars at, 3:362a, 644b
on unauthorized absolution, 6:449b, 450a, 450b
Vox in excelso, 3:644b
Vienne, counts of. *See* Albon, counts of
"Viennese school," Michel Beheim and, 8:306b
Viète, François, *In artem analyticem isagoge,* algebraic notation, 8:213b–214a
Víga-Glúms saga, 4:612b, **12:415b–416a**
Freyr in, 5:297a
fylgja in, 5:335b–336a
Reykdœla saga and, 10:343a, 343b
þættir and, 12:4b
Vigil, cathedral, 1:517a
Vigil the Painter (Vigil Raber). *See* Raber, Vigil
Vigilia crucis, 3:231b
Vigilius, pope, 3:10b, **12:416a-b**
at Second Council of Constantinople, 3:630a-b
on church dedication, 4:130b
Theodora II and, 12:416a
Vigils (canonical hours), 3:67a
Vígkœns saga kúahirðis, 10:394b
Vigla. See Arithmos
Víglundar saga, **12:416b–417a**
sources of, 12:416b
Vignory (basilica: Champagne), 10:478a
Vigueries. See Representative assemblies, French
Viguiers, 3:124b
Vihuela, manuals of, ballad texts and, 11:430a
Vijd (Vijt, Vyd), Jodocus, Ghent Altarpiece and, 4:566b, 5:524a
Viking Age. *See* Vikings
Viking art, 8:373b, **12:417b–419b**, 12:423b
Borre style, 12:418a-b
motifs, 2:332b
depiction of Thor's battle with midgard serpent, 12:45a
influence of on Celtic art, 3:221a-b, 223a
Jellinge style, 12:418a-b, 419a (*illus.*)
Mammen style, 12:418b, 418a, 419a (*illus.*)
Ringerike style, 10:407b, 12:418a, 418b
surviving examples of, 12:417b
tapestry from Oseberg ship, 12:417 (*illus.*)
Urnes style, 12:418b, 418a
woodcarving
animal-head post, 9:285b (*illus.*)
styles of, 9:286a
wagon panel, 9:286 (*illus.*)
see also Mammen style
Viking laws, 12:423b
Viking navigation, **12:419b–422b**, 12:421 (map), 423a
celestial observations and, 12:419b, 420a-b
"latitude" sailing and, 12:420a–422a, 424b
Viking ship, 11:239b–240b (*illus.*)
cog and, 11:242b
Viking sword. *See* Swords
Vikings, **12:422b–437b**
armor of, 1:522b–523a, 523b (*illus.*)
attack on Lindisfarne, 12:424b
attack on Thetford, 12:559b (*illus.*)
in Baltic lands, 2:62b
Carolingian nobility and, 9:148b
in *Coag Gaídel re Gallaib,* 6:539b
conversion of to Christianity, 3:355b
cult of Thor and, 12:46a
defeated by Arnulf, 1:541b
defeated by Baldwin I of Flanders (864), 2:58a
described in *þáttr af Ragnars sonum,* 12:7a
destruction of Cologne by, 3:481a
in England, 11:490a-b, 12:432a–434a
Anglo-Saxon nobility and, 9:148a
monasteries and, 12:683a
tribute to, 4:90a
see also Battle of Maldon, The
etymology of the term, 12:422b–423a
first raids of, 12:424b–425a
in Flanders, Ypres and, 12:731a
in France
defenses against, 10:411b
see also Normans
in Francia, 12:429b–431a, 431b
after 900, 12:431b–432a
Hiberno-Saxon art and, 8:373b
in Iberian Peninsula, 10:38a
invasions by, land reclamation and, 10:277b
in Ireland, 3:397a, 6:516b, 553b, 554a, 12:425a–426a
at Dublin, 4:298b–299a
in the Mediterranean Sea, 12:431a-b
naval raids of, 9:79a-b
navy, military tactics, 12:558b
in New World, 12:428a–429b
in North Atlantic, 12:426a–428a
Ragnarr, king of the Danes, 10:248b–249b
Rhodri Mawr and, 10:366a

Vikings (*cont.*)
  role as merchants, 12:110a-b
  in Russia, 12:434a–436a
    at Novgorod, 12:434a–435a
    fur trade and, 5:328a–329a
  in Scotland, attacks on Dál Riata, 7:229b, 11:490a-b
  ships of, 9:79a-b, 88b–89a, 12:424a-b
  Skrælings and, 11:329a-b
  social structure of, 12:423b
    see also Rígsþula
  tales of, 11:328b
  textile imports by, 4:328a
  tools of, in Mästermyr chest, 8:296a
  urban devastation by, 12:314b
  use of horses, 12:558b
  vs. Charles the Simple, 9:160a
  weapons of, 8:294a
  Welsh raids, 12:516a
  Western European travelers and, 12:153a-b
  see also Scandinavia; Varangians; Viking art
Viktors saga ok Blávus, 10:395a, 395b, 396a
  commendation of King Hákon Magnússon, 10:390a
  Sigurðar saga þögla and, 11:290b
Vilcinasaga, 7:285b
Vilhjálms saga sjóðs, 10:395b, 395a
Villa (farmstead), 12:442b
  see also Estate management
Villa nova de iudaeis, 7:80b
Villa Yprensis. *See* Ypres
Villages
  agricultural organization and, 12:442a
  bylaws of, 12:439b
  centuriation and, 12:443b
  circular, 12:446a
  civitates and, 12:442b
  comital revenues, 10:274a
  "common-field," 12:439b
  as communes, 12:440a
  community development of, 12:438b–439b
  community institutions of, 12:439b–441a
  community structure, **12:437b–441b**
    escarton assemblies (French), 10:325a
    rights of pasture and, 9:455a–456a
    see also Parish; Representative assemblies
  economic development and, 12:444a
  England, 12:443a
  excavations of, 12:444a
  families and, 12:438a, 438b
  field systems and, 12:439b, 444b–446a
  Germany, 12:440b, 441a, 446a
  governance of, 12:440a–441a
  historiography of, 12:437b
  land reclamation and, 10:275a-b
  marshland, 12:446b
  in migration periods, 12:443a, 444b
  mobility of, 12:443a-b
  pioneer, 12:446b
  planned, 12:446b
  population, 12:438a, 442b, 446b
  Provence, 12:442b, 446b
  religious orders and, 12:440a
  Roman, 12:442b, 443a
  seignorial ownership, 11:674b
  settlement of, **12:442a–447a**
    serfdom and, 11:206a
  social structure, 12:437b–438b
  township and, 12:440a, 442b
  warfare and, 12:444a-b
  see also Deserted villages
Villancicos, 11:449a, 452b, 459b, **12:447a–448a**
  Arabic lyrics and, 8:563b
  in *Cancionero general,* 11:424b
  in *cancioneros,* 11:419a
  in *Cantigas de Santa María,* 3:85b
  compared with *kharjas,* 11:408b
  form of, 12:447b
  versification and prosody of Spanish literature and, 11:459b
  see also Spanish literature, dawn and spring songs
Villani, 11:203a
  Orléans, 11:204b
Villani family, Boccaccio and, 2:287b
Villani, Filippo, 6:634b
  on artists' status, 1:579b
  Liber de civitatis Florentiae famosis civibus, 2:240a, 7:325b
Villani, Giovanni
  on assassins, 1:590b
  on Black Death, 2:265a
  carroccio and, 3:117a
  on election of Clement V, 3:438b
  History of Florence, 5:97a-b, 6:264b
  on Latini, 7:382a
  Nuova cronica, 6:634a, 659b
  statistics of, 4:137a
Villani, Matteo, 6:634b, 659b–660a
  on Black Death, 2:266a
Villanova. See Barcelona
Villanova d'Asti, founding of, 12:325b
Villard de Honnecourt, **12:448a-b**
  castle sketches of, 3:145a
  clocktower illustrated by, 3:460a
  drawings of, 5:614a
  on geometry of building design, 3:565b
  Gothic architecture of, 5:587a–588a
  homo quadratus and, 8:580b, 585b, 588b (*illus.*)
  sketchbook, 4:292a
    machines, 11:653a (*illus.*)
    machines and carpenter's tools, 11:644a
    perpetua mobilia, 11:644a, 652a
  use of timber in construction, 3:561a
Villaret, Fulque de, 3:304a
Villasandino, Alfonso Álvarez de, 11:418b–419a
Villefranche-de-Rouergue, 2:128b
Villehardouin, Geoffroi de, 3:247a, **12:448b–449a**
  Conquête de Constantinople, 3:328a, 332a, 12:448b
  death of, 7:378a
  Fourth Crusade and, 4:42a, 43b, 5:256b–257a, 12:389a
  Guy de Thourotte and, 3:277b–278a
  in Morea, 7:376b, 378a, 379b
  as *nuncius,* 4:203b
  Peloponnesian campaign, 12:638a
  Robert de Clari and, 10:431b
Villehardouin, Guillaume II de, Mistra and, 8:446a
Villehardouin princes, duchy of Naxos and, 9:91a
Villeinage
  serfdom and, 11:206b
  see also Serfs and serfdom
Villeins, 4:512b, 11:203a, 205a
  decline of, 11:207a
Villena, Enrique de, 11:420b, **12:449a-b**
  Arte cisoria, 11:441b
  Arte de trovar, 11:441b
  Doce trabajos de Hércules, 11:457a
  lost translations by, 11:443b
  on poetic jousts, 3:170b
Villena, Isabel de, 12:349a
Villena, marquess of (15th century), conversos and, 9:111b
Villers Abbey, 3:458b
Villers-Cotterêts, Ordinance of (1539), 6:442a, 10:178b
Villes neuves, of Henry I of England, 3:498a
Villiers de L'Isle Adam, Philippe, 3:304a
Villon, François, **12:449b–451b**
  at Blois, 3:273a
  autobiographical indications in his work, 2:237a
  "Ballade des pendus," 5:277a
  ballade to the ladies of Paris, 5:236a
  Débat du cuer et du corps, 4:122a
  Grand testament, 5:272a, 276b–277a, 12:450a–451a
    fabliaux and, 4:577a
    identity of poet-narrator, 5:277b
    style of, 5:277b–278a
  independent poems of, 12:451a
  Lais, 5:276b, 12:450a, 450b
  Les contrediz Franc Gontier, 12:482b
  life of, 5:276b, 12:450a
  lyric poetry
    conventionality of, 5:277a, 278a
    subject matter, 5:283a
  Roman de la Rose and, 10:452b
  taverns and, 6:475b
  use of lyric triangle, 5:277b
  use of proverbs, 10:191a
  use of *Rose*-Machaut poetic tradition, 5:280a
  value of work, 5:276b, 277a-b
    influence on later writers, 5:278a-b
  vetula and, 7:367b
Vilmundar saga Viðutan, 10:394b, **12:451b–452a**
  rímur versions of, 12:451b–452a
Vilnius, 7:608b
  established as a diocese, 7:607a
  seat of Algirdas, 7:606a
  seat of Mindaugas, 7:604b
Vim et injuriam. See Trespass
Vimara, **12:452a**
Vímara Peres, 10:37b
Vincennes, Château de, stringcourses on, 11:493b (*illus.*)
Vincent of Beauvais, **12:453b–455b**
  Breviari d'amor and, 4:506b
  cost of his encyclopedia, 7:567b
  De eruditione filiorum nobilium, 8:435a, 12:455a

De moralis principis institutione, 8:435a, 12:455a
Doctrinale, 12:454a, 454b
Epistola consolatoria super morte filii, 12:455a
pedagogical works, 12:455a
Sibylline oracles and, 11:257a
Spanish Alfonsine chronicles and, 11:435b
Speculum doctrinale, 4:572a, 8:644b–645a
Speculum historiale, 4:311b, 572a, 6:69b, 7:219b, 12:454a, 454b
abridged by Jaume Domenec, 3:166b
Catalan adaptation of, 9:511a
in *Libro dei sette savi,* 6:659a
Life of St. Alexis included in, 12:413a
Norwegian translation, 10:391b
Thómas saga erkibyskups and, 12:36a
Speculum maius, 4:247b, 449a, 5:397b–398a, 12:34a, 34b, 453b, 454a-b, 455a
editions of, 12:454b
Speculum morale, 7:300b
Speculum naturale, 12:454a, 454b
study of plants and, 2:245b
Vincent Ferrer, St., 3:646a, 4:250a-b, 12:348a, 349a, **12:452a–453b**
in art, 6:328b (*illus.*)
conversion of Mudejars and, 11:380b
conversion of, 10:5b
Jews and, 7:79a, 82b, 12:453a
missions to Muslims and Jews, 12:453a
in Pero López de Ayala's *Canoniçaçión,* 11:439a
preaching missions of, 12:452b–453a
sermon outlines by, 11:455b
writings of, 3:167b
Vincent of Kielce, rhymed office of St. Stanislaus, 10:367a
Vincent, St. (*d.* 304), as patron of Valencia, 12:348a-b
Vincentius Hilaris. *See* Vincentius Hispanus
Vincentius Hispanus, **12:455b–456b**
work on canon law, 12:456a
Vincentius of Saragossa, bishop, 12:456a
Vindelinus, 10:124b
Vindiciae contra tyrannos, 3:522a
Vindobona. *See* Vienna
Vineam domini Sabaoth. See Innocent III, pope
Vineti, Jean, *Tractatus contra daemonum invocatores,* on devil worship, 8:30a-b
Vinland
discovery of, 4:555a
location of, 12:428b–429b
Vinland Map, 12:429b, 430 (*illus.*)
Vinland sagas, 12:428a-b, **12:456b–458b**
discrepancies in, 12:457a-b
Skrælings in, 11:329a-b
sources of, 12:456b–457a
venue of, 12:457b–458a
see also Viking navigation
Vinodol Statute, heritable property, 11:670a
Viol, 8:561b
Vipiteno (Italy). *See* Sterzing (South Tirol)
Virelai, 4:87a, **12:458b–459a**
Arabic lyrics and, 8:563b
in *Ars nova,* 1:552a-b
French, trecento, 12:218b
in Guillaume de Machaut's work, 8:7a-b
pastoral, 12:458b
"programmatic," 12:458b
of trouvères, 12:218b
see also Ballata
Virga, 8:619 (*illus.*), 625 (*illus.*)
in Franconian notation, 8:628b
Virga prebipunctis. See Scandicus
Virga subbipunctis. See Climacus
Virgate, **12:459a**
Virgil. *See* Vergil
Virgil the Grammarian, 7:361b, **12:459b**
Epitomae, 12:459b
used in Irish biblical commentaries, 2:220a
Virgil of Toulouse. *See* Virgil the Grammarian
Virgin (church: Studenica)
Crucifixion, 11:185 (*illus.*)
wall paintings, 2:446b
Virgin of Ljeviša (church: Prizren), 11:186b
Virgin Mary
annunciation to. *See* Annunciation
in Armenian church, 1:502a, 518a
in art
birth of, by Lorenzetti, 5:604b (*illus.*)
Coronation of, by Boucicaut Master, 5:614b (*illus.*)
by Daddi, 4:75b (*illus.*)–76a
by Dalmaú, 5:612b
by Gentile da Fabriano, 5:387b (*illus.*)
by Gerard David, 4:115 (*illus.*)
by Jan van Eyck, 5:610b (*illus.*)
by Liévin van Lathem, 7:345b (*illus.*)
by Lippo Memmi, 7:587a (*illus.*)
by Lorenzetti, 7:670b (*illus.*)
by Master Wilhelm, 5:608a-b (*illus.*)
Flemish woodcut, 12:693a (*illus.*)
fresco at Pedralbes, Spain, 5:611b (*illus.*)
in *Hours of Mary of Burgundy,* 7:345b (*illus.*)
ivory (Byzantine, mid 10th century), 7:26a (*illus.*)
ivory (French, 13th century), 7:28a
marriage, by Niccolò di Buonaccorso, 9:119b (*illus.*), 119a
Mother of God icon, 10:584b–585a
Platytera type, 2:257a (*illus.*)
portal by Sluter, 5:623b (*illus.*)
cycle of, in the Byzantine church, 7:612b
Eastern homilists and, 12:460a
feasts of, 8:134a-b, 9:714b–9715a
music for, 3:85a
Syrian, 12:460a
iconography of
garden as image of, 5:361b
platytera, 9:255b (*illus.*), 705a-b
Immaculate Conception
in Augustinus Triumphus' work, 2:1a
denied by Aquinas, 12:43a
Duns Scotus and, 4:311a
litanies to the, 7:593a
Orant, in Hagia Sophia (Kiev), 10:583b (*illus.*)
prayer to, 12:460a
rhymed offices to, 10:371a
Rosary, 10:530b–531a
in theology and popular devotion, **12:459b–461a**
in Byzantium, 8:19b–20a
Carmelites and, 3:96a, 96b
cult rejected by Bogomils, 2:294a
Cyril of Alexandria, 4:75a
legends in Dutch literature, 4:320a-b
in Middle English lyrics, 8:340a–341a
in mystery plays, 8:660b, 662b
in mystical spirituality, 9:9a
in N-town plays, 9:49b–50b
pokrov festival, 9:716a
Siena, 11:279b, 280b
see also Assumption of the Virgin; Blessed Virgin Mary, Little Office of; Eleousa; *Glykophilousa;* Lactatio; Lamentation; Marian feasts; Marian hymns; Pietà; Presentation in the Temple; Theotokos; Visitation
Virgin Peribleptos (church: Mistra), wall paintings, 2:450b
Virgin Peribleptos (church: Ochrid)
fresco by Michael Astrapas, 8:303 (*illus.*)
frescoes, 4:524b
wall paintings, 2:448a
Virgin of Strasbourg Cathedral, Erwin and, 4:508a
Virgin of Tenderness. *See Glykophilousa*
Virgin of Vladimir. *See* Vladimir Virgin
Virginal, **12:461a–462a**
see also Eschaquiel
Virgin's Protection (church: Nerl River), architectural elements, 10:580a
Virgo Lactans. *See* Lactatio
Virgula. See Virga
Viribus arte minis. See Pierre de Saintes
Viridarium, 5:362a
Virtues and vices, **12:462a–463a**
in art, 12:462 (*illus.*)
cardinal virtues, 9:669a
Prudence and Strength, 9:668a (*illus.*)
religious instruction on, 10:300b, 301b–302a
in Thomasin von Zerclaere's *Welsche gast,* 12:37b–38a
virtue, in Plotinus' philosophy, 9:96b
see also Prudentius
Vīs u Rāmīn, **12:463a-b**
Georgian translations, 12:463a
Tristan and Isolde and, 12:463a
Visby, 5:460b
commerce, 11:531a
founded, 11:530b

Visby (*cont.*)
founding of, 5:633a
in Hanseatic League, 5:633a
Hanseatic League and, 12:113a
northen European trade and, 9:88b
Visby, Battle of (1361), 5:633a
armor in, 1:525
Vischer, Peter (the Elder), **12:463b**
Visconti, **12:463b–465a**
court of, *see also* Jacobus of Bologna
end of dynasty, 7:9b
Genoese rule, 8:379b
inns and, 6:472b
Milanese rule, 8:379a–380a
Italian expansion, 7:7a, 7b–8a
legitimization of, 7:7b
patronage of music, 12:179b
Petrarch in service to, 9:530a
Visconti, Azzone, 7:7b, 12:464b
reign of, 8:379b
successors of, 8:379b
Visconti, Bernabò, 8:379b, 12:464b
prohibition of 1366, 6:6b
Visconti, Bianca Maria, marriage to Francesco Sforza, 11:216a
Visconti, Filippo Maria, 12:464b
Francesco I Sforza and, 11:216a
marriage of, 8:380a
reign of, 8:379b–380a
Visconti, Galeazzo I (*r.* 1322-1328), duke of Milan, reign of, 8:379b
Visconti, Galeazzo II (*d.* 1378), 8:379b
Visconti, Galeazzo Maria (*d.* 1476), duke of Milan, reign of, 8:380a
Visconti, Gian Galeazzo (*d.* 1402), duke of Milan, 2:390b, 12:464b
astrarium of, 3:462a, 4:261a
Bernardo da Venezia and, 2:196b
Milan Cathedral and, 11:216b
Pisa and, 9:664b
purchase of ducal title, 7:7b
reign of, 8:379b
Siena and, 11:281b
wars with Florence, 5:100a
Visconti, Giovanni, archbishop of Milan, 8:379b, 12:464b
seizure of Bologna, 7:7b
Visconti, Lucchino, 7:7b, 8:379b
Visconti, Matteo, 12:464a-b
Visconti, Matteo I, reign of, 8:379a-b
Visconti, Ottone, archbishop of Milan, 12:464a
administration of, 8:379a
Ghibellines and, 8:379a
Visegrád, trade meeting at (1335), 6:345a
Visentinus, Dominicus Dominici, 4:175b
Višeslav, Croatian prince, reign of, 4:2a
Visigothic architecture, 12:465a–466b (*illus.*)
Visigothic art, **12:465a–468a**
influence on later art forms, 8:511b
metalwork, 12:467a-b
sculpture and, 12:466b
painting, 12:467a
Visigothic law, 12:472a, 474a
administration of, 12:474a-b
Visigothic minuscule script, 9:343a–344b (*illus.*)
Visigoths, 2:90a–91b, **12:468a–475a**
administration of, 12:473a
anointing ceremony of, 7:256b
art, Codex Vigilianus, 12:403b (*illus.*)
Christianity and, 12:469a
coins issued by, 8:427b
in Epiros, 12:469b, 470a
as *foederati,* 12:468b, 470b
in Gaul, 12:470a–471a, 473b
Huns and, 6:352b
in Italy, 6:443a, 12:470a
jewelry of, 5:375b
Jews in Spain and, 11:161b
Julianus of Toledo and, 7:181a-b
language of, 6:435a, 435b, 436a, 437b
laws of
on blasphemy, 2:272a
codes, 7:469a–470b
liturgy of, 6:565b, 7:626a–627a, 8:182b–183a, 9:62b
Merovingians and, 8:278a
migration of, 8:363a
military organization, 12:555a-b
in Moesia, 12:469b
origin of *ghubār* (Toledan) numerals and, 1:393a
origins, 2:90a, 9:289a
polychrome jewelry of, 8:364a
relations with
Byzantine Empire, 12:471a
Ostrogoths, 12:471a
Roman Empire, 12:469a, 469b
Vandals, 12:354b, 354a
Roman Empire and
against Roman cavalry, 3:201a
permitted to cross Danube, 2:90a, 90b
recognized as federate allies, 2:91a
sack of Rome (410), 2:90b, 10:467b
Sidonius and, 11:277a
as slaves, 11:335b
in Spain, 2:91a-b, 10:459a, 465a, 12:471a–474b
active literary life under, 11:405b–406a
anti-Jewish policy of, 7:79b, 85a-b, 95a, 12:472b–473a
Asturias-León, 1:629a, 630a–631a
Barcelona, 2:102a-b
city life, 12:473b
family life, 12:473b–474a
kingship of, 12:472a–474b
social structure, 12:473a-b
sources on, 12:472a
Spanish law and, 7:519b–520b
under Sisebut, 11:314a-b
vs. Basques, 2:126a
vs. Clovis, 3:467a, 7:339a
vs. Franks, 12:470b, 471a
Apollinaris and, 11:277b
vs. Huns, 12:469a
vs. Moors, 12:471b, 472b, 474b
Visio Bernoldi. See Hincmar of Rheims
Visio Philiberti, 6:141b, 7:367a
see also Heinrich von Neustadt
Visio Thurkilli. See Richard of Coggeshall
Visio Tnugdali, 11:439b
Visio Wettini. See Walafrid Strabo
Visioenen. See Hadewijch of Antwerp
Vision. *See* Optics
Vision of Daniel, 8:19a
Vision of Isaiah, 3:182a
Vision of Mac Conglinne, The. See Aislinge meic Con-glinne
Vision of St. Eustace, The. See Pisanello, Antonio
Vision of St. Paul, 12:475b
Vision of Thurkill, visit to hell, 4:278a
Visión de Túngalo, 11:439b
Visions, 1:185b, **12:475a–478a**
of Julian of Norwich, 9:24a-b
as literary form, 12:476a-b
in Middle English literature, 8:319a
parodied in Boccaccio's *Corbaccio,* 2:285b–286a
in Petrarch, 9:537b
Roman de la Rose and, 10:449b
of Sergius of Radonezh, 11:209a
in *Somnium Viridarii,* 11:370a-b
in Spanish literature, 11:439b–440a
see also Amorosa visione; Boccaccio, Giovanni; *Draumkvæde; Pearl; Vision of Thurkill*
Visitatio sepulchri, 11:437a, **12:478a**
Angelica de Christi resurrectione and, 12:648a
incense and, 6:432b
Visitation, **12:478b**
sculpture, Rheims cathedral, 10:309b–310a (*illus.*)
Visor, helmet. *See* Helmet visor
Visp, count of, irrigation projects, 6:559a
Vispertal, irrigation of, 6:559a
Visramiani. See Gurganī
Vita beatae Mariae Aegypticae. See Hildebert of Lavardin
Vita beate virginis Maria rythmica. See Hugo von Trimberg
Vita Beati Dominici. See Grimaldus
Vita Bennonis II episcopi Osnabrugensis. See Norbert of Iburg
Vita Cadoci. See Lifris
Vita Caroli Magni. See Einhard
Vita Constantini. See Eusebius of Caesarea
Vita Dunstani. See Adelard of Ghent
Vita Eigilis. See Candidus of Fulda (Bruun)
Vita et passio. See Ælnoth
Vita Geraldi. See Odo of Cluny
Vita Heriberti. See Lantbert of Deutz
Vita Kentigerni, 8:558b
Vita of Kotor, 11:187a, **12:478b**
Vita Mahumeti. See Embricho of Mainz
Vita Mathildis. See Donizo
Vita Merlini. See Geoffrey of Monmouth
Vita nuova. See Dante Alighieri
Vita prima Brigidae, 2:376b
see also Brigit (Brigid), St.
Vita S. Galli. See Notker Balbulus
Vita St. Malchi. See Reginald of Canterbury
Vita sancti Anscharii, description of Kurland in, 2:62b
Vita sancti Magni, as source for Eiríkr Oddsson's *Hryggjarstykki,* 4:414b
Vita sancti Oswaldi. See Eadmer of Canterbury

Vita sancti Servatti. See Heinrich von Veldeke
Vita santae Radegundis. See Hildebert of Lavardin
Vita Udalrici. See Gerhard of Augsburg
Vita Waltharii manufortis. See Ekkehard I of St. Gall
Vitae fratrum ordinis Praedicatorum. See Gerard de Frachet
Vitae patrum, **12:479a**
French version, 6:659a
Hrotswitha von Gandersheim and, 6:314b
Italian version, 6:660a
Rosweyde's collection, 6:66a
translations of, 5:288b–289a
see also Gregory of Tours
Vitae sororum (Schwesternbücher), 9:13b
Vital of Blois, 7:367a, **12:479b**
Amphitryo, 12:479a
Aulularia, 12:479b
Aulularia and *Querolus,* 10:239b–240a
Geta, 4:283a, 12:479a-b
Vital of Savigny, St., **12:479b–480a**
preaching on Gregorian reform, 6:213b–214a
preaching of, 12:479b–480a
Vital of Tierceville, foundation of Savigny, 10:672b
Vitale II Michiel of Venice, doge, expedition against Byzantines, 12:388b–389a
Vitale da Bologna, 11:299a, **12:480a–481a**
Coronation of the Virgin, 12:480b
Madonna dei Denti, 12:480 (*illus.*)
Vitalian, pope
Theodore of Canterbury and, 12:13b
Theodore of Tarsus and, 2:180b
Vitalienbrüder, 9:82b–83a
conflicts with Lübeck, 7:684a
Vitalis, St. *See* Vital of Savigny, St.
Vitasfratrum. See Jordan of Quedlinburg
Viterbo, vs. Rome, 10:526a
Vitéz de Zredna, Johannes, archbishop, 6:347a, 348a, 348b
Víðarr, 11:27a
Viticulture, 1:78a, 82b, 83b–84a, 85b, 87a, 88a
Aljarafe region, 1:82b
Byzantium, 1:78a
Christian Spain, 1:83b–84a
demand for wine, 5:116b, 125a
France, 5:174a-b
Bas-Languedoc, 1:85b
Italy, pattern of development, 1:87a
see also Wine and winemaking
Vítkof, Battle of (1420), 6:375b
Vitoria, founded, 2:126a
Vitovt. *See* Vytautas (the Great) of Lithuania, prince
Vitruvius
De architectura, 5:588a, 11:515b
Archimedes and, 1:435a
military inventions, 11:641a
sundials and, 3:457b, 11:509a
on water mills, 8:390a–391a
Vitry, Jacques de. *See* Jacques de Vitry
Vitry, Philippe de, **12:481a–483a**
Ars nova, 1:548a–553a, 8:598a, 12:482a
Compendium artis motectorum Marchecti and, 8:646a
influence of, 8:645b
Magister Lambertus and, 8:644a
contemporary references to, 12:481b
music of, 12:481b–482b
musica ficta and, 11:365b
poetry of, 12:482b
politics and, 12:481a-b
Quatuor principalia musice and, **8:646b**
rhythm and, 8:589a
role in secularization movement, 1:551a
Roman de Fauvel, 1:548b
Ulixea fulgens facundia, 12:482b
see also Fauvel, Roman de
Vitulo, abbot, Castile and, 3:127b
Vivaldi, Ugolino, 4:558b, 5:398a
Vivaldi, Vadino, 4:558b, 5:398a
Vivaria. See Fishponds
Vivarium, monastery of
Cassiodorus Senator and, 3:123a–124a
Greek translation and translators, 12:126b
Vivas, Juan, Hispanic version of *Roman du Graal* and, 11:416a
Vives, Joan Lluís, 12:349a
Vizier, 6:589b–590a, 590b, 8:138b, **12:483a**
abolition of by Buyids, 3:50a
origin of name, 3:46b
Samanid court, 10:638b
Shīᶜa and, 11:228a
under Abbasids, 3:44a
under Fatimids, 6:590b–591a
see also Badr al-Jamālī
under Mamluks, 6:591b
see also Barmakids; *Raᵓīs al-ruᵓasā*
Vlach-Bulgarian Empire, 10:577a
decline of, 2:409b–411b
relations with
Epiros, 7:347b
Latin Empire of Constantinople, 7:347a
rise of, 2:407b–409b
Vlachs and, 12:483b
Walachia and, 12:498a
Vlachs, **12:483a–484b**
in Bosnia, 2:340a
caravans, 2:341a
Bulgarians and, 2:407b–408a, 12:483b, 484a
Byzantine Empire and, 12:483b
conversion of, 10:514a, 12:499a, 504a-b
languages of, 12:484a
liturgy, Old Church Slavonic, 12:504a
migration, 12:498b–500a
Vlach-Bulgarian uprising (1186), 9:509b
vs. Isaac II Angelos, 6:559b, 560a
Walachian rule, 12:500b
Vlad II Dracul of Walachia, voivode, 12:484b
Vlad III Ţepeş of Walachia, voivode, 4:211b, 10:514b, **12:484b–485b**, 12:484b, 502b
anti-Ottoman resistance, 12:502b
atrocities of, 12:484b–485a
death of, 12:485b
Dracula tale, 11:347b
invasion of Transylvania, 12:502b
in Michel Beheim's verses, 8:306b
reputation of, 12:485a-b
Vladimir (city)
as capital of Russia, 12:486a-b
taken (1238), 2:131b
Vladimir, (monarchy), 12th century, 8:539a
Vladimir (territory). *See* Poland, Ruthenia and
Vladimir I of Kiev. *See* Vladimir, St.
Vladimir of Bulgaria (889–893), reign of, 2:404a
Vladimir of Bulgaria (brother of Symeon of Bulgaria), 11:554b
Vladimir Cathedral, Greek-cross design of, 4:341a
Vladimir Monomakh, **12:486a**
Kievan Rus under, 7:249a
Vladimir Olgerdovich, prince, coins during rule of, 8:426b
Vladimir, St., 11:338b, **12:485b–486a**
Basil II and, 2:118b
Christianity and, 1:303a, 8:443b, 10:591a, 12:435b, 436a
coinage of, 8:426a
Ilarion and, 6:418b, 419a
khanate of Tmutarakan and, 12:66a
Kievan Rus under, 7:247b–248b
marriage to Anna, 1:303a
patronage of pagan art, 10:582b–583
Yotvingians and, 7:604a
Vladimir Virgin, 6:411 (*illus.*), **12:486a-b**
Vladimir-Suzdal, **12:486b–487b**
Novgorod and, 12:487a
under Mongols, 12:486b, 487a
see also Bogoliubskii, Andrei
Vladimiri, Paul, rector, at Council of Constance, 9:729b
Vladimir's Statute, 7:508a
Vladislav I of Bohemia, king, 2:299b–300a
Vladislav II of Bohemia, king, Henry IV and, 2:299b
Vladislav II of Bohemia, king. *See* Wladislas II of Hungary, king
Wolfram von Eschenbach, courtly language, 6:441a
Vladislav I of Serbia, king, patron of Theodore, 12:14b
Vladislav I of Walachia, voivode, treaty with Louis of Anjou, 12:501a
Vladislav II of Walachia, vs. Vlad Ţepeş, 12:484b, 502b
Vladislav (son of Dragutin of Serbia), 11:474b, 475a
Vladislav (son of Stefan Nemanja), 11:174b–175a
Vladislav (son of Stefan Prvovenčani), 11:473b
Vladislav (son of Stefan Uroš II Milutin), 11:176a, 176b, 177a
Vlastimir, ruler of Serbia, 11:168b
Vocabularius Sancti Galli, 9:233a, **12:487b**
Vogt. *See* Advocate

Voice exchange (polyphony), 12:696a, 696b
Voie d'enfer et de paradis. See Jean de la Motte
Voillé, battle at (507), 7:339a
Voir dit. See Machaut, Guillaume de
Vojislav Vojinoviç, Uroš V and, 11:179a
Volcanoes, climate and, 10:456b–457a
Volga Bulgars, **12:487b–488b**
 Islam and, 12:488a
 languages of, 12:488b
 Russian fur trade and, 5:331a-b
 vs. Kievan Rus, 12:488a-b
 vs. Mongols, 12:488b
Volga River
 Novgorod and, 9:193a
 Vikings and, 12:434a–436b
Völkerwanderungen. See Migration period
Volksepos, 5:444b
Vollbauer. See Peasants, "full"
Vologases V, Arsacid pretender. *See* Valaxš V, Arsacid pretender
Volpaia, Lorenzo della, planetarium of, 3:463b–464a
Vǫlsa þáttr, 12:2b, 4b
Vǫlsung poems, order in Codex Regius, 4:386a-b
Vǫlsunga saga, 9:114a, **12:488b–489b**
 Brynhild in, 2:394b–395a
 flyting and, 9:173a, 174a
 Norna-Gests þáttr and, 9:171a
 Ragnars saga loðbrókar and, 10:249a
 Sigrdrífumál and, 11:288b
 Sigurd and, 11:289a, 289b, 291b, 292a
 Sinfjǫtli in, 11:310a-b
 sources of, 12:488b
 see also Þiðreks saga
Vǫlsungs, Óttarr and, 6:385b
Volta/volte. See Ballata
Volterra
 ambassadors of, 6:474b–475a
 rebellion against Florence, 5:102b
Volto Santo, **12:489b**, 12:490a (*illus.*)
 see also Mandylion
Volumen, 8:98a, **12:489b–490a**
 replaced by codex, 8:100b
Vǫlundarkviða, 6:312b, **12:490a–491a**
 compared with *þiðreks saga,* 12:490b–491a
 comparisons with *Grottasǫngr,* 6:3b
 dating of, 12:490a-b
 order in Codex Regius, 4:386b–387a
Voluntary societies (*ḥevrot*), role in Jewish self-government, 7:69a
Volunteer armies. *See* Warfare
Vǫluspá, **12:491a–492b**
 Codex Regius and, 4:386b
 compared with *Merlínússpá,* 8:276b
 compared with
  Baldrs draumar, 2:56b
  Wessobrunner Gebet, 2:224b
 evidence of Christian influence on, 4:391a
 Grógaldr and, 11:524b
 inclusion in *Hauksbók,* 4:387a
 midgard serpent in, 8:362b, 12:45b
 Mímir in, 8:395b–396a
 Norns and, 9:171b, 172b
 Ragnarǫk and, 10:248a-b
 Surtr and, 11:514a, 515a
 Valkyries in, 12:351a
 on the Vanir, 12:356a-b
Vǫluspá in skamma, 12:492a
 Hyndluljóð and, 6:385b
 preservation in *Flateyjarbók,* 4:387b
 role of Heimdallr in, 6:133b
Volvellae, 4:500a
Vom edlen Menschen. See Eckhart, Meister
Von deutscher Baukunst. See Goethe, Johann von
Von Gottes Zukunft. See Heinrich von Neustadt
Von dem Ritter und von dem Pfaffen. See Heinzelein von Konstanz
Von siben Ingesigeln. See Tilo von Kulm
Von Stahel und Eisen, on iron, 8:285b
Vonones, Parthian king, 1:559a
Vorau Codex, 2:226b, 227a, 227b, 7:206a, 323a, 8:349a
Vorauer Bücher Mosis, 2:227a-b
Vorskla River, Battle of (1399), 5:573a
Vortigern of Britain, Ambrosius Aurelianus and, 2:2b–3a
Vos (fox). *See* Renard the Fox
Vostitsa, under Latins, 7:380a
Votaddio. *See* Wandering Jew legend
Votādīnī. *See* Aneirin, *Gododdin*
Voting rights. *See* Representative assemblies; Suffrage
Votive crown, **12:492b–493a**
Vouge, 7:324 (*illus.*), 325a
Vouillé, Battle of (507), 3:467a, 12:90b
Voulge. *See Vouge*
Voussoir, **12:493a**
 see also Arch; Archivolt; Vault
Vowels, Latin, 12:495a
Vows
 Benedictine, 2:171b–172a
 of chastity, 4:611b
 crusader, 4:16b
 pilgrimage
  Jewish, 9:652b
  Russian Christian, 9:653b–654a
  Western European, 9:655a–656b, 659b–660b
 see also Ex voto; Indulgences; Oaths; Penance
Vox Clamantis. See Gower, John
Vox in excelso. See Vienne, Council of
Vox in Rama (1233), on sorcery, 8:30a
Vox and the Wolf. See Fox and the Wolf
Voyage de Charlemagne à Jérusalem et à Constantinople. See Pélerinage de Charlemagne
Voyage de Saint Brendan, Le, 1:261a, 262a, 11:440a, **12:493a-b**
 modern edition of, 1:271b
Voyage of Trivaile of Sire Jehan de Manderville, Knight. See Archaeology, travelers and their accounts
Voyages et ambassades. See Ghillebert de Lannoy
Vratislav II of Bohemia, king. *See* Vladislav II of Bohemia, king
Vrayes chroniques, Les. See Jean le Bel
Vrelant, Willem, **12:493b**
Vrma giganti, 6:311b
Vrtᶜanēs Kᶜertᶜoł, 1:509a, 509b, 5:540a, 11:582b
 Treatise Against the Iconoclasts, Paulicians and, 9:469a
 Treatise in Defense of Images, condemnation of iconoclasm, 6:188b
Vrtᶜanēs, patriarch of Armenia, 5:540b, 665a
Vsevolod III, grand prince, 8:539a
 theories of rulership reflected in art, 10:584b
Vsevolod I of Kiev, grand prince, 12:486a
Vsevolod of Vladimir-Suzdal, prince, 12:486b
Vuk Brankoviç, Lazar Hrebeljanoviç and, 11:181a, 181b–182a
Vuk (son of Lazar Hrebeljanoviç), Stefan Lazareviç of Serbia and, 11:473a
Vukan of Raška, grand *župan,* 11:171b–172a, 172a-b
Vukan (son of Stefan Nemanja), 11:173b–174a, 473a, 473b
Vukašin Mrnjavčeviç, despot of Serbia, 11:179a-b
Vulgar Latin, **12:493b–495a**
 comparison to Provençal language, 10:157a
 dialects of, 12:494a
 grammar, 7:354b
 Italian language and, 6:621a–622a
 Romance languages and, 7:350b
 sources, 12:490b
 Spanish language and, 11:391a
 vocabulary, 12:495a
Vulgate. *See* Bible
Vulgate cycle, 3:327a
 Estoire de Merlin, 5:259a
 Estoire de saint Graal, 5:259a
 ideological content, 5:259a-b
 importance of, 5:259b
 influence of, 1:571a
 Lancelot del lac, 5:259a
 Mort Artu, consequences of adultery and treason, 5:259a
 origin of, 5:285b–286a
 Queste del saint Graal, spirituality of, 5:259a
 see also Prose Lancelot
Vulpis, Nicholas, 4:176b
Vulture, in British Library MS 3244, 2:204a (*illus.*)
Vuolvinus. *See* Wolvinus
Vyborg, military use, 11:531b, 532a
Vykintas of Lithuania, prince, 7:604b
Vyšehrad, Battle of (1420), 6:376a
Vytautas (the Great) of Lithuania, prince, 2:67a, 7:606b–608a
 characterized by Jan Długosz, 7:608a
 Teutonic Knights and, 7:606b–607b
Vytenis of Lithuania, ruler, 7:605b
Vyvoz. See Peasants, Russia, exportation of

W

- Waccho, Lombard king, 7:654b
- Wace, 1:264b, **12:496a-b**
  - Geoffrey of Monmouth and, 5:389a-b
  - Latin sources, 5:288b
  - Middle English prosody and, 8:344b
  - *Roman de Brut,* 1:565a-b, 2:393a-b, 3:331a, 5:284b, 340b, 8:601a, 12:496b
    - Arthur's retirement to Avalon, 5:244b
    - learned myths and, 5:244b
    - octosyllabic rhyme in, 8:343b
    - on organs, 9:273a
    - recasting in Picard codex, 5:255b
  - *Roman de Rou,* 3:331a, 12:496b
  - *Vie de St. Nicolas,* features of courtly romance narrative, 5:239b
  - *see also Vie de Ste. Marguerite*
- Wade Cup, 6:408b
- *Wāḍiḥ. See* ʿAqīl, Ibn
- Wadi'n Natrun (monastery: Egypt), 11:565a
- Waerferth of Winchester, bishop
  - translation of Gregory's *Dialogues,* 1:284a
    - metrical preface to, 1:281a
- *Wafayāt al-aʿyān wa- anbāʾ al-zamān. See* Khallikān, Ibn
- Wager of law, 3:509a
  - in Exchequer Court, 4:534b
- Wages
  - Black Death and, 2:265a–266a
  - in Bohemia (end of 14th century), 2:303b
- Wagner, Leonhard, *Proba centum scripturarum,* 9:334b
- Wagner, Richard
  - *Die Meistersinger von Nürnberg,* 9:201a
  - *Tannhäuser,* sources for, 5:435b, 12:573b
- Wagon, construction of in antiquity, 12:368a-b
- Wagon fortress, 3:206b
- Wahb, Ibn, *Burhān fī wujūh al-bayān, Al-,* 10:345b
- Wahhabism, iconoclasm and, 6:403a
- Waḥshīya, Ibn, *Kitāb al-sumūm wa'l-tiryāqāt,* 6:179a
- Waifarius. *See* Guaiferius
- Wainfleet, William, bishop of Winchester, dispute about Sir John Fastolf's will and, 9:450b
- Waits, **12:497a-b**
  - employers of, 12:497a
  - functions, 12:497a
  - instruments used, 12:497a-b
- Wakefield Master. *See* Towneley plays
- Wakhtang VI of Georgia, king, 7:222b
- Wakhtang Gurgaslani. *See* Waχtang I Gurgaslani
- Wakīʿ ibn al-Jarrāḥ, 11:511b, 513b
- *Wakīl-al-Tujjar,* 11:250a
- *Waking of Angantýr, The,* insertion in *Hervarar saga ok Heiðreka konungs,* 6:215a
- Walachia, 2:70a, **12:497b–507b**
  - administration
    - ceremonial offices, 12:505b–506a
    - foreign influence, 12:505b
    - *judeţi,* 12:506b
    - *logofat* and *vistier,* 12:505b
    - *vornic,* 12:505b
  - anti-Ottoman resistance, 11:181b, 12:501a
    - Battle of Varna (1444), 4:56a, 56b, 6:347b, 12:502b
  - architecture, 12:505b
  - ban of Severin, 12:500b
  - boundaries, 12:499 (map)
  - class structure, 12:505b–506a
  - culture, Byzantine influence, 12:505a-b
  - Cumans, 12:500a
  - ethnic makeup, 2:399a-b, 10:514a, 12:506b–507a
  - Great and Little, 12:498a
  - history, 10:514b
    - to 1418, 12:500a–501b
    - 15th century, 12:502a–503a
  - as Hungarian dependency, Vlad III Ţepeş and, 10:514b, 12:484b
  - invasion by Stephen the Great, 10:515a
  - linguistic background, 12:498a
  - literature, 10:510b, 11:347b
  - Louis I and, 6:345b, 10:514b
  - Mircea the Old and, 10:514b
  - Moldavian invasions of, 12:503b
  - Neagoe Basarab and, 10:510b
  - as Ottoman dependency, 12:501a–503a
  - religion, 12:504a–505a
    - ecclesiastical provinces, 12:501a, 504b
    - hesychast movement, 12:504b
    - Latin Christianity, 12:504b–505a
    - Mt. Athos connection, 12:504b
    - Orthodox Christianity, 10:510a, 12:504a-b
  - representative assemblies, 12:506a
  - royal charter, 12:500b
  - Transylvanian fiefs, 12:501a
  - voivodes, 6:343b–344a, 10:514b–515a
    - functions and privileges, 12:505b
    - independence from Hungary, 12:501a
- Walad, Bahāʾ al-Dīn, 11:158b
- Walafrid Strabo, 4:542b, 543b, **12:507b–508a**
  - biography of St. Gall, 9:691b–692a
  - Carolingian Latin poetry and, 3:103a
  - on Divine Office, 4:223a
  - *Glossa ordinaria* and, 7:362b
  - *Hortulus,* 5:358b, 360a-b
  - Hrabanus Maurus and, 6:306a
  - hymns of, 6:381b
  - *Liber de cultura hortorum,* 5:358b, 360a-b
  - on liturgy, 7:628b–629a
  - plants cultivated by, 5:360a-b
  - study of animals and, 2:242b–243a
  - on Theganus, 12:7b, 8a
- Walcher of Malvern, 1:611b
- *Waldef, L'estoire de,* 1:267a, **12:508a**
- Waldegrave, Robert, *Whole Prophecie of Scottlande,* Thomas of Erceldoune and, 10:147b
- Waldemar I (the Great) of Denmark, king, 4:153a-b, 154a, 7:280b
  - Wendish campaigns, 10:678b
- Waldemar II of Denmark, king, 4:153b, 154a,b
  - Balts and, 2:65b
  - rule of Lübeck, 7:680b
- Waldemar IV Atterdag of Denmark, king, 4:155b
  - conquest of Gotland, 5:633a, 6:94a
  - Hanseatic League and, 5:464b–465a, 7:682a, 9:82b, 185a
  - Magnus Eriksson and, 11:532b
- Waldemar, duke of Slesvig. *See* Waldemar I (the Great) of Denmark, king
- *Waldemar's Land Book,* 4:149b
- Waldensians, 3:369b–370a, 4:374b, **12:508a–513b**
  - anti-Albigensianism, 3:640a-b, 4:57b, 5:165a, 12:509a
  - believers, 12:511b–512a
  - bishops, 12:511b
  - church reaction to, 12:509a-b, 512a-b
    - papal inquisitions, 6:483a-b, 484b, 488a, 488b, 12:512a-b
  - condemnation of at Lateran IV, 3:640b
  - counterchurch, 3:369b, 12:508a-b
  - *denunciatio* and, 6:478b
  - doctrines, 12:508a, 510a–511a
    - on clerical wealth and power, 12:509a–510b
    - denial of purgatory, 12:510b
    - on indulgences and prayers for dead, 12:510b
    - on poverty, 12:509a, 511a
  - ecclesiastical organization, 12:511b–512a
  - expulsion from Lyons, 7:698b, 12:510a
  - French biblical translations and, 2:218b
  - in Germany, 5:484b
  - as heirs of Peter, 12:511a
  - heretical beliefs, 3:369b, 6:197b, 12:509b–510a
  - Hussitism and, 6:372b–373a
  - increase in, 3:369b
  - influence of, 12:513a
  - Innocent III and, 6:465a
  - in Languedoc, 7:339b
  - legends, 12:511a
  - the "perfect," 12:511b
  - popularity throughout Europe, 6:197b
  - poverty, 12:509a
  - preaching, 6:197a
    - scriptural basis for, 12:509b–510a
  - religious ceremonies, 12:511b
  - social status, 12:512b
  - Trinitarian doctrine and, 12:191a
  - women's role, 12:512b–513a
  - *see also* Bohemian Brethren

Waldere, 1:278b
Walter of Aquitaine legend in, 12:535b
Waldes, 3:369b
conversion experience, 12:508b–509a
Waldglas, 5:554b, 560a–561b
Waldhauser, Konrad, Charles IV and, 6:365b
Waldrammus, 7:363a, **12:513b**
hymns of, 6:381b
Waldstätte. *See* Switzerland
Waleran of Meulan and Worcester, count, heraldic seal of, 11:129b
Wales
Act of Union (1536), 12:525a, 527a
Anglo-Norman colonization, 12:522b–523a, 526a
Battle of Hastings and, 9:165b
border settlements, 12:526a
customs of Breteuil, 12:516b–517a
boundaries, 12:515b (map)
castle fortifications, 12:522b, 528a
creation of principality, 7:637a
culture of, 12:518b, 609b
economy, 12:515a, 520a, 528a-b
English conquest and rule, 12:519a, 520b
Edward II, 12:523a
military and government service, 12:523a
treason and, 12:165b
"Englishries" and "Welshries," 12:517a, 527a
Henry II and, 9:167a
history, **12:513b–525b**
12th century, 12:517b–518b
13th century, 12:521a–522a, 522b–523a
14th century, 12:523a-b
15th through 16th centuries, 12:523b–525a
emerging boundaries, 12:514b
internal divisions, 12:516a-b
see also Maelgwn; Rhodri Mawr; Rhys of Deheubarth; Urien Rheged
kingdoms of, 12:514a–515b
language, 12:513b
Law of the March, 12:527b
Marcher Lords, **12:525b–529a**
absentee lordship, 12:526b
concentration of holdings, 12:526b
control of internal strife, 12:525b–526a
jura regalia, 12:527a–528b
location of, 12:525b
military function, 12:528a
opposition to Llywelyn ap Gruffydd, 12:521b
powers and privileges, 12:517a-b, 528a
relationship with English kings, 12:520b, 524a-b, 528b–529a
source of income, 12:528a-b
tenant rebellions, 12:523b
monarchy
partibility, 12:515a
primogeniture, 12:519a, 520a-b
Norman conquest, 12:516b–517b, 525b–526b
reorganization under Edward I, shires, 12:522b
Treaty of Chester and, 3:299b–230a
Tudor Council of, 12:524b
union with England, 12:524a, 524a–525a
Viking raids, 12:516a
Welsh unity, 12:515b–516b
Wales, National Library of, MS 4973, 12:606a
Wales, prince of, as title, 4:108a
Wales, Statute of (1284), 4:396a, 11:226a, 12:522b, 526b
Walewein, 1:572a, 4:318b–319a
Waleys, Thomas, 7:370a
ars praedicandi of, 1:556a, 557a-b
as exegete, 4:544b
on preaching, 10:363a
Walī (a Sufi saint), 9:44b
Walīd I ibn ᶜAbd al-Malik, al-, Umayyad caliph, **12:529b–530a**
accession to throne, 12:529b
advancement of Islam, 12:530a
on Beirut, 2:164a
building program, 12:529b–530a
internal development of empire, 12:529b
legacy of rule, 12:530a
relationship with al-Ḥajjāj, 6:73a
Walīd II ibn Yazīd, al-, Umayyad caliph
dress of, 3:616b
Khirbat al-Mafjar and, 6:595b
Qays alliance, 8:165a
Walīd, al- (*fl.* 705-715), 4:83a
Wall construction
Romanesque, 10:477a
Normandy, 10:482b
Wall decoration. *See* Fresco; Mosaic; Romanesque art, wall decoration
Wallace, The. See Henry the Minstrel
Wallace, William
execution for treason, 12:165b, 166a
Scottish wars of independence and, 11:109a-b
Wallingford, Richard. *See* Richard of Wallingford
Walo of Autun, **12:530b**
Walpott, Hermann, 3:306a
Wälsche Gast, Der. See Thomasin von Zerclaere
Walsingham, Alan of, **12:530b**
Walsingham, Thomas, 3:327b, 7:370a
Walter of Aquitaine (epic hero), in *Waltharius,* 12:535a-b, 536a
Walter of Bibbesworth, **12:530b–531a**
Tretiz pur aprise de langwage, 1:270b
Tretiz pus aprise de langwage, 12:530b–531a
Walter of Brienne, 7:379b
Catalan Company's service to, 3:156a
in Florence, 12:231a
formation of Arti di Tintori e Saponai, 11:714b
as lord of Florence, 5:98a
Walter of Châtillon, **12:531a–532a**
Alexandreis, 1:150b–151a, 4:496a, 7:367a, 12:531a-b
Alexander compared with Darius, 1:150b
Castilian *Libro de Alexandre* and, 1:152b
influence on Saxo Grammaticus, 10:677a-b
mester de clerecía movement and, 11:412a
Norse adaptation of, 1:152a
sources of, 1:150a, 9:634b
summary, 1:150b
translated into Norwegian, 10:389b, 391b
English humanists and, 12:531a
as goliard, 5:575b
In domino confido, 12:531b
Latin writings of, 7:365a, 370b, 375a, 375b
lyric poetry, 12:531b
Philip the Chancellor and, 7:368b
prose works, 12:531b
role of Fortune, 1:151a
Tractatus contra Judaeos, 12:531b
Walter Chatton, Ockham and, 9:209b
Walter of Colchester, **12:532a-b**
Crucifixion in St. Albans Cathedral, 12:532a (*illus.*)
Walter of Coutances, as justiciar, 7:200a
Walter cycle, flyting and, 9:175a
Walter of England
in Latin pedagogy, 7:352b
Romulus and, 4:572a-b, 573a-b, 10:527b
Walter of Evesham. *See* Odington, Walter
Walter of Henley, **12:532b–534a**
on accounting techniques, 12:533b
Dite de hosbondrie, 12:613a
estate management treatise, 12:532b, 533a
copies of, 12:534a
dating of, 12:532b
on husbandry, 4:513b, 514a
Walter, Hubert, 3:492a, 5:421a, 7:129b, **12:534b–535a**
administrative reforms, 12:534b
criticism of, 12:534b–535a
death of, 7:338a
Exchequer and, 4:534a
as justiciar, 7:200a-b
relations with English monarchy, 4:471a
Richard I (the Lionhearted) and, 10:384a
Walter de Lacy, 6:518b
Walter of Lille. *See* Walter of Châtillon
Walter Map. *See* Map, Walter
Walter of Mauretania, **12:534a-b**
Abelard and, 12:21a
De sacramento conjugii, 12:534a
De Trinitate, 12:534a
Walter de Milemete, on windmill uses, 8:395a
Walter of Mortagne. *See* Walter of Mauretania
Walter of Palear, bishop of Troina, Innocent III and, 11:269b
Walter the Penniless, 4:34a
peasants' crusade, 9:523a-b
Walter of St. Victor
antidialecticism, 9:593b
Contra quattuor labyrinthos Franciae, 4:170a
Walter of Wimborne, 1:255a

Architrenius and, 7:366b
Latin parody and, 9:441a
Marie carmina, 7:368b, 370a
Waltham Abbey, nave of, 1:256a, 257a (*illus.*)
Waltharius, 4:496a, 6:440a, **12:535a–536b**
authorship of, 7:363a, 12:535b
Carolingian cultural aspects, 12:535b
Christian moral, 12:535b–536a
compared with *Biterold und Dietlieb,* 2:253a-b
influenced by Vergil, 9:440a
language and diction, 12:535b
plot summary, 12:535a-b
Þiðreks saga and, 12:30a
see also Waldere
Walther, Bernhard
astronomical observations at Nuremberg and, 11:103a
on astronomy, 1:613b
Walther von Speier, **12:541b–542a**
life of St. Christopher, 12:541b
Walther von der Vogelweide, 6:441a, **12:536b–541b**
at the court of Duke Leopold VI of Austria, 2:7a
biographical sources, 12:536b
compared with Neidhart "von Reuental," 9:93a
criticism of minnesong, 5:440a
criticized by Thomasin von Zerclaere, 12:38a
crusader poetry of, 10:294a
didactic poetry of, 5:442b–443a
Diu minne lât, 8:583a
Elegy, 12:541a
feuds of, 8:351a
financial position of, 10:294a
Gottfried von Neifen and, 5:633b–634a
"Imperial Tune," 5:442b
influence of on Seifrid Helbling, 11:142a, 143a
Johannes Hadlaub and, 7:120b
Kreuzlied, 8:414a
leich to Virgin Mary, 12:541a
lyric technique of, 8:414a
melodies, 12:538a-b
miniature of, 12:537b–538a
musical notations, 12:540b
"Palestine Song," 5:438a
patrons of, 5:435a, 8:349b, 12:537b–539b
professional life of, 8:350b
Reinmar der Alte and, 10:292b, 294a
Reinmar von Haguenau and, 5:438b
Reinmar von Zweter and, 10:295a
rhetorical technique of, 5:436a
Sangspruch and, 8:351b
social status, 12:539b–540a
songs
antipapal, 12:538b–539a
dance, 12:537b
dating of, 12:536b
dawn, 12:537b
didactic, 12:540a-b
lofty love and natural love, 12:536b–537b
naturious, 12:541a
political, 12:538a–540a
on Spervogel, 11:462b
Spruch, 8:414a
sprüche, 12:540b
Tagelied, 8:360a, 414a
Under der linden, 12:537a-b
use of personification, 12:540a-b
use of term *minnesanc,* 5:439a
in *Wartburgkrieg,* 12:573a-b
Wolfger von Erla and, 12:673a
Wolfram von Eschenbach and, 12:674b
on womanhood, 12:537a
Wandalbert of Prüm, hymns of, 6:381b
Wanderer, The, 1:281a
alliterative pattern of, 1:277a
transliteration and translation, 1:282a–283a (*illus.*)
Wanderers. *See* Goliards
Wandering. *See* Migration period
Wandering Jew legend, **12:542a–543b**
Cartaphilan aspects, 12:542a, 543a
ecclesiastical support for, 12:542b
in Iberian Peninsula, 12:543a-b
in Italy and Sicily, 12:542b–543a
Malchean aspects, 12:542a, 542b–543a
origins, 12:542a
surviving accounts, 12:542b
wanderer
characteristics of, 12:543a
names given, 12:542b–543a
as shoemaker, 12:543a-b
Wangara, discovered, 4:561b
Wanj. See Ṣanj (harp)
Wanley, Humfrey, 3:477a
Wapentake, shire and, 11:253b
see also Hundred (land division)
Waq-waq Islands, **12:545b–546a**
in literature, 12:545a
Talking Tree, 12:546 (*illus.*)
Zanj and, 12:739b
Waqf, 8:11b, **12:543b–544b**
administration, 12:544a
concerning schooling, 11:66a, 67a
creation of, 12:543b
documents, 12:544b
family, 12:544a
reservation of, 12:543b–544a
taxation of, 11:669a
under the Seljuks, 11:158a
Wāqidī, Abū ᶜAbd Allāh Muḥammad ibn ᶜUmar al-, **12:544b–545b**
Abbasid service, 12:545a
Al-Taᵓrīkh al-kabīr, 12:545a
historical works, 12:545a-b
Kitāb al-maghāzī, 12:545a
Kitāb al-ṭabaqāt, 12:545a
Waqqār family, physicians at Christian Spanish courts, 11:92b
War Against the Foreigners, The, on Viking attacks on Ireland, 12:426a
War of the Lords. See Levi ben Gershom
"War of St. Sardos" (1323-1325), 2:128b, 129a
Waraqa ibn Nawfal, 6:576b
Warbeck, Perkin, 6:520a
Ward family. *See* Mic an Bhaird
Warda, 11:567b
Warda, George, 11:567b–568a
Wardrobe, royal, **6:299b–306a**
butler and, 2:434a-b
England
books, 6:302a, 304a, 305a
chamber and, 6:301a, 302a
Exchequer and, 4:532b
John and, 6:301b–302a
keeper of, 6:304b–305a
usher of, 6:305a
see also Great wardrobe
wool and, 12:694b
Wardzia, **12:546a-b**
Ware, Sir James, 6:524b
Warendorp, Brun, conquest of Copenhagen, 7:682a
Warfare
against kings, treason definition and, 12:165b–166a
Armenian cavalry, 3:198b–199a
holy
justification of, 4:15b
see also Jihad
just, 4:15b
martial law and, 12:166a-b
naval. *See* Navies
technology of, 11:634a
armor design, 11:659a-b
catapults, 11:634a
gunpowder, 11:638b
gunpowder weapons, 11:638a (*illus.*), 638b
qidr, 11:638b
treatises, 11:638a-b, 641b, 645b–647a, 649a
trebuchet, 11:646 (*illus.*), 646a, 660a-b
travel and, 12:149a, 153a-b
villages and, 12:444a-b
see also Arms and armor; Artillery; Castles and fortifications; Cavalry; Roman Empire, army
Warfare, Byzantine, **12:546b–550b**
Arab invasions, 2:487a, 488a, 490a
barbarian invasions, 2:485b
Avars and Slavs, 2:486b–487a
cavalry, 3:199b–200a
communication of information, 12:547b
defensive conception, 12:546b–547a
divine aid, 12:547a
field commanders, 12:547b–548a
finance, 12:548a, 549b, 550a-b
firearms, 12:549b
foreign mercenaries, 12:549b
frontier militia, 2:484b
Greco-Roman models, 12:547a, 549a, 549b
Greek fire, 5:659b
magister militum, 2:484b
mercenary troops, 2:493b
mobile field armies, 2:484b
Norman conflicts, 2:494a-b, 496b
palace guard, 2:484b
peace negotiations, 12:550a-b
reduction of armed forces, 13th century, 2:500a
religious element, 12:548a
supplies and provisions, 12:548a, 549b
tactics and strategies, 12:547a, 548b
borrowed, 12:549a

Warfare, Byzantine (*cont.*)
tactics and strategies (*cont.*)
evasion of decisive battles, 12:547a-b, 549b–550a
evolution after 11th century, 12:549b
handbooks of, 4:447a, 12:547a
innovations, 12:549a
weaknesses in, 12:547b
technology, 11:634a
trebuchet, 11:660b
under Justinian I, 7:201a, 202b
Venetian naval assistance, 2:494b
see also Cavalry, Byzantine; Diplomacy, Byzantine; Dux; *Magister militum; Strategos; Stratiotai;* Tagmata; Themes
Warfare, Islamic, **12:551a–554a**
battle formations, 12:552a-b
Battle of al-Ḥarra (Umayyads *vs.* Quraysh), 10:242b
Battle of Myriokephalon-Kirkbaş Pass, 10:235b
Battle of Qudayd (Kharijites *vs.* Quraysh), 10:242b
cavalry, 3:208b–209b
development (13th–15th centuries), 12:552b–553a
Egyptian navy, 10:625b
Egyptian Tulinids vs. Abbasid caliphate, 12:224a-b
financing, 6:590a-b, 591a
see also Iqṭāᶜ
firearms, 12:553a
fortifications, 12:553a
jihad, 7:110a–111a
professional soldiers, 8:165a
siege of Huesca, 11:638b
slaves and mercenaries, 10:610a
social structure, 12:551a
staging areas, 8:141b–142a
technology
cannon, 11:638b
gunpowder, 11:638b
rockets and torpedoes, 11:638b
tribal conflicts, Qays-Kalb rivalry, 8:143a, 165a
Turkomans and, 12:226b–227b
use of firearms, 8:76b, 142b
weaponry, trebuchet, 11:660a-b
see also Cavalry, Islamic; Infantry, Islamic
Warfare, Western European, **12:554a–569a**
armor and weapons, 12:564b, 565a-b
gunpowder, 12:566b–567a
in Baltic lands, 2:64a–67a, 67b, 68a
catapults, 3:179b–180a
cavalry, 3:200a–206b
chivalry and, 3:302a
church attitude toward, 11:657a
conscription
Matrikel system (German), 10:330b–331a
of nobility, 9:725a
constable of the realm in, 3:543b–544a
crusader state armies, 12:561a-b
development of representative assemblies and, 10:330b–331a
economic depression and, 12:557a
effect of Arab conquest on, 12:557a-b
equipment requisition, corvées, 3:613b
expenditure, 12:555a
feudal, 12:557a–564a
central and northern Italy, 12:562a-b
crusader states, 12:561a-b
Frankish state, 12:557a–560a
Germany, 12:561b–562a
Normans, 12:560a–561a
fortifications, 12:564a-b
Frankish historiography and, 9:715b–716a
handbooks, 6:11b
Hispano-Mauresque, Reconquest, 10:255b–256a
history, sources for, 12:554a-b, 567b
Hungarian
under Angevins, 6:344b
under Sigismund, 6:346b
Irish
in saga, 6:548b
Vikings and, 6:554a
Italy, condottieri, 3:531a-b, 12:566a
land inheritance customs and, 10:329a
Norman armies, 12:560a
obligation to serve
Anglo-Saxons, 12:556a-b
French, 10:318a
Lombards, 12:555b–556a
Visigoths, 12:555b
organization of field army, 12:555b
plagues and, 9:674a-b, 681b–682b, 684a, 686a
political succession and, 10:329a
postfeudal, 12:564b–567a
private armies, 12:556a, 558a, 569b
role of bridges, 10:411b
siege techniques, 12:564a-b
siege warfare, in Hundred Years War, 6:332b–333a
size of armies, 12:554b–555a
slaves in armies, 12:555b
Swedish, 11:532b
Swiss, 12:565b–566a
tactics and strategies, 12:563b–564a
avoiding decisive battles, 12:561a, 564a, 565a
battle formations, 12:563b–564a, 565b
taxation
Holy Roman Empire, 10:330b–331a
see also Kingship; Representative assemblies; Taxation
technology
armor design, 11:659a-b
crossbow, 11:657a–659b
transportation, 12:376a
tribal, 12:555a–557a
Vegetius' *Epitoma rei militaris,* 12:366b
Viking raids, 12:559b (*illus.*)
volunteer service, 4:18b–19a
see also Arms and armor; Castles and fortifications; Cavalry, Western European; Infantry, Western European; Mercenaries; Peace of God; Scutage; Squire; Truce of God
Warmia, 2:63 (map), 67a
Warmund, bishop of Ivrea, sacramentary of, 10:113b
Warnachar of Burgundy, 8:236a, 278b
Warnerius of Basel, **12:569a**
Warp (unit of measure), 12:593b
Warqa u Gulshāh. See ᶜAyyūqī
Warrens, 6:356b–357a
Wars. See Procopius
Wars of Alexander, The, 8:332a, 333a
Wars of the Lord. See Jacob ben Reuben
Wars of the Lord, The. See Levi ben Gershom
Wars of Religion, French representative assemblies and, 10:316a, 327a
Wars of the Roses, **12:569a–573a**
Barnet-Tewkesbury campaign (1471), 12:554b, 571b
battles, 12:570b, 571a, 572a
causes of, 4:484b, 12:524a, 569a-b
in chronicles, 3:329b
consequences of, 12:572b–573a
history
first phase, 12:569a–571a
second phase, 12:571a-b
third phase, 12:571b–572a
justices of the King's Bench during, 7:194a
Neville-Percy conflict, 12:570a-b
parliamentary attainders, 5:144a
Poynings' Law of 1494 and, 9:437a
in Shakespearean drama, 12:572b
symbolism of roses, 12:572a-b
in Tudor chronicles, 12:572b
Warships, Red Sea and Persian Gulf, 11:247b
Wartburg (castle), Wolfram von Eschenbach and, 12:674a
Wartburgkrieg, **12:573a–574a**
comparison of Austria and Thuringia, 12:573a
melodic and strophic form, 12:573b
polemic dialogue, 12:573b
Praise of Princes, 12:573a
as source of Wagner's *Tannhäuser,* 5:435b
Wolfram von Eschenbach and, 12:674a, 679b
Warwick, earl of, 12:570a, 570b, 571a, 571b
Richard III and, 10:385a
Wash (unit of measure), 12:586b
Washing of the Disciples' Feet (mystery play), 8:661a
Washshāᵓ, al-, on costume, 3:618a
Waṣī, 6:615b
Wāṣil ibn ᶜĀtaᵓ (*d.* 728), 8:655a
Wāṣilīya, 11:139b
Wāsiṭ, **12:574a–575a**
agriculture, 12:574b
cost of construction, 12:574a
decline of, 12:574b
ethnic population, 12:574b
foundation of, 6:511b, 12:574a
internal conflicts and rebellions, 12:574b
al-Kufa and, 7:307a
occupied by Zanj (878), 6:512b
al-Qubba al-Khaḍrāᵓ palace, 12:574a-b
trade and commerce, 12:574b

Wāsiṭī, Yaḥyā ibn Maḥmūd al-, **12:575a-b**
miniatures from *Maqāmāt,* 6:606b (*illus.*), 8:116a (*illus.*), 12:575a (*illus.*)
Muslim merchant ship, 9:86 (*illus.*)
paintings of, 12:575b
Wastell, John, **12:575b–576a**
Bell Harry tower of Canterbury Cathedral, 12:575b (*illus.*)
Water buffalo, 1:296b
domestication of, 1:298a
as food animals, 1:299a-b
spread of in Europe, 1:298a-b
Water clocks. *See* Clocks
Water mill. *See* Mills
Watermarks, **12:576a**, 12:698b
Watermelon, growth of, 1:81b
Water power. *See* Technology, hydraulic
Waterworks, **12:576b–579b**
canals for transport, 12:578b
defensive function, 12:577b
development (early Middle Ages), 12:576b–577a
development (11th to 14th centuries), 12:577a–579a
ecclesiastical projects, 12:576b, 579a
flood control, 12:577a
local variations, 12:578b–579a
Muslim innovations, 12:577a
secular projects, 12:576b, 579a
types of wheel, 12:579a
urban water supply, 12:577b–577a
aqueducts and fountains, 12:577b
pipes, 12:577a
see also Bridges; Canals; Dams; Irrigation
Wāthiq, al-, Abbasid caliph
miḥna and, 8:656a
al-Mu^ctaṣim and, 8:654a
al-Mutawakkil and, 8:654a
Wāthyiq, al-, Abbasid caliph, Ṭāhir II and, 11:575a
Watling Street
Roman bridge over the Medway, 10:415a
Viking raids on England and, 12:432b
Watlings Island. *See* San Salvador
Watriquet de Couvin, *Le mireoirs as princes,* 8:435b
Wattasids
assumption of throne, 8:140b
vs. Muḥammad al-Jūtī, 6:414a
Wauchier de Denain, *Vitae patrum,* translation of, 9:633a-b
Wauquelin, Jean, 5:388a, **12:579b–580a**
Chroniques de Hainaut, Willem Vrelant and, 12:493b
works for Philip the Good, 12:579b
Waw (unit of measure), 12:593b
Wax
bronze casting and, 9:667a-b
in sealing, 11:127b
see also Encaustic
Wax tablets, **12:580a**, 12:699a, 699b, 701 (*illus.*)
see also Stylus
Waχtang I Gurgaslani, 3:308a, **12:580b**
alliance with Byzantium, 5:405a-b
Church of Meteḥi and, 8:298a
foundation of Tbilisi, 11:631b
in *K^cart^clis C^cχovreba,* 7:222b–223a
life of, 5:413b
Sveti Cχoveli and, 11:523b
Way of the Cross. *See* Stations of the Cross
Wayland the Smith, 8:292a (*illus.*), 12:29b–30a
Wazīr. See Vizier
Weaponry. *See* Arms and armor; Artillery; Cannon; Daggers; Lance; Siege weapons; Swords
Wearmouth, monastery of
architectural features, 10:680b
Bede's schooling at, 12:13b
founded, 2:168a
manuscript book production and, 8:102a
Weasel, in medieval animal tales, 2:205a
Weaving
basket or canvas, 11:702a
comb, 11:702a
definition, 11:693b–694a
horizontal treadle loom, 11:703b–704a
odd-numbered weaves, 11:704a
pin beater, 11:702a
plain, tabby, or linen, 11:701b–702a
sword, 11:702a
tablet, 11:702b
twill, 11:702a-b
warping, 11:701a
wefts and warps, yarns for, 11:694a
see also Fulling; Loom
Weaving. *See* Textiles
Web (unit of measure), 12:593b
Wechsel, 9:304b
see also Reinmar der Alte
Wedding at Cana, in art, 11:215a
Week
determining days of, 3:23b
in Islamic calendar, 3:27b
names of days in Latin church, 3:21b
reckoning of in Scandinavia, 3:20b
seven-day, 3:20b, 21b, 25b
Weeper figures. *See* Pleurant
Wegestreit (conflict between the ways), 12:406a–408b
Weiber Schule, 11:557a
Weight-driven alarm device, 3:462b
Weights and measures, Byzantine, **12:580b–582a**
balance weights, 12:581a
bronze, 12:581b
bust weight, 12:581a
coin, 12:581a-b
counterpoise, 11:633a, 12:581a
glass, 12:581b
liquid, 12:581b–582a
listed by Anania Širakac^ci, 12:97a
reforms of Constantine, 12:581a
uncial, 12:581b
weight system, 12:581b
wheat, 12:581b
see also Scale
Weights and measures, Islamic, regulation of, 8:527a
Weights and measures, Persian, listed by Anania Širakac^ci, 12:97a
Weights and measures, Western European, **12:582a–596b**
in animal production, 12:587a
area, 6:223a, 12:583b, 588b–589a
at fairs, 4:586b
bases for, 12:587b–590a
British Isles, 12:585a-b
bushel, 2:433b, 10:238b
capacity measures
heaped, 12:589a-b
shallow, 12:589b
striked, 12:589b
coinage or income basis, 12:586a-b
demi- weights, 12:587b
development of, 12:582a
diminutives for, 12:587b
dry products, 10:604a
England, 12:584b
mile, 8:384a
extra and *intra muros,* 12:585a
food production and tax assessments, 12:586b
France, 12:583b–584a, 585a, 585b, 587b, 594a–596b (table)
development of uniform system, 5:182b
gad, 9:504a
gallon, 5:345b–346a, 10:238b
Italy, 12:585b–586a
journal, 7:153a
land and sea, 12:585a
linear, 12:584a, 588a-b
livre, 12:585b
local units for, 12:584a
metrological proliferation, 12:582b
muid, 8:528b
multiple names, 12:585b–586a
ounce, 9:310b–311a
physical standards, 12:583a
pound, 10:67a-b
quantity measures, 12:590a-b
British Isles, 12:592a–593b (table)
for transport, 12:590a
quart- weights, 12:587b
quarter, 10:238b
regulation of food, 8:146a
Roman system, 8:206b–207a, 12:581b, 582a-b
Scottish, 12:589a
seam, 10:238b
standardization
exception and repeals, 12:583a
official oversight, 12:583b
physical prototypes, 12:583a
role of government in, 12:582b–583b
subunits, 12:585b, 587a-b
trade regulation and, 12:118a-b
units of account, 12:586a
urban and suburban, 12:584b–585a
variations in, 12:583a, 583b–587b
by product, 12:584b
volume measures, 12:583b–584a
wholesale, 12:589b
for wood, 12:589b–590a
work functions and time allotments, 12:586b–587a
see also entries on individual units of measure; Setier
Weingarten (abbey: Constance), 10:508b
Weingarten-Stuttgart MS, 5:436b
Weingärtners Frau und Der Pfaffe, Des, peasantry in, 8:130a
Weinschwelg, Der, **12:596a-b**

Weinschwelg, Der (*cont.*)
drinker's monologue, 12:596a-b
refrain, 12:596a
sources for, 12:596b
Weld (dye), 11:595b
Welf VI of Swabia, duke, 11:527b
Welfs
Bavaria and, 2:134a, 134b
feud of, 5:479b–480a
patronage of literature, 8:349b
territorial lordship of, 5:510a
see also Guelphs and Ghibellines
Wells, St. Cuthbert's Church, John Stowell's reredos to the Virgin, 11:487b–488a (*illus.*)
Wells Cathedral
chapter house, 3:266b (illus.)
star vault of the Lady Chapel at, 5:625b, 626b (*illus.*)
William Joy's work on, 7:153a
William Wynford and, 12:711b
Welsh, in Ireland, 6:517b
Welsh art, influence of on Celtic art, 3:224a-b
Welsh church, 12:524a
"age of saints," 12:514b
cult of St. David's, 10:616a-b, 12:516a
ecclesiastical organization, 12:515a, 517a
English influence, 12:515a, 517a, 525a
influence of on Irish church, 3:227a
monasticism, 12:514b–515a
in twelfth century, 3:232a
Welsh language, 6:436b
grammars, 5:650a
verbal system of, 3:233b
Welsh law, **7:526b–528a**
before 1100, 7:527a-b
after 1282, 7:527b
after 1536, 7:527b
Act of 1543, 12:528b
codifications, 12:516a, 599b, 612a-b
Dictum of Kenilworth (1266), 12:529a
early manuscripts, 7:526b
English applications
replacement by common law, 12:527b, 528b
Treaty of Conway, 12:522a, 526b
Great Sessions, 12:527b
of *gwlad* (territorial unit), 7:527a-b
interpretive problems, 7:527a
jura regalia, 12:527a–528a
kindred, 12:520a
of king's court, 7:527a-b
Law of Hywel Dda, on bards, 2:106a
poetic organization, 12:598b–599a, 604b–605a
sources of, 7:526b
Statute of Westminster (1275), 12:529a
texts, 12:609b
textual variations and contradictions, 7:526b–527a
tribal law, 7:527b
Welsh kings and, 7:527a-b
Welsh literature, **12:597a–601b**
apocryphal, 12:615a
Arthurian legend in, 1:565b–567b, 576b–578a
bards, three grades of, 2:106a
beirdd yr uchelwyr, 12:606a
Celtic mythology and, 9:46b–48b
echtrae and, 6:550a, 552a
eschatological tracts, 12:615a-b
foreign influences, 12:599a, 600a-b, 611a, 611b
French associations, 12:611a, 612a
gnomic literature, 5:568b–569a
Grail legend in, 5:645a
historical, 12:600b–601a, 612b–613a
native cultural development and, 12:609b
oral tradition, 12:602b–603a, 613a-b
patronage, 12:597a, 607b
poetic meter
awdl, 12:598b, 603a, 605b
cywydd, 12:599a, 607a, 608a
englyn, 12:603a, 605b
poetry, 12:514a, **12:601b–609a**
alliteration, 12:603a, 605b, 607a-b
bardic, 12:597b
codification, 12:599b, 607b, 608a, 608b
conventions, 12:604b
court, 6:39b
court poets, 4:76b, 413a-b
cymeriad, 12:603a
dadolychau, 12:605a
debates, 12:608a-b
elegiac, 12:597b, 603a, 604b–605a, 607b–608a
Gododdin, 4:392b
history, 12:597a–609a
humor in, 12:606b–607a
internal rhyme, 12:597b, 603a, 605b, 607a-b
legendary, 12:597b–598a, 603b–604a
love, 12:606b
martial imagery, 12:604b
narrative, 12:598a, 603b
nature, 12:606b
panegyric, 12:604a, 607b
political prophecy, 12:604a, 608b
preservation in manuscripts, 12:605b–606a
professional organizations, 12:598b, 608a
rhieingerddi, 12:605a
satirical, 12:68b
style and diction, 12:605b
subject matter, 12:602a
see also Aneirin; Bardic grammars
preservation of, 1:565b
prose, 12:599b–601a, **12:609a–613b**
categories of, 12:609b
earliest examples, 12:609b
from French and Latin originals, 12:600b
functional, 12:609b, 612a-b
Latin glosses, 12:599b
Latin translations, 12:611b, 612b–613a
Latinate style, 12:613a
learned, 12:609b, 612b–613a
legal texts, 12:609b, 612a-b
literary style, 12:609b
medical texts, 12:612a
romance, 12:611a, 611b
satirical, 12:611a
see also Areithian prose: prose rhetorics
religious, 12:601a, 604a, **12:613b–615b**
for clerical instruction, 12:615a
dialogue poems, 12:614a
didactic, 12:614a-b
for lay people, 12:615a
personal, 12:614a
private prayers, 12:615b
recurring themes, 12:613b–614a
Welsh triads, 1:577b
writers' societies, 4:415a-b
Welsh wars, church taxation and, 11:608b
Welt Lohn, Der. See Konrad von Würzburg
Weltchronik. See Rudolf von Ems; Schedel, Hartmann
Weltliche Klösterlein, Das, 8:411a
Wen (letter), in Old English, 8:310b–311a
Wenceslas, St. *See* Wenceslaus of Bohemia, duke
Wenceslaus I of Bohemia, king, 10:88b, 295a
Wenceslaus II of Bohemia, king, 10:88b
coinage of, 8:430a
Poland and, 9:721a, 723b, 724b
Praguer Groschen issued by, 5:680a
representative assemblies and, 10:330a-b
in Ulrich von Eschenbach's *Wilhelm von Wenden,* 12:250a
Wenceslaus III of Bohemia, king, 10:88b
crowned king of Hungary, 6:344a
Wenceslaus IV of Germany, emperor, 2:300b, 301a, 301b
beginning of Hussite revolution and, 2:303a
conflict with Prague archbishop, 2:304b
Gian Galeazzo and, 12:464b
Gregory XII and, 6:367b
Hussites and, 6:372a, 374a
John XXIII and, 6:368b
reign of, 5:489a
Swabian League and, 5:464a
vs. Bohemian nobility, 6:365a-b
Wenceslaus I of Luxembourg, duke, as benefactor of Froissart, 5:302b
Wenceslaus of Bohemia, duke
Christianity and, 8:443a
in *Passio sancti Venceslai,* 7:386b
Přemysl dynasty and, 10:87b–88a
Wendelgard of Gandersheim, abbess, 6:313b
Wendish language. *See* Lusatian language
Wends, **12:615b–617b**
Christianization, 12:617a
crusade of 1147, 12:647a-b
Danish conquests, 10:678b
departure from Lübeck (12th century), 7:680a
German annexation, 12:617a
in Hanseatic League, 12:616a
Lusatian, 12:616a
Main, 12:616b

in modern times, 12:616a
origins, 12:616a–617a
political history, 12:617a-b
Regnitz, 12:616b
trade and commerce
Danish intrusion, 6:93a, 94a-b
English boycott, 6:95a-b
Holland, 6:96a
tribes encompassed, 12:615b–616a
vs. Knud Lavard, 4:152b
Wenrich of Trier, 10:17a
Wenzel Bible, 2:215b
Werbböczy, István, *Tripartitum opus iuris consuetudinarii Hungariae,* 11:483b
Werewolf, in Icelandic *riddarasögur,* 10:395b
Wergild, 9:148a, **12:617b–618a**
blood feud and, 12:618a
determining amounts, 12:617b
disappearance of, 12:618a
in early Germanic law codes, 7:475b
of a *gesith,* 12:8a
in Hungary under St. Stephen I, 11:479b
in Russian (Muscovite) law, 7:510b
Saxony, 10:682b
social status and amount of, 12:617b
see also Blood money
Werkhop (unit of measure), 12:586b–587a
Werl Altarpiece, 3:61b
Werla, imperial palace of, heating system, 6:119a
Wermund, in *Brevis historia regum Dacie,* 11:522b
Werner II of Bolanden, 8:406a
Werner of Habsburg, 11:539b
Werner, Johann, 1:439a
Werner of Strasbourg, bishop, construction of Habsburg Castle, 6:42a
Wernerius. *See* Irnerius
Wernher, Bruder, 9:93a, 12:619a
Wernher von Elmendorf, **12:619a–620a**
Moralium dogma philosophorum
language of, 12:619a
mirror of princes and, 12:619a-b
preservation in manuscripts, 12:619b–620a
sources for, 12:619b
translation into German, 12:619a
Wernher der Gartenære, **12:618a–619a**
Helmbrecht, 8:353b, 12:618a
dating of, 12:618a-b
influence of, 12:618b
provenance, 12:618b
influence of on Seifrid Helbling, 11:142a
vocation and social status, 12:618b–619a
Wernher, Priester, *Maria,* 8:350a
Werve, Claus de, **12:620a–621a**
Chartreuse de Champmol, 4:186a
Pleurant carving, 12:620b (*illus.*)
Tomb of Philip the Bold, 9:710b
Wessel Gansfort, *via moderna* and, 12:408a
Wessex
period of domination, 2:97a
factors contributing to, 4:455b
reign of Alfred the Great, 4:456a-b
reign of Egbert, 4:455a-b
settlement in 6th century, 4:454a
Vikings and, 12:432b
vs. Charles the Simple, 9:160a
Wessobrunner Gebet, 2:224b, **12:621a**
alliterative verse, 9:233b
West Goths. *See* Visigoths
West Midland Prose Psalter, 4:547a
West Midlands, land tenancy in, 12:438a
West Saxon. *See* English language, Old English
West Saxon Gospels, 8:320a
Hatton MS of, 1:275b
major MSS of, 1:285b
Western Isles, MacDonald lordship, 11:108a
Western Schism. *See* Schism, Great
Westminister, statutes of, 11:468b
Westminster
court of Common Pleas, 11:225b
parliament at, 9:432b
15th-century meeting depicted, 9:430 (*illus.*)
royal treasury at, 4:533a
Westminster Abbey, 1:255b, 10:484a, **12:621b–622a**
chapel of Henry V, 12:29 (*illus.*)
chapel of Henry VII, 5:631a (*illus.*), 12:621b (*illus.*)
fan vault in, 12:365b
see also Vertue, Robert and William
chapter house, 3:267a
construction of, 7:660a
stone used, 7:661a
construction under Henry III, 12:621b
decoration of, 5:625b
design of, 6:167a
establishment of, 1:286b
French models for, 12:621b–622a
Henry VI's tomb, 4:510b
Henry Yevele and, 12:724b
later additions to, 12:622a
municipal administration, seat of, 7:663a
numbers of monks at, 2:173a
Rolf and, 10:449b
rose window of, 3:237a
St. Stephen's Chapel
Hugh of St. Albans and, 5:630b, 6:320b
William Ramsey and, 10:256b
shrine of Edward the Confessor, 12:621b
stained glass in, 5:552b
tomb of Eleanor of Castile, 12:86b (*illus.*)
tomb of Henry VII, 12:88b (*illus.*)
transept of, 5:625b
Wyclif and, 12:706b
see also Thirsk, John
Westminster accounting, 4:514a
Westminster, Council of (1163), 2:151b
Westminster Hall
Henry Yevele and, 12:724b
remodeled by Richard II, 10:384b
Westminster Palace, Hurley and, 6:364b
Westminster Psalter, Christ in Majesty, 5:613 (*illus.*), 614a
Westminster, statutes of, 9:424a, **12:622a-b**
Articuli super cartae (1300), 12:529a
chancellorship, 12:622a-b
De donis conditionalibus, fee tail, 12:622b
feudal land law, 12:622b
protection of foreign merchants, 12:120b
Statute of 1275, monasteries and, 6:468b
Statute of 1285, 4:514b, 7:192a, 195b–196a, 446b, 447b, 452b
De donis conditionalibus, 7:452b
see also Nisi Prius
Westminster, Treaty of (1373), 10:52a-b
Westphalia
ministerials of, 8:406b
power of, 5:460b
Westphalia, duchy of, representative assemblies and, 10:333a
Westwork, **12:622b–623a**
in basilica, 2:124b
of Benedictine abbey church, 10:92a (*illus.*)
in German Romanesque architecture, 10:487b
Münster (Bad Gandersheim), 12:623a (*illus.*)
in Ottonian architecture, 10:477b
St. Étienne (Caen), 10:482b
Wethamstede, John, abbot of St. Albans, 7:370a-b
Wetti, 3:103a
Wettiners, 5:493a
Wettstreit der drei Liebhaber, Der. See Rosenplüt, Hans
Wey (unit of measure), product variations, 12:584b
Wey, William, on the Stations of the Cross in Jerusalem, 11:467b
Weyden, Rogier van der, **12:623a–624b**
atelier, 12:623b
bust portraiture, 12:624b
Campin and, 3:60b, 61a, 61b, 5:86a, 12:623b
Columba Adoration of the Magi Altarpiece, 12:623b
Crucifixion, 5:86b, 611b
Deposition from the Cross, 5:86a, 12:623b, 624 (*illus.*)
Granada-Miraflores Altarpiece of the Virgin, 12:623b
Hans Memling and, 8:271b
Hugo van der Goes and, 5:571b
influence of, 3:324b, 5:86b
invention of new compositional types by, 5:86a
Jorge Inglés and, 7:150a-b
Justice of Herkinbald, 12:623b
Justice of Trajan, 12:623b
Last Judgement polyptych, 5:86a
Last Judgment polyptych, 12:623b
Master I.A.M. of Zwolle and, 6:388b
Miraflores Altarpiece, 5:86a
Nativity Altarpiece, 12:623b
Pietà, 5:611b
pseudo-*Schnitzaltar,* 12:623b
Saint Luke Drawing the Madonna, 12:623b
sculpture of, 12:623b

Weyden, Rogier van der (*cont.*)
see also Flemish art, painting; Master of the Life of Mary
Wharf, Northern European, 11:243b
Wheat, 1:83b, 98b
durum, 2:364b
emmer, 2:364b
growth of
climate and, 3:456a
in Western Europe, 5:645b–646b
hard, 1:86b
see also Grain Crops, Western European
Wheel of Fortune, 3:425a, **12:624b–625b**
in art, 12:625a, 751 (*illus.*)
four shelves, 5:146b–147a
from Machaut's *Livre dou voir dit,* 8:5 (*illus.*)
styles of, 5:146b
Wheel, hydraulic. *See Nā*ᶜ*ūra*
Wheel window, **12:625b–626a**
Notre Dame de Paris, 12:625 (*illus.*)
Wheelbarrow, 12:81a
Wheels
in ancient vehicles, 12:367b
of later medieval vehicles, 12:374a
Wheelwrights, guilds of, 12:374a, 377b
"When Jesus Was Twelve Years Old." *See* Ethelred of Rievaulx, St.
Whetstone, rotary, 11:651b, 660b, 661b (*illus.*)
Whippletree, invention of, 12:371b–372a, 378b
Whirling dervish. *See* Dervish
Whiskey, 4:220a
Whitby, Synod of (663–664), 3:228b, 4:454b, 7:614a, **12:626a-b,** 683a
adoption of Roman liturgical calendar, 3:81b–82a
attendants, 12:626a
celebration of Easter and, 8:369a
clerical tonsure, 12:626b
Colman of Lindisfarne at, 3:480a
English church structure and, 3:373b
Latin church's victory at, 8:371b, 441a
on liturgical calendar, 12:626a-b
resolution of Roman-Celt differences, 4:458b
see also Nechtan
Whitchester, Roger, 7:188a
White Book of Rhydderch, 1:566a, 578a
audience compiled for, 12:613a
Mabinogi, 7:703a, 12:610a
"White Company," vs. Catalans, 7:379b
"White Death of the Saracens." *See* Nikephoros II Phokas, Byzantine emperor
White Elephant, Order of the, 3:305 (*illus.*), 307a
White Guelphs. *See* Guelphs and Ghibellines
White Horde. *See* Golden Horde
White House of St. Ninian. *See Ad candidam casam*
White lead, as cosmetic base, 2:147a, 148a
White Monastery, Missal of, in Alexandrian rite, 1:155a
White Monks. *See* Cistercian order
White Mountain, Battle of the (1621), 6:377a
White Russian language. *See* Byelorussian language
White Sea, discovery of, 4:555a
White Sheep. *See* Aq Qoyunlu
White Stag Chase. *See* Stags
Whiterig, John, 9:26b
Whitsunday. *See* Pentecost
Whitsuntide plays, 3:298b
mystery plays and, 8:657b, 659a
Whittington, Richard, almshouses, 7:665b
Wibald of Stavelot, **12:626b–627a**
register of correspondence, 12:627a
Wibert of Canterbury, **12:627a**
Wibert of Toul, **12:627b**
Wichram of St. Gall, **12:627b**
Computus, 12:627b
Wickram, Jörg, adaptation of Albrecht's Ovid, 1:131b
Wiclif. *See* Wyclif, John
Wide-brimmed pot. *See* Chapel-de-fer
Widows. *See* Women
Widsith, 1:278b
compared with *Norna-Gests þáttr,* 9:171a
Kudrun and, 7:304b
Skjǫldungs and, 6:311a
Widukind of Corvey, 9:717b, 10:70a, **12:627b–628b**
battle descriptions, 12:628a
flyting and, 9:175a
History of the Saxons, 12:627b–628a
sources for, 12:628a
idea of empire, 12:628a
on prayers for the dead, 1:177a
Widukind (Westphalian noble), Saxon rebellion, 10:683a
Wiec. See Freemen, proto-Polish
Wieliczka, saltworks, 10:633a, 634a
Wiener Genesis. See Altdeutsche Genesis
Wiener Oswald, Der. See Oswald, St., German epics about
Wife's Lament, classified as a lyric poem, 8:334b
Wigalois. See Wirnt von Grafenberg, 5:454b
Wigand of Marburg, on the mass suicide at the Pilėnai castle, 7:609b
Wigbodus, **12:628b**
Wigmore Abbey, Chronicle of, **12:628b**
Wigoleis vom Rade, 12:657a
Wiker, abbot of St. Maximin, Sigehard and, 11:285a
Wilars de Honnecourt. *See* Villard de Honnecourt
Wilbrand, count of Oldenburg, 11:314a
Wild, Hans. *See* Hemmel, Peter
Wild Hunt (witchcraft), 12:660a
Wilde Alexander, Der, **12:629a-b**
derivation of "wild," 12:629a
eschatology, 12:629a-b
innovations in lyric poetry, 12:629a
Kindheitslied, 12:629a
melodies, 12:629a
Wilde, John, anthology of, 1:319b
Wildenberc (castle), Wolfram von Eschenbach and, 12:674a
Wilderness cultivation. *See* Reclamation of land
Wildmore Fen, map of, 11:515b
Wilfrid, bishop of York
Saxon church construction, 10:679b
Ripon and Hexham, 10:680b
Wilfrid of Northumbria, bishop, supported by Aldhelm, 1:144a
Wilfrid of Ripon, St. *See* Wilfrid of York, St.
Wilfrid of York, St.
at Synod of Whitby, 12:626a
conversion of Sussex to Christianity, 4:458b
in literature, 7:363a
missions of, 3:344b
Regula sancti Benedicti and, 2:170a
Wilhelm von Bregenz, count, 6:325a
Wilhelm, Master, Madonna and Child with Pea Blossom, 5:608 (*illus.*), 610b
Wilhelm von Österreich. See Johann von Würzburg
Wilhelm von Wenden. See Ulrich von Eschenbach
Wilhelmus. *See* William
Wilhelmus de Cabriano, Hugo and, 6:323b
Wiligelmo da Modena, 10:492a, 501a, **12:630a**
Genesis scenes in Modena Cathedral, 12:630 (*illus.*)
Lanfranc of Modena and, 7:329a
Will, free. *See* Predestination
Will and intellect, in Thomism and competing schools, 12:43a, 43b
Will (testament), 6:460b
Byzantine, 6:452a, 7:596a
English, 6:458b
land inheritance and, 7:453b
French, decline of Roman testamentary law, 7:466a
probated. *See* Probate records
Roman, 6:458a
Willame. *See* Adgar
Wille (priest)
in Bamberg, 8:347b–348a
Ezzolied and, 4:571b
Willegelmus de Modena. *See* Wiligelmo da Modena
Willehalm. See Ulrich von Türheim; Wolfram von Eschenbach
Willehalm von Orlens. See Rudolf von Ems
Willehari, Alamannic duke, vs. Pepin II, 11:526b
Willem, *Van den Vos Reinaerde,* 4:319a, 10:314b
Willem of Hulsterlo, *Reinaert I* and, 2:141b
Willem van Hildegaersberch, didactic poetry of, 4:320a
William II of Achaea, prince, 7:378a, 378b, 379a
defeated at the Battle of Pelagonia (1259), 9:487a
William I of Aquitaine, duke, Cluny and, order of, 3:468b

William IX of Aquitaine, duke, **12:630a–633a**
"Ab la dolchor del temps novel," 12:632a-b
burlesque poems, 12:631b
characterization of Provençal language by, 10:159b
conflict with church, 12:631a
doctrine of free love, 12:631b–632a
fin'amors mode in poetry of, 10:166b–167b
irony in poetry of, 10:166a-b
joi (devoted love) in poetry of, 10:166b, 167a-b
love poems, 12:632a-b
obscenity in poems, 12:631b
poetry of, 3:668b, 669b
sexual behavior, 12:631a
as troubadour, 5:434a, 10:163a, 12:215a
vida of, 10:165a
William X of Aquitaine, duke
Cercamon's lament on death of, 3:240b
court of as cultural center, 8:415b
William II of the Archipelago, duke, 7:381a
William I (the Conqueror) of England, king, 11:160a, **12:633a–634b**
administration, 12:633b
Battle Abbey, 11:657b–658a
Battle of Hastings, crossbowmen, 11:657b
battle of Val-ès-Dunes (1047), 12:633b
Caen under, 3:8b
castles of, 3:145a
cavalry tactics of, 3:203b
charter of London, 7:660a
claim to English throne, 4:461a, 6:111b
conquest of England, 4:461a–462a, 6:111b–112a, 9:79b, 165a, 228a, 12:633b
establishment of earldoms, 4:461b
introduction of feudalism, 4:463b
mercenary troops, 12:559a
oaths of fealty, 4:461b
succession to Edward, 4:395a
coronation at Westminster Abbey, 1:35b, 7:257b, 12:634a
described in Gaimar's *Estoire des Engleis,* 1:265a
Domesday Book, 4:461b, 7:436a-b, 10:29b
evaluation of leadership, 12:634a-b
Franco-Angevin invasions, 12:633b
funeral of, 6:432a
itineracy of, 9:165b–166a
knights of, 7:277b–278a
land disputes and, 7:435a
Lanfranc of Bec and, 7:328b
legal system and
confirmation of existing borough courts, 7:434b
court of common pleas, 3:491a
feudal influence on, 7:433a-b
itinerant justices, 7:183b
justiciar, 7:199b
presentment of Englishry, 4:487a
separation of church and lay courts, 7:434a
writ as used by, 7:435a-b
legfal system and, impartibility, 6:459b
Maine and, 9:164a-b
Malcolm III of Scotland and, 8:56b
marriage to Matilda, 12:634a
military quotas of, 7:277b–278a
minority of, 9:162b, 163b
mint of, 10:66b–67a
nonfeudal systems, 4:464b–465a
provision for succession, 4:461b
relations with church, reform, 4:465b–466a
seal of, 11:128b
shilling and, 11:229a
succession, 12:633b
travels of, 12:159a–160a
unification of Normandy, 12:634a
villages and, 12:444a-b
vs. Stigand, 3:82b
Welsh incursions, 12:516b
Wulfstan of Worcester and, 12:703a
William II of England, king, 4:256a, 9:166b
acquisition of Normandy, 4:462a
conflict with archbishop of Canterbury, 1:253a, 312a-b
coronation of, 7:258b
death of, 6:154b
extortion and bribery, 4:462a
Malcolm III of Scotland and, 8:56b
reign of, 7:199b, 9:166b
Wulfstan of Worcester and, 12:703b
William II of Holland, count, 5:485a
capture of Aachen, 4:59b
election as king of Germany, 4:428a
William I of Poitiers, count, in song, 3:57b
William VII of Poitiers, count, lyric poetry, 8:514a
William VII of Poitiers, count. *See* William IX of Aquitaine, duke
William I of Sicily, king, 11:268b–269a
William II (the Good) of Sicily, king
campaigns of, 11:269a
donor portrait at Monreale, 4:261b
Monreale Cathedral and, 10:504a
reign of, 11:269a
tutored by Peter of Blois, 9:518a
William III of Sicily, king, 11:269b
William IV of Toulouse, count, 12:91b
William of Afflighem, translation of Beatrice of Nazareth's autobiography, 9:12a
William Alnwick of Norwich, bishop, on Lollard movement, 7:647b
William of Apulia, **12:636b**
Gesta Roberti Wiscardi, 7:365b, 12:636b
William of Apulia, duke, Roger II and, 10:440b
William of Auvergne, **12:636b–637a**
on absolution of sin, 9:604a
Aristotle and, 1:462a
on creation by God, 9:596b
Magisterium divinale, 12:636b
on the value of magic, 8:37a
William of Auxerre
on character of sacraments, 9:603a
on sinful concupiscence, 9:600b
Summa aurea, 9:601a, 12:22a
William of Blois, 7:367b
Alda, 4:283a
William Bona Anima, archbishop of Rouen, York tractates and, 12:730b
William de Brailes. *See* Brailes, William de
William of Briane, **12:637a**
William of Canterbury. *See* William the Englishman
William Carver. *See* Carver, William (Bromflet)
William of Champeaux, **12:637a–638a**
Abelard and, 1:16b, 18b
Jewish-Christian polemic treatise of, 10:3b
as master at University of Paris, 9:404a
nominalism and, 9:155a, 155b
retirement at St. Victor, 12:637b
Roscelinus' influence on, 12:637b
theory of universals, 12:637a
William of Champlitte, **12:638a-b**
death of, 7:378a
Peloponnesian campaign, 12:638a
Villehardouin and, 7:376b
William Clito (Robert Curthose's son), 9:166b
William of Conches, 9:702a, **12:638b–639a**
accusations of heresy, 12:638b
Arundel 268 and, 10:473b
cosmological theory, 12:638b
Dragmaticon, 12:638b–639a
Elementorum philosophiae libri IV, 1:607a
on fables, 4:572b
Glossae super Platoneum, 10:270b
glosses, 12:638b
Moralium dogma philosophorum, 7:383a, 9:594a, 12:619b
Philosophia mundi, 12:638b–639a
Tesoretto and, 7:383a
William the Conqueror. *See* William I (the Conqueror) of England, king
William of Dijon, abbot, 5:578b
William the Englishman, **12:645b**
fables of, 7:366b–367a
William of Grosseto, beatification of, 2:143a
William of Hirsau, 11:527b, **12:639a-b**
customs of Cluny, 12:639a
customs of external brothers, 12:639a
modality and, 8:642a
William of Hothum, Thomism and, 12:41b
William Jordan of Cerdagne, count, Tancred and, 11:589b
William of Jumièges, **12:639b**
Gesta Normannorum ducum, 12:639b
sources for history, 4:304a
William of Kirkeby, abbot of St. Albans in Wallingford, Richard of Wallingford and, 10:387b
William Longsword (10th century), assassination of, 9:162a
William of Luxembourg, count, heraldic seal of, 11:129b

William of Macclesfeld
Correctoria corruptorii Thomae and, 12:41a
as defender of Thomism, 12:41b
William of Mainz, archbishop, Hrotswitha and, 6:316a
William of Malmesbury, 7:255a-b, **12:639b–640b**
on Ambrosius Aurelianus, 2:3a
devotional works, 12:639b
on English dialects, 8:311b–312a
Gesta pontificum Anglorum, 6:263b, 12:640a
Gesta regum Anglorum, 1:565a, 6:263b, 12:639b–640a
Historia novella, 12:640a
historiography, 12:639b–640a
modification of Amalarius on liturgy, 7:631b
Recent History, 6:263b
Roger of Salisbury and, 10:443b
stylistic features, 12:640a
on writing as rhetoric, 6:260a
William de la Mare, 7:136b
Correctorium fratris Thomae, 12:40b
William Marshal, 7:130b, **12:635a–636a**
biography of (*Histoire de Guillaume le Maréchal*), 1:266a, 2:236b, 12:635a
comital title, 12:635b
conflict with Llywelyn the Great, 12:519b
estrangement from John, 12:635b–636a
guardian of Henry III, 12:636a
Langton and, 7:338a
marriage, 12:635a-b
model of chivalry, 3:303a
Plantagenet service, 12:635a-b
rise of, 9:150b
role in Magna Carta, 12:636a
William, Master, construction of Rudnitz Bridge, 10:421a
William of Moerbeke, 9:700b, **12:640b–641b**
Aquinas and, 1:463a
Dominican theology and, 4:247b
ecclesiastical career, 12:640b
Geomantia, 12:641a
scientific associations, 12:640b–641a
translations, 10:19b
of Archimedes, 1:434a, 437a–438a, 438b, 439a
of Aristotle, 1:461a, 12:138a, 641a
from Greek, 12:641a
of Proclus' *Elements of Theology,* 9:100a
William of Nassington, 9:26a
William of Newburgh, *Historia rerum Anglicarum,* 1:565b
William of Norwell, royal wardrobe and, 6:304a, 305a
William of Ockham. *See* Ockham, William of
William of Orange, count of Toulouse, 12:90b
Catalonia and, 3:174b
crusading oath of, 3:449b
epics about, 3:258b–259a, 261a, 5:240a-b
misreading as "shortnose," 5:240b–241a
William of Palerne, 8:319b, 332a
William of Paris (royal confessor), 3:535a
William of Perth, martyrdom, 8:159b
William of Poitiers, 7:277a, **12:641b**
Gesta Guillelmi ducis Normannorum, 9:260b, 12:641b
William de la Pole, Hundred Years War and, 6:333b
William des Roches, appointment as seneschal, 5:164b–165a
William of Rubruck, 4:556b–557a
on Armenian settlements in Central Asia, 12:99a
assassin references in work of, 1:591b
Itinerarium, 7:139a
Mandeville's Travels and, 8:82a
on Russian fur trade, 5:332a-b
travels of, 5:398a, 10:28a
William Rufus. *See* William II of England, king
William of St. Amour, 4:251b
on beguines, 2:159b
De periculis novissimis temporum, 12:39b
condemnation of, 1:128a
denunciation of mendicant orders, 2:315a, 5:200b
exile of, 9:408b
Hugh of St. Cher and, 6:321a
Wyclif and, 12:710a
William of St. Bènigne, fake relics and, 10:298a
William of St. Carilef (St. Calais), bishop of Durham, manuscripts made for, 1:256b
William of St. Emmeram in Regensberg, abbacy of monastery at Hirsau, 6:231b
William of St. Thierry, **12:642a–643a**
Abelard and, 1:18a, 2:192a
association with Bernard of Clairvaux, 12:642a
on astrology, 1:607a
as biographer of St. Bernard, 2:191a, 6:69a
Carthusians and, 3:119a
De contemplando deo, 12:642a
De erroribus Guillelmi a Conchis, 12:638b
De natura et dignitate amoris, 12:642a
Epistola ad fratres de Monte Dei, 3:119a, 12:642b
as exegete, 4:543a
Expositio in cantica canticorum, 12:642a-b
influence of on Hadewijch, 9:12a
refutation of Abelard and William of Conches, 12:642b
retirement to Signy, 12:642a-b
works of, 2:174a
William of Saliceto, 8:260a
William of Sens, 8:103b, **12:643a**
work of, on Canterbury Cathedral, 5:582b, 584a
William of Sherwood, *Introductiones in Logicam,* 4:170b
William Tell, Waldstätte and, 11:542a
William (the Lion) of Scotland, king, 7:147b, 11:104b, 106b, 107b
William Torel. *See* Torel, William
William of Tripoli
baptisms by, 4:253a
Itinerary, 4:253a
missions to Arabia, 3:357a
On the State of the Saracens, 4:252b–253a
Refutation of the Koran, 4:253a
William of Tyre, **12:643a–644a**
on assassins, 1:590b–591a
on fairs, 4:589a
Historia rerum transmarinarum, 3:331b, 6:263a
historiography, sources for, 12:643b
history of the Kingdom of Jerusalem, 12:643b
Hugo and, 6:323b
Maronites and, 11:564a
on the Nile, 9:138a
on siege of Beirut (1110), 2:164a
William de Vescy, lord of Kildare, conflict with Kildare Fitzgeralds, 5:75a-b
William of Volpiano, abbot of St. Bénigne-de-Dijon, 2:173b, **12:644a-b**
Montpellier H.159 manuscript and, 8:614b, 615b–616a
Radulphus Glaber and, 10:247a
Richard II of Normandy and, 9:163a
William of Waddington
Manuel des péchés and, 8:96b, 317a
scribe of *Handlyng Synne,* 8:87a
William of Winchester, **12:644a-b**
William of Windsor
in Ireland, 6:519a
Irish parliament and, 9:435b
William of Wykeham, **12:644b–645b**
administrative accomplishments, 12:644b
construction of Winchester College, 12:645a
enlargement of Windsor palace, 12:644b
foundation of New College, Oxford, 12:645a
vs. John of Gaunt, Wyclif and, 12:706b
William Wynford and, 12:711b
Williamites, 5:297b
Willibald, St., biography of St. Boniface, 2:321a
Willibrord, St., 2:172a
Denmark and, 4:151a
missionary work of, 8:441a
Williram von Ebersberg, **12:645b–646b**
allegory of, 5:427b–428a
cathedral schools and, 8:347b
exegetical material, 12:646a
Expositio in Cantica canticorum, 12:646a-b
Latin short poems, 12:646b
Notker Teutonicus and, 9:189b
style of, 8:348b–349a
vernacular prose, 12:646a
version of *Vita S. Aurelii,* 12:646b
Willoughby, Richard, 7:193a
Wilton Diptych, 5:607b (*illus.*), 610a, 628a

symbolism of, 4:476a-b, 477a-b
Wimpergbüchlein. See Roriczer, Mathes
Wimpfen-im-Tal, 5:582a-b
Winchcombe, Richard, **12:646b–647a**
Winchelsea
founding of, 12:324b–325a
medieval streets in, 12:324b–325a
Winchelsea, Thomas, archbishop, 11:609a
Winchelsey, Robert, archbishop of Canterbury, Ockham and, 9:209b
Winchester
as center of Anglo-Saxon art, 1:272b–273a
charges against heard at parliament, 9:424a
in early Middle Ages, 12:320b
foundation of, 12:322b–323b
manuscript illumination in, 8:107b
medieval streets in, 12:323 (*illus.*)
royal treasury at, 4:530b, 6:300b, 301a
scriptoria, 1:276b, 276a
sequence repertory of, 11:165a, 165b
sheepherding in, 12:694a-b
Winchester accounting, 4:514a
Winchester Bible, 1:258a
decorated initials in, 6:462b
drawings in, 4:291a
Winchester Castle, William Wynford and, 12:711b
Winchester Cathedral, 10:484a
Ethelwold and, 4:518a,b
frescoes at, 5:609b
organ, 8:604b
remodeling (1394), 12:645a
use of iron grilles in, 8:286a
William Wynford and, 12:711b
Winchester College
foundation of, 12:645a
William Wynford and, 12:711b
Winchester School
illumination style characterized, 10:108a-b, 109 (*illus.*)
Missal of Robert of Jumièges and, 10:434a
Winchester, Statute of
justices of the peace and, 7:195b–196a
Peasants' Revolt and, 9:479b
Winchester style, 1:273a-b
Anglo-Norman art and, 1:256b, 258a-b
in manuscript book production, 1:258a
Winchester, Treaty of (1153), 6:156b
resolution of succession through, 4:463b
Winchester Troper, 4:518b, 8:44b, 593b, 12:208b, **12:647a–648b**
alphabetic notation in, 8:614b
Cambridge MS, 12:647a
notation of, 12:647b
Oxford MS, 12:647a-b
Wind power. *See* Technology, wind power
Windesheim Congregation, 3:368b
Devotio Moderna and, 4:166b
houses of, 2:366b
resemblance to clergy chapters, 2:367b
Winding sheet of Christ. *See Plashchanitsa;* Turin, Shroud of
Windisch, bishopric of, 11:537a
Windmill. *See* Mills
Windmill Psalter, *Judgment of Solomon,* 6:463a
Window glass, 5:561b–562a
see also Glass, stained; Lancet window; Traceried window
Windsor Castle
Hurley and, 6:364b
Royal Chapel, Berkeley and, 2:188b
William Wynford and, 12:711b
wood for, 3:145b
Windsor, Treaty of (1175), 6:517b
Wine, taxation of, 11:623a
Wine trade, 5:125b, 125a–126a, 12:649b–651b
at fairs, 4:585b, 587a
Bordelais, 2:129a
brokers, 12:121a
Beaune, 12:651a
St. Pourçain, 12:650b–651a
Bruges, 12:650a
Châtillon, 12:650b
early medieval, 12:110a
England/Bordeaux, 12:649b
Hungarian, 6:345b
in London, 7:663a
retail, 12:651a-b
role of criers, 12:121b–122a
transport, 12:152b, 157b, 158b
Western European, 12:111b
Wine and winemaking, **12:648b–654b**
additives to improve taste, 6:283b
adulteration of, 5:125a-b, 12:119b–120a
Beaune, 12:650a, 650b, 651a, 654a
Bordeaux, 12:649b, 650a
customs on, 2:328b
Bordeaux region's rise to prominence, 5:174a-b
Burgundy, 12:649b, 650b
containers for, 12:650a-b
domestic, 12:651b
drinking, 3:98 (*illus.*)
see also Taverns
ecclesiastical, 12:652b
estate management and, 12:652a–653a
fertilizer and, 12:653a
freezing method of, 4:219a
French, *aide* tax and, 10:319b
harvest season, 12:653b
heating method of, 4:219a
in Islam, 2:208b–209a
Islam and, 12:649a
Italy, 12:654a
in Jewish dietary rules, 4:183a
labeling of, 12:120a-b
labor force
contractual, 12:652a
corvée, 12:652b
measurements of, 12:581b
caritas, 12:589b
metayage and, 12:651b–652a
nutritional aspects, 12:650b
preservation of, 12:650b
quality control of, 12:119b–120b
retail sales, regulation of, 5:125a
social class and demand for, 5:125a
surveyors of, enforcement of quality standards, 5:125a-b
use of barrels, 12:122a
Volnay, 12:652a
see also Barrels; Viticulture
Winepresses, 12:653b
Winfrith (Winfrith), St. *See* Boniface, St.
Winged altarpiece. *See* Triptych; Polyptych
"Winged" lance, 7:323b, 324 (*illus.*)
Winileot, 5:433a-b
Winsbecke, Der, 3:662a-b, **12:654b–655b**
additions to, 12:655a-b
contents, 12:655a
sources, 12:654b
Winsbekin, Die, 3:663a
"Winteney Version" (Benedictine Rule), 4:518a
Winterthur
founded, 11:539b
Zurich and, 11:544b
Winwæd, Battle of (654), 4:454b
Wipo of Burgundy, 7:363b, **12:655b–656b**
Cantilena, 12:656a
Deeds of the Emperor Conrad, 10:16a
Gesta Chuonradi imperatoris, 12:655b
lost works, 12:655b
poetical works, 12:656a
political works, 12:656a
Proverbia centum, 12:656a
Rhitmus ad Henricum, 12:656a
in song, 3:58a
Tetralogus, 10:16a, 12:656a
Versus ad mensam regis, 12:656a
Victimae paschali laudes, 6:381b, 9:714a, 12:656a
Wirecker (Wireker), Nigel. *See* Nigel of Longchamp
Wiritto de Grefenberc. *See* Wirnt von Grafenberg
Wirnt von Grafenberg, 9:708a, **12:456b–657b**
Wigalois, 1:572b, 5:454b, 10:315b, 12:656b–657a
plot, 12:656b–657a
sources, 12:657a
Wolfram von Eschenbach and, 12:679b
Wirt, Der, **12:657b–658a**
Wiser, Johannes, scribal work, Trent codices and, 12:183b
Wiślanie tribe, 9:717a
see also Poland
Wisse, Claus, *Neue Parzival,* 5:452b, 12:679b
Wissembourg (10th cent.), *Aesop,* 4:572a
Wit Stwosz. *See* Stoss, Veit
Witan. *See* Witenagemot
Witchcraft, European, **12:658a–665a**
Catharism and, 12:661a
in *Celestina,* 11:423b
craze period, 12:662a–663b, 664b
diabolical, 12:662a-b
early, 8:27a
in England, 12:661b, 663a, 664a
evolution of, 12:659b–662a
folklorist interpretations, 12:659a

Witchcraft, European (*cont.*)
German, 12:664a
historiography of, 12:658b–659b
in Icelandic *riddarasögur,* 10:395b
intellectual interpretations, 12:659b
Italian, 12:661a
late, 8:30a–31a
magic and, 12:658a-b
punishment for, 12:658b, 661b
punishment of, 4:133b
social functions of, 12:663b
social interpretations, 12:659a-b, 663b–664b
sorcery and, 12:658b
theory of, 8:30a
topoi of, 12:660b–661a, 662b–663a
Witches' Hammer, 4:579b
Witelo
influenced by Roger Bacon, 2:39b, 41a
Perpectiva, 1:438b
Witenagemot, **12:665b–666a**
convened at Canterbury, 3:82a
historigraphy of, 12:665b
Witherlogh, Lex castrensis and, 11:522a
Witigis, siege of Rome, 9:292a
Witiza. *See* Benedict of Aniane
Witold (Vytautas) of Lithuania, grand prince, 9:726a-b
Wittelsbach family, 5:493a-b, 9:724a-b, **12:665a**
Bavaria and, 2:134b, 135a, 135b
Frederick I Barbarossa and, 12:665a
Wittenberg, University of, 12:289a
via moderna and, 12:408b
Wittenborg, Johann, mayor of Lübeck, execution of, 7:682a
Wittenwiler, Heinrich, **12:666a–667b**
Der Ring, 2:132b, 12:666a–667b
Wittenwiller, Hugo, *Lehre von den Zeichen des Hirsches,* 4:579b
Wittigsten, 5:463b
Witz, Konrad, **12:668a-b**
Heilspiegel Altarpiece, 12:668a
St. Peter Altarpiece, 5:609 (*illus.*), 611a, 12:668a, 669 (*illus.*)
Speculum of Salvation altarpiece, 5:610b–611a
Wizlaw III von Rügen, 5:438a, 8:414a, **12:668b–669a**
Wlach. See Vlachs
Wladislas II of Hungary, king, 2:300a, 10:88a
Władisław I Łokietek of Poland, king, 9:721a, 722b, 723b–724b
foundation of University of Kraków, 9:729b
Hungarian alliance, 9:629a
restoration of monarchy, 9:628b–629a
Władysław II Jagiełło of Poland, king, 9:725b–727a, 729b
see also Jagiełło dynasty
Władysław III of Poland, king, 6:347b, 9:727a
diet and, 6:335b
Hunyadi and, 6:363b
see also Ladislas I of Hungary, king
Władyslaw Hermann of Poland, king, 9:720a
Woad, 2:146b, 11:595a, 12:694b
preparation of, 4:325b
Wodan (Woden). *See* Odin
Wolf
regarded as demonic by Iranians, 8:16b
see also Fenris wolf
Wolfdietrich, **12:669a–670a**
Ortnit and, 9:283a
plot of, 12:669b–670a
versions of, 12:669b
Wolfenbüttel, Helmstedt MS 628, **12:670b–672a**
collation of, 12:670b–671a
contents of, 12:671a-b
dating of, 12:670b
Wolfenbüttel manuscripts, 8:43a, 44a
Helmstedt MS 628, conductus motets, 8:505b–506a
MS 677, 8:559a
Wolfenbüttel model book, 4:292a
Wolfger von Erla, 5:435a, **12:672a–673a**
at Fourth Lateran Council, 12:673a
involvement in imperial politics, 12:672b–673a
Otto of Brunswick and, 12:672b–673a
Wolfhelm of Cologne, 9:701b
Wolfker von Ellenbrechtskirchen. *See* Wolfger von Erla
Wolfram von Eschenbach, **12:673b–681b**
ceremony and, 9:114a
Chrétien de Troyes and, 5:248b, 448a, 451b
courtly conflicts in works of, 5:449a-b
courtly language, 6:441a
dawn and spring songs, 12:679a-b
erudition of, 12:674b
Gottfried von Strassburg and, 5:634a-b
Hartmann von Aue and, 8:351a
hunting and, 6:359a
influence of, 12:679b
Johann von Würzburg and, 7:117b
Konrad von Stoffeln and, 7:287b
literary fate of, 5:453a
lyric poetry of, 5:441a, 12:679a-b
male-female relationships in, 5:451b–452a
modern editions of, 12:679b–680a
Nibelungenlied and, 9:114b
Parzival, 5:429a, 448a, 451b–452a, 634b, 8:224b, 9:708a
Arthurian legend in, 1:572a
chronology of, 12:676a
plot of, 12:676b–677b
political interpretation, 12:678a
prologue, 12:675a
religious interpretation, 12:677b–678a
as source for *Frauendienst* of Ulrich von Liechtenstein, 12:251b–252a
as source for Wirnt von Grefenberg's *Wigalois,* 12:657a
sources of, 3:311a, 12:677b
style of, 12:676a
personality of, 12:673b–674b
professional life of, 8:350b
religious views of, 12:674b
residences of, 12:673b–674a
in Sachsenheim work, 8:412b
Schüler von Paris and, 11:80a
Seifrid Helbling and, 11:142a
social status of, 12:674a
society depicted by, 5:451b–452a
style of, 5:452a-b, 12:675a–676a
successors of, 5:452b–453a
Titurel, 5:452a, 8:408b, 9:708a, 12:679a
chronology of, 12:676a-b
Ulrich von Eschenbach and, 12:249b
in *Wartburgkrieg,* 12:573a, 573b
Willehalm, 5:452a, 453a, 12:678b–679a
Bataille d'Aliscans and, 12:678b
chronology of, 12:676a, 676b
completion by Ulrich von Türheim, 12:253b
on Neidhart "von Reuental," 9:92b
pessimism of, 12:678b
realism in, 8:351b
Rolandslied and, 10:448a
sources of, 12:676b
Wirt and, 12:657b
Wolgemut, Michael, 9:201 (*illus.*), 710b, **12:681b–682a**
Wolhusen, Lucerne and, 11:544a
Wolsey, Thomas, cardinal, 9:682b
Wolvinus, **12:682a**
see also Paliotto of S. Ambrogio
Women
as actors, 4:270b
aged, in literature, 7:367b
artists, abbess Herrad, 12:160b
beauty aids, *Trotula minor* treatises on, 12:214a-b
Byzantine
cosmetics and, 2:147b
inheritance and, 6:451a, 452a-b
mortality, 4:596a
status of, 4:595b
churching of, 3:382b–383a
costumes. *See* Costume
courtesy books for, 3:663b–665a, 663a–665a
roles and wifely duties described in, 3:662b–664b
decline of status, in late medieval cities, 12:319a
defense of
in Diego de Valera's *Defensa de virtuosas mugeres,* 11:422b
in Teresa de Cartagena's *Admiración operum Dei,* 11:420b
devotional for, *Quinze joies de mariage,* 10:240a
education of, 4:602b
Christine de Pizan on, 3:316a-b
fickleness of, in fabliaux, 4:575a
flyting and, 9:173a, 174a
Frankish, inheritance and, 6:457b
Germanic, 4:600a
inheritance and, 6:457b
hairstyles, Western European, 3:624a
hunting and, 6:357a-b
idealized
in courtesy books, 3:662b–663b
in Italian poetry, 6:646b–647a, 649a, 651b
inheritance, by mother, 6:458a

as innkeepers, 6:473a
Iranian, as poets, 6:507a
Irish lore of. *See Bansenchas*
Islamic
in art, 6:595b (*illus.*), 596 (*illus.*)
costumes worn by, 3:616b
inheritance and, 6:452b
rights of, 3:574a
sexuality, 3:574b
in Shiite law, 11:228b
status of, 4:598b, 6:579a
travel by, 12:148a
Jewish
girls' education, 11:70b
status, 4:607b
in synagogue, 11:557a
veils worn by, 3:619b
legal status, *mundium* (guardianship) in German law, 7:475b
in literature, German lyric poetry, 12:537a
married, status of, 4:603a-b
medical care of, Trota and *Trotula,* 12:213b–214a
noble
cosmetics and, 2:147b
courtesy books for, 3:663b–664a
religious life, 2:158a
in the otherworld, 6:550a, 551b
outlawry of, 9:311b
peasant, 4:604a
physicians, Trota, 12:213b–214a
in poetry, as troubadours' *domna,* 12:207a, 217a-b
prostitutes, 10:154a–155a
religious orders of
Birgittine, 12:689a
Carolingian, 12:683a–684b
Chartreusian, 12:687a
Cistercian, 12:686a-b
decline of, 10:297b
Dominican, 4:251a, 254a–255a, 12:687b–688a
early, 12:682a–683a
in England, 12:685b–686a
Fontevrault and, 12:686b
in France, 12:682b, 684a, 684b, 688b
Franciscan, 12:688a-b
Franciscan, *see also* Poor Clares
in Germany, 12:685a
in Germany, Saxony, 12:685a
Humiliatae, 12:687a
in Italy, 12:684a-b, 685a, 688b
in Italy, Lombardy, 12:684b, 687a
in Italy, Rome, 12:682b
mendicants and, 12:687b–688b
Premonstratensian, 12:685a-b
Roman, cosmetics and, 2:147a-b
saints, 6:69b–70b
single, 3:426a
status of, 3:426a, 4:611a
age of marriage and, 4:146b–147a
among Cathars, 3:185b
Islamic world, 6:99a
in Occitania, 10:163a-b
under feudalism, 4:600b–601a
in Visigothic Spain, 12:474a
see also Femme sole
suffrage denial to, 10:328b
taverns and, 12:651a
troubadours, 3:670a-b
see also Troubadours, women
unmarried, 4:146a, 600a
see also Beguines and beghards
urban, 4:603a-b
as beguines, 2:160a-b
Visigothic, 12:474a
widows, inheritance of, 6:452a
winemaking and, 12:653a, 653b
witchcraft and, 12:661b, 663a, 664a-b
see also Antifeminism; Contraception; Family; Feminism; Marriage; Mysticism
Womens' religious orders, as response to spread of heresy, 6:68b–69a
Women's religous orders, **12:682a–689b**
Wonders of the East, The (Old English text), 1:286a
Wood
as building material. *See* Construction, building materials
use of in European agricultural tools, 12:81a-b
see also Forests; Lumber supply
Wood trade. *See* Lumber trade
Woodcarving
England
in Cornwall, 4:115a-b
early Renaissance style in, 4:263b
Woodcut, **12:689b–694a**
book illustrations, 7:700a
depictions of plows, 12:72b
engraving and, 4:489a, 490a
formularized, 12:692a
painted, 12:692a
signed, 12:692a
stylistic universality of, 12:690a
textile printing and, 12:689b–690a, 692b
see also Block book; *Bois Protat*
Woodford, William, vs. Wyclif, 12:709b
Woodstock, Assize of (1184), 6:356b
Woodstock, Assize of (1198), 5:128b
Woodstock, Treaty of (1247), 7:637a
Welsh rights, 12:520b
Woodville, Elizabeth, marriage to Edward IV, 12:571b
Woodville family
Richard III and, 10:385b
in Wars of the Roses, 12:571b–572a
Woodworking, water mills used for, 8:393b
Wooing of Emer, The, 1:569b
Tristan legend and, 12:199b
Wooing Group, 9:26a
English mysticism and, 9:18b, 19a
Wool, **12:694a–695a**
combing, 11:695a
dyeing of, 12:694b–695a
English, 12:694b
Ypres and, 12:732a-b
fulling process, 11:705a-b
fustians, 11:694a
lubrication, 11:694b–695a
manufacture of iron wire and, 8:293a
merino, 11:694b
preparation, 11:694a–695a, 695b–696a, 707b
see also Bowing; Carding; Fulling; Raising; Shearing
production, 12:694b
in St. Quentin, 12:396a
quality of, age of sheep and, 11:694b
serge, 11:694a
short-stapled, 11:694a-b
in Spain, 8:280b
spinning, regulation of, 11:699a-b, 700b
in tapestries, 11:591a, 593a, 594b–595a
taxation of, 11:615a
wefts and warps
carding of, 11:696a, 696b
spinning of, 11:699a
woolfell, 11:694a
worsteds and
distinctions between, 11:694a
preparation of, 11:694a
Wool trade
ban on exports from France, 12:118a
ban on imports of woolens into Pisa, 12:118a
competition from linen and silk, 12:115b
early medieval, 12:110b, 110a
in England, 7:660b, 663a
with Germany, 6:92a
levy on, in Hundred Years War, 6:334a
in Ghent, 5:521a
in Iceland, 6:394b
packaging of wool cloths, 12:122a
Pisa and, 9:664a-b
Provins, 4:593a
in Scotland, 11:105a, 105b, 111b–112a
Spain and Flanders, 8:280b
Ypres, 12:731a, 731b, 732a
see also Sheep raising
Worcester, mystery plays and, 8:658b
Worcester Castle, Wulfstan of Worcester and, 12:703a
Worcester Cathedral, priory, Wulfstan of Worcester and, 12:703a, 703b
Worcester Fragments, 8:504b
Worcester polyphony, **12:695a–697a**
harmonic aspects, 12:695b, 696b
voice exchange in, 12:696a
Word lists. *See* Encyclopedias and dictionaries; Gloss; Translation and translators, resources and training
Word separation, introduction of, 7:599a, 599b–600a
Words of Hippocrates. See Galen
"World Clock," 3:465a
Worms
commune of, 3:498a
Diet of (1495), provisions of, 10:331a
restoration of its bishop, 3:69a
Worms, Concordat of (1122), 3:352a, 6:499b, **12:697a-b**
Henry V of Germany and, 5:478a
investiture controversy, 4:422a
Lothar of Supplinburg and, 5:478b
ratification of, 3:636b
as traditional concordat, 3:525a
Worms, Diet of (1195), Wolfger von Erla and, 12:672b
Worms, Diet of (1495)
ban on private war, 5:504a

Worms (*cont.*)
  formal reorganization of *Reichstag,* 5:499a
Wrake van Ragisal, Die, 4:319a
Wrap (unit of measure), 12:593b
Wrestling, 5:348a
Writ. *See* English common law
Writing, origins of, according to Nicholas of Cusa, 1:218a
Writing materials
  Byzantine, gold lettering, 11:635b
  diptych, 4:214a
  feathered quill, 11:693a
  inks, pigments, and paints, 11:639a
  Islamic, **12:697b–699a**
    ink, 12:698b
    paper, 12:698a-b
    pens, 12:698b
    see also Dawāt
  regulation of, 11:693b
  Western European, **12:699a–703a**
    ink, 12:700a
    pens, 12:699b
    ruling, 10:554b–555a
    wax tablets, 12:580a
  see also Paper; Parchment; Stylus
Writing systems, European, 6:439a-b
Written documents. *See* Documents
Written records
  in classical Rome, 7:599a
  scarcity of in the High Middle Ages, 7:599a-b
Wrocław, 9:728b
Wuīs u Rāmīn. See Fakhr al-Dīn Gurgānī
Wulf and Eadwacer, 8:327a
Wulfila. *See* Ulfilas
Wulfoald, mayor of the palace in Austrasia, 9:499b
Wulfstan, (9th-century traveler to Scandinavia), 1:284a
  on early Balts, 7:602b
Wulfstan of Winchester
  Life of St. Swithin and, 7:363a
  Winchester Troper and, 12:648a
Wulfstan of Worcester, St., **12:703a–704a**
  as bishop, 12:703a-b
  dispute over *sac* and *soc,* 7:435b
  as prior, 12:703a
  tomb of, 12:703b
Wulfstan of York, archbishop, 1:281b, **12:704a-b**
  adaptations of Aelfric's sermons, 1:284b
  attribution to of a poem in Anglo-Saxon Chronicle, 8:327b–328a
  as homilist, 12:704b
  Institutes of Polity, Civil and Ecclesiastical, 10:16a, 12:704a
  law code of, 12:704a
  legal texts attributed to, 1:286a
  Sermo ad Anglos, 1:285a
  Sermon of the Wolf to the English, 12:704b
  sermons of, 1:284b–285a
    dating of, 1:275b
  on Winchester Cathedral organ, 8:604b
Wunderer, Der, **12:704b–705b**
  versions of, 12:704b–705a
Wurmbunt swords. *See* Swords, pattern-welded
Württemberg, county of, constitution and representative assemblies of, 10:332b–333a
Württemberg dynasty, 11:528a
Würzburg Bridge, construction of, 10:421b
Würzburg, Synod of (1283), on Ave Maria, 2:13b
Würzburg, University of, 12:288a
Wüstungen. See Deserted settlements
Wuzurg Framadār, **12:705b–706a**
Wyclif, John, 8:318a-b, **12:706a–711b**
  against modern logicians, 12:407b, 407a
  banning of books, 7:646a, 647a
  Bible and, 12:708a-b
  censure of ecclesiastical abuses, 3:370b–371a, 6:199b
  on communion under both kinds, 3:505a
  condemnation of teachings, 3:647b, 6:199b
  De ecclesia, 12:706b, 708a
  De eucharistia, 12:708b
  De officio pastorali, on vernacular plays, 4:2855
  De veritate sacrae Scripturae, 12:708a
  dissemination of views, outside Oxford, 7:645b
  doctrines of, 3:370b–371a
  English universities and, 3:59a-b
  as exegete, 4:544b, 547b–548a
    translation, 2:215a, 222a-b
  followers of, merger with Lutheranism, 7:647b
  Hus and, 3:649b–650a, 6:366b, 367a, 12:707a
  on indulgences, 6:450b
  influenced by *Secretum secretorum,* 11:135b
  John Ball and, 9:479a
  John of Gaunt and, 7:135a
  kingship theories of, 7:270a-b
  legal works, 12:707b
  links to Bohemia, 10:384b
  Opus evangelicum, 12:709a
  Oxford disciples, 7:645a
  on papal Avignon, 2:34a
  philosophical works, 12:707a-b
  political activities of, 12:706b
  Postilla super totam bibliam, 12:707b
  predestination and, 3:371a
  private religion, opposition to, 7:648a
  Sermones quadraginta, 12:709a
  Sumula sumulorum magistri Johannis Wiclif, 12:707a
  as teacher, 12:706a-b, 710a
  teachers of, 12:710a
  theological works, 12:707b–709a
  theory of papal authority, 4:376b
  Trialogus, 12:709a, 710b
  Wycliffistae, 7:645b
  see also Lollards
Wycliffite Bible. See Bible, versions
Wynford, William, **12:711b–712a**
Wynfrith. *See* Boniface, St.
Wynkyn de Worde, **12:712a-b**
  Boke of Kervinge, 3:661b
  Book of Margery Kempe and, 9:25a
  Caxton and, 3:211a
  Everyman and, 4:527b–528a
  printer of *Information for Pilgrims unto the Holy Land,* 12:156a-b
  printing of *Ancrene Riwle,* 8:314b
  reprinting of John of Tynemouth's *Sanctilogium,* 6:64a-b
  reprints of Malory's *Morte Darthur,* 8:62a
Wynn. *See* Wen (letter)
Wynnere and Wastoure, 8:319a-b, 332a
Wysbeck, John, **12:712b**

X

Xač^{c}atur Keč^{c}areс^{c}i, 1:511b
Xač^{c}atur of Tarōn, construction of monastery of Hałarcin, 6:76b
Xač^{c}ik I, *kat^{c}ołikos* (973-992), 1:483b
Xač^{c}ik-Gagik, king of the Arcrunis (*fl.* 908), 1:451a
Xač^{c}k^{c}ar, 1:495a (*illus.*), **12:712b–713a**
  Amenap^{c}rkič^{c} type, 12:713a
Xałbakean/Přošean, 1:485b
Xaχuli, **12:713a**
  church at, 5:409a
Xaz. See Musical notation, ekphonetic
Xelami, 8:563a
Xenodochia. See Hospices
Xenophon
  Anabasis, on Karduchoi, 7:310a
  Cyropaedeia, 8:434a
  Hiero, 8:434a
Xenopsylla cheopis. See Flea
Xenos Korones, 8:555b
Ximénez de Cisneros, cardinal
  founded university at Alcalà, 3:644b
  Mozarabic chant and, 5:661b
  revolt against, 11:380b
Ximénez de Rada, Rodrigo, archbishop of Toledo, 11:414a
  De rebus Hispaniae, 11:435b, 435a
  historical works of, 11:406b
Xiphilinos, John, monthly codices, 6:61a
Xlat^{c}, 1:474a, 12:362a, **12:713a-b**
  Armenian trade and, 12:97b, 98b
  under Ayyubids, 1:485a
  under Šah-i Armen, 1:485a
  under Shāh-Arman, 11:220a, 220b
  under T^{c}amt^{c}a, 1:486a
Xorcayn. *See* Khorzanē
Xorjean. *See* Khorzanē
Xoruan, Shirvan and, 11:254a
Xosrov II/III of Armenia, king, in P^{c}awstos Buzand's *History of Armenia,* 9:472b
Xosrov III/IV of Armenia, king, 1:476a
Xosrov Anjewac^{c}i (Armenian writer), 1:511a
Xosrov of Anjewac^{c}ik^{c}, bishop, 5:673b

Xosrovanoyš, Armenian queen, erection of Amenap'rkič^{c}, 10:648a
Xosrovanoyš (queen of Ašot III), 1:589b
Xosroviduχt, princess, 5:668a
Xosroviduxt (sister of Trdat III), 1:519b
Xosrovik, *vardapet*, 1:509b
Xostakdar. See Azat
Xoy
  Armenian trade and, 12:97b
  silk route to the Far East and, 12:99a
Xoyt^{c}. *See* Xut^{c}
Xrami, 7:309b
Xuc^{c}uri alphabet, 5:414b
Xusrō I Anōšarwān, Sasanian king, 4:162a, 7:201b, 11:374b, **12:714a-b**
  administrative reforms, 10:670a-b
  alliance with Turkish khan against Hephthalites, 6:170a
  burning of Melitene, 8:269b
  burning of Sebaste, 11:131b
  Byzantine truce, 10:670a-b
  golden age of Zoroastrian culture and, 12:714a-b
  in Islamic *belles lettres,* 10:670a
  legendary reputation of, 12:714a
  massacre of Mazdakites and, 8:238a
  Naχčawan and, 9:90b
  reforms of, 11:460a
  scholarly patronage, 10:670b
  seals of, 11:122a
  tax system, 10:670a
  vs. Vardan II, 1:477a
  wuzurg framadār and, 12:705b
  see also Letter of Tansar
Xusrō II Abarwēz, Sasanian king, **12:714b–715b**
  Armenian schism and, 1:499b
  in art, 11:597a-b, 598a
  Bahrām VI Čōbēn and, 2:50a-b
  Byzantine conflict, 10:670b
  Emperor Maurice and, 1:477b, 8:230a-b
  Holy Cross and, 12:715a, 715b
  in literature, 6:507a
  Nestorianism and, 9:107a
  Nu^{c}mān III and, 7:320b
  Smbat Bagratuni and, 1:477a
  "Spring of Xusrō," 10:665b
  wealth of, 12:715a
  Xusrō I and, 12:714a
Xusrō II Parvīz. *See* Xusrō II Abarwēz
Xut^{c}, 11:599a
Xwadāy Nāmag, 2:50a, 7:220b, 9:327a-b, **12:715b–716a**
  Shāhnāma and, 11:221a

Y

Yabhalaha II, katholikos, 11:567b
Yabhalaha III, katholikos, 3:313a
Yačaxapatum Čaṙk^{c}, See Maštoc^{c}, St.
Yačhxapatum Girk^{c}. See Gregory the Illuminator, St.
Yad ha-Ḥazakah. See Maimonides, Moses, *Mishneh Torah*
Yādgār Muḥammad, Timurid ruler, rivalry with Abū Sa^{c}īd, 12:342b
Yafurids
  control of San^{c}a, 10:647a
  in San^{c}a, 10:647a
Yaghibasan, Danishmendid ruler, 10:235b
Yahūdiyya, al-, 7:171a
Yaḥyā I, Idrisid ruler, 6:413a, 413b
Yaḥyā II, Idrisid ruler, 6:413a
Yaḥyā III ibn al-Qāsim, Idrisid ruler, 6:413a
Yaḥyā IV ibn Idrīs ibn ^{c}Umar, Idrisid ruler, 6:413a
Yahya of Antioch, **12:716a-b**
Yaḥyā of Antioch, 4:525a
Yahya of Antioch, on Symeon Metaphrastes, 11:554a
Yaḥyā ibn ^{c}Alī ibn Ḥammūd, Hammudid ruler, 6:414a
Yaḥyā ibn Ibrāhīm al-Judālī, leader of the Ṣanhāja, 1:198a-b
Yaḥyā ibn Khālid, Barmakid administrator, 2:110a-b
Yaḥyā ibn Khālid al-Barmakids, translations of Greek scientific treatises into Arabic and, 11:82b
Yaḥyā ibn Sa^{c}īd. *See* Yahya of Antioch
Yaḥyā ibn ^{c}Umar, chief of the Lamtūna, 1:198b
Yalkut Shimoni. See Simon of Frankfurt
Yām, **12:716b**
Yáñez, Rodrigo
  Poema de Alfonso XI, 11:418a
  see also Alfonso XI, Poema de
Yang ch'in, 8:562a
Yannai, use of rhyme and acrostics, 6:131b
Yaozhdāthra ("making whole"), in *Vidēvdād,* 12:411b
Ya^{c}qūb ibn Killis, 5:25b
Ya^{c}qūb ibn Layth, **12:716b–717b**
  defeat of Samanids, 10:637b
  eulogies to, 10:610a
  expansion of Saffarid dynasty, 10:609a
  Shīrāz and, 11:252a
Ya^{c}qūb ibn Sufyān al-Fasawī, *sunna* and, 11:511b, 512a
Ya^{c}qub ibn Yūsuf ibn Killis, 7:104a
Ya^{c}qūb (Saffarid), vs. Muḥammad ibn Ṭāhir, 11:575b
Ya^{c}qūbī, al-, **12:717b–718b**
  Kitāb al-buldān, 12:718a
  lost works, 12:718b
  on al-Maghrib, 8:15a
  Mushākalat al-nās li-zamānihim wa-mā yaghlibu ^{c}alayhim fī kulli ^{c}aṣrin, 12:718a-b
  on Samarra, 10:642a, 642b
  Ta$^{\supset}$rīkh, 12:717b–718a
Yāqūt, Ibn, Abbasid chamberlain, 10:246a
Yāqūt al-Musta^{c}ṣimī, Islamic calligraphy and, 3:54b, 6:606b
Yāqūt al-Rūmī, on Bab al-Mandab, 2:33a
Yarā^{c}, 8:612b
Yarmūk River, Battle of (636), 5:515b, 6:568a, **12:719a-b**
  role of Abū Sufyān, 1:29a-b
Yaropolk II, Kievan Rus under, 7:249a
Yaroslav (the Wise) of Kiev, grand prince, **12:720a-b**
  building program, 10:591b
  campaign into Lithuania, 7:604a
  commemorative art, Hagia Sophia (Kiev), 10:583a
  Khanate of Tmutarakan and, 12:66a
  literature during reign of, 11:346b–347a
  music and, 8:573a
  rule of, 7:248b–249a
  subjugation of Sudovians and, 2:64b
Yaroslavl, **12:720b**
Yaroslav's Statute, 7:508a
Yasa. See Ilkhanids
Yasna, 5:366b
  in Avesta, 2:14b
Yassi Ada ship, 11:231a, 232a, 233b
Yašts, **12:720b–721a**
Yathrib
  Jews in, 7:101b
  Muḥammad in, 6:576b
Yathrib. *See* Medina
Yavuz. *See* Selīm I, Ottoman sultan
Yaws. *See* Plagues, venereal diseases; Slavery and slave trade
Yazatas, 12:747a, 747b
Yazd, mosques, 6:599a
Yazdagird. *See* Yazdegard
Yazdegard I, Sasanian king, religious tolerance, 10:669a
Yazdegard II, Sasanian king
  Armenia and, 1:476b, 498b
  assimilation of Caucasia by, 3:308a
  Hephthalite threat, 10:669b
  Vardan Mamikonean and, 12:360a
Yazdegard III, Sasanian king
  Arab threat, 10:671a
  vs. Arabs, 6:511a
  vs. Muslims, 6:569a
Yazīd I ibn Mu^{c}āwiya, Umayyad caliph, **12:721a–722b**
  accession to caliphate, 12:267b–268a, 721b
  authority over Ḥijāz, 1:16a
  Battle of al-Ḥarra (683), 12:268b
  control in Medina, 1:15b–16a
  frivolity condemned, 5:353a
  revolt against, 12:268b
  struggle for succession after death of, 1:16a
  vs. al-Ḥusayn, 6:370a, 370b, 12:268b
  vs. Medina, 12:722a
Yazīd II, Umayyad caliph, edict of (721), 6:403a
Yazīd III ibn al-Walīd, Umayyad caliph, 12:273b
  in art, 6:595a
Yazīd ibn Abī Sufyān, 6:568a
Yazīd ibn al-Muhallab, revolts, 6:511b
Year 1000, **12:722b–723b**
  expectations of Antichrist, 12:723a
  Hungary and, 6:339a
  terrors of, Romantic vision of, 12:722b–723a
  see also Millennialism

Year
  Annunciation style, 3:20a
  beginning of in Jewish calendar, 3:25b
  Byzantine, 3:19b
  Christmas as start of, 3:19b–20a
  division of
    in Christian calendar, 3:19b–20b
    in Jewish calendar, 3:25a
  January as start of, 3:20a-b
  Lady Day style, 3:20a
  leap, 3:26b
    in Armenian calendar, 3:31a
"Year of the alleluia" (1233), 6:662a
Yehuday Gaon, *Halakhot Pesukot,* 7:169b, 11:584b
Yellow. *See* Safflower; Saffron
Yellow Book of Lecan, 6:523a, 12:140b–141a
  Tadhg Óg and, 9:206a
  see also John of Gaddesden
Yemen, 1:374b–376a, **12:723b–724b**
  Fatimid Empire and, 11:138a
  Ibāḍī communities in, 11:139a
  Ismailism in, 6:614b, 616a, 617a, 618a
  Jewish art in, 7:67a
  Seljuk penetration into, 11:153a
  under Ayyubids, 12:724a
  under Mamluks, 12:724b
  under Rasulids, 12:724a-b
  vs. Sasanians, under Xusrō I, 12:714a
  Zaydis and, 11:138b, 12:741b, 742a
  see also Najrān; San^{c}a
Yemenis, in al-Kufa, 7:306b, 307a
Yemenite Arabs, revolts against Umayyads, 12:273b, 274a
Yenisei Kirghiz, 7:272b–273a
Yeraḥmeel ben Solomon, anthology of Israelite experience, 6:255b
Yersinia pestis, 2:257b
  see also Plagues
Yeshiva. *See* Schools, Jewish
Yesil Cami. *See* Mosque of Mehmed I
Yesügai, role in Kereit power struggle, 8:465a
Yesügei Baghatur, 5:382b
Yevele, Henry, **12:724b–725a**
  professional projects, 8:173b
  reconstruction of Canterbury Cathedral, 3:83b
  social-economic status, 8:173b–147a
Yggdrasill, 11:29a-b
  see also Scandinavian mythology; Tree of Life
Yiddish, 6:441b, **12:725a-b**
  Dukus Horant and, 4:304b
  language, 12:725a-b
  literature, 12:725b
Yildiz (Turkish general), 5:527a
Ylbughā al-Nāširī, governor of Aleppo, rebellion against Sultan Barqūq, 2:113a
Ylias. *See* Simon Chèvre d'Or
Ymage du monde, L', encyclopedic nature of, 4:449a
Ymir, 11:28b–29a
Ymrysonau, 12:608a, 608b
Yngling dynasty, 4:570b, 12:726a
Ynglinga saga. *See* Snorri Sturluson
Ynglingatal, skaldic meter of, 11:320a
Ynglingatal. *See* Þjóðólfr ór Hvini
Yngre Västgötalagen, 7:525a
Yngvars saga Víðförla, **12:726b–727b**
  authorship, 9:216b
  historicity of, 12:727a
  plot of, 12:726b–727a
  protagonist of, 5:138b
Yngvi, 11:328b
Ynys Afallach, 6:552a
Yogh, in Old and Middle English, 8:310b
Yolande, empress, 7:346b, 347b, 349a
Yom Tov ben Abraham Ishbili, 7:81a, 11:586a
York
  barber-surgeons in, 2:99b
  cathedral school of, Alcuin of York and, 1:142a-b
  ecclesiastical courts of, 1:433b
  taken by Vikings, 12:432a
York Breviary, 12:729b
York, Convocation of (1280), 11:608b, 609a
York Manual, 12:729b
York Minster, Great East Window by John Thornton, 12:46b–47a (*illus.*)
York Plays, 8:658a, 658b, 659a, 661a, **12:727b–729a**
  Biblical paraphrase and, 4:547a
  censored, 8:662b
  Creed play, 4:285a
  manuscript of, 12:727b, 728a
  Marriage at Cana, 8:659b
  modern editions of, 12:727b
  modern productions of, 12:728b
  Paternoster play, 4:286a
  public order and, 4:283b
  repertory list, 8:659b
  revived, 8:663a
  staging of, 8:662a, 12:728a
  see also Towneley Plays
York rite, **12:729a-b**
  kiss of peace formula, 12:729a
  "secret" blessing in, 12:729a
York, Statute of (1322), 9:426a, 426b, 11:468b
York tractates, **12:729b–730b**
  authorship of, 12:730a-b
  contents of, 12:730a
  revolutionary ecclesiology in, 4:374b–375a
York, Viking kingdom of, 12:433a-b
Yorkshire, Robin Hood and, 10:436a-b
Yose ben Yose, synagogue poetry, 6:131b
Yosef al-Katīb (the Scribe), earliest datable *kharja* and, 11:408a
Yosippon, 6:255b
  first book, 6:256a
  intended messages, 6:256a
  recensions of text, 6:256a
Yotvingians, subjugated by Vladimir of Kiev, 7:604a
Younger Genesis, The (Old English translation), 2:225a
Younger Metz School, 10:100b
Yovhannēs VI, *kat^{c}ołikos,* Levon II and, 6:312a
Yovhannēs of Armenia, archbishop, identity of, 5:540a
Yovhannēs of Awjun, *kat^{c}ołkos,* 1:501b, 502a, 520b
Yovhannēs of Bagaran, vs. Movsēs (the *kat^{c}ołkos*), 1:499a
Yovhannēs Drasχanakertec^{c}i, *kat^{c}ołkos,* 1:510b, 518b, 519a, 520a
  History, 6:240a
Yovhannēs of Erznka, 1:511b
Yovhannēs Gabełean, *kat^{c}ołikos,* 1:508b, 519a, 5:540a
Yovhannēs (hermit), 1:519b
Yovhannēs, *kat^{c}ołikos, Zwart^{c}noc^{c}* and, 12:749a
Yovhannēs Kozeṙn, 1:511a
Yovhannēs Mamikonean, 1:510b
  on the Armeno-Persian wars, 6:240b
Yovhannēs Mandakuni, *kat^{c}ołikos,* 1:508b, 516b, 5:540a, 540b
Yovhannēs Mayragomec^{c}i, 1:509b
  acceptance of *Ekthesis,* 6:188b
  Hawatarmat, 7:279b
Yovhannēs Ōjneci. *See* John of Ōjun, St.
Yovhannēs Orotnec^{c}i, 1:512a, 520b
Yovhannēs Ovayec^{c}i, *kat^{c}ołikos,* 1:520a
Yovhannēs Sarkawag Vardapet, 1:512a
  calendar reform and, 3:31a
Yovhannēs T^{c}lkuranc^{c}i (Armenian poet), 1:512a
Yovhannēs Vanakan
  Kirakos of Ganjak and, 7:271b–272a
  teacher of Vardan Arewelc^{c}i, 12:359b
Yovhannēs Vardapet of Tawuš, Mχit^{c}ar Goš and, 8:656b
Yovhannēs-Smbat Bagratuni of Armenia, king, 5:339a
  death of, 1:484a
Yovhannēs-Smbat Bagratuni, king, vs. Ašot IV, 1:483a, 484a
Yovsēp^{c} of Constantinople, 1:511a, 520a
Yovsēp^{c}, *kat^{c}ołikos,* 1:518b
Yovsēp^{c} (Qaysite martyr; *d.* 808), 1:519b
Yperperum. *See Hyperpyron*
Ypres, **12:730b–732b**
  ascendancy of, 12:731b–732a
  charter of, 12:731a, 731b
  decline of, 12:732a-b
  government, 12:731b
  population, 12:731a, 732a
Ysengrimus
  episode sequence, 12:733a-b
  influence on *Roman de Renart,* 9:635b
  manuscript sources, 12:733a
  modern interpretations of, 12:734a
  Rainardo e Lesengrino, 10:314a
  style of, 12:733b–734a
  see also Nivardus of Ghent; Renard the Fox
Ysengrimus abbreviatus, 12:734a
Ystorya Bown de Hamtwn. *See Bevers saga*
Ystorya Brenhinedd y Brytanyeit, 12:600b
Ystorya de Carolo Magno, 7:217b, 12:611b
Ystorya Dared, 12:600b
Ystoryaeu Seint Greal, 12:612a

Yuan dynasty, Persian Gulf trade and, 11:247a
Yüan-ch'ao pi-shih. See Secret History of the Mongols
Yuçaf de Écija, 7:82a
Yugoslavia
  glassmaking in, 5:558a-b
  languages of, 6:443b
  see also Bosnia; Croatia; Serbia
Yumurtalik. *See* Āyās
*Yunaban dproc*ᶜ. *See* Armenian Hellenizing School
Yūnus Emre, 9:44b
Yūnus, Ibn, 11:83b
Yūnus al-Kātib (*d. ca.* 765), *Kitāb fī al-aghānī,* 8:565b–566a
Yuri, (son of Vsevolod "Big Nest"), 12:486b
Yuri (son of Andrei Bogoliubskii), Tamar and, 11:587a
Yuri of Galich, prince (15th century)
  siege of Moscow, 8:543b
  struggle for grand princedom, 8:543a-b
Yuri I of Galicia, prince, Metropolitan Peter and, 9:512a
Yuri III Danilovich of Moscow, prince
  assassination of, 8:539b
  Vladimir princedom, 8:539b
Yuri of Kiev, prince (12th century), 5:413b
Yuriev-Polski Cathedral, architectural elements, 10:580a
Yusik, 5:665a
Yūsuf I, Nasrid ruler, Alhambra and, 6:612a
Yūsuf 'As'ar of Ḥimyar, king, 7:101b
Yūsuf of Azerbaijan, emir, Smbat I the Martyr's clashes with, 11:351a
Yūsuf al-Baṣīr. *See* Joseph ben Abraham al-Baṣīr
Yūsuf ibn Tāshfīn, Almoravid ruler, 1:199a-b
  invasion of Spain, 1:199b, 3:73b, 76a, 384a–385b, 387b
Yūsuf, Sājid emir of Azerbaijan, 1:451a, 481b–482a, 519b, 5:339b
  Ašot II and, 1:588b–589a
Yvain, See Chrétien de Troyes, *Chevalier au Lion*
Yves the Breton, 1:591a
Yvette of Huy, 9:11b
Yvo/Yves of Chartres. *See* Ivo of Chartres, St.
Ywain and Gawain, 1:574b

Z

Zāb, 6:414b, 415a
  Ibrāhīm ibn al-Aghlab and, 6:391b
Zabara of Barcelona, Joseph ibn, *Book of Delight,* 8:23a
Zabarella, Francesco, 9:709b, **12:735a-b**
  appointed cardinal, 3:647a
  conciliar theory of, 3:511b–512a, 513a–514b
  disciple of Baldus, 2:57a
  John Hus and, 3:650a
  on *plenitudo potestatis,* 12:735b
  Tractatus de schismate, 12:735b
Zabūr (Arabic word for the Psalms of David), mentioned by Muḥammad, 9:497a
Zaccaria, Benedetto, 4:557b, 558a
Zaccaria family, 7:380a, 381b
Zacharias of Mytilene, **12:735b–736a**
  ecclesiastical histories, 2:512b–513a
Zacharias, pope
  Frankish alliance, 7:657b
  Liutprand and, 10:521b
  Pepin III and, 3:106b, 9:372b, 501a
  reign of, 3:345b–346a
  revival of the papal library, 7:559b
  on slave trade, 11:336b
Zacharias Rhetor. *See* Zacharias of Mytilene
Zacharias Scholasticus. *See* Zacharias of Mytilene
Zachariou (Coptic textile group), 3:590a
Zacher Epitome. See Roman de toute chevalerie
Zacuto, Abraham
  Almanach perpetuum, 1:613a
  solar declination tables, 11:650b
Zadar. *See* Zara
Zadar Cathedral, 10:488b
Zadonshchina, 11:347b
Zagros, Hasanuyids in, 7:310b
Zagros Mountains, 1:470b
Zaharije, ruler of Serbia, 11:170a
Ẓāhir, 6:617b
Ẓāhir, al-, Abbasid caliph, al-Mustanṣir and, 8:650b
Ẓāhir, Barqūq al-. *See* Barqūq, al-Sulṭān al-Malik al-Ẓāhir Sayf al-Dīn
Ẓāhir, Baybars al-, Mamluk sultan, 8:72a
Ẓahīr al-Dīn Bābur, as founder of Great Moghuls, 12:58a
Ẓāhir, al-, Fatimid caliph, 5:27a-b
Ẓahīrī of Samarkand, 6:508b
Ẓāhirīya, 8:72b
Ẓāhiriyya *madrasa,* 6:607b
Zahn, Der, **12:736a-b**
Zähringen dynasty, 5:510a, 11:527b, 538b
  extinction of, 11:539a-b, 540a
  Fraumünster Abbey and, 11:541a
  Lenzburgs and, 11:539a
  literary patronage, 6:102b
  Rudolph of Habsburg and, 11:540a
  vs. Hohenstaufens, in Swabia, 11:539a
  Zurich and, 11:542b
Zahumlje. *See* Hum
Zāᵓiraja, 8:21b
Zajal, 3:85a-b, 8:514b, 563b, 11:449a, 452b
  muwashshaḥ and, 11:448b
  see also Troubadours, poetry, origins and foreign imitations; *Zéjel*
Zakᶜarē, *amir-spasalar,* 1:485b
Zakᶜarē Mχargrzeli, 12:736b, 737a
  Mχitᶜar Goš and, 8:656b
Zakᶜaria of Gnunikᶜ, bishop, 1:511b
Zakᶜaria of Jag, *katᶜołkos,* 1:511a
Zakᶜarids, 1:485b, 514a, **12:736b–737b**
  Armenia and, 1:474a
  Armenian literature and, 1:511b
  Armenian trade and, **12:98b**
  control over Ani in Širak, 1:291a-b, 292a
  Council of Sis (1204) and, 1:501b
  monastic churches of, 1:495b
  Mongols and, 12:737a
  Naχčawan and, 9:91a
  rebuilding of Dwin, 4:324b
  social structure under, 1:490b
  under David the Builder, 12:736a
  see also Mχargrdzeli family; Tigran Honencᶜ
Zakāt, 1:201b–203b
  see also Alms tax, Islamic
Zakāt al-fiṭr. See Alms tax, Islamic
Zákinthos. *See* Zante
Zakon sudnyi liudem, 2:403a, 7:507b
  property transactions, 11:669b–670a
Žale Matki Boskej. See Alexis, St.
Zallaqa. *See* Sagrajas
Zamakh-sharī, al-, 7:296b–297a
  Asās al-balāgha, 4:443b
  Muqaddimat al-adab, 4:444b
Žamatun. *See* Gawitᶜ
Zambra, 8:562b
Zamora Cathedral, 10:487b
Zamora, Treaty of (1143), 10:41a
Zamr, 8:561b
Zamra, 8:562b
Zamrak, Ibn, poetic inscriptions on Alhambra, 6:234a
Zamzam, **12:737b**
Zanāta Berbers, 2:185b
  Almoravids and, 1:198a-b
  vs. Buluggīn, 12:744a
  vs. Idrīs ibn ᶜAbd Allah, 6:413a
  vs. Zirids, in Tripoli, 12:744b
Zand, 12:747a
  Xusrō I and, 12:714b
Zand Āgāhīh. See Bundahishn
Zand ī Vahman Yasht, 9:327a
Zandanījī, **12:737b–738b**
  in Huy, 12:737b, 738a (*illus.*)
Zandīk, 8:237b
Zanga River, 11:214b
Zangī, ᶜImād al-Dīn
  capture of Edessa, 4:30b, 37a
  al-Lādhiqiya and, 7:315b
Zangids, 10:259a
  Ayyubids and, 2:22a
  end of rule, 2:43b
  Islamic art and, 6:607a
  Seljuks of Syria and, 11:155a
  succession struggle after Malikshāh I's death, 11:153b
Zanj, 3:49a, **12:738b–740b**
  Basra and, 2:127b
  land of, 12:739b
  religion of, 12:739b
  revolt, 1:374b, 2:268a-b, 6:512b, 11:331b, 12:574b, 738b–739a
Zankī. *See* Zangī
Zanobi da Strada, 2:277b, 288b
Zante, Orsini and, 7:376a
Zápolyai, János, king of Hungary, 6:349b, 350a

Zapovednye gody. *See* "Forbidden years"
Zara
  conquest by Fourth Crusade, 4:44a-b
  Hungary and, 6:340b
Zara, Treaty of (1202), 4:44b–45a, 46a
Zaragoza. *See* Saragossa
Zarang. *See* Sīstān
Zarathustra. *See* Zoroaster
Zarco, João Gonçalves, 4:559a
Zardušt ī Khwarragān, 8:236b, 237b
Zarduštagān, origins of Mazdakism and, 8:236b
Ẓarīf, court musician as, 8:567a, 568a
Zarqālī, al-, 1:61b
  equatorium and, 4:500b
  stereographic astrolabe, 10:387b
  Toledan Tables and, 12:67a, 68a-b
  Tratado de la azafea, 11:98a-b
  treatises of translated into Hebrew, 11:90b-91a
Zavāra
  a four-*eyvān* mosque of, 11:146b
  mosques, 6:599a, 602b–603a
Zavattari, works in International Style, 5:628a
Zāwi ibn Zīrī (10th–11th centuries), 12:745a
Zāwīya, **12:740b–741a**
  architecture of, 6:611b
Zayd ibn ᶜAlī, 7:307a, 11:138a, 12:741b
Zayd ibn Thābit, Koran and, 6:578b
Zaydis, 6:586b, 11:138a-b, 227a, 12:724a, **12:741b–742b**
  Caspian, 12:741b, 742a
  control of Sanᶜa, 10:647a-b
  founded, 12:741b
  vs. Tahirids, Sanᶜa and, 12:724b
  Yemenite, 12:741b, 742a
Zaydūn, Ibn, 1:401a
  Nūnīya, 6:234a
Zaylah, Ibn, *al-Kāfī,* 8:566a
Zayn al-ᶜĀbidīn, 6:371a
Zaytun (Strait of Formosa), Italian trading colony, 7:15a
Zaytūnīya (mosque: Tunis), 11:514a
Zazal. *See* *Zajal*
Zbyněk of Hazmburk, archbishop of Prague
  Gregory XII and, 6:367b
  Hus and, 6:365a, 368a
Zdeslav of Croatia, prince, reign of, 4:2b
Zealand (in Denmark), 12:423a
Zealots, **12:742b–743b**
  Byzantine, anti-Kantakouzenian rising, 2:501a
  Ignatios and, 6:415b
  in modern historiography, 12:743a
  Nikolaos Kavasilas and, 9:135a
  Thessaloniki and, 12:26b
Zebo da Firenze, 5:629a
Zechin. *See* Ducat
Zegris, feuds with Banū Sarrāj, 5:653b
Zeitblom, Bartholomäus, Hans Schüchlein and, 11:79b
Zéjel, 11:459a, 459b, 459a
  villancico and, 12:447b
  see also Zajal
Želivský, Jan, 6:374a, 376b
Zemeke. *See* Johannes Teutonicus
Zemskii sobor. *See* Russia, National Assembly
Zeneggen, irrigation of, 6:559a
Zengī, ᶜImād al-Dīn. *See* Zangī
Zeno (3rd-century B.C. Stoic philosopher)
  De natura, 1:505b
  School of the Persians and, 11:564b
Zeno the Isaurian, Byzantine emperor, 3:10b, **12:743b–744a**
  conflict with Odoacer, 9:289b–290a
  flood control project, 12:576b
  Henotikon, 1:499a, 508b, 2:486a, 8:477b, 12:743b
  marriage of, 6:560b
  Ostrogoths and, 2:93a-b
  palace library and, 7:561a
  suppression of Nestorianism and, 9:106b
Zeno map, 5:399a
Zeno, Marino, 7:376b
Zeno, Pietro, death of, 7:380b
Zenob Glak, 1:510b
  Patmutᶜiwn Tarōnoy and, 9:457a–458b
Zenobius of Amida, bishop, 1:508a
Zenon (Syrian father), 6:416a
Zenzelinus de Cassanis
  Extravagantes communes, 7:417a
  Extravagantes Johannis papae XXII, 7:417a
Zerbolt of Zutphen, Gerard, *Libellus de modo vivendi hominum simul commorantium,* 4:166b
Zero, evolution of, 1:394a, 394b
Zerubbabel, Book of. *See Book of Zerubbabel*
Zeta
  acquired by Stefan Dečanski, 11:474b
  acquired by Stefan Nemanja, 11:473a
  administered by Stefan Uroš IV Dušan, 11:475a
Ziani, Pietro, doge of Venice, 3:570a, 9:330a-b
Ziani, Sebastiano, of Venice, doge, 12:387b
Zibaldone laurenziano. *See* Boccaccio, Giovanni
Zibaldone magliabechiano. *See* Boccaccio, Giovanni
Žiča (monastery: Serbia), 11:174b, 176a, 184b, 473b
Zīj, 1:611b
Zimām, 6:590a
Zinc
  as alloy, 2:383b
  mining of, 8:397b–398a
Zindīq. *See* Manichaeans
Zingion. *See* Azania
Zingis. *See* Azania
Zinj. *See* Zanj
Zink. *See* Cornett
Zintha, Ganjak of Atropatene and, 5:356a
Zion (church: Ateni), 1:632b
Zīq ī šahriyārān, 10:665b
Zīrī ibn Manād, origins of Zirids and, 12:744a
Zirids, 6:415a, **12:744a–745b**
  at Mahdia, 12:745a
  founded, 6:414b
  of Granada, 12:745a
  Hammadids and, 12:744a-b
  Jews under, 7:98b
  origins of, 12:744a
  al-Qayrawān under, 10:233a
  relations with
    Fatimids, 12:744b
    Zanāta Berbers, 12:744b
  Sicily and, 11:262a, 262b
  succession struggles, 12:744a-b
  in Tunisia, 12:744b
Zischägge, 1:532a
Zither, plucked. *See* Psaltery
Ziyād ibn Abī Sufyān, 6:511b
  al-Kufa and, 7:306b
Ziyada, **12:745b**
Ziyādat Allāh I (Aghlabid ruler of Ifrīqiya), Sicily and, 11:261b
Ziyanids
  conflicts with Hafsids, 6:53a, 53b
  Marinid invasions, 8:138a, 139a
Ẓiyyoni, Menahem, Torah commentary, 9:582a
Žižka, Jan, 3:505b, 6:375a, 375b, 376a
  wagon fortress tactic of, 3:206b
Zlatniki, 8:426a
Znamenny, 8:572b, 573b, 575b
  large, 8:573b
  Old Believers and, 8:576a
Zodiac
  in Islamic astronomy, iconology of, 6:407b–408a
  see also Astrology, Islamic
Zoë, empress dowager, Nikolaos I Mystikos and, 9:135b
Zoë the Macedonian, Byzantine empress, **12:745b**
  marriages, 2:491b, 492a
Zohar, 1:346a, 3:2a-b
  Neoplatonism and, 9:100a
Zonaras, John, **12:745b–746a**
  chronicle of, 6:247b
  Epitome historiarum, 12:745b–746a
  Niketas Choniates and, 9:134a
  world chronicle, 2:55b
Zōrnamak, 3:199a
Zoroaster, 12:746a-b
  composer of Gāthās, 5:366a
  Gāthās, 12:747a
  in Manichaeism, 8:85a
  in *Vidēvdād,* 12:412a
Zoroastrianism, 6:188b, 10:600b, 601a, **12:746a–748a**
  abolition of *dew-yasnih* and *nise-mag i dewan,* 10:662b
  in Armenia, 1:476b, 498a, 6:188b, 8:16a, 78b
  Bundahishn, 2:419a
  church hierarchy, 10:668b
    models for, 10:612a
  cleanliness required of adherents, 10:664a
  clerical offices
    baginapati, 8:447a
    hērbadān hērbad, 8:447a
    hudēnān pēshōbāy, 8:447a
    magupati, 8:447a
    mōbad, 8:447a
  cosmography and cosmology, 10:661b–662a

in Dēnkard, 4:148a-b
doctrines of, 12:746b–747a
erosion of, 12:747b
Gāthās and, 5:366a-b
great fires, 11:628a-b
Indian Parsi community and, 10:665b
in Iraq, 6:513a
Islamic sumptuary laws and, 11:508b
Ka^cba of Zoroaster, 7:204a–205a
Kartīr, 7:221b–222b
Middle Persian and, 6:506a
origins of, 12:746b
in Pahlavi literature, 9:326b–327b
persecution of other religions, 12:747b
Rabbinic Judaism and, 7:160a
on salvation of the world, 12:747a-b
in Sasanian Empire, 1:451b, 452a, 10:600b, 12:747b
centralization of Sasanian authority, 10:662b–663a
church-state relationship, 10:668a
clergy as government servants, 10:663b–664a
exclusion of non-Iranians, 10:663a
Sasanian seals and, 11:122a–123a
in *Shāhnāma,* 11:223a-b
Škand-gumānīg Wizār, 11:324a–325a
temple in Bishapur, 2:252a
under the Arsacids, 9:443b–444a
under Islam, 6:501b, 9:498b
Xusrō I and, 12:714a-b
in *Xwadāy nāmag,* 12:716a
Yašts and, 12:721a
yazatas, 10:662b
Zurvanism and, 12:747b
see also Avesta; *Letter of Tansar;* Mazdakites; *Mōbadān mōbad; Vidēvdād*
Zosimus, 10:467b, **12:748a-b**
New History, 12:748a
pagan histories, 6:243a
Zosimus of Panopolis, innovation in alchemy, 1:135b–136a
Zosimus, pope, Pelagius and, 9:486b
Zrvan. *See* Zurvān
Zubayr, al-. *See* Abd Allāh ibn al-Zubayr
Zubayr ibn al-ᶜAwwām, al-, 6:569b
revolt of, 10:242a
Zubayrids, 6:511b
revolt of al-Mukhtār, 8:166a
Zug, Swiss Confederation and, 11:544a
Zuhr, Abū Marwān ibn, 11:84a
Zuhrī, *ḥadīth* collections, 6:47b
Zülpich, Battle of (496), 11:526a
Župan, 11:473a
Zurārids, in Armenia, 1:513a
Zurich, 11:542b–543a
Germany and, 11:528a
Habsburgs and, 11:540a
Holy Roman Empire and, 11:539b
Kyburgs and, 11:539b
Pfahlburger and, 11:544a
siege (1354), 11:544a
Swiss Confederation and, 11:541b, 543b
vs. Swiss Confederation, 11:544b
Waldstätte and, 11:543b
Zähringens and, 11:538b, 539a
Zurichgau, Rudolph of Habsburg and, 11:540a
Zurna, 8:562a
Zurnā. See Surnāy
Zurvān (god), 12:747b, 748b, 749a
Zurvanism, 12:747b, **12:748b–749a**
compared with Mazdakism, 8:237b–238a
fatalism of, 10:665b
Zuzan, mosque, 6:603a
Zvans, 5:419a
Zvenigorod Deesis, 10:541b
Rublev's icon of Christ, 10:588b
Zvonimir, ban (*fl.* 1065), reign of, 4:6a-b
Zwartᶜnocᶜ (church: Armenia), 9:103a, **12:749a–750b**
architecture of, 12:749b–750a
compared with Bana, 2:70a
as model for church of S. Grigor Lusavoričᶜ, 1:292a
reconstruction of, 12:749b (*illus.*)
Zweite Ambraser Büchlein, 8:409a
Zwentebold of Burgundy, seal wax impression of, 11:125a
Zwolle, Brethren of the Common Life at, 2:367a

Contributors

The Dictionary of the Middle Ages *was conceived in 1975. Most of the articles were written by 1981, then edited and revised between 1981 and 1988 during the course of serial publication. The affiliations listed here are generally those of the time of revision. The names of deceased contributors, where known, are marked with a dagger* †.

UMAR F. ABD-ALLĀH
University of Michigan, Ann Arbor
Fasting, Islamic; Friday Prayer

MUHAMMAD ABDUL-RAUF
International Islamic University
Family, Islamic

DOROTHY ABRAHAMSE
California State University, Long Beach
Hagiography, Byzantine; Magic and Folklore, Byzantine

ROBERT W. ACKERMAN†
Stanford University
Ancrene Riwle; Arthurian Literature; Excalibur; Grail, Legend of; Malory, Sir Thomas

MARILYN McCORD ADAMS
University of California, Los Angeles
Universals

WILLIAM Y. ADAMS
University of Kentucky
Nubia

DOROTHY AFRICA
Aidan of Lindisfarne; Armagh; Bansenchas; Clonard (Cluain-Iraird); Martyrology, Irish; O'Sinaich, Cellach; Patrick, St.

HÉLÈNE AHRWEILER
Université de Paris I
Political Theory, Byzantine

KLAUS AICHELE
Brooklyn College, City University of New York
Ludus de Antichristo

MANSOUR J. AJAMI
Princeton University
Imruʾal-Qays; Jarīr; Maʿarrī, Abū 'l-ʿAlāʾ Ahmad al-; Masʿudī, al-; Nadīm, Ibn al-

F. R. P. AKEHURST
University of Minnesota
Gace Brulé; Sirventes; Troubadour, Trouvère

GUSTAVE ALEF
University of Oregon
Boyar; Dmitrii Ivanovich Donskoi; Duma; Ivan III of Muscovy; Muscovy, Rise of; Novgorod; Primary Chronicle, Russian

JAMES W. ALEXANDER
University of Georgia
Becket, Thomas, St.; Wales: Marcher Lords

JUDSON BOYCE ALLEN†
Marquette University
Accessus ad Auctores

MICHAEL ALTSCHUL
Case Western Reserve University
William Marshal

ROBERT AMIET
Facultés Catholiques, Lyon
Lyonese Rite; Masses, Votive

GEORGE K. ANDERSON†
Brown University
Wandering Jew Legend

GORDON A. ANDERSON
University of New England, New South Wales
Ars Antiqua; Ars Subtilior; Clausula

JEFFREY C. ANDERSON
George Washington University
James the Monk

THEODORE M. ANDERSSON
Stanford University
Atlakviða; Atlamál; Bandamanna Saga; Bjarnar Saga Hítdœlakappa; Brynhild; Droplaugarsona Saga; Fóstbrœðra Saga; Gísla Saga Súrssonar; Grípisspá Gunnlaugs Saga Ormstungu; Guðrúnarkviða III; Hamðismál; Heiðarvíga Saga; Helreið Brynhildar; Hœnsa-Þóris Saga; Irregang und Girregar; Lied vom Hürnen Seyfrid, Das; Ljósvetninga Saga; Nibelungenlied; Norse Kings' Sagas; Oddrun Ar Grátr; Reginsmál and Fáfnismál; Reykdœla Saga; Saga; Sigrdrífumál; Sigurd; Sigurðarkviða in Forna; Sigurðarkviða in Meiri; Sigurðarkviða in Skamma; Þiðreks Saga: Vǫlsunga Saga

GREGORY PETER ANDRACHUK
University of Victoria
Rodríguez del Padrón, Juan

CONTRIBUTORS

AVERY ANDREWS
George Washington University
Caffa; Pera-Galata

RHIAN M. ANDREWS
The Queen's University of Belfast
Meilyr Brydydd; Rhys of Deheubarth

MICHAEL ANGOLD
University of Edinburgh
John III Vatatzes; Laskarids; Nicaea, Empire of; Nymphaion; Theodore I Laskaris; Theodore II Laskaris

MARIA PILAR APARICIO-LLOPIS
Fuero

SARAH ARENSON
Man and Sea Society, Tivon, Israel
Ships and Shipbuilding, Red Sea and Persian Gulf

S. G. ARMISTEAD
University of California, Davis
Alfonso XI, Poema de; Spanish Literature: Ballads

GRACE MORGAN ARMSTRONG
Bryn Mawr College
Fables; Proverbs and Sententiae

MARY-JO ARN
English Institute, Groningen
Groote, Geert; Jean de Meun; Kingis Quair, The; Map, Walter

HOWARD I. ARONSON
University of Chicago
Georgian Language

ŞAHAN ARZRUNI
Music, Armenian

YOM TOV ASSIS
Hebrew University of Jerusalem
Abrabanel, Isaac ben Judah; Oath, More Judaico

ANI P. ATAMIAN
Āyās; Cilician Kingdom; Cilician-Roman Church Union; Guy of Lusignan; Hetʿum I; Hetʿum II; Hetʿumids; Lambron; Leo I/II of Armenia; Leo V/VI of Armenia; Lusignans; Ruben I; Rubenids; Sīs; Tarsus

ESIN ATIL
Freer Gallery of Art
Mamluk Art

AZIZ S. ATIYA†
University of Utah
Copts and Coptic Church

CHARLES M. ATKINSON
Ohio State University
Tropes to the Ordinary of the Mass

LORRAINE C. ATTREED
Cade, Jack/Cade's Rebellion

JUAN BAUTISTA AVALLE-ARCE
University of California, Santa Barbara
Fernán González, Poema de

LEVON AVDOYAN
Library of Congress
Patmutʿiwn (Erkrin) Tarōnoy

PETER J. AWN
Columbia University
Iblīs; Mysticism, Islamic

SUSAN M. BABBITT
American Philosophical Society
Catalan Company; Nicopolis; Robert de Clari; Roger de Flor; Villehardouin, Geoffroi de; William of Tyre

JERE L. BACHARACH
University of Washington
ʿAzīz Biʾllāh Nizār Abū Manṣūr, al-; Ikhshidids; Tulunids

BERNARD S. BACHRACH
University of Minnesota
Alamanni; Alani; Alaric; Burgundians; Jews in Europe: Before 900

GERSHON C. BACON
Bar-Ilan University, Ramat-Gan
Jews in Russia

JULIE O. BADIEE
Western Maryland College
Baḥr al-Muḥīṭ; Waq-Waq Islands

ROGER S. BAGNALL
Columbia University
Roman Egypt, Late

TERENCE BAILEY
Talbot College, University of Western Ontario
Ambrosian Chant; Evovae; Franco of Cologne; Gallican Chant; Gradual; Guido of Arezzo; Intonatio; Mediatio; Mode; Neuma; Noeannoe; Processions, Liturgical; Psalm Tones; Tones, Musical

JÁNOS M. BAK
University of British Columbia
Banat; Banus; Buda; Gerard of Csanád, St.; Hungarian Diet; Hungary; Hunyadi, János; Magyars; Stephen I of Hungary, St.; Stephen, Crown of St.; Székesfehérvár

DEIRDRE BAKER
University of Toronto, Centre for Medieval Studies
Altfrid of Münster; Apollonius of Tyana; Avianus

JOHN W. BALDWIN
The Johns Hopkins University
France: 987–1223; Peter the Chanter; Philip II Augustus

REBECCA A. BALTZER
University of Texas at Austin
Florence, Biblioteca Mediceo-Laurenziana, MS Pluteus 29.1; Wolfenbüttel, Helmstedt MS 628

ANASTASIUS C. BANDY
Lydus

PHILIP J. BANKS
Barcelona

FRANK G. BANTA
Indiana University
Berthold von Regensburg; Wernher der Gartenære

JOHN W. BARKER
University of Wisconsin, Madison
Byzantine Empire: History (1204–1453); Constantine XI Palaiologos; Jean Boucicaut; Mistra; Nikolaos Kavasilas; Thessaloniki; Zealots

CONTRIBUTORS

CARL F. BARNES, JR.
Oakland University, Rochester, Michigan
Abiell, Guillermo; Achard or Aichardus; Amiens Cathedral; Antiquarianism and Archaeology; Archaeology of Medieval Monuments; Bargeboard; Bar Tracery; Bernard of Soissons; Brunsberg, H(e)inrich von; Burghausen, Hanns von; Cathedral; Chartres Cathedral; Cluny, Abbey Church; Collar Beam; Erwin, Master; Eudes of Montreuil; Flèche; Fleuron; Flushwork; Formeret; Gallery; Gargoyle Gayrard, Raymond; Gérard of Clairvaux, St.; Gerhard of Cologne; Golden Section; Grotesque; Harding, Stephen, St.; Hézelon of Liège; Hugh of Semur, St.; Jean (Jehan) d'Andeli; Jean de Beauce; Jean (Jehan) de Chelles; Jean des Champs; Krak des Chevaliers; Mathieu d'Arras; Misericord; Moissac, St. Pierre; Molding; Mouchette; Muldenfaltenstil; Mullion; Notre Dame de Paris, Cathedral of; Oriel Window; Orphrey; Pierre de Montreuil; Pierre des Champs; Regnault de Cormont; Rheims Cathedral; Rib; Robert de Coucy; Robert de Luzarches; Rose Window; St. Denis, Abbey Church; St. Sernin, Toulouse; Ste. Chapelle, Paris; Sondergotik; Strasbourg Cathedral; Thomas de Cormont; Tower; Tribune; Triclinium; Vézelay, Church of La Madeleine; Villard de Honnecourt; Wheel of Fortune; Wheel Window; William of Volpiano; Wysbeck, John; Yevele, Henry

M. P. BARNES
University College, London
Draumkvæde

STEPHEN A. BARNEY
University of California, Irvine
Allegory

ROBERT BARRINGER
St. Michael's College, University of Toronto
Confession; Confessor, Royal; Leo III, Pope; Pope; Seven Deadly Sins

CAROLINE M. BARRON
Royal Holloway College, University of London
London

ELIEZER BASHAN
Bar-Ilan University
Exilarch; Nasi

WILLIAM W. BASSETT
University of San Francisco
Consulate of the Sea; Corporation; Exchequer, Court of

MICHAEL L. BATES
American Numismatic Society
Dinar; Dirham; Mints and Money, Islamic; Seals and Sigillography, Islamic

ÜLKÜ Ü. BATES
Hunter College, City University of New York
Bedestan; Kiosk; Otaq; Qaragūz Figures; Qayṣarīya; Rahle; Sarāy; Selāmlik; Ṣerefe

FRANZ H. BÄUML
University of California, Los Angeles
Biterolf und Dietleib; Dukas Horant; Kudrun

RICHARD BEADLE
Cambridge University
Mystery Plays

ROLAND BECHMANN
Castles and Fortifications; Construction: Building Materials

SILVIO A. BEDINI
Smithsonian Institution
Clocks and Reckoning of Time; Compass, Magnetic; Dondi, Giovanni de'; Portolan Chart; Richard of Wallingford; Scientific Instruments; Sylvester II, Pope

PAUL Z. BEDOUKIAN
Mints and Money, Armenian

ROBERT BEDROSIAN
Aristakēs Lastivert^{c}i; Grigor Aknerc^{c}i; Kirakos of Ganjak; Liparit IV Orbēlean; Orbēlean, Step^{c}anos; Sebēos; Shaddādids;

ROBERT BEDROSIAN (*cont.*)
Sparapet; T^{c}ovma Mecop^{c}ec^{c}i; Vardan Arewelc^{c}i; Zak^{c}arids

JOHN BEELER†
University of North Carolina
Cannon; Warfare, Western European

JEANETTE M. A. BEER
Purdue University
Allegory, French; Chronicles, French; Dialect; Eulalie, La Séquence de Ste.; Fet des Romains, Li; French Language; French Literature: Translations; Gesta Francorum et Aliorum Hierosolimitanorum; Guillaume de Lorris; Picard Language; Picard Literature; Provençal Language; Renaut de Beaujeu; Roman de la Rose; Vegetius

CAROLINE J. BEESON
Khwārizmshāhs; Mashhad

A. F. L. BEESTON
St. John's College, Oxford
Arabia, Pre-Islamic; Arabic Language; Ḥadramawt; Hejaz; Ḥīra, al-

F. BEHRENDS
University of North Carolina at Chapel Hill
Fulbert of Chartres

HAIM BEINART
Hebrew University of Jerusalem
Jews in Christian Spain; New Christians

MALACHI BEIT-ARIÉ
The Jewish National and University Library
Manuscripts and Books: Hebrew

HUGO BEKKER
Ohio State University
Albrecht von Johansdorf; Brant, Sebastian; Friedrich von Hausen; Heinrich von Rugge

HANS BEKKER-NIELSEN
Odense Universitet
Árna Saga Biskups; Bishops' Sagas; Dunstanus Saga; Guðmundar Saga Biskups; Guðmundr Arason; Gyðinga Saga; Hungrvaka; Jón Ögmundarson, St.; Jóns Saga

CONTRIBUTORS

HANS BEKKER-NIELSEN (*cont.*)
HELGA; LAURENTIUS SAGA; PÁLS SAGA BISKUPS

LUIS BELTRÁN
Indiana University
MENA, JUAN DE

ISAAC BENABU
Hebrew University of Jerusalem
JUDEO-SPANISH; SEPHARDIM

ADELAIDE BENNETT
Princeton University
AVILA BIBLE, MASTER OF THE; BRAILES, WILLIAM DE

ANNA G. BENNETT
TAPESTRY, ART OF; TAPESTRY, MILLEFLEURS

BETH S. BENNETT
University of Alabama
CASSIODORUS SENATOR, FLAVIUS MAGNUS AURELIUS

ALEXANDRE BENNIGSEN
University of Chicago
CRIMEA, KHANATE OF

JOHN F. BENTON†
California Institute of Technology
ABELARD, PETER; ARNALD OF VILLANOVA; TROTA AND TROTULA

DAVID BERGER
Brooklyn College, City University of New York
GALUT

ROBERT P. BERGMAN
The Walters Art Gallery
LEO OF OSTIA

DAVID SANDLER BERKOWITZ
Brandeis University
FORTESCUE, SIR JOHN

ROSALIND KENT BERLOW
TRADE, REGULATION OF; WINE AND WINEMAKING

ALDO S. BERNARDO
State University of New York at Binghamton
PETRARCH

CAROL MANSON BIER
The Textile Museum, Washington, D.C.
DĪBĀJ; MULḤAM; ZANDANĪJĪ

LIONEL BIER
Brooklyn College, City University of New York
FĀRS; NAQSH-I RUSTAM; PAIKULI; TAQ-I BOSTAN; TAXT-I SULEIMAN

IRENE A. BIERMAN
University of California, Los Angeles
FATIMID ART; IVORY CARVING, ISLAMIC; KHILᶜA; KISWA; ṬIRĀZ

RAMZI J. BIKHAZI
Kuwait National Museum
HAMDANIDS

SOLOMON A. BIRNBAUM
YIDDISH

GHAZI I. BISHEH
Jordan Archaeological Museum
MIḤRAB; MINBAR; RIWĀQ; ZAMZAM

DALE L. BISHOP
Interchurch Center, New York
AVESTA; BUNDAHISHN; GĀTHĀS; KĀRNĀMAG-I ARDEŠĪR-I BĀBAGĀN; VIDĒVDĀD; YAŠTS; ZURVANISM

JANE BISHOP
The Citadel
ANASTASIUS BIBLIOTHECARIUS; ILLYRICUM; NICHOLAS I, POPE

THOMAS N. BISSON
University of California, Berkeley
ARAGON (800–1137); ARAGON, CROWN OF (1137–1479); CATALONIA (800–1137); FRANCE: TO 987; PEACE OF GOD, TRUCE OF GOD; RAMON BERENGUER IV

JONATHAN BLACK
SARUM USE

BRADFORD B. BLAINE
Scripps College
MILLS

FOSTER W. BLAISDELL†
Indiana University
EREX SAGA; ÍVENS SAGA

N. F. BLAKE
University of Sheffield
ARS MORIENDI; CAXTON, WILLIAM; CHRONICLES

ROBERT J. BLANCH
Northeastern University
GAWAIN AND THE GREEN KNIGHT, SIR; PEARL

CURTIS BLAYLOCK
University of Illinois
BASQUES

A. J. BLISS†
University College, Dublin
SIR ORFEO

HERBERT BLOCH
Harvard University
CONSTANTINE THE AFRICAN

THOMAS W. BLOMQUIST
Northern Illinois University
BANKING, EUROPEAN; LOMBARDS

JONATHAN M. BLOOM
Harvard University
AGHLABID ART; AZHAR, AL-; BĀDGĪR; BADR AL-JAMĀLĪ; FUNDUQ; MASHRA BIYA; MOSQUE; MUṢALLA; QAᶜA

JEROME BLUM
Princeton University
SERFS AND SERFDOM: RUSSIA

RENATE BLUMENFELD-KOSINSKI
Columbia University
AUBADE (AUBE); ELEANOR OF AQUITAINE; TROY STORY

ROGER BOASE
University of Fez
COURTLY LOVE

IMRE BOBA
University of Washington
GREAT (OR OLD) MORAVIA; MORAVIA

M.-C. BODDEN
University of British Columbia
ETHELWOLD AND THE BENEDICTINE RULE

PATRICIA J. BOEHNE
Eastern College
TURMEDA, ANSELM

PERE BOHIGAS
JORDI DE S. JORDI; MARCH, AUSIÀS

SÁNDOR BÖKÖNYI
Hungarian Academy of Sciences
ANIMALS, DRAFT; ANIMALS, FOOD; FOWL, DOMESTIC; FOWLING

HELEN BORELAND
Westfield College, University of London
BERCEO, GONZALO DE

JANE CUYLER BORGERHOFF
MAYOR

DIANE BORNSTEIN†
Queens College, City University of New York
ANTIFEMINISM; BETROTHAL; COURTESY BOOKS; COURTLY LOVE; FAMILY, WESTERN EUROPEAN

C. E. BOSWORTH
University of Manchester
ALAMŪT; ALPTIGIN; COMMANDER OF THE FAITHFUL; GAMES, ISLAMIC; GHĀZĀN (KHAN), MAḤMŪD; GHAZNAVIDS; GHURIDS; ISLAMIC ADMINISTRATION; KURDS; SAFFARIDS; SEBÜKTIGIN; SELJUKS OF RUM; ṬĀHIR IBN AL-ḤUSAYN; TAHIRIDS; TRANSOXIANA; YAᶜQŪB IBN LAYTH

LASKARINA BOURAS
LIGHTING DEVICES

CHARLES BOWEN
University of Massachusetts, Harbor Campus
DINDSHENCHAS

CALVIN M. BOWER
University of Notre Dame
AGNUS CHANT; BOETHIUS, ANICIUS MANLIUS SEVERINUS; PARAPHONISTA; PERFECTIO; PROLATIO; PROPRIETAS; QUADRIVIUM; RHYTHM

GERHARD BÖWERING
Yale University
ISLAM, RELIGION

G. W. BOWERSOCK
Institute for Advanced Study, Princeton
CONSISTORIUM

EDMUND A. BOWLES
CHANSONNIER; MINSTRELS; MUSIC IN MEDIEVAL SOCIETY; MUSICAL INSTRUMENTS, EUROPEAN; ORGAN

WILLIAM M. BOWSKY
University of California, Davis
BERNARDINO OF SIENA, ST.; PODESTA; SIENA

MARY BOYCE
DĒNKARD; PAHLAVI LITERATURE; ZOROASTRIANISM

BEVERLY BOYD
University of Kansas
KEMPE, MARGERY

CLEO LELAND BOYD
LINCOLN, RITE OF YORK RITE

MARJORIE NICE BOYER
York College, City University of New York
ROADS AND BRIDGES, WESTERN EUROPEAN; TRAVEL AND TRANSPORT, WESTERN EUROPEAN; VEHICLES, EUROPEAN

JOHN F. BOYLE
University of Toronto, Centre for Medieval Studies
APOLLINARIUS; APOSTOLIC CONSTITUTIONS

LEONARD E. BOYLE
Vatican Library
VACARIUS

DENIS J. M. BRADLEY
Georgetown University
PHILOSOPHY AND THEOLOGY, WESTERN EUROPEAN: TO MID TWELFTH CENTURY

KATHLEEN J. BRAHNEY
Michigan Technological University
THIBAUT DE CHAMPAGNE

CHARLES M. BRAND
Bryn Mawr College
ALEXIOS I KOMNENOS; ANDRONIKOS I KOMNENOS; ANGELOS; BYZANTINE EMPIRE: HISTORY (1025–1204); DOUKAS; JOHN II KOMNENOS; JOHN KINNAMOS; KOMNENOI; LATIN EMPIRE OF CONSTANTINOPLE; MANUEL I KOMNENOS

PAUL A. BRAND
EXCHEQUER OF THE JEWS

GERARD J. BRAULT
Pennsylvania State University
HUNTING AND FOWLING, WESTERN EUROPEAN; ROLAND, SONG OF

DENIS G. BREARLEY
University of Ottawa
SEDULIUS SCOTTUS

YURI BREGEL
Indiana University
BUKHARA; TIMURIDS; ULUGH BEG

MICHAEL BRETT
University of London, School of African and Oriental Studies
AGHLABIDS; ALMOHADS; BERBERS; CAVALRY, ISLAMIC; FĒS; HAFSIDS; IFRĪQIYA; MAGHRIB, AL-; MARINIDS; MARRAKECH; QAYRAWĀN, AL-; WARFARE, ISLAMIC; ZIRIDS

MARIANNE G. BRISCOE
Newberry Library, Chicago
ARS PRAEDICANDI

SEBASTIAN P. BROCK
The Oriental Institute, Oxford
SYRIAN CHRISTIANITY

CYNTHIA J. BROWN
University of California, Santa Barbara
CHARTIER, ALAIN; COMPLAINTE; DÉBAT; JEAN, DUKE OF BERRY; RHÉTORIQUEURS

JEROME V. BROWN
University of Windsor
DUNS SCOTUS, JOHN; HENRY OF GHENT

KATHARINE REYNOLDS BROWN
Metropolitan Museum of Art, New York
GEMS AND JEWELRY

JEROME V. BROWN
University of Windsor
DUNS SCOTUS, JOHN

S. KENT BROWN
Brigham Young University
AUTOCEPHALOS

CONTRIBUTORS

STEPHEN F. BROWN
Boston College
NEOPLATONISM; PHILOSOPHY AND THEOLOGY, WESTERN EUROPEAN: LATE MEDIEVAL; THEOLOGY, SCHOOLS OF

ROBERT BROWNING
BELISARIOS; BYZANTINE LITERATURE; ENCYCLOPEDIAS AND DICTIONARIES, BYZANTINE; GREEK LANGUAGE, BYZANTINE; JOHN VIII XIPHILINOS, PATRIARCH; JUSTINIAN I; LITERACY, BYZANTINE; RHETORIC: BYZANTINE; SCHOLARSHIP, BYZANTINE CLASSICAL; THEODORA I, EMPRESS; TRANSLATION AND TRANSLATORS, BYZANTINE; UNIVERSITIES, BYZANTINE

KEVIN BROWNLEE
Dartmouth College
PHILIPPE DE NOVARE; ROBERT D'ARBRISSEL

LESLIE BRUBAKER
Wheaton College, Norton, Massachusetts
ABSIDIOLE; AEDICULA; AGAPE; AGNUS DEI; ALBURANUS; ALÉAUME; ALL'ANTICA; ALPHA AND OMEGA; ALTAR, PORTABLE; ALTERNATION (OR ALTERNATING SUPPORTS); AMBO; AMBULATORY; AMPULLA; ANASTASIS; ANCIENT OF DAYS; ANDACHTSBILD; ANDREA DA FIRENZE; ANGEL; ANGILBERT OF MILAN; ANICONISM; ANIMAL STYLE; ANNO; ANNUNCIATION; ANTEPENDIUM; ANTHEMIOS OF TRALLES; APOCALYPSE, ILLUSTRATION OF; APSE; APSE ECHELON; ARABESQUE; ARCH; ARCHANGEL; ARCHIVOLT; ARCOSOLIUM; ARK OF THE COVENANT; ARMA CHRISTI; ARTS, SEVEN LIBERAL; ASCENSION; ASSUMPTION OF THE VIRGIN; ATELIER; ATHOS, MOUNT, MONUMENTS OF; ATRIUM; BALDACHIN; BALL-FLOWER; BAPTISM OF CHRIST; BAS-DE-PAGE; BAPTISTERY; BASILICA; BAY SYSTEM; BAYEUX TAPESTRY; BEATUS MANUSCRIPTS; BEMA; BENEDICTIONAL; BENNO OF OSNABRÜCK; BERKELEY, WILLIAM; BERNARD OF SANTIAGO; BIDUINO; BLACHERNITISSA; BOSS; BOTTEGA; BRATTISHING; BREVIARY OF ALARIC; BROUN, ROBERT; BUTTRESS; CAMPANILE; CANON TABLE; CAPITAL; CARPET PAGE; CARVER,

LESLIE BRUBAKER (*cont.*)
WILLIAM (BROMFLET); CASTRUM; CATACOMBS; CATHEDRA; CENTERING; CHAIRETE; CHALICE; CHANCEL; CHAPEL; CHERUB; CHEVET; CHOIR; CHRISMON; CHRISTOGRAM; CHURCH, TYPES OF; CIBORIUM; CLERESTORY; CLIPEUS (CLIPEATUS); CLOISTER; CODEX AUREUS; COLOBIUM (COLOBION); COLUMN FIGURE; CONSTANTINE (KOSTANDIN) THE ARMENIAN; COOK (COKE), HUMPHREY; CORBEL; CORBEL TABLE; COSMATI WORK; CROCKET; CROSS, FORMS OF; CROSS, PROCESSIONAL; CROSSING; CROWN, MURAL; CROZIER; CRUCIFIXION; CRYPT; CUBICULUM; CUPOLA; CUSP; DALMATIC; DEMETRIOS PRESBYTER; DEPOSITION FROM THE CROSS; DIACONICON; DIAPER PATTERN; DIONYSIOS OF FOURNA; DIONYSIOS THE GREEK; DIPTYCH; DIPTYCH, CONSULAR; DOME; DOME OF HEAVEN; DOME OF THE ROCK; DOMUS ECCLESIAE; DONOR PORTRAIT; DURANDUS; DURROW, BOOK OF; EBO OF RHEIMS; ÉCHOPPE; EGBERT OF TRIER; ELEOUSA; ELEVATION OF THE HOLY CROSS; ÉMAIL BRUN; EMMANUEL, CHRIST; ENAMEL, BASSE-TAILLE; ENAMEL, CHAMPLEVÉ; ENAMEL, CLOISONNÉ; ENAMEL, LIMOGES; ENAMEL, MILLEFIORI; ENAMEL, VERMICULÉ; ENCAUSTIC; ENCOLPIUM; ENTRY INTO JERUSALEM; EPHREM (EPHRAIM); EPIPHANY IN ART; EUTYCHIOS; EVANGELIARY; EVANGELIST SYMBOLS; EX VOTO; EXEDRA; EXONARTHEX; EXULTET ROLL; FALCHION; FIBULA; FINIAL; FLABELLUM; FOLIO; FOUNTAIN OF LIFE; FRANCO-SAXON SCHOOL; FRESCO BUONO; FRESCO SECCO; GEORGE KALLIERGIS; GISLEBERTUS; GLOBUS CRUCIGER; GLYKOPHILOUSA; GOOD SHEPHERD; GOSPELBOOK; GOTHIC, DECORATED; GOTHIC, FLAMBOYANT; GOTHIC, PERPENDICULAR; GOTHIC, RAYONNANT; GRISAILLE; HAMMER BEAM; HANGING BOWL; HEAVENLY JERUSALEM; HETOIMASIA; HEXAEMERON; HIGH CROSSES, CELTIC; HODEGETRIA; HOSIOS LUKAS; HYPOGEUM; ICONODULE; ICONOGRAPHY; IMAGO PIETATIS; INTERLACE; INTRADOS; ISIDOROS OF MILETOS; KASTORIA; KATHOLIKON; KELLS, BOOK OF; LACERTINE; LACTATIO; LINDISFARNE GOSPELS;

LESLIE BRUBAKER (*cont.*)
LIPSANOTHECA; LOCULUS; MACEDONIAN RENAISSANCE; MARTYRIUM; MENOLOGION; MICHAEL ASTRAPAS; MISSAL; OCTATEUCH; OPUS ANGLICANUM; ORANT; PALA D'ORO; PALIMPSEST; PALMETTE; PAROUSIA; PENDENTIVE; PENTATEUCH; POLYPTYCH; PREPENDULIA; PROSKYNESIS; PYXIS; RAVENNA; RELIQUARY; REREDOS; SACRAMENTARY, ILLUMINATION OF; SCREEN, CHANCEL; SCRINIUM; SCRIPTORIUM; SCROLL, INHABITED; SERAPH; STIKARION; SYNAXARY; TABULA ANSATA; TESSERA; THEODORE; TRIBELON; TRIPTYCH; TRULLA; VELLUM; VISITATION; VOLTO SANTO; WESTWORK; WOLVINUS

GENE A. BRUCKER
University of California, Berkeley
ALBERTI, LEON BATTISTA; FLORENCE

JAMES A. BRUNDAGE
University of Wisconsin, Milwaukee
CASUISTRY; CRUSADE PROPAGANDA; TITHES; USURY

LANCE W. BRUNNER
University of Kentucky
FARCING; ITE CHANT; PRECENTOR; RESPONSORY; SANCTUS; SEQUENCE (PROSA)

ANTHONY A. M. BRYER
University of Birmingham, Centre for Byzantine Studies
ALEXIOS I OF TREBIZOND; TREBIZOND, EMPIRE OF

FRANÇOIS BUCHER
Florida State University
PARLER FAMILY

BONNIE BUETTNER
Cornell University
ATHIS UND PROPHILIAS; GRAF RUDOLF

RICHARD W. BULLIET
Columbia University, Middle East Institute
ABODE OF ISLAM—ABODE OF WAR; ᶜIMĀD AL-DAWLA; MUᶜĀWIYA; MUḤTASIB; MUQAFFAᶜ, ᶜABD ALLĀH IBN AL-; MUQTADIR, AL-; MUSTANṢIR, AL-; MUSTAᶜṢIM, AL-; MUᶜTAṢIM, AL-; MUTAWAKKIL, AL-;

RICHARD W. BULLIET (*cont.*)
NISHAPUR; ROADS IN THE ISLAMIC WORLD; TRAVEL AND TRANSPORT, ISLAMIC; VEHICLES, ISLAMIC; VIZIER

VINCENT BURANELLI
LYONS; MANṢŪR, IBN ABĪ ᶜĀMIR AL-; MARSEILLES; MIRROR OF JUSTICES

ROBERT W. BURCHFIELD
Oxford English Dictionaries
ORMULUM

GLYN S. BURGESS
University of Liverpool
ESPURGATOIRE ST. PATRICE; FABLES, FRENCH; MARIE DE CHAMPAGNE; ROMULUS

JAMES F. BURKE
University of Toronto
HISPANO-ARABIC LANGUAGE AND LITERATURE; RUIZ, JUAN; SPANISH LITERATURE: ROMANCES

CHARLES S. F. BURNETT
Warburg Institute, University of London
PLATO OF TIVOLI; TRANSLATION AND TRANSLATORS, WESTERN EUROPEAN

ROBERT I. BURNS, S.J.
University of California, Los Angeles
SPAIN, CHRISTIAN-MUSLIM RELATIONS; SPAIN, MUSLIM KINGDOMS OF; VALENCIA

DAVID BURR
Virginia Polytechnic Institute and State University
JOACHIM OF FIORE; PETER JOHN OLIVI; RICHARDUS DE MEDIAVILLA

ALLEN CABANISS
University of Mississippi
AGOBARD; FLORUS OF LYONS; THEGANUS

ROBERT G. CALKINS
Cornell University
BATAILLE, NICHOLAS; BIBLE MORALISÉE; BIBLIA PAUPERUM; BONDOL, JEAN; BOUCICAUT MASTER; BOURDICHON, JEAN; BROEDERLAM, MELCHIOR; CATHERINE OF CLEVES, MASTER OF; COENE, JAQUES; COLOMBE, JEAN; COLOMBE, MICHEL; DINANDERIE; DROLLERY; FRANKE, MEISTER; GOTHIC ART:

ROBERT G. CALKINS (*cont.*)
PAINTING AND MANUSCRIPT ILLUMINATION; GOTHIC, INTERNATIONAL STYLE; JACQUEMART DE HESDIN; LIMBOURG BROTHERS; MALOUEL, JEAN; PLEURANT; TRÈS RICHES HEURES

DANIEL CALLAM
St. Thomas More College, University of Saskatchewan
CELIBACY; FASTING, CHRISTIAN; MARTYRDOM, CHRISTIAN; PARADISE, WESTERN CONCEPT OF; PURGATORY, WESTERN CONCEPT OF; TRANSLATION OF BISHOPS; TRANSLATION OF SAINTS

ANGUS CAMERON†
University of Toronto, Centre for Medieval Studies
ANGLO-SAXON LITERATURE

AVERIL CAMERON
King's College, University of London
AGATHIAS; HISTORIOGRAPHY, BYZANTINE; JOHN OF EPHESUS; MALALAS, JOHN; PASCHALE CHRONICON; PROCOPIUS; THEOPHYLAKTOS SIMOKATTES; ZOSIMUS

ERIC G. CARLSON
State University of New York at Purchase
ROMANESQUE ARCHITECTURE

ANNEMARIE WEYL CARR
Southern Methodist University
COSTUME BYZANTINE

DEREK C. CARR
University of British Columbia
VILLENA, ENRIQUE DE

EAMON R. CARROLL
Loyola University, Chicago, Illinois
VIRGIN MARY IN THEOLOGY AND POPULAR DEVOTION

JOHN CARSWELL
University of Chicago
GOLDEN HORN WARE; SAᶜD

JOHN CARTWRIGHT
University of Cape Town
HAY, SIR GILBERT

ANTHONY K. CASSELL
University of Illinois
BOCCACCIO, GIOVANNI

VINCENT H. CASSIDY
University of Akron
GEOGRAPHY AND CARTOGRAPHY, WESTERN EUROPEAN

JAMES E. CATHEY
University of Massachusetts, Amherst
BERSERKS; FÁFNIR; FIMBUL WINTER; HEL; NORNS; RÁN; SKAÐI; SURTR; ULLR

MADELINE H. CAVINESS
Tufts University
GLASS, STAINED; HEMMEL, PETER

A. C. CAWLEY
University of Leeds
EVERYMAN; SECOND SHEPHERDS' PLAY; TOWNELEY PLAYS

FRED A. CAZEL, JR.
University of Connecticut
TAXATION, ENGLISH; WALTER, HUBERT

HENRY CHADWICK
Magdalene College, Cambridge
JOHN CHRYSOSTOM, ST.; PRISCILLIAN

GRETEL CHAPMAN
GODEFROID OF HUY; GOZBERTUS; MOSAN ART; NICHOLAS OF VERDUN; RAINER OF HUY; ROGER OF HELMARSHAUSEN

PETER CHARANIS†
Rutgers University
BYZANTINE EMPIRE: ECONOMIC LIFE AND SOCIAL STRUCTURE; MONASTICISM, BYZANTINE; MONEMVASIA

ROBERT J. CHARLESTON
GLASS, WESTERN EUROPEAN

YVES CHARTIER
University of Ottawa
HERMANN VON REICHENAU; HUCBALD OF ST. AMMAND; MUSICAL TREATISES; REGINO OF PRÜM; REMIGIUS OF AUXERRE; SOLESMES; WILLIAM OF HIRSAU

CONTRIBUTORS

COLIN CHASE†
University of Toronto, Centre for Medieval Studies
ACROSTICS—WORDPLAY; ALFRED THE GREAT; ALFRED THE GREAT AND TRANSLATIONS; ANGLO-LATIN POETRY; BEOWULF; CAROLINGIAN LATIN POETRY; FRITHEGOD; MODOIN; PAUL THE DEACON

CHARLES D. CHAVEL
NAḤMANIDES, MOSES

ROBERT CHAZAN
Queens College, City University of New York
ANTI-SEMITISM; ASHKENAZ; EXPULSION OF JEWS; HISTORIOGRAPHY, JEWISH

FREDRIC L. CHEYETTE
Amherst College
ALBIGENSIANS; BASTIDE; BEAUMANOIR, PHILIPPE DE; CATHARS; CHÂTELET; ÉTABLISSEMENTS DE ST. LOUIS; INQUEST, CANONICAL AND FRENCH; LIVRES DE JOSTICE ET DE PLET, LI; SIMON DE MONTFORT; TOULOUSE; VILLAGES: SETTLEMENT

MARJORIE CHIBNALL
Cambridge University
ORDERICUS VITALIS

STANLEY CHODOROW
University of California, San Diego
DECRETALS; DECRETISTS; DECRETUM; LAW, CANNON: AFTER GRATIAN; TANCRED (CANONIST)

V. CHRISTIDES
NAVIES, ISLAMIC

MASSIMO CIAVOLELLA
Carleton University, Ottawa
CAVALCANTI, GUIDO; CECCO ANGIOLIERI; CINO DA PISTOIA; GUINIZZELLI, GUIDO; IACOPO (GIACOMO) DA LENTINI; ITALIAN LITERATURE: DRAMA

MARLENE CIKLAMINI
Rutgers University, New Brunswick
SNORRI STURLUSON; VALLA-LJÓTS SAGA

WANDA CIŻEWSKI
Marquette University
ADAM OF THE LITTLE BRIDGE; BIBLICAL INTERPRETATION; CLEMENS

WANDA CIŻEWSKI (*cont.*)
SCOTUS; COSMAS OF PRAGUE; WILLIAM OF CONCHES; WILLIAM OF MOERBEKE

MARSHALL CLAGETT
Institute for Advanced Study, Princeton
ARCHIMEDES IN THE MIDDLE AGES

DOROTHY CLOTELLE CLARKE
COPLA; DECIR; SPANISH LITERATURE: VERSIFICATION AND PROSODY

JEROME W. CLINTON
Princeton University
ḤĀFIẒ (SHAMS AL-DĪN MUḤAMMAD); RHETORIC: PERSIAN; RŪMĪ (JALĀL AL-DĪN); SHĪRĀZ; TABRĪZ; ᶜUMAR KHAYYĀM

CAROL J. CLOVER
University of California, Berkeley
DARRAÐARLJÓÐ; FAMILY SAGAS, ICELANDIC; HÁRBARÐSLJÓÐ; LAXDŒLA SAGA; LOKASENNA; NJÁLS SAGA; NORSE FLYTING

FRANK M. CLOVER
University of Wisconsin, Madison
ROMAN EMPIRE, LATE

ALAN B. COBBAN
University of Liverpool
CAMBRIDGE, UNIVERSITY OF

MARK R. COHEN
Princeton University
CAIRO GENIZAH; JEWISH COMMUNAL SELF-GOVERNMENT: ISLAMIC WORLD; JEWS IN EGYPT; NADĪM, IBN AL-; NAGID; PEOPLE OF THE BOOK

SIDNEY L. COHEN
Louisiana State University
BIRKA; BRACTEATES; GOTLAND; HEDEBY; OSEBERG FIND; SCANDINAVIA: BEFORE 800; SUTTON HOO

ROSEMARY N. COMBRIDGE
Queen Mary College, University of London
ULRICH VON ZAZIKHOVEN

CHARLES W. CONNELL
University of West Virginia
PROPAGANDA

THOMAS H. CONNOLLY
University of Pennsylvania
OLD ROMAN CHANT

LAWRENCE I. CONRAD
The Wellcome Institute for the History of Medicine
BEIRUT; CALIPHATE; DĪNAWARĪ, ABŪ ḤANĪFA AḤMAD IBN DĀWŪD AL-; FARAZDAQ, AL-; ḤAMĀ; ḤIMṢ; IRAQ; JĀḤIẒ, AL-; KUFA, AL-; MARJ DĀBIQ; MARJ RĀHIṬ; MARWĀN I IBN AL-ḤAKAM; MARWĀN II IBN MUḤAMMAD; MARWĀN, ᶜABD AL-MALIK IBN; NAJD; PLAGUES IN THE ISLAMIC WORLD; QURAYSH; SUYŪṬĪ, AL-; UMAYYADS; WALĪD I IBN ᶜABD AL-MALIK, AL-; WĀQIDĪ, ABU ᶜABD ALLĀH MUḤAMMAD IBN ᶜUMAR AL-; WĀSIṬ; YAᶜQŪBĪ, AL-; YARMUK; YAZĪD I IBN MUᶜĀWIYA

PATRICIA L. CONROY
University of Washington
FÆREYINGA SAGA; FAROESE BALLADS; HOLGER DANSKE

DEMETRIOS J. CONSTANTELOS
Stockton State University
HOSPITALS AND POOR RELIEF, BYZANTINE; MEDICINE, BYZANTINE; ORPHANOTROPHOS; PATRIARCH

JOHN J. CONTRENI
Purdue University
GREGORY OF TOURS, ST.; HAIMO OF AUXERRE; JOHN SCOTTUS ERIUGENA; LUPUS OF FERRIÈRES; PETER OF PISA; PRISCIAN; SCHOOLS, CATHEDRAL; SCHOOLS, PALACE; SMARAGDUS OF ST. MIHIEL; THEODULF OF ORLÉANS; WALAFRID STRABO

ROBERT COOK
Newcomb College
STRENGLEIKAR

DANIEL COQUILLETTE
Boston University
EQUITY

ROBIN CORMACK
Courtauld Institute
BYZANTINE ART

RAYMOND J. CORMIER
Wilson College
ENÉAS, ROMAN D'

ART COSGROVE
University College, Dublin
DUBLIN

MADELEINE PELNER COSMAN
City College of New York
COOKERY, EUROPEAN; COSTUME, WESTERN EUROPEAN; FEASTS AND FESTIVALS, EUROPEAN; HERBS; PHARMACOPEIA

ELIO COSTA
York University, Ontario
LATINI, BRUNETTO

NOËL COULET
Université de Provence
INNS AND TAVERNS

NOEL COULSON
University of London, School of African and Oriental Studies
BLOOD MONEY, ISLAMIC LAW

WILLIAM J. COURTENAY
University of Wisconsin, Madison
ACCIDENT; ACTUALISM; BIEL, GABRIEL; NOMINALISM; OCKHAM, WILLIAM OF; ROSCELINUS; TERMINISM

EDWARD J. COWAN
University of Guelph, Ontario
DURHAM, TREATIES OF; KENNETH I MAC ALPIN; PARLIAMENT, SCOTTISH; ROBERT II OF SCOTLAND

H. E. J. COWDREY
St. Edmund Hall, Oxford
KING'S EVIL

EUGENE L. COX
Wellesley College
BURGUNDY, COUNTY OF; BURGUNDY, DUCHY OF; DAUPHINÉ; PROVENCE; SAVOY, COUNTY OF

JOSÉ LUIS COY
University of Connecticut
LÓPEZ DE AYALA

F. EDWARD CRANZ
Connecticut College
CLASSICAL LITERARY STUDIES

WILLIAM CRAWFORD
University of Toronto, Centre for Medieval Studies
AUDRADUS MODICUS; AUSPICIUS OF TOUL; AUXILIUS; GESTA APOLLONII

GLYNNIS M. CROPP
Massey University, New Zealand
FOLQUET DE MARSEILLES; JEU PARTI; PARTIMEN; TORNADA; VIDAS

BERNARD CULLEN
The Queen's University of Belfast
GODFREY OF FONTAINES; HERESIES, WESTERN EUROPEAN; HERESY; HISTORIOGRAPHY, IRISH; MALACHY, ST.; MARSILIUS OF PADUA; MENDICANT ORDERS; PELAGIUS

SLOBODAN ĆURČIĆ
Princeton University
KONÀK; SERBIAN ART AND ARCHITECTURE; VITA OF KOTOR

MICHAEL CURSCHMANN
Princeton University
MIDDLE HIGH GERMAN LITERATURE

ANTHONY CUTLER
Pennsylvania State University
BYZANTINE MINOR ARTS

GEORGE P. CUTTINO
Emory University
AQUITAINE; BORDEAUX

GILBERT DAGRON
CONSTANTINOPLE

JOSEPH DAN
Hebrew University of Jerusalem
APOCALYPTIC LITERATURE AND MOVEMENT, JEWISH; PHILOSOPHY AND THEOLOGY, JEWISH: IN NORTHERN EUROPE

ABRAHAM DAVID
Hebrew University of Jerusalem
BENJAMIN OF TUDELA

WENDY DAVIES
University College, London
ST. DAVID'S

MICHAEL T. DAVIS
Mount Holyoke College
GUY OF DAMMARTIN; JEAN D'ORBAIS; JEAN DE RAVI; KUENE, KONRAD; LABARUM; LANGLOIS, JEAN; LANX; LAPIDARIUM; LAST SUPPER; LIBERGIER, HUGUES; LOCUS SANCTUS; LOUP, JEAN; MANDORLA; MAPPA MUNDI; PALLIUM; PALUDAMENTUM; PASSION CYCLE; PATEN; PETER URSEOLUS, ST.; PETER VON PRACHTATITZ; PILGRIM'S GUIDE;

MICHAEL T. DAVIS (*cont.*)
RESURRECTION CYCLE; SOUFFLET; TRADITIO CLAVIUM; TRADITIO LEGIS; VERNICLE; VOTIVE CROWN

NORMAN DAVIS
Merton College, Oxford
PASTON LETTERS, THE

JAMES DOYNE DAWSON
Boston University
PRIMITIVE CHURCH, CONCEPT OF

FREDERICK A. DE ARMAS
Louisiana State University
SPANISH LITERATURE: SENTIMENTAL ROMANCES

EDMUND DE CHASCA
CID, HISTORY AND LEGEND OF

FRANCES L. DECKER
FLECK, KONRAD; FLORIS; HEINRICH VON NEUSTADT

ALICIA DE COLOMBÍ-MONGUIÓ
State University of New York at Albany
RAZÓN DE AMOR

GYULA DÉCSY
Indiana University
HUNGARIAN LANGUAGE

HELLE DEGNBOL
FLÓRES SAGA OK BLANKIFLÚR; JÓMSVÍKINGA SAGA

LUKE DEMAITRE
Pace University
INSANITY, TREATMENT OF; MEDICINE, SCHOOLS OF

PETER F. DEMBOWSKI
University of Chicago
AMI ET AMILE; ASSONANCE; BIOGRAPHY, SECULAR; FROISSART, JEHAN; HAGIOGRAPHY, FRENCH; HISTORIA REGUM FRANCORUM; LAISSE; LAI, LAY; MARIE DE FRANCE; PHILIPPE MOUSKET; ST. PATRICK'S PURGATORY

GEORGE T. DENNIS
Catholic University of America
BALDWIN I OF THE LATIN EMPIRE; LATIN STATES IN GREECE

CONTRIBUTORS

DON DENNY
University of Maryland
Charonton (Quarton), Enguerrand; Froment, Nicolas; Moulins, Master of

WALTER B. DENNY
University of Maryland
Caftan; Kilim; Qibla; Rugs and Carpets

LUCY DER MANUELIAN
Ałt^{c}amar; Ani, Monuments of; Armenian Art; Aštarak (Ashtarak); Ereroyk^{c}; Gawit^{c}; Gayianē, Church of; Gelard; Glajor; Gošavank^{c}; Hałarcin; Hałbat; Hoṙomos; Hṙip^{c}imē, Church of St.; Koṙikos; Mastara; Mren, Church of; Noravank^{c} at Amału; Ōjun; Ptłni; Sanahin; Sargis Picak; Skewṙa; T^{c}alin; Tat^{c}ew; Tekor; Tigran Honenc^{c}; T^{c}oros Roslin; T^{c}oros Tarōnec^{c}i; Trdat; Vahka Castle; Xač^{c}k^{c}ar; Zwart^{c}noc^{c}

THÉOPHILE DESBONNETS, O.F.M.
Franciscan Rite

ROBERT DESHMAN
University of Toronto
Anglo-Saxon Art

JEAN DESHUSSES, O.S.B.
Abbaye d'Hautecombe, Saint Pierre de Curtille
Benedict of Aniane

HORACE W. DEWEY
University of Michigan
Agriculture and Nutrition (Slavic); Slavic Languages and Literatures

ALAN DEYERMOND
Westfield College, University of London
Mocedades de Rodrigo; Spanish Literature; Spanish Literature: Translations

JAMES DICKIE
Dervish; Jinn; Rauḍa

WILLIAM J. DIEBOLD
Nomen Sacrum; Pericopes; Prie-Dieu; Rohan Master; St. Philibert, Tournus

WACHTANG DJOBADZE
California State University, Los Angeles
Alaverdi; Atenis Sioni; Bagrat's Cathedral; Bana; Bek^{c}a Opizari; Betania; Bitshvinta (Pitsunda); Bolnisi Seon; Dawid-Garedja; Djvari; Gelat^{c}i; Georgian Art and Architecture; Ikalto; Išḥani; Mc^{c}χet^{c}a; Meteḥi; Nikorc^{c}minda; Oški; Sveti Cxoveli; Tsromi; Urbnisi; Wardzia; Xaχuli

MARIANNE DJUTH
Ripon College
Faustus of Riez

JERRILYNN D. DODDS
Columbia University
Asturian Art; First Romanesque; Hispano-Mauresque Art; Mozarabic Art; Mudéjar Art; Plateresque Style; Santiago de Compostela; Visigothic Art

CHARLES DOHERTY
University College, Dublin
Áedán Mac Gabráin; Ulster

DIANE MARIE DOLAN
Fleury Playbook

MICHAEL W. DOLS
California State University, Hayward
Alchemy, Islamic; Egypt, Islamic; Famine in the Islamic World; Herbs, Middle Eastern; Hospitals and Poor Relief, Islamic

CHARLES DONAHUE, JR.
Harvard University
Law, Civil—Corpus Juris, Revival and Spread

E. TALBOT DONALDSON†
Indiana University
Chaucer, Geoffrey; Langland, William

FRED M. DONNER
University of Chicago
Al-^{c}Abbās ibn ^{c}Abd al-Muttalib ibn Hāshim; ^{c}Abd al-Muttalib; ^{c}Abd Allā ibn al-Zubayr; Abū Bakr; Abū Sufyān; Abū Tālib; ^{c}Ā$^{\supset}$isha; ^{c}Amr ibn al-^{c}Āṣ; Badr, Battle of; Ḥusayn ibn ^{c}Alī, al-; Islam, Conquests of; Khālid ibn al-Walīd; Muezzin

JOHN J. DONOHUE
Université Saint Joseph
Dayr

PENELOPE B. R. DOOB
York University, Toronto
Hoccleve (Occleve), Thomas

ANN DOOLEY
St. Michael's College, University of Toronto
Maelgwn; Munster; Ó Brolcháin, Maol Íosa; Ó Dálaigh, Donnchadh Mór; Ó Dálaigh, Gofraidh Fionn; Ó Dálaigh, Muiredach Albanach; Táin Bó Cuáilnge

AARON DOTAN
Tel-Aviv University
Masoretes

JOHN E. DOTSON
Southern Illinois University at Carbondale
Trade, Western European

LEROY DRESBECK
Western Washington University
Heating

KATHERINE FISCHER DREW
Rice University
Barbarians, Invasions of; Law, German: Early Germanic Codes; Odoacer; Ostrogoths; Theodoric the Ostrogoth; Vandals; Visigoths

MARTHA WESTCOTT DRIVER
Gloss; Pynson, Richard

DIANE L. DROSTE
University of Toronto, Centre for Medieval Studies
Ligature; Mass Cycles, Plainsong; Monophony; Musical Notation: Alphabetic, Daseian, Hufnagel; Plica

EDWARD DUDLEY
State University of New York, Buffalo
Flores, Juan de

LAWRENCE G. DUGGAN
University of Delaware
Representative Assemblies, German

CONTRIBUTORS

A. A. M. DUNCAN
University of Glasgow
Clans, Scottish; Donald III (Donaldbane); Duncan I of Scotland; Edinburgh; Macbeth; Malcolm I of Alba; Malcolm II, III, IV of Scotland; Robert I of Scotland; St. Andrews

WILLIAM HUSE DUNHAM, JR.†
Parliament, English

CHARLES W. DUNN
Harvard University
Middle English Literature: Prosody and Versification

PETER N. DUNN
Wesleyan University
Manuel, Don Juan

WILLIAM DUNPHY
St. Michael's College, University of Toronto
Philosophy and Theology, Western European: Thirteenth-Century Crisis; Siger of Brabant

MANUEL DURAN
Yale University
Misa de Amor, La; Santillana, Marqués de

FRANCIS A. DUTRA
University of California, Santa Barbara
Portugal

STEVEN N. DWORKIN
University of Michigan
Portuguese Language

RICHARD A. DWYER
Florida International University
Ovid in the Middle Ages

WILLIAM EAMON
New Mexico State University
Technology, Treatises on

LAWRENCE M. EARP
University of Wisconsin, Madison
Descort; Isorhythm; Leoninus; Petrus de Cruce; Vitry, Philippe de

BRUCE STANSFIELD EASTWOOD
University of Kentucky
Martianus Capella

PATRICIA J. EBERLE
University of Toronto
Gower, John; Mirror of Princes

PETER W. EDBURY
University College, Cardiff
Assizes of Jerusalem

ANDREW S. EHRENKREUTZ
University of Michigan
Ayyubids; Crusades and Crusader States: Near East; Ḥiṭṭīn; Postal and Intelligence Services, Islamic; Saladin

BJARNI EINARSSON
Handritastofnun Árna Magnússonar
Hallfreðar Saga

E. ROZANNE ELDER
Western Michigan University
Bernard of Clairvaux, St.

STEPHEN R. ELL
University of Iowa
Barbers, Barber-Surgeons; Bedlam; Biology; Leprosy

STEVEN G. ELLIS
University College of Galway
Parliament, Irish

MENACHEM ELON
Supreme Court of Israel
Law, Jewish

JOHN A. EMERSON
University of California, Berkeley
Gregorian Chant

ANNE WHARTON EPSTEIN
Duke University
Cappadocia

MARCIA J. EPSTEIN
University of Calgary
Ballade; Ballata; Caccia; Flexa; Giraut de Bornelh; Jaufré Rudel; Lai, Lay; Madrigal; Marcabru; Peire Vidal; Play of Daniel; Play of Herod; Quodlibet; Rondeau; Rondellus; Rota; Rotrouenge; Tenso; Vers; Virelai

STEVEN EPSTEIN
University of Colorado
Bruni, Leonardo; Guild and Métiers; Italy, Byzantine Areas of; Pisa

JOHN H. ERICKSON
St. Vladimir's Orthodox Theological Seminary
Hiereia, Council of; John Italos; Mark Eugenikos; Nomocanon; Paterikon; Schisms, Eastern-Western Church; Serdica, Council of; Studios Monastery; Synaxary; Synodikon of Orthodoxy; Theodore Balsamon; Theodore of Studios

JOSEPH F. ESKA
University of Toronto, Centre for Medieval Studies
Historiography, Scottish

CLAUDE EVANS
University of Toronto
Breton Literature; Brittany, Celtic

DAVID B. EVANS
St. John's University, New York
Pseudo-Dionysius the Areopagite

ROGER EVANS
Loyola Pastoral Institute
Cantor

THEODORE EVERGATES
Western Maryland College
Ban, Banalité; Champagne, County; Colonus; Hariulf; Nobles and Nobility; Pierre de Fontaines

CHRISTIAN EWERT
Deutsches Archäologisches Institut, Madrid
Almohad Art; Almoravid Art

ROBERT FALCK
University of Toronto
Conductus; Consonance/Dissonance; Contrafactum; Diaphonia; Diastemy; Musical Notation, Bilingual, Western; Organum; O Roma Nobilis; Planctus; Salvatoris Hodie; Viderunt Omnes

ZE'EV W. FALK
Hebrew University of Jerusalem
Family and Family Law, Jewish

CONTRIBUTORS

STEVEN C. FANNING
University of Illinois at Chicago Circle
LOMBARD LEAGUE; LOMBARDS, KINGDOM OF

ANN E. FARKAS
Brooklyn College, City University of New York
ALIMPI; BASMENOYE DELO; CHIN; ICONOSTASIS; ICONS, RUSSIAN; IKONOPISNYI PODLINNIK; PECHERSKAYA LAVRA; POKROV; RUBLEV, ANDREI; RUSSIAN AND SLAVIC ART; TEREM; USHAKOV, SIMON; YAROSLAVL

MARGOT E. FASSLER
Yale University
SEQUENCE, LATE

CHARLES B. FAULHABER
University of California, Berkeley
SPANISH LATIN LITERATURE

T. S. FAUNCE
Princeton University
BODEL, JEAN; GRÉBAN, ARNOUL; GUERNES DE PONT-SAINTE-MAXENCE; MERCADÉ, EUSTACHE

JEFFREY FEATHERSTONE
Harvard University
NIKEPHOROS, PATRIARCH

PAUL J. FEDWICK
Pontifical Institute of Mediaeval Studies, Toronto
BASIL THE GREAT OF CAESAREA, ST.

SEYMOUR FELDMAN
Rutgers University
LEVI BEN GERSHOM

S. C. FERRUOLO
Stanford University
COURSON, ROBERT OF; GERALD OF WALES; INNOCENT III, POPE; JACQUES DE VITRY; NIGEL OF LONGCHAMP; PLACENTINUS; RUFINUS; VITAL OF BLOIS; WALTER OF CHÂTILLON

EDWARD G. FICHTNER
Brooklyn College, City University of New York
ULRICH FÜETRER

PAULA SUTTER FICHTNER
Brooklyn College, City University of New York
BAVARIA; MAXIMILIAN I, EMPEROR; SIGISMUND, EMPEROR

RICHARD S. FIELD
Yale University Art Gallery
BLOCK BOOK; BOIS PROTAT; ETCHING; NIELLO; WOODCUT

JOHN V. A. FINE, JR.
University of Michigan
BOGOMILISM; BORIS; BOSNIA; BOSNIAN CHURCH; BULGARIA; CROATIA; JOHN ASEN II; KALOJAN; KRUM; KULIN; LAZAR HREBELJANOVIĆ; MARKO; PETER AND ASEN; PETER OF BULGARIA; SAMUIL OF BULGARIA; SANDALJ HRANIĆ KOSAČA; SAVA, ST.; SERBIA; STEFAN LAZAREVIĆ; STEFAN NEMANJA; STEFAN PRVOVENČANI; STEFAN TOMAŠ; STEFAN TOMAŠEVIĆ; STEFAN UROŠ II MILUTIN; STEFAN UROŠ IV DUŠAN; STEFAN VUKČIĆ KOSAČA; STJEPAN KOTROMANIĆ; SYMEON OF BULGARIA; TOMISLAV; TVRTKO I; TVRTKO II

EVELYN SCHERABON FIRCHOW
University of Minnesota
EINHARD; NITHARD; POETA SAXO

RUTH H. FIRESTONE
University of Missouri, Columbia
BUCH VON BERN, DAS; ECKENLIED; GOLDEMAR; ORTNIT; WOLFDIETRICH; WUNDERER, DER

JOHN H. FISHER
University of Tennessee
MIDDLE ENGLISH LITERATURE

JOHN F. FITZPATRICK
HASTINGS, BATTLE OF

SEYMOUR L. FLAXMAN
City University of New York
DUTCH LITERATURE; ELCKERLIJC; RUUSBROEC, JAN VAN

JERE FLECK
University of Maryland
ALVÍSSMÁL; GRÍMNISMÁL; HYNDLULJÓÐ; VAFÞRÚÐNISMÁL

DONALD F. FLEMING
SQUIRE

JOHN F. FLINN
University of Toronto
GAUTIER D'ARRAS; RENARD THE FOX

JAROSLAV FOLDA
University of North Carolina
CRUSADER ART AND ARCHITECTURE

PETER G. FOOTE
University College, London
HRÓMUNDAR SAGA GRIPSSONAR; LAW, DANISH; LAW, SWEDISH; SCANDINAVIA: POLITICAL AND LEGAL ORGANIZATION

PATRICK K. FORD
University of California, Los Angeles, Center for the Study of Comparative Folklore and Mythology
MABINOGI; MYTHOLOGY, CELTIC; TALIESIN

CLIVE FOSS
University of Massachusetts, Boston
ANATOLIA; ANTIOCH; CAESAREA; EPHESUS; MELITENE; ROADS AND COMMUNICATIONS, BYZANTINE; SEBASTE; URBANISM, BYZANTINE

ANDRÉ FOURÉ
Archevêché de Rouen
ROUEN, USE OF

GUY FOURQUIN
Université de Lille III
SERFS AND SERFDOM: WESTERN EUROPEAN

DAVID C. FOWLER
University of Washington, Seattle
BALLADS, MIDDLE ENGLISH; BIBLE, OLD AND MIDDLE ENGLISH

DENTON FOX†
University of Toronto
DOUGLAS, GAVIN; DUNBAR, WILLIAM; HENRYSON, ROBERT

CHARLES F. FRAKER
University of Michigan
SPANISH LITERATURE: CHRONICLES

JEROLD C. FRAKES
University of Southern California
HUGH (PRIMAS) OF ORLÉANS; PHILIP THE CHANCELLOR

ANTONIO FRANCESCHETTI
University of Toronto
ITALIAN LITERATURE: EPIC AND CHIVALRIC

ROBERTA FRANK
University of Toronto, Centre for Medieval Studies
BJARNI KOLBEINSSON; BRAGI BODDASON THE OLD; DRÓTTKVÆTT; EDDIC METERS; EGILL SKALLAGRÍMSSON; EILÍFR GOÐRÚNARSON; EINARR HELGASON SKÁLAGLAMM; EYVINDR FINNSSON SKÁLDASPILLIR; FLOKKR; HÁTTALYKILL; HAUKR VALDÍSARSON; KENNING; KORMÁKS SAGA; KVIÐUHÁTTR; LAUSAVÍSA; MÁLKSHÁTTAKVÆÐI; MERLÍNÚSSPÁ; SKÁLDATAL; SKALDIC POETRY; ÞJÓÐÓLFR ÓR HVÍNI; ÚLFR UGGASON

GLADYS FRANTZ-MURPHY
Iona College, New Rochelle
TAXATION, ISLAMIC

JOHN B. FREED
Illinois State University, Normal
AUSTRIA; BABENBERG FAMILY; BILLUNGS; BRANDENBURG; BURGUNDY, KINGDOM OF; CANOSSA; CONSTITUTIO DE FEUDIS; ELECTIONS, ROYAL; GERMANY: 843–1137; GERMANY: 1138–1254; GERMANY: STEM DUCHIES; GORZE; HABSBURG DYNASTY; HENRY III OF GERMANY; HENRY IV OF GERMANY; HENRY THE LION; HIRSAU; HOHENSTAUFEN DYNASTY; HOLY ROMAN EMPIRE; MINISTERIALS; OTTO III, EMPEROR; NUREMBERG; RAINALD OF DASSEL; SAXON DYNASTY; SAXONY; SWABIA; TRANSLATION OF EMPIRE; WITTELSBACH FAMILY; WORMS, CONCORDAT OF

PAUL FREEDMAN
Vanderbilt University
OLIBA

MICHELLE A. FREEMAN
Vanderbilt University
CHRÉTIEN DE TROYES

MARGIT FRENK
El Colegio de Mexico
KHARJA

WALTER FRÖHLICH
THEODORIC OF FREIBERG

EDWARD FRUEH
Columbia University
BRUNO OF MAGDEBURG; DONIZO (DOMNIZO); EMBRICHO OF MAINZ; ERCHAMBERT OF FREISING; EUSEBIUS BRUNO; FARDALFUS ABBAS; FRANCO OF LIÈGE; FRIDUGISUS OF TOURS; GAUFRID (GAUDFRED) MALATERRA; GIBUIN OF LANGRES; GODFREY OF WINCHESTER; GUIDO OF AMIENS; HEINRICH VON AUGSBURG; HERIBERT OF EICHSTADT; ILDEFONSUS, ST.; JOHANNES OF ST. VINCENT; MICON OF ST. RIQUIER; MANFRED OF MAGDEBURG; NORBERT OF IBURG; ONULF OF SPEYER; QUEROLUS; RADULFUS TORTARIUS; RATPERT OF ST. GALL; RICHER OF ST. REMI SIGEHARD OF ST. MAXIMIN; SISEBUT; THEODOFRID OF CORBIE; USUARD; WALO OF AUTUN; WIBERT OF TOUL

CHIARA FRUGONI
Università degli Studi di Pisa
ECCLESIA AND SYNAGOGA

RICHARD N. FRYE
Harvard University
KAᶜBA OF ZOROASTER; SAMANIDS

VICTORIA GABBITAS
Museum of Leathercraft, Northampton
LEATHER AND LEATHERWORKING

ASTRIK L. GABRIEL
University of Notre Dame
PARIS, UNIVERSITY OF; UNIVERSITIES

KARI ELLEN GADE
Indiana University
YNGLINGATAL

JOACHIM E. GAEHDE
Brandeis University
PRE-ROMANESQUE ART

GEDEON GÁL, O.F.M.
St. Bonaventure University, Franciscan Institute
MATTHEW OF AQUASPARTA

AUBREY E. GALYON
Iowa State University
MATTHEW OF VENDÔME

KLAUS GAMBER
Liturgiewissenschaftliches Institut, Regensburg
AQUILEIA, RITE OF; BENEVENTAN RITE; GLAGOLITIC RITE

STEPHEN GARDNER
University of California, Santa Barbara
CANTERBURY CATHEDRAL; CONRAD, PRIOR; DURHAM CATHEDRAL; ERNULF; GEOFFREY OF NOYERS; GERVASE OF CANTERBURY; GLOUCESTER CATHEDRAL; GUNDULF; HALF-TIMBER; HENRY OF REYNES; HERLAND, HUGH; HURLEY, WILLIAM; JOY, WILLIAM; LIERNE; LOCK, ADAM; LOTE, STEPHEN; MICHAEL OF CANTERBURY; NICHOLAS OF ELY; OLD SARUM; ORCHARD, WILLIAM; RAMSEY, JOHN; RAMSEY, WILLIAM; SALISBURY CATHEDRAL; THORNTON, JOHN; TIERCERON; VERTUE, ROBERT AND WILLIAM; WALSINGHAM, ALAN OF; WASTELL, JOHN; WESTMINSTER ABBEY; WIBERT OF CANTERBURY; WILLIAM OF SENS; WINCHCOMBE, RICHARD

NINA G. GARSOÏAN
Columbia University
AŁC; ANI IN DARANAŁIKᶜ; ANI IN ŠIRAK; ARMENIA, GEOGRAPHY; ARMENIA: HISTORY OF; ARMENIA, SOCIAL STRUCTURE; ARMENIAN MUSLIM EMIRATES; ARSACIDS/ARŠAKUNI, ARMENIAN; ARŠAK II; ARTAŠAT (ARTAXATA); AVARAYR; AZAT; BDEŠχ; CAVALRY, ARMENIAN; DWIN; GŌSĀN; GREGORIDS; HERESIES, ARMENIAN; HUNTING, IRANIAN; JOHN OF ŌJUN, ST.; KAMSARAKAN; KARIN (KARNOY KᶜAŁAKᶜ); MAMIKONEAN; MANAZKERT; MARZPANATE; MĀTAKDĀN I HAZĀR DĀTASTĀN; NAχARAR; NAχČAWAN; NERSĒS I THE GREAT, ST.; NERSĒS II AŠTARAKACᶜI; NERSĒS III IŠχANECᶜI; NISIBIS; OSTIKAN; PAHLAWUNI; PAULICIANS; PᶜAWSTOS BUZAND; PᶜILARTOS VARAŽNUNI; ṘAMIK; QIRMIZ; SAHAK, ST.; SEPUH; ŠINAKAN; TANUTĒR; TRADE, ARMENIAN; TRDAT III (IV) THE GREAT, ST.; VARDAN MAMIKONEAN, ST.

ADELHEID M. GEALT
Indiana University
AGNOLO DI VENTURA; AGOSTINO, GIOVANNI D'; ALTARPIECE; ALTICHIERO; ANGELO DA ORVIETO; ANTONIO DA VICENZO; ANTONIO VENEZIANO; ARENA CHAPEL; ARNOLDI, ALBERTO; ARNOLFO DI CAMBIO; ARRICCIO; ASSISI, SAN

ADELHEID M. GEALT (*cont.*)
Francesco; Avanzo, Jacopo; Barna da Siena; Baronzio, Giovanni; Bartolino da Novara; Bartolo di Fredi; Benedetto Antelami; Berlinghieri, Bonaventura; Bernardo da Venezia; Bertuccio; Bonino da Campione; Bonnano da Pisa; Brailes, William de; Brunelleschi, Filippo; Buon, Giovanni and Bartolomeo; Buscheto of Pisa; Cavallini, Pietro; Cennini, Cennino; Cimabue, Cenni di Pepi; Ciuffagni, Bernardo; Conte del Lello Orlandi; Coppo di Marcovaldo; Daddi, Bernardo; Dugento (Duecento) Art; Francesco da Rimini; Fresco Painting; Gaddi, Agnolo; Gaddi, Gaddo; Gaddi, Taddeo; Gano da Siena; Gentile da Fabriano; Gerhardo di Jacopo Starnina; Gesso; Giotto di Bondone; Giovanni d'Ambrogio da Firenze; Giovanni da Fiesole; Giovanni da Milano; Giovanni (Giovannino) de' Grassi; Giovanni (Nanni) di Bartolo; Giovanni di Benedetto da Como; Giovanni di Paolo; Giuliano da Rimini; Giusto de Menabuoi; Goffredo da Viterbo; Guariento di Arpo; Intonaco; Jacopo di Cione; Lippo Memmi; Lorenzetti, Ambrogio; Lorenzetti, Pietro; Lorenzo Monaco; Lorenzo di Niccolò; Lorenzo Veneziano; Lucca di Tommè; Maitani, Ambrogio; Mariotto di Nardo; Maso di Banco; Masolino; Masaccio, Tommaso Cassai; Michelozzo di Bartolomeo; Nanni di Banco; Nardo di Cione; Niccolò di Buonaccorso; Niccolò di Pietro Gerini; Orcagna, Andrea; Panel Painting; Paolo di Giovanni Fei; Paolo Veneziano; Pietro da Rimini; Predella; St. Cecilia Master; Sassetta; Rossello di Jacopo Franchi; Segna di Bonaventura; Semitecolo, Nicoletto; Simone da Bologna; Simone Martini; Sinopia; Spinello Aretino; Stiacciato; Taddeo di Bartolo; Tempera Painting; Torriti, Jacopo; Traini, Francesco; Trecento Art; Uccello, Paolo; Ugolino da Siena; Vanni, Andrea; Vanni, Lippo

DENO J. GEANAKOPLOS
Yale University
Bessarion; Gemistos Plethon, Georgios; Italian Renaissance, Byzantine Influence on; Manuel Chrysoloras; Michael VIII Palaiologos; Pelagonia

PATRICK GEARY
University of Florida
Beatification; Canonization; Capitulary; Carolingians and the Carolingian Empire; Charlemagne; County; Duchy; Merovingians; Mayor of the Palace; Missi Dominici

CHRISTIAN J. GELLINEK
University of Florida
Annolied; Kaiserchronik; Karlmeinet; König Rother; Orendel; Rolandslied

BRUCE E. GELSINGER†
Hanseatic League; Iceland; Viking Navigation

E. MICHAEL GERLI
Georgetown University
Martínez de Toledo, Alfonso

G. H. GERRITS
Acadia University
Jordan of Quedlinburg

STEPHEN GERSH
University of Notre Dame
Conceptualism; Dualism; Essence and Existence; Realism

ALAN GEWIRTH
University of Chicago
Defensor Pacis

HENRI GIBAUD
Vulgate

DOUGLAS GIFFORD
University of St. Andrews
Spanish Literature: Popular Poetry

MOSHE GIL
Tel-Aviv University
Palestine; Pilgrimage, Jewish; Samaritans

JOSEPH GILL, S.J.
Campion Hall, Oxford
Ferrara-Florence, Council of

JAMES L. GILLESPIE
Notre Dame College of Ohio, Ursuline College
Henry IV of England; Henry VI of England; John of Gaunt; Richard II; Richard III

C. M. GILLMOR
United States Naval Academy
Cavalry, European

STEPHEN GILMAN†
Harvard University
Celestina, La

OWEN GINGERICH
Smithsonian Astrophysical Observatory
Alfonsine Tables; Astrolabe; Toledan Tables

DOROTHY F. GLASS
State University of New York at Buffalo
Guglielmo, Fra; Guglielmo da Verona; Niccolò da Verona; Oderisi, Pietro; Vassallettus; Wiligelmo da Modena

THOMAS F. GLICK
Boston University
Agriculture and Nutrition (The Mediterranean Region); Fruits and Nuts; Irrigation; Seville; Toledo; Umayyads of Córdoba

INGEBORG GLIER
Yale University
German Literature: Allegory; Hätzlerin, Klara; Heinrich der Teichner; Minnereden

HANS PETER GLÖCKNER
Johann Wolfgang Goethe Universität
Hugo; Jacobus (de Porta Ravennate); Johannes Andreae; Johannes Monachus

GEOFFREY B. GNEUHS
Vincent Ferrer, St.

JOSCELYN GODWIN
Colgate University
Mystery Religions

HARRIET GOLDBERG
Villanova University
Fortune, Old Spanish

PETER B. GOLDEN
Rutgers University, Newark
ALP ARSLAN; AQ QOYUNLU; ARGUN; ATABEG; AVARS; AZERBAIJAN; BATU; BĀYĀZID I, YILDIRIM; DANISHMENDIDS; EMIR; GENGHIS KHAN; GHĀZĪ; GOLDEN HORDE; HULAGU; HUNS; ILDEGIZIDS; ILKHANIDS; KARAMANIA; MALIKSHĀH; MEHMED (MUḤAMMAD) I; MEHMED (MUḤAMMAD) II; MURAD I; MURAD II; NIẒĀM AL-MULK; QARAKHANIDS; QARA QOYUNLU; RUM; RUSSIA, NOMADIC INVASIONS OF; SARMATIANS; SELJUKS; SHAH-ARMAN; SULTAN; TAMERLANE; TOGHRIL-BEG; TURKOMANS; UZUN ḤASAN; VOLGA BULGARS

DAVID GOLDFRANK
Georgetown University
BOGOLIUBSKII, ANDREI; VLADIMIR-SUZDAL

RAMÓN GONZÁLVEZ
MOZARABIC RITE

JANET E. GORMLEY
The Queen's University of Belfast
UBERTINO OF CASALE

ROBERT S. GOTTFRIED
Rutgers University
BLACK DEATH; BOROUGH (ENGLAND—WALES); CLIMATOLOGY; FAMINE IN WESTERN EUROPE; PLAGUES, EUROPEAN

OLEG GRABAR
Harvard University
ICONOCLASM, ISLAMIC; JERUSALEM; QUBBA; SŪQ; ZĀWĪYA; ZIYADA

ARYEH GRABOIS
University of Haifa
BIBLE; CHRISTIAN HEBRAISTS

JORGE J. E. GRACIA
State University of New York at Buffalo
SCHOLASTICISM, SCHOLASTIC METHOD

ANTHONY GRAFTON
Princeton University
MIDDLE AGES; NICOLAUS DE TUDESCHIS

JAMES A. GRAHAM-CAMPBELL
University College, London
BORRE STYLE; CELTIC ART; JELLINGE STYLE; MAMMEN STYLE; RINGERIKE STYLE; URNES STYLE; VIKING ART

EDWARD GRANT
Indiana University
BURIDAN, JEAN; ORESME, NICOLE

JUDITH GRANT
University of Auckland
VIE SEINT EDMUND LE REI, LA

KATHRYN GRAVDAL
Columbia University
GAUCHIER DE DOURDAN; RAOUL DE HOUDENC

VIVIAN H. H. GREEN
Lincoln College, Oxford University
ELECTIONS, CHURCH; TAXATION, CHURCH

GORDON K. GREENE
Wilfrid Laurier University
ARS NOVA; FAUVEL, ROMAN DE; MA FIN EST MON COMMENCEMENT; MASS CYCLES, EARLY POLYPHONIC; TRECENTO MUSIC

RICHARD LEIGHTON GREENE
CAROLS, MIDDLE ENGLISH; FORTUNE

KATHLEEN GREENFIELD
Albright College
EMBER DAYS; PECKHAM, JOHN

TIMOTHY E. GREGORY
Ohio State University
BYZANTINE EMPIRE: HISTORY (330–1025); CONSTANTINE I, THE GREAT; INHERITANCE, BYZANTINE

JAMES GRIER
Queen's University, Ontario
BENEDICAMUS DOMINO; DISCANTOR; DUPLUM; LIBER USUALIS; NEUME; ST. MARTIAL SCHOOL; SANTIAGO DE COMPOSTELA, SCHOOL OF; TE DEUM

ROBERT GRIGG
University of California, Davis
ICONOCLASM, CHRISTIAN

JOHN L. GRIGSBY†
Washington University, St. Louis
BALLETTE; BLONDEL DE NESLE; CHÂTELAIN DE COUCY; COUTUMES

JOHN L. GRIGSBY† (*cont.*)
DE BEAUVAISIS; GOLDEN LEGEND; GUIOT DE PROVINS; JEAN DE THUIM

KAAREN GRIMSTAD
University of Minnesota
EUFEMIAVISOR; FREYR; FRIGG; FYLGJA; GEFJON; GROTTASǪNGR; HJAÐNINGAVÍG; NJǪRÐR; SINFJǪTLI; STARKAÐR; SVIPDAGSMÁL; VǪLUNDARKVIÐA

MARY GRIZZARD
University of New Mexico
DALMÁU, LUIS; DESTORRENTS, RAMÓN; FERRER I (THE ELDER), JAIME; GALLEGO, FERNANDO; GONSALVES, NUÑO; GUAS, JUAN AND PEDRO; HUGUET, JAIME; JOHN OF S. MARTÍN DE ALBARES; JORGE INGLÉS; JUAN AND SIMÓN DE COLONIA; JUAN DE BURGOS; JUAN DE FLANDES; MAJOLICA; MARTORELL, BERNARDO; MARQUETRY; MARZAL DE SAX, ANDRÉS; NISART, PEDRO; OLIPHANT; POTTERY: REPOUSSÉ; REXACH, JUAN; RODRIGO DE OSONA; SERRA, PEDRO AND JAIME; SITULA; TERRA SIGILLATA

ARTHUR GROOS
Cornell University
CARMINA BURANA; HEINRICH VON VELDEKE (HENDRIK VAN VELDEKE); LAMPRECHT; LOHENGRIN; REINFRID VON BRAUNSCHWEIG; RUDOLF VON EMS

AVRAHAM GROSSMAN
Hebrew University of Jerusalem
GERSHOM BEN JUDAH; KALONYMUS FAMILY

SAMUEL GRUBER
Columbia University
URBANISM, WESTERN EUROPEAN

MINNETTE GRUNMANN-GAUDET
University of Western Ontario
BERTRAND DE BAR-SUR-AUBE; CANTILÈNE; TUROLDUS

FINNBOGI GUÐMUNDSSON
ORKNEYINGA SAGA

BJARNI GUÐNASON
Háskóli Íslands
EIRÍKR ODDSSON; KNYTLINGA SAGA; ORKNEYINGA SAGA; SKJǪLDUNGA SAGA

CONTRIBUTORS

JACQUES GUILMAIN
State University of New York at Stony Brook
Initials, Decorated and Historiated; Manuscript Illumination, European

J. GULSOY
University of Toronto
Catalan Language

LAWRENCE GUSHEE
Augustinus Triumphus; Aurelian of Réôme; Jehan des Murs

JOSEPH GUTMANN
Wayne State University
Jewish Art; Menorah; Synagogue

GREGORY G. GUZMAN
Bradley University
John of Plano Carpini; Vincent of Beauvais

JEAN-MARIE GY, O.P.
Couvent Saint-Jacques, Paris
Papal Curia, Liturgy of

PIERRE-MARIE GY, O.P.
Institut Supérieur de Liturgie, Paris
Benedictional; Benedictions; Collectarium; Ritual

RICHARD F. GYUG
University of Toronto
Consecration of Cemeteries; Milanese Rite

JAMES HAAR
University of North Carolina
Harmony

JEREMIAH M. G. HACKETT
Pontifical Institute of Mediaeval Studies, Toronto
Bacon, Roger

ABRAHAM S. HALKIN
Joseph ben Judah ben Jacob ibn ᶜAknin; Judeo-Arabic Literature

A. RUPERT HALL
The Wellcome Institute for the History of Medicine
Guido da Vigevano

ROBERT HALLEUX
University of Liège
Alchemy

ANDRAS HAMORI
Princeton University
Abū Nuwās; Akhṭak, al-; Arabic Literature, Prose; Arabic Poetry; Mutanabbī, al-; Rhetoric: Arabic, Hebrew

ERIC P. HAMP
University of Chicago, Center for Balkan and Slavic Studies
Aneirin

EMILY ALBU HANAWALT
Boston University
Anna Komnena; Suda

WILLIAM LIPPINCOTT HANAWAY, JR.
University of Pennsylvania
Gulistān; Iranian Literature; Shāhnāma; Vīs u Rāmīn; Xwadāy Nāmag

JAMES HANKINS
Harvard University
Plato in the Middle Ages

NATHALIE HANLET
Bruno of Segni, St.; Cato's Distichs (Latin); Dudo of St. Quentin; Erchenbert of Monte Cassino; Gerhard of Augsburg; Ghislebert of St. Amand; Godzin of Mainz; Gumpold; Hadoardus; Helgaud; Hilduin of St. Denis; Johannes Canaparius; Johannes of St. Arnulf; Landolfus Sagax; Lantbert of Deutz; Meginhart of Fulda; Milo of St. Amand; Oda of Canterbury; Radolf of Liège; Rangerius of Lucca; Rheticius of Autun, St.; Rudolf of Fulda; Sampirus of Astorga; Tatwine of Canterbury; Thiofrid of Echternach; Waldrammus; Warnerius of Basel; Wigbodus

BERT HANSEN
New York University
Magic, Bookish (Western European)

CONRAD HARKINS, O.F.M.
Saint Bonaventure University, Franciscan Institute
Alexander of Hales; Marsh, Adam

JACK R. HARLAN
University of Illinois
Bread; Grain Crops, Western European

PRUDENCE OLIVER HARPER
Metropolitan Museum of Art
Sasanian Art

JOSEPH HARRIS
Harvard University
Eddic Poetry; Eiríksmál and Hákonarmál; Guðrúnarhvǫt; Guðrúnarkviða I; Guðrúnarkviða II; Haraldskvæði; Helgi Poems; Hrólfs Saga Kraka; Norna-Gests Þáttr; Skírnismál; Þættir; Þrymskviða

L. P. HARVEY
University of London, King's College
Aljamiado Literature

AHMAD YUSIF AL-HASSAN
Technology, Islamic; Tools, Agricultural: Islamic

RALPH S. HATTOX
Beverages, Islamic; Dietary Laws, Islamic; Osman I; Samarkand; Selim I

EINAR HAUGEN
Harvard University
Rígsþula; Skrælings; Vinland Sagas

ROBERT K. HAYCRAFT
Paliotto of S. Ambrogio; Retable

EDWARD R. HAYMES
Cleveland State University
Alpharts Tod; König Laurin; Rosengarten; Virginal

HARRY C. HAZEL III
Gonzaga University
William of Auvergne

THOMAS HEAD
Claremont College
Relics

EDWARD A. HEINEMANN
University of Toronto
Chansons de Geste

FREDRIK J. HEINEMANN
Universität Essen
Hrafnkels Saga Freysgǫða

HUBERT HEINEN
University of Texas at Austin
Dietmar von Aist; Eleonore of Austria; Elisabeth of Nassau-Saarbrücken; Gottfried von Neifen; Heinrich von Meissen; Heinrich von Morungen; Henry VI of Germany; Meinloh von Sevelingen; Ulrich von Singenberg; Ulrich von Winterstetten; Wartburgkrieg

KNUT HELLE
University of Bergen, Norway
Norway

LOTTE HELLINGA
The British Library
Gutenberg, Johannes; Printing, Origins of

R. H. HELMHOLZ
Washington University, St. Louis
Annulment of Marriage; Blasphemy; Concubinage, Western; Consanguinity

HEATHER HENDERSON
University of Toronto, Centre for Medieval Studies
Areithian Prose: Prose Rhetorics; Auraicept na nÉces; Ó Huiginn, Tadhg Dall; Ó Huiginn, Tadhg Óg

SCOTT H. HENDRIX
Lutheran Theological Southern Seminary
Brethren of the Common Life

JOHN BELL HENNEMAN
Princeton University Library
Agincourt, Battle of; Cabochien Riots; Charles V of France; Charles VII of France; Enguerrand VII of Coucy; France: 1314–1497; Gabelle; Jacquerie; Law, French: In South; Louis XI of France; Maltolte; Marmousets; Philip VI of Valois; Taxation, French; Valois Dynasty

JOHN HENNIG
Angelus; Ave Maria; Liturgy, Celtic

DAVID HERLIHY
Harvard University
Demography

MICHAEL HERREN
York University, Ontario
Aldhelm; Colman, Bishop of Lindisfarne; Columba, St.; Columbanus, St.; Dicuil; Dubiis Nominibus, De; Gall, St.; Hiberno-Latin; Hisperic Latin; Itinerarium Egeriae; Virgil the Grammarian; Vulgar Latin

JUDITH HERRIN
Warburg Institute, University of London
Constantine V; Isaurians; Leo III, Emperor

ROBERT H. HEWSEN
Glassboro State College
Albania (Caucasian); Araks River; Ararat, Mount; Arčēš; Arcn; Armenian Pentarchy; Ayrarat; Bardhaʿa; Baylaḳān; Berkri; Caucasia; Caucasus Mountains; Cilician Gates; Derbent; Erzincan (Erzinjan); Ganjak; Ganjak of Atropatene; Georgia: Geography and Ethnology; Kabala; Kars; Kura River; Kutʿaisi; Pontus; Sewan, Lake; Shirvan; Širak; Siwnikʿ; Tarōn; Taykʿ; Tbilisi; Urmia, Lake; Van, Lake; Vanand; Vaspurakan; Xlatʿ

P. L. HEYWORTH
University of Toronto
Havelok the Dane; Katherine Group; Middle English Literature: Alliterative Verse

CONSTANCE B. HIEATT
University of Western Ontario
Karlamagnús Saga

BENNETT D. HILL
St. Anselm's Abbey, Washington, D.C.
Benedictines; Camaldolese, Order of; Carthusians; Celestines; Cistercian Order; Dominic, St.; Ethelred of Rievaulx, St.; Grandmont, Order of; Hermits, Eremitism; Missions and Missionaries, Christian; Sack, Friars of the; Savigny; Vital of Savigny, St.; Whitby, Synod of; William of

BENNETT D. HILL (*cont.*)
Wykeham; Wulfstan of Worcester, St.; Wulfstan of York

JOHN HUGH HILL
Baldwin I of Jerusalem; Bohemond I, Prince of Antioch; Clermont, Council of; Crusades and Crusader States: To 1192; Peter the Hermit; Tancred (Crusader)

ROBERT HILLENBRAND
University of Edinburgh
Alhambra; Córdoba; Granada; Khan; Madrasa; Malwiya; Manuscript Books, Binding of: Islamic; Minaret; Pishtaq

J. N. HILLGARTH
Pontifical Institute of Mediaeval Studies, Toronto
Isidore of Seville, St.; Lull, Ramon; Peter IV the Ceremonious

WILLIAM A. HINNEBUSCH†
St. Gertrude Priory
Dominicans

MICHAEL J. HODDER
Sotheby Parke Bernet, Inc.
Allod; Canvas; Cotton; Flax; Wool

GERALD A. J. HODGETT
King's College
Estate Management

RICHARD C. HOFFMANN
York University, Ontario
Fishponds; Tenure of Land, Western European; Tools, Agricultural: European; Villages: Community

ROBERT HOLLANDER
Princeton University
Dante Alighieri

C. WARREN HOLLISTER
University of California, Santa Barbara
Knights and Knight Service

KENNETH G. HOLUM
University of Maryland
Theodosius II the Calligrapher

CONTRIBUTORS

DAVID HOOK
University of London
AUTO DE LOS REYES MAGOS

DAVID L. HOOVER
New York University
OLD ENGLISH LANGUAGE

JASPER HOPKINS
University of Minnesota
ANSELM OF CANTERBURY; NICHOLAS OF CUSA

GEORGE F. HOURANI†
State University of New York at Buffalo
ASHᶜARĪ, AL-; PHILOSOPHY AND THEOLOGY, ISLAMIC

NORMAN HOUSLEY
University of Liverpool
CRUSADES OF THE LATER MIDDLE AGES; PILGRIMAGE, WESTERN EUROPEAN

JOHN HOWE
Texas Tech University
BRUNO OF QUERFURT, ST.; LETALD OF MICY; RICHARD DE BURY; TRANSLATION OF SAINTS

DONALD GWYON HOWELLS
University of Glasgow
LAW, WELSH

ANTONÍN HRUBÝ
University of Washington
ACKERMANN AUS BÖHMEN, DER

ANNE HUDSON
Lady Margaret Hall, Oxford
LOLLARDS; WYCLIF, JOHN

PETER HUENINK
Vassar College
AACHEN, PALACE CHAPEL; BERNWARD; PRE-ROMANESQUE ARCHITECTURE; SAXON ARCHITECTURE

JAY HUFF
JOHN OF AFFLIGHEM; JOHN OF GARLAND

ANDREW HUGHES
University of Toronto
ADAM DE LA BASSÉE; AEVÍA; ANTIPHON; ANTIPHONAL (ANTIPHONER, ANTIPHONARY); CADENCE; CANTATORIUM;

ANDREW HUGHES (*cont.*)
CANTICLE; CAUDA; CLEF; CONTRATENOR; CUSTOS; DIABOLUS IN MUSICA; DIFFERENTIA; MELODY; MUSIC, POPULAR; MUSIC, WESTERN EUROPEAN; MUSICA FICTA; PSALTER; RHYMED OFFICES; TENOR; TONARY; TONES, READING AND DIALOGUE; TROPER; VARIATIO

PENELOPE HUGHES
WAITS

SHAUN F. D. HUGHES
Purdue University
ÁNS SAGA BOGSVEIGIS; RIMUR; SCANDINAVIA IN ARABIC SOURCES; VǪLUSPÁ

KATHRYN HUME
Pennsylvania State University
GRETTIS SAGA ÁSMUNDARSONAR

R. STEPHEN HUMPHREYS
University of Wisconsin, Madison
DAMASCUS; HISTORIOGRAPHY, ISLAMIC; MAMLŪK; MAMLUK DYNASTY

LUCY-ANNE HUNT
University of Birmingham
AXUMITE ART; COPTIC ART

SYLVIA HUOT
University of Chicago
CHANSON DE LA CROISADE CONTRE LES ALBIGEOIS; CHRISTINE DE PIZAN; CONON DE BÉTHUNE

PAUL R. HYAMS
Pembroke College, Oxford
BLOOD LIBEL; HOST DESECRATION LIBEL

J. K. HYDE
University of Manchester
BOLOGNA, UNIVERSITY OF

MAHMOOD IBRAHIM
Birzeit University
JĪLĀNĪ, ᶜABD AL-QĀDIR AL-; ᶜUMAR I IBN AL-KHAṬṬĀB

MOSHE IDEL
Hebrew University of Jerusalem
ABULAFIA, ABRAHAM BEN SAMUEL; CABALA; MOSES BEN SHEM TOV DE LEON

MICHAEL H. IMPEY
University of Kentucky
ROMANIAN LANGUAGE AND LITERATURE

OLGA TUDORICA IMPEY
Indiana University
CALILA E DIGNA; ROMANIAN LANGUAGE AND LITERATURE

HALIL INALCIK
University of Chicago
OTTOMANS

JEAN IRIGOIN
PAPER, INTRODUCTION OF

EPHRAIM ISAAC
Institute of Semitic Studies, Princeton
ABYSSINIA (ETHIOPIA); PRESTER JOHN

ALFRED L. IVRY
Brandeis University
ABRAHAM IBN DAUD; CRESCAS, ḤASDAI; GAONIC PERIOD; ISRAELI, ISAAC; JUDAH HALEVI; MAIMONIDES, ABRAHAM BEN MOSES; PHILOSOPHY AND THEOLOGY, JEWISH: ISLAMIC WORLD; SAADIAH GAON; SOLOMON BEN JUDAH IBN GABIROL

RICHARD A. JACKSON
University of Houston
KINGSHIP, RITUALS OF: CORONATION

WILLIAM E. JACKSON
University of Virginia
JOHANNES HADLAUB; OTTO VON BOTENLAUBEN; REINMAR DER ALTE

W. T. H. JACKSON†
Columbia University
ALEXANDER ROMANCES; BEAST EPIC; BERENGARII IMPERATORIS GESTA; BURCHARD OF WORMS; CAPELLANUS, ANDREAS; EBARCIUS OF ST. AMAND; EPIC, LATIN; ERMENRICH OF ELLWANGEN; FLODOARD OF RHEIMS; FROMUND OF TEGERNSEE; GERHARD OF SOISSONS; GERMAN LITERATURE: ROMANCE; GODFREY OF RHEIMS; GOTTFRIED VON STRASSBURG; GUNZO OF NOVARA; HEINRICH VON FREIBERG; HELPERIC OF AUXERRE; HENRY THE MINSTREL; HILDEBERT OF LAVARDIN; MARBOD OF RENNES; MEINZO OF CONSTANCE; ODO OF MEUN; OTTO OF BAMBERG, ST.; RADBOD OF UTRECHT; RAGIMBOLD OF COLOGNE; REGINALD OF

W. T. H. JACKSON† (*cont.*)
Canterbury; Rimbert, St.; Salomo of Constance; Theodore of Canterbury, St.; Ulrich von Türheim; Verecundus of Junca; Visitatio Sepulchri; Vitae Patrum Walther von Speier; Wichram of St. Gall

FRANK RAINER JACOBY
Brandeis University
Ecbasis Captivi; Ysengrimus

MICHAEL JACOFF
Brooklyn College, City University of New York
Niccolò da Bologna; Pacino di Bonaguida; Pseudo-Niccolò; Tegliacci, Niccolò di Ser Sozzo

C. STEPHEN JAEGER
Bryn Mawr College
Bligger von Steinach

PETER JEFFERY
University of Delaware
Litany; Music, Jewish; Sarum Chant; Tropes to the Proper of the Mass

MICHAEL JEFFREYS
University of Sydney
Byzantine Literature: Popular; Byzantine Poetic Forms; Digenis Akritas

JENNY M. JOCHENS
Towson State University
Denmark

GEORGE JOCHNOWITZ
College of Staten Island, City University of New York
Judeo-Provençal

JAMES J. JOHN
Cornell University
Abbreviator; Alphabets; Bull, Papal; Cartulary; Chancery; Charter; Computus; Datary, Apostolic; Dionysius Exiguus; Paleography, Western European

D. W. JOHNSON
Catholic University of America
Adoptionism; Arianism; Christian Church in Persia; Christianity, Nubian; Docetism; Eutyches; Eutychios the Melchite; Manichaeans; Monophysitism;

D. W. JOHNSON (*cont.*)
Melchites; Nestorianism; Nestorius

ALEXANDRA F. JOHNSTON
Records of Early English Drama
York Plays

CHARLES W. JONES†
Bede; Schools, Monastic

GEORGE FENWICK JONES
University of Maryland
Fachschrifttum; Heinrich von Mügeln; Hugo von Montfort; Oswald von Wolkenstein; Walther von der Vogelweide; Wittenwiler, Heinrich

JENNIFER E. JONES
Daw, John; Down, Roger; Drouet of Dammartin; Geoffroi d'Ainai; Gothic, Manueline; Lazarus, Raising of; Logos; Majestas Domini; Mission of the Apostles; Nativity; Nimbus; Noli Me Tangere; Pentecost; Pietà; Platytera; Presentation in the Temple; Psychopomp; Raymond de Mur; Robert of Jumièges; Seven Sleepers of Ephesus; Sign of the Cross; Spierinc, Claeys; Tetramorph; Transfiguration; Tree of Life; Trinity, Old Testament; Twelve Great Feasts; Virtues and Vices

MICHAEL JONES
University of Nottingham
Brittany, Duchy

CHRISTIANE L. JOOST-GAUGIER
University of New Mexico
Bellini, Jacopo; Pisanello, Antonio

WILLIAM CHESTER JORDAN
Princeton University
Angevins: France, England, Sicily; Bailiff; Bailli; Banking, Jewish, in Europe; Baron; Blanche of Castile; Butler; Chamberlain; Constable of the Realm; Corvée; Crusades and Crusader States: 1212 to 1272; Eudes Rigaud; France: 1223–1328; Joinville, Jean de; Louis IX of France; Mainmort; Margrave, Marquis; Marshal; Mortmain; Ordinance (French and English); Pagus;

WILLIAM CHESTER JORDAN (*cont.*)
Pastoureaux; Pasture, Rights of; Prince; Provost; Seneschal; Sergeant; Song of Lewes; Sumptuary Laws, European

PETER A. JORGENSEN
University of Georgia
Ála Flekks Saga; Drauma-Jóns Saga; Flóres Saga Konungs ok Sona Hans; Samsons Saga Fagra; Sigurðar Saga Fóts; Sigurðar Saga Þögla; Vilmundar Saga Viðutan

JACQUES JOSET
Universitaire Instelling, Antwerpen
Shem Tov

G. H. A. JUYNBOLL
University of Exeter
Ḥadīth; Sunna; Sunnites

BERNICE M. KACZYNSKI
McMaster University
Creeds, Liturgical Use of

WALTER EMIL KAEGI, JR.
University of Chicago
Akritai; Anatolikon, Theme of; Armeniakon, Theme of; Byzantine Empire: Bureaucracy; Cavalry, Byzantine; Constans II, Emperor; Constantine IV; Domestic; Drungarios; Exarchate; Heraklids; Heraklios; Julian the Apostate; Justinian II; Notitia Dignitatum; Opsikion, Theme of; Pronoia; Protospatharios; Scholae; Soldiers' Portions; Strategos; Stratiotai; Tagmata; Themes; Varangian Guard; Warfare, Byzantine

RICHARD W. KAEUPER
University of Rochester
Admiralty, Court of; Aldermen; Arches, Court of; Assize; Asylum, Right of; Constable, Local; Copyhold; Court Leet; Distress; Escheat, Escheator; Felony; Forest Law; Forgery; Homicide in English Law; Impeachment and Attainder; Jail Delivery; Justices of the Peace; Nisi Prius; Oyer and Terminer, Trailbaston; Peasants' Rebellion; Treason; Trespass

CONTRIBUTORS

DANIEL H. KAISER
Grinnell College
LAW, RUSSIAN (MUSCOVITE)

IOLI KALAVREZOU-MAXEINER
University of California, Los Angeles
INTAGLIO; JOSHUA ROLL; PARIS PSALTER

MARIANNE E. KALINKE
University of Illinois at Urbana-Champaign
ELIS SAGA OK ROSAMUNDU; KLÁRI SAGA; MÁGUS SAGA JARLS; MÍRMANNS SAGA; MÖTTULS SAGA; PARCEVALS SAGA; PARTALOPA SAGA; RÉMUNDAR SAGA KEISARASONAR; RIDDARASÖGUR

HOWARD KAMINSKY
Florida International University
BABYLONIAN CAPTIVITY; HUS, JOHN; HUSSITES; PRAGMATIC SANCTION OF BOURGES; PROVISIONS, ECCLESIASTICAL; SCHISM, GREAT

WILLIAM E. KAPELLE
Brandeis University
STRATHCLYDE, KINGDOM OF; THEGN

STEPHEN J. KAPLOWITT
University of Connecticut
ANEGENGE; DER VON KÜRENBERG; EZZOLIED

LLOYD KASTEN
Hispanic Seminary of Medieval Studies
ALFONSO X

TRUDY S. KAWAMI
BISHAPUR; CTESIPHON; FĪRŪZĀBĀD; GUNDĒSHĀPŪR

ALEXANDER P. KAZHDAN
Dumbarton Oaks Research Center
AGRICULTURE AND NUTRITION (BYZANTIUM); CONSTANTINE VII PORPHYROGENITOS; EPARCH, BOOK OF THE; GENESIOS, JOSEPH; GEOPONICA; GEORGE OF CYPRUS; GEORGE THE MONK; HIEROKLES; MENANDER PROTECTOR; SKYLITZES, JOHN; SYMEON METAPHRASTES; THEODORE PRODROMOS; THEOPHANES CONFESSOR; THEOPHANES CONTINUATUS; ZONARAS, JOHN

EDWARD J. KEALEY
College of the Holy Cross
HOSPITALS AND POOR RELIEF, WESTERN EUROPEAN; ROGER OF SALISBURY

SUSAN ANNE KEEFE
BAPTISM

THOMAS KEEFE
Appalachian State University
ANTRUSTIONES

HANS-ERICH KELLER
Ohio State University
GAIMAR, GEFFREI; GEOFFREY OF MONMOUTH; HAGUE FRAGMENT; WACE

JOHN KELLER
University of Kentucky
EXEMPLUM

FRANCIS KELLEY
St. Bonaventure University
PETER AUREOLI

DOUGLAS KELLY
University of Wisconsin, Madison
BENOÎT DE SAINTE-MAURE; FRENCH LITERATURE: ROMANCES; JOHN OF GARLAND

THOMAS E. KELLY
Purdue University
BESTIAIRE D'AMOUR; CHANSON; CHANSONS DE FEMME; CHANSONS DE MALMARIÉE; CHANSONS DE TOILE; CHANT ROYAL; DESCHAMPS, EUSTACHE; GERBERT DE MONTREUIL; PERLESVAUS; RUTEBEUF

ERIC KEMP
CONVOCATIONS OF CANTERBURY AND YORK

MARILYN KAY KENNEY
ARTHURIAN LITERATURE, WELSH; BANGOR (WALES); BERWICK, TREATY OF; CADOC, ST.; CASNODYN; CHESTER, TREATY OF; CONWAY, PEACE OF; CUNEDDA WLEDIG; CYNDDELW BRYDYDD MAWR; DYFED; OWAIN GWYNEDD; RHODRI MAWR

THOMAS KERTH
State University of New York at Stony Brook
TRISTAN, LEGEND OF

HERBERT L. KESSLER
The Johns Hopkins University
CUMDACH; DRAWINGS AND MODEL BOOKS; DURA EUROPOS; EARLY CHRISTIAN ART; MANUALS, ARTISTIC; PSALTER, ILLUMINATION OF; UTRECHT PSALTER

G. L. KEYES
University of Toronto
CHURCH FATHERS; DOCTORS OF THE CHURCH

MAJID KHADDURI
The Johns Hopkins Foreign Policy Institute
DIPLOMACY, ISLAMIC; MOSUL; TENURE OF LAND, ISLAMIC

FRANCES KIANKA
Dumbarton Oaks Research Center
DEMETRIOS KYDONES; NIKEPHOROS GREGORAS

JOSEPH A. KICKLIGHTER
Auburn University
PARLEMENT OF PARIS

RICHARD KIECKHEFER
Northwestern University
FLAGELLANTS; PAPACY, ORIGINS AND DEVELOPMENT OF; REFORM, IDEA OF

MARGOT H. KING
St. Thomas More College, Saskatchewan
HAGIOGRAPHY, WESTERN EUROPEAN

R. P. KINKADE
University of Connecticut
ELUCIDARIUM AND SPANISH LUCIDARIO

DALE KINNEY
Bryn Mawr College
DIOTISALVI (DEOTISALVI); GATTAPONI, MATTEO; GIACOMO DA CAMPIONE; GIOVANNI DI CECCO; JACOPO DI PIERO GUIDI; LANFRANC OF MODENA; LATERAN; MILAN CATHEDRAL; ODO OF METZ; OLD ST. PETER'S, ROME; PISA CATHEDRAL; RAINALDUS; SAN MARCO, VENICE; TALENTI, FRANCESCO

STEVEN D. KIRBY
Niagara University
MESTER DE CLERECÍA

JULIUS KIRSCHNER
University of Chicago
BALDUS; BARTOLO DA SASSOFERRATO; MEDICI

M. JEAN KITCHEL
University of St. Thomas, Houston
BURLEY, WALTER

JOHN M. KLASSEN
Trinity Western College
BOHEMIA-MORAVIA; COMMUNION UNDER BOTH KINDS

DAVID N. KLAUSNER
University of Toronto, Centre for Medieval Studies
DAFYDD AP GWILYM; EISTEDDFOD; IOLO GOCH; LLYWELYN AP GRUFFYDD; MUSIC, CELTIC; URIEN RHEGED; WELSH LITERATURE

CHRISTOPHER KLEINHENZ
University of Wisconsin, Madison
ITALIAN LITERATURE: LYRIC POETRY; ITALIAN LITERATURE: VERSIFICATION AND PROSODY; SICILIAN POETRY

ALAN E. KNIGHT
Pennsylvania State University
CONFRÉRIE; CONGÉ; COURTOIS D'ARRAS; DRAMA, FRENCH; GARÇON ET L'AVEUGLE; JEU; JEU DE LA FEUILLÉE, LE; JEU DE ROBIN ET MARION, LE; MIRACLE PLAYS; PASSION PLAYS, FRENCH; PUY

JAMES E. KNIRK
Universitetet i Oslo
BRETA SQGUR; SVERRIS SAGA

PAUL W. KNOLL
University of Southern California, Los Angeles
JAGIEŁŁO DYNASTY; PIAST DYNASTY; POLAND

JOHN KOENIG
Macquarie University
GUELPHS AND GHIBELLINES

LINDA KOMAROFF
Hamilton College
EYVĀN; GHAZNAVID ART AND ARCHITECTURE; ḤAMMĀM; HĀN; IMĀMZĀDA; SAMANID ART AND ARCHITECTURE; SERDĀB

ELLEN KOSMER
Worcester State College
HONORÉ, MASTER; PUCELLE, JEAN

MARYANNE KOWALESKI
Fordham University
FOOD TRADES; MARKETS, EUROPEAN; MEAD; POLL TAX, ENGLISH

BERND KRATZ
University of Kentucky
BERTHOLD VON HOLLE; BRUDER HANS; HEINRICH VON DEM TÜRLIN; HERBORB VON FRITZLAR

DENNIS M. KRATZ
University of Texas at Dallas
RUODLIEB; WALTHARIUS

HENRY KRATZ
University of Tennessee
PÜTERICH VON REICHERTSHAUSEN, JAKOB III; WOLFRAM VON ESCHENBACH

F. F. KREISLER
DOMESDAY BOOK

BARIŠA KREKIĆ
University of California, Los Angeles
DALMATIA; DUBROVNIK; DYRRACHIUM; MARICA RIVER; OCHRID; VARNA

BARBARA M. KREUTZ
Bryn Mawr College
SHIPS AND SHIPBUILDING, MEDITERRANEAN

THOMAS KUEHN
Clemson University
INHERITANCE, WESTERN EUROPEAN; LAW, SCHOOLS OF

MICHAEL KWATERA, O.S.B.
St. John's Abbey
BOOK OF HOURS; BREVIARY

MARGARET WADE LABARGE
HENRY V OF ENGLAND

NORRIS J. LACY
University of Kansas
GUILLAUME DE DOLE

VALERIE M. LAGORIO
University of Iowa
JULIAN OF NORWICH; MYSTICISM, CHRISTIAN: CONTINENTAL (WOMEN); MYSTICISM, ENGLISH

ANGELIKI E. LAIOU
Harvard University
ANDRONIKOS II PALAEOLOGOS; ANDRONIKOS III PALAEOLOGOS; CHARISTIKION; DUNATOI; FAMILY, BYZANTINE; FARMERS' LAW; JOHN V PALAIOLOGOS; JOHN VI KANTAKOUZENOS; JOHN VIII PALAIOLOGOS; KANTAKOUZENOI; LIUTPRAND OF CREMONA; MANUEL II PALAIOLOGOS; PALAIOLOGOI; PAROIKOI; PENETES; TRADE, BYZANTINE

IAN LANCASHIRE
Erindale College, University of Toronto at Mississauga
N-TOWN PLAYS; WYNKYN DE WORDE

RICHARD LANDES
University of Pittsburgh
RADULPHUS GLABER; YEAR 1000, THE

Y. TZVI LANGERMANN
Hebrew University of Jerusalem
SCIENCE, JEWISH

IRA M. LAPIDUS
University of California, Berkeley
ALEPPO; CAIRO; KHALDŪN, IBN

JOHN LARNER
University of Glasgow
ART, COMMERCIAL TRADE OF; ARTIST, STATUS OF THE; GUILDS OF ARTISTS

JACOB LASSNER
Wayne State University
ABBASIDS; BAGHDAD; BARMAKIDS; HĀRŪN AL-RASHĪD; KHAṬĪB AL-BAGHDĀDĪ, AL-; MAHDĪ, AL-; MA⊃MŪN, AL-; MANṢŪR, ABŪ JA⊂FAR AL-; SAMARRA; ṬABARĪ, AL-

J. DEREK LATHAM
University of Edinburgh
HUNTING AND FOWLING, ISLAMIC

TRAUGOTT LAWLER
Yale University
ENCYCLOPEDIAS AND DICTIONARIES, WESTERN EUROPEAN; TREVISA, JOHN

CONTRIBUTORS

DAMIAN RIEHL LEADER
University of Toronto, Centre for Medieval Studies
ARNOBIUS THE ELDER; ARNOBIUS THE YOUNGER; OXFORD UNIVERSITY

R. WILLIAM LECKIE, JR.
University of Toronto, Centre for Medieval Studies
ALBRECHT VON SCHARFENBERG; GILDAS, ST.; HADAMAR VON LABER; HISTORIA BRITTONUM; MINNEBURG; NENNIUS

LOUIS J. LEKAI
BIBLE, CISTERCIAN

WINFRED P. LEHMANN
University of Texas
INDO-EUROPEAN LANGUAGES, DEVELOPMENT OF

RICHARD LEMAY
City University of New York, Graduate Center
ARABIC NUMERALS; GERARD OF CREMONA; ROMAN NUMERALS

JOHN LE PATOUREL
University of Leeds
NORMANS AND NORMANDY; WILLIAM I OF ENGLAND

JOHANNES LEPIKSAAR
FISHERIES, MARINE

ROBERT E. LERNER
Northwestern University
ALEXANDER OF ROES; ANTICHRIST; BEGUINES AND BEGHARDS; BEGUINS; EIKE VON REPGOWE; EKKEHARD OF AURA; FREE SPIRIT, HERESY OF; FRUTOLF OF MICHELSBERG; GREGORY VII, POPE; HELMOLD OF BOSAU; HUGH OF ST. CHER; INVESTITURE AND INVESTITURE CONFLICT; MILLENNIALISM, CHRISTIAN; OTTO OF FREISING; OTTO I THE GREAT; PASCHAL II, POPE; STEPHEN II, POPE; THIETMAR VON MERSEBURG; VIGILIUS, POPE; WIDUKIND OF CORVEY

ROY F. LESLIE
University of Victoria
BRUT, THE

JOAN LEVIN
Vassar College
ITALIAN LITERATURE: ALLEGORICAL AND DIDACTIC; ITALIAN LITERATURE: POPULAR POETRY

ARTHUR D. LEVINE
University of Toronto
HOCKET; INTROIT; JACOBUS OF BOLOGNA; JUBILUS; MUSICA FICTA; MUTATION; OLD HALL MS; SOLMIZATION; STAFF; SUMER IS ICUMEN IN

KENNETH LEVY
Princeton University
KONTAKION; MUSIC, BYZANTINE

KEITH LEWINSTEIN
Princeton University
MUQADDASĪ, AL-; RĀḌĪ, AL-

ANDREW W. LEWIS
Southwest Missouri State University
CAPETIAN FAMILY ORIGINS

ARCHIBALD R. LEWIS
University of Massachusetts, Amherst
ADMIRAL; BARRELS; CONSULS, CONSULATE; LANGUEDOC; MONTPELLIER

BERNARD LEWIS
Princeton University
ASSASSINS

P. OSMUND LEWRY, O.P.†
Pontifical Institute of Mediaeval Studies, Toronto
DIALECTIC; QUAESTIONES

JOHN LEYERLE
University of Toronto
USK, THOMAS

DAVID C. LINDBERG
University of Wisconsin
LENSES AND EYEGLASSES; OPTICS, WESTERN EUROPEAN

AMNON LINDER
LAW, JEWRY

RUDI PAUL LINDNER
University of Michigan
QAYKHOSRAW I; QILIJ ARSLĀN II

JOHN LINDOW
University of California, Berkeley
BALDR; BALDRS DRAUMAR; FENRIS WOLF; GYLFAGINNING; HÁTTATAL; HÁVAMÁL; HEIMDALLR; HŒNIR; HUGINN AND MUNNIN; IÐUNN; LOKI; MIDGARD SERPENT; MÍMIR; ODIN; RAGNARQK; SKÁLDSKAPARMÁL; SNORRA EDDA; THOR; VALHALLA; VALKYRIE; VANIR

FRANCES RANDALL LIPP
Colorado State University
SEX AETATES MUNDI; WILLIAM IX OF AQUITAINE

CHARLES T. LITTLE
Metropolitan Museum of Art
IVORY CARVING

DONALD P. LITTLE
McGill University
BARQŪQ; CIRCASSIANS; TAYMĪYA, IBN

LESTER K. LITTLE
Smith College
ADRIAN IV, POPE; ANTHONY OF PADUA, ST.; ANTIPOPE; CHURCH, LATIN: 1054 TO 1305; FRANCIS OF ASSISI, ST.; FRANCISCANS; FRIARS; SALIMBENE

ALICE CORNELIA LOFTIN
Virginia Polytechnic Institute
VISIONS

F. DONALD LOGAN
Emmanuel College, Boston
EXCOMMUNICATION; VIKINGS

DEREK W. LOMAX
University of Birmingham
LOPES, FERNÃO; SPANISH LITERATURE: SERMONS

ANNE LOMBARD-JOURDAN
FAIRS; FAIRS OF CHAMPAGNE

MICHAEL P. LONG
Columbia University
BELLS; COUNTERPOINT; LANDINI, FRANCESCO; LAUDA; MARCHETTUS OF PADUA

ERIK LÖNNROTH
Göteborgs Universitet
SWEDEN

LARS LÖNNROTH
Göteborgs Universitet
ALEXANDERS SAGA; KRISTNI SAGA; ODDR SNORRASON; ÓLÁFS SAGA HELGA; ÓLÁFS SAGA TRYGGVASONAR; RÓMVERJA SAGA; TRÓJUMANNA SAGA

ROBERT S. LOPEZ†
Yale University
GENOA

H. R. LOYN
Westfield College, University of London
ANGLO-SAXONS, ORIGINS AND MIGRATION; DANEGELD; DANELAW; ENGLAND: ANGLO-SAXON; ETHELRED THE UNREADY

R. M. LUMIANSKY†
American Council of Learned Societies
MALORY, SIR THOMAS

NIELS LUND
University of Copenhagen
CNUT THE GREAT

MAXWELL LURIA
MIDDLE ENGLISH LITERATURE: LYRIC

JAMES F. LYDON
Trinity College, Dublin
BURGH, DE; FITZGERALDS; IRELAND: EARLY HISTORY; IRELAND: AFTER 1155; WALES: HISTORY

JOHN E. LYNCH
Catholic University of America
OATH

JOSEPH H. LYNCH
Ohio State University
SIMONY

BRYCE LYON
Brown University
BALDWIN I OF FLANDERS; BARONS' WAR; BRUGES; CLARENDON, ASSIZE OF; CLARENDON, CONSTITUTIONS OF; COMMUNE; ÉCHEVIN; ENGLAND: NORMAN-ANGEVIN; EXCHEQUER; FIEF, MONEY; FLANDERS AND THE LOW COUNTRIES; GHENT; GLANVILLE, RANULF DE; HENRY I OF ENGLAND; HENRY II OF ENGLAND; HENRY III OF ENGLAND; HOUSEHOLD, CHAMBER, AND WARDROBE; JOCELIN OF BRAKELOND; JOHN, KING OF

BRYCE LYON (*cont.*)
ENGLAND; JUSTICIAR; LANFRANC OF BEC; LANGTON, STEPHEN; LILLE; PIPE ROLLS; PROVISIONS OF OXFORD; RICHARD I THE LIONHEARTED; SCUTAGE; SIMON DE MONTFORT THE YOUNGER; VERMANDOIS; YPRES

WILLIAM MACBAIN
University of Maryland
VIE DE STE. CATHERINE D'ALEXANDRIE

ROBERT D. MCCHESNEY
Hagop Kevorkian Center for Near Eastern Studies, New York University
AFGHANISTAN; FARGHĀNĀ (FERGANA); QARĀ MUḤAMMAD; YUSUF

MICHAEL MCCORMICK
The Johns Hopkins University
ALGER OF LIÈGE; CHAINED BOOKS; CODEX; COLOPHON; INK; KOLLEMA; KOLLESIS; MANUSCRIPT BOOKS, BINDING OF: EUROPEAN; PAPYRUS; PARCHMENT; PECIA; PHILIP OF HARVENGT; POCKETBOOKS; PRICKINGS; PUNCTUATION; QUIRE; RUDOLF OF ST. TROND; RULING; RUPERT OF DEUTZ; SIGNATURES; STEPHEN OF TOURNAI; STICHOMETRY; STYLUS; VOLUMEN; WALTER OF MAURETANIA; WATERMARKS; WAX TABLETS; WIBALD OF STAVELOT; WRITING MATERIALS, WESTERN EUROPEAN

LAWRENCE J. MCCRANK
Auburn University at Montgomery
LIBRARIES

JOHN M. MCCULLOH
Kansas State University
BRANDEUM; CATACOMBS; MARTYROLOGY

WILLIAM C. MCDONALD
University of Virginia
MICHEL BEHEIM WILDE ALEXANDER, DER

JAMES T. MCDONOUGH, JR.
St. Joseph's College, Philadelphia, Pennsylvania
MACROBIUS; MARTIN OF BRAGA

GEARÓID MAC EOIN
University College, Galway
AISLINGE MEIC CON-GLINNE

TIMOTHY J. MCGEE
University of Toronto
DANCE; DRAMA, LITURGICAL; FAENZA CODEX; MUSICAL ORNAMENTATION; MUSICAL PERFORMANCE

JULIA H. MCGREW
Vassar College
STURLUNGA SAGA

RALPH MCINERNY
University of Notre Dame, Medieval Institute
AQUINAS, ST. THOMAS

CATHERINE A. MCKENNA
Queens College, City University of New York
WELSH LITERATURE: POETRY

JOHN W. MCKENNA
ACCLAMATIONS; ANOINTING

JAMES W. MCKINNON
State University of New York, Buffalo
GALLICAN RITE

DAVID R. MCLINTOCK
University of London
BAPTISMAL VOWS, OLD HIGH GERMAN/OLD SAXON; BIBLICAL POETRY, GERMAN; CHARMS, OLD HIGH GERMAN; CHRISTUS UND DIE SAMARITERIN; GEORGSLIED; HEINRICO (HENRICO), DE; HELIAND; HILDEBRANDSLIED; LUDWIGSLIED; MERIGARTO; MUSPILLI; OLD HIGH GERMAN LITERATURE; OTFRID VON WEISSENBURG; PETRUSLIED; STRASBOURG OATHS; TATIAN; VOCABULARIUS SANCTI GALLI; WESSOBRUNNER GEBET

MARTIN MCNAMARA
Sacred Heart Missionaries, Dublin
AIRDENA BRÁTHA

WILLIAM MACOMBER
St. John's University, Hill Monastic Manuscript Library
ALEXANDRIAN RITE; ANTIOCHENE RITE

MICHAEL MCVAUGH
University of North Carolina
MEDICINE, HISTORY OF; REGIMEN SANITATIS SALERNITANUM

CONTRIBUTORS

WILFERD MADELUNG
The Oriental Institute, Oxford;
Jihad; Millennialism, Islamic; Sects, Islamic; Shīʿa; Zaydis

PAUL MAGDALINO
University of St. Andrews
Postal and Intelligence Services, Byzantine

JOHN C. MAGEE
Pontifical Institute of Mediaeval Studies, Toronto
Angela Merici, St.; Angela of Foligno; Antoninus, St.

HUGH MAGENNIS
The Queen's University of Belfast
Exegesis, Old English

HARRY J. MAGOULIAS
Wayne State University
Niketas Choniates

HENRY MAGUIRE
University of Illinois at Urbana-Champaign
Nikolaos Mesarites

MICHAEL S. MAHONEY
Princeton University
Mathematics; Ptolemaic Astronomy

CLARK MAINES
Wesleyan University
Renaissances and Revivals in Medieval Art

GEORGE P. MAJESKA
University of Maryland
Analoi; Bochka; Chasovnya; Darokhranitelnitsa; Epitrakhil; Fioravanti, Aristotele; Golosniki; Hagia Sophia (Kiev); Icons, Manufacture of; Kamennaya Baba; Kiot; Kleimo; Kliros; Kokoshnik; Kontsovka; Nevsky, Alexander; Oleg; Olga/Helen; Omophorion; Orarion; Papert; Pelena; Peter, Master; Pilgrimage, Russian; Plashchanitsa; Pogost; Prokhor of Gorodets; Rurik; Russian Architecture; Theophanes the Greek; Venets; Vladimir, St.; Vladimir Monomakh; Vladimir Virgin; Yaroslav the Wise

J. RUSSELL MAJOR
Emory University
Representative Assemblies, French

GEORGE MAKDISI
University of Pennsylvania
Schools, Islamic

ALAN MAKOVSKY
Princeton University
Ankara

KRIKOR H. MAKSOUDIAN
Anania Širakacʿi; Archon Ton Archonton; Arcrunis; Armenian Alphabet; Armenian Church, Doctrines and Councils; Armenian Church, Structure; Armenian Hellenizing School; Armenian Language; Armenian Literature; Armenian Saints; Ašot I Mec (the Great); Ašot II Erkatʿ; Ašot III Ołormac (the Merciful); Bagratids (Bagratuni), Armenian; Bible, Armenian; Calendars, Armenian; David of Sasun; David the Invincible; Ēǰmiacin; Eznik of Kołb; Frik; Gagik I; Gagik II; Gagik/Xačʿik-Gagik; Gagik of Kars; Girk Tʿłtʿocʿ; Gregory the Illuminator, St.; Grigor Magistros; Grigor II Vkayasēr; Historiography, Armenian; Homicide in Islamic Law; John I Tzimiskes; Katholikos; Knikʿ Hawatoy; Koriwn; Law, Armenian; Law, Canon: Armenian; Łewond; Lōṙi; Manazkert, Council of; Maštocʿ, St.; Matthew of Edessa; Michael the Syrian; Movsēs Dasχurancʿi; Mχitʿar Goš; Nersēs IV Šnorhali; Nersēs Lambronacʿi; Petros Getadarj; Smbat I the Martyr; Smbat Sparapet; Stepʿanos Asołik Tarōnecʿi; Thaddeus Legend; Tʿovma Arcruni; Vardapet

YAKOV MALKIEL
University of California, Berkeley
Spanish Language

FEDWA MALTI-DOUGLAS
University of Texas at Austin
Biography, Islamic

STEPHEN MANNING
University of Kentucky
Pastourelle; Reverdie

FRANK A. C. MANTELLO
Catholic University of America
Trevet, Nicholas

MAHMOUD MANZALAOUI
University of British Columbia
Secretum Secretorum

IVAN G. MARCUS
Jewish Theological Seminary of America
Circumcision, Jewish; Eleazar ben Judah of Worms; Ḥasidei Ashkenaz; Jewish Communal Self-Government, Europe; Judah ben Samuel he-Hasid; Judeo-Latin; Schools, Jewish

HARRY J. MARGOULIAS
Niketas Choniates

J. Y. MARIOTTE
Archives de la Haute-Savoie
Switzerland

ROBERT MARK
Princeton University
Construction: Engineering

T. L. MARKEY
University of Michigan
Erikskrönikan; Karlskrönikan

RICHARD C. MARKS
The Royal Pavilion, Art Gallery, and Museums, Brighton
Prudde, John

LOUISE MARLOW
Princeton University
Sasanian History

SHAUN E. MARMON
The Johns Hopkins University
Bab al-Mandab; Baḥrayn, al-; Baṭṭūṭa, Ibn; Baybars al-Bunduqdārī; Concubinage, Islamic; Harem; Slavery, Islamic World

MICHAEL E. MARMURA
University of Toronto
Fārābī, al-; Ghazālī, al-; Kindī, al-; Muʿtazila, al-; Rāzī, al-; Rushd, Ibn (Averroës)

STEVEN P. MARRONE
Tufts University
Grosseteste, Robert; Kilwardby, Robert

DENNIS D. MARTIN
Bethany Theological Seminary
Devotio Moderna

JOHN MARTIN
Harvard University
Condottieri

JOHN HILLARY MARTIN, O.P.
John of Paris

JOHN RUPERT MARTIN
Princeton University
Deesis

RICHARD C. MARTIN
Arizona State University
Iḥrām; Mecca; Medina

LAURO MARTINES
University of California, Los Angeles
Italy, Fourteenth and Fifteenth Centuries; Italy, Rise of Towns in

H. SALVADOR MARTÍNEZ
New York University
¡Ay, Iherusalem!; Cuaderna Vía; Mester de Juglaría

JOAQUÍN MARTÍNEZ-PIZARRO
State University of New York at Stony Brook
Adam of Bremen; Ásmundar Saga Kappabana; Bjarkamál; Gríms Saga Loðinkinna; Ketils Saga Hængs; Knud Lavard; Lejre Chronicle; Roskilde Chronicle; Saxo Grammaticus; Sven Aggesen

THOMAS F. MATHEWS
New York University, Institute of Fine Arts
Architecture, Liturgical Aspects; Early Christian and Byzantine Architecture; Parekklesion; Presbyterium

RALPH WHITNEY MATHISEN
University of South Carolina
Desiderius of Monte Cassino; Donatus of Fiesole; Eigel; Endelechius; Engelmodus; Ennodius, Magnus Felix;

RALPH WHITNEY MATHISEN (*cont.*)
Ermoldus Nigellus; Eugenius II of Toledo; Eugenius Vulgarius; Eugippius; Eupolemius; Firmicus Maternus, Julius; Germanus of Auxerre, St.; Germanus of Paris, St.; Hilary of Poitiers, St.; Jordanes; Merobaudes; Orientius; Orosius; Patrician, Roman; Paulinus of Aquileia, St.; Paulinus of Béziers; Paulinus of Nola, St.; Paulinus of Pella; Paulinus of Périgueux; Polemius Silvius; Prosper of Aquitaine; Salvian of Marseilles; Sidonius Apollinaris; Venantius Fortunatus; Victorinus

E. ANN MATTER
University of Pennsylvania
Angel/Angelology; Autpertus, Ambrosius; Origen; Paschasius Radbertus of Corbie, St.

CHRISTOPHER MELCHERT
University of Pennsylvania
Saffāḥ, Abū ʾl-ᶜAbbās al-

DANIEL FREDERICK MELIA
Study Center of the University of California, London
Irish Society; St. Mary's Abbey, Dublin

MARÍA ROSA MENOCAL
University of Pennsylvania
Italian Language

GUY MERMIER
University of Michigan
Cent Nouvelles Nouvelles; Chastelaine de Vergi, La; Comines (Commynes), Philippe de; French Literature, Didactic; Quinze Joies de Mariage, Les; Tristan, Roman de

BRIAN MERRILEES
University of Toronto
Adgar; Amadas et Ydoine; Angier; Anglo-Norman Literature; Anonimalle Chronicle; Arundel Psalter; Blancheflour et Florence; Boeve (Beuves) de Haumtone; Cambridge Psalter; Cato's Distichs (Old French); Chardri; Chroniques de Londres; Crusade and Death of Richard I; Disciplina Clericalis; Donnei des

BRIAN MERRILEES (*cont.*)
Amants; Folies Tristan; Foukes le Fitzwarin (Fitz Waryn); Gui de Warewic; Guischart de Beaulieu; Holkham Bible Picture Book; Hue de Rotelande; Jeu d'Adam; John of Hewden; Jordan Fantosme; Lai del Desiré, Le; Livere de Reis de Brittanie et Livere de Reis de Engleterre; Manière de Langage; Matthew Paris; Orthographia Gallica; Oxford Psalter; Passiun Seint Edmund, La; Petite Philosophie, La; Robert of Greatham; Roman de Toute Chevalerie; Romance of Horn; Scalacronica; Sanson de Nanteuil; Seinte Resureccion, La; Simund de Freine; Urbain le Courtois; Vie d'Edouard le Confesseur, la; Vie de St. Auban; Vie de St. Gilles; Vie de St. Laurent; Vie de St. Thomas Becket; Vie de Ste. Marguerite; Vie de Ste. Modwenne; Voyage de St. Brendan, le; Waldef, l'Estoire de; Walter of Bibbesworth; Wigmore Abbey, Chronicle of; William of Briane

UTA C. MERZBACH
Smithsonian Institution
Calendars and Reckoning of Time

BARRY MESCH
University of Florida
Joseph ibn Caspi

RENÉ METZ
Université de Strasbourg
Clergy; Monasticism, Origins

JAN VAN DER MEULEN
Cleveland State University
Gothic Architecture

JOHN MEYENDORFF
St. Vladimir's Orthodox Theological Seminary
Alexis of Moscow; Archimandrite; Arsenius Autorianus; Athanasius of Alexandria, St.; Athos, Mount; Azymes; Barlaam of Calabria; Byzantine Church; Clergy, Byzantine; Councils (Ecumenical, 325–787); Councils, Byzantine (859–1368); Cyril and Methodios, Sts.; Cyril of Alexandria, St.; Ecumenical

JOHN MEYENDORFF (*cont.*)
Patriarch; Eusebius of Caesarea; Filioque; Gregory of Nazianzus, St.; Gregory of Nyssa, St.; Gregory Palamas; Heresies, Byzantine; Hesychasm; Icon, Theology of; Ilarion; Isidore; John of Damascus, St.; Joseph II, Patriarch; Law, Canon: Byzantine; Liturgy, Byzantine Church; Maximus the Confessor, St.; Metropolitan; Michael Keroularios; Mysticism, Byzantine; Nil Sorsky, St.; Pentarchy; Permanent Synod; Peter; Philotheos Kokkinos; Russian Orthodox Church; Sergius of Radonezh, St.; Symeon the New Theologian, St.; Synkellos; Theodosius of the Caves, St.; Theotokos

MARK D. MEYERSON
University of Toronto, Centre for Medieval Studies
Adalbold of Utrecht; Benzo of Alba; Bernorinus; Bertharius; Bovo II of Corvey

MARILYN S. MILLER
Pontifical Institute of Mediaeval Studies, Toronto
Arnold of Brescia

DAVID MILLS
University of Liverpool
Chester Plays; Drama, Western European; Higden, Ranulf

ALASTAIR J. MINNIS
University of Bristol
Exegesis, Latin; Exegesis, Middle English

ROMUALD J. MISIUNAS
Yale University
Lithuania

LEONEL L. MITCHELL
Seabury-Western Theological Seminary
Confirmation

MICHEL MOLLAT
Institut de France, Académie des Inscriptions et Belles Lettres
Jacques Coeur

THOMAS MONTGOMERY
Tulane University of Louisiana
Spanish Literature: Bible Translations

WALTER L. MOORE
Florida State University
Via Moderna

ANNE M. MORGANSTERN
Ohio State University
Baerze, Jacques de; Beauneveu, André; Georges de la Sonnette; Jean Michel; Morel, Pierre

THERESA MORITZ
William of St. Thierry

MICHAEL MORONY
University of California, Los Angeles
Alids; Ḥajjāj ibn Yūsuf al-Thaqafī, al-; Hāshim ibn ᶜAbd Manāf; Hishām ibn ᶜAbd al-Malik; Muᶜāwiya; Ṣiffīn; ᶜUmar II ibn ᶜAbd al-ᶜAzīz

ROY PARVIZ MOTTAHEDEH
Princeton University
Buyids

JOHN MUENDEL
Lakeland College
Waterworks

ROBERT P. MULTHAUF
Smithsonian Institution
Brewing; Distilled Liquors; Dyes and Dyeing; Salt Trade

MARINA MUNDT
Universitetet i Bergen
Gǫngu-Hrólfs Saga; Hákonar Saga Hákonarsonar; Hákonar Saga Ívarssonar; Hervarar Saga ok Heiðreks; Hlǫðskviða; Konungs; Ragnars Saga Loðbrókar; Sturla Þórðarson

JOHN H. MUNRO
University of Toronto
Hemp; Linen; Silk; Textile Technology; Textile Workers

PETER MUNZ
Victoria University of Wellington
Frederick I Barbarossa

RHOADS MURPHEY
Columbia University
Ṣinf

JAMES J. MURPHY
University of California, Davis
Rhetoric: Western European

STEPHEN MURRAY
Columbia University
Parler Family

B. F. MUSALLAM
Contraception, Islamic

HENRY A. MYERS
Law, German: Post-Carolingian

SANDRA NADDAFF
Harvard University
Thousand and One Nights

JOSEPH FALAKY NAGY
University of California, Los Angeles
Fenian Poetry

FAUZI M. NAJJAR
Michigan State University
Political Theory, Islamic; Ramadan

BEZALEL NARKISS
Hebrew University of Jerusalem
Manuscript Illumination: Hebrew

SEYYED HOSSEIN NASR
Temple University
Sīnā, Ibn

LAWRENCE NEES
University of Delaware
Lombard Art

M. K. NELLIS
Clarkson College
Beauty Aids, Cosmetics

ALAN H. NELSON
University of California, Berkeley
Castle of Perseverance; Medwall, Henry; Morality Play

DANA A. NELSON
University of Arizona
Alexandre, Libro de

LEON NEMOY
Dropsie University
Karaites

COLBERT I. NEPAULSINGH
State University of New York at Albany
IMPERIAL, FRANCISCO; SPANISH LITERATURE: LYRIC POETRY

JOHN W. NESBITT
Dumbarton Oaks Research Center
BESANT; HYPERPYRON; MINTS AND MONEY, BYZANTINE; NOMISMA; SEALS AND SIGILLOGRAPHY, BYZANTINE; TECHNOLOGY, BYZANTINE; WEIGHTS AND MEASURES, BYZANTINE

HELAINE NEWSTEAD†
City University of New York
MANNYNG, ROBERT; MATTER OF BRITAIN, FRANCE, ROME

DONALD M. NICOL
King's College, University of London
EPIROS, DESPOTATE OF; METEORA; MICHAEL I OF EPIROS; MICHAEL II OF EPIROS

STEPHEN G. NICHOLS, JR.
University of Pennsylvania
LAI DU COR, LE; PEIRE CARDENAL

HELMUT NICKEL
Metropolitan Museum of Art
ARMS AND ARMOR; BOW AND ARROW/CROSSBOW; CATAPULTS; CHIVALRY, ORDERS OF; GAMES AND PASTIMES; HERALDRY; LANCE; SWORDS AND DAGGERS

W. F. H. NICOLAISEN
State University of New York at Binghamton
NECHTAN; PICTS

MÁIRÍN NÍ DHONNCHADHA
University College, Cork
ADAMNAN, ST.

JOHN D. NILES
University of California, Berkeley
CÆDMON

MARGARET F. NIMS
Pontifical Institute of Mediaeval Studies, Toronto
ARS POETICA; GEOFFREY OF VINSAUF

THOMAS F. X. NOBLE
University of Virginia
PEPIN I; PEPIN II; PEPIN III AND THE DONATION OF PEPIN; POITIERS, BATTLE OF

JOHN T. NOONAN, JR.
University of California, Berkeley
CONTRACEPTION, EUROPEAN; PAUCAPALEA; ROLANDUS

THOMAS S. NOONAN
University of Minnesota
FURS, FUR TRADE; KIEVAN RUS; MINTS AND MONEY, RUSSIAN; SLAVS, ORIGINS OF

TIMOTHY B. NOONE
University of Toronto, Centre for Medieval Studies
ADALBERT OF BREMEN; ADALBERT, ST.; AGNELLUS OF PISA; AMALRIC OF BÈNE; AVITUS, ST.

VIVIAN NUTTON
The Wellcome Institute for the History of Medicine
HENRY DE MONDEVILLE; MONDINO DEI LUZZI

TORE S. NYBERG
University of Odense
BIRGITTA, ST.

FRANCIS OAKLEY
Williams College
AILLY, PIERRE D'; CHURCH, LATIN: 1305 TO 1500; CONCILIAR THEORY; COUNCILS, WESTERN (1311–1449); ZABARELLA, FRANCESCO

JOSEPH F. O'CALLAGHAN
Fordham University
CALATRAVA, ORDER OF; CORTES; SIETE PARTIDAS; SPANISH ERA

TOMÁS Ó CATHASAIGH
University College, Dublin
CORMAC MAC AIRT; IRISH LITERATURE: SAGA; TARA

SEÁN Ó COILEÁIN
Harvard University
IRISH LITERATURE

DONNCHADH Ó CORRÁIN
University College, Cork
ÁED SLÁNE; CASHEL; CONNACHT; DÁL CAIS; DÁL RIATA; EÓGANACHT; IRISH LITERATURE: HISTORICAL

DONNCHADH Ó CORRÁIN *(cont.)*
COMPOSITIONS; LAW, IRISH; LEINSTER; MAC LONÁIN, FLANN; UÍ NÉILL

BRIAN Ó CUÍV
Dublin Institute for Advanced Studies
ACALLAM NA SENÓRACH

W. A. ODDY
The British Museum
BRONZE AND BRASS; METALSMITHS, GOLD AND SILVER; METALWORKERS

BARBARA OEHLSCHLAEGER-GARVEY
University of Illinois at Urbana-Champaign
KOIMESIS; MANDYLION; MANIERA GRECA; MANUEL EUGENIKOS; MANUEL PANSELINOS; MAPHORION; MICHAEL ATTALEIATES; MISSORIUM; PREPENDULIA; PROSKYNETARION; TABLION

RICHARD O'GORMAN
University of Iowa
ENVOI; NOUVELLE; ROBERT DE BORON; ROBERT LE DIABLE

THOMAS H. OHLGREN
Purdue University
BARD; DUNSTAN, LIFE OF; OSWALD OF RAMSEY; ST. CHAD, BOOK OF

NICHOLAS OIKONOMIDES
Université de Montréal
AUGUSTA; AUTOCRATOR; BASILEUS; BASILICS; CAESAR; CUROPALATES; DESPOT; DUX; ECLOGUE; EPANAGOGE; GEORGE OF PISIDIA; HARMENOPOULOS, CONSTANTINE; ISAPOSTOLOS; KATEPANO; LAW, BYZANTINE; LOGOTHETE; MAGISTROS; NIKEPHOROS II PHOKAS; PHILOTHEOS; PHOKAS; PORPHYROGENITOS; PROCHEIROS NOMOS; PSEUDO-KODINOS; SEBASTOKRATOR; TAXATION, BYZANTINE

BERNARD O'KANE
American University in Cairo
SAHN; ṢUFFA

PÁDRAIG P. Ó NÉILL
University of North Carolina at Chapel Hill
AIRBERTACH MAC COISSE; APROCRYPHA, IRISH; BIBLE, GLOSSES

CONTRIBUTORS

PÁDRAIG P. Ó NÉILL (*cont.*)
AND COMMENTARIES (IRISH); BOOKS, LITURGICAL (CELTIC); BRIGIT (BRIGID), ST.; CELTIC CHURCH; CINÉAL EÓGHAIN; CORMAC MAC CUILENNÁIN; DUODECIM ABUSIVIS SAECULI, DE; GNOMIC LITERATURE; MANUSCRIPTS, CELTIC LITURGICAL; OGHAM; SALTAIR NA RANN

PÁDRAIG Ó RIAIN
University College, Cork
IRISH LITERATURE: RELIGIOUS

ERIC L. ORMSBY
McGill University
ḤAZM, ABŪ MUḤAMMAD ᶜALĪ IBN AḤMAD IBN SAᶜĪD IBN; ISMĀᶜĪLĪYA; PARADISE, ISLAMIC; PURGATORY, ISLAMIC CONCEPT OF

KENAN B. OSBORNE
Franciscan School of Theology, Berkeley, California
TRINITARIAN DOCTRINE

DUANE J. OSHEIM
University of Virginia
MATILDA OF TUSCANY; SUTRI, SYNOD OF

LEAH OTIS
PROSTITUTION

ROBERT G. OUSTERHOUT
University of Illinois at Urbana-Champaign
HAGIA SOPHIA (CONSTANTINOPLE); KARIYE DJAMI, (CONSTANTINOPLE); LAVRA; NAOS; NYMPHAEUM; ORATORY; PASTOPHORY; POLYCANDELON; PROTHESIS; SOLEA; SYNTHRONON; THEODORE METOCHITES

ARSENIO PACHECO-RANSANZ
University of British Columbia
CATALAN NARRATIVE IN VERSE

WALTER PAKTER
University of California, Berkeley
ROGERIUS

HERMANN PÁLSSON
University of Edinburgh
EGILS SAGA EINHENDA OK ÁSMUNDAR BERSERKJABANA; EGILS SAGA SKALLAGRÍMSSONAR; FORNALDARSÖGUR; GAUTREKS SAGA; KONUNGS; HÁLFDANAR SAGA BRÖNUFÓTRA; HÁLFDANAR SAGA

HERMANN PÁLSSON (*cont.*)
EYSSTEINSSONAR; HÁLFS SAGA OK HÁLFSREKKA; HELGA ÞÁTTR ÞÓRISSONAR; HJÁLMÞÉRS SAGA OK ÖLVIS; HRÓLFS SAGA GAUTREKSSONAR; ILLUGA SAGA GRÍÐARFÓSTRA; LANDNÁMABÓK; ÖRVAR-ODDS SAGA; SÖRLA SAGA STERKA; STURLAUGS SAGA STARFSAMA; ÞÁTTR AF RAGNARS SONUM; ÞORSTEINS SAGA VÍKINGSSONAR; ÞORSTEINS ÞÁTTR BÆJARMAGNS; YNGVARS SAGA VÍÐFÖRLA

HERBERT H. PAPER
Hebrew Union College, Jewish Institute of Religion
JUDEO-PERSIAN

ANGELO PAREDI
Biblioteca Ambrosiana, Milan
BUCENTAUR; MILAN; SFORZA; TUSCANY; VISCONTI

PETER D. PARTNER
Winchester College
ALBORNOZ, CARDINAL GIL; ANNATE; COLA DI RIENZO; PAPAL STATES; ROME

LOUIS B. PASCOE
Fordham University
GERSON, JOHN

JOSEPH F. PATROUCH
University of Dayton
PECOCK, REGINALD

PIERRE J. PAYER
PENANCE AND PENITENTIALS

DEREK PEARSALL
Centre for Medieval Studies, University of York, England
LYDGATE, JOHN

OLAF PEDERSEN
University of Aarhus
ARMILLARY SPHERE; ASTROLOGY/ASTRONOMY, EUROPEAN; CLOCKWORK, PLANETARY; CROSS-STAFF; EQUATORIUM; QUADRANT; SUNDIALS

FRANKLIN J. PEGUES
Ohio State University
ASSIZE, ENGLISH; JUSTICES OF COMMON PLEAS; JUSTICES OF THE KING'S BENCH; LAW, ENGLISH

FRANKLIN J. PEGUES (*cont.*)
COMMON: TO 1272; NOGARET, GUILLAUME DE

CLAUDE J. PEIFER, O.S.B.
St. Bede Abbey, Peru, Illinois
BENEDICT BISCOP, ST.; BENEDICT OF NURSIA, ST.; CAESARIUS OF ARLES, ST.; CELESTINE I, POPE; GELASIUS I, POPE; GREGORY I THE GREAT, POPE; LEO I, POPE

CHARLES PELLAT
BASRA

IVANA PELNAR-ZAIKO
MINNESINGERS

DAVID A. E. PELTERET
New College, University of Toronto
ADBO (ABBO) OF ST. GERMAIN-DES-PRÉS; ADELMAN OF LIÈGE; ADÉMAR OF CHABANNES; AEDDI (EDDIUS STEPHANUS); AGIUS OF CORVEY; ASSER; KENTIGERN, ST.; NINIAN, ST.

KENNETH PENNINGTON
Syracuse University
CODEX THEODOSIANUS; CORPUS IURIS CIVILIS; GRATIAN; HUGUCCIO; JOHANNES TEUTONICUS; LAURENTIUS HISPANUS; LAW CODES: 1000–1500; LAW, PROCEDURE OF; MAXIMS, LEGAL; PETRI EXCEPTIONES; VINCENTIUS HISPANUS

RICHARD PERKINS
University College London
FLÓAMANNA SAGA

MOSHE PERLMAN
University of California, Los Angeles
POLEMICS, ISLAMIC-JEWISH

CAROL TALBERT PETERS
SQUARCIONE, FRANCESCO; VITALE DA BOLOGNA

EDWARD PETERS
University of Pennsylvania
DEPOSITION OF RULERS, THEORIES OF; PRISONS; TORTURE

CARL F. PETRY
Northwestern University
QĀᵓITBĀY, AL-ASHRAF; QALĀᵓŪN, AL-MANṢŪR; QĀNṢŪH AL-GHAWRĪ

RICHARD W. PFAFF
University of North Carolina
MARIAN FEASTS

CHRISTOPHER PINET
Montana State University
FARCES; MAISTRE PIERRE PATHELIN

PAUL B. PIXTON
Brigham Young University
COUNCILS, WESTERN (1215–1274)

EDWIN B. PLACE
AMADÍS DE GAULA

ALEJANDRO ENRIQUE PLANCHART
University of California, Santa Barbara
ODINGTON, WALTER; TRENT CODICES; WINCHESTER TROPER

JAMES F. POAG
Washington University
GUTE FRAU, DIE; JOHANN VON WÜRZBURG; KONRAD VON STOFFELN; MAI UND BEAFLOR; ULRICH VON ESCHENBACH

ELIZABETH WILSON POE
Tulane University
ALBA; ARNAUT DANIEL; BERNART DE VENTADORN; BERTRAN DE BORN; CANSO; CERCAMON; CHANSON D'ANTIOCHE

PETER POGGIOLI
University of Melbourne
ROUEN

E. J. POLAK
Queensborough Community College, City University of New York
BONCOMPAGNO (BUONCOMPAGNO) OF SIGNA; DICTAMEN

JANET M. POPE
University of California, Santa Barbara
WITENAGEMOT

H. BOONE PORTER
EXTREME UNCTION

NANCY A. PORTER
University of Toronto, Centre for Medieval Studies
ANGELOMUS OF LUXEUIL; ANGELRAM OF ST. RIQUIER; ANGILBERT, ST.;

NANCY A. PORTER *(cont.)*
ANSELM OF BESATE; ANSELM OF LIÈGE; ARATOR

VENETIA PORTER
The British Council
FAIENCE; GABRI WARE; SAMARKAND WARE

NORMAN J. G. POUNDS
Cambridge University
CHARCOAL; COAL, MINING AND USE OF; MINING; STEELMAKING

JAMES M. POWELL
Syracuse University
BONIFACE, ST.; FREDERICK II OF THE HOLY ROMAN EMPIRE, KING OF SICILY; MELFI, CONSITUTIONS OF; NAPLES; PALERMO; PETER'S PENCE; PIERO DELLA VIGNA; PIRMIN, ST.; ROBERT GUISCARD; ROGER I OF SICILY; ROGER II OF SICILY; SICILIAN VESPERS; SICILY, KINGDOM OF; WILLIAM OF APULIA

DAVID S. POWERS
Cornell University
ALMS TAX, ISLAMIC; INHERITANCE, ISLAMIC; WAQF

JAMES F. POWERS
College of the Holy Cross
ALFONSO I OF ARAGON; NAVARRE, KINGDOM OF

MICHAEL R. POWICKE
University of Toronto
HUNDRED YEARS WAR; PREROGATIVE

WALTER H. PRINCIPE
Pontifical Institute of Mediaeval Studies, Toronto
CHRISTOLOGY; PHILOSOPHY AND THEOLOGY, WESTERN EUROPEAN: TWELFTH CENTURY TO AQUINAS

OMELJAN PRITSAK
Ukrainian Research Institute, Harvard University
KHAZARS

WADĀD AL-QĀḌĪ
American University of Beirut
ᶜALĪ IBN ABĪ ṬĀLIB; BALĀDHURĪ, ABŪ ḤASAN AḤMĀD IBN YAHYA IBN JĀBIR AL-; DRUZES; ḤĀKIM BI-AMR ALLĀH, AL-; ḤASAN IBN ᶜALĪ IBN ABĪ ṬALIB, AL-

DONALD E. QUELLER
University of Illinois at Urbana-Champaign
CRUSADES AND CRUSADER STATES: FOURTH; DIPLOMACY, WESTERN EUROPEAN

J. F. QUINN
Pontifical Institute of Mediaeval Studies, Toronto
BONAVENTURE, ST.

CHARLES RADDING
Loyola University, Chicago, Illinois
COMPURGATION; ORDEALS; WERGILD

JOAN NEWLON RADNER
American University, Washington, D.C.
IRISH LITERATURE: VOYAGE TALES

MARY LYNN RAMPOLLA
ALEXANDER III, POPE; EADMER OF CANTERBURY; MARIANUS SCOTUS; WILLIAM OF MALMESBURY

ROSHDI RASHED
Équipe de Recherche Associée, Histoire des Sciences et de la Philosophie Arabes, Centre d'Histoire des Sciences et des Doctrines, Paris
KARAJI, AL-

ROGER RAY
University of Toledo
HISTORIOGRAPHY, WESTERN EUROPEAN

FRITZ RECKOW
Christian-Albrechts-Universität zu Kiel
COPULA

WILLIAM T. REEDY
State University of New York, Albany
COMMENDATION; COMMON PLEAS, COURT OF

JOSÉ M. REGUEIRO
University of Pennsylvania
SPANISH LITERATURE: DRAMA

THOMAS RENNA
Saginaw Valley State College
CHURCH, LATIN: ORGANIZATION; CLUNY, ORDER OF; DISPUTATIO INTER CLERICUM ET MILITEM;

THOMAS RENNA *(cont.)*
EGIDIUS COLONNA; JEROME, ST.; JONAS OF ORLÉANS; KINGSHIP, THEORIES OF; LEO IX, POPE; ODILO OF CLUNY, ST.; ODO OF CLUNY, ST.; QUAESTIO IN UTRAMQUE PARTEM

GEORGE RENTZ
The Johns Hopkins University
ARABIA, ISLAMIC

NICHOLAS RESCHER
University of Pittsburgh
LOGIC, ISLAMIC

ELIZABETH REVELL
Huron College
PETER OF BLOIS

KATHRYN L. REYERSON
University of Minnesota
LAW, FRENCH: IN SOUTH; URBANISM, WESTERN EUROPEAN

ROGER E. REYNOLDS
Pontifical Institute of Mediaeval Studies, Toronto
ADVENT; ALL SAINTS' DAY; ALL SOULS' DAY; ALTAR—ALTAR APPARATUS; ASCENSION, FEAST OF THE; BANGOR, RITE OF; BLESSED VIRGIN MARY, LITTLE OFFICE OF; CARTHUSIAN RITE; CHRISTMAS; CHURCHING OF WOMEN; CLUNIAC RITE; COLORS, LITURGICAL; CUSTOMARY; DEAD, OFFICE OF THE; DEATH AND BURIAL, IN EUROPE; DIVINE OFFICE; FEET, WASHING OF; FURNITURE, LITURGICAL; HEREFORD RITE; HOLYROOD; HOLY WEEK; INCENSE; KYRIALE; LAW, CANON: TO GRATIAN; LITANIES, GREATER AND LESSER; LITURGY, STATIONAL; LITURGY, TREATISES ON; MASS, LITURGY OF THE; METZ, USE OF; MISSAL; NARBONNE RITE; ORDINALE; ORDINARIUS LIBER; ORDINATION, CLERICAL; ORDINES ROMANI; PONTIFICAL; ROSARY; SACRAMENTARY; ST. PETER, LITURGY OF; STATIONS OF THE CROSS; SYRIAN RITES; VESTMENTS; YORK TRACTATES

BRIGITTE BEDOS REZAK
State University of New York at Stony Brook
SEALS AND SIGILLOGRAPHY, WESTERN EUROPEAN

JEAN RICHARD
Université de Dijon
CYPRUS, KINGDOM OF

D. S. RICHARDS
University of Oxford
ATHĪR, IBN AL-

EARL JEFFREY RICHARDS
University of North Carolina
UNICORN

BENJAMIN Z. RICHLER
Institute for Microfilmed Hebrew Manuscripts, Jerusalem
TRANSLATION AND TRANSLATORS, JEWISH

A. G. RIGG
University of Toronto, Centre for Medieval Studies
ANTHOLOGIES; COMMONPLACE BOOKS; LATIN LANGUAGE; LATIN LITERATURE; LATIN METER; PARODY, LATIN; PETER RIGA

FRANÇOIS RIGOLOT
Princeton University
HEPTAMÉRON, L'; JEAN LEMAIRE DE BELGES

ELIAS L. RIVERS
State University of New York at Stony Brook
MANRIQUE, JORGE

THEODORE JOHN RIVERS
LAW, GERMAN: EARLY GERMANIC CODES; SACHSENSPIEGEL; SCHWABENSPIEGEL

BRYNLEY F. ROBERTS
National Library of Wales
GRUFFUDD AP YR YNAD COCH; GRUFFUDD AP CYNAN; GWALCHMAI AP MEILYR; HYWEL AB OWAIN GWYNEDD; WELSH LITERATURE: PROSE; WELSH LITERATURE: RELIGIOUS

PHYLLIS B. ROBERTS
PREACHING AND SERMON LITERATURE, WESTERN EUROPEAN

TIMOTHY R. ROBERTS
GOTTSCHALK OF ORBAIS; HINCMAR OF RHEIMS; RATRAMNUS OF CORBIE

R. H. ROBINS
University of London
GRAMMAR

IAN S. ROBINSON
Trinity College, Dublin
BERNOLD OF CONSTANCE; POLITICAL THEORY, WESTERN EUROPEAN: TO 1100

ORRIN W. ROBINSON
Stanford University
GERMAN LANGUAGE

ELAINE GOLDEN ROBISON
DEUSDEDIT, CARDINAL; DICTATUS PAPAE; EGBERT OF LIÈGE; EKKEHARD I OF ST. GALL; EKKEHARD IV OF ST. GALL; ENGELBERT OF ADMONT; GUILHEM DE TUDELA; GUTHLAC, ST.; HENRY OF CREMONA; HERMAN THE GERMAN; HERMANN VON CARINTHIA; HUGOLINUS; HUMBERT OF SILVA CANDIDA; JOHN OF CAPESTRANO, ST.; MICHAEL SCOT; NICOLAITISM; ODINGTON, WALTER; PETER OF SPAIN; PETER PEREGRINUS OF MARICOURT; PRUDENTIUS; PTOLEMY OF LUCCA; RAHEWIN; RAIMON DE CORNET; RAIMON DE MIRAVAL; ROBERT OF MELUN; ROFFREDUS DE EPIPHANIIS OF BENEVENTO; SIGEBERT OF GEMBLOUX; THOMAS OF HALES

MAXIME RODINSON
Université de Paris
COOKERY, ISLAMIC

H. ROE
University of Toronto, Centre for Medieval Studies
BARDIC GRAMMARS (IRISH, WELSH); CELTIC LANGUAGES

EDWARD H. ROESNER
BAMBERG MANUSCRIPT; HUELGAS MS, LAS; MAGNUS LIBER ORGANI; MONTPELLIER MS H 196; MOTET MANUSCRIPTS; ST. VICTOR MS

HELEN ROLFSON, O.S.F.
St. John's University, Collegeville, Minnesota
MYSTICISM, CHRISTIAN: LOW COUNTRIES

PAUL ROREM
CANONICAL HOURS; CARNIVAL; CORPUS CHRISTI, FEAST OF; EASTER; LENT

LINDA C. ROSE
ADRIANOPLE (EDIRNE); ALLELENGYON; AMORIANS; AMORION; BAR HEBRAEUS; BARDAS CAESAR; BARI; BONIFACE OF MONTFERRAT; BOSPORUS; BRUSA; CATAPHRACTI; CHRYSOBULLON; COSMAS INDICOPLEUSTES; CRETE; DARDANELLES; DEMES; DIOCESE, SECULAR; DIONYSIOS OF TEL-MAHRÉ; DIYARBAKIR; EDESSA; EKTHESIS; EPARCH; EPIBOLÉ; EUPHRATES RIVER; GEORGE SCHOLARIOS; GERMANOS I; GIRDLED PATRICIAN; GOLDEN HORN; GONZÁLEZ DE CLAVIJO, RUY; GREEK FIRE; HENOTIKON; IGNATIOS, PATRIARCH; IKONION; JEAN DE BRIENNE; JOHN KLIMAKOS, ST.; JOHN IV THE FASTER, PATRIARCH; JOHN OF NIKIU; JOSHUA THE STYLITE; LATEEN SAIL; LEO I, EMPEROR; LEO V THE ARMENIAN, EMPEROR; LEO THE MATHEMATICIAN; LIMITANEI; LUKAS NOTARAS; MAGISTER MILITUM; MAGISTER OFFICIORUM; MICHAEL III; MARIA LEKAPENA; MAURICE, EMPEROR; MESEMBRIA; MONOTHELITISM; MYRIOKEPHALON; NAXOS, DUCHY OF; NIKEPHOROS BRYENNIOS; PALLADIOS; PHILIPPOPOLIS; PHILOSTORGIOS; PRAETORIAN PREFECT; RHODES; ROMANOS I LEKAPENOS; ROMANOS II; ROMANOS IV DIOGENES; SERDICA; SERGIOS I; SIRMIUM; SKANDERBEG; SOCRATES SCHOLASTICUS; SOZOMEN; TABULA PEUTINGERIANA; TAFUR, PERO DE; TARASIOS; THEODORET OF CYR; THEOPHANO, EMPRESS; THOMAS THE SLAV; VICAR; YAHYA OF ANTIOCH; ZACHARIAS OF MYTILENE; ZENO THE ISAURIAN

MIRIAM ROSEN
KHĀNQĀH; WĀSIṬĪ, YAḤYĀ IBN MAḤMŪD AL-

DONALD K. ROSENBERG
Duke University
HERMANN VON SACHSENHEIM

ROY ROSENSTEIN
American College in Paris
DIT; ESTRABOT

CHARLES STANLEY ROSS
Purdue University
BARBOUR, JOHN; VERGIL IN THE MIDDLE AGES

JOEL ROTH
Jewish Theological Seminary
TALMUD, EXEGESIS AND STUDY OF

RHIMAN A. ROTZ
Indiana University Northwest
CLASS STRUCTURE, WESTERN (1000–1300); CLASS STRUCTURE, WESTERN (1300–1500); GERMAN TOWNS; PATRICIAN, URBAN

C. ROUECHÉ
KEKAUMENOS

MARY A. ROUSE
University of California, Los Angeles
ALPHABETIZATION, HISTORY OF; CODICOLOGY, WESTERN EUROPEAN; FLORILEGIA

RICHARD H. ROUSE
University of California, Los Angeles
ALPHABETIZATION, HISTORY OF; CODICOLOGY, WESTERN EUROPEAN; MANUSCRIPT BOOKS, PRODUCTION OF

JAY ROVNER
DIETARY LAWS, JEWISH; LITURGY, JEWISH

STEVEN ROWAN
University of Missouri, St. Louis
GERMANY: ELECTORS; GERMANY: IMPERIAL KNIGHTS; GERMANY: PRINCIPALITIES; SYNDIC

BERYL ROWLAND
York University, Ontario
BESTIARY

GUIDO RUGGIERO
University of Connecticut
VENICE

TEOFILO F. RUIZ
Brooklyn College, City University of New York
ALMOGÁVARES; ANDALUSIA; ASTURIAS-LEÓN (718–1037); AVIZ, ORDER OF; CASTILE; CASTILIAN LANGUAGE; CONVERSO; EULOGIUS OF CÓRDOBA; HERMANDADES; JULIANUS OF TOLEDO; LAW, SPANISH; MESTA; RECONQUEST, THE

DANIEL RUSSELL
University of Pittsburgh
OVIDE MORALISÉ

FREDERICK H. RUSSELL
Rutgers University
CRUSADE, CHILDREN'S; CRUSADE, CONCEPT OF

JAMES R. RUSSELL
Columbia University
ARDEŠĪR (ARDASHIR, ARTAXERES) I; BAHRĀM V GŌR; BAHRĀM VI ČŌBĒN; GRIGOR, NAREKACʿI, ST.; HAZĀRABAD; HEPHTHALITES; KARTĪR; LETTER OF TANSAR; MAGIC AND FOLKLORE: ARMENIAN; MAZDAKITES; MŌBADĀN MŌBAD; PARTHIANS; ŠĀBUHR I; ŠĀBUHR II; ŠĀHAN-ŠĀH; SASANIAN CULTURE; SEALS AND SIGILLOGRAPHY, SASANIAN; ŠKAND-GUMĀNĪG WIZĀR; SPĀHBAD; WUZURG FRAMADĀR; XUSRŌ I ANŌŠARWĀN; XUSRŌ II ABARWĒZ

JEFFREY BURTON RUSSELL
University of California, Santa Barbara
CHURCH, EARLY; CHURCH, LATIN: TO 1054; WITCHCRAFT, EUROPEAN

J. JOSEPH RYAN
St. John's Seminary, Brighton, Massachusetts
IVO OF CHARTRES, ST.

IRINA RYBACEK
PRAGUE

ELIAS N. SAAD
TIMBUKTU

A. I. SABRA
Harvard University
OPTICS, ISLAMIC; SCIENCE, ISLAMIC

PETER SACCIO
Dartmouth College
WARS OF THE ROSES

JOSEPH SADAN
Tel-Aviv University
FURNITURE, ISLAMIC; KURST

PAUL SAENGER
Northwestern University Library
LITERACY, WESTERN EUROPEAN

CONTRIBUTORS

RAYMOND C. ST-JACQUES
University of Ottawa
BIBLE, FRENCH

GEORGE SALIBA
Columbia University
ASTROLOGY/ASTRONOMY, ISLAMIC; BĪRŪNĪ, MUḤAMMAD IBN AḤMAD ABU 'L-RAYḤĀN AL-; TRANSLATION AND TRANSLATORS, ISLAMIC

KAMAL S. SALIBI
American University of Beirut
LEBANON

WILLIAM SAMOLIN
MONGOL EMPIRE

ANTONIO SÁNCHEZ ROMERALO
University of California, Davis
SPANISH LITERATURE: DAWN AND SPRING SONGS; VILLANCICOS

CHRISTOPHER SANDERS
University of Copenhagen
BEVERS SAGA

ERNEST H. SANDERS
Columbia University
MOTET; MUSICAL NOTATION, MODAL; NOTRE DAME SCHOOL; PEROTINUS; WORCESTER POLYPHONY

PAULA SANDERS
Rice University
FATIMIDS; FEASTS AND FESTIVALS, ISLAMIC; IMAM; MUᶜIZZ AL-DAWLA; QĀHIR BI'LLĀH, AL-; QAᵓIM, AL-; SANA; YEMEN

T. A. SANDQUIST
University of Toronto
BRACTON, HENRY DE; FLETA; INNS OF COURT; INQUEST, ENGLISH; JURY; JUSTICES, ITINERANT; OUTLAWRY; STATUTE

MARC SAPERSTEIN
Washington University
MAIMONIDEAN CONTROVERSY

MICHAEL SARGENT
CAPGRAVE, JOHN

BARBARA NELSON SARGENT-BAUR
University of Pittsburgh
COLIN MUSET; FRENCH LITERATURE: LYRIC; GAUTIER DE COINCI; VILLON, FRANÇOIS

NAHUM M. SARNA
Brandeis University
EXEGESIS, JEWISH; HEBREW LANGUAGE, JEWISH STUDY OF

ROGER M. SAVORY
Trinity College, Toronto
IRAN, HISTORY: AFTER 650

GEORGE DIMITRI SAWA
FĀRĀBĪ, AL-; ĪQĀᶜ; MAQĀM; MUSIC, ISLAMIC; MUSIC, ISLAMIC INFLUENCE ON NON-WESTERN; MUSIC, ISLAMIC INFLUENCE ON WESTERN; MUSIC, MIDDLE EASTERN; MUSICAL INSTRUMENTS, MIDDLE EASTERN

JOHN SCARBOROUGH
University of Kentucky
HERBALS: BYZANTINE AND ARABIC

V. J. SCATTERGOOD
Trinity College, Dublin
CLANVOWE, SIR JOHN; PROPHECY, POLITICAL: MIDDLE ENGLISH

PAUL SCHACH
University of Nebraska
EYRBYGGJA SAGA; FINNBOGA SAGA; FLJÓTSDAELA SAGA; GULL-ÞÓRIS SAGA; HARÐAR SAGA GRÍMKELSSONAR (OK GEIRS); HÁVARÐAR SAGA ÍSFIRÐINGS; KJALNESINGA SAGA; SVARFDÆLA SAGA; ÞORÐAR SAGA HREÐU; VÁPNFIRÐINGA SAGA; VÁTNSDŒLA SAGA; VÍGA-GLÚMS SAGA; VÍGLUNDAR SAGA

PETER SCHÄFFER
University of California, Davis
ALBRECHT VON HALBERSTADT

RAYMOND P. SCHEINDLIN
Jewish Theological Seminary of America
ABRAHAM BEN MEÏR IBN EZRA; HEBREW BELLES LETTRES; HEBREW POETRY

JACOB SCHIBY
JUDEO-GREEK

NICOLAS SCHIDLOVSKY
AKATHISTOS; ASMATIKON; HEIRMOS; KANŌN; MUSIC, SLAVIC; MUSIC, SYRIAN; OKTOECHOS; PSALTIKON; STICHERON; TROPARION

ANNEMARIE SCHIMMEL
Harvard University
ANGEL, ISLAMIC; ḤALLĀJ, AL-

BERNHARD SCHIMMELPFENNIG
Universität Augsburg
CORONATION, PAPAL; DEGRADATION OF CLERICS; HOLY YEAR; JUBILEE

JEAN-CLAUDE SCHMITT
École des Hautes Études en Sciences Sociales
MAGIC AND FOLKLORE: WESTERN EUROPEAN

KENNETH R. SCHOLBERG
Michigan State University
SPANISH LITERATURE: SATIRE

JAMES A. SCHULTZ
University of Illinois at Chicago
OSWALD, ST.: GERMAN EPICS; SOLOMON AND MARCOLF

JANICE L. SCHULTZ
Canisius College
ADAM OF ST. VICTOR; ADELARD OF BATH; HONORIUS AUGUSTODUNENSIS; JOHN OF SALISBURY; RICHARD OF ST. VICTOR

ELLEN C. SCHWARTZ
Eastern Michigan University
BULGARIAN ART AND ARCHITECTURE

MARTIN SCHWARTZ
University of California, Berkeley
IRANIAN LANGUAGES

HAIM SCHWARZBAUM
Hebrew University of Jerusalem
MAGIC AND FOLKLORE, JEWISH

SIMON SCHWARZFUCHS
Bar-Ilan University
RABBINATE

ELEANOR SEARLE
California Institute of Technology
WALTER OF HENLEY

ALBERT SEAY
Colorado College
ANONYMOUS IV; JACQUES DE LIÈGE; JOHANNES DE GROCHEO

EDWARD A. SEGAL
ST. GALL, MONASTERY AND PLAN OF; WILLIAM OF JUMIÈGES; WILLIAM OF POITIERS

DAVID H. SELLAR
University of Edinburgh
LAW, SCOTS

DOROTHY SHERMAN SEVERIN
Westfield College, University of London
SPANISH LITERATURE: TROY STORY

IRFAN SHAHĪD
Georgetown University
GHASSANIDS; LAKHMIDS; NAJRĀN

DANUTA SHANZER
University of California, Berkeley
NEMESIANUS, MARCUS AURELIUS OLYMPIUS; RUTILIUS CLAUDIUS NAMATIANUS

ALEXANDER M. SHAPIRO
Oheb Shalom Congregation
RESPONSUM LITERATURE, JEWISH

MARIANNE SHAPIRO
New York University
ERMENGAUD, MATFRE

HARVEY L. SHARRER
University of California, Santa Barbara
ARTHURIAN LITERATURE, SPANISH AND PORTUGUESE

STANFORD J. SHAW
University of California, Los Angeles
BĀYAZĪD II

MICHAEL M. SHEEHAN
Pontifical Institute of Mediaeval Studies, Toronto
DISPENSATION; FAMILY AND MARRIAGE, WESTERN EUROPEAN

DANIEL J. SHEERIN
Catholic University of America
DEDICATION OF CHURCHES

LON R. SHELBY
Southern Illinois University at Carbondale
ARCHITECT, STATUS OF; MASONS AND BUILDERS; PILGRAM, ANTON; RIED, BENEDIKT; RORICZER, CONRAD; RORICZER, MATHES; ULRICH VON ENSINGEN

CARL D. SHEPPARD
University of Minnesota
ROMANESQUE ART

JOHN R. SHINNERS, JR.
St. Mary's College, Notre Dame, Indiana
RELIGIOUS INSTRUCTION

LAURENCE K. SHOOK
Pontifical Institute of Mediaeval Studies, Toronto
ABBO OF FLEURY; ALCUIN OF YORK; AUGUSTINE OF CANTERBURY

LEAH SHOPKOW
University of Toronto, Centre for Medieval Studies
AGNELLUS OF RAVENNA, ST.; ALBERIC OF MONTE CASSINO; ALPERT OF METZ; ALPHANUS OF SALERNO; ARBEO OF FREISING; AYNARD OF ST. ÈVRE; BRAULIO OF SARAGOSSA, ST.

IAN SHORT
Birkbeck College
PSEUDO-TURPIN

BOAZ SHOSHAN
Ben-Gurion University of the Negev
ALEXANDRIA

CHARLES R. SHRADER
NATO Defense College
FOLCWIN OF LOBBES; HERIGER OF LOBBES; NOTGER OF LIÈGE; RATHER OF VERONA

SERGEI A. SHUISKII†
Princeton University
ENCYCLOPEDIAS AND DICTIONARIES, ARABIC AND PERSIAN; KHALLIKĀN, IBN; NAVIGATION: INDIAN OCEAN, RED SEA; NIKITIN, AFANASY; PILGRIMAGE, ISLAMIC

MICHAEL A. SIGNER
Hebrew Union College
PREACHING AND SERMONS, JEWISH

GIULIO SILANO
Pontifical Institute of Mediaeval Studies, Toronto
AZO; GLOSSATORS; IRNERIUS; ITALIAN LITERATURE: CHRONICLES; ITALIAN LITERATURE: RELIGIOUS POETRY; JACOPONE DA TODI; MARTINUS GOSIA; RAYMOND OF PEÑAFORT, ST.; RESCRIPTS

LARRY SILVER
Northwestern University
DANSE MACABRE; ECCE HOMO; GERHAERT, NIKOLAUS; GRASSER, ERASMUS; HAGENAUER (HAGENOWER), NIKOLAUS; HOHENFURTH, MASTER OF; I.A.M. OF ZWOLLE, MASTER; ISENMANN, CASPAR; ISRAEL VAN MECKENEM; KOERBECKE, JOHANN; KONRAD VON SOEST; KRAFFT, ADAM; LIFE OF MARY, MASTER OF THE; LOCHNER, STEPHAN; MEIT, CONRAD; MOSER, LUCAS; MULTSCHER, HANS; OIL PAINTING; NOTKE, BERNT; PACHER, MICHAEL; PLEYDENWURFF, HANS; RIEMENSCHNEIDER, TILMAN; ST. BARTHOLOMEW, MASTER OF; ST. VERONICA, MASTER OF; STOSS, VEIT; SYFER, HANS; THEODORIC, MASTER; VISCHER, PETER (THE ELDER); WITTINGAU MASTER; WITZ, KONRAD; WOLGEMUT, MICHAEL

KATHARINE SIMMS
Trinity College, Dublin
IRISH LITERATURE: BARDIC POETRY

ECKEHARD SIMON
Harvard University
DRAMA, GERMAN; GERMAN LITERATURE: LYRIC; NEIDHART "VON REUENTAL"; RABER, VIGIL; ROSENPLÜT, HANS

MARIANNA S. SIMPSON
National Gallery of Art
MANUSCRIPT ILLUMINATION, ISLAMIC

BARRIE SINGLETON
Courtauld Institute, University of London
ESSEX, JOHN; HICKLING, ROBERT; HOLEWELL, THOMAS; HUGH OF ST. ALBANS; HUGO OF BURY ST. EDMUNDS; HYLL, JOHN; JEAN DE LIÈGE; LAMBESPRINGE, BARTHOLOMEW; MASSINGHAM, JOHN; PARES, JOHN ; POPPEHOWE, THOMAS; PRENTYS, THOMAS; ROLF, THOMAS; STOCKTON, THOMAS; STOWELL, JOHN; SUTTON, ROBERT; THIRSK, JOHN; TOREL, WILLIAM; TORRIGIANO, PIETRO; WALTER OF COLCHESTER; WILLIAM OF WINCHESTER; WILLIAM THE ENGLISHMAN; WYNFORD, WILLIAM

DENNIS SLAVIN
Princeton University
JOGLAR/JONGLEUR

CONTRIBUTORS

LOIS K. SMEDICK
University of Windsor
CURSUS

CYRIL SMETANA
York University
AUGUSTINIAN CANONS; AUGUSTINIAN FRIARS

COLIN SMITH
St. Catherine's College, Cambridge
CANTAR DE MÍO CID

KENNETH SNIPES
Manhattan College
PSELLOS, MICHAEL

JOSEPH T. SNOW
University of Georgia
CANTIGA; DINIS; GALICIAN-PORTUGUESE POETRY

ROBERT J. SNOW
University of Texas at Austin
CANTIGA; DOMINICAN CHANT; LAUDES, ACCLAMATIONS; SANTIAGO DE COMPOSTELA

JAMES SNYDER
Bryn Mawr College
BERMEJO, BARTOLOMÉ; BERRUGUETE, PEDRO; BERTRAM, MEISTER; BORRASSÁ, LUIS; BOUTS, DIRK; CAMPIN, ROBERT; CHRISTUS, PETRUS; DARET, JACQUES; DAVID, GERARD; EYCK, JAN VAN AND HUBERT VAN; FLEMISH PAINTING; GEERTGEN TOT SINT JANS; GHENT ALTARPIECE; GOES, HUGO VAN DER; JOOS VAN GHENT; MEMLING, HANS; OUWATER, ALBERT VAN; WEYDEN, ROGIER VAN DER

JOSEP M. SOLA-SOLÉ
Catholic University of America
CANTIGAS DE AMOR, AMIGO, AND ESCARNIO; DANÇA GENERAL DE LA MUERTE

PAUL SOLON
Macalester College
JOAN OF ARC, ST.; SOMNIUM VIRIDARII

HAYM SOLOVEITCHIK
Yeshiva University
JACOB BEN MEIR; MARTYRDOM, JEWISH; RASHI (RABBI SOLOMON BEN ISAAC); USURY, JEWISH LAW

ROBERT SOMERVILLE
Columbia University
ALEXANDER II, POPE; BERENGAR OF TOURS; COUNCILS, WESTERN (869–1179); THOMAS À KEMPIS; URBAN II, POPE

PRISCILLA P. SOUCEK
New York University, Institute of Fine Arts
AGHKAND WARE; AḤMAD MŪSĀ; ASCENSION OF THE PROPHET; BĀB; BĀDIYA; BAWWĀB, IBN AL-; DAWĀT; ICONOLOGY, ISLAMIC; ISLAMIC ART AND ARCHITECTURE; JUNAYD; KAMKHĀ; KĀRGAH; KITĀBKHĀNA; KŪFĪ; LAQABI WARE; NAQSH; NAQSH ḤADĪDA; NASKHĪ; NASTAᶜLIQ; PALEOGRAPHY, ARABIC AND PERSIAN; RAQQAH; SHADIRVAN; THULUTH; YĀM

SVAT SOUCEK
JANISSARY; KHAN; KIRGHIZ; ULJAYTU KHUDABĀNDA

ERNST H. SOUDEK
University of Virginia
ECKHART, MEISTER; HADEWIJCH OF ANTWERP; HILDEGARD OF BINGEN, ST.; MECHTHILD VON MAGDEBURG; PROSE LANCELOT; SUSO, HEINRICH; TAULER, JOHANNES

JAY L. SPAULDING
Michigan State University
NILE

SUSAN SPECTORSKY
Queens College, City University of New York
BUKHĀRĪ, AL-; ḤANBAL, AḤMAD IBN MUḤAMMAD IBN; MĀLIK IBN ANAS; SHĀFIᶜĪ, AL-

MARY B. SPEER
Rutgers University
ADENET LE ROI

GABRIELLE M. SPIEGEL
University of Maryland
GRANDES CHRONIQUES DE FRANCE; GUILLAUME LE BRETON; LOUIS VI OF FRANCE; RIGORD; SUGER OF ST. DENIS

EDDA SPIELMANN
California State University, Northridge
ERMENRÎKES DÔT

ALAN M. STAHL
American Numismatic Society
GROAT; MINTS AND MONEY, WESTERN EUROPEAN

E. G. STANLEY
Pembroke College, Oxford
OWL AND THE NIGHTINGALE, THE

JERRY STANNARD
University of Kansas
BOTANY

RUTH STEINER
Catholic University of America
AGNUS DEI (MUSIC); COMMUNION CHANT; GLORIA; KYRIE; OFFERTORY; PLAINSONG, SOURCES OF; VENI CREATOR SPIRITUS

WESLEY M. STEVENS
University of Winnipeg
FULDA

PAMELA D. STEWART
McGill University
ITALIAN LITERATURE: PROSE

J. STEYAERT
University of Minnesota
DIJON, CHARTREUSE DE CHAMPMOL; SLUTER, CLAUS

SANDRO STICCA
State University of New York at Binghamton
HROTSWITHA VON GANDERSHEIM

NORMAN A. STILLMAN
State University of New York at Binghamton
JEWS IN MUSLIM SPAIN; JEWS IN NORTH AFRICA; JUDAISM; JUDEO-ARABIC LANGUAGE; MAGIC AND FOLKLORE, ISLAMIC

YEDIDA K. STILLMAN
State University of New York at Binghamton
COSTUME, ISLAMIC; COSTUME, JEWISH; ḤAMĀᵓIL; MAGIC AND FOLKLORE, ISLAMIC; QALANSUWA; SUMPTUARY LAWS, ISLAMIC; ṬAYLASĀN

CHARLES L. STINGER
State University of New York at Buffalo
TRAVERSARI, AMBROGIO

ALAIN J. STOCLET
Adalbero of Laon; Aimoin de Fleury; Amalarius of Metz; Ammianus Marcellinus; André de Fleury; Arnulf; Benedictine Rule; Carmen de Bello Saxonico; Monte Cassino

M. ALISON STONES
University of Minnesota
Anglo-Norman Art

MELVIN STORM
Emporia State University, Kansas
Riddles; Tintagel; Tintern; Trivium

KENNETH R. STOW
University of Haifa
Jews and the Catholic Church; Jews in Europe: After 900; Jews in the Papal States; Servi Camerae Nostrae

SANDRA STOW
University of Haifa
Judeo-French; Judeo-Italian

PAUL W. STRAIT
Florida State University
Cologne

GERALD STRAUSS
Indiana University
Germany: 1254–1493; Germany: Idea of Empire

JOSEPH R. STRAYER†
Princeton University
Advocate; Albert of Saxony; Apostasy; Athanasians; Ausculta Fili; Avignon; Banneret; Benefice, Ecclesiastical; Benefice, Lay; Brick; Britton; Bulgarus; Burgundio of Pisa; Caen; Caesarius of Heisterbach; Caesaropapism; Carroccio; Castellan; Charles Martel; Clerk; Clovis; Commendam; Confessor: Saint; Congé d'Élire; Conrad of Megenberg; Crusades, Political; Curfew; Curia, Lay; Curia, Papal; Dauphin; Diocese, Ecclesiastical; Doctor; Donatism; Dungeon; Feudalism; Fief; George of Trebizond; Gilbert of Poitiers; Gypsies; Hugh of Fleury; Ibelin, Jean d'(of Beirut); Ibelin, Jean d'(of Jaffa); Indiction; James of Viterbo; Jordan of Osnabrück;

JOSEPH R. STRAYER† *(cont.)*
Lambert of Hersfeld; Law, French: In North; Marigny, Enguerran de; Maronite Church; Moat; Neckham, Alexander; Nicholas of Autrecourt; Nicholas of Clamanges; Odofredus; Philip IV the Fair; Pierre Dubois; Plantagenets; Province, Ecclesiastical; William of Champeaux

JAMES H. STUBBLEBINE
Rutgers University
Duccio di Buoninsegna; Guido da Siena; Maestà

LARRY E. SULLIVAN
Lehman College, City University of New York
Paris; Textbooks

RICHARD E. SULLIVAN
Michigan State University
Aachen; Parish

RONALD GRIGOR SUNY
University of Michigan
Amirspasalar; Aznauri; Bagratids (Bagratuni), Georgian; Chosroids (Mihranids); David II (IV) the Builder; David of Tao; Erist$^{\subset}$aw; Georgia: Political History; Georgians (Iberians); Giorgi III; Qma; Tamar; Waχtang I Gurgaslani

RONALD E. SURTZ
Princeton University
Apolonio, Libro de

SANDRA CANDEE SUSMAN
Dalle Masegne, Pierpaolo and Jacobello; Della Robbia, Luca, Andrea, Giovanni; Giovanni da Campione; Giovanni di Balduccio; Guido da Como; Jacopo della Quercia; Piero di Giovanni Tedesco; Pisano, Andrea; Raverti, Matteo; Tino di Camaino

DONALD W. SUTHERLAND†
University of Iowa
Borough-English; Burgage Tenure; Coroner; Englishry, Presentment of; Frankalmoin; Heriot; Law, English Common: After 1272; Liberty and Liberties; Petty Assizes, English;

DONALD W. SUTHERLAND† *(cont.)*
Sac and Soc; Seisin, Disseisin; Sheriff

WIM SWAAN
Werve, Claus de

JUNE SWANN
Central Museum, Northamptonshire
Shoes and Shoemakers

R. N. SWANSON
University of Birmingham
Conclave, Papal; Concordat; Legates, Papal; Nuncio, Papal; Two Swords, Doctrine of

MERLIN SWARTZ
Boston University
Preaching and Sermons, Islamic

JAMES ROSS SWEENEY
Pennsylvania State University
Chivalry; Romanian Principalities; Vlachs; Vlad Ţepeş; Walachia/Moldavia

EDITH DUDLEY SYLLA
North Carolina State University
Physics; Swineshead

EDWARD A. SYNAN
Pontifical Institute of Mediaeval Studies, Toronto
Anselm of Laon; Atto of Vercelli; Augustine of Hippo, St.; Augustinism; Bruno of Würzburg, St.; Bruno the Carthusian, St.; Cassian, John; Clement V, Pope; Fulcher of Chartres; John the Deacon; Philosophy and Theology, Western European: Terminology

JOSEPH SZÖVÉRFFY
Archpoet; Cambridge Songs; Gerhoh of Reichersberg; Hrabanus Maurus; Hymns, Latin; Metellus of Tegernsee; Notker Balbulus; Poetry, Liturgical; Tuotilo; Wipo of Burgundy

EMILY ZACK TABUTEAU
Michigan State University
Champion in Judicial Combat; Custumals of Normandy

KATHRYN MARIE TALARICO
Galeran de Bretagne

CONTRIBUTORS

ALICE-MARY M. TALBOT
Hiram College
Anna (Macedonian Princess); Athanasius I, Patriarch of Constantinople; Attaleiates, Michael; Irene, Empress; Kedrenos, Georgios; Kritovoulos, Michael; Theodora the Macedonian, Empress; Zoë the Macedonian

FRANK TALMAGE†
University of Toronto
Polemics, Christian-Jewish

GEORGE S. TATE
Brigham Young University
Einarr Skúlason; Eysteinn Ásgrímsson; Gamli Kanóki; Leiðarvísan; Líknarbraut; Sólarljóð

ROBERT B. TATE
University of Nottingham
Spanish Literature: Biography; Spanish Literature: Lost Works

GEORGE H. TAVARD
Methodist Theological School
Ecclesiology

PETRUS W. TAX
University of North Carolina, Chapel Hill
Frau Ava; Hartmann von Aue; Heinrich von Melk; Notker Teutonicus; Otloh of St. Emmeram; Pleier, Der; Wernher von Elmendorf; William von Ebersberg

JOHN TAYLOR
University of Leeds
Modus Tenendi Parliamentum; Palatinates; Robin Hood

MICHAEL D. TAYLOR
University of Houston
Maitani, Lorenzo; Pisano, Giovanni; Pisano, Nicola; Tree of Jesse; Ugolino di Vieri

ROBERT TAYLOR
Victoria College, University of Toronto
Comtessa de Dia; Guiraut Riquier; Leys d'Amors; Peire d'Alvernha; Raimbaut d'Aurenga; Raimbaut de Vaqueiras; Raimon Vidal de Besalú; Trobairitz

WILLIAM H. TEBRAKE
University of Maine
Reclamation of Land

ELAINE C. TENNANT
University of California, Berkeley
Ambraser Heldenbuch; Dresdener Heldenbuch

CHRISTOPHER THACKER
University of Reading
Gardens, European

PAUL R. THIBAULT
Franklin and Marshall College
Clement VI, Pope; Gregory IX, Pope; John XXII, Pope

JOAN THIRSK
St. Hilda's College, Oxford
Field Systems

J. WESLEY THOMAS
University of Kentucky
Freidank; Herrand von Wildonie; Herzog Ernst; Konrad von Würzburg; Marner, der; Moriz von Craûn; Steinmar; Tannhäuser; Tristrant; Ulrich von Liechtenstein; Wirnt von Grafenberg; Wizlaw III von Rügen

B. BUSSELL THOMPSON
Spanish Literature: Hagiography

CLAIBORNE W. THOMPSON
Æsir; Bósa Saga ok Herrauðs; Runes

PAULINE A. THOMPSON
University of Toronto, Centre for Medieval Studies
Amaricius; Amatus of Monte Cassino; Anselm II of Lucca

DERICK S. THOMSON
University of Glasgow
Scottish Literature, Gaelic

R. W. THOMSON
Dumbarton Oaks Research Center, Harvard University
Agatʿangełos; Balavariani; Ełišē; Georgian Literature; Kʿartʿlis Cʿχovreba; Movsēs Xorenacʿi; Shotʿa Rustaʿveli

HANS TISCHLER
Indiana University
Franconian Motet

FRANK TOBIN
University of Nevada
Mysticism, Christian: German

M. A. TOLMACHEVA
Washington State University
Geography and Cartography, Islamic; Khurdādhbih, Ibn; Zanj

RICHARD TOPOROSKI
St. Michael's College, University of Toronto
Ambrose, St.

PETER TOPPING
Dumbarton Oaks Research Center, Harvard University
Assizes of Romania; Morea; Morea, Chronicle of; Morea, Despotate of; William of Champlitte

ANTONIO TORRES-ALCALÁ
University of Texas
Mozarabic Literature

DAVID R. TOWNSEND
University of Toronto, Centre for Medieval Studies
Aelfric Bata; Anthologia Latina; Arnulf of Milan; Baudri of Bourgueil; Bebo of Bamberg

IRINA ANDREESCU TREADGOLD
Mosaics and Mosaic Making

WARREN T. TREADGOLD
Hillsdale College
Bardas Phokas; Bardas Skleros; Basil I the Macedonian; Basil II "Killer of Bulgars"; Constantine IX Monomachos; Leo VI the Wise, Emperor; Macedonians; Nikephoros I; Photios; Schism, Photian; Symeon the Logothete; Theodora II, Empress

LEO TREITLER
State University of New York at Stony Brook
Centonization; Melisma; Music, Oral Tradition in

DAVID H. TRIPP
Cathar Liturgy

RALPH V. TURNER
Florida State University
MAGNA CARTA; WESTMINSTER, STATUTES OF

ISADORE TWERSKY
Harvard University
ABRAHAM BEN DAVID OF POSQUIÈRES; MAIMONIDES

AVRAM L. UDOVITCH
Princeton University
BANKING, ISLAMIC; CASBAH; COMMENDA; IDRĪSĪ, AL-; IDRISIDS; SICILY, ISLAMIC; TRADE, ISLAMIC; URBANISM, ISLAMIC

MARY C. UHL
GOLIARDS

KARL D. UITTI
Princeton University
AUCASSIN ET NICOLETTE; FABLIAU AND COMIC TALE; FRENCH LITERATURE: TO 1200; FRENCH LITERATURE: AFTER 1200; PROVENÇAL LITERATURE

RICHARD W. UNGER
University of British Columbia
NAVIES, WESTERN; SHIPS AND SHIPBUILDING, NORTHERN EUROPEAN

WILLIAM L. URBAN
Monmouth College
BALTIC COUNTRIES/BALTS; LÜBECK

KRISTINE T. UTTERBACK
University of Toronto, Centre for Medieval Studies
ARNOLD OF ST. EMMERAM; CANDIDUS OF FULDA (BRUUN); CHRISTIAN OF STABLO; CYPRIAN, ST.

GEORGES VAJDA
Centre National de la Recherche Scientifique, Paris
ABRAHAM BAR ḤIYYA; BAḤYA BEN JOSEPH IBN PAQUDA; DĀWŪD IBN MARWĀN AL-MUQAMMIṢ; JOSEPH BEN ABRAHAM AL-BAṢĪR; JOSEPH IBN SADDIQ

ANNE HAGOPIAN VAN BUREN
Tufts University
AUBERT, DAVID; FILLASTRE, GUILLAUME; FOUQUET, JEAN; JEAN, DREUX; JEAN LE TAVERNIER; JEAN MIÉLOT; LATHEM, LIÉVIN VAN; LEFÈVRE, RAOUL; LIÉDET, LOYSET; MARMION, SIMON; MARY OF

ANNE HAGOPIAN VAN BUREN
(cont.)
BURGUNDY, MASTER OF; VRELANT, WILLEM; WAUQUELIN, JEAN

ARJO VANDERJAGT
Filosofisch Instituut, Groningen
DURAND OF ST. POURÇAIN; HENRY OF LANGENSTEIN; MANEGOLD OF LAUTENBACH; THIERRY OF CHARTRES

AMY VANDERSALL
University of Colorado
LIUTHARD

JOHN VAN ENGEN
University of Notre Dame
BENEDICTUS LEVITA; DECRETALS, FALSE; DONATION OF CONSTANTINE; PRESENTATION, RIGHT OF

MICHEL VAN ESBROECK
Société des Bollandistes
GEORGIAN CHURCH AND SAINTS; HAGIOGRAPHY, GEORGIAN; NINO, ST.

M. F. VAUGHAN
University of Washington
CHARLES OF ORLÉANS

MILOŠ VELIMIROVIĆ
University of Virginia
HYMNS, BYZANTINE; MUSICAL NOTATION, BYZANTINE; MUSICAL NOTATION, EKPHONETIC; OKTOECHOS; PLAINSONG, EASTERN EUROPE; ROMANOS MELODOS

PHILIPPE VERDIER
BOUCHER, GUILLAUME; CERAMICS, EUROPEAN; CHIP CARVING; ENAMEL; METALLURGY

CHARLES VERLINDEN
AZORES; BLACKS; CANARY ISLANDS AND BÉTHENCOURT; EXPLORATION BY WESTERN EUROPEANS; MADEIRA ISLANDS; NAVIGATION, WESTERN EUROPEAN; SLAVERY, SLAVE TRADE

ROSALIE VERMETTE
Indiana University
BARLAAM AND JOSAPHAT

EVELYN BIRGE VITZ
New York University
BIOGRAPHY, FRENCH; VIE DES ANCIENS PÈRES, LA; VIE DE ST. ALEXIS

ELISABETH VODOLA
University of California, Berkeley
HOSTIENSIS; INDULGENCES; INNOCENT IV, POPE; INTERDICT; PRAEMUNIRE; POSTGLOSSATORS

LINDA EHRSAM VOIGTS
University of Missouri, Kansas City
HERBALS, WESTERN EUROPEAN

F. W. VON KRIES
University of Massachusetts, Amherst
HUGO VON TRIMBERG; REINMAR VON ZWETER; THOMASIN VON ZERCLAERE; WINSBECKE; WOLFGER VON ERLA

ERICH VON RICHTHOFEN
University of Toronto
SPANISH LITERATURE: EPIC POETRY

PETER VON SIVERS
University of Utah
SYRIA

SPEROS VRYONIS
University of California, Los Angeles
GUILDS, BYZANTINE

CHRYSOGONUS WADDELL, O.C.S.O.
Abbey of Gethsemani, Kentucky
CARMELITE RITE; CARMELITES; CISTERCIAN CHANT; CISTERCIAN RITE; GILBERTINE RITE; GUIBERT OF NOGENT; PETER THE VENERABLE; PREMONSTRATENSIAN RITE; PREMONSTRATENSIANS

STEPHEN WAGLEY
PLENITUDO POTESTATIS

STEPHEN L. WAILES
Indiana University
FOLZ, HANS; FRAUENLIST; FRESSANT, HERMANN; HÄSLEIN, DAS; MÄREN; RAPULARIUS; SCHRÄTEL UND DER WASSERBÄR, DAS; SPERBER, DER; STRICKER, DER; UNIBOS; WEINSCHWELG, DER; WIRT, DER

WALTER L. WAKEFIELD
State University of New York at Potsdam
INQUISITION

CONTRIBUTORS

JEANETTE A. WAKIN
Radcliffe College
ABŪ ḤANĪFA; CIRCUMCISION, ISLAMIC; FATWĀ; LAW, ISLAMIC; QADI

MUHAMMAD ISA WALEY
The British Library
BURĀQ

PAUL E. WALKER
Columbia University
HERESY, ISLAMIC

ROGER M. WALKER
University of London
CAVALLERO ZIFAR, LIBRO DEL

WILLIAM A. WALLACE
Catholic University of America
ARISTOTLE IN THE MIDDLE AGES; THOMISM AND ITS OPPONENTS

DAVID A. WALSH
University of Rochester
BARISANUS OF TRANI

JOHN K. WALSH
University of California, Berkeley
SPANISH LITERATURE: HAGIOGRAPHY

TERENCE WALZ
American Research Center in Egypt
WRITING MATERIALS, ISLAMIC

SETH WARD
University of Haifa
MALI; POLL TAX, ISLAMIC; USURY, ISLAMIC LAW

ANN K. WARREN
Case Western Reserve University
ANCHORITES; APOSTOLIC SUCCESSION; CHAPLAIN; CHAPTER; CHAPTER HOUSE

MORIMICHI WATANABE
Long Island University
POLITICAL THEORY, WESTERN EUROPEAN: AFTER 1100

ANDREW M. WATSON
University of Toronto
AGRICULTURE AND NUTRITION (THE ISLAMIC WORLD)

W. MONTGOMERY WATT
University of Edinburgh
ALLAH; MUḤAMMAD

EDWIN J. WEBBER
Northwestern University
SPANISH LITERATURE: INSTRUCTIONAL WORKS

RUTH HOUSE WEBBER
University of Chicago
RONCESVALLES

BRUCE WEBSTER
University of Kent
DAVID I OF SCOTLAND; DAVID II OF SCOTLAND

J. R. WEBSTER
St. Michael's College, University of Toronto
EIXIMENIS, FRANCESC; METGE, BERNAT

ELLEN T. WEHNER
University of Toronto, Centre for Medieval Studies
LIVRE DE SEYNTZ MEDICINES, LE; MANUEL DES PÉCHÉS; MELIOR ET YDOINE; MERURE DE SEINTE ÉGLISE; NICOLE BOZON; ORNEMENT DES DAMES; PETER LANGTOFT; PETER PECKHAM; PHILIPPE DE THAON; POLISTORIE; QUATRE LIVRE DES REIS, LI

JUDITH A. WEISE
State University of New York at Potsdam
HONEY

JAMES A. WEISHEIPL†
Pontifical Institute of Mediaeval Studies, Toronto
ALBERTUS MAGNUS; BRADWARDINE, THOMAS

BERNARD G. WEISS
University of Toronto
RESURRECTION, ISLAMIC

ALFORD T. WELCH
Michigan State University
KORAN; LITURGY, ISLAMIC

ANTHONY WELCH
University of Victoria
CALLIGRAPHY, ISLAMIC; ISFAHAN

SUZANNE FONAY WEMPLE
Barnard College
WOMEN'S RELIGIOUS ORDERS

MARTIN WERNER
Temple University
MIGRATION AND HIBERNO-SAXON ART; PICTISH ART

WILLIAM K. WEST
LO CODI; SURVEYING

L. G. WESTERINK
State University of New York at Buffalo
NIKOLAOS I MYSTIKOS, PATRIARCH; PHILOSOPHY AND THEOLOGY, BYZANTINE

HAIJO JAN WESTRA
University of Calgary
BERNARD OF CHARTRES; BERNARD SILVESTER

WINTHROP WETHERBEE
University of Chicago
ALAN OF LILLE

BONNIE WHEELER
Southern Methodist University
CANTERBURY

ESTELLE WHELAN
ABBASID ART AND ARCHITECTURE; AJÍMEZ; AYYUBID ART AND ARCHITECTURE; AZULEJO; BADR AL-DĪN LUʾLUʾ; BARBOTINE; BAYT; BLAZON; CUERDA SECA; KAABA; MUQARNAS; NĀʿŪRA; ORTUQIDS; QAṢR; SABĪL; SELJUK ART AND ARCHITECTURE; TEXTILES, ISLAMIC

KEITH WHINNOM
University of Exeter
CANCIONERO GENERAL; SAN PEDRO, DIEGO DE

LYNN WHITE, JR.†
University of California, Los Angeles
AGRICULTURE AND NUTRITION (NORTHERN EUROPE); TECHNOLOGY, WESTERN; THEOPHILUS

DAVID WHITEHOUSE
Corning Museum
GLASS, ISLAMIC

MARINA D. WHITMAN
CERAMICS, ISLAMIC; KASHI; LAJVARD; LUSTERWARE; MINAI WARE

GREGORY WHITTINGTON
New York University, Institute of Fine Arts
JAMB; LANCET WINDOW; LOMBARD BANDS; MACHICOLATION; MODILLION; MONASTERY; NARTHEX; NAVE; NICHE; OPUS ALEXANDRINUM; OPUS FRANCIGENUM; OPUS MIXTUM; OPUS RETICULATUM; OPUS SECTILE; PILASTER; PILASTER STRIP; PORTCULLIS; QUATREFOIL; REFECTORY; SACRISTY; SCREEN; SEDILIA; SPANDREL; SPOLIA; SQUINCH; STRINGCOURSE; TETRACONCH; TRACERY; TRANSENNA; TRANSEPT; TREFOIL; TRIFORIUM; TRIUMPHAL ARCH; TRUMEAU; TYMPANUM; VAULT; VOUSSOIR

GERNOT WIELAND
University of British Columbia
PAPIAS

SARA HELLER WILENSKY
Haifa University
ISAAC BEN MOSES ARAMA

NIGEL WILKINS
University of Cambridge
ADAM DE LA HALLE

J. E. CAERWYN WILLIAMS
University College of Wales
EINON AP GWALCHMAI; ELIDIR SAIS

JOHN WILLIAMS
University of Pittsburgh
BAÇÓ, JAIME; BASSA, FERRER; CAPILLA MAYOR; DOMINICUS; EMETERIUS OF TÁBARA; ENDE; FLORENTIUS; FRUCTUOSUS; MAIUS; OBECO; PEDRO DE CÓRDOBA; PETRUS; SANCTIUS; SARRACINUS; VIMARA

SARAH JANE WILLIAMS
MACHAUT, GUILLAUME DE

DANIEL WILLIMAN
State University of New York at Binghamton
ARCHIVES; SCHOOLS, GRAMMAR

JOSEPH WILSON
Rice University
WENDS

GABRIELE WINKLER
St. John's University, Collegeville, Minnesota
ARMENIAN RITE; EPIPHANY, FEAST OF

BRUCIA WITTHOFT
Framingham State University
DONATELLO; FRANCESCO DI VALDAMBRINO; GHIBERTI, LORENZO; GORO DI GREGORIO; INTARSIA; LEONARDO DI SER GIOVANNI; NERI DI FIORAVANTI; NIVARDUS OF FLEURY

CURT WITTLIN
University of Saskatchewan
CATALAN LITERATURE

MARTHA WOLFF
Art Institute of Chicago
BURIN; E. S., MASTER; ENGRAVING; HOUSEBOOK, MASTER OF THE; PLAYING CARDS, MASTER OF THE; SCHONGAUER, MARTIN

KLAUS WOLLENWEBER
Memorial University of Newfoundland
ARISTOTELES UND PHYLLIS; BAUERNHOCHZEIT, DIE; BUSSARD, DER; KOTZENMÄRE, DAS; SCHAMPIFLOR; SCHÜLER VON PARIS, DER; ZAHN, DER

CHARLES T. WOOD
Dartmouth College
APPANAGES; BONIFACE VIII, POPE; CELESTINE V, POPE; CLERICIS LAICOS; EDWARD THE CONFESSOR, ST.; EDWARD I OF ENGLAND; EDWARD II OF ENGLAND; EDWARD III OF ENGLAND; EDWARD THE BLACK PRINCE; ENGLAND: 1216–1485; TUDOR, OWEN

KENNERLY M. WOODY†
JOHN GUALBERTI, ST.; PETER DAMIAN, ST.; ROMUALD OF RAVENNA, ST.

ELISABETH PENDREIGH WORK
FLAMENCA, ROMANCE OF

JENNY WORMALD
St. Hilda's College, Oxford
SCOTLAND: HISTORY

FRANK E. WOZNIAK
University of New Mexico
DIPLOMACY, BYZANTINE; ISAAC II ANGELOS; TMUTARAKAN, KHANATE OF

GEORGIA SOMMERS WRIGHT
GOTHIC ART: SCULPTURE

BASIL S. YAMEY
University of London
ACCOUNTING

JAMES L. YARRISON
ALMORAVIDS; ATLAS MOUNTAINS; IBRĀHĪM IBN AL-AGHLAB; LĀDHIQIYA, AL-; MALTA; MEKNES

DAVID YERKES
Columbia University
AELFRIC; HAGIOGRAPHY, MIDDLE ENGLISH; MIDDLE ENGLISH LANGUAGE

ABIGAIL YOUNG
University of Toronto, Centre for Medieval Studies
AURELIANUS, AMBROSIUS; CALBULUS

CHARLES R. YOUNG
Duke University
FORESTS, EUROPEAN

CHRISTIAN K. ZACHER
Ohio State University
MANDEVILLE'S TRAVELS

NORMAN ZACOUR
University of Toronto, Centre for Medieval Studies
CARDINALS, COLLEGE OF

RONALD JOHN ZAWILLA, O.P.
DOMINICAN RITE; DURAND, GUILLAUME; RESERVATION OF THE SACRAMENT

JAROLD K. ZEMAN
Acadia University
BOHEMIAN BRETHREN

VICKIE ZIEGLER
Pennsylvania State University
SEIFRIED HELBLING; SPERVOGEL AND HERGER

CONTRIBUTORS

MARK A. ZIER
University of Toronto, Centre for Medieval Studies
ALEXANDER V; ANDREW OF ST. VICTOR; CLAUDIUS OF TURIN; CORIPPUS; GREGORY OF RIMINI; HOLCOT, ROBERT; NICHOLAS OF LYRA; PETER COMESTOR; PETER LOMBARD; PETER THE DEACON OF MONTE CASSINO

GROVER A. ZINN, JR.
Oberlin College
HUGH OF ST. VICTOR

RONALD EDWARD ZUPKO
Marquette University
ACRE; ALNAGE, AUNAGE; ARPENT; BARREL; BOISSEAU; BOLL; BUSHEL; CHALDER; CLOVE; DUCAT; FLORIN; GALLON; HIDE; HUNDRED (LAND

RONALD EDWARD ZUPKO (*cont.*)
DIVISION); HUNDRED AND HUNDREDWEIGHT; JOURNAL; LAST; LEAGUE; LIVRE; MARC; MILE; MUID; OUNCE; PECK; PENNY; PERCH; POUND, MONEY; POUND, WEIGHT; QUARTER; REEVE; SACK; SETIER; SHILLING; SHIRE; STONE; VIRGATE; WEIGHTS AND MEASURES, WESTERN EUROPEAN

Errata

The first numeral in each entry refers to the page number. The letter identifies the column. The second numeral is the line number from the top of the page or (where specified) from the bottom. These errata exist in the first printing. By 1989 most of the significant errors had been corrected in second or third impressions of individual volumes.

Volume 1

iv, bottom: Patricia A. Rodriguez and Sylvia Lehrman → Joseph Stonehill

xiv(a), 11 from bottom: CARBANISS → CABANISS

xiv(b), 21 from bottom: G. P. CUTTINO → P. CUTTINO

xiv(b), 10 from bottom: AŁTʾAMAR → AŁTʿAMAR

xvii(c), 19: NICHOLAS → NICOLAS

3b, 2–3 from bottom: **AL-ʿABBĀS IBN ʿABD AL-MUTṬALIB IBN HĀSHIM → ʿABBĀS IBN ʿABD AL-MUTṬALIB IBN HĀSHIM, AL-**

7b, 26: 759 → 754

31, map: Matārā → Maṭārā

50a, 24 from bottom: *granaeur* → *grandeur*

50a, 14 from bottom: Hardrada → Hardråde

64, map: ZARANJ → Zaranj *(designating an Afghan town just inside the border)*

66a–67a (*passim*): Agatʿangeł̇os → Agatʿangełos

66b, 1: Ł̣azar → Łazar

66b, 2 from bottom: Korium → Koriwn

67a, 25 from bottom: Agatʿangeł̇ay → Agatʿangełay

67a, 23 from bottom: Ł̇ukasean → Łukasean

67a, 5 from bottom; 67b, 7: Ter-Ghł̇evondyan → Ter-Ghłevondyan

67a, 5 from bottom: *Agatʿangeł̇osi* → *Agatʿangełosi*

67b, 7: Agatʿangeł̇osi → Agatʿangełosi

73a, 8 from bottom: *Add after* "theologies.": He is not to be confused with the ninth-century Andreas Agnellus, author of a *Liber pontificalis ecclesiae Ravennatis.*

73a, 1–3 from bottom: His *Liber pontificalis ecclesiae Ravennatis,* ed. O. Holder-Egger, is in *Monumenta Germaniae historica: Scriptores rerum langobardorum et italicarum seculorum* → The *Liber pontificalis* is in *MGH: Scriptores rerum Langobardorum*

109a, 15: *generatis* → *generalis*

112a, 4 from bottom: See **Apocrypha, Irish.** → See **Irish Literature.**

116b, 11 from bottom: rimur → *rímur*

124, map: *Eliminate* U.S.S.R.; TURKEY → ANATOLIA; Araxes R., Aras R. → Araks R.

134a, 3 from bottom: AŁC → AŁCʿ

144b, 11 from bottom: See **Beer.** → See **Brewing.**

148a, 16–17: probably at → was probably born at

155b, 19: *Degg^{w}a* → *Deggwa*

167b, 17: Pearsal → Pearsall

207a, 14 from bottom: *Ages;* → *Ages* (1967);

220b, running head, 21: AŁTʾAMAR → AŁTʿAMAR

220b, 22: Xačʾ → Xačʿ

220b, 5, 17, 27 from bottom: Ałtʾamar → Ałtʿamar

221a, 18 and 20: *Aghtʾamar* → *Aghtʿamar*

221a, 22: Mnacʾakanyan → Mnacʿakanyan

227a, 24 from bottom: Kühn → Kuhn

227a, 23 from bottom: (1968) → (repr. 1968)

227a, 21 from bottom: Barand → Barend

230b, 12–13: **AMBROGIA, GIOVANNI D'.** See **Giovanni D'Ambrogia.** → **AMBROGIO, GIOVANNI D'.** See **Giovanni d'Ambrogio.**

230b, 14: **AMBROGIO, MAITANI → AMBROGIO MAITANI**

230b, 16: **AMBROGIO, TRAVERSARI → AMBROGIO TRAVERSARI**

234a, 3: **AMBROSIUS AUTOPERTUS.** See **Autopertus, Ambrosius.** → **AMBROSIUS AUTPERTUS.** See **Autpertus, Ambrosius.**

240, map: Ephesus *should appear on the coast, just above the O in* IONIA. *Upper right:* IRAN → CAUCASUS

289b, map: *The words* ANGLO-SAXONS *around the Humber should be deleted.*

307, caption: (Detail), Martini di Simone. 12th Century. → (detail). Simone Martini, 14th century.

310b, 20 from bottom: *loð-inkinna* → *loðinkinna*

311a, 5: teachers → teaches

ERRATA

311a, 9: *Hrafnista-mannasögur* → *Hrafnistumannasögur*
311a, 19–20: *Nordrlanda* → *Norðurlanda*
367, map: *The heavy black boundary marks the English possessions in France. Aquitaine was the region south of the Loire.*
369–376, running heads: PRE-ISLAMIC ARABIA → ARABIA
369b, 10: G. P. CUTTINO → P. CUTTINO
372a–373a (*passim*): Ḳuraysh → Quraysh
372, map: *Shade the Dead Sea, just west of Amman. Locate* Gerra *just left of the initial* A *in* Al-Ḥasa. *Eliminate* (Oqair). *Reverse the labels* SABA *and* HIMYAR. *Eliminate* Qatabān.
381a, 15: Abuᵓl-Faraj → Abu 'l-Faraj
407b, 18 from bottom: Geronimo → Gerónimo
409, map: *A small coastal region under the* o *in* Montpellier *should be shaded as territory to 1204.*
444, caption: Byzantine Icon Screen of the late Middle Ages. DRAWING BY R. NAUMANN → Byzantine iconostasis of the late Middle Ages. Cathedral of the Annunciation, Moscow. FROM L. KOZLOVA, *CATHEDRAL SQUARE IN THE MOSCOW KREMLIN: A GUIDE*
452a, 22 from bottom: Šābulhr → Šābuhr
453a, 17: See **Dionysius, the Pseudo** → See **Pseudo-Dionysius the**
463a, bottom: indivdual → individual
471, map: *Upper half, center:* Araxes → Araks. Karin/ Theodosiopolis → Karin/ Erzurum/Theodosiopolis. *Eliminate* Erzerum *and* Kalikala.
482a, 9 and 22 from bottom: Lastivertcᶜi → Lastivercᶜi
489b, 3 and 9: *na$_{\chi}$arars* → *naχarars*
489b, 7: *$_{\chi}$ostakdars* → *χostakdars*
489b, 8 and 11: *$_{\chi}$ostaks* → *χostaks*
523b: *The circular shield is the Viking shield. The oblong at top right is the knightly shield.*
534a, upper caption: Typical 15th-century armor → Tournament armor, late 16th century
564a, 7 from bottom: rehearsed → rehashed
582b, 13–12 from bottom: **ASHᶜARĪ, AL-, ABU'L-ḤASAN ᶜALĪ IBN ISMAᶜĪL** → **ASHᶜARĪ, ABU 'L-ḤASAN ᶜALĪ IBN ISMAᶜĪL AL-**
587b, 25–26: *For-naldarsögur* → *Forn-aldarsögur*
598b, 7 from bottom; 599a, 5 and 8 from bottom: Navara → Novare
600a, 6: **Navara** → **Novare**
600b, 13: *del* → *de*
614a, 13: Ackropolites → Akropolites
615a, 2: Corpernicus → Copernicus
618a, 6 from bottom: Ghazzālī → Ghazālī
634a, 23: ABŪ ᵓL-ḤASAN → ABU' L-ḤASAN
634b, 10: Dīn → Dīn
634b, 17: of ᶜ Izz → of ᶜIzz
634b, 10 from bottom: ABŪ ᵓL-FATḤ → ABU 'L-FATḤ
635a, 20: ABŪ ᵓL-SA → ABŪ 'L-SA
635a, 7 from bottom: *at-ta'rikh* → *al-taᵓrīkh*
635a, 5 from bottom: *al-Ta'rikh* → *al-Taᵓrīkh*
635b, 12: *Diya'* → *Diyaᵓ*

Volume 2

9b, 2 from bottom: αὐτοχέφαλος → *αὐτοκέφαλος*
12a, 2 and 17 from bottom: Ephthalite → Hephthalite
19a, running head and 1: LOPEZ → LÓPEZ
19b, 14: **Mamluks** → **Mamluk Dynasty**
23b, 25: Yūsuf → Yūsuf II
25a, 8 from bottom: *Egypten* → *Ägypten*
41a, 10 from bottom: 1879 → 1897
49a, 1 from bottom: **Tamara** → **Tamar**
49b, 1: *Eliminate* **BAHOU.** See **Qbou.**
63, map: *Center:* SAMOGITHIA → SAMOGITIA
64b, 16: Magdeburg → Querfurt
68b, 4: **Political; Lithuania; Military Orders.→Political; Lithuania.**
79a, 27–29: **in Europe; Commerce, European; Exchequer, Finance; Lombards (Bankers); Mints and Coinage, Western European; Usury.→ in Europe; Exchequer; Lombards (Bankers); Mints and Money, Western European; Trade, Western European; Usury.**
94b, 4 from bottom: lofing → lolfing
113a, 14 from bottom: govenor → governor
135b, 4 from bottom: Abū ᵓl-Ḥasan → Abu 'l-Ḥasan
140a, 13: *eyvan* → *eyvān*
140a, 23: **Eyvan; Islamic Architecture.** → **Eyvān; Islamic Art and Architecture.**
140a, 24 from bottom: **BDEŠχ** → **BDEŠX**
140a, 23 from bottom: *aptahšā* → *aptahšā*
166a, 6: tenth → twelfth
168a, 7: cogomen → cognomen
174a, 11 from bottom: Byrhth- → Byrht-
189a, 23 from bottom: *altarmenishchen* → *altarmenischen*
198a, 17 from bottom: *Eliminate* **BERRIES OF FINGEN.** See **Apocrypha, Irish.**
231a, 19 from bottom: srict → strict
234a, 20–21: John Scotus Erigena → John Duns Scotus
234a, 19 from bottom: John Scotus → Duns Scotus
252b, 13 from bottom: 2 vols. → 3 vols.
276a, 19: *Eliminate* **Trovadores.**
276a, 2 from bottom: Trachtenburg → Trachtenberg
290b, 12–13: **Italian Prose; Italian Versification and Prosody** → **Italian Literature**
300b, 13: Charles VI → Charles IV
312a, 22: *juris* → *iuris*
333a, upper caption: Gripping beast brooch → Gripping beast pendant
333a, lower caption: Aron-Slab with ring chain detail. DRAWING BY KIRK MICHAEL. → Cross-slab ring

chain motif from Kirk Michael, Isle of Man.
385a, 21: **BROT AF SIGURDHARKVIDHU** → **BROT AF SIGURÐARKVIÐU**
413a, 11: 1369 → 1361
434a, 5 from bottom: *Eliminate* **BUSTAN.** See **Garden, Islamic.**
470, 5 from bottom: *theologische* → *theologischen*
471a, 10: *des* → *der*
471a, 11: *altkirchliche* → *altkirchlichen*
471a, 16 from bottom: *byzantinishen* → *byzantinischen*
521–525: *Note that the second printing retitles and reorders the last two articles:* BYZANTINE LITERATURE: POETIC FORMS *and* BYZANTINE LITERATURE: POPULAR

Volume 3

xiii(a), 21 from bottom: *du Sorbonne* → *de Paris*
1b, 4 from bottom: Nakman → Nahman
17a, 6 from bottom: **DENG** → **OENGUS**
54b, 17 from bottom: Yaqut → Yaqūt
55b, 13 from bottom: *Eliminate* **Eclogue.**
76a, 26–25 from bottom: Sir Ben Abu Béker → Sir ibn Abi Bakr
93a, running head: CAPRINI, JOHN DE PLANO → CAPPADOCIA
93a, 4–3 from bottom: **CAPRINI, JOHN DE PLANO.** See **Plano Caprini, John of.** → **CARPINI, JOHN OF PLANO.** See **John of Plano Carpini.**
103a, 7: Scotus Erigena → Scottus Eriugena
103a, 6: Scotus → Scottus
106b, 25: he ritually served the king as stirrup holder → he apparently showed marked deference to Pepin
115b, 19: *Personlichkeit* → *Persönlichkeit*
193b, 16 from bottom: *Ubersetzungen* → *Übersetzungen*
194, map: *Center left:* **AZEBAIJAN** → **AZERBAIJAN**
205b, 17 from bottom: Bouvet's → Bonet's
209b, 2: *wa ᵓl farr* → *wa 'l-farr*
222a, upper caption: Tara brooch, gilt bronze. → Tara brooch, gilt silver.
222b, upper caption: Ardagh chalice, silver and millefiori glass. → Ardagh chalice, silver.
222b, lower caption: Nigg stone. Class III Pictish slab, late 9th century. → Nigg stone. Class II Pictish slab, *ca.* 800.
240a, 20 from bottom: Forthingham → Frothingham
263b, 1: See individual articles. → See **Ambrosian Chant; Gregorian Chant.**
301a, 8: **Millenialism.** → **Millennialism.**
306a, 9: Hopsitalers → Hospitalers
306a, 10: Hermann Walpott (1199) → Hermann (or Heinrich) Walpott (1198–1200)
306a, 10 from bottom: last grand master → last medieval grand master
306a, 6 from bottom: the duke of Prussia. → the duke.
306a, 4 from bottom: its fighting → its prime fighting
316b, 10: Christine's → Christine
319a, 25: saracophagi → sarcophagi
437b, 1 from bottom: **Gonzalez** → **González**
467b, 14: **To 937** → **To 987**
557a, 15: *Bayerische* → *Bayerischen*
564a, 19: *le maison* → *la maison*
595b, 6–5 from bottom: Pro-vençal → Pro-vençal
627a, 16: **Robert of Coucy** → **Robert de Coucy**
677b, 2: liturgische → liturgischen

Volume 4

41a, 4 from bottom: 1979 → 1879
49a, 19 from bottom: *in* → *im*
64b, 10: **Russian Nomads, Invasions of** → **Russia, Nomadic Invasions of**
115b, 1: Cornwall between → Cornwall, between
124a, 11 from bottom: Römisch → römisch
127a, 1: *Realencyclopädie* → *Realenzyklopädie*
136a, 14: *wiener* → *Wiener*
156b, 19 from bottom: *Danemark* → *Dänemark*
156b, 9 from bottom: *Königtum* → *Königstum*
162b, 5 from bottom: *Eliminate* **DERRY.** See **Columba, St.**
165b, 8 from bottom: *Kanonessammlung* → *Kanonensammlung*
167b, 23: *Eliminate* **DHIMMA.** See **Minorities.**
192b, 7 from bottom: **Dionisios** → **Dionisius**
215b, 2: *Consulardiptychen* → *Konsulardiptychen*
234b, 15–16: (the most recent and only → (with Teresa of Ávila the only
259b, 15: **Pepin** → **Pepin III**
267a, 22, and 11 from bottom: Benediktbeuren → Benediktbeuern
268a, 15: Bozon → Bozen
270a, 9: Apallonia → Apollonia
270a, 6 from bottom: *Eliminate* (see illustration)
270a, 5 from bottom: 1538 → 1583
271b, 20: five → twenty-five
272b, 8 and 11: *Mittelalterliche* → *mittelalterliche*
272b, 17: *den* → *der*
272b, 19: *mittelalterliche* → *mittelalterlichen*
278b, 13 from bottom: F. M. Robinson → F. N. Robinson
293b, 11–12: **Girart de Roussillon, Master of the.** → **Jean, Dreux.**
304a, 8: Furstentitel → Fürstentitel
328a, 24: Osnaberg → Oseberg
336b, 1 from bottom: *Anastasis* → Anastasis
338, caption: 1834. COURTESY OF ROYAL INSTITUTE OF BRITISH ARCHITECTS, DUMBARTON OAKS. → 1834, Royal Institute of British Architects, London. PHOTO COURTESY OF DUMBARTON OAKS CENTER FOR BYZANTINE STUDIES, WASHINGTON, D.C.
347a, 18 from bottom: Sopočani → Sopocani
366b, 12: exmple → example

382b, 5 from bottom: **Gottschalk of Orbais → Latin Literature**

384a: *The article* **EDESSA** *should be moved to page 392, after* **EDDIC POETRY.**

419a, 22 from bottom: **ELDIGÜZ.** See **Ildiguizid (Eldigüz).** → **ELDIGÜZIDS.** See **Ildegizids.**

427a, 18 from bottom: Lothair III → Lothair II

447a, 17 from bottom: and the *Taktikon* of Pseudo-Kodinos → and the Pseudo-Kodinos

449b–450a (*passim*): Hugutio → Huguccio

449b, 7 from bottom: Hugguccio → Huguccio

449b, 17 from bottom; 450a, 10: *Magnae derivationes → Liber derivationum*

450b, 6: *Insert* **Huguccio** *between* **St. Victor** *and* **Isidore of Seville**

536a, running head and 1: EXICIDIS → EXCIDIO

539a, 19 from bottom: Ḥushiʾel → Ḥushi'el

539b, 21 from bottom: Abū'l Walid → Abu 'l-Walid

551a, 6 from bottom: *Rómanorum → Romanorum*

577b, 23 from bottom: Augustodenensis' → Augustodunensis'

578b, 16 from bottom: *Secreta → Secretum*

580a, 17 from bottom: **Scandinavia, Arabic Sources in. → Scandinavia in Arabic Sources.**

619b, 3: *Insert* **Fornaldarsögur;** *between* **Fljótsdæla Saga;** *and* **Fostbrœðra Saga;**

619b, 9: *Eliminate* **Sagas, Legendary;**

Volume 5

xi(c), 23 from bottom: HOFFMAN → HOFFMANN

29a, 2 from bottom: Ṭalāʾiʿibn → Ṭalāʾiʿ ibn

64b, 13 from bottom: *Vatnsdæla → Vatnsdœla*

84b, 1 from bottom: **FLEMALLE → FLÉMALLE**

152a, 4 from bottom: **Fiesole, Giovanni da. → Giovanni da Fiesole.**

230a, 22: *épéron → éperon*

274b, 24: fabliaux → *fabliaux*

365b, 16 from bottom; 357, 24: Saʿadya → Saadiah

369a, 12: *other medieval tales → Other Medieval Tales*

383a, 1 from bottom: *Eliminate* of **Atropatene**

384b, 14 from bottom: Almeria → Almería

388a, 15: Cornwell → Cornwall

422a: *The article* **GERARD OF CSANAD, ST.** *should be moved to page 423, after* **GERARD OF CREMONA.**

429a, 13: *Erec → Erek*

435a, 21 from bottom: or Erla → von Erla

513b, 18: **Gerson → Gershom**

527a, 2: Din → Dīn

544a, 19: Taronacʿi → Tarōnecʿi

569b, 6 from bottom: Sigrdŕfumál → Sigrdrífumál

569b, 5 from bottom: *Eliminate* **GNOSTICISM.** See **Mysticism.**

604a, 12 from bottom: Haguenau → Hagenauer

612a, 24: Andés Marzal → Andrés, Marzal

627a, 21: ser. **29** → ser., **29**

632a, 17 and 9 from bottom: Øland → Öland

665b, 8 from bottom: **GREGORIUS, ABU'L FARAJ → GREGORIUS**

669a, 13: 598 → 568

673b–674a: *The article* **GRIGOR NAREKACʿI, ST.** *should be moved to page 675, after* **GRIGOR MAGISTROS.**

677a, 17 from bottom: **GRIMS → GRÍMS**

Volume 6

ix(a), 1: ABRAHAMSON → ABRAHAMSE

ix(a), 17: LUSIGAN → LUSIGNAN

ix(a), 22: BACHRACH → BACHARACH

xiii(b) 21: Þ ÁTTR → ÞÁTTR

37a, 12: *südgermanisches → südgermanischen*

105a, 23: *story, Gregorius → story: Gregorius*

161b, 10 from bottom: III's fifth → III's third son and in the male line from Edward III's fifth

187b, 11: Zervanite → Zurvanite

188a, 3 from bottom; 188b, 1 and 24: Yovannēs → Yovhannēs

229b, 19 and 18 from bottom: **Mystical Writings, Middle English → Mysticism, English**

246b, 23: Miketas → Niketas

253b, 23: *taʾrikh → taʾrīkh*

312a, 6 from bottom: *Hálf-danar → Hálfdanar*

318b: *The article* **HUGH OF SEMUR, ST.** *should be moved to page 323, before* **HUGINN AND MUGINN.**

338, map: *Left-center:* Poszony → Pozsony

385a, 6 from bottom: regius → Regius

387b, running head and 1 from bottom: HYWELL DA → HYWELL DDA

399b, 2 from bottom: Inconoclasm → Iconoclasm

418a, 9: BACHRACH → BACHARACH

422, map: *Boundaries are incorrect. From the fourth century, the northern boundary of the region and prefecture of Illyricum was the Danube River. The eastern boundary ran approximately due north from the Aegean to the Danube near Nicopolis, 175 miles west of the Black Sea. The province known as Dacia after the 290's was included within the region of Illyricum, south of the Danube.*

438a, 20 from bottom: vocabulary → Vocabulary

573, map: *Center left:* Fez → Fēs

602a, 6: *khanaqāh → khānqāh*

621a, running head and 1: ISXAN ISXANACᶜ → IŠXAN IŠXANACᶜ

632a, 18: *Psycomachia → Psychomachia*

635a, 6 from bottom: Ranieri → Raniero

651b, 11 from bottom: *sopra le → sopra la*

662b, 2: a old friar → an old friar

662b, 2: Fasano → Fasani

Volume 7

xi(b), 6 from bottom: *Wilfred* → *Wilfrid*

20a, running head and 1: IUDICA → IUDICIA

36b, 17 from bottom: *del'Academie* → *de l'Academie*

396, 9: **Philippe de Vitry → Vitry, Philippe de**

46b, 12: *Eliminate* **JANDUN.** See **Jean de Jandun.**

54a, 5 from bottom: **Master of Moulins → Moulins, Master of**

55b, 1 from bottom: *Geschied-en* → *Geschied- en*

87, table: The total at the bottom right should be 53,800,000.

95b, 18 from bottom: ADALUSIAN → ANDALUSIAN

99a, 6 and 8: Al-Da'ri → al-Da'ri

146a, 20 from bottom: **French Language. → Picard Literature.**

118b, 5: *canonischen* → *kanonischen*

152–153: *The article* **JOSHUA ROLL** *should come before the article* **JOSHUA THE STYLITE.**

176a, 4 from bottom: zealot → Zealot

204b, 1: Naqsh-e → Naqsh-i

205a, 2: Naqsh-e → Naqsh-i

211b, 16: **KARAJĪ, AL → KARAJĪ, AL-**

211b, 16: **Muhammad → Muḥammad**

221a, 10 from bottom: (Kars-cay) → (Kars-çay)

221a, 5 from bottom: Mušeḷ → Mušeł

236a, 25: *wa-anbāᵓ* → *wa- anbāᵓ*

244a, 3 from bottom: 1120 → 1220

276a, 12: **Hrebeljanovic → Hrebeljanović**

320b, 18: Eyed"), → Eyed")

361b, 3: Perigueux → Périgueux

489a, 8: Shāfiᶜī al-; → Shāfiᶜi, al-;

539b, 10: Freiburg → Freiberg

553a, 1 from bottom: **LETTER WRITING, FRENCH. → LETTER WRITING.**

618b, 20 from bottom: prophet → Prophet

634b, 15 from bottom: **BRITTANIE → BRITANNIE**

692b, 17 from bottom: *vorum* → *rorum*

706a, 7: do Troyes → de Troyes

Volume 8

ix(a), 5: ACKERMANN → ACKERMAN

xi(a), 21 from bottom: GRAFFTON → GRAFTON

xi(a), 14 from bottom: *Wilfred* → *Wilfrid*

47b, 10 from bottom: **Rasīd → Rashīd**

47b, 9 from bottom: Ja ᶜfar → Jaᶜfar

56b, 24 from bottom: Bendectine → Benedictine

78–79: *The article* **MAMIKONEAN** *should appear on page 68, following* **MALWIYA.**

90a, 23 from bottom: al-Zāhira → al-Ẓāhira

96b: *The article* **MANUEL DES PÉCHÉS** *should appear on page 94a, before* **MANUEL.**

99b, 1 from bottom; 100a, 3: Harāt → Herāt

109b, 6: Andrè → André

141a, 2 from bottom: **ADAE → ADAM**

144a, 4: RECOURCE → RESOURCE

197b, 3 from bottom: **ments Responsory; → ment; Responsory**

284, photograph: *Reverse image, so that the Crucifixion appears on the left door.*

300b, 1: (1340–1346–1413) → (1340/1346–1413)

306b, 9 from bottom: Neumark → Neumarkt

309b, 4: GRAFFTON → GRAFTON

311b, 8: *se* → *þe*

362b, 24 from bottom: Ragnarǫk → Ragnarǫk

365b, 2 from bottom: ODLSAK- → OLDSAK-

437b: *Eliminate* **MISSAL.** See **Mass.**

479a, 24: ᵓl-Barakāt → 'l-Barakāt

481b, 5 from bottom: **Pierre of → Pierre de**

534a, 15: *ᵓl-Ṣaḥāba* → *'l-Ṣaḥāba*

564b, 1 from bottom: Budapest → Budapest. The American Academy for Jewish Research, New York.

605a, 4 from bottom: business → buisines

611a, 17 from bottom: *tār* → *ṭār*

620, table: *Add footnote to square quilisma:* *Not found in medieval sources.

Volume 9

ix(a), 15: NIEBELUNGENLIED → NIBELUNGENLIED

xv(c), 8: *Amherst* → *Buffalo*

4b, 9 from bottom: Encylopedia → Encyclopedia

31b, 20 and 21: Mechtild → Mechthild

40a, 12; 40b, 14: Abu → Abū

68a, 5 from bottom: Banu → Banū

71a, 16 from bottom: Evreux → Évreux

88a, 2: *Tacuini sanitatis of Ibn Buṭlān.* → *Tacuinum sanitatis im medicina.*

95b, 6: 135–31 → 135–51

104b, 16: Frederick II → Frederick I

136a, 3: KLAUS G. BEYER, WEIMAR → FROM WACHTANG BERIDSE/EDITH NEUBAUER, *DIE BAUKUNST DES MITTELALTERS IN GEORGIEN* © UNION VERLAG (VOB), BERLIN, 1981. Foto Klaus G. Beyer, Weimar.

140b, 11: MICHAEL → MICHEL

142a, 6 from bottom: Baṭṭūṭā → Baṭṭūṭa

243b, 4: *Eliminate* vol. I,

245b, 2: presumably based on an original in Ibn al-Haytham. → representing Kamāl al-Dīn's understanding of the structure of the eye.

245b, 3: III.A. → AHMET III

247a, 8: *Auzsätze* → *Aufsätze*

248a, 6 from bottom: ontological → ontological,

308b, 21: replaced by more → replaced by the more

330a, 4: **Bahya ben Joseph ibn Paqūdā. → Baḥya ben Joseph ibn Paquda.**

392b, 3: **PAQŪDĀ . . . Paqūdā → PAQUDA . . . Paquda**

453, caption: Plan of St. Savior in Chora, Constantinople, *ca.* 1050, showing the prothesis (1) and diaconicon (2), which together constitute the pastophory. → The Kariye Djami (St. Savior in Chora), Constantinople, 12th–14th centuries. Plan showing pastophories: prothesis (1) and location of former diaconicon (2), converted to private chapel. *[Second and later printings show a different illustration and caption.]*
466b, 17 from bottom; 481a, 2: **Russian Nomads, Invasions of.** → **Russia, Nomadic Invasions of.**
515b, 1: *catholocae* → *catholicae*
520b, 1: *and Sygerium* → *ad Sygerium*
582a, 1: Ziyyoni → Ẓiyyoni
651b, 6 from bottom: Abu al-Baqāᵓ → Abu 'l Baqāᵓ
671a, 10 from bottom: *Eliminate* **PIYYUT.** See **Hebrew Poetry.**
672a, 25: among on canonists → among canonists
705a, 3: Abūᵓl-Qāsim → Abu 'l Qāsim
710b, 12: **Claus.**→ **Claus; Werve, Claus de;** and illustration overleaf.

Volume 10

ix(a), 10: REYKDOELA→ REYKDŒLA
3b, 10: *Annu-* → *Anu-*
42b, 24 from bottom: Yusuf Yaᶜqub → Yūsuf Yaᶜqūb
85b, 7 from bottom: Loan → León
101a, 3–4: "Paliotto of S. Ambrogio.") → "Metalsmiths.")
226a, 9: *Eliminate* **QALI.** See **Rugs and Carpets.**
226b, 26 from bottom: al- Ghawrī's → al-Ghawrī's
270a, 1: *divevsis* → *diversis*
314b, 14 from bottom: *Historie* → *Histoire*
330a, 15 from bottom: Repgow → Repgowe
340a, 23: Mileševa → Mileševo
395b, 12 from bottom: *Samons saga* → *Samsons saga*
422b, 13: MAJORIE → MARJORIE
510b, 7–8: hospodar, or ruler, of → ruler of
511a, 19 from bottom: with its → in spite of its
512a, 8 from bottom: *învăţaţiva* → *învăţaţi-va*
512a, 6 from bottom: *secrerat* → *secerat*
512b, 24: rhotocism → rhotacism
512b, 16 from bottom: *Ioanei* → *Ionaei'*
513a, 25: *intro* → *inter*
513a, 15 from bottom: [laui] → [law]
513a, 7 from bottom: *venirăti* → *venirăţi*
513b, 23: *iveaşte, ivi* → *scîrbit* (suffering), *iveaşte, ivi*
513b, 25–26: *steble* (branches), seven words out of a total of 148. → *glasure* (voices); *sfîrşit* (end); *steble* (branches), a total of only eleven words.
514a, 5: Lorgu Lordan y María Manolin → Iorgu Iordan y María Manoliu
525a, 26 from bottom: *petri* → *Petri*
624b, 15 from bottom: **SAJJADA** → **SAJJĀDA**
671b, 12: **Zarvanism; Zoroastrianism.]** → **Zoroastrianism; Zurvanism.]**
707a, 2 from bottom: runī → rūnī

Volume 11

x(a), 4: FREDERICK → FREDERIC
xi(b), 18 from bottom: HOFFMAN → HOFFMANN
xii(c), 19: *Add* SCARLET;
37a, 16–19: While all medieval scarlets were dyed with kermes "in the grain," that is, as yarn or fiber rather than as woven material, some also contained additional dyes, especially → While all medieval scarlets were dyed "in grain" with kermes, some also contained additional dyes, especially
126a, 5: Philip I France → Philip I of France
282a, 3: 1325 → 1525
295a, 12: industries. → industries, and under Justinian a state monopoly, though one later restricted to just the finest silk fabrics (*kekolymena*).
322a, 21: *r. ca.* → *ca.*
347b, 1: *Yusskyia* → *Russkyia*
407b, 15 from bottom: **Eugenias** → **Eugenius**
429b, 19 from bottom: *viejo* → *viejos*
441b, 20 from bottom: (1475). → *ciencia* (1475).
446a, 22: Gunicelli → Guinizzelli
574a–b (*passim*): TĀHIR . . . Tāhir → ṬĀHIR . . . Ṭāhir
714a, 22: 1223 → 1323

Volume 12

ix(a), 15: GEORGE R. → GEORGE K.
xiii(c), 18 from bottom: ROGER → ROBERT
xv(c), 4: TERRENCE → TERENCE
45a, 19: **Kildwardby, Richard** → **Kildwardby, Robert**
366b, 14: **Renatus Flavius Vegetius** → **Flavius Vegetius Renatus**
379b, 12 from bottom: sevaral → several
462a, 2: Kemnaten → Kemenaten
471a, 25: Follwing → Following
558: *Add running head:* WARFARE, WESTERN EUROPEAN
611a, 15: *Efrog* → *Efrawg*
656a, 9: documentat → document
674b, 10: Hartman → Hartmann
676a, 8 from bottom: Herman → Hermann
676b, 15 from bottom: land → hand
679b, 15: Gravenberg → Grafenberg
706a, 6: Xusro → Xusrō
711b, 19 from bottom: **YNFORD** → **WYNFORD**
717a, 19 from bottom: Sistan → Sīstān
722b, 20 from bottom; 723a, 19 from bottom: apocalpytic → apocalyptic
728a, 19: firty-one → fifty-one
731a, 11: castellon → castellan

ERRATA

731a, 2 from bottom: charger → charter
732b, 13: prinicpal → principal
744a, 18: 1972 → 972
744a, 19: Abū 'l-Futūḥ → Abu 'l-Futūḥ
745a, 6 from bottom: Allah → Allāh